RHS PLANT FINDER 2012-2013

Devised by Chris Philip
and Realised by Tony Lord

Editor-in-Chief
Janet Cubey

RHS Editors
James Armitage   Dawn Edwards
Neil Lancaster   Christopher Whitehouse

Compiler
Judith Merrick

Royal
Horticultural
Society

Published by
The Royal Horticultural Society
80 Vincent Square
London SW1P 2PE

First edition April 1987
Twenty-sixth edition April 2012

British Library Cataloguing Publication Data.
A Catalogue record for this book is available from the British Library.

ISBN 978-1-907057-25-0

Compiled by
The Royal Horticultural Society
80 Vincent Square,
London SW1P 2PE
Registered charity no: 222879/SC038262

www.rhs.org.uk

Illustrations by Sarah Young
Maps by Alan Cooper

Produced for The Royal Horticultural Society by

COOLING BROWN

Printed and bound by CPI Group (UK) Ltd, Croydon, CR0 4YY

The Compiler and the Editors of the *RHS Plant Finder* have taken every care, in the time available, to check all the information supplied to them by the nurseries concerned. Nevertheless, in a work of this kind, containing as it does hundreds of thousands of separate computer encodings, errors and omissions will, inevitably, occur. Neither the RHS, the Publisher nor the Editors can accept responsibility for any consequences that may arise from such errors.

If you find mistakes we hope that you will let us know so that the matter can be corrected in the next edition.

Front cover photograph: Display of tulips at RHS Garden Wisley (RHS/Neil Hepworth)
Spine: *Clivia miniata* (RHS/Rebecca Ross)
Back cover from left to right: *Gerbera* Garvinea Rachel = 'Garrachel' (RHS/Christopher Whitehouse), *Arisaema* seedhead (RHS/Mike Sleigh), *Tigridia pavonia* (RHS/Carol Sheppard), *Crocosmia* 'Lucifer' (RHS/Christopher Whitehouse)

www.rhs.org.uk

CONTENTS

INTRODUCTION

The *RHS Plant Finder* exists to put enthusiastic gardeners in touch with suppliers of plants. The book is divided into two related sections – **PLANTS** and **NURSERIES. PLANTS** includes an A–Z Plant Directory of about 70,000 plant names, against which are listed a series of nursery codes. These codes point the reader to the full nursery details contained in the **NURSERIES** section towards the back of the book.

The *RHS Plant Finder* is comprehensively updated every year and provides the plant lover with the richest source of suppliers known to us.

As you will see from the entries in the **NURSERY DETAILS BY CODE** many nurseries do not now publish a printed catalogue but produce an online version only. This is a growing trend, fuelled by the cost of printing a full catalogue.

It is important to remember when ordering that many of the nurseries listed in the book are small, family-run, businesses that propagate their own material. They cannot therefore guarantee to hold large stocks of the plants they list. Some will, however, propagate to order.

NEW IN THIS EDITION

In this edition's essay RHS Horticultural Scientist, Tijana Blanusa, discusses "Urban Greening" and how it affects us all.

Major changes to nomenclature in this edition reflect the decisions made by the RHS Advisory Committee on Nomenclature and Taxonomy (ACONAT). These include: following the American Iris Society in their recognition of Siberian irises (Sib) as one of the classification groups for *Iris* rather than listing them all as cultivars of *Iris sibirica*; inclusion of *Chamaecytisus* within *Cytisus* (following the classification of *Genistae* in *Legumes of the World*); inclusion of *Ledum* with *Rhododendron;* recognition of *Prunus* × *incam* for *P. campanulata* × *P. incisa* hybrids*; inclusion of Seriphidium* within *Artemisia;* following Janis Ruksans' treatment of *Crocus*, *C. ligusticus* is now considered the correct name for *C. medius* and *C. albiflorus* and *C. heuffelianus* are recognised as species rather than being included within *C. vernus*; *Prosartes* has been accepted as distinct from *Disporum*.

If there is a botanical or nomenclatural issue that you wish to bring to the attention of the editors or wish ACONAT to discuss, please contact us.

AVAILABLE FROM THE COMPILER

APPLICATION FOR ENTRY

Nurseries appearing in the *RHS Plant Finder* for the first time this year are printed in bold type in the *Nursery Index by Name* starting on p.895.

If you wish your nursery to be considered for inclusion in the next edition of the *RHS Plant Finder* (2013-2014), contact the Compiler at the address below. Entries to the book are free.

PLANTS LAST LISTED IN EARLIER EDITIONS

Plants cease to be listed for a variety of reasons. For more information turn to *How to Use the Plant Directory* on p.18. A listing of the 50,000 or so plants listed in earlier editions, but for which we currently have no known supplier, is available online at www.rhs.org.uk/rhsplantfinder/documents.asp.

LISTS OF NURSERIES FOR PLANTS WITH MORE THAN 30 SUPPLIERS

To prevent the book from becoming too big, we do not print the nursery codes where more than 30 nurseries offer the same plant. The plant is then listed as being "Widely available". This is detailed more fully in *How to Use the Plant Directory* on p.18.

If any readers have difficulty in finding such a plant, we will be pleased to send a full list of all the nurseries that we have on file as stockists. All such enquiries must include the full name of the plant being sought, as shown in the *RHS Plant Finder*, together with an A5 size SAE.

The above may be obtained from:
The Compiler, *RHS Plant Finder*, RHS Garden Wisley, Woking, Surrey GU23 6QB
Email: plantfinder@rhs.org.uk

This information is also available online.

THE RHS PLANT FINDER ONLINE

The *RHS Plant Finder* is available on the Internet. Visit the Royal Horticultural Society's website **www.rhs.org.uk** and search the *RHS Plant Finder Online.*

ACKNOWLEDGEMENTS

Judith Merrick compiled this edition with help from June Skinner and Gill Skilton. Richard Sanford managed the editing of the plant names on the database. Rupert Wilson and Julia Barclay administered the Horticultural Database, using the BG-Base™ Collection Management Software.

RHS Botanists James Armitage, Dawn Edwards, Neil Lancaster and Christopher Whitehouse have undertaken the task of editing the new plant names in this edition of the book.

As always, we are greatly indebted to Peter Cooling of Cooling Brown Ltd, for his skill in enabling us to turn our mass of raw data into a published format.

We should also like to acknowledge the contributions of Simon Maughan, Rae Spencer Jones, Diana Levy and Louise Bowering of RHS Media; John David, RHS Chief Scientist; Sharon McDonald, RHS Int. Cultivar Registrar; Deborah Chubb, RHS Hort. Informatics; Carol Sheppard, RHS Images Support Manager; Kerry Walter of BG-BASE (UK) Ltd.; Max Phillips of Strange Software Ltd.; Alan Cooper and Tony Lord.

Our colleagues on the RHS Advisory Committee on Nomenclature and Taxonomy, along with the RHS International Cultivar Registrars, have all provided valuable guidance and information. Many nurseries have supplied helpful information on plants, which has proved useful in verifying some of the more obscure names, and have suggested corrections to existing entries. Some of these remain to be checked and will be entered in the next edition, although those that contravene the Codes of Nomenclature may have to be rejected. We appreciate your patience while these checks are made. We are also grateful to all our regular correspondents and to the many readers who have made comments and suggestions.

Clematis	D. Donald, Int. Cultivar Registrar, RHS
Chrysanthemum	J. Barker (2007–08)
Conifers	S. McDonald, Int. Cultivar Registrar, RHS
Dahlia	R. Hedge, (Hon. Asst. Cultivar Registrar), S. McDonald, Int. Cultivar Registrar, RHS Wisley
Dianthus	Dr A.C. Leslie, Int. Cultivar Registrar, RHS
Heathers	Dr E.C. Nelson, Int. Cultivar Registrar
Ilex	S. Andrews (2006)
Iris	J. Hewitt (2005, 2007–08)
Lilium	D. Donald, Int. Cultivar Registrar, RHS
Meconopsis	Dr E. Stevens (2003,'05 & 2007)
Narcissus	S. McDonald, Int. Cultivar Registrar, RHS
Nerine	Dr J.C. David (2009)
Rhododendron	Dr A.C. Leslie, Int. Cultivar Registrar, RHS
Sorbus	Dr H. McAllister
Thymus	M. Easter (2003–11)
Viburnum	C. Sanders

Janet Cubey
RHS Chief of Horticultural Informatics
February 2012

Conservation and the Environment

Invasive Plants
As the *RHS Plant Finder* demonstrates, gardens in Britain have been greatly enriched by the diversity of plants introduced to cultivation from abroad. While the vast majority of those introduced have enhanced our gardens, a few have proved to be highly invasive and to threaten native habitats. Once such plants are established it is very difficult, costly and potentially damaging to native ecosystems to eradicate or control the invasive "alien" species. Gardeners can help by choosing not to buy or distribute non-native invasive plants and by taking steps to prevent them escaping into the wild and by disposing of them in a responsible way.

Ten of the most serious invasive non-native species are no longer listed in the *RHS Plant Finder*. Any cultivars or varieties of them that are listed are believed to be less invasive than the species themselves. These 10 plants are:

Azolla filiculoides – fairy fern
Crassula helmsii – New Zealand pygmy weed
Elodea nuttalli – Nuttall's waterweed
Fallopia japonica – Japanese knotweed
Heracleum mantegazzianum – giant hogweed
Hydrocotyle ranunculoides – floating pennywort
Impatiens glandulifera – Himalayan balsam
Lagarosiphon major – curly waterweed
Ludwigia grandiflora – water primrose
Myriophyllum aquaticum – parrot's feather

Further species are considered to present a threat to UK habitats and gardeners are encouraged to grow alternative plants. Guidance on this can be found in three booklets:

Gardening without harmful invasive plants
Landscaping without harmful invasive plants
Keeping ponds and aquaria without harmful invasive plants

These are available on the Plantlife website (www.plantlife.org.uk) or by post from Plantlife. For further information on non-native invasive species see the GB non-native species secretariat website (www.nonnativespecies.org)

Bringing plants back from abroad
Travelling can be a great source of inspiration for gardeners and often provides an opportunity to encounter new and interesting plants. Anyone wishing to bring plants back into Britain from overseas must realise, however, that this is a complex matter. Various regulations are in force that apply to amateur gardeners as well as to commercial nurseries. The penalties for breaking these can be serious.

Some of the most important regulatory instruments are listed below.

Plant Health regulations are in place to control the spread of pests and diseases. Plants are divided into the categories of prohibited, controlled and unrestricted, but there are also limits that vary according to the part of the world you are travelling from. For full details contact the Food and Environment Research Agency, (www.fera.defra.gov.uk/plants/plantHealth/index.cfm).

The Convention on International Trade in Endangered Species (CITES) affects the transport of animal and plant material across international boundaries. Its aim is to prevent exploitative trade and thereby to prevent harm and the ultimate extinction of wild populations. A tighter regime on trade in species of wild fauna and flora exists in the EU that requires export permits for any plants listed in Appendices A, B & C and import permits for Appendices A & B. There is a further Appendix D for non-CITES listed species that the EU consider to be endangered. A broad range of plants is covered in these Appendices, including *Cactaceae* and *Orchidaceae* and, although species are mentioned in the convention title, the restrictions cover all cultivars and hybrids of listed species too, except for specific exclusions, where there are annotations in the Appendices. Details of the plants listed in the Appendices can be found on the website of the UK's CITES Management Authority, Animal Health, (www.defra.gov.uk/animalhealth/cites/legislation.html).

The Convention on Biological Diversity (CBD or the "Rio Convention") recognises the property rights of individual countries in relation to their own biodiversity. It exists to enable access to that biodiversity, but equally to ensure the sharing of any benefit derived from it. In principle it is possible to collect plant material from other countries that have asserted their rights under the CBD, by ensuring that you have obtained documentary evidence of prior informed consent on the basis of mutually agreed terms for any uses that the material will be put to in the future. In practice the legal requirements for collecting plant material varies from country to country and it is advisable to contact the National Focal Point for further information. These details and other information on the Convention can be found on the CBD website (www.cbd.int).

European Habitats Directive. The full implementation of this Directive into UK law in 2007 extended protection to all of the European

Protected Species (EPS) listed in the Appendices of that Directive (these are Appendices II(b) and IV(b) for plants) whether they are native to the UK or not. This requires a licence for material of any of these species collected in the wild after 1994. These are issued by Natural England (for England), the Countryside Council for Wales (in Wales) and Scottish Natural Heritage (for Scotland), (www.jncc.gov.uk/page-1374).

Contact addresses:

Plantlife
14 Rollestone Street
Salisbury
Wiltshire
SP1 1DX
Tel: (01722) 342730

Wildlife Licensing and Registration Service (WRLS)
Animal Health
1/17 Temple Quay House
2 The Square
Temple Quay
Bristol
BS1 6EB
Tel: 0117 372 8774

Plant Health
Room 10GA01
The Food and Environment Research Agency
Sand Hutton
York
YO41 1LZ
Tel: (01904) 465625

Joint Nature Conservation Committee
Monkstone House
City Road
Peterborough
PE1 1JY
Tel: (01733) 562626

Department for Environment, Food & Rural Affairs (Defra)
Nobel House
17 Smith Square
London
SW1P 3JR
Email for general biodiversity queries:
biodiversity@defra.gsi.gov.uk

URBAN GREENING: MORE THAN MEETS THE EYE

Even in the busiest and most populous of western cities, a surprisingly high proportion of the surface is covered in vegetation (almost 50% in some cases). In the UK, almost half of these urban green areas consist of private gardens. Hence what we do in our gardens and how we manage them can really impact upon our environment, both positively and negatively.

Being a scientist by training, my focus is largely on establishing where clear evidence exists for the environmental benefits (and costs) of urban vegetation, more specifically in our private gardens, and where uncertainties still remain. My job is to question general assumptions about what urban green spaces (and domestic gardens in particular) do and don't do and to challenge advice given to people involved in managing any sort of green space.

In discussions of how vegetation impacts upon the environment, terms such as 'ecosystem functions' and 'ecosystem services' are frequently used. Very broadly speaking, 'ecosystem services' can be thought of as benefits that humans derive from resources and processes supplied by ecosystems. In some scientific literature, the term 'ecosystem disservice' is also used to balance the arguments and describe functions of ecosystems that are perceived as negative for human well-being.

Benefits of urban vegetation

There is very sound scientific evidence about a number of the 'services' that urban vegetation can provide. It is well established for example that vegetation moderates air temperature, helps insulate buildings against the extremes of weather and supports and enriches urban biodiversity and human health. So the common public perception that parks, street trees and green domestic spaces help lower summer temperatures locally is supported by largely unanimous scientific evidence. The scientific questions that remain lie, for example, in the need to tease out how vegetation works at various spatial scales (e.g. locally, next to an individual house, or on neighbourhood or whole-city scale) and how various 'services' provided by the vegetation can be best combined.

Less beneficial effects

On the 'disservices' side of the equation, scientific literature is quite clear that urban vegetation, in consuming water, pesticides and fertilisers, causes – directly and indirectly – carbon cost (i.e. can cause more carbon emissions than it can capture). The way our urban green spaces and private gardens are managed (i.e. how much water, energy, etc. is consumed in their management) greatly influences the level of their potential environmental benefits. That said, although some scientific literature on the environmental impact of urban vegetation deals with private gardens, the majority of the literature deals with other forms of urban greening (e.g. urban trees and forests, public green spaces, green roofs). This implies that we have to be cautious when extrapolating the information about different forms of urban vegetation.

Areas of uncertainty: the role of vegetation in reducing pollution

In addition to environmental 'services' and 'disservices' where the positive or negative role of urban vegetation is established with a high degree of certainty, there are also areas where there is significantly more scientific debate as to vegetation's true impact. One such 'service' is the role of urban vegetation in the removal of airborne pollutants, both gases and particles. The debate here becomes particularly complex as the plants themselves can, in addition to removing pollutants, also emit them in the form of so-called biogenic volatile organic compounds (BVOCs). These compounds can, through a series of reactions, form greenhouse gases which contribute to global warming. For example, most broad-leaved species from the genera *Eucalyptus, Liquidambar, Liriodendron, Populus* and *Quercus*, as well as conifers in general, are emitters of BVOCs in significant quantities. This list of species continues to expand as we acquire more knowledge about the process.

Broadly speaking, the perception of non-scientists is that plants act to clean up polluted air. Indeed, some scientific evidence supports the notion that urban trees and shrubs (particularly the species which emit only low levels of BVOCs) contribute to the removal of air pollutants (gaseous and particulate) and so improve environmental quality and human health. While the role of herbaceous garden vegetation in air pollutant removal has not been quantified specifically, extrapolations from the effects of herbaceous green-roof vegetation suggest that there could be a significant improvement in air quality above this type of vegetation compared to non-vegetated patches. This comes about because the plants reduce concentrations of gases such as ozone and sulphur dioxide and remove larger particles (≤10 mm) from the air.

Trees remove gaseous air pollutants primarily by uptake through leaf stomata (small 'pores', mostly found on the underside of leaves, which regulate water loss from, and CO^2 uptake into, the plant) but some specific issues surround urban trees. For example, urban trees are able to capture significantly less methane than rural forest but have higher capture capacity than lawns. Recent findings also suggest that relatively dense or extensive belts of vegetation may be required to elicit specific benefits, e.g. protecting housing from pollutant sources associated with arterial roadways. This implies the need to think carefully about the extent and type of vegetation used in order for it to be effective.

Trees also remove airborne particulate pollutants by interception and retention on plant surfaces. The intercepted particles can be released and re-suspended in the atmosphere, washed off by rain, or dropped to the ground with leaf fall, so this route provides only temporary retention of airborne particulate pollutants. Greater pollutant capture is recorded with a greater degree of homogeneous tree cover; therefore only gardens with multiple tree cover would provide any measurable particulate retention. Also, a longer growing season, complex foliage structure in evergreen species, hairiness of leaves and higher wind speeds are linked with better particulate retention. There is a suggestion, however, that smaller particles (≤2.5 mm), which can penetrate to the deepest parts of lungs and cause health problems, are not removed as efficiently as the larger (≤10 mm) particles.

On balance, there is a significant level of scientific uncertainty about the role of urban vegetation in air pollutant removal; this is particularly the case with domestic gardens, where there is no direct evidence available. The contribution of gardens to this 'service' will strongly depend on a garden's make-up and location, as well as local climatic influences.

Conclusion

Overall, I hope to have conveyed the message that urban vegetation systems are varied and complex but that when implemented with thought and in a site-specific manner they are able to help ameliorate many urban problems. We need to understand their complexity while retaining a critical approach in order to continue to benefit from them in the fast-changing urban environment.

Dr Tijana Blanusa
RHS Senior Horticultural Scientist

Additional Reading

Lyytimäki, J., Sipilä, M. 2009. Hopping on one leg – The challenge of ecosystem disservices for urban green management. *Urban Forestry & Urban Greening* 8(4):309–315.

Millennium Ecosystem Assessment (MEA). 2005. *Ecosystems and Human Well-Being: Synthesis.* Island Press, Washington.

Niinemets, U., Peñuelas, J. 2008. Gardening and urban landscaping: Significant players in global change. *Trends in Plant Science* 13(2):60–65.

Pataki, D.E., Carreiro, M.M., *et al.* 2011. Coupling biogeochemical cycles in urban environments: ecosystem services, green solutions, and misconceptions. *Frontiers in Ecology and the Environment* 9(1):27–36.

RHS Plant Trials Bulletins

The Trials Bulletins give the results and findings of RHS Trials. The detailed descriptions and images of the plants that have been given the Award of Garden Merit are included, as well as updates on nomenclature, cultivation details and a table comparing the different characteristics of the entries in the trial.

Begonia Rex Cultorum Group
Canna
Clematis alpina and *C. macropetala*
Dahlia
Daisies (yellow perennial)
Delphinium
Fuchsia, hardy
Geranium, hardy (Stage 1)
Geranium, hardy (Stage 2)
Geranium, hardy (Stage 3)
Hyacinthaceae (little blue bulbs)
Hydrangea paniculata
Iris, bearded
Lavandula, hardy
Miscanthus
Peppers, chilli
Peppers, sweet
Potatoes, salad
Potentilla, shrubby
Rhododendron yakushimanum and hybrids
Runner Beans
Saxifraga, silver
Sedum, herbaceous

If you would like a copy of any of these, please contact:
The Trials Office, RHS Garden Wisley, Woking, Surrey GU23 6QB. Please enclose an A4 SAE and a cheque for £2.00 per copy (as a donation towards costs) made out to the Royal Horticultural Society.

In addition to the above there are four bulletins that are only available on the RHS Website: *Caryopteris*, *Perovskia*, *Pittosporum* and *Spiraea japonica*.
To view and download any of these RHS Plant Trials Bulletins online, please visit:
www.rhs.org.uk/trials

EXTENDED GLOSSARY

This glossary combines some of the helpful introductory sections from older editions in an alphabetical listing. A fuller, more discursive account of plant names, *Guide to Plant Names*, and a detailed guide to the typography of plant names, *Recommended Style for Printing Plant Names*, are both available as RHS Advisory Leaflets. To request a copy of either please send an A4 sae to The Compiler at the contact address given on page 5.

ADVISORY COMMITTEE ON NOMENCLATURE AND TAXONOMY

This Panel advises the RHS on individual problems of nomenclature regarding plants in cultivation and, in particular, use of names in the *RHS Horticultural Database*, reflected in the annual publication of the *RHS Plant Finder*.

The aim is always to make the plant names in the *RHS Plant Finder* as consistent, reliable and stable as possible and acceptable to gardeners and botanists alike, not only in the British Isles but around the world. Recent proposals to change or correct names are examined with the aim of creating a balance between the stability of well-known names and botanical and taxonomic correctness. In some cases the Panel feels that the conflicting views on the names of some groups of plants will not easily be resolved. The Panel's policy is then to wait and review the situation once a more obvious consensus is reached, rather than rush to rename plants only to have to change them again when opinions have shifted.

The Panel is chaired by Dr Alan Leslie (RHS) with Dr Janet Cubey (RHS) (Vice-Chair) and includes: Dr Crinan Alexander (RBGE), Susyn Andrews, Chris Brickell, Dr James Compton, Dr John David (RHS), Mike Grant (RHS Publications), Dr John Grimshaw, Dr Stephen Jury (University of Reading), Dr Tony Lord, Prof David Mabberley (corresponding member, Australia), Dr Charles Nelson, Chris Sanders, Julian Shaw (attending RHS staff), with Dr Christopher Whitehouse (RHS) as Secretary.

AUTHORITIES

In order that plant names can be used with precision throughout the scientific world, the name of the person who coined the name of a plant species (its author, or authority) is added to the plant name. Usually this information is of little consequence to gardeners, except in cases where the same name has been given to two different plants or a name is commonly misapplied. Although only one usage is correct, both may be encountered in books, so indicating the author is the only way to be certain about which plant is being referred to. This can happen equally with cultivars. Authors' names, where it is appropriate to cite them, appear in a smaller typeface after the species or cultivar name to which they refer and are abbreviated following Brummitt and Powell's *Authors of Plant Names*.

🏆 AWARD OF GARDEN MERIT

The Award of Garden Merit (AGM) is intended to be of practical value to the ordinary gardener and is therefore awarded only after a period of assessment by the Society's Standing and Joint Committees. An AGM plant:

- must be available
- must be of outstanding excellence for garden decoration or use
- must be of good constitution
- must not require highly specialist growing conditions or care
- must not be particularly susceptible to any pest or disease
- must not be subject to an unreasonable degree of reversion

The AGM symbol is cited in conjunction with the **hardiness** rating. A full list of AGM plants may be found on the RHS website at www.rhs.org.uk/plants/plant-trials-and-awards/plant-awards.

The AGM plant list has, to date, been re-examined every 10 years. It is currently under review and a new list will be published in 2013.

BOTANICAL NAMES

The aim of the botanical naming system is to provide each different plant with a single, unique, universal name. The basic unit of plant classification is the species. Species that share a number of significant characteristics are grouped together to form a genus (plural **genera**). The name of a species is made up of two elements; the name of the genus followed by the specific epithet, for example, *Narcissus romieuxii*.

Variation within a species can be recognised by division into subspecies (usually abbreviated to subsp.), varietas (or variety abbreviated to var.) and forma (or form abbreviated to f.). Whilst it is unusual for a plant to have all of these, it is possible, as in this example, *Narcissus romieuxii* subsp. *albidus* var. *zaianicus* f. *lutescens*.

The botanical elements are always given in italics, with only the genus taking an initial capital letter. The rank indications are never in italics. In instances where the rank is not known it is necessary to form an invalid construction by quoting a second epithet without a rank. This is an unsatisfactory situation, but requires considerable research to resolve.

In some genera, such as *Hosta*, we list the cultivar names alphabetically with the species or **hybrid** to which they are attributed afterwards in parentheses. For example, *Hosta* 'Reversed' (*sieboldiana*). In other situations where the aim is not to create a list alphabetically by cultivar name we would recommend styling this as *Hosta sieboldiana* 'Reversed'.

Classification of Genera

Genera that include a large number of species or with many cultivars are often subdivided into informal horticultural classifications or more formal Cultivar Groups, each based on a particular characteristic or combination of characteristics. Colour of flower or fruit and shape of flower are common examples and, with fruit, whether a cultivar is grown for culinary or dessert purposes. How such groups are named differs from genus to genus.

To help users of the *RHS Plant Finder* find the plants they want, the classifications used within cultivated genera are listed using codes and plants are marked with the appropriate code in brackets after its name in the Plant Directory. To find the explanation of each code, simply look it up under the genus concerned in the **Classification of Genera** starting on p.29. The codes relating to edible fruits are also listed here, but these apply across several genera.

Collectors' References

Abbreviations (usually with numbers) following a plant name refer to the collector(s) of the plant. These abbreviations are expanded, with a collector's name or expedition title, in the section **Collectors' References** starting on p.20.

A collector's reference may indicate a new, as yet unnamed range of variation within a species. The inclusion of collectors' references in the *RHS Plant Finder* supports the book's role in sourcing unusual plants.

The Convention on Biological Diversity calls for conservation of biodiversity, its sustainable use and the fair and equitable sharing of any derived benefits. Since its adoption in 1993, collectors are required to have prior informed consent from the country of origin for the acquisition and commercialisation of collected material.

Common Names

In a work such as this, it is necessary to refer to plants by their botanical names for the sake of universal comprehension and clarity. However, at the same time we recognise that with fruit and vegetables most people are more familiar with their common names than their botanical ones. Cross-references are therefore given from common to botanical names for fruit, vegetables and the commoner culinary herbs throughout the Plant Directory.

Cultivar

Literally meaning cultivated variety, cultivar names are given to denote variation within species and that generated by hybridisation, in cultivation. To make them easily distinguishable from botanical names, they are not printed in italics and are enclosed in single quotation marks. Cultivar names coined since 1959 should follow the rules of the International Code of Nomenclature for Cultivated Plants (**ICNCP**).

Descriptive Terms

Terms that appear after the main part of the plant name are shown in a smaller font to distinguish them. These descriptive elements give extra information about the plant and may include the **collector's reference**, **authority**, or what colour it is. For example, *Clematis henryi* B&SWJ 3402, *Penstemon* 'Sour Grapes' M. Fish, *Lobelia tupa* dark orange-flowered.

Families

Genera are grouped into larger groups of related plants called families. Most family names, with the exception of eight familiar names, end with the same group of letters, *-aceae*. While it is still acceptable to use these eight exceptions, the modern trend adopted in the *RHS Plant Finder* is to use alternative names with *–aceae* endings. The families concerned are *Compositae* (*Asteraceae*), *Cruciferae* (*Brassicaceae*), *Gramineae* (*Poaceae*), *Guttiferae* (*Clusiaceae*), *Labiatae* (*Lamiaceae*), *Leguminosae* (split here into *Caesalpiniaceae*, *Mimosaceae* and *Papilionaceae*), *Palmae* (*Arecaceae*) and *Umbelliferae* (*Apiaceae*).

Apart from these exceptions we now follow (from 2010) *Mabberley's Plant Book* (3rd edition).

GENUS (plural – GENERA)

Genera used in the *RHS Plant Finder* are almost always those given in Brummitt's *Vascular Plant Families and Genera.* For spellings and genders of generic names, Greuter's *Names in Current Use for Extant Plant Genera* has also been consulted. See **Botanical Names**.

GREX

Within orchids, hybrids of the same parentage, regardless of how alike they are, are given a grex name. Individuals can be selected, given cultivar names and propagated vegetatively. For example, *Pleione* Versailles gx 'Bucklebury', where Versailles is the grex name and 'Bucklebury' is a selected **cultivar**.

GROUP

This is a collective name for a group of cultivars within a genus with similar characteristics. The word Group is always included and, where cited with a cultivar name, it is enclosed in brackets, for example, *Actaea simplex* (Atropurpurea Group) 'Brunette', where 'Brunette' is a distinct cultivar in a group of purple-leaved cultivars.

Another example of a Group is *Rhododendron polycladum* Scintillans Group. In this case *Rhododendron scintillans* was a species that is now botanically 'sunk' within *R. polycladum*, but it is still recognised horticulturally as a Group.

Group names are also used for swarms of hybrids with the same parentage, for example, *Rhododendron* Polar Bear Group. These were formerly treated as **grex** names, a term now used only for orchids. A single clone from the Group may be given the same cultivar name, for example, *Rhododendron* 'Polar Bear'.

HARDINESS

Hardiness ratings are shown for **Award of Garden Merit** plants. The categories used are as follows:

H1 = plants requiring heated glass in the British Isles

H2 = plants requiring unheated glass in the British Isles

H3 = plants hardy outside in some regions of the British Isles or in particular situations, or which, while usually grown outside in summer, need frost-free protection in winter (eg. dahlias)

H4 = plants hardy throughout the British Isles

H1-2, H2-3, H3-4 = plants intermediate between the two ratings given

H1+3 = requiring heated glass; may be grown outside in summer

To assist gardeners to determine more clearly which plants are hardy in their local area, the RHS is working towards introducing a new, enhanced, hardiness rating scheme in 2013, to coincide with the publication of the new **Award of Garden Merit** plant list.

HYBRIDS

Some species, when grown together, in the wild or in cultivation, are found to interbreed and form hybrids. In some instances a hybrid name is coined, for example hybrids between *Primula hirsuta* and *P. minima* are given the name *Primula* × *forsteri*, the multiplication sign indicating hybrid origin. Hybrid formulae that quote the parentage of the hybrid are used where a unique name has not been coined, for example *Rhododendron calophytum* × *R. praevernum*. In hybrid formulae you will find parents in alphabetical order, with the male (m) and female (f) parent indicated where known. Hybrids between different genera are also possible, for example × *Mahoberberis* is the name given to hybrids between *Mahonia* and *Berberis*.

There are also a few special-case hybrids called graft hybrids, where the tissues of two plants are physically rather than genetically mixed. These are indicated by an addition rather than a multiplication sign, so *Laburnum* + *Cytisus* becomes + *Laburnocytisus*.

ICNCP

The ICNCP is the International Code of Nomenclature for Cultivated Plants. First published in 1959, the most recent (8th) edition was published in 2009.

Cultivar names that do not conform to this Code, and for which there is no valid alternative, are flagged I (for invalid). This code states that the minimum requirement is for a cultivar name to be given in conjunction with the name of the genus. However, in the *RHS Plant Finder* we choose to give as full a name as possible to give the gardener and botanist more information about the plant, following the Recommendation in the Code.

NOTES ON NOMENCLATURE AND IDENTIFICATION

The **Notes on Nomenclature and Identification**, starting on p.24, give further information for names that are complex or may be confusing. See also **Advisory Committee on Nomenclature and Taxonomy**.

PLANT BREEDERS' RIGHTS

Plants covered by an *active* grant of Plant Breeders' Rights (PBR) are indicated throughout the Plant Directory. Grants indicated are those awarded by both UK and EU Plant Variety Rights offices. Because grants can both come into force and lapse at any time, this book can only aim to represent the situation at one point in time, but it is hoped that this will act as a useful guide to growers and gardeners. UK grants represent the position as of the end of December 2011 and EU grants as of the end of December 2011. We do not give any indication where PBR grants may be pending.

To obtain PBR protection, a new plant must be registered and pass tests for distinctness, uniformity and stability under an approved name. This approved name, under the rules of the **ICNCP**, established by a legal process, has to be regarded as the cultivar name. Increasingly however, these approved names are a code or "nonsense" name and are therefore often unpronounceable and meaningless, so the plants are given other names designed to attract sales when they are released. These secondary names are often referred to as selling names but are officially termed **trade designations**.

For further information on UK PBR contact:
Plant Variety Rights Office,
Whitehouse Lane,
Huntingdon Road,
Cambridge CB3 0LF
Tel: (01223) 342350
Website: www.fera.defra.gov.uk/plants/plantVarieties/

For details of plants covered by EU Community Rights contact:
Community Plant Variety Office (CPVO),
3 Boulevard Maréchal Foch, BP 10121,
FR-49101 Angers Cedex 02, France
Tel: 00 33 (02) 41 25 64 00
Fax: 00 33 (02) 41 25 64 10
Website: www.cpvo.europa.eu

The *RHS Plant Finder* takes no responsibility for ensuring that nurseries selling plants with PBR are licensed to do so.

Reverse Synonyms

It is likely that users of this book will come across names in certain genera that they did not expect to find. This may be because species have been transferred from another genus (or **genera**). A list of **Reverse Synonyms** is available online at www.rhs.org.uk/rhsplantfinder/documents.asp. Alternatively, a copy can be requested by sending a sae (1 × 2nd class letter stamp) to The Compiler at the address given on page 5.

Selling Names

See **Trade Designations**

Series

With seed-raised plants and some popular vegetatively-propagated plants, especially bedding plants and pot plants such as *Petunia* or *Impatiens*, Series have become increasingly popular. A Series contains a number of similar cultivars, but differs from a **Group** in that it is a marketing device, with cultivars added to create a range of flower colours in plants of similar habit. Individual colour elements within a Series may be represented by slightly different cultivars over the years.

The word Series is always included and, where cited with a cultivar name it is enclosed in brackets, for example *Aquilegia* 'Robin' (Songbird Series). The Series name usually follows the rest of the plant name, but sometimes in this book we list it before the cultivar name in order to group members of a Series together when they occur next to one another on the page.

Species

See under **Botanical Names**

Subspecies

See under **Botanical Names**

Synonyms

Although the ideal is for each species or cultivar to have only one name, anyone dealing with plants soon comes across a situation where one plant has received two or more names, or two plants have received the same name. In each case, only one name and application, for reasons of precision and stability, can be regarded as correct. Additional names are known as synonyms. Further information on synonyms and why plants change names is available in *Guide to Plant Names*. See the introduction to this glossary for details of how to request a copy.

See also **Reverse Synonyms**.

Trade Designations

A **trade designation** is the name used to market a plant when the cultivar name is considered unsuitable for selling purposes. It is styled in a different typeface and without single quotation marks.

In the case of **Plant Breeders' Rights** it is a legal requirement for the cultivar name to appear with the trade designation on a label at the point of sale. Most plants are sold under only one trade designation, but some, especially roses, are sold under a number of names, particularly when cultivars are introduced from other countries.

Usually, the correct cultivar name is the only way to ensure that the same plant is not bought unwittingly under two or more different trade designations. The *RHS Plant Finder* follows the recommendations of the **ICNCP** when dealing with trade designations and PBR. These are always to quote the cultivar name and trade designation together and to style the trade designation in a different typeface, without single quotation marks, for example *Choisya* × *dewitteana* Goldfingers = 'Limo'PBR. Here Goldfingers is the trade designation and 'Limo' is the cultivar name that has been granted **Plant Breeders' Rights**. This may also be styled in other ways, such as *Choisya* × *dewitteana* GOLDFINGERS ('Limo')PBR.

TRANSLATIONS

When a cultivar name is translated from the language of first publication, the translation is regarded as a **trade designation** and styled accordingly. We endeavour to recognise the original cultivar name in every case and to give an English translation where it is in general use.

VARIEGATED PLANTS

Following a suggestion from the Variegated Plant Group of the Hardy Plant Society, a (v) is cited after those plants which are "variegated". The dividing line between variegation and less distinct colour marking is necessarily arbitrary and plants with light veins, pale, silver or dark zones, or leaves flushed in paler colours, are not shown as being variegated unless there is an absolutely sharp distinction between paler and darker zones.

For further details of the Variegated Plant Group, please write to:

Brian Dockerill
19 Westfield Road
Glyncoch
Pontypridd
Mid-Glamorgan
CF37 3AG

VARIETY

See under **Botanical Names** and **Cultivar**

'The question of nomenclature is always a vexed one. The only thing certain is, that it is impossible to please everyone.'

W.J. BEAN – PREFACE TO FIRST EDITION OF *Trees & Shrubs Hardy in the British Isles*

HORTAX
The Horticultural Taxonomy Group

If you have an interest in the names of garden plants and wish to learn more or would like to make a comment about the International Code of Nomenclature for Cultivated Plants (ICNCP) visit the HORTAX website: www.hortax.org.uk

SYMBOLS AND ABBREVIATIONS

SYMBOLS APPEARING TO THE LEFT OF THE NAME

*	Name not validated. Not listed in the appropriate International Registration Authority checklist nor in works cited in the Bibliography. For fuller discussion see p.11
I	Invalid name. See *International Code of Botanical Nomenclature 2006* and *International Code of Nomenclature for Cultivated Plants 2009*. For fuller discussion see p.11
N	Refer to Notes on Nomenclature and Identification on p.24
§	Plant listed elsewhere in the Plant Directory under a synonym
×	Hybrid genus
+	Graft hybrid genus

SYMBOLS APPEARING TO THE RIGHT OF THE NAME

✿	Plant Heritage (NCCPG) National Plant Collection® exists for all or part of this genus. Provisional Collections appear in brackets. Full details of the Plant Heritage Collections are found in the *2011 National Plant Collections® Directory* available from: www.plantheritage.com or Plant Heritage, 12 Home Farm, Loseley Park, Guildford, Surrey GU3 1HS
♀H4	The Royal Horticultural Society's Award of Garden Merit, see p.11
(d)	double-flowered
(F)	Fruit
(f)	female
(m)	male
(v)	variegated plant, see p.15
PBR	Plant Breeders Rights see p.13
new	New plant entry in this edition

For abbreviations relating to individual genera see **Classification of Genera** p.29

For **Collectors' References** see p.20

For symbols used in the **Nurseries** section see p.801

SYMBOLS AND ABBREVIATIONS USED AS PART OF THE NAME

×	hybrid species
aff.	affinis (akin to)
agg.	aggregate, a single name used to cover a group of very similar plants, regarded by some as separate species
ambig.	ambiguous, a name used by two authors for different plants and where it is unclear which is being offered
cf.	compare to
cl.	clone
f.	forma (botanical form)
gx	grex
sensu lato	in the broadest sense
sp.	species
subsp.	subspecies
subvar.	subvarietas (botanical subvariety)
var.	varietas (botanical variety)

It is not within the remit of this book to check that nurseries are applying the right names to the right plants or to ensure nurseries selling plants with Plant Breeders' Rights are licensed to do so.

Please, never use an out of date edition

PLANTS

WHATEVER PLANT YOU ARE LOOKING FOR, MAYBE AN OLD FAVOURITE OR A MORE UNUSUAL CULTIVAR, SEARCH HERE FOR A LIST OF THE SUPPLIERS THAT ARE CLOSEST TO YOU.

How to Use the Plant Directory

Nursery Codes

Look up the plant you require in the alphabetical Plant Directory. Against each plant you will find one or more four-letter codes, for example WCru, each code represents one nursery offering that plant. The first letter of each code indicates the main area of the country in which the nursery is situated. For this geographical key, refer to the **Nursery Codes and Symbols** on p.800.

Turn to the **Nursery Details by Code** starting on p.804 where, in alphabetical order of codes, you will find details of each nursery which offers the plant in question. If you wish to visit any nursery, you may find its location on one of the maps (following p.901). Please note, however, that not all nurseries, especially mail order only nurseries, choose to be shown on the maps. For a fuller explanation of how to use the nursery listings please turn to p.801. **Always check that the nursery you select has the plant in stock before you set out.**

Plants with more than 30 Suppliers

In some cases, against the plant name you will see the term 'Widely available' instead of a nursery code. If we were to include every plant listed by all nurseries, the *RHS Plant Finder* would become unmanageably bulky. We therefore ask nurseries to restrict their entries to those plants that are not already well represented. As a result, if more than 30 nurseries offer any plant the Directory gives no nursery codes and the plant is listed instead as being 'Widely available'.

You should have little difficulty in locating these in local nurseries or garden centres. However, if you are unable to find such plants, we will be pleased to send a full list of all the nurseries that we have on file as stockists. To obtain a list, please see the Introduction on p.4 or go to www.rhs.org.uk/rhsplantfinder/.

Finding Fruit, Vegetables and Herbs

You will need to search for these by their botanical names. Common names are cross-referenced to their botanical names in the Plant Directory.

If you have Difficulty Finding your Plant

If you cannot immediately find the plant you seek, look through the various species of the genus. You may be using an incomplete name. The problem is most likely to arise in very large genera such as *Phlox* where there are a number of possible species, each with a large number of cultivars. A search through the whole genus may well bring success. Please note that, for space reasons, the following are not listed in the Plant Directory: annuals, orchids, except hardy terrestrial orchids; cacti, except hardy cacti.

Cross-references

It may be that the plant name you seek is a synonym. Our intention is to list nursery codes only against the correct botanical name. Where you find a synonym you will be cross-referred to the correct name. Occasionally you may find that the correct botanical name to which you have been referred is not listed. This is because it was last listed in an earlier edition as explained below.

Plants Last Listed in Earlier Editions

It may be that the plant you are seeking has no known suppliers and is thus not listed.

The loss of a plant name from the Directory may arise for a number of reasons – the supplier may have gone out of business, or may not have responded to our latest questionnaire and has therefore been removed from the book. Such plants may well be still available but we have no current knowledge of their whereabouts. Alternatively, some plants may have been misnamed by nurseries in previous editions, but are now appearing under their correct name.

To obtain a listing of plants last listed in earlier editions please see the Introduction on p.4 or go to our website where it is available as a pdf.

Please, never use an out of date edition

USING THE PLANT DIRECTORY

The main purpose of the Plant Directory is to help the reader correctly identify the plant they seek and find its stockist. Each nursery has a unique identification code which appears to the right of the plant name. Turn to Nursery Details by Code on p.804 for the address, opening times and other details of the nursery. The first letter of each nursery code denotes its geographical region. Turn to the map on p.800 to find your region code and then identify the nurseries in your area.

Another purpose of the Directory is to provide more information about the plant through the symbols and other information. For example, if it has an alternative names, is new to this edition or has received the RHS Award of Garden Merit.

Euonymus (*Celastraceae*)

	B&L 12543	EPla EWes
	B&SWJ 4457	WPGP
	CC 4522	CPLG
	alatus ♀H4	Widely available
	- B&SWJ 8794	WCru
	- var. ***apterus***	EPfP
	- Chicago Fire	see *E. alatus* 'Timber Creek'
	- 'Ciliodentatus'	see *E. alatus* 'Compactus'
§	- 'Compactus' ♀H4	Widely available
§	- 'Fire Ball'	EPfP
	- Little Moses = 'Odom'	MBlu
*	- 'Macrophyllus'	EPfP
	- 'Rudy Haag'	CPMA EPfP
	- 'Select'	see *E. alatus* 'Fire Ball'
	- 'Silver Cloud' **new**	EPfP
§	- 'Timber Creek'	CPMA EPfP MBlu MBri NLar
	americanus	EPfP GIBF MBlu NLar
	- 'Evergreen' **new**	EPfP
	- narrow-leaved	EPfP NLar
	atropurpureus	EPfP
	'Benkomoki' **new**	MGos
	bungeanus	CMCN EPfP EPla NLar
	- 'Dart's Pride'	CPMA EPfP NLar
	- 'Fireflame'	EPfP NLar
*	- var. ***mongolicus***	EPfP
	- 'Pendulus'	EPfP MBlu SIFN
	- var. ***semipersistens***	CPMA EPla
	carnosus	EPfP NLar
	'Copper Wire'	EMil SPoG
	cornutus var. ***quinquecornutus***	CPMA EPfP LPan MBlu NBhm NLar SIFN SPoG WPGP WPat
	'Den Haag'	EPfP MBri
	echinatus	EPfP EPla
	- BL&M 306	SLon
	europaeus	Widely available
	- f. ***albus***	CPMA CTho EPfP LTwo NLar
	- 'Atropurpureus'	CMCN CTho EPfP MBlu MBri NLar SIFN
	- 'Atrorubens'	CPMA
	- 'Aucubifolius' (v)	EPfP
*	- 'Aureus'	CNat
	- 'Brilliant' **new**	EPfP
*	- f. ***bulgaricus***	EPfP
	- 'Chrysophyllus'	EPfP MBlu NLar
	- 'Howard'	EPfP
	- var. ***intermedius***	ENot EPfP MAsh MBlu NLar
	- 'Miss Pinkie'	CEnd CMCN
	- 'Pumilis' **new**	EPfP
	- 'Red Cascade' ♀H4	Widely available
	- 'Scarlet Wonder'	CPMA EPfP MBri NLar
	- 'Thornhayes'	CTho EPfP
I	- 'Variegatus' **new**	EPfP
	farreri	see *E. nanus*
	fimbriatus	EPfP
	fortunei Blondy = 'Interbolwi'PBR (v)	Widely available

ABBREVIATIONS
To save space a dash indicates that the previous heading is repeated. If written out in full the name would be Euonymus alatus *'Fire Ball'.*

NEW
Plant new to this edition.

DESCRIPTIVE TERM
See p.12.

SYMBOLS TO THE LEFT OF THE NAME
Provides information about the name of the plant. See p.16 for the key.

SYMBOLS TO THE RIGHT OF THE NAME
Tells you more about the plant itself, e.g. (v) *indicates that the plant is variegated,* (F) *= fruit. See p.16 for the key.*

SELLING NAMES
See p.14.

♀H4
This plant has received the RHS Award of Garden Merit. See p.11.

CROSS-REFERENCES
Directs you to the correct name of the plant and the nursery codes. See p.18.

NURSERY CODE
A unique code identifying each nursery. Turn to p.804 for details of the nurseries.

WIDELY AVAILABLE
Indicates that more than 30 Plant Finder nurseries supply the plant, and it may be available locally. See p.18.

PBR
Plant Breeders' Rights. See p.13.

SUPPLEMENTARY KEYS TO THE DIRECTORY

COLLECTORS' REFERENCES

Abbreviations following a plant name, refer to the collector(s) of the plant. These abbreviations are expanded below, with a collector's name or expedition title. For a fuller explanation, see p.12.

A&JW	Watson, A. & J.
A&L	Ala, A. & Lancaster, Roy
AB&S	Archibald, James; Blanchard, John W. & Salmon, M.
AC	Clark, Alan J.
AC&H	Apold, J.; Cox, Peter & Hutchison, Peter
AC&W	Albury; Cheese, M. & Watson, J.M.
ACE	AGS Expedition to China (1994)
ACL	Leslie, Alan C.
AER	Robinson, Allan
AGS/ES	AGS Expedition to Sikkim (1983)
AGSJ	AGS Expedition to Japan (1988)
AH	Hoog, A.
AIM	Avent, Tony Mexico (1994)
Airth	Airth, Murray
Akagi	Akagi Botanical Garden
AL&JS	Sharman, Joseph L. & Leslie, Alan C.
APA	Cox, K.; Hootman, S.; Hudson, T.; et al, Expedition to Arunchal Pradesh (2005)
ARG	Argent, G.C.G.
ARGS	Alaska Rock Garden Society trip to China
ARJA	Ruksans, J. & Siesums, A.
B	Blanchard, John
B&F MA	Brown, Robert & Fisher, Rif & Middle Atlas (2007)
B L.	Beer, Len
B&L	Brickell, Christopher D. & Leslie, Alan C.
B&M & BM	Brickell, Christopher D. & Mathew, Brian
B&S	Bird P. & Salmon M.
B&SWJ	Wynn-Jones, Bleddyn & Susan
B&V	Burras, K. & Vosa, C.G.
BB	Bartholomew, B.
BC	Chudziak, W.
BC&W	Beckett; Cheese, M. & Watson, J.M.
Beavis	Beavis, Derek S.
Berry	Berry, P.
Berry & Brako	Berry, P. & Brako, Lois
BKBlount	Blount, B.K.
BL&M	University of Bangor Expedition to NE Nepal
BM	Mathew, Brian F.
BM&W	Binns, David L.; Mason, M. & Wright, A.
BOA	Boardman, P.
Breedlove	Breedlove, D.
BR	Rushbrooke, Ben
BS	Smith, Basil
BSBE	Bowles Scholarship Botanical Expedition (1963)
BSSS	Crûg Expedition, Jordan (1991)
Bu	Bubert, S.
Burtt	Burtt, Brian L.
BWJ	Wynn-Jones, Bleddyn
C	Cole, Desmond T.
C&C	Cox, P.A. & Cox, K.N.E.
C&Cu	Cox, K.N.E. & Cubey, J.
C&H	Cox, Peter & Hutchison, Peter
C&K	Chamberlain & Knott
C&R	Christian & Roderick
C&S	Clark, Alan & Sinclair, Ian W.J.
C&V	K.N.E. Cox & Vergera, S.
C&W	Cheese, M. & Watson, J.M.
CC	Chadwell, Christopher
CC&H	Chamberlain, David F.; Cox, Peter & Hutchison, P.
CC&McK	Chadwell, Christopher & McKelvie, A.
CC&MR	Chadwell, Christopher & Ramsay
CCH&H	Chamberlain, D.F.; Cox, P.; Hutchison, P. & Hootman, S.
CCH&H	Chamberlain, Cox, Hootman & Hutchison
CD&R	Compton, J.; D'Arcy, J. & Rix, E.M.
CDB	Brickell, Christopher D.
CDC	Coode, Mark J.E.; Dockrill, Alexander
CDC&C	Compton; D'Arcy; Christopher & Coke
CDPR	Compton; D'Arcy; Pope & Rix
CE&H	Christian, P.J.; Elliott & Hoog
CEE	Chengdu Edinburgh Expedition China (1991)
CGG	Glendoick Gardens Expedition to Guizou (2009)
CGV	Vosa, Canio

CGW	Grey-Wilson, Christopher
CH	Christian, P. & Hoog, A.
CH&M	Cox, P.; Hutchison, P. & Maxwell-MacDonald, D.
CHP&W	Kashmir Botanical Expedition
CL	Lovell, Chris
CLD	Chungtien, Lijiang & Dali Exped. China (1990)
CM&W	Cheese M.; Mitchel J. & Watson, J.
CN&W	Clark; Neilson & Wilson
CNDS	Nelson, C. & Sayers D.
Cooper	Cooper, R.E.
Cox	Cox, Peter A.
CPC	Cobblewood Plant Collection
CPN	Compton, James
CS	Stapleton, Christopher
CSE	Cyclamen Society Expedition (1990)
CT	Teune, Carla
CWJ	Colley, Finlay; Wynn-Jones, Bleddyn, Taiwan (2007)
Dahl	Dahl, Sally
DBG	Denver Botanic Garden, Colorado
DC	Cheshire, David
DF	Fox, D.
DG	Green, D.
DHTU	Hinkley, D.; Turkey (2000)
DJH	Hinkley, Dan
DJHC	Hinkley, China
DJHV	Hinkley, Dan, Vietnam
DM	Millais, David
Doleshy	Doleshy, F.L.
DS&T	Drake, Sharman J. & Thompson
DWD	Rose, D.
DZ	Zummell, D.
ECN	Nelson, E. Charles
EDHCH	Hammond, Eric D.
EGM	Millais, T.
EKB	Balls, Edward K.
EM	East Malling Research Station
EMAK	Edinburgh Makalu Expedition (1991)
EMR	Rix, E.Martyn
EN	Needham, Edward F.
ENF	Fuller, E. Nigel
ETE	Edinburgh Taiwan Expedition (1993)
ETOT	Kirkham, T.S.; Flanagan, Mark
F	Forrest, G.
F&M	Fernandez & Mendoza, Mexico
F&W	Watson, J. & Flores, A.
Farrer	Farrer, Reginald
FK	Kinmonth, Fergus W.
FMB	Bailey, F.M.
G	Gardner, Martin F.
G&K	Gardner, Martin F. & Knees, Sabina G.
G&P	Gardner, Martin F. & Page, Christopher N.
GDJ	Dumont, Gerard
GG	Gusman, G.
GS	Sherriff, George
Green	Green, D.
Guitt	Guittoneau, G.G.
Guiz	Guizhou Expedition (1985)
GWJ	Goddard, Sally; Wynne-Jones, Bleddyn & Susan
G-W&P	Grey-Wilson, Christopher & Phillips
H	Huggins, Paul
H&B	Hilliard, Olive M. & Burtt, Brian L.
H&D	Howick, C. & Darby
H&M	Howick, Charles & McNamara, William A.
H&W	Hedge, Ian C. & Wendelbo, Per W.
Harry Smith	Smith, K.A.Harry
Hartside	Hartside Nursery
HCM	Heronswood Expedition to Chile (1998)
HECC	Hutchison; Evans; Cox, P.; Cox, K.
HEHEHE	Zetterlund, H. et al, Gothenburg Botanic Gardens Expedition to northern China
Hird	Hird
HH&K	Hannay, S & S & Kingsbury, N.
HLMS	Springate, L.S.
HM&S	Halliwell, B.; Mason, D. & Smallcombe
HOA	Hoog, Anton
Hummel	Hummel, D.
HW&E	Wendelbo, Per; Hedge, I. & Ekberg, L.
HWEL	Hirst, J.Michael; Webster, D.
HWJ	Crûg Heronswood Joint Expedition
HWJCM	Crûg Heronswood Expedition
HWJK	Crûg Heronswood Expedition, East Nepal (2002)
HZ	Zetterlund, Henrik
ICE	Instituto de Investigaciónes Ecológicas Chiloé & RBGE
IDS	International Dendrological Society
ISI	Int. Succulent Introductions
J&JA	Archibald, James & Jennifer
J. Jurasek	Jurasek, J.
JCA	Archibald, James
JE	Jack Elliott
JJ	Jackson, J.
JJ&JH	Halda, J. & Halda, J.
JJH	Halda, Joseph J.
JLS	Sharman, J.L.
JM-MK	Mahr, J.; Kammerlander, M.
JMT	Mann Taylor, J.
JN	Nielson, Jens
JR	Russell, J.
JRM	Marr, John
JW	Watson, J.M.
K	Kirkpatrick, George
K&LG	Gillanders, Kenneth & Gillanders, L.
K&Mc	Kirkpatrick, George & McBeath, Ronald J.D.
K&P	Josef Kopec & Milan Prasil
K&T	Kurashige, Y. & Tsukie, S.
KC	Cox, Kenneth
KEKE	Kew/Edinburgh Kanchenjunga Expedition (1989)
KGB	Kunming/Gothenburg Botanical Expedition (1993)

KM	Marsh, K.
KR	Rushforth, K.D.
KRW	Wooster, K.R. (distributed after his death by Kath Dryden)
KW	Kingdon-Ward, F.
KWJ	Crûg-World of Ferns Joint Expedition, Vietnam (2007)
L	Lancaster, C. Roy
L&S	Ludlow, Francis & Sherriff, George
LA	Long Ashton Research Station clonal selection scheme
LB	Bird P.; Salmon, M.
LEG	Lesotho Edinburgh/Gothenburg Expedition (1997)
Lismore	Lismore Nursery, Breeder's Number
LM&S	Leslie, Mattern & Sharman
LP	Palmer, W.J.L.
LS&E	Ludlow, Frank; Sherriff, George & Elliott, E. E.
LS&H	Ludlow, Frank; Sherriff, George & Hicks, J. H.
LS&T	Ludlow, Frank; Sherriff, George & Taylor, George
M&PS	Mike & Polly Stone
M&T	Mathew & Tomlinson
Mac&W	McPhail & Watson
McB	McBeath, R.J.D.
McLaren	McLaren, H.D.
MDM	Myers, Michael D.
MECC	Scottish Rock Garden Club, Nepal (1997)
MESE	Alpine Garden Society Expedition, Greece (1999)
MF	Foster, Maurice
MH	Heasman, Matthew T.
MK	Kammerlander, Michael
MP	Pavelka, Mojmir
MPF	Frankis, M.P.
MS	Salmon, M.
MS&CL	Salmon, M. & Lovell, C.
MSF	Fillan, M.S.
NAPE	Hootman, S.; et al, Expedition to Naglaland and Arunachal Pradesh (2003)
NICE	North India Expedition (1997)
NJM	Macer, N.J.
NN	Nielsen & Nielsen (2009)
NNS	Ratko, Ron
NS	Turland, Nick
NVD	Expedition to Vietnam
NVFDE	Northern Vietnam First Darwin Expedition
Og	Ogisu, Mikinori
OS	Sonderhousen, O.
P. Bon	Bonavia, P.
P&C	Paterson, David S. & Clarke, Sidney
P&W	Polastri & Watson, J. M.
PAB	Barney, P.A.
PB	Bird, Peter
PC&H	Pattison, G.; Catt, P. & Hickson, M.
PD	Davis, Peter H.
PF	Furse, Paul
PJC	Christian, Paul J.
PJC&AH	P.J. Christian & A. Hogg
PNMK	Nicholls, P.; Kammerlander, M.
Polunin	Polunin, Oleg
Pras	Prasil, M.
PS&W	Polunin, Oleg; Sykes, William & Williams, John
PW	Wharton, Peter
R	Rock, J.F.C.
RB	Brown, R.
RBS	Brown, Ray, Sakharin Island
RCB AM	Brown, Robert, Expedition to Armenia
RCB/Arg	Brown, Robert, Argentina, (2002)
RCB E	Brown, Robert, Expedition to Spain (Andalucia)
RCB/Eq	Brown, Robert, Ecuador, (1988)
RCB RA	Brown, Robert
RCB RL	Brown, Robert, Expedition to Lebanon
RCB/TQ	Brown, Robert, Turkey (2001)
RE	Evans, Ron
RH	Hancock, R.
RKMP	Ruksans, J.; Krumins, A.; Kitts, M.; Paivel, A.
RM	Ruksans, J. & Kitts, M.
RMRP	Rocky Mountain Rare Plants, Denver, Colorado
RS	Suckow, Reinhart
RSC	Richard Somer Cocks
RV	Richard Valder
RWJ	Crûg Farm-Rickards Ferns Expedition to Taiwan (2003)
S&B	Blanchard, J.W. & Salmon, M.
S&F	Salmon, M. & Fillan, M.
S&L	Sinclair, Ian W.J. & Long, David G.
S&SH	Sheilah & Spencer Hannay
Sandham	Sandham, John
SB&L	Salmon, Bird & Lovell
SBEC	Sino-British Expedition to Cangshan
SBEL	Sino-British Lijiang Expedition
SBQE	Sino-British Expedition to Quinghai
Sch	Schilling, Anthony D.
SD	Sashal Dayal
SDR	Rankin, Stella & David
SEH	Hootman, Steve
SEP	Swedish Expedition to Pakistan
SF	Forde, P.
SG	Salmon, M. & Guy, P.
SH	Hannay, Spencer
Sich	Simmons, Erskine, Howick & Mcnamara
SJ	Johansson, Stellan
SLIZE	Swedish-Latvian-Iranian Zagros Expedition to Iran (May 1988)
SOJA	Kew/Quarryhill Expedition to Southern Japan

SS&W	Stainton, J.D. Adam; Sykes, William & Williams, John
SSNY	Sino-Scottish Expedition to NW Yunnan (1992)
T	Taylor, Nigel P.
T&K	Taylor, Nigel P. & Knees, Sabina
TH	Hudson, T.
TS&BC	Smythe, T. & Cherry, B.
TSS	Spring Smyth, T.L.M.
TW	Tony Weston
USDAPI	US Department of Agriculture Plant Index Number
USDAPQ	US Dept. of Agriculture Plant Quarantine Number
USNA	United States National Arboretum
VHH	Vernon H. Heywood
VV	Victor, David
W	Wilson, Ernest H.
WM	McLewin, William
Woods	Woods, Patrick J.B.
Wr	Wraight, David & Anke
WWJ	Wharton, Peter; Wynn-Jones, Bleddyn & Susan
Yu	Yu, Tse-tsun

Notes on Nomenclature and Identification

These notes refer to plants in the Plant Directory that are marked with a 'N' to the left of the name. 'Bean Supplement' refers to W.J. Bean *Trees & Shrubs Hardy in the British Isles* (Supplement to the 8th edition) edited by D L Clarke 1988.

***Acer davidii* 'Ernest Wilson' and *A. davidii* 'George Forrest'**
These cultivars should be grafted in order to retain the characteristics of the original clones. However, many plants offered under these names are seed-raised.

***Acer palmatum* 'Sango-kaku' / 'Senkaki'**
Two or more clones are offered under these names. *A. palmatum* 'Eddisbury' is similar with brighter coral stems.

***Achillea ptarmica* The Pearl Group / *A. ptarmica* (The Pearl Group) 'Boule de Neige' / *A. ptarmica* (The Pearl Group) 'The Pearl'**
In a past trial of achilleas at Wisley, only one of the several stocks submitted as 'The Pearl' matched the original appearance of this plant according to Graham Stuart Thomas, this being from Wisley's own stock. At rather less than 60cm (2ft), this needed little support, being the shortest of the plants bearing this name, with slightly grey, not glossy dark green, leaves and a non-invasive habit. This has been designated as the nomenclatural standard for this cultivar and only this clone should bear the cultivar name 'The Pearl'. The Pearl Group covers all other double-flowered clones of this species, including seed-raised plants which are markedly inferior, sometimes scarcely double, often invasive and usually needing careful staking. It has been claimed that 'The Pearl' was a re-naming of Lemoine's 'Boule de Neige' but not all authorities agree: all plants submitted to the Wisley trial as 'Boule de Neige' were different from each other, not the same clone as Wisley's 'The Pearl' and referrable to The Pearl Group.

***Anemone nemorosa* 'Alba Plena'**
This name is used for several double white forms including *A. nemorosa* 'Flore Pleno' and *A. nemorosa* 'Vestal'.

***Artemisia ludoviciana* subsp. *ludoviciana* var. *latiloba* / *A. ludoviciana* 'Valerie Finnis'**
Leaves of the former are glabrous at maturity, those of the latter are not.

***Artemisia stelleriana* 'Boughton Silver'**
This was thought to be the first validly published name for this plant, 'Silver Brocade' having been published earlier but invalidly in an undated publication. However, an earlier valid publication for the cultivar name 'Mori' has subsequently been found for the same plant. A proposal to conserve 'Boughton Silver' has been tabled because of its more widespread use.

***Aster amellus* Violet Queen**
It is probable that more than one cultivar is sold under this name.

Aster dumosus
Many of the asters listed under *A. novi-belgii* contain varying amounts of *A. dumosus* blood in their parentage. It is not possible to allocate these to one species or the other and they are therefore listed under *A. novi-belgii.*

***Aster* × *frikartii* 'Mönch'**
The true plant is very rare in British gardens. Most plants are another form of *A.* × *frikartii*, usually 'Wunder von Stäfa'.

Aster novi-belgii
See note under *A. dumosus*. *A. laevis* is also involved in the parentage of most cultivars.

***Berberis buxifolia* 'Nana' misapplied / 'Pygmaea'**
See explanation in Bean Supplement.

Brachyscome
Originally published as *Brachyscome* by Cassini who later revised his spelling to *Brachycome*. The original spelling has been internationally adopted.

***Calamagrostis* × *acutiflora* 'Karl Foerster'**
C. × *acutiflora* 'Stricta' differs in being 15cm taller, 10–15 days earlier flowering with a less fluffy inflorescence.

Calceolaria integrifolia sensu lato
Christine Ehrhart (*Systematic Botany*. (2005. 30(2):383–411) has demonstrated that this is a complex involving nine distinct species (*C. andina*, *C. angustifolia*, *C. auriculata*, *C. georgiana*, *C. integrifolia sensu stricto*, *C. rubiginosa*, *C. talcana*, *C. verbascifolia* and *C. viscosissima*). However, it is not yet clear to which species plants in cultivation belong or whether they are hybrids.

Caltha polypetala
This name is often applied to a large-flowered variant of *C. palustris*. The true species has more (7–10) petals.

***Camassia leichtlinii* 'Alba'**
The true cultivar has blueish-white, not cream flowers.

***Camassia leichtlinii* 'Plena'**
This has starry, transparent green-white flowers; creamy-white 'Semiplena' is sometimes offered under this name.

***Campanula lactiflora* 'Alba'**
This refers to the pure white-flowered clone, not to blueish- or greyish-white flowered plants, nor to seed-raised plants.

Canna
Species names marked 'N' are among those sometimes included within *Canna indica* L. See *Blumea* 53:247–318 for a complete list.

***Carex morrowii* 'Variegata'**
C. oshimensis 'Evergold' is sometimes sold under this name.

Carya illinoinensis
The correct spelling of this name is discussed in *Baileya*, 10(1) (1962).

Cassinia retorta
Now included within *C. leptophylla*. A valid infraspecific epithet has yet to be published.

***Ceanothus* 'Italian Skies'**
Many plants under this name are not true to name.

***Chamaecyparis lawsoniana* 'Columnaris Glauca'**
Plants under this name might be *C. lawsoniana* 'Columnaris' or a new invalidly named cultivar.

Clematis chrysocoma
The true *C. chrysocoma* is a non-climbing erect plant with dense yellow down on the young growth, still uncommon in cultivation.

Clematis montana
This name should be used for the typical white-flowered variety only. Pink-flowered variants are referable to *C. montana* var. *rubens*.

***Clematis* 'Victoria'**
Raised by Cripps (1867). There is also a Latvian cultivar of this name with petals with a central white bar in the collection of Janis Ruplēns which is probably, though not certainly, of his own raising.

***Colchicum* 'Autumn Queen'**
Entries here might refer to the slightly different *C.* 'Prinses Astrid'.

***Cornus* 'Norman Hadden'**
See note in Bean Supplement, p.184.

Cotoneaster dammeri
Plants sold under this name are usually *C. dammeri* 'Major'.

***Cotoneaster frigidus* 'Cornubia'**
According to Hylmø this cultivar, like all other variants of this species, is fully deciduous. Several evergreen cotoneasters are also grown under this name; most are clones of *C.* × *watereri* or *C. salicifolius*.

Crataegus coccinea
C. intricata, *C. pedicellata* and *C. biltmoreana* are occasionally supplied under this name.

***Crocus cartwrightianus* 'Albus'**
The plant offered is the true cultivar and not *C. hadriaticus*.

***Dianthus* fringed pink**
D. 'Old Fringed Pink' and *D.* 'Old Fringed White' are also sometimes sold under this name.

***Dianthus* 'Musgrave's Pink' (p)**
This is the registered name of this white-flowered cultivar.

***Epilobium glabellum* misapplied**
Plants under this name are not *E. glabellum* but are close to *E. wilsonii* Petrie or perhaps a hybrid of it.

Erodium glandulosum
Plants under this name are often hybrids.

Erodium guttatum
Doubtfully in commerce; plants under this name are usually *E. heteradenum*, *E. cheilanthifolium* or hybrids.

***Fagus sylvatica* Atropurpurea Group / Cuprea Group**
It is desirable to provide a name, Cuprea Group, for less richly coloured forms, used in historic landscapes before the purple clones appeared.

***Fagus sylvatica* 'Pendula'**
This name refers to the Knap Hill clone, the most common weeping form in English gardens. Other clones occur, particularly in Cornwall and Ireland.

Fuchsia loxensis
For a comparison of the true species with the hybrids 'Speciosa' and 'Loxensis' commonly grown under this name, see Boullemier's Check List (2nd ed.) p.268.

***Geum* 'Borisii'**
This name refers to cultivars of *G. coccineum* Sibthorp & Smith, especially *G.* 'Werner Arends' and not to *G.* × *borisii* Kelleper.

Halimium halimifolium
Plants under this name are sometimes *H.* × *pauanum* or *H.* × *santae*.

***Hebe* 'Carl Teschner'**
See note in Bean Supplement, p.264.

***Hedera helix* 'Caenwoodiana' / 'Pedata'**
Some authorities consider these to be distinct cultivars while others think them different morphological forms of the same unstable clone.

***Hedera helix* 'Oro di Bogliasco'**
Priority between this name and 'Jubiläum Goldherz' and 'Goldheart' has yet to be finally resolved.

***Hedychium* 'Tara'**
The attribution of this cultivar to *H.* × *moorei* or *H. coccineum* is currently under discussion.

***Helleborus* × *hybridus* / *H. orientalis* misapplied**
The name *H.* × *hybridus* for acaulescent hellebore hybrids does not seem to follow the *International Code of Botanical Nomenclature* Article H.3.2 requiring one of the parent species to be designated and does not seem to have been typified, contrary to Article 7 of the Code. However, the illustration accompanying the original description in Vilmorin's *Blumengärtnerei* 3(1): 27 (1894) shows that one parent of the cross must have been *H. guttatus*, now treated as part of *H. orientalis*. Taking this illustration as the type for this hybrid species makes it possible to retain *H.* × *hybridus* formally as a hybrid binomial (rather than *H. hybridus* as in a previous edition), as the Code's requirement to distinguish one parent is now met.

***Hemerocallis fulva* 'Kwanso', 'Kwanso Variegata', 'Flore Pleno' and 'Green Kwanso'**
For a discussion of these plants see *The Plantsman*, 7(2).

***Heuchera villosa* 'Palace Purple'**
This cultivar name refers only to plants with deep purple-red foliage. Seed-raised plants of inferior colouring should not be offered under this name.

Hosta montana
This name refers only to plants long grown in Europe, which differ from *H. elata*.

***Hydrangea macrophylla* Teller Series**
This is used both as a descriptive common name for Lacecap hydrangeas (German *teller* = plate, referring to the more or less flat inflorescence) and for the series of hybrids raised by Wädenswil in Switzerland bearing German names of birds. It is not generally possible to link a hydrangea described by the series name plus a colour description (e.g. Teller Blau, Teller Rosa, Teller Rot) to a single cultivar.

Hypericum fragile
The true *H. fragile* is probably not available from British nurseries.

Ilex* × *altaclerensis
The argument for this spelling is given by Susyn Andrews, *The Plantsman*, 5(2) and is not superseded by the more recent comments in the Supplement to Bean's Trees and Shrubs.

***Iris histrioides* 'Major'**
Two clones are offered under this name, the true one pale blue with darker spotting on the falls, the incorrect one violet-blue with almost horizontal falls.

Juniperus* × *media
This name is illegitimate if applied to hybrids of *J. chinensis* × *J. sabina*, having been previously used for a different hybrid (P.A. Schmidt, *IDS Yearbook 1993*, 47–48). Because of its importance to gardeners, a proposal to conserve its present use was tabled but subsequently rejected.

Lavandula spica
This name is classed as a name to be rejected (*nomen rejiciendum*) by the *International Code of Botanical Nomenclature*.

Lavatera olbia* and *L. thuringiaca
Although *L. olbia* is usually shrubby and *L. thuringiaca* usually herbaceous, both species are very variable. Cultivars formerly ascribed to one species or the other have been shown to be hybrids and are referable to the recently-named hybrid species *L.* × *clementii*.

***Lobelia* 'Russian Princess'**
This name, originally for a pink-flowered, green-leaved cultivar, is now generally applied to a purple-flowered, dark-leaved cultivar that seems to lack a valid name.

***Lonicera periclymenum* 'Serotina'**
See note in Bean Supplement, p.315.

Lonicera sempervirens* f. *sulphurea
Plants in the British Isles usually a yellow-flowered form of *L. periclymenum*.

***Malus domestica* 'Dummellor's Seedling'**
The phonetic spelling 'Dumelow's Seedling' contravenes the ICBN ruling on orthography, i.e. that, except for intentional latinisations, commemorative names should be based on the original spelling of the person's name (Article 60.11). The spelling adopted here is that used on the gravestone of the raiser in Leicestershire.

***Meconopsis* Fertile Blue Group**
This Group comprises seed-raised and intrinsically perennial tall blue poppies of as yet indeterminate origin.

***Meconopsis napaulensis* misapplied**
In his revision of the evergreen monocarpic species, Dr C. Grey-Wilson has established that *M. napaulensis* DC., a dwarfish yellow-flowered species not usually more than 1.1m tall and endemic to C Nepal, is not currently in cultivation. The well-known plants of gardens which pass for *M. napaulensis* are hybrids, for the present to be known as *M. napaulensis* misapplied. The parents of the hybrids are *M. staintonii* (from W Nepal) and *M. paniculata* (a yellow-flowered species with a purple stigma) or *M. staintonii* and *M. regia* or a complex mixture of all three species. *M. staintonii*, newly described by C. Grey-Wilson (*Bot. Mag.* (2006) 23(2):176–209), is a tall (to 2.5m), robust species with red or pink flowers and a dark green stigma, near in appearance to *M. napaulensis* of gardens, but less so to true *M. napaulensis*. As *M. staintonii*, like its near relatives, readily hybridises in cultivation, it is rarely seen in an unadulterated form.

***Melissa officinalis* 'Variegata'**
The true cultivar of this name has leaves striped with white.

***Pelargonium* 'Lass o' Gowrie'**
The American plant of this name has pointed, not rounded leaf lobes.

Pelargonium quercifolium
Plants under this name are mainly hybrids. The true species has pointed, not rounded leaf lobes.

***Penstemon* 'Taoensis'**
This name for a small-flowered cultivar or hybrid of *P. isophyllus* originally appeared as 'Taoense' but must be corrected to agree in gender with *Penstemon* (masculine). Presumably an invalid name (published in Latin form since 1958), it is

not synonymous with *P. crandallii* subsp. *glabrescens* var. *taosensis*.

Pernettya
Botanists now consider that *Pernettya* (fruit a berry) is not separable from *Gaultheria* (fruit a capsule) because in some species the fruit is intermediate between a berry and a capsule. For a fuller explanation see D. Middleton, *The Plantsman*, **12(3)**.

Pinus ayacahuite
P. ayacahuite var. *veitchii* (syn. *P. veitchii)* is occasionally sold under this name.

***Pinus nigra* 'Cebennensis Nana'**
A doubtful name, possibly a synonym for *P. nigra* 'Nana'.

Polemonium archibaldiae
Usually sterile with lavender-blue flowers. A self-fertile white-flowered plant is sometimes sold under this name.

***Prunus laurocerasus* 'Castlewellan'**
We are grateful to Dr Charles Nelson for informing us that the name 'Marbled White' is not valid because although it has priority of publication it does not have the approval of the originator who asked for it to be called 'Castlewellan'.

Prunus serrulata* var. *pubescens
See note in Bean Supplement, p.398.

***Prunus* × *subhirtella* 'Rosea'**
Might be *P. pendula* var. *ascendens* 'Rosea', *P. pendula* 'Pendula Rosea', or *P.* × *subhirtella* 'Autumnalis Rosea'.

Rheum* × *hybridum
The name *R.* × *cultorum* was published without adequate description and must be abandoned in favour of the validly published *R.* × *hybridum*.

***Rhododendron* (azaleas)**
All names marked 'N' refer to more than one cultivar.

Rhus hirta and R. typhina
Linnaeus published both *R. typhina* and *R. hirta* as names for the same species. Though *R. hirta* has priority, it has been proposed that the name *R. typhina* should be conserved.

Rosa gentiliana
Plants under this name are usually the cultivar 'Polyantha Grandiflora' but might otherwise be *R. multiflora* 'Wilsonii', *R. multiflora* var. *cathayensis, R. henryi* or another hybrid.

***Rosa* 'Jacques Cartier' misapplied**
For a discussion on the correct identity of this rose see *Heritage Rose Foundation News*, Oct. 1989 & Jan. 1990.

***Rosa* 'Kazanlik'**
For a discussion on the correct identity of this rose see *Heritage Roses,* Nov. 1991.

***Rosa* Sweetheart**
This is not the same as the Sweetheart Rose, a common name for *R.* 'Cécile Brünner'.

Rosa wichurana
This is the correct spelling according to the ICBN 1994 Article 60.11 (which enforces Recommendation 60C.1c) and not *wichuraiana* for this rose commemorating Max Wichura.

***Rubus fruticosus* L. agg.**
Though some cultivated blackberries do belong to *Rubus fruticosus* L. *sensu stricto,* others are more correctly ascribed to other species of *Rubus* section *Glandulosus* (including *R. armeniacus, R. laciniatus* or *R. ulmifolius)* or are hybrids of species within this section. Because it is almost impossible to ascribe every cultivar to a single species or hybrid, they are listed under *R. fruticosus* L. agg. (i.e. aggregate) for convenience.

***Salvia officinalis* 'Aurea'**
S. officinalis var. *aurea* is a rare variant of the common sage with leaves entirely of gold. It is represented in cultivation by the cultivar 'Kew Gold'. The plant usually offered as *S. officinalis* 'Aurea' is the gold variegated sage *S. officinalis* 'Icterina'.

***Sambucus nigra* 'Aurea'**
Plants under this name are usually not *S. nigra.*

***Skimmia japonica* 'Foremanii'**
The true cultivar, which belongs to *S. japonica* Rogersii Group, is believed to be lost to cultivation. Plants offered under this name are usually *S. japonica* 'Veitchii'.

***Spiraea japonica* 'Shirobana'**
Shirobana-shimotsuke is the common name for *S. japonica* var. *albiflora*. Shirobana means white-flowered and does not apply to the two-coloured form.

Staphylea holocarpa* var. *rosea
This botanical variety has woolly leaves. The cultivar 'Rosea', with which it is often confused, does not.

***Tricyrtis* Hototogisu**
This is the common name applied generally to all Japanese *Tricyrtis* and specifically to *T. hirta*.

Tricyrtis macropoda
This name has been used for at least five different species.

Uncinia rubra
This name is also misapplied to *U. egmontiana* and *U. uncinata*.

***Viburnum opulus* 'Fructu Luteo'**
See note below.

***Viburnum opulus* 'Xanthocarpum'**
Some entries under this name might be the less compact *V. opulus* 'Fructu Luteo'.

Viburnum plicatum
Entries may include the 'snowball' form, *V. plicatum* f. *plicatum* (syn. *V. plicatum* 'Sterile'), as well as the 'lacecap' form, *V. plicatum* f. *tomentosum*.

Viola labradorica
See Note in *The Garden*, **110(2)**: 96.

Vitis **'Fragola'**
This appears to refer to *uva fragola*, the strawberry grape, and therefore plants under this name may be found to be either *V. labrusca* or *V.* × *labruscana*.

Wisteria floribunda **'Violacea Plena' and *W. floribunda* 'Yae-kokuryū'**
We are grateful to Yoko Otsuki, who has established through Engei Kyokai (the Horticultural Society of Japan) that there are two different double selections of *Wisteria floribunda*. 'Violacea Plena' has double lavender/lilac flowers, while 'Yae-kokuryū' has more ragged and tightly double flowers with purple/indigo centres. Each is distinctive but it is probable that both are confused in the British nursery trade. 'Yae-fuji' might be an earlier name for 'Violacea Plena' or a Group name covering a range of doubles but, as *fuji* is the Japanese common name for the species, it would not be a valid name under the ICNCP.

CLASSIFICATION OF GENERA

Genera including a large number of species, or with many cultivars, are often subdivided into informal horticultural classifications, or formal cultivar groups in the case of *Clematis* and *Tulipa*. The breeding of new cultivars is sometimes limited to hybrids between closely-related species, thus for *Saxifraga* and *Primula*, the cultivars are allocated to the sections given in the infrageneric treatments cited. Please turn to p.12 for a fuller explanation.

ACTINIDIA

(s-p) Self-pollinating

BEGONIA

(C) Cane-like
(R) Rex Cultorum
(S) Semperflorens Cultorum
(T) × *tuberhybrida* (Tuberous)

CHRYSANTHEMUM

(By the National Chrysanthemum Society)
(1) Indoor Large (Exhibition)
(2) Indoor Medium (Exhibition)
(3a) Indoor Incurved: Large-flowered
(3b) Indoor Incurved: Medium-flowered
(3c) Indoor Incurved: Small-flowered
(4a) Indoor Reflexed: Large-flowered
(4b) Indoor Reflexed: Medium-flowered
(4c) Indoor Reflexed: Small-flowered
(5a) Indoor Intermediate: Large-flowered
(5b) Indoor Intermediate: Medium-flowered
(5c) Indoor Intermediate: Small-flowered
(6a) Indoor Anemone: Large-flowered
(6b) Indoor Anemone: Medium-flowered
(6c) Indoor Anemone: Small-flowered
(7a) Indoor Single: Large-flowered
(7b) Indoor Single: Medium-flowered
(7c) Indoor Single: Small-flowered
(8a) Indoor True Pompon
(8b) Indoor Semi-pompon
(9a) Indoor Spray: Anemone
(9b) Indoor Spray: Pompon
(9c) Indoor Spray: Reflexed
(9d) Indoor Spray: Single
(9e) Indoor Spray: Intermediate
(9f) Indoor Spray: Spider, Quill, Spoon or Any Other Type
(10a) Indoor, Spider
(10b) Indoor, Quill
(10c) Indoor, Spoon
(11) Any Other Indoor Type
(12a) Indoor, Charm
(12b) Indoor, Cascade
(13a) October-flowering Incurved: Large-flowered
(13b) October-flowering Incurved: Medium-flowered
(13c) October-flowering Incurved: Small-flowered
(14a) October-flowering Reflexed: Large-flowered
(14b) October-flowering Reflexed: Medium-flowered
(14c) October-flowering Reflexed: Small-flowered
(15a) October-flowering Intermediate: Large-flowered
(15b) October-flowering Intermediate: Medium-flowered
(15c) October-flowered Intermediate: Small-flowered
(16) October-flowering Large
(17a) October-flowering Single: Large-flowered
(17b) October-flowering Single: Medium-flowered
(17c) October-flowering Single: Small-flowered
(18a) October-flowering Pompon: True Pompon
(18b) October-flowering Pompon: Semi-pompon
(19a) October-flowering Spray: Anemone
(19b) October-flowering Spray: Pompon
(19c) October-flowering Spray: Reflexed
(19d) October-flowering Spray: Single
(19e) October-flowering Spray: Intermediate
(19f) October-flowering Spray: Spider, Quill, Spoon or Any Other Type
(20) Any Other October-flowering Type
(21a) Korean: Anemone
(21b) Korean: Pompon
(21c) Korean: Reflexed
(21d) Korean: Single
(21e) Korean: Intermediate
(21f) Korean: Spider, Quill, Spoon, or any other type
(22a) Charm: Anemone
(22b) Charm: Pompon
(22c) Charm: Reflexed
(22d) Charm: Single
(22e) Charm: Intermediate
(22f) Charm: Spider, Quill, Spoon or Any Other Type
(23a) Early-flowering Outdoor Incurved: Large-flowered

(23b)	Early-flowering Outdoor Incurved: Medium-flowered
(23c)	Early-flowering Outdoor Incurved: Small-flowered
(24a)	Early-flowering Outdoor Reflexed: Large-flowered
(24b)	Early-flowering Outdoor Reflexed: Medium-flowered
(24c)	Early-flowering Outdoor Reflexed: Small-flowered
(25a)	Early-flowering Outdoor Intermediate: Large-flowered
(25b)	Early-flowering Outdoor Intermediate: Medium-flowered
(25c)	Early-flowering Outdoor Intermediate: Small-flowered
(26a)	Early-flowering Outdoor Anemone: Large-flowered
(26b)	Early-flowering Outdoor Anemone: Medium-flowered
(27a)	Early-flowering Outdoor Single: Large-flowered
(27b)	Early-flowering Outdoor Single:Medium-flowered
(28a)	Early-flowering Outdoor Pompon: True Pompon
(28b)	Early-flowering Outdoor Pompon: Semi-pompon
(29a)	Early-flowering Outdoor Spray: Anemone
(29b)	Early-flowering Outdoor Spray: Pompon
(29c)	Early-flowering Outdoor Spray: Reflexed
(29d)	Early-flowering Outdoor Spray: Single
(29e)	Early-flowering Outdoor Spray: Intermediate
(29f)	Early-flowering Outdoor Spray: Spider, Quill, Spoon or Any Other Type
(29Rub)	Early-flowering Outdoor Spray: Rubellum
(30)	Any Other Early-flowering Outdoor Type

Clematis

(Cultivar Groups as per Matthews, V. (2002) *The International Clematis Register & Checklist 2002*, RHS, London.)

(A)	Atragene Group
(Ar)	Armandii Group
(C)	Cirrhosa Group
(EL)	Early Large-flowered Group
(F)	Flammula Group
(Fo)	Forsteri Group
(H)	Heracleifolia Group
(I)	Integrifolia Group
(LL)	Late Large-flowered Group
(M)	Montana Group
(T)	Texensis Group
(Ta)	Tangutica Group
(V)	Viorna Group
(Vb)	Vitalba Group
(Vt)	Viticella Group

Dahlia

(Classification according to The International Dahlia Register (1969), 20th Supp. (2009) formed through consultation with national dahlia societies.)

(Sin)	1 Single
(Anem)	2 Anemone-flowered
(Col)	3 Collerette
(WL)	4 Waterlily (unassigned)
(LWL)	4B Waterlily, Large
(MWL)	4C Waterlily, Medium
(SWL)	4D Waterlily, Small
(MinWL)	4E Waterlily, Miniature
(D)	5 Decorative (unassigned)
(GD)	5A Decorative, Giant
(LD)	5B Decorative, Large
(MD)	5C Decorative, Medium
(SD)	5D Decorative, Small
(MinD)	5E Decorative, Miniature
(SBa)	6D Small Ball
(MinBa)	6E Miniature Ball
(Pom)	7 Pompon
(C)	8 Cactus (unassigned)
(GC)	8A Cactus, Giant
(LC)	8B Cactus, Large
(MC)	8C Cactus, Medium
(SC)	8D Cactus, Small
(MinC)	8E Cactus, Miniature
(S-c)	9 Semi-cactus (unassigned)
(GS-c)	9A Semi-cactus, Giant
(LS-c)	9B Semi-cactus, Large
(MS-c)	9C Semi-cactus, Medium
(SS-c)	9D Semi-cactus, Small
(MinS-c)	9E Semi-cactus, Miniature
(Misc)	10 Miscellaneous
(Fim)	11 Fimbriated
(SinO)	12 Single Orchid (Star)
(DblO)	13 Double Orchid
(B)	Botanical
(DwB)	Dwarf Bedding
(Lil)	Lilliput (in combination)

Dianthus

(By the RHS)

(b)	Carnation, border
(M)	Carnation, Malmaison
(pf)	Carnation, perpetual-flowering
(p)	Pink
(p,a)	Pink, annual

Fruit

(B)	Black (*Vitis*), Blackcurrant (*Ribes*)
(Ball)	Ballerina (*Malus*)
(C)	Culinary (*Malus, Prunus, Pyrus, Ribes*)

(Cider)	Cider (*Malus*)
(D)	Dessert (*Malus, Prunus, Pyrus, Ribes*)
(F)	Fruit
(G)	Glasshouse (*Vitis*)
(O)	Outdoor (*Vitis*)
(P)	Pinkcurrant (*Ribes*)
(Perry)	Perry (*Pyrus*)
(R)	Red (*Vitis*), Redcurrant (*Ribes*)
(S)	Seedless (*Citrus, Vitis*)
(W)	White (*Vitis*), Whitecurrant (*Ribes*)

FUCHSIA

(E)	Encliandra
(T)	Variants and hybrids of F. *triphylla*

GLADIOLUS

(B)	Butterfly
(E)	Exotic
(G)	Giant
(L)	Large
(M)	Medium
(Min)	Miniature
(N)	Nanus
(P)	Primulinus
(S)	Small
(Tub)	Tubergenii

HEPATICA NOBILIS

(Adapted from the International Hepatica Society classification for *Hepatica nobilis*)

(1)	Hyoujun (normal)
(2)	(degenerated anther)
(3)	Otome (degenerated stamen)
(4)	Henka (petal deformity)
(5/d)	Herashibe (semi double, primitive)
(5A/d)	Choji (semi-double, primitive)
(6/d)	Nidan (semi-double, advanced)
(7/d)	Sandan (double, primitive)
(8/d)	Karako (double, advanced)
(9/d)	Sene-e (double, completed)

HYDRANGEA MACROPHYLLA

(H)	Hortensia
(L)	Lacecap

IRIS

(Adapted from the American Iris Society Classification)

(AB)	Arilbred
(BB)	Border Bearded
(Cal-Sib)	Series *Californicae* × Series *Sibiricae*
(CH)	Californian Hybrid
(DB)	Dwarf Bearded (not assigned)
(Dut)	Dutch
(IB)	Intermediate Bearded
(J)	Juno (subgenus *Scorpiris*)
(La)	Louisiana Hybrid
(MDB)	Miniature Dwarf Bearded
(MTB)	Miniature Tall Bearded
(Rc)	Regeliocyclus (Section *Regelia* × Section *Oncocyclus*)
(SDB)	Standard Dwarf Bearded
(Sib)	Siberian
(Sino-Sib)	Series *Sibiricae*, chromosome number 2n=40
(SpH)	Species Hybrid
(Spuria)	Spuria
(TB)	Tall Bearded

LILIUM

(Classification according to *The International Lily Register* (ed. 4, 2007))

(I)	Asiatic hybrids derived from *L. amabile, L. bulbiferum, L. callosum, L. cernuum, L. concolor, L. dauricum, L. davidii, L.* × *hollandicum, L. lancifolium, L. lankongense, L. leichtlinii, L.* × *maculatum* and *L. pumilum, L.* × *scottiae, L. wardii* and *L. wilsonii.*
(II)	Martagon hybrids derived from *L. dalhansonii, L. hansonii, L. martagon, L. medeoloides and L. tsingtauense*
(III)	Euro-Caucasian hybrids derived from *L. candidum, L. chalcedonicum, L. kesselringianum, L. monadelphum, L. pomponium, L. pyrenaicum* and *L.* × *testaceum.*
(IV)	American hybrids derived from *L. bolanderi, L.* × *burbankii, L. canadense, L. columbianum, L. grayi, L. humboldtii, L. kelleyanum, L. kelloggii, L. maritimum, L. michauxii, L. michiganense, L. occidentale, L.* × *pardaboldtii, L. pardalinum, L. parryi, L. parvum, L. philadelphicum, L. pitkinense, L. superbum, L. vollmeri, L. washingtonianum* and *L. wigginsii.*
(V)	Longiflorum lilies derived from *L. formosanum, L. longiflorum, L. philippinense and L. wallichianum.*
(VI)	Trumpet and Aurelian hybrids derived from *L.* × *aurelianense, L. brownii, L.* × *centigale, L. henryi, L.* × *imperiale, L.* × *kewense, L. leucantheum, L. regale, L. rosthornii, L. sargentiae, L. sulphureum* and *L. sulphurgale* (but excluding hybrids of *L. henryi* with all species listed in Division VII).
(VII)	Oriental hybrids derived from *L. auratum, L. japonicum, L. nobilissimum, L.* × *parkmanii, L rubellum* and *L. speciosum* (but excl. all hybrids of these with *L. henryi*).
(VIII)	Other hybrids not covered by any of the previous divisions (I-VII)
(IX)	Species and cultivars of species

a/	upward-facing flowers
b/	outward-facing flowers
c/	downward-facing flowers
/a	trumpet-shaped flowers
/b	bowl-shaped flowers
/c	flat flowers (or with only tepal tips recurved)
/d	recurved flowers

MALUS *SEE* FRUIT

NARCISSUS

(By the RHS, revised 1998)

(1)	Trumpet
(2)	Large-cupped
(3)	Small-cupped
(4)	Double
(5)	Triandrus
(6)	Cyclamineus
(7)	Jonquilla and Apodanthus
(8)	Tazetta
(9)	Poeticus
(10)	Bulbocodium
(11a)	Split-corona: Collar
(11b)	Split-corona: Papillon
(12)	Miscellaneous
(13)	Species

NYMPHAEA

(H)	Hardy
(D)	Day-blooming
(N)	Night-blooming
(T)	Tropical

PAPAVER

(Not a horticultural classification, used to save space in this publication)

(SPS)	Super Poppy Series

PAEONIA

(S)	Shrubby

PELARGONIUM

(A)	Angel
(C)	Coloured Foliage (in combination)
(Ca)	Cactus (in combination)
(d)	Double (in combination)
(Dec)	Decorative
(Dw)	Dwarf
(DwI)	Dwarf Ivy-leaved
(Fr)	Frutetorum
(I)	Ivy-leaved
(Min)	Miniature
(MinI)	Miniature Ivy-leaved
(R)	Regal
(Sc)	Scented-leaved
(St)	Stellar (in combination)
(T)	Tulip (in combination)
(U)	Unique
(Z)	Zonal

PRIMULA

(Classification by Section as per Richards. J. (2002) *Primula* (2nd edition). Batsford, London)

(Ag)	*Auganthus*
(Al)	*Aleuritia*
(Am)	*Amethystinae*
(Ar)	*Armerina*
(Au)	*Auricula*
(A)	Alpine Auricula
(B)	Border Auricula
(S)	Show Auricula
(St)	Striped Auricula
(Bu)	*Bullatae*
(Ca)	*Capitatae*
(Cf)	*Cordifoliae*
(Ch)	*Chartaceae*
(Co)	*Cortusoides*
(Cr)	*Carolinella*
(Cu)	*Cuneifoliae*
(Cy)	*Crystallophlomis*
(Da)	*Davidii*
(De)	*Denticulatae*
(Dr)	*Dryadifoliae*
(F)	*Fedtschenkoanae*
(G)	*Glabrae*
(Ma)	*Malvaceae*
(Mi)	*Minutissimae*
(Mo)	*Monocarpicae*
(Mu)	*Muscarioides*
(Ob)	*Obconicolisteri*
(Or)	*Oreophlomis*
(Pa)	*Parryi*
(Pe)	*Petiolares*
(Pf)	*Proliferae*
(Pi)	*Pinnatae*
(Pr)	*Primula*
(Poly)	Polyanthus
(Prim)	Primrose
(Pu)	*Pulchellae*
(Py)	*Pycnoloba*
(R)	*Reinii*
(Si)	*Sikkimenses*
(So)	*Soldanelloides*
(Sp)	*Sphondylia*
(Sr)	*Sredinskya*
(Su)	*Suffrutescentes*
(Y)	*Yunnannenses*

PRUNUS *SEE* FRUIT

PYRUS *SEE* FRUIT

RHODODENDRON

(A)	Azalea (deciduous, species or unclassified hybrid)

(Ad)	Azaleodendron
(EA)	Evergreen azalea
(G)	Ghent azalea (deciduous)
(K)	Knap Hill or Exbury azalea (deciduous)
(M)	Mollis azalea (deciduous)
(O)	Occidentalis azalea (deciduous)
(R)	Rustica azalea (deciduous)
(V)	Vireya rhododendron
(Vs)	Viscosa azalea (deciduous)

RIBES *SEE* FRUIT

ROSA

(A)	Alba
(Bb)	Bourbon
(Bs)	Boursault
(Ce)	Centifolia
(Ch)	China
(Cl)	Climbing (in combination)
(D)	Damask
(DPo)	Damask Portland
(F)	Floribunda or Cluster-flowered
(G)	Gallica
(Ga)	Garnette
(GC)	Ground Cover
(HM)	Hybrid Musk
(HP)	Hybrid Perpetual
(HT)	Hybrid Tea or Large-flowered
(Min)	Miniature
(Mo)	Moss (in combination)
(N)	Noisette
(Patio)	Patio, Miniature Floribunda or Dwarf Cluster-flowered
(Poly)	Polyantha
(Ra)	Rambler
(RH)	Rubiginosa hybrid (Hybrid Sweet Briar)
(Ru)	Rugosa
(S)	Shrub
(SpH)	Spinosissima Hybrid
(T)	Tea

SAXIFRAGA

(Classification by Section from Gornall, R.J. (1987). *Botanical Journal of the Linnean Society,* 95(4): 273-292)

(1)	*Ciliatae*
(2)	*Cymbalaria*
(3)	*Merkianae*
(4)	*Micranthes*
(5)	*Irregulares*
(6)	*Heterisia*
(7)	*Porphyrion*
(8)	*Ligulatae*
(9)	*Xanthizoon*
(10)	*Trachyphyllum*
(11)	*Gymnopera*
(12)	*Cotylea*
(13)	*Odontophyllae*
(14)	*Mesogyne*
(15)	*Saxifraga*

TULIPA

(Classification by Cultivar Group from *Classified List and International Register of Tulip Names* by Koninklijke Algemeene Vereniging voor Bloembollencultuur 1996)

(1)	Single Early Group
(2)	Double Early Group
(3)	Triumph Group
(4)	Darwin Hybrid Group
(5)	Single Late Group (including Darwin Group and Cottage Group)
(6)	Lily-flowered Group
(7)	Fringed Group
(8)	Viridiflora Group
(9)	Rembrandt Group
(10)	Parrot Group
(11)	Double Late Group
(12)	Kaufmanniana Group
(13)	Fosteriana Group
(14)	Greigii Group
(15)	Miscellaneous

VERBENA

(G)	Species and hybrids considered by some botanists to belong to the separate genus *Glandularia*.

VIOLA

(C)	Cornuta Hybrid
(dVt)	Double Violet
(ExVa)	Exhibition Viola
(FP)	Fancy Pansy
(PVt)	Parma Violet
(SP)	Show Pansy
(T)	Tricolor
(Va)	Viola
(Vt)	Violet
(Vtta)	Violetta

VITIS *SEE* FRUIT

THE PLANT DIRECTORY

A

Abelia ✿ (*Caprifoliaceae*)

biflora	LRHS
chinensis misapplied	see *A.* × *grandiflora*
§ ***chinensis*** R.Br.	CBcs CExl CMac EBee ELan EPfP EWTr LRHS MAsh MMuc SEND SHil SKHP SPer SPoG SRms WGrn WPat
'Edward Goucher' ♀H4	CBar CDoC CDul CMac CWSG CWib EBee ELan EPfP LBMP LRHS LSRN MAsh MBri MGos MRav MSwo NBir SEND SGol SPer SPlb SWvt WPat WSHC
engleriana	CExl EPfP LHop LRHS MAsh MBlu NLar NSoo SEND SLon SSpi
floribunda ♀H3	CBcs CDul CExl CHel CMac CWib EBee ECre ELan ELon EPfP LHop LRHS MAsh MRav NLar NSoo SEND SGol SKHP SPer SPoG SRms SSpi WGob WPat
§ × ***grandiflora*** ♀H4	Widely available
- 'Aurea'	see *A.* × *grandiflora* 'Gold Spot'
- 'Brockhill Allgold' **new**	EPfP
- 'Compacta'	LRHS
- Confetti = 'Conti'PBR (v)	CBcs CDoC CMac CSBt CWSG EBee ELan EPfP LAst LRHS LSRN MAsh MGos MRav MSwo NEgg NLar SGol SLim SPer SPoG SWvt WCot
§ - 'Francis Mason' (v)	Widely available
§ - 'Gold Spot' (v)	EPfP LRHS MGos MWat NLar SGol WGob WPat
- 'Gold Strike'	see *A.* × *grandiflora* 'Gold Spot'
- Golden Panache = 'Minpan'	MRav
- 'Goldsport'	see *A.* × *grandiflora* 'Gold Spot'
- 'Hopleys'PBR (v) ♀H4	CBcs CDoC CMac CSBt CTri CWib EBee ELan EPfP LHop LRHS MAsh MGos MRav NLar SEND SLon SPoG SRms SWvt WCot WGrn WHar
- 'Kaleidoscope'PBR (v)	CAbP CDoC CMac CWGN EBee EHoe ELan EPfP EShb LAst LRHS LSRN MAsh MBri MGos MPkF NLar SGol SHil SLim SPoG SWvt WCot WGob WGrn
- 'Panache' (v)	CDoC LLHF WCot
- 'Prostrate White'	LRHS NLar
- 'Semperflorens'	EBee EMil LRHS
- 'Sherwoodii'	CDoC EBee EMil EPfP LRHS MAsh MGos SLim WPat
- 'Sunrise' (v)	EPfP NLar SLim
- Sunshine Daydream = 'Abelops'PBR (v)	MPkF
- 'Variegata'	see *A.* × *grandiflora* 'Francis Mason'
mosanensis	ELan EPfP LLHF LRHS MBlu MBri NCGa NLar SLon SPoG SSpi WSHC
parvifolia 'Bumblebee'	IDee
Petite Garden = 'Minedward'PBR	CDoC LLHF LRHS MBri
rupestris misapplied	see *A.* × *grandiflora*
rupestris Lindl.	see *A. chinensis* R.Br.
schumannii ♀H4	CAbP CBcs CExl CMHG CMac CSBt CTri ECrN ELan EPfP LHop LRHS MAsh MBri MMuc MRav NLar SKHP SLim SLon SPer SWvt WGrn WPat
spathulata	WGob
triflora	CAbP CExl CWib ECre EPfP LAst LHop LRHS MMuc NLar NSoo SEND SKHP SPhx WGob WSHC

Abeliophyllum (*Oleaceae*)

distichum	CBcs CDoC CEnd CWib EBee ECrN ELan ELon EPfP LAst LBMP LRHS MAsh MBlu MBri MGos NSoo SGol SPer SSpi SWvt WCFE WSHC
- Roseum Group	CBcs CDoC CExl CJun EBee ELan ELon EPfP EWTr LHop LRHS MAsh MGos MMuc MRav SKHP SLon SPoG

Abelmoschus (*Malvaceae*)

esculentus	SVic

Abies (*Pinaceae*)

alba	CDul NWea
- 'Bystricka'	MAsh
- 'Compacta'	CKen
- 'Green Spiral'	NLar
- 'King's Dwarf'	CKen
- 'Microphylla'	CKen
- 'Münsterland'	CKen
- 'Nana' misapplied	see *Picea glauca* 'Nana'
- 'Nana' ambig.	CKen
- 'Pendula'	CKen
- 'Pyramidalis'	NLar
amabilis	GLin
- 'Spreading Star'	SLim
arizonica	see *A. lasiocarpa* var. *arizonica*
balsamea	CDul GKin
- 'Cook's Blue'	CKen
- Hudsonia Group ♀H4	CDoC CKen CMac EHul EPot LRHS NWad SLim WIce
- 'Jamie'	CKen MAsh NLar
- 'Le Feber'	CKen
- 'Nana'	CKen EHul MAsh MBri MJak NPCo NWad WGor
- var. ***phanerolepis*** 'Bear Swamp'	CKen NHol NLar
- 'Piccolo'	CDoC CKen LRHS NLar WGor
- 'Prostrata'	MBri
- 'Renswoude'	CKen
- 'Tyler Blue'	CKen NLar
- 'Verkade's Prostrate'	CKen

*	***borisii-regis*** 'Pendula'	CKen
	brachyphylla dwarf	see *A. homolepis* 'Prostrata'
	cephalonica	CDul CKen CMCN
	- 'Greg's Broom'	CKen
§	- 'Meyer's Dwarf'	CMac LRHS NLar NPCo SLim
	- 'Nana'	see *A. cephalonica* 'Meyer's Dwarf'
	cilicica 'Spring Grove'	CKen
	colimensis NJM 09.074	WPGP
	concolor ♀H4	CBcs CDul CTho MJak MMuc NWea SEND
	- 'Archer's Dwarf'	CKen NLar SLim
	- 'Argentea' Niemetz, 1903	CKen
	- 'Aurea'	NLar
	- 'Birthday Broom'	CKen
	- 'Blue Sapphire'	CKen
§	- 'Compacta' ♀H4	CDoC CKen LRHS MGos NHol NLar NWea SLim
	- 'Fagerhult'	CKen
	- 'Gable's Weeping'	CKen
	- 'Glauca'	see *A. concolor* Violacea Group
	- 'Glauca Compacta'	see *A. concolor* 'Compacta'
	- 'Hillier Broom'	see *A. concolor* 'Hillier's Dwarf'
§	- 'Hillier's Dwarf'	CKen
	- 'Husky Pup'	CKen
	- (Lowiana Group) 'Creamy'	CKen NLar
	- 'Masonic Broom'	CKen NLar
	- 'Mike Stearn'	CKen
	- 'Mora'	CKen
	- 'Ostrov nad Ohri'	CKen
	- 'Piggelmee'	CKen
	- 'Pygmy'	CKen
	- 'Scooter'	CKen NLar
§	- Violacea Group	CKen MAsh MGos SLim
	prostrate	EUJe LRHS NHol NLar
	- 'Wattez Prostrate'	LRHS
	- 'Wattezii'	CKen
	- 'Wintergold'	CKen MGos NHol NLar NPCo SLim
	delavayi	CDul EPfP
	- var. ***delavayi*** Fabri Group	see *A. fabri*
I	- 'Nana'	CKen
§	***fabri***	CDul CKen
	fargesii	CKen NLar
	forrestii	CKen
	fraseri	CDul CTho NWea
	- 'Blue Bonnet'	CKen NLar
	- 'Piglet's' witches' broom	NLar
	- 'Raul's Dwarf'	CKen
	grandis	CBcs CDoy CDul CJun ELan EPfP NWea
	- 'Compacta'	CKen
	- 'Van Dedem's Dwarf'	CKen NLar SLim
	homolepis	CKen
§	- 'Prostrata'	CKen
	kawakamii	CKen
	koreana	CBcs CDoC CDul CJun CKen CMac CTho EHul ELan EPfP GKin LAst LRHS MAsh MBlu MGos MJak MMuc NEgg NHol NPCo NWea SGol SLim SPer SPoG SWvt WHar WMou
	- 'Alpin Star'	CKen MAsh NLar
	- 'Aurea'	see *A. koreana* 'Flava'
	- 'Blaue Zwo'	CKen
	- 'Blauer Eskimo'	CKen MAsh NLar SLim
	- 'Blauer Pfiff'	CKen
	- 'Blinsham Gold'	CKen
	- 'Blue Emperor'	NLar
	- 'Blue Magic'	CKen NLar
	- 'Blue 'n' Silver'	NLar
	- 'Bonsai Blue'	IVic
I	- 'Brevifolia' **new**	NLar
	- 'Brilliant' **new**	CKen NLar
	- 'Cis'	CDoC CKen LRHS NHol NLar SLim
	- 'Compact Dwarf'	NLar
	- 'Crystal Globe'	CKen
	- 'Dark Hill'	NLar
	- 'Doni-tajuso'	CKen NLar WGor
	- 'Eisregen'	CKen
	- 'Festival'	NHol NLar
§	- 'Flava'	CMac NLar NPCo
	- 'Fliegender Untertasse'	IVic
	- 'Frosty'	SLim
	- 'Gait'	CKen
	- 'Golden Glow'	NLar SLim
	- 'Goldener Traum'	CKen NLar
	- 'Green Carpet'	CKen LRHS
	- 'Horstmann'	CKen
	- 'Ice Breaker'	MAsh SLim
	- 'Inverleith'	CKen
	- 'Kohout'	CKen
	- 'Kohout's Icebreaker'	CKen
	- 'Lippetal'	CKen
	- 'Luminetta'	CKen LRHS NHol
	- 'Nadelkissen'	CKen NHol
	- 'Nisbet'	LRHS NHol NLar NPCo SCoo SLim
	- 'Oberon'	CDoC CKen MAsh MBri NHol NLar NWad SLim
	- 'Piccolo'	CKen
	- 'Pinocchio'	CDoC CKen NHol NLar
	- 'Ry'	NLar
	- 'Schneestern'	NLar
	- 'Sherwood Compact'	CKen
	- 'Shorty' **new**	CKen
	- 'Silberkugel'	CKen CMen NLar NWad SLim
	- 'Silberlocke' ♀H4	CDoC CDul CKen GKin LRHS MAsh MBlu MBri MGos NEgg NLar SCoo SLim SPer SPoG WGor
	- 'Silbermavers'	CKen
	- 'Silberperl'	CKen CMen LRHS MBri NLar
	- 'Silberzwerg'	NHol NLar
	- 'Silver Show'	CDoC CDul CKen NHol NLar
	- 'Threave'	CKen NHol NLar
	- 'Verdener Dom'	NLar
	- 'Wellenseind' **new**	CKen
	lasiocarpa 'Alpine Beauty'	CKen
§	- var. ***arizonica***	CDul
	- - 'Compacta' Hornibr. ♀H4	CDoC CKen CMac EHul ELan MBri MGos NHol NLar SLim SPoG WGor
	- - 'Kenwith Blue'	CKen SLim
	- 'Compacta' Beissn.	LRHS MAsh
	- 'Day Creek'	CKen NLar
	- 'Duflon'	CKen
	- 'Elaine'	CKen
	- 'Green Globe'	CKen LRHS NLar
	- 'Joe's Alpine'	CKen
	- 'Kyle's Alpine' **new**	CKen
	- 'Logan Pass'	CKen
	- 'Mulligan's Dwarf'	CKen
	- 'Prickly Pete'	CKen NLar
I	- 'Prostrata'	CMac
	- 'Stevens Blue'	MAsh NLar
	- 'Toenisvorst'	CKen
	- 'Utah'	CKen
I	***magnifica*** 'Nana'	CKen
	- witches' broom	CKen
	nebrodensis	CKen
	nobilis	see *A. procera*

nordmanniana ♀H4	CCVT CDul CJun CMac CTho EHul ELan EPfP MJak MMuc NEgg NWea SEND SPoG WMou
- 'Arne's Dwarf'	CKen
- 'Barabits' Compact'	MBri NLar
- 'Barabits' Spreader'	CKen
- 'Dahlheim'	MAsh
- subsp. ***equi-trojani***	CDul NWea
- - 'Archer'	CKen NPCo
- 'Golden Spreader' ♀H4	CDoC CKen CMac LRHS MAsh MBlu MBri MGos NHol NLar NPCo SCoo SLim SPoG WThu
- 'Hasselt'	CKen
- 'Jakobsen'	CKen
- 'Silberspitze'	CKen
numidica	CKen
- 'Glauca'	CKen
- 'Lawrenceville'	NPCo
pinsapo 'Atlas'	MAsh NLar
- 'Aurea'	CKen LRHS MPkF NHol NLar SLim
I - 'Aurea Nana'	CKen
- 'Fastigiata'	MPkF NLar SGol
- 'Glauca' ♀H4	CDoC CDul CKen CTho ELan LRHS MBlu NLar SLim
- 'Hamondii'	CKen
I - 'Horstmann'	CKen NHol NLar NPCo SLim
- 'Kelleriis'	EUJe NLar
- 'Pendula'	CKen NLar
- 'Quicksilver'	CKen
- 'San Pedro' new	CKen
§ ***procera*** ♀H4	CBcs CDul MJak NWea
- 'Bizarro'	NLar
- 'Blaue Hexe'	CKen IVic LRHS MAsh SLim
- 'Delbar Cascade' new	CKen
- Glauca Group	CDoC CDul CTho ECrN EPfP GKin LRHS MAsh MBlu MBri NHol NLar SLim
- - 'Glauca Prostrata'	EUJe GKin SLim
- 'La Graciosa'	NLar
- 'Noble's Dwarf'	SLim
- 'Obrighofen'	NLar
- 'Prostrata'	MAsh
- 'Sherwoodii'	CKen SLim
Rosemoor hybrid	CKen
sachalinensis	CKen
sibirica	EPfP
spectabilis	EPfP
veitchii	CDul CTho
- 'Heddergott'	CKen NHol NLar SLim
- 'Heine'	CKen NLar
- 'Kramer'	CKen NLar
I - 'Pendula'	CKen IVic
- 'Rumburk'	CKen SLim
- 'Syców'	CKen
vejarii new	SLim

Abromeitiella see *Deuterocohnia*

Abrotanella (*Asteraceae*)

sp.	ECho

Abutilon ✿ (*Malvaceae*)

'Amiti'	ELar GFai
'Apricot Belle'	SMDP
'Ashford Red'	CBcs CCCN EBee ELan LRHS SKHP SMDP SVen WCot WKif
'Boule de Neige'	MOWG SMrm
'Canary Bird' ♀H2	CBcs CCCN CHEx CHll SMDP SVen WKif
'Cannington Carol' (v) ♀H2	CCCN CHll ELan LLHF LSRN SEND SLim WCot
'Cannington Peter' (v) ♀H2	CCCN LSRN
'Cannington Sonia' (v)	SMDP
'Cloth of Gold'	CMac
'Cynthia Pike' (v)	LRHS
'Flamenco'	CCCN CWGN LRHS NEgg
'Heather Bennington'	SMDP
'Henry Makepeace'	ELar SMDP
'Hinton Seedling'	CCCN CRHN
× ***hybridum*** apricot-flowered	CHEx
- red-flowered	CHEx
indicum	WCot
'Ines'	WPGP
'Jacqueline Morris'	LRHS SMrm
'John Thompson'	CCCN CWGN LSRN WCot
'Kentish Belle' ♀H2-3	Widely available
'Kreutzberger'	ELar
'Lemon Queen'	ELar
'Linda Vista Peach' ♀H2	ELar SMDP
'Louis Marignac'	ELar GFai
'Marion' ♀H2	CRHN ELar LRHS LSRN MOWG SMDP SMrm
'Master Michael'	CMac SEND
megapotamicum ♀H3	Widely available
- 'Variegatum' (v)	CBcs CCCN CMac EBee ELan ELar EPfP LRHS MAsh MGos MOWG MSCN NEgg SEND SKHP SLim SLon SPer SPoG SWvt WCot WGrn XLum
- 'Wisley Red'	CBcs CRHN CSPN EBee LRHS SKHP SMDP
× ***milleri*** hort. ♀H2	CCCN CMac CRHN WCot WWlt
- 'Variegatum' (v)	CCCN CHEx CHel CMac LRHS NEgg WCot
- 'Ventnor Gold'	SVen
'Nabob' ♀H2	CCCN CDoC CExl CHGN CHel CRHN EBee EUJe MOWG SMDP SMrm SPoG WGob
'Old Rose Belle'	GFai SMDP
'Orange Hot Lava'	CExl WPGP
'Orange Vein'	EShb SMDP
'Patrick Synge'	CCCN CHGN CHll CMHG EBtc EShb MOWG SPhx SVen WPGP
pictum 'Thompsonii' (v)	CCCN CHEx EShb SVen
'Pink Lady'	CCCN
'Red Bells'	ELar GFai SVen
'Red Queen'	ELar
'Russels Dwarf'	CCCN
'Savitzii' (v) ♀H2	MSCN SVen
'Silver Belle'	CCCN
'Simcox White'	CCCN
'Snow Boy'	ELar
'Souvenir de Bonn' (v) ♀H2	CCCN CHll ELar EShb LSou SMDP SMrm
× ***suntense***	CBcs CCCN CMHG CSBt ELan EPfP LRHS MAsh MOWG MSCN NPer SChF SEND SMDP
- 'Jermyns' ♀H3	CAbP CExl ELan EPfP GCra LRHS LSRN MBri MGos SCoo SKHP SPoG SSpi SVen SWvt WCot
'Tango'	CCCN CWGN EUJe LRHS SEND SLim
variegated, salmon-flowered (v)	LAst
'Victory'	CCCN CWGN SKHP SLim
vitifolium	CBcs CCCN CDTJ CWib EPfP NEgg SPad SVen WBor WHil WKif
- 'Album'	CBcs CCCN CDul CExl CHll ELan EWTr GCal LEdu SEND SPer SSpi WSpi

- 'Tennant's White' ♀H3	CAbP CCCN CExl EBee EPfP GGal LRHS MBri SKHP
- 'Veronica Tennant' ♀H3	CExl SMrm WGwG WKif
'Waltz'	CCCN CWGN EUJe LLHF LRHS SEND WCot
'Westfield Bronze' (v)	CRHN SMDP

Acacia (*Mimosaceae*)

sp.	LSRN
acinacea	IDee SPlb
adunca	SPlb
angustissima	SPlb
armata	see *A. paradoxa*
axillaris	SPlb
baileyana ♀H2	CBcs CCCN CDul CEnd CGHE CMac CSBt CTsd EBee EHoe ELan EPfP LRHS LSRN MAsh MGos MOWG MWat SBig SCoo SEND SLim SPer SPlb SWvt WPat
- var. ***aurea***	SPlb
- 'Purpurea' ♀H2	Widely available
- 'Songlines'	LRHS MBri MGos SHil
boormanii	SPlb WPGP
cardiophylla	SEND
caven NJM 08.0021	WPGP
covenyi	WPGP
cultriformis	CCCN CTsd ESwi SEND
dealbata ♀H2	Widely available
- 'Argentea'	LRHS MGos SHil
- 'Gaulois Astier'	CSBt ELon LRHS LSRN MBri MGos SHil SPoG SSpi SWvt WPGP
- subsp. ***subalpina***	WPGP
'Exeter Hybrid'	CDoy CSBt
fimbriata	CRHN
floribunda 'Lisette'	LRHS SHil
gregorii	SPlb
julibrissin	see *Albizia julibrissin*
karroo	CArn CDTJ SPlb
longifolia	CBcs CCCN CDTJ EPfP LRHS SHil
- subsp. ***sophorae***	CCCN
macradenia	SPlb
mearnsii	CCCN EBee
melanoxylon	CBcs CDTJ CTsd ESwi IGor MTPN SEND SLim SPlb
nanodealbata new	SPad
§ ***paradoxa*** ♀H2	ELon ESwi NSoo
pataczekii	CSBt EPfP EWes WPGP
pendula	SPlb
podalyriifolia	CCCN SPlb
pravissima ♀H2-3	Widely available
- 'Bushwalk Baby'	MOWG
retinodes ♀H2	CBcs CCCN CDTJ CDoC CRHN CTsd EBee EPfP ESwi LRHS MTPN SEND SLim SPad SWvt
- blue-leaved	ESwi
riceana	CCCN CTsd SVen
rubida	CTsd IDee MREP SPlb
sentis	see *A. victoriae*
spectabilis	CCCN SPlb
suaveolens	SPlb
verticillata	CBcs CCCN CDTJ CHGN CHll CTsd EPfP MOWG MTPN
- riverine form	CExl CHel EBee EPfP LRHS
§ ***victoriae***	SPlb

Acaena (*Rosaceae*)

adscendens misapplied	see *A. affinis*, *A. saccaticupula* 'Blue Haze'
adscendens ambig. 'Glauca'	EHoe NBir
§ ***affinis***	EBee SDix
anserinifolia misapplied	see *A. novae-zelandiae*
buchananii	CTri EBee ECho EDAr EHoe GAbr GBin MBrN MMuc NLar SRms
caerulea hort.	see *A. caesiiglauca*
§ ***caesiiglauca***	CTri GAbr GQue MLHP
eupatoria	EBee
fissistipula	EDAr
inermis	SPlb
- 'Purpurea'	CSam EBee EHoe EWes GAbr GBin GKev GQue LRHS NDov NHol NLar NRya SPlb WHoo WMoo WPtf
macrocephala	EBee
magellanica	GCal GKev
microphylla ♀H4	CSam CTri EBee ECho EDAr GBin MBel MBrN NLar SPlb SRms WMoo
- 'Braune Feder'	EBee
- Copper Carpet	see *A. microphylla* 'Kupferteppich'
- 'Glauca'	see *A. caesiiglauca*
§ - 'Kupferteppich'	CHel CSam ECho ECtt EHoe EPPr GAbr GBin GCal GQue LHop MBri MRav NBir NBro NLar NPnk WMoo WPat WWEG
minor var. ***antartica***	GBin
myriophylla	ECho
§ ***novae-zelandiae***	CTri EBee SDix WMoo
'Pewter'	see *A. saccaticupula* 'Blue Haze'
'Purple Carpet'	see *A. microphylla* 'Kupferteppich'
'Purple Haze'	CSpe
§ ***saccaticupula*** 'Blue Haze'	EBee ECho EDAr EHoe EHyd LHop LRHS MBrN MRav SPer SPlb SRms WMoo WPtf WWEG
splendens	SPlb
tesca new	GBin

Acalypha (*Euphorbiaceae*)

'Mini Red' new	LAst
pendula	see *A. reptans*
§ ***reptans***	CCCN

Acanthocalyx see *Morina*

Acantholimon (*Plumbaginaceae*)

acerosum	XSen
androsaceum	see *A. ulicinum*
armenum	XSen
glumaceum	LLHF
trojanum	XSen
§ ***ulicinum***	WAbe XSen

Acanthopanax see *Eleutherococcus*

ricinifolius	see *Kalopanax septemlobus*

Acanthus ✿ (*Acanthaceae*)

arboreus new	XLum
balcanicus misapplied	see *A. hungaricus*
'Candelabra'	WHil
caroli-alexandri	see *A. spinosus* L.
dioscoridis	GCal WHil
- var. ***perringii***	CCon CDes CMea CRDP GBin LRHS MNrw WCot WHil XLum
eminens	WCot
hirsutus	CMea EPri IFoB SBig WCot WHil
- subsp. ***syriacus***	GCal NLar SMrm WCot WHil
'Hollande du Nort'	EBee GBin WHil XLum
§ ***hungaricus***	CHid CMHG CMac EBee ECtt ELan EShb GBin LRHS MBel MRav NLar SDix SPer SWat WCot WHil WMnd WWEG XLum XSen

	– AL&JS 90097YU	WHil
	– MESE 561	EPPr WHil
	longifolius Host	see *A. hungaricus*
	mollis	Widely available
	– from Turkey	WHil
	– 'Fielding Gold'	see *A. mollis* 'Hollard's Gold'
	– free-flowering	GCal MAvo WHil XLum
§	– 'Hollard's Gold'	CBct CCon CExl CHEx CHel CMac EBee ECtt ELan EPPr EPfP GBuc GCal GKin GMaP LHop LPio LRHS MAsh NCGa NEgg NLBP NLar SPoG SWat WCot WHil WWEG
	– 'Jefalba'	see *A. mollis* (Latifolius Group) 'Rue Ledan'
	– Latifolius Group	MRav SRms WHil WHoo
§	– – 'Rue Ledan'	EBee EShb GBin LHop LRHS MAvo NGdn SPhx WCot WHil WWEG XLum
	– – 'Sjaak'	WHil
	– 'Long Spike'	GCal WHil
	– 'Niger'	GKev LRHS WHil
	– 'Tasmanian Angel' (v)	ECtt WCot XLum
	'Morning's Candle'	ECtt MBri NGdn NLar SGol WHil XLum
	sennii	CAby CCse CDes SMad SPhx WSHC XLum
	spinosus misapplied	see *A. spinosus* Spinosissimus Group
§	***spinosus*** L. ♀H4	Widely available
	– Ferguson's form	WCot WHil XLum
	– 'Lady Moore' (v)	WHil XLum
	– 'Royal Haughty'	EWes MAvo XLum
§	– Spinosissimus Group	CBct CCon CMHG CTsd ELan ELon GBin GCal GCra IBoy LEdu MRav SWat WCot WHil WMnd
	'Summer Beauty'	EBee ECtt EWes GBin LHop WCot WHil WWEG XLum
	'Whitewater' (v)	CBct CWGN EBee ECtt LBuc LRHS MAvo MHol MSCN NSti NWad SBig WCot

Acca (*Myrtaceae*)

sellowiana (F)	CBcs CDTJ CDul CExl CHel CMac CTsd EBee ECrN ELan EPfP LAst LHop LRHS MGos MREP NPla SLPl SLim SPer SPlb SPoG SVic SWvt WSHC XSen
– 'Apollo' (F)	LRHS
– 'Coolidge' (F)	CAgr
– 'Gemini' (F)	LRHS
– 'Mammoth' (F)	CAgr CBcs CCCN
– 'Triumph' (F)	CAgr CBcs CCCN
– 'Unique' (F)	CAgr EUJe
– 'Variegata' (F/v)	CCCN

Acer ✿ (*Sapindaceae*)

	albopurpurascens CWJ 12361	WCru
	amoenum B&SWJ 10916	WCru
	– 'Firecracker'	see *A. palmatum* var. *dissectum* 'Firecracker'
	barbinerve	EPfP
	buergerianum	CBcs CDul CJun CMCN CMen MMuc MPkF NEgg NLar SGol WMou
	– var. ***formosanum*** CWJ 12477	WCru
	– 'Himcode'	NLar
	– 'Mino-yatsubusa'	MPkF
	– 'Miyasama-yatsubusa'	MPkF
	– 'Naruto'	CMCN MPkF
	campbellii	WCru
	subsp. ***campbellii*** GWJ 9360	
	– 'Exuberance'	CJun
	campestre ♀H4	Widely available
	– 'Carnival' (v)	CCVT CDul CEnd CJun EBee ECrN ELon MAsh MBlu MPkF NLar NPCo SGol SMad SPoG SWvt WCot WHar
	– 'Eco Sentry' PBR **new**	EBee
	– 'Elsrijk'	CCVT EBee SCoo SGol
	– 'Evelyn'	see *A. campestre* 'Queen Elizabeth'
	– 'Evenly Red'	MBlu WPGP
	– 'Pendulum'	CEnd
	– 'Postelense'	CJun CMCN EBee MBlu
	– 'Pulverulentum' (v)	CJun CMCN NPCo
§	– 'Queen Elizabeth'	MGos SGol SKHP
	– 'Red Shine'	SGol
	– 'Royal Ruby'	CJun MGos SKHP
*	– 'Ruby Glow'	CEnd ECrN
	– 'Schwerinii'	CDul
I	– 'Silver Celebration' (v)	CJun
	– 'William Caldwell'	CEnd CTho EBee ECrN MBri
	capillipes ♀H4	CBcs CDul CLnd CMCN CTho CWib EBee ECrN GKin LRHS MGos MJak MMuc NSoo NWea SPer SPlb WHCr WHar WPGP
	– 'Antoine'	MBri NLar
	– 'Candy Stripe'	see *A.* × *conspicuum* 'Candy Stripe'
	– 'Honey Dew'	CJun
	aff. ***capillipes***	MWat
	cappadocicum	CCVT CDul CEnd CMCN ECrN MMuc MSnd NWea WMou
	– 'Aureum' ♀H4	CBcs CCVT CDoC CDul CEnd CMCN CTho EBee ECrN ELan EPfP GBin GKin IArd MAsh MBlu MBri MGos MRav NLar SGol SLim SPer SPoG SSpi SWvt WHar
	– var. ***mono***	see *A. pictum*
	– 'Rubrum' ♀H4	CBcs CDul CLnd CMCN EBee ECrN EPfP GBin GKin IDee MBlu MGos MRav SGol SLim SPer WHar WHer
	– var. ***sinicum***	EPfP
	– var. ***tricaudatum***	CExl
	carpinifolium	IArd MBlu MPkF NLar
	– B&SWJ 10955	WCru
	– B&SWJ 11124	WCru
§	***caudatifolium*** CWJ 12403	WCru
	– RWJ 9843	WCru
§	***caudatum*** GWJ 9279	WCru
	– GWJ 9317	WCru
	– HWJK 2240	WCru
	– HWJK 2338	WCru
	– subsp. ***ukurunduense***	MPkF
	– – B&SWJ 8658	WCru
	circinatum	CBcs CCVT CDoC CDul CJun CMCN EBee ECrN EPfP IVic MBlu MMuc MSnd NLar NWea SPlb WMou WPat
	– B&SWJ 9565	WCru
	– 'Burgundy Jewel'	CJun
	– 'Little Gem'	CJun
	– 'Monroe'	CJun SGol
	– 'Pacific Fire'	CJun
	– 'Sunglow'	CJun NLar
	circinatum × ***palmatum***	SBig
	cissifolium	CMCN EPfP IArd NLar
	– B&SWJ 10801	WCru

§	× ***conspicuum*** 'Candy Stripe'	CBcs CJun NLar SLim WPGP
	- 'Elephant's Ear'	CJun EPfP NLar
	- 'Mozart'	CJun MBlu MBri MPkF NLar SSta
	- 'Phoenix'	CEnd CJun CMCN CTho EPfP GKin IVic MBlu NLar SSta WHar WPGP WPat
	- 'Silver Ghost'	MPkF
§	- 'Silver Vein'	CDoC CEnd CJun CMCN EPfP LRHS NLar SSta SWvt WPGP
	crataegifolium B&SWJ 11036	WCru
	- B&SWJ 11355	WCru
	- 'Ittai-san-nishiki'	SSta
	- 'Meuri-keade-no-fuiri' (v)	MPkF
	- 'Meuri-no-ōfu' (v)	MPkF
	- 'Veitchii' (v)	CJun CMCN EBee EPfP MBlu MPkF NLar SBig SSpi SSta
	creticum misapplied	see *A. sempervirens*
	dasycarpum	see *A. saccharinum*
	davidii	CBcs CDoC CDul CExl CLnd CMCN CTsd ECrN MBlu MGos MRav SGol SLim SPer SSta WPat
	- AC 1471 **new**	MSnd
§	- 'Canton'	CJun
	- 'Cantonspark'	see *A. davidii* 'Canton'
	- 'Cascade'	CJun MBlu SSta
	- 'Chinese Temple'	SBir
N	- 'Ernest Wilson'	CBcs NLar SSta
N	- 'George Forrest' $\mathbb{Y}^{H4}$	CDoC CDul CExl CJun CLnd CMCN CMac CTho EBee ECrN ELan EPfP GBin LAst LRHS MMuc NLar NWea SEND SLim SPer SPoG SSta WHar WMou
	- 'Hagelunie'	SBir SSta
	- 'Hansu-suru' (v)	SSta
	- 'Karmen'	CBcs CDul CGHE CJun SSta WPGP
	- 'Madeline Spitta'	CMCN MBri
	- 'Purple Bark'	CExl CJun MBri NLar SBir SSta
	- 'Rosalie'	CBcs CJun EPfP MBlu MBri NLar SBir SSta
	- 'Serpentine' $\mathbb{Y}^{H4}$	CBcs CDoC CJun CMCN CNWT EBee ELan EPfP GBin IDee MBlu MBri NEgg NLar SChF SSta WPGP
	- 'Silver Vein'	see *A.* × *conspicuum* 'Silver Vein'
	discolor	CMCN
	elegantulum	CDoC CExl CJun GBin IDee WPGP
	erianthum	CMCN
	erythranthum B&SWJ 11733	WCru
	- DJHV 06147	WCru
	fabri	CDul CExl
	- WWJ 11614	WCru
	flabellatum	CMCN
	- var. ***yunnanense***	EBee MSnd
	forrestii	CExl CMCN EPfP MBri
	- BWJ 7515	WCru
	- 'Alice'	CEnd CJun SSta
	- 'Sirene'	CJun SSta
	- 'Sparkling'	CJun
	× ***freemanii***	CMCN
	- 'Armstrong'	CCVT SGol
	- Autumn Blaze = 'Jeffersred'	CBcs CCVT CDoC CDul CMCN EBee EPfP IArd LRHS MBlu MGos MMuc NLar SBir SCoo SGol SPer SPoG WHar WMou
	- Celebration = 'Celzam'	CCVT CDul MGos
	- 'Indian Summer'	see *A.* × *freemanii* 'Morgan'
§	- 'Morgan'	CJun NLar

	fulvescens	see *A. longipes*
	ginnala	see *A. tataricum* subsp. *ginnala*
	globosum	see *A. platanoides* 'Globosum'
	grandidentatum	see *A. saccharum* subsp. *grandidentatum*
	griseum $\mathbb{Y}^{H4}$	Widely available
	grosseri	CDul CMCN CTri IGor SGol
	- var. ***hersii*** $\mathbb{Y}^{H4}$	CBcs CDoC CDul CLnd CMac CWib EBee ECrN ELan EPfP GBin LRHS MBri MMuc MRav NLar NWea SLim SPer SSta SWvt WHar
	- 'Leiden'	EPfP
	heldreichii	CMCN
	henryi	CBcs CDul EPfP NEgg NLar
	heptaphlebium B&SWJ 11695	WCru
	- B&SWJ 11713	WCru
	- DJHV 06063	WCru
	japonicum	CMCN MMuc SEWo
	- B&SWJ 8417	WCru
§	- 'Aconitifolium' $\mathbb{Y}^{H4}$	Widely available
	- 'Aki-hi' **new**	NLar
	- 'Ao-jutan'	CJun
	- 'Attaryi'	CMCN LRHS MPkF NLar
	- 'Aureum'	see *A. shirasawanum* 'Aureum'
	- 'Emmit's Pumpkins'	CJun
	- 'Ezo-no-momiji'	see *A. shirasawanum* 'Ezo-no-momiji'
	- 'Fairy Lights'	NLar
	- 'Filicifolium'	see *A. japonicum* 'Aconitifolium'
	- 'Green Cascade'	CEnd CJun CMCN CMac CMen IVic LRHS MGos MPkF NLar NPCo SBig SGol WPGP WPat
	- 'Kalmthout'	NLar
	- 'King's Copse'	CJun LRHS
	- 'Laciniatum'	see *A. japonicum* 'Aconitifolium'
	- f. ***microphyllum***	see *A. shirasawanum* 'Microphyllum'
	- 'Ogurayama'	see *A. shirasawanum* 'Ogurayama'
	- 'Ō-isami'	EPfP MPkF NLar SBig
	- 'Ō-taki'	CJun
	- 'Vitifolium' $\mathbb{Y}^{H4}$	CDoC CDul CEnd CJun CMCN CMac CSBt ELan EPfP GBin LRHS MBlu MBri MGos MPkF NEgg NLar NPCo SBig SBod SGol SPer SSta WCFE WPGP
	kawakamii	see *A. caudatifolium*
	laevigatum B&SWJ 11684	WCru
§	- var. ***reticulatum*** B&SWJ 11698	WCru
§	***longipes***	CMCN
	macrophyllum	CDul CMCN EPfP MBlu
	mandschuricum	CDul MBlu
§	***maximowiczianum***	CBcs CMCN CTho ELan MMuc MPkF SGol
	maximowiczii	MPkF WHCr
	micranthum	CDoC CGHE CMCN EBee EPfP GKin MBlu NLar SSpi WHar WPGP
	miyabei	MPkF
	mono	see *A. pictum*
	monspessulanum	CDul CMCN SEND
	morifolium B&SWJ 11473	WCru
	morrisonense	see *A. caudatifolium*
	negundo	CDul CMCN CTho CWib ECrN SWvt
	- 'Auratum'	CMCN SGol
	- 'Aureomarginatum' (v)	ECrN SGol
	- 'Aureovariegatum' (v)	CBcs
§	- 'Elegans' (v)	CDul CEnd CMCN ECrN SCoo WHar

- 'Elegantissimum'	see *A. negundo* 'Elegans'
- 'Flamingo' (v)	CBcs CCVT CDoC CDul CEnd CMac CWSG CWib ECrN ELan ELon EPfP LHop LRHS MAsh NLar NWea SGol SHil SLim SPer SPoG SWvt WHar
- 'Kelly's Gold'	CBcs CTho NLar NWea SGol SLim WHar
- 'Sensation'	NLar
- 'Variegatum' (v)	ECrN SGol
- var. ***violaceum***	CEnd CMCN SVen
- 'Winter Lightning'	CJun CTho NLar
nikoense	see *A. maximowiczianum*
'Norwegian Sunset'	CCVT
oblongum	CMCN
- KWJ 12232	WCru
- WWJ 11851 **new**	WCru
oliverianum	CExl EPfP
- subsp. ***formosanum*** CWJ 12437	WCru
opalus	CMCN SEND
orientale misapplied	see *A. sempervirens*
orizabense	EBee
Pacific Sunset = 'Warrenred'	NLar
palmatum	CBar CBcs CCVT CDoy CDul CMCN CMHG CMen CSBt CTri CWib EPfP EWTr GKin MBlu MGos NEgg NWea SAPC SEWo SGol SPlb SWvt WHar WPat
- 'Akane'	CMen
§ - 'Aka-shigitatsu-sawa'	CBcs CJun CMCN CMac CMen LRHS MGos MJak MPkF NLar SGol
- 'Akegarasu'	CMen NLar
- 'Akita-yatsubusa'	MPkF
- 'Alpenweiss'	CJun
- 'Amagi-shigure'	CJun MPkF
- 'Amber Ghost'	CJun
- 'Aoba-jo'	CJun CMen MPkF NLar NPCo
- 'Ao-kanzashi' (v)	MPkF NLar
- 'Ao-seigen'	CJun
- 'Aoshime-no-uchi'	see *A. palmatum* 'Shinobuga-oka'
- 'Aoyagi'	CEnd CJun CMCN CMen LRHS MGos MPkF NHol NLar NPCo SSta WPat
§ - 'Arakawa'	CEnd CMCN CMac CMen MPkF NLar NPCo
- 'Arakawa-ukon'	CJun NLar
- 'Aratama'	CJun CMen LRHS MJak MPkF NLar
- 'Ariadne' (v)	CEnd CJun CWib MBri MGos MPkF NLar SBig SCoo SPoG WPat
- 'Ariake-nomura'	CMen MPkF
- 'Asahi-zuru' (v)	CBcs CDoC CJun CMCN CMen LRHS MBri MGos MPkF NLar NPCo SBod SHil
- 'Ashurst Wood'	SBig
- 'Atrolineare'	CMen MPkF NLar WPat
- 'Atropurpureum'	Widely available
- 'Atropurpureum Novum'	MPkF NLar SGol
- 'Attraction'	CMCN CMen NPCo
- 'Aureum'	CMCN CMac CMen CWib ELan EPfP IBoy LMil LRHS MAsh MBlu MGos MPkF NHol NLar NPCo SPoG SSpi WCFE
- Autumn Glory Group	CEnd CJun CMac CMen
- 'Autumn Red'	CMen NPCo
* - 'Autumn Showers'	CEnd CJun
- 'Azuma-murasaki'	CJun CMen MPkF NLar
- 'Beni-chidori'	CMen NLar

- 'Beni-gasa'	CJun MPkF WPat
- 'Beni-hime'	MBri MPkF NLar WPat
- 'Beni-hoshi'	MPkF
- 'Beni-kagami'	CEnd CJun CMCN EPfP MPkF NLar SGol
- 'Beni-kawa'	CJun CMen LRHS MPkF NPCo SBig SGol WPat
- 'Beni-komachi'	CBcs CEnd CJun CMCN CMen EPfP LRHS MBri MGos MPkF NLar NSoo SSta WPat
- 'Beni-maiko'	CEnd CJun CMCN CMen CWib EBee EPfP LRHS MBri MGos MJak MPkF NLar NPCo NSoo SBig SCoo SHil SPoG SWvt WPat
- 'Beni-musume'	MPkF
- 'Beni-otake'	CBcs CJun CMen ELan EPfP EUJe IVic LMil LRHS MBri MGos MPkF NLar NPCo SBig
- 'Beni-otome'	MPkF
- 'Beni-schichihenge' (v)	CBcs CEnd CJun CMCN CMen CWCL CWGN GKin LMil LRHS MAsh MBri MGos MJak MPkF NHol NPCo SBig SCoo SGol SHil SSta WPat
- 'Beni-shi-en'	CJun MPkF NLar WPat
- 'Beni-shigitatsu-sawa'	see *A. palmatum* 'Aka-shigitatsu-sawa'
- 'Beni-tsukasa' (v)	CEnd CJun CMen EPfP LRHS MAsh MPkF NLar NPCo SChF SSpi SSta
- 'Beni-tsuru'	MPkF
- 'Beni-ubi-gohon'	CJun MJak MPkF NLar
- 'Beni-zuru'	WPat
- 'Berry Broom'	MPkF NLar
- 'Berry Dwarf'	CJun MPkF
- 'Bi Hō'	CJun IVic NLar SGol
- 'Bloodgood' 🏆^{H4}	Widely available
- 'Bonfire' misapplied	see *A. palmatum* 'Seigai'
- 'Bonfire' ambig.	CJun
- 'Bonnie Bergman'	CJun
- 'Boskoop Glory'	GKin
- 'Brandt's Dwarf'	WPat
- 'Burgundy Lace' 🏆^{H4}	CBcs CDoC CEnd CJun CMCN CMen CWib EBee ELan ELon EPfP EUJe GKin LMil LRHS LSRN MAsh MBri MGos MJak MPkF NPCo SBig SBod SCoo SGol SPer SPoG SSta WPat
- 'Butterfly' (v)	Widely available
- 'Calico'	CJun
- 'Caperci Dwarf'	MPkF
- 'Carlis Corner'	CJun MPkF
- 'Carminium'	see *A. palmatum* 'Corallinum'
- 'Chikuma-no'	CMen MPkF
- 'Chirimen-nishiki' (v)	MPkF
- 'Chitose-yama' 🏆^{H4}	CDul CEnd CJun CMCN CMac CMen CWCL EPfP GBin GKin LBuc LRHS MAsh MBri MGos MPkF MRav NHol NLar NPCo SGol SHil SLim SSta WPat
§ - 'Chiyo-hime'	ELan EPfP NLar NPCo NSoo SPoG
- 'Collingwood Ingram'	SGol
- 'Coonara Pygmy'	CJun CMCN CMac CMen GKin LRHS MGos MPkF NLar NPCo SCoo
- 'Coral Pink'	CJun CMen MPkF SGol SSta
§ - 'Corallinum'	CEnd CJun CMCN CMen EPfP LRHS MPkF NLar NPCo WCFE WPat
- var. ***coreanum*** B&SWJ 8606	WCru
- - 'Korean Gem'	CJun CMen MPkF NPCo

	- 'Crimson Prince'	CJun MPkF SCoo
	- 'Crippsii'	CBcs CMac CMen EUJe GBin LRHS MGos MPkF SBod SCoo SGol
	- 'Curtis Strapleaf'	MPkF
	- 'Deshōjō'	CMCN CMen CWSG CWib MBlu MGos MPkF NLar SCoo SGol
	- 'Diana'	CMen MPkF NLar SGol
	- 'Diane Verkade'	MPkF
	- var. ***dissectum*** ♀H4	Widely available
	- - 'Ao-shidare'	CJun
	- - 'Autumn Fire'	CJun
	- - 'Baby Lace'	CJun CWGN IVic SSta
	- - 'Balcombe Green'	SBig
	- - 'Baldsmith'	CJun CLnd EUJe LBuc LMil LRHS MGos MPkF NLar WPat
	- - 'Barrie Bergman'	CJun WPat
	- - 'Beni-fushigi'	MPkF
	- - 'Beni-shidare Tricolor' (v)	CMen MPkF NLar
	- - 'Beni-shidare Variegated' (v)	CJun CMCN
	- - 'Berrima Bridge'	CJun
	- - 'Bewley's Red'	CJun
	- - 'Brocade'	CJun IVic MPkF WPat
	- - 'Bronzewing'	CJun
	- - 'Chantilly Lace'	CJun IBoy MPkF
	- - 'Crimson Princess'	CBcs LBuc LMil LRHS MJak MPkF
	- - 'Crimson Queen' ♀H4	Widely available
	- - Dissectum Atropurpureum Group	CBcs CJun CMac CTri ELan EPfP LRHS MGos NWea SBig SCoo SLim SReu SSta SWvt
	- - 'Dissectum Flavescens'	CEnd CJun CMac CMen LMil MBlu MPkF NPCo
§	- - 'Dissectum Nigrum'	CJun CMac CMen ELon LRHS MPkF NLar NPCo WPat
	- - 'Dissectum Palmatifidum'	CDoC CMen LRHS MPkF NPCo SCoo SGol SPer
	- - 'Dissectum Rubrifolium'	MPkF
§	- - 'Dissectum Variegatum' (v)	CJun MPkF NPCo
	- - Dissectum Viride Group	CBcs CJun CLnd CMCN CMac CMen CSBt ELan ELon EPfP LAst LMil LRHS MAsh MBlu MGos MSwo NEgg NPCo NWea SBod SLim SPer SSta SWvt
	- - 'Ellen'	CJun MPkF WPat
	- - 'Emerald Lace'	CJun GKin LBuc LRHS MBri MPkF NLar NSoo SHil SSta WCFE WPat
	- - 'Felice'	CJun MPkF WPat
	- - 'Filigree' (v)	CJun CMCN CMen EPfP LRHS MAsh MGos MPkF NLar NPCo SBig SSta WCFE WPat
§	- - 'Firecracker' PBR	MPkF NLar
	- - 'Garnet' ♀H4	Widely available
	- - 'Goshiki-shidare' (v)	CEnd CJun CMen MPkF
	- - 'Green Globe'	CJun LRHS
	- - 'Green Hornet'	CJun
	- - 'Green Lace'	CMen LRHS MPkF
	- - 'Green Mist'	CJun LRHS WPat
	- - 'Hanzel'	WPat
	- - 'Inaba-shidare' ♀H4	Widely available
	- - 'Jeddeloh Orange'	MPkF
I	- - 'Kawaii'	CJun
	- - 'Kiri-nishiki'	CJun CMen LRHS MPkF NLar NPCo
	- - 'Lace Lady' **new**	LRHS
*	- - 'Lionheart'	CJun CMen CWGN LRHS MGos MPkF NLar SCoo
	- - 'Nomura-nishiki' (v)	CMen
	- - 'Octopus'	CJun NLar
	- - 'Orangeola'	CJun CLnd CMen CSBt EUJe IBoy IVic LRHS MAsh MGos MJak MPkF NHol NLar NPCo SBig SBod SCoo SGol SPoG SSta WPat
	- - 'Ornatum'	CMCN CMen CWCL CWib EPfP GBin LAst LSRN MGos MPkF NEgg NLar NPCo NPri SCoo WCFE
	- - 'Otto's Dissectum'	CJun
	- - 'Pendulum Julian'	CMCN LRHS MPkF NLar
	- - 'Pink Ballerina' (v)	CJun
	- - 'Pink Filigree'	CJun CMen EPfP MPkF NLar
	- - 'Raraflora'	CJun
	- - 'Red Autumn Lace'	CJun WPat
	- - 'Red Dragon'	CDoC CJun CMen CWGN LMil LRHS MAsh MPkF NLar NPCo SBig SBod WPat
	- - 'Red Feather'	CJun
	- - 'Red Filigree Lace'	CEnd CJun CMCN CMen CWGN LRHS MGos MPkF NPCo SBig WPat
	- - 'Red Select'	LRHS MPkF
	- - 'Seiryū' ♀H4	Widely available
§	- - 'Shōjō-shidare'	CEnd CJun CMen LRHS MPkF
	- - 'Shu-shidare'	CJun
	- - 'Spring Delight'	CJun MPkF NLar
	- - 'Suisei' (v)	MPkF
	- - 'Sunset'	CJun MPkF
	- - 'Tamukeyama'	CJun CMCN CMen EBee ELan EUJe LMil LRHS MBri MGos MJak MPkF NLar NPCo SBod SCoo SGol SLau WPat
	- - 'Toyama-nishiki' (v)	CMCN CMen CWGN LRHS MPkF NLar NPCo
	- - 'Waterfall'	CJun CMCN
	- - 'Watnong'	CJun LRHS MPkF
	- - 'Zaaling'	CMen NPCo
	- 'Doctor Tilt'	MPkF
	- 'Donzuru-bo'	CJun
	- 'Dormansland'	SBig
	- 'Dragon's Fire'	CJun
	- 'Earthfire'	LRHS MJak MPkF WPat
I	- 'Ebbingei'	CMac
	- 'Eddisbury'	CEnd CJun CMen CSBt EPfP GBin MBlu MPkF NLar SSta WPGP WPat
	- 'Edna Bergman'	CJun
	- 'Effegi'	see *A. palmatum* 'Fireglow'
	- 'Eimini'	MPkF
	- 'Elegans'	CMen EPfP MPkF NLar NPCo
	- 'Elizabeth'	CJun MPkF
	- Emperor 1	see *A. palmatum* 'Wolff'
	- 'Englishtown'	MPkF WPat
	- 'Enkan'	CEnd CJun CMen CWGN LRHS MBri MGos MPkF NLar NPri SGol WPat
	- 'Eono-momiji'	CMen
	- 'Ever Red'	see *A. palmatum* var. *dissectum* 'Dissectum Nigrum'
	- 'Fairy Hair'	CJun
	- 'Fall's Fire'	CJun NLar
	- 'Fascination'	CJun
	- 'Fior d'Arancio'	CJun IVic MPkF NLar NPCo WPat
	- 'Fireball'	CJun
§	- 'Fireglow'	CBcs CDoC CEnd CJun CMCN CMen CSBt CWCL CWib GBin LMil LRHS MBri MGos MJak MPkF NEgg NLar NPCo SBod SCoo SGol SPer WPat
	- 'First Ghost'	CJun
	- 'Fjellheim'	CJun MPkF

	– 'Frederici Guglielmi'	see *A. palmatum* var. *dissectum* 'Dissectum Variegatum'
	– 'Garyū'	MPkF
	– 'Geisha'	CJun MPkF
	– 'Geisha Gone Wild' (v)	CJun MPkF
	– 'Gentaku'	CJun
	– 'Germaine's Gyration'	CJun
	– 'Ghost'	CJun
	– 'Gibbsii'	CMen NPCo
I	– 'Globosum'	IBoy MPkF
	– 'Glowing Embers'	CJun MPkF WPat
	– 'Golden Pond'	CJun
	– 'Goshiki-kotohime' (v)	CJun CMCN MPkF NLar SBod
	– 'Goten-nomura'	NLar
	– 'Grace'	CJun
	– 'Grandma Ghost'	CJun
	– 'Green Flag'	CJun
	– 'Green Star'	WPat
	– 'Green Trompenburg'	CJun CMen GBin MPkF NEgg NLar NPCo
	– 'Groundcover'	MPkF
§	– 'Hagoromo'	CMac CMen MPkF NPCo SCoo
	– 'Hamano-maru'	MPkF
	– 'Hana-matoi'^{PBR} (v)	CMCN MPkF
	– 'Hanami-nishiki'	CMen MPkF NEgg WPat
	– 'Haru-iro'	CJun
	– 'Harusame' (v)	MPkF NLar WPat
	– 'Hazeroino' (v)	CMen MPkF
	– 'Heartbeat'	CJun LRHS MPkF
	– 'Heffner's Red'	CJun MPkF
	– 'Helena'	see *A. shirasawanum* 'Helena'
	– var. ***heptalobum***	CMCN
§	– 'Heptalobum Elegans'	LRHS
	– 'Heptalobum Elegans Purpureum'	see *A. palmatum* 'Hessei'
	– 'Heptalobum Rubrum'	NLar
	– 'Herbstfeuer'	CJun MPkF
§	– 'Hessei'	CEnd CMen CWCL MPkF NLar
	– 'Higasayama' (v)	CBcs CEnd CJun CMCN CMen CWGN IVic LRHS MGos MPkF NLar NPCo SGol WPat
	– 'Hino-tori-nishiki'	CMen NLar SGol
	– 'Hōgyoku'	CJun CMCN CMen LRHS MPkF
	– 'Hondoshi'	NLar
	– 'Honō-o'	MPkF NLar
	– 'Hoshi-kuzu'	MPkF NLar
	– 'Hupp's Dwarf'	CJun MPkF
	– 'Hupp's Red Willow'	NLar
	– 'Ibo-nishiki'	CMen MPkF
	– 'Ichigyōji'	CEnd CJun CMen IVic MAsh NLar NPCo SBig SChF WPGP WPat
	– 'Ightham Gold'	SSta
	– 'Iijima-sunago'	CMen MPkF
	– 'Inazuma'	CBcs CDoC CJun CMCN CMen LMil LRHS MGos MPkF NLar SBod SCoo SGol SLau WPat
	– 'Irish Lace'	CJun
	– 'Iso-chidori'	MPkF
	– 'Issai-nishiki'	CMen MPkF NPCo
*	– 'Issai-nishiki-kawazu'	MPkF
	– 'Jane'	MPkF NLar
	– 'Japanese Sunrise'	CJun LRHS MPkF WPat
	– 'Jerre Schwartz'	LBuc LRHS MGos MPkF NLar SHil WPat
	– 'Jirō-shidare'	CJun EPfP MPkF NLar SBig
	– 'JJ'	CJun
	– 'Julia D.'	CJun
	– 'Kaba'	CMen IVic MPkF
	– 'Kagero' (v)	MPkF
§	– 'Kagiri-nishiki' (v)	CJun CMCN CMac CMen CWGN IVic LRHS MPkF NEgg NLar
	– 'Kamagata'	CBcs CEnd CJun CMCN CMen GKin IVic LRHS MAsh MGos MPkF NLar NPCo SCoo WPGP WPat
	– 'Kandy Kitchen'	CJun CMen LRHS
	– 'Karaori-nishiki' (v)	CMen MPkF NLar SPer
	– 'Karasugawa' (v)	CJun CMen CWGN MPkF NLar NPCo
	– 'Kasagiyama'	CEnd CJun CMen LRHS MPkF
	– 'Kasen-nishiki'	CMen MPkF
	– 'Kashima'	CEnd CJun CMCN CMen LRHS MPkF NLar NPCo WPat
	– 'Kashima-yatsubusa'	MPkF
	– 'Katja'	CJun CMen MPkF
	– 'Katsura' ♀^{H4}	Widely available
	– 'Katsura-nishiki'	MPkF
	– 'Kawahara Rose'	MPkF NLar
	– 'Ki-hachijō'	CJun CMCN CMen MPkF NLar WPat
	– 'Killarney'	CJun
	– 'Kingsville Variegated' (v)	MPkF
	– 'Kinky Krinkle'	CJun MPkF
	– 'Kinran'	CMen LRHS MPkF NPCo SChF
	– 'Kinshii'	CEnd CJun CMCN CMen EPfP GBin IVic LRHS MPkF NHol NLar NPCo WPat
	– 'Kiyohime'	CDoC CMCN CMen MPkF WPat
	– 'Koba-shōjō'	MPkF
	– 'Kogane-nishiki'	CMen NLar SGol
	– 'Kogane-sakae'	CJun MPkF
	– 'Kokobunji-nishiki' (v)	MPkF
	– 'Komache-hime'	CJun CMen MPkF WPat
	– 'Komon-nishiki' (v)	CJun CMen MPkF
	– 'Koriba'	CJun MPkF NLar
	– 'Koshibori-nishiki'	MPkF
§	– 'Koshimino'	CJun
	– 'Kotohime'	CJun CMCN CMen GKin IVic LRHS MGos MPkF NLar SBig SCoo SHil SPoG
	– 'Koto-ito-komachi'	CJun CMen EPfP LRHS MPkF NPCo
	– 'Koto-maru'	MPkF NLar SGol
	– 'Koto-no-ito'	CMCN LMil LRHS MGos MPkF NLar SGol WPat
	– 'Koya-san'	CMen MPkF NLar
	– 'Kurabu-yama'	CMen MPkF
	– 'Kuro-hime'	WPat
	– 'Kurui-jishi'	MPkF
	– 'Kyōryū'	MPkF
	– 'Kyra'	CMen MPkF
	– 'Leather Leaf'	MPkF
§	– 'Linearilobum'	CBcs CDoC CMen EBee EPfP GBin IVic LMil LRHS MGos MPkF NLar NPCo SCoo SLau
	– 'Little Princess'	see *A. palmatum* 'Chiyo-hime'
	– 'Lozita'	NLar WPat
	– 'Lutescens'	CMen MPkF NPCo
	– 'Lydia'	MPkF NLar
	– 'Maiko'	CMen MPkF
	– 'Mallet' **new**	NLar
	– 'Mama'	CMen NPCo
	– 'Mapi-no-machihime'	CEnd CJun CMCN CMen ELan LRHS MAsh MGos MPkF NHol WPGP WPat
	– 'Marakumo'	MPkF
	– 'Marasaki-yama'	MPkF
	– 'Mardi Gras'	CJun
	– 'Margaret'	MPkF WPat
	– 'Margaret Bee'	CJun

	- 'Marjan'	CJun MPkF NLar
	- 'Marlo'^{PBR}	MAsh MRav NLar NPri NSoo
	- 'Masamurasaki'	CMen MPkF
	- 'Masukagami' (v)	CEnd CJun MPkF
	- 'Matsuga-e' (v)	CMen MPkF NPCo
	- 'Matsukaze'	CJun CMCN CMen
	- var. ***matsumurae***	WCru
	B&SWJ 11100	
	- 'Matsuyoi'	CJun MPkF NLar
	- 'Meihō-nishiki'	CJun
	- 'Melanie'	CJun SBig
	- 'Meoto'	CJun
	- 'Midori-no-teiboku'	CJun MPkF
	- 'Mikawa-yatsubusa'	CMCN CMac CMen EUJe IVic
		MGos MPkF NLar NPCo SGol WPat
	- 'Mikazuki' (v)	CJun
	- 'Mimaye'	CJun
	- 'Mini Mondo'	MPkF
	- 'Mirte'	CJun CMen MPkF SBig SBod SGol
	- 'Mizuho-beni'	CJun CMen NLar NPCo
	- 'Mizu-kuguri'	MPkF NLar
§	- 'Momenshide' **new**	NLar
	- 'Momoiro-koya-san'	CJun MPkF NLar SGol WPat
	- 'Mon Papa'	CJun CMen NLar
	- 'Monzukushi'	CJun MPkF
	- 'Moonfire'	CJun CMCN ELan EPfP LRHS MAsh
		MGos MPkF NLar SGol WPat
	- 'Mr Sun'	CJun
*	- 'Muncaster'	SBig
	- 'Murasaki-hime'	MPkF
	- 'Murasaki-kiyohime'	CEnd CJun CMCN CMen LRHS
		MPkF NLar NPCo WPGP WPat
	- 'Mure-hibari'	CJun CMen MPkF
	- 'Murogawa'	CJun CMen NPCo
	- 'Musashino'	CJun SGol
	- 'Nakata'	NLar
	- 'Nanase-gawa'	MPkF
	- 'Nicholsonii'	CMen IVic MPkF NLar NPCo WPat
	- 'Nigrum' 🏆^{H4}	CMCN CTri WPat
	- 'Nishiki-gasane' (v)	CMen MPkF
§	- 'Nishiki-gawa'	CEnd CJun CMen LRHS MPkF
		NPCo
	- 'Nishiki-momiji'	CMen
	- 'Nishiki-yamato'	NLar
	- 'Nomura'	CJun CMen
	- 'Nomurishidare'	see *A. palmatum* var. *dissectum*
	misapplied	'Shōjō-shidare'
	- 'Nomurishidare' Wada	SSpi
	- 'Nuresagi'	CEnd CJun MPkF WPat
	- 'Ogi-nagashi' (v)	MPkF NLar
	- 'Ōgi-no-sen'	MPkF
	- 'Ōgon-sarasa'	CJun MPkF
	- 'Ojishi'	CMen MPkF
	- 'Ō-kagami'	CBcs CDoC CEnd CJun CMac
		CMen CSBt EPfP LRHS MAsh MGos
		MPkF NLar NPCo SCoo WCFE WPat
	- 'Okukuji-nishiki'	CJun
	- 'Okushimo'	CEnd CJun CMCN CMen IVic LRHS
		MPkF NLar NPCo SSta WPat
	- 'Omato'	CJun MAsh MPkF SBig
	- 'Omure yama'	CBcs CDoC CEnd CJun CMCN
		CMen EPfP LMil LRHS MGos MPkF
		NLar NPCo SBod SCoo SGol SPer
		SSta
	- 'Orange Dream'	Widely available
	- 'Oranges and Lemons'	CJun NLar SGol
	- 'Oregon Sunset'	CJun MPkF NLar WPat
	- 'Oridono-nishiki' (v)	CBcs CDoC CEnd CJun CMCN
		CMac CMen CWCL CWGN EBee
		ELan EPfP LRHS MAsh MBlu MGos
		MPkF NEgg NLar NPCo SLim SPoG
		SSta
	- 'Oriental Mystery'	CJun
	- 'Ōsakazuki' 🏆^{H4}	Widely available
	- 'Ōshio-beni'	CJun CMen NPCo
	- 'Ōshū-shidare'	CJun CMen IBoy MPkF
	- 'Oto-hime'	CJun CMen LRHS MPkF NPCo
	- 'Otome-zakura'	CJun CMen LRHS MPkF WPat
	- 'Peaches and Cream' (v)	CBcs CJun CMen LRHS MPkF NLar
		NPCo SGol SPer SSta WPat
	- 'Peve Chameleon'	MPkF NLar
	- 'Peve Dave'	MPkF NLar
	- 'Peve Multicolor'	CJun MPkF NLar
	- 'Peve Ollie'^{PBR}	GKin MPkF NLar
	- 'Peve Stanley'	MPkF NLar
	- 'Peve Starfish'	NLar
	- 'Phoenix'	CJun EBee LBuc MAsh MBri MPkF
		NLar NPri NSoo SHil
	- 'Pine Bark Maple'	see *A. palmatum* 'Nishiki-gawa'
	- 'Pixie'	CJun CMen ELon EUJe IVic LRHS
		MGos MPkF NLar WPat
	- 'Princetown Gold'	NLar
	- 'Pung-kil'	IVic MPkF
	- 'Purple Ghost'	CJun NLar
	- 'Red Baron'	CJun IBoy
	- 'Red Blush'	CJun
	- 'Red Cloud'	CJun MPkF NLar
	- 'Red Elf'	MPkF
	- 'Red Emperor'	CBcs ELan EUJe IBoy LMil LRHS
		MBri MPkF NLar SPer WPat
	- 'Red Flame'	NLar
	- 'Red Flash'	CJun CMen MPkF
	- 'Red Jonas'	MPkF NLar
	- 'Red Pygmy' 🏆^{H4}	Widely available
	- 'Red Spider'	CJun
	- 'Red Wood'	CDoC CJun MPkF SBod SGol
		SLau
	- 'Redwine'^{PBR}	GBin LRHS MPkF NLar
	- 'Renjaku-maru'	MPkF
	- 'Reticulatum'	see *A. palmatum* 'Shigitatsu-sawa'
	- 'Ribesifolium'	see *A. palmatum* 'Shishigashira'
	- 'Rising Sun'	CJun NLar
	- 'Rokugatsu-en-nishiki'	WPat
	- 'Roseomarginatum'	see *A. palmatum* 'Kagiri-nishiki'
	- 'Rough Bark Maple'	see *A. palmatum* 'Arakawa'
	- 'Royle'	CJun
	- 'Rubrum'	CMen
I	- 'Rubrum Kaiser'	CJun
	- 'Ruby Ridge'	CJun
	- 'Ruby Star'	CJun MPkF
	- 'Rufescens'	MPkF
	- 'Ryokū-ryū'	CMen MPkF
	- 'Ryusen'	CJun NLar
	- 'Ryuzu'	CJun MPkF
	- 'Sagara-nishiki' (v)	CEnd CJun CMen LRHS MPkF
		NPCo
	- 'Sai-ho'	MPkF
	- 'Saint Jean'	MPkF
	- 'Samidare'	CJun MPkF NLar
	- 'Sandra'	CMen MPkF
N	- 'Sango-kaku' 🏆^{H4}	Widely available
	- 'Saoshika'	CJun CMen MPkF NLar
	- 'Sa-otome'	CMen MPkF
	- 'Satsuki-beni'	CJun CMen MPkF NPCo
	- 'Sazanami'	CDoC CEnd CJun CMen MPkF NLar
		WPat
	- 'Scolopendriifolium'	see *A. palmatum* 'Linearilobum'
§	- 'Seigai'	CJun MPkF

	- 'Seigen'	CEnd CJun CMCN CMen LRHS MPkF NPCo
	- 'Seiun-kaku'	CJun CMen MPkF WPat
	- 'Sekimori'	CJun NLar SBig
	- 'Sekka-yatsubusa'	CMCN CMen MPkF NLar
	- 'Semi-no-hane'	CJun NLar
N	- 'Senkaki'	see *A. palmatum* 'Sango-kaku'
	- 'Septemlobum Elegans'	see *A. palmatum* 'Heptalobum Elegans'
	- 'Septemlobum Purpureum'	see *A. palmatum* 'Hessei'
	- 'Sessilifolium' dwarf	see *A. palmatum* 'Hagoromo'
	- 'Sessilifolium' tall	see *A. palmatum* 'Koshimino'
	- 'Shaina'	CBcs CDoC CEnd CJun CMen CSBt CWGN CWib EBee EPfP IVic LRHS MBlu MBri MGos MPkF NLar NPCo NSoo SCoo SGol SHil SLim WMou
	- 'Sharon'	WPat
	- 'Sharp's Pygmy'	CJun CMen LRHS MPkF NPCo SGol WPat
	- 'Sherwood Flame'	CDoC CJun CMen CWib LRHS MAsh MBlu MGos MPkF NLar NPCo SCoo SGol
	- 'Shichigosan'	CMen
	- 'Shidava Gold'	CJun MPkF WPat
	- 'Shi-en'	MPkF
	- 'Shigarami'	CJun CMen MPkF
§	- 'Shigitatsu-sawa' (v)	CEnd CJun CMCN CMac CMen LRHS MGos MPkF NLar NPCo SBig
	- 'Shigure-bato'	CJun MPkF
	- 'Shigurezome'	MPkF NLar
	- 'Shikageori-nishiki'	CJun CMen MPkF
	- 'Shime-no-uchi'	CJun MPkF SBig
	- 'Shimofuri-nishiki'	MPkF
	- 'Shin-chishio'	CJun
	- 'Shindeshōjō'	Widely available
§	- 'Shinobuga-oka'	CBcs CJun CMCN CMen EUJe LRHS MPkF SBod SGol SLau
	- 'Shinonome'	CJun CMen MPkF NLar
	- 'Shirazz' (v)	CDoC CWGN IBoy LMil LRHS LSRN MBri MGos MPkF NLar SPer SPoG
§	- 'Shishigashira'	CDoC CJun CMCN CMac CMen EBee EPfP EUJe GKin IArd IVic LRHS MBlu MBri MGos MPkF NLar NPCo SCoo SGol SPoG WPat
	- 'Shishio'	CBcs CMCN CMen LMil LRHS MPkF NPCo SBig SSpi WPat
	- 'Shishio Improved'	CEnd CJun CMCN CMac CMen ELon EPfP LRHS MAsh MGos MPkF NHol NLar NPCo SBig SWvt
	- 'Shishio-hime'	MPkF
	- 'Shishi-yatsubusa'	CJun MPkF
	- 'Shōjō'	CJun CMCN NLar
	- 'Shōjō-no-mai'	CJun
	- 'Shōjō-nomura'	CEnd CMen MPkF NLar WPat
	- 'Sister Ghost'	CJun
	- 'Skeeter's Broom'	CBcs CJun CMen EBee ELan EPfP GBin IArd IBoy LBuc LMil LRHS MBri MGos MPkF NPCo SBig SCoo WPGP WPat
*	- 'Sode-nishiki'	CJun MPkF NLar
	- 'Starfish' **new**	MPkF
	- 'Stella Rossa'	CEnd CJun LRHS MPkF
	- 'Sumi-nagashi'	CBcs CDoC CMen CWCL EBee GBin LMil LRHS MGos MJak MPkF NLar NPCo SBod SCoo SGol SLau WPat
I	- 'Summer Gold'	CJun MPkF NLar SWvt
	- 'Sunshine'	MPkF

	- 'Susan'	MPkF
	- 'Taiyō-nishiki'	CJun MPkF
	- 'Takao'	CMen
	- 'Tama-hime'	CJun CMen LRHS MPkF NPCo
	- 'Tana'	CJun CMCN CMen EPfP MPkF NLar WPat
	- 'Tarō-yama'	CJun MPkF WPat
	- 'Tatsuta'	CMen MPkF
	- 'Taylor' PBR (v)	CEnd CWGN EPfP IVic LRHS MAsh MGos MPkF NLar NPri NSoo SCoo SHil SPoG
	- 'Tennyo-no-hoshi'	CMen MPkF NLar NPCo
	- 'Tiger Rose'	CJun
	- 'Tiny Tim'	CJun MPkF
	- 'Tobiosho'	CJun
	- 'Trompenburg' ♀H4	Widely available
	- 'Tsuchigumo'	CJun CMen MPkF NLar
	- 'Tsukasa Silhouette'	CJun
	- 'Tsukuma-no'	MPkF
	- 'Tsukushigata'	MPkF SGol WPat
	- 'Tsuma-beni'	CMCN CMen EPfP LRHS MPkF NLar NPCo
	- 'Tsuma-gaki'	CDoC CJun CMen LRHS MBri MGos MPkF NLar NPCo WPat
	- 'Tsuri-nishiki'	CJun CMen MPkF
	- 'Twombly's Red Sentinel'	CJun MBlu MPkF
	- 'Ueno-homare'	CMen MPkF
	- 'Ueno-yama'	CBcs CJun EUJe MPkF SGol WPat
	- 'Ukigumo' (v)	CBcs CEnd CJun CLnd CMCN CMac CMen CWib ELan GKin LMil LRHS MGos MPkF MRav NHol NLar NPCo SBig SCoo SPer SPoG SSta
	- 'Ukon'	CJun CMen LMil LRHS MJak MPkF NPCo SCoo
	- 'Umegae'	CJun
	- 'Uncle Ghost'	CJun
	- 'Usu-midori'	CJun
	- 'Utsu-semi'	CJun MPkF
	- 'Van der Akker'	CJun
	- 'Versicolor' (v)	CJun CMCN MPkF
	- 'Vic Pink'	CJun
	- 'Victoria'	SGol
	- 'Villa Taranto'	CDoC CEnd CJun CMCN CMen CWSG EPfP EUJe IVic LMil LRHS MAsh MBri MGos MPkF NHol NLar NPCo SCoo SGol SSta WPGP WPat
	- 'Volubile'	CMCN CMen MPkF NPCo
	- 'Wabito'	CJun CMen MPkF
	- 'Waka-midori'	CMen
	- 'Waka-momiji' (v)	CJun
	- 'Wakehurst Pink' (v)	CMCN MPkF WPat
	- 'Wendy'	CJun CMen IVic MPkF NLar SGol WPat
	- 'Wetumpka Red'	CJun
	- 'Whitney Red'	CMen
	- 'Wildgoose'	MPkF
	- 'Will D'	CJun
	- 'Wilson's Pink Dwarf'	CEnd CJun CMen CWib EBee GKin IVic LRHS MBri MGos MPkF NLar NPCo NSoo SChF SCoo SLim SPoG WPGP WPat
	- 'Winter Flame'	CJun GBin LMil LRHS MPkF NHol SBod WPat
§	- 'Wolff'	MPkF
	- 'Wolff's Broom'	MPkF WPat
	- 'Wou-nishiki'	CMCN CMen MPkF NPCo
	- 'Yana-gawa'	CMen
	- 'Yasemin'	CJun CMen CWGN IVic MPkF NLar NPCo SBig

- 'Yatsubusa'	MPkF NLar
- 'Yezo-nishiki'	CMen LRHS MBlu MPkF NLar
- 'Yūba-e'	MPkF NLar WPat
- 'Yūgure'	IVic MPkF
- 'Yuri-hime'	MPkF
- 'Yushide'	see *A. palmatum* 'Momenshide'
papilio	see *A. caudatum*
pauciflorum 'Blaze Away'	CJun LRHS
pectinatum GWJ 9354	WCru
- subsp. ***pectinatum*** B&SWJ 8270	WCru
- - HWJ 569	WCru
- - HWJ 944	WCru
pensylvanicum 🏆^{H4}	CBcs CDul CLnd CMCN CTho ECrN ELan EPfP MGos MMuc MRav NWea SEND SLim SPer SSpi SSta WPat
- 'Erythrocladum'	CEnd CJun CMCN EPfP MAsh MBri NEgg NHol NLar SBig SLim WPGP
pentaphyllum	SBig
* ***phlebanthum*** B&SWJ 9751	WCru
§ ***pictum***	CMCN
- subsp. ***okamotoanum***	CMCN
- - B&SWJ 8516	WCru
- - B&SWJ 12623 **new**	WCru
- subsp. ***pictum*** f. ***ambiguum*** B&SWJ 8806	WCru
- 'Shufu-nishiki'	CMCN
- 'Usugomo'	WPat
aff. ***pictum*** MCN0931	CMCN
- MCN0951	CMCN
platanoides 🏆^{H4}	CBcs CCVT CDoC CDul CLnd CMCN CSBt CTri CWib ECrN ELan EPfP MGos MMuc MSwo NWea SEND SEWo SGol SPer WHar WMou
- 'Cleveland'	CBcs CCVT
- 'Columnare'	CCVT CMCN CWib SCoo
- 'Crimson King' 🏆^{H4}	Widely available
- 'Crimson Sentry'	CCVT CDoC CDul CEnd CLnd CTri EBee ELan EPfP IArd IVic LAst LRHS LSRN MAsh MGos MRav SEWo SGol SPoG SWvt WHar
- 'Deborah'	CBcs CDul CTho EWTr SGol
- 'Dissectum'	WPat
- 'Drummondii' (v)	Widely available
- 'Emerald Queen'	CCVT ECrN
- 'Faassen's Black'	CJun
§ - 'Globosum'	CLnd CMCN EBee ECrN NLar SWvt
- 'Goldsworth Purple'	CLnd NEgg
- 'Laciniatum'	CMCN GBin WPat
- 'Marit'	WPat
- Princeton Gold = 'Prigo'^{PBR}	CBcs CDoC CDul EBee ECrN ELan EMil LBuc LRHS MAsh MBri MGos SCoo SEWo SGol SLim SPer SPoG WHar
- 'Reitenbachii'	CDul
- 'Royal Red'	CDul CWib ECrN MRav NLar SCoo SEWo
- 'Schwedleri' 🏆^{H4}	CMCN EPfP SGol
- 'Stollii' **new**	WPat
- subsp. ***turkestanicum***	SSta
pseudoplatanus	CBcs CCVT CDul CLnd CMCN CSBt CTri ECrN ELan LBuc MGos NWea SGol SPer WHar WMou
§ - 'Atropurpureum'	CDul ECrN NWea SEWo WHar
- 'Brilliantissimum' 🏆^{H4}	Widely available
- 'Erythrocarpum'	CMac
- 'Gadsby'	CDul EBee
- 'Leopoldii' misapplied	see *A. pseudoplatanus* f. *variegatum*
- 'Prinz Handjéry'	CBcs CDul CEnd CMCN CTri CWib MGos NHol NLar NWea SGol SPer WHar
- 'Spaethii' misapplied	see *A. pseudoplatanus* 'Atropurpureum'
§ - f. ***variegatum*** (v)	NEgg
- - 'Esk Sunset' (v)	CLnd EBee ELan LRHS LSRN MGos MPkF NLar SPoG WHar
- - 'Leopoldii' ambig. (v)	CBcs CCVT CDul CLnd CMCN ECrN ELan SPer SWvt
- - 'Simon-Louis Frères' (v)	CBcs CCVT CDul CLnd CMCN CWib EBee ECrN LAst MAsh MGos NEgg NLar SBod SCrf SGol SWvt WHar
- 'Worley'	CBcs CDul CLnd CMCN CMac EBee ECrN MRav NWea SGol SLim SPer
pseudosieboldianum	CJun CMCN IArd MBlu MPkF
- B&SWJ 8468	WCru
- B&SWJ 8746	WCru
- B&SWJ 8769	WCru
- var. ***microsieboldianum*** B&SWJ 8766	WCru
- subsp. ***takesimense*** B&SWJ 8500	WCru
- - B&SWJ 8540	WCru
pycnanthum	EPfP
'Red Flamingo' (v)	CJun CWSG LRHS MBlu MGos MPkF NLar SGol SHil SPoG
reticulatum	see *A. laevigatum* var. *reticulatum*
rubescens	CJun
- CWJ 12438	WCru
- RWJ 9840	WCru
- variegated (v)	CJun WPGP
rubrum	CAgr CBcs CCVT CDul CLnd CMCN CSBt CTho CTri EBee ELan EPfP EWTr MGos MMuc NWea SCoo SEWo SGol SLim SPer WCFE WHar WMoo WMou
- Autumn Flame	see *A. rubrum* 'Pete's Red'
- 'Autumn Flame'	CLnd
- 'Autumn Spire'	CJun
- 'Bowhall'	SBir
- 'Brandywine'	CDul CJun CTho EBee EPfP LRHS MAsh MBlu MBri NLar NWea SBir SCoo SPoG WHar
- Candy Ice' (v)	CJun
- 'Columnare'	EPfP
- 'Embers'	CJun NLar
- Fairview Flame	see *A. rubrum* 'Pete's Fairview'
- Fireball = 'Firzam'	CJun
- 'Firedance'	CJun
- 'Joseph' **new**	NLar
- 'New World'	SCoo
- 'Northwind'	CJun
- 'Northwood'	CJun
- 'October Glory' 🏆^{H4}	Widely available
§ - 'Pete's Fairview'	SPer
§ - 'Pete's Red'	MPkF
- 'Red King'	CJun
- Red Sunset = 'Franksred'	CCVT CDul CEnd CJun CLnd CMCN CTho EBee ELan EPfP NLar SBir SCoo SGol SLim SPoG SSta
- 'Scanlon'	CBcs CDul CEnd CJun CMCN CTho ELan EPfP LAst MBlu SLim SPer
- 'Schlesingeri'	CEnd CJun CLnd CMCN CMac EPfP
- 'Somerset'	CDul CJun CTho CTri EBee LRHS SCoo SLim WHar

	- Summer Red = 'Hosr'	CJun EBee SCoo SLim
	- 'Sun Valley'	CJun EBee LRHS MAsh SCoo SLim WHar
	- 'Tilford'	CJun SCoo SSta
§	***rufinerve*** 𝕐H4	CCVT CDoC CDul CLnd CMCN CTho CTri EBee ECrN ELan EPfP EWTr LRHS MAsh MBri MMuc NEgg NLar NWea SCoo SGol SPer SWvt WHar
	- B&SWJ 10845	GKin WCru
	- B&SWJ 10924	WCru
	- B&SWJ 10959	WCru
	- B&SWJ 11571	WCru
	- 'Albolimbatum'	see *A. rufinerve* 'Hatsuyuki'
	- 'Erythrocladum'	CBcs CJun SKHP
§	- 'Hatsuyuki' (v)	CEnd CJun CMCN EBee MBri SBig SSta
	- 'Ko-fuji-nishiki'	SSta
	- 'Winter Gold'	CJun EPfP SSta
	- 'Yakushima-nishiki'	SSta
§	***saccharinum***	CBcs CCVT CDul CLnd CMCN CTri CWib EBee ECrN ELan EPfP MGos MMuc MSnd NWea SCoo SGol SPer WHar
	- 'Born's Gracious'	CJun
	- 'Fastigiatum'	see *A. saccharinum* f. *pyramidale*
	- f. ***laciniatum***	CCVT EBee MBlu MGos MMuc SGol SPer
	- 'Laciniatum Wieri'	CDul CMCN SGol
	- f. ***lutescens***	CDul
§	- f. ***pyramidale***	CLnd ECrN NWea SPer
	saccharum	CAgr CBcs CDul CMCN CTho ECrN EPfP MBlu
	- 'Brocade'	CJun
	- 'Fiddlers Creek'	CJun
§	- subsp. ***grandidentatum***	EPfP
§	***sempervirens***	CJun EPfP LEdu MPkF SChF WPGP
	'Sensu'	CJun
	serrulatum CWJ 12437	WCru
	shirasawanum	CMCN
§	- 'Aureum' 𝕐H4	Widely available
	- 'Autumn Moon'	CBcs CJun CMCN CMen CWGN EPfP LRHS MBri MPkF NLar NPCo NPri SCoo SGol SLim SPoG WPat
§	- 'Ezo-no-momiji'	CJun CMen MPkF NPCo
	- 'Gloria'	LRHS MPkF NLar SGol
§	- 'Helena'	MPkF NLar WPat
	- 'Jordan'[PBR]	CDul CEnd CWGN EBee LRHS LSRN MBri MGos MPkF NLar SHil SLim SPoG
	- 'Lovett'	CJun
§	- 'Microphyllum'	MPkF
§	- 'Ogurayama'	CJun CMen NPCo
	- 'Palmatifolium'	CJun EUJe
	- 'Red Dawn'	CJun
	- 'Susanne'	CJun CMen MPkF SGol
	- var. ***tenuifolium*** B&SWJ 11073	WCru
	sieboldianum	CDul CMen CTho CTri ECrN MAsh MMuc SGol WHCr WHar WMou WPGP WPat
	- B&SWJ 10849	WCru
	- B&SWJ 11049	WCru
	- B&SWJ 11090	WCru
	- 'Sode-no-uchi'	CJun CMen MPkF NPCo
	- var. ***tsushimense*** B&SWJ 10962	WCru
	sikkimense B&SWJ 11613	WCru
	- B&SWJ 11689	WCru
	- B&SWJ 11703	WCru
	- DJHV 06152	WCru
	- WWJ 11601	WCru
	- WWJ 11613	WCru
	- WWJ 11853	WCru
	'Silver Cardinal' (v)	CBcs CEnd CJun CMCN EPfP MGos MPkF NLar WHar
	'Silver Vein'	see *A.* × *conspicuum* 'Silver Vein'
	sinense	CMCN
	spicatum	EPfP NLar
§	***stachyophyllum***	GQui
	- BWJ 8101	WCru
	sterculiaceum	NLar
	subsp. ***franchetii***	
	tataricum	CCVT CMCN
	- subsp. ***aidzuense*** B&SWJ 10958	WCru
§	- subsp. ***ginnala***	CBcs CCVT CDul CLnd CMCN CNWT CTri GKin MBlu MGos NLar NWea SGol
	- - 'Flame'	CDul CJun EBee ECrN ELan EPfP MGos MMuc MSnd NLar NWea
	- - 'Red Wing'	CJun EBee
	tegmentosum	CDul CJun CMCN EBee EPfP MBlu NLar
	- B&SWJ 8421	WCru
	- subsp. ***glaucorufinerve***	see *A. rufinerve*
	tetramerum	see *A. stachyophyllum*
	tonkinense subsp. ***liquidambarifolium*** DJHV 06173	WCru
	trautvetteri	CMCN EPfP
	triflorum 𝕐H4	CBcs CCVT CDul CJun CMCN EBee EPfP MBlu NLar SSpi
	truncatum	CDul MBlu MPkF
	- B&SWJ 8914	WCru
	- 'Akikaze-nishiki' (v)	CJun MPkF
	tschonoskii subsp. ***koreanum***	MPkF
	velutinum	CMCN
	'Viper' **new**	GQue LRHS
	'White Tigress'	CBcs CDoC CDul CJun CTho EBee EPfP GQue LRHS MBri NLar NWea SPoG WHar WPGP WPat
	× ***zoeschense***	CMCN MPkF
	- 'Annae'	SGol

Aceriphyllum see *Mukdenia*

× *Achicodonia* (*Gesneriaceae*)

'Dark Velvet'	WDib

Achillea (*Asteraceae*)

	ageratifolia 𝕐H4	CMea ECho ECtt EDAr LPio LRHS NGdn SRms
§	***ageratum***	CArn CPrp ECho ELau GPoy LEdu MHer MNHC SIde SRms WGwG WHer WJek XLum
	'Alabaster'	NDov SPhx
	Anthea = 'Anblo'[PBR]	CKno CWCL EBee ECtt IBoy LBMP LPio LRHS LSRN MAsh MCot MRav MSpe NHol NLar SRGP SRms SWvt
§	'Apfelblüte' (Galaxy Series)	CAby CWCL EBee ECtt EHyd ELan EPfP EWTr GKin LRHS LSRN MBel MMuc MRav MSpe NDov NGdn NHol NLBP NSti NWad SEND SPer WMnd WWEG
	Appleblossom	see *A.* 'Apfelblüte'
	'Apricot Beauty'	ECtt GMaP GQue SBod

	'Apricot Delight' (Tutti Frutti Series)	MNrw NCGa
	argentea misapplied	see *A. clavennae*, *A. umbellata*
	argentea Lamarck	see *Tanacetum argenteum*
I	***argentifolia*** hort.	WKif
	aurea	see *A. chrysocoma*
	'Bahama'	GBin GQue NBro
	'Belle Epoque' ♀H4	WWEG
	biebersteinii	XLum
	'Breckland Bouquet'	ECtt EWes
	'Breckland Ruby'	EWes
	'Carmina Burana'	CMea
	'Christine's Pink' ♀H4	MSpe MTis
§	***chrysocoma***	ECho MMuc MWat WMoo
	- 'Grandiflora'	LPla NGdn
§	***clavennae***	ECho EPot GKev MWat SBch SRms WAbe XSen
	clypeolata misapplied	COlW
	clypeolata Sibth. & Sm.	EBee EPPr LRHS NLar SPlb SRms
	coarctata	NBir XSen
	Colorado Group	CWCL LRHS NChi SPav
	'Coronation Gold' ♀H4	CDoC CPrp CWCL EBee ECtt ELan EPfP GBuc LAst LRHS MAsh MNFA MRav MWat NDov SDys SPer SWvt WCAu WCot WWEG XLum
	'Credo' ♀H4	CPrp ECtt ELon EPPr EPfP EWTr GBin IBoy LPio LPla LRHS MBel MNFA MRav MSpe NGdn NHol NLar NSti NWad SBea SMad SMrm SPer SWat WMnd WWEG
	crithmifolia	XLum
	decolorans	see *A. ageratum*
	erba-rotta subsp. ***moschata***	NBro
§	'Fanal'	CAby CMea COlW CPrp CWCL EBee ECtt EHyd ELan EPfP GBuc GKin IBoy LRHS MAsh MCot MRav MSpe NBir NDov NEgg NHol NLar NWad SPer SPoG SWvt WCot WMnd WWEG
	'Faust'	ELon MNrw SMrm
	'Federsee'	MArl
	'Feuerland'	CMac CSam EBee ECtt ELon EPPr EPfP GBin GKin LRHS MRav MSpe NBir NDov NGdn NSti SMrm SPer SPoG WWEG
	filipendulina	WHrl
	- 'Cloth of Gold' ♀H4	Widely available
	- 'Gold Plate' ♀H4	CAby CDoC CMac CSam CWCL EBee ECtt ELan EPfP GMaP LHop LRHS MAvo MBel MBri MMuc MRav NDov NOrc SEND SMrm SPer SPoG SRms SWvt WCot WJek WMnd WWEG
	- 'Parker's Variety' ♀H4	EBee GQue NBre WMoo XLum
	'Fleur van Zonneveld'	MSpe MTis NDov
	Flowers of Sulphur	see *A.* 'Schwefelblüte'
	(Forncett Series) 'Forncett Beauty'	SWvt
	- 'Forncett Candy'	WWEG
	- 'Forncett Citrus'	MAvo
	- 'Forncett Fletton'	CCon CWCL ECtt ELon EPPr EPfP EShb GBin GKin LHop MBel MNFA MNrw MRav MSpe MTis NCGa NGdn NHol NWad WPtf WWEG WWlt
	- 'Forncett Ivory'	EPPr MAvo WPtf
	fraasii	XSen
	(Galaxy Series) red-flowered	WSpi
	'Gloria Jean'	SHar SPhx
	'Gold and Grey'	SMrm WWEG
	grandifolia misapplied	see *Tanacetum macrophyllum* (Waldst. & Kit.) Sch.Bip.
§	***grandifolia*** Friv.	CElw COlW CSam LPla MRav NBro SPhx WBor WHer WMnd WMoo WOut
	'Great Expectations'	see *A.* 'Hoffnung'
	'Heidi' ♀H4	CCVN WPtf WWEG
	'Heinrich Vogeler'	EBee
	'Hella Glashoff' ♀H4	CMea CWCL EBee ELon GBin LRHS NDov
§	'Hoffnung'	CPrp CWCL MRav MSpe WWEG
	× ***huteri***	ECho ECtt EDAr EPfP MRav NGdn SBch SEND SRms WAbe WNew
	'Inca Gold'	CCVN CWCL ECGP ECtt EPPr EShb GBuc GQue LRHS MCot MRav MSpe MTis NHol NSti NWad WCFE WGwG WHoo WWEG
	'Jacqueline'	EWll MSpe MTis
	'Judity'	WOut
	× ***kellereri***	XSen
	'King Alfred'	CMea EPfP
	× ***kolbiana***	MWat SRms
§	'Lachsschönheit' (Galaxy Series) ♀H4	Widely available
	× ***lewisii*** 'King Edward' ♀H4	ECho EDAr EPfP GMaP NBir SBch SRms WAbe WIce
	ligustica	WCot
	'Lucky Break' ♀H4	MSpe MTis SDix WCot
	macrophylla	MBNS NBre
	'Marie Ann'	ECtt GQue LSRN MNrw NLar NPnk SPhx SRGP
	'Marmalade'	MTis SMrm WCFE WTGP WWEG
	'Martina' ♀H4	CDoC ECtt EPPr GBin GBuc GKin LAst LBMP LHop LPio MAsh MBNS MBel MCot MRav NCGa NDov NGdn NHol NOrc NWad SRGP WCot WWEG
	'McVities'	CWCL ECtt EPPr MSpe MTis WMnd WWEG
	millefolium	CArn CHab ELau GPoy MNHC NMir SPlb SRms WHer WJek WOut WSFF XLum
	- 'Bloodstone'	ECtt EWes MRav WPtf
	- 'Cassis'	CCVN CSpe GQue LDai LRHS MCot MNHC NGBl NLar SPet WBor WBrk WMoo WPtf
§	- 'Cerise Queen'	Widely available
	- 'Chamois'	MNrw
	- 'Cherry King'	NBir
	- 'Christel'	CCVN EWes GBin
	- 'Circus'	XLum
	- 'Kelwayi' ♀H4	WPtf
	- Kirschkönigin	see *A. millefolium* 'Cerise Queen'
	- 'Lansdorferglut' ♀H4	EBee LPla LRHS MTis NDov SPhx WWEG
	- 'Laura'	CSam CWGN LSou MAsh MNrw NCGa WHil
	- 'Lavender Beauty'	see *A. millefolium* 'Lilac Beauty'
§	- 'Lilac Beauty'	CBar COlW CPrp EHyd ELon EPfP EWTr GBin GBuc IBoy IPot LBMP LPio LRHS LSRN MHol MRav MSpe NBir NDov NEgg NLar NWad SHil SRms WWEG XLum
*	- 'Lilac Queen'	MArl
	- 'Little Suzie'	CWGN MAsh MBri
	- 'Lollypop'	LDai
	- 'Old Brocade'	EShb MTis WWEG

	- Pastel Shades	IFoB
	- 'Peggy Sue'	CWGN MBri NCGa
	- 'Pomegranate' (Tutti Frutti Series)	CWGN IPot LHop LLHF MNrw MTis NCGa NLar SHar XLum
	- 'Pretty Woman'	CSam CWGN MBri NCGa
	- 'Raspberry Ripple'	GBin
	- 'Red Beauty'	CWCL EBee ELan EPfP GBin MBNS MSpe SRms WWEG XLum
	- 'Red Salmon'	EWes
	- 'Red Velvet'	Widely available
	- 'Rose Madder'	CPrp CWCL ECtt EHoe EPPr EPfP GKin GMaP LPla LRHS MAsh MCot MHol MNrw MSpe NBir NCGa NGdn NHol NLar NSti SMrm SWvt WCot WGwG WHoo XLum
	- 'Salmon Pink'	IBoy ITim
	- 'Salmon Queen'	NHol
	- 'Sammetriese'	ELon LRHS MNrw NCGa SMad SPhx WWEG
	- 'Schneetaler'	GBin
	- 'Serenade'	EBee ECtt MAsh MSpe
	- 'Sue's Pink'	CSam MSpe
	- 'White Queen'	EBee
	- 'Wonderful Wampee'	EBee MNrw MTis NLar WCot
	'Mondpagode' ♀H4	EPPr EWTr LPla LRHS MAvo MBNS MCot MNFA MRav NGdn NHol SPhx WGwG WHoo WKif
*	'Moonbeam'	GKin SEND
	'Moonshine' ♀H3	Widely available
	'Moonwalker'	CAbP EBee EPfP NBre SPav WBrk WCot XLum
	nobilis	WOut
	- subsp. ***neilreichii***	CSpe ECGP EHoe EWTr GCal GQue IKil LAst LRHS MNrw NSti SPer SWvt WGwG WHal WPtf WWEG
*	***odilis***	LRHS
	'Paprika' (Galaxy Series)	Widely available
	'Peardrop'	NBre
	'Petra'	MNrw XLum
	pindicola subsp. ***integrifolia***	EWes
	pink-flowered from Santa Cruz Island	CKno CWCL
	'Pink Grapefruit' (Tutti Frutti Series)	MNrw MTis NCGa NLar WCAu
	'Pink Lady'	GBBs
	'Pretty Belinda'	EBee ECtt EPfP IPot LAst LPla LRHS LSRN LSou MBNS MBel MBri MCot MSpe NLar NSti SKHP SPoG STes WWlt
	'Prospero'	WCot WWEG
	ptarmica	CArn CBre ELau MHer NMir NPri SRms XLum
*	- 'Ballerina'	MBNS MWhi NBre NDov NGdn NLar
	- Innocence	see *A. ptarmica* 'Unschuld'
	- 'Major'	WCot
	- 'Nana Compacta'	CSpe EPPr GBin IBoy LRHS NBir NCGa SPlb WCFE WWEG
	- 'Perry's White' (d)	CBcs CBre IPot MNrw NGdn SRGP WCot
	- 'Stephanie Cohen'	see *A. sibirica* 'Stephanie Cohen'
N	- The Pearl Group seed-raised (d)	CTri ELan MMuc SGbt SPlb SWat WMoo
N	- - 'Boule de Neige' (clonal) (d)	GKin IBoy MRav MSpe NBre NPer NSti SPer SPet XLum
N	- - 'The Pearl' (clonal) (d) ♀H4	CMac CSBt CWCL EPfP IBoy IFoB LHop LPot LRHS LSRN MBel MHol MLHP MRav MWat NBid NBir NBro NLar SRms WBor WBrk WCot WHer WHil WJek
§	- 'Unschuld'	NBir
	pyrenaica	XLum
	'Rougham Salmon'	WPtf
	'Safran'	LRHS XLum
	salicifolia 'Silver Spray'	GQue NLar SPav WOut
	'Sally'	EPPr MSpe
	Salmon Beauty	see *A.* 'Lachsschönheit'
	'Sandstone'	see *A.* 'Wesersandstein'
	'Saucy Seduction' (Tutti Frutti Series)	ELon LLHF MAsh MTis NCGa NLar
§	'Schwefelblüte'	MRav NBir SBch SMrm
	'Schwellenburg'	CDes NBre WCot
	sibirica	WPtf
	subsp. ***camschatica***	
	- - 'Love Parade'	CHid EBee EPfP ITim LEdu LHop LRHS MBNS MMuc MNrw MRav NGdn NLar SGbt SPer STes WMoo WWEG XLum
§	- 'Stephanie Cohen'	CPrp GBee GBin WWEG
	'Stephanie'	ECtt EPPr EWes LSRN MSpe
	Summer Berries Group	LPio LRHS
	Summer Pastels Group	EPfP IBoy LRHS NLar NOrc SPav SPoG SRms
	'Summerwine' ♀H4	Widely available
	'Sunbeam'	SHar
	'Sunny Seduction'	ELon NCGa
I	'Taygetea'	ECtt ELan EPPr EPfP MBNS NPnk SDix SPer SPet SRkn WCot WSHC WWEG
	'Terracotta'	Widely available
	'The Beacon'	see *A.* 'Fanal'
	'Tissington Flame'	MAvo MTis
	'Tissington Old Rose'	MAvo MNrw MSpe MTis WBrk
	tomentosa ♀H4	CTri ECho ECtt WCot
§	- 'Aurea'	ECho LRHS NBro
	- 'Goldie'	EDAr MAsh
	- 'Maynard's Gold'	see *A. tomentosa* 'Aurea'
	'Tri-colour'	NGdn NWad
§	***umbellata***	WAbe WBrk XSen
	'W.B. Childs'	ELan MCot MNrw MRav NDov SHar WCot
	'Walther Funcke'	Widely available
§	'Wesersandstein'	CWCL ECtt EPPr GBin GMaP LPla LRHS MNrw NBir SGbt WWEG
	'Wilczekii'	SRms
	'Yellowstone'	EWes LDai MAsh

× *Achimenantha* (*Gesneriaceae*)

'Aries'	EABi WDib
'Inferno' ♀H1	EABi WDib
'Pisces' **new**	WDib
'Texas Blue Bayou' **new**	WDib
'Texas Spotted Leopard'	EABi
'Tyche'	EABi

Achimenes (*Gesneriaceae*)

'Addano'	WDib
'Ambroise Verschaffelt' ♀H1	EABi WDib
'Ami Van Houtte'	WDib
'Apricot Glow'	EABi
'Aquamarine'	WDib
'Ballerina'	WDib
'Blue David'	EABi
'Blue Sparkles'	EABi SDeJ
'Boy David'	EABi
'Caligula'	EABi
'Cameo Rose'	WDib

'Camille Brozzoni'	EABi
'Cascade Fashionable Pink'	WDib
'Cascade Rose Red'	WDib
'Cascade Violet Night'	WDib
'Charity'	WDib
'Charm'	SDeJ
'Cherry Blossom'	EABi
'Claret'	EABi WDib
'Clouded Yellow'	EABi
'Coral Cameo Mix'	EABi
'Cornell Favourite'	EABi
'Côte d'Ivoire'	EABi
'Crackerjack'	WDib
'Crummock Water'	EABi WDib
'Derwentwater'	EABi
'Donna'	EABi
'Dot'	EABi
'Double Pink Rose' (d)	WDib
'Electra'	EABi
'English Waltz'	EABi
erecta	EABi WDib
'Erlkönig'	WDib
'Extravaganza'	WDib
'Flamenco'	WDib
'Flaming Embers'	EABi
'Glory'	EABi WDib
grandiflora 'Robert Dressler'	EABi
'Grape Wine'	EABi
'Hard to Get'	EABi
'Harry Williams'	EABi WDib
'Hilda Michelssen' ♀H1	EABi WDib
'Jay Dee Coral'	WDib
'Jay Dee Large White'	WDib
'Jay Dee Pink'	WDib
'Jay Dee Purple'	WDib
'Jennifer Goode'	EABi WDib
'Johanna Michelssen'	WDib
'Jubilee Gem'	EABi
'Just Divine'	EABi WDib
'Kim Blue'	WDib
'Light Lilac'	WDib
'Little Beauty'	WDib
longiflora	EABi
- 'Major'	WDib
'Luneberg'	EABi
'Menuett'	WDib
mexicana	SDeJ
'Mozelle'	EABi
'Opal'	WDib
'Orange Delight'	EABi WDib
'Orange Queen'	EABi
'Palette Salmon' (Palette Series)	EABi
'Pally'	WDib
'Patens Major'	EABi WDib
'Peach Blossom'	SDeJ WDib
'Peach Glow'	EABi WDib
'Pearly Queen'	EABi
pedunculata	EABi
'Petite Fadette'	EABi
'Pink Beauty'	EABi
'Pink Rose' (d)	EABi
'Platinum'	EABi
'Primadonna'	SDeJ WDib
'Pulcherrima'	SDeJ
I 'Purple Hybrid'	EABi
'Purple King'	WDib
'Purple Queen'	WDib
'Purple Triumph'	WDib
'Queen of Queens'	WDib
'Rainbow'	EABi WDib
'Red Elfe'	EABi
'Red Giant'	EABi
'Red Hilda Michelssen'	WDib
'Rhino'	EABi
'Rosa Charm'	EABi
'Rose Dream'	EABi
'Serge Saliba'	EABi
'Show-off'	WDib
'Snow Princess'	SDeJ
'Stan's Delight' (d) ♀H1	EABi WDib
'Sterntaler'	WDib
'Summer Sunset'	EABi
'Sweet & Sour'	EABi
'Tango'	WDib
'Tarantella'	EABi WDib
'Teresa'	EABi
(Tetra Series) 'Tetra Verschaffelt'	EABi
- 'Tetra Wine Red Charm'	EABi
'Tiger Eye'	WDib
'Trailing Yellow'	EABi
'Vie-en-Rose'	EABi
'Violacea Semiplena'	WDib
'Vivid'	EABi WDib
'Weinrot Elfe'	WDib
'Wetterlow's Triumph'	EABi WDib
'Yellow Beauty'	WDib

Achlys (*Berberidaceae*)

japonica	WCru
triphylla	WCru

Achnatherum see *Stipa*

Achyranthes (*Amaranthaceae*)

bidentata	CArn

Acidanthera see *Gladiolus*

Acinos (*Lamiaceae*)

§ ***alpinus***	EBee EDAr GJos ITim LLHF SBch SPhx WJek XLum
§ ***corsicus***	WHoo WKif

Aciphylla (*Apiaceae*)

aurea	GBin GCal GKev SPlb
colensoi	CMen
congesta	CMen EPot
crosby-smithii	CMen
dieffenbachii	CBrP EUJe
glaucescens	EUJe GKev SPlb
hectorii	CMen
horrida	CMen
kirkii	CMen
lecomtei new	CMen
'Lomond'	EBee
montana	CMen EPot GLin
pinnatifida	CMen
simplex	CMen
spedenii new	CMen
subflabellata	GKev

Acis (*Amaryllidaceae*)

§ ***autumnalis*** ♀H4	CAby CAvo CBro CDes CElw CTca CTri ECho EPot EWes GKev LEdu

	LRHS NBir SBch SMrm SRms SRot WAbe WHil WHoo WPGP
- 'Cobb's Variety'	WCot
- var. ***oporantha***	CWCL EPri
- - from Morocco	ECho
- var. ***pulchella***	ECho
- 'September Snow'	GKev
nicaeensis ♀H2-3	CDes ECho EPot GCal GKev LLHF LRHS WAbe WCot WThu
§ ***rosea***	ECho WAbe WThu
§ ***tingitana***	CBro ECho
§ ***trichophylla***	ECho LLHF WCot
- J&JA 630.501	LWst
- f. ***purpurascens***	CDes ECho WCot
§ ***valentina***	ECho SRot WCot

Acmella (*Asteraceae*)

§ ***oleracea***	CArn

Acmena (*Myrtaceae*)

smithii	EShb

Acnistus (*Solanaceae*)

australis	see *Iochroma australe*

Aconitum (*Ranunculaceae*)

B&SWJ 2954 from Nepal	WCru
CNDS 036 from Burma	WCru
GWJ 9417 from northern India	WCru
alboviolaceum	LLHF WCot
- var. ***alboviolaceum*** f. ***albiflorum*** B&SWJ 4105	WCru
- - - B&SWJ 8444	WCru
- var. ***purpurascens*** B&SWJ 8477	WCru
'Album' **new**	WMnd
altissimum	see *A. lycoctonum* subsp. *vulparia*
anglicum	see *A. napellus* subsp. *napellus* Anglicum Group
§ ***anthora***	CArn EPfP EWTr IKil LRHS MHol NLar
arcuatum	see *A. fischeri* var. *arcuatum*
austroyunnanense	WSHC
- BWJ 7902	WCru
autumnale misapplied	see *A. carmichaelii* Wilsonii Group
autumnale Rchb.	see *A. fischeri* Rchb.
× ***bicolor***	see *A.* × *cammarum* 'Bicolor'
'Blue Lagoon'PBR	CWGN EBee IPot
'Blue Opal'	CDes EBee ECtt EWes WPGP
'Blue Sceptre'	GBin LDai LRHS NLar
'Bressingham Spire' ♀H4	Widely available
bulbilliferum HWJK 2120	WCru WSHC
§ × ***cammarum*** 'Bicolor' ♀H4	Widely available
- 'Eleanora'	CCon ECtt EPfP EWes GBuc GCra LHop LRHS LSou MBri MNrw NLar SPoG SRms WCot
- 'Grandiflorum Album'	CAby LPio LPla MNrw
- 'Pink Sensation'PBR	CAby EPfP GQue LLHF MBNS NBre NCGa NDov NLar NPnk
§ ***carmichaelii***	CArn CHel CMea CSam ELan EPfP GBin GBuc GCra GKin IFoB IFro LAst LRHS LSou MBri MNrw NBro NChi NEgg NGdn NOrc NSoo SGol SRms WCot WHoo
- Arendsii Group	ECtt GKev LAst LRHS SPhx SRot
- - 'Arendsii' ♀H4	Widely available
- - 'Cloudy'PBR	NDov NLar
- 'Moody Blues' **new**	EBee
- 'Redleaf'	see *A. carmichaelii* 'Royal Flush'
- 'River Arrow'	WCot
- 'River Avon'	WCot
- 'River Dee'	WCot
- 'River Devon'	WCot
- 'River Finn'	WCot
- 'River Lugg'	WCot
- 'River Lune'	WCot
- 'River Medway'	WCot
- 'River Nene'	WCot
- 'River Ouse'	WCot
- 'River Spey'	WCot
- 'River Tees'	WCot
- 'River Teifi'	WCot
- 'River Trent'	WCot
- 'River Welland'	WCot
§ - 'Royal Flush'PBR	COIW CWGN EBee ECtt EPfP GBin IBoy MBNS MNrw NLar SPer WCot
- var. ***truppelianum***	WCot
- - HWJ 732	EBee WCot WCru
§ - Wilsonii Group	CPrp EBee ECGP GMaP LPio LPla LRHS MCot MRav MWat MWhi NCGa NDov NEgg WHoo XLum
- - 'Barker's Variety'	CCon CKno ELon EPfP GBuc GCal GQue LHop LRHS NGdn NLar NSti WCot WSpi
- - 'Kelmscott' ♀H4	ECtt EWes MCot MRav SDix WRHF WSpi
- - 'Spätlese'	CAbP CSam CWGN EBee ECtt ELon EPfP GCal LBMP LEdu LRHS LSou MCot MNFA NBir NDov NGdn NLar SGbt SMrm WCot
chasmanthum	LRHS
chiisanense B&SWJ 4446	WCru
cilicicum	see *Eranthis hyemalis* Cilicica Group
'Cloudy'	CPrp EBee ECtt MBri NGdn WCot
compactum	see *A. napellus* subsp. *vulgare*
confertiflorum	see *A. anthora*
delphiniifolium	CExl
elliotii	EBee
elwesii	EBee LRHS NBre
episcopale	WCru
aff. ***episcopale***	WWEG
- CLD 1426	GBuc
excelsum	see *A. lycoctonum* subsp. *lycoctonum*
ferox	EBee ELon EWes LLHF
- HWJK 2217	WCru
fischeri misapplied	see *A. carmichaelii*
§ ***fischeri*** Rchb.	CWib EBee MMuc MSCN NCGa NLar WCot
- B&SWJ 8809	WCru
§ - var. ***arcuatum*** B&SWJ 774	WCru
formosanum	LEdu
- B&SWJ 3057	WCru
fukutomei B&SWJ 337	MRav WCru
gammiei GWJ 9418	WCru
gmelinii	see *A. lycoctonum* subsp. *lycoctonum*
grossedentatum	LPla NLar
§ ***hemsleyanum***	CExl CHVG CMea CRHN CWGN ECtt EPfP GCra GKev NBid WCru
- dark blue	MLHP
- 'Red Wine'	CMea LRHS WWEG
hyemale	see *Eranthis hyemalis*

'Ivorine'	CSam CTri EBee ELan ELon EPfP GAbr GBuc GCra GMaP LAst LEdu LHop LRHS LSRN MCot MHol NGdn NLar NPri NSti SPer WPnP
jaluense B&SWJ 8741	WCru
japonicum	EBee GCal LRHS NLar WCot
- var. ***hakonense***	CExl
- var. ***montanum*** B&SWJ 5507	WCru
§ - subsp. ***napiforme***	EWes WCot
- - B&SWJ 943	CDes EBee ELon WCru
§ - subsp. ***subcuneatum*** B&SWJ 6228	WCru
krylovii	WCot
kusnezoffii	WCot
laciniatum GWJ 9254	WCru
- GWJ 9324	WCru
lamarckii	see *A. lycoctonum* subsp. *neapolitanum*
lasianthum	see *A. lycoctonum* subsp. *vulparia*
loczyanum B&SWJ 11529	WCru WSHC
longecassidatum B&SWJ 4277	WCru
- B&SWJ 8486	WCru
- B&SWJ 8488	WCru
lycoctonum	LRHS NLar NOrc WSpi
- 'Darkeyes'	CAbP WCot
- 'Graupe'	WCot
§ - subsp. ***lycoctonum***	CCon SRms WCot
- - var. ***rubicundum***	LRHS
§ - subsp. ***moldavicum***	LRHS WCot
§ - subsp. ***neapolitanum***	EBee ECtt GCal GMaP MMuc NLar
- 'Russian Yellow'	EWld GCal
§ - subsp. ***vulparia***	CArn CCon CMac GPoy MNrw MRav NEgg NGdn WCot
mairei	see *A. vilmorinianum*
moldavicum	see *A. lycoctonum* subsp. *moldavicum*
nagarum	WCot
- KR 7589	CDes WPGP
napellus	CArn CHel CMHG CPrp CSpe ECtt EPfP GAbr GKev GPoy LAst LEdu LRHS MBel MCot MHoo MMuc MNHC MWat NEgg SPet SRms SWat WBor WHoo WShi XLum
- 'Bergfürst'	CAby CMea EBee LPla LRHS MNFA NDov
- 'Blue Valley'	EPfP EWes SPoG WHil
- subsp. ***fissurae***	LRHS
- 'Gletschereis'	EBee
- subsp. ***napellus***	SRms
§ - - Anglicum Group	CSev EBee MCot WCot
- 'Rubellum'	ECtt ELan GQue IBoy LRHS MCot NBir NBro NEgg NPri SPoG WMnd
- 'Schneewittchen'	CSpe EBee EWes GQue IPot
- subsp. ***vulgare*** 'Albidum'	CMea CPrp ELan ELon EPfP GAbr GMaP LEdu LRHS MBel NBid NHol NLar NPri SBea SGol SMrm SPer SPet WBor
- - 'Carneum'	GCra LRHS WHer WKif
napiforme	see *A. japonicum* subsp. *napiforme*
neapolitanum	see *A. lycoctonum* subsp. *neapolitanum*
'Newry Blue'	EBee EPfP GBuc IMou LRHS NBir NLar SRms WSpi
orientale misapplied	see *A. lycoctonum* subsp. *vulparia*
orientale ambig.	NPro
paniculatum misapplied	see *A. variegatum* subsp. *paniculatum*
piepunense	EBee GKev
proliferum B&SWJ 4107	WCru
pseudohuiliense	CExl
pseudolaeve B&SWJ 8663	WCru
- var. ***erectum*** B&SWJ 8466	WCru
pubiceps new	WCot
- white-flowered	GCal
pyrenaicum misapplied	see *A. lycoctonum* subsp. *neapolitanum*
ranunculifolius	see *A. lycoctonum* subsp. *neapolitanum*
sachalinense	WCot
- subsp. ***yezoense***	EBee GCal NLar WCot
senanense var. ***incisum*** B&SWJ 11032	WCru
seoulense B&SWJ 694	WCru
- B&SWJ 864	WCru
- BWJ 4107 new	IMou
septentrionale	see *A. lycoctonum* subsp. *lycoctonum*
'Spark's Variety' $\mathbb{Y}^{H4}$	Widely available
spicatum GWJ 9393	WCru
- GWJ 9394	WCru
'Stainless Steel'	Widely available
subcuneatum	see *A. japonicum* subsp. *subcuneatum*
× ***tubergenii***	see *Eranthis hyemalis* Tubergenii Group
uchiyamae B&SWJ 1005	WCru
- B&SWJ 1216	ELon EPPr WCru
- B&SWJ 4446	NLar
variegatum	EBee GCal
§ - subsp. ***paniculatum***	MLHP WCot
§ ***vilmorinianum*** BWJ 8055	WCru
volubile misapplied	see *A. hemsleyanum*
volubile Pall	CCon
vulparia	see *A. lycoctonum* subsp. *vulparia*
yamazakii	WCru
zigzag var. ***ryohakuense*** B&SWJ 0906	WCru

Aconogonon see *Persicaria*

Acorus ✿ (*Acoraceae*)

calamus	CArn CBAq CKno CWat EHon ELau GPoy MNHC MSKA MWts NPer SWat WHer WMAq
- subsp. ***angustatus***	GPoy
- 'Argenteostriatus' (v)	CBAq CRow CWat EBee EHon MCot MMuc MWts NOrc SEND SRms SWat WMAq WWEG
* ***christophii***	ELon EPPr EWes
gramineus	ELau GPoy MSKA NPer SWat WHer WMoo
- 'Golden Edge' (v)	ELon EWes MBri
- 'Hakuro-nishiki' (v)	EHoe EPPr EPot GBin LRHS MGos MMoz NBid NHol NWad SRms SWvt WMoo XLum
- 'Kinchinjunga' (v)	IFro
- 'Licorice'	EBee EPPr GBin GCal MBNS SPoG WGrn
- 'Masamune' (v)	EWes GBin GCal WMoo
- 'Minimus Aureus'	CBre GCal
- 'Oborozuki' misapplied	see *A. gramineus* 'Ōgon'
- 'Oborozuki' (v)	EHoe
§ - 'Ōgon' (v)	Widely available
- 'Omogo'	MJak
- var. ***pusillus***	NBro WWEG

- 'Variegatus' (v)	Widely available
- 'Yodo-no-yuki' (v)	EBee
'Intermedius'	NPer

Acradenia (*Rutaceae*)

frankliniae	CBcs CMHG CMac CTsd EBee IDee MBlu SKHP SPlb WHor WPGP

Actaea (*Ranunculaceae*)

alba misapplied	see *A. pachypoda*, *A. rubra* f. *neglecta*
arizonica	EBee GCal LPla LRHS SPhx WCru
asiatica	CDes EBee
- B&SWJ 616	WCru
- B&SWJ 6351 from Japan	WCru
- B&SWJ 8694 from Korea	WCru
- BWJ 8174 from China	WCru
biternata B&SWJ 5591	WCru
- B&SWJ 8917	WCru
- B&SWJ 11190	WCru
'Chocoholic'	CLAP EBee ECtt GBin IKil IPot MCot NCGa
§ ***cimicifuga***	CLAP GCal GPoy LRHS
- B&SWJ 2657	WCru
§ ***cordifolia***	EBee GBin GMaP LAst LHop LRHS MSCN NGdn NLar SBod SMrm SWvt WBor
- variegated (v)	EBee LRHS
dahurica	CArn EBee GBin GQue LRHS SWat WCot
- B&SWJ 8426	WCru
- B&SWJ 8573	WCru
- tall	GBin
erythrocarpa	see *A. rubra*
frigida B&SWJ 2966	WCru
heracleifolia B&SWJ 8843	WCot WCru
§ ***japonica***	CLAP GCal
- B&SWJ 5828	WCru
- B&SWJ 11136	WCru
- var. ***acutiloba*** B&SWJ 6257	WCru
- compact	GBin
- - B&SWJ 8758A	WCot WCru
I - 'Minima'	LRHS
mairei	GCal LRHS
- BWJ 7635	WCru
- BWJ 7939	WCru
§ ***matsumurae***	CExl
- B&SWJ 11187	WCru
- B&SWJ 11528	WCru
- 'Elstead Variety' ♀H4	CExl GCal MRav
- 'Frau Herms'	LRHS
- 'White Pearl'	Widely available
§ ***pachypoda*** ♀H4	CBro CExl EBee ECGP EPfP GBin GCal GLog GPoy IGor LRHS NBid NLar WCru
- 'Misty Blue'	CWGN ECtt ESwi IPot LBMP LSou MHol NLar NMyG SHar SMad SPoG WCot
- f. ***rubrocarpa***	GCal
§ ***podocarpa***	SPlb SRms WCru
racemosa ♀H4	CArn CMac ELan EPfP EWTr GBin GCal GPoy LRHS MHoo NBid NGdn NLar NSti SPer SWvt WMnd
§ ***rubra*** ♀H4	CBro EBee ELan GCal LRHS MCot MMHG MNrw NBid SMad WCru
- B&SWJ 9555	WCru
- ***alba***	see *A. pachypoda*, *A. rubra* f. *neglecta*
§ - f. ***neglecta***	GAbr GCal GQue SKHP WCot WCru
simplex	EBee GCra LRHS NEgg SEND SWat WCot
- B&SWJ 8653	WCru
- B&SWJ 8664	WCru
- B&SWJ 10957	WCru
- B&SWJ 11133	WCru
§ - Atropurpurea Group	Widely available
- - 'Bernard Mitchell'	CCon
- - 'Black Negligee'	CExl CLAP CWGN ECtt EUJe GAbr GQue IBoy LLHF LPla LRHS LSou MAvo MBel MBri MHol NCGa NLar NMyG SPad SPoG SWat WCot WMoo WWEG
- - 'Brunette' ♀H4	Widely available
- - 'Carbonella'	ECtt WHlf
- - 'Hillside Black Beauty'	CCVN CLAP ECtt GBin GMaP LRHS MNrw NBir NPnk WCot
- - 'James Compton'	CCVN CExl CLAP CPar EBee ECtt EHoe EPfP GCal GMaP IBoy IKil IPot LRHS MAsh MAvo MBNS MNHC NBir NDov NGdn NLar NOrc SWvt WCAu WCFE WMoo WWlt
- - 'Mountain Wave'	CLAP ECtt WCot WPGP
- 'Pink Spike'	Widely available
§ - 'Prichard's Giant'	CLAP EBee GBin GCal LRHS MRav MSpe NDov NLar
- ***ramosa***	see *A. simplex* 'Prichard's Giant'
- 'Silver Axe'	GCal LRHS NBre NGdn
- variegated (v)	CDes WCot
spicata	EPPr GBin GCra GPoy LRHS NLar WCru
- from England	GCal WCru
taiwanensis B&SWJ 3413	WCru
- RWJ 9996	WCru
yesoensis B&SWJ 6355	WCru
- B&SWJ 10860	WCru
yunnanensis	EBee GCal

Actinella see *Tetraneuris*

Actinidia (*Actinidiaceae*)

BWJ 8161 from China	WCru
arguta (f/F)	CAgr NLar
- 74-32 (m)	CAgr
- B&SWJ 4455 from Jejudo, South Korea	WCru
- B&SWJ 4823 from Japan	WCru
- B&SWJ 8529 from Ulleungdo, South Korea	WCru
- 'Ananasnaya' (f/F)	CAgr
- var. ***cordifolia*** (f/F)	CAgr
- 'Geneva 2' (f/F)	CAgr
- 'Issai' (s-p/F)	CAgr CBcs CCCN EPfP EPom EUJe LRHS MGos NLar SVic WCot
- 'Jumbo' (f/F)	SVic
- 'Ken's Red' (F)	CAgr SVic
- 'Kiwai Vert' (f/F)	CAgr
- LL#1 (m)	CAgr
- LL#2 (f/F)	CAgr
- LL#3 (m)	CAgr
- 'Meader' (m)	CAgr
- 'MSU' (F)	CAgr
- 'Purpurna Sadowa' (f/F) **new**	LRHS MCoo
- 'Shoko' (f)	WCru
- 'Unchae' (m)	WCru

- 'Weika' (m) new	MCoo
- 'Weiki' (m)	LRHS SVic
chinensis misapplied	see *A. deliciosa*
chinensis ambig.	CDoy
§ ***deliciosa***	MGos MRav WSHC
- 'Atlas' (m)	CAgr NLar SDea
* - 'Boskoop'	EUJe MCoo MGos
- 'Hayward' (f/F)	CAgr CBcs CCCN CDoC CHEx CHel CMac EBee EPfP LHop LRHS LSRN MCoo MREP NLar SDea SWvt
- hermaphrodite (F)	ELan
- 'Jenny' (s-p/F)	CAgr CHEx CMac CSut CTri EPfP EPom LAst LBuc LRHS MBri MGos SDea SLim SPer SPoG SPre SVic
- 'Saanichton' (f/F) new	CAgr
- 'Solo' (s-p/F)	CBcs CCCN CDoC CMac CSBt EBee EPfP LRHS LSRN MCoo NLar NPri SLim SPer SWvt WPGP
- 'Tomuri' (m)	CBcs CCCN CDoC CHEx CMac EBee EPfP LRHS LSRN MCoo NLar SWvt
hypoleuca B&SWJ 5942	WCru
kolomikta ♀H4	Widely available
- (m)	MBlu NPla
- B&SWJ 4243	LSRN WCru
- 'Pasha' (m) new	CAgr
- 'Red Beauty' (F)	CAgr
- 'September Sun' (f/F) new	CAgr
- 'Tomoko' (f/F)	WCru
- 'Yazuaki' (m)	WCru
latifolia B&SWJ 3563	WCru
melanandra	SPlb
petelotii HWJ 628	WCru
pilosula misapplied	see *A. tetramera* var. *maloides*
pilosula (Finet & Gagnep.) Stapf ex Hand.-Mazz. new	GGal LRHS
polygama	GCal
- B&SWJ 5444	WCru
- B&SWJ 8525 from Korea	WCru
- B&SWJ 8923 from Japan	WCru
- 'Vera's Pride' (f/F) new	CAgr
rufa B&SWJ 3525	WCru
aff. ***strigosa*** HWJK 2367	WCru
tetramera B&SWJ 3564	WCru
§ - var. ***maloides***	CBcs CDoC CExl CHel CSPN CWGN EBee EPfP EUJe EWTr GCal GGal LHop MGos NLar SBrt SCoo SHil SKHP SPoG WCru WPGP WSHC

Adansonia (*Malvaceae*)

grandidieri	SPlb
gregorii	SPlb
madagascariensis	SPlb
rubrostipa	SPlb
za	SPlb

Adelocaryum see *Lindelofia*

Adenanthos (*Proteaceae*)

sericeus	SVen

Adenium (*Apocynaceae*)

obesum ♀H1	LToo
- subsp. ***boehmianum***	LToo
- subsp. ***swazicum***	LToo

Adenocarpus (*Papilionaceae*)

decorticans	SPlb SVen

Adenophora (*Campanulaceae*)

sp. new	MHol
BWJ 7696 from China	WCru
'Afterglow'	see *Campanula rapunculoides* 'Afterglow'
'Amethyst'	EDif
asiatica	see *Hanabusaya asiatica*
aurita	CRDP WCot
bulleyana	CCon CHVG ELan GCra GJos IKil LRHS NBid NGdn SPav SPlb WCot
capillaris	WCot
subsp. ***leptosepala***	
- - BWJ 7986	WCru
coelestis	CExl NBid
- B&SWJ 7998	WCru
confusa	GAbr LDai WHer WSHC
* ***cymerae***	LDai
grandiflora B&SWJ 8555	WCru
jasionifolia BWJ 7946	WCru
khasiana	CExl LLHF NLar XLum
lamarkii B&SWJ 8738	WCru
latifolia misapplied	see *A. pereskiifolia*
latifolia ambig. white-flowered	MMuc
liliifolia	EPfP GAbr GCal LHop LRHS MMuc NPer SMrm XLum
maximowicziana B&SWJ 11008	WCru
morrisonensis RWJ 10008	WCru
§ ***nikoensis***	ECtt NBid
§ ***pereskiifolia***	EWes SHar SPlb WCot
polyantha	NLar SRms
polymorpha	see *A. nikoensis*
potaninii	CCon EBee ELan MMuc SEND WHal WPtf
- pale flowered	LPla MMuc SEND WHal
remotiflora B&SWJ 8714	WCru
- B&SWJ 11016	WCru
takedae B&SWJ 11424	WCru
- var. ***howozana***	MLHP
tashiroi	CPrp XLum
trachelioides B&SWJ 8614	WCru
triphylla B&SWJ 8608	WCru
- B&SWJ 10916	WCru
- var. ***hakusanensis***	LLHF
- var. ***japonica***	LDai
- - B&SWJ 8835	WCru
- - B&SWJ 10933	WCru
uehatae B&SWJ 126	SKHP WCru

Adesmia (*Papilionaceae*)

longipes new	SPlb

Adiantum ✿ (*Pteridaceae*)

sp.	CMac
aethiopicum	XBlo
§ ***aleuticum*** ♀H4	CLAP MMoz NBro NLar SPlb WFib WPGP
- 'Imbricatum'	CBty CElw CLAP ELon IKil ISha IVic LRHS MAvo MGos NBid NLar NMyG SDix WCot WFib XLum
§ - 'Japonicum'	CDes NBir WHal WPGP
- 'Miss Sharples'	CBty CDTJ CLAP ELan LBMP LRHS MGos NBid NLar NMyG SRms WPGP
§ - 'Subpumilum' ♀H4	CLAP LRHS NBid WAbe WFib
bonatianum	CExl

	capillus-veneris	CBty ISha WFib
	- 'Mairisii'	see *A.* × *mairisii*
	hispidulum	CBty CCCN ISha LRHS
	- 'Bronze Venus'	CCCN LRHS
§	× ***mairisii*** ♀H3	CBty ISha LRHS
	pedatum misapplied	see *A. aleuticum*
	pedatum ambig.	CBty ISha
	pedatum L. ♀H4	CBcs CHEx CLAP EFer ELan ELon EPfP GMaP LAst LPot LRHS MBri SPer SWat WPGP
	- Asiatic form	see *A. aleuticum* 'Japonicum'
	- 'Japonicum'	see *A. aleuticum* 'Japonicum'
	- 'Roseum'	see *A. aleuticum* 'Japonicum'
	- var. ***subpumilum***	see *A. aleuticum* 'Subpumilum'
	raddianum 'Fragrans'	see *A. raddianum* 'Fragrantissimum'
§	- 'Fragrantissimum'	EShb
	venustum ♀H4	CBty CExl CFil CGHE CHEx CHVG CLAP EFer EPot EWTr ISha IVic MCot MWat SChr SKHP SRms SWat WAbe WCot WFib WHal WPGP

Adina (*Rubiaceae*)

	rubella	NLar

Adlumia (*Papaveraceae*)

	fungosa	CSpe EDAr LRHS

Adonis (*Ranunculaceae*)

	amurensis misapplied	see *A.* 'Fukujukai', *A. multiflora*
	amurensis ambig.	CMea EBee LEdu LLHF LRHS WCot
	- 'Pleniflora'	see *A. multiflora* 'Sandanzaki'
	annua	CRDP
	brevistyla	GBuc
§	'Fukujukai'	EBee
§	***multiflora***	SRot
§	- 'Sandanzaki' (d)	EBee LRHS
	ramosa **new**	EPot
	vernalis	CHel EBee GPoy LRHS NLar

Adoxa (*Adoxaceae*)

	moschatellina	CDes CSpe NMir NRya WHer WSFF WShi

Aechmea (*Bromeliaceae*)

	sp.	XBlo
	caudata var. ***variegata***	CHEx
	fasciata ♀H1	XBlo
	ramosa	XBlo
	victoriana	XBlo

Aegle (*Rutaceae*)

	sepiaria	see *Poncirus trifoliata*

Aegopodium (*Apiaceae*)

	podagraria 'Dangerous' (v)	CHid
	- gold-margined (v)	EPPr
	- 'Variegatum' (v)	EBee EHoe EPPr EShb GMaP LHop LRHS LSou MBel MHoo MRav MWhi NBid NPri NSti SEND SPer SPoG WCFE WCot WMoo WSHC WWEG XLum

Aeonium (*Crassulaceae*)

	sp.	CArn
	arboreum ♀H1	CAbb CDTJ CHEx CHel EShb GCal SEND SMrm
	- 'Atropurpureum' ♀H1	CAbb CCCN CDTJ CHEx CSuc EAmu EShb NEgg NPer SEND SPer SPoG WCot WNew
	- var. ***holochrysum*** **new**	CSuc
I	- 'Magnificum'	ESwi GBin SAPC
	- 'Variegatum' (v)	CSuc NPer
	balsamiferum	CCCN CDTJ CHEx CHel CSuc SChr
	'Black Cap'	CCCN
	'Black Magic' **new**	CSuc
	'Blushing Beauty'	CAbb CSuc EShb
	'Bronze Medal' **new**	CSuc
	canariense	CCCN CDTJ CHEx CSuc SVen
	- var. ***palmense***	SVen
	castello-paivae	EShb SChr
	ciliatum	CSuc SPlb
	'Copper Kettle' **new**	CSuc
	'Cristata Sunburst'	CDTJ WCot
	cuneatum	SEND
	'Cyclops' **new**	CSuc
	davidbramwellii **new**	CSuc
*	***decorum*** 'Variegatum' (v)	WCot
	'Dinner Plate'	CDTJ CHEx
	'Dinner Plate' × ***haworthii***	CHEx
	× ***domesticum***	see *Aichryson* × *aizoides* var. *domesticum*
*	***escobarii*** **new**	CSuc
	'Garnet' **new**	CSuc
	glandulosum	CSuc SVen
	glutinosum **new**	CSuc
	goochiae	CSuc SBch
	gorgonium **new**	CSuc
	haworthii ♀H1	CDTJ CHEx SBHP SEND SVen
	- 'Variegatum' (v)	CDTJ CSuc EShb SChr SVen
	hierrense	CSuc SPlb WCot
	holochrysum Webb & Berth.	CAbb
	'Lemon-Lime' **new**	CSuc
	leucoblepharum **new**	CSuc
	lindleyi	CSuc SChr
	× ***mascaense*** **new**	CSuc
*	***multiflorum*** 'Variegatum' (v)	CDTJ
	nobile	CBrP CSuc
	percarneum	EShb
	'Plum Purdy' **new**	CSuc
I	'Pygmaeum' **new**	CSuc
	sedifolium **new**	CSuc
	simsii	CSuc
	- variegated (v)	EShb
	simsii × 'Zwartkop' **new**	CCCN CSuc
	spathulatum	CSuc
	'Sunburst' (v) **new**	CSuc
	'Suncup' **new**	CSuc
	tabuliforme ♀H1	CCCN CDTJ CSpe CSuc EUJe SMad SPlb WCot
	- 'Cristatum'	WCot
	urbicum	CHEx
	valverdense **new**	CSuc
	'Velour' **new**	CSuc
	'Voodoo'	CSuc EAmu WCot
	'Zwartkin' **new**	CSuc
	'Zwartkop' ♀H1	CAbb CBcs CCCN CHEx CHVG CHel CHll CSpe ECtt EShb EUJe EWll GBin LSou MCot MSCN MSem NPer NPla SAPC SChr SEND SMad SMrm SRot SWvt WCot WWFP

Aeschynanthus (*Gesneriaceae*)

	'Big Apple'	WDib
	Black Pagoda Group	WDib

buxifolius KR 7798	WAbe WCot
'Fire Wheel'	WDib
hildebrandii	WDib
'Hot Flash'	WDib
'Little Tiger'	WDib
longicalyx	WDib
§ ***longicaulis*** ♀H1	WDib
marmoratus	see *A. longicaulis*
radicans ♀H1	WDib
'Scooby Doo'	WDib
speciosus ♀H1	WDib

Aesculus ✿ (*Sapindaceae*)

arguta	see *A. glabra* var. *arguta*
× ***arnoldiana***	CDul CMCN NLar
assamica	EGFP
- NJM 10.030 new	WPGP
- WWJ 11886	WCru
'Autumn Splendor'	EPfP
§ × ***bushii***	CDul CMCN NLar
californica	CBcs CDul CHel CMCN CMac EPfP ERod SKHP WPGP
× ***carnea***	CDul SGol WHar
- 'Aureomarginata' (v)	ERod LLHF WHar
- 'Briotii' ♀H4	CBcs CCVT CDoC CDul CEnd CHel CLnd CMac CSBt CTho CWib EBee ECrN ELan EPfP LBuc LRHS MBri MGos MMuc NLar NWea SCoo SEND SEWo SLim SPer SPoG WHar
- 'Plantierensis'	CDul MBri
* - 'Variegata' (v)	CDul CMCN
chinensis	CMCN
flava ♀H4	CDul CLnd CMCN CTho EBee EGFP ELan EPfP EWTr MBri MMuc SEND SLim
f. ***vestita***	CDul MBlu MBri NLar
georgiana	see *A. sylvatica*
glabra	CDul CMCN CTho EGFP
§ - var. ***arguta***	CMCN NLar
- 'Autumn Blaze'	EPfP
- 'October Red'	EPfP MBri
glaucescens	see *A.* × *neglecta*
hippocastanum ♀H4	CBcs CCVT CDul CLnd CMac CSBt CTho CTri CWib EBee ECrN ELan EPfP GAbr LAst LBuc MGos MMuc MSwo NLar NWea SEND SEWo SGol SLim SPer WHar
- 'Aureomarginata' (v)	CMac
§ - 'Baumannii' (d) ♀H4	CDoC CDul CLnd CMCN ECrN ELan EPfP ERod MGos MSwo NWea SPer
- 'Digitata'	CDul CMCN WPat
- 'Flore Pleno'	see *A. hippocastanum* 'Baumannii'
- 'Hampton Court Gold'	CDul CMCN CMac
- f. ***laciniata***	CDul CMCN ERod IArd MAsh NLar SMad WCot WPat
- 'Monstrosa'	WPat
- 'Wisselink'	CDul CMCN ECrN WCot WPat
indica	CDul CHEx CMCN EBee ECrN ELan EPfP SEND SGol
- 'Sydney Pearce' ♀H4	CBcs CDul CEnd CJun CMCN EPfP ERod GKin MBlu MBri NLar SBrt SLim WPat
× ***marylandica***	CDul WPat
× ***mississippiensis***	see *A.* × *bushii*
× ***mutabilis*** 'Harbisonii'	WPat
- 'Induta'	CDul CMCN EBee EPfP GBin IArd MBri SKHP
§ - 'Penduliflora'	CDul
§ × ***neglecta***	CMCN NLar
- 'Autumn Fire'	EBee EPfP GBin MBlu MBri SLim WPat
- 'Erythroblastos' ♀H4	CBcs CDul CEnd CJun CMCN EBee EPfP ERod MAsh MBlu MBri MRav SCoo SMad SPoG WCot WPat
parviflora ♀H4	CBcs CDul CLnd CMCN CMac CTri EBee ELan EPfP EUJe EWTr GKin LRHS MBlu MGos MMuc MPkF MRav NEgg NLar SEND SGol SLPl SLim SMad SPer SWvt WHar
§ ***pavia*** ♀H4	CBcs CDul CLnd CMCN EPfP
- 'Atrosanguinea'	CEnd CLnd CMCN EPfP ERod MBlu MBri SKHP
I - 'Biltmore Buckeye'	MPkF
- var. ***discolor*** 'Koehnei'	CMCN EPfP MBlu MBri NLar SPoG
- 'Penduliflora'	see *A.* × *mutabilis* 'Penduliflora'
- 'Purple Spring'	MBri WPat
- 'Rosea Nana'	CMCN WPat
splendens	see *A. pavia*
§ ***sylvatica***	CMCN
turbinata	CBcs CDul EGFP
wilsonii	CExl

Aethionema (*Brassicaceae*)

armenum	ECho EDAr LLHF SBch
capitatum	CPBP ECho
glaucinum	ECho
§ ***grandiflorum*** ♀H4	ECho LRHS NBro NRya SRms WRHF XLum XSen
- Pulchellum Group ♀H4	GKev
iberideum	MWat SRms
* ***kotschyi*** hort.	EDAr WAbe
oppositifolium	GKev LLHF MWat
pulchellum	see *A. grandiflorum*
schistosum	LLHF
thomasianum	EPot
'Warley Rose' ♀H4	ECho EHyd ELan EPot GJos GMaP LHop LRHS MAsh MSCN NBir SBch SRms WIce WThu XSen
'Warley Ruber'	CMea ECho NBir SBch WAbe

Aethusa (*Apiaceae*)

cynapium	CSpe

Aextoxicon (*Aextoxicaceae*)

punctatum	CBcs

Afrocarpus (*Podocarpaceae*)

falcatus	ECou

Afrocrocus (*Iridaceae*)

unifolius from Roggeveld	ECho

Agapanthus ✿ (*Agapanthaceae*)

sp.	XPde
'Aberdeen'	XPde
'Adonis'	IBlr
'African Moon'	CPen CPrp
africanus misapplied	CElw CExl CHel CTsd CWCL CWib EBee ELan EPfP EPot EUJe GBBs GKev LRHS MWat SAPC SChr SPer SRot SVic WBor WSpi WWEG XLum
- 'Albus' misapplied	CBcs CDoC CExl CHel CWCL EBee ELan EPfP EPot GKev LRHS LSRN MGos NSoo SDeJ SEND SGol SPer WBor WWEG XLum
'Aimee'	CBro
'Albus' ambig.	GKev GMaP MGos MHer MWat

	'Alice Gloucester'	CPrp
	'Amsterdam'	CPen EBee XPde
	'Angela'	CPen CPrp IBal XPde
	'Anthea'	XPde
	'Aphrodite'	IBlr
	'Apple Court'	XPde
	'Aquamarine'	CAvo
	'Arctic Star'	CCCN CExl CKno CPen CPou CPrp CTca CWCL EBee ELon IBal LRHS LSRN LSou MAvo SDys SFai XPde
	Ardernei hybrid	CAvo CExl CPrp ECtt EWes GAbr GCal IBal IBlr LSou MAvo NEgg SMrm WCot WGwG WPGP WWEG XPde
§	'Argenteus Vittatus' (v) ♀H1	CPen CPrp
	'Atlas'	IBlr
	'Aureovittatus' (v)	IBal
	'Baby Blue'	see *A.* 'Blue Baby' Rom.
	'Baby Pete'[PBR]	CPen
	Back in Black = 'B in B'[PBR]	CCCN CExl CWCL ELan EPfP EWes MBNS MBri NBid SMrm
	'Ballyrogan'	IBlr
	'Bangor Blue'	IBlr
	'Basutoland'	EBee LRHS
	'Beatrice'	XPde
	'Beeches Dwarf'	ELan
	'Ben Hope'	CBro CPrp IBal IBlr WCot XPde
	'Beth Chatto'	see *A. campanulatus* 'Albovittatus'
	'Bianco'	XPde
	'Bicton Bell'	IBal IBlr
	'Big Blue'	CCCN CHel CMac CPrp EBee EPfP GKev LSou SEND SRkn
	'Black Beauty'	LRHS WSpi
	'Black Buddhist'	CCCN CHel CPen CWCL ECtt EPri GBuc LSou MGos NGdn SFai SGol SPer
	'Black Pantha'[PBR]	Widely available
§	'Blue Baby' Rom.	CCCN CPen ELan ELon IBlr LRHS XPde XTur
	'Blue Bird'	LRHS SHil XPde
	'Blue Boy'	XPde
	'Blue Brush'	CAbb CMac CPen CPrp CSBt EPfP IBal LRHS LSou SCoo SEND SFai
	'Blue Cascade'	IBlr
	'Blue Companion'	CPrp IBal IBlr WMnd
	'Blue Diamond' ambig.	CMac
	'Blue Dot'	CPrp ECtt EPfP LLHF LRHS LSou NGdn SDys
	'Blue Formality'	IBal IBlr
	'Blue Giant'	CBro CCCN CHel CKno CPen CPrp EBee EPfP IBlr LRHS MGos MNFA SWat WPGP WWEG
	'Blue Globe'	CHid CPen EPri GMaP LRHS
	'Blue Haze'	XPde
	'Blue Heaven'[PBR]	EWoo LHop MBri NPnk
	'Blue Horizons'	CCCN LBuc
	'Blue Ice'	CPen CPou IBal
	'Blue Imp'	CBro IBlr
	'Blue Jay'	CPen
	'Blue Lakes'	XPde
	'Blue Méoni'	XPde
	'Blue Moon'	CAbP CAvo CBro CPen EBee ECtt EWoo IBlr LLWG LRHS MAvo MCot MHol NLar SFai SPer WCot WRHF
	'Blue Nile'	XPde
	'Blue Prince'	CPen EBee LRHS
	'Blue Ribbon'	XPde
	'Blue Rinse' **new**	CAvo
	'Blue Skies' ambig.	NCGa XPde
I	'Blue Skies' Dunlop	IBlr
	'Blue Spear'	CPen
	'Blue Triumphator'	CTca EPfP EWll GBin GKev GMaP IBlr LRHS MHer WSpi WWEG XPde
	'Blue Umbrella'	SRkn
	'Blue Velvet'	XPde
	blue-flowered	WCFE
	Bluestorm = 'Atiblu'[PBR]	EPfP LBuc LRHS SAPC
	'Bluety'[PBR]	CPen XPde
	'Bressingham Blue'	CBro CPrp CTri EWes GCal IBal IBlr LRHS MRav SFai SWat WSpi XPde
	'Bressingham Bounty'	EBee IBal LRHS SFai XPde
	'Bressingham White'	LRHS MBri MRav NCGa SWat WSpi XPde
	'Bridal Bouquet' **new**	GBin LSRN
	'Bristol'	XPde
	'Buckingham Palace'	CBro CDes CPrp EWes GAbr IBlr WCot WPGP XPde
	'Cally Blue'	GAbr GCal IBal
	'Cally Longstem'	EBee GCal
	'Cally Pale Blue'	IBal
	'Cambridge'	XPde
	campanulatus	CMac CPrp ELan EPfP EWTr GKin IBal IBlr IGor LRHS MCot MMuc MRav NEgg SEND SWat WPGP
	- var. ***albidus***	CHel ELan EPfP EShb GKin IBlr LHop LPio LRHS MMuc NBid NGdn NSoo SEND SPer WGwG WHoo WPGP XPde
§	- 'Albovittatus' (v)	CPrp ECho IBal LRHS LSou
	- bright blue-flowered	GCal
	- 'Buckland'	IBlr
	- 'Cobalt Blue'	GBin GKin LRHS LSou MAsh MAvo MNrw NGdn
	- dark blue-flowered	WSpi XPde
	- 'Nanus' **new**	LRHS
	- 'Oxford Blue'	CPrp IBal IBlr LRHS WSpi XPde
	- subsp. ***patens*** ♀H3	CPrp EBee EPfP IBal LRHS MRav SWat WPGP WSpi
	- - deep blue-flowered	CCon IBlr LRHS WWEG XPde
	- 'Profusion'	CBro CPrp IBal IBlr LRHS XPde
	- variegated (v)	EBee NPer
	- 'Wedgwood Blue'	CPrp EBee IBal IBlr LRHS WSpi XPde
	- 'Wendy'	IBal IBlr LRHS XPde
	- 'White Hope'	IBal IBlr
	'Carefree'	CPrp IBal
	'Castle of Mey'	CBro CExl CFil CHel CPen CPrp GAbr IBlr LPla LRHS WPGP XPde
	'Catharina'	XPde
§	***caulescens*** ♀H1	IBal IBlr LRHS WPGP XPde
	- subsp. ***angustifolius***	CHid CPrp EBee ELon EUJe IBlr MHol SMad SPer WCot WPGP
	- subsp. ***caulescens***	IBlr SWat
	'Cedric Morris'	CPen IBlr XPde
	'Chandra'	IBlr
	'Charlotte'[PBR]	CMac CPen EBee EPfP LRHS SPoG XPde
	'Cherry Holley'	ELon XPde
	'Chika's Blue'	MAvo
	'Clarence House'	CBro CPen CPrp XPde
	coddii	CExl EWes IBlr SMrm WCot XPde
	'Columba'	CPen EBee ELon IBal LDai NBid XPde
	comptonii	see *A. praecox* subsp. *minimus*
	'Cool Blue'	XPde
	'Corina'	EBee
	'Crystal Drop'	CExl CPen CPou CPrp EPri SWat WPGP

	Danube	see *A.* 'Donau'
	'Dawn Star'	XPde
	'Debbie'	XPde
	'Delft'	CPrp IBal IBlr
	Dell Garden hybrids	LRHS
	'Density'	IBlr
	'Diana'	XPde
	'Dnjepr'	CBro EBee XPde
	'Dokter Brouwer'	CPen ECtt GKev IBoy IKil LRHS LSRN MCot XPde
§	'Donau'	CBro CPen EPri EShb EWoo GKev IBal NBir NOrc NSoo SGol SWat WCot XPde
	'Dorothy Edwards'	SFai
	Double Diamond = 'Rfdd'	CPen CWCL CWGN EPri EWes IBal LRHS LSRN LSou NPri SFai SPoG WSpi
	'Duivenbrugge Blue'	XPde
	'Duivenbrugge White'	XPde
	dyeri	see *A. inapertus* subsp. *intermedius*
	'Early Blue'	EWTr EWoo
	'Ed Carman' (v)	LSou
	'Elisabeth'	XPde
	'Enigma'	CAbb CBro CCCN CExl CHel CPen CPrp CSpe CWCL CWGN EBee EPri EWoo GBin IBal LRHS NLar SFai SLon SPoG SRkn SWat WCot WSpi
	'Ethel's Joy'	CPen
	'Eve'	IBlr XPde
	'Evening Star'	XPde
	'Finnline' (v)	CPen
	'Flanders Giant'	XPde
	'Flore Pleno' (d)	Widely available
	'Gayle's Lilac'	CBcs CCCN CElw CExl CPen CPrp ECtt ELan ELon EPfP EWoo GKin LHop LPio LRHS LSou MRav NGdn SEND SMrm WGwG WWEG
	'Gem'	ELon MAvo
I	'Giganteus Albus'	XPde
	'Glacier Stream'	CBro CPen EBee EPri GBuc IKil XTur
	'Glen Avon'	CAbb CBro CCCN CCon CExl CPen CPrp EBee EPfP EWoo GBin IBal LRHS NLar SCoo SFai SLon WSpi XPde
	'Golden Rule' (v)	CPrp EHoe GBuc IBal IBlr XPde
	'Grey Ruler'	LSou MAvo
	'Hanneke'	CPen
	'Harvest Blue'	XPde
§	Headbourne hybrids	Widely available
	- dark blue-flowered	EHyd GBuc LRHS
	- dwarf	GBuc LRHS
	'Headbourne White'	CAvo EHyd EPri
	'Heavenly Blue'	CCCN
	'Helen'	IBlr
	'Holbeach'	CPen XPde
	'Holbrook'	CSam XPde
	'Hydon Mist'	XPde
	'Ice Blue Star'	CBro XPde
	'Ice Lolly'	CBro CPen IKil XPde
	inapertus	CAvo CBro CFil CPrp CSpe EWes GGal SWat WCot WPGP WSpi XPde
	- dwarf	IBlr
	- subsp. ***hollandii***	CPom EBee GCal IBal IBlr SWat WCot XPde
	- - 'Zealot'	IBlr
	- 'Ice Cascade'	CCCN CPen EBee IBal LRHS SWat
	- 'Icicle'	GCal
	- subsp. ***inapertus***	IBlr SWat
I	- - 'Albus'	IBlr LRHS
	- - 'Cyan'	IBlr
	- - 'White'	CPrp IBal
§	- subsp. ***intermedius***	CBro CPrp EBee EPfP GKev IBlr SWat
	- - 'Long Tom'	CExl EPri WPGP
	- - white-flowered	CPen CPou
	- large	IBal
	- 'Little Black Number'	CPen
	- 'Margaret'	CCCN EBee MBri
	- 'Midnight Cascade'	CCCN CExl CPar CPen EBee IBal LRHS LSou MCot NBid SWat
I	- 'Nigrescens'	CPen
	- subsp. ***parviflorus***	IBlr
	- subsp. ***pendulus***	CCon IBlr LRHS WPGP
	- - 'Graskop'	CAbb CBcs CCCN CCon CExl CHel CPen CSpe EBee EPfP EPri EWoo GBin IBal IBlr LRHS LSou NPri SFai SKHP SPer WCot WPGP XPde
	- - 'Violet Dusk'	IBlr
	- 'Sapphire Cascade'	CPen IBal LSou SWat
	'Inkspots'	CAbb CCCN CMac CPen CSpe CWCL EPfP GBin IBal LRHS LSou LSqu SFai SPoG
	'Innocence'	IBlr
	'Intermedius' Leichtlin	CWCL IBal XPde
I	'Intermedius' van Tubergen	EBee NBid XTur
	'Isis'	CAvo CBro CCon CPrp CSam CTri GBuc IBal IBlr LRHS WSpi XPde
	'Jacaranda' **new**	SPer
	'Jack Elliott'	MAvo
	'Jack's Blue'	Widely available
	'Jersey Giant'	LEdu XPde
	'Jodie'	ELon MAvo XPde
	'Johanna'	CPen XPde
	Johannesberg hybrids	EPfP
	'Jolanda'	CPrp EBee ELon
	'Kingston Blue'	IBal IBlr IGor NBid WWEG XPde
	'Kobold'	CBro
	'Lady Edith'	IBlr
§	'Lady Grey'	IBlr
	'Lady Moore'	CBro IBlr IGor XPde
	'Lapis'	CHel CHid CPrp IBal SFai
	'Latent Blue'	IBlr
	'Lavender Haze'	CCCN CHel CPen EPfP IBal LRHS SFai WSpi
	'Leicester'	CPen XPde
	'Liam's Lilac'	CCCN CExl CKno CPar CPen CPou EBee ELon EWoo IBal LRHS NLar SFai WCot
	'Lilac Flash'	CPen
	'Lilac Time'	CExl CPrp IBlr WCot XPde
	'Lilliput'	CBcs CBro CCCN CMac CMea CPrp CSpe ECtt ELan EPfP EShb GBuc GMaP IBal LHop LRHS MAvo MRav NGdn SPer WMnd XPde
	'Limoges'	XPde
	'Little White'	CPen
	'Littlecourt'	CBro
	'Loch Hope' ♀H3	CBro CDoC CPrp CSam ELon EPfP EUJe EWoo GCal IBal LRHS LSou MAvo MHol MRav SFai SPer WCot XPde
	'Lowland Nursery'	XPde
	'Luly'	CPen CPrp EPfP IBal LRHS MAvo SHil SWat XPde

'Luna'	EBee
'Lydenburg'	CPen CPrp EPri IBal IBlr
'Mabel Grey'	see *A.* 'Lady Grey'
'Magnifico'	CPrp IBal IBlr
'Malaga'	XPde
'Malvern Hills'	XPde
'Margaret'	IBal LSRN
'Marianne'	XPde
'Mariètte'	CPen XPde
'Marjorie'	XPde
'Martine'	CPen EBee
'May Snow' (v)	WCot
'Megan's Mauve'	CKno CPou ELon EPri SFai
'Meibont' (v)	IBal WCot XPde
'Mercury'	IBlr
Midknight Blue = 'Monmid'	LRHS XTur
'Midnight'	CPen EWes WSpi
'Midnight Blue' ambig.	CAby CMea CPen ELan IBal IGor MGos MHer SFai
'Midnight Blue' P. Wood	GCal IBlr
'Midnight Dream'	CPen STPC
§ 'Midnight Star'	Widely available
'Miniature Blue'	SWat
'Misty Dawn' (v)	EBee IBal MHol SFai WCot
mixed seedlings	EPfP IBal MGos NOrc XPde
mixed white-flowered	WCFE
'Montreal'	XPde
'Moonshine'	CPen
I 'Mooreanus' misapplied	EBee EPfP IBal IGor NBid XPde
'Mount Stewart'	IBal IBlr
'Navy Blue'	see *A.* 'Midnight Star'
'New Orleans'	XPde
'Newa'	EBee XPde
'Nikki'	CMea
'Norman Hadden'	IBlr
'Northern Light'	CPen LLHF
'Northern Star'PBR	CAbb CCon CDoC CExl CHVG CKno CPen CPrp ELon EWes EWoo IBal LBMP LRHS LSRN LSou NPri NSti SFai SLon SPer SPoG WPGP WWlt
nutans	see *A. caulescens*
'Nyx'	IBlr
'NZ Blue'	XPde
'NZ White'	XPde
'Oslo'	XPde
'Oxbridge'	IBlr
'Pacific Blue'	EBee
Palmer's hybrids	see *A.* Headbourne hybrids
'Paris'	CPen XPde
'Patent Blue'	CPrp IBlr
'Patriot'	EPfP LRHS MBri
'Penelope Palmer'	CPrp IBlr
'Penny Slade'	XPde
'Peter Pan' ambig.	Widely available
'Peter Pan' Giridlion	LLWG
'Phantom'	CAbb CDes GCal IBal IBlr SFai SPer WPGP XPde
'Pinchbeck'	XPde
'Pinky'	XPde
'Pinocchio'	CPen CWib SDeJ XPde
'Plas Merdyn Blue'	CPrp IBlr
'Plas Merdyn White'	CPrp IBlr XPde
'Podge Mill'	IBlr XPde
'Polar Ice'	CCon CPen CPrp EBee ELon EPri EWoo IBal IBlr IBoy LRHS LSRN SMad WCAu WSpi XPde XTur
'Porcelain'	IBal IBlr
praecox	CPrp EShb IBal IBlr LRHS
- 'Albiflorus'	CBcs CBro CPou CPrp CTri EPri IBal LRHS NEgg SEND WSpi XPde
- 'Floribundus'	SWat
- 'Maximus Albus'	CPou IBal IBlr
§ - subsp. ***minimus***	CElw CPou EBee IBal IBlr SWat XPde
- - 'Adelaide'	CPrp
- - blue-flowered	SWat
- - white-flowered	SWat
- 'Neptune'	IBlr
§ - subsp. ***orientalis***	CBro CCCN CSut IBlr SWat
- - 'Cape Blue'	CPrp
- - 'Mount Thomas'	CPrp
- - 'Silver Star' (v)	CPen
- subsp. ***praecox***	IBlr
- - azure-flowered	CPrp SWat
- - 'Variegatus'	see *A.* 'Argenteus Vittatus'
- 'Saturn'	IBlr
- Slieve Donard form	IBlr
- 'Uranus'	IBlr
- 'Venus'	IBlr
'Premier'	CPrp IBal IBlr LRHS
'Princess Margaret'	XPde
'Proteus'	XPde
§ 'Purple Cloud'	Widely available
'Purple Haze'	CPen
'Purple Star'	CCCN CKno
'Queen Mother'	CHid LRHS XPde
Queen Mum = 'Pmn06'PBR	CCCN CDoC CExl CHVG CHel CPen CPrp ELon EPfP EPri GBin IBal LSRN MBri SFai SHil SMrm STPC XTur
'Radiant Star'	IBal LRHS
'Raveningham Hall'	XPde
'Regal Beauty'	CPen CPrp CSBt CSev EShb EWoo IBal LRHS LSRN NBid NLar SFai WSpi
'Rhone'	CBro IBlr XPde
rich blue-flowered	XPde
'Rosemary'	XPde
'Rosewarne'	CBcs CCCN CExl CMac EPfP GBin IBal IBlr NLar XPde
'Rotterdam'	CPen XPde
'Royal Blue'	CBro GMaP
'Royal Lodge'	XPde
'Royal Purple'	XPde
'San Gabriel' (v)	XPde
'Sandringham'	CDes CHel CPen CPrp EWes IBlr WPGP XPde
'Sapphire'	IBlr XPde
'Sarah'PBR	CCCN CPen IBal LSRN LSou
'Sea Coral'	CCCN CCon CMac CPrp EBee EPfP EPri LRHS MAvo WGwG
'Sea Foam'	CMac CPen IBal NLar XPde
'Sea Mist'	CCCN EBee IBal
'Sea Spray'	CCCN CKno EBee EPri IBal LRHS XPde
'Selma Bock'	CPen
'Senna'PBR	CCCN CExl IBal LRHS LSou
'Septemberhemel'	CPen XPde
'Sevilla'	XPde
'Silver Baby'	CKno CPen CPrp CWGN ELon EPfP LRHS
'Silver Jubilee'	XPde
'Silver Lining'	EBee ECtt IBal LRHS SFai
'Silver Mist'	CPen IBlr LRHS SWat XPde
Silver Moon = 'Notfred'PBR (v)	CAbb CCCN CPen EBee ELan EPfP EWes EWoo IBal LBMP LRHS LSou MGos NPri NSti SFai SPoG XPde

	'Silver Sceptre'	IBlr
	'Sky'	CAbb CPar CSBt EPfP EWoo IBal IBlr LRHS LSRN LSou NBid SFai SKHP SPoG SRkn SRms SWat WCot WSpi XPde
	'Sky Pendulous' **new**	CBcs
	'Sky Rocket'	IBal IBlr
	'Sky Star'	XPde
	'Slieve Donard'	IBlr
	'Sneeuwwitje'	XPde
	'Snow Cloud'	CAbb CBro CExl CPen CSBt EBee EPfP LRHS NEgg SFai SLon XPde
	'Snow Pixie'	CBro CSpe CWGN EBee IBal LSRN LSou SFai WSpi
	'Snow Princess'	CPen ELon EPfP IBal LRHS
	'Snow Shadows'	CBro
	'Snowball'	CBcs CDoC CExl CHel CPen EBee LRHS LSou WWEG XPde
	'Snowdrops'	CCCN EBee IBal LHop SKHP
	'Snowstorm'PBR	IBal LBuc
	'Sofie'PBR	CPen EWoo STPC
	'Sophie' **new**	XTur
	'Southern Cross' **new**	IBal SFai
	'Spokes'	IBlr
	'Star Quality' **new**	IBal
	'Starburst'	IBlr
	'Stardust' **new**	IBal
	'Stargazer' **new**	WHlf
	'Stars and Stripes'	IBal LRHS NPri SFai
	'Stéphanie'	XPde
	'Stéphanie Charm'	CPen XPde
	'Stockholm'	CPrp GAbr
	'Storm Cloud' Reads	see *A.* 'Purple Cloud'
	'Storm Cloud' (d)	CBro CCon
	'Streamline'	CBcs CBro CDoC CElw CHel CKno CMea CTca EBee ECtt ELon EPfP EShb GKin GMaP IBal LAst LRHS LSou MGos MRav SDys WWEG XPde
	'Summer Clouds'	ELan
	'Summer Skies'	IBal
	'Sunfield'	CKno CPen CPrp EPfP GAbr IBal LRHS NLar NPer XPde
	'Super Star'	CBro XPde
I	'Supreme'	IBlr
	'Suzan'	XPde
	'Sylvine'	CPen XPde
	'Tall Boy'	IBal IBlr
	'Tarka'	CExl CPen CPrp CWCL ELon IBal LSou NLar SDys SFai
	'Taw Valley'	CAbb CHVG CKno CPen CPrp ELon IBal SFai SLon SPoG WPGP
	'Thumbelina'	CBro CKno CMac CSev CWCL EBee EPfP EWoo IBal LSou SFai XLum
	'Timaru'	CBro CCVN CCon CDoC CElw CPen CPrp EBee ECtt ELan ELon EPfP EWoo GAbr GMaP IBal LAst LPla LRHS MBri MHol NEgg NGdn NLar SFai SMrm WCot WWEG XPde
	'Tinkerbell' (v)	CBcs CBro CCCN CPrp EBee EHoe ELan EPfP EPri EShb IBal LEdu LHop LRHS LSou MGos MRav NPer SPoG SRms SWvt XPde
	'Tiny Tim'	CSpe XPde
	'Titan'	IBlr
	'Tom Thumb'	CAvo CExl CHel COIW ECtt EPfP EPot GBin IBal LBMP LRHS LSou SFai SRkn SRot WGor
	'Torbay'	CElw CHel CPrp ECtt ELon EShb GAbr GCal GKin IBal IBlr LLWG LPio LRHS MNrw NCGa NEgg NHol WHoo WWEG XPde
	'Tornado'	CPen EBee ECGP ECtt ELon IBal LPla LRHS MNrw WCot
	Tresco hybrid	CHEx
	'Triangle'	CPen
	'Trudy'	XPde
	'Twilight'	IBlr
	umbellatus L'Hérit.	see *A. africanus*
	umbellatus Redouté	see *A. praecox* subsp. *orientalis*
	'Underway'	EBee EWes GCal GKev IBal IBlr XPde
	'Vague Bleue'	XPde
	'Vallée Bleue' **new**	XTur
	'Vallée de la Loire' **new**	XTur
	'Vallée de la Sarthe' **new**	XTur
	'Vallée de l'Authion' **new**	XTur
	'Vallée du Cap' **new**	XTur
	'Velvet Night'	CPen
	'Virginia'	XPde
	'Wavy Navy'	CPen
	'White Avon'	CPen
	'White Baby' **new**	XTur
	'White Dwarf'	see *A.* white flowered, dwarf
	'White Heaven'PBR	Widely available
	'White Ice'	CBcs CPen LRHS
	'White Smile'	EPri
	'White Star'	XPde
	'White Starlet'	XPde
	'White Superior'	CPen GMaP LAst SPet XPde
	'White Triumphator'	WSpi
	'White Umbrella'	LRHS
	white-flowered	CHEx
§	white-flowered, dwarf	CBro CPen EBee ECtt EPfP EShb GBuc IBal LRHS MAsh NBir NGdn NHol
	'Whitney'PBR	CPen IBlr
	'Windlebrooke'	CCCN EPri XPde
	'Windsor Castle'	CPen CPrp IBal IBlr XPde
	'Windsor Grey'	Widely available
	'Winsome'	IBlr
	'Winter Sky'	XPde
	'Wolga'	CBro EWll
	'Wolkberg' Kirstenbosch	IBlr
	'Yellow Tips'	XPde
	'Yves Klein'	CPrp IBlr
	'Zachary'	CPen CPou CPrp ELon IBal LRHS
	'Zella Thomas'	XPde

Agapetes (*Ericaceae*)

'Ludgvan Cross' ♀H1-2	CCCN CTsd EBee SSpi
serpens ♀H1	CCCN CHEx CWib EShb SLon
- 'Scarlet Elf'	CCCN EBee LRHS
smithiana var. ***major***	GGGa

Agastache (*Lamiaceae*)

'After Eight'	IBoy LRHS NCGa NDov
anethiodora	see *A. foeniculum* (Pursh) Kuntze
anisata	see *A. foeniculum* (Pursh) Kuntze
aurantiaca	SMrm SPhx
- 'Apricot Sprite'	EPfP LDai LPio MBri MHer MNHC MSCN NEgg NGdn NSoo SMad SRkn SRms WHar
- (Cocktail Series) 'Lavender Martini' **new**	LRHS
- - 'Peach Margarita' **new**	LRHS
- - 'Raspberry Daiquiri' **new**	LRHS

'Blackadder'	Widely available
'Blue Boa' **new**	CWGN
'Blue Delight'	SBch
'Blue Fortune' ♀$^{H3-4}$	CBcs EBee LHop MAvo MBri MCot NDov NLar NSoo SMad SMrm SPer SPhx SWvt WWEG
'Bolero' **new**	CSpe LHop LRHS MAvo
§ ***cana***	LDai SPhx
- 'Heatwave'^{PBR}	NCGa WCot
- 'Purple Pygmy'	EPfP LHop SRot
'Cotton Candy'^{PBR}	EBee IBoy
'Firebird'	EBee ECtt ELan GKin LHop LSou MBri NSoo SPer SWat SWvt
foeniculum misapplied	see *A. rugosa*
§ ***foeniculum*** (Pursh) Kuntze	CArn CMea ELan GMaP GPoy MCot MHer MHoo MNHC SPav SPhx SRms WJek WWEG XLum
- 'Alabaster'	CBcs EBee NLar
- 'Alba'	NBre SHDw SPav
'Globetrotter'	SPhx
'Glowing Embers'	ECtt
'Kolibri'	LHop MAvo NDov
'Linda'	CSpe NDov WCot
§ ***mexicana***	LDai SPav
- 'Red Fortune'^{PBR}	CAbP CWGN ECtt LHop LPio MBri MCot MSCN NEgg NLar NSti SMad SPad WCot
- 'Rosea'	see *A. cana*
- 'Sangria'	EBee EDif ELon LHop LRHS MCot NGdn SBch SPad SPhx SRms
nepetoides	SPav
'Painted Lady'	CSpe ECtt
pallidiflora	EPfP MRav
var. ***neomexicana*** 'Lavender Haze'	
'Pink Beauty'	GBBs NLar
'Pink Pop'	EPfP SPhx
'Purple Haze'	NDov
'Raspberry Summer'^{PBR}	CWGN EBee ECtt LHop LSou NCGa NDov NLar
'Rose Mint'	CSpe
§ ***rugosa***	CAby CArn ELau GPoy LEdu LHop LPio MHoo MNHC NEgg SPav SPhx SPlb SRms SWat WJek WMoo
- B&SWJ 4187 from Korea	WCru
- f. ***albiflora***	NBre NEgg
- - 'Alabaster' **new**	MAvo NDov
- - 'Liquorice White'	EBee EPfP MBel MHoo NLar SMrm SPer SPlb WGwG
- 'Golden Jubilee'	CAby CSpe EBee ECtt ELan EPfP IBoy LDai MHer MSpe NLar NOrc NSti NWad SBea SPoG SRms WHil WJek WMoo WWEG XLum
- Heronswood strain	CSpe
- 'Honey Bee Blue'	NWad
- 'Korean Zest'	WCru
- 'Liquorice Blue'	CKno CTsd EPfP MBel MSpe NEgg NGBl NGdn NOrc NWad SPer SPoG SWvt WMoo
rupestris	CSpe EWTr SPhx XLum
- 'Apache Sunset'	ELon MBri SPlb
'Serpentine'	CSpe NDov SPhx
'Summer Fiesta'^{PBR}	IBoy LSou MNrw NCGa
'Summer Glow'^{PBR}	CWGN ECtt GBin LBuc LLHF LSou MBel NCGa SPoG WHlf
'Summer Love'^{PBR}	CSpe EBee LSou MNrw NCGa NDov NLar
'Summer Sky'^{PBR}	LRHS NCGa NDov
'Summer Sunset' **new**	CWGN LSou
'Tangerine Dreams' ♀^{H3}	ECtt EDif EPfP LHop LSou NCGa NEgg NGdn SBch SCoo WHil
'Tango' **new**	MAvo SGbt
'Tutti-frutti'	ECtt NCGa SPhx
urticifolia	CSpe
- 'Alba'	CSpe

Agathaea see *Felicia*

Agathis (*Araucariaceae*)

australis	CBrP CDoC

Agathosma (*Rutaceae*)

ovata	CCCN

Agave ✿ (*Asparagaceae*)

albomarginata	CDTJ EGri
americana ♀^{H1}	CAbb CBcs CDoC CHEx CHel EAmu EGri EPfP EShb EUJe LRHS SAPC SBod SBst SEND SMad SPlb SPre SVen SWvt
- 'Marginata' (v) ♀$^{H3-4}$	CBrP CDTJ CFil CHII MREP NLBP SEND SVen WCot WSFF
- 'Mediopicta' misapplied	see *A. americana* 'Mediopicta Alba'
- 'Mediopicta' (v) ♀^{H1}	CDTJ CFil CHEx SAPC SBig
§ - 'Mediopicta Alba' (v) ♀^{H1}	CBrP CDTJ CFil CJun EAmu EShb ESwi SEND WCot
- 'Mediopicta Aurea' (v)	CFil WCot
- var. ***oaxacensis***	WPGP
- subsp. ***protamericana***	CDTJ EGri
- subsp. ***protamericana*** × ***scabra*** F&M 310	WPGP
- 'Striata' (v)	EShb WCot
- 'Variegata' (v) ♀^{H1}	CAbb CBcs CDoC CFil CHEx EAmu EGri EPfP EShb EUJe EWes LRHS MAvo MBel MGos MRav MSem NPer NPla NSoo SAPC SBst SChr SMad SPlb SWvt WCot
angustifolia	see *A. vivipara* var. *vivipara*
- var. ***marginata*** hort.	SBig WCot
applanata	CFil CJun EGri WPGP
× ***arizonica***	EGri
asperrima	CDTJ CHel EGri
§ - subsp. ***maderensis***	SPlb
atrovirens	WCot
- var. ***mirabilis***	CDTJ CFil EGri
- - F&M 245	WPGP
attenuata	CAbb CBrP CDTJ EAmu SBig SPlb WCot WPGP
avellanidens	EGri
beauleriana	EAmu EGri SBig
'Bloodspot' **new**	WCot
boldinghiana	WCot
bovicornuta	WCot
bracteosa	CCCN CDTJ EGri WCot
celsii	see *A. mitis* var. *mitis*
cerulata subsp. ***nelsonii***	CDTJ
chiapensis	EGri
chrysantha	CCCN CDTJ EBee EGri WCot WGrn WPGP
- 'Black Canyon'	WCot
chrysoglossa	WPGP
colimana	see *A. ortgiesiana*
colorata	CCCN CDTJ CJun WCot
'Cornelius'	WCot
cupreata	CDTJ EGri
datylio	EGri
de-meesteriana	EAmu
- var. ***marginata*** (v)	EAmu

	deserti	CDTJ CDoC CHel CJun LRHS WCot
	difformis	CDTJ EGri
	- NJM 05.034	WPGP
	durangensis	SPlb
	elongata	see *A. vivipara* var. *vivipara*
	ensifera	CJun
	felgeri	CDTJ
	ferdinandi-regis	see *A. victoriae-reginae*
	ferox	see *A. salmiana* var. *ferox*
	filifera ♀H1	CCCN CDTJ CHEx CJun EAmu SChr SPlb WCot
	flexispina	EGri SPlb
	garciae-mendozae	CDTJ
	- NJM 05.073	WPGP
	geminiflora	CCCN CDTJ CFil CHel CJun EAmu EShb
	gentryi	CDTJ CFil EGri SPlb
	- F&M 213A	WPGP
	ghiesbreghtii	EGri
	gigantea	see *Furcraea foetida*
	goldmaniana	see *A. shawii* subsp. *goldmaniana*
	× ***gracilipes***	WPGP
	guadalajarana	CDTJ EGri WCot WPGP
	guttata new	WCot
	havardiana	CFil EAmu EGri EUJe WCot WPGP XSen
	- DJH 1326	WCot
	horrida	CDTJ CFil CJun EGri SBig
	- subsp. ***horrida***	SPlb
	- 'Perotensis'	EGri EShb
	hurteri	CDTJ EGri
	impressa	WCot
	kerchovei	WCot
	lechuguilla	CDTJ EGri SChr WCot WPGP XSen
	lophantha	see *A. univittata*
	- var. ***caerulescens***	see *A. univittata*
	'Macha Mocha'	WCot
	macroacantha	CDTJ
	maculosa	WCot WPGP
	marmorata	CJun WCot
	maximilliana	SPlb
	mitis var. ***albidior***	EGri
§	- var. ***mitis***	CDTJ CDoC EAmu EGri
	- var. ***mitis*** × ***variegata***	WCot
	mitriformis	EGri
	montana	CDTJ CFil EAmu EGri EUJe SBst SChr SMad SPlb WCot
	- F&M 221	WPGP
	- F&M 209	WPGP
	neomexicana	CCCN CDTJ CFil EAmu EBee EGri EUJe WPGP XSen
	- S&B 948	WCot
	× ***nigra*** hort.	EAmu EGri
	nizandensis	CHEx
§	***obscura***	CDTJ EGri WCot
	ocahui	EGri
	oroensis	WCot
§	***ortgiesiana***	WCot
	ovatifolia	CDTJ CFil CJun EGri SKHP SPlb
	- NJM 09.002	WPGP
	palmeri	CCCN CFil EBee WCot WPGP
	panamana	see *A. vivipara* var. *vivipara*
	parrasana	CDTJ EAmu EGri EUJe WPGP
	parryi	CDTJ CDoC CHel EAmu EGri GKev SBst SPlb WPGP XSen
	- var. ***couesii***	SKHP XSen
	- 'Cream Spike' (v)	CFil EAmu WCot
	- var. ***huachucensis***	CDTJ WCot
	- 'Ohi-kissho-ten-nishiki' (v)	WCot
	- subsp. ***parryi***	CDTJ WCot WPGP
	- - JCA 1.035.000	WPGP
	- small	EGri
	- small, variegated (v)	EGri
	- var. ***truncata***	EAmu EGri
	- - variegated (v) new	WCot
	parviflora ♀H1	EGri WCot
	pendula	EGri
	polyacantha var. ***xalapensis***	see *A. obscura*
	potatorum ♀H1	EGri
	- 'Gary Fisher' new	WCot
	- var. ***verschaffeltii***	EAmu
	salmiana	CDTJ CFil EAmu EGri SBig SPlb
	- F&M 290	WPGP
	- subsp. ***crassispina***	SPlb
§	- var. ***ferox***	CDTJ CDoC CHel EAmu EGri MREP SAPC SBig SPlb WCot
	scabra	CCCN CDoC CHel EGri WCot
	- subsp. ***maderensis***	see *A. asperrima* subsp. *maderensis*
	schidigera	EGri WCot
	- 'Shira-ito-no-ohi' (v)	WCot
	schottii	CDTJ EGri WCot
	'Sharkskin'	WCot
§	***shawii*** subsp. ***goldmaniana***	EGri
	shrevei subsp. ***magna***	EGri SPlb
	sileri	WCot
	sisalana	EAmu
	- 'Variegata' (v)	EAmu
	stictata	WCot
	striata	EAmu EGri
*	- ***rubra***	CDTJ SPlb
	stricta ♀H1	CCCN CDTJ EAmu EGri MREP WCot
	- dwarf	CBrP
	- 'Nana'	CDTJ
	tequilana variegated (v)	WCot
	toumeyana	CAbb EGri WCot
	- var. ***bella***	CDTJ XSen
	triangularis	CDTJ EGri
	undulata new	WCot
	- 'Chocolate Chips' new	WCot
§	***univittata***	CDTJ CJun EGri WCot
	- 'Quadricolor' (v)	CDTJ SMad SPlb WCot
	utahensis ♀H1	EGri SEND WCot XSen
	- var. ***eborispina***	EGri WCot XSen
	- subsp. ***kaibabensis***	WCot XSen
	- var. ***nevadensis***	EGri
	variegata	WCot
	- B&SWJ 10234	WCru
§	***victoriae-reginae*** ♀H1	CBrP CCCN CDTJ CJun EAmu EGri SChr
	- variegated (v)	EGri
	virginica	WCot
§	***vivipara*** var. ***vivipara***	EGri SBig WCot
	vizcainoensis	EGri
	weberi	EAmu
	wocomahi	EGri WCot
	xylonacantha	EGri SChr SPlb WCot
	- blue-leaved	EGri
	zebra	EGri

Ageratina (*Asteraceae*)

§	***altissima***	CHid CMac ELan EPfP LRHS MCot
	- 'Braunlaub'	CPrp ECtt LPla LRHS MMuc NBir NBre SEND SHar SWat WMnd WPtf
	- 'Chocolate' ♀H4	Widely available

§	***aromatica***	MRav NBro SWat
§	***ligustrina*** 🏆^{H3}	CExl CHel CMHG CRHN CTri EBee EHoe ELan EPfP GCal LHop LRHS MBlu NCGa SDix SEND SLim SPer SPoG SRkn WMnd WPGP WPat WSFF
§	***occidentalis*** NNS 94-53	WCot

Ageratum (*Asteraceae*)

	'Blue Champion'	LAst NPri
	corymbosum	CHll CSpe EShb
	houstonianum 'Blue Danube' 🏆^{H3} **new**	CWCL
	- 'High Tide Blue'	NPri

Agonis (*Myrtaceae*)

	flexuosa	CCCN

Agrimonia (*Rosaceae*)

	eupatoria	CArn CHab GPoy MHer MHoo MNHC NMir SWat WHer WHfH
*	- var. ***alba***	NLar
	grandiflora	EBee
	odorata misapplied	see *A. procera*
	odorata (L.) Mill.	see *A. repens*
	pilosa	CArn EBee
§	***procera***	EBee
§	***repens***	WMoo

Agropyron (*Poaceae*)

	glaucum	see *Elymus hispidus*
	magellanicum	see *Elymus magellanicus*
	pubiflorum	see *Elymus magellanicus*

Agrostemma (*Caryophyllaceae*)

	coronaria	see *Lychnis coronaria*
	githago	CHab MNHC
	- 'Ocean Pearl'	CSpe MCot SPhx

Agrostis (*Poaceae*)

	calamagrostis	see *Stipa calamagrostis*
§	***canina*** 'Silver Needles' (v)	LRHS NBir WWEG
	capillaris	CHab
§	***montevidensis***	NWsh SMad
	nebulosa	CKno SPhx
	- 'Fibre Optics'	see *Panicum* 'Fibre Optics'
	stolonifera 'Julia Ann' (v)	WCot

Aichryson (*Crassulaceae*)

§	× ***aizoides*** var. ***domesticum***	CSuc
	- - 'Variegatum' (v) 🏆^{H1}	EBak WCot
	villosum	CFil

Ailanthus (*Simaroubaceae*)

§	***altissima***	CBcs CCVT CDul CExl CMac EBee EPfP EUJe IDee LEdu MBlu NWea SAPC SEND SPer SPlb SWvt
	- var. ***tanakae*** CWJ 12452	WCru
	- - RWJ 9906	WCru
	glandulosa	see *A. altissima*

Ainsliaea (*Asteraceae*)

	acerifolia B&SWJ 4795	WCru
	- var. ***subapoda*** B&SWJ 11537	WCru
	apiculata B&SWJ 11397	WCru
	- var. ***acerifolia*** B&SWJ 6059	WCru
	nervosa B&SWJ 11344	WCru
	tonkinensis B&SWJ 11819	WCru
	uniflora B&SWJ 11336	WCru

Ajania (*Asteraceae*)

§	***pacifica***	EBee
	- 'Mimosa White'	EBee
	- 'Silver Edge'	XLum

Ajuga (*Lamiaceae*)

	ciliata var. ***villosior***	CCon MAvo
	genevensis	LRHS SPhx
	incisa	EWld GBin GCal
	- 'Bikun' (v)	CDes CLAP EBee SRGP WCot
	- 'Blue Enigma'	CExl CLAP EWes IMou NCGa NLar
	- 'Blue Ensign'	LDai
	'Little Court Pink'	see *A. reptans* 'Purple Torch'
	lupulina	EBee
	metallica hort.	see *A. pyramidalis*
	'Pink Spires'	NCot
§	***pyramidalis***	CArn LRHS
	- 'Metallica Crispa'	CBct EBee ECho ELan EPPr EPfP EPri EWes GKin LRHS NBir NHol NLar SMad SRms SWvt
	reptans	CArn CHab CTri ECtt GKev GPoy LRHS MCot MHer MHoo MNHC NMir WJek WOut XLum
	- f. ***albiflora***	CBar CRow LRHS WHfH
	- - 'Alba'	CArn CBre ECtt ELon EPfP MRav NBro SRms WCAu WMoo
	- 'Arctic Fox' (v)	ECho LSou MRav MSCN SWvt
	- 'Argentea'	see *A. reptans* 'Variegata'
§	- 'Atropurpurea'	CBar EBee ECho ELan EPfP GAbr LRHS MGos MLHP MSpe NWad SEND SGol SPer SPlb SRms SWvt WBrk WJek WWEG XLum
	- Black Scallop = 'Binblasca'^{PBR}	Widely available
	- 'Braunherz'	CBct CCVN CTri EBee ECho ECtt EHoe ELan EPfP EShb GAbr GMaP IGor LHop LRHS MAsh MBri MHer MWat NBir NPri SGol SPer SWvt WHar WHil WHoo WMoo
	- 'Burgundy Glow' (v)	CBcs CBct CHel CWCL ECho EHoe EHyd ELan EPfP EShb GMaP LAst LBuc LRHS MAsh MGos MHer MJak NPri SGol SPad SPer SPlb SPoG SRms SWvt WCAu WGwG WMoo
§	- 'Catlin's Giant' 🏆^{H4}	Widely available
	- 'Chocolate Chip'	see *A. reptans* 'Valfredda'
	- 'Delight' (v)	ECho
	- 'Dixie Chip'	EPfP
	- 'Ebony'	LSRN
	- 'Evening Glow'	WMoo
	- 'Flisteridge'	CNat
	- 'Golden Beauty'	ECho ECtt WOut
	- 'Golden Glow' (v)	LRHS SHil
	- 'Grey Lady'	GBuc
	- 'Harlequin' (v)	SWvt
	- 'John Pierpoint'	SHar
	- 'Jumbo'	see *A. reptans* 'Jungle Beauty'
§	- 'Jungle Beauty'	EPfP MRav XLum
	- 'Macrophylla'	see *A. reptans* 'Catlin's Giant'
§	- 'Multicolor' (v)	CBcs CBct ECho ELan LRHS MRav SPer SPlb SPoG SRms SWvt WMoo WNew
	- 'Palisander'	ECtt NEgg
	- 'Party Colours'	CLAP
	- 'Pink Elf'	CMHG ECho GCra MRav NBro SWat WWEG

	– 'Pink Splendour'	NBre
	– 'Pink Surprise'	EHoe EPri MHer MLHP NRya WWEG
	– 'Purple Brocade'	EHoe LRHS
§	– 'Purple Torch'	EBee NBir NLar SRms WCAu
	– 'Purpurea'	see *A. reptans* 'Atropurpurea'
	– 'Rainbow'	see *A. reptans* 'Multicolor'
	– 'Rosea'	EBee ELon NPnk WCAu WMoo XLum
	– 'Rowden Amethyst'	CRow
	– 'Rowden Appleblossom'	CRow
	– 'Rowden Royal Purple'	CRow EBee
	– 'Toffee Chip'PBR (v)	LSou SGol
	– 'Tricolor'	see *A. reptans* 'Multicolor'
§	– 'Valfredda'	ECho ECtt EPfP GKev LRHS NEgg NLar WBrk WCot WGwG WMoo WWEG
§	– 'Variegata' (v)	CBct ECho ECtt EPfP MHol SEND SPer SPoG SRms SWat
	Sugar Plum = 'Binsugplu'PBR	ELon EShb

Akebia ✿ (*Lardizabalaceae*)

	sp.	GGal
	longeracemosa	NLar
	– B&SWJ 3606	CExl LEdu WCot WCru WPGP
	× ***pentaphylla***	CRHN ELan EPfP EWTr LRHS MAsh MRav NLar SPer WGob
	– B&SWJ 2829	WCru
	quinata	Widely available
	– B&SWJ 4425	WCru
	– 'Alba'	CBcs CHll CMen CSPN CWGN NLar SMDP WPat
	– 'Amethyst'	EBee EMil SKHP
	– 'Amethyst Glow'	EPfP LRHS NLar SPer SPoG
	– cream-flowered	CHel CRHN EBee EPfP EWld LRHS LSRN MRav SKHP SPer SSta SWvt WCru WPGP
	– 'Shirobana'	MBlu
	– variegated (v)	CBcs LLHF SMad WCot WPat
	– 'White Chocolate'	ESwi NLar WCru WSHC
	trifoliata	CBcs ELan EPfP EWld LRHS SEND SLim SLon WOld
	– B&SWJ 2829	WCru
	– B&SWJ 5063	WCru

Alangium (*Cornaceae*)

	platanifolium	CAbP CBcs CExl SBrt WPGP
	– var. ***macrophyllum***	EPfP SEND SPoG WBor
	– var. ***platanifolium***	NLar

Albizia (*Mimosaceae*)

	chinensis	EBee EPfP LRHS
	distachya	see *Paraserianthes lophantha*
§	***julibrissin***	CArn CDTJ CWib EAmu EPfP NEgg WOut
	– 'Ernest Wilson'	EBee MTPN WCFE WGrn
	– 'Evy's Purple' **new**	SGol
	– Ombrella = 'Boubri'PBR	ELan EPfP LRHS MBri SCoo SPoG WHar WPGP
	– f. ***rosea*** ♀H2-3	Widely available
	– 'Rouge d'Été'	EBee
I	– 'Rouge Selection'	LRHS SLim
	– 'Shidare' **new**	LRHS
	– 'Summer Chocolate'PBR	CBcs CDul CWGN EBee ELan EPfP LRHS LSqu MPkF NPri SCoo SHil SLim SMad SPer SPoG WHar WPGP
	kalkora	SPlb
	lophantha	see *Paraserianthes lophantha*

Albuca ✿ (*Asparagaceae*)

	JCA 15856	CTca
	from Lesotho	GCal
§	***abyssinica***	EBee
	angolensis	CPou
	aurea	CTca
	bainesii	see *A. abyssinica*
*	***batliana***	ECho
	batteniana	CCon ECho
	canadensis (L.) F.M. Leight.	CPou EBee MAvo WCot WHil
	cooperi	ECho
	'Dirk Wallace'	CExl
	fastigiata	ECho
	– f. ***floribunda***	WCot
	flaccida	MAvo
	fragrans	EBee
	glauca	EBee ECho
	humilis	CDes CExl ECho LLHF NRya WAbe WCot WHil
	longifolia	ECho
	namaquensis **new**	WHil
	nelsonii	CAvo CDes CPrp CTca EBee ECho WCot WHil
	setosa	CTca EBee ECho
	shawii	CBro CCon CDes CPou CTca EBee ECho EPri GKin LAst LRHS MHer NCGa SPet SPoG WAbe WCot WGwG WHil
	spiralis	WHil
	trichophylla	WHil

× *Alcalthaea* (*Malvaceae*)

	suffrutescens	CAbP CSpe ECtt ELan ELon
	'Parkallee' (d)	GAbr LDai LHop LPla LRHS MAvo MNrw MPie NGdn NLar SPad SPhx WBrk WCot WHoo WWFP XLum
	– 'Parkfrieden' (d)	CSpe EBee ECtt ELon MAvo MNrw SPhx XLum
	– 'Parkrondell' (d)	CDes ECtt ELan ELon LHop LPla MAvo MNrw SHar WCot XLum
	– white-flowered	IFro

Alcea (*Malvaceae*)

	'Apple Blossom' (d)	EPfP
	'Arabian Nights'	SPav
	'Blackcurrant Whirl'	SPav
	ficifolia	NChi SPav WHil WMoo
	'Happy Lights'	ELon
	'Peaches 'n' Dreams'	EPfP LHop NGBl WRHF
§	***rosea***	SVic
	– 'Blacknight' (Spotlight Series)	NPri SVic
	– Chater's Double Group (d)	ECtt EPfP IBoy MBri MHol SPoG SRms WHar WRHF
	– – chamois (d)	EPfP
	– – chestnut brown-flowered (d)	EPfP
	– – pink-flowered (d)	ELan EPfP NSoo
	– – purple-flowered (d)	EPfP LAst SPoG
	– – red-flowered (d)	ELan EPfP SPoG
	– – salmon pink-flowered (d)	ELan EPfP
	– – scarlet-flowered (d)	EPfP NSoo SPoG
	– – violet-flowered (d)	EPfP
	– – white-flowered (d)	ELan EPfP MWat NSoo SMrm SPoG
	– – yellow-flowered (d)	EPfP NSoo SPoG
	– Cottage Mixed	WHil

- 'Crème de Cassis' ELan EPfP LPot LRHS NGBl SPav
- double yellow-flowered (d) EBee
- 'Mars Magic' (Spotlight Series) MWat NPri SVic WCot
- 'Nigra' CSpe EBee ECtt ELan EPfP IBoy LAst LBMP LHop LRHS LSRN MHer MNHC MSpe MWat NGBl NGdn NPri SPer WCAu WHar WWEG XEll XLum
- 'Polarstar' (Spotlight Series) NPri SVic
- single-flowered SBod
- Spring Celebrities Group (d) new CWCL
- Summer Carnival Group CWib SRms
- 'Sunshine' (Spotlight Series) CHVG EBee EPfP MWat NPri SVic

§ ***rugosa*** MSpe SHar SPav XSen
'The Watchman' NSoo

Alcea × *Althaea* see × *Alcalthaea*

Alchemilla ✿ (*Rosaceae*)

abyssinica WHrl
alpina misapplied see *A. conjuncta, A. plicatula*
alpina ambig. MCot
alpina L. CMea ECho EHoe ELan EPfP EWTr GKev GPoy LEdu LHop LRHS MMuc MRav MWat NChi SBch SRms SWat WMoo WSHC
§ ***conjuncta*** CArn CMac COlW CPrp CSam ELan EPfP EShb GAbr GMaP LHop LLWP LRHS MHer MLHP MNFA MRav NBid NChi NDov NEgg NRya SPlb SRms WCAu WJek WKif
ellenbeckii ECho EPfP GAbr WPGP WWFP
epipsila EBee ELan EShb LRHS NLar SPad SPhx
erythropoda ♀H4 Widely available
faeroensis LRHS WMoo WPtf XLum
- var. ***pumila*** WAbe
glaucescens CNat
hoppeana misapplied see *A. plicatula*
iniquiformis EBee WPGP
lapeyrousei EBee NChi
mollis ♀H4 Widely available
* - 'Robusta' MMuc SEND SPlb SWat WMoo WPnP
- 'Thriller' EPfP LRHS
'Mr Poland's Variety' see *A. venosa*
pedata CHid NChi
peristerica EBee
§ ***plicatula*** NLar
psilomischa LRHS
pumila NBre
saxatilis LRHS MWhi NLar
sericata 'Gold Strike' IMou MWhi SHar SMad WHil
speciosa LRHS SBch
straminea MRav NBre
valdehirsuta new EBee
§ ***venosa*** EBee LRHS
vetteri EBee WHrl
vulgaris misapplied see *A. xanthochlora*
§ ***xanthochlora*** CArn GPoy NLar SRms WHer

Aldrovanda (*Droseraceae*)

vesiculosa EFEx

alecost see *Tanacetum balsamita*

Alectorurus (*Liliaceae*)

yedoensis var. ***platypetalus*** EBee

Alectryon (*Sapindaceae*)

excelsus ECou

Aletris (*Melanthiaceae*)

farinosa CArn

Alisma (*Alismataceae*)

lanceolatum MSKA MWts
plantago-aquatica CBAq CHab CRow CSpe EHon MSKA MWts NPer SWat WMAq XBlo
- var. ***parviflorum*** CBAq MSKA MWts SPlb SWat WMAq

Alkanna (*Boraginaceae*)

tinctoria CArn

Allamanda (*Apocynaceae*)

cathartica CCCN

Alliaria (*Brassicaceae*)

petiolata CArn GPoy NMir WHer WOut WSFF

Allium (*Alliaceae*)

RCB UA 5 WCot
§ ***acuminatum*** CPom ECho GBin NBir
I - 'Album' ECho LRHS
aflatunense misapplied see *A. hollandicum*
aflatunense ambig. ECho LRHS LSRN SDeJ SEND WCot WWEG
I - 'Alba' ECho
'Akbulak' EBee ECho
albopilosum see *A. cristophii*
altaicum ECho
altissimum 'Goliath' CGrW CTca EBee GKev LRHS WCot
amabile see *A. mairei* var. *amabile*
'Ambassador' CBro CMea CTca ERCP LRHS MAvo MNrw SPhx
ampeloprasum CPrp ECho SEND SPlb SVic WHer WShi
- var. ***babingtonii*** CAgr CArn CPom CPrp CTca GPoy LEdu WHer WShi
§ - 'Elephant' LEdu
amphibolum ECho EPot
amplectens ECho LLHF
- 'Graceful Beauty' new ERCP
§ ***angulosum*** CAvo CTca ECho EWld LEdu LPla WCot
aschersonianum ERCP SDeJ
atropurpureum CAby EBee ELan EPfP ERCP LRHS MCot MWat SDeJ SPer SPhx
atropurpureum* × *schubertii LSRN
atroviolaceum ECho
azureum see *A. caeruleum*
balansae ECho
barszczewskii ECho
'Beau Regard' ♀H4 CTca CWCL EBee ELan ERCP NLar
beesianum misapplied see *A. cyaneum*
beesianum W.W. Smith CDes CPom LRHS NBir NRya
- 'Album' ECho
blandum see *A. carolinianum*
bodeanum see *A. cristophii*

	brevicaule	ECho
	bucharicum	ECho
	bulgaricum	see *Nectaroscordum siculum* subsp. *bulgaricum*
§	***caeruleum*** ♀H4	CAby CArn CAvo CBro CPom CSpe CTca CTri EBee ECho ECtt ELon EPfP EPot ERCP LHop LPot LRHS MBri MGos MNrw MWat NBir NLar NRya SDeJ SPer SPhx
	- ***azureum***	see *A. caeruleum*
	caesium ♀H4	CAvo ECho ERCP GAbr
	caespitosum	ECho
	callimischon	ECho EPot
	subsp. ***callimischon***	
	- subsp. ***haemostictum***	CDes ECho WAbe WCot
	canadense	CArn ECho
§	***carinatum***	ECho GKev
§	- subsp. ***pulchellum*** ♀H4	CBro EBee ECho ELon EPot LHop LLWP LRHS MHer MNFA MNrw MWat SPhx
	- - f. ***album*** ♀H4	CBro EBee ECho ELon LEdu LLWP MNrw MWat SBch SPhx WPtf
	- - 'Tubergen'	ECho
§	***carolinianum***	ECho
	cepa	SVic
	- Aggregatum Group	ELau GPoy
	- - 'Golden Gourmet' ♀H3	SVic
	- - 'Matador' ♀H3	SVic
	- - 'Pikant' ♀H3	SVic
	- 'Perutile'	CArn CHby GPoy LEdu MHer SHDw
	- Proliferum Group	CArn CHby CPrp CSev EOHP GAbr GPoy LEdu MHer MHoo MNHC SIde WGwG WHer WJek XLum
	- 'Red Brunswick'	SVic
	- var. ***viviparum***	ECho
	- 'White Lisbon' ♀H4	SVic
	cernuum	CAby CAvo CBro CDes CMea CTca EBee ECho EPfP EPot ERCP GBin GKev LEdu LHop LRHS MBel MCot MLHP MNrw SDeJ SKHP SPhx SRms
§	- 'Hidcote' ♀H4	CSam WKif
	- 'Major'	see *A. cernuum* 'Hidcote'
	- var. ***obtusum***	ECho
	- pink-flowered	NBir
	- 'White Dwarf'	EBee ECho
	chinense	GPoy LEdu
	cirrhosum	see *A. carinatum* subsp. *pulchellum*
	commutatum	ECho
	cowanii	see *A. neapolitanum* Cowanii Group
	crenulatum	CPom ECho
§	***cristophii*** ♀H4	Widely available
	cupanii	ECho
	cupuliferum	ECho
	curtum RCB RL 13	WCot
§	***cyaneum*** ♀H4	CPBP CPom ECho LBee LRHS MHer NRya WCot
	cyathophorum	ECho EWld LRHS
§	- var. ***farreri***	CArn CBre CBro CPom ECho EPot LEdu LLWP LRHS MLHP MNrw MRav NChi NRya SBch WCot
	darwasicum	ECho
	- RM 8274	ECho
	decipiens	ECho
	dichlamydeum	ECho
§	***drummondii***	ECho LRHS
	'Early Emperor'	CBro CWCL ERCP
	elatum	see *A. macleanii*
	'Emir'	CBro
	ericetorum	CPom ECho WCot
	falcifolium	ECho EPot LLHF NMin WCot
	farreri	see *A. cyathophorum* var. *farreri*
	fimbriatum	ECho
	- var. ***abramsii***	ECho
	- var. ***purdyi***	ECho
	'Firmament'	CAvo CBro CPom ECho ERCP LRHS SDeJ SPhx
	fistulosum	CArn CHby ECho ELau GBin GPoy LEdu MHer MHoo MMuc MNHC NPri SIde SRms SVic WGwG WJek XLum
	- 'Red Welsh'	CPrp SRms WJek
	- red-flowered	CHby
	flavum ♀H4	CAby CArn CBro CTca ECGP ECho EPot ERCP GKev MRav NSla SDeJ WGwG WThu WWEG
§	- 'Blue Leaf'	ECho LEdu NBir SMrm
	- subsp. ***flavum***	EBee ECho
	- - var. ***minus***	ECho
	- 'Glaucum'	see *A. flavum* 'Blue Leaf'
	- var. ***nanum***	ECho EPot
	- subsp. ***tauricum***	CSpe EBee ECho SPhx WCot
	'Forelock'	CAvo CBro CTca EBee ERCP LRHS MNrw WCot
	forrestii	ECho WCot
	geyeri	EBee ECho GBin LLHF WCot
	giganteum ♀H4	CAvo CBcs CTca CWCL EBee ECtt ELan EPfP ERCP GKev GPoy IBoy LRHS LSRN MBri MNHC MWat NLar NOrc SDeJ SMrm SPer SPoG SRms SWat SWvt WWEG
	'Gladiator' ♀H4	CAvo CCon CTca CWCL EBee ECtt ERCP GAbr GMaP LRHS LSRN MNrw MRav NOrc SDeJ SPad WWEG
	glaucum	see *A. senescens* subsp. *glaucum*
	'Globemaster' ♀H4	CAby CAvo CBro CMea CTca CWCL EBee ECtt ELan EPfP EPot ERCP LEdu LRHS LSRN MAvo MBri MMHG MNrw NLar SDeJ SPer SPhx WCot WWEG
	'Globus'	CTca EBee
	goodingii	EBee ECho
	guttatum	ECho
	subsp. ***dalmaticum***	
	- - HOA 9114	ECho
	- subsp. ***sardoum*** CH 859	ECho
	haemanthoides	WCot
	haematochiton	ECho
	'Hair'	see *A. vineale* 'Hair'
	heldreichii	EBee ECho
*	***hirtifolium*** var. ***album***	EBee ECho LRHS
	'His Excellency'	CCon EBee ERCP LRHS
§	***hollandicum*** ♀H4	CAvo CBro CTca EBee ECGP ECtt EPfP GKev NEgg NOrc SPer SPlb
	- 'Purple Sensation' ♀H4	Widely available
	- 'Purple Surprise' ♀H4	WCot
	hookeri	LEdu
	- ACE 2430	EBee EPot LEdu WCot
	- var. ***muliense***	LEdu
	- 'Zorami' **new**	LEdu
	humile	ECho
	hyalinum pink-flowered	EBee
	hymenorrhizum	ECho
§	***insubricum*** ♀H4	CDes ECho LWst MNrw NBir WAbe
	'Jackpot' **new**	ERCP

	jajlae	see *A. rotundum* subsp. *jajlae*
	jesdianum 'Michael Hoog'	see *A. rosenorum* 'Michael H. Hoog'
	- 'Purple King'	ERCP LRHS MNrw
	- 'White Empress'[PBR]	CAvo EBee SPhx
	kansuense	see *A. sikkimense*
	karataviense ♀H3	CAby CAvo CBro CTca EBee ELan EPfP EPot GAbr GKev LHop LRHS MBri MCot NBir NLar SDeJ SMrm SWvt
	- 'Ivory Queen'	CAby CAvo CBro CTca EBee EPfP ERCP GAbr GKev LRHS LSRN NLar SDeJ SMrm SPad SPlb WWFP
	komarovianum	see *A. thunbergii*
	ledebourianum	ECho
	lenkoranicum	CAvo CPom EBee ECho WCot
§	***lineare***	ECho
	litvinovii	ECho
	longicuspis	ECho
	'Lucy Ball'	ERCP LRHS NBir NLar SDeJ
§	***lusitanicum***	CBro CTca ECho ERCP NBre SDix WAbe WCot
§	***macleanii***	CAvo EBee ECho LRHS
	macranthum	CPom EBee ECho EPot GBin LRHS
	macrochaetum	ECho
	macropetalum	ECho
	mairei	ECho EHyd LHop LLWP LRHS NRya
§	- var. ***amabile***	ECho NRya NSla WThu
	- - pink-flowered	ECho
	- - red-flowered	ECho
	maximowiczii	ECho
	- white-flowered	ECho
	'Mercurius'[PBR]	EBee ERCP LRHS MNrw SPhx WCot
	'Miami' **new**	ERCP
	'Millennium' **new**	WCot
	moly	CArn CWCL EBee ECho GKev LRHS MBri MMuc MRav MWat NRya SDeJ SRms WCot XLum
	- 'Jeannine' ♀H4	CBro CTca EBee ECho EPot GAbr GBin LRHS MMHG WShi
	'Mont Blanc'	CMea EBee ELan ERCP GBin GQue LRHS MNrw NLar
	multibulbosum	see *A. nigrum*
	murrayanum misapplied	see *A. unifolium*
	murrayanum Regel	see *A. acuminatum*
	narcissiflorum misapplied	see *A. insubricum*
§	***narcissiflorum*** Vill.	CRDP CSpe EBee ECho MNrw
	neapolitanum	EBee ECho EPot MBri MCot SEND SPer SRms WGwG
§	- Cowanii Group	CBro ECho LRHS SDeJ WCot
	- 'Grandiflorum'	ECho
	nevskianum	ECho EPot SKHP
§	***nigrum***	CAvo CBro ECGP EPfP EPot ERCP LRHS MCot MRav NBir SDeJ SPhx WCot
	nutans	CPrp EBee LEdu MHer MNHC SHDw WHal WHil WJek
	nuttallii	see *A. drummondii*
§	***obliquum***	CAvo CBro CPom ECho ERCP SPhx WCot
	ochotense	WCot
	odorum L.	see *A. ramosum* L.
	oleraceum	EBee ECho WHer
	olympicum	CDes
§	***oreophilum***	CSam ECho EPfP LRHS MLHP SMrm SPer SRms WCot WHoo
	- 'Agalik'	ECho
	- 'Zwanenburg' ♀H4	ECho EPot
	ostrowskianum	see *A. oreophilum*
	ovalifolium var. ***leuconeurum***	WCot
	pallasii	ECho
	pallens	CBre ECho NBir
§	***paniculatum***	LWst
*	- var. ***minor***	ECho
	paradoxum	ECho LEdu NBir
	- var. ***normale***	CBro CDes CPom CRDP ECho EPot ERCP EWld MRav NBir WCot
	pedemontanum	see *A. narcissiflorum* Vill.
	pendulinum	ECho
	'Pinball Wizard'	CBro CTca CWCL ERCP LRHS
	'Pink Jewel'	ERCP WCot
	platycaule	ECho SKHP WCot
	plummerae	EBee ECho SKHP
	plurifoliatum	ECho
	polyphyllum	see *A. carolinianum*
	porrum 'Musselburgh'	NPri
	przewalskianum	EBee LEdu
	pskemense	WCot
	pulchellum	see *A. carinatum* subsp. *pulchellum*
	'Purple Rain'	ERCP
	pyrenaicum misapplied	see *A. angulosum*
	pyrenaicum Costa & Vayr.	SEND
	ramosum Jacq.	see *A. obliquum*
§	***ramosum*** L.	EBee ECho LEdu MHoo
	rosenbachianum misapplied	see *A. stipitatum*
	rosenbachianum Regel	CBro EBee LRHS
	- 'Album'	ERCP LRHS
	- 'Michael Hoog'	see *A. rosenorum* 'Michael H. Hoog'
	- 'Shing'	EBee IBal MNrw
§	***rosenorum*** 'Michael H. Hoog'	EBee ECho EPot LRHS
	roseum	CMea ECho EPfP EPot SDeJ
§	***rotundum*** subsp. ***jajlae***	ECho
	'Round and Purple'	EBee ERCP LRHS
	sativum	CArn ECho MHer NPri SIde SPoG SRms
	- 'Albanian Late' **new**	LEdu
	- 'Elephant'	see *A. ampeloprasum* 'Elephant'
	- var. ***ophioscorodon***	ECho GPoy SPlb
	saxatile	ECho
	schmitzii	CPom ECho
	schoenoprasum	Widely available
	- f. ***albiflorum***	CArn CPbn CPrp ECho LEdu MHer NBir NCGa SIde WCot WHer
	- 'Black Isle Blush'	CDes CPbn CTca EBee GPoy LEdu LPla MHer
	- 'Corsican White'	LEdu
	- fine-leaved	ELau
	- 'Forescate'	CPrp CTca EBee EWes LEdu LHop LRHS MRav NBir SIde SPet WHoo XLum
	- medium-leaved	ELau NPri
	- 'Netherbyres Dwarf'	CArn
	- 'Pink Perfection'	GPoy LEdu LPla MHer
	- 'Polyphant'	CBre
	- 'Shining Silver' **new**	LEdu
	- var. ***sibiricum***	SDix WShi
	- 'Silver Chimes'	CAvo CDes EBee MRav SHDw
	- thick-leaved	ECho ELau
	- 'Wallington White'	LEdu
	- 'Wilau'	ELau
	schubertii	CAby CAvo CBro CHVG CSpe CTca CWCL ECtt ELan EPfP EPot ERCP GKev LPio LRHS MBri MNrw NDov SDeJ SPer SPhx WCot

scorodoprasum	EBee ECho SIde
- 'Art' **new**	ERCP
- subsp. ***jajlae***	see *A. rotundum* subsp. *jajlae*
- 'Passion'	ERCP
- subsp. ***scorodoprasum***	ECho
senescens	CArn CBro CDes CTca CTri ECGP EPot LEdu LRHS MRav SBch SEND SMrm SRms XLum XSen
§ - subsp. ***glaucum***	CArn CAvo CMea CPBP CPom CPrp CSpe EBee ECho LAst LEdu LPio LRHS MNFA NDov NGdn NRya SPet SWat WCot XSen
- subsp. ***senescens***	ECho LEdu
serra	WCot
sessiliflorum	ECho
shelkovnikovii **new**	WCot
sibthorpianum	see *A. paniculatum*
siculum	see *Nectaroscordum siculum*
§ ***sikkimense***	CCon CPom EBee ECho EWTr GBin LEdu LRHS NSla SPet WCot
'Silver Spring'	EPot ERCP LRHS MNrw SDeJ
sphaerocephalon	Widely available
'Spider'	CAvo CBro ERCP SPhx
splendens	ECho GAbr
stellatum	LRHS WGwG
stellerianum	WAbe WThu
var. ***kurilense***	
§ ***stipitatum***	ECho ERCP LRHS SPhx WCot
- 'Album'	CBro ECho LRHS
- 'Mars'	EBee EPfP ERCP LRHS
- 'Mount Everest'	CAvo CBro CCon CHid CTca EPfP EPot ERCP GBin GKev GMaP LRHS LSRN MNrw SDeJ SMrm SPer SPhx WCot WShi
- 'Violet Beauty'	[illegible] CWCL GKev WCot
- 'White Giant'	CTca EBee ERCP LRHS
stracheyi	WCot
'Stratos'	EBee ERCP LRHS
strictum misapplied	see *A. lineare*
subhirsutum	CPom XLum
'Summer Beauty'	see *A. lusitanicum*
'Summer Drummer'	CTca EBee ERCP SDeJ SPhx
'Sweet Discovery'	EBee LRHS
tanguticum	LRHS
taquetii	see *A. thunbergii*
§ ***thunbergii*** ♀H4	EBee ECho NBir NRya SPhx WAbe WWEG
- PAB 3821 **new**	LEdu
- 'Album'	CDes ECho WAbe
- 'Ozawa'	CDes EBee ECho LEdu SRms WAbe WCot WOld
tibeticum	see *A. sikkimense*
* ***tournefortii***	EBee ECho
triquetrum	ECho EDAr ELan ELau EPfP EPot LEdu NBir SEND WCot WHer WMoo XLum
tschimganicum	SKHP
tuberosum	CArn CAvo CBro CHby CPrp CSev CSpe CTca EBee ECho ELau GPoy LEdu LPot LRHS MHer MHoo MNHC NDov NGdn SDeJ SEND SIde SPoG SRms SVic WCot WJek XLum XSen
- B&SWJ 8881	WCru
- purple/mauve-flowered	CHby ECho ELau
§ ***unifolium*** ♀H4	CAvo CPom EBee ECho EPfP EPot ERCP GAbr GBin GKev LRHS MHer MRav NBir NLBP SDeJ SEND SMrm
ursinum	CArn CHab CHby ECho EOHP GPoy LEdu LRHS MHoo WJek WPtf WSFF WShi
'Valerie Finnis'	CPBP
validum NNS 06-41	WCot
victorialis	ECho
- 'Cantabria'	CDes EBee
- 'Kemerovo'	EBee
vineale	CArn LEdu NMir WHer
- PAB 2763 **new**	LEdu
- 'Dready'	ECho GKev
§ - 'Hair'	CAby CTca EBee EPfP ERCP GKev LRHS MCot NBir
violaceum	see *A. carinatum*
virgunculae	CMea WAbe
wallichii	EWes GMaP GQue LEdu LLHF MBNS NBir NChi SKHP WCot XLum
- PAB 2976 **new**	LEdu
- dark-flowered	CHel CPom WCot
zaprjagajevii	WCot
zebdanense	EBee ECho

almond see *Prunus dulcis*

Alnus ✿ (*Betulaceae*)

cordata ♀H4	CBcs CCVT CDoC CDul CLnd CMCN CMac CSBt CSto CTho CTri EBee ECrN ELan EPfP EWTr LBuc MGos NEgg NLar NWea SEND SEWo SGol SPer SPlb WMou
cremastogyne	CMCN EBtc
fauriei from Niigata, Japan	CSto
firma	CSto
glutinosa	CBcs CCVT CDoC CDul CHab CLnd CMac CSBt CSto CTho CTri EBee ECrN EPfP LBuc MGos MJak NWea SEWo SGol SPer WHar WMou WSFF
- 'Aurea'	CDul CEnd CTho CWib MBlu MGos
- var. ***barbata***	CSto
- 'Imperialis' ♀H4	CCVT CDoC CDul CEnd CLnd CTho EBee ECrN ELan EPfP EWTr GBin LHop LRHS MBlu MBri MMuc MPkF NBro NLar NWea SEND SEWo SGol SKHP SPer WHar
- 'Laciniata'	CCVT CDoC CDul CMac CTho ECrN MGos
- 'Pyramidalis'	CDul
hirsuta	CSto NWea
incana	CBcs CCVT CDoC CDul CLnd CMCN CTho CWib EBee ECrN LBuc MGos NLar NWea SGol SPer WHar WMou
- 'Aurea'	CBcs CDul CEnd CLnd CMac CTho EBee ECrN ELan EPfP IArd MBlu MBri MGos MRav NBro NEgg NLar NWea SEWo SGol SPer WHar
- 'Laciniata'	CTho MGos NLar SCoo WMou
- 'Pendula'	CTho
japonica	CSto NLar
aff. ***jorullensis*** NJM 09.070	WPGP
maximowiczii	CSto
- from Ulleungdo	WCru
oregana	see *A. rubra*
pendula	CSto
- B&SWJ 10895	WCru
rhombifolia	EBtc

§	***rubra***	CCVT CDoC CDul CLnd CMCN CTho ECrN ELan NWea WMou
	- f. ***pinnatisecta***	CMCN CTho
	sieboldiana	WCru
	× ***spaethii***	MMuc
	subcordata	CSto
	viridis	CAgr CSto EBtc EGFP NWea
	- subsp. ***sinuata***	CAgr CSto EGFP NWea

Alocasia ✿ (*Araceae*)

× ***amazonica*** ♀H1	XBlo
'Aurora'	EAmu
'Black Stem'	EAmu
'Calidora'	CDTJ NSoo SPlb
cucullata	XBlo
gageana	CDTJ
lauterbachiana	EAmu
macrorrhiza	CCon CDTJ EAmu SAPC SBig SBst SPlb
- 'Variegata' (v) ♀H1	EAmu
'Mayan Mask'	EAmu
odora	CAbb CDTJ EAmu SPlb XBlo
plumbea	XBlo
'Portodora'	EAmu
sarawakensis 'Yucatan Princess' **new**	EAmu
'Stingray'	EAmu
wentii	CDTJ EAmu WCot
- 'Aline'PBR (v)	EAmu
- 'Victory' (v)	EAmu

Aloe ✿ (*Asphodelaceae*)

	aculeata	CAbb EShb
	africana	CAbb
	arborescens	CAbb CBrP CDTJ CDoC CHEx EAmu EShb EUJe SBst SEND SPlb
	aristata ♀H1	CHEx EGri EUJe SAPC SChr SEND SPlb WPGP XLum
	- 'Green Pearl'PBR **new**	SMad
	barbadensis	see *A. vera*
	barberae	CCCN
	betsileensis	LToo
	brevifolia ♀H1	CAbb CBrP EAmu EShb EUJe SAPC SBst
	broomii	CAbb CCCN CDoC EPfP LToo SPlb
	camperi 'Maculata'	SEND
	castanea	CAbb
	ciliaris	CHll EShb
	comptonii	CAbb EShb
	cooperi	CCCN CDTJ CDoC
	dawei	EShb
	descoingsii ♀H1	LToo
	descoingsii × ***haworthioides***	CSuc
	dichotoma	CAbb CSuc SPlb
	dinteri **new**	CSuc
	ecklonis	CCCN CSuc SPlb
	elegans	LToo
	excelsa	CSuc
	ferox	CAbb CBrP CCCN CDTJ CDoC CSuc EAmu SBig
	fosteri	CDTJ CSuc
	gerstneri **new**	CSuc
	greatheadii	CSuc
	- var. ***davyana***	SChr
	humilis	CBrP CSuc SChr SEND
	juvenna	EShb
	kedongensis	SEND
	krapohliana	CAbb
	lineata	CAbb
	littoralis	CAbb
	lutescens	CAbb
	maculata	CDTJ CDoC CSuc
	marlothii	CAbb CCCN CSuc EShb SPlb
	melanacantha ♀H1	CAbb
	microstigma	CCCN CDoC
	mitriformis	CBrP EPfP SEND
	mutabilis	CHEx SChr SEND
	peglerae	CAbb
	petricola	CAbb
	plicatilis	CCCN CDTJ CSuc EShb
	pluridens	CAbb
	polyphylla	CAbb CSuc EAmu WPGP
	pratensis	CCCN CDTJ
	reitzii	CAbb SPlb
	rivae **new**	CSuc
	rugosifolia **new**	CSuc
	sheilae **new**	CSuc
	sinkatana	CSuc
	'Snowflake'	CSuc
	somaliensis ♀H1	SMad
	speciosa	CAbb
	spectabilis	CSuc
	spicata	CAbb
	× ***spinosissima***	CDoC SChr
	striata	CAbb CCCN CSuc EShb LToo
	striatula	CAbb CBrP CDTJ CDoC CGHE CHEx CSam CSuc CTca EAmu EBee EGri EShb EUJe IBlr LEdu SAPC SBHP SBig SChr SEND SKHP SPlb SVen WCot WPGP
	succotrina	CAbb
	suprafoliata	CAbb
	tenuior	CSuc
	thraskii	CAbb CSuc
	tomentosa	LToo
	vanbalenii **new**	CSuc
	variegata (v) ♀H1	EShb
§	***vera*** ♀H1	CArn CCCN CDoC CHby CSpe EOHP EUJe GPoy MHoo MNHC NPer NPla NPri SBch SChr SEND SIde SMad SPlb SPre SVic WJek
	wickensii	CAbb LToo
	yavellana	SPlb

Aloe × *Haworthia* see × *Alworthia*

Alonsoa (*Scrophulariaceae*)

	'Bright Spark'	CSpe WKif
	incisifolia	CCCN CSpe
	meridionalis	CCCN
	- 'Rebel'	LAst MSCN SRkn WBor
*	- 'Salmon Beauty'	LRHS
	'Pink Beauty'	CSpe
	'Scarlet Lucky Lips' (v)	LSou
	warscewiczii	CCCN
	- 'Peachy-keen'	CSpe

Alopecurus (*Poaceae*)

	alpinus	see *A. borealis*
§	***borealis***	LRHS
	- subsp. ***glaucus***	ELan EPPr SPer
	pratensis	CHab NOrc
	- 'Aureovariegatus' (v)	EHoe EPPr GMaP NBid SLim SPer XLum
	- 'Aureus'	MRav NBro SPlb WWEG
	- 'No Overtaking' (v)	EPPr

Alophia (*Iridaceae*)

lahue	see *Herbertia lahue*

Aloysia (*Verbenaceae*)

chamaedrifolia	EPfP
citriodora	see *A. citrodora*
§ ***citrodora*** ΨH2	Widely available
gratissima	WJek
triphylla	see *A. citrodora*

Alpinia (*Zingiberaceae*)

formosana	LEdu
galanga	CArn
japonica	CExl LEdu
- B&SWJ 8889	WCru
nutans misapplied	see *A. zerumbet*
speciosa	see *A. zerumbet*
§ ***zerumbet***	EAmu
- B&SWJ 11512	WCru
- 'Variegata' (v)	CDTJ EAmu EUJe XBlo

Alsobia see *Episcia*

Alstroemeria (*Alstroemeriaceae*)

'Adonis'^{PBR}	LRHS SPer
'Aimi'	CCon ELan SPer SWvt
'Aliénor' (Duchesses d'Anjou Series) **new**	XTur
'Angelina'	LRHS SWvt
'Anne' (Duchesses d'Anjou Series) **new**	XTur
'Antoine' (Ducs d'Anjou Series) **new**	XTur
'Apollo' ΨH4	CBcs CTsd ELan MBNS MNrw NBre SWvt
'Arthur' (Duc d'Anjou Series) **new**	XTur
'Athena'	LRHS
'Aubance' (Jardin Series) **new**	XTur
aurantiaca	see *A. aurea*
§ ***aurea***	MRav SRms XLum
- 'Apricot'	GCal
- 'Dover Orange'	IGor
- 'Lutea'	NLar SDeJ SPlb
- 'Orange King'	CTsd ELan EPfP NLar SDeJ
'Authion' (Jardin Series) **new**	XTur
'Baracé' (Jardin Series) **new**	XTur
'Baugé' (Jardin Series) **new**	XTur
'Béatrice' (Duchesses d'Anjou Series) **new**	XTur
'Blanche' (Duchesses d'Anjou Series) **new**	XTur
'Blushing Bride'	CCon ELon MBNS SWvt
'Bonanza'	SLon SPer
brasiliensis	CCon CTsd GCal WCot WSHC XLum
- 'Cally Star' (v)	GCal
'Briançon' (Jardin Series) **new**	XTur
'Brissac' (Jardin Series) **new**	XTur
'Cahors'	LRHS MBri
'Camille' (Pitchounes Series) **new**	XTur
'Candy Floss'	EPfP
'Caroline' (Duchesses d'Anjou Series) **new**	XTur
'Charles' (Ducs d'Anjou Series) **new**	XTur
'Charm'	LRHS SPer
'Chartrené' (Jardin Series) **new**	XTur
'Chi Chi'	WCot
'Chinon' (Jardin Series) **new**	XTur
§ 'Christina'^{PBR}	LRHS MBNS SLon SWvt
'Christine' (Duchesses d'Anjou Series) **new**	XTur
'Coronet' ΨH4	MBNS
'Dandy Candy'	ELon EWll LAst MCot NGdn NLar SPoG WBrk WCot
'Dayspring Delight' (v)	CRDP
'Diane' (Duchesses d'Anjou Series) **new**	XTur
diluta subsp. ***chrysantha*** F&W 8700	WCot
'Distré' (Jardin Series) **new**	XTur
Doctor Salter's hybrids	SRms
'Dorotheé' (Duchesses d'Anjou Series) **new**	XTur
'Douceur d'Automne'	LRHS MBri
'Elvira'	LRHS
'Evening Song'	CCon LRHS MBNS SLon SPer SWvt
'Flaming Star'	CBcs
'Fougeré' (Jardin Series) **new**	XTur
'Frances' (v)	CAvo CBro
'Freedom'	CDoC CWGN ECtt ELon LSou MAvo MBNS MBri MHol NEgg NLar NSti SMad SPoG WCot
'Friendship' ΨH4	CBcs CTsd ELan NBre SPlb SWvt
'Gaspard' (Pitchounes Series) **new**	XTur
'Gée' (Jardin Series) **new**	XTur
'Gloria'	MBNS SWvt
'Glory of the Andes' (v)	CWGN NLar
'Golden Delight'	ELan LRHS SPer
I 'Hatch Hybrid'	GCal
'Hawera'	GCal SMrm
'Héloïse' (Pitchounes Series) **new**	XTur
'Henri' (Ducs d'Anjou Series) **new**	XTur
hookeri	ECho
- subsp. ***cummingiana***	WCot
'Hyrôme' (Jardin Series) **new**	XTur
Inca Adore = 'Koadore'	CExl MBri
Inca Avanti = 'Koncavanti'	LBuc
Inca Azure = 'Konazur'^{PBR}	CDoC MHol
Inca Classic = 'Konclassic'	WHlf
Inca Devotion = 'Koncvotio'^{PBR}	EBee LHop MBri NLar NMir
Inca Exotica = 'Koexotica'^{PBR}	EBee LHop LRHS MBri MGos NMir SPoG
Inca Glow = 'Koglow'^{PBR}	CExl CWGN EBee ELon EWTr MGos MHol NLar NPri SDeJ
Inca Ice = 'Koice'	CWGN LHop LRHS MGos NLar SPoG
Inca Joli = 'Koncajoli'	LBuc
Inca Lake = 'Koncalake'	EBee LBuc
Inca Milk = 'Koncamilk'	WHlf
Inca Obsession = 'Koobsion'	LRHS
Inca Pulse = 'Konpulse'^{PBR}	CWGN EBee ELon GBin LHop LRHS MBri MHol NLar NPri SDeJ SPoG
Inca Serin = 'Koserin'^{PBR}	LHop LRHS
Inca Tropic = 'Kotrop'	CExl EBee LRHS MBri MGos SPoG WHlf

Inca Yuko = 'Koncayuko'	CWGN LBuc NPri SPoG
Indian Summer = 'Tesronto' **new**	NPri
Inticancha Creamy Dark Pink = 'Tescreda'	SDeJ
Inticancha Dark Purple = 'Tesdarklin'PBR	LBuc
Inticancha Maya = 'Tesmaya'	CWGN LBuc
Inticancha Navayo = 'Tesnava'	LBuc
Inticancha Purple = 'Tespurplin'PBR	CWGN
Inticancha Red = 'Tesrobin'PBR	CWGN LBuc
Inticancha White Pink Heart = 'Tesheartin'	LBuc
Isabella = 'Stalis'	LSRN
'Isabelle' (Duchesses d'Anjou Series) **new**	XTur
'Jalesne' (Jardin Series) **new**	XTur
'Layon' (Jardin Series) **new**	XTur
ligtu hybrids	CAvo CBcs ELan EPfP MNrw NHol NLar NPer SDeJ SRms SWvt WBrk WHoo XLum
'Liré' (Jardin Series) **new**	XTur
'Little Miss Christina'	see *A.* 'Christina'
'Little Miss Davina'	LRHS
'Little Miss Isabel'	LRHS
'Little Miss Lucy'	LRHS
'Little Miss Roselind'	see *A.* 'Roselind'
'Little Miss Sophie'	see *A.* 'Sophie'
'Little Miss Tara'	see *A.* 'Tara'
'Little Miss Veronica'	MBNS
'Louis' (Ducs d'Anjou Series) **new**	XTur
'Louise'	LSRN
'Louise' (Duchesses d'Anjou Series) **new**	XTur
'Lovet' (Jardin Series) **new**	XTur
'Lucinda'	CBcs SWvt
magnifica subsp. ***maxima***	WCot
'Margot' (Pitchounes Series) **new**	XTur
'Marguerite' (Duchesses d'Anjou Series) **new**	XTur
'Marie' (Duchesses d'Anjou Series) **new**	XTur
'Marina'	MBNS
'Marissa'	GMaP
'Mars'	LRHS
'Mathilde' (Duchesses d'Anjou Series) **new**	XTur
'Mauve Majesty'	CDoC ELon IBoy LSou MAvo MHol NLar NPri WCot
'Mazé' (Jardin Series) **new**	XTur
'Montsoreau' (Jardin Series) **new**	XTur
'Moulin Rouge'	ELan LRHS MBNS SLon
'Neptune'	LRHS MBri
'Nicolas' (Ducs d'Anjou Series) **new**	XTur
'Orange Gem' ♀H4	MBNS
'Orange Glory' ♀H4	ELon GMaP MBNS SWvt WWlt
'Orange Supreme'	LRHS
'Oriana'	ELan SWvt
'Oudon' (Jardin Series) **new**	XTur
patagonica	ECho WAbe
'Pauline' (Pitchounes Series) **new**	XTur
pelegrina	ECho
'Philippe' (Ducs d'Anjou Series) **new**	XTur
philippii	WCot
'Phoenix' (v)	CCon LRHS SLon SWvt
'Pink Perfection'	NLar
'Polka'	MBNS
presliana RB 94103	WCot
- subsp. ***australis***	SMrm
Princess Angela = 'Staprilan'	CBcs ELan MBNS NLar
Princess Anouska = 'Zaprinous'PBR	ELan NLar SLon SPer
Princess Ariane = 'Zapriari'PBR	LRHS
Princess Camilla = 'Stapricamil'PBR	CBcs LRHS SLon SPer SPoG
Princess Daniela = 'Stapridani'PBR	SCoo SPoG
Princess Ella = 'Staprirange'	NLar
Princess Fabiana = 'Zaprifabi'PBR	ELan LRHS SPoG
Princess Felicia = 'Zapricia'PBR	ELan LRHS SPer
Princess Isabella = 'Zapribel'PBR	LRHS LSRN NLar
Princess Ivana = 'Staprivane'PBR	ELan LRHS NLar SPoG
Princess Juliana = 'Staterpa'	SPoG
Princess Julieta = 'Zaprijul'PBR	NLar SPoG
Princess Letizia = 'Zaprilet'PBR	LRHS
Princess Leyla = 'Stapriley'PBR	CBcs LRHS MBNS SLon SPer SPoG
Princess Louise = 'Zaprilou'PBR	LRHS LSRN
Princess Margaret	NLar
Princess Marilene = 'Staprilene'PBR	LRHS MBNS
Princess Mary = 'Zaprimary'PBR	LRHS NLar
Princess Mathilde = 'Zaprimat'PBR	LRHS
Princess Monica = 'Staprimon'PBR	LRHS MBNS SPoG
Princess Oxana = 'Staprioxa'PBR	LRHS NLar
Princess Paola = 'Stapripal'PBR	MBNS SCoo
Princess Ragna	see *A.* Princess Stephanie
Princess Sara = 'Staprisara'PBR	SPoG
Princess Sarah = 'Stalicamp'	MBNS
Princess Sissi = 'Staprisis'	SPoG
§ Princess Sophia = 'Stajello'	SPoG
§ Princess Stephanie = 'Stapirag'	NLar
Princess Susana = 'Staprisusa'PBR	SCoo SPoG
Princess Theresa = 'Zapriteres'PBR	EPfP LRHS NLar

Princess Zavina = 'Staprivina'PBR	CBcs CCon ELan LRHS MBNS NLar SPer
§ ***psittacina***	CAvo CBro CGHE CHll CSam ELan EPfP GBin GBuc GCal GCra LHop MCot MHer SRms WSHC XLum
- 'Mona Lisa'	EWll GBuc LLHF LSou
- 'Royal Star' (v)	CBro CExl CWCL ELan ELon EPfP EWTr GBuc GCal LHop LRHS LSou MAsh MAvo SHar SPoG SRms WCot WHoo WSHC WWEG WWlt XLum
pulchella Sims	see *A. psittacina*
'Purple Rain'	ELan LRHS MNrw SLon SWvt
'Querré' (Jardin Series) **new**	XTur
'Red Beauty' (v)	see *A.* 'Spitfire'
'Red Beauty'	ELan GMaP LRHS MBNS SPer SWvt WCot
'Red Coat'	NLar
'Red Elf'	IBoy MBNS SWvt
'René' (Ducs d'Anjou Series) **new**	XTur
'Rhubarb and Custard'	EPfP
Rock 'n' Roll = 'Alsdun01' (v) **new**	LBuc NSoo
§ 'Roselind'	CCon ELan LRHS MBNS SWvt
'Rosie' (Pitchounes Series) **new**	XTur
'Saturne'	EPfP LBuc LRHS MBri
'Selina'	LRHS MBNS NBre
'Serenade'	CBcs CCon ELan
'Serrant' (Jardin Series) **new**	XTur
'Short Purple'	LSou
§ 'Sophie'PBR	ELan MBNS SLon SWvt
§ 'Spitfire' (v)	CRDP EPfP IBoy LRHS SLon SWvt
'Spring Delight' (v)	CRDP WCot
'Strawberry Lace'	EPfP
'Sunrise'	WWlt
'Sunstar'	GMaP
'Sweet Laura'PBR	CAbP CDoC ELon LLHF LSRN MAvo MBri MPie NEgg NGdn NLar NPri NSti SPoG WCot
'Tanya'	LRHS
§ 'Tara'PBR	MBNS SPlb SWvt
'Tessa'	LRHS MBNS NBre SLon
'Thorigné' (Jardin Series) **new**	XTur
'Tiercé' (Jardin Series) **new**	XTur
'Turkish Delight'	EPfP
'Uranus'	LBuc LRHS MBri
'William' (Ducs d'Anjou Series) **new**	XTur
'Yellow Friendship' ♀H4	MBNS NLar SWvt
Yellow King	see *A.* Princess Sophia
'Zoé' (Pitchounes Series) **new**	XTur

Althaea (*Malvaceae*)

armeniaca	EBee LPla NLar WCot WOut
cannabina	CArn CFis CSpe ELan GCal GQui IPot LHop LPio LPla MBel MHer MNrw NGBl SPhx WBor WHal WOld
officinalis	CArn CHab CPrp CSev ELan GPoy MHer MHoo MNHC NLar SIde SRms WHfH WJek WOut XLum
- ***alba***	LSou NLar
§ - 'Romney Marsh'	GCal MRav SEND WKif
rosea	see *Alcea rosea*
rugosostellulata	see *Alcea rugosa*

Althaea × *Alcea* see × *Alcalthaea*

Altingia (*Hamamelidaceae*)

poilanei B&SWJ 11756	WCru

× *Alworthia* (*Asphodelaceae*)

'Black Gem'	EPfP EShb SEND

Alyogyne (*Malvaceae*)

'Attraction'	ECou
hakeifolia	ECou
- 'Elle Maree'	CSpe ECou MOWG
- 'Melissa Anne'	ECou MOWG
§ ***huegelii***	CCCN CSpe EBee ECou SRkn SRms
- 'Lavender Lass'	ECou
- 'Santa Cruz'	CCCN CHll CSpe ECou LHop MOWG SEND SLon WPGP
- 'White Delight'	ECou
'Joy'	ECou
Magic Moments = 'Hutwow'	CSpe LBuc NSoo SLon
'Shepherds Delight'	ECou

Alyssoides (*Brassicaceae*)

utriculata	WHil XSen

Alyssum (*Brassicaceae*)

argenteum	ECho
corymbosum	see *Aurinia corymbosa*
montanum	ECho MWat SPlb SRms
§ - 'Berggold'	ECtt EPfP MMuc XLum
- 'Luna'	WHil
- Mountain Gold	see *A. montanum* 'Berggold'
obovatum	WIce
oxycarpum	EPot
saxatile	see *Aurinia saxatilis*
spinosum	EPot
- 'Roseum' ♀H4	CMea CTri ELan EPot MLHP MSCN MWat NSla SBch WAbe
* - 'Roseum Variegatum'	EPot
stribrnyi	LLHF
tortuosum	SEND
wulfenianum	EDAr GAbr IFoB LLHF WIce XLum

Amaranthus (*Amaranthaceae*)

'Autumn Palette'	CSpe
hypochondriacus 'Pygmy Torch' ♀H3	CSpe
tricolor **new**	SRms

× *Amarcrinum* (*Amaryllidaceae*)

'Dorothy Hannibal'	WCot
memoria-corsii	CPrp ECho
- 'Howardii'	CCon CDes ECho EShb LEdu SDeJ

× *Amarine* (*Amaryllidaceae*)

tubergenii 'Zwanenburg'	WCot

× *Amarygia* (*Amaryllidaceae*)

parkeri	ECho
§ - 'Alba'	CAvo CBro CPrp ECho WCot
- 'Rosea'	WCot

Amaryllis (*Amaryllidaceae*)

§ ***belladonna*** ♀H2-3	CAby CBcs CBro CHEx CPrp CTca CTsd ECho EPfP ERCP EShb SDeJ SEND SPav WCot
- 'Parkeri Alba'	see × *Amarygia parkeri* 'Alba'

- white-flowered	CDes ECho SDeJ WCot

Ambrosina (*Araceae*)

bassii from Tunisia	ECho

Amelanchier ✿ (*Rosaceae*)

alnifolia	CSpe CTho EBtc
- 'Forestburg'	NLar
- 'Obelisk'PBR	CDoC CDul EPfP GKin GQue LBuc LHop LLHF LRHS LSRN MAsh MBri MGos MJak NCGa NLar SCoo SPoG SSta WHar
- pink-fruited	NLar
§ - var. ***pumila***	LHop MMHG
- 'Smokey'	CDul
§ ***arborea***	CTho
'Autumn Glory' new	NLar
bartramiana	CTho SSta
- 'Eskimo'	NLar
canadensis K. Koch	see *A. lamarckii*
canadensis Sieb. & Zucc.	see *A. arborea*
canadensis ambig.	CDul IBoy NLar NPri SEWo SPoG WHar
canadensis (L.) Medik.	CAgr CDoC CJun CLnd CMac CSBt CSam CTho CTri CWSG CWib EBee ECrN ELan EPfP LEdu LHop LRHS MGos MRav MSwo NCGa NWea SPer WMoo WPat
§ - 'Glenn Form'	EBee LRHS MBlu MBri MGos SGol SPoG SSta WHar
- 'Prince William'	CAgr MCoo NLar SSta
- Rainbow Pillar	see *A. canadensis* 'Glenn Form'
× ***grandiflora*** 'Autumn Brilliance'	CEnd CJun NHol SGol
- 'Ballerina' ♀H4	Widely available
- 'Cole's Select'	LRHS SKHP
- 'Forest Prince'	NLar
- 'Princess Diana'	MAsh MBlu NLar SCoo
- 'Robin Hill'	CBcs CCVT CDul CMac EBee ECrN ELan EMil EPfP LAst LBuc MBlu MGos MRav NEgg NLar NWea SCoo SEWo SGol WHar
- 'Rubescens'	CEnd CJun EBee EPfP NLar SLon
'La Paloma'	EBee EPfP LRHS MBri MGos SCoo SLim WHar
laevis	CBcs CDul CTri EPfP MGos MSwo NLar
- 'Cumulus'	NLar
- 'Prince Charles'	NLar
- 'R.J. Hilton'	MBri SCoo WHar
- 'Snow Cloud'	CDoC
- 'Snowflakes'	CEnd CJun EBee LRHS MAsh MGos NHol NLar SEWo SLim SPer SPoG WHar
§ ***lamarckii*** ♀H4	Widely available
ovalis misapplied	see *A. spicata* (Lam.) K. Koch
ovalis Medik.	SPlb
- 'Edelweiss'	CJun IArd NEgg NLar SCoo
- 'Helvetia'	MBri
pumila	see *A. alnifolia* var. *pumila*
rotundifolia ambig.	CNWT MCoo
sanguinea 'Chimney Rock'	NLar
sinica	CBcs NLar
§ ***spicata*** (Lam.) K. Koch	MCoo SSta
stolonifera	CTri

× *Amelasorbus* (*Rosaceae*)

raciborskiana	MBlu MBri

Amicia (*Papilionaceae*)

zygomeris	CAbb CCse CHEx CHGN CHll CPom CSpe EBee EUJe EWes EWll GCal LHop MCot SDix SEND SMad SMrm SPoG WCot WPGP
- 'John's Big Splash' (v)	WCot

Amitostigma (*Orchidaceae*)

Enomotoe gx 'Kou Itten'	LWst

Ammi (*Apiaceae*)

majus	CArn CSam CSpe LEdu MNHC SDix SPhx WHfH WJek
visnaga	CArn CBre CHby CSam CSpe ELau MNHC SPhx WHal WJek

Ammobium (*Asteraceae*)

calyceroides	ECou

Ammocharis (*Amaryllidaceae*)

coranica	ECho WCot

Ammophila (*Poaceae*)

arenaria	CKno EBee IMou SMea XLum
breviligulata	IMou SPhx XLum

Amomyrtus (*Myrtaceae*)

§ ***luma***	CAgr CBcs CDoC CDul CHEx CTri CTsd EBee ELan GGal GQui IDee SAPC WJek

Amorpha (*Papilionaceae*)

canescens	EBee LRHS SPhx SPlb
fruticosa	CBcs EBtc EWTr MBlu MMuc NLar SEND SPlb
herbacea	NLar
nana new	XLum
paniculata	NLar

Amorphophallus ✿ (*Araceae*)

albus	CDTJ EBee LEdu WCot
bulbifer	CDTJ EAmu ESwi SBig SBst SDeJ SPlb XLum
dunnii	CDTJ LEdu
kerrii	CExl WCot
kiusianus B&SWJ 4845	WCru
konjac	CCon CDTJ CDes CExl CFil CGHE CHEx CSpe EAmu EUJe LEdu SChF SPlb WPGP XLum
nepalensis	EAmu SBst
rivieri	CPom EBee GCal LEdu LRHS SDeJ WCot
stipitatus	LEdu WCot

Ampelocalamus (*Poaceae*)

§ ***mocrophyllum***	ERod WJun
scandens	WPGP

Ampelocissus (*Vitaceae*)

sikkimensis HWJK 2066	WCru

Ampelodesmos (*Poaceae*)

mauritanica	CHid CKno COIW CSam EBee EHoe EShb EWes MWhi SEND SMad SPlb WCot WWEG XLum

Ampelopsis (*Vitaceae*)

aconitifolia	NLar

- 'Chinese Lace'	CHel EBee EUJe LRHS MRav NLar
arborea	WCru
brevipedunculata	ELan MMHG SCoo SKHP SLim SPer SPhx SPoG WHar
- var. ***maximowiczii*** 'Elegans' (v)	CBcs CHEx CMac CWib EBee ELan EPfP EShb LAst LHop LRHS MGos MRav NBro SPer SPoG SWvt WCot WPat WSHC
delavayana	CDoy EBee MMuc
henryana	see *Parthenocissus henryana*
megalophylla	ELan EShb GCal NCGa NLar SKHP SPer
sempervirens hort. ex Veitch	see *Cissus striata*
tricuspidata 'Veitchii'	see *Parthenocissus tricuspidata* 'Veitchii'

Amphicome see *Incarvillea*

Amsonia (*Apocynaceae*)

'Blue Ice'	IPot
ciliata	EBee ELan GKev IDee IKil LEdu MBri NLar SKHP XLum
- 'Spring Sky' new	EBee
§ ***elliptica***	LRHS
'Ernst Pagels'	LHop
hubrichtii	CAby CCon CCse CHid CSpe EBee ELon EPPr LEdu LHop LRHS SMad SMrm SPad SPhx SWvt WHoo WPtf WSHC
illustris	CAbP CSpe EBee EPPr GCal LEdu LRHS NLar SHar SPhx WHoo WSHC
§ ***orientalis***	CCon CHll CMea CTri GCal LEdu LHop LRHS MCot MLHP MMuc MRav NCGa NDov NLar SMrm SPhx SPoG SVen SWvt WBor WPtf XEll
sinensis	see *A. elliptica*
tabernaemontana	Widely available
- 'Montana' new	SWvt
- var. ***salicifolia***	CAby CSpe EWll IPot LEdu WCAu
- 'Stella Azul'	IPot

Amygdalus see *Prunus*

Amyris (*Rutaceae*)

madrensis new	CFil

Anacamptis (*Orchidaceae*)

§ ***laxiflora***	NLAp
§ ***morio***	NLAp
papilionacea	NLAp
pyramidalis	EFEx NLAp WHer
sancta	NLAp

Anacyclus (*Asteraceae*)

pyrethrum	GPoy
- var. ***depressus***	CTri ECho ELan EPfP GMaP MAsh MHol SPlb SRot XLum
- - 'Garden Gnome'	CTri ECho SRms WHil
- - 'Silberkissen'	CMea EDAr NSla SBch

Anagallis (*Primulaceae*)

monellii 🏆H4	GKev
- Blue Compact = 'Wesanacomp'	LSou
- subsp. ***linifolia*** 'Blue Light'	CSpe
- 'Skylover'	CCCN LAst
tenella	LLWG
- 'Studland'	EPot WAbe

Ananas (*Bromeliaceae*)

comosus (F)	CCCN SPre
- 'Champaca' (F)	CCCN SPre

Anaphalioides (*Asteraceae*)

§ ***bellidioides***	CTri ECou

Anaphalis (*Asteraceae*)

alpicola	EPot NBre
margaritacea	CBcs EBee ECtt GMaP NBid SRms WHar WMoo WPtf
§ - 'Neuschnee'	CTri EPfP NBre WWEG XLum
- New Snow	see *A. margaritacea* 'Neuschnee'
- var. ***yedoensis*** 🏆H4	CTri MCot MLHP NBre SDix
§ ***nepalensis*** var. ***monocephala***	MCot NBre NSti
nubigena	see *A. nepalensis* var. *monocephala*
subumbellata	LRHS
transnokoensis	EBee EWes
§ ***trinervis***	CExl GCra XLum
triplinervis 🏆H4	CHel EHoe ELan ELon EPfP GAbr GMaP IBoy IFoB LRHS MCot MRav NBid NLar NPri NSti SBod SPer WHoo WMoo WWEG
- CC 1620	EBee EPPr NBir
§ - 'Sommerschnee' 🏆H4	CMac EBee ECtt EHoe EPfP IBoy LBMP LPot LRHS MCot MHol MRav NEgg NLar SPer WMnd WPtf
- Summer Snow	see *A. triplinervis* 'Sommerschnee'

Anchusa (*Boraginaceae*)

sp.	CHab
§ ***azurea***	NLar
- 'Dropmore'	CTri EPfP NEgg NLar NOrc SRms WWEG
- 'Feltham Pride'	EBee ELan EPfP SRms SWvt WHoo
- 'Little John'	SRms
- 'Loddon Royalist' 🏆H4	Widely available
- 'Opal'	EPfP LRHS
capensis 'Blue Angel'	CWCL MNHC SWvt
cespitosa Lam.	ECho ELan EWes LLHF WAbe
italica	see *A. azurea*
laxiflora	see *Borago pygmaea*
myosotidiflora	see *Brunnera macrophylla*
officinalis	CArn MNHC
sempervirens	see *Pentaglottis sempervirens*

Ancylostemon (*Gesneriaceae*)

convexus B&SWJ 6624	WCru

Andrachne (*Phyllanthaceae*)

colchica	EBee WCot

Androcymbium (*Colchicaceae*)

cuspidatum 'Karoopoort'	ECho
dregei 'Locricsfontein'	ECho
eucomoides 'Varsputs'	ECho
gramineum	ECho
- from Morocco	ECho
melanthioides	ECho
volutare 'Tanqua'	ECho

Andromeda (*Ericaceae*)

glaucophylla f. ***latifolia***	IVic
polifolia	ECho

- 'Alba'	EBee ECho LRHS MAsh SPer SPlb SWvt
- 'Blue Ice'	EBee ELan EPfP IDee LRHS MAsh NHar NLar SLim SPer SPoG SSpi WAbe WPat
- 'Compacta' ♀H4	CDoC CMac ECho EPfP EPot LSRN MAsh NWad SRms SWvt WGwG WSHC
- 'Compacta Alba' ♀H4	ECho
- 'Grandiflora'	ECho
- 'Kirigamine'	LRHS MAsh NHar
- 'Macrophylla' ♀H4	ECho EPot NHar WPat WThu
- 'Nana'	EPfP LRHS
- 'Nikko'	CMac
- 'Shibutsu'	NHar

Andropogon (*Poaceae*)

gerardii	CAby CKno EBee EHoe EPPr LEdu MWhi NWsh SPhx WWEG XLum
glomeratus new	COIW
scoparius	see *Schizachyrium scoparium*

Androsace (*Primulaceae*)

adenocephala new	GKev
alpina	WAbe
bisulca var. ***aurata***	CPBP
brachystegia	GKev
brahmaputrae new	GKev
bulleyana	CPBP
caduca	WAbe
carnea	ECho IFoB
- SDR 6357	GKev
- subsp. ***brigantiaca***	GKev NSla WAbe WHoo
- var. ***halleri***	see *A. carnea* subsp. *rosea*
- subsp. ***laggeri*** ♀H4	ECho LLHF NSla WAbe
- - 'Andorra'	NHar
§ - subsp. ***rosea*** ♀H4	ECho IFoB WAbe
carnea × ***pyrenaica***	ECho EPot LLHF
chaixii	IFoB
chamaejasme	ECho GKev
- subsp. ***carinata***	GKev
ciliata	WAbe
cylindrica	CPBP ECho ITim LRHS WAbe
cylindrica × ***hirtella***	ECho LLHF LRHS WAbe
delavayi	EPot WAbe
- ACE 1786	WAbe
elatior	WAbe
euryantha new	GKev
fedtschenkoi	GKev
geraniifolia	EBee GKev SRms WAbe
globifera	WAbe
halleri	see *A. carnea* subsp. *rosea*
hausmannii	WAbe
hedraeantha	WAbe
himalaica	CPBP EPot WAbe
hirtella	IFoB ITim LLHF WAbe
idahoensis	GKev WAbe
idahoensis × ***laevigata***	WAbe
jacquemontii	see *A. villosa* var. *jacquemontii*
lactea	WAbe
laevigata	CPBP ITim SIgm WAbe
- 'Gothenburg'	WAbe
- 'Saddle Mount'	CPBP WAbe
lanuginosa ♀H4	CMea CSpe ECho ECtt EDAr EHoe EPot GBin MWat NHar NHol SBch SRms SRot WAbe WIce
- 'Wisley Variety'	SIgm
lehmanniana	WAbe
- 'Gotëborg Yellow'	WAbe
limprichtii	see *A. sarmentosa* var. *watkinsii*
mariae	WAbe
× ***marpensis***	EPot WAbe
microphylla	see *A. mucronifolia* G.Watt
'Millstream'	IFoB
minor	EPot GKev WAbe
montana	WAbe
mucronifolia misapplied	see *A. sempervivoides*
§ ***mucronifolia*** G.Watt	WAbe
mucronifolia G.Watt × ***sempervivoides***	EPot NHar WAbe
muscoidea	WAbe
- SEP 132	CPBP
- 'Breviscapa'	EPot
- Schacht's form	EPot WAbe
nivalis Chumstick form	LLHF
ochotensis	WAbe
primuloides	see *A. studiosorum*
pubescens	ECho LLHF LRHS
pyrenaica	ECho LLHF LRHS WAbe
rigida	EPot GKev LLHF WAbe
robusta	EPot
- subsp. ***purpurea***	WAbe
- - 'Dolpo Dwarf'	WAbe
sarmentosa misapplied	see *A. studiosorum*
sarmentosa ambig.	GJos GKev XLum
sarmentosa Wall.	SRms WHoo
- CC 5557 new	GKev
- from Namche, Nepal	WAbe
- Galmont's form	see *A. studiosorum* 'Salmon's Variety'
- 'Sherriffii'	ECho EPot GKev SIgm SRms WIce
§ - var. ***watkinsii***	EPot
- var. ***yunnanensis*** misapplied	see *A. studiosorum*
selago	WAbe
- 'Red Eye'	WAbe
§ ***sempervivoides*** ♀H4	ECho EDAr EHyd EPot GBin GJos GKev GMaP LHop LRHS NHol NSla SBch SIgm SPlb SRms WAbe WIce WPat
- CC 4631	GKev
- CC 5299	GKev
- 'Greystone'	EPot
- 'Susan Joan'	EPot GKev WAbe
strigillosa	WAbe
§ ***studiosorum*** ♀H4	EPot GAbr GKev IFoB NSla WAbe
- 'Chumbyi'	EPot LLHF SHar SIgm SRms WIce WPat WThu
- 'Doksa'	CPBP EPot IFoB SHar WAbe WIce
§ - 'Salmon's Variety'	CMea CTri SBch SIgm WAbe
tangulashanensis	CPBP LLHF WAbe
tapete ACE 1725	WAbe
vandellii	WAbe
villosa	GKev IFoB WAbe
- SDR 5445	GKev
- var. ***arachnoidea***	GKev
§ - var. ***jacquemontii***	CPBP NHar SHar
- - lilac-flowered	EPot WAbe
- - pink-flowered	EPot SIgm WAbe
- subsp. ***taurica***	WAbe
vitaliana	see *Vitaliana primuliflora*
wardii	WAbe
watkinsii	see *A. sarmentosa* var. *watkinsii*
yargongensis	EPot GKev WAbe
zambalensis	WAbe
zayulensis	GKev

Andryala (*Asteraceae*)

	lanata	see *Hieracium lanatum*

Anemanthele (*Poaceae*)

§	***lessoniana*** ♀^{H4}	Widely available
	- 'Autumn Tints'	EHoe
	- 'Gold Hue'	CKno EHoe

Anemarrhena (*Asparagaceae*)

	asphodeloides	CArn WCot

Anemone ✿ (*Ranunculaceae*)

	Chen Yi T49	WCot
	aconitifolia Michx.	see *A. narcissiflora*
	altaica	LWst NLar SRms
	amurensis	CExl
	apennina ♀^{H4}	CAvo CLAP ECGP ECho WShi
	- var. ***albiflora***	CLAP ECho EPPr EPot
	- double white-flowered (d)	LRHS
	- double-flowered (d)	ECho EPPr MAvo WCru
	- 'Petrovac'	CLAP EBee LLHF LWst SPhx WCot
	baicalensis	WOut WSHC
	baldensis	ECho GBuc GKev IGor SRms
	barbulata	CExl EBee EWes GBuc GKev NLar
	biflora new	ECho
	blanda ♀^{H4}	ECho LRHS MAsh MAvo MBri MLHP MNHC MWat NLar SEND WBor WShi
I	- 'Alba'	LRHS
	- blue-flowered	CAvo CBro CHVG CHel CMea CTri ECGP ECho ELan EPfP EPot ERCP GAbr GKev GMaP IGor LEdu LRHS MBri NPnk SDeJ SMrm SPer SPhx SPoG SRms WCot WHoo
	- 'Charmer'	CGrW ECho EPot SDeJ
	- 'Ingramii'	LWst WCot
	- pink-flowered	LEdu
	- var. ***rosea*** ♀^{H4}	ECho ELan EPfP GKev LRHS SBch SDeJ SPer SPoG
	- - 'Pink Charmer'	ECho
	- - 'Pink Star'	CAvo ECho ERCP GKev NBir
	- - 'Radar' ♀^{H4}	CAvo CMea ECho EPot ERCP LRHS MNrw NBir SDeJ WAbe
	- 'Violet Star'	ECGP GKev SDeJ SPhx WCot
	- 'White Charmer'	ECho
	- 'White Splendour' ♀^{H4}	CAvo CBro CHVG CMea CTri ECho ELan EPfP EPot ERCP GAbr GKev LPio LRHS NBir NLar SDeJ SMrm SPer SPhx SPoG SRms WCot WWFP
	caerulea	LEdu LWst
	canadensis	CSpe ECGP ELon EPPr GBuc LRHS WCot
	caroliniana	ECho LRHS
	caucasica	ECho
	chapaensis HWJ 631	WCru
	coronaria	SVic
	- De Caen Group	CHid EPfP GKev LRHS SPoG
	- - 'Bicolor'	CHid GKev SDeJ
§	- - 'Die Braut'	ERCP NBir NPnk SDeJ
	- - 'His Excellency'	see *A. coronaria* (De Caen Group) 'Hollandia'
§	- - 'Hollandia'	LPot SDeJ WHil
	- - 'Mister Fokker'	CTca ERCP NPnk SDeJ
	- - The Bride	see *A. coronaria* (De Caen Group) 'Die Braut'
	- - 'The Governor'	CTca GKev SDeJ
	- (Harmony Series) 'Harmony Orchid' new	LRHS
	- - 'Harmony Pearl' new	LRHS
	- - 'Harmony Scarlet' new	LRHS
	- Saint Bridgid Group (d)	EPfP GKev LRHS NHol
	- - 'Lord Lieutenant' (d)	CMea EPfP ERCP GKev NBir SDeJ
	- - 'Mount Everest' (d)	ERCP GKev NBir SDeJ WHil
	- - 'Saint Bridgid' (d)	CHid
	- - 'The Admiral' (d)	EPfP GKev NBir SDeJ
	- 'Sylphide' (Mona Lisa Series)	ERCP LPot NBir SDeJ WCot
	crinita	NLar
	cylindrica	EBee NBre NLar XEll
	dahurica new	CHid
	'Danish White'	MNrw
	decapetala	GBuc LLHF MHer
	demissa	WCot WSHC
	- SDR 3307	EBee
	- var. ***major***	EBee
	drummondii	GKev LRHS
	eranthoides	ECho
	fanninii	GCal
	fasciculata	see *A. narcissiflora*
	flaccida	CLAP ECho EPPr GBin LRHS MAvo MMHG MNFA MNrw SBch WCot WCru WHal WSHC
	globosa	see *A. multifida* Poir.
	'Guernica'	ECho EWes
	'Hatakeyama Double' (d)	GCal WSHC
	'Hatakeyama Single'	CDes
	hepatica L.	see *Hepatica nobilis*
§	***hortensis***	CDes EBee ECho
§	***hupehensis***	CExl EBee GMaP NOrc
	- BWJ 8190	WCru
	- f. ***alba***	CExl CLAP CSpe IFro WPGP
§	- 'Bowles's Pink' ♀^{H4}	CElw CEnd ECho SPet WCru WPGP
	- 'Crispa'	see *A.* × *hybrida* 'Lady Gilmour' Wolley-Dod
	- 'Eugenie'	ECtt GBuc LRHS NBir NDov
	- 'Hadspen Abundance' ♀^{H4}	Widely available
	- var. ***hupehensis***	WSpi
§	- var. ***japonica***	CPou XLum
	- - B&SWJ 4886	WCru
	- - 'Bodnant Burgundy'	CDes LRHS WPGP
§	- - 'Bressingham Glow'	CExl CMHG CMac CSam ECtt ELan EPfP EPot GKin LRHS MRav NBir NDov NOrc SPet WBrk WWEG
§	- - 'Pamina' ♀^{H4}	Widely available
	- - Prince Henry	see *A. hupehensis* var. *japonica* 'Prinz Heinrich'
§	- - 'Prinz Heinrich' ♀^{H4}	Widely available
§	- - 'Rotkäppchen'	CHVG ECtt GBin GKin GQue IVic LRHS LSou MAvo MCot MHol NGdn NHol NLBP NLar NSti SMrm SWvt WCot WPtf WRHF WSHC
	- - 'Splendens'	CHel CMHG EPfP GBBs LAst LHop LRHS MBri MCot MMuc NEgg NGdn NLar SHil SPer SWvt WHal WWEG XLum
	- 'Little Princess'^{PBR}	EBee ECtt MNrw
	- 'Ouvertüre'	ECtt GBuc GQue MAvo WCot WPGP
	- 'Praecox'	CHel CMea EHyd EPfP GBBs LRHS LSou MBNS NBir NCGa NSti SHil SWvt WHal WHil WMnd WWEG
	- 'September Charm'	see *A.* × *hybrida* 'September Charm'
	- 'Superba'	EBee GBin WKif
§	× ***hybrida***	ECho LRHS NChi NEgg WMoo
	- 'Alba' misapplied (UK)	see *A.* × *hybrida* 'Honorine Jobert'

	- 'Alba Dura'	see *A. tomentosa* 'Albadura'
	- 'Albert Schweitzer'	see *A.* × *hybrida* 'Elegans'
	- 'Alice'	LRHS
	- 'Andrea Atkinson'	Widely available
	- 'Bowles's Pink'	see *A. hupehensis* 'Bowles's Pink'
	- 'Bressingham Glow'	see *A. hupehensis* var. *japonica* 'Bressingham Glow'
	- 'Coupe d'Argent'	EBee IKil
§	- 'Elegans' ♀H4	CSam EBee ECtt GMaP LHop LRHS MMuc NBir SEND SWat SWvt WSpi
§	- 'Géante des Blanches'	EBee SMrm
§	- 'Honorine Jobert' ♀H4	Widely available
§	- 'Königin Charlotte' ♀H4	Widely available
	- 'Lady Gilmour' misapplied	see *A.* × *hybrida* 'Montrose'
	- 'Lady Gilmour' ambig.	CHel GAbr GMaP MBel MPie SPad WGwG WHoo XLum
§	- 'Lady Gilmour' Wolley-Dod	CSam ECtt EPfP GCra LEdu LRHS MRav NBir NChi NEgg WCot WCru WWEG XLum
	- 'Loreley'	EBee EPfP GBuc LRHS NLar STPC SWvt WWEG
	- 'Luise Uhink'	CPou LRHS
	- 'Märchenfee'	EBee MAvo
	- 'Margarete' Kayser & Seibert	CExl CPar ECtt ELan EPfP LRHS MGos NGdn WCot WCru
	- 'Max Vogel'	see *A.* × *hybrida* 'Elegans'
	- 'Monterosa'	see *A.* × *hybrida* 'Montrose'
§	- 'Montrose'	CPou EWes GCal GMaP LRHS LSou MBri NBir NLar SRms SWat
	- 'Pamina'	see *A. hupehensis* var. *japonica* 'Pamina'
	- (Pretty Lady Series) 'Pretty Lady Diana'	ECtt LBuc LRHS LSou SWvt WHil
	- - 'Pretty Lady Emily'	ECtt LBuc LRHS LSou SHar SWvt WHil
	- - 'Pretty Lady Julia' **new**	LBuc LRHS
	- - 'Pretty Lady Susan'	ECtt LBuc LRHS LSou SHar SWvt WHil
	- Prince Henry	see *A. hupehensis* var. *japonica* 'Prinz Heinrich'
	- 'Profusion'	CTri LBuc LRHS WHal
	- Queen Charlotte	see *A.* × *hybrida* 'Königin Charlotte'
	- 'Richard Ahrens'	ECtt EPfP GBuc GCal GMaP LAst LHop LRHS LSRN MGos MLHP MSCN NEgg NGdn NLar NOrc SPad SWat SWvt WCru WMnd WWEG
§	- 'Robustissima'	EBee EPfP GBBs GMaP LPio LRHS LSRN MCot MGos MNrw MRav NBir NDov NGdn NLar NSoo NSti SEND SPer SWat SWvt WMnd WMoo WWEG
	- 'Rosenschale'	EBee LRHS MNrw WCru
	- 'Rotkäppchen'	see *A. hupehensis* var. *japonica* 'Rotkäppchen'
§	- 'September Charm' ♀H4	Widely available
	- 'Serenade'	CHel CSam EBee ECtt EPfP GBBs LRHS LSRN MAsh MBri MRav NBir NCGa NLar SMrm SPoG SRkn WCAu WMoo XLum
	- Tourbillon	see *A.* × *hybrida* 'Whirlwind'
§	- 'Whirlwind'	Widely available
	- 'White Queen'	see *A.* × *hybrida* 'Géante des Blanches'
	- Wirbelwind	see *A.* × *hybrida* 'Whirlwind'
	japonica	see *A.* × *hybrida*, *A. hupehensis*, *A. hupehensis* var. *japonica*
	- 'Crustata' **new**	CMac
	keiskeana	WCru
§	× ***lesseri***	CBro CCon CSpe ECho ELan GKev LHop MHer SPhx SRms
	leveillei	CAby CElw CLAP CSpe CWCL EPPr EWTr GBuc IPot LAst LPla LRHS LSou MNFA NBir NGdn NLar NPnk NSti SPhx SPoG WAbe WCru WKif WPtf WSHC WSpi WWlt
	- BWJ 7919	WCru
§	× ***lipsiensis***	CBro CDes ECho EPPr EPfP EPot EShb GAbr GBBs GBin GMaP IFro LRHS MAvo MMoz MNrw NLar NRya SBch SMrm WCot WCru WHal WPGP WSHC
	- 'Pallida' ♀H4	CSam CSpe EBee ECho ELon GBuc GKev IGor LEdu LLWP LWst MAvo NLar SKHP WCot WShi XEll
	- 'Vindobonensis'	MAvo WCot
	lithophila	LLHF
	magellanica hort. ex Wehrh.	see *A. multifida* Poir.
	matsudae B&SWJ 1452	WCru
	multifida misapplied, red-flowered	see *A.* × *lesseri*
§	***multifida*** Poir.	CPrp ECho EPfP GJos LHop LRHS NBir NSti SPoG SRms WHoo
	- Annabella Series	EPfP GAbr GKev SMrm
	- - 'Annabella Deep Rose'	WHrl
	- 'Major'	CCon CFis CMea CSpe EPfP SMrm SPhx WIce
	- f. ***polysepala***	NEgg
	- 'Rubra'	EBee EPfP GAbr GBin GKev LRHS MCot NBir NEgg NLar NPnk SMrm SPoG WHoo
	- white-flowered	LRHS NPnk WBor
	- yellow-flowered	CBro MCot NSum
§	***narcissiflora***	CSpe ECho GKev LRHS MMHG NBir NChi
	- var. ***citrina***	LRHS
	nemorosa ♀H4	Widely available
N	- 'Alba Plena' (d)	CSam ECho EPPr GBuc LWst NGdn NLar NPnk WSHC
	- 'Allenii' ♀H4	CBro ECho ELon EPPr EPot GBin GBuc GMaP ITim LRHS LWst MAvo MMoz MNFA MRav NRya WShi
	- 'Amy Doncaster'	CLAP ECho
	- 'Atley'	EBee LWst MAvo
	- 'Atrocaerulea'	CLAP GBuc IBlr NLar
	- 'Ballyrogan Blue'	MNrw
	- 'Bill Baker's Pink'	CDes CLAP LEdu
	- 'Blue Beauty'	CLAP EBee ELon GBuc GMaP IBlr LWst MAvo SBch
	- 'Blue Bonnet'	ECho GBuc IGor MAvo MNrw
	- 'Blue Eyes' (d)	CDes CElw CLAP EBee GBuc GMaP IBlr IGor LWst MAvo MMoz NBir WCot WSHC
	- 'Bowles's Purple'	ECho ELon GBBs GBuc GMaP IBlr LRHS MNrw NBid NHar NRya SBch SKHP WBor WCot WPnP
	- 'Bracteata'	CBro ECho EHyd GBuc LRHS MMHG MMoz
	- 'Bracteata Pleniflora' (d)	CLAP ECho ELon EPot GBuc GKev GMaP IBlr IGor LHop LWst MAvo MNrw NBir NPnk SBch WCot WHal
	- 'Buckland'	CLAP EBee EPfP EPot IBlr LWst MAvo SKHP
	- 'Caerulea'	EPot ITim
	- 'Cedric's Pink'	CLAP EPPr IBlr LLHF MNrw
	- 'Celestial'	EBee ECho ELan EPPr GBuc

	- 'Dee Day'	CLAP EBee GBuc MAvo MNrw
	- 'Dell Garden'	EPPr
	- 'Evelyn Meadows' ♀H4	CLAP
	- 'Flore Pleno' (d)	CDes ECho GAbr IFro MMoz NBir WBor
	- 'Frühlingsfee'	MAvo NLar
	- 'Gerda Ramusen'	CDes CLAP ECho ELan ELon EWes GBuc LLHF
I	- 'Gigantea Rubra'	WCot
	'Good Blue' **new**	MAvo
	- 'Green Fingers'	CLAP EBee ECho EPPr EPot GBuc GMaP LWst MAvo MMHG MNrw WCot WSHC
	- 'Hakumane Senjuizaki'	WCot
	- 'Hannah Gubbay'	CLAP IBlr MAvo
	- 'Hilda'	EBee ECho EPot GBuc MNrw NBir NPnk NRya
	- 'Kassari Kirju'	LWst
	- 'Kentish Pink'	GBBs GBin GMaP NPnk
	- 'Knightshayes Vestal' (d)	CExl CLAP MAvo MRav WCot
	- 'Kyffhäuser Rote'	WCot
	- 'Lady Doneraile'	CDes CLAP EPot GBuc NBir
	- 'Latvian Pink'	EBee ECho EPot LWst MAvo
	- 'Leeds' Variety'	CLAP EPot GAbr GBin GBuc GMaP ITim LWst MAvo MNrw NPnk
	- 'Lionel Bacon'	LWst
	- 'Lismore Blue'	EBee ECho EPPr EPot
	- 'Lucia'	EBee EPot LWst
	- 'Lychette'	EBee ECho EPPr EPot GAbr GBuc IBlr ITim LWst MAvo MNrw
	- 'March Blue' **new**	EPfP
	- 'Marie Rose'	EPot
	- 'Mart's Blue'	EBee GBuc
	- 'Miss Eunice'	CDes CLAP
	'Monstrosa'	ECho GBuc GKev MAvo
	- 'New Pink'	CLAP IBlr
	- 'Parlez Vous'	CExl EBee ECho EPPr LEdu MAvo MNrw NPnk
	- 'Pat's Pink'	WShi
	- 'Pentre Pink'	EPot IBlr MNrw
	- 'Picos Pink'	GBuc LWst
	- pink-flowered	CLAP ECho
	- 'Ploeger's Plena' (d) **new**	EBee
	- 'Polar Star'	CLAP
	- 'Robinsoniana' ♀H4	Widely available
	- 'Rosea'	CLAP EBee ECho MNrw
	- 'Royal Blue'	CBro CHel CLAP ECho EPPr EPot GAbr GBin GMaP LEdu LWst MAvo NPnk WCot WPnP
	- 'Rubra'	MNrw
	- 'Stammheim' (d)	CLAP EPPr
	- 'Super Allenii'	GBuc MAvo
	- 'Tinney's Blush'	CLAP
	- 'Tomas'	CLAP EBee ECho ELon EPot GBuc NHar
	- 'Vestal' (d) ♀H4	Widely available
	- 'Virescens' ♀H4	CAvo CLAP CPBP CWCL EBee ECho ELon EPPr EPot GAbr GBuc GKev GMaP LWst MAvo MMoz NBir NHar WPtf WShi
	- 'Viridiflora'	CExl CLAP ECho EPfP GAbr GBuc LHop MNrw NBir NSti WCot WSHC
	- 'Westwell Pink'	CLAP ECho EPPr LLHF MNrw SPhx WBor WCot WShi
	- 'Wilks' Giant'	MAvo
	- 'Wilks' White'	ELon EPPr
	- 'Wisley Pink'	EPot MAvo
	- 'Wyatt's Pink'	CLAP ELon EPot LWst MAvo NCGa
	- 'Yerda Ramusem'	EBee ECho EPPr GBuc MAvo

	nemorosa* × *ranunculoides	see *A.* × *lipsiensis*
	nikoensis	ECho
	obtusiloba	CLAP GBuc NSla SRms WAbe
	- blue-flowered	WAbe
I	- 'Sulphurea'	WCot
	- yellow-flowered	WAbe
	palmata	EWes LDai LEdu NBre NPnk SBea SMad WCot
	parviflora	ECho GKev
	patens	see *Pulsatilla patens*
	pavonina	CMea CSpc IBoy LRHS NBir SLon SPoG WAbe WCot
	- lilac-flowered	NBir
	- pink-flowered	NBir
	petiolulosa	EPot
	prattii	CExl CLAP EPPr WHal
	pseudoaltaica	WCru
	pulsatilla	see *Pulsatilla vulgaris*
	quinquefolia	WCot
	raddeana	ECho LWst
	ranunculoides ♀H4	Widely available
	- 'Bill Baker' **new**	LEdu
	- 'Frank Waley'	WCot
	- 'Fuchsis Traum' **new**	WCot
*	- ***laciniata***	CLAP GBuc WCot
	- 'Pleniflora' (d)	CLAP CPBP ECho EPPr EPot GBBs GBuc GKev LEdu LRHS LWst MAvo NLar WCot
	- subsp. ***ranunculoides***	ECho GKev WHil
	- 'Semi Plena'	CDes ECho
	- subsp. ***wockeana***	CDes CSam EBee ECho GBuc LEdu MAvo
	reflexa	EBee GKev LLHP
	riparia	see *A. virginiana* var. *alba*
	rivularis	CAvo CLAP CMea CPar CSpe CTsd CWCL EBee GBin GBuc GKev GPoy IPot LEdu LHop LRHS NBir NChi NHar NLar NPnk NWad SBrt SMad WCru WHoo WKif WMoo
	- BWJ 7611	WCru
	- CC 4587	GKev
	- CC 4588	CExl
	- PAB 2477 **new**	LEdu
	- 'Blue Back'	GCal
	- 'Glacier'	MPie NEgg NLar WSpi
	aff. ***rivularis***	WPtf WSpi
	rupicola	IGor NBir
	× ***seemannii***	see *A.* × *lipsiensis*
	stellata Lam.	see *A. hortensis*
	stolonifera double-flowered (d)	EBee MAvo WCot WSHC
	sulphurea misapplied	see *Pulsatilla alpina* subsp. *apiifolia*
	sumatrana B&SWJ 11265	WCru
	sylvestris	Widely available
	- 'Elise Fellmann' (d)	CSpe EBee EPfP GBin GBuc WHal WHil
	- 'Macrantha'	EPfP GAbr NGdn SMrm WCot
	tetrasepala	WCot
§	***tomentosa***	EBee LRHS NBre SDix SRms SWat
§	- 'Albadura'	EBee
	- 'Robustissima'	see *A.* × *hybrida* 'Robustissima'
	trifolia L.	EPPr GBuc NBid NLar SRms WCot
	trullifolia	CDes GBee GBin GCra NSla WAbe
	vernalis	see *Pulsatilla vernalis*
	virginiana	EBee GAbr IPot LDai LEdu LPla NBid NPnk WHrl WWEG

§	- var. ***alba***	NLar NSti WPtf
	vitifolia misapplied	see *A. tomentosa*
	'Wild Swan' **new**	CSpe IBoy LBMP LBuc NPnk STPC WNPC

Anemonella (*Ranunculaceae*)

thalictroides	CCon CElw CLAP CWCL EBee ECho EFEx ELon EPot GAbr GBuc GKev ITim MAvo MMoz NHar NPnk NRya WAbe WCru WHlf WSpi XLum
- 'Alba Plena' (d)	ECho GBuc
- 'Amelia'	CLAP EPPr GBuc NHar WAbe
- 'Babe'	LWst WCot
- 'Betty Blake' (d)	ECho EPot MMHG NRya WCot
- 'Big'	LWst
- 'Cameo'	CLAP ECho EFEx EPPr LLHF LWst MAvo NHar NRya WCot WCru
- 'Diamante'	WCot
- 'Double Green' (d)	EFEx LWst
- 'Flore Pleno' (d)	GBuc
- 'Full Double White' (d)	ECho EFEx LWst
- 'Green Hurricane' (d)	ECho EFEx LLHF LWst MAvo NLar
- 'Jade Feather'	CElw EPot
- large-white-flowered **new**	CDes
- f. ***rosea***	CElw CLAP CRDP EBee ECho ELan GBuc IPot LLHF WAbe WCru
- - 'Oscar Schoaf' (d)	CLAP ECho GBuc ITim LWst WAbe
- - semi-double pink-flowered (d)	CElw CLAP CRDP LWst MAvo NLar
- semi-double white-flowered (d)	CElw CLAP CRDP EPPr WAbe
- 'Tairin'	LWst
- 'XXL'	WCot

Anemonopsis (*Ranunculaceae*)

macrophylla	CExl CLAP CPBP CPom CRDP CSpe EBee ECho EWes GAbr GCal LRHS MNrw MRav NLar SBch SBea SMad SPhx SRms WAbe WCru WPGP WSHC
- 'White Swan'	GBin WCru WSHC

Anemopsis (*Saururaceae*)

sp. **new**	CArn
californica	EBee EWay GBin IFoB LLWG MSKA MWts NLar WCot WPGP

Anethum (*Apiaceae*)

graveolens	CArn GPoy MHer MHoo MNHC NPri SIde SRms SVic
- 'Dukat'	CSev ELau MHoo
- fern-leaved	MHoo

angelica see *Angelica archangelica*

Angelica (*Apiaceae*)

	sp.	CHab
	acutiloba	MMHG
	- var. ***iwatensis*** B&SWJ 11197	WCru
	anomala B&SWJ 10886	WCru
	archangelica	Widely available
	atropurpurea	ECtt EPfP GKev GQue LRHS MHer MHoo MNrw MRav NCGa SWat SWvt WWEG WWlt
	dahurica	MHoo WOut XLum
	- B&SWJ 8603	WCru
	decursiva	CArn
	- B&SWJ 5746	WCru
	'Ebony'	CBre CSpe GAbr LEdu LHop LPio LRHS MHer NCGa WBor WCot
	edulis B&SWJ 10968	LEdu WCru
	gigas	Widely available
	- B&SWJ 4170	WCru
	hispanica	see *A. pachycarpa*
	japonica B&SWJ 11480	WCru
	montana	see *A. sylvestris*
	morii RWJ 9802	WCru
§	***pachycarpa***	CArn CSpe EBee ELan EPri GBin GKev GMaP LHop LRHS MHer MHoo NBir NLar NPnk SPhx WJek WWEG XLum
	pubescens B&SWJ 5593	WCru
	- B&SWJ 11129	WCru
	- var. ***matsumurae*** B&SWJ 6387	WCru
	sachalinensis	CSpe
	sinensis	CArn GPoy LEdu MHoo
	'Summer Delight'	see *Ligusticum scoticum*
§	***sylvestris***	CArn CHab LLWG
*	- 'Purpurea'	CSpe EWes GQue WPGP
	- 'Vicar's Mead'	CDes CSev LEdu LPla LRHS MBel NBir NChi NLar NPnk SHar SPhx SWvt WBor WCot WPtf WSpi
	taiwaniana	CArn CBre CDTJ CSam ELan ESwi LRHS NLar
	ursina B&SWJ 10829	WCru

Angelonia (*Plantaginaceae*)

(Angelface Series) Angelface Blue Improved	NPri
- Angelface Wedgwood Blue = 'Anwedg'PBR	NPri

Anigozanthos (*Haemodoraceae*)

'Bush Ranger' (Bush Gems Series)	CCCN
flavidus	EAmu ECre SPlb
- 'Ember'	CCCN
- 'Illusion'	CCCN
- 'Opal'	CCCN
- 'Pearl'	CCCN
- red-flowered	SPlb
- 'Splendour'	CCCN
- 'Yellow Gem'	CCCN
manglesii ♀H1	SPlb

Anisacanthus (*Acanthaceae*)

quadrifidus var. ***wrightii***	WCot

anise see *Pimpinella anisum*

Anisodontea (*Malvaceae*)

§	***capensis***	CCCN CHGN CHll EBee ELan EPri GBee LAst MCot MOWG SChF SLim SMrm SPlb SRkn SRms SVen SWvt
	- 'Tara's Pink'	CSpe EWes SMrm
	'Crystal Rose' **new**	LRHS
	'Donatella' **new**	SLim
	'El Royo'	CAbP CSpe CWGN ECtt LHop LSou MHol MPie SPad WCot XLum
	'Elegant Lady'	CSpe GFai
	huegelii	see *Alyogyne huegelii*
	× ***hypomadara*** misapplied	see *A. capensis*

julii SPlb SVen
Lady in Pink LHop
= 'Nuanilaninp'
'Large Magenta' LSou SWvt
malvastroides LHop WWlt
scabrosa CSev GFai

Anisodus (*Solanaceae*)

carniolicioides BWJ 7501 WCru
§ ***luridus*** EWld GCal

Anisotome (*Apiaceae*)

lyallii EBee

Annona (*Annonaceae*)

cherimola (F) CCCN XBlo

Anoiganthus see *Cyrtanthus*

Anomalesia see *Gladiolus*

Anomatheca (*Iridaceae*)

cruenta see *Freesia laxa*

Anopterus (*Escalloniaceae*)

glandulosus CFil WSHC

Anredera (*Basellaceae*)

§ ***cordifolia*** CRHN ECho EShb LEdu

Antennaria (*Asteraceae*)

aprica see *A. parvifolia*
dioica CArn CTri ECtt EDAr GAbr GBin GJos GPoy MJak NSla SPlb SRms XLum
- 'Alba' EHoe
- 'Alex Duguid' EPot
- 'Aprica' see *A. parvifolia*
- 'Minima' ECho EPot ITim MWat NBro NHar WAbe
- 'Nyewoods Variety' EPot
- red-flowered ECho
- var. ***rosea*** see *A. rosea*
- 'Rotes Wunder' CMea EPot SBch WAbe
* - 'Rubra' ECho ECtt EDAr LRHS MHer WIce WRHF XLum
'Joy' EPot WAbe
macrophylla hort. see *A. microphylla*
§ ***microphylla*** SRms
§ ***parvifolia*** CTri ECho NPri SRms SRot
- var. ***rosea*** see *A. microphylla*
plantaginifolia EBee
§ ***rosea*** ♀H4 ECho GMaP MAsh SPlb SRms WHoo WIce

Antenoron see *Persicaria*

Anthemis ✿ (*Asteraceae*)

from Turkey ECtt EWes LLWP
arvensis CHab
§ 'Beauty of Grallagh' GBuc GCal SDix
'Cally Cream' GCal NCGa SMrm SPhx
'Cally White' GBin GCal WWFP
carpatica LRHS NBro
- 'Karpatenschnee' LRHS NBre WWEG
cretica subsp. ***columnae*** WAbe
§ - subsp. ***cretica*** CMea
- subsp. ***pontica*** NLar
'Daisy Bee' EBee MAvo
frutescens Voss see *Argyranthemum frutescens*
'Grallagh Gold' misapplied, orange-yellow see *A.* 'Beauty of Grallagh'
'Grallagh Gold' ECtt EWes LDai MWat NPer
§ ***marschalliana*** CMea ECho ECtt EDAr EHyd LRHS SMrm SPlb WCot
- subsp. ***pectinata*** **new** NSla
montana see *A. cretica* subsp. *cretica*
nobilis see *Chamaemelum nobile*
punctata WNew
- subsp. ***cupaniana*** ♀H3-4 Widely available
- - 'Nana' NPer SHar
rudolphiana see *A. marschalliana*
sancti-johannis CMHG CWib EPfP LDai LRHS LSou NDov NPer NWad SMrm SPer SRms WMoo
Susanna Mitchell = 'Blomit' CMea EBee ECtt ELon EPfP EWll GMaP LRHS LSRN MAvo MNrw NBir NDov NPnk SMrm SRGP SWvt WMnd WSHC WWEG XLum
'Tetworth' ECtt ELan EPfP WWEG
tinctoria CArn CHby CMac EBee GPoy LRHS MHer NPer SRms SWvt WHfH WJek WSFF XLum
- 'Alba' EBee LRHS NLar WWEG XLum
- 'Charme'PBR EPfP LAst LRHS MHol NLar SPoG SWvt WCot WMnd
- 'Compacta' EWes GCal MNrw XLum
- dwarf SBri
- 'E.C. Buxton' Widely available
- 'Eva' NBre NDov WWEG
I - 'Golden Rays' SDix WWEG
- 'Hall Farm Frilly' **new** ECtt
- 'Kelwayi' CSBt CTri EPfP LRHS NBro NLar NPer SPer SRms SWat WMoo WWEG XLum
- 'Lemon Ice' GMaP
- 'Lemon Maid' CCon ECtt ELon EPfP GBin LRHS SMrm
- 'Sauce Hollandaise' Widely available
- subsp. ***tinctoria*** SMrm
- 'Waddow Gold' **new** NWad
- 'Wargrave Variety' CElw CMac CSam CWCL ECtt ELan EPfP LBMP LRHS LSou MAvo MNFA NBir NBro NCGa NChi NEgg NGdn NPnk NWad SDix SPhx SWvt WMnd
'Tinpenny Sparkle' CAbP CSam EBee ECtt EWll GMaP LSou MAvo MHol MPie NDov NLar NSti WBrk WCot WHoo WMnd WRHF WWEG
triumfettii NPer NPnk WCot
tuberculata NChi SBch
'White Water' WAbe
zyghia **new** EBee

Anthericum (*Asparagaceae*)

algeriense see *A. liliago*
* ***bovei*** CBro
§ ***liliago*** CSpe ECho ELan GCal GMaP IFoB LHop LRHS MCot MRav NCGa NLar WPtf WWEG XEll
- 'Major' ♀H4 CAvo CBro CDes EBee ECGP ECho IGor MLHP WPGP
plumosum see *Trichopetalum plumosum*
ramosum CAby CDes CSpe ECho ELan EPot EPri EWes GCal GKev LRHS MBrN NBid NBir NCGa NLar SMrm SPhx WPGP

Antholyza (*Iridaceae*)

coccinea	see *Crocosmia paniculata*
× ***crocosmioides***	see *Crocosmia* × *crocosmioides*
paniculata	see *Crocosmia paniculata*

Anthoxanthum (*Poaceae*)

odoratum	CHab ELau GPoy XLum

Anthriscus (*Apiaceae*)

cerefolium	CArn CHby ELau EPfP GPoy MHer MHoo MNHC SRms WJek
sylvestris	CArn CHab NMir SPhx WOut WSFF
- 'Ravenswing'	Widely available

Anthurium (*Araceae*)

andraeanum 'Glowing Pink'	XBlo
- 'Red Heart'	XBlo
- 'Tivolo'	XBlo
'Aztec'	XBlo
Baleno = 'Anthauf4'[PBR]	XBlo
'Caribo'	XBlo
crenatum	XBlo
'Crimson'	XBlo
'Magenta'	XBlo
'Mikra'	XBlo
'Octavia'	XBlo
'Pico Bello'	XBlo
Pink Champion = 'Antinkeles'[PBR]	XBlo
'Porcelaine White'	XBlo
Red Champion = 'Anthbnena'[PBR]	XBlo
'Vitara'	XBlo
White Champion = 'Anthefaqyr'[PBR]	XBlo

Anthyllis (*Papilionaceae*)

aurea	LLHF
barba-jovis	LRHS
hermanniae 'Compacta'	see *A. hermanniae* 'Minor'
§ - 'Minor'	WAbe
montana	XSen
- subsp. ***atropurpurea***	EHyd LRHS
- 'Rubra' 🏆H4	ECho EDAr EWes LHop LLHF NSla
- 'Rubra Compacta'	WAbe
vulneraria	CHab NMir NRya SEND SPhx WSFF
- var. ***coccinea***	CPom ELan GAbr GBin ITim MBel NSla SEND SPhx WCFE WHal WHil WIce
- dark red-flowered	CSpe

Antirrhinum (*Plantaginaceae*)

asarina	see *Asarina procumbens*
barrelieri	SEND
braun-blanquetii	GCra SEND WCot WMoo
'Eternal'	LRHS
hispanicum 'Avalanche'	ECtt
- subsp. ***hispanicum*** 'Roseum'	CMea LPot
majus	WCot
- 'Black Prince'	CSpe ECtt LHop SPhx
- 'Bronze Dragon'	EWTr
- 'Cheerio' (mixed) **new**	CWCL
- 'June Blake' (v) **new**	WCot
- Liberty Classic Series	NPri
- - 'Liberty Classic Scarlet'	NPri
- - 'Liberty Classic Yellow'	NPri
- 'Night and Day'	CSpe WMoo
- (Sonnet Series) 'Sonnet Pink'	NPri
- - 'Sonnet White'	NPri
- - 'Sonnet Yellow'	NPri
molle	CSpe ECtt GKev MCot NPer NSla SChF WAbe
- pink-flowered	MCot SRms WAbe
- white-flowered	GKev WAbe
sempervirens	MHer WAbe XLum
siculum	WCot

añu see *Tropaeolum tuberosum*

Aphelandra (*Acanthaceae*)

squarrosa 'Citrina'	XBlo

Aphyllanthes (*Asparagaceae*)

monspeliensis	ECho SBrt XLum

Apios (*Papilionaceae*)

§ ***americana***	CAgr CCon CPom EBee ECho EWes GBin LEdu NBir WCot WCru WSHC
tuberosa	see *A. americana*

Apium (*Apiaceae*)

graveolens	CArn CHab CPrp ELau GPoy MHer MNHC SIde SRms SVic WJek
- var. ***rapaceum*** 'Prinz' 🏆H3	SVic
- (Secalinum Group) 'Par-cel'	MHer SRms

Apium × *Petroselinum* (*Apiaceae*)

hybrid, misapplied	see *A. graveolens* Secalinum Group

Apocynum (*Apocynaceae*)

cannabinum	CArn GPoy

Apodolirion (*Amaryllidaceae*)

macowanii	ECho

Aponogeton (*Aponogetonaceae*)

desertorum	EWay LLWG
distachyos	CBAq CRow CWat EHon EWay MSKA MWts NPer SCoo SVic SWat WMAq XLum

apple see *Malus domestica*

apricot see *Prunus armeniaca*

Aptenia (*Aizoaceae*)

cordifolia 🏆H1-2	CCCN NPer SChr SEND SPet SPlb SVen
- 'Variegata' (v)	CCCN

Aquilegia ✿ (*Ranunculaceae*)

sp.	SVic
akitensis misapplied	see *A. flabellata* var. *pumila*
'Alaska' (State Series) 🏆H3-4	LBuc LRHS SHil SMrm
* ***alba variegata*** (v)	ECho
alpina	CMea CPrp ECho ECtt EPfP IPot MAsh MNHC NGdn SPer SRms WCAu WMoo WTou XLum
'Alpine Blue'	SPet
amaliae	see *A. ottonis* subsp. *amaliae*
'Apple Blossom'	NBir WTou

	aragonensis	see *A. pyrenaica*
§	***atrata***	CCon CLAP CPou EBee ECho LRHS WTou
	aurea misapplied	see *A. vulgaris* golden-leaved
	aurea Janka	GKev
	bertolonii 🏆^{H4}	CMea ECho GKev LHop LRHS NRya NSla SRms WHoo
	- 'Blue Berry'	WThu
	Biedermeier Group	ECho EPfP LRHS NGdn NNor NOrc SBod SPoG SRot WTou
	'Blackcurrant'	CWCL
	'Blue Jay' (Songbird Series)	LRHS
	'Blue Star' (Star Series)	EBee ELan EPfP GBin LRHS NEgg NPnk WTou
	'Bluebird' (Songbird Series) 🏆^{H2}	LBuc LRHS NBir NPer NPri
	brevistyla	EBee NNor
	'Fruit and Nut Chocolate'	CDes EBee EUJe MBNS MBel MHol NMyG WCot
	buergeriana	SPhx WAbe
	- 'Calimero'	CHel CTsd LHop LRHS MBNS NLar SBea
	- var. ***oxysepala***	see *A. oxysepala*
	'Bunting' (Songbird Series) 🏆^{H2}	CWGN MHer NPri SGbt
	canadensis 🏆^{H4}	CLAP CSpe EHoe ELan GAbr LRHS NBir NBro SRms WGwG WTou XLum
	- 'Little Lanterns'	EPPr LHop LRHS NLar WHil WIce
	- 'Nana'	GKev WThu
	- 'Pink Lanterns'	LRHS
	'Cardinal' (Songbird Series)	LBuc LRHS
	chaplinei	GBin GKev NBir SBch
	chrysantha	CHel GBin GKev NBre SRms SWvt WKif WTou
	- 'Yellow Queen'	CExl COlW CWCL EBee EPPr EPfP GBin GMaP LBMP LHop LRHS MBri MWat NBre NGdn NPnk NPri SBea SGbt SMrm SPad SPhx STes WCFE WHil XLum
	clematiflora	see *A. vulgaris* var. *stellata*
	Clementine Series	EPfP LRHS
	coerulea 🏆^{H4}	GKev NNor SRms
	- var. ***coerulea***	GKev
	- 'Himmelblau'	NBre
	'Colorado' (State Series)	LBuc LRHS MBri SHil
	'Crimson Star'	ELan EPfP GJos LRHS SPer SPoG WMoo WTou WWEG
	dichroa	EBee WPGP
	discolor	EPot GKev LLHF WThu WTou
	'Double Rubies' (d)	ELan LSRN SMrm WMoo
	'Dove' (Songbird Series) 🏆^{H2}	CWGN EWll LBuc LRHS MHer NPri SGbt
I	'Dragonfly'	CBcs CWib ELan EPfP LRHS MBel MJak NGdn SPer SPet SPoG WTou WWEG
	'Dragon's Breath' (mixed) **new**	WTou
	ecalcarata	see *Semiaquilegia ecalcarata*
	einseleana	LLHF
	'Elegance'	WTou
	'Elegant Moonstone'	WTou
	'Elegant Opal'	WTou
	'Elegant Ruby'	WTou
	elegantula	GKev
	flabellata 🏆^{H4}	EWTr GCra WTou
	- f. ***alba***	CTri ECho ELan
	- - 'White Jewel' (Jewel Series)	GKev

	- 'Blackcurrant Ice'	EPfP LRHS MBri MHer
	- Cameo Series	GMaP WGor
	- - 'Cameo Blue and White'	CWib NCGa SRot
	- - 'Cameo Pink and White'	MHer NCGa SRot
	- - 'Cameo White'	SRot
	- 'Georgia' (State Series) 🏆$^{H3-4}$	LBuc LRHS MBri SHil SMrm
	- Jewel Series	ECho
	- 'Ministar'	ECho EDAr WHil XLum
	- 'Nana Alba'	see *A. flabellata* var. *pumila* f. *alba*
§	- var. ***pumila*** 🏆^{H4}	CCon CWCL ECho EDAr EHyd GKev LHop LRHS NGdn WTou
§	- - f. ***alba*** 🏆^{H4}	ECho EDAr GKev LHop LRHS SRms WTou
	- - 'Atlantis'	EPPr GBBs LRHS
	- - 'Flore Pleno' (d)	ECho
I	- - f. ***kurilensis*** 'Rosea'	CCon EDAr GKev WAbe
	- 'Vermont' (State Series)	SMrm
	'Flamboyant'	WTou
	'Florida' (State Series) 🏆^{H2}	LBuc LRHS SHil
	formosa	CMea NChi WKif WTou
§	***fragrans***	CCon CLAP CTsd ELan EWTr GJos LRHS SGbt SMrm SPad WHoo WTou
	glandulosa	LLHF
	glauca	see *A. fragrans*
	'Golden Guiness'	WPnP
	'Goldfinch' (Songbird Series)	CWGN LBuc LRHS MHer NBir SGbt SMrm
	'Heavenly Blue'	EBee LRHS SPhx WTou
	'Hensol Harebell' 🏆^{H4}	SHar SRms
	japonica	see *A. flabellata* var. *pumila*
	jonesii	GKev SPlb
	jonesii × saximontana	GKev
	'Kansas' (State Series)	MBri
	karelinii	EBee
	'Koralle'	NBre WTou
	'Kristall'	NBre SGbt SPhx STes XLum
	laramiensis	CPBP
	'Leprechaun Gold' (v)	EPfP LAst NGdn
	longissima 🏆^{H4}	CMea GKev MHer NPnk SHar WHil WHoo
	'Louisiana' (State Series) 🏆^{H2}	LBuc LRHS MBri SHil SMrm
	'Magpie'	see *A. vulgaris* 'William Guiness'
	'Maxi'	NBre WHil WTou
	McKana Group	Widely available
	'Milk and Honey'	WTou
	'Montana' (State Series)	MBri
	Mrs Scott-Elliot hybrids	CSBt EPfP SPet
	Music Series 🏆^{H4}	SRms
	'Nightingale' (Songbird Series)	NPri SGbt
	nigricans	see *A. atrata*
	nivalis	LLHF
	olympica	EWes WTou
	'Oranges and Lemons'	SMrm WCot
	(Origami Series) 'Origami Red and White' 🏆^{H2}	NPri
	- 'Origami Rose and White' 🏆^{H2}	NPri
	- 'Origami Yellow' 🏆$^{H3-4}$	NPri
§	***ottonis*** subsp. ***amaliae***	CPBP LLHF WAbe
§	***oxysepala***	CExl CHel GCal WTou
	- B&SWJ 4775	WCru
	Perfumed Garden Group	CPla LRHS
	'Pink Star' (Star Series)	NPnk
	pleated burgundy-flowered	LRHS
	'Purple Emperor'^{PBR}	EPfP LRHS
§	***pyrenaica***	GKev

'Red Hobbit'	CBct CSpe ELan EPfP IBoy LHop LRHS LSou MBel MHer MHol MSpe NBre NEgg NGdn SBea SHil WBor WGwG WHoo
'Red Star' (Star Series)	CHel CPrp EPfP LRHS NEgg WHil WTou
'Robin' (Songbird Series)	CWGN MHer SGbt
rockii	CCon CHel CLAP EWes GCal GJos GKev SBrt
- B&SWJ 7965	WCru
'Roman Bronze'	see *Aquilegia* × *Semiaquilegia* 'Roman Bronze'
'Rose Queen'	EBee EPfP NBre NNor WHoo WTou
saximontana	EPot GKev NSla WTou
§ 'Schneekönigin'	CWCL GMaP LRHS WCFE
scopulorum	EBee GKev LLHF WAbe
shockleyi	CDes
Shooting Stars (mixed)	WTou
sibirica	CCon GKev LLHF
'Silver Queen'	ELan LHop
skinneri	CExl CSpe ELan EWTr LRHS WKif WMnd
- 'Tequila Sunrise'	CSpe CWCL CWib ELan GBin LSou MHer NNor SPad
Snow Queen	see *A.* 'Schneekönigin'
'Spitfire'	LBuc LRHS NCGa NPri
Spring Magic Series	LRHS
- Spring Magic Blue and White	LRHS WTou
- Spring Magic Navy and White **new**	LRHS
- Spring Magic Pink and White	WTou
- Spring Magic Rose and Ivory	WTou
- Spring Magic White **new**	LRHS
- Spring Magic Yellow **new**	WTou
State Series	WWEG
stellata	see *A. vulgaris* var. *stellata*
'Sunburst Ruby'	CPla LRHS WMoo WTou
'Sweet Rainbows' (d)	CPla
triternata	NNor
'Virginia' (State Series)	LBuc LRHS MBri SHil
viridiflora	CLAP EBee ELan EPfP GCal LPio MBel WAbe WCot WHil WKif WMnd WTou
- 'Chocolate Soldier'	CHel CSpe CWCL
'Volcano!' (mixed)	WTou
vulgaris	CArn CHab CMHG CWCL EPfP GKev GPoy LLWP LPio LRHS MHer MMuc MNHC NBro NGdn NMir SPlb WMoo WShi WWEG
- 'Adelaide Addison'	LRHS WHoo WTou
- var. ***alba***	CMea EPPr EPfP LRHS WGwG WTou
- 'Altrosa'	NBre
- 'Aureovariegata'	see *A. vulgaris* Vervaeneana Group
- 'Blackbird' (Songbird Series) (d)	CWCL
- 'Burnished Rose'	CPla
- ***clematiflora***	see *A. vulgaris* var. *stellata*
- (Clementine Series) 'Clementine Blue' (d)	EPfP WCot WTou
- - 'Clementine Dark Purple' (d)	EPfP SPoG
- - 'Clementine Red' (d)	EPfP SPoG
- - 'Clementine Rose' (d) **new**	WTou
- - 'Clementine Salmon Rose' (d)	EPfP LRHS SPoG WTou
- - 'Clementine White' (d)	EPfP SPoG
- 'Crystal Star'	LRHS
- var. ***flore-pleno*** (d)	LLWP WTou
- - bicolour	WTou
- - black-flowered (d)	WCot WTou
- - blue-flowered (d)	WTou
- - 'Dorothy Rose' (Dorothy Series) (d)	LHop SPad
- - 'Double Pleat' (d)	EPfP
- - 'Double Pleat' blue/white-flowered (d)	CPrp
- - 'Double Pleat' pink/white-flowered (d)	CPrp CWCL
- - 'Jane Hollow' (d)	CPou
- - pale blue-flowered (d)	WCot WTou
- - pink-flowered (d)	WTou
- - purple-flowered (d)	WTou
- - red-flowered (d)	WTou
- - 'Strawberry Ice Cream' (d)	NBro NNor
* - - 'White Bonnet' (d)	CWCL
- - white-flowered (d)	WTou
- 'Foggy Bottom Blues'	LRHS
§ - golden-leaved	ECho WTou
- 'Heidi'	NBre
- 'Mellow Yellow'	CPla CTsd EHoe LBuc LRHS SDix WMoo
- Munstead White	see *A. vulgaris* 'Nivea'
§ - 'Nivea' ♀H4	CPou CSpe EBee EDif ELan EPfP MBri NChi SPoG
- 'Pink Spurless'	see *A. vulgaris* var. *stellata* pink-flowered
- 'Pom Pom Crimson' (Pom Pom Series)	NBro WCot
- scented	WTou
§ - var. ***stellata***	CMea ELan GKev LRHS LSou MWhi NBir NBro NNor WKif WMoo WTou
- - Barlow Series (d)	CHVG WTou WWEG
- - - 'Black Barlow' (d)	Widely available
- - black-flowered	WTou
- - 'Blue Barlow' (Barlow Series) (d)	CAby CSpe ECtt EPfP GMaP LRHS LSRN MWat NBre NPri SHil SPer SPhx SWvt WCot WMnd WTou WWEG XLum
- - 'Blue Fountain'	WTou
- - blue-flowered	LRHS WTou
- - 'Bordeaux Barlow' (Barlow Series) (d)	EBee LRHS WTou WWEG
- - 'Christa Barlow' (Barlow Series) (d)	EPfP LRHS MBel NBre NGdn NLar SPer WTou
- - double-flowered (d)	WTou
- - 'Firewheel'	WMoo
- - 'Greenapples' (d)	CAbP CAby CBre CHVG CPrp CWCL EBee ELan GBin GKev GQue LAst LBMP LPla LRHS MCot MPie SMrm WCot WHoo WTou WWFP
* - - 'Iceberg'	LRHS
- - 'Nora Barlow' (Barlow Series) (d) ♀H4	Widely available
- - 'Pink Barlow' (Barlow Series) (d) **new**	GKev
§ - - pink-flowered	LRHS WTou
- - red-flowered	WTou
- - 'Rose Barlow' (Barlow Series) (d)	EBee EPfP GBin LRHS LSRN WMnd WTou
- - 'Royal Purple' (d)	NBro NNor WMoo WTou
- - 'Ruby Port' (d)	Widely available

	- - 'Ruby Port' crimped (d)	WPnP
	- - 'Touchwood Dreamtime'	WTou
	- - 'White Barlow' (Barlow Series) (d)	CAby EBee EPfP IBoy LRHS SHil SPer SWvt WTou
	- - white-flowered	CSpe GCra LRHS NBro WTou
	- variegated foliage	see *A. vulgaris* Vervaeneana Group
§	- Vervaeneana Group (v)	CMHG CWCL ELan EPfP LRHS NBir NDov NPer SPlb SRms SWat WBor WHoo WMoo WTou
	- - 'Lime Frost' (v)	WTou
	- - 'Woodside Blue' (v)	LRHS NWad WTou WWEG
	- - 'Woodside White' (v)	NBir WBrk WTou
§	- 'William Guiness'	Widely available
	- 'William Guiness Doubles' (d)	WMoo WTou
	- 'Winky Wooh' (Winky Series)	CBct GBBs GBin WBor
	'White Star' (Star Series)	CHel CPrp ELan EPfP LAst LPio LRHS MRav NEgg NPnk SPer WHil WTou WWEG
	white-flowered	WTou
	Winky Series	ELan NCGa NNor SWvt WHil WTou
	- 'Winky Blue-White'	GBin LRHS NPri SMrm WCFE WTou
	- 'Winky Double Red-White' (d)	LRHS
	- 'Winky Purple-White'	NPri SMrm
	- 'Winky Red-White'	CHel LRHS NPri SRot SWvt WTou
	- 'Winky Rose-Rose'	LRHS
	yabeana	GKev ITim MWhi WMoo
	'Yellow Star' (Star Series) ♀H3-4	CHel EPfP EWTr MAvo NPnk SPer WPtf WWEG

Aquilegia × *Semiaquilegia* (*Ranunculaceae*)

	hybrid, blue-flowered	NGdn
§	'Roman Bronze'	CPla LRHS WMoo WTou

Arabis (*Brassicaceae*)

	albida	see *A. alpina* subsp. *caucasica*
	alpina	MAsh SPlb
§	- subsp. ***caucasica***	ECho
	- - 'Corfe Castle'	ECtt
	- - 'Douler Angevine' (v)	CMea ECtt ELon MHol NPri SPoG WIce
	- - 'Flore Pleno' (d) ♀H4	CElw CHid CSpe CTri CWCL ECho ECtt ELan EWld GAbr GJos GMaP MAvo SBch SIgm SRms WHoo WNew
	- - 'Pinkie'	ECho GKev
	- - 'Pixie Cream'	EDAr LBMP NGdn SBch
	- - 'Rosea'	GJos LRHS NBir SRms
§	- - 'Schneehaube' ♀H4	CTri CWib ECho ECtt EPfP GMaP LRHS MJak NBir NGdn SPoG SRms
	- - Snowcap	see *A. alpina* subsp. *caucasica* 'Schneehaube'
	- - 'Variegata' (v)	ECho ECtt ELan ELon GMaP LAst NPri SPoG SRms
	androsacea	EPot GKev SRms
	× ***arendsii*** 'Compinkie'	GJos LBMP SPlb SRms
	blepharophylla	EPfP WSHC
§	- 'Frühlingszauber' ♀H4	CTri ELan EPfP GJos NBir NGdn NPri SPoG SRms
	- 'Rose Delight'	LRHS
	- 'Rote Sensation'	ELan GKev NGdn
	- Spring Charm	see *A. blepharophylla* 'Frühlingszauber'
	carduchorum	XLum
	caucasica	see *A. alpina* subsp. *caucasica*
	ferdinandi-coburgi	ECho MWat NHol WNew
	- 'Aureovariegata' (v)	CMea CTri ECho ECtt ELan SPet SWvt
	- 'Old Gold'	ECho EHoe EPfP LPot MAsh MHer NHol NRya SPoG SRms SRot SWvt WCFE WHil
	- 'Variegata'	see *A. procurrens* 'Variegata'
§	***procurrens*** 'Variegata' (v) ♀H4	CTri ECho ECtt EHoe ELan EPfP EWes GKev MBrN MHer MJak MSCN SPlb SRms SRot WNew
	Snow Cap	see *A. alpina* subsp. *caucasica* 'Schneehaube'
	× ***wilczekii***	EPot

Arachniodes (*Dryopteridaceae*)

	davalliaeformis	CBty ISha LRHS
	miqueliana	ISha
	simplicior (v)	CBty CCCN CKel ISha WCot
	standishii	CBty ISha

Araiostegia (*Davalliaceae*)

	faberiana	CExl
	hymenophylloides	SKHP WCot
	parvipinnata	see *A. perdurans*
§	***perdurans***	CFil WCot WPGP
	- B&SWJ 1608	WCru
	pulchra HWJ 1007	WCru

Aralia ✿ (*Araliaceae*)

	apioides	IMou
	- EDHCH 9720	WCru
	armata RWJ 10060	WCru
	bipinnata RWJ 10101	WCru
	cachemirica	CDTJ CLAP EWes GCal MBrN NBid NLar SDix SMad SPlb WCru WHal WMoo
	californica	EBee GCal GPoy IGor LEdu NLar SDix SKHP WCru
	castanopsidicola CWJ 12411	WCru
	chapaensis B&SWJ 11812	WCru
	- HWJ 723	WCru
	chinensis misapplied	see *A. elata*
	chinensis L. BWJ 8102	WCru
	continentalis	CLAP IGor NLar
	- B&SWJ 4152	WCru
	- B&SWJ 8524	WCru
	cordata	EWes GCal GKev LEdu NLar
	- B&SWJ 5511	CBcs WCru
	- B&SWJ 5596	WCru
	- 'Sun King'	ECtt ESwi EUJe LLWG LRHS MSCN NLar NSti WCot WHil
	decaisneana RWJ 9910	WCru
§	***elata*** ♀H4	CBcs CCVT CDoC CDul CExl CHel CHll CMac CTsd EBee ELan EPfP GKev IDee LRHS LSRN MBlu MGos MMuc NBid SAPC SGol SHil SLim SPer SPoG SWvt
	- B&SWJ 5480	WCru
	- 'Albomarginata'	see *A. elata* 'Variegata'
	- 'Aureo-marginata' (v)	CMac
	- 'Aureovariegata' (v)	CBcs ELan EWes NLar
	- 'Golden Umbrella' (v)	EUJe LSRN NLar
	- 'Silver Umbrella' (v)	EUJe NLar
§	- 'Variegata' (v) ♀H4	CBcs ELan EPfP MGos NLar SWvt
	foliolosa B&SWJ 8360	WCru
	kansuensis BWJ 7650	WCru
	- CD&R 2289	WCru
	leschenaultii B&SWJ 9515	WCru
	- B&SWJ 11789	WCru

papyrifera	see *Tetrapanax papyrifer*
racemosa	CArn GPoy GQue LEdu LPla NLar SRms
- B&SWJ 9570	WCru
searelliana B&SWJ 11736	WCru
sieboldii de Vriese	see *Fatsia japonica*
spinosa L.	CArn EBtc GKev GQue LEdu MBlu NLar SPlb
subcordata HWJK 2385	WCru
verticillata B&SWJ 11797	WCru
vietnamensis B&SWJ 12349E	WCru

Araucaria (*Araucariaceae*)

angustifolia	WPGP
angustifolia* × *araucana	CFil WPGP
§ ***araucana***	Widely available
cunninghamii	ECou
excelsa misapplied	see *A. heterophylla*
§ ***heterophylla*** 🏆[H1]	CCCN CDoC MBri SAPC SEND
imbricata	see *A. araucana*

Araujia (*Apocynaceae*)

sericifera	CHll CMac CRHN CSpe SVen WCot WSHC

Arbutus ✿ (*Ericaceae*)

andrachne	EPfP
× ***andrachnoides*** 🏆[H4]	CAbP CHGN CJun CTho ELan EPfP GGal LRHS LSRN MRav SAPC SMad SPer SPoG WPGP WPat
menziesii 🏆[H3]	CBcs CDoC CMCN EBee EPfP IGor LRHS MGos MMuc NSoo SMad SPer
× ***reyorum*** 'Marina'	CAbP CDoC CJun ELan EPfP IVic LHop MAsh MBlu SEND SPer SPoG SSpi WPGP WPat
unedo 🏆[H4]	Widely available
- 'Atlantic'	CCCN CJun EPfP LRHS LSRN MAsh MBri MGos SBig SGol SHil SLim SWvt WPGP WPat
- 'Compacta'	CBcs CCCN CDoC EBee IArd LRHS MAsh MGos NLar SLon SPoG SWvt
- 'Elfin King'	ELan EPfP LRHS MAsh NLar SLon SPoG
- 'Quercifolia'	CAbP CHll CJun ELan LLHF MAsh NLar WPat
- Roselily = 'Minlily'[PBR]	SBig
- f. ***rubra*** 🏆[H4]	Widely available
xalapensis	SPlb

Archontophoenix (*Arecaceae*)

alexandrae	EAmu
cunninghamiana 🏆[H1]	CBrP EAmu XBlo

Arctanthemum (*Asteraceae*)

§ ***arcticum***	NLar
- 'Polarstern'	EBee
- 'Schwefelglanz'	NCGa

Arcterica see *Pieris*

Arctium (*Asteraceae*)

lappa	CArn GPoy SIde SRms SVic WSFF
- 'Takinogawa Long'	MNHC
minus	NMir

Arctostaphylos (*Ericaceae*)

glandulosa	SAPC
uva-ursi	GBin GPoy NLar SPlb
- 'Massachusetts'	EBee NLar
- 'Snowcap'	MAsh
- 'Vancouver Jade'	CDoC EBee GKin LRHS LSRN MAsh SCoo SLon SPer SPoG SRms SWvt

Arctotis (*Asteraceae*)

Hannah = 'Archnah'[PBR]	CSpe ECtt MBNS WHil
Hayley = 'Archley'[PBR]	CCCN COIW ECtt MBNS SMrm WHil
'Heidi' **new**	MBNS NPri WHil
'Hello'	COIW NPri WHil
'Holly'	COIW LAst MBNS NPri
'Hope' **new**	MBNS
× ***hybrida*** hort. 'Apricot'	CCCN COIW ECtt EDif LAst SVen
- 'Flame' 🏆[H1+3]	CAby CCCN COIW ECtt LAst MBNS SCoo SMrm SRms SVen
- 'Red Devil'	CCCN COIW LAst LSou MBNS SCoo SMrm SVen
- 'Wine'	CCCN COIW EDif LAst LSou MBNS SCoo SMrm SRkn
venusta **new**	SMrm

Ardisia (*Primulaceae*)

japonica B&SWJ 1032	WCru
- var. ***angusta***	WCot
- var. ***minor*** B&SWJ 1841	WCru
- - B&SWJ 3809	WCru

Areca (*Arecaceae*)

triandra	XBlo

Arecastrum see *Syagrus*

Arenaria (*Caryophyllaceae*)

aggregata **new**	GKev
- subsp. ***erinacea***	GKev
§ ***alfacariensis***	EPot NLar
balearica	CWCL ECho EDAr EWes LLWG MAsh NRya NSla SPlb SRms
capillaris	CTri
grandiflora	XLum
kansuensis	NLar
ledebouriana	EDAr MWat NLar
montana 🏆[H4]	CMea ECho ECtt EDAr EPfP EWTr GAbr GMaP ITim LHop LRHS MGos MLHP NPri SPet SPhx SPlb SRms WAbe WIce WWFP
- 'Avalanche'	ECtt
- 'Blizzard'	EPfP
pulvinata	see *A. alfacariensis*
purpurascens	CMea CPBP ECho EPot EWes ITim LLHF NLar SRms SRot WAbe
tetraquetra	SIgm
- subsp. ***amabilis***	EPot
verna	see *Minuartia verna*

Arenga (*Arecaceae*)

engleri	EAmu
micrantha	WCot

Argania (*Sapotaceae*)

spinosa	CFil WPGP

Argemone (*Papaveraceae*)

grandiflora	CSpe SBch
hunnemannii	WHil

Argyranthemum ✿ (*Asteraceae*)

'Anastasia'	MAJR

	'Beth'	GBee MAJR
	'Blanche' (Courtyard Series)	MAJR
	Blazer Rose = 'Supaglow' (Daisy Crazy Series)	MAJR
§	'Blizzard' (d)	MAJR
	Blushing Rose = 'Supaellie' (Daisy Crazy Series)	MAJR
	'Bofinger'	MAJR
	'Bon Bon'	MAJR
	'Bridesmaid'	MAJR
	Bright Carmine = 'Supalight'^{PBR} (Daisy Crazy Series)	MAJR
	broussonetii	MAJR
	Butterfly = 'Ulyssis' ♀$^{H1+3}$	LAst
	canariense hort.	see *A. frutescens* subsp. *canariae*
	'Champagne'	MAJR
	Cherry Harmony = 'Supa532' (Daisy Crazy Series) (d)	MAJR MCot
	Cherry Love = 'Supacher'^{PBR} (Daisy Crazy Series) (d)	CCCN EPfP MAJR
	'Citronelle'	CBcs MAJR
	'Comtesse de Chambord'	MAJR
	'Cornish Gold' ♀$^{H1+3}$	CBcs CCCN MAJR WGor
	coronopifolium	MAJR
	- primrose-flowered **new**	MAJR
	'Dana'	LAst
	'Donington Hero' ♀$^{H1+3}$	MAJR MHom
	double pink-flowered (d)	SVen
	double white-flowered (d)	MAJR
	'Edelweiss' (d)	MAJR
	'Flamingo'	see *Rhodanthemum gayanum*
§	***foeniculaceum*** misapplied	CTri ELan
	- pink-flowered	see *A.* 'Petite Pink'
§	***foeniculaceum*** (Willd.) Webb & Sch.Bip.	MAJR MCot
	- 'Royal Haze' ♀$^{H1+3}$	CCCN CHll MAJR NPer
	'Frosty'	MAJR
§	***frutescens***	CHEx MAJR WKif
§	- subsp. ***canariae*** ♀$^{H1+3}$	CCCN MAJR
	- subsp. ***foeniculaceum*** (Pit. & Proust) Humphries **new**	MAJR
	- subsp. ***succulentum*** 'Margaret Lynch'	MAJR
	'Fuji Sundance'	MAJR
	'George'	MAJR
	'Gill's Pink'	MAJR MHom WPnn
	gracile	CHll
	- 'Chelsea Girl' ♀$^{H1+3}$	CCCN CHEx MAJR MCot MHom SPhx WKif
	'Guernsey Pink'	MAJR MHom
	Gypsy Rose = 'M9/18d'	CCCN MAJR
	'Icknield Jubilee'	MAJR
	'Icknield Lemon Ice'	MAJR
	'Icknield Pink'	MAJR
	'Icknield Surprise'	MAJR
	'Icknield Sylvia'	MAJR
	'Icknield Yellow'	MAJR
	'Jamaica Primrose' ♀$^{H1+3}$	CSpe CTri ECtt SDix WCot WPnn
	aff. 'Jamaica Primrose' **new**	CAby
	'Jamaica Snowstorm'	see *A.* 'Snow Storm'
	'Julieanne'	MAJR
	LaRita Red (LaRita Series) **new**	LAst
	lemsii	MAJR
	'Levada Cream' ♀$^{H1+3}$	MAJR MHom
	'Libby Brett'	MAJR
	'Lilliput'	MAJR
	(Madeira Series) Madeira Crested Ivory = 'Bonmadcivy' (d) **new**	CWGN
	- Madeira Crested Merlot = 'Bonmadmerlo'^{PBR} (d) **new**	CWGN SVen
§	***maderense*** ♀$^{H1+3}$	CHll GCal MAJR SVen
	'Mary Wootton' (d)	ECtt MAJR
	mawii	see *Rhodanthemum gayanum*
	Meteor Red = 'Supa742' (Daisy Crazy Series)	CBcs CHel MBNS MCot
	'Mike's Pink'	MAJR
	'Millennium Star'	MAJR
	'Mini-snowflake'	see *A.* 'Blizzard'
§	'Mrs F. Sander' (d)	MAJR
	ochroleucum	see *A. maderense*
	Pacific Gold = 'Pacargone'^{PBR} (d)	CBcs
§	'Petite Pink' ♀$^{H1+3}$	CCCN ECtt MAJR
	Ping-Pong = 'Innping'^{PBR} (d)	CCCN CHel
	'Pink Australian' (d)	MAJR MHom
	'Pink Delight'	see *A.* 'Petite Pink'
	'Pink Pixie'	MAJR
	pinnatifidium subsp. ***succulentum***	MAJR
	Pomponette Pink = 'Supa392'^{PBR} (d)	CBcs
	'Porto Moritz'	MAJR
	'Powder Puff' (d)	ECtt MAJR
	'Primrose Petite' (Courtyard Series)	MAJR
	prostrate double pink-flowered (d)	MAJR
	Renaissance Daisies = 'Summer Melody'^{PBR}	CBcs CCCN CHel MAJR
	'Rising Sun'	MAJR
	'Saimi'	MAJR
	São Vicente = 'Ohmadsavi'^{PBR} (Madeira Series)	MAJR
	'Shirley's Yellow' **new**	MHom
	'Silver Leaf'	MAJR
	'Silver Queen'	see *A. foeniculaceum* misapplied
§	'Snow Storm' ♀$^{H1+3}$	MAJR MHom WPnn
	'Snowball'	MAJR
	'Snowflake' misapplied	see *A.* 'Mrs F. Sander'
	Sole Mio = 'Supa3047' (d)	CWCL MAJR
	'Starlight'	MAJR MCot
	'Starlight Red' (Daisy Crazy Series)	MAJR
	Strawberry Pink = 'Suparosa' (Daisy Crazy Series)	EPfP
	'Sugar and Ice' (d)	CCCN MAJR
	'Sugar Baby' (d)	CCCN
	Sugar Cheer = 'Cobeer' (d)	MAJR
	'Sugar Lace'	MAJR
	Sultan's Dream = 'Supadream' (Daisy Crazy Series)	EPfP
	Sultan's Lemon = 'Supalem'^{PBR} (Daisy Crazy Series)	EPfP MAJR
	Sultan's Pride = 'Cosupri' (Daisy Crazy Series)	MAJR
	'Summer Angel' (d)	MAJR

'Summer Pink'	CCCN MAJR
'Summer Stars' (Daisy Crazy Series) (d)	MAJR
Summersong Blush Pink (Daisy Crazy Series) (d) **new**	MCot
Summersong Lemon = 'Supa601' (Daisy Crazy Series) (d)	MAJR
Summersong White = 'Supa594' (Daisy Crazy Series) (d)	MAJR
'Summertime'	MAJR
Summit Pink = 'Cobsing'PBR (Daisy Crazy Series)	EPfP MAJR
'Sweety'	MAJR
'Tweeny' (d)	MAJR
'Vancouver' (d) ♀H1+3	CCCN CHll CWCL ECtt SBHP
Vanilla Ripple = 'Supabright' (Daisy Crazy Series)	MAJR
* 'Vera'	CCCN
'Weymouth Pink'	MAJR
'Weymouth Surprise'	MAJR
White Blush = 'Supamorni' (Daisy Crazy Series)	MAJR
White Crystal = 'Supagem' (Daisy Crazy Series)	MAJR
'White Spider'	CCCN ELan MAJR MHom
'White Star' (d)	MAJR
'Whiteknights' ♀H1+3	MAJR
'Yellow Australian' (d)	MAJR

Argyrocytisus (*Papilionaceae*)

battandieri ♀H4	Widely available
- 'Yellow Tail' ♀H4	CEnd CHel ELan EPfP LRHS MBri MGos SKHP SSta WHar

Arisaema ✿ (*Araceae*)

C&H 7026	LWst
CC 2792	WCot
CC 4904	CExl
CC 5511	CExl
Chen Yi 97	WCot
album	XLum
amurense	CElw CFil CLAP EBee ECho GBuc GCal MMoz
§ - subsp. ***robustum***	ECho
brevipes	CExl
candidissimum ♀H4	CBro CCon CDes CElw CFil CHel CLAP CWCL EAmu ELon EPfP EPot GBuc GCra LRHS LWst MAvo MRav NHar NLar NSla SDeJ SKHP WBor WCot WHal WIvy WPGP
- white-flowered	CFil
ciliatum	CDes ELon GBuc MAvo MMoz NHar NLar SRot
- var. ***liubaense***	CAby CFwr CWCL EPfP EPot EWld GBuc MMoz WIvy
- - CT 369	CExl CLAP EBee EPfP LWst SDys SKHP WPGP WSHC
- variegated (v)	WCot
concinnum	CCon EAmu EWld GBin SBst WPnP XLum
consanguineum	CAby CDes CExl CFwr CHEx CLAP EPfP GBin GCal GKev LWst MAvo MMoz NHar NLar SMrm WPGP WPnP XLum
- B&SWJ 071	WCru
- CLD 1519	ECho GBuc
- subsp. ***kelung-insulare*** B&SWJ 256	WCru
- variegated (v)	WCot
costatum	CCCN CFil CHEx EAmu ECho EPfP EPot EUJe GBin LRHS LWst MMoz NHol SBst WCot WPGP XLum
dracontium	EAmu ECho XLum
elephas	ECho
erubescens	GBin
- white-lined-leaved	WCot
exappendiculatum	CDes CExl CFil MMoz
fargesii	CExl CFil CHel ECho LWst MMoz SChF SKHP WCot XLum
flavum	CDes CFil CPom CWCL ECho ELon EPfP EPot EWld GBuc GCal MMoz NHar SPlb
- CC 6303	ITim
- subsp. ***abbreviatum***	GBin GBuc
- - CC 6300	ITim
- tall	ECho
formosanum B&SWJ 280	WCru
§ ***franchetianum***	CExl LWst
galeatum	EAmu EBee ECho EPot GBin NHol WCot XLum
grapsospadix B&SWJ 7000	WCru
§ ***griffithii***	CBro CHel EAmu ECho EUJe GBin GBuc LRHS MMoz NBid NLar NSoo SDeJ WCot XLum
- 'Numbuq'	GCra
- var. ***pradhanii***	EBee GBin XLum
helleborifolium	see *A. tortuosum*
intermedium	ECho GBin MMoz MNrw XLum
jacquemontii	CAby CFil CLAP EBee ECho EWld GCra GLog NLar XLum
- CC 5184	ITim
japonicum Komarov	see *A. serratum*
jinshajiangense	CExl
kiushianum	EFEx MMoz NLar WCot
leschenaultii	EBee
lichiangense	EBee LWst
§ ***lobatum***	CExl EBee
§ ***nepenthoides***	CBcs CFil EAmu ECho EPot EUJe GBin GKev ITim LRHS MMoz NLar NSoo WPnP XLum
ochraceum	see *A. nepenthoides*
onoticum	see *A. lobatum*
petelotii B&SWJ 9706	WCru
polyphyllum B&SWJ 3904	WCru
propinquum	ECho GBin LWst NHol WCot XLum
purpureogaleatum	see *A. franchetianum*
ringens misapplied	see *A. amurense* subsp. *robustum*
ringens ambig.	SKHP
ringens (Thunberg) Schott	EFEx LEdu
- f. ***praecox*** B&SWJ 1515	WCru
- f. ***sieboldii*** B&SWJ 551	WCru
aff. ***ringens*** **new**	CHel
robustum	see *A. amurense* subsp. *robustum*
§ ***serratum***	ECho MMoz MNrw
sikokianum	CBcs CBro EAmu ECho EFEx EPot LRHS NLar SKHP WPnP
speciosum	CExl CFil CHEx EAmu ECho EWld GBin LRHS MMoz NSoo SDeJ SPlb WPnP XLum
* - var. ***magnificum***	GBin NHol WPnP XLum
- var. ***mirabile***	XLum
taiwanense	CLAP SKHP
- B&SWJ 269	WCru

- var. ***brevipedunculatum*** B&SWJ 1859 — WCru
- f. ***cinereum*** B&SWJ 19121 — WCru
thunbergii — EFEx LRHS
- subsp. ***autumnale*** B&SWJ 1425 — WCru
- subsp. ***urashima*** — EBee EFEx
§ ***tortuosum*** — CExl CFil EAmu ECho EUJe EWld GBin GBuc LEdu LWst MNrw NEgg NSoo SChF WPGP WPnP XLum
- 'Black Rod' new — CFil
- var. ***helleborifolium*** — NBid XLum
triphyllum — CElw CExl CHel CLAP EAmu ECho EPot GPoy LRHS MMoz NLar SPlb WPnP
- subsp. ***triphyllum*** var. ***atrorubens*** — CLAP
§ ***utile*** — EAmu ECho EPot GBin XLum
verrucosum — see *A. griffithii*
- var. ***utile*** — see *A. utile*
yunnanense — CLAP

Arisarum (*Araceae*)

proboscideum — Widely available
vulgare — ECho EPot WCot
- from Crete — ECho
* - f. ***maculatum*** — ECho
- subsp. ***simorrhinum*** — ECho
- subsp. ***vulgare*** — ECho

Aristea (*Iridaceae*)

sp. — GGal
africana 'Worcester' — ECho
angolensis — EBee
§ ***capitata*** — CHel CHll CPrp CSpe WHil
- pink-flowered — CHel CPrp EPri
ecklonii — CExl CHEx CPou CPrp CTca CTsd EBee EPri EShb IGor MHer
- GWJ 9469 — WCru
ensifolia — ELan
grandis — CCon
spiralis 'Paarl' — ECho
thyrsiflora — see *A. capitata*
woodii 'Clarens' — ECho

Aristolochia (*Aristolochiaceae*)

baetica — CExl
californica — LEdu SKHP
chilensis — CCCN SPlb
clematitis — CArn ECho GPoy LEdu LPla
cucurbitifolia B&SWJ 7043 — WCru
delavayi — CHEx SVen
durior — see *A. macrophylla*
gigantea — CCCN CHll
grandiflora — CCCN CHll
griffithii B&SWJ 2118 — WCru
heterophylla — see *A. kaempferi* f. *heterophylla*
kaempferi — CCCN
- B&SWJ 293 — WCru
§ - f. ***heterophylla*** B&SWJ 3109 — WCru
× ***kewensis*** — CCCN
liukiuensis B&SWJ 4960 — WCru
§ ***macrophylla*** — CArn CBcs CCCN CMac EBee EPfP MRav NEgg SLim
manshuriensis B&SWJ 12557 new — WCru
moupinensis BWJ 8181 — WCru
onoei B&SWJ 4960 — WCru
rotunda — SKHP
sempervirens — SBrt SKHP WCru WSHC
sipho — see *A. macrophylla*
tomentosa — SKHP

Aristotelia (*Elaeocarpaceae*)

§ ***chilensis*** — IVic LEdu
- 'Variegata' (v) — CCCN CMCN CMac CWib EBee GQui SBod SPlb
fruticosa — IGor
- (f) — ECou
- (m) — ECou
- black-fruited (f) — ECou
- white-fruited (f) — ECou
macqui — see *A. chilensis*
peduncularis — CExl
serrata — ECou SVen
- (f) — ECou
- (m) — ECou

Armeria (*Plumbaginaceae*)

§ ***alliacea*** (Cav.) Hoffmanns. & Link — LRHS
- f. ***leucantha*** — SRms WMoo
'Bloodgood' — ECho ECtt
'Brutus' — CDes
caespitosa — see *A. juniperifolia*
- 'Bevan's Variety' — see *A. juniperifolia* 'Bevan's Variety'
(Joystick Series) 'Joystick Lilac Shades' — COlW EBee EHyd ELan EPfP EShb LRHS
- 'Joystick Red' — EHyd ELan EPfP EShb EWll LRHS WHil WWFP
- 'Joystick White' — EBee EHyd ELan EPfP EWll LRHS WHil
§ ***juniperifolia*** ♀H4 — CMea ECho EHyd ELan EPfP GMaP LRHS MHer NSla SBch SPoG SRms WIce XLum
- 'Alba' — CMea ECho ELan EPfP EPot GMaP MAsh MHer SBch SPoG SRms SRot WAbe WHoo WThu
§ - 'Bevan's Variety' ♀H4 — ECho ECtt ELan EPfP EPot GMaP LEdu MMuc NLar NRya SPoG SRms SRot WAbe WHoo WNew
- 'Brookside' — GJos
- dark-flowered — WAbe
- rose-flowered — ITim
juniperifolia × ***maritima*** — [illegible]
§ ***maritima*** — CArn CHab ECho EHyd EPfP GJos LAst LPot LRHS MBel MNHC MSCN NEgg SPet SWvt WCFE WHfH WJek WMoo WNew
- 'Alba' — CBcs COlW CTri ECho EHyd ELan EPfP GJos GMaP LBMP LEdu LRHS MCot MMuc NRya SPet SPlb SPoG WCFE WMoo WNew
- 'Armada Rose' — LRHS
- 'Bloodstone' — CTri ECho ECtt ELan MWat
- 'Corsica' — CTri NBir SBch
- Düsseldorf Pride — see *A. maritima* 'Düsseldorfer Stolz'
§ - 'Düsseldorfer Stolz' — CElw ECho ECtt EDAr ELan EPfP GKev GMaP LHop LRHS MCot MLHP NDov NPri SPoG SWvt WIce WNew XLum
- 'Laucheana' — SBch WHoo WMoo
- 'Nifty Thrifty' (v) — CMea CTri ECho ECtt EHoe EWes MHer SPoG SRot
* - 'Pink Lusitanica' — LBMP LRHS

	- 'Rosa Stolz'	NDov
I	- 'Rubrifolia'	CAby CCon CMea CSpe ECho ECtt EHoe EPPr EShb GCal GMaP LAst LBMP LEdu MAvo MHer MMuc NHol NLar NRya SBch SPoG SRot SWvt WAbe WHoo WIce WNew
I	- 'Rubrifolia Compacta'	WAbe
	- 'Ruby Glow'	CTri SBch
	- 'Schöne von Fellbach'	XLum
	- 'Splendens'	CBcs COIW CTri ECho EDAr EPfP GMaP LAst LRHS MAsh MGos MHer MJak MMuc NMir NRya SBch SPoG WMoo XLum
	- 'Splendens Alba'	XLum
	- 'Vindictive' 🏆H4	CMea CTri EPfP
	plantaginea	see *A. alliacea* (Cav.) Hoffmanns. & Link
	pseudarmeria	EBee ECho ELan EPfP LPot MWhi XLum
	- hybrids	CTri ELan
	'Vesuvius'	WCot XLum
	vulgaris	see *A. maritima*
	welwitschii	IFoB SRms
	'Westacre Beauty'	EWes

Armoracia (*Brassicaceae*)

§	***rusticana***	CArn CHby CPrp CSev CTri ELau EPfP GAbr GPoy MHer MHoo MMuc MNHC NPer NPri SIde SPoG SRms SVic WHer WJek
	- 'Variegata' (v)	EBee ELau GCal IFoB LEdu LHop MAvo NSti SMad SRms WHer WJek WMoo

Arnica (*Asteraceae*)

	angustifolia subsp. ***alpina***	SRms
	- subsp. ***iljinii***	NBir
	chamissonis Schmidt	see *A. sachalinensis*
	chamissonis Less.	CHby EBee MNHC NLar WJek XLum
	montana	CArn EOHP GPoy MHer MHoo MNHC SRms SWat WHfH
§	***sachalinensis*** RBS 0206	EPPr

Arnoglossum (*Asteraceae*)

	atriplicifolium	LRHS

Aronia (*Rosaceae*)

	arbutifolia	CBcs CDul CTri EPfP LSRN MBlu SGol SLon SPlb
	- 'Erecta'	CDul EBee ELan EPfP GBin LHop LRHS MBlu MBri MMuc NLar SLPl SPoG SRms SWvt WCFE
	melanocarpa	CDul CMCN CPom CSpe CTsd CWib ELan EPfP EWTr GKin IGor LEdu LRHS MAsh WGrn
	- 'Autumn Magic'	CBcs CDoC CJun EBee ELan EPfP GBin LAst LHop LRHS MAsh MMuc NLar SCoo SLPl SLon
	- var. ***grandifolia***	CJun
	- 'Hugin'	CAgr CJun LEdu MCoo NLar
	× ***prunifolia***	CDoC GAbr LEdu WGrn
	- 'Aron' (F)	CJun
	- 'Brilliant'	CDoC CTri EPfP GBin GKin LRHS NEgg NLar SGol SPer WHar
	- 'Nero' (F)	CAgr GBin GGGa LEdu MCoo NLar
	- 'Serina' (F)	CJun NLar
	- 'Viking' (F)	CAgr CDul CJun ECrN EPfP EPom EWTr GBin GGGa LBuc LEdu LHop LRHS MBlu NBro NLar SGol

Arrhenatherum (*Poaceae*)

	elatius	CHab
	- var. ***bulbosum*** 'Variegatum' (v)	EBee EHoe ELan EPPr GBin GKev GMaP LBMP MMoz MMuc MWhi NBid NOak NOrc NWad SEND WMoo WPtf WWEG

Artemisia ✿ (*Asteraceae*)

	RBS 0207	CExl
	from Taiwan	WHer
§	***abrotanum*** 🏆H4	Widely available
	absinthium	CArn CEls CHab CSev ELan GPoy MHer MHoo MNHC NLar NSti SIde SRms SVic WJek XLum XSen
	- 'Lambrook Giant'	CEls
	- 'Lambrook Mist' 🏆H3-4	CEls CFis CMac CPrp CSev EBee ECtt ELan EPfP GCal GQue LRHS MRav NDov SMrm SWat WMnd WWEG XLum
	- 'Lambrook Silver' 🏆H4	CArn CEls CExl CSam EBee ELan EPfP GCal GMaP LHop LPot LRHS LSRN MHer MMuc MRav NBro SEND SLim SPer SWat SWvt WMnd WWEG
	- 'Silver Ghost'	CEls
	afra	CArn CEls XSen
§	***alba***	CEls GPoy MHer SRms WJek XSen
§	- 'Canescens' 🏆H4	CEls CSam CTri EBee ECtt ELan EPfP GMaP LAst LBMP LRHS MHer MRav SDix SEND SMrm SPer WCFE WCot WMnd WWEG XSen
	annua	CArn CEls
	anomala	CArn CEls
	arborescens 🏆H3	CArn CEls LRHS NEgg SDix SPer WKif
	- 'Brass Band'	see *A.* 'Powis Castle'
	- 'Faith Raven'	CEls EBee EPfP GBin MBNS NLar
	- 'Porquerolles'	CEls
	argentea L'Hér. **new**	CEls
	argyi	CEls
§	***armeniaca***	CEls ECho XSen
	assoana	see *A. caucasica*
	atrata	CEls
	barrelieri	CEls
	caerulescens subsp. ***gallica***	CEls
	californica	CEls
	- 'Canyon Gray'	CEls
	campestris	XLum XSen
	- subsp. ***borealis***	CEls
	- subsp. ***campestris***	CEls
	- subsp. ***maritima***	CEls
	- - from Wales	CEls
	camphorata	see *A. alba*
	cana	CEls MHer
	canariensis	see *A. thuscula*
	canescens misapplied	see *A. alba* 'Canescens'
	canescens Willd.	see *A. armeniaca*
	capillaris	CEls XLum
§	***caucasica*** 🏆H3-4	CEls CFis ECho EPot EWes MHer SChF SPhx SRms SRot
	- ***caucasica***	CEls
	chamaemelifolia	CEls MHer NBre SRms WJek XSen
	cretacea	see *A. nutans*
	discolor Dougl. ex Besser	see *A. michauxiana*

	douglasiana	CEls
	- 'Valerie Finnis'	see *A. ludoviciana* 'Valerie Finnis'
	dracunculus	MJak MNHC MRav SPlb SRms WBrk WHfH
	- French	CArn CEls CHby CSev CTsd ELau GPoy LEdu MHer MHoo NPri SEND SIde WGwG WJek XLum
	- Russian	CEls SVic
	- 'Thüringen' **new**	IMou
	ferganensis	CEls
	filifolia	CEls XSen
	fragrans Willd.	CEls
	frigida $\mathbb{Y}^{H3-4}$	CEls XSen
	genipi	CEls MHoo
	glacialis	CEls
	gmelinii	CEls
	gnaphalodes	see *A. ludoviciana*
	gorgonum	CEls SEND
	gracilis hort.	see *A. scoparia*
	'Hausserman'	XLum
	herba-alba	CEls XSen
	japonica	CEls
	kawakamii B&SWJ 088	WCru
	kitadakensis	CEls
	- 'Guizhou'	see *A. lactiflora* Guizhou Group
	laciniata	CEls
	lactiflora $\mathbb{Y}^{H4}$	CDoy CEls CPrp EBee ECtt ELan GBee GMaP MHoo MRav NGdn NOrc SDix SMrm SPer SRms WHfH WMoo XLum
	- 'Elfenbein'	GCal IMou LHop LPla
§	- Guizhou Group	Widely available
	- - 'Dark Delight'	EBee ECtt EWes
	- 'Jim Russell'	CDes CElw EBee ECtt EWes NBre SPhx WWFP
	- ***purpurea***	see *A. lactiflora* Guizhou Group
	- 'Weisses Wunder'	EBee
	lanata Willd.	see *A. caucasica*
	lanata Lam.	XSen
	laxa	see *A. umbelliformis*
	'Little Mice'	CEls EBee WWEG
§	***ludoviciana***	CEls ELan GBee IFoB MCot NLar NOrc NPer SRms WCFE XLum
	- var. ***latifolia***	see *A. ludoviciana* subsp. *ludoviciana* var. *latiloba*
	- subsp. ***ludoviciana*** var. ***incompta***	CEls LAst
N	- - var. ***latiloba***	CEls EBee EHoe LHop NBro NPnk SWvt WCot WHoo
	- subsp. ***mexicana*** var. ***albula***	CEls SMrm
	- 'Silver Queen' $\mathbb{Y}^{H4}$	Widely available
N	- 'Valerie Finnis' $\mathbb{Y}^{H4}$	Widely available
	maritima	CArn MHer
	- var. ***maritima***	CEls
	mauiensis	CEls
§	***michauxiana***	CEls EBee NSti XSen
	molinieri	CEls XSen
	mutellina	see *A. umbelliformis*
	niitakayamensis	CEls
	nitida	CEls
§	***nutans***	CEls MCot MRav
	palmeri hort.	see *A. ludoviciana*
	pamirica	CEls
	aff. ***parviflora*** CLD 1531	CEls
	pedemontana	see *A. caucasica*
	pontica	CArn CEls EBee EHoe ELan GMaP GPoy LEdu LRHS MAvo MBNS MHer MNHC MRav NBro NLar NSti SRms WCAu WHfH WHoo WJek WWEG XSen
§	'Powis Castle' $\mathbb{Y}^{H3}$	Widely available
	princeps	CArn CEls ELau GPoy SIde
	procera Willd.	see *A. abrotanum*
	purshiana	see *A. ludoviciana*
	pycnocephala	CEls
	- 'David's Choice'	CEls SMad
	ramosa	CEls
	'Rosenschleier'	EWes LPla MAvo NBre WPGP WWEG
	schmidtiana $\mathbb{Y}^{H4}$	CEls CFis MWat NOrc SRms WKif
	- 'Nana' $\mathbb{Y}^{H4}$	Widely available
	- 'Nana Attraction'	LRHS NLar SRot
§	***scoparia***	MHoo
	'Sea Foam'	EPfP LRHS
	selengensis	CEls
	splendens misapplied	see *A. alba* 'Canescens'
	splendens Willd.	SPhx
	- var. ***brachyphylla***	MAsh
	stelleriana	CArn CEls CTri EDAr GBee GKev IFoB LHop MAvo MCot MHer MNFA NBro NPri SPer SRms
	- RBS 0207	CEls NLar
N	- 'Boughton Silver'	CEls EBee ECtt EHoe ELan EPfP GBBs GMaP IKil LDai LRHS MAsh MCot MRav NLar NSti NWad SMrm SPhx SRms SWvt WWEG
N	- 'Mori'	see *A. stelleriana* 'Boughton Silver'
	- 'Nana'	CEls SWvt
	- 'Prostrata'	see *A. stelleriana* 'Boughton Silver'
	- 'Silver Brocade'	see *A. stelleriana* 'Boughton Silver'
	taurica	CEls
§	***thuscula***	CEls
	tridentata	CArn WHer
§	***umbelliformis***	CEls
	vallesiaca $\mathbb{Y}^{H4}$	CEls
	verlotiorum	CEls
	vulgaris L.	CArn CEls ELau GPoy MHer MHoo MNHC WHer
	- 'Cragg-Barber Eye' (v)	EBee NBld
	- Oriental Limelight = 'Janlim' (v)	CEls COIW EBee ECtt EHoe EPfP GAbr LHop MJak MNHC MWhi NBir NEgg NLar SWvt WHer WJek
	- 'Variegata' (v)	CEls EBee EPfP NBir WHer WMoo XLum
	× ***wurzellii***	CEls

Arthropodium (*Asparagaceae*)

candidum	ECGP ECho ECou EHoe MMuc MPie
- 'Cappuccino'	CBcs
- 'Capri'	LPot
- 'Maculatum'	ECho LEdu SBrt SPlb
- ***purpureum***	ECho IKil
cirratum	CHel CHll CSpe ECho ECou IKil MHer MPie
- 'Matapouri Bay'	CAbb CBcs CHEx EBee ECre
milleflorum	SBrt
minus	CExl ECou

artichoke, globe see *Cynara cardunculus* Scolymus Group

artichoke, Jerusalem see *Helianthus tuberosus*

Arum (*Araceae*)

alpinum	see *A. cylindraceum*
besserianum	ECho LWst

byzantinum	EChoLWst
'Chameleon'	CDes EPPr MAvo NBir SKHP SMad SPer WCot WWEG
§ ***concinnatum***	ECho SChr SKHP
- black-spotted	ECho
- 'Mount Ida'	ECho SKHP
- purple	ECho
- variegated (v)	WCot
concinnatum* × *cyrenaicum	ECho
concinnatum* × *cyrenaicum from Crete	LWst
cornutum	see *Sauromatum venosum*
creticum	CBro CCon CFil CMea CSpe ECho GCal LRHS MNrw MRav SKHP SRot WBor
- 'Karpathos'	CExl ECho GKev LWst MMoz SKHP WCot
- 'Marmaris White'	CDes WCot
- yellow-spotted	NBir WIvy
creticum* × *italicum	CDes
§ ***cylindraceum***	ECho
cyrenaicum	CFil CPom EBee ECho LEdu LWst WCot
- MS 696 from Crete	WCot
- from Crete	ECho
dioscoridis	CPom ECho EWes GCra GKev MMoz WCot
- JCA 195.197	WCot
- var. ***cyprium***	ECho GKev LWst
§ - var. ***dioscoridis*** JCA 5396A	LWst
- var. ***liepoldtii***	see *A. dioscoridis* var. *dioscoridis*
- var. ***philistaeum*** HKEP 9263	LWst
- var. ***smithii***	see *A. dioscoridis* var. *dioscoridis*
- var. ***syriacum***	LWst
dracunculus	see *Dracunculus vulgaris*
elongatum	CPom LWst
- RS 274/87	EBee LWst
hygrophilum	CPom LWst WCot
italicum	CArn CLAP CTri ECho IBoy NLar SDeJ SWat WCot WShi
- subsp. ***albispathum***	EBee ECho MMoz WCot
- 'Black Spot'	EPPr
- black-spotted	ECho
- 'Edward Dougal'	WCot
- giant	ECho
- 'Green Marble'	SEND WWEG
- subsp. ***italicum***	ECho EShb WBrk
- - 'Cyclops'	WWEG
§ - - 'Marmoratum' ♀H4	Widely available
- - 'Sparkler'	WCot
- - 'Spotted Jack'	MAvo WCot WWEG
- - 'Tiny'	CCon CDes CExl GCal SWvt WWEG
§ - - 'White Winter'	CDes CElw MAvo WBrk WCot WWEG
- 'Nancy Lindsay'	MMoz
- subsp. ***neglectum***	SChr
- - 'Miss Janay Hall' (v)	CAvo LLHF MMoz WCot
- 'Pictum'	see *A. italicum* subsp. *italicum* 'Marmoratum'
- 'Tresahor Beauty'	MAvo
italicum* × *maculatum new	WHer
jacquemontii	ECho
korolkowii	LWst WCot
maculatum	CArn EBee ECho EPot GKev GPoy MHer MRav NLar WHer WShi
- 'Painted Lady' (v)	WCot
- 'Pleddel'	MRav
nickelii	see *A. concinnatum*
§ ***nigrum***	CPom ECho EWes LLHF WCot WGwG
- 'Trebinje'	LWst
orientale	EPot WCot
- VV RR.55	LWst
palaestinum	EBee LWst
petteri misapplied	see *A. nigrum*
pictum	CExl CLAP CMac ECho EWes LEdu LLHF WCot
- 'Taff's Form'	see *A. italicum* subsp. *italicum* 'White Winter'
purpureospathum	CFil CPom ECho EPPr WCot WPGP
- VV CR.543	LWst
rupicola var. ***rupicola***	ECho LWst
- var. ***virescens***	ECho LWst

Aruncus ✿ (*Rosaceae*)

aethusifolius ♀H4	Widely available
- 'Little Gem'	ECho WCru
asiaticus B&SWJ 8624	WCru
dioicus	Widely available
§ - (m) ♀H4	CDoC CMac CRow EHoe ELan IBoy MBNS MRav MWts NBro NSti SMad SPer SRms SWat WMoo
- var. ***acuminatus***	EBee
- Child of Two Worlds	see *A. dioicus* 'Zweiweltenkind'
- 'Glasnevin'	CSev EBee ECtt GBee LRHS MRav
- var. ***kamtschaticus***	EWes LRHS NBre NLar WHrl
- - RBS 0208	NGdn
- 'Kneiffii'	Widely available
§ - 'Zweiweltenkind'	GCal IPot LRHS NBre NLar SMad WCot XLum
'Guinea Fowl'	GQue LEdu MAvo MBri NCGa NGdn NHar NLar NSti SMrm
'Horatio'	CSam EBee ELan GBin IMou IPot LEdu LHop LPla MHol MMuc MPie NDov NLar SMad SPhx WCot WRHF
'Johannifest'	CDes ECtt IMou IPot WCot
'Misty Lace'	GBin MAvo MBri NCGa NGdn NHar NLar SMrm
'Noble Spirit'	MBel NGdn NLar SWat
'Perlehuhn'	EBee IMou
plumosus	see *A. dioicus*
sinensis	NBre
sylvestris	see *A. dioicus*
- 'Sommeranfang' new	IMou
'Woldemar Meier'	EBee GBin IMou WCot

Arundinaria (*Poaceae*)

anceps	see *Yushania anceps*
auricoma	see *Pleioblastus viridistriatus*
disticha	see *Pleioblastus pygmaeus* 'Distichus'
falconeri	see *Himalayacalamus falconeri*
fargesii	see *Bashania fargesii*
fastuosa	see *Semiarundinaria fastuosa*
fortunei	see *Pleioblastus variegatus*
funghomii	see *Schizostachyum funghomii*
§ ***gigantea***	CDTJ MWht
- subsp. ***tecta***	CBcs
hindsii	see *Pleioblastus hindsii*
hookeriana misapplied	see *Himalayacalamus falconeri* 'Damarapa'

hookeriana Munro	see *Himalayacalamus hookerianus*
humilis	see *Pleioblastus humilis*
japonica	see *Pseudosasa japonica*
jaunsarensis	see *Yushania anceps*
maling	see *Yushania maling*
marmorea	see *Chimonobambusa marmorea*
murielae	see *Fargesia murielae*
nitida	see *Fargesia nitida*
oedogonata	see *Clavinodum oedogonatum*
palmata	see *Sasa palmata*
pumila	see *Pleioblastus argenteostriatus* f. *pumilus*
pygmaea	see *Pleioblastus pygmaeus*
quadrangularis	see *Chimonobambusa quadrangularis*
simonii	see *Pleioblastus simonii*
spathiflora	see *Thamnocalamus spathiflorus*
tessellata	see *Thamnocalamus tessellatus*
vagans	see *Sasaella ramosa*
variegata	see *Pleioblastus variegatus*
veitchii	see *Sasa veitchii*
viridistriata	see *Pleioblastus viridistriatus*
'Wang Tsai'	see *Bambusa multiplex* 'Floribunda'

Arundo (*Poaceae*)

donax	CAbb CHEx CKno COIW CPla EAmu ELan EPPr EUJe EWes GCra GGal GMaP IDee LRHS MBlu MBrN MNrw MRav NSoo SAPC SDix SEND SMad SPer SPlb SPoG WHal WWEG
- 'Golden Chain' (v)	CKno ELan EPPr EShb EWes LRHS SMad
- 'Macrophylla'	CExl CFil CHGN CKno LEdu WPGP
- 'Variegata'	see *A. donax* var. *versicolor*
§ - var. ***versicolor*** (v)	CAbb CBcs CHEx CKno CPrp EAmu ELan ELon EPPr EPfP EShb EUJe EWes GCal LEdu LHop LLWG LRHS MMoz MREP MRav SEND SMad SPer SPlb SPoG WCot WWEG XLum
I - - 'Aureovariegata' (v)	CDTJ
formosana	CKno EPPr
- 'Golden Showers'	ESwi EUJe SEND

Asarina (*Plantaginaceae*)

barclayana	see *Maurandya barclayana*
erubescens	see *Lophospermum erubescens*
lophantha	see *Lophospermum scandens*
lophospermum	see *Lophospermum scandens*
§ ***procumbens***	CHel CTri ECho IBoy NBir NRya SPhx SRms WBrk WKif
- 'Alba'	IFro

Asarum (*Aristolochiaceae*)

Chen Yi 5	WCot
albomaculatum	ECho
- B&SWJ 1726	WCru
arifolium	EBee EPPr
campaniflorum	EBee ECho WCot WCru
canadense	CArn EBee ECho EWld GBBs GPoy LEdu MMoz NLar WCru WWEG
cardiophyllum B&SWJ 11742 new	WCru
caudatum	CHEx CLAP EBee ECho EPfP LEdu NBro NLar SRms WCot WCru WWEG
- deciduous	WCru
- white-flowered	SKHP WCru
caudigerum	WCot
- B&SWJ 1517	WCru
- HWJ 641 from Vietnam	WCru
caulescens	ECho EPPr WCru
- B&SWJ 5886	WCru
delavayi	ECho LEdu NLar WCot WCru
epigynum B&SWJ 3443	WCru
- 'Silver Web'	WCru
europaeum ♀H4	Widely available
- PAB 4377 new	LEdu
fauriei	WCru
forbesii	EBee ECho MMoz
geophilum	MMoz
hartwegii	CLAP IGor WCru WThu
himalaicum GWJ 9341	WCru
hypogynum B&SWJ 3628	WCru
infrapurpureum B&SWJ 1994	WCru
- 'Taroko Web'	WCru
kumageanum	WCot
lemmonii	LEdu LRHS
leptophyllum B&SWJ 1983	WCru
longirhizomatosum	WCru
macranthum	WCot
- B&SWJ 1691	WCru
maculatum B&SWJ 1114	WCru
magnificum	CHel MMoz WCru
maximum	CCon CLAP ECho MMoz WCru
- 'Silver Panda'	CExl ECtt ESwi EUJe MCot MSCN NLar NPnk SKHP SMad WCot
naniflorum 'Eco Decor'	CLAP WCot
nipponicum B&SWJ 2830	WCru
petelotii HWJ 1043	WCru
pulchellum	CAby WCot WCru
sieboldii	GPoy WCru
splendens	CBct CBro CHid EBee ECho ELan EPfP GBin GMaP LEdu MHol MPie MRav NGdn NLar NPnk NSti SKHP SMad SPlb WCot WCru XLum
taipingshanianum B&SWJ 1688	WCot WCru
- 'Elfin Yellow'	WCru
wulingense	CExl WCru

Asclepias (*Apocynaceae*)

californica new	SBrt
'Cinderella'	SGol
cordifolia new	SBrt
curassavica	CCCN EShb LLWG SRkn XLum
- 'Red Butterfly'	SLon
- 'Silky Gold'	SPet
- 'Silky Red'	SPet
exaltata	SBrt
§ ***fascicularis***	CPom SBrt
fasciculata	see *A. fascicularis*
incarnata	ELan IFoB LRHS MRav NBre SBea SBrt SMrm SPlb XLum
- 'Alba'	CPom
- 'Ice Ballet'	CAbP CPrp ELan IFoB LHop LLWG LRHS NLar SPer SPet SPoG
* - 'Iceberg'	SGol
- 'Soulmate'	EBee ELan EPfP LPot MMuc NOrc SPer SPet WHil WKif
physocarpa	see *Gomphocarpus physocarpus*
purpurascens	CArn CPom EBee
rubra new	SBrt
speciosa	NBre SBea SBrt SPhx WPGP

sullivantii	EBee SBrt
syriaca	CArn EBee LRHS MBel NBre XLum
tuberosa	CArn CBcs CPrp CWib EBee ECtt GPoy LAst LSou MAsh MHer MNHC NEgg NOrc SBea SMad SPoG WGwG XLum
- Gay Butterflies Group	LRHS

Asimina (*Annonaceae*)

triloba (F)	CBcs CDTJ MBlu NLar SGol SPlb
- 'Davis' (F)	CAgr
- 'Nc-1' (F)	CAgr
- 'Pennsylvania Golden' (F)	CAgr
- 'Prolific' (F)	CAgr
- 'Sunflowers'	CCCN

Asparagus (*Asparagaceae*)

RCBAM 23	WCot
from Malawi, hardy	SKHP
asparagoides 🏆H1	EShb
densiflorus 'Mazeppa'	EShb
- 'Myersii' 🏆H1	EShb SEND
- Sprengeri Group 🏆H1	SEND
falcatus	SEND
filicinus	XBlo
- var. ***giraldii***	WCot
aff. ***meioclados*** B&SWJ 8309	WCru
officinalis 'Argenteuil'	LEdu
- 'Ariane'	WHar
- 'Backlim' 🏆H4	ECrN EMil EPom
- 'Connover's Colossal' 🏆H4	CHid CSBt LHop LSRN MNHC SEND SVic WHar
- 'Crimson Pacific'	SVic
- 'Dariana'	EMil SDea
- 'Gijnlim' 🏆H4	ECrN EMil EPom SDea
- 'Guelph Millennium'	EPom
- 'Jersey Knight'	SVic
- 'Mary Washington'	LEdu
- 'Pacific 2000'	EPom LSRN SPoG
- 'Pacific Purple'	EPom SPoG
- 'Stewart's Purple'	EPom WHar
pseudoscaber 'Spitzenschleier'	CDes EShb SDix SMad WCot
schoberioides	LEdu
- B&SWJ 8814	WCru
virgatus	EShb WCot WPGP

Asperula (*Rubiaceae*)

§ ***arcadiensis*** 🏆H3	ECho WAbe WThu
aristata subsp. ***scabra***	CSpe WCot
- subsp. ***thessala***	see *A. sintenisii*
boissieri	ECho WThu
daphneola	ECho EWes WAbe
gussonei	CMea ECho SIgm WAbe
lilaciflora	ECho
- var. ***caespitosa***	see *A. lilaciflora* subsp. *lilaciflora*
§ - subsp. ***lilaciflora***	ECho
nitida	ECho EPot
- subsp. ***puberula***	see *A. sintenisii*
odorata	see *Galium odoratum*
§ ***sintenisii*** 🏆H2-3	CMea CPBP ECho ITim WAbe WHoo WThu
suberosa misapplied	see *A. arcadiensis*
taurina subsp. ***caucasica***	NLar WBor
tinctoria	CArn GPoy MHer SRms

Asphodeline (*Asphodelaceae*)

§ ***brevicaulis***	WCot XSen
liburnica	CBro CSam ELan GAbr SMad SPhx WCot WHoo XSen
§ ***lutea***	Widely available
§ - 'Gelbkerze'	EBee EPfP LRHS
- Yellow Candle	see *A. lutea* 'Gelbkerze'
taurica	ECho MBNS WCot XSen

Asphodelus (*Asphodelaceae*)

acaulis	ECho LLHF WCot XLum
§ ***aestivus***	EBee EWes GCal MBel WCot
- Cally Spear strain	GCal
albus	CArn CAvo CSpe EPPr IFoB LRHS MLHP NBid SPlb SRms WWEG XLum
brevicaulis	see *Asphodeline brevicaulis*
cerasiferus	see *A. ramosus*
fistulosus	LEdu
lusitanicus	see *A. ramosus*
luteus	see *Asphodeline lutea*
microcarpus	see *A. aestivus*
§ ***ramosus***	CPar ECho GCal WCot

Aspidistra (*Asparagaceae*)

Chen Yi 135	WCot
from China	WCot
attenuata	IBlr
- B&SWJ 377	WCru
caespitosa 'Jade Ribbons'	EShb IBlr WCot
'China Star'	CHEx IBlr WCot
daibuensis	IBlr
- B&SWJ 312b	WCru
- 'Totally Dotty' (v)	WCru
elatior 🏆H1	CBct CHEx CTsd EBak EShb ESwi IBlr LEdu MRav NPla SAPC SEND SMad WCot WWFP
- 'Akebono' (v)	WCot
- 'Asahi' (v)	IBlr WCot
- 'Hoshi-zora' (v)	IBlr WCot
- 'Milky Way' (v)	EShb ESwi IBlr MMoz SEND WCot
- 'Okame' (v)	WCot
- 'Variegata' (v) 🏆H1	CBct CHEx IBlr IFoB IFro NBir SEND WCot
- 'Variegata Exotica' (v)	XBlo
leshanensis (v)	IBlr
linearifolia 'Leopard'	ESwi IBlr WCot
lurida	EBee EShb
- 'Ginga Giant' (v)	WCot
- 'Irish Mist' (v)	IBlr
minutiflora	WCot
mushaensis B&SWJ 1953	WCru
aff. ***mushaensis*** 'Spotty Dotty' (v)	WCru
omeiensis	WCot
patentiloba	WCot
saxicola 'Uan Fat Lady'	see *A. zongbayi* 'Uan Fat Lady'
sutepensis B&SWJ 5216	WCru
typica 'China Sun'	IBlr WCot
zongbayi	WCot
§ - 'Uan Fat Lady'	ESwi WCot WCru

Asplenium ✿ (*Aspleniaceae*)

antiquum	CBty
- 'Osaka' **new**	CBty
bulbiferum misapplied	see *A.* × *lucrosum*
bulbiferum ambig. × ***oblongifolium***	GBin
bulbiferum Forst.f.	ESwi GBin
§ ***ceterach***	EFer WAbe WHer XLum

difforme* × *dimorphum	CBty
× ***ebenoides***	CBty WCot
§ × ***lucrosum*** ♀H1-2	CBty CKel ESwi
'Maori Princess'	GBin WFib
nidus ♀H1	XBlo
oblongifolium	GBin
§ ***scolopendrium*** ♀H4	Widely available
- 'Angustatum'	CBty CLAP CWCL ELon EPPr EPfP ERod EShb GBin GKev LRHS MBri MGos MMoz NEgg NHol NLar NWad SEND SPoG SRms WMoo WPnP WPtf WWEG
- Crispum Group	CLAP EFer ELan MRav MWat NBid NHol SRms SRot WFib WPGP WPtf
- - 'Crispum Bolton's Nobile' ♀H4	WFib
- - 'Golden Queen'	CLAP
- Crispum Cristatum Group	CLAP MMuc SEND
- Crispum Fimbriatum Group	CLAP
- Cristatum Group	CBty CLAP CWCL EBee ELan ELon EPfP LAst LRHS MBri MGos MMoz MRav MWhi NHol NLar SPad SPer SPoG SRms SRot SWat WFib WMoo WPnP WWEG
- Fimbriatum Group	CLAP LRHS
- 'Furcatum'	CBty CDTJ CLAP EBee NHol NLar SBod
- 'Kaye's Lacerated' ♀H4	CLAP EFer WFib
- Laceratum Group	CLAP
- Marginatum Group	EFer
- 'Muricatum'	CLAP ELan GBin MRav MWhi NBid NHol WFib
- 'Ramocristatum'	CLAP
- Ramomarginatum Group	CLAP ELan
- 'Sagittatoprojectum Sclater'	WFib
- Undulatum Group	CBty CDTJ CLAP EBee EPfP EUJe LRHS MMoz MMuc NBir NEgg NHol NLar SEND SRms WIvy WPnP XLum
- Undulatum Cristatum Group	CLAP
trichomanes ♀H4	Widely available
- Cristatum Group	SRms
- Incisum Group	EBee EFer NOrc SRms WAbe
- 'Ramocristatum'	WAbe

Astartea (*Myrtaceae*)

fascicularis	ECou

Astelia (*Asteliaceae*)

alpina	IBlr
banksii	CBcs CDoC CHEx CSpe EBee IBal LRHS LSRN MGos SBod SCoo SHil SLim WCot
§ ***chathamica*** ♀H3	Widely available
- 'Silver Spear'	see *A. chathamica*
chathamica* × *fragrans	ECou
cunninghamii	see *A. solandri*
fragrans	CBcs CCon EBee ECou GCal IBlr LEdu
graminea	GCal
grandis	CBcs IBlr LEdu
nervosa	ECou IBlr LEdu LSRN SAPC
- 'Alpine Ruby'	IBlr
- 'Bronze Giant'	IBlr
- 'Silver Sabre'	IBlr
- 'Westland'	CBcs CDoC CKno COlW CTsd EBee GCal IBlr LEdu LHop LRHS LSRN MGos MRav NSoo NSti SEND SHil SLim SPad SPlb SPoG SWvt WCot
nivicola 'Golden Gem'	IBlr
- 'Red Gem'	GCal LEdu
petriei	IBlr
'Red Devil'	CDoC CSpe ECou GBin IBoy LRHS MHol SHil WCot WHer
'Silver Mound'	EPfP
'Silver Shadow' **new**	CDoC WCot
§ ***solandri***	ECou IBlr

Aster ✿ (*Asteraceae*)

acris	see *A. sedifolius*
ageratoides	CPou CPrp LRHS WOld
- 'Ashvi'	WCot WOld
- 'Asran'	CHVG ECtt EHoe EPPr EWes LSou MMuc MPie WBrk WCot WOld XLum
- 'Ezo Murasaki' **new**	NDov WCot
- 'Harry Smith'	NDov WWEG
- 'Little Theo' **new**	EBee
- 'Stardust'	WOld
- 'Starshine'PBR	ECtt EPPr IBoy MPie WCot
alpigenus* var. *alpigenus	LLHF
- var. ***haydenii***	LLHF
alpinus ♀H4	EBee ECho EPfP GJos LPot MAsh SRms XSen
- var ***albus***	EDAr EPfP GKev LRHS NBro NLar SPoG
- Dark Beauty	see *A. alpinus* 'Dunkle Schöne'
§ 'Dunkle Schöne'	EBee EDAr LDai LRHS SBea SPoG SRms
- 'Goliath'	EBee EPfP LRHS NBro NLar SPlb
- 'Happy End'	NBre NLar SPoG SRms XLum
- 'Pinkie'	EBee EDAr EPfP LRHS NLar
- 'Trimix'	ECho NBir SRms
- 'White Beauty'	SRms
amelloides	see *Felicia amelloides*
amellus	CArn LRHS LSou WMoo
- 'Blue King'	EBee GBuc MAvo NWsh SMrm SWvt
- 'Breslau'	LRHS MAvo
- 'Brilliant'	CPrp ECtt EPPr GBuc LAst LRHS LSou MAvo MBNS MNFA MRav MWat SMrm SMrs SPer SRGP WHoo WOld
- 'Forncett Flourish'	WCot WOld
- 'Framfieldii' ♀H4	MNFA NDov WCot WOld
- 'Gründer'	LRHS MAvo WHil WOld
- 'Jacqueline Genebrier' ♀H4	ELon GBuc NDov WOld
- 'Jubilee'	LRHS
- 'King George' ♀H4	Widely available
- 'Kobold'	LRHS WOld
- 'Lac de Genève'	LRHS WCot
- 'Lady Hindlip'	CSam
- 'Louise'	MBrN SBch
- 'Mira'	MNrw
- 'Moerheim Gem'	LRHS WOld
- 'Nocturne'	WCot WOld
- Pink Zenith	see *A. amellus* 'Rosa Erfüllung'
§ - 'Rosa Erfüllung'	CMac ECtt ELan ELon EPPr EPfP GBin GBuc GMaP IVic LAst LHop LRHS LSou MCot MRav NWsh SPhx SRGP SWvt WCot WMnd WOld
- 'Rotfeuer'	ELon GQue WCot

	- 'Rudolph Goethe'	ECtt ELan EMil EPPr EPfP GBee IKil LAst LRHS SBHP SRGP WMoo WOld WSpi WWEG
	- 'Silbersee'	CSam LRHS
	- 'Sonia'	GBuc LRHS MNFA MRav WOld
	- 'Sonora'	EBee LHop LPla MNrw SMrm SPhx SRGP WKif WOld
	- 'Sternkugel'	WOld
	- 'Vanity'	LRHS WOld
§	- 'Veilchenkönigin' ♀H4	Widely available
N	- Violet Queen	see *A. amellus* 'Veilchenkönigin'
	- 'Weltfriede'	WOld
	× ***amethystinus***	MNrw WCot
	'Anita Pfeiffer'	LRHS
	'Anja's Choice'	EBee LHop MSpe WOld
	asperulus misapplied	see *A. peduncularis*
	'Blue Autumn'	NCGa
	'Blue Moon' PBR **new**	WOld
	'Blütenregen'	WCot
	capensis 'Variegatus'	see *Felicia amelloides* variegated
§	***carolinianus***	EShb XEll
	'Cassandra'	NCGa
	'Cheavers'	LRHS
	'Chesters Star'	MAvo WOld
	ciliolatus	LRHS
	'Claudia'	WBrk
	'Climax' misapplied	see *A. laevis* 'Arcturus', *A. laevis* 'Calliope'
	'Climax' ambig.	CAby CElw ELan GCal GQue MMuc MRav NBid SMrm XLum
	'Climax' Vicary Gibbs	WOld
	coelestis	see *Felicia amelloides*
	coloradoensis	GKev LLHF NSla
	'Connecticut Snow Flurry'	see *A. ericoides* f. *prostratus* 'Snow Flurry'
	conspicuus	EBee
	'Coombe Fishacre' ♀H4	CAby COlW CSam EBee ELan GBuc GCal LPla LRHS MCot MNFA MNrw MRav NCGa NLar SMrs WCot WHoo WOld WSpi
	cordifolius	LRHS
	- 'Aldebaran'	NDov WOld
	- 'Chieftain' ♀H4	CAby MNrw SPhx WOld
	- 'Elegans'	CSam EBee LRHS WMnd WOld
	- 'Ideal'	NLar XLum
	- 'Silver Spray'	CKno CPrp ECtt ELon GMaP GQue MHom MWat NBre SRGP WOld XLum
	- 'Sweet Lavender' ♀H4	EBee LRHS WOld
	- 'White Chief'	WOld
	corymbosus	see *A. divaricatus*
	'Cotswold Gem'	WCot WOld
	diffusus	see *A. lateriflorus*
	diplostephioides	EDAr EPPr EPfP GBin GBuc IKil LRHS MBNS MMHG NBre NLar SPlb WPtf
§	***divaricatus***	Widely available
§	- 'Eastern Star'	NCGa WCot WOld
	- Raiche form	see *A. divaricatus* 'Eastern Star'
	- 'Tradescant'	IMou MNrw
	'Duchess' (mixed) **new**	CWCL
N	***dumosus***	CExl
	- 'Biteliness'	NBre NLar
	- Sapphire = 'Kiesapphire' PBR	CHel CPrp ELon EWTr LHop LRHS LSRN MBri MHol NEgg SRGP SRkn SWvt
	'Dwarf Barbados'	EPfP LRHS
	'Early Blue' **new**	IBoy
	ericoides	CKno MCot NBre NOrc WWEG
	- 'Blue Star' ♀H4	CPrp CSam EBee LRHS NLar WMnd WOld WWEG
	- 'Blue Wonder'	XLum
	- 'Brimstone' ♀H4	MRav NBre WOld
	- 'Cinderella'	CPrp EBee LRHS NSti WOld WWEG
	- 'Constance'	WOld
	- 'Erlkönig'	ECGP EPri EShb GCal GQue LAst LRHS NGdn NLar NPnk SPer SWat WCot WMnd WOld XLum
	- 'Esther'	CPrp ELan NCGa SMrm WOld
	- 'First Snow' **new**	WCot
	- 'Golden Spray' ♀H4	EBee EPfP GMaP GQue NLar NSoo WMnd WOld
	- 'Herbstmyrte'	CSam LRHS
	- 'Hon. Edith Gibbs'	WOld
	- 'Monte Cassino'	see *A. pilosus* var. *pringlei* 'Monte Cassino'
	- 'Pink Cloud' ♀H4	CHVG COlW CPrp ECtt EPfP EPri EShb GBuc GCal LAst LEdu LRHS MNFA MSpe NCGa NHol NOrc NWad SRGP SWat WMnd WOld WSpi WWEG
	- f. ***prostratus***	EPot GBuc GQue XSen
§	- - 'Snow Flurry' ♀H4	CAby CMea EBee ECtt GBuc IMou LEdu LPla MAvo MNrw MWat NLar SMrm WCot WHoo WMnd WOld WOut XLum
	- 'Rosy Veil'	MHom NBir NGdn
	- 'Schneegitter'	LRHS WCot XSen
	- 'Schneetanne'	NBre
	- 'Star Shower'	LRHS
	- 'Sulphurea'	MWat
	- 'Vimmer's Delight'	WCot
	- 'White Heather'	CPrp NLar WMnd WOld WSpi
	- 'Yvette Richardson'	MHom WOld WWEG
	falcatus	EBee WCot
	- var. ***commutatus***	WCot
	'Fanny's Fall'	see *A. oblongifolius* 'Fanny's'
§	***flaccidus***	LRHS
	foliaceus from Montana	EPPr
	- var. ***parryi***	EBee
	× ***frikartii***	CMac EBee ELan EPfP EShb LPio MRav SMrm SWvt
	- 'Eiger'	WOld
	- 'Flora's Delight'	GCal LRHS MNrw MSpe NLar WOld WWEG
	- 'Jungfrau'	CWGN EPPr GBuc GMaP GQue LRHS MCot MRav NLar SPhx WOld WWEG
N	- 'Mönch' ♀H4	Widely available
	- Wonder of Stafa	see *A.* × *frikartii* 'Wunder von Stäfa'
§	- 'Wunder von Stäfa' ♀H4	CEnd CExl CKno ECtt ELan ELon EPfP GBuc GMaP IPot LHop LPio LRHS LSRN LSou MBNS MCot MHol MRav NBir NDov NLar SWvt WCot WMnd WOld WWEG XLum
	furcatus	XLum
	'Glow in the Dark'	CDes MAvo MSpe WCot WOld
	greatae	EBee
	'Herfstweelde'	CPrp EBee WOld
§	× ***herveyi***	CCon CPrp CSam ECtt ELan EPfP GCal GLog LEdu LLWP LRHS MMuc MNFA MSpe NLar NSti SDix SPer SPhx SPoG SRGP WBor WCot WMnd WOld WPtf
	himalaicus	GKev
	'Hon. Vicary Gibbs' (*ericoides* hybrid)	WOld WOut
	hybridus luteus	see *Solidago* × *luteus*

	'Ivy House'	ECtt
	'Kylie' ♀H4	CAby CDes CHVG CPrp ECtt LRHS LSRN MHom NCGa SPhx SRGP WBor WBrk WCot WHil WOld
	laevis	LEdu NBre NLar SPhx
§	- 'Arcturus'	CCon CElw LRHS MAvo MHom MNrw NBir NCGa NSti WCot WMnd WOld WWEG WWlt XLum
	- 'Blauhügel'	LPla NDov
§	- 'Calliope'	Widely available
	- 'Cally Compact'	GQue NLar
	- var. ***geyeri***	MNrw WOut
	- 'Nightshade'	MAvo MNrw WBrk WOld
	- 'Vesta'	WOld
	- white-flowered	WOld
	lanceolatus Willd.	EPPr NCGa
	- 'Edwin Beckett'	CBre MHom MNrw WOld
§	***lateriflorus***	WOld
	- 'Bleke Bet'	WCot WOld
	- 'Buck's Fizz'	ELan NLar WOld
	- 'Chloe'	CSam NCGa
	- 'Datschi'	XLum
	- var. ***horizontalis*** ♀H4	CCon CMHG CPrp CSam EBee ECtt EHoe ELan EPfP GAbr LRHS MBri MCot MNFA MRav MWat NBro NCGa NGdn NWad SDix SPer SPlb SRms SRot SWat WKif WOld WPtf
	- 'Jan'	WOld
	- 'Lady in Black'	Widely available
	- 'Lovely'	CSam LRHS NBre SRGP WCot
	- 'Prince'	Widely available
	laterifolius 'Snow Flurry'	see *A. ericoides* f. *prostratus* 'Snow Flurry'
	'Les Moutiers'	MHom MNrw WBrk WOld
§	***linosyris***	EPfP EWes GBin LRHS MAvo NLar SPhx WHer WOld XLum
	- 'Gold Dust' **new**	GBin
	- 'Goldilocks'	see *A. linosyris*
	'Little Carlow' (*cordifolius* hybrid) ♀H4	Widely available
	'Little Dorrit' (*cordifolius* hybrid)	ECtt NWsh WOld
	macrophyllus	ELan GBee LRHS MSpe NLar WOld
	- 'Albus'	EPPr WOld
	- 'Twilight'	see *A.* × *herveyi*
	mongolicus	see *Kalimeris mongolica*
	'Mrs Dean'	ECtt
	natalensis	see *Felicia rosulata*
	'Natasha'	LSRN
	(Newstars Series) 'Newstars Fantasy' **new**	WCot
	- 'Newstars Glory' **new**	WCot
	'Nicholas' **new**	WCot
	'Noreen'	MAvo
	novae-angliae	CArn WOld
	- 'Alex Deamon'	ELon MAvo WOld
	- 'Anabelle de Chazal'	ECtt ELon MAvo SMrs WBrk WOld
	- 'Andenken an Alma Pötschke'	Widely available
	- 'Andenken an Paul Gerber'	ECtt ELon LHop MAvo MHom MNrw NDov WOld
	- 'Augusta'	ELon MAvo WBrk WOld
	- Autumn Snow	see *A. novae-angliae* 'Herbstschnee'
	- 'Barr's Blue'	CAby CMac EBee ECtt ELon EPfP GCra MAvo MHom MMuc MWat NLar NWsh SEND SMrs SPer SRms WBrk WMoo WOld
	- 'Barr's Pink'	CBre CMac EBee ECtt ELon EPfP MAvo MCot MHom MLHP MMuc MPie MWat NLar SEND WBrk WOld WSFF WSpi
*	- 'Barr's Purple'	ECtt WBrk WCFE WOld
	- 'Barr's Violet'	CHVG ECtt MAvo MHom SRms WBrk WCot WHal WHoo WHrl WMoo WOld WWEG
	- 'Bishop Colenso'	CAby
	- 'Brockamin'	MNrw WBrk
	- 'Brockamin Margaret'	WOld
	- 'Christopher Harbutt'	LEdu SRGP WBrk
	- 'Colwall Century'	MAvo WBrk WOld
	- 'Colwall Constellation'	MAvo WBrk WOld
	- 'Colwall Galaxy'	MAvo WBrk WHrl WOld
	- 'Colwall Orbit'	ECtt ELon MAvo WOld
	- 'Connie' **new**	MNrw
	- 'Crimson Beauty'	CAby ELon MAvo MHer MHom MNrw MWat WBrk WOld
	- 'Dapper Tapper'	WCot
	- 'Evensong'	ECtt MAvo WBrk WOld
	- 'Festival'	WBrk
	- 'Foxy Emily'	ECtt MAvo WOld
	- 'Harrington's Pink' ♀H4	Widely available
	- 'Helen Picton'	CSam ECtt ELon MAvo MBrN MHer MHom MWat NWsh WBrk WOld
§	- 'Herbstschnee'	Widely available
	- 'James Ritchie'	ELon LLHF MAvo WHoo WOld
	- 'John Davies'	MAvo MNrw WHil WOld
	- 'Jon Baker' **new**	WBrk
	- 'Kate Deamon'	WOld
	- 'Lachsglut'	ELon MAvo WCot WOld
	- 'Ladies Day'	WOld
	- 'Little Bella' **new**	WOld
	- 'Lou Williams'	CAby ECtt ELon MAvo MNrw MWat SMrs WHil WOld
I	- 'Lucida'	MAvo WHal WOld
	- 'Lucinda'	ECtt
	- 'Lye End Beauty'	CKno ECtt ELon LLWP MAvo MHom MNFA MNrw MWat SBch SMrs WBrk WCot WHoo WMoo WOld
	- 'Mabelle' **new**	NDov
	- 'Marina Wolkonsky'	CAby EBee ECtt ELon EWes LHop MAvo MNrw NLar SMrs SPhx WBrk WCot WKif WOld WWEG
	- 'Millennium Star'	ECtt ELon MAvo WOld
	- 'Miss K.E. Mash'	ECtt MAvo MHom SRGP WBrk WOld WWTO
	- 'Mrs S.T. Wright'	CAby CPrp CTri ECtt EWes MAvo MBrN MHom MNFA MNrw SMrs SRGP WOld WWEG
	- 'Mrs S.W. Stern'	WOld
	- 'Naomi'	MAvo WOld
	- 'Pink Parfait'	CSam ECtt LRHS MAvo NBre NGdn SMrs SRms WBrk WCot WOld
	- 'Pink Victor'	CTri MAvo SRms WMoo
	- 'Pride of Rougham'	EWes WBrk
	- 'Primrose Upward'	CAby MAvo MNrw NDov NWsh WCot WOld
	- 'Purple Cloud'	CSam ELon LHop MAvo MHer MHom MWat NBre NGdn WBrk WHal WOld WWEG
I	- 'Purple Dome'	Widely available
	- 'Quinton Menzies'	CSam ELon MAvo WBrk WOld WWEG
	- 'Red Cloud'	ELon MAvo MHer NBre SMrm WBrk WOld
	- 'Rosa Sieger' ♀H4	CAby CBre CPrp CSam ECtt ELon GMaP GQue MAvo MHom MNrw

		NGdn SPhx WBor WBrk WHoo
		WOld WWEG XLum
	- 'Rose Williams'	MAvo SBch WOld WOut
	- 'Röter Stern'	ECtt MAvo WBrk WOld
	- 'Rougham Pink' **new**	WBrk
	- 'Rougham Purple'	EWes
	- 'Rougham Violet' **new**	WBrk
	- 'Rubinschatz'	MAvo MHom MWat NBre NWsh
		SRms WOld XLum
	- 'Rudelsburg'	EBee ECtt MAvo WBrk
	- 'Saint Michael's'	WOld
	- 'Sayer's Croft'	ECtt ELon LRHS MHom MWat
		WCot WHil WHoo WOld WOut
	- September Ruby	see *A. novae-angliae*
		'Septemberrubin'
§	- 'Septemberrubin'	CMea ECtt ELon EPfP EWTr IFoB
		LEdu LHop LSou MBel MNFA MRav
		NWsh SMrs SPhx SRGP WOld WSpi
		XLum
	- 'Treasure'	CBre EBee ECtt ELon EWes LRHS
		MAvo NBre SMrm SMrs SPhx SRGP
		WBrk WMoo WOld
	- 'Vibrant Dome'PBR	MAvo NLar
	- 'Violet Dusk' **new**	WBrk
	- 'Violet Haze'	CMea ELon WBrk
	- 'Violetta'	ECtt ELon LRHS LSou MAvo MHom
		MNFA MNrw NWsh SMrs SPhx
		WHil WHoo WKif WOld
	- 'W. Bowman'	ECtt MNrw WOld
	- 'Wow'	CAby ELon SMrm
	'Novemberlaan' **new**	MSpe
N	***novi-belgii***	WHer
	- 'Ada Ballard'	CFis CMac EBee LDai LHop LRHS
		LSRN NBre NEgg SMrm SMrs SPer
		SRGP WMoo WOld WSpi WWEG
	- 'Albanian'	WOld
	- 'Alderman Vokes'	WOld
	- 'Algar's Pride'	ECtt WOld WWEG
	- 'Alice Haslam'	CMac EBee ECtt ELan LRHS MJak
		NEgg NLar NOrc SRGP SRms WCAu
		WOld WWEG
	- 'Angela Peel'	EBee LRHS
	- 'Anita Ballard'	WOld
	- 'Anita Webb'	NBir WOld
	- 'Anneke'	LRHS NLar NSoo SRGP SRkn WOld
	- 'Apollo'	LRHS MWat NEgg NLar WOld
	- 'Applc Blossom'	WOld
	- 'Audrey'	CMac ECtt GMaP LRHS LSRN MBNS
		NEgg NGdn NOrc SBea SRGP SRms
		WOld
	- 'Autumn Beauty'	WOld
	- 'Autumn Days'	WOld
	- 'Autumn Glory'	WOld
	- 'Autumn Rose'	SMrs WOld
	- 'Baby Climax'	WOld
	- 'Bahamas' (Island Series)	EPfP EWll LBMP LRHS LSou NLar
		NWsh SRms SWvt WCot WHil
	- 'Barbados' (Island Series)	EPfP LRHS LSou MBri NLar SWvt
		WCot
	- 'Beauty of Colwall'	WOld
	- 'Beechwood Challenger'	MPie WOld
	- 'Beechwood Charm'	WOld
	- 'Beechwood Rival'	CTri EBee LRHS MBri WOld XEll
	- 'Blandie'	CTri EPfP SRGP WOld
	- 'Blauglut'	WOld
	- 'Blue Baby'	CMac
	- 'Blue Bouquet'	CTri SRms WOld
	- 'Blue Boy'	WOld WWEG
	- 'Blue Danube'	SMrs WOld

- 'Blue Eyes'	SMrs WOld
- 'Blue Gown'	CCse GCal GQue WOld WOut
- 'Blue Lagoon'	CFis CMea ELan LSRN MBri NPnk
	SMrs SRGP WBrk WOld
- 'Blue Patrol'	WOld
- 'Blue Radiance'	WOld
- 'Blue Spire'	WOld
- 'Boningale Blue'	WOld
- 'Boningale White'	NDov WOld
- 'Bridesmaid'	WOld
- 'Bridgette'	NPnk
- 'Bright Eyes'	SRGP WOld
- 'Brightest and Best'	WOld
- 'Brigitte'	NLar
- 'Cameo'	WOld
- 'Cantab'	WOld
- 'Carlingcott'	WOld
- 'Carnival'	CMac EBee ECtt IVic LDai LRHS
	MMHG NEgg NOrc SMrs SRGP
	WOld
- 'Cecily'	WOld WWEG
- 'Charles Wilson'	CFis WOld
- 'Chatterbox'	ELan EPfP LPot LRHS MRav MWat
	NEgg NLar WHar WOld
- 'Chelwood'	WOld
- 'Chequers'	CElw EBee MBNS NEgg SRGP WOld
- 'Christina'	see *A. novi-belgii* 'Kristina'
- 'Christine Soanes'	WOld
- 'Cliff Lewis'	WOld
- 'Climax Albus'	see *A.* 'White Climax'
- 'Cloudy Blue'	WOld
- 'Colonel F.R. Durham'	WOld
- 'Coombe Gladys'	WOld
- 'Coombe Margaret'	WOld
- 'Coombe Radiance'	WOld
- 'Coombe Ronald'	MWat WOld
- 'Coombe Rosemary'	ECtt LRHS NLar WBor WOld
- 'Coombe Violet'	MWat WOld
- 'Countess of Dudley'	CFis WOld
- 'Court Herald'	WOld
- 'Crimson Brocade'	CCon EBee ECtt ELan EPfP LRHS
	MBri NDov NLar NSoo SPoG SRGP
	WSpi
- 'Dandy'	CMac ELan LRHS NBir NEgg NGdn
	SRGP WOld
- 'Daniela'	SRms WBrk WOld
- 'Daphne Anne'	WOld
- 'Dauerblau'	WOld
- 'Davey's True Blue'	CTri SMrs WOld XLum
- 'David Murray'	WOld
- 'Dazzler'	ECtt WOld WWEG
- Debbie = 'Dasdebi'	LRHS
(Mystery Lady Series) (d)	
- Demi = 'Dasdem'PBR	LRHS
(Mystery Lady Series) (d)	
- 'Destiny'	WOld
- 'Diana'	NWsh
- 'Diana Watts'	WOld
- 'Dietgard'	ELon WOld WWEG
- 'Dolly'	CElw NBir SRms WOld WWEG
- 'Dora Chiswell'	WOld
- 'Dusky Maid'	ELon WOld
- 'Dwarf Ibiza'	LRHS
- 'Elizabeth'	CAby CElw
- 'Elizabeth Hutton'	WOld
- 'Elsie Dale'	WOld
- 'Elta'	WOld
- 'Erica'	CElw MWat WOld
- 'Ernest Ballard'	WOld

- 'Eva'	ELon SRms WOld
- 'Eventide'	CElw CTri LSRN WOld
- 'Fair Lady'	LRHS MWat WOld
- 'Faith'	WOld
- 'Farncombe Lilac'	NCot
- 'Farncombe Wine Red'	NCot
- 'Fellowship' ♀H4	CCon CDes CHVG COIW ECtt ELon LEdu MAvo MBri MMuc MNrw NCGa SHar SMrs SRGP SRms WBrk WCot WOld WWEG
- 'Flamingo'	EBee LRHS WOld
- 'Freda Ballard'	CFis ECtt GMaP LHop LRHS MWat SRGP WCAu WNew WOld WWEG
- 'Freya'	CElw LSRN WOld WSHC
- 'Fuldatal'	WOld
- 'Gayborder Blue'	WOld
- 'Gayborder Royal'	CCon WOld
- 'Goliath'	WOld
- 'Grey Lady'	WOld WWEG
- 'Guardsman'	WOld
- 'Gulliver'	WOld WWEG
- 'Gurney Slade'	WOld
- 'Guy Ballard'	WOld
- 'Harrison's Blue'	MWat SMrs WOld
- 'Heinz Richard'	CFis COIW LRHS MHer NBir NBre NGdn SBch SMrs SRGP SRms WOld WWEG
- 'Helen'	ELon WOld
- 'Helen Ballard'	SRms WOld
- 'Herbstgruss vom Bresserhof'	NBre NLar WOld
- 'Herbstpurzel'	WOld
- 'Hilda Ballard'	WOld
- 'Ibiza'	LRHS WCot
- 'Ilse Brensell'	WOld WWEG
- Ingrid = 'Dasing' (Mystery Lady Series) (d)	LRHS
- 'Irene'	WOld
- 'Janet Watts'	WOld
- 'Jean'	ELon MWat SRms WOld
- 'Jean Gyte'	WOld
- 'Jeanette'	SRms WOld
- 'Jenny'	Widely available
- Jessica = 'Dasjes'PBR (Mystery Lady Series) (d)	LRHS
- 'Jollity'	WOld
- 'Jugendstil' **new**	XLum
- 'Julia'	WOld
- 'Karminkuppel'	NBre
- 'Kassel'	SRms WOld
- Katharine = 'Daskat' (Mystery Lady Series) (d)	LRHS
- 'King of the Belgians'	WOld
§ - 'Kristina'	COIW EPPr ITim LRHS MRav NBir WCot WOld WWEG
- 'Lady Frances'	SRms WOld
- 'Lady in Blue'	CSBt EBee ECtt ELan EPPr EPfP LAst LEdu LHop LRHS MBNS MBri MLHP MWat NEgg NGdn NSoo NWad SGbt SPer SPoG SRGP SRms SWat SWvt WCAu WHar WOld WWEG
- 'Lassie'	CElw MWat WOld
- 'Lavender Dream'	WOld
- 'Lawrence Chiswell'	WOld
- 'Lederstrumpf'	NDov
- 'Lisa Dawn'	ECtt SMrs WOld
- 'Little Boy Blue'	LRHS NBre SRms WOld XLum
- 'Little Man in Blue'	WOld WWEG

- 'Little Pink Beauty'	COIW ECtt ELan EPfP EWTr IBoy ITim LAst LHop LRHS MBNS MJak NEgg NGdn NWad SBea SPer SRGP SRms STes WHar WHil WOld WWEG
- 'Little Pink Lady'	LRHS SRms WOld
- 'Little Pink Pyramid'	SRms WOld WWEG
- 'Little Red Boy'	WOld
- 'Little Treasure'	WOld
- 'Madge Cato'	SRms WOld
- 'Mammoth'	WOld
- 'Margery Bennett'	WOld
- 'Marie Ballard'	Widely available
- 'Marie's Pretty Please'	WOld
- 'Marjorie'	LSRN SPoG SRGP WOld XLum
- 'Mary Ann Neil'	SMrs SRms
- 'Mary Deane'	WOld
- 'Mauve Magic'	MWat SRms WOld WWEG
- 'Melbourne Belle'	WOld
- 'Melbourne Magnet'	WOld
- 'Midget'	WOld
- 'Mistress Quickly'	ECtt MCot SMrs WOld WWEG
- 'Mittelmeer'	NDov WOld XLum
- 'Mount Everest'	LHop NCGa NSoo SPhx WOld WWEG
- 'Mrs Leo Hunter'	WOld
- 'Neron'	MNrw NDov
- 'Nesthäkchen'	WOld
- 'Newton's Pink'	WOld
- 'Niobe'	WOld
- 'Norman's Jubilee'	EBee EPfP LRHS NBir NEgg SMrs WOld WWEG
- 'Nursteed Charm'	WOld
- 'Oktoberschneekuppel'	WOld
- 'Pamela'	WOld
- 'Patricia Ballard'	CBcs CCon CHab CMac CSBt EBee GCra GMaP LRHS MHer MWat MWhi NBir NLar NPer NSoo NWad SGol SMrs SPer SRGP WNew WOld WWEG
- 'Peace'	WOld
- 'Percy Thrower'	ECtt SMrs WOld
- 'Peter Chiswell'	SRms WOld
- 'Peter Harrison'	GMaP NBir WMnd WOld XLum
- 'Peter Pan'	LRHS NLar
- 'Picture'	NBre
- 'Pink Lace'	MBNS WOld
- 'Plenty'	WOld
- 'Porzellan'	CElw CFis COIW EBee ECtt MAvo MBNS MNrw NGdn SMrs SRGP WCot WOld
- 'Pride of Colwall'	SRms WOld
- 'Priory Blush'	CElw WOld
- 'Professor Anton Kippenberg'	CFis EPfP GMaP LLWP LRHS MNrw MRav NBre NLar SPer SRGP SRms SWvt WMnd WOld WWEG XLum
- 'Prosperity'	NBre WOld
- 'Purple Dome'	CFis ELan LEdu LSRN MHer MWat SHar SRkn WOld WOut
- 'Queen Mary'	WOld
- 'Ralph Picton'	WOld
- 'Rector'	see *A. novi-belgii* 'The Rector'
- 'Red Robin'	MSpe MWat
- 'Red Sunset'	SRms WOld
- 'Rembrandt'	ECtt LDai NEgg NGdn SMrs SRGP
- 'Remembrance'	MWat SRms WOld WWEG
- 'Reverend Vincent Dale'	WOld
- 'Richness'	WOld
- 'Rose Bonnet'	CSBt SPlb WOld
- 'Roseanne'	WOld

- 'Rosebud' ambig.	WOld WWEG
- 'Rosenquartz'	NLar
- 'Rosenwichtel'	LRHS NLar WOld WWEG
- 'Royal Ruby'	CFis EBee ECtt LRHS NLar WOld WWEG
- 'Royal Velvet'	WOld
- 'Rozika'	WOld
- 'Rufus'	WOld
- 'Sailor Boy'	NCGa
- 'Saint Egwyn'	WOld
- 'Sam Banham'	MNrw WOld
- 'Samoa' (Island Series)	CTsd EPfP EUJe EWll LRHS LSou MBri NLar NPri SRms WCot
- 'Sandford White Swan'	GBuc MHom WOld WWEG
- 'Sarah Ballard'	LRHS SRGP WOld
§ - 'Schneekissen'	ECtt ELan EPfP EWTr GMaP LRHS MBNS MHer MJak NSoo NWsh SPer SRGP SWvt WHar WOld WWEG XLum
- 'Schneezicklein'	GBin
- 'Schöne von Dietlikon'	CKno MWat WOld XLum
- 'Schoolgirl'	WOld WWEG
- 'Sheena'	WOld
- 'Silberblaukissen'	WOld
- Snow Cushion	see *A. novi-belgii* 'Schneekissen'
- 'Snowsprite'	CSBt ELan LRHS MWat NEgg NLar NOrc SGbt SGol SMrs SRGP SRms SWat WOld
- 'Sonata'	GMaP WOld
- 'Sophia'	MWat SMrs WOld
- 'Starlight'	ECtt IBoy NLar NSoo WRHF
- 'Steinebrück'	WOld
- 'Sterling Silver'	WOld
- 'Sun Queen' **new**	WOld
- 'Sunset'	WOld
- 'Susan'	WOld
- 'Sweet Briar'	CElw WOld
- 'Tapestry'	WOld
- 'Terry's Pride'	EBee SRGP WOld WWEG
- 'The Archbishop'	ECtt WOld XEll
- 'The Bishop'	WOld
- 'The Cardinal'	WOld
- 'The Dean'	WOld
§ - 'The Rector'	WOld
- 'The Sexton'	WOld
- 'Thundercloud'	CAby WOld
- 'Timsbury'	CElw SRms WOld WWEG
- 'Tovarich'	WOld
- 'Trudi Ann'	NBir WOld
- 'Twinkle'	WOld
- 'Victor'	WOld
- 'Vignem'	NSti
- 'Violet Lady'	WOld
- 'Violetta'	SMrs
- 'Waterperry'	MWat WBrk WOld
- 'White Ladies'	CBcs CHab ECtt GCra GMaP LRHS MMuc MWat NLar NOrc SPer SRGP XLum
- 'White Swan'	ECtt
- 'White Wings'	MWat WOld
- 'Winston S. Churchill'	CTri ELan EPfP GMaP IKil LRHS MCot MWat SPer SPlb SPoG SRGP WOld WSpi
oblongifolius	NWsh WOld XSen
§ - 'Fanny's'	CAby CPrp ECtt GCal GQue MNFA NWad SPoG SRGP WCot WOld
- 'October Skies' **new**	EBee MNrw
occidentalis KM Z-80-02 **new**	EBee
'Ochtendgloren' (*pringlei* hybrid) ♀^{H4}	CDes CPrp CSam EBee ECtt EPPr EWes GBuc MHom MNrw MSpe NCGa SMrm WCot WHal WOld WWEG
Octoberlight	see *A.* 'Oktoberlicht'
§ 'Oktoberlicht'	LRHS MNrw NCGa SMrm WOld
oolentangiensis	LRHS NLar
'Orchidee'	EBee EPri EWTr EWes MAvo
'Orpheus'	MNrw WBrk
pappei	see *Felicia amoena*
'Pearl Star'	WOld
§ ***peduncularis***	CAby EBee EPPr LPla LRHS MBri NDov WOld
petiolatus	see *Felicia petiolata*
'Photograph' ♀^{H4}	CAby CHVG CSam EBee ECtt ELon LRHS MAvo MHom NPnk SMrm WOld
§ ***pilosus*** var. ***demotus*** ♀^{H4}	EBee EWes MRav NWad WOld
§ - var. ***pringlei*** 'Monte Cassino' ♀^{H4}	CHid CSBt EPfP GQue IPot LHop LPot LRHS MBNS MRav MWat SMrm SPer SPhx SRGP WOld WSpi WWEG XLum
- - 'October Glory'	CCse NDov
- - 'Phoebe'	WOld
- - 'Pink Cushion'	WCot
'Pink Star'	CMea ECtt ELon GMaP LRHS MNFA MRav MWat NDov NSti SBch SPhx WHoo WOld WOut XLum
'Pixie Dark Eye' (*ericoides* hybrid)	CDes EBee WCot
'Pixie Red Eye' (*ericoides* hybrid)	WCot
'Prairie Lavender'	WOld
'Prairie Pink'	WOld
'Prairie Purple'	WOld
'Prairie Violet'	WOld
'Primrose Path'	EBee LEdu MNrw NCGa WBrk WCot WOld
ptarmicoides	see *Solidago ptarmicoides*
puniceus	NBre XLum
purdomii	see *A. flaccidus*
pyrenaeus 'Lutetia'	CPrp EBee GBuc GCal GMaP MAvo MHom MNFA MNrw MWat NCGa NDov NLar SPoG SRGP WCAu WKif WOld WWEG XLum
radula	CSam EPPr EWes IMou LPla MAvo MNrw NBre NLar WOld WSHC
- 'August Sky' **new**	WCot
'Ringdove' (*ericoides* hybrid) ♀^{H4}	CKno CPrp MAvo MCot MHom MNFA NCGa NSti SRGP WCot WOld
'Rosa Star'	WOld
'Rose Queen'	MAvo
rotundifolius 'Variegatus'	see *Felicia amelloides* variegated
rugulosus 'Asrugo'	EBee
sagittifolius Wed.	XLum
× ***salignus***	WOld
- Scottish form	WOld
* ***sativus atrocaeruleus***	LRHS
§ ***scaber***	EBee NWsh WCot
scandens	see *A. carolinianus*
schreberi	CCon EPPr EWes LEdu MAvo MSpe NBre NCGa NWsh WBor WCot WOld
'Sea Spray' **new**	WCot
§ ***sedifolius***	ECtt ELan ELon GAbr GQue LEdu MAvo MWat NBid NSti SDix SEND SPoG WCot WMnd WOld WWlt

– RCB AM -5	WCot
– 'Nanus'	CExl ELan GCal LRHS MHom MNFA MRav NBir NLar NWsh SPer WCot WMnd WOld WSpi XLum XSen
– 'Roseus'	IMou LRHS
§ ***sibiricus***	NBre NLar WOld
'Snow Flurry'	see *A. ericoides* f. *prostratus* 'Snow Flurry'
'Snow Star'	WOld
'Soft Lass' **new**	WCot
spathulifolius	WCot XLum
spectabilis	EBee IMou LRHS WOld
subcaeruleus	see *A. tongolensis*
'Sunhelene'	CDes WCot
'Sunqueen'	WCot
tataricus	LPla
– 'Jindai'	EBee
thomsonii	WCot WOld
– 'Nanus'	CAby GBee GMaP LRHS MCot SBch SPhx WCot WOld WSHC WSpi
tibeticus	see *A. flaccidus*
'Tina'	NDov
Tonga = 'Dasfour'	EPfP EWTr LRHS LSou MHol NBir NLar NPri SRms SWvt WCot
§ ***tongolensis***	SBHP
– 'Berggarten'	LDai LRHS MPie NPnk WOld
– 'Dunkleviolette'	SRms
– 'Napsbury'	LRHS WOld
– 'Wartburgstern'	CCon EHyd EPfP SGbt WWEG XLum
tradescantii misapplied	see *A. pilosus* var. *demotus*
tradescantii L.	ELan MBNS MRav NSti SMad WBrk WCot WOld
'Treffpunkt'	IMou
trinervius var. ***harae***	WOld
tripolium	WHer
'Triumph'	WCot
turbinellus misapplied 🏆^{H4}	CAby CKno EPfP GCal GGal IKil LPla NGdn NWsh SPhx SRkn WOld WWEG
turbinellus Lindl.	CSam EBee EPfP EWTr GBee MWat NCGa NDov NLBP NLar WOld WSpi
– hybrid	WOld
umbellatus	CBre CKno GQue NBir NDov NLar WCot WOld
'Vasterival'	MAvo MSpe NCGa NDov WOut WWEG
vimineus Lam.	see *A. lateriflorus*
* ***vimineus*** Lour.	MAvo
– 'Ptarmicoides'	see *Solidago ptarmicoides*
§ 'White Climax'	CAby MHom WBrk WCot
'Wood's Blue' **new**	LRHS
'Wood's Pink'	WHil
'Wood's Purple'	WHil
'Yvonne'	CBre

Asteranthera (*Gesneriaceae*)

ovata	CExl CFil CGHE EBee EPfP GGGa LRHS LSou MAsh SLon SPoG WAbe WPGP WSHC

Asteriscus (*Asteraceae*)

'Gold Coin'	see *Pallenis maritima*
maritimus	see *Pallenis maritima*

Asteromoea (*Asteraceae*)

mongolica	see *Kalimeris mongolica*
pinnatifida	see *Kalimeris pinnatifida*

Asterotrichion (*Malvaceae*)

discolor	ECou SPlb SVen

Astilbe ✿ (*Saxifragaceae*)

CC 5201	CExl
'Alive and Kicking'	MBri
'Amerika' (× *arendsii*)	CMHG CSBt
'Amethyst' (× *arendsii*)	CMHG CMac ELon EPfP LLWG LRHS MRav NBir NBre NHol NSoo SPer SPoG WHoo WMoo WWEG
'Angel Wings' (× *arendsii*)	NPro
'Anita Pfeifer' (× *arendsii*)	CMHG ELon GBin IBoy NLar XLum
'Aphrodite' (*simplicifolia* hybrid)	CBcs GCal LRHS MLHP NBre WGor
× ***arendsii***	EPfP IFoB NBre WHar WMoo
(Astary Series) 'Astary Pink' (× *arendsii*) **new**	LRHS
– 'Astary Red' (× *arendsii*) **new**	LRHS
– 'Astary White' (× *arendsii*)	LRHS
astilboides	CMHG SWvt
'Atrorosea' (*simplicifolia* hybrid)	LRHS SRms
'Avalanche'	GBin NHol SPad WMnd WWEG
§ 'Beauty of Ernst' (× *arendsii*)	LRHS LSou MSCN SLon SPoG SRms WHil WMoo
§ 'Beauty of Lisse' (× *arendsii*)	LRHS LSou MSCN WOut
Bella Group (× *arendsii*)	NBre SPet WMnd
'Bergkristall' (× *arendsii*)	CMHG
'Betsy Cuperus' (*thunbergii* hybrid)	CMHG EBee GBin MRav NBre
'Bonn' (*japonica* hybrid)	CWCL CWat LRHS NLBP SCoo SRms
'Boogie Woogie'^{PBR} (× *arendsii*)	MAsh
§ 'Brautschleier' (× *arendsii*) 🏆^{H4}	CExl CMHG CMac CPrp CTri EBee ECtt EPfP GBin GCra GKev LRHS LSRN MSCN NGdn NLBP NLar WPnP WPtf XLum
'Bremen' (*japonica* hybrid)	CMHG GBin LRHS
'Bressingham Beauty' (× *arendsii*)	Widely available
Bridal Veil (× *arendsii*)	see *A.* 'Brautschleier'
§ 'Bronce Elegans' (*simplicifolia* hybrid) 🏆^{H4}	CCon CMHG CPrp ELon EPfP GBin GBuc GMaP LRHS MRav NHol NLar NPro WMoo WOut WWEG
'Bronzelaub' (× *arendsii*)	CMHG
* ***bumalda*** 'Bronze Pygmy'	MMoz NHol
'Bumalda' (× *arendsii*)	CCon CSBt CWCL GBin GMaP IBoy LRHS NChi NGdn NPro SPlb WGwG WMoo
'Bunter Zauber' (× *arendsii*) **new**	XLum
'Burgunderrot' (× *arendsii*)	EBee EPfP MBri MNrw NLar SMrm
'Carminea' **new**	CMHG
'Carnea' (*simplicifolia* hybrid)	CMHG
'Catherine Deneuve'	see *A.* 'Federsee'
'Cattleya Dunkel' (× *arendsii*)	CMHG
'Cattleya' (× *arendsii*)	CMHG CSam GBuc LRHS NLar NSoo WMoo
'Ceres' (× *arendsii*)	CMHG
'Cherry Ripe'	see *A.* 'Feuer'
chinensis	CMHG ECho LRHS NBre WSHC
– B&SWJ 8178	WCru
– from Russia	GCal
– 'Brokat'	GBin

- 'Christian'	GBin
- var. ***davidii***	CMHG
- - B&SWJ 8583	WCru
- - B&SWJ 8645	WCru
- 'Diamonds and Pearls'PBR	CWGN GAbr LSou MBri WHil
- 'Finale'	ELon NHol SPer WOut
- 'Frankentroll'	CMHG
- 'Intermezzo'	GBin GCal GMaP LRHS NLar
- 'Little Vision in Pink'PBR	MBri MSCN WHil
- 'Love and Pride'	LSou MBri
- 'Milk and Honey'PBR	ECtt EWTr LSou MBNS NSoo SGol
§ - var. ***pumila*** ♀H4	Widely available
- - 'Serenade'	CMac NGdn
- 'Purple Glory'	CMHG EWll IKil
- 'Spätsommer'	CMHG EBee
- var. ***taquetii***	CMac ELan EPfP LRHS NBre NSti SRms
- - Purple Lance	see *A. chinensis* var. *taquetii* 'Purpurlanze'
§ - - 'Purpurlanze'	CKno CMHG CPrp EBee ECtt ELon EShb GBin GCra GMaP LAst LLWP LRHS LSRN MNrw MRav NBid NBir NBro NDov NGdn NHol NLar SPhx SPoG SWvt WBor WCAu WGwG WMoo
§ - - 'Superba' ♀H4	CMHG CMac CRow CTri EBee GBin IBoy LRHS MLHP NBro NWad SDix SPer SRms WMoo
- 'Troll'	GBin
- 'Veronika Klose'	CMHG GBin NLar NPro WWEG
- 'Vision in Pink'PBR	CWCL ELan EWll LSou MBNS MHol NPri WHil
- 'Vision in Red'PBR	CMil CWCL CWat ECtt ELan EPfP EWll IBoy LHop LRHS LSou MBNS MBri MHol MNrw NLar NSoo SGbt SPoG WHil WMoo
- 'Vision in White'	MBri NSoo SPoG WHil
- 'Visions'	CMHG CMac CWCL IBoy LRHS LSou MBNS MBri NBro NGdn NPro
'Colette's Charm' **new**	LRHS
Cologne	see *A.* 'Köln'
Color Flash	see *A.* 'Beauty of Ernst'
Color Flash Lime	see *A.* 'Beauty of Lisse'
'Country and Western'PBR (× *arendsii*)	LSou
'Crimson Feather'	see *A.* 'Gloria Purpurea'
× ***crispa***	ECho
- 'Gnom'	NHar
- 'Lilliput'	ECtt GBee NBir NHar NLar NPro NRya
§ - 'Perkeo' ♀H4	CBcs CCon EBee ECho ECtt ELan EPfP GMaP LRHS NBir NHar NLar NMyG NPro SRms WCot WMoo WWEG
- 'Peter Pan'	see *A.* × *crispa* 'Perkeo'
- 'Red Rog'	NPro
- 'Snow Queen'	NBir NHar NPro
'Darwin's Dream'	IBoy NLar NPro
'Darwin's Favourite' (× *arendsii*)	CWCL
'Delft Lace'	LBuc LRHS
'Deutschland' (*japonica* hybrid)	CBcs CCon CHVG CMHG CSam CWCL EBee ECtt EPfP GMaP IBoy LPot LRHS LSRN MBNS MGos MLHP MMuc MRav NBir NHol NLar SPer SPoG SRms SWat WHoo WMnd WMoo WWEG
§ 'Diamant' (× *arendsii*)	CHel CMHG LRHS LSRN MMuc NGdn NHol

Diamond	see *A.* 'Diamant'
'Drayton Glory' (× *arendsii*)	see *A.* × *rosea* 'Peach Blossom'
'Drum and Bass'PBR	IBoy LSou MAsh NLar NSoo
'Dunkelachs' (*simplicifolia* hybrid)	EBee LRHS MSCN NMyG
'Dusseldorf' (*japonica* hybrid)	CMHG CSam CWCL LRHS NHol
'Eden's Odysseus'	GBin IBoy NHol
'Eden's Twinkle' **new**	EBee
'Elegans' (*simplicifolia* hybrid)	CMHG CMac
Elizabeth Bloom = 'Eliblo'PBR (× *arendsii*)	CHVG ELon LLWG LRHS MHol MRav NDov NEgg NGdn NHol SGol
'Elizabeth' (*japonica* hybrid)	CMHG
'Ellie' (× *arendsii*)	CMHG CMac CWCL GBin GQue LRHS LSRN LSou MAsh MBNS MBri NGdn NHol NLar SMrm WPtf
'Erica' (× *arendsii*)	CExl CMHG CTri EWll NLar NPnk NPro SPad WMoo WWEG
'Etna' (*japonica* hybrid)	CBcs CMHG CSam IBoy LRHS MMuc NEgg NGdn NHol NLar SMrm SRms WHar WPnP
'Europa' (*japonica* hybrid)	CMHG CMac ECtt GBin LRHS MGos NGdn NLar SPoG WHar WMoo
'Fanal' (× *arendsii*) ♀H4	Widely available
'Fata Morgana' (× *arendsii* hybrid)	CMHG
§ 'Federsee' (× *arendsii*)	CBcs CHVG CMHG CWCL EBee ECtt ELan LRHS MBNS NBre NBro NGdn NPro XLum
§ 'Feuer' (× *arendsii*)	CMHG CMac CPrp ECtt ELan EPfP GBin GBuc LBMP LRHS NEgg NGdn NHol NLar NOrc NPro WBor WGwG WMoo
Fire	see *A.* 'Feuer'
'Fireberry'PBR (Short 'n' Sweet Series)	LSou MAsh NLar
'Flamingo'PBR (× *arendsii*)	GBin MBNS NSoo
§ ***formosa*** B&SWJ 10946	WCru
'Gertrud Brix' (× *arendsii*)	CBcs CWat MMuc NBir NGdn XLum
§ ***glaberrima***	NBid
§ - var. ***saxatilis*** ♀H4	EPfP GBin IFro NHar NSla WAbe WHal WThu
- ***saxosa***	see *A. glaberrima* var. *saxatilis*
'Gladstone' (× *arendsii*)	see *A.* 'W.E. Gladstone'
§ 'Gloria Purpurea' (× *arendsii*)	CMHG ELon NLBP WMoo
'Gloria' (× *arendsii*)	CMHG CMac CTri ECtt MRav
Glow	see *A.* 'Glut'
§ 'Glut' (× *arendsii*)	CCon CMHG CWCL ECtt EWTr LLWG LRHS MMuc NGdn NHol SRms WHil
'Granat' (× *arendsii*)	CFis CMHG CMac GBuc NBir NBre NDov NEgg NGdn NHol NLar WMoo
* Grande Group (× *arendsii*)	NBre
grandis	CMHG GBee WHer
'Grete Püngel' (× *arendsii*)	GBin WWEG
'Harmony' (× *arendsii*)	CMHG
'Heart and Soul'PBR	EPfP LSou MBri
'Hennie Graafland' (*simplicifolia* hybrid)	CBcs CMHG CWCL GBin LRHS LSou NLar
'Henry Noblett'	GBin
'Hip Hop' **new**	MAsh
'Holden Clough' (*japonica* hybrid)	NHol NWad
Hyacinth	see *A.* 'Hyazinth'

§	'Hyazinth' (× *arendsii*)	CExl CMHG CPrp EBee GMaP LBMP LLWG LRHS LSou NHol
	'Inshriach Pink' (*simplicifolia* hybrid)	CBcs CCVN CMHG CPrp EHoe ELan LRHS MBri NBir NHar NHol NLar SBch WHal WOut
	'Irrlicht' (× *arendsii*)	CMHG CMac EBee ELan EPfP EShb EWTr GBin GBuc IBoy LHop LRHS NWad SPer SWat WWEG
	'Isa Hall' new	CMHG
	japonica	CExl GKev
*	- 'Pumila'	NBir NGdn
	- var. ***terrestris***	see *A. glaberrima*
	'Jo Ophorst' (*davidii* hybrid)	CMHG EBee ECtt GBuc LRHS NEgg NGdn NHol NLar
	'Jump and Jive'PBR	LSou NSoo
	'Juno' new	XLum
	'Koblenz' (*japonica* hybrid)	CMHG CWCL
§	'Köln' (*japonica* hybrid)	CMHG CWat ELon GBin LRHS NMyG
	koreana	WCot
	- B&SWJ 8611	WCru
	- B&SWJ 8680	WCru
	'Kriemhilde'	CMHG MSCN
	'Kvële' (× *arendsii*)	CMHG WMoo
§	'Lachskönigin' (× *arendsii*)	CMHG
	'Lilli Goos' (× *arendsii*)	CMHG GBin GCal
	'Lollipop'	MBNS NPro SRms
	longicarpa B&SWJ 6711	WCru
	macroflora	GCal
	'Magenta' new	CMHG
	'Maggie Daley'	IBoy NBro NPro WMoo
	'Mainz' (*japonica* hybrid)	CHVG CMHG ECtt
	'Mars' (× *arendsii*)	CMHG
	microphylla	CMHG
	- B&SWJ 11085	WCru
	- pink-flowered	CMHG
	'Midnight Arrow' (*davidii* hybrid) new	CMHG
	'Moerheim Glory' (× *arendsii*)	GBin IBoy NBre NGdn NLar
	'Moerheimii' (*thunbergii* hybrid)	CMHG
	'Mont Blanc' (× *arendsii*)	CMHG
	'Montgomery' (*japonica* hybrid)	CMHG CWCL CWGN EBee ELon EShb GAbr GBin IKil LBMP LRHS LSRN MBNS MBri MMuc NBro NCGa NEgg NGdn NHol
	'New Wave' new	MAsh
	'Nikki'	NCGa NLar NPro
§	***okuyamae*** B&SWJ 10975	WCru
	'Opal' new	CMHG
	Ostrich Plume	see *A.* 'Straussenfeder'
	'Paul Gaärder' (× *arendsii*)	CMHG
	'Peaches and Cream'	MMHG NBro NLar NPnk
	'Peter Barrow' (*glaberrima* hybrid)	GBin SRms
	'Pink Fanal'	LRHS
	'Pink Lightning'PBR (*simplicifolia* hybrid)	CWCL EBee MBNS MBri NLar NOrc SMrm SPoG
	Pink Pearl (× *arendsii*)	see *A.* 'Rosa Perle'
	'Poschka'	CCon NPro
	'Professor van der Wielen' (*thunbergii* hybrid)	CCon CMHG EBee GQue LRHS NHol NLar SPer SRms WWEG
	pumila	see *A. chinensis* var. *pumila*
	'Purple Rain'PBR (× *arendsii*) new	NSoo
	'Radius'	MSCN NGdn NLar WHil WPnP
	'Red Baron'	SPad
	Red Light	see *A.* 'Rotlicht'

	'Red Sentinel' (*japonica* hybrid)	CBcs CCon CHel CWCL CWat EBee ELon EPfP GBin GMaP IBoy LRHS MAsh MBri NBro NCGa NGdn NHol NLar NPro WHil WHrl
	'Rheinland' (*japonica* hybrid) $♀^{H4}$	CBcs CMHG CWCL ELon GBin LRHS MBel MMuc NGdn SHil SRot WHoo WMnd WPnP
	'Rhythm and Blues'PBR	EBee ECtt NLar
	rivularis	CMHG WCot
	- CC 5201	GKev
	- GWJ 9366	WCru
I	- 'Grandiflora'	EBee GBin
§	- var. ***myriantha***	NBre
	- - BWJ 8076a	WCru
	- - SICH 757	CExl
	'Robinson's Pink'	NGdn
	'Rock and Roll'PBR	LSRN MSCN WHil
§	'Rosa Perle' (× *arendsii*)	CHVG CMHG CSam NHol
§	× ***rosea*** 'Peach Blossom'	CBcs CMHG CPrp ELon GCra IBoy LRHS NBir NGdn NPro SGbt SPoG SWvt WHoo WMnd WMoo
	'Rosea' (*simplicifolia* hybrid)	NHol
	'Rot Straussenfeder' (× *arendsii*)	GBin
§	'Rotlicht' (× *arendsii*)	CMHG CMac LRHS NGdn NHol NLar NPro WGor
	'Salland'	EBee LRHS
	Salmon Queen	see *A.* 'Lachskönigin'
	'Salmonea' (*simplicifolia* hybrid)	CMHG
	'Saxosa'	see *A. glaberrima* var. *saxatilis*
	'Sheila Haxton' (*chinensis* hybrid)	LRHS NHar
	Showstar Group (× *arendsii*)	LRHS MSnd WHil
	simplicifolia $♀^{H4}$	SKHP
	- 'Alba'	CMHG
	- Bronze Elegance	see *A.* 'Bronce Elegans'
	- 'Darwin's Snow Sprite'	CMac GBin MWts NHol NLar
	- 'Jacqueline'	LSou MAsh NHol
*	- 'Nana Alba'	NPro
	- 'Praecox Alba'	GBin NEgg WWEG
	- 'Rose of Cimarron'	NPro
	- 'White Sensation'PBR	EBee GQue LRHS NLar
	'Snowdrift' (× *arendsii*)	CHid CMHG CWat GMaP IKil LBMP LLWG LRHS MBNS MBel MMuc MWat NBir NEgg NOrc NPro SPer SWat WWEG
	'Solferino' (× *arendsii*)	CMHG
	'Spartan' (× *arendsii*)	see *A.* 'Rotlicht'
	'Spinell' (× *arendsii*)	CWCL GBuc LRHS NBre WMoo WPnP WWEG
	'Sprite' (*simplicifolia* hybrid) $♀^{H4}$	Widely available
	'Stand and Deliver'PBR	ECtt
§	'Straussenfeder' (*thunbergii* hybrid) $♀^{H4}$	CMHG CMac CTri ECtt EPfP GBin GMaP LBMP LHop LRHS NBid NBir NBro NGdn NHol NLar NOrc SPer SPoG WCAu WMoo WPtf WWEG
	'Sugar Plum' (*simplicifolia* hybrid)	NGdn
	'Sugarberry'PBR (Short 'n' Sweet Series)	NLar
	'Superba'	see *A. chinensis* var. *taquetii* 'Superba'
	thunbergii	CExl LRHS
	- var. ***congesta*** B&SWJ 10961	WCru
	- var. ***formosa***	see *A. formosa*

	- var. ***hachijoensis***	EBee
	- - B&SWJ 5622	WCru
	- var. ***okuyamae***	see *A. okuyamae*
	- var. ***sikokumontanum*** B&SWJ 11164	WCru
	- var. ***terrestris*** B&SWJ 6125	WCru
	'To Have and To Hold'	LSou
	'Venus' (× *arendsii*)	ECtt GMaP LRHS MBNS MCot NGdn NHol NOrc SPer SWat WMoo
	'Vesuvius' (*japonica* hybrid)	CBcs LRHS NBro NLar
	virescens	see *A. rivularis* var. *myriantha*
§	'W.E. Gladstone' (*japonica* hybrid)	WGor
	'Walküre' (× *arendsii*)	CMHG
	'Walter Bitner'	GBin LLWG LRHS MAsh MBNS NBre NHol SRGP
	'Washington' (*japonica* hybrid)	LAst NBre NGdn WPnP
§	'Weisse Gloria' (× *arendsii*)	CHVG CMHG CMac CPrp GAbr GBin GBuc LLWG LRHS NBro NDov NEgg NHol NMyG NOrc NPro SCoo SHil SMrm WBor WCAu WMoo
	White Gloria	see *A.* 'Weisse Gloria'
	'White Wings' PBR (*simplicifolia* hybrid)	NLar
	'William Reeves' (× *arendsii*)	CMHG NHol
	'Willie Buchanan' (*simplicifolia* hybrid)	CBcs CHid CMHG CPrp EHoe GAbr GBin GMaP LBMP LRHS NEgg NGdn NHar NHol SPer SRms WAbe WCFE WGwG WMoo WNew WWEG
	Younique Carmine = 'Verscarmine' PBR	LSou MAsh WHil
	Younique Lilac = 'Verslilac' PBR **new**	MAsh
	Younique Pink = 'Verspink' PBR	WHil
	Younique Silvery Pink = 'Versilverypink' PBR	WHil
	Younique White = 'Verswhite' PBR	MAsh NCGa
	'Zuster Theresa' (× *arendsii*)	CHel CMHG EBee IBoy LRHS MBNS MNrw NBro

Astilboides (*Saxifragaceae*)

§	***tabularis***	Widely available

Astragalus (*Papilionaceae*)

	angustifolius **new**	XSen
	canadensis	LRHS SPhx
	glycyphyllos	CArn SPhx
	looseri **new**	WCot
	membranaceus	CArn
	- var. ***mongholicus***	WSHC
	purshii	ECho
	utahensis	CPBP

Astrantia ✿ (*Apiaceae*)

	'Atomic Sunburst'	GQue
	bavarica	GCal MFie
	'Berendien Stam'	EBee ECGP MAvo MFie
	'Bloody Mary'	CWCL EBee ELan GBuc MFie NGdn NLar NPnk
	'Buckland'	Widely available
	'Burgundy Manor' **new**	SHar
	'Bury Court'	NDov
	carniolica	NEgg
	- ***major***	see *A. major*
	- 'Rubra'	CBcs GMaP MFie
	- 'Variegata'	see *A. major* 'Sunningdale Variegated'
	'Clear Pink'	NDov
	'Dark Shiny Eyes'	CExl CLAP EBee ECtt GBin IBoy LHop LLHF MBNS NCGa NGdn NLar NSti SPoG SWvt
	'Hadspen Blood'	Widely available
	'Helen'	NLar
	helleborifolia misapplied	see *A. maxima*
	Hidcote hybrid **new**	LRHS
	'Larch Cottage Clear Pink'	NLar
	'Madeleine'	see *A. major* 'Madeleine van Bennekom'
§	***major***	Widely available
	- 'Abbey Road' PBR	CBct CExl CKno CLAP CSev CWCL EBee ECtt GBin IBoy IKil LBMP LHop LSou MBri MFie NEgg NLar SMrm SPoG SRkn SRms WCAu WWlt
I	- 'Alba'	CBcs CMHG CWCL EBee GKev IBal IKil LRHS MCot MFie MRav NBir NGdn NPer WGwG WMnd WMoo
	- subsp. ***biebersteinii***	LRHS MFie NBir
	- 'Bo-Ann'	CWCL IBoy MFie NLar
	- 'Celtic Star'	CSpe EBee MFie SWvt
	- 'Claret'	Widely available
	- Cliff's form	MFie
	- 'Elmblut'	MAvo MFie
	- 'Florence' PBR	EBee ECtt EPfP GBin LRHS MAvo MBri MTis NCGa NDov NLar SPoG
	- 'Gill Richardson'	CDes CExl CLAP CPom CPrp CSam CSpe CWCL EPri EShb EWTr GBuc GCal IBoy IPot LHop LLWG LRHS LSRN MAvo MBel MFie MRav MWhi NDov NGdn NHol NOrc SGbt WMoo
	- 'Greenfingers'	EWes
	- subsp. ***involucrata***	LRHS MFie SWat
	- - 'Barrister'	CSam GBuc LRHS MAvo MFie NLar
	- - 'Canneman'	EBee EWes LPla MFie NLar WCot
	- - 'Jumble Hole'	NDov
	- - 'Margery Fish'	see *A. major* subsp. *involucrata* 'Shaggy'
	- - 'Moira Reid'	CBct CExl CLAP CSam ECtt ELan EShb GCal GMaP LAst LRHS LSRN MAvo MCot MFie MRav NPnk
	- - 'Orlando'	CLAP MFie
§	- - 'Shaggy' 🏆H4	Widely available
	- - 'Snape Cottage'	CDes
	- 'Jitse'	EBee MAvo
	- 'Lars'	CExl CWib ECtt ELan ELon EPfP GBin GCra IBal IFoB LPio LRHS LSRN MBri MFie MHol MNrw MWhi NBid NGdn NLar NPnk NSoo SPer SPet SPoG SRot SWvt WCAu
	- 'Lola'	EBee GBuc NCGa NLar SMrm
§	- 'Madeleine van Bennekom'	CLAP EBee GBin MAvo NCGa
	- 'Penny's Pink'	CWCL EBee ELan MFie NPnk WCot
	- 'Percy Picton'	MAvo
	- 'Pink Crush'	EBee LRHS
	- 'Pink Pride'	IFro LSou MHol NCGa SHar WCAu
	- 'Pink Sensation'	EBee
	- 'Pink Surprise' **new**	MAvo
	- 'Primadonna'	EBee EPri GMaP MFie MHol NHol NLar SPlb WMnd WWEG

	- 'Princesse Sturdza'	EBee LSou MBri NCGa WHil WWlt
	- 'Reverse Sunningdale Variegated' (v)	LSou MAvo MFie
	- 'Rosa Lee'	CWCL MFie NPnk
	- var. ***rosea***	CBre CHel CWCL EPfP GKev LHop LRHS LSRN MFie MLHP MRav MSpe MWat MWhi NGdn WCAu WMoo WWEG
	- - George's form	CBct CHel CKno CLAP CPrp CWCL ECtt LHop LRHS LSRN MFie NCGa NEgg NPnk
	- 'Rosensinfonie'	CWCL EBee GMaP MFie NBro NPnk
§	- 'Rubra'	CSBt CSpe CWCL ECtt ELan EPfP IBoy LAst LRHS MFie MGos MHol MSpe NBir NChi NPer NPnk SPad SRms SWat WBor WCAu WCru WHal WMoo WWEG
	- 'Ruby Cloud'	CHVG CHel CHid CWCL ECtt ELon EPri GBuc LBMP LPio LRHS MFie MNrw NBro NGdn NSti SBod SRot WBor WMnd
	- 'Ruby Giant' **new**	EBee
	- 'Ruby Glow'	LRHS MFie
	- 'Ruby Star'[PBR]	CLAP CMil EBee ECGP ECtt ELon GAbr GMaP IBoy IPot LRHS MAvo MBel MFie MHol NDov NLar NSti SMrm SPer SWvt WBor WCot WHoo WMnd
	- 'Ruby Wedding'	Widely available
	- 'Silver Glow'	EBee ECtt IBal
	- 'Star of Beauty'[PBR]	CLAP CWCL ECtt ELan GBin IBoy LLWG LSou MBri MFie MMHG NCGa NGdn NLar NSti SMrm SPet SRms SRot WHil
	- 'Star of Billion'[PBR]	CLAP EBee ECtt ELan GBin IBoy LLWG NDov SGol
	- 'Star of Fire'[PBR]	CBct LLWG LSou MBel MBri NCGa SRot
	- 'Star of Royals'[PBR]	CLAP ECtt GBin IPot LLWG LSou MBri SMrm
	- 'Star of Summer'	EBee LSou
	- 'Starburst'	EBee MFie
	- 'Sue Barnes' (v)	EBee GCal MAvo MFie
§	- 'Sunningdale Variegated' (v) 🏆[H4]	Widely available
	- 'Titoki Point'	MFie WCot
	- 'Venice'[PBR]	CHel CLAP CWCL CWGN ECtt GBuc IBoy IPot LRHS LSou MAvo MCot MSCN MTis MWhi NCGa NDov NLar NSti SMrm SRms STPC WWlt
§	***maxima*** 🏆[H4]	Widely available
	- 'Mark Fenwick'	MFie NBir
*	- ***rosea***	ECtt GQue MNrw MWhi NBir NGdn WWEG
	minor	EBee WCru
	'Moulin Rouge'[PBR]	Widely available
	'Queen's Children'	CBct GBuc SGol
	'Rainbow'	MFie NLar
	'Roma'[PBR]	Widely available
	rubra	see *A. major* 'Rubra'
	'Sheila's Red'	IPot LRHS LSRN MBNS NDov
	'Snow Star'[PBR]	CWCL CWib EBee EPfP GBin LRHS MBNS MFie NCGa NLar NPnk SHil SPoG
	'Star of Heaven'	NLar
	'Superstar'[PBR]	CMea CMil EBee ECGP ECtt ELon EPfP GBin IBoy IPot LLWG LRHS MAvo MBNS MBel MHol MTis NDov NLar NSti SMrm SPer SWvt WCot WHoo
	'Warren Hills'	CCVN CLAP GMaP MFie NLar NPnk
	'Washfield'	MTis NCGa NDov

Astrodaucus (*Apiaceae*)

	orientalis	SPhx

Asyneuma (*Campanulaceae*)

	canescens	LRHS LSou NBre
	compactum **new**	CPBP
	limonifolium	WAbe
§	***prenanthoides***	SMrm
	- 'Cambell Blue'	LRHS
	pulvinatum	CPBP WAbe

Asystasia (*Acanthaceae*)

	bella	see *Mackaya bella*
§	***gangetica***	CSev
	violacea	see *A. gangetica*

Athamanta (*Apiaceae*)

	cretensis	CArn
	macedonica	LEdu
	turbith	CSpe LEdu MNrw
	- subsp. ***haynaldii***	EBee
	vestina	SPhx

Athanasia (*Asteraceae*)

§	***parviflora***	MOWG SPlb SVen
	pinnata **new**	SVen

Atherosperma (*Atherospermataceae*)

	moschatum	CBcs CDoC CFil CHll SKHP WSHC

Athrotaxis (*Cupressaceae*)

	cupressoides	CDoC CDul CKen WThu
	laxifolia	CDoC CKen WThu
	selaginoides	CDoC IGor

Athyrium ✿ (*Woodsiaceae*)

	'Branford Beauty'	CCCN CDes CLAP ISha NLar WPGP
	'Branford Rambler'	CLAP ISha
	filix-femina 🏆[H4]	Widely available
§	- subsp. ***angustum***	CBty CLAP ELan GBin LRHS MMoz NGdn WMoo
	- - f. ***rubellum*** 'Lady in Red'	CCCN CDes CElw CKel CLAP CWCL EBee ELon ESwi ISha LEdu LLWG LRHS LSRN MGos NBid NLar SPoG WMoo WWEG
	- 'Corymbiferum'	SRms
	- 'Crispum Grandiceps Kaye'	NGdn SRms
	- Cristatum Group	CLAP EFer ELan LSRN MMoz NGdn SWat WFib
	- 'Dre's Dagger'	NLar
	- 'Fieldii'	CLAP SRms
	- 'Frizelliae' 🏆[H4]	Widely available
	- 'Frizelliae Capitatum'	CLAP WFib WPGP
	- 'Frizelliae Cristatum'	SRms
	- 'Grandiceps'	CLAP SRms
	- 'Lady Victoria'	CLAP
	- 'Lady-in-Lace'	CLAP LLHF LLWG MCot MHol SMad WCot
	- 'Minutissimum'	CBty CDes CGHE CLAP EBee ELan ISha MMoz
*	- 'Nudicaule'	SRms

- Plumosum Group	CLAP WFib XLum
- 'Plumosum Axminster'	CLAP EFer NLar
- 'Plumosum Divaricatum'	SRms
- 'Plumosum Druery'	CLAP
- Red Stem	see *A. filix-femina* 'Rotstiel'
§ - 'Rotstiel'	CDTJ CLAP EBee MMoz WMoo WPnP WWEG
- 'Vernoniae' ♀H4	CBty CDTJ CLAP ELan MMoz NLar
- 'Vernoniae Cristatum'	CLAP WFib
- 'Victoriae'	CBty CCCN CDTJ CDes CWCL EFer GMaP ISha LRHS MMuc NBid NGdn NLar NMyG SEND WMoo WPat WWEG XLum
- - seedling	MBri WPtf
- Victoriae Group	see *A. filix-femina* subsp. *angustum*
'Ghost'	CBty CCCN CDes CLAP ISha LRHS LSou MGos NCGa NLar NSti WCot WPat WPtf
goeringianum 'Pictum'	see *A. niponicum* var. *pictum*
niponicum	LRHS NMyG WHal
- f. ***metallicum***	see *A. niponicum* var. *pictum*
§ - var. ***pictum*** ♀H3	Widely available
- - 'Apple Court'	CBty CCCN ISha LRHS NLar
- - 'Burgundy Lace'	CBty CLAP LLWG LRHS MCot MPnt NLar WCot WPat WPtf
* - - 'Cristatoflabellatum'	CLAP EBee LRHS
- - 'Pewter Lace'	CBty NLar
- - 'Red Beauty'	CBty CDTJ CLAP EPfP GBin LRHS LSRN NHol NLar SGol SPoG SRkn WCot WMoo WPat WPnP
- - 'Regal Red'	CBty ISha LRHS
- - 'Silver Falls'	CBty CLAP EAmu EShb LRHS NMyG WCot WHal WPGP
- - 'Soul Mate'	CLAP
- - 'Ursula's Red'	CBcs CBty CCVN CElw CLAP EShb LHop LLWG LRHS LSRN LSou MSCN NBid NBir NEgg NLar NPnk SMrm WCot WPGP
- - 'Wildwood Twist'	CLAP NMyG WCot
'Ocean's Fury'	CLAP
otophorum ♀H4	ISha MRav NBid SRms WPGP
- var. ***okanum***	Widely available
vidalii	CDTJ CLAP EBee ISha LLWG LRHS LSou MMoz NEgg NLar NMyG SMrm WCot WFib WWEG XLum

Atractylodes (*Asteraceae*)

japonica	EFEx
macrocephala	CArn EFEx

Atragene see *Clematis*

Atriplex (*Amaranthaceae*)

canescens	NLar
cinerea	ECou
halimus	CArn CBcs ECre EHoe ELau EPPr MBri MRav NLar SDix SLon SPer SPlb WCot
hortensis var. ***rubra***	CArn CSpe ELan LSou MHer MNHC SHDw SIde SMrm SRms WCot WJek
- - 'Oriental Red' **new**	WCot

Atropa (*Solanaceae*)

acuminata	CArn
bella-donna	CArn GPoy SEND
mandragora	see *Mandragora officinarum*

Aubrieta (*Brassicaceae*)

sp. **new**	MLHP
'Alba'	see *A.* 'Fiona'
albomarginata	see *A.* 'Argenteovariegata'
'Alix Brett'	CMea
'Ann Kendall'	ECtt
§ 'Argenteovariegata' (v) ♀H4	ECho ELan LRHS MJak
(Audrey Series) 'Audrey Blue' **new**	WIce
- 'Audrey Red' **new**	WIce
§ 'Aureovariegata' (v) ♀H4	ECho ELan NPer XLum
Axcent Series	LRHS
- 'Axcent Antique Magenta'	LRHS WGor
- 'Axcent Antique Rose'	LRHS WGor
- 'Axcent Blue with Eye' **new**	LBuc LRHS
- 'Axcent Dark Red' **new**	LRHS
- 'Axcent Deep Purple' **new**	LBuc LRHS
- 'Axcent Lilac' **new**	LRHS
- 'Axcent Violet with Eye' **new**	LRHS
bicolour	CMea
Blaue Schönheit	see *A.* 'Blue Beauty'
'Blaumeise'	LRHS WSpi
§ 'Blue Beauty'	CMea ECtt EPfP GAbr GBin MHol NLar WHil WHoo WSpi
'Blue Emperor'	WSpi
* 'Blue Mist'	EDAr
'Blue Whale'	ECtt LHop SRot SWvt
§ 'Bob Saunders' (d)	CFis CMea NCGa
'Bressingham Pink' (d) ♀H4	CMea ECtt ELan EPfP SPoG
'Bressingham Red'	ECtt ELan EPfP LHop SPoG
'Bubble Purple'	EPfP
canescens	CPBP XSen
- subsp. ***cilicica***	EPot
Cascade Series	CWCL GJos SPoG
- 'Blue Cascade'	MBNS SPlb SPoG WGor
- 'Lilac Cascade'	SPoG
- 'Purple Cascade'	CTri CWib LBMP LSRN MAsh MBNS MJak SPlb SPoG SRms WGor
- 'Red Cascade' ♀H4	CTri CWib ECtt LBMP LSRN MBNS MJak SPlb SPoG
deltoidea	SVic XSen
- Variegata Group (v)	ECtt MHol NPri NSla
- - 'Nana Variegata' (v)	CMea WGor
'Doctor Mules' ♀H4	ECtt SRms
'Doctor Mules Variegata' (v)	ECho ECtt EHoe ELan ELon EPfP LAst MAsh MHer NLar NWad SPoG SWvt WHoo
double pink-flowered (d)	EPfP MHol
'Downers Variegata' (v)	ECtt EPot NWad
'Elsa Lancaster'	NSla
§ 'Fiona'	ECtt
glabrescens	CPBP EPot WAbe
'Gloria'	CMea ECtt EPot GAbr MHol NLar SRot WBor WHoo WIce
'Gloriosa'	MAsh
'Golden Emperor'	MHer
'Golden King'	see *A.* 'Aureovariegata'
gracilis 'Kitte Rose'	ECtt LBuc LRHS
'Greencourt Purple' ♀H4	CFis CMea ECho ELan MHer MWat
'Hamburger Stadtpark'	CWCL ECtt ELan EPfP LHop SRot
'Kati'	NCGa
'Kitte'	ECtt ELan EPfP EPot GBin LRHS NLar NPri SPoG SRms
'Kitte Blue'	LBuc LRHS
'Kitte Purple'	ELan LRHS
'Leichtlinii'	XLum
macedonica	EPot
pinardii	XSen

'Pink Beauty'	ECtt WIce
'Purple Charm'	SRms
'Red Carpet'	ECtt ELan EPot MAsh MHer SRms
'Red Carpet Variegated' (v)	CMea
'Rose Queen'	CMea
Royal Series ♀H4	COlW
- 'Royal Blue'	EPfP EPot MJak NEgg NLar SRot WMoo XLum
- 'Royal Red'	EPfP SBch WGor WMoo
- 'Royal Violet'	EPfP SBch WMoo XLum
'Schofield's Double'	see *A.* 'Bob Saunders'
'Silberrand'	NSla
'Somerfield Silver'	ELan EPfP
'Somerford Lime' (v)	ECtt ELan EPfP LSou MHol SRms
'Swan Red' (v)	ECtt EHoe ELon EPot LAst MHer MHol NEgg NLar NSla SRot WHil WIce
thessala	CPBP
'Triumphante'	ECtt
'Valerie' (v)	ECtt EPot
'Westacre Gold' new	ECtt
'Whitewell Gem'	WMoo XLum

Aucuba ✿ (*Garryaceae*)

himalaica	CFil
var. ***dolichophylla*** new	
japonica	CCVT CDul SEWo
- 'Angelon'	LRHS SHil
- 'Crassifolia' (m)	EBtc GBin SAPC
- 'Crotonifolia' (f/v) ♀H4	Widely available
- 'Crotonifolia' (m/v)	CMac MAsh SGol SRms WRHF
- 'Dentata'	CHEx WCru
- 'February Star' (f/v)	SDix
'Golden King' (m/v) ♀H4	CDoC CMac CWib EBee ELan ELon EPfP LRHS LSRN MAsh MGos NLar NSoo SGol SLim SPer SPoG
- 'Golden Spangles' (f/v)	CBcs CDoC EBee IVic NLar SLim SWvt
- 'Goldstrike' (v)	EBee LRHS LSRN MAsh NEgg SMad
'Hillieri' (f)	EBtc
- f. ***longifolia*** ♀H4	CMac NLar SAPC SDix WCot WCru
- - 'Salicifolia' (f)	ESwi LAst MRav NLar WCru
- 'Maculata' hort.	see *A. japonica* 'Variegata'
- 'Marmorata'	LRHS MBri MGos SHil
- 'Mr Goldstrike' (m/v)	EPfP LRHS SVen
- Pepper Pot = 'Shilpot' (m/v)	CHEx EPfP LRHS MAsh SLon SPoG
- 'Picturata' (m/v)	CDul CMac CSBt ELan ELon LRHS MAsh MGos NLar SEND SHil SLim SPer
- 'Rozannie' (f/m) ♀H4	CBar CBcs CDoC CDul CEnd CMac CSBt EBee ECrN ELan ELon EPfP IVic LRHS LSRN MAsh MBlu MGos MRav NLar SHil SLim SPer SPoG SVen SWvt WMoo
- 'Sulphurea Marginata' (f/v)	CBcs CMac CTri EBee EPfP EShb ESwi LRHS NLar SHil SPer
§ - 'Variegata' (f/v)	Widely available
omeiensis	CExl CFil
- B&SWJ 2864	WCru
- BWJ 8048	WCru
- L 614	CFil WPGP

Aulax (*Proteaceae*)

cancellata	SPlb

Aurinia (*Brassicaceae*)

§ ***corymbosa***	ECho
§ ***saxatilis*** ♀H4	ECho EPfP MMuc NPri SPlb WNew
- 'Argentea'	ECho
- 'Citrina' ♀H4	ECtt MWat SBch SRms
- 'Compacta'	CTri ECtt GJos WIce
- 'Dudley Nevill Variegated' (v)	ECho ECtt ELon EWes MHer
- Gold Ball	see *A. saxatilis* 'Goldkugel'
- 'Gold Dust'	ECho ECtt NRya SRms
- 'Golden Queen'	MHer
§ - 'Goldkugel'	ECho EPfP NPri SPoG
- 'Variegata' (v)	NPri SPoG

Austrocedrus (*Cupressaceae*)

§ ***chilensis***	CKen CMen IGor SBig

Avena (*Poaceae*)

candida	see *Helictotrichon sempervirens*

Avenula see *Helictotrichon*

Averrhoa (*Oxalidaceae*)

carambola (F)	CCCN

avocado see *Persea americana*

Azalea see *Rhododendron*

Azara ✿ (*Salicaceae*)

sp.	NEgg
dentata	CBcs CHll CMac GGal
- 'Variegata'	see *A. integrifolia* 'Variegata'
* ***integerrima***	GQui
integrifolia	CBcs CCCN
'Uarie'	UUUN
§ - 'Variegata' (v)	CWib LRHS NEgg
lanceolata	CDul CExl CMCN CTri GBin GGal LEdu WGrn
microphylla ♀H3	CBcs CDoy CDul CExl CHel CMCN CMac CTri EBee ELon EPfP EUJe GGal IVic LRHS LSRN MAsh MGos NSoo SAPC SEND SHil SLim SPer SPlb SSpi WPGP
* - 'Albovariegata' (v) new	CTri
- 'Gold Edge' (v)	EBee EPfP LRHS
- 'Variegata' (v)	CBcs CDoC CExl CJun CMac CWib EBee EHoe EPfP GQui LBMP LRHS MAsh MRav NLar SEND SLon SPoG SSpi WPat WSHC
* ***patagonica***	MBlu
petiolaris	CMCN CTri LEdu
serrata ♀H3	CBcs CDul CEnd CHel CMCN CTsd CWib EBee EPfP EShb GBin LHop LRHS MSCN NCGa NLar SDix SEND SGol SPer SPoG SRms SVen WBor WHar WKif WSHC
uruguayensis	CCCN CExl EBtc GBin

Azorella (*Apiaceae*)

filamentosa	ECou WAbe
glebaria misapplied	see *A. trifurcata*
glebaria A. Gray	see *Bolax gummifer*
gummifer	see *Bolax gummifer*
lycopodioides	WAbe
§ ***trifurcata***	CPar CSpe CTri ECho EPot GAbr MMuc NBir SIgm SPlb
- 'Nana'	ECho MWat WThu XLum

Azorina (*Campanulaceae*)

§ ***vidalii***	SPlb

B

Babiana (*Iridaceae*)

angustifolia	ECho
'Blue Gem'	ECho
fragrans 'Porterville'	ECho
- 'Rawsonville'	ECho
patersoniae **new**	SPlb
'Purple Star' **new**	CHel
pygmaea	WCot
ringens	WCot
stricta ♀H1-2	CCCN ECho SDeJ
- 'Purple Star'	CExl ECho
- 'Tubergen's Blue'	ECho
villosa	ECho WCot
- 'Tulbagh'	ECho
'Zwanenburg's Glory'	CPrp ECho

Baccharis (*Asteraceae*)

halimifolia	CBcs GLin SEND XLum
patagonica	LRHS MMuc SAPC SPhx SVen

Backhousia (*Myrtaceae*)

citriodora	CArn

Bacopa (*Plantaginaceae*)

sp. **new**	SWvt
monnieri	LLWG
'Snowflake'	see *Sutera cordata* 'Snowflake'

Baeckea (*Myrtaceae*)

gunniana	CExl
linifolia	SPlb
virgata	ECou SPlb

Baeometra (*Colchicaceae*)

uniflora 'Malmesbury'	ECho

Balbisia (*Ledocarpaceae*)

peduncularis	CCCN

Baldellia (*Alismataceae*)

sp. **new**	CBAq
ranunculoides	CRow WMAq
- f. ***repens***	LLWG

Ballota ✿ (*Lamiaceae*)

acetabulosa ♀H3-4	CMHG EWes WCot XSen
'All Hallow's Green'	see *Marrubium bourgaei* var. *bourgaei* 'All Hallows Green'
hirsuta	XSen
nigra	CArn GPoy MHer MHoo MNHC NMir SRms WHfH
§ - 'Archer's Variegated' (v)	LDai MAvo
- 'Variegata'	see *B. nigra* 'Archer's Variegated'
pseudodictamnus ♀H3-4	CBcs EBee EHoe ELan EPfP GMaP LBMP LHop LRHS LSRN MBel MCot MRav NPer NSti SDix SEND SLon SMrm SPer SPoG WCFE WSHC XLum XSen
- B&M 8119	WCot
rupestris 'Frogswell Carolyn' (v)	IFro XSen

Balsamita see *Tanacetum*

Balsamorhiza (*Asteraceae*)

incana	SBrt
sagittata	ECho

Bambusa (*Poaceae*)

glaucescens	see *B. multiplex*
§ ***multiplex***	XBlo
- 'Alphonso-Karrii'	ERod SBig
- 'Elegans'	see *B. multiplex* 'Floribunda'
- 'Fernleaf'	see *B. multiplex* 'Floribunda'
§ - 'Floribunda'	EShb XBlo
- 'Golden Goddess'	XBlo
- 'Silverstripe'	see *B. multiplex* 'Variegata'
§ - 'Variegata' (v)	XBlo
- 'Wang Tsai'	see *B. multiplex* 'Floribunda'
pubescens	see *Dendrocalamus strictus*
ventricosa	SBig XBlo
vulgaris	XBlo
- 'Vittata'	ERod XBlo

banana see *Ensete*, *Musa*

Banksia (*Proteaceae*)

aemula	MOWG
canei	SPlb
ericifolia	CDTJ
- var. ***ericifolia***	CCCN
- var. ***macrantha***	SPlb
grandis	CBcs CCCN
integrifolia	CBcs CCCN CDTJ SPlb WPGP
marginata	SPlb
media	SPlb
oblongifolia	SPlb
paludosa	SPlb
robur	CBcs CCCN SPlb
serrata	SPlb
speciosa	SPlb
spinulosa var. ***collina***	SPlb
- var. ***spinulosa***	CBcs CCCN
violacea	SPlb

Baptisia (*Papilionaceae*)

§ ***alba***	EPfP GBBs LRHS
- var. ***alba*** 'Wayne's World'	EBee
§ - var. ***macrophylla***	CCse EBee EWes LPla LRHS SPhx
australis ♀H4	Widely available
- 'Caspian Blue'	CExl CHel CWCL LEdu LHop WSHC
- 'Exaltata'	LHop LRHS WCot
- var. ***minor***	SPhx WSHC
× ***bicolor*** 'Starlite' (Prairieblues Series)	MBri SKHP SPoG
bracteata	LRHS
- var. ***leucophaea***	LEdu LRHS LSou SPhx
'Carolina Moonlight'	EWes IPot LHop SKHP SPoG
'Chocolate Chip' **new**	LHop
lactea	see *B. alba* var. *macrophylla*
leucantha	see *B. alba* var. *macrophylla*
megacarpa	LRHS SKHP
pendula	see *B. alba*
'Purple Smoke'	CAbP CAby CDes CExl CSpe ECtt EPPr GBuc LEdu LHop LRHS MHol MMuc MNrw NBre NSti SEND SPad SPhx WCot
sphaerocarpa	EBee SPhx WCot
- 'Screamin' Yellow'	LRHS
tinctoria	CArn SPhx
× ***variicolor*** 'Twilite' (Prairieblues Series)	EPfP EWes MBri SKHP SPoG WNPC

Barbarea (*Brassicaceae*)

	praecox	see *B. verna*
§	***verna***	GPoy MHer SVic
	vulgaris 'Variegata' (v)	LDai NBro WHer WMoo
	- 'Variegated Winter Cream' (v)	WHil

Barleria (*Acanthaceae*)

	albostellata new	WHil
	cf. ***crassa*** new	WHil
	garden selection new	WHil
	gueinzii new	WHil
	micans	CCCN
	obtusa	WHil
	ovata new	WHil
	repens	MOWG
	suberecta	see *Dicliptera sericea*

Barosma see *Agathosma*

Bartlettina (*Asteraceae*)

§	***sordida***	CCCN EBee EUJe

Basella (*Basellaceae*)

	rubra	SHDw SVic

Bashania (*Poaceae*)

§	***fargesii***	ENBC ERod MRav MWht SEND WJun
I	***qingchengshanensis***	ERod MWht WJun

basil see *Ocimum basilicum*

Bauera (*Cunoniaceae*)

	rubioides	CTsd MOWG

Bauhinia (*Caesalpiniaceae*)

	galpinii	SPlb
*	***lutea***	CCCN
	natalensis	SPlb
	purpurea L.	CCCN SPlb
	scandens new	MOWG
	tomentosa	CCCN
	'White Lady'	CCCN
	yunnanensis	EDif

Baumea see *Machaerina*

bay see *Laurus nobilis*

Beaucarnea (*Dracaenaceae*)

	recurvata ♀^{H1}	EGri SEND SPlb

Beaufortia (*Myrtaceae*)

	sparsa	CTsd MOWG
	squarrosa	SPlb

Beauverdia see *Leucocoryne*

Beckmannia (*Poaceae*)

	eruciformis	XLum

Bedfordia (*Asteraceae*)

	linearis	SPlb SVen

Beesia (*Ranunculaceae*)

	calthifolia	CBct CCon CDTJ CLAP CMHG CPom CSpe EPfP IGor IMou LHop LLHF WCru WPGP WSHC
	- DJHC 98447	CDes CExl CLAP
	deltophylla	EBee EWld WCot

Begonia ✿ (*Begoniaceae*)

	B&SWJ 2692 from Sikkim, India	WCot
	B&SWJ 10279	CHEx
	BWJ 7840 from China	WCru
	Chen Yi 5	WCot
	Chen Yi 7	WCot
	DJHC 580	WCot
	'Abel Carrière' (R)	WDib
	aconitifolia (C)	EShb EUJe
	albopicta (C)	EBak
	- 'Rosea' (C)	MOWG WDib
	'Amazon Delta' (R)	SBrm
§	***annulata*** HWJK 2424	ESwi WCru
	'Arctic Breeze'^{PBR} (R)	SBrm
	'Argentea' (R)	EBak
	'Argenteo-guttata'	EShb
	'Axel Lange' (R)	SBrm
	'Aya' (C)	WDib
	'Baronessa'	SBrm
	'Beatrice Haddrell'	WDib
	(Belleconia Series) Belleconia Apricot Blush = 'Innbellab'	ESwi
	- Belleconia Rose = 'Innbellro'^{PBR}	ESwi
	- Belleconia Soft Orange = 'Imbellpea'	ESwi SMrm
	'Benitochiba' (R)	CLAP ESwi EUJe LLWG LRHS LSou MAvo NLar WCot WDib WGrn
	'Bethlehem Star'	WDib
§	'Bettina Rothschild' (R)	SBrm WDib
	'Blackberry Swirl' (R)	WDib
	'Blue Sky Pink' (Blue Sky Series) new	LAst
	'Bokit'	WDib
	'Bokit' × ***imperialis***	WDib
	boliviensis (T)	CDes ESwi GCal
	- 'Firecracker'	WDib
	Bonfire = 'Nzcone'^{PBR} ♀$^{H3-4}$	EPfP LBuc SPoG
	'Bouton de Rose' (T)	SDeJ
	'Brown Twist'	WDib
	'Burgundy Velvet'	WDib
	'Burle Marx' ♀^{H1}	EShb SDix WDib
	'Candy Floss'	CDes WCru
	'Captain Nemo' (R)	SBrm
	carolineifolia	WDib
	'Casey Corwin' (R)	SBrm WDib
	cathayana 'Tie-Dye' new	GCal
	'Cathedral'	CDoC WDib
I	***chapaensis*** HWJ 642	WCru
	'China Curl' (R) ♀^{H1}	WDib
	chitoensis B&SWJ 1954	WCru
	chloroneura	WDib
	'Cleopatra' ♀^{H1}	WDib
	coccinea (C)	WDib
	'Coconut Ice'	EShb
	'Connee Boswell'	WDib
§	***corallina*** (C)	EBak
	cucullata	CFil CSpe EShb ESwi SEND SKHP
	var. ***arenosicola*** (S)	WCot
	'Curly Fireflush' (R)	MSCN SBrm WDib
	'David Blais' (R) ♀^{H1}	WDib
	'Dawnal Meyer' (C)	WDib
I	'De Elegans'	WDib

Devil Series (S)	NPri
- 'Devil Red' (S)	LAst
- 'Devil Rose' (S)	LAst
- 'Devil White' (S)	LAst
'Dewdrop' (R) ♀H1	WDib
'Dibleys Pink Showers'PBR	WDib
discolor	see *B. grandis* subsp. *evansiana*
'Don Miller' (C)	WDib
'Elda Haring' (R)	SBrm
Elegance = 'Yagance'PBR (Million Kisses Series) ♀H3-4	LSou
emeiensis	CSpe SKHP
'Emerald Beauty' (R) ♀H1	SBrm
'Emerald Giant' (R)	WDib
'Erythrophylla'	EShb
'Escargot' (R) ♀H1	WDib
'Etna' (R)	SBrm
Fimbriata Group (T)	SDeJ
'Fire Flush'	see *B.* 'Bettina Rothschild'
'Fireworks' (R) ♀H1	WDib
'Flo'Belle Moseley' (C)	WDib
§ ***foliosa*** var. ***miniata*** ♀H1	CDoC CHll CSpe EBak EShb MArl SDix WDib
- - pink-flowered	CDTJ MOWG
- - red-flowered	CDTJ
- - 'Rosea'	CDoC
fuchsioides	see *B. foliosa* var. *miniata*
'Glowing Embers'	LBuc SMrm SPoG
gracilis (T) F&M 266	CFil WPGP
- F&M 337	CFil WPGP
grandis (T)	XLum
§ - subsp. ***evansiana*** ♀H3-4	CAby CCon CHEx CSpe CTsd EBee EShb EUJe GCal LAst LEdu LPla SBch SDix SEND SKHP SPlb WCot WCru WMoo
- - B&SWJ 11188	WCru
- - var. ***alba*** hort.	CAby CCon CFil CLAP CSpe EBee EShb ESwi EWld EWll GCal LEdu LPla LRHS SBch SKHP SPoG SSpi WCot WMoo WPGP XLum
- - 'Claret Jug'	CExl CFil EBee EShb ESwi WCot WGrn WPGP WWEG
- - 'Pink Parasol'	CLAP EBee ESwi WCru
- - 'Simsii'	EBee
- - 'Sublime'	LEdu
- 'Sapporo'	CFil EBee EPPr ESwi GCal WCru
§ - subsp. ***sinensis***	WCot
I - - 'Red Undies'	CLAP EBee ESwi WCru
aff. ***grandis*** subsp. ***sinensis*** (T)	SKHP
- - BWJ 8133	WCru
'Green Gold' (R)	SBrm WDib
griffithii	see *B. annulata*
'Gryphon'	LAst LSqH
haageana hort. ex W. Watson	see *B. scharffii*
hatacoa silver-leaved	EShb WDib
Heaven Series (S)	LAst NPri
'Helen Teupel' (R)	WDib
'Hilo Holiday' (R) ♀H1	WDib
Honeymoon = 'Yamoon' (Million Kisses Series)	LAst
'Houston Fiesta' (R)	SBrm
(Illumination Series) 'Illumination Apricot' (T/d)	SCoo WGor
- 'Illumination Rose' (T/d)	SCoo WGor
- 'Illumination Salmon Pink' (T/d) ♀H2-3	SCoo
- 'Illumination Scarlet' (T/d)	WGor
- 'Illumination White' (T/d)	SCoo
'Inca Fire'PBR (R)	SBrm
incarnata 'Metallica'	see *B. metallica*
'Indian Summer'PBR (R)	SBrm
× ***intermedia*** Veitch ex Van Houtte 'Bertinii' (T)	SDeJ
'Ironstone' (R) ♀H1	SBrm
'La Paloma' (C)	WDib
Large-flowered Double Group (T/d)	SDeJ
'Lime Swirl'	WDib
'Limeade'	WDib
listada ♀H1	WDib
'Little Brother Montgomery' ♀H1	EShb SDix WDib
'Lois Burks' (C)	WDib
'Looking Glass' (C)	WDib
'Lucerna' (C)	EBak
'Lucky Colours' (R)	SBrm
luxurians ♀H1	CHEx CHll CSpe EAmu ESwi EUJe LLWG WCot
macduffieana	see *B. corallina*
maculata 'Wightii' (C)	CSpe WDib
'Magma' (R)	SBrm
Marginata Group (T) **new**	SDeJ
'Marmaduke' ♀H1	WCot WDib
'Marmorata' (T)	SDeJ
'Martin Johnson' (R) ♀H1	WDib
masoniana ♀H1	GCal WDib WSFF
'Merry Christmas' (R) ♀H1	WDib
'Metallic Mist'PBR	CSpe ESwi EUJe LBMP LSou NSti WGrn
§ ***metallica*** ♀H1	EShb
'Midnight Magic' (R) ♀H1	WDib
Million Kisses Series	LBuc
'Mishmi Silver'	GCal
'Mr Kartuz' (R) **new**	SBrm
'Munchkin' ♀H1	WDib
'My Best Friend'	WDib
'Namur' (R) ♀H1	WDib
Nonstop Series (T/d) ♀H2-3	LAst SDeJ
'Organdy' (mixed)	LAst
'Pachea' (R)	SBrm
palmata	CDTJ CExl CHEx EBee EShb GCal SKHP WPGP
panchtharensis **new**	CFil
Passion = 'Yabos' (Million Kisses Series)	LBuc LSou
'Peardrop'PBR	LBuc
pedatifida	CCon SKHP
- DJHC 98473	WCru
Pendula Group (T)	SDeJ
'Picotee' (T)	CSut SDeJ
'Pink Champagne' (R) ♀H1	WDib
I 'Pink Lady'	WCru
'Pink Pop' (R) **new**	SBrm
'Pollux'	WDib
'Princess of Hanover' (R) ♀H1	WDib
putii B&SWJ 7245	WCru
'Queen Olympus'	WDib
'Raspberry Swirl' (R) ♀H1	WDib
ravenii (T)	CHEx SKHP
- B&SWJ 1954	GCal WCot
'Razzmatazz' (R)	WDib
'Red Dragon' (R)	WDib
'Red Kiss' (R)	SBrm

'Red Robin' (R)	SBrm WDib
'Red Undies' (*grandis*)	see *B. grandis* subsp. *sinensis* 'Red Undies'
'Regal Minuet' (R)	SBrm WDib
'Richard Galle'	LAst
'Richmondensis' (S)	EShb
'Ricinifolia'	EShb GCal
'Rocheart' (R) 𝕐^{H1}	SBrm WDib
'Sal's Comet' (R) 𝕐^{H1}	WDib
'Sal's Moondust'	WDib
§ ***scharffii***	EBak SDix
'Scherzo'	WDib
serratipetala	EBak WDib
'Shamus'	WDib
* ***shepherdii***	WDib
Sherbet Bon Bon = 'Yabon' 𝕐$^{H3-4}$	LBuc
sikkimensis	GCal
- B&SWJ 2692	WCru
silletensis subsp. ***mengyangensis***	GCal
'Silver Cloud' (R) 𝕐^{H1}	WDib
'Silver Jewell'	WDib
'Silver Lace'	WDib
'Silver Splendor'	CLAP CSpe WCot
'Silver Spray' (R)	SBrm
sinensis	see *B. grandis* subsp. *sinensis*
sizemoreae	WDib
'Snow Storm'	WDib
* 'Snowcap' (C) 𝕐^{H1}	EShb WDib
solananthera A. DC. 𝕐^{H1}	EShb WDib
'Solid Silver' (R) **new**	WDib
soli-mutata	WDib
sonderiana (T)	GCal
'Stained Glass'	WDib
(Summerwings Series)	WGor
Summerwings Deep Red = 'Insumdered' **new**	
- Summerwings Orange = 'Innbolora'^{PBR}	ESwi WBor
- Summerwings White = 'Innbolwhi'^{PBR}	ESwi SMrm
sutherlandii (T) 𝕐^{H1}	CCCN CExl CFil CPom EABi EBak EBee EWld IGor LRHS NBir NPer SBch SDix SEND SVen WCot WDib WPGP
- 'Papaya' (T)	CSpe
'Switzerland' (T)	SDeJ
taliensis	SKHP
- EDHCH 042	WCru
- 'White-boned Demon'	SKHP
'Texastar'	WDib
'Thrush' (R)	SBrm
'Thurstonii' 𝕐^{H1}	EShb
'Tiger Paws' 𝕐^{H1}	EShb
'Tim Anderson' (R)	SBrm
* ***tripartita*** (T)	WDib
'Two Face'	WDib
'Vesuvius' (R)	WDib
'Wavy Green' **new**	GCal
'Wild Swan'	WCru

Belamcanda see *Iris*

Bellevalia (*Asparagaceae*)

atroviolacea	ECho
brevipedicellata	ECho
ciliata	ECho
'Cream Pearl'	ECho WCot
desertorum JCA 0.227.690	WCot
dubia	CDes CPom EBee ECho EWld WCot
- subsp. ***hackelii***	ECho
- var. ***maura***	see *B. mauretanica*
hyacinthoides	ECho WCot
longipes	ECho
§ ***mauretanica***	ECho
§ ***paradoxa***	CAby CHid CMea EBee ECho ERCP LPio MNrw SDeJ WCot
- white-flowered	ECho
pycnantha misapplied	see *B. paradoxa*
- 'Green Pearl' **new**	ECho SDeJ
romana	CPom EBee ECho ERCP GKev SDeJ WCot
sarmatica	ECho
sessiliflora	ECho
tabriziana	CDes ECho WCot
trifoliata	ECho
webbiana	ECho

Bellis (*Asteraceae*)

§ ***caerulescens***	GAbr
perennis	CArn
- 'Alice'	GAbr WCot
- 'Dresden China'	EWes GAbr
- 'Galaxy White' (Galaxy Series)	EPfP
- Hen and Chickens	see *B. perennis* 'Prolifera' single-flowered
- old strain **new**	WCot
§ - 'Prolifera' single-flowered	GAbr LRHS WCot
- 'Rusher Rose'	EPfP
- 'Single Blue'	see *B. caerulescens*
- 'The Pearl'	GAbr WCot
- 'White Pearl'	LRHS
rotundifolia 'Caerulescens'	see *B. caerulescens*
sylvestris	CArn WCot

Belloa (*Asteraceae*)

chilensis **new**	SPlb

Beloperone see *Justicia*

guttata	see *Justicia brandegeeana*

Bensoniella (*Saxifragaceae*)

oregona	CExl

Benthamiella (*Solanaceae*)

nordenskjoldii	WAbe
patagonica	WAbe
- F&W 9345	ITim WAbe
- white-flowered	WAbe
- yellow-flowered	WAbe

Berberidopsis (*Berberidopsidaceae*)

corallina	CBcs CDoC CDoy CMac CTri CWSG EBee ELan EPfP GGal IArd IDee IVic LBMP LHop LRHS MGos MOWG NLar SLim SPer SPoG SWvt WCru WHar WSHC

Berberis ✿ (*Berberidaceae*)

CC 4730	CExl
aggregata	MJak NBir SEND SPer SRms
amurensis var. ***latifolia*** B&SWJ 8539	WCru
aquifolium	see *Mahonia aquifolium*

	- 'Fascicularis'	see *Mahonia* × *wagneri* 'Pinnacle'
	aristata ambig.	CArn
	asiatica	CExl GPoy
	'Baby Bear'	CJun
	bealei	see *Mahonia japonica* Bealei Group
	× ***bristolensis***	SRms
N	***buxifolia*** 'Nana' misapplied	see *B. microphylla* 'Pygmaea'
	candidula C.K. Schneid.	CDul EPfP LRHS MSwo NLar SLon SPer
	- 'Jytte'	see *B.* 'Jytte'
	× ***carminea*** 'Pirate King'	CHel CSBt EBee EPfP LRHS MAsh MBlu SPoG SWvt WPat
	darwinii ♀H4	Widely available
I	- 'Compacta'	CDoC CMac CRos EBee ECrN EPfP LAst LBuc LHop LRHS MAsh NEgg NLar NSoo SHil SLim SPoG WCot
	deinacantha AC 1010 **new**	MSnd
	dictyophylla ♀H4	CDul CJun EBee EPfP LHop LRHS MGos MMuc NLar SKHP SLon SPer SPoG SSpi WSHC WSpi
	dulcis 'Nana'	see *B. microphylla* 'Pygmaea'
	dumicola	MSnd
	empetrifolia	LEdu
	× ***frikartii*** 'Amstelveen' ♀H4	CCVT CDoC EBee ECrN ELan EPfP LAst LRHS MBNS MRav NLar SEND WMoo
	- 'Telstar'	EBtc EWTr MRav NLar NPro WMoo
	gagnepainii misapplied	see *B. gagnepainii* var. *lanceifolia*
	gagnepainii C.K. Schneid.	CDul CMac
§	- var. ***lanceifolia***	CTri MGos MMuc NWea SEND SGol WHar
	- - 'Fernspray'	EPfP MRav SRms
	- 'Purpurea'	see *B.* × *interposita* 'Wallich's Purple'
	'Georgei' ♀H4	CWib EPfP GQui LRHS
	'Goldilocks'	CJun EBee EPfP LSRN MBlu
	goudotii B&SWJ 10769	WCru
	heterophylla	GKev
	hypokerina	CMac
	insignis	GCal
	- subsp. ***insignis*** var. ***insignis***	ELon LLHF WPat
	- - B&SWJ 2432	WCru
§	× ***interposita*** 'Wallich's Purple'	CCVT EBee EPfP MRav MSwo SPer WMoo
	jamesiana	LLHF MSnd WPat
	julianae ♀H4	CBcs CDul CHab CMac EBee ELan EPfP MGos MJak MMuc MSwo NWea SEND SGol SLPl SPer SRms SWvt WHar WSHC
§	'Jytte'	EBee EMil
	kawakamii	SLPl
	koreana	CDul EPfP NLar
	- 'Rubin'	CAgr
	'Little Favourite'	see *B. thunbergii* f. *atropurpurea* 'Atropurpurea Nana'
	× ***lologensis*** 'Apricot Queen' ♀H4	CBcs CMac EPfP GBin LRHS MAsh MGos MRav NLar SPer SPoG WPat
	- 'Mystery Fire'	IArd MAsh MBri MGos MJak NHol NLar SGol SWvt WHar WMoo
	- 'Stapehill'	CMac ELan EPfP LRHS MAsh
	× ***media*** 'Dual Jewel' **new**	NLar
	- Park Jewel	see *B.* × *media* 'Parkjuweel'
§	- 'Parkjuweel'	CBcs CMac EBee IArd MRav WMoo
	- 'Red Jewel' ♀H4	CDoC CMac ECrN EPfP LRHS MAsh MGos MRav SEND SPer SPoG WCFE WMoo
	microphylla	EPfP WCFE

§	- 'Pygmaea'	CBcs CSBt EBee EPfP LRHS MAsh MGos MRav SLim SPer
	mitifolia	NLar
	montana	WPGP WPat
	morrisonensis	GBin
	× ***ottawensis*** 'Auricoma'	SGol SWvt
	- f. ***purpurea***	CCVT CMac CWib LRHS WHar
§	- - 'Superba' ♀H4	Widely available
§	- 'Silver Miles' (v)	EHoe MRav NLar WHar WPat
§	***panlanensis***	LEdu
	- 'Cally Rose'	GCal
	poiretii	CExl
	polyantha var. ***polyantha***	CTri
	'Red Tears'	CJun MMHG MRav NLar SPer WMoo
	× ***rubrostilla*** 'Cherry Ripe'	CMac
	- 'Rubrostilla'	EBee
	- 'Wisley'	LRHS
	sanguinea misapplied	see *B. panlanensis*
	sargentiana	SLPl
	sieboldii	ELon LLHF MAsh MRav WPat WSpi
§	***soulieana***	EPfP LRHS
	stenophylla Hance	see *B. soulieana*
	× ***stenophylla*** Lindl. ♀H4	CCVT CDoC CDul CSBt CTri EBee EPfP LBuc MBri MRav NWea SEND SGol SPer WHar WMoo
	- 'Claret Cascade'	EBee MRav NLar SPer
	- 'Corallina Compacta' ♀H4	CHel CMac CMea EBee ECho ELan EPfP EPot LHop LRHS MAsh SPoG SRms WPat WThu
	- 'Crawley Gem'	GBin NLar
	- 'Etna'	ELan LRHS MAsh SCoo
	- 'Irwinii'	CMac LRHS SPer
	- 'Nana'	LRHS SRms
	- 'Pink Pearl' (v)	CMHG
	subacuminata NJM 09.165 **new**	WPGP
	taliensis	CExl
	temolaica ♀H4	CGHE CJun EBee EBtc EPfP MAsh MGos MRav MSnd NEgg NLar NWea SChF SMad SSta WCFE WPGP WPat WSpi
	- SF 95186	NSti
	thunbergii ♀H4	CBar CBcs CDoC CDul CMac EPfP LBuc NLar NWea SPer SWvt WMou
	- f. ***atropurpurea***	CBar CBcs CCVT CMac CRos CSBt CTri EBee EPfP LBuc MGos MRav MSwo NEgg NLar NWea SCoo SGol SPer SPlb WHar WMoo WMou
	- - 'Admiration' PBR ♀H4	CBcs CDoC CSBt ELan EPfP LBMP LBuc LLHF LRHS LSRN LSqu MAsh MBri MGos MJak MMHG NEgg NHol NLar SCoo SLim SLon SPer SPoG SWvt WGob WPat
§	- - 'Atropurpurea Nana' ♀H4	Widely available
	- - 'Aurea'	CBcs CDoC CDul CMac EBee EHoe ELan EPfP EPot LBMP LRHS LSRN MAsh MBlu MGos MRav MWat NLar SLim SPlb SSpi SWvt WMoo
	- - 'Bagatelle' ♀H4	CDoC EBee ELan EPfP EPot IArd IVic LAst LHop LRHS LSRN MAsh MBri MGos MRav NEgg NLar SLim SPer SPoG SWvt WCFE WHar WMoo WPat
	- - 'Concorde'	EPfP LRHS
	- - 'Dart's Red Lady' ♀H4	CExl CJun CSBt CWib EHoe ELan EPfP LRHS MAsh NLar NPro SLim SPer SPoG SWvt WPat

- - 'Erecta'	CMac EPfP MRav SPer WCFE
- - 'Golden Ring' (v) ♀H4	CBcs CDoC CDul CMac EBee EHoe ELan EPfP LBMP LHop LRHS MAsh MGos MRav NEgg NHol SLim SPer SPoG SWvt WMoo WPat
- - 'Harlequin' (v) ♀H4	CBcs CDoC CRos EBee ELan EPfP LRHS LSRN MAsh MBri MGos NEgg NLar SGol SHil SLim SPer SPoG SWvt WHar WPat
- - 'Helmond Pillar'	Widely available
- - 'Pink Queen' (v)	CDul ELan EPfP EWTr LHop LRHS MAsh NLar WMou WPat
- - 'Red Chief' ♀H4	CBcs CMac CRos EBee EHoe ELan EPfP LRHS MAsh MGos MJak MSwo NEgg SGol SHil SLim SLon SPer SPoG SWvt WHar WMoo WPat
- - 'Red Pillar'	CDoC CMac CRos EBee EHoe ELan EPfP IVic LAst LRHS MAsh MBri MGos MWat NEgg SHil SLim SWvt WPat
- - 'Red Rocket'	EPfP LRHS NLar WMoo
- - 'Rose Glow' (v) ♀H4	Widely available
- - 'Rosy Rocket'PBR (v)	CWGN EBee ECrN EPfP LRHS MAsh MBri SPer SPoG
- 'Atropurpurea Superba'	see *B.* × *ottawensis* f. *purpurea* 'Superba'
- Bonanza Gold = 'Bogozam'PBR	CBcs CDoC EBee ELan EPfP LRHS MAsh MRav NLar SLim SPer SPoG WPat
- 'Carpetbagger'	WHar
- 'Crimson Pygmy'	see *B. thunbergii* f. *atropurpurea* 'Atropurpurea Nana'
- 'Diabolic'	CRos LBuc LRHS MAsh MGos NHol SHil SPer SPoG WGrn
- 'Fireball'PBR ♀H4	EPfP LRHS MAsh
- 'Golden Rocket'PBR	CRos EPfP LHop LLHF LRHS MAsh MGos MJak MWat SPer WGob
- 'Golden Torch'	CRos CSBt ELan EPfP LRHS LSRN MAsh MBri MRav NEgg SHil SLim SWvt WPat
- 'Green Carpet'	CDul CMac LHop LRHS MBlu NLar SGol SPoG
- 'Green Mantle'	see *B. thunbergii* 'Kelleriis'
- 'Green Marble'	see *B. thunbergii* 'Kelleriis'
- 'Green Ornament'	NHol
§ - 'Kelleriis' (v)	LHop LRHS MGos MRav NHol NLar SLon
- 'Kobold'	CMac EPfP LHop LRHS MAsh MGos NEgg NLar SLim SPer SPoG WMoo
- 'Maria'PBR ♀H4	CWGN ELon GBin LLHF LRHS LSou MBri MGos MJak NCGa NEgg NHol NLar NPri NSoo SHil SLim SPoG WHar WMoo
- 'Orange Rocket'PBR	CRos EPfP LRHS MAsh MBri NHol SHil SPer SPoG WGob WPat
- 'Pink Attraction' (v)	NLar
- 'Pow-wow'	CDoC EBee LRHS MAsh MBri MGos NEgg NLar SCoo SLim SPoG SWvt WPat
- 'Red Torch' **new**	MMHG
- 'Silver Beauty' (v)	CBcs CMHG EBee MBri
- 'Silver Mile'	see *B.* × *ottawensis* 'Silver Miles'
- 'Somerset'	CMac
- 'Starburst'PBR (v)	CBcs CDoC CDul CRos CSBt EBee EPfP LRHS LSRN MAsh MBri MGos NEgg NPri SCoo SHil SLim SLon SPoG SWvt WGob
- 'Tiny Gold'PBR	EBee GBin LAst LBuc LRHS MAsh MGos NLar SLim SLon SPoG SWvt WGob
* - 'Tricolor' (v)	CMac MRav WPat
trigona 'Orange King'	CBcs CMac CTri EBee ELan EPfP MAsh MGos NEgg NLar SPer SPoG WHar WPat
valdiviana	CExl CGHE CJun CMHG EBee EPfP IArd IDee SKHP SMad SSpi WPGP WPat
verruculosa ♀H4	CBcs CDul EBee EPfP EWTr LAst LHop LRHS MGos NLar NWea SCoo SPer SRms SWvt
- 'Hard's Rob'	NLar
aff. ***verticillata*** B&SWJ 10672	WCru
virescens B&SWJ 2646D	WCru
vulgaris	CArn CHab CNat EPfP GPoy MCoo NWea
- 'Wiltshire Wonder' (v)	CNat
wilsoniae	CBcs CDul CMac CTri ECre ELan EPfP LHop MMuc NLar NWea SPer WCFE
- blue-leaved	MAsh
- var. ***guhtzunica***	EWes

Berchemia (*Rhamnaceae*)

racemosa	CMen NLar WSHC

bergamot see *Citrus bergamia*

Bergenia ✿ (*Saxifragaceae*)

'Abendglocken'	CMac ECGP ECtt EPfP GQue LRHS NSti WCot
§ 'Abendglut'	Widely available
'Admiral'	CBct MLHP MNFA WCot
afghanica	XLum
* ***agavifolia***	CBct XLum
'Andrea'	WCot
'Autumn Magic'	CBct COIW ELon EPfP GQue LAst LHop LRHS LSou NEgg NPri
'Baby Doll'	Widely available
'Bach'	ECtt GAbr GQue LSou MAsh MCot NLar NSti WCAu WCot WHil
§ 'Ballawley' clonal ♀H4	GCal IBlr IGor IMou LRHS MLHP MRav NEgg WCot WMnd WWEG XLum
§ Ballawley hybrids	CMac SDix
'Ballawley Red'	NEgg
'Ballawley' seed-raised	see *B.* Ballawley hybrids
'Bartók'	CDes CLAP ECtt ESwi GQue NLar WCot
beesiana	see *B. purpurascens*
'Beethoven'	CBct CDes EBee GCra IGor MRav NBir NBre WCot WPGP
Bell Tower	see *B.* 'Glockenturm'
'Bizet'	CBct XLum
'Borodin'	CBct
'Brahms'	CBct WCot
'Bressingham Bountiful'	CBct
'Bressingham Ruby'PBR	CBct CLAP EBee ECtt ELon IPot LBMP LRHS LSRN MBel MGos MHol MRav NBir NEgg SGol STPC SWvt WCot WHil WPGP
'Bressingham Salmon'	EBee ECtt ELan ELon GMaP LRHS LSRN MRav NLar SRms WCot WMnd
'Bressingham White' ♀H4	Widely available
'Britten' ♀H4	WCot

ciliata	CBct CDes CHEx CLAP CMac CTca EShb EUJe GCra LEdu LPio LRHS MLHP MRav NHol NLar SDix WKif WPGP WSHC XLum
- f. ***ligulata***	see *B. pacumbis*
- 'Patricia Furness'	CLAP
- 'Wilton'	CBct CDes CLAP WCot WWEG
ciliata × crassifolia	see *B.* × *schmidtii*
'Claire Maxine' ♀H4	CBct CLAP EBee ECtt GBin GCal MPie NLar SHar WCot
cordifolia	Widely available
- 'Jelle'	EBee
- 'Lunar Glow'	CBct COlW EBee ECtt ELon EPfP LHop LSou MBri NLar NPri SPoG WHil
- 'Purpurea' ♀H4	CBcs CDoC CMac CWCL EBee ECrN ELan EPfP LBuc LRHS MLHP MRav NBir NEgg SPer SRms SWvt XLum
- 'Rosa Zeiten' ♀H4	GBin
- 'Rose'	LRHS
- 'Tubby Andrews' (v)	CBct CMac EBee EShb LEdu LRHS MAvo MBel MBrN NEgg NLar NPro SRms WHrl WWEG
- 'Vinterglöd'	EBee ELan ELon EPfP GMaP GQue IFoB LAst LRHS NBre NGdn NLar SWvt WPnP XLum
crassifolia	EBee EPfP GKev NBre SRms WWEG XLum
- DF 90028	GBin
- 'Autumn Red'	CBct EBee WWEG
- 'Orbicularis'	see *B.* × *schmidtii*
I - var. ***pacifica***	XLum
- - 'Cally Gem'	EBee GCal
* ***cyanea***	CLAP WCot
'David'	EWes WWEG
'Delbees'	see *B.* 'Ballawley' clonal
'Doppelgänger'	EBee
'Eden's Dark Margin'	CBct CDoC ECtt ELon GBin GQue LDai LRHS LSou MBri MNrw NCGa NLar NMyG NPro SPoG WCot WHil
'Eden's Magic Giant' ♀H4	CBct CCon EBee ECGP ECtt ELon EWll GBin LPla LRHS MBNS MBri MPie NCGa NLar SPoG SRms WCot
emeiensis	CDes CLAP GCal IGor IMou LEdu WCot WPGP
- hybrid	CBct
'Eric Smith' ♀H4	CBct GCal GCra MBri MNFA WCAu WCot WMnd
'Eroica' ♀H4	CBct COlW CSpe EBee ECtt ELan ELon EPfP GBin IBoy LHop LRHS LSou MBri MMuc MRav NBre NLar NSti SPer SWvt WHoo WMnd WPtf WSpi
'Evening Glow'	see *B.* 'Abendglut'
§ 'Glockenturm'	CBct NEgg
'Goldfisch'	EBee
'Harzkristall'	CBct CDoC COlW GBin LHop LRHS SPoG
'Hellen Dillon'	see *B. purpurascens* 'Irish Crimson'
'Herbstblute'	WCAu
'Ice Queen'	CBct CMil LLHF LLWG WCot
'Jo Watanabe'	CBct MRav
'Kashmir'	XLum
'Lambrook'	see *B.* 'Margery Fish'
§ 'Margery Fish'	CBct CFis SPer
milesii	see *B. stracheyi*
§ 'Morgenröte' ♀H4	CBcs CBct CMac EBee ELon EPfP GMaP LHop LRHS LSRN MGos MNFA MRav NHol NLar NSti SPer SRms SWvt WCFE WCot WWEG
'Morning Light'	ECtt ELon NPro
Morning Red	see *B.* 'Morgenröte'
'Mrs Crawford'	CBct
'Oeschberg'	CBct GBin GCal
'Opal'	CBct EBee GBin
'Overture'	Widely available
§ ***pacumbis***	CHEx CLAP EBee GBin GCal NBid NBre NSti
- B&SWJ 2693	WCru
- CC 1793	SBch WCot
- CC 3616	CBct CDes WCot WPGP
'Perfect'	WMnd
'Pink Dragonfly'	CMac EBee ECtt ELon EPfP GBin LRHS NLar SPoG WCAu
'Pink Frostwork' **new**	WCot
'Pinneberg'	GBin
'Pugsley's Pink' ♀H4	CBct
'Purple Queen'	LRHS
§ ***purpurascens*** ♀H4	CMac EBee EHyd EPfP GMaP IGor LRHS MBrN SPer WWEG
- SDR 4548	GKev
- var. ***delavayi*** ♀H4	EBee LRHS NBre NLar SRms
§ - 'Irish Crimson' ♀H4	CAby WCot
aff. ***purpurascens***	NGdn
- ACE 2175	WCot
'Purpurglocken'	EBee ECtt GCal LRHS WCAu
'Red Beauty'	COlW EHoe EPfP IBoy LRHS MSnd
'Red Rush'	EBee
'Rietheim'	EBee GBin
'Rosi Klose'	CLAP EBee ECtt EHoe ELon EWes GBin GCra LHop LRHS MBri MNFA MRav NBre NGdn WCot WGwG WWEG
'Rosi Ruffles'	EBee MBNS
'Rotblum'	CBct CNec ECtt EHoe ELon EPfP GMaP LEdu MSCN NBir NGdn NOrc WHar WWEG
§ × ***schmidtii*** ♀H4	CBct CMac GBin LRHS MRav NBir NBre NLar WCot WWEG
'Schneekissen'	CBct CMac CPrp ECGP ECtt LRHS MCot MRav WCAu
§ 'Schneekoenigin'	CBct GBin GCal MRav
§ 'Silberlicht' ♀H4	Widely available
Silverlight	see *B.* 'Silberlicht'
'Simply Sweet'	WCot
Snow Queen	see *B.* 'Schneekoenigin'
§ ***stracheyi***	CBct CCon CExl GBin GCal MLHP NBid NLar SDix WCot WWEG
- CC 4609	EBee
- Alba Group	GCal WPGP WWEG
'Sunningdale' ♀H4	CBcs CMac ELan EPfP GCra GMaP LHop LRHS MRav NBir NGdn SPer SWvt WMnd WWEG
tianquanensis	EBee WPGP
'Tim' **new**	EBee
'Walter Kienli'	EBee GBin
Winter Fairy Tales	see *B.* 'Wintermärchen'
§ 'Wintermärchen' ♀H4	CBct CPrp ECtt ELan ELon EPfP EShb GBin GCra LAst LRHS MLHP MMuc MRav NHol NPro SWvt WCAu WCot WMnd WWEG

Bergeranthus (*Aizoaceae*)

multiceps	SChr

Berkheya (*Asteraceae*)

multijuga	CSpe EPfP EWld LRHS SBHP

purpurea	CBcs CCVN CSpe EBee ELon EPfP EPri IBoy LEdu LRHS MHol MNrw MPie NEgg SBch SBea SMrm SPet SPlb WCot WHer WKif WMnd WSHC
- 'Silver Spike'	EPfP GBin LSRN NGdn
- 'Zulu Warrior'	CMac NGBl SBHP SRkn

Berlandiera (*Asteraceae*)

lyrata	CArn

Berneuxia (*Diapensiaceae*)

thibetica	WCot

Berula (*Apiaceae*)

erecta	NPer

Berzelia (*Bruniaceae*)

galpinii	SPlb

Beschorneria (*Asparagaceae*)

albiflora	CFil CSpe EBee WPGP
septentrionalis	CAbP CAby CCon CDTJ CDoC CFil CGHE CHEx CSpe EBee EGri ESwi EUJe IBoy LRHS LSou MBNS MBel MHol SEND SPad WCot WGrn WPGP
septentrionalis* × *yuccoides	CFil CHll WPGP
tubiflora	CDTJ CFil CHEx
wrightii	CFil
yuccoides ♀H3	CAbb CBcs CExl CFil CHEx EAmu EBee EGri EMil ESwi LEdu SAPC SEND
- subsp. ***dekosteriana***	CFil
- 'Quicksilver'	CBcs CCCN CDoC CEnd CExl CKno CMHG CSBt EBee ELan EPfP IVic LRHS MBri NSoo SLim SSpi WGrn WPGP

Bessera (*Asparagaceae*)

elegans	CAvo CCon CGrW EBee ECho EPot MHer SDeJ

Beta (*Amaranthaceae*)

vulgaris	SHDw SVic WHer
- 'Bull's Blood'	CSpe WJek
- subsp. ***cicla***	SVic
var. ***flavescens*** Bright Lights ♀H3	
- - - 'Rhubarb Chard' ♀H3	WJek
- subsp. ***maritima***	CAgr

Betonica see *Stachys*

Betula ✿ (*Betulaceae*)

	alba L.	see *B. pendula*, *B. pubescens*
	albosinensis misapplied	see *B. utilis*
	albosinensis Burkill ♀H4	CDul CLnd CMCN EBee EPfP
	- W 4106	CSto
	- from Gansu, China	CSto
	- 'Bowling Green'	CExl CJun MBlu WPGP
	- 'China Rose'	see *B. albosinensis* 'China Ruby'
§	- 'China Ruby'	CJun EBee EPfP SSpi WPGP
	- 'Chinese Garden'	CJun
	- clone F	see *B. albosinensis* 'Ness'
	- 'Fascination'	CCVT CMCN EBee IDee MBlu MGos NLar SKHP WHar WMou
	- 'K.Ashburner'	CJun CTho
§	- 'Ness'	CJun CTho
	- 'Pink Champagne'	CJun CSto EPfP WPGP
	- 'Red Panda'	CJun EBee GQue
	- 'Rhinegold'	MBlu
	- 'Sable'	SLim
	- var. ***septentrionalis*** ♀H4	CBcs CCVT CDoC CDul CEnd CLnd CSto CTho CWib EBee ECrN ELon EPfP EWTr GBin GKin LAst MBlu MGos MRav MSwo NWea SCoo SGol SLim SPer WMou WPGP
	- - 'Kansu'	CEnd CJun CLnd CTsd EBee LRHS MBri NLar NWea SBig SCoo WHar
	- - 'Purdom'	CJun CLnd SBig
§	***alleghaniensis***	CCVT CDul CMCN CSto EPfP GBin MMuc NLar NWea SGol WCru
	apoiensis 'Mount Apoi'	CJun SBig
	chichibuensis	CSto MMHG MSnd WHer
	chinensis	CMCN
	'Conyngham'	CJun CTho MBlu SLau
	cordifolia	see *B. papyrifera* var. *cordifolia*
	costata misapplied	see *B. ermanii* 'Grayswood Hill'
	costata ambig.	CMCN ECrN MMuc SGol
	costata Trautv.	CTho EBee MSwo
*	- 'Fincham Cream'	CJun SBig
	'Crimson Frost'	EBee
	cylindrostachya	EBee
	dahurica Pall.	CSto
	- 'Maurice Foster'	CDoC CJun CTho EBee WPGP
	- 'Stone Farm'	CJun
	delavayi	EBee
	divaricata	CJun
	ermanii	CBcs CCVT CDoC CDul CMCN CMac CSBt CTri ECrN ELan EWTr GBin GQui LAst LRHS MBlu MGos MMuc MRav NEgg NLar NWea SGol WMou
	- B&SWJ 8801 from South Korea	WCru
	- from Hokkaido, Japan	CSto
	- 'Blush'	CJun MBlu SBig SCoo
	- var. ***ermanii***	LSRN
	- - MSF 825	EBee
	- - MSF 865	WPGP
§	- 'Grayswood Hill' ♀H4	CDul CEnd CJun CLnd CMCN CMHG CSBt CTho CTri EBee EPfP GQui MAsh MBlu MGos SCoo SLim SMad SPer SWvt WPGP
	- 'Hakkoda Orange'	CJun CTho MBri SCoo WHar WPGP
	- 'Holland'	IArd IDee NLar
	- 'Moonbeam'	WHar
	- 'Mount Zao'	CJun CSto IVic WPGP
*	- 'Pendula'	CJun EBee GBin LLHF LRHS MBlu SBig SBir SCoo
	- 'Polar Bear'	CJun EBee GBin MBlu MBri NLar SCoo SSta WPGP
	- 'Zao Purple'	CDul
	'Fetisowii'	CDul CEnd CJun EBee EBtc LRHS MBlu NLar SBig WHar
	fruticosa	see *B. humilis*
	globispica	CJun
	'Hergest'	CDoC CJun EBee ECrN EPfP MAsh MBri MGos SCoo SLau WHar
§	***humilis***	GKev
	insignis	CSto
	- B&SWJ 11751	WCru
	'Inverleith'	see *B. utilis* var. *jacquemontii* 'Inverleith'
	jacquemontii	see *B. utilis* var. *jacquemontii*
	kamtschatica	see *B. humilis*

	lenta	CDul CMCN CSto EPfP IArd MBlu MMuc NWea
	luminifera	CJun EBee EBtc NLar
	lutea	see *B. alleghaniensis*
§	***mandshurica***	CSto NEgg
§	- var. ***japonica***	MMuc MSnd NWea
	- - 'Whitespire Senior'	CDul
	maximowicziana	CDul CLnd CMCN CSto CWib EPfP IDee NLar SGol
	medwedewii	CDul CJun CLnd CMCN CSto EBee EPfP NLar NWea
	- 'Gold Bark'	CJun CMCN EPfP MBlu
	michauxii	NLar WCru
	nana	CDul GQue MGos MRav NHar NWea
	- 'Glengarry'	EPot GBin NLar
	nigra	CBcs CCVT CDoC CDul CEnd CLnd CMCN CTho CTri EWTr MAsh MBri SEWo SGol WMou
	- 'Black Star' **new**	LRHS
§	- 'Cully' ♀H4	CDoC CDul CLnd CTho EBee ECrN LHop MGos MRav NWea SBig SCoo SGol WMou
	- Dura-Heat = 'Bnmtf'	MGos NLar
	- Heritage	see *B. nigra* 'Cully'
	- 'Little King'	CJun MGos MPkF SKHP
	- 'Peter Collinson'	CJun
	- 'Summer Cascade'	CDoC EBee LSRN MAsh SKHP SLon
	- Tecumseh Compact = 'Studetec'	MPkF SGol
	- Wakehurst form	EPfP SPer SPoG
	papyrifera	CCVT CDul CLnd CMCN CMac CSBt CSto CTri EBee ECrN ELan EPfP EWTr LBuc LSRN MBlu MGos MMuc MRav MSwo NWea SEND SGol SPer WHar WMou
	- 'Belle Vue'	CSto EBee WPGP
§	- var. ***cordifolia***	CSto
	- - 'Clarenville'	CJun EBee WPGP
	- 'Saint George'	CJun CTho
	- 'Vancouver'	CJun CTho MBlu
§	***pendula*** ♀H4	Widely available
	- 'Bangor'	CJun SSta
	- f. ***crispa***	see *B. pendula* 'Laciniata'
	- 'Dalecarlica' misapplied	see *B. pendula* 'Laciniata'
	- 'Dalecarlica' ambig.	CBcs CCVT CSBt EBee ECrN LRHS MRav SCrf SWvt
	- 'Dark Prince'	CJun
	- 'Fastigiata'	CCVT CDul CLnd CSBt CTho EBee ECrN ELan MGos MJak NEgg NWea SCoo SGol SPer
*	- 'Golden Beauty'	CDoC CDul CMac EBee LAst MAsh MGos NLar SCoo SLim SPoG SSpi WHar
	- 'Golden Cloud'	GKin MJak
§	- 'Laciniata' ♀H4	CDul CMCN CMac CTho CWib EBee ELan EPfP EWTr IDee MAsh MBlu MGos MRav MSwo NWea SCoo SGol SPer WCFE WHar WMou
	- 'Long Trunk'	CDul EBee ECrN LAst LLHF MAsh MBlu SGol SLim WHar
	- 'Purpurea'	CCVT CDul CMCN CSBt CWib EBee ECrN ELan ELon EPfP EWTr GKin LAst LSRN MGos MSwo NLar NWea SCoo SGol SPer
	- 'Silver Grace'	CJun EBee ECrN LSRN SKHP
	- 'Tristis' ♀H4	CBcs CCVT CDoC CDul CEnd CJun CLnd CMCN CMac CSBt CSto CTho CTri EBee ECrN EPfP LAst LSRN MAsh MGos MRav MSwo NLar NWea SGol SLim SPer WHar WMou
	- 'Youngii'	Widely available
	- 'Zwitsers Glorie'	SKHP
§	***pendulata*** 'Spider Alley' PBR	LRHS
	platyphylla misapplied	see *B. mandshurica*
	platyphylla Sukaczev subsp. ***kamtschatica***	see *B. mandshurica* var. *japonica*
	- Dakota Pinnacle = 'Fargo'	EBee NLar SCoo WHar
	- subsp. ***platyphylla***	MSnd
	populifolia	CSto
	potaninii	MSnd
§	***pubescens***	CCVT CDul CHab CSto CTri EBee ECrN GQue SEND WMou
	raddeana	EBtc
	'Royal Frost'	CDul CJun EBee GQue IArd IDee MAsh MBlu NLar SLim WHar
	'Silver Trestles'	see *B. pendulata* 'Spider Alley'
	szechuanica	NEgg NPCo
	- W 983	WPGP
	- 'Liuba White'	CJun CTho
	- 'Moonlight'	SLau
§	***utilis***	CDul CMCN CSBt CSto ECrN MAsh MMuc SEND SSta
	- BL&M 100 from central Nepal	CSto
	- GWJ 9259	WCru
	- H&M 1480 from Sichuan, China	CSto
	- HWJK 2250	WCru
	- HWJK 2345	WCru
	- Sch 2168	EBee
	- SICH 667 from Sichuan, China	CSto
	- S&L from Nepal	CDul
	- Yu 10163 from Yunnan, China	CSto
	- from eastern Nepal	CSto
	- 'Bhutan Sienna' **new**	CSto
	- 'Buddha' **new**	WPGP
	- 'China Bronze'	WPGP
	- 'Darkness'	SLon
	- 'Fascination'	CDul CJun EBee EPfP IArd MBri MGos NWea SCoo SLim SSpi SSta WHCr WSpi
*	- 'Fastigiata'	CJun SBig SSta
	- 'Forrest's Blush'	CDul CJun CSto EBee LSRN MBri SBig WHar WPGP
	- var. ***jacquemontii***	Widely available
	- - Polunin	WPGP
	- - 'Doorenbos' ♀H4	Widely available
	- - 'Grayswood Ghost' ♀H4	CDoC CDul CEnd CJun CLnd CMCN CMHG CTho CTri ELan EPfP LRHS MBlu MBri NLar NWea SBig SBir SLau SLim SMad SSta WHar WPGP WSpi
§	- - 'Inverleith'	CDul CJun EBee GBin GQue MAsh SBig SBir SCoo SLim WPGP
	- - 'Jermyns' ♀H4	CDul CEnd CJun CLnd CMHG CMac CTri EBee EPfP IVic LRHS LSRN MBlu MBri SCoo SLau SPer SSta SWvt WHCr WHar
	- - 'McBeath'	SLau
	- - 'Silver Shadow' ♀H4	CDul CEnd CJun CLnd CTho EPfP LRHS LSRN MBlu NLar NWea SBig SBir SCoo SKHP SLau SLim SPer SPoG SSta WSpi

	- - 'Trinity College'	CDul CJun CTri EBee LRHS MBri SBig SBir SSpi SSta WHCr WHar
	- 'Knightshayes'	CTho
	- 'Moonbeam'	CDul CJun CSBt GQue LRHS MBri SBig SCoo SPoG WHar
	- 'Mount Luoji'	CSto WPGP
	- 'Nepalese Orange'	CSto WPGP
	- var. ***occidentalis*** 'Kyelang'	CJun CTho IVic
	- 'Polar Bear'	LRHS
	- var. ***prattii***	CEnd CJun CTho
	- - Park Wood 1123	CSto EBee WPGP
	- 'Ramdana River'	CDoC CMHG EBee WPGP
	- 'Schilling'	CJun
	- 'Sichuan Red' **new**	CSto
	- 'Wakehurst Place Chocolate'	CDul CJun CSBt CTho EBee GBin MBlu MBri NWea SBig SCoo SLim SSpi SSta WHCr WHar WSpi
*	- var. ***yunnanensis***	CSto
	cf. ***utilis***	CTri SGol
	verrucosa	see *B. pendula*

Biarum (*Araceae*)

	S&L 604	WCot
	SB&L 597	WCot
	bovei	ECho WCot
	- LB 351	WCot
	carratracense	WCot
	- from Spain	WCot
	davisii	ECho EPot LWst WCot
	dispar	WCot
	- S&L 290/2	WCot
	- SB&L 294	WCot
	- SB&L 564	WCot
	ditschianum	WCot
	- from Turkey	WCot
	marmarisense	EBee ECho LWst WCot
	ochridense hort.	see *B. tenuifolium* subsp. *abbreviatum* autumn-flowering
	tenuifolium	EBee ECho WCot
	- LB 223	WCot
	- LB 295	WCot
	- PB 357	WCot
	- S&L 174	WCot
	- subsp. ***abbreviatum***	LWst
	- - MS 974	WCot
	- - from Greece	ECho
§	- - autumn-flowering	WCot
	- subsp. ***arundanum***	WCot
	- subsp. ***galianii*** PB 435	WCot
	- subsp. ***idomenaeum*** MS 738	WCot
	- subsp. ***zelebori***	ECho WCot
	- - CRL 502	WCot
	- - LB 300	WCot
	- - PB 224	WCot
	- - PB 334	WCot

Bidens (*Asteraceae*)

	B&SWJ 10276 from Mexico	WCru
	atrosanguinea	see *Cosmos atrosanguineus*
§	***aurea***	ECtt EWes LAst LEdu MNrw MSpe NPer NPri SMrm SPet WBor WOld XLum
	- B&SWJ 9049 from Guatemala	WCru
	- 'Cream Streaked Yellow'	GQue
	- cream-flowered	MNrw
	- 'Golden Drop'	LSou
	- 'Hannay's Lemon Drop'	CAby CCVN CKno EBee ECtt ELon EPfP EShb LHop LPio LPla LPot LSou MNrw MSpe SGbt SPoG SRms WBor WPGP
*	- 'Lemon Queen' **new**	SMad
	- 'Rising Sun'	EWes
	- white-flowered	GCal
	ferulifolia ♀H1+3	ECtt NPer
	- Peter's Gold Rush = 'Topteppich'PBR	LSou
	- Solaire = 'Bidtis 1'PBR	WGor
	- 'Yellow Charm'	LSou
	heterophylla Ortega	see *B. aurea*
	heterophylla misapplied	CAby CPrp ECtt MCot MRav MWat WHal WMoo XLum
	- CD&R 1515	LPla
	humilis	see *B. triplinervia* var. *macrantha*
	integrifolia	SMad
	'Pirate's Treasure'	ECtt
	triplinervia B&SWJ 10413	WCru
	- B&SWJ 10696	WCru
§	- var. ***macrantha***	ELon LHop

Bignonia (*Bignoniaceae*)

	capreolata	CCCN CRHN WSHC
	- 'Dragon Lady'	SKHP
	lindleyana	see *Clytostoma calystegioides*
	tweedieana	see *Macfadyena unguis-cati*
	unguis-cati	see *Macfadyena unguis-cati*

Bilderdykia see *Fallopia*

Billardiera (*Pittosporaceae*)

	cymosa	CTsd MOWG
	longiflora ♀H3	CBcs CHid CMac CSBt CTri CWib EBee ECou ELan EPfP IArd ITim LRHS LSRN MAsh MGos MOWG MRav NLar NSoo SEND SLim SPer SPoG SWvt WKif WPGP WPat WSHC
	- 'Cherry Berry'	CBcs CFlo CMac EBee ELan EPfP LRHS LSRN NLar SLim SPoG SRms SWvt WSHC
	- ***fructu-albo***	CBcs CFlo EBee ELan EPfP EWes NLar SLon SPer SWvt

Billbergia (*Bromeliaceae*)

	nutans	CHll EBak ESwi EUJe IBlr IMou LEdu MRav SChr SEND SPlb WGwG WSFF
	- var. ***schimperiana***	EShb
*	- 'Variegata' (v)	CCon CHll EShb EUJe SChr WCot
	pyramidalis ♀H1	XBlo
I	- 'Variegata' (v)	IBlr
	× ***windii*** ♀H1	CCon CHEx EBak

Biserrula (*Papilionaceae*)

	pelecinus	WCot

Bismarckia (*Arecaceae*)

	nobilis	CCCN EAmu

Bistorta see *Persicaria*

Bituminaria (*Papilionaceae*)

	bituminosa HH&K 174	WSHC

blackberry see *Rubus fruticosus*

blackcurrant see *Ribes nigrum*

Blackstonia (*Gentianaceae*)

perfoliata	CRDP

Blechnum (*Blechnaceae*)

alpinum	see *B. penna-marina* subsp. *alpinum*
brasiliense 🏆H1	ISha
§ ***chilense*** 🏆H3	CBcs CBty CDTJ CDes CGHE CHEx CLAP EAmu EPfP GBin GCal GCra IArd IBlr LEdu LRHS MMoz SAPC SBig SKHP SPlb WCru WMoo WPGP
discolor	CLAP
fluviatile	CBcs CDTJ CLAP MMoz
gibbum	CBty
- 'Silver Lady'	ISha
magellanicum misapplied	see *B. chilense*
magellanicum (Desv.) Mett.	CKel EAmu SBig SKHP WPGP
minus	CBty
novae-zelandiae	CBcs CDTJ
nudum	CBty CDTJ CKel EAmu ESwi
penna-marina 🏆H4	CBty CCCN CElw CExl CKel CLAP EFer GAbr GBin GCal GMaP LEdu LRHS MRav NBir NWad WFib WMoo WWEG XLum
§ - subsp. ***alpinum***	CLAP SKHP WMoo
- 'Cristatum'	CLAP GAbr
punctulatum	ISha
spicant 🏆H4	Widely available
tabulare misapplied	see *B. chilense*
tabulare (Thunb.) Kuhn 🏆H1	CBcs CDTJ CKel EAmu EPfP GGal WPGP
wattsii	CDes EAmu

Blepharocalyx (*Myrtaceae*)

§ ***cruckshanksii***	CCCN CExl EBee ELon IArd LHop LRHS NLar WBor
- 'Heaven Scent'	see *B. cruckshanksii*

Blephilia (*Lamiaceae*)

ciliata	SPhx

Bletilla ✿ (*Orchidaceae*)

sp.	NDav
Brigantes gx	NLAp
Coritani gx	NLAp
formosana	NLAp
hyacinthina	see *B. striata*
ochracea	CExl GKev NLAp WCot
Penway Imperial gx	NLAp
Penway Majestic gx	NLAp
Penway Pixie gx	NLAp
Penway Sunset gx	NLAp WCot
sinensis	CExl
§ ***striata***	CAby CBct CCon CDes CExl CHel CTri CTsd EBee ECho EPot GKev LEdu LRHS MNrw NLAp SDeJ SPer WCot WPGP XLum
- ***alba***	see *B. striata* f. *gebina*
- 'Albostriata'	CBct CCon CExl EBee ECho ELan LRHS NLAp WCot XLum
§ - f. ***gebina***	CCon CCse CDes CExl CHel CTri CTsd EBee ECho EPot GKev LEdu LRHS NLAp SDeJ SPer WPGP XLum
- - variegated (v)	EPot LEdu
- 'Gotemba Stripes' **new**	NLAp
- var. ***japonica***	IGor
- 'Junpaku'	LWst NLAp
- 'Kuchi-beni'	GKev LWst NLAp
- 'Lips'	LWst NLAp
- 'Soryu'	NLAp
- variegated (v)	LRHS
szetschuanica	GKev NLAp

Bloomeria (*Asparagaceae*)

crocea	ECho GKev
- var. ***aurea***	ECho GKev GLin
- var. ***montana***	ECho

blueberry see *Vaccinium corymbosum*

Blumea (*Asteraceae*)

balsamifera	CHab

Bocconia (*Papaveraceae*)

cordata	see *Macleaya cordata* (Willd.) R. Br.
frutescens F&M 358	WPGP
microcarpa	see *Macleaya microcarpa*

Boehmeria (*Urticaceae*)

nivea	WCot
platanifolia	IMou
tricuspis	IMou SBrt

Boenninghausenia (*Rutaceae*)

albiflora	CRDP
- B&SWJ 1479	WCru
- BWJ 8141 from China	WCru
- pink-flowered B&SWJ 3112	WCru
japonica B&SWJ 11186	WCru

Bolax (*Apiaceae*)

glebaria	see *B. gummifer*
§ ***gummifer***	ECho WAbe

Bolboschoenus (*Cyperaceae*)

§ ***maritimus***	SMea

Boltonia (*Asteraceae*)

asteroides	GCra LRHS MMuc SMrm SPer SWat WRHF XLum
- var. ***latisquama***	GMaP GQue LSou MAvo MRav MWat NCGa NLar SHar SMad WBor WHal WHil
- - 'Nana'	MRav NBre
- - 'Snowbank'	ELan GCal LHop LRHS MSpe NDov
- 'Pink Beauty'	LHop
decurrens	EBee GCal IMou NBre WBor
- 'Warrior's Blush' **new**	MNrw
incisa	see *Kalimeris incisa*

Bolusanthus (*Papilionaceae*)

speciosus	SPlb

Bomarea (*Alstroemeriaceae*)

F&M 130	WPGP
acutifolia	CFil SKHP
- B&SWJ 9094	WCru
- B&SWJ 9130	WCru
- B&SWJ 10388	WCru
aff. ***andreana*** B&SWJ 10617	WCru
boliviensis	WCru
caldasii	see *B. multiflora*

	costaricensis B&SWJ 10467	WCru
	distichifolia	CExl WCot
§	***edulis***	CGHE CRHN CWGN WCot WKif WPGP
	- B&SWJ 9017	LEdu WCru
	- F&M 104	CExl WPGP
	frondea	see *B. multiflora*
	aff. ***frondea*** B&SWJ 10681	WCru
	hirsuta B&SWJ 10774	WCru
	hirtella	see *B. edulis*
§	***multiflora*** 🏆H1	CBcs CCCN CCon CExl EBee EShb GCal IKil SKHP WBor WCot WCru WPGP WSHC
	salsilla	CAvo CCCN CFil SKHP WPGP WSHC

Bombax (*Malvaceae*)

	ceiba	SPlb

Bongardia (*Berberidaceae*)

	chrysogonum	CAvo ECho EPot GKev LLHF LRHS WCot WHal

Bonia (*Poaceae*)

§	***solida***	CHEx ERod MMoz MMuc MWht SEND WJun

Boophone (*Amaryllidaceae*)

	disticha	WCot

borage see *Borago officinalis*

Borago (*Boraginaceae*)

	laxiflora	see *B. pygmaea*
	officinalis	CArn CHby CSev ELau EPfP GPoy MHer MHoo MNHC NBir NPri SBch SRms SVic WJek
	- 'Alba'	CBre CSev ELau MHoo MNHC SBch SIde SRms WJek
	- 'Bill Archer' (v)	CNat
§	***pygmaea***	CArn CExl CHid CSpe ELan GCal MHer MHoo MNrw NBir NSti SRms WGwG WJek WMoo

Borinda (*Poaceae*)

	KR 4558	ERod
	KR 5600 **new**	MWht
	KR 5950	ERod
	KR 7346 **new**	MWht
	from Muli County, Sichuan	WJun
	albocerea	EPfP ERod MWht WJun
	- Yunnan 1	ERod WJun WPGP
	- Yunnan 2	CDTJ CEnt ERod MMoz WJun WPGP
	- Yunnan 3a	CDTJ CEnt ERod WJun WPGP
	- Yunnan 3b	ERod WJun
	- Yunnan 4	CDTJ CEnt WPGP
	boliana	SBig WJun
	edulis	WJun
	frigida	CDTJ CEnt WJun WPGP
	- KR 4059	ERod MWht
	fungosa	EAmu ESwi IBoy WJun WPGP
	grossa KR 5931	MWht
	lushuiensis	WJun
	macclureana KR 5050	WJun
	- KR 5051	MWht
	- KR 5177 from Gyala, Nepal	ERod ESwi MWht WJun
	- KR 5602	ERod
	- KR 5950	ERod
	- KR 6236	ESwi
	- KR 6243	ERod WJun
	- KR 6400 from Show La	ESwi
	- KR 6438 from Pasm Tso	ESwi
	papyrifera	CEnt ERod WJun WPGP
	- CS 1046	MAvo WJun
	- KR 3968	WJun
	- KR 7613	MWht WJun
	scabrida	CDTJ CEnt ERod MAvo MMoz MWht WJun WPGP
	- 'Asian Wonder'	LRHS MBlu NLar SPoG

Boronia (*Rutaceae*)

	heterophylla	CBcs CCCN CTsd EPfP IDee IVic LRHS MOWG
	- 'Ice Charlotte'	CBcs CCCN IDee
	serrulata	CBcs

Bossiaea (*Papilionaceae*)

	riparia	SPlb

Bothriochloa (*Poaceae*)

§	***bladhii***	CKno EPPr
	caucasica	see *B. bladhii*

Bougainvillea (*Nyctaginaceae*)

	'African Sunset' **new**	SPlb
	'Alexandra'	SPre
	'Brilliant' misapplied	see *B.* × *buttiana* 'Raspberry Ice'
§	× ***buttiana*** 'Raspberry Ice' (v)	EShb
	glabra 🏆H1	CMen SPre
	'Purple Robe'	MREP
	'Tropical Rainbow'	see *B.* × *buttiana* 'Raspberry Ice'

Boussingaultia (*Basellaceae*)

	baselloides Hook.	see *Anredera cordifolia*

Bouteloua (*Poaceae*)

	curtipendula	LRHS
§	***gracilis***	CAby EBee EHoe LEdu LRHS MWhi NWsh SMad SMea SMrm WPGP WWEG XLum

Bouvardia (*Rubiaceae*)

	ternifolia	CAbP CAby CSpe CWGN ESwi ELJc LSou MHol MNrw SPad WCot

Bowiea (*Asparagaceae*)

	volubilis	EBee EShb

Bowkeria (*Stilbaceae*)

	sp.	CCCN
	cymosa	SPlb
	verticillata	CHII WBor

Boykinia (*Saxifragaceae*)

	aconitifolia	CMac EWld IMou LRHS MRav NLar NRya SMad WCru WMoo
	elata	see *B. occidentalis*
	heucheriformis	see *B. jamesii*
§	***jamesii***	LRHS WAbe
	lycoctonifolia	EBee NLar
	major	EBee
§	***occidentalis***	MMHG WCru WMoo WPtf XLum
	rotundifolia	EBee EWld GJos NBir WCru WMoo
	tellimoides	see *Peltoboykinia tellimoides*

boysenberry see *Rubus* 'Boysenberry'

Brachychilum see *Hedychium*

Brachychiton (*Malvaceae*)

acerifolius	SPlb
populneus	SPlb

Brachyelytrum (*Poaceae*)

japonicum	EPPr LRHS NLar

Brachyglottis ✿ (*Asteraceae*)

§ ***bidwillii***	CBcs IVic WHor
§ ***compacta***	ECou ELan EPfP LRHS MAsh SLon SPer SPoG
compacta* × *monroi	ECou
'County Park'	ECou ELon
Dunedin Group new	WHar
- 'Drysdale'	EBee ELan EPfP LRHS MAsh SBod SKHP SLon SRGP SWvt
§ - 'Moira Reid' (v)	CExl CTsd
§ - 'Sunshine' ♀H4	CBar CDoC CDul CSBt CTri CWib EBee ECrN ELan EPfP IVic LRHS MGos MJak MRav MSwo MWat NPer NPri NSoo NWea SEND SLim SPer SPlb SPoG SRGP SRms SWvt
'Frosty'	EBee ECou ECrN
greyi misapplied	see *B.* (Dunedin Group) 'Sunshine'
§ ***greyi*** (Hook. f.) B. Nord.	CMac EPfP MWhi SGol
greyi* × *repanda	CDoC EShb
huntii	SVen
huntii* × *stewartii	SEND
laxifolia misapplied	see *B.* (Dunedin Group) 'Sunshine'
§ ***monroi*** ♀H4	CBcs CMac CSBt CTsd CWib EBee ECou EHoe ELan EPfP IVic LRHS MAsh MRav SGol SKHP SLon SPer SVen
- 'Clarence'	ECou
repanda	CBcs
- 'Purpurea'	CBcs
- var. ***rangiora***	CTsd
§ ***rotundifolia***	CCCN CDoC
'Silver Waves'	ECou
I 'Sunshine Improved'	CBcs EHoe
'Sunshine Variegated'	see *B.* (Dunedin Group) 'Moira Reid'
Walberton's Silver Dormouse = 'Walbrach'PBR	EPfP LBuc LRHS NPri SLim SPoG SRkn STPC WCot WHil

Brachypodium (*Poaceae*)

pinnatum	EPPr
sylvaticum	CHab SEND

Brachyscome (*Asteraceae*)

'Blue Mist'	SPet
iberidifolia 'Brachy Blue'	LAst
'Magenta Delight' new	NPri
'Metallic Blue'	NPri
'Pink Mist'	SPet
rigidula	CPBP ECou GKev
'Strawberry Mousse'	SPet
Surdaisy Strawberry Pink = 'Bonbrapi'	LAst NPnk NPri

Brachystachyum (*Poaceae*)

densiflorum	ERod

Brachystelma (*Asclepiadaceae*)

bracteolatum	LToo
bruceae new	LToo
foetidum	LToo
meyerianum	LToo
nanum	LToo
pygmaeum	LToo

Bracteantha see *Xerochrysum*

Brahea (*Arecaceae*)

aculeata	EAmu
armata	CBrP CDTJ CPHo EAmu EPfP EShb MREP SAPC SBst SPlb WCot
calcarea new	EAmu
decumbens new	EAmu
dulcis	EAmu
edulis	CBrP CPHo EAmu EGri
'Super Silver'	EAmu WCot

Brassaia see *Schefflera*

Brassica (*Brassicaceae*)

juncea 'Red Giant' new	CSpe
nigra	CArn
oleracea	SVic WHer
- 'Nine Star Perennial'	CAgr SVic
- 'Palmifolia'	SVic
* ***rapa*** var. ***japonica***	MNHC SHDw

Bravoa (*Agavaceae*)

geminiflora	see *Polianthes geminiflora*

Brighamia (*Campanulaceae*)

insignis	CCCN

Brillantaisia (*Acanthaceae*)

kirungae	CCCN

Brimeura (*Asparagaceae*)

§ ***amethystina*** ♀H4	CExl CPom ECho GBin GKev LEdu LRHS SDeJ SPhx WCot WThu
- 'Alba'	ECho GKev SDeJ SPhx WCot

Briza (*Poaceae*)

maxima	CKno CTri EHoe LEdu LHop NGdn NSti SPhx WHal WHer WTou
media	CHab CKno CPrp EBee EHoe ELan EPfP LBMP LBuc LPot LRHS MBlu MCot MMuc MWhi NLar NMir NWad NWsh SEND SMrm SPer SPhx SWvt WHal WHoo WMnd WWEG XLum
- 'Golden Bee'	CKno EHoe ELon EPPr EPfP LEdu LRHS MMHG NLar
- 'Limouzi'	CCon CElw CKno EBee EHoe ELon EPPr EPfP GCal LEdu LRHS MAvo NSti SMad SMea XLum
- 'Russells'PBR	CHid CKno EBee EHoe ELan EPPr EPfP LHop LPot LRHS MAvo MBri NCGa NWsh SHil SMea SPer SPoG SWvt WGrn
subaristata	EPPr LRHS MWhi WHrl
triloba	EWes MMHG NWsh SMea

Brodiaea (*Asparagaceae*)

§ ***californica***	ECho GKev WCot
- NNS 00-109 new	WCot
- NNS 06-102	WCot

coronaria	WCot
'Corrina'	see *Triteleia* 'Corrina'
elegans	ECho
ida-maia	see *Dichelostemma ida-maia*
laxa	see *Triteleia laxa*
pallida	WCot
peduncularis	see *Triteleia peduncularis*
stellaris	ECho

Bromus (*Poaceae*)

erectus	CHab
inermis 'Skinner's Gold' (v)	EBee EHoe EPPr NLar SMea WCot WWEG

Broussonetia (*Moraceae*)

kazinoki	CArn LHop
papyrifera	CAbP CBcs CDul EBtc EGFP ELan GBin IVic WPGP
- 'Billardii'	NLar
- 'Laciniata'	EBee IDee SMad

Browallia (*Solanaceae*)

from Sikkim	CSpe

Bruckenthalia see *Erica*

Brugmansia ✿ (*Solanaceae*)

§	***arborea***	CDTJ
§	- 'Knightii' (d) ♀H1	CDTJ
	aurea	CCCN CHEx EUJe
	× ***candida***	CCCN CHEx
	- 'Blush'	EUJe
§	- 'Grand Marnier' ♀H1	CDTJ CHEx CHII
	- 'Plena'	see *B. arborea* 'Knightii'
§	- 'Variegata' (v)	CCCN CDTJ CHII CSam
	× ***cubensis*** 'Charles Grimaldi'	CSam
	'Flowerdream' (d)	EUJe
§	× ***insignis***	CHII
§	- pink-flowered	SEND
	meteloides	see *Datura inoxia*
	rosei	see *B. sanguinea* subsp. *sanguinea* var. *flava*
§	***sanguinea***	CCCN CHEx CHII EShb EUJe IDee SEND SPlb
	- red-flowered	CHEx
	- 'Rosea'	see *B.* × *insignis* pink-flowered
§	- subsp. ***sanguinea*** var. *flava*	CHEx
§	***suaveolens*** ♀H1	CHII ELan EUJe
	- pink-flowered	EShb
	- ***rosea***	see *B.* × *insignis* pink-flowered
	- 'Variegata' (v)	EShb
	- yellow-flowered	EShb
	suaveolens × ***versicolor***	see *B.* × *insignis*
	'Variegata Sunset'	see *B.* × *candida* 'Variegata'
	versicolor misapplied	see *B. arborea*
§	***versicolor*** Lagerh.	CCCN

Brunfelsia (*Solanaceae*)

	americana	CCCN MOWG
	calycina	see *B. pauciflora*
	jamaicensis	MOWG
	lactea	CCCN
§	***pauciflora*** ♀H1	CCCN ELan
	- 'Floribunda'	MOWG

Brunia (*Bruniaceae*)

albiflora	SPlb

Brunnera ✿ (*Boraginaceae*)

§	***macrophylla*** ♀H4	Widely available
	- 'Alba'	see *B. macrophylla* 'Betty Bowring'
§	- 'Betty Bowring'	Widely available
	- 'Blaukuppel'	CLAP EWes GBin LRHS NBir WPtf
	- 'Dawson's White' (v)	CBcs CLAP CWCL ECtt ELan EPfP EPri GBuc GJos GMaP IKil LBMP LHop LRHS LSRN MCot MGos MLHP MRav NBid NBir NGdn NLar SPer SRGP SWvt WPtf
	- 'Diane's Gold'	EBee ECtt MPnt NLar
	- 'Emerald Mist' (v)	CHel ECtt EPfP GBin MBri NLar NSti SPad SWvt
	- 'Gordano Gold' (v)	EHoe EPPr NBir WCot
	- 'Green Gold' (v)	EBee MBri NLar NSti
	- 'Hadspen Cream' (v) ♀H4	Widely available
	- 'Hopley's Gold'	LHop
	- 'Inspector Morse'	SWvt
	- 'Jack Frost'PBR ♀H4	Widely available
	- 'King's Ransom' (v)	ECtt MAsh NLar NSti SPoG
	- 'Langford Hewitt' (v)	MNrw
	- 'Langtrees'	CBct CMac EBee ECtt EHoe GBin GBuc GCal GCra LHop LRHS MCot MHol MMuc MRav MWhi NBir NGdn NOrc SEND SPer SWat WKif WPtf WWEG
	- 'Looking Glass'PBR	Widely available
	- 'Marley's White'	CLAP ELan LLHF NEgg NLar SBch SGbt
§	- 'Mister Morse'PBR (v)	Widely available
	- 'Silver Wings'	CElw CWCL ECtt EPfP EWTr EWll GKev LRHS MBel MBri MWhi NBir NGdn NLar NSti NWad SGol SHar SPoG SWat WCAu
	- 'Spring Yellow'	ECtt NLar
	'Mrs Morse'	see *B. macrophylla* 'Mister Morse'
	sibirica	CLAP EBee EPPr EWes NBid

Brunsvigia (*Amaryllidaceae*)

bosmaniae	ECho WCot
gregaria	WCot
josephinae LAV 30394 **new**	WCot
marginata	ECho
pulchra	ECho WCot
radula 'Vanrhynsdorp'	ECho
radulosa	ECho WCot
rosea 'Minor'	see *Amaryllis belladonna*
striata	ECho

Bryonia (*Cucurbitaceae*)

dioica	CArn GPoy NMir

Bryophyllum see *Kalanchoe*

Buddleja ✿ (*Scrophulariaceae*)

HCM 98.017 from Chile	WPGP
agathosma	CExl MOWG SLon WKif WLav WPGP WSHC
albiflora	SLon WLav
alternifolia ♀H4	Widely available
- 'Argentea'	CBcs CDoC EBee ELan EPfP EWTr LBMP LRHS MBNS MRav NLar SKHP SRGP WCot WLav WSHC XSen
asiatica ♀H2	CHid MOWG SLon WLav
- B&SWJ 11278	WCru
auriculata	CBcs CDul CExl CWib EBee ELan EPfP EShb LRHS MOWG MRav SDix

	SKHP SLon SPlb SPoG SVen WCru WLav
'Autumn Surprise'	SLon
'Blue Chip' (Lo and Behold Series)	CDoC EBee EPfP GBin LBuc LRHS MAsh MBri MGos NSoo SLim SLon SPoG SRms WLav
* 'Blue Trerice'	CExl
caryopteridifolia	EBtc GQui SEND SLon WCot
colvilei	CBcs CDoC CHel ECre ELan EPfP GCal GGal GKin IArd IDee LAst NSoo SBrt SLon WSpi
- B&SWJ 2121	WCru
- GWJ 9399	WCru
- 'Kewensis'	CExl CHGN CHid EBee EWes GCal GGal NLar SLon SVen WBor WCFE WCru WGob WLav WPat WSHC WSpi
cordata	SLon
- B&SWJ 10433	WCru
- F&M 220	WPGP
coriacea	SLon WSpi
§ ***crispa***	CExl CHel CHid CSpe ELan EPfP GCal LRHS MOWG SEND SLon SPer SRkn SVen WKif WPGP WSHC WSpi XSen
- var. ***farreri***	CHGN CHid SLon
- Moon Dance = 'Hulmoon'	EBee
crotonoides subsp. ***amplexicaulis***	SLon
curviflora f. ***venenifera***	SLon
- - B&SWJ 6036	WCru
'David Griffin'	LRHS
davidii	CArn CCVT NPol NWea
- B&SWJ 8083	WCru
- Adonis Blue = 'Adokeep'^PBR^	CBcs CNec LBuc LRHS MBri NPri SLon STPC WLav
- 'African Queen'	CAni LRHS SLim SLon SRGP WLav
- var. ***alba***	CWib
§ - 'Autumn Beauty'	CAni SLon WLav
- 'Bath Beauty'	CAni
- 'Beijing'	see *B. davidii* 'Autumn Beauty'
- 'Bishop's Velvet'	CAni
- 'Black Knight' ♀H4	Widely available
- 'Blue Horizon' ♀H4	CAni NLar SLon SRGP WCot WLav WMoo WRHF
- 'Border Beauty'	CAni CNec SLon WLav
- 'Boskoop Beauty'	CAni
- 'Brown's Beauty'	CAni
- 'Butterfly Heaven'^PBR^ **new**	WLav
- Buzz Series	LBuc NHol
- - Buzz Ivory = 'Tobuivo'	CBct CNec ELan LRHS LSRN NHol NPri SHil SLim SMDP WHil
- - Buzz Lilac	ELan LRHS NHol
- - Buzz Magenta = 'Tobudpipur'	CBct CMea CNec ELan ELon LRHS NHol NPri SHil SLim WHil WLav
- - Buzz Sky Blue = 'Tobuskyblu'	ELon EPfP LBMP LRHS NHol NPri SHil SLim SMDP SPad
- - Buzz Violet = 'Tobudviole'	CBct CHid CMea ELan EPfP GBin LRHS NHol NPri SHil SLim WLav
- Camberwell Beauty = 'Camkeep' (English Butterfly Series) ♀H4	CDoC CHll CNec CSBt LBuc LRHS MBri NHol SLon WLav
- 'Car Wash'	CAni
- 'Castle Blue'	SLon
- 'Castle School'	CAni CSam WLav
§ - 'Charming'	WMoo WSHC WWlt
- 'Clive Farrell'	see *B. davidii* 'Autumn Beauty'
- 'Corinne Tremaine'	WHer
- 'Darent Valley' **new**	SLon

- 'Dartmoor' ♀H4	CAni CDul CEnd CExl CHll CMac CTri CWCL EBee ECre ECtt ELan EPfP GBin GCal LRHS MAsh MGos MRav NLar NPer SDix SLim SPer SPlb SPoG SRms WLav WSHC
- 'Dart's Ornamental White'	MRav SLon WLav
- 'Dart's Papillon Blue'	CAni SLon WLav
- 'Dart's Purple Rain'	CAni CNec SLon WLav
- 'Dubonnet'	CAni SLon WLav
- 'Dudley's Compact Lavender'	CAni
- 'Ecolonia'	CAni SLon WLav
- 'Ellen's Blue'	CExl CFil LRHS WLav
- 'Empire Blue' ♀H4	CAni CBar CBcs CDoC CDul CHab CNec CSBt EBee ECtt EPfP GKin LRHS LSRN MGos MRav NBir NPer NSoo NWea SEND SPer SPlb SPoG SRGP SRms SWat SWvt WWlt
- 'Fair Lady' **new**	WLav
- 'Fascinating'	CAni CNec GCal MRav NBir SLon WLav
- 'Flaming Violet'	CAni SLon WLav
- 'Florence'	LLHF LRHS LSRN MBri MWat NEgg NLar SLon SRGP WMoo
- 'Fortune'	CAni
- 'Foxtail' **new**	WLav
- 'Glasnevin Hybrid'	CAni CNec LRHS NLar SDix SLon WLav
- 'Gonglepod'	CAni SLon WLav
- 'Greenway's River Dart'	CAni SLon
- 'Grey Dawn'	WLav
- 'Griffin Blue' **new**	MAsh WLav
- 'Gulliver'^PBR^	NLar SGol SLon WLav
- 'Harlequin' (v)	Widely available
- 'Heath'	SPhx
- 'Ile de France'	CAni CBcs CWib NLar NWea SLon SRms WLav
- 'Leela Kapila'	SLon
- 'Les Kneale'	CAni SLon WLav
- 'Lilac Moon' **new**	WLav
- 'Lyme Bay'	CAni
- Marbled White = 'Markeep'^PBR^ (English Butterfly Series)	CNec CSBt LBuc MBri SLon STPC WLav WMoo
- Masquerade = 'Notbud' (v)	MRav SLon WGor
§ - Nanho Blue = 'Mongo' ♀H4	CAni CMHG CMac CNec CSBt EBee ECrN ECtt ELan EPfP GKin LAst LRHS MAsh MGos MJak MLHP MMuc MRav MSwo MWat NBir NLar SGol SLim SPoG SRGP WMoo XSen
- 'Nanho Petite Indigo'	see *B. davidii* Nanho Blue
- 'Nanho Petite Plum'	see *B. davidii* Nanho Purple
- 'Nanho Petite Purple'	see *B. davidii* Nanho Purple
§ - Nanho Purple = 'Monum' ♀H4	CAni CDoC CMHG CMac CTri CWib EBee ELan EPfP LAst LRHS LSRN MBri MGos MRav NLar SGol SLim SLon SPer SPlb SPoG SRGP SRms XSen
- Nanho White = 'Monite' ♀H4	EBee EHoe ELan EPfP LRHS SGol SLon SPer SPoG SRms
- var. ***nanhoensis***	CAni CDul MAsh SEND SGol WLav
- - blue-flowered	NWad SLon
- 'Orchid Beauty'	CAni SLon WLav
- 'Orpheus'	CAni SLon WLav
- 'Panache'	EPfP LRHS MAsh SLon WLav
- 'Peace'	CMac CTri EPfP LSRN MRav NLar SLon SPoG WLav

- Peacock = 'Peakeep' PBR (English Butterfly Series)	CNec CSBt LBuc LRHS MBri SPoG STPC WLav
- 'Persephone'	SLon WLav
- 'Petite Indigo'	see *B. davidii* Nanho Blue
- 'Pink Beauty'	LAst LSRN MBlu SRGP
- 'Pink Charming'	see *B. davidii* 'Charming'
- 'Pink Pearl'	CAni CNec LRHS SEND SLon WLav
- 'Pink Spreader'	CAni LRHS SLon WLav
- 'Pixie Blue'	CAni LBMP LRHS MAsh SLon WLav
- 'Pixie Red'	CAni LBMP LRHS MAsh MHer NEgg NLar SEND WLav
- 'Pixie White'	LRHS MAsh NLar SEND WLav
- Purple Emperor = 'Pyrkeep' (English Butterfly Series)	LBuc MBri NBir SLon SPoG STPC WLav
- 'Purple Friend'	CAni SLon WLav
- 'Purple Prince'	CAni
- 'Red Admiral'	CAni LLHF LRHS MAsh SLon SPoG SRGP
- Rêve de Papillon Blue = 'Minpap3'	EMil WLav
- Rêve de Papillon = 'Minpap'	CNec EMil LRHS MAsh WLav
- Rêve de Papillon White = 'Minpap2'	EMil
- 'Royal Purple'	CAni SLim SWvt
- 'Royal Red' ♀H4	Widely available
- 'Royal Red Variegated' (v) **new**	CTsd
- 'Saith Ffynnon Early'	WSFF
- 'Santana' (v)	CAni CDul CMac CNec EHoc ELon EPfP EWes LAst LRHS LSou MRav NEgg NHol NLar NWad SGol SPoG SWvt WCFE WCot WMoo WPat WSpi XSen
- 'Shapcott Blue'	CAni
- 'Shire Blue'	WLav
- 'Southcombe Splendour'	CAni
- 'Summer Beauty'	CAni CDul CWib LRHS MBlu MRav SLon WLav
- 'Summer House Blue'	LRHS SLon WLav
- 'Twotones'	WLav
- 'Variegata' (v)	CAni LRHS MAsh SLon SWvt WLav
- 'White Ball'	EHoe ELan EPfP NLar SLon WLav
- 'White Bouquet'	CAni CCVT CDul CSBt EPfP GKin LAst LRHS MHer MSwo MWat NWea SEND SPer SRGP SWvt WLav XSen
- 'White Cloud'	CAni ECrN GQui SRms WGwG
- 'White Harlequin' (v)	SLon WCFE
- 'White Profusion' ♀H4	CAni CBar CBcs CDul CHab CNec CSam EBee ECtt ELan EPfP GBin LPot LRHS MBlu MGos MJak MRav NBir NEgg NLar NPri NWea SGol SLim SWat SWvt WCFE
- 'White Wings'	SLon WLav
- 'Widecombe'	CAni
- 'Windtor' **new**	CNec
§ ***delavayi***	CExl ECre SEND WCru
fallowiana misapplied	see *B.* 'West Hill'
fallowiana Balf. f. & W.W. Sm	ELan GQui LRHS WLav WSpi
- ACE 2481	LRHS
- BWJ 7803	WCru
- var. ***alba*** ♀H3	CDoC CHGN CMac ECrN ELan EPfP LRHS MAsh MRav NLar SLon SPoG WPGP WSHC
- 'Bishop's Violet' **new**	CTsd

'Flower Power'	see *B.* × *weyeriana* 'Bicolor'
forrestii	WCru
- PAB 4198 **new**	LEdu
globosa ♀H4	Widely available
- RCB/Arg C-11	WCot
- 'Cally Orange'	GCal WGwG
- 'Lemon Ball'	MBlu NPer SLon WLav
glomerata	EBee EShb SLon WPGP
- 'Silver Service'	ELan LRHS SKHP WCot
heliophila	see *B. delavayi*
indica	SLon
japonica	SLon
- B&SWJ 8912	WCru
× ***lewisiana*** 'Margaret Pike'	MOWG SLon
'Lilac Chip' (Lo and Behold Series) **new**	LRHS NSoo
limitanea	SLon
lindleyana	Widely available
aff. ***lindleyana***	EWTr WSpi
- B&SWJ 11478	WCru
'Lochinch' ♀H3-4	Widely available
longifolia	SLon XScn
'Longstock'	SLon
'Longstock Silver'	SLon
loricata	CDoC CExl CHGN CTsd CWib EBee EMil EPfP GBin GQui IDee LRHS MOWG NSoo SKHP SLon SPlb WCot WGob WLav WPGP
macrostachya	GLin
- HWJ 602	WCru
- WWJ 12016	WCru
§ ***madagascariensis*** ♀H1	CRHN MOWG NLar SLon SPlb SVen
'Malvern Blue'	CAni
megalocephala B&SWJ 9106	WCru WPGP
'Miss Ruby' **new**	CDoC LBuc LRHS
§ 'Morning Mist' PBR	CDoC CExl CMHG CWGN EBee EHoe ELan EPfP GBin LLHF LRHS LSRN MBri MOWG NBir NEgg NHol NLar NPri SLon SPoG SRms WCot WPGP
myriantha	CExl SLon XSen
nappii	SLon
nicodemia	see *B. madagascariensis*
nivea	CDoy CExl CHid CMHG MOWG NSoo SLon WGob WLav XSen
- B&SWJ 2679	WCru
- pink-flowered	SLon
officinalis ♀H2	CExl MOWG SLon
paniculata	SLon
parvifolia	SLon
- MPF 148	WLav
× ***pikei*** 'Hever'	SRms XSen
'Pink Delight' ♀H4	Widely available
'Pink Perfection'	CAni
'Pride of Hever'	MOWG SDys
'Pride of Longstock'	LBuc LRHS SLon SPoG
'Red Chip' (Lo and Behold Series) **new**	LRHS
saligna	SLon
'Salmon Spheres'	SLon
salviifolia	CBcs CExl CHid CTsd EBee ELan GGal IDee LRHS MBlu NSoo SEND SPlb SVen WGob WGwG WHer WLav WPGP
- white-flowered	SLon WPGP
Silver Anniversary	see *B.* 'Morning Mist'
stachyoides	MOWG WLav

stenostachya	CExl SLon
sterniana	see *B. crispa*
'Sugar Plum'	LRHS SLon
tibetica	see *B. crispa*
tubiflora	MOWG SLon WLav
venenifera B&SWJ 895	WCru
§ 'West Hill'	SLon WLav
× ***weyeriana***	CDul ECtt EPfP GGal GQui MMuc MNrw MSwo NBir NSoo SPad SPlb SWvt WOut
§ - 'Bicolor'	CNec EPfP LRHS MNrw NLar SRms WLav
- 'Boy Blue' **new**	SLon
- 'Golden Glow' (v)	CTri ECrN EPfP GBin LSRN NLar SLon WLav WSFF
- 'Honeycomb'	GBin MGos NLar
- 'Lady de Ramsey'	SEND
- 'Moonlight'	CBcs CExl CNec ELan GBin IFro LAst LRHS SLon WCot WLav WSpi
- 'Pink Pagoda'	LRHS SLon
- 'Sungold' 🏆^{H4}	Widely available
'Winter Sun'	SLon
yunnanensis	GCal NLar SLon
- B&SWJ 8146	WCru

Buglossoides (*Boraginaceae*)

§ ***purpurocaerulea***	CHll CSpe EBee ELan EPfP LHop MLHP MWhi NBid NChi WCot WSHC XLum

Bukiniczia (*Plumbaginaceae*)

cabulica	CSpe GKev WAbe

Bulbine (*Asphodelaceae*)

SH 74	CCse
abyssinica	ECho
alooides	ECho
annua misapplied	see *B. semibarbata*
bulbosa misapplied	see *B. semibarbata*
capitata 'Bloemfontein'	ECho
caulescens	see *B. frutescens*
§ ***frutescens***	CDoC CHll EShb MHer SBHP SVen WJek XLum
- 'Hallmark'	CCCN
latifolia	CCCN EShb
narcissifolia 'Ladybrand'	ECho
§ ***semibarbata***	CCCN

Bulbinella (*Asphodelaceae*)

angustifolia	ECho
cauda-felis 'Tulbagh'	ECho
eburnifolia	ECho
elata	WCot
gibbsii var. ***balanifera***	ECho
graminifolia 'Clanwilliam'	ECho
hookeri	CExl CHel CPom EBee ECho EWld GBee GBin GKev ITim LRHS MHer SRms WHal WThu
latifolia	ECho
- subsp. ***doleritica***	ECho
- subsp. ***latifolia***	IBlr
nutans	EBee ECho WPGP
punctulata 'Piketberg'	ECho

Bulbinopsis see *Bulbine*

Bulbocodium (*Colchicaceae*)

vernum	ECho EPot GKev LLHF LRHS NMin SDeJ

bullace see *Prunus insititia*

Bunias (*Brassicaceae*)

orientalis	CAgr ELau

Bunium (*Apiaceae*)

bulbocastanum	CSpe IMou LEdu SDix SHDw XLum

Buphthalmum (*Asteraceae*)

salicifolium	CSam EBee ELan EPfP MMuc NBro NGdn SEND SPer SRms SWat WCot XLum
- 'Alpengold'	GMaP LRHS MNFA NBre NLar
- 'Dora'	CSam ECtt LRHS WCot
- 'Sunwheel'	LRHS SRms
speciosum	see *Telekia speciosa*

Bupleurum (*Apiaceae*)

angulosum	LRHS NBir
- copper-leaved	see *B. longifolium*
falcatum	ECGP LRHS NDov WCot
fruticosum	CBcs CFil CSpe EBee ELan EPfP GBin LPla LRHS MAsh NSoo SDix SEND SKHP SLon SMad SPer SPhx SPoG SSpi WCot WPGP WPat XSen
§ ***longifolium***	CElw CMea CPom CSpe EBee EWes LEdu LRHS MNrw NChi SKHP SMrm
- subsp. ***aureum***	SPhx
ranunculoides	XLum
rotundifolium	CSpe GAbr LEdu MCot SPhx
- 'Copper'	WCot
spinosum	WHil XSen
tenue	CArn

Burchellia (*Rubiaceae*)

capensis	SPlb

Bursaria (*Pittosporaceae*)

spinosa	CCCN CHll ECou

Butia (*Arecaceae*)

capitata	CAbb CBcs CBrP CCCN CDTJ CPHo EAmu EGri MREP SAPC SBst
§ - var. ***odorata***	EAmu SPlb
eriospatha	EAmu
odorata	see *B. capitata* var. *odorata*
yatay	EAmu SBig

Butia × *Jubaea* (*Arecaceae*)

B. capitata × ***J. chilensis*** **new**	EAmu

Butomus (*Butomaceae*)

umbellatus 🏆^{H4}	CBAq CRow CWat EHon EPfP EWay GQue MNrw MRav MSKA MWts NBir NPer SWat WMAq XLum
- f. ***albiflorus***	MSKA
- 'Rosenrot'	CRow EWay LLWG
- 'Schneeweisschen'	CRow EWay GQue LLWG MNrw MWts NLar

butternut see *Juglans cinerea*

× *Butyagrus* (*Arecaceae*)

nabonnandii	EAmu

Buxus ✿ (*Buxaceae*)

	sp. new	MJak
	aurea 'Marginata'	see *B. sempervirens* 'Marginata'
	balearica ♀H4	MBlu
	'Green Gem'	NHol NWad
	'Green Mound'	LBMP
	'Green Velvet'	EPfP WSpi
	harlandii hort.	CMen SRiv
	japonica 'Nana'	see *B. microphylla*
§	***microphylla***	MHer NWad NWea SGol
	- 'Asiatic Winter'	see *B. microphylla* var. *japonica* 'Winter Gem'
§	- 'Compacta'	CMen LLHF MHer NWad SRiv WCot WPat WThu
	- 'Curly Locks'	MHer NWad
	- 'Faulkner'	CCVT EBee ELan EPfP LBuc LHop LRHS LSRN MAsh MBNS MGos MJak MREP SGol SHil SPer SPoG SRiv WMoo
	- Golden Dream = 'Peergold'PBR	NLar
	- 'Golden Triumph'PBR	EPfP
	- 'Green Pillow'	EPfP MHer SRiv WSpi
	- 'Herrenhausen'	WSpi
	- var. ***japonica*** 'Green Jade'	WSpi
	- - 'Morris Midget'	NWad
	- - 'National'	WSpi
§	- - 'Winter Gem'	MHer MRav NLar SLPl WSpi
	- 'John Baldwin'	SRiv
	- var. ***microphylla***	WSpi
	sempervirens ♀H4	Widely available
§	- 'Angustifolia'	MHer MRav NWad SMad
	- 'Arborescens'	CNWT
	- 'Argentea'	see *B. sempervirens* 'Argenteo-variegata'
§	- 'Argenteo-variegata' (v)	EPfP IFoB MJak NEgg SGol
	- 'Aurea'	see *B. sempervirens* 'Aureovariegata'
	- 'Aurea Maculata'	see *B. sempervirens* 'Aureovariegata'
	- 'Aurea Marginata'	see *B. sempervirens* 'Marginata'
	- 'Aurea Pendula' (v)	CJun
§	- 'Aureovariegata' (v)	EPfP EShb LRHS MGos MHer MRav SBod SPer SRiv WMoo
	- 'Bentley Blue'	NWea
	- 'Blauer Heinz'	ELan EWTr IVic MHer MRav SRiv WSpi
	- 'Bowles's Blue'	EWes
I	- 'Brilliantissima'	WMoo WSpi
	- clipped ball	CWib EPfP LSRN MGos NLar SGol SLim SRiv
	- clipped bird	SRiv
	- clipped cone	LSRN SGol SRiv
	- clipped pyramid	CWib EPfP LSRN MGos NLar SGol SLim SRiv
	- clipped spiral	LSRN SGol SRiv
	- 'Elegans'	IFoB LRHS
§	- 'Elegantissima' (v) ♀H4	Widely available
	- 'Gold Tip'	see *B. sempervirens* 'Notata'
	- 'Golden Frimley' (v)	LHop
§	- 'Graham Blandy'	IVic MHer SGol SRiv WSpi
	- 'Green Balloon'	EPfP LBuc
	- 'Greenpeace'	see *B. sempervirens* 'Graham Blandy'
	- 'Handsworthiensis'	CLnd CTri NHol NLar NWea SEND SRms WMoo WSpi
	- 'Japonica Aurea'	see *B. sempervirens* 'Latifolia Maculata'
	- 'Kensington Gardens'	WSpi
	- 'King Midas'	IVic
	- 'Kingsville'	see *B. microphylla* 'Compacta'
	- 'Kingsville Dwarf'	see *B. microphylla* 'Compacta'
	- 'Latifolia Aurea Maculata'	WSpi
	- 'Latifolia Macrophylla'	SLon
§	- 'Latifolia Maculata' (v) ♀H4	CAbP CDoC CWib EPfP LRHS MHer NPer SEND SPoG SRiv WJek
	- 'Longifolia'	see *B. sempervirens* 'Angustifolia'
§	- 'Marginata' (v)	CArn IFoB LHop LRHS SGol SLon WHar WSpi
	- 'Memorial'	MHer NWad SRiv WSpi
	- 'Myosotidifolia'	NPro SRiv WCot WSpi
	- 'Myrtifolia'	MHer
§	- 'Notata' (v)	IFoB MAsh SBod WHar WMoo
	- 'Parasol'	MHer
	- 'Prostrata'	NWad
	- 'Rosmarinifolia'	MHer MRav
	- 'Rotundifolia'	ELan SEND WMoo
	- 'Silver Beauty' (v)	NEgg
	- 'Silver Variegated'	see *B. sempervirens* 'Elegantissima'
	- 'Suffruticosa' ♀H4	Widely available
*	- 'Suffruticosa Covent Garden'	MREP
	- 'Suffruticosa Variegata' (v)	SRms SWvt
	- 'Vardar Valley'	NPro SRiv WSpi
*	- 'Variegata' (v)	ECrN ELan MSwo
	- 'Waterfall'	MHer
	- 'Wisley Blue'	WSpi
	sinica var. ***insularis*** 'Justin Brouwers'	MHer SRiv
	- - 'Tide Hill'	MHer SRiv WSpi

C

Cachrys (*Apiaceae*)

	alpina	SPhx

Caesalpinia (*Caesalpiniaceae*)

	gilliesii	CBcs CSpe EBee EDif EGri LSRN MOWG SPlb
	mexicana	CSpe
	pulcherrima	CCCN SPlb
	spinosa	CBcs SPlb

Caiophora (*Loasaceae*)

	coronata	SPlb

Caladium (*Araceae*)

	'Candidum' (v)	SDeJ
	'Carolyn Whorton' new	SDeJ
	'Florida Cardinal' (v)	SDeJ
	'Freida Hemple'	SDeJ
	'White Christmas' (v)	SDeJ

Calamagrostis (*Poaceae*)

	sp. new	MAsh
	from Korea	NDov
	× ***acutiflora***	XLum
	- 'Avalanche'	CKno EHoe EPPr EWes LHop LRHS MWhi NWsh
	- 'Eldorado' (v)	WCot
N	- 'Karl Foerster'	Widely available
	- 'Overdam' (v)	Widely available
	- 'Stricta'	EBee EPPr NWsh

	- 'Waldenbuch'	CKno NDov
	argentea	see *Stipa calamagrostis*
	arundinacea	CElw CExl CMac COIW CSpe ECou SDix SPlb WMoo WPGP XLum
	'Avalanche'	CKno GBin GCal GQue MAsh NOak
§	***brachytricha*** ♀H4	Widely available
	canadensis	EPPr
	emodensis	CCVN CKno CMea CSam CSpe CWCL EBee EHoe MAvo MMoz MWhi NOak NWsh SMad WCot WGrn WMoo WPGP
	epigejos	CKno LEdu WHrl
	nutkaensis	EPPr
	splendens misapplied	see *Stipa calamagrostis*
	splendens Trin.	LPla NDov
	varia	CKno EBee EHoe GBin SMrm WHrl

Calamintha (*Lamiaceae*)

	alpina	see *Acinos alpinus*
§	***ascendens***	CArn EBee WMoo
	clinopodium	see *Clinopodium vulgare*
*	'Fritz Kuhn'	WWEG
§	***grandiflora***	CArn CMea EBee ELan GJos GPoy ITim LEdu LRHS MHer MMuc MNHC MRav MWat MWhi NBir NPer SMrm SPer SPlb SRms WCAu WJek WMoo
	- 'Elfin Purple'	EBee EPfP
	- 'Variegata' (v)	CPrp ECtt ELan EPPr EPfP MPie SPoG WCAu WGrn
	'Harrogate'	NDov
§	***menthifolia***	MHoo NBre NLar WJek
§	***nepeta***	CArn CHab CMea ECtt EWTr GMaP LAst LPio LRHS MHer MNFA MNHC NBro SBch SEND SPhx SPlb SPoG SRms SWat WCAu WJek WMoo WOut
	- subsp. ***glandulosa***	ECGP WMoo
	- - ACL 1050/90	EBee WHoo
	- - 'White Cloud'	CSpe EBee ECGP ECtt ELan GQue LLWP MRav NBir SPoG WCAu WMoo
	- 'Gottfried Kuehn'	LPla MRav
§	- subsp. ***nepeta***	CPrp ELan ELon EPfP MCot MHer MLHP MRav MWat NDov NSti SPer WHal WWEG XLum
	- - 'Blue Cloud'	CFis CSam CSpe EBee EPfP LRHS MAvo MSpe MWat NBir NCGa NDov SPhx WCAu WMoo WWEG
	- 'Weisse Riese'	SPhx
	nepetoides	see *C. nepeta* subsp. *nepeta*
	officinalis misapplied	see *C. ascendens*
	sylvatica	see *C. menthifolia*
I	- 'Menthe'	LPla
	vulgaris	see *Clinopodium vulgare*

calamondin see × *Citrofortunella microcarpa*

Calandrinia (*Portulacaceae*)

	grandiflora	LLHF
*	***ranunculina***	CPBP
	sibirica	see *Claytonia sibirica*
	umbellata	EDAr LBMP MAsh WIce
	- 'Ruby Tuesday'	NPri XLum

Calanthe (*Orchidaceae*)

	alismifolia	EBee EFEx
	arcuata	EFEx
	arisanenesis	EFEx
	aristulifera	EFEx NLAp
	bicolor	see *C. striata*
	discolor	CDes EBee EFEx NLAp WCot
	- subsp. ***amamiana***	EFEx
	- var. ***flava***	see *C. striata*
	- subsp. ***tokunoshimensis***	EFEx
	fargesii	WCot
	graciliflora	EFEx
	Kozu gx	LEdu
	mannii	EFEx
	nipponica	CBct EBee EFEx LWst NLAp
	reflexa	EBee EFEx LWst NLAp
	sieboldii	see *C. striata*
§	***striata***	CBct EFEx NLAp WCot
	sylvatica	EBee NLAp
	- pink-flowered	WCot
	Takane gx	LWst NLAp
	tricarinata	CBct EBee EFEx NLAp

Calathea (*Marantaceae*)

	argyrophylla 'Exotica'	XBlo
	louisae 'Maui Queen'	XBlo
§	***majestica*** ♀H1	XBlo
	makoyana ♀H1	XBlo
	oppenheimiana	see *Ctenanthe oppenheimiana*
	ornata	see *C. majestica*
	picturata 'Argentea' ♀H1	XBlo
	roseopicta ♀H1	XBlo
	- 'Rosastar' **new**	XBlo
	rufibarba	XBlo
*	***stromata***	XBlo
	veitchiana 'Medaillon' **new**	XBlo
	zebrina ♀H1	XBlo
	'Zoizia'	XBlo

Calceolaria (*Calceolariaceae*)

	acutifolia	see *C. polyrhiza* Cav.
	arachnoidea	EBee SKHP SPlb
§	***biflora***	ECho EPfP GKev MAsh NLar
	- 'Goldcap'	ECho SMrm
	- 'Goldcrest Amber'	SPlb
	corymbosa	GKev
	falklandica	ECho GBin LLHF SRms
	fothergillii	GKev WAbe
	'Goldcrest'	ECho LRHS SRms
N	***integrifolia*** ♀H3	CAbb CDTJ CExl CHel CSpe CTri ECtt ELan EPfP MSCN NSoo SEND SPer SRms WAbe WGob WWlt
	- bronze	MSCN SPer
	- 'Gaines' Yellow'	EBee GCal
	'John Innes'	ECho
	'Kentish Hero'	CSpe CTsd GBin GCal SDys WAbe
	mollissima **new**	GKev
	aff. ***pavonii***	CRHN
	perfoliata B&SWJ 10638	WCru
	plantaginea	see *C. biflora*
§	***polyrhiza*** Cav.	ECho
	rugosa	see *C. integrifolia*
	'Sunset Red Bicolor' (Sunset Series) **new**	CHel
	tenella	ECho NSla WAbe
	uniflora	CPBP
	- var. ***darwinii***	ECho GKev NSla WAbe
	'Walter Shrimpton'	ECho EWes WAbe

Calendula (*Asteraceae*)

	arvensis	CCCN
	'Bronze Beauty'	CSpe

officinalis	CArn ELau GPoy MHer MHoo MNHC SIde SPav SRms SVic SWvt WJek WSFF
- 'Art Shades' **new**	CWCL
- (Calypso Series) 'Calypso Orange'	CWCL MHoo
- - 'Calypso Yellow'	MHoo
- Fiesta Gitana Group ♀H4	CPrp WJek
- 'Touch of Red Buff' (Touch of Red Series)	CSpe
'Tarifa'	SEND

Calibanus (*Asparagaceae*)

hookeri	EShb

Calibrachoa (*Solanaceae*)

(Cabaret Series) Cabaret Apricot = 'Balcabapt'	NPri
- Cabaret Deep Blue = 'Balcabdebu'	NPri
- Cabaret Hot Pink = 'Balcabhopi'PBR	NPri
- Cabaret Red Improved = 'Balcabimred'PBR	NPri
- Cabaret White Improved = 'Balcabwitim'	NPri
- Cabaret Yellow = 'Balcabyelow'PBR	NPri
(Can-can Series) Can-can Apricot = 'Balcanapt' **new**	NPri
- Can-can Rose Star = 'Balcanrost' **new**	NPri
(Million Bells Series) Million Bells Cherry = 'Sunbelchipi'PBR	WGor
- Million Bells Trailing Blue = 'Sunbelkubu'PBR	LAst
- Million Bells Trailing Ice = 'Sunbelkuriho'PBR	LAst
- Million Bells Trailing Lavender Vein = 'Sunbelbura'PBR	LSou
- Million Bells Trailing Lemon	LSou
- Million Bells Trailing Plum = 'Sunbelkufepi'	LSou
(MiniFamous Series) MiniFamous Double Blush Pink = 'Kleca08164' **new**	LAst
- MiniFamous Double Lemon = 'Kleca09204' **new**	LAst
- MiniFamous Double Nostalgia **new**	LAst
(Superbells Series) Superbells Apricot Punch = 'Uscali41308'	LAst
- Superbells Imperial Purple = 'Uscali100'PBR	LSou
- Superbells Orange = 'Uscali41109'	LSou
- Superbells Pink = 'Uscali11'PBR ♀H3	LSou
- Superbells Red = 'Uscali28'PBR	WGor
- Superbells Yellow = 'Uscali53002'	WGor

Calibrachoa × *Petunia* see × *Petchoa*

Calla (*Araceae*)

aethiopica	see *Zantedeschia aethiopica*
palustris	CBAq CRow CWat EBee EHon EWay MSKA MWts NPer SWat WMAq

Calliandra (*Mimosaceae*)

'Dixie Pink'	CCCN
eriophylla	SPlb
portoricensis	CCCN
surinamensis	CCCN
tweediei	CCCN MOWG

Callianthemum (*Ranunculaceae*)

anemonoides	LLHF WAbe WCot
kernerianum	WAbe

Callicarpa (*Lamiaceae*)

acuminata **new**	CFil
americana	CExl NLar
- var. ***lactea***	CMCN
bodinieri	NBir
- var. ***giraldii***	GBin MRav NLar SGol
- - 'Profusion' ♀H4	Widely available
cathayana	NLar
dichotoma	CBcs CExl NLar
- 'Issai'	ESwi LLHF WPat
- 'Variegata' (v)	CJun
japonica	CExl CMen NLar
- B&SWJ 12621 **new**	WCru
- f. ***albibacca***	ESwi LRHS NLar
- 'Heavy Berry'	NLar
- 'Koshima-no-homate'	NLar
- 'Leucocarpa'	CBcs CExl CMac EBee ELan EPfP ESwi MRav NLar SPer SPoG WGob
- var. ***luxurians*** B&SWJ 8521	WCru
kwangtungensis	CBcs EPfP ESwi
mollis	CBcs CExl NLar
shikokiana	NLar
× ***shirasawana***	NLar
aff. ***tikusikensis*** B&SWJ 7127	WCru
Van den Broek selection	NLar
yunnanensis	NLar

Callirhoe (*Malvaceae*)

involucrata	SBrt SMad WHrl XLum
- var. ***tenuissima***	GCal

Callisia (*Commelinaceae*)

fragrans	EOHP EShb

Callistemon (*Myrtaceae*)

acuminatus	CCCN
'Awanga Dam'	ECou
brachyandrus	SVen
'Burgundy'	MOWG
'Candy Pink'	MOWG
citrinus	CHel CHll CTri CWSG EBee ECou EPfP EPri MREP SPlb SRms WGrn WHar
- 'Albus'	see *C. citrinus* 'White Anzac'
- 'Angela'	MOWG
- 'Firebrand'	LRHS MAsh
- 'Splendens' ♀H3	CBar CBcs CCCN CDoC CDul CHEx CMac CSBt CWib ELan ELon EPfP

		EUJe IArd LRHS MAsh MBri MGos MOWG NSoo SCoo SEND SHil SLim SPer SPoG SSta SVen SWvt WGwG
§	- 'White Anzac'	CDoC CMac ELan EPfP MOWG SEND SPoG SSta
	comboynensis	CCCN
	'Eureka'	MOWG
	glaucus	see *C. speciosus*
	'Hannah's Child'	MOWG
	'Happy Valley'	ECou MOWG
	'Havering Gold'	ECou
	'Havering Pink'	ECou
	'Havering Red'	ECou
	'Inferno'	LRHS
	'Injune'	MOWG
	'Kings Park Special'	MOWG
	laevis hort.	see *C. rugulosus*
	linearifolius	LSRN
	linearis ♀H3	CBcs CMac CTri ECou ECrN ELan EPfP LRHS LSRN MAsh MHer MOWG SEND SLim SLon SPlb SRms SWvt WSHC
	macropunctatus	SPlb SVen
	'Masotti'PBR	LRHS MPkF SHil
	'Mauve Mist'	CCCN CDoC ELan EPfP EPri GBin LRHS MOWG SPoG SVen WGrn
	'Millie Marsden'	MOWG
	pachyphyllus	ECou MOWG
	- var. ***viridis***	MOWG
	pallidus	CBcs CCCN CHEx CHel CMac CTsd CWib EBee ECou ELan EPfP LRHS MAsh MOWG MRav SDys SEND SPer SPlb SPoG SVen
	- 'Candle Glow'	MOWG
	- 'Father Christmas'	MOWG
	paludosus	see *C. sieberi* DC.
	pearsonii 'Rocky Rambler'	MOWG
	'Perth Pink'	CBcs CCCN CDoC ELan EPfP LHop LRHS MOWG SLim SVen
	phoeniceus	ECou MOWG
	- 'Pink Ice'	MOWG
	pinifolius	SPlb SVen
	- 'Sockeye'	MOWG
	'Pink Champagne'	MOWG
§	***pityoides***	CExl ECou MOWG
	- from Brown's Swamp, Australia	ECou
	recurvus	MOWG
	'Red Clusters'	CHel CMac EBee ELan EPfP IArd LRHS MAsh MOWG NEgg NPri SWvt
	'Reeve's Pink'	MOWG
	rigidus	CBcs CDoC CHEx CMHG CTri CTsd CWib ELan EPfP EPri IArd LRHS LSRN MGos MMuc MRav NLar SPer SVen SWvt
§	***rugulosus***	CBcs CCCN MOWG SVen SWvt
	salignus ♀H3	CBcs CCCN CDoC CDul CMac CTri CTsd EPfP GLin LRHS MHer MOWG MRav NEgg NLar SLim SPer SVen
	sieberi misapplied	see *C. pityoides*
§	***sieberi*** DC.	CBcs CDoC CHel CTsd ECou ELan EPfP LRHS MMuc MOWG NBir NLar SEND SLim SPlb
	- purple-flowered	MOWG
§	***speciosus***	CDul MOWG NLar SPlb
	subulatus	CHEx ECou GGal MOWG NLar SAPC SPlb WMoo
	- 'Crimson Tail'	EBee NLar SEND
I	- 'Packer's Selection'	ECou MOWG
	'Taree Pink'	MOWG
	viminalis	CBcs CCCN MOWG SPlb
	- 'Captain Cook'	CMac ECou IDee LRHS LSRN MOWG NLar SRms SVen SWvt WGrn
	- 'Endeavor'	CCCN SLim
	- 'Hannah Ray'	EUJe MOWG
	- Hot Pink = 'Kkho1'PBR	EBee LRHS MPkF NPri SCoo SLim
	- 'Little John'	LRHS LSRN MAsh MOWG SPad SWvt
	- 'Malawi Giant'	MOWG
	'Violaceus'	SPlb SVen
	viridiflorus	CMCN ECou GGal SEND SPlb WGwG
	- 'County Park Dwarf'	ECou
	'White Anzac'	see *C. citrinus* 'White Anzac'

Callistephus (*Asteraceae*)

	chinensis	SVic

Callitriche (*Plantaginaceae*)

	sp.	WSFF
	autumnalis	see *C. hermaphroditica*
	brutia	LLWG
	subsp. ***hamulata*** new	
§	***hermaphroditica***	CBAq
§	***palustris***	MSKA MWts
	stagnalis	WMAq
	verna	see *C. palustris*

Callitris (*Cupressaceae*)

	rhomboidea	IGor

Calluna ✿ (*Ericaceae*)

	vulgaris	SPer SWhi WOut
	- 'Adrie'	SWhi
	- 'Alba Elongata'	see *C. vulgaris* 'Mair's Variety'
	- 'Alexandra'PBR (Garden Girls Series) ♀H4	IVic SCoo SPoG
	- 'Alicia'PBR (Garden Girls Series) ♀H4	CBcs SCoo SPoG SWhi
	- 'Allegro' ♀H4	EPfP MMuc SCoo SWhi
	- 'Amethyst'PBR (Garden Girls Series)	CBcs MJak MMuc SPoG SWhi
	- 'Amilto'	SPer SWhi
	- 'Anette'PBR (Garden Girls Series) ♀H4	MJak SCoo SWhi
	- 'Annegret'	see *C. vulgaris* 'Marlies'
	- 'Annemarie' (d) ♀H4	CSBt EPfP SCoo SPlb SWhi
	- 'Anthony Davis' ♀H4	SWhi
	- 'Aphrodite'PBR (Garden Girls Series)	SWhi
	- 'Arina'	MAsh SCoo
	- 'Athene'PBR (Garden Girls Series)	SWhi
	- 'Aurea'	MJak
	- 'Beoley Crimson'	SCoo
	- 'Beoley Gold' ♀H4	CSBt CTri EPfP MAsh NHol SCoo SWhi
	- 'Beoley Silver'	SCoo SWhi
	- 'Blazeaway'	CTri EPfP MAsh MJak SCoo SWhi
	- 'Bonfire Brilliance'	CSBt NHol
	- 'Bonita'PBR (Garden Girls Series)	SWhi
	- 'Boskoop'	IVic MAsh NHol SWhi
	- 'C.W. Nix'	CSBt
	- 'Con Brio'	SCoo SWhi

	- 'Cottswood Gold'	SCoo
	- 'County Wicklow' (d) ♀H4	CBcs CTri EPfP MMuc NHol SCoo SWhi
	- 'Cuprea'	EPfP MJak SCoo SWhi
	- 'Dark Beauty'PBR (d) ♀H4	CBcs EPfP IVic MAsh NHol SCoo SWhi
	- 'Dark Star' (d) ♀H4	EPfP MAsh MMuc NHol SCoo SWhi
	- 'Darkness' ♀H4	CBcs CTri EPfP MAsh MJak NHol SCoo SWhi
	- 'David Hagenaars'	SWhi
	- 'Dunnet Lime'	SPlb
	- 'Easter-bonfire'	SCoo SWhi
	- 'Elsie Purnell' (d) ♀H4	EPfP MAsh NHol SCoo SPlb SWhi
	- 'Feuerwerk'	SCoo
	- 'Firefly' ♀H4	CBcs CSBt EPfP MJak MMuc NHol NWea SCoo SPer SWhi
	- 'Flamingo'	MMuc SCoo SWhi
	- 'Forest Fire'	SWhi
	- 'Foxii Lett's Form'	see *C. vulgaris* 'Mousehole'
	- 'Foxii Nana'	NHol SWhi
	- 'Fred J. Chapple'	MJak SWhi
	- Garden Girls Series	MMuc
	- 'Glenfiddich'	CSBt MAsh
	- 'Gold Haze' ♀H4	CTri MAsh NHol SCoo SWhi
	- 'Gold Knight'	EPfP MAsh SCoo
	- 'Golden Carpet'	CSBt MAsh NHol
	- 'Golden Turret'	MAsh
	- 'Grey Carpet'	SPer
	- 'Guinea Gold'	MAsh
§	- 'H.E. Beale' (d)	CTri EPfP MJak NHol SCoo
	- 'Hammondii Aureifolia'	SPlb SWhi
	- 'Hammondii Rubrifolia'	SWhi
	- 'Highland Rose'	SPlb
	- 'Humpty Dumpty'	NHol
	- 'J.H. Hamilton' (d) ♀H4	CTri MAsh NHol SCoo SWhi
	- 'Jan Dekker'	MAsh SWhi
	- 'Johnson's Variety'	SCoo
	- 'Josefine'	SWhi
	- 'Joy Vanstone' ♀H4	EPfP
	- 'Kerstin' ♀H4	MMuc NHol SCoo SPer SPlb SWhi
	- 'Kinlochruel' (d) ♀H4	CBcs CSBt CTri EPfP MAsh NHol SPer SPlb SWhi
	- 'Kirby White'	MAsh SPlb SWhi
	- 'Klaudine'PBR (Garden Girls Series)	IVic
	- 'Leprechaun'	NHol SWhi
	- 'Leslie Slinger'	SCoo SWhi
	- 'Little John'	LSRN
	- 'Long White'	SWhi
	- 'Madonna'PBR (Garden Girls Series)	SWhi
§	- 'Mair's Variety' ♀H4	SCoo
	- 'Marleen'	MJak SWhi
§	- 'Marlies'	SWhi
	- 'Melanie' (Garden Girls Series)	NHol SCoo SWhi
§	- 'Mousehole'	NHol
	- 'Mrs Pat'	MAsh NHol
	- 'Multicolor'	MAsh NHol
§	- 'My Dream' (d) ♀H4	CSBt EPfP SCoo
	- 'Orange Queen'	CSBt
	- 'Peter Sparkes' (d) ♀H4	CBcs CSBt EPfP MAsh MMuc NHol SCoo SWhi
	- 'Pink Beale'	see *C. vulgaris* 'H.E. Beale'
	- 'Purple Passion'	EPfP SCoo
	- 'Radnor' (d) ♀H4	CSBt
	- 'Ralph Purnell'	SCoo
	- 'Red Beauty'	CBcs SWhi
	- 'Red Favorit' (d)	SPer SWhi
	- 'Red Fred'	SCoo
	- 'Red Haze'	EPfP NHol SCoo
	- 'Red Pimpernel'	EPfP SCoo SWhi
	- 'Red Star' (d)	NHol
	- 'Reini'	SWhi
	- 'Robert Chapman' ♀H4	CSBt CTri MAsh NHol SPer SWhi
	- 'Rosalind' ambig.	EPfP
	- 'Rosalind, Underwood's'	EPfP NHol
	- 'Roter Oktober'	SWhi
	- 'Ruby Slinger'	NHol SWhi
	- 'Ruth Sparkes' (d)	NHol
	- 'Sandy'PBR (Garden Girls Series)	SPoG SWhi
	- 'Schurig's Sensation' (d)	IVic
	- 'Serlei Aurea' ♀H4	CSBt EPfP MAsh
	- 'Silver Knight'	CSBt EPfP MAsh MJak NHol SCoo SPer SPlb SWhi
	- 'Silver Queen' ♀H4	MAsh MJak NHol SWhi
	- 'Silver Rose' ♀H4	SWhi
	- 'Sir John Charrington' ♀H4	CSBt EPfP MAsh NHol SWhi
	- 'Sister Anne' ♀H4	CSBt EPfP MMuc SCoo SWhi
	- 'Snowball'	see *C. vulgaris* 'My Dream'
	- 'Sonja' (d)	IVic
	- 'Spitfire'	MAsh
	- 'Spring Cream' ♀H4	MAsh MMuc NHol SCoo SPoG SWhi
	- 'Spring Torch'	CSBt MAsh MJak NHol SCoo SPoG SWhi
	- 'Stefanie'	SWhi
	- 'Strawberry Delight' (d)	EPfP SCoo
	- 'Sunrise'	EPfP
	- 'Sunset' ♀H4	SWhi
	- 'Tib' (d) ♀H4	CSBt MAsh SWhi
	- 'Tricolorifolia'	EPfP MAsh SCoo SWhi
	- 'Velvet Fascination' ♀H4	EPfP NHol SCoo SWhi
	- 'White Coral' (d)	EPfP IVic SCoo SWhi
	- 'White Lawn' ♀H4	MMuc NHol SWhi
	- 'Wickwar Flame' ♀H4	CBcs CSBt EPfP MAsh MJak MMuc NHol SCoo SPer SPlb SWhi
	- 'Winter Chocolate'	CSBt EPfP MAsh NHol SCoo SWhi
	- 'Yvette's Gold'	SWhi

Calocedrus (*Cupressaceae*)

§	***decurrens*** ♀H4	CBcs CDoC CDul CLnd CMac CMen CTho EHul EPfP LRHS MBlu NPCo NWea SLim SPoG
	- 'Aureovariegata' (v)	CBcs CWib EHul LRHS MBri SCoo
	- 'Berrima Gold'	CDoC LRHS NLar SLim
§	- 'Depressa'	CKen
	- 'Intricata'	CKen NLar SLim
	- 'Maupin Glow' (v)	NLar SLim
	- 'Nana'	see *C. decurrens* 'Depressa'
	- 'Pillar'	CKen NLar

Calocephalus (*Asteraceae*)

brownii	see *Leucophyta brownii*

Calochortus (*Liliaceae*)

albus	ECho
- var. ***rubellus***	ECho
aureus	ECho
caeruleus	ECho
'Cupido'PBR	CExl ECho GKev
invenustus	ECho
luteus Douglas ex Lindl.	EPot
- 'Golden Orb'PBR	CExl CGrW ECho GKev SDeJ
splendens 'Violet Queen'	CGrW ECho GKev
superbus	ECho EPot GKev SDeJ
'Symphony'PBR	CExl ECho EPot GKev SDeJ

	venustus	CGrW ECho EPot GKev SDeJ
	- 'Burgundy' **new**	ECho EPot GKev SDeJ
	vestae	WCot

Calomeria (*Asteraceae*)

§	***amaranthoides***	WJek

Calonyction see *Ipomoea*

Calopogon (*Orchidaceae*)

	tuberosus	NLAp

Caloscordum (*Alliaceae*)

§	***neriniflorum***	WAbe

Calothamnus (*Myrtaceae*)

	quadrifidus	ECou
	- yellow-flowered	MOWG
	validus	SPlb

Calotropis (*Apocynaceae*)

	procera	SPlb

Calpurnia (*Papilionaceae*)

	aurea	SPlb

Caltha ✿ (*Ranunculaceae*)

	howellii	see *C. leptosepala* subsp. *howellii*
	introloba	SWat
	laeta	see *C. palustris* var. *palustris*
	leptosepala	CLAP CRow EBee EWTr EWay LLHF NLar
§	- subsp. ***howellii*** NNS 07-87	GKev
	natans	EWay LLWG
	palustris 🏆H4	Widely available
	- var. ***alba***	Widely available
	- 'Auengold' **new**	EBee LLWG
	- 'Auenwald'	CLAP EBee LLWG
	- 'Flore Pleno' (d) 🏆H4	Widely available
	- 'Honeydew'	CDes CLAP CRow EWay LLWG LRHS MWts WCot WSHC
	- 'Marilyn'	LLWG
	- 'Multiplex' (d)	ECtt GBin GBuc GKev SRot
	- Newlake hybrid	LLWG
§	- var. ***palustris***	CBAq CBre CRow EHon ELan EWay MWts SWat
	- - 'Plena' (d)	CBAq CWat EPfP EWay LRHS MCot MSKA SGol SPoG
	- var. ***radicans***	CRow
	- - 'Flore Pleno' (d)	CRow
	- 'Stagnalis'	CRow MSKA MWts
	- 'Yellow Giant'	MSKA
N	***polypetala*** misapplied	see *C. palustris* var. *palustris*
N	***polypetala*** Hochst. ex Lorent	CCon CWat GCal MSCN MSKA NPer SMad SWat WMAq
	sagittata	WSHC

Calycanthus (*Calycanthaceae*)

	fertilis	see *C. floridus* var. *glaucus*
	floridus	CAgr CArn CBcs CDul CJun CMCN CWib EBee ELan EPfP EWTr IDee ITim LAst LEdu LRHS MBNS MBlu MBri MGos MMuc NLar SPer SPlb SPoG SSpi SWvt WCFE
	- 'Athens'	CBcs CJun NLar
§	- var. ***glaucus***	EPfP LRHS NLar SHil WSHC
	- - 'Purpureus'	CBcs CJun MBlu MBri NLar
	- var. ***laevigatus***	see *C. floridus* var. *glaucus*
	- 'Michael Lindsay'	CJun MBri NLar
	mohrii	NLar
	occidentalis	CAgr CArn CDul CMCN CSpe CWib EBee EPPr MBlu MMuc WCFE

Calystegia (*Convolvulaceae*)

	'Angel's Trumpets'	SKHP
§	***hederacea*** 'Flore Pleno' (d)	SMad WCot
	japonica 'Flore Pleno'	see *C. hederacea* 'Flore Pleno'
	soldanella NNS 99-85	WCot

Calytrix (*Myrtaceae*)

	tetragona	SPlb

Camassia ✿ (*Asparagaceae*)

	'Blue Candle' **new**	EPot ERCP
	'Blue Heaven'	EBee ERCP LRHS SDeJ
	cusickii	Widely available
	- white-flowered	IFoB
	- 'Zwanenburg'	CTca EBee ERCP GKev LRHS WCot
	esculenta Lindl.	see *C. quamash*
	leichtlinii misapplied	see *C. leichtlinii* subsp. *suksdorfii*
N	***leichtlinii*** (Baker) S.Watson	see *C. leichtlinii* subsp. *leichtlinii*
	'Alba' misapplied	
*	- 'Alba Plena'	MNrw MWat NBir
I	- 'Atrocaerulea'	GMaP STes
	- 'Blue Wave'	ERCP NHol NWad SBch
§	- subsp. ***leichtlinii*** 🏆H4	Widely available
	- 'Sacajawea'	CAvo CMea CTca EBee ECtt ERCP LBuc LRHS SBch SDeJ
	- 'Semiplena' (d)	CAvo CBro CMea CRDP CTca EBee ECtt ERCP LHop LRHS MBel MCot MNrw NSti SDix SPhx WBor WCot WHoo WShi
	- 'Sky Blue'	CMea LRHS
§	- subsp. ***suksdorfii***	GCra WCot
	- - 'Alba'	CHel LRHS
	- - Caerulea Group	Widely available
	- - 'Electra'	CAvo
§	***quamash***	CArn CAvo CBro CTca CWCL EBee ELan EPfP EPot ERCP GKev ITim LEdu LPio LRHS MBel MBri MCot NBir NCGa SDeJ SRms WShi XLum
	- 'Blue Melody' (v)	CAvo CBro CSam CTca EBee ECtt EPot ERCP GKev GMaP LEdu LRHS SDeJ
	- subsp. ***maxima*** NNS 06-119	GKev
	- 'Orion'	CBro EBee GKev WCot

Camellia ✿ (*Theaceae*)

	'Adorable' (*pitardii* hybrid)	LRHS LSRN
	'Alpen Glo'	MPkF
	'Annette Carol'	CDoC
	'April Blush'	SCog
	'Ariel's Song'	CDoC
	'Auburn White'	see *C. japonica* 'Mrs Bertha A. Harms'
	'Baby Bear'	CDoC MPkF SCam
	'Barbara Clark' (*reticulata* × *saluenensis*)	CDoC LRHS LSRN SCog SCoo
	'Bertha Harms Blush'	see *C. japonica* 'Mrs Bertha A. Harms'
	'Bett's Supreme'	CDoC
	'Black Lace' 🏆H4	CTrh CTri EPfP LRHS LSRN MAsh MBri MMuc SAPC SCam SCog SCoo SEND SHil
	'Blissful Dawn'	CBcs

	'Bonnie Marie'	CDoC MGos SCam SCog
	'Canterbury'	CDoC LRHS
	'Champêtres Spring Awakening'	MPkF
	'China Lady' (*granthamiana* × *reticulata*)	SCam
	'Christmas Daffodil' (*japonica* hybrid)	MPkF
	'Cinnamon Cindy'	CDoC LRHS SCog
	'Cinnamon Sensation'	SCog
	'Confucius' (*reticulata* hybrid)	SCam
	'Congratulations'	CSBt LSRN
	'Contessa Lavinia Maggi'	see *C. japonica* 'Lavinia Maggi'
	'Cornish Snow' (*cuspidata* × *saluenensis*) ♀H4	CBcs CDoC CSBt CTri ELan EPfP GGal MGos NLar NSoo SCam SCog SPer SSpi
	'Cornish Spring' (*cuspidata* × *japonica*) ♀H4	CCCN CDoC CHel CSBt CTrh CTsd EPfP LRHS MAsh MGos SCam SCog SPer
	'Crimson Candles'	LRHS MPkF SCam
	cuspidata	SCam SCog
	'Czar'	see *C. japonica* 'The Czar'
	'Dainty Dale'	CDoC SCam
	'Delia Williams'	see *C.* × *williamsii* 'Citation'
	'Den Burton' (*japonica* × *reticulata*)	SCam
	'Diamond Head' (*japonica* × *reticulata*)	LSRN
	'Diana's Charm'	CDoC LSRN
	'Doctor Clifford Parks' (*japonica* × *reticulata*) ♀H2	CDoC SCam SCog
	'Donckelaeri'	see *C. japonica* 'Masayoshi'
	edithae	LRHS
	'El Dorado' (*japonica* × *pitardii*)	CDoC
	'Elizabeth Bolitho'	SCam
	'Extravaganza' (*japonica* hybrid)	CHel CTrh IArd SCam
	'Fairy Blush'	CDoC LRHS MPkF
	'Fairy Wand'	CDoC LRHS MPkF
	'Fascination' **new**	SWvt
	'Felice Harris' (*reticulata* × *sasanqua*)	CDoC SCam SCog
	'Festival of Lights'	MPkF
	'Fiesta Grande'	SCam
	'Fire 'n' Ice'	CDoC SCam
	'Forty-niner' (*japonica* × *reticulata*)	CBcs MAsh
	'Fox's Fancy'	CDoC
	'Fragrant Pink'	CDoC CTrh SCam
	'Francie L' (*reticulata* × *saluenensis*) ♀H3-4	CDoC EPfP SCam SCog SSta
	'Free Spirit'	CTrh
	'Freedom Bell' ♀H4	CDoC CHel CMHG CTrh EPfP GGal GKin LRHS MAsh MBri MPkF NPri SCam SCog SCoo
	'Gael's Dream' (*reticulata* hybrid)	SCam
	'Gay Baby'	CDoC MPkF
	'Golden Anniversary'	see *C. japonica* 'Dahlohnega'
	grijsii	CExl CTrh SCam
	handelii	CExl
	'Happy Anniversary'	CSBt LSRN SWvt
§	***hiemalis*** 'Bonanza'	LRHS MPkF SCam
	- 'Chansonette'	CDoC ELon MGos SCam SCog
§	- 'Dazzler'	CBcs LRHS SCam SCog
	- 'Interlude'	MPkF
	- 'Kanjirō'	CDoC SCam
	- 'Shōwa-no-sakae'	CDoC LRHS MPkF SCog
§	- 'Sparkling Burgundy' ♀H3	CBcs CDoC ELon EPfP LRHS MGos NPri NSoo SCam SCog SMDP
	'High Fragrance'	LRHS MPkF
	'Hooker'	CDoC LRHS SCoo
	'Ice Follies'	SCam
	'Imbricata Rubra'	see *C. japonica* 'Imbricata'
	'Inspiration' (*reticulata* × *saluenensis*) ♀H4	CDoC CMac CSam CTrh EPfP GKin LSRN MBri MGos NLar NSoo SCam SCog SPer SSpi
	japonica	SEWo SPrc
	- 'Aaron's Ruby'	CDoC ELon LRHS SCog
	- 'Ada Pieper'	CTrh
	- 'Adelina Patti' ♀H4	CBcs CDoC CMHG CTrh ELon SCam SCog
	- 'Adolphe Audusson' ♀H4	Widely available
	- 'Adolphe Audusson Special'	LSRN
§	- 'Akashigata' ♀H4	CBcs CDoC CMac ELon EPfP LRHS LSRN SCam SCog SLim SPoG SSta
	- 'Alba Plena' ♀H4	CTrh LRHS NSoo SCam SCog SWvt
	- 'Alba Simplex'	CDoC CMac CTrh ELan EPfP IVic MJak SCam SCog SSta
	- 'Alexander Hunter' ♀H4	CDoC LRHS MAsh SCog
	- 'Alison Leigh Woodroof'	CDoC
§	- 'Althaeiflora'	CBcs CDoC ELon LRHS MGos SCam SCog
	- 'Amazing Graces'	CDoC
	- 'Anemoniflora'	CBcs CDoC EPfP LRHS SCam SCog
	- 'Angel'	LSRN SCam WBor
	- 'Angello'	CWSG
	- 'Ann Sothern'	CBcs
	- 'Annie Wylam' ♀H4	CTrh
	- 'Apollo' ambig.	CBcs CDoC LRHS MBri
	- 'Apollo' Paul, 1911	MSwo SCam SCog
§	- 'Apple Blossom' ♀H4	CTsd LRHS
	- 'Arajishi' misapplied	see *C. japonica* subsp. *rusticana* 'Beni-arajishi'
*	- 'Augustine Supreme'	CMac
	- 'Australis' ♀H4	SCam
	- 'Ave Maria' ♀H4	CDoC CTrh LRHS
	- 'Baby Pearl'	LSRN SCam
	- 'Baby Sis'	CDoC LRHS
	- 'Ballet Dancer' ♀H4	CDoC ELon LSRN SCam SCog
	- 'Bambino'	CDoC
	- 'Baron Gomer'	see *C. japonica* 'Comte de Gomer'
	- 'Baronne Leguay'	SCam
	- 'Beau Harp'	CDoC LRHS SCam
	- 'Bella Lambertii'	SCog
	- 'Bella Romana'	SCam
	- 'Benten-kagura' (v)	CDoC
	- 'Berenice Boddy' ♀H4	CDoC LRHS
	- 'Berenice Perfection'	CDoC SCog
	- 'Betty Foy Sanders'	CTrh
	- 'Betty Robinson'	CDoC LRHS
	- 'Betty Sheffield'	CDoC SCog
	- 'Betty Sheffield Pink'	LRHS SCam
	- 'Betty Sheffield Supreme'	CBcs
	- 'Betty's Beauty'	LRHS
	- 'Billie McCaskill'	SCam
	- 'Black Magic'	CTrh LRHS MAsh
	- 'Black Tie'	CDoC CWSG ELan ELon LRHS MGos NSoo SCam SCog
	- 'Blackburnia'	see *C. japonica* 'Althaeiflora'
	- 'Blaze of Glory'	SCog
§	- 'Blood of China'	CBcs CDoC CSBt ELan LRHS LSRN MBri MGos MMuc NSoo SCam SCog SCoo SHil

	- 'Bob Hope' ♀H4	CBcs CDoC CTrh CTri LRHS MAsh
	- 'Bob's Tinsie' ♀H4	CDoC CMHG CSBt EPfP LRHS LSRN MAsh MPkF NLar
§	- 'Bokuhan' ♀H4	CDoC MPkF
	- 'Bonomiana'	SAPC
	- 'Bright Buoy'	CDoC
	- 'Brushfield's Yellow' ♀H4	CBcs CDoC CMHG CSBt CTsd CWSG ELan ELon EPfP IArd LMil LRHS LSRN MAsh MBri MGos NEgg NLar SCam SCog SCoo SPer SSta
	- 'Bush Hill Beauty'	see *C. japonica* 'Lady de Saumarez'
§	- 'C.M. Hovey' ♀H4	CMHG CMac
	- 'C.M. Wilson'	CDoC CMac SCog
	- 'Campsii Alba'	CDoC CTsd
	- 'Can Can'	CDoC ELon MGos SCam SCog
	- 'Candy Apple'	CTrh
	- 'Candy Stripe'	CDoC SCam
	- 'Captain Blood'	CDoC
	- 'Cara Mia'	CDoC CTsd LRHS SCam
	- 'Carter's Sunburst' ♀H4	CBcs CDoC ELan EPfP SCog
	- 'Cassandra'	EPfP SHil
	- 'Chandleri Elegans'	see *C. japonica* 'Elegans'
	- 'Charlotte de Rothschild'	CTrh CTri
	- 'Cheryll Lynn'	CDoC
	- 'Christmas Beauty'	SCam
	- 'Cinderella'	CDoC LRHS MAsh SCog SSta
	- 'Clarke Hubbs'	CDoC
	- Classique = 'Kerguelen'PBR	LRHS MPkF
	- 'Colonel Firey'	see *C. japonica* 'C.M. Hovey'
	- 'Commander Mulroy' ♀H4	CDoC CTrh SCam
§	- 'Comte de Gomer'	CDoC ELan ELon EPfP LRHS MBri SCog
	- 'Conspicua'	CBcs
	- 'Contessa Samailoff'	CDoC
§	- 'Coquettii' ♀H4	CBcs LRHS MAsh SCam
	- 'Coral Pink Lotus'	CDoC
	- 'Coral Queen'	CDoC SCam
	- 'Cornish Excellence'	CDoC CHel SCam
	- 'Curly Lady'PBR	MMuc MPkF NPri WMoo
§	- 'Dahlohnega'	CDoC CSBt CTrh ELon LRHS LSRN MPkF SCam
	- 'Daikagura'	CBcs CDoC
	- 'Dainty'	CBcs
	- 'Daitairin'	see *C. japonica* 'Dewatairin'
	- 'Daphne du Maurier'	LRHS
	- 'Dark of the Moon'	CDoC LRHS
	- 'Dear Jenny'	CBcs
	- 'Debutante'	CBcs CDoC CMac ELon MGos SCam SCog
	- 'Deep Secret' ♀H4	CDoC
	- 'Desire' ♀H4	CBcs CDoC CHel CMHG CSBt CTrh CTsd EPfP LRHS LSRN MAsh MBri MPkF SCam SCog SCoo SPoG WGob
	- 'Devonia'	CBcs SCog
§	- 'Dewatairin' (Higo)	CBcs CDoC SCam SCog
	- 'Diddy's Pink Organdie' **new**	LRHS
	- 'Dixie Knight'	CBcs CDoC LRHS MGos SCam SCog
	- 'Dobreei'	CMac
	- 'Doctor Burnside'	CDoC CHel CTrh LRHS SCam SCog
	- 'Doctor King'	EPfP MBri NSoo
	- 'Doctor Tinsley' ♀H4	CDoC LRHS MAsh NPri SCoo
	- 'Dolly Dyer'	CDoC MPkF
	- 'Dona Herzilia de Freitas Magalhaes'	CBcs CDoC ELon MGos SCam SCog

	- 'Dona Jane Andresson'	SCam
	- 'Donckelaeri'	see *C. japonica* 'Masayoshi'
	- 'Donnan's Dream'	CTrh
	- 'Drama Girl' ♀H2	CBcs CDoC CTsd EPfP LRHS SBod SCam SCog
	- 'Dream Time'	CBcs
	- 'Duc de Bretagne'	SCog
	- 'Duchesse Decazes'	CBcs
	- 'Ed Combatalade'	CDoC
	- 'Edelweiss'	CDoC SCam SCog
	- 'Effendee'	see *C. sasanqua* 'Rosea Plena'
§	- 'Elegans' ♀H4	CBcs CDoC ELon EPfP LMil LRHS MBri NEgg SCam SCog SCoo SLim SPer SPoG SWvt
	- 'Elegans Champagne'	EPfP
	- 'Elegans Splendor'	CDoC
	- 'Elisabeth'	CDoC LRHS
	- 'Elizabeth Arden'	CTsd
	- 'Elizabeth Cooper'	CTrh LSRN
	- 'Elizabeth Dowd'	CBcs SCog
	- 'Elizabeth Hawkins'	CTrh LRHS MMuc NCGa
	- 'Emily Wilson'	CDoC
	- 'Emmett Barnes'	SCam
	- 'Emmett Pfingstl'	SCam
	- 'Emperor of Russia'	CBcs CDoC LRHS
	- 'Eric Baker'	CDoC SCam
	- 'Eugène Lizé'	SCam
	- 'Eximia'	EPfP LRHS SCam SCog
	- 'Fanny'	SCog
	- 'Fashionata'	CDoC SCam
	- 'Feast Perfection'	CDoC
	- 'Finlandia Variegated'	CDoC ELon MGos SCam SCog
	- 'Fire Dance'	CDoC
	- 'Fire Falls' ♀H4	CDoC CMHG
	- 'Firebird'	CBcs
	- 'Flamingo'	CDoC
	- 'Flashlight'	CDoC EPfP LRHS
§	- 'Fleur Dipater'	LRHS SCam
	- 'Flowerwood'	SCog
	- 'Forest Green'	CDoC MAsh
	- 'Fortune Teller'	CBcs
	- 'Frans van Damme'	CBcs
	- 'Fred Sander'	CBcs CDoC ELon LRHS MGos SCam SCog
	- 'Frosty Morn'	CDoC
	- 'Furo-an'	MAsh
§	- 'Gigantea'	LRHS SCam
	- 'Giuditta Rosani'	CDoC LRHS
	- 'Gladys Wannamaker'	SCog
	- 'Glen 40'	see *C. japonica* 'Coquettii'
	- 'Gloire de Nantes' ♀H4	CTrh SCam SCog
	- 'Gold Tone'	CDoC SCam
*	- 'Golden Wedding' (v)	SCog
	- 'Goshozakura'	CDoC
	- 'Grace Bunton'	CBcs CDoC ELon MGos SCam SCog
	- 'Granada'	SCog
	- 'Grand Prix' ♀H4	CDoC ELon LSRN MGos NLar SCam SCog SPer
	- 'Grand Slam' ♀H2	CBcs CDoC MAsh SCam
	- 'Grand Sultan'	CDoC
	- 'Guest of Honor'	CBcs CDoC
	- 'Guilio Nuccio' ♀H4	CBcs CDoC CHel CTri ELan ELon EPfP IArd LMil LRHS LSRN NEgg SCam SCog SCoo SLim SPer
	- 'Gus Menard'	SCam
	- 'Gwenneth Morey'	CBcs CDoC
	- 'H.A. Downing'	CDoC SCam
§	- 'Hagoromo' ♀H4	CBcs CDoC CTrh CTsd ELan SCam SCog SPer

- 'Hakugan' EPfP NLar NSoo
§ - 'Hakurakuten' ♀^{H4} CDoC CTri SCog
- 'Hanafūki' CDoC LRHS MAsh MGos SCam SCog
- 'Happy Birthday' LSRN
- 'Haru-no-utena' CTrh
- 'Hatsuzakura' see *C. japonica* 'Dewatairin'
- 'Hawaii' CDoC CMac CTrh LRHS SCog
- 'Her Majesty Queen Elizabeth II' CDoC
- Herme see *C. japonica* 'Hikarugenji'
- 'High Hat' CBcs SCog
- 'High, Wide 'n' Handsome' CDoC
§ - 'Hikarugenji' CDoC SCog
- 'Hinomaru' CDoC CMac
- 'Hiryū' **new** MBri
- 'Holly Bright' CTrh
- 'Honeyglow' CDoC
- 'Ichisetsu' SCog
§ - 'Imbricata' LRHS MMuc SCog
- 'Incarnata' SCam
- 'Italiana Vera' LRHS MAsh
- 'J.J. Whitfield' CMac SCam
- 'Jack Jones Scented' CMHG
- 'Janet Waterhouse' CBcs SCam
§ - 'Japonica Variegata' (v) CDoC LRHS SCam
- 'Jean Clere' CDoC SCog
- 'Jennifer Turnbull' CDoC
- 'Jessie Katz' CDoC
- 'Jingle Bells' CBcs
- 'Jitsugetsusei' CDoC
'Joseph Pfingstl' ♀^{H4} CDoC CTri EPfP LRHS MMuc NLar NPri SCam SCog SEND
- 'Jovey Carlyon' CBcs LRHS
- 'Joy Sander' see *C. japonica* 'Apple Blossom'
- 'Julia France' SCog
- 'Juno' CBcs LRHS SCam SCoo
- 'Jupiter' Paul, 1904 ♀^{H4} CBcs CDoC CHel CMac CTri EPfP LSRN MGos SCam SCog SPer
- 'Kellingtoniana' see *C. japonica* 'Gigantea'
- 'Kentucky' LRHS SCam
- 'Kick-off' CBcs CTrh SCog
- 'Kimberley' CBcs CDoC LSRN SCog
- 'King Size' CDoC MGos
- 'King's Ransom' CDoC CMac CTsd LRHS
- 'Kingyoba-shiro-wabisuke' CDoC CHll
- 'Kingyo-tsubaki' CDoC SCam SSta
- 'Kitty Berry' CTrh
- 'Kokinran' CDoC SCam
§ - 'Konronkoku' ♀^{H4} CBcs CDoC LRHS SCog
- 'Kouron-jura' see *C. japonica* 'Konronkoku'
- 'Kramer's Supreme' CBcs CCCN CDoC CDul ELon LRHS LSRN MBri MGos SCam SCog SCoo SGol SHil
§ - 'Kumasaka' CTri LRHS MBri
- 'La Pace Rubra' SCam
- 'Lady Campbell' CTri EPfP NSoo SCam SPad
- 'Lady Clare' see *C. japonica* 'Akashigata'
§ - 'Lady de Saumarez' CBcs CDoC CMac
- 'Lady Erma' CBcs
- 'Lady Loch' CTrh SCam
- 'Lady Marion' see *C. japonica* 'Kumasaka'
- 'Lady McCulloch' LRHS
- 'Lady Saint Clair' CDoC
- 'Lady Vansittart' CDoC CTrh ELan EPfP GGal LRHS LSRN MBri MPkF SCam SCog SCoo SLim SPer SPoG SSta
§ - 'Lady Vansittart Pink' CMac
- 'Lady Vansittart Red' see *C. japonica* 'Lady Vansittart Pink'
- 'Lady Vansittart Shell' see *C. japonica* 'Yours Truly'
- 'Lady Vere de Vere' (d) CDoC
- 'Latifolia' SCam
- 'Laura's Red' CTsd
- 'Laurie Bray' NSoo SCog
§ - 'Lavinia Maggi' ♀^{H4} CBcs CDoC CTri ELan ELon EPfP LMil LRHS LSRN MBri NPri SCam SCog SCoo SHil SPoG SReu SRms SSta
- 'L'Avvenire' SCog
§ - 'Le Lys' SCam
- 'Lemon Drop' CTrh
- 'Leonora Novick' CDoC SCog
- 'Lillian Rickets' CDoC
- 'Lily Pons' ♀^{H4} CDoC CTrh
- 'Little Bit' CBcs CDoC CMHG CTrh ELon SCam SCog SSta
- 'Little Man' **new** LRHS
- 'Lovelight' ♀^{H4} CHel CTrh LRHS SCam
- 'Lucy Hester' CDoC
- 'Ludgvan Red' LRHS
- 'Lulu Belle' SCog
- 'Mabel Blackwell' SCam
- 'Madame de Strekaloff' CMac CSBt SCam
- 'Madame Hahn' CDoC
- 'Madame Lebois' CDoC SCam
- 'Madame Martin Cachet' SCog
- 'Magnoliiflora' see *C. japonica* 'Hagoromo'
- 'Maiden's Blush' CMac
- 'Man Size' CDoC
- 'Manuroa Road' LRHS MPkF
- 'Margaret Davis' CCCN CDoC CHel CSBt CWSG ELan ELon EPfP LRHS LSRN MBri MGos MPkF NEgg NSoo SCam SCoo SHil SLim SPoG WGob
- 'Margaret Davis Picotee' ♀^{H4} CBcs CMHG CTrh SCog SPer
- 'Margaret Rose' SCam
'Margaret Short' CDoC CTsd
- 'Marguérite Gouillon' CDoC SSta
- 'Marian Mitchell' SCam
- 'Mariana' CDoC SCog
- 'Marjorie Magnificent' LRHS SCoo
- 'Mark Alan' CDoC LRHS LSRN MPkF
- 'Maroon and Gold' CDoC LRHS LSRN SCog
- 'Mars' ♀^{H4} SCam SCog SPer
- 'Mary Alice Cox' CDoC
- 'Mary Costa' CBcs CDoC CTrh
'Mary J Wheeler' LSRN
§ - 'Masayoshi' ♀^{H4} CBcs CSBt LRHS SCam SCog
- 'Mathotiana Alba' ♀^{H4} CDoC CMac CTri CTsd ELan EPfP LSRN MMuc SCam SCog SPer
§ - 'Mathotiana Rosea' ♀^{H4} CMac SCam
- 'Mathotiana Supreme' CDoC MGos SCam SCog
- 'Matterhorn' CTrh
- 'Mattie Cole' CDoC SCam
- 'Mercury' ♀^{H4} CBcs CMac EPfP GGGa SCog
- 'Mercury Variegated' (v) CMHG
- 'Mermaid' CDoC LRHS
- 'Midnight' CBcs CDoC CMHG LRHS SCoo
- 'Midnight Magic' CBcs CTrh CTri
- 'Midnight Serenade' CDoC LRHS
- 'Midnight Variegated' **new** MPkF
- 'Midsummer's Day' CBcs
§ - 'Mikenjaku' CBcs CDoC LRHS MAsh MBri NPri SCog
- 'Miriam Stevenson' SCam
- 'Miss Charleston' CHel SCog
- 'Miss Lyla' MMuc
- 'Modern Art' MPkF

- 'Momiji-gari'	CDoC SCam
- 'Monstruosa Rubra'	see *C. japonica* 'Gigantea'
- 'Monte Carlo'	CDoC SCam SCog
- 'Moonlight'	CDoC
- 'Moonlight Bay'	CTrh
- 'Moshe Dayan'	CDoC LRHS MAsh MGos SCog SCoo
- 'Moshio'	CDoC
§ - 'Mrs Bertha A. Harms'	CDoC LRHS MAsh SCam SCog
- 'Mrs Charles Cobb'	LRHS
- 'Mrs D.W. Davis'	CBcs CDoC EPfP SCam
- 'Mrs William Thompson'	LRHS SCam
§ - 'Mystic'	CDoC
- 'Nagasaki'	see *C. japonica* 'Mikenjaku'
- 'Nigra'	see *C. japonica* 'Konronkoku'
- 'Nioi-fubuki' (Higo)	CDoC
- 'Nobilissima'	CBcs CDoC CMac CTrh CTri CWSG EPfP MBlu MBri MMuc NSoo SCam SCog SCoo SPer SPoG
- 'Nokogiriba-tsubaki'	MPkF SCam
- 'Nuccio's Amigo'	MAsh
- 'Nuccio's Cameo'	CDoC CTrh LMil LRHS MAsh SCoo WGob
- 'Nuccio's Carousel'	MPkF
- 'Nuccio's Gem' ♀H4	CDoC CMHG ELan EPfP LRHS SCoo SGol SSta
- 'Nuccio's Jewel' ♀H4	CDoC CSBt CTrh ELon EPfP LRHS LSRN MAsh MPkF SCam SCog WMoo
- 'Nuccio's Pearl'	CBcs CDoC EPfP LRHS LSRN MAsh MBri NEgg SCam SCog SCoo
- 'Nuccio's Pink Lace'	CDoC CTri LRHS
- 'Olga Anderson'	CDoC
- 'Onetia Holland'	CDoC EPfP LSRN SCam SCog SLim
- 'Oo-La-La'	CTrh LRHS MPkF
- 'Optima'	CBcs CDoC ELon LRHS SCam SCog SCoo
- 'Optima Rosea'	SPoG
- 'Orandakō'	MBri SHil
- 'Paeoniiflora Alba'	SCam
- 'Patricia Ann'	LSRN
- 'Paul Jones Supreme'	CDoC
- 'Paulette Goddard'	SCam
- 'Paul's Apollo'	see *C. japonica* 'Apollo' Paul, 1911
- 'Peachblossom'	see *C. japonica* 'Fleur Dipater'
- 'Pearl Harbor'	SCam
- 'Pensacola Red'	CDoC
- 'Pink Champagne'	NPri
- 'Preston Rose'	CBcs
- 'Primavera'	CTrh SCam SCog
- 'Prince Murat'	CDoC LRHS
- 'Princess Baciocchi'	CBcs NLar SCam
- 'Princess du Mahe'	CMac
- 'R.L. Wheeler' ♀H4	CBcs CDoC CSBt CTri EPfP LRHS LSRN MBri NPri SCog SCoo
- 'Raspberry Ripple'	MPkF
- 'Red Dandy'	CDoC MGos SCam SCog
- 'Red Red Rose'	CDoC LRHS
- 'Reg Ragland'	CDoC SCam SCog
- 'Roger Hall'	CBcs CDoC CTrh LRHS LSRN MPkF SCog SCoo SPoG
- 'Rosa Baroveira Nella'	NSoo
- 'Rosularis'	CDoC ELon SCam SCog SPer
- 'Royal Velvet'	CDoC CTrh
- 'Rubescens Major' ♀H4	CBcs
- 'Ruddigore'	CTrh
§ - subsp. ***rusticana***	CBcs CDoC MGos SCog
- - 'Arajishi' misapplied	see *C. japonica* subsp. *rusticana* 'Beni-arajishi'

- - 'Arajishi' Ko'emon	SCam
- - 'Beni-arajishi' **new**	LRHS
- - 'Reigyoku' (v)	CBcs CDoC
- 'Sabiniana'	LRHS
- 'Saint André'	CMac LRHS SCoo
- 'Sally Harrell'	SCam
- 'San Dimas' ♀H4	CDoC CTrh LRHS MGos SCam SCog
- 'Saturnia'	CDoC ELon LRHS MMuc WBor
- 'Sawada's Dream'	CDoC SCog
- 'Scented Red'	CDoC
- 'Scentsation' ♀H4	CDoC CMHG CTri MBri SCog SHil
- 'Sea Foam'	LRHS
- 'Sea Gull'	CTrh
- 'Senator Duncan U. Fletcher'	CDoC
- 'Shikibu'	CTrh
- 'Shiragiku'	CBcs CDoC EPfP SCog
- 'Shiro Chan'	CDoC ELon MGos SCog
- 'Shirobotan'	CDoC ELon LRHS MAsh MGos SCam SCog SCoo
- 'Silver Anniversary'	CBcs CDoC CMHG CSBt CTrh CTri ELan ELon EPfP LMil LRHS LSRN MAsh MGos NEgg NLar NPri NSoo SCam SCog SCoo SLim SPer SPoG SReu SWvt
- 'Silver Ruffles'	CDoC LRHS
- 'Silver Waves'	MPkF
- 'Something Beautiful'	CDoC
- 'Souvenir de Bahuaud-Litou' ♀H4	CBcs CDoC SCam SCog
- 'Spencer's Pink'	CDoC
- 'Splendens Carlyon'	LRHS SCoo
- 'Spring Fever'	SCam
- 'Spring Fling'	CTrh
- 'Spring Formal'	CTrh
- 'Spring Frill'	SCam SCog
- 'Stacy Susan'	MPkF
- 'Stardust'	SCam
- 'Strawberry Blonde'	SCog WGob
- 'Strawberry Parfait'	CDoC
- 'Strawberry Swirl'	SCog
- 'Sugar Babe'	CDoC CTrh LRHS SCam SCog SCoo
- 'Suibijin' **new**	SSpi
- 'Sunset Glory'	SCam
- 'Sweetheart'	SCog
- 'Sylva' ♀H4	GGGa GGal NSoo SBod SSpi
- 'Sylvia'	CMac
- 'Takanini'	CDoC
- 'Tama Electra' **new**	MPkF
- 'Tama-no-ura'	CDoC
- 'Tammia'	CDoC LRHS MAsh
- 'Tarō'an'	CDoC GGal
- 'Teresa Ragland'	CDoC SCam
- 'Teringa'	CDoC
§ - 'The Czar'	CBcs
- 'The Mikado'	CDoC LRHS SCog
- 'Tickled Pink'	CDoC
- 'Tiffany'	CBcs CDoC LRHS MGos SCam SCog SCoo
- 'Tinker Bell'	CDoC ELon MGos SCam SCog
- 'Tom Pouce'	LRHS MPkF
- 'Tom Thumb' ♀H4	CDoC CTrh LRHS MAsh SRms SSta
- 'Tomorrow'	CDoC CTsd MMuc NEgg SCam SCog
- 'Tomorrow Park Hill'	CBcs SCog
§ - 'Tomorrow Variegated' (v)	SCam
- 'Tomorrow's Dawn'	CDoC
- 'Touchdown'	SCam

	- 'Trewithen White'	CDoC
§	- 'Tricolor' ♀H4	CBcs CDoC CMHG CMac CSBt ELon LRHS MAsh MMuc SCam SCog SCoo
	- 'Tricolor Red'	see *C. japonica* 'Lady de Saumarez'
	- 'Trinkett'	CDoC
	- 'Valtevareda'	CDoC
	- variegated (v)	SCog
	- 'Victor de Bisschop'	see *C. japonica* 'Le Lys'
	- 'Victor Emmanuel'	see *C. japonica* 'Blood of China'
	- 'Ville de Nantes'	LRHS
	- 'Virginia Carlyon'	CBcs CDoC
	- 'Virginia Robinson'	SCam
	- 'Virgin's Blush'	SCam
	- 'Visconti Nova'	LRHS
	- 'Vittorio Emanuele II'	CDoC CTrh LRHS MAsh SCoo
	- 'Volcano'	CDoC MPkF
	- 'Vosper's Rose'	CDoC
	- 'Warrior'	CDoC SCog
	- 'Wheel of Fortune' **new**	LRHS MAsh
	- 'White Nun'	CBcs SCog
	- 'White Perfection'	SAPC
	- 'White Swan'	CSBt LRHS MAsh SCoo
	- 'White Tinsie' **new**	LRHS
	- 'Wilamina' ♀H4	CDoC CMHG
	- 'Wildfire'	LRHS SCam
	- 'William Bartlett'	CTrh
	- 'William Honey'	CTrh
	- 'Wisley White'	see *C. japonica* 'Hakurakuten'
	- 'Witman Yellow'	CTrh
§	- 'Yours Truly'	CDoC CMac CTrh CTsd LRHS LSRN MAsh SCog
	- 'Yukimi-guruma'	CDoC
	'John Tooby'	CDoC
	'Jury's Yellow'	see *C.* × *williamsii* 'Jury's Yellow'
	'Kichō' **new**	MPkF
	'Larry Piet' (*reticulata* hybrid)	SCam
	'Lasca Beauty' (*japonica* × *reticulata*)	CBcs SCam
	'Lavender Queen'	see *C. sasanqua* 'Lavender Queen'
	'Leonard Messel' (*reticulata* × (× *williamsii*)) ♀H4	CBcs CDoC CMHG CMac CTri EPfP GGal LRHS MAsh MGos MPkF NLar SCam SCog SCoo SPer SReu
	'Liz Henslowe'	CTsd
	'Madame Victor de Bisschop'	see *C. japonica* 'Le Lys'
	'Magic Mum'	LSRN
	'Mandalay Queen' (*reticulata* hybrid)	SCam
	'Maud Messel' (*reticulata* × (× *williamsii*))	SCam
	'Milo Rowell'	CDoC
	'Mimosa Jury'	CDoC LRHS
	'Monticello'	CDoC
	'Mystique'	see *C. japonica* 'Mystic', *C. reticulata* 'Mystique'
	'Nicky Crisp' (*japonica* × *pitardii*)	CDoC LRHS MPkF
	'Nijinski' (*reticulata* hybrid)	CDoC
	'Nikisi Kerin'	NSoo
	'Nonie Haydon' (*pitardii* hybrid)	CDoC
	oleifera	CExl NLar SCog
	'Phyl Doak' (*reticulata* × *saluenensis*)	CDoC
	'Pink Goddess'	MPkF
	'Pink Spangles'	see *C. japonica* 'Mathotiana Rosea'
	pitardii	CDoC
	- 'Snippet'	CDoC
	'Polar Ice'	CDoC SCog
	'Polyanna'	CDoC SCog
	'Portuense'	see *C. japonica* 'Japonica Variegata'
	'Quintessence' (*japonica* × *lutchuensis*)	CDoC CTrh LRHS SCam SCog
	reticulata 'Captain Rawes'	SCam
	- 'Jean Morel'	SCam
	- 'Mary Williams'	NLar NSoo SCoo
	- 'Miss Tulare'	CDoC
§	- 'Mystique'	CDoC
	- 'Satsuma kurenai'	LRHS
	- 'Simpatica'	SCam
	- 'Songzilin'	SCam
	'Rose du Steir' (*reticulata*) hybrid	MPkF SCam
	rosiflora 'Roseaflora Cascade'	CDoC
	rusticana	see *C. japonica* subsp. *rusticana*
	'Salutation' (*reticulata* × *saluenensis*)	SCam
I	***sasanqua*** 'Alba'	CTri
I	- 'Apple Blossom'	MAsh
	- 'Baronesa de Soutelinho'	ELon SCam SCog
	- 'Bettie Patricia'	SCog
	- 'Bonanza'	see *C. hiemalis* 'Bonanza'
	- Borde Hill form	SCam
	- 'Brocéliande'	MPkF
	- 'Cleopatra'	EPfP MAsh NSoo
	- 'Cotton Candy'	CDoC
	- 'Crimson King' ♀H3	CDoC SCam
	- 'Dazzler'	see *C. hiemalis* 'Dazzler'
	- 'Early Pearly'	CDoC LRHS SCam
I	- 'Exquisite'	CDoC
	- 'Flamingo'	see *C. sasanqua* 'Fukuzutsumi'
	- 'Fragrans'	ELon SCam SCog SMDP
	- 'Fuji-no-mine'	ELon SCam SCog
§	- 'Fukuzutsumi'	CSBt SCam
	- 'Gay Border' **new**	LRHS
	- 'Gay Sue'	CDoC CTrh SCam
	- 'Hiryū'	LRHS SCam
	- 'Hugh Evans' ♀H3	CAbP CBcs CDoC CTrh ELan ELon EPfP LRHS SCam SCog SCoo SMDP SSta
	- 'Jean May' ♀H3	CDoC ELan ELon EPfP LRHS MBri NPri NSoo SCam SCog SCoo SPer
	- 'Kenkyō'	ELon SCam SCog SPer SSta
§	- 'Lavender Queen'	SCam
	- 'Maiden's Blush'	LRHS MBri SCam SCog
	- 'Narumigata'	CAbP CBcs CDoC CHll CMac CTrh CTsd ELon EPfP LRHS MBlu MBri MGos NPri NSoo SCam SPoG SSta
	- 'New Dawn'	SCam SCog
	- 'Nyewoods'	CMac
	- 'Papaver'	SCam SCog
	- 'Paradise Audrey'	LMil LRHS
	- 'Paradise Belinda' PBR	CDoC EPfP LMil LRHS
	- 'Paradise Blush'	CBcs CDoC LRHS SCog
	- 'Paradise Glow'	CBcs CDoC LMil LRHS SCam SCog
	- 'Paradise Helen'	LRHS SCam
	- 'Paradise Hilda'	CBcs CDoC LRHS SCam
	- 'Paradise Joan'	CDoC
	- 'Paradise Little Liane' PBR	CDoC SCam SCog
	- 'Paradise Pearl'	CBcs CDoC EPfP LMil LRHS SCam SCog
	- 'Paradise Petite' PBR	SCog
	- 'Paradise Sayaka'	CDoC
	- 'Paradise Venessa' PBR	CBcs CDoC EPfP LRHS SCam SCog
	- 'Peach Blossom'	CBcs

	- 'Plantation Pink'	ELan EPfP LRHS MBri NPri NSoo SCam SCog SRkn
	- 'Rainbow'	CAbP CDoC CTrh ELan ELon EPfP GGal LRHS MBri MPkF SCam SCoo SSta
	- 'Rosea'	ELon SCam SCog
§	- 'Rosea Plena'	CBcs CMac SCam
	- 'Sasanqua Rubra'	CMac SCam SCog SMDP
	- 'Sasanqua Variegata' (v)	ELon MPkF SCam SCog
	- 'Setsugekka'	CDoC LRHS SCog
	- 'Shishigashira' Nihon Engei Kai Zasshi, 1894	SCog
	- 'Silver Dollar'	CDoC
	- 'Snowflake'	SCam SSta
	- 'Souvenir de Claude Brivet'	CDoC
	- 'Sparkling Burgundy'	see *C. hiemalis* 'Sparkling Burgundy'
	- 'Tanya'	CDoC
	- 'Versicolor'	EPfP MBri MPkF NSoo
	- 'Winter's Snowman'	CBcs CDoC EPfP LRHS SCam SCog
	'Satan's Robe' (*reticulata* hybrid)	CDoC MGos SCog
	'Scented Gem'	MPkF SCam
	'Scented Sun'	CTrh
	'Scentuous' (*japonica* × *lutchuensis*)	CDoC CTrh
	'Show Girl' (*reticulata* × *sasanqua*)	SCam SCog
§	***sinensis***	CBcs CCCN CTrh CTsd GPoy LRHS NLar SCam SPlb SPre
	- var. ***assamica***	CCCN SPre
	- var. ***sinensis***	CCCN
	'Sir Victor Davis'	CDoC
	'Snow Flurry'	CBcs LRHS SCam SCog
	'Spring Festival' (*cuspidata* hybrid) ♀H4	CDoC CMHG CTrh MMuc MPkF SCog
	'Spring Mist' (*japonica* × *lutchuensis*)	CDoC CMHG CTrh
	'Sugar Dream'	CDoC CTrh SCam
	'Superscent'	CTrh
	'Survivor'	LRHS MPkF SCam
	'Swan Lake'	NPri SCog WGob
	'Sweet Emily Kate' (*japonica* × *lutchuensis*)	CDoC LRHS MPkF
	'Sweet Jane'	LRHS MPkF SCam SCog
	'Tarōkaja' (wabisuke)	SCam
	thea	see *C. sinensis*
	'Tinsie'	see *C. japonica* 'Bokuhan'
	'Tiny Princess' (*fraterna* × *japonica*)	CMac
	'Tom Knudsen' (*japonica* × *reticulata*) ♀H3	CDoC LRHS SCam
	'Tomorrow Supreme'	see *C. japonica* 'Tomorrow Variegated'
	transnokoensis	CExl CMac CTrh MPkF SCam
	'Tricolor Sieboldii'	see *C. japonica* 'Tricolor'
	'Tristrem Carlyon' (*reticulata* hybrid) ♀H4	CDoC CTri EPfP LRHS NPri SCam
	'Valley Knudsen' (*reticulata* × *saluenensis*)	SCog
	× ***vernalis***	SCam
	- 'Ginryû'	SCam
	- 'Star Above Star'	CMHG
	- 'Yuletide'	CDoC CTrh LRHS LSRN MPkF SCam SCog
	'Volcano'	CDoC
	'White Retic' (*japonica* × *reticulata*)	SCam

	× ***williamsii*** 'Angel Wings'	LRHS
	- 'Anticipation' ♀H4	CBcs CDoC CDul CHel CMHG CMac CSBt CSam CTrh ELan EPfP GGGa GGal GKin LMil LRHS MBri MGos MSwo NEgg NPri NSoo SCam SCog SLim SPer SPoG SSpi SWvt
	- 'Ballet Queen'	CBcs CDoC CSBt SCam
	- 'Ballet Queen Variegated'	CDoC MGos SCog
	- 'Bartley Number Five'	CMac
	- 'Beatrice Michael'	CMac
	- 'Bow Bells'	CDoC CTri ELan SCam
	- 'Bowen Bryant' ♀H4	GGGa GGal NPri SCog WGob
	- 'Brigadoon' ♀H4	CBcs CDoC CTrh CTri EPfP GGGa GGal GKin MBri NPri SCam SCog
	- 'Burncoose'	CBcs
	- 'Burncoose Apple Blossom'	CDoC
	- 'Buttons 'n' Bows'	CDoC MPkF SCog
	- 'C.F. Coates'	CDoC SCam SCog
	- 'Caerhays'	CBcs SCam
	- 'Carolyn Williams'	CBcs SCam
	- 'Celebration'	CBcs CSBt LSRN
	- 'Charlean'	CDoC SCam
	- 'Charles Colbert'	CDoC LRHS
	- 'China Clay' ♀H4	CDoC CHel EPfP LRHS
§	- 'Citation'	CBcs CMac SCog
	- 'Clarrie Fawcett' ♀H4	CDoC
	- 'Contribution'	CTrh
	- 'Coral Delight'	MPkF
	- 'Crinkles'	CDoC SCam
	- 'Daintiness' ♀H4	CDoC SCog
	- 'Dark Nite'	CMHG
	- 'Debbie' ♀H4	Widely available
	- 'Debbie's Carnation'	CDoC
	- 'Donation' ♀H4	Widely available
	- 'Dream Boat'	CDoC LRHS MPkF
	- 'E.G. Waterhouse'	CBcs CDoC CTrh CTri ELan ELon EPfP GKin LRHS MBri MGos NSoo SCam SCog SSta
	- 'E.T.R. Carlyon' ♀H4	CDoC CTrh CTri EPfP LRHS MAsh MBri MPkF NLar NPri SCog SCoo SLim
	- 'Elegant Beauty' ♀H4	CBcs CDoC ELon NLar SCam SCog SPer
	- 'Elizabeth Anderson' ♀H4	CTrh CTsd SCam
	- 'Elizabeth de Rothschild'	GGGa NSoo
	- 'Ellamine'	CBcs
	- 'Elsie Jury' ♀H3	CBcs CDoC CMac CTri ELan GKin LRHS MGos NLar SCam SCog SGol SPer
	- 'Exaltation'	CDoC SCam SCog
	- 'Fiona Colville'	CDoC
	- 'Francis Hanger'	CDoC CTrh LRHS MGos SCam SCog SPer
	- 'Galaxie' ♀H4	CBcs CDoC SCog
	- 'Gay Time'	LRHS SCog
	- 'George Blandford' ♀H4	CBcs CMac GGal
	- 'Glenn's Orbit' ♀H4	CBcs CDoC NLar SCam SCog
	- 'Golden Spangles' (v)	CBcs CDoC CMac ELan EPfP GKin LRHS MMuc SCam SCog SLim SPer
	- 'Grand Jury'	LRHS
	- 'Gwavas'	CBcs CCCN CDoC LRHS MAsh SCam SCog SCoo
	- 'Hilo'	CDoC SCam
	- 'Hiraethlyn'	CBcs
	- 'J.C. Williams' ♀H4	CBcs CMac CTri EPfP MMuc SCog SEND

	- 'Jamie'	CDoC
	- 'Jean Claris'	CDoC
	- 'Jenefer Carlyon'	CBcs CDoC
	- 'Joan Trehane' ♀H4	SCam
	- 'John Pickthorn' **new**	CBcs
	- 'Julia Hamiter' ♀H4	CBcs CDoC
§	- 'Jury's Yellow' ♀H4	Widely available
	- 'Laura Boscawen'	CDoC SCam
	- 'Les Jury' ♀H4	CDoC CGHE CMHG CSBt CTrh LMil LSRN NEgg SCog SLim
	- 'Little Lavender'	CDoC
	- 'Margaret Waterhouse'	CDoC MGos SCam SCog
	- 'Marjorie Waldegrave'	LRHS
	- 'Mary Christian' ♀H4	CBcs GGal SCam SSta
	- 'Mary Phoebe Taylor' ♀H4	CDoC GGal MBri MPkF NLar SCam SCog SCoo SLim
	- 'Mildred Veitch'	CDoy
	- 'Mirage'	CDoC SCam
	- 'Moira Reid'	CDoC
	- 'Monica Dance'	CBcs CDoC
	- 'Muskoka' ♀H4	CBcs
	- 'New Venture'	CBcs
	- 'Night Rider'	CDoC MPkF
	- 'November Pink'	CBcs
	- 'Palaxie'	SCam
	- 'Phillippa Forward'	CBcs CMac
	- 'Pink Dahlia'	SCam
	- 'Pink Wave' **new**	LRHS
	- 'Rendezvous'	CDoC MGos SCam SCog
	- 'Rose Bouquet'	CDoC
	- 'Rosemary Williams'	CBcs
	- 'Ruby Bells'	CMHG
	- 'Ruby Wedding' (d)	CBcs CDoC CSBt CTrh CTsd EPfP LMil LRHS LSRN MAsh NEgg NPri NSoo SCog SCoo SLim SPoG SWvt WGob
	- 'Saint Ewe' ♀H4	CBcs CDoC CHel CSBt CTri ELan EPfP GGal LRHS MBri MGos NPri SCam SCog SCoo SPer
	- 'Saint Michael'	CBcs CDoC
	- 'Sayonara'	CBcs SCam SCog
	- 'Senorita' ♀H4	CDoC ELon GKin MBri NLar NPri SCam SCog
	- 'Simon Bolitho'	SCog
	- 'Sun Song'	SCog
	- 'Taylor's Perfection'	SCam
	- 'The Duchess of Cornwall'	CDoC SCam
	- 'Tiptoe'	CDoC GKin
	- 'Tulip Time'	LRHS MPkF
	- 'Waltz Time'	CDoC SCam
	- 'Water Lily' ♀H4	CBcs CDoC CTri ELon EPfP LRHS MGos NLar SCam
	- 'Wilber Foss' ♀H4	CDoC ELon GKin LRHS MGos MMuc SCam SCog SEND
	- 'Wynne Rayner'	CDoC SCam
	- 'Yesterday'	MMuc
	'Winter's Charm'	SCog
	'Winter's Dream'	SCog
	'Winter's Interlude'	CDoC LRHS SCam SCog
	'Winter's Joy'	SCog
	'Winter's Toughie'	CBcs SCam SCog
	'Winton' (*cuspidata* × *saluenensis*)	CBcs CDoC
	'Yoimachi' (*fraterna* × *sasanqua*)	CDoC CTrh

Camissonia (*Onagraceae*)

bistorta 'Sunflakes'	CSpe

Campanula ✿ (*Campanulaceae*)

	sp.	WCot
	RCB AM 13	WCot
	abietina	see *C. patula* subsp. *abietina*
	alaskana	see *C. rotundifolia* var. *alaskana*
§	***alliariifolia***	Widely available
	- DHTU 0126	WCru
	- 'Ivory Bells'	see *C. alliariifolia*
I	***alpestris*** 'Silver Bells' **new**	LAst MAsh MBri MSCN
	americana	EWTr XLum
	argaea	GKev
	arvatica	EACa ECho EPot GMaP LRHS NHar
	- 'Alba'	GMaP
	aucheri	see *C. bellidifolia* subsp. *aucheri*
	barbata	CCon EACa ECho EPfP MWat WAbe WMoo
	'Belinda'	CPBP EPot
	bellidifolia	LLHF NBir NSla
§	- subsp. ***aucheri***	EPfP ITim
	- subsp. ***saxifraga***	GKev ITim
§	***betulifolia*** ♀H4	CSam EACa EPot NSla
	'Birch Hybrid' ♀H4	CFis EACa ECho ECtt ELan EPfP LRHS MMuc XLum
	'Blithe Spirit' **new**	WAbe
	bononiensis	LLHF NWad SRms XLum
	'Bumblebee'	WAbe
	'Burghaltii' ♀H4	CDes ELan GBee GCal LRHS NLar SHar WOut
	'Cantata'	CPBP EPot WAbe
§	***carnica***	ECho XLum
	carpatica ♀H4	ECho EPfP NBrc NBro NGdn SPlb SRms SWat XLum
	- f. ***alba***	ECho LRHS NBre NGdn SPlb SWat XLum
	- - 'Bressingham White'	EACa
§	- - 'Weisse Clips'	CBar ECho ECtt ELan EPfP GBin GKin LAst LHop LRHS MAsh NEgg NGdn NHol NPri SPer SPoG SRms SWvt
§	- 'Blaue Clips'	CBar CBcs EBee ECho ECtt ELan EPfP GKin GMaP IFoB LAst LHop LRHS MAsh MGos NEgg NGdn NPri SPer SPoG SRms SWvt
	- Blue Clips	see *C. carpatica* 'Blaue Clips'
	- 'Blue Moonlight'	EACa ECho LHop LRHS
	- 'Chewton Joy'	CTri EACa ECho LLHF LRHS
	- dwarf	EACa
	- 'Karpatenkrone'	EACa GBin NBre
	- 'Kathy'	EPot GBuc
	- 'Silberschale'	NBre
	- var. ***turbinata***	ECho SRms WAbe
	- - 'Foerster'	EACa ECho LRHS XLum
	- - 'Isabel'	EACa ECho LLHF LRHS XLum
	- - 'Jewel'	EACa ECho EHyd LHop LRHS
	- White Clips	see *C. carpatica* f. *alba* 'Weisse Clips'
	cashmeriana 'Blue Cloud'	CWib
	cephallenica	see *C. garganica* subsp. *cephallenica*
§	***chamissonis***	ECho EPot LLHF NWad
	- 'Major'	EWes
	- 'Oyobeni'	EACa
§	- 'Superba' ♀H4	EACa ECho NRya WAbe
	choruhensis	LLHF SPlb
§	***cochlearifolia*** ♀H4	CSpe CTri EBee ECho EDAr EPfP GJos GMaP LRHS MAsh MMuc SBch SPoG SVic WHoo WSpi XLum

	- var. ***alba***	CSpe CTri EDAr MHer NRya SBch SRms WHoo XLum
	- - 'Bavaria White'	ECho
	- - 'White Baby' (Baby Series)	ECho ECtt ELon EPfP EPot GJos LRHS SPet SPoG XLum
	- 'Bavaria Blue'	ECho ELon GJos NHol SMrm SPet XLum
	- 'Blue Baby' (Baby Series)	ECho ECtt EPfP GJos LRHS MHer SPoG SRms SRot
	- 'Blue Wonder'	GBin ITim
	- 'Cambridge Blue'	EACa
	- 'Elizabeth Oliver' (d)	CCon CTri CWGN EACa ECho ECtt EDAr EHyd EPot GAbr GCal GMaP LHop LRHS MHer MHol NBir SPlb SRms WAbe WHil WHoo WIce WRHF
	- 'Oakington Blue'	LLHF
	- var. ***pallida*** 'Silver Chimes'	ECho
	- 'R.B. Loder' (d)	LRHS MHer
	- 'Tubby'	EACa ECho EPot GJos LLHF LRHS MHer SRms
	- 'Warleyensis'	see *C.* × *haylodgensis* W. Brockbank 'Warley White'
	collina	CTri EACa LLHF WCFE XLum
	'Covadonga'	CMea EACa ECho LHop LLHF LRHS SBch WAbe WThu
	cretica	MHol
	'Crystal'	ECtt MAvo MNrw MSpe
	dasyantha	see *C. chamissonis*
	dolomitica	EACa EBee GKev ITim LLHF
	'E.K. Toogood'	CCon CElw EACa ECho ECtt GJos MWat SRms XLum
	elatines	LRHS
	ephesia	GKev
	- SDR 1111	GKev
	eriocarpa	see *C. latifolia* 'Eriocarpa'
	'Faichem Lilac'	GCra LLHF NPro
	fenestrellata	EACa SRms WAbe XLum
§	- subsp. ***istriaca***	GKev
	finitima	see *C. betulifolia*
	foliosa	EACa
	fragilis	ECho IFoB
	- 'Hirsuta'	ECho
	garganica ♀H4	EACa ECho EHyd EPfP GKev GMaP LAst LRHS MAsh MMuc MRav NEgg SEND SMrm SPet SWvt WMoo XLum
	- 'Aurca'	scc *C. garganica* 'Dickson's Gold'
	- 'Backhouse'	LRHS
	- 'Blue Diamond'	EACa ECho IVic LHop
§	- subsp. ***cephallenica***	CElw EACa NBro
§	- 'Dickson's Gold'	Widely available
	- 'Erinus Major'	EACa IVic XLum
	- 'Hirsuta'	ECho
	- subsp. ***istriaca***	see *C. fenestrellata* subsp. *istriaca*
	- 'Major'	ECho LAst SPoG
	- 'Mrs Resholt'	ECtt ESwi LAst SWvt WGor
	- 'W.H. Paine' ♀H4	EACa ECho ECtt IFoB IGor NSla WAbe WHoo
	'Glandore'	EACa XLum
	glomerata	CExl GAbr GJos LSRN NBir NBro NGBl NMir WBrk XSen
	- var. ***acaulis*** hort.	EACa EBee EPfP GKev LEdu LRHS MNHC NLar SPet WSpi XLum
	- var. ***alba***	CBcs CCon CSpe EACa EBee ECtt ELan EPfP EWTr GJos GMaP LBMP LRHS MLHP MRav SMrm SPer SPlb SPoG SWat WCAu WGwG WMnd WWEG XLum
§	- - 'Schneekrone'	LRHS NBre

	- 'Caroline'	Widely available
	- Crown of Snow	see *C. glomerata* var. *alba* 'Schneekrone'
	- var. ***dahurica***	CCon ELon LRHS NBre NLar SMrm SPet XLum
	- 'Emerald'	EACa EBee LRHS MBri MHer NLar
	- 'Freya' **new**	WHil
	- 'Joan Elliott'	EBee ECtt GBuc LEdu LSRN MNFA MWat WSpi
	- 'Purple Pixie'	LRHS
	- 'Superba' ♀H4	Widely available
	grossekii	CCon EBee LLHF LRHS WHrl
	hakkiarica	EBee MPie WCot
	'Hannah'	EACa ECho LHop LRHS
	× ***haylodgensis*** misapplied	see *C.* × *haylodgensis* 'Plena'
§	× ***haylodgensis*** W. Brockbank 'Marion Fisher' (d)	CPBP ECtt EDAr EPot WAbe WHoo
§	- 'Plena' (d)	ECho ECtt EDAr ELan EPot LHop LRHS NPri SRms WAbe WCot WHoo WKif
§	- 'Warley White' (d)	ECho XLum
	- 'Yvonne'	EACa ECtt EPot LHop WHil WNew
	hercegovina 'Nana'	CPBP EPot ITim WAbe
	'Hilltop Snow'	NHar
	hofmannii	CTsd ELan GKev ITim MBNS NLar NWad
§	***incurva***	CSpe EACa EBee ELan EWld GJos GKev LHop WMoo
	× ***innesii***	see *C.* 'John Innes'
	isophylla ♀H2	ECho
	- 'Alba' ♀H2	ECho
	- Starina Bicolor Star = 'Camp Bulewhit'PBR	LRHS
	Jenny = 'Harjen'PBR	CWGN EBee SHar
	'Joe Elliott' ♀H2-3	CPBP NSla WAbe
§	'John Innes'	CPBP
	kemulariae	EDAr LLHF XLum
	- 'Alba'	ITim
	'Kent Belle' ♀H4	Widely available
	khasiana	EBee GKev
	lactiflora	CAby CElw CHel CMac EACa EBee EPfP GAbr GCra IFoB ITim LRHS MCot MLHP MSCN NEgg SPer WHoo WMoo WSpi WWEG XLum
	- ***alba***	see *C. lactiflora* white-flowered
N	- 'Alba' ♀H4	EBee EPfP GBin GMaP IBoy IVic MAvo MSCN WMnd
	- 'Avalanche'	ECtt LRHS MBNS NLar NOrc WHil
	- 'Blue Cross'	EBee LRHS
	- 'Border Blues' **new**	MBri
	- dwarf pink-flowered	EACa EBee EPfP WSpi
	- 'Favourite'	CCon CSpe ECtt MNrw NGdn
	- hybrids	GJos
	- 'Lidie's Choice' **new**	CSam
	- 'Loddon Anna' ♀H4	Widely available
	- 'Macrantha'	WSpi
	- 'Moorland Rose'	WMoo
	- 'Pouffe'	CHid CPrp EACa EBee ECtt ELan EPfP EWTr GMaP IVic LRHS MHol MNrw MRav NBro NGdn NLar SGbt SMrm SPer SWat SWvt
	- 'Prichard's Variety' ♀H4	Widely available
	- 'Superba' ♀H4	ECtt IVic SMad WSpi
	- 'Violet'	SWat WSpi
	- 'White Pouffe'	EACa EBee ECtt ELan EPfP GBin GMaP IVic LRHS LSRN MLHP NLar SGbt SPer SPoG SWat

§	- white-flowered	GBin NBir SMrm SPer SWat WSpi
	latifolia	EACa GJos LPot LRHS MCot MLHP NBid NOrc SPer SRms WMoo WShi
	- var. ***alba***	EBee ELan EPfP EWTr GCra GJos LRHS MBri MMuc NGdn SEND SPav SPer SRms WHal WSpi WWEG
	- - 'White Ladies'	LRHS
*	- 'Amethyst'	WSpi
	- blue-flowered	WSpi
	- 'Brantwood'	CFis GAbr LRHS MRav NLar SRms SWat WCot WMnd WSpi
	- 'Buckland'	CDes
§	- 'Eriocarpa'	LRHS
	- 'Gloaming'	ECtt GBBs LRHS NPnk
	- var. ***macrantha***	CAby EBee ELan ELon EPfP GMaP LHop LRHS MAvo MBri MNHC MWat NLar NSoo NSti SPer SWat SWvt WCot WMoo WSpi WWEG
	- - 'Alba'	ECtt EWTr GMaP IPot LHop MHol MRav NLar WCot WMoo WWEG
	- 'Misty Dawn'	MAvo WCot
	latiloba	CElw CMHG WBrk WCot WKif WSpi
§	- 'Alba' ♀H4	CElw EBee ELan GCal GCra MCot NEgg NLar NWad WBrk WSpi
	- 'Hidcote Amethyst' ♀H4	CPrp CSpe CWGN EACa EBee ECtt ELan ELon EPfP EWII GAbr GBuc GCal IKil LRHS MCot MRav MSpe MTis MWhi NBid NBir NGdn NLar WCot WMnd WSpi WWEG
	- 'Highcliffe Variety' ♀H4	ECtt ELan EPfP EShb GBuc GCra LRHS MHol MRav MTis NLar WCot WMnd WSpi WWEG
*	- 'Highdown'	GBuc
	- 'Percy Piper' ♀H4	EACa ELan GBuc LRHS MAsh MRav NBre NBro NLar WSpi
	- 'Splash'	MAvo
	'Linda'	LSRN
	linifolia	see *C. carnica*
	'Lynchmere'	CMea WAbe
	makaschvilii	CHid CPla CSpe EACa EBee GKev LHop LRHS MHer MPie MSpe NLar SMrm SRkn WCot WHrl XSen
	'Marion Fisher'	see *C. × baylodgensis* W. Brockbank 'Marion Fisher'
	medium	EPfP LAst
	'Mevr. V. Vollenhove'	EBee WCot
	'Monic'	EPfP
	muralis	see *C. portenschlagiana*
	nitida	see *C. persicifolia* var. *planiflora*
	'Norman Grove'	EPot
	ochroleuca	CMea CPom CSpe EBee GBin LHop MBri SWat WCFE WCot WHrl WNPC
	- 'White Beauty'	CWib
	- 'White Bells'	MWhi
	odontosepala	EBee
	- from Iran	EPPr NLar
	'Oliver's Choice'	WHrl
	olympica misapplied	see *C. rotundifolia* 'Olympica'
	ossetica	EBee ECtt ELan MLHP
	patula	EACa NLar WKif XLum
§	- subsp. ***abietina***	NLar
	'Paul Furse'	EBee ECtt LRHS MSpe NBre NCGa NSti SHar WWEG
	pendula	EPfP EWes GBee MBNS XLum
	persicifolia	CBcs CMac CSBt CTri EBee EHon EPfP GAbr GBBs GJos GMaP IBoy ITim LRHS MBel MCot MLHP MMuc NBro NEgg NMir NPri SDix SPer SPoG WCFE WCot WHoo WMoo XLum
	- var. ***alba***	CBcs CPrp CSBt CSpe CTri EPfP GBBs GCra GJos GMaP LPot LRHS MBel MBri MLHP MMuc NMir SMrm SPer SPlb SPoG SWat SWvt WCAu WCFE WHoo WMoo WPtf WWEG
§	- 'Alba Coronata' (d)	GAbr WSpi
	- 'Alba Plena'	see *C. persicifolia* 'Alba Coronata'
	- 'Azure Beauty'	CSpe EBee ECtt ELan NCGa NLar WCot WSpi
	- 'Beau Belle'	LSou NLar
§	- 'Bennett's Blue' (d)	EPfP MRav SRms SWat
	- 'Blue Bloomers' (d)	CElw CLAP ECtt EPri EWes GBin IKil LRHS MAvo MBel MNFA MRav MSCN NLBP NWad SMrm WBrk WCFE WCot WHal WSpi XLum
	- blue cup-in-cup (d)	ELon WPtf
	- 'Blue-eyed Blonde' PBR (v)	ECtt LSou NDov NLar
	- blue-flowered	IFoB SPlb WSpi
	- 'Boule de Neige' (d)	LRHS WSpi WWEG
	- 'Caerulea Coronata'	see *C. persicifolia* 'Coronata'
§	- 'Chettle Charm' PBR ♀H4	CMac CPrp CTri CWCL ECtt ELan EPfP EShb GAbr LRHS LSou MAvo MBel MBri MCot MHer MRav MWhi NBir NChi NLar SMrm SPer SWat SWvt WCot WMnd WSpi WWEG
	- 'Cornish Mist'	CCon CExl EBee ECtt ELan EPfP GBin LPla MCot MPie NLar WCot
§	- 'Coronata' (d)	GCra LRHS NLar
	- cup and saucer blue (d)	GCra
	- double blue-flowered (d)	NBro
	- double white-flowered (d)	ELan
	- 'Fleur de Neige' (d) ♀H4	NBre WCot WWEG
	- 'Frances' (d)	CLAP WCot
	- 'Gawen'	CMac CWCL EBee ECtt GMaP MCot MTis NBre SGbt SMrm
	- 'George Chiswell'	see *C. persicifolia* 'Chettle Charm'
	- 'Grandiflora Alba'	NLar NWad SMrm XLum
§	- 'Hampstead White' (d)	GCal NBro WHil WMnd WSpi WWEG
	- 'Hetty'	see *C. persicifolia* 'Hampstead White'
	- 'Kelly's Gold'	CCon ELon EPfP LRHS NBir NLar WWEG
	- 'La Belle'	CWGN EBee ECtt LSou MNrw NLar WCot
	- 'La Bello' PBR	CWGN EBee ECtt MAsh MNrw
	- 'La Bonne Amie' (d)	EBee ECtt IBoy IKil MAsh NDov NLar SBod XEll
	- 'Moerheimii' (d)	EPfP
	- 'Perry's Boy Blue'	NPer
§	- var. ***planiflora***	CPBP EPot MWat
	- - f. ***alba***	MWat WAbe
	- - 'Coerulea' **new**	WAbe
	- 'Powder Puff' (d)	EBee EPfP GBin NEgg SMrm WCot
	- 'Pride of Exmouth' (d)	ELan EShb IBoy LPot MHer MSpe WMnd WSpi WWEG
	- subsp. ***sessiliflora*** 'Alba'	see *C. latiloba* 'Alba'
	- 'Snowdrift'	SRms
	- Takion Series	CSpe
	- - 'Takion Blue'	EBee EHyd GBin LRHS MSCN
	- - 'Takion White'	EHyd EPfP LRHS
	- 'Telham Beauty' misapplied	CSBt EBee ELan EPfP MRav SMrm SPer SRms SWvt WMnd
	- 'Telham Beauty' ambig.	LBMP LRHS MCot MSCN NEgg NGBl SPad SRkn SWvt WWEG XLum

	- 'Telham Beauty' D.Thurston	MWhi NLar
	- 'Wortham Belle' misapplied	see *C. persicifolia* 'Bennett's Blue'
	- 'Wortham Belle' ambig.	CWCL CWGN
	- 'Wortham Belle' Blooms	ECtt LRHS MBNS NDov NEgg WGwG
	petrophila	WAbe
	pilosa	see *C. chamissonis*
	- 'Superba'	see *C. chamissonis* 'Superba'
	'Pink Octopus'[PBR]	CCVN CPrp CWGN ECtt ELon GBin IBoy IPot LLHF MBNS MBri MCot MHol MMoz MPie MPnt MTis NCGa NGdn NLar NPnk SMad SMrm SPad SRkn SRms WCot WPtf WSpi XLum
	piperi	CPBP
	planiflora	see *C. persicifolia* var. *planiflora*
§	***portenschlagiana*** ♀H4	Widely available
	- 'Biokovo'	XLum
	- 'Blue Ocean' **new**	GBin
	- 'Catharina'	EACa EBee LRHS SHil SPoG
	- 'Lieselotte'	CElw CPBP LLHF SBch
	- 'Major'	LAst LBMP WMoo
	- 'Resholdt's Variety'	CBar CMea CSam EACa EBee ECho ECtt EDAr EHyd ELan EPfP EPot GMaP LHop LRHS MMuc MRav NPri WMoo XLum
	poscharskyana	Widely available
	- 'Blauranke'	EACa EWes XLum
	- 'Blue Gown'	EACa GMaP MNFA XLum
	- 'Blue Waterfall'	CCVN CWGN EACa LRHS MBNS NCGa NDov SPoG WCot XLum
	- 'E.H. Frost'	CElw EACa ECho ECtt EDAr EHyd ELan EPPr EPfP EWTr GKev GMaP IBoy LHop MBri MCot MMuc MWat NBro NRya SEND SPer SRGP SRms SWvt WBrk WMnd WMoo XLum
I	- 'Freya'	XLum
	- 'Lilacina'	EPPr
	- 'Lisduggan Variety'	CElw EACa EBee ECtt EDAr EPPr EWes GMaP IBoy LHop LRHS MBri MHer MNFA NBro WCot WIce WMoo XLum
	- 'Nana Alba'	EACa EPPr
	- 'Pinkins'[PBR]	EACa
	- 'Stella' ♀H4	EACa ECho ECtt ELan EPPr EPfP IBoy LRHS LSRN MAvo MRav NBro NDov SPer SRGP SWvt WHoo WMoo XLum
	- 'Trollkind'	EPPr XLum
	- variegated (v)	EHoe
	- white-flowered	CTri ECho ELan
	prenanthoides	see *Asyneuma prenanthoides*
	primulifolia	ELan LRHS MNrw NBir SRms SWat WMoo XLum
	× ***pseudoraineri*** hort.	EACa ECho EWes LRHS
	pulla	CPBP CSpe EACa ECho ECtt EDAr EHyd ELan ELon EPot GMaP LRHS NSla SPoG SRot WAbe WIce
	- 'Alba'	EACa ECho ECtt EDAr LRHS NSla WAbe
	× ***pulloides*** hort. 'G.F.Wilson' ♀H4	EACa ECho ECtt EPot EWld SRkn
	- 'Jelly Bells'[PBR]	ECtt IPot NDov NLar WCot
	punctata	CMHG CSpe GJos GKev LEdu LRHS MCot NBro NSti SWat WGwG WMoo
	- f. ***albiflora***	MNrw MSpe WMnd
	- - 'Alba'	CCVN

	- 'Alina's Double' (d)	MBel MNrw MSCN MSpe NLar WCot WWEG
	- 'Cherry Pie'	EPfP LRHS
	- dwarf	CPBP GKev
	- 'Einhorn JP'	IVic
	- 'Golddrache JP'	IVic
	- 'Hexe JP'	IVic
	- var. ***hondoensis***	EBee MLHP
	- hose-in-hose (d)	MMHG WGwG
	- 'Hot Lips'	CMac ELan EPPr EPfP LRHS NPro SRGP WWEG
*	- var. ***howozana***	GKev
	- var. ***microdonta*** B&SWJ 5553	WCru
	- 'Milky Way'	EPPr
	- 'Milly'	IVic
	- 'Moorgeist JP'	IVic
*	- 'Nana'	CCVN
	- 'Nasachtal'	IVic
	- 'Pantaloons' (d)	CMac CSpe ECtt LRHS NLar SRms WCot
	- 'Pink Chimes'	EBee IVic LSou MBNS MHol NLar
	- 'Plum Wine'	MSpe
	- 'Pumpernickel JP'	IVic
	- 'Reifrock'	IVic SMrm
	- 'Rosea'	SRms
	- f. ***rubriflora***	CCVN CSpe EBee ECtt ELan EPfP GCra GJos LBMP LHop LRHS MCot MNrw MWat NEgg NOrc NSoo SMrm SPer SRms WMnd WWEG XLum
	- - 'Beetroot'	IKil IVic MHer MTis NLar WHrl
	- - 'Bowl of Cherries'[PBR]	CSpe ECtt ELan EPPr EPfP ESwi IVic LLHF LRHS LSou MMHG NLar NPnk SRkn SRot
	- - 'Cherry Bells'	ECtt EPfP IVic LSRN
	- - 'Vienna Festival'	CSBt NLar WCot
	- - 'Wine 'n' Rubies'	ECtt GBee LSRN MAvo MSCN WCot
	- 'Seejungfrau JP'	IVic
I	- 'Silver Bells' **new**	WHil WHlf
	- 'Troll JP'	IVic
	- 'Twilight Bells'	NBre
	- 'Wedding Bells'	CPrp EACa EBee ELan EPri LAst LDai LPio LRHS LSRN MHer MHol MSpe MTis NCGa NLar NSti SRkn SRms WCAu WWEG
	- 'Weisser Schwan JP'	IVic
	- 'Weisser Turm JP'	IVic
I	- 'White Bells'	ELan EPPr MJak
	- white hose-in-hose (d)	MNrw WBrk XLum
	'Purple Sensation'[PBR]	CSpe ECtt EPfP LSou MBel MBri MNrw NCGa NLar NPnk NSti WCot
	pusilla	see *C. cochlearifolia*
	pyramidalis	CSpe EACa EBee ELan EPfP GJos LRHS NGBl SPav SPlb WSpi WWEG XLum
	- 'Alba'	CSpe CWib EACa ELan EPfP GJos LRHS NGBl SPav SPlb WSpi WWEG XLum
	- lavender blue-flowered	CWib
	raddeana	EACa SBrt WBrk
	raineri ♀H4	ECho EPot NSla WAbe
*	- 'Alba'	ECho WAbe
	- 'Nettleton Gold'	ECho EPot LRHS
§	***rapunculoides***	GJos GKev LHop SWat WCFE XLum
§	- 'Afterglow'	MAvo WCot
	- 'Alba'	EACa XLum
	rapunculus	CArn XLum
	recurva	see *C. incurva*

	rhomboidalis Gorter	see *C. rapunculoides*
	rhomboidalis L.	XLum
	rigidipila	WHer WOut
	rotundifolia	CArn EACa ECho ELan EPfP GAbr GJos GLog MCot MHer MNHC NBre NGBl SIde SPlb SWat WBrk WPtf XLum
§	- var. ***alaskana***	LRHS
	- var. ***alba***	CElw EWes WAbe
§	- 'Olympica'	IGor MMuc WHoo
	- 'Superba'	ECho
	- 'White Gem'	CMea EACa EHyd EPfP GJos LBMP LRHS NBre WHoo WPtf
	'Royal Wave'	CAbP ECtt IPot MAvo MHol NDov NLar WCot
	rupestris	LLHF
	rupicola	WAbe
	'Samantha'	EACa ECtt GBin IBoy LHop LRHS LSRN SHar SMrm SRGP WCot WHoo XEll
	'Sarastro'	Widely available
	sarmatica	EPfP GAbr GKev LRHS MNFA NBid SRms WKif
	- 'Hemelstraling'	NLar
	'Senior'	EPPr IVic SHar
	'Serafinental'	IVic
	speciosa	EBee MWhi
	'Stansfieldii'	CPBP EACa ECho LLHF LRHS
	suanetica new	GMaP
	'Summer Nights'	NCGa
	'Summer Pearl'	CPBP ECtt
	'Summertime Blues'PBR	ECtt IBoy NDov NLar
§	'Swannables'	CPou EACa EBee LLHF MAvo MNFA NCGa NChi WOut
	takesimana	CBro CDoC CPrp CSpe ECtt EDAr ELan EPfP GAbr GKev GKin LEdu LHop LRHS MCot MLHP NBro NEgg NSti SPad SPer SPet SRms SWvt WMnd WMoo WWEG XLum
	- B&SWJ 8499	WCru
I	- 'Alba'	GBBs LBMP NBre WMoo
	- 'Beautiful Trust'	CCVN CLAP EBee LHop MCot MSpe NPnk WCot WSpi
	- 'Elizabeth'	Widely available
	- 'Elizabeth II' (d)	ECtt EPPr WCot WPtf WSpi
	thyrsoides	GKev SPav XLum
	'Timsbury Perfection'	NHar WAbe
	'Tiny Bells'	LLHF
	tommasiniana ♀H4	WAbe
	trachelium	CMHG EBee ELon GJos GKev LRHS MRav NMir SWat WCot WHer WMoo WOut WWEG XLum
	- f. ***alba***	CLAP LRHS NLar SGbt SWat WCot WMoo
	- - 'Alba Flore Pleno' (d)	CLAP LEdu
	- 'Bernice' (d)	Widely available
	- lilac-blue-flowered	SWat
	- 'Snowball'	CMac EShb LSRN
	troegerae	NSla
	'Tymonsii'	CPBP ECho LLHF NBir
	'Van-Houttei'	CDes EWes WCot WSpi
	versicolor	CPBP CSpe
	vidalii	see *Azorina vidalii*
	'Viking'PBR	IPot
	waldsteiniana	CPBP WAbe
	wanneri	EPfP
	- 'Violet Belle' new	LRHS
	'Warley White'	see *C.* × *baylodgensis* W. Brockbank 'Warley White'
	'Warleyensis'	see *C.* × *baylodgensis* W. Brockbank 'Warley White'
	× ***wockei*** 'Puck'	CHid EACa ECho ECtt EPot LHop LLHF LRHS WAbe
	zangezura	EACa EDAr EPfP GKev IKil NGdn SGbt STes XLum
	zoysii	EPot

Campanula × *Symphyandra* see *Campanula*

Campanumoea see *Codonopsis*

Campsis (*Bignoniaceae*)

	grandiflora	CArn CBcs CFlo CSBt CSPN CWGN ELan EPfP LRHS LSRN MJak SPer SRms SWvt WCFE
	radicans	CArn CBcs CDul CMac CRHN CWib ECrN ELan EPfP LRHS LSRN MJak MSwo SLon SPer SPlb
	- 'Atrosanguinea'	SVen
	- 'Flamenco'	CBcs CDoC CMac CSPN CWCL EBee ELan EUJe LRHS LSRN NLar SCoo SLim SVen SWvt
§	- f. ***flava*** ♀H4	CBcs CDoC CFlo CMac CTri EBee ELan ELon EPfP LHop LRHS MBlu MGos MJak NLar NPla SLim SPer SPoG SVen SWvt WSHC
	- 'Indian Summer'	CBcs CFlo CSBt CSPN CWGN EBee EPfP LRHS LSRN LSou MBri MGos MREP NLar SCoo WHar
	- 'Stromboli'	EPfP
	- 'Yellow Trumpet'	see *C. radicans* f. *flava*
	× ***tagliabuana*** Dancing Flame = 'Huidan'PBR	CWGN LRHS
	- 'Madame Galen' ♀H4	Widely available

Camptosema (*Papilionaceae*)

	pracandinum	WPGP

Camptosorus see *Asplenium*

Camptotheca (*Nyssaceae*)

	acuminata	WPGP

Campylandra see *Tupistra*

Campylotropis (*Papilionaceae*)

	macrocarpa	EPfP WSHC

Canarina (*Campanulaceae*)

	canariensis ♀H1	CCCN CFil ECho MOWG WPGP

Candollea see *Hibbertia*

Canna ✿ (*Cannaceae*)

	'Adam's Orange'	CDTJ CHEx XBlo
	'Alaska' ♀H3	EAmu SCan
N	***altensteinii***	CDTJ SCan SHaC SPlb XBlo
	'Ambassador'	SCan SDeJ
	'Ambassadour'	SCan SHaC
	'Annaeei' ♀H3	EAmu
	'Annei-Rubra'	SCan
	'Anthony and Cleopatra' (v)	WCot
	'Argentina'	SCan SHaC
	'Assaut'	SCan SHaC
	'Atlantis'	XBlo
	'Australia'	CDTJ EAmu EPfP SCan SHaC WCot XBlo
	'Austria'	SCan

	'Baron Seguier' **new**	XLum
	'Bethany' ♀H3	SCan
	'Black Knight'	CCon ECGP LAst LSRN MSCN SCan SDeJ WHil XBlo
	'Bonfire'	CDTJ CHEx EAmu
	brasiliensis	CCon CHll CRHN SCan SHaC XBlo
	'Brillant'	SCan SDeJ SHaC
	'Caballero'	XLum
	'Canary'	XBlo
	'Centenaire de Rozain-Boucharlat'	SCan SDeJ SHaC SPlb XLum
	'Champion'	SCan
I	'Citrina'	XBlo
§	'Cleopatra'	CCCN EAmu SCan SHaC XBlo
N	***coccinea***	SAPC
	'Corrida'	XLum
	'Corsica' (Island Series)	SCan
	'Creamy White'	SHaC XBlo
	'Di Bartolo'	XBlo
	'Durban' Hiley, orange-flowered	see *C.* 'Phasion'
	'Durban' ambig.	CWGN EPfP LSRN
	'E. Neubert'	SCan SHaC
N	***edulis***	CDTJ CHEx EUJe SCan
	- purple-leaved	SCan
§	× ***ehemanii*** ♀H3	CDTJ EUJe SCan SDix SHaC WPGP
	'En Avant'	SPlb
	'Endeavour'	CHEx EUJe MSKA SCan SHaC
	'Erebus' ♀H3	MSKA SCan SDix SHaC
	'Étoile du Feu'	XBlo
	'Fatamorgana'	SHaC
	'Fiesta' **new**	SHaC
	Firebird	see *C.* 'Oiseau de Feu'
	flaccida	SCan SHaC
	'Flame'	XBlo
§	'Florence Vaughan'	SCan
	'Foulquier' **new**	XLum
	'General Eisenhower' ♀H3	EAmu SCan SHaC
	generalis × ***indica***	SHaC
	glauca	SCan SDix SHaC
	'Gnom'	SCan SDeJ SHaC
	'Golden Girl'	SCan
	'Golden Orb'	SHaC
	'Gran Canaria'	SCan
	'Grand Large' **new**	XLum
	'Grande'	CCon SCan SHaC
	'Heinrich Seidel'	CHll SCan
	Henlade hybrids	CDTJ
	'Henlade Pink'	SCan
	'Henlade Red'	SCan
	'Hercule'	SCan
	'Hossegor' **new**	XLum
	'Hungaria'	SCan
	hybrids	SHaC
	'Ibis'	EAmu EPfP
	'Ibiza' (Island Series)	SCan
	indica	CAbb CDTJ CHel SAPC SCan SHaC SPlb
	- 'Kreta' (Island Series)	SCan
	- 'Purpurea'	CDTJ CHEx EAmu EUJe SCan SDix SHaC SPlb WPGP
	- 'Red King Rupert'	CCCN
	- 'Russian Red' ♀H3	SCan SHaC
	- Tropicanna Gold = 'Mactro'PBR	CCCN EPfP SCan SPoG
	'Intrigue'	EAmu SCan
	iridiflora misapplied	see *C.* × *ehemanii*
	iridiflora Ruiz & Pav.	CDTJ CHEx CSpe SAPC
	'Italia'	SCan
	jacobiniflora	SCan SHaC
	'Kalimpong'	CDTJ
I	'King Humbert' (blood-red)	CBcs CDTJ CHEx EPfP WHil XBlo
	King Humbert (orange-red)	see *C.* 'Roi Humbert'
	'King Midas'	see *C.* 'Richard Wallace'
	'Königin Charlotte'	SCan SDeJ SHaC
	'La France'	SCan
	latifolia	SHaC
	'Lesotho Lil'	CHll SCan SHaC
	'Libération'	XLum
	'Liberté'	see *C.* 'Wyoming'
	'Lion Rouge' **new**	XLum
	'Lippo's Kiwi'	SCan
	'Llanthony'	SCan
	'Louis Cayeux' ♀H3	SDix
	'Louis Cottin'	CBcs CCCN CDTJ EPfP
	'Lucifer'	CCCN CHEx NEgg NPer XLum
N	***lutea***	CHEx SHaC XBlo
	'Madame Angèle Martin'	XBlo
	'Madeira' (Island Series)	EUJe SCan
	'Malawiensis Variegata'	see *C.* 'Striata'
	'Marabout'	SBst SCan
	'Maudie Malcolm'	EPfP
	'Montaigne'	XLum
	'Moonshine'	CCCN
	'Musifolia' ♀H3	CDTJ CHEx EAmu EUJe EWes SCan SDix SHaC XBlo
	'Mystique' ♀H3	EWes SCan SDix
	'Ointment Pink'	XBlo
§	'Oiseau de Feu'	XLum
	'Oiseau d'Or'	XLum
	'Orange Beauty'	SCan
	'Orange Perfection'	CCon SCan
	'Orange Punch'	EAmu SCan WCot
	'Osric'	CSpe
	'Panache'	CDTJ CHEx EUJe SCan SHaC WCot
	paniculata	SHaC
	'Payton' **new**	LLWG
	'Peach Pink'	XBlo
	'Pearlescent Pink'	XBlo
	'Perkeo'	SHaC
§	'Phasion' (v) ♀H3	CCCN CHll CSpe ELan EPfP EUJe EWes LSRN MSCN NPer NPla SBst SCan SDix SHaC SPoG WCot XBlo
	'Picasso' ♀H3	CBcs CCCN CDTJ CExl CHEx XBlo
	'Pink Champagne'	XBlo
	'Pink Futurity' (Futurity Series)	CCCN
	'Pink Perfection'	SHaC
	'Pink Sunburst' (v)	CDTJ SCan WHil
	'Plaster Pink'	XBlo
	'President'	SCan SHaC XBlo XLum
	'Pretoria'	see *C.* 'Striata'
	'Pretoria Variegata'	see *C.* 'Striata'
	'Pringle Bay' (v)	SCan
	'Professor Lorentz'	see *C.* 'Wyoming'
	'Ra' ♀H3	MSKA SHaC
§	'Richard Wallace'	CExl SCan SHaC SPlb XBlo
	'Robert Kemp'	SHaC
§	'Roi Humbert'	SCan SHaC
	'Roi Soleil' ♀H3	XLum
	'Roitelet'	CHEx
	'Roma'	SCan SHaC
	'Rosemond Coles'	CHEx SCan SHaC XBlo
	'Saladin'	SHaC XLum
	'Sémaphore'	EUJe MAvo SCan SPad WCot XBlo
	'Shenandoah' ♀H3	SCan SHaC
	'Singapore Girl'	SCan SHaC
	'Snow-white'	XBlo

	'Soudan'	CDTJ SCan
N	***speciosa***	CDTJ XBlo
	'Statue of Liberty'	SCan
	'Strasbourg'	NPer SCan XLum
	'Strawberry Pink'	XBlo
	'Striata' misapplied	see *C.*'Stuttgart'
§	'Striata' (v) ♀H3	CCCN CDTJ CHEx CSpe CWGN EPfP EUJe LSRN MREP NPla SCan SEND SHaC SMad WCot XBlo
	'Striped Beauty' (v)	CCCN CDTJ EUJe LAst SCan
§	'Stuttgart' (v)	CDTJ CSpe EAmu EWes SCan SHaC WHil
	'Summer Gold'	XBlo
	'Summer Joy'	SHaC
	'Sunset'	WCot
	'Tali'	SCan
	'Talisman'	XBlo
	'Taney'	EUJe MSKA SHaC
	'Taroudant'	XLum
	'Tenerife'	SCan
	'Tricarinata'	CHEx
	(Tropical Series) 'Tropical Bronze Scarlet'	SCan SHaC WHil
	- 'Tropical Red'	SCan SHaC
	- 'Tropical Rose'	SCan SHaC
	- 'Tropical Salmon'	SCan SHaC
	- 'Tropical White'	SCan SHaC WHil
	- 'Tropical Yellow'	SCan SHaC
	Tropicanna	see *C.*'Phasion'
	Tropicanna Black = 'Lon01'PBR	EPfP SCan
	tuerckheimii	SCan SHaC
	'Valentine'	EAmu ECGP WCot
	'Vanilla Pink'	XBlo
	'Verdi' ♀H3	SCan SHaC
N	***warscewiczii***	CDTJ CExl SCan SHaC
	'Weymouth'	CDTJ SCan
	'Whithelm Pride' ♀H3	SCan SDeJ SHaC
	'Wintzer's Colossal'	SCan
	'Woodbridge Pink'	XBlo
§	'Wyoming' ♀H3	CBcs CCCN CDTJ CHEx ECGP EUJe SCan SDeJ SEND SHaC WHil XBlo
	'Yara'	SCan SDeJ SHaC
	'Yellow Humbert' misapplied	see *C.*'Richard Wallace', *C.*'Cleopatra', *C.*'Florence Vaughan'
	'Yellow Humbert'	LAst SCan

Cantua (*Polemoniaceae*)

	buxifolia ♀H2-3	CAbb CBcs CCCN CDoy CExl CHel CHll EBee ECre LRHS MOWG WPGP
	- 'Alba'	CCCN EBee ESwi
	- 'Dancing Oaks'	WCot

Cape gooseberry see *Physalis peruviana*

Capnoides see *Corydalis*

Capparis (*Capparaceae*)

	spinosa	CCCN
	- subsp. ***rupestris***	SPlb WJek

Capsicum (*Solanaceae*)

	annuum	CCCN
	- var. ***annuum*** (Longham Group) cayenne	CCCN
	- - 'Prairie Fire' ♀H2	CCCN
	- 'Apache' ♀H2	CCCN SEND SPre

Caragana (*Papilionaceae*)

	CC 3945	CExl
	arborescens	CAgr CArn CDul CMCN EBee ELan EPfP NWea SEND SPer SPlb
	- 'Lorbergii'	CEnd GBin MBlu SPer
	- 'Pendula'	CMac CWib ELan ESwi GBin LAst NEgg NLar SCoo SLim SPer
	- 'Walker'	CEnd CMac CWib ELan EPfP GBin MBlu MBri MGos NHol NLar NWea SCoo SLim SPer
	pygmaea	NLar

carambola see *Averrhoa carambola*

caraway see *Carum carvi*

Cardamine ✿ (*Brassicaceae*)

	angustata	WCru
	asarifolia misapplied	see *Pachyphragma macrophyllum*
	asarifolia L.	LRHS
	bulbifera	CLAP EBee ELon EPPr LEdu MAvo NRya WCot WCru WSHC
	bulbosa	GBuc
	californica	EPPr MAvo NRya WCru WMoo
	concatenata	WCru
	digitata	EBee NCGa
	diphylla	CDes CLAP LEdu SKHP WCot WCru
	- 'American Sweetheart'	CExl
	- 'Eco Cut Leaf'	CDes CExl EBee WCru
	- 'Eco Moonlight'	WCru
	aff. ***diphylla*** **new**	WCot
	enneaphylla	CLAP EBee EWld NBid NDov
	glandulifera	CElw ELon EPPr GBuc LEdu MAvo MMoz MNrw NSla SMrm WCot WCru WSHC
§	***heptaphylla***	CAvo CLAP ECho ELon GBin IGor WSHC
	- from the Pyrenees **new**	GCal
	- 'Big White'	GBuc GCal NCGa
	- Guincho form	CLAP EPPr WCot
	- white-flowered	CLAP GMaP
§	***kitaibelii***	CLAP GCal LEdu WCru
	latifolia Vahl	see *C. raphanifolia*
	macrophylla	CLAP EBee LEdu SWat WCot WSHC
	- CD&R 561	NCGa
	- 'Bright and Bronzy'	CExl GBin WCru
	maxima	LEdu WCru
	pachystigma	GBuc
	pentaphylla ♀H4	CBro CSpe EBee ECho ELan ELon EPPr GAbr GBin GBuc GMaP IFro IGor LEdu MCot NBir NHar WCot
	- bright pink-flowered	CLAP WCot
	pratensis	CArn CBAq CWat EHon LRHS MCot MHer MNHC MSKA NMir NPri SWat WHer WMoo WSFF WShi
	- 'Diane's Petticoat'	MHer MNrw WHoo
	- 'Edith' (d)	CLAP EBee LRHS MMoz MNrw
	- 'Flore Pleno' (d)	CAby CBct CBre EBee EPfP GBuc GCal GMaP IFro LEdu MHer MHol MNrw NBid NBir NBro NCGa NLar NPnk NPri NSla SWat WCot WSFF
	- 'William' (d)	MNrw
	quinquefolia	CDes CElw CLAP CMea CPom ELon GBuc LEdu MCot MMoz MNrw NCGa SDys SMrm WBrk WCot WCru WOut WPGP
§	***raphanifolia***	CBre CDes CExl CRow EBee GAbr GBin GCal IFro IMou LLWG LRHS

	NBid NBro NRya NSti SKHP SWat WMoo WOut WPGP
- PAB 204 **new**	LEdu
trifolia	CAby CMac EBee EPPr GBin GCal GMaP IFro IMou LRHS MRav NBir NBro NRya SWat WCot WCru WMoo
waldsteinii	CDes CElw CExl CLAP CSpe EBee ECho EPPr GBuc LEdu NCGa SBch WCru WSHC
yezoensis B&SWJ 4659	EBee WCru

cardamon see *Elettaria cardamomum*

Cardiandra (*Hydrangeaceae*)

alternifolia	LLHF
- B&SWJ 5719	WCru
- B&SWJ 5845	WCru
- B&SWJ 6177	WCru
- B&SWJ 6354	WCru
- subsp. ***moellendorffii***	CExl CFil WPGP
- 'Pink Geisha'	WCru
amamiohshimensis	WCru
formosana	CExl CFil WPGP
- B&SWJ 2005	WCru
- 'Crûg's Abundant'	WCru
- 'Hsitou'	WCru
- 'Hsitou Splendour'	WCru

Cardiocrinum ✿ (*Liliaceae*)

cathayanum	GCal
cordatum	ECho
- B&SWJ 2812	WCru
- B&SWJ 4841	WCru
- B&SWJ 5427	WCru
- B&SWJ 6336	WCru
- var. ***glehnii***	CCCN ECho GBuc
- - B&SWJ 4722	WCru
- - B&SWJ 4758	WCru
- red-veined	MNrw
giganteum	CBcs CBct CBro CCCN CDes CHEx CHid CSpe CTca ECho EPot GAbr GBin GBuc GCal GCra LRHS MNrw NLar WAbe WCot WCru WPnP XLum
- B&SWJ 2419	WCru
- GWJ 9219 from Sikkim	WCru
- HWJK 2158 from Nepal	WCru
- var. ***yunnanense***	ECho EPfP GAbr GBuc GGGa GLin LRHS NBid WCot WCru WPGP

cardoon see *Cynara cardunculus*

Carduus (*Asteraceae*)

benedictus	see *Cnicus benedictus*

Carex (*Cyperaceae*)

acuta	MSKA
- 'Variegata' (v)	CBAq CMac CRow CWat EHoe EShb GMaP IFro LLWG MMoz MWts NBro NOak WCot WMoo
acutiformis	NMir
alba	CKno EPPr WCot
'Amazon Mist'	LHop MBri NWsh
appalachica	EPPr
arenaria	CKno GBin
atrata	EHoe WHrl
§ - subsp. ***pullata***	CDes GCal
- - KEKE 494	EBee
aurea	EPPr IFoB
baccans	CExl GCal SBrt
bebbii	EPPr
berggrenii	ECou EHoe ELan EPPr GBin LPot LRHS NLar SPlb
brizoides	IMou
brunnea	CMac SHDw
- 'Jenneke' (v)	EPfP LRHS MAsh SHDw SLim SWvt
- 'Variegata' (v)	EHoe SHDw
buchananii 🏆H4	Widely available
- 'Green Twist'	EShb LPla
- 'Red Rooster'	MWat WRHF
- 'Viridis'	ELan EPPr GBin XLum
chathamica	GKev LRHS SVen
'China Blue'	MMoz
ciliatomarginata 'Treasure Island' (v)	EPPr WCot
colchica **new**	XLum
comans	EPPr EPfP NBro
- from Dunedin, New Zealand	EPPr
- 'Bronze Perfection'	SMea XLum
- bronze-leaved	Widely available
- 'Bronzita'	LRHS
- 'Copper Green'	SMea
- 'Dancing Flame'	CWCL ELon NWsh
- 'Frosted Curls'	Widely available
- red-leaved	CBcs CWCL NLar SRms
- 'Small Red'	see *C. comans* 'Taranaki'
§ - 'Taranaki'	EPPr EPfP MBNS SCoo
conica	MWat
- 'Hime-kan-suge'	see *C. conica* 'Snowline'
- 'Kiku-sakura' (v)	EPPr
§ - 'Snowline' (v)	CMac EHoe ELan EPfP GAbr GKev GMaP LEdu LLWP LRHS MMoz NBro NLar NWsh SGol SWvt XLum
crinita	EPPr
cristatella	EPPr
dallii	WHrl
davalliana	EBee
davisii	EPPr
depauperata	EHoe
dipsacea	CKno CMac CWCL EHoe EPPr EShb GMaP LRHS MMoz MNrw NWsh SBch SBea WHal
- 'Dark Horse'	CKno EHoe LLHF LRHS SEND SMea WPtf
divulsa	CKno
- subsp. ***leersii***	EPPr
§ ***dolichostachya*** 'Kaga-nishiki' (v)	CSBt EPPr GKev LEdu LHop LRHS SLim
duthiei	see *C. atrata* subsp. *pullata*
ebenea	LRHS
§ ***elata*** 'Aurea' (v) 🏆H4	Widely available
- 'Bowles's Golden'	see *C. elata* 'Aurea'
- 'Knightshayes' 🏆H4	CKno EBee EWes MWhi NLar WCot
'Evergold'	see *C. oshimensis* 'Evergold'
firma 'Variegata' (v)	MWat WThu
flacca	CHab CKno EHoe EPPr GBin XLum
- 'Bias' (v)	MMoz
- 'Blue Zinger'	CKno WWEG
§ - subsp. ***flacca***	EBee EWes MMoz NSti SMea
flagellifera	CBcs CHEx CMac CSpe CTri CWCL EBee EHoe ELon EPPr EPfP EShb GCal GMaP LRHS LSRN MBrN MBri MLHP MMuc MWhi NBir SEND SMrm SPlb WWEG
- 'Auburn Cascade'	LHop LRHS NWad WPtf
- 'Coca-Cola'	NOak WRHF
- 'Kiwi' **new**	EShb

	flava	CBAq CKno EHoe EPPr
	fortunei	see *C. morrowii* Boott
	fraseri	see *Cymophyllus fraserianus*
	fraserianus	see *Cymophyllus fraserianus*
	glauca Bosc. ex Boott	see *C. glaucescens*
	glauca Scop.	see *C. flacca* subsp. *flacca*
§	***glaucescens***	CWCL EPPr
	'Gold Fountains'	see *C. dolichostachya* 'Kaga-nishiki'
	granularis	EPPr
I	'Grayassina'	EPPr
	grayi	CDes CWCL EHoe LEdu LLWG LRHS MBlu MSKA NCGa NLar NOak NPnk SPlb WBor XLum
	'Happy Wanderer'	SLPl
	hystricina	LRHS
	'Ice Dance' (v)	CKno EBee EPPr EPfP GBin GQue LEdu LPot LRHS MAsh MBri MJak MMoz MSCN NHol NOak NOrc NWad SBch SEND SGol SHil SWvt WCot WPtf WWEG
	kaloides	EHoe EPPr LRHS XLum
	'Kan-suge'	see *C. morrowii* Boott
*	***leformeri***	XLum
	lupulina	GBin NOak
	lurida	EPfP MBNS XLum
	- 'Silver'	EPPr MBNS
	mertensii NNS 07-98	EPPr
	Milk Chocolate = 'Milchoc'[PBR] (v)	EPfP NOak
	morrowii misapplied	see *C. oshimensis*
§	***morrowii*** Boott	CWCL EPPr NWad
I	- 'Fisher's Form' (v)	CKno CTri ELan EPPr LHop MMoz MRav NHol NLar NWsh SWvt WGrn WWEG
	- 'Gilt' (v)	EHoe EPPr MBNS NHol NWad
	- 'Nana Variegata' (v)	CTri NBir
	- 'Pinkie'	WPtf
	- var. ***temnolepis***	IMou
	- - 'Silk Tassel' (v)	EPPr
N	- 'Variegata' (v)	EHoe ELan EPPr GCal GMaP LAst MJak MMoz MMuc NBir NSti SGol SLPl SRms XLum
	muehlenbergii	EPPr
	muricata	EPPr
	muskingumensis	CBAq CExl CKno CWCL CWib EHoe ELan EPPr EPfP EShb GBin GCal LEdu LLWP LRHS NBro NOak NWsh SDix SLim SMad WMoo WPnP WWEG
	- 'Ice Fountains' (v)	CBAq EPPr WWEG
	- 'Little Midge'	CKno CMac EPPr GBin GCal LEdu NOak WCot WWEG
	- 'Oehme' (v)	CKno CWCL EBee EPPr EShb GBin GCal LEdu LLWG LRHS NBid NHol NWad WPtf WWEG
	- 'Silberstreif' (v)	CKno EBee EPPr GBin LEdu MMuc NLar XLum
	nigra (L.) Reichard	CBAq EHon EPPr XLum
§	- 'On-line' (v)	CKno EPPr MBNS MMoz
	- 'Variegata'	see *C. nigra* 'On-line'
	No 1, Nanking (Greg's broad leaf)	MMoz
	No 4, Nanking (Greg's thin leaf)	EPPr MMoz
	normalis	EPPr
	obnupta	CKno EPPr
	ornithopoda 'Aurea'	see *C. ornithopoda* 'Variegata'
§	- 'Variegata' (v)	EBee EPPr GBin NBro NHol NOak NWsh SBch WMoo WWEG
§	***oshimensis***	EPPr MMoz
	- Everest = 'Fiwhite'[PBR] (v)	CKno GBin LBMP LHop SPoG WCot
§	- 'Evergold' (v) ♀H4	Widely available
	- 'Everillo'[PBR]	ESwi WCot
	- 'Variegata' (v)	NBir
	otrubae	CHab XLum
	panicea	CKno CSBt CWCL EBee EHoe EPPr LLWG MMoz MSKA WMoo
	paniculata	XLum
	parviflora	SMea
	pendula	Widely available
	- 'Cool Jazz' (v)	EPPr MSKA
	- 'Moonraker' (v)	CWCL EHoe EPPr ESwi MBNS MSKA NOak NWad SLPl WCot WWEG
	petriei	CWCL EBee LLWP MBNS WCot XLum
	phyllocephala 'Sparkler' (v)	EHoe EPfP EUJe LRHS SPad SWvt XLum
	plantaginea	EBee EHoe EPPr GBin LEdu WCot WMoo WWEG
	praegracilis	CKno EPPr
	Pritchard's selection (v)	IFro
	projecta	EPPr
	pseudocyperus	CBAq CPom EHoe EHon GBin MMoz MSKA MWts NPer NWsh SWat WMoo WPnP
	punctata	XLum
	remota	CKno EHoe EPPr SMea
	riparia	CBAq MMoz MMuc MSKA NPer SMea SWat WShi
	- 'Bowles's Golden'	see *C. elata* 'Aurea'
	rostrata	MMuc SEND
	sabynensis	see *C. umbrosa* subsp. *sabynensis*
	secta	CKno ECou EPPr EPfP GBin GMaP IMou LRHS MNrw SHDw WMoo
	- from Dunedin, New Zealand	EPPr
	siderosticha 'Banana Boat'	see *C. siderosticha* 'Golden Falls'
	- 'Echigo-nishiki' (v)	EPPr
§	- 'Golden Falls' (v)	LEdu LRHS NOak SMad
	- 'Golden Fountains'	WCot
	- 'Old Barn'	EBee
	- 'Shima-nishiki' (v)	CJun EBee EPPr EPfP LRHS MBNS NOak WWEG
	- 'Variegata' (v)	CHEx CPrp CTsd EBee EHoe ELan ELon EPPr EPfP EShb GCal LEdu LRHS NBir NBro NLar NOak NSti NWsh SLim WBor WWEG
	'Silver Sceptre' (v)	EHoe EPPr EShb GMaP LRHS MBNS MBri MGos NHol NSti NWsh SEND SLim SPlb SWvt WBrk WMoo
	'Silver Streams'	WWEG
	solandri	CKno LEdu LPla NWsh SHDw XLum
	spissa	MNrw
	stricta Gooden. 'Bowles's Golden'	see *C. elata* 'Aurea'
	sylvatica	EHoe
	tenuiculmis	CWCL EBee EPPr EShb LHop NOak NSti NWad NWsh WCot WWEG XLum
	- 'Cappucino'	CKno
	testacea	Widely available
	- dark-leaved	EPfP
	- 'Old Gold'	ELan EPPr EWes LRHS NOak SMad SPlb WGrn WMoo
	- 'Prairie Fire'	CSpe LHop LRHS

texensis	EPPr
'The Beatles'	EHoe EPPr NBir
'Triffid'	WPtf
trifida	CHEx CKno EHoe MNrw
- 'Chatham Blue'	CHid GBin LRHS MMoz SEND
* - 'Glauca'	CWCL
- 'Rekohu Sunrise'PBR (v)	CBct CKno EBee ELon EPfP ESwi LRHS MBri SLon SPoG
umbrosa subsp. ***sabynensis*** 'Thinny Thin' (v)	EBee EPPr EShb
vulpina	EPPr LRHS
vulpinoidea	EPPr LRHS

Carica (*Caricaceae*)

papaya (F)	XBlo
- 'Babaco'	CCCN
pubescens	SPlb

Carissa (*Apocynaceae*)

grandiflora	see *C. macrocarpa*
§ ***macrocarpa*** (F)	CCCN
- 'Boxwood Beauty' **new**	NSoo

Carlina (*Asteraceae*)

acaulis	CArn ECho ELan SPlb
- subsp. ***acaulis***	GPoy
- bronze-leaved	LDai
- var. ***caulescens***	see *C. acaulis* subsp. *simplex*
§ - subsp. ***simplex***	EBee NPri
- - bronze-leaved	SMad SPhx
vulgaris 'Silver Star'	SPhx

Carmichaelia (*Papilionaceae*)

'Abundance'	ECou
'Angie'	ECou
angustata 'Buller'	ECou
appressa	ECou
- 'Ellesmere'	ECou
astonii	ECou
- 'Ben More'	ECou
- 'Chalk Ridge'	ECou
australis	WSHC
'Charm'	ECou
'Clifford Bay'	ECou
corrugata	ECou
curta	ECou
enysii	LLHF
fieldii 'Westhaven'	ECou
flagelliformis 'Roro'	ECou
'Hay and Honey'	ECou
kirkii	ECou WThu
'Lilac Haze'	ECou
monroi	ECou
- 'Rangitata'	ECou
- 'Tekapo'	ECou
odorata	CExl ECou
- 'Lakeside'	ECou
- 'Riverside'	ECou
ovata 'Calf Creek'	ECou
'Parson's Tiny'	ECou
petriei	ECou SMad
- 'Aviemore'	ECou
- 'Lindis'	ECou
- 'Pukaki'	ECou
'Porter's Pass'	ECou
'Spangle'	ECou
'Tangle'	ECou
uniflora	ECou
- 'Bealey'	ECou
williamsii	ECou

× *Carmispartium* see *Carmichaelia*

Carpenteria (*Hydrangeaceae*)

californica ♀H3	CJun CSBt CTri EBee ELan EPfP EWTr GKev LAst LRHS MBri MGos MWat NPri SEND SSpi SWvt WPat WSpi
- 'Bodnant'	CDul EBee ELan LRHS LSRN MBri MGos NSoo SHil SPer SPoG SWvt WPGP WSpi
- 'Elizabeth'	CAbP CBcs CJun CSBt CWGN EBee ELan EPfP LRHS LSRN MAsh SPoG SSpi SSta WCFE WPGP WPat
- 'Ladhams' Variety'	CBcs CDul CJun CMac EBee EPfP LRHS MGos MRav SRkn SWvt WSpi

Carpinus ✿ (*Betulaceae*)

sp.	CMen LSRN SWvt
betulus ♀H4	Widely available
* - 'A. Beeckman'	SGol
- 'Columnaris'	CDul CLnd CTho EBee
* - 'Columnaris Nana'	LLHF MPkF WPat
§ - 'Fastigiata' ♀H4	Widely available
- 'Frans Fontaine'	CCVT CDoC CDul CEnd CLnd CMCN CTho EBee EPfP IArd LHop MBlu MBri MGos NLar NWea SCoo SEWo SGol SLim SPer WHar
- 'Globus'	MBlu
- 'Incisa'	WMou
- 'Lucas'	SGol SSta WMou
- 'Monument'	MPkF
- 'Pendula'	CDul CEnd CTho EBee IArd IDee MBlu SPoG SWvt
- 'Purpurea'	CDul CEnd MBlu MGos NLar
- 'Pyramidalis'	see *C. betulus* 'Fastigiata'
- 'Quercifolia'	CDul EBee
caroliniana	CDul CLnd CMCN EPfP SBir SMad WMou
- 'Sentinel Dries'	MBlu MBri
cordata	MBlu SSta
coreana	CMCN SBir
fangiana	CBcs CEnd CExl CTho EPfP IVic MBlu SKHP SSta WPGP WPat
fargesii	see *C. viminea*
henryana	CExl CMen EBtc SBir
japonica ♀H4	CDul CEnd CLnd CMCN CMen EBee EPfP LLHF MBlu MBri NLar SBir SCoo SEWo SMad SSta
- B&SWJ 10803	WCru
- B&SWJ 11072	WCru
kawakamii CWJ 12412	WCru
- CWJ 12449	WCru
laxiflora	CExl CMen WPGP
- B&SWJ 10809	WCru
- B&SWJ 11035	WCru
- var. ***longispica*** B&SWJ 8772	WCru
- var. ***macrostachya***	see *C. viminea*
orientalis	SBir
- PAB 3865 **new**	LEdu
polyneura	SBir SSta
pubescens	WPGP
- 'Abbotsbury'	SSta
rankanensis	SSta
- RWJ 9839	WCru
× ***schuschaensis***	EBtc

shensiensis	CDul
tschonoskii B&SWJ 10800	WCru
turczaninowii ♀H4	CDul CMCN CMen EGFP NLar SBir SSta WPGP
§ ***viminea***	CEnd CExl SSta

Carpobrotus (*Aizoaceae*)

§ ***edulis***	CCCN CDTJ SAPC SEND SVen WHer XLum
- var. ***edulis***	CHEx
- var. ***rubescens***	CCCN CHEx
muirii	CCCN SVen
sauerae	CCCN

Carpodetus (*Rousseaceae*)

serratus	CBcs IVic

Carrierea (*Salicaceae*)

calycina	IVic WPGP

carrot see *Daucus carota*

Carthamus (*Asteraceae*)

tinctorius	CArn MNHC SPav SRms

Carum (*Apiaceae*)

carvi	CArn ELau GPoy MHer MHoo MNHC SIde SRms SVic WJek
petroselinum	see *Petroselinum crispum*

Carya ✿ (*Juglandaceae*)

cordiformis	CTho MBlu
N ***illinoinensis*** (F)	CAgr CBcs EGFP MBri
- 'Carlson No 3' seedling (F)	CAgr
- 'Colby' seedling (F)	CAgr
- 'Cornfield' (F)	CAgr
- 'Lucas' (F)	CAgr
laciniosa (F)	CTho EGFP EPfP
- 'Henry' (F)	CAgr
- 'Keystone' seedling (F)	CAgr
ovata (F)	CAgr CBcs CDul CLnd CMCN CTho EPfP MBlu SSpi
- 'Grainger' seedling (F)	CAgr
- 'Neilson' seedling (F)	CAgr
- 'Weschcke' seedling (F)	CAgr
- 'Yoder No 1' seedling (F)	CAgr
tomentosa	EPfP NLar

Caryophyllus see *Syzygium*

Caryopteris ✿ (*Lamiaceae*)

× ***clandonensis***	CMac ECtt MWat NBir
- 'Arthur Simmonds' ♀H4	CTri ELan EPfP LHop SPer WGor
- 'Dark Knight'	CMea CSpe CTsd EBee ECtt ELan EPfP LAst LBuc LRHS MAsh MBri NPnk SHil SPoG SWvt WHil WHoo
- 'Ferndown'	CWib ELon EPfP NLar SEND SPoG SRms
- 'First Choice' ♀H3-4	CDul CMac EBee ECtt ELan EPPr EPfP EShb LAst LHop LRHS LSRN LSqu MAsh MGos NSoo SDys SLim SPoG SRkn SWvt
- 'Gold Giant'	LRHS MAsh
- Grand Bleu = 'Inoveris'PBR	CDoC CDul CMac CSBt EBee ELan EPfP EShb LRHS LSRN MBri MGos MSwo NLar SGol SWvt WHil WPat WRHF
- 'Heavenly Baby' ♀H3-4	EPfP LRHS MAsh SKHP SLon SPoG WHar
- 'Heavenly Blue'	Widely available
- Hint of Gold = 'Lisaura'PBR ♀H3-4	CDoC ELan EPfP LRHS MAsh MBri SPoG STPC
- 'Kew Blue'	CBcs CDul CMac CSBt EBee EHoe ELan EPfP EShb IVic LBMP LRHS LSRN MAsh MGos MHer MSwo MWat SCoo SGol SLim SLon SPer SPoG SSta SWvt WSHC XSen
- 'Longwood Blue'	EPfP LRHS MAsh SRms
- Petit Bleu = 'Minbleu'PBR	EBee LRHS
- Sterling Silver = 'Lissilv'PBR	CDoC EBee EHoe EPfP LRHS LSRN MAsh SPer SPoG SRms
- 'Summer Gold'	MAsh MRav
- 'Summer Sorbet'PBR (v) ♀H3-4	CDoC CWGN EBee EHoe ELan EPfP EWes LHop LRHS MAsh MGos MTPN NEgg NLar NPnk SCoo SEND SLim SPer SPoG SWvt WHar
- 'White Surprise'PBR	CWGN EBee EHoe ELan EMil EPfP LRHS MBri MPkF SPoG
- 'Worcester Gold' ♀H3-4	Widely available
divaricata	CMCN SBrt WHil
- 'Electrum'	CDes LSou
- 'Jade Shades'	EBee LSou
§ ***incana***	EPfP SPer
- 'Autumn Pink'PBR	EPfP
- 'Blue Cascade'	EBtc ELan MRav NLar SRms WGrn WPat
§ - 'Jason'PBR	ELon EPfP MBri MPkF NEgg NLar SPoG SWvt WHil
- Sunshine Blue	see *C. incana* 'Jason'
mastacanthus	see *C. incana*

Caryota (*Arecaceae*)

mitis ♀H1	CCCN EAmu
- 'Himalaya'	EAmu

Cassandra see *Chamaedaphne*

Cassia (*Caesalpiniaceae*)

corymbosa Lam.	see *Senna corymbosa*
marilandica	see *Senna marilandica*
nemophila new	SPlb

Cassinia (*Asteraceae*)

fulvida	CBcs EHoe SVen
leptophylla	CBcs
- 'Avalanche Creek'	ECou
- subsp. ***vauvilliersii***	EBee SEND SVen
'Ward Silver'	ECou EHoe EWes

Cassinia × *Helichrysum* (*Asteraceae*)

hybrid	WKif

Cassiope ✿ (*Ericaceae*)

'Askival Arctic Fox'	ITim
'Askival Freebird'	see *C.* Freebird Group
'Askival Snowbird'	ITim NHar
'Askival Snow-wreath'	see *C.* Snow-wreath Group
'Askival Stormbird'	ITim
'Badenoch'	ECho GBin
'Edinburgh' ♀H4	ECho EPot GBin NHar NWad
fastigiata	WAbe
§ Freebird Group	NHar
lycopodioides 'Beatrice Lilley'	GBin NHar WThu
- 'Jim Lever'	NHar WAbe
- 'Rokujō'	ITim
mertensiana	ECho EPot
- 'California Pink'	NHar NWad

- var. ***californica***	ITim NWad WThu
- var. ***gracilis***	ITim NHar NWad WThu
'Muirhead' ♀H4	ECho NHar WThu
'Randle Cooke' ♀H4	ECho NHar WIce WThu
selaginoides	GBin
- LS&E 13284	WAbe WThu
§ Snow-wreath Group	ITim
tetragona	ITim WAbe
wardii	ITim

Castanea ✿ (*Fagaceae*)

'Bouche de Bétizac' (F)	CAgr CMam
crenata	CAgr CDul
'Maraval' (F)	CAgr CTho MBlu MBri MCoo SGol WHar
'Maridonne' (F)	CAgr CMam
'Marigoule' (F)	CAgr CMam EPom ERea MCoo WHar
'Marlhac' (F)	CAgr CMam
'Marsol' (F)	CAgr MCoo SGol
mollissima	CBcs
'Précoce Migoule' (F)	CAgr
sativa ♀H4	CBcs CCVT CDoC CDul CLnd CSBt CTho CTri CWib ECrN ELan EPfP ERea EWTr LAst LBuc MBri MGos MMuc NPri NWea SEND SEWo SGol SLim SPer WHar WMou
§ - 'Albomarginata' (v) ♀H4	CDul CEnd EBee EPfP LHop MBlu MBri SPoG
- 'Anny's Red'	MBlu
- 'Anny's Summer Red'	CDul
- 'Argenteovariegata'	see *C. sativa* 'Albomarginata'
- 'Aspleniifolia'	CDul
- 'Aureomarginata'	see *C. sativa* 'Variegata'
- 'Belle Epine' (F)	CAgr
- 'Bournette' (F)	CAgr CMam
* - 'Doré de Lyon'	CAgr
- 'Marron Comballe' (F)	CAgr
- 'Marron de Goujounac' (F)	CAgr
- 'Marron de Lyon' (F)	CAgr CDul CEnd CTho EPfP EPom IVic MBri SVic
- 'Regal' (F)	EPom
§ - 'Variegata' (v)	CBcs CLnd CMCN ELan

Castanopsis (*Fagaceae*)

sclerophylla	CBcs WPGP

Castanospermum (*Papilionaceae*)

australe	CArn

Castilleja (*Orobanchaceae*)

integra new	GKev
miniata	SPlb WAbe

Casuarina (*Casuarinaceae*)

cunninghamiana	SPlb

Catalpa ✿ (*Bignoniaceae*)

bignonioides ♀H4	CBcs CCVT CDul CHEx CHab CLnd CMCN CSBt CTho CTri CTsd EBee ECrN ELan EPfP EWTr GKin LEdu MBri MSwo NWea SEND SGol SPad SPer SPlb SWvt
- 'Aurea' ♀H4	Widely available
* - 'Aurea Nana'	CEnd MBri
- 'Nana'	EBee LRHS MBri SLim WHar WPat
- 'Purpurea'	see *C.* × *erubescens* 'Purpurea'
- 'Variegata' (v)	ELon EPfP LHop LRHS MAsh NWea WPat
bungei	CTho MBlu SAPC SGol
§ × ***erubescens***	CBcs CDul CEnd CLnd CMac CTho
'Purpurea' ♀H4	EAmu EBee ELan ELon EPfP EUJe EWTr LAst LRHS MAsh MBlu MBri MGos MRav NLar SHil SLim SPer SPoG SWvt WHar WPGP WPat
fargesii f. ***duclouxii***	CBcs CDul CEnd EBee EPfP IVic MBlu MBri NLar WPGP
ovata	CMCN CTho
- 'Slender Silhouette'	NLar
speciosa	CDul CTho EWTr MBlu SVen
- 'Frederik'	NLar
- 'Pulverulenta' (v)	CDul CEnd CMCN EBee LLHF SBig WPat
* ***szechuanica***	NLar

Catananche (*Asteraceae*)

caerulea	CDoC CMea CSBt CTri EHyd ELan EPfP EShb LPot LRHS MBel MBri MHer MNHC MSpe NEgg NPri SBea SMrm SPad SPer SPoG SWvt WHoo WMoo XLum
- 'Alba'	CMea EHyd ELan EPfP IFoB LRHS MBel MNrw NBir SMrm SPer SPoG SWvt WMoo
- 'Amor Blue'	EPfP LRHS
- 'Bicolor'	MHer MSpe WMoo
- 'Major' ♀H4	ELan LDai LRHS SHil SRms
caespitosa	SIgm

Catha (*Celastraceae*)

edulis	CArn GPoy WHfH WJek

Caulokaempferia (*Zingiberaceae*)

petelotii B&SWJ 11818	WCru

Caulophyllum (*Berberidaceae*)

thalictroides	EBee EPPr IMou IPot LEdu SRot WCru WMoo WPnP WSHC
- subsp. ***robustum***	WCru

Cautleya ✿ (*Zingiberaceae*)

cathcartii	CExl LEdu
- 'Tenzing's Gold'	CDes WCru
§ ***gracilis***	CDTJ CExl EBee EPfP EUJe GCal IBlr MMoz MNrw NSoo SBig XLum
- B&SWJ 7186	LEdu WCru
- NJM 09.105	WPGP
- 'Edinburgh Lemon'	IBlr
lutea	see *C. gracilis*
spicata	CAby CBct CCCN CDTJ CDoC CHEx CHel CSpe CTsd ECho EUJe IBlr MMoz NSoo SBHP SBig SBst XLum
- CC 3676	CExl
- 'Arun Flame'	LEdu WCru
- 'Crûg Canary'	LEdu WCru
* - var. ***lutea***	CBct CHEx LEdu WBor
- 'Robusta'	CAvo CExl CHEx EAmu EBee GCal GCra IBlr LEdu LRHS MNrw SChF SMad WBor WCru WPGP

Cayratia (*Vitaceae*)

japonica B&SWJ 6636	WCru
§ ***thomsonii*** BWJ 8123	WCru

Ceanothus ✿ (*Rhamnaceae*)

'A.T. Johnson'	EBee ECrN EPfP SGol SPer SRms
americanus	CArn

	arboreus	SAPC
	- 'Trewithen Blue' ♀H3	CBcs CDul CMac CSBt CTsd CWib EBee ELan EPfP LAst LHop LRHS LSRN MAsh MBri MGos MRav MSwo NPri NSoo SEND SHil SLim SPer SPlb SPoG SWvt WSHC
	'Autumnal Blue' ♀H3	Widely available
	'Blue Cushion'	CBcs CDoC CTri CWSG LRHS MAsh MGos MJak MRav NHol SLim SLon SWvt
	'Blue Diamond'PBR	LSRN NLar
	'Blue Jeans'	EBee LRHS MMuc NLar
	'Blue Mound' ♀H3	Widely available
	'Blue Sapphire'PBR	CBcs CDoC CWGN ELan ELon EPfP LRHS LSRN MAsh MGos MRav NEgg NLar NPri SWvt
	'Burkwoodii' ♀H3	CBcs CDoC CDul CHab CSBt EBee EPfP LAst LRHS MAsh MGos MRav NEgg SLim SPer SPoG SWvt
	'Cascade' ♀H3	CBcs CHab EBee LRHS LSRN MGos MWat SLim SLon SPer SPlb WHar
	'Centennial'	MRav
	'Concha' ♀H3	Widely available
§	***cuneatus*** var. ***rigidus***	WSHC
	'Cynthia Postan'	EBee EPfP LRHS MAsh MWat NLar SCoo
	'Dark Star' ♀H3	CDoC CMHG CTri CWGN CWSG EBee ELon EPfP LBMP LRHS LSRN MAsh MGos MOWG NHol SCoo SEND SLim SPoG SSta SWvt
	'Delight'	CBcs EPfP
	× ***delileanus*** 'Gloire de Versailles' ♀H4	CBcs CDoC CDul CTri CWib EBee ELan ELon EPfP LAst LBMP LHop LRHS MGos MRav MSwo NLar SGol SPer SWvt WSHC
	- 'Henri Desfossé'	ELan EPfP LRHS LSRN MRav MSwo NLar SPer SPoG
	- 'Indigo'	EPfP
	- 'Topaze' ♀H4	CDul EBee ELan EPfP LRHS MOWG MRav NLar SGol SLon WHar WKif
	dentatus misapplied	see *C.* × *lobbianus*
	dentatus Torr. & A. Gray	SPlb
	- var. ***floribundus***	EBee
	'Diamond Heights'	see *C. griseus* var. *horizontalis* 'Diamond Heights'
	'Edinburgh' ♀H3	EPfP
	El Dorado = 'Perado' (v)	NLar
	gloriosus	EWes
	- 'Anchor Bay'	EPfP LRHS
	- 'Emily Brown'	CBcs CDoC CRos LAst LSRN MRav NLar
	griseus	MAsh
§	- var. ***horizontalis*** 'Diamond Heights' (v)	CMac EPfP LSRN MAsh MBri SPer
	- - 'Silver Surprise'PBR (v)	EBee ELan EPfP LBuc LRHS LSRN MAsh MGos NEgg NLar SLim
	- - 'Yankee Point'	CBcs CDoC CMac CSBt CWib EBee ECrN EPfP LRHS LSRN MAsh MGos MRav MSwo MWat NLar NSoo SCoo SEND SLim SPlb SPoG SVen SWvt
	- 'Kurt Zadnik'	LRHS
	impressus	CTri EPfP LRHS MAsh SHil SLPl SPer SVen SWvt
	- 'Victoria'	EBee LSRN MWat NLar NSoo SRGP WHar
N	'Italian Skies' ♀H3	CBcs CDoC CDul CHab CRos CSBt CWib EBee ELan EPfP LAst LBMP LHop LRHS LSRN MAsh MGos MSwo NEgg NLar NSoo SCoo SGol SLim SLon SPer SPlb SPoG SWvt
	'Joan Mirov'	NLar
	'Lemon and Lime'	LBuc LRHS
§	× ***lobbianus***	CDul CTri
	'Madagascar'	EBee EPfP LRHS SCoo SPoG
	× ***pallidus***	WHar
	- 'Marie Simon'	CBcs CWib EBee ELan EPfP LAst LRHS LSRN MGos SGol SPer SPoG SRms SWvt WCFE WHar WKif
	- 'Perle Rose'	CBcs CDul EPfP LLHF LRHS MGos MOWG NLar SPer SPoG WKif
	papillosus	IArd
§	'Pershore Zanzibar'PBR (v)	CBcs CMac CSBt EBee EHoe ELan EPfP EShb LAst LBuc LRHS LSRN MGos MRav MSwo NEgg NLar NPri SCoo SGol SLim SPer SPoG SWvt
	'Pin Cushion'	CWSG CWib EPfP LRHS MAsh NHol
	'Point Millerton'	see *C. thyrsiflorus* 'Millerton Point'
	'Popcorn'	CDoC
	prostratus	SMad
	'Puget Blue' ♀H4	Widely available
	'Ray Hartman'	NLar
	repens	see *C. thyrsiflorus* var. *repens*
	rigidus	see *C. cuneatus* var. *rigidus*
	'Snow Flurries'	see *C. thyrsiflorus* 'Snow Flurry'
	'Southmead' ♀H3	CDoC CTri ECrN ELan EPfP LBMP LRHS MAsh MGos MSwo SHil SLim SPer WHar WRHF
	thyrsiflorus	CTri CWib MAsh SPer SRms SWvt WHar
§	- 'Millerton Point'	EBee EPfP LRHS MGos NLar SCoo SLim SPoG WHar
	- 'Mystery Blue' **new**	LRHS SHil SPoG STPC
§	- var. ***repens*** ♀H3	Widely available
	- 'Skylark' ♀H3	Widely available
§	- 'Snow Flurry'	CWib EPfP LBMP MSwo
	'Tilden Park'	LRHS MAsh
	'Tuxedo'PBR	MAsh SPer
	× ***veitchianus***	CDoC CSBt EBee ELan EPfP LRHS MAsh SEND SPer
	'Zanzibar'	see *C.* 'Pershore Zanzibar'

Cedrela (*Meliaceae*)

	sinensis	see *Toona sinensis*

Cedronella (*Lamiaceae*)

§	***canariensis***	CArn CPrp GPoy MHer MNHC SWat WJek
	mexicana	see *Agastache mexicana*
	triphylla	see *C. canariensis*

Cedrus (*Pinaceae*)

	atlantica	CDul CJun CLnd CMac CMen EHul NWea SEND SGol WMou
	- 'Aurea'	CDul MBri MGos NLar NPCo NWea SSta WHar
	- 'Fastigiata'	CDul EHul LRHS MAsh MGos NLar SCoo SLim
	- Glauca Group ♀H4	Widely available
	- - 'Glauca Fastigiata'	CKen CMen
	- - 'Glauca Pendula'	CCVT CDoC CDul CMen ECrN EHul EPfP LRHS MBlu MBri MGos NEgg NPCo NWea SGol SLim SSta WHar
	- - 'Silberspitz'	CKen
	- 'Pendula'	MAsh SMad
	- 'Sahara Frost'	NLar

– 'Saphir Nymph'	CKen MAsh NLar SLim
brevifolia	NLar
– 'Epstein'	NLar
– 'Hillier Compact'	CKen NLar
– 'Kenwith'	CKen NLar
deodara ♀H4	Widely available
– 'Albospica' (v)	MAsh SWvt
– 'Aurea' ♀H4	CDoC CKen CTho EHul EPfP LRHS MAsh MBri MGos NEgg NLar SGol SLim WHar
– 'Blue Dwarf'	CKen
* – 'Blue Mountain Broom'	CKen
– 'Blue Snake'	CKen IVic
– 'Blue Surprise'	SLim
– 'Bush's Electra'	CJun NLar SMad
– 'Devinely Blue'	CKen LRHS SLim
– 'Feelin' Blue'	CDoC CKen EHul LRHS MAsh MBri MJak NEgg NLar NPCo SCoo SLim SWvt
– 'Gold Cascade'	SLim
– 'Golden Horizon'	CDoC CKen CMac CMen EHul LRHS MAsh MBri NEgg NPCo SCoo SLim SPoG
– 'Golden Jubilee' **new**	SGol
– 'Karl Fuchs'	EWTr NLar WGor
– 'Klondyke'	MAsh
– 'Lime Glow'	SLim
– 'Miles High'	CJun
– 'Mountain Beauty'	CKen
– 'Nana'	CKen
– 'Nivea'	CKen
– 'Pendula'	CKen EHul NWea SLim WGor
– 'Pygmy'	CKen
– 'Raywood's Prostrate'	CKen
– 'Roman Candle'	NPCo
– 'Scott'	CKen
– 'Silver Mist'	CKen
– 'Silver Spring'	NLar
libani ♀H4	CCVT CDoC CDul CLnd CMCN CTho ECrN EHul ELan EPfP EUJe EWTr LRHS MAsh MBlu MBri MMuc NLar NWea SEND SGol SLim SPer SPlb SWvt WHar WMou
– 'Blue Angel'	NLar SLim
– 'Comte de Dijon'	NLar
– 'Fontaine'	NLar
– 'Hedgehog'	NLar
– 'Home Park'	CKen NLar
– 'May'	NLar
– Nana Group	CKen NPCo
– 'Sargentii'	CKen EHul NLar NPCo
– 'Taurus'	NLar

Ceiba (*Malvaceae*)

pentandra	SPlb

Celastrus (*Celastraceae*)

dependens CWJ 12478	WCru
flagellaris B&SWJ 8572	WCru
hookeri B&SWJ 11667	WCru
kusanoi CWJ 12445	WCru
orbiculatus	CBcs CDoC ELan EPPr IGor LHop LRHS MRav SLon SPer WBor
– 'Diana' (f)	CMac
– 'Hercules' (m)	CMac
– Hermaphrodite Group ♀H4	EBee SDix SEND SKHP WSHC
– var. ***papillosus*** B&SWJ 591	WCru
– var. ***punctatus*** CWJ 12439	WCru
scandens	CMac GKev SPhx SPlb
stephanotiifolius B&SWJ 4727	WCru

Celmisia (*Asteraceae*)

allanii	EPot IBlr WAbe
angustifolia	GKev
argentea	WAbe
bellidioides	EWes NHar NSla WAbe
bonplandii	GKev
brevifolia	EPot
coriacea misapplied	see *C. semicordata*
coriacea (G. Forst.) Hook. f.	GBin
dallii	EPot
'David Shackleton'	IBlr
densiflora	IBlr
– silver-leaved	IBlr
discolor	EPot
'Eggleston Silver'	NBir NEgg
glandulosa	GCra
gracilenta	GKev WAbe
hectorii	IBlr WAbe
hectorii × ***ramulosa***	WAbe
holosericea	GKev
hookeri	GBin LRHS
petiolata	GKev
prorepens	EPot GKev
ramulosa var. ***tuberculata***	IBlr NSla
§ ***semicordata***	GCra IBlr NSla
– subsp. ***semicordata*** **new**	EPot GKev
– subsp. ***stricta***	IBlr
sessiliflora	WAbe
spectabilis	EPot GKev
– subsp. ***magnifica***	EPot
– subsp. ***spectabilis*** **new**	GKev
traversii	EPot
verbascifolia	GKev
§ ***walkeri***	IBlr
webbiana	see *C. walkeri*

Celosia (*Amaranthaceae*)

argentea var. ***cristata*** Plumosa Group Kimono Series	LAst
– – – 'Smart Look Red' ♀H3	NPri

Celsia see *Verbascum*

× *Celsioverbascum* see *Verbascum*

Celtica see *Stipa*

Celtis (*Cannabaceae*)

australis	CBcs EBtc MGos SEND
biondii	NLar
bungeana	NLar
caucasica	CFil
occidentalis	CDul ELan EWTr
sinensis	CMen

Cenolophium (*Apiaceae*)

denudatum	CDes CSam CSpe GBin LEdu LRHS NChi WPGP WPtf

Centaurea ✿ (*Asteraceae*)

HH&K 271	NBid

	RCB AM-6	WCot
	alba	LDai
	albonitens new	WCot
	alpestris	MSpe NLar SPhx WPGP
	'Amethyst on Ice'	LBuc LRHS
§	***atropurpurea***	CDes CSpe EPfP EWes GQue LDai LPot LRHS MSpe NBid NLar SHar SMrm SPhx SPlb WHrl WPGP
	bagadensis	MSpe
	bella	CDes CPrp EBee ECtt ELon GCal LBMP LHop LPla LRHS MAvo MBel MCot MLHP MNFA MRav MSpe NBro NSti SEND SPet SPhx SPoG SWat WKif WMnd XLum XSen
	- 'Katherine' (v)	MSpe
	benoistii misapplied	see *C. atropurpurea*
	benoistii ambig.	CSpe
	benoistii* × *orientalis ambig.	SPhx
	'Blewit'	CDes CElw MAvo MSpe WPGP
	cana	see *C. triumfettii* subsp. *cana*
	candidissima misapplied	see *C. cineraria*
	'Caramia'	CDes EBee MSpe NBid
	carniolica SDR 5443	CHel GKev
	cheiranthifolia	CDes EPPr MAvo MNrw MSpe NBid NBir NLBP SHar WPGP XSen
	- var. ***purpurascens***	CDes
§	***cineraria***	ECre LDai SPhx WHil WOut
	- subsp. ***cineraria*** ♀H3	CSpe SEND WCot
	cyanus	CHab MHer MNHC SVic WJek
	- 'Black Ball'	CSpe MNHC
	- 'Blue Ball'	CSpe
	- 'Pinkie' (d) new	MNHC
	cynaroides	see *Stemmacantha centaureoides*
	dealbata	CKno CMac COIW CPrp CWib ELon EPfP GJos IFoB LRHS MLHP MSpe NBro NLar NMir NOrc NPri SEND SMrm WCot WMoo WWEG XLum
	- 'Steenbergii'	CMac ELan GCal LLWP MSpe NBid NBir NGdn NPer NSti SBch SPer SPoG WCot WMnd
	- 'Steenbergii' variegated (v)	LDai
	debeauxii subsp. ***nemoralis***	LDai MAvo NLar
	declinata RCB UA 18 new	WCot
	drabifolia subsp. ***austro-occidentalis***	GKev
	- subsp. ***cappadocica*** new	GKev
	fischeri Willd.	MSpe WPGP
	glastifolia	CDes EBee GCal LRHS MSpe WPGP
	gymnocarpa	see *C. cineraria*
	hypoleuca	LRHS NBid
	jacea	GKev GQue MSpe NBid NLar WCot
	'John Coutts'	Widely available
	'Jordy'	CWGN ECtt EPPr GBin GBuc IPot LDai MAvo MBri MSpe NCGa NChi NLar SPhx WCAu WHil WKif WPtf
	karabaghensis	EBee GCal WPGP
	kotschyana	CDes EBee WPGP
	macrocephala	Widely available
	mollis	NBid
	montana	Widely available
	- 'Alba'	Widely available
	- 'Amethyst Dream' PBR	IPot NLar
	- 'Amethyst in Snow'	CHel ECtt GBin IPot MAvo MBri NHol NLar NWad SPoG
	- 'Black Sprite'	ECtt MAvo MBri NDov NLar NPnk NSti STPC WHil WNPC
§	- 'Carnea'	CCVN CDes CElw CPom CSam GCra GMaP MAvo MBel MCot MSpe NBir NChi NLBP NLar SPhx WBrk WCAu WMoo WWEG
	- 'Elworthy Glacier'	CElw
	- 'Gold Bullion'	CPrp CSpe EBee ECtt ELan ELon EPfP EWes GMaP LDai LRHS MAvo MHer MHol MRav MSpe NBid NBir NLar NPro SMad SMrm WSHC
	- 'Grandiflora'	EBee MBri MJak MPie
	- 'Joyce'	CElw CPom LDai MAvo MSpe NBid NLar WSHC
	- 'Lady Flora Hastings'	CBre CCse CDes CElw CKno CPom CSam CSpe EBee LDai MAvo MSpe NBid WPGP WWEG
	- 'Lilac Heart'	MTis
	- lilac-flowered	NBid
	- 'Ochroleuca'	CDes CElw EBee LDai MBel MSpe NBid NBre WPGP
	- 'Parham'	CPrp CSev ECtt ELan ELon GCal LBMP LLWP LRHS MBel MBri MCot MNrw MRav MSpe MWat NEgg NSti SPer SPlb SPoG WMnd WMoo WSHC
	- 'Purple Heart'	CDes ECtt ELon IPot LSou MBel MHer MNrw MSpe MTis NLar NPri SMrm SRot WCAu WCot
	- 'Purple Prose'	CElw MAvo
	- 'Purpurea'	CDes CElw CPom MSpe WOut
	- 'Rosea'	see *C. montana* 'Carnea'
*	- ***violacea***	NBid
	- 'Violetta'	IPot MAvo MSpe MTis NBid NBir SBch WMoo
	montana* × *triumfettii	CElw SHar WSHC
	nervosa	see *C. uniflora* subsp. *nervosa*
	nigra	CArn CHab EPfP GJos MNHC MSpe NMir SMrm SPhx WMoo WOut WSFF
	- var. ***alba***	CBre NBid
	- 'Elstead'	MSpe
	- subsp. ***rivularis***	LDai MMuc NBid XLum
	nogmovii	MAvo MSpe
	orientalis	CFis CSpe EBee ECGP EWes GCal IBoy LRHS MSpe NBre NLar SPhx SPoG WHoo
	pannonica subsp. ***pannonica*** HH&K 259	NBid WSHC
	pestalozzae	GKev
	phrygia	COIW MSpe
	pulcherrima	LRHS MSpe NBre SPhx XSen
	'Pulchra Major'	see *Stemmacantha centaureoides*
	rupestris	EBee EPfP MSpe NBre SPhx
	ruthenica	LRHS SKHP SPer SPhx SPlb WCot
	salicifolia	MSpe NBir
	salonitana RCB AM 1	WCot
	scabiosa	CArn CHab CWib IBoy MHer MNHC MSpe NBid NBir NBre NLar NMir SPhx
	- f. ***albiflora***	LRHS
	'Silver Feather' new	LBuc SHil
	simplicicaulis	CSam LRHS MAsh MSpe SBch SHar SMrm SRms WHoo WSHC XSen
	thracica	CDes EBee WCot
	triumfettii	CPBP
	- 'Blue Dreams'	LDai
§	- subsp. ***cana***	XSen
I	- - 'Rosea'	WBrk
	- 'Hoar Frost'	CDes MAvo MSpe NDov WPGP
	- subsp. ***stricta***	CPrp MSpe

	uniflora	EBee XSen
§	- subsp. ***nervosa***	MSpe NBid NBre NBro NLar XLum
	vallesiaca new	WOut
	woronowii	MAvo MSpe

Centaurium (*Gentianaceae*)

erythraea	CArn GPoy MHer MHoo
scilloides	NSla WAbe

Centella (*Apiaceae*)

§	***asiatica***	CArn EOHP GPoy LEdu WJek

Centradenia (*Melastomataceae*)

sp. new	LAst
inaequilateralis	CCCN
- 'Cascade'	MBri SPet

Centranthus (*Caprifoliaceae*)

§	***lecoqii***	ECtt EWes LPla SPhx WCot
§	***ruber***	Widely available
§	- 'Albus'	Widely available
	- 'Atrococcineus'	MAvo MMuc
	- var. ***coccineus***	CBcs CHab EBee EHyd ELan EPfP EWTr GAbr GBin GKin GMaP LBMP LRHS MCot MJak MRav MWat NPri NSoo SEND SHil SMrm SPhx SRot SWat WCAu WCot WWEG
	- mauve-flowered misapplied	see *C. lecoqii*
	- mauve-flowered	NBir
	- 'Nettleton'	CNat
	- 'Roseus'	EPfP WMoo
	- 'Snowcloud'	ECtt EHyd EPfP MNHC SRms
	'White Cloud'	WJek

Centropogon (*Campanulaceae*)

§	***ayavacensis*** subsp. ***ayavacensis*** B&SWJ 10663	WCru
	cordifolius B&SWJ 10282	WCru
	costaricae B&SWJ 10455	WCru
	ferrugineus B&SWJ 10665	WCru
	hirsutus B&SWJ 10657	WCru
	aff. ***valerii*** B&SWJ 10341	WCru
	willdenowianus	see *C. ayavacensis* subsp. *ayavacensis*

Cephalanthera (*Orchidaceae*)

falcata	EFEx
longibracteata	EFEx

Cephalanthus (*Rubiaceae*)

occidentalis	CWib EBee GBin IVic LRHS LSou MBNS MBlu MBri NLar SLim SPoG WBor WCFE

Cephalaria (*Caprifoliaceae*)

§	***alpina***	COIW EBee EPPr EPfP LBMP LRHS MAsh MHer MNFA MNrw MRav SPhx SRms SWat WCot XLum
	ambrosioides MESE 503	EBee
	caucasica	see *C. gigantea*
	dipsacoides	LPio LPla MSpe SKHP SPhx WMoo
§	***flava***	EBee LRHS NBre
	galpiniana	SPlb
§	***gigantea***	Widely available
	graeca	see *C. flava*
	leucantha	CArn CFis EBee GBin NBre NLar SPhx WMoo
	litvinovii	CElw SPhx
	tatarica hort.	see *C. gigantea*
	tchihatchewii	EBee NLar WCot

Cephalaria × Scabiosa (*Caprifoliaceae*)

C. alpina × S. cinerea	LRHS

Cephalotaxus (*Taxaceae*)

fortunei 'Prostrate Spreader'	SLim
harringtonia var. ***drupacea***	CDoC
- 'Fastigiata'	CDoC EHul IArd IDee LRHS MAsh MBri MGos NLar NWea SPoG
- 'Gimborn's Pillow'	NLar NWea
- 'Korean Gold'	LRHS NLar
- 'Prostrata'	LRHS
sinensis	CMCN

Cerastium (*Caryophyllaceae*)

alpinum	ECho IFoB SRms
- var. ***lanatum***	ECho EWes XLum
arvense 'Compactum' new	XLum
biebersteinii new	XLum
fontanum	CHab
tomentosum	CBar ECho EPfP GBin MMuc NPri SEND SPer SPet SPlb SPoG
- var. ***columnae***	ECho EHoe EWes XLum

Ceratonia (*Caesalpiniaceae*)

siliqua	CBcs SPlb

Ceratophyllum (*Ceratophyllaceae*)

demersum	CBAq CWat EHon EWay MSKA MWts SWat WMAq WSFF
submersum new	LLWG

Ceratostigma ✿ (*Plumbaginaceae*)

	abyssinicum	ELan GCal LHop
	asperrimum B&SWJ 7260	WCru
	'Autumn Blue'	EPfP LRHS
	capensis	CMac
	griffithii	CBcs CDoC CDul CHll CMac EBee ECtt EHoe EHyd ELan EPfP EWTr LBMP LRHS MRav MSwo NLar SCoo SGol SHil SLim SMad SPer SPoG SRms SVen WGwG WKif XLum XSen
	- wild-collected	GCal
§	***plumbaginoides*** ♀H3-4	Widely available
	willmottianum ♀H3-4	Widely available
	- BWJ 8140	WCru
	- Desert Skies = 'Palmgold'PBR	CBcs ELan EPfP MBlu NLar SGol SLim SPer SPoG SWvt
	- Forest Blue = 'Lice'PBR	CDoC CMac CSBt EBee ELan EPPr EPfP LAst LRHS LSRN MBri MGos MRav NLar NPri SCoo SHil SLim SPer SPoG SWvt WPat

Cercidiphyllum ✿ (*Cercidiphyllaceae*)

japonicum ♀H4	Widely available
- HEHEHE 316	GKev
- 'Boyd's Dwarf'	CJun CRos LLHF LRHS MAsh NLar SPoG SSta WAbe
- 'Chameleon' (v) new	NLar
- 'Herkenrode Dwarf'	NLar
- 'Heronswood Globe'	CJun EPfP MBlu NLar SSta WSpi
- 'Kreukenberg Dwarf'	CJun SSta
- f. ***miquelianum***	GKev NLar

– 'Morioka Weeping'	CDoC CJun CTho MPkF NLar SChF SSta WPGP
– 'Peach'	CJun NLar
§ – f. ***pendulum*** ♀H4	CDoC CDul CEnd CExl CJun CMCN CMHG CMac CRos CTri EBee ELan EPfP GBin GKin IArd IDee LRHS MAsh MBlu MGos NEgg NLar SCoo SLim SPoG SSpi SSta WHar
– – 'Amazing Grace'	CTho MBlu NLar
– 'Raspberry'	CJun NLar SSta
– Red Fox	see *C. japonicum* 'Rotfuchs'
§ – 'Rotfuchs'	CBcs CEnd CJun CLnd CMCN CMac CRos EBee ELan EPfP EWTr GBin GKin IVic LRHS MAsh MBlu MBri MGos MPkF NCGa NLar NPCo SHil SPoG SSpi SSta WHar WPat
– 'Ruby'	CJun MBlu NLar SChF WPGP
– 'Strawberry'	CBcs CJun LHop MBlu NLar SSta
– 'Tidal Wave'	CJun NLar SSta
– 'Titania'	SSta
magnificum	CDoC CEnd CExl CMCN EPfP IDee MBlu NEgg NLar SSta WPGP
– f. ***pendulum***	see *C. japonicum* f. *pendulum*

Cercis (*Caesalpiniaceae*)

canadensis	CBcs CDul CLnd CMCN CWGN EPfP MGos MMuc NEgg NLar NWea SCoo SLim SPer WPat
– 'Ace of Hearts'PBR	MPkF NLar NTre SSta
– f. ***alba***	CBcs ESwi LSRN WMou
– – 'Royal White'	CJun EPfP IArd LRHS MBlu NTre
– 'Appalachian Red'	CJun CTho ESwi LSRN MBlu MGos NLar NTre SGol SKHP
– 'Cascading Hearts'	CBcs ESwi NLar NTre
– 'Flame'	CJun NLar NTre SKHP SSta WPGP WPat
– 'Forest Pansy' ♀H4	Widely available
– 'Hearts of Gold'PBR	CRos CTho CWGN EBee EPfP EWTr LRHS MAsh MBlu MBri MGos MPkF MRav NLar NTre SHil SKHP SLon SPoG WHar WMou
– Lavender Twist = 'Covey'	CBcs CWSG EBee EPfP ESwi LRHS LSRN MBlu MBri MGos NLar NTre SGol SKHP SLon SPoG WHar WMou
– Little Woody = 'Litwo'PBR	MPkF NLar NTre SGol
– 'Melon Beauty'	ESwi NLar SKHP WPat
– var. ***mexicana*** 'Sanderson'	WPGP
§ – var. ***occidentalis***	LEdu SSta
– 'Pauline Lily'	NLar NTre
– 'Pink Heartbreaker'	SGol
– 'Ruby Falls' **new**	NTre
– 'Rubye Atkinson'	CJun NLar SSpi
– 'Silver Cloud' (v) **new**	NTre
– 'Tennessee Pink'	CJun NLar NTre
– var. ***texensis*** 'Oklahoma'	CJun EBee ESwi LSRN MGos MPkF NLar NPCo NTre SKHP WHar WMou
– – 'Texas White'	CBcs CJun EBee EPfP MBri MPkF NLar NTre SGol SKHP SLim SPoG WHar WPat
– – 'Traveller'	NTre SGol
chinensis	LLHF NLar SPer
– f. ***alba***	CTho MGos
– 'Avondale'	Widely available
– 'Don Egolf'	CJun EUJe LSRN MBlu MGos MPkF NLar NTre SGol SKHP SSta
– 'Shirobana' **new**	NTre
chingii	CExl WPGP
gigantea	NLar
griffithii	LLHF NLar SSta
'Merlot' **new**	NTre
occidentalis	see *C. canadensis* var. *occidentalis*
racemosa	CExl IDee WPGP
siliquastrum ♀H4	Widely available
– f. ***albida***	CTho ECrN ELan EPfP EPri EWes LRHS SKHP SPer SSpi WSpi
– 'Bodnant'	CTho EBee EPfP EWes IArd LLHF LRHS LSRN MBlu MBri MGos NLar NTre SHil SSta WHar WPGP WPat
– 'White Swan'	CJun CTho EBee EWes NTre

Cerinthe (*Boraginaceae*)

glabra	SPlb
major	SWvt
– 'Kiwi Blue'	CHll
– 'Purpurascens'	CSpe CWCL ELan EPfP LBMP LRHS MNHC NWad SEND SMrm SPer SPhx SPoG WKif WWEG
– 'Yellow Gem'	ELan
retorta	LDai

Ceropegia (*Apocynaceae*)

barklyi	LToo
conrathii	LToo
§ ***linearis*** subsp. ***woodii*** ♀H1	EShb
multiflora	LToo
rendallii	LToo
woodii	see *C. linearis* subsp. *woodii*

Cestrum (*Solanaceae*)

aurantiacum	EShb
auriculatum	MOWG
× ***cultum***	CHll EShb
– 'Cretan Pink'	CCCN MOWG
– 'Cretan Purple'	CBcs CCCN CHGN CHel CHll EBee ELan ELon EPfP EShb LHop LRHS MOWG NSoo SEND SPoG WKif WSHC
diurnum × ***nocturnum***	EShb
§ ***elegans***	CDoC CExl CHEx CHel CHll CRHN CTsd EBee ELan ELon EPfP IDee LHop LRHS MOWG NEgg NSoo SEND SLon
fasciculatum	EShb MOWG
'Newellii' ♀H2	CBcs CCCN CExl CHel CMHG CWCL CWib EBak EBee ELan ELon EPfP EShb EUJe LRHS MOWG NSoo SEND SPlb SVen WKif WSHC
nocturnum	CCCN CHll EBak EOHP EShb MOWG
parqui ♀H3	CAbb CBcs CCCN CHel CHll CTsd CWib EBee ELan EPfP EUJe LHop LRHS MOWG SDix SEND SLon SMad WJek WKif WSHC
psittacinum	CExl
purpureum (Lindl.) Standl.	see *C. elegans*
roseum	CExl
– B&SWJ 10255 from Oaxaca State, Mexico	WCru
– 'Ilnacullin'	EBee
* ***splendens***	MOWG

Ceterach (*Aspleniaceae*)

officinarum	see *Asplenium ceterach*

Chaenomeles (*Rosaceae*)

	sp. new	CWSG
	cathayensis	CAgr CTho NLar WHer
§	***japonica***	MMuc SEND
	- 'Chojubai'	CMen
	- 'Cido'	CAgr LBuc MCoo
	- 'Orange Beauty'	LRHS NHol SPer
	- 'Sargentii'	CMac EPfP MBri NBro SGol
	lagenaria	see *C. speciosa*
	Madame Butterfly = 'Whitice'	CDoC EBee EPfP LRHS LSRN MAsh MBri MMuc MRav NEgg SLim SPer SPoG
	maulei	see *C. japonica*
	'Orange Star'	CEnd NLar
	sinensis	see *Pseudocydonia sinensis*
§	***speciosa***	NWea SMrm
	- 'Apple Blossom'	see *C. speciosa* 'Moerloosei'
	- 'Brilliant'	EPfP
	- 'Cardinalis'	CMac
	- 'Contorta'	LRHS MAsh
	- 'Eximia'	LRHS
	- 'Falconnet Charlet' (d)	EBee LRHS MBri MRav
	- 'Flocon Rose'	EPfP LRHS
	- 'Friesdorfer'	LRHS
	- 'Geisha Girl' (d) ♀H4	CBcs CDoC CEnd CHel CMac CSBt EBee EPfP LAst LHop LRHS LSRN MAsh MBri MGos MRav MSwo MWat NPri SGol SHil SLim SMrm SPer SPoG SRms SWvt
	- 'Grayshott Salmon'	NPro
	- Hot Fire = 'Minvesu'	CDoC EBee EPfP LRHS MBri
	- 'Kinshiden'	EPfP LRHS
	- 'Knap Hill Radiance'	SLim
§	- 'Moerloosei' ♀H4	Widely available
	- 'Nivalis'	Widely available
	- 'Rubra Grandiflora'	LRHS
	- 'Simonii' (d)	CBcs EPfP MRav NWea
	- 'Snow'	LBMP MAsh MSwo SRms
	- 'Umbilicata'	MBlu NLar SPer SRms
	- 'Winter Snow' (d)	SPer
	- 'Yukigotan'	CDoC EBee LLHF LRHS MBri MMuc NLar SGol SHil SWvt WPat
	× ***superba***	IBoy
	- 'Boule de Feu'	CTri CWib MCoo
	- 'Cameo' (d)	CEnd EBee ELon EPfP LHop LRHS MAsh MBNS MRav MWat NLar NSoo SGol SLPl
	- 'Clementine'	CWib
	- 'Crimson and Gold' ♀H4	Widely available
	- 'Elly Mossel'	CMac CWib NLar
	- 'Fascination'	NLar
	- 'Fire Dance'	CHll CWib MSwo NLar SGol SPer WRHF
	- 'Fusion'	CAgr
	- 'Hever Castle'	CJun
	- 'Hollandia'	SRms
	- 'Issai White'	MRav
	- 'Jet Trail'	CBcs CMac CSBt EBee ECrN ELan EPfP LAst LRHS LSRN MAsh MBri MGos MJak MRav MSwo NLar SGol SHil SLim SPoG SWvt
	- 'Knap Hill Scarlet' ♀H4	CDoC CDul CHel EBee ELan EPfP GGal LRHS MAsh MBri MGos NSoo SEND SLim SPer SPoG SRms SWvt
	- 'Lemon and Lime'	ELan EPfP LRHS MAsh MGos MRav SLon SPer SRms
	- 'Nicoline' ♀H4	CBcs CDoC CDul EBee EPfP IBoy LRHS MGos NEgg SLim WMoo
	- 'Orange Trail'	MBri
	- 'Pink Lady' ♀H4	Widely available
	- 'Pink Trail'	MBri
	- 'Red Joy'	EBee EPfP LRHS MBri NLar WGrn
	- 'Red Trail'	MRav
	- 'Rowallane' ♀H4	CHll ELan EPfP MRav MWat
	- 'Salmon Horizon'	EPfP EWTr IArd NLar
	- 'Tortuosa'	EBee LHop NLar WGrn
	'Toyo-nishiki'	MBlu

Chaenorhinum (*Plantaginaceae*)

§	***origanifolium***	ECho SBch SPlb
	- 'Blue Dream'	CSpe ECho EPfP GKev IPot MAsh SPoG SWvt WMoo
	- 'Dreamcatcher'	EPfP
	- 'Summer Skies'	NPri SPet

Chaerophyllum (*Apiaceae*)

hirsutum	CRow IMou
- 'Roseum'	Widely available

Chamaebatiaria (*Rosaceae*)

millefolium	SBrt

Chamaecyparis ✿ (*Cupressaceae*)

	formosensis	CKen
	lawsoniana	CDul EHul NWea WMou
	- SIN 1820	GLin
	- 'Allumii Aurea'	see *C. lawsoniana* 'Alumigold'
	- 'Allumii Magnificent'	CDul
§	- 'Alumigold'	MAsh MGos SCoo
	- 'Alumii'	CMac EHul MAsh MGos MJak NWea
	- 'Aurea'	CDul
	- 'Aurea Densa' ♀H4	CKen CMac CSBt CTri EHul EPfP MAsh MGos NEgg WGor
	- 'Bleu Nantais'	CKen CMac EHul LBee LRHS MAsh MGos SCoo SLim SPoG WGor
	- 'Blom'	CKen EHul
§	- 'Blue Gown'	EHul LBee
	- 'Blue Surprise'	CKen EHul MJak
	- 'Brégéon'	CKen NLar
	- 'Broomhill Gold'	CDoC CSBt EHul LBee LRHS MAsh MGos NPri SCoo SLim SPer SPoG WBor
	- 'Caudata'	CKen NLar
	- 'Chantry Gold'	EHul
§	- 'Chilworth Silver' ♀H4	CSBt EHul LBee LRHS MAsh SCoo SLim SPer SRms
	- 'Columnaris'	CBcs CDoC EPfP LAst LBee LRHS MBri MJak NEgg NWea SCoo SPoG
	- 'Columnaris Aurea'	see *C. lawsoniana* 'Golden Spire'
N	- 'Columnaris Glauca'	CDul CMac CWib EHul MAsh MGos NEgg NLar NWea SCoo SPer
	- 'Crawford's Compact'	CMac
	- 'Cream Crackers'	EHul
	- 'Cream Glow'	CKen CSBt LRHS MAsh MGos SCoo WGor
	- 'Croftway'	EHul
	- 'Dik's Weeping'	CDoC NLar NWea SLim
	- 'Duncanii'	EHul
	- 'Dutch Gold'	EHul MAsh MGos
	- 'Dwarf Blue'	see *C. lawsoniana* 'Pick's Dwarf Blue'
	- 'Eclipse'	CKen
	- 'Elegantissima' ambig.	CKen CMac
	- 'Ellwoodii' ♀H4	CDul CMac CSBt CTri CWib EHul EPfP LAst LRHS MGos MJak NPri NWea SCoo SLim SPer SRms
I	- 'Ellwoodii Glauca'	SPlb

	– 'Ellwood's Empire'	EHul
	– 'Ellwood's Gold' ♀H4	CBcs CDoC CDul CMac CSBt CWib EHul ELan EPfP LBee LRHS MAsh MBri MGos MJak NPri NWea SPer SPlb SPoG SRms WMoo
	– 'Ellwood's Gold Pillar'	EHul LBee LRHS MAsh MBri MGos NHol SLim SPoG WBor WGor
§	– 'Ellwood's Nymph'	CKen LRHS SLim
	– Ellwood's Pillar = 'Flolar'	CDoC CMac EHul LAst LBee LRHS MBri MGos NLar SCoo SLim WCFE
	– 'Ellwood's Pygmy'	CMac
	– 'Ellwood's Silver'	MAsh
	– 'Ellwood's Silver Threads'	CMac LBee
	– 'Ellwood's Variegata'	see *C. lawsoniana* 'Ellwood's White'
§	– 'Ellwood's White' (v)	CKen CMac CSBt EHul EPfP SPoG
I	– 'Emerald'	CKen
	– 'Emerald Spire'	MAsh
	– 'Erecta Aurea'	EHul
	– 'Erecta Viridis'	CBcs MJak NEgg NWea
	– 'Ericoides'	EHul
	– 'Filiformis Compacta'	EHul
	– 'Filip's Golden Tears'	MAsh SLim
	– 'Fleckellwood'	CWib EHul MAsh
	– 'Fletcheri' ♀H4	CMac EHul NWea
	– 'Fletcheri Aurea'	see *C. lawsoniana* 'Yellow Transparent'
	– 'Fletcher's White'	EHul
	– 'Forsteckensis'	CKen EHul NLar NWea
I	– 'Forsteckensis Aurea'	CDoC
	– 'Fraseri'	NWea
	– 'Gimbornii' ♀H4	CDul EHul LBee SCoo SLim
	– 'Glauca'	CDul
	– 'Globosa'	MGos
	– 'Gnome'	CDoC CKen CMac EHul LAst LRHS NHol SCoo SLim SPoG WGor WThu
§	– 'Golden Pot'	CDoC CMac CSBt CWib EHul LBee LRHS SCoo
§	– 'Golden Queen'	EHul
	– 'Golden Showers'	EHul
§	– 'Golden Spire'	MGos
	– 'Golden Triumph'	EHul
	– 'Golden Wonder'	EHul MAsh MJak NEgg NLar NWea SCoo
	– 'Goldfinger'	NLar
	– 'Grayswood Feather'	CDoC EHul LBee LRHS MAsh SCoo SPlb
	– 'Grayswood Gold'	EHul
	– 'Grayswood Pillar' ♀H4	EHul MGos
	– 'Green Globe'	CDoC CKen CMen CSBt EHul LBee MAsh SLim WThu
§	– 'Green Hedger' ♀H4	CDul CSBt NWea
§	– 'Green Pillar'	CDul CWib LAst LBee NEgg SCoo
	– 'Green Spire'	see *C. lawsoniana* 'Green Pillar'
	– 'Hogger's Blue Gown'	see *C. lawsoniana* 'Blue Gown'
	– 'Imbricata Pendula'	CDoC CKen NLar SLim SMad WBor
	– 'Ivonne'	EHul MGos MJak
	– 'Jackman's Green Hedger'	see *C. lawsoniana* 'Green Hedger'
	– 'Jackman's Variety'	see *C. lawsoniana* 'Green Pillar'
	– 'Jeanette'	CKen
	– 'Kelleriis Gold'	EHul
	– 'Killarny Salmon'	CMac
	– 'Kilmacurragh' ♀H4	CDul CMac MAsh MGos NWea WCFE
	– 'Kilworth Column'	CDoC NLar NWea
	– 'Kingswood'	CDoC
	– 'Knowefieldensis'	CMac
	– 'Lane' misapplied	see *C. lawsoniana* 'Lanei Aurea'
	– 'Lane' den Ouden	CWib MRav NEgg
§	– 'Lanei Aurea' ♀H4	EHul MGos MJak SPoG
	– 'Lemon Queen'	CDul EHul LBee
	– 'Little Spire' ♀H4	CDoC EUJe LRHS MBri MGos NHol NLar SCoo SLim SPoG WGor
	– 'Lutea' ♀H4	CMac EHul MGos
§	– 'Lutea Nana' ♀H4	CMac EHul MAsh NLar
	– 'Luteocompacta'	LBee
*	– 'MacPenny's Gold'	CMac
	– 'Minima Argentea'	see *C. lawsoniana* 'Nana Argentea'
	– 'Minima Aurea' ♀H4	CDoC CDul CKen CMac CSBt CWib EHul EPfP EPot LAst LBee LRHS MAsh MBri MGos MJak NEgg NWea SLim SPer SPoG WBor WCFE WMoo
	– 'Minima Glauca' ♀H4	CMac EHul EPfP LAst LRHS MJak NEgg NWea SCoo SLim SRms
*	– 'Moonsprite'	CKen EHul LAst LRHS NLar SCoo SLim SPoG WGor
	– 'Nana'	CMac
	– 'Nana Albospica' (v)	EHul LBee MGos SCoo SPoG WGor
§	– 'Nana Argentea'	CKen CMac EHul SPoG WGor
	– 'Nana Lutea'	see *C. lawsoniana* 'Lutea Nana'
	– 'Nicole'	EHul LAst MAsh MBri MGos NWea SCoo WGor
	– 'Nidiformis'	EHul
	– 'Nyewoods'	see *C. lawsoniana* 'Chilworth Silver'
	– 'Nymph'	see *C. lawsoniana* 'Ellwood's Nymph'
	– 'Pagoda'	MAsh
§	– 'Pelt's Blue' ♀H4	CBcs CDoC CDul CKen CSBt EHul LRHS MGos NLar SCoo SLim SPoG
	– 'Pembury Blue' ♀H4	CDoC CDul CWib EHul EPfP LBee LRHS MAsh MGos MJak MRav NEgg NLar NWea SCoo SLim SPer SPoG
§	– 'Pick's Dwarf Blue'	LRHS
	– Pot of Gold	see *C. lawsoniana* 'Golden Pot'
	– 'Pottenii'	CMac EHul LBee MAsh MGos NWea
	– 'Pygmaea Argentea' (v) ♀H4	CKen CMac CSBt CWib EHul ELan LBee MAsh MBri MGos NEgg NWea SLim SPer SPoG WBor WCFE
	– 'Pygmy'	EHul LRHS NLar NWea
	– 'Rijnhof'	EHul LBee
	– 'Rimpelaar'	CDoC
	– 'Royal Gold'	EHul
	– 'Silver Queen' (v)	CKen
	– 'Silver Threads' (v)	EHul ELan LBee MAsh MGos SPoG
	– 'Silver Tip' (v)	EHul LRHS SLim
	– 'Snow Flurry' (v)	CKen EHul WGor
	– 'Snow White' PBR (v)	EHul LBee LRHS MAsh MBri MGos NHol SCoo SLim SPoG WGor
	– 'Springtime' PBR	CSBt EHul LBee MAsh MBri SCoo
	– 'Stardust' ♀H4	CBcs CDoC CDul CSBt CWib EHul ELan LRHS MAsh MGos MJak NEgg NPri NWea SCoo SLim SPoG
	– 'Stewartii'	CDul NEgg NWea SCoo
*	– 'Summer Cream'	EHul
	– 'Summer Snow' (v)	CDoC EHul EPfP LBee LRHS MGos NHol NPri SCoo SLim
	– 'Sunkist'	LRHS SCoo SLim
	– 'Tamariscifolia'	CDoC EHul WCFE
	– 'Tilford'	EHul
	– 'Treasure' (v)	CSBt EHul LRHS MAsh MGos SLim
	– 'Van Pelt'	see *C. lawsoniana* 'Pelt's Blue'
	– 'Waterfall'	SMad
	– 'Westermannii' (v)	CMac MGos
	– 'White Spot' (v)	EHul MGos NPri
	– 'Winston Churchill'	CMac MGos NWea
	– 'Wisselii' ♀H4	CDoC CKen CMac EHul LAst MGos NLar NWea SCoo SRms WCFE
	– 'Wisselii Nana'	CKen EHul

	- 'Wissel's Saguaro'	CDoC CKen IVic MGos NLar SLim
	- 'Witzeliana'	CDul NLar
	- 'Yellow Queen'	see *C. lawsoniana* 'Golden Queen'
	- 'Yellow Success'	see *C. lawsoniana* 'Golden Queen'
§	- 'Yellow Transparent'	CMac
	- 'Yvonne'	CDoC CDul EPfP LRHS MAsh MBri NEgg NLar SCoo SLim SPoG
	leylandii	see × *Cuprocyparis leylandii*
	obtusa 'Albovariegata' (v)	CKen
	- 'Arneson's Compact'	CKen
	- 'Aurea'	CDoC SCoo
	- 'Aurora'	CKen ELan MAsh SLim
	- 'Bambi'	CDoC CKen NLar WAbe WThu
	- 'Barkenny'	CKen
	- 'Bartley'	CKen
	- 'Bassett'	CKen
	- 'Bess'	CKen
	- 'Brigitt'	CKen
	- 'Buttonball'	CKen
	- 'Caespitosa'	WAbe
	- 'Chabo-yadori'	CDoC EHul LRHS NLar SLim
	- 'Chilworth'	CDoC CKen NLar
	- 'Chima-anihiba'	CKen
	- 'Chirimen'	CDoC CKen NLar NWad SLim
	- 'Clarke's Seedling'	CDoC
	- 'Confucius'	CDoC EHul MGos
	- 'Corley Gold'	NLar
§	- 'Crippsii' 🏆H4	CBcs CDoC CMac LRHS SCoo
	- 'Crippsii Aurea'	see *C. obtusa* 'Crippsii'
	- 'Dainty Doll'	CDoC CKen NHol NLar
	- 'Densa'	see *C. obtusa* 'Nana Densa'
	- 'Draht'	CDoC MGos NLar
	- 'Draht Hexe'	CKen
	- 'Elf'	CKen
	- 'Ellie B'	CKen
	- 'Ericoides'	CKen
	- 'Erika'	NLar
	- 'Fernspray Gold'	CDoC CDul CKen CMac CTri EHul EPfP LRHS MAsh MBri MGos NEgg NLar SCoo SLim SPer SPoG
	- 'Flabelliformis'	CKen
	- 'Gnome'	CKen CMen
	- 'Gold Fern'	CKen
	- 'Golden Fairy'	CDoC CKen NLar
	- 'Golden Filament' (v)	CKen
	- 'Golden Nymph'	CDoC CKen NLar
	- 'Golden Sprite'	CDoC CKen NLar WAbe
	- 'Goldilocks'	EHul
	- 'Gracilis Aurea'	CKen CMac
	- 'Green Cushion' **new**	CKen
	- 'Green Diamond'	CKen
	- 'Hage'	CKen
	- 'Hypnoides Nana'	CKen
	- 'Intermedia'	CDoC CKen WAbe
	- 'Ivan's Column'	CKen
	- 'Junior'	CKen
	- 'Juniperoides'	CKen WThu
	- 'Juniperoides Compacta'	WAbe
	- 'Kamarachiba'	CDoC CKen CSBt EHul LBee LRHS MAsh NLar SCoo SPoG WGor
	- 'Kerdalo'	NLar
	- 'Konijn'	EHul
	- 'Kosteri'	CDoC CKen CMac EHul ELan LBee LPot MAsh NEgg NHol SCoo WGor
	- 'Kyoto Creeper'	CKen
	- 'Leprechaun'	NLar WAbe
	- 'Limerick'	CKen
	- 'Little Markey'	CKen
	- 'Lucas'[PBR]	CDoC NLar
	- 'Marian'	CKen NLar
§	- 'Mariesii' (v)	CKen
	- 'Melody'	CKen
	- 'Meroke'	NLar
	- 'Minima'	CKen
	- 'Nana' 🏆H4	CDoC CKen CMac CMen LBee NHol NWad
	- 'Nana Aurea' 🏆H4	CDoC CMac CSBt EHul EPfP MAsh NHol
§	- 'Nana Densa'	CDoC CKen CMac
	- 'Nana Gracilis' 🏆H4	CDoC CDul CKen CMen CSBt EHul ELan EPfP EUJe IVic LAst LRHS MAsh MBri MGos MJak NEgg NWad NWea SCoo SLim SPoG
I	- 'Nana Gracilis Aurea'	CMen EHul
I	- 'Nana Lutea'	CDoC CKen EHul EPfP EPot LBee LRHS MAsh MGos NHol SCoo SLim WBor
	- 'Nana Rigida'	see *C. obtusa* 'Rigid Dwarf'
	- 'Nana Variegata'	see *C. obtusa* 'Mariesii'
	- 'Pygmaea'	CSBt EHul LRHS MGos SCoo SLim
§	- 'Rigid Dwarf'	CDoC CKen EHul LBee LPot SPoG
	- 'Saffron Spray'	LRHS
	- 'Snowflake' (v)	CDoC CKen NWad
	- 'Snowkist' (v)	CKen
	- 'Spiralis'	CKen
	- 'Split Rock' **new**	NLar
	- 'Stoneham'	CKen
	- 'Tempelhof'	CKen EHul LRHS MAsh NEgg NLar SCoo SLim
	- 'Tetragona Aurea'	CBcs CMac EHul LRHS SLim
	- 'Timothy'	CMac
	- 'Tonia' (v)	CKen EHul LRHS SLim WGor
	- 'Topsie'	CKen
	- 'Tsatsumi'	CDoC NLar
	- 'Tsatsumi Gold'	CDoC CKen EHul LRHS MPkF NLar SCoo SLim SPoG
	- 'Verdon'	CKen
	- 'Wissel'	CKen
	- 'Wyckoff'	CKen
	- 'Yellowtip' (v)	CKen EPfP MAsh
	pisifera 'Aurea Nana' misapplied	see *C. pisifera* 'Strathmore'
	- 'Avenue'	EHul
	- 'Baby Blue'	EHul ELan EPfP LRHS MGos SCoo SLim WGor
	- 'Blue Globe'	CKen
	- 'Boulevard' 🏆H4	CBcs CDoC CDul CJun CMac CSBt CWib EHul ELan EPfP EPot LAst LBee LRHS MAsh MGos MJak NEgg NPri NWea SLim SPer WBor WMoo
	- 'Compacta Variegata' (v)	MAsh NEgg
	- 'Curly Tops'	CSBt EHul LRHS NHol SCoo SLim WGor
	- 'Devon Cream'	NEgg SCoo
	- 'Filifera'	CMac CSBt LRHS SCoo
	- 'Filifera Aurea' 🏆H4	CKen CMac CWib EHul EPfP LBee MGos MJak NEgg NHol NWea SCoo SPer WCFE
	- 'Filifera Aureovariegata' (v)	EHul LRHS
	- 'Filifera Nana'	EHul ELan LRHS MGos SLim SPoG
	- 'Filifera Nana Aurea'	see *C. pisifera* 'Golden Mop'
	- 'Filifera Sungold'	see *C. pisifera* 'Sungold'
	- 'Fuiri-tsukomo'	CKen
	- 'Gold Cushion'	CKen
	- 'Gold Dust'	see *C. pisifera* 'Plumosa Aurea'
	- 'Gold Spangle'	CKen EHul
§	- 'Golden Mop' 🏆H4	CKen EHul NLar
	- 'Green Pincushion'	CKen CMen

	- 'Hime-himuro'	CKen
	- 'Hime-sawara'	CKen CMen
	- 'Lime Tart' **new**	CKen
	- 'Margaret'	CKen
	- 'Nana'	CKen CMen EHul MAsh MBri NHol
I	- 'Nana Albovariegata' (v)	CDoC MAsh WThu
	- 'Nana Aureovariegata' (v)	CDoC CSBt EHul LBee LRHS MBri
I	- 'Nana Compacta'	CMac SRms
	- 'Nana Variegata' (v)	CMac LBee NWad
I	- 'Parslorii'	CKen
	- 'Pici'	CKen
§	- 'Plumosa Aurea'	CKen EHul MAsh NWea
	- 'Plumosa Aurea Compacta'	CKen
	- 'Plumosa Aurea Nana'	MAsh
I	- 'Plumosa Aurea Nana Compacta'	CMac
	- 'Plumosa Aurescens'	CDoC CMac
§	- 'Plumosa Compressa'	CDoC CKen EHul EUJe NWad SCoo WGor
	- 'Plumosa Densa'	see *C. pisifera* 'Plumosa Compressa'
	- 'Plumosa Flavescens'	EHul
I	- 'Plumosa Juniperoides'	CKen EHul MBri SCoo WGor
§	- 'Plumosa Rogersii'	EHul
I	- 'Pygmaea Tsukumo'	NLar
	- 'Rogersii'	see *C. pisifera* 'Plumosa Rogersii'
	- 'Silver and Gold' (v)	EHul
	- 'Silver Lode' (v)	CKen
	- 'Snow' (v)	CKen
	- 'Snowflake'	CKen EHul
	- 'Spaan's Cannon Ball'	CKen
	- 'Squarrosa Dumosa'	CKen EHul
I	- 'Squarrosa Lombarts'	CSBt EHul
	- 'Squarrosa Lutea'	CKen
	- 'Squarrosa Sulphurea'	CSBt EHul EPfP LRHS MBri SLim
§	- 'Strathmore'	EHul NWad
§	- 'Sungold'	CDoC CKen CSBt EHul LRHS MAsh MGos SCoo SLim SPoG
	- 'Tama-himuro'	CKen
	- 'Teddy Bear'	MBri NLar
	- 'True Blue'	EHul
	- 'Winter Beauty'	LRHS
	thyoides 'Andelyensis'	CMac CSBt EHul MBri NEgg SCoo
	- 'Aurea'	EHul
	- 'Conica'	CKen MAsh
	- 'Ericoides' ♀H4	CKen CTri EHul LBee SPlb
	- 'Little Jamie'	CKen
	- 'Red Star'	see *C. thyoides* 'Rubicon'
§	- 'Rubicon'	CMac CSBt EHul EPfP LBee LRHS MBri NEgg SLim SPoG
	- 'Top Point'	LAst LBee LRHS MAsh SCoo SPoG
	- 'Variegata' (v)	EHul

Chamaecytisus (*Papilionaceae*)

	purpureus 'Incarnatus'	see *Cytisus purpureus* 'Atropurpureus'

Chamaedaphne (*Ericaceae*)

	calyculata	CBcs
	- 'Nana'	NHar

Chamaedorea (*Arecaceae*)

	costaricana	EAmu
	metallica misapplied	see *C. microspadix*
§	***microspadix***	CPHo EAmu SChr
	radicalis	CBrP CPHo EAmu SChr

Chamaemelum (*Asteraceae*)

§	***nobile***	CArn CHby CPrp CSev CTri ELau EPfP GPoy MBri MHer MHoo MMuc MNHC NGdn NPri SEND SPlb SRms SVic WJek
	- dwarf	SMor SVic
	- dwarf, double-flowered (d)	LEdu
	- 'Flore Pleno' (d)	CBre CMea CPrp CSev CTri ELau EPfP GPoy LAst MBri MHer MHol MHoo MNHC MRav MSCN NBro NCot NDov NGdn SIde SPer SRms WAbe WHal WJek WWEG
	- 'Treneague'	Widely available

Chamaenerion (*Onagraceae*)

§	***angustifolium***	SWat WSFF
§	- 'Album'	CDes CElw CMea CSpe EBee ELan EPfP LEdu LRHS MMuc MNrw MRav NBid NBir NSti SPer SPhx SPoG SWat WCot WHal WMoo WPGP WSFF WSHC
	- 'Isobel'	MRav WCot
	- 'Stahl Rose'	CElw CHid CMea EPfP EWes LPla MCot NPri NSti SGbt SMrm SPhx SPoG SWat WCot WSHC
§	***dodonaei***	CFis ELan EWes IMou LPla SPhx WCot WSHC

Chamaepericlymenum see *Cornus*

Chamaerops (*Arecaceae*)

	excelsa misapplied	see *Trachycarpus fortunei*
	excelsa Thunb.	see *Rhapis excelsa*
	humilis ♀H3	CAbb CBcs CBrP CHEx CWSG EGri EPfP ESwi EUJe LRHS MGos MREP NPla NPri NSoo SAPC SChr SEND SHil SPlb SPoG STrG WPGP
§	- var. ***argentea***	CBrP CDTJ CPHo EAmu LRHS MGos SChr SHil SPlb WCot
	var. ***cerifera***	see *C. humilis* var. *argentea*
	- 'Vulcano'	CDTJ EAmu MBri MGos SChr

Chamaespartium see *Genista*

Chamaesphacos (*Lamiaceae*)

	ilicifolius misapplied	see *Siphocranion macranthum*

Chambeyronia (*Arecaceae*)

	macrocarpa	EAmu

Chamelaucium (*Myrtaceae*)

	uncinatum	CCCN MOWG

Chamerion see *Chamaenerion*

Chasmanthe (*Iridaceae*)

	aethiopica	EBee
	bicolor	CDes CExl CPrp CTca EBee IDee WOut
	floribunda	CHEx CPrp CTca EBee
	- var. ***duckittii***	CCon CPrp EBee ECho EPfP
	- 'Saturnes'	EBee

Chasmanthium (*Poaceae*)

§	***latifolium***	CKno EHoe ELan ELon EPPr EPfP EShb EUJe LRHS MBrN MBri MMoz SGol SMrm SPoG WBor WCot WWEG WWFP XLum
	- 'Golden Spangles'	CKno
	- 'River Mist' (v)	CAbP EBee ELon MAvo SPoG STPC
	- 'Variegatum' (v)	WCot

laxum	SMea

Cheilanthes (*Pteridaceae*)

argentea	ISha
distans	ISha SRms
lanosa	CBty CCCN CHid CLAP EBee EFer EWes ISha LRHS WCot
myriophylla	WAbe
siliquosa NNS 00-83	WCot
sinuata	ISha
tomentosa	CBty CCCN CLAP ISha LRHS
wrightii	ISha

Cheiranthus see *Erysimum*

Cheirolophus (*Asteraceae*)

benoistii misapplied	see *Centaurea atropurpurea*
benoistii (Humb.) Holub	CSpe MRav SKHP WSHC
teydis	SPlb

Chelidonium (*Papaveraceae*)

japonicum	see *Hylomecon japonica*
majus	CArn GPoy GQui MHer NMir WHer WSFF
- 'Flore Pleno' (d)	CBre NBid NBro WHer WTou
- var. ***laciniatum***	NBir WCot

Chelone (*Plantaginaceae*)

barbata	see *Penstemon barbatus*
§ ***glabra***	Widely available
lyonii	EBee ELan NBre NLar SPad SPhx WMoo WShi
- 'Hot Lips'	LHop WCAu
- 'Pink Temptation'	MSCN SPet
obliqua	Widely available
- var. ***alba***	see *C. glabra*
- 'Forncett Foremost'	GQui
- 'Forncett Poppet'	NBre
- 'Ieniemienie'	EBee LEdu
- 'Pink Sensation'	NBre
* - ***rosea***	WGwG
I 'Pink Turtle' **new**	GBin

Chelonopsis (*Lamiaceae*)

moschata	CLAP EBee GBin LEdu LHop MHer SBrt SMad WMoo WPGP
yugiharana	CAby CDes MCot NBid NPnk SHar WMoo

Chengiopanax (*Araliaceae*)

sciadophylloides B&SWJ 4728	WCru

Chenopodium (*Amaranthaceae*)

ambrosioides	CArn
bonus-henricus	CAgr CArn CHab CHby GPoy LPot MCoo MHer MNHC SIde SRms WHer WJek
giganteum	MNHC SHDw WJek

cherimoya see *Annona cherimola*

cherry, Duke see *Prunus* × *gondouinii*

cherry, sour or morello see *Prunus cerasus*

cherry, sweet see *Prunus avium*

chervil see *Anthriscus cerefolium*

chestnut, sweet see *Castanea sativa*

Chiastophyllum (*Crassulaceae*)

§ ***oppositifolium*** 🏆H4	CBcs CSam CTri ECho EDAr EHyd ELan EPfP GAbr GJos GKev LAst LRHS MHol MLHP MRav MSCN NBid SPlb SRms WHlf WKif WMoo WSHC XLum
- 'Frosted Jade'	see *C. oppositifolium* 'Jim's Pride'
- 'Jane's Reverse' (v)	EBee WCot
§ - 'Jim's Pride' (v)	EBee ECho ECtt EHoe EWes GAbr GBuc GKev GMaP LRHS MHer MRav NHar NPer NPri SPlb SRGP SRms SRot WAbe WMoo WSHC
simplicifolium	see *C. oppositifolium*

Chiliotrichum (*Asteraceae*)

diffusum (G. Forst.) Kuntze	CWib
- 'Siska'	CBcs SMad

Chilopsis (*Bignoniaceae*)

linearis (Cav.) Sweet	CArn
- var. ***linearis*** **new**	SPad

Chimonanthus ✿ (*Calycanthaceae*)

fragrans	see *C. praecox*
nitens	CBcs CMCN NLar
§ ***praecox***	Widely available
- 'Brockhill Goldleaf'	NLar
- 'Grandiflorus' 🏆H4	CEnd CJun EPfP LRHS MAsh SPoG SSta WPGP WPat
- 'Luteus' 🏆H4	CEnd CJun ELan EPfP LRHS LSRN MAsh MGos SPoG SSpi SSta WPGP WPat
- 'Sunburst'	CJun
- 'Trenython'	CEnd CJun WPGP WPat
yunnanensis W.W. Sm.	see *C. praecox*
yunnanensis misapplied	IArd

Chimonobambusa (*Poaceae*)

KR 7592	MWht
hookeriana misapplied	see *Himalayacalamus falconeri* 'Damarapa'
§ ***marmorea***	CDTJ CEnt ERod MMoz MWht SBig
- 'Variegata' (v)	CDTJ ERod ESwi MMoz SLPl
§ ***quadrangularis***	CBcs CDTJ CDoC CEnt EPfP ERod ESwi IMou MMoz MWht SBig WPGP
- 'Nagaminei' (v)	ERod
- 'Suow' (v)	CDTJ WPGP
- 'Tatejima'	ERod
tumidissinoda	CDTJ CEnt EPfP ERod ESwi IMou MMoz MWhi MWht SBig SGol WJun WPGP

Chinese chives see *Allium tuberosum*

Chiogenes see *Gaultheria*

Chionanthus (*Oleaceae*)

retusus	CBcs CDul CMCN EBee EPfP LRHS MBri MPkF NLar SHil SKHP SPer SSpi
- 'Tokyo Tower'	CJun
virginicus	CBcs CDoC CDul CJun CMCN EBee ECrN ELan EPfP EWTr GBin GKin IArd IDee LHop LRHS MBlu MBri MMuc MRav NEgg NLar SKHP SPer SPlb SSpi WPGP

Chionochloa (*Poaceae*)

conspicua	CKno EBee GBee GBin GCal GKev MAvo NBid NBir SMea WPGP
- 'Rubra'	see *C. rubra*
flavescens	EHoe GBin
flavicans	CSpe IMou LRHS MAvo SMad SMea
§ ***rubra***	CBcs CElw CGHE CKno CSpe EBee EHoe ELan EWes GBin GCal GMaP IMou LHop LRHS MAsh MAvo MMoz MRav NChi SMad WCot WMoo WPGP
- PAB 67 new	LEdu
- subsp. ***cuprea***	GBin WCot

Chionodoxa ✿ (*Asparagaceae*)

cretica	see *C. nana*
§ ***forbesii***	CBro CWCL ECGP ECho EPfP EPot GKev NBir SDeJ SPer SRms WRHF WShi
- 'Alba'	ECho
- 'Blue Giant'	ECho ELan EPot ERCP
- 'Rosea'	ECho
- Siehei Group	see *C. siehei*
- 'Tmoli'	ECho
- 'Violet Beauty'	ECho GKev SDeJ
- 'Zwanenburg'	ECho
gigantea	see *C. luciliae* Gigantea Group
luciliae misapplied	see *C. forbesii*
luciliae ambig.	CAvo ECho EHyd SEND
luciliae Boiss. 🏆H4	CAby CBro EPfP MBri SPer
- 'Alba'	CHVG ECho LRHS SDeJ SMrm SPer
§ - Gigantea Group	ECho GKev
'Alba'	EPot GKev
§ ***nana***	ECho
'Pink Giant'	CAvo CBro CMea ECho ELan EPfP EPot ERCP EWTr GKev LRHS SBch SDeJ SMrm WBor WCot XLum
sardensis 🏆H4	CBro CHVG CPrp ECho EHyd EPot ERCP GKev LRHS SDeJ SPhx WCot WShi
§ ***siehei*** 🏆H4	CBro ECho

Chionographis (*Melanthiaceae*)

japonica	EFEx WCru

Chionohebe (*Plantaginaceae*)

pulvinaris	NSla WAbe

× *Chionoscilla* (*Asparagaceae*)

§ ***allenii***	ECho EPot SPhx WCot

Chirita (*Gesneriaceae*)

'Aiko'	WDib
'Candy'	WDib
'Chastity'	WDib
'Diane Marie'	WDib
'Erika'	WDib
flavimaculata	WDib
heterotricha	WDib
'Keiko'	WDib
linearifolia	WDib
linearifolia × ***sinensis***	WDib
linearifolia × ***sinensis*** 'Latifolia'	WDib
longgangensis	WDib
'New York'	WDib
sinensis 🏆H1	WDib
- 'Hisako'	WDib
speciosa 'Crûg Cornetto'	WCru
'Stardust'	WDib
'Sweet Dreams'	WDib
tamiana	WDib

Chironia (*Gentianaceae*)

baccifera	SPlb

× *Chitalpa* (*Bignoniaceae*)

tashkentensis	CBcs CEnd EBee EPfP ESwi MTPN WPGP
- 'Morning Cloud'	MBlu
- 'Pink Dawn'	ESwi LRHS MBlu MBri SPad
- Summer Bells = 'Minsum'	CDoC ELon LHop SBig WCot

chives see *Allium schoenoprasum*

Chlidanthus (*Amaryllidaceae*)

fragrans	CCCN ECho EShb SDeJ SEND XLum

Chloranthus (*Chloranthaceae*)

fortunei	CDes CLAP WPGP
- 'Domino'	WCot
japonicus	GBuc WCru
oldhamii	CBct
- B&SWJ 2019	LEdu WCru
serratus	WCru

Chloris (*Poaceae*)

distichophylla	see *Eustachys distichophylla*

Chlorogalum (*Asparagaceae*)

pomeridianum	CFil CLak

Chlorophytum (*Asparagaceae*)

comosum	EShb SEND SVic
- 'Aureomarginata' (v)	SEND
- 'Variegatum' (v) 🏆H1+3	EShb SEND SPre SRms
- 'Vittatum' (v) 🏆H1+3	EShb SRms
krookianum	CCon EBee WCot
macrophyllum	EShb
nepalense B&SWJ 2528	WCru
orchidastrum 'Green Orange'	WCot
saundersiae	CExl

Choisya (*Rutaceae*)

× ***dewitteana*** 'Aztec Pearl' 🏆H4	Widely available
- Golden Gift = 'Lismarty'PBR	LRHS SSpi
- Goldfingers = 'Limo'PBR	CBcs CDul CWGN EBee ELan ELon EPfP EShb LAst LHop LRHS LSRN MBri MGos MRav NEgg NHol NLar NPri SCoo SLim SLon SPer SPoG SWvt
- White Dazzler = 'Londaz'PBR	CDoC CSBt CWGN EBee ELan ELon EPfP EWTr GBin LBuc LHop LLHF LRHS LSRN MBri MGos MPkF NLar NPri NSoo SHil SLim SLon SPoG SRkn WCot WGrn
dumosa	LHop
ternata 🏆H4	Widely available
- Moonshine = 'Walcho'PBR	NLar
- Moonsleeper	see *C. ternata* Sundance
- Snow Flurries = 'Lisflurry'PBR	ELan EPfP LLHF LRHS SPoG
§ - Sundance = 'Lich'PBR 🏆H3	Widely available

Chondrosum (*Poaceae*)

gracile see *Bouteloua gracilis*

Chordospartium see *Carmichaelia*

Chorisia (*Bombacaceae*)

speciosa CCCN EShb SPlb

Chorizema (*Papilionaceae*)

cordatum ♀H1 ECou SVen
dicksonii SPlb

Chronanthus see *Cytisus*

Chrysalidocarpus see *Dypsis*

Chrysanthemopsis see *Rhodanthemum*

Chrysanthemum ✿ (*Asteraceae*)

E.H.Wilson s.n. **new** WCot
'Action Bronze' (22) EPfP
'Agnes Ann' (21d) EWoo MNrw
'Alan Foxall Yellow' (3b) MCms
'Albert's Yellow' (21d) EWoo
'Alec Bedser' (25a) NHal
'Alehmer Rote' (21) LDai MNrw WWEG
'Alex Young' (25b) MCms
'Aline' (21) EShb EWoo MNrw
'Alison' (29c) EWoo MNrw
'Alison's Dad' MNrw
'Allouise' (25b) ♀H3 NHal
'Allouise Pink' (25b) MCms
'Allyson Peace' (14a) MCms NHal
alpinum see *Leucanthemopsis alpina*
'Amber Gigantic' (1) NHal
'Amber Matlock' (24b) MCms
'American Beauty Lemon' (5b) MCms
'American Beauty White' (5b) MCms
'Anastasia' (21c) CHid EBee ECtt ELon GCal LDai LRHS MNrw MRav NSti WHoo WWEG
'Angela Blundell' (19b) WCot
'Angela Cosimini' (25b) MCms
'Angelic' (28) EWoo
'Anne Ratsey' (21) CHVG CPrp CSam MNrw
'Anne, Lady Brocket' (21d) ECtt EWoo MNrw NWsh
'Anthony Peace' (25b) MCms NHal
'Antigua'PBR MCms
'Apollo' H. Shoesmith EWoo LLHF MNrw WCot
'Apollo' (21) EWll LDai NCGa SMrs SPhx WHoo
'Apricot' see *C.* 'Cottage Apricot'
'Apricot Chessington' (25a) MCms NHal
'Apricot Courtier' (24a) MCms NHal
'Apricot Enbee Wedding' see *C.* 'Bronze Enbee Wedding'
arcticum L. see *Arctanthemum arcticum*
argenteum see *Tanacetum argenteum*
'Astro' (25b) NHal
'Aunt Millicent' (21d) ♀H4 EWoo LLHF MNrw NHal SPhx WCot
'Balcombe Perfection' (5a) MCms NHal
balsamita see *Tanacetum balsamita*
Barbara = 'Yobarbara' (22) NHal
'Beacon' (5a) ♀H2 NHal
'Beechcroft' (29Rub) **new** MNrw
'Belle' (21d) EWoo MNrw
'Beppie Bronze' (29e) GBBs MCms
'Beppie Pink' (29c) **new** GBBs
'Beppie Purple' (29e) GBBs MCms
'Beppie Red' (29e) GBBs MCms
'Beppie Rose' (29e) MCms
'Beppie Yellow' (29e) MCms
'Best Man' (29d) MCms
'Betty' (21) EWoo
'Bill Holden' (14a) MCms NHal
'Bill Wade' (25a) NHal
'Billy Bell' (15a) MCms NHal
'Blanche Poitevene' (5b) EMal
'Bob Green' (13b) MCms
'Bobby Swinburn' (13b) NHal
'Branroyal'PBR **new** NLar
Bravo = 'Yobra' (22c) ♀H3 NHal
* 'Breitner's Supreme' MNrw WWEG
'Brennpunkt' EWoo MNrw SMrs
'Bretforton Road' MNrw WCot
'Brierton Violet' (17b) NHal
'Brightness' (21) EWoo MNrw
'Bronze Cassandra' (5b) ♀H2 MCms NHal
'Bronze Dee Gem' (29c) MCms NHal
§ 'Bronze Elegance' (28b) CTri EBee ECtt EWoo LDai LRHS MNrw NBir NGdn NSti NWsh SMrs SRms WBor
§ 'Bronze Enbee Wedding' (29d) ♀H3 NHal
'Bronze Gigantic' (1) NHal
'Bronze Matlock' (24b) NHal
'Bronze Max Riley' (23b) ♀H3 MCms NHal
'Bronze Mayford Perfection' (5a) ♀H2 NHal
'Bronze Mei-kyo' see *C.* 'Bronze Elegance'
'Bronze William Florentine' (15a) MCms
'Brown Eyes' (21) EWoo
'Bunty' (28) SMad
burnt orange-flowered CAby CPrp MNrw
'Burntwood Belle' (3b) **new** MCms
'Buxton Ruby' EWoo
'Capel Manor' EBee EWoo MNrw WCot
'Carlene Welby' (25b) MCms
'Carmine Blush' (21) ♀H4 EBee EWoo MNrw SMrs SPhx WCot
'Casablanca' (25a) **new** NHal
'Cassandra' (5b) ♀H2 MCms NHal
'Charles Tandy Yellow' (15b) MCms
'Chelsea Physic Garden' CAby EWoo IGor LLHF MNrw SMrs SPhx WCot WWEG
'Chempak Rose' (14b) MCms
'Cherry Chessington' (25a) MCms NHal
'Cherry Riley's Dynasty' (14a) MCms
Chesapeake = 'Yochesapeake'PBR (10a) MCms NHal
'Chestnut Talbot Maid' (29c) MCms
'Chestnut Talbot Parade' (29c) ♀H3 MCms
'Chloe Ball' (13b) **new** MCms
'Christopher Lawson' (24b) MCms NHal
'Cinderella' WMnd
cinerariifolium see *Tanacetum cinerariifolium*
'Clapham Delight' (23a) MCms NHal
'Clara Curtis' (21d) Widely available
'Clare Louise' (24b) MCms
'Clarksdale' (15b) MCms
'Colsterworth' MNrw

	'Contralto' (22)	EWoo
	'Coral Reef' (10b)	MCms NHal
	'Corinna' (21d) **new**	GBin
	'Cornetto' (25b)	MCms NHal
	corymbosum	see *Tanacetum corymbosum*
§	'Cottage Apricot' (21)	EBee ECGP EWoo LDai LRHS MBNS MLHP MNrw MRav
	'Cottage Bronze'	MNrw
	'Cottage Lemon'	MNrw
	'Cottage Pink'	see *C.* 'Emperor of China'
	'Cottage Yellow'	EWoo SMrs
	'Coup de Soleil'	WCot
	'Courtier' (24a)	NHal
	'Cousin Joan'	EWoo LDai LLHF MNrw NCGa WCot
	'Cream Duke of Kent' (1)	NHal
	'Cream Elegance' (9c)	NHal
	'Cream John Hughes' (3b)	MCms
	'Cream Patricia Millar' (14b)	NHal
	'Cream Talbot Maid' (29c)	MCms
	'Cream West Bromwich' (14a)	MCms
	Dana = 'Yodana' (25b) ♀H3	NHal
	Dance = 'Fidance' PBR	MCms
	'Dance Red' **new**	MCms
	Dance Salmon = 'Fidancesal' PBR	MCms
	'Dance Sunny'	MCms
	'Dance White'	MCms
	'Daniel Cooper' (21)	EWoo MNrw SBch
	'Daphne' (21d)	EWoo
	'Darren Pugh' (3b)	MCms NHal
	'Dee Gem' (29c) ♀H3	MCms NHal
	'Delta' (5b)	NHal
	'Delta Copper Bronze'	NHal
	'Delta Crimson' (29d)	NHal
	'Delta Yellow' (29)	NHal
	'Dennis Gill' (25b)	MCms
	'Deva Glow' (25a)	MCms
	'Dezianne'	MCms
	'Dezianne Yellow'	MCms
	'Dixter Orange'	GCal SMad
§	'Doctor Tom Parr' (21c)	CExl ELan EWoo LHop MNrw
	'Don't Start' (7a)	MCms
	'Doreen Hall' (15a)	NHal
	'Doreen Statham' (4b)	MCms NHal
	'Doris Ozols' (25a)	NHal
	'Dorothy Stone' (25b)	NHal
	'Dorridge Crystal' (24a)	MCms NHal
	'Dublin'	MCms
	'Duchess of Edinburgh' (21d)	CFis CPrp ECtt ELan EPfP EShb EWoo GBin LRHS MNrw NSoo SDys SMrs SPhx XLum
	'Duke of Kent' (1)	NHal
	'Dulwich Pink'	EWoo WCot
	'Dutchy' PBR	MCms
	'Early Yellow'	EWoo MNrw WCot
	'Edelweiss' (21)	CAby
	'Edward Shaw' (5a)	MCms
	'Egret' (23b)	MCms NHal
	'Elegance' (9c)	NHal
	'Elizabeth Lawson' (5b)	NHal
	'Elizabeth Shoesmith' (1)	NHal
	'Ellen' (29c)	NHal
§	'Emperor of China' (21)	CAby CElw ECtt EWoo IGor MNrw MRav NHal SMrs SPhx WBor WCot WMnd WWEG XLum
	'Enbee Wedding' (29d) ♀H3	MCms NHal
	'Energy' PBR	MCms
	'Esther' (21d)	EWoo MNrw NCGa SMad SMrs
	'Ethel Edwards' (25b)	NHal
	'Eva Allen' (25b)	MCms
	'Fairweather' (3b)	MCms NHal
	'Fairweather Peach' (3b)	MCms
	'Feeling Green Dark' PBR	MCms
	foeniculaceum misapplied	see *Argyranthemum foeniculaceum* misapplied
	foeniculaceum (Willd.) Desf.	see *Argyranthemum foeniculaceum* (Willd.) Webb & Sch. Bip.
	'Fondant'	NHal
	'Foxtrot' PBR ♀H3	NLar
	'French Rose' **new**	MNrw
	'Froggy' PBR	MCms
	frutescens	see *Argyranthemum frutescens*
	'Gala Burgundy'	EPfP NLar
	'Gambit' (24a)	NHal
	'Geof Brady' (5a)	NHal
	'Geoff Aird' (15b) **new**	NHal
	'Geoff Amos' (3b)	MCms NHal
	'Geoff Brady' (5a)	MCms
	'Geoff Sylvester' (25a)	NHal
	'George Griffiths' (24b) ♀H3	MCms NHal
	'Gigantic' (1)	NHal
	'Gillette' (23b)	MCms
	'Ginger Nut' (25b)	MCms
	'Ginger Nut Yellow' (25b)	MCms
I	'Gladys' (12a)	EBee
	'Gladys Emerson' (3b)	MCms NHal
	'Gold Enbee Wedding' (29d) ♀H3	MCms
	'Gold Marianne'	XLum
	'Golden Cassandra' (5b) ♀H2	MCms NHal
	'Golden Chalice' (12a)	NHal
	'Golden Courtier' (24a)	MCms NHal
	'Golden Gigantic' (1)	NHal
	'Golden Mayford Perfection' (5a) ♀H2	MCms NHal
	'Golden Plover' (22)	NHal
	'Golden Rain' (10a) ♀H2	MCms NHal
	'Golden Wedding' (21)	MNrw
	'Golden William Florentine' (15a)	MCms
	'Golden Woolman's Glory' (7a)	NHal
	'Goldengreenheart' (21)	ECtt EShb EWoo LLHF MNrw SMrs WHoo
	'Goldmarianne' (21)	GBin
	'Grandchild' (21c) ♀H4	LLHF MNrw NHal SMrs
	'Hanenburg'	NHal
	haradjanii	see *Tanacetum haradjanii*
	'Harold Lawson' (5a)	MCms NHal
	'Harry Gee' (1)	NHal
	'Harry Tolley' (14b)	MCms
*	'Hazel' (21)	EWoo
	'Heather James' (3b)	MCms NHal
	'Heide' (29c) ♀H3	NHal
	'Helen Louise' (25b) **new**	MCms
	'Herbstbrokat'	GBin XLum
	'Hesketh Knight' (5b) ♀H2	MCms NHal
	'Hoagy' (29d) **new**	NHal
	'Holly Elizabeth' (14a) **new**	MCms
	Holly = 'Yoholly' (22b) ♀H3	NHal
	'Honey Enbee Wedding' (29d)	NHal
	'Horningsea Pink' (19d)	ECGP WBor
	'Imp' (21e)	EWoo

'Innocence' (21)	CFis ECtt ELan EWoo IGor MNrw MRav NGdn WHoo
'Isabellrosa' (21)	GBin
'Janet South'	EWoo MNrw
'Jante Wells' (21b)	MNrw WBor WWEG
'Jenny Wren' (12a)	NHal
'Jessie Cooper' misapplied	see *C.* 'Mrs Jessie Cooper' (21)
'Jessie Habgood' (1)	NHal
'Jimmy Tranter' (14b)	NHal
'Joan Waugh' (14b) **new**	MCms
'John Harrison' (25b)	MCms NHal
'John Hughes' (3b)	MCms NHal
'John Lowry' (24a)	MCms NHal
'John Riley' (14a)	NHal
'John Wingfield' (14b)	MCms NHal
'John Wingfield Honey' (14b)	MCms
'John Wingfield Pearl' (14b)	MCms
'Jolie Rose' **new**	WCot
'Joyce Fountain' (24a)	MCms NHal
'Joyce Frieda' (13b)	MCms NHal
'Julia' (28)	EPfP MNrw
'Julia Peterson'	MHer WCot WHoo
'Julie Lagravère' (28)	EWoo MNrw SMrs WPtf XLum
'Karen Taylor' (29c) ♀H3	NHal
'Kath Stephenson' (7b)	MCms NHal
'Kath Stephenson Honey' (7b)	MCms
'Kath Stephenson Peach' (7b)	MCms
'Kath Stephenson Primrose' (7b)	MCms
'Kath Stephenson Rose' (7b)	MCms NHal
'Kath Stephenson Salmon' (7b)	MCms
'Katie Jane' (7b)	NHal
'Kay Woolman' (13b)	MCms NHal
'Kay Woolman Yellow' (13b)	MCms
'Killerton Tangerine' **new**	MNrw
'Kiyominomeisui'	MCms NHal
'Kleiner Bernstein'	MNrw WCot
'La Damoiselle' **new**	WCot
§ 'Lady in Pink' (21)	EWoo LDai MNrw
'Lady Manito'	EWoo
'Lakelanders' (3b)	NHal
'Lancashire Fold' (1)	NHal
'Leo' (21b)	EWoo
leucanthemum	see *Leucanthemum vulgare*
'Lexy'PBR	MCms
'Lexy Red'PBR	MCms
'Lilac Chessington' (25a)	MCms NHal
Linda = 'Lindayo' (22c) ♀H3	NHal
'L'Innocence' (21)	CAby
'Little Dorrit' (21f)	EWoo
'Lollipop'PBR	MCms
'Lorna Wood' (13b)	MCms NHal
'Louise' (25b)	MNrw
'Louise Park' (24a)	MCms
'Lucy' (29a) ♀H3	MCms NHal
'Lucy Simpson' (21d)	EWoo SBch
'Lundy' (2)	NHal
'Lydia Mannion' (7b)	MCms
'Lynn Johnson' (15a)	MCms NHal
Lynn = 'Yolynn' (22c) ♀H3	NHal
macrophyllum	see *Tanacetum macrophyllum* (Waldst. & Kit.) Sch.Bip.

'Malcolm Perkins' (25a)	MCms
'Mancetta Comet' (29a)	NHal
'Mancetta Symbol' (5a)	MCms
'Mandarin'	EWoo
maresii	see *Rhodanthemum hosmariense*
'Margaret' (29c) ♀H3	NHal WCot
'Margery Fish' **new**	MNrw
'Marion' (25a)	LDai MNrw WCot
'Mark Woolman' (1)	NHal
'Mary' (21f)	EWoo LDai MNrw NHal
'Mary Stoker' (21d)	CAby ECtt ELan ELon EPfP EWoo LPio LRHS MNrw MPie MRav NCGa NHal NLar NSoo WCAu WMnd WWEG
'Mary's Miracle' (24a) **new**	MCms
'Matador' (14a)	NHal
'Matlock' (24b)	NHal
'Mauve Gem' (21f) ♀H3	MNrw NHal
mawii	see *Rhodanthemum gayanum*
'Max Riley' (23b) ♀H3	MCms NHal
maximum misapplied	see *Leucanthemum* × *superbum*
maximum Ramond	see *Leucanthemum maximum* (Ramond) DC.
'Maxine Charlton' (24b) **new**	MCms
'Maxine Johnson' (25b)	NHal
'May Shoesmith' (5a) ♀H2	NHal
'Maybach' **new**	MCms
'Mayford Perfection' (5a) ♀H2	MCms NHal
'Mei-kyō' (28b)	CFis CMea CTri ECtt EWoo IGor MNrw SMrs SRms WBor WHil WWEG
'Membury' (24b)	NHal
'Michelle Preston' (13b)	NHal
'Millennium' (25b) ♀H3	MCms NHal
'Millie Mathews' (14b) **new**	MCms
'Misty Cream' (25b)	MCms
'Misty Golden' (25b)	MCms
'Misty Lemon' (25b)	MCms
'Moonlight' (29d/K)	MRav
'Morning Star' (12a)	NHal
§ 'Mrs Jessie Cooper' (21)	CAby CHGN EWoo GBee GQue LDai MNrw NBir NLar SDys SMrm SMrs SRms WCot WHoo WPtf
'Mrs Jessie Cooper No 1'	NCGa NWsh
'Mrs Jessie Cooper No 2'	MNrw
'Muriel Odell' (7b)	MCms
'Music' (23b)	NHal
'Muxton Sable' (10a)	MCms NHal
'Myss Carol' (29c) ♀H3	NHal
'Myss Debbie' (29e)	NHal
'Myss Dorothy' (29c) **new**	NHal
'Myss Eliza' (29c) **new**	MCms
'Myss Goldie' (29c)	MCms
'Myss Jem' (29e)	NHal
'Myss Jem Red' (29e)	NHal
'Myss Marion' (29c) ♀H3	EWoo NHal
'Myss Rihanna' (29c) **new**	MCms
'Myss Saffron' (29c) ♀H3	NHal
'Nancy Perry' (21d)	CSam EWoo GBee MNrw MRav XLum
'Nantyderry Sunshine' (28b) ♀H4	CPrp EBee ELon LLHF LRHS MNrw NWsh SPhx WBor WCot WMnd WWEG
'Naru' (9c)	NHal
'Natalie Sarah' (29d) ♀H3	MCms NHal
'Nell Gwynn' (21d) ♀H3	EWoo MNrw NHal
Nicole = 'Yonicole' (22c) ♀H3	NHal

nipponicum	see *Nipponanthemum nipponicum*
'Olwyn' (4b)	MCms
'Orange Allouise' (25b)	MCms NHal
'Orange Enbee Wedding' (29d)	NHal
pacificum	see *Ajania pacifica*
'Paloma Redeye' (29d) **new**	NHal
'Paloma Regent' (29d) **new**	NHal
parthenium	see *Tanacetum parthenium*
'Patricia Millar' (14b)	MCms NHal
'Patricia Millar Cerise' (14b)	MCms
'Patricia Millar Coral' (14b)	MCms
'Patricia Millar Orange' (14b)	MCms NHal
'Patricia Millar Yellow' (14b)	MCms NHal
'Paul Boissier' (30Rub)	CAby CFis ECtt EWoo LDai MNrw NSti SMrs SPhx WMnd
'Pauline White' (15a)	MCms
'Peach Courtier' (24a)	NHal
'Peach Enbee Wedding' (29d) ♀H3	NHal
'Peach John Wingfield' (14b)	MCms NHal
'Peach Patricia Millar' (14b)	MCms
'Pearl Celebration' (24a)	MCms
'Pennine Bullion'	NHal
'Pennine Gift' (29c)	NHal
'Pennine Marie' (29a) ♀H3	MCms
'Pennine Oriel' (29a) ♀H3	MCms NHal
'Pennine Point' (19c)	NHal
'Pennine Polo' (29d) ♀H3	NHal
'Pennine Ranger' (29d)	NHal
'Pennine Swan' (29c)	NHal
'Pennine Sweetheart' (29c) ♀H3 **new**	MNrw
'Pennine Toy' (19d)	NHal
'Penny's Yellow'	LHop LLHF
'Perry's Peach' (21a) ♀H4	EWoo LDai LLHF MNrw NCGa NHal NPer SPhx
'Peter Rowe' (23b)	MCms NHal
'Peter Sare' (21d)	LRHS
'Peterkin'	CMac ECtt ELon EWoo LRHS WWEG
'Pink Anemone'	EWoo
'Pink Duke of Kent' (1)	NHal
'Pink John Wingfield' (14b)	NHal
'Pink Progression'	see *C.* 'Lady in Pink'
'Pink Splendour' (10a) ♀H2	NHal
'Poesie' **new**	WCot
'Polar Gem' (3a)	MCms NHal
'Pot Black' (14b)	MCms NHal
'President Osaka'	MNrw
'Primrose Allouise' (24b) ♀H3	NHal
'Primrose Chessington' (25a)	MCms
'Primrose Courtier'	see *C.* 'Yellow Courtier'
'Primrose Dorothy Stone' (25b)	NHal
'Primrose Enbee Wedding' (29d) ♀H3	MCms NHal
'Primrose Fairweather' (3b)	MCms
'Primrose Jessie Habgood' (1)	NHal
'Primrose John Hughes' (3b)	MCms NHal
'Primrose Mayford Perfection' (5a) ♀H2	NHal
'Primrose Sam Vinter' (5a)	NHal
'Primrose West Bromwich' (14a)	MCms NHal
'Princess' (21d)	LLHF
'Promise' (25a)	NHal
'Purleigh White' (28b)	ECtt ELon EWoo LDai MLHP MNrw NSti SMrs WCot WWEG
'Purple Chempak Rose' (14b)	MCms NHal
'Ralph Lambert' (1)	NHal
'Raquel' (21)	MNrw
'Red Balcombe Perfection' (5a)	MCms NHal
'Red Chempak Rose' (14b)	MCms
'Red Louise Park' (14a) **new**	MCms
'Red Mayford Perfection' (5a)	MCms NHal
'Red Pennine Gift' (29c)	NHal
'Red Regal Mist' (25b)	MCms
'Red Shirley Model' (3a)	MCms NHal
'Redbreast' (12a)	NHal
'Regal Mist Purple' (25b)	MCms NHal
I 'Rhumba' **new**	WCot
'Riley's Dynasty' (14a)	MCms
'Ringdove' (12a)	NHal
'Rita McMahon' (29d) ♀H3	NHal
'Robeam' (9c) ♀H2	NHal
Robin = 'Yorobi' (22c)	NHal
'Roen Sarah' (29c)	NHal
'Rose Enbee Wedding' (29d)	MCms NHal
'Rose Madder'	EWoo LPot MNrw WCot
'Rose Mayford Perfection' (5a) ♀H2	MCms NHal
'Rose Patricia Millar' (14b)	NHal
'Rosetta'	MNrw WCot
'Rosy Yoigloo'PBR	SHar
'Roy Bevan' (29d)	MCms
'Roy Coopland' (5b) ♀H2	MCms
'Royal Command' (21a)	MNrw SMrs WCot
'Royal Sport'	EWoo
rubellum	see *C. zawadskii*
'Ruby Enbee Wedding' (29d) ♀H3	MCms NHal
'Ruby Glow' (7b)	MCms
'Ruby Mound' (21c) ♀H3	CAby EWoo LLHF MNrw NHal SDys SHar SMrs SPhx WCot
'Ruby Raynor' (21) ♀H4	EWoo MNrw NHal SDys SMrs WCot
'Rumpelstilzchen' (21d)	CMea ECtt EWoo MNrw NWsh
'Salhouse Dream' (10a) **new**	NHal
'Salhouse Joy' (10a)	MCms NHal
'Salmon Allouise' (25b)	NHal
'Salmon Enbee Wedding' (29d) ♀H3	NHal
'Salmon Fairweather' (3b)	MCms
'Salmon John Wingfield' (24b)	MCms
'Salmon Pauline White' (15a)	MCms
'Salmon Talbot Maid' (29c)	MCms
'Salmon Talbot Parade' (29c) ♀H3	MCms
'Sam Vinter' (5a)	NHal
'Samba' **new**	WCot
'Sarah Louise' (25b)	NHal
'Savanna Charlton' (25a)	MCms
'Sea Urchin' (21f) ♀H3	MNrw NHal SDys
'Seatons Galaxy' (10a) **new**	NHal
'Senkyo Kenshin' (10a) **new**	MCms

'Sheena' (9f/10)	NHal
'Sheffield'	EWoo
'Sheila Coles' (7b)	MCms NHal
'Sheila Harris' (3b) **new**	MCms
'Shenley Orange'	EWoo
'Shining Light' (21f)	EWoo LLHF MNrw
'Shirley Primrose' (1)	NHal
'Sonnenschein'	LHop
'Sound'	MCms
'Southway Sheba' (29d) 🏆^{H3}	MCms NHal
'Southway Sheba Bronze' (29d)	MCms NHal
'Southway Shimmer' (29d)	NHal
'Southway Shiraz' (29d)	NHal
'Southway Sloe' (29d) **new**	MCms
'Southway Snoopy' (29d)	NHal
'Southway Spectacular' (29d) **new**	NHal
'Southway Strontium' (29d)	NHal
'Spartan Canary'	EWoo
'Spartan Display'	EWoo
'Spartan Linnet'	EWoo
'Spartan Raspberry' (21d)	EWoo
'Spartan Seagull' (21d)	EWoo MNrw
'Stallion'^{PBR}	MCms
'Starlet' (21f)	EWoo LLHF NHal
'Stockton' (3b) 🏆^{H2}	MCms NHal
'Stratford Pink' (21d)	EWoo
'Suffolk Pink'	ECtt EShb EWoo MNrw
'Sundae'^{PBR} (22c)	EPfP
Sundoro = 'Yosun' (22d)	NHal
Sunny Igloo = 'Sunny Yoigloo'^{PBR}	SHar
Swan = 'Fiswan'^{PBR}	MCms
'Syllabub' 🏆^{H3}	ECtt MNrw
'Symphony' (10a)	MCms NHal
'Talbot Maid' (29c)	MCms
'Talbot Parade' (29c) 🏆^{H3}	MCms
'Talbot Parade Pink' (29c)	MCms
'Tapestry Rose' (21d)	CMea EWoo LDai MNrw NCGa SPhx WBor WHoo
'Terracotta' (29c) **new**	NHal
'Terry Brook' (29e)	MCms NHal
'Terry Morris' (7b)	MCms
'Thoroughbred' (24a)	NHal
'Tickle Pink' (29f/K)	MNrw
'Tom Parr'	see *C.* 'Doctor Tom Parr'
'Tom Snowball' (3b)	MCms NHal
'Topsy' (21c)	ELon EWoo
'Tracy Waller' (24b)	NHal
'Trident' (2) **new**	NHal
Triumph = 'Yotri' (22)	NHal
uliginosum	see *Leucanthemella serotina*
'Uri'	CAby CFis EWoo SPhx
'Vagabond Prince'	ELon EWoo MNrw NCGa WBor WHoo
'Venice' (24b)	NHal
'Venus' (21)	NCGa WCot
'Venus One'	EWoo LDai MNrw NHal SPhx
'Vibrant' (9c) 🏆^{H2}	NHal
'Viking' **new**	MCms
'Vulcano Dark'	MCms
'Warm Yoigloo'^{PBR}	SHar SPoG
'Wedding Day' (29k)	EWoo MNrw
'Wedding Sunshine' (21)	LDai MNrw
welwitschii	see *Glebionis segetum*
'Wembley' (24b)	MCms NHal
'Wendy Tench' (21d)	ECtt EWoo NWsh
'West Bromwich' (14a)	NHal
weyrichii	EBee ECho LEdu NLar SBch SRms WWEG
'White Allouise' (25b) 🏆^{H3}	MCms NHal
'White Beppie' (29e)	GBBs MCms
'White Cassandra' (5b)	MCms NHal
'White Enbee Wedding' (29d)	MCms NHal
'White Fairweather' (3b)	MCms NHal
'White Gem' (21f)	NHal
'White Gloss' (21e)	LLHF MNrw
'White Pearl Celebration' (24a)	MCms
'White Tower' (27)	EWoo MNrw
'William Florentine' (15a)	MCms NHal
'Wills Wonderful' (21d)	EWoo
'Win' (9c)	NHal
'Winning's Red' (21)	EWoo LHop NCGa SMad WCot
'Wizard'^{PBR}	EPfP
'Woolman's Glory' (7a)	MCms NHal
'Woolman's Glory Red' (7a)	MCms
'Woolman's Star' (3a)	MCms NHal
'Woolman's Venture' (14b)	MCms NHal
'Yellow Allouise' (25b)	MCms
'Yellow American Beauty' (5b) 🏆^{H2}	MCms
'Yellow Billy Bell' (15a)	NHal
'Yellow Clapham Delight' (23a)	MCms NHal
§ 'Yellow Courtier' (24a)	MCms NHal
'Yellow Duke of Kent' (1)	NHal
'Yellow Egret' (23b)	NHal
'Yellow Ellen' (29c)	NHal
'Yellow Enbee Wedding' (29d)	MCms NHal
'Yellow Heide' (29c) 🏆^{H3}	NHal
'Yellow John Hughes' (3b) 🏆^{H2}	MCms NHal
'Yellow John Wingfield' (14b)	MCms NHal
'Yellow May Shoesmith' (5a)	NHal
'Yellow Mayford Perfection' (5a) 🏆^{H2}	NHal
'Yellow Pennine Oriel' (29a) 🏆^{H3}	MCms NHal
'Yellow Spider' (10a)	MCms
'Yellow Starlet' (21f)	EWoo LLHF MNrw
'Yellow Woolman's Glory' (7a)	MCms
yezoense 🏆^{H4}	LRHS MNrw SRms
- B&SWJ 10872	WCru
- 'Roseum'	ECtt
'Yonashville'	SRms
§ ***zawadskii***	CMac

Chrysogonum (*Asteraceae*)

virginianum	CMea CPrp EBee EWes LRHS MRav SBch SPer WWEG

Chrysolepis (*Fagaceae*)

chrysophylla	CMCN

Chrysopogon (*Poaceae*)

gryllus	EBee WPGP

Chrysopsis (*Asteraceae*)

§ ***mariana***	WOld
villosa (Pursh) Nutt. ex DC.	see *Heterotheca villosa*

Chrysosplenium (*Saxifragaceae*)

davidianum	CBre CSam EBee EWld GCal GJos GKev IMou ITim LRHS NBir NLar NSla WBor WCot WCru WMoo WPtf WSHC
- SBEC 233	CExl
flagelliferum B&SWJ 8902	WCru
hebetatum B&SWJ 9835	WCru
lanuginosum var. ***formosanum*** B&SWJ 6979	ESwi WCru
macrophyllum	CDes CExl EBee EPPr EWld GCal GKev GMaP IGor IMou LEdu MMHG MPie MTPN SHar WBor WCot WCru WSHC
macrostemon var. ***shiobarense*** B&SWJ 6173	WCru
oppositifolium	NMir WSFF WShi

Chusquea (*Poaceae*)

breviglumis misapplied	see *C. culeou* 'Tenuis'
culeou ♀H4	CAbb CBcs CDoC CEnd CEnt CHEx CHid EAmu ENBC EPfP EUJe IDee LEdu MAvo MGos MMoz MWht SBig SPlb SSta WJun
- 'Breviglumis'	see *C. culeou* 'Tenuis'
- 'Purple Splendour'	WJun
§ - 'Tenuis'	ERod
- weeping	CDTJ
cumingii	CBcs WJun WPGP
delicatula from Machu Picchu, Peru	CExl CFil
gigantea	CDTJ CEnt CExl CFil EPfP ERod ESwi MMoz MWht SBig WJun WPGP
montana	CBcs
mulleri F&M 104A from Mexico	CExl WPGP
nigricans	CFil
quila	MMoz

Cibotium (*Cibotiaceae*)

barometz new	EAmu

Cicerbita (*Asteraceae*)

BWJ 7891 from China	CSpe WCru
CC 6912 new	ITim
§ ***alpina***	GAbr NBid SPlb
bourgaei	LRHS
macrorhiza CC 6912 new	GKev
plumieri	EWes GAbr IFro WCot WMoo WPtf
- 'Blott' (v)	WCot

Cichorium (*Asteraceae*)

intybus	CArn CHby CPom CPrp CSpe ELan ELau GPoy LHop MBel MHoo MNHC NBir NCGa NMir NPri SIde SPer SPlb SPoG SRms SVic WHrl WJek WMoo WSHC
- f. ***album***	EBee ECtt EWTr GKin LHop LRHS MBel MCot MHoo NBir NCGa SBea SHar SWat
- 'Palla Rossa' ♀H3 new	SRms
- 'Roseum'	ECtt ELan EWTr GKin LHop LRHS MHoo NBir NCGa NPnk SBea SHar SPoG SWat WHrl

Cicuta (*Apiaceae*)

virosa	LLWG

Cimicifuga see *Actaea*

acerina	see *Actaea japonica*
americana	see *Actaea podocarpa*
cordifolia (DC.) Torrey & A.Gray	see *Actaea cordifolia*
cordifolia Pursh	see *Actaea podocarpa*
foetida	see *Actaea cimicifuga*
racemosa var. ***cordifolia***	see *Actaea cordifolia*
- 'Purpurea'	see *Actaea simplex* Atropurpurea Group
ramosa	see *Actaea simplex* 'Prichard's Giant'
rubifolia	see *Actaea cordifolia*
simplex var. ***matsumurae***	see *Actaea matsumurae*

Cineraria (*Asteraceae*)

maritima	see *Senecio cineraria*

Cinnamomum (*Lauraceae*)

camphora	CBcs CExl CHEx IGor SPlb WHfH

Cionura (*Asclepiadaceae*)

oreophila	ELan GCal SKHP WPGP WSHC

Circaea (*Onagraceae*)

alpina	EBee
lutetiana	WHer
- 'Caveat Emptor' (v)	NBid WCot

Cirsium (*Asteraceae*)

anartiolepis F&M 252	WPGP
arvense	WSFF
I ***atroroseum***	SWat
canum new	GQue
diacantha	see *Ptilostemon diacantha*
eriophorum	LDai
helenioides	see *C. heterophyllum*
§ ***heterophyllum***	CHid CPom EBee EWld GQue LDai LEdu MAvo NChi NLar SHar WHil WPGP
- PAB 067 new	LEdu
japonicum 'Early Pink Beauty'	LDai
- 'Mura-kumo' (v)	WCot
- 'Pink Beauty'	MHol SPhx WWEG
- 'Rose Beauty'	EBee LRHS
'Mount Etna'	CMHG EBee ELan GKin GQue LHop LRHS MBNS MMuc MSpe NDov NGdn SEND WPGP WWEG
oleraceum	LEdu LRHS NBid NLar
purpuratum	WPGP
rivulare 'Atropurpureum'	Widely available
spinosissimum	SBrt
tuberosum	CAby LEdu NDov SKHP SPhx
vulgare	WSFF

Cissus (*Vitaceae*)

antarctica ♀H1	CCCN EShb SEND
pedata B&SWJ 2371	WCru
rhombifolia ♀H1	EOHP EShb SEND
§ ***striata***	CBcs CDoC CHEx CMac CWCL EBee ELon EShb IBoy LRHS MRav SEND SLim SWvt WSHC

Cistus ✿ (Cistaceae)

	acutifolius misapplied	see *C. inflatus, C.* × *pulverulentus*
	× ***aguilarii***	CBcs CHEx CSBt CTri LAst MRav SPhx WSHC
	- 'Maculatus' ♀H3	CDoC CDul CExl CHel CSam EBee ELan EPfP LRHS LSRN MMuc NLar SCoo SMad SPer SPoG SWvt WKif WPGP WSpi
	albidus	CArn SVen WKif XSen
	algarvensis	see *Halimium ocymoides*
	'Ann Baker'	SLPl
	'Anne Palmer'	see *C.* × *fernandesiae* 'Anne Palmer'
	× ***argenteus*** 'Blushing Peggy Sammons'	ELan NLar SVen XSen
	- Golden Treasure = 'Nepond' (v)	SWvt
	- 'Paper Moon'	EBee LSRN NLar SVen
§	- 'Peggy Sammons' ♀H3	CDoC EBee ELan EPfP EWTr LBMP LPot LRHS LSRN MAsh MGos MOWG MWat NLar SCoo SEND SLim SPer SWvt WHar WSHC XSen
	- 'Silver Ghost'	EPfP LRHS SLim SVen
	- 'Silver Pink' ambig.	CBar CBcs CDoC CDul CWib EBee ECtt ELan EPfP LRHS MAsh MBri MGos MRav MSwo MWat NBir NLar NPri SEND SHil SLim SPer SPoG SSta
	- 'Stripey'	XSen
	'Blanche'	see *C. ladanifer* 'Blanche'
	× ***bornetianus*** 'Jester'	CSBt EBee EPfP LRHS MAsh MBri NLar SHil SVen
	× ***canescens***	SVen XSen
	- f. ***albus***	CWib WKif XSen
§	***clusii***	NLar
	- subsp. ***multiflorus***	XSen
	× ***corbariensis***	see *C.* × *hybridus*
	creticus	CDoC CExl CMac CSam ELau LAst LRHS MAsh MBri MGos MOWG NLar SHil SLon SPoG SRms SVen SWvt WKif WPGP WSpi
	- subsp. ***corsicus***	XSen
§	- subsp. ***creticus***	EBee ELan ELon EPfP MRav SCoo SPer
	× ***crispatus***	XSen
§	- 'Warley Rose'	GMaP SIgm WKif XLum
	crispus misapplied	see *C.* × *pulverulentus, C.* × *purpureus*
§	***crispus*** L.	EBee ELan SEND SGol
	- 'Prostratus'	see *C. crispus* L.
	- 'Sunset'	see *C.* × *pulverulentus* 'Sunset'
§	× ***cyprius*** ♀H4	CArn ELan EPfP GBin LRHS MGos MJak MRav MWat SDix SEND SPer SRms SWvt WSpi
§	- var. ***ellipticus*** 'Elma' ♀H3	ELan EPfP LRHS MAsh NLar SPer XSen
§	× ***dansereaui***	CMac CSBt CWib LRHS NLar SVen SWvt
	- 'Decumbens' ♀H4	CDul CTri CTsd EBee ELan EPfP LHop LRHS MAsh MBNS MBri MJak MRav MSwo NLar SAPC SCoo SHil SPer SPhx SPoG SWvt WPGP
	- 'Jenkyn Place'	CDoC EBee GMaP IVic LSRN MBNS NLar SLPl SPer SPoG WKif
	× ***dubius***	SVen XSen
	'Elma'	see *C.* × *cyprius* var. *ellipticus* 'Elma'
	'Enigma'	CDoC
§	× ***fernandesiae*** 'Anne Palmer'	EBee EPfP LLHF LRHS MAsh NLar SPoG SRGP
	× ***florentinus*** misapplied	see × *Halimiocistus* 'Ingwersenii'
	× ***florentinus*** ambig.	SVen XLum
§	× ***florentinus*** Lam.	GMaP XSen
	- 'Fontfroide'	MMuc SEND SVen
*	- 'Tramontane'	XSen
	'Gordon Cooper'	EBee LSRN MMuc SPoG
	× ***heterocalyx*** 'Chelsea Bonnet'	EBee EPfP GMaP MBNS SCoo SEND SLim SPoG XSen
	heterophyllus	SVen
	'Highlights' new	EPfP
	hirsutus Lam. 1786	see *C. inflatus*
	- var. ***psilosepalus*** misapplied	see *C. inflatus*
§	× ***hybridus***	Widely available
	- 'Gold Prize' (v)	CMHG CWGN CWSG ELan MGos NEgg NLar SWvt WGrn
	- Little Miss Sunshine = 'Dunnecis' (v)	EBee LBMP LBuc LRHS MAsh MBri SHil SPoG SRms SWvt
	- Rospico = 'Rencis'PBR (v)	LRHS SIgm
§	***inflatus***	XSen
	ingwerseniana	see × *Halimiocistus* 'Ingwersenii'
	'Jessamy Beauty'	SLPl SVen WIce
	'Jessamy Bride'	SLPl SVen
	'Jessamy Charm'	SPhx
	ladanifer misapplied	see *C.* × *cyprius*
	ladanifer ambig.	CMac SAPC WKif
	ladanifer L. ♀H3	CDoC CDul CSBt CTri ELan EPfP GPoy MRav MSwo SPer SWvt WHar WSpi
§	- 'Blanche'	EBee EPfP EWTr LLHF LSRN NLar SEND SPer SSpi SWvt WKif WSpi
§	- 'Paladin'	LRHS
	- Palhinhae Group	see *C. ladanifer* var. *sulcatus*
	- 'Pat'	ELan EPfP LRHS LSRN MAsh NBir SPer SPoG SSpi
§	- var. ***sulcatus***	ELan EPfP LHop LRHS WCot
	- - f. ***bicolor***	EBee
	lasianthus	see *Halimium lasianthum*
	laurifolius ♀H4	EBee EPfP MGos NBir NEgg NLar SEND SKHP SLPl SPer SVen SWvt WSpi XLum XSen
	- subsp. ***atlanticus***	XSen
	× ***laxus*** 'Snow White'	CDoC CWGN EBee EPfP LAst MGos NLar NPer SLPl SLim SLon
	× ***ledon***	XSen
§	× ***lenis*** 'Grayswood Pink' ♀H4	CDoC CExl CTri CWSG EBee ECrN ELan EPfP EWTr LHop LRHS LSRN MAsh MGos MSwo NLar NSoo SBch SBod SEND SIgm SLim SPer SPlb SVen SWvt XLum
	libanotis	SVen
	- 'Major'	WSpi XSen
	× ***longifolius***	see *C.* × *nigricans*
	× ***loretii*** misapplied	see *C.* × *dansereaui*
	× ***loretii*** Rouy & Foucaud	see *C.* × *stenophyllus*
	× ***lucasii***	XSen
	× ***lusitanicus*** Maund	see *C.* × *dansereaui*
	'Merrist Wood Cream'	see × *Halimiocistus wintonensis* 'Merrist Wood Cream'
	monspeliensis	CAbP CMac EPfP LRHS MAsh MBNS SEND SLon SPer XSen
	- 'Vicar's Mead'	CCCN EPfP MBNS SEND
	monspeliensis × ***salviifolius***	see *C.* × *florentinus* Lam.
§	× ***nigricans***	XSen
	× ***oblongifolius***	XSen
	× ***obtusifolius*** misapplied	see *C.* × *nigricans*
	× ***obtusifolius*** ambig.	EBee ELan LRHS MRav SKHP
	× ***obtusifolius*** Sweet	EPfP EWes WPGP XSen

§	- 'Thrive'	EPfP LRHS MBri MGos SCoo SHil
	ocymoides	see *Halimium ocymoides*
	× ***pagei***	XSen
	'Paladin'	see *C. ladanifer* 'Paladin'
	palhinhae	see *C. ladanifer* var. *sulcatus*
	parviflorus misapplied	see *C.* × *lenis* 'Grayswood Pink'
	parviflorus Lam.	WSHC
	aff. ***parviflorus*** new	MOWG
*	× ***pauranthus*** 'Natacha'	XSen
	'Peggy Sammons'	see *C.* × *argenteus* 'Peggy Sammons'
	× ***platysepalus***	SPhx
	populifolius	CMHG CMac EPfP EWTr LLHF LRHS NLar SGol SPer SWvt
	- var. ***lasiocalyx***	see *C. populifolius* subsp. *major*
§	- subsp. ***major*** 🏆H3	EBee EPfP LRHS LSRN MOWG SKHP WPGP WSpi
	psilosepalus misapplied	see *C. inflatus*
§	× ***pulverulentus***	CExl CTri EBee EPfP MMHG SVen XSen
*	- Delilei Group	XSen
	- - 'Fiona'	XSen
§	- 'Sunset' 🏆H3	Widely available
	- 'Warley Rose'	see *C.* × *crispatus* 'Warley Rose'
§	× ***purpureus*** 🏆H3	Widely available
	- 'Alan Fradd'	CBcs CMac CWSG EBee ECrN ELan EPfP EUJe LHop LPot LRHS LSRN MAsh MCot MGos MSwo MWat NLar NSoo SCoo SEND SGol SHil SLim SPoG SRGP SWvt XLum XSen
	- var. ***argenteus*** f. ***stictus***	EPfP LRHS LSRN SVen XSen
	- 'Betty Taudevin'	see *C.* × *purpureus*
	× ***rodiaei*** 'Jessabel'	EBee EMil EPfP LRHS MAsh NLar SCoo SPer SWvt WPGP
	- 'Jessica'	NLar WSpi
	rosmarinifolius	see *C. clusii*
	'Ruby Cluster'	CCCN LRHS LSRN MMuc NLar
	sahucii	see × *Halimiocistus sahucii*
	salviifolius	CAbP CArn CCCN MOWG SVen XSen
	- 'Avalanche'	MRav WAbe
	'Gold Star'	ELan NLar
	- 'May Snow'	EHoe LBuc LRHS MAsh
	- 'Prostratus'	EBee ELan EPfP LRHS SWvt WPGP WSpi
	'Silver Pink' misapplied	see *C.* × *lenis* 'Grayswood Pink'
	'Silver Pink' ambig.	CHel CMac CWSG EBee ELan NSoo SMad WKif
	× ***skanbergii*** 🏆H3	CHEx CMac CTri CWib ELan EPfP LHop MGos MLHP MOWG MRav MWat NBir NLar SDix SEND SMrm SPer SPoG XLum XSen
	'Snow Fire' 🏆H4	CCCN CDoC EBee ELan EPfP LRHS LSRN MAsh MGos MMuc MWat NLar NPro NSoo SBod SCoo SLPl SWvt WGrn
§	× ***stenophyllus***	CWib EPfP MMuc
	'Stripey'	SVen
	× ***tephreus***	XSen
	'Thrive'	see *C.* × *obtusifolius* 'Thrive'
	tomentosus	see *Helianthemum nummularium* subsp. *tomentosum*
	× ***verguinii***	LHop SDix XSen
	villosus	see *C. creticus* subsp. *creticus*
	wintonensis	see × *Halimiocistus wintonensis*

Citharexylum (*Verbenaceae*)

	quadrangulare Jacq.	see *C. spinosum*
	spicatum	CExl CFil WBor WPGP
§	***spinosum***	CHll

× *Citrofortunella* (*Rutaceae*)

	sp.	CCCN
	floridana 'Eustis' (F)	SPre
§	***microcarpa*** (F) 🏆H1	CCCN CDoC EPfP LRHS NLar SPre
	mitis	see × *C. microcarpa*

citron see *Citrus medica*

Citronella (*Icacinaceae*)

§	***gongonha***	SVen
	mucronata	see *C. gongonha*

Citrullus (*Cucurbitaceae*)

	colocynthis	CArn

Citrus (*Rutaceae*)

	aurantiifolia (F)	CCCN EPfP EUJe SPre SVic
	aurantium 'Seville' (F)	LSRN
	calamondin	see × *Citrofortunella microcarpa*
	'Fukushu' (F)	CCCN
	hystrix	CCCN CDoC ELan LSRN NPla SPre
	jambhiri 'Otahcite' (F)	CCCN
	japonica	see *Fortunella japonica*
	'Kulci' (F)	CCCN
	kumquat	see *Fortunella margarita*
	'La Valette' (F)	CCCN LSRN SEND SPre
	× ***latifolia*** (F/S)	CCCN CDoC EPfP LRHS MREP SPre
	- variegated (v) new	SPre
	limetta	CCCN
	limettoides (F)	CArn
	limon (F)	CHEx EPfP EUJe LRHS LSRN MREP SHil
	'Eureka' (F)	CCCN
	- 'Fino' (F)	CCCN
	- 'Four Seasons' (F)	CCCN LSRN NLar SPre
§	- 'Garey's Eureka' (F)	CDoC ELan EPfP
	- 'Quatre Saisons'	see *C. limon* 'Garey's Eureka'
	- 'Variegata' (F/v) 🏆H1	CCCN
	- 'Verna' (F)	CCCN
	- 'Villa Franca' (F)	SVic
	'Lipo' (F)	CCCN NLar SPre
	madurensis	see *Fortunella japonica*
	medica 'Cidro Digitado'	see *C. medica* var. *digitata*
§	- var. ***digitata*** (F)	SPre
	- 'Ethrog' (F)	SPre
	- var. ***sarcodactylis***	see *C. medica* var. *digitata*
	× ***meyeri***	CHEx
	- 'Meyer' (F) 🏆H1	CBcs CCCN CHll CTri ELan EPfP LRHS LSRN NLar SPer SPre
	microcarpa Philippine lime	see × *Citrofortunella microcarpa*
	mitis	see × *Citrofortunella microcarpa*
	× ***nobilis*** Ortanique Group (F)	CCCN
	× ***paradisi*** (F)	CCCN EUJe MREP SPre SVic
	- 'Golden Special' (F)	SVic
	- 'Star Ruby' (F/S)	CCCN
	'Pursta' (F)	CCCN
	reticulata (F)	CCCN LRHS MREP SPre SVic
	- 'Hernandina' (F)	CCCN
	- Mandarin Group (F)	CDoC EPfP
	- - 'Clementine' (F)	CDoC EPfP LRHS SPre
	- - 'Esbal' (F)	CCCN
	- - 'Nules' (F/S)	CCCN
	- 'Nova'	see *C.* × *tangelo* 'Nova'
	- Satsuma Group	see *C. unshiu*
	- 'Suntina'	see *C.* × *tangelo* 'Nova'
	sinensis (F)	CCCN LRHS SHil SPre SVic

	- 'Fukumoto' (F)	CCCN
	- 'Lane Late' (F)	CCCN
	- 'Navelina' (F/S)	CCCN CDoC SPre
	- 'Sanguinelli' (F)	CCCN
	- 'Valencia' (F)	CCCN SVic
§	× ***tangelo*** 'Nova' (F/S)	CCCN
§	***unshiu*** (F)	SPre
	- 'Miyagawa'	CCCN
	- 'Okitsu' (F/S)	CCCN

Cladium (*Cyperaceae*)

	mariscus	XLum

Cladrastis (*Papilionaceae*)

§	***kentukea***	CBcs CDul CLnd CMCN CTho EBee ELan EPfP EUJe EWTr LAst LRHS MBlu MBri MRav NLar SSpi WHar
§	- 'Perkins Pink'	MBlu MBri
	- 'Rosea'	see *C. kentukea* 'Perkins Pink'
	lutea	see *C. kentukea*
	sikokiana **new**	CFil
	sinensis	CBcs CExl CFil CGHE EPfP MBlu SKHP WPGP

Clarkia (*Onagraceae*)

*	***repens***	CSpe

Clavinodum (*Poaceae*)

§	***oedogonatum***	MWht

Claytonia (*Portulacaceae*)

	alsinoides	see *C. sibirica*
	megarhiza var. ***nivalis***	WCot
§	***perfoliata***	CArn GPoy MNHC WHer
§	***sibirica***	CAgr CArn CElw IMou LSou MMoz WBor XLum
	- f. ***albiflora***	CElw MMoz MPie WBor WCot WMoo
	virginica	LRHS MMoz WMoo

Clematis ✿ (*Ranunculaceae*)

	BWJ 7630 from China	WCru
	BWJ 8169 from China	WCru
	CC 711	CExl
	CC 4710	CExl
	CC 5904	GKev
	SDR 6151	GKev
	'Abigail' (Vt)	NHaw
	Abilene = 'Evipo027'	CFlo EPfP ETho LBuc LRHS LSqu NTay SPoG SWCr
	'Abundance' (Vt) ♀H4	CDoC CFlo CRHN CSPN CWCL EBee ETho LBMP LRHS LSRN MAsh MBri NHol NTay SDix SPer
	acuminata var. ***sikkimensis*** B&SWJ 7202	WCru
	addisonii	CBcs CSPN NHaw
	afoliata	ECou WThu
	afoliata × ***forsteri***	ECou
	'Ai-Nor' (EL)	ETho
	'Akaishi' (EL)	ETho NTay
	akebioides	NHaw
	- SDR 6110	GKev
	Alabast = 'Poulala'PBR (EL) ♀H4	CLng CSPN EBee ETho LRHS MBri NHaw SCoo
	Alaina = 'Evipo 056' **new**	ETho LBuc LRHS LSqu NPri SLon SPoG
	'Alba Luxurians' (Vt) ♀H4	CBcs CCon CDoC CDoy CElw CFlo CRHN CSPN CSam CTri CWCL EBee ELan ELon EPfP ETho LPio LRHS LSRN MAsh MBri MGos MRav NHol NTay SDix SLim SPer SPoG SWCr
	'Albatross' (EL)	LSRN
	'Albert' (A)	NTay
	'Albiflora' (A)	CLng CSPN NTay
	'Albina Plena' (A/d)	ETho LRHS MGos NPri SLon
	'Aleksandrit' (EL)	NHaw
	'Alice Fisk' (EL)	CSPN EBee ETho LRHS LSRN MBri MSwo NHaw SLim WGor
	'Alionushka' (I) ♀H4	CRHN EBee ELan EPfP ETho LRHS LSRN MBri MGos NLar SLim SPoG SWCr
	'Allanah' (LL)	EBee ETho LRHS LSRN MGos NHaw SCoo SLim SPoG
	alpina ♀H4	GGal GKin IBoy LSRN MAsh MJak MRav MWhi NHaw NPer SEWo SPlb SPre SWvt
	- 'Albiflora'	see *C. sibirica*
	- 'Columbine White'	see *C.* 'White Columbine'
I	- 'Odorata' (A)	CSPN NHaw
§	- 'Pamela Jackman' (A) ♀H4	CDoC CMac CSPN CWSG EBee ELan IBal LBMP LRHS LSRN MAsh MBri MMuc NEgg NTay SCoo SDix SEND SLim SPer SPoG SRkn SWCr SWvt
	- pink-flowered	GKev
	- 'Stolwijk Gold' (A)	CSPN ETho MBlu NHaw NTay SRms
	alternata	CWGN ETho
	'Amelia' (I)	SMDP
	'Amelia Joan' (Ta)	MWat
	'Ameshisuto' (EL)	ETho
	'Amethyst Beauty' (A)	EPfP LBuc LRHS
	Amethyst Beauty = 'Evipo043'	ETho LSqu NTay SLon
	'Andromeda' (EL)	CSPN ETho LRHS MBri NHaw NTay SWCr
	Aneta = 'Evipo055' **new**	CFlo
	Angela = 'Zoang' (EL) **new**	NTay
	Angelique = 'Evipo017' (EL)	CFlo CLng CRos CSPN EPfP ETho LBuc LRHS LSqu NTay SCoo SLon SPer SWCr
	'Anita' (Ta)	CFlo ETho LSRN NHaw NTay SLim SMDP
	Anna Louise = 'Evithree'PBR (EL) ♀H4	CLng CRos CSPN CWCL EBee EPfP ETho LBuc LRHS LSRN LSqu MBri NTay SCoo SLim SLon SPer SWCr
	'Annabel' (EL)	CSPN LSRN MAsh
	Anniversary = 'Pynot' (EL)	LSRN SCoo
	'Aotearoa' (LL)	EBee IPot MBri NHaw
	'Aphrodite' (I) **new**	CCon
	'Aphrodite Elegafumina' (I)	CCon CRHN CWGN LRHS NHaw SWCr
	'Apple Blossom' (Ar) ♀H4	Widely available
	'Arabella' (I) ♀H4	CFlo CRHN CSPN CWCL CWGN EBee ELan EPfP EShb ETho LRHS LSRN MAsh MBri NLar NPri NTay SLim SPoG SWCr SWvt WSHC
§	Arctic Queen = 'Evitwo'PBR (EL) ♀H4	CFlo CLng CRos CSPN CWCL EBee EHyd EPfP ETho LBuc LRHS LSRN LSqu MAsh MBri NPri NTay SCoo SLon SPoG SWCr
	armandii	Widely available
	- 'Enham Star'	LRHS MBri MGos
§	- 'Little White Charm'	EBee LRHS MBri SKHP
	- 'Meyeniana'	see *C. armandii* 'Little White Charm'

I	- 'Snowdrift'	CBcs CFlo CSBt CSPN CWSG EBee ELan EPfP ETho LRHS LSRN MAsh MGos MSwo NEgg NLar NTay SKHP SPer SPoG SRms SWCr
	× ***aromatica***	CBcs CCon CFlo CSPN CWGN EBee ELan EPfP ETho LPio LRHS MRav NTay SCoo
§	'Asagasumi' (EL)	ETho
	'Asao' (EL)	CLng EBee ELan EPfP ETho IBoy LRHS MBri MGos MRav NTay SCoo SPer SPoG SWCr
	'Ascotiensis' (LL)	CLng CRHN CSPN EBee EPfP ETho LRHS MBri NHaw NTay SCoo SLim SLon SPer SPoG SWCr
	'Aureolin' (Ta)	CSPN
	Avant-garde = 'Evipo033'^{PBR} (Vt)	CFlo CLng CRos CSPN CWCL CWGN EBee EPfP ETho EUJe LRHS LSqu NTay SLon
§	Aztek = 'Daihelios' (Ta)	CSPN ETho LRHS MGos NTay SCoo
	Baby Doll = 'Zobadol' (EL) **new**	ETho
	Baby Star = 'Zobast' (EL) **new**	ETho
§	'Bagatelle' (LL)	CLng CSPN LRHS MBri NHaw
	'Bal Maiden' (Vt)	CRHN NHaw
§	'Ballerina in Blue' (A/d)	IPot NHaw
	'Ballet Skirt' (A/d) 🏆^{H4}	NHaw
	'Barbara' (LL)	ETho LSRN MRav NHaw NTay
	'Barbara Dibley' (EL)	CFlo CLng CTri CWSG LRHS MAsh NHaw SCoo SLim
	'Barbara Harrington'^{PBR} (LL)	CLng LRHS LSRN NHaw SLon SWCr
	'Barbara Jackman' (EL)	CLng CMac EBee ETho LRHS LSRN MAsh MRav MSwo NTay SCoo SLon SPer SWCr
	'Basil Bartlett' (Fo)	ECou
	'Beata' (LL)	ELMC MGos NHaw
	'Beauty of Worcester' (EL)	CCon CMac CSPN CWSG EBee ELan ELon EPfP ETho LRHS LSRN MAsh MSwo NHaw NTay SCoo SDix SLim SPer SPet WSpi
	'Bees' Jubilee' (EL)	CBcs CMac CWSG EBee ELan ELon ETho LRHS LSRN MAsh MGos MRav MSwo NBir NLar NTay SLim SPer SPet SPoG SWvt
	'Bella' (EL)	LSRN NHaw
	'Belle Nantaise' (EL)	NTay SCoo SPet SRms
	'Belle of Woking' (EL)	CLng CSPN CWSG EBee ELan ELon ETho LRHS LSRN MAsh MRav NTay SCoo SLim SPer SPoG SWCr SWvt
	'Bells of Emei Shan'	ETho
	'Ben's Beauty' (A) **new**	CFlo
	'Berry Red' (A)	CWGN
	'Best Wishes'^{PBR} **new**	LRHS
§	'Beth Currie' (EL)	CLng CSPN EPfP LRHS SWCr
	'Betina'	see *C.* 'Red Beetroot Beauty'
	'Betty Corning' (Vt) 🏆^{H4}	CFlo CLng CRHN CSPN CWGN EBee ELan EPfP ETho LPio LRHS LSRN MBri NTay SCoo SLon SRms SWCr SWvt
	'Betty Risdon' (EL)	ETho
	Bijou	see *C.* Thumbelina
	'Bill MacKenzie' (Ta) 🏆^{H4}	Widely available
	'Black Prince' (Vt)	CFlo CRHN CWGN EBee ELan EPfP ETho IPot LRHS LSRN MBri MGos NHaw NLar NTay SLim SLon SMDP SRms
	'Black Tea' (LL)	CDul CSPN ELMC IPot LRHS LSRN NHaw NTay SLim SLon SWCr
§	'Błękitny Anioł' (LL) 🏆^{H4}	CFlo CLng CMac CRHN CSPN ELon ETho LRHS MAsh MBri MGos NLar NTay SCoo SPer SPet SWCr WBor
	Blue Angel	see *C.* 'Błękitny Anioł'
	'Blue Belle' (Vt)	CRHN ELan SLon
	'Blue Bird' (A/d)	CBcs CWCL EBee IPot MAsh NTay SMDP SPoG SRms
	Blue Blood	see *C.* 'Königskind'
	'Blue Boy' (EL)	see *C.* 'Elsa Späth'
	'Blue Boy' (I)	see *C.* × *diversifolia* 'Blue Boy' (I)
	'Blue Dancer' (A)	CBcs CLng EBee EPfP ETho LRHS MBri MGos NLar NTay SWCr
	'Blue Eclipse' (A)	CFlo CSPN CWGN MBri MGos NHaw NHol NTay
	'Blue Eyes' (EL)	CSPN ELMC ELon ETho LSRN MBri NHaw NTay SLim
§	'Blue Light'^{PBR} (EL/d)	CFlo CSPN ELan LRHS MGos NLar NTay
	Blue Moon = 'Evirin'^{PBR} (EL)	CLng EPfP ETho LRHS LSRN MBri NLar NTay SCoo SLon SWCr
	Blue Pirouette = 'Zobluepi'^{PBR} (I)	MBri MJak SMDP
	Blue Rain	see *C.* 'Sinii Dozhd'
	'Blue Ravine' (EL)	EBee EPfP LRHS MBri MGos NLar NTay SCoo
	Blue River = 'Zoblueriver'^{PBR}	CWGN ELan
	'Blue Tapers' (A)	NHaw
§	'Blushing Ballerina' (A/d)	MBri
	Bonanza = 'Evipo031'^{PBR}	CLng CRos EHyd EPfP ETho LRHS LSqu MBri NLar NTay SCoo SDix SLon SPer SPoG SWCr
	× ***bonstedtii*** 'Crépuscule' (H)	LRHS MCot SMDP
	'Boskoop Beauty' (EL)	NHaw
	Bourbon = 'Evipo018'^{PBR}	EPfP ETho LBuc LRHS LSqu NPri NTay SCoo SLon SPoG SWCr
	brachyura B&SWJ 8854	WCru
	'Brocade' (Vt)	CRHN CSPN NHaw
	'Broughton Bride' (A)	CFlo CLng CSPN CWGN ETho MBri NHol NTay SMDP
	'Broughton Star' (M/d) 🏆^{H4}	CFlo CMac CRHN CSBt CSPN CWCL CWib ELan EPfP ETho IBoy LRHS LSRN MAsh MBlu MBri MGos MRav MSwo NBir NHol NTay SLim SLon SPoG SRkn SRms SWvt WBor
	'Brunette' (A)	CFlo CSPN EBee ELan EPfP ETho IPot LRHS MBri MGos NHaw NLar NTay SLon SPoG SWCr
	buchananiana Finet & Gagnep.	see *C. rehderiana*
	buchananiana DC. B&SWJ 8333a	WCru
	'Buckland Beauty' (V)	CFlo CLng CSPN CWGN ETho NHaw SMDP
	'Buckland Cascade'	SMDP
	'Burford Bell' (V)	NHaw
	'Burford Princess' (Vt)	CRHN NHaw
	'Burford White' (A)	CSPN MBri NLar
	'Burma Star' (EL)	CFlo CWGN ETho LRHS MBri NHaw NTay
	'By the Way' (M) **new**	SMDP
	Caddick's Cascade = 'Semu' (LL)	CSPN CWGN ELMC ETho NHaw
	calycina	see *C. cirrhosa* var. *balearica*
	campaniflora	see *C. viticella* subsp. *campaniflora*
	'Candida' (EL)	MBri
	'Candleglow' (A)	MBri NHaw

	Name	Suppliers
	'Candy Stripe'	CLng LRHS NTay SCoo SPoG
	'Capitaine Thuilleaux'	see *C.* 'Souvenir du Capitaine Thuilleaux'
	'Cardinal Wyszynski'	see *C.* 'Kardynał Wyszyński'
	'Carmencita' (Vt)	CRHN CSPN EBee LRHS LSRN NHaw SCoo SLon
	'Carnaby' (EL)	CBcs CSPN CWCL EBee ELan ELon EPfP ETho LRHS LSRN MAsh MBri MGos MJak NPri NTay SCoo SLim SPoG SWCr SWvt
	'Carnival Queen' (EL)	CSPN
	'Carol Leeds' (Vt)	NHaw
	'Caroline' (LL)	CSPN CWGN ETho LSRN NHaw NTay SMDP
	× ***cartmanii*** hort. 'Avalanche'PBR (Fo/m) ♀H3	CFlo CSPN ELan EPfP ETho GBin LRHS MBri NLar NPri NTay SCoo SLim SLon SPoG SWCr SWvt
	- 'Joe' (Fo/m)	CBcs CFlo EBee ELan EPfP ETho EWes LRHS LSRN MGos NTay SCoo SPoG SWCr SWvt WIce
	- 'Joe' × ***marmoraria*** (Fo)	ECho MGos SWCr
	- 'Joe' × 'Sharon'	LSRN
	- 'White Abundance'PBR (Fo/f)	ETho LRHS NLar SPoG
	× ***cartmanii*** hort. × ***petriei*** (Fo)	ECho
	Cassis = 'Evipo020'PBR	CSPN CWGN EBee EPfP ETho LBuc LRHS LSRN LSqu MBri NTay SCoo SLon SPer SWCr
	'Catherine Clanwilliam' (T) **new**	CWGN SMDP
	'Celebration' Caddick (EL)	see *C.* 'Pink Celebration'
	'Celebration'PBR Godfrey (EL)	CFlo LBuc LRHS NTay SLim
	Cezanne = 'Evipo023'PBR (EL)	CFlo CLng CRos CSPN EPfP ETho LBuc LRHS LSqu NPri NTay SCoo SLon SPer SWCr
	'Chacewater' (Vt)	CRHN
	'Chalcedony' (EL)	CSPN CWGN EBee ELMC ETho MGos NTay
	Chantilly = 'Evipo021'PBR	CFlo CSPN EHyd EPfP ETho LBuc LRHS LSRN LSqu NTay SCoo SLon SPer SWCr
	'Charissima' (EL)	CSPN CWGN EPfP LRHS MGos NLar SCoo SPet
	'Charlie Brown' (LL)	CRHN NHaw
	'Chatsworth' (Vt)	CRHN CWGN EPfP LRHS NHaw SLon SWCr
	Cherokee	see *C.* Ooh La La
	Chevalier = 'Evipo040'	EHyd EPfP ETho LRHS NTay SLon SPer SPoG SWCr
	chiisanensis	WSHC
	- B&SWJ 4560	WCru
	- B&SWJ 8706	WCru
	- B&SWJ 8800	WCru
	- 'Lemon Bells' (A)	ELan EPfP LRHS MAsh SCoo SLon SWCr
	- 'Love Child' (A)	ELan NTay
	chinensis misapplied	see *C. terniflora*
	chinensis Osbeck PAB 3751 **new**	LEdu
	- RWJ 10042	WCru
	Chinook = 'Evipo013'PBR	CLng LRHS SLim
	chrysantha	see *C. tangutica*
	chrysocoma misapplied	see *C. spooneri*
N	***chrysocoma*** Franch.	SMDP
	'Cicciolina' (Vt)	CRHN ETho NHaw
	cirrhosa	CTri ELan LRHS MAsh MGos MWhi SWCr
§	- var. ***balearica***	CBcs CDoC CFlo CMac CSPN CTri CWCL CWSG EBee ELan EPfP ETho LHop LRHS LSRN MAsh MBri MGos MRav MSwo NTay SDix SEND SLim SPer SPoG SWCr SWvt
	- 'Jingle Bells'	CFlo CLng CMac EBee EPfP ETho LBMP LRHS LSRN MAsh MBri NPri NTay SCoo SLim SLon SPoG SWCr WSpi
	- 'Ourika Valley'	EBee ELMC EPfP ETho LRHS MAsh MBri NLar NTay
	- var. ***purpurascens*** 'Freckles' ♀H3	Widely available
	- - 'Lansdowne Gem'	CFlo CMac CSPN CWGN CWib LRHS NTay SKHP SMDP SPoG SWCr SWvt WSpi
	- 'Wisley Cream' ♀H3	CBcs CFlo CMac CSPN CWCL CWib EBee ELan EPfP ETho LRHS LSRN MAsh MBri MGos MSwo NTay SCoo SEND SKHP SLim SPer SPoG SRms SWCr SWvt
	clarkeana misapplied	see *C. urophylla* 'Winter Beauty'
	columbiana	SPer
	- var. ***tenuiloba*** 'Ylva' (A)	NHaw WAbe
	'Columbine' (A)	CWSG EBee ETho LRHS MBri MSwo NTay SDix SPer
	'Columella' (A)	ETho MGos NHaw NLar
	'Comtesse de Bouchaud' (LL) ♀H4	CDoC CFlo CMac CSPN CTri CWCL CWSG EBee ELan ELon EPfP EShb ETho LRHS LSRN MAsh MBri MGos MRav NPri NTay SDix SEND SLim SPer SPoG SWCr WBor
	Confetti = 'Evipo036'PBR	CFlo CLng EBee EPfP ETho LRHS LSRN MBri NTay SLim SLon
	'Congratulations' (EL)	ELon LRHS LSRN SLim
	connata	GQui
	- GWJ 9386	WCru
	- HWJCM 132	WCru
	aff. ***connata*** GWJ 9431 from West Bengal	WCru
	aff. ***connata*** HWJK 2176 from Nepal	WCru
	'Constance' (A) ♀H4	CFlo CMac CSPN CWCL EBee EPfP ETho LRHS LSRN MBri NHaw NLar NTay SCoo SPer SPre SRms SWCr
	'Continuity' (M)	CWGN
	'Cora' (I)	CWGN
	'Cornish Spirit' (Vt)	CRHN
	'Corona' (EL)	CLng CSPN ELon EPfP LRHS MBri NHaw SCoo
	'Corry' (Ta)	NLar
	'Côte d'Azur' (H)	CBcs CCse CExl CMac GCal LRHS MNrw
	'Countess of Lovelace' (EL)	CBcs CSPN CWSG EBee ELan EPfP ETho LSRN MBri MGos NTay SCoo SPet
	Countess of Wessex = 'Evipo073' **new**	ETho LRHS LSqu
	County Park hybrids (Fo)	ECou
	'Cragside' (A)	EBee ETho MMuc
§	'Crimson King' (LL)	MBri NHaw NLar WGor
	'Crinkle'PBR (M)	CCCN CLng
§	***crispa***	CElw NHaw
§	Crystal Fountain = 'Evipo038'PBR (EL)	CFlo CLng CSPN CWCL CWGN EBee EHyd EPfP ETho LBuc LRHS LSRN LSqu MBri NTay SCoo SLim SLon SPer SPoG SWCr
	'Danae' (Vt)	NHaw

	Dancing Dorien = 'Zodado' PBR (EL)	WCot
	Dancing Queen = 'Zodaque' PBR (EL)	ETho MBri NTay WSpi
	Dancing Smile = 'Zodasmi' **new**	NTay WCot
	'Daniel Deronda' (EL) 🏆H4	CDoC CFlo CSPN CWCL CWSG ELan ELon ETho IBoy LBMP LRHS LSRN MAsh MBri MGos NBir NTay SCoo SDix SLim SPoG SWCr
	'Dark Eyes' (Vt)	CSPN CWGN ETho
	'Dark Secret' (A)	MBri NHaw NHol NTay
	'Dawn' (EL)	CCCN CFlo CLng CSPN ETho LRHS LSRN MBri NTay SCoo SPer
	'De Vijfhoeven' (Vt) **new**	NHaw
	'Débutante' (EL)	NHaw
	'Denny's Double' (EL/d)	CSPN CWGN CWSG ELMC ETho LRHS NTay
	'Destiny' (EL) **new**	CWGN
	Diamantina = 'Evipo039' PBR	CFlo EHyd EPfP ETho LBuc LRHS LSqu NPri NTay SLon SPer SPoG SWCr
	'Diana' (LL)	ETho LSRN NHaw
	Diana's Delight = 'Evipo026'	EHyd EPfP ETho LRHS LSRN LSqu NTay SLon SPer SPoG SWCr
	dioscoreifolia	see *C. terniflora*
§	× ***diversifolia***	CRHN EBee MGos NHaw SDix SWvt
§	- 'Blue Boy' (I)	CRHN CSPN EBee MGos NHaw SLon
	- 'Heather Herschell' (I)	CFlo CRHN CSPN EBee ELon NHaw SMDP
§	- 'Hendersonii' (I)	CFlo CWCL EBee ELan EPfP ETho GBuc LHop LRHS LSRN MBri MCot MRav MSwo NBir SDix SPer SWat SWvt WCot
§	- 'Olgae' (I)	CExl CSPN EBee NHaw SMDP
	'Doctor Ruppel' (EL)	CDul CFlo CMac CSPN CWCL CWSG ELon EPfP ETho IBoy LRHS LSRN MAsh MBri MGos MRav MSwo NBir NPri NTay SDix SLim SPer SWCr
	'Dominika' (LL)	NHaw
	'Dorath'	ELMC ELon LRHS NHaw NTay SPoG
	'Dorothy Barbara' (M) **new**	SMDP
	'Dorothy Tolver' (LL)	ETho
	'Dorothy Walton'	see *C.* 'Bagatelle'
	'Double Cross'	ECou
	'Double Delight' (M)	CFlo CWGN WNPC
	'Duchess of Albany' (1882) (LL)	MAsh MBri
	'Duchess of Albany' (1897) (T)	CFlo CSPN CTri CWSG CWib EBee ELan EPfP ETho LRHS LSRN MAsh MGos NEgg NHol SPer
	'Duchess of Edinburgh' (EL)	CBcs CMac CWSG EBee ELan ELon EPfP IBoy LRHS LSRN MAsh MBri MGos MSwo NEgg NHol NTay SDix SEND SLim SPer SPoG SWCr SWvt
	'Duchess of Sutherland' (EL)	MGos NHaw SDix
	'Dulcie'	NHaw
	× ***durandii*** 🏆H4	CBcs CFlo CRHN CSPN CSpe CWCL EBee ELan EPfP ETho LRHS LSRN MAsh MBri MRav NTay SCoo SPer SPoG SWCr SWvt WCot
	'Dutch Sky' (LL)	ETho MBri
	'Early Sensation' (Fo/f)	CBcs CFlo CSPN CTri CWSG CWib EBee ELan ELon EPfP ETho EUJe LRHS LSRN MAsh MBri MGos NTay SCoo SLim SPer SPoG SPre SWCr SWvt
	'East Malling' (M)	NHaw
	East River = 'Zoeastri' PBR (I)	ELan IPot
	'Eclipse' (H)	NHaw SMDP
	'Edith' (EL) 🏆H4	ETho LSRN MBri NHaw NLar NTay WGor
	'Edomurasaki' (EL)	MBri
	'Edouard Desfossé' (EL)	CLng MBri
	'Edward Prichard'	CFlo CSPN EBee MAsh MGos NHaw NTay SDix SMDP
	'Eetika' (LL)	CRHN ETho NHaw
	'Ekstra' (LL)	NHaw
	'Eleanor' (Fo/f)	ECou
	'Elf' (Vt)	CWGN SMDP
	'Elfin' (Fo/v)	ECou
	'Elizabeth' (M) 🏆H4	Widely available
§	'Elsa Späth' (EL)	CExl CMac CSPN CTri EBee ELan EPfP ETho LRHS LSRN MAsh MBri MGos NTay SLim SPer SWCr SWvt
	'Elten' (M)	CSPN
	'Elvan' (Vt)	CRHN NHaw NLar
	'Ember' (T) **new**	CWGN
	'Emilia Plater' (Vt)	CRHN EBee ETho LRHS MBri MGos NHaw SLon
	Empress = 'Evipo011' PBR (EL)	CFlo CLng CSPN EBee ELan EPfP ETho LBuc LRHS LSqu NTay SLon SWCr
	'Entel' (Vt)	CRHN NHaw
	× ***eriostemon***	see *C.* × *diversifolia*
	'Ernest Markham' (LL) 🏆H4	CBcs CDoC CMac CSPN CWCL EBee ELan EPfP ETho IBoy LRHS LSRN MAsh MBri MGos MJak MSwo NEgg NPri NTay SDix SLim SPer SPoG SWCr SWvt
	'Essex Star' (Fo)	ECou
	'Étoile de Malicorne' (EL)	MBri WGor
	'Étoile de Paris' (EL)	EBee MBri
	'Étoile Rose' (Vt)	CCon CMac CRHN CSPN CTri CWCL ELan EPfP ETho LBMP LRHS LSRN MAsh MGos NHaw NHol NTay SCoo SDix SLim SLon SPer SPoG SWCr
	'Étoile Violette' (Vt) 🏆H4	Widely available
	Evening Star = 'Evista' (EL)	EPfP MBri
	'Eximia'	see *C.* 'Ballerina in Blue'
	'Fair Rosamond' (LL)	EBee MBri MGos NHaw NLar NTay
	'Fairy' (Fo/f)	ECou
	Fairy Blue	see *C.* Crystal Fountain
	'Fairydust' (Vt) **new**	NHaw
	× ***fargesioides***	see *C.* 'Paul Farges'
	fasciculiflora	CMHG
	- KWJ 12160	WCru
	- L 657	WCru WPGP
	'Fascination' PBR (I)	CFlo CWGN MBri NHaw NTay SMDP
	fauriei	WSHC
	Filigree = 'Evipo029' PBR	CFlo CRos CSPN LBuc LRHS NTay SPoG SWCr
	'Fireworks' (EL)	CFlo CSPN CWGN EBee EPfP ETho IBoy LRHS LSRN MAsh MBri MGos MRav NEgg NLar NTay SLim SPer SPoG SWCr WGor
	'Flamingo' (EL)	CWCL CWSG
	flammula	CFlo CMac CSPN CWib EBee ELan EPfP LRHS LSRN MAsh MBlu MBri MRav NTay SDix SPer SPoG SWCr SWvt WSpi

	- 'Rubra Marginata'	see *C.* × *triternata* 'Rubromarginata'
	Fleuri = 'Evipo042' (EL)	CFlo CLng CSPN CWCL EPfP ETho LBuc LRHS NTay SCoo SLon SPoG SWCr
	florida	CWGN SWvt
	- 'Bicolor'	see *C. florida* var. *florida* 'Sieboldiana'
	- var. ***flore-pleno*** (d)	CCCN CFlo CSPN CWCL EBee ELan EPfP ETho LRHS LSRN MAsh NEgg NTay SPoG SWCr
§	- var. ***florida*** 'Sieboldiana' (d)	CBcs CFlo CSPN CWCL CWSG EBee ELan EPfP ETho LRHS LSRN MAsh MBri MGos MJak NTay SLim SPoG SRkn SWCr SWvt
	- var. ***normalis*** Pistachio = 'Evirida'^{PBR} (LL)	CCCN CFlo CLng CSPN CWCL CWGN EBee EPfP ETho LRHS LSRN LSqu MAsh NLar NTay SLim SLon SWCr
	- - 'Thorncroft' (LL)	ETho
	'Floris V' (I)	NHaw NLar
	'Fluffy Duck' (Vt/d) **new**	NHaw
	foetida × 'Lunar Lass' (Fo)	ECho ECou
	foetida* × *petriei	ECho ECou
	'Fond Memories' (EL)	CFlo EBee EPfP ETho LSRN MBri NLar NTay SLon
	Forever Friends = 'Zofofri'^{PBR} (LL)	CWGN ETho IPot
I	'Forget-me-not'	LSRN MBri NLar
	forrestii	see *C. napaulensis*
§	***forsteri***	CBcs CSPN
	'Foxtrot' (Vt)	CRHN NHaw
	'Foxy' (A) ♀^{H4}	CFlo CLng EBee MBri NHaw NLar NTay SLon
	'Fragrant Joy' (Fo/m)	ECou
	'Fragrant Oberon' (Fo)	CFlo ECou NTay SMDP SWvt WSpi
	'Fragrant Spring' (M)	CSBt CSPN CWGN ETho IBoy LRHS MGos MMuc NHaw NLar SEND SLim SMDP SWCr WSpi
	'Frances Rivis' (A) ♀^{H4}	CFlo CMac CSPN CSam CWCL EBee ELan EPfP ETho LRHS LSRN MAsh MBlu MBri MGos MMuc MRav MSwo NLar NTay NWea SDix SPer SPoG SRms SWCr WSpi
	'Francesca' (A)	LSRN
	'Frankie' (A) ♀^{H4}	CFlo CLng CSPN ELan EPfP ETho LRHS LSRN MAsh MBri NTay SCoo SWCr
	Franziska Maria = 'Evipo008' (EL)	CFlo CLng EPfP LBuc LRHS LSqu MAsh MBri NTay SCoo SLon SWCr
	'Frau Mikiko' (EL)	ETho MGos
	'Frau Susanne' (EL)	ETho
	'Freda' (M) ♀^{H4}	CRHN CTri CWGN CWSG EBee ELan EPfP ETho LRHS LSRN MBlu MBri MGos MRav NHol NTay SDix SLim SPer SWCr
	fremontii	NHaw
	fruticosa	SBrt
	'Fryderyk Chopin' (EL)	CSPN ELMC NHaw NLar
	'Fujimusume' (EL) ♀^{H4}	CFlo CSPN CWGN EBee ETho IPot LRHS MAsh NHaw NTay SPoG SWCr
	fujisanensis B&SWJ 11370	WCru
	'Fukuzono'	ETho LRHS LSRN NHaw NTay SWCr
	fusca misapplied	see *C. japonica*
	fusca Turcz.	EBee GBin SBrt WIvy
	- dwarf	CWGN NHaw
§	- var. ***fusca***	ETho WSHC
	- var. ***kamtschatica***	see *C. fusca* Turcz. var. *fusca*
	'Fuyu-no-tabi' (EL)	ETho

	'Gabrielle' (EL)	EBee LSRN MBri NHaw
	Galore	see *C.* Vesuvius
	'Garnet' (V) **new**	NHaw
	Gazelle = 'Evipo014'^{PBR}	CLng LRHS NTay SKHP
	'Gemini' (EL)	MGos
	'Generał Sikorski' (EL)	CBcs CFlo CMac CSPN CWSG EBee ELan EPfP ETho LBMP LRHS LSRN MAsh MBri MGos NTay SCoo SLim SPer SWCr SWvt
	gentianoides	SBrt
	'Geoffrey Tolver' (LL)	ETho NHaw
	'Georg' (A/d)	NHaw
	'Georg Ots' (LL)	NHaw
	Giant Star = 'Gistar'^{PBR} (M)	CLng ELMC IBoy LRHS MGos NEgg NLar NPer SLim SPoG SRkn WMoo WNPC
	'Gillian Blades' (EL) ♀^{H4}	CFlo CLng CSPN EBee ELan EPfP ETho LRHS LSRN MAsh MBri NHaw NTay SCoo SWCr SWvt
§	'Gipsy Queen' (LL) ♀^{H4}	CBcs CMac CSPN CWCL CWSG EBee ELan ELon EPfP ETho IBoy LRHS LSRN MAsh MBri NTay SDix SLim SPer SPoG SWCr SWvt
	'Gladys Picard' (EL)	EBee MBri NHaw
	glauca Turcz.	see *C. intricata*
	glaucophylla	WCru WSHC
	'Gojōgawa' (EL)	ETho
	'Golden Harvest' (Ta)	NLar
	Golden Tiara = 'Kugotia'^{PBR} (Ta) ♀^{H4}	CSPN CWGN EBee ETho GBin LSRN MBri MGos NLar NTay SRms
	'Gothenburg' (M)	EBee MBri NHaw
	'Grace' (Ta)	CRHN NHaw NLar
	grandiflora	SLim SRms
I	'Grandiflora' (F)	LRHS
	'Grandiflora Sanguinea' Johnson	see *C.* 'Södertälje'
	'Grandiflora Sanguinea' (Vt)	NTay
	grata misapplied	see *C.* × *jouiniana*
	'Gravetye Beauty' (T)	CFlo CMac CRHN CSPN EBee ELan EPfP ETho LRHS LSRN MAsh MBri MGos NHol NTay SDix SLon SPer SPoG SRms SWCr SWvt WSpi
§	'Grażyna' (LL)	ETho NTay
	'Green Velvet' (Fo/m)	ECou
	grewiiflora B&SWJ 2956	WCru
	'Guernsey Cream' (EL)	CCon CFlo CSPN CWCL CWSG EBee EPfP ETho LRHS LSRN MAsh MBri MGos NLar NTay SCoo SDix SLim SRkn SWCr
	Guiding Promise = 'Evipo053'	CLng LRHS NTay
	'Guiding Star' (EL)	NHaw
	'H.F. Young' (EL)	CFlo CLng CSPN CWSG EBee ELan EPfP ETho LRHS LSRN MAsh MBri MGos MMuc NLar NTay SCoo SDix SPer SWCr SWvt
	haenkeana	NHaw
	'Hagley Hybrid' (LL)	CDoC CDul CMac CSPN CWCL EBee ELan EPfP ETho LRHS LSRN MAsh MBri MGos MJak MMuc MRav NEgg NLar NTay SDix SLim SPer SPet SPoG SRms SWCr SWvt
	'Hakuōkan' (EL)	CSPN ELMC EPfP ETho LRHS LSRN MBri NLar SCoo
	'Hakuree' ambig.	LRHS
	'Hakuree' K. Ozawa (I)	ETho SMDP
	'Hanaguruma' (EL)	CSPN EBee ETho LSRN MBri NHaw
	'Hanajima' (I)	ETho SMDP

'Hania' (EL)	ETho
'Happy Anniversary' (EL)	EBee LBuc LSRN MBri NLar NTay
§ Happy Birthday = 'Zohapbi'^{PBR} (LL)	LSRN NTay
Harlow Carr = 'Evipo004'^{PBR}	CLng CMac EBee EPfP LRHS MBri NTay SCoo SDix SLim SRms SWCr
'Haru Ichiban' (EL)	ETho
Havering Hybrids (Fo)	ECou
'Helen Cropper' (EL)	ETho
'Helios'	see *C.* Aztek
'Helsingborg' (A) ♀^{H4}	CFlo CLng CSPN EBee ELan EPfP ETho LRHS MAsh MBri NPri NTay SCoo SPoG SRms SWCr
hendersonii Koch	see *C.* × *diversifolia* 'Hendersonii'
hendersonii Stand.	see *C.* × *diversifolia*
I 'Hendersonii' (I)	CFlo GBuc LSRN MNFA
I 'Hendersonii Rubra' (Ar)	CSPN
'Hendryetta'^{PBR} (I)	EBee EPfP LPio MBri SMDP SWvt
henryi	EShb LSRN MBri NTay
- B&SWJ 3402	WCru
- var. ***morii*** B&SWJ 1668	WCru
'Henryi' (EL) ♀^{H4}	CFlo CMac CSPN CTri CWCL CWSG EBee ELan EPfP ETho LRHS LSRN MBri MGos MRav MSwo NEgg SDix SPer SPet SPoG SWCr
heracleifolia	CCon CMac CPou ECtt LRHS MWhi NLar WBor WWEG XLum
- Alan Bloom	see *C. tubulosa* Alan Bloom
- 'Blue Dwarf'	ETho MGos SMDP WAbe
- 'Cassandra'	CFlo CWGN ECtt ELon EPfP EShb ETho GCal LRHS LSRN MCot MGos NBro NCGa NOrc SChF SMDP WGwG
'China Purple'	CEnd GBin LRHS LSou MSCN NLar SMDP WHoo
- var. ***davidiana***	see *C. tubulosa*
- 'Pink Dwarf' (H)	CWGN ETho NLar NTay SMDP WAbe
'Roundway Blue Bird' (H)	LHop NHaw SMDP
hexapetala Forster	see *C. forsteri*
hexasepala	see *C. forsteri*
'Hikarugenji' (EL)	NHaw
'Honora' (LL)	CFlo CSPN CWGN LRHS MAsh MBri NTay SCoo
'Horn of Plenty' (EL)	LRHS MBri NHaw
'Huldine' (LL) ♀^{H4}	CBcs CLng CRHN CSPN EBee ELan EPfP ETho LRHS LSRN MAsh MBri MRav NTay SDix SLon SPer SPet SWCr SWvt WSHC
'Huvi' (LL)	CWGN ETho NHaw
'Hybrida Sieboldii' (EL)	EUJe SCoo
Hyde Hall = 'Evipo009'^{PBR} (EL)	CFlo CLng CMac CRos CSPN CWGN EBee EHyd ELan EPfP LRHS LSqu MAsh MBri NTay SCoo SLim SLon SPer SWCr
'Hythe Egret' (Fo)	ECho LLHF
I Am a Little Beauty = 'Zolibe' (Vt)	CRHN NHaw NTay
I am Lady J = 'Zoiamlj' (Vt) new	NHaw
I Am Lady Q = 'Zoiamladyq'^{PBR} (Vt)	CRHN CWGN NHaw
I Am Red Robin = 'Zorero'^{PBR} (A)	CSPN IPot MBri NTay WIce
I am Stanislaus = 'Stanislaus' (H)	SMDP
ianthina	SMDP
- var. ***kuripoensis***	NHaw
- - B&SWJ 700	WCru
'Ibi' (EL)	CWGN

Ice Blue = 'Evipo003'^{PBR} (Prairie Series) (EL)	CLng CRos EHyd ELan EPfP ETho LBuc LRHS LSqu MBri NPri NTay SCoo SLim SLon SPer SWCr
'Ice Queen' (EL)	MAsh
'Imperial' (EL)	NHaw
'Ingrid Biedenkopf' (Vt)	NHaw
Inspiration = 'Zoin'^{PBR} (I)	CSPN EBee ELan MBri MGos NLar SCoo
integrifolia	CElw CExl CPou CSpe EBee ELan EPfP IFoB LHop LPio MBel MBri MGos MHer NLar NPer NTay SRms WCot WHoo WWEG
- RCB UA 10	WCot
I - 'Alba'	CBcs CCon CFlo CSPN EBee ECtt ELon LPio LRHS LSRN MBri NBir NHaw NSti NTay SCoo WWlt
- 'Blue Ribbons' (I) new	EDAr
- 'Budapest' (I)	NHaw
- 'Hendersonii' Koch	see *C.* × *diversifolia* 'Hendersonii'
- 'Olgae'	see *C.* × *diversifolia* 'Olgae'
- 'Ozawa's Blue' (I)	CWGN EBee ETho MBNS
- white-flowered	see *C. integrifolia* 'Alba'
'Intermedia Rosea' (I) new	NChi
§ ***intricata***	CExl MGos
'Iola Fair' (EL)	NHaw
ispahanica	NHaw
'Ivan Olsson' (EL)	ETho IPot MGos
'Jackmanii' (LL) ♀^{H4}	CBcs CMac CTri EBee EPfP ETho IBoy LRHS LSRN MAsh MBri MGos MJak NWea SCoo SEND SLim SPet SPoG SWCr SWvt
'Jackmanii Alba' (EL)	ELan ELon EPfP ETho LRHS LSRN MAsh MBri SCoo SLim SPet SPoG WSpi
Jackmanii Purpurea = 'Zojapur'^{PBR} (LL)	ETho LRHS
'Jackmanii Rubra' (EL)	ETho
'Jackmanii Superba' misapplied	see *C.* 'Gipsy Queen'
'Jackmanii Superba' ambig. (LL)	CFlo CMac CSPN CWCL CWSG ELan EPfP ETho LRHS MAsh MBri MGos MMuc MRav MSwo NEgg NPer NPri NTay SDix SLim SPer SPoG SWCr WSpi
'Jacqueline du Pré' (A) ♀^{H4}	CBcs CFlo CMac CSPN CWCL EBee ELan EPfP ETho MBri MGos NHaw NLar NTay SMDP
'Jacqui' (M/d)	MGos NHaw
'James Mason' (EL)	CSPN EBee ETho LSRN MBri NHaw
'Jan Fopma'^{PBR} (I)	CWGN ETho LRHS NTay SMDP
'Jan Lindmark' (A/d)	CLng EBee ETho LRHS MAsh MBri MGos NLar NTay SCoo SPre
§ 'Jan Paweł II' (EL)	EBee ELan ETho LRHS MBri SCoo SPer
'Janny' (A)	IPot
§ ***japonica***	NHaw SMDP WSHC
- B&SWJ 11204	WCru
§ - var. ***obvallata*** B&SWJ 8900	WCru
'Jean Caldwell' (Vt) new	NHaw
'Jenny' (M/d)	CFlo ETho LSRN MGos NHaw SMDP SPoG SWCr
'Jenny Caddick' (Vt)	ETho NHaw
'Jerzy Popiełuszko' (EL)	ETho
I 'Jessica'	NTay
Jewel of Merk	see *C.* Happy Birthday
'Joan Baker' (Vt)	CRHN
John Howells = 'Zojohnhowells'^{PBR} (Vt)	CFlo ETho LSRN MBri NTay SLon

	'John Huxtable' (LL) ♀H4	CFlo CLng EPfP ETho LRHS MBri NHaw NTay WGor
	John Paul II	see *C.* 'Jan Paweł II'
	'John Treasure' (Vt)	CRHN LRHS NHaw NLar SMDP
	'John Warren' (EL)	CWSG EBee LRHS MAsh MBri NHaw NTay SCoo SLim SPer SWCr
	Jolly Good = 'Zojogo'PBR (LL)	NTay
	'Jolly Jake' (Vt) **new**	CFlo
	Josephine = 'Evijohill'PBR (EL) ♀H4	CFlo CLng CSPN CWCL EBee EHyd EPfP ETho EUJe LRHS LSRN LSqu MAsh MBri NLar NPri NTay SCoo SLim SPer SPoG SRkn SWCr SWvt
§	× ***jouiniana***	MRav SEND SWCr SWvt WSHC
	- 'Chance' (H)	NHaw NTay
	'Julka' (EL)	CFlo EBee ELMC ETho NHaw NTay
	'June Pyne' (EL)	ETho MBri
	'Justa' (Vt)	NHaw
	'Juuli' (I)	LRHS LSRN MBri
	'Kaaru' (LL)	CRHN CSPN ELMC
	'Kacper' (EL)	ETho MGos NHaw
	'Kaen' (EL)	ETho NTay
	'Kaiu' (V)	CFlo CSPN CWGN EBee LRHS NHaw SLim SMDP SWCr
§	'Kakio' (EL)	CLng ETho LRHS LSRN MAsh MBri MGos NTay SDix SLim SPer SPoG SWCr
	'Kalina' (EL)	ETho NHaw
I	'Kamilla' (EL)	CWGN IPot
§	'Kardynał Wyszyński' (EL)	ETho MBri MGos
§	'Kasmu' (Vt)	NHaw
	'Kathleen Dunford' (EL)	LSRN MBri NHaw NTay SCoo
	'Kathryn Chapman' (Vt)	CRHN NHaw
	'Ken Donson' (EL) ♀H4	EBee EPfP MBri MGos SCoo
	'Ken Pyne' (LL)	CFlo
	'Kermesina' (Vt) ♀H4	CCon CRHN CWCL EBee ELan EPfP ETho IBoy LRHS MAsh MBri MGos SCoo SDix SLim SPer SPoG SRms SWCr
	'Kiev' (Vt)	NHaw
	'Killifreth' (Vt)	CRHN NHaw
	'King Edward VII' (EL)	EBee MBri NTay WGor
	Kingfisher = 'Evipo037'PBR (EL)	CFlo CRos CSPN EHyd ELan EPfP ETho LBuc LRHS LSqu NPri NTay SCoo SLon SPer SPoG SWCr
	'Kinju Atarashi' (LL)	ETho WHlf
	'Kiri Te Kanawa' (EL)	CSPN EBee ELon ETho LRHS LSRN MBri MGos NHaw NLar NTay SMDP
	'Kommerei' (LL)	ETho NHaw
§	'Königskind' (EL)	CSPN ETho MGos NLar
	koreana	MAsh WCru
	'Küllus' (LL)	CWGN
	ladakhiana	CElw GQui NHaw SMDP WPGP
	'Lady Betty Balfour' (LL)	CLng CMac CSPN CWSG ETho LRHS MBri NTay SCoo SPet SPoG SWvt
	'Lady Bird Johnson' (T)	CFlo EBee ELon EPfP LRHS LSRN NTay SCoo
	'Lady Caroline Nevill' (EL)	MBri
	'Lady Londesborough' (EL)	EBee EPfP MBri NHaw NTay SCoo SDix
	'Lady Northcliffe' (EL)	CLng CSPN CTri CWSG ETho LRHS MAsh MBri NTay SDix SPet WSpi
	'Lambton Park' (Ta) ♀H4	CCon CRHN ETho LRHS LSRN NHaw NLar NTay SMDP
	lasiandra	NHaw
	'Last Dance' (Ta)	CRHN
	Lasting Love	see *C.* 'Grażyna'
	'Lasurstern' (EL) ♀H4	CBcs CExl CFlo CMac CSPN CTri EBee ELan EPfP ETho LRHS LSRN MAsh MBri NTay SDix SPer SPoG SWCr SWvt
	'Laura' (LL)	NHaw
	'Laura Denny' (EL)	ETho
	'Lavender Twirl'	CRHN
	'Lawsoniana' (EL)	CMac EBee MBri WSpi
	'Łech Wałęsa' (EL)	ETho
	'Lemon Chiffon' (EL)	CLng CSPN ETho LRHS NHaw NTay
	Liberation = 'Evifive'PBR (EL)	CLng EBee LRHS MBri NLar NTay SCoo SLim SLon SPoG SWCr
§	***ligusticifolia***	NHaw
	'Lilacina Floribunda' (EL)	NHaw
	'Lilactime' (EL)	NHaw
	'Lincoln Star' (EL)	CLng CMac EBee ELon LRHS MAsh MBri MGos SDix SLim SPer SPet SPoG SWvt
	'Little Bas' (Vt)	CRHN MBri NHaw NLar SLon
	'Little Butterfly' (Vt)	CRHN MGos NHaw
	'Little Mermaid' (EL)	CFlo ETho
	'Little Nell' (Vt)	CCCN CRHN CSPN EBee ELan EPfP ETho LSRN MAsh NTay SCoo SDix SLon WSpi
I	'Longiflora' **new**	CFlo
	'Lord Herschell'	CFlo CSPN CWGN ETho LRHS MBri SMDP
	'Lord Nevill' (EL)	CWSG EPfP LRHS MBri SPer
	'Louise Pummell' (Fo)	ECou
	'Louise Rowe' (EL)	CFlo CLng EBee ELan ETho LRHS LSRN MBri MGos NHaw NTay SDix SWCr
	loureiroana HWJ 663	WCru
	'Love Jewelry' (EL)	ETho NHaw NTay
	'Loving Memory'	ETho
	'Lunar Lass' (Fo/f)	CFlo ECho ETho ITim LRHS WAbe
I	'Lunar Lass Variegata' (Fo/v)	ECho LLHF
	'Luxuriant Blue' (Vt)	CRHN NHaw NTay
	'M. Koster' (Vt)	CDoC CRHN EBee ETho NHaw SLon SRms
	macropetala (d)	CBcs CDoy CSBt EBee ELan EPfP ETho LAst LRHS MAsh MGos MRav MWhi NTay SDix SPer SWCr
	- 'Alborosea'	see *C.* 'Blushing Ballerina'
	- 'Blue Lagoon'	see *C. macropetala* 'Lagoon' Jackman 1959
	- 'Lagoon' Jackman 1956	see *C. macropetala* 'Maidwell Hall' Jackman
	- 'Lagoon' ambig.	LSRN SWCr
§	- 'Lagoon' Jackman 1959 (A/d) ♀H4	CSPN EBee ETho LRHS LSRN MBri MSwo NHol NTay SCoo SPoG
§	- 'Maidwell Hall' Jackman (A/d)	CSPN CTri CWSG EPfP ETho IPot LSRN MAsh MGos NTay WSpi
	- 'Maidwell Hall' O.E.P. Wyatt (A)	MRav SCoo SPer
	- 'Wesselton' (A/d) ♀H4	CFlo CSPN CTri ELMC EPfP ETho LBMP LRHS MAsh MBri NHaw NTay SPre SWCr
	- 'White Moth'	see *C.* 'White Moth'
	'Madame Baron-Veillard' (LL)	CLng ELMC LRHS MBri NEgg SCoo
	'Madame Edouard André' (LL)	CLng CSPN EPfP LRHS MAsh MBri NTay SCoo SPet SPoG SWCr
	'Madame Grangé' (LL) ♀H4	CSPN EPfP LRHS MBri NHaw SCoo SPoG
	'Madame Julia Correvon' (Vt) ♀H4	Widely available
	'Madame le Coultre'	see *C.* 'Mevrouw Le Coultre'
	'Madame Michiko' (EL) **new**	LSqu

	'Majojo' (Fo)	LLHF
	mandschurica	ETho GCal GKev LPio NHaw NLar XLum
	marata	WThu
	'Margaret Hunt' (LL)	CSPN ELan ETho IBoy LSRN MBri NHaw NTay
	'Margaret Jones' (M/d)	NHaw
	'Maria Cornelia'PBR (Vt)	CRHN CWGN ETho NTay
	'Marie Boisselot' (EL) 🏆H4	CBcs CFlo CMac CSPN CTri CWCL CWSG EBee ELan EPfP ETho IBoy LRHS LSRN MAsh MBri MGos MRav MSwo NPri NTay SDix SEND SPer SPet SPoG SWCr SWvt
	'Marjorie' (M/d)	CBcs CDoC CSPN CTri CWSG ELan EPfP ETho GKin IBoy LRHS LSRN MAsh MBri MGos MRav NEgg NTay SLim SPer SPoG SRms SWCr
	'Markham's Pink' (A/d) 🏆H4	Widely available
	marmoraria 🏆H2-3	ECho EDAr EHyd LHop LRHS
	marmoraria* × *petriei	ECho
	'Marmori' (LL)	CWGN ETho NHaw
	'Mary Rose'	see *C. viticella* 'Flore Pleno'
	'Mary Whistler' (A)	MGos
§	'Maskarad' (Vt)	MBri
	Masquerade (Vt)	see *C.* 'Maskarad'
I	'Masquerade' (EL)	MBri
	'Maureen' (LL)	CWGN CWSG
	maximowicziana	see *C. terniflora*
	'Mayleen' (M) 🏆H4	CPou CSBt CTri CWSG EBee EPfP ETho IBoy LRHS MAsh MBri MGos MRav NEgg NTay SCoo SLim SPer SPoG SRms SWCr SWvt
	'Mazury' (LL)	ETho
	Medley = 'Evipo012'PBR	CLng LRHS
	'Melodie' (Vt)	NHaw
§	'Mevrouw Le Coultre' (EL)	MJak
	meyeniana* var. *insularis B&SWJ 6700	WCru
	microphylla	ECou
	Mienie Belle = 'Zomibel'PBR (T)	CWGN ETho IPot NHaw
	'Mikelite' (Vt)	NHaw
	'Miniseelik' (LL)	NHaw
	'Minister' (EL)	MBri
	'Minuet' (Vt) 🏆H4	CRHN CSPN EBee EPfP ETho LRHS MAsh NTay SCoo SDix SLon SPer SWvt WSpi
	'Miranda' (I)	CWGN SMDP
	'Miriam Markham' (EL)	MBri NHaw
	'Miss Bateman' (EL) 🏆H4	CDoC CFlo CMac CSPN CTri CWCL CWSG EBee ELan EPfP ETho LRHS LSRN MAsh MBri MMuc NTay SDix SEND SLim SPer SPet SPoG SWCr WBor
	'Miss Christine' (M)	CFlo EBee ETho LSRN NTay SMDP
	'Miss Crawshay' (EL)	NHaw
	'Mister Hans Horn' (Vt) **new**	NHaw
	Mon Amour = 'Zomea' (EL) **new**	CWGN
	'Moniuszko' (EL)	CWGN
N	***montana***	CExl CSBt GGal MAsh MGos SDix SEWo SPet
	- B&SWJ 6724 from Taiwan	WCru
	- B&SWJ 6930	WCru
	- BWJ 8189b from China	WCru
	- HWJK 2156 from Nepal	WCru
	- var. ***alba***	see *C. montana* var. *montana*
	- 'Alexander' (M)	CPou CWSG EPfP LRHS SWCr
	- var. ***grandiflora*** (M) 🏆H4	CDoy CDul CMac CSam CWSG EBee ELan EPfP ETho GKin LBuc LHop LPot LRHS MBri MJak MMuc NBir NPri NTay SEND SLim SPer SPet SPoG SRms SWCr SWvt
§	- var. ***montana***	CBar CDoy MAsh SPoG
I	- 'Peveril'	CSPN
	- var. ***rubens*** misapplied	see *C. montana* var. *montana*
	- var. ***rubens*** E.H.Wilson	CDoC CSBt CTri ELan EPfP ETho GGal LRHS MBri MSwo NHol NWea SDix SPlb
I	- - 'Odorata' (M)	EBee ETho GKin LRHS MRav SCoo SLim SPoG WGor
	- - 'Pink Perfection' (M)	CDoC CMac CWSG EBee ELan EPfP GKin LRHS LSRN MAsh MBri NEgg NTay SCoo SLim SPer SPoG SWCr SWvt
	- - 'Tetrarose' (M) 🏆H4	Widely available
I	- 'Rubens Superba' (M)	CTri CWSG GKin MAsh NPri SRms SWCr
	- var. ***sericea***	see *C. spooneri*
	- 'Superba' (M) **new**	MBri
§	- var. ***wilsonii***	CFlo CSPN CSam EBee ELan EPfP ETho GKin LRHS LSRN MBri MGos MNHC MRav MSwo NTay SDix SMDP SPoG SRms SWCr SWvt
	'Monte Cassino' (EL)	CSPN CWGN EBee NTay
	'Moonbeam' (Fo)	CJun ECou ITim MGos MRav NOrc
	Moonfleet = 'Evipo046' (LL)	CLng NTay
§	'Moonlight' (EL)	MAsh
	'Moonman' (Fo)	ECou LLHF
	Morning Cloud	see *C.* 'Yukikomachi'
	'Morning Heaven' (Vt)	NHaw
	Morning Star = 'Zoklako'PBR (EL)	CWGN ETho
	Morning Yellow = 'Cadmy'PBR (M)	CCCN EBee IBoy LRHS NEgg
	'Mrs Cholmondeley' (EL) 🏆H4	CMac CSPN CWSG EBee ELan ELon EPfP ETho LRHS LSRN MAsh MBri MGos MSwo NPri NTay SLim SPer SPoG SWCr
	'Mrs George Jackman' (EL) 🏆H4	CFlo CLng CSPN CWCL ETho LRHS MGos NLar NTay SCoo
	'Mrs James Mason' (EL)	NHaw
	'Mrs N.Thompson' (EL)	CMac CSPN CTri CWCL EBee ELan ELon ETho IBoy LRHS LSRN MAsh MBri NBir NEgg NHol NPer NTay SDix SLim SPer SPoG SWCr
	'Mrs P.B.Truax' (EL)	LRHS NTay SMDP
	'Mrs Robert Brydon' (H)	ECtt LSRN NLar NTay SRms WHil
	'Mrs Spencer Castle' (EL)	CSPN ETho
	'Mrs T. Lundell' (Vt)	CRHN CSPN MGos NHaw
	'Multi Blue' (EL)	CBcs CFlo CWSG EBee ELan ELon EPfP ETho EUJe IBoy LRHS LSRN MAsh MBri MGos MRav NTay SLim SPer SPoG SRkn SRms SWCr
	'My Angel'PBR (Ta)	CSPN ELan NHaw NLar NTay
	'Myōjō' (EL)	EBee
§	***napaulensis***	CFlo CSPN CTri CWCL EPfP ETho LPio NHaw NTay SMDP WCru WSHC
I	'Natacha' (EL)	EBee NHaw NTay SCoo
	'Natascha' (EL)	CLng CSPN LRHS LSRN MBri SWvt
	'Negritianka' (LL)	CSPN EBee ELMC EPfP LRHS LSRN MBri NHaw
	'Negus' (LL)	MGos
	'Nelly Moser' (EL) 🏆H4	Widely available
	'Nelly Moser Neu' (EL)	NTay
	'New Dawn' (M)	CSPN NHaw

	Name	Suppliers
	'New Love'[PBR] (H)	CSPN ETho LSRN NHaw NLar NTay
	New Zealand hybrids (Fo)	ECou
	'Night Veil' (Vt)	ETho
	'Niobe' (EL) ♀H4	CBcs CMac CSPN CWCL CWSG EBee ELan EPfP EShb ETho EUJe IBoy LRHS LSRN MAsh MBri MGos MMuc MSwo NHol NPri NTay SDix SLim SPer SPoG SRms SWCr
	North Star (LL)	see *C.* 'Põhjanael'
	'North Star' (EL)	EPfP NTay
	'Nunn's Gift' (Fo)	ETho
	nutans var. ***thyrsoidea***	see *C. rehderiana, C. veitchiana*
	obvallata	see *C. japonica* var. *obvallata*
	'Ocean Pearl' (A)	CFlo EBee ETho LSRN MBri NLar NTay
	Octopus = 'Zooct'[PBR] (A)	CFlo NTay
	'Odoriba' (V)	CRHN CWGN ETho NHaw SMDP
	'Omoshiro' (EL)	CWGN ETho LRHS NHaw NTay
§	Ooh La La = 'Evipo041' (EL)	CFlo CLng CRos CSPN CWCL EHyd EPfP ETho LBuc LRHS NPri NTay SCoo SPer SPoG SWCr
	'Oonagare Ichigoo' (Vt)	MGos
	Opaline	see *C.* 'Asagasumi'
	orientalis misapplied	see *C. tibetana* subsp. *vernayi*
	orientalis L.	CElw GCra SCoo SWvt
	- 'Orange Peel'	see *C. tibetana* subsp. *vernayi* var. *vernayi* 'Orange Peel'
*	- 'Rubromarginata' (Ta)	MBri
	- 'Sherriffii'	see *C.* 'Sherriffii'
	orientalis* × *tangutica new	SWvt
	'Paddington' (EL)	ETho
	'Pagoda' (Vt) ♀H4	CDoC CRHN EBee EPfP MBri MRav SCoo SLon SMDP SRms
	Palette = 'Evipo034'[PBR] (Vt)	CLng LRHS MBri NTay SLon
	'Pamela' (F)	ETho NHaw NTay
	'Pamela Jackman'	see *C. alpina* 'Pamela Jackman', *C.* 'Pamela Jackman' (Vt)
§	'Pamela Jackman' (Vt)	MBri
	'Pamiat Serdtsa' (I)	ETho NHaw
	'Pamina' (EL)	ETho
	'Pangbourne Pink' (I) ♀H4	CFlo CSPN CWCL EBee EPfP ETho LRHS MBri NHaw NTay SCoo SWCr
	paniculata Thunb.	see *C. terniflora*
	paniculata J.G.Gmel (f)	ETho
	'Paradise Queen' (EL)	EBee LBuc MBri NLar
	'Parasol' (EL)	MBri
	Parisienne = 'Evipo019'[PBR] (EL)	CFlo CLng CSPN EPfP ETho LRHS LSqu NTay SCoo SLon SPer SPoG SWCr
	parviflora DC.	see *C. viticella* subsp. *campaniflora*
	parviloba var. ***bartlettii*** B&SWJ 6788	WCru
	'Pastel Blue' (I)	ETho SMDP
	'Pastel Pink' (I)	SMDP
	'Pastel Princess' (EL)	NHaw
	'Pat Coleman' (EL)	ETho
	patens	CCse CElw
	- 'Korean Moon' (EL)	WCru
§	- 'Manshuu Ki' (EL)	CFlo CSPN EBee ELon EPfP ETho LRHS NTay SPer
	- 'Yukiokoshi' (EL)	ETho
	Patricia Ann Fretwell = 'Pafar' (EL)	SMDP
§	'Paul Farges' (Vb) ♀H4	CSPN CWGN ETho MBri MNrw NHaw NTay SMDP
	'Pauline' (A/d) ♀H4	CBcs CWSG EBee LRHS LSRN MBri MGos NTay SCoo SLim SWCr
	'Pearl Rose' (A/d)	CWSG
	'Pendragon' (Vt)	CRHN NHaw
	'Pennell's Purity' (LL)	CFlo NHaw NTay
	Peppermint = 'Evipo005'[PBR] (d)	CFlo CLng CRos CSPN ELan EPfP LRHS LSqu NTay SCoo SLon SWCr
	'Perida' (LL)	CWGN
	'Perle d'Azur' (LL)	CBcs CMac CRHN CSPN CTri CWCL CWSG EBee ELan ELon EPfP ETho LAst LRHS LSRN MAsh MBri MGos MRav MSwo NEgg NTay SDix SLim SPer SPet SPoG SRms SWCr
	'Perrin's Pride' (Vt)	CLng LRHS MBri MGos NHaw NLar NTay SCoo SWCr
	Petit Faucon = 'Evisix'[PBR] (I) ♀H4	CFlo CLng CWCL EBee EPfP ETho LRHS LSRN LSqu MBri NLar SCoo SDix SLim SPer SWCr SWvt
	petriei	ECou WThu
	- 'Princess' (Fo/f)	ECou
	- 'Steepdown' (Fo/f)	ECou
	'Peveril Pearl' (EL)	ETho
	'Peveril Pristine' (Vt)	CWGN
	'Peveril Profusion' (T)	SMDP
	Picardy = 'Evipo024'[PBR] (EL)	CFlo CLng CRos CSPN EHyd EPfP ETho LBuc LRHS LSqu NPri NTay SCoo SLim SPer SPoG SWCr
I	'Picton's Variety' (M)	CSPN CTri MBri NHaw
	'Piilu' (EL)	CSPN CWGN EBee ELan ETho LBuc LRHS LSRN LSou MAsh MBNS MBri MGos NHaw NLar NTay SCoo SLim SMDP SPoG SRkn SWCr
§	'Pink Celebration' (EL)	ETho
	Pink Champagne	see *C.* 'Kakio'
	'Pink Fantasy' (LL)	CFlo CLng CRHN CSPN CTri EBee ETho LRHS MAsh MBri MGos NLar NTay SCoo SLim SRkn SWCr
	'Pink Flamingo' (A) ♀H4	CLng CSPN CWCL EBee ELan EPfP ETho LRHS MBri NTay SCoo SLim SPoG SRkn SWCr WBor
	'Pink Ice' (I)	CSPN EBee LRHS NHaw
	'Pirko' (Vt)	NHaw
§	***pitcheri***	NHaw SMDP
	'Pixie' (Fo/m)	CFlo CSPN ECou ELan ELon EPfP ETho LRHS MGos NHaw NLar NTay SCoo SLim SPoG
I	'Pleniflora' (M/d)	NHaw
§	'Plum Beauty' (A)	NHaw
	pogonandra new	NHaw
§	'Põhjanael' (LL)	CSPN MBri NLar
	Polar Bear	see *C.* Arctic Queen
	'Poldice' (Vt)	CRHN
	'Polish Spirit' (LL) ♀H4	CBar CDoC CFlo CMac CRHN CSPN CTri EBee ELan EPfP ETho LAst LBMP LRHS LSRN MBri MMuc NHol NTay SEND SLon SPer SPoG SRkn SWCr SWvt
	potaninii	CCon GCra NChi WPtf WSHC
	- 'Summer Snow'	see *C.* 'Paul Farges'
	'Praecox' (H) ♀H4	CRHN CWCL EBee ELan EPfP ETho LHop LRHS MBri MCot MWhi NBir NSti NTay SDix SPer SPoG SWCr WCot
	Pretty in Blue = 'Zopre'[PBR] (F)	MBri SWvt
	'Primrose Star'	see *C.* 'Star'
	'Prince Charles' (LL) ♀H4	CFlo CPou CRHN CSPN CTri EBee ELan EPfP ETho LRHS LSRN MAsh MBri MGos MJak MMuc NHaw NLar NTay SCoo SDix SLim SPer SPet SPoG SWCr SWvt

§	'Princess Diana' (T) ♀H4	CFlo CRHN CSPN CSam CTri CWGN CWSG EBee ELan ETho LBuc LRHS LSRN MAsh MBel MBlu MGos MJak MSwo NHol NTay SCoo SLim SPer SPoG SRms SWCr SWvt
	Princess Kate = 'Zoprika' (T) **new**	CWGN ETho IPot
§	'Princess of Wales' (1875) (EL)	EPfP LSRN NLar SLon SWvt
	'Prins Hendrik' (EL)	WGor
	'Prinsesse Alexandra'PBR (EL)	ETho NTay
	'Propertius' (A)	CFlo CSPN CWGN ETho LRHS MGos NHaw NTay SMDP
	'Prosperity' (M)	ETho
	'Proteus' (EL)	CLng CSPN EBee ELan EPfP ETho LRHS MAsh MBri MGos NTay SCoo SLim SWCr
	'Pruinina'	see *C.* 'Plum Beauty'
	psilandra CWJ 12377	WCru
	'Purple Haze' (Vt)	CRHN NHaw
	'Purple Princess' (H)	CMac NTay
	'Purple Spider' (A/d)	CFlo CMac CSPN EBee EPfP ETho IPot MAsh MBlu MBri NHaw NLar NTay SCoo
	'Purpurea Plena' (Vt/d) **new**	LPio
	'Purpurea Plena Elegans' (Vt/d) ♀H4	Widely available
	quadribracteolata	NHaw
	Queen Mother = 'Zoqum' (Vt) **new**	ETho IPot
	'Radiance' **new**	CWGN
	'Ragamuffin' (EL/d)	MGos
	'Rahvarinne' (LL)	ETho
	'Ramona' (LL)	CLng LRHS LSRN NHaw SWCr
	ranunculoides	NHaw
	'Rapture' (T)	MBri
	'Rasputin' (LL)	ETho
	Rebecca = 'Evipo016'PBR (EL)	CFlo CSPN CWCL EHyd ELan EPfP LBuc LRHS LSRN LSqu MBri NPri NTay SCoo SLon SPer SPoG SWCr
	recta	CSPN ECtt LPio MNrw MWhi NLar WHil
	- 'Lime Close' seedlings	CAby
	- 'Purpurea' (F)	CFlo CMea EHoe ELan EPfP EWTr GKev LHop LPio LRHS MNrw NBid NBir NChi NSti NTay SChF SDix SEND SPer SWCr WHoo XLum
	'Velvet Night' (F)	CSpe ECtt ESwi ETho GBuc MAvo MBNS MBel MCot NEgg NLar SMDP WCot
§	'Red Beetroot Beauty' (A)	CSPN
	'Red Cooler'	see *C.* 'Crimson King'
	'Red Pearl' (EL)	CFlo EBee ETho LRHS LSRN MBri MGos NTay SPoG SWCr
I	'Red Star' (d)	EPfP NTay WCot
	Reflections = 'Evipo035' (LL)	EPfP ETho LRHS LSqu NTay SLon SWCr
§	***rehderiana*** ♀H4	CCon CRHN CSPN CSam ELan EPfP ETho LRHS MBlu MBri MRav NBir NSti NTay SChF SDix SPer SWvt WPGP WSHC
	'Remembrance' (LL)	CFlo EPfP ETho LSRN MBri
	repens Finet & Gagn.	see *C. montana* var. *wilsonii*
	'Rhapsody' ambig.	CLng EBee EPfP ETho LRHS MAsh MBri NTay SCoo SWCr
	'Rhapsody' B. Fretwell (EL)	CSPN LSRN NHaw
	'Richard Pennell' (EL) ♀H4	EBee LRHS MAsh SLim SWCr
	'Richard's Picotee' (Vt) **new**	NHaw
	'Rising Star'	LRHS NHaw
	'Robud'PBR (M/d)	NPer
	'Roelie' (Vt)	NHaw
	'Roko-Kolla' (LL)	EBee ETho
	'Romance' (Vt)	MBri
	'Romantika' (LL)	CFlo CSPN EBee ELMC ELan ELon ETho IBoy IPot LRHS LSRN MAsh MBri NHaw NTay SCoo
	'Rooguchi' (I)	CFlo CLng CWGN EBee ETho IPot MBri NHaw SMDP SPoG
	'Rooran' (EL)	ETho
	'Rosa Königskind' (EL)	ETho
	'Rosamunde' (LL)	ETho
	'Rose Supreme' (EL)	ETho
I	'Rosea' (I) ♀H4	CSPN EPfP ETho LHop LRHS LSRN NTay
I	'Rosea' (Vt)	NHaw
	Rosemoor = 'Evipo002'PBR (EL)	CFlo CLng CRos CSPN CWCL CWGN EBee EPfP ETho IBal LBuc LRHS LSqu MAsh MBri NTay SCoo SDix SLim SLon SWCr SWvt
	'Rosy O'Grady' (A) ♀H4	CWCL MAsh MBri NLar NTay SRms
	'Rosy Pagoda' (A)	EBee ELan LRHS MBri NBir NHaw NLar NTay SLim
	'Rouge Cardinal' (LL)	CFlo CMac CSPN CWSG EBee ELan ELon EPfP ETho IBoy LRHS LSRN MAsh MBri MGos MJak NEgg NTay SDix SLim SPer SPet SPoG SRms SWCr
	'Royal Velours' (Vt) ♀H4	CDoC CFlo CRHN CSPN CTri EBee ELan EPfP ETho LRHS LSRN MAsh MBri MGos NHol SCoo SDix SLim SPer SPoG SWCr
	Royal Velvet = 'Evifour'PBR (EL)	CSPN EPfP LRHS LSRN MBri NTay SCoo
	'Royalty' (EL) ♀H4	CLng CSPN ELan EPfP LRHS LSRN MAsh MBri MJak NBir NTay SCoo SPer SPoG SWCr
	'Rubens Superba'	see *C. montana* 'Rubens Superba'
	'Rubra' (Vt)	MBlu
	'Ruby' (A)	CSPN CWSG EBee ELan EPfP ETho LRHS LSRN MAsh NTay SCoo SPer SRms
	'Ruby Glow' (EL)	CLng EPfP LRHS LSRN NTay SCoo SPoG SWCr
	'Ruby Wedding' (T)	CFlo CWGN EPfP LBuc LSRN MBri NTay SMDP SWvt
	'Rüütel' (EL)	CFlo ELon ETho LRHS MAsh MBri MGos NHaw NTay SCoo SMDP
	'Sally Cadge' (EL)	NHaw
	'Samantha Denny' (EL)	CSPN NHaw
	'Sander' (H)	ETho SMDP
	Saphyra Indigo = 'Cleminov 51'PBR (I)	CLng
	Savannah = 'Evipo015'PBR (Vt)	CLng LRHS SLim
	'Scartho Gem' (EL)	CLng LRHS MBri SCoo
	'Sealand Gem' (EL)	MBri NHaw
	'Serenata' (EL)	MBri
	serratifolia	ETho GLog MWhi SDix SPlb
	- B&SWJ 8458 from Korea	WCru
	'Sheila Thacker' (EL)	ETho
I	'Sherriffii' (Ta)	SWvt
	'Shikoo' (EL) **new**	ETho
	Shimmer = 'Evipo028' (LL)	EPfP LBuc LRHS LSqu NTay SLon SWCr
	'Shirayukihime' (EL)	NLar
§	'Shiva' (A)	MBri
	'Shooun' (EL)	MBri
	'Sialia' (A/d)	CFlo CSPN

§	***sibirica***	EPfP MBri
	'Signe' (Vt)	see *C.* 'Kasmu'
	'Silver Moon' (EL)	CFlo CLng CSPN EPfP ETho LRHS MAsh MBri NLar NTay SCoo
	simensis	LEdu
	'Simplicity' (A)	CSPN MBri
	simsii Small	see *C. pitcheri*
	simsii Sweet	see *C. crispa*
	'Sinee Plamia' (LL)	NHaw
§	'Sinii Dozhd' (I)	CWCL EPfP NHaw
	'Sir Eric Savill' (M)	ETho SMDP
	'Sir Garnet Wolseley' (EL)	MBri SDix
	'Sir Trevor Lawrence' (T)	CSPN EBee ETho LRHS NHaw
	'Sizaia Ptitsa' (I)	ETho
	'Snow Queen' (EL)	CCon CFlo CLng CSPN EBee EPfP ETho LRHS MBri NTay SLim SPet SPoG SRms
	'Snowbird' (A/d)	CFlo CSPN EBee EPfP LRHS NHaw NTay SPer SPoG
	'Snowdrift'	see *C. armandii* 'Snowdrift'
§	'Södertälje' (Vt)	CRHN EBee EPfP ETho MBri SCoo
	'Solidarność' (EL)	ETho
	'Sonnette' (V)	CFlo CWGN NHaw
	'Southern Cross' (Fo)	ECou
§	'Souvenir du Capitaine Thuilleaux' (EL)	LRHS MBri NTay
	'Special Occasion' (EL)	CLng CSPN CWGN EBee ETho LRHS LSRN MBri NHaw NLar NTay SCoo SPoG SWCr
	Spiky = 'Zospi' (A/d) **new**	CFlo
§	***spooneri***	CTri SCoo SLim SWvt WSpi
	'Sputnik' (I)	CWGN NHaw
	stans	CElw CExl CHel CPou EBee EPfP IFro LRHS NLar SMDP SWCr WSHC
	- B&SWJ 5073	WCru
	- B&SWJ 6345	WCru
§	'Star' PBR (M/d)	CSPN EPfP LRHS MBri MSwo NLar NTay SPer
	'Star of India' (LL)	CLng EBee EPfP ETho LRHS MBri MGos NTay SCoo SLim SPer WBor
	Star River = 'Zostarri' PBR (I)	ELan
I	'Starfish' (EL)	MGos NHaw
	'Starlight' (M)	EBee ELon LRHS NTay SLim
	'Stasik' (LL)	NHaw
	'Stephanie' (A)	CFlo CSPN
	Still Waters = 'Zostiwa' PBR (EL)	CSPN CWGN ETho NTay
	Sugar Candy = 'Evione' PBR (EL)	CLng LRHS MAsh MBri NTay SCoo SLim
	Summer Snow	see *C.* 'Paul Farges'
	Summerdream = 'Zosumdre' (EL)	ETho IPot NTay
	'Sundance' (Ta)	CSPN SMDP
	Sunny Sky = 'Zosusk' PBR (Vt)	CFlo NHaw NTay
	'Sunrise' PBR (M/d)	CSPN CWGN EBee ETho LRHS MBri MSwo NHaw NLar NTay
	'Sunset' (EL) ♀H4	CLng EBee ELon LRHS LSRN MBri NLar NTay SCoo SLim SPoG SWCr
	'Swedish Bells' (I)	CWGN ETho
	'Sweet Scentsation' (F)	CFlo EPfP MBri NHaw NLar
I	'Sweetheart' (I) **new**	ELan EPfP NTay
	'Sylvia Denny' (EL)	CWSG EBee ELan EPfP ETho MAsh MBri NTay SPet
	'Sympatia' (LL)	NHaw
	'Syrena' (LL)	NHaw
	szuyuanensis B&SWJ 6791	WCru
	- CWJ 12455	WCru

	'Tae' (EL)	ETho
	'Tage Lundell' (A)	CFlo CSPN EBee EPfP MBri NLar SMDP
	Tai Yang = 'Evipo045' **new**	LRHS
	'Tango' (Vt)	CRHN NHaw
§	***tangutica***	Widely available
	'Tapestry' (I)	NHaw SMDP
	tashiroi purple-flowered B&SWJ 7005	WCru
	- 'Yellow Peril'	WCru
	'Teksa' (LL)	NHaw
	Temptation = 'Zotemp' PBR (EL)	CSPN NTay
§	***terniflora***	CBcs EBee EPfP ETho NHaw SKHP
	- B&SWJ 5751	WCru
	'Teshio' (EL)	IPot NHaw
	texensis	WSHC
	- 'The Princess of Wales'	see *C.* 'Princess Diana'
	'The Bride' (EL)	CSPN CWGN EBee ETho LRHS LSRN MGos NHaw NTay
	'The First Lady' (EL)	CSPN ETho MBri
	'The President' (EL) ♀H4	CDul CMac CSPN CTri CWCL CWSG EBee ELan EPfP ETho IBoy LBMP LRHS LSRN MAsh MBri MGos MJak MRav MSwo NEgg NPri NTay SDix SLim SPer SPet SPoG SRms SWCr
	'The Princess of Wales' (EL)	see *C.* 'Princess of Wales' (1875) (EL)
	'The Princess of Wales' (T)	see *C.* 'Princess Diana' (T)
	'The Vagabond' (EL)	CSPN ELan ELon EPfP ETho LRHS LSRN MAsh MBri NHaw NLar NTay SCoo SLim SPoG SWCr
	'The Velvet' (EL)	ELMC
§	Thumbelina = 'Evipo030' PBR (EL)	CLng CWCL LBuc NTay SPoG SWCr
	thunbergii misapplied	see *C. terniflora*
	'Tibetan Mix' (Ta)	SMDP
	tibetana	NHaw
	- 'Black Tibet' (Ta)	CWGN SMDP
§	- subsp. ***vernayi***	CMHG
	- - 'Glasnevin Dusk' (Ta) **new**	SMDP WSHC
§	- - var. ***vernayi*** 'Orange Peel' LS&E 13342 (Ta)	CBcs CDoC ETho MRav SEND
	'Tie Dye' (LL)	ELan EPfP ETho NTay
	'Tinkerbell'	see *C.* 'Shiva'
	'Toki' (EL)	CWGN
	tongluensis GWJ 9358	WCru
	- HWJK 2368	WCru
	'Tranquility' **new**	CWGN SMDP
	'Treasure Trove' (Ta)	CSPN SMDP
	'Triinu' (Vt)	NHaw
	× ***triternata***	LSRN
§	- 'Rubromarginata' ♀H4	CCon CDoC CFlo CMac CRHN CSPN CSam CWGN EBee ELan ELon EPfP ETho LRHS LSRN MAsh MBri MGos MJak MRav NTay SDix SLim SLon SPer SPoG SRkn SRms SWCr
	'Tsunami Child' (M) **new**	IMou
	'Tsuzuki' (EL)	CSPN
§	***tubulosa***	CSPN ETho SMDP
§	- Alan Bloom = 'Alblo' PBR (H)	LRHS
	- 'Wyevale' (H) ♀H4	CFlo CHel CMac CSPN ELan ELon EPfP LHop LRHS MCot MRav NSti NTay SCoo SDix SMDP SPer WCot WWlt

	'Twilight' (EL)	CFlo CLng CSPN EPfP LRHS MAsh MBri NTay SWCr
	Twinkle Bell = 'Wer01'	NTay
	Twinkle = 'Zotwi' (I) **new**	CWGN
	uncinata B&SWJ 11368	WCru
	- CWJ 12373	WCru
§	***urophylla*** 'Winter Beauty'	CDoC CFlo EBee ETho LSRN MBri NTay SBrt SMDP SPoG
	urticifolia B&SWJ 8651	WCru
	- B&SWJ 8852	WCru
	'Utopia' (EL)	CSPN CWGN
	'Valge Daam' (LL)	CWGN ETho NHaw
	'Van Gogh' (M) **new**	SMDP
	'Vanessa' (LL)	CRHN
	'Vanso'	see *C.* 'Blue Light'
	× ***vedrariensis*** 'Hidcote' (M)	NHaw
	- 'Highdown' (M)	EBee
§	***veitchiana***	NHaw
	'Venosa Violacea' (Vt) 𝕐^{H4}	CCon CFlo CMac CRHN CSPN EBee ELan EPfP ETho LRHS LSRN MAsh MRav NHaw NHol NTay SCoo SDix SPer SPoG SRms SWCr
	'Vera' (M)	CSPN LRHS LSRN NTay SCoo SLim
	vernayi	see *C. tibetana* subsp. *vernayi*
	'Veronica's Choice' (EL)	CFlo CSPN EBee ELan LRHS MBri MGos MRav NHaw NTay SPet
	Versailles = 'Evipo025'^{PBR} (EL)	CLng EPfP LRHS NTay SLim
	versicolor	WSHC
§	Vesuvius = 'Evipo032'^{PBR} (Vt)	CLng EPfP LRHS MBri NTay SCoo SLim SLon
	'Vetka'^{PBR} (LL)	NHaw
	Victor Hugo = 'Evipo007'^{PBR} (LL)	CFlo CLng EBee EPfP LRHS NLar NTay SCoo
N	'Victoria' (LL) 𝕐^{H4}	CRHN CSPN ETho LRHS LSRN MBri MRav NHaw NTay SCoo SWCr
	Viennetta = 'Evipo006'^{PBR} (d)	CFlo CSPN EPfP ETho LRHS LSqu NTay SCoo SLon SPer SRms SWCr
	'Ville de Lyon' (LL)	CBcs CFlo CMac CRHN CSPN CWCL EBee ELan EPfP GGal IBoy LRHS LSRN MAsh MBri MGos MJak NEgg NTay SDix SLim SPer SPoG SWCr
	'Vince Denny' (Ta)	EBee MBri NHaw SMDP
	Vino = 'Poulvo'^{PBR} (EL)	CLng EBee LRHS MBri NHaw NTay SCoo SLim SWCr
I	'Viola' (LL)	CFlo CSPN CWGN EBee ELMC ELon ETho LRHS LSRN MBri MGos NHaw NTay SMDP
	'Violet Charm' (EL)	MBri
	'Violet Elizabeth' (EL)	MRav
I	'Violet Purple' (A)	NHaw
	viorna	NHaw WCru
	virginiana misapplied	see *C. vitalba*
	virginiana Hook.	see *C. ligusticifolia*
	virginiana L.	CElw
§	***vitalba***	CArn CDul ECrN ETho NHaw NTay NWea WHer WSFF
	- SDR 6610	GKev
	viticella 𝕐^{H4}	CRHN CWib ETho GKev MBri NHaw
§	- subsp. ***campaniflora***	CSPN EShb ETho GCal NHaw
§	- 'Flore Pleno' (Vt/d)	CFlo CRHN CSPN EBee ELon EPfP ETho LRHS LSRN NHaw NTay SLon SWCr
	- 'Hågelby Blue' (Vt)	NHaw
	- 'Hågelby Pink' (Vt)	CRHN CWGN NHaw
	- 'Hågelby White' (Vt)	CWGN NHaw SMDP
	- 'Hanna' (Vt)	CRHN LSRN NHaw
	- 'Mary Rose'	see *C. viticella* 'Flore Pleno'
	'Vivienne'	see *C.* 'Beth Currie'
	'Voluceau' (Vt)	CLng CPou CRHN EBee ELan LRHS LSRN MRav SRms SWCr
	'Vostok' (LL)	MGos NTay
	'Vyvyan Pennell' (EL)	CBcs CFlo CMac CSPN CTri EBee ELan EPfP ETho EUJe IBoy LBMP LRHS LSRN MAsh MBri MGos MSwo NEgg NLar NTay SLim SPer SPoG SWCr SWvt
	'W.E. Gladstone' (EL)	ETho LRHS SDix SPer
	Wada's Primrose	see *C. patens* 'Manshuu Ki'
	'Walenburg' (Vt)	CRHN CWGN ETho NHaw SLon
	'Walter Pennell' (EL)	CBcs EBee LRHS SCoo WGor
	'Warsaw' (Ta)	NLar SWCr
	'Warszawska Nike' (EL) 𝕐^{H4}	CLng CMac CRHN EBee ELan EPfP ETho LBMP LRHS MAsh MBri MGos NTay SCoo SLim SPer SPoG
	'Warszawska Olga' (EL)	ETho
	'Warwickshire Rose' (M)	CFlo CLng CRHN CSPN CTri CWGN CWSG ETho LRHS LSRN MAsh NHaw NTay SLim SPoG SWCr WSHC
	'Waterperry Star' (Ta)	MWat
	'Wedding Day' (EL)	CFlo ETho LSRN NLar NTay
	'Wee Willie Winkie' (M)	LRHS SCoo
	'Westerplatte' (EL)	CFlo CLng CRHN CSPN CWGN EBee EPfP ETho LRHS MAsh MBri MGos NHaw NTay SLim SMDP SPoG SWCr
	'Whirligig' (A)	CSPN
§	'White Columbine' (A) 𝕐^{H4}	ELan ETho LRHS MBri MGos NTay SDix SLim
	'White Lady' (A/d)	NHaw
	'White Magic'^{PBR} (Vt)	CRHN ETho
§	'White Moth' (A/d)	CSPN ELan ETho LSRN MAsh MGos MRav NHaw NHol NTay SLim SPer SPoG WSpi
	'White Satin' (A)	SWCr
	'White Swan' (A/d)	CSPN MAsh MBri NHol NLar SCoo
	'White Wings' (A/d)	CFlo LSRN
	'Will Goodwin' (EL) 𝕐^{H4}	CBcs CLng CMac CWCL ELan EPfP LRHS MBri SLim SRms
	'William Kennett' (EL)	CLng CWSG ELan EPfP ETho IBoy LRHS MBri MGos MJak
	williamsii	SMDP
	'Willy' (A)	CBcs CSPN EBee ELan EPfP ETho LBMP LRHS MAsh MBri MSwo NLar NTay SDix SLim SPer SRms SWCr
	Wisley = 'Evipo001'^{PBR} (Vt)	CBcs CLng CSPN EPfP LRHS MBri NLar NTay SLim SLon SWCr
	'Xerxes' misapplied	see *C.* 'Elsa Späth'
	'Yatsuhashi' ambig.	CCon ELMC LRHS
	'Yellow Queen' Holland	see *C. patens* 'Manshuu Ki'
	'Yellow Queen' Lundell/Treasures	see *C.* 'Moonlight'
§	'Yukikomachi' (EL)	CSPN ETho NHaw NTay
	'Yvette Houry' (EL)	NHaw
	'Yvonne Hay'	SMDP
	Zara = 'Evipo062' **new**	ETho LRHS LSqu NPri SLon SPoG
	'Zephyr' (Vt)	NHaw

Clematopsis see *Clematis*

Clementsia see *Rhodiola*

Cleome (*Cleomaceae*)

	hassleriana 'Helen Campbell' 𝕐^{H} 3	CSpe SPhx

'Odyssee Deep Rose'	NPri
'Odyssee White'	NPri
Senorita Rosalita = 'Inncleosr'PBR	NPri

Clerodendrum (*Lamiaceae*)

bungei	Widely available
- 'Pink Diamond' (v)	CCCN CDoC CWGN EBee ELan EPfP EThi EUJe EWes LRHS LSRN MGos MPkF NLar SEND SKHP SLim SPoG
§ ***chinense*** var. ***chinense*** (d) ♀H1	CCCN CHll
- 'Pleniflorum'	see *C. chinense* var. *chinense*
fragrans var. ***pleniflorum***	see *C. chinense* var. *chinense*
* ***mutabile*** B&SWJ 6651	WCru
myricoides	CCCN CHll CRHN MOWG SMrm
'Ugandense' ♀H1	WSFF
philippinum	see *C. chinense* var. *chinense*
speciosissimum	MOWG
aff. ***subscaposum*** WWJ 11735	WCru
thomsoniae ♀H1	WSFF
trichotomum	CBcs CDul CElw CEnd CExl CLnd CMCN CSam CSpe CTri CWib EPfP EUJe IArd LRHS SLPl SLim SLon SPer SSta WBor WHar
- 'Carnival' (v)	CAbP CBcs CCCN CDul CExl CJun CMac EBee ELan EPfP EWes LRHS MAsh MGos NLar SEND SKHP SLim SMDP SPer SPoG SWvt WCot WPat
- var. ***fargesii*** ♀H4	Widely available
- 'Purple Blaze'	EPfP
- 'Purple Haze'	CJun NLar
- 'Shiro'	WCru
wallichii	CSpe EShb

Clethra ✿ (*Clethraceae*)

acuminata	EPfP GKin NLar
alnifolia	CBcs CDul CExl CMHG EBee MPkF SRms WCFE WCot
- 'Anne Bidwell'	EWTr MBlu NLar
- 'Creel's Calico' (v)	NLar
- 'Fern Valley Pink'	CCCN CMac EBee ELon GKin LLHF LRHS NLar
- 'Hokic Pink'	GKin NLar
- 'Hummingbird'	CCCN CDoC CEnd CExl CMac CWib EBee ELan EPfP GKin IDee LRHS MAsh MBlu NLar NPCo SLim SPad SPoG SSpi SWvt
- 'Paniculata' ♀H4	CDoC ELon EPfP LRHS MMuc MNHC SBod WBor
- 'Pink Spire'	CDoC CExl CWCL ECrN EPfP GKin MMHG MMuc MRav NEgg NLar SCoo
- 'Rosea'	CTri GKin GQui MMHG MPkF SPer
- 'Ruby Spice'	CBcs CCCN CEnd CExl CMac CWib EBee ELan ELon EPfP GBin GGGa GKin IDee LAst LRHS LSRN MBlu NCGa NEgg NLar SLim SPer SPoG SWvt WGob
- 'September Beauty'	NLar
- 'Sixteen Candles'	GGGa GKin NLar
arborea	CBcs NLar
barbinervis ♀H4	CBcs CDoC CExl EBee EPfP GGGa GKin IDee IVic LRHS MBlu NLar SPer SSpi WSHC
- B&SWJ 11562	WCru
delavayi Franch.	CBcs CCCN CDoC EBee EPfP GGGa GQui IDee NLar SKHP SSpi
- SBEC 1513	CExl
- Stone's hardy strain	SKHP
fargesii	CExl EPfP GKin NLar WPGP
mexicana new	CFil
monostachya	CExl GGGa NLar
pringlei	CFil NLar WPGP WSHC
tomentosa 'Cottondale'	NLar

Cleyera (*Pentaphylacaceae*)

fortunei	see *C. japonica* 'Fortunei'
- 'Variegata'	see *C. japonica* 'Fortunei'
japonica	CDoC
§ - 'Fortunei' (v)	CCCN CMHG CMac CWib LRHS SHil SSta
- var. ***japonica***	WPGP
- 'Tricolor' (v)	CBcs CDoC MPkF
- var. ***wallichii***	EBee WPGP

Clianthus ✿ (*Papilionaceae*)

maximus	SVen
§ ***puniceus*** ♀H2	CAbb CBcs CDoy CExl CHel CHll CMHG CPom CSBt CSpe CTsd CWib EBee EGri EPfP IBoy LHop LRHS MOWG NSoo SEND SPer SPlb SPoG SVen SWvt WCot WPGP WSHC
§ - 'Albus' ♀H2	CBcs CExl CHEx CHGN CHel CHll CSpe CWib EBee EPfP IBoy IDee LRHS MOWG SPer SPoG SVen SWvt WCot WPGP
- 'Flamingo'	see *C. puniceus* 'Roseus'
- 'Kaka King'	CBcs EWes MREP SPoG
- 'Red Admiral'	see *C. puniceus*
- 'Red Cardinal'	see *C. puniceus*
§ - 'Roseus'	CBcs CExl CHel EPfP EUJe IVic LRHS SPer SPoG WCot WPGP
- 'White Heron'	see *C. puniceus* 'Albus'

Clinopodium (*Lamiaceae*)

ascendens	see *Calamintha ascendens*
calamintha	see *Calamintha nepeta*
grandiflorum	see *Calamintha grandiflora*
§ ***vulgare***	CArn CHab CSpe MHer MNHC NMir WJek WMoo WOut WPtf

Clintonia (*Liliaceae*)

andrewsiana	CLAP ECho EWes WCru
udensis	WCru
- HWJK 2339 from Nepal	WCru
umbellulata	CLAP GCal LRHS WCru
uniflora	CLAP ECho EWes

Clivia ✿ (*Amaryllidaceae*)

caulescens	WCot
gardenii × ***miniata***	WCot
miniata ♀H1	CAbb CBcs CTca CTsd ECho EWoo SMrm SRms WCot
- 'Aurea' ♀H1	CSpe EWoo
- 'Beverley's Delight'	WCot
- broad-leaved	EWoo
- - dark orange-flowered	EWoo
- var. ***citrina*** ♀H1	CTca ECho WCot
- 'Citrina Spider'	CFwr
- Daruma Group	WCot
- green-centred	EWoo WCot
- hybrids	SEND
- 'Light of Buddha' (v)	WCot

- 'Orange Spider'	CFwr
- pastel shades	CFwr EWoo WCot
- 'Vico Yellow'	CTsd EWoo
- 'Wide Leaf Monk'	WCot
nobilis 🏆^{H1}	WCot
'San Marcus Yellow' × 'Solomone Yellow'	WCot

Clusia (*Clusiaceae*)

rosea	CCCN

Clypeola (*Brassicaceae*)

jonthlaspi	WCot

Clytostoma (*Bignoniaceae*)

§ ***calystegioides***	CCCN CHII CRHN EShb

Cneorum (*Rutaceae*)

tricoccon	SKHP

Cnicus (*Asteraceae*)

§ ***benedictus***	CArn

Cnidium (*Apiaceae*)

officinale	GPoy

Cobaea (*Polemoniaceae*)

pringlei	CRHN WPGP WSHC
- CD&R 1323	WCot
scandens 🏆^{H3}	CCCN CDTJ CSpe ELan NPri SPer SVen WHlf
- f. ***alba*** 🏆^{H3}	CSpe SPer

cobnut see *Corylus avellana*

Coccoloba (*Polygonaceae*)

uvifera **new**	SPlb

Cocculus (*Menispermaceae*)

laurifolius	EUJe
§ ***orbiculatus***	CExl
- B&SWJ 535	WCru
trilobus	see *C. orbiculatus*

Cochlearia (*Brassicaceae*)

armoracia	see *Armoracia rusticana*
officinalis	CArn ELau MHer WHer

Cocos (*Arecaceae*)

plumosa	see *Syagrus romanzoffiana*
weddelliana	see *Lytocaryum weddellianum*

Codonanthe (*Gesneriaceae*)

gracilis	WDib
'Paula'	WDib

× *Codonatanthus* (*Gesneriaceae*)

'Golden Tambourine'	WDib
'Sunset'	WDib
'Tambourine'	WDib

Codonopsis (*Campanulaceae*)

ACE 1625 **new**	EPot
HWJK 2105 from Nepal	WCru
affinis HWJCM 70	WCru
- HWJK 2151	WCru
benthamii GWJ 9352	WCru
bhutanica	NEgg
cardiophylla	CHel EWld GCal
clematidea	CCon CHel CSpe EBee ECho EPfP EWld GCal GKev LRHS MNrw NEgg NLar NSum SPhx SPlb SWvt WWEG
convolvulacea misapplied	see *C. grey-wilsonii*
convolvulacea Kurz	NSla
- 'Alba'	see *C. grey-wilsonii* 'Himal Snow'
- Forrest's form	see *C. forrestii* Diels
- var. ***hirsuta*** B&SWJ 7812	WCru
'Dangshen'	see *C. pilosula*
dicentrifolia	CHel
- HWJCM 267	WCru
forrestii misapplied	see *C. grey-wilsonii*
§ ***forrestii*** Diels	ECho NHar
- BWJ 7776	WCru
- BWJ 7847	WCru
§ ***grey-wilsonii*** 🏆^{H4}	CAby CBro CCon ECho EWld GKev NSum WIvy
- B&SWJ 7532	WCru
§ - 'Himal Snow'	CAby ECho EWld NCGa
handeliana	see *C. tubulosa*
inflata GWJ 9442	WCru
kawakamii	EPot
- B&SWJ 1592	WCru
- RWJ 10007	WCru
§ ***lanceolata***	CAby SBrt
- B&SWJ 562	WCru
meleagris ambig.	CCon
meleagris Diels	GKev
mollis	ECho NLar NSum
nepalensis Grey-Wilson	see *C. grey-wilsonii*
obtusa	EWld
ovata	NBro SPhx
§ ***pilosula***	EWld GKev GPoy SBrt WSHC
- BWJ 7910	WCru
§ ***rotundifolia*** var. ***angustifolia***	EWld WCru
- var. ***grandiflora***	EWld GKev
silvestris	see *C. pilosula*
subsimplex BWJ 7502	WCru
tangshen misapplied	see *C. rotundifolia* var. *angustifolia*
tangshen Oliv.	CArn GKev
§ ***tubulosa***	LRHS
ussuriensis	see *C. lanceolata*
vinciflora	ECho GKev WIvy
viridiflora	CCon WCru
viridis HWJK 2435	WCru

Coffea (*Rubiaceae*)

arabica	CCCN SPre

coffee see *Coffea*

Coincya (*Brassicaceae*)

wrightii PJL 20098	CHid

Colchicum ✿ (*Colchicaceae*)

agrippinum 🏆^{H4}	CAvo CBro CTca ECho EPot GBin GKev LWst MRav NBir NRya WHoo
'Antares'	NBir
asteranthum	LWst
atropurpureum	ECho EPot
- Drake's form	ECho
'Autumn Herald'	ECho ELan GKev
N 'Autumn Queen'	CTca ECho GKev
§ ***autumnale***	CArn CAvo CBro CHab ECho EPot GKev GPoy NRya SDeJ WShi
* - 'Albopilosum'	NBir
- 'Alboplenum'	CTca ECho ERCP GKev LRHS

	– 'Album'	CAvo CBro CTca ECho EPot ERCP GKev LRHS NBir SPer WShi
	– 'Atropurpureum'	ECho
	– var. ***major*** hort.	see *C. byzantinum* Ker Gawl.
	– var. ***minor*** hort.	see *C. autumnale*
§	– 'Nancy Lindsay' ♀H4	CBro ECho EPot LLHF LRHS WCot WShi
	– 'Pannonicum'	see *C. autumnale* 'Nancy Lindsay'
§	– 'Pleniflorum' (d)	ECho GKev
*	– ***roseum***	ECho
	– 'Roseum Plenum'	see *C. autumnale* 'Pleniflorum'
	baytopiorum	ECho LWst
	– from Turkey	ECho
§	***bivonae***	ECho EPot
	– HOA 9139	LWst
	– 'Apollo'	ECho GKev LWst
	– 'Mount Giona' **new**	GKev
	– 'Petrovac'	LWst
	– 'Vesta'	LWst
§	***boissieri***	ECho LWst
	bornmuelleri misapplied	see *C. speciosum* var. *bornmuelleri* hort.
	bornmuelleri Freyn	CBro ECho EPot GKev
	bowlesianum	see *C. bivonae*
	brachyphyllum OS 1030	LWst
§	***byzantinum*** Ker Gawl. ♀H4	CBro EPot GKev NBir SDeJ
	– ***album***	see *C. byzantinum* 'Innocence'
§	– 'Innocence'	ECho EPot GKev
	chalcedonicum subsp. ***punctatum***	LWst
	cilicicum	ECho EPot
	– Bowles's form	ECho
	– 'Purpureum'	CTca ECho GKev LLHF
	'Conquest'	see *C.* 'Glory of Heemstede'
	corsicum	ECho GKev LWst WThu
	cupanii	ECho
	– var. ***pulverulentum***	ECho
	davisii	ECho
	'Dick Trotter'	ECho EPot
	'Disraeli'	ECho EPot GKev
	falcifolium	ECho LWst
§	***giganteum***	ECho LRHS SPer
§	'Glory of Heemstede'	ECho GKev
	graecum	ECho
	– HOA 9141	LWst
	'Harlekijn'	ECho EPot ERCP
	hungaricum	ECho EPot LWst
	– f. ***albiflorum***	ECho EPot GKev LWst
	– 'Valentine'	EPot LWst
	– 'Velebit Star'	ECho GKev LWst
	illyricum	see *C. giganteum*
	'Jochem Hof'	ECho LEdu
	'Jolanthe'	LWst
	kesselringii	ECho EPot GKev LWst
	kotschyi	LWst
	laetum misapplied	see *C. parnassicum*
	'Lilac Bedder'	ECho
	'Lilac Wonder'	ECho ELan EPfP GKev MRav SDeJ SEND WCot
	longifolium	see *C. neapolitanum*
	luteum	ECho LWst
	macrophyllum	ECho
	– HOA 9806	LWst
	micranthum	ECho
	minutum	ECho LWst
	munzurense	LWst
§	***neapolitanum***	LWst
	parlatoris	ECho LWst
§	***parnassicum***	ECho LWst WThu
	– CH 835	LWst
	'Pink Goblet' ♀H4	CBro
	'Poseidon'	ECho
	procurrens	see *C. boissieri*
	pusillum	GKev
	– VV CR.441	LWst
	'Rosy Dawn' ♀H4	CBro CTca ECho GKev
	sanguicolle	LWst
	sfikasianum	ECho LWst
	sibthorpii	see *C. bivonae*
	speciosum ♀H4	CAvo CBro ECho ELan EPot GKev NBir
	– 'Album' ♀H4	CAvo CBro ECho EPfP EPot ERCP GAbr GKev LRHS MBri NBir SDeJ
	– 'Atrorubens'	ECho MBri
I	– var. ***bornmuelleri*** hort.	ECho LWst
	– var. ***illyricum*** hort.	see *C. giganteum*
	– 'Ordu'	ECho
	– 'Rubrum'	ECho
	szovitsii Fisch. & B. Mey.	ECho
	– pink-flowered	LWst
	– 'Snow White'	LWst
	– 'Tivi'	ECho LWst
	– 'Vardaovit' **new**	LWst
	– white-flowered	ECho LWst
	tenorei ♀H4	ECho EPot GKev LLHF NBir
	'The Giant'	CBro ECho EPfP EPot GKev SDeJ WCot
	triphyllum	ECho GKev LWst
	troodi ambig.	ECho
	variegatum	ECho LWst
	'Violet Queen'	ECho EPot GAbr GKev
	'Waterlily' (d) ♀H4	CAvo CBro CTca ECho ELan EPfP EPot ERCP GBin GKev LRHS NBir SDeJ WCot WHoo
	'William Dykes'	ECho
	'Zephyr'	ECho

Coleonema (*Rutaceae*)

§	***pulchellum***	CCCN CHEx CHel CSpe SVen
	pulchrum misapplied	see *C. pulchellum*
	'Sunset Gold'	CSpe SPlb

Coleus see *Solenostemon*

Colignonia (*Nyctaginaceae*)

	ovalifolia B&SWJ 10644	WCru

Colletia (*Rhamnaceae*)

	armata	see *C. hystrix*
	cruciata	see *C. paradoxa*
§	***hystrix***	CBcs CMac CTri CTsd ELon IVic NLar SAPC SMad
	– RCB RA S-3	WCot
	– 'Rosea'	CMac GCal MBlu SKHP
§	***paradoxa***	CBcs CCCN CDoC CWib EBee ELan EPfP LAst SAPC SKHP SMad SPoG
	paradoxa × ***spinosissima***	SMad
	ulicina	SVen

Collinsonia (*Lamiaceae*)

	canadensis	CArn

Collomia (*Polemoniaceae*)

	grandiflora	WCot WWFP

Colocasia (*Araceae*)

	affinis var. ***jeningsii***	CCon CDTJ EAmu

	antiquorum	see *C. esculenta*
§	***esculenta*** 🏆H1	CCon CDTJ CHEx EAmu EBee EUJe MSKA SPlb XBlo
	- 'Black Beauty'	EAmu
	- 'Black Magic'	CAbb CBct CDTJ CHll EAmu ECtt EUJe IKil LRHS MSKA NSoo SAPC SBig SBst SDix SEND SPad WCot XBlo
	- 'Blue Hawaii'	LRHS WCot
	- burgundy-stemmed	CDTJ SBig SBst
	- 'Chicago Harlequin'	EAmu
	- 'Diamond Head'	CWGN EAmu ESwi EUJe LRHS WCot
	- 'Fontanesii'	CDTJ CHEx EAmu MPkF SBst WCot
	- 'Hawaiian Eye'	LRHS WCot
	- 'Hilo Bay'	EAmu ESwi LRHS MBel WCot
	- 'Hilo Beauty'	EAmu XBlo
	- 'Illustris'	CAbb CDTJ LLWG WCot
	- 'Jack's Giant'	EAmu
	- 'Mojito' (v)	EAmu
	- 'Nancy's Revenge'	EAmu
	- 'Nigrescens'	EAmu
	- 'Pineapple Princess' (v)	LRHS WCot
	- 'Pink China'	EAmu
	- 'Ruffles'	EUJe
	- 'Sangria'	EAmu
	- 'Tea Cup'	EAmu
	fallax	CCon CHEx EAmu
	formosana B&SWJ 6909	WCru
	gaoligongensis	CCon
	gigantea	CDTJ EAmu
	'Himalayan Dragon'	SKHP
	'Madeira' **new**	EAmu

Colquhounia (*Lamiaceae*)

	coccinea	CArn CHel CHll CMHG EShb GGal MBlu MRav NLar SBrt SLon WSHC
	- Sch 2458	WPGP
§	- var. ***mollis*** B&SWJ 7222	WCru
	- var. ***vestita*** misapplied	see *C. coccinea* var. *mollis*
	- var. ***vestita*** ambig.	CBcs CTsd EBee EPfP LRHS SEND

Columnea (*Gesneriaceae*)

	'Aladdin's Lamp'	WDib
	× ***banksii*** 🏆H1	WDib
§	'Broget Stavanger' (v)	WDib
	'Chanticleer' 🏆H1	WDib
I	'Firedragon'	WDib
	'Gavin Brown'	WDib
	gloriosa	EBak
	'Inferno'	WDib
	'Katsura'	WDib
	'Merkur'	WDib
I	'Midnight Lantern'	WDib
	'Rising Sun'	WDib
	schiedeana	WDib
	'Sherbert'	WDib
	'Stavanger' 🏆H1	WDib
	'Stavanger Variegated'	see *C.* 'Broget Stavanger'

Colutea (*Papilionaceae*)

	arborescens	CBcs CExl CWib EBee ELan LRHS MBlu MGos MMuc NWea SEND SPer SPlb SPoG
	cilicica **new**	EGFP
	× ***media***	CPom CTsd ECre MBlu
	- 'Copper Beauty'	CBcs ELan LRHS NLar SMad SPer WPat
	orientalis	CCCN

Colvillea (*Caesalpiniaceae*)

	racemosa	SPlb

Comarum see *Potentilla*

Combretum (*Combretaceae*)

	fruticosum	CCCN

Commelina (*Commelinaceae*)

	coelestis	see *C. tuberosa* Coelestis Group
	dianthifolia	SRms WPtf
	- 'Electric Blue'	ELan EPfP LRHS SVic
	robusta	CSpe SBrt WCot
	tuberosa	NWad XLum
	- B&SWJ 10353	WCru
	- 'Alba'	ELan
	- blue-flowered	SDeJ
§	- Coelestis Group	CAby CSpe IGor LHop LLWG LRHS NSti SDys SRms WKif WSHC
	- - 'Sleeping Beauty'	MSpe

Comptonia (*Myricaceae*)

	peregrina	WCru

Conandron (*Gesneriaceae*)

	ramondioides B&SWJ 8929	WCru

Conanthera (*Tecophilaeaceae*)

	campanulata	EBee

Coniogramme (*Pteridaceae*)

	japonica	WFib

Conium (*Apiaceae*)

	maculatum	CArn
	- 'Golden Nemesis' (v)	WCot

Conoclinium (*Asteraceae*)

§	***coelestinum***	EWes LHop LRHS SBrt XLum

Conopodium (*Apiaceae*)

	majus	SRms WShi

Conostylis (*Haemodoraceae*)

	candicans	ECou

Convallaria (*Asparagaceae*)

	japonica	see *Ophiopogon jaburan*
	keiskei	EPPr WHil WWEG
I	- 'Marginata' (v) **new**	WCot
	majalis 🏆H4	Widely available
	- 'Albostriata' (v)	CBct CFwr CLAP CRDP CRow EBee ECho EHoe ELan EPPr EPfP GAbr GMaP LRHS LWst MAvo MCot MHol MNrw MRav NBir NPnk NSti WCot WHer WPnP WWFP
	- 'Berlin Giant'	MAvo NBre NRya SDeJ
	- 'Blush'	CAvo
	- 'Bordeaux'	CExl EBee EPPr MHer NLar WCot
	- 'Bridal Choice'	EBee ELan GBin NLar
	- 'Dorien'	CBct CBre EPPr MAvo
	- 'Flore Pleno' (d)	EBee WWEG
	- 'Géant de Fortin'	CAvo CBct CBro CCon CExl CLAP CRow ECho EPot GCal MMoz MRav NBir NBre NLar NMyG SBch WCot WWEG
	- 'Gerard Debureaux'	see *C. majalis* 'Green Tapestry'
	- 'Gold Leaf' **new**	CAvo

§	- 'Green Tapestry' (v)	CBct CLAP CRow MAvo
	- 'Haldon Grange' (v)	CDes CLAP EPPr MAvo
	- 'Hardwick Hall' (v)	CBct CCse CExl CLAP CRow EBee ECho EHoe EPot MAvo NBre NMyG WCot WWEG XEll
	- 'Hitschberger Riesenperle' **new**	XLum
	- 'Hofheim' (v)	CLAP CRow LEdu MAvo WCot WWEG
	- 'Prolificans'	CBct CCon CCse CLAP CRDP EBee ECho ECtt EPPr EPfP LSou MRav NBir NLar NPnk NSti WCot WHil WPnP
	- var. ***rosea***	Widely available
	- 'Variegata' (v)	CAvo EPot LBMP LHop LRHS MLHP NMyG SBch SMad WHil WThu WWEG
	- 'Vic Pawlowski's Gold' (v)	CBct CDes CExl CLAP CMac CRow ELon EPPr LWst MAvo MMoz NSla
	transcaucasica	EBee

Convolvulus (*Convolvulaceae*)

	althaeoides	CFis CMea ECho ELan EPri SEND SPhx
§	- subsp. ***tenuissimus***	CSpe EWes WCFE WCot
§	***boissieri***	EPot WAbe XEll XSen
	cantabricus	LRHS SPhx XLum XSen
	chilensis	CCCN
	cneorum ♀^{H3}	Widely available
	- 'Snow Angel'	EBee LRHS LSou SWvt
	compactus	GKev XSen
	elegantissimus	see *C. althaeoides* subsp. *tenuissimus*
	humilis	ECho
	lineatus	ECho EWes
	mauritanicus	see *C. sabatius*
	nitidus	see *C. boissieri*
§	***sabatius*** ♀^{H3}	CCCN CHEx CHel CSam CTri ECho ECtt ELan EPfP EPot LAst LHop LRHS MCot SEND SLim SPer SPlb SPoG SVen SWvt WCFE XLum XSen
	- dark-flowered	CCCN CSpe ECho SMrm
	- 'Moroccan Beauty'^{PBR}	CSpe LSou
	suendermannii ambig.	GKev

× *Cooperanthes* see *Zephyranthes*

Cooperia see *Zephyranthes*

Copernicia (*Arecaceae*)

alba	EAmu

Coprosma (*Rubiaceae*)

	acerosa 'Hawera'	CBcs
	- 'Live Wire' (f)	ECou
	atropurpurea (f)	ECou
	- (m)	ECou
	'Autumn Orange' (f)	ECou
	'Autumn Prince' (m)	ECou
	baueri misapplied	see *C. repens*
	'Beatson's Gold' (f/v)	CBcs CDTJ CExl CHGN CHll CTsd EBee ELan EPfP EShb IVic LRHS SEND SLim SWvt WGrn WSHC
	'Black Cloud'	EBee LRHS
	'Blue Pearls' (f)	ECou
	'Blue Skies'	NHar WThu
	brunnea	ECou WThu
	- (f)	WThu
	- (m)	WThu
	- 'Blue Beauty' (f)	ECou
	- 'Violet Fleck' (f)	ECou
	'Bruno' (m)	ECou
	'Cappuccino'	CBcs EShb LSou
	cheesemanii (f)	ECou
	- (m)	ECou
	- 'Hanmer Red' (f)	ECou
	- 'Mack' (m)	ECou
	- 'Red Mack' (f)	ECou
	'Coppershine'	CExl
	crassifolia × ***repens*** (m)	ECou
	× ***cunninghamii*** (f)	ECou
	× ***cunninghamii*** × ***macrocarpa*** (m)	ECou
	'Cutie' (f)	ECou
	'Dark Purple'	LRHS
	depressa	ECou WThu
	- 'Orange Spread' (f)	ECou
	'Evening Glow'^{PBR} (f/v)	CCCN CDTJ CDoC CSBt EBee ELan EPfP EShb EUJe IVic LBuc LRHS LSou MAsh MPkF NSoo SEND SHil SLim SRms WHar
	'Fire Burst'^{PBR} (f/v)	CBcs CCCN EBee ELan EPfP EShb EUJe LBuc LRHS LSou MAsh MBri MPkF MRav SHil SLim SLon SRms WHar
	grandifolia	ECou
	'Green Girl' (f)	ECou
	'Green Globe'	CHll
	'Hinerua' (f)	ECou
	'Indigo Lustre' (f)	ECou
	'Jewel' (f)	ECou
	'Karo Red'^{PBR} (v)	CBcs ELan ELon EPfP LBuc MPkF SLim SRms
	× ***kirkii*** 'Gold Edge'	ECou
I	- 'Kirkii' (f)	CHll ECou
	- 'Variegata' (f/v)	CBcs CTsd EBee ECou EPfP EShb LRHS SEND SLim
	'Kiwi' (m)	ECou
	'Kiwi-gold' (m/v)	ECou
	'Lemon and Lime'^{PBR} (v)	CDoC EBee ELan EPfP EUJe LRHS MAsh MBri MPkF NSoo SHil SPoG SRms WHar
	'Lemon Drops' (f)	ECou
	linariifolia (m)	ECou
	lucida	IDee
	macrocarpa (f)	ECou
	- (m)	ECou
	'Midnight Martini' **new**	LBuc LRHS SHil
	nitida (f)	ECou
	parviflora (m)	ECou
	- red-fruited (f)	ECou
	- white-fruited (f)	ECou
	'Pearl Drops' (f)	ECou
	'Pearl's Sister' (f)	ECou
	'Pearly Queen' (f)	ECou
	petriei	ECou WThu
	- 'Don' (m)	ECou
	- 'Lyn' (f)	ECou
	- 'White Pearls'	WThu
	propinqua (f)	ECou
	- (m)	ECou
	- var. ***latiuscula*** (f)	ECou
	- - (m)	ECou
	'Prostrata' (m)	ECou
	pseudocuneata (m)	ECou
	quadrifida	ECou
	'Rainbow Surprise'^{PBR} (v)	CCCN CExl CSBt EBee ELan LRHS LSou MBri MPkF MRav NSoo SHil SLim SRms WHar

§ ***repens***	CBcs CExl EShb SPlb SVen
- (f)	ECou
- (m)	ECou
- 'County Park Plum' (v)	CBcs ECou ELon
- 'County Park Purple' (f)	ECou ELon
- 'County Park Red'	ECou ELon
- 'Exotica' (f/v)	ECou
- 'Marble King' (m/v)	ECou
- 'Marble Queen' (m/v) ♀H1-2	CBcs ECou
- 'Orangeade' (f)	ECou
- 'Pacific Lady'	EBee ECou
- Pacific Night = 'Hutpac'PBR (m)	CDoC CSBt ECou ELan EPfP EUJe IVic LBuc LRHS MAsh MBri MPkF NPri SHil SLon SPoG
- Pacific Sunset = 'Jwncopps' (v)	EPfP LBuc LRHS NSoo SLon
- 'Painter's Palette' (m)	EBee ECou EShb SVen
- 'Picturata' (m/v) ♀H1-2	ECou EShb SEND
- 'Pina Colada' (v)	LBuc LRHS SHil
- 'Pink Splendour' (m/v)	CBcs ECou
- 'Rangatiri' (f)	ECou
- 'Silver Queen' (m/v)	ECou
- 'Variegata' (m/v)	ECou
rigida	ECou
- 'Ann' (f)	ECou
- 'Tan' (m)	ECou
robusta	CBcs ECou
- 'Sally Blunt' (f)	ECou
- 'Steepdown' (f)	ECou
- 'Tim Blunt' (m)	ECou
- 'Variegata' (m/v)	ECou
- 'William' (m)	ECou
- 'Woodside' (f)	ECou
'Roy's Red' (m)	EBee EShb LRHS LSRN SEND SPoG
rugosa	CExl
- (f)	ECou
'Snowberry' (f)	ECou
'Tequila Sunrise' **new**	LBuc LRHS SHil
'Translucent Gold' (f)	ECou
'Violet Drops' (f)	ECou
virescens (f)	ECou
'Walter Brockie'	CHGN CHII
'White Lady' (f)	ECou
'Winter Bronze' (f)	ECou

Coptis (*Ranunculaceae*)

japonica	WCru
- var. ***dissecta***	WCru
- var. ***major***	CDes EBee WCru WSHC
omeiensis	WCru
quinquefolia B&SWJ 1677	WCru
ramosa B&SWJ 6000	WCru
- B&SWJ 6030	WCru
trifolia	WCru

Corallospartium see *Carmichaelia*

Cordyline ✿ (*Asparagaceae*)

australis ♀H3	Widely available
- 'Albertii' (v) ♀H3	CCCN MBri SAPC SEND
- 'Atlantic Green'	SHil
- 'Atropurpurea'	CCCN EUJe MWat SEND
- 'Black Night'	CCCN LRHS
- Burgundy Spire = 'Jel01'PBR	EPfP LBuc LRHS
- 'Claret'	CBcs
- 'Coffee Cream'	CCCN EPfP
- 'Olive Fountain'	CCCN
- 'Peko'PBR	CCCN
- 'Pink Champagne'	CCCN EBee ELan LBuc LRHS MGos MSwo NEgg SLim
- Pink Passion = 'Seipin'PBR	CCCN CWSG EBee EPfP LRHS NSoo
- 'Pink Stripe' (v)	CCCN CDoC ELan EPfP LSRN MBri SLim SWvt
- 'Purple Heart'	CCCN MSwo
- Purpurea Group	CBcs CDTJ EBee ELan EPfP MGos SEND SPer SPlb
- 'Red Sensation'	CCCN CHEx SWvt
- 'Sparkler'	CCCN EPfP LRHS MBri MGos SHil
- 'Sundance' ♀H3	CBcs CDoC CEnd CMac CWib EBee EPfP LRHS MAsh MBri MGos MSwo NPer SEND SLim SPoG SRms SWvt
- 'Torbay Dazzler' (v) ♀H3	CAbb CBcs CDoC CEnd CHEx CSBt EBee ELan ELon EPfP EUJe IVic LRHS LSRN MAsh MBri MGos MJak NEgg NPla NPri SEND SHil SLim SPer SPoG SWvt
- 'Torbay Red' ♀H3	CCCN CDoC CMac EBee EPfP LRHS LSRN MBri NPri SPer SWvt
- 'Torbay Sunset'	CCCN
- 'Variegata' (v)	MWat
'Autumn'	CCCN
banksii	CTsd IDee
'Cardinal'PBR	CBcs
'Cherry Sensation' (v) **new**	LBuc LRHS SHil
'Dark Star'	CBcs CCCN CDTJ CMac COIW SLim
'Eurostar'	CCCN
'Eurostripe'PBR	LRHS MBri SHil
Festival Grass = 'Jurred'	EAmu LRHS
'Firecracker'	CCCN LRHS MBri SHil
fruticosa 'Red Edge' ♀H1	XBlo
§ ***indivisa***	CBcs CCCN CDTJ CTsd EAmu ELon IDee SAPC SPlb WPGP
kaspar	CCCN CTsd EAmu SAPC
obtecta	CCCN CTsd
- bronze-leaved	CTsd
pumilio	LRHS
'Purple Sensation'	CBcs CCCN EUJe LRHS NPri
'Purple Tower' ♀H3	EBee MJak
'Red Bush'	XBlo
'Red Heart'	CCCN CWSG
'Red Star'	CAbb CBcs CCCN COIW CSBt CWGN CWSG CWib EBee EPfP LRHS MBri MJak MSwo NPer SHil SPoG SWvt
Renegade = 'Tana'PBR	LBuc LRHS NPri
'Southern Splendour'	CCCN EAmu ELan EPfP ESwi LBuc LRHS MBri MGos NPri SHil SPoG
§ ***stricta***	CHEx
'Sunrise' (v)	CWGN EAmu EUJe LRHS MBri SHil
terminalis	see *C. fruticosa*

Coreopsis (*Asteraceae*)

'Astolat'	LSou MRav SPer
auriculata Cutting Gold	see *C.* 'Schnittgold'
- 'Elfin Gold'	EDAr EHyd
- 'Nana'	MNrw NBre
- 'Superba'	LRHS MRav
- 'Zamphir'	EBee EPfP MNrw WCot
'Autumn Blush'	NLar
'Baby Gold'	see *C. lanceolata* 'Sonnenkind' (unblotched)
Baby Sun	see *C.* 'Sonnenkind' (red-blotched)
'Calypso' (v)	EWes LBuc LRHS SMad
'Cha Cha Cha' **new**	LSou

'Cosmic Eye' (Big Bang Series) NCGa
'Cranberry Ice' CWGN NLar
'Dream' SRkn
'Fruit Punch' **new** LRHS
'Full Moon'PBR (Big Bang Series) NLar STPC XLum
'Garnet' **new** NLar
'Golden Pompom'PBR (d) LSou
grandiflora NEgg SHar
- 'Bernwode' (v) CMac LSou NLar SWvt
- 'Domino' EHyd LRHS SMrm
- 'Early Sunrise' ♀H4 CSBt EBee ECtt EHyd EPfP EShb IBoy LBMP LDai LPot LRHS MAsh MBri NBir NGBl NPer SGbt SPet SPhx SPoG SWvt WWEG XLum
- Flying Saucers = 'Walcoreop'PBR EPfP LBuc LRHS SCoo SPoG
- 'Heliot' LPot MAvo MBri SPhx
- 'Illico' MBri
- 'Mayfield Giant' CCon CSBt EBee ELan EShb LHop MNrw NPri SPer SRms SWvt WHrl
- 'Rising Sun' EHyd ELan MBri NPri SPhx
- 'Sunburst' EPfP NBre XLum
- 'Sunfire' LRHS MBri MHer SHil SPhx
- 'Sunray' CBcs CDoC CSBt CWib ECtt EHyd EPfP EShb LRHS LSRN MAvo MBri MGos NGdn NPri SHil SMrm SPad SPlb SPoG SRms SWvt WMoo XLum
- 'Tetra Riesen' NBre
integrifolia LRHS
'Jethro Tull' SPoG
'Jive' (Coloropsis Series) CSpe CWGN LSou
lanceolata NBre
- 'Goldfink' LRHS MRav SRms
- 'Goldteppich' LRHS
- 'Little Sundial' LSou MBri
§ - 'Sonnenkind' (unblotched) GMaP XLum
- 'Walter' LSou NDov NEgg SPoG WCot WGwG WWEG XLum
'Limbo' (Coloropsis Series) **new** LSou
'Limerock Passion'PBR EPfP LRHS LSou MAvo MBNS NPnk SHar SRkn
'Limerock Ruby'PBR CSev ECtt EPau EPfP GMaP LHop LRHS LSou MHol NEgg NPnk SRkn SWvt WSpi XLum
'Mango Punch' CSpe LHop MAvo NPnk
maximiliani see *Helianthus maximiliani*
'Moonlight'PBR CSev
'Pink Lady'PBR LHop
'Pinwheel' LSou
pubescens LSou
- 'Sunshine Superman' ELan
pulchra LRHS
rosea CPom
- 'American Dream' CSBt EHyd ELan EPfP GBBs GMaP LAst LRHS LSRN MHer NBir NGdn NLar SPer SPlb SRms SWvt WGwG WMnd XLum
- 'Heaven's Gate'PBR LAst
- 'Nana' XLum
- 'Sweet Dreams'PBR CSev LHop LRHS LSRN SPer SRkn
'Ruby Frost' **new** CCVN MHol NLar NPnk
'Rum Punch'PBR CSpe LHop
'Salsa' (Coloropsis Series) **new** LSou
'Sangria'PBR LHop SPoG
§ 'Schnittgold' NBre SHar
I 'Sonnenkind' (red-blotched) LRHS NBre
'Star Cluster' (Big Bang Series) **new** STPC
'Sterntaler' CCon CMea EBee ECtt ELon EPPr EPau EPfP EShb LHop LRHS MBri NPri SMrm SPad SPet SPoG SWvt WWEG XLum
Sun Child see *C.* 'Sonnenkind' (red-blotched)
'Tequila Sunrise' (v) MNrw NLar
tinctoria CArn MNHC SRms
tripteris CAby ELan EPfP LPio LPla LRHS MMuc NBre SMad SPhx WMoo XLum
- 'Mostenveld' EBee
verticillata CMac EBee GCal LRHS MBrN MGos MHer MWat NPer SDix SRms WCAu WHal
- Crème Brûlée = 'Crembru'PBR ECtt EWes LPio LRHS NEgg NPnk SCoo SMrm SRkn WSpi
I - 'Golden Gain' ECtt LHop MArl NGdn WGwG WMnd WWEG
- 'Golden Shower' see *C. verticillata* 'Grandiflora'
§ - 'Grandiflora' ♀H4 CBcs CPrp EBee ELan EPfP GMaP LRHS MRav NCGa NGdn NHol NWad SPer WMnd XLum
- 'Limerock Dream'PBR LRHS LSou MBNS SHar
- 'Moonbeam' ♀H4 Widely available
- 'Old Timer' ♀H4 SDix
- 'Ruby Red' CAbP LRHS MAvo MBri
- 'Sunbeam' ELon
- 'Tweety' **new** MAsh
- 'Zagreb' ♀H4 Widely available

coriander see *Coriandrum sativum*

Coriandrum (*Apiaceae*)

* ***citratus*** ELau
sativum CArn GPoy MHer MHoo MNHC NPri SIde SPoG SRms
- 'Confetti' MHoo
- 'Leisure' MHoo SVic
- 'Santo' ELau
- 'Slobolt' ELau

Coriaria ✿ (*Coriariaceae*)

arborea WCru
intermedia B&SWJ 019 WCru
japonica NLar SVen WCru
- B&SWJ 2833 WCru
- subsp. ***intermedia*** B&SWJ 3877 WCru
kingiana WCru
§ ***microphylla*** WCru
- B&SWJ 8999 WCru
myrtifolia NLar WCru
nepalensis NLar WCru
- BWJ 7755 WCru
pteridoides WCru
ruscifolia WCru
- HCM 98178 WCru
sarmentosa WCru
terminalis var. ***xanthocarpa*** EPfP GCal WCru
- - GWJ 9204 WCru
- - HWJK 2112c WCru
thymifolia see *C. microphylla*

Cornus ✿ (*Cornaceae*)

alba L. CBar CCVT CDoC CDul CLnd ECrN MHer MRav NWea SEWo SRms WMou
- 'Alleman's Compact' CJun

	- 'Argenteovariegata'	see *C. alba* 'Variegata'
	- 'Aurea' ♀H4	Widely available
	- Baton Rouge = 'Minbat'^{PBR}	CNec EBee ELon EMil EPfP LRHS SWvt
	- 'Cream Cracker'^{PBR} (v)	EBee MRav
	- 'Elegantissima' (v) ♀H4	Widely available
	- 'Gouchaultii' (v)	CBcs CDul CJun CMac CRos EBee EPfP GKin LRHS MRav NLar NSoo SGol SHil SLim SPer SRms WMoo
	- 'Hessei' misapplied	see *C. sanguinea* 'Compressa'
	- 'Hessei' Hesse	CJun WPat
	Hutchinson's form	WCot
	- Ivory Halo = 'Bailhalo'^{PBR}	EBee EMil EPfP LSRN MAsh MRav NLar NWea SLim SPer SPoG
	- 'Kesselringii'	Widely available
	- Red Gnome = 'Regnzam'	ELon LLHF MAsh WPat
	- 'Ruby'	CJun
	- 'Siberian Pearls'	CBcs CJun ELan GKin MBlu MBri NLar
§	- 'Sibirica' ♀H4	Widely available
	- 'Sibirica Variegata' (v)	CDoC CJun CMac EBee ELon EPfP GCra GKin LRHS LSRN MAsh MBlu MGos NCGa NEgg SHil SLim SPer SPoG SSpi SWvt WCFE WHar WMoo
	- 'Snow Pearls'	CJun
	- 'Spaethii' (v) ♀H4	Widely available
§	- 'Variegata' (v)	LAst
	- 'Westonbirt'	see *C. alba* 'Sibirica'
	- 'Wintersun' **new**	NLar
	alternifolia	CBcs CCVT CMCN CTho ELan WMou
§	- 'Argentea' (v) ♀H4	Widely available
	- 'Brunette'	CJun NLar
	- 'Golden Surprise'	CJun
	- 'Silver Giant' (v)	CJun GBin MBri NLar
	- 'Variegata'	see *C. alternifolia* 'Argentea'
	- 'Yellow Spring'	CJun MBri NLar
	amomum	CAbP EBtc NLar
	- 'Blue Cloud'	CJun
	- 'Lady Jane'	NLar
	angustata	CMCN SKHP SSpi
	'Full Moon'	CJun
	'Ascona'	CBcs CEnd CJun EPfP NLar SSta
	Aurora = 'Rutban' (Stellar Series)	CJun MBlu NLar SGol
	canadensis ♀H4	Widely available
	candidissima Marshall	see *C. racemosa*
	capitata	CBcs CDoC CHel CJun CMac CTsd EBee EPfP GKev IDee LRHS MGos SEND SKHP SPoG SSpi WCru WPGP
	- ACE 2033	SSpi
	- subsp. ***emeiensis***	CJun
	- 'Foreness Fog' (v)	SEND
§	Celestial = 'Rutdan' (Stellar Series)	CJun LRHS NLar SGol SKHP
	'Celestial Shadow'	LBuc MGos MPkF SGol
	'Centennial'	LRHS
	chinensis	SSta SWvt
	'Constellation' (Stellar Series)	CJun MAsh SGol
	controversa	CBcs CCVT CDul CLnd CMCN CTri ECrN ELan EPfP EWTr GBin MBlu MBri MWat NLar SEND SEWo SGol SLPl SLim SSpi SSta SWvt WHar
I	- 'Aurea' **new**	LRHS
	- 'Candlelight'	MBlu NLar
§	- 'Frans Type' (v)	CJun LSRN SSta
I	- 'Marginata Nord'	NLar
	- 'Pagoda'	CJun EPfP MBlu MBri MGos NLar
	- 'Troya Dwarf'	CJun NLar
	- 'Variegata' (v) ♀H4	Widely available
	- 'Variegata' Frans type	see *C. controversa* 'Frans Type'
	- 'Winter Orange'	CJun NLar
	'Dorothy'	CJun NLar
	'Eddie's White Wonder' ♀H4	Widely available
	florida	CDul CLnd CMCN CTho EWTr LAst MMHG MMuc NWea SPer WHCr WHar
	- 'Alba Plena' (d)	CJun
	- 'Appalachian Spring'	CTho
	- 'Apple Blossom'	CJun CMac CMen NPCo
	- 'Aurea' × ***kousa***	MPkF
	- 'Autumn Gold'	SSta
	- Cherokee Brave = 'Comco No 1'	CBcs CJun CMen CTho ESwi LMil LRHS MAsh MGos NPCo SGol SPoG SSta WGob
	- 'Cherokee Chief' ♀H4	CBcs CDul CEnd CJun CMac CMen CTri EBee GKin IVic LAst LSRN MGos MPkF NPCo SLim WGob WHar
	- 'Cherokee Daybreak'	see *C. florida* 'Daybreak'
	- 'Cherokee Princess'	CJun LRHS MAsh SGol SPoG SSta
	- 'Cherokee Sunset'	see *C. florida* 'Sunset'
	- 'Cloud Nine'	CBcs CDoC CJun CMac CMen EBee GKin MGos MPkF NPCo WGob WHar
§	- 'Daybreak' (v)	CBcs CEnd CJun ESwi LRHS LSRN MAsh MBri MGos MPkF SHil SSta WHar
	- 'Eternal Dogwood' (d)	ESwi LSRN SGol
	- 'First Lady' (v)	CJun CMac CMen NPCo WGob
	- 'Fragrant Cloud'	SWvt
	- 'G.H. Ford' (v)	NLar
	- 'Golden Nugget' (v)	CJun
	- 'Granary Gold'	SSta
	- 'Junior Miss'	CEnd
	- 'Moonglow'	CJun
	- 'Pendula'	CJun
	- 'Pink Flame' (v)	CJun SSta
	- f. ***pluribracteata*** (d)	NLar
	- var. ***pringlei***	CJun
	- 'Purple Glory'	CBcs CJun LRHS NLar
	- 'Pygmaea'	NLar
	- 'Rainbow' (v)	CAbP CBcs CJun CMac CWib GKin LRHS MAsh MBri MGos MPkF SHil SLim SPoG SSpi WHar
	- 'Red Giant'	CAbP CBcs CJun
	- f. ***rubra***	CBcs CDul CTri CWib ELan GKin LRHS MGos MMuc MRav NPCo SPer
	- 'Spring Day'	CMac CMen NPCo WGob
	- 'Spring Song'	CJun CMac CMen NPCo WGob
	- 'Springtime'	CJun
	- 'Stoke's Pink'	CEnd CJun CMac CMen NPCo WGob
§	- 'Sunset' (v)	CEnd CJun CMen CWib LRHS MAsh MGos NLar NPCo SPer SSta SWvt WHar
	- 'Sweetwater'	CEnd CJun
	- 'Tricolor'	see *C. florida* 'Welchii'
	- subsp. ***urbiniana*** **new**	WPGP
	- 'Variegata'	GKin
§	- 'Welchii' (v)	CMac
	- 'White Cloud'	CJun
	'Gloria Birkett'	CAbP CJun ELan EPfP LMil LRHS MAsh NPCo SSpi WGob
	hemsleyi	SKHP

hessei misapplied	see *C. sanguinea* 'Compressa'
hongkongensis	LRHS MAsh NLar WPGP
- B&SWJ 11700	WCru
- HWJ 1033	WPGP
- aff. subsp. ***gigantea*** KWJ 12225	WCru
- subsp. ***melanotricha***	WPGP
- aff. subsp. ***tonkinensis*** B&SWJ 11791	WCru
'Jerry Mundy'	CMac IVic
'Kelsey Dwarf'	see *C. sericea* 'Kelseyi'
'Kenwyn Clapp'	CJun
kousa	CCVT CDoC CMCN CMHG CMac CTho ELan EPfP GKin MJak NEgg NLar SPer SPlb WHar WMou
- B&SWJ 12610 from Korea **new**	WCru
- 'Akabana'	CJun
- 'Akatsuki'	MPkF SSta
- 'All Summer'	CJun
- 'Angyo Issai'	NLar
- 'Autumn Rose'	CJun EPfP NLar
- 'Beni-fuji'	CJun NLar
- 'Big Apple'	CJun LLHF LRHS MAsh NLar
- 'Blue Shadow'	CJun MBri NLar SSta
- 'Boldre Beauty'	SSpi
- 'Bonfire' (v)	CJun
- 'Bultinck's Beauty'	NLar
- 'Bultinck's Giant'	NLar
- 'Bush's Pink'	CJun
- 'Cherokee'	CJun
- 'China Dawn' (v)	CJun SSta
- var. ***chinensis*** ♀^{H4}	Widely available
- - 'Bodnant Form'	CEnd CJun CMac NLar NPCo SSta WBor
- - 'China Girl'	CDul CEnd CJun EBee ELan EPfP EWTr GKin IArd IDee LAst LMil LRHS LSRN MAsh MBlu MBri MGos MRav MSwo NLar SHil SLim SPer SPoG SSpi SSta WPat
- - 'Claudia'	IVic NLar SSta
- - 'Great Star'	MAsh
- - 'Greta's Gold' (v)	CJun SSta
- - 'Ikone'	IVic
- - 'Snowflake'	CJun
- - 'Spinners'	CJun MBri
- - 'Summer Stars'	CJun
- - 'White Dusted' (v)	CJun EPfP MBlu NLar
- - 'White Fountain'	EPfP LRHS MBri MPkF MPnt NLar WHar
- - 'Wieting's Select'	CJun IDee IVic MBlu MBri MPkF NLar
- - 'Wisley Queen'	CAbP CJun CMHG EPfP LRHS MAsh SSta
- 'Claudine'	CJun
- 'Doctor Bump'	CJun
- 'Doubloon'	CJun LRHS WPat
- 'Dwarf Pink'	CJun
- 'Ed Mezitt'	CJun NLar
- 'Eline'^{PBR}	MBlu NLar
- 'Elizabeth Lustgarten'	CJun MBlu MPkF SSta
- 'Eurostar'	IArd IVic NLar
- 'Eva'^{PBR}	MBlu MPkF
- 'Fanfare'	CJun NLar
- 'Fernie's Favourite'	CJun
- Galilean = 'Galzam'	CJun MPkF
- 'Gay Head'	CJun
I - 'Girard's Nana'	CJun
- 'Gold Cup' (v)	CJun MPkF SSta
- 'Gold Star' (v)	CBcs CEnd CJun CMac CWGN ELan EPfP LMil MAsh MBlu MGos MPkF NLar NPCo SPoG SSta WGob
- 'Greensleeves'	CJun EPfP LLHF LRHS MAsh SSta
- 'Heart Throb'	CJun MGos NLar SGol
- 'Highland'	CJun
- 'John Slocock'	CJun MBri NLar
- 'Kim'	NLar
- 'Kreutzdame'	CJun MBlu MBri NLar
- 'Laura'	SSta
- 'Little Beauty'	CJun
- 'Lizzie P' **new**	NLar
- 'Lustgarten Weeping'	CJun NLar
- 'Madame Butterfly'	CJun IDee LRHS MBlu MBri NLar NPCo
- 'Marwood Dawn'	CMHG SSta
- 'Marwood Twilight'	CMHG
- 'Melanie'^{PBR}	GQue LRHS MBlu
- 'Milky Way'	CDul CJun CLnd CMCN CTho ESwi EWTr GBin LSRN MAsh MBlu MGos MPkF NLar NPCo SGol SPoG SSpi WPat
- 'Milky Way Select'	CBcs CJun LRHS MGos
- 'Minuma'	NLar
- 'Miss Petty'	CJun MPkF NLar
- 'Miss Satomi' ♀^{H4}	Widely available
- 'Moonbeam'	CJun NLar WPat
- 'Mount Fuji'	CJun CMHG MBlu NLar SSta
- 'National'	CJun EPfP LMil LRHS MAsh MGos MPkF NLar SSta WPat
- 'Nicole'	CDoC EBee LRHS NLar WGob WPat
- 'Ohkan'	CJun
- 'Pevé Limbo' (v)	CJun NLar
- 'Pevé Satomi Compact'	NLar
- 'Polywood'	CJun NLar
- 'Radiant Rose'	CJun MPkF NLar SSpi SSta
- 'Rasen'	CJun NLar
- 'Rel Whirlwind'	CJun NLar
* - 'Robert'	NLar
- 'Rosea'	CJun
- Samaratin = 'Samzam' (v)	CBcs CEnd CJun LSRN MGos MPkF SGol SKHP SSta
- 'Satomi Akatuki' (v)	NLar
- 'Schmetterling'	CJun MBlu NLar WPat
- 'Snowbird'	CJun
- 'Snowboy' (v)	CBcs CDul CEnd CJun CMac MBlu NPCo SMad
- 'Snowflurries'	CJun
- 'Southern Cross'	CJun GBin
- 'Square Dance'	CJun
- 'Steeple'	CJun
- 'Summer Fun'	CJun LRHS SPoG SSta
- 'Summer Gold' (v)	MPkF
- 'Summer Majesty'	CJun
- 'Sunsplash' (v)	CJun SSta
- 'Temple Jewel' (v)	CJun
- 'Teutonia'	CJun IArd IDee IVic MBri MGos NLar SHil SSta
- 'Trinity Star'	CJun
- 'Triple Crown'	CJun WPat
- 'Tsukubanomine'	CJun CLnd NLar
- 'Vale Milky Way' (v)	NLar
- 'Weaver's Weeping'	CJun MPkF NLar
- 'Weisse Fontäne'	CJun NLar
- 'White Dream'	CJun NLar
- 'White Giant'	CJun
- 'Willy Boy' **new**	CLnd
- 'Wolf Eyes' (v)	CBcs CJun MAsh MBlu MPkF NLar SGol SSpi SSta

	macrophylla Wall.	EPfP
	- MSF 821	WPGP
	mas	Widely available
	- 'Aurea' (v)	CAbP CJun ELan ELon EPfP LRHS MAsh MBlu MBri MGos MRav NEgg NLar NPCo SGol SLim SPer SPoG SSpi SSta WPat
§	- 'Aureoelegantissima' (v)	CEnd CJun CMac EBee LRHS MAsh MBri NEgg NLar SPer SSpi WPat
	- 'Devin'	NLar
	- 'Elegant' (F)	CAgr
	- 'Elegantissima'	see *C. mas* 'Aureoelegantissima'
	- 'Golden Glory' ♀H4	CJun CLnd EPfP MBri NLar SKHP
	- 'Gourmet' (F)	CAgr
	- 'Happy Face'	NLar
	- 'Hillier's Upright'	CJun
	- 'Jolico' (F)	CAgr CJun MBlu NLar SKHP
	- 'Kasanlaker' (F)	CAgr NLar
	- 'Pancharevo' (F) **new**	CAgr
	- 'Pioneer' (F)	CJun
	- 'Redstone' (F)	CJun
	- 'Schönbrunner Gourmet Dirndl' (F)	MCoo
	- 'Shan' (F) **new**	CAgr
	- 'Shumen' (F) **new**	CAgr
	- 'Spring Glow'	CJun NLar
	- 'Titus' (F)	NLar
	- 'Variegata' (v) ♀H4	CAbP CBcs CJun CMCN CMac EBee EPfP LRHS MAsh MBlu MBri MGos NLar NPCo SKHP SPer SPoG SSpi
	- 'Xanthocarpa'	CJun NLar
	- 'Yellow'	CAgr
N	'Norman Hadden' ♀H4	Widely available
	nuttallii	CDul CTho CTri CWib EBee ELan EPfP GLin MGos SPer SWvt
	- 'Colrigo Giant'	CJun
	- 'Gold Spot' (v)	CJun CMac NPCo NWea SHil
	- 'Monarch'	CJun CTho SKHP SSpi WPat
	- 'North Star'	CJun NLar
	- 'Portlemouth'	CEnd CJun LRHS NLar
	- 'Zurico'	CJun MPkF NLar
	officinalis	CAgr CDul CMCN CMac EPfP LRHS NLar SKHP SWvt
	- 'Ellen'	NLar
	- 'Kintoki'	ESwi MBri SKHP
	'Ormonde'	CJun CWGN EPfP NLar NPCo SSpi SSta WGob
	'Pink Blush'	CJun NLar
	'Porlock' ♀H4	CDul CJun CMCN EPfP IArd LRHS LSRN MAsh MBri NLar SHil SWvt WPat
	pumila	CJun NLar
§	***racemosa***	EBtc NLar
	rugosa	EBtc NLar
I	× ***rutgersiensis***	LRHS
	- Galaxy	see *C.* Celestial
	Ruth Ellen = 'Rutlan' (Stellar Series)	CJun NLar WPat
	sanguinea	CBcs CCVT CDul CHab CLnd CTri ECrN EPfP LBuc MJak MMuc MRav MSwo NWea SEWo SGol SPer SVic WHar WMou
	- 'Anny'	CJun MAsh MBlu WPat
	- 'Anny's Winter Orange'	CJun
	- 'Atrosanguinea' **new**	SWvt
§	- 'Compressa'	EPfP MRav NLar
	- 'Magic Fire' **new**	SWvt
	- 'Magic Flame'	CJun ELon EPfP LRHS MBri NLar WPat
	- 'Midwinter Fire'	Widely available
	- 'Winter Beauty'	CJun CSBt CWib ELon EPfP EUJe LBMP MAsh MBlu NEgg NLar NSoo NWea SLon SWvt WCFE WHar WPat
§	***sericea***	MSCN SRms WMoo
	- 'Bud's Yellow'	LRHS MBlu MBri SHil
	- 'Cardinal'	CHGN CRos EPfP LRHS MAsh MBri NLar SHil
	- 'Coral Red'	CJun
	- 'Flaviramea' ♀H4	Widely available
	- 'Hedgerows Gold' (v)	CJun CRos EBee ELan ELon EMil EPfP LHop LRHS MAsh MBri SHil SPoG WCot WPat
	- 'Isanti'	CJun
§	- 'Kelseyi'	CJun CMac EBee EPfP MBrN MRav NLar SLPl WMoo
	- Kelsey's Gold = 'Rosco'	MAsh WPat
	- subsp. ***occidentalis*** 'Sunshine'	CJun NPro
§	- 'White Gold' (v) ♀H4	CDoC CJun EHoe ELon EPfP EWTr MBri MRav NLar NPro NSoo SLon SPer SPoG WMoo
	- 'White Spot'	see *C. sericea* 'White Gold'
	Stardust = 'Rutfan' (Stellar Series)	CJun
	Stellar Pink = 'Rutgan' (Stellar Series)	CBcs CJun CTho LRHS MAsh MBri MGos MPkF NLar SGol SKHP WGob
	stolonifera	see *C. sericea*
	× ***unalaschkensis***	EBee LLHF
	- NNS 08-101	GKev
	Venus = 'Kn30 8'PBR	CJun ELan EPfP LBuc LRHS MAsh MBlu MBri MPkF SLon SSta
	waltari	CBcs EBtc
	- B&SWJ 8776	WCru

Corokia (*Argyrophyllaceae*)

	buddlejoides	CBcs CHGN CMHG CTsd EBee ECou NLar NPnk SEND
	'Coppershine'	CMHG
	cotoneaster	CAbP CBcs CDul CMac CTri EBee ECho ECou ECre ELan EPfP EUJe LRHS MAsh MGos MPkF NLar SBod SIgm SMad SPer SPoG SWvt WCot WGrn WPat
	- 'Boundary Hill'	ECou
	- 'Brown's Stream'	ECou
	- 'Hodder River'	ECou
	- 'Ohau Scarlet'	ECou
	- 'Ohau Yellow'	ECou
	- 'Swale Stream'	ECou
	- 'Wanaka'	ECou
*	***daphnoides***	NPnk
	macrocarpa	ECou
	× ***virgata***	CAbP CTri CTsd ECou ELan EPfP GBin GGal LRHS NLar SAPC SWvt WSHC
	- 'Bronze King'	EBee EPfP LRHS MOWG MPkF SPer SVen
	- 'Bronze Lady'	ECou
	- 'Cheesemanii'	ECou
	- 'County Park Lemon'	ECou
	- 'County Park Orange'	ECou
	- 'County Park Purple'	ECou
	- 'County Park Red'	ECou
	- 'Frosted Chocolate'	CBcs CMHG CTsd EBee ECou ELan EPfP IVic LHop LLHF LRHS MOWG MPkF SEND SKHP SLim SPoG SVen SWvt WGrn

	- 'Geenty's Green'	EBee ECou LRHS
	- 'Havering'	ECou
	- 'Pink Delight'	ECou EPfP ESwi MAsh MRav
	- 'Red Wonder'	CMHG CMac EBee ELan EPfP IVic LRHS MMHG MPkF SEND SLim SPoG SVen WGrn
	- 'Sandrine'	ECou
	- 'Silver Ghost'	ECou
	- 'Sunsplash' (v)	CBcs CDoC CMac CTsd EBee ECou EPfP ESwi LBMP LHop LLHF LRHS MAsh MPkF NLar NPnk SEND SPoG SWvt WGrn
I	- 'Virgata'	ECou
	- 'Wingletye'	ECou
	- 'Yellow Wonder'	CBcs CMHG EBee ESwi LRHS NLar SEND SLim SWvt

Coronilla (*Papilionaceae*)

	comosa	see *Hippocrepis comosa*
	emerus	see *Hippocrepis emerus*
	glauca	see *C. valentina* subsp. *glauca*
	minima	XSen
	'Nan Hicks' new	EWld
	valentina	CDoC CRHN CSPN EBee LHop SDix WSHC
	- 'Clotted Cream' new	CHid
	- 'Creamed Corn'	WCot
§	- subsp. ***glauca*** ♀H3	CDul CMac CSBt CTri CWib EBee ELan EPfP LRHS LSRN MMuc SBch SEND SLim SPer SPoG SRms SVen SWvt WAbe WPat XLum XSen
	- - 'Brockhill Blue'	EBee EMil IVic LRHS WCot
	- - 'Citrina' ♀H3	Widely available
*	- - 'Pygmaea'	LRHS WCot
	- - 'Variegata' (v)	CBcs CDoC CMac CSPN CTri CWib EBee EHoe ELan EPfP LRHS MAsh MCot SEND SLim SLon SMad SMrm SPer SPoG SVen WCot
	varia	see *Securigera varia*

Correa (*Rutaceae*)

	aemula new	MOWG
	alba	CCCN CDoC CExl ECou EPfP
	- 'Pinkie' ♀H2	CExl CTsd ECou MOWG WCot
	alba* × *backhouseana	MOWG
	backhouseana ♀H2	CAbb CBcs CCCN CDoC CExl CHll CMac CTri CTsd EBee ECou ELan EPfP GCal IDee IVic LHop LPot LRHS MOWG NLar SBrt SVen WSHC
	- 'Mount Congreve' new	MOWG
	- 'Peaches and Cream'	CCCN IVic SRkn
	decumbens	ECou MOWG
	'Dusky Bells' ♀H2	CAbb CBcs CCCN CDoC CHll CTri CTsd EBee ECou EPfP IVic LHop LRHS MAsh MOWG SEND SHil SLim SMrm SPlb SPoG SRkn SVen
	'Dusky Maid'	CCCN CExl
	'Federation Belle'	CCCN CDoC ECou MOWG SPlb SVen
	glabra	MOWG
	'Gwen'	CDoC ECou
	'Harrisii'	see *C.* 'Mannii'
	'Inglewood Gold'	ECou
	'Ivory Bells'	ECou EPfP
	lawrenceana	CExl CFil CTsd ECou SEND SVen WPGP
§	'Mannii' ♀H2	CBcs CCCN CDoC CExl CTsd EBee ECre ELan ELon EPfP IVic LRHS MOWG SPoG WSHC
	'Marian's Marvel' ♀H2	CCCN CDoC CExl CTsd EBee ECou ECre EPfP IDee LBMP MAsh MOWG SEND SPoG SRkn SVen
	'Peachy Cream'	CAbb CCCN CDoC CTsd EPfP LRHS
	'Poorinda Mary'	ECou MOWG
	pulchella ♀H2	CDoC CExl CTri
	- orange-flowered	MOWG
	- 'Pink Mist'	CDoC ECou MOWG
	reflexa ♀H2	CDoC CExl ECou SBrt
	- var. ***nummulariifolia***	ECou MOWG SBrt WAbe
	- var. ***reflexa***	CExl
	- - 'Mary's Choice'	CDoC
*	- ***virens***	CExl
	schlechtendalii	CCCN ECou LHop

Cortaderia ✿ (*Poaceae*)

	argentea	see *C. selloana*
	fulvida misapplied	see *C. richardii* (Endl.) Zotov
§	***fulvida*** (Buchanan) Zotov ♀H3-4	CKno EWes IArd NWsh SMad WCot
	jubata 'Candy Floss'	see *C. selloana* 'Candy Floss'
	richardii misapplied	see *C. fulvida* (Buchanan) Zotov
	richardii ambig.	CCon CExl EHoe GBin IMou MMuc NBir SMad WHrl WWEG
§	***richardii*** (Endl.) Zotov ♀H3-4	CAby CBcs CKno EBee EPPr ESwi EWes IMou MAvo MWhi SAPC WCru WMnd WPGP
	- Brown's strain	WCot
§	***selloana***	CBcs CDul CHEx CTri CWib IBoy MGos MJak MRav NBir SAPC SGol SPlb
§	- 'Albolineata' (v)	CBcs CBct ELon EWes MMuc MWht NOak SEND SLim SPer SPoG SWvt
§	- 'Aureolineata' (v) ♀H3-4	CBcs CBct CDoC CMac CWCL ELan EPfP GMaP IVic LRHS MGos MMuc NBid NOak SEND SLim SPer SPoG SWvt
§	- 'Candy Floss'	CKno
	- 'Evita' PBR ♀H3-4	CKno SMad
	- 'Gold Band'	see *C. selloana* 'Aureolineata'
	- 'Icalma'	EPPr
	- 'Monstrosa' ♀H3-4	MMuc SEND SMad
	- 'Patagonia' ♀H3-4	EHoe EPPr
	- 'Pink Feather'	CTsd EHyd EPfP MMuc SEND
	- 'Pumila' ♀H4	Widely available
	- 'Rendatleri'	CBcs CDoC ELan LSRN SCoo SLim SPer SPoG
	- 'Rosea'	EPfP MAsh MGos MJak NGdn NLar SGol WWEG
	- 'Silver Fountain' (v)	ELan EPfP LRHS MAsh
	- 'Silver Stripe'	see *C. selloana* 'Albolineata'
	- 'Splendid Star' PBR (v)	CBcs EHoe LHop LRHS MAsh MBri MGos MJak MREP NLar NOak SLim SMad SPoG SWvt WCot
	- 'Sunningdale Silver' ♀H3-4	CDoC CMac ECtt ELan ELon EPfP LRHS LSRN MBri MGos MMuc SEND SLim SMad SPer SPoG SWvt
*	- 'White Feather'	NGdn SLim WWEG
	Toe Toe	see *C. richardii* (Endl.) Zotov

Cortiella (*Apiaceae*)

	aff. ***hookeri*** HWJK 2291	WCru

Cortusa (*Primulaceae*)

	brotheri	EBee ECho
*	***caucasica***	EBee GKev
*	- 'Alba'	GKev
	matthioli	ECho GBin GKev SRms
	- 'Alba'	CCon ECho SRms

	- var. ***congesta***	GKev
	- subsp. ***pekinensis***	CCon ECho EDAr GKev MLHP MPnt NBid NLar SPet SRms WPnP
	turkestanica	ECho LLHF

Corydalis ✿ (*Papaveraceae*)

	anthriscifolia	CLAP EWes MMHG WCot
	'Blackberry Wine'	CExl EBee ECtt EPfP GBuc LRHS MPnt NLar NPnk
	'Blue Panda'	see *C. flexuosa* 'Blue Panda'
	bracteata	LWst
	'Bronze Beauty'	WMoo
	bulbosa misapplied	see *C. cava*
	bulbosa (L.) DC.	see *C. solida*
	buschii	CLAP CPBP EBee ECho ELon GBin GBuc NHar NMyG
	calcicola	GKev
	'Canary Feathers' PBR	ECtt MBNS MHol NLar NMyG NPnk NPri SPoG
	cashmeriana	LRHS NBid NHar WAbe WHal
	- 'Kailash'	LRHS
	cashmeriana × ***flexuosa***	CBro CLAP ECho LHop WAbe
	caucasica	ECho GBuc LWst
	- var. ***alba*** misapplied	see *C. malkensis*
§	***cava***	CLAP EBee ECho EPot SPhx WShi
	- 'Albiflora'	CLAP ECho SPhx
	- subsp. ***cava***	ECho
	cheilanthifolia	CDoy CExl CRow CSpe EBee EPfP LEdu LPla LRHS SRms XLum
	'Craigton Blue'	CLAP EBee EPPr GBuc IPot NHar WAbe
	curviflora	GKev
	- subsp. ***rosthornii***	CExl EWes
	- - 'Blue Heron'	CSpe ECtt MPnt
	darwasica	LWst
	davidii	CExl
	decipiens Schott, Nyman & Kotschy	see *C. solida* subsp. *incisa*
I	***decipiens*** misapplied ♀H4	CPom ECho EPot
I	- purple-flowered	EBee ECho
	densiflora	ECho
	'Early Bird'	ECtt
	elata	CLAP CSpe EWes GBin GBuc IFro LHop LRHS LSou MArl MBel MBri MCot MNrw NBid NBir SPhx SPoG WCru WHal WPtf WSHC
	- 'Blue Summit'	CLAP EBee ECtt EPPr IMou LRHS
	elata × ***flexuosa***	IMou
	elata × ***flexuosa*** clone 1	CCse CExl CLAP
	flexuosa ♀H4	CSpe ECho EPfP GBin MArl MNrw NSla WAbe WBor WSHC XLum
	- CD&R 528	IFro NRya
	- 'Balang Mist'	CExl CLAP NHar
	- 'Blue Dragon'	see *C. flexuosa* 'Purple Leaf'
§	- 'Blue Panda'	CExl EBee EPPr EPot EWes GBuc GMaP NHar NLar WCru
	- 'China Blue'	Widely available
	- 'Golden Panda' (v)	CBct MBNS NPnk
	- 'Hale Cat'	EBee ECtt EPPr
	- 'Hidden Purple'	CHid
	- 'Nightshade'	CExl LLHF LRHS NBid WCot WHoo
I	- 'Norman's Seedling'	EBee EPPr IVic WPGP
	- 'Père David'	CMac CSBt CSpe CWCL EBee ECho ELan EPPr EPfP GBin ITim LRHS MHer MWat NBir NCGa NMyG SPlb SPoG SWvt WCru WSHC WWEG XLum
§	- 'Purple Leaf'	CAvo CElw CHel CMac ECho EHoe ELan EPPr EPfP GAbr GMaP LHop LRHS MBNS MHol NCGa NLar NPnk NPri SMad SMrm SPad SPer SPlb SPoG WAbe WCot WMoo WPGP WWEG
	'Foundling'	LWst
	glaucescens	LWst
	- 'Early Beauty'	LWst
	aff. ***glaucescens*** from Ihnachsai Gorge, Uzbeckistan **new**	LWst
	'Golden Spinners'	IVic
	'Heavenly Blue'	GKev
	heterocarpa	IMou
	incisa	ECho ERCP
	- B&SWJ 4417	WCru
	'Kingfisher'	CDes CLAP CPom LRHS NHar NLar NSla WAbe
	kusnetzovii	LWst
	ledebouriana	LWst
	leucanthema DJHC 752	CDes CExl CLAP
	- 'Silver Spectre' (v)	CExl EBee LLHF LRHS WMoo
	linstowiana	CSpe LRHS
	- CD&R 605	CExl CLAP
§	***lutea***	CBcs EBee EPfP IFoB IFro MMuc NBir NPer NPri NWad SEND SRms WCot WMoo
	magadanica	LRHS MMoz
§	***malkensis*** ♀H4	CPom EBee ECho EPot GBin GBuc GKev LLHF LRHS NBir NRya WCot WThu
	'Maya' (v)	XLum
	moorcroftiana	CExl
	'New Contender'	LWst
	nobilis	CPom CSpe ECho IFoB LLHF SPhx
	ochotensis	IMou LRHS
§	***ochroleuca***	CElw CPom CRow CSpe GCal LPla LRHS NLar WMoo
	ophiocarpa	CSpe EHoe ELan GCal WHil WMoo
	ornata	LWst
	pachycentra	CExl WAbe
	paczoskii	ECho GBuc GKev LRHS MNrw
	popovii	LWst
	pseudofumaria alba	see *C. ochroleuca*
	pumila	ECho
	'Rainier Blue'	IVic
	rosea 'American Dream'	CWCL
	scandens	see *Dactylicapnos scandens*
	schanginii	GKev LWst
	subsp. ***ainii*** ♀H2	
	- - from Sjasu Valley, Kazakhstan	LWst
	- subsp. ***schanginii***	LWst
	scouleri	IMou NBir
	shimienensis	CPom
	- 'Berry Exciting' PBR	CBct CLAP CWGN ECtt ELon EPfP GBuc LHop LRHS LSou MBNS MHol NLar NPnk NPri SPoG
	siamensis	IFoB IMou
	- B&SWJ 7200	WCru
§	***solida***	CAby CAvo CBro CPom EBee ECho ECtt ELan EPfP EPot GAbr ITim LEdu LHop LRHS MPie MRav NLar NPnk NRya SDeJ SPhx WCot WShi
	- 'Crane' **new**	LWst
	- 'Fire Bird'	ECho LWst
	- 'Firecracker'	CBro ECho LLHF LRHS SPhx
	- 'Galah' **new**	ECho LWst

§	- subsp. ***incisa*** 🏆H4	EBee ECho EPot GKev SDeJ SPhx WCot
	- - white-flowered	LWst
	- lilac-flowered	IFoB
	- 'Moonlight Shade'	ECho
	- Nettleton seedlings	EPot
	- 'Night Heron'	LWst
	- 'Pink Discovery'	LWst
	- 'Pipit'	LWst
	- 'Purple Beauty'	ECho GKev LWst MNrw SPhx
	- 'Purple Bird'	CAvo EPot LWst
	- 'Redpoll' **new**	LWst
	- 'Redwing'	LWst
	- 'Rosefinch' **new**	LWst
§	- subsp. ***solida***	CLAP ECho EPot GBin GKev NBir NRya SPhx WCot
	- - from Penza, Russia	LLHF LWst
	- - 'Beth Evans'	CAvo CBro CWCL EBee ECho ECtt ELon EPPr EPot ERCP GAbr GBin GBuc GKev LEdu LLHF LRHS MBel MCot MNrw NBir NCGa NHar NLar NWad SDeJ SMad SPhx WCot WWEG
	- - 'Blushing Girl'	ECho
	- - 'Dieter Schacht' 🏆H4	EBee EPPr GKev ITim LLHF NLar WAbe WCot
	- - 'Evening Shade'	ECho
	- - 'George Baker' 🏆H4	Widely available
	- - 'Lahovice'	WAbe WCot
	- - Prasil Group	EPot GKev SPhx WBor
	- - 'White Knight'	EBee WCot
	- 'Spoonbill'	LWst
	- f. ***transsylvanica***	see *C. solida* subsp. *solida*
	- 'White King'	WCot
	- 'White Swallow'	EPot LWst
	- 'Zwanenberg'	LWst
	'Spinners'	CDes CElw CFis CHel CLAP EBee ECtt ELon EPPr GCal GKev GLog IVic NMyG SBch WSHC WWEG XLum
	stipulata B&SWJ 2951	WCru
	taliensis	CExl GLog
	temulifolia 'Chocolate Stars'	CSpe CWGN EBee ECtt LEdu LHop LLHF LPla MBNS MHol MPie NCGa NSti WCot WSHC
	'Tory MP'	CBct CDes CExl CHid CLAP CPom CSam CSpe EBee EPPr GAbr IFro LRHS MNrw MPie NBid NCGa NHar NMyG WHoo WMnd WPGP
	transsylvanica hort.	see *C. solida* subsp. *solida*
	turtschaninovii	SKHP
	- 'Gorin'	LWst
	vittae	ECho IFoB LWst
	- 'Goliath'	LWst
	wendelboi	IFoB
	'Wildside Blue'	CLAP
	wilsonii	CExl IFoB IGor

Corylopsis ✿ (*Hamamelidaceae*)

	glabrescens	CHGN CJun LRHS
	- var. ***gotoana***	CJun EPfP LRHS MAsh NLar SSpi SSta WPat
	- - 'Chollipo'	CAbP CBcs LRHS NLar SSta
	- 'Lemon Drop'	NLar
	glandulifera	SSpi
	himalayana	WAbe
	multiflora	SSpi
	pauciflora 🏆H4	CBcs CDoC CDul CEnd CJun CMHG CTri CWib EBee ELan EPfP IDee IVic LRHS LSRN MAsh MRav NEgg NLar NPCo NPri SChF SGol SKHP SLim SPer SPoG SSpi WPGP
	platypetala	see *C. sinensis* var. *calvescens*
	- var. ***laevis***	see *C. sinensis* var. *calvescens*
§	***sinensis*** var. ***calvescens***	CBcs CJun EPfP
§	- - f. ***veitchiana*** 🏆H4	CDoy CJun CSam EPfP IArd LRHS NLar SSpi
§	- var. ***sinensis*** 🏆H4	CDoC CHel CJun EBee ELon EPfP IVic LAst LRHS MAsh NLar SLon WAbe
	- - 'Spring Purple'	CAbP CBcs CEnd CGHE CJun CMac EBee EPfP IVic LRHS NLar SChF SHil SKHP SSpi SSta WPGP WPat
	- 'Veitch's Purple'	CJun NLar
	spicata	CBcs CDul CJun IArd IDee IGor LRHS MBlu MRav NEgg NLar SGol SLim SSpi WPat
	- 'Golden Spring'	EPfP
	- 'Red Eye'	IVic
	veitchiana	see *C. sinensis* var. *calvescens* f. *veitchiana*
	willmottiae	see *C. sinensis* var. *sinensis*
	'Winterthur'	SSta

Corylus ✿ (*Betulaceae*)

	avellana (F)	CBcs CCVT CDoC CDul CHab CLnd CMac CTho CTri ECrN EPfP EPom EWTr GAbr LAst LBuc MBri MGos MJak NEgg NLar NWea SEWo SPer SPre SVic WHar WMou
	- 'Anny's Red Dwarf'	IArd
	- 'Aurea'	CBcs CDoC CDul CEnd CSBt CTho CTri EBee ECrN ELan EPfP GBin LBuc LRHS MAsh MBlu MBri MGos MRav NLar NWea SLim SPer SSta SWvt
	- 'Bollwylle'	see *C. maxima* 'Halle'sche Riesennuss'
§	- 'Butler' (F)	CAgr CDul CMac CMam CTho CTri ERea IArd MBri MJak SDea SKee SPoG WHar
	- 'Casina' (F)	CAgr CTho
	- 'Contorta'	Widely available
	- 'Corabel' (F)	CAgr CMam MBri
	- 'Cosford' (F)	CAgr CCVT CDul CMac CSBt CTho CTri ECrN EPom ERea GTwe IArd LBuc LRHS MBlu MBri MGos NLar SDea SEWo SGol SKee SPer SWvt WHar
§	- 'Ennis' (F)	CAgr CDul CMam MBri NOra SDea SKee WHar
	- 'Fortin' (F)	ECrN
§	- 'Fuscorubra' (F)	CJun EPom MRav NLar SWvt
	- 'Gustav's Zeller' (F)	CAgr
§	- 'Heterophylla'	CDul EBee EPfP MBri NLar SSta WHar WPat
	- 'Laciniata'	see *C. avellana* 'Heterophylla'
§	- 'Lang Tidlig Zeller' (F)	CAgr ERea LRHS MBri MCoo NWea
	- 'Louis Berger' (F)	MCoo NLar
	- 'Merveille de Bollwyller'	see *C. maxima* 'Halle'sche Riesennuss'
	- 'Nottingham Prolific'	see *C. avellana* 'Pearson's Prolific'
	- 'Pauetet' (F)	CAgr
§	- 'Pearson's Prolific' (F)	CAgr CSBt GTwe LBuc MMuc NLar SDea SEND SGol SKee
	- 'Pendula'	MAsh MBlu SCoo WHar WPat
	- 'Purpurea'	see *C. avellana* 'Fuscorubra'
	- 'Red Dwarf'	NLar

- 'Red Majestic'PBR	Widely available
- 'Tonda di Giffoni' (F)	CAgr MCoo
- 'Webb's Prize Cob' (F)	CAgr CDul CLnd ECrN ERea GBin GTwe IArd MBlu MJak MMuc NLar SDea SEND SGol SKee SVic WMou
colurna ♀H4	CCVT CDul CLnd CMCN CMac EBee ECrN EPfP EWTr IArd MBlu MGos NLar NWea SCoo SGol SPer WHar WMou
× ***colurnoides*** 'Chinoka' (F)	CAgr MCoo WHar
- 'Freeoka' (F)	CAgr MCoo WHar
- 'Laroka' (F)	ECrN
Early Long Zeller	see *C. avellana* 'Lang Tidlig Zeller'
maxima (F)	CMac CTri EPom GTwe MSwo NWea SDea
- 'Butler'	see *C. avellana* 'Butler'
- 'Ennis'	see *C. avellana* 'Ennis'
- 'Fertile de Coutard'	see *C. maxima* 'White Filbert'
- 'Frühe van Frauendorf'	see *C. maxima* 'Red Filbert'
- 'Garibaldi' (F)	NLar
- 'Grote Lambertsnoot'	see *C. maxima* 'Kentish Cob'
- 'Gunslebert' (F)	CAgr CCVT CDul CMac CMam CSBt CTho CTri ECrN ERea GTwe LRHS MBri NOra SDea SKee SPoG WHar
- Halle Giant	see *C. maxima* 'Halle'sche Riesennuss'
§ - 'Halle'sche Riesennuss' (F)	CAgr CMam ECrN ERea GTwe MBri MMuc NLar NOra SEND SKee WHar
§ - 'Kentish Cob' (F)	CAgr CBcs CDul CMac CSBt CTho ECrN ELan EPfP EPom ERea GTwe IArd LBuc LRHS MBlu MBri MGos MWat NLar SDea SEWo SKee SLim SPer SPoG SRms SWvt WHar
'Lambert's Filbert'	see *C. maxima* 'Kentish Cob'
- 'Longue d'Espagne'	see *C. maxima* 'Kentish Cob'
- 'Monsieur de Bouweller'	see *C. maxima* 'Halle'sche Riesennuss'
- 'Purple Filbert'	see *C. maxima* 'Purpurea'
§ - 'Purpurea' (F) ♀H4	Widely available
§ - 'Red Filbert' (F)	CDul CEnd CTho EPom ERea GTwe IArd MAsh MBlu MBri NLar NOra SCoo SGol SKee SLim SSta WHar WPat
- 'Red Zellernut'	see *C. maxima* 'Red Filbert'
- 'Spanish White'	see *C. maxima* 'White Filbert'
§ - 'White Filbert' (F)	GTwe SKee WHar
- 'White Spanish Filbert'	see *C. maxima* 'White Filbert'
'Witpit Lambertsnoot'	see *C. maxima* 'White Filbert'
'Nottingham Early' (F)	NLar
sieboldiana B&SWJ 11056 **new**	WCru
'Te Terra Red'	CDul CJun CMCN EBee MBlu MBri NLar SLon SSpi WHar

Corymbia see *Eucalyptus*

Corynabutilon see *Abutilon*

Corynephorus (*Poaceae*)

canescens	NBir WWEG

Corynocarpus (*Corynocarpaceae*)

laevigatus	ECou MBri

Cosmos (*Asteraceae*)

§ ***atrosanguineus***	Widely available
- Chocamocha = 'Thomocha'PBR	CBcs CCCN CHel CHid CSpe CWCL CWGN ECtt EPfP EUJe GMaP IBoy LHop LSRN LSou NCGa NDov NLar NPri SMrm SPer SRot WBor
bipinnatus 'Antiquity'	NPri SPhx
- 'Double Click'	SPhx
- 'Purity'	CSpe SPhx
- 'Sea Shells' (mixed) **new**	CWCL
- Sensation Series	SPhx
- Sonata Series 'Sonata Carmine'	LSou NPri SPoG
- - 'Sonata Pink'	LSou NPri SPoG
- - 'Sonata White'	CSpe LAst LSou NPri SPoG
caudatus	WJek
peucedanifolius	CAvo CSpe
- 'Flamingo'	CGrW EPfP ERCP SDeJ WHil
sulphureus Bright Lights (mixed)	CSpe

Cosmos × *Dahlia* (*Asteraceae*)

'Mexican Black'	ECtt ERCP WCot

costmary see *Tanacetum balsamita*

Cotinus ✿ (*Anacardiaceae*)

americanus	see *C. obovatus*
§ ***coggygria*** ♀H4	CArn CBcs CDoC CMCN CMac CWSG EBee ECrN ELan EPfP LHop MBri MMuc MRav MSwo MWat NWea SEND SGol SPer SWvt WHar
- Golden Spirit = 'Ancot'PBR	Widely available
- 'Kanari'	CJun NLar WPat
- 'Nordine'	NLar WPat
- 'Notcutt's Variety'	MRav
- 'Old Fashioned'	MGos MPkF NLar WMou
- 'Pink Champagne'	CBcs CJun EPfP MAsh NLar SSta WPat
- Purpureus Group	EPfP SGol
- 'Red Beauty'	CJun
- 'Royal Purple' ♀H4	Widely available
- Rubrifolius Group	CBcs EPfP SGol SPer SWvt
- Selection **new**	EPfP
- Smokey Joe = 'Lisjo'PBR	EPfP LRHS MAsh NCGa SLon SPoG SSta SWvt WHar
- 'Smokey Joe Purple'	LSou
- 'Velvet Cloak'	CAbP CJun ELan EPfP GKin LRHS MGos MPkF MRav NLar SGol SLon SWvt WHar WMou
- 'Young Lady'PBR	CBcs CDoC CMac CSBt EBee ELon EPfP EUJe EWes GBin LAst LHop LRHS MAsh MBlu MBri MPkF NCGa NEgg NHol NLar NPro SCoo SGol SPer SWvt WHar WPat
Dusky Maiden = 'Londus'PBR	ELon EPfP GBin LLHF LRHS MAsh MBri MGos NLar SLon SPoG WPat
'Flame' ♀H4	CDul CJun EBee ELan ELon EPfP EUJe EWTr LRHS MAsh MBri MGos MRav SHil SKHP SLim SPer SPoG SWvt WPat
'Grace'	Widely available
§ ***obovatus*** ♀H4	CJun CMCN EBtc ELon EPfP IArd LLHF LRHS MBlu MPkF MRav SSpi SSta WPGP WPat

Cotoneaster ✿ (*Rosaceae*)

SDR 5804	GKev
SDR 5841 **new**	GKev
acuminatus	SRms
§ ***adpressus*** 'Little Gem'	ECho NHar NLar
- var. ***praecox***	see *C. nanshan*

	- 'Tangstedt'	SGol
	- 'Tom Thumb'	see *C. adpressus* 'Little Gem'
	affinis	SRms
	albokermesinus	SRms
	amoenus	SLPl SRms
	- AC 829 **new**	MSnd
	- 'Fire Mountain'	NPro
§	***apiculatus***	SRms
§	***ascendens***	SRms
	assamensis	SRms
§	***astrophoros***	CMac MBlu NHar
	atropurpureus	SRms
§	- 'Variegatus' (v) Υ^{H4}	Widely available
	boisianus	SRms
	bradyi	SRms
§	***bullatus*** Υ^{H4}	CDul CTri EPfP IGor MMuc NLar SPer SRms WHil
	- 'Firebird'	see *C. ignescens*
	- f. ***floribundus***	see *C. bullatus*
	- var. ***macrophyllus***	see *C. rehderi*
	bumthangensis	SRms
	buxifolius blue-leaved	see *C. lidjiangensis*
	- 'Brno'	see *C. marginatus* 'Brno'
	- f. ***vellaeus***	see *C. astrophoros*
	camilli-schneideri	SRms
	canescens	SRms
	cinnabarinus	SRms
§	***cochleatus***	CDul LAst SRms
§	***congestus***	CSBt CWib MSwo MWat SPlb SRms WHar XLum
	- 'Nanus'	CMea ELan
	conspicuus	CBcs LAst SRms
	- AC 3176 **new**	MSnd
	- 'Decorus' Υ^{H4}	CDoC CDul CSBt EPfP LAst LHop LRHS MBri MGos MJak MMuc MSwo NEgg NLar NWea SGol SHil SLim SPer SPlb SPoG SWvt WHar WMoo
	- 'Leicester Gem'	SRms
	- 'Red Glory'	CMac
	cooperi	SRms
	cordifolius	MBlu SRms
	cornifolius	SRms
	cuspidatus	MBlu
N	***dammeri*** Υ^{H4}	Widely available
§	- 'Major'	CBar LBuc SPoG
§	- 'Mooncreeper'	CWSG SEND WHar
	- 'Oakwood'	see *C. radicans* 'Eichholz'
	- var. ***radicans*** misapplied	see *C. dammeri* 'Major'
	dielsianus	NLar NWea SRms
	distichus var. ***tongolensis***	see *C. splendens*
	divaricatus	EPfP NLar NWea SPer SRms
	duthieanus 'Boer'	see *C. apiculatus*
	elatus	SRms
	elegans	SRms
	emeiensis	SRms
	'Erlinda'	see *C.* × *suecicus* 'Erlinda'
	'Exburiensis'	CBcs CCVT CDoC CDul EBee EPfP LAst MBri MGos MMuc MRav MWat NLar SEND SGol WHar
	falconeri	SRms
	fastigiatus	SRms
	flinckii	SRms
	floccosus	NWea
	floridus	SRms
	forrestii	SRms
	franchetii	CBar CCVT CDul CMac CSBt EBee ECrN ELan EPfP LBuc LHop LRHS MGos MJak MMuc MSwo MWat NLar NWea SCoo SGol SLim SPer SPoG SRms SVic SWvt WCFE WHar
	frigidus	SRms
N	- 'Cornubia' Υ^{H4}	Widely available
	- 'Saint Monica'	MBlu
	gamblei	SRms
	ganghobaensis	SRms
	- B&L 12234 **new**	WCru
	glabratus	SLPl SRms
	glacialis	SRms
	glaucophyllus	IArd SEND SRms
§	***glomerulatus***	SRms
	gracilis	SRms
	granatensis	SRms
	harrovianus	NLar SLPl SRms
I	***hedegaardii*** 'Fructu Luteo'	SRms
	henryanus	SRms
	- 'Corina'	SRms
	'Herbstfeuer'	see *C. salicifolius* 'Herbstfeuer'
	'Highlight'	see *C. pluriflorus*
§	***hjelmqvistii***	LBuc SRms
	- 'Robustus'	see *C. hjelmqvistii*
	- 'Rotundifolius'	see *C. hjelmqvistii*
	hodjingensis	SRms
	horizontalis Υ^{H4}	Widely available
	- 'Variegatus'	see *C. atropurpureus* 'Variegatus'
	- var. ***wilsonii***	see *C. ascendens*
	hualiensis	SRms
	- B&SWJ 3143 **new**	WCru
	humifusus	see *C. dammeri*
	hummelii	SRms
§	'Hybridus Pendulus'	Widely available
§	***hylmoei***	SLPl SRms
	hypocarpus	SRms
	ignavus	SRms
§	***ignescens***	NWea SRms
	ignotus	SRms
	induratus	SLPl SRms
	insculptus	SRms
	integerrimus	SRms
§	***integrifolius*** Υ^{H4}	MAsh SPoG SRms WMoo
	- 'Silver Shadow'	NLar
	kangdingensis	SRms
	lacteus Υ^{H4}	CBcs CCVT CDul CSam CTri EBee ECrN ELan EPfP EWTr LBuc LHop LRHS MGos MJak MMuc MRav MWat NEgg NLar NWea SCoo SEND SGol SLon SPer SPoG SRms SWvt WCFE
	lancasteri	SRms
	langei	SRms
	laxiflorus	SRms
§	***lidjiangensis***	SRms
§	***linearifolius***	GCra
	lucidus	CDul NLar SRms
	- 'Mini'	SLPl
	ludlowii	SRms
	magnificus	SRms
§	***mairei***	NWea SRms
	marginatus Lindl. ex Loudon	SRms
§	- 'Blazovice'	SRms
§	- 'Brno'	SRms
	marquandii	SRms
§	***meiophyllus***	MBlu
	meuselii	SRms
	microphyllus misapplied	see *C. purpurascens*
	microphyllus ambig.	CBcs

microphyllus Wall. ex Lindl.	CDul CTri EBee LRHS MGos NWea SDix SPer SPoG WMoo
- NICE 004	WCFE
- var. ***cochleatus*** (Franch.) Rehd. & Wils.	see *C. cochleatus*
- var. ***cochleatus*** ambig.	EPot NSla
- 'Donard Gem'	see *C. astrophoros*
- 'Teulon Porter'	see *C. astrophoros*
- var. ***thymifolius*** misapplied	see *C. linearifolius*
- var. ***thymifolius*** (Lindl.) Koehne	see *C. integrifolius*
- var. ***thymifolius*** ambig.	LRHS
milkedandaensis	SRms
miniatus	SRms
mirabilis	SRms
monopyrenus	SRms
'Mooncreeper'	see *C. dammeri* 'Mooncreeper'
morrisonensis	SRms
moupinensis	SRms
- BWJ 8167	WCru
mucronatus	SRms
multiflorus Bunge	NLar
§ ***nanshan***	CAbP NWea SRms WHar
- 'Boer'	see *C. apiculatus*
naoujanensis	EPfP MBri
- 'Berried Treasure'	EPfP LRHS SHil
newryensis	SRms
nitens	SRms
nitidifolius	see *C. glomerulatus*
nohelii	SRms
notabilis	SRms
nummularioides	SRms
nummularius	SRms
obscurus	SRms
obtusus Wall. ex Lindl.	SRms
pangiensis	SRms
pannosus	SLPl SRms
paradoxus	SRms
parkeri	SRms
pekinensis	SRms
permutatus	see *C. pluriflorus*
perpusillus	SRms
§ ***pluriflorus***	CDul SRms
poluninii	SRms
polycarpus	SRms
praecox 'Boer'	see *C. apiculatus*
procumbens	SRms
- 'Queen of Carpets'	CDoC EBee ELan EPfP IBoy LHop LRHS LSRN MAsh MBri MGos MRav MWhi SCoo SHil SLim SPoG SRms SWvt WMoo
- 'Streib's Findling'	see *C.* 'Streib's Findling'
prostratus	SRms
przewalskii	SRms
pseudo-obscurus	SRms
§ ***purpurascens***	CSBt
pyrenaicus	see *C. congestus*
qungbixiensis	SRms
racemiflorus	SRms
§ ***radicans*** 'Eichholz'	NHol NWad SPoG
§ ***rehderi***	CMHG SRms
roseus	SRms
'Rothschildianus' ♀^{H4}	Widely available
rugosus	SRms
salicifolius	CTri MSwo NLar NWea SEND SRms
- Autumn Fire	see *C. salicifolius* 'Herbstfeuer'
§ - 'Avonbank'	CDoC CEnd NLar WHar
- 'Brno Orangeade'	SRms
- 'Gnom'	CDul CMac ELan EPfP LRHS MAsh MGos MRav NBir NEgg SPer SPoG SRms WHar WMoo
§ - 'Herbstfeuer'	MRav MSwo SRms WMoo
- Park Carpet	see *C. salicifolius* 'Parkteppich'
§ - 'Parkteppich'	NWea
- 'Pendulus'	see *C.* 'Hybridus Pendulus'
- 'Repens'	CDoC CWib EPfP MWhi NHol NPla NPri NWad NWea SGol SLim SPer SPoG SRms WHar
- var. ***rugosus***	see *C. hylmoei*
- 'Scarlet Leader'	CMac
salwinensis	SLPl SRms
sandakphuensis	SRms
scandinavicus	SRms
schantungensis	SRms
schlechtendalii 'Blazovice'	see *C. marginatus* 'Blazovice'
- 'Brno'	see *C. marginatus* 'Brno'
schubertii	SRms
serotinus misapplied	see *C. meiophyllus*
serotinus Hutchinson	NLar SLPl SRms
shannanensis	SRms
shansiensis	SRms
sherriffii	SRms
sikangensis	SRms
simonsii ♀^{H4}	CBcs CCVT CDoC CDul CLnd CMac EBee ECrN ELan EPfP LBuc LRHS MGos MJak MMuc NHol NLar NWad NWea SGol SPer SPoG SRms WHar
§ ***splendens***	SRms
- 'Sabrina'	see *C. splendens*
spongbergii	SRms
staintonii	SRms
sternianus ♀^{H4}	EPfP SLPl SRms
- ACE 2200	EPot
§ 'Streib's Findling'	IBoy MAsh NLar SGol
suavis	SRms
subacutus	SRms
subadpressus	SRms
× ***suecicus*** 'Coral Beauty'	CCVT CDoC CHab CTri CWib EBee EPfP EShb LAst LBuc LHop LRHS MAsh MGos MJak MSwo MWat NEgg NHol NLar NPri SBod SGol SLim SPer SPoG SRms SWvt WHar WMoo
§ - 'Erlinda' (v)	NLar SRms
- 'Ifor'	SLPl SRms
- 'Juliette' (v)	EHoe LRHS LSRN MAsh NLar SCoo SLim WHar
- 'Skogholm'	CBcs CDul CWib EBee EPfP LRHS MAsh MGos NWea SPer SRms WHar
taoensis	SRms
tardiflorus	SRms
tauricus	SRms
teijiashanensis	SRms
tengyuehensis	SRms
thimphuensis	SRms
tomentellus	WCFE
tomentosus	SRms
turbinatus	SLPl SRms
'Valkenburg'	SRms
vandelaarii	SLPl SRms
veitchii	NLar SRms
verruculosus	SRms
villosulus	SRms
vilmorinianus	SRms
wardii misapplied	see *C. mairei*
wardii W.W. Sm.	GGal SRms

	× ***watereri***	CCVT CWib ECrN ELon LAst MJak MMuc MSwo NWea SEND WJas
	- 'Avonbank'	see *C. salicifolius* 'Avonbank'
	- 'Cornubia'	see *C. frigidus* 'Cornubia'
	- 'John Waterer' ♀H4	EPfP SPer SPoG
	- 'Notcutt's Variety'	EPfP
	- 'Pendulus'	see *C.* 'Hybridus Pendulus'
	- 'Pink Champagne'	CMac MRav
	wilsonii	SRms
	yalungensis	SRms
	yinchangensis	SRms
	zabelii	SRms

Cotula (*Asteraceae*)

	coronopifolia	CBAq CWat NPer SWat
	hispida ambig.	EBee GKev SIgm
§	***hispida*** (DC.) Harv.	CMea CTri ECho EDAr EHoe EPot GMaP MAsh MHer MWat NPer NRya SPoG SRms WIce WJek XLum
	lineariloba (DC.) Hilliard	ECho EWes
	minor	see *Leptinella minor*
	'Platt's Black'	see *Leptinella squalida* 'Platt's Black'
	potentilloides	see *Leptinella potentillina*
	pyrethrifolia	see *Leptinella pyrethrifolia*
	rotundata	see *Leptinella rotundata*
	squalida	see *Leptinella squalida*

Cotyledon (*Crassulaceae*)

	chrysantha	see *Rosularia chrysantha*
	gibbiflora var. ***metallica***	see *Echeveria gibbiflora* var. *metallica*
	oppositifolia	see *Chiastophyllum oppositifolium*
	orbiculata	CHEx SDix SPlb
	- var. ***oblonga***	EShb SPlb WCot
	- var. ***orbiculata***	EShb
	simplicifolia	see *Chiastophyllum oppositifolium*

Crambe (*Brassicaceae*)

	cordifolia ♀H4	Widely available
	maritima ♀H4	CArn CHel CSev CSpe EBee EPfP GMaP GPoy LPio LRHS MCoo MCot MRav NEgg NLar NPnk NSti SEND SMad SPer SWat WCot WJek WMnd WPGP WWEG XLum
	- 'Lilywhite'	CAgr LEdu SVic
	orientalis	LRHS

cranberry see *Vaccinium macrocarpon, V. oxycoccos*

Crassula (*Crassulaceae*)

	anomala	see *C. atropurpurea* var. *anomala*
	arborescens	EShb EUJe SChr
	argentea	see *C. ovata*
§	***atropurpurea*** var. ***anomala***	SChr
	- subsp. ***arborescens*** 'Blue Mist'	SEND
	'Buddha's Temple'	CSuc
	coccinea	EShb SPlb
	columella	CSuc
	elegans subsp. ***elegans***	CSuc
	multicava	CHEx CHel
	muscosa	CSuc SChr SPlb SRot
	obtusa	SRot
	orbicularis	WCot
§	***ovata*** ♀H1	CDoC CHEx EBak EPfP NPer NPla SChr SEND SPlb SPre SVen WThu
	- 'Blue Bird'	LToo
	- 'Horn Tree' **new**	CSuc
	- 'Variegata' (v)	EBak WCot
	perfoliata var. ***falcata*** ♀H1	EOHP EShb EUJe SRot WCot
	perforata	EUJe
	- 'Variegata' (v)	SRot
	portulacea	see *C. ovata*
§	***sarcocaulis***	CBcs CHEx CHVG CTri ECho ELan ELon GMaP ITim MAsh MSCN SEND SPlb SPoG SRms SRot SVen WAbe WIce WSHC XSen
	sedifolia	see *C. setulosa* 'Milfordiae'
	sediformis	see *C. setulosa* 'Milfordiae'
	setulosa	SPlb
§	- 'Milfordiae'	CTri ECho EPot NBir NRya
	socialis	WAbe
	- 'Major'	SChr
	tetragona	SEND
*	***tomentosa*** 'Variegata' (v)	EShb

+ *Crataegomespilus* (*Rosaceae*)

	'Jules d'Asnières'	NLar

× *Crataegosorbus* (*Rosaceae*)

	miczurinii 'Ivan's Belle'	CAgr

Crataegus (*Rosaceae*)

	sp.	SWvt
	F&M 196	WPGP
	arnoldiana	CAgr CDul CLnd CTri EBee ECrN EPfP MCoo MMuc NWea SCoo SEND SLPl
	'Autumn Glory'	CEnd CLnd EBee ECrN
	azarolus	EPfP
	champlainensis	CLnd
	chrysocarpa	EPfP
	chungtienensis SDR 5104	GKev
N	***coccinea*** misapplied	see *C. intricata*
N	***coccinea*** ambig.	NWea
§	***coccinea*** L.	CAgr CLnd CNWT CTho MAsh SCoo
	coccinioides	EPfP
	cordata	see *C. phaenopyrum*
	crus-galli misapplied	see *C. persimilis* 'Prunifolia'
	crus-galli L.	CCVT CDul CLnd ECrN EPfP IGor LAst MAsh MBri NLar NWea SPer WJas
	dahurica	EPfP
	× ***dippeliana***	EPfP
	dsungarica	EPfP
	× ***durobrivensis***	CAgr CDul CLnd EPfP MBri
	ellwangeriana	CAgr ECrN EPfP SDix
	- 'Fire Ball'	MBlu
	eriocarpa	CLnd
	gemmosa	CEnd MAsh NLar NWea
	greggiana	EPfP IGor
	× ***grignonensis***	CBcs CDul CLnd CTho ECrN MBri SPer WJas
§	***intricata***	EPfP NWea
	irrasa	EPfP
	jonesiae	EPfP
	korolkowii	IGor
	laciniata Ucria	see *C. orientalis*
§	***laevigata***	CCVT CDul NWea
	- 'Coccinea Plena'	see *C. laevigata* 'Paul's Scarlet'
	- 'Crimson Cloud'	Widely available
	- 'Gireoudii'	CDul CWib LAst MGos NSti WJas
	- 'Mutabilis'	CTri SGol

§	– 'Paul's Scarlet' (d) ♀H4	Widely available
	– 'Pink Corkscrew'	EPfP LLHF MBlu WPat
	– 'Plena' (d)	CBcs CDoC CDul CLnd CMac CSBt CTri CWib EBee ECrN EPfP LAst MGos MRav MSwo MWat NWea SCrf SEWo SGol SLim SPer SWvt WHar
	– 'Rosea'	GKin SEND
	– 'Rosea Flore Pleno' (d) ♀H4	Widely available
	× ***lavalleei***	CCVT CDul CLnd CTri ECrN ELan EPfP LAst MMuc MRav MSwo NWea SCoo SEND SLon SPer
	– 'Aurora' **new**	NLar
	– 'Carrierei' ♀H4	CDul CTho EBee EPfP EWTr IVic LHop LSRN MAsh MBri NWea SCoo SEWo SPoG WCot WMou
	lobulata	EPfP
	× ***media*** **new**	MJak
	mexicana	see *C. pubescens* f. *stipulacea*
	mollis	CAgr CTho ECrN EPfP WSpi
	monogyna	Widely available
§	– 'Biflora'	CDul CEnd CLnd CTho CTri EBee ECrN MAsh MCoo MGos NLar SLim
	– 'Compacta'	LLHF MBlu WPat
	– 'Flexuosa'	WCot
	– 'Praecox'	see *C. monogyna* 'Biflora'
	– 'Stricta'	CCVT CDul CLnd CSBt EBee ECrN EPfP IDee MMuc SEND SGol
	– 'Variegata' (v)	ECrN
	× ***mordenensis*** 'Toba' (d)	CDul CLnd EPfP SGol
	nigra	EPfP IGor
§	***orientalis***	CCVT CDul CEnd CLnd CMCN CTho CTri EBee ECrN EPfP IArd MAsh MBri MCoo MGos NLar NWea SCoo SLim WHar WJas WMou
	oxyacantha	see *C. laevigata*
	pedicellata	see *C. coccinea* L.
	pentagyna	EPfP
§	***persimilis*** 'Prunifolia' ♀H4	Widely available
	– 'Prunifolia Splendens'	CCVT EBee EWTr GBin LBuc MBri MCoo SCoo WPat
§	***phaenopyrum***	CDul CLnd CTho EPfP MBri SLPl
	pinnatifida	EPfP
	– var. ***major***	CDul CEnd EPfP LEdu MBri MCoo
	– – 'Big Golden Star'	CAgr CLnd CTho ECrN EPfP LRHS MAsh MBlu MCoo NLar SCoo
	'Praecox'	see *C. monogyna* 'Biflora'
	prunifolia	see *C. persimilis* 'Prunifolia'
	pseudoheterophylla	EPfP
§	***pubescens*** f. ***stipulacea***	CDul CTho ECrN EPfP
	punctata	CTho EPfP SLPl
	– f. ***aurea***	EPfP MBri
	sanguinea	EPfP
	schraderiana	CAgr CDoC CDul CLnd CTho EBtc EPfP IVic MBri NLar NWea SCoo WHar
	sorbifolia	EPfP
	submollis	IGor
	succulenta	EPfP
	– 'Jubilee'[PBR]	EBee MCoo
	– var. ***macracantha***	CMCN EPfP
	suksdorfii	EPfP
	tanacetifolia	CAgr CDul CTho EPfP MBlu MBri
	tracyi	MBri
	turkestanica	EPfP
	viridis 'Winter King'	EPfP SLim
	wattiana	CLnd EBee ELan EPfP

× *Crataemespilus* (*Rosaceae*)

grandiflora	CDul CLnd WSpi

Cremanthodium (*Asteraceae*)

CC 6525	GKev
arnicoides	EBee

Crenularia see *Aethionema*

Crepis (*Asteraceae*)

aurea	ECho
incana ♀H4	CMea CPla ECho ECtt MAvo NChi NSla NWad SPhx SRms
– 'Pink Mist'	GBin NLar

Crinitaria see *Aster*

Crinodendron (*Elaeocarpaceae*)

hookerianum ♀H3	Widely available
– 'Ada Hoffmann'	Widely available
patagua	CBcs CCCN CDoy CExl CHid CTsd CWib EBee ELon EPfP EPri ESwi GBin LRHS MMuc NEgg NLar NSoo SBrt SPlb SPoG SVen WSHC

Crinum (*Amaryllidaceae*)

	sp. **new**	CMac
	amoenum	CCCN EBee ECho GBin WCot
	asiaticum	WCot
§	***bulbispermum***	CPrp EBee ELan GCal LRHS WCot
	capense	see *C. bulbispermum*
	'Carolina Beauty'	WCot
	'Cintho Alpha'	EBee SDeJ SPer
	'Elizabeth Traub'	WCot
	'Ellen Bosanquet'	CCCN CCon CTca EBee ELan GBin WCot
	'Emma Jones'	WCot
	'Hanibal's Dwarf'	CFil WCot WPGP
	moorei	CAvo CBro CCon CTca ECho IVic LEdu SChr WPGP
	– f. ***album***	CCCN CFil CTca EBee
	'Ollene'	WCot
§	× ***powellii*** ♀H3	CBcs CBro CExl CPrp CTca CTsd EAmu EBak ECho ELan ELon EPfP GCal LEdu LHop LPio LRHS MNrw MRav NLar SHod SDeJ SEND SMad SPer SRms WCot WPGP WWFP XLum
	– 'Album' ♀H3	CAvo CBro CDes CHEx CPrp CTca CTri EBee ECho ELan ELon EPfP EWes GCra LEdu LPio LRHS MRav NWad SDeJ SEND SMad SPer SRms SSpi WCot WPGP
	– 'Harlemense'	CDes
	– 'Longifolium'	see *C. bulbispermum*
	– 'Roseum'	see *C.* × *powellii*
	'Sangria'	WCot
	'Summer Nocturne'	WCot
	variabile	EBee WCot
	'White Queen'	WCot
	yemense misapplied	IMou

Criogenes see *Cypripedium*

Crithmum (*Apiaceae*)

maritimum	CArn GPoy MHoo MNHC SBHP SPlb SRms WJek

Crocosmia ✿ (*Iridaceae*)

	'Anniversary'	IBlr
	'Apricot'	CTca ECrc IBal
	'Apricot Surprise'	ELon
	aurea misapplied	see *C.* × *crocosmiiflora* 'George Davison' Davison
	aurea ambig.	EShb GCal
	aurea (Pappe ex Hook.f.) Planch.	CPou IBlr
	- from Swaziland **new**	GCal
	- subsp. ***aurea***	CTca IBlr
	- - 'Maculata'	IBlr
	- subsp. ***pauciflora***	IBlr
	'Auricorn'	CTca IBlr
	'Auriol'	IBlr NCot
	'Aurora'	NGdn
	'Beth Chatto'	CTca ECrc IBal
	'Bowland Blaze' **new**	MAvo
	Bressingham Beacon = 'Blos'	IBlr LRHS MSpe
	'Bressingham Blaze'	CBre CMHG CPrp CTca ECrc ECtt IBlr LRHS NGdn NHol WCot WHil
	Bridgemere hybrid	ECrc NHol
	Bright Eyes = 'Walbreyes'PBR	EPfP LBuc LRHS
	'Buttercups'	CMea EPot MBri
	'Cadenza'	IBal IBlr NHol
	'Carnival'	IBlr
	'Cascade'	IBal IBlr
	'Chinatown'	IBal IBlr NHol WHil
	'Chrome'	CSam
	'Chrome Spray' **new**	IBlr
	'Citronella' misapplied	see *C.* × *crocosmiiflora* 'Honey Angels'
	'Comet' Knutty	CTca ECrc GCal IBlr LRHS MAvo WMoo
	'Cornish Copper'	CTca
	× ***crocosmiiflora***	CHEx CTca CTri IBlr MCot SPlb SRms WBrk WMoo WShi
	- 'A.E. Amos'	ECrc
	- 'A.J. Hogan'	CPrp CTca IBal IBlr NHol
	- 'African Glow'	CDes CTca ECrc IBal LEdu
	- 'Amber Sun'	IBlr
	- 'Amberglow'	CElw CExl IBal IBlr MAvo NHol NPer
	- 'Apricot Queen'	CTca IBlr NHol
	- 'Autumn Gold'	IBlr
	- 'B.A. Walker'	ECrc
	- 'Baby Barnaby'	CBre CDes
	- 'Babylon'	Widely available
	- 'Bicolor'	CTca IBal IBlr WHil
	- 'Burford Bronze'	CTca IBal IBlr NHol
	- 'Buttercup'	CSam CTca ECrc ECtt EPfP EWll IBal IBlr IKil LRHS MAvo MCot NBre NHol SRkn STes WMoo WWEG
	- 'Canary Bird'	CBro CSam ECtt IBal IBlr LRHS NGdn NHol WBrk WSpi
	- 'Cardinale'	IBlr
§	- 'Carmin Brillant' ♀H3-4	CBro CPrp CSam CTca CWCL EBee ECtt ELon EPfP ERCP GKev IBlr LEdu LRHS LSou MBri NHol NPnk NSoo SHil SPoG SRms WMoo WWEG
	- 'Challa'	CTca ECtt
	- 'Citrina'	CTca MNrw WSpi
	- 'Citronella' J.E. Fitt	CBro CExl CSam CTri ECrc EPfP GMaP GQue LRHS MBel MRav NGdn NHol WCot WGwG
§	- 'Coleton Fishacre'	Widely available
§	- 'Columbus'	CAvo CSam CTca EBee ECrc ELon EPfP EPri IBal IBlr LHop LRHS LSou MAsh MAvo MSCN NHol SPer SRms WHil WMoo WWEG
	- 'Colwall'	IBal IBlr
	- 'Constance'	CBro CSam CTca ECrc ECtt IBal IBlr LRHS MAvo MBri NBid NGdn NHol WBrk WHil
	- 'Corona'	CPrp CTca IBal IBlr MAvo NHol
	- 'Corten'	IBlr
§	- 'Croesus'	CTca IBal IBlr MRav
	- 'Custard Cream'	CPrp CSpe CTca ECrc IBlr LRHS NHol
	- 'D.H. Houghton'	IBlr
	- 'Daisy Hill' **new**	IBlr
	- 'David Fitt' **new**	MAvo
	- 'Debutante'	CDes CTca ECrc EPri IBal IBlr LRHS NHol SHar WSHC
§	- 'Diadème'	CSam CTca
	- 'Dusky Maiden'	CMac CTca ECrc ECtt EHoe ELon EPri EWTr GCal GKin GMaP IBal IBlr LAst LRHS LSou MRav MSwo NHol NPnk SRms SWvt WSpi WWEG WWlt
	- 'Dwarf Gold'	IBal
§	- 'E.A. Bowles'	CPou CTca EBee ECrc IBlr LRHS
	- 'Eastern Promise'	CBre CTca ELon IBal IBlr MAvo
	- 'Eclatant'	IBlr
	- 'Elegans'	ECrc ECtt IBal IBlr LRHS
§	- 'Emily McKenzie'	Widely available
	- 'Étoile de Feu'	IBlr
	- 'Fantasie'	ECrc IBal
	- 'Festival Orange'	ECrc IBlr
	- 'Fire Jumper'	CDes CTca IBal MAvo WPGP
	- 'Firebrand'	IBlr
	- 'Fireglow'	CTca ECtt IBal IBlr
	- 'Flamethrower'	IBlr
	- 'George Davison' misapplied	see *C.* × *crocosmiiflora* 'Golden Glory' ambig., *C.* 'Sulphurea'
§	- 'George Davison' Davison	Widely available
	- 'Gillian'	ECrc
	- 'Gloria'	CTca ECrc IBal MAvo
	- 'Golden Glory' misapplied	see *C.* × *crocosmiiflora* 'Diadème'
§	- 'Golden Glory' ambig.	CExl COlW CTca CWCL EBee ELan GBuc IBal IBlr LPio MAsh MSCN MSwo NBir SRms WCot
	- 'Goldfinch'	EBee ECrc IBlr NHol WHil WWEG
	- 'Goldie'	CTca ECrc MAvo
	- 'Hades'	IBlr
	- 'Harvest Sun'	IBlr
	- 'Heligan'	EPfP
	- 'His Majesty'	CBro CSam CSpe CTca ECrc IBal IBlr LRHS NHol WHil
	- 'Hoey Joey'	ECrc
§	- 'Honey Angels'	Widely available
	- 'Honey Bells'	ECrc LRHS WBrk
	- 'Irish Dawn'	ECrc IBal IBlr NBre NHol NWad
§	- 'Jackanapes'	CDes CTca ECtt ELan GCal IBal IBlr LRHS MBri MLHP STPC WPGP
	- 'Jackanapes VI'	IBal
	- 'James Coey' misapplied	see *C.* × *crocosmiiflora* 'Carmin Brillant'
	- 'James Coey' J.E. Fitt	COlW EHoe EPfP GKin IFoB MLHP NDov NGdn NHol NLar SMrm WMoo
§	- 'Jessie'	CTca IBlr LRHS
	- 'Judith'	CTca IBlr
	- 'Kapoor'	IBlr

	- 'Kiautschou'	CTca CWCL EBee IBal IBlr LRHS NGdn NHol
	- 'Lady Hamilton'	CCon CElw CExl CSam CTca GCal GCra IBal IBlr LRHS MAvo MBri MRav NCGa NHol WHil WMoo WWEG
	- 'Lady McKenzie'	see *C.* × *crocosmiiflora* 'Emily McKenzie'
	- 'Lady Oxford'	CTca ECrc IBlr LRHS NHol WHil
	- 'Lambrook Gold'	CAvo ECrc IBlr
	- 'Lemon Fleece'	CCVN
	- 'Lord Nelson'	CExl CTca IBal NHol
	- 'Loweswater'	ECrc MAvo
	- 'Lutea'	ECtt IBal IBlr LRHS
	- 'Marjorie'	ECrc
	- 'Mars'	CElw ECrc EWes EWll IBal IFoB LRHS MAvo NGdn SRkn WWEG
	- 'Mephistopheles'	CTca IBlr MAvo NHol
	- 'Merryman'	CTca ECrc IBal
	- 'Météore'	CHel EPfP GQue LRHS MBNS MBri NBre WWEG
	- 'Morgenlicht'	CTca IBlr NHol WBrk
	- 'Moses'	CTca
	- 'Mount Usher'	CCon CCse CTca ECrc GCal IBal IBlr NHol
§	- 'Mrs Geoffrey Howard'	CSam CTca CWCL IBal IBlr LEdu LRHS NHol SHar SRms WBrk WCru WPGP
	- 'Mrs Morrison'	see *C.* × *crocosmiiflora* 'Mrs Geoffrey Howard'
	- 'Newry Seedling'	see *C.* × *crocosmiiflora* 'Prometheus'
	- 'Nimbus'	CTca IBal IBlr WHil
§	- 'Norwich Canary'	CMHG CTca EPfP EPri GBuc GCra IBal IBlr LEdu LRHS MBri MRav NBir NGdn NHol WBrk WCot WHil WMoo WOut WWEG
	- 'Olympic Fire'	ECrc IBlr NHol
	- 'Olympic Sunrise'	CTca
	- 'Pepper'	IBlr
	'Ping Pong'	CTca
	- 'Plaisir'	CTca IBal IBlr LRHS NBid NHol WWEG
	- 'Polo'	CSam CTca CWCL
	- 'Princess'	see *C. pottsii* 'Princess'
§	- 'Princess Alexandra'	IBlr
	- 'Prolificans'	ECrc IBlr
§	- 'Prometheus'	CTca IBal IBlr NHol
	- 'Queen Alexandra' misapplied	see *C.* × *crocosmiiflora* 'Princess Alexandra'
§	- 'Queen Alexandra' J.E. Fitt	CTca IBlr WHal WMoo
	- 'Queen Charlotte'	CTca ECrc IBal IBlr
	- 'Queen Mary II'	see *C.* × *crocosmiiflora* 'Columbus'
	- 'Queen of Spain'	CTca IBal IBlr LRHS WHil WWEG
	- 'Rayon d'Or'	EBee ECrc IBlr WPGP
	- 'Red King'	EBee EPfP IBal IBlr LHop LRHS MBri NLar WHil WMoo WRHF WWEG
	- 'Red Knight'	IBlr
	- 'Rheingold' misapplied	see *C.* × *crocosmiiflora* 'Diadème'
	- 'Rose Queen'	IBlr
	- 'Saint Clements'	CTca EBee IBlr NHol
	- 'Saracen'	CMac CTca ECtt ELon GBuc GCal GKin IBal IBlr IBoy LEdu LRHS LSou MBNS NBre SKHP SMrm WMoo
	- 'Severn Seas'	ECrc ECtt WSpi
	- 'Sir Mathew Wilson'	EBee IBal IBlr LRHS WPGP
	- 'Solfatare' ♀H3	Widely available
	- 'Solfatare Coleton Fishacre'	see *C.* × *crocosmiiflora* 'Coleton Fishacre'
	- 'Star of the East' ♀H3	Widely available
	- 'Starbright'	IBlr
	- 'Starfire'	ECrc
	- 'Sultan'	CExl IBlr WMoo
	- 'Tiger's Eye'	CTca
	- 'Venus'	CBre CHel CTca ECtt ELon EShb IBal IBlr LPla LRHS MAvo NBre NHol WHil WMoo
	- 'Vesuvius'	ECrc GCal IBlr LRHS NCGa WSHC
	- 'Vic's Yellow'	ECrc
	- 'Voyager'	ECtt ELon ERCP IBal IBlr LRHS MBri NHol NLar SDeJ WRHF
	- Wasdale strain	ECrc
	- 'Zeal Tan'	CElw CExl CMHG CSam CTca CWCL ECtt ELan ELon EPri GBin GCal IBal IBlr LEdu LRHS MBNS MNFA NEgg NLar NSti SMrm WBrk WCot WMoo
§	× ***crocosmioides***	CTca IBlr WHil
	- 'Castle Ward Late'	CPrp CTca ECrc ECtt GBin GCal GCra GQue IBal IBlr LRHS NHol NLar SMrm SRms WMoo
	- 'Mount Stewart Late'	IBlr
§	- 'Vulcan' Leichtlin	CMac CTca IBlr LRHS WHil
	'Darkleaf Apricot'	see *C.* × *crocosmiiflora* 'Coleton Fishacre'
	'Devil's Advocate'	CTca
	'Doctor Marion Wood'	EBee
	'Eldorado'	see *C.* × *crocosmiiflora* 'E.A. Bowles'
	'Elegance'	IBlr
	'Ellenbank Canary'	CTca MAvo
	'Ellenbank Firecrest'	CDes CTca EBee MAvo NCGa WPGP
	'Ellenbank Goldcrest'	NLar
	'Ellenbank Skylark'	MAvo
	'Emberglow'	Widely available
	'Fandango'	IBal IBlr NHol
	'Fernhill'	ECrc IBlr
	'Fire King' misapplied	see *C.* × *crocosmiiflora* 'Jackanapes'
	'Fire King' ambig.	EBee ECrc EPot ERCP IBal LRHS NLar NSti SWvt WHil
	'Fire Sprite'	IBlr
	'Firecracker' **new**	IBlr
	'Firefly'	IBlr
	'Fireworks'	EBee
	'Flaire'	IBlr
	'Fleuve Jaune'	CTca ECrc ECtt LRHS
	'Forest Fire'	IBal LLHF LSou
	fucata	IBlr
	- 'Jupiter'	see *C.* 'Jupiter'
	fucata* × *paniculata	CTca IBal
	'Fugue'	CTca IBlr NCot
	'Fusilade'	IBlr
	'Gold Sprite'	IBlr
	'Golden Ballerina' PBR	ECtt EWes GBin IBal LRHS LSou MBri NCGa SPoG SRkn WWlt
	'Golden Dew'	CTca ECrc ECtt EPfP GQue MBNS NCGa NEgg SKHP WCot WMoo
	Golden Fleece *sensu* Lemoine	see *C.* × *crocosmiiflora* 'Coleton Fishacre'
	'Harlequin'	CElw CTca IBal MAvo
	'Harmonia'	CDes CTca
	'Hellfire'	CHVG CMea CPar CSam CTca ECtt ELon EUJe GAbr IBal LEdu LLHF LRHS MAvo MBNS MBri MNrw MTis NGdn NSti SMad SPer SRms WCot WWlt

'Highlight'	ECrc IBal IBlr MAvo NHol
'Jennine'	IBal LRHS NHol
'Jenny'	MAvo
Jenny Bloom = 'Blacro'PBR	LRHS NChi
'John Boots'	CHel EBee ECtt ELon GBuc IBal LRHS MCot NBid NHol NLar SRms WHil
§ 'Jupiter'	CBre CSam CTca CWCL GCal IBal LRHS MAvo MRav NCGa NHol NLar WHil
'Kathleen'	ECrc LRHS
'Krakatoa'	CHVG CHll CPrp CTca ECrc GBin IBal LLHF MAvo MBel SKHP SPoG SRkn SWvt WMoo
'Lady Wilson' misapplied	see *C.* × *crocosmiiflora* 'Norwich Canary'
'Lana de Savary'	CPrp CTca EBee EWes GCal IBal IBlr LRHS NBid NHol NWad
'Late Cornish'	see *C.* × *crocosmiiflora* 'Queen Alexandra' J.E. Fitt
'Late Lucifer'	CHEx CTca CTri GCal IBlr SDix
× ***latifolia***	see *C.* × *crocosmioides*
'Lemon Spray' **new**	CTca IBlr
'Limpopo'	CCVN CDes CMac CMea CPar CTca EBee ECtt ELon EPri EShb GAbr GQue IBal LEdu LPio LRHS MAvo MBNS MBri MNrw MSCN NEgg NLar NPnk SMrm SPer WCot WWFP WWlt
'Lowen Daa' **new**	CTca
'Lucifer' ℣H4	Widely available
'Lucifer's Children' **new**	EPfP
'Malahide Castle Red'	SMad
'Mandarin'	ECrc IBlr
'Marcotijn'	CTca IBal IBlr IGor LRHS
masoniorum ℣H3	Widely available
- from Satan's Nek, South Africa	CTca
- 'African Dawn'	CTca ECrc ECtt
- 'Amber'	IBlr
- 'Dixter Flame'	IBlr IFoB SDix WOut
- 'Firebird'	CTca GCra IBlr IGor LRHS NBre NHol SRms WSpi
- 'Flamenco'	IBlr
- 'Golden Swan'	SRms
- Holehird strain	ECrc
- 'Kiaora'	IBlr
- 'Moira Reid'	IBlr NHol
- red-flowered	IBlr
- 'Rowallane Apricot'	IBlr
- 'Rowallane Orange'	CTca IBlr NHol
- 'Rowallane Yellow' ℣H3-4	CPrp CTca EBee GCal IBal IBlr IGor IMou LRHS MBri NCGa NHol WCot WSHC
- Slieve Donard selection	CTca ECrc IBal
- 'Sunflare' **new**	IBlr
- 'Tropicana'	IBlr
mathewsiana	IBlr
mathewsiana × ***paniculata***	CTca
'Minotaur'	IBlr
'Miss Scarlet'	EPfP LBuc LRHS
'Mistral'	CCCN CHel CTca ECtt EPfP EPot GBuc GKev IBal IBlr LAst LRHS NBre NHol NLar WMoo
'Moorland Blaze'	WMoo
'Mount Stewart'	see *C.* × *crocosmiiflora* 'Jessie'
'Mr Bedford'	see *C.* × *crocosmiiflora* 'Croesus'
'Mullard Pink'	CTca ECrc
'Okavango'PBR	CBre CBro CMac CPrp CTca ECtt ELon EPri GAbr GQue IBal MAvo MBNS MBri MCot MHol MNrw NLar SKHP SMrm WCot WHil
Old Hat	see *C.* 'Walberton Red'
'Orange Devil'	CBre ECtt GKin IBal IBlr LLHF MBNS WHil
'Orange Lucifer'	NBre
'Orange River'	MAvo
'Orangeade'	CTca ECtt IBal IBlr LRHS NHol SRms
'Pageant'	ECrc
§ ***paniculata***	CMac CPou CTca ECtt GAbr GBin MNFA NBid NHol SAPC SPet WBrk WMoo WOut WShi
- from Howick	CTca
- from Kologha	CTca
- brown/orange-flowered	IBlr
- 'Cally Greyleaf'	GCal
- 'Cally Sword'	GCal
- 'Major'	CTri IBlr
- 'Natal'	CPrp CTca ECtt IBal NHol
- red-flowered	CTca IBlr LRHS SWvt
- triploid	IBlr
aff. ***paniculata***	ECtt IBlr
'Paul's Best Yellow'	CDes CEnd CSam CTca ECGP ECtt ELon EWes GAbr IBal LLHF LLWG LRHS MAvo MBNS MTis NSti SBod SHar SMad SMrm SPer SWvt WCot WHoo
pearsei	CTca IBlr
'Phillipa Browne'	CTca ECtt IBal LSou NEgg WCot WMoo
pottsii	CTca ECtt IBal IBlr LRHS NHol WHil WPtf WWEG
- CD&R 109	CPou
- 'Culzean Pink'	CElw CExl CHVG COIW CPrp CTca EBee GBin GCal IBal IBlr LPla LRHS MLHP NBid NBir NCot NHol NLar WOut
- deep pink-flowered	IBlr IGor WMoo
- 'Grandiflora'	IBlr
§ - 'Princess'	ECrc IBal
- tall	CTca
'Quantreau'	EBee IBlr
'Queen Alexandria'	LRHS
'R.W. Wallace'	CTca IBal
'Red Star'	IBal
rosea	see *Tritonia disticha* subsp. *rubrolucens*
'Rowden Bronze'	see *C.* × *crocosmiiflora* 'Coleton Fishacre'
'Rowden Chrome'	see *C.* × *crocosmiiflora* 'George Davison' Davison
'Ruby Velvet'	IBlr
'Rubygold'	CPrp IBlr
'Saffron Queen'	IBlr
'Saturn'	see *C.* 'Jupiter'
'Scarlatti'	CTca IBal IBlr NHol
'Scarlet Wonder' **new**	CTca
'Severn Sunrise' ℣H3-4	Widely available
'Shocking'	EBee IBlr MAvo
'Sonate'	CTca
'Sorento' **new**	IBlr
'Spitfire'	CExl CPrp CSam CTca ECtt ELan GAbr GQue IBal IBlr LHop LRHS MArl MAvo MRav NHol SWvt
§ 'Sulphurea'	CExl CPou CSam ECtt EPfP IBal IBlr MSpe NHol SDix WBrk WHal

	'Sunzest'	CTca ECrc MAvo
	'Tamar Double Red' **new**	CTca
	'Tamar Glow'	CTca
	'Tamar New Dawn'	CTca
	'Tamar Peace'	CTca
	'Tangerine'	ECrc
	'Tangerine Dream' **new**	IBlr
	'Tangerine Queen'	CTca ECrc IBal IBlr LRHS NHol WHil WMoo
	'Tiger'	CElw CTca ECrc
	'Toccata' **new**	IBlr
I	'Vulcan' A. Bloom	CTca IBal IBlr MAvo WCot
	'Vulcan' Leichtlin	see *C.* × *crocosmioides* 'Vulcan' Leichtlin
§	'Walberton Red'	CDes CTca ECrc EWes IBal IBlr LRHS MAvo MBri NWad SKHP SMad
	Walberton Yellow = 'Walcroy'PBR	CHVG EPfP LRHS MAsh
	'Zambesi'PBR	CDes CMac CTca ECtt ELon EUJe GQue IBal LHop MAvo MBNS MBri MCot MNrw MTis NCGa NLar SKHP SPer WCot WHil WPGP
	'Zeal Giant'	CRow CTca ECrc ECtt IBlr NHol
	'Zeal Remembrance'	CTca
	'Zeal Unnamed'	CPrp CTca EBee ECrc GBee IBal IBlr NHol

Crocus ✿ (*Iridaceae*)

	'Advance'	CBro ECho EPot ERCP MBri SDeJ WShi
	alatavicus	ECho
§	***albiflorus***	ECho EPot
	ancyrensis	ECho EPot GKev SDeJ
	- 'Golden Bunch'	ECho SDeJ WShi
§	***angustifolius*** ♀H4	ECho EPot GKev SDeJ
	- bronze-tinged	NMin
	- 'Minor'	ECho EPot
	antalyensis	ECho LWst
	- white-flowered	LWst
	- yellow flowered	LWst
	'Ard Schenk'	ECho GKev LRHS
	asturicus	see *C. serotinus* subsp. *salzmannii*
	asumaniae	ECho
	'Aubade'	ECho EPot GKev
	aureus	see *C. flavus* subsp. *flavus*
	banaticus ♀H4	ECho EPot GKev LLHF LWst NHar
	- 'Snowdrift'	NHar
	baytopiorum	ECho
	biflorus	ECho
	- subsp. ***adamii***	ECho
	- subsp. ***biflorus***	ECho
	- 'Blue Pearl' ♀H4	CAvo CBro ECho EPfP EPot GKev LPio MBri NBir SDeJ SPer SPhx WCot WShi
	- subsp. ***crewei***	ECho
	- subsp. ***isauricus***	ECho
	- subsp. ***melantherus***	ECho
	- 'Miss Vain'	ECho EPot ERCP GKev MBri
	- subsp. ***punctatus***	ECho
	- 'Serevan'	EPot LWst
	- subsp. ***tauri***	ECho LWst
	- subsp. ***weldenii***	ECho
	- - 'Albus'	ECho EPot
	- - 'Fairy'	ECho EPot
	'Blue Bird'	ECho EPot
	boryi	ECho
	- VV GR.1410	LWst
	cambessedesii	ECho
	cancellatus **new**	SDeJ
§	- subsp. ***cancellatus***	ECho EPot GKev LLHF
	- var. ***cilicicus***	see *C. cancellatus* subsp. *cancellatus*
	- subsp. ***lycius***	ECho EPot LWst
	- subsp. ***mazziaricus***	EPot
	- - large-flowered	LWst
	- - 'Menalo'	LWst
	- - 'Parnassus'	LWst
	- - 'Pilion'	LWst
	- - 'Rendina'	LWst
	candidus 'Lune'	LWst
	- var. ***subflavus***	see *C. olivieri* subsp. *olivieri*
	cartwrightianus ♀H4	ECho GKev LLHF LRHS WShi
	- CE&H 613	LWst
	- 'Albus' misapplied	see *C. hadriaticus*
N	- 'Albus' Tubergen ♀H4	ECho EPot GKev SDeJ
	- 'Halloween'	LWst
	- white-flowered clone	LWst
	chrysanthus ♀H4	CHab
	- 'Afyon'	LWst
	- 'Blue Peter'	ECho
	- 'Cream Beauty' ♀H4	CAvo CBro CMea ECho EPfP EPot GKev LRHS MBri NBir SDeJ WShi
	- 'E.A. Bowles' ♀H4	ECho
	- 'E.P. Bowles'	ECho MBri
	- 'Early Gold'	ECho
	- var. ***fuscotinctus***	ECho EPfP EPot MBri SDeJ
	- 'Milea'	LWst
	- 'Sunspot'	EPot
	- 'Uschak Orange'	ECho
	- 'Warley'	ECho
	- 'Zwanenburg Bronze' ♀H4	ECho EPfP GKev LPio SDeJ WShi
	'Cloth of Gold'	see *C. angustifolius*
	clusii	see *C. serotinus* subsp. *clusii*
	corsicus ♀H4	ECho EPot LWst
	× ***cultorum*** 'Fantasy'	ECho WShi
	- 'Flower Record'	ECho GKev NBir SDeJ
	- 'Grand Maître'	CAvo MBri SDeJ
	- 'Haarlem Gem'	ECho
	- 'Jeanne d'Arc'	CAvo CBro ECho EPfP EPot GKev MBri NBir SDeJ WShi
	- 'King of the Striped'	ECho SDeJ SPer
	- 'Negro Boy'	ECho EPot
	- 'Peter Pan'	CAby
	- 'Pickwick'	CAby CAvo ECho EPfP EPot MBri NBir SDeJ WShi
§	- 'Purpureus Grandiflorus'	CBro EPot SDeJ
	- 'Queen of the Blues'	CBro EPot WShi
	- 'Remembrance'	CAby CAvo CBro ECho EPfP EPot GKev NBir SDeJ WShi
	dalmaticus	EPot
	- 'Petrovac'	LWst
	danfordiae	ECho
	'Dorothy'	ECho EPot GKev
	'Dutch Yellow'	see *C.* × *luteus* 'Golden Yellow'
	'Ego'	ECho LWst
	etruscus ♀H4	ECho LWst
	- 'Rosalind'	ECho
	- 'Zwanenburg' ♀H4	ECho EPot GKev SDeJ
	flavus	ECho
§	- subsp. ***flavus*** ♀H4	ECho EPot GKev WShi
	fleischeri	ECho EPot
	gargaricus subsp. ***herbertii***	LWst
	'Gipsy Girl'	CAvo ECho EPfP EPot ERCP MBri
	'Golden Mammoth'	see *C.* × *luteus* 'Golden Yellow'
	'Goldilocks' ♀H4	ECho EPot GKev SDeJ

goulimyi ♀H4	CBro ECho EPot GKev LLHF SDeJ
- from Sikea, Greece **new**	GKev
- subsp. ***leucanthus*** HOA 0183	LWst
§ ***hadriaticus*** ♀H4	ECho EPot GKev LLHF
- 'Alepohori'	LWst
- var. ***chrysobelonicus***	see *C. hadriaticus*
- subsp. ***hadriaticus*** f. ***lilacinus***	EPot LWst
- 'Jumbo'	LWst
'Herald'	CAvo ECho
heuffelianus subsp. ***heuffelianus***	ECho EPot WShi
imperati subsp. ***imperati*** var. ***albus***	WAbe
- subsp. ***suaveolens***	ECho EPot
- - 'De Jager'	ECho ERCP
'Janis Ruksans'	CAvo LWst
'Jeannine'	ECho EPot SDeJ
× ***jessoppiae***	ECho LWst
karduchorum	ECho EPot
korolkowii	CGrW ECho GKev LWst
- 'Golden Nugget'	EPot
- 'Kiss of Spring'	ECho EPot
kosaninii	ECho NMin
- CH 801	LWst
- 'April View'	EPot NMin
kotschyanus ♀H4	ECho
- 'Albus'	ECho SDeJ
§ - subsp. ***kotschyanus***	ECho EPot SDeJ
- 'Reliance'	ECho LWst
kotschyanus × ***ochroleucus***	ECho
'Ladykiller' ♀H4	CAvo CBro ECho EPot ERCP GKev MBri NMin SPhx WShi
laevigatus ♀H4	ECho
- CE&H 612	LWst
- HOA 0138	LWst
- HOA 0153	LWst
- 'Fontenayi'	ECho EPot ERCP GKev
- white-flowered	ECho
'Large Yellow'	see *C.* × *luteus* 'Golden Yellow'
§ ***ligusticus*** ♀H4	CAvo CBro ECho EPot
'Little Amber'	LWst
longiflorus ♀H4	ECho EPot LLHF
§ × ***luteus*** 'Golden Yellow' ♀H4	CAvo EPfP EPot GKev WShi
§ - 'Stellaris' ♀H4	ECho
malyi ♀H4	ECho NMin
- 'Ballerina'	ECho LWst
- 'Sveti Roc'	EPot LWst
mathewii	ECho EPot WCot
- HKEP 9291	LWst
- 'Dream Dancer'	LWst
medius	see *C. ligusticus*
minimus	ECho EPot ERCP LLHF
niveus	CBro ECho EPot GKev LLHF WAbe WCot
- VV GR.1410	LWst
- VV KA.2312	LWst
nudiflorus	ECho EPot GKev LLHF
ochroleucus ♀H4	ECho EPot GKev LLHF SDeJ
olivieri	ECho
- subsp. ***balansae***	ECho
- - 'Zwanenburg'	ECho EPot
- subsp. ***istanbulensis***	LWst
§ - subsp. ***olivieri***	ECho
- - HOA 0156	LWst
- - 'Little Tiger'	ECho LWst

oreocreticus	ECho
pallasii	ECho
- VV KR.75	LWst
- subsp. ***pallasii***	ECho
- subsp. ***turcicus*** VV TW.855	LWst
- white-flowered	LWst
paschei HKEP 9034	LWst
pestalozzae	ECho
- var. ***caeruleus***	ECho
- - CRO 401	LWst
'Prins Claus'	ECho EPfP EPot ERCP MBri SBch SDeJ SPer
'Prinses Beatrix'	ECho NMin
pulchellus ♀H4	CAvo ECho EPot ERCP GKev
- 'Albus'	ECho EPot
- 'Inspiration'	ECho
- 'Michael Hoog'	ECho
'Purple Heart'	LWst
'Purpureus'	see *C.* × *cultorum* 'Purpureus Grandiflorus'
reticulatus	ECho
- VV YY.306	LWst
- subsp. ***reticulatus***	ECho EPot
robertianus HOA 9856	EPot LWst
'Romance'	CAvo EPot GKev MBri SDeJ
'Ruby Giant'	CAvo CBro ECho EPfP EPot ERCP GKev MBri NBir SDeJ SPer SPhx WShi
rujanensis	ECho LWst
salzmannii	see *C. serotinus* subsp. *salzmannii*
sativus	CArn CAvo CBro CPrp CTca CTsd ECho ELan EPot ERCP GKev GPoy NBir SDeJ SVic
'Saturnus'	EPot
scardicus	LWst
§ ***serotinus*** subsp. ***clusii***	ECho
§ - subsp. ***salzmannii***	ECho LLHF
- - HOA 9911	LWst
- - KPW 9425	LWst
- - KPW 9432	LWst
sibiricus	see *C. sieberi*
§ ***sieberi*** ♀H4	EPot
- 'Albus'	see *C. sieberi* 'Bowles's White'
- subsp. ***atticus***	ECho GKev
- - 'Firefly'	ECho EPot GKev SDeJ
- - 'Stunner'	LWst
§ - 'Bowles's White' ♀H4	CAvo CBro ECho EPot GKev SDeJ
- 'Hubert Edelsten' ♀H4	ECho
- 'Ronald Ginns'	EPot
- subsp. ***sublimis*** 'Tricolor' ♀H4	CAvo CBro CTca ECho EPfP EPot GKev MBri NBir NWad SDeJ SPer
- 'Vardousia'	LWst
- 'Violet Queen'	ECho
'Snow Bunting' ♀H4	CAvo CBro CTca ECho EPfP EPot GKev LPio NBir SDeJ SPer WShi
speciosus ♀H4	CAvo CBro CTca EPfP MLHP NBir SDeJ SPer WCot WShi
- 'Aino'	ECho LWst
- 'Aitchisonii'	ECho EHyd EPot GKev LRHS
- 'Albus' ♀H4	CAvo CBro ECho EPot ERCP GKev SDeJ
- 'Artabir'	ECho EHyd EPot GKev LRHS SDeJ
- 'Cassiope'	ECho EHyd EPot GKev LRHS SDeJ
- 'Conqueror'	CBro ECho EPfP EPot ERCP GKev LRHS SDeJ WBor
- 'Oxonian'	CBro ECho GKev
- subsp. ***speciosus***	ECho EPot NBir SDeJ
- subsp. ***xantholaimos***	LWst
'Spring Beauty'	CAvo EPfP ERCP SDeJ SPer

× ***stellaris***	see *C.* × *luteus* 'Stellaris'
susianus	see *C. angustifolius*
suterianus	see *C. olivieri* subsp. *olivieri*
tommasinianus ♀H4	CAvo CBro CGrW CHab CMea CTca ECho EPot LLWP MBri MRav NBir SDeJ SPhx SRms WShi
- 'Albus'	CMea ECho EPot GKev WShi
- 'Barr's Purple'	CAby ECho EPot GKev SDeJ
- 'Claret'	ECho
- 'Eric Smith'	EPot
- 'Lilac Beauty'	ECho EPfP EPot SPer
- 'Pictus'	ECho LLHF WShi
- 'Roseus'	CAvo CDes ECho EPot ERCP GKev NMin SPhx WCot WShi
- 'Whitewell Purple'	CAvo CBro ECho EPot ERCP GKev MBri NBir SDeJ WShi
tournefortii ♀H2-4	ECho
* - 'Albus'	ECho
vallicola	LWst
'Vanguard' ♀H4	CAvo CBro ECho EPfP EPot SDeJ
veluchensis	ECho
veneris	ECho
vernus	ECho GKev
- subsp. ***albiflorus***	see *C. albiflorus*
- garden hybrids	see *C.* × *cultorum*
- 'Graecus'	ECho EPot
- 'Krasno Polje'	LWst
- 'Michael's Purple'	ECho
- 'Tatra Shades'	ECho
- Uklin strain	ECho
- subsp. ***vernus*** 'Grandiflorus'	see *C.* × *cultorum* 'Purpureus Grandiflorus'
- - var. ***neapolitanus***	LWst
versicolor	ECho
- 'Picturatus'	ECho EPot ERCP LLHF NMin SDeJ
vitellinus	ECho EPot LWst
- white-flowered	LWst
'Yalta'	CAvo ECho ERCP GKev
'Yellow Giant'	SDeJ
'Yellow Mammoth'	see *C.* × *luteus* 'Golden Yellow'
'Zenith'	ECho EPot
'Zephyr' ♀H4	CBro ECho EPot
zonatus	see *C. kotschyanus* subsp. *kotschyanus*

Croomia (*Stemonaceae*)

heterosepala	WCru

Crotalaria (*Papilionaceae*)

laburnifolia	CCCN

Crowea (*Rutaceae*)

exalata* × *saligna	CExl

Crucianella (*Rubiaceae*)

stylosa	see *Phuopsis stylosa*

Cruciata (*Rubiaceae*)

§ ***laevipes***	NMir

Crusea (*Rubiaceae*)

coccinea	CSpe
- 'Crûg Crimson'	WCru

Cryptocarya (*Lauraceae*)

alba	GBin SVen

Cryptogramma (*Pteridaceae*)

crispa	WHer

Cryptomeria ✿ (*Cupressaceae*)

japonica ♀H4	CDul CMen CTho ELau EPfP MBlu MMuc SEND SWvt WMou
- Araucarioides Group	EHul NLar
- 'Atawai'	NLar
- 'Aurea'	EUJe
- 'Bandai'	LBuc
- 'Bandai-sugi' ♀H4	CKen CMac CMen EHul EPfP GKin MGos NHol NLar SCoo SLim WGor
- 'Barabits Gold'	MGos
- 'Birodo'	CKen
- 'Black Dragon'	SLim
- 'Compressa'	CDoC CKen EHul EPfP LBee MAsh MGos WGor
§ - 'Cristata'	CBcs CDoC CMac ELan LRHS MAsh MGos MPkF SLim
- 'Dacrydioides'	CDoC GKin NLar SLim
- 'Dinger' **new**	CKen
- Elegans Group	CBcs CDoy CDul CMac CSBt EHul ELan EPfP LRHS MBri MGos NEgg NLar NWea SCoo SEND SLim SPer SPoG
- 'Elegans Aurea'	EHul ELan MAsh SWvt
- 'Elegans Compacta' ♀H4	CDoC CMac CSBt CWib EHul ELan GBin LBee LRHS MBri MMuc NLar NWea SCoo SLim SPoG SWvt
- 'Elegans Nana'	LBee LRHS NEgg SRms WBor
- 'Elegans Viridis'	ELan LRHS MJak NEgg SBod SLim SPer SPoG
- 'Globosa Nana' ♀H4	EHul EPfP LAst LBee MGos NEgg NHol SAPC SCoo SLim SPoG WGor
- 'Golden Promise'	MAsh NHol NWad SCoo SLim SWvt WGor
- Gracilis Group	CDoC
- 'Jindai-sugi'	GKin NLar
- 'Karl Fuchs'	SLim
- 'Kilmacurragh'	CKen EHul NWea SLim
- 'Knaptonensis' (v)	CDoC NLar
- 'Kohui-yatsubusa'	CKen
* - 'Konijn-yatsubusa'	CKen
- 'Koshiji-yatsubusa'	NLar
- 'Koshyi'	CKen
- 'Little Champion'	CDoC CKen NLar SLim
- 'Little Diamond'	CKen
- 'Little Sonja'	CKen SLim
- 'Little Yoko' **new**	CKen
- 'Littleworth Dwarf'	see *C. japonica* 'Littleworth Gnom'
§ - 'Littleworth Gnom'	NLar
- 'Lobbii Nana' hort.	see *C. japonica* 'Nana'
- 'Monstrosa'	NLar
§ - 'Nana'	CDoC CMac EHul EPfP
- 'Osaka-tama'	CKen
- 'Pipo'	CKen
- 'Pygmaea'	NHol NLar NWad SRms
- 'Rasen-sugi'	GKin IVic LRHS MGos NLar SCoo SLim SMad
- 'Rein's Dense Jade'	SLim
- 'Sekkan-sugi'	CBcs CDoC CDul CMac EHul EPfP ESwi GBin GKin IArd LAst LBee LRHS MGos NLar SCoo SLim SPoG SWvt WBor
- 'Sekka-sugi'	see *C. japonica* 'Cristata'
§ - 'Spiralis'	CDoC CKen CMac EHul ELan EPfP GKin LAst LBee LRHS MAsh MGos NEgg NHol NLar NWad NWea SCoo SLim SPer SPoG SWvt
§ - 'Spiraliter Falcata'	CDoC NLar
§ - 'Tansu'	CDoC CKen WGor

- 'Tenzan-sugi'	CDoC CKen MGos NHol NLar NWad SLim WThu
- 'Tilford Gold'	EHul MGos NEgg NHol WGor
- 'Toda'	CKen
- 'Vilmorin Gold'	CKen MGos NHol
- 'Vilmoriniana' 🏆^{H4}	CDoC CKen CMen CTri EHul EPfP EPot GKin MBri MGos NEgg NHol NLar SCoo SLim SPer SPoG SWvt WMoo
- 'Winter Bronze'	CKen
- 'Yatsubusa'	see *C. japonica* 'Tansu'
- 'Yore-sugi'	see *C. japonica* 'Spiralis', 'Spiraliter Falcata'
- 'Yoshino'	CKen SLim

Cryptostegia (*Apocynaceae*)

grandiflora	CCCN

Cryptotaenia (*Apiaceae*)

japonica	CHby CPou MHer MNHC SRms WHer WJek
- f. ***atropurpurea***	CSpe EBee EHoe LEdu MNrw SDix SPhx

Ctenanthe (*Marantaceae*)

lubbersiana 🏆^{H1}	XBlo
§ ***oppenheimiana***	XBlo

Cucubalus (*Caryophyllaceae*)

baccifer	CArn EWld NLar

Cudrania see *Maclura*

cumin see *Cuminum cyminum*

Cuminum (*Apiaceae*)

cyminum	CArn ELau MNHC SVic

Cunninghamia (*Cupressaceae*)

konishii	CExl
- 'Coolyns Compact'	WThu
§ ***lanceolata***	CBcs CDTJ CDoC CDul CGHE CKen CMCN CMac CTho EPfP GKin LRHS SMad SSpi SSta WBor WPGP
- 'Glauca'	CExl CJun CTho IVic
- 'Little Leo'	LRHS
sinensis	see *C. lanceolata*
unicaniculata	see *C. lanceolata*

Cunonia (*Cunoniaceae*)

capensis	CExl

Cuphea (*Lythraceae*)

caeciliae	WWlt
cyanea	CMHG SDix WWlt
'Firecracker'	LAst NPri
hyssopifolia 🏆^{H1}	CHll SWvt
- 'Alba'	CCCN SWvt
- pink-flowered	CCCN
- red-flowered	CCCN
- 'Rosea'	SEND SWvt
§ ***ignea*** 🏆^{H1}	SVen SVic WWlt
§ ***llavea*** 'Georgia Scarlet'	CCCN LAst LSou WWlt
- 'Tiny Mice'	see *C. llavea* 'Georgia Scarlet'
I ***macrophylla*** hort.	CHll WWlt
maculata	CCCN
platycentra	see *C. ignea*
'Regal Purple' **new**	CPla
'Torpedo'	LSou
viscosissima	CSpe MCot

× *Cupressocyparis* see × *Cuprocyparis*

Cupressus (*Cupressaceae*)

arizonica var. ***arizonica*** 'Arctic'	CDoC
- var. ***glabra*** 'Angaston'	SLim
- - 'Aurea'	CMac EHul LRHS MAsh NPCo SGol SLim
- - 'Blue Ice' 🏆^{H3}	CBcs CDoC CDul CMac CTho EHul LRHS MAsh MGos NPCo SCoo SLim SPer SPoG SWvt WMou
- - 'Compacta'	CKen
I - - 'Fastigiata'	CCVT CDoC EHul EPfP
- - 'Glauca'	EPfP MBlu
* - - 'Lutea'	SPoG
- 'Pyramidalis' 🏆^{H3}	EPfP SEND SGol
cashmeriana 🏆^{H2}	CBcs CDTJ CDoC CTho ELan IGor IVic LRHS NPCo SLim SMad
lusitanica 'Brice's Weeping'	CKen LRHS SLim
- 'Glauca Pendula'	CDoC
- 'Pygmy'	CKen
macrocarpa	CBcs CCVT CDoC CDul CTho EHul SEND
- 'Compacta'	CKen
- 'Gold Spread'	EHul LRHS SLim
- 'Goldcrest' 🏆^{H3}	CBcs CCVT CDoC CDul CMac ECrN EHul ELan LBee LRHS MBri MGos NBir NPri NSoo NWea SEWo SGol SLim SPer SPoG SWvt WCFE WMou
- 'Golden Cone'	CKen NPCo
- 'Golden Pillar' 🏆^{H3}	CDoC CMac EHul SWvt
- 'Greenstead Magnificent'	LRHS SLim
- 'Horizontalis Aurea'	EHul
- 'Lohbrunner'	CKen
- 'Lutea'	CDoC
I - 'Pendula'	SLim
- 'Pygmaea'	CKen
- 'Sulphur Cushion'	CKen
- 'Wilma'	CSBt EHul LAst LBee LRHS MAsh MGos NEgg SCoo SGol SLim SPoG SWvt
- 'Woking'	CKen
sempervirens	CDul CMCN CTsd EAmu EHul ELan LRHS SPlb
- 'Bolgheri'	SBig
- 'Garda'	CDoC
- 'Green Pencil'	CKen
- 'Pyramidalis'	see *C. sempervirens* Stricta Group
- var. ***sempervirens***	see *C. sempervirens* Stricta Group
§ - Stricta Group 🏆^{H3}	CBcs CCVT CDul CKen CMCN CTho EHul EPfP EWTr MREP NLar SAPC SEND SEWo SGol WCFE
- 'Swane's Gold'	CBcs CDoC CDul CKen EHul EPfP LRHS MAsh NPCo SLim WCFE
- 'Totem Pole'	CCVT CKen CSBt CTho CTri EHul ELan EPfP EUJe LBee LRHS MAsh MGos NEgg SCoo SEND SPoG SWvt

× *Cuprocyparis* (*Cupressaceae*)

§ ***leylandii*** 🏆^{H4}	CBcs CCVT CDoC CDul CMac CSBt CTri ECrN EHul EPfP LBuc LRHS LSRN MAsh MBri MGos MJak MMuc NEgg NPri NSoo NWea SGol SLim SPer SPoG SWvt WHar WMou

I - '2001' CCVT CDoC SGol SLim WMou
§ - 'Castlewellan' CBcs CCVT CDoC CDul CMac CSBt CTri EHul EPfP LBuc LRHS LSRN MAsh MBri MGos MJak MMuc NPri NSoo NWea SEND SGol SLim SPer SPoG SWvt WHar WMou
- Excalibur Gold = 'Drabb'PBR CDoC NWea
- 'Ferngold' MAsh
- 'Galway Gold' see × *C. leylandii* 'Castlewellan'
- 'Gold Rider' 𝕐H4 CDoC EHul MAsh MGos MMuc NEgg NWea SCoo SEND SMad SPer SPoG SWvt WHar
§ - 'Harlequin' (v) CMac SEND SWvt
- 'Herculea' CDoC NPri
- 'Leighton Green' WMou
- 'Naylor's Blue' CMac
- 'Olive's Green' SWvt
- 'Robinson's Gold' 𝕐H4 CMac EHul GQui LRHS MMuc NWea SGol SLim WMou
- 'Variegata' see × *C. leylandii* 'Harlequin'
- 'Winter Sun' NLar WCFE

Curculigo (*Hypoxidaceae*)

capitulata XBlo
crassifolia B&SWJ 2318 WCru

Curcuma ✿ (*Zingiberaceae*)

alismatifolia EPfP SDeJ
longa CArn
roscoeana SDeJ
zedoaria 'Bicolor Wonder' CCCN SBst
- 'Pink Wonder' CCCN
- 'White Wonder' CCCN SDeJ

Curtonus see *Crocosmia*

Cussonia (*Araliaceae*)

paniculata CDTJ CWGN EShb EUJe WCot
spicata CDTJ SPlb

custard apple see *Annona cherimola*

Cyananthus (*Campanulaceae*)

§ ***chungdienensis*** GKev
integer misapplied see *C. microphyllus*
lobatus 𝕐H4 LLHF
- 'Albus' EPot WAbe
- dark WAbe
- giant EPot NHar WAbe
lobatus* × *microphyllus EPot WAbe
§ ***microphyllus*** 𝕐H4 EPot GJos NHar NSla WAbe
microphyllus × 'Sherriff's Variety' **new** NHar
sherriffii EPot GJos IFoB WAbe
spathulifolius WAbe
zhongdienensis see *C. chungdienensis*

Cyanotis (*Commelinaceae*)

somaliensis 𝕐H1 EShb

Cyathea (*Cyatheaceae*)

australis CBty CDTJ CKel EAmu ESwi
brownii ISha
cooperi CDTJ CKel EAmu ESwi WFib
* - 'Brentwood' ISha
cunninghamii EAmu
dealbata CDTJ CKel EAmu GBin
dregei SPlb
medullaris CKel EAmu
smithii CDTJ CKel EAmu
tomentosissima CDTJ CKel EAmu

Cyathodes (*Ericaceae*)

colensoi see *Leucopogon colensoi*
fraseri see *Leucopogon fraseri*
parviflora see *Leucopogon parviflorus*

Cycas (*Cycadaceae*)

circinalis EAmu
panzhihuaensis CBrP EAmu SPlb
revoluta 𝕐H1 CAbb CBrP CCCN CDoC EAmu EPfP EUJe MBri MREP SAPC SBst SChr SEND SMad SPlb STrG WCot XBlo
revoluta* × *taitungensis CBrP
§ ***rumphii*** CBrP
taitungensis CBrP
thouarsii see *C. rumphii*

Cyclamen ✿ (*Primulaceae*)

abchasicum see *C. coum* subsp. *caucasicum*
africanum CBro ECho EPot GKev LRHS MAsh
africanum* × *hederifolium ECho
§ ***alpinum*** CBro ECho EPot GKev LLHF LRHS MAsh SDeJ
- 'Nettleton White' MAsh
balearicum CBro ECho EPot LRHS MAsh
cilicium 𝕐H2-4 CBro ECho EHyd EPfP EPot ERCP GBuc GKev LRHS MAsh MHer WCot WHoo WIvy WSHi
- f. ***album*** CBro ECho EPot GBuc LLHF LRHS MAsh
- patterned-leaved ECho NBir
colchicum ECho MAsh
§ ***coum*** 𝕐H4 Widely available
- var. ***abchasicum*** see *C. coum* subsp. *caucasicum*
§ - subsp. ***caucasicum*** GKev MAsh
- subsp. ***coum*** CBro ECho LEdu MAsh
- - f. ***albissimum*** GBuc
- - - 'George Bisson' MAsh
- - - 'Golan Heights' MAsh WIvy
- - f. ***coum*** Nymans Group MAsh
- - - Pewter Group 𝕐H2-4 ECho GBuc MAsh WCot WIvy
- - - - 'Blush' GBuc
- - - - 'Maurice Dryden' CBro CLAP ECho EHyd EPot LHop LRHS MAsh WHoo
- - - - red-flowered WPat7
- - - - 'Tilebarn Elizabeth' MAsh NBir WHoo
- - - - white-flowered MAsh
- - - 'Roseum' CAvo GBuc LRHS
- - - Silver Group CAvo CBro ECho LHop LRHS NPnk NRya WHoo
- - - - red-flowered WHoo
- - magenta-flowered CWCL WHoo
- - f. ***pallidum*** 'Album' CAvo ECho EPot GKev MAsh SDeJ SMrm SPer WHlf WHoo WPat
- dark pink-flowered CAvo CLAP ECho WHoo
- hybrid ERCP
- marble-leaved ECho LHop WHoo
- plain-leaved CLAP
- red-flowered CLAP ECho
I - 'Rubrum' GKev
- 'Something Magic' **new** LSou
- 'Tilebarn Graham' MAsh
creticum ECho MAsh

cyprium	CBro ECho LRHS MAsh
- 'E.S.'	ECho MAsh WThu
- 'Galaxy'	MAsh
elegans	MAsh
europaeum	see *C. purpurascens*
fatrense	see *C. purpurascens* subsp. *purpurascens* from Fatra, Slovakia
graecum	CBro ECho GKev LLHF LRHS MAsh WCot WIvy WThu XEll
- subsp. ***anatolicum***	MAsh
- subsp. ***candicum***	MAsh
- subsp. ***graecum*** f. ***album***	CBro ECho EPot LRHS MAsh
- - f. ***graecum*** 'Glyfada'	EPot MAsh
§ ***hederifolium*** ♀H4	Widely available
- S&L 175/1	WCot XLum
- arrow-head	CLAP ECho SBea
- var. ***confusum***	MAsh WCot
- var. ***hederifolium*** f. ***albiflorum***	CAvo CBro CTri ECho EWTr GKev LEdu LRHS NPnk NWad SDeJ WCot WHoo WPat WPnP XLum
- - - 'Album'	CHel CWCL MAsh
- - - Bowles's Apollo Group	GBuc
§ - - - - 'Artemis'	MAsh
- - - - 'White Bowles's Apollo'	see *C. hederifolium* var. *hederifolium* f. *albiflorum* (Bowles's Apollo Group) 'Artemis'
- - - 'Daley Thompson'	WCot
- - - 'Linnett Stargazer'	WCot
- - - 'Nettleton Silver'	see *C. hederifolium* var. *hederifolium* f. *albiflorum* 'White Cloud'
- - - 'Perlenteppich'	GMaP
- - - silver-leaved	SDys
§ - - - 'White Cloud'	CLAP ECho MAsh WCot WHoo WIvy
- - f. ***hederifolium*** Bowles's Apollo Group	CHid CLAP GBuc MAsh
- - - 'Fairy Rings'	MAsh
- - - red	NWad
- - - 'Ruby Glow'	CWCL GBuc LRHS MAsh NBir WCot WPat WThu
- - - Silver Cloud Group	CBro CHid CLAP GBuc GKev MAsh NBir WHoo WIvy WPat
- - - 'Silver Shield'	MAsh
- - - 'Stargazer'	LLHF MAsh
- - 'Tilebarn Silver Arrow'	MAsh
- island scented strain	WCot
- 'Lysander' **new**	EPot
- 'Red Sky'	NWad
- 'Rose Pearls'	SRot
- Silver-leaved Group	ECho EHyd EPot GKev LHop MAsh SBea SRot
- - 'Silver Leaf Pink'	CHel NWad
- - 'Silver Leaf White'	NWad
× ***hildebrandii***	LLHF
ibericum	see *C. coum* subsp. *caucasicum*
intaminatum	CBro ECho EHyd EPot LLHF LRHS MAsh WIvy XEll
- patterned-leaved	MAsh
- pink-flowered	MAsh
- plain-leaved	MAsh WThu
latifolium	see *C. persicum*
libanoticum	CBro ECho EPot LRHS MAsh XEll
mirabile ♀H2-3	CBro ECho EHyd EPot GBuc GKev LLHF LRHS MAsh SDeJ WIvy WThu
- f. ***mirabile*** 'Tilebarn Anne'	MAsh
- - 'Tilebarn Nicholas'	ECho MAsh
- f. ***niveum*** 'Tilebarn Jan'	ECho MAsh
neapolitanum	see *C. hederifolium*
orbiculatum	see *C. coum*
parviflorum	MAsh
§ ***persicum***	CAby CBro CWCL ECho GBuc LRHS MAsh
- 'Silverado White' **new**	WPtf
- white-flowered	ECho MAsh
pseudibericum ♀H2-3	CBro ECho EHyd EPot GKev LHop LLHF LRHS MAsh SDeJ WThu
- f. ***roseum***	MAsh
§ ***purpurascens*** ♀H4	CBro ECho GBuc GKev LLHF MAsh WHoo WIvy WPat WThu
- var. ***fatrense***	see *C. purpurascens* subsp. *purpurascens* from Fatra, Slovakia
- 'Lake Garda'	MAsh
§ - subsp. ***purpurascens*** from Fatra, Slovakia	GKev MAsh
repandum	CAvo CBro ECho EPot GKev LLHF LRHS MAsh WHer
- 'Pelops' misapplied	see *C. rhodium* subsp. *peloponnesiacum*
- subsp. ***repandum*** f. ***album***	MAsh
rhodium ♀H2-3	MAsh
§ - subsp. ***peloponnesiacum***	ECGP
- subsp. ***rhodium***	MAsh
- subsp. ***vividum***	MAsh
rohlfsianum	CBro ECho GKev LRHS MAsh
× ***saundersiae***	MAsh
× ***schwarzii***	MAsh
trochopteranthum	see *C. alpinum*
× ***wellensiekii***	MAsh

Cyclea (*Menispermaceae*)

polypetala KWJ 12157	WCru

Cydonia ✿ (*Rosaceae*)

japonica	see *Chaenomeles speciosa*
oblonga (F)	ECrN
- 'Agvambari' (F)	SKee
- 'Aromatnaya' (F)	ERea WHar
- 'Bereczki'	see *C. oblonga* 'Bereczki'
§ - 'Bereczki' (F) **new**	NLar
- 'Champion' (F)	CAgr CBcs CHab CMam ECrN ERea GTwe LBuc MCoo NEgg NLar NOra SKee SVic WHar
- 'Early Prolific' (F)	SEND
- 'Ekmek' (F)	SKee
- 'Isfahan' (F)	ERea SKee
- 'Krymsk' (F)	CAgr
- 'Leskovac' (F)	CAgr EPom ERea NLar NOra
§ - 'Lusitanica' (F)	CAgr CHab ECrN ELan ERea GTwe LRHS NLar NOra SEWo SKee WHar
- 'Meech's Prolific' (F)	CAgr CDul CHab CLnd CTho CTri ECrN EMil EPom ERea GTwe LRHS MBlu MBri MGos MRav MWat NLar NOra NWea SDea SFam SKee SLim SPer SPoG WHar
- pear-shaped (F)	CHab ECrN NEgg SPer
- Portugal	see *C. oblonga* 'Lusitanica'
- 'Rea's Mammoth' (F)	CHab ERea NLar
- 'Seibosa' (F)	SKee
- 'Serbian Gold' (F)	CDoC CDul CTho EPom ERea GQue GTwe LRHS MBri NLar NOra WHar

- 'Shams' (F)	SKee
- 'Smyrna' (F) **new**	NLar WHar
- 'Sobu' (F)	SKee
- 'Vranja' misapplied	see *C. oblonga* 'Bereczki'
- 'Vranja' Nenadovic (F) 🏆^{H4}	Widely available

Cylindropuntia (*Cactaceae*)

imbricata **new**	SPlb XLum XSen
leptocaulis **new**	XSen
versicolor **new**	XSen
× ***viridiflora*** **new**	XSen

Cymbalaria (*Plantaginaceae*)

	aequitriloba 'Alba'	GAbr
§	***hepaticifolia***	EPot SBrt
§	***muralis***	ECho ECtt GAbr MHer WBor WGor WHer WIce XLum
	- 'Albiflora'	see *C. muralis* 'Pallidior'
	- 'Kenilworth White'	WMoo
	- 'Nana Alba'	MSCN
§	- 'Pallidior'	ECho
§	***pallida***	CPBP MMuc SBch SEND SPlb WMoo
	- 'Alba'	WMoo
§	***pilosa***	ECtt NLar
	'Snow Wave' **new**	LSou

Cymbopogon (*Poaceae*)

citratus	CArn CCCN CTsd GPoy MNHC SHDw SIde SRms SVic WJek
flexuosus	CCCN ELau MHer MHoo WJek
martini	GPoy
nardus	CArn GPoy

Cymophyllus (*Cyperaceae*)

§	***fraserianus***	CDes CFil CHEx GBin

Cynanchum (*Apocynaceae*)

acuminatifolium	GCal
ascyrifolium	WCot

Cynara (*Asteraceae*)

§	***baetica*** subsp. ***maroccana***	LDai SBrt
	cardunculus 🏆$^{H3-4}$	Widely available
	- ACL 380/78	SWat
I	- 'Cardy'	NCGa
	- var. ***ferocissima***	LRHS
I	- 'Florist Cardy'	IGor NLar
	- 'Gobbo di Nizza'	ELau ERea LEdu SVic WHer
§	- Scolymus Group	CBcs CHEx CMea EHoe EWes GPoy IBoy IGor LRHS LSRN MBri MNHC NPri SEND SPav SPer SPhx SPoG SVic WHer WWEG
	- - 'Carciofo Violetto Precoce'	LEdu WHer
	- - 'Gigante di Romagna'	WHer
	- - 'Gros Camus de Bretagne'	MAvo WCot XLum
	- - 'Gros Vert de Lâon'	CBcs ELan ELau LRHS WCot
	- - 'Imperial Star'	ELau SMad SVic
	- - 'Large Green'	NLar
	- - 'Monica Lynden-Bell'	WCot
	- - 'Purple Globe'	CArn CPrp ELau LEdu SMrm
	- - 'Romanesco'	ELau SVic
	- - 'Tavor' **new**	GCal LRHS
	- - 'Vert Globe'	CSBt CSev ELau ERea LEdu MRav MWat NPer NPri SMrm SPad SVic SWvt
	- - 'Violet de Provence'	CSBt ELau LEdu
	- - 'Violetto di Chioggia'	CSev ELau ERea LEdu WHer
	hystrix misapplied	see *C. baetica* subsp. *maroccana*
	scolymus	see *C. cardunculus* Scolymus Group
	syriaca	XSen

Cynodon (*Poaceae*)

aethiopicus	EBee EHoe LEdu SHDw WCot

Cynoglossum (*Boraginaceae*)

amabile f. ***roseum*** 'Mystery Rose'	CHVG
dioscoridis	SPhx
grande	SBrt
nervosum	EBee ELan EPfP LAst LHop LRHS MLHP MMuc MRav NChi NEgg SEND SPer WCot WWEG
officinale	CArn MHer WSFF

Cynosurus (*Poaceae*)

cristatus	CHab NMir
- viviparous	CNat

Cypella (*Iridaceae*)

	aquatilis	LLWG
§	***coelestis***	WPGP
	herbertii	CDes CPom
	peruviana	WHil
	plumbea	see *C. coelestis*

Cyperus (*Cyperaceae*)

§	***albostriatus***	CCCN EShb
	alternifolius misapplied	see *C. involucratus*
	alternifolius L.	CBAq EAmu EPfP EUJe MSKA SAPC WMAq
	- 'Compactus'	see *C. involucratus* 'Nanus'
	'Chira'	MBNS NWsh
	diffusus misapplied	see *C. albostriatus*
§	***eragrostis***	CArn CBAq EHoe GCal MWts SDix SPlb SWat WGrn WMAq WMoo
	esculentus	CArn LEdu
	fuscus	NWsh WHal WMoo
	glaber	IBoy LDai MAsh MBNS
	haspan misapplied	see *C. papyrus* 'Nanus'
	haspan L.	MSKA
§	***involucratus*** 🏆^{H1}	CHEx EBak EShb EWay MSKA MWts SEND SMad SWat WMoo
§	- 'Nanus'	EShb
	longus	CBAq CWat EHoe EHon EPPr GCal MMuc MWts NPer SEND SWat WHal WMAq XLum
	papyrus 🏆^{H1}	CDTJ CKno EAmu MSKA SAPC SBig XBlo
§	- 'Nanus' 🏆^{H1}	XBlo
	- 'Perkamentus'^{PBR}	LLWG
	prolifer	LLWG
	rotundus	MBri
	ustulatus	CKno
	vegetus	see *C. eragrostis*

Cyphanthera (*Solanaceae*)

tasmanica	ECou

Cyphomandra see *Solanum*

Cypripedium (*Orchidaceae*)

acaule	NLAp
Achim gx	XFro

Aki gx	LWst NLAp XFro
- 'Pastel'	LWst NLAp XFro
- 'Pastel' × ***kentuckiense*** new	NLAp
Alois gx new	NLAp
× ***andrewsii***	NLAp
× (× ***ventricosum***) new	
Annegret gx new	NLAp
Annette gx new	NLAp
Bärbel Schmidt gx	NLAp
× ***barbeyi***	see *C.* × *ventricosum*
Bernd gx	NLAp
Bill gx new	NLAp
Birgit gx pastel-flowered	NLAp XFro
calceolus	CCon LRHS NLAp
calceolus* × *segawae new	NLAp
californicum	LRHS NLAp
Chauncey gx new	NLAp
Cleo Pinkepank gx	NLAp
× ***columbianum***	NLAp
cordigerum	NLAp
corrugatum	see *C. tibeticum*
Dietrich gx	XFro
Emil gx	NLAp XFro
Erika gx	NLAp
× ***fasciolatum*** new	
fasciolatum	NLAp
fasciolatum* × *montanum new	NLAp
flavum	GBin LRHS NLAp
- S008-1 from Hengduan Mts, China	NLAp
- white-flowered	LRHS NLAp
formosanum	NLAp SKHP
franchetii	NLAp
Gabriela gx	NLAp
Gisela gx	LWst NLAp XFro
- 'Pastel'	LWst
- 'Yellow'	CAvo
Hank Small gx	LWst NLAp XFro
Hans Erni gx	NLAp
henryi	NLAp
henryi* × *montanum	NLAp
Inge gx	NLAp XFro
Ingrid gx	XFro
Ivory gx new	NLAp
japonicum	NLAp
Kathleen Anne Green gx new	NLAp
kentuckiense	CCCN CCon LRHS NLAp
kentuckiense* × *montanum new	NLAp
Kristi Lyn gx	NLAp XFro
Lady Dorine gx new	NLAp
Lothar Pinkepank gx	NLAp
Lucy Pinkepank gx	NLAp
macranthos	LRHS NLAp
- 'Hotei'	NLAp
- var. ***speciosum*** new	NLAp
Maria gx	LWst XFro
Memoria Gerd Kohls gx	NLAp
Memoriam Shawna Austin gx new	NLAp
Michael gx	LWst NLAp XFro
- 'Pastel'	LWst
montanum × ***reginae*** new	NLAp
montanum × ***tibeticum*** new	NLAp
Otto gx new	NLAp
parviflorum	NLAp
§ - var. ***pubescens***	LRHS NLAp
'Parville' new	LRHS NLAp
Paul gx	LWst NLAp XFro
Peter gx	XFro
Philipp gx	LWst NLAp XFro
Pixi gx	NLAp
Pluto gx	NLAp XFro
pubescens	see *C. parviflorum* var. *pubescens*
'Pueblo' new	LRHS NLAp
Rascal gx	NLAp
reginae	CCCN CCon EBee EWes GKev LRHS MBri NLAp SKHP
- f. ***album***	LRHS NLAp
Renate gx pastel-flowered	XFro
Sabine gx	LWst NLAp XFro
- pastel-flowered	LWst XFro
Schoko gx new	NLAp
Sebastian gx	XFro
Sunny gx	NLAp
§ ***tibeticum***	NLAp
- S028-1 from Hengduan Mts, China	NLAp
Tilman gx	XFro
Ulla Silkens gx	LWst MBri NLAp XFro
Ursel gx	NLAp XFro
§ × ***ventricosum***	LRHS NLAp XFro
- 'Pastel'	XFro
Victoria gx	NLAp XFro

Cyrilla (*Cyrillaceae*)

racemiflora	CMac

Cyrtanthus (*Amaryllidaceae*)

'Alaska'	ECho
§ ***brachyscyphus***	ECho EShb
breviflorus	ECho WPGP
'Edwina'	CCCN ECho
§ ***elatus*** ♀H1	CSpe ECho EWll LEdu LRHS WCot
- 'Cream Beauty'	ECho
- 'Pink Diamond'	ECho
- pink-flowered	ECho
'Elizabeth'	CCCN ECho
mackenii	ECho EShb WPGP
- var. ***cooperi***	CAby
- cream white-flowered	CCCN ECho
- 'Himalayan Pink'	CCCN EBee ECho
- orange-flowered	ECho
- pink-flowered	CAbb
- red-flowered	CAbb CCCN EBee ECho
- white-flowered	ECho
- yellow-flowered	ECho
montanus	ECho WCot
obliquus	WCot
parviflorus	see *C. brachyscyphus*
purpureus	see *C. elatus*
sanguineus	ECho WCot
smithiae	ECho
speciosus	see *C. elatus*

Cyrtomium (*Dryopteridaceae*)

§ ***caryotideum***	CBty CLAP ISha WWEG
§ ***falcatum*** ♀H3	CBty CCon CDoy CHEx CLAP CMHG EAmu EFer ELan ELon EPfP EWTr GBin GMaP IVic LRHS NOrc SEND SPoG SRms SRot WCot WMoo XBlo XLum

- 'Rochfordianum'	CBty CCCN GBin ISha LRHS MWat WFib
§ ***fortunei*** ♀H4	CHel CHid CLAP EFer ELan ELon EPfP EUJe GBin IDee LRHS MGos MRav NBid NGdn SPer SPoG SRms WCFE WFib WMoo WPnP WWEG XLum
- var. ***clivicola***	CBty CKel CWCL EBee EPfP EShb ISha LPot LRHS MGos MMoz MRav NLar SPad WCot XLum
macrophyllum	CLAP GLin

Cystopteris ✿ (*Woodsiaceae*)

bulbifera	CLAP MNFA WCot
dickieana	CLAP GBin WFib
fragilis	EFer WFib
moupinensis B&SWJ 6767	WCru

Cytisus (*Papilionaceae*)

'Amber Elf'PBR	MBri
'Andreanus'	see *C. scoparius* f. *andreanus*
'Apricot Gem'	LRHS NLar
'Baronscourt Amber' new	MAsh
× ***beanii*** ♀H4	CDul ELan EPfP LRHS MAsh SLon
'Boskoop Glory'	NLar
'Boskoop Ruby' ♀H4	CDoC CMac CSBt EBee EPfP LBMP LRHS LSRN MAsh MJak NEgg NHol NPri NSoo SHil SPer SWvt WBor WHar
'Burkwoodii' ♀H4	CBcs CDoC CDul EBee ELan EPfP LAst LRHS LSRN MSwo MWat NEgg SPoG
canariensis	see *Genista canariensis*
'Compact Crimson'	LRHS
§ ***decumbens***	MAsh
'Donard Gem'	LRHS
'Dukaat'	NHol
'Golden Cascade'	CBcs CWCL ELan LBMP LRHS MAsh NEgg SLim
'Golden Sunlight'	CSBt EPfP MJak MSwo
'Goldfinch'	CDoC CSBt ELan LRHS MBri MJak MSwo NHol NLar NSoo SPad
§ ***hirsutus***	CExl SRms WPGP
'Hollandia' ♀H4	CBcs CSBt EBee EPfP LBMP MGos MMuc MRav SGol
× ***kewensis*** ♀H4	ELan EPfP LRHS MAsh MGos MRav NHol NWea SPer SRms
- 'Niki'	EPfP LRHS MAsh MMuc SPer
'Killiney Red'	EBee ELan MBri
'Killiney Salmon'	LSRN MMuc MRav
'La Coquette'	EPfP LRHS SPlb
'Lena' ♀H4	CDoC CMac CSBt EBee EPfP LRHS LSRN MBri MGos MMuc MWat NBir NEgg NHol NLar NPri NSoo SGol SHil SLim SPoG WHar
'Luna'	EPfP MGos SHil
maderensis	see *Genista maderensis*
'Maria Burkwood'	NLar NSoo
'Minstead'	EBee ELan NEgg SPer
'Moonlight'	EWTr
'Moyclare Pink'	EBee
'Mrs Norman Henry'	NLar
'Newry Seedling'	CMac
nigricans 'Cyni'	EBee ELan ELon IArd LAst LRHS MAsh MMuc SPer SPoG SSpi
'Palette'	MMuc
'Porlock'	see *Genista* 'Porlock'
× ***praecox***	CMac ELon LAst LRHS MAsh NEgg SGol SPlb SPoG WHar
- 'Albus'	CBcs CDoC CDul CMac EBee ELan EPfP LAst LRHS LSRN MAsh MGos MJak MRav NHol NSoo SHil SPer WHar
- 'Allgold' ♀H4	CBcs CDoC CDul CMac CSBt CTri CWCL EBee ELon EPfP LRHS LSRN MAsh MBri MMuc MRav NEgg NHol NPri NWea SEND SGol SHil SLon SPer SPoG SRms SWvt
- 'Canary Bird'	see *C.* × *praecox* 'Goldspeer'
§ - 'Goldspeer'	MWat
- 'Lilac Lady'	LRHS
- 'Warminster' ♀H4	EPfP MBri MMuc MRav NWea SEND SPer SRms
proliferus	CExl
purpureus	ELan EPfP LHop MRav SPer WPat
- f. ***albus***	EPfP
§ - 'Atropurpureus' ♀H4	EPfP NWea WGob
racemosus	see *Genista* × *spachiana*
Red Favourite	see *C.* 'Roter Favorit'
'Red Wings'	MMuc NHol SPer
§ 'Roter Favorit'	EPfP MWat WGor WRHF
scoparius	CArn CDul NWea
§ - f. ***andreanus*** ♀H4	CDoC CTri EPfP SPer
- 'Cornish Cream'	CDul CSBt EBee ELan EPfP LRHS SPer
- 'Firefly'	CBcs CMac
- 'Fulgens'	CWCL EPfP
§ - subsp. ***maritimus***	SLPl
- Monarch strain	GJos
- var. ***prostratus***	see *C. scoparius* subsp. *maritimus*
× ***spachianus***	see *Genista* × *spachiana*
supinus	see *C. hirsutus*
'White Lion'	CMac
'Windlesham Ruby'	CExl ELan EPfP LRHS LSRN NLar SLim SPer
'Zeelandia' ♀H4	CMac EPfP LRHS MWat NEgg NHol SPer

D

Daboecia ✿ (*Ericaceae*)

§ ***cantabrica***	MMuc
§ - f. ***alba***	CSBt MBri NWad SWhi
- - 'David Moss' ♀H4	MMuc
- 'Alberta White'	IVic
- 'Amelie'PBR	IVic SWhi
- 'Atropurpurea'	CSBt NWad SWhi
- 'Blueless'	SWhi
- f. ***blumii*** 'White Blum'	SPer SWhi
- 'Charles Nelson' (d)	SWhi
- 'Cinderella'	IVic SWhi
- 'Cupido'	CTsd IVic
- 'Glamour'	SPer
- 'Hookstone Purple'	NWad SWhi
- 'Praegerae'	CTri SWhi
- 'Rainbow' (v)	SWhi
- subsp. ***scotica*** 'Golden Imp'	SWhi
- - 'Goscote'	MGos
- - 'Jack Drake' ♀H4	MBri SWhi
- - 'Katherine's Choice'	CBcs SWhi
- - 'Silverwells' ♀H4	CBcs MAsh MBri NHol SWhi
- - 'William Buchanan' ♀H4	GJos MAsh MBri NHol NWad SCoo SWhi

- - 'William Buchanan Gold' (v)	MBri
- 'Tinkerbell'	GJos SWhi
- 'Vanessa'PBR	IVic
- 'Waley's Red' ♀H4	NHol NWad SWhi

Dacrycarpus (*Podocarpaceae*)

§ ***dacrydioides***	CBcs CBrP ECou LEdu
- 'Dark Delight'	ECou

Dacrydium (*Podocarpaceae*)

bidwillii	see *Halocarpus bidwillii*
cupressinum	CBcs CDoC SMad SPlb WThu
franklinii	see *Lagarostrobos franklinii*
laxifolium	see *Lepidothamnus laxifolius*

Dactylicapnos (*Papaveraceae*)

§ ***lichiangensis***	WCru
macrocapnos	CCon CSpe EPfP IDee IFro WCru WTou
§ ***scandens***	CHel CRHN EPfP IRos MSCN SBrt SMad
- GWJ 9438	WCru
- 'Shirley Clemo'	CExl
torulosa	WTou
- B&SWJ 7814	WCru
§ ***ventii*** GWJ 9376	WCru

Dactylis (*Poaceae*)

glomerata	CHab WSFF
- 'Variegata' (v)	MMuc NBid SEND SHDw

Dactylorhiza (*Orchidaceae*)

sp.	NDav
alpestris	CCon CLAP SKHP
aristata	EFEx
§ ***elata*** ♀H4	GAbr IBlr
- Duguid's	NLAp WThu
§ ***foliosa*** ♀H4	CCCN CTsd GCra IBlr NLAp
§ ***fuchsii***	CCCN CCon CMil EPot GBin GKev LEdu LRHS MMoz MNrw NLAp NRya NSla SKHP WHer
- 'Bressingham Bonus'	LRHS
- pink-flowered	CCon
× ***grandis***	CLAP IBlr
- Blackthorn hybrid	CLAP
hybrid **new**	LEdu
incarnata	NBid NLAp
lapponica	NLAp
§ ***maculata***	CCon CHid EBee ELan EPfP NLAp WBor WHer
- subsp. ***ericetorum***	LRHS NLAp
- 'Madam Butterfly'	LRHS
maderensis	see *D. foliosa*
§ ***majalis***	CCon CLAP EPot LRHS MNrw NLAp WSFF
- subsp. ***occidentalis***	NLAp
- subsp. ***sphagnicola***	CLAP
mascula	see *Orchis mascula*
praetermissa	CCCN CCon CLAP LRHS NLAp SKHP
- subsp. ***praetermissa*** hybrid	SKHP
purpurella	CCon CLAP GAbr GJos LRHS NLAp NRya
sambucina	NLAp

Dahlia ✿ (*Asteraceae*)

'Abacus Red Star' **new**	WAba
'Abacus Sol'	WAba
'Abacus Trinidad Sunset' **new**	WAba
'Abba' (SD)	ECtt WAba
'Abbie' (SD)	NHal
'Abingdon Ace' (SD)	SGbt
'Abridge Ben' (MinD)	SGbt
I 'Acapulco' (S-c)	ERCP
'Admiral Rawlings' (SD)	WWlt
'Aitara Caress' (MinC)	NHal SGbt
'Akita' (Misc)	CSut EPfP SGbt WAba
'Alauna Clair-Obscur' (Fim)	CSut ERCP
'Albert Schweitzer' (MS-c)	SGbt
'Alfred Grille' (MS-c)	SDeJ SGbt SMrm SPer
'Alf's Mascot' (MD)	WAba
'Allan Snowfire' (MS-c)	LAyl NHal WAba
'Alloway Candy' (Misc)	ERCP
'Alloway Cottage' (MD)	NHal SGbt
'Almand's Climax' (GD) ♀H3	SGbt
'Alva's Doris' (SS-c) ♀H3	LAyl
'Alva's Supreme' (GD) ♀H3	LAyl NHal WAba
'Amaran Relish' (LD)	SGbt
'Amber Banker' (MC)	SGbt
'Amber Festival' (SD)	NHal
'Amber Quartz' (Misc)	SMrm
'Amberglow' (MinBa)	LAyl
'Ambition' (SS-c)	ERCP
American Pie = 'Vdtg26'PBR (Dark Angel Series) (Sin)	LRHS SDeJ
'Amgard Delicate' (LD)	SGbt
'Amira' (SBa)	NHal
'Amy Cave' (SBa)	NHal
'Andrea Clark' (MD)	NHal
'Andrea Lawson'	GBin NHal
'Andrew Mitchell' (MS-c)	NHal WAba
'Andries' Orange' (MinS-c)	ECtt LRHS LYaf
'Anelog' (MinBa)	NHal
'Angora' (SD/Fim)	SGbt
'Ann Breckenfelder' (Col) ♀H3	ECtt ERCP EUJe GBin LRHS NEgg NHal SDix SMrm WWEG
'Annette' (MC) **new**	WAba
'Annika' (Sin) **new**	SDeJ
'Anniversary Ball' (MinBa)	LAyl
'Apache' (MS-c/Fim)	ERCP SDeJ SGbt SPer WAba
'Apache Blauw'	ERCP
'Apple Blossom' (MC)	SGbt
'April Heather' (Col) ♀H3	NHal WWEG
'Arabian Night' (SD)	CAvo CBcs CHel CSpe CSut ECtt ELan ERCP GBin LAyl LRHS LSRN MNrw NHal NLar SDeJ SEND SGbt SPer WCot WWEG
'Arlequin' (LD)	SGbt
I 'Atlanta' (SD) **new**	SGbt
'Audacity' (MD)	LAyl SGbt
'Aurora's Kiss' (MinBa)	ERCP NHal SGbt
'Aurwen's Violet' (Pom)	LAyl NHal
australis	CSpe WPGP
- B&SWJ 10208	WCru
- B&SWJ 10358	WCru
- B&SWJ 10389	WCru
'Autumn Fairy' (D)	ERCP SDeJ
'Autumn Shadows' (MD) **new**	SGbt
'Avignon' (LD)	CSut SDeJ WBrk
'Avoca Amanda' (MD)	NHal WAba
'Avoca Comanche' (SS-c)	NHal
'Avoca Salmon' (MD)	NHal

	'Avon Snowflake' (MinC) **new**	NHal
	'B.J. Beauty' (MD)	LAyl NHal
	'Babette' (S-c)	LYaf SMrm
	'Babylon' (GD)	SGbt
§	'Babylon Brons' (LD)	CSut ERCP SGbt SMrm WAba
	'Babylon Bronze'	see *D.* 'Babylon Brons'
§	'Babylon Paars' (MD)	LRHS SDeJ SGbt
	'Babylon Purple'	see *D.* 'Babylon Paars'
	'Babylon Rose' (GD)	LRHS SGbt
	'Ballego's Glory' (MD)	SGbt
	'Bantling' (MinBa)	ECtt ERCP SGbt
	'Barbara's Pastelle' (MS-c)	SGbt
	'Barbarry Banker' (MinD)	LAyl
	'Barbarry Bluebird' (MinD)	NHal SGbt
	'Barbarry Melody' (SD)	NHal
	'Barbarry Monitor' (MinBa)	SGbt
	'Barberry Maverick' (MinBa)	GBin
	'Baret Joy' (LS-c)	NHal WAba
	'Bargaly Blush' (MD)	NHal
	'Barry Williams' (MD)	SGbt
	'Bayou'^{PBR} (Misc)	ERCP SGbt
I	'Bea' (SWL)	WAba
	'Bednall Beauty' (Misc/DwB) ♀^{H3}	CHll CSpe CWCL ECtt ELan EUJe EWes LHop LRHS LSRN MRav NEgg WAba WCot WWEG
	'Bell Boy' (MinBa)	SGbt
	'Berliner Orange' (MD)	ERCP
	'Berwick Wood' (MD)	NHal SGbt
	'Beth's Chaplet' (Sin)	WCot
	'Biddenham Strawberry' (SD)	SGbt
	'Bill Homberg' (GD)	SGbt
	'Bingo' (MinD)	SGbt
	'Bishop of Auckland'^{PBR} (Misc)	CWGN ECtt EPfP EPot ERCP LRHS MCot NEgg SDeJ SGbt SHil SMrm SPoG WCot
	'Bishop of Cambridge' (Sin)	EHyd
	'Bishop of Canterbury'^{PBR} (Misc)	CPrp ECtt EPfP LPio LRHS MBri NHal NSoo SDeJ SGbt SHil SPoG
	'Bishop of Dover' (Sin)	EPfP EPot LRHS SDeJ SGbt
	'Bishop of Leicester' (Misc)	ECtt EHyd EPfP EPot LPio LRHS NSoo SDeJ SGbt SHar SPet
	'Bishop of Llandaff' (Misc) ♀^{H3}	Widely available
	'Bishop of Oxford' (Misc)	CHVG COlW ECtt ELan EPfP EPot ERCP LRHS MBri SDeJ SGbt SHil SPet SPoG
	'Bishop of York' (Misc)	CAvo COlW CPrp CSpe ECtt EPfP EPot LRHS MBri NGdn NSoo SDeJ SGbt SHil SMrm SPet SPoG WBrk
	'Bitsa' (MinBa)	SMrm
	'Black Beauty' ambig.	CSpe
	'Black Fire' (SD)	ECtt
	'Black Jack' (SD) **new**	ERCP NHal
	'Black Monarch' (GD)	NHal SGbt
	'Black Narcissus' (MC)	EPfP SGbt SMrm SPer
	'Black Star' (Sin)	EPfP
	'Black Touch' (Fim)	ERCP
	'Black Wizard' (MS-c)	EPfP
	'Blackberry Ripple' (SS-c)	ERCP LBuc
	'Bloodstone' (SD)	SGbt
	'Bloom's Kenn' (MD)	SGbt
	'Blue Bell' (MD)	ERCP
	'Blue Boy' (SD)	ERCP SPer
	'Blue Record' (MS-c/DwB)	ERCP
	'Blyton Lady in Red' (MinD)	NHal

	'Blyton Softer Gleam' (MinD) ♀^{H3}	NHal SGbt WAba
	'Bonaventure' (GD)	NHal
	'Bonesta' (MinD)	LRHS
	'Boogie Woogie' (Anem)	SDeJ
	'Boom Boom Red' (MinBa) **new**	EPfP
	'Boom Boom White' (MinBa) **new**	ERCP
	'Border Princess' (SC/DwB)	SGbt
	'Brackenridge Ballerina' (SWL)	LAyl NHal SGbt WAba
	'Brandaris' (MS-c)	SGbt
	'Brandon James' (MinD)	ERCP SDeJ
	'Brandysnap' (SD)	SGbt
	Braveheart = 'Vdtg67'^{PBR} (Dark Angel Series) (Sin)	LRHS SDeJ
	'Brian's Dream' (MinD)	LAyl NHal
	'Bride's Bouquet' (Col)	ERCP WAba
	'Bridge View Aloha' (MS-c) ♀^{H3}	SGbt
	'Bright Eyes' (Sin) **new**	CAvo ERCP
	'Bronze Glints' (MS-c)	WAba
	'Brookfield Delight' **new**	WWlt
	'Bryn Terfel' (GD)	NHal SGbt WAba
	'Butterball' (MinD/DwB)	SDeJ
	'Caballero' (SWL)	LBuc
	'Café au Lait' (GD)	EPfP ERCP IPot SDeJ SEND SGbt SPer WAba
	'Camano Sitka' (MS-c)	WAba
	'Cameo' (WL)	LAyl NHal SGbt
	'Canary Fubuki' (Fim)	ERCP SDeJ SGbt
I	'Candlelight' (GD)	NHal
	'Candy Cupid' (MinBa) ♀^{H3}	WAba
	Candy Eyes	see *D.* 'Zone Ten'
	'Candy Keene' (LS-c)	NHal
	'Caribbean Fantasy' (SD)	NSoo SMrm SPet WAba
	'Carolina Moon' (SD)	LAyl NHal SGbt
	'Carol's Spanish Dancer' (MinC) **new**	NHal
	'Carreg Cyril's Girl' (Col) **new**	WAba
	'Carstone Firebox' (Col)	NHal
	'Carstone Ruby' (SD)	NHal
	'Carstone Suntan' (MinC)	NHal
	'Carstone Valiant' (MinBa)	NHal
	'Cascade Kerr' (Col) ♀^{H3}	WAba
	'Catherine Deneuve' (Misc)	CAvo CWGN SGbt
	'Cha Cha' (SS-c)	SGbt
	'Champion' (SDec) **new**	LBuc
	'Charlie Briggs' (SBa)	NHal
	'Charlie Dimmock' (SWL) ♀^{H3}	LAyl NHal SGbt WAba
	'Charlie Two' (MD)	NHal
	'Chat Noir' (MS-c)	CAvo ECtt ERCP LRHS SGbt
	'Cheerio' (SS-c)	LRHS
	'Cherwell Goldcrest' (SS-c)	NHal SGbt WWEG
	'Cherwell Siskin' (MD)	WAba
	'Cherwell Skylark' (SS-c) ♀^{H3}	NHal
	'Chessy' (Sin/Lil) ♀^{H3}	WAba
	'Cheyenne Chief' (Fim) **new**	WAba
	'Chic' (MinBa)	ECtt
	'Chic en Rouge' (Misc)	LSou
	'Chilson's Pride' (SD)	SGbt
	'Chimborazo' (Col)	LAyl SDix SGbt
	'Chocolate and Candy' (D)	SMrm
	'Christine' (SD)	SPer

I 'Christine' (SWL)	SGbt
'Christmas Carol' (Col)	ECtt GBin WAba
'Christmas Star' (Col)	SGbt
'Christopher Nickerson' (MS-c)	SGbt
'Christopher Taylor' (SWL)	NHal SGbt
'Citizen' (MS-c)	WAba
'Clair de Lune' (Col) ♀H3	CWCL ECtt ERCP LRHS MCot NHal NLar NSti SGbt SMrm WAba WCot
I 'Clarion' (Sin)	CHVG LRHS
'Classic Poème'PBR (Misc)	ERCP
'Classic Rosamunde'PBR (Misc)	CHVG NHal
'Classic Swanlake'PBR (Misc)	ERCP
'Claudette' (D)	ECtt
'Clearview Irene' (MS-c)	NHal
'Clearwater David' (SD)	GBin
coccinea (B)	CExl CFil CGHE CSpe EPfP GBin MCot SDix SGbt WAba WPGP
- NJM 05.072	WPGP
- hybrids	WHil
- var. ***palmeri***	CAvo CFil WPGP XEll
coccinea × ***merckii*** (B)	CFil
'Color Spectacle' (LS-c)	MBri
'Confection' (MinD)	NHal
'Contessa' (SWL)	SDeJ
'Coral Jupiter' (GS-c)	NHal
'Cornel' (SBa)	ERCP LAyl LYaf NHal SGbt WAba
'Cornel Brons' (MinBa)	ERCP
'Cornish Ruby'	CCon CHel EPfP
'Corona' (SS-c/DwB)	SDeJ
'Coronella' (MD)	SGbt
'Corrine' (SWL)	WAba
'Craigowan' (MS-c)	NHal
'Crazy Legs' (MinD)	SGbt
'Crazy Love' (SD)	WAba
'Cream Moonlight' (MS-c)	SGbt
'Croydon Superior' (GD)	SGbt
'Culdrose' (SD) **new**	SGbt
'Currant Cream' (SBa)	SGbt
'Czardas'	GCal
Dahlietta Becky (Dahlietta Surprise Series) (Col) **new**	LRHS
Dahlietta Jenny	see *D.* 'Jenny'
'Daleko Jupiter' (GS-c)	NHal WAba
'Dana' (SS-c)	WAba
I 'Dandy' (Col) **new**	CWCL
'Danjo Doc' (SD)	SGbt
'Dannevirke' (Sin) **new**	LRHS
'Danum Gail' (LD)	WAba
'Danum Meteor' (GS-c)	WAba
'Danum Torch' (Col)	ECtt SGbt
'Dark Desire'PBR (Sin/DwB)	CCon CSpe CWCL CWGN ECtt LHop NSti WCot
'Dark Fubuki' (Fim) **new**	ERCP
'Dark Spirit' (MinD)	CHVG ECtt SGbt WAba
'Darkarin' (Misc)	SPer
'Dave's Choice' (MinBa) **new**	NHal
'Dave's Snip' (MinD)	WAba
'David Digweed' (SD)	NHal SGbt
'David Howard' (MinD) ♀H3	CBcs CHVG CHel CPrp ECtt ELan EPfP ERCP EUJe GBin LAst LAyl LHop LPio LRHS MBri MRav MSpe NHal NSoo SDix SGbt SMrm SPer SWvt WAba WCot WWEG WWlt
'Dawn Sky' (SD)	LAyl
'Deborah's Kiwi' (SC)	NHal SGbt
'Debra Anne Craven' (GS-c)	NHal WAba
'Decorette' (DwB/SD)	SGbt
'Deepest Yellow' (MinBa)	SDeJ SGbt
'Denise Willow' (Pom)	WAba
'Diamond Jubilee' (MinD) **new**	SPer
'Diamond Wedding' (SD) **new**	SGbt
'Diamond Years' (SD) **new**	SGbt
'Diana Gregory' (Pom)	SGbt
'Diana's Memory' (Min/Dec)	CSut
'Dikara Jodie' (MD)	NHal
'Dikara Kent' (MinBa) **new**	WWEG
'Dikara Moon' (MD)	NHal
'Dikara Superb' (MinD) **new**	NHal
I 'Disneyland' (Col) **new**	SGbt
dissecta	CExl CFil EBee WAba
- F&M 191	WPGP
'Doctor Caroline Rabbitt' (SD)	SGbt
'Doctor John Grainger' (MinD)	LRHS
'Doktor Hans Ricken' (SD)	WAba
'Don Hill' (Col) ♀H3	NHal WAba WCot
'Doris Day' (SC)	LYaf NHal SGbt
'Doris Knight' (SC)	LYaf
'Double Dream Fantasy' (Misc)	LRHS
'Downham Royal' (MinBa)	ERCP
Dracula = 'Vdtg17'PBR (Dark Angel Series) (Sin)	EPfP LRHS
Dragon Ball = 'Vdtg31'PBR (Dark Angel Series) (Sin)	EPfP LRHS SDeJ
'Dream Fantasy' (Dream Series) (Misc)	CWCL
'Dreamy Inspire'	NLar
'Dreamy Moonlight' (Dreamy Series) (Sin)	NLar WHil
'Duddon Grace' (SWL)	NHal
'Duet' (MD)	ECtt GBin SGbt
'Dusky Harmony' (SWL)	SGbt
'Dutch Explosion' (SS-c)	GBin
'Early Harvest' (MD) **new**	SGbt
'Easter Sunday' (Col)	CHVG
'Eastwood Moonlight' (MS-c)	NHal SGbt
'Eastwood Star' (MS-c)	WAba
'Edge of Joy'	SPer
'Edinburgh' (SD)	ERCP SDeJ SGbt
'Edith Jones' (Col)	WAba
'Edwins Sunset' (WL) **new**	NHal
'Elga' (SS-c)	ERCP
'Elgico Leanne' (MC)	SGbt
'Ella Britton' (MinD)	LRHS
'Ellen Huston' (Misc/DwB) ♀H3	CHVG ECtt ERCP NHal SGbt WCot
'Elma E' (LD)	LAyl NHal
'Elmbrook Chieftain' (GD)	SGbt
'Embrace' (SC)	LAyl NHal WAba
'Emma's Coronet' (MinD)	WAba
'Emory Paul' (LD)	ERCP
'Engelhardt's Matador' (MD)	CHll ECtt ERCP EUJe LRHS MCot NSti SGbt SMrm WCot
'Eveline' (SD)	CHVG ERCP SGbt WAba
'Evelyn Rumbold' (GD)	SGbt
excelsa (B)	CHll WPGP
- B&SWJ 10238	WCru

- 'Penelope Sky'	WCru
'Excentrique' (Misc)	ECtt
'Exotic Dwarf' (Sin/Lil) ♀H3	CWGN ECtt NHal WHoo
'Eye Candy' (Sin)	LRHS
'Fabula' (Col)	LRHS
'Fairfield Frost' (Col)	NHal
'Fairway Spur' (GD)	NHal WAba
'Fairy Queen' (MinC)	SGbt
'Famoso' (Col)	ERCP
'Fantastico' (Col)	ERCP
'Fascination' (Misc) ♀H3	CBcs CHVG COIW ECGP ECtt ERCP LAyl MCot MSCN NEgg NGdn NLar SDeJ SGbt SMrm SPet WHoo WWEG
'Fashion Monger' (Col)	ECtt ERCP NEgg NHal SGbt
'Fata Morgana' (Anem)	SGbt
'Ferncliffe Illusion' (LD)	ERCP SGbt
'Festivo' (Col)	LRHS
'Fidalgo Magic' (MD)	WAba
'Fidalgo Supreme' (MD)	LAyl
'Fiesta' (Pom)	SDeJ
Figaro Series (Misc/DwB) ♀H3	NPri
'Figurine' (SWL) ♀H3	WAba
'Fille du Diable' (LS c)	SGbt
'Finchcocks' (SWL) ♀H3	LAyl
'Fire and Ice' ambig.	CHVG MAsh WHil
'Fire Mountain' (MinD)	CHVG NHal
'Firebird' (MS-c)	see *D.* 'Vuurvogel'
'Firebrand' ambig. (S-c)	SGbt
'Firepot' ambig.	ERCP SGbt SMrm
'Flaming Torch' (MinD) new	LBuc
'Fleur' (MinD/Fim)	SMrm SPer
'Fleurel'PBR (GD)	ERCP SDeJ
'Floorinoor' (Anem)	SGbt WAba
'Fontmell Irene' (Col) new	SGbt
'Fontmell Kaz' (Col) new	SGbt
'Formby Supreme' (MD)	SGbt
'Fortuna' (Col)	ERCP
'Frank Holmes' (Pom)	WAba
'Franz Kafka' (Pom)	ERCP LRHS SDeJ
'Freak of Nature' (Misc)	WAba
'Freelancer' (LC)	SGbt
'Freestyle' (SC)	WAba
§ 'Freya's Paso Doble' (Anem) ♀H3	LAyl
'Frigoulet' (SC)	CSut ERCP SGbt WAba
'Funny Face' (Misc)	WAba
'Fusion' (MD) ♀H3	SGbt SHar WCot
'Fuzzy Wuzzy' (MD)	ERCP WAba
'G.I. Joe' (LD) new	SGbt
'Gainesville' (MinD)	EPfP
(Gallery Series) 'Gallery Art Deco'PBR (SD) ♀H3	ERCP LRHS NHal SGbt SHil
- 'Gallery Art Fair'PBR (MinD) ♀H3	ERCP LRHS NHal SDeJ SHil
- 'Gallery Art Nouveau'PBR (MinD) ♀H3	ERCP LRHS NHal NSoo SHil WCot
- 'Gallery Bellini'PBR (SD)	SDeJ
- 'Gallery Cézanne'PBR (MinD)	LRHS SGbt SHil
- 'Gallery Cobra'PBR (MinD) ♀H3 new	ERCP
- 'Gallery La Tour'PBR (MinD)	SDeJ
- 'Gallery Leonardo'PBR (SD) ♀H3	LRHS SDeJ
- 'Gallery Matisse'PBR (SD)	LRHS
- 'Gallery Monet'PBR (SD) ♀H3	NSoo
- 'Gallery Pablo'PBR (SD) ♀H3	LRHS SGbt SHil
- 'Gallery Rembrandt'PBR (MinD) ♀H3	LRHS NSoo
- 'Gallery Renoir'PBR (SD) ♀H3	LRHS NHal SHil
- 'Gallery Rivera'PBR (MinD)	ERCP LRHS SDeJ SHil
- 'Gallery Salvador'PBR (SD)	ERCP SGbt
- 'Gallery Singer'PBR (MinD) ♀H3	LRHS
- 'Gallery Vermeer'PBR (MinD)	LRHS SGbt
- 'Gallery Vincent'PBR (MinD) ♀H3	LRHS
'Garden Festival' (SWL)	ERCP WAba
'Garden Party' (MC/DwB) ♀H3	LAyl
'Garden Princess' (SC/DwB)	SGbt
'Garden Wonder' (SD)	SDeJ
'Garnet Quartz' (Misc)	MAsh
Gateshead Festival	see *D.* 'Peach Melba' (SD)
'Gay Princess' (SWL)	LAyl
'Geerlings' Babette' (SBa) new	ERCP
'Geerlings' Cupido' (SWL)	NHal SGbt WAba
'Genova' (MinBa)	ERCP
'Geoffrey Kent' (MinD) ♀H3	NHal
'Gerrie Hoek' (SWL)	ECtt ERCP IPot LRHS LYaf SDeJ SGbt
'Gillwood Terry G' (SC) new	NHal
'Gina Lombaert' (MS-c)	SEND WAba
'Gipsy Night' (MinBa)	ERCP SDeJ
'Giraffe' (DblO)	ERCP LRHS SGbt WAba
'Giselle' ambig.	SPet
'Gitts Perfection' (GD)	SGbt
'Glenbank Honeycomb' (Pom)	WWEG
'Glorie van Heemstede' (SWL) ♀H3	ERCP LAyl LYaf NHal SDeJ SEND SGbt
'Glorie van Noordwijk' (MinS-c)	ERCP SDeJ SGbt WAba
'Go American' (GD)	NHal
'Gold Crown' (LS-c)	SDeJ
'Golden Emblem' (MD)	ECtt SDeJ
'Golden Scepter' (MinD)	ERCP SDeJ SGbt WAba
'Good Earth' (MC)	SDeJ
'Gracie S' (MinC)	NHal
'Grand Prix' (GD)	ERCP SDeJ SGbt
'Grand Willo' (Pom)	WAba
'Grayval Gem' (Pom)	NHal
'Grenadier' (SD) ♀H3	ECtt ERCP LRHS NLar SDix SGbt SMrm WAba WBrk WCot WWEG
'Grenidor Pastelle' (MS-c)	NHal WAba
'Gurtla Twilight' (Pom)	NHal WWEG
'Gwyneth' (SWL)	WAba WWEG
'Gypsy Boy' (LD)	LAyl
'Gypsy Girl' (SD)	SGbt
'Hamari Accord' (LS-c) ♀H3	LAyl
'Hamari Girl' (GD)	NHal SGbt
'Hamari Gold' (GD) ♀H3	NHal SGbt WAba
'Hamari Katrina' (LS-c)	WAba
'Hamari Rosé' (MinBa) ♀H3	NHal SGbt
'Hamari Sunshine' (LD) ♀H3	NHal SGbt
'Hamilton Lillian' (SD) ♀H3	WAba
'Hapet Charmant' (WL) new	NHal
'Hapet Ideal' (SS-c) new	NHal

	'Hapet Pearl' (MinBa) **new**	NHal
	'Hapet Pom' (Pom) **new**	NHal
	'Happy Days Red' (Sin)	EPfP
	(Happy Single Series) Happy Single Date = 'HS Date'PBR (Sin)	ERCP NSoo SDeJ WHil
	- Happy Single First Love = 'HS First Love'PBR (Sin)	ERCP SDeJ
	- Happy Single Flame = 'HS Flame'PBR (Sin) ♀H3	ERCP MBri NSoo WHil
	- Happy Single Juliet = 'HS Juliet'PBR (Sin)	ERCP LRHS SDeJ
	- Happy Single Kiss = 'HS Kiss'PBR (Sin)	LRHS
	- Happy Single Party = 'HS Party'PBR (Sin)	LRHS MBri SDeJ
	- Happy Single Princess = 'HS Princess'PBR (Sin) ♀H3	CHel ERCP
	- Happy Single Romeo = 'HS Romeo'PBR (Sin)	LRHS NPri NSoo SDeJ WHil
	- Happy Single Wink = 'HS Wink'PBR (Sin)	EPfP ERCP LRHS LSou NPri NSoo SDeJ WHil
	'Happy Tip Purple' (Sin)	LRHS
	'Happy Tip Red' (Sin) **new**	LRHS
	'Haresbrook' (Sin)	NGdn
	'Harriet G' (SWL) **new**	NHal
§	'Harvest Samantha' (Sin/Lil) ♀H3	NHal
	'Hawai'PBR	CSut
	'Hayley Jayne' (SC)	ERCP SGbt WAba
	'Helga' (MS-c)	ECtt
	'Herbert Smith' (D)	SEND
	'Hexton Copper' (SBa)	SGbt
	'Hillcrest Amour' (SD)	SGbt
	'Hillcrest Candy' (MS-c) **new**	NHal SGbt
	'Hillcrest Cheryl' (SinO) **new**	NHal
	'Hillcrest Delight' (MD)	NHal SGbt
	'Hillcrest Desire' (SC) ♀H3	LAyl WAba
	'Hillcrest Embers' (LD)	WAba
	'Hillcrest Hannah' (MinD)	NHal
	'Hillcrest Heights' (LS-c)	WAba
	'Hillcrest Jake' (MS-c)	NHal
	'Hillcrest Kismet' (MD)	LAyl NHal
	'Hillcrest Regal' (Col) ♀H3	SGbt WAba
	'Hillcrest Royal' (MC) ♀H3	LAyl NHal SDix SGbt
	'Holland Festival' (GD)	SGbt
	'Hollyhill Big Pink' (GS-c) **new**	SGbt
	'Hollyhill Cotton Candy' (MC)	WAba
	'Hollyhill Flamingo' (MS-c)	WAba
	'Honeypot' (MinBa) **new**	SGbt
	'Honka' (SinO) ♀H3	ECtt ERCP LAyl LRHS NHal NSti SDeJ WAba WCot
	'Honka Fragile' (SinO) **new**	ERCP
	'Honka Red' (Misc)	EPfP ERCP NHal
	'Honka Surprise' (SinO)	ECtt EPfP ERCP EUJe MCot NHal SDeJ SMrm WCot
	'Honka White' (Misc)	ERCP
	'Honor Francis' (Misc)	WCot WWEG
I	'Hootenanny' (Col) **new**	NHal
	'Hot Chocolate' (MinD)	SGbt
	'Hugh Mather' (MWL)	GBin
	'Hugs and Kisses' ambig.	EPfP
	'Icarus' (SS-c)	WAba
	'Ice Cube' (MD)	ERCP SDeJ
	'Ice Queen' (SWL)	SGbt
	'Imagion' (SD)	EPfP
	'Imperial Palace' (C) **new**	CHVG
	imperialis (B)	CCon CDTJ CHEx CHll LEdu LRHS SBig SDix SGbt WAba
	- B&SWJ 8997	WCru
	- 'Alba' (B)	CCon WPGP
	- pink double-flowered (B)	CExl CFil WPGP
	'Inca' (Anem)	WAba
	'Inca Dambuster' (GS-c)	NHal SGbt
	'Independence' (LD) **new**	SGbt
	'Indian Summer' (SC)	NHal
	'Ivanetti' (MinBa)	EPfP NHal SGbt WAba
	'Jack Hood' (SD)	SGbt
	'Jackie's Baby' (MinD)	WAba
	'Jamaica' (SD)	WAba
I	'Jan van Schaffelaar' (Pom)	ERCP SDeJ
	'Janal Amy' (GS-c)	NHal SGbt WAba
	'Jane Horton' (Col)	SGbt
	'Jason' (SS-c)	WAba
	'Jean Fairs' (MinWL) ♀H3	LYaf SGbt
	'Jean Marie'PBR (MD)	ERCP
	'Jean Shaw' (GD) **new**	NHal
	'Jeanne d'Arc' (GC)	EPfP
§	'Jenny'PBR (Dahlietta Select Series) (Misc) **new**	SGbt
	'Jescot Jess' (MinD)	LYaf
	'Jescot Julie' (DblO)	ERCP GBin LAyl
	'Jescot Lingold' (MinD)	SGbt
	'Jessica Willows' (SWL)	NHal
	'Jill Day' (SC)	LYaf
	'Jim Branigan' (LS-c)	NHal WAba
	'Jive' (Anem)	SDeJ WAba
	'Jocondo' (GD)	NHal SGbt WAba
	'Johann' (Pom)	NHal
	'Jomanda' (MinBa) ♀H3	GBin LYaf NHal SGbt
	'Jo's Choice' (MinD)	LYaf
	'Josie Gott' (MinBa) ♀H3 **new**	SGbt
	'Jowey Linda' (MinBa) **new**	WAba
	'Joyce Green' (GS-c)	SGbt
	'Jules Dyson' (Misc)	SDys
	'Julie One' (DblO)	SGbt
	'Jura' (SS-c)	EPfP MBri
	'Karenglen' (MinD) ♀H3	LYaf NHal SGbt
	'Karma Amanda'PBR (SD)	LRHS MBri WAba
	'Karma Bon Bini'PBR (SC)	SGbt WAba
	'Karma Choc'PBR (SD)	CSpe EPfP ERCP IPot LPio LRHS MSCN SEND SGbt SMrm SPer WAba WHoo
	'Karma Corona'PBR (SC)	MBri SGbt WAba
	'Karma Fuchsiana' (SD)	ERCP LRHS MBri NPri SGbt WAba
	'Karma Irene'PBR (SD)	ERCP
	'Karma Lagoon'PBR (SD)	ERCP LRHS SGbt WAba
	'Karma Maarten Zwaan'PBR (SWL)	WAba
	'Karma Naomi'PBR (SD)	ERCP SGbt SMrm WAba
	'Karma Pink Corona'PBR (SC)	WAba
	'Karma Prospero'PBR (SD)	ERCP MBri SMrm WAba
	'Karma Red Corona'PBR (SC)	MBri SDeJ SGbt WAba
	'Karma Sangria'PBR (SC)	LRHS MBri SDeJ SGbt WAba
	'Karma Serena'PBR	SDeJ WAba
	'Karma Yin Yang' (SD)	SGbt WAba
	'Kate Mountjoy' (Col)	SGbt
	'Kate's Pastelle' (MS-c)	WAba
I	'Katie' (SD)	NHal
	'Katie Dahl' (MinD)	NHal

	'Kayleigh Spiller' (Col)	SGbt
	'Keith's Choice' (MD)	NHal SGbt WAba
	'Keith's Pet' (Sin) ♀H3	SGbt
	'Kelsea Carla' (SS-c) ♀H3	WAba
	'Kelvin Floodlight' (GD)	CHVG LBuc SDeJ SGbt SMrm SPer
	'Kenn Emerland' (MS-c)	EPfP SDeJ SGbt
	'Kenora Challenger' (LS-c)	NHal SGbt WAba
	'Kenora Fireball' (MinBa)	WAba
	'Kenora Frills' (MD/Fim)	NHal
	'Kenora Jubilee' (LS-c)	NHal SGbt
	'Kenora Lisa' (MD)	WAba
	'Kenora Macop-B' (MC/Fim)	CSut IPot NHal WAba
	'Kenora Sunset' (MS-c) ♀H3	LAyl LYaf NHal SGbt
	'Kenora Superb' (LS-c)	NHal SGbt
	'Kenora Valentine' (LD) ♀H3	LAyl NHal SGbt
	'Ken's Flame' (SWL)	SGbt
	'Ken's Rarity' (SWL)	SGbt
	'Kidd's Climax' (GD) ♀H3	ERCP
	'Kikoski' (GC) **new**	SGbt
	'Kilburn Fiesta' (MS-c)	NHal
	'Kilburn Rose' (WL) **new**	NHal
	'Kilmorie' (SS-c)	NHal
	'Kingston' (MinD)	SGbt
	'Kiss Me' (SD)	EPfP
	'Kiwi Gloria' (SC)	GBin NHal
	'Klankstad Kerkrade' (SC)	SGbt
	'Klondike' (MS-c)	ERCP WAba
I	'Knockout' (Sin) ♀H3	EPfP ERCP GBin LRHS LSRN LSou MBri MGos NSoo SHar SPoG
I	'Kyoto' (SWL)	LRHS SGbt
	'L.A.T.E.' (MinBa)	GBin NHal SGbt WAba
	'La Recoleta' (D)	ERCP
	'La Rouvre' (SS-c)	GBin
	'Lady Linda' (SD)	LYaf NHal SGbt WAba
	'Lady Sandra' (MD) **new**	SGbt
	'L'Ancresse' (MinBa)	GBin LAyl NHal WAba
	'Larkford' (SD)	SGbt
	'Lavender Line' (SS-c)	NHal
	'Le Baron' (SD)	ERCP
	'Le Castel' (SWL) ♀H3	SDeJ
	'Lemon Cane' (Misc)	WAba
	'Lemon Elegans' (SS-c) ♀H3	LYaf NHal
	'Lemon Meringue' (SD)	ECtt SGbt
	'Lemon Zing' (MinBa)	LAyl NHal SGbt
	'Leslie's Willo' (Pom) **new**	WWEG
	'Life Force' (GD)	SGbt
	'Life Style' (Anem)	SPer
	'Lilac Bull' (MinD)	LRHS
	'Lilac Marston' (MinD) ♀H3	NHal
	'Lilac Taratahi' (SC) ♀H3	CSam LAyl
	'Lilac Time' (MD)	ERCP SDeJ SGbt
	'Lilian Alice' (Col)	CHVG NHal
	'Linda's Chester' (SC)	LYaf
	'Lismore Canary' (SWL)	WAba
	'Lismore Carol' (Pom)	NHal
	'Lismore Moonlight' (Pom)	LAyl NHal
	'Lismore Robin' (MinD)	NHal
	'Lismore Sunset' (Pom)	SGbt
	'Lismore Willie' (SWL) ♀H3	LYaf WAba
	'Little Matthew' (Pom)	SGbt
	'Little Robert' (MinD)	EPfP ERCP SGbt
	'Little Sally' (Pom)	SGbt
	'Little Snowdrop' (Pom)	SGbt
	'Little Treasure'	EPfP
I	'Little William' (MinBa)	SGbt
	'Lorona Dawn' (SinO)	ERCP WAba
	'Louis V' (LS-c/Fim)	SGbt
	'Lucky Number' (MD)	ERCP
	'Ludwig Helfert' (S-c)	SEND
	'Mabel Ann' (GD)	LAyl NHal WAba
	'Madame de Rosa' (LS-c)	LAyl NHal
	'Madame J. Snapper'	WWEG
	'Madame Simone Stappers' (WL)	ECtt LRHS
	'Madame Vera' (SD)	LYaf
	'Magenta Magenta' (MinD) **new**	SGbt
	'Magenta Magic' (Sin/DwB)	NHal
	'Magenta Star' (Sin) ♀H3	GBin SGbt
	'Maggie C' (MS-c)	NHal
	'Malham Portia' (SWL)	WAba
I	'Mambo'	SDeJ
	'Manhattan Island' (MD)	ERCP
	'Marble Ball' (MinD)	ERCP SDeJ SGbt
	'Marie Schnugg' (Misc) ♀H3	CAvo SGbt
	'Marlene Joy' (MS-c/Fim)	SGbt WAba
	'Mars' (Col)	SGbt
	'Martina' (SD)	NHal
	'Martin's Yellow' (Pom)	NHal
	'Mary Eveline' (Col)	ECtt LAyl NHal
	'Mary Evelyn' (SC)	LPio MSCN SGbt SMrm SPer
	'Mary Pitt' (MinD)	SGbt
	'Mary's Jomanda' (SBa) ♀H3	GBin NHal SGbt WWEG
	'Matador' (D)	EPfP
	'Matilda Huston' (SS-c)	LAyl NHal
	'Maureen Hardwick' (GD)	SGbt
	(Maxi Series) 'Maxi Romero' (D)	MBri
	– 'Maxi Tampico' (Misc)	LRHS MBri
	'Maxime' (SD) **new**	ERCP
	'Maya' (SD)	IPot
	'Mayan Glory' (LD) **new**	SGbt
	'Mayan Pearl' (O) ♀H3 **new**	SGbt
	'Mayan Swan' (SS-c) **new**	SGbt
	'Medal Winner' (SS-c) **new**	LBuc
	'Megan Dean' (MinBa)	NHal
	'Melody Harmony'PBR (SD) ♀H3	EPfP
	merckii (B)	CCon CExl CFil CGHE CSpe EUJe EWes LPio LRHS MCot MNrw MRav SEND SHar WAba WPGP
	– F&M 222	WPGP
	– 'Alba' (B)	CExl CFil CSpe LPio
	– compact (B)	CFil WPGP
	– 'Edith Eddleman' (B)	CFil
	'Mermaid of Zennor' (Sin)	CCon
	'Mevrouw Clement Andries' (MS-c/Fim)	ERCP
	'Mexican Wow' (LD) **new**	SGbt
	'Mexico Million' (SBa) **new**	SGbt
	'Mexico Mogul' (MD) **new**	SGbt
	'Mick's Peppermint' (MS-c)	SGbt
	'Midnight' (Pom)	SGbt
	'Mingus Gregory' (LS-c)	WAba
	'Mingus Max' **new**	ERCP
	'Mingus Randy' (LS-c)	SPer
	'Mingus Toni' (SD) **new**	ERCP
	'Mingus Wesley' (LD)	WAba
	'Minley Carol' (Pom) ♀H3	LAyl NHal WAba
	'Misterton' (MD)	SGbt
	'Mistral' (MS-c/Fim)	ECtt
	mollis **new**	CFil
	'Mom's Special' (LD)	ERCP
	'Monet Mystique' (SWL) **new**	SGbt
	'Monet Sunlight' (SWL) **new**	SGbt

'Moonfire' (Misc/DwB) ♀H3 CHel CWCL CWGN ECtt ELan EPfP ERCP EUJe LAyl LBMP LRHS MBri NEgg NHal NPri SDix SGbt SMrm SPer WCot WHoo WWEG
'Moonglow' (LS-c) ERCP
'Moor Place' (Pom) NHal SGbt WAba WWEG
'Moray Susan' (SWL) WAba
'Mr Optimist' (SD) SPer
'Mrs Eileen' (GD) ERCP SGbt
'Mrs H. Brown' (Col) SGbt
'Mrs McDonald Quill' (LD) SGbt
'München' (MinD) LBuc NGdn SDeJ SGbt
'Murdoch' ambig. ECtt LRHS WCot
'Murillo' ambig. LAyl
'Musette' (MinD) SGbt
'My Beverley' (Fim) LAyl NHal
'My Love' (SS-c) CSut ERCP SEND SGbt SMrm WAba
'My Neddy' (SD) **new** SGbt
'Myama Fubuki' (Fim) ERCP
'Myrtle's Folly' (Fim) ERCP
'Mystery Day' (MD) SMrm
Mystic Desire see *D.* 'Scarlet Fern'
'Mystic Enchantment' **new** LRHS
'Mystic Haze' **new** LRHS
Mystic Mars see *D.* 'Scarlet Fern'
'Nagano' (MinD) SDeJ SGbt
'Nargold' (MS-c/Fim) LAyl
'Narrow's Tricia' (MS-c) WAba
'Natal' (MinBa) ECtt ERCP SDeJ
'Nathalie's Wedding' (SWL) ERCP
'Nepos' (SWL) GBin SGbt
'Nescio' (Pom) ERCP SDeJ
'New Baby' (MinBa) ERCP SGbt
I 'Night Queen' (MinBa) ERCP
'Nippon' (Sin) EHyd EPfP LRHS
'Nonette' (SWL) CWGN ECtt LRHS NEgg SGbt WCot
'Noreen' (Pom) NHal
* 'Nuit d'Eté' (MS-c) CAvo CHVG CSpe EPfP ERCP LRHS SEND SGbt SPad WAba WBrk
'Nurse Nightingale' (MD) **new** SGbt
'Oakwood Goldcrest' (SS-c) NHal
'Old Gold' (SD) SGbt
'Omo' (Sin/Lil) ♀H3 WAba
'Onesta' (SD) ERCP LRHS SDeJ
'Opus' (SD) SGbt
'Orange Explosion' (Misc) **new** SGbt
'Orange Fubuki' (SD) ERCP
'Orange Nugget' (MinBa) SDeJ
I 'Orange Queen' (MC) SGbt
'Orchid Princess' (MS-c) ERCP
'Orel' (Col) SGbt WAba
'Oreti Bliss' (SC) LAyl NHal
'Oreti Classic' (MD) NHal
'Orfeo' (MC) CHVG ECtt ERCP MNrw SDeJ SGbt WAba
'Oriental Dream' (D) LRHS
'Osirium' (SD) ERCP SGbt SPer
'Ossie Latham' (Sin) **new** LRHS SGbt
'Otto's Thrill' (LD) ERCP SMrm
'Pacific Argyle' (SD) NHal
'Painted Girl' (D) ERCP
'Pam Howden' (SWL) NHal SGbt
'Park Princess' (SC/DwB) CHVG LAyl NGdn NHal NSoo SDeJ SGbt SMrm
'Paso Doble' misapplied see *D.* 'Freya's Paso Doble'
'Paso-Doble' (MD) **new** SGbt
'Pat Knight' (Col) WAba
'Pat Mark' (LS-c) LAyl
'Pat 'n' Perc' (Col) **new** SGbt
'Patricia' (Col) NHal
'Peace Pact' (SWL) WAba
'Peach Brandy' (MinWL) SMrm
'Peach Delight' (MS-c) **new** SGbt
§ 'Peach Melba' (SD) SGbt
'Peaches and Cream' PBR (MinD) NSoo
'Peachess' (MinBa) **new** WAba
'Pearl of Heemstede' (SD) ♀H3 LAyl NHal
'Pearl Sharowean' (MS-c) WAba
'Pembroke Levenna' (MinBa) NHal
'Penhill Autumn Shade' (LS-c) **new** SGbt
'Penny Lane' **new** SPer
'Peter' (MinD) ECtt SGbt
'Pfitzer's Joker' (SC) WAba
I 'Phoenix' (MD) WAba
'Pianella' (SS-c) SGbt
'Pinelands Pixie' (Fim) NHal
'Pinelands Princess' (Fim) ERCP SGbt
'Pink Giraffe' (O) ♀H3 ERCP LRHS SGbt
'Pink Jupiter' (GS-c) NHal SGbt
'Pink Pastelle' (MS-c) ♀H3 NHal SGbt WAba
'Pink Shirley Alliance' (SC) LAyl
'Pink Skin' (MD) ECtt LRHS SDeJ
pinnata B&SWJ 10240 WCru
'Piperoo' (MC) SGbt
'Piper's Pink' (SS-c/DwB) ECtt LAyl LRHS SGbt
'Playa Blanca' (SC/DwB) NSoo SGbt
'Polka' (Anem) **new** SDeJ SGbt WAba
'Pontiac' (SC) LAyl SGbt
'Pooh' see *D.* 'Pooh - Swan Island'
§ 'Pooh - Swan Island' (Col) ♀H3 CHVG ERCP EUJe GBin LAyl MAvo NHal SMrm WCot
'Preference' (SS-c) ERCP SDeJ SGbt
'Preston Park' (Sin/DwB) ♀H3 LAyl NHal
Pretty Woman = 'Vdtg43' PBR (Dark Angel Series) (Sin) LRHS WHil
Pride of Berlin see *D.* 'Stolz von Berlin'
'Primrose Pastelle' (MS-c) NHal
I 'Princess' (Col) SDeJ
'Princesse Elisabeth' (MinD) ERCP
'Princesse Gracia' (MinD) ERCP
'Princesse Laetitia' (MinD) ERCP
'Procyon' (SD) NSoo SGbt WAba
'Promise' (MS-c/Fim) ECtt ERCP
aff. ***pteropoda*** F&M 312 WPGP
'Purple Gem' (SS-c) ERCP LAst NSoo SGbt SMrm WAba
'Purple Haze' (Misc) EPfP ERCP LBuc
'Purple Pearl' (MD) **new** ERCP
'Purple Puff' (Anem) WAba
aff. ***purpusii*** B&SWJ 10321 WCru
'Radfo' (SS-c) WAba
'Raffles' (SD) LAyl
'Ragged Robin' (Misc) CSpe CWGN ECtt LRHS
'Raiser's Pride' (MC) NHal
'Raymond Guernsey' ECtt LRHS
'Red and White' (SD) SGbt
'Red Carol' (Pom) NHal
'Red Diamond' (MD) NHal
'Red Fubuki' (SD) SDeJ
'Red Majorette' (SS-c) SDeJ
'Red Pygmy' (SS-c) SDeJ

	'Reginald Keene' (LS-c)	NHal
	'Reputation' (LC)	SGbt
	'Requiem' (SD)	ECtt ERCP
	'Reverend P. Holian' (GS-c)	SGbt
	'Rhonda' (Pom)	NHal WWEG
	'Richard S' (LS-c)	NHal
	'Ridlings Annette'	WAba
	'Ridlings Salmon Wheels' (Col)	WAba
	'Ridlings Wicked' (SWL)	WAba
	'Riisa' (MinBa)	WAba
	'Rip City' (SS-c)	CSpe ERCP MCot WCot
	'Rita Shrimpton' (Misc)	WAba
	'Rocco' (MinBa)	ERCP SGbt
	'Rose Jupiter' (GS-c)	NHal
	'Rose Quartz' (Misc)	SMrm
	'Rosella' (MD)	SDeJ SGbt
	'Rosemary Webb' (SD)	SGbt
	'Rossendale Lewis' (MinD)	NHal
	'Rossendale Natasha' (MinBa)	NHal SGbt
	'Rossendale Peach' (SD)	WAba
	'Rothesay Robin' (SD)	GBin
I	'Roxy' (Sin/DwB)	CBcs CHel ECtt EHyd ELan EPfP ERCP EUJe LAst LAyl LRHS LSRN MAvo MBri MCot MNrw NEgg NGdn NHal SGbt SMrm WCot WHoo
	'Royal Mail' (MinD) **new**	SGbt
	'Royal Visit' (SD)	SGbt
	'Ruby Wedding' (MinD)	SGbt
	rudis	CExl CFil WPGP
	'Ruskin Amanda' (MS-c)	WAba
	'Ruskin Andrea' (SS-c)	NHal
	'Ruskin Bride' (MS-c)	NHal WAba
	'Ruskin Buttercup' (MinD)	SGbt
	'Ruskin Charlotte' (LS-c)	LAyl WAba
	'Ruskin Diana' (SD)	NHal
	'Ruskin Harmony' ambig.	NHal WAba
	'Ruskin Limelight' (MC)	NHal WAba
	'Ruskin Marigold' (SS-c)	LAyl NHal WAba
	'Ruskin Michelle' (MS-c)	GBin
	'Ruskin Myra' (SS-c)	LAyl NHal
	'Ruskin Respectable' (SS-c)	WAba
	'Ruskin Sensation' (MS-c)	NHal
*	'Ruskin Tangerine' (SBa)	NHal SGbt
	'Ryecroft Brenda T' (SD)	NHal
	'Ryecroft Claire' (MinD)	NHal
	'Ryecroft Crystal' (SS-c)	NHal
	'Ryecroft Delight' (MinBa)	NHal
	'Ryecroft Gem' (MinBa)	NHal
	'Ryecroft Ice' (LD)	NHal SGbt
	'Ryecroft Jan' (MinBa) ♀H3	NHal
	'Ryecroft Jim' (Anem)	NHal
	'Ryecroft Laura' (MinBa)	NHal
	'Ryecroft Rebel' (MD)	NHal
	'Ryecroft Sparkler' (MinC)	NHal SGbt
	'Ryecroft Zoe' (SS-c)	NHal
	'Saint-Saëns' (S-c)	ERCP SDeJ SEND
	'Sakura Fubuki' (Fim)	ERCP
	'Salmon Keene' (LS-c)	WAba
	'Salmon Symbol' (MS-c)	WAba
	'Sam Hopkins' (SD)	LAyl NHal
	'Sam Huston' (GD)	SGbt
	'Samantha'	see *D.* 'Harvest Samantha'
	'Sandra' (MinD)	ERCP
	'Santa Claus' (MD)	SGbt SPer
	'Sarah' (MinS-c)	ECtt LRHS
	'Sascha' (SWL) ♀H3	LAyl NHal
	'Sassy' (MinD)	SGbt
§	'Scarlet Fern' (Sin)	LRHS LSRN
	'Scarlett Claire' (Col)	WAba
	'Scaur Swinton' (MD)	LAyl NHal SGbt
	'Scura' (DwSin)	ERCP
	'Seattle' (SD)	WWEG
	'Seduction' (MinD)	EPfP ERCP
	'Seikeman's Feuerball' (MinD)	WAba
	'Seirō' (MS-c) **new**	SGbt
	'Serano' (MC)	CAvo
	'Shandy' (SS-c)	LAyl
I	'Sheila' (MinBa) **new**	WAba
	'Shooting Star' (LS-c)	CSut
	'Show 'n' Tell' (Fim)	ERCP SGbt
	'Silver City' (LD)	NHal SGbt
	'Sir Alf Ramsey' (GD)	LAyl NHal SGbt
	'Sister Lake' (MC) **new**	SGbt
	'Small World' (Pom) ♀H3	LAyl NHal WAba WWEG
	'Smokey' (MD)	SEND WAba
	'Snip' (MinS-c)	WAba
	'Snow Cap' (SS-c)	SDeJ
	'Snowbound' (LD) **new**	SGbt
	'Snowflake' (SWL)	ERCP SDeJ WAba
	'Snowstorm' (MD)	SGbt
	'So Dainty' (MinS-c) ♀H3	LAyl
I	'Sorbet' (MS-c)	LAyl NHal
	'Sorrento Fiesta' (SS-c)	WAba
	'Sorrento Flush' (SD)	WAba
	'Soulman' (Anem)	CSpe SGbt WBrk
	'Souvenir d'Été' (Pom)	SDeJ
	'Spanish Conquest' (MinD) **new**	SGbt
	'Sparkler' ([illegible])	ERCP
	'Spartacus' (LD)	LAyl NHal
	'Spectacular' (SD)	SGbt
	'Spike' (LS-c) **new**	SGbt
	'Staleen Condesa' (MS-c) ♀H3	NHal SGbt
	'Star Child' (SinO)	WAba
	'Star Surprise' (SC)	SDeJ
	Star Wars (Dark Angel Series)	EPfP LRHS SDeJ WHil
	'Star's Favourite' (MC)	CHVG ERCP
	'Steven's Vanda' (MinD)	WAba
	'Stevie D' (SD) ♀H3	SGbt
§	'Stolz von Berlin' (MinBa)	ERCP SDeJ SGbt
	'Stoneleigh Cherry' (Pom)	LAyl
	'Suffolk Punch' (MD)	LAyl
	'Sugar Diamond' (SC) **new**	ERCP
	'Summer Festival' (SD)	SGbt
I	'Summer Night' (SC)	CHVG ECGP LAyl NHal
	'Sunlight Pastelle' (MS-c)	WAba
	'Sunray Glint' (MS-c)	WAba
	'Sunset' (WL)	WAba
I	'Sunshine' (Sin)	ECtt LRHS WAba
	'Superfine' (SC)	WAba
	'Susan Carey' (LS-c) ♀H3	WAba
	'Susan Gilliott' (MS-c)	NHal
	'Suzette' (SD/DwB)	SGbt
	'Swan Lake' (SD)	SPet
	'Swanvale' (SD)	SGbt
	'Sweet Content' (SD)	SGbt
	'Sweet Irene' (SBa) **new**	SGbt
I	'Sylvia' (SBa)	ERCP SMrm WAba
	'Tahoma Tom Tom' (MS-c)	NHal
	'Tally Ho' (Misc) ♀H3	CHVG CHel ECGP ECtt EPfP LRHS MRav SDys SGbt WCot WWEG
	'Tam Tam' (MinBa)	EPfP SPer

'Tapestry' (Sin)	SGbt
'Taratahi Ruby' (SWL) ♀H3	ERCP GBin LAyl LYaf NHal WAba
Taxi Driver = 'Vdtg57' PBR (Dark Angel Series) (Sin)	EPfP LRHS
'Teesbrooke Audrey' (Col)	ECtt LAyl NHal WAba
'Teesbrooke Red Eye' (Col) ♀H3	ERCP GBin NHal SGbt WAba
tenuicaulis	CCon CDTJ CExl GGal SBig
- F&M 99	WPGP
- F&M 257	CFil WPGP
- F&M 355	CFil WAba WPGP
- F&M 369	WPGP
'Terracotta' (DwB)	NHal
'The Phantom' (Anem)	ERCP
'Thomas A. Edison' (MD)	ERCP MBri SDeJ SGbt
'Tiger Eye' (MD)	SGbt
I 'Tiptoe' (MinD)	LAyl NHal
'Tisa' (Pom) **new**	NHal
'Tohsuikyoh' (Misc)	SGbt
'Tomo' (SD)	LAyl NHal
'Top Totty' (MinD)	NHal
'Topmix' (Sin)	SDeJ
'Topmix Pink' (Sin) **new**	SDeJ
'Topmix Red' (Sin) **new**	SDeJ
'Topmix White' (DwB)	SDeJ
'Topmix Yellow' (DwB)	SDeJ
'Toto' (Anem)	ERCP
'Trelyn Kiwi' (SS-c) ♀H3	GBin NHal SGbt
'Trelyn Rebecca' (Col)	NHal
'Trelyn Rhiannon' (SC) ♀H3	NHal
'Trelyn Seren' (SinO)	NHal
'Trengrove Autumn' (MD)	SGbt
'Trengrove Millennium' (MD)	NHal SGbt
'Trevor' (Col)	SGbt
'Tricolor'	MSCN
'Troy Dyson' (Misc)	SDys
'Truly Scrumptious' (MS-c) **new**	SGbt
'Tu Tu' (MS-c)	SGbt
tubulata **new**	CFil
'Tudor 1' (Misc/DwB)	NHal
'Tui Orange' (SS-c)	WAba
'Twiggy' (SWL)	SGbt
'Twilight Time' (MD)	SDeJ
'Twinklc Stars' **new**	SDeJ
'Twyning's After Eight' (Sin) ♀H3	CExl CHVG CSpe CWGN ECtt ELan EPfP ERCP GBin LRHS MBri MCot NEgg NHal NSti SDix SDys SGbt SMrm SPer WBor WCot WHoo
'Twyning's Aniseed' (Sin)	EPfP
'Twyning's Revel' (Sin)	CSam
'Twyning's Smartie' (Sin) ♀H3	GBin
'Tyrell'	EPfP
'Uchuu' (GD)	SGbt
'Vancouver' (Misc)	ERCP SDeJ SMrm WAba
'Veritable' (MS-c)	CSut SGbt
'Vicky Crutchfield' (SWL)	WCot
'Vulcan' (LS-c)	SGbt
'Vulkan' (MS-c)	ERCP
§ 'Vuurvogel' (MS-c)	ERCP LBuc SDeJ
'Waltzing Mathilda' (Misc)	ERCP
'Wanda's Aurora' (GD)	NHal
'Wanda's Capella' (GD)	WAba
'Wandy' (Pom) ♀H3	WAba
'War of the Roses' (SD)	WHer
'Westerton Folly' (SBa) **new**	NHal
'Weston Buccaneer' (MinC) **new**	NHal
'Weston Dove' (MinS-c)	WAba
'Weston Miss' (MinS-c)	NHal
'Weston Nugget' (MinC)	WAba
'Weston Pirate' (MinC) ♀H3	NHal WAba WWEG
'Weston Spanish Dancer' (MinC) ♀H3	LAyl LYaf NHal SGbt
'Weston Stardust' (MinC) **new**	NHal
'Wheels' (Col)	WAba
'White Alva's' (GD) ♀H3	LAyl NHal SGbt
'White Ballerina' (SWL)	LAyl NHal SGbt
'White Ballet' (SD) ♀H3	LAyl SGbt
'White Charlie Two' (MD)	NHal
'White Katrina' (LS-c)	WAba
'White Knight' (MinD)	NHal
'White Linda' (SD)	NHal
'White Moonlight' (MS-c)	LAyl NHal
'White Nettie' (MinBa)	SGbt
'White Onesta' (SD) **new**	SDeJ
'White Perfection' (LD)	ECtt EPfP ERCP SDeJ
'White Star' (MS-c)	ERCP SDeJ WAba
'Who Dun It' (MD)	ERCP
'Willo's Borealis' (Pom)	NHal
'Willo's Surprise' (Pom)	NHal SGbt WWEG
'Willo's Violet' (Pom)	NHal SGbt WAba WWEG
'Wine & Roses' (SWL)	SGbt
'Winholme Diane' (SD)	NHal WAba
'Winston Churchill' (MinD)	LYaf
'Winter Springs' (S-Sc)	ERCP
'Wishes n Dreams' (Sin)	SPer
'Witteman's Best' (LS-c)	ERCP MCot SGbt
'Witteman's Superba' (SS-c) ♀H3	NHal SDix
'Wizard of Oz' (MinBa)	ERCP
'Woodbridge' (Sin) ♀H3	SGbt
'Woodside Finale' (MinD)	NHal
'Wootton Impact' (MS-c) ♀H3	NHal
'Worton Blue Streak' (SS-c)	ERCP SGbt
'Yellow Galator' (MC)	SGbt
'Yellow Hammer' (Sin/DwB) ♀H3	LAyl NHal SGbt
'Yellow Passions' (MD)	ERCP
'Yellow Star' (MS-c)	ERCP SDeJ
'Yelno Enchantment' (SWL)	LAyl
'Yin Yang'	SGbt
'York and Lancaster' (MD)	SGbt
I 'Yvonne' (MWL)	WAba
§ 'Zone Ten' PBR (Sin/DwB)	CWGN EPfP GBin LRHS LSRN LSou MGos SHar SPoG WBor
'Zorro' (GD) ♀H3	ERCP NHal SGbt WAba

Daiswa see *Paris*

Dalea (*Papilionaceae*)

candida	EBee
purpurea	EBee SPhx
- 'Stephanie'	EWll MHer

damson see *Prunus insititia*

Danae (*Asparagaceae*)

§ ***racemosa***	CBcs CFil CTri EBee ELan EPfP MGos MRav SAPC SEND SRms SSpi SWvt WCot WCru WPGP WPat

Daphne ✿ (*Thymelaeaceae*)

	DJHC 98164 from China	WCru
	acutiloba	CJun WSpi
	- 'Fragrant Cloud'	CExl CJun EWes SChF
	albowiana	CJun EWes LLHF LRHS WSpi
	alpina	CJun GKev NEgg NHol WAbe
	altaica	CJun
	arbuscula ♀^{H4}	CJun EPot LLHF MWat SIgm WThu
	- subsp. ***arbuscula*** f. ***albiflora***	CJun
	- 'Diva'	CJun
	- 'Muran Pride'	CJun
	- f. ***radicans***	CJun
	arbuscula × ***cneorum*** var. ***verlotii***	CJun
	arbuscula × 'Leila Haines'	see *D.* × *schlyteri*
	arisanensis B&SWJ 6983	WCru
	bholua	CAbP CHll CJun EPfP GCal GGal LRHS SSpi
I	- 'Alba'	CJun CMac EPfP LRHS SSta WPGP WSpi
	- 'Darjeeling'	CExl CHll CJun EPfP LRHS SKHP SLim WPGP WSpi
	- var. ***glacialis*** 'Gurkha'	CExl CGHE CJun EPfP SChF SKHP WPGP
	- 'Jacqueline Postill' ♀^{H3}	Widely available
	- 'Limpsfield'	CJun LRHS SChF SCoo SSta
	- 'Peter Smithers'	CExl CJun LRHS LSRN SPer SSta WPGP
	- 'Wisley Purple'	CJun
	blagayana	CJun ECho NBir SIgm SRms WThu
	- 'Brenda Anderson'	CJun EPot WAbe
	'Bramdean'	see *D.* × *napolitana* 'Bramdean'
	× ***burkwoodii*** ♀^{H4}	CMea EBee ECrN LSRN
	- 'Albert Burkwood'	CJun
	- 'Astrid' (v)	CBcs CJun LRHS MGos MJak NLar SLon
§	- 'Carol Mackie' (v)	CJun LRHS SIgm
	- 'G.K.Argles' (v) ♀^{H4}	CJun
I	- 'Gold Sport'	CJun SChF
	- 'Gold Strike' (v)	CJun
	- 'Golden Treasure'	CJun MAsh SChF
	- 'Lavenirei'	CJun
	- 'Somerset'	CBcs CJun EBee ELan MGos MRav MSwo NLar NWea WThu
§	- 'Somerset Gold Edge' (v)	CJun
§	- 'Somerset Variegated' (v)	SChF WThu
	- 'Variegata' broad cream edge	see *D.* × *burkwoodii* 'Somerset Variegated'
	- - broad gold edge	see *D.* × *burkwoodii* 'Somerset Gold Edge'
	- - narrow gold edge	see *D.* × *burkwoodii* 'Carol Mackie'
	calcicola 'Gang-ho-ba'	CJun WAbe
	- 'Sichuan Gold'	CJun
	caucasica	CJun
	circassica	CJun SChF
	cneorum	CBcs CJun IVic MGos MWat
	- f. ***alba***	CJun
	- 'Benaco'	CJun
	- 'Blackthorn Triumph'	CJun WAbe
	- 'Eximia' ♀^{H4}	CJun EPot WAbe WThu
	- 'Klaus Patzner'	CJun
	- 'Lac des Gloriettes'	CJun
	- 'Puszta'	CJun WAbe
	- var. ***pygmaea***	CJun EPot WAbe
	- - 'Alba'	CJun
	- 'Rubra'	LRHS
	- 'Ruby Glow'	CJun
	- 'Variegata' (v)	CJun EPot GKev
	- 'Velký Kosir'	CJun MWat SChF WAbe
	- var. ***verlotii***	EPot
	collina	see *D. sericea* Collina Group
	× ***eschmannii*** 'Jacob Eschmann'	CJun
	'Forarch'	CJun
	genkwa	CJun SKHP WThu
	giraldii	CJun GKev
	gnidioides	CJun
	'Guardsman'	CJun MAsh
	× ***hendersonii***	CJun
	- 'Appleblossom'	CJun SChF WAbe
	- 'Aymon Correvon'	CJun WThu
	- 'Blackthorn Rose'	CJun
	- 'Ernst Hauser'	CJun WAbe WIce WThu
	- 'Fritz Kummert'	CJun WAbe WThu
	- 'Jeanette Brickell'	CJun WAbe WThu
	- 'Kath Dryden'	CJun SChF SIgm WAbe
	- 'Marion White'	CJun WAbe
	- 'Rosebud'	CJun WThu
	- 'Solferino'	CJun
	'Hinton'	CJun
	× ***houtteana***	CJun
	× ***hybrida***	CJun
	japonica 'Striata'	see *D. odora* 'Aureomarginata'
	jasminea	CJun ECho WAbe
	jezoensis	CJun LRHS SSta
	× ***jintyae*** 'Pink Cascade'	CJun
	juliae	CJun WAbe
	kamtschatica	CJun
	'Kilmeston Beauty'	CJun
	kosaninii	CJun
	× ***kalymeri*** 'Spring Sonnet'	CJun SChF SIgm
	laureola	CBcs CJun EPfP GPoy MMHG NBid NBir NLar NPer SPer WSpi
	- 'Kingsley Green'	CJun
	- 'Margaret Mathew'	CJun EPfP SChF
	- subsp. ***philippi***	CHel CJun CMac ELan EPfP LRHS MAsh MBlu MGos NLar SKHP WSpi
	'Leila Haines'	CJun
	× ***mantensiana*** 'Audrey Vockins'	CJun
	- 'Manten'	CJun
	× ***mauerbachii*** 'Perfume of Spring'	CJun ECho SChF
	'Meon'	see *D.* × *napolitana* 'Meon'
	mezereum	CTri ECho GKev GMaP GPoy IFoB ITim LRHS MAsh MBri MGos NChi NWea SChF SGol SLim SWvt WCFE WHar WPGP
	- f. ***alba***	CBcs CJun ECho GKev MAsh MGos NChi SChF SRms SWvt WAbe WCFE
	- - 'Bowles's Variety'	CJun EPot
	- 'Rosea'	ECho SRms
	- var. ***rubra***	CBcs CJun CMac CWSG CWib ELan GKin LRHS MGos MJak MRav MSwo SPer WAbe
	× ***napolitana*** ♀^{H4}	CJun EPfP SChF
§	- 'Bramdean'	CJun WThu
§	- 'Meon'	CJun MAsh WAbe WPat WThu
	odora	CJun CWSG EBee EPfP LRHS LSRN MSwo SLim
§	- f. ***alba***	CCCN CJun CMac
	- - 'Sakiwaka'	CCCN CExl CJun SKHP WPat
§	- 'Aureomarginata' (v) ♀$^{H3-4}$	Widely available
	- 'Clotted Cream' (v)	CJun

- 'Geisha Girl' (v)	CJun MAsh MGos
- var. ***leucantha***	see *D. odora* f. *alba*
- 'Limelight' (v)	CJun
- 'Mae-jima' (v)	CExl CHel CJun EBee ELan EPfP LLHF LRHS MAsh NLar SCoo SLon SPoG
- 'Marginata'	see *D. odora* 'Aureomarginata'
- Marianni = 'Rogbret' (v) **new**	CWSG ELon EUJe NLar SGol SWvt WCot
- Rebecca = 'Hewreb' (v)	LBuc LRHS MAsh MBri SPoG
- var. ***rubra***	CCCN CCon CJun LLHF
- 'Sunshine' **new**	SSta
- 'Walberton' (v)	EPfP LRHS MBri
oleoides	CJun GKev
- var. ***buxifolia*** **new**	GKev
papyracea	CExl CFil
petraea	CJun WAbe
- 'Cima Tombea'	CJun
- 'Corna Blacca'	CJun
- 'Garnet'	CJun WAbe
- 'Grandiflora'	CJun WAbe
- 'Lydora'	CJun
- 'Persebee'	CJun
- 'Punchinello'	CJun
- 'Tuflungo'	CJun
'Pink Star'	CJun
pontica ♀^{H4}	CBcs CJun EBee EPfP LRHS MBri SDix SKHP SSpi WPGP WSpi
retusa	see *D. tangutica* Retusa Group
'Richard's Choice'	CJun
× ***rollsdorfii*** 'Arnold Cihlarz'	CJun WAbe
- 'Wilhelm Schacht'	CAbP CJun IVic MAsh SChF WAbe WThu
'Rossetii'	CJun
'Rosy Wave'	CJun SChF
§ × ***schlyteri***	CJun
- 'Lovisa Maria'	CJun EPot SIgm WAbe
sericea	CJun
§ - Collina Group	CAbP CJun EPfP WIce
'Spring Beauty'	CJun SPer
'Spring Herald'	CJun
'Stasek' (v)	CJun
× ***suendermannii*** 'Franz Suendermann'	MAsh WAbe
× ***susannae*** 'Anton Fahndrich'	CJun GKev NLar WThu
- 'Cheriton'	CJun EPfP EPot LRHS NHol WAbe WThu
- 'Tage Lundell'	CJun IVic
- 'Tichborne'	CAbP CJun EPot SChF WAbe WThu
tangutica ♀^{H4}	CBcs CExl CJun CMac CTri ECho ELan EPfP EWTr GAbr GKev LRHS LSRN MAsh MGos NBir NHol NPCo SBrt SCoo SEND SKHP SPoG SRkn SRms SSpi WAbe WKif WSpi
- 'Aureomarginata' (v) **new**	WPat
§ - Retusa Group ♀^{H4}	CExl CJun CWCL ECho ELan ELon EPot GAbr GBin GKev LEdu LHop LRHS NBir NLar NRya NSla SIgm SPer SRms WSpi
× ***transatlantica*** 'Beulah Cross' (v)	CAbP CJun ELan LLHF LRHS MAsh SChF SLon
- Eternal Fragrance = 'Blafra'^{PBR}	CAbP CCCN CEnd CExl CWGN EBee ELan ELon EPfP EPot EUJe LLHF LRHS LSqu MAsh MBri MGos NLar SCoo SKHP SLim SLon SMad SPer SPoG SSpi SSta WPGP
- 'Jim's Pride'	SChF WPat
- Spring Pink Eternal Fragrance = 'Blapink' **new**	EPfP MAsh SPer
'Valerie Hillier'	CJun LRHS
velenovskyi	CJun
× ***whiteorum*** 'Beauworth'	CJun WAbe
- 'Kilmeston'	CJun WAbe
- 'Warnford'	CJun
wolongensis 'Kevock Star'	CExl GKev

Daphniphyllum (*Daphniphyllaceae*)

KWJ 12244 from northern Vietnam	WCru
aff. ***angustifolium*** B&SWJ 8225	WCru
- B&SWJ 11804	WCru
- WWJ 12020	WCru
glaucescens	WCru
subsp. ***oldhamii*** var. ***kengii*** B&SWJ 6872	
- - - B&SWJ 7119	WCru
- - var. ***oldhamii*** B&SWJ 7056	WCru
- - - CWJ 12351	WCru
humile	see *D. macropodum* var. *humile*
aff. ***longeracemosum*** B&SWJ 11788	WCru
macropodum	CBcs CCCN CFil CGHE CHEx CWib EBee EPfP GBin LRHS NLar SAPC SDix SKHP SSpi SVen WCru WPGP
- B&SWJ 581	WCru
- B&SWJ 2898	WCru
- B&SWJ 6809 from Taiwan	WCru
- B&SWJ 8507 from Ulleungdo, South Korea	WCru
- B&SWJ 8763 from Cheju-do, Korea	WCru
- B&SWJ 11489 from Yakushima, Japan	WCru
- dwarf	WCru
§ - var. ***humile*** B&SWJ 11232	WCru
majus B&SWJ 11744	WCru
paxianum B&SWJ 9755	WCru
pentandrum B&SWJ 6888	WCru
- B&SWJ 7056	WCru
- CWJ 12393	WCru
- RWJ 9836	WCru
teysmannii B&SWJ 11110 from Japan	WCru
- B&SWJ 11112	WCru
- B&SWJ 11358 from Japan	WCru
aff. ***teysmannii*** CWJ 12350 from Taiwan	WCru

Darlingtonia (*Sarraceniaceae*)

californica ♀^{H1}	EFEx WSSs

Darmera (*Saxifragaceae*)

peltata ♀^{H4}	Widely available
- 'Nana'	CHEx EPfP GBuc LBMP LRHS LSou MWts NBid NHol NLar NMyG SWat WMoo

Darwinia (*Myrtaceae*)

taxifolia	MOWG

Dasylirion (*Asparagaceae*)

§ ***acrotrichum***	CDTJ CExl EGri EShb SAPC
berlandieri	CExl

- NJM 05.048	WPGP
cedrosanum	CDTJ CJun SPlb
durangense	EGri
glaucophyllum	CJun EAmu MREP
gracile Planchon	see *D. acrotrichum*
leiophyllum	WPGP
longissimum	CBrP EAmu EShb SChr
lucidum	EGri
miquihuanense	EAmu SMad
- F&M 301A	WPGP
- F&M 321	WPGP
- NJM 05.062	WPGP
quadrangulatum	EAmu EGri SPlb
- NJM 05.064	WPGP
serratifolium	EAmu EUJe
texanum	EGri IDee LEdu
wheeleri ♈H1	CBrP EAmu EGri SPlb

date see *Phoenix dactylifera*

Datisca (*Datiscaceae*)

cannabina	CArn CDTJ EBee EPPr GBin GCal IMou LPio LPla NChi NLar SBrt SDix SMad SMrm SPhx WMoo WPGP

Datura (*Solanaceae*)

arborea	see *Brugmansia arborea*
cornigera	see *Brugmansia arborea*
'Double Blackcurrant Swirl' **new**	CSpe
ferox	CArn
§ ***inoxia*** ♈H3	CSpe
meteloides	see *D. inoxia*
rosea	see *Brugmansia* × *insignis* pink-flowered
rosei	see *Brugmansia sanguinea*
sanguinea	see *Brugmansia sanguinea*
stramonium	CArn
suaveolens	see *Brugmansia suaveolens*
versicolor	see *Brugmansia versicolor* Lagerh.
- 'Grand Marnier'	see *Brugmansia* × *candida* 'Grand Marnier'

Daubenya (*Asparagaceae*)

alba	ECho
aurea	ECho
- var. ***coccinea***	ECho
marginata	ECho
namaquensis	ECho

Daucus (*Apiaceae*)

carota	CArn CHab LEdu NMir SVic WHer WSFF

Davallia (*Davalliaceae*)

canariensis ♈H1	CMen SEND
mariesii ♈H3	CMen ISha WCot
- B&SWJ 4448	WCru
- var. ***stenolepis***	CMen
tasmanii	CMen
trichomanoides	CBty CMen
- f. ***barbata***	CMen

Davidia (*Nyssaceae*)

involucrata ♈H4	Widely available
- 'Sonoma'	MBlu
- var. ***vilmoriniana*** ♈H4	CBcs CDoC CWCL ELan EPfP LRHS MAsh MBlu MGos SLim SPer

Daviesia (*Papilionaceae*)

cordata	SPlb
* ***ovalifolia***	SPlb
pectinata	SPlb

Debregeasia (*Urticaceae*)

longifolia	SVen
- WWJ 11686	WCru

Decaisnea (*Lardizabalaceae*)

fargesii	Widely available
- B&SWJ 8070	WCru

Decodon (*Lythraceae*)

verticillatus	LLWG

Decumaria (*Hydrangeaceae*)

barbara	CBcs CMac EBee MMuc NLar SLim WCru WSHC
- 'Vicki'	NBro NLar
sinensis	EBee EPfP ESwi LRHS MMuc SHil SKHP SLon SPoG SSpi WCru WSHC

Degenia (*Brassicaceae*)

velebitica	GKev

Deinanthe (*Hydrangeaceae*)

bifida	CDes CExl CMil EBee EPfP EWes LRHS WCru WPGP
- B&SWJ 5436	EWld SBig WCru
- B&SWJ 5551	WCru
- B&SWJ 5655	LEdu NLar WCru
- 'Pink Kii'	WCru
- 'Pink-Shi'	EWld WCru WSHC
bifida × ***caerulea***	CLAP WCru
'Blue Blush'	WCru
caerulea	CLAP CMil GCra IGor IMou LEdu LHop LRHS NLar NPnk SKHP WCru WPGP WSHC
- 'Blue Wonder'	CExl CLAP LLHF

Delonix (*Caesalpiniaceae*)

decaryi	SPlb
regia	SPlb

Delosperma (*Aizoaceae*)

LEG 037	ITim
from Graaf Reinet, South Africa	NSla
from Sani Pass, South Africa	EPot NSla WAbe
§ ***aberdeenense*** ♈H1	CHEx SChr XLum
alpinum	EPot EWes
ashtonii	CCCN EWes XLum
basuticum	NSla
'Basutoland'	see *D. nubigenum*
'Beaufort West' **new**	EPot WIce XLum
congestum	CCCN CMea CPBP ECho EDAr EPot EWll NRya WAbe WIce XLum
- 'Album' **new**	WIce
- 'Gold Nugget'	ECho EHyd LRHS
* - white-flowered	ECho EDAr EPot WAbe
cooperi	CCCN CTri ECho ECtt EDAr EHyd EPfP EPot GBin ITim LAst LRHS LSou MSCN SChr SIgm SPlb SVen WIce WPnn XLum XSen
dyeri Red Mountain = 'Psdold' **new**	XLum
ecklonis	GKev

	floribundum 'Starburst'	EDAr EWll MHol NRya
§	'John Proffitt'	CCCN GKev SPlb XLum
	lavisiae	NSla SPlb
	'Lesotho Pink' **new**	EWes
	lineare	XLum
	Mesa Verde = 'Kelaidis'	ECtt
§	***nubigenum***	CTri ECho ECtt EPot GKev ITim SEND SPlb SPoG
	'Ruby Coral'	EPot
	sphalmanthoides	CPBP EPot WAbe
	sutherlandii	ECho EDAr EPfP GBin NPri XLum
	- 'Peach Star'	CCCN EDAr EWll LRHS WIce
	Table Mountain	see *D.* 'John Proffitt'

Delphinium ✿ (*Ranunculaceae*)

	sp.	SVic
	'After Midnight'	CNMi
	'Ailsa'	CNMi
	'Alice Artindale' (d)	CDes EWes EWld IFoB WCot
	'Ann Woodfield'	CNMi
	'Apollo'	WSpi
	'Ariel' ambig.	LRHS
	Astolat Group	CBcs CSBt CTri CWib ELan EPfP GMaP IBoy LBMP LRHS MBri MGos MWat NBir NHol NLar NSoo SPer SPoG SWvt WCAu WHar XLum
	'Atholl' ♀H4	CNMi ELar
	(Aurora Series) 'Aurora Dark Blue'	LRHS
	- 'Aurora Deep Purple'	LRHS
	- 'Aurora Lavender'	LRHS
	'Bambi'	CNMi
	'Basil Clitheroe'	LRHS
	Belladonna Group	CWCL ELan EPfP MAvo WHar
	- 'Atlantis' ♀H4	ELar LRHS NLar SMrm WSpi
	- 'Balaton'	ELar
	- 'Blue Bees'	LRHS
	- 'Casa Blanca'	ELar EPfP GMaP LRHS NLar WSpi XLum
	- 'Cliveden Beauty'	CWCL EPfP GMaP LHop LRHS MAvo NLar XLum
§	- 'Janny Arrow'	LRHS
	- 'Moerheimii'	LRHS WSpi
	- 'Peace'	LRHS
	- 'Piccolo'	LRHS NLar
	- 'Pink Sensation'	see *D.* × *ruysii* 'Pink Sensation'
	- 'Völkerfrieden' ♀H4	ELar IBoy LRHS MNrw MRav WSpi
	× ***bellamosum***	EPfP GMaP LRHS MAvo MNrw NLar XLum
	'Berghimmel'	LRHS
	'Beryl Burton'	CNMi
	'Black Arrow'	WCot
	Black Knight Group	Widely available
	'Black Pearl'	ECtt IKil
	'Black Velvet'	CBcs
	'Black-eyed Angels' (New Millennium Series) **new**	SGbt STes
	'Blue Arrow'	see *D.* 'Blue Max Arrow', *D.* (Belladonna Group) 'Janny Arrow', *D.* 'Kings Blue Arrow'
	Blue Bird Group	CBcs CSBt CTri ELan EPfP GMaP LBMP LRHS MGos MWat NLar NMir NSoo SGbt SPer SPoG WCAu WHoo XLum
	'Blue Butterfly'	see *D. grandiflorum* 'Blue Butterfly'
	'Blue Dawn' ♀H4	CNMi ELar
	Blue Fountains Group	CSBt EPfP LSRN SPer SPoG SRms
	'Blue Jay'	CBcs CTri EPfP LSRN MWat NBir NHol SPer WSpi XLum
	'Blue Lace'	LRHS WSpi
§	'Blue Max Arrow'	LRHS
	'Blue Mirror'	SRms
	'Blue Nile' ♀H4	CNMi
	'Blue Oasis'	CNMi
	Blue River	CBcs
	'Blue Skies'	NLar
	Blue Springs Group	NGdn
	'Blue Tit'	CNMi
	'Bob Geldof'	CNMi
	'Boudicca'	CNMi
	'Bruce' ♀H4	CNMi ELar
	brunonianum	WThu
	'Butterball'	CNMi ELar WSpi
	Cameliard Group	CBcs CSBt ELan EPfP LBMP LHop LRHS MWat NLar SPer SPoG
	'Can-Can' ♀H4	CNMi ELar
	cardinale	SPlb
	ceratophorum var. ***ceratophorum*** BWJ 7799	WCru
	'Chelsea Star'	CNMi LRHS
	'Cher'	CNMi
	'Cherry Blossom'	EPfP NLar WRHF
	'Cherub' ♀H4	ELar
	'Christel'	LRHS LSRN NLar
	'Christine Harbutt'	ELar
	'Claire' ♀H4	CNMi ELar
	'Clifford Sky' ♀H4	EHyd ELar LRHS
	'Conspicuous' ♀H4	CNMi ELar
	'Constance Rivett' ♀H4	ELar
	'Coral Sunset' PBR (d)	MBri
	'Crown Jewel'	ELar
	'Cupid'	ELar
	'Dark Blue White Bee' (Excalibur Series) **new**	NHol
	'Darling Sue'	CNMi
	'Darwin's Blue Indulgence' PBR	MBri
	'Darwin's Pink Indulgence' PBR	MBri
	delavayi	LRHS
	'Desante Blue'	LRHS
	'Diamant' PBR	EWll IKil LRHS
	'Dreaming Spires'	SRms
	drepanocentrum HWJK 2263	WCru
	'Dunsden Green'	CNMi
	Dusky Maidens Group	CMea ELan IFoB LRHS SGbt SPoG STes WSpi
	dwarf, dark blue-flowered	LRHS
	elatum	GCal
	- SDR 6391	GKev
	- 'Dasante Blue'	NPri
	- (New Millennium Series) 'Blushing Brides' **new**	SPoG
	- - 'Double Innocence' (d)	IPot LRHS STes
	- - 'Morning Lights'	SPoG
	- - 'Sweethearts' ♀H4 **new**	CMea
	- 'Sweet Sensation' **new**	IBoy LRHS NLar
	'Elisabeth Sahin' ♀H4	ELar
	'Elizabeth Cook' ♀H4	CNMi ELar
	'Elmfreude'	IBoy LRHS WSpi
	'Emily Hawkins' ♀H4	CNMi
	'Etonian'	LRHS
	exaltatum	LBMP LPla
	'Fanfare'	CNMi ELar
	'Faust' ♀H4	CNMi ELar EWll LRHS
	'Fenella' ♀H4	CNMi ELar LRHS

	'Finsteraarhorn'	GBin IKil LRHS MAvo MNrw WSpi
	'Florestan'	CNMi
	'Foxhill Nina' 🏆^{H4}	CNMi ELar
	'Franjo Sahin'	CNMi ELar
	Galahad Group	CBcs CSBt CTri CWCL CWib ECtt ELan EPfP GMaP LHop LRHS MBri MJak MWat NBir NGdn NHol NLar NSoo SMrm SPer SPlb SPoG WCAu WHar WHoo
	'Galahad' (Pacific Hybrids Series)	CHel XLum
	'Galileo' 🏆^{H4}	CNMi
	'Garden Party'	WSpi
	'Gemini'	CNMi
	'Gemma'	CNMi
	'Gillian Dallas' 🏆^{H4}	ELar
	glaciale HWJK 2299	WCru
	'Gossamer'	CNMi ECtt IKil
§	***grandiflorum*** 'Blauer Zwerg'	SPoG
§	- 'Blue Butterfly'	CSpe EPfP LBMP LHop LRHS SPlb SPoG WSHC
	- Blue Dwarf	see *D. grandiflorum* 'Blauer Zwerg'
	- 'Delfix'	LRHS
	- (Summer Series) 'Summer Blues'	LRHS MBri SHil SRot
	- - 'Summer Nights'	EPfP LRHS MBri SHil WHar
	- - 'Summer Stars'	LRHS MBri SHil
*	- 'Tom Pouce'	EHyd EPfP
	'Green Twist' (New Millennium Series)	EWll LRHS SPoG WSpi
	(Guardian Series) 'Guardian Blue'	LRHS NPri
	- 'Guardian Lavender'	LRHS NPri
	- 'Guardian White'	LRHS NPri
	Guinevere Group	CBcs CSBt CWib ECtt EPfP LRHS MBri NBir NLar SPer SPoG XLum
	- 'Lady Guinevere'	IBoy
	'Guy Langdon'	CNMi
	halteratum	CSpe
	hansenii	LLHF
	'Highlander Blueberry Pie'	IBoy LRHS WHlf
	'Highlander Crystal Delight'	LRHS WHlf
	'Highlander Morning Sunrise'	WHlf
	'Honey Pink'	CNMi
I	'Independence'	IKil LRHS
	'Innocence'	CMea
	'Jenny Agutter'	CNMi
	'Jill Curley' 🏆^{H4}	ELar LRHS
	'Kathleen Cooke'	CNMi
	'Kestrel' 🏆^{H4}	CNMi ELar
	King Arthur Group	CBcs CSBt CWCL ELan EPfP LBMP LHop LPot LRHS LSRN MGos MWat NLar NSoo SPer SPoG XLum
§	'Kings Blue Arrow'^{PBR}	LRHS
	'La Bohème'	CWCL NLar STes WCot
§	'Langdon's Royal Flush' 🏆^{H4}	ELar LRHS
	'Lanzenträger'	LRHS
	'Leonora'	CNMi ELar
	'Lily Radley'	ELar
	'Loch Leven' 🏆^{H4}	CNMi
	'Lord Butler' 🏆^{H4}	CNMi ELar LRHS
	'Lucia Sahin' 🏆^{H4}	CNMi
	maackianum	GCal LLHF NLar WCot
	Magic Fountains Series	IFoB LRHS NGBl SPet SPlb SPoG WGor
	- 'Magic Fountains Cherry Blossom'	EPfP SPoG
	- 'Magic Fountains Dark Blue'	EPfP GMaP LSRN NEgg NLar SPoG
	- 'Magic Fountains Deep Blue'	NLar
	- 'Magic Fountains Lavender'	EPfP
	- 'Magic Fountains Lilac Pink'	EPfP SPoG
	- 'Magic Fountains Lilac Rose'	NLar WGor
	- 'Magic Fountains Pure White'	EPfP NEgg NLar
	- 'Magic Fountains Sky Blue'	EPfP SPoG
	'Margaret' 🏆^{H4}	CNMi ELar
	'Marilyn Clarissa'	CNMi
	'Merlin' ambig.	LRHS LSRN
	'Michael Ayres' 🏆^{H4}	CNMi ELar
	micropetalum CNDS 031	WCru
	'Mighty Atom'	CNMi EWll IKil
	'Min' 🏆^{H4}	CNMi ELar
	'Misty Mauves' (New Millennium Series) (d)	LRHS WSpi
	'Molly Buchanan'	CNMi
	'Moon Light' (Highlander Series) (d) **new**	LRHS NLar
	'Moonbeam'	ELar
	'Moonlight Blues' (New Millennium Series) **new**	SGbt STes
	'Morgentau'	LRHS
	'Mother Teresa'	CNMi
	'Mrs Newton Lees'	EWll IKil LRHS
	'Ned Wit'	IKil
	New Century hybrids	CBcs
	'Nobility'	ELar WSpi
	nudicaule 'Laurin'	LRHS
	'Oliver' 🏆^{H4}	CNMi ELar
	'Our Deb' 🏆^{H4}	ELar
	oxysepalum	LLHF
	Pacific hybrids	EPfP LSRN MHer NLar SRms SWvt WHar
	'Pagan Purples' (New Millennium Series) (d)	IFoB WSpi
	'Patricia Johnson'	CNMi ELar
	Percival Group	EPfP
	'Pericles'	CNMi LRHS
	'Pink Punch' (New Millennium Series)	ELan
	Pink River = 'Barfourtythree'^{PBR}	CBcs
	'Pink Ruffles'	CNMi ELar
	'Plagu Blue'^{PBR}	WSpi
	Princess Caroline = 'Odabar'^{PBR}	CBcs
	'Purple Passion' (New Millennium Series)	ELan EPfP IPot LRHS SPoG STes
	'Purple Velvet' 🏆^{H4}	ELar
	pylzowii	EWld
	'Raymond Lister' **new**	MAvo
	'Red Caroline'	CBcs
	requienii	CSpe EWld NSti
	'Rona'	CNMi
	'Rosemary Brock' 🏆^{H4}	ELar
	Round Table Mixture	CTri
	'Royal Aspirations' (New Millennium Series)	CMea ELan IPot LRHS SGbt SPoG STes
	'Royal Flush'	see *D.* 'Langdon's Royal Flush'

	'Ruby'	CNMi
	'Ruby Tuesday'	CNMi
§	× ***ruysii*** 'Pink Sensation'	EBee EWTr LRHS NLar WSpi
	'Sandpiper' ♀H4	CNMi
	'Schönbuch'	LRHS
	'Secret'PBR	LRHS WCot
	'Silver Jubilee'	CNMi ELar
	'Sky Sensation'	IBoy
	'Snow Crown'	WSpi
	'Snow Queen Arrow'	LRHS
	'Sommerabend'	LRHS
	'Sooty'	CNMi
	'Spindrift' ♀H4	CNMi ELar
	stapeliosmum B&SWJ 2954	WCru
	- HWJK 2179	WCru
	staphisagria	CArn
	'Stardust'	WSpi
	'Starlight'PBR	LRHS
	'Strawberry Fair'	LRHS
	Summer Skies Group	CBcs CSBt CTri CWCL ELan EPfP LHop LRHS MBri MWat NBir NLar NSoo SPer SPoG WCAu WHoo XLum
	'Summer Wine'	ELar
	'Summerfield Diana'	CNMi
	'Summerfield Oberon'	ELar WCot
	'Sungleam' ♀H4	ECtt ELar IKil WSpi
	'Sunkissed' ♀H4	CNMi ELar
	'Sunny Skies' (New Millennium Series)	CMea ELan LRHS SPoG
	'Susan Edmunds'PBR (d) ♀H4	CNMi
	sutchuenense	CPom EWld
	- BWJ 7867	WCru
	tatsienense	IFoB SRms
	'Tiddles' ♀H4	ELar
	'Tiger Eye'	CNMi ELar
	'Trudy'	CNMi
	'Vanessa Mae'	CNMi
	'Walton Benjamin'	CNMi
	'Walton Gemstone' ♀H4	ELar
	White River = 'Barfourtyfive'PBR	CBcs
	'White Swan'	EPfP
	'Wishful Thinking'PBR	MBri
	Woodfield strain	WHrl
	'Yvonne'	LRHS LSRN
	'Zauberflöte'	EBee LRHS

Dendranthema see *Chrysanthemum*

pacificum	see *Ajania pacifica*

Dendriopoterium see *Sanguisorba*

Dendrobenthamia see *Cornus*

Dendrocalamus (*Poaceae*)

	asper	XBlo
	calostachys	SPlb
	giganteus	XBlo
§	***strictus***	XBlo

Dendromecon (*Papaveraceae*)

rigida	CBcs EPfP LRHS SChF SKHP WPGP WSHC

Dendropanax (*Araliaceae*)

trifidus B&SWJ 11230	WCru

Dennstaedtia (*Dennstaedtiaceae*)

punctilobula	CLAP

Dentaria see *Cardamine*

pinnata	see *Cardamine heptaphylla*
polyphylla	see *Cardamine kitaibelii*

Deparia (*Woodsiaceae*)

okuboana	ISha

Dermatobotrys (*Scrophulariaceae*)

saundersii	ECre

Derwentia see *Parahebe*

Deschampsia (*Poaceae*)

	cespitosa	CKno COIW CWib EPPr EPfP LPot LRHS MWat SPlb WCot WGwG WMoo WWEG XLum
	- Bronze Veil	see *D. cespitosa* 'Bronzeschleier'
§	- 'Bronzeschleier'	CMea CPrp CWCL EBee EHoe ELan EPPr EPfP GMaP LEdu LRHS MAsh MAvo MBel MBrN MBri NGdn NOak NWsh SPer SPhx SRms SWvt WMoo WPtf WWEG XLum
	- 'Coral Cloud'	GQue
	- 'Fairy's Joke'	see *D. cespitosa* var. *vivipara*
	- 'Garnet Schist' **new**	GQue
	- Gold Dust	see *D. cespitosa* 'Goldstaub'
	- Golden Dew	see *D. cespitosa* 'Goldtau'
	- Golden Pendant	see *D. cespitosa* 'Goldgehänge'
	- Golden Shower	see *D. cespitosa* 'Goldgehänge'
	- Golden Veil	see *D. cespitosa* 'Goldschleier'
§	- 'Goldgehänge'	CSam EHoe MMHG NBir WWEG XLum
§	- 'Goldschleier'	CAby CPrp CSam EBee EPPr EPfP GBin GCal GMaP GQue LEdu LHop LRHS NGdn NWsh SPhx SWvt WMoo WPGP XLum
§	- 'Goldstaub'	EPPr
§	- 'Goldtau'	Widely available
	- 'Mill End'	CKno
	- 'Northern Lights' (v)	ELan ELon EPfP LRHS MBel MBri MMuc NBro NSti SLim SPad SPer SPoG SRms SWvt WPGP WPtf WWEG
	- 'Pixie Fountain'	CKno EDAr EPPr GQue LHop NOak WWEG
	- 'Schottland'	CKno ELon EPPr GBin LEdu NDov
	- 'Tauträger'	ELon GQue XLum
§	- var. ***vivipara***	EHoe EPPr GBin LRHS NBro
	- 'Willow Green'	GCal SCoo
	flexuosa	EHoe NBir NWsh
	- 'Tatra Gold'	CSBt CWCL EHoe ELan ELon EPfP EShb GMaP LBMP LRHS MAsh MMuc MRav NBir NBro NGdn NOak NPri NSti SLim SPer SPoG SRot SWvt WWEG
	holciformis 'Marin'	CKno

Desfontainia (*Loganiaceae*)

§	***spinosa*** ♀H3	Widely available
	- 'Harold Comber'	CMac GKin WCru WHor
	- f. ***hookeri***	see *D. spinosa*

Desmodium (*Papilionaceae*)

callianthum	CMac LRHS WSHC
canadense	CDes CPom EBee LRHS NLar

cuspidatum	SPhx
var. ***longifolium*** new	NPro SGol SHil SPlb SPoG SWvt WKif WSHC
§ ***elegans*** ♀H4	CBcs CExl CHEx EBee ELan EPfP LRHS MBri NLar SBrt SKHP SVen WHer WPGP WSHC
- f. ***albiflorum***	SBrt
paniculatum	CPom SBrt WSHC
praestans	see *D. yunnanense*
sessilifolium new	SPhx
tiliifolium	see *D. elegans*
§ ***yunnanense***	CExl CHEx WSHC

Deuterocohnia (*Bromeliaceae*)

brevifolia ♀H1	CFil EBee WCot WPGP
longipetala RCB/Arg L-5	WCot

Deutzia ✿ (*Hydrangeaceae*)

CC 4548	CExl
CC 4550	CExl
calycosa	GQui
- B&SWJ 7742	WPat
- BWJ 8007	WCru
- 'Dali'	CDoC CExl CFil SDys
aff. ***calycosa*** SIN 1878	GLin
chunii	see *D. ningpoensis*
compacta	CMCN SLon WPGP
- GWJ 9202	WCru
- GWJ 9203	WCru
- GWJ 9339	WCru
- 'Lavender Time'	CDoC CExl CMac EBee EPfP EWTr NLar SWvt WCFE
cordatula B&SWJ 3720	WCru
- B&SWJ 6917	WCru
crenata B&SWJ 8886	WCru
- B&SWJ 8896	WCru
- B&SWJ 8924	WCru
- 'Flore Pleno'	see *D. scabra* 'Plena'
- var. ***heterotricha*** B&SWJ 5805	WCru
- - B&SWJ 8879	WCru
- var. ***nakaiana***	WPat
- - B&SWJ 11184	WCru
- - 'Nikko'	see *D. gracilis* 'Nikko'
§ - 'Pride of Rochester' (d)	CBcs CMCN CWib EBee ECrN GKin LRHS LSou MBri MGos MRav NLar SGol SLim SPoG SWvt WGrn
'Dark Eyes'	CExl CFil
discolor 'Major'	CExl CFil WPGP WPat
× ***elegantissima***	SRms
- 'Fasciculata'	EBee ELan EPfP LRHS SPer SWvt
- 'Rosealind' ♀H4	CBar CBcs CDul CExl CHel CTri EBee ELan EPfP GKin IArd LHop LRHS LSRN MGos MMuc MRav SEND SLim SPer SRms SWvt WCFE WKif WPat WSHC
glabrata B&SWJ 617	GQui WCru
- B&SWJ 8427	WCru
glomeruliflora BWJ 7742	WCru
gracilis	CDoC CDoy CSBt ELan EPfP EWTr GGal GKin GQui IArd LPot MAsh MGos MRav MSwo NSoo SPad SPer SPoG WHar WSpi
- B&SWJ 8927	WCru
- 'Aurea'	CBcs EPfP NLar
- 'Carminea'	see *D.* × *rosea* 'Carminea'
§ - 'Marmorata' (v)	SLon
§ - 'Nikko'	CBcs CExl CHel CMCN CMac CMea EBee ECho ELan EShb EWes GKin LRHS MBri MGos MHer MWhi NLar NPro SGol SHil SPlb SPoG SWvt WKif WSHC
- var. ***ogatae*** B&SWJ 8911	WCru
- 'Rosea'	see *D.* × *rosea*
- 'Variegata'	see *D. gracilis* 'Marmorata'
grandiflora	NChi WPGP
'Hillieri' new	CFil
hookeriana	EPfP LBuc LLHF LRHS MBri SHil SWvt
× ***hybrida*** 'Contraste'	CMac SPer
- 'Joconde'	CExl WKif
- 'Magicien'	CDoC CDul CExl CMHG CMac CSBt CWib ECrN ELan EPfP EShb GQui LHop LRHS MAsh MBri MRav MSwo NBir SKHP SLon SMrm SPer SPoG SRms SWvt WKif WPat WSHC
- 'Mont Rose' ♀H4	Widely available
§ - 'Strawberry Fields' ♀H4	Widely available
'Iris Alford'	CDoC CExl CGHE EBee LBuc LRHS MBri SHil SLon WPGP
× ***kalmiiflora***	CExl CJun CMac CSBt CTri EBee GBin GKin GQui LRHS MAsh MJak NLar SLPl SPer SRms
× ***lemoinei***	MJak
longifolia	CMCN WGob WPGP WPat
- 'Veitchii' ♀H4	CDoy CSBt GQui MRav
- 'Vilmoriniae'	MRav
× ***magnifica***	CBcs CDul EBee GQui SRms
- 'Nancy'	GKin
- 'Rubra'	see *D.* × *hybrida* 'Strawberry Fields'
× ***maliflora*** new	CFil
maximowicziana B&SWJ 11567	WCru
monbeigii	CDoC CExl CFil EPfP LLHF LRHS MRav WKif
- BWJ 7728	WCru
multiradiata	CExl CFil WPGP
§ ***ningpoensis*** ♀H4	CExl CFil EBee EPfP GQui SLPl SMrm SPer WPGP
paniculata B&SWJ 8592	WCru
parviflora var. ***barbinervis*** B&SWJ 8478	WCru
'Pink Pompon'	see *D.* 'Rosea Plena'
prunifolia B&SWJ 8588	WCru
pulchra	CAbP CDoC CMCN CPom EBee EPfP IDee LRHS MRav SLon SMrm SPer SSpi WGob WPGP WPat WSpi
- B&SWJ 3870	WCru
- B&SWJ 6908	WCru
purpurascens BWJ 7859	WCru
rehderiana	CFil
§ × ***rosea***	CDul CWib EPfP LAst LRHS MAsh SRms WKif WRHF
- 'Campanulata'	CExl EPfP MAsh MSwo
§ - 'Carminea'	SPlb SRms WGob WPat
§ 'Rosea Plena' (d)	CDoC CExl CMac CSBt CWib EBee ECrN EPfP EWTr GKin LBuc LRHS MAsh MBri MGos NEgg NLar SLim SWvt WGob WPat
rubens	LLHF WPat
scabra	CDul CTri
- B&SWJ 11127	WCru
- B&SWJ 11168	WCru
- B&SWJ 11178	WCru
§ - 'Candidissima' (d)	CDul CMac GQui MRav NLar SPer WGob WPat WRHF
- 'Codsall Pink'	CFil MRav
§ - 'Plena' (d)	CExl EBee ECrN ELan EPfP GKin NSoo SPer WCFE WKif

	– 'Pride of Rochester'	see *D. crenata* 'Pride of Rochester'
	– 'Punctata' (v)	EHoe EShb MMuc SRms
	– 'Robert Fortune'	SPlb
	– 'Variegata' (v)	CDul CMac
	setchuenensis	CMac GQui SSpi WPat WSHC
	– var. ***corymbiflora*** 🏆H4	CBcs CDoC CDul CExl CGHE CHel CSam CTri EBee EPfP EWTr IArd IDee LHop LRHS MBri MSwo SPoG SWvt WKif WPGP
	staminea HWJK 2180	WCru
	taiwanensis	SGol WPat
	– B&SWJ 6858	WCru
	– CWJ 12443	WCru
	– CWJ 12459	WCru
	'Tourbillon Rouge'	EBee EPfP LRHS LSRN NLar WGob
*	***vidalii***	GGal
	× ***wellsii***	see *D. scabra* 'Candidissima'
	× ***wilsonii***	SRms

Dianella (*Hemerocallidaceae*)

	brevicaulis	ECou
	caerulea	CHel CMac EBee ECou ELan EPri IBoy IGor IMou LEdu MNrw MOWG NBir SMrm
	– Breeze = 'Dcnco' PBR	NOak
	– Cassa Blue = 'Dbb03' PBR	EPfP LAst LHop LRHS NOak NSoo SPad SPer SPoG
	– 'Kulnura'	ECou
	– Little Jess = 'Dcmp01' PBR	CExl EBee NOak SPoG
	– 'Variegata'	see *D. tasmanica* 'Variegata'
	ensifolia	LEdu
	intermedia 'Variegata' (v)	IBlr
	nigra	CBcs CExl ECou IFro IMou LEdu
	– 'Margaret Pringle' (v)	CBcs CExl ECou NOak
	revoluta	CCon ECou
	– Baby Bliss = 'Dtn03' PBR	CKno NOak WCot
	– 'Hartz Mountain'	ECou
	– Little Rev = 'Dr5000' PBR	EBee EPfP ESwi NOak NSoo
	'Silver Streak' (v)	NSoo
	tasmanica	CAbb CBcs CCon CElw CEnd CExl CHEx CHel CHll CKno CMac CSpe CTri CTsd ECou ECre ELan EPfP EShb GBin GGal IBlr LEdu LHop MOWG SAPC SEND SMad SRms SSpi
	– from Logan	GCal
	– 'Emerald Arch'	ELan ESwi NOak SPer
	– 'Prosser'	ECou
	– Tasred = 'Tr20' PBR	CExl EBee ELan EPfP ESwi NOak NSoo SPer SPoG
§	– 'Variegata' (v)	CCCN CCon CDTJ CExl ECou ELan EPfP LHop SEND

Dianthus ✿ (*Caryophyllaceae*)

	sp.	SVic
	AC&W 2116	ECtt
	'Aicardi' (pf)	CNMi
	'Alan Titchmarsh' (p)	CWCL ECtt EPfP LRHS LSRN MGos MTis NCGa NEgg SPoG SWvt
	'Aldridge Yellow' (b)	SAll
	'Alfriston' (b) 🏆H4	SAll
	'Alice' (p)	LSRN SAll
	'Alice Lever' (p)	WAbe
	Alicia = 'Baralicia' (pf) **new**	NDar
§	'Allen's Maria' (p)	SAll
	'Allspice' (p)	MRav WHoo
	Allwoodii Group (p)	NNor
	– 'Doris' (p) **new**	SHil
	Allwoodii Alpinus Group (p)	NGdn SRms XLum
	'Allwood's Celebration' (p)	SAll
	'Allwood's Crimson' (pf)	SAll
	'Allwood's Delight' (p)	SAll
	alpinus 🏆H4	GJos NSla WNew
	– 'Albus' (p)	NWad
	– 'Joan's Blood' (p) 🏆H4	ECho ELon GBuc LSRN WAbe
	'Alyson' (p)	SAll
	amurensis	ECho EPPr GCal MLHP NNor SPhx WSHC
	– 'Andrey' (p)	NNor
	anatolicus	CTri ECho EDAr MHer NGdn XLum
	'Anders Apollo' (p)	CNMi
	'Anders Cream Princess' (pf)	CNMi
	'Anders Eileen Gamble' (pf) **new**	NDar
	'Anders Fay Seagrave' (p) **new**	NDar SAll
	'Anders Irene Ann' (pf)	CNMi
	'Anders Kate Murray' (pf) **new**	NDar
	'Anders Kath Phillips' (pf) 🏆H4	CNMi
	'Anders Kyrenia Sunset' (pf) **new**	NDar
	'Anders Melody' (p)	SAll
	'Anders My Love' (pf) **new**	NDar
	'Anders Patricia Griffiths' (p)	CNMi SAll
	'Anders Pluto' (p) **new**	NDar
	'Anders Pure Joy' (pf) **new**	NDar
	'Anders Remember Me' (pf) **new**	NDar
	'Anders Royal Purple' (pf)	CNMi NDar
	'Anders Scipio' (pf) **new**	NDar
	'Anders Sundance' (pf)	CNMi
	'Anders Verdant' (p) **new**	NDar
	'Anders White Joanne' (pf) **new**	NDar
	'Andrew Morton' (b)	SAll
	'Angela Carol' (pf)	CNMi
	'Angelo' (b)	SAll
	'Ann Franklin' (pf) 🏆H1	CNMi
	'Annabelle' (p)	SAll
	'Anne Jones' (b)	EPfP
	'Anne S. Moore' (b) **new**	NDar
	'Annette' (p)	CPBP ECho EDAr EHyd LRHS LSRN NGdn SRGP SWvt
	'Annie Claybourne' (pf)	CNMi
	'Apricot Sue' (pf)	CNMi SAll
	Arctic Star	see *D.* 'Devon Arctic Star'
	arenarius	CCon EDAr GKev LEdu NGdn SPlb XLum
	– 'Little Maiden' (p)	EDif NCGa NGdn SPhx WIce
	'Argus'	IGor SAll
	armeria	CFis WHer WOut
	arpadianus	GKev NGdn
	– var. ***pumilus***	EPot GKev LLHF
	'Arthur Holmes' (pf) **new**	NDar
	'Arthur Leslie' (b)	SAll
§	× ***arvernensis*** (p) 🏆H4	ECho EPot SBch
	– 'Albus'	ECho
	'Audrey Robinson' (pf)	CNMi
	'Aurora' (b)	SAll
	'Auvergne'	see *D.* × ***arvernensis***
	'Averiensis'	see *D.* 'Berlin Snow'
	'B9/114' (b) **new**	NDar

	'B9/139' (b) **new**	NDar
	'Baby Treasure' (p)	ECtt
	'Bailey's Celebration' (p)	ECtt EPfP LRHS MSpe MTis NCGa SRGP WMnd
	'Barbara Norton' (p)	ECtt
	barbatus	MNrw SVic
	- SDR 6404	GKev
	- Barbarini Series	WGor
	- 'Black Adder'	CSpe
I	- 'Darkest of All'	CSpe
	- (Diabunda Series) 'Diabunda Purple Picotee' **new**	SPav
	- - 'Diabunda Red' **new**	SPav
	- Nigrescens Group (p,a) 🏆^{H4}	CBre CHVG CMea CSpe MNHC SPhx
I	- 'Sooty' (p,a)	CTsd EDAr
	- 'Super Parfait Strawberry' (Super Parfait Series) 🏆^{H3}	LRHS
	- 'Tuxedo Black'	WMoo
	'Barley Sugar' (pf) **new**	CNMi
§	'Bat's Double Red' (p)	SAll
	'Becky Robinson' (p) 🏆^{H4}	CNMi NDar SAll
	'Belmont Duchess' (p) **new**	SAll
	'Belmont Ruby Wedding' (p)	CNMi
§	'Berlin Snow' (p)	CPBP EPot EWes
I	'Betty Dee Sport' (pf) **new**	NDar
	'Betty Miller' (b)	SAll
	'Betty Morton' (p) 🏆^{H4}	ECtt IFoB WKif
	'Betty's Choice' (pf)	CNMi
	'Betty's Delight' (pf)	NDar
	'Bill Smith' (pf)	CNMi
	'Blue Hedgehog'	ECtt
	'Blue Hills' (p)	ECho GKev
	'Blue Ice' (b)	SAll
	'Blush'	see *D.* 'Souvenir de la Malmaison'
	'Bobby' (p)	SAll
	'Bob's Highlight' (pf)	CNMi
	'Bofield Boy' (b) **new**	NDar
	'Bofield Emily' (b) **new**	NDar
	'Bofield Lisa' (b) **new**	NDar
	'Bofield Marie' (b) **new**	NDar
	'Bombardier' (p)	ECtt
	'Bookham Gleam' (b)	SAll
	'Bookham Grand' (b)	SAll
	'Bookham Heroine' (b)	SAll
	'Bookham Lad' (b)	SAll
	'Border Special' (b)	SAll
	'Bouquet Purple' (p)	CSpe
	'Bovey Belle' (p) 🏆^{H4}	SAll
	'Bressingham Pink' (p)	ECtt
	brevicaulis	WAbe
	- subsp. ***brevicaulis***	LLHF
	'Brian Tumbler' (b) 🏆^{H4}	SAll
	'Bridal Veil' (p)	SAll SBch WHer
	'Brigadier' (p)	ECtt
	'Brilliance' (p)	MSCN WMoo
	'Brilliant'	see *D. deltoides* 'Brilliant'
	'Brilliant Star' (p) 🏆^{H4}	ECho ECtt LRHS MWat SEND SWvt WIce
	'Brympton Red' (p)	CFis SAll
	'Bryony Lisa' (b) 🏆^{H4}	SAll
	caesius	see *D. gratianopolitanus*
	callizonus	LLHF
	'Calypso' (pf)	CTri
	'Calypso Star' (p) 🏆^{H4}	ECho ECtt NGdn SPoG
	'Camilla' (b)	CNMi
	'Can-can' (pf)	ECho ECtt

	'Candy Clove' (b)	SAll
	Candy Floss	see *D.* 'Devon Flavia'
	'Candy Spice' (p)	MRav
	Capri = 'Kocapri' (pf) 🏆^{H1}	SAll
§	'Carmine Letitia Wyatt'^{PBR} (p) 🏆^{H4}	ECtt LRHS NCGa SPoG
I	'Caroline' (pf) **new**	NDar
	carthusianorum	CAby CArn CKno CSpe EWTr GQue LDai LEdu LPio LPla MCot MNFA NDov NGdn NSti SAll SPhx SPlb SRms SWat SWvt WKif WPGP WWEG WWFP XLum
I	- 'Rupert's Pink' (p)	NGdn SWvt
	caryophyllus	CArn ELau
	- 'Citrien'^{PBR} (pf)	LRHS
	- Limoni = 'Kolim' (pf) **new**	LBuc
	- 'Milky Way' (pf)	SAll
	- 'Princess'^{PBR} (pf) **new**	LBuc NPri
	'Charles' (p)	SAll
	'Charles Edward' (p)	SAll
	'Charles Musgrave'	see *D.* 'Musgrave's Pink'
	Charlie = 'Hilcharly' (pf)	NDar SAll
	'Chastity' (p)	LLHF SAll WHoo
	Cheddar pink	see *D. gratianopolitanus*
	'Cherly'	LSRN
	'Cherry Clove' (b)	SAll
	'Cherry Pie' (p)	ECtt LRHS
	'Cheryl'	see *D.* 'Houndspool Cheryl'
	'Chesswood Dorothy Cottam' (b) **new**	SAll
	'Chesswood Margaret Alison' (b) 🏆^{H4} **new**	NDar
	'Chetwyn Ruth Gillies' (pf)	CNMi
	'Chianti Double' (p)	SAll
	chinensis (p,a)	WHil
	- 'Black and White' (p,a)	CSpe
	'Chris Crew' (b) 🏆^{H4}	SAll
	'Clara' (pf)	CNMi NDar
	'Clara's Lass' (pf)	CNMi NDar
	'Clare' (p)	SAll
	'Claret Joy' (p) 🏆^{H4}	CBcs ECtt EPfP LRHS MMuc NEgg SAll SEND
	'Clifford Joy' (pf) **new**	NDar
	'Clifford Pipperoo' (pf) **new**	NDar SAll
	'Clunie' (b)	SAll
§	'Cockenzie Pink' (p)	SAll SBch WHer
	Coconut Sundae = 'Wp05 Yves' (p)	ECtt ELan ELon EPfP EWII GBin LAst LHop LRHS LSRN MAvo MSCN NCGa NNor NPri SRot WGor WHil
	'Constance' (p)	SAll
	'Constance Finnis'	see *D.* 'Fair Folly'
	'Consul' (b)	SAll
	'Conwy Silver' (p)	WAbe
	'Conwy Star' (p)	CPBP WAbe
	'Coquette' (pf) 🏆$^{H2-3}$ **new**	NDar
	'Coral Reef'^{PBR} (p)	ECtt ELan NNor SPoG
	'Coronation Ruby' (p) 🏆^{H4}	SAll
	'Cosmic Swirl Pink' (p)	MHol WHil
	'Cosmic Swirl Red' (p)	WHil
	'Coste Budde' (p)	WSHC
	Cracker = 'Wp10 Sab06' (Early Bird Series) (p)	ECho GAbr
	'Cranmere Pool' (p) 🏆^{H4}	CBcs ECtt ELan EPfP LRHS NGdn NNor SPoG SWvt WRHF WWEG
	'Cream Sue' (pf)	CNMi
	'Crimson Chance' (p)	EPot NSla
	'Crimson Warrior' (pf)	CNMi
	'Crock of Gold' (b)	SAll
	'Crompton Bride' (pf)	CNMi

	'Crompton Classic' (pf)	CNMi NDar
	'Crompton Princess' (pf)	CNMi NDar
	cruentus	CAby LPio NDov SPhx SWvt WWEG
	'D.D.R.'	see *D.* 'Berlin Snow'
	'Dad's Favourite' (p)	CFis SAll WHer
	'Dainty Dame' (p) ♀^{H4}	CSpe CTri ECho EPfP LRHS MNHC SAll SBch SRot
	'Dancing Queen'^{PBR} (p)	CMea MTis NNor WWFP
	'Daphne' (p)	SAll
	'Dark Star' (p)	ECho
	'Dartington Double' (p)	ECho SEND
	'David' (p)	LSRN NSoo SAll SBch
	'David Russell' (b) ♀^{H4}	SAll
	'David Saunders' (b) ♀^{H4}	SAll
	'Dawn' (b)	SAll
	'Dawn' (pf)	ECho
	'Daydream' (pf)	MNrw
	'Dedham Beauty'	MPie WCot WWEG
	deltoides ♀^{H4}	CArn ECho EPfP LEdu MAsh MMuc MNHC SPlb SRms WJek WPtf
	- 'Albus' (p)	EPfP GKev MNHC NGdn WMoo
	- 'Arctic Fire' (p)	CWib ECho EDAr EPfP NGdn NHol WMoo
	- 'Bright Eyes' (p)	ECho LRHS MTis MWat
§	- 'Brilliant' (p)	CTri ECho EPau GJos LAst MNHC NGdn NHol SAll SRms WGor WWEG
	- 'Dark Eyes' (p)	EWes
	- 'Erectus' (p)	EPfP
	- Flashing Light	see *D. deltoides* 'Leuchtfunk'
§	- 'Leuchtfunk' (p)	ECho ECtt EDAr EPfP LAst MJak NNor SPoG WMoo WRHF WWEG
I	- 'Luneburg Heath Maiden Pink' (p)	NGdn
	- Microchips Group (p)	WMoo
	- 'Nelli' (p)	ECho NGdn WMoo
	- red-flowered (p)	SVic
	- 'Shrimp' (p)	NGdn
	'Dennis' (p)	LSRN SAll
	'Desert Song' (b)	SAll
	'Desmond'	EPfP LHop
§	'Devon Arctic Star' (p)	CMea CTri ECho ELan ELon GBin GMaP NEgg SPoG SRms SRot SWvt
	'Devon Blush' (p)	ECtt
	'Devon Cream'^{PBR} (p)	ECtt ELan GAbr LAst LRHS LSou MWat NEgg WHil WMnd
	'Devon Dove'^{PBR} (p) ♀^{H4}	CMea CSBt CTri ECGP ECtt ELan EPfP LHop LRHS LSou MRav MWat NCGa NDov NEgg
§	'Devon Flavia'^{PBR} (Scent First Series) (p) ♀^{H4}	ECtt ELan GBin LAst LBMP LRHS MAvo MTis NEgg NPri SEND SHil SPoG WGor WHil
	'Devon General'^{PBR} (p)	CTri
	'Devon Glow' (p) ♀^{H4}	EPfP
	'Devon Magic'^{PBR} (p)	ECtt ELan
§	'Devon Sapphire' (p) ♀^{H4}	CMea ECho ELan EWTr MAvo WIce
§	'Devon Siskin' (p) ♀^{H4}	NEgg
	'Devon Wizard'^{PBR} (p) ♀^{H4}	CSBt ECtt EPfP LRHS MMuc MRav MSpe NCGa NDov NEgg NNor SEND
§	'Devon Xera' (p) ♀^{H4}	ECho SHil SRms
	'Dewdrop' (p)	CMea CTri ECho ECtt EPfP MAsh MHer MMuc NBir NGdn SAll SBch SEND
	'Diamond Scarlet' (Diamond Series)	LRHS
	'Diana'	see *D.* Dona
	'Diana Lavender Picotee' (p, a) **new**	LRHS
	'Diane' (p) ♀^{H4}	ELan EPfP LRHS NEgg SAll SPoG SWvt WMnd
*	'Diane Cape'	SAll
	'Diplomat' (b)	SAll
	'Doctor James Dennison' (pf) **new**	CNMi
§	Dona = 'Brecas' (pf)	LSRN SRGP
	'Dora' (p)	ECho LRHS
	'Doreen Hodgson' (p) **new**	SAll
	'Doris' (p) ♀^{H4}	Widely available
	'Doris Allwood' (pf)	CNMi CSBt EMal NDar SAll
	'Doris Elite' (p)	SAll
	'Doris Galbally' (b)	SAll
	'Doris Majestic' (p)	SAll
	'Doris Ruby'	see *D.* 'Houndspool Ruby'
	'Doris Supreme' (p)	SAll
	'Double Lace'	LRHS
	'Double North' (p)	ELon
	'Dubarry' (p)	CTri ECtt
	'Duchess of Fife' (p)	ECtt EPfP
	'Duchess of Roxburghe' (pf)	EMal SAll
	'Duchess of Westminster' (M)	EMal SAll
	'Duke of Norfolk' (pf)	EMal SAll
	'Dunkirk Spirit' (pf) ♀^{H1}	CNMi
	'Dusky' (p)	CNMi
	'Dusky Janelle' (pf)	CNMi
	'Earl of Essex' (p)	SAll
	'Edenside Scarlet' (b)	SAll
	'Edenside White' (b)	SAll
	'Edna' (p)	SAll
	'Edward Allwood' (pf)	SAll
	'Edwin Cross' (b)	SAll
	'Eileen' (p)	SAll
	'Eileen Lever' (p)	CPBP IFoB MWat WAbe
	'Eileen Neal' (b) ♀^{H4}	SAll
	'Eileen O'Connor' (b) ♀^{H4}	SAll
	'Eira Wen' (p) **new**	WAbe
	'Eleanor Parker' (p)	WAbe
	'Eleanor's Old Irish' (p)	CAbP ECtt ELon LRHS MBel MHol MPie MWhi WCot WHoo WMnd WRHF WWEG
	'Elfin Star' (p)	ECho
	'Elizabeth Nelson' (b) **new**	NDar
	'Elizabethan' (p)	CFis CSpe MCot SDys
*	'Elizabethan Pink' (p)	SAll
	'Ellen Ladd' (pf)	CNMi NDar
	'Elsie Ketchen' (pf)	CNMi NDar
	'Emile Paré' (p)	CFis
	'Emjay' (b)	NDar SAll
	Emma = 'Barmane' (pf)	NDar SAll
	'Emma West' (pf)	CNMi
	'Emperor'	see *D.* 'Bat's Double Red'
	erinaceus	ECho GJos
	- var. ***alpinus***	EPot GBin
	- Duguid's	WAbe WThu
	'Erycina' (b)	SAll
	'Ethel Hurford' (p)	WHoo
	'Eva Humphries' (b)	SAll
	'Evening Star' (p) ♀^{H4}	CTri ECho GAbr GBin LRHS NEgg SPoG SWvt WIce
	'Eve's Holly' (pf) **new**	CNMi
	'Exquisite' (b)	SAll
§	'Fair Folly' (p)	IGor SAll SBch WHer
	Falicon = 'Barfalicon'^{PBR} (pf) **new**	NDar
	'Fanal' (p)	NBir

	Fancy Fuego = 'Bargofanfu' (pf) **new**	NDar
	'Farnham Rose' (p)	SAll
	'Fenbow Nutmeg Clove' (b)	SDix
	'Fettes Mount' (p)	LPla MWhi WCot
	'Feuerhexe' (p)	EPot
	'Fimbriatus' (p)	WHoo
	'Fiona' (p)	SAll
	Fire Star	see *D.* 'Devon Xera'
	'Firestar' (p)	CTri ELan LRHS MAsh MWat SRot SWvt
	'First Lady' (b)	SAll
	Fizzy = 'Wp08 Ver03'PBR (Early Bird Series) (p)	CMea ECho ELan LBMP
	'Flanders' (b) ♀H4	SAll
	'Flashdance' (pf) **new**	CNMi
	'Fleur' (p)	SAll
	'Florence Franklin' (pf) **new**	CNMi
	'Floristan Mix' (p,a)	NNor
	'Forest Princess' (b)	NDar SAll
	'Forest Sprite' (b)	SAll
	'Forest Treasure' (b)	SAll
	'Forest Violet' (b)	SAll
	'Forge Pink'	LLHF
	'Fortuna' (p)	SAll
	'Fountain's Abbey' (p)	IGor
	'Fragrant Ann' (pf) ♀H1	CNMi SAll
	'Fragrant Phyllis' (pf)	CNMi
	'Frances Isabel' (p)	SAll
	'Frank Bruno' (pf)	CNMi
	'Freda' (p)	SAll
	'Freda Woodliffe' (p)	ECtt EPot SBch WAbe
	freynii	ECho EPot EWes GKev WAbe
*	- var. ***nana***	GKev
*	'Frilly'	LBMP SHil
	Frilly = 'Wp08 Ulr03'PBR (Early Bird Series) (p)	ECho
N	fringed pink	see *D. superbus*
	furcatus	GKev
	'Fusilier' (p)	CTri ECho ECtt EDAr EHyd EPfP GBuc GKev GMaP LHop LRHS MAsh SAll SEND SHar SRot SWvt
	'Gail Graham' (b)	SAll
	'Gail Tilsley' (b)	SAll
	'Garland' (p)	CMea CTri
	'Gaydena' (b)	SAll
	giganteus	GKev
	'Gingham Gown' (p)	ECtt EPot NBir SAll
	glacialis subsp. ***gelidus***	EPot GKev
	'Gold Dust' (p)	SAll
	'Gold Flake' (p)	SBch
	'Gold Fleck' (p)	ECtt EPot EWTr
	'Golden Cross' (b) ♀H4	NDar SAll
	'Grace's Scarlet Clove' (b) **new**	SAll
	'Grandma Calvert' (p)	SAll SBch
	'Grange Classic Choice' (pf) **new**	NDar
	'Gran's Favourite' (p) ♀H4	CBcs CSBt CTri CWCL ECtt ELan EPfP GAbr LAst LHop LPot LRHS LSRN MBel MCot MMuc MTis MWat NEgg NGdn NNor SAll SEND SHil SPlb SPoG SRGP SWvt
	'Gransole' (pf) **new**	NDar
§	***gratianopolitanus*** ♀H4	CArn CPBP CTri EDAr EPfP GJos GKev LEdu MHer MNHC MRav NBid SAll WGwG
	- 'Albus'	MHer
	- dwarf	WAbe
*	- 'Karlik' (p)	GKev
§	- 'Tiny Rubies' (p)	EDAr SDys WAbe
	'Green Lane' (p)	CHll
	'Greensides' (p)	SAll
	'Grey Dove' (b) ♀H4	SAll
	'Greytown' (b)	GCal
	'Gypsy Star' (p)	ECho SPoG
	haematocalyx 'Alpinus'	see *D. haematocalyx* subsp. *pindicola*
§	- subsp. ***pindicola***	GKev LLHF WAbe
	'Hannah Gertsen' (p)	SAll
	'Hannah Louise' (b) ♀H4	SAll
	'Harkell Special' (b)	SAll
	'Hayden' (pf) **new**	CNMi
	'Hayley's Choice' (b) **new**	NDar SAll
	'Haytor Rock' (p) ♀H4	EPfP LRHS NCGa NNor WGwG
	'Haytor White' (p) ♀H4	CBcs CTri CWib EPfP MRav MWhi NSoo SAll WWEG
	'Hazel Ruth' (b) ♀H4	SAll
	'Heath' (b)	SAll
	'Helen' (p)	ELon LSRN SAll
	'Helena Hitchcock' (p)	SAll
	'Héraclès' (pf) **new**	NDar
	'Hereford Butter Market' (p)	EBee
	'Hidcote' (p)	CTri LLHF LRHS SIgm
	'Hidcote Red'	ECho
	'Highland Fraser' (p)	WKif
	Highland hybrids	SGbt
	'Hope' (p)	SAll SBch
	'Hot Spice' (p) ♀H4	SPoG
§	'Houndspool Cheryl' (p) ♀H4	CTri EPfP SAll SRGP
§	'Houndspool Ruby' (p) ♀H4	CBcs EPfP LBMP LSRN SAll
	hyssopifolius	CArn
	'Ian' (p)	LSRN SAll WWEG
	Iced Gem = 'Wp06 Fatima'PBR (Scent First Series) (p)	ELan ELon EPfP LBMP LHop LRHS LSRN NNor SHil SPoG SRot
	'Icomb' (p)	WHoo
	'Inchmery' (p)	SAll SBch WHer WHoo
	'India Star'PBR (p) ♀H4	CTri ECho EPfP LBMP LRHS MWat NEgg SEND SRms SRot WIce
	'Indiana' (pf) **new**	NDar
	'Inglestone' (p)	CTri
	Inka = 'Barinka'PBR (pf)	NDar
	'Inshriach Dazzler' (p) ♀H4	ECho ECtt EPot GMaP LRHS MAsh MHer NEgg NHar NHol SRot WAbe
	'Inshriach Startler' (p)	CMea WNew
	'Irene Della-Torré' (b) ♀H4	NDar SAll
	'Jack's Lass' (pf)	CNMi
	'Jacqueline Ann' (pf) ♀H1	CNMi
	'James Portman' (p)	ELon
	'Janelle Welch' (pf)	CNMi
	'Janet Walker' (p)	GMaP
	'Jean Knight' (b) ♀H4 **new**	NDar
	'Jess Hewins' (pf)	CNMi NDar SAll
	'Joan Schofield' (p)	SBch
	'Joanne' (pf)	CNMi
	'Joanne's Highlight' (pf)	CNMi NDar
	'Joe Vernon' (pf)	CNMi
	'Johnny' (pf)	SAll
	'Joy' (p) ♀H4	EPfP LAst SAll SPoG WWEG
	'Julian' (p)	SAll
	'Julie Ann Davis' (b)	SAll
	'Kathleen Hitchcock' (b) ♀H4	SAll
	'Kessock Charm' (p)	MNrw

'Kessock Rose Blush' (p) **new**	NDar
'Kesteven Kirkstead' (p) ♀H4	GAbr MNrw SAll
'Kim' (p)	NDov
Kiro = 'Lonkirok'PBR (pf) ♀H1	NDar
knappii	CFis GKev LDai LPio SPhx WHer WMoo XLum
- 'Yellow Harmony' (p,a)	ELon SAll
'Kristina' (pf) ♀H1	NDar SAll
'La Bourboule' (p) ♀H4	CMea CTri ECho ECtt EDAr GAbr LRHS MWat SBch
'La Bourboule Alba' (p)	CTri ECho ECtt EDAr EPot MAsh SBch WGor
'Laced Joy' (p)	SAll
'Laced Monarch' (p)	CBcs ECtt ELan EPfP GCra LHop LRHS MCot MMuc NCGa NEgg NNor SAll SEND SMrm SPlb SPoG WWEG
'Laced Mrs Sinkins' (p)	CNMi SAll
'Laced Prudence'	see *D.* 'Prudence'
'Laced Romeo' (p)	SAll
'Laced Treasure' (p)	SAll
'Lady Granville' (p)	IGor SAll SBch
Lady in Red = 'Wp04 Xanthe'PBR (p)	CSBt ECtt ELan EPfP LRHS LSou MTis MWhi NNor
Lady Madonna = 'Wp04 Opal'PBR (p) ♀H4	ELan MTis
'Lady Wharncliffe' (p)	SBch
'Lady Windermere' (M)	EMal SAll
'Lakeside Trinity' (p) **new**	NDar
'Lancashire Jubilation' (p) **new**	NDar
'Lancing Monarch' (b)	SAll
'Lancing Supreme' (p)	SAll
'Laura' (p)	SAll
'Lavender Lady' (pf)	CNMi
'Leatham Pastel' (pf)	CNMi
'Lemsii' (p) ♀H4	NGdn
'Leslie Rennison' (b)	SAll
'Letitia Wyatt' (p) ♀H4	CMea EPfP LRHS MRav MWat MWhi SBch SPoG SRGP
'Leuchtkugel' (p)	CPBP ECho LLHF WAbe
leucophaeus var. ***leucophaeus***	LLHF
'Liberty' (pf)	NDar
'Lillie Brooks' (p) **new**	NDar
'Lily Lesurf' (b)	SAll
Lily the Pink = 'Wp05 Idare'PBR (p) ♀H4	ELan LRHS MTis
'Lime Crush' (pf) **new**	CNMi
'Linfield Annie's Fancy' (pf)	CNMi
'Linfield Doreen Ashmore' (p)	SAll
'Linfield Dorothy Perry' (p) ♀H4	SAll
'Linfield Isobel Croft' (p)	SAll
'Linfield Julie' (p)	SAll
'Linfield Kathy Booker' (p) ♀H4	SAll
'Linfield Pink Margaret' (p)	CNMi SAll
Lisa = 'Kolisa' (pf) **new**	NDar
'Little Ben' (p)	SAll
'Little Jock' (p)	ECho ECtt EDAr EHyd LRHS MAsh MHer MWat SAll SBch SPlb
'Little Miss Muffet' (p)	CHll
'Liz Rigby' (b)	SAll
'London Brocade' (p)	SAll
'London Glow' (p)	CNMi SAll SBch
'London Lovely' (p)	SAll
'London Poppet' (p)	CNMi SAll
'Lord Nuffield' (b)	SAll
lumnitzeri	GKev LLHF NGdn
'Lustre' (b)	SAll
'Madonna' (pf)	EPfP WHer
'Maggie' (p)	LSRN
'Maisie Neal' (b) ♀H4	SAll
'Mambo' (pf) ♀H4	SAll
'Mandy' (p)	SAll
'Manon des Sources' (pf)	CNMi NDar
'Margaret Taylor' (p)	CNMi SAll
'Maria'	see *D.* 'Allen's Maria'
'Marielle' (pf) **new**	NDar
'Marjery Breeze' (p)	SAll
'Marmion' (M)	EMal SAll
'Mars' (p)	ECho
'Ma's Choice' (p)	SAll
'Matthew' (p)	WHoo
'Maudie Hinds' (b)	NDar SAll
'Maybole' (b)	SAll
Memories = 'WP11 Gwe04' (p) **new**	LBuc LRHS
'Mendip Hills' (b)	SAll
Mendlesham Minx = 'Russmin'PBR (p)	ECho EDAr ELan EPfP LRHS SAll SRms SWvt
'Merlin'	see *D.* 'Devon Siskin'
'Messines Pink' (p)	SAll
'Michael Saunders' (b) ♀H4	SAll
'Mickail Gorbachev' (pf) **new**	NDar
microlepis	ECho EDAr GKev NGdn NSla WAbe
- f. ***albus***	GKev NSla
- ED 791562	NGdn
- var. ***musalae***	ECho LLHF
- 'Rivendell' (p)	ECho WAbe
'Mike Briggs' (b)	SAll
'Milky Way' (pf) ♀H2-3 **new**	NDar
'Mini-Charlie' (pf) **new**	NDar
'Miss Farrow' (p) **new**	LRHS
'Miss Sinkins' (p)	CTri IFoB
'Mona Lisa' (pf) **new**	NDar
'Monica Wyatt' (p) ♀H4	CBcs ECtt ELan EPfP LRHS NCGa NEgg SPoG WWEG
'Montrose Pink'	see *D.* 'Cockenzie Pink'
'Monty Allwood' (p)	SAll
'Moor Editha' (p)	CNMi
'Moore Maurice Alison' (b) **new**	NDar
'Mo's Doris' (pf) **new**	NDar
Mother of Pearl = 'WP10 Ele04' (Perfume Pinks Series) (p)	ELan EWll LBMP MTis
'Moulin Rouge' (p) ♀H4	CTri CWCL ECtt ELan EPfP GAbr GCra LHop LRHS MSpe MTis NDov SPoG WWEG
'Mrs Gumbly' (p)	CNMi
'Mrs Macbride' (p)	SAll
'Mrs Roxburgh' (p)	CSam
'Mrs Sinkins' (p)	Widely available
'Murray's Laced Pink' (p)	MWhi
N 'Musgrave's Pink' (p)	CFis MRav SAll SBch
'Musgrave's White'	see *D.* 'Musgrave's Pink'
myrtinervius	CCon ECho EDAr NGdn WHoo
'Mystic Dawn' (b) **new**	NDar SAll
Mystic Star	see *D.* 'Devon Sapphire'

	'Napoleon III' (p)	SAll
	Napoli = 'Hilpoli' (pf)	WHil
	nardiformis	XLum
	'Natalie Saunders' (b) ♀H4	SAll
	'Nautilus' (b)	SAll
	neglectus misapplied	see *D. pavonius*
	'Neon Star'PBR (p) ♀H4	CTri ECho EDAr EHyd ELan GBuc GKev LRHS MWat SHil SPoG SRms SRot
	'Night Star' (p) ♀H4	ECho ELan EPfP GBin GKev GMaP LHop LPot LRHS MHol NEgg SBch SEND SRot WHil WPtf
	'Nika' (pf)	SAll
	nitidus	NBir
	noeanus	see *D. petraeus* subsp. *noeanus*
	'Nomie' (pf) **new**	CNMi
	'Northland' (pf)	CNMi EMal SAll
	'Nyewoods Cream' (p)	CMea CTri ECho MHer NGdn SBch
§	'Oakington' (p)	CTri MRav
	'Oakington Rose'	see *D.* 'Oakington'
	'Oakwood Billy Boole' (p)	CNMi NDar
	'Oakwood Candy' (p)	CNMi
	'Oakwood Erin Mitchell' (p)	CNMi NDar
	'Oakwood Margaret Gee' (p) **new**	NDar
	'Oakwood Romance' (p) ♀H4	CNMi
	'Oakwood Sweetheart' (p)	SAll
	'Old Blush'	see *D.* 'Souvenir de la Malmaison'
	'Old Clove Red' (b)	LPio
	'Old Crimson Clove' (b)	SBch
	'Old Dutch Pink' (p)	SBch
	'Old French Red' (pf)	EMal
	'Old Mother Hubbard' (p)	CHll
	'Old Red Clove' (p)	CHVG CSpe ECtt MBel MCot NSti WCot
§	'Old Square Eyes' (p)	MNrw SAll SHar
	'Old Velvet' (p)	CNMi GCal MNrw SAll SBch
	'Oliver' (p)	SAll
	'Omagio' (pf)	SBch
	'Orange Maid' (b)	SAll
	Osiris = 'Barorisis' (pf) **new**	NDar
	'Owston Coral Dream' (p) **new**	NDar
	'Owston Rose' (p) **new**	NDar
	'Owston Third Avenue' (p)	NDar SAll
	'Oxford Magic' (p)	SAll
	'Paddington' (p)	CNMi
	'Painted Lady' (p)	SAll
	'Paisley Gem' (p)	SAll SBch
	'Pamela Flett' (p)	CNMi
	Passion = 'Wp Passion'PBR (Scent First Series) (p)	CMea EBee ECtt ELan EPfP GBin LSou MBel MHer MHol MPie MTis NNor SHil SPoG WCot WHil
§	***pavonius*** ♀H4	CPBP EWes NGdn SBch
	'Pax' (pf)	SAll
	'Peach' (p)	SEND
	'Pendle Doris Delight' (p) **new**	SAll
	'Pendle Mrs Riley' (p)	CNMi
	'Pennine Reflections' (b) **new**	SAll
	'Peter Wood' (b) ♀H4	SAll
§	***petraeus***	EWes NGdn WThu
§	- subsp. ***noeanus***	LHop LLHF WHal
	'Petticoat Lace' (p)	SAll
	'Phantom' (b)	SAll
	'Pheasant's Eye' (p)	SAll SBch WHer
*	'Picton's Propeller' (p)	GBuc
	Pierrot = 'Kobusa' (pf)	CNMi
	'Pike's Pink' (p) ♀H4	CSpe CTri ECho ECtt EDAr EHyd ELan EPfP LHop LRHS MAsh MHer MMuc MRav MWat NBir NGdn SAll SBch SEND WAbe
	pindicola	see *D. haematocalyx* subsp. *pindicola*
	pinifolius	IFro SBrt
	'Pink Devon Pearl'PBR (p)	LPot
	'Pink Doris' (pf)	CNMi
	'Pink Fantasy' (b)	SAll
	'Pink Fizz'	LRHS MTis
	'Pink Jacqueline Ann' (pf)	CNMi
	'Pink Jewel' (p)	CMea CPBP EDAr GKev MAsh MNHC SAll SBch
	'Pink Mrs Sinkins' (p)	MHer MLHP MNrw SAll
	'Pink Pearl' (b)	SAll
	'Pixie Star'PBR (p) ♀H4	ECho EPfP SPoG SRot WIce
	plumarius	CArn MLHP SAll WHer XLum
	- 'Albiflorus'	XLum
	- Ipswich Pink Group (p)	GJos MNHC
	- 'Sonata'	GJos
	Popstar = 'Wp04 Esther' (p)	ECho EWll SGbt SRms
	'Pretty' (p)	SAll
	Pretty Flamingo	see *D.* 'Carmine Letitia Wyatt'
	'Prince Charming' (p)	ECho ECtt MAsh
	'Princess of Wales' (M)	EMal SAll
	'Priory Pink' (p)	SAll
§	'Prudence' (p)	SAll
	'Pudsey Prize' (p)	CPBP EPot WAbe
	'Purple Jenny' (p)	SAll
	'Queen of Hearts' (p)	CTri ECho MMuc SEND
§	'Queen of Henri' (p)	ECho ECtt LRHS
	'Queen of Sheba' (p)	IGor SAll SBch WHer WKif
	'Rachel' (p)	SAll
	'Raggio di Sole' (pf)	CNMi
	'Rainbow Loveliness' (p,a)	SAll
	'Ralph Gould' (p)	ECho
	'Raspberry Parfait' (p,a)	LRHS
	'Raspberry Sundae' (p)	ECtt ELan EPfP GBin LBMP LRHS LSRN NCGa SEND SHil SPoG WBor WRHF
	Rebekah = 'Wp09 Mar05'PBR (Early Bird Series) (p)	CMea LBMP LRHS SHil
	'Red Fuego' (pf) **new**	NDar
	'Red Star'PBR (p) ♀H4	ECho ELan GJos LRHS SRot WIce
	'Reine de Henri'	see *D.* 'Queen of Henri'
	'Richard Pollak' (b)	NDar SAll
	'Richmond Margaret's Choice' (p) **new**	NDar
	'Rizalene' (p) **new**	CNMi
	'Robert Allwood' (pf)	SAll
	'Robert Smith' (b) **new**	NDar
	'Robin Ritchie' (p)	WHoo
	'Robina's Daughter'	GAbr
	Romance = 'Wp09 Wen04'PBR (Scent First Series) (p)	ELan LRHS MTis SHil
	'Roodkapje' (p)	XLum
	'Rose de Mai' (p)	CFis CNMi CSam SAll SBch WHoo
	'Rose Joy' (p) ♀H4	EPfP
§	'Rose Monica Wyatt'PBR (p) ♀H4	LRHS NCGa
	Rosebud = 'Wp08 Ros03'PBR (Early Bird Series) (p)	LBMP SHil
	'Rötkappchen' (p) **new**	WCot

'Ruby'	see *D.* 'Houndspool Ruby'
'Ruby Doris'	see *D.* 'Houndspool Ruby'
'Ruby Wedding' (p)	LSRN
rupicola	WCot
'Sam Barlow' (p)	SAll SBch
'Santa Claus' (b)	SAll
scopulorum perplexans	ITim
'Seren Wen' (p)	WAbe
serotinus	WCot XLum
Sherbet = 'Wp08 Ros03'PBR (Early Bird Series) (p)	ELan GAbr SHil
Shooting Star = 'Wp04 Flores'PBR (p)	ECho ELan LRHS SRms
'Shot Silk' (pf)	SAll
'Show Aristocrat' (p)	SAll
'Show Beauty' (p)	SAll
Show Girl = 'Hilshow' (pf)	LRHS
Show Girl = 'Wp08 Uni02'PBR (Scent First Series) (p)	ELan EWll
'Show Glory' (p)	SAll
'Show Harlequin' (p)	SAll
'Show Satin' (p)	SAll
'Shrimp' (b)	CWib
Silver Star = 'Wp10 Hel01' (p)	ECho LRHS SHil
'Singapore Girl' (Kiwi Series) (p)	CWGN
Slap 'n' Tickle = 'Wp05 Pp22'PBR (Scent First Series) (p)	ECtt ELon LRHS LSRN MAvo MTis NCGa NPri SHil SPoG SRot
'Solomon' (p)	IGor SAll
'Solway Star' (pf) **new**	NDar
'Sops-in-wine' (p)	CSam ECtt MSCN SAll
§ 'Souvenir de la Malmaison' (M)	EMal SAll
'Spangle' (b)	SAll
'Spencer Bickham' (p)	MNrw
spiculifolius	CFis EPot SBch
'Spinfield Joy' (b) ♀H4 **new**	NDar SAll
'Spirit' (pf)	SAll
'Spring Star' (p)	ECtt SRot WJek
'Square Eyes'	see *D.* 'Old Square Eyes'
squarrosus	ECho EPot WAbe
* - ***alpinus***	ECho
- 'Nanus'	see *D.* 'Berlin Snow'
'Starburst'PBR (p)	CMea ECho ELon EWll GAbr GBin LRHS NCGa SHil WIce
Stardust = 'Wp07 Opr04'PBR (Early Bird Series) (p)	ECho LBMP WIce
Starlight = 'Hilstar' (pf)	CMea LRHS NCGa SRms
Starlight = 'Wp 06 Parnia'PBR (p)	ECho
'Starry Eyes' (p) ♀H4	CSam ECho EHyd ELan GBin GMaP LRHS NEgg NPri SBch SRms SRot SWvt
'Storm' (pf)	CNMi EMal SAll
stramineus	GKev
'Strawberries and Cream' (p)	CBcs ECtt LRHS NEgg NOrc SPoG
strictus **new**	WCot
subacaulis	EDAr GAbr IFoB NGdn XLum
- subsp. ***brachyanthus***	GJos
- - 'Murray Lyon'	CPBP WThu
suendermannii	see *D. petraeus*
Sugar Plum = 'Wp08 Ian04'PBR (Scent First Series) (p)	ELan EPfP EWll LBMP LBuc MHer MTis WGor

'Summerfield Adam' (p)	SAll
'Summerfield Amy Francesca' (p)	SAll
'Summerfield Blaze' (p)	SAll
'Summerfield Blush' (p) **new**	SAll
'Summerfield Daniel' (b)	SAll
'Summerfield Debbie' (p)	SAll
'Summerfield Emma Louise' (p)	SAll
'Summerfield Jo' (p) **new**	SAll
'Summerfield Rebecca' (p)	SAll
Summertime	see *D.* 'Rose Monica Wyatt'
'Sunburst' (p)	ELon
(Sunflor Series) 'Sunflor Bianca'	WHil
- 'Sunflor Citrien'	WHil
- 'Sunflor Crystal' **new**	WHil
'Sunray' (b)	SAll
'Sunstar' (b)	SAll
§ ***superbus***	CMHG GBBs MNFA MNrw NNor SBch SHar SPhx WMoo WRHF XLum
- 'Crimsonia' (p)	MBrN
I - 'Primadonna'	GQue
'Supernova' (pf) **new**	CMea
'Susan' (p)	SAll
'Susannah' (p)	SAll
* 'Susan's Seedling' (p)	SAll
'Sutton Amethyst' (p) **new**	NDar
'Sutton Brierley Grace' (p)	NDar
'Sutton Obsession' (p) **new**	NDar
'Sutton Pamela Flett Supreme' (p)	NDar
'Swanlake' (p)	SAll
'Sweet Cecille' (pf) **new**	CNMi
'Sweet Sophie' (pf)	CNMi NDar
'Sweet Sue' (b)	SAll
'Sweetheart Abbey' (p)	CNMi IGor
I 'Sweetness Mix' (p)	GJos
sylvestris	WOut
'Tamsin Fifield' (b) ♀H4	SAll
'Tatra Blush' (p)	GCal
'Tatra Fragrance' (p)	CCse GCal SAll SBch
'Tatra Ghost' (p)	SAll SDys
'Tayside Red' (M)	EMal SAll
'Terranova' (pf)	CNMi
'Thora' (M)	EMal SAll
Tickled Pink = 'Devon Pp 11' (Scent First Series) (p)	CMea ECtt ELan ELon EPfP EWll LBMP LRHS LSRN MTis NPri SHil SPoG WHil
'Tiny Rubies'	see *D. gratianopolitanus* 'Tiny Rubies'
'Tony's Choice' (pf)	CNMi
'Tracy Jardine' (pf)	CNMi
'Treasure' (p)	SAll
'Trevor' (p)	SAll
tristis **new**	XLum
'Tropic Butterfly' (p)	LPot
'Tudor'	MNrw
turkestanicus	NNor SVen WPtf
Tyrolean trailing carnations	SAll
'Uncle Teddy' (b) ♀H4	SAll
'Unique' (p)	IGor SAll SBch
'Ursula Le Grove' (p)	WHer
'Valda Wyatt' (p) ♀H4	CBcs ELan EPfP LAst LRHS MCot NCGa NEgg NNor NSti SAll SEND SPoG SWvt WMnd
Viana = 'Kovian'PBR (pf) ♀H1	SAll

'Vic Masters'	SBch
'Violet Clove' (b)	SAll
'W.A. Musgrave'	see *D.* 'Musgrave's Pink'
'Waithman Beauty' (p)	CTri ECtt GMaP SAll WAbe WHoo
'Waithman's Jubilee' (p)	SAll
'Warden Hybrid' (p)	CTri ECho ECtt EHyd GAbr GMaP LAst LRHS MNHC NGdn NWad SBch SPoG SWvt WAbe
'Waterloo Sunset'PBR (p)	CMea CSBt LRHS MTis
'Weetwood Double' (p)	MWhi SBch
'Welton Beauty' (p) **new**	NDar
'Welton Ice Man' (p) **new**	NDar
'Welton Ivory' (pf) **new**	NDar
'Welton Raspberry Ice' (p)	SAll
'Welton Red' (b) **new**	NDar
'Welton Star' (p)	NDar
weyrichii	ECho
'Whatfield Anona' (p)	SAll
'Whatfield Beauty' (p)	ECho ECtt
'Whatfield Brilliant' (p)	ECho
'Whatfield Cancan' (p) ♀H4	CMea ECho ECtt EHyd ELan EPot EWTr GMaP LHop LRHS MNHC NEgg NGdn NHol NPri SAll SBch SMrm SPoG SWvt WJek WNew WWFP
'Whatfield Cyclops' (p)	ECho SAll
'Whatfield Dawn' (p)	ECho
'Whatfield Dorothy Mann' (p)	ECho SAll SBch
'Whatfield Fuchsia Floss' (p)	SAll
'Whatfield Gem' (p)	ECho ECtt ELan EPfP LRHS MNHC MWat NGdn SAll SIgm SWvt WHoo WNew
'Whatfield Joy' (p)	ECho ECtt ELan EPfP LRHS MHer NGdn SAll
'Whatfield Magenta' (p) ♀H4	CSam ECho ECtt EHyd ELan EPfP EPot LHop LRHS MWat SAll SBch SPoG WAbe
'Whatfield Mini' (p)	SAll SBch
'Whatfield Miss' (p)	SAll SBch
'Whatfield Misty Morn' (p)	ECho SAll
'Whatfield Nine Star' (p)	ECho
'Whatfield Peach' (p)	SAll SBch
'Whatfield Pretty Lady' (p)	ECho SAll
'Whatfield Rose' (p)	ECho
'Whatfield Ruby' (p)	ECho ELan GJos SAll
'Whatfield Supergem' (p)	ECho ECtt
'Whatfield White' (p)	ECho ECtt SAll
'Whatfield White Moon' (p)	ECho
'Whatfield Wisp' (p)	CPBP CTri ECho EPfP EPot MRav NBir SBch WNew
'White and Crimson' (p)	SAll
'White Joy'PBR (p) ♀H4	ELan MRav
'White Kath Phillips' (pf) **new**	NDar
'White Ladies' (p)	MRav SAll
'White Liberty'PBR (pf)	SAll
'Whitehill' (p) ♀H4	ECho MHer
'Whitesmith' (b) ♀H4	SAll
'Widecombe Fair' (p) ♀H4	CTri ELan EPfP SAll SPoG
'William Brownhill' (p)	CNMi
'Yellow Alice' (b) **new**	SAll
'Zebra' (b)	SAll
'Zurigo' (pf) **new**	NDar

Diapensia (*Diapensiaceae*)

lapponica var. ***obovata***	NHar WAbe

Diarrhena (*Poaceae*)

japonica	MMoz

Diascia (*Scrophulariaceae*)

	'Alice Cap'	SBch
	'Andrew'	SBch
	'Appleby Appleblossom'	SBch
	'Appleby Apricot'	NDov
	barberae 'Belmore Beauty' (v)	EWes
	- 'Blackthorn Apricot' ♀H3-4	CBar CHel EBee ECtt EHyd ELan EPfP GBin GMaP LRHS LSRN NDov SMrm SPer SPlb SPoG SRms SWvt WGwG WWlt XEll
§	- 'Fisher's Flora' ♀H3-4	EPyc NDov
§	- 'Ruby Field' ♀H3-4	CBar CMea EBee EHyd ELan EPfP LHop LRHS LSRN NEgg SPer SPoG SRms SWvt
	'Blue Belle' **new**	LAst
	Blue Bonnet = 'Hecbon'	SBch SWvt
	'Blush'	see *D. integerrima* 'Blush'
	Breezee Apricot = 'Diaspritwo'PBR	LHop
	Breezee Snow = 'Inndiabzsno'PBR	LHop SMrm
	'Candy Floss'	SBch
	Coral Belle = 'Hecbel'PBR ♀H3-4	ECtt EHyd GBin LHop LRHS LSou SMrm
	cordata misapplied	see *D. barberae* 'Fisher's Flora'
	cordifolia	see *D. barberae* 'Fisher's Flora'
	'Denim Blue'	CSpe EPfP LBuc NLar SPoG WPtf
	elegans misapplied	see *D. fetcaniensis*, *D. vigilis*
	'Elizabeth' ♀H3-4	WHil
	'Emma'	NDov SWvt
	felthamii	see *D. fetcaniensis*
§	***fetcaniensis***	CMea CPrp EPfP EShb GMaP LRHS MCot MHer NEgg SPer WCFE WHal WKif
	- 'Daydream'	LBuc SBch WHrl
	flanaganii misapplied	see *D. vigilis*
	(Flying Colours Series) Flying Colours Appleblossom = 'Diastara'	EPfP SPoG
	- Flying Colours Apricot = 'Diastina'	EPfP
	- Flying Colours Red = 'Diastonia'	EPfP SPoG
	'Frilly' ♀H3-4	ECtt
	'Hector Harrison'	see *D.* 'Salmon Supreme'
	Ice Cracker = 'Hecrack'	CMea ELan LHop LRHS SBch SRms
	Ice Cream = 'Icepol'	SCoo
	Iceberg = 'Hecice'PBR	NDov SWvt
§	***integerrima*** ♀H3-4	MCot SIgm
	- 'Alba'	see *D. integerrima* 'Blush'
§	- 'Blush'	CSpe NDov
	- 'Ivory Angel'	see *D. integerrima* 'Blush'
	integrifolia	see *D. integerrima*
	'Jacqueline's Joy'	CMea NPer SBch
	'Joyce's Choice' ♀H3-4	EHyd LRHS SRms
	'Katherine Sharman' (v)	EWes
	'Lilac Belle' ♀H3-4	CMea EHyd ELan LHop LRHS NBir NEgg SPlb SPoG SRms
	'Lilac Gem'	SBch
	'Lilac Mist' ♀H3-4	NPer
	lilacina × ***rigescens***	GBee
	Little Dancer = 'Pendan'PBR	EPot GBin LAst LSou MSCN NLar SCoo SLon SMrm

	'Little Dazzler'	EPfP GBin
	Little Dreamer = 'Pender'^PBR	LAst NLar
	Little Drifter = 'Pendrif'^PBR	LSou NLar
	Little Maiden = 'Penmaid'^PBR	GBin LAst NLar WGor
	Little Tango = 'Pentang'^PBR	CPrp LAst LHop LSou NLar SRms SVen WCot WRHF
	personata	CAby CHll CMea CPrp CSpe ECtt ELon GBin LBMP LLHF LPio LPla LSou MCot MHer MNrw NDov SPer SPhx WBrk WCot WPtf WSHC
	- 'Hopleys'	ECre EWes LHop MAvo NCGa SHar WWEG
	'Peter'	NDov
	Pink Panther = 'Penther'	NLar SCoo SWvt
	'Pitlochrie Pink'	GBin
	Red Ace = 'Hecrace'^PBR	EPfP LAst LHop NPer SWvt
	Redstart = 'Hecstart'	NGdn SWvt
	rigescens ♀H3	CCon CHEx CPrp CSpe CWCL ECtt ELan GBin LHop MHer MRav NPer NSoo SPer SPlb SPoG SWvt WBor WCFE WSHC WSpi
§	- 'Anne Rennie'	LRHS MCot SWvt
	- pale-flowered	see *D. rigescens* 'Anne Rennie'
	Romeo Orange = 'Balromor' (Romeo Series)	NPri
	'Ruby Field'	see *D. barberae* 'Ruby Field'
	'Rupert Lambert' ♀H3-4	EWes NDov SBri
§	'Salmon Supreme'	ELan LRHS NGdn NPer SPoG SRms
	tetcaniensis 'African Queen'	EDif
	'Twinkle' ♀H3-4	EHyd LRHS NBir NPer SRms
*	'Twins Gully'	EWes SMrm
§	***vigilis*** ♀H3	CExl CMea EPfP EPot GBee LHop LRHS NBro SRms WHal WPnn WWEG
	- 'Jack Elliott'	MRav WCFE
	(Whisper Series) Whisper Apricot Improved = 'Balwhisaptim'^PBR	SCoo
	- Whisper Cranberry Red = 'Balwhiscran'^PBR	SCoo
	White Belle = 'Penbel'^PBR	LAst

Dicentra ✿ (*Papaveraceae*)

	CC 4452	CExl
	'Adrian Bloom'	CExl EBee ECtt EPfP GBuc LRHS MCot SMrm SPer SWvt WMoo
	'Aurora'	EBee ECtt ELon EPfP GBin GBuc LAst LRHS LSou MRav NGdn NLar NSti SPer SPoG SWvt WMoo
	'Boothman's Variety'	see *D.* 'Stuart Boothman'
	'Bountiful'	CMac ECtt EPau LSou MCot MRav NGdn SWvt
	'Brownie'	GBuc
	'Burning Hearts'^PBR	CWCL CWGN ECtt EPot IKil IPot LHop LLHF LRHS LSou MAsh MBri MPnt NCGa NDov SPer WHil
	canadensis	CLAP EBee GBuc MAvo NLar WAbe WCru WHal
	'Candy Hearts'^PBR	EBee ECtt ELan EPfP LHop LRHS MBri MCot NBro NGdn NLar SGol WHil
	cucullaria	CAby CElw CHel CLAP CPBP CWCL EBee ECho ELon EPPr EPot GAbr GBuc ITim LRHS MNrw MRav NLar WAbe WCru
	- 'Pink Punk' **new**	EBee LLHF MNrw
	- 'Pittsburg'	CRDP EBee EPPr GBuc MNrw
	eximia misapplied	see *D. formosa*
	eximia ambig.	MHol
	eximia (Ker Gawl.) Torr.	EBee
	- 'Alba'	see *D. eximia* 'Snowdrift'
§	- 'Snowdrift'	CLAP EBee ECtt ELan EPfP MCot SRms WMoo
	'Fire Island'	ECtt MBri
	'Firecracker'	ECtt MBri MPnt
§	***formosa***	CBcs CHel CTri EBee ELan EPfP GKev IFro LAst LPio LRHS MLHP NBro NGdn NOrc NPri NSoo SPlb SRms WMoo
	- f. ***alba***	GAbr GCra GLog GMaP LPio NBir SRms WCru WKif
	- 'Bacchanal' ♀H4	Widely available
	- 'Cox's Dark Red'	CExl CLAP EWes GBuc LLHF LWst SKHP
	- 'Langtrees' ♀H4	CMac CRow CSam EPau EPfP GBuc LHop LRHS MLHP MRav NBro SRms SWvt WCru WHrl WMoo WOut
	- subsp. ***oregana***	CLAP EPPr IGor SKHP WHal
	- - NNS 00-233	CLAP
	- - 'Rosea'	EPPr
	- Snowflakes = 'Fusd'	EWes LRHS MRav
	- 'Spring Gold'	ELon EPPr LBuc LRHS NLar WMoo
	- 'Spring Magic'	EPPr LBuc LRHS NLar
	'Ivory Hearts'^PBR	CWGN EBee ECtt ELan EPfP IKil LHop LRHS MAsh MAvo MBri MCot NBro NCGa NLar NPnk NSti SPer WCAu WHil
§	'Katie'	EPPr
	'Katy'	see *D.* 'Katie'
	'King of Hearts'	Widely available
	lichiangensis	see *Dactylicapnos lichiangensis*
	'Luxuriant' ♀H4	CBcs CSBt ECtt ELan EPfP GBuc LAst LHop LRHS LSRN MCot MGos MHol MRav SMrm SPer SPoG SRms SRot SWvt WMoo WPnP
	macrantha	see *Ichthyoselmis macrantha*
	'Pearl Drops'	ELan GLog GMaP LRHS MCot MMoz MRav NBid SRms WHil WMoo
	peregrina	WAbe
	'Red Fountain'^PBR	CWCL ECtt IPot LHop LRHS MBri NCGa NLar NPnk NSti
	scandens	see *Dactylicapnos scandens*
	spectabilis	see *Lamprocapnos spectabilis*
	'Spring Morning'	CElw CMHG CSam ECtt EPPr EPau LBMP LRHS LSou NDov NOrc WHoo
§	'Stuart Boothman' ♀H4	CMac CSam CSpe CWCL EBee ECtt ELan ELon EPfP EShb GBuc GMaP LAst LHop LRHS MCot MLHP MRav MSpe NBro NCGa NGdn NLar SPer SPoG SRms SWvt WKif WMoo
	thalictrifolia	see *D. scandens*
	ventii	see *Dactylicapnos ventii*

Dichelachne (*Poaceae*)

	crinita	SMea

Dichelostemma (*Asparagaceae*)

	congestum	CAvo ECho LRHS SDeJ
§	***ida-maia***	CAvo CGrW CWCL ECho EPot LRHS MCot SDeJ
	- 'Pink Diamond'	CGrW EBee ECho SDeJ

volubile	ECho
- 'Pink Giant'	SDeJ

Dichocarpum (*Ranunculaceae*)

§ ***dicarpon*** B&SWJ 11555	WCru

Dichondra (*Convolvulaceae*)

argentea 'Silver Falls'	CSpe EShb ESwi LAst LSou LSqH NPri SCoo SPer SPoG
§ ***micrantha***	EShb
repens misapplied	see *D. micrantha*

Dichopogon (*Anthericaceae*)

strictus	ECou WSFF

Dichroa (*Hydrangeaceae*)

febrifuga	CAbb CBcs CDoC CExl CHEx CHGN CHll CMil CTsd CWib EBee ELan EPfP LRHS SWvt WCru WPGP
- B&SWJ 2367	WCru
- HWJK 2430	WCru
- pink-flowered	CHEx
hirsuta B&SWJ 8207 from Vietnam	WCru
aff. ***hirsuta*** B&SWJ 8371 from Laos	WCru
versicolor B&SWJ 6565	WCru
- B&SWJ 6605 from Thailand	WCru
aff. ***yunnanensis*** B&SWJ 9734	WCru

Dichromena see *Rhynchospora*

Dichrostachys (*Mimosaceae*)

cinerea	SPlb

Dicksonia ✿ (*Dicksoniaceae*)

antarctica ♀H3	Widely available
fibrosa ♀H3	CBcs CDTJ CKel EAmu EExo ISha
lunata new	EAmu
sellowiana	CDTJ CKel
squarrosa ♀H2	CBcs CCCN CDTJ CKel EAmu SAPC

Dicliptera (*Acanthaceae*)

§ ***sericea***	CHll EShb IKil LHop MSCN SBch SMrm SRkn WCot WHil WVaU WPGP
suberecta	see *D. sericea*

Dicoma (*Asteraceae*)

anomala	SPlb

Dictamnus ✿ (*Rutaceae*)

albus	CArn CBcs CHll CPrp CTri EBee ELan EPfP EWTr GMaP LAst LEdu LHop LRHS MBri MCot MNrw MRav NSti SBrt SKHP SPer SPoG SWat SWvt WHil WSHC WWEG WWlt
- var. ***albus*** ♀H4	IBoy MAvo NPnk SWvt
§ - var. ***purpureus*** ♀H4	Widely available
* - ***turkestanicus***	GCal
fraxinella	see *D. albus* var. *purpureus*

Didymochlaena (*Dryopteridaceae*)

lunulata	see *D. truncatula*
§ ***truncatula***	XBlo

Dierama ✿ (*Iridaceae*)

sp.	WHil
adelphicum	EBee
ambiguum	CWCL EBee IGor XLum
argyreum	CCCN CElw CMac CPla CTsd CWCL EBee EPri GBin LRHS NLar SBrt SPad SPoG SRot XLum
'Ariel'	IBlr
'Ballyrogan Red'	IBlr
Barr hybrids new	WHil
'Black Knight'	CExl IBlr
'Blackberry Bells'	CSam CWCL CWGN ELon GBin MBri NLar SPoG WHil
'Blue Belle'	IBal IVic LBMP LBuc LRHS LSou
'Blush'	IBlr
'Buckland White'	WPGP
'Candy Stripe'	CBcs CPla CWCL EBee IBal WHil
'Carmine'	CWCL
'Cherry Chimes'	EPfP
'Cinnamon Fairy'	IBal MBri
cooperi	CElw CPou CTca EBee IBlr NBir WWEG
'Coral Bells'	CDes EBee GCal IBal
'Cosmos'	CExl CWCL EPri LRHS MHer MWhi SBod
'Dark Angel'	NCGa
'Delicacy'	IBlr
'Desire'	IBlr
dissimile	EBee IGor
'Donard Legacy'	IBlr NLar
§ ***dracomontanum***	Widely available
- JCA 3.141.100	WPGP
- dwarf, pale pink-flowered	LRHS
- Wisley Princess Group	MBri
dracomontanum × ***pulcherrimum***	SMad
dubium	EBee IBlr
ensifolium	see *D. pendulum*
erectum	CBcs CCCN CHel CHid CMac CTsd CWCL EBee EPri GBin IBlr LRHS NLar SRot
floriferum	IBlr
formosum	CCon EBee WPGP
galpinii	CCCN CHel CPla CWCL EBee ELan EPri IGor LLHF LRHS WPGP
grandiflorum	CPou IBlr IGor
'Guinevere'	Widely available
igneum	Widely available
- CD&R 278	CExl CPou ELon GBuc
insigne	CCCN CHel CHid CWCL EBee ESwi EWTr GBin LRHS NLar
'Iris'	IBlr
jucundum	CHel CWCL EBee GBuc
'Juno' new	CMac
'Knee-high Lavender'	CDes WPGP
'Lancelot'	CElw CExl ECtt IBal IBlr LRHS MBNS MBri MRav NBir NCGa NEgg NGdn NPnk SWvt WCot WKif
latifolium	CHid IBlr MNrw
'Mandarin'	IBlr
medium	EBee ELon SWat WPGP WWEG
'Milkmaid'	CExl IBlr
'Miranda'	CAbP EBee ECtt EPri IBal LRHS MBNS NEgg NGdn NLar NPnk WCot
mossii	CBcs CCCN CCon CExl CHel CHid CMHG CMac CTsd CWCL EBee ELan EPri GBin IBlr IGor LHop

	LRHS NLar SPlb SRot SVen WPGP XLum
nixonianum	IBlr
'Painted Lady'	CWCL IBal LBuc LRHS MBri SKHP SLon
'Pamina'	CExl CPrp IBlr
'Papagena'	IBlr
'Papageno'	IBlr
pauciflorum	CAbb CCCN CCon CExl CGHE CHel CHid CPrp CWCL CWib EPri GBin IKil MNrw NBir NLar SRot SWat WPGP WSHC WWEG
§ ***pendulum***	CBro EBee ELan EPfP GBBs IBlr LRHS LSRN MNrw MRav SWvt WWEG
pictum	IBlr
'Pink Rocket'	MHer NHol
Plant World hybrids	ELon
Plant World Jewels	CWCL
'Pretty Flamingo'	CExl CHel CPrp IBlr
'Puck'	CDes EBee GCal IBlr IGor MRav WHil WPGP
pulcherrimum	Widely available
- var. ***album***	CCCN CHel CWCL ELan IBlr LRHS MBel MHer MNrw MWhi WHil WPGP
- 'Blackbird'	Widely available
- dark pink-flowered	IBoy
- 'Falcon'	IBlr
- 'Flamingo'	IBlr
- 'Merlin'	CElw CExl CPou CWCL EBee ECtt ELon GMaP IBal IBlr IBoy LRHS MBri NBir NGdn NPnk SVen SWvt WGwG
- 'Peregrine'	IBoy
- purple-flowered	LRHS
- red-flowered **new**	SMrm
- 'Redwing'	IBlr
- Slieve Donard hybrids	CWCL EBee GBuc LAst LRHS NEgg SMad WHil WHrl WMnd WPtf
pumilum misapplied	see *D. dracomontanum*
'Queen of the Night'	IBlr
reynoldsii	CAbb CCCN CCon CExl CHel CHid CMac CPla CTsd CWCL EBee ELan EPri GAbr IBlr IVic LBMP LHop LRHS MBel MWhi NLar SPlb SPoG SRkn SVen WKif WMnd WPnP
robustum	CAbb CExl CPou CWCL IBlr LRHS MNrw SMad WPGP
'Sarastro'	CExl IBlr
'September Charm'	IBlr
sertum	EBee
'Spring Dancer'	EHoe NHol
'Tamino'	IBlr
'Tiny Bells'	EBee EDAr GBin GCal MBri
'Titania'	GCal IBal IBlr NSti
trichorhizum	CCCN CCon CExl CHel CPla CPrp CWCL EBee ELan EPri GBin IBlr LHop LRHS WPGP WWEG
'Tubular Bells'	IBlr
'Violet Ice'	IBlr
'Westminster Chimes'	IBlr
'Zulu Bells'	ELon

Diervilla ✿ (*Caprifoliaceae*)

middendorffiana	see *Weigela middendorffiana*
rivularis 'Troja Black'	EPPr NLar
§ ***sessilifolia***	CBcs CHGN CMac EPPr IDee LAst MRav NLar SLon WCot WMoo
- 'Butterfly'	CMac EPPr NLar WMoo
- Cool Splash = 'Lpdc Podaras' (v)	CMHG CWGN EBee ELan EMil EPPr LBuc LRHS MAsh SPoG SWvt
× ***splendens***	CExl CMHG CWib EBee EHoe ELan EPPr EPfP IDee LHop LRHS MBNS MBlu MRav MSwo SEND SLPl SPer SPoG SWvt

Dietes (*Iridaceae*)

bicolor	CAbb CExl CHEx CPrp CTca EPri LEdu LSou SChr
grandiflora	CAbb CArn CCse CExl CHEx CPrp CTca ECho
§ ***iridioides***	CHel CPrp CTca EBee ECho ESwi LRHS WCot
robinsoniana	CSpe

Digitalis ✿ (*Plantaginaceae*)

sp.	SVic
'Albino'	EPfP LRHS
ambigua	see *D. grandiflora*
apricot hybrids	see *D. purpurea* 'Sutton's Apricot'
canariensis	CAbb CBcs CCCN CDTJ CHEx CHel CHll CRHN CSpe EWll LRHS SDix SEND SPlb SVen WCFE WWlt
cariensis	GKev
ciliata	GKev
'Danielle' **new**	CSpe
davisiana	CExl EWld MNHC WMoo
dubia	EPfP WAbe
'Elsie Kelsey'	ECtt NBir SWvt WHil
eriostachya	see *D. lutea*
ferruginea ♀H4	CLAP CSam ECtt ELan EPPr EPfP GCra IBoy IFoB LEdu LRHS MHer MNHC MRav MWat NBir NBro NCGa NDov NGdn SKHP SPav SPer SRms SWat WBrk WKif WMnd WMoo XLum
- subsp. ***ferruginea***	WSpi
- 'Gelber Herold'	CLAP GMaP NLar SHar SPhx
- 'Gigantea'	CLAP ECtt ELan GBin GQue LAst LEdu MBNS NChi SPlb SWat WWEG
fontanesii	NBir SBrt
'Foxtrot'	EPfP LRHS MBri SHil
× ***fulva***	NBir
'Glory of Roundway'	CLAP ECtt LBMP LSou NLar SPer SPoG STPC WCot
§ Goldcrest = 'Waldigone' PBR	LRHS
§ ***grandiflora*** ♀H4	CBcs CHab CHel CMea COlW CPom CTri EBee ELan EPPr EPfP GMaP IFoB LAst LBMP LRHS MLHP MNHC MRav MWat MWhi NGdn SHil SPer SRms SWvt WHoo WMoo WWEG
- 'Carillon'	EBee ELan EPfP GBin IFoB LAst LDai LRHS MBel NBir NLar SRot WHil
- 'Cream Bell'	EPfP LRHS MHol
- 'Dwarf Carillon'	EWld
aff. ***grandiflora*** **new**	IBoy
heywoodii	see *D. purpurea* subsp. *heywoodii*
'Illumination'	LBuc LRHS SPoG
isabelliana	CCCN LDai WHlf
'John Innes Tetra'	MNrw SPad WHoo
kishinskyi	see *D. parviflora*
laevigata	CCon EPfP GBin LEdu LRHS NBro SEND SPav SPet WMnd WMoo
- white-flowered	WCot
lamarckii misapplied	see *D. lanata*

§	***lanata***	CArn ECtt ELan EPfP GKev LAst LBMP LRHS MBNS MNFA MNHC NGdn NOrc SBea SPav SPer SPhx SPlb SRms WMnd WWEG
	- 'Café Crème'	CLAP MCot SPet
§	***lutea***	Widely available
	- SDR 6377	GKev
	- SDR 6413	GKev
I	- 'Aurea'	LPla
§	- subsp. ***australis***	LDai
	- 'Flashing Spires' (v)	CPla
	× ***mertonensis*** Υ^{H4}	Widely available
	- 'Raspberry'	CLAP
	- 'Summer King'	ECtt ELan EWld LSRN NBre NPri SMrm WHil
	micrantha	see *D. lutea* subsp. *australis*
	nervosa	LHop
	obscura	CFis ECho GCal IFoB LBMP LRHS MHer SPet SPlb WMnd
*	- 'Dusky Maid'	LHop LRHS SPet
	orientalis	see *D. grandiflora*
§	***parviflora***	CCVN CDes CSam EBee ECtt ELan EPPr EPfP GAbr GBin GCra GJos GKev IBoy LEdu LRHS MAvo MBNS NBro NChi SBea SEND SPav WHoo WMnd WMoo WPGP WWEG
	- 'Milk Chocolate'	CBcs CLAP CMHG CSpe ECtt ELan EPfP GBin GBuc GJos GQue LHop LPio LRHS LSRN LSou MCot MHer MNHC NBir NBre NEgg NLar NPri SBHP SKHP SMrm SPet
	'Pink Chapel'	ECtt WCot
	'Polkadot Pippa'	MBri WHlf
	purpurea	CArn CHab ELan EPfP GPoy LRHS MHer MLHP MMuc MNHC NMir NPri SIde SMrm SPlb SPoG WBrk WJek WMoo WOut WSFF WWFP
	- 'Alba'	see *D. purpurea* f. *albiflora*
§	- f. ***albiflora***	Widely available
	- - 'Anne Redetzky'^{PBR}	CSpe LRHS WCot
	- Camelot Series	LRHS
	- - 'Camelot Cream'	ELan EPfP LBMP LRHS MBri MCot NLar NPri SWvt
	- - 'Camelot Lavender'	EHyd ELan EPfP LBMP LRHS MBri NEgg NLar SWvt
	- - 'Camelot Rose'	EHyd ELan EPfP LBMP LRHS MBri NEgg NLar NPri SMrm SWvt
	- - 'Camelot White'	EHyd ELan EPfP LRHS MBri NEgg NLar
*	- 'Campanulata Alba'	MBel
	- 'Chedglow' (v)	CNat
	- 'Dalmatian Purple'	LRHS MBri SHil
	- 'Dalmatian White'	LAst MBri NPri SHil WHlf
	- Excelsior Group	CBcs CMac CSBt CTri CWCL ECtt EPfP GJos GMaP IBoy LAst LHop LRHS MBri MJak MWat NHol NMir SBod SPer SPoG SRms SWvt WGor WHar WWEG XLum
	- - (Suttons; Unwins) Υ^{H4}	ECtt MRav
	- Foxy Group	CWib EPfP LRHS MJak SPet SPoG WWEG
	- - 'Foxy Apricot'	SWvt
	- - 'Foxy Pink'	ELan GBin LHop
	- Giant Spotted Group	ECtt EPfP LRHS SPoG
	- Glittering Prizes Group	SWat
	- (Gloxinioides Group) 'The Shirley' Υ^{H4}	WMoo
§	- subsp. ***heywoodii***	ELan WMoo WWEG
	- - 'Silver Fox'	LRHS LSRN WCot
	- subsp. ***mariana***	EBee
	- 'Pam's Choice'	Widely available
	- 'Pam's Split'	CHid
	- 'Primrose Carousel'	NEgg NLar SMrm
	- 'Snow Thimble'	CLAP ELan EShb LHop LRHS MAvo MBri MNFA NLar WBor WWEG
§	- 'Sutton's Apricot' Υ^{H4}	Widely available
	- white cen-type mutant	NChi
	purpurea × ***thapsi***	EBee WWEG
	'Red Skin'	CLAP CPom GBin SPad WMoo
	'Saltwood Summer'	EPfP LRHS MBri SHil
	sceptrum	CCCN CExl CHEx SPlb SVen WPGP
	'Serendipity'	EPfP LRHS MBri SHil
	× ***sibirica***	EBee
	'Spice Island'	CLAP ECtt ELon ESwi GBin IBoy LEdu LRHS LSou MAvo MCot MHol NCGa NDov NLar NSti SPer SPoG STPC WCot WWlt
*	***stewartii***	ELan EWes GCra LDai WMoo
	'Strawberry Fayre'	GJos
	thapsi	EDif ELan EPfP GKev LRHS SBrt SEND WMoo WWEG XLum
	- 'Spanish Peaks'	CHid LSou
	trojana	ECtt GKev IFoB SDix
	- 'Helen of Troy'	CLAP ELan LHop SKHP WSpi
	viridiflora	CExl ECtt NBro
	'Walberton's Goldcrest'	see *D.* Goldcrest

Dilatris (*Haemodoraceae*)

ixioides new	CLak
pillansii new	CLak

dill see *Anethum graveolens*

Diocirea (*Scrophulariaceae*)

violacea	ECou

Dionaea ✿ (*Droseraceae*)

muscipula	CHew EECP SKHP SPlb WSSs
- 'Akai Ryu'	EECP WSSs
- 'B52'	EECP WSSs
- (Dentate Traps Group) 'Dentate Traps'	WSSs
- 'Royal Red'	CHew WSSs
- 'Sawtooth'	EECP WSSs
- shark-toothed	EECP
- 'Spider'	EECP

Dionysia (*Primulaceae*)

'Annielle'	WAbe
archibaldii	WAbe
- 'Tora'	WAbe
aretioides Υ^{H2}	WAbe
- 'Bevere'	WAbe
- 'Phyllis Carter'	ECho
bryoides	WAbe
- 'Esselmont'	WAbe
'Charlson Emma'	WAbe
'Charlson Gem'	WAbe
'Charlson Jake'	WAbe
'Charlson Moonglow'	WAbe
'Charlson Petite'	WAbe
'Charlson Pip'	WAbe
'Charlson Primrose'	WAbe
'Charlson Thomas'	WAbe
'Corona' new	WAbe
curviflora	WAbe
'Emmely'	WAbe
'Eric Watson'	WAbe

'Ewesley Iota'	WAbe
'Ewesley Kappa'	WAbe
'Ewesley Theta'	WAbe
'Geist' **new**	WAbe
'Harlekin'	WAbe
janthina	WAbe
'Judith Bramley'	WAbe
'Lycaena'	WAbe
'Monika'	WAbe
'Pascal'	WAbe
'Schneeball'	WAbe
tapetodes	WAbe
- 'Brimstone'	WAbe
- 'Peter Edwards'	WAbe
'Tess'	WAbe
'Yellowstone'	WAbe

Dioon (*Zamiaceae*)

califanoi	CBrP
caputoi	CBrP
edule ♀H1	CBrP SBst SPlb
- var. ***angustifolium***	CBrP
mejiae	CBrP
merolae	CBrP
rzedowskii	CBrP
spinulosum	CBrP SBig

Dioscorea (*Dioscoreaceae*)

CC 5622	EWld
araucana	LSou
batatas	CAgr CArn LEdu
deltoidea	CExl
japonica	CAgr EShb LEdu
quinqueloba	WCru
villosa	CArn

Diosma (*Rutaceae*)

ericoides	SEND SWvt
- 'Pink Fountain'	CAbb EBee LBuc LRHS SPoG
- 'Sunset Gold'	CAbb CSpe CWGN EBee EPfP LBuc LRHS SCoo SPoG
hirsuta 'Silver Flame'	EBee

Diosphaera (*Campanulaceae*)

asperuloides	see *Trachelium asperuloides*

Diospyros (*Ebenaceae*)

austroafricana	CFil SPlb
* ***hyrcanum***	EGFP NLar
kaki (F)	CBcs CMCN EPfP MREP NLar NPla SEWo WPGP
- 'Fuyu' (F)	CAgr
- 'Kostata' (F)	CAgr
- 'Mazelii' (F)	CAgr WPGP
lotus	CAgr CBcs CMCN ESwi LEdu NLar SPlb
- (f)	CAgr
- (m)	CAgr
lycioides	SPlb
'Nikita's Gift'	CAgr
ramulosa	SPlb
rhombifolia	NLar
'Russian Beauty'	CAgr
virginiana (F)	CAgr CBcs CMCN NLar SPlb SSpi
- 'Early Golden' (F)	CAgr
- 'Meader' (F)	CAgr

Dipcadi (*Asparagaceae*)

ciliare	CLak
marlothii 'Bloemfontein'	ECho
serotinum	ECho
- subsp. ***lividum***	WPGP
viride	CLak
white-flowered	CLak

Dipelta (*Caprifoliaceae*)

floribunda ♀H4	CBcs CDoy CDul CExl CFil CJun CMCN CMac ELan EPfP LRHS MBlu MBri NLar SKHP WPGP WPat
ventricosa	CAbP CBcs CExl CFil CGHE CJun ELan EPfP LRHS MAsh MBlu NLar SChF SSpi WPGP WPat
yunnanensis	CBcs CExl CHel CJun EBee ELan EPfP LRHS NLar SKHP SSpi SWvt WPGP WPat

Diphylleia (*Berberidaceae*)

cymosa	CAby CLAP EBee GCal MRav SPhx WCot WCru
- red-marked	CDes
grayi	CLAP WCru
sinensis	CExl WCru

Dipidax see *Onixotis*

Diplacus see *Mimulus*

Dipladenia see *Mandevilla*

Diplarrena (*Iridaceae*)

§ ***latifolia***	GBBs GCal IBlr IGor LRHS WKif WPtf
- Helen Dillon's form	IBlr
moraea	CAbP CHel CMac EBee ECho GAbr GBBs GBin GCal IBlr IKil LEdu LRHS MBel NCGa NLBP WPGP WSHC
- ***minor***	IBlr
- 'Slieve Donard'	IBlr
- West Coast form	see *D. latifolia*

Diplotaxis (*Brassicaceae*)

muralis	CArn ELau WJek
tenuifolia	ELau MNHC SRms

Dipsacus (*Caprifoliaceae*)

§ ***fullonum***	CArn CHab EPfP GKev MBri MHer MNHC NMir NPri SEND SIde SRms WHer WJek WSFF
inermis	CElw CSam NBid NLar
japonicus	SKHP
- HWJ 695	SPhx WCru
pilosus	CPom
sativus	NLar
strigosus	SPhx
sylvestris	see *D. fullonum*

Dipteracanthus see *Ruellia*

Dipteronia (*Aceraceae*)

sinensis	CBcs CMCN MBri NLar WPGP

Disa (*Orchidaceae*)

aurata	NDav
Bride's Dream gx **new**	NDav
Child Safety Transvaal gx **new**	NDav
Constantia gx **new**	NDav

Diores gx	NDav
- 'Inca City' **new**	NDav
- 'Inca Gold' **new**	NDav
- 'Inca Princess' **new**	NDav
- 'Inca Warrior' **new**	NDav
Diorosa gx **new**	NDav
Foam gx **new**	NDav
Ivan Watson gx **new**	NDav
Kalahari Sands gx **new**	NDav
Kewbett gx **new**	NDav
Kewdior gx **new**	NDav
Kewensis gx 'Alice' **new**	NDav
- 'Ann' **new**	NDav
- 'May' **new**	NDav
- 'Milkmaid' **new**	NDav
- 'Ruth' **new**	NDav
Reheat gx **new**	NDav
Riette gx **new**	NDav
Sealord gx **new**	NDav
Tracey Parkinson gx **new**	NDav
tripetaloides	NDav
uniflora	NDav
- carmine-flowered **new**	NDav
- pink-flowered **new**	NDav
Unifoam gx **new**	NDav
- 'Firebird' **new**	NDav
Unilangley gx **new**	NDav
Watsonii gx 'Bramley' **new**	NDav
- 'Candy' **new**	NDav
- 'Sandra' **new**	NDav

Disanthus (*Hamamelidaceae*)

cercidifolius ♀H4	CAbP CBcs CJun CMCN CMac EPfP
	GBin GKin IArd IDee LRHS MAsh
	MBlu MBri MPkF NLar SPer SPoG
	SSpi WPGP
- 'Ena-nishiki' (v)	NLar

Discaria (*Rhamnaceae*)

chacaye	LEdu WPGP
toumatou	SVen

Diselma (*Cupressaceae*)

archeri	CDoC CKen SCoo SLim
- 'Read Dwarf'	CKen

Disphyma (*Aizoaceae*)

crassifolium	SChr

Disporopsis (*Asparagaceae*)

	B&SWJ 229 from Taiwan	WCru
	B&SWJ 1864 from Taiwan	WCru
	aspersa	CHEx CLAP CSpe EBee ECho EPPr
		EWld LEdu MAvo NBir WCru WPGP
	- tall	CBct CExl WCru
	fuscopicta	CBct CLAP EBee EPPr MAvo MPie
		WCru WWEG
	longifolia	CLAP
	- B&SWJ 5284	WCru
	- HWJ 861	CDes LEdu
	luzoniensis B&SWJ 3891	CBct CExl ESwi LEdu WCru
	'Min Shan'	CExl ELon
*	***nova***	EPPr
§	***pernyi***	Widely available
	- B&SWJ 1864	CBct EPPr MAvo
	- 'Bill Baker'	CBct EBee LEdu MAvo
	aff. ***pernyi***	WWlt
	taiwanensis	CHel IMou
	- B&SWJ 3388	CBct CHel WCru
	undulata	CBct EPPr IMou LEdu NBid WCru

Disporum (*Colchicaceae*)

	austrosinense B&SWJ 9777	LEdu WCru
	bodinieri	CBct CExl LEdu LWst WPnP
	- BWJ 8128	WCru
	- DJHC 765	WCru
	cantoniense	CBct CCon EPPr EPri LEdu LWst
		WCru XLum
	- B&L 12512	CExl CLAP
	- B&SWJ 1424	WCru
	- B&SWJ 9715	WCru
	- DJHC 98485	CLAP LEdu MMoz SKHP
I	- 'Aureovariegata'	CBct LEdu WCot
	- var. ***cantoniense*** f. ***brunneum*** B&SWJ 5290	WCru
	- var. ***multiflorum*** B&SWJ 11252	WCru
	- - B&SWJ 11291	WCru
	- var. ***sikkimense*** B&SWJ 2337	WCru
	- - B&SWJ 2358	LEdu WCru
	- var. ***y-tiense*** HWJ 1045	WCru
	hookeri	see *Prosartes hookeri*
	kawakamii B&SWJ 350	WCru
	- RWJ 10103	CBct WCru
	lanuginosum	see *Prosartes lanuginosa*
	leschenaultianum B&SWJ 9484	WCru
	- B&SWJ 9505	WCru
	leucanthum	LWst WCru
	- B&SWJ 2389	WCru
	longistylum	LEdu
	- B&SWJ 2859	WCru
	- L 1564	CBct ESwi WCru
	- 'Green Giant'	CBct CDes CExl CLAP EBee EPfP
		IFoB LEdu LSou LWst MSCN NLar
		WHil WPnP WPtf
	- 'Night Heron'	CBct CExl CLAP EBee IFoB IMou
		LEdu WCot WPnP
	lutescens	WCru
	maculatum	see *Prosartes maculata*
	megalanthum	CBct CDes CExl CLAP IFoB MMoz
		WCru
	- CD&R 2412B	CExl CLAP EPPr
	montanense B&SWJ 559	CBct LEdu WCru
	- B&SWJ 6812	WCru
	oreganum	see *Prosartes hookeri* var. *oregana*
	sessile	EBee ECho LEdu WCru
	- AGSJ 146	GBuc
	- B&SWJ 2824	WCru
I	- 'Aureovariegatum' (v)	ECho WCru
	- 'Kinga' (v)	EBee
	- f. ***macrophyllum*** B&SWJ 4316	WCru
I	- 'Robustum Variegatum' (v)	EBee
	- 'Variegatum' (v)	CAby CExl CHEx CHel CPom EBee
		ECho ELan ELon EPPr EPfP GBBs
		GMaP IMou LEdu LRHS MRav NLar
		SPhx WBor WCru WPGP WPnP
	- var. ***yakushimense***	ECho LEdu
	- yellow-margined variegated (v)	CBct
	shimadae B&SWJ 399	WCru
	smilacinum	LWst NLar WCru
	- B&SWJ 713	CBct WCru
*	- 'Aureovariegatum' (v)	LEdu WCru

- pink-flowered	WCru
smithii	see *Prosartes smithii*
taiwanense B&SWJ 1513	WCru
- B&SWJ 2018	WCru
tonkinense B&SWJ 11672	WCru
- B&SWJ 11814	WCru
- HWJ 882	WCru
trabeculatum	CBct WCru
- 'Nakafu'	IMou LEdu WCru
trachycarpum	see *Prosartes trachycarpa*
uniflorum	CAby CBct CGHE CLAP CPom ECho EPfP LEdu LRHS LWst MMHG MNrw NBid WPnP WSHC
- B&SWJ 651	CBct LEdu WCru
- B&SWJ 872	WCru
- B&SWJ 4100	WCru
viridescens	CBct EBee EPPr LEdu SKHP WCru
- B&SWJ 4598	WCru

Distylium (*Hamamelidaceae*)

myricoides	CMCN NLar
racemosum	CBcs CMac EPfP IGor IVic MBlu NLar SLPl SSta

Dittrichia (*Asteraceae*)

viscosa new	WCot

Diuranthera see *Chlorophytum*

Dizygotheca see *Schefflera*

Dobinea (*Anacardiaceae*)

vulgaris B&SWJ 2532	WCru

Dodecatheon (*Primulaceae*)

alpinum	GKev NHar
- subsp. ***alpinum***	EBee
- - NNS 02-132	GKev
amethystinum new	GKev
'Aphrodite'PBR	LLWG NLar
austrofrigidum	GKev NCGa NHar
clevelandii var. ***alba*** new	GKev
- subsp. ***insulare***	LLHF
- subsp. ***patulum***	ECho LRHS
conjugens	LLHF
cusickii	see *D. pulchellum* subsp. *cusickii*
dentatum ♀H4	CElw CPBP GKev LEdu NHar WAbe
- subsp. ***utahense***	NHar
frigidum	WAbe
§ ***hendersonii*** ♀H4	EPot
integrifolium	see *D. hendersonii*
§ ***jeffreyi***	EBee ECho EPPr GBuc GKev LEdu LRHS MNrw NCGa NLar NPnk NSum WAbe
- NNS 07-168	GKev
- NNS 08-119 new	GKev
- subsp. ***pygmaeum***	GKev
- 'Rotlicht'	EBee
* × ***lemoinei***	WAbe
§ ***meadia*** ♀H4	Widely available
- from Cedar County, USA	WAbe
- f. ***album*** ♀H4	CBro ECho EHyd ELan EPfP EPot GAbr LEdu LHop LRHS MBel MMoz MNrw NCGa NHol NLar NMyG NPnk NSum NWad SKHP SPer SWvt
- 'Aphrodite'	EPfP LSou
* - 'Goliath'	GAbr NSum
- membranaceous	WAbe
- 'Queen Victoria'	ECho GBuc LEdu NLar NPnk SKHP
- red shades	GBuc NSum SMrm
pauciflorum misapplied	see *D. pulchellum*
pauciflorum (Dur.) E. Greene	see *D. meadia*
poeticum	CPBP
- NNS 00-259	NCGa
§ ***pulchellum*** ♀H4	CBro EBee ECho EDAr GKev IBoy LHop LLWG LRHS MNrw WIce
- ***album***	ECho
§ - subsp. ***cusickii***	LEdu
- subsp. ***pulchellum*** 'Red Wings'	ECho EPot IBoy LLHF LRHS NBir NHar NLar NPnk SKHP
- ***radicatum***	see *D. pulchellum*
- 'Sooke Variety'	WAbe
radicatum	see *D. pulchellum*
redolens	GBuc
tetrandrum	see *D. jeffreyi*

Dodonaea (*Sapindaceae*)

viscosa	CBcs ECou SPlb
- (f)	ECou
- (m)	ECou
- 'Purpurea'	CBcs CDoC CExl CHGN CHel CTsd EAmu EBee ECre EHoe EUJe IVic LRHS SLim SVen

Doellingeria (*Asteraceae*)

scabra	see *Aster scaber*

Dolichos (*Papilionaceae*)

purpureus	see *Lablab purpureus*

Dombeya (*Malvaceae*)

wallichii	CCCN

Dondia see *Hacquetia*

Doodia (*Blechnaceae*)

media	CBty GBin ISha LRHS

Doronicum (*Asteraceae*)

austriacum	NBid
caucasicum	see *D. orientale*
§ ***columnae***	CBcs
cordatum	see *D. columnae*
§ × ***excelsum*** 'Harpur Crewe'	CPrp LEdu LRHS MRav NPer
'Finesse'	GCal LRHS SRms
§ 'Frühlingspracht' (d)	LRHS
'Little Leo'	CAby EBee ELan EPfP EShb GJos LRHS LSRN MBrN NLar NPri NSoo SPoG SRGP SRms WHil WRHF
§ ***orientale***	EBee ELan EPfP GJos LRHS SEND SPer SPoG SWat
- 'Leonardo'	LBuc WHar
- 'Leonardo Compact'	LPot
- 'Magnificum'	CSBt EBee EPfP GMaP LRHS MBNS MBri NEgg NGBl NMir SMrm SPoG SRms WHar WHoo
pardalianches	CArn CFis CMea MMuc WRHF
plantagineum 'Excelsum'	see *D.* × *excelsum* 'Harpur Crewe'
Spring Beauty	see *D.* 'Frühlingspracht'

Doryanthes (*Doryanthaceae*)

excelsa	CHEx
palmeri	CBrP

Dorycnium see *Lotus*

Douglasia see *Androsace*

	vitaliana	see *Vitaliana primuliflora*

Dovyalis (*Salicaceae*)

	caffra (F)	XBlo

Doxantha see *Macfadyena*

Draba (*Brassicaceae*)

	acaulis	WAbe
	aizoides	ECho EDAr GKev LRHS MAsh SPlb SRms XLum
	aizoon	see *D. lasiocarpa*
	bruniifolia	EWes
	bryoides	see *D. rigida* var. *bryoides*
	'Buttermilk'	WAbe
	cretica	EDAr
	cusickii	GKev
	densifolia	IFoB
	fladnizensis	LLHF
	var. ***pattersonii***	
	imbricata	see *D. rigida* var. *imbricata*
	'John Saxton'	WAbe
§	***lasiocarpa***	XLum
	longisiliqua ♀H2	LLHF WAbe
	mollissima	WAbe
	- 'Göteborg'	EPot
	oligosperma	EDAr IFoB
	oreades	CPBP
	ossetica	WAbe
	polytricha	WAbe
§	***rigida*** var. ***bryoides***	WThu
*	- var. ***imbricata***	NSla
	- - f. ***compacta***	EPot
	rosularis	EDAr
	× ***salomonii***	EPot
	scardica	see *D. lasiocarpa*
	ventosa	WAbe
	yunnanensis	WAbe

Dracaena ✿ (*Asparagaceae*)

	cochinchinensis	SPlb
	draco ♀H1	CArn EShb SPlb WCot XBlo
	fragrans Deremensis Group	XBlo
	indivisa	see *Cordyline indivisa*
	'Lemon Lime Tips'	XBlo
	marginata (v) ♀H1	XBlo
	- 'Tricolor' (v) ♀H1	XBlo
	stricta	see *Cordyline stricta*

Dracocephalum (*Lamiaceae*)

	argunense	SBch SPhx SRms
*	- 'Album'	GKev
	- 'Blue Carpet'	LEdu NLar
	- 'Fuji Blue'	CExl EDAr EPfP EWes LRHS NBre SPoG WIce
	- 'Fuji White'	CExl EBee SPhx SPoG
	austriacum	SBrt
	botryoides	LLHF SPhx
	forrestii	EBee GKev MAvo
	aff. ***forrestii***	LLHF
	grandiflorum	GJos LLHF MMHG SBHP SBch SBrt SPhx XLum
	- 'Altai Blue'	LRHS
	hemsleyanum	LLHF
	isabellae	LRHS
	mairei	see *D. renatii*
	nutans	LRHS
	peregrinum	SBrt
	- 'Blue Dragon'	SPhx
	prattii	see *Nepeta prattii*
§	***renatii***	LLHF SPhx
	rupestre	EBee SPhx
	ruyschiana	ELan EWes LRHS MMHG MRav SPhx
	- 'Blue Moon'	NLar
	sibiricum	see *Nepeta sibirica*
*	***tataricum***	LRHS
	virginicum	see *Physostegia virginiana*
	wendelboi	NBir

Dracunculus (*Araceae*)

	canariensis	WCot
	muscivorus	see *Helicodiceros muscivorus*
§	***vulgaris***	CAby CHel CHid CPom EBee ECho EPfP EPot ESwi EUJe GKev LRHS MMoz MRav SDix SEND SMad SPlb WCot

Dregea (*Apocynaceae*)

	sinensis	CBcs CCCN CHel CHll CRHN ELan EPfP EShb EWes LRHS MOWG MRav SEND SKHP SPer SPoG WPGP WSHC
	- 'Brockhill Silver'	LRHS SKHP
	- 'Variegata' (v)	EWes

Drepanostachyum (*Poaceae*)

	falconeri J.J.N. Campbell. ex D. McClintock	see *Himalayacalamus falconeri*, *Himalayacalamus falconeri* 'Damarapa'
	hookerianum	see *Himalayacalamus hookerianus*
§	***khasianum***	CExl WPGP

Drimia (*Asparagaceae*)

	angustifolia ambig.	ECho
	anomala	CLak
	basutica	CLak
	elata	CLak
	involuta	CLak
	mzimvubuensis	CLak
	sphaerocephala	CLak
	uniflora	CLak

Drimiopsis (*Asparagaceae*)

	maculata	LToo MPie WCot

Drimys (*Winteraceae*)

	andina	CExl EBee EPfP
	aromatica	see *D. lanceolata*
	colorata	see *Pseudowintera colorata*
	granadensis	WCru
	var. ***grandiflora*** B&SWJ 10777	
§	***lanceolata***	Widely available
	- (f)	ECou EUJe SPer
	- (m)	CDoC ECou SPer
	- 'Mount Wellington'	GCal
	- 'Red Spice'	EPfP ESwi
	- 'Suzette' (v)	LRHS MBlu
*	***latifolia***	CBcs CHEx IDee
	winteri ♀H4	Widely available
§	- var. ***chilensis***	CExl EPfP LRHS SSpi WCru WPGP
	- Latifolia Group	see *D. winteri* var. *chilensis*

Drosanthemum (*Aizoaceae*)

hispidum	ECho EHyd ELan EPfP LRHS MAsh SBHP SPlb SPoG WAbe WNew
speciosum	ECho
* ***sutherlandii***	ECho

Drosera ✿ (*Droseraceae*)

admirabilis	CHew
aliciae	CHew EECP
andersoniana	EFEx
androsacea	CHew
ascendens	CHew
binata	CHew EECP
§ - subsp. ***dichotoma***	CHew
- 'Extrema'	CHew
- 'Multifida'	CHew
browniana	EFEx
bulbigena	EFEx
bulbosa subsp. ***bulbosa***	EFEx
- subsp. ***major***	EFEx
callistos	CHew
capensis	CHew SPlb
- 'Albino'	CHew EECP
dichotoma	see *D. binata* subsp. *dichotoma*
dichrosepala	CHew EECP
echinoblastus	CHew
enodes	CHew
ericksoniae	CHew
erythrorhiza	EFEx
- subsp. ***collina***	EFEx
- subsp. ***erythrorhiza***	CHew EFEx
- subsp. ***magna***	EFEx
- subsp. ***squamosa***	EFEx
filiformis var. ***filiformis***	CHew EECP
gigantea	EFEx
graniticola	EFEx
helodes	CHew
heterophylla	EFEx
lasiantha	CHew
leioblastus	CHew
loureiroi	EFEx
macrantha	EFEx
- subsp. ***macrantha***	EFEx
macrophylla subsp. ***macrophylla***	EFEx
mannii	CHew
marchantii subsp. ***prophylla***	EFEx
menziesii subsp. ***basifolia***	EFEx
- subsp. ***menziesii***	EFEx
- subsp. ***thysanosepala***	EFEx
modesta	EFEx
nidiformis	CHew
orbiculata	EFEx
paleacea subsp. ***trichocaulis***	CHew
peltata	EFEx
platypoda	EFEx
pulchella	CHew
pycnoblasta	CHew
pygmaea	CHew
ramellosa	EFEx
roseana	CHew
rosulata	EFEx
rotundifolia	WHer
salina	EFEx
sargentii	CHew
scorpioides	CHew EECP
slackii	CHew
stelliflora	CHew
stolonifera subsp. ***compacta***	EFEx
- subsp. ***humilis***	EFEx
- subsp. ***porrecta***	EFEx
- subsp. ***rupicola***	EFEx
- subsp. ***stolonifera***	EFEx
tubaestylus	EFEx
zonaria	EFEx

Drosophyllum (*Drosophyllaceae*)

lusitanicum	CHew

Dryandra (*Proteaceae*)

formosa	SPlb

Dryas (*Rosaceae*)

drummondii	ECho LLHF WAbe
integrifolia 'Greenland Green'	WAbe
octopetala 🏆^{H4}	CArn CMea ECho EHyd GJos GKev LHop LRHS MWat NChi SPoG SRms SWvt WAbe WHil
- subsp. ***hookeriana***	LLHF
§ - 'Minor' 🏆^{H4}	EPot WAbe
× ***suendermannii*** 🏆^{H4}	CMea EBee EPfP EPot GMaP NHar NSla SBch WAbe
tenella misapplied	see *D. octopetala* 'Minor'

Dryopteris ✿ (*Dryopteridaceae*)

aemula	EFer SRms
§ ***affinis*** 🏆^{H4}	CBty CLAP CMac EPfP ERod GMaP LBuc LRHS MCot MGos MMoz NPri SPer SPoG SRms WCot WFib WShi WWEG XLum
- subsp. ***affinis***	WSpi
§ - subsp. ***borreri***	SRms
- subsp. ***cambrensis***	ISha
- - 'Crispa Barnes'	WPGP
- - 'Insubrica'	EFer
- 'Congesta'	CLAP WWEG
- 'Congesta Cristata'	CLAP EFer GMaP SRot
- Crispa Group	CLAP EHon GBBs MMoz WSpi WWEG
§ - 'Crispa Gracilis' 🏆^{H4}	CKel CLAP ELan ERod GBin ISha MMoz NBir NEgg NMyG WWEG
* - 'Crispa Gracilis Congesta'	CBty CWCL NGdn NWad WCot WFib WPat
§ - 'Cristata' 🏆^{H4}	Widely available
- 'Cristata Angustata' 🏆^{H4}	CBty CLAP EFer ELan EPfP MMoz NBid NGdn NHol SRms WBor WFib WMoo WPGP WRHF
- 'Cristata The King'	see *D. affinis* 'Cristata'
- 'Grandiceps Askew'	EFer SRms WFib
- 'Pinderi'	CBty CLAP EBee GBin ISha NMyG SRms WWEG
- Polydactyla Group	CLAP WSpi
- - 'Polydactyla Dadds'	CBty CLAP LLHF NLar NMyG SEND WWEG
- - 'Polydactyla Mapplebeck' 🏆^{H4}	CLAP NBid SRms WFib
- 'Revolvens'	CLAP EFer
atrata misapplied	see *D. cycadina*
atrata (Wall. ex Kunze) Ching	CDTJ CKel CWCL EWTr SPoG XLum
× ***australis***	CDes CLAP ISha
austriaca	see *D. dilatata*

	bissetiana	ISha
	blanfordii	WPGP
	- from Kashmir	ISha
	borreri	see *D. affinis* subsp. *borreri*
	buschiana	CBty CDTJ CLAP EBee MRav NLar WCot WWEG
	carthusiana	CLAP EFer GBin NLar WPtf WSpi XLum
	- 'Cristata'	EFer
	celsa	ISha
	championii	CCCN CLAP ISha LRHS
	clintoniana	CLAP EFer GBin LRHS MMoz NMyG WCot WPGP
	× ***complexa***	CBty ISha
	- 'Stablerae'	CLAP EFer GBin MWhi WFib WPGP
	- 'Stablerae' crisped	NMyG WFib
	coreanomontana	CBty
	crassirhizoma	CCCN CKel CLAP EBee GBin ISha LRHS MMoz NMyG WSpi
	cristata	CLAP CWCL EBee EPfP WMoo WSpi XLum
§	***cycadina*** 🏆H4	CLAP EBee EFer ELan EPPr EPfP ERod EShb EUJe GBin ISha LRHS MBri MGos MMoz MWat NBid NBir NMyG WFib WMoo WPnP
	cystolepidota **new**	EFer
§	***dilatata*** 🏆H4	EFer ELan EPfP ERod LRHS MRav SRms WFib WHal WShi WSpi
	- 'Crispa Whiteside' 🏆H4	CBty CLAP CWCL EBee EFer EPfP ERod LBMP LRHS MBri MMoz MWhi NLar SHil SPlb WCot WFib WMoo WPGP WPat WSpi WWEG
	- 'Cristata'	WSpi
	- 'Grandiceps'	CLAP CMac EFer WFib
	- 'Jimmy Dyce'	CLAP ISha
	- 'Lepidota Crispa Cristata'	CLAP EBee WPat
	- 'Lepidota Cristata' 🏆H4	CBty CLAP CWCL ELan EPPr ERod NGdn NMyG SRms WFib WMoo
	- 'Lepidota Grandiceps'	CLAP
*	- 'Recurvata'	CLAP ISha LLHF NLar
	erythrosora 🏆H4	Widely available
	- 'Brilliance'	CCCN CLAP GQue ISha LRHS LSou NLar SMrm WCot
	- var. ***koidzumiana***	ISha
	- var. ***prolifica*** 🏆H4	CBty CKel CLAP EBee ELan EPfP GMaP ISha LRHS MGos MMoz NBir NEgg NLar NPri SPoG WFib WPat WSpi WWEG
	filix-mas 🏆H4	CSBt CTri CWCL ELan EPfP ERod GMaP LAst LEdu LRHS MCot MMoz MMuc MRav MWat NHol SEND SGol SPer SRms WFib WSFF WShi WSpi WWEG XLum
	- 'Angustata Cristata'	WSpi
	- 'Barnesii'	CLAP CWCL EFer ERod GBin ISha LRHS MMuc NLar SGol SHil SPlb WWEG
	- 'Crispa'	CBty CLAP EHon LRHS SGol SRms WFib WSpi
	- 'Crispa Congesta'	see *D. affinis* 'Crispa Gracilis'
	- 'Crispa Cristata'	CBty CLAP CWCL EBee EFer ELan EPfP ERod EUJe GMaP IKil LHop LRHS MBri NBid NBir SEND SPoG SRms WFib WGor WWEG XLum
	- 'Crispatissima'	EBee
	- 'Cristata' 🏆H4	CLAP EBee EFer ELan EPfP LPot MJak MMoz NMyG NOrc SEND SRms WMoo
	- Cristata Group	EFer
*	- - 'Cristata Grandiceps'	EFer
	- - 'Cristata Jackson'	CLAP MWhi SPlb
	- - 'Cristata Martindale'	CLAP NBid NMyG SRms WFib
	- - 'Fred Jackson'	CLAP WFib
	- 'Depauperata'	CLAP WPGP
	- 'Euxinensis'	CLAP
	- 'Furcans'	CLAP EBee
	- 'Grandiceps Wills' 🏆H4	NBid WFib
	- 'Linearis'	EFer EHon ELan ISha LAst MCot MGos MWhi SRms WFib
	- 'Linearis Congesta'	WPGP
	- 'Linearis Polydactyla'	CBty CDes CHel CLAP CMac CWCL EFer ELan EPPr EPfP LRHS MMoz MMuc MRav NGdn NHol NMyG SBod SEND SPoG WMoo WPnP WPtf WSpi XLum
	- 'Parsley'	CLAP ISha
*	- Polydactyla Group	MGos MRav MWat NEgg
I	- 'Revolvens'	MWhi WFib
	goldieana	CDTJ CLAP EBee EFer EWTr GMaP ISha LRHS NBid NBir NLar NMyG WFib WMoo WPnP WSpi WWEG XLum
	hirtipes misapplied	see *D. cycadina*
	intermedia	ISha
	labordei	ISha LRHS
	lacera	ISha
	lepidopoda	CBty GLin
	ludoviciana	CBty ISha
	marginalis	CDTJ CKel CLAP GBin LRHS MMoz NLar WMoo WSpi
	pacifica	CLAP
	paleacea	CLAP
	pseudofilix-mas	ISha
	pseudomas	see *D. affinis*
	× ***remota***	ISha
	× ***separabilis***	ISha
	sieboldii	CBty CCon CLAP CWCL EFer ELan ERod EShb EUJe ISha LRHS NBid NBir NCGa NGdn NLar NMyG SEND SRms WMoo WPGP WWEG XLum
	stewartii	CLAP LLHF NLar WWEG
	tokyoensis	CDTJ CKel CLAP GBin ISha LRHS MMoz NLar NMyG WPGP WSpi
	uniformis	CLAP EFer
	wallichiana 🏆H4	Widely available
	- F&M 107	WPGP

Duchesnea (*Rosaceae*)

	chrysantha	see *D. indica*
§	***indica***	LEdu MRav SEND WMoo WOut XLum
§	- 'Harlequin' (v)	CExl EBee
*	- 'Snowflake' (v)	WMoo
	- 'Variegata'	see *D. indica* 'Harlequin'

Dugaldia (*Asteraceae*)

	hoopesii	see *Hymenoxys hoopesii*

Dulichium (*Cyperaceae*)

	arundinaceum	LLWG
	- 'Tigress'	LLWG

Dunalia (*Solanaceae*)

	australis	see *Iochroma australe*
	- blue-flowered	see *Iochroma australe* 'Bill Evans'
	- white-flowered	see *Iochroma australe* 'Andean Snow'

Duranta (*Verbenaceae*)

§ ***erecta***	CCCN CHll EShb
§ - 'Geisha Girl'	CCCN EShb
- 'Sapphire Swirl'	see *D. erecta* 'Geisha Girl'
- 'Variegata' (v)	CCCN EShb
- white-flowered **new**	SVen
plumieri	see *D. erecta*
repens	see *D. erecta*
serratifolia	CCCN

Duvernoia see *Justicia*

Dyckia (*Bromeliaceae*)

brevifolia **new**	WCot
'Cherry Coke' **new**	WCot
frigida	EGri WCot WGrn
leptostachya	WCot WGrn
marnier-lapostollei	WCot
'Morris Hobbs'	WCot
remotiflora	CBrP EGri SChr
velascana	EGri

Dypsis (*Arecaceae*)

§ ***decaryi***	CCCN EAmu XBlo
decipiens	CBrP
lutescens ♀H1	MBri XBlo

Dysosma see *Podophyllum*

E

Ecballium (*Cucurbitaceae*)

elaterium	CArn CDTJ CFil LEdu SIde WPGP

Eccremocarpus (*Bignoniaceae*)

scaber	CBcs CWCL EBee ELan EPfP GKev LBMP LHop LRHS MBri MNrw NPer SEND SLim
- 'Carmineus'	EPfP EWld
- 'Coccineus' **new**	EUJe
- cream-flowered	ESwi NLar
- orange-flowered	ESwi
- red-flowered	NLar SPoG
- 'Tangerine' **new**	CSpe
- 'Tresco Cream'	CSpe

Echeandia (*Asparagaceae*)

formosa B&SWJ 9147	WCru

Echeveria ✿ (*Crassulaceae*)

affinis	CDTJ EUJe SRot
'Afterglow' **new**	CSuc
agavoides ♀H1	CDTJ MRav WCot
albicans	CSuc SPlb
amoena	CDoC
* 'Black Knight'	CDoC
* 'Black Prince'	CAbb CDTJ CDes CDoC ELan NPer SPet SPlb SRot WCot WPGP
'Blue Boy'	CDoC
'Blue Prince'	CDoC
'Blue Waves'	CSuc WCot
* ***cana***	CDTJ CDoC EWll SRot
cante	SPlb
carnicolor	CSuc
- RE 37	CDoC
'Chrissy 'n' Ryan'	CDoC
coccinea	ELan
colorata	WCot
- f. ***brandtii***	CDoC
colorata × ***peacockii*** RE 240	CDoC
'Corymbosa'	WCot
'Crûg Ice'	WCru
'Curly Locks'	WCot
cuspidata × ***setosa*** var. ***ciliata*** **new**	CSuc
'Derenceana'	CDoC
× ***derosa***	CDTJ EPfP
'Dondo' **new**	CSuc
'Doris Taylor'	CSuc MSCN
'Duchess of Nuremberg'	CDoC CHel EUJe SMrm SPlb SRot
elegans ♀H1	CDTJ CDoC CHEx CHel EPfP EUJe LSou SAPC SPlb WNew
'Galaxy Mars' (Galaxy Hybrids Series)	CDoC
'Ghost Buster' **new**	WPGP
§ ***gibbiflora*** var. ***metallica*** ♀H1	EPfP
× ***gilva***	CSuc
* - 'Red' ♀H1	WCot
glauca Baker	see *E. secunda* var. *glauca*
harmsii ♀H1	CDoC CSuc WGwG
'Hens and Chicks'	CHEx
hyalina RE 614	CDoC
'Ileen'	CDoC
'J. van Keppel'	CDoC
lilacina	CDoC EUJe SMrm SPlb SRot WPGP
lutea RE 502	CDoC
'Mahogany'	CDoC WCot WGrn
'Mauna Loa'	CAbb CDTJ CDoC EBee EWes WCot WGrn
maxonii B&SWJ 10396	WCru
'Meridian'	CHEx
'Mexico City'	CDoC
minima **new**	CSuc
montana B&SWJ 10277	WCru
- RE 431	CDoC
multicaulis	CSuc MSCN
nodulosa	CSuc WCot
nuda **new**	CSuc
'Paul Bunyon'	CSuc
peacockii	MHer MSCN SMrm SPet SPlb WNew
'Perle d'Azur'	CHEx
'Perle von Nürnberg' ♀H1	CAbb SMad SPet SPlb
prolifica	CSuc
pulidonis ♀H1	CDoC EPfP MHer WCot
purpusorum	SPlb
'Ramillette' **new**	CSuc
'Ron Evans'	CDoC
rosea	WCot
runyonii 'Topsy Turvy'	CDTJ CDoC CHEx EPfP SPet SRot
secunda	CAbb SPlb
§ - var. ***glauca*** ♀H1	CDTJ CDes CDoC CHEx EAmu ELan EShb NBir WPGP
* - - 'Gigantea'	NDov NPer WCot WPGP
setosa ♀H1	CDTJ EPfP WCot
- var. ***ciliata***	EShb
- var. ***deminuta***	CSuc
shaviana	CDTJ EUJe SRot WCot
- RE 581	CDoC
subsessilis	WCot
- RE 163	CDoC
'Violet Queen'	CDoC

Echinacea ✿ (*Asteraceae*)

§ 'Adam Saul'	STPC
§ 'After Midnight' PBR (Big Sky Series)	CBcs EBee ECtt IBoy IPot LRHS NLar
'Aloha' **new**	NLar
'Amazing Dream' **new**	ECtt IBoy
angustifolia	CArn CHel EPfP GPoy LRHS MHer MHoo SPhx WJek
§ 'Art's Pride' PBR	EPfP LRHS LSRN MGos MPie MRav NBir NEgg NPnk
'Coral Reef'	ECtt
'Cranberry Cupcake' (d) **new**	ECtt
Crazy Pink	see *E.* 'Adam Saul'
Crazy White	see *E.* 'Noam Saul'
'Daydream' **new**	ECtt LSou
Double Scoop Bubblegum = 'Balscblum' **new**	MAsh
Double Scoop Orangeberry = 'Balscoberr' **new**	WHlf
'Emily Saul'	see *E.* 'After Midnight'
'Evan Saul'	see *E.* 'Sundown'
'Firebird'	ECtt LRHS MNrw SGbt
'Flame Thrower'	CWGN EBee ECtt LRHS NLar
'Gemini Pink' **new**	MBri
'Green Envy' PBR	CBcs CWGN ECtt ELan EPfP EWll GQue IBoy LRHS LSou MAvo MBNS MBel MBri MNrw NEgg NLar NPnk NSti SKHP SMrm SPer SPoG WCot
'Green Jewel'	CWGN EBee ECtt EUJe LRHS MBel MBri MCot NDov SMrm WCot
'Guava Ice' **new**	LLHF
§ 'Harvest Moon' PBR (Big Sky Series)	CHel CHid CKno CMac CWGN EBee ECtt EPfP EWTr LBMP LHop LRHS LSRN MBel MBri MCot NDov NEgg NPnk NSti SKHP SMad SMrm SPer SPhx SPoG SWvt WCot WMnd WWEG
'Heavenly Dream'	ELon WWEG
'Hot Lava'	CWGN ECtt LHop LSou NDov SPoG
'Hot Papaya' (d)	CWCL CWGN ECtt EWll IBoy IPot LLHF LRHS LSou MBNS MBri MHol SMad SPer WCot
'Hot Summer' PBR	CBcs CHel CPar EBee ECtt IPot LRHS MBri MPie NCGa NDov NLar SGbt SPoG STPC
'Irresistible' (d)	CWGN EBee IPot MBri NPnk
'Jupiter' (Big Sky Series) **new**	STPC
'Katie Saul'	see *E.* 'Summer Sky'
'Mac 'n' Cheese'	LRHS WCot
'Mama Mia'	CPar ECtt NLar SGbt
Mango Meadowbrite = 'CBG Cone3'	EBee EPfP LRHS SPoG
'Marmalade' **new**	CWGN LLHF LSou
'Matthew Saul'	see *E.* 'Harvest Moon'
'Maui Sunshine'	ECtt SHar SMad
'Meditation' **new**	WCot
§ 'Noam Saul' **new**	STPC
Orange Meadowbrite	see *E.* 'Art's Pride'
pallida	CAby CArn CKno CMea CPrp CSpe CWib EBee ELan EPfP EPri EShb GPoy LHop LRHS MHoo MNFA MWhi NDov NGdn NPri SKHP SPer SPhx SWvt WJek WPtf WWEG XLum
- 'Hula Dancer'	CHel NGdn NPri SHar SPhx WWEG
paradoxa	CAby CArn CHid CNec EBee ELan EPfP EPri GPoy LDai LHop LRHS LSRN MCot NGdn NPri SMrm SPav SPhx SPlb SWvt WWEG XLum
- var. ***paradoxa***	MHoo
- 'Yellow Mellow'	EPfP
paradoxa* × *purpurea **new**	IBoy
'Piccolino'	CAbP CWGN EBee ECtt LLHF MHol MPie WCot
'Pink Mist' (Mistical Series)	EBee
Pixie Meadowbrite = 'CBG Cone 2'	CAbP CDes CWGN ECtt GQue IKil LRHS SHar WCot WPGP
§ ***purpurea***	Widely available
- 'Alaska' PBR	EBee IBoy LRHS LSou NGdn NLar SGol
- 'Alba'	EPfP LBMP LRHS SHil SMrm WCot XLum
- 'Augustkönigin'	CKno EBee LRHS MNrw NBir NDov
- 'Avalanche' PBR	EBee ELon LRHS LSou
- 'Baby Swan Pink'	LRHS SPhx
- 'Baby Swan White'	EHyd ELon GBin LBMP LRHS NLar WCot WWEG
- Bressingham hybrids	CHel CNec LRHS MRav MWat SMrm SPer
- 'Catharina' PBR **new**	EBee
- 'Coconut Lime' PBR	CWGN ECtt EPfP LRHS LSou NPnk
- Doppelganger	see *E. purpurea* 'Doubledecker'
§ - 'Doubledecker'	CHel CWCL EPfP GBin IBoy LLHF LRHS MHol NGdn NPri NSoo SBod SGbt SGol SWat XLum
- Elton Knight = 'Elbrook' PBR ♀H3	EBee ECtt LRHS LSRN MBri SDix SKHP SRkn STPC SWvt
- 'Fancy Frills'	EBee ECtt LSou
- 'Fatal Attraction' PBR	CBcs CMea CPar CWGN ECtt ELon EPfP GQue IBoy IPot LBMP LRHS LSRN LSou MAsh MAvo MBNS MBel MBri MNrw MRav NDov NEgg NPnk SPad SPer SPhx SPoG SWvt WCot
- 'Fragrant Angel' PBR	CHid CMac EBee ECtt ELon EPfP LHop LRHS LSRN MBel MCot NLar SKHP SPoG SRkn SWat SWvt WCot
- 'Green Eyes'	ECtt NLar
- 'Green Jewel' PBR	GBin LSou SGbt SGol
- 'Happy Star' **new**	LRHS MAsh
- 'Hope' PBR	CPar EBee ECtt LRHS LSou MAsh MMHG NLar WCAu
- 'Jade'	CAbP EBee ECtt GQue LRHS LSRN LSou MBNS MCot NEgg NGdn NLar NPnk SWat
- 'Kim's Knee High' PBR	CKno CMea EBee ECtt ELan EPfP GMaP LBMP LRHS LSou MBel MCot MRav NBir NGdn NLar NPnk SGol SPer SWat SWvt WCot WPGP
- 'Kim's Mop Head'	CKno CMea ECtt ELan ELon EPfP EWes LRHS LSou MCot MRav NGdn NLar NOrc NPnk WCot
§ - 'Leuchtstern'	CKno EHyd EPfP LRHS NBir NGdn SWat WWEG XLum
- 'Lilliput' PBR	ECtt NLar
- 'Little Giant'	ELon
- 'Little Magnus' PBR	CHel CKno LRHS MAsh SPoG
- 'Lucky Star'	EPfP LRHS NCGa SBea SPhx WCFE
- 'Magnus' ♀H4	Widely available
- 'Magnus Superior'	CAby CHel CNec LRHS NDov SBea SPhx WHoo

- 'Mars'	EBee
- 'Maxima'	CAbP ECtt LRHS MNrw WWEG
- 'Meringue'PBR	IBoy LRHS SPoG
- 'Merlot'PBR	ECtt LRHS LSou
- 'Milkshake'PBR **new**	CWGN LSou
- 'Mistral'	LRHS
- 'Pica Bella'	CWGN EBee ECtt EPfP LRHS LSou MSCN NLar
- 'Pink Double Delight'PBR	EBee LHop LRHS MRav NGdn SWat WHlf
- 'Pink Glow'	NDov
- 'Pink Poodle'PBR	CPar EPri IBoy
- 'Pink Sorbet'PBR **new**	NLar
- 'Polar Breeze' **new**	EBee LRHS
- PowWow Wild Berry = 'Pas702917' (PowWow Series) **new**	LAst LRHS
- 'Prairie Splendor'	EBee EPfP LRHS MHol SPhx
- 'Primadonna Deep Rose'	IFro LEdu NBre NGBl SRot SVic
- Primadonna (mixed)	ELon
- 'Primadonna White'	CHel EHyd LEdu LRHS NPri SRot
- 'Purity'PBR	ECtt LRHS
- 'Razzmatazz'PBR (d)	CAbP CMac CWGN EBee ECtt ELan EUJe EWes IBoy LHop MBri MGos MNrw MPie MRav NEgg NGdn NPnk NSti SGol SPer SWat SWvt WCot
- 'Red Baron' **new**	MSCN
- 'Red Knee High'	ECtt LRHS MBri
- 'Robert Bloom'	CAbP EBee ECtt GQue LHop MRav NBir SWvt
- 'Rubinglow'	ECtt IBoy LSou MTis NBir NLar SWvt WCAu
- 'Rubinstern' ♀H4	Widely available
- 'Ruby Giant' ♀H4	CCon CKno CWGN ECtt ELan EUJe GBin GMaP IBoy LHop LRHS LSRN LSou MBel MCot MGos MNFA MTis NEgg NLar NPri NSti SGbt SMad SPer SPoG STes WCot WWEG
- 'The King'	NGdn NLar
- 'Verbesserter Leuchtstern'	NLar
- 'Vintage Wine'PBR	CCon CKno CMac CWGN EBee ECtt ELan ELon EPfP GAbr GMaP GQue IKil LPla LRHS LSou MBel MNrw MTis NEgg NLar NPnk NSti SPer SPoG SWvt WCot WWEG
- 'Virgin'PBR	EBee IPot MAvo NCGa NDov NLar SPhx
- 'White Lustre'	EPfP NBre SRms
- 'White Snow' **new**	CHel
- 'White Swan'	Widely available
'Quills and Thrills' (Prairie Pillars Series) **new**	IPot
'Raspberry Tart'	ECtt LRHS LSou
'Secret Lust' (d)	ECtt LSou
'Secret Passion'	CWGN ECtt SGbt
'Secret Romance' **new**	LSou
simulata	SPhx
'Solar Flare' (Big Sky Series) **new**	CPar MBri
(Sombrero Series) 'Sombrero Hot Coral' **new**	MAsh
- 'Sombrero Salsa Red' **new**	MAsh
- 'Sombrero Sandy Yellow' **new**	MAsh
'Starlight'	see *E. purpurea* 'Leuchtstern'
'Strawberry Shortcake'	EBee LHop WHlf
'Summer Breeze' **new**	NDov
'Summer Cocktail'	EBee IPot NCGa
'Summer Passion' **new**	SGol
'Summer Salsa'	CAbP EBee IPot LLHF MHol MPie SMrm WCot
§ 'Summer Sky'PBR (Big Sky Series)	ECtt IPot LRHS MBNS NDov NLar NPnk SPhx
'Summer Sun'	EBee NCGa NLar
§ 'Sundown'PBR (Big Sky Series)	CMac CPar CSev CWCL EBee ECtt EPfP IPot LRHS MBNS MRav MWhi NLar NPnk SGbt SPoG SRkn WCAu
'Sunrise'PBR (Big Sky Series)	Widely available
'Sunset'PBR (Big Sky Series)	CAbP ECtt ELon EWes GBin LDai LLHF LRHS LSRN MBNS MBri MGos NEgg NPnk SMrm SPoG SWat SWvt
'Tangerine Dream'	ECtt LSou NLar
tennesseensis	CArn SPhx WPGP
- 'Rocky Top'	CBcs CHel EBee EPfP LRHS MNFA SKHP SPhx
'Tiki Torch'PBR	CMea CPar CWGN EBee ECtt ELon EWes LRHS MAvo MTis NLar NPri SMrm SPer SPoG SRkn WCot WWEG
'Tomato Soup'PBR	Widely available
'Twilight'PBR (Big Sky Series)	EBee ECtt LRHS LSou MBri MNrw NOrc NPnk
'White Mist' (Mistical Series)	EBee

Echinops (*Asteraceae*)

RCB AM -14	WCot
RCB/TQ H-2	WCot
albus	see *E.* 'Nivalis'
§ ***bannaticus***	CBcs CSBt NBid WWEG
* - 'Albus'	EBee
- 'Blue Globe'	CMHG CMea CSev EBee EHoe ELan ELon EPfP EShb GCal IBoy LRHS LSRN MGos MHol NCGa NChi NGdn NHol SPhx SPoG WMnd WWEG XLum
- 'Star Frost'	EBee ELan EPfP GQue LRHS NLar SMrm SPhx
- 'Taplow Blue' ♀H4	Widely available
commutatus	see *E. exaltatus*
§ ***exaltatus***	LPla NBir
maracandicus	EBee GCal WCot
§ 'Nivalis'	CBre SEND
* ***perringii***	GCal
ritro misapplied	see *E. bannaticus*
§ ***ritro*** L. ♀H4	CElw CMea CTri CWib ECtt ELan ELon EPfP GJos LAst LRHS MArl MBel MCot MMuc MWat NBro NGBl NPri SEND SMrm SPer SPlb SPoG SRms SWvt WBrk XLum XSen
- 'Blue Cloud'	LRHS
- subsp. ***ruthenicus*** ♀H4	ELan EWTr MNFA MRav
- - 'Platinum Blue'	ECtt ELon EWTr LRHS NEgg SPet SPhx WMnd
- 'Veitch's Blue' misapplied	see *E. ritro* L.
- 'Veitch's Blue'	Widely available
sphaerocephalus	NBir SMrm SPlb
- 'Arctic Glow'	CMHG CMac CPou ECtt EHoe EHyd ELan EPfP GBin GMaP LRHS MBri MCot MWhi NDov NGdn NLar SPer SPlb SPoG SWvt WCAu WMnd WWEG XLum
terscheckii	EAmu
tjanschanicus	LDai LRHS WWEG

Echinospartum (*Papilionaceae*)

sp.	CArn

Echium (*Boraginaceae*)

	acanthocarpum	XPde
	aculeatum	XPde
	- 'Bicolor'	XPde
	- 'Rosea'	XPde
	boissieri	CCCN ELan WOut XPde
	brevirame	XPde
	callithyrsum	XPde
§	***candicans*** ♀H2-3	CAbb CBcs CCCN CCon CHEx CSpe EBee ECre ELan EShb IBoy IDee SAPC SEND SVen XPde
	- 'Ciel'	XPde
	- 'Marine'	XPde
§	- 'Rouge'	XPde
	decaisnei	XPde
	subsp. ***decaisnei***	
	famarae	XPde
	fastuosum	see *E. candicans*
	gentianoides	SPlb SVen XPde
	- 'Dark Globe'	XPde
	- 'Maryvonne'	XPde
	- 'Pablina'	XPde
	giganteum	XPde
	handiense	XPde
	italicum	CCCN WOut XPde
	lusitanicum	CCCN
	- subsp. ***polycaulon***	XPde
	onosmifolium	XPde
	pininana ♀H2-3	CAbb CBcs CBct CDoC CHEx CPla CTsd EAmu ECre EGri ELan EUJe EWll IBoy IDee LRHS SAPC SBst SChr SEND SIde SMad SPav SVen WKif XPde
	- 'Snow Tower'	CCCN CDTJ CPla EAmu ELan SBst SMad SVen XPde
	'Pink Fountain'	CCCN CDTJ CPla ECre ELan SBst XPde
	plantagineum	XPde
	rosulatum	CCCN XPde
	russicum	CAby CArn CBct CCCN CFis CSpe EBee EWll IBoy IDee LHop LRHS MHoo MSpe SPad SPav SPhx SPlb WCot XPde
	simplex	XPde
	strictum	CCCN XPde
	sventenii	SPlb XPde
	tuberculatum	SPhx WMoo XPde
	vulgare	CArn CBct CCCN CHab ELan MHer MHoo MNHC NLar NMir NPri SBch SIde WHer WHfH WJek WSFF
	- 'Blue Bedder' ♀H4	SPhx WSFF
	- Drake's form	SPhx
	webbii	MMHG XPde
	wildpretii ♀H2-3	CCCN CCon CDTJ CPla ELan EUJe SPlb SVen XPde
	- subsp. ***wildpretii***	SPav

Edgeworthia (*Thymelaeaceae*)

§	***chrysantha***	CBcs CExl CHGN CJun CWib EBee ELan EPfP GBin GKin LRHS MGos MTPN NLar SBig SChF SHil SPer WSHC
I	- 'Grandiflora'	CJun GBin LRHS MBri MGos NLar
§	- 'Red Dragon'	CJun NLar
	- f. ***rubra*** hort.	see *E. chrysantha* 'Red Dragon'
	papyrifera	see *E. chrysantha*

Edraianthus (*Campanulaceae*)

	croaticus	see *E. graminifolius*
	dalmaticus	EPot
§	***graminifolius***	EPot XLum
	- subsp. ***graminifolius*** new	EPot
	owerinianus	CPBP WAbe
§	***pumilio*** ♀H4	EPot GKev NSla SRms WAbe
	serbicus	EPot
§	***serpyllifolius***	NSla
	- 'Major'	WAbe
	tenuifolius 'Albus'	GKev
	wettsteinii	CPBP

Ehretia (*Boraginaceae*)

	anacua	CBcs
	dicksonii	CBcs CHEx IVic
	rigida new	SPlb

Eichhornia (*Pontederiaceae*)

	crassipes	CBAq MSKA MWts SCoo
	- 'Major'	NPer

Elaeagnus (*Elaeagnaceae*)

	angustifolia	CAgr CBcs CDul EPfP MCoo MGos NLar NWea SPer SRms
	- Caspica Group	see *E.* 'Quicksilver'
	argentea	see *E. commutata*
§	***commutata***	CBcs CDul CMac ECrN EHoe EPfP LHop MBlu MWhi NLar SPer WHar
§	× ***ebbingei***	Widely available
	- 'Coastal Gold' (v)	CBcs CDoC CDul EPfP LBMP LRHS LSRN MAsh MGos MJak SGol SLim SRms
I	- 'Compacta'	LRHS SHil
	- 'Gilt Edge' (v) ♀H4	Widely available
*	- 'Gold Flash'	LAst
	- Gold Splash = 'Lannou' (v)	CDoC CMac EBee EPfP SGol SPoG SWvt
	- 'Lemon Ice' (v)	NLar
	- 'Limelight' (v)	Widely available
	- 'Moonlight'	LRHS MAsh
	- 'Salcombe Seedling'	CCCN
	- 'Viveleg' PBR (v)	EPfP LRHS MBri SEWo SHil
	glabra	GGal
	- 'Reflexa'	see *E.* × *reflexa*
	macrophylla	CMac
	multiflora	CDoC CDul SPer
	parvifolia	CCCN
	pungens	NBir
	- 'Argenteovariegata'	see *E. pungens* 'Variegata'
	- 'Aureovariegata'	see *E. pungens* 'Maculata'
	- 'Dicksonii' (v)	CWib LRHS MAsh NLar SLon SPer SRms
	- 'Forest Gold' (v)	ELan EPfP LRHS MAsh
	- 'Frederici' (v)	CBcs CDoC CMac EBee EHoe ELan EPfP LAst LHop LRHS MAsh MRav NLar SPer SPoG SWvt
	- 'Goldrim' (v) ♀H4	EPfP
	- 'Hosuba-fukurin' (v)	EBee ELan GKin LBuc LLHF LRHS MAsh SLon
§	- 'Maculata' (v)	Widely available
§	- 'Variegata' (v)	CBcs CMac NBir SPer
§	'Quicksilver' ♀H4	Widely available
§	× ***reflexa***	WPGP
	× ***submacrophylla***	see *E.* × *ebbingei*
	umbellata	CBcs CDul CExl CTho EPfP EWTr LEdu MAsh MBlu NLar SPer WPat WSHC

- 'Amber' (F) new	CAgr
- 'Big Red' (F)	CAgr
- 'Brilliant Rose' (F)	CAgr
- 'Garnet' (F)	CAgr
- 'Hidden Springs' (F)	CAgr
- 'Jewel' (F)	CAgr
- 'Late Scarlet' (F) new	CAgr
- 'Newgate' (F)	CAgr
- 'Red Cascade' (F)	CAgr
- 'Ruby' (F)	CAgr
- 'Sweet 'n' Tart' (F)	CAgr

Elaeocarpus (*Elaeocarpaceae*)

aff. ***griseopuberulus*** WWJ 12110 new	WCru
sylvestris var. ***ellipticus***	LEdu WPGP

Elatostema (*Urticaceae*)

rugosum	CHEx

Elegia (*Restionaceae*)

capensis	CAbb CCCN CCon CDTJ CDoC CExl CHEx CPrp EAmu SPlb SPoG WPGP
cuspidata	CHel
hookeriana	NEgg
macrocarpa	CCCN SPlb
spathacea	CCon
tectorum	CAbb CCon CHEx CPrp EAmu EPfP EUJe LRHS MGos NOak NPla SHDw SPlb SPoG

Eleocharis (*Cyperaceae*)

acicularis	CBAq CWat MSKA
parvula new	MSKA

Eleorchis (*Orchidaceae*)

japonica	LWst NLAp

Elettaria (*Zingiberaceae*)

cardamomum	CArn EOHP EShb GPoy LEdu SHDw WJek

Eleutherococcus (*Araliaceae*)

sp. new	CArn
hypoleucus B&SWJ 5532	WCru
nakaianus B&SWJ 5027	WCru
pictus	see *Kalopanax septemlobus*
senticosus	GCal GPoy
- B&SWJ 4568	WCru
septemlobus	see *Kalopanax septemlobus*
sessiliflorus B&SWJ 4528	WCru
- B&SWJ 8457	WCru
sieboldianus	CBcs MRav SEND
- 'Variegatus' (v)	CBcs CSpe EBee EHoe ELan ELon EPfP EShb EUJe GBin LAst LRHS MRav NEgg NLar WHer
trifoliatus RWJ 10108	WCru

Elingamita (*Primulaceae*)

johnsonii	ECou

Elisena (*Amaryllidaceae*)

longipetala	see *Hymenocallis longipetala*

Ellisiophyllum (*Plantaginaceae*)

pinnatum	WSHC
- B&SWJ 197	CDes EBee WCot WCru WPGP

Elmera (*Saxifragaceae*)

racemosa	EPau WPtf

Elodea (*Hydrocharitaceae*)

canadensis	CBAq MSKA NBir WMAq

elderberry see *Sambucus nigra*

Elsholtzia (*Lamiaceae*)

fruticosa	CArn
stauntonii	CArn CBcs CHel EBee ELan GPoy IVic LRHS MHer NLar SBch SBrt SLon SPer SRms SWvt WBor WJek XLum

Elymus (*Poaceae*)

arenarius	see *Leymus arenarius*
canadensis	EHoe EPPr
- f. ***glaucifolius***	CCon
cinereus from Washington State, USA	WPGP
glaucus misapplied	see *E. hispidus*
§ ***hispidus***	CSpe EPPr MBlu MBri MLHP SPer WCFE WCot
§ ***magellanicus***	Widely available
- 'Blue Sword'	LRHS MBri MGos SHil SLon SRkn SRms
riparius	EPPr
sibiricus	EPPr
villosus	EPPr
- var. ***arkansanus***	EPPr
virginicus	EBee EPPr

Embothrium ✿ (*Proteaceae*)

coccineum	CBcs CDoy CFil CGHE CHel EBee EPfP GKin SPlb WPGP WPat
- Lanceolatum Group	CAby CDoC CDul CEnd CHel CTsd EBee ECre ELon EPfP EUJe GKin LRHS MBlu MMuc MPkF ŞAPC SLim SPer SSpi SSta SWvt WAbe WBor
- - 'Inca Flame'	CCCN EPfP LRHS MAsh SPoG SWvt
- - 'Ñorquinco' ♀H3	CBcs GGal
- Longifolium Group	CCCN EPfP IBlr WPGP

Eminium (*Araceae*)

lehmannii new	LWst
regelii	LWst

Emmenopterys (*Rubiaceae*)

henryi	CBcs CDul CGHE EPfP IArd IDee MBlu NLar SMad WCot WPGP

Empetrum (*Ericaceae*)

nigrum	GPoy

Empodium (*Hypoxidaceae*)

plicatum	EPot

Encephalartos ✿ (*Zamiaceae*)

altensteinii	CBrP
caffer	CBrP
cycadifolius	CBrP
ferox	CBrP
horridus	CBrP
lanatus	CBrP
lebomboensis	CBrP
lehmannii	CBrP
natalensis	CBrP

villosus	CBrP

Endymion see *Hyacinthoides*

Enkianthus ✿ (*Ericaceae*)

campanulatus ♀H4	Widely available
- var. ***campanulatus*** f. ***albiflorus***	CBcs GKin IVic NLar
I - 'Hollandia'	CBcs GKin
I - 'Pagoda' **new**	MBri
- var. ***palibinii***	EPfP GGGa GKin LRHS MAsh SSpi
- 'Red Bells'	CDoC CDul CMac EPfP GBin GKin LRHS MAsh NLar SSpi SSta SWvt
- 'Red Velvet'	CBcs GKin NLar
- 'Ruby Glow'	CBcs IVic
- var. ***sikokianus***	EPfP GGGa GKin NLar
* - 'Variegatus' (v)	LRHS MAsh SPoG
- 'Venus'	CBcs GKin NLar
- 'Victoria'	CBcs NLar
- 'Wallaby'	CBcs LRHS NLar WAbe
cernuus f. ***rubens*** ♀H4	CBcs CMac EPfP GBin GGGa GKin NLar
chinensis	CBcs EPfP GGGa LRHS MAsh
deflexus	EBee GGGa LRHS MAsh SSpi WPGP
perulatus ♀H4	CBcs CDul CMac EBee GKin LRHS MGos MRav NLar SPer SSpi SSta
serrulatus	GGGa

Ensete (*Musaceae*)

gilletii	XBlo
- from Malawi	XBlo
- from Mozambique	XBlo
glaucum	CDTJ CDoC EAmu EUJe GCal SBst
superbum	EAmu
§ ***ventricosum*** ♀H1+3	CCCN CDTJ CDoC CHII EAmu EUJe SAPC SEND XBlo
§ - 'Maurelii'	CBrP CCCN CDTJ CDoC CHEx CHel CHII CSpe EAmu ESwi EUJe NPla NSoo SAPC SDix SEND SPer SPoG WCot WPGP
- 'Rubrum'	see *E. ventricosum* 'Maurelii'
- 'Tandarra Red'	CAbb CDoC ESwi

Entelea (*Malvaceae*)

arborescens	CHEx ECou EShb SPlb

Eomecon (*Papaveraceae*)

chionantha	CCon CDes CExl CHEx CSam CSpe EСho GAbr GBuc GCal GCra LEdu LRHS MLHP MRav NBid WCru WHer WMoo WPGP WPtf WWEG XLum

Epacris (*Ericaceae*)

impressa	WAbe
microphylla	ITim
serpyllifolia	WThu

Ephedra (*Ephedraceae*)

sp.	SAPC
chilensis	XLum
- 'Mellow Yellow'	EBee
- 'Quite White'	EBee
distachya	GPoy
equisetina	CArn IFro
fedtschenkoi	XSen
gerardiana	IFro LRHS
- var. ***sikkimensis***	WOld XLum
intermedia RCB/TQ K-1	WCot
§ ***major***	XSen
minuta	MSCN
monosperma	WThu
nebrodensis	see *E. major*
nevadensis	CArn GPoy WHfH
sinica	CArn GPoy
viridis	CArn XSen

Epigaea (*Ericaceae*)

asiatica	WAbe
gaultherioides	GGGa

Epigeneium (*Orchidaceae*)

acuminatum **new**	EWTr NLar

Epilobium (*Onagraceae*)

angustifolium	see *Chamerion angustifolium*
- f. ***leucanthum***	see *Chamaenerion angustifolium* 'Album'
californicum misapplied	see *Zauschneria californica*
canum	see *Zauschneria californica* subsp. *cana*
dodonaei	see *Chamerion dodonaei*
garrettii	see *Zauschneria californica* subsp. *garrettii*
N ***glabellum*** misapplied	MSCN NSla WCFE WWlt
glabellum G. Forst.	CMea CSpe WKif
hirsutum 'Album'	EWTr LPio
microphyllum	see *Zauschneria californica* subsp. *cana*
rosmarinifolium	see *Chamerion dodonaei*
septentrionale	see *Zauschneria septentrionalis*
villosum	see *Zauschneria californica* subsp. *mexicana*

Epimedium ✿ (*Berberidaceae*)

Chen Yi 8 from Jian Xi, China	WCot
from Yunnan, China	CDes CLAP CPom IFoB WPGP
acuminatum	CCon CCse CElw CFil CGHE CLAP EFEx LEdu MNrw NMyG WMoo WPGP WSHC XPou
- L 575	CDes CElw CExl CFil EBee
- 'Galaxy'	CDes CExl CFil CJun CLAP CMil WPGP
- 'Night Mistress' **new**	XPou
- 'Quinquin' **new**	IMou
- yellow-flowered CC 011415 **new**	XPou
'Akakage'	CExl CLAP GBuc
'Akebono'	CAbP CDes CHid CJun CLAP CMil CSpe EBee ECtt EPPr EPfP IFoB LLHF LSou MBel MNrw NCGa NLar SDix SMrm SPad SPoG WCot XEll
Alabaster = 'Conalba' **new**	SGol
alpinum	CFil CFis CMac EBee EPPr EWTr LEdu SHar WMoo XLum
'Amanogawa'	CDes CJun CLAP CMil CPom IFoB LEdu MAvo WPGP XPou
'Amber Queen'PBR	CAbP CLAP CMil EPfP EWTr IFoB LLHF LLWG MMHG NCGa NHar NPnk NSti SMrm SPhx WCAu WCot
'Arctic Wings'PBR	CLAP CMil LLWG MBNS NGdn SMrm
'Asiatic Hybrid'	CJun CLAP WHal
'Autumn Raspberry'	CJun
'Beni-kujaku'	CDes CJun CLAP EBee IFoB NLar
'Black Sea'	CElw CJun CLAP CSpe EPPr EPot GBuc IFoB IMou LHop MNrw NCGa NLar NPnk SGol XPou

borealiguizhouense CC 020711 **new**	XPou
brachyrrhizum	CDes CExl CJun CLAP CMil CPom LLHF NLar WPGP
- CPC 940447 **new**	XPou
- 'Elfin Magic' **new**	IFoB
brevicornu	CLAP CPom WPGP
- Og 82.010	CExl CFil CJun CLAP XPou
- Og 88.010	CJun CLAP XPou
'Buckland Spider'	CDes CLAP EBee EPPr IFoB MNrw WPGP
campanulatum	CGHE LLHF
- Og 93.087	CExl CFil CJun
× ***cantabrigiense***	CBro CMac ECtt ESwi GBuc GKev GMaP MRav NBre SRms WWEG XLum
chlorandrum	CAby CLAP IFoB LEdu WPGP
- Og 94.003	CDes EBee XPou
creeping yellow	EBee LSou MBri WHil
cremeum	see *E. grandiflorum* subsp. *koreanum*
davidii	CDes CFil CGHE EPPr LEdu MNrw NLar NMyG SKHP WHal WPGP WSHC
- CPC 960079	CExl EBee XPou
- EMR 4125	CElw CExl CJun CLAP NCGa XPou
- dwarf	CExl
dewuense **new**	XPou
diphyllum	CDes CExl CFil CGHE CPom CTsd EBee IFoB IVic WHal WPGP XPou
dolichostemon	CElw CLAP IFoB LHop NLar
- Og 81.010	CJun XPou
'Domino' **new**	XPou
ecalcaratum	CDes CLAP CMil CPom EBee LEdu MNrw WPGP
- Og 93.082	CExl CJun XPou
- spurred **new**	XPou
elongatum	CLAP
- CC 12906 **new**	XPou
'Emperor'	see *E.* 'Phoenix'
'Enchantress'	CDes CElw CJun CLAP CMil CPom EWTr EWld IFoB MNrw NLar WHal
epsteinii	CAby CDes CFil CLAP CMil CPom EBee EPPr IFoB LEdu LLHF MNrw SMad WCot WPGP
- CPC 940347	CExl CJun IVic XPou
fangii	CExl IFoB
- CC 022008 **new**	XPou
fargesii	CDes CExl CFil EBee IFoB LEdu MAvo MNrw NCGa WCot WPGP
- Og 93.057	XPou
- 'Pink Constellation'	CDes CExl CFil CJun CLAP CPom LEdu LHop SBch WPGP XPou
'Fire Dragon'[PBR]	CLAP CWCL EPfP IFoB LLHF MAvo MBNS NHar SMrm WCAu WHil
flavum	CFil EBee SKHP WPGP
- Og 92.036	CDes CExl CJun CLAP
'Flowers of Sulphur'[PBR]	CLAP EBee
franchetii	CCon CExl CGHE IFoB SKHP
- 'Brimstone Butterfly'	CDes CExl CFis CJun CLAP EBee EPPr LHop MAvo NLar WCot WHoo WPGP XPou
'Fukujuji'	CLAP
'Golden Eagle'	CDes CExl CJun CLAP CPom EWes EWld MNrw
§ ***grandiflorum*** ♀[H4]	CBcs CElw COlW CPla CTri ELan ELon EPfP EWTr GBuc GLog NBir NLar NMyG NPnk SPer WPnP WPtf WSpi WWEG
- 'Akagiza Kura' **new**	XPou
- 'Album'	CLAP
- 'Bandit' **new**	IFoB XPou
- 'Beni-chidori'	CJun CLAP
- 'Circe' **new**	XPou
- 'Crimson Beauty'	CJun CLAP MRav WHal WHoo WSHC WSpi
- 'Crimson Queen'	CDes EBee IFoB LEdu MNrw WPGP
- f. ***flavescens*** Aomori forms **new**	XPou
- - Number 1 CC 940549 **new**	XPou
- 'Freya'	CDes CExl IFoB WSHC XPou
§ - var. ***higoense***	CDes CJun WHal WPGP XPou
- 'Jennie Maillard'	WCot
- 'Koji'	CLAP EBee IFoB NLar WSHC
§ - subsp. ***koreanum***	CLAP CPla EFEx IFoB
- 'La Rocaille'	CLAP EBee XPou
- lilac-flowered	CLAP WHal
- 'Lilafee'	Widely available
- 'Mount Kitadake'	CLAP WAbe XPou
- 'Mugawa-gen-pan' **new**	XPou
- 'Nanum' ♀[H4]	CDes CJun CPBP CSpe EBee ECho EPot GBuc MNrw NHar SKHP WAbe WPGP WThu XPou
- pink-flowered	MCot
- 'Purple Pixie'[PBR] **new**	EBee
- 'Purple Prince'	CDes CExl CLAP EBee WPGP XPou
- 'Queen Esta'	CDes CExl CJun CLAP CMil EBee IFoB LEdu MAvo MNrw SBch WPGP WSHC XPou
- 'Red Beauty'	CLAP CWCL EBee ELan ELon EWTr IFoB LSou MAvo MCot NLar WGrn WSpi
- 'Rose Queen' ♀[H4]	CHel CSam ELan ELon EPfP EThi GMaP LBMP LRHS MBri MRav NBir NMyG NSti SWvt WMoo WWEG
- 'Roseum'	CLAP CMac CMil ESwi IFoB SWvt WSpi
- 'Rubinkrone'	GBuc GMaP IMou MNrw NMyG
- 'Sirius'	CJun CLAP MNrw
- f. ***violaceum***	CJun CLAP EBee LRHS WCFE WSHC
- 'White Beauty'	WSHC
- 'White Queen' ♀[H4]	CCon CElw CJun EBee EPPr IFoB LLHF WCot WHal
- 'Wildside Red'	CJun
- 'Yellow Princess'	CDes CJun CLAP EBee XPou
- 'Yubae'	IFoB
'Heavenly Purple'	CJun
higoense	see *E. grandiflorum* var. *higoense*
hunanense **new**	XPou
ilicifolium	CDes CFil CJun EBee LEdu WPGP
- Og 93.020	XPou
'Jean O'Neill'	CDes CLAP EBee LEdu WCot WPGP
'Jenny Pym'	EBee
'Kaguyahime'	CJun CLAP CMil EPPr IFoB WSHC XPou
'King Prawn' **new**	CDes
koreanum 'Harold Epstein' **new**	XPou
'Kotobuki'	XPou
'Kozakura'	XPou
latisepalum	CDes CLAP CPom EBee LEdu MNrw NCGa NLar WCot WPGP
- Og 91.002	CJun
- Og 93.009	XPou
- OgY 44 **new**	XPou
'Lemon Meringue Pie'	CJun

leptorrhizum	CDes CElw CExl CFil CGHE CJun CLAP EBee EPPr EWTr EWld GBuc IFoB IVic LEdu MNFA MNrw NCGa NHar NLar NMyG SBch SKHP WCot WHal
- Og Y44	CExl WSHC
- 'Mariko'	CDes CExl CJun CLAP CMil CPom LEdu WPGP XPou
lishihchenii	CDes CExl CFil CJun CLAP WPGP
- CC 95007 new	XPou
- Og 96.024	XPou
'Little Shrimp'	CJun CTri EBee GMaP LLHF LRHS MNFA MNrw NLar
macranthum	see *E. grandiflorum*
macrosepalum new	XPou
membranaceum	CAby CCon CFil CGHE CLAP CMil EBee EWTr LEdu LLHF NCGa WHal WPGP XPou
- Og 93.047	CExl CJun EPPr
mikinorii	CExl CPom
- CC 990001 new	XPou
myrianthum	CDes CJun LEdu WPGP XPou
ogisui	CAby CDes CLAP CMil CPom IFoB LEdu WPGP WThu
- Og 91.001	CExl CFil CJun EBee MNrw SKHP XPou
§ × ***omeiense*** 'Akame'	CDes CExl CGHE CJun CLAP CMil EPPr WPGP XPou
- 'Emei Shan'	see *E.* × *omeiense* 'Akame'
- 'Myriad Years'	CLAP XPou
- 'Pale Fire Sibling'	CDes CJun
- 'Stormcloud'	CDes CExl CFil CGHE CJun CLAP CMil CPom EBee EPPr EWTr MNrw WPGP XPou
parvifolium new	XPou
pauciflorum	CFil EBee EPPr EWTr LEdu NHar NMyG SMad WPGP XPou
- Og 92.123	CExl CJun CLAP
× ***perralchicum*** Υ^{H4}	CBro CJun CMac CTri GKev LRHS MLHP NLar SLPl WPnP WSHC
- 'Fröhnleiten'	Widely available
- 'Lichtenberg'	CDes EBee XPou
- 'Wisley'	CElw CJun CSam EWes
perralderianum	CHEx CMac CSam EPot GMaP MBel MCot MNrw SRms WHal WPnP WSpi XLum
- 'Weihenstephan'	LRHS MMoz WPnP
aff. ***perralderianum***	WSpi
§ 'Phoenix'	CDes CExl EBee WPGP
'Pink Champagne'	EBee EPfP LEdu MAvo NCGa SMrm
'Pink Elf'^{PBR}	CLAP CMil EBee ECGP EPfP EWTr IFoB LLHF MBel MNrw NCGa NLar NOrc NPnk NSti SRms WCAu WCot WHil
pinnatum	ECho GMaP WHal WSpi XLum
§ - subsp. ***colchicum*** Υ^{H4}	CHel CJun CLAP CMac CWCL ELan EPfP EWTr GBBs GBuc LEdu LRHS MCot MRav NGdn NLar SDix WCAu WCot WPnP WSpi WWEG
- - L 321	CDes WPGP
- ***elegans***	see *E. pinnatum* subsp. *colchicum*
platypetalum	CFil CLAP CMil WCot WPGP
- Og 93.085	CExl CJun XPou
pubescens	EBee IFoB
- Og 91.003	CExl CFil CJun WPGP
pubigerum	CJun CSam EWTr GAbr GBuc LEdu LRHS MNFA NLar NMyG SEND SWvt WHal WPtf WSpi WWEG XEll XPou

rhizomatosum	CLAP EPPr GMaP LLHF NMyG WPGP WSHC
- Og 92.114	CJun EBee WCot XPou
× ***rubrum*** Υ^{H4}	Widely available
sagittatum	CLAP EFEx
- 'Warlord' new	XPou
'Sasaki'	CLAP EPot EWTr GBin GBuc IFoB MAvo NLar WSpi XEll
sempervirens	CJun CLAP WHal
- 'Okuda's White'	CDes EBee WPGP
- var. ***sempervirens***	CLAP
- 'White Purity' new	XPou
× ***setosum***	CJun NLar WHal
'Shiho'	EBee EWTr GBin
shuichengense CC 030175 new	XPou
'Sphinx Twinkler'	see *E.* 'Spine Tingler'
§ 'Spine Tingler' new	CMil ESwi MSCN WCot XPou
'Starcloud'	GBin LRHS NCGa
stellulatum long-leaved CC 970051 new	XPou
- 'Wudang Star'	CDes CExl CFil CGHE CJun CLAP CMil CPom EWes IFoB IMou IVic WPGP WSpi XPou
- 'Yukiko' new	XPou
sutchuenense	CLAP
- CC 990394 new	XPou
'Suzuka'	LEdu
'Tama-no-genpei'	CDes CJun CPom IFoB
'The Giant' new	XPou
'Totnes Turbo' new	CDes
trifoliolatobinatum new	XPou
× ***versicolor***	CExl LRHS
- 'Cherry Tart'	CLAP
- 'Cupreum'	CJun CLAP EBee GBuc LRHS WCAu
§ - 'Discolor'	CAby CDes CElw CFis CLAP CPom EPPr EWld NBir XPou
- 'Neosulphureum'	CBro CDes CLAP EPPr SLPl WPGP WSHC WThu XPou
- 'Sulphureum' Υ^{H4}	Widely available
- 'Versicolor'	see *E.* × *versicolor* 'Discolor'
× ***warleyense***	Widely available
- 'Orangekönigin'	Widely available
'William Stearn'	CDes CExl CJun CLAP XPou
wushanense	CFil CLAP EPPr EWTr LEdu XPou
- CC 014193 new	XPou
- Og 93.019	CExl CJun XPou
- 'Caramel'	CDes CExl CJun CLAP CMil CPom EBee IFoB LEdu SKHP WPGP WSHC XPou
- spiny-leaved CC 014631 new	XPou
× ***youngianum***	CMac IFoB NEgg
- 'Merlin'	CElw CJun CLAP CMil EBee EPfP EPot GBuc IFoB MBri NHar NLar NSti WHal WSHC XPou
- 'Niveum' Υ^{H4}	Widely available
- 'Roseum'	Widely available
- 'Shikinomai'	CExl CJun CLAP EPPr EPot
- 'Tamabotan'	CDes CLAP CMil MNrw MRav XPou
§ - 'Typicum'	CElw CLAP GBuc LRHS WSHC
- 'Yenomoto'	CJun CLAP
- 'Youngianum'	see *E.* × *youngianum* 'Typicum'
zhushanense	LEdu

Epipactis (*Orchidaceae*)

gigantea	CAvo CBro CCon CHel EBee ECho ELan EPot GBin GKev LRHS MNrw MRav NCGa NChi NDav NLAp WPGP

	gigantea* × *veratrifolia	see *E.* Lowland Legacy gx
	helleborine	WHer
	Lizzy Lou gx	LWst
§	**Lowland Legacy gx**	NLAp
	- 'Irène'	LWst
	palustris	ECho LRHS NDav NLAp NPnk WHer WPnP
	royleana	NLAp
	Sabine gx	CAby
	- 'Frankfurt'	EWld MNrw
	thunbergii	EFEx NLAp

Epipremnum (*Araceae*)

pinnatum 'Marble Queen' (v)	XBlo

Episcia (*Gesneriaceae*)

dianthiflora	WDib
'San Miguel'	WDib

Equisetum ✿ (*Equisetaceae*)

	arvense	CArn
	'Bandit' (v)	CDes CNat SMad WMoo
	× ***bowmanii***	CNat
*	***camtschatcense***	CDes EWay SAPC SBig SMad SPlb XLum
	× ***dycei***	CNat
	fluviatile	CNat MSKA
	giganteum	LLWG
	hyemale	CBAq CKno EHoe EPfP GQue MSKA MWts NOak NPer NSti SAPC SPlb WCot WMoo XLum
§	- var. ***affine***	CNat CRow ELan EWll LEdu LSou MBlu MSKA WMAq
	- var. ***robustum***	see *E. hyemale* var. *affine*
	pratense	CNat
	ramosissimum var. ***japonicum***	LEdu NPla SWat
	scirpoides	CBAq EBee EFer EHoe EWay MAvo MSKA MWts NPer NWad SPlb SWat WMAq WMoo WPnP XLum
	telmateia	LEdu SMad
	variegatum	EFer

Eragrostis (*Poaceae*)

RCB/Arg S-7	EBee
airoides misapplied	see *Agrostis montevidensis*
airoides ambig.	GAbr WMoo
chloromelas	EPPr
curvula	CAby CElw CKno CMea CWCL EHoe EPPr GAbr LRHS MAvo MBel MRav MWhi NBir NChi NGdn NOak NWsh SEND SPhx WMoo XLum
- S&SH 10	CDes CElw CKno EPPr WPGP
- 'Totnes Burgundy'	CAby CDes CExl CKno CWCL EBee EHoe EPPr EPfP LRHS MAvo MNrw NOak SMea SRms WMoo WPGP
elliottii	CKno EPPr EShb LBMP LRHS MAvo NWsh SEND SHDw SMea SMrm WWEG
- 'Wind Dancer'	EPPr LRHS
prolifera new	IMou
'Silver Needles'	see *Agrostis canina* 'Silver Needles'
spectabilis	CCon CKno CSBt EBee ELan EPfP LBMP LDai LRHS MMHG MWhi NGdn NLar NWsh SDix SMea SMrm WMoo WWEG XLum
trichodes	CCon CKno EBee EHoe LDai LEdu NWsh SMea SMrm WCot

Eranthemum (*Acanthaceae*)

pulchellum 🏆H1	ECre

Eranthis (*Ranunculaceae*)

	cilicica	see *E. hyemalis* Cilicica Group
§	***hyemalis*** 🏆H4	CBro CMea CSpe CTca ECho ELan ELon EPfP GBin GKev LRHS MBel MCot MRav MWat SDeJ SMrm SPer SPhx SWvt WBor WCot WHoo WShi
§	- Cilicica Group	CBro CHel ECho ELan EPot GKev GMaP LRHS MBel NLar SDeJ SPhx WCot WShi
	- 'Flore Pleno' (d)	ECho EPot
	- 'Grünling'	CAvo ECho EPot
	- 'Orange Glow'	ECho
	- 'Schwefelglanz'	CAvo CBro ECho EPot
§	- Tubergenii Group	CBro ECho EPot
	- - 'Guinea Gold' 🏆H4	CMea CTca ECho
	pinnatifida	EFEx WCru
	× ***tubergenii***	see *E. hyemalis* Tubergenii Group

Ercilla (*Phytolaccaceae*)

volubilis	CExl CFil CHel CRHN CWGN EBee EWes IDee LHop LRHS SEND WCru WSHC

Eremophila (*Scrophulariaceae*)

§	***debilis***	ECou
	glabra	SVen
	'Kilbara Carpet'	ECou
	longifolia	SPlb
	maculata	ECou
	- pale pink-flowered	MOWG
	- 'Peaches and Cream'	MOWG
	'Yellow Trumpet'	ECou

Eremostachys (*Lamiaceae*)

laciniata	XSen

Eremurus (*Asphodelaceae*)

altaicus JCA 0.443.809	WCot
'Brutus'	EBee
bungei	see *E. stenophyllus* subsp. *stenophyllus*
cristatus JCA 0.444.029	WCot
'Disco'	EBee
'Emmy Ro'	EBee LRHS WCot
'Flamengo'	EBee
fuscus JCA 0.444.043	WCot
'Helena'	EBee LRHS
himalaicus	CAvo CBro CCon EBee ELan EPot ERCP GBin LRHS MHer NLar SDeJ SPer SPhx WCot
'Image'	EBee LRHS
× ***isabellinus*** 'Cleopatra'	CAvo CMea CWCL EBee EPfP EPot ERCP EWTr GMaP LPio LRHS MBNS MBel MGos MHer SDeJ SPer SPhx SPoG
- 'Obelisk'	ELan
- 'Pinokkio'	CAvo CWCL EBee EPot LPio LRHS MHer SDeJ
- Ruiter hybrids	CMea ELan EPfP GKev GMaP LAst LRHS MGos MNrw SEND SPer SPhx
- Shelford hybrids	CAvo CBcs ELan GKev SDeJ SPhx
'Jeanne-Claire'	LRHS NLar
'Joanna'	LRHS LSRN NLar

lactiflorus	WCot
'Line Dance'	EBee
'Luca Ro'	EBee NLar
'Moneymaker'	CAvo CWCL EBee EPot
'Oase'	ELan MAvo SDeJ
'Paradiso'	EBee
regelii JCA 444.083	WCot
'Rexona'	EBee MBNS SDeJ
robustus ♀H4	CAvo CBcs CBro CCon CMea CWCL ELan EPot ERCP LRHS MAvo MHer MNrw NLar SDeJ SPer SPhx SPlb
'Roford'	MNrw
'Romance'	EBee EPot ERCP LPio MBNS MBel MNrw NLar SDeJ
'Rumba'	EBee
stenophyllus ♀H4	CBro CTri CWCL CWib EPot ERCP GBin LHop LPio LRHS MPkF NLar SDeJ SPhx SPoG WCot
§ - subsp. ***stenophyllus***	CAvo CBcs EBee EPfP GMaP IBoy LAst MHer MNrw NLBP NPer NPri SPer
'Tap Dance'	EBee MAvo
'White Beauty Favourite'PBR	ERCP EWTr MAvo SPhx
'Yellow Giant'	EBee
zenaidae JCA 0.444.409	WCot

Erepsia (*Aizoaceae*)

lacera	SPlb

Erianthus see *Saccharum*

Erica ✿ (*Ericaceae*)

aestiva	SPlb
alopecurus	SPlb
arborea	CBcs SPlb
- var. ***alpina*** ♀H4	CDoC CTri EPfP GGal SPer SPoG SWhi
§ - - f. ***aureifolia*** 'Albert's Gold' ♀H4	CSBt CTri ELan EPfP GAbr LRHS MAsh MBri NHol SCoo SPer SPoG SWhi
- 'Arbora Gold'	see *E. arborea* var. *alpina* f. *aureifolia* 'Albert's Gold'
- 'Arnold's Gold'	see *E. arborea* var. *alpina* f. *aureifolia* 'Albert's Gold'
- 'Estrella Gold' ♀H4	CBcs CDoC CSBt CTri ELan EPfP LRHS MAsh SCoo SPer SPoG SWhi
australis ♀H4	ELon
- f. ***albiflora*** 'Mr Robert' ♀H3	GCal
- 'Riverslea' ♀H4	CTri GCal MAsh SPoG SWhi
caffra	SPlb
canaliculata ♀H3	CBcs
carnea 'Adrienne Duncan' ♀H4	SCoo SRms SWhi
- f. ***alba*** 'C.J. Backhouse'	SRms
- - 'Golden Starlet' ♀H4	CSBt CTri EPfP MAsh MJak NHol NWea SCoo SPer SRms SWhi
- - 'Ice Princess' ♀H4	CBcs ELan EPfP MAsh NHol SCoo SRms SWhi
- - 'Isabell' ♀H4	CSBt CSam EPfP IVic MAsh SCoo SRms SWhi
- - 'Rosalinde Schorn'	SRms
- - 'Schneekuppe'	SWhi
- - 'Schneesturm'	SRms
- - 'Snow Queen'	SRms
- - 'Springwood White' ♀H4	CSBt CTri ELan EPfP MAsh NHol SEND SLon SRms SWhi
- - 'Whitehall'	SCoo SRms SWhi
- - 'Winter Snow'	CSBt ELan SCoo SPer SRms SWhi
- 'Amy Doncaster'	see *E. carnea* 'Treasure Trove'
- 'Ann Sparkes' ♀H4	CSBt CTri ELan EPfP MAsh NHol SCoo SPer SRms SWhi
- 'Atrorubra'	SWhi
- f. ***aureifolia*** 'Aurea'	SCoo SRms
- - 'Barry Sellers'	SRms
§ - - 'Bell's Extra Special'	EPfP SRms
- - 'Foxhollow' ♀H4	CBcs CTri EPfP IArd MAsh MJak NHol SCoo SRms SWhi
- - 'Gelber Findling'	SRms
- - 'Hilletje'	SRms SWhi
- - 'January Sun'	SRms
- - 'Westwood Yellow' ♀H4	CSBt CSam MAsh NHol SRms SWhi
- 'Beoley Pink'	SRms
- 'Challenger' ♀H4	ELan EPfP MAsh NHol SCoo SLon SRms SWhi
- 'Clare Wilkinson'	SRms
- 'December Red'	ELan EPfP MAsh MMuc SCoo SEND SRms SWhi
- 'Diana Young'	SCoo SWhi
- 'Dømmesmoen'	SRms
- 'Early Red'	SRms
- 'Eileen Porter'	SEND
- 'Eva'	CBcs IVic SRms SWhi
- 'Foxhollow Fairy'	SPer SRms
- 'Gracilis'	SRms
- 'Heathwood'	CBcs MAsh SRms SWhi
- 'James Backhouse'	CTri
- 'Jason Attwater'	SRms
- 'Jennifer Anne'	SRms
- 'John Kampa'	SRms
- 'John Pook'	SCoo SRms
- 'King George'	CTri SRms SWhi
§ - 'Kramer's Rubin'	SRms
- 'Lena'	see *E.* × *darleyensis* 'Lena'
- 'Lohse's Rubin'	NWea SRms SWhi
- 'Loughrigg' ♀H4	CTri MAsh MJak NHol SCoo SRms SWhi
- 'March Seedling'	EPfP MAsh NHol SCoo SLon SPer SRms SWhi
- 'Margery Frearson'	SRms
I - 'Martin'	SRms
- 'Memory'	SWhi
- 'Myretoun Ruby' ♀H4	CBcs CSBt CTri EPfP MAsh NHol SCoo SPer SRms SWhi
- 'Nathalie' ♀H4	CSBt CSam IVic MAsh NHol SCoo SRms SWhi
- 'Pink Mist'	SRms SWhi
- 'Pink Spangles' ♀H4	CBcs CSBt CSam CTri MAsh MJak SCoo SPer SRms SWhi
- 'Pirbright Rose'	SRms
- 'Polden Pride'	SRms
- 'Praecox Rubra' ♀H4	EPfP NHol SCoo SRms
- 'Queen Mary'	SRms
- 'Queen of Spain'	MAsh SRms
- 'R.B. Cooke' ♀H4	EPfP MAsh MJak SCoo SRms
- 'Robert Jan'	SRms
- 'Rosalie' ♀H4	CSam EPfP IArd MAsh MMuc SCoo SRms SWhi
- 'Rosantha'	SRms
- 'Rosea'	SPlb
- 'Rosy Morn'	SRms
- 'Rotes Juwel'	SRms
- 'Rubinteppich'	SRms
- 'Ruby Glow'	MJak NHol
- 'Scatterley'	SRms
- 'Schatzalp'	SRms

	- 'Sherwood Creeping'	SRms
	- 'Smart's Heath'	SRms
	- 'Springwood Pink'	CSBt CTri NHol SRms SWhi
	- 'Tanja'	SWhi
§	- 'Treasure Trove'	SWhi
	- 'Vivellii' ♀H4	CTri MAsh MJak NHol SCoo SRms SWhi
	- 'Walter Reisert'	SRms
	- 'Wentwood Red'	SRms
	- Whisky	see *E. carnea* f. *aureifolia* 'Bell's Extra Special'
	- 'Winter Beauty'	MJak NHol
	- Winter Rubin	see *E. carnea* 'Kramer's Rubin'
	- 'Winterfreude'	CSam
	- 'Wintersonne'	CBcs CSam EPfP MMuc SRms SWhi
	ciliaris 'Bretagne'	SWhi
	- 'Corfe Castle'	SWhi
	- 'David McClintock'	SWhi
	- 'Globosa'	SWhi
	- 'Ram'	SWhi
	cinerea	SWhi
	- f. ***alba*** 'Alba Minor' ♀H4	MAsh SWhi
	- - 'Celebration'	NHol SWhi
	- - 'Domino'	MAsh
	- - 'Hookstone White' ♀H4	SWhi
	- 'Atropurpurea'	MAsh
	- f. ***aureifolia*** 'Apricot Charm'	CSBt
	- - 'Fiddler's Gold' ♀H4	MAsh SWhi
	- - 'Golden Charm'	NHol SWhi
	- - 'Golden Drop'	CSBt MAsh
	- - 'Golden Hue' ♀H4	MAsh NHol
	- - 'Summer Gold'	SWhi
	- 'C.D. Eason' ♀H4	CBcs CSBt CTri EPfP IVic MAsh SCoo SWhi
	- 'Cevennes'	SWhi
	- 'Cindy' ♀H4	NHol
	- 'Eden Valley' ♀H4	SCoo SWhi
	- 'Glasnevin Red'	IVic
	- 'Glencairn'	MMuc SWhi
	- 'Katinka'	CBcs IVic SWhi
	- 'Lime Soda' ♀H4	SWhi
	- 'Mrs E.A. Mitchell'	SPlb
	- 'My Love'	SWhi
	- 'P.S. Patrick' ♀H4	SWhi
	- 'Pentreath' ♀H4	MMuc SWhi
	- 'Pink Ice' ♀H4	CTri EPfP MAsh NHol SWhi
	- 'Purple Beauty'	SWhi
	- 'Purple Robe'	SWhi
	- 'Rosita'	SWhi
	- 'Roter Kobold'	SWhi
	- 'Sherry'	NHol SWhi
	- 'Stephen Davis' ♀H4	NHol SCoo SWhi
	- 'Velvet Night' ♀H4	CSBt MAsh MMuc NHol SWhi
	- 'Vivienne Patricia'	SWhi
	cooperi	SPlb
	curviflora	SPlb
	× ***darleyensis***	GGal
	- 'Alba'	see *E.* × *darleyensis* f. *albiflora* 'Silberschmelze'
	- f. ***albiflora*** 'Ada S. Collings'	MAsh SRms
	- - 'Bing'	SCoo
	- - 'N.R. Webster'	SRms
§	- - 'Silberschmelze'	CSBt CTri EPfP MAsh MJak MMuc SCoo SEND SRms SWhi
	- - 'White Glow'	CTri MAsh SRms
	- - 'White Perfection' ♀H4	CBcs CSBt EPfP IArd IVic MAsh MJak NHol SCoo SPer SPoG SRms SWhi

	- 'Archie Graham'	SRms
	- 'Arthur Johnson' ♀H4	CSBt CTri MAsh SRms SWhi
§	- f. ***aureifolia*** 'Eva Gold' PBR	SWhi
	- - 'Jack H. Brummage'	CSBt CTri MAsh SRms SWhi
	- - 'Mary Helen'	CSBt EPfP MAsh NHol SCoo SRms SWhi
	- - 'Moonshine'	SRms SWhi
	- - 'Tweety'	CBcs SRms
	- 'Aurélie Brégeon'	SRms
	- 'Bert'	SCoo
	- 'Cherry Stevens'	see *E.* × *darleyensis* 'Furzey'
§	- 'Darley Dale'	CSBt ELan EPfP MAsh MJak MMuc SCoo SEND SLon SPoG SRms SWhi
	- 'Epe'	SRms
	- 'Eva'	see *E.* × *darleyensis* f. *aureifolia* 'Eva Gold'
§	- 'Furzey' ♀H4	CSBt EPfP MAsh NHol NWea SCoo SRms SWhi
	- 'George Rendall'	CSBt CTri EPfP MAsh SCoo SRms
	- 'Ghost Hills' ♀H4	CSBt EPfP MAsh MJak SCoo SPoG SRms SWhi
	- 'J.W. Porter' ♀H4	EPfP MJak MMuc SCoo SEND SLon SRms SWhi
	- 'James Smith'	SRms
	- 'Jenny Porter' ♀H4	CSBt ELan EPfP SCoo SLon SWhi
	- 'Katia' PBR (Winter Belles Series)	SPer SWhi
	- 'Kramer's Rote' ♀H4	CBcs CSBt CTri ELan EPfP MJak NHol SCoo SPoG SRms SWhi XLum
§	- 'Lena'	SPer
	- 'Lucie' PBR (Winter Belles Series)	SWhi
	- 'Margaret Porter'	EPfP MAsh SCoo SWhi
	- Molten Silver	see *E.* × *darleyensis* f. *albiflora* 'Silberschmelze'
	- 'Phoebe' PBR	SPer SWhi
	- 'Pink Perfection'	see *E.* × *darleyensis* 'Darley Dale'
	- 'Spring Surprise' PBR	EPfP SCoo SPer SWhi
	- 'W.G. Pine'	SRms
	- 'White Spring Surprise'	SWhi
	- 'Winter Surprise'	SWhi
	erigena f. ***alba*** 'W.T. Rackliff' ♀H4	CBcs CSBt EPfP MAsh NHol SCoo SRms SWhi
	- f. ***aureifolia*** 'Golden Lady' ♀H4	CSBt MAsh NHol SCoo SRms SWhi
	- - 'Thing Nee'	SRms SWhi
	- 'Brightness'	CSBt EPfP MAsh NHol SCoo
	- 'Irish Dusk' ♀H4	CBcs CSBt CTri EPfP MAsh NWea SCoo SEND SRms SWhi
	- 'Superba'	MAsh SRms SWhi
	glauca var. ***elegans***	CDes
	- var. ***glauca***	SPlb
	gracilis	SPoG
§	× ***griffithsii*** 'Heaven Scent'	SWhi
	- 'Jacqueline'	SWhi
	- 'Valerie Griffiths'	NHol SWhi
	'Heaven Scent'	see *E.* × *griffithsii* 'Heaven Scent'
	× ***krameri*** 'Rudi'	IVic
	lusitanica ♀H3	LRHS SPoG
	- f. ***aureifolia*** 'George Hunt'	ELan EPfP LRHS MAsh SLon SPer SPoG
	- 'Sheffield Park'	EPfP LRHS MAsh SPer SPoG
	mackayana f. ***eburnea*** 'Shining Light'	SWhi
	- 'Galicia'	SWhi
	- f. ***multiplicata*** 'Plena' (d)	WHer
	mammosa	SPlb

	mediterranea	see *E. erigena*
	× ***oldenburgensis*** 'Ammerland'	SCoo SRms SWhi
	patersonii	SPlb
	perspicua	SPlb
	spiculifolia 'Balkan Rose'	GCal
	'Spring Field White'	MMuc
	straussiana	SPlb
	× ***stuartii*** 'Irish Lemon' ♀H4	CSBt EPfP NHol SWhi
	- 'Irish Orange'	CSBt NHol SWhi
	terminalis 'Thelma Woolner'	SWhi
	tetralix	SWhi
	- f. ***alba*** 'Alba Mollis' ♀H4	CSBt MAsh SWhi
	- f. ***aureifolia*** 'Ruth's Gold'	NHol
	- 'Con Underwood' ♀H4	CSBt SWhi
	- 'Riko'	SWhi
	- 'Silver Bells'	CSBt
	- f. ***stellata*** 'Pink Star' ♀H4	NHol SWhi
	vagans f. ***alba*** 'Cornish Cream' ♀H4	EPfP NHol SWhi
	- - 'Diana's Gold'	SRms
	- - 'Golden Triumph'	SWhi
	- - 'Kevernensis Alba' ♀H4	NWad SWhi
	- f. ***aureifolia*** 'Valerie Proudley' ♀H4	CSBt MAsh NHol
	- - 'Yellow John'	SRms SWhi
	- 'Birch Glow' ♀H4	EPfP SWhi
	- 'Fiddlestone'	SWhi
	- 'Keira'	SRms SWhi
	- 'Lyonesse' ♀H4	MAsh MMuc NHol SWhi
	- 'Mrs D F Maxwell' ♀H4	CBcs CSBt MAsh NHol SWhi
	- 'Saint Keverne'	CSBt IArd IVic NHol SWhi
	× ***veitchii***	MMuc
	- 'Exeter' ♀H3	CDoy CSBt CTsd ELan EPfP GAbr MAsh SWhi
	- 'Gold Tips' ♀H4	CSBt EPfP SWhi
	- 'Pink Joy'	SWhi
	versicolor	SPlb
	× ***watsonii*** 'Claire Elise'	SWhi
	- 'Dawn' ♀H4	SWhi
	- 'H. Maxwell'	SWhi
	- 'Mary'	SWhi
	- 'Pink Pacific'	SWhi
	× ***williamsii*** 'Ken Wilson'	SWhi
	woodii	SPlb

Erigeron ✿ (*Asteraceae*)

	acris subsp. ***angulosus***	GKev
	'Adria'	EBee ECtt LLHF LRHS MBNS MSpe SPer WMnd WWEG
	annuus	CSpe NDov
	aurantiacus	NBre NBro NPri WCot
	aureus 'Canary Bird' ♀H4	EPfP EPot NSla WAbe
	- 'The Giant'	WAbe
	'Azure Beauty'	ELan EPfP
	Azure Fairy	see *E.* 'Azurfee'
§	'Azurfee'	CSBt EBee ELan EPfP GMaP MBNS MHol NBir NLar NPri SPer SPhx SPoG SWvt WMoo WWEG
	Black Sea	see *E.* 'Schwarzes Meer'
	'Blue Beauty'	CMac EPfP LRHS
	caespitosus	EDAr
	'Charity'	MRav WBrk
	chrysopsidis 'Grand Ridge'	ECho EHyd LHop LLHF LRHS WAbe
	compositus	CTri GKev SRms
§	- var. ***discoideus***	EDAr NSla SPlb WHoo
	- 'Rocky'	ECho
	Darkest of All	see *E.* 'Dunkelste Aller'
	deep pink-flowered	CHEx
	'Dignity'	EBee ECGP ELan GBuc LHop LLHF LRHS MBrN MRav MSpe NSoo SMrm SPer SPet WBrk WWEG
	'Dimity'	CMea NBir NBre WAbe WBrk WHal
	divergens	EBee
	'Dominator'	MNrw
I	'Dunkelste Aller' ♀H3	CPrp CSam ELan EPfP GBin GMaP LHop LRHS LSou MAvo MRav MSpe NLar NPri SGbt SPoG SRms SWvt WCAu WWEG
	elegantulus	CMea
*	***ereganus***	NBre WBrk
	'Felicity'	WBrk
	flettii	ECho GKev
	'Foersters Liebling' ♀H4	EBee ELon GBin LHop MBel WCot WWEG
	formosissimus	GBin
	'Four Winds'	CAbP ECho ECtt ELan EWes GKev LRHS MRav NGdn WBrk WWEG
	'Gaiety'	LRHS NBre
	glaucus	CCCN CSBt ECho GBee GJos GKev LRHS MBNS MRav NBre NGdn SEND SMad WBrk WHoo
	- 'Albus'	ELon LHop LRHS MBNS WBor
	- 'Elstead Pink'	CTri ECtt ELan LRHS
	- 'Roger Raiche'	CMea MRav SMrm
	- 'Rose Purple'	CFis
	- 'Roseus'	CBcs SEND
	- 'Sea Breeze'	CCCN CNec COIW CPrp ECtt ELon EWll GJos GMaP LHop LRHS MBNS MBri MHol NDov NPri SGbt SHil SPoG SRms STes WBor WNew
	- 'Sennen' new	WBrk
	- 'Viewpoint Blue'	ELon LRHS
	howellii	NBre
§	***karvinskianus*** ♀H3	Widely available
	- 'Stallone'	NPri
	leiomerus	GKev LBee LLHF
	linearis	EDAr LLHF
	'Mrs F.H. Beale'	LSou MSpe SRGP
	mucronatus	see *E. karvinskianus*
	multiradiatus	GCal
	'Nachthimmel'	NBre NGdn
	ochroleucus var. ***scribneri***	LLHF
	oreganus	LRHS
	philadelphicus	CDes CElw IGor MNrw NBir NBro
	'Pink Beauty'	SKHP
	Pink Jewel	see *E.* 'Rosa Juwel'
	pinnatisectus	CPBP
	poliospermus var. ***poliospermus***	LLHF
	'Profusion'	see *E. karvinskianus*
	pygmaeus	LLHF
	pyrenaicus Rouy	see *Aster pyrenaeus*
	'Quakeress'	CElw CPrp ECtt EPfP EPri EShb GBin GBuc GMaP IKil LBMP LHop LRHS MNrw MRav MSpe NGdn SMrm WBrk WWEG XLum
§	'Rosa Juwel'	CSBt CTri ECtt ELan EPfP GBin GMaP LRHS MBNS MHol MRav NBir NHol NPri SPer SPoG SRms SWvt WMnd WMoo
	'Rosenballett'	LRHS

'Rotes Meer'	CMac MRav MSpe
rotundifolius 'Caerulescens'	see *Bellis caerulescens*
salsuginosus misapplied	see *Aster sibiricus*
§ 'Schneewittchen'	CSam EBee ELan EPfP LHop LPio MBNS MBel MPie MRav MSpe NCGa SPet SPoG SRms SWvt WWEG
§ 'Schwarzes Meer'	EBee LPla MBel SPer SPoG WCot
scopulinus	ITim LLHF WAbe
'Serenity'	LRHS
simplex	ECho EHyd LRHS
'Sincerity'	WBrk XLum
Snow White	see *E.* 'Schneewittchen'
'Sommerabend'	WBrk
'Sommerneuschnee'	EBee GBin LPio LPla NDov SPhx WCAu WCot WMnd
speciosus 'Grandiflora'	MHol
'Strahlenmeer'	MSpe NBre
trifidus	see *E. compositus* var. *discoideus*
uniflorus	LLHF MAsh SRms
'Unity'	LRHS
vagus	ITim
'Wayne Roderick'	EBee ELan EPfP LAst LRHS NPri SRGP
'White Quakeress'	CElw CFis CMea MRav SMrm WCot
'Wuppertal'	MSpe

Erinacea (*Papilionaceae*)

§ ***anthyllis*** ♀H4	WThu
pungens	see *E. anthyllis*

Erinus (*Plantaginaceae*)

alpinus ♀H4	CTri ECho ECtt EDAr GAbr GJos GKev MAsh MLHP MWat NBir NHol NSla SRms WCot XLum
- var. ***albus***	ECho GJos SRms WHoo XLum
- 'Doktor Hähnle'	ECho EDAr GMaP NRya SRms WHoo XLum

Eriobotrya (*Rosaceae*)

'Coppertone'	see × *Rhaphiobotrya* 'Coppertone'
deflexa	CBcs CHEx
japonica (F) ♀H3	CAbb CArn CBcs CCCN CDul CHEx CTho CWGN EAmu EBee ELan EPfP EUJe LRHS MGos MREP NPla SAPC SBst SCoo SEND SPer SPlb SSta SVic WHer WPGP
- 'Baffico' (F)	CAgr
- 'BB' (F)	CAgr
- 'Gold Nugget' (F)	XBlo
- 'Mrs Cookson' (F)	MBri
- 'Oliver' (F)	MBri
- 'Ottaviana' (F)	CAgr

Eriocapitella see *Anemone*

Eriocephalus (*Asteraceae*)

africanus	SPlb WJek

Eriogonum (*Polygonaceae*)

alatum **new**	WCot
alleni	WCot
cespitosum	LLHF WAbe
ovalifolium Wellington form **new**	GKev
umbellatum	ECho GKev
- subsp. ***covillei***	CPBP
- var. ***torreyanum***	CMea

Eriophorum (*Cyperaceae*)

angustifolium	CBAq CWat EHoe EHon ELon MSKA MWts SPlb SWat WMAq WPnP XLum
chamissonis	MWts
latifolium	LLWG MSKA MWts XLum
rousseauianum	MSKA
vaginatum	CRow EHoe EWay LLWG MSKA XLum

Eriophyllum (*Asteraceae*)

lanatum	CFis EBee EPfP NBid NGBl SHar WWEG XLum

Eritrichium (*Boraginaceae*)

aretioides **new**	SPlb

Erodium (*Geraniaceae*)

absinthoides	LRHS XSen
- var. ***amanum***	see *E. amanum*
'Almodovar'	EFar
§ ***amanum***	CSpe EWes
balearicum	see *E.* × *variabile* 'Album'
'Bidderi'	EPot GJos IPot NChi XSen
'Candy Store'	LRHS
'Carmel'	EFar XSen
'Caroline'	CMea EFar SBch WHoo
carvifolium	CHid EFar
§ ***castellanum***	EBee LLHF SMrm
celtibericum	EFar XSen
- 'Javalambre'	XSen
- 'Peñagolosa'	XSen
'Cézembre'	EFar XSen
chamaedryoides	see *E. reichardii*
- 'Roseum'	see *E.* × *variabile* 'Roseum'
§ ***cheilanthifolium***	XSen
- 'David Crocker'	EPot IGor
chrysanthum	CElw CSam CTri ECho ECtt EDAr EPfP EPot EWTr GBuc GJos GMaP ITim LHop LRHS MCot MPnt MRav NChi NLar SEND SMrm SRot SWvt XLum XSen
- (f) **new**	EFar
- (m) **new**	EFar NRya
- 'Arcadia' **new**	CMea EFar SPhx
- pink-flowered	CSpe ECtt LHop SMrm SRot
corsicum	ECho
- 'Album'	ECho LLHF
'County Park'	IPot MLHP SRms XSen
daucoides misapplied	see *E. castellanum*
daucoides Boiss.	EBee
'Elizabeth'	EFar
'Fran's Delight'	CMea CPBP ECtt EFar EPot GJos SBch WHoo
'Freedom'	XEll
'Fripetta'	WAbe WIce XSen
'Géant de Saint Cyr'	ECtt
'Gini's Choice'	WCot
N ***glandulosum*** ♀H4	CMea ECho EPfP MAsh MMuc SBch SEND SRms SRot WPat XLum XSen
- 'Marie Poligné'	XSen
'Grey Blush'	WKif
gruinum	CHid SPhx
guicciardii	XSen
- 'Jolivot' **new**	EFar
- 'Peter Smith' **new**	EFar
guttatum misapplied	see *E.* 'Katherine Joy'
N ***guttatum*** (Desf.) Willd.	EWTr LHop MAsh SRms

	hymenodes L'Hér.	see *E. trifolium*
	'Isabel'	EFar
	'Julie Ritchie'	CMea WHoo
§	'Katherine Joy'	ECtt EWes MHer NRya SBch SRGP SRot WAbe XSen
	'Kew' **new**	EFar
	× ***kolbianum***	WAbe WCot WHoo WPnn XSen
	- 'Nadia'	EFar
	- 'Natasha'	CMHG ECtt EPot EWes GBuc GMaP MHer NSla SPoG SRGP WAbe WIce WKif XSen
	'Las Meninas'	CRDP ECtt NLar WCot
	× ***lindavicum***	NChi WPnn XSen
	- 'Greengrass Cream' **new**	EFar
	'Lucy' **new**	EFar
	macradenum	see *E. glandulosum*
	manescavii	Widely available
	'Marchants Mikado'	WKif
	'Maryla'	EFar SBch WIce
	'Merstham Pink'	EFar GMaP SMrm SRms XLum XSen
	'Mesquita'	CMea
	'Moon Man' **new**	EFar
	'Pallidum'	CSam
	pelargoniiflorum	CFis CHid CSpe ELan EPfP EWTr LRHS MCot SEND SMrm SRms SWvt WHil WKif WPnn
	'Peter Vernon'	EFar MHer XSen
	petraeum subsp. ***crispum*** misapplied	see *E. cheilanthifolium*
	- subsp. ***petraeum***	EPot MSpe
	'Pippa Mills'	CMea
	'Princesse Marion'	EFar MLHP XSen
*	'Purple Haze'	MSCN SMrm SRms SRot
§	***reichardii***	CTri ECho ECtt EHyd LRHS MBrN MHer SPoG SRms WCFE WPnn
	- 'Album'	ECho LRHS MAsh MSCN SMrm SPoG WHoo WPnn
	- 'Bianca'	EPfP
*	- 'Rubrum'	CElw ECho
	'Robertino'	WAbe
	'Robin'	EFar
	rodiei	EWes WKif
§	***rupestre***	ECho ECtt SRms SRot WIce
	'Sans-culottes' **new**	EFar
	'Sarck'	XSen
	sibthorpianum	XSen
	'Souvenir d'Hélène' **new**	XSen
	'Spanish Eyes'	CWGN ECtt IPot LAst LRMP LRHS LSou MBel MCot NEgg NLar NPri SMrm SRot SWvt WCot WHoo WKif
	'Stephanie'	CFis CMHG ECho ECtt EFar ELan EWes LSRN WAbe WIce XSen
	supracanum	see *E. rupestre*
	'Tiny Kyni'	XSen
	trichomanifolium misapplied	see *E. cheilanthifolium*
	trichomanifolium L'Hér.	EWes
§	***trifolium***	ECho ELan EPfP EWld LRHS MHer SBch SPhx
	'Turkish Delight' **new**	EFar
	× ***variabile***	ECtt
§	- 'Album'	CMea ECho EPfP EPot GMaP LAst LRHS MHer NEgg NPri NSla SRms SRot SWvt WAbe WBrk
I	- 'Bishop's Form'	CMea ECho ECtt ELon EPfP GJos GMaP IPot LAst LRHS MAsh MHer NEgg NLBP NPri NRya SMrm SPoG SRGP SRms SRot SWvt WAbe WBrk WCFE WHoo WIce WNew
	- 'Candy'	ELon MHer
	- 'Derek'	ECho SRGP
	- 'Flore Pleno' (d)	ECho ELan EPfP EWes GMaP ITim LRHS MHer SPoG SRms WBrk
	- 'Red Rock'	CTri
§	- 'Roseum' ♀H4	ECho ECtt ELan ELon EPfP MMuc MSCN NSla SPlb SRms WBrk
	- 'Timpany Seedling' **new**	ITim
	'Whiteleaf'	EFar
	'Whitwell Superb'	XSen

Erpetion see *Viola*

Eruca (*Brassicaceae*)

	vesicaria subsp. ***sativa***	CSpe ELau GPoy MHer MHoo MNHC SIde SVic

Eryngium ✿ (*Apiaceae*)

	NJM 09.072	WPGP
§	***agavifolium***	Widely available
	- giant **new**	WPGP
	alpinum ♀H4	CBcs CHel CSpe ECho ELan GKev GMaP IBoy LAst LHop LRHS MGos MSCN NBir SKHP SPer SPet SRms SRot WCAu
	- 'Amethyst'	IPot LRHS LSRN NBro
	- 'Blue Jacket'	NSti
	- 'Blue Star'	CExl CHel CSpe EBee ECtt ELan ELon EPfP GBin GBuc LRHS NLar SMad WCFE WWEG
	- 'Holden Blue'	MAvo
	- 'Slieve Donard'	see *E.* × *zabelii* 'Donard Variety'
	- 'Superbum'	CSpe ECtt GJos GLog LRHS MNrw SDod SRms SWat
	amethystinum	CCse ELon EPri LRHS SEND SMrm WHoo WWEG XLum
	biebersteinianum	see *E. caeruleum*
	'Blue Jackpot'	EWes MAvo MBel NCGa
	'Blue Steel'	EWTr GKev LLHF
	bourgatii	Widely available
	- Graham Stuart Thomas's selection	CBcs CDes CEnd CExl CMHG CSpe ECtt ELan ELon EPPr EWes GAbr LHop LRHS MAvo MBel MCot MNFA NBir SMad SPad SPer WCot WHoo WHrl WPGP WWEG
	- 'Oxford Blue' ♀H4	CRDP GBin GMaP MHer NLar SKHP SWvt
	- 'Picos Amethyst'	CBcs CMac CWCL ELon LHop LRHS LSRN LSou MBel MGos NCGa NLar NSti SCoo SKHP
	- 'Picos Blue' PBR	Widely available
	- 'Silver Blue'	LRHS
	bromeliifolium misapplied	see *E. agavifolium*, *E. eburneum*
	bromeliifolium ambig.	LRHS
§	***caeruleum***	MNrw
	campestre	CArn MAvo WWEG
	caucasicum	see *E. caeruleum*
	'Cobalt Star'	MAvo NLar
	creticum	NBro NChi
	cymosum B&SWJ 10267	WCru
	decaisneanum misapplied	see *E. pandanifolium*
	deppeanum F&M 54	WPGP
	- NJM 05.031	LEdu
	Dove Cottage hybrid	NDov
	ebracteatum	MAvo
	- var. ***poterioides***	LPla SMad SPhx
§	***eburneum***	CCon EPfP EWes GCal GMaP LRHS MSpe NBro NChi SKHP SMad
	aff. ***eburneum***	CMac

'Electric Haze'	CSam ECtt GBuc LHop LRHS LSou NPnk NSti NWad SPoG
elegans var. **elegans**	CCon
foetidum	CArn
§ **giganteum** ♀H4	CBcs CSev CSpe ELan EPfP EWTr GCal GKev IBoy LAst LEdu LRHS MLHP MWat NBir NBro NGdn NLar SBod SDix SKHP SRms SWvt WMnd
- 'Silver Ghost' ♀H4	CAby CExl CMea CSam CSpe ECtt EWll LBMP LHop LRHS MBel NChi NDov NGdn NSti SKHP SPer SWat SWvt WCot WWEG
gracile B&SWJ 10205	WCru
- B&SWJ 10351	WCru
- B&SWJ 10441	WCru
'Green Jade'	LRHS
guatemalense B&SWJ 8989	WCru
- B&SWJ 10322	WCru
- B&SWJ 10420	WCru
horridum misapplied	see *E. eburneum*
horridum ambig.	EWes MNrw NChi NLar SAPC WMnd
horridum Malme	CCVN WCot
humile B&SWJ 10464	WCru
'Indigo Star'	MAvo
leavenworthii	CHel LRHS
maritimum	CArn CPom CPou EBee GPoy MHer MNHC NLar SMrm SPlb
Miss Willmott's ghost	see *E. giganteum*
× **oliverianum** ♀H4	CMea CSpe ECtt ELan EPfP GBuc GCal GKev LHop LRHS MAvo MBel MLHP MNFA MRav MTis NBir NChi NLar SDix SMrm SPer SWat SWvt WCot WHoo
palmatum	NChi
§ **pandanifolium** ♀H4	CCon CHEx CKno ELan EPfP EUJe EWTr EWes LEdu LHop NSoo SAPC SEND SKHP SMad SPlb SPoG SWvt WMnd WWEG
- 'Physic Purple'	CAby CSpe MAvo SPhx
planum	Widely available
- 'Azureum' **new**	EWTr
- 'Bethlehem' ♀H4	NLar SWat
§ - 'Blauer Zwerg'	CKno EBee MAvo
- 'Blaukappe'	CExl CMea COIW ELon EPfP LDai LRHS MNFA NLar SBod SEND SKHP SMrm SPet SPhx WWEG
* - 'Blue Candle'	NLar
- Blue Dwarf	see *E. planum* 'Blauer Zwerg'
- 'Blue Glitter'	ELon LRHS NLar SPhx SWvt
- 'Blue Hobbit'	CExl CHel CMea CSpe EBee ELon EPfP GBin LBMP LBuc LHop MBri MHer NGdn NLBP NLar NWad SPad SPet SWvt WHar
- 'Blue Ribbon'	LRHS LSou
- 'Flüela'	CBct EWTr EWes GBuc LRHS LSRN MBel NEgg SWat
- 'Jade Frost' PBR (v)	CAbP CBct CExl CWGN ELon EPfP EWes LBMP LHop LLHF LRHS LSou MAvo MBNS MBel MHol MNrw MRav MTis NLar NSti SKHP SMrm SPad SPoG SRms SWvt WCot XLum
- 'Little Blue Wonder' PBR	CBct NHol
- 'Naughty Jackpot' (v)	EBee NLar
- 'Paradise Jackpot' PBR	SPer
- 'Seven Seas'	CCon LRHS MBNS MBel NEgg
- 'Silver Salentino'	ELon SPhx WHil WOut
- 'Silver Stone'	EBee LDai LRHS
- 'Sunny Jackpot' PBR	NSti
- 'Tetra Blau'	LRHS
- 'Tetra Petra'	LHop LRHS NEgg
- 'Tiny Jackpot'	IBoy NLar NPnk
- 'White Glitter'	EBee SPhx
proteiflorum	EPfP EUJe IGor LRHS SKHP SMad SPhx SPlb
- F&M 224	WPGP
serbicum	GCal MAvo WCot
serra	EWes LDai LRHS
strotheri B&SWJ 9109	WCru
- B&SWJ 10392	WCru
tricuspidatum	ECtt LRHS
× **tripartitum** ♀H4	CTri ECtt ELan EPPr EPfP GMaP LAst LHop LRHS LSRN MBri MNFA MRav MWat NBro NEgg NLar SPhx SPoG SRkn SWat SWvt WWlt
* **umbelliferum**	GCal MBNS NPri SKHP
variifolium	Widely available
- 'Miss Marbel'	EPfP WSHC
venustum	EUJe LRHS SMad
yuccifolium	CCon EPfP EWes GCal LEdu LRHS NLar SDix SMrm SPhx SPlb SWvt XLum
× **zabelii**	CAby CRDP NBir NChi
- 'Big Blue'	ECGP ELon GBin LPio LRHS MAvo MBri MHol MSCN MTis NCGa NLar WCot WHil
- 'Blaue Ritter'	SKHP SWat
§ - 'Donard Variety'	CHel EBee ECtt GBuc GCal IPot ITim LEdu LRHS MAvo NLar SWat
- 'Forncett Ultra'	GCal MAvo
- 'Jewel'	MAvo SWat
- 'Jos Eijking' PBR	Widely available
- 'Violetta'	IGor NLar SWat

Erysimum ✿ (*Brassicaceae*)

'Andy's Oranges and Lemons' (v)	WCot
'Anne Marie'	EPfP
'Apricot Delight'	see *E.* 'Apricot Twist'
§ 'Apricot Twist'	Widely available
arkansanum	see *E. helveticum*
asperum	GJos IFro
'Audrey's Pink'	CSev WHoo
'Bowles's Mauve' ♀H3	Widely available
'Bowles's Purple'	SRms SWvt
'Bowles's Yellow'	GCal WCot
'Bredon' ♀H3	EPfP NPer
'Butterscotch'	MMHG WHoo
capitatum var. **purshii**	GKev LLHF NSla WAbe
- - pink/purple-flowered **new**	GKev
caricum	WAbe
cheiri	CArn MHer
- 'Baden-Powell' (d)	GCal
- 'Bloody Warrior' (d)	CElw ECtt GCal
- 'Harpur Crewe' (d)	ECtt EPfP GMaP NPer SRms WHer
- 'Orange Bedder' (Bedder Series)	NBir
'Chelsea Jacket'	EPfP
'Constant Cheer'	CMea CPrp CSBt CWCL EBee ECtt ELan ELon EPfP IFoB LRHS MAvo MCot NPer SEND SPer SPoG SRGP SRkn SWvt WCAu WHil WKif
'Cotswold Gem' (v)	ECtt EHoe ELan EPfP LDai LSou NPer SBri SLim SWvt WCot
'Dawn Breaker'	ECtt LRHS WCot

'Dorothy Elmhirst'	see *E.* 'Mrs L.K. Elmhirst'
dwarf, lemon-flowered	WHoo
'Emm's Variety'	ECtt
'Gold Rush'	GJos
'Gold Shot'	GJos
'Golden Gem'	ECho ELan EPfP
'Golden Jubilee'	ECho ECtt GBuc WIce
'Hector's Gatepost'	EWTr LRHS SRGP
§ ***helveticum***	ECho EDAr LRHS SRms
'Jacob's Jacket'	ECtt MBNS MHer NPer
'Jenny Brook'PBR	NCGa
'John Codrington'	GBin LHop NPer WKif
'Jubilee Gold'	WWEG
kotschyanum	ECho EPot NSla SRms WIce
linifolium	SRms WGor
- 'Little Kiss Lilac'	GJos
§ - 'Variegatum' (v)	CCCN CSBt ECtt ELan ELon EPfP LRHS NEgg NLar NPer NPri SPer SPoG SRot WCAu XLum
- 'Variegatum' peach-flowered (v)	MAsh NLBP SPad
'Moonlight'	EBee EPot GBuc GMaP MHer MRav NBir SRms WHoo
§ 'Mrs L.K. Elmhirst'	ECtt ELon MMHG NPer WHoo
mutabile	CTri EHyd EPfP MRav WHal
'My Old Mum'	CWGN LRHS LSRN LSou MRav WHlf
'Orange Flame'	CMea ECho ELon EPot LHop MHer NPer WHoo WNew
'Orange King'	WIce
'Orange Zwerg' **new**	WIce
'Parish's'	CElw CHVG CSpe MRav WWFP
'Parkwood Gold'	ECho EPot GJos GKev
'Pastel Patchwork'	CSpe LRHS LSou
perofskianum	GKev
Perry's hybrid	NPer
'Perry's Peculiar'	NPer
'Perry's Surprise'	NPer
'Perry's Variegated' (v)	NPer
'Plant World Lemon'	CHGN CNec ELon NLar
'Poppet'	CSpe
'Poppet Heaton'	CHll
§ ***pulchellum***	GKev
pumilum DC.	see *E. helveticum*
pusillum	WAbe
'Ray's Early Giants' (mixed) **new**	CPla
'Roddy's Own'	IBlr
rupestre	see *E. pulchellum*
Rysi Bronze = 'Innrysibro'PBR	LSou WHil
Rysi Gold = 'Innrysigol'PBR	SPoG
Rysi Moon	CWGN GBin
'Sissinghurst Variegated'	see *E. linifolium* 'Variegatum'
'Spice Island'	EBee EPfP NCGa
'Sprite'	CMea CTri NPer SEND
'Starbright'	CWCL LRHS
'Stars and Stripes' (v)	EPfP LRHS LSou SRkn
'Sunbright'	EPot
Sunburst = 'Listrace'	CAby CMea CWGN ECtt ELon LSou SPoG WCot WHil WWlt
'Sweet Sorbet'	ELon EPfP NEgg NLar SRkn SWvt WHil
Walberton's Fragrant Star = 'Walfrastar' (v)	EPfP LBuc LRHS SPoG
Walberton's Fragrant Sunshine = 'Walfrasun'	CHll EPfP LRHS MBri SCoo SPoG
'Wenlock Beauty'	CFis LDai SRms
'Winter Joy'	ELon LLHF LSou MBNS NLar
Winter Orchid	CSpe CWGN GBin LRHS NDov WCot
Winter Rouge	CWCL ELon LBMP LRHS
Winter Sorbet = 'Inneryws'PBR	ECtt ELon EPfP LBMP

Erythraea see *Centaurium*

Erythrina (*Papilionaceae*)

abyssinica	SPlb
amazonica	SPlb
arborescens	SPlb
× ***bidwillii***	CCCN WPGP
crista-galli	CBcs CCCN CDTJ CHel CHll CPom CSpe EAmu EBee ELan EPfP ESwi EUJe LEdu LRHS MPie SPlb WPGP
guatemalensis	SPlb
herbacea	SPlb
§ ***humeana***	SPlb
latissima	SPlb
lysistemon	SPlb
princeps	see *E. humeana*
rubrinervia	SPlb
speciosa	SPlb
vespertilio	SPlb

Erythronium ✿ (*Liliaceae*)

albidum	CHel CLAP EBee ECho GAbr GBuc GKev IBlr LWst MMoz
americanum	CArn CHel CLAP ECho EPot IBlr LWst MMoz MNrw WAbe
'Apple Blossom'	ECho LWst
'Ballyrogan's Blaze' **new**	IBlr
'Beechpark'	IBlr
'Blush'	ECho IBlr
'Bronze Beauty'	IBlr
'Californian Star'	IBlr
californicum ♀H4	CCon CLAP ECho GBuc IBlr LWst
- J&JA 13216	CLAP
- JCA 1.350.200	LWst
- 'Brimstone'	IBlr
- 'Brocklamont Inheritance' **new**	IBlr
- 'Bronze Edge'	IBlr
- 'Dark Delight'	IBlr
- Plas Merdyn form	IBlr
- 'Stellar' **new**	IBlr
- 'White Beauty' ♀H4	Widely available
californicum* × *hendersonii	IBlr
'Carol Scott' **new**	IBlr
caucasicum	CLAP LWst
citrinum	GBuc LLHF
- J&JA 13462	CLAP
- subsp. ***citrinum***	GBuc
citrinum* × *hendersonii	IBlr
'Citronella'	CBro CCon CLAP GBuc GKev IBlr LWst WAbe
cliftonii hort.	see *E. multiscapideum* Cliftonii Group
'Craigton Cover Girl'	IBlr
'Delicacy'	IBlr
dens-canis ♀H4	Widely available
- JCA 470.001	CLAP
- from Slovenia	CLAP
- 'Charmer'	ECho MNrw
- 'Frans Hals'	CLAP EBee ECho EPot GBuc GCra GKev IPot MNrw SKHP WHal
- large-flowered	IBlr

	– 'Lilac Wonder'	EBee ECho EPot GBuc GKev GMaP IPot LEdu MAvo MNrw NWad SDeJ
*	– 'Moerheimii' (d)	ECho EPot GKev IBlr
	– var. ***niveum***	IBlr LWst NEgg
	– 'Old Aberdeen'	CAvo CLAP IBlr LWst MNrw
	– 'Pink Perfection'	EBee ECho GKev LEdu MNrw NMin SDeJ
	– 'Purple King'	EBee ECGP ECho EPot GBuc GKev GMaP IPot LWst MAvo MMoz MNrw NHol NWad SDeJ
	– 'Rose Queen'	ECho EPot GBuc GKev GMaP IPot MAvo MNrw NMin NWad SDeJ SPhx WHal
*	– 'Semi-plenum' (d)	IBlr
	– 'Snowflake'	CAvo CBro CLAP ECho EPot GBuc GKev IPot MBel MMoz MNrw NBir NHol NMin NWad SDeJ SKHP SMrm SPhx SPoG WAbe
	– 'White Splendour'	ECho IBlr LWst MNrw
	– white-flowered, from Serbia	ECho
	'Eirene' **new**	IBlr
	elegans	ECho GBuc LWst
	'Flash'	IBlr
§	***grandiflorum***	CLAP ECho
	– M&PS 007	CLAP
	– subsp. ***chrysandrum***	see *E. grandiflorum*
	'Harvington Snowgoose'	CAvo CLAP EHyd IBlr LLHF LRHS LWst MBri SKHP SPoG
	helenae	CLAP ECho IBlr
	hendersonii	CAvo CLAP EBee ECho GBuc LWst SKHP WAbe
	– J&JA 12945	CLAP
	howellii	CLAP
	– J&JA 13441	CLAP
	'Janice'	LWst
	japonicum	CHel EBee ECho EFEx EPot MBel MNrw
	'Jeanette Brickell'	CLAP GBuc IBlr LWst
	'Jeannine'	GBuc IBlr LWst
	'Joan Wiley'	LWst
	'Joanna'	GBuc IBlr LWst MNrw
	'John Brookes'	LWst
	'Keith'	LWst
	'Kinfauns Pink'	CWCL GBuc IBlr LLHF LWst
	klamathense	EPot
	'Kondo'	CCon CHel CTri EBee ECho EPfP EPot GKev GMaP IBlr LWst NBir NHol NLar NWad SPer WAbe WCot
	'Lavender Eye' **new**	IBlr
	'Margaret Mathew'	CLAP IBlr LWst WAbe
	'Minnehaha'	GBuc LWst
	montanum	ECho
§	***multiscapideum***	CLAP ECho GBuc LLHF LWst WCot
	– NNS 02-166	WCot
§	– Cliftonii Group	CLAP GBuc LWst SKHP WCot
	'Oregon Encore'	IBlr
	oregonum	CHel CLAP ECho EHyd GBuc IBlr LLHF LRHS LWst MNrw SKHP
	– subsp. ***leucandrum***	CLAP LWst
	– – 'The Giant' **new**	IBlr
	– subsp. ***oregonum*** NNS 01-202	WCot
I	– 'Sulphur Form'	CLAP
	'Pagoda' 🏆H4	Widely available
	purdyi	see *E. multiscapideum*
	revolutum 🏆H4	CBro CHel CLAP CWCL EBee ECho EPot GBuc GKev GMaP IBlr LRHS LWst MNrw SChF SKHP SRot WCru
	– from God's Valley	IBlr MNrw
	– 'Dark Dapple'	IBlr
	– 'Guincho Splendour'	IBlr
I	– 'Inshriach Form'	IBlr
	– Johnsonii Group	ECho LWst WCru
	– 'Knightshayes'	CAvo EBee EHyd GBuc IBlr LRHS MBri SKHP
	– 'Knightshayes Pink'	CHel CLAP IBlr LLHF LWst NBir SPoG WShi
	– 'Pink Beauty'	GKev LWst
	– Plas Merdyn form	IBlr
	– 'Rose Beauty'	ECho
	– 'Wild Salmon'	CLAP EBee EHyd LLHF LRHS LWst MBri SPoG
	revolutum × ***californicum*** 'Purple Heart'	IBlr
	'Rippling Waters'	IBlr
	'Rosalind'	IBlr LWst
	sibiricum	ECho
	'Sundisc'	ECho GBuc IBlr LWst WAbe
	'Sunshine' **new**	IBlr
	'Susannah'	IBlr LWst
	taylorii	LWst
	tuolumnense 🏆H4	CBro CCon CLAP CWCL EBee ECho EPot GBuc GKev GMaP IBlr MCot MMoz MNrw NWad SDeJ SMrm SPhx WCot
	– EBA clone 2	IBlr LWst
	– EBA clone 3	IBlr
	– 'Edgar Klein'	LWst
	– Plas Merdyn form	IBlr
	– 'Spindlestone'	EBee EHyd GBuc IBlr LRHS LWst
	umbilicatum	EBee ECho IBlr LWst
	'White Star' **new**	IBlr

Escallonia ✿ (*Escalloniaceae*)

	'Alice'	EBee SLPl SPer
§	***alpina*** SDR 7016 **new**	GKev
	'Apple Blossom' 🏆H4	Widely available
§	***bifida*** 🏆H3	CDoC CDul CHGN ECre LRHS SDix
	'C.F. Ball'	CBcs CTri ELan EPfP GKin LBMP LBuc LRHS MAsh MSwo NEgg NPla NWea SEND SGol SRms WHar WMoo
	'Compacta Coccinea'	LRHS MBri
	'Dart's Rosy Red'	MBri SLPl WHar WMoo
	'Donard Beauty'	NEgg SRms
	'Donard Brilliance'	SGol SRms WHar
	'Donard Radiance' 🏆H4	CBcs CDoC CDul CMac CSBt CWib EBee ELan EPfP EShb LHop LRHS LSRN NLar NWad NWea SGol SLim SPer SPoG SRms SWvt WHar WMoo
	'Donard Seedling'	CBcs CCVT CDoC CDul CHab EBee ECrN ELan EPfP GKin LAst LBuc LRHS MAsh MGos MSwo NPer NWea SGol SLPl SLim SPer SRms SWvt WHar WMoo
	'Donard Star'	CWib EPfP NLar NWad NWea WCFE WHar
	'Donard White'	EPfP NLar SPoG
	'Edinensis'	EBee EPfP NLar SLim SRms WMoo
	'Everest'	EPfP LRHS MAsh NEgg SLon
	× ***exoniensis***	SRms
	fonkii	see *E. alpina*
	'Gwendolyn Anley'	SLPl
	'Hopleys Gold'	see *E. laevis* 'Gold Brian'
	illinita	EBee NLar
	'Iveyi' 🏆H3	Widely available
	'Jamie'^{PBR}	EShb LLHF LSRN WMoo
§	***laevis***	LRHS

§ - 'Gold Brian'PBR	CDul CMac EHoe ELan EPau EPfP LRHS LSRN MAsh MGos MJak MWat NLar SCoo SGol SPer WHar
- 'Gold Ellen' (v)	CSBt CTri EBee EHoe ELan ELon EPfP LRHS LSRN MAsh MBri MGos MRav MSwo NEgg NHol NLar NSoo SCoo SEND SHil SLim SPer SPoG SRms SWvt WHar WMoo
'Langleyensis' ♀H4	CHab CMac CTri CWib GGal SGol SRms WHar
montevidensis	see *E. bifida*
organensis	see *E. laevis*
'Peach Blossom' ♀H4	CBar CDoC CDul CWib EBee ELan ELon EPfP GKin LHop LRHS MAsh MLHP MMuc MSwo NBir SCoo SEND SGol SLPl SLim SPer SPoG SRms
'Pink Pyramid'	LRHS
'Pride of Donard' ♀H4	CHab CSBt EBee EPfP GKin LRHS MGos SRms WHar
punctata	see *E. rubra*
Red Carpet = 'Loncar'PBR	ELon LAst LRHS NSoo SLon WHar WMoo WNPC
'Red Dream'	CSBt CWSG EBee EPfP LRHS MAsh MBlu MBri MGos MSCN MSwo NLar NWad SCoo SEWo SHil SPoG SRms SWvt
'Red Elf'	CMac EBee ELan EPfP GKin LAst LRHS MBri MGos MWat NEgg SCoo SHil SLPl SPer SPlb SPoG SRms SWvt
'Red Hedger'	CHab CSBt CTsd CWib ELan EShb GGal MRav NSoo SCoo SRms WMoo
'Red Knight'	MAsh
'Red Robin'	SPoG
resinosa	CExl CTsd SAPC SPlb SRms SVen WJek
revoluta	CTri
§ ***rubra*** SDR 7052	GKev
- 'Crimson Spire' ♀H4	CBar CBcs CDoC CDul CSBt CTri CWib EBee ECrN EPfP GKin LRHS LSRN MAsh MBri MGos MMuc MRav MWat NBir NEgg NWea SEND SHil SLim SPer SPlb SPoG SRms WMoo
- 'Ingramii'	CWib NWea SEND
- var. ***macrantha***	Widely available
* - - ***aurea***	NPla
- 'Pygmaea'	see *E. rubra* 'Woodside'
§ - 'Woodside'	ECho EPfP LLHF NWad SGol SRms WHil
'Silver Anniversary'	MSwo
'Slieve Donard'	CMac EPfP MRav NEgg NWad NWea SLPl SLim SLon SRms WHar
tucumanensis	SPlb SVen
'Ventnor'	SPlb SVen WPGP

Eschscholzia (*Papaveraceae*)

californica ♀H4	MBel
- 'Alba'	CSpe
- 'Gini's Cream'	CSpe
- 'Ivory Castle'	SMrm SPhx
- 'Jersey Cream'	CSpe
- 'Red Chief'	SMrm SPhx

Espeletia (*Asteraceae*)

aff. ***summapacis*** B&SWJ 10766	WCru

Esterhuysenia (*Aizoaceae*)

alpina	CPBP WAbe

Eucalyptus ✿ (*Myrtaceae*)

aggregata	SAPC SKin
alpina	SPlb
amygdalina	SPlb
approximans new	SKin
archeri	CDTJ CDul CTho ELan EPfP LRHS MBri MGos MMuc MWhi NLar NSoo SEND SHil SKin WCot
baeuerlenii	SKin
caesia	SPlb
camaldulensis	SPlb
camphora	CCCN CTsd EBee ESwi SKin
cinerea	SBig SKin SPlb
citriodora	EOHP MHer SKin SPlb
coccifera	CBcs CSBt CTsd ELan EPfP EUJe LRHS MMuc NEgg NPer SBig SEND SKin SPlb WCot
cordata	ELan SKin
crenulata	SKin
crucis subsp. ***crucis***	SPlb
curtisii	SPlb
cypellocarpa	SPlb
dalrympleana ♀H3	CMHG CMac EBee ELan EPfP EUJe LRHS LSRN MGos MSwo NLar NPer SBig SEND SHil SKin SLim SPer SPlb SRms WHar WPGP
debeuzevillei	see *E. pauciflora* subsp. *debeuzevillei*
delegatensis	CMHG GLin NPer SKin
divaricata	see *E. gunnii* subsp. *divaricata*
erythrocorys	SPlb
eximia	SPlb
* - 'Nana'	SPlb
ficifolia	CBcs CDTJ
fraxinoides	SPlb
gamophylla	SPlb
glaucescens	CMHG ELan EPfP EWes LRHS SAPC SEWo SKin SPer
globulus	CWCL SPlb
goniocalyx	EPfP
§ ***gregsoniana***	EPfP GGal SKin SPlb
gunnii ♀H3	Widely available
- Azura = 'Cagire'PBR	LRHS LSRN MPkF SLon
§ - subsp. ***divaricata***	EPfP MBri SKin
johnstonii	CDul NSoo SKin SPer
kitsoniana	ELan SKin
kruseana	SPlb
kybeanensis	SKin WCot
leucoxylon subsp. ***megalocarpa***	SPlb
ligustrina	SKin
'Little Boy Blue'	CWib LSRN
macarthurii	SKin
macrocarpa	SPlb
mannifera subsp. ***elliptica***	SKin
mitchelliana	SKin
* ***moorei nana***	CDTJ
neglecta	SKin
nicholii	CBcs CDul CSpe EHoe ELan EPfP EUJe EWes LRHS MGos NSoo SCoo SKin SLim SPoG WCot
niphophila	see *E. pauciflora* subsp. *niphophila*
nitens	CDTJ CTsd SBig SKin SPlb
§ ***nitida***	SKin

	nova-anglica	SKin
	parviflora	SKin
	parvifolia ♀H4	CCCN CDoC CMac EPfP LRHS MWhi NLar SCoo SEND
	pauciflora	CCCN CDoC CSBt CTsd ELan EUJe MGos MMuc SPer
§	- subsp. ***debeuzevillei***	CDoC EPfP EWes SAPC SBig SKin
	- subsp. ***hedraia***	SKin
	- var. ***nana***	see *E. gregsoniana*
§	- subsp. ***niphophila*** ♀H4	Widely available
	perriniana	CBcs CDul CMHG EBee ELan EPfP EUJe LRHS MBri MGos MWhi NEgg NSoo SBig SCoo SHil SKin SLim SPer SPlb SPoG SWvt
	pulverulenta	CMac SKin SPlb
	- 'Baby Blue'	LHop LRHS SHil SKin SWvt
	regnans	SKin
	risdonii	SKin
	rodwayi	SKin
	rossii	SPlb
	rubida	CCCN CMHG SKin
	sideroxylon	SPlb
	- 'Rosea'	SPlb
	simmondsii	see *E. nitida*
	stellulata	SKin
	stricta	SKin
	subcrenulata	ELan EPfP GLin SKin
	tetraptera	SPlb
	torquata	SPlb
	urnigera	LHop SKin
	vernicosa	SKin
	viminalis	LRHS SKin

Eucharidium see *Clarkia*

Eucharis (*Amaryllidaceae*)

§	***amazonica*** ♀H1	CCCN ECho SDeJ SPav
	grandiflora misapplied	see *E. amazonica*

Eucodonia (*Gesneriaceae*)

	'Adele'	EABi

Eucomis ✿ (*Asparagaceae*)

	Aloha	see *E.* 'Leia'
	autumnalis misapplied	see *E. zambesiaca*
§	***autumnalis*** (Mill.) Chitt. ♀H2-3	CAvo CBro CHEx CTsd EBee ECho EPot ERCP GKev LRHS SDeJ SPav SPer SPlb
	- subsp. ***autumnalis*** 'Peace Candles'	CTca
	'Baby Coral' **new**	CAvo
	bicolor ♀H2-3	Widely available
	- 'Alba'	CAvo CExl CTca EAmu EBee ECho GKev LPio LRHS
	- 'Stars and Stripes'	WCru WHil
	'Cabernet Candles'	CTca WHil
§	***comosa***	CAvo CBro CHEx CHll CPrp CSam CTca EBee ERCP EShb GKev LEdu LRHS SDeJ SMad SPav WHil WWEG
	- 'Cornwood'	CAvo CPrp CTca WHil
	- 'First Red'	WPGP
	- green-leaved	CTca
	- 'Kilimanjaro'	CTca EBee GKev WHil
	- 'Lotte'	CTca GKev
	- 'Oakhurst'	CAby CBct CDoC CHel CKno ECtt ESwi LHop WHil
	- purple-leaved	CAvo CHEx EShb
	- 'Sparkling Burgundy'	Widely available
	- 'Sparkling Rosy'	ERCP GKev
	- var. ***striata***	CAby CDes
	- 'Tarzan's Tail'	WHil
	'Frank Lawley'	CDes LPio
	'Freckles' **new**	LSou
	humilis	CTca XEll
	- 'Twinkle Stars'	EBee EPot MBri
	hybrid	SDix
	'John Huxtable'	GCal LPio
	'John Treasure'	WHil
	'Joy's Purple'	CBro CPar CTca EPri LRHS
§	'Leia'PBR	CTca LRHS
	'Louis Wain' **new**	WHil
	montana	CBro CPar CPrp CTca EBee EPot GKev WCot WPGP
	pallidiflora ♀H4	CAvo CHEx LEdu WPGP
	'Pink Gin'	CAvo
	'Playa Blanca' **new**	CTca
	pole-evansii	CBro CCon CExl CPar CTca EAmu ELan EPri EUJe GKev IGor IVic LHop LPio LRHS MMHG MRav SDeJ SMrm WCru WWEG
	- 'Burgundy'	GBin
I	- 'Purpurea'	CExl GCal
	punctata	see *E. comosa*
	regia	CTca
	- JCA 3.230.709	WCot
*	***reichenbachii***	CDTJ SPlb
	'Swazi Pride'	CTca
	'Tugela Ruby'PBR **new**	CTca
	undulata	see *E. autumnalis* (Mill.) Chitt.
	vandermerwei	CAvo CBro CDes CHel CTca EBee EPot ERCP GKev SDeJ SKHP WPGP
	- 'Octopus'	CCCN CExl CJun CKno CPrp CTca EAmu EBee ELan EPfP ESwi EUJe GBin GKev LRHS LSou MAvo MGos MHer SPad SPer WCot WWEG
§	***zambesiaca***	CTca EBee GCal LPio WWEG
	- JCA 3.230.709	WCot
	- JCA 3.231.010 **new**	WCot
	- 'White Dwarf'	ECho EShb SPer
	'Zeal Bronze'	CMHG CTca ELan EPfP GCal GCra LPio LRHS

Eucommia (*Eucommiaceae*)

	ulmoides	CBcs CDul CMCN EBtc EPfP IArd IDee NLar WPGP

Eucryphia ✿ (*Cunoniaceae*)

	cordifolia	CAbP CBcs CDoC CGHE CHel CMac CWib GKin MBlu
	- Crarae hardy form	GGGa
§	***cordifolia*** × ***lucida***	CBcs CCCN ELan GGal MSnd
	glutinosa ♀H4	CCCN EPfP GGGa GKev GKin LRHS MAsh SSpi
	- 'Miniature'	EBee EPfP SChF WPGP
	× ***hillieri***	WSpi
	- 'Winton'	CMHG GQui
	× ***intermedia***	CExl CMac CWSG EBee EPfP GKin NLar SRms SSpi SSta
	- 'Rostrevor' ♀H3	CBcs CDul CExl CMHG CMac CTho ELan EPfP GBin GGGa GGal GQui LRHS LSRN MBlu MGos NLar SReu SSta WSHC WSpi
	'Leatherwood Cream'	GKin WSpi
	lucida	CCCN CTho ELan LLHF NLar WSpi
	- 'Ballerina'	CMHG CMac CTho ELon GKin LRHS MAsh MGos SChF SCoo SPoG SSpi WPGP
	- 'Dumpling'	CExl CGHE WPGP

	- 'Gilt Edge' (v)	CBcs CWGN GKin LLHF LRHS
	- 'Pink Cloud'	CBcs CDoC CDul CEnd CExl CMac CTho ELan EPfP GGGa GKin GQui IVic LHop LRHS LSRN MBlu NLar SLim SSpi SSta SWvt WPGP
	- 'Pink Whisper'	see *E. milliganii* subsp. *pubescens* 'Pink Whisper'
	- 'Spring Glow' (v)	CExl CWGN LLHF LRHS MAsh SPoG
	milliganii	CAbP CDoC CFil CMac ELan EPfP GGGa GQui LHop LRHS MBlu SBrt SRms SSpi SSta WPGP
§	- subsp. ***pubescens*** 'Pink Whisper'	WPGP
	moorei	CBcs CCCN CExl CMac GGGa GQui
	× ***nymansensis***	CHab CWib SAPC SReu SRms SSpi
	- 'George Graham'	CMHG GGGa
	- 'Nymans Silver' (v)	ELan GGGa LLHF LRHS MAsh SPoG SSpi WPat
	- 'Nymansay' ♀^{H3}	Widely available
	'Penwith' misapplied	see *E. cordifolia* × *lucida*
	'Penwith' ambig.	CTsd GKin GQui MMuc

Eugenia (*Myrtaceae*)

uniflora	CCCN

Eumorphia (*Asteraceae*)

sericea	CFis

Eunomia see *Aethionema*

Euodia (*Rutaceae*)

daniellii	see *Tetradium daniellii*
hupehensis	see *Tetradium daniellii* Hupehense Group

Euonymus ✿ (*Celastraceae*)

	B&L 12543	EWes
	CC 4522	CExl
	alatus ♀^{H4}	Widely available
	- B&SWJ 8794	WCru
	- var. ***apterus***	EPfP MBri WGrn
	- - B&SWJ 11051	WCru
	- Chicago Fire	see *E. alatus* 'Timber Creek'
	- 'Compactus' ♀^{H4}	Widely available
§	- 'Fire Ball'	CJun EPfP
	- Little Moses = 'Odom'	NLar
*	- 'Macrophyllus'	CJun EPfP MBri
	- 'Rudy Haag'	CJun EPfP NLar
	- 'Select'	see *E. alatus* 'Fire Ball'
	- 'Silver Cloud'	CJun EPfP NLar
§	- 'Timber Creek'	CJun EPfP IDee LLHF MBlu NLar WPat
	americanus	EPfP MBlu NLar
	- 'Evergreen'	EPfP
	- narrow-leaved	CJun EPfP
	atropurpureus	EPfP
	bungeanus	EPfP WPat
	- 'Dart's Pride'	CJun EPfP NLar
	- 'Fireflame'	CJun EPfP WPat
*	- var. ***mongolicus***	EPfP
	- 'Pendulus'	CJun EPfP MBlu SCoo
	- var. ***semipersistens***	CJun
	carnosus	CJun EPfP
	chibae B&SWJ 11159	WCru
	'Copper Wire'	EHoe
	cornutus var. ***quinquecornutus***	CJun CMCN ELan EPfP GKev IDee IGor MBlu MMHG NLar WPGP WPat
	'Den Haag'	CJun EPfP NLar
	echinatus	EPfP
	europaeus	Widely available
	- from Slovakia	WCru
	- f. ***albus***	CJun CTho EPfP LRHS NLar
	- 'Atropurpureus'	CMCN CTho EPfP NLar
	- 'Atrorubens'	CJun
	- 'Aucubifolius' (v)	CMac
*	- 'Aureus'	CNat
	- 'Brilliant'	CJun EPfP NLar
*	- f. ***bulgaricus***	EPfP
	- 'Chrysophyllus'	EPfP MBlu
	- 'Howard'	EPfP
	- var. ***intermedius***	CJun EPfP MBlu MBri NLar
	- 'Miss Pinkie'	CEnd
	- 'Red Cascade' ♀^{H4}	Widely available
	- 'Scarlet Wonder'	CJun EPfP
	- 'Thornhayes'	CTho EPfP NLar
I	- 'Variegatus' (v)	EPfP
	europeaus 'Pumilis'	EPfP
	farreri	see *E. nanus*
	fimbriatus	CJun EPfP SEND
	fortunei	LEdu NWad
	- Blondy = 'Interbolwi'^{PBR} (v)	CDoC CDul CTri CWib EBee ELan EPfP LAst LRHS MAsh MBri MGos MJak MMuc MRav MSwo NEgg NLar NPri NWad SCoo SEND SGol SLim SPer SPoG
	- 'Canadale Gold' (v)	EBee EPfP LRHS MAsh NHol NPri SLon SPoG
	- 'Coloratus'	CMac EPfP MBlu MSwo SEND SPer
	- 'Dart's Blanket'	CDul EBee ELan EPPr EPfP MRav SEND
	- 'Emerald Gaiety' (v) ♀^{H4}	Widely available
	- 'Emerald 'n' Gold' (v) ♀^{H4}	Widely available
	- 'Emerald Surprise' (v) ♀^{H4}	EPfP SRGP
	- 'Gaiety Silver' **new**	IBoy
	- 'Gold Spot'	see *E. fortunei* 'Sunspot'
	- 'Gold Tip'	see *E. fortunei* 'Golden Prince'
	- Golden Harlequin = 'Hoogi'^{PBR} (v)	CSBt LHop LRHS MAsh MPkF NWad SPoG SWvt
§	- 'Golden Pillar' (v)	EHoe
§	- 'Golden Prince' (v)	CMac EHoe MRav MSwo SRms
	- Goldy = 'Waldbolwi'^{PBR}	LRHS NLar NSoo SGol SHil
	- 'Harlequin' (v)	CBar CBcs CMac CSBt CWGN EBee EHoe ELan ELon EPfP EShb LBuc LRHS LSRN MAsh MBlu MGos MJak MRav NBir NPro SGol SLim SPer SPoG SRms SWvt
	- 'Heins Silver' **new**	NSoo
	- 'Hort's Blaze'	EPPr
	- 'Kewensis'	CDoC CHid CMac CWib EBee EUJe GCal LRHS MWhi SAPC SPoG WCru
	- 'Minimus'	CDul CTri EPPr MSwo NPro WBor WPGP XLum
*	- 'Minimus Variegatus' (v)	ECho EPPr EShb SPlb
	- 'Perrolino'	EBee
§	- var. ***radicans***	EWld
	- 'Sheridan Gold'	CMac CTri MRav NWad
	- 'Silver Gem'	see *E. fortunei* 'Variegatus'
	- 'Silver Pillar' (v)	EHoe
	- 'Silver Queen' (v)	Widely available
	- 'Silverstone'^{PBR} (v)	EPfP LRHS NPro SPoG
	- 'Sunshine' (v)	EBee ELan EPfP LRHS MAsh NWad SLon SPoG
§	- 'Sunspot' (v)	CBcs CMac ELan MGos MJak MMuc MSwo SEND SRms WHar
	- 'Tustin' ♀^{H4}	EPPr

§ - 'Variegatus' (v) SRms
- 'Wolong Ghost' CDoC CExl EBee EMil EPPr GKin IArd IDee LRHS MBlu MGos NLar SGol SKHP SWvt WCot

frigidus EPfP
grandiflorus CJun EPfP NLar SCoo
- 'Red Wine' CJun CTho ELon EMil EPfP ESwi LHop LRHS NLar SKHP WPGP WPat
- f. ***salicifolius*** CJun EPfP

hamiltonianus CMCN EBee EBtc ECrN EPfP SEND SSpi
- 'Fiesta' CJun EPfP
- subsp. ***hians*** see *E. hamiltonianus* subsp. *sieboldianus*
- 'Indian Summer' CJun ELon EPfP LRHS MAsh MBri MMHG NLar SCoo SKHP SPoG SSpi WPGP WPat
- 'Koi Boy' CJun MAsh
- 'Miss Pinkie' CJun EPfP IVic MAsh NLar SCoo WPat
- 'Pink Delight' CJun
- 'Poort Bulten' CJun EPfP NLar
- 'Popcorn' CJun EPfP WPat
- 'Rainbow' CJun EPfP
- 'Red Chief' CJun EPfP NLar
- 'Red Elf' CJun EPfP NLar
- 'Rising Sun' CJun EBee EPfP MBri NLar
§ - subsp. ***sieboldianus*** CDul CExl CJun EPfP GBin MRav NPCo WPat
- - B&SWJ 10941 WCru
- - 'Calocarpus' CJun EPfP SCoo
- - 'Coral Charm' CJun EPfP NLar
- - Semiexsertus Group EPfP
* - - var. ***yedoensis*** f. ***koehneanus*** EPfP
- 'Snow' CJun EPfP WCot WPat
- 'Winter Glory' CJun MMHG NLar WPat
- var. ***yedoensis*** see *E. hamiltonianus* subsp. *sieboldianus*

japonicus CBcs CDoC CDul CMac CTri ECrN EPfP SAPC SBod SEND SEWo SPer
- 'Albomarginatus' CBcs CDul CTri EHoe EPfP LRHS MJak SEND SRms
§ - 'Aureomarginatus' LRHS
- 'Aureopictus' see *E. japonicus* 'Aureus'
- 'Aureovariegatus' see *E. japonicus* 'Ovatus Aureus'
§ - 'Aureus' (v) CBcs CDoC CSBt CTsd CWib EBee LAst LRHS NPri NSoo SCoo SLon SPer WHar
- 'Benkomasaki' EPfP
- 'Bravo' CDoC CDul EBee EHoe EPfP IVic LRHS MAsh MGos NLar SCoo SEWo SHil SLim SPer SPoG SWvt
- 'Chollipo' 𝕐H4 EBee ELan EPfP LRHS MAsh SEND SHil SPoG
- 'Compactus' SCoo
- 'Duc d'Anjou' misapplied see *E. japonicus* 'Viridivariegatus'
- 'Duc d'Anjou' Carrière (v) EBee EHoe ELan EPfP EWes MRav SEND SPoG
- 'Elegantissimus Aureus' see *E. japonicus* 'Aureomarginatus'
- Exstase = 'Goldbolwi' PBR (v) SPoG WCot
- 'Francien' (v) LBuc LRHS SHil
- 'Gold Queen' PBR LRHS
- 'Golden Maiden' EBee ELan EPfP LRHS MAsh SLim SLon SPoG SWvt
- 'Golden Pillar' see *E. fortunei* 'Golden Pillar'
- 'Green Rocket' EBee EPfP EShb LRHS MBri SGol SHil SLim SPoG
- 'Green Spider' SPoG
- 'Grey Beauty' ELon EShb NLar
- 'Happiness' PBR **new** MPkF SLim
- 'Hibarimisake' EPfP
- 'Kathy' PBR ELon EPfP LRHS LSqu MAsh NSoo SHil SLim SPoG SRGP
§ - 'Latifolius Albomarginatus' (v) CTsd EBee ELan EPfP MRav MSwo SPer SWvt
- 'Luna' see *E. japonicus* 'Aureus'
- 'Macrophyllus Albus' see *E. japonicus* 'Latifolius Albomarginatus'
- 'Maiden's Gold' CSBt
- 'Marieke' see *E. japonicus* 'Ovatus Aureus'
- 'Microphyllus' CDoC MRav
§ - 'Microphyllus Albovariegatus' (v) CBcs CDoC CDul CMac CSBt CTri ELan EPfP LAst LRHS MGos NSoo SHil SLim SPoG SRms SWvt
§ - 'Microphyllus Aureovariegatus' (v) CDoC ELan EPfP LRHS MAsh NLar NSoo SHil WHar
- 'Microphyllus Aureus' see *E. japonicus* 'Microphyllus Pulchellus'
§ - 'Microphyllus Pulchellus' (v) CBcs CDoC CMac CSBt EBee ECrN EPfP LRHS MAsh MGos SEND SHil SWvt
- 'Microphyllus Variegatus' see *E. japonicus* 'Microphyllus Albovariegatus'
§ - 'Ovatus Aureus' (v) 𝕐H4 CBar CDoC CDul CExl CMac CSBt CTri EBee ELon EPfP LAst LRHS MGos MRav NLar NSoo SEND SGol SHil SLim SPer SPlb SPoG SRms SWvt
- 'Président Gauthier' (v) CBar CDoC EBee MGos SCoo SLim SWvt WCFE
- 'Pulchellus Aureovariegatus' see *E. japonicus* 'Microphyllus Aureovariegatus'
I - 'Pyramidatus' EPfP
- 'Robustus' EPfP
- 'Silver King' CMac
- 'Silver Krista' (v) NLar
- 'Susan' (v) CDoC CMac EShb MAsh SRGP
§ - 'Viridivariegatus' (v) LRHS

kachinensis B&SWJ 11668 WCru
kiautschovicus EPfP
- 'Berry Hill' EPfP NLar
- 'Manhattan' EPfP NLar
latifolius CJun CMCN EPfP IMou WPat
lucidus CExl CHll SSpi
maackii MBri NWea
macropterus CJun EPfP
maximowiczianus EPfP NLar WPat
mexicanus **new** CFil
morrisonensis EPfP
- B&SWJ 3700 WCru
myrianthus CJun EPfP EWes MAsh MBlu NLar
§ ***nanus*** CJun CWib EPfP NLar WThu
- var. ***turkestanicus*** CFil EBee EPfP GKin LHop LRHS SLon SRms WOld
obovatus EPfP NLar
occidentalis EPfP
oresbius EPfP
oxyphyllus CDul CJun CMCN CTho EPfP IArd NLar WCru WPat
- 'Angyo Elegant' (v) EPfP
- 'Waasland' CJun EPfP
pauciflorus EPfP
phellomanus 𝕐H4 CDoC CDul CTho EBee EPfP GKin LHop LRHS MAsh MBlu MBri MGos MPkF MRav NLar SCoo SEND SKHP SPoG SWvt WCot WPGP

	- 'Silver Surprise' (v)	CJun ELon EPfP WPat
	Pierrolino = 'Heespierrolino'PBR	LRHS MRav SCoo
§	***planipes*** ♀H4	Widely available
	- 'Dart's August Flame'	CJun EPfP
	- 'Gold Ore'	EPfP
	- 'Sancho'	CJun EPfP MBri WPat
	quelpaertensis	EPfP
	radicans	see *E. fortunei* var. *radicans*
	'Rokojō'	LLHF WPat
	'Rokojō Variegated' (v)	WCot
	rongchuensis	CJun EPfP
	rosmarinifolius	see *E. nanus*
	sachalinensis misapplied	see *E. planipes*
	sachalinensis (F. Schmidt) Maxim. B&SWJ 10835	WCru
	sacrosanctus	CJun EPfP
	sanguineus	CJun EPfP SSpi
	sieboldianus	WCru
	var. ***sanguineus*** B&SWJ 11140	
	- - B&SWJ 11386	WCru
	spraguei	EPfP NLar
	- CWJ 12446	WCru
	theifolius GWJ 9377	WCru
	tingens	CJun EPfP NLar
	trapococcus	EPfP
	vagans	EPfP WCot
	verrucosus	CJun MAsh NLar
	vidalii	EPfP
	wilsonii	CDoC
	yedoensis	see *E. hamiltonianus* subsp. *sieboldianus*

Eupatoriadelphus see *Eupatorium*

Eupatorium ✿ (*Asteraceae*)

	B&SWJ 9052 from Guatemala	WCru
	album misapplied	see *Ageratina altissima*
	album L.	NBid SWat
	altissimum	SRms
	aromaticum	see *Ageratina aromatica*
	atrorubens	see *Bartlettina sordida*
	cannabinum	CArn CHab EHon ELan EShb GLog GPoy IFoB MBNS MHer MMuc MNHC MRav NBir NMir NPer SEND SPav SWat WHrl WSFF
§	- f. ***albiflorum***	CAby SPhx
	- 'Album'	see *E. cannabinum* f. *albiflorum*
	- f. ***cannabinum*** 'Flore Pleno' (d)	CAby CMac CPrp CSev ECtt ELan ELon EPfP IBoy LHop LRHS MAvo MBel MHer MRav NBir NEgg NGdn SPhx SWat WCot WMnd WPtf WSFF XLum
	- - 'Spraypaint' (v)	WSFF
	capillifolium ♀H3	CAby EBee ECtt ESwi EWes LHop LPio SBod SDix SHar SMrm SPhx WCot WWEG
	chinense	CSpe
	coelestinum	see *Conoclinium coelestinum*
	dubium 'Baby Joe'PBR	CWGN EBee IPot MNrw NPnk
	- 'Little Joe'	CKno EBee EPPr EShb LEdu NPnk WWEG
	fistulosum	EBee
	- f. ***albidum*** 'Bartered Bride'	CKno EBee ECtt EWTr EWes GCal LRHS MAvo WCot
	- - 'Ivory Towers'	LBMP MSpe WWEG
	- - 'Massive White' ♀H4	CCon GCal NBir NSti
	- 'Berggarten'	GCal
	- 'Carin'	WSFF
	fortunei	CArn
	- 'Fine Line' (v)	CKno EPPr LSou WSFF WWEG
	- 'Pink Elegance' (v)	EBee ECtt EShb LHop LPio LRHS MMHG SPoG WMnd WWEG
	hyssopifolium	LRHS
	japonicum	GPoy
	ligustrinum	see *Ageratina ligustrina*
	lindleyanum	CKno EBee
	maculatum	NGdn NLar NPnk WHrl
	- Atropurpureum Group ♀H4	Widely available
	- - 'Gateway'	EBee ECtt ELon GCal LPio LRHS NBre NLar SWvt WHil WHoo WMnd WMoo WPtf WSFF
	- - 'Glutball'	CKno ELon GCal LBMP LPla LRHS MNrw NChi SMad WWEG
	- - 'Little Red'	GBin WSFF
	- - 'Phantom'PBR	EBee ECtt ELon GQue IPot LBMP LRHS MBri MWts NCGa NLar SPoG WMoo WPtf
	- - 'Purple Bush' ♀H4	CKno EBee ECtt EHyd ELon EPPr EWTr GBee GBin GCal GQue LRHS NBre NEgg NPnk SPad SPhx SWvt WCAu WSFF WWEG
	- - 'Red Dwarf'	EBee ECtt GQue IPot LEdu MAsh MSCN STPC WHil WWEG
	- - 'Riesenschirm' ♀H4	Widely available
	makinoi var. ***oppositifolium***	EBee
	- - B&SWJ 8449	WCru
	micranthum	see *Ageratina ligustrina*
	occidentale	see *Ageratina occidentalis*
	perfoliatum	CArn CKno GPoy LRHS MNrw NBre NLar SPhx WSFF
	purpureum	Widely available
	- 'Album'	CTri MBel SPhx SWvt
	rugosum	see *Ageratina altissima*
	weinmannianum	see *Ageratina ligustrina*

Euphorbia ✿ (*Euphorbiaceae*)

	'Abbey Dore'	WCot
	ambovombensis	LToo
	amygdaloides	ECtt SWat SWvt WOut
	- 'Bob's Choice'	EWes
	- 'Craigieburn'	CDes EWes GBuc GCra LRHS MAsh MGos MRav NDov WPGP
	- 'Frosted Flame'PBR	CSpe
§	- 'Purpurea'	Widely available
§	- var. ***robbiae*** ♀H4	Widely available
	- - dwarf	EWes
	- - 'Pom Pom'	LSou WPGP
	- - 'Redbud'	EWes LSou SLPl
	- 'Rubra'	see *E. amygdaloides* 'Purpurea'
	- 'Winter Glow'	CSpe
	baselicis	CPla CPom CSpe
	biglandulosa Desf.	see *E. rigida*
	Blackbird = 'Nothowlee'PBR	Widely available
	'Blue Dome'	CSpe
	'Blue Haze'	CAby CDes CPom LRHS MAvo WCot WPGP
	Breathless Blush = 'Balbreblus'	WCot
	caerulescens	LToo
	canariensis	EPfP
	capitulata	EWes
	cashmeriana CC&McK 607	EWes

ceratocarpa	CFil CGHE CSpe ECtt EWes GMaP LPla LRHS LSou NEgg NWit SEND SIgm SMad WCot WPGP WSHC
characias	CArn CBcs CHEx CMac ECtt EPfP IBoy LPio LRHS MCot MJak MLHP MRav NPer SBod SPer SPhx SRms SWvt WBrk WCot WMnd WWEG XLum XSen
- 'Black Pearl'	CBcs COlW CRos EBee ECrN ECtt EPfP LAst LHop LRHS MBri MGos MPnt NEgg NLBP NPnk SGbt SGol SHil SLim SMrm SPer SPoG SRkn SWvt WSpi WWEG
- 'Blue Wonder'	CExl ECtt ELan EPfP GAbr GBin GMaP LBMP LRHS LSou MAvo MGos MHol NCGa NEgg NGdn NLar NWit WCot
- subsp. ***characias***	COlW GMaP MAsh SEND
- - 'Blue Hills'	ECtt WWEG
- - 'Burrow Silver' (v)	CCon EPfP LDai LHop MRav NEgg SPer SWvt
- - 'Humpty Dumpty'	CExl CHel CSev EBee ECrN ECtt ELan ELon EPfP EWTr GMaP IBoy LPio LRHS LSRN MAsh MBri MGos MNHC NGdn NLar NPer NSoo SMrm SPer SRms SWvt WCot WWEG
- 'Dwarf Black Pearl'	ECtt WWEG
- 'Forescate'	CSev EPfP GBin LHop LRHS LSRN
- 'Glacier Blue'	CSpe CWGN LRHS MAvo SPoG STPC WNPC
- 'Goldbrook'	CWCL EBee ECtt EHoe EPfP LRHS MRav NCGa NGdn WSpi
- 'Kestrel' (v)	WCot
- 'Portuguese Velvet' ♀H4	CExl CHel COlW CPrp CWCL ECtt ELan EPfP EUJe LAst LHop LPio LPla LRHS MAsh MCot NCGa NLar NPri NWit SKHP SLim SMrm SPhx SPoG WCot WGwG WMnd WWEG
- Silver Swan = 'Wilcott'PBR (v)	Widely available
- 'Spring Splendour'	EWes LRHS
- 'Tasmanian Tiger'PBR (v)	CWGN ECtt EUJe EWes LHop LRHS LSou MBri MGos MPnt NBir SGol SKHP SWvt WCot WHil
- subsp. ***wulfenii*** ♀H3-4	Widely available
- - 'Bosahan' (v)	CBcs CExl
- - 'Emmer Green' (v)	CExl ECtt ELon EPfP EWes GAbr GMaP LRHS LSou MMHG MPie NWit SMrm WCot WWEG
- - 'Jimmy Platt'	SRms WCot
§ - - 'John Tomlinson' ♀H3-4	LSRN MRav WSpi
- - Kew form	see *E. characias* subsp. *wulfenii* 'John Tomlinson'
- - 'Lambrook Gold' ♀H3-4	CSam CWCL EPfP GCra LRHS MRav NLar NPer SMad WCot WMnd WWEG
- - 'Lambrook Gold' seed-raised	see *E. characias* subsp. *wulfenii* Margery Fish Group
- - 'Lambrook Yellow'	WSpi
§ - - Margery Fish Group	CWCL LRHS MCot NBir NCGa
- - 'Perry's Tangerine'	EWes NPer
§ - - 'Purple and Gold'	ECtt EWes MAvo NWit SWvt WWEG
- - 'Purpurea'	see *E. characias* subsp. *wulfenii* 'Purple and Gold'
- - var. ***sibthorpii***	IBoy
- - 'Silver Shadow'	WCot
- - 'Thelma's Giant'	MAvo NWit
- - 'Westacre Giant'	EWes
clavarioides var. ***truncata***	WCot
'Copton Ash'	CSpe EBee EWes GBin MBri SKHP WNPC XSen
corallioides	IFro LRHS NPer NSti WHer
§ ***cornigera*** ♀H4	CElw EPfP GBin GBuc LRHS MMuc MRav MSpe NBid NGdn NLar NSti NWit SEND SPhx SWat WCru
- 'Goldener Turm'	CAby ECtt ESwi GBin GBuc GCal LPio LPla LRHS LSou MBri MCot MNrw NDov NWit SDix SMrm SPer WCot
corollata	EBee
croizatii	LToo
cylindrifolia var. ***tubifera***	LToo
cyparissias	CBcs ELan EPot LRHS MLHP MRav NBir NGdn NLar SMrm SPav SRms WBrk WCot XLum XSen
- 'Betten'	see *E.* × *gayeri* 'Betten'
- 'Bushman Boy'	SMrm
- 'Clarice Howard'	see *E. cyparissias* 'Fens Ruby'
§ - 'Fens Ruby'	Widely available
- 'Orange Man'	CNec CTca ECtt EPfP EWes LBMP LRHS LSou NBro NEgg NGdn NLar SMrm SPoG SVen SWat SWvt WBrk WWEG
- 'Purpurea'	see *E. cyparissias* 'Fens Ruby'
- 'Red Devil'	NWit SMrm WWEG
- 'Tall Boy'	EWes
decaryi var. ***cap-saintemariensis***	LToo
decidua new	LToo
deflexa	EBee EWes MAvo
'Despina'PBR	LBuc LRHS SMrm
§ ***donii***	EWes NWit SDix
- HWJK 2405	WCru
- 'Amjillasa'	SDix
dulcis	CBre NBro NWit SBod
- 'Chameleon'	CEnd CSBt EBee ECtt EHoe ELan ELon EPfP GMaP LAst MGos MRav NBid NBir NEgg NLar NPer SGol SPlb SRot SWat SWvt WBrk WCot WMoo WSpi WWEG
'Efanthia'PBR	CEnd CKno CSev EPfP EWes GBin LAst LHop LRHS LSou MAvo NLar SMrm
enopla	EPfP
enormis	LToo
epithymoides	see *E. polychroma*
esculenta	LToo
esula Baker's form	NWit
Excalibur = 'Froeup'PBR ♀H4	CExl CKno CMac CWCL EBee ELan ELon GBin IVic LHop LRHS LSRN MBNS MBri MMuc MNrw MRav NBir NEgg NLar NSti SBod SEND SPoG SRkn WSpi
fischeriana B&SWJ 8575 new	WCru
flavicoma	GCal WSHC
fragifera	NWit
§ × ***gayeri*** 'Betten'	EBee LPla
glauca	ECou SKHP
'Golden Foam'	see *E. stricta*
graniticola new	LToo
'Grey Hedgehog' new	LSou
griffithii	CHll GGal IFoB NBro SWat WMoo
- 'Dixter' ♀H4	Widely available
- 'Dixter Flame'	IFoB NWit

	- 'Fern Cottage'	CElw EWes MAvo MSpe WMnd WWEG
	- 'Fireglow'	Widely available
	- 'King's Caple'	ELon EWes GBin SPoG WCru WSpi
	- 'Wickstead'	COlW CPom GAbr GBin MLHP WSpi
	groenewaldii	LToo
	'Helena'PBR (v)	CExl EPfP LRHS LSRN NLar NPnk SWvt WHil
	horrida ♀H1	SPlb
	hyberna	SWat
	hypericifolia Diamond Frost = 'Inneuphe'PBR	CCVN CSpe ESwi LBMP LHop LSou SRkn WCot
	ingens	CAbb SPlb
	jacquemontii	IFoB NChi
	'Jade Dragon'	LRHS SWvt WWEG
	'Jessie'	NCGa
	jolkinii	CExl
	Kalipso = 'Innkalff'	NLar SRot
	knobelii	LToo
	'Lambrook Silver'	SRkn
	lathyris	CArn CBre LRHS MLHP NLar NPer NWit SBod SRms SVic
	longifolia misapplied	see *E. cornigera*
	longifolia D. Don	see *E. donii*
	longifolia Lam.	see *E. mellifera*
	margalidiana	EWes MAvo NWit WCot
	× ***martini*** ♀H3	Widely available
	- 'Aperitif'PBR	EPfP MNHC SMrm
	- 'Ascot Rainbow'	CRos EPfP EWes LBMP LBuc LHop LLHF LRHS LSou MAsh MBri NCGa NLar NSoo NSti SHar SHil SLim SMad SPad SPer SPoG SSta WNPC WSpi
	- 'Baby Charm'	EBee ECtt ELon GBin GCal GKin IPot LHop LRHS LSRN MBri NGdn NLar NPnk SMrm WNPC
	- dwarf	CCon
	- 'Helen Robinson'	WCot WPGP
	- Helena's Blush = 'Inneuphhel' (v)	EPfP EWll
	- 'Kolibri'	EPfP SPoG SWvt
	- 'Little John'	CRos LRHS MBri SHil
	- Rudolph = 'Waleuphrud'	EPfP LRHS
	- Tiny Tim = 'Waleutiny'	ELon EPPr EPfP GBin LRHS LSRN MAsh SPoG SWvt
§	***mellifera*** ♀H3	Widely available
	meloformis ♀H1	LToo
	milii ♀H1	EBak
	moratii	LToo
	myrsinites ♀H4	Widely available
	- 'Washfield'	SBrt
	nereidum	EWes NWit
	nicaeensis	GCal LPla LRHS SEND SPer SPhx WCot XLum XSen
	- subsp. ***glareosa***	NWit
	obesa ♀H1	LToo
	oblongata	EWes GBin LRHS NWit SEND
	palustris ♀H4	Widely available
	- 'Walenburg's Glorie'	CWCL EBee ELan EWTr GBin GQue IBoy MAvo MBri MNrw MRav NSti NWit SMad SWat WCot WKif
	- 'Woodchippings' **new**	WCot
	- 'Zauberflöte'	ELon SRms
	paralias	WCot WHer
	× ***pasteurii***	CCon CDTJ EPfP EUJe EWes GCal LPio LSou MNHC MNrw MSpe NBir NLar NWit SPhx WPGP
	- 'Devil's Honey'	CHid

	- 'John Phillips'	CExl CGHE CMHG CPom EBee EPfP IVic LRHS SChF WPGP WSpi
	- 'Phrampton Phatty'	WPGP
	pekinensis	SKHP
	pentagona	SVen
	perangusta	LToo
	pilosa 'Major'	see *E. polychroma* 'Major'
	pithyusa	CSpe EBee ELan EPfP MRav SEND WCot WSHC XLum XSen
	platyclada	LToo
§	***polychroma*** ♀H4	Widely available
	- 'Bonfire'PBR	ECtt LRHS MBri NCGa NLar SPoG
§	- 'Candy'	EBee EPfP LRHS MAvo SMrm
	- compact	NWit
	- 'First Blush' (v)	NWit
	- 'Golden Fusion'	EPfP LRHS MAsh MAvo MBri SHil
§	- 'Lacy' (v)	CDoC EWes LRHS NBir NGdn NWit SKHP
§	- 'Major' ♀H4	CExl EBee LRHS WCot WKif
	- 'Midas'	CWCL GBin MNrw NWit SDix SMrm
	- 'Purpurea'	see *E. polychroma* 'Candy'
*	- 'Senior'	GBin LRHS MBri
	- 'Sonnengold'	LRHS
	- 'Variegata'	see *E. polychroma* 'Lacy'
	portlandica	SVen WHer
§	× ***pseudovirgata***	SMrm
	pulcherrima	SPre
	pulvinata	LToo
	'Red Flush'	EPfP LRHS
	Redwing = 'Charam'PBR ♀H4	CBcs CKno CMac ECtt ELan EPfP IKil LBuc LRHS LSou MAsh MAvo MBri MGos MHol MPic MRav NDov NLar NPri NSti NWit SGol SLim SPer SPoG SWvt WCot
	reflexa	see *E. seguieriana* subsp. *niciciana*
§	***rigida*** ♀H4	CAby CBro CDes CPom CSpe EHoe ELan EPfP EUJe EWes LPla LRHS MAvo SIgm SMrm SPhx WCot WPGP WSpi WWEG XSen
	robbiae	see *E. amygdaloides* var. *robbiae*
	rothiana GWJ 9479a	WCru
	'Roundway Titan'	EBee EMil LRHS SSpi SWvt
	sarawschanica	GQue LPla LRHS NWit SMad SPhx
	schillingii ♀H4	CPom EHoe ELan EPfP GCra GMaP LHop LRHS LSRN MBri MRav SDix SMrm SPer SPhx SPlb SPoG SWvt WCru WSpi WWEG
	schoenlandii	LToo
	seguieriana	SPhx
§	- subsp. ***niciciana***	GBin IMou WHoo
	serrulata Thuill.	see *E. stricta*
	sikkimensis ♀H4	CExl CMHG CPom CWCL ELan EWTr GCal LRHS NEgg NPer SRms WCru
	- 'Crûg Contrast'	WCru
	soongarica	NWit
	spinosa	NWit SPlb XSen
	stellispina	LToo
§	***stricta***	CFil CPom GAbr IFro LRHS NWad SBod
	stygiana	CCon CExl CHel CPom CSam CSpe ELon EShb EWes GBin GCal LRHS SMrm SPlb WCru
	- subsp. ***santamariae*** **new**	CFil
	- subsp. ***stygiana***	CFil CGHE EBee WPGP
	symmetrica	LToo
	Thalia = 'Innthal'	EPfP
	tirucalli	EShb

tortirama LToo
umfoloziensis LToo
uralensis see *E.* × *pseudovirgata*
valdevillosocarpa SPhx WCot
'Velvet Ruby' CSev GBin LSRN LSou MAvo NWit SWvt WCot WNPC
viguieri 🏆H1 LToo
villosa Waldst. & Kit. ex Willd. GBin MSpe NWit
§ ***virgata*** EWes NWit
× ***waldsteinii*** see *E. virgata*
wallichii misapplied see *E. donii*
wallichii Kohli see *E. cornigera*
wallichii ambig. CSam MRav NPnk WCAu
wallichii Hook. f. CExl EPfP GCal MNrw NOrc SKHP SPhx
- 'Lemon and Lime' CWib
'Whistleberry Garnet' CMac CWCL EBee EPfP LBMP LLHF LRHS LSou NGdn NSti SDix SEND SKHP SLim SPoG SWvt WNPC WWlt

Euptelea (*Eupteleaceae*)

franchetii see *E. pleiosperma*
§ ***pleiosperma*** IArd IDee NLar SSpi
polyandra EPfP NLar SBrt

Eurya (*Pentaphylacaceae*)

japonica WPGP
- 'Variegata' misapplied see *Cleyera japonica* 'Fortunei'

Euryops (*Asteraceae*)

abrotanifolius CCCN SVen
§ ***acraeus*** 🏆H4 CMea CSBt ECho EPot EWes WAbe
§ ***chrysanthemoides*** CCCN CDoC CHEx EShb SEND SVen
- 'Sonnenschein' SPet
evansii see *E. acraeus*
lateriflorus SPlb
pectinatus 🏆H2 CBcs CCCN CDTJ CDoC CExl CHEx CHel CTca CTri CTsd ELan EPfP EShb GGal IVic LAst LRHS MOWG MRav SEND SVen SWvt
tysonii CTca EPot EWes SPlb SVen WAbe
virgineus CCCN CDoC CExl SPlb SVen

Eustachys (*Poaceae*)

§ ***distichophylla*** NWsh

Eustrephus (*Philesiaceae*)

latifolius ECou

Eutaxia (*Papilionaceae*)

obovata ECou

Eutrochium see *Eupatorium*

Ewartia (*Asteraceae*)

planchonii EPot NSla WAbe

Exochorda (*Rosaceae*)

alberti see *E. korolkowii*
giraldii var. ***wilsonii*** CExl CMac EBee EPfP LHop LRHS MBlu MRav NLar NSoo SSta SWvt
§ ***korolkowii*** LRHS NLar
× ***macrantha*** LRHS
- 'Irish Pearl' CExl
§ - 'Niagara' **new** GBin NPnk
- 'The Bride' 🏆H4 Widely available
racemosa EPfP MMuc NLar SPer
serratifolia CBcs EPfP LRHS SPoG
- 'Snow White' CJun EPfP EWes GKin IArd MBlu NLar SLon SPoG SWvt
Snow Day Surprise see *E.* × *macrantha* 'Niagara'

F

Fabiana (*Solanaceae*)

imbricata CAbP CHel ELon EPfP LLHF LRHS SLon SPer SPlb
- 'Prostrata' CBcs EBee EPfP LRHS SSpi SVen WThu
- f. ***violacea*** 🏆H3 CExl CSBt CTri CTsd EBee EPfP LLHF LRHS MMuc SEND SPer SPoG SWvt WKif

Fagopyrum (*Polygonaceae*)

from India **new** GCal
cymosum see *F. dibotrys*
§ ***dibotrys*** EBee ELan EWld

Fagus ✿ (*Fagaceae*)

§ ***crenata*** CMen
- 'Mount Fuji' CMen LLHF SBir
engleriana CExl SBir
grandifolia subsp. ***mexicana*** SBir
japonica SBir
- var. ***multinervis*** SBir
longipetiolata CExl
lucida CExl
orientalis CMCN SBir
- 'Iskander' IArd MBlu NLar
sieboldii see *F. crenata*
sylvatica 🏆H4 Widely available
§ - 'Albomarginata' (v) CLnd CMCN EBee
- 'Albovariegata' see *F. sylvatica* 'Albomarginata'
- 'Aniek' **new** SGol
- 'Ansorgei' CEnd EBee LAst LLHF MBlu MPkF WCot
- 'Arcuata' SBir
N - Atropurpurea Group Widely available
- 'Aurea Pendula' CEnd CMCN MBlu SBir WPat
- 'Bicolor Sartini' MBlu
- 'Birr Zebra' CEnd
- 'Black Swan' CLnd CMCN EBee IArd LLHF LSRN MAsh MBlu MGos NEgg NHol NLar NPCo SBir SLon SPoG
- 'Cochleata' CMCN
- 'Cockleshell' MBlu SBir
- 'Comptoniifolia' see *F. sylvatica* var. *heterophylla* 'Comptoniifolia'
- 'Cristata' MBlu
N - Cuprea Group NWea
§ - 'Dawyck' 🏆H4 CBcs CDoC CDul CLnd CMac CSBt CTho EBee ECrN ELan EPfP MBri MGos NEgg NLar NPCo NWea SBir SGol SLau SLim SPer
- 'Dawyck Gold' 🏆H4 CBcs CDoC CDul CEnd CLnd CMCN CMac CTri EBee GKin IVic LRHS MAsh MBlu MBri MGos MSwo NEgg NPCo NWea SBir SGol SLau SPer WHar
- 'Dawyck Purple' 🏆H4 CBcs CDoC CDul CEnd CLnd CMCN CMac CTho CTri CWib EBee EPfP EWTr GKin IVic LAst

		LHop LSRN MAsh MBlu MBri MGos NEgg NLar NWea SBir SGol SPer
	- 'Eugen'	SBir
	- 'Fastigiata' misapplied	see *F. sylvatica* 'Dawyck'
	- 'Felderbach'	MBlu SBir
	- 'Franken' (v)	LLHF MBlu SBir
	- 'Greenwood'	LLHF MBlu
	- var. ***heterophylla***	CLnd CSBt CTho NWea
	- - 'Aspleniifolia' ♀H4	CBcs CDul CEnd CMCN CMac EBee ECrN ELan EPfP GKin MBlu MBri MGos NPCo SBir SCoo SGol SLau SPer SPoG WMou
§	- - 'Comptoniifolia'	SBir
	- - f. ***laciniata***	MBlu
	- 'Horizontalis'	MBlu
	- 'Incisa'	MBlu
	- 'Luteovariegata' (v)	CEnd CMCN
	- 'Mercedes'	CDoC CMCN LLHF MBlu NPCo WPat
N	- 'Pendula' ♀H4	CBcs CDoC CDul CEnd CLnd CMCN CSBt CTho EBee ECrN ELan EPfP MGos MSwo NEgg NPCo NWea SGol SLau SPer WHar WMou
	- 'Prince George of Crete'	CDul CMCN SBir
	- 'Purple Fountain' ♀H4	CDoC CDul CEnd CMCN EBee ELan LAst LHop LRHS MAsh MBlu MBri MGos MWat NLar SBir SLau SLim
	- Purple leaved Group	see *F. sylvatica* Atropurpurea Group
	- 'Purpurea Latifolia'	EWTr
	- 'Purpurea Pendula'	CBcs CCVT CEnd CMCN CSBt CTri CWib ELan EPfP GKin IVic LAst MAsh MBri MGos MJak MSwo NEgg NPCo NWea SCoo SGol SLau SLim SPer SPoG WHar
§	- 'Purpurea Tricolor' (v)	CDul CEnd CMCN ECrN MAsh MBlu MGos NWea SBir SCoo WMou
	- 'Quercifolia'	MBlu
	- 'Red Obelisk'	see *F. sylvatica* 'Rohan Obelisk'
	- 'Riversii' ♀H4	CBcs CDoC CDul CEnd CLnd CMCN CTho CTri CWib ECrN ELan EPfP GKin LAst MAsh MBri MGos NEgg NWea SPer SPoG WHar
	- 'Rohan Gold'	CEnd CMCN EBee MBlu SGol
	- 'Rohan Minaret' **new**	SGol
§	- 'Rohan Obelisk'	CDul CEnd CMCN CTho ELan EWTr IArd MBlu SBir SGol
I	- 'Rohan Pyramidalis'	CEnd
	- 'Rohan Trompenburg'	CMCN MBlu
	- 'Rohan Weeping'	MBlu SBir
	- 'Rohanii'	CBcs CDoC CDul CEnd CLnd CMCN CTri EBee ELan EPfP GKin LAst LHop MGos NPCo SBir SLau SPer WHar WMou
	- 'Roseomarginata'	see *F. sylvatica* 'Purpurea Tricolor'
	- 'Rotundifolia'	CDul MBlu SGol
	- 'Spaethiana'	GKin
	- 'Striata'	LLHF NPCo SBir
	- 'Sychrov'	SBir
	- f. ***tortuosa***	MPkF
	- - 'Rot Süntel'	CDul MBlu
	- 'Tricolor' misapplied (v)	see *F. sylvatica* 'Purpurea Tricolor'
	- 'Tricolor' ambig. (v)	SLau
	- 'Tricolor' (v)	CBcs CLnd CMac CSBt CWib EBee ELan LLHF NEgg NHol SGol
	- 'Viridivariegata' (v)	CMCN
	- 'Zlatia'	CBcs CDul CLnd CMCN CSBt CWib ELan EPfP MBlu MGos MPkF MSwo NWea SBir SGol SLau SPer

Fallopia (*Polygonaceae*)

	aubertii	see *F. baldschuanica*
§	***baldschuanica***	CBcs CMac CSBt CTri CWib EBee ELan EPfP LBuc LRHS MAsh MGos MJak MMuc MSwo NEgg NPri NWea SEND SLim SLon SPer SPlb SPoG SWvt WHar
	- Summer Sunshine = 'Acofal'PBR	ELan
§	***japonica*** var. ***compacta***	NLar WMoo XLum
	- - 'Fuji Snow'	see *F. japonica* var. *compacta* 'Milk Boy'
§	- - 'Milk Boy' (v)	EShb
	- - 'Variegata' misapplied	see *F. japonica* var. *compacta* 'Milk Boy'
§	***multiflora***	CArn LEdu
	- var. ***hypoleuca***	SCoo SLim SPoG
	- - B&SWJ 120	EBee WCru
	sachalinensis	NLar

Farfugium (*Asteraceae*)

§	***japonicum***	CHEx MBel
	- B&SWJ 884	WCru
	- 'Argenteum' (v)	SMad
§	- 'Aureomaculatum' (v) ♀H1	CCon CHEx CHll EAmu ECtt EPfP LEdu LRHS
	- 'Bumpy Ride'	WCot
	- 'Crispatum'	CAbP CCon EAmu ECtt ELan EPfP LAst LEdu WCot WWEG
	- double-flowered (d)	WCru
	- var. ***formosanum*** B&SWJ 7125	WCru
	GWJ 10356	WCru
	- 'Kagami-jishi' (v)	WCot
	- 'Kaimon Dake'	WCot
	- 'Kinkan' (v)	WCot
I	'Nanum'	CHEx
	- 'Ryuto'	WCot
I	- 'Tsuwa-buki'	WCot
	'Last Dance'	NLar
	tussilagineum	see *F. japonicum*

Fargesia (*Poaceae*)

	from Jiuzhaigou, China	CDTJ CEnt EAmu EPfP ERod EUJe GBin MAvo MBri MMoz MMuc MWht NLar NWsh SBig WJun WPGP
	adpressa	WJun
	angustissima	CDTJ CEnt CExl CFil EPfP ERod MMuc MWht SBig WJun
	confusa	CDTJ
	denudata	CDTJ CEnt CFil ENBC ERod MAvo SBig WJun
	- L 1575	CExl MMoz MWht
	- Xian 1	CDTJ MMoz WPGP
	dracocephala	CDoC CEnt CExl CFil EPfP ERod ESwi GBin LEdu LRHS MBrN MMoz MMuc MWht SBig SLPl WJun WMoo WPGP
	- 'White Dragon'	CExl CFil SMad WPGP
	ferax	WJun
§	***murielae*** ♀H4	CDoC CEnt CFil CHEx ELan ENBC EPau EPfP ERod MGos MJak MMoz MMuc MWhi MWht NGdn SAPC SPlb SPoG WJun WMoo WPGP
	- 'Amy'	NLar
	- 'Bimbo'	CEnt EPfP ERod ESwi LRHS MAvo MWhi MWht NLar WJun WMoo WPGP

- 'Dana Jumbo'	LRHS
- 'Grüne Hecke'	ERod MWht SBig
- 'Harewood'	CFil MMoz MWht SWvt WPGP
- 'Joy'	GBin NLar WMoo
- 'Jumbo'	CEnt CSBt EAmu ELan ELon ENBC EPfP ERod ESwi EUJe LRHS MAvo MBri MGos MMoz MWhi MWht NGdn NWsh SBig SPer SPoG SRms SWvt WJun
- 'Kranich'	NLar
- 'Lava'	MBri
- 'Mae'	CDTJ MWht
- 'Pinocchio'	MBri
- 'Simba' ♀H4	Widely available
- 'Vampire'	ERod EUJe LRHS MBri SBig
- 'Willow'	MBri
murieliae	EAmu
'Superjumbo'PBR new	
* ***nepalensis***	ESwi
§ ***nitida***	CAbb CBcs CDoC CDoy CEnd CEnt CSBt ELan ENBC EPfP ERod IFro LRHS MAvo MBlu MBri MGos MJak MMoz MRav MWht SPoG SRms SWvt WHer WJun WMoo WPGP
- 'Eisenach'	MMoz
- 'Great Wall'	EAmu MBri MGos MWht
- Jiuzhaigou 1	see *F.* Red Panda
- 'Jiuzhaigou 2'	WJun
- 'Jiuzhaigou 4'	CExl CFil WPGP
- 'Jiuzhaigou 8'	WPGP
- 'Jiuzhaigou Genf'	CFil WPGP
- 'Nymphenburg' ♀H4	CEnd MBri MMoz SBig
perlonga	WJun
- Yunnan 6	ERod MMoz WPGP
§ Red Panda = 'Jiu'	CExl CFil LRHS SPoG WJun
robusta	CAbb CDTJ CEnd CEnt ENBC EPfP ERod GCal MAvo MBrN MBri MMoz MMuc MWhi MWht NGdn NLar SBig SEND SLPl WJun
- 'Campbell'	EAmu
- 'Ming Yunnan'	LEdu WJun
- 'P. King'	ERod MWht
- 'Pingwu'	CDTJ CEnt EAmu ERod GBin MGos MWht SBig WJun
- 'Red Sheath'	CEnt CExl ERod MMoz MWht WJun WPGP
- 'Wolong'	CDoC CExl ERod MMoz MWht WJun WPGP
rufa	CAbb CEnt CExl CFil CHEx EAmu ENBC EPPr EPfP ERod GCal LRHS LSRN MAvo MBlu MBrN MGos MJak MMoz MMuc MWhi MWht NLar SBig WJun WPGP
spathacea misapplied	see *F. murielae*
utilis	CEnt ERod MMoz MMuc MWht SEND WJun
yulongshanensis	ERod MWht WJun
yunnanensis	EAmu

Farsetia (*Brassicaceae*)

clypeata	see *Fibigia clypeata*

Fascicularia (*Bromeliaceae*)

andina	see *F. bicolor*
§ ***bicolor***	Widely available
§ - subsp. ***bicolor***	CFil CMac EGri IBoy SMad
§ - subsp. ***canaliculata***	CAbP CFil CHEx CHid IBlr LEdu SChr SKHP SPad WCot WPGP
kirchhoffiana	see *F. bicolor* subsp. *canaliculata*
litoralis	see *Ochagavia litoralis*
pitcairniifolia misapplied	see *F. bicolor* subsp. *bicolor*
pitcairniifolia (Verlot) Mez	see *Ochagavia litoralis*

× *Fatshedera* (*Araliaceae*)

lizei ♀H3	CBcs CDoC CDul CHEx CMac CTri EBee ECrN ELon EPfP EUJe LRHS MAsh MBel MRav NEgg SAPC SDix SEND SPer SPlb SPoG SWvt
§ - 'Annemieke' (v) ♀H3	CBcs CDoC CHEx CMac CRHN EBee ELan EPfP EUJe LHop LRHS MAsh MMuc MRav NEgg SEND SPer SPoG WBor
- 'Lemon and Lime'	see × *F. lizei* 'Annemieke'
- 'Maculata'	see × *F. lizei* 'Annemieke'
- 'Variegata' (v) ♀H3	CMac EBee EBtc ELan EPfP LAst LRHS MAsh MBel MGos MMuc NEgg SDix SEND SPer SWvt WCFE

Fatsia (*Araliaceae*)

§ ***japonica*** ♀H4	Widely available
- 'Annelise' (v)	SEND
- 'Moseri'	CExl ECtt ELan ESwi EUJe LHop NGdn NLar SWvt WCot
- 'Spider's Web' (v)	CAbb CExl CHid CWGN EAmu ECtt ELan ELon ESwi EUJe LBMP LRHS LSou MRav MSCN SMad SPad SPer SPoG WCot WGrn
- 'Variegata' (v) ♀H3	CAbb CBcs CMac EAmu ELan EPfP ESwi LRHS MAsh MBri MGos MPie MRav SEND SLim SLon SPer SPoG WCot
papyrifera	see *Tetrapanax papyrifer*
polycarpa	CDTJ CExl EAmu WPGP
- B&SWJ 7144	CExl WCru
- RWJ 10133	WCru
- deeply cut leaf new	WCru
- - BWJ 12499 new	WCru

Faucaria (*Aizoaceae*)

felina	WCot
subsp. ***tuberculosa*** new	
tigrina ♀H1	EPfP

Fedia (*Valerianaceae*)

cornucopiae	CArn

Feijoa see *Acca*

Felicia (*Asteraceae*)

§ ***amelloides***	CCCN LAst MCot SEND SPlb
- 'Blue Eyes'	LAst
- 'Santa Anita' ♀H3	CTri SVen
§ - variegated (v)	CCCN ECtt LAst LSou MBri MCot MSCN NPer SDix SEND SPet
§ ***amoena***	CTri
- 'Variegata' (v)	CCCN CTri
capensis	see *F. amelloides*
coelestis	see *F. amelloides*
echinata	CCCN
filifolia	SPlb
- blue-flowered	SVen
fruticosa	CHll
natalensis	see *F. rosulata*
pappei	see *F. amoena*
§ ***petiolata***	CTri EWes MNrw NSti
§ ***rosulata***	CMea CPBP ECho GAbr MBrN MHer NBro SBrt SRot WIce
uliginosa	EWes WIce

Fenestraria (*Aizoaceae*)

	rhodalophylla subsp. ***aurantiaca*** ♀H1	LToo

fennel see *Foeniculum vulgare*

fenugreek see *Trigonella foenum-graecum*

Ferraria (*Iridaceae*)

	LP 18095	WCot
§	***crispa***	ECho WCot
	- var. ***nortieri***	WCot
	divaricata	CDes WCot
	schaeferi	WCot
	undulata	see *F. crispa*

Ferula (*Apiaceae*)

	assa-foetida	LDai
	chiliantha	see *F. communis* subsp. *glauca*
§	***communis***	CArn CMea CSpe EBee ECGP ELan EPfP EWTr GBin GCra IBoy LRHS SDix SEND SPav SPhx SPlb WJek
	- 'Gigantea'	see *F. communis*
§	- subsp. ***glauca***	CArn CMea EWes SDix WPGP
	'Giant Bronze'	see *Foeniculum vulgare* 'Giant Bronze'
	tingitana 'Cedric Morris'	GCra SDix

Ferulago (*Apiaceae*)

	sylvatica	SPhx

Festuca (*Poaceae*)

	actae	XLum
	amethystina	CKno CWib EHoe LEdu LRHS MNFA NGdn SEND SMea SRot WMoo WWEG XLum
	- 'Aprilgrün'	XLum
	arundinacea	CHab MMoz SEND
	californica	CKno EPPr
	coxii	CHid WCot
	curvula subsp. ***crassifolia***	EShb
	durissima new	XLum
	elegans	EPPr XLum
	eskia	EHoe EPPr LRHS XLum
	filiformis	CHab
	gamisansii new	XLum
§	***gautieri***	EPPr GBin SMea XLum
	- 'Pic Carlit'	GBin
	gigantea	CHab SEND XLum
	glacialis	XLum
	glauca Vill.	CBar CBcs CWib ELan EPfP EShb GMaP LPot MBNS MGos MRav MWat NGdn NOak SLim SPer SPlb SRms WWEG
I	- 'Auslese'	CExl EPPr NGdn
	- 'Azurit'	EHoe EPPr EWes NWad NWsh SPoG
§	- 'Blaufuchs' ♀H4	EHon ELan EPfP EWes GMaP LRHS MAsh MAvo MBlu MGos MRav NWad SLim SPer SPlb SWvt WWEG XLum
§	- 'Blauglut'	EBee EPfP LRHS MBri MRav
	- Blue Fox	see *F. glauca* 'Blaufuchs'
	- Blue Glow	see *F. glauca* 'Blauglut'
	- 'Elijah Blue'	Widely available
	- 'Euchre'	LSRN
	- 'Golden Toupee'	CTsd EHoe ELan EPfP EWes LRHS MAsh MBlu MGos NBir NEgg NHol SLim SPer SPlb SPoG SVen SWvt WWEG
	- 'Harz'	EHoe
	- 'Intense Blue'	CKno EWes SMad SPoG STPC
*	- ***minima***	CCCN NWsh WGrn WWEG
	- 'Pallens'	see *F. longifolia*
	- Sea Urchin	see *F. glauca* 'Seeigel'
§	- 'Seeigel'	EPPr LRHS NWad
	- Select	see *F. glauca* 'Auslese'
	- 'Seven Seas'	see *F. valesiaca* 'Silbersee'
	- 'Silberreiher'	EPPr WWEG
	- 'Solling'	XLum
	- 'Uchte'	CWCL ELan EPPr LHop WWEG
	'Hogar'	EPPr
	idahoensis	EShb
	- 'Tomales Bay'	CKno
§	***longifolia***	EPPr
	mairei	CKno EBee EHoe EPPr SPhx XLum
	novae-zelandiae	CWCL
	ovina	CHab EPfP GBin WSFF
	- var. ***gallica***	NWsh
	- 'Söhrewald'	EPPr
*	- 'Tetra Gold'	SWvt
	paniculata	CKno EHoe EPPr XLum
	- subsp. ***spadicea***	XLum
	pratensis	CHab
	punctoria	MMuc SMea
	rubra	CHab CKno WSFF XLum
	scoparia	see *F. gautieri*
	'Siskiyou Blue'	CKno EPPr WWEG
	tatrae	EBee WCot
	tolucensis NJM 09.071	WPGP
	valesiaca	SMea
	- var. ***glaucantha***	CWib EPPr NGdn NLar WWEG XLum
§	'Silbersee'	EHoe EPPr GBin NWsh SRms
	- Silver Sea	see *F. valesiaca* 'Silbersee'
	violacea	EPPr
	vivipara	CPrp EHoe LEdu NBid
*	'Willow Green'	SPlb

Fibigia (*Brassicaceae*)

§	***clypeata***	LDai
I	- 'Select'	CSpe

Ficus ✿ (*Moraceae*)

	afghanistanica	ERea
	benjamina 'Alij'	WCot
	carica (F)	CCCN EUJe MBri MREP SAPC SEWo SLon SPad
	- 'Abicou' (F)	ERea
	- 'Adam' (F)	CCCN ERea LEdu
	- 'Alma' (F)	ERea
	- 'Angélique' (F)	ERea
I	- 'Bauern Feige' (F) new	SRms
	- 'Beall' (F)	CCCN
	- 'Bellone' (F)	CCCN
	- 'Black Ischia' (F)	CCCN CHel ERea SDix
	- 'Black Jack' (F)	ERea
	- 'Black Mission' (F)	EAmu
	- 'Black Neck Lady' (F)	MGos SHil
	- 'Bornholm' (F)	LSRN NLar SPre
	- 'Bourjassotte Grise' (F)	CAgr CHel ERea SDea
	- 'Brogiotto' (F)	CCCN
	- 'Brown Turkey' (F) ♀H3	Widely available
	- 'Brunswick' (F)	CAgr CCCN CDul CHel CHll CRHN ELan ELon EPfP EPom ERea EWTr

		GTwe LEdu LRHS NLar SDix SEND SLim SPoG SRms WCot WHar
	- 'Califfo Blue' (F) new	CSut SRms
	- 'Castle Kennedy' (F)	CCCN CHel ERea GTwe
	- 'Celeste' (F)	CBcs CCCN
	- 'Colummaro Black Apulia' (F)	CCCN
	- 'Colummaro White Apulia' (F)	CCCN
	- 'Continental' (F)	MGos SHil
	- 'Dalmatie' (F)	CAgr CCCN ELan EPfP ERea LRHS MGos SEND SRms WPGP
§	- 'Desert King' (F)	ERea
I	- 'Digitata' (F)	MBlu
	- 'Digredo' (F)	CCCN
	- 'Dorée de Porquerolles' (F)	CCCN
	- 'Drap d'Or' (F)	ERea
	- 'Excel' (F)	ERea
	- 'Figue d'Or' (F)	ERea
	- 'Filacciano' (F)	CCCN
	- 'Flanders' (F)	CCCN
	- 'Goutte d'Or' (F)	CAgr CCCN EPfP ERea SDea
	- 'Green Ischia' (F)	CCCN
	- 'Grise de Marseille' (F)	CCCN
	- 'Grise de Saint Jean' (F)	CCCN
	- 'Ice Crystal' (F)	ELan EPfP ERea LRHS MBlu SPoG SRms WHar WPGP
	- 'Jordan' (F)	IDee LBuc
	- 'Kadota' (F)	CCCN IDee LBuc
	- 'King'	see *F. carica* 'Desert King'
*	- 'Laciniata' (F)	MBri
	- 'Lisa' (F)	ERea
	- 'LSU Purple' (F)	ERea
	- 'Malta' (F)	GTwe
	- 'Marseillaise' (F)	GTwe SDea
	- 'Melanzana' (F)	CCCN
	- 'Monstreuse' (F) new	ERea
	- 'Morena' (F) new	CSut
	- 'Moscatel' (F)	CCCN
	- 'Neck Lady White' (F)	MGos SHil
	- 'Negrétte de Porquerolles' (F)	CCCN
	- 'Nero' (F)	ELon SGol
	- 'Newlyn Harbour' (F)	ELon
	- 'Noire de Caromb' (F)	CAgr CCCN EPfP ERea LRHS SRms
	- 'Noire de Provence'	see *F. carica* 'Reculver'
	- 'Osborn's Prolific' (F)	ECrN EPfP MAsh SEND SGol SWvt WPGP
	- 'Panachée' (F)	CCCN CSut EPom ERea SRms
	- 'Peter's Honey' (F)	ERea
	- 'Petite Nigra' (F)	ERea
	- 'Pied de Boeuf' (F)	CCCN
	- 'Pinet' (F)	MGos SHil
	- 'Porthminster' (F)	CHEx
	- 'Précoce de Dalmatie' (F)	NLar SRms
	- 'Précoce Ronde de Bordeaux' (F)	ERea SEND
	- 'Quinta' (F)	CCCN
§	- 'Reculver' (F)	SEND
	- 'Ronde de Bordeaux' (F)	CCCN
	- 'Rouge de Bordeaux' (F)	CCCN EPom ERea MAsh SDea SPlb
	- 'Safi' (F)	CCCN
	- 'Saint Johns' (F)	CHel
	- 'San Pedro Miro' (F)	ERea
	- 'Sugar 12' (F)	ERea
	- 'Sultane' (F)	CAgr ERea
	- 'Texas Everbearing' (F)	ERea
	- 'Verte d'Argenteuil' (F)	CCCN
	- 'Violetta' PBR (F)	MBri WHar
	- 'Violette Dauphine' (F)	CHel EPfP ERea
	- 'Violette de Bordeaux' (F) new	ERea
	- 'Violette de Sollies' (F)	ERea
	- 'Violette Normande' (F)	MAsh SEND
	- 'Violette Sepor' (F)	ERea
	- 'White Adriatic' (F)	CBcs
	- 'White Genoa'	see *F. carica* 'White Marseilles'
	- 'White Ischia' (F)	CHel ERea
§	- 'White Marseilles' (F)	CAgr CCCN CRHN CWib ECrN ERea LRHS MBri SDea SEND SRms WPGP
	- 'Zidi' (F)	CCCN
	pubigera	CExl
	pumila 🏆H1	CHEx
	- 'Variegata' (v)	CHEx EShb
	tikoua new	CFil

fig see *Ficus carica*

filbert see *Corylus maxima*

Filipendula ✿ (*Rosaceae*)

	alnifolia 'Variegata'	see *F. ulmaria* 'Variegata'
	camtschatica	CCon CRow ELan LEdu LRHS MCot NBid NLar WPGP
	- B&SWJ 10987	WCru
	- RBS 0224	NLar
	- 'Rosea'	LHop MRav SMad
	digitata 'Nana'	see *F. multijuga*
	formosa B&SWJ 8707	WCru
	hexapetala	see *F. vulgaris*
	- 'Flore Pleno'	see *F. vulgaris* 'Multiplex'
	'Kahome'	CPrp CRow ELon EShb GMaP IFoB LLWG LRHS MSCN NBir NGdn NLar NOrc SPer SPet SPhx SWat WHil WMoo WPnP WWEG
	kiraishiensis	EBee
	- B&SWJ 1571	WCru
§	***multijuga***	GCal IFoB LLWG LRHS NHol NLar NWad WBor WMoo
	- var. ***yezoensis*** B&SWJ 10828 new	IMou SMrm WCru
	palmata	LLWG MLHP NBre SWat WMoo
	- 'Digitata Nana'	see *F. multijuga*
	- dwarf	CDes CLAP
	- 'Elegantissima'	see *F. purpurea* 'Elegans'
	- 'Göteborg'	EBee
	- 'Nana'	see *F. multijuga*
	- 'Rosea'	CMac LLWG NBir
	- 'Rubra'	CTri GCra LRHS MRav NGdn
	purpurea 🏆H4	CKno CRow CSBt ELon EPfP IBlr LRHS MBri MMuc SBod SEND WCru WMoo
	- f. ***albiflora***	LLWG MBri NPri WMoo
§	- 'Elegans'	CRow EBee ELon GBin LLWG LRHS MLHP NBid NHol SPer SPet SWat WMoo WPnP
	- 'Pink Dreamland'	SPhx
*	- 'Plena' (d)	NLar
	'Queen of the Prairies'	see *F. rubra*
	'Red Umbrellas'	LSou
§	***rubra***	CRow IFro LSRN MCot WSFF
§	- 'Venusta' 🏆H4	Widely available
	- 'Venusta Magnifica'	see *F. rubra* 'Venusta'
	rufinervis B&SWJ 8611	WCru
§	***ulmaria***	CArn CHab CHby EHon ELau GMaP GPoy MCot MHer MHoo MNHC

	MWts NMir SIde SWat WHfH WJek WMoo WOut WPnP WSFF WShi XLum
- 'Aurea'	CCon CMac CRow CTri EBee ECtt EHoe ELan GAbr GMaP LPio LRHS MLHP MRav NBid NLar SPer SRms WCot WMoo WSHC WWEG
- 'Flore Pleno' (d)	CBre EBee LHop LLWG LRHS MRav NBid NBre SPer SWat WCot WHil
- 'Rosea'	CDes EBee IBlr MBel MHer
§ - 'Variegata' (v)	CPrp EBee ECtt EHoe ELan GBuc IFoB LBMP LRHS NBid NGdn NLar SPer WHfH WMoo WPGP WPnP WWEG WWFP
§ ***vulgaris***	CArn CHab LRHS MBel MLHP MMuc MNHC NBro NLBP NMir SWat WHer WHfH WJek WWEG
- 'Flore Pleno'	see *F. vulgaris* 'Multiplex'
- 'Grandiflora'	CBre EBee
§ - 'Multiplex' (d)	CMac CSpe ELan GMaP LLWG LRHS MHer MMuc MRav MSpe MWts NBid NBir NLar NPri NRya SEND SPer SRms WMoo XLum
- 'Plena'	see *F. vulgaris* 'Multiplex'
- 'Rosea'	NBre

Firmiana (*Malvaceae*)

simplex	EShb ESwi EUJe IDee SPad WPGP

Fitzroya (*Cupressaceae*)

cupressoides	CBcs CDoC CMac CTho GBin IArd IDee LRHS SCoo SLim WThu
- 'Borde Hill' (f) **new**	WThu
- 'Westonbirt' (m) **new**	WThu

Foeniculum (*Apiaceae*)

vulgare	CArn CHEx CHby CPrp ECrN ELan ELau EPfP GPoy LRHS MGos MHer MHoo MNHC NPri SEND SIde SPer SPhx SPlb SPoG SRms SVic SWvt WHfH WJek WWEG
- 'Bronze'	see *F. vulgare* 'Purpureum'
- var. ***dulce***	CSev SIde
§ - 'Giant Bronze'	EBee LRHS MAvo SPhx WGrn WSpi
§ - 'Purpureum'	Widely available
- 'Smokey'	MRav
- 'Sweet Florence'	SVic

Fontanesia (*Oleaceae*)

fortunei **new**	EBtc
phillyreoides	CBcs

Fontinalis (*Fontinalaceae*)

antipyretica	CBAq

Forsythia (*Oleaceae*)

'Arnold Dwarf'	ECrN NBir SRms
'Beatrix Farrand' ambig.	CTri MWat NWea SEND SRms
'Beatrix Farrand' K. Sax	MMuc NLar
'Fiesta' (v)	CJun EPfP LAst LRHS MAsh MGos MRav MSwo SPer SPoG WCot
giraldiana	MSwo SLon SRms
Gold Tide	see *F.* Marée d'Or
'Golden Bells'	WHar
'Golden Nugget'	CMac ELan EPfP LBuc LRHS MAsh SCoo SLon SPoG WCFE
'Golden Times' (v)	CMac EBee EWes LAst LBuc LPot LSRN MAsh MGos MSwo NSoo NWea SCoo SPoG SWvt
× ***intermedia***	IBoy
- 'Arnold Giant'	MBlu
- 'Goldrausch'	LRHS MAsh NLar SHil
- 'Goldzauber'	NWea
- 'Josefa' (v)	ELon WPat
- 'Lynwood Variety' ♀H4	Widely available
- 'Lynwood Variety' variegated (v)	CWib
- Minigold = 'Flojor'	CHel CMac CSBt EBee MSwo MWat NSoo SRms
- 'Spectabilis'	CDul EBee EPfP LBuc NSoo NWea SCoo SGol SLim
- 'Spectabilis Variegated' (v)	CMHG MBNS NPro
- 'Spring Glory'	MHer WSpi
- Week End = 'Courtalyn'PBR ♀H4	CWSG EBee EPfP LBuc LRHS LSou MAsh MBri MMuc NHol NLar NSoo SEND SGol SHil SLon SPlb
§ Marée d'Or = 'Courtasol'PBR ♀H4	ELon IVic LRHS MAsh MGos MRav NLar NWea SLon SPer SPoG
Mêlée d'Or = 'Courtaneur'	SCoo SGol
Melissa = 'Courtadic'	NWea
ovata 'Tetragold'	EBee NWea
'Paulina'	NLar WAbe
* 'Spring Beauty'	WSpi
suspensa	CMac CTri CWib EPfP NWea SPlb SRms
- 'Nymans'	MBri MRav NSti SEND
§ - 'Taff's Arnold' (v)	CExl CJun WSpi
- 'Variegata'	see *F. suspensa* 'Taff's Arnold'
'Tremonia'	NEgg
viridissima	NWea
- 'Bronxensis'	CMac ECho ELon LHop LLHF MAsh NBir NLar WAbc WCot WPat
- var. ***koreana*** 'Kumson' (v)	EBee SLim SPoG
- 'Weber's Bronx'	NLar WAbe

Fortunatia see *Oziroë*

Fortunella (*Rutaceae*)

§ ***japonica*** (F)	EPfP
§ ***margarita*** (F)	CDoC ELan LRHS SPre
- 'Nagami' (F)	SPre
- 'Obovata' (F) **new**	SPre

Fothergilla (*Hamamelidaceae*)

gardenii	CBcs CJun ELan EPfP LRHS MBlu MGos MRav NLar SPer SWvt WGob
- 'Blue Mist'	CAbP CDoC CEnd CExl CHel CJun EBee ELan ELon EPfP GQue IVic LRHS MAsh MPkF NLar SKHP SPer SPoG SSta WPat
- 'Harold Epstein'	NLar
- 'Suzanne'	NLar
- 'Zundert'	NLar
'Huntsman'	CCCN EBee EPfP
× ***intermedia*** Beaver Creek = 'Klmtwo'	NLar
- 'Blue Shadow'	CBcs CJun EPfP EUJe LRHS LSRN MGos MPkF MRav NLar SGol SKHP
- 'Mount Airy'	CDoC CJun CMCN EBee EPfP LRHS MBri MPkF NLar SKHP SSta
- 'Red Licorice'	CJun EPfP NLar
- 'Sea Spray'	CJun NLar
- 'Windy City'	CJun MBri NLar
major ♀H4	CBcs CDul CJun CWib EBee ELan EPfP GKin IDee LRHS LSRN MAsh MBlu MGos MJak NEgg NLar NPri SHil SPer SPoG SReu SWvt WPat

- 'Bulkyard'	CJun
- Monticola Group	CDoC CDul CEnd CJun EBee ELan EPfP LRHS MAsh MGos NSoo SLim SPer SSpi SSta WGob

Fouquieria (*Fouquieriaceae*)

columnaris new	SPlb
splendens	EAmu SPlb

Fragaria (*Rosaceae*)

from Taiwan	WHer
alpina	see *F. vesca* 'Semperflorens'
- 'Alba'	see *F. vesca* 'Semperflorens Alba'
× ***ananassa*** 'Albion'PBR (F)	CSBt CSut LSRN NPri SPer
- 'Alice'PBR (F) ♀H4	CAgr CMac EPom ERea LBuc LEdu LRHS MCoo
- 'Anablanca' (F) new	CSut
- 'Aromel' (F) ♀H4	EPfP LBuc LRHS MAsh
- 'Bogota' (F)	LRHS
- 'Bolero' (F)	LRHS MBri
- 'Calypso' (F)	CSBt LBuc LRHS MCoo SDea SEND
- 'Cambridge Favourite' (F) ♀H4	CAgr CMac CSBt CTri EMil EPfP EPom GTwe LBuc LRHS MAsh MBri MCoo MGos MJak NEgg NPri SDea SEND SPlb WHar
- 'Cambridge Vigour' (F)	LRHS MAsh
- 'Christine' (F)	CAgr CSut EMil EPom LRHS
- 'Darselect'PBR (F)	EPom
- 'Elegance' (F)	EPom GTwe SRms
- 'Elsanta' (F)	CSBt CTri EMil EPfP EPom GTwe IArd LBuc LEdu LRHS NEgg NPri SDea SPer WHar
- 'Elvira' (F)	EPfP LRHS
- 'Eros'PBR (F)	LBuc
- 'Fenella' (F)	CMac EPom GTwe MCoo
- 'Flamenco'PBR (F)	EPom LEdu LRHS
- 'Florence'PBR (F)	CAgr CSBt CTri EMil EPfP EPom ERea GTwe LBuc LEdu LRHS MBri SPer
- Fraise des Bois	see *F. vesca*
- 'Frau Mieze Schindler' (F) new	EPom
- 'Fruitful Summer' (F)	LBuc LRHS
- 'Hapil' (F) ♀H4	CTri EMil EPfP EPom GTwe LBuc LEdu LRHS MAsh
- 'Honeoye' (F) ♀H4	CAgr CSBt EMil EPfP EPom GAbr GTwe LBuc LEdu LRHS MAsh MBri MCoo NWad SEND SPer WHar
- 'Judibell'PBR (F)	LBuc LRHS
- 'Korona'PBR (F)	CMac EPom MCoo
- 'Loran' (F)	LRHS
- 'Malling Opal'PBR (F)	EPom
- 'Malwina'PBR (F)	CSut EPom SVic
- 'Mount Everest' (F)	LBuc
- 'Pandora' (F)	LEdu LRHS
- 'Pegasus'PBR (F) ♀H4	CAgr CSBt EPfP EPom GTwe LBuc LRHS NPri
- Pink Panda = 'Frel'PBR (F)	CMac CTri EBee ELan LHop LRHS MBel MGos MRav NDov NEgg NGdn NLar SPer SPoG WCAu WJek WWFP
- pink-flowered (F)	GAbr LPot MBel
- 'Rabunda' (F)	LRHS
- Red Ruby	see *F. × ananassa* 'Samba'
- 'Redgauntlet' (F)	EPfP GTwe LBuc LRHS MAsh
- 'Rhapsody' (F) ♀H4	GTwe LRHS LSRN
- 'Rosie'PBR (F)	SDea
- 'Royal Sovereign' (F)	CMac CTri EPom GTwe LEdu LRHS MCoo NBir SVic
§ - 'Samba'PBR (F)	CMac GLog LHop LRHS MBel MNrw NDov NEgg NGdn NLar SPer SPoG WCAu
- 'Senga Sengana' (F)	SVic
- 'Sonata'PBR (F)	CSut EPom LRHS
- 'Sophie'PBR (F)	EMil LEdu LRHS
- 'Sweetheart' (F)	LRHS
- 'Symphony'PBR (F) ♀H4	CAgr CSBt EPfP EPom LBuc LRHS LSRN MBri SPer
- 'Totem' (F)	GTwe LRHS
§ - 'Variegata' (v)	CTri EBee LDai LHop MHoo MRav SPer SPoG WMoo
- 'White Dream' (F) new	LBuc
'Bowles's Double'	see *F. vesca* 'Multiplex'
chiloensis (F)	LEdu
- 'Chaval' (F)	CHid EPPr IMou MRav NChi WMoo
- 'Variegata' misapplied	see *F. × ananassa* 'Variegata'
daltoniana	GCra
'Delican'	SHar
indica	see *Duchesnea indica*
'Lipstick'	LHop NLar
moschata	CAgr
nubicola	CAgr GPoy
'Roman'	LRHS
'Variegata'	see *F. × ananassa* 'Variegata'
§ ***vesca*** (F)	CAgr CArn CBcs ELan EPfP GPoy MHer MNHC NMir NPri SIde SPlb SVic WGwG WJek WOut WSFF WShi
- 'Alexandra' (F)	CArn CPrp ELau EPPr ERea SHar SIde WHar
- 'Baron Solemacher' (F)	SHDw SPhx WHer
- 'Flore Pleno'	see *F. vesca* 'Multiplex'
- 'Fructu Albo' (F)	CAgr CArn CBre CRow GLin WMoo
- 'Golden Alexandra' (F)	ELau EWes MHer NPro WHer WOut
- 'Golden Surprise'	SHDw
- 'Mara des Bois'PBR (F)	EPom
- 'Mignonette'	NDov SHar
- 'Monophylla' (F)	CRow SIde WHer
§ - 'Multiplex' (d)	CRow MRav NChi WBor WHer WOut
§ - 'Muricata'	CBre CRow LEdu
- 'Pineapple Crush' (F)	WHer
- 'Plymouth Strawberry'	see *F. vesca* 'Muricata'
§ - 'Semperflorens' (F)	WRHF
§ - 'Semperflorens Alba' (F)	CAgr
- 'Variegata' misapplied	see *F. × ananassa* 'Variegata'
* - 'Variegata' ambig. (v)	EHoe LLWG LRHS NEgg WWEG
virginiana	CAgr
- subsp. ***glauca***	EPPr
viridis	CAgr

Francoa (*Francoaceae*)

appendiculata	GAbr GKev GQui NBir WHer WMoo
- red-flowered	LHop
Ballyrogan strain	IBlr
'Confetti'	CAbP CExl ELan WCot
'Purple Spike'	see *F. sonchifolia* Rogerson's form
ramosa	CCVN CCon CTri IBlr LRHS NBro SDix WKif WMoo
* - 'Alba'	CSpe EDif
sonchifolia	Widely available
- 'Alba'	GKev WMoo
- 'Culm View Lilac'	CCVN
- 'Lynda Windsor'	CRDP
- 'Pink Bouquet'	CKno CMac EBee GBin SHar WOut
- 'Pink Giant'	CKno GBin GBuc GCal GKev MHer SMrm WHil WMoo

§ – Rogerson's form	CAby CCVN CElw CRDP CSam CTri EBee ELon IVic LBMP LHop LRHS MAvo MBel MBri NBir NChi SDix WMoo WWEG

Frangula (*Rhamnaceae*)

§ ***alnus***	CArn CCVT CDul CHab CTri ECrN EShb LBuc MBlu MGos NWea SEWo WMou WSFF
– 'Aspleniifolia'	EBee EPfP LRHS MBlu MMuc MPkF NLar SMad WPat
– 'Columnaris'	SLPl
– 'Fine Line'	NLar
– 'Minaret'	MBlu
– 'Ron Williams'	MBlu

Frankenia (*Frankeniaceae*)

laevis	SRms
thymifolia	CTri ECho MAsh MHer MWat SEND SIgm SPlb XLum

Franklinia (*Theaceae*)

alatamaha	CBcs IVic MBlu MBri WPGP

Fraxinus ✿ (*Oleaceae*)

americana	CDul CMCN EWTr NEgg NWea
– 'Autumn Purple'	CDul CEnd CMCN CTho EBee EPfP MAsh MBlu NWea WMou
angustifolia	CMCN
– 'Raywood' ♀H4	Widely available
anomala	EGFP
bungeana	IArd
chinensis	CDul CLnd CMCN
excelsior	CBcs CCVT CDoC CDul CHab CLnd CMac CSBt CTho CTri CWib ECrN EPfP LBuc MAsh MBri MGos MJak MMuc NWea SEND SEWo SGol SPer WMou
– 'Aurea Pendula'	CDul CEnd CMac CWib MBlu MGos
– 'Crispa'	MBlu NLar
– f. ***diversifolia***	CDul CLnd MBri
– 'Jaspidea' ♀H4	CBcs CCVT CDoC CDul CEnd CLnd CMCN CMac CTho CWib EBee ECrN ELan EPfP ERod LAst LHop MAsh MBlu MBri MGos MMuc MRav MSwo NWea SEND SGol SPer
– 'Nana'	LLHF WPat
– 'Pendula' ♀H4	CCVT CDul CEnd CLnd CMac CTsd EBee ECrN ELan MBlu NEgg NWea SGol SPer WMou
– 'R.E. Davey'	CDul
– variegated (v)	CMac
– 'Westhof's Glorie' ♀H4	CCVT CDoC CDul CLnd ECrN
hopeiensis	MBlu
insularis var. ***henryana***	CDul CMCN
latifolia	CMCN MBlu
mariesii	see *F. sieboldiana*
nigra	CMCN
– 'Fallgold'	CEnd
ornus ♀H4	CArn CCVT CDul CLnd CMCN CMac CTri EBee ECrN ELan EPfP EWTr LAst LEdu MMuc MSnd MSwo NWea SEND SPer WMou
– 'Arie Peters'	CDul
– 'Mecsek'	MBlu
– 'Obelisk'	EBee EBtc EWTr MAsh MBlu MBri NLar SPoG
– 'Rotterdam'	EBee
pennsylvanica	CDul CLnd CMCN
– Cimmaron = 'Cimmzam'	CDul
– 'Variegata' (v)	CLnd EBee
quadrangulata	CDul
§ ***sieboldiana***	CDul CLnd CMCN EPfP MBri SSpi
sogdiana Potamophila Group **new**	CFil
velutina	CDul CLnd SLPl
xanthoxyloides	CDul MBlu NEgg
– var. ***dumosa***	EBee

Freesia (*Iridaceae*)

alba Foster	see *F. lactea*
'Fragrant Sunburst'	SPoG
fucata	ECho
grandiflora	CExl CHll ECho WCot
grandiflora × ***laxa***	CDes
§ ***lactea***	CDes ECho
§ ***laxa*** ♀H2-3	CAvo CExl CRHN CSev CSpe CTri ECho EPri LEdu LRHS MCot WAbe WCot WPat
– var. ***alba*** ♀H2-3	CExl CPom CRHN CSev CSpe ECho EPri MCot WAbe
– blue-flowered	ECho WAbe
– 'Joan Evans'	CRHN CSpe ECho LLHF SBch
– red-spotted	CExl ECho
– ***viridiflora***	ECho
refracta 'Worcester'	ECho
viridis	CDes CExl ECho
xanthospila	WCot

Fremontodendron (*Malvaceae*)

sp. **new**	CHel
'California Glory' ♀H3	CBcs CDoC CDul CMac CWSG EBee ELon EPfP EUJe LAst LBMP LHop LRHS LSRN MAsh MBlu MGos MWat NEgg NPla NPri NSoo SAPC SGol SHil SMad SPer SPoG SVen SWvt
californicum	CDoy CTri CWib ELan MBri NLar SEND SLim SPlb
'Dara's Gold'	LRHS
'Pacific Sunset'	CBcs EPfP LSRN MGos MRav NEgg SGol
'Tequila Sunrise'	CBcs CDoC CJun CWGN EUJe LHop LLHF WPGP

Freylinia (*Scrophulariaceae*)

cestroides	see *F. lanceolata*
§ ***lanceolata***	CBcs CCCN CWib EBee SPlb SVen
tropica	CHll GFai
visseri	GFai MOWG

Fritillaria ✿ (*Liliaceae*)

acmopetala ♀H4	CAvo CBro CCon CHid CPom CWCL ECho EPot ERCP GBuc GKev ITim LRHS MNrw NMin SDeJ SPhx WCot WIce
– 'Brunette'	EPot
– 'Paul Furse' **new**	GKev
– subsp. ***wendelboi***	ECho EPot WCot
– – 'Zwanenburg'	LWst
affinis	CWCL ECho EPot GBin GBuc ITim
– NNS 00-336	WCot
– 'Sunray'	GKev
§ – var. ***tristulis***	CWCL GKev ITim
– 'Vancouver Island'	ECho

	amana	CTca CWCL ECho EPot ERCP GKev LLHF NMin WCot
	- 'Cambridge' ♀H4	WCot
	- 'Goksan Gold'	ECho
	- yellow-flowered	EPot
	arabica	see *F. persica*
	armena	GKev
	- MP 8146	LWst
	assyriaca	EPfP EPot GBuc
	aurea 'Golden Flag'	ECho EPot GKev LLHF
	biflora	ECho EPot
	- 'Martha Roderick'	ECho GKev SDeJ
§	***bithynica***	ECho
	- from Turkey	WCot
	bucharica	ECho EPot GKev NMin
	- 'Nurek Giant'	ECho GKev
	camschatcensis	CAvo CBro CHel CPom CWCL ECho EFEx EPfP EPot ERCP GBin GBuc GKev GMaP LRHS NBir NHar NLar NSla SDeJ SPhx WAbe WCot WCru
	- 'Alaska'	NHar
	- 'Aurea'	ECho GBuc LWst NHar SPhx
	- black-flowered	ECho NHar
	- double-flowered (d)	CCon ECho GBuc LWst
	- f. ***flavescens***	EFEx GBuc
	- green-flowered	CAby
	carduchorum	see *F. minuta*
	carica	ECho EPot
	- brown-flowered	ECho
	caucasica	ECho
	cirrhosa	LWst
	- brown-flowered	LWst
	- green-flowered	LWst
	citrina	see *F. bithynica*
	'Craigton Cascade' new	GKev
	crassifolia subsp. ***hakkarensis*** new	GKev
§	- subsp. ***kurdica***	ECho GKev ITim
	davisii	ECho EPot GKev LLHF LRHS WCot
	davisii × ***graeca***	WCot
	eduardii	ECho EPot GKev LRHS LWst WCot
	elwesii	ECho EPot ERCP GKev ITim LLHF LPio LRHS LWst SDeJ SPhx
*	***glauca*** 'Golden Flag'	ECho
	- 'Goldilocks'	ECho SDeJ
	graeca	ECho EPot GBuc GKev ITim NMin SDeJ
	- subsp. ***graeca***	GBuc
	hispanica	see *F. lusitanica*
	imperialis	ECGP MBri
	- 'April Flame'	CHel
	- 'Aureomarginata' (v)	LRHS
	- 'Aurora'	EPot ERCP GKev LPio LRHS MBri NLar NPer SDeJ
	- 'Garland Star'	GAbr GKev LRHS NLar
	- var. ***inodora***	GKev LRHS
	- 'Lutea'	CAvo CHel CTca ELan EPfP ERCP GKev LRHS SPhx SPoG
	- 'Maxima'	see *F. imperialis* 'Rubra Maxima'
	- 'Maxima Lutea' ♀H4	CBro ELan EPfP EPot ERCP GKev MBri NLar SDeJ SPer SPoG
	- 'Prolifera'	GKev NLar SDeJ
	- 'Rubra'	CTca ERCP GKev NLar SPer
§	- 'Rubra Maxima'	CBro CTca ELan EPfP EPot ERCP GKev LRHS SDeJ
	- 'Slagzwaard'	GKev
	- 'Striped Beauty'	EPot GKev SDeJ
	- 'Sulpherino'	GKev
	- 'The Premier'	GKev LRHS SDeJ
	- 'William Rex'	CAvo CHel EPfP EPot ERCP GKev LRHS SDeJ SPhx SPoG
	involucrata	ECho WCot
	japonica var. ***koidzumiana***	EFEx
	karadaghensis	see *F. crassifolia* subsp. *kurdica*
	kotschyana	ECho EPot LWst WCot
	- subsp. ***grandiflora***	WCot
	lanceolata	see *F. affinis* var. *tristulis*
	latakiensis	ECho EPot
§	***lusitanica***	ITim
	meleagris	Widely available
	- 'Artemis'	GBuc
	- var. ***unicolor*** subvar. ***alba*** ♀H4	CAvo CBro ECho ERCP GBuc GKev MBri MWat NHol SDeJ SMrm SPer SPhx WCot WPnP WShi
	- - - 'Aphrodite'	EPot NBir
	meleagroides	WCot
	messanensis subsp. ***gracilis***	LWst
	michailovskyi ♀H2	CAby CHel CHid CTri CWCL ECho EPfP EPot ERCP GBuc GKev LHop LRHS MNrw NPnk SDeJ SRms
	minima	ECho
§	***minuta***	ECho EPot ERCP NMin
	montana	ECho WCot
	nigra Mill.	see *F. pyrenaica*
	olivieri	ECho
	pallidiflora ♀H4	CBro CLAP CTca CWCL ECho EPot ERCP GBuc GCra GKev LPio MBri NBir NPnk SDeJ SPhx WCot
§	***persica***	CAvo ECho EPfP EPot ERCP GKev LHop LPio LRHS MBri MNrw SPhx
	- 'Adiyaman' ♀H4	ELan LRHS SDeJ
	- 'Alba'	GKev
	- 'Chocolate'	CWCL
	- 'Ivory Bells'	CAvo ELan EPot ERCP LPio LRHS SDeJ SKHP SPhx
	- 'Ivory Queen'	CBro
	- 'Midnight Bells' new	ECho GKev
*	- 'Senkoy'	LRHS
	pinardii	ECho EPot
	- 'Ole Sonderhause' new	ECho
	pontica ♀H4	CAvo CBro CCon CLAP CWCL ECho EPot ERCP GBuc GKev ITim MNrw SDeJ SPhx WCot WCru
	pudica	ECho WAbe WCot
*	- 'Fragrant'	ECho
	- 'Giant'	ECho EPot GKev NMin SDeJ
	purdyi	ECho
§	***pyrenaica*** ♀H4	CLAP CWCL ECho GCra LLHF SPhx WCru
	- 'Cedric Morris'	WCot
	- var. ***lutescens*** new	WCot
	raddeana	ECho EPot ERCP GKev LRHS LWst SDeJ SPhx
	reuteri new	ECho
	rhodocanakis	NMin WCot
	rubra major	see *F. imperialis* 'Rubra Maxima'
	ruthenica	ECho GKev
	sewerzowii	CHel ECho EPot GKev
	- 'Black Bear'	LWst
	- 'Brown Eyes'	LWst
	- 'Gulliver'	LWst
	sinica	LLHF WCot
	stenanthera	CHel ECho EPot
	tachengensis	see *F. yuminensis*
	thunbergii	ECho GKev LLHF SPhx WCot

tuntasia subsp. ***tuntasia***	WCot
uva-vulpis	CAby CCon CMea CTca ECtt EHyd ELon EPot ERCP GKev LHop LPio LRHS MNrw NBir SDeJ SPhx WCru
verticillata	CBro EPot GKev SPhx WCru
whittallii	ECho EPot GKev
- PW 72-64B	LWst
- 'Green Light'	NMin
§ ***yuminensis***	WCot

Fuchsia ✿ (*Onagraceae*)

'A.M. Larwick'	CSil EBak
'A.W. Taylor'	EBak
'Aalt Hillie van de Veen' **new**	WOth
'Abbé Farges' (d)	CDoC CLoc CSil CWVF EBak EPts SVic WRou
'Abigail' ambig.	CWVF
'Abigail Storey'	CSil
'Abundance'	CSil
'Achievement' ♀H4	CDoC CLoc CSil LCla MJac SVic
'Adalbert Bogner' (d)	CDoC
'Adelaide Hoodless'	WRou
'Adinda' (T) ♀H1	CDoC EPts LCla WRou
'Admiration'	CSil
'Ailsa Garnett' (d)	EBak
'Aintree'	CWVF
'Airedale'	CWVF
'Aisen'	WRou
'Aladna's Sander' (d)	CWVF
'Alan Ayckbourn'	CWVF
'Alan Titchmarsh'	CDoC EPts LCla SLBF
'Alaska' (d)	CLoc EBak SVic
'Albertina'	SVic
'Albertus Schwab'	LCla
'Alde'	CWVF
'Alderford'	SLBF
'Alf Thornley' (d)	CWVF WOth
'Alfred Rambaud' (d)	CDoC CSil
'Alice Ashton' (d)	EBak
'Alice Blue Gown' (d)	CWVF
'Alice Doran'	CDoC CSil LCla
'Alice Hoffman' (d) ♀H3-4	CAby CCCN CDoC CLoc CMac COIW CSBt CSil CWVF EBak EBee ELan EPfP EPts LAst LRHS MAsh MGos MJac NEgg NLar SEND SHil SLBF SLim SPer SPet SPoG SVic WRou
'Alice Mary' (d)	EBak
'Alice Sweetapple' (d)	CWVF
'Alice Travis' (d)	EBak
'Alicia Sellars' **new**	SLBF WRou
'Alipat'	EBak
'Alison Ewart'	CLoc CWVF EBak MJac SPet SVic
'Alison Patricia' ♀H3	CWVF EBak LAst MJac SLBF SVic WOth WRou
'Alison Reynolds' (d)	CWVF
'Alison Ruth Griffin' (d)	MJac
'Alison Ryle' (d)	EBak
'Alison Sweetman' ♀H1+3	CSil CWVF MJac
'Allure' (d)	CWVF
'Aloha' **new**	WOth
alpestris	CDoC CSil EBak GCal LCla SVic
'Alton Waters' (d/v)	WOth
'Alwin' (d)	CWVF
'Alyce Larson' (d)	CWVF EBak MJac SVic
'Alyssa May Garcia' (d) **new**	SLBF WRou
'Amazing Grace' (d)	MJac
'Amazing Maisie' (d)	SLBF
'Ambassador'	EBak SVic
'Amelie Aubin'	CLoc CWVF EBak SVic
'America'	CWVF
'Amerika' (d) **new**	WOth
'Amethyst Fire' (d)	CSil
'Amigo' ambig.	EBak
§ ***ampliata***	CDoC LCla
'Amy'	MJac
'Amy Lye'	CLoc CSil EBak SVic
'Amy Ruth'	CWVF
§ 'Andenken an Heinrich Henkel' (T)	CDoC CLoc CWVF EBak WRou
'André Le Nostre' (d)	CWVF EBak SVic
'Andreas Schwab'	LCla
andrei	CDoC LCla
'Andrew'	EBak
'Andrew Carnegie' (d)	CLoc
'Andrew Hadfield'	CWVF SVic
'Andromeda' De Groot	CSil
'Angela' ^{PBR} **new**	WOth
'Angela Dawn'	WRou
'Angela King' **new**	WRou
'Angela Leslie' (d)	CLoc CWVF EBak SVic
'Angela Rippon'	CWVF MJac
'Angel's Flight' (d)	EBak
'Angel's Kiss' (E)	CDoC LCla SLBF
'Angie Baby' **new**	WOth
'Anita' (d)	CLoc CWVF EPts LAst MJac SLBF SVic WGor WOth WRou
'Anjo' (v)	CWVF
'Ann Howard Tripp'	CDoC CLoc CWVF EPts MJac SVic WRou
'Ann Lee' (d)	EBak
'Ann Marie McManus'	CSil
'Anna Louise'	WOth
'Anna of Longleat' (d)	CWVF EBak LAst MJac SPet
'Anna Silvena'	LSou
'Annabel' (d) ♀H3	CCCN CDoC CLoc CTri CWVF EBak EPts LAst MJac SLBF SPet SVic WRou
'Anneke de Keijzer'	CDoC LCla WOth
'Annie Geurts'	CDoC
'Annie M.G. Schmidt'	EPts WRou
'Another Little Cracker'	WRou
'Another Storey'	CSil
'Ant and Dec' (d/v)	MJac
'Anthea Day' (d)	CLoc
'Anthonie Sherwood' (T) **new**	WRou
'Antigone'	SLBF WOth
'Aphrodite' (d)	CLoc CWVF EBak
'Applause' (d)	CLoc CWVF EBak EPts SPet SVic
aprica misapplied	see *F.* × *bacillaris*
aprica Lundell	see *F. microphylla* subsp. *aprica*
'Apricot Ice'	CLoc SVic
'Arabella'	CWVF
'Arabella Improved'	CWVF SVic
arborea	see *F. arborescens*
§ ***arborescens***	CBcs CDoC CHll CLoc CSil CWVF EBak EWld LCla MCot SDys SMrm SVic WJek WRou WWlt
- B&SWJ 10475	WCru
'Arcadia Gold' (d)	CWVF SVic
'Arcady'	CLoc CWVF
'Ariel' (E)	CDoC CSil LRHS SVen SVic WOth WRou
'Arkie'	MJac
'Arlendon' (d)	CWVF
'Army Nurse' (d) ♀H4	CDoC CLoc CSil CWVF ELan ELon EPfP EPts LRHS MGos NBir NLar

		SEND SHil SLBF SLim SPet SVic WRou
	'Arthur Baxter'	EBak
	'Ashley'	CDoC LCla
	'Ashley and Isobel'	CWVF
	'Ashtede'	SLBF
	'Ashville'	SLBF WRou
	'Atahualpa' (T)	CDoC WOth
	'Athela'	EBak
	'Atlantic Star'	CWVF MJac
	'Atlantis' (d)	CWVF
	'Atomic Glow' (d)	EBak SVic
	'Aubergine'	see *F.* 'Gerharda's Aubergine'
	'Audrey Hepburn'	CWVF
	'Auenland'	MJac
	'Aunt Hilda'	CSil
	'Aunt Juliana' (d)	EBak
	'Auntie Jinks'	CDoC CWVF EBak LAst MJac SLBF SPet SVic WOth
	'Aurora Superba'	CLoc CWVF EBak SLBF
	'Australia Fair' (d)	CWVF EBak
§	***austromontana***	EBak
	'Autumnale' 🏆H1+3	CDoC CLoc CWVF EBak EPts SLBF SPet SPoG SVic WRou
	'Avalanche' ambig. (d)	CDoC CLoc EBak LRHS SLBF
	'Avocet'	CLoc EBak
	'Avon Celebration' (d)	CLoc
	'Avon Gem'	CLoc CSil
	'Avon Glow' (d)	CLoc
	'Avon Gold'	CLoc
	ayavacensis	CDoC LCla
	'Aylisa Rowan' (E)	SLBF
	'Azure Sky' (d)	MJac
	'Baby Blue Eyes' 🏆H3-4	CDoC CSil CWVF ELan ELon EPfP LRHS LSRN MAsh SVic WRou
	'Baby Blush'	CSil
	'Baby Bright'	CWVF LCla WRou
	'Baby Brooke' **new**	WRou
	'Baby Chang'	WOth
	'Baby Pink' (d)	CWVF
	'Baby Thumb' (v)	EPts
	'Babyface' Tolley (d)	SVic
§	× ***bacillaris*** (E)	CAbb CDoC CHGN CSil EBak EBee EWes GCal SEND SLBF SPoG
§	- 'Cottinghamii' (E)	CDoC CSil EWld SPlb WSHC
	- 'Oosje'	see *F.* 'Oosje'
§	- 'Reflexa' (E)	CAbP CCCN LSou
	'Baden Powell' (E)	SVic
	'Bagworthy Water'	CLoc
	'Baker's Tri' (T)	EBak
	'Balkonkönigin'	CLoc CWVF EBak
	'Ballerina'	CDoC
	'Ballerina Dreams'	LAst
	'Ballerina Girl' (E)	SLBF
	'Ballet Girl' (d) 🏆H1+3	CLoc CWVF EBak SLBF
	'Bambini'	CWVF EPts
	'Banks Peninsula'	GBin GQui
	'Barbara'	CLoc CSil CWVF EBak EPts LCla MJac SPet SVic WRou
	'Barbara Evans'	SLBF
	'Barbara Pountain' (d)	CWVF
	'Barbara Windsor'	CWVF MJac
	'Barry's Queen'	see *F.* 'Golden Border Queen'
	'Bart Comperen' (d)	WRou
	'Bartje'	SLBF
	'Bashful' (d)	CDoC CSil EPts LCla SPet SVic
	'Beacon'	CDoC CLoc CMac CSil CWVF EBak EPfP EPts LAst LCla LRHS MJac SLBF SPet SPoG SVic WRou
	'Beacon Rosa'	CDoC CLoc CSil CWVF ELon EPfP EPts LAst LCla LRHS MJac SLBF SPet SPoG SVic WRou
	'Beacon Superior'	CSil
	'Bealings' (d)	CWVF SVic
	'Beauty of Bath' (d)	CLoc EBak
	'Beauty of Clyffe Hall' Lye	CSil EBak
	'Beauty of Exeter' (d)	CWVF EBak
	'Beauty of Meise' (d)	CDoC
	'Beauty of Prussia' (d)	CLoc CSil CWVF
	'Beauty of Swanley'	EBak
	'Beauty of Trowbridge'	CWVF LCla WOth
	'Becky Jane'	CSil
	'Bella Forbes' (d) 🏆H1+3	CSil EBak
	'Bella Rosella' (California Dreamers Series) (d)	EPts LAst MJac SCoo SLBF
	'Belsay Beauty' (d)	CWVF MJac
	'Belvoir Beauty' (d)	CLoc
	'Ben de Jong'	CDoC LCla SLBF WRou
	'Ben Jammin'	CLoc CSil CWVF EPfP EPts LRHS SEND SVic WRou
	'Beninkust'	WOth
	'Béranger' Lemoine, 1897 (d)	CSil EBak
	'Berba's Happiness' (d)	CWVF
	'Berba's Trio'	WOth
	'Berliner Kind' (d)	CSil CWVF EBak
	'Bermuda' (d)	CWVF
	'Bernadette' (d)	CWVF
	'Bernie's Big-un' (d)	MJac
	'Bernisser Hardy' 🏆H3-4	CDoC CSil EPts LCla LRHS SLBF SLim WOth
	'Beryl Clarke' (v)	EPts
	'Bessie Kimberley' (T)	CDoC LCla
	'Beth Robley' (d)	CWVF
	'Betsy Huuskes'	SLBF
	'Betsy Ross' (d)	EBak
	Betty = 'Shabetty'PBR (Shadowdancer Series)	LAst
	'Beverley'	CWVF EBak EPts
	'Beverley Sisters' (d)	MJac
	'Bewitched' (d)	EBak
	'Bianca' (d)	CWVF SVic
	'Bicentennial' (d)	CLoc CWVF EBak EPts LAst MJac SPet SVic
	'Big Slim'	WOth
	'Billy'PBR	CDoC WOth WRou
	'Billy Green' (T) 🏆H1+3	CDoC CLoc CWVF EBak EPts LCla MHer MJac SVic WRou
	'Billy P'	LAst
	'Bilton'	CSil
	'Bishop's Bells' (d)	CWVF SVic
	'Bittersweet' (d)	SVic
	'Black Beauty' (d)	CWVF
	'Black Country 21'	SLBF
	'Black Prince'	CDoC CWVF SVic
	'Blackmore Vale' (d)	CWVF
	'Blacky' (d)	CCCN EBak EUJe GBin LAst LSou MSCN NPri SDys SEND SMrm SPet SVic
I	'Blanche Regina' (d)	CWVF MJac
	'Bland's New Striped'	EBak EPts LSou SLBF
	'Blaze Away' (d)	LAst MJac WGor
	'Blood Donor' (d)	MJac
	'Blowick'	CWVF MJac SPet
	'Blue Angel' (d) **new**	LAst WOth
	'Blue Beauty' (d)	CSil EBak
	'Blue Bush'	CSil CWVF EPts MJac SVic
	'Blue Butterfly' (d)	CWVF EBak SVic
	'Blue Eyes' (d)	CDoC SPet

'Blue Gown' (d)	CDoC CLoc CSil CWVF EBak SVic WRou
'Blue Lace' (d)	CSil SVic
'Blue Lagoon' ambig. (d)	CWVF
'Blue Lake' (d)	CWVF
'Blue Mink'	EBak
'Blue Mirage' (d)	CLoc CWVF LAst SVic
'Blue Mist' (d)	EBak
'Blue Pearl' (d)	CWVF EBak
'Blue Pinwheel'	CWVF EBak
'Blue Satin' (d)	LAst
'Blue Sleighbells'	WOth
'Blue Tit'	CSil LCla
'Blue Veil' (d)	CLoc CWVF MJac SCoo SVic
'Blue Waves' (d)	CLoc CSBt CWVF EBak MJac SVic
'Blush o' Dawn' (d)	CLoc CWVF EBak EPts SVic
'Bob Bartrum'	EPts SLBF
'Bob Pacey'	CWVF
'Bobby Boy' (d)	EBak
'Bobby Dazzler' (d)	CWVF
'Bobby Shaftoe' (d)	EBak
'Bobby Wingrove'	EBak
'Bobby's Girl'	EPts
'Bobolink' (d)	EBak
'Bob's Best' (d)	CWVF EPts MJac
'Boerhaave'	EBak
boliviana Britton	see *F. sanctae-rosae*
boliviana ambig.	CBcs WRou
§ ***boliviana*** Carrière	CDoC CHEx CHll CLoc CWVF EBak LCla
§ - var. ***alba*** ♀H1+3	CDoC CHll CLoc EBak EPts LCla MREP SVic WOth
- var. ***boliviana***	CRHN SVic
- var. ***luxurians*** 'Alba'	see *F. boliviana* Carrière var. *alba*
- f. ***puberulenta*** Munz	see *F. boliviana* Carrière
'Bon Accorde'	CLoc CWVF EBak EPts SLBF WRou
'Bon Bon' (d)	CWVF EBak SVic
'Bonita' (d)	CWVF SVic
'Bonnie Lass' (d)	EBak
'Bora Bora' (d)	CWVF EBak SVic
'Borde Hill' (d)	EPts
'Border Princess'	EBak
'Border Queen' ♀H3-4	CDoC CLoc CSil CWVF EBak EPts MJac MSCN SLBF SPet SVic WOth
'Border Raider'	WRou
'Border Reiver'	CWVF EBak SVic
'Börnemann's Beste'	see *F.* 'Georg Börnemann'
'Bouffant'	CLoc SVic
'Bountiful' Munkner (d)	CLoc CWVF
'Bouquet' (d)	CDoC CSil
'Bow Bells'	CDoC CLoc CWVF MJac SPet SVic
'Boy Marc' (T) ♀H1	LCla
'Braamt's Glorie'	CDoC WRou
bracelinae	CDoC CSil
'Brandane' **new**	WRou
'Brandt's 500 Club'	CLoc EBak
'Breckland'	EBak
'Breeders' Delight'	CSil CWVF
'Breeder's Dream' (d)	EBak
'Breevis Minimus'	SLBF
'Brenda' (d)	CWVF EBak
'Brenda White'	CLoc CWVF EBak SVic WOth WRou
'Brentwood' (d)	EBak
brevilobis	CSil
'Brian C. Morrison' (T)	LCla
'Brian G. Soanes'	EBak
'Brian Kimberley' (T)	LCla
'Brian McFetridge' (d) **new**	WRou
'Bridal Veil' (d)	EBak

'Bridesmaid' (d)	CWVF EBak SPet SVic
'Brigadoon' (d)	EBak
'Brighton Belle' (T)	CDoC CWVF
'Brilliant' ambig.	CWVF
'Brilliant' Bull, 1865	CDoC CLoc CSil EBak LCla
'Briony Caunt'	CSil
'British Jubilee' (d)	CWVF SVic WOth
'British Sterling' (d)	WOth
'Brixham Orpheus'	CWVF
'Broadway' **new**	WRou
'Brodsworth'	CSil
'Bronze Banks Peninsula'	CDoC CSil
'Brookwood Belle' (d)	CWVF EPts LCla MJac SLBF
'Brookwood Joy' (d)	CWVF
'Brutus' ♀H4	CDoC CLoc CSil CWVF EBak EPfP EPts LRHS MAsh MSCN MWat NGBl SCoo SLBF SPet SPoG SVic WRou
'Bryan Breary' (E)	LCla WRou
'Buddha' (d)	EBak
'Bugle Boy'	LCla WRou
'Bunny' (d)	CWVF EBak SLBF SVic
'Burstwick'	CSil
'Buster' (d)	LCla
'Buttercup'	CLoc CWVF EBak SVic
'C.J. Howlett'	CSil EBak
'Caballero' (d)	EBak
'Caesar' (d)	CWVF EBak
'Caledonia'	CSil EBak
'Callaly Pink'	CWVF
'Cambridge Louie'	CWVF EBak SPet
campos-portoi	CDoC CFil CSil LCla WPGP WRou
'Candlelight' (d)	EBak
'Candy Bells' (d)	CSBt
canescens misapplied	see *F. ampliata*
'Canny Bob'	MJac
'Canopy' (d)	CWVF
'Capri' (d)	CWVF EBak
'Cara Mia' (d)	CLoc SPet
'Caradela' (d)	CLoc MJac WRou
'Cardinal'	CLoc
'Cardinal Farges' (d)	CLoc CWVF SLBF SVic
'Careless Whisper'	CDoC LCla SLBF
'Carioca'	EBak
'Carl Drude' (d)	CSil SVic
'Carla Johnston' ♀H1+3	CDoC CLoc CWVF EPts MJac SVic WRou
'Carl's Brummagem Beauty'	MJac
'Carmel Blue'	CCCN CDoC CLoc EPfP LAst LRHS SVic WGor
'Carmen' Lemoine (d)	CDoC CSil
'Carmine Bell'	CSil
'Carnea'	CSil CWib
'Carnoustie' (d)	EBak
'Carol Grace' (d)	CLoc
'Carol Nash' (d)	CLoc
'Caroline'	CLoc CWVF EBak EPts SVic WRou
'Caroline's Joy'	MJac SCoo SPet
'Cascade'	CDoC CLoc CWVF EPts LBMP MJac SLBF SPet
'Caspar Hauser' (d)	CWVF SLBF SVic
'Catharina' (T)	CDoC
'Catherine Bartlett'	CWVF
'Cathie MacDougall' (d)	EBak
'Cecile' (d)	CCCN CDoC CWVF EPts LAst MJac SLBF SVic
'Celadore' (d)	CWVF
'Celebration' (d)	CLoc CWVF
'Celia Smedley' ♀H3	CDoC CLoc CWVF EBak EPts LAst LCla MJac SLBF SPet SVic WRou

'Centerpiece' (d)	EBak
'Ceri'	CLoc
'Cerrig'	SVic
'Champagne Celebration'	CLoc WOth
'Chancellor' (d)	CWVF
'Chandleri'	CWVF SLBF SVic
'Chang' ♀$^{H1+3}$	CDoC CLoc CWVF EBak LCla SLBF SVic WOth WRou
'Chantelle Garcia' (d)	CDoC SLBF WRou
'Chantry Park' (T)	LCla
'Chapel Rossan' (E) **new**	SLBF WRou
'Charisma'	SVic
'Charles Edward' (d)	CSil
'Charles Welch'	EPts
Charlie Dimmock = 'Foncha'^{PBR} (d)	CLoc LAst
'Charlie Gardiner'	CWVF EBak
'Charlie Girl' (d)	EBak SVic
'Charming'	CDoC CLoc CSil CWVF EBak LRHS MAsh MJac SVic
'Chartwell'	WOth
'Chatt's Delight'	SLBF
'Checkerboard' ♀^{H3}	CLoc CWVF EBak EPts LAst LCla MJac MSCN SLBF SPet SVic WOth WRou
'Cheers' (d)	CWVF
'Chelsea Louise'	EPts
'Cherry Pop' (E) **new**	WRou
'Chessboard'	CLoc
'Chillerton Beauty' ♀^{H3}	CLoc CSil CTri CWVF ELan ELon EPfP EPts LCla LRHS MJac NLar SEND SLBF SPer SPet SVic WMnd WOth WRou
'Chilli Red' **new**	EPts
'China Doll' (d)	CWVF EBak
'China Lantern'	CLoc CSil CWVF EBak SVic
'Chor Echo'	CDoC
'Chris Bright'	MJac WRou
'Chris Joiner' **new**	WRou
'Chris Nicholls' (d)	CSil
'Chris Tarrant' (d)	EPts
'Christina Becker'	SVic
'Christine Bamford'	CDoC CSil CWVF
'Christine Rogers'	CDoC
'Churchtown'	CWVF
cinerea	CDoC LCla
'Cinnabarina' (E)	CLoc
'Cinque Port Liberty' (d)	SLBF
'Cinvenu'	LCla
'Cinvulca'	LCla
'Circe' (d)	CWVF EBak
'Circus'	EBak
'Circus Spangles' (d)	CLoc
'Citation'	CLoc CWVF EBak
'City of Adelaide' (d)	CLoc
'City of Leicester'	CWVF MHer SPet
'Clair de Lune'	CDoC CWVF EBak SVic
'Claire Evans' (d)	CWVF
'Claire Oram'	CLoc
'Claudia' (d)	CDoC LAst LCla MJac SLBF WRou
'Cliantha' (d)	CDoC WRou
'Clifford Gadsby' (d)	EBak
'Cliff's Hardy'	CDoC CSil LCla SVic
'Cliff's Own'	SVic
'Cliff's Unique' (d)	CWVF EPts
'Clifton Beauty' (d)	CWVF MJac
'Clifton Belle' (d)	CWVF
'Clifton Charm'	CSil EPts LCla MJac SVic
'Clipper'	CSil CWVF
'Cloth of Gold'	CLoc CWVF EBak MHer MJac SPet SVic
'Cloverdale Jewel' (d)	CDoC CWVF EBak SPet SVic
'Cloverdale Joy'	EBak
'Cloverdale Pearl'	CDoC CWVF EBak SPet SPoG SVic
'Coachman' ♀^{H4}	CLoc CWVF EBak EPts LAst LCla SLBF SPet SVic WOth WRou
coccinea	CDoC CSil CTsd WOth
'Codringtonii'	CSil
× ***colensoi***	CDoC CSil ECou LCla WRou
'Collingwood' (d)	CLoc CWVF EBak
'Colne Fantasy' (v)	CDoC
'Come Dancing' (d)	CDoC CWVF SPet SVic
'Comet' Banks	CWVF
I 'Comet' Tiret (d)	CDoC CLoc EBak
'Comperen Lutea' (d)	CDoC
'Conchetta Garcia' **new**	CDoC SLBF WRou
'Conchilla' (d)	EBak
'Connie' (d)	EBak SVic
'Connor's Cascade'	SLBF
'Conspicua' ♀$^{H3-4}$	CDoC CSil CWVF EBak ELon SLBF SVic
'Constable Country' (d)	CWVF
'Constance' (d)	CDoC CLoc CSil CWVF LCla MJac SLBF SPet SVic
'Constance Comer'	MJac WRou
'Constellation' ambig.	CWVF
'Constellation' Schnabel, 1957 (d)	CLoc EBak
'Coombe Park'	MJac
'Copycat'	CSil
'Coquet Bell'	CWVF EBak
'Coquet Dale' (d)	CWVF EBak
'Coral Baby' (E)	LCla SLBF WRou
'Coral Rose' (d)	SVic
'Coral Seas'	EBak
'Coralle' (T)	CCCN CDoC CLoc CWVF EBak EPts LCla MHer MJac MSCN SLBF SVic WOth WRou
'Corallina' ♀$^{H3-4}$	CDoC CLoc CSil EBak SEND SVic WPnn
I 'Corallina Variegata' (v)	CSil
* ***cordata*** B&SWJ 9095	WCru
- B&SWJ 10325	WCru
cordifolia misapplied	see *F. splendens*
'Core'ngrato' (d)	CLoc CWVF EBak
'Cornelia Smith' (T)	CDoC LCla
'Cornwall Calls' (d)	EBak
'Corsage' (d)	CWVF SVic
'Corsair' (d)	EBak SVic
corymbiflora misapplied	see *F. boliviana* Carrière
corymbiflora Ruíz & Pav.	CDoC EBak SVic
'Cosmopolitan' (d)	EBak
'Costa Brava'	CLoc EBak
'Cotta Bright Star'	CDoC CWVF LCla
'Cotta Carousel'	LCla
'Cotta Christmas Tree'	CDoC LCla SLBF WRou
'Cotta Fairy'	CWVF
'Cotta Vino'	SVic
'Cottinghamii'	see *F.* × *bacillaris* 'Cottinghamii'
'Cotton Candy' (d)	CLoc CWVF SVic WRou
'Countdown Carol' (d)	EPts
'Countess of Aberdeen'	CWVF EBak SLBF
'Countess of Maritza' (d)	CLoc CWVF
'County Park'	ECou
'Court Jester' (d)	CLoc EBak
'Cover Girl' (d)	EBak EPts
'Coxeen'	EBak
'Crackerjack'	CLoc EBak

	'Crescendo' (d)	CLoc CWVF
	'Crinkley Bottom' (d)	EPts MJac SLBF
	'Crinoline' (d)	EBak
	'Crosby Serendipity'	CLoc
	'Crosby Soroptimist'	CWVF MJac
	'Cross Check'	CWVF
	'Crusader' (d)	CWVF
	'Crystal Blue'	EBak SVic
	'Crystal Stars' (d)	SVic
	'Cumbrian Lass' **new**	WRou
	'Cupid'	EBak
	'Curly Q'	EBak SVic
	'Curtain Call' (d)	CWVF EBak SVic
	cylindracea misapplied	see *F.* × *bacillaris*
	cylindracea Lindl. (E)	CSil
	- B&SWJ 10294 (E/f)	WCru
	'Cymon' (d)	CWVF
	'Cymru' (d)	SVic
	cyrtandroides	CSil
	'Dainty'	EBak
	'Dainty Lady' (d)	EBak
	'Daisy Bell'	CDoC CLoc CWVF EBak LCla MJac SPet SVic
	'Dalton'	EBak
	'Dana Samantha'	EPts
	'Dancing Bloom'	EPts
	'Dancing Flame' (d) ♀H1+3	CLoc CWVF EBak EPts LAst LBMP MJac SLBF SVic WRou
	'Daniel Pfaller' (d)	MJac
	'Danielle'	WRou
	'Danish Pastry'	CWVF SPet
	'Danny Boy' (d)	CLoc CWVF EBak SVic
	'Dark Eyes' (d) ♀H4	CCCN CLoc CSil CWVF EBak LAst LBMP MJac SLBF SPer SPet SVic WOth
	'Dark Mystery' (d)	WOth
	'Dark Night' (d)	CSil
	'Dark Secret' (d)	EBak
	'Dark Treasure' (d)	CDoC
	'Daryn John Woods'	CDoC LCla
	'David' ♀H3-4	CDoC CLoc CSil CWVF ELon EPfP EPts LAst LCla LSRN MJac SEND SLBF SLPl WGor WHil WRou
	'David Alston' (d)	CLoc CWVF EBak
	'David Lockyer' (d)	CLoc CWVF SVic
	'David Savage' (d)	LCla
	'David Ward' (d)	NEgg
	'Dawn'	EBak
	'Dawn Fantasia' (v)	CLoc EPts
	'Dawn Redfern' (d)	CWVF
	'Dawn Sky' (d)	EBak
	'Dawn Star' (d)	CLoc CWVF MJac SVic
	'Dawn Thunder' (d)	SVic
	'Day by Day'	CSil
	'Day Star'	EBak
	'De Groot's Dream'	WOth
	'De Groot's Floriant'	LCla
	'De Mijnlamp' (d)	CDoC
	'Debby' (d)	EBak
	'Deben Petite' (E)	LCla
	'Deborah Jane'	SLBF
	'Deborah Street' (d)	CLoc
§	***decussata*** Ruíz & Pav.	EBak
	'Dee Copley' (d)	EBak
	'Deep Purple' (d)	CDoC CLoc CWVF LAst LBMP MJac SCoo SLBF
	'Delia Smith' (d)	EPts
	'Delicate Purple' **new**	WRou
	'Delilah' (d)	CWVF

	'Delta's Bride'	SLBF WRou
	'Delta's Dream'	CWVF
	'Delta's Drop'	SVic
	'Delta's Fellow' **new**	WOth
	'Delta's Groom'	LCla SLBF WRou
	'Delta's Ko' (d)	SVic
	'Delta's Parade' (d)	CDoC WOth
	'Delta's Rien'	SVic
	'Delta's Sara'	CDoC CSil EPfP LAst LBuc LRHS MJac SHil SLim SPoG WHar WRou
	'Delta's Song'	WRou
	'Delta's Symphonie' (d)	CWVF
	'Delta's Wonder'	CSil SVic
	'Dennis Cartwright' **new**	MJac
§	***denticulata***	CDoC CLoc CWVF EBak EPfP EPts LCla MHer SLBF SVic WOth
	'Derby Imp'	CWVF
	'Desperate Daniel'	EPts
	'Devonshire Dumpling' (d)	CCCN CLoc CTsd CWVF EBak EPts LAst MJac SLBF SPet SVic WRou
	'Diablo' (d)	EBak
	'Diamond Celebration' (d)	WOth
	'Diamond Wedding'	SVic
	'Diana' (d)	EBak
	'Diana Wills' (d)	CWVF
	'Diana Wright'	CDoC CSil LPla
	Diana, Princess of Wales = 'Fucdpw'PBR	LAst MJac
	'Diane Brown'	CWVF
	'Diane Marie'	WRou
	'Diane Stephens'	SLBF WRou
§	'Die Schöne Wilhelmine'	SVic
	'Dilly-Dilly' (d)	CWVF
	'Dimples' (d)	CSil
	'Dipton Dainty' (d)	CLoc EBak SVic
	'Display' ♀H4	CDoC CLoc CSil CWVF EBak EPfP EPts LAst LCla LRHS MAsh MJac NPer SHil SLBF SPet SPoG SVic
	'Doc'	CDoC CSil EPts SPet SVic
	'Docteur Topinard'	CLoc EBak
	'Doctor'	see *F.* 'The Doctor'
	'Doctor Becky Reynolds' (d)	WRou
	'Doctor Foster' ♀H4	CDoC CLoc CSil CTri EBak EPfP SPoG SVic
	'Doctor Mason'	CWVF
	'Doctor Olson' (d)	CLoc EBak
	'Doctor Robert'	CWVF EPts MJac SVic
	'Doctor Sat Sandilands' (d) **new**	WRou
	'Dodo'	LCla SLBF
§	'Dollar Prinzessin' (d) ♀H4	CDoC CLoc CMac CSil CWVF EBak EPfP EPts LAst LCla LRHS MAsh MGos MJac NPer SHil SLBF SLim SMrm SPet SPlb SVic WRou
	'Dominyana'	EBak LCla
	'Don Peralta'	EBak
	'Dopy' (d)	CDoC EPts SPet SVic
	'Doray' **new**	SLBF WRou
	'Doreen Redfern'	CLoc CWVF MJac SPet SVic
	'Doreen Stroud' (d)	CWVF
	'Doris Joan'	SLBF
	'Dorothea Flower'	CLoc CWVF EBak WOth
	'Dorothy'	EPts LCla SLBF SPet
	'Dorothy Ann'	LCla SLBF
	'Dorothy Cheal'	CWVF
	'Dorothy Clive'	WRou
	'Dorothy Day' (d)	CLoc

Name	Suppliers
'Dorothy Hanley' (d)	CCCN CLoc EPts LAst LRHS LSou MAsh MJac SEND SLBF SPet SVic WOth WRou
'Dorothy Oosting' (d)	CDoC
'Dorothy Shields' (d)	CWVF MJac WOth
'Dorrian Brogdale' (T)	LCla
'Dorset Abigail'	CWVF
'Dorset Delight' (d)	CWVF
'Dotti' (d)	SLBF
'Douglas Boath' (d)	WRou
'Drake 400' (d)	CLoc
'Drama Girl' (d)	CWVF
'Drame' (d)	CDoC CSil CWVF EBak SVic
'Drum Major' (d)	EBak
'Du Barry' (d)	EBak
'Duchess of Albany'	CLoc EBak
'Duchess of Cornwall' (d)	EPts
'Duet' (d)	SVic
'Duke of Wellington' Haag, 1956 (d)	CLoc
'Dulcie Elizabeth' (d)	CWVF EBak MJac SPet
'Dunrobin Bedder'	CSil
'Dusky Beauty'	CWVF SVic WRou
'Dusky Rose' (d)	CLoc CWVF EBak MJac SVic
'Dutch Kingsize'	WOth
'Dutch Mill'	CLoc CWVF EBak
'Dutch Rosemarieke' **new**	WOth
'Duyfken'	CWVF
'Dying Embers'	CLoc MSCN SVen WOth WRou
'Dymph Werker van Groenland' (E)	LCla
'East Anglian'	CLoc EBak
'Easter Belle'	LRHS
'Easter Bonnet' (d)	CLoc CWVF
'Ebb 'n' Flow'	EBak
'Ebbtide' (d)	CLoc EBak
'Echo'	CWVF
'Ed Largarde' (d)	EBak
'Eden Lady'	CDoC CLoc SPet
'Eden Princess'	CWVF MJac
'Eden Rock' (d)	CLoc WGor WOth
'Edith' ambig.	EPts WRou
'Edith' Brown (d)	CSil LCla SLBF
'Edith Emery' (d)	SPet
'Edna May'	CWVF
'Edna W. Smith'	CWVF
'Eileen Raffill'	EBak
'Eileen Saunders'	CSil EBak
'El Camino' (d)	CWVF
'El Cid'	CLoc CSil EBak SVic
'Elaine Ann'	EPts MJac
'Elaine Taylor' (d)	MJac
'Eleanor Clark'	WOth
'Eleanor Leytham'	CWVF EBak SVic WRou
'Eleanor Rawlins'	CSil EBak WRou
'Elf'	CSil
'Elfin Glade'	CLoc CSil CWVF EBak SVic
'Elfrida' (d)	CSil
'Elfriede Ott' (T) ♀H1	CLoc EBak LCla
'Elisabeth Schnedl' (d)	WRou
'Elizabeth' ambig.	WOth
'Elizabeth' Whiteman, 1941	EBak
'Elizabeth Honnorine'	SVic
'Elizabeth Travis' (d)	EBak
'Ellen Morgan' (d)	CWVF EBak
'Elma'	LCla MJac
'Elsa' (d)	CWVF SVic
'Elsie Maude' (d)	CWVF
'Elsie Mitchell' (d)	CWVF SPet

	Name	Suppliers
	'Elysée'	CSil
§	'Emile de Wildeman' (d)	CWVF EBak SPet
	'Emile Zola'	CSil
	'Emily'	WOth
	'Emily Austen'	CWVF
	'Emma Alice' (d)	CWVF
	'Emma Louise' (d)	WOth
	'Empress of Prussia' ♀H4	CDoC CLoc CSil CWVF EBak EPts SLBF SVic WMnd WOth
	'Enchanted' (d)	CWVF EBak
	encliandra (E)	WRou
	- subsp. ***encliandra*** (E)	CDoC
*	- var. ***gris*** (E)	CSil
§	'Enfant Prodigue' (d)	CDoC CLoc CSil SDix SLBF SMrm WMnd
	'English Rose' (d)	CWVF
	'Enstone'	see *F. magellanica* var. *molinae* 'Enstone'
	'Erich Mehlis' **new**	WOth
	'Eric's Hardy' (d)	CDoC
	'Eric's Majestic' (d)	MJac
	'Erika Köth' (T)	LCla
	'Ernest Rankin'	CSil SVic
	'Ernie' PBR	EPts LAst SLBF
	'Ernie Bromley'	CSil CWVF
	'Ernie Wise' (d)	MJac SCoo
	'Eroica'	SVic
	'Eruption'	CDoC CLoc LAst MCot
	'Esmerelda'	MJac
	'Estelle Marie'	CLoc CWVF EBak SPet SVic
	'Eternal Flame' (d)	CWVF EBak EPts SVic
	'Ethel May' (d)	MJac
	'Ethel Wilson'	CSil
	'Eusebia' (d)	SVic
	'Eva Boerg'	CCCN CLoc CSil CTri CWVF EBak LAst SPet SVic WKif
	'Evelyn Stanley' (d)	CWVF
§	'Evelyn Steele Little'	EBak
	'Evening Sky' (d)	EBak
	'Evensong'	CLoc CWVF EBak SVic
	excorticata	CAbb CBcs CDoC CExl CSil CTsd ECre GBin MCot SPlb
	'Exmoor Paths'	CSil
	'Exmoor Pearl'	CSil
	'Exmoor Rose'	CSil
	'Exmoor Silver'	CSil
	'Exmoor Woods'	CSil
	'Fabian Franck' (T)	CDoC LCla WRou
	'Fairy Floss'	SLBF
	'Fairy Lavender' **new**	LAst
	'Falklands' (d)	CSil EPts SLBF WRou
	'Falling Stars'	CLoc CWVF EBak SVic
	'Falmouth' **new**	CDoC
	'Fan Dancer' (d)	EBak
	'Fancy Pants' (d)	CLoc CWVF EBak SVic
	'Fanfare'	CDoC EBak LCla SVic
	'Fascination'	see *F.* 'Emile de Wildeman'
	'Fashion' (d)	EBak
	'Favourite'	EBak
	'Felicity Kendal' (d)	SCoo
	'Feltham's Pride'	CWVF
	'Fenman'	CWVF SVic
	'Festival Lights' (E)	SLBF WRou
	'Festoon'	EBak
	'Fey' (d)	CWVF
	'Ffion'	CDoC EPts WOth
	'Fiery Spider'	EBak SVic
	'Finn'	CDoC CWVF EPts
	'Fiona'	CDoC CLoc CWVF EBak SPet SVic

'Fiorelli Flowers' (d)	CDoC
'Fire Mountain' (d)	CLoc SVic
'Firecracker'	see *F.* 'John Ridding'
'Firefly'	SVic
'Firelite' (d)	EBak
'Firenza' (d)	CWVF
'First Kiss' (d)	CWVF
'First Lady' (d)	CWVF
'First Lord'	CWVF
'First Success' (E)	CDoC CWVF LCla SVic WRou
'Flair' (d)	CLoc CWVF
'Flame'	EBak
'Flamenco Dancer' (California Dreamers Series) (d)	CLoc
'Flamingo' (d)	SVic
'Flash' ♀$^{H3-4}$	CLoc CSil CTri CWVF EBak ELan EPfP EPts LCla MJac SLBF SPet SPoG SVic WOth WRou
'Flashlight'	CDoC CSil CWVF EPfP EWld LAst LCla LRHS MJac SCoo WOth
'Flashlight Amélioré'	CSil
'Flat Jack o' Lancashire' (d)	CSil SLBF
'Flavia' (d)	EBak
'Fleur de Picardie'	SLBF
'Flirtation Waltz' (d)	CLoc CWVF EBak MJac SVic
'Flocon de Neige'	CSil EBak
'Flogman'	LCla
'Floral City' (d)	CLoc EBak
'Florence May Joiner' **new**	WRou
'Florence Taylor' (d)	CWVF
'Florence Turner'	CSil EBak
'Florentina' (d)	CLoc CWVF EBak SVic
'Florrie's Gem' (d)	SLBF
'Flowerdream' (d)	CWVF
'Flyaway' (d)	EBak
'Fly-by-night' (d)	CWVF
'Flying Cloud' (d)	CDoC CLoc CSil CWVF EBak SVic WOth WRou
'Flying Scotsman' (d)	CDoC CLoc CWVF EBak EPts SCoo SVic WRou
'Folies Bergères' (d)	EBak
'Foolke'	CSil EBak
'Forfar's Pride' (d)	CSil
'Forget-me-not'	CLoc CWVF EBak SVic
'Fort Bragg' (d)	CWVF EBak
'Fountains Abbey' (d)	CWVF
'Four Farthings' (d)	EPts
'Foxgrove Wood' ♀$^{H3-4}$	CSil CWVF EBak EPts SLBF WOth WRou
'Foxtrot' (d)	CWVF
'Foxy Lady' (d)	CWVF
'Frances Haskins'	CSil WRou
'Frank Saunders'	CWVF LCla SLBF
'Frank Unsworth' (d)	CWVF EPts MJac SPet
'Frankfurt 2006'	MJac
'Frankie's Magnificent Seven' (d)	EPts
'Franz von Zon'	LCla SLBF WRou
'Frau Hilde Rademacher' (d)	CDoC CSil CWVF EBak EPts SLBF SVic
'Frauke'	SVic
'Fred Hansford'	CDoC CSil CWVF
'Fred Swales' (T)	WOth
'Fred's First' (d)	CDoC CSil
'Freefall'	EBak
'Friendly Fire' (d)	CLoc
'Frosted Flame'	CLoc CWVF EBak LAst LCla MJac SLBF SPet
'Frühling' (d)	CSil EBak
'Fuchsiade '88'	CLoc CSil CWVF EBak SLBF WRou
'Fuchsiarama '91' (T) ♀^{H1}	CWVF WRou
'Fudzi San' (T) **new**	WRou
'Fuji-san'	CDoC ELon EPts
'Fuksie Foetsie' (E)	CDoC CSil
fulgens (T) ♀$^{H1+3}$	CDoC GCal LCla LRHS WRou
* - 'Variegata' (T/v)	CDoC CLoc EPts LCla WOth WRou
'Fulpila'	LCla SLBF
'Für Elise' (d)	EBak
'Gala' (d)	EBak
'Galadriel'	WOth
'Garden News' (d) ♀$^{H3-4}$	CDoC CLoc CSil CWVF EPfP EPts LAst LCla LRHS MAsh MJac MSCN NGBl NPer SHil SLBF SPet SVic WHar WMnd WRou
'Garden Week' (d)	CDoC CWVF SVic
'Gartenmeister Bonstedt' (T) ♀$^{H1+3}$	CDoC CLoc CWVF EBak EWld LCla SVic
'Gary Rhodes' (d)	EBak MJac SCoo
'Gay Fandango' (d)	CLoc CWVF EBak
'Gay Parasol' (d)	LAst MJac SVic
'Gay Paree' (d)	EBak
'Gay Senorita'	EBak
'Gay Spinner' (d)	CLoc
gehrigeri	EBak
'Gemma Fisher' (d)	EPts
Gene = 'Goetzgene'^{PBR} (Shadowdancer Series)	LAst LSou SCoo
'Général Monk' (d)	CDoC CSil CWVF EBak EPts LAst SVic
'Général Voyron'	CSil
'General Wavell' (d)	SVic
'Genii' ♀^{H4}	Widely available
'Geoff Oke'	CDoC SLBF
'Geoffrey Smith' (d)	CSil EPts
§ 'Georg Börnemann' (T)	CLoc EBak
'George Allen White' (d)	CWVF
'George Barr'	EPfP LRHS
'George Johnson'	CDoC
'George Travis' (d)	EBak
'Gerald Drewitt'	CSil
§ 'Gerharda's Aubergine'	CLoc CSil CWVF
'Gesneriana'	CLoc EBak
'Ghislaine' (d)	CDoC
'Giant Pink Enchanted' (d)	CLoc EBak
'Gilda' (d)	CWVF MJac SVic
'Gillian Althea' (d)	CWVF
'Gilt Edge' (v)	CLoc
'Gina Bowman' (E)	CDoC EPts LCla SLBF WRou
Ginger = 'Goetzginger'^{PBR} (Shadowdancer Series)	LAst LSou SCoo
'Gipsy Princess' (d)	CLoc
'Girls' Brigade'	CWVF
'Glad B' **new**	WRou
'Gladiator' (d)	CMac EBak SVic
'Gladys Godfrey'	EBak
'Gladys Lorimer'	CDoC CWVF EPfP EPts LRHS
'Gladys Miller'	CLoc
glazioviana	CDoC CSil CWVF EPts GCal LCla LHop MHer SLBF SVen WRou
'Glenby' (d)	CWVF
'Glendale'	CWVF
'Glitters'	CWVF EBak
§ 'Globosa'	CAgr CSil EBak
'Glow'	CSil EBak
'Glowing Embers'	EBak
'Glowing Lilac' (d)	EPts
'Gold Brocade'	ELan EPfP

'Gold Crest'	EBak
'Gold Leaf'	CWVF
'Golden Anniversary' (d)	CLoc CWVF EBak MJac SVic WRou
'Golden Arrow' (T)	LCla SVic
§ 'Golden Border Queen'	CLoc EBak SPet
'Golden Dawn'	CLoc CWVF EBak SVic
'Golden Girl'	SLBF
'Golden Herald'	CSil SLBF
'Golden la Campanella' (d/v)	CLoc
'Golden Lena' (d/v)	CSil CWVF
'Golden Marinka' (v) ♀H3	CLoc EBak LSou SPet SVic
'Golden Swingtime' (d)	MJac SPet SVic
'Golden Treasure' (v)	CLoc CSil CWVF
'Golden Vergeer' (v)	SLBF
'Golden Wedding'	SVic
'Goldsworth Beauty'	CSil
'Golondrina'	CSil CWVF EBak
'Good Girl' **new**	WOth
'Goody Goody'	EBak SVic
'Gordon Boy' (d)	CSil
'Gordon Thorley'	CSil
'Gordon's China Rose'	LCla
'Gota'	CDoC WRou
'Göttingen' (T)	EBak
'Governor Pat Brown' (d)	EBak
'Grace Darling'	CWVF EBak
gracilis	see *F. magellanica* var. *gracilis*
'Graf Witte'	CDoC CSil CWVF SPet SVic
'Grand Duke' (T/d)	CWVF
'Grand Prix' (d)	SVic
'Grandad Hobbs' (d)	LCla SLBF WRou
'Grandma Sinton' (d)	CLoc CWVF
'Grandpa Jack' (d)	SLBF
'Granny Charlton'	WCFE
'Grasmere'	WOth
'Grayrigg'	CDoC CSil ELon EPts LCla LSRN SEND SLBF WOth
'Great Ouse' (d)	EPts
'Great Scott' (d)	CLoc
'Green 'n' Gold'	EBak
'Greenpeace'	CDoC SLBF SVic
'Grey Lady' (d)	CSil SVic
'Grietje' (E)	WOth
'Groene Kan's Glorie'	SVic
'Grumpy'	CWVF EPts SPet SVic
'Gruss aus dem Bodethal'	CLoc CWVF EBak EPts SLBF
'Guinevere'	CWVF EBak
'Gunar Reich' (d) **new**	WOth
'Gustave Doré' (d)	CSil EBak
'Guy Dauphine' (d)	EBak
'Gwen Dodge'	SVic
'Gypsy Girl' (d)	CWVF
'H.G. Brown'	CSil EBak
'Hage Pinokkio' **new**	WOth
'Hampshire Blue'	CDoC CWVF SVic
'Hanna' (d)	LRHS
'Hannah Louise' (d)	EPts
'Hans Callaars'	LCla
'Happiness' (d)	SVic
'Happy'	CDoC CSil CWVF EPts LCla MSCN SPet SVic
'Happy Anniversary'	CLoc SVic
'Happy Fellow'	CDoC CLoc CSil EBak WOth
'Happy Wedding Day' (d)	CLoc CWVF EPts LAst MJac SCoo SPet SVic
'Hapsburgh'	EBak
'Harbour Lites'	SLBF WRou
'Harlow Car'	CDoC CWVF EPts

'Harlow Perfection'	CDoC
'Harmony' Niederholzer, 1946	EBak
'Harry Dunnett' (T)	EBak
'Harry Gray' (d)	CLoc CWVF EBak EPts LAst MJac SLBF SPet SVic
'Harry Pullen'	EBak
'Harry Taylor' (d)	EPts
'Harry's Sunshine'	SLBF
'Harti's Olivia'	CDoC
hartwegii	CDoC CSil LCla MHer
'Harvey's Reward'	SLBF
'Hathersage' (d)	EBak
hatschbachii	CDoC CSil CTsd EWes GCal LCla LRHS MCot MHer SBrt SDix SLon SPlb SPoG SVen WHil WOth WPnn
'Haute Cuisine' (d)	CLoc SVic
'Hawaiian Sunset' (d)	CLoc CWVF EPts SLBF WRou
'Hawkshead' ♀H3-4	Widely available
'Hayley Jay' (d)	CDoC SLBF WRou
'Hazel' (d)	CWVF SVic
'Heart Throb' (d)	EBak
'Heavenly Hayley' (d)	SLBF
'Hebe'	EBak
'Heidi Ann' (d) ♀H3	CDoC CLoc CSil CWVF EBak EPts LAst LRHS MAsh SLBF SPet SVic
'Heidi Blue' (d)	SLBF
'Heidi Joy'	CSil
§ 'Heidi Weiss' (d)	CDoC CLoc CSil CWVF SPet
'Heinrich Henkel'	see *F.* 'Andenken an Heinrich Henkel'
'Helen Clare' (d)	CLoc CWVF EBak
'Helen Gair' (d)	CWVF
'Helen Lang'	EPts
'Hellen Devine'	CWVF
'Hemsleyana'	see *F. microphylla* subsp. *hemsleyana*
'Hendrikje Stoffels' (d) **new**	WOth
'Henkelly's Chloris' **new**	WOth
'Henkelly's Gitano' **new**	WOth
'Henning Becker' ♀H3	CWVF ELan ELon
'Henri Poincaré'	EBak
'Henrieke Dimi' (d)	CDoC
'Herald' ♀H4	CDoC CSil CWVF EBak EPfP LRHS LSou MAsh SHil SLBF SVic WOth
'Herbé de Jacques'	see *F.* 'Mr West'
'Heri Shusui' (d)	CDoC
'Heri Trevally' **new**	WOth
'Heritage' (d)	CLoc CSil EBak
'Herman de Graaff' (d)	SLBF
'Hermiena'	CLoc CWVF EPts SLBF SVic WOth WRou
'Heron'	CSil EBak
'Herps Kipkar' **new**	WOth
'Herps Martina' **new**	WOth
'Herps Pierement'	SLBF WRou
'Hessett Festival' (d)	CWVF EBak
'Heston Blue' (d)	CWVF
'Heydon'	CWVF
'Hi Jinks' (d)	EBak
hidalgensis	see *F. microphylla* subsp. *hidalgensis*
'Hidcote Beauty'	CLoc CWVF EBak LCla SLBF SPet SVic
'Hidden Treasure'	WRou
'Highland Pipes'	LCla SVic
'Hilary' **new**	WRou
'Hilda May Salmon'	CWVF
'Hindu Belle'	EBak

'Hinnerike' (E)	CSil CWVF LCla SVic
'Hiroshige' (T)	LCla
'His Excellency' (d)	EBak
'Hobo' (d)	CSil
'Hobson's Choice' (d)	CWVF SLBF
'Holly's Beauty' (d)	CLoc EPts LAst
'Hollywood Park' (d)	EBak
'Horsforth Beauty' **new**	WRou
'Horsforth in Bloom' **new**	WRou
'Hot Coals'	CWVF EPts MJac SVic WRou
'Howerd Hebden'	CDoC
'Howlett's Hardy' ♀H3-4	CDoC CLoc CSil CWVF EBak NLar SVic WMnd
'Huet's Baraketh'	WOth
'Huet's Kwarts'	CDoC
'Huet's Turkoois'	CDoC
'Hula Girl' (d)	CDoC CWVF EBak MJac SPet
'Huntsman' (d)	CCCN CDoC
'Ian Leedham' (d)	EBak
'Ian Storey'	CDoC CSil
'Ice Cream Soda' (d)	EBak
'Iceberg'	CWVF EBak SVic
'Icecap'	CWVF SVic
'Iced Champagne'	CLoc CWVF EBak MJac
'Ichiban' (d)	CLoc
'Ida' (d)	EBak
'Igloo Maid' (d)	CLoc CWVF EBak SVic
'Imogen Faye' (d)	SLBF WRou
'Impala' (d)	CWVF
'Imperial Fantasy' (d)	CWVF
'Impudence'	CLoc CWVF EBak
'Impulse' (d)	CLoc
'Independence' (d)	SVic
'Indian Maid' (d)	CDoC CWVF EBak
'Insulinde' (T)	CDoC CWVF EPts LCla MHer MJac SLBF
'Interlude' (d)	EBak
'Iolanthe' (T)	CWVF
'Iona' **new**	WRou
'Irene L. Peartree' (d)	CWVF LCla
'Irene Sinton' (d)	MJac
'Iris Amer' (d)	CLoc CWVF EBak
'Irving Alexander' (d)	CDoC
'Isabel Ryan'	CSil
'Isis' Lemoine	CSil WRou
'Isle of Mull'	CSil
'Isle of Purbeck'	SVic
'Italiano' (d)	CWVF MJac SVic
'Ivana van Amsterdam'	WRou
'Ivy Grace'	CSil
'Jack Acland'	CWVF
'Jack Shahan' ♀H3	CCCN CDoC CLoc CSil CWVF EBak LAst LCla MJac SLBF WOth WRou
'Jack Siverns' **new**	WRou
'Jack Stanway' (v)	CDoC CWVF WOth
'Jack Wilson'	CSil
'Jackie Bull' (d)	CWVF EBak
'Jackpot' (d)	EBak
'Jackqueline' (T)	CWVF
'Jamboree' (d)	EBak
'James Bamber' **new**	WRou
'James Lye' (d)	CWVF EBak
'James Travis' (E/d)	CDoC CSil EBak LCla WRou
'Jan Bremer'	SVic
'Jandel'	CWVF
'Jane Humber' (d)	CWVF
'Jane Lye'	EBak
'Janice Perry's Gold' (v)	CLoc MJac
'Janie' (d)	EPfP MAsh SVic
'Jap Vantveer' (T)	LCla
'Jasper Marnix' **new**	WOth
'Jaunty Jack'	SLBF WOth
'Javelin'	CDoC WOth
'Jean Baker'	CDoC
'Jean Campbell'	EBak
'Jean Frisby'	CLoc
'Jean Taylor'	EPts WRou
'Jean Webb' (v)	WCot
'Jennifer'	EBak MJac
'Jennifer Ann'	LAst SLBF
'Jennifer Lister' (d)	CSil
'Jenny May'	CLoc EPts LCla
'Jenny Sorensen'	CWVF
'Jess'	LCla SLBF
'Jessie Pearson'	CWVF
'Jessimae'	CWVF SPet
'Jester' Holmes (d)	CLoc CSil WOth
'Jet Fire' (d)	EBak
'Jezebel' (d)	SVic
'Jiddles' (E)	LCla WRou
'Jill Holloway' (T)	SLBF
'Jill Whitworth'	CDoC WPnn
'Jim Coleman'	CWVF SVic
'Jim Dodge' (d)	EPts
'Jim Hawkins'	EBak
'Jim Muncaster'	CWVF
'Jim Watts'	CDoC WOth
jimenezii	CDoC WOth
'Jimmy Cricket' (E)	CDoC SLBF
'Joan Barnes' (d)	CWVF
'Joan Cooper'	CLoc CSil CWVF EBak SLBF SVic
'Joan Goy'	CWVF MJac SVic WRou
'Joan Knight'	CLoc
'Joan Margaret' (d)	MJac
'Joan Morris'	SLBF
'Joan Pacey'	CDoC CWVF EBak
'Joan Read'	WRou
'Joan Smith'	EBak
'Joan Waters' (d)	CWVF
'Joanna Lumley' (d)	EPts MJac
'Jo-Anne Fisher' (d)	EPts
'Joan's Delight'	SVic WOth
'Joe Kusber' (d)	CWVF EBak
'John Bartlett'	CLoc
'John Grooms' (d)	CLoc SVic WRou
'John Lockyer'	CLoc CWVF EBak
'John Maynard Scales' (T)	CDoC CWVF LCla MJac WRou
'John Nicholass' **new**	SLBF
§ 'John Ridding' PBR (T/v)	CLoc EPts LBuc SPoG
'John Suckley' (d)	EBak
'John Wright'	LCla
'Jomam' ♀H3	CWVF
'Jon Oram'	CLoc CWVF
'Jonny Wilkinson'	MJac
'Jose's Joan' (d)	CWVF SVic
'Jotu' **new**	WOth
'Joy Patmore'	CLoc CWVF EBak SLBF SPet
'Joyce Adey' (d)	CWVF
'Joyce Sinton'	CLoc CWVF
'Joyce Wilson' (d)	EPts
'Joycey' **new**	WRou
'Judith Coupland'	CWVF
'Juella'	WRou
'Jülchen'	CWVF
'Jules Daloges' (d)	EBak
'Julie Marie' (d)	CWVF MJac
'June Gardner'	CWVF

	'Jungle'	LCla SLBF WOth
I	'Juno' Kennett	EBak
	juntasensis	WOth
	'Jupiter Seventy'	EBak
	'Just Pilk'	SLBF
	'Just Pink' (E)	CDoC
	'Justin's Pride'	CDoC CSil
	'Kaleidoscope' (d)	EBak
	'Kaley Jackson'	WRou
	'Kames Bay' **new**	WRou
	'Karen Isles' (E)	CDoC LCla SLBF
	'Karen Louise' (d)	CLoc
	'Kate Taylor' (d)	SLBF
	'Kate Wieteska' (E) **new**	WRou
	'Kate Wylie'	WRou
	'Kath van Hanegem'	CLoc SLBF WRou
	'Kath Wilson'	LAst
	'Kathryn Maidment'	SVic
	'Katie Rogers'	EPts
	'Katie Susan'	SLBF
	'Katinka' (E)	CDoC CWVF LCla SLBF
	'Katjan'	CSil LCla SLBF WOth WRou
	'Katrina' (d)	CLoc EBak
	'Katrina Thompsen'	CLoc CWVF EPts SLBF WRou
	'Katy Flynn'	CLoc CWVF SLBF WRou
	'Katy James'	WRou
	'Keepsake' (d)	EBak
	'Kegworth Carnival' (d)	CWVF
	'Ken Goldsmith' (T)	CWVF
	'Ken Jennings'	CWVF
	'Ken Tudor' **new**	MJac
	'Kenny Dalglish' (d)	CSil
	'Kenny Holmes'	CWVF
	'Kenny Walkling'	LCla SLBF WRou
	'Kernan Robson' (d)	CLoc CWVF EBak
	'Keystone'	EBak
	'Kilili' **new**	WOth
	'Kim Joiner' **new**	WRou
	'Kimberly' (d)	EBak
	'King of Bath' (d)	EBak
	'King of Hearts' (d)	EBak
	'King's Ransom' (d)	CLoc CWVF EBak SPet SVic
	'Kiss 'n' Tell'	CWVF MJac
	'Kit Oxtoby' (d)	CDoC CWVF MJac SLBF WOth
	'Kiwi' (d)	EBak
	'Knockout' (d)	CWVF SVic
	'Kobold'	SLBF
	'Kolding Perle'	CWVF SLBF WRou
	'Komeet'	CDoC
	'Kon-Tiki' (d)	SPet
	'Krommenie'	WRou
	'Kuniko Atarashi' (d)	EPts
	'Kwintet'	CWVF EBak MJac SPet
	'La Bianca'	EBak
	'La Campanella' (d) ♀H3	CCCN CDoC CLoc CWVF EBak EPts LAst MJac SPet SVic
	'La Fiesta' (d)	EBak
	'La France' (d)	EBak
	'La Neige' ambig.	CWVF
	'La Neige' Lemoine (d)	EBak
	'La Porte' (d)	CLoc CWVF
	'La Rosita' (d)	EBak
I	'La Traviata' Blackwell (d)	EBak
	'Lace Petticoats' (d)	EBak SVic
	'Lady Beth' (d)	SVic
	'Lady Boothby'	Widely available
	'Lady Framlingham' (d)	EPts
	'Lady in Grey' (d)	MJac SVic
	'Lady in Red' (d) **new**	WRou

	'Lady Isobel Barnett'	CLoc CWVF EBak MJac SLBF SPet SVic WOth
	'Lady Kathleen Spence'	CWVF EBak SPet SVic
	'Lady Patricia Mountbatten'	CWVF SVic WOth WRou
	'Lady Ramsey'	EBak
	'Lady Rebecca' (d)	CLoc
	'Lady Thumb' (d) ♀H3	Widely available
	'Laepines'	WOth
	'Laing's Hybrid'	CWVF EBak WOth
	'Lakeland Princess'	EBak
	'Lakeside'	EBak
	'Lambada'	LAst SLBF WRou
	'Lancambe'	CSil
	'Lancashire Lass'	CWVF
	'Lancelot'	EBak
	'Lapshead White'	CExl
	'Lark' (T)	CWVF
	'Lassie' (d)	CDoC CLoc CWVF EBak
	'Last Chance' (E)	SLBF
	'Laura' ambig.	CWVF SPet SVic WOth WRou
I	'Laura' (Dutch)	CLoc EPts LCla SLBF
	'Laura Cross' (E)	CDoC SLBF WOth WRou
	'Lauren'	CDoC WRou
	'Lavender Kate' (d)	CWVF EBak
	'Lazy Lady' (d)	CWVF EBak
	'Lechlade Apache'	CDoC LCla
	'Lechlade Bullet'	LCla
	'Lechlade Chinaman'	CDoC SVic
	'Lechlade Debutante'	CDoC LCla WOth
	'Lechlade Fairy' (E) **new**	WRou
	'Lechlade Fire-eater' (T)	CDoC
	'Lechlade Gorgon'	CDoC CWVF LCla SLBF
	'Lechlade Magician'	CDoC CSil EPts LCla SLBF SPet SVic
	'Lechlade Maiden'	CDoC CWVF
	'Lechlade Martianess'	LCla SVic WOth
	'Lechlade Potentate'	LCla
	'Lechlade Tinkerbell' (E)	CDoC LCla
	'Lechlade Violet' (T)	CSil LCla SVic
	lehmanii	LCla
	'Len Bielby' (T)	CDoC CWVF LCla
	'Lena' (d) ♀H3	CDoC CLoc CMac CSil CTri CWVF EBak EPts MJac SLBF SMrm SPer SPlb SVic
	'Lena Dalton' (d)	CLoc CWVF EBak SVic
	'Leonhart von Fuchs'	WOth
	'Leonora'	CDoC CLoc CWVF EBak SLBF SPet SVic WRou
	'Lesley' (T)	CWVF LCla
	'Lesley's Wonder'	MJac
	'Leslie Bowman'	LCla SLBF
	'Lett's Delight' (d)	CWVF EPts
	'Letty Lye'	EBak
	'Leverhulme'	see *F.* 'Leverkusen'
§	'Leverkusen' (T)	CDoC CLoc EBak LCla MJac WOth
I	'Liebesträume' Blackwell (d)	EBak
	'Liebriez' (d) ♀H3-4	CSil EBak SPet SVic
	'Liemers Lantaern'	CWVF
	'Likalin'	CWVF
	'Lilac'	EBak
	'Lilac Dainty' (d)	CSil
	'Lilac Lustre' (d)	CLoc CWVF EBak SPet SVic
	'Lilac Mist'	SLBF
	'Lilac Queen' (d)	EBak
	'Lilian'	WOth
	'Lillian Annetts' (d)	CDoC CWVF MJac SLBF WRou
	'Lillibet' (d)	CLoc CWVF EBak
	'Lime Lite' (d)	MJac
	'Linda Goulding'	CWVF EBak SVic
	'Linda Grace'	MJac

	'Linda Hinchliffe'	MJac
	'Linda Rosling' (d)	CDoC
	'Lindisfarne' (d)	CLoc CWVF EBak MJac SPet WOth
	'Lindsey Victoria' (d)	SVic
	'Lionel'	CSil WOth WRou
	'Lipstick'	SLBF WRou
	'Lisa' (d)	EPts SPet
	'Little Beauty'	CDoC CSil CWVF SVic
	'Little Boy Blue'	EPts
	'Little Brook Gem'	SLBF
	'Little Catbells' (E)	SLBF WRou
	'Little Cracker'	LBuc
	'Little Gene'	EBak WRou
	'Little Margaret' **new**	WRou
	'Little Nan'	SLBF
	'Little Ouse' (d)	CWVF
	'Little Scamp'	SLBF
	'Liz' (d)	CSil EBak
	Liza = 'Goetzliza'^{PBR} (Shadowdancer Series)	LSou
	'Lochinver' (d)	CWVF
	'Loeky'	CDoC CLoc CWVF EBak SVic WOth
	'Logan Garden'	see *F. magellanica* 'Logan Woods'
	'Lolita' (d)	CWVF EBak
	'London 2000'	CDoC LCla MJac SLBF WRou
	'London Eye'	WOth WRou
	'London in Bloom'	SLBF
	'Lonely Ballerina' (d)	CLoc CWVF
	'Long Distance' (T)	CDoC LCla
	'Long Wings'	LCla SVic
	'Lord Byron'	CLoc EBak
	'Lord Derby'	CSil
	'Lord Jim'	CDoC LCla
	'Lord Lonsdale'	CWVF EBak EPts LCla SVic WRou
	'Lord Roberts'	CLoc CWVF SLBF
	'Lorelei'	CDoC
	'Lorna Fairclough'	MJac
	'Lorna Swinbank'	CWVF SVic
	'Lorraine's Delight' (d)	SVic
	'Lottie Hobby' (E) ♀$^{H1+3}$	CDoC CLoc CMac CSil CTsd CWVF EHyd EPfP EPts LCla MLHP SVic WCot WRou
	'Louise Emershaw' (d)	CWVF EBak MJac SVic
	'Louise Nicholls'	MJac
	'Loulabel'	SVic
	'Lovable' (d)	EBak
	'Loveliness'	CLoc CWVF EBak SVic
	'Lovely Linda'	SLBF
	'Love's Reward' ♀$^{H1+3}$	CLoc CWVF MJac SLBF SVic WRou
	'Lower Raydon'	EBak
N	***loxensis*** misapplied	see *F.* 'Speciosa', *F.* 'Loxensis'
I	'Loxensis'	CDoC CWVF EBak SVic
	'Loxhore Herald'	CSil
	'Loxhore Lullaby' (E)	CSil LCla
	'Loxhore Minuet' (T)	CDoC LCla
	'Loxhore Posthorn' (T)	CDoC LCla
	'Lucinda'	CWVF
	'Lucky Strike' (d)	EBak
	Lucy = 'Goetzlucy' (Shadowdancer Series)	EBak
	'Lucy Locket'	MJac
	'Lunter's Klokje'	WOth
	'Lustre'	CWVF EBak SVic
	lycioides misapplied	see *F.* 'Lycioides'
§	***lycioides*** Andrews	EBak WOth
I	'Lycioides'	LCla
	'Lye's Excelsior'	EBak
	'Lye's Own'	EBak SLBF SPet

	'Lye's Unique' ♀$^{H1+3}$	CDoC CLoc CWVF EBak EPts LCla MJac SLBF SPet SVic WOth
	'Lynette' (d)	CLoc
	'Lynn Cunningham'	CDoC
	'Lynn Ellen' (d)	CDoC CWVF EBak
	'Lynne Marshall'	WOth
	'Lynne Patricia' (d)	EPts SLBF WRou
	'Mabel Greaves' (d)	CWVF
	'Mac Wagg'	WRou
	'Machu Picchu'	CLoc CWVF EPts LCla SVic WOth WRou
	macrophylla	CDoC WMoo
	'Madame Aubin'	CSil
	'Madame Butterfly' (d)	CLoc
	'Madame Cornélissen' (d) ♀^{H3}	CDoC CLoc CMac CSBt CSil CTri CWVF EBak EBee EHyd ELan EPfP EPts LAst LRHS MAsh MBri MRav NLar SCoo SHil SLBF SLim SPer SPet SPoG SVic WRou
	'Madame Eva Boye'	EBak
	'Maes-y-Groes'	CSil
	magellanica	CDoC CSil CTsd CWib GKev MLHP NPer NWea SPer SVic WMoo WPnn
	- 'Alba'	see *F. magellanica* var. *molinae*
I	- 'Alba Aureovariegata' (v)	CDoC CMac EPfP SPer SVic
	- 'Alba Variegata' (v)	CSil
	- 'Americana Elegans'	CDoC CSil
	- 'Angel's Teardrop'	CDoC
	- 'Comber'	CSil
	- var. ***conica***	CDoC CSil
	- var. ***discolor***	CSil
	- 'Duchy of Cornwall'	CDoC
	- 'Exmoor Gold' (v)	CSil
§	- var. ***gracilis*** ♀^{H3}	CAgr CDoC CHEx CLoc CSil CTri CWVF EPfP LRHS MLHP NBro SCoo SVic WMoo WPnn WRou
	- - 'Aurea' ♀$^{H3-4}$	CBcs CDoC CMac CSil CTsd CWVF EBee ELan EPfP LCla LRHS MHer MRav SCoo SDix SLBF SPer SPet SPoG WMoo WSpi
	- - 'Purple Mountain'	EPfP LRHS SPoG
§	- - 'Tricolor' (v) ♀^{H3}	CDoC CSil CTsd EPfP EPts EWes LBMP LCla LRHS NLar SEND SLBF SRms WCFE WPnn
	- - 'Variegata' (v) ♀^{H3}	CDoC CSil CTsd EBak EPfP LCla LRHS MGos MRav SDix SPer SPet WPnn WSpi
	- 'Guiding Star'	CDoC
	- 'Lady Bacon'	CDoC CSil ELon EPts EWes GCal LHop MCot SDys SEND SLBF WOth WRou WSHC
§	- 'Logan Woods'	CAby CDoC CSil ELon GKin SLBF SMrm WRou
	- 'Longipedunculata'	CDoC CSil SLPl
	- 'Lyonesse Lady'	CDoC
	- var. ***macrostema***	CSil
	- var. ***magellanica***	WSpi
§	- var. ***molinae***	Widely available
§	- - 'Enstone' (v)	ELon
	- - 'Golden Sharpitor' (v)	CCCN LAst WRou
	- - 'Mr Knight's Blush'	CDul
§	- - 'Sharpitor' (v)	CDoC CSil CTsd EBak EBee ELan ELon EPfP LRHS MAsh NPer SBch SPer SVic WKif WMoo WOth WRou WSHC
	- 'Mountain Gold' **new**	LAst WOth
	- var. ***myrtifolia***	CDoC CSil CTsd
*	- var. ***prostrata***	CSil

	- 'Pumila'	CAby CDoC CSil EWes GCal MHer MLHP SCoo SRot SVic WAbe
	- ***purpurea***	LRHS SBch
	- 'Red Mountain'	EWes
	- 'Sea King'	CDoC
	- 'Sea Spray'	CDoC
	- 'Seahorse'	CDoC
§	- 'Thompsonii' ♀H3-4	CDoC CSil ECGP SBch
	- 'Threave'	CDoC
§	- 'Versicolor' (v)	Widely available
	'Magenta Flush'	CDoC CWVF
	'Magic Flute'	CLoc CWVF MJac SVic
	'Maharaja' (d)	EBak
	'Major Heaphy'	CWVF EBak MHer
	'Making Waves'	WRou
	'Malibu Mist' (d)	CWVF
	'Mama Bleuss' (d)	EBak
	'Mancunian' (d)	CWVF
I	'Mandarin' Schnabel	EBak
	'Mandi Oxtoby' (T)	LCla
	'Mantilla' (T)	CDoC CLoc CWVF EBak LCla MJac SVic
	'Maori Pipes' (T)	WOth
	'Marbled Sky'	SVic
	'Marcel Michiels' (d)	CDoC
	'Marcia'PBR (Shadowdancer Series)	CLoc LAst LSou
	'Marcus Graham' (d)	CLoc CWVF EBak SCoo SVic WRou
	'Marcus Hanton' (d)	CWVF
	'Mardi Gras' (d)	EBak
	'Margaret' (d) ♀H4	CDoC CDul CLoc CSil CTri CWVF EBak EPts SEND SLBF SPet SVic WRou
	'Margaret Bird'	LCla
	'Margaret Brown' ♀H4	CDoC CLoc CSil CTri CWVF EBak LCla LRHS SLBF SPet SVic WOth WRou
	'Margaret Davidson' (d)	CLoc
	'Margaret Pilkington'	CWVF SVic WOth
	'Margaret Roe'	CSil CWVF EBak MJac SPet
	'Margaret Susan'	EBak
	'Margarite Dawson' (d)	CSil SVic
	'Margery Blake'	CSil EBak
	'Maria Landy'	CWVF MJac SLBF
	'Maria Mathilde' (d)	SLBF
	'Marilyn Olsen'	CWVF
	'Marin Belle'	EBak
	'Marin Glow' ♀H3	CLoc CWVF EBak SLBF SVic
	'Marina Kelly'	WRou
	'Marinka' ♀H3	CLoc CWVF EBak EPts LAst LBMP LCla MJac SLBF SPet SVic
	'Mark Kirby' (d)	CWVF EBak
	'Marlies de Keijzer' (E)	CDoC EPts LCla SLBF SVen
	'Marry Perry'	WRou
	Martha = 'Goetzmart'PBR (Shadowdancer Series)	LAst LHop WBor
	'Martina'	SLBF
	'Martin's Choice'	WOth
I	'Martin's Choice Improved' **new**	WOth
	'Martin's Inspiration'	CDoC LCla WOth
	'Martin's Little Beauty'	CDoC
	'Martin's Yellow Surprise' (T)	LCla SLBF SVic
	'Marty' (d)	EBak
	'Mary' (T) ♀H1+3	CDoC CLoc CWVF EPts LCla SLBF SVic WRou
	'Mary Lockyer' (d)	CLoc EBak
	'Mary Poppins'	CWVF SVic
	'Mary Reynolds' (d)	CWVF
	'Mary Thorne'	CSil EBak
	'Mary's Millennium'	CWVF
	'Masquerade' (d)	EBak
	'Mauve Beauty' (d)	CSil CWVF SLBF
	'Mauve Lace' (d)	CSil
	'Mauve Wisp' (d)	SVic
	'Mavis Enderby'	SLBF
	'Max Jaffa'	CWVF
I	'Maxima'	CDoC EPts LAst LCla SLBF
	'Maxima's Baby'	CDoC
	'Mayblossom' (d)	CWVF
	'Mayfield'	CWVF
	'Mazda'	CWVF
	'McGee's Chocolate Mint' **new**	SLBF
	'Meadowlark' (d)	CWVF EBak
	'Medard's Botsaert' (d)	CDoC
	'Meditation' (d)	CLoc CSil
	'Melanie'	SVic
	'Melissa Heavens'	CWVF
	'Melody'	EBak SPet SVic
	'Melody Ann' (d)	EBak
	'Melting Moments' (d)	SCoo WRou
	'Mendocino Rose'	SVic
	'Mephisto'	CSil CWVF
	'Mercurius'	CSil
	'Merlin'	CDoC CSil LCla
	'Merry Mary' (d)	CWVF EBak
	'Mersty' (d) **new**	SLBF
I	'Mexicali Rose' Machado	CLoc
	'Michael' (d)	CWVF EPts
	'Michael Wallis' (T)	CDoC LCla SLBF
	'Michelle Wallace'	SVic
	michoacanensis misapplied	see *F. microphylla* subsp. *aprica*
	michoacanensis Sessé & Moç. (E) B&SWJ 9027	WCru
	- B&SWJ 9148	WCru
	'Micky Goult' ♀H1+3	CLoc CWVF EPts MJac SLBF SPet SVic WOth WRou
	'Microchip' (E)	CSil LCla
	microphylla (E)	CAby CBcs CDoC CElw CExl CLoc CSil CWVF EBak ELon GCal IDee NBro SIgm SVic WRou
	- B&SWJ 10331	WCru
§	- subsp. ***aprica*** (E)	CDoC LCla
	- - B&SWJ 9101	WCru
	- - 'Dolly's Dress'	WCru
	- 'Cornish Pixie'	CDoC
§	- subsp. ***hemsleyana*** (E)	CDoC CExl CSil LCla
	- - B&SWJ 10478	WCru
	- - 'Silver Lining'	LHop WCru WSHC
	- - 'Sprite' (E/v) **new**	WRou
§	- subsp. ***hidalgensis*** (E)	CDoC CSil LCla WRou
	- subsp. ***microphylla*** (E)	CSil
§	- subsp. ***minimiflora*** (E)	SVic
	- subsp. ***quercetorum*** (E)	CDoC CSil CTsd
	- 'Variegata' (E/v)	EWes
	'Midas'	CWVF
	'Midnight Sun' (d)	CWVF EBak
	'Midwinter'	CWVF SVic
	'Mieke Meursing' ♀H1+3	CDoC CLoc CWVF EBak MJac SPet
	'Miep Aalhuizen'	CDoC LCla WOth
	'Mike Oxtoby' (T)	CWVF
	'Millennium'	CLoc EBak EPts MJac SCoo SVic WRou
	'Millie Butler'	CWVF

'Ming'	CLoc
'Miniature Jewels' (E)	SLBF
minimiflora misapplied	see *F.* × *bacillaris*
minimiflora Hemsl.	see *F. microphylla* subsp. *minimiflora*
'Minirose'	CDoC CWVF EPts SLBF WOth
'Minnesota' (d)	EBak
'Miramere'	EPts
'Mischief'	SVic
'Miss California' (d)	CDoC CLoc CWVF EBak
'Miss Great Britain'	CWVF
'Miss Lye'	CSil
'Miss Muffett' (d)	CSil EPts
'Miss Vallejo' (d)	EBak
'Mission Bells'	CDoC CLoc CWVF EBak EPts SPet SVic
'Misty Blue' (d)	SVic
'Misty Haze' (d)	CWVF SVic
'Molesworth' (d)	CWVF EBak MJac
'Money Spinner'	CLoc EBak
'Monsieur Thibaut' ♀H4	CSil SPer
'Monte Rosa' (d)	CWVF
'Montevideo' (d)	CWVF
'Monument' (d)	CSil
'Mood Indigo' (d)	CWVF MJac SLBF SVic WOth
'Moonbeam' (d)	CLoc
'Moonglow'	MJac
'Moonlight Sonata'	CLoc CWVF EBak SPet
'Moonraker' (d)	CWVF SVic
'More Applause' (d)	CLoc
'Morning Light' (d)	CLoc EBak SVic
'Morning Mist'	EBak
'Morrells' (d)	EBak
'Moth Blue' (d)	CWVF EBak
'Mountain Mist' (d)	CWVF SVic
'Moyra' (d)	CWVF
'Mr A. Huggett'	CLoc CSil CWVF EPts SLBF WOth
'Mr W. Rundle'	EBak SVic
§ 'Mr West' (v)	LRHS LSou MBri MCot WMoo
'Mrs Churchill'	CLoc
'Mrs John D. Fredericks'	CSil
'Mrs Lawrence Lyon' (d)	EBak
'Mrs Lee Belton' (E)	CDoC LCla SLBF
'Mrs Lovell Swisher' ♀H4	CWVF EBak LCla SVic
'Mrs Marshall'	CWVF EBak SLBF
'Mrs Popple' ♀H3	Widely available
'Mrs W. Castle'	CDoC CSil SVic
'Mrs W.P. Wood' ♀H3	CDoC CLoc CSil CWVF ELon LRHS MSCN SVic WOth WRou
'Mrs W. Rundle'	CLoc CWVF EBak SLBF
'Muriel' (d)	CLoc CWVF EBak
'Murru's Pierre Marie' (d)	SLBF
'My Delight'	CWVF
'My Fair Lady' (d)	CLoc CWVF EBak
'My Kath' (d) **new**	WRou
'My Little Cracker'	CDoC WRou
'My Mum'	LCla SLBF WRou
'My Pat'	SLBF WRou
'My Reward' (d)	CWVF
'Naaldwijk 800'	WOth
'Nan Hay' **new**	WRou
'Nancy Lou' (d)	CDoC CLoc CWVF MJac SLBF SPet SVic
'Nanny Ed' (d)	CWVF
'Natasha Lynn' (d) **new**	WRou
'Natasha Sinton' (d)	CCCN CWVF LAst MJac SPet
'Nathan Rhys' **new**	SLBF WRou
'Native Dancer' (d)	CWVF EBak
'Nautilus' (d)	EBak
'Neapolitan' (d)	CDoC SLBF
'Neck'	LCla
'Nell Gwyn'	CLoc CWVF EBak SVic
'Nellie Nuttall' ♀H3	CLoc CWVF EBak EPts SLBF SPet SVic
'Neopolitan' (E)	CLoc CSil EPts SVic WRou
'Nettala'	CDoC SVic WOth
'Neue Welt'	CSil CWVF EBak
'New Fascination' (d)	EBak
'New Millennium'	CDoC
'Niamh Jane Allen' (d) **new**	WRou
'Nice 'n' Easy' (d)	LRHS MJac
'Nicki Fenwick-Raven' (E)	LCla
'Nicki's Findling'	CDoC CWVF EPts LCla MJac WRou
'Nicola'	EBak
'Nicola Jane' (d)	CDoC CSil CWVF EBak EPts LCla MJac SHar SLBF SPet SVic WRou
'Nicolette'	CWVF MJac
'Nightingale' (d)	CLoc EBak
§ ***nigricans***	CDoC
- B&SWJ 10664	WCru
'Nina Wills'	EBak
'Niobe' (d)	EBak
'Niula'	CDoC LCla
'No Name' (d)	EBak
'Nonchalance' (T)	LCla
'Noor' **new**	WOth
'Norman Welton'	SLBF
'Normandy Bell'	EBak SVic
'Northern Jewel'	SLBF
'Northilda'	SVic
'Northumbrian Belle'	EBak
'Northumbrian Pipes'	LCla WOth
'Northway'	CLoc CWVF MJac SPet SVic
'Norvell Gillespie' (d)	EBak
'Novato'	EBak
'Novella' (d)	CWVF EBak
'Nuance'	LCla WOth
'Nunthorpe Gem' (d)	CDoC CSil
'O Sole Mio'	SVic
obconica (E)	CDoC CSil WOth WRou
'Obcylin' (E)	CDoC EPts LCla
'Obergärtner Koch' (T) ♀H1	CDoC
'Ocean Beach'	CDoC EPts
'Oetnang' (d)	CTri SCoo
'Oh Carol' (E)	LCla SLBF WOth WRou
'Old Somerset' (v)	CCCN CDoC SVic
'Olga Storey'	CDoC
'Olive Smith'	CWVF EPts LCla MJac WRou
'Olympic Lass' (d)	EBak WOth
'Olympic Sunset'	SVic WOth
'Onward'	CSil
§ 'Oosje' (E)	CDoC CSil LCla SLBF SVic WRou
'Opalescent' (d)	CLoc CWVF SVic
'Orange Crush'	CLoc CWVF EBak MJac SPet WOth
'Orange Crystal'	CWVF EBak MJac SLBF SVic
'Orange Drops'	CLoc CWVF EBak EPts SVic
'Orange Flare'	CLoc CWVF EBak SLBF SVic
'Orange Heart'	LCla
'Orange King' (d)	CLoc CWVF LAst
'Orange Mirage'	CLoc CWVF EBak LAst SLBF SPet SVic
'Orange Star' (E)	CDoC WRou
'Orangeblossom'	SLBF WOth
'Oranje van Os'	CWVF
'Orient Express' (T) ♀H1	CDoC CLoc CWVF MJac SVic
'Oriental Sunrise'	CWVF
'Ornamental Pearl' (v)	CLoc CWVF EBak WOth

'Orwell' (d)	CWVF
'Oso Sweet'	CWVF
'Other Fellow'	CWVF EBak EPts LCla MJac SLBF SPet SVic WOth
'Oulton Empress' (E)	LCla SLBF WRou
'Oulton Fairy' (E)	SLBF
'Oulton Painted Lady'	WRou
'Oulton Red Imp' (E)	LCla SLBF
'Oulton Travellers Rest' (E)	SLBF
'Oulton Tu-Fu' (E) **new**	WOth
'Our Carol'	SLBF
'Our Claire' **new**	WRou
'Our Darling'	CWVF
'Our Hilary'	SLBF
'Our Kid' **new**	SLBF
'Our Nan' (d)	MJac
'Our Pamela'	MJac
'Our Shep' (d)	WRou
'Our Spencer'	SLBF
'Our Ted' (T)	EBak EPts
'Our William'	SLBF
'Overbecks'	see *F. magellanica* var. *molinae* 'Sharpitor'
'P.E. King' (d)	SLBF
'Pabbe's Kirrevaalk'	WOth
'Pabbe's Klompnoagel'	WOth
'Pabbe's Wikwief'	CDoC
'Pacific Grove' Greene	see *F.* 'Evelyn Steele Little'
'Pacific Grove' Niederholzer (d)	EBak
'Pacific Queen' (d)	EBak
'Pacquesa' (d)	CWVF EBak SPet SVic
'Padre Pio' (d)	CWVF EBak MJac
'Pallas'	CSil
'Pam Plack'	CDoC CSil LCla SLBF
'Pamela Knights' (d)	EBak
'Pamela Wallace'	WOth
'Pam's People'	LCla
'Pan' (T)	WOth
'Pan America' (d)	EBak
'Panache' (d)	LCla
'Pangea' (T)	LCla
paniculata (T) ♀$^{H1+3}$	CCCN CDoC CRHN CWVF EBak EPts IDee LCla MCot MHer MREP SLBF WCru
'Panique'	CDoC LCla WRou
'Pantaloons' (d)	EBak
'Pantomine Dame' (d)	CWVF
'Panylla Prince'	CDoC LCla SLBF WRou
'Papa Bleuss' (d)	CWVF EBak
'Papoose' (d)	CDoC CSil EBak LCla SEND SLBF SVic
'Parkstone Centenary' (d)	CWVF
'Party Frock'	CDoC CLoc CWVF EBak
parviflora misapplied	see *F.* × *bacillaris*
parviflora Lindl.	see *F. lycioides* Andrews
'Pastel'	EBak
'Pat Meara'	CLoc EBak
'Pathétique' (d)	CLoc
'Patience' (d)	CDoC CWVF EBak SLBF
'Patio King'	EBak
'Patio Princess' (d)	CLoc CWVF EPts LAst
'Patricia' Wood	EBak
'Patricia Hodge'	WOth WRou
'Patty Evans' (d)	CWVF EBak
'Patty Sue' (d)	WRou
'Paul Cambon' (d)	EBak
'Paul Fisher'	CDoC
'Paul Roe' (d)	MJac

'Paul Storey'	CDoC CSil
'Paula Jane' (d)	CDoC CWVF LAst MJac SLBF SVic WGor
'Pauline Rawlins' (d)	CLoc EBak
'Paulus'	WRou
'Peace' (d)	EBak
'Peachy' (California Dreamers Series) (d)	CDoC CLoc LAst SCoo WRou
'Peachy Keen' (d)	EBak
'Peacock' (d)	CLoc
'Pearly Queen' (d)	WOth
'Peasholm' **new**	WRou
'Pee Wee Rose'	CSil EBak SVic
'Peggy Burford' (T)	LCla
Peggy = 'Goetzpeg'^{PBR} (Shadowdancer Series)	LAst LSou SCoo
'Peggy King'	CDoC CSil EBak SPet SVic
'Peloria' (d)	CLoc EBak
'People's Princess'	MJac
'Peper Harow'	EBak
'Pepi' (d)	CWVF EBak
'Peppermint Candy' (d)	CDoC CWVF MJac
'Peppermint Stick' (d)	CDoC CLoc CWVF EBak SPet SVic
'Perky Pink' (d)	EBak EPts
'Perry Park'	CWVF EBak MJac SVic
'Perry's Jumbo'	NPer
perscandens	CExl CSil LCla WGwG
'Personality' (d)	EBak
'Peter Bielby' (d)	CWVF
'Peter Crookes' (T)	CWVF
'Peter Grange'	EBak
'Peter James' (d)	CSil
'Peter Meredith'	MJac WOth WRou
'Peter Pan'	CSil CWVF
petiolaris	CDoC LCla
- B&SWJ 10675	WCru
'Petit Four'	CWVF WOth
'Petite' (d)	EBak
'Phaidra'	CDoC LCla WRou
'Pharaoh'	CLoc
'Phénoménal' (d)	CSil CWVF EBak
'Phil's Pill'	SLBF
'Phryne' (d)	CSil EBak SVic
'Phyllis' (d) ♀^{H4}	CAgr CDoC CLoc CSil CWVF EBak EPts LCla LRHS MJac SEND SLBF SPet SVic WRou
'Piet G. Vergeer'	WRou
'Piet van der Sande'	CDoC LCla
'Piggelmee'	CDoC
'Pinch Me' (d)	CWVF EBak SPet SVic
'Pink Aurora'	CLoc
'Pink Ballet Girl' (d)	CLoc EBak SVic
'Pink Bon Accord'	CLoc CWVF SVic
'Pink Cloud'	CLoc EBak
'Pink Cornet'	LCla
'Pink Darling'	CLoc EBak
'Pink Dessert'	EBak
'Pink Domino' (d)	CSil
'Pink Fairy' (d)	EBak SPet
'Pink Fandango' (d)	CLoc
'Pink Fantasia'	CDoC CLoc CWVF EBak EPts LAst LCla MJac SLBF SVic WOth WRou
'Pink Flamingo' (d)	EBak
'Pink Galore' (d)	CLoc CWVF EBak LAst MJac SLBF SPet
'Pink Goon' (d)	CDoC CSil SLBF SVic
'Pink Haze'	CSil SVic
'Pink Jade'	CWVF EBak
'Pink la Campanella'	CWVF EBak LAst WGor

	'Pink Lace' (d)	SPet
	'Pink Marshmallow' (d) ♀H1+3	CDoC CLoc CWVF EBak MJac SLBF SPet SVic
	'Pink Pearl' Bright (d)	CSil EBak
	'Pink Profusion'	EBak
	'Pink Quartet' (d)	CLoc CWVF EBak
	'Pink Rain'	CWVF MJac
	'Pink Slippers'	CLoc
	'Pink Spangles'	CWVF SVic
	'Pink Sprite' **new**	WRou
	'Pink Temptation'	CLoc CWVF EBak SVic
	'Pinto de Blue' (d)	WRou
	'Pinwheel' (d)	CLoc EBak
	'Piper' (d)	CDoC CWVF
	'Piper's Vale' (T)	CDoC LAst MJac SLBF WOth
	'Pirbright'	CWVF
	'Pixie'	CDoC CLoc CSil CWVF EBak MJac SLBF SPet SVic
	'Playboy' (d)	SVic
	'Playford'	CWVF EBak
	'Plenty'	EBak SVic
	'Plumb Bob' (d)	CWVF
	'Pole Star'	CSil
	'Polskie Fuksji'	CDoC
	'Pop Whitlock' (v)	CWVF MCot SPet SVic
	'Poppet'	CWVF
	'Popsie Girl'	CDoC SLBF WOth WRou
	'Port Arthur' (d)	CSil EBak
	'Postiljon'	CWVF EBak
	'Postman'	CDoC
	'Powder Puff' ambig.	CWVF SPet
	'Powder Puff' Hodges (d)	CLoc SVic
I	'Powder Puff' Tabraham (d)	CSil
	'Prelude' Blackwell	CLoc CSil
I	'Prelude' Kennett (d)	EBak
	'President'	CDoC CSil EBak LRHS
	'President B.W. Rawlins'	EBak
	'President Barrie Nash'	CLoc
	'President Carol Gubler' (d) **new**	SLBF
§	'President Elliot'	CSil
	'President George Bartlett' (d)	CDoC CLoc CSil EPts MJac SLBF WRou
	'President Jim Muil'	SLBF
	'President Joan Morris' (d)	SLBF
	'President John Porter'	SLBF
	'President Leo Boullemier'	CWVF EBak MJac SPet SVic
	'President Margaret Slater'	CLoc CWVF EBak SPet SVic
	'President Moir' (d)	SLBF WOth
	'President Norman Hobbs'	CWVF
	'President Roosevelt' (d)	CDoC
	'President Stanley Wilson' (d)	CWVF EBak EPts
	'President Wilf Sharp' (d)	SVic
	'Preston'	CMac
	'Preston Guild' ♀H1+3	CDoC CLoc CSil CWVF EBak NPer SDys SLBF SPet SVic WOth WRou
	'Pride of the West'	EBak
	'Prince of Orange'	CLoc CWVF EBak SVic
	'Princess Dollar'	see *F.* 'Dollar Prinzessin'
	'Princessita'	CWVF EBak SPet WOth
	procumbens	CBcs CCCN CDoC CExl CLoc CSil CWVF EBak ECou EPfP EPts EUJe GCal IDee LCla MCot MHer SBrt SLBF WOth WRou
	- 'Argentea'	see *F. procumbens* 'Wirral'
	- 'Variegata'	see *F. procumbens* 'Wirral'
§	- 'Wirral' (v)	CDoC CLoc CSil CTsd ITim WOth WRou

'Prodigy'	see *F.* 'Enfant Prodigue'
'Profusion' ambig.	SVic
'Prosperity' (d) ♀H3	CDoC CLoc CSil CWVF EBak EPfP EPts LCla LRHS MJac SLBF SPet SVic WOth WRou
'Pumila'	CExl CMac CWib EBee ELan EPfP EPts LRHS SDix SPet SVic
'Purbeck Mist' (d)	CWVF
'Purperklokje'	CSil CWVF EBak SVic
'Purple Emperor' (d)	CLoc
'Purple Heart' (d)	CLoc EBak
'Purple Lace'	CSil SVic
'Purple Rain'	EPts
'Purple Splendour' (d)	CDoC CSil
'Pussy Cat' (T)	CLoc CWVF EBak SVic
'Putney Pride'	EPts
'Put's Folly'	CWVF EBak MJac SPet WOth
putumayensis	CSil EBak
'Quasar' (d)	CCCN CDoC CLoc CWVF EPts LAst MJac SLBF SVic
'Queen Mabs'	EBak
'Queen Mary'	CLoc CSil EBak
'Queen of Bath' (d)	EBak SVic
'Queen of Derby' (d)	CSil CWVF
'Queen of Hearts' Kennett (d)	SVic
'Queen's Park' (d)	EBak
'Query'	CSil EBak SVic
'R.A.F.' (d)	CLoc CWVF EBak EPts SPet SVic WRou
'Rachel Amber' **new**	WRou
'Rachel Ann' **new**	WRou
'Rachel Craig' (d)	WRou
'Radcliffe Bedder' (d)	CSil
'Radings Gerda' (E)	LCla SLBF WRou
'Radings Inge' (E)	CDoC
'Radings Karin'	CDoC WRou
'Radings Mia' (T)	SLBF
'Radings Michelle'	CSil CWVF WRou
'Rahnee'	CWVF
'Rainbow'	CWVF
'Ralph's Delight' (d)	CWVF
'Rambling Rose' (d)	CLoc CWVF EBak MJac
'Rams Royal' (d)	CDoC CWVF
'Raspberry' (d)	CLoc CWVF EBak SVic
'Raspberry Ripple' (d)	WRou
'Raspberry Sweet' (d)	CWVF
'Ratae Beauty'	CWVF
ravenii	CSil
'Ravensbarrow'	CSil
'Ravenslaw'	CSil
'Ray Redfern'	CWVF
'Razzle Dazzle' (d)	EBak
'Razzmatazz' **new**	WRou
'Reading Show' (d)	CSil CWVF EPts SLBF
'Rebecca Williamson' (d)	CWVF MJac
'Rebeka Sinton' (v)	CLoc EBak
'Red Ace' (d)	CSil WOth
'Red Imp' (d)	CSil
'Red Jacket' (d)	CWVF EBak
'Red Petticoat'	CWVF
'Red Rain'	CWVF
'Red Ribbons' (d)	EBak
'Red Rover'	WRou
'Red Rum' (d)	SPet
'Red Shadows' (d)	CLoc CWVF EBak
'Red Spider'	CCCN CLoc CWVF EBak LAst SCoo SPet SVic
'Red Wing'	CLoc

	'Reflexa'	see *F.* × *bacillaris* 'Reflexa'
	'Reg Gubler'	SLBF
	'Regal'	CLoc
	'Regal Robe' (d)	CDoC
	regia	CSil
	- var. ***radicans***	CSil
	- subsp. ***regia***	CSil LCla
	- subsp. ***reitzii***	CDul CSil EWes LCla
	- subsp. ***serrae***	CDoC CSil WOth
	'Remember Carole Anne' (d) **new**	WRou
	'Remember Eric'	CDoC CSil WOth
	'Remembrance' (d)	CSil EPts LCla SLBF WRou
	'Remus' (d)	SVic
	'Rene Schwab'	LCla
	'Renee-Madeleine'	WOth
	'Requiem'	CLoc
	'Reverend Doctor Brown' (d)	EBak
	'Reverend Elliott'	see *F.* 'President Elliot'
	'Reverend Frank Pagden' **new**	WRou
	'Rhapsody' ambig.	SVic
I	'Rhapsody' Blackwell (d)	CLoc
	'Rhombifolia'	CSil
	'Riccartonii' ♀H3	Widely available
	'Richard John' (v)	SVic
	'Richard John Carrington'	CSil
	'Ridestar' (d)	CLoc CWVF EBak
	'Rigoletto'	SVic
	'Rijs 2001' (E)	CDoC SLBF WRou
	'Rina Felix'	CDoC WOth
	'Ringwood Gold'	SVic
	'Ringwood Market' (d)	CSil CWVF EPts MJac SCoo SPet SVic
	'Rise and Shine'	WRou
	'Rivendell'	EPts
	'Riverdancer Claire'	CDoC WOth
	'Robert Lutters'	SVic
	'Robin Hood' (d)	CSil
	'Rocket Fire' (California Dreamers Series) (d)	SVic
	'Roesse Blacky'	CDoC
	'Roesse Callisto'	CDoC
	'Roesse Duck' **new**	WOth
	'Roesse Juliet'	CDoC
	'Roesse Meton' **new**	WOth
	'Roesse Peacock' (d)	CDoC
	'Roesse Sextans'	WRou
	'Roger de Cooker' (T)	CLoc EPts LCla WOth WRou
	'Rohees Lava'	SLBF
	'Rohees Leada' (d)	SLBF
	'Rohees New Millennium' (d)	SLBF
	'Rohees Tethys' (d)	SLBF
	'Rolla' (d)	CWVF EBak
	'Rolt's Ruby' (d)	CSil CWVF SVic
	'Roman City' (d)	CLoc SVic
	'Romance' (d)	CWVF
	'Romany Rose'	CLoc
	'Ron Ewart'	WRou
	'Ron Venables'	WRou
	'Ronald L. Lockerbie' (d)	CLoc CWVF SVic
	'Rondo'	MJac
	'Ronnie Barker' (d)	MJac
	'Ron's Ruby'	CSil
	'Roos Breytenbach' (T)	CCCN CDoC LAst LCla MJac WOth WRou
	'Rosamunda' (d)	CLoc
	'Rose Aylett' (d)	EBak
	'Rose Bradwardine' (d)	EBak
	'Rose Churchill' (d)	MJac
	'Rose Fantasia'	CDoC CLoc CWVF EPts LAst MJac SLBF WRou
	'Rose of Castile'	CDoC CLoc CSil EBak EPts LCla MJac SLBF SVic WRou WWlt
	'Rose of Castile Improved' ♀H4	CSil CWVF EBak LCla MJac SPet WOth
	'Rose of Denmark'	CCCN CLoc CSil CWVF EBak MJac SCoo SLBF SPet WGor
	'Rose Reverie' (d)	EBak
	'Rose Winston' (d)	SCoo
	rosea misapplied	see *F.* 'Globosa'
	rosea Ruíz & Pav.	see *F. lycioides* Andrews
	'Rosebud' (d)	EBak
	'Rosecroft Beauty' (d)	CSil CWVF EBak SVic
	Rosella = 'Goetzrose'PBR (Shadowdancer Series)	LAst
	'Roselynne'	WRou
	'Rosemarie Higham'	MJac SCoo WOth
	'Rosemary Day'	CLoc
	'Ross Lea' (d)	CSil
	'Roswitha'	SLBF
	'Rosy Bows'	CWVF
	'Rosy Frills' (d)	CWVF MJac SVic
	'Rosy Morn' (d)	CLoc EBak
	'Roualeyn's White Gold' (d) **new**	WRou
	'Rough Silk'	CLoc CWVF EBak
	'Roy Castle' (d)	CWVF
	'Roy Walker' (d)	CWVF
	'Royal Academy' (d)	EPts WRou
	'Royal and Ancient'	CWVF
	'Royal Mosaic' (California Dreamers Series) (d)	CDoC MJac
	'Royal Orchid'	EBak
	'Royal Purple' (d)	CSil EBak
	'Royal Serenade' (d)	CWVF
	'Royal Touch' (d)	EBak
	'Royal Velvet' (d) ♀H3	CCCN CLoc CWVF EBak EPts LAst LRHS MAsh MJac SLBF SPet SVic WRou
	'Royal Welsh'	WRou
	'Rubra Grandiflora'	CWVF EBak LCla SDys SLBF WRou
	'Ruby Wedding' (d)	CWVF SLBF
	'Ruddigore'	CWVF
	'Ruffles' (d)	CWVF EBak
	'Rufus' ♀H3-4	CDoC CLoc CMac CSil CWVF EBak ELan EPfP EPts LCla MJac SLBF SPet SVic WRou
	'Ruth'	CSil SVic
	'Ruth Brazewell' (d)	CLoc
	'Ruth King' (d)	CWVF EBak
	'Rutland Water'	CDoC
	'S'Wonderful' (d)	CLoc EBak
	'Sabrina'	WRou
	'Sailor'	EPts SVic
	'Sally Bell'	CSil
	'Salmon Cascade'	CWVF EBak EPts LCla MJac SLBF
	'Salmon Glow'	CWVF MJac SVic
	'Sam Sheppard'	SLBF
	'Samson' (d/v)	EBak
	'San Diego' (d)	CWVF
	'San Francisco'	EBak
	'San Leandro' (d)	EBak
	'San Mateo' (d)	EBak
§	***sanctae-rosae***	CDoC EBak LCla
	'Sandboy'	CWVF EBak

'Sanguinea'	CSil
'Sanrina'	CDoC
'Santa Cruz' (d)	CMac CSil CWVF EBak SLBF SVic
'Santa Lucia' (d)	CLoc EBak
'Santa Monica' (d)	EBak
'Sapphire' (d)	EBak
'Sara Helen' (d)	CLoc EBak
'Sarah Brightman' (d)	CLoc MJac
'Sarah Eliza' (d)	SCoo
'Sarah Jane' (d)	CSil EBak SVic
'Sarah Louise'	CWVF
'Sarong' (d)	EBak
'Satellite'	CLoc CWVF EBak SVic
'Saturnus'	CSil CWVF EBak LRHS MAsh SEND SPet SPoG
'Saxondale Sue'	SVic
'Scabieuse'	CSil
scabriuscula	CDoC LCla
scandens	see *F. decussata* Ruíz & Pav.
'Scarcity'	CDoC CSil CWVF EBak SVic
'Schneeball' (d)	CDoC CSil EBak SVic
'Schneewitcher'	CDoC CSil EPts
'Schneewittchen' Klein	CSil EBak
'Schönbrunner Schuljubiläum' (T)	EBak
'Schöne Hanaurin'	SLBF
'Schöne Wilhelmine'	see *F.* 'Die Schöne Wilhelmine'
'Scotch Heather' (d)	CWVF
'Sea Shell' (d)	CWVF EBak
'Seaforth'	EBak
'Sealand Prince'	CDoC CSil CWVF LCla SVic
'Seattle Blue' (T/d) **new**	SLBF
'Sebastopol' (d)	CLoc
'Selma Lavrijsen'	CDoC WOth
serratifolia Hook.	see *F. austromontana*
serratifolia Ruiz & Pav.	see *F. denticulata*
'Seventh Heaven' (d)	CLoc CWVF LAst MJac SCoo WRou
'Shady Blue'	CWVF
'Shangri-La' (d)	EBak
'Shanley'	CWVF SVic
'Sharon Allsop' (d)	CWVF
'Sharon Caunt' (d)	CSil
'Sharon Leslie'	WRou
'Sharpitor'	see *F. magellanica* var. *molinae* 'Sharpitor'
'Shawna Ree' (E)	CDoC
'Sheila Crooks' (d)	CDoC CWVF EBak
'Sheila Kirby'	CWVF
'Sheila Steele' (d)	CWVF
'Sheila's Love'	MJac
'Shelford'	CDoC CLoc CWVF EBak EPts MJac SLBF SVic WOth WRou
'Shell Pink'	SVic
'She's a Beauty'	MJac
'Shirley Halladay' (d)	LCla
'Shirley'^{PBR} (Shadowdancer Series)	LAst LSou SCoo
'Shooting Star' (d)	EBak
'Showfire'	EBak
'Showtime' (d)	CWVF
'Shrimp Cocktail'	CLoc MSCN WHar WRou
'Shuna Lindsay'	LCla WOth
'Siberoet' (E)	CDoC LCla SLBF
'Sierra Blue' (d)	CDoC CLoc CWVF EBak
'Silver Anniversary' (d)	SVic
'Silver Dollar'	SVic
'Silver Pink'	CSil
'Silverdale'	CDoC CSil EPts
'Simon J. Rowell'	LCla
simplicicaulis	CDoC EBak LCla
'Sincerity' (d)	CLoc SVic
'Siobhan'	CWVF
'Siobhan Evans' (d)	SLBF WRou
'Sir Alfred Ramsey'	CWVF EBak
'Sir David Attenborough' (d)	MJac
'Sir David Jason'	MJac
'Sir Ian Botham' (d)	MJac
'Sir Matt Busby' (d)	EPts LAst MJac WRou
'Siren' Baker (d)	EBak
'Sister Ann Haley'	EPts
'Sister Sister' (d)	SLBF WRou
'Sleepy'	CDoC CSil EPts SPet SVic
'Sleigh Bells'	CLoc CWVF EBak SVic WOth
'Small Pipes'	CWVF
'Smarty' **new**	WRou
'Smokey Mountain' (d)	SVic
'Sneezy'	EPts SVic
'Snow Burner' (California Dreamers Series) (d)	CDoC CLoc LAst
'Snow White' (d)	SVic
'Snowbird' (d)	SLBF
§ 'Snowcap' (d) ♀H3-4	CCCN CDoC CLoc CSil CWVF EBak EPfP EPts GKin LAst LCla LRHS MAsh MGos MJac NPer SCoo SHil SLBF SLim SPet SPoG SVic WRou
'Snowdon' (d)	CWVF
'Snowdrift' Colville (d)	CLoc
'Snowdrift' Kennett (d)	EBak
'Snowfall'	CWVF
'Snowfire' (d)	CLoc CWVF SCoo SVic
'Snowflake' (E)	CDoC EPts LCla SLBF WBor WRou
'Son of Thumb' ♀H4	CDoC CLoc CSil CWVF EPfP EPts LAst LBMP LRHS MAsh MJac SLBF SLim SPet SVic WRou
'Sonata' (d)	CLoc CWVF EBak SVic
'Sophie Grace' **new**	WRou
'Sophie Louise'	CWVF EPts SLBF WRou
'Sophie Strawson' **new**	WRou
'Sophisticated Lady' (d)	CLoc CWVF EBak EPts SPet SVic
'South Gate' (d)	CLoc CWVF EBak EPts LAst LBMP SPet SVic
'South Lakeland'	CSil
'South Seas' (d)	EBak
'Southlanders'	EBak
'Space Shuttle'	CLoc LCla SLBF WRou
'Sparky' (T)	CLoc CWVF EPts LCla WOth WRou
'Sparky Bright' **new**	EPts
§ 'Speciosa'	CDoC EBak LCla WRou
'Spion Kop' (d)	CCCN CDoC CWVF EBak LAst SPet WGor
§ ***splendens*** ♀H1+3	CCCN CDoC CLoc CSil EBak IDee LCla MCot NPer SLBF SVic
- B&SWJ 10469	WCru
- 'Karl Hartweg'	CDoC
'Squadron Leader' (d)	CWVF EBak EPts
'Stanley Cash' (d)	CLoc CWVF SPet SVic
'Star Wars'	CDoC CLoc EPts MJac WOth WRou
'Stardust'	CDoC CWVF EBak
'Steeley' (d)	SVic
'Stella Ann' (T)	CWVF EBak EPts LCla WRou
'Stella Marina' (d)	EBak
'Straat Cumberland'	LCla
'Straat Fuknoka'	CDoC LCla
'Straat Futami' (E)	CDoC EPts LCla
'Straat Kobe' (T)	CDoC LCla
'Straat La Plata'	LCla
'Straat Magelhaen'	LCla

'Straat Messina'	LCla
'Straat of Plenty'	CDoC LCla
'Strawberry Daiquiri' (d)	WOth
'Strawberry Delight' (d)	CLoc CWVF EBak MJac SPet SVic
'Strawberry Sundae' (d)	CLoc CWVF EBak
'Strawberry Supreme' (d)	CSil
'String of Pearls'	CLoc CWVF MJac SLBF SPet SVic
'Stuart Joe'	CWVF
'Sue'	SLBF WOth
'Sue Joiner' **new**	WRou
'Suffolk Splendour' (d)	EPts
'Sugar Almond' (d)	CWVF
'Sugar Blues' (d)	EBak
'Sugar Plum Fairy' (E)	WRou
'Summerdaffodil'	WOth
'Sunbeam Hillary' (Sunbeam Series)	WOth
'Sunkissed' (d)	EBak
'Sunny Jim'	SVic
'Sunny Smiles'	CSil CWVF
'Sunray' (v)	CDoC CLoc COlW CWVF EBak ELon LBuc LRHS MAsh MGos NEgg SCoo SHil SLim SPoG SVen WCot WOth
'Sunset'	CLoc CWVF EBak
'Supersport' (d)	SVic
'Superstar'	CWVF EPts SVic
'Susan Ford' (d)	CWVF SPet
'Susan Green'	CSil CWVF EBak MJac
'Susan McMaster'	CLoc
'Susan Olcese' (d)	CWVF EBak
'Susan Travis'	CLoc CSil CWVF EBak SVic
'Swanley Gem' ♀^{H3}	CLoc CWVF EBak SLBF SPet SVic
'Swanley Pendula'	CLoc
'Swanley Yellow'	CWVF EBak SVic
'Sweet Hollie' **new**	SLBF WRou
'Sweet Leilani' (d)	EBak
'Sweet Sarah' (E)	EPts
I 'Sweetheart' van Wieringen	EBak
'Swingtime' (d) ♀^{H3}	CCCN CLoc CWVF EBak EPts LAst LCla MJac SLBF SPet SVic WRou
sylvatica misapplied	see *F. nigricans*
sylvatica Benth.	CDoC
'Sylvia Barker'	CWVF LCla SLBF WRou
'Sylvia Rose' (d)	CWVF
'Sylvia's Choice'	EBak
'Symphony'	CLoc CWVF EBak
'T.S.J.' (E)	CDoC LCla
'T'Vöske' (d/v)	WOth
'Taco'	CDoC LCla
'Taddle'	CWVF SLBF
'Taffeta Bow' (d)	CLoc SVic
'Taffy' (d)	EBak
'Tamerus Nandoe'	WRou
'Tamworth'	CLoc CWVF EBak MJac SVic
'Tangerine'	CLoc CWVF EBak SVic WCot
'Tanya Bridger' (d)	EBak
'Tarra Valley'	LCla SVic WOth
'Task Force'	CWVF SVic
'Taudens Heil'	WOth
'Tausendschön' (d)	CLoc
'Ted Perry' (d)	CWVF
'Ted's Tribute'	WRou
'Temptation' ambig.	CWVF
'Temptation' Peterson	CLoc EBak
'Tennessee Waltz' (d) ♀^{H3}	CDoC CLoc CSil CWVF EBak EPts SLBF SPet SVic WRou
'Tessa Jane'	CSil
tetradactyla misapplied	see *F.* × *bacillaris*

'Texas Longhorn' (d)	CLoc CWVF EBak SVic
'Thalia' (T) ♀$^{H1+3}$	CCCN CDoC CHEx CLoc CWVF EBak EPfP EPts EUJe LAst LCla LSRN MBri MCot MHer MJac NEgg NPri SLBF SMrm SPer SPlb SPoG SVic WOth WRou WWlt
'Thamar'	CDoC CLoc CWVF EPts SVic WOth WRou
'That's It' (d)	EBak SVic
'The Aristocrat' (d)	CLoc EBak
§ 'The Doctor'	CLoc CSil CWVF EBak
'The Jester' (d)	EBak
'The Madame' (d)	CWVF EBak
'The Tarns'	CSil CWVF EBak SVic WOth
'Thelma Vint'	CDoC
'Therese Dupois'	CSil
'Théroigne de Méricourt'	EBak
'Thilco'	CDoC CSil
'Thistle Hill' (d)	CDoC CSil
'Thomas' (d)	EPts
'Thomas Berge'	WRou
'Thompsonii'	see *F. magellanica* 'Thompsonii'
'Thornley's Hardy'	CSil MRav SVic
'Three Cheers'	CLoc EBak
'Three Counties'	EBak
'Thunderbird' (d)	CLoc CWVF EBak
thymifolia (E)	CWVF EBee GCra LRHS MHer SBch SDys WKif
- subsp. ***minimiflora*** (E)	CSil
- subsp. ***thymifolia*** (E)	CDoC CSil CTsd
'Tiara' (d)	EBak
'Tickled Pink'	WRou
'Tiffany' Reedstrom (d)	EBak
'Tillingbourne' (d)	CSil SLBF
'Time After Time'	CLoc WRou
'Timlin Brened' (T)	CWVF EBak WRou
'Timothy Titus' (T) ♀^{H1}	LCla
'Ting-a-ling'	CLoc CWVF EBak SPet SVic
'Tinker Bell' Hodges	EBak SVic
'Tintern Abbey'	CWVF
'Tjinegara'	CDoC LCla
'Toby Bridger' (d)	CLoc EBak
'Toby Foreman'	SLBF
'Tolling Bell'	CWVF EBak SPet
'Tom Goedeman'	LCla
'Tom H. Oliver' (d)	EBak
'Tom Knights'	EBak SPet WOth
'Tom Thorne'	EBak
'Tom Thumb' ♀^{H3}	Widely available
'Tom West' misapplied	see *F.* 'Mr West'
'Tom West' Meillez (v)	CDoC CHEx CLoc CMHG CSBt CSil CWVF CWib EBak EHoe EPts LAst LCla LHop LSRN MAsh MHer MJac MSCN SDix SLBF SLim WOth WRou
'Tom Woods'	CWVF
'Tomarama' (E) **new**	WRou
'Ton Ten Hove'	CDoC LCla
'Tony Talbot'	MJac
'Tony's Treat' (d)	EPts
'Toos'	SVic
'Topaz' (d)	CLoc EBak
'Topper' (d)	CWVF
'Torch' (d)	CLoc CWVF EBak SVic
'Torchlight'	CWVF EPts LCla
'Torvill and Dean' (d)	CLoc CWVF EPts LAst MJac SLBF SPet WGor
'Tosca'	CWVF
'Town Crier'	SLBF
'Tracid' (d)	CSil SVic

'Trail Blazer' (d)	CLoc CWVF EBak MJac
'Trailing King'	WOth
'Trailing Queen'	EBak MJac
'Trase' (d)	CDoC CSil CWVF CWib EBak SVic WRou
'Traudchen Bonstedt' (T) ♀H1	CDoC CLoc CWVF EBak LCla SVic
'Traviata'	see *F.* 'La Traviata' Blackwell
'Treasure' (d)	EBak
'Tresco'	CSil
'Tricolor'	see *F. magellanica* var. *gracilis* 'Tricolor'
'Trientje'	LCla SLBF
'Trimley Bells'	EBak WRou
triphylla (T)	EBak MHer
'Trish's Triumph'	EPts WOth
'Tristesse' (d)	CLoc CWVF EBak
'Troika' (d)	EBak
'Troon'	CWVF
'Tropicana' (d)	CLoc CWVF EBak SVic
'Troubador' Waltz (d)	CLoc
'Troutbeck'	CSil
'Trudi Davro'	LAst MJac SCoo
'Trudy'	CDoC CSil CWVF EBak EPts SVic
'Truly Treena' (d)	SLBF
'Trumpeter' ambig.	CDoC CWVF
'Trumpeter' Fry	SVic
'Trumpeter' Reiter (T)	CLoc EBak EPts LCla MJac WRou
'Tubular Bells' (T)	LCla WOth
'Tuonela' (d)	CLoc CWVF EBak
'Turkish Delight'	WRou
'Tutti-frutti' (d)	CLoc
'Twinkling Stars'	CWVF MJac SVic
'Twinny'	CWVF EPts WRou
'Two Tiers' (d)	CSil CWVF WRou
'U.F.O.'	CWVF SVic
'Ullswater' (d)	CWVF EBak
'Ultramar' (d)	EBak
'Uncle Charley' (d)	CDoC CSil EBak SVic
'Uncle Jinks'	SPet
'Uncle Steve' (d)	EBak SVic
'University of Liverpool'	CLoc MJac
'Upward Look'	EBak
'Valda May' (d)	CWVF
'Vale of Belvoir'	SVic
'Valentine' (d)	EBak
'Valerie Ann' (d)	EBak SPet SVic
'Valerie Bradley'	EPts
'Valiant'	EBak
'Vanessa Jackson'	CLoc CWVF MJac SVic
'Vanity Fair' (d)	CLoc EBak
'Variegated Lottie Hobby' (E/v)	CSil WOth
'Variegated Pink Fascination' (v)	WRou
'Variegated Pixie' (v)	CSil
'Variegated Procumbens'	see *F. procumbens* 'Wirral'
'Variegated Swingtime' (v)	EBak LAst SLBF
'Variegated Waveney Sunrise' (v)	MBri
'Veenlust'	EBak
'Velvet Crush'	EPts LAst WRou
'Vendeta'	CDoC LCla
'Venus Victrix'	CSil EBak WOth
venusta	CDoC EBak LCla
'Vera Garcia'	CDoC SLBF WRou
'Versicolor'	see *F. magellanica* 'Versicolor'
'Victory' Reiter (d)	EBak
'Vielliebchen'	CDoC CSil

'Vintage Dovercourt'	LCla
'Violet Bassett-Burr' (d)	CLoc EBak
'Violet Gem' (d)	CLoc
'Violet Lace' (d)	CSil
'Violet Rosette' (d)	CWVF EBak SVic
Violetta = 'Goetzviol' (Shadowdancer Series)	CDoC LAst LSou SCoo WRou
'Viva Ireland'	EBak
'Vivien Colville'	CLoc SVic
'Vobeglo'	CWVF
'Vogue' (d)	EBak
'Voltaire'	CSil EBak
'Voodoo' (d)	CCCN CDoC CLoc CWVF EBak EPts LAst SCoo SVic WRou
vulcanica André	CDoC LCla
'Vyvian Miller'	CWVF
'W.P. Wood'	CDoC CSil
'Wagtails White Pixie'	CSil EBak EPfP WRou
'Waldfee' (E)	CCVN CDoC CSil LCla WRou
'Waldis Alina'	WRou
'Waldis Billy'	SLBF WRou
'Waldis Grafin' **new**	WRou
'Waldis Isobel' **new**	WRou
'Waldis Junella' (d)	SLBF
'Waldis Maja'	WRou
'Waldis Ovambo'	SLBF
'Waldis Spezi'	CDoC LCla
'Waldis Speziella'	SLBF
'Walsingham' (d)	CWVF EBak
'Walton Jewel'	EBak
'Walz Bella'	LCla
'Walz Blauwkous' (d)	CDoC CWVF
'Walz Estaffette' (d)	SVic
'Walz Fluit'	MJac
'Walz Freule'	CWVF MJac
'Walz Harp'	CWVF WOth
'Walz Jubelteen'	CDoC CLoc CWVF ELon EPts LCla MJac SLBF SVen SVic WOth WRou
'Walz Lucifer'	CWVF LCla SLBF WRou
'Walz Mandoline' (d)	CWVF SVic
'Walz Panfluit'	LCla
'Walz Polka'	CDoC LCla SLBF
'Walz Sitar'	WOth
'Walz Sprietje'	CDoC
'Walz Triangel' (d)	SVic
'Walz Tuba'	CDoC
'Wapenveld 150'	LCla
'Wapenveld's Bloei'	CDoC EPts LCla SLBF
'War Paint' (d)	CLoc EBak
'Warton Crag'	CWVF SVic
'Water Nymph'	CLoc LAst SLBF SVic WOth WRou
'Wattenpost'	SLBF
'Wave of Life'	CWVF
'Waveney Gem'	CDoC CLoc CWVF EBak LCla MJac SLBF WOth
'Waveney Queen'	CWVF SVic
'Waveney Sunrise'	CWVF MJac SPet SVic WOth
'Waveney Unique'	CWVF
'Waveney Valley'	CWVF EBak
'Waveney Waltz'	CWVF EBak
'Wedding Bells' ambig.	SVic
'Welsh Dragon' (d)	CLoc CWVF EBak
'Wendy' Catt	see *F.* 'Snowcap'
'Wendy Bendy' **new**	SLBF
'Wendy Hebdon'	WRou
'Wendy's Beauty' (d)	CLoc EBak EPts MJac
'Wentworth'	CWVF SVic
'Wessex Belle' (d/v)	CWVF
'Wessex Hardy'	CSil

'Westham'	LCla
'Westminster Chimes' (d)	CLoc CWVF SPet SVic
'Wharfedale' ♀H3	CSil ELon EPts MJac SLBF SVic WOth
'What's-it' (E) **new**	SLBF
'Whickham Blue'	CWVF
'Whirlaway' (d)	CLoc CWVF EBak SVic
'White Ann'	see *F.* 'Heidi Weiss'
'White Bride' (d)	SVic
'White Clove'	CDoC CSil SVic WRou
'White Galore' (d)	CWVF EBak SVic
'White Général Monk' (d)	CDoC CSil
'White Gold' (v)	EBak
'White Heidi Ann' (d)	CSil
'White Joy'	EBak
'White King' (d)	CLoc CWVF EBak LAst SVic WRou
'White Lace'	CSil
'White Pixie' ♀H3-4	CDoC CSil EPts MJac SLBF SPet SVic
'White Queen' ambig.	CWVF EPfP
'White Queen' Doyle	EBak
'White Spider'	CLoc CWVF EBak SVic
'White Veil' (d)	CWVF
'Whiteknights Amethyst'	CDoC CSil
'Whiteknights Blush'	CCse CDoC CExl CSil EBee EPfP EWes GCal GQui LRHS SMrm
'Whiteknights Cheeky' (T)	CWVF EBak EPts LCla SVic
'Whiteknights Green Glister'	CSil EPfP
'Whiteknights Pearl' ♀H1+3	CSil CTsd CWVF EPfP EPts LAst LCla LRHS MLHP SDys SEND SLBF SPet SVic WOth
'Whitton Starburst'	CDoC LCla
'Wicked Queen' (d)	CSil SVic
'Widnes Wonder'	SLBF WRou
'Widow Twanky' (d)	CWVF
'Wigan Pier' (d)	EPts MJac SLBF WRou
'Wight Magic' (d)	MJac
'Wild and Beautiful' (d)	CWVF SVic
'Wilf Langton'	SLBF WOth WRou
'Wilhelmina Schwab'	CDoC LCla
'Willow Tinsdale'	LSou SLim
'Willy Nijhuis' **new**	WOth
'Wilma van Druten'	CDoC LCla
'Wilson's Colours'	EPts LCla
'Wilson's Joy'	MJac
'Wilson's Pearls' (d)	CWVF SLBF SPet
'Wilson's Sugar Pink'	EPts LCla MJac WOth
'Win Oxtoby' (d)	CWVF
'Windhapper'	LCla SLBF
'Windmill'	CWVF
'Wine and Roses' (d)	EBak
'Wingrove's Mammoth' (d)	SVic
'Wings of Song' (d)	CWVF EBak
'Winjim' (T) **new**	WRou
'Winston Churchill' (d) ♀H3	CLoc CWVF EBak LAst LRHS MJac SCoo SPet SVic
'Winter's Touch'	WOth
'Witchipoo'	SLBF
'Woodnook' (d)	CWVF
'Woodside' (d)	CSil SVic
'Wyre Light' (E) **new**	SLBF
'Ymkje'	EBak
'Yolanda Franck'	CDoC LAst
'York Manor'	CDoC
'Yvonne Schwab'	CDoC LCla
'Zeebrook'	SVic
'Zellertal'	CDoC
'Zets Bravo'	CDoC
'Ziegfield Girl' (d)	EBak SVic
'Zifi'	SLBF
'Zulu King'	CDoC CSil SVic WOth
'Zulu Queen'	SVic WOth
'Zus Liebregts' (d)	WOth
'Zwarte Snor' (d)	CWVF

Fumaria (*Papaveraceae*)

capreolata	WSFF
lutea	see *Corydalis lutea*
officinalis	CArn

Furcraea (*Asparagaceae*)

bedinghausii	see *F. parmentieri*
§ ***foetida***	CCCN SBig
§ - var. ***mediopicta*** (v)	SBig
- 'Variegata'	see *F. foetida* var. *mediopicta*
gigantea	see *F. foetida*
longaeva misapplied	see *F. parmentieri*
macdougalii	SPlb
§ ***parmentieri***	CBcs CCCN CCon CDTJ CExl CHEx CHGN CHll CTsd EAmu EBee EGri GBin LEdu SAPC SBst SPlb WPGP
- NJM 05.081	WPGP
selloa var. ***marginata*** (v)	CDoC CHEx EAmu

G

Gahnia (*Cyperaceae*)

sieberiana	SPlb

Gaillardia (*Asteraceae*)

aristata 'Maxima Aurea'	EBee EHyd EPfP MSpe NBre SPhx
'Arizona Sun'	ECtt EHyd LRHS MAsh MHer NPri SHil SMrm SPad SPet SVic WCAu
'Bijou'	EBee MSpe NBre SWvt
'Dwarf Goblin'	NGBl SPet
§ 'Fackelschein'	IBoy MSpe NBre XLum
'Fanfare' PBR	CMac CWGN EBee ECtt LHop LRHS LSou MGos NPri SCoo SMrm SPer
Goblin	see *G.* × *grandiflora* 'Kobold'
'Golden Queen'	XLum
× ***grandiflora*** 'Amber Wheels'	EBee EPfP MSpe NGdn SPhx WWEG
- 'Bremen'	MSpe XLum
- 'Burgunder'	CPrp CSBt CSpe EBee EHyd ELan EPfP EShb LAst LHop LRHS LSou MBri MPie MSpe NGBl NPri NSoo SPer SPhx SPoG SWvt WCAu WWEG XLum
- 'Dazzler' ♀H4	CSBt EBee ELan EPfP LAst LRHS SMrm SPer SPoG WMoo WWEG XLum
§ - 'Goldkobold'	XLum
- 'Granada'	LRHS
§ - 'Kobold'	CBcs CMac CSBt CTsd EBee EHyd ELan ELon EPfP GMaP IBoy LAst LRHS MBri MSpe NBre NEgg NHol NLar NPri NSoo SPer SPlb SPoG SWvt WHar WWEG XLum
- 'Mesa Yellow'	NPri
- (Sunburst Series) Sunburst Burgundy Picotee = 'Granretip' PBR	LRHS

	- - Sunburst Burgundy	SHil SPet
	- - Sunburst Orange **new**	LRHS SHil
	- - Sunburst Yellow = 'Granyel'[PBR]	SHil
	- 'Tizzy'[PBR]	MPie
	- 'Tokajer'	EBee ELan EPfP LRHS MSpe NBre SPhx XLum
	'Naomi Sunshine'	SHar
§	'Oranges and Lemons'[PBR]	CPrp EBee ECtt LHop LSou NLar SHar SMrm WCAu
	'Red Sun' **new**	NLar
	Saint Clements	see *G.* 'Oranges and Lemons'
	Torchlight	see *G.* 'Fackelschein'
	Yellow Goblin	see *G.* × *grandiflora* 'Goldkobold'

Galactites (*Asteraceae*)

	tomentosa	EHoe ELan EPfP EPyc EWTr LDai SPav
	- white flowered	CPla

Galanthus ✿ (*Amaryllidaceae*)

	'Acton Pigot No. 3'	CAvo
	'Ailwyn' **new**	CAvo
	'Alan's Treat' **new**	CAvo
	× ***allenii***	CAvo CBro
	alpinus	CAvo
	var. ***bortkewitschianus***	
	'Anne of Geierstein'	CDes IFoB WCot
	'Annette'	NMyG
	'Armine'	CAvo CElw IFoB WCot
	'Art Nouveau' **new**	CAvo
	'Atkinsii' 🏆H4	CAvo CBgR CBro CElw CLAP CWCL ECho EPot EWoo GAbr GKev IFoB IGor LRHS MAsh MRav MWat NBir NMyG WCot WHoo WShi
	'Autumn Beauty'	CBro LRHS
	'Backhouse Spectacles'	ITim
	'Barbara's Double' (d)	CAvo CBgR CLAP MAsh
	'Benhall Beauty'	CAvo EWoo
	'Benton Magnet'	EWoo
	'Bertram Anderson'	EWoo MAsh WCot
	'Bess'	CAvo CElw CSna IFoB MAsh
	'Bill Bishop'	CAvo CDes EWoo IFoB IPot LRHS MAsh
	'Bitton' ambig. **new**	NPol
	'Blewbury'	IFoB
	'Brenda Troyle'	CBro CElw CLAP ELon EPot GAbr GKev IGor IPot LRHS MHom NMyG NPol WCot WIvy
	'Byfield Special'	CAvo IFoB
	byzantinus	see *G. plicatus* subsp. *byzantinus*
	'Castlegar'	CAvo IFoB
	caucasicus misapplied	see *G. elwesii* var. *monostictus*
	caucasicus ambig.	GAbr IFoB NPol
	- 'Comet'	see *G. elwesii* 'Comet'
	- var. ***hiemalis*** Stern	see *G. elwesii* Hiemalis Group
	'Cicely Hall'	CDes IFoB
	'Clare Blakeway-Phillips'	CLAP
	corcyrensis spring-flowering	see *G. reginae-olgae* subsp. *vernalis*
	- winter-flowering	see *G. reginae-olgae* subsp. *reginae-olgae* Winter-flowering Group
	'Cordelia' (d)	CLAP IFoB IPot LRHS NMyG
	'Cornwood Gem'	IFoB
	'Cottisford' **new**	CDes
	'Cowhouse Green'	CAvo
	'Curly'	CDes EWoo IFoB MAsh
	'David Baker' **new**	CDes
	'Desdemona' (d)	CBgR CBro CLAP EPot LLHF LRHS NMyG WCot WIvy
	'Ding Dong'	CAvo IFoB
	'Dionysus' (d)	CBgR CBro CExl CLAP EPot EWes EWoo GKev IGor LLHF MAsh MHom NBir NMyG WBrk WShi
	'Drummond's Giant'	IFoB
	'Ecusson d'Or' **new**	CAvo
§	***elwesii*** 🏆H4	CBro CTri CWCL ECho ELan ELon EPfP EPot ERCP IFoB IGor LPio LRHS MWat NBir NPol SDeJ SPoG SRms WCot WHoo WShi
	- 'Abington Green'	CSna
	- 'Broadleigh Gardens'	LRHS
	- 'Cedric's Prolific'	CDes EWoo IFoB IGor NMyG
§	- 'Comet'	CAvo CDes CElw ELon EWoo GBuc IFoB MAsh
	- 'Daphne's Scissors'	CAvo CBgR CElw CSna
	- 'David Shackleton'	CAvo CElw EWoo IFoB LRHS MAsh
	- 'Early Twin'	WCot
	- Edward Whittall Group	CLAP
	- 'Elmley Lovett' **new**	CDes
	- var. ***elwesii*** 'Big Boy' **new**	CAvo
	- - 'Fenstead End'	EWoo
	- - 'Kite'	EWoo LRHS
	- - 'Magnus'	CLAP NBir
	- - 'Maidwell L'	CBro CSna LRHS MAsh
	- - 'Sibbertoft Magnet'	CAvo IFoB
*	- 'Flore Pleno' (d)	NPol
	- 'Godfrey Owen'	CDes IFoB
	- 'Green Brush'	CAvo IFoB
§	- Hiemalis Group	CBro EPot LRHS LWst MHom WCot
	- - 'Barnes'	WCot
	- 'J. Haydn'	ECho MAsh NMyG
	- 'Jessica'	CAvo IFoB
	- 'Long 'drop'	IFoB
	- 'Mandarin'	CElw
	- 'Marielle'	EPPr
	- 'Marjorie Brown'	CFis NMyG
	- 'Milkwood'	see *G. elwesii* 'Mrs Macnamara'
§	- var. ***monostictus*** 🏆H4	CAvo ECho EWoo IFoB LLHF LRHS WBrk WIvy
	- - 'G. Handel'	ECho IFoB LLHF LRHS NMyG
	- - 'Green Tips'	CAvo
	- - 'H. Purcell'	ECho LLHF LRHS
	- - late-flowering	LWst
	- - 'Miller's Late'	CAvo
	- - 'Rogers Rough'	SDys
	- - 'Warwickshire Gemini'	CDes
§	- 'Mrs Macnamara'	CAvo CDes EWoo IFoB LRHS MAsh
	- 'Peter Gatehouse' **new**	CDes
	- 'Selborne Green Tips'	CAvo
	- 'Sickle'	CAvo CDes CSna
	- 'Sir Edward Elgar'	LLHF LRHS
I	- 'Snowwhite' **new**	GKev
	- 'Three Leaves'	CAvo IFoB
	- 'Washfield Colesbourne'	see *G.* 'Washfield Colesbourne'
	'Erway'	MHom
	'F63'	IFoB
	'Falkland House'	CElw
	'Faringdon Double' (d)	LRHS
	'Fieldgate Prelude'	CAvo
	'Fieldgate Superb'	IFoB
	fosteri	CBro ECho LRHS
	'G71' (d)	IFoB
	'Galadriel' **new**	CAvo
	'Galatea'	CBro CLAP CSna EWes EWoo LRHS MAsh MHom SDys WIvy
	'George Elwes'	CAvo

'Ginns'	CDes CLAP ELon EWoo IFoB ITim
§ ***gracilis***	CAvo CBre CBro CExl CLAP LRHS NPol
- 'Highdown'	CElw CLAP IFoB LWst MHom
- Kew	CElw
- 'Vic Horton'	WThu
graecus misapplied	see *G. gracilis*
graecus Orph. ex Boiss.	see *G. elwesii*
'Grande Juge'	IFoB
'Grayling'	see *G. plicatus* 'Percy Picton'
Greatorex double (d)	CLAP
'Green Man'	CAvo IFoB
'Green Necklace' **new**	CAvo
'Greenfields'	CBgR CSna IFoB IGor
'Heffalump' (d)	CAvo CDes IFoB MAsh
'Hill Poë' (d)	CBro CDes CElw CLAP EPot IFoB IPot MAsh MHom MWat NMyG
'Hippolyta' (d)	CAvo CBro CElw CLAP ELon EPot EWoo GAbr GKev IFoB IGor LRHS MAsh MHom NMyG NPol SKHP WCot WIvy WShi
'Hobson's Choice'	LRHS
'Honeysuckle Cottage'	CAvo
× ***hybridus*** 'Merlin'	CAvo CBro CElw IFoB IGor LRHS MHom NMyG WCot WIvy
- 'Robin Hood'	CAvo CDes CLAP IFoB LRHS
'Icicle'	CAvo
§ ***ikariae*** Bak.	CBgR CElw EPfP
- subsp. ***ikariae*** Butt's form	NPol
- Latifolius Group	see *G. platyphyllus*
- subsp. ***snogerupii***	see *G. ikariae* Bak.
'Imbolc'	CAvo IFoB
'Irish Green'	CAvo IFoB
'Jacquenetta' (d)	CAvo CBro CElw CLAP CSna EWoo IFoB IGor ITim LRHS MHom NMyG
'Jade' **new**	CAvo
'James Backhouse'	WHoo WShi
'John Gray'	CAvo CBro CDes CSna EWoo IFoB MAsh
'June Boardman' **new**	CAvo
'Ketton'	CBro CElw CSna EWoo IFoB LRHS NRya WIvy
'Kildare'	CAvo CDes IFoB
'Kingston Double' (d)	CAvo CBgR CLAP
'Lady Beatrix Stanley' (d)	CAvo CBro CElw CLAP EPot GAbr IFoB LLWP LRHS MAsh MHom NMyG WCot
lagodechianus	MPhe
'Lapwing'	CAvo IFoB
latifolius Rupr.	see *G. platyphyllus*
'Lavinia' (d)	CAvo CElw CLAP LRHS MHom
'Lerinda'	IFoB
'Limetree'	CBgR CElw CLAP EPri EWoo LRHS MHom NCot NPol
'Little Ben'	CAvo
'Little John'	LRHS WBrk
'Little Magnet'	CAvo
'Louise Ann Bromley' **new**	CAvo
lutescens	see *G. nivalis* Sandersii Group
'Lyn'	CBro LRHS NBir
'Magnet' ♀H4	CAvo CBgR CBro CElw CLAP ECho ELon EPot EWoo GAbr GKev IGor ITim LRHS LWst MAsh MHom MWat NBir NMyG NPol SKHP WBrk WCot WHoo WShi
aff. 'Magnet'	SMrm
'Maidwell'	IFoB
'Melanie Broughton'	CAvo IFoB

'Mighty Atom'	CDes CLAP WBrk
'Moccas'	CBgR CElw CSna MHom
'Modern Art'	CAvo EWoo IFoB
'Mrs Backhouse No 12'	IFoB LRHS
'Mrs Thompson'	CAvo CDes CElw IFoB LRHS WIvy
'Natalie Garton'	CAvo IFoB
'Neill Fraser'	MHom
nivalis ♀H4	Widely available
- 'Alice's Late' **new**	CBgR
- 'Anglesey Abbey'	CAvo CElw EWes EWoo IFoB MAsh MHom
- 'April Fool'	MHom
- 'Ballynahinch' **new**	ITim
- 'Bitton'	CLAP
- 'Blonde Inge'	CAvo IFoB MAsh
- 'Chedworth'	CElw WBrk
- 'Cornwood'	CAvo EWoo
- 'Dreycott Greentip'	IFoB
- 'Elfin'	CElw IFoB
- 'Fuzz'	CAvo
- 'Greenish'	EWoo
- subsp. ***imperati***	CExl
- 'Lutescens'	see *G. nivalis* Sandersii Group
- 'Major Pam'	IFoB
- 'Maximus'	LRHS WShi
- 'Melvillei'	EWoo
- f. ***pleniflorus*** (d)	CTca GKev MAsh SPoG
- - 'Bagpuize Virginia' (d)	CAvo
- - 'Blewbury Tart' (d)	CAvo CBro CElw CLAP CSna EWoo IFoB WBrk
- - 'Flore Pleno' (d) ♀H4	CBro CExl CWCL EPfP EPot ERCP IFoB ITim LHop LLWP LPio LRHS MMuc NCot NRya SDeJ SEND SMrm SPer SRms WBrk WCot WHoo WPnP WShi
- - 'Lady Elphinstone' (d)	CAvo CBro CDes CLAP CRow CSna IFoB LLHF MAsh MHom NMyG NPol NRya WCot WIvy
- - 'Pusey Green Tips' (d)	CAvo CBro CElw CLAP EPot IFoB IPot LRHS NMyG NPol WCot
§ - - 'Wonston Double' (d)	CAvo IFoB
- Poculiformis Group	CLAP
- - 'Angelique'	CAvo
§ - Sandersii Group	CRDP IFoB MAsh
§ - Scharlockii Group	CAvo CBgR CElw IGor MAsh MHom WBrk
- 'Tiny'	IFoB MHom NBir
- 'Virescens'	CLAP IFoB
- 'Viridapice'	CAvo CBgR CBro CElw CExl ECho EPot GKev IFoB IGor LRHS MAsh MWat NBir NPol SDeJ SKHP WCot WHoo WShi
- 'White Dream'	IFoB WShi
'Ophelia' (d)	CAvo CBro EPot EWoo GAbr IGor LRHS MHom MWat NMyG NPol SKHP WBrk WHoo
'Orion'	CDes
'Orleton' **new**	CDes
'Peg Sharples'	CAvo IFoB MHom
peshmenii	EPot
§ ***platyphyllus***	CExl
plicatus ♀H4	CAvo CBro CElw EPot GAbr LRHS MCot MHom NMyG NPol WBrk WCot WHoo WShi
- 'Augustus'	CAvo CBro CElw ELon EPot EWes IFoB IGor LRHS MAsh MHom NMyG WCot WIvy
- 'Baxendale's Late'	CAvo CLAP EWoo
- 'Bill Clark'	CDes IFoB MAsh

	- 'Bolu Shades'	IFoB LWst
§	- subsp. ***byzantinus***	CBro MHom WThu
	- 'Colossus'	CBro IFoB MAsh
	- 'Diggory'	CAvo IFoB MAsh
	- 'Duckie' **new**	CAvo
	- 'Gerard Parker'	CAvo IFoB
	- 'Green Hayes'	CAvo
	- 'Greenpeace'	CSna
	- 'John Long' **new**	CAvo
	- 'Lambrook Greensleeves'	CAvo
	- late flowering	LWst
	- 'Limey'	EWoo
	- 'Oreanda'	IPot
§	- 'Percy Picton'	CAvo MAsh
	- 'Sally Pasmore'	CAvo
	- 'Sophie North'	CLAP IFoB NPol
	- 'The Pearl'	IFoB
	- 'Three Ships'	CAvo CDes EWoo IFoB
	- 'Trym'	CDes IFoB MAsh NPol
	- 'Warham'	CBro EPot GAbr IFoB IGor LRHS MHom NMyG WCot
	- 'Warham Rectory'	LRHS
	- 'Wendy's Gold'	CBro CDes CSna IFoB MAsh
	- 'Woodtown' **new**	IMou
	'Pride o' the Mill'	CAvo
	'Primrose Warburg'	CAvo CDes IFoB
	reginae-olgae	CBro GKev IFoB MHom
	- subsp. ***reginae-olgae*** ♀H2-4	EPot
	- - 'Cambridge'	MHom
§	- - Winter-flowering Group	CBro
§	- subsp. ***vernalis***	EPot IFoB NMyG WCot
	'Reverend Hailstone'	IFoB LRHS
	'Richard Ayres' (d)	CAvo IFoB LRHS
	rizehensis	CAvo CLAP IFoB LRHS MHom NMyG
	Baytop 34474	IFoB
	'Rodmarton'	IFoB MAsh
	'S.Arnott' ♀H4	CAvo CBro CElw CExl CLAP ECho ELon EPot ERCP EWoo GAbr GBuc GKev IFoB IGor LRHS MAsh MWat NBir NPol NRya SDeJ WBrk WCot WHoo
	'Saint Anne's'	CAvo CDes CElw CSna IFoB MHom
	'Scharlockii'	see *G. nivalis* Scharlockii Group
	'Seagull'	CAvo CElw
	'Sentinel'	CAvo
	'Silverwells'	CSna IFoB LRHS
	'Sir Herbert Maxwell' **new**	ITim
	'Spindlestone Surprise'	CAvo EWoo
§	'Straffan'	CAvo CBro CElw EPot IFoB IGor LRHS MHom NMyG NPol WBrk WCot
	'Sutton Courtenay'	CAvo CSna
	'The O'Mahoney'	see *G.* 'Straffan'
	'Titania' (d)	CBro ELon IFoB IGor LRHS MHom
	'Tubby Merlin'	CElw CLAP EWoo IFoB LRHS MAsh WIvy
	'Uncle Dick'	CAvo
	× ***valentinei*** 'Compton Court'	CBro IFoB ITim
§	'Washfield Colesbourne'	CElw EWoo
	'Washfield Warham'	CAvo EWoo ITim LRHS MAsh NMyG
	'Wasp'	CDes
	'White Admiral'	SKHP
	'White Dreams'	IFoB LRHS
	'White Swan' Ballard (d)	CElw LRHS
	'William Thomson'	CSna
	'Winifrede Mathias'	CBgR CElw CLAP LRHS MAsh
	'Wisley Magnet'	LRHS
	'Wonston Double'	see *G. nivalis* f. *pleniflorus* 'Wonston Double'
	woronowii ♀H4	CAvo CBro CElw CLAP CTca CTri ECho EPfP EPot GKev IFoB ITim LPio LRHS MAsh MBri MHom MWat NBir NMyG SDeJ SPer WBrk WCot

Galax (*Diapensiaceae*)

	aphylla	see *G. urceolata*
§	***urceolata***	ECho IBlr WSHC

Galega (*Papilionaceae*)

	bicolor	NBir NChi SRms SWat
	'Duchess of Bedford'	EBee GBin
	× ***hartlandii***	CExl LRHS
	- 'Alba' ♀H4	ELon EWes GBin IBlr LRHS MArl MCot SWat WCot WSHC
	- 'Candida'	NBir
	- 'Lady Wilson' ♀H4	CPom ECtt ELon EWes EWld GBin MArl MLHP WCot WHoo WOut
	- 'Spring Light' (v)	LSou
	'Her Majesty'	see *G.* 'His Majesty'
§	'His Majesty'	CDes CKno EBee ECtt IFro MCot MLHP MRav SMrm WCot WHoo WPGP
	officinalis	Widely available
	- 'Alba' ♀H4	CPom CPrp ECtt ELan EPfP LEdu LPot MAvo MBrN MHer MNHC NPnk SPer WHer WHrl WKif WMoo
	- Coconut Ice = 'Kelgal' (v)	CAbP
	- 'Lincoln Gold'	MTPN
	orientalis	CDes EBee ECtt EWes LEdu LRHS MArl MCot WCot WMoo WPGP WSHC

Galeobdolon see *Lamium*

Galeopsis (*Lamiaceae*)

	tetrahit	WSFF

Galium (*Rubiaceae*)

	cruciata	see *Cruciata laevipes*
	mollugo	CArn CHab
§	***odoratum***	Widely available
	verum	CArn CHab GJos GPoy MCoo MHer MNHC NMir SIde

Galtonia (*Asparagaceae*)

	candicans ♀H4	Widely available
	- 'Moonbeam' (d)	CRDP EBee
	princeps	CBro CSam CTca EBee GBin GCra LRHS WHil WPGP
	regalis	CExl CTca WPGP
	viridiflora	CAvo CBro CTca EBee ELan EPot ERCP GBin GCal GGal IBoy LEdu LPio LRHS MNrw NChi SDeJ WCot WHil XLum

Galvezia (*Plantaginaceae*)

	speciosa	MCot

Gamblea (*Araliaceae*)

	pseudoevodiifolia B&SWJ 11707	WCru

Garcinia (*Clusiaceae*)

mangostana	CCCN

Gardenia (*Rubiaceae*)

augusta	see *G. jasminoides*
florida L.	see *G. jasminoides*
grandiflora	see *G. jasminoides*
§ ***jasminoides*** ♀H1	CArn CBcs CCCN EBak MBri
- 'Kleim's Hardy'	Widely available
magnifica	MOWG
'Perfumed Petticoats'	WHlf

garlic see *Allium sativum*

garlic, elephant see *Allium ampeloprasum* 'Elephant'

Garrya ✿ (*Garryaceae*)

congdonii	NLar
elliptica	CBcs CDul CMac EBee EPfP GGal LRHS LSRN MBri MGos NPri NWea SEND SPlb WHar WPat
- (f)	MJak MSwo SWvt
- (m)	CDoC CTri ELon LAst MBlu NLar SGol SLim
- 'James Roof' (m) ♀H4	Widely available
× ***issaquahensis*** 'Glasnevin Wine'	CAbP CDul CJun ELan ELon EPfP IArd LRHS MAsh MBri MGos SCoo SLim SPer SPoG
- 'Pat Ballard' (m)	EPfP
× ***thuretii***	CBcs LAst MBri NLar SPer

Gasteria ✿ (*Asphodelaceae*)

bicolor var. ***liliputana***	SPlb
carinata var. ***verrucosa***	CHel EShb MSCN
ellaphieae	LToo
excelsa	LToo
nitida var. ***nitida*** variegated (v)	WCot
'Smokey'	EShb

× *Gaulnettya* see *Gaultheria*

Gaultheria ✿ (*Ericaceae*)

adenothrix	WThu
antarctica	WThu
crassa 'John Saxton'	WAbe
cuneata ♀H4	ECho EPot LRHS MAsh NHar WThu
forrestii	CExl
hispidula	ECho
itoana	ECho GJos GKev NHar WThu
miqueliana	WThu
§ ***mucronata***	CDul EPfP MAsh MJak NWea
- (m)	CBcs CMac CSBt CTri CWSG EPfP LRHS MGos NEgg NWad SPer SRms
- SDR 7051 <u>**new**</u>	GKev
- 'Alba' (f)	MJak
- 'Bell's Seedling' (f/m) ♀H4	CBcs CDoC CDul CTri EBee ELan EPfP LRHS MAsh NBir NEgg SPer SPoG
- 'Cherry Ripe' (f)	CMac MMuc
- 'Crimsonia' (f) ♀H4	CBcs CMac EPfP SPer SRms
- 'Indian Lake'	NWad
- 'Lilacina' (f)	CMac MAsh
- 'Lilian' (f)	CSBt EPfP NWad
- Mother of Pearl	see *G. mucronata* 'Parelmoer'
- 'Mulberry Wine' (f) ♀H4	CSBt CTri ELan NEgg NHol SPer
§ - 'Parelmoer' (f)	CSBt NEgg SPer
- 'Pink Pearl' (f) ♀H4	SRms
- red-berried (f)	MJak
- 'Rosea' (f)	MJak
§ - 'Signaal' (f)	CBcs EBee EPfP MAsh NEgg NWad SPer
- Signal	see *G. mucronata* 'Signaal'
§ - 'Sneeuwwitje' (f)	CBcs EPfP MAsh NBir SPer
- Snow White	see *G. mucronata* 'Sneeuwwitje'
- 'Thymifolia' (m)	EPfP
- white-berried (f)	MMuc
- 'Wintertime' (f) ♀H4	CMac SRms
§ ***myrsinoides***	GKev WThu
nana Colenso	see *G. parvula*
nummularioides	NLar
§ ***parvula***	WThu
'Pearls'	NHar WAbe WThu
procumbens ♀H4	CAgr CBcs CDoC CMac CWSG EBee ECho EPfP GJos GMaP GPoy LRHS MAsh MBlu MBri MGos MJak NEgg NWea SLim SPer SPlb SPoG SRms SWvt
- 'Very Berry'	EShb NHol NWad
prostrata	see *G. myrsinoides*
pumila	GAbr LEdu NHar
schultesii	WThu
shallon	CAgr CBcs CSBt EPfP MGos MJak SPer SRms SWvt
sinensis	NHar
- lilac-berried	WThu
tasmanica	ECou
tetramera	CExl
thymifolia	NWad
trichophylla	EDAr NHar
× ***wisleyensis***	LRHS SLon SRms
- 'Pink Pixie'	LRHS MAsh NLar
- 'Ruby'	CMac
- 'Wisley Pearl'	CBcs IBlr NLar SCoo
yunnanensis	CExl

Gaura (*Onagraceae*)

lindheimeri ♀H4	CAby CMea COIW CSBt CSpe CWib EBee ELan EPfP EShb EWTr LHop LRHS MCot MHer NEgg SBch SEND SPer SPhx SWvt WHar WHoo WMnd WMoo XLum XSen
- 'Ballerina Blush'	LPio
- 'Ballerina Rose'	SPet
- Belleza Series	CWCL EPfP LRHS MBri MNrw SHil
- 'Blaze'PBR	LHop
- Cherry Brandy = 'Gauchebra'PBR	EBee ECtt EHyd ELan EPfP IPot LRHS MBri MCot SHil SWvt WHar
- 'Corrie's Gold' (v)	CAby EBee ECtt EHoe EHyd ELan EPfP LRHS MHer SPer SPet WMnd
- 'Crimson Butterflies'PBR	EHyd EPfP LRHS
- (Geyser Series) Geyser Pink = 'Gaudros'PBR <u>**new**</u>	EBee
- - Geyser White = 'Gaudwwhi'PBR <u>**new**</u>	EBee
- 'Grace' <u>**new**</u>	WGor
§ - 'Heather's Delight'	MRav
- In the Pink	see *G. lindheimeri* 'Heather's Delight'
- 'Jo Adela' (v)	EPfP
- Karalee Petite = 'Gauka'	CWCL EPfP
- Karalee Petite Improved	see *G. lindheimeri* Lillipop Pink
- Karalee Pink	LSRN MBri
- Karalee White = 'Nugauwhite'PBR	CHel CWCL EPfP LAst LHop LRHS LSRN MBri NLar SCoo SHil SPer SPoG

§	- Lillipop Pink = 'Redgapi'^{PBR}	CAby CPrp ELon EPfP LBMP LHop LRHS LSou MAvo MBrN MBri NEgg NLar SMrm SPoG
	- 'My Melody'^{PBR} (v)	CWCL LPot
	- 'Occitania' (v)	XLum
	- Papillon = 'Nugaupapil'^{PBR}	ECtt ELon LBMP LHop MAvo SMrm SPer SPoG
	- 'Passionate Blush'^{PBR}	CBcs EPfP LRHS LSRN LSou SLon SPad SPoG SRms
	- 'Passionate Rainbow'^{PBR} (v)	CWCL EHoe EPfP LRHS LSou SPoG SRms
	- 'Pink Dwarf'	EPfP IPot LRHS
	- 'Pink Gin' **new**	LRHS LSou
	- 'Rosyjane'	CAby CHel CKno CSpe CWCL ECtt EHoe EPfP EWTr LAst LBMP LHop LRHS LSRN LSou MBel MBri MRav NSoo SHar SHil SLon SMrm SPad SPer SPoG SRms SWvt
	- 'Ruby Ruby'	SHar
	- short	EBee
	- 'Siskiyou Pink'	CBcs CSBt CWCL ECtt EHoe EHyd ELan EPfP LRHS LSRN MWat NSoo SEND SMad SPer SWat SWvt WCFE WMnd WWEG XLum
	- Snow Fountain = 'Walsnofou'	LRHS
	- 'Summer Breeze'	EBee NGBl SBea SPhx
	- 'The Bride'	CTri CWCL EBee ECtt EHyd EPfP LRHS LSRN LSou MBel MMuc MRav MWat SGbt SPav SPet SWvt WMnd
	- 'Tutti Frutti'^{PBR}	LRHS LSou SPoG
	- 'Vanilla'^{PBR}	CKno CWCL LBMP LRHS LSou SPoG
I	- 'Variegata' (v)	CWCL LRHS SHil SRms
	- 'Whirling Butterflies'	CKno CSpe CWCL ECtt ELan ELon EPfP GMaP LRHS MWat SMad SPer SWat SWvt WWEG
	- 'White Dove'	EPfP IPot LBuc
	- 'White Heron'	MNrw
	sinuata	CAby SHar

Gazania (*Asteraceae*)

'Apache' **new**	LBuc
'Aztec' Υ^{H1+3}	CCCN
'Bicton Orange'	CCCN COIW CSam ECtt SCoo SVen
(Kiss Series) 'Big Kiss White Flame'	SVen
- 'Big Kiss Yellow Flame'	SVen
'Blackberry Ripple'	CCCN COIW SCoo SMrm SVen
'Blackcurrant Ice'	MCot
'Christopher'	SCoo
'Christopher Lloyd'	CCCN ECtt SMrm SVen
'Cookei' Υ^{H1+3}	CSpe
'Cornish Pixie'	CCCN
'Cream Beauty'	MCot
(Daybreak Series) 'Daybreak Rose Stripe'	NGBl
- 'Daybreak Red Stripe'	NGBl
Gazoo Series	LBuc SPoG
'Jamaica Ginger'	SMrm
'Kiss Bronze Star' (Kiss Series)	SVen
krebsiana	CCCN
'Lemon Beauty'	ECtt
'Magic'	CCCN NPri SCoo
Nahui = 'Suga119' (Sunbathers Series)	CCCN
'Orange Beauty'	ELan
rigens 'Variegata' (v) Υ^{H1+3}	CCCN ELan
Rumi = 'Suga116' (Sunbathers Series)	CCCN
Sunset Jane Lemon Spot = 'Sugajale' (Sunbathers Series)	CCCN
Sunset Jane = 'Sugaja'^{PBR} (Sunbathers Series)	CCCN
'Talent'	SEND
Tiger Eye = 'Gazte'^{PBR} (v)	CCCN CWGN LAst LSou
Toptokai = 'Suga407' (Sunbathers Series)	CCCN
Totonaca = 'Suga212' (Sunbathers Series)	CCCN

Geissorhiza (*Iridaceae*)

aspera	ECho
bracteata	ECho
brehmii 'Rawsonville'	ECho
darlingensis	ECho
imbricata	ECho
- subsp. ***bicolor***	ECho
inequalis	ECho
inflexa	ECho
monanthos	ECho
ornithogaloides	ECho
- subsp. ***marlothii***	ECho
radians	ECho
rosea	ECho
splendidissima	ECho

Gelasine (*Iridaceae*)

	azurea	see *G. elongata*
§	***coerulea***	SBrt WSHC
§	***elongata*** **new**	WHil

Gelidocalamus (*Poaceae*)

fangianus	see *Ampelocalamus mocrophyllum*

Gelsemium (*Gelsemiaceae*)

rankinii	EBee LRHS
sempervirens Υ^{H1+3}	CArn CCCN CHII CRHN EBee EShb ESwi LRHS LSRN MOWG SBrt SLim SPoG

Genista (*Papilionaceae*)

	aetnensis Υ^{H4}	CDul EBee ELan EPfP EUJe NLar SAPC SEND SPer SRms WPat WSHC
§	***canariensis***	CExl CSBt CWib
	cinerea	WCFE
	decumbens	see *Cytisus decumbens*
	'Emerald Spreader'	see *G. pilosa* 'Yellow Spreader'
	fragrans	see *G. canariensis*
	hispanica	CBcs CDul CSBt ELan EPfP GGal MGos NLar SEND SLim SPer SRms SWvt WCFE WHar
	humifusa	see *G. pulchella*
	lydia Υ^{H4}	Widely available
§	***maderensis***	LRHS SHil
	pilosa	MAsh
	- 'Goldilocks'	LRHS MMuc
	- 'Lemon Spreader'	see *G. pilosa* 'Yellow Spreader'
	- var. ***minor***	NLar NSla SBch WAbe
	- 'Procumbens'	CMea MHer
	- 'Vancouver Gold'	CBcs CMac ELan EPfP MBri MGos MRav SMad SPer SRms WGor
§	- 'Yellow Spreader'	CBcs MAsh MSwo
§	'Porlock' Υ^{H3}	CBcs CDoC CDul CExl CMac CSBt CTri CWib EBee EPfP GGal LRHS

		MAsh MBri MMuc MRav SEND SHil SLim
§	***pulchella***	CTri
	sagittalis	CTri EBee LRHS MMuc NBir SPer WWFP
§	× ***spachiana*** ♀H1	CTri EBee NSoo SPoG
	tenera 'Golden Shower'	SLPl
	tinctoria	CArn CHab EOHP GPoy MHer WHer
§	- 'Flore Pleno' (d) ♀H4	ECho NPro
	- 'Moesiaca'	WAbe
	- 'Plena'	see *G. tinctoria* 'Flore Pleno'
	- 'Royal Gold' ♀H4	CWib EBee EPfP MRav NWad SPer SPlb
	villarsii	see *G. pulchella*

Gentiana ✿ (*Gentianaceae*)

	sp.	LLWG
§	***acaulis*** ♀H4	CMea CPla ECho EDAr EHyd ELan EPfP EPot GKev GMaP LHop LRHS MAsh MWat NGdn NHar NLar NSla SPlb SRms WAbe WPat
	- f. ***alba***	WThu
	- 'Belvedere'	EPot WAbe
	- 'Coelestina'	WThu
	- 'Dinarica'	see *G. dinarica*
	- 'Holzmannii'	IVic WAbe
	- 'Krumrey'	EPot GKev
	- 'Max Frei'	NHar
	- 'Rannoch'	EPot GKev
	- 'Stumpy'	EPot
	- 'Trotter's Variety'	WAbe
	- 'Undulatifolia'	EPot
	- 'Velkokvensis'	IVic
	affinis	LHop
	'Alex Duguid'	IVic NHar
	'Amethyst'	EPot GMaP LRHS SPoG WAbe
	angulosa misapplied	see *G. verna* 'Angulosa' hort.
	angustifolia	WAbe XEll
I	- 'Alba'	EPot
	- Frei hybrid	GKev
	asclepiadea ♀H4	CLAP CSpe CTri EBee ECho ELan GAbr GCra GKev LEdu LRHS MBri MNrw NBid NBir NCGa NLar SMad SPoG SRms SSpi WBor WHoo WKif WSHC
	- 'Alba'	CCon CLAP EBee GCal IGor LEdu MNrw NBid SRms WCFE WHoo
	- 'Knightshayes'	CCon CLAP EBee GKev LLHF NLar
	- 'Pink Swallow'	CLAP EBee GAbr GQue MSCN NLar WWEG
	- 'Rosea'	GKev MNrw
	atuntsiensis	EPot
	'Balmoral' PBR	GMaP NHar
	'Barbara Lyle'	WAbe
	bavarica var. ***subacaulis***	SPlb
	× ***bernardii***	see *G.* × *stevenagensis* 'Bernardii'
	'Berrybank Dome'	CSam GMaP LRHS
	'Berrybank Sky'	GMaP LRHS NCGa
	'Berrybank Snowflakes'	GMaP
	'Berrybank Star'	GMaP
	bisetaea	SRms
	'Blauer Stern'	IVic
	'Blue Magic' PBR	LRHS
	'Blue Sea'	LRHS
	'Blue Silk'	EWes GKev IVic LRHS NHar SPoG WAbe
	brachyphylla	WAbe
	'Braemar' PBR	GMaP NHar
	'Cairngorm'	LRHS NHar
	× ***caroli***	WAbe
	clausa	GKev
	clusii	WAbe
	'Compact Gem'	EPot NHar WAbe
§	***cruciata***	EWTr LHop MMHG NLar
§	***dahurica***	ECho NGdn NLar XLum
	decumbens	GKev
	depressa	EPot WAbe
	'Devonhall'	IVic NHar NWad
	'Diana' PBR	LRHS
§	***dinarica***	ECho EPot NHar
	- 'Colonel Stitt'	WThu
	- 'Frocheneite'	EPot
	'Elehn'	NHar
	'Elizabeth'	CSam
	'Ettrick'	IVic NHar NHol
	'Eugen's Allerbester' (d)	GKev GMaP IVic LRHS NHar NHol NWad SPer SPoG WAbe
	'Eugen's Bester'	NHar
	farreri Silken Star Group	WAbe
	fetissowii	see *G. macrophylla* var. *fetissowii*
	'Gellerhard'	NHar
	'Gewahn'	IVic NHar
I	'Glamis Strain'	LRHS NHar
	'Glen Isla'	EWes
	'Glendevon'	WAbe
§	***gracilipes***	GKev MWat SPlb SRms XLum
	- 'Yuatensis'	see *G. macrophylla* var. *fetissowii*
	'Henry'	WAbe
	Inshriach hybrids	LRHS
	'Inverleith' ♀H4	EWes LRHS NHol SPlb
	'Iona' PBR	GAbr GMaP NCGa NHar
	'Joan Ward'	LRHS SPer SPoG
	kochiana	see *G. acaulis*
	kurroo	LHop
	- var. ***brevidens***	see *G. dahurica*
	lagodechiana	see *G. septemfida* var. *lagodechiana*
	ligustica	EPot
	'Little Diamond' PBR	LRHS NLar
	'Lucerna'	EPfP GKev LRHS NHol
	lutea	EBee GKev GPoy LLHF LRHS NBid NChi SMad SRms
	- subsp. ***symphyandra*** new	GKev
	× ***macaulayi*** ♀H4	CPla
	- 'Elata'	IVic NWad
	- 'Kidbrooke Seedling'	EWes GKev GMaP LRHS WAbe
	- 'Kingfisher'	CPla IVic LRHS NBir WAbe
§	- 'Wells's Variety'	LRHS
§	***macrophylla*** var. ***fetissowii***	ECho GKev LLHF
	makinoi 'Marsha' PBR	CHll LRHS MMHG NCGa NLar SPoG WCot
	- 'Royal Blue'	GAbr GCal WWEG
	'Margaret'	WAbe
	'Multiflora'	LRHS
	occidentalis	EPot
	olgae	EBee LHop
	olivieri	LLHF
	paradoxa	GKev LLHF NSla SBrt WAbe
	paradoxa × ***septemfida*** new	GKev
	phlogifolia	see *G. cruciata*
	pneumonanthe	EBee LRHS SPlb
	pumila subsp. ***delphinensis***	WAbe
	purdomii	see *G. gracilipes*
	robusta	GKev
	saxosa	EPfP ITim LRHS NBir NSla WAbe

scabra	LRHS
- 'Zuikorindo'	NLar
'Selektra'	IVic
septemfida ♀H4	EDAr EHyd GKev LHop LRHS MAsh MBri MJak MWat NBir SPlb SRms WGwG WHoo WKif
- 'Alba'	LLHF
- var. ***kolakovskyi***	LLHF
§ - var. ***lagodechiana*** ♀H4	LLHF LRHS SRms XLum
- - 'Select'	GKev
'Serenity'	IVic LRHS NWad WAbe
'Shot Silk'	CSam EWes GJos GMaP LRHS MGos NBir NCGa NHar NHol SPoG WAbe
'Silken Giant'	WAbe
'Silken Night'	NHar WAbe
'Silken Seas'	NHar WAbe
'Silken Skies'	NHar WAbe
'Silken Surprise'	WAbe
sino-ornata ♀H4	CPla CTri EBee ECho GKev GMaP LSRN MAsh MBri NCGa SRms WAbe
- SDR 5127	GKev LRHS MGos
- 'Alba'	CPla
- 'Angel's Wings'	LRHS
- 'Bellatrix'	IVic NHar
- 'Blautopf'	IVic
- 'Brin Form'	SRms
- 'Downfield'	GKev LRHS
- 'Edith Sarah'	IVic
- 'Oha'	IVic
- 'Purity'	LRHS WAbe
- 'Starlight'	NHar
I - 'Trotter's Form'	EWes
- 'Weisser Traum'	IVic LRHS NHol NLar SPer
- 'White Wings'	EWes
siphonantha	WAbe
'Sir Rupert'	IVic NHar
'Sternschuppe'	GKev
× ***stevenagensis*** ♀H4	CPla LRHS
§ - 'Bernardii'	NHar WAbe
- dark-flowered	WAbe
straminea	LLHF
'Strathmore' ♀H4	CSam EWes GKev GMaP LRHS NBir NCGa NHar NHol SPlb WAbe
'Suendermannii'	GKev
syringea	WAbe
ternifolia 'Cangshan'	WAbe
- 'Dali'	NHar
'The Caley' **new**	GMaP
tibetica	CArn CCon GPoy LRHS XLum
- PAB 2357 **new**	LEdu
triflora	LRHS
- 'Alba'	GKev LRHS
- var. ***japonica***	NLar WWEG
- 'Royal Blue'	LRHS
veitchiorum	WAbe
verna	ECho EDAr EHyd EPfP EWes LHop LRHS LSRN NPri NSla SPoG WAbe WPat
- 'Alba'	ITim WAbe WPat
- subsp. ***angulosa*** (Bieb.) V.E.Avet.	WIce
§ - 'Angulosa' hort. ♀H4	MAsh
- subsp. ***balcanica***	WPat
- subsp. ***oschtenica***	WAbe
- slate blue-flowered	LLHF
- subsp. ***tergestina***	WAbe
villosa	LHop
'Violette'	LRHS NHol
waltonii	EWes
wellsii	see *G.* × *macaulayi* 'Wells's Variety'
wutaiensis	see *G. macrophylla* var. *fetissowii*

Gentianella (*Gentianaceae*)

campestris **new**	GKev

Geranium ✿ (*Geraniaceae*)

from Bambashata, Altai Mountains	NCot
aconitifolium misapplied	see *G. palmatum*
aconitifolium L'Hér.	see *G. rivulare*
'Adam Moreland' **new**	WOut
'Alan Mayes'	CElw CMac CNec CSev ECtt EPPr EWoo GBin GBuc GKin LRHS LSou MNFA NGdn SRGP WCra WPtf
'Alan's Blue'	NChi
albanum	CElw EPPr LLWP MMuc MNrw SDix SRGP WMoo WPtf
albiflorum	WSpi
anemonifolium	see *G. palmatum*
'Ann Folkard' ♀H4	Widely available
'Ann Folkard' × ***psilostemon***	LSRN
'Anne Thomson' ♀H4	Widely available
× ***antipodeum*** 'Chocolate Candy' PBR	LBuc LRHS
- 'Kahlua'	EPfP
- 'Pink Spice' PBR	CWGN EBee EWoo GKin LBuc LRHS MGos SRms
- 'Sea Spray'	CMHG NBro WMnd
- 'Stanhoe'	ECtt
- (*G. sessiliflorum* subsp. *novae-zelandiae* 'Nigricans' × *G. traversii* var. *elegans*)	SRms
antrorsum	ECou
aristatum	EPPr EWes GCal MNFA MNrw MRav NBir SGbt SRGP WCru WMoo
armenum	see *G. psilostemon*
asphodeloides	CBre CElw CSev IFro MBNS MNrw MWhi NBid NBir NCot SGbt SPav SRGP WBrk WMnd WMoo WPnP
- subsp. ***asphodeloides*** white-flowered	CElw SRGP WMoo
- 'Starlight'	NBid
atlanticum Hook. f.	see *G. malviflorum*
'Aussie Gem'	EBee
'Azzurro' **new**	MAsh WHil
'Baby Blue'	see *G. himalayense* 'Baby Blue'
'Benjamin Browne'	CSev
'Bertie Crûg'	EBee ECtt EHoe ELon GKev LLHF NBir NLar SMrm SPer SPoG SRms SRot SWat SWvt WBor WCru
biuncinatum	IFro
'Blue Boy'	NLar
'Blue Cloud' ♀H4	Widely available
'Blue Pearl'	EPPr NBir NSti SRGP WMoo
§ Blue Sunrise = 'Blogold' PBR ♀H4	Widely available
'Blushing Turtle' **new**	NLar WHlf
'Bob's Blunder'	ECtt EPfP LLWG LRHS MBNS MBel MNrw MSCN SMrm SPoG SRGP SWvt WCot WCra WHoo WRHF
bohemicum	SRGP WHer
- 'Orchid Blue'	CSpe EPfP SWvt
'Breathless' **new**	NCot
'Brookside' ♀H4	Widely available
'Buckland Beauty'	CElw CExl

'Buxton's Blue'	see *G. wallichianum* 'Buxton's Variety'
caeruleatum	EPPr GCal NLar
caespitosum	LLHF
caffrum	CPla IFro SPlb SRGP
canariense	see *G. reuteri*
candicans misapplied	see *G. lambertii*
§ × ***cantabrigiense***	CMac CSBt ECtt IFro LPio LRHS MHer MNrw NBir NBro NPer NSti SMrm SRms WBrk WCru WMoo
- 'Berggarten'	EBee EPPr GBin SRGP WBrk WPtf
- 'Biokovo'	Widely available
- 'Cambridge'	CBcs CMHG CNec CPrp EBee ECtt ELan EPPr EPfP GAbr GKin LHop LRHS MCot MRav MSwo MWhi NCot SPer SWat SWvt WBrk WCra WMnd WMoo WPnP WPtf
- 'Harz'	EBee EPPr
- 'Karmina'	CFis EPPr EPfP LRHS MNFA MWhi SBod SHil SWat WBrk WHoo WMoo WPtf WWEG XLum
- 'Rosalina'	EPPr
- 'St Ola'	Widely available
- 'Vorjura'	EBee EPPr WBrk
- 'Westray' PBR	CHVG CMac CMea CNec COIW EBee ECtt EPPr EPfP EShb GAbr GBuc GLog GMaP LAst LSou MBel MHol MMuc NGdn NLar NPri NSti SEND SMrm SRkn SRms SWvt WCra WIce
'Catherine Deneuve'	STPC
'Chantilly'	CFis CLAP CSev EBee ECGP ECtt EPPr EPfP EWTr LRHS MAvo MNrw NBir NCGa NChi WCru WGwG WMoo WPtf
'Chipchase Castle'	NChi
christensenianum B&SWJ 8022	WCru
cinereum	CNec ECho WSpi
- 'Apple Blossom'	see *G.* × *lindavicum* 'Apple Blossom'
- 'Elizabeth'	ECtt GBuc LSRN
- subsp. ***nanum***	see *G. nanum*
- 'Sateene' PBR	EBee EPPr GMaP LRHS NDov SRot WCra
(Cinereum Group) 'Alice' PBR	EBee EPPr GMaP IPot LLHF LSRN MAsh MBNS NHar NLar NSti SRot WCra
- 'Ballerina' ♀H4	Widely available
- 'Carol'	CWGN ECtt EPPr EWes GKin LRHS LSRN LSou MBNS MSpe NCGa NHar NLar NSti SWvt WCra WHoo WSpi
- 'Lambrook Helen'	CExl CFis
- 'Laurence Flatman'	CExl CKno CPla ECtt EPfP EPri GBuc GMaP LAst LBMP LRHS LSou MAsh MGos NBid NEgg NHar NRya NSla SRms SRot SWat WAbe WHoo WMnd
- 'Lizabeth' PBR	ECtt EPPr GBin IPot LSou NHar NLar SMrm WCra WHil
- 'Prima Ballerina'	NLar
- 'Purple Pillow'	Widely available
- René Macé = 'Progera'	LRHS SRkn
- Rothbury Gem = 'Gerfos' PBR ♀H4	CWGN ECtt LLHF LRHS NChi SKHP SWvt
- 'Signal'	ECtt EPPr EPot MAsh MSCN NCGa NHar NLar
§ - 'Thumbling Hearts'	CHel CWGN IPot MBri
- Thumping Heart	see G. (Cinereum Group) 'Thumbling Hearts'
'Claridge Druce'	see *G.* × *oxonianum* 'Claridge Druce'
clarkei 'Kashmir Pink'	Widely available
§ - 'Kashmir White' ♀H4	Widely available
- 'Mount Stewart'	CExl WCru WPGP
- (Purple-flowered Group) 'Kashmir Purple'	Widely available
- Raina 82.83	MNrw
clarum B&SWJ 10246	WCru
collinum	EPPr NBir NCot SRGP WCru
'Colour Carousel'	EBee GBin
'Coombland White'	CCon CExl ECtt GBuc LBMP LSou MAvo MBel MCot MNrw NLar NSti SKHP SMrm SPer SRGP WCot WCra WMoo WPnP
'Criss Canning'	EPPr
'Cyril's Blue'	NChi
'Cyril's Fancy'	EBee EPPr
dahuricum	WCru
dalmaticum ♀H4	Widely available
- 'Album'	CHel EBee ECho ECtt ELan EPPr EPfP EPot GBuc LRHS MRav MSpe NDov NRya SBch SRGP SRms SWat WAbe WCra WCru
- 'Bressingham Pink'	ECtt EPPr
- 'Bridal Bouquet'	EPot LLHF NChi NCot NSla
- 'Stades Hellrosa'	EPPr
dalmaticum × ***macrorrhizum***	see *G.* × *cantabrigiense*
'Danny Boy' ♀H4 **new**	EBee
delavayi misapplied	see *G. sinense*
delavayi Franch.	WSpi
'Devon Pride'	CElw EBee EPPr
'Dilys' ♀H4	CElw CPrp ELan EPPr GBuc LPio MCot MLHP MNFA MNrw NBir NChi NDov NGdn NLar SRGP WCra WCru WHal WMoo WPnP
'Distant Hills'	CDes EBee EPPr SRGP
'Diva'	CSam EBee EPPr EPfP LLHF SRGP
'Doctor Geert Lambrecht' **new**	EBee
donianum	NSla
'Double Jewel'	see *G. pratense* 'Double Jewel'
Dragon Heart = 'Bremdra' PBR	CLAP CSev EBee ECtt EPPr EWoo IPot LSRN MAvo MBri MPnt NCGa NSti SKHP SPoG STPC WCAu WCra WHil WPtf
'Dusky Crûg'	CElw CLAP CSBt CSam ECtt EHoe ELan ELon EPPr EPfP EWTr GBBs GKin LAst MBel MCot MNrw MPie NEgg NOrc SMrm SPoG SWvt WCot WCra WCru WMnd
'Dusky Rose'	CHel CLAP CPrp CSpe ECtt ELan EPfP EWoo MBri NCGa NLar SRGP SRot WSpi
'Edith May'	EBee
'Elizabeth Ross'	MAvo
'Elke'	Widely available
'Ella'	CWGN
'Elworthy Eyecatcher'	CDes CElw CLAP EBee EPPr MNrw SRGP WPGP
'Elworthy Tiger'	CElw
'Emily'	SRGP
endressii ♀H4	CBre CElw CNec CSev ECho EPfP GAbr GLog GMaP LPot MBNS MCot MHer MMuc NBro NPer NPol SEND

		SPlb SRGP SRms SWvt WCra WHar WMoo WPtf WSpi WWEG XLum
	– 'Album'	see *G.* 'Mary Mottram'
	– 'Castle Drogo' ♀H4	EPPr SRGP
	– 'Prestbury White'	see *G.* × *oxonianum* 'Prestbury Blush'
	– 'Rose'	MAvo
	– 'Wargrave Pink'	see *G.* × *oxonianum* 'Wargrave Pink'
	erianthum	GMaP IMou MLHP NLar SRGP WCru WMoo
	– 'Axeltree'	WCot
	– 'Cally Pearl'	GCal
	– 'Calm Sea'	CDes WCru WMoo
	– 'Neptune'	CDes MNFA WCru WWEG
	– 'Pale Blue Yonder' **new**	EBee
	eriostemon Fischer	see *G. platyanthum*
	'Eureka Blue'	ECtt NCot NLar
	'Eva'	WPnP
	'Expression'	see *G.* 'Tanya Rendall'
	'Extravaganza'	EBee
	'Farncombe Cerise Star'	CElw
§	***farreri***	CExl ECho EPot LHop LLHF LRHS NBir
	'Fay Anna'	EPfP MBri NCGa WHil
	'Foundling'	NDov
	fremontii	EWld
	'Glenyell' **new**	SBch
	goldmannii	SKHP
	gracile	CFis EBee GMaP LRHS LSou MNrw NBir SRGP WBrk WCru WMoo WPtf
	– 'Blanche'	EPPr MNrw
	– 'Blush'	CElw EPPr LPla MNFA
	– 'Golden Gracile'	see *G.* 'Mrs Judith Bradshaw'
	grandiflorum	see *G. himalayense*
	'Grasmere'	ECtt
	'Gwen Thompson'	WOut
	gymnocaulon	CMac EPPr GKin LRHS SRGP WCru
	gymnocaulon* × *platypetalum	NCot
	'Harmony'	EBee EPPr
	harveyi	CMea ELan EWes LRHS NChi SPhx SRGP WKif WSpi
	hayatanum	WSpi
	– B&SWJ 164	NLar WCru WMoo
§	***himalayense***	CBcs CMHG COIW ELan EPfP LAst LPio LRHS MBNS MLHP MMuc MRav MWat NBir NBro SEND SPlb SRGP SRms SRot SWat WCot WMoo WPnP WSpi WWEG XLum
	– CC 1957 from Tibetan border	CExl EPPr
	– ***alpinum***	see *G. himalayense* 'Gravetye'
§	– 'Baby Blue'	CElw EBee ECtt ELon EPPr GBuc GCal GCra IFro LRHS MAvo MNFA MNrw NCot NGdn NLar NSti SBch SRGP WBrk WCAu WCra WCru WMoo WPnP WPtf
	– 'Birch Double'	see *G. himalayense* 'Plenum'
	– 'Derrick Cook'	CDes CElw CLAP CPrp EBee ECtt EPPr GBuc LPio MAvo MNFA MSpe MWhi NCot STPC WBrk WHoo
	– 'Devil's Blue'	EPPr SRGP WPtf
§	– 'Gravetye' ♀H4	Widely available
	– 'Irish Blue'	CElw EBee EPPr EWoo GBee GBuc GCal GCra IGor MSpe NCot NLar NPol NSti SRGP WCra WCru WMoo WPnP WPtf
	– ***meeboldii***	see *G. himalayense*
	– 'Pale Irish Blue'	EBee GCal NCot
§	– 'Plenum' (d)	Widely available
	ibericum misapplied	see *G.* × *magnificum*
	ibericum Cav.	CSBt CTri NBre NLar SPav SRGP
	– 'Blue Springs'	ECtt
	– subsp. ***ibericum***	CMac EPPr WPtf
	– subsp. ***jubatum***	EPPr LRHS MNrw SGbt SRms WCru WSpi
	– – 'White Zigana'	CDes CFis CNec CPrp EBee ECGP ECtt EPPr EPfP EWoo LRHS LSRN MAvo MNFA NLar WBor WPtf
	– subsp. ***jubatum* × *renardii***	SWvt
	– var. ***platypetalum*** misapplied	see *G.* × *magnificum*
	– var. ***platypetalum*** Boiss.	see *G. platypetalum* Fisch. & C.A. Mey.
§	– 'Ushguli Grijs'	EBee EPPr NCot NLar WCot WPtf
	ibericum* × *libani	CDes EBee
	incanum	CAbP CMHG ELon EShb EWes NBir SBrt SRGP SVen WSpi
	– white-flowered	SRGP
	'Ivan' ♀H4	CElw CLAP EBee ECtt EPPr GBuc LRHS NChi NLar SRGP WCru WMoo WPnP
	'Ivybridge Eyeful' **new**	CDes
	'Jean Armour'	CDes EBee ECtt GBuc LRHS NLar SPoG SRGP WCra WGwG WPGP
	'Johnson's Blue' ♀H4	Widely available
	'Jolly Bee'	see *G.* Rozanne = 'Gerwat'
	'Joy'	CLAP COIW CPrp EBee ECtt ELon EPPr GBin GBuc LRHS LSou MAvo MCot MNrw MRav NBir NCGa NChi NDov NEgg NLar NSti NWad SRGP SRms WCot WCra WMoo WPnP
§	'Kanahitobanawa'	EBee MAvo WCot
	'Karen Wouters'	EPPr NCot
	'Kashmir Blue'	CExl ECtt ELan EPPr EPfP GMaP LRHS NCot NGdn NLar NPnk SWat SWvt WKif WMoo WPnP WPtf WWEG
	'Kashmir Green'	CLAP EBee ECtt EPPr EPfP EWTr LLHF MAvo MBNS NSti WMoo WPnP
§	'Khan'	CFis EPPr IFro IPot LRHS MAvo NCot NPro SDys SRGP WBrk WCru
	'Kirsty'	EBee
	kishtvariense	GCal IMou LRHS MNrw MRav NSti WCru
	koraiense	NBre WMoo WPtf
	– B&SWJ 797	WCru
	– B&SWJ 878	CExl EBee WCru
	koreanum ambig.	CPla NLar WMoo
	– B&SWJ 602	CExl WCru
	krameri	IMou NLar
	– B&SWJ 1142	CExl WCru
	'Lakwijk Star'	EBee IPot MBri NCot NLar WCra
§	***lambertii***	EWes GBuc GCal LRHS NBir
	– 'Swansdown'	GBuc WCru
	lanuginosum	LRHS
I	***libani***	ELon EPPr LLWP LRHS MCot NBid NChi NSti WBrk WCot WSHC
	– RCB RL B-2	WCot
	libani* × *peloponnesiacum	WPGP
	'Libretto'	WCru
	'Light Dilys'	EPPr NDov
	'Lilac Ice' **new**	NLar

§	× ***lindavicum*** 'Apple Blossom'	CMea LRHS MAsh MSCN NSla
	- 'Gypsy' 🏆H4	CMea SBch
	linearilobum subsp. ***transversale***	SRot WCru WPnP
I	- - 'Laciniatum'	LWst
	- - 'Rose Foundling'	LWst
§	'Little David'	CElw EBee NLar
	'Little Devil'	see *G.* 'Little David'
	'Little Gem'	CMea EBee EPPr LRHS MAvo NChi NLar SBch WHoo WMoo
	lucidum	NCot WOut WPtf WSFF
	'Luscious Linda'	EBee MAvo NLar WPnP
	'Lydia'	SRGP
§	***macrorrhizum***	CArn CSBt ECrN ELon EPfP GKev GKin IFro LEdu MBNS MCot MLHP MRav MWat MWhi NBro NCGa NPnk SRms SWat WCAu WHar WHil WSpi WWEG XLum
	- AL & JS 90179YU	CHid EPPr
	- 'Album' 🏆H4	CBre CElw CSam ELan ELon EPPr EPfP GMaP LRHS MAsh MBel MBri MHer MNFA MSpe MSwo MWat NBid NBro NChi SPhx SWat WBrk WCot WCru WMoo WPtf WWEG
	- 'Bevan's Variety' 🏆H4	Widely available
	- 'Bulgaria'	EPPr WBrk
	- 'Cham-ce'	EPPr WBrk
	- 'Czakor'	Widely available
I	- 'De Bilt'	EWes WBrk
	- 'Freundorf'	EBee EPPr EWes GCal NCot WBrk
	- 'Ingwersen's Variety' 🏆H4	Widely available
	- 'Lohfelden'	CLAP EBee EPPr EWes GBuc GCal SRGP WCru
	- 'Mount Olympus'	see *G. macrorrhizum* 'White-Ness'
	- 'Mytikas' 🏆H4	EPPr WBrk WPtf
	- 'Pindus'	CLAP CPrp EBee EPPr GAbr GBuc LRHS MBNS MNFA NBre NDov NLar NSti SPoG SRGP WCra WCru WPtf
	- 'Prionia'	EPPr NCot WBrk
	- 'Purpurrot'	WBrk WWEG
	- 'Ridsko'	EPPr GCal LPla LRHS NBro SRGP WBrk WCru
	- ***roseum***	see *G. macrorrhizum*
	- 'Rotblut'	EPPr SRGP WBrk
	- 'Sandwijck'	EBee EPPr SBch WBrk
	- 'Snow Sprite'	CMea CPla EPPr EPot EPyc LLHF MHer NLar NPro WBrk WHrl
	- 'Spessart'	CBar CSev EBee ELan ELon EPPr EPfP EWoo GMaP LHop LRHS MBri MGos MMuc NLar SEND SGbt SPer SPhx SWvt WBrk WCra WHar WRHF WSpi WWEG XLum
	- 'Variegatum' (v)	CNec EBee ELan GMaP LEdu MNFA NBir SRGP SRms WBrk WCot WMnd WWEG
	- 'Velebit'	EPPr SRGP WBrk WCru XLum
§	- 'White-Ness' 🏆H4	Widely available
	- 'Witoscha'	LRHS
	macrostylum	WCot WCru
I	- 'Caeruleum'	WPtf
	- 'Leonidas'	EPPr WCot WPnP
	- 'Talish'	EPPr
	- 'Uln Oag Triag'	EPPr
	maculatum	CArn CElw CSev EPfP LRHS MAvo MCot MMHG MNrw MRav NSti SRGP SWat WCru WHal WPnP WSpi
	- from Kath Dryden	EPPr
	- f. ***albiflorum***	CLAP EBee ELan ELon EPPr EPfP EWoo LRHS MAsh MBel MNFA MNrw MWhi NChi NLar NSti SMrm SRGP WBrk WCru WMoo WPnP
	- 'Beth Chatto'	Widely available
	- 'Elizabeth Ann'PBR 🏆H4	CElw CLAP CMac COlW CSam CSev CWGN EBee ECtt EPPr EWoo GAbr LBMP LSou MTis NCGa NGdn NLar NSti SMrm SPoG WCot WCra WMoo WPGP WPnP WPtf WWEG
	- 'Espresso'	Widely available
	- 'Putnam County'	EPPr
	- 'Shameface'	EPPr WMoo
	- 'Silver Buttons'	CDes EBee
	- 'Smoky Mountain'	EPPr
	- 'Spring Purple'	CElw EBee EPPr MAvo NChi NLar
	- 'Sweetwater'	EPPr
	- 'Vickie Lynn'	CLAP EBee EPPr MAvo NChi
	maderense 🏆H2	CAbb CBcs CCon CHEx CPla CSpe CTsd ECre ELan EPfP EShb EUJe EWes IBoy LRHS NBir NPer SAPC SDix SPav SPhx SRGP SRkn SVen SWvt WCru
	- 'Guernsey White'	CCon SMrm SVen WCot WOut
	- white-flowered	CSpe LDai
	maderense × ***palmatum***	CHII
§	× ***magnificum*** 🏆H4	Widely available
	- 'Blue Blood'	CElw CLAP CSev EBee ECtt EPPr GAbr LRHS LSou MAsh MBNS MCot NGdn NSti SMrm SWvt WCot WCra WWEG
	- 'Ernst Pagels'	NCot
	- 'Hylander'	EPPr
	- 'Peter Yeo'	EBee EPPr MNFA SRGP WPtf
	- 'Rosemoor'	CElw CHid CNec EBee ECtt ELan EPPr EPfP GBin GCal IKil LRHS MWhi NPro SMrm SPer WCot WCra WMnd WPtf XLum
	- 'Vital'	XLum
	magniflorum	EWes GKev NBid NGdn WSpi
	'Maître Hugo'	EBee NCot
§	***malviflorum***	CFis CMHG ELan EPPr LLWP NCot SBch SBrt WCot WCru
	- from Spain	EWes WSHC
	- pink-flowered	EPPr
§	'Mary Mottram'	CElw EPPr LDai LPio WCot
	'Mavis Simpson' 🏆H4	Widely available
	maximowiczii	SBch WPtf
	'Maxwelton'	EBee
	'Melinda'PBR	CWGN EBee ECtt EPPr EWoo IPot MHol MNrw MTis NCot NDov NLar NMir WCot WCra
	'Memories'PBR	ECtt LRHS LSRN MBNS
	'Menna Bach'	MAvo
	'Meryl Anne'	SRGP WPtf
	microphyllum	see *G. potentilloides*
	'Midnight Clouds'	ECtt EPfP MAsh MAvo NCGa NSti STPC WCra WHil WPtf
	molle	NBir WSFF
	× ***monacense***	CPrp EBee ELan IFoB LEdu LRHS MBNS MWat SRGP SWat WCra WCru WMoo WPnP
	- var. ***anglicum***	CCon ECtt EPPr GMaP LRHS MRav MWhi NLar WMoo
	- 'Anne Stevens'	EBee WPtf
	- 'Claudine Dupont'	CElw EPPr IFro NCot NWad WCot
	- dark-flowered	WMoo
	- 'Emma White'	EBee EPPr NCot SBch
	- var. ***monacense***	NEgg WSpi

	– – 'Breckland Fever'	EBee EPPr NCot SRGP
§	– – 'Muldoon'	EPPr EPfP LRHS NBir SRGP WMoo WPnP
*	'Money Peniche'	XEll
	'Mourning Widow'	see *G. phaeum* 'Lady in Mourning'
	'Mrs Jean Moss'	EBee EPPr EWes NCot
§	'Mrs Judith Bradshaw'	EBee MNrw NChi NCot
§	***nanum***	WAbe
	napuligerum misapplied	see *G. farreri*
	'Natalie'	EBee EPPr LRHS LSRN MAvo NChi WPtf
	nepalense	SRGP SRms
	'Nicola'	CElw EBee EPPr IFro MAvo MNFA NLar SBch SRGP
	'Nimbus' ♀H4	Widely available
	nodosum	Widely available
	– 'Blueberry Ice'	CElw MAvo
	– 'Clos du Coudray'	EBee EPPr EWoo MAvo NCot NLar WCra
	– 'Dark Heart' **new**	MCot
	– dark-flowered	see *G. nodosum* 'Swish Purple'
	– 'Hexham Big Eyes'	CElw EWes MAvo
	– 'Hexham Face Paint' **new**	EPPr
	– 'Hexham Freckles'	EBee EPPr
	– 'Hexham Lace'	CElw EPPr
	– 'Julie's Velvet'	CDes CElw LEdu SBch WBor WHoo WPGP
	– pale-flowered	see *G. nodosum* 'Svelte Lilac'
	– 'Pascal'	EPPr
	– 'Saucy Charlie'	SBch
	– 'Silverwood'	CElw CLAP CWGN EBee EPPr EWoo LSou MAvo MNFA MTis NChi NLar NSti SBch SMrm SPoG WCot WCra WHoo WWFP
	– 'Simon'	SRGP
§	– 'Svelte Lilac'	CElw EPPr EPfP LAst LRHS LSou MNFA MNrw NBro NHol SRGP SWat WBrk WCAu WCru WMoo WPnP
§	– 'Swish Purple'	CElw EPPr NLar SRGP WCru WMoo WPGP WPnP
	– 'Tony's Talisman' **new**	EBee
	– 'Whiteleaf'	CElw CMac CMea EPPr GCal MNFA NChi SMrs SRGP WCru WHal WMoo WPGP WPnP
	'Northumberland Lavender Queen' **new**	EBee
	'Nunwood Purple'	EBee EPPr MAvo MNFA WPtf
	ocellatum	IFro
	'Old Rose'	LRHS MNFA SRGP WCru
§	***orientalitibeticum***	CCon CExl CMHG CSpe ECtt EPPr GAbr GKev IFro MCot MHer MMuc MSpe NBid NLar SEND SKHP SMad WCot WMoo WPtf WSpi WWEG
	'Orion' ♀H4	Widely available
	'Orkney Blue'	CElw EPPr WCru
	Orkney Cherry = 'Bremerry'PBR	CMac EBee ECtt EPPr EPfP EWTr GBin LLHF MBel NDov NSti SPoG SRkn SRms STPC
	'Orkney Dawn'	WCru WPnP
	'Orkney Mist' **new**	EBee
	'Orkney Pink'	EBee ECtt EHyd EPPr EPfP LEdu LHop LSRN MLHP NSti SPoG SRGP SWat
	'Out of the Blue'	WOut
	× ***oxonianum***	LRHS NCot WMoo
	– 'A.T. Johnson' ♀H4	CBcs EBee ECtt ELan EPPr EPfP GKin LAst LHop LRHS MNFA MRav MWat MWhi NBir NEgg NGdn NSoo NSti SMrm SPer SRGP SRms SWat SWvt WCra WCru WMnd WMoo WWEG
	– 'Andy's Star'	EBee NCot
	– 'Ankum's White'	CLAP
	– 'Anmore'	SRGP
	– 'Beholder's Eye' ♀H4	CPrp EPPr GAbr NLar SBch SRGP WPnP WPtf WWEG
	– 'Breckland Sunset'	EBee EPPr SBch SRGP
	– 'Bregover Pearl'	CBre CElw EPPr SRGP WMoo
	– 'Bressingham's Delight'	ECtt SRGP
	– 'Buttercup'	EBee EPPr SRGP
	– Caborn hybrids **new**	LLWP
I	– 'Cally Seedling'	EBee EWes GCal
	– 'Chocolate Strawberry'	EBee EPPr EWes
§	– 'Claridge Druce'	Widely available
	– 'Coronet'	CCon GCal SRGP WMoo
	– 'David Rowlinson'	EPPr SBch
	– 'Diane's Treasure'	EBee SBch
	– 'Elworthy Misty'	CElw EPPr SBch SRGP
	– 'Frank Lawley'	LLWP NBid NChi SBch SRGP WMoo
§	– 'Fran's Star' (d)	SRGP WBrk WCru
	– 'Hexham Pink'	EBee EPPr EWes NChi SBch SRGP
	– 'Hollywood'	EBee ELan EPPr EPfP NLar NPer SRGP SRms WMoo WPtf WWEG
	– 'Iced Green Tea' **new**	EPPr
	– 'Julie Brennan'	EBee GAbr SMrs
	– 'Kate Moss'	EPPr EWes NSti SRGP
	– 'Katherine Adele'	EBee ECtt EPPr EPfP EWes GCal LPla LSou MAvo MSpe MTis NCot NLar NSti SRGP SRms
§	– 'Kingston'	CElw EBee EPPr
	– 'Königshof'	EPPr EWes
	– 'Kurt's Variegated'	see *G.* × *oxonianum* 'Spring Fling'
	– 'Lace Time'	CBre CCon CPrp CSev EBee ECtt EPPr GBuc GKin LRHS LSRN MBri MSpe NEgg NHol SPer SPoG SRGP SRms WCra WMnd WMoo
	– 'Lady Moore'	LRHS NBro SRGP WMoo
	– 'Lambrook Gillian'	CFis EPPr SRGP WBrk
	– 'Lasting Impression'	EPPr SRGP
	– 'Laura Skelton'	CElw EBee NCot SBch
	– 'Little John'	EWes
	– 'Maid Marion'	EPPr EWes
	– 'Maurice Moka'	MAsh WCra
	– 'Miriam Rundle'	CElw EPPr LRHS SRGP WCru WMoo WWEG
	– 'Moorland Jenny'	CElw WMoo
	– 'Moorland Star'	WMoo
	– 'Mrs Molly Kisby' **new**	EBee
	– 'Music from Big Pink'	EBee EPPr EWes
	– 'Pat Smallacombe'	EBee WMoo
	– 'Patricia Josephine'	WCAu
	– 'Pearl Boland'	EBee EPPr SRGP
	– 'Phantom'	EBee EPPr
	– 'Phoebe Noble'	CBre CElw CPrp EBee EPPr LRHS MNrw NLar SRGP WMoo
	– 'Phoebe's Blush'	EPPr GCal GQue SRGP
	– 'Pink Cluster'	CLAP
	– 'Pink Lace'	LSou
§	– 'Prestbury Blush'	CElw EPPr NCot SRGP
	– 'Prestbury White'	see *G.* × *oxonianum* 'Prestbury Blush'
	– 'Raspberry Ice'	EBee EWes
	– 'Rebecca Moss'	CPrp EBee ECtt ELan EPPr GAbr GCra LRHS LSRN NCot NSti SMrm SRGP WCra WCru WOut WPtf WWEG

- 'Robin's Ginger Nut'	EBee EWes
- 'Robin's Red Eye' **new**	EPPr
- 'Rose Clair'	CCon ELan EPPr EPfP MBri MWhi NBir NLar SRGP WCru WMnd WMoo WWEG
- 'Rosemary'	SBch
- 'Rosemary Verey'	SBch
- 'Rosenlicht'	CPrp EBee EPPr EWoo GKin LRHS MAsh MRav NLar SRGP WCru WHoo WMnd WMoo WPtf XLum
- 'Rothbury Sarah'	EBee
- 'Sandy'	EWes
§ - 'Spring Fling' (v)	ECtt EWes LPla NSti NWad SRGP
- 'Stillingfleet Keira'	EBee NSti SRGP
- 'Summer Surprise'	EPPr EWes SBch WCru
- 'Susan'	EPPr EWes
- 'Susie White'	EPPr SRGP WCru
§ - f. ***thurstonianum***	Widely available
- - 'Armitageae'	EPPr SRGP
- - 'Breckland Brownie'	CElw EBee EPPr EWes SRGP
- - 'Crûg Star'	WCru
- - 'David McClintock'	EBee SBch SRGP WMoo
- - 'Peter Hale'	CMea
- - 'Red Sputnik'	EBee EPPr SRGP
- - 'Sherwood'	EPPr GCal GQue MBel MSpe NBro NEgg NSti SRGP WMoo
- - 'Southcombe Double' (d)	CLAP CNec CPla CWCL ECtt ELan EPPr EPfP GCra LRHS LSou MBri SBea SPer SPoG SRGP SRms WCra WCru WMoo WPtf WWEG
§ - - 'Southcombe Star'	EBee EPPr GAbr GCal LRHS NBro NGdn SRGP WCru WMoo WWEG
- - 'Sue Cox'	EPPr
- - 'White Stripes' **new**	EBee
- 'Trevor's White'	CLAP EBee EPPr LLWP LRHS MNFA SBch SRGP WCru
- 'Wageningen' ♀H4	CBre EBee EPPr GCal LPla LRHS LSou MBri MNFA NGdn NLar SEND SMrm SRGP SRms WCot WCra WCru WHoo WMoo WPtf
- 'Walter's Gift'	CNec ECtt EPPr EPri EShb EWoo LLWP LRHS LSou MAvo MHer MRav MWhi NBir NBro NCGa NDov NLar NPer SMrm WBrk WCru WHoo WMoo
§ - 'Wargrave Pink' ♀H4	Widely available
- 'Waystrode'	EPPr SRGP
- 'Westacre White'	EWes
- 'Whitehaven'	SRGP
- 'Whiter Shade of Pale'	EBee EPPr
- 'Winscombe'	EPfP GCal SRGP WMnd WMoo WWEG
§ ***palmatum*** ♀H3	CAbb CBcs CExl CHEx CMac CPla CSpe EHoe ELan EWoo GAbr GBin GBuc IBoy IFro IKil LRHS MPie NBro NPer SChr SDys SMrm SPhx SRkn WCru WKif WMoo WPGP
palustre	CElw EBee EPPr LRHS MMuc MNrw NCot SRGP WMoo WPtf
Patricia = 'Brempat' ♀H4	Widely available
peloponnesiacum	CElw EPPr EWes GQue LPio LRHS MAsh MNFA NOrc NWad WMoo WPtf
'Perfect Storm'	CLAP CWGN ECtt LLHF NCGa NLar STPC
phaeum	Widely available
- from Ploeger **new**	NCot
- 'Acorn Bank' **new**	EBee
- 'Advendo'	EBee EPPr NCot
- 'Album'	Widely available
- 'Alec's Pink'	EBee EPPr LLWP NCot SHar WOut WPtf
- 'All Saints'	EBee EPPr LEdu SRGP
- 'Angelina'	EBee EPPr NCot WPtf
- 'Aureum'	see *G. phaeum* 'Golden Spring'
- 'Blauwvoet'	EPPr LBMP NChi NCot
- 'Blue Shadow'	CDes CElw CLAP EBee EPPr LEdu LLWP SRGP WPtf
- 'Caborn Lilac'	LLWP
- 'Calligrapher'	CElw EPPr LLHF NChi NCot SMrs SRGP WMoo WPtf
- 'Chocolate Chip'	EPPr NCot WPtf
- 'Conny Broe' (v)	CLAP SBch
- 'Countess of Grey'	SMrs
- 'Dark Dream'	EBee
- dark-flowered	NCot
- 'David Bromley'	NCot WCru WPtf
- 'David Martin'	EBee EPPr NCot
- 'Enid'	EPPr
- 'George Stone'	EPPr LLHF WPtf
- 'Golden Samobor'	CElw EPPr SBch
§ - 'Golden Spring'	EBee EPPr MAvo NCot NPro SRGP
- 'Green Ghost' **new**	EBee EPPr
- 'Hannah Perry'	LLWP
- 'Hector's Lavender'	EBee NCot SRGP
- var. ***hungaricum***	EBee EPPr LLWP SRGP WPtf
- 'James Haunch'	EPPr
- 'Judith's Blue'	EBee EPPr NChi NCot
- 'Klepper'	EPPr GBin
§ - 'Lady in Mourning'	CExl EBee EPPr GCal MNFA NChi SRGP SRms SWat WCru WMoo
- 'Lavender Pinwheel'	CPrp EBee EPfP MBri MSpe NCot SPer SPoG WHil WPtf
- 'Lilacina'	WPtf
- 'Lily Lovell'	Widely available
- 'Lisa' (v)	CLAP EPPr MAvo MNrw NCot SBch WCot
- 'Little Boy'	EBee EPPr
- var. ***lividum***	CBre CPrp GMaP LLWP MRav NCot SRGP SRms WPnP XLum
- - 'Joan Baker'	CBre CFis CSam EBee EPPr LPla MNFA NChi NCot NGdn NSti SDys SPer SRGP WCru WMoo WPnP WWEG
- - 'Majus'	EBee ECtt ELan EPPr EPfP EPyc LLWP LPla LRHS WMoo
- 'Maggie's Delight' (v)	SRGP
- 'Marchant's Ghost'	IFro NGdn
- 'Margaret Wilson' (v)	CCon CDes CWGN EBee ECtt EPPr EShb EWes GAbr GCal LEdu LRHS MAvo MCot MNrw MSpe NEgg NGdn NLar NSti SBch SMrs SPer SPoG SRGP WCot WCra WMoo WPnP WSHC
- 'Mierhausen'	EBee EPPr NCot WPtf
- 'Mojito' (v)	WCot WCra
- 'Moorland Dylan'	WMoo WPtf
- 'Mottisfont Rose'	CLAP NCot SBch
- 'Mourning Widow'	see *G. phaeum* 'Lady in Mourning'
- 'Mrs Charles Perrin'	CElw CFis WPtf
- 'Night Time'	EBee EPPr WPtf
- 'Nightshade'	EBee EPPr WPtf WSpi
- 'Our Pat' ♀H4	CLAP EBee EPPr MAvo NChi WCot
- var. ***phaeum***	WPtf WSpi
- - 'Langthorns Blue'	CWCL EBee ELan EPPr EWes LEdu LRHS MNrw SRGP SWvt WPtf
- - 'Samobor'	Widely available
- 'Phantom of the Opera' (v)	EBee EPPr NCot

I	- 'Ploeger de Bilt'	EPPr WPtf
	- purple-flowered	NCot NPnk
	- 'Rachel's Rhapsody'	CElw EPPr MAvo NCot SRGP WPtf
	- 'Raven'	CLAP EBee ECtt EPPr EWoo MAvo NChi NCot NLar WCra WHlf WPtf
	- 'Ray of Light' **new**	EPPr
	- red-flowered	MRav
	- 'Rise Top Lilac'	EBee NCot WPGP WPtf
	- 'Robin's Angel Eyes' **new**	EBee
	- 'Rose'	LRHS
	- 'Rose Air'	EPPr MAvo SRGP WMoo
	- 'Rose Madder'	CCon CElw COlW EPPr EPyc GBuc GCal LEdu LLWP LPla MNrw NChi SBch SPhx SRGP WCru WMoo
	- 'Saturn'	EPPr WPtf
	- 'Séricourt'	CDes WCot
	- 'Shadowlight'	EPPr MTis NCot NLar WCra
	- 'Slatina'	EPPr WPtf
	- 'Springtime' [PBR]	EBee EPPr EPfP LLHF MBNS NChi NCot NGdn NLar
	- 'Stillingfleet Ghost'	EBee EPPr LEdu LRHS MNrw NChi NCot NSti
	- 'Taff's Jester' (v)	LPla NHol SRGP WCot
	- 'Trevor's Recall' **new**	EBee
	- 'Tyne Mist' **new**	EPPr
§	- 'Variegatum' (v)	CBre CMac EBee EHoe ELan EPPr GMaP IFro LRHS MCot MRav MSpe NBir NBro NCot NEgg NPro SRGP WCru WHer WMoo
	- 'Vintage Dave'	WOut
	- 'Walküre'	CSev EPPr EWes EWoo NCot NLar WPtf
	'Philippe Vapelle'	Widely available
	'Pink Carpet'	NDov
	'Pink Delight'	CElw CMea LPio MNrw SBch
	'Pink Penny'	CLAP EBee EPPr EPfP LRHS NCGa SRGP STPC WCra WMoo WPtf
§	***platyanthum***	EPPr MNrw MWhi SRGP WCru WPtf
	- var. ***reinii***	WCru
	- 'Russian Giant'	EPPr
	platypetalum misapplied	see *G. × magnificum*
	platypetalum Franch.	see *G. sinense*
§	***platypetalum*** Fisch. & C.A. Mey.	EPPr LRHS NBir SRGP WCru XLum
	- 'Genyell'	EBee EPPr
	- 'Georgia Blue'	WCru
	- 'Turco'	EBee EPPr NLar
§	***pogonanthum***	CHid GLog NBir
§	***potentilloides***	NBir SRGP WMoo
	pratense	CArn CBre CHab CMac CNec EBee ECtt ELan EPPr GJos GMaP MHer MLHP MNHC NCot NMir SPer SPlb SPoG SRGP SRms SWat WCot WMoo WPnP WSFF WWEG XLum
	- 'Akaton'	NLar
	- 'Bittersweet'	EPPr
	- Black Beauty = 'Nodbeauty' [PBR]	CBcs CExl CSBt CSev CWCL CWGN ECtt EPfP EWes IPot LRHS LSRN MGos MPnt NCGa NLar NPri SMrm SPer SPoG SRkn SRot SWat WCot WHoo WSpi
	- 'Blue Lagoon'	EBee EPPr MAsh
*	- 'Blue Skies'	LSou WSpi
	- 'Cluden Sapphire'	EBee EPPr GQue MAsh MWhi NChi NHol NPro WCru WSpi
§	- 'Double Jewel' (d)	CWCL CWGN EBee EPfP IPot LLHF LRHS MAsh MBNS MBri NCGa NLar WBor WCra WPtf
	- 'Else Lacey' (d)	CDes EBee
	- 'Flore Pleno'	see *G. pratense* 'Plenum Violaceum'
I	- 'Himalayanum'	NLar
	- 'Hocus Pocus'	CWGN ECtt ELan EPfP EWoo LRHS MAsh MAvo MBNS MBri NBro NLar NSti WCra
	- 'Ilja'	EBee
	- 'Janet's Special'	WHoo
	- 'Midnight Blues'	GBin MAsh NCGa NSti SMrm WCra
	- Midnight Reiter strain	Widely available
	- 'Milk Cow Blues' **new**	EBee
	- 'Mrs Kendall Clark' ♀H4	Widely available
	- 'New Dimension'	CBcs EBee ELan MAsh MBri NSti WHoo
	- 'Okey Dokey'	EBee
	- 'Pennine Cloud'	CSev
	- 'Pink Splash'	EPPr LSou WMoo WPtf
	- 'Plenum Album' (d)	CLAP ECtt ELan EPPr EPfP EWes GBin LLHF MBel MNrw NEgg NGdn NLar SGbt SPer SWvt WBor WCra WPtf WWEG
	- 'Plenum Caeruleum' (d)	CMHG ECtt EPPr GCra MRav NBid NEgg NLar SWat WSHC
§	- 'Plenum Violaceum' (d) ♀H4	Widely available
	- var. ***pratense*** f. ***albiflorum***	CElw CSam EPPr EWTr EWoo GCra GMaP IFro LRHS MNrw NBid NOrc SGbt SMrm WMnd WMoo WPtf
	- - - 'Galactic'	CLAP CMea COlW ECtt EPPr LRHS MHol NBir NCot NLar SMrm SPhx WCot WCra WCru WMoo WPnP WSpi
	- - - 'Laura' [PBR] (d)	CExl CWCL EBee EPPr EWes LRHS LSRN LSou NSti SKHP SMrm SPoG WCra
	- - - 'Plenum Album' (d)	CDes EBee EPPr STes WCot WPnP
	- - - 'Silver Queen'	EBee ECtt EPPr GQue LRHS LSou NBir NBre SRGP WCra WMoo WPGP WPtf
	- 'Purple Heron'	CDes LSRN
*	- 'Purple-haze'	CPla CTca MCot WMoo WTou
	- 'Rectum Album'	see *G. clarkei* 'Kashmir White'
	- 'Robin's Grey Beard' **new**	EBee
§	- 'Rose Queen'	EPPr MRav NBir NHol SGbt SRGP WCru
	- 'Roseum'	see *G. pratense* 'Rose Queen'
	- 'Splish-splash'	see *G. pratense* 'Striatum'
	- 'Stanton Mill'	NBid
	- var. ***stewartianum***	EBee MRav
	- - 'Elizabeth Yeo'	CLAP ECGP ECtt EPPr EWoo NLar NWad WCra WCru
	- - 'Purple Silk'	EPPr
	- - 'Raina' **new**	EBee
§	- 'Striatum'	Widely available
	- 'Striatum' dwarf	WCru
	- 'Striatum' pale-flowered	CBre
	- variegated, white-flowered (v)	WCot
§	- Victor Reiter Junior strain	CPrp CSev CSpe ELan GKev LEdu LRHS MLHP MMHG MNFA NBir NGdn SPoG SRot WCot WCru WPtf
	- 'Wisley Blue'	EPPr SBch SRGP WHal
	- 'Yorkshire Queen'	EBee EPPr NGdn NSti WCru
	'Prelude'	CBre CElw CSev EBee ELon EPPr NBir NCot NPro SRGP WPtf
	procurrens	CBre CElw COlW CTri EPPr EShb GAbr GCal GCra LLWP LRHS WBor WBrk WCru WMoo WPtf
§	***psilostemon*** ♀H4	Widely available

- 'Bressingham Flair'	CCon CKno CLAP EPfP GAbr GBuc GCra LRHS MRav NBid NLar SPer SRms WCru WMoo
- 'Coton Goliath'	EPPr EWes NCot
- 'Jason Bloom'	EPPr LRHS
- 'Madelon'	CElw EBee NCot
- 'Moorland Jack'	WMoo
'Midnight Star'	EBee EWes
pulchrum	CFil CSpe EBee EWes EWld LRHS SRGP WPGP
punctatum hort.	see *G.* × *monacense* var. *monacense* 'Muldoon'
- 'Variegatum'	see *G. phaeum* 'Variegatum'
'Purple Rain'	EBee EPPr NChi
pylzowianum	MRav NBid NRya SBch WMoo
pyrenaicum	GAbr NBre NCot NSti WTou
- f. ***albiflorum***	GAbr IFro MNrw NBir SRGP WBrk WCot WTou
- 'Barney Brighteye'	SRGP
- 'Bill Wallis'	Widely available
- 'Bright Eyes'	LLWP NCot
- 'Isparta'	EPPr IFro LPla NCot SBch SHar SPhx SRGP WBrk WTou
- 'Summer Sky'	GBin SPav SRGP
- 'Summer Snow'	CCon NLar
'Rainbow'PBR	EWoo MBNS WCra
Rambling Robin Group	CSpe ECre EHoe EPri EWes LLHF NLBP
'Ray's Pink'	CPla
rectum	EPPr NBre NLar WCru
- 'Album'	see *G. clarkei* 'Kashmir White'
'Red Admiral'	EBee ECtt EPPr GBuc GCal LRHS MAvo NCot NSti SRGP
reflexum	CFis CPrp EPPr WCru
- 'Katara Pass'	EPPr
refractum	CExl
regelii	EPPr LRHS WCru WMoo WPtf
renardii ♀H4	Widely available
- 'Beldo'	MAvo
- blue-flowered	see *G. renardii* 'Whiteknights'
- 'Rothbury Hills'	EBee EPPr
- 'Sarah Comish' **new**	EBee
- 'Tcschelda'	CMHG CNec ECtt EPPr EShb GBuc LRHS NBir SMrm SRms WCra WMoo WPtf
§ - 'Whiteknights'	EBee NBir WCru
- 'Zetterlund'	CFis EBee ELan EPPr EPfP EPri EWTr LHop LPio LRHS NEgg NSoo NSti WBrk WCra WMnd WMoo WPtf
§ ***reuteri***	CPla LDai SRGP WCru WOut
'Richard Nutt'	EBee
richardsonii	CSpe EBee EPPr GCal LRHS MCot NBir NBre NDov NWad SRGP WCra WCru WPtf
- pink-flowered	MAvo
- white-flowered	NChi
× ***riversleaianum*** 'Russell Prichard' ♀H4	Widely available
§ ***rivulare***	GLog NBre NLar WMnd WPtf
robertianum	CArn EPPr LLHF MHer SRms WSFF
§ - 'Album'	EPPr SHar SRGP SRms WHer
- f. ***bernettii***	see *G. robertianum* 'Album'
- 'Celtic White'	CBre EPPr GCal IFro SPav SRGP
robustum	EPri LRHS MGos NBir NBro SKHP SPav SPlb SRGP WKif
'Rosetta'PBR	EBee LRHS NCGa NLar
'Rosie Crûg'	SWvt
rosthornii	WCru
'Rothbury Red'	LLHF MBri NChi SBch
§ Rozanne = 'Gerwat'PBR ♀H4	Widely available
rubescens	see *G. yeoi*
rubifolium	MNFA WCru
§ 'Ruprecht'	LRHS
ruprechtii misapplied	see *G.* 'Ruprecht'
ruprechtii (Grossh.) Woronow	EPPr MNrw NBre SRGP
Sabani Blue = 'Bremigo'PBR	CAbP CLAP CMac CSev CSpe EBee ECtt EPPr EWes EWoo GAbr LBMP LPla MHol NLar NSti SPer SPoG WCot WHil
'Salome'	CAby CBcs CLAP CSev EBee ECtt ELan EPfP GAbr LHop LRHS MCot NBir NPri NSti SPoG SRms SRot SWat SWvt WCot WCra WGwG WHoo WMoo WPnP WWEG
'Sandrine'PBR	CBcs CLAP CSev CWCL CWGN EBee EPfP GBin IPot LLHF LRHS LSou MHol MNrw NDov NPri NSti SGol SMrm SPoG SRms WCot WCra WPnP
sanguineum	Widely available
- Alan Bloom = 'Bloger'PBR	EBee EPPr LHop LRHS
- 'Album' ♀H4	Widely available
- 'Alpenglow'	EBee EPPr SRGP WBrk
- 'Ankum's Pride' ♀H4	CElw CPrp EPPr EPfP LHop LRHS LSou MNFA MTis NCGa NDov NGdn NHar NLar NSti SBch SMrs SRGP SWat WBrk WCra WCru WMoo WPnP WPtf
- 'Apfelblüte'	EPPr GJos IPot NLar
- 'Aviemore' ♀H4	CElw CFis EPPr GCal
- 'Barnsley'	CElw CPrp EPPr NBro NPro WHrl
- 'Belle of Herterton'	EPPr MAvo NBid NPro WBrk WCru
- 'Bloody Graham'	EPPr MAvo MNFA WBrk WMoo
- 'Canon Miles'	CElw EPPr IPot LRHS NLar SRGP
- 'Catforth Carnival'	EBee EPPr MAvo
- 'Cedric Morris'	CElw ELon EPPr GCra LRHS MAvo MNFA NBid SBch SMrs SRGP WBrk WCru
- 'Compactum'	EBee WMoo XLum
§ - 'Droplet'	SRGP
- 'Elsbeth'	CElw CNec CPrp EBee ECtt ELan EPPr EWes GCal LRHS MSpe NDov NGdn NLar NSti SPoG SRGP WBrk WCru WHal WMoo WPnP WWEG XLum
- 'Feu d'Automne'	EBee EPPr
- 'Fran's Star'	see *G.* × *oxonianum* 'Fran's Star'
- 'Glenluce'	CElw CMea CPrp EBee ECtt EPPr EPfP GBuc GCal LHop LRHS MAsh MRav MSpe NDov NOrc NWad SRGP SRms SWat WBrk WCra WHal WMnd WSpi
- 'Hampshire Purple'	see *G. sanguineum* 'New Hampshire Purple'
- 'Holden'	CElw EBee EPPr WBrk
- 'Inverness'	EBee EPPr XLum
- 'Joanna'	CFis MAvo
- 'John Elsley'	CPrp EBee ECtt EHoe EPPr LAst LLWP LRHS LSou MAsh MNFA MSpe MWhi NBro NDov NGdn SRGP SWat WMnd WPnP WWEG
- 'John Innes'	EPPr
- 'Jubilee Pink'	GCal WCru
- 'Kristin Jacob'	EPPr
- var. ***lancastrense***	see *G. sanguineum* var. *striatum*
- 'Leeds Variety'	see *G. sanguineum* 'Rod Leeds'

§	– 'Little Bead' ♀H4	ECho NWad WBrk XLum
	– 'Max Frei'	Widely available
	– 'Minutum'	see *G. sanguineum* 'Droplet'
	– 'Nanum'	see *G. sanguineum* 'Little Bead'
§	– 'New Hampshire Purple'	CLAP CPrp ECtt EPPr GLog IPot LAst MAvo MNFA NBro NGdn NLar NSti WCra
	– 'Nyewood'	CNec CPrp EBee ECGP ECtt EPPr EWll LRHS MSpe NDov SEND SRGP WBrk WCru
I	– 'Plenum' (d)	EPPr
	– 'Prado'	XLum
	– 'Pride of Coombland'	SMrs
	– var. ***prostratum*** (Cav.) Pers.	see *G. sanguineum* var. *striatum*
	– 'Purple Flame'	see *G. sanguineum* 'New Hampshire Purple'
§	– 'Rod Leeds'	CFis CLAP EBee MNFA SRGP
	– 'Sara'	MAvo
§	– 'Shepherd's Delight' **new**	EPPr
	– 'Shepherd's Warning' misapplied	see *G. sanguineum* 'Shepherd's Delight'
	– 'Shepherd's Warning' ♀H4	CTri ECtt GCal MMuc NBir NLar SEND SRGP SWat WCru WHoo WIce
	– 'Shooting Star'	NCot
	– 'South Nutfield'	CElw
§	– var. ***striatum*** ♀H4	Widely available
	– – deep pink-flowered	CSBt MSwo SWvt
	– – 'Mottisfont'	SBch
	– – 'Reginald Farrer'	WCru
	– – 'Splendens' ♀H4	CElw CSev CWib EBee EPPr GCal LHop LRHS NBid NCot WCru
	– 'Tirol' **new**	EBee
	– 'Vision Light Pink'	EPPr
	– 'Vision Violet'	CSpe EBee EPPr IFoB MAvo MSpe SWvt WBrk XLum
	– 'Westacre Poppet'	EWes
	'Sanne'	EWoo MAsh MAvo MBri MHol NLar SMrm WCot WCra WRHF
	saxatile	EBee EPPr
	'Scapa Flow'	EBee EPPr GCal MAvo
	schlechteri	EWes
	sessiliflorum	ECou
I	– subsp. ***novae-zelandiae*** 'Nigricans'	CFis ECho ELan GAbr GKev MHer NLar SBch SRGP
§	– – 'Porters Pass'	ECho EHoe EWes SBch SPlb WHoo
	– – red leaved	see *G. sessiliflorum* subsp. *novae-zelandiae* 'Porters Pass'
	shikokianum	CLAP EBee GKev NLar SRGP WHrl WPtf
	– var. ***kaimontanum***	WCru
	– var. ***quelpaertense***	CDes CFis MAvo
	– – B&SWJ 1234	WCru
	– var. ***yoshiianum*** B&SWJ 6147	WCru
	'Shocking Blue'	EPPr NLar NSti
	'Shouting Star'	see *G.* 'Kanahitobanawa'
	'Silva'	CElw ECtt EPPr MNFA MNrw MRav SWat WCru
*	'Silver Shadow'	SPhx
§	***sinense***	CCon CExl ECtt EPfP GBuc GCal LRHS MCot MNrw NGdn SRGP WCra WGwG XLum
	'Sirak' ♀H4	Widely available
	soboliferum	ELan EPPr LRHS NBir SBch SPer SRGP WCru WMoo WPtf
	– Cally strain	CDes EBee EPPr GCal MAvo
	– var. ***kiusianum***	CElw

	– 'Starman'	EBee ECtt EPPr EPfP EWoo LSou MBri MSwo NCGa NLar SKHP SPoG STPC WCra WMoo
	'Solitaire'	CDes CFil CGHE EBee WCot
	'Southcombe Star'	see *G.* × *oxonianum* f. *thurstonianum* 'Southcombe Star'
	'Spinners'	Widely available
	stapfianum var. ***roseum***	see *G. orientalitibeticum*
	'Stephanie'	CDes CElw CSev EBee EPPr EPfP EWes GBuc LPio LRHS LSRN MAvo MBNS MNFA MNrw MSpe NCot NGdn NLar NSti WCra WPnP WPtf
	'Storm Chaser'	CLAP CMac CSpe GBin LRHS NSti
	'Strawberry Frost'	LLHF
	subcaulescens ♀H4	Widely available
	– from Mount Kithairon, Greece **new**	EFar
	– 'Giuseppii' ♀H4	CExl CHel EBee ECtt ELon EPot GAbr GBuc GKev LSou MAsh MHer MRav NDov NLar NPnk NPri SMrm SRGP SRot SWvt WHrl
	– 'Splendens' ♀H4	CSpe CTri ECtt EPPr GBuc LHop LRHS LSou MCot MHer NEgg NPri NSla SRms SWat WGwG WSpi
	'Sue Crûg'	CHel CPrp ECtt ELan EPfP EShb GCra LAst LLWG LLWP LRHS LSou MNFA MWhi NDov NEgg NHol NLar NSti SBch SPer SPoG SRGP SRkn WCru WHoo WMoo
	'Sue's Sister'	WCru
	'Summer Cloud'	EPPr MNFA SRGP WOut
	Summer Skies = 'Gernic'PBR (d)	Widely available
	suzukii	WTuf
	– B&SWJ 016	CExl WCru
	'Sweet Heidy'PBR	CSev EBee ECtt EPPr LBMP LLHF LRHS MSwo NCGa NLar NSti SPoG WBor WCra WHil
	sylvaticum	LPio NBid NGdn NMir WMoo WShi
	– 'Afrodite'	EPPr
	– f. ***albiflorum***	CBre CElw ELan EWoo NSti WCru
	– – 'Cyril's Superb White' **new**	EBee
	– 'Album' ♀H4	Widely available
	– 'Amanda'	EBee EPPr
	– 'Amy Doncaster'	Widely available
	– 'Angulatum'	CElw EPPr MNFA WMoo
	– 'Birch Lilac'	CElw CLAP EBee EPPr EPfP GBuc GCal LRHS NLar NPnk WMoo
	– 'Caeruleum'	GCal
	– 'Coquetdale Lilac'	EBee EPPr NChi
	– 'Greek Fire' **new**	EBee EPPr
	– 'Ice Blue'	EBee EPPr MNFA NChi
	– 'Immaculée'	EPPr MRav
	– 'Kanzlersgrund'	CElw EPPr
	– 'Lilac Time'	EPPr
	– 'Mayflower' ♀H4	Widely available
	– 'Meran'	EPPr LRHS
	– 'Nikita'	CLAP EPPr SBch
	– f. ***roseum***	CFis EPPr NBre NLar WPtf
	– – 'Baker's Pink'	CLAP EBee EPPr GCra MNFA MNrw MRav NBir SBch SRGP WCru WMoo
	– subsp. ***sylvaticum*** var. ***wanneri***	EPPr WCru
§	'Tanya Rendall'PBR	CMHG CSam EBee ECtt ELan ELon EPPr GBin IPot LRHS MBri MHol NDov NLar SPer SPoG SRms WCot WCra WPnP WWEG
	'Terre Franche'	EPPr MAvo NLar SMrs WWEG

§ ***thunbergii***	CCon CHid EWes EWll LSou NLar SRGP WMoo WPnP XLum
- 'Jester's Jacket' (v)	CPla LRHS MAvo MGos MLHP MNrw SRGP WCot WOut WSpi
- pink-flowered	SRGP
- white-flowered	EPPr SRGP
thurstonianum	see *G.* × *oxonianum* f. *thurstonianum*
'Tinpenny Mauve'	WHoo
'Tiny Monster'	CFis EBee ECtt EPPr EWes GBin GQue IBoy IKil MAvo MNFA MNrw MWhi NDov NGdn NSti SPhx WBrk WCot XLum
transbaicalicum	CFis EPPr LRHS XLum
traversii	CWib
- var. ***elegans***	CWib LRHS
tuberosum	CElw CHid EBee ECho ELan EShb MRav NBir NBro NCot NGdn NLBP SBch SKHP SPhx WSpi
- 'Richard Hobbs' **new**	EPPr
- 'Rosie's Mauve'	MAvo
'Ushguli Grijs'	see *G. ibericum* Cav. 'Ushguli Grijs'
'Verguld Saffier'	see *G.* Blue Sunrise
versicolor	CMac CMea COIW EBee EPPr EPfP GAbr LRHS MHer MMuc NCot SRms WMoo
- 'Kingston'	see *G.* × *oxonianum* 'Kingston'
§ - 'Snow White'	EPPr MNrw SRGP WCru WMoo
- 'The Bride'	CMea
- 'White Lady'	see *G. versicolor* 'Snow White'
'Victor Reiter'	see *G. pratense* Victor Reiter Junior strain
violareum	see *Pelargonium* 'Splendide'
viscosissimum	EBee SRGP WMnd
- var. ***incisum***	LRHS
wallichianum	CFis CMac CPou EBee IFro NBir NSti WMoo
§ - 'Buxton's Variety' ♀H4	Widely available
- 'Chris'	EWes SRGP
- 'Crystal Lake'PBR	CHel CWGN ECtt EPfP EWoo IPot LAst LSou MBNS NBir NSti WCra WHil WPtf
- 'Havana Blues'	EPPr EWoo GBin MBri STPC WCot
- magenta-flowered	GBuc
- pale blue-flowered	CElw
- 'Pink Buxton'	EWes NLar
- pink-flowered	CLAP GBuc GCal WCru
- 'Rise and Shine'PBR	EBee EWTr EWoo WCot
- 'Rosetta'	EPPr
- 'Rosie'	LRHS SRGP
- 'Syabru'	CMea LRHS MNrw NLar WMoo
- 'Sylvia's Surprise'PBR	CLAP
wilfordii misapplied	see *G. thunbergii*
Wisley hybrid	see *G.* 'Khan'
wlassovianum	Widely available
- 'Blue Star'	IPot MRav NPro SRGP
§ ***yeoi***	CSpe NBir NBro NSti SRGP WCru WOut
yesoense	EBee NBir NSti SRGP
- var. ***nipponicum***	WCru
yoshinoi misapplied	see *G. thunbergii*
yunnanense misapplied	see *G. pogonanthum*
yunnanense ambig.	CCon

Gerbera (*Asteraceae*)

(Everlast Series) Everlast Carmine = 'Amgerbcar'	ELon EUJe LHop LRHS LSou MBNS SMrm
- Everlast Honey **new**	MBNS WHil WHlf
- Everlast Orange = 'Amgerbora'	LRHS
- Everlast Pink = 'Amgerbpink'	LRHS LSou MBNS SHar WHil
- Everlast White = 'Amgerbwhi'	LHop LRHS SHar SMrm
- Everlast Yellow	LHop LSou
(Garvinea Series) 'Fleurie'PBR	MBNS WHil
- Garvinea Lisa = 'Garlisa'PBR	WHlf
- Garvinea Orangina = 'Orangina'PBR	SPoG WHlf
- Garvinea Rachel = 'Garrachel'PBR	MNrw WCot WHlf
- Garvinea Sylvana = 'Garsylvana'PBR	WCot
- Garvinea Valerie	WHlf
- 'Sunny'PBR **new**	WHlf

Gesneria (*Gesneriaceae*)

cardinalis	see *Sinningia cardinalis*

Gethyllis (*Amaryllidaceae*)

afra 'Paarl'	ECho
barkerae	ECho
- 'Nardouwsberg'	ECho
- subsp. ***paucifolius***	ECho
britteniana 'Rietputs'	ECho
ciliaris	ECho
- 'Porterville'	ECho
grandiflora	ECho
gregoriana	ECho
hallii 'Komiesberg'	ECho
linearis 'Piketburg'	ECho
oligophylla 'Moedverloor'	ECho
transkarooica 'Waboomsberg'	ECho
verticillata	ECho
- 'Pikenierskloof'	ECho
villosa	ECho

Gethyum (*Alliaceae*)

atropurpureum	WCot

Geum ✿ (*Rosaceae*)

'Abendsonne'	CDes CElw EBee MAvo MSpe NPro SBri WOut WWEG
aleppicum	NBre
alpinum	see *G. montanum*
andicola	NBre
'Apricot Beauty'	CWCL
'Apricot Delight'	LLHF NPro
'Beech House Apricot'	CAby CElw CLAP ECtt EPri GCra LRHS MAvo MNFA MNrw MRav NCGa NChi NHol NLar NPro SBri SPoG WMoo WPnP WWEG
'Bell Bank'	Widely available
'Birkhead's Creamy Lemon'	CElw EBee MAvo NBir SBri
'Blazing Sunset' (d)	Widely available
'Blood Orange'	MAvo NPro
N 'Borisii'	Widely available
'Bremner's Gold'	NPro SBri
'Bremner's Nectarine'	CElw MNrw MSpe MTis NChi NPro WWEG
'Broomrigg Beauty'	MAvo NPro
bulgaricum	CElw EBee MRav NBir NLar NPro NRya WWEG XLum
'Butterscotch'	EBee SBri
calthifolium	EPPr LRHS MRav NBre NBro

capense	NBre NPro SPlb
§ ***chiloense***	LEdu
– 'Farncombe'	NCot
– 'Red Dragon'	CBre CWCL ELon LLHF LSRN NBre SWvt WOut WWEG
'Chipchase'	MAvo NChi NPro SBri SHar WHoo WWEG
coccineum misapplied	see *G. chiloense*
coccineum ambig.	NCGa
coccineum Sibth. & Sm.	EPri MSpe
'Ann'	
– 'Cooky'	CElw CHel EPfP GJos LBMP LRHS MSCN NGBl NLar NPro SHil SPad SPoG SRms SWvt WRHF WWEG
– 'Eos'	CDes CElw CSpe CWCL EBee ECtt ELon EPPr EWes GAbr LEdu LHop MAsh MAvo MHol MNrw MPnt NGdn NLar NPri NPro SPoG WCot WMoo WWEG
– 'Koi'	LBuc
– 'Queen of Orange'	CBre CNec GBin MAsh NPro SRot
– 'Werner Arends'	CMHG GAbr GCal MAvo MBri MNrw MRav NDov SBri WMoo WWEG
'Copper Pennies'	NPro
'Coppertone'	CElw CLAP CPla CWCL ELan EPri LRHS MRav NBir NBro NCGa NChi NRya SBri XEll
'Cotton Candy'	MAvo NPro WWEG
'Country Rock Star' **new**	NPro
'Cream Crackers'	NPro
'Custard Pie'	NPro WWEG
'Dawn'	SBri
'Deano's Delight'	NPro
'Diana'	EBee MAvo MNrw NLar NPro SBri WWEG
'Dingle Apricot'	CElw ECtt GAbr GBin MNrw MRav NBir WWEG
'Dolly North' (d)	CCVN EBee EPyc GAbr MArl MCot MNrw MRav MSpe NBro NGdn SBri SHar WCAu WHal WWEG
'Eden Valley Angel' **new**	NPro
'El Wano' **new**	NPro
elatum	GKev
'Elizabeth'	SBri
'Elworthy Amber'	CElw MAvo
'Emory Quinn'	NPro WWEG
'Fancy Frills'	CElw WWEG
'Farmer John Cross'	CAby CBre CDes CElw CLAP EBee ECtt ELon EPri GJos LPla MAvo MNrw MSpe MTis NCGa NCot NLar SBri WHal WMoo WWEG
fauriei* × *kamtschatica	EBee
'Feuermeer'	CElw NLar NPro SBri
'Fire Opal' (d) ♀H4	CDes CElw CWCL EBee LPla MNrw NBir NBre NPro SBri WMoo WWEG
'Fire Storm' **new**	CWGN MBel MPnt MTis NLar WCot
'Fireball'	ECtt EShb LRHS LSou MAvo NBre NLar
'Flame'	NPro SBri WWEG
'Flames of Passion'[PBR]	Widely available
'Fresh Woods'	WWEG
'Georgeham'	CPla
'Georgenberg'	CElw CLAP CPrp CSam ECtt EPfP EPri GMaP LAst LRHS MBel MCot MHer MNrw MRav NBir NBre NGdn NHol NLar NWad SBea SBri SRms SWvt WCAu WGwG WHoo WMoo WWEG
'Glencoe'	CElw
'Golden Joy'	WHoo WWEG
'Hannay's'	MAvo MNrw MSpe NPro SBri SHar WWEG
'Herterton Primrose'	CCon CDes CElw CLAP CWCL EBee ECtt EPPr GBuc GCal LLHF LLWG MAvo MSpe NCGa NSti SBri WHal WHoo WWEG
'Hilltop Beacon' (d)	CElw LLHF MAvo NPro SBri WHoo
* ***hybridum luteum***	NSti SBri
× ***intermedium***	CBre EPPr NGdn NLar NPro SBri WMoo WWEG
– 'Diane'	CDes GJos MSpe NBre NChi SBri
– 'Hofrennydd'	NWad
'Jolly Roger'	EBee NPro WWEG
'Karlskaer'	CDes CElw CWCL ECtt EPri EWes GBin GBuc GQue LHop LRHS MAsh MBel MBri MCot MNrw MSpe NGdn NLar SBea SBri WCot WGwG WMoo WNew WPtf WWEG
'Kashmir'	SBri
'Kath Inman'	SBri WWEG
'Kathryn'	CDes
'Lady Stratheden' (d) ♀H4	Widely available
'Lemon Delight'	CElw
'Lemon Drops'	Widely available
'Lionel Cox'	CElw COIW CPla CPrp CWCL ECtt ELan EPPr EWTr GCal GCra GMaP LAst LBMP MBNS MCot MNFA MRav NBir NBro NChi NGdn NLar NPnk SRGP SRms WWEG
'Lipstick Sunset' **new**	NPro
'Lisanne'	CElw CSam EBee IPot MAsh MAvo MSpe NCGa NDov SBri WWEG
'Little Lottie'	NPro
'Little Twister'	NPro WWEG
macrophyllum	EBee
magellanicum	EWes NBre NLar
'Magic Toybox'	NPro
'Mai Tai'	CHel IBoy MAvo MTis WCAu WHlf
'Mandarin' (d)	CCon CCse CDes GAbr GCal SBri
'Mango'	SBri
'Mango Lassi'	CElw MAvo WCAu
'Marmalade'	CSev ECtt EPri GAbr GJos LLWG MAvo MNrw MSpe NBre NCGa NLar NPnk NPro WHrl WKif WMoo WOut WWEG
'McClure's Magic' **new**	NPro
§ ***montanum*** ♀H4	EBee ECho EDAr GBin GCra GKev LRHS MMuc NBir NBro NPri NRya NSla SEND SPet SRms WWEG XLum
– SDR 5495	GKev
'Moonlight Serenade'	EBee NPro WWEG
'Moorland Sorbet'	NPro SBri WMoo WPtf WWEG
'Mrs J. Bradshaw' (d) ♀H4	Widely available
'Mrs W. Moore'	CBre CDes CElw CLAP CWCL EBee ECtt EPPr EShb GAbr GJos LDai MHer MNrw NBir NCGa NChi NLBP NLar NPnk NPro SBri SRGP WHoo WMoo WWEG
'Nordek'	CElw ECtt GAbr GBuc GCal GJos LAst LRHS MAsh MNFA MNrw MRav NEgg NGdn SBri SPoG WWEG
'Norwell Yellow Lamp'	MAvo
'Octavie'	SBri
'Orangeman'	MNrw
parviflorum	NBre NBro

	'Peachy Proud'	NPro WWEG
	'Pear Drops' **new**	NPro
	pentapetalum	see *Sieversia pentapetala*
	- 'Flore Pleno' (d)	WAbe
	'Pink Frills'	CElw CWCL ECtt EPPr EPri EWTr EWes GAbr GBin GBuc GQue LLWG LPla MAvo MPnt MRav MSpe MTis NCGa NLar SBri SGbt SMrm WWEG
	'Poco'	EBee MAvo NPro SBri
	'Pomelos'	SBri
	'Present'	CElw ECtt MAvo NBre NCGa NChi NPro SBri WWEG
	'Primrose'	GAbr GJos GQue NGdn NLar NPro SBri
	'Prince of Orange' (d)	CElw GAbr LRHS MNrw MRav NBre SBri WHrl WWEG
	'Prinses Juliana'	Widely available
	pyrenaicum	EBee NBre NCGa
	quellyon	see *G. chiloense*
I	'Rearsby Hybrid'	CElw LLHF MRav NPro SPlb WHoo WWEG
	'Red Wings' (d)	EPPr GBin GBuc GCal GMaP GQue LRHS MAsh MCot MRav NBir NCGa NDov NSoo SBri SHar SPoG WGwG WWEG
§	***reptans***	GBin
	rhodopeum	EBee LLHF
	'Rijnstroom'	ELan EPPr LDai MNrw SHar WCAu WPtf
	rivale	CArn CBAq CHab COlW EHon EPfP MCot MHer MHol MNHC MWts NBro NMir NPer SPet SPlb SRms SWat WMAq WMoo WOut WWEG
	- 'Album'	Widely available
	- 'Apricot'	SBri
	- 'Barbra Lawton'	MSpe SBri WWEG
	- 'Cream Drop'	CElw LLWG MAvo MCot MSpe NCGa NChi NPnk NPro SBri SMrm WWEG
*	- ***islandicum***	SBrt
	- 'Leonard's Double' (d)	CPrp CSev WWEG
	- 'Leonard's Variety'	Widely available
	- 'Marika'	CCVN CHid EBee EPri LRHS NBre NCGa SBri SMrm SRGP WMoo WWEG
	- 'Marmalade'	CAby CBre CElw CWCL EBee IPot MPnt NChi NPro SBri WPtf WWEG
	- 'Snowflake'	CElw MAvo MSpe NPro WWEG
	'Rubin'	ECtt EPPr EPyc GCra IPot NBre NBro NDov SBri
	'Rusty Young'	MAvo NPro
	'Savanna Sunset'	MAvo NPro WWEG
	'Sigiswang'	CDes CElw EBee EWes GAbr GJos MNrw MRav NBre NPro SBri SMrm WCAu WWEG
	'Spider Muffin' **new**	NPro
	'Stacey's Sunrise'	NPro SBri
	'Star of Bethlehem'	NPro WWEG
I	'Starker's Magnificum'	WCot WWEG
	'Strawberries and Cream'	NPro
	'Sundrud Star' **new**	NPro
	'Sunrise' (d)	EDAr
	'Sweet Angel Dar'	NPro WWEG
	'Tangerine'	EPri LSou MRav MSpe NPro SBri WWEG
	'Tango Dream'	WWEG
	'Tequila Sunrise' **new**	MTis
	'Tinkerbell' **new**	NPro
	'Tinpenny Orange'	CElw NPro SBri WWEG
	× ***tirolense***	EBee MAvo NBre NCGa NPro
	'Totally Tangerine'PBR	CSpe EPfP EWTr LBuc LRHS MCot SHar
	'Trevor's Lemon'	MAvo
	triflorum	CElw EShb MAvo MNrw NLar NPnk SPhx WOut
	- var. ***campanulatum***	CCon NPro WWEG
	'Turbango'	NPro
	'Turnpike Troubadour'	NPro
	urbanum	CArn CHab GJos SWat WHer WHfH WMoo
	'Wallace's Peach'	SBri

Gevuina (*Proteaceae*)

avellana	CBcs CHEx CHel WPGP

Gilia ✿ (*Polemoniaceae*)

achilleifolia	SPhx
californica	see *Leptodactylon californicum*
tricolor	NPol

Gillenia (*Rosaceae*)

stipulata	CLAP IPot LEdu MNrw SPhx
trifoliata ♀H4	Widely available
- 'Pink Profusion'	STPC

Ginkgo (*Ginkgoaceae*)

	biloba ♀H4	Widely available
	- B&SWJ 8753	WCru
	- 'Anny's Dwarf'	MAsh NLar SBig
	- 'Autumn Gold' (m)	CBcs CDul CEnd CMCN EBee ECrN LAst LLHF MBlu MGos MPkF NLar SBig SLim
	- 'Barabits' Fastigiata' **new**	ESwi
I	- 'Barabits Nana'	SBig
	- 'Beijing Gold'	IVic MBlu MPkF NLar SBig
	- 'Broom with Tubes' **new**	SMad
	- 'California Sunset'	MBlu SBig
	- 'Chase Manhattan'	MPkF
	- 'Chi-chi'	MPkF SBig SLim
	- 'Chotek'	SBig
	- 'Chris' Dwarf'	NLar
	- 'Doctor Causton' (f)	CAgr
	- 'Doctor Causton' (m)	CAgr
	- 'Eastern Star' (f)	CAgr
	- 'Elsie'	SBig
	- 'Everton Broom'	NLar SLim
	- 'Fairmount' (m)	MBlu SBig
	- 'Fastigiata' (m)	CMCN EBee EPfP ESwi MBlu MGos SBig
	- 'Globosa'	MBlu
	- 'Gnome'	ESwi LSRN MGos MPkF
	- 'Golden Globe'	ESwi MPkF
	- 'Gresham'	MPkF
	- 'Horizontalis'	MBlu SBig
	- 'Jade Butterflies'	MBlu MBri MPkF NLar SBig SLim
	- 'Jehosaphat' **new**	NLar
	- 'Jerry Vercade'	MPkF
	- 'King of Dongting' (f)	CAgr ESwi MBlu SBig
	- 'Lakeview' (m)	MPkF SBig
	- 'Mariken'	ELan EPfP ESwi GKin LRHS MPkF NLar SBig SLim SLon
	- 'Mayfield' (m)	SBig
	- 'Menhir'	ELan MBri MPkF
	- 'Montezuma'	SBig
	- 'Obelisk' **new**	NLar
	- Ohazuki Group (f)	CAgr SBig

- Pendula Group	CEnd CMCN ESwi MAsh MBlu MPkF SBig SGol
- 'Pendula Gruga'	SBig
- 'Pixie'	SBig
- 'Princeton Sentry' (m)	EBee IVic LLHF NLar SBig SMad
- 'Robbie's Twist'	MPkF SBig
- 'Santa Cruz'	SBig
- 'Saratoga' (m)	CAgr CBcs CEnd CJun CMCN EBee EPfP ESwi LRHS MBlu MBri MPkF SBig SEND SLim SMad SSpi
- 'Shangri-La' (m)	MBlu
- 'Sinclair'	MPkF
- 'Survivor' **new**	SMad
- 'Tit'	CEnd CMCN EPfP ESwi NLar SBig
- 'Tremonia'	CMCN EPfP MBlu MPkF NLar SBig SLim
- 'Troll'	CDoC MAsh MBlu NLar SBig SCoo SLim SMad
- 'Tubifolia'	CMCN ESwi MBlu MPkF NLar SBig
- 'Umbrella'	SBig
- Variegata Group (v)	CBcs CJun ESwi MGos MPkF NLar SBig SPoG
- 'W. B.'	MPkF SBig
- 'Weeping Wonder' (f)	SBig

ginseng see *Panax ginseng*

Gladiolus (*Iridaceae*)

sp.	MNrw
acuminatus	WCot
'Akuta' (M/E)	CGrW
alatus	ECho
- 'Rawsonville'	ECho
'Alba' (N)	CGrW
'Alexandra' (P)	WCot
'Amanda Mahy' (N)	GKev
'Amsterdam' (G)	CGrW
angustus	CDes WCot
antakiensis	CPou
'Anyu S' (L)	CGrW
'Atom' (S/P)	CAvo CBro CGrW ECho EPot WCot
aureus	WCot
Barnard hybrids	CGrW
'Beautiful Angel'	CGrW
'Beauty Bride' (L)	CGrW
'Big Boss' (G)	CGrW
'Black Star'	EPfP ERCP SPer
'Blackbird' (S)	CGrW
'Blue Frost' (L)	SDeJ
'Bonfire' (G)	CGrW
'Boone'	GBin SMrm WCot
'Break of Dawn'	SDeJ
brevifolius 'Somerset West'	ECho
- 'Villiersdorp'	ECho
byzantinus	see *G. communis* subsp. *byzantinus*
caeruleus	WCot
- 'Saldanha'	ECho
callianthus	see *G. murielae*
'Cardinal' **new**	SPer
cardinalis	CDes CRDP GCal IBlr LEdu SKHP WCru
carinatus	CDes CGrW ECho WCot
carinatus* × *huttonii 'Purple Spray'	WCot
carinatus* × *orchidiflorus	WCot
'Carine' (N)	EBee GKev SDeJ
carmineus	CGrW ECho WCot
carneus	CGrW EBee ECho EPot GCal SDeJ
caryophyllaceus	CGrW ECho
'Charm' (N/Tub)	CBro EPot LEdu SDeJ
'Charming Beauty' (Tub)	ECho EPot SDeJ
'Charming Lady' (Tub)	ECho
'Cindy' (B)	ECho
citrinus	see *G. trichonemifolius*
'Claudia' (N)	CGrW EBee GKev
'Columbine' (P)	SDeJ
× ***colvillii***	CMea IBlr
- 'Albus'	ERCP GKev
- 'The Bride' ♀H3	CAvo CBro CElw CHel EBee GKev LDai LEdu LSRN SDeJ SPhx
§ ***communis***	Widely available
subsp. ***byzantinus*** ♀H4	
'Coral Lace' (L) **new**	SDeJ
'Côte d'Azur' (G)	CGrW
'Cotton Queen' (L)	CGrW
crassifolius	ECho
'Cream Perfection' (L)	CGrW SDeJ
'Creamy Yellow' (S)	CGrW
'Cristabel'	WCot
cunonius	WHil
§ ***dalenii***	CGrW CPou EBee ECho IBlr WCot
- 'Apricot Delight' (v)	IBlr
- 'Citrone Spectrum' (v)	IBlr
- subsp. ***dalenii***	CPrp IBlr
- green-flowered	IBlr
- 'Guardsman' (v)	IBlr
* - f. ***rubra***	IBlr
- yellow-flowered	EBee
'David Hills' (*papilio* hybrid)	CDes NCGa WCot WHal
'Delirium'	CGrW
densifolius	ECho
'Dion' (M)	CGrW
'Dixon' (L)	CGrW
ecklonii	ECho
- 'Mount Thomas'	ECho
'Elvira' (N)	ECho GKev
'Emerald Spring' (S)	WCot
'Esta Bonita' (G)	CGrW
'Excel' (L)	CGrW
'Extasy'PBR (L)	CGrW
'Farondole'	SDeJ
'Felicita' (L)	CGrW
'Fidelio' (L)	CSut SDeJ
'Finishing Touch'PBR (L)	CGrW
flanaganii	CDes CExl CMea CPBP CSpe EBee ECho GCal LLHF NSla SChr WAbe WCot
- JCA 261.000	SKHP
'Flevo Cosmic' (Min)	CGrW SMrm
'Flevo Dancer' (S)	CGrW
'Flevo Eclips'PBR (G)	CGrW
'Flevo Frizzle'	CGrW
'Flevo Junior' (S)	CGrW
'Flevo Libre'PBR (L)	CGrW
'Flevo Primo'PBR (S)	CGrW
'Flevo Shine' (M)	CGrW
'Flevo Smile' (S)	WCot
'Flevo Souvenir'PBR (L)	CGrW
'Flevo Spirit'	CGrW
'Flevo Sunset'PBR (L)	CGrW
floribundus hort.	ECho
- subsp. ***fasciatus***	CGrW
fourcadei	CGrW ECho
'Frangine' (L)	CGrW
'French Silk' (L)	CGrW
× ***gandavensis*** hort.	GBin
geardii	WCot

'Gold Struck' (L)	CGrW
'Good Luck' (N)	CBro
gracilis	ECho WCot
grandis	see *G. liliaceus*
'Green Star' (L)	CGrW EBee ERCP SDeJ
'Green Woodpecker' (M)	EBee
gueinzii 'Mossel Bay'	ECho
'Halley' (N)	ECho GKev
'Happy Weekend' (L)	SDeJ
hirsutus	CGrW ECho
'Holland Pearl' (B)	ERCP SDeJ
'Huron Silk' (L)	CGrW
huttonii	CDes CGrW ECho WCot
huttonii* × *liliaceus	CDes
huttonii* × *tristis	CPou
huttonii* × *tristis var. ***concolor***	CDes WCot
hyalinus	CGrW
'Ibadan'[PBR] (L)	CGrW
'Ice Cream'	SPer
illyricus	ECho GCal WShi
imbricatus	ECho
'Impressive' (N)	CBro GKev SDeJ
'Indian Summer'[PBR]	CGrW
inflatus	CGrW ECho
- 'Ceres'	ECho
involutus	CGrW
- 'Mossel Bay'	ECho
§ ***italicus***	CGrW CHid EBee ELan EPfP GCal GKev SKHP WHil XLum
'Jacksonville Gold' (L)	SDeJ
'Jayvee' (S)	CGrW
'Jester' (L)	SDeJ
kotschyanus	EBee ECho
'Kristin' (L)	CGrW
'Lady Lucille' (M)	CGrW
'Las Vegas'	GKev
'Lavender Flare' (S)	CGrW
'Lavy Linda' (L)	CGrW
'Lemon Drop' (S)	CGrW
leptosiphon	CGrW
- 'Molenaars River'	ECho
§ ***liliaceus***	CGrW ECho WCot
- 'Caledon'	ECho
'Little Wiggy' (P)	CGrW
longicollis	ECho
'Loulou' (G)	CGrW
'Mademoiselle de Paris'	ERCP
'Marj S' (L)	CGrW
'Match Point' (L)	SDeJ
meliusculus	ECho
'Mexico'	CSut SDeJ
miniatus	CDes
'Mirella' (N)	CAvo GKev MRav
'Mon Amour'[PBR]	CGrW SDeJ
monticola	EBee
mortonius	GCal
'Mr Chris' (S)	CGrW
§ ***murielae*** 🏆H3	CAvo CBro CGrW CMea CPrp ECho EPfP EPot ERCP EWll LRHS MCot SCoo SDeJ SHil SPer SPet SPhx SPlb STes WHal WHoo
natalensis	see *G. dalenii*
'Nathalie' (N)	CGrW EBee GKev SDeJ
'Nori' (M)	ERCP
'Nova Lux' (L)	SDeJ
'Nymph' (N)	CAvo CHel EPot GKev LDai LEdu LPio SDeJ
'Oasis'[PBR] (G)	CGrW
ochroleucus	WHil
§ ***oppositiflorus***	CDes IBlr LEdu SChr SPlb WHil
- subsp. ***salmoneus***	see *G. oppositiflorus*
orchidiflorus	CGrW ECho
'Oscar' (G)	ERCP
palustris	CDes CRDP
papilio	Widely available
§ - Purpureoauratus Group	CBro EBee IBlr SRms
- yellow-flowered	CMea SMad
'Parade' (G)	CGrW
'Passos'[PBR]	CSut EPfP ERCP
'Peach Blossom' (N)	IBlr
'Peach Melba' (L)	CGrW
'Perseus' (P/Min)	ERCP
'Perth Pearl' (M)	CGrW
'Peter Pears' (L)	CSut SDeJ
'Phyllis M' (L)	CGrW
Pilbeam hybrids	CGrW WCot
'Plum Tart' (L)	ERCP
'Pop Art'	SDeJ
primulinus	see *G. dalenii*
'Prins Claus' (N)	CBro CTca EPot GKev
'Prinses Margaret Rose' (Min)	CSut SDeJ
priorii 'Dasberg'	ECho
'Priscilla' (L)	MLHP SDeJ
pritzelii	CGrW
- 'Quaggasfontein'	ECho
'Purple Flora'	ERCP SPer
'Purple Prince' (M)	CGrW
purpureoauratus	see *G. papilio* Purpureoauratus Group
quadrangularis	CGrW ECho
'Raspberry Swirl' (L/E)	CGrW
recurvus	CGrW ECho
'Robinetta' (*recurvus* hybrid) 🏆H3	CWCL ECho EPot LDai SDeJ
'Roma' (L)	CGrW
'Ruby' (*papilio* hybrid)	CAby CAvo CBro CDes CMea CPen CPou CPrp CTca EPri LEdu LSRN NCGa NChi SMad WHil WHoo
'Rusty Red' (P)	CGrW
'Ruth Ann'	CGrW
Sancerre (B/L)	EPfP
saundersii	CDes GCal WHil
'Scarlet Lady' (P)	CGrW
scullyi	CGrW
- 'Ceres Karoo'	ECho
segetum	see *G. italicus*
sericeovillosus	IBlr
'Slick Chick' (S)	CGrW
'Smoke 'n' Mirrors'	CGrW
'Solveiga' (L/E)	CGrW
'Sophie'[PBR]	CGrW
'Spic and Span' (L)	SDeJ
'Spinners'	CDes IBlr WCot
splendens	CDes CGrW WPGP
- 'Roggeveld'	ECho
'Stiena' (L)	CGrW
'Tan Royale' (P)	CGrW
'Teamwork' (L)	CGrW
'Terry' (G)	CGrW
'That's Love' (L) **new**	SDeJ
'Trader Horn' (G)	CGrW SDeJ
§ ***trichonemifolius***	CGrW ECho
tristis	CAvo CBro CDes CElw CGHE CGrW CPou CPrp ECho ELan ELon GCal GKev WHal WHil WPGP
- var. ***concolor***	CGrW CPou CPrp WCot
undulatus	CDes CGrW ECho WCot

uysiae	CGrW ECho
- 'Gannaga'	ECho
vandermerwei	CGrW ECho
'Velvet Eyes' (M)	SDeJ
venustus	CGrW ECho
'Video' (L)	CGrW
'Violetta' (M)	CGrW SDeJ SMrm
virescens	CGrW
- 'Ceres'	ECho
watermeyeri	CGrW
watsonioides	SKHP WCot
'Wax Ruffles' (L/E)	CGrW
'White Prosperity' (L)	CSut ERCP SDeJ
'Yellow Gem'	SDeJ
'Zamora' (L)	CGrW

Glandularia see *Verbena*

Glaucidium (*Ranunculaceae*)

palmatum ♀H4	CExl CWCL EBee EFEx EPot GBuc GKev NSla WCru WHal
- 'Album'	see *G. palmatum* var. *leucanthum*
§ - var. ***leucanthum***	EFEx GKev

Glaucium (*Papaveraceae*)

§ ***corniculatum***	CAbP CCon CSpe EWld LRHS SPhx
flavum	CArn CCon CSpe ELan MHer SMrm SPav XSen
- ***aurantiacum***	see *G. flavum* f. *fulvum*
- f. ***flavum***	LLHF
§ - f. ***fulvum***	LRHS SDix SMrm WCot XSen
- orange-flowered	see *G. flavum* f. *fulvum*
- red-flowered	see *G. corniculatum*
phoenicium	see *G. corniculatum*

Glebionis (*Asteraceae*)

coronaria	MNHC
§ ***segetum***	CHab

Glechoma (*Lamiaceae*)

hederacea	CArn GPoy MHer NMir WHer
- 'Barry Yinger Variegated' (v)	EBee
§ - 'Variegata' (v)	SPer SPet XLum

Gleditsia (*Caesalpiniaceae*)

caspica	CArn LEdu
japonica	EPfP NLar
koraiensis	LEdu
triacanthos	CDul CWib IDee LEdu SPlb
- 'Calhoun'	CAgr
- 'Emerald Cascade'	CBcs CEnd EBee
- 'Goofy' **new**	SMad
- f. ***inermis*** Spectrum = 'Speczam'	LRHS MAsh MBri WHar
- 'Millwood'	CAgr
- 'Rubylace'	CBcs CCVT CDul CEnd CLnd CMCN CSBt EBee ECrN ELan EPfP EWTr IVic LAst LSRN MBlu MBri MGos MRav MSwo NLar NPri SGol SKHP SLim SPer
- 'Sunburst' ♀H4	Widely available

Globba ✿ (*Zingiberaceae*)

racemosa var. ***hookeri*** HWJCM 471	WCru

Globularia (*Plantaginaceae*)

albiflora	EPot
bellidifolia	see *G. meridionalis*
bisnagarica	GKev
cordifolia ♀H4	ECho EDAr EPot GKev LRHS NBir WCot XSen
- 'Alba'	NHar
incanescens	XSen
§ ***meridionalis***	ECho EPot EWes GKev GMaP MWat SIgm
- 'Blue Bonnets'	NHar
- 'Hort's Variety'	NSla WAbe
nana	see *G. repens*
nudicaulis	ECho GKev
punctata	CCon SRms XSen
pygmaea	see *G. meridionalis*
§ ***repens***	ECho NHar WAbe
stygia	XSen
trichosantha	SRms XSen
valentina	EPot GKev
vulgaris	XSen

Gloriosa (*Colchicaceae*)

lutea	see *G. superba* 'Lutea'
rothschildiana	see *G. superba* 'Rothschildiana'
superba ♀H1	ERCP SDeJ
- 'Carsonii'	ERCP SDeJ
- 'Greenii'	ERCP SDeJ
§ - 'Lutea'	SDeJ
§ - 'Rothschildiana'	CBcs CGrW SDeJ SRms WCot
- 'Simplex'	CLak
- 'Verschuurii'	CLak

Gloxinia (*Gesneriaceae*)

sp.	EABi
nematanthodes **new**	CDrt
sylvatica 'Bolivian Sunset'	WDib

Glyceria (*Poaceae*)

aquatica variegata	see *G. maxima* var. *variegata*
maxima	MMuc MSKA NPer SPlb
§ - var. ***variegata*** (v)	CBAq CWCL CWat EHoe EHon ELan EPfP EShb EWay GCra GMaP IBoy LHop LRHS MBlu MMuc MWhi NGdn NOrc NWsh SMrm SPer SRms SVic SWat WMAq WMoo WWEG XLum
notata	SVic
spectabilis 'Variegata'	see *G. maxima* var. *variegata*

Glycyrrhiza (*Papilionaceae*)

§ ***glabra***	CArn CCCN CHby EBee ELau GPoy MHer MHoo MNHC NLar SDix SRms WHfH WJek
glandulifera	see *G. glabra*
uralensis	CArn EBee ELau GPoy MHer NLar SPhx
yunnanensis	CSpe

Glyptostrobus (*Cupressaceae*)

pensilis	CExl CFil SLim WPGP

Gmelina (*Lamiaceae*)

hystrix	CCCN

Gnaphalium (*Asteraceae*)

'Fairy Gold'	see *Helichrysum thianschanicum* 'Goldkind'
trinerve	see *Anaphalis trinervis*

Godetia see *Clarkia*

Gomphocarpus (*Apocynaceae*)

§	***physocarpus***	CArn CDTJ

Gomphostigma (*Scrophulariaceae*)

	virgatum	CAbP CExl CFis CSpe EPPr IDee LLWG LSou MHol MNFA SMrm SPlb WCFE WCot
	- 'White Candy'	NLar SVen

Gomphrena (*Amaranthaceae*)

	globosa	CCCN

Goniolimon (*Plumbaginaceae*)

	collinum 'Sea Spray'	CFis EDAr WHil
§	***incanum***	SMrm
	speciosum	EDAr LLHF
§	***tataricum*** var. ***angustifolium***	SRms
	- 'Woodcreek'	NLar

Goodia (*Papilionaceae*)

	lotifolia	CCCN

Goodyera (*Orchidaceae*)

	biflora	EFEx
	pubescens	EFEx
	schlechtendaliana	EFEx

gooseberry see *Ribes uva-crispa*

Gordonia (*Theaceae*)

	axillaris	see *Polyspora axillaris*

granadilla see *Passiflora quadrangularis*

granadilla, purple see *Passiflora edulis*

granadilla, sweet see *Passiflora ligularis*

granadilla, yellow see *Passiflora laurifolia*

grape see *Vitis*

grapefruit see *Citrus* × *paradisi*

Graptopetalum (*Crassulaceae*)

	filiferum	CDoC EUJe SPlb
§	***paraguayense***	CDoC SEND SVen
	'Superbum'	CDoC

× *Graptoveria* (*Crassulaceae*)

	'Acaulis'	CDoC
	'Caerulescens'	CDoC
	'Mrs Richards'	CDoC CSuc
	'Ron Ginns'	CDoC
	'Titubans'	CDoC
	'Van Keppel'	CDoC

Gratiola (*Plantaginaceae*)

	officinalis	CArn CBAq EHon LLWG MHer MHoo MSKA

Greenovia (*Crassulaceae*)

	aizoon	CSuc
§	***aurea***	CSuc CWil SPlb
	diplocycla 'Gigantea'	SPlb

Grevillea (*Proteaceae*)

	alpina 'Olympic Flame'	CBcs CCCN CDoC CExl CHel CSBt CTsd CWib EBee EPfP LEdu LRHS MOWG SCoo SEND SPoG SVen WBor WGrn
	aquifolium	MOWG
	australis	ECou
	banksii 'Canberra Hybrid'	see *G.* 'Canberra Gem'
	- var. ***forsteri***	SPlb
	barklyana	MOWG
	'Bronze Rambler'	MOWG
§	'Canberra Gem' $\mathbb{Y}^{H3-4}$	Widely available
	'Clearview David'	CCCN CWGN LRHS LSRN MOWG SCoo SLim SSpi SVen
	'Cranbrook Yellow'	EPfP
	crithmifolia	SPlb
	'Evelyn's Coronet'	MOWG
	iaspicula	MOWG
	johnsonii	CMac EUJe MOWG
	juniperina	CBcs CCCN CExl CMac EBee EPfP SLim SVen
	- prostrate, yellow-flowered **new**	MOWG
	- f. ***sulphurea***	CCCN CExl CHll CTsd ELon EPfP LRHS MOWG SBod SPlb SPoG WPat WSHC
	lanigera	EUJe
I	- 'Lutea'	MOWG
	- 'Mount Tamboritha'	CBcs CCCN CDoC CExl CMac EBee EPfP IDee LRHS SBod SLim SPoG SVen
	- prostrate	MAsh MOWG WGrn WPat
§	- 'Red Salento'^{PBR}	LRHS
	leucopteris	SPlb
	'Long John'	MOWG
	'Mason's Hybrid'	MOWG
	olivacea 'Apricot Glow'	MOWG
	paniculata	SPlb
	'Pink Lady'	CCCN CMHG CWGN EBee ECou ELon EPfP LRHS MOWG SCoo
	'Poorinda Constance'	MOWG
	'Red Dragon' (v)	LRHS
	'Red Hooks' **new**	MOWG
	rhyolitica	MOWG
	robusta $\mathbb{Y}^{H1+3}$	EShb MOWG SPlb SSta WCot
	- 'Red Salento'	see *G. lanigera* 'Red Salento'
	'Robyn Gordon'	MOWG
	'Rondeau'	CCCN
	rosmarinifolia $\mathbb{Y}^{H3}$	CBcs CCCN CDoC CExl CHll CMac CSBt CTri CWib EBee EPfP EShb GKin IDee MOWG MWat NSoo SAPC SBod SCoo SIgm SLim SLon SPer SPlb SPoG SSta WGwG
	- 'Desert Flame'	CExl
	- 'Jenkinsii'	CCCN CExl CMac CSBt EBee EPfP EUJe MOWG SLim SSpi
	'Scarlet Sprite'	MOWG
§	× ***semperflorens***	CWib LRHS MOWG SPlb WGrn
	'Splendour'	MOWG
	thelemanniana Spriggs' form	MOWG
	thyrsoides	GGal
	tolminsis	see *G.* × *semperflorens*
	victoriae	CCCN CDoC CHel CTsd EPfP IVic MOWG SCoo WCot WPGP
	- 'Mount Annan'	MOWG
	- subsp. ***victoriae***	CExl

- yellow-flowered LRHS
williamsonii ECou LRHS SCoo WPat

Grewia (*Malvaceae*)

occidentalis CDoC MOWG

Greyia (*Melianthaceae*)

sutherlandii MOWG SPlb

Grindelia (*Asteraceae*)

§ ***camporum*** CCon IMou SPlb
chiloensis CAbb
- F&W 9390 WCot
integrifolia XLum
robusta see *G. camporum*
squarrosa WHil
stricta CArn

Griselinia ✿ (*Griseliniaceae*)

littoralis 🏆H3 Widely available
- 'Bantry Bay' (v) CAbP CCCN CDoC CTsd EBee EHoe ELan ESwi LRHS MAsh NCGa SLim SPer SPoG SWvt
- 'Brodick Gold' CExl ELon GKin
- 'Dixon's Cream' (v) CBcs CCCN CDul CMac CSBt EBee EPfP EUJe LRHS SGol SLim SLon SPoG SVen
- Green Horizon = 'Whenuapai'[PBR] CDoC LBuc SLim SPer STPC
- 'Green Jewel' (v) CCCN CWib ESwi NLar
- 'Variegata' (v) 🏆H3 Widely available
ruscifolia LEdu
scandens CCCN

guava, common see *Psidium guajava*

guava, purple or strawberry see *Psidium littorale* var. *longipes*

Guichenotia (*Sterculiaceae*)

macrantha new SPlb

Gunnera ✿ (*Gunneraceae*)

chilensis see *G. tinctoria*
cordifolia LLWG
densiflora LLWG
dentata CPla
flavida CPla LLWG
hamiltonii CAby CPla GAbr LLWG NBir
killipiana B&SWJ 9009 new WCru
magellanica Widely available
- 'Muñoz Gamero' WShi
- 'Osorno' EBee MMoz
manicata 🏆H3-4 Widely available
monoica LLWG
perpensa CBcs CCCN CDes EBee EWTr IMou LLWG
prorepens CExl CMac CPla LLWG NBir WGwG WWEG
scabra see *G. tinctoria*
§ ***tinctoria*** 🏆H4 CCCN CExl CHEx CHel CMac CWib EHon ELan EPfP EUJe GBin IBoy IVic LRHS NCot NLar SDix SWat SWvt WPGP

Gymnadenia (*Orchidaceae*)

conopsea ECho EFEx LWst NLAp
× ***densiflora*** NLAp
odoratissima NLAp

Gymnocarpium (*Woodsiaceae*)

dryopteris 🏆H4 CLAP EFer EShb GKev GMaP ISha MMoz MMuc NLar WAbe WFib WOut WPtf WShi
- PAB 1757 new LEdu
- 'Plumosum' 🏆H4 CBty CKel CLAP EPfP ERod LRHS NHar NLar WFib WHal WMoo WWEG
oyamense CLAP EFer SKHP
robertianum EFer EWld

Gymnocladus (*Caesalpiniaceae*)

dioica CBcs CDul CLnd CMCN EBee EBtc ELan EPfP EUJe LRHS MBlu MBri SHil SMad SPer SSpi WPGP

Gymnocoronis (*Asteraceae*)

spilanthoides LLWG

Gymnospermium (*Berberidaceae*)

§ ***albertii*** LWst
sylvaticum LWst

Gynandriris see *Moraea*

Gynerium (*Poaceae*)

argenteum see *Cortaderia selloana*

Gynostemma (*Cucurbitaceae*)

pentaphyllum CAgr
- B&SWJ 570 WCru

Gypsophila (*Caryophyllaceae*)

aretioides ECho EPot LHop LRHS
§ - 'Caucasica' CPBP ECho EPot LLHF
- 'Compacta' see *G. aretioides* 'Caucasica'
cerastioides CMea CTri ECho ECtt EDAr EPfP EWTr GAbr GBin LBMP LHop LRHS MAsh MRav NGdn NLar SPlb SRms SWvt WAbe WHoo WIce WNew XLum
- silver variegated (v) new MHol NOrc
dubia see *G. repens* 'Dubia'
fastigiata 'Silverstar' LRHS LSou
(Festival Series) 'Festival' SGbt
- 'Festival Pink' ECtt GBee LBuc LRHS SPoG STPC
gracilescens see *G. tenuifolia*
'Jolien' (v) EBee ELan WIce
muralis 'Garden Bride' SWvt
- 'Gypsy Deep Rose' EPfP LBuc LRHS
- 'Gypsy Pink' (d) EPfP SWvt
- 'Pink Sugardot' SBch
'Pacific Rose' MRav
pacifica NBre NLar
paniculata EPfP MHol NBre NEgg SMrm SRms XLum
- 'Bristol Fairy' (d) 🏆H4 CSBt EBee ELan EPfP GMaP LRHS MJak NLar SHar SPoG SWvt WCAu WWEG XLum
- 'Compacta Plena' (d) ECtt ELan EPfP GMaP LHop MRav NEgg NGdn SRms
- double white-flowered (d) XLum
- (Festival Series) 'Festival Snow' new LBuc
- - Festival Star = 'Danfestar'[PBR] LAst
- 'Flamingo' (d) CBcs LHop NLar SWvt XLum
- 'Pacific Pink' EBee

	– 'Perfekta'	CBcs SPer
§	– 'Schneeflocke' (d)	EPfP GMaP LRHS MBel NBre NLar SRms WWEG
	– Snowflake	see *G. paniculata* 'Schneeflocke'
	repens ♀H4	ECtt EPfP GBin GJos MAsh MWat SBch SPlb SWvt XLum
	– 'Dorothy Teacher'	CMea ECho ECtt MAsh SBch WGor
§	– 'Dubia'	ECho ECtt EHyd EPot MAsh MHer MMuc NLar SRms WSHC
	– 'Fratensis'	ECho ECtt LLHF WIce
	– Pink Beauty	see *G. repens* 'Rosa Schönheit'
§	– 'Rosa Schönheit'	EPot LRHS NDov SPer XLum
	– 'Rosea'	CPBP CTri CWib ECho ECtt EDAr EPfP GJos GMaP ITim LBMP MHol MMuc MWat NGdn SPoG SRms SWvt WHoo WIce XLum
	– white-flowered	CMea CWib ECho ELan EPfP NGdn SWvt
§	'Rosenschleier' (d) ♀H4	CMea EBee ECtt ELan EPfP LBMP LHop MBel MCot MRav NCGa NDov NEgg NGdn SBch SPer SRms SRot SWvt WHoo WSHC WWEG XLum
I	'Rosenschleier Variegata' (v)	WWEG
	'Rosy Veil'	see *G.* 'Rosenschleier'
§	***tenuifolia***	ECho EPot GMaP MWat
	Veil of Roses	see *G.* 'Rosenschleier'
	'White Festival'[PBR] (Festival Series) (d)	LRHS SPoG

Gyptis (*Asteraceae*)

commersonii	LHop

H

Haberlea (*Gesneriaceae*)

ferdinandi-coburgii	CLAP ECho
rhodopensis ♀H4	CDes CElw EBee ECho GKev MWat NSla SBch SRms WAbe WPGP XLum
– 'Virginalis'	CElw CLAP ECho NSla WAbe WThu

Habranthus ✿ (*Amaryllidaceae*)

	andersonii	see *H. tubispathus*
	brachyandrus	GCal SRms
	gracilifolius	ECho
	howardii	ECho
	martinezii	CPBP ECho EDif WCot
	mexicanus	ECho
§	***robustus*** ♀H1	CCCN CExl ECho EPot EShb LHop WPGP
§	***tubispathus*** ♀H1	ECho GCal WCot

Hacquetia (*Apiaceae*)

	epipactis ♀H4	Widely available
§	– 'Thor' (v)	CLAP EBee ECho EWes LLHF NBir NChi WCot WPGP
	– 'Variegata'	see *H. epipactis* 'Thor'

Haemanthus (*Amaryllidaceae*)

albiflos ♀H1	CHEx CPrp CTca ECho EOHP EShb SRms
amarylloides subsp. ***polyanthes***	ECho
barkerae	ECho
carneus	ECho
coccineus ♀H1	CLak ECho WCot
crispus	ECho
humilis	ECho
– subsp. ***hirsutus***	WCot
kalbreyeri	see *Scadoxus multiflorus* subsp. *multiflorus*
katherinae	see *Scadoxus multiflorus* subsp. *katherinae*
lanceifolius	ECho
montanus	ECho
natalensis	see *Scadoxus puniceus*
pauculifolius	ECho
pubescens subsp. ***leipoldtii***	ECho
sanguineus	ECho

Hakea (*Proteaceae*)

	epiglottis	ECou
	laurina	SPlb
§	***lissosperma***	CDoC ECou EPfP SPlb WPGP
	microcarpa	ECou
	nodosa	CCCN
	platysperma	SPlb
§	***salicifolia***	CBcs CCCN NPri SPlb
	saligna	see *H. salicifolia*
	sericea misapplied	see *H. lissosperma*
	sericea Schrad. & J.C.Wendl.	ECou WCot
	– pink-flowered	SPlb WCot
	victoriae	SPlb

Hakonechloa ✿ (*Poaceae*)

	macra	CFil CGHE CKno CMac CPla CSam EHoe ELan EPPr EShb GBin GCal LRHS MAvo MMoz MNFA MRav NDov NOak NPol SMad SPhx SPoG WPGP WSHC
§	– 'Alboaurea' (v) ♀H4	CBcs CExl CKno CTsd CWGN ELan EPfP LAst LRHS LSRN MGos MMuc NCGa NPla SHil
	– 'Albovariegata' (v)	CKno EPPr GCal LEdu MAsh MAvo
	– 'All Gold'	CExl CFil CKno EBee ECtt EPPr EWes GQue IBoy ITim LBMP LEdu LRHS MAsh MBri MGos SMad SPad SPoG WCot WPGP
	– 'Aureola' ♀H4	Widely available
	– 'Mediovariegata' (v)	CGHE CWCL EBee EPPr WPGP
	– 'Naomi' (v)	EBee EPfP LRHS MBri SPer SPoG
	– 'Nicolas'	CExl CKno CSam EBee ECtt ELan ELon EPfP EWes GBin LLHF LLWG LRHS LSRN LSou MBel MBri MCot MSCN NLBP NSti SPer SPoG
	– 'Samurai' (v)	CKno LRHS
	– 'Stripe It Rich' (v)	EWes SGol
	– 'Variegata'	see *H. macra* 'Alboaurea'

Halesia (*Styracaceae*)

§	***carolina***	Widely available
	– Monticola Group	CBcs CCVT CDul CMCN ELan EPfP IVic LRHS MAsh NLar SPer SSpi SWvt WHar WMou
I	– 'Variegata' (v)	NLar SSta
	– 'UConn Wedding Bells'	CJun MBlu SKHP
	– Vestita Group ♀H4	CDoC CDul CJun CTho EPfP LRHS MAsh MBlu MGos MRav NLar SPer SSpi SSta WGob WPat
	– 'Rosea'	CJun EPfP MBlu NLar SKHP
	diptera	MBlu NEgg SKHP
	– Magniflora Group	CJun EPfP MBlu MBri
	tetraptera	see *H. carolina*

× *Halimiocistus* (*Cistaceae*)

	algarvensis	see *Halimium ocymoides*
§	'Ingwersenii'	CBcs CDoC ECho EDAr ELan EWes SPer SPoG SRms XLum
	revolii misapplied	see × *H. sahucii*
§	***sahucii*** ♀^{H4}	CBcs CDoC CSBt CTri EBee ELan EPfP EUJe LBMP LRHS MAsh MBNS MRav MSwo MWat NPri SEND SPer SPoG SRms SWvt XLum
	- Ice Dancer = 'Ebhals'^{PBR} (v)	CDoC EBee EPfP LAst MAsh SPer SWvt
	'Susan'	see *Halimium* 'Susan'
§	***wintonensis*** ♀^{H3}	CBcs CDoC EBee ELan EPfP GMaP LRHS MAsh SLon SPer SRms WHar WSHC
§	- 'Merrist Wood Cream' ♀^{H3}	CBcs CDoC CMac CSBt EBee ELan EPfP LAst LRHS LSRN MAsh MRav MSwo NBir SLim SPer SPoG SWvt WSHC

Halimium (*Cistaceae*)

§	***calycinum***	CDoC EBee ELan EPfP IVic LRHS MAsh MBri SCoo SEND SHil SLim SPer SPoG SWvt WAbe WCFE WGob
	commutatum	see *H. calycinum*
N	***halimifolium*** misapplied	see *H.* × *pauanum*
§	***lasianthum*** ♀^{H3}	CBcs CMac CSBt CWib ELan EPfP LRHS MRav SLim
	- 'Concolor'	CWib EBee LRHS MAsh MSwo SWvt
	- subsp. ***formosum*** 'Sandling'	ELan EPfP LRHS MAsh MMuc SLon SPoG SRms
	libanotis misapplied	see *H. calycinum*
§	***ocymoides*** ♀^{H3}	CBcs CDoC CWib ELan EPfP IVic LRHS MSwo WHar WKif
§	× ***pauanum***	LRHS MMuc
§	'Susan' ♀^{H3}	CDoC ELan EPfP GKev LRHS MMHG SCoo SLim SPer WAbe
§	***umbellatum***	EPfP LHop SPer
	wintonense	see × *Halimiocistus wintonensis*

Halimodendron (*Papilionaceae*)

	halodendron	CArn CBcs CDul MBlu SPer

Halleria (*Stilbaceae*)

	lucida	CCCN SVen

Halocarpus (*Podocarpaceae*)

§	***bidwillii***	CDoC ECou

Haloragis (*Haloragaceae*)

	erecta	SPlb SVen XLum
	- 'Rubra'	WCot
	- 'Wellington Bronze'	CExl CHel CSpe EHoe EUJe LEdu LHop LRHS MLHP WHer WMoo XLum

Hamamelis ✿ (*Hamamelidaceae*)

	'Amethyst'	CJun NLar SGol
	'Brevipetala'	CBcs CEnd CJun NLar
	'Danny'	CJun NLar
	'Dishi'	CJun
	'Doerak'	CJun MBlu
	'Fire Blaze'	CJun MBlu
	'Girard Orange'	EPfP
	× ***intermedia*** <u>**new**</u>	CDul
	- 'Advent'	CJun
	- 'Angelly' ♀^{H4}	CEnd CJun MBlu NLar SPoG
	- 'Aphrodite' ♀^{H4}	CDoC CJun CRos EPfP LRHS MAsh MBlu MBri MGos MRav NCGa NLar SHil SPer SPoG
	- 'Arnhem'	NLar
	- 'Arnold Promise' ♀^{H4}	Widely available
	- 'Aurora' ♀^{H4}	CJun CRos EPfP LRHS MBlu MBri MGos NHol SHil SPoG
	- 'Barmstedt Gold' ♀^{H4}	CJun CRos EPfP LRHS LSRN MAsh MGos SHil SPoG
	- 'Bernstein'	CJun
	- 'Birgit'	NLar
	- 'Carmine Red'	CJun CMac MGos NLar
	- 'Copper Beauty'	see *H.* × *intermedia* 'Jelena'
	- 'Cyrille'	NLar
	- 'Diane' ♀^{H4}	Widely available
§	- 'Feuerzauber'	CEnd CMac CSBt CTri EBee LBuc MGos NLar SPer SPoG SWvt
	- Fire Cracker	see *H.* × *intermedia* 'Feuerzauber'
	- 'Foxy Lady' <u>**new**</u>	CRos LRHS MAsh SPoG
	- 'Frederic'	CJun EPfP LRHS MAsh
	- 'Gimborn's Perfume'	NLar
	- 'Gingerbread'	CJun EBee EPfP LLHF LRHS MAsh
	- 'Glowing Embers'	CJun LRHS MAsh
	- 'Harlow Carr'	LRHS MAsh
	- 'Harry'	CJun LRHS LSRN MAsh
	- 'Heinrich Bruns'	CJun
	- 'Hiltingbury'	MGos
§	- 'Jelena' ♀^{H4}	Widely available
	- 'John'	LRHS LSRN MAsh
	- 'Limelight'	CJun MBlu NLar
	- 'Livia'	CJun EPfP LRHS MAsh MBri SCoo SHil SPoG SSpi
	- Magic Fire	see *H.* × *intermedia* 'Feuerzauber'
	- 'Moonlight'	CJun NLar
	- 'Nina'	EPfP LRHS MAsh MGos NHol NLar
	- 'Ninotchka'	CJun
	- 'Old Copper'	NLar
	- 'Orange Beauty'	CBcs LRHS MBlu MGos SCoo SGol SHil
	- 'Orange Peel'	CJun EPfP LLHF LRHS MAsh MBri SHil
	- 'Ostergold'	CJun NLar
	- 'Pallida' ♀^{H4}	Widely available
	- 'Primavera'	CJun CLnd IArd LRHS MGos NPCo
	- 'Ripe Corn'	CJun CRos EPfP LRHS MAsh
	- 'Robert'	CJun EPfP LRHS LSRN MAsh SHil SPoG
	- 'Rubin'	CJun CRos EPfP GKir LRHS MAsh MBri MGos NLar SCoo SHil SPer SPoG
	- 'Rubinstar'	CJun
	- 'Ruby Glow'	CBcs CMac CWGN CWib LSRN MGos NLar NPCo NWea SCoo SLim SPer SPoG SWvt
	- 'Savill Starlight'	CJun
	- 'Spanish Spider'	MBlu NLar
	- 'Strawberries and Cream'	CJun MAsh NLar
	- 'Sunburst'	CJun LRHS NLar SGol SHil
	- 'Twilight'	CJun NLar
	- 'Vesna' ♀^{H4}	CJun CMac CRos EPfP LRHS MAsh MBlu NLar SCoo SHil SPoG
	- 'Westerstede'	CJun EBee EPfP IArd LSRN MGos NHol NLar NPla NWea SCoo SEWo SGol SLim WHar
	- 'Wiero'	CJun NLar
	- 'Zitronenjette'	CJun
	japonica 'Pendula'	CJun MBlu NLar
	- 'Rubra'	NPCo
	- 'Zuccariniana'	MGos NLar

mollis ♀H4	Widely available
- 'Boskoop'	CJun GKin
- 'Coombe Wood'	CJun EPfP LRHS MGos SPoG
- 'Emily' **new**	LRHS MAsh
- 'Goldcrest'	CJun
- 'Imperialis'	CJun LRHS SPoG
- 'Iwado'	CJun
- 'Jermyns Gold' ♀H4	CJun LRHS SHil SPoG
- 'Kort's Yellow'	CJun
- var. ***pallida*** **new**	SEWo SWvt
- 'Wisley Supreme'	CJun ELan EPfP LLHF LRHS MAsh SGol SHil SPoG SSpi
'Rochester'	CJun NLar NPCo
vernalis 'Lombarts' Weeping'	NLar
- purple	MBlu NLar
- 'Sandra' ♀H4	CBcs CMCN ELan EPfP LRHS MAsh MBlu MGos MRav NLar SLon SPer SPoG
virginiana	CAgr GPoy IDee MMuc NWea
- 'Mohonk Red'	CJun

Hamelia (*Rubiaceae*)

patens	CCCN

Hanabusaya (*Campanulaceae*)

§ ***asiatica***	NCGa NChi SBrt

Haplocarpha (*Asteraceae*)

rueppellii	SRms SRot

Haplopappus (*Asteraceae*)

coronopifolius	see *H. glutinosus*
§ ***glutinosus***	ECho ECtt EDAr EPot NLar SPlb SRms
prunelloides var. ***mustersii*** F&W 9384	WCot
'Purple Carpet' **new**	EBee
rehderi	GJos MWat

Hardenbergia (*Papilionaceae*)

comptoniana ♀H1	CExl WCot
- 'Rosea'	SPer
violacea ♀H1	CCCN CHel CHll CRHN ELan IDee MHer SBch SEND SHil SLim SPer WCot
- f. ***alba***	CHll ECou SEND
- - 'White Crystal'	SPer
- - 'White Wanderer'	CCCN
- dwarf	ECou
- 'Happy Wanderer'	CCCN MOWG SChF SPoG
- f. ***rosea***	CCCN SPer

Harpephyllum (*Anacardiaceae*)

caffrum (F)	XBlo

Hastingsia (*Asparagaceae*)

alba	WSHC

Haworthia ✿ (*Asphodelaceae*)

attenuata	EShb
'Black Prince'	EPfP EShb SBch
cymbiformis	EPfP
fasciata	EPfP SEND
glabrata var. ***concolor***	EPfP EShb
pumila ♀H1	SEND
radula	EPfP
tesselata	see *H. venosa* subsp. *tesselata*
§ ***venosa***	SEND
subsp. ***tesselata*** ♀H1	

hazelnut see *Corylus*

Hebe ✿ (*Plantaginaceae*)

albicans ♀H4	CBcs CMac ELan EPfP GKin LAst LPot LRHS LSRN MAsh MBri MGos MJak MRav NPri NWea SCoo SHil SLim SPer SPoG SRms SWvt WHar XLum
- prostrate	see *H. albicans* 'Snow Cover'
* - 'Snow Carpet'	CCCN LRHS
§ - 'Snow Cover'	EWes LRHS
- 'Snow Drift'	see *H. albicans* 'Snow Cover'
- 'Snow Mound'	SHea
§ 'Alicia Amherst'	LRHS SHea
'Amanda Cook' (v)	NPer SGol SPoG
'Amethyst'	SHea
§ 'Amy'	ELon GGal LRHS NPer SHea SPer SWvt
× ***andersonii***	EPfP LRHS SHea
§ - 'Andersonii Variegata' (v)	LRHS SRms
- 'Argenteovariegata'	see *H.* × *andersonii* 'Andersonii Variegata'
'Andressa Paula'	CCCN LRHS
'Anna'	EPfP
anomala misapplied	see *H.* 'Imposter'
anomala (Armstr.) Cockayne	LRHS SHea
§ ***armstrongii***	ECho
'Arthur'	ECou
'Autumn Glory'	CSBt CTsd CWSG ELan EPfP LAst LRHS LSRN MAsh MBri MGos MJak MSwo NBir NPri SGol SLim SPer SPlb SPoG SVen SWvt XLum
'Autumn Joy'	SWvt
azurea	see *H. venustula*
'Baby Blush' PBR	LRHS SLim
'Baby Boo' (v)	LRHS SLon
'Baby Marie'	CAbP CSBt ECho ECou ELan ELon EPfP GKin LBMP LBuc LRHS LSRN MBri MSwo NLar NPer SCoo SLim SPoG SRGP SRms SRot SWvt
'Beatrice'	SHea
'Beverley Hills' PBR	CSBt LRHS
'Bicolor Wand'	CCCN CTsd LRHS SHea
bishopiana	ECou EPfP
'Black Beauty'	LBMP LRHS MJak
'Black Knight'	LBuc LRHS SLim
'Black Panther'	ELon NSoo
'Blue Clouds' ♀H3	EPfP LAst LLHF LRHS MBri MSwo SPer WCFE
§ 'Blue Gem'	LBuc SLim
'Blue Shamrock'	SWvt
Blue Star = 'Vergeer 1' PBR	EPfP LRHS MAsh MBri NLar SLon SPoG SRms
'Bluebell'	SHea
'Blush Wand'	SHea
'Blushing Bride' (v)	LRHS
bollonsii	SHea
'Boscawenii'	ECre SHea WHer
'Bouquet' PBR	NEgg
§ 'Bowles's Hybrid'	CCCN LRHS MRav MSwo SEND SHea SRms
brachysiphon	CTri MRav SEND SHea SPer SRms SVen
'Bracken Hill'	SHea
brevifolia	LRHS SLim

	breviracemosa	SHea
	Bronze Glow = 'Lowglo'	LBuc LRHS
	'Bronzy Baby'PBR (v)	SPoG
	buchananii	ECho MHer NPer
§	- 'Fenwickii'	ECho
	- 'Minima'	ECho
	- 'Minor' Hort. NZ	ECho GBin NBir
	buxifolia misapplied	see *H. odora*
	buxifolia (Benth.) Andersen	CMac ELan LHop MMuc NWea SEND WHar
	'C.P. Raffill'	SHea
§	'Caledonia' ♀H3	CCCN CSBt EPfP LBMP LRHS LSRN MAsh MBri MGos NPer NPri SCoo SHea SLim SPoG SRms SWvt WHoo XLum
	'Candy'	SHea
§	***canterburiensis***	ECou
N	'Carl Teschner'	see *H.* 'Youngii'
	'Carnea'	SHea
	'Carnea Variegata' (v)	EPfP EShb LRHS SLim SPer SPoG SRms
	carnosula	NBir SPer WHar
	catarractae	see *Parahebe catarractae*
	'Celine'	EPfP LBuc LRHS SRGP
	'Champagne'	CCCN EPfP LAst LPot LRHS LSRN MBlu MBri NLar NSoo SCoo SEND SLim SRms XLum
	Champion = 'Champseiont'PBR	LRHS MSwo SCoo
	'Charming White'	LRHS LSRN
	chathamica	ECou LRHS
	'Christabel'	LRHS
	'Clear Skies'PBR	ECou LBuc LRHS NEgg SLim SRms
	'Colwall'	ECho
	'Conwy Knight'	SRms WAbe
	corriganii	SHea
	corstorphinensis	SHea
	'County Park'	ECou EWes
	'Cranleighensis'	CTsd SHea
	cupressoides	CFis LRHS MSCN
	- 'Boughton Dome'	CTri ECho EPfP MAsh MHer WAbe WHoo
	darwiniana	see *H. glaucophylla*
	'Dazzler' (v)	CAbP
	decumbens	EWes
	'Denise'	LRHS
	'Diamond'	LRHS LSRN SLon SRms
	dieffenbachii	SHea
	diosmifolia	CDoC EPfP LRHS SHea SLim
	- 'Wairua Beauty'	SLim
	divaricata	ECou SHea
*	- 'Marlborough'	ECou
	- 'Nelson'	ECou
	'Dorothy Peach'	see *H.* 'Watson's Pink'
	'E.B. Anderson'	see *H.* 'Caledonia'
	'Eclipse'	LAst
	'Edington'	LRHS SHea SPer WCFE
	'Ellie'	LRHS
	elliptica	ECou SHea
	- 'Anatoki'	SHea
	- 'Charleston'	SHea
	- 'Kapiti'	ECou
	- 'Variegata'	see *H.* 'Silver Queen'
	'Emerald Dome'	see *H.* 'Emerald Gem'
§	'Emerald Gem' ♀H3	CMac CTri ECho EPfP EShb LBMP LRHS LSRN MAsh MBri MGos MHer MJak MMuc MSwo NLar SEND SHil SPer SPlb SPoG WHar
	'Emerald Green'	see *H.* 'Emerald Gem'
	epacridea	EWes
§	'Eveline'	CSBt CTri LRHS MJak NBir SLim SPer
	evenosa	SHea
	'Eversley Seedling'	see *H.* 'Bowles's Hybrid'
	'Fairfieldii'	WPat WSHC
	'First Light'PBR	CWSG LRHS NPri SGol SRms
	'Fragrant Jewel'	CAbP CWib LRHS SEND SLim SPhx
	× ***franciscana***	ECou SHea
	- 'Blue Gem' ambig.	CTsd ELan EPfP LRHS MRav NBir NPer SEND SGol SPer SPlb SPoG SRms WHar
	- 'Lavender Queen'	LRHS SHea
	- 'Purple Tips' misapplied	see *H. speciosa* 'Variegata'
	- 'Variegata'	see *H.* 'Silver Queen'
I	- 'White Gem'	SRms
	- yellow variegated (v)	SPer
	'Franjo'	ECou
	'Frozen Flame' (v)	ELan LBuc LRHS SPoG
	Garden Beauty Blue = 'Cliv'PBR	LBuc LRHS SLim SRms
	Garden Beauty Pink = 'Lowink'	SLim SRms
	Garden Beauty Purple = 'Nold'PBR	LBuc LRHS SLim
	'Garden Elegance Blue'	LBuc LRHS NPri SLim SPoG
	'Garden Elegance Blush'	LBuc LRHS
	'Garden Elegance Pastel'	LBuc SLim
	'Garden Elegance Pink'	LBuc NPri SLim
	'Garden Elegance Purple'	LBuc SLim SPoG
	'Garden Elegance Rose'	LBuc SLim
	'Gauntlettii'	see *H.* 'Eveline'
	'Gibby'	LRHS
§	***glaucophylla***	SHea
	- 'Clarence'	ECou
	- 'Joan Hunwick'	SHea
I	'Glaucophylla Variegata' (v)	CTri EPfP LBuc LRHS NBir SCoo SLim SPer
	'Gnome'	LRHS
	'Goethe'	SEND
	'Gold Beauty' (v)	LRHS SPoG SRms
	'Golden Nugget'	LRHS
	'Goldrush'PBR (v)	LBuc SPoG
	gracillima	SHea
	'Gran's Favourite'	LRHS LSRN
	'Great Orme' ♀H3	CDul CWib ECou ELan EPfP GBin GGal LAst LRHS LSRN MAsh MGos MJak MRav MSwo NPri SEND SLim SPer SPlb SPoG SRms SWvt WAbe WSFF
	'Green Globe'	see *H.* 'Emerald Gem'
	'Greensleeves'	LRHS
	'Grethe'	SPoG
	'Hadspen Pink'	LRHS
	'Hagley Park'	LRHS
§	'Hartii'	EPfP LBuc LRHS MRav SLim
	'Headfortii'	SHea
	'Heartbreaker'PBR (v)	ELan LAst LBuc LRHS MAsh MGos NLar NPri SCoo SLim SPoG SWvt
	HebeDonna Diana = 'Zenia'PBR **new**	ELan
	'Heidi'	SHea
	'Hidcote'	LRHS
	'Hielan Lassie'	LRHS SHea
	'Highdown Pink'	SHea
	'Highdownensis'	LRHS
	'Hinderwell'	NPer
	hulkeana ♀H3	LRHS LSou MHer WAbe WKif
§	'Imposter'	SRms

	'Inspiration'	LRHS SHea
	insularis	ECou
	'James Stirling'	see *H. ochracea* 'James Stirling'
	'Jane Holden'	LRHS
	'Joanna'	ECou
§	'Johny Day'	LRHS
	'Judy'	LRHS
	'Karo Golden Esk'	EPfP LRHS
	'Killiney Variety'	SHea
	'Kirkii'	EPfP LAst MSwo NLar SHea SPer XLum
	'Knightshayes'	see *H.* 'Caledonia'
	'La Favorite'	CTsd SHea
	'La Séduisante'	CTri ECou LRHS SEND SHea SRms
	'Lady Ann' PBR (v)	CSBt EPfP LRHS NEgg NLar NPri SPoG
	'Lady Ardilaun'	see *H.* 'Amy'
	laevis	see *H. venustula*
	latifolia	see *H.* 'Blue Gem'
	'Lavender Spray'	see *H.* 'Hartii'
	leiophylla	SHea SVen
	Leopard = 'Lowand'	LBuc LRHS
	'Lewisii'	SHea
	'Lilac Wand'	CTsd SHea
	'Lindsayi'	ECou LRHS SHea
	'Lisa'	EPfP
	'Lopen' (v)	ECou
	lyallii	see *Parahebe lyallii*
	lycopodioides 'Aurea'	see *H. armstrongii*
	'Lynash'	LRHS
	mackenii	see *H.* 'Emerald Gem'
	macrantha ♀H3	GBin LRHS SDix SPer SRms WAbe
	macrocarpa	ECou LRHS
	- var. ***latisepala***	ECou LBuc LRHS SLim
	- var. ***macrocarpa***	SLim
	'Magic Summer'	LBuc LRHS MBri SPoG
	'Margery Fish'	see *H.* 'Primley Gem'
	'Margret' PBR ♀H4	CSBt EPfP LAst LBMP LRHS LSRN MAsh MBrN MBri MGos NPri NSoo SCoo SHea SLim SPoG SRGP SRms
	'Marie Antoinette'	LRHS
	'Marilyn Monroe' PBR **new**	LRHS
	'Marjorie'	CDul CMac ELan EPfP GBin LAst LRHS LSRN MJak MSwo NLar NPer NWea SPer SPoG SRms SWvt
	'Mauve Queen'	LRHS
	'McKean'	see *H.* 'Emerald Gem'
	'Megan'	ECou
	'Mercury'	ECou
	'Mette'	LLHF
	Midnight Sky = 'Lowten' PBR	LBuc LRHS NPri SCoo SLim SPoG
	'Midsummer Beauty' ♀H3	CWCL ECou ECrN EPfP LAst LRHS LSRN MBri MGos MJak MRav NBir SEND SHea SLim SPer SPlb SPoG SRms SWvt WHar WSFF XLum
	'Milmont Emerald'	see *H.* 'Emerald Gem'
	'Miss Fittall'	SHea
*	'Moppets Hardy'	SPer
	'Mrs E.Tennant'	SHea
§	'Mrs Winder' ♀H4	CCCN CDul EHoe ELan EPfP EUJe LAst LPot LRHS LSRN MAsh MCot MGos MJak MRav MSwo MWat NBir NCot NEgg NLar NPer NPri SCoo SEND SGol SLim SPer SPoG SWvt
	'Mystery'	ECou
	'Nantyderry'	LRHS SHea
§	'Neil's Choice' ♀H4	ECou ELon LRHS SHea
	'Neopolitan'	LBuc LRHS SPoG

	'New Zealand'	XLum
	'Nicola's Blush' ♀H4	CCVN CSBt ECou ELon EPfP EShb LAst LRHS LSRN MCot MMuc MRav MWat NBir NCot NHol NLar SCoo SEND SGol SPer SPoG SRGP SRms SWvt WKif
	ochracea	EPfP LRHS
§	- 'James Stirling' ♀H4	CBcs CMac CSBt ECho ELan EPfP EShb GKin LRHS LSRN MAsh MGos MJak MSwo NLar NPri NWad SCoo SLim SPer SPlb SPoG SWvt WHar
	'Oddity'	LRHS
§	***odora***	ECou EPfP MJak
I	- 'Nana'	EPfP LBuc
	- 'New Zealand Gold'	LRHS MAsh MMuc SCoo SHil
	- 'Summer Frost'	LRHS
	'Oratia Beauty' ♀H4	LRHS LSRN MRav NLar SEND SLim
	'Orphan Annie' PBR (v)	LRHS LSRN
	parviflora misapplied	see *H.* 'Bowles's Hybrid'
	parviflora (Vahl) Cockayne & Allan var. ***angustifolia***	see *H. stenophylla*
	- 'Holdsworth'	LRHS
	- 'Palmerston'	SHea
	'Pascal' ♀H4	ELan EPfP LRHS LSRN MAsh MBri MGos SCoo SLim SLon SPer SPoG SRms SWvt
	'Pastel Elegance'	LRHS
	'Patti Dossett'	see *H. speciosa* 'Patti Dossett'
	pauciramosa	GCal SRms
	'Pearl of Paradise' PBR	SPoG
	perfoliata	see *Parahebe perfoliata*
	'Perry's Rubyleaf'	NPer
	'Petra's Pink'	CCCN LRHS SLim
	'Pewter Dome' ♀H4	CMac CSBt ECou EHoe EPfP LHop LRHS MGos MRav SDix SHea SPer SRms SWvt
	pimeleoides	ECou
	- 'Glauca'	NPer SGol
	- 'Glaucocaerulea'	ECou
	- 'Quicksilver' ♀H4	CAbP CSBt CTri ECou EDAr ELan EPfP LAst LRHS LSRN MGos MMuc MRav MSwo NBir NPer SCoo SLim SPer SRms WHar
	pinguifolia	ECou SPlb
	- 'Dobson'	LRHS
	- 'Pagei' ♀H4	Widely available
	- 'Sutherlandii'	CBcs CDoC ECho LRHS LSRN MGos MJak NSoo NWea SCoo SHea SWvt
	'Pink Elegance'	LRHS
	'Pink Elephant' (v) ♀H3	LBuc LRHS MAsh MJak MWat NLar NPri SLim SPoG
	'Pink Fantasy'	LRHS MRav
	'Pink Goddess'	EPfP LRHS SRGP
	'Pink Lady' PBR	SGol SPoG
	'Pink Paradise' PBR	CAbP ELan EPfP LRHS MJak SPoG SRms
	'Pink Payne'	see *H.* 'Eveline'
	'Pink Pixie'	MBri MGos SCoo SRms
	'Pink Princess'	LRHS
	'Pink Wand'	CTsd SHea
	poppelwellii	GBin
	'Porlock Purple'	see *Parahebe catarractae* 'Delight'
	'Pretty in Pink'	LRHS
§	'Primley Gem'	CFis LRHS
I	'Prostrata'	CSBt
	'Purple Elegance'	LRHS
	'Purple Emperor'	see *H.* 'Neil's Choice'
	'Purple Paradise' PBR	LRHS MBri NEgg SPoG

	'Purple Picture'	ELon
	'Purple Princess'	LRHS SGol
	'Purple Queen'	EPfP EShb LRHS MJak SEND SPoG
	Purple Shamrock = 'Neprock'^{PBR} (v)	EPfP LAst LBuc LRHS LSRN MBri MGos NEgg NLar SCoo SLim SPer SPoG SRms SWvt
	'Purple Tips' misapplied	see *H. speciosa* 'Variegata'
	'Rachel'	LRHS LSRN SLon
§	***rakaiensis*** 🏆^{H4}	Widely available
	- 'Golden Dome'	see *H. rakaiensis*
	raoulii	SIgm SRms WAbe
	'Raven'	LRHS
	recurva	CSam CTri EPfP LPot LRHS MCot MMuc SHea SRms
	- 'Boughton Silver' 🏆^{H3}	ELan LRHS SEND SLim
	'Red Edge' 🏆^{H4}	Widely available
	'Red Rum'	LBuc
	'Red Ruth'	see *H.* 'Eveline'
	'Reine des Blanches'	SHea
	rigidula	LRHS MMuc SEND
	'Ronda'	ECou
	'Rose Elegance'	LRHS
	'Rosie'^{PBR}	CSBt LRHS LSRN SCoo SPer SWvt
	'Royal Blue'	LRHS SLim
	'Royal Purple'	see *H.* 'Alicia Amherst'
	salicifolia	CCCN CMac CTri ECou ELan EPfP LAst LRHS MGos MJak MRav NWad SEND SHea SPer SPlb SRms XLum
	'Sandra Joy'	LRHS
	'Sapphire' 🏆^{H4}	ECou EPfP LRHS MAsh NPri SCoo SHea SLim SRms SWvt
	'Sarana'	LRHS
	'Shiraz'	LRHS
	'Silver Dollar' (v)	CAbP CCCN CMac CSBt ELan LRHS MJak MMuc NEgg NWad SLim SPer SPoG SRms
§	'Silver Queen' (v) 🏆^{H2}	CSBt ECou ELan EPfP EShb GBin LRHS MAsh MJak MRav NEgg NLar NPer SEND SPer SPoG SRms
	'Silver Swallow' **new**	LRHS
	'Simon Délaux'	ECou LRHS SEND SPer
I	'Southlandii'	ECho MWhi SGol
	'Sparkling Sapphires' **new**	LBuc
	speciosa	SHea
	- 'Johny Day'	see *H.* 'Johny Day'
§	- 'Patti Dossett'	LRHS
	- 'Rangatira'	ECou
§	- 'Variegata' (v)	NPer NSoo
	'Spender's Seedling' misapplied	see *H. stenophylla*
	'Spender's Seedling' ambig.	MCot MMuc MSCN
	'Spender's Seedling' Hort.	ECou LRHS MRav SEND SHea SPoG SRms
	'Spring Glory'	LRHS
§	***stenophylla***	EShb GGal SAPC SDix
	stricta	ECou LRHS SEND
	- var. ***egmontiana***	LRHS
	- var. ***macroura***	SHea
	- var. ***stricta***	SHea
	subalpina	CSBt ECho SHea
	'Summer Blue'	LRHS MBlu MRav
	'Super Red'	CSBt LRHS MBri SLim SPoG
	'Sweet Kim' (v)	CMac LBuc LRHS MBri SLim SPoG
	'Tina'	ECou
	'Tom Marshall'	see *H. canterburiensis*
	topiaria 🏆^{H4}	CAbP CSBt CSam ECho ECou EPfP GCal LHop LRHS MBrN MMuc MRav MSwo NBir SCoo SEND SPer SPoG WHoo
	- 'Doctor Favier'	LRHS SRms
	townsonii	ECou LHop LRHS
	traversii	ECou SEND SHea SRms
	- 'Mason River'	ECou
	- 'Woodside'	ECou
	'Tricolor'	see *H. speciosa* 'Variegata'
	'Trixie'	ECou LRHS
	'Twisty'	LRHS
	'Valentino'^{PBR}	LRHS NEgg SCoo SLim
	'Veitchii'	see *H.* 'Alicia Amherst'
§	***venustula***	ECou LRHS MMuc SEND
	- 'Patricia Davies'	ECou
	vernicosa 🏆^{H3}	CDul ECho EPfP LRHS MGos MHer NWad SCoo SPer SPlb SRot SVen SWvt WAbe
	'Violet Wand'	LRHS SHea
	'Vogue'	LRHS
	'Waikiki'	see *H.* 'Mrs Winder'
§	'Warley'	LRHS
	'Warley Pink'	LRHS
	'Warleyensis'	see *H.* 'Warley'
§	'Watson's Pink'	LRHS SHea SPer WKif
	'White Gem' (*brachysiphon* hybrid) 🏆^{H4}	LRHS NPer SEND SHea SPer
	'White Heather'	EPfP LRHS NBir SHea
	'White Paradise'^{PBR}	SPoG
	'Wild Romance'	LBuc
	'Willcoxii'	see *H. buchananii* 'Fenwickii'
	'Wingletye' 🏆^{H3}	CCCN ECou LRHS WAbe
	'Winter Glow'	CCCN LRHS SCoo
	'Wiri Blush'	LRHS SLim SWvt
	'Wiri Charm'	CAbP CBcs CMac CSBt ELon EPfP LRHS MGos MSwo NEgg SEND SHea SLim SPoG
	'Wiri Cloud' 🏆^{H3}	CBcs CMac EPfP LRHS MGos MMuc MSwo SEND SRms
	'Wiri Dawn' 🏆^{H3}	ELan EPfP EWes LBuc LRHS SEND SLim SRms SWvt
	'Wiri Desire'	CCCN LRHS
	'Wiri Gem'	LRHS
	'Wiri Icing Sugar'	LRHS
	'Wiri Image'	CBcs CSBt EPfP LRHS MRav SEND SPoG
	'Wiri Joy'	LRHS SEND SPoG
	'Wiri Mist'	CBcs LRHS MJak SPoG
	'Wiri Prince'	LRHS
	'Wiri Splash'	EPfP LRHS SGol SPoG
	'Wiri Vision'	CSBt LRHS SEND
	'Wiri Vogue'	LRHS SLim
§	'Youngii' 🏆$^{H3-4}$	CMac CSBt CTri ELan EPfP GKin LAst LBMP LPot LRHS MAsh MHer MJak MRav NBir NPri SEND SGol SLim SPer SPlb SPoG SRms SWvt WCFE WHoo

Hebenstretia (*Scrophulariaceae*)

	dura	CPBP
*	***quinquinervis***	LSou

Hechtia (*Bromeliaceae*)

	sp.	WCot
	texensis	EGri

Hedeoma (*Lamiaceae*)

	ciliolata	WAbe
	hyssopifolia	SPhx

Hedera ✿ (*Araliaceae*)

§	***algeriensis***	CDoC SAPC WFib

	– 'Bellecour'	WFib XLum
§	– 'Gloire de Marengo' (v) ♀H3	Widely available
§	– 'Gloire de Marengo' arborescent (v)	SPer
	– 'Marginomaculata' (v) ♀H3	CDoC EPfP EShb LRHS MAsh SMad WFib
	– 'Montgomery'	LRHS LSRN
	– 'Ravensholst' ♀H3	CMac EShb MRav SGol WFib
§	***azorica***	EShb WFib
	– 'Pico'	EShb WFib
	– 'Variegata' (v)	WCot
	canariensis misapplied	see *H. algeriensis*
	– var. ***azorica***	see *H. azorica*
	– 'Cantabrian'	see *H. maroccana* 'Spanish Canary'
	– 'Variegata'	see *H. algeriensis* 'Gloire de Marengo'
	chinensis	see *H. sinensis* var. *sinensis*
	– typica	see *H. sinensis* var. *sinensis*
§	***colchica*** ♀H4	CDul ECrN NWea SPer WCFE WFib
	– 'Batumi'	MBNS WFib
	– 'Dentata' ♀H4	CHEx MRav MWhi NEgg SGol WFib
	– 'Dentata Aurea'	see *H. colchica* 'Dentata Variegata'
§	– 'Dentata Variegata' (v) ♀H4	Widely available
	– 'My Heart'	see *H. colchica*
	– 'Paddy's Pride'	see *H. colchica* 'Sulphur Heart'
§	– 'Sulphur Heart' (v) ♀H4	Widely available
	– 'Variegata'	see *H. colchica* 'Dentata Variegata'
	cristata	see *H. helix* 'Parsley Crested'
§	***cypria***	CDoC EWld WFib
	helix	CArn CCVT CMac CTri NWea WSFF XLum
	– 'Adam' (v)	CWib EBee LSRN MBri WFib
	– 'Amberwaves'	MBri WFib
	– 'Angularis Aurea' ♀H4	EPfP NBir WFib
	– 'Anita'	GBin WFib
§	– 'Anna Marie' (v)	CMac MBri SRms WFib
	– 'Anne Borch'	see *H. helix* 'Anna Marie'
	– 'Arborescens'	WSFF XLum
	– 'Ardingly' (v)	MWhi WFib
	– 'Atropurpurea'	EBee EPPr GBin WFib
	– 'Baden-Baden'	EShb
	– var. ***baltica***	WFib
	– 'Bill Archer'	GBin WFib
	– 'Bird's Foot'	see *H. helix* 'Pedata'
	– 'Boskoop'	WFib
	– 'Bredon'	MRav
	– 'Brimstone' (v)	WFib
§	– 'Brokamp'	SLPl WFib
	– 'Buttercup'	CBcs CMac CTri EBee EHoe ELan EPfP EShb LAst LRHS LSRN MAsh MBri MGos MJak MWhi NBid SLim SPoG SRms WCFE WFib
	– 'Caecilia' (v) ♀H4	EPfP LRHS MSwo SWvt WCot WFib
N	– 'Caenwoodiana'	see *H. helix* 'Pedata'
	– 'Caenwoodiana Aurea'	WFib
	– 'Calico' (v)	WFib
	– 'Calypso'	WFib
	– 'Carolina Crinkle'	MWhi
	– 'Cathedral Wall'	WFib
§	– 'Cavendishii' (v)	SRms WFib
	– 'Cavendishii Latina'	WCot
§	– 'Ceridwen' (v) ♀H4	MBri SDys SPlb WFib
	– 'Cheeky'	WFib
	– 'Cheltenham Blizzard' (v)	CNat
	– 'Chester' (v)	LRHS WFib
	– 'Chicago'	CWib WFib
	– 'Chicago Variegated' (v)	WFib
	– 'Chrysophylla'	MSwo
	– 'Clotted Cream' (v)	CMac EBee ECGP ECrN ELon LBMP LRHS MAsh WFib
	– 'Cockle Shell'	WFib
	– 'Colin'	GBin
§	– 'Congesta' ♀H4	CMac GCra MLHP NBir SRms WFib
	– 'Conglomerata'	CBcs ELan MMoz NBir SRms WFib
	– 'Conglomerata Erecta'	EPfP WCFE WFib
	– 'Courage'	WFib
	– 'Crenata'	WFib
	– 'Crispa'	MRav
	– 'Cristata'	see *H. helix* 'Parsley Crested'
	– 'Curleylocks'	see *H. helix* 'Manda's Crested'
	– 'Curley-Q'	see *H. helix* 'Dragon Claw'
	– 'Curvaceous' (v)	WCot WFib
	– 'Cyprus'	see *H. cypria*
	– 'Dainty Bess'	CWib
	– 'Dead Again'	WCot
§	– 'Dealbata' (v)	CMac WFib
	– 'Deltoidea'	see *H. hibernica* 'Deltoidea'
	– 'Discolor'	see *H. helix* 'Minor Marmorata', *H. helix* 'Dealbata'
§	– 'Donerailensis'	MBlu WFib
	– 'Don's Papillon'	CNat
§	– 'Dragon Claw'	SDys WFib
	– 'Duckfoot' ♀H4	CDoC EShb MWhi WCot WFib
	– 'Eileen' (v)	WFib
	– 'Elfenbein' (v)	WFib
	– 'Erecta' ♀H4	CDul CTca EPPr EPfP GCal LAst LRHS MBlu MGos NHol NWad SDys SHil SPer SPlb WFib XLum
	– 'Erin'	see *H. helix* 'Pin Oak'
	– 'Ester' (v)	CBar LAst SRGP WHar
§	– 'Eva' (v)	WFib
	– 'Fantasia' (v)	EShb MBri WFib
	– 'Feenfinger'	SDys WFib
	– 'Filigran'	WFib
	– 'Flashback' (v)	WFib
	– 'Flavescens'	WFib
	– 'Fluffy Ruffles'	WFib
I	– 'Francis Ivy'	WFib
	– 'Frosty' (v)	WFib
	– 'Garland'	WFib
	– 'Gavotte'	WFib
	– 'Gilded Hawke'	WFib
	– 'Glache' (v)	MRav WFib
	– 'Glacier' (v) ♀H4	CBar CBcs CDoC CTri CWib EBee ELan EPfP LBMP LHop LRHS MAsh MBri MGos MJak MMuc MRav MSwo MWhi NBro NHol NWea SEND SLim SPer SPoG SRms SWvt WFib
	– 'Glymii'	EBee WFib
	– 'Gold Harald'	see *H. helix* 'Goldchild'
	– 'Gold Ripple'	NLar SEND
§	– 'Goldchild' (v) ♀H3-4	CBar CBcs CDoC CMac EHoe ELon EPfP EShb LAst LRHS MAsh MGos MJak MRav MSwo MWat NBir NEgg NHol SLim SPer SPoG SWvt WFib WHar
	– 'Golden Ann'	see *H. helix* 'Ceridwen'
*	– 'Golden Arrow'	ELan LRHS MAsh
	– 'Golden Curl' (v)	CMac EPfP LRHS
	– 'Golden Ester'	see *H. helix* 'Ceridwen'
	– 'Golden Girl'	SDys WFib
	– 'Golden Ingot' (v) ♀H4	ELan EShb MWhi SDys WFib
	– 'Golden Jytte' (v)	WFib
	– 'Golden Kolibri'	see *H. helix* 'Midas Touch'
	– 'Golden Mathilde' (v)	GBin

	- 'Golden Medal'	WCot
	- 'Goldfinch'	MBri WFib
	- 'Goldfinger'	EShb MBri WFib
	- 'Goldheart'	see *H. helix* 'Oro di Bogliasco'
	- 'Goldstern' (v)	MRav MWhi WFib
	- 'Gracilis'	see *H. hibernica* 'Gracilis'
	- 'Green Finger'	see *H. helix* 'Très Coupé'
	- 'Green Ripple'	CBcs CTri EBee ELan EPfP EShb LRHS MBlu MGos MJak MSwo MWht NBro SEND SLim SPer SPlb SRms WFib
	- 'Greenman'	SDys WFib
	- 'Halebob'	EShb MBri SDys WFib
	- 'Hamilton'	see *H. hibernica* 'Hamilton'
	- 'Harald' (v)	CTri CWib WFib
*	- 'Hazel' (v)	WFib
	- 'Heise' (v)	WFib
	- 'Heise Denmark' (v)	WFib
	- 'Helvig'	see *H. helix* 'White Knight'
	- 'Henrietta'	WFib
	- 'Hispanica'	see *H. iberica*
	- 'Hite's Miniature'	see *H. helix* 'Merion Beauty'
	- 'Holly'	see *H. helix* 'Parsley Crested'
	- 'Hullavington'	CNat
	- 'Humpty Dumpty'	CExl
	- 'Imp'	see *H. helix* 'Brokamp'
	- 'Itsy Bitsy'	see *H. helix* 'Pin Oak'
	- 'Ivalace' ♀H4	CBcs EPfP EShb MGos MSwo MWhi SDys SRms WFib XLum
	- 'Jake'	EShb MBri WFib
	- 'Jasper'	WFib
	- 'Jersey Doris' (v)	WFib
	- 'Jerusalem'	see *H. helix* 'Schäfer Three'
	- 'Jester's Gold'	EPfP MBri
	- 'Jubilee' (v)	WFib
	- 'Kaleidoscope'	WFib
	- 'Kevin'	WFib
	- 'Kolibri' (v)	CDoC EBee EPfP EShb LAst MBri WFib
§	- 'Königer's Auslese'	EShb WFib
	- 'Lalla Rookh'	MRav WFib WRHF
	- 'Leo Swicegood'	MWhi WFib
	- 'Light Fingers'	ELon EPfP LRHS SDys WFib
	- 'Little Diamond' (v)	CDoC CMac CTri EBee ELan EPfP LBuc LRHS MBri SLon SWvt WFib WHrl
	- 'Little Luzii'	EShb WFib
	- 'Lia'	see *H. helix* 'Eva'
	- 'Luzii' (v)	WFib
	- 'Maculata'	see *H. helix* 'Minor Marmorata'
§	- 'Manda's Crested' ♀H4	ELan NLar WFib
	- 'Maple Leaf' ♀H4	EShb SDys WFib
	- 'Maple Queen'	MBri
	- 'Marginata Elegantissima'	see *H. helix* 'Tricolor'
	- 'Marginata Minor'	see *H. helix* 'Cavendishii'
I	- 'Marmorata' Fibrex	WFib
	- 'Masquerade' (v)	EBee WGor
	- 'Mathilde' (v)	WFib
	- 'Melanie' ♀H4	SRGP WFib
	- 'Meon'	WFib
§	- 'Merion Beauty'	WFib
§	- 'Midas Touch' (v) ♀H3-4	CWib EPPr EPfP MBri WFib
	- 'Minature Needlepoint'	EBee
	- 'Mini Ester' (v)	MBri
	- 'Mini Heron'	MBri
	- 'Minikin' (v)	WCot
	- 'Minima' misapplied	see *H. helix* 'Spetchley'
	- 'Minima' Hibberd	see *H. helix* 'Donerailensis'
	- 'Minima' M.Young	see *H. helix* 'Congesta'
§	- 'Minor Marmorata' (v) ♀H4	XLum
	- 'Mint Kolibri'	EHoe MBri
	- 'Minty' (v)	WFib
	- 'Misty' (v)	WFib
	- 'Needlepoint'	XLum
	- 'Niagara Falls'	LRHS
	- 'Nigra Aurea' (v)	WFib
	- 'Obovata'	WFib
N	- 'Oro di Bogliasco' (v)	CDul CMac CTri EBee ECrN EPfP EShb GKin LRHS MAsh MBri MJak MRav MSwo NWad NWea SEND SLim SPer SPlb SPoG SRms SWvt WFib
	- 'Ovata'	WFib
§	- 'Parsley Crested' ♀H4	CMac EPfP EShb LRHS NBid SGol WFib
	- 'Patent Leather'	WFib
N	- 'Pedata'	MSwo SDys WFib
	- 'Perkeo'	WFib
	- 'Peter' (v)	WFib
§	- 'Pin Oak'	EBee
	- 'Pink 'n' Curly'	WCot WFib
	- 'Pink 'n' Very Curly'	WCot
§	- 'Pittsburgh'	EShb WFib
	- 'Plume d'Or'	WFib
§	- f. ***poetarum***	MBlu WCot WFib
	- - 'Poetica Arborea'	SDix
	- 'Poetica'	see *H. helix* f. *poetarum*
	- 'Raleigh Delight' (v)	WCot
	- 'Ray's Supreme'	see *H. helix* 'Pittsburgh'
	- subsp. ***rhizomatifera***	WFib
	- 'Richard John'	WFib
	- 'Ritterkreuz'	WFib
	- 'Romanze' (v)	WFib
	- 'Russelliana'	WFib
	- 'Sagittifolia' misapplied	see *H. helix* 'Königer's Auslese'
	- 'Sagittifolia' Hibberd	see *H. hibernica* 'Sagittifolia'
	- 'Sagittifolia' ambig.	ECrN LRHS MAsh MBlu MMuc
	- 'Sagittifolia Variegata' (v)	MBri WFib WRHF
	- 'Saint Agnes'	LRHS
	- 'Sally' (v)	WFib
	- 'Salt and Pepper'	see *H. helix* 'Minor Marmorata'
§	- 'Schäfer Three' (v)	CWib WFib
	- 'Seabreeze'	WFib
	- 'Shamrock'	EPfP WFib
	- 'Shannon'	WFib
	- 'Silver Ferny'	WFib
	- 'Silver King' (v)	MRav WFib
	- 'Silver Queen'	see *H. helix* 'Tricolor'
§	- 'Spetchley' ♀H4	CMac GCal GKev MAsh MRav MWhi NPer NWad WCot WFib WHrl WWFP
	- 'Splashes'	WFib
	- 'Sunrise'	WFib
	- 'Suzanne'	see *H. nepalensis* 'Suzanne'
	- 'Tanja'	WFib
	- 'Teardrop'	WFib
	- 'Telecurl'	WFib
	- 'Temptation' (v)	WFib
	- 'Tenerife' (v)	WFib
	- 'Topazolite' (v)	WFib
§	- 'Très Coupé'	CDoC EShb LRHS SAPC SEND
§	- 'Tricolor' (v)	CMac CTri EPfP EShb WCFE WFib
	- 'Trinity' (v)	WFib
	- 'Tripod'	SDys WFib
	- 'Triton'	EPfP WFib
	- 'Troll'	WFib
	- 'Ursula' (v)	EShb WFib

	- 'Very Merry'	SDys WFib
*	- 'Vitifolium'	WFib
§	- 'White Knight' (v) ♀H4	WFib
	- 'White Mein Herz' (v)	WFib
	- 'White Ripple' (v)	WFib
	- 'Williamsiana' (v)	WFib
	- 'Winter Purple Vein' **new**	CNat
	- 'Woerneri'	NLar WFib
	- 'Yellow Ripple'	EShb MBri SDys WFib
	- 'Zebra' (v)	WFib
	hibernica ♀H4	CCVT CDul CSBt EPfP LBuc LRHS MJak MRav MSwo MWhi NWea SEWo SGol SPer WFib
	- 'Anna Marie'	see *H. helix* 'Anna Marie'
I	- 'Arbori Compact'	EPfP
	- 'Betty Allen'	WFib
§	- 'Deltoidea' ♀H4	MWht WCFE WFib
I	- 'Digitata Crûg Gold'	WCot WCru
	- 'Ebony'	WFib
	- 'Glengariff'	WFib
§	- 'Gracilis'	WFib
§	- 'Hamilton'	WFib
	- 'Lobata Major'	SRms
	- 'Maculata' (v)	SLPl WSHC
	- 'Palmata'	WFib
	- 'Rona'	WFib
§	- 'Sagittifolia'	CTri EPfP
	- 'Sulphurea' (v)	WFib
	- 'Variegata' (v)	WFib
§	***iberica***	WFib
	maderensis	WFib
	maroccana 'Morocco'	WFib
§	- 'Spanish Canary'	WFib
	nepalensis	WFib
	- 'Marble Dragon'	see *H. sinensis* var. *sinensis* 'Marble Dragon'
§	- 'Suzanne'	WFib
	pastuchovii	CDoC EShb WFib
	- from Troödos, Cyprus	see *H. cypria*
	- 'Ann Ala'	CDoC CFil EPfP GBin MBlu WCot WFib WGwG
	- 'Lagocetti'	WFib
§	***rhombea***	WCot WFib
	- 'Eastern Dawn'	WFib
	- 'Japonica'	see *H. rhombea*
I	- f. ***pedunculata*** 'Maculata'	CWib
	- var. ***rhombea*** 'Variegata' (v)	WFib
§	***sinensis*** var. ***sinensis***	WFib
	- - KWJ 12345 **new**	WCru
§	- - 'Marble Dragon'	WFib

Hedychium ✿ (*Zingiberaceae*)

	'Anne Bishop'	SEND
	aurantiacum	CBcs CBct CCCN CHEx CTsd EAmu EBee LEdu NPla SBig XLum
	brevicaule B&SWJ 7171	WCru
	'C.P. Raffill'	see *H.* × *moorei* 'Raffillii'
	chrysoleucum	CCCN SBst
*	'Clarkei'	CTsd
	coccineum ♀H1	CDTJ CTsd EAmu EPfP EUJe IKil MNrw SBig XLum
	- B&SWJ 5238	WCru
	- PAB 4636 **new**	LEdu
	- var. ***angustifolium***	CFil EPfP WPGP
	- 'Disney'	CDTJ
	coronarium	CAbb CAvo CBct CCCN CDTJ CExl CFil CHll CTsd EAmu EBee EPfP EUJe IKil LLWG SBig WPGP XBlo XLum
	- B&SWJ 3745	WCru
	- 'Gold Spot'	CBct CCCN CTsd EUJe SKHP
	- 'Orange Spot'	EAmu
	- var. ***urophyllum***	IBlr
	- - HWJ 604	WCru
	densiflorum	CAbb CCCN CDTJ CDes CExl CHEx CHll CTsd EAmu EPfP EUJe IBlr LEdu NPla SDix SSpi WCot WCru WPGP XLum
	- EN 562	CExl CFil
	- LS&H 17393	CExl CFil WPGP
	- Sch 582	CDes
	- 'Assam Orange'	CAvo CCCN CDoC CExl CHEx CSam CTsd EAmu EBee EPPr GCal IBlr IDee LEdu LRHS MNrw SBig SChr SDix SEND SMad SPlb WCru WPGP
	- 'Sorung'	CExl CFil LEdu SChr WPGP
	- 'Stephen'	CAvo CBct CCCN CCon CDTJ CDes CExl CFil CHEx EAmu EPfP EUJe LEdu LRHS MNrw SChr SPlb WPGP
	'Devon Cream'	CCCN CDTJ CExl CHll EAmu LRHS SChr
	'Doctor Moy' (v)	CDTJ EUJe
	'Elizabeth'	CCon EAmu EBee
	ellipticum	CAbb CAvo CCCN CDTJ CTsd EAmu EUJe GCal SBig XLum
	- B&SWJ 8354	WCru
	'Filigree'	CExl
§	***flavescens***	CBcs CBct CCCN CDTJ CTsd EAmu EBee EPfP EUJe SChr WCru
	flavum misapplied	see *H. flavescens*
	flavum Roxb.	CAbb CBcs EBee XLum
	forrestii misapplied	CCCN EUJe
	forrestii Diels	CDes CExl EAmu GCal IBlr IDee MNrw MREP SAPC SPlb WPGP
	gardnerianum ♀H1	CAbb CBcs CCon CExl CHEx CHll CTsd EBee EPfP EUJe IDee IKil LEdu LRHS MNrw NBir NPla NSoo SAPC SChr SDeJ SMad WCru WPGP XLum
	'Gold Flame'	CDes EBee
	gracile	EAmu EUJe WCru
	greenii	CBcs CBct CCCN CCon CHEx CHll CTsd EPfP EUJe LEdu MNrw NPla NSoo SBig SDix WBor WCru XLum
	griffithianum	CCCN CTsd EAmu EBee EPfP IKil SBig XLum
	- white-flowered	CCCN
	'Hardy Exotics 1'	CHEx
	'Luna Moth'	CFil WPGP
	luteum	CTsd
	maximum	CFil EAmu SChr SKHP WPGP
	- B&SWJ 8261A	WCru
	- HWJ 810	WCru
§	× ***moorei*** 'Raffillii'	MNrw SBig WCru
	'Pink Princess' **new**	CBct
	'Pink V'	CCon
	'Pradhan'	CCon
	'Samsheri'	CCCN CHll SChr
	spicatum	CAbb CCCN CCon CDTJ CExl CHEx CTsd EUJe GCal GPoy IBlr LEdu MNrw WPGP
	- B&SWJ 7231	WCru
	- BWJ 8116 from Sichuan, China	WCru
	- CC 1705	CExl

- P.Bon. 57188 — CExl CFil WPGP
- PAB 4578 **new** — LEdu
- from Salween Valley, China — CExl
- 'Liberty' — WCru
- 'Singalila' — WCru
'St Martin's' — CCCN
stenopetalum B&SWJ 7155 — WCru
'Tahitian Flame' (v) — EUJe
'Tai Pink Princess' (Tai Series) — CTsd
N 'Tara' ♀H3 — CAbb CBct CDes CDoC CExl CHEx CHll CSam EAmu EBee EPfP EUJe IBlr LBMP LEdu LRHS MNrw SAPC SBst SChr SPlb SPoG WCru WPGP
thyrsiforme — CTsd EAmu EUJe NSoo SBig WCru XLum
'Vanilla Ice' (v) **new** — EAmu
villosum — CDTJ
wardii — CExl CFil CTsd EUJe WPGP
× ***wilkeanum*** — SPer
yunnanense — CCon CDes CHll LEdu SBig WPGP
- B&SWJ 9717 — WCru
- BWJ 7900 — WCru
- L 633 — CExl IBlr
- from Cally Gardens — GCal

Hedysarum (*Papilionaceae*)

coronarium — CSpe ELan MCot WCot WKif WWFP
hedysaroides — IKil
multijugum — CBcs EBee MBlu SPer WSHC
tauricum — SPhx
varium — CPBP
subsp. ***pestalozzae*** **new**

Heimia (*Lythraceae*)

salicifolia — CArn ECre

Helenium ✿ (*Asteraceae*)

'Abbey Dore Bronze' **new** — MSpe
'Adios' — MAvo MSpe
autumnale — CSBt CTri LDai LPot LSRN MLHP NChi SPet SWvt WGwG WHar WMoo WPtf XLum
- 'All Gold' — SWvt
I - 'Cupreum' — SBch
§ - Helena Series — SWvt
§ - - 'Helena Gold' — EPfP NBre
- - 'Helena Rote Töne' — EPfP LBMP LRHS MWhi
'Baronin Linden' — MAvo MSpe
'Baudirektor Linne' ♀H4 — CSam LEdu LRHS MSpe MTis SHar
'Beatrice' — MSpe
'Biedermeier' — CWCL ECtt EShb LRHS MRav MSpe NEgg WCAu
bigelovii — XLum
'Blanche Royale' — MSpe
'Blütentisch' misapplied — see *H.* 'Riverton Beauty'
'Blütentisch' Foerster ♀H4 — CHVG CMea COIW GMaP LRHS MSpe MTis NCGa NLar WMnd WWEG
'Bressingham Gold' — LRHS MNrw MSpe WHrl WWEG
'Bruno' — CAby ELan ELon LRHS MArl MSpe NLar SMrm
'Butterpat' ♀H4 — ECtt GBee GCra GMaP LRHS MArl MRav MSpe NSti WWEG
'Can Can' — CSam EBee ECtt EPfP LSou MAvo MSCN MSpe MTis NGdn SPer
'Chelsey' — CPrp CTsd ECtt ELan EPfP GQue LHop LRHS LSRN LSou MBri MNrw MSpe NLar NSti WBor WWlt
'Chipperfield Orange' — CAby CElw CSam EBee ECtt GMaP MArl MRav MSpe NBre NGdn WOld WWEG
'Coppelia' — LRHS MRav MSpe MTis NBir NGdn
Copper Spray — see *H.* 'Kupfersprudel'
'Crimson Beauty' — ECtt ELan LRHS
Dark Beauty — see *H.* 'Dunkle Pracht'
'Dauerbrenner' — CSam LEdu MAvo MSpe MTis
'Die Blonde' — MSpe NBre
'Double Trouble'PBR — ECtt EPfP IBoy IKil LLHF LRHS MBNS MBri MSpe NGdn NPri SGbt SPer SPoG STes WCAu WCot WHil
§ 'Dunkle Pracht' — CHVG CPrp CSam ECtt LSRN MCot MPie MSpe NEgg NLar NPri WCot WOld WWEG
'El Dorado' — CSam MAsh MAvo MSpe MTis NCGa SHar WCot
'Fata Morgana' — EBee ECtt LHop LLHF MSpe MTis NBre WCAu
'Feuersiegel' ♀H4 — CAby CSam ECtt LRHS MSpe NBre WOld WWEG
'Fiesta' — ECtt MBri MSpe NDov WHoo
'Flammendes Käthchen' — CSam EBee LRHS MAvo MSpe NBre NCGa NDov SHar SMrm SPhx
'Flammenrad' — CAby CSam EBee MSpe
'Flammenspiel' — EBee LRHS MCot MNrw MSpe NLar
flexuosum — SPhx
'Françoise' — CSam
'Gartensonne' ♀H4 — CSam MSpe SMrm WWEG
'Gay-go-round' — CSam MSpe
'Gelbe Waltraut' — MSpe
Gold Fox — see *H.* 'Goldfuchs'
'Gold Intoxication' — see *H.* 'Goldrausch'
Golden Youth — see *H.* 'Goldene Jugend'
§ 'Goldene Jugend' — CMea ELan LRHS MSpe MTis WCot WWEG
§ 'Goldfuchs' — CWCL LRHS MSpe WCot
'Goldkugel' — EBee MSpe
§ 'Goldlackzwerg' — LEdu LRHS MSpe MTis NBre
§ 'Goldrausch' — CAby CMac CSam CWCL EBee ECtt EPfP GBee GCra LRHS LSou MSpe MTis MWat NBre NGdn NSti WMoo WOld WWEG
'Goldreif' — MSpe
'Goldriese' — MSpe
'Hartmut Rieger' — CSam MSpe
'Helena' misapplied — see *H. autumnale* 'Helena Gold'
'Helena' Foerster — MSpe NLar
'Herbstgold' — MSpe
hoopesii — see *Hymenoxys hoopesii*
'Indianersommer' — CCVN CElw CSam ECtt GMaP LDai LRHS MSpe NDov NLar NOrc SPer WWEG
'Jam Tarts' — MSpe WCot
'Julisamt' — LEdu MSpe
'July Sun' — NBir
'Kanaria' — CAby CHVG CPrp EBee ECtt EWll GBin GQue LHop LRHS MAvo MSpe MTis NDov NEgg NLar WMnd
'Karneol' ♀H4 — CSam LRHS MSpe
'Kleine Aprikose' — MSpe
'Kleiner Fuchs' — MHer MSpe NLar WWEG
'Kokarde' — CSam MAvo MSpe WWEG
'Königstiger' — CSam ECtt LRHS LSou MNrw MSpe NBre NDov SMrm
'Kugelsonne' — MSpe NBre
§ 'Kupfersprudel' — CSam LRHS MAvo MSpe MTis
'Kupferziegel' — CSam MSpe MTis

'Kupferzwerg'	CWCL EBee ELan IPot MSpe NBre NDov SPhx
'Lambada'	IPot MSpe
'Louise Beacock' **new**	MSpe
'Loysder Wieck'	EBee ECtt EPfP LRHS MAvo MSpe MTis NDov NGdn SHil SPet
'Luc'	MSpe MTis WCot
§ 'Mahagoni'	CSam MSpe
'Mahogany'	see *H.* 'Goldlackzwerg'
Mahogany	see *H.* 'Mahagoni'
'Mardi Gras'	CMac ECtt LRHS LSou MBel MBri MSpe MTis NCGa NDov SPoG
'Margot'	CAby CSam CWCL MSpe MTis NBre
'Marion Nickig'	CSam MSpe MTis NDov
'Meranti'	CMea MAvo MSpe NDov WCot
'Mien Ruys'	MSpe
'Moerheim Beauty' ♀H4	Widely available
'Moth'	MSpe
'Oldenburg'	MSpe
'Orange Beauty'	MSpe
'Patsy'	MSpe
Pipsqueak = 'Blopip'	EBee LLHF LRHS MAvo MSpe NBre SPoG
'Potter's Wheel'	CAby MSpe MTis NDov WWEG
puberulum	LRHS NBir NLar
'Puck'	MSpe MTis
'Pumilum Magnificum'	CWCL ELan EPfP GQue IBoy LEdu LHop LRHS MSpe MTis WPGP XLum
'Ragamuffin'	CSam MSpe MTis WCot
'Rauchtopas'	CAby CSam EBee GQue IPot LSou MAvo MSpe MTis NCGa NDov SMrm WHoo WPGP
Red and Gold	see *H.* 'Rotgold' Foerster
'Red Army'	CAby CHVG CPrp EBee ELan IPot LEdu LPio LRHS LSou MAsh MAvo MBri MNrw MSpe MTis NCGa NGdn SPet
'Red Glory'	MSpe
'Red Jewel'	CMea EBee ECtt ELon IBoy LBMP LLHF LPla LRHS LSou MAvo MHol MNrw MPie MSpe MTis NDov NEgg NGdn NLar NPnk NSti SKHP SMad SMrm WCot WMnd WMoo WPGP WWEG
'Ring of Fire' ♀H4	MSpe
§ 'Riverton Beauty'	CSam LLHF MNrw MSpe MTis WCot WHoo
'Riverton Gem'	CSam ECtt LLHF MNrw MSpe MTis NChi WHoo
'Rotgold' misapplied	see *H. autumnale* Helena Series
§ 'Rotgold' Foerster	CMea ECtt LSRN MSpe NBre NChi SRms WMoo
'Rotkäppchen'	MSpe
'Rubinkuppel'	LRHS MSpe NCGa
'Rubinzwerg' ♀H4	Widely available
§ 'Ruby Thuesday'	CAby CTsd EBee ECtt ELan EPfP IBoy IKil LLHF LRHS LSRN MBNS MBel MHer MNrw MSpe MTis NEgg NGdn NHol NLar NSti SMad SPoG SWvt
'Ruby Tuesday'	see *H.* 'Ruby Thuesday'
'Sahin's Early Flowerer' ♀H4	Widely available
'Samtjuwel'	MSpe MTis
'Schokoladenkönigin'	MSpe
'Septemberfuchs'	EBee LEdu LPla MCot MTis NDov SPhx WWEG
'Septembergold'	MSpe
'Sonnenkringel'	MSpe
'Sonnenwunder'	MLHP MSpe NBre
'Sophie zur Linden'	CSam MSpe MTis WCot
'Sunshine'	MSpe
'Sunshine Superman' **new**	MSpe
'The Bishop'	COlW CPrp EBee ECtt EHyd ELon EPfP GCra LAst LBMP LHop LRHS MBri MRav MSCN MSpe NHol NPri NSoo SGbt SGol SPer SPet SWvt WHil WMnd WWEG
'Tie Dye' **new**	SMrm SPoG
'Tijuana Brass'	ECtt NLar
'Tura' **new**	MSpe
'Two Faced Fan'	MSpe MTis
'Vicky'	MAvo MSpe
'Vivace'	LEdu MSpe WCot
'Wagon Wheel'	MSpe WCot
'Waldhorn'	LRHS MSpe MTis
'Waltraut' ♀H4	CElw CKno CPrp CSam CWCL ECtt ELan EPfP GBBs LBMP LEdu LHop LRHS MAvo MCot MPie MRav MSpe MTis NBir NDov NHol NPri SBea SMrm SPer SWvt WCAu WWEG
'Wesergold' ♀H4	EBee GBBs LLHF LSou MBel MHer MSpe MTis NDov NLar
'Westerstede'	MSpe MTis
'Wonnadonga'	GBin MSpe MTis
'Wyndley'	Widely available
'Zimbelstern'	CCse ECtt ELon IPot LHop LRHS MAvo MCot MNFA MSpe MTis NLar SMrm SPhx WCot WPGP WWEG

Helianthella (*Asteraceae*)

§ ***quinquenervis***	EBee GCal LLHF LRHS MHer NLar SMad SPer

Helianthemum ✿ (*Cistaceae*)

sp.	SVic
'Alice Howorth'	WHoo WIce
alpestre serpyllifolium	see *H. nummularium* subsp. *glabrum*
'Amabile Plenum' (d)	GAbr GCal
'Amy Baring' ♀H4	CTri ECho ECtt GAbr LRHS NWad
'Annabel' (d)	ECho ECtt GAbr LHop LRHS NHol NSla
apenninum	LLHF SRms XLum
'Apricot'	CTri ECtt
'Apricot Blush'	WAbe
'Baby Buttercup'	CMea GAbr
'Beech Park Red'	CTri EPot MHer NHol WAbe WHoo WIce WKif
'Ben Afflick'	ECho ECtt LHop LRHS SRms
'Ben Alder'	ECtt GAbr MHer
'Ben Dearg'	CMea ECho ECtt SRms
'Ben Fhada'	CBcs CMea COlW CSam CTri ECho ECtt EHyd ELan ELon EPfP GMaP LBMP LBee LHop LRHS MAsh MHer MLHP NEgg SEND SPoG SRGP SRms WAbe XLum
'Ben Heckla'	CSam ECho ECtt EPfP GAbr LHop LPot LRHS MAsh XLum
'Ben Hope'	CTri ECho ECtt ELan EPfP MJak SGol SRGP XLum
§ 'Ben Ledi'	CBcs COlW ECho ECtt ELan ELon EPfP GAbr GMaP LHop MAsh MHer MSCN NHol NSla SPoG SRms SRot WAbe WNew
'Ben Lomond'	GAbr
'Ben Macdhui'	GAbr

	'Ben More'	CBcs CMea COlW ECho ECtt EHyd ELan ELon EPfP GAbr GJos GMaP LHop LRHS MAsh MSwo NBir SEND SIgm SPoG SRGP SRms SRot WHoo WIce
	'Ben Nevis'	CTri ECho ECtt GAbr SRms
	'Ben Vane'	ECho ECtt GAbr LRHS
	'Boughton Double Primrose' (d)	ECho ECtt GMaP WAbe WHoo WSHC
	'Bronzeteppich'	LLHF
	'Broughty Beacon'	ECtt WGor
	'Broughty Sunset'	CSam ECtt GAbr NBir
	'Bunbury'	ECtt ELon GAbr MWat NBir SDix SPoG SRms WIce WRHF
	canum subsp. ***balcanicum***	WAbe
	'Captivation'	ECtt GAbr NHol
	'Cerise Queen' (d)	CTri ECtt EPfP GAbr GKev LAst LBMP LHop MSwo SDix SEND SRms WHoo
	chamaecistus	see *H. nummularium*
	'Cheviot'	GAbr NBir SBch WHoo WSHC XLum
I	'Chloe's Variegata' (v)	EWes
	'Chocolate Blotch'	ECho GAbr GCra LHop LRHS NWad SEND SRms
	'Cornish Cream'	ECtt GAbr LBee NHol
	croceum	LLHF
	cupreum	ECtt GAbr GKev
	'David'	NHol
	'David Ritchie'	LLHF WHoo
	'Diana'	CMea SBch
	double apricot-flowered (d)	GAbr
	- orange-flowered (d)	LHop
	- primrose-flowered (d)	GAbr
	- red-flowered (d)	NChi
	'Dunwich' **new**	GGal
	'Ellen' (d)	CMea
	'Everton Ruby'	see *H.* 'Ben Ledi'
	'Fairy'	EHyd ELan EPfP GAbr LLHF
§	'Fire Dragon' ♈H4	CMea ECho ECtt ELan EPfP GAbr GMaP GQue LRHS NBir SRms WAbe WRHF XLum XSen
	'Fireball'	see *H.* 'Mrs C.W. Earle'
	'Firegold' (v)	WAbe
	'Georgeham'	CMea ECtt ELon EPfP GAbr NBir NHol SRms WGor WHoo WRHF XLum
§	'Golden Queen'	ECtt EPfP GAbr LAst MAsh MSwo WRHF
	'Hampstead Orange'	CTri
	'Hartswood Ruby'	GMaP MBNS
	'Henfield Brilliant' ♈H4	CExl CHVG CSam CSpe ECho ECtt EHyd ELan EPfP GAbr LHop LRHS MRav NBir NHol NSla SDix SMad SRms WHoo XLum
	'Highdown'	GAbr SRms
	'Highdown Apricot'	ECho ECtt LHop LLHF LRHS SPoG
	'Honeymoon'	ECtt EPfP GAbr NWad
	hymettium **new**	ITim
	'Jeanie' (d)	ECho
	'Jubilee' (d) ♈H4	CHVG CTri ECho ECtt ELan ELon EPfP GAbr LHop MAsh MBNS NBir NChi NHol SPoG SRms WHil WKif
	'Karen's Silver'	WAbe
	'Kathleen Druce' (d)	ECho ECtt EWes GAbr NWad WHoo
	'Kathleen Mary'	CMea
	'Lawrenson's Pink'	ECho ECtt GAbr LHop LRHS MCot MLHP SRGP
	'Lemon Queen'	NWsh
	lunulatum	CMea ECho LLHF LRHS NWad WAbe
	'Magnificum'	MWat
§	'Mrs C.W. Earle' (d) ♈H4	COlW CTri ECho ECtt ELan EPfP GCra LRHS MBNS MWat NEgg NSla SRms
	'Mrs Clay'	see *H.* 'Fire Dragon'
	'Mrs Hays'	ECtt
	'Mrs Lake'	GAbr
	'Mrs Moules'	SRms
	mutabile	SPhx SPlb
§	***nummularium***	ECho GPoy MHer MNHC NMir WAbe WIce WSFF XSen
§	- subsp. ***glabrum***	GAbr
§	- subsp. ***tomentosum***	GAbr MWat
	oelandicum	NSla NWad SRms WAbe
	- subsp. ***piloselloides***	WAbe
	'Old Gold'	ECtt GAbr SRms WAbe
	'Orange Phoenix' (d)	ECtt EPfP MBNS NWad
	'Ovum Supreme'	GAbr NHol
	pilosum	LLHF
	'Pink Angel' (d)	ECtt ELon MBNS
	'Praecox'	CMea CTri ECho GAbr SRms WHoo
	'Prima Donna'	EHyd ELan EPfP NBir
	'Prostrate Orange'	SRms
	'Raspberry Ripple'	ECho ECtt ELan EPfP EPot EWTr LRHS SPoG SRms
	'Razzle Dazzle' (v)	CMea ECtt ELon LLHF SLon SRms
	'Red Dragon'	EPot MLHP MSCN WAbe
	'Red Orient'	see *H.* 'Supreme'
	'Regenbogen' (d)	CPBP GCal SEND
§	'Rhodanthe Carneum' ♈H4	CBar CMac CMea COlW CSam CTri ECho ECtt ELan EPfP GMaP LBee LHop LRHS MRav MSwo NBir NWad SEND SPer SPhx SPoG SRot WAbe WHil WHoo WNew
§	'Rosakönigin'	ECtt GAbr MHer NHol WAbe WRHF
	'Rose of Leeswood' (d)	CMea CTri ECtt LBee NChi NEgg SPoG SRms WHoo WKif WSHC XLum
	Rose Queen	see *H.* 'Rosakönigin'
	'Roxburgh Gold'	SRms
	'Ruth'	SEND
	'Saint John's College Yellow'	CSam ECho LRHS
	'Salmon Beauty'	NHol
	'Salmon Queen'	ECho ECtt EWTr GAbr LHop LRHS SEND SRms
*	***scardicum***	CMea
	serpyllifolium	see *H. nummularium* subsp. *glabrum*
	'Shot Silk'	ECtt EWes
	'Snow Queen'	see *H.* 'The Bride'
	'Sterntaler'	GAbr LLHF SRms
	'Sudbury Gem'	CTri ECho EHyd LRHS SEND SGol
	'Sulphur Moon'	ECho EHyd LHop LLHF LRHS
	'Sulphureum Plenum' (d)	SGol
	'Sunbeam'	CSam ECho SRms
§	'Supreme'	ECho EHyd ELan EPfP EWes LHop SRms XLum
	'Tangerine'	ECtt GAbr
§	'The Bride' ♈H4	Widely available
	'Tigrinum Plenum' (d)	ECho EWes
	'Tomato Red'	NSla SEND XLum
	tomentosum	see *H. nummularium* subsp. *tomentosum*
	umbellatum	see *Halimium umbellatum*
	'Voltaire'	ECtt EPfP GAbr LLHF NWad XLum
	'Watergate Rose'	MWat NBir

'Welsh Flame'	NHol WAbe
'Whenday'	CMea
'Wisley Pink'	see *H.* 'Rhodanthe Carneum'
'Wisley Primrose' ♀H4	Widely available
'Wisley White'	CTri ECho ECtt ELan EPfP MAsh
'Wisley Yellow'	ECtt ELan
'Yellow Queen'	see *H.* 'Golden Queen'

Helianthus (*Asteraceae*)

sp.	SVic
atrorubens	LHop MRav NBro
'Bitter Chocolate'	CAby MAvo
'Capenoch Star' ♀H4	CElw CPrp EBee ECtt GMaP IBoy LEdu LPio LRHS MBri MRav MSpe MTis NBro NLar SDix SLPl SMrm WCAu WWEG
'Capenoch Supreme'	EBee ECtt LRHS
'Carine'	MAvo MLHP MNrw MTis
'Cosmic Whisper'	MAvo
decapetalus	MBel
- Morning Sun	see *H.* 'Morgensonne'
'Dorian Roxburgh'	MAvo
× ***doronicoides***	LRHS
giganteus	SHar
- 'Sheila's Sunshine'	CAby CBre CElw GBin LHop LRHS NDov SHar WOld
'Gullick's Variety' ♀H4	CBre ECtt LLWP NBro NChi NLar SPhx WOld WWEG XLum
'Happy Days'	CAby CBre CElw EBee ECtt ELon EWes LBMP LSou MAvo MPie MTis NCGa NSti SPoG WCot
'Hazel's Gold'	EBee ECtt LRHS NBre
hirsutus	EBee
× ***kellermanii***	EBee MTis NBre NDov SPhx
§ × ***laetiflorus***	MWhi NBre NLar NOrc
- 'Grandiflora'	LRHS
§ 'Lemon Queen' ♀H4	Widely available
'Limelight'	see *H.* 'Lemon Queen'
'Loddon Gold' ♀H4	ECtt ELan EPfP LRHS MAvo MBel MRav MSCN MSpe MTis NBir SRGP SWvt WBrk WCot WWEG
§ ***maximiliani***	ELon EWll LDai LHop LRHS SPhx WPtf
microcephalus	CAby CSam EBee ELon MTis NDov
- 'JS Straffe Prairie Gast'	EBee
'Miss Mellish' ♀H4	EBee MSCN WBrk WCot WHoo WWEG
mollis	CSam LRHS SBrt SPav
'Monarch' ♀H4	CMea CSam EBee GBee MAvo MBel MRav MSpe NBre NCGa NLar SMrm WCot WHil WOld WWEG
§ 'Morgensonne'	ECtt MTis MWat WCot
× ***multiflorus*** 'Meteor'	EBee LRHS NBre WCot WWEG
'O Sole Mio'	WCot
occidentalis	LRHS SMad
orgyalis	see *H. salicifolius*
quinquenervis	see *Helianthella quinquenervis*
rigidus misapplied	see *H.* × *laetiflorus*
§ ***salicifolius***	Widely available
- 'Low Down'PBR	LRHS
- 'Table Mountain'PBR	CSpe EBee MAvo SWvt WCot
scaberrimus	see *H.* × *laetiflorus*
'Soleil d'Or'	ECtt EWll WHal WWEG
strumosus	WCot
tomentosus	LRHS
'Triomphe de Gand'	LRHS MTis MWat NDov
tuberosus	CArn EBee GPoy SVic
- 'Fuseau'	SVic
- 'Garnet'	LEdu
- 'Sugarball'	LEdu

Helichrysum (*Asteraceae*)

from Drakensberg Mountains, South Africa	GAbr
adenocarpum	SPlb
alveolatum	see *H. splendidum*
ambiguum	EPfP
amorginum 'Pink Sapphire'PBR	LRHS
- Ruby Cluster = 'Blorub'PBR	EPfP LRHS NPri
angustifolium	see *H. italicum*
- from Crete	see *H. microphyllum* (Willd.) Cambess.
§ ***arwae***	WAbe
aucheri new	CPBP
bellidioides	see *Anaphalioides bellidioides*
'Coco'	see *Xerochrysum bracteatum* 'Coco'
confertum	SPlb
coralloides	see *Ozothamnus coralloides*
'County Park Silver'	see *Ozothamnus* 'County Park Silver'
'Dargan Hill Monarch'	see *Xerochrysum bracteatum* 'Dargan Hill Monarch'
'Elmstead'	see *H. stoechas* 'White Barn'
frigidum	CPBP
hookeri	see *Ozothamnus hookeri*
§ ***hypoleucum***	SDix
'Icicles'	GBin
§ ***italicum*** ♀H3	CArn CPrp ECrN EPfP GBin GPoy LPot MHer MMuc MNHC NPri SEND SPet SPoG SRms SVen WGwG WHer WHfH WJek XLum
- 'Dartington'	GBin WJek
I - 'Glaucum'	CWib
- 'Korma'PBR	EBee EHoe ELan EPfP EWTr GBin LRHS LSRN LSou MGos NPri SLon SPoG SRms WJek
- subsp. ***microphyllum***	see *H. microphyllum* (Willd.) Cambess.
- 'Nanum'	see *H. microphyllum* (Willd.) Cambess.
§ - subsp. ***serotinum***	CBcs EHoe EPfP GPoy LRHS MCot MHoo MRav SLim SPer SRms SWvt XSen
lanatum	see *H. thianschanicum*
ledifolium	see *Ozothamnus ledifolius*
marginatum misapplied	see *H. milfordiae*
marginatum DC. new	GKev
microphyllum ambig.	SPer SRms
§ ***microphyllum*** (Willd.) Cambess.	MNHC SEND WJek
§ ***milfordiae*** ♀H2-3	EPot ITim NSla NWad SIgm SRms WAbe
orientale	EPot XSen
pagophilum	EPot WAbe
petiolare ♀H2	EBak ECtt LAst MCot SPer SPoG
- 'Aureum'	see *H. petiolare* 'Limelight'
- 'Goring Silver' ♀H2-3	SPet SPoG
§ - 'Limelight' ♀H2	ECtt LAst MCot NPri SPer SPet SPoG
- 'Variegatum' (v) ♀H2	ECtt LAst MCot NPri SPet SPoG
plicatum	WCot
populifolium misapplied	see *H. hypoleucum*
rosmarinifolium	see *Ozothamnus rosmarinifolius*
§ 'Schwefellicht'	EPfP EShb MLHP MRav SPer WCAu WKif WSHC WWEG

	selago	see *Ozothamnus selago*
	serotinum	see *H. italicum* subsp. *serotinum*
	sessilioides	EPot WAbe
§	***sibthorpii***	WAbe
	'Skynet'	see *Xerochrysum bracteatum* 'Skynet'
§	***splendidum*** ♀H3	EPfP LRHS NBro SKHP SLon XSen
	stoechas	CArn
§	- 'White Barn'	CSpe WCot XLum
	Sulphur Light	see *H.* 'Schwefellicht'
§	***thianschanicum***	SRms XLum XSen
	- Golden Baby	see *H. thianschanicum* 'Goldkind'
§	- 'Goldkind'	NBir XLum
	trilineatum	see *H. splendidum*
	tumidum	see *Ozothamnus selago* var. *tumidus*
	virgineum	see *H. sibthorpii*
	wightii B&SWJ 9503	WCru
	witbergense	GKev WAbe
	woodii	see *H. arwae*

Helicodiceros (*Araceae*)

§	***muscivorus***	CHid WCot

Heliconia ✿ (*Heliconiaceae*)

	caribaea 'Burgundy'	see *H. caribaea* 'Purpurea'
§	- 'Purpurea'	XBlo
	'Golden Torch'	XBlo
	indica 'Spectabilis'	XBlo
	latispatha 'Orange Gyro'	XBlo
*	- 'Red Gyro'	XBlo
	metallica	XBlo
	psittacorum	CCCN
	rostrata	CCCN SBst XBlo
	schiedeana	CHll
	- 'Fire and Ice'	EAmu

Helictotrichon (*Poaceae*)

	pratense	CHab EHoe
§	***sempervirens*** ♀H4	Widely available
I	- 'Pendulum'	EBee GBin MAvo MSpe WRHF
	- 'Saphirsprudel'	CCse EBee EPfP LRHS SHil WCot WPGP WWEG

Heliophila (*Brassicaceae*)

	coronopifolia	CSpe

Heliopsis (*Asteraceae*)

	Golden Plume	see *H. helianthoides* var. *scabra* 'Goldgefieder'
	helianthoides	LRHS MLHP NBre
	- 'Limelight'	see *Helianthus* 'Lemon Queen'
	- Loraine Sunshine = 'Helhan'PBR (v)	CWGN LBMP LRHS LSou MPie MSCN NSti SMad SPoG WCot
	- var. ***scabra***	NHol SRot WMnd XLum
	- - 'Asahi'	ECtt ELan EWll GMaP MAvo MBri NLar NPri SMrm SPoG WHoo
	- - Ballerina	see *H. helianthoides* var. *scabra* 'Spitzentänzerin'
	- - 'Benzinggold' ♀H4	LSou MRav SMrm
	- - 'Bressingham Doubloon' (d)	ECtt LRHS
	- - 'Desert King'	LRHS
	- - 'Gigantea'	LRHS
	- - Golden Plume	see *H. helianthoides* var. *scabra* 'Goldgefieder'
§	- - 'Goldgefieder' ♀H4	EBee EPfP LRHS NBre
	- - Goldgreenheart	see *H. helianthoides* var. *scabra* 'Goldgrünherz'
§	- - 'Goldgrünherz'	LRHS
	- - 'Hohlspiegel'	LRHS
	- - 'Jupiter'	LRHS
	- - 'Lohfelden'	LRHS
	- - 'Patula'	EBee
	- - 'Prairie Sunset'PBR	ECtt MBri WWlt
§	- - 'Sommersonne'	CSBt ECtt EPfP EWll LRHS MSpe MWhi NGBl NLar NPer SMrm SPer SPoG SRms WMnd WWEG
§	- - 'Spitzentänzerin' ♀H4	ECtt
	- - 'Summer Nights'	CMea EBee EPfP LBMP LDai LRHS LSou MBri MCot MNrw MPie MSpe SBea SMrm SPhx SPoG
	- - Summer Sun	see *H. helianthoides* var. *scabra* 'Sommersonne'
	- - 'Sunburst' (v)	LRHS SPav
	- - 'Venus'	ECtt EWll LRHS LSou MBri NLar WHoo
	- 'Summer Pink'	SPoG
	- 'Super Dwarf'	LSou
	- 'Tuscan Sun'PBR	CMea EBee ECtt MBri NPri WHil
	orientalis	LLHF

Heliotropium ✿ (*Boraginaceae*)

§	***amplexicaule***	SDys
	anchusifolium	see *H. amplexicaule*
§	***arborescens***	CArn EPfP EShb MCot MHom
	- 'Chatsworth' ♀H1	CAby CCCN CSpe ECre ECtt MHom
	- 'Dame Alice de Hales'	ECtt MHom
	- 'Gatton Park'	MHom
	- 'Lord Roberts'	ECtt MHom WWlt
	- 'Marine'	CSam ECtt NPri WGor
	- 'Mary Fox'	MHom
	- 'Mrs J.W. Lowther'	MHom
	- pale lilac-flowered **new**	CSam
	- 'President Garfield'	MHom
	- 'Princess Marina' ♀H1	EPfP LAst LSou NLar
	- 'Reva'	ECtt MHom
	- 'The Queen'	ECtt
	- 'The Speaker'	MHom
	- 'White Lady'	CCCN CSpe ECtt MHom NLar
	- 'White Queen'	ECtt MHom
	- 'Woodcote'	MHom
	'Butterfly Kisses'	EPfP
	peruvianum	see *H. arborescens*

Helipterum see *Syncarpha*

Helleborus ✿ (*Ranunculaceae*)

	abruzzicus WM 0227	MPhe
	abschasicus	see *H. orientalis* Lam. subsp. *abchasicus*
	'Angel Glow'	LRHS MBri
§	***argutifolius*** ♀H4	Widely available
	- 'Janet Starnes' (v)	MAsh
	- 'Little 'Erbert'	MAsh
	- mottled-leaved	see *H. argutifolius* 'Pacific Frost'
§	- 'Pacific Frost' (v)	CPla LRHS MAsh MMHG
	- 'Red Riding Hood'	LRHS
	- 'Silver Lace'	CCon ELan EPfP GKev IBoy LDai LHop LRHS LSRN MBel MHol NBir NLar NPnk NSti NWad SKHP SPer SPoG WMoo
	atrorubens misapplied	see *H. orientalis* Lam. subsp. *abchasicus* Early Purple Group
	atrorubens Waldst. & Kit.	CDes MRav
	- WM 9028 from Slovenia	MPhe

- WM 9805 from Croatia	GBuc MPhe
- WM 9825	LWst
- spotted form	MPhe
× ***ballardiae***	CLAP
- 'Candy Love'PBR	CRos LRHS MBri NLar SHil
- 'HGC Cinnamon Snow'	ESwi LRHS
- 'HGC Pink Frost'	LRHS
'Blue Moon'	IBoy
bocconei	GCal LWst
- subsp. ***bocconei***	see *H. multifidus* subsp. *bocconei*
colchicus	see *H. orientalis* Lam. subsp. *abchasicus*
corsicus	see *H. argutifolius*
- 'Marble' (v)	CSpe
croaticus	LWst MAsh
- WM 9313	MPhe
- WM 9810	MPhe
cyclophyllus	MPhe SPer
- HOA 8934	LWst WSpi
- HOA 9144	LWst
dumetorum	GBuc GCal WSpi
- WM 0023	LWst
- WM 9209	MPhe
- WM 9627 from Croatia	GBuc MPhe
- WM 9832	LWst
§ × ***ericsmithii***	CAby CDes CExl CLAP CMHG CMil CSpe ELon EPfP GAbr GBuc GMaP LAst LHop LLHF LRHS LSRN LSou MAsh MNFA NBir NGdn NLar NPnk WHoo WPGP WSpi
- 'Bob's Best'	CEnd CExl CHid CLAP ECtt ESwi GBin LBMP LPla LRHS MBNS MHol MNrw MPie NPnk NWad SHar SKHP SPer SPoG SWvt WCot WRHF
- 'HGC Silvermoon'PBR	IBoy LRHS MAsh NLar SPoG
- 'Ruby Glow'	EPfP LRHS
- 'Snow Love'PBR	CRos EPfP LRHS MBri NLar SHil
- 'Winter Moonbeam'PBR	CLAP CSpe EPfP LRHS MBri MCot NCGa SKHP SLon SPoG
- 'Winter Sunshine'PBR	CLAP EPfP LBuc LRHS MBri SKHP SPoG
foetidus ♀H4	Widely available
- from Italy	IFoB
- 'Chedglow'	CNat EBee
- 'Gold Bullion'	CPla ECtt ELon GBuc MAsh SPoG WWEG
- 'Harvington Pewter'	CLAP EHyd LRHS MAsh
- 'Pewter'	CLAP
- 'Ruth'	MAsh
- 'Sopron'	CLAP NLar
- sweet-scented	MHom
- Wester Flisk Group	CExl ECtt EPfP GBuc IFoB LAst LHop LRHS MAsh MBri MRav MSwo NHol NPer NPnk WHar WPGP
- 'Yorkley'	LSRN
Gold Collection	see *H.* cultivars with names starting HGC
'Golden Sunrise' (Winter Jewels Series)	MPnt NCGa
'Harlequin Gem' (Winter Jewels Series) (d)	MPnt
'HGC Jericho'PBR	IVic
N × ***hybridus***	Widely available
- 'Amber Queen' (Queen Series)	WSpi
- anemone-centred	CHid CLAP GBin IFoB LHel MNrw SHil
- 'Apple Blossom'	IFoB

- 'Apricot Blush' (Winter Jewels Series) **new**	CWGN NPnk
- apricot-flowered	CLAP EPfP GBuc IFoB LBMP WSpi
- Ashwood Garden hybrids	ELan EPPr EPfP LRHS MAsh MMuc MRav SEND SLon SRms WSpi WWEG
- - anemone-centred	MAsh
- - double-flowered (d)	MAsh
- Ballard's Group	CLAP IBoy LRHS MWat NCGa SPer WPnP
- best greens **new**	IFoB
- 'Black Beauty'	IFoB NEgg NPnk WSpi
- 'Black Knight' **new**	IFoB
- black-flowered	CLAP GBuc GKev GMaP IFoB NChi
- 'Blue Lady' (Lady Series)	CBcs EPfP GBin IFoB LRHS MBNS MGos NGdn SMad SMrm SPer WSpi
- 'Blue Metallic Lady' (Lady Series)	CExl CWCL EPfP GAbr GKev IBoy IFoB LAst LBMP LHop MBNS MHol MWhi NEgg NGdn NPnk SMrm SPer WGwG WSpi WWEG
- Bradfield hybrids	MCot
- - anemone-centred	MCot
- - double-flowered (d)	MCot
- - picotee	MCot
- Caborn hybrids	LLWP
- 'Cherry Blossom' (Winter Jewels Series)	CWGN MPnt NCGa NPnk
- 'Cinderella' (d)	LRHS
- 'Clare's Purple'	LSRN WSpi
- 'Cosmos'	MBNS
- cream-flowered	CLAP IFro
- dark-flowered	WSpi
- dark purple-flowered	IFoB LHel
- dark red-flowered	IFoB LHel
- 'David's Star' (d)	CCon
- deep red-flowered	CLAP GBuc NChi NHol
- double (d)	CLAP CMea COlW CSpe GBuc IFoB LHop MNrw NPnk
- - black-flowered (d)	CExl IFoB
- - green-flowered (d)	IFoB LHel
- - pink-flowered (d)	IFoB LHel
- - purple-flowered (d)	LHel
- - red-flowered (d)	CExl
- - white-flowered (d)	CExl IFoB LHel WSpi
- - yellow-flowered (d)	CExl IFoB IFro LHel
- 'Double Ellen Picotee' (d)	GBin WHlf
- 'Double Ellen Red' (d)	GBin WHlf
- 'Double Ellen White' (d)	GBin WHlf
- Double Ladies, mixed (d)	GAbr WCot
- 'Double Vision' (d)	EPPr
- Elizabeth Town anemone-centred	IFro
- - double-centred (d)	IFro
- - picotee-centred	IFro
- - red-centred	IFro
- 'Emerald Queen' (Queen Series)	ELan GBin GQue WSpi
- Field of Blooms hybrids **new**	IFoB
- - anemone-centred **new**	IFoB
- - double-flowered (d) **new**	IFoB
- - picotee **new**	IFoB
- 'Gala Queen' (Queen Series)	CHel ELon
- 'Golden Lotus' (d)	CWGN MPnt NPnk
- 'Harvington Apricots'	CRos EHyd LRHS NBir NLar NPri SKHP SLon SPoG
- Harvington double apricot-flowered (d)	LRHS NPri SPoG

- - - chocolate (d)	CLAP EHyd NPri SPoG
- - - dark purple (d)	LRHS NPri
- - - lime-green (d)	CLAP LRHS NPri
- - - pink (d)	CHel CLAP CRos EHyd LRHS NPri SKHP SLon SPoG
- - - pink speckled (d)	CHel EHyd LRHS NPri SPoG
- - - purple (d)	CHel CLAP EHyd LRHS NBir NLar NPri SKHP SPoG
- - - red (d)	CHel CLAP CRos EHyd LRHS NBir NLar NPri SLon SPoG
- - - speckled (d)	LRHS NPri SPoG
- - - white (d)	CHel CLAP CRos EHyd LRHS NBir NLar NPri SKHP SLon SPoG
- - - yellow (d)	CHel CLAP EHyd LRHS NBir NLar NPri SKHP SLon SPoG
- - - yellow speckled (d) **new**	LRHS SPoG
- - picotee	CLAP EHyd LRHS NBir NLar NPri SKHP SLon SPoG
- - pink	CRos EHyd LRHS NLar NPri SLon SPoG
- - - speckled	CHel EHyd LRHS NLar NPri SLon SPoG
- - red	CHel CRos EHyd LRHS MHer NLar NPri SLon SPoG
- - speckled	EHyd LRHS MHer NPri SLon
- - - white	EHyd NPri SKHP SLon SPoG
- - white	CHel CRos EHyd LRHS MHer NLar NPri SKHP SLon SPoG
- - yellow	CHel CRos EHyd LRHS MHer NLar NPri SKHP SLon SPoG
- - - speckled	CRos EHyd LRHS MHer NLar NPri SLon SPoG
- 'Harvington Shades of the Night'	EHyd LRHS MHer NLar NPri SKHP SLon SPoG
- 'Harvington Smokey Blues'	CHel LRHS NPri SKHP SLon SPoG
- 'Harvington Smokey Double' (d)	NPri
- Hillier hybrids anemone-centred	CRos SHil
- - - pink **new**	LRHS
- - burgundy	LRHS MBri SHil
- - clear white	CRos LRHS SHil
- - double (d)	SHil
- - - pink (d)	CRos LRHS
- - pink and white	LRHS
- - single	SHil
- - slate	CRos LRHS SHil
- - spotted, double-pink (d)	LRHS
- - - green	LRHS
- - - pink	CRos LRHS MBri
- - - white	CRos LRHS MBri
- - yellow	CRos MBri
- Homelea hybrids, anemone-centred	CRDP
- - double (d)	CRDP
- 'Ice Queen' (Queen Series)	ELan WSpi
- Kaye's garden hybrids	LRHS
- Kochii Group	LRHS
- 'Lady in Red' **new**	IBoy
- Lady Series	IFoB NSum
- large, pink-flowered	IFoB IFro
- mauve freckled, double (d)	IFro
- 'Mrs Betty Ranicar' (d)	CBro EPfP IFoB LRHS MBNS MBri NCGa
- 'Onyx Odyssey'	CSpe CWGN MPnt NCGa
- 'Pale Picotee'	GBuc
- pale pink-flowered	GBuc
- 'Pamina'	IFoB
§ - Party Dress Group (d)	CHel CHid ELan ELon GBin IFoB LRHS LSRN NLar WBor
- - 'Party Dress Pink' (d)	CWCL
- 'Picotee'	CLAP GBuc IFoB LHel WCru WHoo
- 'Picotee' double-flowered (d)	CWCL LHel
- Picotee Group	NLar
- pink freckled, double (d)	IFro
- 'Pink Lady' (Lady Series)	CBcs EPfP GQue IFoB NEgg NGdn NPri SPer
- 'Pink Upstart'	IFoB
- pink-flowered	CLAP GBuc LHel MBNS WHoo
- pink-red-flowered	LHel
- plum-flowered	CLAP GBuc MMuc SEND
- primrose-flowered	CLAP ECGP ELan GBuc MCot MMuc NEgg SEND
- 'Purple Haze'	NPnk
- purple-flowered	CLAP WHoo
- (Queen Series) 'Queen of Hearts'	CHel ELan WSpi
- - 'Queen of Spades'	CHel ELan SMad WSpi
- - 'Queen of the Night'	CExl CHel CLAP CWCL ELan EPfP IBal MWhi WSpi
- 'Red Lady' (Lady Series)	CBcs CExl EPfP EPot GAbr IBal IFoB LHop LRHS LSRN MBNS MWhi NEgg NOrc SMrm SPer
- 'Red Spotted'	EPfP LRHS MWhi WWEG
- 'Red Upstart'	IFoB
- red-flowered	GBuc
- slaty blue-flowered	CLAP GBuc IFoB LHel
- slaty purple-flowered	GBuc
- 'Smokey Blue'	IFoB LRHS NPnk SEND WSpi
- smokey purple-flowered	ELan LSRN MMuc SGbt
- 'Speckled Draco'	CExl
§ - spotted	CLAP EPfP GBuc GMaP IFoB NEgg WCot WCru WHoo WWEG
- - cream	CLAP IFoB NBir
- - double, pink (d)	LHel
- - - white (d)	IFoB LHel
- - - yellow (d)	IFoB
- - green	CLAP
- - ivory	CLAP
- - pink	CLAP IFro LHel LRHS MBNS NBir SEND SHil WHoo
- - primrose	CLAP ELan SGbt
- - white	GBuc IFro LHel MMuc NBir SHil
- - yellow	LHel SHil
- 'Spotted Lady'	GBin
- Sunshine selections	GKev IBal
- 'Swirling Skirts'	GBin
- 'Tricastin'	IBoy
- 'Tutu'PBR	EPfP LBuc LRHS MBri NCGa SPer SPoG
- 'Ushba'	CLAP IFoB
- Washfield double-flowered (d)	CSpe EPfP NCGa SPer SRkn WRHF WSpi
- - white (d)	IFoB
- 'White Lady' (Lady Series)	CExl EPot IFoB LHop LPio MBNS NEgg NPri SMrm SPer WSpi
- 'White Lady Spotted' (Lady Series)	CHVG ELon EPfP GBin GQue MHol NEgg SPer
- white-flowered	GBuc IFoB LHel WCFE WHoo
- Winter Queen strain	WWEG
- yellow freckled, double (d)	IFro
- 'Yellow Lady' (Lady Series)	CBcs CCon EPfP EPot LHop LRHS MBNS MWhi NEgg SMrm SPer WSpi WWEG
- yellow-flowered	GMaP IFoB LHel WHoo

	– Zodiac Group	MBNS NPnk
§	'Ivory Prince'PBR	EPfP LBuc LRHS MAsh SPoG
	'Jade Star' (Winter Jewels Series)	MPnt
	'Kiwi Black Velvet'	IBal
	liguricus	GCal MAsh
	– WM 0230	MPhe
	lividus ♀H2-3	CBro CLAP EHyd EPfP EWes IFoB LHop LRHS NBir SDeJ SKHP SWat
	– subsp. ***corsicus***	see *H. argutifolius*
	– 'Silver Edge'	EPfP NPnk
	– 'White Marble'	LRHS NPnk SKHP
	'Moonshine'PBR	CLAP ELon MHol NHol NLar NWad SLon
	multifidus	EPPr IFoB NBir
§	– subsp. ***bocconei***	GCal LWst
	– – WM 9719 from Italy	MPhe
	– – WM 9905 from Sicily	MPhe
	– subsp. ***hercegovinus*** WM 0020	MPhe
	– – WM 0622	MPhe
	– subsp. ***istriacus***	CBro MAsh
	– – WM 9322	MPhe
	– – WM 9324	MPhe
	– subsp. ***multifidus*** WM 9529	MPhe
	– – WM 9833 from Croatia	MPhe
	niger ♀H4	Widely available
	– Ashwood strain	CLAP MAsh
	– Blackthorn Group	CDes CLAP NLar
	– 'Christmas Carol'	CHel
	– 'David'	IVic
	– 'Double Fashion'PBR	EBee LRHS
	– double-flowered (d)	CDes CHel ELan MAsh
	– 'Eifelturm'	IVic
	– Harvington hybrids	CLAP EHyd LRHS MAsh MBri MHer NPri SPoG
	– – double-flowered (d) **new**	SPoG
	– 'HGC Jacob'PBR	IVic LBuc LRHS LSRN
	– 'HGC Josef Lemper'PBR	IVic LRHS LSRN MBri
	– 'HGC Joshua'PBR	IVic
	– 'Innocence' **new**	CRDP
	– 'Ivory Prince'	see *H.* 'Ivory Prince'
	– Lynda Windsor Group	CRDP
	– 'Marion' (d)	IFoB
	– 'Maximus'	CLAP EWes
	– 'Potter's Wheel'	CLAP EPfP LRHS NBir
	– 'Praecox'	EPPr EPfP EWes LRHS
	– 'Schneeball'	IVic
	– 'White Christmas'	LRHS MBri SHil
	– 'White Magic'	WSpi
	× ***nigercors*** ♀H4	CSpe ECtt GBin GMaP LHop LPla LRHS MAsh MCot WCot WPGP
	– double-flowered (d)	GBin LSou MBNS WCot
	– 'HGC Green Corsican'PBR	EBee LRHS
	– 'Morning's Pride'PBR	LRHS
	– 'Pink Beauty'	LBuc NLar SPoG
	× ***nigristern***	see *H.* × *ericsmithii*
	odorus	GCal IFoB MAsh MPhe NPnk SPer WSpi XLum
	– WM 0312 from Bosnia	MPhe
	– WM 9415	MPhe
	– WM 9728 from Hungary	MPhe
N	***orientalis*** misapplied	see *H.* × *hybridus*
	orientalis ambig.	CBar CHab CTsd ECho EHyd LAst LPio LRHS MWat NPri WPtf
	orientalis Lam.	CBcs EWes LRHS MJak MPhe MSwo XLum
§	– subsp. ***abchasicus***	LRHS
	– – WM 9607	LWst
§	– – Early Purple Group	CTri GCal MRav SRms
	– subsp. ***guttatus*** misapplied	see *H.* × *hybridus* spotted
	– subsp. ***guttatus*** (A. Braun & Sauer) B. Mathew	NChi SRkn
	– – IBT 9401-7	SEND
	– subsp. ***orientalis*** from the Caucasus	LWst
	'Pink Beauty'PBR	EPfP LRHS MBri NCGa NLar SLon SPoG
	'Pirouette'PBR	CLAP EPfP LRHS MBri
	purpurascens	EPPr GBuc GMaP IFoB LRHS MAsh MRav MWat NBir SPer WSpi XEll
	– WM 0815 from Romania	MPhe
	– WM 9211 from Hungary	MPhe
	– WM 9412	MPhe
	– WM 9922	LWst
	(Rodney Davey Marbled Group) 'Anna's Red'	CRDP
	– 'Penny's Pink'	CBcs CRDP
	'Silver Dollar'	EPfP EWes LRHS LSRN NPnk SPer SPoG
	'Snow White'	MAsh
	× ***sternii***	CBcs CHel CSpe CTri CWCL EHyd ELan EPfP EWTr GMaP IFro LRHS MCot MMoz MNrw MWat NEgg NLar SPer SPoG WMoo
	– Aberconwy strain	CLAP
	– Ashwood strain	MAsh NLar
	– 'Beatrice le Blanc'	MAsh
	– Blackthorn Group ♀H3-4	ELon EPfP EUJe EWTr IFoB LHop LRHS MCot MRav SPer SWvt WBrk WPGP
	– Blackthorn dwarf strain	CHel CLAP
	– Boughton Group	MRav
	– 'Boughton Beauty'	CHel CLAP ELan GBuc WSpi
	– pewter-flowered	CSpe ECho
	thibetanus	CCon CExl CHel CLAP ECho EFEx EPot EWes MAsh MPhe NPnk
	torquatus	CBro GBuc LRHS MAsh MPhe SPer
	– HOA 9115	LWst
	– LD 308 from Serbia	LWst
	– WM 0609 from Montenegro	MPhe
	– WM 0617 from Serbia	MPhe
	– WM 9106 from Montenegro	GBuc MPhe
	– WM 9820 from Bosnia	MPhe
	– Caborn hybrids	LLWP
	– 'Dido' (d)	CExl
	– double-flowered, WM 0620 from Montenegro (d)	MPhe
	– hybrids	IFoB
	– Party Dress Group	see *H.* × *hybridus* Party Dress Group
	'Verboom Beauty'	LRHS
	vesicarius	MAsh
	viridis	GCal GPoy IFoB LRHS MAsh SRms XLum
	– WM 0444	MPhe
	– WM 9723 from Italy **new**	MPhe
	– subsp. ***occidentalis***	CBro MAsh
	Walberton's Rosemary = 'Walhero'PBR	EPfP LBuc LRHS MAsh SHar SPoG
	'Washfield Queen' (Queen Series)	CHel CWCL
	'White Beauty'PBR	EPfP LBuc LRHS MBri NCGa NLar SPer SPoG

Helonias (*Melanthiaceae*)

bullata	EBee LRHS

Heloniopsis (*Melanthiaceae*)

acutifolia	CDes
- B&SWJ 218	WCru
- B&SWJ 6817	WCru
- B&SWJ 6836	WCru
japonica	see *H. orientalis*
§ ***kawanoi***	CDes EBee SKHP WCot WCru
koreana B&SWJ 4173	WCru
leucantha B&SWJ 11148	WCru
§ ***orientalis***	CBro CLAP ECho GBuc GCal WCot WCru
- B&SWJ 6278	WCru
- B&SWJ 6327	WCru
- B&SWJ 6380 from Japan	WCru
- from Korea	EPfP SChF SKHP
- var. ***breviscapa***	EBee EPfP LEdu SChF SMad WCru WPGP
- - B&SWJ 5635	WCru
- - B&SWJ 5873	WCru
- - B&SWJ 5938	WCru
- - 'A-so'	LEdu WCru
- var. ***flavida*** B&SWJ 11400	WCru
- variegated (v)	WCru
- var. ***yakusimensis***	see *H. kawanoi*
tubiflora B&SWJ 822	WCru
- 'Temple Blue'	CDes CLAP WCru WPGP
umbellata	EBee EPfP LHop SKHP SMad WMoo
- B&SWJ 1839	CLAP WCru
- B&SWJ 3732	WCru
- B&SWJ 6836	WCru
- B&SWJ 6846	WCru
- B&SWJ 7117	WCru

Helwingia (*Helwingiaceae*)

chinensis	ESwi NLar SSpi WBor WPGP
himalaica	CExl CFil ESwi WPGP
japonica	CHGN EFEx

Helxine see *Soleirolia*

Hemerocallis ✿ (*Hemerocallidaceae*)

from Gansu **new**	MPhe
'Aabaa'	EWoo
'Aabachee'	CBgR
'Above the Clouds'	EWoo
'Absolute Treasure'	CFwr
'Absolute Zero'	SPol
'Adah'	SDay
'Adamas' **new**	CFwr
'Addie Branch Smith'	SDay
'Adeline Goldner'	CFwr
'Admiral's Braid'	EWoo
'Adorable Tiger' **new**	CFwr
'Adoration'	SPer
'African Chant'	ELan
'Age of Miracles'	SPol
'Ahoya'	CBgR SPol
'Airs and Graces'	SDay
'Alabama Jubilee'	WNHG
'Alabama Wildfire' **new**	CFwr
'Alakazam'	EWoo
'Alan'	ECtt LRHS MRav
'Alaqua'	CCon GBuc LRHS MBNS
'Alberene' **new**	CFwr
'Alec Allen'	SDay
'Alexander the Great'	WHrl
'Alien Encounter'	SPol
'All American Baby'	CWat MBNS MSpe SPol
'All American Eagle' **new**	SPol
'All American Magic'	SPol
'All American Plum'	CWCL EPfP IBoy MBNS MSpe WHrl
'All American Tiger'	MSpe SDay
'All American Windmill'	CFwr EWoo
'All Fired Up'	SDay SPol
'All I Want for Christmas' **new**	CFwr
'Allegiance'	WNHG
'Almost Paradise'	SPol
'Alpine Mist'	SDay
'Alpine Rhapsody'	SPol
'Alpine Snow'	EWoo
'Alternate Universe' **new**	CFwr
altissima	CHEx LPla MNrw SDix SPhx XSen
'Always Afternoon'	CBgR CKel EWoo GBuc MBNS MNrw MSpe NCGa SPol WCAu WHrl WWEG XSen
'Amadeus'	GBuc
'Amazon Amethyst'	WCAu
'Ambassador'	CBgR
'Amber Classic'	ELon
'American Freedom'	EWoo
'American Revolution'	CBgR CCVN CPar EBee ELon EWoo GBin LPio MBNS MBel MCot MGos MHol MNFA MWat NChi SDys SPol WCot WHrl WMoo WPnP WSpi XLum XSen
'Amersham'	MNFA
'Amethyst Squid'	EWoo
'Among Us' **new**	CFwr
'Amy'	WWEG
'Anatomically Correct'	EWoo
'Andrew Christian'	SPol
'Android'	CFwr
'Andy Candy'	CFwr
'Angel Artistry'	SDay
'Aniakchak'	EWoo
'Ann Kelley'	SDay
'Anna Warner'	ELon MMuc SEND
'Annabelle's Ghost'	CBgR SPol
'Annette's Magic' **new**	CFwr
'Annie Welch'	ELon EPfP MBNS NBre
'Answering Angels' **new**	CFwr
'Antarctica'	SPol
'Antique Rose'	CKel SDay
'Anzac'	COlW CTsd ECtt IBoy LRHS MBNS MBel NBre NGdn SGol SWvt WMoo
'Apache Bandana'	EWoo
'Apache Beacon'	EWoo
'Apache War Feather'	EWoo
'Apollo'	XSen
'Apollodorus'	SDay WHrl
'Apple Court Chablis'	SPol
'Apple Court Champagne'	SPol
'Apple Court Damson'	SPol
'Apple Court Ruby'	SPol
'Apple Of My Eye'	EWoo
'Apple Swirl' **new**	SPol
'Apple Tart'	SDay
'Applique'	CFwr
'Après Moi'	MBNS NLar
'Apricot Beauty' (d)	CPrp LHop MBNS NSoo SGol
'Apricotta'	WCot WPnP
'Apron Strings'	CFwr
'Arachnephobia'	EWoo

'Arctic Snow'	CBgR CBro CHel CMac ECrc ECtt ELon EWoo LRHS MBNS MNrw NLar SPol WPnP
'Armed and Dangerous' **new**	CFwr
'Arms to Heaven'	EWoo
'Arriba'	MNFA NBro
'Arthur Moore'	SDay
'Asian Artistry'	WNHG
'Asiatic Pheasant'	SPol
'Asterisk'	SDay
'Astral Voyager'	CFwr
'Aten'	SDay
'Athlone'	EWoo
'Atlanta Cover Girl' **new**	SDay
'Atlanta Fringe Benefit'	SDay
'August Frost'	SPol
'Aunt Wimp'	EWoo
'Authur Vincent'	SPol
'Autumn Jewels'	EWoo SPol
'Autumn Minaret'	EWoo
'Autumn Prince'	EWoo
'Autumn Red'	CBcs GKin MBNS MMuc MNrw NBir SEND SPol WCot
'Ava Michelle'	SDay
'Avant Garde'	SPol WCAu
'Avon Crystal Rose'	WNHG
'Awesome Blossom'	LSou MBNS MNrw SMrm WCAu WHrl
'Awesome Candy'	EWoo LSRN
'Aztec Firebird'	CFwr EWoo
'Aztec Furnace'	CBro SDay
'Baby Blues'	SDay SPol
'Baby Darling'	SDay
'Baby Talk'	CCon
'Baja'	MNFA
'Bakabana' **new**	MSCN
'Bald Eagle'	MNrw WWEG
'Bali Hai'	COlW MBNS SRms WHrl
'Bamboo Blackie'	CBgR EWoo SPol XSen
'Banana Cream Beauty' **new**	SDeJ
'Banbury Cinnamon'	MBNS MSpe
'Bangkok Belle'	CWat
'Banned in Boston'	EWoo MSpe
'Barbara Dittmer'	SPol
'Barbara Mitchell'	EWoo GBuc MBNS MNFA SDay SDeJ WCAu XSen
'Barbaresco'	SPol
'Barbary Corsair'	MNFA SDay
'Bark At Me'	CFwr
'Barnegat Orange Twister'	CFwr
'Barney Barnes' **new**	CFwr
'Baronet's Badge'	SPol
'Bat Signal'	CFwr EWoo
'Bathsheba'	SPol
'Battle Hymn'	WCAu
'Beagle Bess' **new**	CFwr
'Beaming Blessings' **new**	CFwr
'Beat the Barons'	SPol
'Beautiful Edgings'	EWoo SPol
'Beauty to Behold'	SDay
'Becky Lynn'	ECtt MBNS
'Bed of Roses'	MNFA
'Before Night Falls' **new**	CFwr
'Bela Lugosi'	CAbP CBgR CHel CMac CWat EBee ECrc ELon EPfP EWoo GQue LRHS LSRN MBNS MCot MNrw MSpe MWhi NBro NEgg SPad SPer SPol WCot WHrl WNHG
'Believe It'	WNHG
'Ben Lee'	SDay
'Ben Webster' **new**	CFwr
'Benchmark'	WHrl
'Bengal Bay'	EWoo
'Bengal Fire'	WNHG
'Berlin Lemon' ♀H4	MNFA
'Berlin Red' ♀H4	CWCL ELon GBee GKin LBMP LRHS MNFA MNrw SDay
'Berlin Red Velvet' ♀H4	MNFA
'Berlin Watermelon'	MBNS
'Bernard Thompson'	MNFA
'Berrylicious' **new**	EPfP
'Bertie Ferris'	EWoo NLar SDay
'Bess Ross'	CMHG MNFA XSen
'Bess Vestal'	MWat
'Best Kept Secret'	EWoo SPol
'Bette Davis Eyes'	CBgR CWat SDay SPol
'Betty Warren Woods'	SDay
'Betty Woods' (d)	SDay
'Betty's Pick'	EWoo
'Beware the Wizard'	CFwr
'Beyond 2000'	CFwr
'Big Apple'	SDay SPol
'Big Bird'	EWoo LSRN MBNS
'Big City Eye'	MBNS
'Big Golden'	WWEG
'Big Kiss' (d)	SPol
'Big Ross'	CFwr
'Big Smile'	CWCL CWGN MBNS MNrw NBro NSoo SDeJ
'Big Snowbird'	CFwr
'Big Time Happy'	LRHS MBNS SPoG
'Big World'	CBgR
'Bigcabin Neon Beacon' **new**	CFwr
'Bill Norris'	SDay
'Bird Bath Pink'	SPol
'Birdwing Butterfly'	EWoo SPol
'Bite the Bullet' **new**	CFwr
'Bitsy'	ELon LRHS SPet WCot WMnd WWEG
'Black Ambrosia'	SPol
'Black Arrowhead' **new**	CFwr SPol
'Black Emanuelle'	CExl CHel EWTr IKil LAst LDai MBNS MNrw
'Black Eye'	SDay WNHG
'Black Eyed Stella'	CKel MBNS WCot
'Black Eyed Susan'	ECtt MBNS MSpe
'Black Falcon Ritual' **new**	CFwr
'Black Friar'	EWoo
'Black Ice'	CFwr EWoo SPol
'Black Knight'	EWoo NLar SRms
'Black Magic'	CBro CTri CWat ELan EPfP GKin GMaP IPot LHop LRHS LSRN MHer MRav MWhi NBir NEgg NGdn SMrm SPer WHer WHrl WMoo
'Black Plush'	EWoo SPol
'Black Prince'	CBgR CCon EWll EWoo IBoy LRHS MBNS NBre NBro
'Black Stockings'	EWes IPot MBri MWhi SDeJ
'Blackberry Candy'	CHel CSam ECtt GKin MBNS MNrw MSpe NHol NWad WCAu
'Blackeye Belle'	EWoo
'Blessed Again'	SDay
'Blessing'	SPol
'Blonde Ambition' **new**	CFwr
'Blonde is Beautiful'	SDay
'Blue Beat' **new**	CFwr
'Blue Happiness'	SDay

'Blue Sheen'	CCon CMac COIW EBee ECtt GMaP MBNS WMoo
'Blue Venom' **new**	CFwr
'Blueberry Candy'	ECtt EWoo IBoy MBNS
'Blueberry Cream'	CWCL ELon EPfP MBNS MMHG MNrw MSpe
'Blueberry Frost'	CBgR
'Blueberry Sundae'	CHel CWat EBee ELon NSoo SGol
'Blue eyed Butterfly'	SPol
'Blue-eyed Curls'	CFwr
'Blushing Belle'	MBNS NBro NEgg
'Blutorange'	CFwr
'Bobby Martin' **new**	CFwr
'Bobo Anne'	CWat
'Bogie and Becall'	SPol
'Bold Courtier'	CBgR
'Bold Encounter'	CFwr
'Bold One'	CMHG SPol
'Bold Ruler'	SPol
'Bonanza'	Widely available
'Boney Maroney'	CBgR CFwr EWoo
'Bonheur'	WHrl
'Bonnie Boy'	XLum XSen
'Bonnie Holley' **new**	CFwr
'Boogie my Woogie Baby'	CFwr EWoo
'Booroobin Magic'	EWoo
'Border Baby'	ECtt
'Border Lord'	EWoo
'Both Sides Now' **new**	ECtt
'Boulderbrook Serenity'	SDay
'Bourbon Kings'	EHyd MBNS MSpe NBre SDeJ WHrl
'Bradley Bernard'	SPol
'Braided Edgings'	CFwr
'Brand New Lover'	SDay
'Brass Buckles'	see *H.* 'Puddin'
'Brasstown'	SPol
'Brazilian Orange' **new**	XSen
'Breed Apart'	SPol
'Brenda Newbold'	SDay SPol
'Brer Rabbit's Baby'	EWoo
'Bridge of Dreams' **new**	CFwr
'Bridget'	ELan
'Bright Beacon'	SDay SPol
'Bright Island' **new**	XSen
'Bright Side' **new**	CBgR
'Bright Spangles'	MSpe SDay
'Brilliant Circle'	ECtt
'Bring It On' **new**	CFwr
'Broadway Bold Eyes'	SPol
'Broadway Valentine'	XSen
'Brocaded Gown'	ELan SDay
'Brown Billows'	EWoo
'Brown Exotica'	CFwr EWoo
'Brown Witch'	EWoo
'Brown-Eyed Girl' **new**	SPol
'Bruno Müller'	MNFA
'Brushed with Bronze'	SPol
'Brutus'	WHrl
'Bubbly'	SDay
'Bud Producer'	SPol
'Buddha'	WCAu
'Buenos Aires' **new**	XSen
'Buffy's Doll'	MBNS
'Bugs Ear'	SDay
'Bumble Bee'	CWat ECtt MBNS NBre
'Bumble Bee Boogie' **new**	CFwr
'Burlesque'	SDay SPol WCot
'Burning Daylight' ♀H4	CBgR EBee ECtt EPfP LRHS MNFA MNrw MRav MWat NBre NEgg SGol SPer SRms WCAu WCFE WCot WPtf
'Bus Stop'	SPol
'Butterfly Charm'	CWat
'Butterpat'	SDay
'Butterscotch Ruffles'	SDay
'Buzz Bomb'	CWat ECGP ECrc ECtt GBee GKin LRHS LSRN MBNS MCot MNFA NEgg NGdn NHol SPer WWEG
'By Myself'	XSen
'Cabbage Flower'	SDay XSen
'Cabriolet' **new**	XSen
'Cajun Christmas'	CFwr
'Calico Spider'	SPol XSen
'California Sunshine'	SPol
'Call Girl'	SDay
'Calypso'	EWoo
'Camden Ballerina'	SDay
'Camden Gold Dollar'	SDay
'Camelot Green'	WNHG
'Cameroons'	SDay SPol
'Canadian Border Patrol'	CWCL IPot MBNS MNrw NLar SPer SPol WCAu WHrl
'Canary Glow'	CTri IBoy SMrm
'Canary Wings'	CBgR
'Candid Colors' **new**	CFwr
'Candide'	SDay
'Candied Popcorn Perfection'	CFwr
'Candy Cane Dreams' **new**	CFwr
'Cantique'	SDay SPol
'Capernaum Cocktail'	SPol
'Capulina'	EWoo
'Cara Mia'	CBgR MBNS NBir SPol
'Caribbean Jack Dolan'	EWoo
'Carlotta'	SDay
'Carmen Marie' **new**	XSen
'Carnival in Mexico' **new**	CFwr
'Carnival Mask' **new**	CFwr
'Carolicolossal'	ELon SDay SPol
'Carolina Cranberry'	ELan
'Carolina Low Country'	CFwr
'Carolina Red Bug' **new**	CFwr
'Caroline Taylor'	WHrl
'Carrick Wildon'	CFwr
'Cartwheels' ♀H4	EPfP EShb GBuc GKin GMaP LRHS MBNS MBel MSpe NBro SBch SPer WCAu WMoo
'Carved Pumpkin Pie' **new**	CFwr
'Casa des Juan' **new**	CFwr
'Castile'	SDay
'Castle Pinkney' **new**	CFwr
'Castle Strawberry Delight'	SPol
'Catapult Sam' **new**	CFwr
'Catch a Falling Star' **new**	CFwr
'Catherine Neal'	SDay SPol
'Catherine Woodbery'	Widely available
'Cathy Cute Legs' **new**	CFwr
'Cathy's Sunset'	CKel CSam ECtt GKin LRHS LSRN MBNS MSpe MWat NBre NBro NEgg NGdn NWad SRGP
'Cat's Cradle'	SDay
'Caviar'	SDay
'Cayenne' **new**	SPol
'Cedar Waxwing'	MNrw
'Cedric Morris'	LRHS
'Celestial City'	SDay
'Celtic Christmas'	CFwr SPol
'Cenla Crepe Myrtle'	EWoo

'Cerulean Star'	EWoo SPol
'Challenger'	EWoo
'Chamonix' **new**	XSen
'Chance Encounter'	MBNS NHol SPol
'Chang Dynasty' **new**	CFwr
'Changing Latitudes'	SPol
'Charlene Moore'	SPol
'Charles Johnston'	CBgR CKel EWoo MBNS SDay
'Charlie Pierce Memorial'	SPol
'Charon the Ferryman'	CFwr
'Chartreuse Magic'	CMHG
'Chartwell'	EWoo
'Chasing the Sun'	CFwr
'Château Lafite'	SPol
'Cheerful Note'	WNHG
'Cherokee Patterns'	SPol
'Cherokee Vision' **new**	CFwr
'Cherry Candy'	MSpe
'Cherry Cheeks'	CCon ECtt ELan ELon EPfP LRHS MBNS MBri MHol MNrw MRav NHol SPol WCAu WCot WMoo WWEG
'Cherry Eyed Pumpkin'	EWoo SDay WCAu
'Cherry Kiss'	IVic
'Cherry Lace' **new**	XSen
'Cherry Ripe'	MNFA
'Cherry Tiger'	MBNS MSpe
'Cherry Valentine'	CBcs MBNS MSpe
'Chesapeake Crablegs' **new**	CFwr
'Chesières Lunar Moth'	ELon SPol
'Chester Cyclone'	SDay
'Chevron Spider'	SDay
'Chicago Antique Tapestry'	SDay
'Chicago Apache'	CCon EBee ELon EPfP EWoo MBNS MNFA NBir NCGa SBch SMad SPer SPol
'Chicago Aztec'	ELon
'Chicago Blackout'	CCon CWat EBee ECtt WCot
'Chicago Cattleya'	CCon
'Chicago Cherry'	WNHG
'Chicago Fire'	EBee EPfP LPio MBNS SDay
'Chicago Firecracker'	XLum XSen
'Chicago Heirloom'	CCon MBNS
'Chicago Jewel'	CCon ELon NSti
'Chicago Knobby'	EBee MBNS MNrw SDay
'Chicago Knockout'	CCon EHyd ELan EPfP EWoo SPer WWEG
'Chicago Mist'	WNHG
'Chicago Peach'	NBir
'Chicago Picotee Lace'	WWEG
'Chicago Picotee Memories'	EBee LRHS MBNS
'Chicago Picotee Promise'	WNHG
'Chicago Princess'	EWoo
'Chicago Queen'	SDay WMnd WNHG
'Chicago Rainbow'	CBgR MBNS
'Chicago Royal Crown'	ECtt
'Chicago Royal Robe'	CWCL CWat ELon EWll LRHS MBNS NBid NCGa SPer SWat WCot
'Chicago Silver'	CCon COIW MBNS
'Chicago Star'	WNHG
'Chicago Sugarplum'	SDay
'Chicago Sunrise'	CBgR GMaP IBoy LRHS MBNS MRav NGdn NOrc SPet SWvt WCot WWEG
'Chief Four Fingers'	EWoo
'Child of Fortune'	SDay
'Children's Festival'	CMac ECtt GMaP LRHS MBNS MRav MSpe NLar SWvt WMoo

'China Bride'	EWoo SDay SPol
'Chinese Coral'	EWoo
'Chinese Imp'	NLar SDay
'Chocolate Candy'	CWGN EBee EPfP EWTr IPot MBNS
'Choctaw Chick'	CFwr
'Chokecherry Mountain'	EWoo
'Chorus Line'	SDay SPol WNHG
'Chorus Line Kid'	SPol
'Christine Lynn'	WNHG
'Christmas Is'	CBgR CHel CMac COIW CWGN EBee ELon GBin GKin LPot LRHS LSou MBNS MBel MNrw MSpe NBre NCGa NHol SDay SPol WCot WHrl WWEG XSen
'Ciarra Vonnie'	SDay
'Cimarron Knight'	EWoo SPol WCAu
'Cindy's Eye'	WCot
'Cinnamon Pleasure'	WCAu
'Circle of Beauty'	SPol
citrina	CBgR CExl CHid CMac EBee EWTr EWoo GQue IBoy IMou LRHS MCot WCot WHrl WRHF XLum XSen
citrina × (× ***ochroleuca***)	WCot
'Civil Law'	SDay
'Civil Rights'	SDay
'Classic Caper'	WNHG
'Claudine'	ELon
'Cleo'	EWoo
'Cleopatra'	ELon EWoo SPol
'Clothed in Glory'	EWoo MBNS WCot WWEG
'Cluster Muster' **new**	CFwr
'Coburg Fright Wig'	EWoo
'Cocktail Party'	MBri
'Colonel Joe'	EWoo
'Comanche Eyes'	SDay
'Comet Flash'	SPol
'Coming Up Roses'	ELon
'Concorde Nelson'	CFwr
'Condilla' (d)	SPol
'Connie Abel' **new**	CFwr
'Connie Can't Have It' **new**	CFwr
'Conspicua'	SPol
'Contessa'	CBro GBin LRHS SPer
'Cool It'	CKel LHop MBNS MPie NBre NCGa SDeJ WHrl
'Cool Jazz'	SDay SPol
'Cool Summer Breeze' **new**	SPol
'Copper Dawn'	NChi
'Copper Windmill'	CBgR SDay SPol
'Copperhead'	SPol
'Coral Crab'	EWoo
'Coral Eye Shadow'	EWoo
'Coral Mist'	ECrc MBNS NBre
'Coral Sparkler'	WNHG
'Coral Spider'	SPol
'Coral Taco'	EWoo
'Corky' ♀^{H4}	CBro CCon EBee ECGP EHyd ELan EPfP GBuc GCal GMaP LPot LRHS LSRN MBel MNFA MNrw MSpe MWat NEgg NGdn NLar SDix SPer SPhx WCAu WPnP WWEG XLum XSen
'Corryton Pink'	SPol
'Corsican Bandit'	SDay
'Cosmic Hummingbird'	SDay
'Cosmopolitan'	MBNS
'Country Club'	EBee GMaP MBNS NHol SPol WWEG
'Country Melody'	SDay

'Court Magician'	EWoo
'Court Troubadour'	ELon SPol
'Coyote Moon'	SDay
'Craig Green' **new**	CFwr
'Cranberry Baby'	SDay WHoo WNHG
'Cranberry Coulis'	CWat MBNS
'Crawleycrow'	XSen
'Crazy Crane' **new**	CFwr
'Crazy Ivan' **new**	CFwr
'Crazy Pierre'	EWoo SPol WHrl XSen
'Cream Drop'	CPrp ECtt GBuc GMaP IBoy LRHS MCot MHer MRav NBro NGdn NLar NSti SPer WCot WHrl WMoo
'Creation'	CFwr EWoo
'Cricket Call' **new**	CFwr
'Crimson Flood'	EWoo
'Crimson Icon'	SDay
'Crimson Pirate'	CBgR CBre CHel CMac EBee ECrc ELon EPfP EWoo GKev IBoy LHop LSRN MBNS MSpe NBir NHol NOrc NPro SPer SPlb SPol SWat WCAu WHar WHrl WMoo XLum
'Crintonic Shadowlands'	SPol
'Cripple Creek'	CFwr EWoo
'Croesus'	SRms
'Crooked House' **new**	CFwr
'Crystal Cupid' **new**	XSen
'Crystal Pinot'	ELon
'Cupid's Gold'	SDay
'Curls'	MBNS SDay
'Curly Brick Road'	SPol
'Curly Cinnamon Windmill'	SDay SPol
'Curly Pink Ribbons'	EWoo
'Curly Rosy Posy'	SDay
'Custard Candy'	CWCL CWGN EWoo GKin MBNS MSpe NHol WCAu WNHG
'Cynthia Mary'	ECtt GKin LHop MBNS MSpe NBro SRGP
'Cypriana' **new**	XSen
'D.R. McKeithan'	CFwr
'Daily Dollar'	LRHS MBNS MSpe NGdn
'Dallas Spider Time'	MNFA SDay
'Dallas Star'	SPol WHrl
'Dan Mahony'	MBNS NSoo
'Dan Tau'	CKel
'Dance Among the Stars'	CFwr
'Dance Ballerina Dance'	EBee SDay
'Dancing Crab'	EWoo SPol
'Dancing Dwarf'	SDay
'Dancing Lions'	SDay
'Dancing Shiva'	SDay SPol
'Dancing Summerbird'	ELon SPol
'Dancing with Julie' **new**	CFwr
'Daring Deception'	CCon CKel ECtt ELon EPfP IPot LRHS MBNS MNrw MSpe SPad WHrl
'Daring Dilemma'	SPol
'Daring Reflection'	MSpe SDay
'Darius'	WNHG
'Dark and Handsome'	MBNS
'Dark Angel'	MSpe
'Dark Avenger'	MBNS MSpe
'Dark Elf'	SDay
'Dark Monkey' **new**	CFwr
'Dark Sprite'	MSpe
'Date Book'	EWoo
'David Holman'	WNHG
'David Kirchhoff'	NSoo
'Davidson Update'	WNHG
'Dazzling Spider'	CFwr
'Debary Canary'	EWoo
'Debussy'	EWoo
'Decatur Ballerina'	WNHG
'Decatur Captivation'	WNHG
'Decatur Cherry Smash'	SDay
'Decatur Dictator'	WNHG
'Decatur Elevator'	EWoo
'Decatur Imp'	WHrl
'Decatur Jewel'	WNHG
'Decatur Rhythm'	WNHG
'Decatur Supreme'	WNHG
'Decatur Treasure Chest'	WNHG
'Deep in My Heart' **new**	CFwr
'Delicate Design'	SPol
'Delightful David' **new**	CFwr
'Delightsome'	SDay
'Demetrius'	CWat MNFA
'Dena Marie's Sister'	CFwr
'Derrick Cane'	SPol
'Desdemona'	SPol XLum
'Desert Dreams'	WCot
'Desert Icicle'	EWoo
'Designer Gown'	SDay
'Designer Jeans'	SPol
'Destination Y' **new**	XSen
'Destined to See'	CBcs CBro CCVN CCon COIW CPar ECtt ELon IPot LDai LHop LRHS LSRN LSou MBNS MNrw NBir NBro NEgg SPer SPol WCot WHrl
'Devil's Footprint'	SDay SPol
'Devon Cream'	SPer
'Devonshire'	SDay
'Dewberry Candy'	ELon MSpe
'Diabolique'	EWoo
'Diamond Dust'	CKel ECtt GBee LRHS MBNS NLar SPer
'Dick Kitchingman'	SPol
'Dido'	CTri
'Dipped in Ink'	SPol
'Distant Star'	EWoo
'Distinctive Elegance' **new**	CFwr
'Divertissment'	CBgR ELon EWoo SDay WHrl
'Dixie Rooster' **new**	CFwr
'Dizzy Miss Lizzy' **new**	CFwr
'Do the Twist'	EWoo
'Do You Know Doris'	SDay
'Dominic'	CBgR COIW CPar EWoo IBoy MSpe SPol WCot WMoo
'Don Stevens'	WHrl
'Don't Know Jack' **new**	CFwr
'Dont Mess with Me'	CFwr
'Dorethe Louise'	CBgR SDay SPol
'Dorothy McDade'	COIW EWoo MNrw
'Dot Paul'	ELan
'Double Action' (d)	SDay SPol
'Double Charm' (d) **new**	XSen
'Double Coffee' (d)	SPol
'Double Corsage' (d)	SPol
'Double Cream' (d)	WCot
'Double Cutie' (d)	NBre NLar SDay
'Double Delicious' (d)	WCot
'Double Doubloon' (d)	XLum
'Double Dream' (d)	WHrl
'Double Firecracker' (d)	CCVN CWat EBee MBNS NBro NLar XSen
'Double Glitter' (d) **new**	XSen
'Double Oh Seven' (d)	ELon SPol
'Double Passion' (d)	MBNS

'Double Pop Art' (d) **new**	XSen
'Double Red Royal' (d)	MAvo XSen
'Double River Wye' (d)	CBgR CCon COIW CWat ECtt EHyd EPfP EShb GBin IBoy MBNS MHer MNrw NGdn SPol SWat WBrk WCot WHoo WHrl WMnd WWEG
§ 'Doubloon' (d)	COIW LRHS NHol
'Dowager Queen' **new**	WNHG
'Dragon Dreams'	SPol
'Dragon Fire Breath'	CFwr
'Dragon Heart'	EWoo
'Dragon King'	SPol
'Dragon Lore'	MBNS
'Dragon's Eye'	CWat EWoo MSpe SDay SPol
'Dragon's Orb'	CKel SDay
'Dream Baby'	NBre
'Dream Catcher'	EWoo
'Dream Keeper'	EWoo
'Dresden Doll'	EBee SPer
'Droopy Drawers'	SPol
'Druid's Chant'	EWoo LRHS MSpe
'Duke of Durham'	EWoo MBNS MSpe SPhx
dumortieri	CBro ELan LRHS MCoo MCot MRav NBid NBir NSti SPer WCot WHrl WWEG XSen
– B&SWJ 1283	WCru
'Dune Buggy' **new**	XSen
'Dune Needlepoint'	SPol WHrl
'Duplex' (d) **new**	XSen
'Dutch Gold'	LRHS MNrw NBro
'Earl of Warwick'	CBgR SPol
'Earlianna'	SPol
'Earnest Yearwood' **new**	SDay
'Earth Angel'	SPol
'Earth Fire' **new**	SDay
'Easy Ned'	ELon EWoo SDay SPol
'Easy Street'	SDay
'Eat Our Wake Pintaheads'	CFwr
'Ebony Prince'	EWoo
'Echo Canyon'	EWoo
'Ed Murray'	MNFA WCAu
'Edgar Brown'	MBNS SPol WCot
'Edge Ahead'	CMac ECtt GKin LRHS MBNS MSpe NHol
'Edge of Darkness'	CKel CWGN EPfP MBNS NBro NLar NSti
'Edge of Frenzy' **new**	CFwr
'Edna Spalding'	LRHS SDay
'Eenie Allegro'	CBro ECtt MBNS SPer WMnd
'Eenie Fanfare'	MBNS NBir WWEG
'Eenie Weenie'	CBro ECtt EHyd ELon GKev IBoy LRHS MBNS NBro SRms WWEG
'Eenie Weenie Non-stop'	EPPr
'Eggplant Ecstasy'	CFwr
'Eggplant Electricity'	EWoo
'Eggplant Escapade'	CBgR MSpe SPol
'Egyptian Ibis'	EWoo SPol WMnd WNHG
'Egyptian Queen'	CBgR
'El Desperado'	CBcs CBgR CPar CSam ECtt ELon EPfP EWoo GBin GBuc IPot LHop LRHS LSRN MBNS MHol MLHP MNrw NCGa NEgg SPav WCAu WCFE WCot WWEG
'El Glorioso'	CWat
'Elaine Strutt'	MBNS MNFA MNrw SDay SWvt WCot
'Eleanor Marcotte'	SDay
'Elegant Candy'	CBgR CKel CMac MAvo MBNS MSpe NCGa WCAu
I 'Elegantissima'	SPol
'Eleonor'	EBee EPfP MBNS SMrm
'Elfin Daydream'	SPol
'Elf's Cap'	SDay
'Elijah Sain'	SPol
'Elizabeth Anne Hudson'	SDay
'Elizabeth Salter'	CWCL MBNS NLar SPol WCAu
'Elmore James'	EWoo
'Eloquent Cay'	CFwr
'Elva White Grow'	SDay
'Elves' Watermark'	SPol
'Emerald Eye'	SDay
'Emerald Lady'	SPol
'Emily Anne'	SPol
'Emily's Fiery Horse' **new**	CFwr
'Emperor's Choice' **new**	SDay
'Enchanted April'	SPol
'Enchanted Circle'	SDay
'Enchanter's Spell'	SDay
'English Cameo'	SPol
'Enigma Variations' **new**	SPol
'Entransette'	SDay
'Entrapment'	IBoy MBNS MBel MSpe SDeJ
'Envoyé Spécial' **new**	XSen
'Envy Me'	SPol
'Erica Nichole Gonzales'	SDay
'Erlo' **new**	CFwr
'Eskimo Kisses'	CFwr
'Etched Eyes'	EWoo SPol
'Eternal Blessing'	SPol
'Ethel Buccola' **new**	CFwr
'Etruscan Tomb'	SPol
'Euro-mazing' **new**	CFwr
'Evelyn Claar'	CMac
'Evelyn Kloeris' **new**	CFwr
'Evelyn Lela Stout'	SDay
'Even Stephen' **new**	SPol
'Evening Gown'	SPol
'Ever So Ruffled'	SDay
'Exotic Dancer'	CFwr
'Exotic Design' **new**	CFwr
'Exotic Love'	MSpe SDay
'Exotic Treasure' **new**	CFwr
'Eye Catching'	EWoo
'Eye of Horus' **new**	CFwr
'Eye of Round'	CFwr
'Eye on America'	EBee WCAu
'Eyes Right Jones' **new**	CFwr
'Eyes Wide Shut'	CFwr
'Eye-yi-yi'	SPol
'Ezekiel'	SPol XSen
'Fabergé'	SDay
'Fairest Love'	EBee LDai MBNS MNrw
'Fairest of Them'	CBgR
'Fairy Charm'	SDay
'Fairy Frosting'	SDay
'Fairy Summerbird'	SPol
'Fairy Tale Pink'	EWoo MNFA SDay SPol
'Fairy Wings'	SPer
'Faith Nabor'	SPol
'Falcon'	SPol
'Fall Farewell'	WNHG
'Fandango'	LPla
'Fantasia'	EWoo
'Farmer's Daughter'	CBgR EWoo
'Fashion Police' **new**	CFwr
'Fat Lady Sings' **new**	SPol
'Father's Day Gift' **new**	CFwr
'Feather Down'	SPol

	'Fellow'	SPol
	'Femme Fatale' **new**	SDay
	'Feria' **new**	XSen
	'Ferris Wheel'	EWoo
	'Festive Art'	SPol
	'Final Touch'	CBgR EBee MBNS NBro SGol SPol
	'Finlandia'	MNFA
	'Fire and Fog'	CFwr CHel EPfP MAvo MBNS
	'Fire and Wind'	CFwr
	'Fire Dance'	ELon
	'Fire from Heaven'	WHrl
	'Fire Tree'	CBgR ELon SPol
	'Fireborn'	CFwr
	'Fires of Fuji'	CFwr
	'Firestorm'	EWoo SPol
	'First Formal'	SMrm SPer
	'First Knight' **new**	SDay
	'Fitzasaurus' **new**	CFwr
	'Flaming Sword'	NHol WBrk WRHF
	flava	see *H. lilioasphodelus*
	'Florida Sunshine' (d) **new**	XSen
	'Flower Pavilion'	SDay SPol
	'Floyd Cove'	SDay
	'Fly Catcher'	CBgR
	'Flyaway Home'	SPol
	'Flying Frisbee' **new**	CFwr
	'Flying Saucer'	EWoo
	'Fol de Rol'	EWoo
	'Fooled Me'	EBee MBNS MBri MSpe NCGa SDay SPad SPol
	'Foolscap'	EWoo
	'For the Good Times'	EWoo
	'Forbidden Dreams'	EWoo
	'Forestlake Ragamuffin' **new**	SPol
	'Forgotten Dreams'	EBee MBNS MSpe
	forrestii	CExl
	'Forsyth Ace of Hearts'	CBgR
	'Forsyth Frostbound'	SPol
	'Forsyth Lemon Drop'	SDay
	'Forsyth White Sentinel'	CFwr
	'Forty Second Street'	CCon LHop LRHS MBNS
	'Fox Ears'	EWoo
	'Fox Hunter' **new**	CFwr
	'Foxhaven Enigma' **new**	CFwr
	'Fragrant Pastel Cheers'	SDay
	'Fragrant Treasure'	ERCP
	'Frances Busby' **new**	CFwr
	'Frances Fay'	SPol
	'Frances Joiner'	EWoo
	'Francis of Assisi'	EWoo
	'Francois Verhaert'	EWoo
	'Frank Gladney'	MNFA XSen
	'Frans Hals'	Widely available
	'Fred Ham'	XSen
	'Fred Manning' **new**	CFwr
	'Free Wheelin''	CWGN MBri MSCN NSoo
	'French Cavalier'	CFwr
	'French Connection'	SDay
	'French Porcelain'	SDay
	'French Twist' **new**	CFwr
	'Fresh Air'	MNrw
	'Frosted Encore'	SDay
	'Frosted Pink Ice'	SPol
	'Frosted Vintage Ruffles'	CHel MBri NCGa
	'Frosty White'	SDay
	'Fuchsia Beauty'	SPol
	'Fuchsia Four'	SPol
	fulva	CTri ELan LPot NBir NBre SPol SRms WBrk WHrl XSen
	- B&SWJ 8647	WCru
N	- 'Flore Pleno' (d)	CDoy CMHG CMac ECtt EHon ELan EPfP LHop LRHS MHer MRav MSpe NBir NBro NGdn NSti SMad SPav SPer SRms SWat WBrk WCAu WMoo WWEG XSen
N	- 'Green Kwanso' (d)	CAvo CBgR CExl ECGP LRHS MMHG WPnP
	- var. ***kwanso*** B&SWJ 6328	WCru
	- 'Kwanso' ambig. (d)	LRHS NOrc
	- var. ***littorea***	CMac XLum XSen
	- var. ***rosea***	LRHS SPol WCot XSen
§	- 'Variegated Kwanso' (d/v)	CBro CRow CWCL EBee EWoo GCra MRav NBir SBod SMad WBor WCot WHer WHil WHoo WHrl
	'Fun Fling'	SPol
	'Funky Fuchsia'	SPol
	'Gadsden Firefly'	CFwr
	'Gadsden Goliath'	CFwr SPol
	'Gadsden Light'	SDay SPol
	'Gala Greetings' **new**	XSen
	'Gale Storm'	WNHG
	'Garden Crawler'	CBgR
	'Garden Portrait'	EWoo SDay SPol
	'Gay Music'	MBNS
	'Gay Octopus'	SPol
	'Gay Rapture'	SPer
	'Gay Troubadour'	EWoo
	'Gemini Jack' **new**	CFwr
	'Geneva Chainsaw' **new**	CFwr
	'Geneva Firetruck'	CFwr
	'Gentle Country Breeze'	SDay SPol
	'Gentle Rose'	SDay
	'Gentle Shepherd'	Widely available
	'George Cunningham'	ECtt ELan LRHS MRav NBir SMrs SPol
	'George David'	WHrl
	'Georgette Belden'	ECGP ECtt GKin LRHS MBNS MBri MSpe MWat NHol SPol
	'Georgia Cream' (d)	NLar
	'Gerard Deschenes' **new**	CFwr
	'German Ballerina'	SPol
	'Get All Excited'	SPol
	'Giant Moon'	CBgR CMHG ECtt ELan LRHS MBNS SRms WHal
	'Giant on the Mountain' **new**	CFwr
	'Giddy Go Round'	EWoo SPol
	'Gilded by Grace' **new**	CFwr
	'Girouette' **new**	XSen
	'Give Me Eight'	SPol
	'Glacier Bay'	CBgR CWat MBNS
	'Glacier Gleam'	MSpe
	'Glass Menagerie' **new**	CFwr
	'Glittering Treasure'	LRHS XLum
	'Glowing Heart'	SDay
	'Go Seminoles' **new**	CFwr
	'Going Bananas'PBR	WCot
	'Gold Elephant'	SDay
	'Gold Imperial'	NBre
	'Golden Bell'	NGdn
	'Golden Change'	CFwr
	'Golden Chimes' ♀H4	Widely available
	'Golden Ginkgo'	MBri MSpe
	'Golden Marvel'	EWoo
	'Golden Orchid'	see *H.* 'Doubloon'
	'Golden Prize'	EWoo GQue NGdn SDay WCot XSen

'Golden Scroll'	SDay
Golden Zebra ='Malja'^{PBR} (v)	CWGN ELan EPfP IBoy LHop MBNS MRav NLar NSti WCot
'Golliwog'	CBgR
'Graal' **new**	XSen
'Grace and Favour'	SPol
'Grace and Grandeur'	EWoo
'Graceful Eye'	SDay
'Graceland'	SDay
'Graces of Ganymede' **new**	CFwr
'Grand Masque' **new**	CFwr
'Grand Masterpiece'	NGdn SDay SPet
'Grand Palais'	SDay
'Grandma Kissed Me'	SPol
'Grandma's Smile' **new**	CFwr
'Granite City Towhead'	CFwr ELon
'Grape Arbor' **new**	WNHG
'Grape Harvest'	WNHG
'Grape Magic'	WCot
'Grape Twizzler' **new**	CFwr
'Grape Velvet'	CSpe EWoo MNFA NBre NSti SBch SPol SRms WCAu WMnd WWEG
'Green Canary'	SPol
'Green Dolphin Street'	SDay
'Green Dragon'	SPol
'Green Eyed Lady'	SDay
'Green Eyes Wink' **new**	MHol
'Green Flutter' $\mathbb{Y}^{H4}$	CBgR EBee EWoo GCal GQue LPio LPla LSRN MBNS MBri MNFA NBir NBre NGdn NSti SPhx SPol WCot WWEG
'Green Goddess'	XLum
'Green Gold'	CMHG
'Green Mystique'	EBee MBri
'Green Puff'	NBir SDay
'Green Spider'	CBgR SDay
'Green Warrior'	CFwr EWoo
'Green Widow'	EWoo SDay
'Grey Witch'	SPol
'Greywoods Nautical Nellie'	CFwr
'Grumbly'	ELan WPnP
'Guadalajara' **new**	CFwr
'Guardian Angel'	WCFE
'Gypsy Cranberry'	SPol
'Gypsy Prince'	MNFA
'Hail Mary'	SDay
'Halloween Costume' **new**	CFwr
'Halloween Harvest' **new**	CFwr
'Hamlet'	SDay WNHG
'Happy Returns'	CBgR CHel CHid CSBt CTri ELan EWoo GBin GBuc LPot LRHS LSRN MBNS MBel MBri NEgg NGdn NHol SGol SRGP SRms WCAu WWEG XLum
'Harbor Blue'	SDay
'Harry Barras'	XLum
'Hawaiian Nights'	EWoo
'Hawk'	ELon SDay SPol
'Heady Wine'	MSpe SDay
'Heart's Glee' **new**	XSen
'Heat of the Moment' **new**	CFwr
'Heat Wave'	CFwr
'Heavenly Angel Ice' **new**	CFwr
'Heavenly Beginnings' **new**	CFwr
'Heavenly Curls'	SPol
'Heavenly Dragon Fire' **new**	CFwr
'Heavenly Fire Arrow' **new**	CFwr

'Heavenly Flight of Angels' **new**	CFwr
'Heavenly Mr Twister'	EWoo
'Heavenly Starfire'	CFwr EWoo SPol
'Heavenly Treasure'	SPol
'Heidi Eidelweiss'	CExl
'Heirloom Lace'	SDay
'Helix'	CFwr
'Helle Berlinerin' $\mathbb{Y}^{H4}$	MNFA SDay SPol
'Hello Screamer' **new**	CFwr
'Helter Skelter'	SDay SPol
'Her Majesty's Wizard'	CBgR ELan ELon EWoo MBNS SPol
'Hercules'	NBre
'Heron's Cove'	EWoo
'Hesperus'	EWoo
'Hey There'	SDay
'High Tor'	GQui MNFA SPol WHrl
'Higher Ambition' **new**	CFwr
'Highland Lord' (d)	EBee EPfP MBNS SDay XSen
'Hightower'	CFwr
'Hillbilly Heart'	CFwr
'Hint of Blue'	SPol
'Hippie Chic' **new**	CFwr
'Holiday Delight'	MBNS
'Holiday Mood'	ELan
'Holly Dancer'	EWoo SPol
'Honey Jubilee'	SPol
'Honey Redhead'	SPol
'Hope Diamond'	SDay
'Hornby Castle'	CBro LRHS NHol
'Hot Chocolate'^{PBR}	EBee SRGP
'Hot Town'	ELan
'Hotter than the Fourth of July' **new**	CFwr
'Houdini'	MSpe WMnd
'House Music' **new**	XSen
'House of Bluelights'	SPol
'House of Orange'	SPol
'Howlin' Wolf' **new**	CFwr
I 'How's the Weather up There?'	EWoo
'Hubbles Buddy'	CFwr EWoo
'Humdinger'	WCot
'Hunker Down' **new**	CFwr
'Hyperion'	CBgR CMac COIW CPrp CTri EBee ECtt EPfP EShb EWoo GKin LAst LEdu LRHS MHol MNFA MRav MSpe NBid NGdn SMrs SPer SPoG WCot WWEG
'I Luv Lucy' **new**	CFwr
'Ice Carnival'	CKel EBee ELon EPfP LDai MBNS NBre NGdn NOrc SHar SPet
'Ice Castles'	CTri SDay
'Icecap'	WMoo
'Icy Lemon'	SDay
'Ida Duke Miles'	SDay
'Igor'	CFwr
'Imperator'	NHol
'Impromptu'	SDay
'In Depth' (d)	EPfP EWoo MBNS NBro NLar WCot WHrl
'In Search of Angels'	CFwr
'In Strawberry Time'	WNHG
'Indian Fandango'	EWoo
'Indian Fires'	CFwr
'Indian Giver'	SPol
'Indian Paintbrush'	ELon EWoo MBri NBir SPol
'Indigo Moon'	SPol XSen
'Indy Envy'	CFwr

	'Inimitable' **new**	CFwr
	'Inky Fingers'	SPol
	'Inner View'	ECtt ELon EWoo MBNS NLar SDay WMnd
	'Instant Zéro' **new**	XSen
	'Invitation to Immortality'	EWoo
	'Iowa Greenery'	SPol
	'Iridescent Jewel'	SDay
	'Irish Elf'	ELon SDay SHar
	'Irish Handshake' **new**	CFwr
	'Iron Gate Glacier'	MBNS MNFA XLum
	'Irresistible Charm' **new**	EPfP
	'Isle of Dreams'	SPol
	'Isleworth'	EWoo
	'Isolde'	MSpe
	'Itsy Bitsy Spider'	CFwr EWoo
	'Ivelyn Brown'	SDay SPol
	'Ivory Coast' **new**	SDay
	'Jake Russell'	MBNS MNFA
	'Jam All Night' **new**	CFwr
	'Jamaican Jammin''	SPol
	'Jamaican Magic' **new**	CFwr
	'Jamaican Me Happy'	CFwr
	'James Clark'	EWoo
	'James Marsh'	CBgR EWes EWoo GBin MBNS MBri MNFA MNrw MSpe NSti WCAu WCot WMnd
	'Jammin' with Jane' **new**	CFwr
	'Jan Kay'	SDay
	'Janet Gordon'	SPol
	'Janice Brown'	CKel CWCL CWGN EWoo LAst LSou MBNS MNFA MSpe NCGa NHol NLar SDay SPol WHrl
	'Jan's Twister'	MNrw SPol WHrl
	'Jason Salter'	NCGa SDay
	'Jay Turman'	SDay
	'Jazz at the Wool Club'	CFwr
	'Jean'	SDay
	'Jean Swann'	MBNS NSoo
	'Jedi Dot Pierce'	MNFA
	'Jedi Tequila Sunrise'	CFwr
	'Jellyfish Jealousy'	EWoo
	'Jenny Wren'	EPPr EWoo MBNS NBre NBro SRGP WWEG
	'Jersey Jim'	SPol
	'Jersey Spider'	EWoo SDay SPol
	'Jerusalem'	SDay
	'Jesse James'	SPol
	'Jeu de Piste' **new**	XSen
	'Jeune Tom' **new**	CBgR
	'Jewel Case'	WNHG
	'Joan Senior'	Widely available
	'Jockey Club' (d)	ECtt MBNS
	'Joe Marinello'	SPol
	'Johanna Klein Strack' **new**	CFwr
	'John Benoot' **new**	CFwr
	'Johnny Come Lately'	SPol
	'Joie de Vivre'	EWoo
	'Jolly Red Giant'	EWoo
	'Jolyene Nichole'	SDay
	'Jordan'	LSRN
	'Journey to Oz'	EWoo
	'Journey's End'	SDay
	'Judah'	SPol
	'Judge Roy Bean'	EWoo SPol
	'Julie Newmar'	IPot
	'Jumping Jack Flash' **new**	CFwr
	'June Melody'	WNHG
	'Jungle Beauty'	CBgR SPol
	'Jungle Jack Joiner' **new**	CFwr
	'Just a Tease' **new**	CFwr
	'Just Kiss Me'	SPol
	'Justin Brent' **new**	XSen
	'Justin George'	SPol
	'Justin June'	WHrl
	'Kachina Firecracker'	CFwr EWoo
	'Kalahari Jewel' **new**	CFwr
	'Kamadeva' **new**	CFwr
	'Kansas Kitten'	EWoo
	'Karateake'	CFwr
	'Karen's Curls'	EWoo SPol
	'Kasia'	WHrl
	'Katahdin'	EWoo
	'Kate Carpenter'	SDay SPol
	'Katherine Harris'	CFwr
	'Kathleen Salter'	EWoo
	'Kathryn June Wood'	EWoo
	'Kathy Macartney'	CFwr EWoo
	'Kathy's Cat Spooky' **new**	CFwr
	'Kecia'	MNFA
	'Keene'	EWoo
	'Kelly's Girl'	SPol
	'Kenyan Sun'	EWoo
	'Kevin Michael Coyne'	EWoo SPol
	'Key to my Heart'	CBgR
	'Key West'	CFwr
	'Killarney Castle' **new**	CFwr
	'Kindly Light'	EWoo MNFA SPol
	'King James'	EWoo
	'King's Throne'	WNHG
	'Kiowa Sunset'	MSpe
	'Kisses for Cinderella'	CFwr
	'Klaatu Barada Nikto' **new**	CFwr
	'Kokopelli' **new**	CFwr
N	'Kwanso Flore Pleno'	see *H. fulva* 'Green Kwanso'
N	'Kwanso Flore Pleno Variegata'	see *H. fulva* 'Variegated Kwanso'
	'La Peche'	SDay
	'Lace Cookies'	EWoo
	'Lacy Dolly'	LLHF MBri WCAu
	'Lacy Marionette'	ELon EWoo SDay SPol
	'Lady Cynthia'	CKel
	'Lady Fingers'	CBgR MNFA SDay SPol
	'Lady Liz'	MNFA
	'Lady Mischief'	SDay
	'Lady Neva'	CBgR ELon EWoo SDay
	'Lady Tiger' **new**	WNHG
	'Ladykin'	ELon SDay SPol
	'Lake Effect'	EWoo
	'Lake Norman Spider'	EWoo SPol
	'Land of Cotton'	XSen
	'Land of Enchantment' **new**	CFwr
	'Lark Song'	LRHS WHrl
	'Last Song' **new**	CFwr
	'Laughing Feather'	CFwr EWoo
	'Laura Lambert'	SPol
	'Lauradell'	SDay
	'Laurena'	SPol
	'Lavender Blue Baby'	EPfP
	'Lavender Deal'	LRHS MNrw WNHG
	'Lavender Illusion'	CSev
	'Lavender Light'	EWoo
	'Lavender Memories'	SDay
	'Lavender Plicata'	SPol
	'Lavender Showstopper'	WCAu
	'Lavender Silver Cords'	SPol
	'Lavender Spider'	CBgR SPol
	'Lavender Tonic'	SPol

'Layers of Gold' (d) **new**	XSen
'Ledgewood Cinnamon Lace' **new**	CFwr
'Lee Reinke'	SPol
'Legs Limmer'	CFwr EWoo
'Lemon Bells' ΥH4	CWat EBee ECGP EPfP EWoo GKev GKin GMaP LEdu LRHS MBNS NBro NCGa NSoo SDay WCAu
'Lemon Dessert'	ELon
'Lemon Fellow'	EWoo
'Lemon Madeline'	EWoo
'Lemon Meringue Twist'	EWoo
'Lemon Mint'	ELon
'Lemonora'	SDay
'Lenox'	SDay
'Leonard Bernstein'	EWoo SPol
'Leslie Renee'	CFwr
'Let it Rip'	EWoo SPol
'Let Loose' **new**	CFwr
'Lexington Avenue'	SPol
'Licorice Candy'	SPol
'Licorice Twist'	EWoo
'Lies and Lipstick' **new**	CFwr
'Light the Way'	GBin
'Light Years Away'	ELon MBNS MNrw NBro
§ ***lilioasphodelus*** ΥH4	Widely available
- 'Rowden Golden Jubilee' (v)	CRow
'Lilly Dache'	EWoo
'Lilting Belle'	SPol
'Lilting Lady'	SDay SPol
'Lilting Lavender'	ELon SPol WCAu WCot
'Lime Frost'	CBgR SDay SPol
'Lime Painted Lady'	CBgR
'Limited Edition'	EWoo
'Lin Wright'	EWoo
'Linda'	MRav NHol
'Linda Agin'	EWoo
'Lines of Splendor'	EWoo
'Little Bee'	NBre
'Little Big Man'	SDay
'Little Bugger'	ELon NLar WWEG
'Little Bumble Bee'	CCon COIW LRHS MBNS WWEG
'Little Business'	COIW MBNS MNFA SDay
'Little Cadet'	XLum
'Little Carpet'	MBNS SPer SPet
'Little Deeke'	MNFA SDay WHrl
'Little Dream Red'	SDay
'Little Fat Cat'	CBgR
'Little Fat Dazzler'	ELon SPol
'Little Fellow'	MBNS
'Little Grapette'	COIW ELon EPfP ERCP GCra GQue LPla LRHS MBNS MNFA MSpe NLar NSti WCAu WWEG
'Little Greenie'	SDay
'Little Gypsy Vagabond'	CWat SDay SPol
'Little Heavenly Angel'	COIW SPol
'Little Judy'	SPol
'Little Kiki'	SDay
'Little Maggie'	SDay SPol
'Little Men'	WCAu
'Little Miss Manners' **new**	MAsh NLar
'Little Missy'	CBgR COIW CWat MBNS NBre SPet WHoo WNHG
'Little Monica'	SDay
'Little Pumpkin Face'	CWat
'Little Rainbow'	WWEG
'Little Red Hen'	CHel CSam ECGP GKin LRHS MBNS MSpe NBir NBro NEgg NGdn
'Little Show Stopper'	EWoo MBNS NBro NLar
'Little Swain'	SDay
'Little Sweet Sue'	MNFA
'Little Sweet Talk'	ELon
'Little Tawny'	ELon
'Little Toddler'	SDay
'Little Violet Lace'	SDay
'Little Wart'	SDay WHrl
'Little Wine Cup'	CMHG CMac CSam CWat ECrc ECtt ELon EPfP GKin GMaP LBMP LRHS MNFA MRav MSpe MWat MWhi NBir NEgg NGdn NOrc SEND SPer SPol SRms WMoo WWEG
'Little Women'	MBNS SDay
'Little Zinger'	SDay
'Littlest Angel'	SDay
'Littlest Clown'	SDay
'Liz Schreiner' **new**	CFwr
'Lizard's Purple Fashion'	CFwr
'Lobo Lucy'	ELon
'Lochinvar'	GBuc MRav
'Lois Burns'	EWoo SDay SPol
'Lonesome Dove'	SPol
'Long John Silver'	ELon
'Long Legged Lap Dancer' **new**	CFwr
'Long Stocking'	EWoo SPol WCot
'Longfield's Anwar'	EWoo
'Longfield's Bandit'	EWoo
'Longfield's Beauty'	EWoo MBNS MSpe NCGa
'Longfield's Glory'	MBNS MSpe NBre
'Longfield's Mandy'	MSpe
'Longfield's Maxim' (d)	MBNS SDeJ
'Longfield's Pride'	ECho IBoy MBNS SRms WBor
'Longfield's Purple Eye'	NLar
'Longfield's Tropica'	MBNS
'Longfield's Twins'	MBNS WCot
longituba AIK 284	WCot
- B&SWJ 4576	WCru
'Look at Me'	ELan
'Look Lucky'	CFwr
'Loose as a Goose' **new**	CFwr
'Loose Reins' **new**	CFwr
'Lord Camden'	MNFA
'Lori Goldston'	EWoo MBNS
'Lorita Wadsworth' **new**	CFwr
'Loth Lorien'	CFwr
'Louis Burnes'	SPol
'Louis McHargue'	SDay
'Louise Lemly'	CFwr
'Love Glow'	CCon
'Love or Else'	EWoo
'Love Will Find a Way' **new**	CFwr
'Lucille Lennington'	WNHG
'Lucretius'	MNFA
'Lullaby Baby'	CWat ELan EWoo MBNS NLar SDay SPol
'Luna' **new**	SPol
'Luscious Honeydew'	WNHG
'Lusty Lealand'	MBNS MNFA SDay
'Luxury Lace'	CPrp CWat ECtt EHyd ELan EPfP GBin GKin LRHS LSRN MSpe NBir NGdn NHol NWad SPer SPol WHrl WMoo WPnP XLum XSen
'Lynn Hall'	EHyd EMil MBNS NLar
'Lyric Opera'	SDay
'Mabel Fuller'	CBgR MRav SPer WHrl
'Macbeth'	MBNS
'Mad Max'	EWoo MSpe SPol

'Made from Scratch' **new**	CFwr
'Maestro Puccini'	SDay
'Maggie Fynboe'	CBgR SPol
'Magic Amethyst'	CBgR
'Magic Attraction' **new**	CFwr
'Magic Carpet Ride'	SPol
'Magic Lace'	EWoo
'Magic Masquerade' **new**	SDay
'Magnificent Eyes'	SPol
'Magnificent Rainbow'	CBcs
'Malachite Prism'	CWGN
'Malaysian Monarch'	WMnd WNHG
'Malaysian Spice'	WNHG
'Maleny Bright Eyes'	MSpe
'Maleny Mite'	EWoo
'Maleny Piecrust'	EWoo
'Maleny Tapestry'	MSpe
'Maleny Think Big'	EWoo
'Mallard'	CBgR CWat ECGP ECtt LLWP LRHS MBNS MNFA MRav NBir SPer SWat WCot
'Mambo Maid' **new**	XSen
'Man on Fire'	MBNS WNHG
'Manchurian Apricot'	SDay
'Mandalay Bay Music'	EWoo
'Marble Faun'	SDay
'Margaret McWhorter' **new**	SPol
'Margaret Perry'	CPrp ECrc MNrw
'Margo Reed Indeed'	SPol
'Marietta Charmer' **new**	SDay SPol
'Marilyn Siwik'	EWoo
'Marion Caldwell'	SPol
'Marion Vaughn' Υ^{H4}	CSev ECtt ELan EPfP EWoo GBuc GKin GMaP LBMP LHop LRHS MBel MNFA MSpe NSti SDix SPer SRGP SSpi WCot WHar WHoo WPtf WWEG
'Mariska'	EWoo SDay WNHG
'Marked by Lydia'	CFwr ELon SPol
'Marse Connell'	MSpe
'Martha Adams'	SDay
'Martie Everest'	EWoo
'Martina Verhaert'	CWGN EBee
'Mary Ethel Anderson'	EWoo
'Mary Todd'	EBee MBNS WMnd XSen
'Mary's Gold'	SDay SPol
'Masquerade Show' **new**	CFwr
'Mata Hari'	SDay SPol
'Matisse'	SPol
'Mauna Loa'	CSBt GQue LRHS MBNS MNFA MNrw MSpe NBre NOrc SDeJ WCAu WCot
'May May'	CBgR SPol
'Meadow Mist'	ELon
'Meadow Sprite'	SDay WCot
'Medicine Feather'	EWoo
'Medusa's Glance'	EWoo
'Megatrend'	CFwr
'Mema's Dingbat' **new**	CFwr
'Mephistopheles'	EWoo
'Merry Moppet'	EWoo
'Metaphor'	SDay XSen
'Michele Coe'	ECtt GKin LPio LPla LRHS MBNS MNFA MSpe NBre NBro NEgg NGdn SRGP WHrl WMoo
'Mico'	ELon
middendorffii	CMac GMaP LPla LRHS MCoo NSti WHrl WPnP WThu
'Midnight Dynamite'	MBNS
'Midnight Love'	EWoo
'Midnight Magic'	EWoo
'Midnight Mantis'	SPol
'Midnight Raider'	EWoo
'Mighty Highty Tighty'	CFwr
'Mighty Mogul'	MNFA
'Mikado'	CBgR CMac
'Milady Greensleeves'	EWoo SDay SPol
'Milanese Mango'	EWoo
'Mildred Mitchell'	CBgR CWat ELon MBNS NLar SPol
'Millie Schlumpf'	SPol
'Mimosa Umbrella'	SPol
'Ming Lo'	MSpe SDay
'Ming Porcelain'	SPol WCAu
'Mini Pearl'	CHel COIW ELon EWTr LRHS MBNS SPer
'Mini Stella'	CBro ECtt MBNS NBre NOrc NSoo SPet
miniature hybrids	SRms
'Minnie Wildfire'	SPol
minor	CBro EBee EDAr EPPr GKev LRHS SRms XSen
- B&SWJ 8841	WCru
'Minstrel's Fire' **new**	CFwr
'Miracle Maid'	WNHG
'Miss Jessie'	EWoo MNFA SPol
'Missenden' Υ^{H4}	CBgR MNFA MNrw
'Missouri Beauty'	IBoy MBNS SPol
'Missouri Memories'	SPol
'Misty Twisty'	CFwr
'Moment in the Sun' **new**	CFwr
'Moment of Truth'	NBre
'Mont Royal Demitasse'	ELon SPol
'Moon Witch'	SDay SPol
'Moonlight Masquerade'	CBgR CWat ECtt EPfP GBuc MMuc NLar SRms
'Moonlight Mist'	SDay SPol
'Moonlit Caress'	CBgR EBee MBNS NBro
'Moonlit Crystal'	SPol
'Moonlit Masquerade'	CPar CWGN EWoo GBin MBNS MBel MNrw MSpe NCGa SBch SEND SPer SPet SPol WCAu WHrl
'Moonlit Summerbird'	SDay SPol
'Moontraveller'	WCot
'Mormon Spider'	MSpe SPol
'Morning Dawn'	WWEG
'Morning Sun'	MBNS NBre NLar WCot
'Morocco'	SPol
'Morocco Red'	CBro CCse CTri ELan NBre WWEG
'Morrie Otte'	SPol
'Mosel'	SDay
'Moses' Fire'	ECtt EPfP MBNS MSCN NLar
'Mossy Glade' **new**	CBgR
'Mount Echo Sunrise'	EWoo
'Mount Joy'	SPer
'Mountain Laurel'	ECGP ECtt ELon GKin LDai LRHS LSRN MBNS MCot MRav NEgg SPol
'Moving Forward' **new**	CFwr
'Mr Spaceman' **new**	CFwr
'Mrs David Hall'	CCse
'Mrs Hugh Johnson'	EBee GCra NHol WHrl
* 'Mrs Lester'	SDay
'Muddy Waters' **new**	CFwr
'Muffet's Little Friend'	SPol
'Mulberry Frosted Edge'	EWoo
multiflora	LRHS MNFA NHol XSen
'Muscle Man' **new**	XSen
'Music of the Master' **new**	CFwr
'My Belle'	SDay

'My Darling Clementine'	SDay
'My Friend Floyd' **new**	CFwr
'My Heart Belongs to Daddy' **new**	CFwr
'My Hope'	SPol
'My Melinda'	SDay
'Mynelle's Starfish'	CPar SPol WHrl
nana	CCon
'Nanuq'	ELon
'Naomi Ruth'	MBNS MSpe
'Nashville'	CBro ELan WHrl
'Nashville Lights'	CBgR SPol
'Nathan Sommers'	EWoo
'Natural Veil'	SPol
'Navajo Princess'	CWat MBNS MNrw
'Navajo Rodeo'	EWoo
'Neal Berrey'	SDay
'Nefertiti'	ELon MBNS NBir NCGa SPer WCAu
'Neon Rose'	GKin MWat
'New Direction'	CFwr EWoo
'Neyron Rose' ♀^{H4}	COlW EPfP GBuc GKin GQue LHop LRHS MBNS MCot NBre NEgg NGdn WMoo
'Nick's Faith'	WHrl
'Nicole Joyce'	SPol
'Night Beacon'	CBgR ECho ECtt ELon EWes EWoo GBuc GKin LPot MBNS MNFA MNrw MPie MSpe NLar SDay SDeJ SPol WCAu WHrl
'Night Embers'	ECtt EWTr EWoo NLar
'Night Raider'	CBgR SDay
'Night Wings'	EWoo
'Nigrette'	NHol
'Nile Crane'	CBgR ELon MBNS MNrw MSpe SDay SPer
'Nile Plum'	EWoo SDay SPol
'Ninja Throwing Star' **new**	CFwr
'Ninth Millennium'	CFwr
'Nob Hill'	CCse ELon LRHS SPol WHrl XLum
'Noble Warrior'	MSpe
'Nona's Garnet Spider'	ELon SPol
'Noonday Dreams'	CFwr
'Nordic Night'	CBgR SDay SPol
'North Wind Dancer'	EWoo
'Northbrook Star'	MNFA
'Norton Beauté'	WCot
'Norton Eyed Seedling'	WNHG
'Norton Orange'	MNFA
'Nosferatu'	SDay SPol
'Not Forgotten'	WNHG
'Nouveau Riche'	SPol
'Nova' ♀^{H4}	CPrp ELon
'Novarlis' **new**	CFwr
'Nuclear Meltdown'	EWoo
'Nuka'	XLum
'Numinous Moments'	SDay
'Nutmeg Elf'	CBgR EWoo SPol
'Nuttin Bugs Me' **new**	CFwr
'Oakes Love'	MNrw
'Ocean Rain'	SDay SPol
'Octopus Hugs'	SPol
'Official Curse'	SPol
'Ojo de Dios'	EWoo
'Oklahoma Kicking Bird'	SDay
'Old Tangiers'	EWoo
'Old Time Memories' **new**	CFwr
'Olive Bailey Langdon'	SDay SPol WCot
'Oliver Billingslea'	EWoo
'Olly Olly Oxen Free' **new**	CFwr
'Olympic Gold' **new**	XSen
'On and On'	GQue LHop MBNS NCGa
'On Pointe'	EWoo
'On Silken Thread'	SPol
'On the Border' **new**	CFwr
'On the Web'	CFwr
'One Fire' **new**	XSen
'Oodles'	WHrl
'Open Hearth'	SPol WHrl
'Open my Eyes'	EWoo
'Orange Clown' **new**	CFwr
'Orange Dream'	SDay
'Orange Exotica'	CBgR
'Orange Prelude'	XSen
'Orange Splash' **new**	CFwr
'Orangeman' misapplied	LRHS MBNS NGdn
'Orchid Beauty'	MLHP WMoo
'Orchid Candy'	EWoo MBNS NBir SPol
'Orchid Corsage'	ELon SPol
'Orchid Lady Slipper'	EWoo
'Orchid Moonrise'	EWoo
'Oriental Ruby'	SDay
'Orion's Band'	EWoo
'Orphée' **new**	XSen
'Ostrich Plume'	SDay
'Ouachita Beauty'	SPol
'Our Kirsten'	SDay
'Out of Darkness'	EWoo
'Outrageous'	WNHG
'Outrageous Ramona'	WNHG
'Over the Top'	MBNS
'Paige's Pinata'	EBee MBNS
'Painted Lady'	MNFA
'Painted Peach' **new**	SPol
'Painted Pink'	SDay
'Painting the Roses Red'	CFwr
'Palace Garden Beauty'	EWoo
'Palace Guard'	MNFA
'Pale Moon Windmill'	CFwr
'Pandora's Box'	CExl CMHG CTri CWat ECtt ELan EPfP MBNS MMuc MNFA MNrw NBir NGdn NLar SDay SDeJ SEND SPet SPol STes WBor WCAu WHoo WMoo WWEG
'Panic in Detroit' **new**	CFwr
'Pantherette'	SPol
'Paper Butterfly'	SDay SPol
'Papoose'	XLum
'Pardon Me'	CBro CMHG ELan ELon EWoo GKin GMaP LRHS MBNS MBel MNFA MSpe NCGa NGdn NHol SDeJ SPol SRGP WBor WCAu
'Pardon Me Boy'	SPol
'Parfait'	CBgR EWoo SPol
'Parrot Jungle' **new**	CFwr
'Passion for Red'	SDay
'Pastel Ballerina'	SDay
'Pastilline'	SPol
'Pat Mercer'	XSen
'Patchwork Puzzle'	EWoo SPol
'Patricia'	MBNS
'Patricia Fay'	XSen
'Patricia Gentzel Wright'	EWoo
'Patricia Snider Memorial' **new**	CFwr
'Patsy Bickers'	EWoo
'Patterns'	SPol
'Pawn of Prophecy'	SDay
'Peace be Still'	EWoo

'Peach Float'	EWoo
'Peach Jubilee'	SPol
'Peach Yum Yum'	CFwr
'Peacock Curls'	EWoo
'Peacock Maiden'	EWoo SDay SPol XSen
'Pear Ornament'	SDay
'Pearl Lewis'	SPol
'Pearl Sherwood'	EWoo
'Penelope Vestey'	GBuc MBNS MNFA NBir SDay SPol SRGP
'Penny's Worth'	LEdu LRHS MBNS NOrc WCot WHoo XLum
'Perfect Pleasure'	MBNS
'Persian Melon Plus'	WCAu
'Persian Ruby'	SPol
'Persian Shrine'	SPol
'Persimmons Cinnamon and Marmalade' **new**	CFwr
'Petite Ballerina'	SDay
'Phyllis Cantini'	SPol
'Piano Man'	MBNS NLar WNHG
'Piccadilly Princess'	SDay
'Picket Fences'	CFwr
'Picotee Rippled Ruffles' **new**	CFwr
'Pinebelt Darkeyes' **new**	CFwr
'Pink Ambrosia'	EWoo
'Pink Charm'	CHel CMac COIW ECtt EPPr GKin GMaP LRHS MBNS NBro NHol SPol
'Pink Circle'	SDay
'Pink Cotton Candy'	EWoo SDay SPol
'Pink Damask' ♀H4	Widely available
'Pink Dazzler'	WNHG
'Pink Dream'	MBNS NBir NBre SPol
'Pink Flirt'	SDay
'Pink Grace'	SPol
'Pink Lady'	MNrw MRav SRms
'Pink Monday'	SDay WNHG
'Pink Pajamas'	CFwr
'Pink Prelude'	GBee MBNS MWat NBro
'Pink Puff'	MBNS NBir NBre NLar
'Pink Rain Dance'	SPol
'Pink Spider'	SDay
'Pink Sundae'	WHrl
'Pink Super Spider'	EWoo SDay SPol
'Pink Whip Tips' **new**	CFwr
'Pink Windmill'	ELon EWoo SPol
'Piping Rock'	CFwr
'Pirate Treasure'	MBNS
'Pirate's Patch'	EWoo SPol WCot
'Pixie Parasol'	WMnd WNHG
'Pixie Pipestone'	SPol
'Pizza'	SDay
'Planet Golden Orange Ruffy' **new**	CFwr
'Planet Sunshine' **new**	CFwr
'Plum Beauty'	NLar
'Plum Candy'	EWoo
'Plumburst' **new**	EPfP
'Poetic Dance'	EWoo
'Point of Honor'	EWoo
'Pojo'	SDay
'Pony'	CWat SDay SPol
'Prague Spring'	MNFA MSpe SDay SPol WCAu
'Prairie Belle'	MBNS NBre NLar SPol
'Prairie Blossoms'	CFwr
'Prairie Blue Eyes'	ECtt IBoy MBNS NPri SPlb SPol WCot WHrl WMnd WWEG
'Prairie Charmer'	MMuc SEND WHrl

'Precious d'Oro'	EBee GQue
'Pretty Miss'	ECtt EWTr LRHS
'Preview Party'	WNHG
'Primal Scream'	SPol WCot
'Primrose Mascotte'	NBir
'Prince of Purple'	ELon
'Prince Redbird'	SDay
'Princess Blue Eyes'	SPol
'Princess Lilli'	MBNS
'Princeton Eye Glow'	SDay
'Prissy Frills'	SPol
'Prize Picotee Deluxe'	SPol
'Prize Picotee Elite'	SDay SPol
'Promising Future'	CFwr
'Protocol'	MSpe SDay SPol
'Proud Mary'	SDay
§ 'Puddin'	CWat SDay
'Pueblo Dreamer'	CFwr EWoo
'Puff the Magic Dragon' **new**	CFwr
'Pug Yarborough'	SPol
'Pumpkin Kid'	SDay SPol
'Pumpkin Pie Spice' **new**	SPol
'Pumpkin Prince'	CFwr
'Pumpkins Gone Wild' **new**	CFwr
'Punxsutawney Phil' **new**	CFwr
'Puppet Show'	SDay
'Pure and Simple'	ELon SPol
'Purple Arachne'	SPol
'Purple Bicolor'	WHrl
'Purple Grasshopper'	EWoo
'Purple Many Faces' **new**	SPol
'Purple Oddity'	EWoo SPol
'Purple Pinwheel'	EWoo SPol
'Purple Rain'	CWat LRHS MBNS MNFA SPol SWvt
'Purple Rain Dance'	SPol
'Purple Sombrero' **new**	CFwr
'Purple Waters'	MBNS NBre NOrc SPol WPnP
'Purpleicious' **new**	SMrm
'Pygmy Plum'	SDay XSen
'Queen Empress'	WNHG
'Queen Lily'	WNHG
'Queen of Can Do' **new**	CFwr
'Queen of May'	MNrw WCot
'Quick Results'	SDay
'Quilt Patch'	SPol
'Quinn Buck'	SDay
'Ra Hansen'	SDay
'Rachael My Love' (d) **new**	XSen
'Racing Stripes'	CFwr
'Radiant'	CBcs
'Radiant Greetings'	MNFA XSen
'Radiation Biohazard'	CFwr SPol
'Radioactive Curls' **new**	CFwr
'Raging Tiger'	WHrl
'Rags to Riches'	CFwr
'Rainbow Candy'	CWGN LLHF MBNS SPad
'Rainbow Drive'	CFwr
'Rainbow Gold' **new**	XSen
'Rainbow Serpent' **new**	CFwr
'Raining Violets'	EWoo
'Rajah'	CBgR CMac MBNS MSpe NBro WHrl
'Randall Moore'	SPol
'Rander's Pride'	EWoo
'Rapid Eye Movement'	CFwr
'Raspberry Butterflies'	EWoo
'Raspberry Candy'	CBro GCra IBoy MBNS MNrw MSpe NBro NCGa NHol NOrc SRms WHrl

'Raspberry Masquerade'	CFwr
'Raspberry Pixie'	SDay SPol
'Raspberry Star'	EWoo
'Raven Woodsong'	EWoo
'Real Wind'	CFwr SPol
'Red Admiral'	LRHS
'Red Butterfly'	SPol
'Red Eyed Fantasy' **new**	CFwr
'Red Eyed Shocker'	CFwr
'Red Hill'	EWoo
'Red Precious' ♀H4	MNFA MNrw WCot
'Red Rain'	EWoo WHrl XSen
'Red Resplendence'	EWoo
'Red Ribbons'	ELon EWoo MNFA SDay SPol
'Red Ruby'	ERCP
'Red Rum'	EWll MNFA MSpe NBro WMoo
'Red Squirrel' **new**	CFwr
'Red Suspenders'	ECtt MBNS
'Red Twister'	ELon SDay SPol
'Red Volunteer'	SDay SPol
'Redheaded Hussy' **new**	CFwr
'Reflections in Time'	EWoo
'Regal Giant'	EWoo
'Regency Dandy'	SDay SPol XSen
'Renee'	MNrw
'Return Trip'	SPol
'Revolute'	SDay
'Rhode Island Red'	CFwr
'Ribbonette'	EBee MBNS MSpe
'Ricky Rose'	XSen
'Rigamarole'	SPol
'Riley Barron'	SDay
'Roaring Jellyfish' **new**	CFwr
'Robespierre'	SDay
'Rock Solid' **new**	CFwr
'Rocket City'	ELan SPol WNHG
'Rocky Horror'	CFwr
'Rocky Mountain Pals' **new**	CFwr
'Rococo'	SDay
'Rodeo Sweetheart'	CFwr
'Roger Grounds'	CBgR SPol
'Roll Up Candy' **new**	CFwr
'Rolling Hill' **new**	CFwr
'Rolling Raven' **new**	CFwr
'Roman Toga'	CBgR
'Romanian Rendevous'	CFwr EWoo
* 'Romantic Rose'	ELon MBNS NLar WHrl
'Ron Rousseau'	SPol
'Root Beer'	WHrl
'Rose Claire'	LPla
'Rose Corsage'	EWoo
'Rose Emily'	SDay SPol
'Rose Fever'	EWoo
'Rose Roland'	NBre
'Roseate Spoonbill'	EWoo
'Roses in Snow'	IBoy MBNS SPol
'Roswitha'	CWat SPol
'Rosy Lights'	EWoo SPol
'Rosy Returns'	EPfP LRHS MBNS NLar SHar
'Round Midnight'	SPol
'Royal Braid'	EPfP MBNS MSpe NLar SPer WCot
'Royal Celebration'	WCot
'Royal Elk'	EWoo
'Royal Emperor' **new**	CFwr
'Royal Eventide' **new**	CFwr XSen
'Royal Heritage'	SDay
'Royal Hunter'	CFwr
'Royal Robe'	CTri
'Royal Russian Rendezvous' **new**	CFwr
'Royal Saracen'	SDay
'Royal Thornbird'	CBgR
'Royal Trophy'	WNHG
'Royalty'	GCra
'Ruby Moon'	CFwr
'Ruby Sentinel'	SDay
'Ruby Spider'	ELon EWoo SDay SPol
'Ruby Storm' **new**	CFwr
'Rue Madelaine'	SPol
'Ruffled Antique Lavender'	WCAu
'Ruffled Apricot'	CKel MBNS MNFA MSpe SDay WNHG
'Ruffled Carousel'	WNHG
'Rumble Seat Romance'	WNHG
'Russian Rhapsody'	CKel SDay SPol
'Sabine Baur'	CWat EBee EWoo IPot LRHS MBNS MNrw NLar
'Sabra Salina'	EWoo SDay
'Saffron Glow'	SDay
'Saintly'	EWoo MSpe
'Salmon Pagoda'	EWoo
'Salmon Sheen'	SDay SPer
'Sammy'	SDay
'Sammy Russell'	Widely available
'Samuel Bell'	EWoo
'San Luis Halloween'	CFwr
'Sanford Code Red'	CFwr
'Sanford Star Search'	CFwr
'Santa's Little Helper'	CFwr
'Santiago'	SPol
'Saratoga Pinwheel'	SPol
'Satin Glass'	LRHS MNFA
'Satin Glow'	MLHP
'Scapes from Hell'	EWoo
'Scarlet Butterfly'	SPol
'Scarlet Flame'	WMoo
'Scarlet Orbit'	EWoo SDay SPol
'Scarlet Pimpernel' **new**	CFwr
'Scarlet Prince'	WNHG
'Scarlet Ribbons'	SPol
'Scatterbrain'	CKel SPol
'Schnickel Fritz'	EBee
'School Girl'	LRHS
'Scorpio'	CBgR SPol
'Scout's Honor' **new**	CFwr
'Screaming Demon'	SPol
'Sea Siren'	CWat
'Seabiscuit' **new**	CFwr
'Seal of Approval'	EBee
'Sebastian'	MNFA
'Secret Splendor'	SPol
'Secretary's Sand'	EWoo
'Selma Longlegs'	SPol
'Seminole Blood'	SPol
'Seminole Princess' **new**	CFwr
'Seminole Wind'	EWoo SPol
'Sentinel Solar Burst' **new**	CFwr
'Serena Sunburst'	SPol
'Serenade'	EWoo
'Serene Madonna'	CCon GBin SPoG
'Serenity Bay'	CFwr
'Serenity Morgan'	EPfP MBNS
'Sergeant Major'	EWoo
'Shadowed Pink'	WNHG
'Shady Lady'	SDay
'Shake the Mountains'	CFwr
'Shaman'	SDay SPol

'Shangri La Truffle'	CFwr
'She Devil'	CFwr
'Shelly Victoria'	SDay
'Sherry Lane Carr'	SDay SPol
'Sherwood Gladiator'	WNHG
'Shibui Splendor'	SPol
'Shimek September Morning'	SPol
✶ 'Shocker'	EWoo
'Shogun'	MBNS
'Shotgun'	SPol
'Shuffle the Deck'	CFwr EWoo
'Sidewinder Oh Seven' **new**	CFwr
'Sigudilla'	WNHG
'Silken Fairy'	SDay
'Silken Touch'	CBgR SPol
'Siloam Amazing Grace'	SDay
'Siloam Baby Doll'	SDay
'Siloam Baby Talk'	ELon GBuc NBir WMoo WPnP
'Siloam Bertie Ferris'	MBNS
'Siloam Bo Peep'	SDay
'Siloam Button Box'	MBNS SDay WHrl
'Siloam Bye Lo'	EWoo MSpc SDay
'Siloam Cinderella'	SDay SPol
'Siloam David Kirchhoff'	EBee MBNS MSpe SDay XSen
'Siloam Doodlebug'	CBgR CWat MSpe
'Siloam Double Classic' (d)	SPol
'Siloam Dream Baby'	ELon MBNS MSpe NCGa
'Siloam Ethel Smith'	SDay SPol
'Siloam Fairy Tale'	CWat SDay
'Siloam Flower Girl'	SDay
'Siloam French Doll'	MBNS NLar
'Siloam French Marble'	SDay
'Siloam Frosted Mint'	SPol
'Siloam Gold Coin'	SDay
'Siloam Grace Stamile'	CCon MBNS SDay
'Siloam Helpmate'	WNHG
'Siloam Jack Spratt' **new**	CFwr
'Siloam Jim Cooper'	MSpe
'Siloam Joan Senior'	MBNS
'Siloam John Yonski'	SDay
'Siloam June Bug'	CBgR ELan WCot
'Siloam Justine Lee'	MBNS
'Siloam Little Angel'	SPol
'Siloam Little Girl'	CWat ECtt SDay
'Siloam Mama'	SDay
'Siloam Merle Kent'	EWoo MSpe SPol
'Siloam Orchid Jewel'	SDay
'Siloam Paul Watts'	SPol
'Siloam Pink Glow'	SWat
'Siloam Plum Tree'	SPol
'Siloam Pocket Size'	SDay
'Siloam Queen's Toy'	SPol
'Siloam Ribbon Candy'	SDay WNHG
'Siloam Rose Dawn'	SDay SPol
'Siloam Rose Queen'	SDay
'Siloam Royal Prince'	EPfP MSpe
'Siloam Show Girl'	CWGN EWoo GKin MBNS
'Siloam Spizz'	SDay
'Siloam Theresa Moore'	SDay
'Siloam Tiny Mite'	SDay WHrl
'Siloam Tom Thumb'	CBgR MBNS MSpe WCAu
'Siloam Ury Winniford'	CBro CMac EMil MBNS MSpe NBre NLar WHoo WHrl WPnP
'Siloam Virginia Henson'	EWoo NCGa WWEG
'Silver Ice'	EWoo SDay SPol
'Silver Lance'	SDay SPol
'Silver Quasar'	SDay SPol
'Silver Trumpet'	WWEG

'Silver Veil'	SDay
'Simmering Elephants' **new**	CFwr
'Simplicity in Motion' **new**	CFwr
'Simply Divine'	CFwr
'Sinbad Sailor'	NLar
'Singing in the Sunshine'	EWoo
'Sir Blackstem'	ELon GCal
'Sir Francis Drake' **new**	CFwr
'Sir Modred'	SPol WNHG
'Sirius'	NHol
'Sixth Sense'	ELon MBNS WHrl
'Skeezix' **new**	CFwr
'Skinny Dipping' **new**	CFwr
'Skinwalker'	EWoo
'Slapstick'	ELon SDay SPol
'Slender Lady'	CFwr ELon SDay XSen
'Small Town'	EWoo
'Small World Tornado'	EWoo
'Smith Brothers'	SPol
'Smoke Scream' **new**	CFwr
'Smokestack Lightning' **new**	CFwr
'Smoky Mountain Autumn'	EWoo SPol
'Smuggler's Gold'	ECtt
'Smuggler's Temptation'	SPol
'Snappy Rhythm'	MNFA
'Snowed In'	EWoo
'Snowy Apparition'	EBee ECrc ECtt GKin LHop LRHS MBNS MNFA MWhi NWad SPol WCAu
'Snowy Eyes'	CHid GKin MBNS NCGa NHol SWat WHrl
'So Excited'	SDay
'So Lovely'	EWoo XLum
'So Many Stars'	CFwr
'Soft Cashmere'	XLum
'Solano Bull's Eye'	MLHP
'Sombrero Way'	SDay
'Someone Special'	SDay SPol
'Song In My Heart'	EWoo
'Song Sparrow'	CBro
'Soraya Seline' **new**	CBgR
'Sorcerer's Song'	SDay
'South Seas'	LRHS
'Southern Prize'	SDay
'Sovereign Queen'	WNHG
'Spacecoast Color Scheme' **new**	CFwr
'Spacecoast Cranberry Kid' **new**	CFwr
'Spacecoast Dragon Prince'	EWoo
'Spacecoast Peach Fringe'	CFwr
'Spacecoast Royal Ransom' **new**	CFwr
'Spacecoast Scrambled'	CBcs CWGN EPfP MBNS NLar SMrm
'Spacecoast Starburst'	CBcs MBNS NBro WCAu WCot
'Spanish Fandango'	SPol
'Spanish Glow'	SPol
'Spice Hunter'	CFwr
'Spider Breeder'	ELon EWoo
'Spider Man'	ELon MNFA SDay SPol WCAu XSen
'Spider Miracle'	SDay SPol
'Spider Red'	CWGN EWoo
'Spilled Milk'	SPol
'Spindazzle'	CBgR CFwr SPol
'Spinne in Lachs'	SPol
'Spirit of Sapelo'	EWoo
'Spock's Ears' **new**	CFwr
'Spock's Sun'	CFwr

	'Spooner'	CBgR
	'Spring Willow Song'	SDay
	'Square Dancer's Curtsy' **new**	CFwr
	'Squash Dolly'	EWoo
	'Stafford'	Widely available
	'Staghorn Sumac'	GKin LEdu LRHS MBNS NHol WCAu
	'Star Asterisk' **new**	CFwr SPol
	'Star of India'	SPol
	'Stargate Corridor' **new**	SPol
	'Starling'	COlW CPar EWoo MNFA WWEG
	'Starman's Quest'	SPol
	'Stars and Stripes'	MNFA
	'Starstruck'	WNHG
	'Startle'	ELon EPfP MBNS MNrw WCot WHrl
	'Startling Creation'	CFwr
	'Statuesque'	EWoo
	'Stella de Oro'	Widely available
	'Stella in Red'	EPfP
	'Stinnette'	WCot
	'Stippled Starlight' **new**	CFwr
	'Stoke Poges' ♀H4	CAvo CBgR CBro EBee ELon EPfP EWTr GBin LAst LBMP LHop LPot LRHS LSRN MBNS MNFA MSpe NPri SPer STes SWat WHrl
	'Stone Beacon' **new**	CFwr
	'Stone Island' **new**	CFwr
	'Stoplight'	CBgR ELon SDay SPol
	'Storm of the Century'	MNrw
	'Storm Over Toledo'	CFwr
	'Strasbourg'	CMac
	'Strawberry Candy'	CHel CMac COlW CSBt ECtt ELon EPfP EWll EWoo IBoy LSRN MBNS MSpe NGdn SPer SPet STes WCAu WHoo WHrl WMoo WWEG
	'Strawberry Fields Forever'	EWoo MBNS MBri NLar SPol
	'Strawberry Swirl'	MNFA
I	'Streaker' B. Brown (v)	XSen
	'Street Urchin'	SPol
	'Streets of Heaven'	EWoo
	'Strikingly Dramatic' **new**	CFwr
	'String Theory' **new**	CFwr
	'Strutter's Ball'	EWoo LPla MBNS MNFA MSCN MSpe NGdn SDay SPer SPol SWat WCAu WHrl WMnd
	'Stu's Old Pink Spider' **new**	CBgR
	'Sugar Cookie'	EWoo SDay SPol
	'Summer Dragon'	MBNS
	'Summer Fireworks'	EWoo
	'Summer Interlude'	WMoo
	'Summer Wine'	Widely available
	'Sunday Gloves'	SPol WNHG
	'Sunray Brilliance'	EWoo
	'Super Purple'	CKel
	'Superlative'	SPol
	'Susan Weber'	EWoo SPol
	'Suzie Wong'	MNFA
	'Suzy Cream Cheese' **new**	CFwr
	'Svengali'	SDay SPol
	'Swallow Tail Kite' **new**	SPol
	'Swashbuckler Bay Boy' **new**	CFwr
	'Sweet Charlotte'	SPol
	'Sweet Hot Chocolate'	LRHS MBNS
	'Sweet Pea'	SDay
	'Sweet Sugar Candy'	ECtt EWoo SDeJ
	'Swirling Spider'	CBgR EWoo SPol
	'Swirling Water'	SDay
	'Taj Mahal'	ELon EWoo
	'Tammy Faye Eyes' **new**	CFwr
	'Tang'	CHid MBNS WCAu
	'Tangerine Tango'	EWoo
	'Tango Noturno'	SPol
	'Tani'	SDay
	'Tarantula'	ELon SPol
	'Taruga'	EWoo SDay
	'Tasmania'	SPer
	'Tchao Pantin'	XSen
	'Teacup Fingers' **new**	CFwr
	'Technical Knockout'	EWoo
	'Tejas'	CElw ELon NBre SPer
	'Témoin' **new**	XSen
	'Tennessee Flycatcher'	EWoo SPol
	'Tennessee Williams'	SPol
	'Tennyson'	CFwr
	'Tequila Mockingbird' **new**	CFwr
	'Tet Set'	WNHG
	'Tetraploid Stella de Oro'	SDay
	'Tetrina's Daughter' ♀H4	CBgR LRHS NHol
	'Texas Sunlight'	CHel
	'Thanks a Bunch'	SPol
	'The Band Played On' **new**	CFwr
	'The Tingler'	CFwr EWoo
	'Thelma Perry' **new**	LEdu
	'Thin Man'	CFwr
	'Third Witch'	CFwr EWoo
	'Thomas Tew' **new**	CFwr
	'Three Diamonds'	SPol
	'Thumbelina'	WMoo XLum
§	***thunbergii***	GCal MCoo
	- 'Ovation'	MBNS
	'Thundering Ovation'	CWGN
	'Thy True Love'	SDay
	'Tiger Swirl' **new**	CFwr
	'Tigereye Spider'	EWoo
	'Tigerland' **new**	CFwr
	'Tigerling'	EWoo MSpe SPol
	'Tigger'	SPol
	'Time Lord'	SDay XSen
	'Time to Believe'	SPol
	'Tiny Talisman'	SDay
	'Tiny Temptress'	SDay
	'Tis Midnight'	WNHG
	'Titanic Tower' **new**	CFwr
	'Tom Collins'	SDay
	'Tom Wise'	SPol
	'Tomorrow's Song'	SPol
	'Tone Poem'	WNHG
	'Tonia Gay'	SDay SPol
	'Toodleloo Kangaroo'	EWoo
	'Toothpick'	EWoo SPol
	'Tootsie'	SDay
	'Tootsie Rose'	SDay SPol
	'Top Honors'	SPol
	'Topaz Gem'	SPol
	'Topguns Aleah Kaye' **new**	CFwr
	'Topguns Anita Causey' **new**	CFwr
	'Topguns Bandit's Bandana' **new**	CFwr
	'Topguns Butterball' **new**	CFwr
	'Topguns Cactus Jack' **new**	CFwr
	'Topguns Cherokee Dancer' **new**	CFwr
	'Topguns Cherry Limeade' **new**	CFwr
	'Topguns Citrine Dream' **new**	CFwr

'Topguns Copper Butterflies' new	CFwr
'Topguns Dragonfly Sunset' new	CFwr
'Topguns Dream Catcher' new	CFwr
'Topguns Eye Popper' new	CFwr
'Topguns Grim Reaper' new	CFwr
'Topguns Harlequin Ruffles' new	CFwr
'Topguns Jennifer Hankins' new	CFwr
'Topguns Lemon Ruffles' new	CFwr
'Topguns Linda Farris' new	CFwr
'Topguns Molten Lava' new	CFwr
'Topguns Okie Twister' new	CFwr
'Topguns Orange Fizz' new	CFwr
'Topguns Orange Marmalade' new	CFwr
'Topguns Pawnee Princess' new	CFwr
'Topguns Pinwheel' new	CFwr
'Topguns Rising Sun' new	CFwr
'Topguns Ruffled Amazement' new	CFwr
'Topguns Stop 'n' Go' new	CFwr
'Topguns Tilt-A-Whirl' new	CFwr
'Torpoint'	CBgR GBee MBNS MRav NEgg
'Towhead'	MRav SDay WCot
'Toyland'	EPfP MBNS NBir NGdn NLar SPol
'Trahlyta'	CBgR EWoo MSpe SDay SPol WHrl
'Treasure of Love'	EWoo
'Trevi Fountain'	EWoo
'Trond'	SDay
'Tropical Breeze' new	CFwr
'Tropical Depression'	CFwr EWoo
'Tropical Toy'	SDay
'Troubled Sleep'	EWoo
'Truchas Sunrise'	CFwr EWoo
'True Gertrude Demarest'	WHrl
'True North'	CFwr
'True Pink Beauty'	EWoo
'Truffle Heritage'	CFwr
'Tune the Harp'	SPol
'Tuolumne Fairy Tale'	SPol
'Turkey Lurkey' new	CFwr
'Turkish Turban'	SDay SPol
'Tuscawilla Blackout'	XSen
'Tuscawilla Tigress'	GKin IKil MBNS MNrw NCGa SMad SPol WHrl
'Tutti Frutti Truffle'	CFwr
'Tuxedo'	SPol
'Twenty Third Psalm'	WHal
'Twiggy'	CFwr MSpe
'Twilight Secrets'	LRHS MBNS SGol
'Twilight Swan' new	WNHG
'Twirling Pinata'	CFwr EWoo
'Twirling Wings' new	CFwr
'Twist and Shout'	CFwr
'Twist and Spin' new	CFwr
'Twist of Lemon'	CFwr EWoo SDay
'Twisted Mint Julep' new	CFwr
'Twister Time'	CFwr
'Two Faces of Love'	SPol
'Two Part Harmony'	CFwr
'Tylwyth Teg'	CFwr SPol
'Ultimate Destiny'	CWat
'Unchartered Waters'	MBNS
'Unforgetable Fire'	EWoo
'Unique Purple'	SPol
'Uniquely Different'	SPol
'Valiant'	EWoo MBNS WHrl
'Valley Monster'	SPol
'Vanilla Candy'	MSpe
'Variegated Woottens' (v)	EWoo
'Varsity'	CExl CWat LRHS NBir SPer
'Veins of Truth'	CBgR EBee
'Velvet Onyx' new	CFwr
'Velvet Ribbons' new	CFwr
'Vendetta'	WNHG
'Venusian Heat' new	CFwr
'Venus's Fire' new	CFwr
'Vera Biaglow'	MSpe SPol
'Very Berry Ice'	SPol
'Vespers'	CAbP WPnP
vespertina	see *H. thunbergii*
'Veuve Joyeuse'	XSen
'Victoria Aden'	CBro
'Victoria Elizabeth Barnes'	WNHG
'Victorian Lace'	EWoo
'Victorian Ribbons'	SPol
'Victorian Violet'	SDay
'Video'	SDay
'Vintage Bordeaux'	ELan
'Vintage Burgundy'	CBgR WNHG
'Violent Thunder' new	CFwr
'Violet Hour'	SDay
'Viracocha'	WMnd WNHG
'Virgil Earp' new	CFwr
'Virgin's Blush'	SPer
'Vohann'	SDay
'Volcano Queen' new	CFwr
'Walking on Sunshine'	WCot
'Walt Disney'	GKin
'War Paint'	SDay
'Warrior Victorious'	CFwr
'Watch Tower'	CBgR
'Watchyl Christmas Widow'	CFwr
'Watchyl Dancing Spider'	SPol
'Watchyl Digital Scream'	CFwr
'Watchyl Digital Spider'	CFwr
'Watchyl Lavender Blue'	CFwr
'Water Witch'	CWat SDay STes
'Watermelon Man'	EWoo
'Watership Down'	EWoo
'Watson Park Tempest' new	CFwr
'Wayside Green Imp'	MNrw
'We Love'	EWoo
'Weaver's Art'	SPol
'Web Browser'	CFwr
'Web Dancer'	SPol
'Wedding Band'	SDay
'Wee Willie Wonka'	WNHG
'Wekiwa'	EWoo
'Welchkins'	SDay
'Welfo White Diamond'	SPol
'Westward Wind'	EWoo
'Whammer Jammer' new	CFwr
'What a Day for a Daydream'	CFwr
'Whichford' ♀H4	CBgR CBro CSam ECrc ECtt ELan EPfP EWoo GBuc GKin LRHS MBNS MNFA MSpe NEgg SPhx WGwG WHrl WPtf
'Whirling Fury'	ELon EWoo
'White Coral'	EWTr LRHS LSRN MBNS MNFA NBro

'White Edged Madonna'	SBch WHrl
'White Perfection'	EWoo
'White Temptation'	CCon EPfP IBoy NCGa NGdn NOrc WHoo WMnd WNHG XSen
'White Tie Affair'	EWoo
'White Zone'	EWoo
'Whooperee'	SDay
'Wideyed'	XLum
'Wild about Sherry'	CFwr SPol
'Wild and Wonderful'	EPfP EWoo MBri NCGa WWlt
'Wild Child' **new**	CFwr
'Wild Horses'	CHel CWGN EBee EPfP EWes LRHS MNrw NLar SPad SPol WHrl
'Wild Mustang'	MBNS MSpe
'Wild Rose Fandango'	CFwr EWoo
'Wild Winter Wine'	CFwr
'Wild Wookie'	CFwr
'Wildest Dreams'	EWoo
'Wilson Spider'	SPol
'Wind Beneath My Sails'	EWoo
'Wind Frills'	SPol XSen
'Wind Song'	ELon
'Windmill Yellow'	EWoo
'Window Dressing'	EWoo
'Winds of Love'	EWoo
'Wine Delight'	SDay
'Wine Merchant'	MNFA
'Wineberry Candy'	EWoo LHop MBNS MSpe NLar SDay
'Winged Migration'	CFwr EWoo
'Wings on High'	EWoo
'Winnie the Pooh'	SDay
'Winsome Lady'	ECGP ECtt GKin MBNS WHrl
'Wisest of Wizards'	MBNS MNrw NCGa SPol WHrl
'Wishing Well'	WCot
'Witch Hazel'	WCAu
'Witch Stitchery'	SDay
'Witches Brew'	CBgR
'Witches Wink'	EWoo MSpe
'Witch's Stick' **new**	CFwr
'Without Warning'	CBgR
'Woodside Ruby'	WNHG
'Written on the Wind' **new**	CFwr
'Wyoming Wildfire' **new**	CBgR
'Xia Xiang'	EWoo
'Xochimilco'	WNHG
'Ya Ya Girl'	EWoo
'Yabba Dabba Doo'	MNrw SPol
'Yazoo Green Octopus'	EWoo
'Yellow Angel'	ELon SPol WCot
'Yellow Finch' **new**	CFwr
'Yellow Lollipop'	SDay
'Yellow Rain'	WCot
'Yellow Ribbon'	SPol
'Yellow Submarine'	MBNS
'Yesterday Memories'	SDay
yezoensis	EBtc
'Yo-rick Yost' **new**	CFwr
'You Angel You'	MBNS MSpe
'Yuma'	WNHG
'Zagora'	WCAu
'Zampa'	CBgR SDay
'Zara'	SPer
'Zuni Thunderbird'	EWoo

Hepatica ✿ (*Ranunculaceae*)

acutiloba	CBro CRDP ECho GBBs GBuc MMoz NBir WAbe XEll
- blue-flowered	MAsh
- white-flowered	MAsh
americana	EBee ECho ELan ITim LHop MAsh NBir NPnk
angulosa	see *H. transsilvanica*
(Forest Series) 'Forest Pink'	ELan XEll
- 'Forest Purple' (Forest Series)	XEll
- 'Forest Red' (Forest Series)	ELan XEll
- 'Forest White' (Forest Series)	ELan XEll
henryi	MAsh NLar NSla
insularis	GBuc MAsh
- B&SWJ 859	WCru
maxima	GBuc MAsh
- B&SWJ 4344	WCru
× ***media*** 'Ballardii'	GBuc IBlr LLHF MNFA
- 'Harvington Beauty'	CLAP IBlr IFoB LRHS MAsh MHom NBir
§ ***nobilis*** ♀^{H4}	CBro CWCL EBee ECho EHyd EPfP EPot GBBs GCra GKev IBlr ITim LHop LPio LRHS MAsh MBel MCot MHer MRav NBir NCGa NPnk NSum SPer SPhx SRms WAbe WCot WPnP
- var. ***asiatica***	MAsh NPnk
- blue-flowered	ECho IFoB MAsh NSla WAbe WGwG
- 'Cobalt'	CLAP ECho NSla WAbe
- 'Cremar'	MAsh
- dark-blue-flowered	CLAP
- dwarf white-flowered	IFoB
- var. ***japonica***	EPfP EWes IFoB LHop MAsh NBir NSla
- - 'Akane' (1)	ECho
- - 'Gyousei' (1)	ECho GBuc
- - Herashibe Group (5/d)	GBuc
- - 'Isaribi' (1)	ECho
- - 'Kasumino'	ECho
- - f. ***magna***	MAsh
- - 'Ō-murasaki' (1)	ECho
- - 'Ryougetsu' (1)	LLHF
- - 'Sougetsu' (6/d)	ECho
- large, pale blue-flowered	NSla
- 'Lilac Picotee'	NSla
- mottled leaf	ECho
- patterned leaf	NSla
- pink-flowered	CLAP ECho MAsh
- var. ***pubescens***	MAsh
* - var. ***pyrenaica***	GBuc LEdu MAsh NSla WThu
* - - 'Apple Blossom'	GBuc MAsh NBir WAbe
- 'Pyrenean Marbles'	CLAP GBin
- red-flowered	ECho
- var. ***rubra***	CLAP ECho NSla
- 'Rubra Plena' (d)	CWCL NHar NSla WPnP
- white-flowered	CLAP ECho GAbr MAsh
'Sakaya'	ECho
'Shunrin' (d)	CRDP
§ ***transsilvanica*** ♀^{H4}	CBro CLAP ECho EPot GAbr GBin MAsh MCot MMoz NPnk SMrm WPnP
- 'Blue Eyes'	EBee ECho EPot GKev MHom NCGa
- 'Blue Jewel'	CCon CLAP CWCL EBee ECho ELan MCot MHol MHom NCGa NLar WCot WPnP
- blue-flowered	IBlr IFoB MAsh
- 'Buis'	CLAP ECho IFoB LRHS MHom NLar WPnP
- 'Eisvogel'	CLAP ECho
- 'Elison Spence' (d)	IBlr MCot

	- 'Lilacina'	ECho MAsh NSla
	- 'Loddon Blue'	IBlr
	- pink-flowered	CLAP ECho MAsh
	- 'Sieben Bergen'	IBlr
	- white-flowered	ECho MAsh
	triloba	see *H. nobilis*
	yamatutai	EBee GBuc NLar
	aff. ***yamatutai***	MAsh

Heptacodium (*Caprifoliaceae*)

	jasminoides	see *H. miconioides*
§	***miconioides***	Widely available

Heptapleurum see *Schefflera*

Heracleum (*Apiaceae*)

	lehmannianum	WCot

Herbertia (*Iridaceae*)

§	***lahue***	CDes ECho

Hereroa (*Aizoaceae*)

	glenensis	ECho EDAr EHyd LRHS SPlb

Hermannia (*Malvaceae*)

I	***ciliaris***	EDif
	flammea	SPlb
	stricta	CPBP SDys WAbe

Hermodactylus see *Iris*

Herniaria (*Caryophyllaceae*)

	glabra	CArn GPoy WHfH

Hertia see *Othonna*

Hesperaloe (*Asparagaceae*)

	F&M 311.1	WPGP
	'Mamulique' **new**	WCot
	'New Blue' **new**	WCot
	parviflora	EAmu LEdu SBig SPlb XSen
	- creamy yellow-flowered **new**	WCot

Hesperantha (*Iridaceae*)

§	***baurii***	ECho GBuc GLin LLHF WAbe
	coccinea	Widely available
	- from Giants Castle	CTca
	- f. ***alba***	Widely available
	- 'Ballyrogan Giant'	CCon CPrp CTca GBuc IBlr MAvo NHol WHer WPGP
	- 'Big Moma'	CPrp MAvo WWEG
	- 'Brick Red'	MAvo
	- 'Cardinal'	CPrp NHol WMoo
	- 'Cindy Towe'	MAvo
	- 'Countesse de Vere'	EBee
	- early-flowering	CPrp
	- 'Elburton Glow'	CPrp MAvo
	- 'Fenland Daybreak'	CCVN CHel CKno COlW CTsd EBee ECtt ELan ELon EPfP LAst LRHS LSou MBri MGos MHol NCGa NEgg NLar NPri SPet SRms SRot SWvt WHil WHoo WMnd WMoo WNew WWEG
	- 'Good White'	NBir NCGa
	- 'Hilary Gould'	CPrp GBuc MAvo NCGa WHal
	- 'Jack Frost'	EBee NCGa WMoo WWEG
	- 'Jennifer' ♀H4	CBro CPrp CTca CTri EBee ELon EPfP EShb GAbr GBin GBuc LPot LRHS LSou MAvo MRav NCGa NLar SRms SWvt WMoo WWEG XLum
	- late-flowering	NCot
	- 'Maiden's Blush'	CPrp ELan LRHS LSou MCot NHol NLar SPet SRms
§	- 'Major' ♀H4	Widely available
	- 'Marietta'	NWad
	- 'Mollie Gould'	CPrp CTca ECtt ELon EShb GBuc GCra LBMP LHop LSou MHer MMHG NCGa NHol NLar NPnk SCoo SPoG SRms WHil WMoo WWEG
	- 'Mrs Hegarty'	Widely available
	- 'November Cheer'	CMac CPrp IBlr LLHF NBir NLar WWEG XLum
	- 'Oregon Sunset'	CPrp MAvo
	- 'Pallida'	CPrp CSam ELan MLHP MRav NBir
	- 'Pink Marg'	CPrp MAvo
	- 'Pink Princess'	see *H. coccinea* 'Wilfred H. Bryant'
	- 'Professor Barnard'	CCCN CPrp CSpe CTca EBee ECho ECtt ELon EPfP EPri EShb GAbr MAvo MBNS NBir NEgg SRot WMoo WWEG
	'Red Arrow' **new**	EWes
	- 'Red Dragon'	GAbr GBuc LLHF NCGa NHol
I	- 'Rosea'	SDeJ
	- 'Salmon Charm'	ECtt GBuc LLHF LRHS NCGa WMoo
	- 'Silver Pink'	IBlr
	- 'Snow Maiden'	CElw CHel CWCL EBee ECtt
	- 'Strawberry'	CPrp
§	- 'Sunrise' ♀H4	Widely available
	- 'Tambara'	CCsc CPou CPrp CSam GAbr GBuc MAvo XLum
	- 'Viscountess Byng'	CBcs CHel CTca CTri CWCL EBee EPau LRHS NBir SMrm SPer WWEG
§	- 'Wilfred H. Bryant'	Widely available
	- 'Zeal Salmon'	CCon CPou CPrp GAbr MAvo NBir NCGa
	cucullata	ECho
	falcata	ECho
	grandiflora	ECho
	huttonii	ECho LLHF MHer NBir
	mossii	see *H. baurii*
	oligantha 'Kamiesberg'	ECho
	pauciflora	ECho

Hesperis (*Brassicaceae*)

	dinarica	LRHS
	lutea	see *Sisymbrium luteum*
	matronalis	CArn CBre CSev CSpe EBee ELan ELau EPfP GMaP IFro LPio LPot LRHS MBNS MCot MNHC NGdn NPri SGbt SIde SPer SPoG SRms SWat WJek WMnd WMoo WSFF
	- ***alba***	see *H. matronalis* var. *albiflora*
§	- var. ***albiflora***	CSpe CTri ELau EPfP LRHS MCot MMuc MNHC NGdn NPnk SIde SPer SPoG SWat WBrk WMnd WMoo
	- - 'Alba Plena' (d)	CAbP ELan ELon IBoy LRHS MBel MCot MHol MNrw NBir NCGa NPri WCot WHer
	- - 'Edith Harriet' (d/v)	WCot
	- 'Cally Dwarf' (d)	GCal
	- 'Lilacina'	SWat
	steveniana	SBch

Hessea (*Amaryllidaceae*)

	breviflora	ECho

incana 'Pendoornhoek'	ECho
mathewsii	ECho
pulcherrima	ECho
speciosa	ECho
stellaris	ECho

Heteromorpha (*Apiaceae*)

arborescens	CExl SPlb SVen

Heteropyxis (*Myrtaceae*)

natalensis	EShb

Heterotheca (*Asteraceae*)

camporum	LHop
var. ***glandulissimum***	
mariana	see *Chrysopsis mariana*
§ ***villosa***	EPPr WCot
- 'Golden Sunshine'	CPrp

Heuchera ✿ (*Saxifragaceae*)

'Alan Davidson'	MPnt
'Alison'	MPnt
'Amber Waves'[PBR]	CExl ELan EPfP LRHS LSRN MJak MPnt NBir SGol SRGP SWvt
§ ***americana***	MNFA MRav NBir SHeu SWvt
- var. ***americana***	MPnt
- Dale's strain	EHoe IFoB MPnt NLar SHeu SPlb SWvt WPnP
- 'Harry Hay'	CDes CLAP EPPr LPla MPnt SHeu WPGP WSHC
- 'Ring of Fire'	EBee ECtt LHop LRHS NPri SHeu SWvt
'Amethyst Myst'	CAby CHid CLAP COlW ECtt EPfP LHop LRHS LSRN MPnt NPla SGol SHeu SLim SPer
'Apple Crisp'	ECtt MAsh MPnt SHeu WNPC
'Autumn Haze'[PBR]	MPnt SHeu
'Autumn Leaves'	CHid CLAP CMea ECtt ELan ELon ESwi EWll LBMP LRHS LSou MPnt NCGa NLar NPri NWad SHeu SMrm SPoG SRot SWvt WCot WSpi
'Baby's Breath'	ECho MPnt
'Beaujolais'[PBR]	CAbP CLAP ECtt ESwi LRHS LSou MAsh MBNS MBri MNrw MPnt NBir NCGa NLar NSti SHeu WBrk WCot
'Beauty Colour'	CAbP CLAP CMac CRos ECtt ELan ELon EPfP GMaP LHop LRHS LSRN MBri MJak MPie MRav NGdn NHol NWad SHeu SHil SWvt WMnd
'Belle Notte' **new**	SHeu
'Berry Marmalade'	ECtt GBin LSou MAsh MPnt NWad SHeu SWvt WNPC
'Berry Smoothie'[PBR]	Widely available
'Binoche'	ECtt MPnt SHeu
'Birkin'	EBee LRHS MPnt SHeu
'Black Negligee' **new**	LRHS
'Blackberry Crisp'	ECtt MAsh MPnt SHeu WNPC
'Blackberry Jam'	CHel CLAP COlW CSev CSpe ECtt ELan ELon ESwi GBin LBMP LRHS MAsh MPnt NBir NHol NSti SFai SHeu SWvt WGor
'Blackbird' ♀[H4]	CLAP CMac LRHS MPnt MWat SFai SHeu SWvt WMnd
'Blackout'	CAbP ECtt ESwi MAsh MNrw MPnt SEND SHeu WBrk WCot WNPC WWEG
'Blood Red'	CLAP LSou MPnt NWad SHeu SLim
'Blood Vein'	MPnt SHeu
'Bouquet'	MPnt
bracteata	MPnt XLum
'Bressingham Glow'	MPnt SHeu
Bressingham hybrids	CWib GJos IFoB MLHP NBir SPer SRms WWEG
'Bressingham Spire' **new**	MPnt
'Bronze Beauty'	CMil MPnt SHeu WCot
'Brown Sugar'	EBee ECtt MPnt SHeu WNPC
'Brownfinch'	MPnt SHeu
'Brownies'	CAbP CLAP ECtt ESwi GAbr LPla MBNS MPie MPnt SHeu WCot WPtf
'Burgundy Frost' ♀[H4]	MPnt
'Café Olé'	ECtt ELon LSou MAsh MPnt NLar SHeu WHer WNPC
'Cajun Fire' **new**	MAsh MPnt SHeu WNPC
'Can-can' ♀[H4]	CTri ECtt ELon EPfP ITim LRHS LSRN MAsh MAvo MCot MNrw MPnt NBir NEgg NGdn NLar NPri SHeu SPer SRot SWvt WBrk WCot WWEG
'Canyon Duet'	LHop MBNS MPnt SHeu
'Canyon Pink'	NSti
'Cappuccino'	EBee ECtt ELan EPfP IBoy MPnt MRav SGol SHeu SWvt
'Caramel'[PBR]	Widely available
'Carmen'	MPnt
'Cascade Dawn'	CLAP CWCL EBee ECtt EPfP LSRN MPnt NBir SWvt WNPC
'Champagne Bubbles'	MLHP SHeu
Charles Bloom = 'Chablo'	MPnt
'Chatterbox'	MPnt SHeu
'Cherries Jubilee'[PBR]	CAbP CCon CLAP ELon EPfP GMaP LSRN LSou MPnt NWad SLim WNPC
'Cherry Cola'	ECtt LSou MPnt NLar SHeu WNPC
'Chiqui'	MPnt
chlorantha	MPnt
- 'Burnt Sienna' **new**	GCal
'Chocolate Ruffles'[PBR]	Widely available
'Chocolate Veil' ♀[H4]	EPfP LSRN MPnt WWEG
'Christa'	MPnt SHeu
'Cinnabar Silver'[PBR]	CLAP ECtt LRHS LSou MPnt NBir NCGa NDov SHeu WNPC
'Circus' **new**	MPnt SHeu
'Citronelle'	CSev CWGN EBee ECtt ITim LSou MBNS MPnt NPnk SHeu SWvt WCot
'City Lights'	LSou SHeu
'Color Dream'[PBR]	MPnt SHeu
coral bells	see *H. sanguinea*
'Coral Bouquet'	MPnt SHeu
'Coral Cloud'	MPnt
'Corallion' **new**	MPnt
Crème Brûlée = 'Tnheu041' (Dolce Series)	Widely available
'Crème Caramel'	CExl IFoB MPnt SHar
'Creole Nights' **new**	MPnt SHeu WNPC
'Crimson Curls'	CLAP EBee ECtt EPfP LBuc LRHS LSou MAsh MPnt SFai SHeu SRms SWvt
'Crispy Curly'	MPnt SHeu
cylindrica	EPfP LLWP LRHS MPnt SHeu WWEG
- var. ***alpina***	GKev LLHF
- 'Cream' **new**	MPnt
- 'Francis'	MPnt
- 'Greenfinch'	CFis ELan EPfP GKev GMaP LPio LRHS LSRN MPnt MRav NBir SHeu SWat WMnd XLum

- 'Hyperion'	MPnt
'Damask'	MPnt
'Dark Beauty'PBR	CCVN CLAP ECtt ELon LRHS LSRN LSou MAsh MBNS NLar NPri NWad SHeu SMad SRot WCot
'Dark Secret'PBR	MPnt SHeu
'David'	MPnt SHeu WBrk
'Delta Dawn' **new**	LSou MPnt SFai SHeu WNPC
'Dennis Davidson'	see *H.* 'Huntsman'
'Dingle Mint Chocolate'	ECtt
Ebony and Ivory = 'E and I'PBR	CAbP CLAP CRos EBee ECtt EHoe EShb GKev GMaP LBMP LHop LRHS LSRN MBri MGos MPnt NBir NHol NLar SHar SHil SRot SWvt WWEG
'Eden's Aurora'	MPnt
'Electra'PBR	CLAP CMea ECtt ELon ESwi EUJe EWll LHop LRHS LSou MBNS MBri MPnt NDov NHol NLar NPnk NPri NWad SHeu SMrm SPoG SRot SWvt WBor WCot WHlf WSpi
'Electric Lime'	CLAP ECtt EHoe ELan ESwi GBin MPnt NPri NWad SHeu WNPC
elegans NNS 05-372	WCot
'Elworthy Rusty'	CElw
'Emperor's Cloak'	LEdu NLar SHeu SPad SWvt WMoo
'Encore'PBR	MNrw MPnt SHeu
Eton Mess	see *H.* 'Raspberry'
'Fantasia'	SHeu
'Fire Alarm' **new**	MPnt SHeu
'Fire Chief'PBR	CHel CLAP CWCL CWGN ECtt ESwi EWll GBin LBMP LHop LRHS LSou MAsh MPnt NHol NLar NPri NWad SFai SHeu SMrm SPer SPoG SRkn SRot SWvt
'Firebird'	MPnt NBir
Firefly	see *H.* 'Leuchtkäfer'
'Fireworks'PBR ♀H4	CAbP CCVN CRos ECtt LRHS MBNS MPnt NLar NPri SHil SLim SPer SRot
'Florist's Choice'	MNFA SHeu
'French Quarter'	MPnt SHeu
'Frosted Violet'	see *H.* 'Frosted Violet Dream'
§ 'Frosted Violet Dream'PBR	CLAP ECtt EPfP LHop LRHS LSRN LSou MAsh MPnt NCGa NLar SHeu SWvt WNPC
'Georgia Peach'PBR	Widely available
'Georgia Plum' **new**	SHeu
'Ginger Ale'PBR	CBct CLAP COIW CWGN ECtt ELan EPfP ESwi EWes LBMP LHop LRHS LSou MAsh MBNS MPnt NBir NGdn NHol NLar NPnk NPri NWad SFai SHeu SMad SPer SWvt WWEG
'Ginger Peach'	CLAP ECtt LSou MPnt NDov NPnk NWad SHeu WNPC
glabra	MPnt
glauca	see *H. americana*
'Gloire d'Orléans'	MPnt XLum
'Gotham' **new**	SHeu
'Green Ivory'	MPnt MRav SHeu XLum
'Green Sashay' **new**	MPnt
'Green Spice'	CLAP COIW CWCL ECtt EHoe ELan ELon EPfP ESwi EUJe LBMP LHop LRHS LSou MBri MPnt NBir NCGa NHol NPla NPnk NPri NWad SFai SHeu SPer SPoG SRkn SWvt WGwG
'Green Spire'	CHel
grossulariifolia	GMaP
'Guardian Angel'	CLAP CMac LSou MPnt SHeu SPoG SRGP
'Gypsy Dancer'PBR (Dancer Series)	CLAP ECtt EPfP MPnt SHeu WNPC
'Hailstorm' (v)	MPnt
hallii	CPBP MPnt
'Havana'	LSou MPnt SHeu
'Helen Dillon' (v)	EShb GCal GMaP LAst MPnt NBir NPnk SRGP SWvt WGwG WWEG
'Hercules'PBR	ECtt MAsh MPnt SHeu
hispida	MPnt
'Hollywood'PBR	CHel CWCL EBee ECtt ELon EPfP ESwi LAst LBMP LHop LRHS LSRN LSou MBri MPnt NBir NDov NHol NPri NWad SHeu SMrm SPoG SRkn SRot
§ 'Huntsman'	MBNS MPnt MRav
'Jade Gloss'PBR	CLAP CRos EPfP GBin LRHS MBri MPnt SHeu SHil SWvt WNPC WWEG
'June Bride' **new**	MPnt
'Kadastra' **new**	MPnt
'Kassandra'	EBee ECtt LRHS MPnt SGol SHeu STPC
Key Lime Pie = 'Tnheu042'PBR (Dolce Series)	CBcs CExl CRos CWGN ECtt EPfP EWll LHop LRHS LSRN MAsh MBri MGos NBir NBro NHol NLar NPla SHeu SHil SPer SRot SWvt WBor
Kira Series **new**	MPnt
'Lady in Red'	NBre
'Lady Marmalade' **new**	MBri
'Lady Romney'	XLum
'Lemon Chiffon'PBR	ECtt MPnt NDov SHeu
§ 'Leuchtkäfer'	Widely available
Licorice = 'Tnheu044'PBR (Dolce Series)	COIW CRos CWCL ECtt ELon ESwi EUJe EWll GBin LRHS MAsh MBNS MBri MGos MPnt NBir NLar NPri SHeu SHil SLim SRot SWvt WHoo WWEG
'Lime Marmalade'	Widely available
'Lime Rickey'PBR	Widely available
'Lipstick'	CWGN EBee ECtt ELon MAsh MPnt NDov SHeu SWvt
'Little Tinker'	MPnt
'Lune Rousse'	SHeu
'Magic Color'PBR	WCot
'Magic Wand' ♀H4	CAbP ELon MBNS NEgg SHeu
'Magnum'	CWGN EBee ECtt ESwi MPnt SHeu STPC WCot
'Mahogany'PBR	CLAP EBee EPfP EUJe GBin LRHS LSou MAsh MJak MPnt NBir NGdn NPri SHeu SLim SWvt WHoo
'Malachite'	EPfP LRHS MPnt SHeu
'Marmalade'PBR	Widely available
'Mars'	EPfP LRHS MPnt SHeu
'Mary Rose'	MPnt
'Melting Fire'	EBee GJos LRHS LSou MPnt NLar SGol SHeu WNPC
'Mercury'	SHeu
'Metallic Shimmer' (Fox Series)	MPnt
'Metallica'	NGBl SHeu WMoo
micans	see *H. rubescens*
micrantha	GCal MLHP MNFA MPnt SHeu SRms
- var. ***diversifolia*** misapplied	see *H. villosa*
- 'Martha's Compact'	MPnt WCot
§ - 'Ruffles'	MPnt

'Midas Touch'	CLAP CWGN EBee ECtt ELon LSou MPnt NCGa NLar SHeu WNPC
'Midnight Bayou'	CHel EBee ECtt ELan ELon ESwi EWll GBin LBMP LHop LRHS MAsh MBri MPnt NPer NPri SFai SHeu SRot SWvt WNPC
'Midnight Rose'	Widely available
'Midnight Rose Select' **new**	MPnt NWad
'Milan'PBR	ECtt ELon MPnt SFai SHeu WNPC
'Mini Mouse'	LRHS MPnt SHeu
'Mint Frost'PBR	EBee ECtt ELan EPfP LHop LPot LRHS LSou MPnt MRav NBir NCGa SHeu SWvt WWEG
'Mint Julep'	ECtt MBri MPnt SHeu WNPC
'Miracle'PBR	CLAP ECtt EPfP MPnt SHeu WNPC
'Mocha'PBR	CLAP EBee MBNS MNrw MPnt SHeu STes SWvt
'Molly Bush' ♀H4	LRHS MBri MPnt MWhi SHeu
'Mother of Pearl'	MPnt
'Muscat'	MAsh MPnt SHeu
'Mysteria'PBR	ELon LSou MPnt SHeu WNPC
'Mystic Angel'	MPnt SHeu
'Neptune'	ECtt LRHS MPnt SHeu
'Oakington Jewel'	EBee LRHS
'Obsidian'PBR	Widely available
'Orphée'	MPnt
'Paprika' **new**	MPnt SHeu
'Paris'PBR	CLAP COlW CRos ECtt EPfP GBin LRHS LSou MBri MPnt NDov NHol NPri SHeu SHil SMad SPoG WWEG
parishii NNS 93384	MPnt
parvifolia var. ***nivalis***	MPnt
- var. ***utahensis***	MPnt
'Peach Crisp'	CWGN ECtt LSou SHeu WNPC
'Peach Flambé'PBR	Widely available
'Peach Pie'	ECtt MPnt
'Peachy Keen'	SHeu
'Pear Crisp'	ECtt MAsh MPnt SHeu WNPC
'Penelope' **new**	MPnt
'Peppermint Spice'PBR (21st Century Collection Series)	MPnt NPnk SGol SHeu
'Persian Carpet'	CHEx CWCL ECtt GMaP LRHS MPnt NBir SHeu SWvt WPtf
(Petite Series) 'Petite Marbled Burgundy'	EBee ECtt EHoe LLHF LRHS MPnt NDov SHeu SWvt
- 'Petite Pearl Fairy'	CAbP EHoe ELan MPnt SHeu SWvt
- 'Petite Pink Bouquet'	EHoe MPnt SHeu
'Pewter Moon'	CBcs EBee ELan GMaP MGos MRav MSpe NBir SHeu XLum
'Pewter Veil'	LRHS SHeu WMnd
pilosissima	XLum
'Pinot Bianco'	MAsh SHeu
'Pinot Gris'PBR	CLAP CSpe CWGN EBee ECtt ESwi LRHS LSou MAsh MNrw MPnt SHeu WBrk WCot
'Pinot Noir'	MAsh MPnt SHeu WOut
'Pistache'	CAbP ECtt LBMP LSou MPnt NPnk SHeu SPer WCot
§ 'Pluie de Feu'	CCon EBee ECtt EPPr GBuc LRHS MPnt MRav XLum
'Plum Pudding'PBR	Widely available
'Plum Royale'PBR	CLAP CMac CRos CWGN ECtt ELon EPfP LBMP LRHS LSou MAvo MBri MCot MPnt NCGa NDov NLar NPnk NPri NSti NWad SFai SHeu SHil SPer SRkn SWvt WCot WWEG
'Pretty Perinne'	EBee MPnt SHeu WNPC
'Pretty Polly'	MPnt
'Prince'	CCVN EHyd ELan EPfP LRHS LSRN MBNS MBel MPnt SFai SHeu SPoG SWvt
'Prince of Silver'	LRHS MPnt MWhi SHeu
pringlei	see *H. rubescens*
pubescens	ECho MPnt SHeu XLum
- 'Alba'	MPnt
pulchella	CPBP EDAr LLHF MHer MPnt MWat SBch SHeu SRms
'Purple Petticoats' ♀H4	CBcs EBee ECtt ELan EPfP GBin LRHS LSou MLHP MNFA MPnt NLar NPnk NPri SHeu SLim SRot
'Quick Silver'	LRHS MNFA MPnt NBir SHeu SWvt
'Rachel'	CAbP CCVN EHyd ELan EPfP GBuc GMaP IFoB LRHS LSRN MPnt MRav NBir NGdn NPnk SRGP SWvt XLum
Rain of Fire	see *H.* 'Pluie de Feu'
§ 'Raspberry' (Fox Series)	MPnt
'Raspberry Ice'PBR	MPnt SHeu
'Raspberry Regal' ♀H4	ECtt MPnt MRav NBir SHeu SWvt WCot WSHC
'Rave On'PBR	Widely available
'Red Dress' **new**	SHeu
'Red Spangles'	EPfP LRHS NBir SHeu WWEG
'Regina' ♀H4	CAbP EBee EHyd EPfP LHop LSRN MPnt NBro SHeu SWvt
'Rhapsody'	LRHS
richardsonii	MNrw MPnt XLum
'Rickard'	MPnt
'Rio' **new**	SHeu
'Robert'	MPnt
'Root Beer'	ECtt LRHS LSou MPnt NDov SHeu
Rosemary Bloom = 'Heuros'PBR	EBee LRHS SHeu
§ ***rubescens***	CAbP ECho NBro WThu
'Ruffles'	see *H. micrantha* 'Ruffles'
'Sanbrot'	MPnt
§ ***sanguinea***	CMac CSBt MPnt MRav NBir
- 'Alba' ♀H4	CSpe EPPr LPla MPnt
- 'Geisha's Fan'	CHid CWCL ECtt MPnt MSpe NEgg SHeu SPer SWvt
- 'Monet' (v)	MLHP MPnt SHeu
- 'Petworth' **new**	EBee
- var. ***pulchra***	CPBP
- 'Ruby Bells'	CCVN CMea EPPr EPfP LRHS LSRN MCot MPnt NLar SHeu
- 'Sioux Falls'	MBNS NBre SHeu
- 'Snow Storm' (v)	ELan EPfP MPnt SHeu SPlb WMnd
- 'Splendens'	MPnt XLum
- 'Taff's Joy' (v)	MPnt
- 'White Cloud' (v)	EBee EPfP LRHS MPnt NBre SHeu SRms XLum
'Sashay' ♀H4	CLAP ELon IBoy LSou MHol MPnt NLar NSoo SGol SHeu SPoG WNPC
'Saturn'	LBuc LRHS MPnt SHeu SWvt WNPC
'Schneewittchen'	EBee EPfP MPnt MRav
'Scintillation' ♀H4	MPnt NBre
'Shamrock'	NBre
'Shanghai'PBR	ECtt EPfP EWTr GBin LRHS LSou MAsh MPnt NWad SHeu SMad WNPC
'Shenandoah Mountain'	MPnt
'Silver Indiana'	LRHS LSRN MPnt SHeu
'Silver Light'PBR	EPfP LRHS MPnt SHeu
'Silver Lode'PBR	MPnt SHeu
'Silver Scrolls'PBR	Widely available
'Silver Shadows'	MBrN MPnt SHeu

	'Silver Streak'	see × *Heucherella* 'Silver Streak'
	'Sioux Falls'	MPnt
	'Snow Angel'	CWGN EPfP LBMP LSou MPnt SHeu SPoG WCot
	'Snowfire' (v)	MPnt SHeu
	'Southern Comfort'PBR	CLAP CWGN ECtt ESwi LRHS MBNS MPnt NCGa NDov NHol NLar NPer NPnk NPri NWad SGol SHeu SLim SPoG SRot SWvt WCot
	'Sparkler' **new**	MPnt
	'Sparkling Burgundy'	ECtt EPfP LRHS MPnt NDov NPri SHeu SWvt
	'Spellbound' **new**	MAsh MPnt SFai SHeu WNPC
	'Starry Night'PBR	MPnt
	'Steel City'	MPnt SHeu
	'Stormy Seas'	ELan EPfP EWTr GCra LRHS MLHP MPnt MRav NBir SHeu SWvt
	'Strawberries and Cream' (v)	EShb MPnt SHeu
	'Strawberry Candy'PBR	CMac CWCL CWGN ELon GBin GJos LHop LSRN MBNS MPnt NBir NLar NWad SHeu SLim SRkn
	'Strawberry Swirl'	ECtt EPfP EWTr GMaP LRHS MGos MPnt MRav NBir NLar NSti SHeu SWvt WNPC
	Sugar Frosting = 'Pwheu0104'PBR	CHid CRos ECtt EHoe GBin GKev LHop LRHS MAvo MBri MPnt NCGa NHol NPri SHeu SHil SRot SWvt
	'Sugar Plum'	CSpe ECtt ELon EPfP EUJe EWTr LRHS MBNS MPnt NPri SHeu SRot WCot WNPC WSpi
	'Swirling Fantasy'PBR	EShb GJos LSou MAsh MPnt SHeu
	'Tangerine Wave' (Fox Series)	MPnt
	'Tara'	MPnt SHeu WNPC
	'Tiramisu'PBR	CAbP CHid CLAP CWGN ECtt ELon ESwi IBoy ITim LBMP LHop LRHS MBNS MJak MNrw MPnt NBir NPnk NSti SFai SHeu SPer SPoG SWvt WBrk WCot
	'Van Gogh'	SHeu
	'Vanilla Spice'	MPnt SHeu
	'Veil of Passion'	NBre
	'Velvet Night'	EPfP LRHS LSou MJak MPnt NBir SHeu SPlb WMnd WWEG
	'Venus'	CMea CWGN EBee ECtt EPfP EShb LBMP LRHS MBNS MBel MNrw MPkF MPnt NOrc NSti SEND SHeu SPer WBrk WCot WHoo
	'Vesuvius'	MPnt NCGa SHeu WNPC
	'Vienna'	MPnt SFai SHeu WNPC
§	***villosa***	LRHS MPnt MRav SVic XLum
	- 'Autumn Bride'	MPnt SHeu
	- Bressingham Bronze = 'Absi'PBR	LRHS MPnt SHeu
	- 'Chantilly'	MPnt SHeu
	- var. ***macrorhiza***	EShb LBMP MPnt NBre WPnP XLum
N	- 'Palace Purple'	Widely available
	- 'Palace Purple Select'	CBcs CMac CTri CWat CWib LAst MCot MJak NEgg SLim SWvt WHar
	'Virginale'	MPnt
	'Vulcano' **new**	LSou MAsh WBrk WCot
	'White Marble'	MPnt SHar
	'White Spires'	LRHS MPnt SHar SHeu
	'White Swirls'	MPnt
	'William How'	MPnt
	'Winter Red'	EBee LRHS MBNS MPnt NEgg SHeu
	'Zabeliana'	MPnt

× *Heucherella* ✿ (*Saxifragaceae*)

	'Alabama Sunrise'PBR	CHid CLAP CMHG ECtt ELan ESwi GBin LHop LSou MBri MPkF MPnt NCGa NHol NPer NPnk NPri NWad SGol SHeu SMad SPoG SRot SWvt WBor
	alba 'Bridget Bloom'	EBee ELan EPfP EWTr GMaP LRHS MNFA MPnt MRav NOrc SHeu SPer SRms XLum
§	- 'Rosalie'	EBee LRHS MPnt MRav NBir NBro NPnk SHeu SPlb WSHC
	'Art Deco' **new**	SHeu
	'Berry Fizz'	MPkF MPnt SHeu STPC WGor WNPC
	'Birthday Cake'	MPnt SHeu
	'Brass Lantern'	CSpe CWGN ECtt GBin LBMP LSou MAsh MBel MBri MPnt NPnk NPri SHeu SRot STPC WNPC WSpi
	'Burnished Bronze'PBR	ECtt ELon GBin GKev LRHS LSou MBri MPkF MPnt NBro NEgg NHol NLar NPla NWad SHeu SPer SRot SWvt WCot
	'Chocolate Lace'PBR	MPnt SHeu
	'Cinnamon Bear'	MPnt SHeu
	'Citrus Shock'	MPnt SHeu
	'Dayglow Pink'PBR	CLAP ECtt EShb GBin GMaP LHop LSRN MPkF MPnt NBro NLar NPnk SHeu STes WBor WNPC
	'Fan Dancer'	CLAP MPnt SHeu
	'Freefolk Stars' **new**	SHar
	Gold Strike = 'Hertn041'PBR	CLAP ECtt GJos LRHS MBNS MPnt NPnk SHeu
	'Golden Zebra'	CAbP CLAP CWCL CWGN ECtt ELan LLWG LSou MBNS MBri MNrw MPkF MPnt NDov NHol NLar NPnk NSoo NWad SHeu STes SWvt WCot WGor WSpl
	'Great Smokies' **new**	MPnt SHeu
	'Gunsmoke'	CLAP ECtt GBin LSou MAsh MBri MPkF MPnt NPnk SHeu WNPC
	'Heart of Darkness'PBR	MPnt SHeu
	'Kimono'PBR ♀H4	Widely available
	'Ninja'	see *Tiarella* 'Ninja'
	'Party Time'PBR	SHeu
	Pink Whispers = 'Hertn042'PBR	LPot MPnt SHeu
	'Quicksilver'	CBcs GMaP MBri MPnt SHeu SWvt
	'Redstone Falls'	ECtt LBMP MPnt NLar NPnk NPri SFai SHeu SPoG STPC SWvt WNPC
	'Ring of Fire'	SWvt
§	'Silver Streak'	LRHS MPnt NBro SHeu SWvt
	'Solar Eclipse'	ECtt MAsh MPkF MPnt NLar SHeu WNPC
	'Solar Power'	CWGN EBee ECtt MPnt NLar SHeu WNPC
	'Stoplight'PBR	Widely available
	'Sunrise Falls' **new**	MAsh MPkF MPnt SHeu WNPC
	'Sunspot'PBR (v)	CLAP ECtt EPfP MGos NBro NSti SGol SHeu WHer
	'Sweet Tea'PBR	Widely available
	'Tapestry'PBR	Widely available
	tiarelloides ♀H4	CMac EPfP
§	'Viking Ship'PBR	CSev ECtt GKev LRHS MPnt MRav MTPN NBir SHeu
	'Yellowstone Falls'	CWGN LBMP MPnt NPnk SFai SHeu SRot STPC SWvt WNPC

Hexastylis see *Asarum*

Hibanobambusa (*Poaceae*)

'Kimmei'	MMuc
tranquillans	CEnt ERod MBrN MMoz MMuc MWht SEND WJun
- 'Shiroshima' (v) ♀H4	CAbb CDTJ CDoC CEnt EAmu ENBC EPfP ERod EUJe MBrN MBri MJak MMoz MMuc MWhi MWht SBig SEND WJun

Hibbertia (*Dilleniaceae*)

aspera	CAbb CBcs CCCN CRHN CTsd EBee ECre IVic LRHS MOWG WCFE WSHC
§ ***cuneiformis***	CCCN
procumbens	ITim WAbe
§ ***scandens*** ♀H1	CBcs CCCN CHll CRHN ECou ECre ELan MOWG SEND
'Spring Sunshine'	CHel ESwi LHop
tetrandra	see *H. cuneiformis*
volubilis	see *H. scandens*

Hibiscus ✿ (*Malvaceae*)

coccineus	EShb SBrt SMad
coccineus* × *moscheutos	SBrt
'Fireball'PBR	EUJe
hamabo	ELan
huegelii	see *Alyogyne huegelii*
'Kopper King'PBR	EUJe MAsh MBNS
leopoldii	SRms
militaris	SBrt
moscheutos	CArn CCon EBee SBrt SMad SVic XLum
- 'Galaxy'	XLum
- 'Robert Fleming'PBR	EUJe
mutabilis	EDif LEdu MOWG
paramutabilis	EWes SMad
'Resi' **new**	LRHS
rosa-sinensis	EBak MOWG SPlb SPre
- 'Arcadian Spring'	MOWG
- 'Big Tango'	MOWG
- 'Blues Man'	MOWG
- 'Byron Metts'	MOWG
- 'Cajun Cocktail'	see *H. rosa-sinensis* 'Jambalaya'
- 'Candy Floss' (d)	MOWG
- 'Carmen Keene'	MOWG
- 'Cloud Nine'PBR	MOWG
- 'Cockatoo'	MOWG
- 'Cooperi' (v) ♀H1	WCot
- 'Courier Mail'	MOWG SPlb
- 'Dorothy Brady'	MOWG
- 'Enid Lewis' (d)	MOWG
- 'Erin Rachael'	MOWG
- 'Expo'	MOWG
- 'Gwen Mary'	MOWG
- 'Helene'	LSRN
- 'Holly's Pride'	MOWG
- 'Hot Bikini'	MOWG
§ - 'Jambalaya'	MOWG
- 'June's Joy'	MOWG
- 'Key West Thunderhead' (d)	MOWG
- 'Lady Bug'	MOWG
- 'Lady Flo'	MOWG
- 'Lemon Chiffon'	MOWG
- 'Linda Pear' (d)	MOWG
- 'Madame Dupont'	MOWG
- 'Mrs Andreasen' (d)	MOWG
- 'Rhinestone'	MOWG
- 'Soft Shoulders'	MOWG
- 'Spanish Lady'	MOWG
- 'Sprinkle Rain'	MOWG
- 'Tarantella'	MOWG
- 'The Path'	MOWG
- 'Vermillion Queen'	MOWG
- 'Weekend'	MOWG
- 'White Swan'	MOWG
schizopetalus ♀H1	MOWG
sinosyriacus 'Lilac Queen'	CExl LRHS SKHP WPGP
- 'Ruby Glow'	CExl LRHS LSRN SKHP WPGP
syriacus 'Aphrodite'	EPfP LRHS MAsh
- 'Ardens' (d)	CEnd CSBt LAst NLar SPer
- Blue Bird	see *H. syriacus* 'Oiseau Bleu'
- Blue Chiffon = 'Notwood3'PBR	LBuc LRHS MBri MGos SPoG
- 'Boule de Feu' (d)	ELan
- China Chiffon = 'Bricutts'	LRHS MAsh MBri MGos SEND SHil SPoG
- 'Diana' ♀H4	EBee EPfP LRHS LSRN MAsh MGos MRav SCoo SKHP SLon
- 'Dorothy Crane'	EBee LRHS SKHP
- 'Duc de Brabant' (d)	CSBt ELon EPfP MBlu SPer
- 'Elegantissimus'	see *H. syriacus* 'Lady Stanley'
- 'Hamabo' ♀H4	CDul CSBt CTri EBee EPfP EUJe LAst LRHS LSRN MBri MGos MWat NLar NPri SCoo SEND SGol SHil SLim SPer SPoG SWvt WHar
- 'Helene'	ELan LSRN MBlu
- 'Jeanne d'Arc' (d)	SGol
§ - 'Lady Stanley' (d)	CMac CSBt EBee SCoo SPer
- Lavender Chiffon = 'Notwoodone'PBR ♀H4	EBee ELan ELon EPfP EWes LRHS LSRN MBri MGos NLar SCoo SEND SHil SPer SPoG
- 'Leopoldii'	SKHP
- 'Marina'	EBee EPfP EUJe MBlu MRav NLar SGol
- 'Mauve Queen'	SSta
- 'Meehanii' misapplied	see *H. syriacus* 'Purpureus Variegatus'
- 'Meehanii' (v) ♀H4	CEnd CSBt EBee EMil EPfP LRHS SCoo SKHP SPer
- 'Monstrosus'	MGos NLar
§ - 'Oiseau Bleu' ♀H4	Widely available
- Pink Chiffon **new**	SLon
- Pink Giant = 'Flogi'	CMac EBee ELan EPfP LAst LRHS MGos MWat SPad SPer
- Purple Ruffles = 'Sanchoyo' (d)	EPfP LRHS MBri SHil SPoG
§ - 'Purpureus Variegatus' (v)	CMac CSBt LAst LRHS SPoG
- 'Red Heart' ♀H4	CDul CEnd CMac CSBt CTri EBee ELan EPfP LAst LRHS MAsh MBri MGos MMuc MRav NLar SEND SHil SKHP SLim SPad SPer SPoG SRms SWvt WCFE
- Rosalbane = 'Minrosa'	SGol
- Russian Violet = 'Floru'	CEnd EBee ELan EPfP LAst LRHS SKHP
- 'Shintaeyang'	MBri
- 'Speciosus'	SPer
- 'Totus Albus'	CMac CSBt
- Ultramarine = 'Minultra'PBR	EPfP LRHS SKHP
- 'Variegatus'	see *H. syriacus* 'Purpureus Variegatus'
- 'Violet Clair Double' (d)	CMac
- White Chiffon = 'Notwoodtwo'PBR (d) ♀H4	EBee ELan EPfP EWes LRHS LSRN MAsh MBri MGos MRav NLar SCoo SHil SPer SPoG

- 'William R. Smith' 🏆H4	EBee ELan LRHS MBri MMuc MSwo SEND SPer
- 'Woodbridge' 🏆H4	CBcs CEnd CMac CSBt CTri EBee ELan EPfP EUJe LRHS LSRN MAsh MBri MGos MMuc MSwo NLar NPri SEND SGol SHil SKHP SLim SPer SPlb SPoG SRms SSpi SWvt
trionum	CSpe SBch WKif
- 'Sunny Day'	ELan

hickory, shagbark see *Carya ovata*

Hieracium (*Asteraceae*)

aurantiacum	see *Pilosella aurantiaca*
britannicum	WOut
brunneocroceum	see *Pilosella aurantiaca* subsp. *carpathicola*
§ ***lanatum***	ECho NBir
maculatum	see *H. spilophaeum*
pilosella	see *Pilosella officinarum*
× ***rubrum***	LRHS
scullyi	EPPr
§ ***spilophaeum***	EHoe MMuc NBid NPer NSti WOut
- 'Blue Leaf'	WCot
umbellatum	WOut
villosum	CPBP ECho EHoe LRHS NBro WHer
welwitschii	see *H. lanatum*

Hierochloe (*Poaceae*)

odorata	EPPr GPoy MBNS XLum

hildaberry see *Rubus* 'Hildaberry'

Himalayacalamus (*Poaceae*)

asper	CDTJ ERod
§ ***falconeri***	CEnt SDix
§ - 'Damarapa'	CEnt EPfP MMoz WJun
§ ***hookerianus***	CExl EAmu EPfP IMou SBst WJun
- 'Himalaya Blue'	CDTJ
porcalus	WJun WPGP

Himantoglossum (*Orchidaceae*)

hircinum	NLAp

× *Hippeasprekelia* (*Amaryllidaceae*)

sp. **new**	CDes
'Red Beauty'	WCot
'Red Star'	CCCN

Hippeastrum (*Amaryllidaceae*)

× ***acramannii***	GCal WCot
'Apple Blossom'	SDeJ
'Baby Star'	SDeJ
'Benfica'	CSpe
'Charisma'	SDeJ
'Fairytale'	SDeJ
× ***johnsonii*** hort.	CExl WCot
'Liberty'	SDeJ
'Mont Blanc'	SDeJ
papilio 🏆H1	MMHG SDeJ
'Picotee'	SDeJ
'Red Peacock' (d)	SDeJ
'Rilona'	SDeJ
'San Antonio Rose'	WCot
striatum	WCot
'Toughie'	CDes EBee LLHF WPGP
yungacense 'Kiara' **new**	XTur

Hippocrepis (*Papilionaceae*)

§ ***comosa***	EDAr SPhx SSpi
§ ***emerus***	CBcs CCCN CExl CMHG EBee ELan EPfP LAst LHop MGos NLar SEND SVen WSHC

Hippophae (*Elaeagnaceae*)

rhamnoides 🏆H4	CArn CBcs CCVT CDul CHab CLnd CMac CSpe CTri ECrN EHoe ELan EPfP EPom LBuc LEdu MBlu MCoo MMuc NWea SEND SEWo SGol SPlb
- (m)	EPom
- 'Askola' (f)	MBri
- 'Dorana'	CAgr
- 'Frugna' (f)	CAgr NLar
- 'Hergo' (f)	CAgr MCoo NLar
- 'Hikul'	MBri NLar
- 'Juliet' (f)	CAgr
- 'Leikora' (f)	CAgr ELan EPfP IVic MBlu MCoo MGos NLar SPer
- 'Orange Energy' (f/F)	CAgr MBri MCoo NSoo
- 'Pollmix' (m)	CAgr ELan EPfP IVic MBlu MBri MCoo MGos NLar NSoo SPer
- 'Pollmix 3' (m)	MCoo
- 'Sirola'	CAgr MCoo
salicifolia	CAgr
- GWJ 9221	WCru

Hippuris (*Plantaginaceae*)

vulgaris	CBAq CWat EHon EWay MSKA NPer WMAq XLum

Hirpicium (*Asteraceae*)

armerioides	SPlb

Hoheria ✿ (*Malvaceae*)

'Ace of Spades'	CAbb CMHG EBee EPfP EWTr LRHS SKHP WPGP
§ ***angustifolia***	ECou EPfP SVen WPGP
angustifolia × ***sexstylosa***	WPGP
'Borde Hill'	CAbb CJun CMHG CMac CTho EBee ECou EPfP IVic LHop LRHS MAsh SKHP SLim SPer SSpi WPGP
'County Park'	ECou
glabrata	CMac ECou EPfP GGGa GGal IDee NBir SKHP WPGP
'Glory of Amlwch' 🏆H3	CAbb CBcs CDoC CDul CJun CSam CTho EBee ECou ELan EPfP GGGa GQui LRHS LSRN SChF SKHP SSpi WPGP
'Hill House'	CHII
§ ***lyallii*** 🏆H4	CCCN CDoC CExl CHel EBee ECou ELan EPfP GCra IDee LRHS LSRN SPer SSpi SVen
- 'Chalk Hills'	ECou
- 'Swale Stream'	ECou
microphylla	see *H. angustifolia*
populnea	CBcs CCCN CTsd
- 'Alba Variegata' (v)	ECou
- 'Holbrook'	CSam
- 'Moonlight'	CHGN
- 'Purple Shadow'	ECou
- 'Variegata' (v)	ECou
'Purple Delta'	ECou
sexstylosa	CAbb CDul CHEx CHid CMHG CTho CTri CWSG ECou ELan EPfP EWTr LHop LRHS LSRN MGos

NEgg SDix SEND SKHP SPer SVen SWvt
- 'Crataegifolia' CAbb CHel EWTr NSoo
- 'Pendula' CBcs CMac
- 'Stardust' ♀H4 Widely available

Holboellia (*Lardizabalaceae*)

angustifolia NLar WCru
- subsp. ***linearifolia*** BWJ 8004 WCru
- subsp. ***obtusa*** DJHC 506 WCru
brachyandra HWJ 1023 WCru
aff. ***chapaensis*** B&SWJ 7250 WCru
coriacea CBcs CCCN CHEx CHll CRHN CSPN CSam EBee ELan EPfP LRHS MGos MOWG MRav NLar SAPC SKHP SPer WCFE WCru
- B&SWJ 2818 WCru
fargesii EBee LRHS SKHP WCot WCru
latifolia CBcs CCCN CHll CMac CTri EBee ELan EPfP GCal LRHS MOWG SEND SHil SKHP SLim SPer SPoG WCFE WCot WCru WPGP
- HWJCM 008 WCru
- HWJK 2014 WCru
- HWJK 2213 WCru
- SF 95134 EPfP
- dark-flowered HWJK 2213 WCru

Holcus (*Poaceae*)

lanatus WSFF
mollis 'Albovariegatus' (v) CWCL EHoe ELan EPPr EPfP GMaP LBMP MWhi NBid NBro NPer NSti SPlb SRms WCot WWEG XLum
- 'Jackdaw's Cream' (v) EPPr
- 'White Fog' (v) EBee EPPr MMuc NWad

Holmskioldia (*Lamiaceae*)

* ***lutea*** CCCN
sanguinea CCCN

Holodiscus (*Rosaceae*)

discolor CBcs EBee ELan EPfP EWes GCal IDee LEdu LRHS MBlu MBri MMuc MRav NLar SCoo SHil SKHP SLon SMad SPer SPlb SSpi WBor
- var. ***ariifolius*** CDul EPfP

Homalocladium (*Polygonaceae*)

§ ***platycladum*** EShb LEdu

Homeria (*Iridaceae*)

breyniana var. ***aurantiaca*** see *Moraea collina*

Homoglossum see *Gladiolus*

Hoodia (*Asclepiadaceae*)

dregei new LToo

Hordeum (*Poaceae*)

chilense EBee
jubatum CKno CSpe CWCL EHoe EWes MSCN MWhi NChi NGdn SEND SMrm SPhx
- 'Early Pink' NDov
secalinum CHab

Horkeliella (*Rosaceae*)

purpurascens NNS 98-323 WCot

Horminum (*Lamiaceae*)

pyrenaicum CPom CPrp EBee ECho LBMP MMuc SEND SRms WMoo WPtf
I - f. ***alboviolaceum*** EDAr
- dark-flowered ECho GCal
- 'Roseum' new ECho
- white-flowered ECho

Hornungia (*Brassicaceae*)

alpina new XLum

horseradish see *Armoracia rusticana*

Hosta ✿ (*Asparagaceae*)

AGSJ 302 CDes WPGP
'A Many-Splendored Thing' EMic IBal NSue
'Abba Dabba Do' (v) COIW ECtt EGol ELon EMic IBal LBuc LPla NEgg NHol NSue
'Abba Showtime' IBal
'Abby' (v) EGol EMic IBal WWEG
'Abiqua Ariel' EMic IBal
'Abiqua Blue Crinkles' EMic IBal NBir
'Abiqua Blue Edger' EMic IBal
'Abiqua Delight' (v) IBal
'Abiqua Drinking Gourd' EGol EMic GMaP IBal IFoB MHom NMyG NSue WWEG
'Abiqua Elephant Ears' new IBal
'Abiqua Ground Cover' EGol IBal
'Abiqua Moonbeam' (v) CCon EMic IBal MSwo NGdn
'Abiqua Recluse' EGol EMic IBal
'Abiqua Trumpet' EGol EMic IBal NGdn NLar NNor
'Abraham Lincoln' IBal
'Academy Blushing Recluse' (v) IBal
'Academy Devon Moor' IBal
'Academy Fire' (v) IBal
'Ada Reed' IBal
'Adorable' new IBal
aequinoctiiantha EGol
'Aksarben' EMic
'Alakazaam' (v) EGol EMic IBal NSue
'Alan Titchmarsh' IBal
albomarginata see *H.* 'Paxton's Original'
§ 'Albomarginata' (*fortunei*) (v) CBcs CMac EGol GKev IBal IFoB LRHS MNrw NBir NGdn SPoG SWvt
'Alex Summers' EMic IBal NMyG
'All That Jazz' (v) EMic IBal
'Allan P. McConnell' (v) EGol EMic GCra IBal LRHS MHom NSue WHal WWEG
'Allegan Emperor' (v) IBal
'Allegan Fog' (v) EGol EMic IBal IFoB LRHS NSue
'Alligator Shoes' (v) EGol EMic IBal
'Alpine Aire' EMic
'Alpine Dream' IBal
'Alternative' IBal
'Alvatine Taylor' (v) EGol EMic IBal LAst NGdn NSue
'Amanuma' EGol EMic IBal MHom
'Amazing Grace' (v) EMic IBal
'Amber Maiden' (v) IBal
'Amber Tiara' EMic IBal
'American Dream' (v) EGol EMic IBal LRHS
'American Gothic' (v) new IBal
'American Great Expectations' (v) IFoB

'American Halo'	EMic IBal LRHS NLar NSti
'American Hero' (v)	EMic
'American Icon'	EMic IBal
'American Sweetheart'PBR	EMic IBal
'Americana' (v)	EMic IBal
'Amethyst Gem'	EGol IBal
'Amy Elizabeth' (v)	EMic IBal
'Andorian'	IBal
'Andy Taylor'	LRHS
'Angel Feathers' (v)	IBal
'Anglo Saxon' (v)	IBal
'Ann Kulpa' (v)	EMic IBal NGdn
'Anne' (v)	IBal LRHS LSRN NSue
'Ansly' (v)	IBal
'Antioch' (*fortunei*) (v)	EGol EMic GLog IBal MRav NLar NSue
'Aoba Tsugaru'	IBal
'Aoki' (*fortunei*)	EMic IBal
'Aphrodite' (*plantaginea*) (d)	GAbr IBal LRHS LSou MBNS NGdn NLar WCot WGwG WWEG
'Apollo'	NNor
'Apple Green'	EMic GKev IBal
'Apple Pie'	IBal
'Aqua Velva'	EGol IBal
'Arc de Triomphe'	EMic IBal
'Archangel'	EGol IBal
'Arctic Blast'	EMic IBal
'Argentea Variegata' (*undulata*)	see *H. undulata* var. *undulata*
'Aristocrat' (Tardiana Group) (v)	EBee EGol EMic IBal LRHS MBri NGdn NSue
'Asian Beauty'	EGol
'Asian Pearl' (v)	IBal
'Aspen Gold' (*tokudama* hybrid)	EMic
'Atlantis'PBR (v)	EMic IBal NGdn NSue
'Atom Smasher' **new**	IBal
'August Beauty'	EMic IBal
'August Moon'	Widely available
'Aureafolia'	see *H.* 'Starker Yellow Leaf'
'Aureoalba' (*fortunei*)	see *H.* 'Spinners'
'Aureomaculata' (*fortunei*)	see *H. fortunei* var. *albopicta*
'Aureomarginata' ambig. (v)	SCoo
'Aureomarginata' (*montana*) (v)	CMac EGol EHoc ELan EMic GCal GMaP IBal MMuc NCGa NEgg NGdn NHol NLar WWEG
'Aureomarginata' (*rohdeifolia*) (v)	EMic
§ 'Aureomarginata' (*ventricosa*) (v) ♀H4	EGol EMic EPfP IBal MWat NGdn
'Aureostriata' (*tardiva*)	see *H.* 'Inaho'
'Aurora Borealis' (*sieboldiana*) (v)	EGol
'Austin Dickinson' (v)	ECtt EGol EMic IBal LBuc LRHS NEgg
'Avalanche'	IBal
'Avocado'	ELon EMic EWTr IBal NSue
'Azure Mediterranean'	IBal
'Azure Snow'	EGol IBal
'Azuretini' **new**	IBal
'Babbling Brook'	EGol IBal
'Baby Blue' (Tardiana Group)	EMic
'Baby Blue Eyes'	IBal NSue
'Baby Bunting'	EGol EMic IBal IFoB NBro NLar NNor NPro NSue
'Baby Doll' (v) **new**	IBal
'Bailey's Cream' (v) **new**	IBal
'Bali-Hai'	IBal
'Ballerina'	EGol IBal NSue
'Banana Boat' (v)	EGol IBal
'Banana Muffins'	IBal
'Band of Gold'	EMic IBal
'Banyai's Dancing Girl'	EGol EMic IBal
'Barbara Ann' (v)	EBee EMic IBal MHom NGdn NMyG WWEG
'Barbara May'	IBal
'Barbara White'	IBal
'Barney Fife'	IBal
'Battle Star' (v)	EMic IBal
'Bea's Colossus'	IBal
'Beauty Little Blue'	EGol IBal
'Beauty Substance'	EGol EMic IBal NNor
'Beckoning'	IBal NSue
'Bedford Blue'	EMic IBal
'Bedford Rise and Shine' (v)	EGol EMic IBal
'Bedford Wakey-Wakey'	EGol IBal
'Bell Bottom Blues'	IBal
bella	see *H. crassifolia*
'Bells of Edinburgh'	IBal
'Bennie McRae'	EGol IBal
'Betcher's Blue'	EGol EMic IBal
'Betsy King'	CMac EGol MRav NMyG
'Bette Davis Eyes'	EGol IBal
'Betty'	EGol IBal
'Biddy's Blue'	IBal
'Big Boy' (*montana*)	EGol IBal LRHS NSue
'Big Daddy' (*sieboldiana* hybrid) (v)	Widely available
'Big John' (*sieboldiana*)	IBal
'Big Mama'	EGol EMic IBal MBNS MNrw NGdn NLar NPnk NSue
'Big Top'	IBal
'Bigfoot'	EGol IBal
'Biggie'	IBal
'Bill Brinka' (v)	EGol EMic IBal LRHS
'Birchwood Blue'	EGol
'Birchwood Blue Beauty'	IBal
'Birchwood Gem'	IBal
§ 'Birchwood Parky's Gold'	EBee ECtt EGol EMic EPfP GMaP IBal LBMP MBNS NGdn NHol NNor
'Birchwood Ruffled Queen'	EGol EMic IBal
'Bitsy Gold'	EGol EMic IBal
'Bitsy Green'	EGol
'Bix Blues'	IBal
'Bizarre'	EMic IBal
'Black Beauty'	EGol IBal
'Black Hills'	EGol EMic IBal
'Black Pearl'	IBal
'Blackfoot'	EGol EMic IBal
'Blackjack' (*sieboldiana*)	IBal
'Blaue Venus'	EGol IBal
'Blauspecht'	IBal
'Blaze of Glory'	IBal
'Blazing Saddles' (v)	EMic IBal MBNS
'Blonde Elf'	EGol EMic IBal MPnt NEgg NGdn NHol NNor NSue WWEG
'Blue Angel' misapplied	see *H. sieboldiana* var. *elegans*
'Blue Angel' (*sieboldiana*) ♀H4	Widely available
'Blue Arrow'	EGol IBal LRHS NNor NSue
'Blue Baron'	EMic IBal
'Blue Beard'	IBal
'Blue Belle' (Tardiana Group)	EGol EMic IBal NGdn NPro WWEG
'Blue Blush' (Tardiana Group)	EGol EMic IBal NGdn
'Blue Boy'	EGol EMic EWes IBal NMyG NNor

	'Blue Cadet'	CBcs CMac EBee EGol EHoe EMic EShb GQue IBal IBoy IFoB LRHS MLHP MWhi NBir NGdn NLar NSue NWad SPoG WMnd WWEG
	'Blue Canoe'	EMic IBal
	'Blue Cascade'	EMic IBal
	'Blue Chip'	EMic IBal
	'Blue Circle'PBR **new**	IBal
	'Blue Clown'	IBal
	'Blue Cup' (*sieboldiana*)	EMic MRav
	'Blue Danube' (Tardiana Group)	EGol EMic IBal MHom
	'Blue Diamond' (Tardiana Group)	EGol EMic NNor WWEG
	'Blue Dimples' (Tardiana Group)	ECtt EGol EMic IBal
	'Blue Edger'	EMic IBal NBir
	'Blue Eyes'	IBal NSue
	'Blue Flame'	EMic IBal
	'Blue Frost'	IBal
	'Blue Haired Lady'	IBal
	'Blue Hawaii'	EMic IBal
	'Blue Heart' (*sieboldiana*)	EMic IBal
	'Blue Ice' (Tardiana Group)	EGol IBal
	'Blue Impression'	EMic
	'Blue Ivory' (v)	CBcs EBee ECtt LRHS MAsh NSue SGol SMrm
	'Blue Jay' (Tardiana Group)	EGol EMic IBal
	'Blue Lady'	EMic IBal
	'Blue Lollipop' **new**	NSue
	'Blue Mammoth' (*sieboldiana*)	EGol EMic IBal NSue
	'Blue Maui'	EMic IBal
	'Blue Monday'	EMic IBal
	'Blue Moon' (Tardiana Group)	EGol EMic EPfP GKev IBal MJak NGdn NNor
	'Blue Mountains'	IBal LBuc
	'Blue Mouse Ears'	EBee EGol EMic EPfP GBin IBal IBoy LLWG LRHS MBNS MBri MHom MPnt NBro NGdn NHar NMyG NNor NSla NSue SPoG WCot WWEG
	'Blue Plate Special'	IBal
	'Blue River' (v)	EMic IBal
	'Blue Seer' (*sieboldiana*)	EGol EMic
	'Blue Shadows' (*tokudama*) (v)	EMic ESwi IBal NLar
	'Blue Skies' (Tardiana Group)	EGol IBal MHom
	'Blue Splendor' (Tardiana Group)	IBal
	'Blue Umbrellas' (*sieboldiana* hybrid)	EGol ELan EMic EPfP GMaP IBal LRHS MHom NGdn NLar NNor
	'Blue Veil'	EGol IBal
	'Blue Vision'	EMic IBal MWhi
	'Blue Wedgwood' (Tardiana Group)	EGol ELan EMic GQue IBal LRHS MGos NGdn WWEG
	'Blue Wonder'	IBal
	'Blueberry à la Mode'	EMic IBal
	'Blueberry Muffin'	EMic IBal
	'Blueberry Tart'	IBal
	'Bluetooth' **new**	IBal
	'Bob Deane' (v)	EMic IBal
	'Bob Olson' (v)	EGol IBal
	'Bobbie Sue' (v)	EGol IBal
	'Bogie and Bacall' (v)	IBal
	'Bold Edger' (v)	EGol EMic IBal
	'Bold Intrigue' (v)	IBal
	'Bold Ribbons' (v)	EGol EMic GAbr IBal
	'Bold Ruffles' (*sieboldiana*)	EGol
	'Bolt out of the Blue'	EMic
	'Bonanza'	EMic
	'Border Bandit' (v)	EGol IBal
	'Border Favorite'	EMic
	'Border Street' (v)	IBal
§	'Borwick Beauty' (*sieboldiana*) (v)	EGol EMic IBal LSou NCGa NGdn NLar NPnk SPer WWEG
	'Bottom Line' (v)	IBal
	'Bountiful'	EGol EMic IBal
	'Bouquet'	EGol
	'Boyz Toy'	EMic NSue
	'Brandywine'	IBal
	'Brash and Sassy'	IBal
	'Brave Amherst' (v)	IBal
	'Brenda's Beauty' (v)	EGol EMic IBal NMyG
	'Bressingham Blue'	EBee ECtt EGol EMic GQue IBal LRHS MRav NLar NNor SWvt WMnd
	'Bridal Veil'	EMic IBal
	'Bridegroom'	EGol EMic IBal
	'Bridgeville'	IBal
	'Brigadier'	EGol IBal
	'Brigham Blue'	IBal
	'Bright Glow' (Tardiana Group)	EGol EMic IBal
	'Bright Lights' (*tokudama*) (v)	EGol EMic IBal NGdn
	'Brim Cup' (v)	CHel EBee ECtt EGol ELon GAbr GBuc IBal LAst LSou MBNS NBro NGdn NMyG NNor NOrc SPer WWEG
	'Brooke'	EGol EMic IBal NMyG WWEG
	'Brother Ronald' (Tardiana Group)	EGol EMic IBal
	'Brother Stefan'	EMic IBal
	'Bruce's Blue'	EGol
	'Brutus' **new**	IBal
	'Bubba'	IBal
	'Buckshaw Blue'	EGol IBal NBir NGdn NPro WHrl
	'Buckwheat Honey'	IBal
	'Bulletproof'	IBal
	'Bunchoko'	IBal NNor
	'Burke's Dwarf'	IBal
	'Butter Rim' (*sieboldii*) (v)	EGol IBal
	'Cadillac' (v)	EMic
*	'Caerula' (*ventricosa*)	IFoB
	'Cally Atom'	GCal IBal
	'Cally Colossus' **new**	GCal
I	'Cally Strain' (*nigrescens*) **new**	MHer
	'Cally White' (*nigrescens*)	GCal IBal NCGa
	'Calypso' (v)	EGol EMic IBal WWEG
	'Camelot' (Tardiana Group)	EGol IBal LRHS NGdn
	'Cameo'	EMic IBal NSue
	'Camouflage'	EMic IBal
	'Canadian Blue'	EMic MWhi
	'Candy Dish'	IBal
	'Candy Hearts'	CSam EGol EMic IBal MHom NNor
	capitata	NNor
	- B&SWJ 588	WCru
	'Captain Kirk' (v)	EMic IBal NGdn NMyG NSue
	'Captain's Adventure' (v)	EMic NGdn NSue
	caput-avis	see *H. kikutii* var. *caput-avis*
	'Carder Blue'	EMic
	'Carnival' (v)	CHel EGol EMic IBal IFoB LRHS NEgg NGdn NSue
	'Carol' (*fortunei*) (v)	EGol EMic IBal NEgg NGdn NLar NMyG NNor

	'Carolina Blue'	IBal
	'Carousel' (v)	EGol IBal
	'Carrie' (*sieboldii*) (v)	EGol
	'Cascades' (v)	EGol EMic IBal NGdn SPoG
	'Cat and Mouse'	EGol IBal
	'Cathedral Windows' (v)	EMic IBal
	'Catherine'	IBal LLWG NSue
	'Cat's Eyes' (*venusta*) (v)	EGol EMic IBal NNor
	'Cavalcade' (v)	EMic
	'Celebration' (v)	EGol ELan EMic IBal LRHS WWEG
	'Celestial'	IBal
	'Celtic Dancer' **new**	EMic
	'Celtic Uplands'	EMic
	'Center of Attention'	EMic IBal NGdn
	'Cha Cha Cha'	IBal
	'Chain Lightning' (v)	EMic IBal
	'Challenger'	EMic
	'Chameleon' (v)	EMic
	'Change of Tradition' (*lancifolia*) (v)	EMic
	'Chantilly Lace' (v)	EGol EMic WWEG
	'Chariots of Fire' (v)	IBal
	'Chartreuse Waves'	EGol IBal
	'Chartreuse Wiggles' (*sieboldii*)	EGol IBal NSue
	'Cheatin' Heart'	EGol EMic IBal NMyG NSue WWEG
	'Chelsea Babe' (*fortunei*) (v)	EGol IBal
	'Cherish'	EGol IBal NGdn
	'Cherry Berry' (v)	EGol EMic EPfP GBin IBal IFoB LRHS MBNS MNrw MPie NBro NCGa NEgg NGdn NLar NMyG NPro NWad SPoG WWEG
	'Cherry Tart'	EMic IBal NSue
	'Cherub' (v)	EGol EMic IBal LRHS
	'Chesapeake Bay'	EMic IBal NSue
	'Chesterland Gold'	IBal
	'China Girl'	EMic
	'Chinese Gold'	IBal
	'Chinese Sunrise' (v)	CWCL EGol EMic GBin IBal LBuc MHom NNor SRms
	'Chiquita'	EGol IBal
	'Chi-town Classic' (v)	IBal
	'Chodai Ginba'	IBal
§	'Chōkō-nishiki' (*montana*) (v)	EGol EMic IBal LRHS NGdn NNor
	'Choo Choo Train'	EGol EMic
	'Chopsticks'	EMic IBal
	'Christmas Candy'PBR	EMic GAbr IBal LRHS MBri
	'Christmas Cookies'	IBal
	'Christmas Lights' (v)	IBal
	'Christmas Pageant' (v)	EMic IBal
	'Christmas Tree' (v)	EBee EGol EMic IBal IFoB LPla LRHS NEgg NGdn NSue WMoo WWEG
	'Cinderella'	EMic IBal
	'Cinnamon Sticks'	IBal
	'Citation' (v)	EGol IBal
	'City Lights'	ECtt EGol EMic IBal NEgg
	'City Slicker' (v)	IBal
	'Claudia'	IBal
	clausa	EMic
	– var. ***normalis***	GQui IBal NBir NGdn NLar
	'Clear Fork River Valley'	EMic IBal
	'Cleopatra' (v)	IBal
	'Clifford's Forest Fire'	EMic IBal LRHS NLar
	'Clifford's Stingray' (v)	EMic IBal NSue
	'Climax' (v)	EMic IBal IBoy NMyG NSue
	'Cloudburst'	EMic IBal
	'Clovelly'	EMic IBal

	'Clown's Collar' (v)	EMic IBal
	'Coal Miner' **new**	EMic
	'Coconut Custard'	EMic NSue
	'Cody'	EGol IBal
	'Cold Heart'	EMic
	'Collector's Banner'	EGol IBal
	'Collector's Choice'	EGol IBal
	'Color Festival' (v)	EMic IBal NSue
	'Color Glory'	see *H.* 'Borwick Beauty'
	'Colossal'	EGol EMic IBal
	'Columbus Circle' (v)	EGol EMic IBal
	'Confused Angel' (v)	IBal
	'Cookie Crumbs' (v)	EGol EMic IBal
	'Cool Hand Luke' (*tokudama*) (v)	IBal
	'Coquette' (v)	EGol EMic GAbr IBal
	'Corkscrew'	EMic NSue
	'Corn Belt' (v)	EMic IBal
	'Corn Muffins'	EMic
	'Cotillion' (v)	EGol EMic IBal NSue
	'Count Your Blessings' (v)	EMic
	'Country Mouse' (v)	EGol EMic IBal
	'County Park'	EGol EMic IBal
	'Cowrie' (v)	IBal
	'Cracker Crumbs' (v)	EGol EMic GKev IBal MHom NHar NMyG NNor NSla NSue WWEG
	'Craig's Temptation'	IBal
§	***crassifolia***	EMic LRHS XLum
	'Cream Cheese' (v)	EGol IBal
	'Cream Delight' (*undulata*)	see *H. undulata* var *undulata*
	'Crepe Soul' (v)	EGol IBal
	'Crepe Suzette' (v)	EGol IBal NNor
	'Crested Reef'	EGol EMic IBal NMyG
	'Crested Surf' (v)	EGol EMic IBal
	'Crinoline Petticoats'	EGol IBal
§	***crispula*** (v) ♀H4	EGol EMic EPfP IBal MCot MHom MRav NChi NMyG
	'Crown Prince' (v)	EGol IBal NGdn
	'Crown Royalty'	EMic
§	'Crowned Imperial' (*fortunei*) (v)	EMic
	'Crumb Cake' **new**	EGol
	'Crumples' (*sieboldiana*)	EGol IBal
	'Crusader' (v)	EGol ELon EMic IBal LRHS WWEG
	'Crystal Chimes'	IBal
	'Crystal Dixie'	EGol EMic IBal NSue
	'Cumulonimbus' **new**	LRHS
	'Curlew' (Tardiana Group)	EGol IBal
	'Curls'	EMic IBal
	'Curly Fries' **new**	EMic
	'Curtain Call'	IBal
	'Cutting Edge'	EMic IBal
	'Cuyahoga' (v)	IBal
	'Dab a Green'	IBal
	'Daisy Doolittle' (v)	EMic IBal
	'Dance with Me' (v)	EMic IBal
	'Dancing in the Rain' (v)	CWGN EBee EMic LLWG MBri NBro NGdn NSue
	'Dancing Mouse' (v) **new**	EGol
	'Dancing Queen'	IBal
	'Dark Shadows'	EMic NGdn NSti
	'Dark Star' (v)	EGol EMic IBal NGdn NSue
	'Dark Victory'	IBal
	'Dawn'	EGol EMic IBal
	'Dawn's Early Light'	EMic
	'Dax'	IBal
	'Daybreak'	EGol EMic IBal MBri NBro
	'Day's End' (v)	EGol EMic IBal

'Deane's Dream'	EMic IBal NSue
decorata	EGol EMic
'Deep Blue Sea'	EMic IBal
'Deep Pockets'	IBal
'Dee's Golden Jewel'	EMic
'Déjà Blu' (v)	EMic IBal
'Deliverance'	IBal NSue
'Delta Dawn' (v)	EMic IBal LRHS NGdn
'Delta Desire'	IBal
'Deluxe Edition'	IBal
'Desert Mouse'[PBR] (v) **new**	EGol
'Designer Genes'	EMic IBal NSue
'Devon Blue' (Tardiana Group)	EGol LRHS NNor
'Devon Desire' (*montana*)	IBal NLar
'Devon Discovery'	IBal
'Devon Giant'	EMic IBal NNor
'Devon Gold'	EMic GAbr IBal
'Devon Green'	CRos ELan EMic GBin IBal IPot LRHS MBel MHom MMuc NBro NEgg NGdn NLar NMyG NPro NSue SEND WHal WHoo WWEG
'Devon Mist'	IBal NNor
'Devon Tor'	IBal
'Dew Drop' (v)	EMic WWEG
'Dewed Steel'	IBal
'Diamond Tiara' (v)	EGol EMic IBal LRHS NBir NGdn WWEG
'Diana Remembered'	EGol EMic IBal NGdn
'Dick Ward'	EMic IBal
'Dilithium Crystal'	IBal
'Dillie Perkeo'	IBal
'Dilys'	EMic MNrw
'Dimple'	EMic IBal
'Dinky Donna'	EMic IBal NMyG NSue
'Dinner Jacket'	ELan IBal LRHS
'Dixie Chick' (v)	EGol EMic IBal NNor NSue
'Dixie Chickadee' (v)	EGol EMic
'Dixieland Heat'	IBal
'Doctor Fu Manchu'	IBal
'Domaine de Courson'	EMic IBal
'Don Stevens' (v)	EGol IBal
'Dorothy'	EMic
'Dorset Blue' (Tardiana Group)	EMic IBal
'Dorset Charm' (Tardiana Group)	EGol EMic
'Dorset Flair' (Tardiana Group)	EGol EMic IBal
'Doubled Up' **new**	IBal
'Doubloons'	EGol EMic NMyG
'Dragon Tails'	EGol EMic IBal NHar NMyG NSue
'Dream Queen' (v)	ECtt EMic IBal
'Dream Weaver' (v)	EGol EMic IBal IFoB IPot LRHS MHom MNrw NBro NGdn NSue SPer SPoG WWEG
'Dress Blues'	CMac EMic IBal
'Drummer Boy'	EGol EMic IBal WWEG
'Duchess' (*nakaiana*) (v)	IBal
'Duke of Cornwall' (v)	IBal
'DuPage Delight' (*sieboldiana*) (v)	EGol EMic IBal NGdn NLar
'Dust Devil' (*fortunei*) (v)	EGol IBal
'Earth Angel'[PBR] (v)	EMic IBal NGdn NSue
'Ebb Tide' (*montana*) (v)	IBal
'Ebony Towers'	EMic
'Edge of Night'	EGol EMic IBal
'Edwin Bibby'	EMic
'El Capitan' (v)	EGol EMic IBal IFoB LRHS
'El Niño'[PBR] (Tardiana Group) (v)	CWGN EGol EMic IBal IPot LRHS MHom MNrw NBro NCGa NGdn NMyG WWEG
§ 'Elata'	EGol EMic IBal
'Elatior' (*nigrescens*)	EMic IBal
'Elbridge Gerry' (v) **new**	IBal
'Eldorado'	see *H.* 'Frances Williams'
'Eleanor Lachman' (v)	EGol EMic IBal NSue
'Eleanor Roosevelt'	IBal
'Electrocution' (v) **new**	NSue
'Elegans'	see *H. sieboldiana* var. *elegans*
'Elfin Power' (*sieboldii*) (v)	EGol
'Elisabeth'	EMic IBal LSRN
'Elizabeth Campbell' (*fortunei*) (v)	EGol EMic
'Elkheart Lake'	EMic
'Ellen'	EMic
'Ellerbroek' (*fortunei*) (v)	EMic IBal
'Elsley Japan'	IBal
'Elsley Runner'	EGol IBal NSue WWEG
'Elvis Lives'	EGol EMic IBal NEgg NGdn NLar NMyG NNor NPro NSue
'Emerald Carpet'	EGol IBal
'Emerald Crown'	IBal
'Emerald Necklace' (v)	EGol EMic IBal
'Emerald Ruff Cut'	EMic IBal
'Emerald Tiara' (v)	EGol EMic IBal LRHS MLHP NLar NMyG WWEG
'Emeralds and Rubies'	EGol EMic IBal NSue
'Emily Dickinson' (v)	EGol EMic IBal LRHS MMuc NNor SEND WWEG
'Empress Wu'	EBee EMic EUJe IBal IBoy NGdn NSue WCot
'Encore'	IBal
'English Sunrise' (Tardiana Group)	IBal
'Enterprise'	EBee EMic IBal LLWG NGdn NSue
'Eola Sapphire'	EMic
'Eos'	NLar
'Eric Smith' (Tardiana Group)	EGol EMic IBal MHom
'Eric's Gold'	IBal
'Erie Magic' (v)	EGol IBal
'Eskimo Pie' (v)	EBee EMic MBri NGdn NSue
'Essence of Summer'	EMic EPfP IBal
'Eternal Flame'	EMic IBal
'Evelyn McCafferty' (*tokudama* hybrid)	EGol IBal
'Eventide' (v)	EGol IBal
'Everlasting Love' (v)	EGol
'Excitation'	EGol EMic IBal
'Exotic Presentation' (v) **new**	EMic
'Extasy' (v)	EMic IBal NGdn NSue
'Eye Candy' (v)	IBal
'Eye Catcher'	EMic
'Eye Declare' (v)	IBal
'Faith'	EMic
'Faithful Heart' (v)	IBal
'Fall Bouquet' (*longipes* var. *hypoglauca*)	EGol
'Fall Emerald'	EMic
'Fan Dance' (v)	EGol EMic IBal
'Fantabulous' (v)	IBal
'Fantastic' (*sieboldiana* hybrid)	EGol
'Fantasy Island' (v)	EGol EMic IBal
'Fat Boy'	IBal
'Fatal Attraction'	IBal

'Feather Boa'	EGol EMic IBal IFoB NHar NSue WWEG
'Fenman's Fascination'	EMic IBal
'Fiesta' (v)	IBal
'Final Summation' (v)	EMic IBal NSue
'Finlandia' **new**	IBal
'Fire and Ice' (v)	Widely available
'Fire Island'	CHel ECtt EGol EMic GBin IBal MHom MNrw NGdn NMyG NSue
'Fireworks' (v)	EGol EMic EPfP GBin IBal LRHS MBNS MBri NBro NGdn NMyG NSue SPoG
'First Frost' (v)	EBee EMic IBal LRHS MAsh MBri NCGa NGdn NMyG NSue WWEG WWlt
'First Love' (*montana*)	EMic
'First Mate' (v)	EMic IBal NSue
'First Moon'	IBal
'Five O'Clock Shadow' (v)	IBal
'Five O'Clock Somewhere' (v)	IBal
'Flame Stitch' (*ventricosa*) (v)	IBal
'Flapjack' (v)	IBal
'Fleet Week'	EMic IBal
'Flemish Angel' (v)	IBal
'Flemish Gold'	IBal
'Flemish Sky'	EMic IBal IFoB MBri NGdn
'Floradora'	EGol EMic IBal
'Flower Power'	EGol IBal NNor
'Fluted Fountain'	EMic
'Fool's Gold' (*fortunei*)	EMic IBal
'Forest Fireworks' (v)	IBal
'Forest Shadows'	IBal
'Formal Attire' (*sieboldiana* hybrid) (v)	EGol EMic IBal LRHS
'Forncett Frances' (v)	EGol IBal
'Fortis'	see *H. undulata* var. *erromena*
fortunei	EGol EMic NNor
§ - var. ***albopicta*** (v) ♀H4	CSam EGol EHoe ELan EMic EPfP EUJe GMaP IFoB LEdu LPot LRHS MRav NEgg NGdn NMyG NNor SBod SPer WBrk WHoo WMnd WWEG
- - f. ***aurea*** ♀H4	CMac EGol EHoe ELan EMic NEgg NLar SRms WHal
- - - dwarf	EMic
- - f. ***viridis***	NNor
§ - var. ***aureomarginata*** (v) ♀H4	CPrp CSam CTri EGol EHoe ELan ELon EMic EPfP EShb GMaP IBal LBMP LPot LRHS MLHP MMuc MSwo NGdn NLar NNor SBod SEND SPer SPlb SPoG WMnd WWEG
- var. ***gigantea***	see *H. montana*
- var. ***hyacinthina*** ♀H4	EGol EMic EPfP LRHS MRav NGdn NLar WPtf XLum
- - variegated	see *H.* 'Crowned Imperial'
- var. ***rugosa***	EMic
- var. ***stenantha***	EMic
'Fountain of Youth' (*kikutii*)	IBal
'Fourteen Carats'	EMic IBal
'Fourth of July'	EGol IBal NSue
'Fragrant Blue'	EBee EGol EMic IBal LRHS NBro NGdn NSue SPoG XLum
'Fragrant Blue Ribbons' (v) **new**	EMic
'Fragrant Bouquet' (v)	ECtt EGol ELan EMic IBal LAst LRHS LSRN MMuc NCGa NGdn NHol NLar NMyG NSue SEND WPtf WWEG

'Fragrant Dream'	EGol EMic IBal NLar WWEG
'Fragrant Fire'	EMic IBal
'Fragrant Gold'	EGol EMic
'Fragrant King'	IBal
'Fragrant Queen'PBR (v)	EMic IBal
'Fragrant Star'	EMic IBal
'Fragrant Surprise' (v)	IBal
'Fran Godfrey'	EMic IBal NMyG
'Francee' (*fortunei*) (v) ♀H4	Widely available
§ 'Frances Williams' (*sieboldiana*) (v) ♀H4	Widely available
'Frances Williams Improved' (*sieboldiana*) (v)	EGol EPfP GBuc IFoB MWat
'Francheska' (v)	EMic IBal
'Fresh' (v)	EGol EMic IBal
'Fried Bananas'	EGol EMic IBal MBri WWEG
'Fried Green Tomatoes'	EGol EMic IBal NLar NMyG NNor
'Friends' (v)	EMic
'Fringe Benefit' (v)	EGol EMic GAbr IBal WWEG
'Frost Giant' (v)	IBal
'Frosted Dimples'	EMic IBal
'Frosted Frolic' (v)	EMic IBal
'Frosted Jade' (v)	EBee EGol EMic EPfP IBal NLar
'Frosted June'	EMic IBal
'Frosted Mouse Ears'PBR	EGol EMic IBal MAsh NSue
'Frozen Margarita'	EMic IBal
'Frühlingsgold' (v)	IBal
'Fruit Punch'	EMic IFoB
'Fujibotan' (v)	EGol EMic IBal IFoB
'Fulda'	EMic IBal
'Funky Monkey'	EMic
'Gaiety' (v)	EGol EMic IBal
'Gaijin' (v)	EGol IBal NSue
'Garden Party' (v)	IBal
'Garden Treasure'	EGol
'Garnet Prince'	EGol IBal
'Gay Blade' (v)	EGol IBal LRHS
'Gay Feather' (v)	EMic IFoB
'Gay Search' (v)	IBal
'Geisha' (v)	EGol IBal LBMP LRHS NGdn NNor NPro NSue WWEG
'Geisha Satin Ripples'	IBal
'Gemini Moon' (v)	IBal
'Gemstone'	IBal
'Gene's Joy'	IBal
'Gentle Giant'	IBal
'Gentle Spirit' (v)	IBal
'George M. Dallas' (v)	IBal
'George Smith' (*sieboldiana*)	EMic IBal
'Georgeous George'	IBal
'Ghost Spirit'	IBal NSue
'Ghostmaster' (v)	EMic IBal LRHS NSue WWlt
'Gig Harbor'	IBal
'Gigantea' (*sieboldiana*)	see *H.* 'Elata'
'Gilt by Association'	IBal
'Gilt Edge' (*sieboldiana*) (v)	EMic NMyG WWEG
'Gingee'	IBal
'Ginko Craig' (v)	CMac EGol EHoe ELan EMic EPfP GKev GMaP IBal IFoB LRHS MRav MWhi NBir NGdn NLar NMyG NNor NSti SPer SPoG WMnd WWEG
'Ginrei'	IBal
'Ginsu Knife' (v)	EMic IBal
'Glad Rags' (v)	IBal
'Glad Tidings' **new**	IBal
'Glamour' **new**	EMic

	'Glass Hearts'	EMic IBal
	glauca	see *H. sieboldiana* var. *elegans*
	'Glitter'	EMic IBal
	'Glockenspiel'	EGol EMic
I	'Gloriosa' (*fortunei*) (v)	EGol IBal IFoB LRHS
	'Glory'	EGol IBal
	'Glory Hallelujah'	EMic
	'Goblin'	EMic
	'Goddess of Athena' (*decorata*) (v)	EGol IBal
	'Gold Drop' (*venusta* hybrid)	EGol EMic NHol WWEG
	'Gold Edger'	CBcs CMac CPrp EBee EGol EHoe ELan EMic EPfP GKev GMaP IBal LRHS MRav NBir NGdn NLar NNor NSti WWEG
	'Gold Edger Surprise' (v)	EMic
	'Gold Flush' (*ventricosa*)	EMic
§	'Gold Haze' (*fortunei*)	EGol EMic IBal MHom NBir NCGa NMyG WWEG
	'Gold Leaf' (*fortunei*)	EGol IBal
	'Gold Pressed Latinum'	IBal
	'Gold Regal'	EBee EGol EMic GBin IBal IFoB LRHS MHom NMyG WMnd
	'Gold Rush'	NMyG
	'Gold Standard' (*fortunei*) (v)	Widely available
	'Goldbrook' (v)	EGol EMic IBal
	'Goldbrook Galleon'	EGol IBal
	'Goldbrook Gayle' (v)	EGol
	'Goldbrook Gaynor'	EGol IBal
	'Goldbrook Genie'	EGol IBal
	'Goldbrook Ghost' (v)	EGol
	'Goldbrook Girl'	EGol IBal
	'Goldbrook Glamour' (v)	EGol IBal
	'Goldbrook Gleam' (v)	EGol IBal
	'Goldbrook Glimmer' (Tardiana Group) (v)	EGol IBal LRHS
	'Goldbrook Glory'	EGol EMic IBal
	'Goldbrook Gold'	EGol IBal
	'Goldbrook Good Gracious' (v)	EGol IBal
	'Goldbrook Grace'	EGol
	'Goldbrook Gratis' (v)	EGol IBal
	'Goldbrook Grayling'	EGol EMic IBal
	'Goldbrook Grebe'	EGol IBal
	'Goldbrook Greengage' (v) **new**	EGol
	'Goldbrook Greenheart'	IBal
	'Golden Age'	see *H.* 'Gold Haze'
	'Golden Anniversary'	EGol
	'Golden Ben'	ITim
	'Golden Essence'	IBal
	'Golden Fascination'	EGol
	'Golden Fountain'	EMic
	'Golden Friendship'	EGol IBal
	'Golden Gate'	EGol IBal
	'Golden Goal'	IBal
	'Golden Guernsey' (v)	EMic
	'Golden Isle'	EGol EMic IBal
	'Golden Meadows'[PBR] (*sieboldiana*)	ECtt EMic IBal NGdn NSue SGol SMrm
	'Golden Medallion' (*tokudama*)	ECtt EGol ELan EMic IBal LRHS NEgg NGdn
	'Golden Nakaiana'	see *H.* 'Birchwood Parky's Gold'
	'Golden' (*nakaiana*)	see *H.* 'Birchwood Parky's Gold'
	'Golden Oriole'	EGol EMic IBal NNor WWEG
	'Golden Prayers' (*tokudama*)	EBee ECtt EHoe ELan LRHS MRav NBir NBro NEgg NGdn NLar WHal WSHC
	'Golden Scepter'	EGol EMic IBal LRHS NNor
	'Golden Sculpture' (*sieboldiana*)	EGol EMic IBal
	'Golden Spider'	EGol EMic IBal WWEG
	'Golden Sunburst' (*sieboldiana*)	CPrp EGol ELan IBal NEgg NGdn NLar XLum
	'Golden Tiara' (v) ♀H4	Widely available
	'Golden Tusk'	IBal
	'Golden Waffles'	EMic IBal NEgg
	'Goldsmith'	EGol
	'Goober'	IBal
	'Good as Gold'	EMic IBal
	'Gorgon'	IBal
	'Gosan Leather Strap'	IBal
	'Gosan' (*takahashii*)	EGol IBal
	gracillima	IBal NRya WWEG
	'Granary Gold' (*fortunei*)	EGol MHom
	'Grand Canyon'	EMic
	'Grand Finale'	IBal
	'Grand Forks'	IBal
	'Grand Marquee' (v)	EMic IBal MBri NGdn NLar SGol WWEG
	'Grand Master'	EGol IBal
	'Grand Prize' (v)	IBal
	'Grand Rapids'	EMic IBal
	'Grand Slam'	EGol EMic IBal
	'Grand Tiara' (v)	EGol EMic IBal NGdn
	'Grand Total'	IBal
	'Grant Park'	IBal
	'Grape Fizz' **new**	IBal
	'Gray Cole' (*sieboldiana*)	EGol EMic IBal
	'Great Arrival'	EMic IBal
	'Great Escape'[PBR] (v)	EMic IBal LLWG
	'Great Expectations' (*sieboldiana*) (v)	CHid CMac EGol EMic EPfP GAbr IBal IBoy IFoB IVic LRHS LSRN MBNS MHer MNrw MWhi NBro NCGa NGdn NLar NNor NSti SHil SMrm WWEG
	'Great Lakes Gold'	IBal
	'Green Acres' (*montana*)	EMic IBal LEdu
	'Green Angel' (*sieboldiana*)	EGol IBal
	'Green Blade'	IBal
	'Green Eyes' (*sieboldii*) (v)	EGol EMic IBal
	'Green Fountain' (*kikutii*)	EGol EMic IBal NMyG WWEG
	'Green Gold' (*fortunei*) (v)	EMic
	'Green Lama'	IBal
	'Green Mouse Ears'	EGol EMic IBal MAsh NMyG
	'Green Piecrust'	EGol IBal NNor
	'Green Power'	IBal
	'Green Sheen'	EGol EMic
	'Green Summer Fragrance'	IBal
	'Green Velveteen'	EGol IBal
	'Green with Envy' (v)	EGol EMic IBal NNor NSue WWEG
	'Greensleeves' (v)	IBal
	'Grey Ghost'	EMic IBal
	'Grey Goose' (Tardiana Group)	EMic
	'Grey Piecrust'	EGol
	'Groo Bloo'	IBal
	'Ground Master' (v)	CMac EBee ECtt EGol ELan EPfP GCra GMaP IBal IFoB MRav MSwo NBro NGdn NNor NSti WMoo WPtf WWEG
	'Ground Sulphur'	EGol EMic IBal
	'Grover Cleveland'	IBal
	'Grünherz'	IBal
	'Grunspecht' (Tardiana Group)	IBal

'Guacamole' (v)	CBcs ECtt EGol EMic EPfP IBal LRHS MBri NGdn NLar NMyG NNor NPnk NSue WHoo WWEG
'Guardian Angel' (*sieboldiana*)	EGol EMic IBal NLar
'Gum Drop'	EMic NNor
'Gun Metal Blue'	EGol IBal
'Gypsy Rose'	EPfP IBal NGdn NMyG NSue
'Hacksaw'	EMic IBal NSue
'Hadspen Blue' (Tardiana Group)	CSBt CWCL EBee EGol ELan EMic EPfP GBin GKev GMaP IBal IBoy LRHS MBel MBrN MGos MRav NBir NBro NEgg NGdn NHol NNor SPer SPoG WMnd WPtf WWEG
'Hadspen Hawk' (Tardiana Group)	IBal NMyG
'Hadspen Heron' (Tardiana Group)	EGol EMic MHom MWat WCot XLum
'Hadspen Nymphaea'	EGol IBal
'Hadspen Rainbow'	EMic IBal
'Hadspen Samphire'	EGol EMic IBal LRHS MHom NBir NBro
'Hadspen White' (*fortunei*)	EMic IBal NLar
'Haku-chu-han' (*sieboldii*) (v)	IBal
'Hakujima' (*sieboldii*)	EGol IBal NSue
'Hakumuo' (v)	IBal
§ 'Halcyon' (Tardiana Group) ♀H4	Widely available
'Halcyon Gold' **new**	SGol
'Half and Half'	EMic IBal
'Halo'	EGol
'Hampshire County' (v)	EMic IBal
'Hanky Panky' (v)	EMic IBal LRHS NCGa NGdn NMyG NSti NSue
'Hannibal Hamlin' (v)	IBal
'Happily Ever After' (v)	IBal
'Happiness' (Tardiana Group)	EGol EHoe EMic IBal MHom MRav NMyG
'Happy Camper' (v)	IBal
'Happy Hearts'	EGol EMic
'Happy Valley' (v)	IBal
'Harmony' (Tardiana Group)	EGol EMic
'Harpoon' (v)	EMic IBal
'Harriette Ward'	IBal
'Harry van de Laar'	EMic IBal IPot
'Harry van Trier'	EMic GBin
'Hart's Tongue'	IBal
'Harvest Delight'	EMic
'Harvest Glow'	EGol IBal
'Hawkeye' (v)	IBal
'Hazel'	EMic IBal
'Heart Ache'	EGol IBal
'Heart and Soul' (v)	EGol EMic IBal
'Heart Broken'	IBal
'Heart of Chan'	IBal
'Heart Throb'	EMic
'Heartbeat' (v)	IBal
'Heartleaf'	EMic
'Heart's Content' (v)	EGol IBal
'Heartsong' (v)	EGol EMic IBal NMyG
'Heat Wave'PBR (v)	EMic IBal
'Heavenly Beginnings' (v)	IBal
'Heavenly Tiara' (v)	IBal
'Heideturm'	EGol IBal
'Helen Doriot' (*sieboldiana*)	EGol EMic IBal
'Helen Field Fischer' (*fortunei*)	CPrp IBal

helonioides misapplied f. ***albopicta***	see *H. rohdeifolia*
'Herifu' (v)	EGol EMic
'Herkules'	IBal
'Hertha' (v)	EMic
'Hidden Cove' (v)	EGol IBal
'Hidden Treasure' (v) **new**	IBal
'Hideout' (v) **new**	EGol IBal
'High Kicker'	EGol IBal
'High Society' (v)	CBcs ELan EMic EPfP IBal IFoB MHom MNrw NGdn NNor
'High Tide'	IBal
'Hi-ho Silver' (v)	EMic IBal NSue WWEG
'Hilda Wassman' (v)	EGol IBal
'Hillbilly Blues' (v)	IBal
'Hippodrome' (v)	EMic IBal
'Hirao Elite'	EMic IBal
'Hirao Majesty'	EGol IBal
'Hirao Splendor'	EGol
'Hirao Supreme'	EGol EMic IBal
'His Honor' (v)	EMic IBal
'Holly's Dazzler' **new**	IBal
'Holly's Honey'	EGol IBal
'Hollywood Lights' (v)	EMic EPfP IBal NGdn
'Holstein'	see *H.* 'Halcyon'
'Holy Molé' (v)	EMic IBal
'Holy Mouse Ears'PBR	EGol EMic IBal NSue
'Honey Moon'	EGol IBal NNor
'Honeybells' ♀H4	CBcs CMac CTri EBee EGol ELan EMic EPfP IBal LEdu LHop LRHS MCot MRav NBid NGdn NNor NSti SPer WPtf WWEG XLum
'Honeysong' (v)	EGol EMic IBal NNor
'Hoosier Dome'	EMic
'Hoosier Harmony' (v)	EGol EMic
'Hope' (v)	EGol IBal
'Hotcakes'	IBal
'Hotspur' (v)	EMic
'Hush Puppie'	EGol EMic IBal NSue
'Hyacintha Variegata' (*fortunei*) (v)	CMac NNor
'Hydon Gleam'	EGol EMic IBal
'Hydon Sunset'	EBee ECtt EGol EMic GCra IBal LRHS NBir NHol NMyG NNor NRya NSti NSue WHal WMnd WPtf WWEG
hypoleuca	EGol EMic IBal
'Hyuga-urajiro' (v)	EMic IBal NSue
'Ice Age Trail' (v)	IBal
'Ice Cream' (*cathayana*) (v)	EGol IBal NGdn
'Ice Prancer'	EMic
'Iced Lemon' (v)	EGol EMic IBal NNor NSue
'Illicit Affair'	EGol EMic IBal NSue
'Imp' (v)	EMic IBal
§ 'Inaho'	EGol LRHS
'Inca Gold'	EGol IBal
'Independence' (v)	EBee EMic IBal MBri NBro NMyG NSue SPoG
'Independence Day' (v)	EMic
'Innisjade'	IBal
'Inniswood' (v)	CWCL ECtt EMic IBal IPot LRHS MBNS NBro NGdn NLar NSti WMnd WWEG
'Invincible'	ECtt EGol EMic IBal LAst LPot NBid NEgg NGdn NLar NMyG NNor SPoG WPtf WWEG
'Invincible Spirit'	IBal

	'Iona' (*fortunei*)	EGol EMic IBal NMyG NNor
	'Irische See' (Tardiana Group)	EGol IBal
	'Irish Eyes' (v)	EMic IBal
	'Irish Luck'	EMic
	'Iron Gate Delight' (v)	NNor
	'Iron Gate Glamour' (v)	EGol
	'Iron Gate Special' (v)	EMic
	'Iron Gate Supreme' (v)	EMic
	'Island Charm' (v)	EGol EMic IBal LRHS NHar NLar NMyG
	'Island Forest Gem'	IBal
	'Itsy Bitsy Spider'	EGol
	'Ivory Coast' (v)	EMic IBal NSue
	'Ivory Necklace' (v)	IBal
	'Iwa Soules'	EGol
	'Iwa Yara Moto' **new**	IBal
	'Jack of Diamonds'	IBal
	'Jade Cascade'	EGol ELan EMic GBin IBal NBir NEgg NLar WWEG
	'Jade Scepter' (*nakaiana*)	EGol EMic
	'Jadette' (v)	EGol
	'Janet Day' (v)	EMic IBal
	'Janet' (*fortunei*) (v)	EGol EMic IBal NGdn NNor
	'Japan Girl'	see *H.* 'Mount Royal'
	'Jaws'	EMic IBal NSue
	'Jaz'	IBal
	'Jennifer Bailey' (v) **new**	IBal
	'Jerry Landwehr'	IBal
	'Jewel of the Nile' (v)	EMic IBal
	'Jim Mathews'	IBal
	'Jimmy Crack Corn'	EGol EMic IBal LRHS NGdn
	'Jingle Bells'	IBal
	'John Wargo'	EGol IBal
	'Johnny Angel'	EMic
	'Joker' (*fortunei*) (v)	NNor
	'Jolly Green Giant' (*sieboldiana* hybrid)	EMic
	jonesii	EMic
	'Joseph'	EGol IBal
	'Josephine' (v)	NNor
	'Journeyman'	EGol EMic IBal LRHS
	'Journey's End' (v)	EMic IBal
	'Joyce Trott' (v)	EMic IBal
	'Joyful' (v)	IBal
	'Jubilee' (v)	EMic IBal
	'Judy Rocco'	IBal
	'Juha' (v)	EMic
	'Jules'	IBal
	'Julia' (v)	EGol EMic IBal
	'Julie Morss'	EGol EMic GMaP IBal MHom NEgg WWEG
	'Jumbo' (*sieboldiana*)	MAsh
	'June' PBR (Tardiana Group) (v) ♀H4	Widely available
	'June Fever' PBR (Tardiana Group)	EMic ESwi IBal MBri NBro NGdn NLar NSue
	'Jurassic Park'	EBee EMic GBin IBal LLWG MNrw NLar
	'Just June' (Tardiana Group) (v)	WWlt
	'Just So' (v)	EGol EMic IBal
	'Justine'	EMic NSue
	'Kabitan'	see *H. sieboldii* var. *sieboldii* f. *kabitan*
	'Kabuki'	IBal
	'Kalamazoo' (v)	EMic
	'Kaleidochrome' (v)	IBal
	'Karin'	EGol EMic IBal
	'Katherine Lewis' (Tardiana Group) (v)	ECtt EMic IBal LSRN NHol
	'Kath's Gold'	EMic
	'Katie Q' (v)	EMic IBal
	'Katsuragawa-beni' (v)	EMic IBal
	'Kelsey'	EGol EMic
	'Kenzie' (v)	EMic
	'Key Lime Pie'	EMic IBal
	'Key West'	EMic
	'Kifukurin' (*kikutii*)	see *H.* 'Kifukurin-hyuga'
	'Kifukurin' (*pulchella*) (v)	EGol
	'Kifukurin' (*venusta*) (v)	EMic
§	'Kifukurin-hyuga' (v)	IBal
	'Kifukurin-ko-mame' (*gracillima*) (v)	EMic NSue
	'Kifukurin-ubatake' (*pulchella*) (v)	EGol EMic IBal
	kikutii	EGol EMic IBal IMou LRHS
§	– var. ***caput-avis***	EGol EMic
§	– var. ***yakusimensis***	CPBP IBal SMad
	'Ki-nakafu-otome' (*venusta*)	IBal
	'Kinbotan' (v)	EGol EMic
	'Kinbuchi Tachi' (*rectifolia*) (v)	IBal
	'King James'	IBal
	'King of Spades'	IBal
	'King Tut'	EMic
	'Kingfisher' (Tardiana Group)	EGol
§	'Kirishima'	EMic NSla NSue
	'Kisuji'	see *H.* 'Mediopicta'
	'Kitty Cat'	EMic IBal NSue
	'Kiwi Black Magic'	EGol IBal
	'Kiwi Blue Baby'	EGol EMic IBal
	'Kiwi Blue Ruffles'	IBal
	'Kiwi Blue Sky'	IBal
	'Kiwi Canoe'	IBal
	'Kiwi Cream Edge' (v)	EMic IBal
	'Kiwi Forest'	IBal
	'Kiwi Full Monty' (v)	EBee EMic IBal LRHS MSCN NSue
	'Kiwi Gold Rush'	IBal
	'Kiwi Hippo'	EGol IBal
	'Kiwi Jordan'	IBal
	'Kiwi Kaniere Gold'	IBal
	'Kiwi Minnie Gold'	IBal
	'Kiwi Parasol'	IBal
	'Kiwi Skyscraper'	IBal
	'Kiwi Sunlover'	IBal
	'Kiwi Sunshine'	IBal
	'Klopping Variegated' (v)	EGol EMic
	'Knight's Journey'	IBal
	'Knockout' (v)	EGol IBal MBNS MNrw MRav NBro NEgg NGdn NLar NMyG NNor
	'Komodo Dragon'	EMic IBal SKHP
	'Kong'	IBal
	'Konkubine'	EMic
	'Korean Snow'	IBal
I	'Koreana Variegated' (*undulata*)	EMic
	'Koriyama' (*sieboldiana*) (v)	EMic IBal
	'Krossa Cream Edge' (*sieboldii*) (v)	IBal
	'Krossa Regal' ♀H4	Widely available
	'Krugerrand'	IBal
	'La Donna' **new**	IBal
	'Lacy Belle' (v)	CSBt EBee EGol EMic EPfP IBal NBro NGdn NPro NSue
	'Lady Godiva'	IBal
	'Lady Guineverre'	EMic IBal

'Lady Helen'	EMic
'Lady in Red'	IBal
'Lady Isobel Barnett' (v)	IBal
laevigata	EGol IBal
'Lahn'	IBal
'Lake Hitchock'	EGol IBal
'Lake Huron'	IBal
'Lakeside Accolade'	EGol IBal
'Lakeside Alex Andra' (v)	IBal
'Lakeside April Snow' (v)	EMic IBal
'Lakeside Baby Face' (v)	EGol EMic IBal NSue
'Lakeside Banana Bay' (v)	IBal
'Lakeside Beach Captain' (v)	EMic
'Lakeside Black Satin'	EMic IBal
'Lakeside Blue Cherub'	EMic IBal
'Lakeside Breaking News' (v)	EMic IBal
'Lakeside Butter Ball'	IBal
'Lakeside Cha Cha' (v)	EGol EMic IBal MWhi
'Lakeside Cindy Cee' (v)	IBal
'Lakeside Coal Miner'	EMic IBal NGdn
'Lakeside Color Blue'	IBal
'Lakeside Contender'	IBal
'Lakeside Cupcake' (v)	EMic IBal LRHS
'Lakeside Cupid's Cup' (v)	IBal
'Lakeside Dimpled Darling' (v)	EGol
'Lakeside Dividing Line' (v)	IBal
'Lakeside Doodad' (v)	EGol IBal
'Lakeside Down Sized' (v)	EGol EMic IBal NSue
'Lakeside Dragonfly' (v)	EMic EPfP IBal LLWG LRHS NMyG NSue
'Lakeside Elfin Fire'	EGol EMic IBal
'Lakeside Fancy Pants' (v)	IBal
'Lakeside Feather Light' (v)	IBal
'Lakeside Foaming Sea'	IBal
'Lakeside Full Tide' **new**	IBal
'Lakeside Hazy Morn' (v)	IBal
'Lakeside Hoola Hoop' (v)	IBal
'Lakeside Iron Man'	IBal
'Lakeside Jazzy Jane' (v)	IBal
'Lakeside Kaleidoscope'	EGol EMic IBal NGdn
'Lakeside Keepsake' (v)	IBal
'Lakeside Legal Tender'	IBal
'Lakeside Lime Time'	IBal
'Lakeside Little Gem'	EGol IBal
'Lakeside Little Tuft' (v)	EGol EMic IBal MBri NMyG NSue
'Lakeside Lollipop'	EGol EMic IBal
'Lakeside Looking Glass'	EMic
'Lakeside Love Affaire'	EGol EMic
'Lakeside Maestro'	IBal NLar
'Lakeside Maverick' **new**	IBal
'Lakeside Meadow Ice' (v)	IBal
'Lakeside Meter Maid' (v)	IBal
'Lakeside Midnight Miss'	IBal
'Lakeside Miss Muffett' (v)	EGol IBal
'Lakeside Neat Petite'	EGol IBal
'Lakeside Ninita' (v)	EGol EMic IBal NSue
'Lakeside Old Smokey'	IBal
'Lakeside Paisley Print' (v)	IBal NSue
'Lakeside Pebbles'	IBal
'Lakeside Premier'	EGol EMic
'Lakeside Prissy Miss' (v) **new**	EGol
'Lakeside Prophecy Fulfilled' (v)	IBal
'Lakeside Rhapsody' (v)	EMic IBal
'Lakeside Ring Master' (v)	IBal
'Lakeside Ripples'	IBal
'Lakeside Rocky Top' (v)	IBal
'Lakeside Roy El' (v)	IBal
'Lakeside Sassy Sally'	IBal
'Lakeside Scamp' (v)	EGol EMic NSue
'Lakeside Shadows' (v)	IBal
'Lakeside Shoremaster' (v)	IBal
'Lakeside Sir Logan'	IBal
'Lakeside Slick Chick' (v)	IBal
'Lakeside Sophistication' (v) **new**	IBal
'Lakeside Sparkle Plenty' (v)	IBal
'Lakeside Spellbinder' (v)	IBal
'Lakeside Spruce Goose' (v)	EMic IBal
'Lakeside Storm Watch'	EMic IBal
'Lakeside Symphony' (v)	EGol EMic
'Lakeside Tee Ki' (v)	IBal
'Lakeside Tycoon'	IBal
'Lakeside Whizzit' (v) **new**	EGol IBal
'Lakeside Zesty Zeno' (v)	IBal
'Lakeside Zinger' (v)	EGol EMic IBal NSue
lancifolia ♀H4	CMac EGol ELan EMic GMaP IBal LRHS MRav NGdn NMyG NSti SBod SRms WKif WSHC
'Last Dance' (v)	IBal
'Laura Lanier' **new**	EMic
'Laura Z'	IBal
'Lavender Doll'	IBal
'Leading Lady'	IBal
'Leather Sheen'	EGol EMic
'Leatherneck'	IBal
'Lederhosen'	EMic IBal
'Lee Armiger' (*tokudama* hybrid)	EGol
'Lemon Delight'	EGol EMic IBal LRHS NNor NSue WWEG
'Lemon Frost'	EMic IBal
'Lemon Juice'	NMyG
'Lemon Lime'	EGol EMic IBal MHom MNrw NNor NPro NSue WWEG
'Lemon Twist'	IBal
'Lemonade'	GBin IBal
'Leola Fraim' (v)	EGol EMic IBal LRHS
'Let Me Entertain You'	EMic
'Leviathan'	EMic
'Lewis and Clark' **new**	IBal
'Libby'	EMic IBal
'Liberty'PBR (v)	CWGN EMic IBal LRHS MAsh MBri NBro NGdn NNor NSue
'Li'l Abner' (v)	IBal
'Lily Blue Eyes'	EMic
'Lime Fizz'	EGol EMic IBal NSue
'Lime Piecrust'	EGol IBal
'Lime Shag' (*sieboldii* f. *spathulata*)	EGol IBal NSue
'Limey Lisa'	EGol EMic IBal NSue WWEG
'Linda Sue' (v)	IBal
'Lionheart' (v)	EMic IBal
'Little Aurora' (*tokudama* hybrid)	EGol EMic IBal WWEG
'Little Bit'	IBal
'Little Black Scape'	EGol EMic IBal LSRN MHom NEgg NGdn NHol NLar NPro NSue
'Little Blue' (*ventricosa*)	EGol EMic
'Little Bo Beep' (v)	EGol IBal NSue WWEG
'Little Boy'	IBal
'Little Caesar' (v)	EGol EMic IBal NGdn NSue
'Little Devil'	EGol EMic IBal NSue

'Little Doll' (v)	EGol IBal
'Little Jay' (v)	EGol EMic IBal NSue
'Little Maddie'	EGol EMic
'Little Miss Magic'	IBal
'Little Miss Muffett'	EGol
'Little Razor'	EGol IBal
'Little Red Joy'	EGol EMic IBal
'Little Red Rooster'	EMic IBal NGdn NMyG NNor NSue WWEG
'Little Stiffy'	EGol EMic NSue
'Little Sunspot' (v)	EGol EMic IBal NHar NSue
'Little Treasure' (v)	EGol EMic NSue
'Little White Lines' (v)	EGol EMic GKev IBal NSue
'Little Willie' (v)	EGol
'Little Wonder' (v)	EGol EMic IBal NSue WWEG
'Living Water' **new**	EMic
'Lizard Lick'	IBal NSue
'Lollapalooza' (v)	IBal
'London Fog' (v)	IBal NSue
'Lonesome Dove' (v)	EMic
longipes	EGol
- B&SWJ 10806	WCru
'Lothar the Giant'	IBal
'Louisa' (*sieboldii*) (v)	LRHS
'Love Pat' ♀^{H4}	CCon EGol EMic EPfP GAbr IBal LRHS LSRN MRav NGdn NLar NNor WCAu
'Loyalist'^{PBR} (v)	EMic LRHS NGdn NLar SPoG WWEG
'Lucky Mouse'^{PBR} (v) **new**	EGol MAsh NMyG NSue
'Lucy Vitols' (v)	EGol EMic IBal
'Lullabye'	EMic
'Lunar Eclipse' (v)	CHid EMic NEgg WWEG
'Machete'	IBal
'Mack the Knife'	EMic IBal
'Maekawa'	EGol EMic IBal
'Magic Fire'^{PBR} (v)	EMic EPfP IBal MNrw
'Magic Island'	IBal NSue
'Majesty'	EGol EMic IBal MBri NGdn
'Malabar' (v)	EMic IBal
'Mama Mia' (v)	EGol EMic EPfP IBal LRHS MBNS NBro NGdn NHol NWad
'Manhattan'	EMic
'Manzo' (v)	EGol
'Maraschino Cherry'	EGol EMic EWTr IBal NEgg NGdn NMyG
'Marble Rim' (v)	EGol IBal
'Mardi Gras' (v)	EMic IBal
'Marge' (*sieboldiana* hybrid)	EMic
'Margie's Angel' (v) **new**	NSue
'Margin of Error' (v)	EGol IBal NMyG
'Marginata Alba' misapplied	see *H.* 'Albomarginata' (*fortunei*), *H. crispula*
'Marginata Alba' ambig. (v)	NNor
'Marilyn'	EGol EMic IBal
'Marilyn Monroe'	EMic IBal NSue
'Marmalade on Toast'	EMic
'Marquis' (*nakaiana* hybrid)	EGol IBal
'Marrakech'	EMic IBal NSue
'Mary Joe'	EMic IBal
'Mary Marie Ann' (*fortunei*) (v)	EGol EMic IBal
'Masquerade' (v)	EGol EMic IBal NHar WHal WThu
'Maui Buttercups'	EMic IBal
'May'	EMic IBal
'Maya' (*fortunei*) (v)	EMic IBal
'Medieval Age' (v)	IBal
§ 'Mediopicta' (*sieboldii*)	EMic IBal NSue
'Mediovariegata' (*undulata*)	see *H. undulata* var. *undulata*
'Medusa' (v)	EGol EMic IBal NGdn NSue
'Memories of Dorothy'	EMic IBal
'Mentor Gold'	EGol
'Mesa Fringe' (*montana*)	EMic IBal
'Mid Afternoon'	IBal
'Midas Touch'	NEgg NLar NNor
'Middle Ridge'	EMic
'Midnight at the Oasis' (v) **new**	EMic IBal
'Midnight Ride'	IBal
'Midwest Gold'	MHom
'Midwest Magic' (v)	EGol EMic IBal NLar
'Mieke' (v)	IBal
'Mighty Mite'	EGol NSue
'Mighty Mouse' (v)	IBal
'Mikawa-no-yuki'	IBal
'Mike Shadrack' (v) **new**	EMic
'Miki'	IBal
'Mildred Seaver' (v)	EGol EMic IBal LRHS MHom
'Millennium'	EMic
'Minnie Bell' (v)	EGol IBal
'Minnie Klopping'	EMic
minor misapplied f. ***alba***	see *H. sieboldii* var. *alba*
§ ***minor*** Maekawa	EBee EGol ITim WCot XLum
- B&SWJ 1209 from Korea	WCru
- B&SWJ 8775 from Korea	WCru
- B&SWJ 11103 from Japan	WCru
- from Korea	EGol IBal
- Goldbrook form	EGol
'Minor' (*ventricosa*)	see *H. minor* Maekawa
'Mint Candy'	IBal
'Mint Julep' (v)	IBal
'Minuet' (v)	IBal
'Minuteman' (*fortunei*) (v)	CCon ECtt EMic EPfP GBin IBal IPot LRHS MBNS MMuc NGdn NLar NMyG NNor NOrc NPnk WGor WWEG
'Miss Linda Smith'	EMic IBal
'Miss Ruby'	EMic IBal
'Miss Saigon' (v)	IBal
'Miss Tokyo' (v)	EMic IBal
'Mississippi Delta'	EMic
'Mister Watson'	EMic IBal
'Misty Waters' (*sieboldiana*)	EMic
'Moerheim' (*fortunei*) (v)	EGol EMic IBal LRHS WHal WWEG
'Mohegan'	EMic
'Moi Marleen'	IBal
N ***montana***	EGol EMic
- B&SWJ 4796	WCru
- B&SWJ 5585	WCru
- 'Hida-no-hana' (v)	IBal
- f. ***macrophylla***	EGol IBal NSue
'Moody Blues' (Tardiana Group)	EMic
'Moon Glow' (v)	EGol
'Moon Lily'	EMic
'Moon River' (v)	EGol EMic IBal NSue
'Moon Shadow' (v)	EGol
'Moon Split' (v)	EMic EPfP NGdn
'Moon Waves'	EGol
'Moonbeam'	EShb
'Moongate Flying Saucer'	EMic
'Moonlight' (*fortunei*) (v)	EGol EMic GMaP IBal LRHS NNor
'Moonlight Sonata'	EGol EMic IBal
'Moonstruck'^{PBR} (v)	ECtt EGol EMic IBal
'Morning Light'^{PBR}	ECtt EGol EMic EPfP GBin IBal LBMP LLWG MAvo MBNS MBri NBro NGdn NLar NPnk SRkn
'Morning Star'	EMic IBal NSue

	'Moscow Blue'	EGol EMic
	'Mount Everest'	EMic IBal
	'Mount Fuji' (*montana*)	EGol IBal
	'Mount Hope' (v)	EGol
	'Mount Kirishima' (*sieboldii*)	see *H.* 'Kirishima'
§	'Mount Royal' (*sieboldii*)	IBal
	'Mount Tom' (v)	EGol EMic IBal
	'Mountain Snow' (*montana*) (v)	EGol EMic LRHS
	'Mountain Sunrise' (*montana*)	EGol
	'Mourning Dove' (v)	EMic IBal
	'Mouse Trap' (v) **new**	IBal NSue
	'Mr Big'	IBal NGdn WCot
	'Mrs Minky'	EBee EMic LRHS
	'Muffie' (v)	EMic IBal
	'Munchkin' (*sieboldii*)	LLHF
	'My Claire' (v)	IBal
	'My Cup of Tea'	IBal
	'My Friend Nancy' (v)	EGol IBal
	'Mystic Star'	IBal
	nakaiana	EBee EMic IBal
	'Nakaimo'	IBal NHol
	'Nameoki'	NHol
	'Nana' (*ventricosa*)	see *H. minor* Maekawa
	'Nancy'	EMic
§	'Nancy Lindsay' (*fortunei*)	CTri EMic IBal NGdn NLar
	'Nancy Minks'	EMic IBal
	'Neat and Tidy'	IBal
	'Neat Splash' (v)	CWCL NBir WWEG
	'Neat Splash Rim' (v)	IBal
	'Neelix'	IBal
	'Nemesis' (v)	IBal
	'Neptune'	EMic IBal NSue
	'Niagara Falls'	CCon EGol EMic IBal NGdn NSue
	'Nicola'	EGol EMic IBal MHom NSue
	'Night before Christmas' (v)	CCon CHid EGol EMic IBal LRHS MNrw NBro NCGa NEgg NGdn NHol NMyG NNor NPnk WHoo WWEG
	'Night Life'	EMic IBal
	nigrescens	EGol EMic GGal IBal LRHS
	'Niko' (v)	IBal
	'Nokogiryama'	EMic
	'None Lovelier' (v)	EMic IBal
	'Nor'easter' (v)	IBal
	'North Hills' (*fortunei*) (v)	EGol EMic IBal MHom NBir NGdn SWvt WWEG
	'Northern Exposure' (*sieboldiana*) (v)	CCon EBee EGol EMic IBal NCGa NGdn
	'Northern Halo' (*sieboldiana*) (v)	EMic
	'Northern Sunray' (*sieboldiana*) (v)	IBal
	'Norwalk Chartreuse'	IBal
	'Nutty Professor' (v)	IBal
	'Oberon'	EGol
	'Obscura Marginata' (*fortunei*)	see *H. fortunei* var. *aureomarginata*
	'Obsession'	EGol IBal
	'Ocean Isle' (v)	IBal
	'October Sky'	EMic
	'Oder'	IBal
	'Ogon-chirifu-hime'	IBal
	'Ogon-hime-tokudama'	IBal
	'Ogon-koba'	IBal
	'Ogon Tachi' (*rectifolia*) (v)	EMic IBal
	'Oh Cindy' (v)	EMic IBal
	'O'Harra'	EGol EMic IBal
	'Old Faithful'	EGol EMic IBal
	'Old Glory'PBR (v)	ECtt EGol EMic IBal
	'Olga's Shiny Leaf'	EGol EMic
	'Olive Bailey Langdon' (*sieboldiana*) (v)	EMic IBal
	'Olive Branch' (v)	EGol EMic IBal
	'Olympic Edger'	EMic IBal
	'Olympic Glacier' (v)	EMic IBal
	'Olympic Gold Medal'	EMic IBal
	'Olympic Silver Medal'	EMic IBal
	'Olympic Sunrise' (v)	EMic IBal
	'Olympic Twilight'	EMic IBal
	'On Stage'	see *H.* 'Chōkō-nishiki'
	'On the Border' (v)	IBal
	'One Man's Treasure'	EMic IBal IPot MBel NGdn
	'Ooh La La' (v)	IBal
	'Ophir'	EMic IBal
	'Ops' (v)	EGol EMic IBal NSue
	'Orange Crush' (v)	IBal
	'Orange Marmalade' (v)	ECtt EMic IBal LRHS NGdn NSue SGol SPoG
	'Oriana' (*fortunei*)	EGol EMic
	'Orion's Belt' (v)	IBal
	'Osprey' (Tardiana Group)	EGol
	'Oxheart'	EMic IBal
	'Oze' (v)	EMic IBal NSue
	pachyscapa	EMic
	'Pacific Blue Edger'	CCon EGol EMic NGdn NNor WWEG
	'Painted Lady' (*sieboldii*) (v)	GKev
	'Pamela Lee' (v)	IBal NGdn NMyG NSue
	'Pandora's Box' (v)	EGol NHar NSue WCot
	'Paradigm' (v)	EBee EGol EMic IBal LRHS NGdn
	'Paradise Backstage' (v)	EMic IBal
	'Paradise Beach'	EMic IBal
	'Paradise Blue Sky'	IBal
	'Paradise Expectations' (*sieboldiana*) (v)	EMic IBal SPoG
	'Paradise Glory'	EMic IBal
	'Paradise Gold Line' (*ventricosa*) (v)	IBal
	'Paradise Island'PBR (*sieboldiana*) (v)	EMic EPfP IBal NGdn NSue
	'Paradise Joyce'PBR	EGol EMic IBal IPot LRHS NLar NNor NSue WWEG
	'Paradise Ocean'	EMic
	'Paradise on Fire' (v)	EMic IBal
	'Paradise Parade' (v)	IBal
	'Paradise Passion' (v)	IBal
	'Paradise Power'PBR	EMic
	'Paradise Puppet' (*venusta*)	EMic GKev IBal NNor NSue WWEG
	'Paradise Red Delight' (*pycnophylla*)	EMic IBal
	'Paradise Sandstorm'	IBal
	'Paradise Standard' (d)	EMic IBal
	'Paradise Sunset'	EGol EMic IBal NSue
	'Paradise Sunshine'	EMic
	'Paradise Surprise' (v)	IBal
	'Paradise Tritone' (v) **new**	EMic
	'Parhelion'	EMic
	'Parky's Prize' (v)	EGol IBal
	'Pastures Green'	EGol IBal
	'Pastures New'	EGol EMic MHom WWEG
	'Pathfinder' (v)	EGol EMic IBal
	'Patricia'	EMic
	'Patrician' (v)	EGol EMic IBal
	'Patriot' (v)	Widely available
	'Patriot's Fire' (v)	IBal
	'Patriot's Green Pride'	IBal

'Paul Revere' (v)	IBal
'Paul's Glory' (v)	EGol EMic EPfP GMaP IBal LRHS MBri NBir NGdn NMyG NNor NSue WWEG
§ 'Paxton's Original' (*sieboldii*) (v) ♀H4	EGol IFoB WWEG
'Peace' (v)	EGol EMic IBal LRHS
'Peacock Strut'	IBal
'Peanut'	EGol IBal NSue
'Pearl Lake'	EGol EMic IBal MHom NBir NEgg NGdn NHol NLar NMyG NNor SRGP
'Peedee Absinth'	EMic
'Peedee Laughing River' (v)	IBal
'Pelham Blue Tump'	EGol EMic
'Peppermint Cream' (*cathayana*)	IBal
'Peppermint Ice' (v)	EGol EMic IBal NGdn
'Percy'	EMic IBal
'Peridot' (Tardiana Group)	IBal
'Permanent Wave'	EGol IBal
'Perry's True Blue'	EMic
'Peter Pan'	EGol EMic IBal
'Peter the Rock'	IBal
'Pete's Dark Satellite'	EMic IBal NSue
'Pewterware'	EMic IBal
'Phantom'	IBal
'Philadelphia'	EMic IBal
'Phoenix'	EGol EMic IBal NLar
'Photo Finish' (v)	EGol EMic
'Phyllis Campbell'	see *H.* 'Sharmon'
'Picta' (*fortunei*)	see *H. fortunei* var. *albopicta*
'Piecrust Power'	IBal
'Piedmont Gold'	CHid EHoe EMic GBin IBal LHop LRHS WPtf
'Pilgrim' (v)	EGol EMic IBal LRHS NBro NGdn NMyG NSue
'Pineapple Poll'	EGol EMic NNor NSue WWEG
'Pineapple Upside Down Cake' (v)	EMic IBal NBro NLar NSue
'Pinky'	IBal
'Pinwheel' (v)	IBal
'Pistache' (v)	EMic IBal NSue
'Pixie Vamp' (v)	EGol EMic
'Pizzazz' (v)	EGol EMic IBal LRHS MHom NGdn NHol NLar WWEG
plantaginea	EMic IBal LEdu LPla LRHS SSpi WKif
- var. ***grandiflora***	see *H. plantaginea* var. *japonica*
§ - var. ***japonica*** ♀H4	CAby CAvo EBee LRHS MNrw MRav NLar SMrm WCFE WPGP WWEG
'Platinum Tiara' (v)	EGol EMic IBal NBir
'Plug Nickel'	EMic IBal
'Polar Moon' (v)	IBal
'Pole Cat' (v)	IBal
'Pooh Bear' (v)	EGol EMic IBal NSue
'Popcorn'	EMic IBal NSue
'Popo'	EGol EMic IBal NSue
'Porter' (*venusta*)	IBal
'Pot of Gold'	EMic
'Potomac Pride'	EGol EMic LRHS NMyG
'Powder Blue' (v)	IBal
'Powderpuff'	IBal
'Prairie Glow'	IBal
'Prairie Moon' **new**	NSue
'Prairie Sky'	EMic IBal MBri NGdn
'Praying Hands' (v)	EGol EMic EPfP GBin GKev IBal IBoy IFoB IPot LBMP LRHS LSou MBNS NMyG NSue SMrm SPoG WWEG
'Prestige and Promise' (v)	IBal
'Pretty Flamingo'	EMic IBal
'Prima Donna'	EMic
'Prince of Wales'	EMic IBal LRHS LSqu NNor SPoG SRkn
'Princess Anastasia' (v)	IBal
'Proud Sentry'	EMic NSue
'Puck'	EGol
'Punky' (v)	EMic IBal
'Purple Boots'	EMic IBal
'Purple Dwarf'	EGol EMic IBal NLar WCru WHal WWEG
'Purple Glory'	EMic
'Purple Haze'	EMic IBal LRHS NCGa NGdn NMyG NSue SHar WCot
'Purple Heart' **new**	ECtt GBin NMyG NSue
'Purple Lady Finger'	IBal WWEG
'Purple Passion'	EGol EMic IBal NSue
'Purple Profusion'	EGol EMic IBal
'Quarter Note' (v)	IBal
'Queen Josephine' (v)	EGol EMic EPfP IBal LRHS MBNS MHom NCGa NGdn SRGP
'Queen of the Seas'	EMic IBal
'Quill'	EMic NSue
'Quilting Bee'	EGol EMic IBal
'Radiant Edger' (v)	EGol EMic GCra IBal NHol WWEG
'Radio Waves'	EMic IBal
'Rain Dancer'	EMic IBal
'Rain Forest'	EMic IBal
'Rainbow's End' (v)	IBal
'Rainforest Sunrise' (v)	ELon EMic IBal LLWG LSou NGdn NSue
'Rascal' (v)	EGol EMic
'Raspberries and Cream' (v)	IBal
'Raspberry Sorbet'	EGol EMic IBal NSue
'Raspberry Sundae' (v) **new**	NMyG NSue
rectifolia	NNor
'Red Cadet'	EMic IBal
'Red Dog'	EMic
'Red Dragon'	IBal
'Red Hot Flash' (v)	EMic IBal
'Red Hot Poker'	IBal
'Red Neck Heaven' (*kikutii* var. *caput-avis*)	IBal
'Red October'	EBee ECtt EMic EPfP EUJe GAbr IBal IBoy LBMP LEdu LRHS LSou MBNS MHol MPie NGdn NLar NPnk NSue WCot WWEG
'Red Salamander'	EGol EMic IBal
'Red Sox'	IBal
'Red Stepper'	EMic
'Red Tubes' (*venusta*)	IBal
'Red Wing' (v)	IBal
'Regal Chameleon'	IBal
'Regal Rhubarb'	EGol EMic IBal
'Regal Splendor' (v)	EGol ELon EMic IBal LRHS MHom NBro NCGa NGdn NMyG NNor WHoo WMnd
'Regal Supreme' (v)	EMic
'Reginald Kaye'	EMic
'Rembrandt Blue' **new**	EMic IBal
'Remember Me'[PBR]	CWCL ELan ELon GBin IBal LRHS LSRN MBNS MBri MPnt NGdn NHol NLar NMyG NNor NSue NWad WGor WWEG
'Reptilian'	EGol EMic IBal
'Resonance' (v)	NGdn NLar

'Restless Sea'	EMic
'Reversed' (*sieboldiana*) (v)	EGol EMic IBal LRHS NBro NGdn NNor NSue WHal
'Revolution'PBR (v)	EGol EMic GKev IBal LRHS LSRN NBro NEgg NGdn NLar NMyG NSue SPoG WWEG
'Rhapsody' (*fortunei*) (v)	EGol EMic
'Rhapsody in Blue'	EGol IBal
'Rhein' (*tardiana*)	IBal
'Rheingold' (v)	IBal
'Rhinestone Cowboy' (v)	IBal
'Rhythm and Blues'	IBal
'Rich Uncle'	IBal
'Richland Gold' (*fortunei*)	EGol EMic
'Rickrack'	IBal
'Rim Rock'	EMic
'Ringtail'	EMic IBal
'Rippled Honey'	COIW EGol EMic IBal NMyG NPro
'Rippling Waves'	EGol EMic
'Riptide'	NGdn
'Risa'	IBal
'Rising Sun'	EGol
'Risky Business'PBR (v)	EBee EMic IBal NSue SMrm
'Robert Frost' (v)	EGol EMic IBal
'Robin Hood'	EMic IBal
'Robin of Loxley'	EMic
'Robusta' (*fortunei*)	see *H. sieboldiana* var. *elegans*
'Robyn's Choice' (v)	GKev IBal
'Rock and Roll' **new**	EMic
'Rock Island Line' (v)	EMic IBal NSue
'Rock Princess'	IBal
§ ***rohdeifolia*** (v)	LRHS
'Roller Coaster Ride'	IBal NSue
'Ron Damant'	IBal
'Rootin'-Tootin'' (v)	IBal
'Roseann Walter' (v) **new**	EMic
'Rosedale Golden Goose'	EMic IBal
'Rosedale Knox'	IBal
'Rosedale Lost Dutchman'	IBal
'Rosedale Melody of Summer' (v)	IBal
'Rosedale Misty Magic' (v)	IBal
'Rosedale Richie Valens'	IBal
'Rosedale Spoons'	IBal
'Rosemoor'	EGol IBal
'Rotunda'	EGol
'Roxsanne'	EMic
'Roy Klehm' (v)	EMic IBal
'Royal Charm'	IBal
'Royal Flush' (v)	IBal
'Royal Golden Jubilee'	EMic IBal NCGa
'Royal Mouse Ears' **new**	IBal
§ 'Royal Standard' ♀H4	Widely available
'Royal Tapestry' (v)	IBal
'Royal Tiara' (*nakaiana*) (v)	EGol IBal
'Royalty'	EGol IBal
rupifraga	EGol IBal
'Rusty Bee'	IBal
'Ryan's Big One'	IBal
§ 'Sagae' (v) ♀H3-4	EGol EMic IBal IPot LRHS MBri MHom MNrw NGdn NNor NPnk SDix WHoo WWEG
'Saint Elmo's Fire' (v)	EGol EMic IBal LRHS
'Saint Paul'	EMic IBal MNrw NSue
'Saishu-jima' (*sieboldii* f. *spathulata*)	EMic WCru
'Saishu-yahite-site' (v)	EGol
'Salute' (Tardiana Group)	EGol EMic
'Samual Blue'	EGol
'Samurai' (*sieboldiana*) (v)	EGol EMic IBal MRav NBir NBro NGdn NLar NNor NSue
'Sandhill Crane' (v)	IBal
'Sarah Kennedy' (v)	IBal
'Sara's Sensation' (v)	IBal
'Satisfaction' (v)	EMic
'Savannah'	EGol IBal
'Sazanami' (*crispula*)	see *H. crispula*
'Scallion Pancakes'	EMic
'Schwan'	GBin
'Scooter' (v)	EGol IBal
'Sea Beacon' (v)	EGol
'Sea Bunny'	EGol
'Sea Dream' (v)	EGol EMic LRHS NEgg NGdn NNor
'Sea Drift'	EGol
'Sea Fire'	EGol NGdn
'Sea Frolic'	EGol IBal
'Sea Gold Star'	EGol
'Sea Gulf Stream'	EMic
'Sea Hero'	EGol
'Sea Lotus Leaf'	EGol EMic LLWP NLar NNor
'Sea Monster'	EGol IBal
'Sea Octopus'	EGol
'Sea Sapphire'	EGol IBal
'Sea Thunder' (v)	EGol EMic IBal NGdn
'Sea Yellow Sunrise'	EGol EMic IBal
'Second Wind' (*fortunei*) (v)	EGol EMic NMyG
'Secret Ambition'PBR (v)	EMic IBal
'Secret Love'	EMic IBal
'Seducer' (v)	EMic IBal
'See Saw' (*undulata*)	EGol EMic
'September Sun' (v)	EGol EMic IBal LRHS NNor
'Serena' (Tardiana Group)	IBal
'Serendipity'	EGol EMic GAbr IBal MHom
'Shade Beauty' (v)	EGol IBal
'Shade Fanfare' (v) ♀H4	ECtt EGol EHoe ELan EMic EPfP IBal LAst LPla LRHS MBNS MRav MWhi NBir NGdn NLar NSti SPer WMnd WWEG
'Shade Finale' (v)	IBal
'Shade Master'	EGol EMic IBal
'Shade Parade' (v)	EMic IBal
§ 'Sharmon' (*fortunei*) (v)	EGol ELon EMic IBal MBNS NEgg NLar
'Sharp Dressed Man'	EMic IBal NGdn
'Shazaam'	EMic
'Sheila West'	EMic IBal
'Shelleys' (v)	EGol IBal
'Sherborne Profusion' (Tardiana Group)	EMic IBal
'Sherborne Songbird' (Tardiana Group)	EGol IBal
'Sherborne Swallow' (Tardiana Group)	IBal
'Sherborne Swan' (Tardiana Group)	EGol IBal
'Sherborne Swift' (Tardiana Group)	EGol EMic IBal LRHS
'Shere Khan' (v)	EGol
'Shimmy Shake'	EMic
'Shining Tot'	EGol LLHF
'Shiny Penny' (v)	EGol EMic IBal NSue WWEG
'Shirley Levy' **new**	IBal
'Shirley Vaughn' (v)	EGol IBal
'Shogun' (v)	EGol IBal
'Showboat' (v)	EGol EMic IBal LRHS
sieboldiana	CMac CSBt EGol ELan EMic GCra GMaP LBMP LLWP LPio LRHS MRav

		MSwo NChi SPlb SRms WMoo WWEG XLum
§	– var. ***elegans*** ♀H4	Widely available
	– var. ***mira***	EMic
	– var. ***sieboldiana***	NGdn
	sieboldiana* × *venusta	NGdn
	sieboldii	GBin MRav
§	– var. ***alba***	EGol IBal
§	– var. ***sieboldii*** f. ***kabitan*** (v)	EGol EMic IBal NGdn NHar WWEG
	– – f. ***shiro-kabitan*** (v)	EGol EMic LRHS
	– f. ***spathulata***	EMic
	'Silberpfeil'	EMic IBal NSue
	'Silk Kimono' (v)	EGol
	'Silver Bay'	EMic IBal
	'Silver Bowl'	EGol
	'Silver Crown'	see *H.* 'Albomarginata'
	'Silver Heart' (v)	IBal
	'Silver Lance' (v)	EGol EMic IBal
	'Silver Lining'	IBal
	'Silver Lode' (v)	IBal
	'Silver Moon'	EMic
	'Silver Shadow' (v)	CHid EMic GBin IBal NBir NGdn NHol NNor NWad
	'Silver Spray' (v)	EGol IBal
	'Silver Star' (v)	IBal
	'Silver Threads and Gold Needles' (v)	IBal NSue
	'Silverado' (v)	IBal
	'Silvery Slugproof' (Tardiana Group)	LRHS WWEG
	'Singin' the Blues'	IBal
	'Singing in the Rain' (v)	IBal
	'Sitting Pretty' (v)	EGol
	'Sky Dancer'	EMic IBal MBri
	'Sleeping Beauty'	CWGN EMic IBal NGdn NMyG NSue
	'Slick Willie'	EGol EMic
	'Slim and Trim'	EGol EMic IBal NSue
	'Small Parts'	EGol EMic IBal NSue
	'Small Sum'	IBal
	'Smooth Sailing' (v)	IBal
	'Snow Cap' (v)	EGol EMic IBal NGdn NLar NNor NPro WWEG
	'Snow Crust' (v)	EGol EMic
	'Snow Flakes' (*sieboldii*)	CMac EGol NBro NGdn NLar NPro WWEG
	'Snow Mound'	IBal
	'Snow Mouse' (v)	EGol EMic IBal MAsh NMyG NSue
	'Snow White' (*undulata*) (v)	EGol IBal
	'Snowbound' (v)	IBal
	'Snowden'	CPrp EGol EMic GMaP IBal LRHS MWat NBir NGdn NHol NNor SSpi WCru WWEG
	'Snowy Lake' (v)	IBal
	'So Sweet' (v)	COIW EBee ECtt EGol EHoe ELan EMic EPfP GBin LRHS MHom MSwo NBro NGdn NHol NMyG NNor SPad SPoG WWEG
	'Solar Flare'	EGol EMic
	'Something Blue'	EMic
	'Something Different' (*fortunei*) (v)	EGol IBal
	'Something Else'	EMic
	'Sophistication' (v)	EGol
	'Southern Gold'	EMic
	'Sparkling Burgundy'	EGol EMic NSue
	'Sparky' (v)	EGol IBal
	'Spartacus' (v)	EMic IBal
	'Spartan Arrow' **new**	NSue

	'Spartan Glory' (v)	IBal
	'Special Gift'	EGol EMic WWEG
	'Spellbound' (v)	IBal
	'Spilt Milk' (*tokudama*) (v)	EBee EGol EMic IBal LRHS SPoG WHoo
§	'Spinners' (*fortunei*) (v)	EGol EMic LRHS NNor
	'Spinning Wheel' (v)	EGol
	'Spock's Ears'	IBal
	'Spring Break' (v)	EMic
	'Spring Fling'	EMic IBal
	'Spritzer' (v)	EGol EMic IBal MNrw NSue
	'Squash Casserole'	EGol
	'Squiggles' (v)	EGol
	'Stained Glass'	CBcs ECtt EGol ELon EMic EPfP IBal MBri NGdn NMyG NNor NSue WRHF
	'Stand by Me' (v) **new**	EMic NSue
	'Star Kissed'	IBal
	'Starburst' stable (v)	IBal
	'Stardust'	IBal
	'Stargate'	IBal
§	'Starker Yellow Leaf'	EMic
	'Starship' (v)	EMic IBal
	'Steffi' (v) **new**	IBal
	'Step Sister'	EMic IBal
	'Stepping Out' (v)	EMic IBal
	'Stetson' (v)	EMic IBal
	'Stiletto' (v)	CCon CHel EGol EHoe ELon EMic EShb GAbr GCra GKev IBal LBMP LRHS MBNS MBel MHom MNrw NBro NGdn NLar NMyG NNor NPro NSue SPoG SWvt WPtf WWEG
	'Stimulation'	IBal
	'Stirfry'	EMic
	'Stitch in Time' (v)	IBal
	'Stonewall'	IBal
	'Strawberry Surprise' (v) **new**	EMic
	'Striker' (v)	EGol IBal NSue
	'Striptease' (*fortunei*) (v)	CMac EGol EMic IBal LPio LRHS MBNS MBri MNrw NGdn NHol NLar NPnk NSue WWEG
	'Sugar and Cream' (v)	EGol EMic IBal LRHS NGdn NNor
	'Sugar and Spice' (v)	EMic IBal
	'Sugar Daddy'	EMic
	'Sultana' (v)	EMic WWEG
	'Sum and Substance' ♀H4	Widely available
	'Sum and Subtle' (v)	EMic IBal
	'Sum Cup-o-Joe' (v)	EMic
	'Sum it Up' (v)	EMic
	'Sum of All' (v)	NSue
	'Summer Breeze' (v)	EGol EMic IBal NGdn NSue
	'Summer Fragrance'	EBee ECtt EGol EMic GBin LRHS
	'Summer in Georgia'	IBal
	'Summer Lovin'' (v)	IBal
	'Summer Music' (v)	CWCL EGol EMic IBal WWEG
	'Summer Serenade' (v)	EGol EMic IBal NGdn
	'Summer Squall' **new**	IBal
	'Sun Catcher'	EMic
	'Sun Glow'	EGol
	'Sun Power'	EBee EGol EMic EPfP LRHS MBNS NBro NGdn NLar NMyG NSti SMrm
	'Sun Worshipper'	IBal
	'Sundance' (*fortunei*) (v)	EGol
	'Sunlight Child'	EGol IBal
	'Sunny Smiles' (v)	EMic
	'Sunshine Glory'	EGol EMic IBal
	'Super Bowl'	EGol
	'Super Nova' (v)	EGol EMic IBal SPoG

'Super Sagae'	EMic IBal
'Surprised by Joy' (v)	EGol EMic IBal NNor NSue WWEG
'Susy'	IBal
'Sutter's Mill'	IBal
'Suzuki Thumbnail'	EMic
'Swamp Thing' (v) **new**	IBal
'Sweet Bo Beep'	EGol IBal LRHS
'Sweet Bouquet'	EMic
'Sweet Home Chicago' (v)	EGol EMic IBal NSue
'Sweet Innocence' (v)	EMic IBal
'Sweet Marjorie'	EGol
'Sweet Sunshine'	EGol EMic
'Sweet Susan'	EGol EMic LPla LRHS LSRN MBNS SPer SWvt
'Sweet Tater Pie'	EGol EMic
'Sweetheart'	EMic
'Sweetie' (v)	EMic IBal LRHS NSue WWEG
'Sweetness'	IBal
'Swirling Hearts'	EGol IBal
'Swizzle Sticks'	IBal
'T. Rex'	EBee EMic IBal NSue
'Tall Boy'	EGol GBin IBal NBir NNor
'Tamborine' (v)	EGol IBal LRHS
'Tango'	EMic IBal NSue
'Tappen Zee' (v)	EMic IBal
Tardiana Group	EGol MHom NGdn
tardiflora	CExl CFil EGol IBal WCot WPGP
tardiva	LRHS
'Tattle Tails' **new**	EMic
'Tattoo'^{PBR} (v)	CWGN EGol EMic LSRN MBNS MNrw NLar WWEG
'Tea and Crumpets' (v)	IBal
'Tea at Betty's'	IBal
'Tears of Joy' **new**	NSue
'Teaspoon'	EMic IBal NNor NSue
'Teatime' (v)	EMic IBal
'Teeny-weeny Bikini' (v)	EMic IBal NSue
'Templar Gold'	IBal
'Temple Bells'	EGol
'Temptation'	EMic IBal
'Tenryu'	EGol
'Tequila Sunrise'	IBal
'Terpsichore'	EMic
'Terracotta'	MCri
'Terry Wogan'	IBal NNor
'Tet a Poo'	IBal
'The King' (v)	IBal
'The Leading Edge' (v)	IBal
'The Queen' (v)	IBal
'The Razor's Edge'	IBal
'The Right One' (v)	IBal
'The Shining'	IBal
'The Twister'	EGol IBal
'Theo's Blue'	EMic IBal
'Thomas Hogg'	see *H. undulata* var. *albomarginata*
'Thumb Nail'	EGol EMic IBal NNor
'Thumbelina'	EGol EMic IBal NGdn
'Thunderbolt'^{PBR} (*sieboldiana*)	EGol EMic IBal MBNS NGdn NLar SMrm
'Tick Tock' (v)	EMic IBal NSue
'Tickle Me Pink'	EMic IBal
'Tidewater'	IBal
'Time Tunnel' (*sieboldiana*) (v)	EMic IBal
'Timeless Beauty' (v) **new**	LLWG
'Tiny Tears'	EGol GAbr IFoB
'Titanic'^{PBR}	EMic IBal
tokudama	EGol EMic IBal MHom NBir NGdn NHol NNor NSti XLum
§ - f. ***aureo-nebulosa*** (v)	EGol EMic IBal NGdn NSti SRms WMnd
'Tokudama Blue'	IBoy
tokudama f. ***flavocircinalis*** (v)	CPrp EGol EMic EPfP GMaP IBal NBro WHoo WMnd
'Toledo'	IBal
'Tom Schmid' (v)	EGol EMic IBal NMyG NSue
'Tom Thumb'	EGol EMic IBal
'Topaz'	IBal
'Topscore'	NNor
'Torchlight' (v)	EGol EMic IBal LRHS MHom NSue
tortifrons	EMic IBal
'Tortilla Chip'	IBal NSue
'Tot Tot'	EGol EMic IBal NSue
'Touch of Class'^{PBR} (v)	ECtt EMic GBin IBal LRHS NGdn NHol NMyG NNor NSue WWEG
'Touchstone' (v)	IBal SWvt WWEG
'Toy Soldier'	EMic IBal NGdn NSue
'Tranquility' (v)	EMic
'Tremors'	EMic IBal
'Trill'	IBal
'Trixi' (v)	IBal
'Tropical Dancer'	EMic IBal
'True Blue'	EBee EGol EMic IBal WWEG
'Tsugaru Komachi'	EMic
'Tsugaru Komachi Kifukurin' (v)	IBal
tsushimensis	LRHS
'Turnabout' (v) **new**	IBal
'Turning Point'	EGol IBal
'Tutu'	EGol
'Twiggie'	EMic
'Twilight' (*fortunei*) (v)	ECtt EGol EMic EShb IBal LRHS MBNS MBri NGdn NLar SWvt WRHF WWEG
'Twilight Time'	IBal LRHS
'Twinkle Toes'	EGol EMic IBal
'Twist of Lime' (v)	EGol EMic GKev IBal LRHS NGdn NNor NSue WWEG
'UFO'	EMic IBal NSue
'Ultramarine'	IBal
'Ultraviolet Light'	EGol IBal
'Ulysses S. Grant' **new**	IBal
'Unchained Melody'	IBal
undulata	NNor
§ - var. ***albomarginata***	CBcs CMac CSam EGol ELan EMic EPfP GMaP IBoy LRHS LSRN MRav MWat NBid NBir NGdn NLar SPer SRms SWvt WMnd WPtf WWEG XLum
§ - var. ***erromena*** ♀^{H4}	EMic GMaP NNor WHrl XLum
§ - var. ***undulata*** (v) ♀^{H4}	EBee ELan EPfP GMaP IBal LPot LRHS MCot MRav MSwo NEgg NGdn NLar NNor SPer WWEG
- var. ***univittata*** (v) ♀^{H4}	EGol EMic GKev LAst MHom MWhi NBir NPro WMoo
'Unforgettable'	EMic IBal
'Upper Crust' (v)	IBal
'Urajiro' (*hypoleuca*)	EGol IBal
'Urajiro-hachijo' (*longipes* var. *latifolia*)	EGol IBal
'Valentine Lace'	EGol EMic GKev IBal
'Valley's Cathedral'	IBal
'Valley's Chute the Chute'	EMic IBal
'Valley's Glacier' (v)	EMic IBal NSue
'Valley's Vanilla Sticks'	EMic IBal
'Van Wade' (v)	EGol EMic IBal
'Vanilla Cream' (*cathayana*)	EGol EMic IBal
'Variegata' (*gracillima*)	see *H.* 'Vera Verde'

	'Variegata' (*tokudama*)	see *H. tokudama* f. *aureo-nebulosa*
	'Variegata' (*undulata*)	see *H. undulata* var. *undulata*
	'Variegata' (*ventricosa*)	see *H.* 'Aureomarginata' (*ventricosa*)
	'Variegated' (*fluctuans*)	see *H.* 'Sagae'
	'Velvet Moon' (v)	EMic IBal
	ventricosa ♀H4	CBcs CMac EGol EMic GMaP IBal MWhi NGdn XLum
	- BWJ 8160 from Sichuan	WCru
	- var. ***aureomaculata***	EGol EMic LRHS NBir NNor NSti
I	'Venucosa'	EGol
	'Venus' (d)	CAby ECtt EMic IBal LRHS MHol NGdn SMrs WCot
	'Venus Star'	EGol EMic IBal
	venusta ♀H4	CCon EBee ECho EGol EMic GCra IBal LRHS MHer MRav NBid NBir NNor NRya NSti SRot WWEG
	- B&SWJ 4389	WCru
	- ***yakusimensis***	see *H. kikutii* var. *yakusimensis*
§	'Vera Verde' (v)	GCra GQui LRHS NBir NSue
	'Verdi Valentine'	IBal
	'Verkade's No 1'	IBal
	'Verna Jean' (v)	EGol EMic IBal
	'Veronica Lake' (v)	EGol EMic IBal LRHS NNor NSue WHal
	'Victory'	EMic IBal
	'Viking Ship'	EMic
	'Vilmoriniana'	EGol EMic IBal
	'Vim and Vigor'	EMic IBal
	'Vina'	IBal
	'Viridis Marginata'	see *H. sieboldii* var. *sieboldii* f. *kabitan*
	'Vulcan' (v)	EMic IBal
	'Wagtail' (Tardiana Group)	EGol EMic IBal
	'Wahoo' (*tokudama*) (v)	EGol IBal
	'War Paint'	EMic IBal NSue
	'Warwick Ballerina'	EGol IBal
	'Warwick Comet' (v)	IBal
	'Warwick Curtsey' (v)	EGol EMic IBal
	'Warwick Delight' (v)	EGol IBal
	'Warwick Edge' (v)	EGol EMic IBal
	'Warwick Essence'	EGol EMic IBal
	'Warwick Sheen'	IBal
	'Waukon Glass'	EMic IBal
	'Waukon Thin Ice'	EMic IBal
	'Waukon Water'	EMic IBal
	'Waving Winds' (v)	EGol IBal LRHS NSue
	'Waving Wuffles'	EMic IBal
	'Wayside Blue'	EMic
	'Wayside Perfection'	see *H.* 'Royal Standard'
	'Weihenstephan' (*sieboldii*)	EGol EMic IBal
	'Well Shaked' (v)	IBal
	'Weser'	EGol
	'Wheaton Blue'	EMic LRHS
	'Whirligig' (v)	EMic
	'Whirling Dervish' (v)	IBal
	'Whirlwind' (*fortunei*) (v)	EBee EGol EMic GBin GQue IBal LBMP LRHS MBri MNrw MRav NBro NEgg NGdn NMyG NNor NOrc NSue SMrm SPad WBor WMnd WWEG
	'Whirlwind Tour' (v)	EGol IBal
	'Whiskey Sour'	IBal
	'White Bikini' (v)	IBal NSue
	'White Ceiling'	IBal
	'White Christmas' (*fortunei*) (v)	NGdn
	'White Christmas' (*undulata*) (v)	EGol EMic
	'White Dove' (v)	EMic IBal
	'White Edger'	EMic
	'White Elephant' (v) **new**	IBal
	'White Fairy' (*plantaginea*) (d)	EMic
	'White Feather' (*undulata*)	CHid CWGN EBee ELon EPfP LRHS MNrw NBir NGdn NLar NMyG NNor SMad
	'White Gold'	EGol IBal
	'White Knight'	IBal
	'White On' (*montana*)	EMic
	'White Ray'	IBal
	'White Triumphator' (*rectifolia*)	EGol EMic GBin IBal
	'White Trumpets'	EMic
	'White Vision'	EGol IBal
	'Wide Brim' (v) ♀H4	Widely available
	'Wiggle Worms' (v)	IBal
	'William Lachman' (v)	NLar
	'Wily Willy'	IBal
	'Wind River Gold'	EGol EMic IBal
	'Windsor Gold'	see *H.* 'Nancy Lindsay'
	'Winfield Blue'	EGol EMic IBal
	'Winfield Gold'	EGol EMic IBal
	'Winfield Mist' (v)	IBal
	'Winsome' (v)	EGol IBal
	'Winter Lightning' (v)	NNor
	'Winter Snow' (v)	EMic IBal NGdn NSue
	'Winter Vision' (v)	IBal
	'Winter Warrior' (v)	EMic IBal
	'Wintergreen' (v)	IBal
	'Wogon' (*sieboldii*)	EMic GKev GMaP ITim NSti
	'Wogon's Boy'	EGol EMic LRHS WWEG
	'Wolverine' (v)	EBee ECtt EGol EHoe EMic GAbr LRHS LSou MHom NGdn NLBP NSue SWvt WCot WWEG
	'Woodland Elf' (v) **new**	IBal
	'Woolly Mammoth' (v)	IBal
	'Woop Woop' (v)	EMic IBal
	'World Cup'	IBal
	'Worldly Treasure'	IBal
	'Wrinkles and Crinkles'	EMic
	'Wylde Green Cream'	EGol EMic IBal NGdn
	'Xanadu' (v)	IBal
	'X-rated' (v)	IBal
	'Yakushima-mizu' (*gracillima*)	EMic IBal NMyG
*	***yakushimana***	NHar
	'Yellow Boa'	EGol EMic IBal NSue
	'Yellow Edge' (*fortunei*)	see *H. fortunei* var. *aureomarginata*
	'Yellow Edge' (*sieboldiana*)	see *H.* 'Frances Williams'
	'Yellow Polka Dot Bikini' (v) **new**	NSue
	'Yellow River' (v)	EGol EMic IBal LRHS NGdn NMyG NNor NSue
	'Yellow Splash' (v)	EMic LRHS MHom NNor
	'Yellow Splash Rim' (v)	EGol EMic NCGa
	'Yellow Splashed Edged' (v)	EMic
	'Yellow Submarine'	IBal
	'Yesterday's Memories' (v)	EMic
	'Yin' (v)	EMic IBal
	yingeri	EGol WPGP WSHC
	- B&SWJ 546	WCru
	'Yucca Ducka Do' (v)	IBal
	'Zager Blue'	EMic
	'Zager Green'	EMic
	'Zager White Edge' (*fortunei*) (v)	EGol EMic IBal
	'Zebra Stripes' (v)	IBal

	'Zion's Hope' **new**	EMic
	'Zitronenfalter'	EGol IBal
	'Zodiac' (*fortunei*) (v)	IBal
	'Zounds'	EBee ECtt EGol EMic EPfP EShb IBal LRHS MRav NGdn NLar NSti SRms WWEG

Hottonia (*Primulaceae*)

	palustris	CBAq EHon MSKA MWts NPer SWat

Houstonia (*Rubiaceae*)

	caerulea misapplied	see *H. michauxii*
	caerulea L.	ECho
	- var. ***alba***	SPlb
§	***michauxii***	GAbr
	- 'Fred Mullard'	EWes

Houttuynia (*Saururaceae*)

	cordata	CBAq GKev GPoy LPot SDix SWat WWEG XLum
§	- 'Boo-Boo' (v)	CMac EPfP NBro SMrm WWEG
§	- 'Chameleon' (v)	Widely available
	- 'Fantasy'	EBee LLWG
	- 'Flame' (v)	CHel CMac EBee LBMP LRHS MBri SHil SMrm WWEG
	- 'Flore Pleno' (d)	CBAq CMac CRow CWat EHon ELan EPfP MRav MSCN NBir NPer SPer SPlb SRms SWat WHrl WPnP XLum
	- 'Joker's Gold'	CHel CMac EBee ECtt EPPr EPfP SMrm SPoG
	- 'Pied Piper'	CDoC NBir SGol SPad
	- 'Tequila Sunrise'	CHEx
	- 'Terry Clarke'	see *H. cordata* 'Boo-Boo'
	- 'Tricolor'	see *H. cordata* 'Chameleon'
	- Variegata Group (v)	CBAq NBro

Hovea (*Papilionaceae*)

	celsii	see *H. elliptica*
§	***elliptica***	SPlb
	montana	SPlb

Hovenia (*Rhamnaceae*)

	dulcis	CAgr CBcs EPfP LEdu NLar
	- B&SWJ 11024	WCru

Howea (*Arecaceae*)

§	***belmoreana*** ♀H1	XBlo
§	***forsteriana*** ♀H1	CCCN NPla XBlo

Hoya (*Apocynaceae*)

§	***australis***	CBcs MOWG
	bella	see *H. lanceolata* subsp. *bella*
	carnosa ♀H1	CBcs EBak EOHP WCot WWFP
	- 'Compacta Regalis' (v)	NPer
	- 'Krinkle 8'	NPer
	- 'Tricolor' (v)	NPer
*	***compacta*** 'Tricolor'	NPer
	darwinii misapplied	see *H. australis*
	lacunosa	CCCN
§	***lanceolata***	CBcs
	subsp. ***bella*** ♀H1	

huckleberry, garden see *Solanum scabrum*

Hugueninia (*Brassicaceae*)

	alpina	see *H. tanacetifolia*
§	***tanacetifolia***	WOut

Humata (*Davalliaceae*)

	tyermannii	CMen EShb ISha WFib

Humea see *Calomeria*

	elegans	see *Calomeria amaranthoides*

Humulus ✿ (*Cannabaceae*)

	lupulus	CArn CBcs EPfP GPoy NLar NMir SIde WHer
	- 'Aureus' ♀H4	Widely available
	- 'Aureus' (f)	CRHN ELon GCal GKev SPoG WBor WCot WWFP
*	- ***compactus***	GPoy
	- 'Fuggle'	CAgr GPoy SDea
	- 'Golden Tassels' (f)	CSPN EBee ECrN ELon LHop LRHS MBri MCoo MGos MJak NLar NPri SEND SPer SPoG
	- (Goldings Group) 'Cobbs'	SDea
	- - 'Mathons'	CAgr SDea
	- 'Hallertauer'	SDea
	- 'Prima Donna'	CAgr LHop MCoo NLar SCoo SPer SPoG SWvt
	- 'Taff's Variegated' (v)	EWes MAvo WSHC
	- 'Wye Challenger'	CAgr GPoy MHer
	- 'Wye Northdown'	CAgr SDea

Hunnemannia (*Papaveraceae*)

	fumariifolia	CSpe WHil XSen

Huodendron (*Styracaceae*)

	biaristatum	WPGP
	tibeticum	CFil WPGP

Hutchinsia see *Pritzelago*

Hyacinthella (*Asparagaceae*)

	acutiloba	ECho
	dalmatica	ECho
	glabrescens	WCot
	heldreichii	ECho WCot
	lazulina	LWst
	leucophaea	ECho
	lineata	WCot
	millingenii	ECho WCot
	pallens	ECho

Hyacinthoides (*Asparagaceae*)

	aristidis	ECho WCot
§	***hispanica***	ECho LPio NBir SEND
	- 'Alba'	ECho
	- subsp. ***algeriensis***	WCot
	- 'Dainty Maid'	ECho WCot
	- 'Excelsior'	ECho
	- 'Miss World'	ECho WCot
	- 'Mount Everest'	ECho
	- 'Queen of the Pinks'	ECho WCot
	- 'Rosea'	ECho
	- 'White City'	ECho WCot
§	***italica*** ♀H4	CPom ECho WShi
	mauritanica	ECho
§	***non-scripta***	CAvo CBro CHab CTca CTri ECho EPot GKev LPot LRHS MCot MHer MMuc NBir NPri SDeJ SEND SPer SRms SVic WHer WShi XLum
	- 'Alba'	ECho MMuc NBir SEND
	- 'Backkum's Blue'	NMin
	- 'Bracteata'	CNat
	- cleistogamous	CNat

	- 'Rosea'	ECho
§	***vincentina***	WCot

Hyacinthus ✿ (*Asparagaceae*)

	amethystinus	see *Brimeura amethystina*
	azureus	see *Muscari azureum*
	comosus 'Plumosus'	see *Muscari comosum* 'Plumosum'
	orientalis 'Aiolos'	SPer
	- 'Anastasia'	CAvo
	- 'Anna Liza'	MBri
	- 'Anna Marie' ♀H4	CBro MBri SDeJ
	- 'Blue Festival' ♀H4	SDeJ
	- 'Blue Giant'	SDeJ
	- 'Blue Jacket' ♀H4	CBro MBri SDeJ
	- 'Blue Magic'	SDeJ
	- 'Blue Pearl' PBR	SDeJ
	- 'Carnegie'	CAvo CBro EPfP ERCP MJak SPhx
	- 'Chestnut Flower' (d) **new**	SDeJ
	- 'China Pink'	SDeJ SPer
	- 'City of Haarlem' ♀H4	CAvo CBro EPfP MBri MJak SDeJ
	- 'Crystal Palace' (d)	SDeJ
	- 'Delft Blue' ♀H4	CAvo CBro EPfP MBri MJak SDeJ SPer SPhx
	- 'Fondant'	SDeJ
	- 'General Köhler' (d)	SDeJ
	- 'Gipsy Queen' ♀H4	EPfP MBri SDeJ WCot
	- 'Hollyhock' (d) ♀H4	ERCP SDeJ
	- 'Jan Bos' ♀H4	LPio MBri SDeJ SPer
	- 'Kronos'	CAvo
	- 'Lady Derby'	SDeJ
	- 'L'Innocence' ♀H4	CAvo CBro
	- 'Miss Saigon' ♀H4	ERCP
	- multi-flowered	ERCP SDeJ
	- 'Odysseus'	SDeJ
	- 'Ostara' ♀H4	MBri
	- 'Paul Hermann' ♀H4	SDeJ
	- 'Peter Stuyvesant'	EPfP ERCP SDeJ
	- 'Pink Festival' ♀H4	SDeJ
	- 'Pink Pearl' ♀H4	EPfP MBri SDeJ
	- 'Purple Sensation' PBR	CAvo SPhx
	- 'Red Magic'	SDeJ
	- 'Rosette' (d)	SDeJ
	- 'Splendid Cornelia'	CAvo ERCP SDeJ
	- 'White Festival' ♀H4	CAvo SDeJ
	- 'White Pearl'	MBri SDeJ
	- 'Woodstock'	CAvo CBro EPfP ERCP SDeJ SPer

Hydrangea ✿ (*Hydrangeaceae*)

	angustipetala	see *H. scandens* subsp. *chinensis* f. *angustipetala*
	anomala subsp. ***anomala*** BWJ 8052 from China	WCru
	- - HWJK 2065 from Nepal	WCru
§	- - 'Winter Glow'	ESwi MTPN WCot WCru
	- subsp. ***glabra*** B&SWJ 6804	WCru
	- - 'Crûg Coral'	WCru
§	- subsp. ***petiolaris*** ♀H4	Widely available
	- - B&SWJ 5457	WCru
	- - B&SWJ 5996 from Yakushima	WCru
	- - from Yakushima	CFil
§	- - var. ***cordifolia***	NBro NLar
	- - - B&SWJ 6081 from Yakushima	WCru
	- - - B&SWJ 11487	WCru
§	- - - 'Brookside Littleleaf'	EBee GKin IDee MBri NBro NLar
	- - dwarf	see *H. anomala* subsp. *petiolaris* var. *cordifolia*
	- - 'Firefly' (v)	WPat
*	- - var. ***minor*** B&SWJ 5991	WCru
	- - 'Mirranda'	CBcs CRHN EBee EPfP ESwi NBro SGol SPoG SWvt WBor
*	- - var. ***tiliifolia***	EBee ESwi EWTr LRHS WSHC
	- - - B&SWJ 4400	WCru
	- - - B&SWJ 8497	WCru
*	- subsp. ***quelpartensis***	CMil CRHN GQui
	- - B&SWJ 8799	WCru
	- - B&SWJ 8846	WCru
	- Semiola = 'Inovalaur' PBR	EBee ESwi LLHF LRHS SGol SKHP SLim WPGP
	- 'Winter Surprise'	see *H. anomala* subsp. *anomala* 'Winter Glow'
§	***arborescens***	CArn CExl MRav WPGP
	- 'Annabelle' ♀H4	Widely available
	- 'Bounty'	MAsh WPat
§	- subsp. ***discolor***	LEdu WPat
	- - 'Sterilis'	CFil GBin GGGa SHyH WPGP
	- -	WPat
	- Endless Summer Bella Anna = 'Piiha-I' (Endless Summer Series) **new**	LBuc MBri NSoo
	- 'Grandiflora' ♀H4	CBcs ELan EPfP IBoy MSwo NBro NEgg WPGP
	- 'Hayes Starburst' PBR	CDoC CMil CWGN EBee GGGa LLHF LRHS SCoo SHyH SKHP SPoG SSpi WPGP WPat
	- 'Hills of Snow'	IVic NLar
	- Incrediball = 'Abetwo'	ELan EPfP LRHS LSqu MBlu SLon SPoG
§	- Invincibelle Spirit = 'Ncha1'	CDoC ELan EPfP GBin LLHF LRHS LSqu MBlu SLon SPer SPoG
	- 'Invincible Spirit'	see *H. arborescens* Invincibelle Spirit
	- 'Picadilly'	NLar
	- 'Pink Annabelle'	see *H. arborescens* Invincibelle Spirit
	- 'Pink Pincushion'	NBro NLar
	- 'Puffed Green'	NLar
	- subsp. ***radiata***	EBee LRHS MRav SPoG WCru WPGP
	- - 'Samantha'	EPfP LLHF LRHS WPGP
	- 'Ryan Gainey'	EUJe MPkF
	- 'Vasterival'	NLar
	- 'Wesser Falls'	CMil
	- White Dome = 'Dardom' PBR	NBro
	aspera	CMac CTri EUJe SHyH SLon SSpi SSta WCru WKif WPGP
	- HWJCM 452	WCru
	- from Gongshan, China	CExl CFil CMil WPGP
	- 'Anthony Bullivant'	EBee GKin IArd IDee LRHS NLar SHyH SKHP WPat
	- 'Bellevue'	IVic
	- Farrell form	CFil
	- Kawakamii Group	CExl CGHE CHEx CMil CSpe EBee ESwi EWTr LRHS NCGa NLar SGol SKHP WCru WPGP WPat
	- - B&SWJ 3456	WCru
	- - B&SWJ 3527	WCru
	- - B&SWJ 6702	WCru
	- - B&SWJ 6714	WCru
	- - B&SWJ 6827	WCru
	- - B&SWJ 6996	WCru
	- - B&SWJ 7101	WCru
	- - 'August Abundance'	WCru
	- - 'Formosa'	WCru
	- - 'Maurice Mason'	CExl CFil

	- - 'September Splendour'	WCru
	- Kawakamii Group	CFil WPGP
	× ***involucrata***	
	- 'Macrophylla' ♀H3	CFil CWib EBee EPfP EWTr GCal GKin IVic MBri MGos MRav SHil SHyH SPer WCru WPGP
	- 'Mauvette'	CMil ECre EPfP GKin LRHS MBlu NBro NLar SGol SPer SSpi WCru WGob
	- 'Peter Chappell'	CExl CMac CMil LRHS NLar WPat
	- 'Pink Cloud' **new**	CFil
§	- subsp. ***robusta***	CExl SLPl WCru WPGP
	- - GWJ 9430	WCru
	- - WWJ 11888	WCru
	- 'Rocklon'	CMil ESwi NLar WCru
	- 'Rosthornii'	see *H. aspera* subsp. *robusta*
	- 'Sam MacDonald'	CExl LRHS NLar SKHP SSpi WPGP WPat
§	- subsp. ***sargentiana*** ♀H3	Widely available
	- - 'La Fosse' **new**	WPGP
	- - large-leaved	CExl CFil WCru
	- subsp. ***strigosa***	CDul CExl EPfP EWTr LRHS SHyH SSpi WCru WPGP WPat
	- - B&SWJ 8201	WCru
	- - HWJ 653	WCru
	- - HWJ 737	WCru
	- - from Gong Shan, China	CExl EBee
	- aff. subsp. ***strigosa*** **new**	CFil
	- 'Taiwan Pink'	EPfP IArd NLar
	- 'The Ditch' **new**	ESwi
	- 'Trelissick Blue Skies' **new**	CFil
	- 'Velvet and Lace'	LRHS MBri NLar SHil
§	- Villosa Group ♀H3	Widely available
	- - 'Trelissick' **new**	CFil
	asterolasia B&SWJ 10481 **new**	WCru
	cinerea	see *H. arborescens* subsp. *discolor*
	'Dark Angel' **new**	LRHS NPri
	'Garden House Glory'	CExl CFil CGHE WPGP
	glabrifolia	see *H. scandens* subsp. *chinensis*
	glandulosa B&SWJ 4031	WCru
	'Glyn Church'	WPGP
	aff. ***gracilis*** B&SWJ 3942	WCru
§	***heteromalla***	CGHE CMHG GGGa GGal SLPl WPGP
	- B&SWJ 2142 from India	WCru
	- B&SWJ 2602 from Sikkim	WCru
	- BWJ 7657 from China	WCru
	- GWJ 9337 from Sikkim	WCru
	- HWJ 938 from Vietnam	WCru
	- HWJCM 180	WCru
	- HWJK 2127 from Nepal	WCru
	- SBEC	GGGa
	- Bretschneideri Group	EBee EPfP GKin GQui SHyH WCru WPGP
	- 'Fan Si Pan'	WCru
	- 'Nepal Beauty'	ESwi EUJe IVic SGol WPGP
	- 'Snowcap'	EPfP GQui IArd LRHS NLar SHyH SKHP SLPl SSpi WPGP
	- f. ***xanthoneura*** 'Wilsonii'	WKif
	hirta B&SWJ 5000	WCru
	- B&SWJ 11022	WCru
	indochinensis	CExl ESwi
	- B&SWJ 8307	WCru
	- B&SWJ 11717	WCru
*	- f. ***purpurascens*** KWJ 12233B	WCru
	integerrima	see *H. serratifolia*
	integrifolia B&SWJ 022	WCru
	- B&SWJ 6967	NLar WCru
	involucrata	EPfP LLHF LRHS MBri MMHG SBrt SHil SHyH
	- B&SWJ 4790	WCru
	- dwarf	CExl CFil WCru
	- 'Hortensis' (d) ♀H3-4	CMil EPfP MRav NLar SMad SSpi WCru WKif WPGP WSHC
	- 'Mihara kokonoe'	WPGP
	- 'Multiplex'	WCru
	- 'Oshima'	WPGP
	- 'Plena' (d)	EBee LRHS MRav NLar WCru WPGP
	- 'Sterilis'	CMil WCru
	- 'Tokada Yama' **new**	NLar
	- 'Viridescens'	LLHF LRHS NLar SHyH WCru WPGP
	- 'Yohraku-tama'	CFil NLar WPGP
	- 'Yokudanka' (d)	CMil GQui MAsh NLar WPGP
	kawagoeana var. ***grosseserrata*** B&SWJ 11500	WCru
	kwangsiensis B&SWJ 11717	WCru
	- WWJ 11609	WCru
	lingii B&SWJ 11790	WCru
	lobbii	see *H. scandens* subsp. *chinensis*
	longifolia B&SWJ 6883	WCru
	- CWJ 12413	WCru
	longipes	CExl CMil GQui WCru WPGP
	- var. ***fulvescens*** B&SWJ 8188	WCru
	- var. ***longipes*** **new**	CExl CFil
	luteovenosa	WCru
	- B&SWJ 5647	WCru
	- B&SWJ 5929	WCru
	- B&SWJ 6220	WCru
	- B&SWJ 6317	WCru
	macrophylla (H)	GGal
	- 'AB Green Shadow'PBR (H)	MAsh MMHG SPoG
	- 'Adria' (H)	MBri NLar SHyH
	- 'Aduarda'	see *H. macrophylla* 'Mousmée'
	- 'All Summer Beauty' (H)	CDoC ELon GGGa MAsh SHyH WGob
	- Alpen Glow	see *H. macrophylla* 'Alpenglühen'
§	- 'Alpenglühen' (H)	CBcs CExl CSBt IVic LRHS SHyH SLim
	- 'Altona' (H) ♀H3-4	CBcs EPfP GGGa IArd LRHS MAsh MGos MRav NBir NLar SHyH SPer
	- 'Ami Pasquier' (H) ♀H3-4	CBcs CDoC CMac COlW CSBt CTri CTsd EBee ELan EPfP GGal IVic LRHS LSRN MMuc MRav MSwo NEgg SBod SCoo SEND SHyH SLim SSpi SWvt
*	- 'Aureomarginata' (v)	SHyH WCot
	- 'Ave Maria' (H)	GGGa MAsh
§	- 'Ayesha' (H)	Widely available
	- 'Bachstelze' (Teller Series) (L)	IVic MAsh WPGP
	- 'Bavaria' (H)	GKin
	- 'Beauté Vendômoise' (L)	LRHS NLar SHyH SSpi WPGP
	- 'Bela'PBR (H)	LRHS
	- 'Benelux' (H)	CBcs SHyH
	- 'Bicolor'	see *H. macrophylla* 'Harlequin'
	- 'Black Steel Zambia' (H)	LBuc NPri SLon
	- 'Black Steel Zebra' (H)	NPri SLon
§	- 'Blauer Prinz' (H)	MAsh SHyH
§	- 'Bläuling' (Teller Series) (L)	CDoC EPfP GKin LSRN MBri SHyH SLim WHar

§	- 'Blaumeise' (Teller Series) (L)	CDoC CFil CMHG ELon EPfP GGGa LRHS MAsh MBri MGos MRav NEgg SCoo SHyH SLim SLon SPoG SSpi SWvt WPGP
	- 'Blue Bonnet' (H)	CDul EPfP LRHS LSRN MRav SHyH SPer
	- Blue Butterfly	see *H. macrophylla* 'Bläuling'
	- Blue Prince	see *H. macrophylla* 'Blauer Prinz'
	- Blue Sky	see *H. macrophylla* 'Blaumeise'
	- Blue Tit	see *H. macrophylla* 'Blaumeise'
	- 'Blue Wave'	see *H. macrophylla* 'Mariesii Perfecta'
	- 'Bluebird' misapplied	see *H. serrata* 'Bluebird'
	- Bluebird	see *H. macrophylla* 'Bläuling'
§	- 'Blushing Bride' PBR (H)	ELan GKin LBuc MAsh MBri NPri SLon SPoG
	- 'Bodensee' (H)	MBri MMuc SEND SHyH
	- 'Bouquet Rose' (H)	CWib ECtt MJak MMuc SEND SHyH
	- 'Brestenburg' (H)	MAsh
	- 'Brügg' (H)	EBee LRHS MAsh SHyH SLim SPer WPGP
	- 'Buchfink' (Teller Series) (L)	SHyH
	- Cardinal	see *H. macrophylla* 'Kardinal' (Teller Series)
§	- 'Cardinal Red' (H)	ECre EPfP
	- 'Cendrillon' (H)	CMil LLHF STPC WGob
	- 'Chaperon Rouge' (H)	LRHS
	- Color Fantasy (H)	EBee MBrN
	- 'Cordata'	see *H. arborescens*
	- 'Dandenong' (L)	GQui MAsh
	- 'Dart's Romance' (L)	SHyH
	- 'Dart's Song' (L)	NLar
	- 'Deutschland' (H)	CTri
	- Dolce Gipsy = 'Dolgip' (L)	EPfP LRHS
	- Dolce Kiss = 'Dolkis' (L)	CDoC EPfP LRHS
	- 'Domotoi'	see *H. macrophylla* 'Setsuka-yae'
	- Dragonfly	see *H. macrophylla* 'Libelle'
§	- 'Early Sensation' (Forever and Ever Series) (H)	CMac GKin LBuc LLHF
	- 'Eldorado' (H)	SHyH
	- Endless Summer = 'Bailmer' (H)	ELan EPfP LBuc LRHS MAsh MGos NPri SPoG
	- Endless Summer Blushing Bride	see *H. macrophylla* 'Blushing Bride'
	- Endless Summer Twist-n-Shout = 'Piihm-I' (L)	EPfP LBuc LRHS MBri
§	- 'Enziandom' (H)	CBcs CExl CFil CSBt GGal MAsh SHyH WPGP
	- 'Etoile Violette' (L)	ESwi LRHS
	- 'Europa' (H) ♀H3-4	CBcs CExl LRHS SHyH SVen
	- 'Fantasia' PBR (H)	NPnk
§	- 'Fasan' (Teller Series) (L)	MAsh SDix WHar
	- Firelight	see *H. macrophylla* 'Leuchtfeuer'
	- Fireworks	see *H. macrophylla* 'Hanabi'
	- Fireworks Blue	see *H. macrophylla* 'Jōgasaki'
	- Fireworks Pink	see *H. macrophylla* 'Jōgasaki'
	- Fireworks White	see *H. macrophylla* 'Hanabi'
	- Forever and Ever	see *H. macrophylla* 'Early Sensation'
	- 'Forever Pink' (H)	GGGa MAsh NLar
§	- 'Frau Fujiyo' (Lady Series) (H)	CExl
§	- 'Frau Katsuko' (Lady Series) (H)	SPer
§	- 'Frau Mariko' (Lady Series) (H)	MRav
§	- 'Frau Taiko' (Lady Series) (H)	SPer
	- 'Freudenstein' (H)	ESwi
	- 'Frillibet' (H)	CAbP MRav NLar SVen
	- 'Ganku Bo Chokens' (H)	WCot
	- 'Gartenbaudirektor Kühnert' (H)	SHyH
§	- 'Générale Vicomtesse de Vibraye' (H) ♀H3-4	CDoC CDul CEnd COlW CTri EBee ELon EPfP GGal LRHS MAsh SHyH SLim SPer SSpi
	- Gentian Dome	see *H. macrophylla* 'Enziandom'
	- 'Geoffrey Chadbund'	see *H. macrophylla* 'Möwe'
	- 'Gerda Steiniger' (H)	SHyH
	- 'Gertrud Glahn' (H)	SHyH
	- 'Gimpel' (Teller Series) (L)	MAsh
	- 'Glowing Embers' (H)	IArd
	- Goldrush = 'Nehyosh' (L/v)	CDul EBee LRHS NEgg SLim
	- 'Goliath' (H)	ELon EPfP
§	- 'Grant's Choice' (L)	NBro SHyH
	- Great Star = 'Blanc Bleu' (L)	EPfP LSRN MAsh SLim
	- 'Hamburg' (H)	CBcs CTri EBee ECtt EPfP MGos SDix SHyH SLim
§	- 'Hanabi' (L/d)	CBcs CDoC CEnd ECre GGal LRHS MBlu NLar SHyH
§	- 'Harlequin' (H)	GGGa WCot
	- 'Harry's Red' (H)	MAsh SHyH
	- 'Hatsu-shime' (L)	NLar
	- 'Heinrich Seidel' (H)	CBcs CTri SHyH WMoo
	- 'Hobella' PBR (Hovaria Series) (L)	CWCL
	- 'Hobergine' PBR (Hovaria Series) (H)	SHyH
	- 'Holehird Purple' (H)	MAsh
	- 'Homigo' PBR (Hovaria Series) (H)	SHyH
	- 'Izu-no-hana' (L/d)	CAbb CBcs CFil CHel CMil ELon ESwi LHop MAsh MBlu NLar SHyH WBor WPGP
	- 'James Grant'	see *H. macrophylla* 'Grant's Choice'
	- 'Joan Rose' **new**	MGos
	- 'Jofloma' (H)	ESwi NLar
§	- 'Jōgasaki' (L/d)	CBcs CExl CMil LRHS MAsh MBlu NLar SDys SHyH SVen WPGP
	- 'Joseph Banks' (H)	CBcs CTri SHyH
	- 'Kardinal'	see *H. macrophylla* 'Cardinal Red' (H)
§	- 'Kardinal' (Teller Series) (L)	MAsh SGol
	- 'King George' (H)	CBar CBcs CDoC CDul COlW CSBt EBee EPfP LRHS MGos MMuc MSCN NEgg NHol SGol SHyH SLim SPer SPoG SVen SWvt WMoo
§	- 'Klaveren' (L)	CMil GGGa MAsh NBro SHyH
	- 'Kluis Superba' (H)	CBcs CTri GGal SHyH
	- 'La France' (H)	COlW CTri IVic LRHS SHyH SLim
	- 'Lady Fujiyo'	see *H. macrophylla* 'Frau Fujiyo'
	- 'Lady in Red' (L)	CMil EPfP LRHS SPoG
	- Lady Katsuko	see *H. macrophylla* 'Frau Katsuko'
	- 'Lady Mariko'	see *H. macrophylla* 'Frau Mariko'
	- 'Lady Taiko Blue'	see *H. macrophylla* 'Frau Taiko'
	- 'Lady Taiko Pink'	see *H. macrophylla* 'Frau Taiko'
	- 'Lanarth White' (L) ♀H3-4	Widely available
	- 'Lemon Wave' (L/v)	NLar
§	- 'Leuchtfeuer' (H)	ELon LRHS MBri SHyH WMoo
§	- 'Libelle' (Teller Series) (L)	CBcs CDoC CMil EBee ELon EPfP GGGa LRHS MGos MRav NEgg NLar SGol SHyH SLim SPer SSpi SVen

	- 'Lilacina'	see *H. macrophylla* 'Mariesii Lilacina'
	- 'Love You Kiss'PBR (Hovaria Series) (L)	CBcs CMil LBuc LRHS NLar SCoo SHyH SPoG SRGP STPC
§	- 'Maculata' (L/v)	ELan GQui WGwG
	- 'Madame A. Riverain' (H)	EBee EPfP NLar SHyH
	- 'Madame Emile Mouillère' (H) ♀H3-4	Widely available
	- Magical Jade = 'Hortmaja'PBR (H)	EPfP MBlu WCot
	- 'Maréchal Foch' (H)	CTri GGal NLar SVen
	- 'Mariesii' (L)	CDoy CMHG COIW CTri EBee ELan GGal LRHS MSwo NLar SHyH SPer
§	- 'Mariesii Grandiflora' (L) ♀H3-4	EPfP GGal LRHS NBro SEND SHyH SPer SRms SVen WMoo
§	- 'Mariesii Lilacina' (L) ♀H3-4	EPfP MMuc SEND SHyH SLon SPer SSpi WMoo
§	- 'Mariesii Perfecta' (L) ♀H3-4	Widely available
	- 'Mariesii Variegata' (L/v)	CWib
	- 'Masja' (H)	CBcs EBee ELon GKin IArd IVic LAst MAsh MGos MMuc MRav MSwo NBro NLar SEND SGol SHyH SLim WBor
	- 'Mathilde Gütges' (H)	CDoC GGal
	- 'Max Löbner' (H)	SHyH
	- 'Merveille Sanguine' (H)	Widely available
	- 'Messalina' (L)	MAsh SHyH
	- 'Mirai'PBR (H)	CBcs CDoC CMil ESwi SHyH WCot WPGP
	- 'Miss Belgium' (H)	CMac CTri GKin MAsh
§	- 'Mousmée' (L)	IArd SHyH SSpi
	- 'Mousseline' (H)	CFil
§	- 'Möwe' (L) ♀H3-4	CBcs CDoC CEnd CExl CMil COIW EBee ECtt ELon EPfP GGal LHop LSRN MAsh MMuc NLar SCoo SDix SEND SGol SHyH SLim SPer SRms SSpi SSta WPat
	- 'Mrs W.J. Hepburn' (H)	CSBt SHyH SPer
§	- 'Nachtigall' (Teller Series) (L)	GGal IVic MAsh SHyH WPGP WPat
	- 'Nanping'PBR (Sturdy Series) (L)	EPfP
	- 'Niedersachsen' (H)	CDoC CTri MRav SHyH
	- Nightingale	see *H. macrophylla* 'Nachtigall'
	- 'Nigra' (H) ♀H3-4	Widely available
	- 'Nikko Blue' (H)	CBcs EBee EPfP GKin MJak MMuc NLar SHyH
	- var. ***normalis*** (L)	CExl
§	- 'Nymphe' (H)	MBri SHyH
	- 'Oregon Pride' (H)	CFil GGGa MAsh WPGP
	- 'Otaksa' (H)	NLar
	- 'Papagei' (Teller Series) (L)	SPer
	- 'Parzifal' (H) ♀H3-4	CDul SHyH
	- 'Pax'	see *H. macrophylla* 'Nymphe'
	- 'Pfau' (Teller Series) (L)	CHel CMil ELon MAsh SHyH
	- Pheasant	see *H. macrophylla* 'Fasan'
	- 'Pia' (H)	CDoC CExl CMil CPla ELan LBMP LBuc LRHS MAsh MGos MMuc MRav SHyH SMad SPer SRms WBor WCru WGrn
	- Pigeon	see *H. macrophylla* 'Taube'
	- 'Pink Wave' (L)	SVen
	- 'Pirate's Gold' (v)	CMil EHoe GGGa WHar WMoo
	- 'Prinses Beatrix' (H)	SHyH
	- 'Quadricolor' (L/v)	CExl CHII CMac CMil CTsd EHoe GCal GGal MGos MRav SDix SHyH SLim SPer SPlb SRms WCot WSHC
	- 'Queen Elizabeth' (H)	GKin
	- 'R.F. Felton' (H)	CBcs SHyH
	- 'Red Baron'	see *H. macrophylla* 'Schöne Bautznerin'
	- 'Red Red' (H)	MAsh
	- Redbreast	see *H. macrophylla* 'Rotkehlchen'
	- 'Regula' (H)	SHyH
	- 'Renate Steiniger' (H)	CDoC LRHS MBri MGos MMuc MRav SHyH SLim
	- 'Romance'	LBuc WCot
	- 'Rosea'	MCri
	- 'Rosita' (H)	MAsh MBri NBir
§	- 'Rotkehlchen' (Teller Series) (L)	CDoC EPfP NEgg NLar SLim SPlb SPoG SWvt
	- 'Rotschwanz' (Teller Series) (L)	CFil CMil EBee ESwi LLHF LRHS MAsh SHyH WPGP WPat
	- 'Sabrina'PBR (H)	CBcs CMil LLHF MBri SPoG SRkn
	- 'Saint Claire' (H)	CBcs
	- 'Salsa'	CMil LLHF MAsh MBri
	- 'Sandra' (Dutch Ladies Series) (L)	CBcs CMil ELon STPC
	- 'Schneeball' (H)	MAsh MBri SHyH
§	- 'Schöne Bautznerin'	LRHS MBri NCGa SHyH SLim WGob WMoo
	- 'Sea Foam' (L)	NLar
	- 'Selina'	CBcs CDoC EPfP LAst LBuc LLHF LSRN MBri SCoo SPoG
	- 'Selma'PBR (Dutch Ladies Series) (L)	CBcs MBri
§	- 'Setsuka-yae' (L/d)	CMil NLar
	- 'Shakira' (H)	LLHF
	- 'Sheila' (Dutch Ladies Series) (L)	CBcs EPfP LSRN MBri
	- 'Shin-ozaki' (H)	NLar
	- 'Sibilla' (H)	MJak SPlb
	- 'Sindarella' (H)	MBri
	- Sister Therese	see *H. macrophylla* 'Soeur Thérèse'
§	- 'Soeur Thérèse' (H)	CBar CBcs EPfP MAsh MMuc NLar SEND SGol SWvt WGwG
	- 'Soraya' (Dutch Ladies Series) (L)	CBcs
	- 'Sumida-no-hanabi' (L/d)	WPGP
*	- 'Sunset' (L)	CBcs SVen
	- 'Sweet Fantasy' (Hovaria Series) (H) new	ELan EPfP
§	- 'Taube' (Teller Series) (L)	CBcs CDoC CExl CMHG EPfP GGal GQui MAsh MGos SCoo SHyH SLim SWvt
	- 'Teller Pink'	see *H. macrophylla* 'Taube'
	- 'Teller Red'	see *H. macrophylla* 'Rotkehlchen'
N	- Teller variegated	see *H. macrophylla* 'Tricolor'
N	- Teller Weiss	see *H. macrophylla* 'Libelle'
	var. ***thunbergii***	see *H. serrata* var. *thunbergii*
	- 'Tokyo Delight' (L) ♀H3-4	CExl CGHE CTsd EBee LRHS MAsh SDys SHyH WPGP
§	- 'Tricolor' (L/v)	CBcs CDoC CDul CTri EBee ELan ELon ESwi LAst LRHS MGos SHyH SLon SPer WMoo
	- 'Variegata'	see *H. macrophylla* 'Maculata'
	- 'Veitchii' (L) ♀H3-4	CBcs CDoy CDul CExl CMHG CMil CSBt EBee ECre EPfP GGal LPot LRHS MGos MRav MSwo SDix SHyH SPer SSpi WPGP
	- 'Vicomte de Vibraye'	see *H. macrophylla* 'Générale Vicomtesse de Vibraye'
	- 'Westfalen' (H) ♀H3-4	CMac IArd SDix
I	- 'White Lace' (L)	GKin
	- 'White Mop' (H)	CWib
	- 'White Wave'	see *H. macrophylla* 'Mariesii Grandiflora'

	- 'Zaunkoenig' (L)	MAsh
	- 'Zebra'PBR (H)	ELan EPfP ESwi LBuc MGos WCot
	- 'Zhuni Hito' (L)	NLar
	- 'Zorro'PBR (L)	CBcs CDoC CMil EBee EPfP ESwi GGGa GKin LBuc LRHS MAsh MCri SCoo SLim SLon SPoG SSpi WCot
	- 'Zsasa' (H) **new**	LBuc
	- 'Zulu' (H)	ELan
	aff. ***mangshanensis*** BWJ 8120	WCru
	paniculata	CMCN
	- B&SWJ 3556 from Taiwan	WCru
	- B&SWJ 5413 from Japan	WCru
	- B&SWJ 8894 from Japan	WCru
	- from Taiwan	SKHP
	- 'Ammarin'	GQui LLHF NLar WPat
	- Angel's Blush	see *H. paniculata* 'Ruby'
	- 'Big Ben' ♀H4	EPfP GGGa GQui LRHS MBri NLar SKHP
	- 'Bombshell'	ESwi LRHS NLar SPoG
	- 'Brussels Lace'	CAbP CAbb CDul EPfP EWTr GBin LRHS LSRN MBri MRav NLar SGol SHyH SLon SPoG SSta WGob WGrn WPat
	- 'Burgundy Lace'	CBcs EBee MBlu MBri NLar
	- 'Chantilly Lace'	CMHG CMil LRHS MBri SHil
	- Dart's Little Dot = 'Darlido'PBR	IVic LLHF LSRN NLar SLim WPGP WPat
	- 'Dharuma'	GKin LLHF LRHS SGol
	- Diamant Rouge = 'Rendia' **new**	SGol
	- 'Dolly'	EPfP GQui LRHS LSRN MAsh SHyH
	- Early Sensation = 'Bulk'PBR	ESwi EThi GBin GKin LRHS MSwo NSoo SHyH SKHP SMDP SPoG WGrn WMoo
	- 'Everest'	CAbP CMil EBee EPfP LRHS MAsh SHyH SPoG WGob WPat
	- 'Floribunda'	CGHE EBee ELan EPfP LRHS MAsh SHyH WPGP
	- 'Grandiflora' ♀H4	Widely available
	- 'Great Escape'	NLar
	- 'Greenspire'	EPfP LRHS MAsh MBlu MRav SHyH WPat
	- 'Harry's Souvenir'	NLar
	- 'Kyushu' ♀H4	Widely available
	- 'Last Post'	GQui
	- 'Limelight'PBR ♀H4	Widely available
	- Magical Candle = 'Bokraflame'PBR	EPPr EPfP WCot
	- Magical Fire = 'Bokraplume'PBR **new**	NLar
	- 'Mathilde'	NLar
	- Mega Mindy = 'Ilvomindy'	SKHP
	- 'Mega Pearl'	LSRN NLar
	- 'Melody'	NLar
	- 'Mount Aso'	EWld GQui NBro WPGP
	- 'October Bride'	CEnd GQui MBri NLar WPGP
	- 'Papillon'	WPGP WPat
	- 'Pee Wee'	LLHF NLar
	- 'Phantom' ♀H4	CBcs CDoC CMCN CMil EBee ELan ELon EMil EPfP EUJe GGGa GKin LRHS LSRN LSqu MAsh MBri MRav NBro NCGa NLar NPri SCoo SHyH SPoG WCot WKif WPGP WPat WWFP
	- 'Pink Beauty'PBR (H)	CTri LSRN
	- Pink Diamond = 'Interhydia' ♀H4	Widely available
	- 'Pink Jewel'	CWib LLHF WPat
	- 'Pink Lady'	EUJe NBro
	- Pinky-Winky = 'Dvppinky'PBR ♀H4	CWGN EBee EPPr EPfP ESwi GBin GKin GQui IArd IVic LBuc LLHF LRHS MBlu NLar SGol SHyH SKHP SLim SPoG SSta
	- 'Praecox'	GQui MRav WKif
	- Prim'White = 'Dolprim' **new**	CDoC LRHS
	- 'Rosy Morn'	LRHS
§	- 'Ruby'	CBcs IArd LSRN MAsh NLar
	- 'Silver Dollar' ♀H4	CDoC EBee EPfP LRHS LSRN MBri SHyH
	- Sundae Fraise = 'Rensun' **new**	CDoC LRHS LSqu MAsh SGol
	- 'Tardiva'	CBcs EBee EPfP GGal GKin GQui LRHS MGos MRav NBro SDix SHyH SPer SRms SWvt WGob WPGP WPat
	- 'Tender Rose'	NLar
	- 'Unique' ♀H4	Widely available
	- Vanille Fraise = 'Renhy'PBR	CBcs CDoC CEnd CMHG CWGN EBee ELon EPfP EThi GBin GGGa LAst LBuc LRHS LSRN MAsh MBlu MBri MRav MSwo NCGa NLar SGol SHil SHyH SPoG SWvt WGrn WPGP
	- 'White Goliath'	GQui IArd NLar
	- 'White Lace'	NLar
	- 'White Lady'	CBcs
	- 'White Moth'	CAbP CBcs EBee EPfP GGGa LLHF LRHS NBro NLar SHyH WPat
	- 'Wim's Red'PBR	ELan ESwi MMHG NLar SGol SPoG
	- 'Yuan-Yang'	WCru
	peruviana* × *seemanii	CEnd GKin IArd IDee SSta
	peruviana* × *serratifolia	WPGP
	petiolaris	see *H. anomala* subsp. *petiolaris*
	'Preziosa' ♀H3-4	Widely available
	quercifolia ♀H3-4	Widely available
	- 'Alice'	CJun EBee EPfP ESwi LRHS LSRN MAsh NLar SGol SHyH SSpi WPGP
	- 'Alison'	EPfP SGol
I	- 'Amethyst' Dirr	NLar SGol
	- 'Applause'	LRHS NLar
	- 'Back Porch'	GBin NLar SGol
	- 'Burgundy'	CBcs CJun CMil EBee EPfP ESwi GBin IArd IDee IVic LRHS NCGa NLar SGol WPGP
	- 'Flore Pleno'	see *H. quercifolia* Snowflake
	- 'Harmony'	CJun CMil EBee ELon EPfP ESwi IArd LRHS NLar SHil SHyH SKHP SSta WPGP WPat
	- 'Ice Crystal'	IVic SGol WPGP
	- 'Lady Anne'	EBee EPfP MRav WPGP
	- 'Little Honey'PBR	NLar SGol SSpi
	- Little Honey = 'Brihon'	CAbP EPfP IVic LRHS MAsh
*	- 'Pee Wee'	CAbP CBcs CDoC CJun EBee ELan EPfP LRHS MAsh MPkF NLar SGol SHyH SKHP SLon SMDP SPoG SSta WPGP WPat
	- 'Sike's Dwarf'	CJun IVic MPkF MRav SGol WCot WPat
	- 'Snow Giant'	CJun
	- Snow Queen = 'Flemygea'	Widely available
	- 'Snowdrift'	CJun CMil
§	- Snowflake = 'Brido' (d)	CAbP CBcs CDoC CEnd CMil CWGN ELan EPfP LRHS MAsh MGos MRav NLar SHyH SKHP SLon SPer SPoG SSpi SSta WPGP WPat
	- 'Stardust'	MMHG

	- 'Tennessee Clone'	CJun ESwi LRHS NLar SKHP
	sargentiana	see *H. aspera* subsp. *sargentiana*
	scandens	CFil NBro
	- B&SWJ 5448	WCru
	- B&SWJ 5481	WCru
	- B&SWJ 5496	WCru
	- B&SWJ 5523	WCru
	- B&SWJ 5602	WCru
	- B&SWJ 5893	WCru
	- B&SWJ 5929	WCru
	- B&SWJ 6159	WCru
	- B&SWJ 6317	WCru
§	- subsp. ***chinensis***	CBcs CExl
	- - B&SWJ 1488	WCru
	- - B&SWJ 3214	WCru
	- - B&SWJ 3410 from Taiwan	WCru
	- - B&SWJ 3420	WCru
	- - B&SWJ 3423 from Taiwan	WCru
	- - B&SWJ 3487 from Taiwan	WCru
	- - B&SWJ 3869	WCru
	- - BWJ 8000 from Sichuan	WCru
§	- - f. ***angustipetala*** B&SWJ 3454	WCru
	- - - B&SWJ 3553	WCru
	- - - B&SWJ 3667	WCru
	- - - B&SWJ 3733	WCru
	- - - B&SWJ 3814	WCru
	- - - B&SWJ 6038 from Yakushima	WCru
	- - - B&SWJ 6041 from Yakushima	WCru
	- - - B&SWJ 6056 from Yakushima	WCru
	- - - B&SWJ 6787	WCru
	B&SWJ 6802	WCru
	- - - B&SWJ 7121	WCru
	- - - B&SWJ 7128	WCru
	- - f. ***formosana*** B&SWJ 1488	WCru
	- - - B&SWJ 3271	WCru
	- - - B&SWJ 7058	NLar WCru
	- - - B&SWJ 7097	NLar WCru
	- - f. ***macrosepala*** B&SWJ 3423	ESwi WCru
	- - - B&SWJ 3476	WCru
	- - - CWJ 12441	WCru
	- - f. ***obovatifolia*** B&SWJ 3487b	WCru
	- - - B&SWJ 3683	WCru
	- - - B&SWJ 7121	WCru
	- subsp. ***liukiuensis***	WCru
	- - B&SWJ 6022	WCru
	- - B&SWJ 11471	WCru
	- 'Splash' (v)	CMil
	seemannii	Widely available
	- 'Roger Grounds' (v)	WCot
	aff. ***seemannii*** **new**	GKin
	serrata	CExl CTri CWib WKif
	- B&SWJ 6184	WCru
	- B&SWJ 6241	WCru
	- 'Acuminata'	see *H. serrata* 'Bluebird'
	- 'Aigaku' (L)	CExl CFil CMil
	- 'Aka Beni-yama'	GQui
	- 'Akabe-yama'	NBro NLar
	- 'Akishino-temari'	WPGP
	- Amacha Group	CGHE
	- - 'Amagi-amacha' (L)	CMil GQui NBro NLar
	- - 'Ō-amacha'	CMil GQui WPGP
	- 'Amagyana' (L)	CExl CGHE
	- subsp. ***angustata***	WCru
	- 'Ao-yama'	WPGP
	- 'Belladonna'	GQui
	- 'Belle Deckle'	see *H. serrata* 'Blue Deckle'
	- 'Beni-gaku' (L)	CExl CFil CMil ECre LRHS MAsh NBro NLar SHyH WPGP
	- 'Beni-temari' **new**	NBro
	- 'Beni-yama' (L)	CFil CGHE CMil GQui WPGP
	- 'Besshi-temari' **new**	CFil
	- 'Blue Billow' (L)	GGGa NBro NLar
§	- 'Blue Deckle' (L)	CAbb CMHG CMac GGal MAsh MGos MRav NBro SDys SHyH WPGP
§	- 'Bluebird' (L) ♀H3-4	Widely available
	- 'Cap Sizun'	WPGP
	- 'Chiba Cherry-lips'	ESwi WCru
	- 'Chiri-san Sue' (d)	CFil WCru
	- 'Crûg Cobalt'	WCru
	- 'Diadem' (L) ♀H3-4	CAbb CDoC CExl CMil EPfP GQui LRHS NBro SHyH WPGP
	- dwarf white-flowered (L)	WCru
	- 'Forget Me Not'	GQui
	- 'Fuji Snowstorm' (v)	CMil
	- 'Fuji Waterfall'	see *H. serrata* 'Fuji-no-taki'
	- 'Fuji-no-shirayuki' (L/d)	CMil
§	- 'Fuji-no-taki' (L/d)	CAbP CMil ELon ESwi LLHF NCGa NEgg WPGP WWFP
	- 'Golden Showers' (L)	NBro
	- 'Golden Sunlight'PBR (L)	CDoC SWvt
	- 'Graciosa' (L)	LLHF WPGP WPat
	- 'Grayswood' (L) ♀H3-4	CBcs CDul CExl CHel CMac COlW CSBt EBee EPfP GGal GQui LRHS MAsh MRav NBro SDix SGol SHyH SLim SPer SSpi WBor WKif WPGP
	- 'Hakucho' (L/d)	NBro WPGP
	- 'Hallasan' misapplied	see *H. serrata* 'Maiko', 'Spreading Beauty'
	- 'Hallasan' ambig.	CMil
	- 'Hallasan' R. & J. de Belder (L)	CMil WPGP
	- 'Hime-benigaku' (L)	CMil MAsh
	- 'Impératrice Eugénie' (L)	GQui NLar
	- 'Intermedia' (L)	CExl NBro
	- 'Isusai-jaku' (L)	GQui
	- 'Kiyosumi' (L)	CDoC CEnd CExl CFil CGHE CLAP CMil ECre ELon GGal GQui NBir NLar SBrt SHyH WBor WCot WCru WPGP WPat
	- 'Klaveren'	see *H. macrophylla* 'Klaveren'
	- 'Koreana' (L)	MAsh
	- 'Kurenai' (L)	NBro NLar WPGP
	- 'Kurohime' (L)	NBro WPGP
	- 'Macrosepala' (L)	CDoC SHyH WPGP
§	- 'Maiko' (L)	IArd
	- 'Midori' (L)	CExl SHyH
	- 'Mikata Yae'	CMil WPGP
	- 'Miranda' (L) ♀H3-4	CDoC CExl CMil CSam EPfP LRHS MAsh NBro NLar SDys SHyH SSpi
	- 'Miyama-yae-murasaki' (L/d)	CExl CFil CGHE CLAP CMil CSpe ESwi MAsh SHyH WPGP
	- 'Momo-beni-yama'	CMil
	- 'Mont Aso'	CMil NLar
	- 'Niji' (L) **new**	WPGP
	- 'Odoriko-amacha'	WPGP
	- 'Otsu-hime' **new**	NLar
	- 'Pretty Maiden'	see *H. serrata* 'Shichidanka'
	- 'Professeur Iida' (L)	WPGP
§	- 'Prolifera' (L/d)	CGHE CMil LLHF WPGP WPat

	- 'Pulchella'	see *H. serrata* 'Prolifera'
	- 'Ramis Pictis' (L)	CBcs GQui NBro NLar SHyH WPGP
	- 'Rosalba' (L) 🏆$^{H3-4}$	CExl CLAP ECre GGal IVic NBro WSHC
	- 'Santiago' (L) **new**	CDoC
	- 'Sapphirine' (L)	GQui
	- 'Sekka'	WPGP
§	- 'Shichidanka' (L/d)	CFil EBee LLHF LRHS NBro WPat
	- 'Shichidanka-nishiki' (L/d/v)	CDoC CExl ECre ESwi GQui SHyH WBor
	- 'Shinonome' (L/d)	CExl CMil GQui WPGP
	- 'Shirofuji' (L/d)	CFil CLAP CMil EWld LLHF MAsh WPGP WPat
	- 'Shiro-gaku' (L)	MAsh NBro NLar
	- 'Shiro-maiko'	WPGP
	- 'Shirotae' (L/d)	CExl CFil CMil EBee MAsh SHyH WPGP
	- 'Shōjō'	CMil ELon MAsh WPGP WPat
§	- 'Spreading Beauty' (L)	WPGP
	- 'Suzukayama-yama'	WPGP
§	- var. ***thunbergii*** (L)	GQui
*	- - 'Plena' (L/d)	GQui WCru
	- 'Tiara' (L) 🏆$^{H3-4}$	CAbb CDoC CDul CExl CFil CMil EBee ELon EPfP GGGa GGal IVic LRHS LSRN MAsh NBir NBro NLar SDix SDys SHyH SLim WPGP WPat
	- 'Tosa-no-akatsuki' **new**	CFil
	- 'Uzu-azisai'	WPGP
	- 'Veerle' (L) **new**	NBro
	- 'Woodlander' (L)	WPat
	- 'Yae-no-amacha' (L/d)	CBcs CExl NBro NLar SHyH WPGP
	- subsp. ***yezoensis***	CMil GQui NLar
	- - 'Hime-gaku'	CMil
§	***serratifolia***	CExl CHEx EPfP IArd IDee SSpi SSta WPGP
	- HCM 98056	WCru
	sikokiana	CLAP
	- B&SWJ 5035	WCru
	- B&SWJ 5855	WCru
	- B&SWJ 11174	WCru
	- B&SWJ 11381	WCru
	'Silver Slipper'	see *H. macrophylla* 'Ayesha'
	tiliifolia	see *H. anomala* subsp. *petiolaris*
	villosa	see *H. aspera* Villosa Group
	xanthoneura	see *H. heteromalla*
	'Zambia'	EPfP LBuc MGos WCot

Hydrastis (*Ranunculaceae*)

canadensis	CArn GPoy LEdu MNrw

Hydrocharis (*Hydrocharitaceae*)

morsus-ranae	CBAq CHab CRow CWat EHon EWay MSKA MWts NPer SWat

Hydrocleys (*Alismataceae*)

nymphoides	LLWG XBlo

Hydrocotyle (*Araliaceae*)

asiatica	see *Centella asiatica*
sibthorpioides 'Crystal Confetti' (v)	LLWG
vulgaris	CWat

Hydrophyllum (*Boraginaceae*)

canadense	IMou
'Spring Silver'	SKHP

Hylomecon (*Papaveraceae*)

hylomeconoides	WCru
§ ***japonica***	CLAP ECho ELan EWld GBBs GCra GKev IMou LEdu LRHS NBir NLBP NRya WCru

Hylotelephium see *Sedum*

Hymenanthera see *Melicytus*

Hymenocallis (*Amaryllidaceae*)

	'Advance'	ECho
§	***caroliniana***	ECho
	× ***festalis*** 🏆^{H1}	CCCN ECho SDeJ SPav
	- 'Zwanenburg'	CGrW ECho
	harrisiana	CCCN CTca ECho EPfP SDeJ
§	***longipetala***	ECho
	occidentalis	see *H. caroliniana*
	'Sulphur Queen' 🏆^{H1}	CGrW ECho SDeJ SPav

Hymenolepis (*Asteraceae*)

parviflora	see *Athanasia parviflora*

Hymenosporum (*Pittosporaceae*)

flavum	EShb EUJe MOWG

Hymenoxys (*Asteraceae*)

	grandiflora	see *Tetraneuris grandiflora*
§	***hoopesii***	CMac EBee ELan EPfP GMaP LHop LRHS NBir NChi NEgg NLar NPri SPer SPoG SRms WCot WHar WMnd WWEG XLum

Hyoscyamus (*Solanaceae*)

niger	CArn GPoy MNHC

Hypericum ✿ (*Hypericaceae*)

	CC 4131	CExl
	CC 4544	CExl
	SDR 6106	GKev
	aegypticum	ECho EPot MHer SBrt SIgm SVen WAbe WThu
	amblycalyx	WAbe
	androsaemum	CArn EDAr ELan GAbr MHer MRav MSwo NPer WHfH WMoo WOut
§	- 'Albury Purple'	ELan EShb LDai MRav NLar WHrl WMoo XLum
	- 'Autumn Blaze'	CBcs MBri
§	- 'Dart's Golden Penny'	SPer
	- 'Excellent Flair'	MBri NLar
§	- f. ***variegatum*** 'Mrs Gladis Brabazon' (v)	NBir NLar WCot WHrl
	athoum	WAbe WIce WThu
	balearicum	WAbe XSen
	bellum	EBee GCal SLon
	calycinum	CBcs CDul CMac CTri EBee ELan ELon EPfP LAst LBuc MGos MMuc MRav MWat NWea SEND SGol SPer SWvt WMoo XLum
	- 'Brigadoon'	LRHS MAsh SGol
	- 'Senior'	LAst
	cerastioides	CMea CTri CWib EDAr EDif NGdn NSla SIgm SRms WAbe XSen
	coris	EWes SRms WAbe
	cuneatum	see *H. pallens*
	× ***cyathiflorum*** 'Gold Cup'	CMac LRHS MAsh
	× ***dummeri*** 'Peter Dummer'	MAsh MBri NLar
	'Eastleigh Gold'	CMac
	'Elite Baby Green'	EPfP

	'Elite Mayor'	EPfP
	'Elite Sweet Lion'	EPfP
	elodes	CBAq CWat LLWG MSKA
	empetrifolium	see *H. empetrifolium*
	'Prostratum'	subsp. *tortuosum*
§	- subsp. ***tortuosum***	EWes
	foliosum NJM 08.031	WPGP
	forrestii ♀H4	MMuc SEND
N	***fragile*** misapplied	see *H. olympicum* f. *minus*
	frondosum 'Buttercup'	NLar SLim
	- 'Sunburst'	EBee
	'Gemo'	EBee SLim
	'Gold Penny'	see *H. androsaemum* 'Dart's Golden Penny'
	Golden Beacon = 'Wilhyp'PBR	CEnd CSpe ESwi GAbr LAst LHop LRHS LSou MNrw NEgg NLar SPad WCot WHrl
	grandiflorum	see *H. kouytchense*
	grandifolium new	EDAr
	henryi	SLPl
	- L 753	SRms
	- subsp. ***hancockii*** NJM 10.092 new	WPGP
	'Hidcote' ♀H4	Widely available
	'Hidcote Variegated' (v)	LRHS MAsh SLim SRms
	hirsutum	CHab NMir
	(Hypearls Series) Hypearls Annelies	SHil
	- Hypearls Jacqueline	SHil
	- Hypearls Olivia new	SHil
	× ***inodorum*** 'Albury Purple'	see *H. androsaemum* 'Albury Purple'
	- 'Autumn Surprise'PBR	NEgg
	- 'Dream'	NLar
	- 'Elstead'	ECtt ELan EPfP MRav MWat NLar NWea
	- Magical Cherry = 'Kolmcherrip'PBR	ELan EPfP NSoo
	- Magical Limelight = 'Kolmalimeli' new	ELan NSoo
	- Magical White = 'Kolmawhi'PBR	ELan EPfP SPoG
	- 'Rheingold'	MAsh
	- 'Ysella'	MRav
	japonicum	ECho
	kamtschaticum	XLum
§	***kouytchense*** ♀H4	CDul EBee EPfP EWes GQui LRHS MAsh MMuc MRav SEND SPoG WCot WPat
	lancasteri	EPfP LRHS MAsh SPoG
	leschenaultii misapplied	see *H.* 'Rowallane'
	linarioides	EBee
	maclarenii	EWes
	Magical Beauty = 'Kolmbeau'PBR	ELon MJak NLar NPnk NSoo SPoG WCot
	Magical Red = 'Kolmred'PBR	EPfP MJak NLar NSoo SPoG
	Miracle Fantasy = 'Hymirfan'	NLar
	Miracle Summer = 'Hymirsum'	EPfP NLar
	Miracle Wonder = 'Hymirwon'	NLar
	× ***moserianum*** ♀H4	CBar CDul CMac EPfP LRHS MGos MJak MRav NPer SHil SLon SPer SRms
	- 'Daybreak'	EBee LRHS MAsh SPoG WRHF
§	- 'Tricolor' (v)	Widely available
	- 'Variegatum'	see *H.* × *moserianum* 'Tricolor'
	'Mrs Brabazon'	see *H. androsaemum* f. *variegatum* 'Mrs Gladis Brabazon'
	nummularium	WAbe
	oblongifolium	CExl
	olympicum ♀H4	CArn CEnt CTri ECho ELan GJos LRHS MAsh MBrN MMuc MWat SEND SPer SRms SWvt WAbe WIce WSHC XLum XSen
	- 'Grandiflorum'	see *H. olympicum* f. *uniflorum*
§	- f. ***minus***	CTri ECho ECtt GKev NGdn SPlb SRms WHrl
§	- - 'Sulphureum'	CPrp ECho ELon EWTr EWes GMaP LRHS MLHP NBir SPer SRms SWvt WCFE
	- - 'Variegatum' (v)	EWes NBir SPoG SWvt
§	- f. ***uniflorum***	ECho NBro NRya
	- - 'Citrinum' ♀H4	CMea CSpe ECtt EPfP GBuc MRav MWat NBro SIgm SRot WAbe WCot WHoo WKif WRHF
	orientale	EWes GLog
§	***pallens***	ECho WAbe
	perforatum	CArn CHab CHby EPfP GPoy IRos MHer MHoo MNHC NMir SEND SIde SRms WHer WHfH WJek WMoo WSFF
	polyphyllum	see *H. olympicum* f. *minus*
	- 'Citrinum'	see *H. olympicum* f. *minus* 'Sulphureum'
	- 'Grandiflorum'	see *H. olympicum* f. *uniflorum*
	prolificum	MMHG WCFE
	quadrangulum L.	see *H. tetrapterum*
	reptans misapplied	see *H. olympicum* f. *minus*
	reptans Dyer	CMea EWes SBrt
	revolutum	LEdu
§	'Rowallane' ♀H3	CTri GCal SDix SMrm SSpi
	'Sonnenbrut'	SLPl
	subsessile	CExl
	'Sungold'	see *H. kouytchense*
	'Sweet Lion'	CMac
§	***tetrapterum***	CArn LLWG
	trichocaulon	ECho EWes
	uralum HWJ 520	WCru
	xylosteifolium	SLon

Hypocalyptus (*Papilionaceae*)

sophoroides	SPlb

Hypochaeris (*Asteraceae*)

radicata	CHab NMir

Hypocyrta see *Nematanthus*

Hypoestes (*Acanthaceae*)

aristata	CExl EShb

Hypolepis (*Dennstaedtiaceae*)

millefolium	LRHS WCot

Hypoxis (*Hypoxidaceae*)

	hemerocallidea	WCot
	- 'Bloemfontein'	ECho
	hirsuta	CCCN ECho WCot
	hygrometrica	ECho ECou IBal WThu
	krebsii	ECho
	obtusa 'Harrismith'	ECho
	parvula	XLum
§	- var. ***albiflora*** 'Hebron Farm Biscuit'	CBro CCCN ECho EWes NWad WAbe
	rigidula 'Harrismith'	ECho

villosa	ECho

Hypoxis × Rhodohypoxis see × *Rhodoxis*

H. parvula × R. baurii	see × *Rhodoxis hybrida*

Hypsela (*Campanulaceae*)

longiflora	see *H. reniformis*
§ ***reniformis***	ECho LLWG MRav

Hyssopus ✿ (*Lamiaceae*)

from Georgia	EWes
officinalis	Widely available
- f. ***albus***	ELau EPfP GPoy MHer MHoo MNHC SPer SPlb SRms WHfH WJek XLum XSen
- subsp. ***aristatus***	CArn EBee ELau ELon EPfP GPoy LLWP MHer MHoo MNHC SPoG WJek XLum XSen
- 'Roseus'	ELau EPfP GPoy LLWP MHer MHol MHoo MNHC SEND SIde SPer SPoG WJek XLum XSen

Hysterionica (*Asteraceae*)

pulchella	CPBP

Hystrix (*Poaceae*)

patula	CKno EBee EHoe EPPr EShb GCal LLWP MBel MMoz MNrw MWhi SPlb XLum

Iberis (*Brassicaceae*)

Absolutely Amethyst ='Ib2401'	CBct CMea ECtt ELon GBin MHol NPri SMrm WIce
aurosica subsp. ***cantabrica***	GKev
candolleana	see *I. pruitii* Candolleana Group
commutata	see *I. sempervirens*
gibraltarica	ECho EWTr SRms WGor
- 'Betty Swainson'	EWTr SBch SMrm SPhx
jordanii	see *I. pruitii*
'Masterpiece'	LRHS WHlf
§ ***pruitii***	WAbe
§ - Candolleana Group	ECho
saxatilis	ECho ITim LHop LRHS WThu
semperflorens	WCFE
§ ***sempervirens*** ♀H4	CHVG CMea CTri CWib ECho ELan EPfP IFoB LAst MAsh MMuc MWat NBro NOrc NSoo SEND SRms WCFE WHar WRHF
- 'Compacta'	ECho
- 'Elfenreigen'	GCal
- 'Fischbeck'	SRot
- 'Golden Candy'	CTri EHoe MAvo SPoG
- 'Little Gem'	see *I. sempervirens* 'Weisser Zwerg'
- 'Pygmaea'	ECho
- Schneeflocke	see *I. sempervirens* 'Snowflake'
- 'Snow Cushion'	EPfP NHol
§ - 'Snowflake' ♀H4	CBar ECho EPfP GBin IFoB LHop LPio MBel MHer MWat NPri NRya SPer SPoG SWvt WIce XLum
- 'Tahoe'	LPot
§ - 'Weisser Zwerg'	CMea ECho ECtt ELan MHer MRav NRya SRms WThu

Ichthyoselmis (*Papaveraceae*)

§ ***macrantha***	EPfP GCra IMou LHop MNrw WCru WPGP

Idesia (*Salicaceae*)

polycarpa	CBcs CDul CMCN EBee EBtc EPfP IVic LHop NLar
- CWJ 12837 **new**	WCru

Ilex ✿ (*Aquifoliaceae*)

§ × ***altaclerensis*** 'Belgica Aurea' (f/v) ♀H4	CBcs CDoC CJun CTho EBee EPfP MBri MSwo NHol
- 'Camelliifolia' (f) ♀H4	CTho EBee ELan EPfP MBlu NEgg NPCo SGol
- 'Camelliifolia Variegata' (f/v)	CMac
- 'Golden King' (f/v) ♀H4	Widely available
- 'Hendersonii' (f)	NPCo
- 'Hodginsii' (m) ♀H4	CTri
- 'James G. Esson' (f)	CRos LRHS SHil
- 'Lawsoniana' (f/v) ♀H4	CDoC CJun CMac CRos CSBt CTri EBee EHoe ELan EPfP LRHS MAsh MBlu MMuc NEgg NHol NLar NPCo NWea SEND SGol SHil SLim SLon SPer SPoG SRms WHar WMou WPat
- 'Purple Shaft' (f)	CMCN MRav
- 'Ripley Gold' (f/v)	CLnd LRHS MAsh MBri NWea
- 'Silver Sentinel'	see *I.* × *altaclerensis* 'Belgica Aurea'
- 'Wilsonii' (f)	EPfP NLar NPCo NWea
aquifolium ♀H4	CBar CBcs CCVT CDul CHab CJun CSBt CTho CTri CWib EBee ECrN EPfP MBri MGos MJak MMuc MRav MSwo NLar NPri NWea SEND SEWo SGol SHil SPer WHar WMoo WMou
- 'Alaska' (f)	CCVT CDoC CDul CJun CMCN CRos EBee LBuc LRHS MAsh MBri NLar NSoo NWea SGol SHil SWvt
- 'Amber' (f) ♀H4	CTri NLar NPCo NWea
- 'Angustifolia' (f)	WCFE
- 'Angustifolia' (m or f)	EPfP MAsh SPoG
- 'Angustimarginata Aurea' (m/v)	MAsh NPCo
§ - 'Argentea Marginata' (f/v) ♀H4	Widely available
§ - 'Argentea Marginata Pendula' (f/v)	CDoC CMac CTri ELan EPfP LRHS MAsh MRav NWea SPer SRms WPat
- 'Argentea Pendula'	see *I. aquifolium* 'Argentea Marginata Pendula'
- 'Argentea Variegata'	see *I. aquifolium* 'Argentea Marginata'
- 'Atlas' (m)	CBcs CDoC LBuc
- 'Aurea Marginata' (f/v)	CLnd CMac EPfP LBuc MGos NPCo SEWo WCFE WHar WPat
- 'Aurea Marginata Pendula' (f/v)	CDoC WPat
- 'Aurea Regina'	see *I. aquifolium* 'Golden Queen'
- 'Aureovariegata Pendula'	see *I. aquifolium* 'Weeping Golden Milkmaid'
- 'Aurifodina' (f)	CJun NPCo
- 'Bacciflava' (f)	CBcs CDoC CMac CTho CTri EBee ELan ELon EPfP IArd MBlu MGos MRav NEgg NLar NPCo NWea SLim SPer SRms SWvt WCFE
- 'Bowland' (f/v)	NHol
- 'Chris Whittle'	NHol
- 'Crassifolia' (f)	CWib IArd SMad WPGP
- 'Elegantissima' (m/v)	CJun SCoo

	- 'Fastigiata Sartori'	NLar
	- 'Ferox' (m)	CJun EBee ELan EPfP LRHS NLar SPer
	- 'Ferox Argentea' (m/v) ♀^{H4}	Widely available
	- 'Ferox Aurea' (m/v)	CDoC CJun CWib ELan ELon EPfP MAsh NEgg NPCo
§	- 'Flavescens' (f)	MBlu NPCo
	- 'Fructu Luteo' (f) **new**	WHar
	- 'Gold Flash' (f/v)	LRHS MAsh NEgg NLar
I	- 'Golden Hedgehog'	LRHS SPer
	- 'Golden Milkboy' (m/v)	CLnd CMac ELan EPfP SGol WPat
§	- 'Golden Queen' (m/v) ♀^{H4}	CDoC CMac CWib IArd MGos NBir NPCo SRms WPat
	- 'Golden van Tol' (f/v)	CBcs CDoC CSBt CTri CWSG ECrN ELan ELon EPfP LRHS MAsh MBlu MGos MSwo NEgg NLar NPCo SCoo SGol SRms WMoo
	- 'Green Minaret'	IVic
§	- 'Green Pillar' (f)	EPfP
	- 'Green Spire'	see *I. aquifolium* 'Green Pillar'
	- 'Handsworth New Silver' (f/v) ♀^{H4}	Widely available
	- 'Harpune' (f)	IArd
§	- 'Hascombensis'	CDoC LHop NWea
	- 'Hastata' (m)	CWib IArd IDee
	- 'J.C. van Tol' (f) ♀^{H4}	Widely available
	- 'Lichtenthalii' (f)	IArd IVic NPCo
	- 'Madame Briot' (f/v) ♀^{H4}	Widely available
	- 'Marijo'	CRos LRHS SHil
	- moonlight holly	see *I. aquifolium* 'Flavescens'
	- 'Myrtifolia' (f)	NEgg NPCo
	- 'Myrtifolia' (m)	CMac ELan EPfP GCal MGos NEgg NLar NPCo SMad WMoo
	- 'Myrtifolia Aurea' (m/v)	NEgg SWvt WGob
	- 'Myrtifolia Aurea Maculata' (m/v) ♀^{H4}	CDoC CJun CTri ELan EPfP LRHS MAsh MRav NEgg NPCo NWea SMad SPoG SWvt WPat
	- 'Northern Lights' (v)	EBee ELMC EPfP MSwo
	- 'Pendula' (f)	MRav NWea
	- 'Pendula Mediopicta'	see *I. aquifolium* 'Weeping Golden Milkmaid'
	- 'Pyramidalis' (f) ♀^{H4}	CDoC CDul CMac CTri ELan LRHS MAsh MBri MGos NLar NPCo NWea SGol SHil SRms WMoo
	- 'Pyramidalis Aureomarginata' (f/v)	CDoC NLar
	- 'Pyramidalis Fructu Luteo' (f) ♀^{H4}	MAsh MBri
	- 'Recurva' (m)	CMac
	- 'Rubricaulis Aurea' (f/v)	NLar NPCo
	- Siberia = 'Limsi'^{PBR} (f)	IVic
	- 'Silver King'	see *I. aquifolium* 'Silver Queen'
	- 'Silver Milkboy' (f/v)	EBee ELan EPfP MBlu
	- 'Silver Milkmaid' (f/v)	CDoC EPfP LRHS MAsh MJak NEgg NHol NSoo SLim SPer SWvt WGob WMoo WMou
§	- 'Silver Queen' (m/v) ♀^{H4}	Widely available
	- 'Silver Sentinel'	see *I.* × *altaclerensis* 'Belgica Aurea'
	- 'Silver van Tol' (f/v)	CDoC CJun CLnd EBee ELan LRHS MAsh NEgg NLar NPCo NPer SPer
	- 'Somerset Cream' (f/v)	CJun CTri CWib
	- 'Sterntaler'	IVic
§	- 'Watereriana' (m/v)	MAsh
	- 'Waterer's Gold'	see *I. aquifolium* 'Watereriana'
§	- 'Weeping Golden Milkmaid' (f/v)	MRav WPat
	- 'White Cream' (m/v)	IVic MBri
	- 'Wichtel'	IVic
	- 'Yellow Star' (f/v)	IVic
	× ***aquipernyi*** Dragon Lady = 'Meschick' (f)	CDoC NPCo
	× ***attenuata*** 'Sunny Foster' (f/v)	CDoC EPfP
§	***bioritsensis***	CMCN CTri
	'Brilliant' (f)	NPCo
	'Clusterberry' (f)	NPCo
	colchica	CMCN IDee
	cornuta	EPfP
	- B&SWJ 8756	WCru
	- 'Burfordii' (f)	NLar
	- 'Ira S. Nelson' (f/v)	IArd IDee
	crenata	CDul CMCN CTri EPfP EShb GCra MGos MRav NHol NWea SAPC STrG
	- 'Aureovariegata'	see *I. crenata* 'Variegata'
	- 'Convexa' (f) ♀^{H4}	CDul EPfP MAsh MRav NEgg NPCo NWea WGwG WMoo WPat
	- 'Convexed Gold' (f/v)	LRHS MBri NSoo NWad
	- 'Dwarf Pagoda' (f)	IVic
	- 'Fastigiata' (f)	CDoC EPfP LRHS MAsh MBri MGos NLar SPer SPoG
*	- 'Glory Gem' (f)	CBcs
	- 'Golden Gem' (f/v) ♀^{H4}	CDoC CMac CRos CSBt CTri ELan ELon EPfP IVic LRHS MAsh MGos MSwo NSoo NWea SCoo SGol SHil SPer SPoG SWvt WPat
	- 'Golden Rock'^{PBR}	EBee
*	- 'Green Hedge'	EPfP LBuc
	- 'Helleri' (f)	EPfP MAsh WPat
	- 'Ivory Tower' (f)	NEgg NPCo
	- 'Luteovariegata'	see *I. crenata* 'Variegata'
	- 'Mariesii' (f)	CMac MBlu
I	- 'Pyramidalis' (f)	MRav NWea
§	- 'Shiro-fukurin' (f/v)	CMCN ELan EPfP LRHS SLon
	- 'Sky Pencil' (f)	CMCN
	- 'Snowflake'	see *I. crenata* 'Shiro-fukurin'
	- 'Stokes' (m)	NLar
§	- 'Variegata' (v)	CMac EPfP LRHS NLar
	dimorphophylla	CMac
	dipyrena	IArd
	'Doctor Kassab' (f)	CMCN
	'Elegance' (f)	MBlu
	hascombensis	see *I. aquifolium* 'Hascombensis'
	'Indian Chief' (f)	NPCo
	× ***koehneana***	CDul
	- 'Chestnut Leaf' (f) ♀^{H4}	CAVT CDoC CLnd CMCN EBee EPfP EWTr MRav NLar NPCo NSoo SSta WGrn WMou
	laevigata	CMCN
	latifolia	CHEx CMCN NLar WPGP
*	'Little Diamond'	LSRN
	'Lydia Morris' (f)	CSam
	× ***meserveae***	NSoo
	- Blue Angel = 'Conang' (f)	CBcs CDoC CDul CMac EBee ELan EPfP IFoB LRHS MAsh MBri MRav NEgg NLar NPCo NWea SPoG SRms
	- Blue Bunny = 'Meseal' (f)	IVic
	- 'Blue Girl' (f)	CTri
	- Blue Maid = 'Mesid' (f)	NLar NPCo
	- Blue Prince = 'Conablu' (m)	CBcs CDoC CDul CLnd CMCN CMac EBee ELan LBuc LRHS MAsh MBlu MJak NEgg NHol NLar NSoo NWea SLim SPer SPoG
	- Blue Princess = 'Conapri' (f)	CBcs CDul CMCN CMac EBee ELan EPfP LBuc LRHS MAsh MBlu MJak MRav NLar NPCo NPri NWea SCoo SLim SPer SPoG

- Castle Spire = 'Hachfee'PBR	EBee NLar
- Castle Wall = 'Hecken Star'PBR	EBee IVic
- 'Heckenpracht'PBR	EBee IVic
myrtifolia	CMac MAsh MRav NHol
'Nellie R. Stevens' (f)	CDoC ECrN EPfP NLar NWea SEWo
opaca	CMCN
perado subsp. ***azorica***	WPGP
- - B&SWJ 12526 **new**	WCru
- subsp. ***perado***	CBcs NPCo
- subsp. ***platyphylla***	CBcs CMCN MBlu SAPC
pernyi	CDoC CMCN CMac CTri EPfP LRHS MAsh MJak SLon SPoG
- var. ***veitchii***	see *I. bioritsensis*
'September Gem' (f)	CMCN NPCo
serrata	CMac CMen
- 'Koshobai'	CMen
- 'Leucocarpa'	CMen
suaveolens	CMCN
verticillata	CMCN EBee LRHS NEgg
- (f)	CBcs EBtc ELon EPfP MMHG NLar NWea
- (m)	EBtc ELon EPfP MMHG NLar NWea
- f. ***chrysocarpa*** (f)	NLar
- 'Maryland Beauty' (f)	CJun NLar
- 'Southern Gentleman' (m)	CJun MBlu NLar
- 'Winter Gold' (f)	CJun MBlu
- 'Winter Red' (f)	CJun CMCN MBlu
vomitoria	CMCN EBtc
yunnanensis	GQui IArd

Iliamna see *Sphaeralcea*

Illicium (*Schisandraceae*)

anisatum	CBcs CDoC CExl CFil CMac EPfP IGor NLar WPGP WPat WSHC
floridanum	CBcs EBee EPfP GKin LEdu NLar SBrt SSpi WPat
- f. ***album***	EPfP
- 'Halley's Comet'	CExl CFil NLar
aff. ***griffithii*** **new**	WCru
henryi	CDoC CExl CGHE CWib EBee EPfP IVic NLar SSpi WPGP WSHC
aff. ***henryi***	CBcs
jiadifengpi	NLar
lanceolatum	CExl CFil
- KWJ 12245 **new**	WCru
majus WWJ 11919	WCru
aff. ***majus*** **new**	WCru
mexicanum	CFil
oligandrum	CExl NLar
parviflorum	CFil
simonsii	CExl CFil IVic MBlu WPGP
- BWJ 8024	WCru
'Woodland Ruby'	NLar

Ilysanthes see *Lindernia*

Impatiens ✿ (*Balsaminaceae*)

CC 4980	CExl
DJHC 98415	CDes WCru WPGP
apiculata	EBee GCal
arguta	CCon CDes CExl CLAP CSam CSpe EShb GCal MPie SBrt WPGP
- 'Alba'	CSpe
Athena Series (d)	NPri
auricoma	WCot
auricoma × ***bicaudata***	WDib
balfourii	CPla
bicaudata	CSpe MPie
congolensis	CCCN
'Emei Dawn'	WCru
flanaganae	CCon CFil WPGP
forrestii	CLAP
gomphophylla	CCon CFil
(Harmony Series) Harmony Dark Red = 'Danhardkrd'	WGor
- Harmony Orange Star	WGor
- Harmony Pink Smile = 'Danhar267'	WGor
- Harmony Raspberry Cream = 'Danharras'	WGor
- Harmony Violet = 'Danharvio'	WGor
keilii	WDib
kerriae B&SWJ 7219	WCru
kilimanjari subsp. ***kilimanjari***	CCon CDoC CSpe GCal MPie
kilimanjari × ***pseudoviola***	CDes CDoC CSpe MPie WDib
langbianensis HWJ 1054	WCru
(LaTina Series) 'LaTina Appleblossom' **new**	LAst
- 'LaTina Electric Purple' **new**	LAst
- 'LaTina Red Orange' **new**	LAst
macrophylla B&SWJ 10157	WCru
namchabarwensis	CDes CSpe MCot WCot WPGP
niamniamensis	CHll EBak EShb WCot WDib
- 'Congo Cockatoo'	CDTJ CDoC NPer SRms
- 'Golden Cockatoo' (v)	CDTJ CDoC CHll EBak EShb
noli-tangere	WSFF
omeiana	CCCN CCon CDes CHEx CHel CLAP CPom CSpe EBee EPPr ESwi EUJe EWld GCal IGor LEdu LRHS MNrw MSCN NLar SBch SBig WBor WCot WCru WPGP WPtf WSHC
- DJH C98492	WCru
- 'Ice Storm'	EBee GCal LEdu WCru
- silver-leaved	CDes CHEx CLAP WCru WPGP
- variegated (v) **new**	LEdu
parasitica	WDib
platypetala B&SWJ 9722	WCru
puberula	CCon CSam MPie
- HWJK 2063	CDes EBee SBrt WCru WPGP
repens 🏆H1	WDib
rothii	CCon CDes CSpe EShb GCal
scabrida	CPla CSpe
§ 'Secret Love'	CCCN WDib
sodenii	CCon CDTJ CSpe GCal SBHP WDib
stenantha	CCon CDes MPie
(Sunpatiens Series) Sunpatiens Spreading Variegated Salmon = 'Sakimp005' (v) **new**	LSou
- Sunpatiens Spreading Variegated White = 'Sakimp018'PBR (v) **new**	LSou
tinctoria	CCon CExl CFil CGHE CHEx CHel CHll CPom CSpe GCal GCra LPio MNrw WCot WPGP
- from Cherangani, Kenya	GCal

- subsp. ***tinctoria***	IFro
tuberosa	WDib
ugandensis	GCal
uniflora	CCon EBee GCal SBrt WPGP
Velvetea	see *I.* 'Secret Love'
walleriana DeZire Series	NPri
- - 'DeZire Lavender Splash'	LAst
- (Musica Series) 'Musica Bicolor Cherry' **new**	LAst
- - 'Musica Pink Aroma' (d) **new**	LAst
- - 'Musica Salmon' (d) **new**	LAst

Imperata (*Poaceae*)

cylindrica	CMen XLum
- 'Red Baron'	see *I. cylindrica* 'Rubra'
§ - 'Rubra'	Widely available

Incarvillea (*Bignoniaceae*)

arguta	LLHF XLum
brevipes	see *I. mairei*
compacta	EBee LLHF
- BWJ 7620	WCru
delavayi	CBcs CHel CSBt CWib ECho ELan EPfP EPot GBuc GKev GMaP IBoy LPot MGos MSCN MWhi NBir NLar NSoo SDeJ SGol SPad SPer SRms SVen SWvt WHil WWEG XLum
- SDR 4711	GKev
- 'Alba'	see *I. delavayi* 'Snowtop'
- 'Bees' Pink'	CHel EBee EDAr EPfP EPot GBuc LRHS NLar
- 'Rose'	LRHS
§ - 'Snowtop'	CHel EBee ELan EPfP EPot GKev IBoy LRHS NBir NLar NSoo SDeJ SGol SPer SWvt WWEG
cf. ***delavayi*** SDR 6715	GKev
forrestii	EBee GKev
grandiflora	EBee ELan GKev
lutea	EBee GKev
§ ***mairei***	CTsd ECho EDAr GKev LRHS NLar
- SDR 1812	GKev
- SDR 4336	GKev
- var. ***mairei***	GBuc
- - f. ***multifoliata***	see *I. zhongdianensis*
olgae	EBee EPfP
sinensis 'Churon'	CHel EDif
younghusbandii	LLHF
§ ***zhongdianensis***	CFis CPBP EBee ECho EPot GKev LLHF LRHS SPhx
- ACE 1600	GBuc
- BWJ 7692	WCru
- BWJ 7978	EDAr WCru
- white-flowered **new**	GKev

Indigofera (*Papilionaceae*)

amblyantha ♀H4	CBcs CCCN CExl ELon EPfP LRHS MAsh MBlu MBri NLar SEND SKHP SPlb SSpi WSHC
australis	MOWG
balfouriana BWJ 7851	WCru
cassioides	WCru
decora f. ***alba***	EPfP
dielsiana	CCCN EBee ELan EPfP LRHS WKif WPGP
'Dosua'	SEND
gerardiana	see *I. heterantha*
hancockii	SKHP WSHC
hebepetala	EBee EPfP SBrt SKHP WPGP WSHC
§ ***heterantha*** ♀H4	Widely available
- from China	MBri
heterophylla **new**	CCCN
himalayensis	CExl CMHG EBee SKHP
- Yu 10941	WPGP
- 'Silk Road'	CCCN ELan EPfP LRHS MBlu MBri MGos SHil SKHP
howellii	CMHG SChF SKHP WPGP
howellii × ***pendula*** **new**	WSHC
kirilowii	EPfP IVic MBri MOWG NLar SKHP WPGP WSHC
pendula	CCCN CExl CHel CMHG CSpe CWGN EBee EPfP GKev LRHS MOWG SEND SKHP SPoG SSpi WKif WPGP WSHC
- B&SWJ 7741	WCru
potaninii	CExl CHel CMac EPfP LHop LRHS MOWG WHer
pseudotinctoria	CCCN CPom EPfP SEND SRms
aff. ***pseudotinctoria*** **new**	CCCN
subverticillata	WSHC
szechuensis	SKHP
tinctoria	CArn CCCN

Indocalamus (*Poaceae*)

latifolius	EPPr ERod EUJe MMoz MMuc MWht WJun
solidus	see *Bonia solida*
§ ***tessellatus*** ♀H4	CAbb CDoC CEnt CHEx EAmu ELon ENBC EPfP ERod GCal IDee MBri MMoz MWht NGdn SEND SMad WJun WMoo WPGP
- f. ***hamadae***	ERod MMoz MWht WJun

Indosasa (*Poaceae*)

gigantea	ERod

Inula (*Asteraceae*)

acaulis	WCot
afghanica	EBee
barbata	GCal LRHS
conyzae	WHer
cordata	LRHS
dysenterica	see *Pulicaria dysenterica*
ensifolia	CBcs ELan EPfP GJos MNFA NBro XLum
- 'Compacta'	ECho GCal LRHS
- 'Gold Star'	CMac EBee ECho MBNS MRav NBid NBir NEgg SPoG
glandulosa	see *I. orientalis*
helenium	CArn CHab CHby CPrp CSev ELau GAbr GPoy IBoy LEdu MHer MHoo NBid NBir NLar NMir SPoG SRms WGwG WHer WHfH WJek WMoo
hirta	XLum
hookeri	CBre CMea CSam ELan GBin GCal GJos GMaP IFro LEdu LLWG MBel MHol MLHP MMuc MNFA NBid NChi NDov NPer NSti SDix SEND WBrk WWEG
- GWJ 9033	WCru
macrocephala misapplied	see *I. royleana*
magnifica	Widely available
- 'Sonnenstrahl' ♀H4	GQue NLar SEND SPhx
oculus-christi	EBee EWes NBre WCot
§ ***orientalis***	EPfP GAbr GJos MBri NGBl NLar NSoo SMad SPad SRms WJek WWEG XLum

racemosa	CTca EPPr EWes GBin GCal IBlr LHop MNrw SMrm SPlb WBor
- 'Sonnenspeer'	GBin NBid NLar SLPl WPtf
§ ***royleana***	GCal MNrw MRav
salicina	EBee

Iochroma (*Solanaceae*)

§ ***australe***	CCCN CHll CSpe EDif EWld MOWG SPlb SVen
§ - 'Andean Snow'	CExl CHll EShb
§ - 'Bill Evans'	CExl EShb
cyaneum	CCCN CDoC CHll MOWG
- purple-flowered	CCCN CHll
gesnerioides	WCot
- 'Coccineum'	CCCN CDoC CHll WCot
§ ***grandiflorum***	CCCN CDoC CHll CSev SEND
warscewiczii	see *I. grandiflorum*

Ipheion ✿ (*Alliaceae*)

'Alberto Castillo'	CAby CAvo CBro CDes CHid CMea CPom ECho ELan ELon EPot ERCP EWes GBuc GKev LHop LLHF LPio LRHS MNrw NMin NPnk SDeJ SDys SPhx WCot WHoo WIvy WPGP WWFP
dialystemon	ECho EPot LLHF NPnk WAbe
- JCA 2420010	WPGP
hirtellum	CDes
'Jessie'	CAby CBro CDes CMea CPom CPrp EBee ECho EPot ERCP GBuc GKev LHop LLHF LRHS MNrw NMin NPnk WCot
'Rolf Fiedler' ♀H2-3	CAvo CBro CHel CPom CPrp CTri EBee ECho ELan EPPr EPfP EPot ERCP EWes GBuc GKev LHop LPio LRHS MNrw NHol NPnk SDeJ SMrm SPer SPhx WHoo
sellowianum	CAby CDes WCot
sessile	CDes EBee ECho
'Tessa' 'PBR **new**	ERCP GKev LLHF
§ ***uniflorum***	CBro CTri ECho MMoz MNrw SBch SEND SMrm SPer SRms WBrk WCot XLum
- f. ***album***	CBro CPom CPrp EBee ECho EPPr EPot EWes GKev LEdu LRHS MNrw WCot WHal WHil
- 'Charlotte Bishop'	CAvo CBro CCon CDes CMea CPom CPrp EBee ECho EHyd ELon EPPr EPot ERCP EWes GBuc GKev LHop LLHF LPio LRHS MNrw NBir NMin NPnk NRya SDeJ SMrm WCot WHoo
- 'Froyle Mill' ♀H4	CBro CMea CPom CPrp EBee ECho ELon EPPr EPot ERCP EWes GKev LHop LLWP LPio LRHS MNrw NPnk WCot WHil WHoo
- subsp. ***tandiliense***	CDes
- 'Wisley Blue' ♀H4	CBro CCon CExl CMea CPom CPrp CTri EBee ECho ELan ELon EPfP EPot ERCP GBuc GKev LHop LLWP LPio LRHS MRav NPnk NRya SDeJ SMrm SRms WCot WHoo

Ipomoea (*Convolvulaceae*)

acuminata	see *I. indica*
alba	CCCN
batatas 'Blackie'	EShb ESwi
- 'Margarita'	EShb ESwi
- 'Pink Frost' (v)	EShb
- Suntory Black Tone = 'Kyuikukan 1' PBR	EShb
- (Sweet Caroline Series) 'Sweet Caroline Bewitched Purple' PBR **new**	SMrm
- - 'Sweet Caroline Bronze' PBR	ESwi EUJe SMrm
- - 'Sweet Caroline Purple' PBR	EUJe
- - 'Sweet Caroline Sweetheart Light Green' PBR	ESwi
- - 'Sweet Caroline Sweetheart Purple' PBR	CSpe ESwi
carnea	CCCN
coccinea var. ***hederifolia***	see *I. hederifolia*
§ ***hederifolia***	CCCN
× ***imperialis*** 'Sunrise Serenade'	CCCN
§ ***indica*** ♀H1	CCCN CHEx CHVG CHll CRHN CSam EShb MOWG MREP SPer
learii	see *I. indica*
§ ***lobata*** ♀H3	CSpe LSou
'Milky Way'	CCCN
muellerii	CCCN
× ***multifida***	CSpe
purpurea 'Grandpa Otts'	CWCL
- 'Kniola's Black Night'	CSpe
quamoclit	CSpe
versicolor	see *I. lobata*

Iresine (*Amaranthaceae*)

Blazin' Lime	see *I.* 'Lime'
Blazin' Rose	see *I.* 'Rose'
herbstii	EShb EUJe
- 'Aureoreticulata'	EShb
§ 'Lime' **new**	EUJe
§ 'Rose' **new**	EUJe

Iris ✿ (*Iridaceae*)

'Abbey Chant' (IB)	CIri WCAu XSen
'About Town' (TB)	WCAu
'Abracadabra' (SDB)	SMrm
'Absolute Treasure' (TB)	EWoo
'Ace' (MTB)	LMin
'Acoma' (TB)	WCAu
'Action Front' (TB)	ECGP EIri EPfP ESgI EWoo LHop LPio LRHS MLHP SDeJ SHil SMrm WCAu WGwG WWEG
'Actress' (TB)	CMac CWGN EBee EPfP LRHS LSRN SHil
acutiloba	LWst
'Adobe Rose' (TB)	ESgI SIri XSen
'Adventuress' (TB)	EWoo XSen
'After Dark' (TB)	CKel
'Afternoon Delight' (TB)	ESgI EWoo WCAu
'Afternoon in Rio' (TB)	WCAu
'Again and Again' (TB)	EWoo
'Agatha Christie' (IB)	WCAu
'Age of Innocence' (TB)	WCAu
'Aglow Again' (MTB)	SDys
'Agnes James' (CH) ♀H3	CBro
'Agua Fresca' (TB/v)	WCAu
'Ahwahnee Princess' (SDB)	EWoo
'Aichi-no-kagayaki' (SpH)	EBee WCot WHil XLum
'Alabaster Unicorn' (TB)	ESgI
'Albatross' (TB)	SMrm

albicans ♀H4	CMea CPBP ECho LEdu
– 'Blue Pygmy' **new**	CAby
albomarginata	ECho LWst
'Alcazar' (TB)	EWoo LSRN SWat WMnd WWEG
'Aldo Ratti' (TB)	ESgI
'Alene's New Love' (SDB)	EWoo
'Alene's Other Love' (SDB)	WCAu
'Alenette' (TB)	WCAu
'Alexia' (TB) ♀H4	CKel
'Alice Harding' (TB)	ESgI
'Alida' (Reticulata)	CBro ECho EPot ERCP GKev LLHF SDeJ
'Alizes' (TB) ♀H4	CPar ESgI LRHS WCAu XSen
'Allegiance' (TB)	WCAu
'Amadora' (TB)	CKel EIri
'Amas' (TB)	WCAu
'Amazing Grace' (TB)	EWoo
'Ambassadeur' (TB)	EWoo
'Amber Beauty' (Dut) **new**	GKev
'Amber Queen' (DB)	ECtt ELan NBir SDeJ SPer
'Ambersand' (IB)	SIri
'Ambroisie' (TB) ♀H4	ESgI EWoo
'Amelia Bedeila' (IB)	SIri
'American Patriot' (IB)	CKel WCAu
'Amethyst Dancer' (TB)	WCAu
'Amethyst Flame' (TB)	ECho ESgI NBre SRms WCAu
'Amherst Blue' (IB)	EIri SIri
'Amherst Bluebeard' (SDB)	ESgI SIri
'Amherst Caper' (SDB)	EIri ESgI
'Amherst Glacier' (IB)	WCAu
'Amherst Jester' (BB)	SIri
'Amherst Purple Ribbon' (SDB)	WCAu
'Amigo' (TB)	EWoo
'Amphora' (SDB)	CBro LBuc
'Amy Remy' (TB) **new**	CIri
'Ancient Echoes' (TB)	ESgI
'Andalou' (TB) ♀H4	CWCL EWoo XSen
'Angel Heart' (IB)	EWoo
'Angel Unawares' (TB)	WCAu
'Angel's Tears'	see *I. histrioides* 'Angel's Tears'
'Angel's Touch' (TB)	ESgI
anglica	see *I. latifolia*
'Ann Dasch' (Sib)	WWEG
'Annabel Jane' (TB)	CHid CKel COIW ELon WCAu
'Anne Elizabeth' (SDB)	CBro
'Annemarie Troeger' (Sib) ♀H4	ELon SMrm
'Annikins' (IB) ♀H4	CKel
'Anniversary Celebration' (TB)	CKel
'Announcement' (TB)	CIri
'Antarctique' (IB)	ESgI
'Antiope' (Rc)	GKev
'Anvil of Darkness' (TB)	EWoo
'Aphrodisiac' (TB)	XSen
aphylla	GBin WThu
– 'Slick'	SDys
'Apollo' (Dut)	CAvo GKev
'Appledore' (SDB)	CBro
'Appointer' (SpH)	NChi
'Apricorange' (TB) ♀H4	CKel WCot
'Apricot Blaze' (TB)	ESgI
'Apricot Drops' (MTB) ♀H4	ESgI LMin WCAu
'Apricot Frosty' (BB)	ESgI WCAu XSen
'Apricot Silk' (IB)	CCCN IBoy SEND SMrm WWEG
'Apricot Topping' (BB)	WCAu
'Arab Chief' (TB)	CKel
* 'Arabic Night' (IB)	WCAu

'Arcobaleno' (TB)	CIri
'Arctic Age' (TB)	WCAu
'Arctic Fancy' (IB) ♀H4	CKel
'Arctic Sunrise' (TB)	ESgI
'Arctic Wind' (IB) **new**	WCAu
'Argus Pheasant' (TB)	ESgI WCAu
'Armageddon' (TB)	ESgI
'Arms Wide Open' (TB)	CIri
'Around Midnight' (TB)	LRHS WCAu
'Arpège' (TB)	XSen
'Art Deco' (TB)	SIri XSen
'Art School Angel' (TB)	CIri
'Arts Alive' (Spuria)	EWoo
'As de Coeur' (TB)	XSen
'As You Were' (TB)	CIri
'Ascension Crown' (TB)	ESgI
'Ask Alma' (IB)	ESgI XSen
'Astrid Cayeux' (TB)	ESgI
'Astro Flash' (TB)	ESgI
'Astrology' (TB)	WCAu
'Athaenos' (IB) **new**	CIri
'Atlantic Crossing' (Sib)	SIri
'Atlantic Sky' (TB)	ESgI
* 'Atlantique' (TB)	CKel
'Attention Please' (TB)	CKel ELan SMrm WWEG
attica	CBro CPBP ECho LLHF LWst NRya WCot WThu
– lemon-flowered	WThu
§ ***aucheri*** ♀H2	ECho EPot GKev LLHF LWst NMin
– 'Blue Jay'	LWst
– 'Blue Tit'	LWst
– indigo-flowered	LWst
– 'Leylek Ice'	LWst
– 'Leylek Lilac'	LWst
– 'Olof'	LWst
– 'Snow Princess'	ECho LWst
– 'Snow White'	ECho LWst
– 'Turkish Ice'	LWst
– white-flowered	LWst
'Aunt Josephine' (TB)	ESgI
'Aurean' (IB)	CKel
'Austrian Sky' (SDB)	CMac EBee ECtt LHop LRHS NSoo SDeJ WCot
'Autumn Apricot' (TB)	EWoo
'Autumn Circus' (TB)	EWoo WCAu
'Autumn Echo' (TB)	ESgI XSen
'Autumn Embers' (SDB)	WCAu
'Autumn Encore' (TB)	EWoo MHer
'Autumn Riesling' (TB)	WCAu
'Autumn Tryst' (TB)	ESgI EWoo WCAu
'Avalon Sunset' (TB)	EIri
'Awesome Blossom' (TB)	ESgI
'Az Ap' (IB)	ELon WCAu WHil
'Babbling Brook' (TB)	XSen
'Baby Bengal' (BB)	XSen
'Baby Blessed' (SDB)	CBro WCAu
'Baby Prince' (SDB)	ESgI
'Baby Sister' (Sib)	CMHG EBee EWoo GAbr GBin GBuc LRHS LSRN NBre NBro SRGP SWat
'Baccarat' (TB)	WCAu
'Bach Toccata' (MTB)	SDys
'Back in Black' (TB)	CKel
'Badlands' (TB)	WCAu
'Bal Masqué' (TB)	ESgI XSen
'Ballistic' (SDB)	WCAu
'Ballyhoo' (TB)	WCAu XSen
'Baltic Star' (TB)	EWoo WCAu

	'Banbury Beauty' (CH) ♀H3	MAvo
	'Banbury Gem' (CH)	MAvo
	'Banbury Ruffles' (SDB)	ESgI WCAu
	'Bandera Waltz' (TB)	WCAu
	'Bang' (TB)	CKel
	'Bangles' (MTB) ♀H4	LMin SDys WCAu
	'Banish Misfortune' (Sib)	CIri WCAu
	'Banker Dave' (TB) new	CIri
	'Bar de Nuit' (TB)	ESgI EWoo
	'Barbara My Love' (TB)	WCAu
	'Barbara's Kiss' (Spuria)	CIri
	barbatula BWJ 7663	WCru
	barnumae	LWst
	'Baroque Prelude' (TB)	CKel WCAu
	'Batik' (BB)	SIri WCot XSen
	'Battlestar Atlantis' (TB)	CIri
	'Baubles and Beads' (MTB)	LMin
	'Bayberry Candle' (TB)	WCAu
	'Be Mine' (TB)	CIri
	'Be My Baby' (BB)	WCAu
	'Beach Girl' (TB)	EWoo
	'Bedtime Story' (IB)	SWat WWEG XSen
	'Beechfield'	LRHS
	'Bee's Knees' (SDB) ♀H4	SIri
	'Before the Storm' (TB)	CKel ELon ESgI GBin WCAu XSen
	'Beguine' (TB)	ESgI
	'Being Busy' (SDB)	ESgI
	'Bel Azur' (IB)	ESgI EWoo LRHS
	'Bel Esprit' (TB)	WCAu
	'Belgian Princess' (TB)	WCAu
	'Belise' (Spuria) ♀H4	WCot
	'Belle de Nuit' (TB)	EWoo
	'Ben a Factor' (MTB)	ESgI LMin
	'Benton Arundel' (TB)	EMal
	'Benton Bluejohn' (TB) new	EMal
	'Benton Caramel' (TB)	EMal EWoo
	'Benton Cordelia' (TB)	EMal
	'Benton Daphne' (TB)	EMal
	'Benton Dierdre' (TB)	EBee ELon EMal SRms
	'Benton Evora' (TB)	EMal
	'Benton Lorna' (TB)	EMal
	'Benton Nigel' (TB)	EMal EWoo WCAu
	'Benton Olive' (TB)	EMal
	'Benton Opal' (TB) new	EMal
	'Benton Pearl' (TB) new	EMal
	'Benton Primrose' (TB)	EMal EWoo
	'Benton Sheila' (TB)	ELon
	'Benton Susan' (TB)	EMal EWoo
	'Beotie' (TB)	EWoo
	'Bering Sea' (IB)	WCAu
	'Berkeley Gold' (TB)	CSBt ECtt ELan EShb EWes LRHS NOrc SDeJ SPer SWat WWEG
	'Berlin Bluebird' (Sib)	CGHE
	'Berlin Purple Wine' (Sib)	EPri
	'Berlin Ruffles' (Sib) ♀H4	CIri EWes EWoo
	'Berlin Sky' (Sib)	ESgI EWes
	'Berlin Tiger' (SpH) ♀H4	CRow EBee EPPr EPfP LLWG MSCN MWts NLar SGol WHil
	'Bermuda Triangle' (BB)	SDys
	'Best Bet' (TB)	ESgI EWoo WCAu
	'Bethany Claire' (TB)	ESgI WCAu
	'Betty Cooper' (Spuria)	WCAu
	'Betty Simon' (TB)	CKel CWCL EWoo XSen
	'Beverly Sills' (TB)	EBee EPfP EWoo GBin LSou MRav SBea SDeJ SRGP WCAu WGwG XSen
	'Bewilderbeast' (TB)	XSen
	'Bianco' (TB)	WWEG
	'Bibury' (SDB) ♀H4	WCAu
	'Bickley Cape' (Sib)	WWEG
	'Big Dipper' (TB)	ECtt
	'Big Melt' (TB)	CKel
	'Big Squeeze' (TB)	WCAu
	biglumis	see *I. lactea*
	biliottii	CBro
	'Bishop's Robe' (TB)	ESgI
	'Black as Night' (TB)	XSen
	'Black Beauty' (Dut)	EPfP
	'Black Beauty' (TB)	MWat SPer
	'Black Cherry Delight' (SDB)	ESgI
	'Black Dragon' (TB)	CCCN CHid MAvo NLar XSen
	'Black Flag' (TB)	XSen
	'Black Gamecock' (La)	CCon CHel CWCL EBee ECtt ELan MBNS MNrw MSCN MWts NBro NLar SKHP SMrm WMAq
	'Black Hope' (TB)	CIri EWoo
	'Black Ink' (TB)	COIW
	'Black Knight' (TB)	MRav NLar WHrl WKif
	'Black Magic' (IB)	EWoo
	'Black Night' (IB)	SRGP WWEG
	'Black Sergeant' (TB) ♀H4	CKel
	'Black Stallion' (MDB)	ESgI
	'Black Swan' (TB)	CMac ECtt ELan EPfP ESgI EShb EUJe EWoo GCal LSRN MNrw NBre NGdn SBea SPer SPoG WCAu WCot WHil XSen
	'Black Taffeta' (TB)	CKel
	'Black Tie Affair' (TB)	EPfP ESgI EWoo XSen
	'Blackbeard' (BB) ♀H4	CKel WCAu
	'Blackberry Tease' (TB) new	WCAu
	'Blackberry Towers' (TB)	ESgI
	'Blackcurrant' (IB)	WCAu
	'Blackout' (TB)	ESgI EWoo
	'Blast' (IB)	CKel
	'Blatant' (TB)	ESgI EWoo WCAu XSen
	'Blazing Light' (TB)	XSen
	'Blenheim Royal' (TB)	ESgI WCAu XSen
	'Blessed Again' (IB)	EBee
	'Blitzen' (IB)	WCAu
	'Blue Admiral' (TB)	GBin
	'Blue Boy' (IB)	EWoo
I	'Blue Butterfly' (Sib)	CPrp EBee EPfP LLWG LPio MNrw NGdn
	'Blue Denim' (SDB)	ECho ECtt EPfP GCal GMaP MRav NBir NPnk WBor WCAu WCot WHil WWEG
	'Blue Eyed Blond' (IB)	MNrw
	'Blue Eyed Brunette' (TB)	WCAu
	'Blue Gown' (TB)	EWoo
	'Blue Hendred' (SDB)	NBir WCAu
	'Blue King' (Sib)	CHel CHid CKel EHyd ELan EPfP GBin GKev GMaP MRav NBro NGdn SMrm SPer WMnd WMoo WWEG
	'Blue Lamp' (TB)	CKel
	'Blue Line' (SDB) ♀H4	CDes NBre
	'Blue Meadow Fly' (Sino-Sib)	LLHF
	'Blue Mere' (Sib)	MCot
	'Blue Moon' (Sib)	CPrp EBee GBuc GQue MJak
*	'Blue Mystery'	LLHF
	'Blue Note Blues' (TB)	WCAu
	'Blue Note' (Reticulata)	CBro LLHF NMin
	'Blue Pigmy' (SDB)	CPBP CWat EBee ECtt EPfP LRHS NGdn NLar SDeJ SPer
	'Blue Pools' (SDB)	MBri NBir
	'Blue Reverie' (Sib)	ELon ESgI EWoo

	'Blue Rhythm' (TB)	CAby CKel ELan ELon EPfP EWoo GMaP LRHS MRav SCoo SDeJ SPer WCAu WMnd WWEG
	'Blue Sapphire' (Dut) **new**	MAvo
	'Blue Sapphire' (TB)	ESgI WCAu
	'Blue Sceptre' (Sib)	IBlr
	'Blue Shimmer' (TB)	CSBt EBee ELan EPfP ESgI EShb EWoo LRHS LSRN NCGa SDeJ SPer SWat WCAu WGwG WWEG
	'Blue Staccato' (TB)	CKel WCAu XSen
	'Blue Suede Shoes' (TB)	ESgI EWoo LSRN XSen
	'Blue Warlsind' (J)	LWst
	'Bluebeard's Ghost' (SDB) ♀H4 **new**	CIri WCAu
	'Blueberry Fair' (Sib)	CIri
	'Bluebird Wine' (TB)	WCAu
	'Bob Nichol' (TB) ♀H4	CKel
	'Bob's Fancy'	SDeJ
	'Bockingford' (MTB)	LMin SIri
	'Bohemia Sekt' (TB)	CKel
	'Bohemian' (TB)	CWCL
	'Bold Encounter' (TB) **new**	WCAu
	'Bold Pretender' (La)	CHel ECtt ELan EPfP LLWG MBNS MSCN NLar SKHP WHil
	'Bold Print' (IB)	ELon IPot LRHS LSRN NCGa SBea SHil SPoG WCAu WWEG
	'Bollinger'	see *I.* 'Hornpipe'
	'Bonnie Davenport' (TB)	CIri
I	'Bonny' (MDB)	CBro
	'Bonus Bucks' (TB)	CKel
	'Boo' (SDB)	CKel CPBP WCAu XSen
	'Border Happy' (TB)	WCAu
	'Bottled Sunshine' (IB) **new**	LRHS
	'Bouzy Bouzy' (TB)	ESgI XSen
	'Bracknell' (Sib)	WBor
	bracteata	EBee GBuc IGor
	- NNS 04-223	GBuc
	bracteata* × *thompsonii	IGor
	'Braithwaite' (TB)	CAby CKel CWGN ECGP ELan ESgI EShb EWoo LRHS MSpe NSoo SDeJ SPer SRms SWat WCAu WGwG
	'Brandaris' (TB)	ESgI
	'Brannigan' (SDB)	CBro NBir NSti
	'Brasero' (TB)	CWCL EWoo
	'Brash and Bold' (AB)	WCAu
	'Brasilia' (TB)	NBir NBre
	'Brassie' (SDB)	CBro MBNS NBro WHil WWEG XSen
	'Brave New World' (TB) ♀H4	CIri
	'Breakers' (TB) ♀H4	CKel EWoo WCAu
	'Breezy Blue' (SDB)	WCAu
	'Bridal Icing' (TB) **new**	WCAu
	'Bridal Jig' (Sib)	EBee
§	'Bride' (DB)	WMnd
	'Bride's Halo' (TB)	LSRN WCAu XSen
	'Bright Button' (SDB)	CKel ESgI EWoo
	'Bright Fire' (TB)	EIri
	'Bright Vision' (SDB)	ESgI
	'Bright White' (MDB)	CBro CKel ECho SMrm
	'Bright Yellow' (DB)	MRav
	'Brighteyes' (IB)	LRHS SRms
	'Brindisi' (TB)	XSen
	'Brise de Mer' (TB)	XSen
	'Bristo Magic' (TB)	XSen
	'Bristol Gem' (TB)	XSen
	'Broad Shoulders' (TB)	WCAu
	'Broadband' (TB)	WCAu
	'Broadleigh Angela' (CH)	CBro
	'Broadleigh Ann' (CH)	CBro
	'Broadleigh Carolyn' (CH) ♀H3	CBro CElw
	'Broadleigh Clare' (CH)	CBro
	'Broadleigh Dorothy' (CH)	CBro MAvo
	'Broadleigh Eleanor' (CH)	CBro
	'Broadleigh Elizabeth' (CH)	CBro
	'Broadleigh Emily' (CH)	CBro
	'Broadleigh Fenella' (CH)	CBro
	'Broadleigh Jean' (CH)	CBro
	'Broadleigh Joan' (CH)	CBro
	'Broadleigh Lavinia' (CH)	CBro MRav
	'Broadleigh Mitre' (CH)	CBro CElw
	'Broadleigh Nancy' (CH)	CBro MAvo
	'Broadleigh Peacock' (CH)	CBro CElw MAvo WSHC
	'Broadleigh Penny' (CH)	CBro
	'Broadleigh Rose' (CH)	CBro CElw EPri EPyc LRHS MBrN MRav SMrm WSHC
	'Broadway Baby' (IB)	ESgI SIri
	'Bronzaire' (IB) ♀H4	CKel EIri WCAu WGwG
	'Bronze Age' (AB)	LWst
	'Bronze Beauty' (Dut)	ERCP GKev
	'Bronze Beauty' (TB)	SDeJ
	'Bronze Beauty' van Tubergen (*boogiana* hybrid)	EPfP NBir SDeJ
	'Bronze Perfection' (Dut)	WRHF
	'Bronzed Violet' (TB)	CKel
	'Brother Carl' (TB)	XSen
	'Brown Chocolate' (TB)	WCAu
	'Brown Lasso' (BB) ♀H4	WCAu
	'Bruce' (TB)	WCAu
	'Brummit's Mauve' (TB)	WCAu
	'Bruno' (TB)	LSRN NLar
	'Brussels' (TB)	ESgI
	bucharica misapplied	see *I. orchioides* Carrière
	bucharica ambig.	ECho ELon MNrw SDeJ WBor
§	***bucharica*** Foster ♀H3-4	CBro ECho EPfP EPot GKev
*	- 'Baldschuan Yellow' (J)	LWst
	- 'Princess'	EBee ECho
*	- 'Top Gold'	ECho
	bucharica* × *orchioides	ECho
	'Buckwheat' (TB)	EWoo SIri
	'Buisson de Roses' (TB)	XSen
	bulleyana	CHel ECho GKev SRms
	- BWJ 7912	WCru
	- from Dali, Yunnan, China **new**	SBrt
	- black-flowered	CExl GKev
	- - SDR 1792	EBee
	- - SDR 4775	GKev
	'Bumble Boogie' (MTB) **new**	WCAu
	'Bumblebee Deelite' (MTB) ♀H4	CJun CKel LMin WCAu
	'Burgermeister' (TB)	XSen
	'Burgundy Party' (TB)	XSen
	'Burka' (TB)	ESgI
	'Burnt Toffee' (TB)	ESgI XSen
	'Burst' (TB)	CKel WCAu
	'Buto' (TB)	EWoo
	'Butter and Sugar' (Sib) ♀H4	Widely available
	'Butter Pecan' (IB)	WCAu
	'Buttercup Bower' (TB)	WCAu
	'Buttermere' (TB)	SRms
	'Butterpat' (IB)	ESgI
	'Butterscotch Carpet' (SDB)	WCAu

	'Butterscotch Kiss' (TB)	CMac ECGP ELan EPfP GMaP LDai LHop LRHS MBNS MRav NBir NLar SHil SPer
	'Buzzword' (SDB)	WCAu
	'Bye Bye Blues' (TB)	ESgI XSen
	'Byzantine Purple' (TB)	EWoo
	'Cabaret Royale' (TB)	ESgI XSen
	'Cable Car' (TB)	CKel CWCL ESgI EWoo SMrm WCAu
	'Caesar' (Sib)	CRow EWoo SDys SRms
	'Caesar's Brother' (Sib)	CCon CHid CPrp ELan EPfP EWoo GBin GBuc LRHS MBri MNFA NBro NHol NLar SPer SPet SWat WCAu WHoo WNew WWEG WWlt
	'Cajun Rhythm' (TB)	XSen
	'Calgary' (TB)	WCAu
	'Caliente' (TB)	COIW CWGN MRav MWhi WCAu XSen
	'California Dreamin'' (TB)	CIri
	'California Gold' (TB)	WWEG
	'California Style' (IB)	XSen
§	Californian hybrids	CElw CMac CPBP GCra LRHS NBir WCot
	'Calligrapher' (IB) **new**	WCAu
	'Calm Stream' (TB) $\mathbb{Y}^{H4}$	CKel WCAu
	'Calypso Mood' (TB)	XSen
	'Cambridge' (Sib) $\mathbb{Y}^{H4}$	CAby EHoe EIri GBuc LRHS MWat NBre NGdn SWat WHoo WWlt
	'Camelot Rose' (TB)	WCAu XSen
	'Cameo Blush' (BB)	XSen
	'Cameo Wine' (TB)	CJun ESgI MNrw XSen
	'Cameroun' (TB)	ESgI EWoo
	'Campbellii'	see *I. lutescens* 'Campbellii'
	canadensis	see *I. hookeri*
	'Canadian Kisses' (SDB)	ESgI
	'Canadian Streaker' (TB/v)	WCot
	'Canary Bird' (TB)	ESgI
	'Candy Rock' (IB)	CIri EWoo WCAu
	'Candylane' (MTB)	CKel
	'Cannington Apricot' (IB)	CKel
	'Cannington Bluebird' (TB)	WCAu
	'Cannington Ochre' (SDB)	CBro
	'Cannington Skies' (IB)	CKel
	'Can't Touch This' (TB)	WCAu
	'Cantab' (Reticulata)	CAby CBro ECho EPot ERCP GBin GKev LPio LRHS SDeJ
	'Caprice' (TB)	EWoo
	'Capricious Candles' (TB)	CIri
	'Captain Gallant' (TB)	ESgI
	'Captain Indigo' (IB)	CKel ESgI WCAu
	'Captive Sun' (SDB)	EPfP LRHS NSoo SIri
	'Caramba' (TB)	WCAu
	'Caramel' (TB)	XSen
	'Careless Sally' (Sib) **new**	CIri
	'Carenza' (BB)	CKel
	'Caribbean Dream' (TB)	EWoo XSen
	'Carnaby' (TB)	ESgI IPot LRHS MRav MSpe NCGa SDeJ WCAu WWEG XSen
	'Carnival Ride' (TB) **new**	WCAu
	'Carnival Song' (TB)	WCAu
	'Carnival Time' (TB)	CMac CWGN EBee ECtt EShb LBuc LDai LRHS MSpe NCGa SBea SMrm SPer WHoo XSen
	'Carol Lee' (TB)	EBee
	'Carolina Gold' (TB)	XSen
	'Carolyn Rose' (MTB) $\mathbb{Y}^{H4}$	EBee SMrm
*	'Caronte' (IB)	ESgI
	'Carriage Trade' (TB) **new**	LRHS
	'Carriwitched' (IB)	CKel
	'Casbah' (TB)	XSen
	'Cascade Rhythm' (TB)	WCAu
	'Cascade Springs' (TB)	XSen
	'Cascade Sprite' (SDB)	SRms
	'Casual Joy' (TB)	CIri
	'Catalyst' (TB)	XSen
	'Cat's Eye' (SDB)	CIri ESgI SIri
	caucasica	CMac
	'Cayenne Capers' (TB)	ESgI
	'Cedric Morris'	EWes
	'Cee Jay' (IB) $\mathbb{Y}^{H4}$	EWoo
	'Cee Tee'	EWoo XSen
	'Celebration Song' (TB)	ESgI SIri WCAu XSen
	'Celestial Glory' (TB)	XSen
	'Cerdagne' (TB)	XSen
	'Chalkhill' (SDB)	WCAu
	chamaeiris	see *I. lutescens* subsp. *lutescens*
	'Champagne Elegance' (TB)	EIri EPri LAst NBir WCAu XSen
	'Champagne Encore' (IB)	ESgI EWoo
	'Champagne Frost' (TB)	XSen
	'Champagne Music' (TB)	WCAu
	'Champagne Waltz' (TB)	XSen
	'Champagne Wishes' (TB) **new**	WCAu
	'Chance Beauty' (SpH) $\mathbb{Y}^{H4}$	WCAu
	'Chandler's Choice' (Sib)	EWes
	'Change of Pace' (TB)	ESgI WCAu XSen
	'Chanted' (SDB)	EWoo WCAu XSen
	'Chantilly' (TB)	CHid EBee ELan EPfP EWoo LRHS MRav NBir NGdn NLar SPer SWat
	'Chapeau' (TB)	ESgI WCAu
	'Chapel Bells' (TB)	CKel
	'Charlotte Maria' (TB)	CKel
	'Charmaine' (TB)	XSen
	'Chartreuse Bounty' (Sib)	EPri EWes NLar NSti
	'Chartreuse Ruffles' (TB)	ECtt
	'Chasing Rainbows' (TB)	SDys WCAu
	'Château d'Auvers-sur-Oise' (TB)	SIri
	'Cheap Frills' (TB) **new**	WCAu
	'Cher' (TB)	LSRN
	'Cherished' (TB)	WWEG
	'Cherry Blossom Special' (TB)	CIri
	'Cherry Garden' (SDB)	CAby CBro CDes CHel CKel CPBP CWat ECho ECtt ELan EPfP EShb EWes GBuc GMaP LAst LEdu LPio LRHS MAsh MBNS MRav NBir NGdn NPnk SDeJ WBor WCot WWEG WWFP
	'Cherrywood' (SDB)	CBro
	'Cherub's Smile' (TB)	XSen
	'Cheryl Ann O'Leary' (TB)	CIri
	'Chevalier de Malte' (TB)	ESgI
	'Chickee' (MTB) $\mathbb{Y}^{H4}$	CKel
	'Chicken Little' (MDB)	CBro
	'Chief Moses' (TB)	WCAu
I	'Chieftain' (SDB)	MRav
	'Chilled Wine' (Sib)	ELon
	'China Dragon' (TB)	SWat XSen
	'China Nights' (TB)	ESgI
	'China Seas' (TB)	NBre
	'Chinese Coral' (TB)	XSen
	'Chinese Treasure' (TB)	XSen
	'Chinook Winds' (TB)	ESgI WCAu
	'Chivalry' (TB)	ESgI
	'Chorus Girl' (TB)	CKel
	'Christine Mullins' (Sib) **new**	WBor

	'Christmas Angel' (TB)	WCAu
	chrysographes 🏆^{H4}	CBro CHid CMac CTsd CWCL EPfP EPri EWll IBoy IKil LAst LLWG LRHS MBel MHer MLHP MMuc MRav NPnk NPri NSti SRot
I	- 'Black Beauty'	CCon ECho EPfP
	- 'Black Gold'	EPri MHol
I	- 'Black Knight'	CCse CExl ELon EPfP GBuc GCal GCra ITim LHop NChi NLar SMad SWat WGwG WMnd
	- black-flowered	CDes CExl CFil EBee ELan GAbr GBin GBuc GCal GKev GKin LRHS MNrw MSCN MWhi NGdn NPnk NSoo SPer SPoG WCot WCru WMoo WPGP WPnP WSHC WWEG
	- dark-flowered	CHel GKev
	- 'Goldvein'	CMac
	- 'Inshriach'	IMou LEdu
	- 'Kew Black'	CExl ECho LEdu NBir WHer WWEG
	- 'Kilmurry Black' **new**	IKil
	- 'Mandarin Purple'	GCal MBri MSpe SWat
	- 'Rob'	ECho
§	- 'Rubella'	ECho GCra
	- 'Rubra'	see *I. chrysographes* 'Rubella'
	chrysographes* × *forrestii	GBin NBir
	chrysophylla	IGor
	'Chubby Cheeks' (SDB)	CKel WCAu
	'Church Stoke' (SDB)	WCAu
	'Cider Haze' (TB)	CKel
	'Cimarron Rose' (SDB)	ESgI
	'Cimarron Strip' (TB)	EPfP WWEG XSen
	'Cimarron Trail' (TB)	WCAu
	'Cinnamon Stick' (Spuria)	CIri
	'Circle of Light' (TB) **new**	WCAu
	'Circle Round' (Sib)	CSpe
	'Circus Stripes' (TB)	XSen
	'Cirrus Veil' (SDB)	WCAu
	'Citoyen' (TB)	XSen
	'Citronnade' (TB)	ESgI
	'City Lights' Harrell (TB)	WCAu
	'City of Paradise' (TB)	ESgI
	'Claire Doodle' (MTB)	LMin
	'Clairette' (Reticulata)	ECho EPot GKev NMin SDeJ WRHF
	'Clara Garland' (IB) 🏆^{H4}	CKel WCAu
	'Clarence' (TB)	CKel ESgI EWoo XSen
	clarkei	CHel CPrp EBee ECho GBin
	- B&SWJ 2122	WCru
	- CC 2751	CExl
	- SDR 3819	GKev
	'Classic Look' (TB)	ESgI
	'Classic Navy' (BB)	ESgI
	'Clear Choice' (TB)	WCAu
	'Clear Morning Sky' (TB) 🏆^{H4}	EPot
	'Clearwater River' (TB)	WCAu
	'Cleo' (TB)	CKel NSti
	'Cleo Murrell' (TB)	ESgI EWoo
	'Cleve Dodge' (Sib)	EPri ESgI EWoo SIri XLum
	'Cliffs of Dover' (TB)	CKel EIri ESgI EWoo GCal MCot SRms
	'Close Shave' (TB)	CIri
	'Cloud Ballet' (TB)	EWoo
	'Cloud Mistress' (IB)	ESgI
	'Cloud Pinnacle' (IB)	CKel
	'Cloudcap' (TB)	SRms
	'Clown Around' (TB)	CIri
	'Clownerie' (TB)	EWoo
	'Clyde Redmond' (La) 🏆^{H4}	WMAq
	'Coalignition' (TB)	EWoo WCAu
	'Codicil' (TB)	EIri EWoo XSen
	'Colery'	LRHS
	'Colette Thurillet' (TB)	WCAu XSen
	collettii	ECho
	'Color Carnival' (TB)	ESgI
	'Color Me Blue' (TB)	WCAu
	'Color Splash' (TB)	XSen
	'Colorific' (La)	EPfP NBro NLar WHil
	'Colortart' (TB)	XSen
	'Combo' (SDB)	CKel
	'Come to Me' (TB)	CIri
	'Coming Up Roses' (TB)	XSen
	'Con Fuoco' (TB)	XSen
	'Concertina' (IB)	CIri EWoo WCAu
	confusa 🏆^{H3}	CHEx CPla CSev EUJe GGal IFro SAPC SBig SEND SMad XSen
	- 'Martyn Rix'	CAbb CAby CBct CDes CGHE CHEx CHel CHid CPou ELon EPfP GCal IGor LRHS MLHP SBrt SEND WGwG WHer WMnd WPGP
	'Conjuration' (TB)	ESgI EWoo SIri
	'Connect the Dots' (MTB)	LMin WCAu
	'Connection' (TB) **new**	WCAu
	'Constant Wattez' (IB)	CKel EBee ESgI NLar
	'Constantine Bay' (TB)	ESgI
	'Consummation' (MTB)	SGol
	'Contrast in Styles' (Sib)	EPri GAbr LLWG LSou MSCN WBor WCAu WHil
	'Cookies Bright Spot' (MTB)	WCAu
	'Cool Spring' (Sib)	MSpe
	'Copatonic' (TB)	ESgI WCAu
	'Copper Capers' (TB)	ESgI
	'Copper Classic' (TB)	ESgI LSRN WCAu
	'Coquet Waters' (Sib)	NBid
	'Coquetteric' (TB)	EWoo
	'Coral Carpet' (SDB)	WCAu
	'Coral Point' (TB)	WCAu
	'Coral Sunset' (TB)	WCAu XSen
	'Cordoba' (TB)	WCAu XSen
	'Coronation Anthem' (Sib)	EWoo
	'Côte d'Or' (TB)	XSen
	'County Town Red' (TB)	SIri
	'Coup de Soleil' (TB)	EWoo
	'Cozy Calico' (TB)	WCAu
	'Crackles' (TB)	CKel
	'Cracklin Burgundy' (TB)	XSen
	'Craithie' (TB)	EMal
	'Cranapple' (BB) 🏆^{H4}	ESgI
	'Cranberry Ice' (TB)	ELon EWoo XSen
	'Cranberry Sauce' (TB)	WCAu
	'Cranbrook' (IB) 🏆^{H4}	SIri
	'Cream Beauty' (Dut)	GKev SDeJ
	'Cream Pixie' (SDB)	WCAu
	'Cream Soda' (TB) 🏆^{H4}	CKel
	cretensis	see *I. unguicularis* subsp. *cretensis*
	'Crimson King' (IB)	EWoo
	'Crimson Snow' (TB)	WCAu
	'Crinoline' (TB)	CKel XSen
	'Crispette' (TB)	WCAu
	cristata 🏆^{H4}	NHar NLar SRms
	- 'Alba'	EBee GCal WThu
	crocea 🏆^{H4}	GKev
	'Croftway Lemon' (TB)	COIW ELon
	'Cross Current' (TB)	WCAu
	'Crowned Heads' (TB)	CKel WCAu XSen
	'Crownette' (SDB)	CKel
	'Crushed Velvet' (TB)	WCAu

'Crystal Fountain' (TB)	CIri
'Crystal Gazer' (TB)	ESgI
'Crystal Glitters' (TB)	ESgI
'Crystal Phoenix'	CRow
'Cumulus' (TB)	EWoo
cuniculiformis	ECho WCot
'Cup Race' (TB)	WCAu XSen
'Cupid's Arrow' (TB) **new**	WCAu
'Curlew' (IB)	WCAu
'Cutie' (IB)	ESgI EWoo WCAu
'Cyanea' (DB)	ECho
cycloglossa	ECho EPot GKev WCot
'Dakota Smoke' (TB)	EWoo
'Dale Dennis' (DB)	XSen
'Dance Away' (TB)	ESgI
'Dance Ballerina Dance' (Sib)	CCon CHid CWCL EPfP EPri LLWG MRav NLar SMrm
'Dance for Joy' (TB)	XSen
'Dance the Night Away' (TB)	WCAu
'Dancer's Veil' (TB)	CKel CMac EBee ECtt ELon ESgI LRHS MRav SPer WCAu
'Dancing Bunnies' (SDB)	WCAu
'Dancing Gypsy'	WCAu
'Dancing Lilacs' (MTB)	ESgI LMin
'Dancing Nanou' (Sib)	ECtt SWat
danfordiae	CAvo CBro ECho EPfP EPot GKev LRHS SDeJ SPer
'Dangerous Mood' (TB)	EWoo
'Dante's Inferno' (TB)	EWoo
'Dardanus' (Rc)	ECho EPot ERCP GKev LLHF SDeJ
'Dark Crystal' (SDB)	ESgI EWoo
'Dark Desire' (Sib)	MRav
'Dark Spark' (SDB)	WCAu
'Dark Vader' (SDB)	ESgI
'Darkness' (IB)	SIri
'Darkside' (TB)	XSen
'Dash Away' (SDB)	ESgI SIri
'Dashing' (TB)	EWoo
'Dauber's Delight'	CIri
'Dauber's Surprise' (TB) **new**	CIri
'Daughter of Stars' (TB)	ESgI EWoo
'Dauntless' (TB)	ESgI
'David Guest' (IB)	CKel
'Dawn of Fall' (TB)	ESgI
'Dawn Waltz' (Sib)	EBee WCAu
'Dawning' (TB) ♀H4	ESgI EWoo
'Dazzle Time' (TB) **new**	CIri
'Dazzling' (IB) **new**	WCAu
'Dazzling Gold' (TB)	ESgI WCAu XSen
'Death by Chocolate' (SDB)	ESgI
'Dear Delight' (Sib)	LLHF LLWG LRHS NLar WBor
'Dear Dianne' (Sib)	CHid CKel
'Decadence' (TB) **new**	WCAu
'Deep Black' (TB)	CAby CKel CPar CWGN EBee ELan EPfP ESgI EUJe GBin IPot LRHS LSRN MBNS MCot MRav MWat NCGa NLar NOrc NWad SDeJ SPer SPoG SWat WGwG WWEG
'Deep Pacific' (TB)	WCAu
'Deep Space' (TB)	WCAu
'Deft Touch' (TB)	CKel WCAu XSen
delavayi ♀H4	EBee ECho EWes GMaP MBel WRHF
- SDR 50	CExl GKev
- 'Didcot'	EBee LRHS
'Delicate Lady' (IB) ♀H4	CKel
'Delirium' (IB)	WCAu
'Delta Blues' (TB)	EWoo
'Delta Butterfly' (La)	WMAq
'Demelza' (TB)	CKel
'Demi-Deuil' (TB)	EWoo
'Demon' (SDB)	CJun CKel XSen
'Denys Humphry' (TB)	CKel WCAu
'Deputé Nomblot' (TB)	EWoo
'Derwentwater' (TB)	SRms
I 'Desert Dream' (Sino-Sib)	GAbr
'Desert Echo' (TB)	COIW MHer XSen
'Desert Song' (TB)	CKel WCAu
'Devil David' (TB)	CIri
'Devil May Care' (IB)	ESgI EWoo
'Devilry' (SDB)	EWoo
'Devil's Spoon' (TB)	CIri
'Devonshire Cream' (TB)	CIri WCAu
'Devoted' (SDB) **new**	WCAu
'Dewful' (Sib)	EBee
'Diabolique' (TB) ♀H4	XSen
'Diamond Ring' (TB)	SDys
dichotoma	EWes
- from Shaanxi Province, China **new**	SBrt
'Diligence' (SDB) ♀H4	CKel
'Dinky Circus' (MDB) **new**	CPBP
'Dinky Doodle' (SDB) **new**	WCAu
'Dirigo Black Velvet' (Sib)	CIri
'Disco Jewel' (MTB)	ESgI LMin
'Discovered Treasure' (TB)	WCAu
'Ditzy' (SDB) **new**	SIri
'Diversion' (TB)	ESgI
'Divine' (TB)	CKel
'Dixie Darling' (TB)	ESgI XSen
'Dixie Pixie' (SDB)	WCAu
'Doctor No' (TB)	CIri
'Dogrose' (TB)	EWoo
'Dolce' (SpH)	WCAu
'Doll' (IB)	EWoo
'Doll Ribbons' (MTB)	EPfP
'Dolly Madison' (TB)	ESgI
domestica	CArn CBro CHll EHyd ELan EPfP GKev SMrm SPav SPlb SRms WHer WOut WSHC
- B&SWJ 8692B	WCru
- 'Crûg Colossal'	WCru
- 'Freckle Face'	CMac LSou WHil
- 'Hello Yellow'	EShb
'Don Juan' (TB)	EWoo
'Dorcas Lives Again' (TB)	WHil
'Dotted Swiss' (TB)	XSen
'Double Bubble' (TB)	EWoo
'Double Byte' (SDB)	XSen
'Double Click' (TB)	EWoo
'Double Espoir' (TB)	XSen
'Double Lament' (SDB)	CBro
'Double Mini'	EWoo
'Double Standards' (Sib)	EBee EPri WHil
'Double Vision' (TB)	ESgI EWoo XSen
douglasiana ♀H4	ECho GCal GKev MHer WOut
- 'Cape Ferrelo'	SKHP
'Dover Beach' (TB)	SIri
'Draco' (TB)	ESgI XSen
'Drake Carne' (TB)	CKel
'Drama Queen' (TB)	CIri
'Dream Indigo' (IB)	CKel EWoo WCAu XSen
'Dreaming Green' (Sib)	EBee
'Dreaming Orange' (Sib)	ECtt EPri
'Dreaming Spires' (Sib) ♀H4	ESgI SIri WCot

'Dreaming Yellow' (Sib) ♀^{H4} CBre CIri CMHG COIW CSam EPfP EPri EShb GBuc GKin LEdu LRHS MLHP MMuc MRav NGdn SEND SPer SVic WCAu WMoo WNew WWlt
'Dreamsicle' (TB) EWoo
'Dresden Candleglow' (IB) WCAu
'Drive Me Wild' (TB) WCAu
'Dualtone' (TB) CKel
'Dude Ranch' (TB) WCAu
'Dunkler Wein' (Sib) EBee EWes
'Dunlin' (MDB) CBro ECho NBir
'Dural White Butterfly' (La) CHid EPfP MSCN
'Durham Dream' (TB) CIri
'Dusky Challenger' (TB) CJun CKel ESgI EWoo WCAu XSen
'Dusky Evening' (TB) XSen
'Dutch Chocolate' (TB) ESgI EWes EWoo WCAu XSen
'Dwight Enys' (TB) ♀^{H4} CKel
'Dynamite' (TB) ESgI EWoo XSen
'Dyonisos' (TB) SIri
'Eagle's Flight' (TB) CKel XSen
'Earl of Essex' (TB) WCAu XSen
'Early Frost' (IB) CKel ESgI
'Early Light' (TB) ♀^{H4} ESgI LPot WCAu
'East Indies' (TB) WCAu
'Easter' (SDB) SIri
'Eastertime' (TB) ESgI EWoo
'Easy' (MTB) EIri SIri
'Easy Grace' (TB) EWoo
'Ebony Echo' (TB) EWoo
'Echo de France' (TB) ESgI EWoo XSen
'Edge of Winter' (TB) CKel SIri XSen
'Edith Wolford' (TB) CCCN CWCL ECtt ESgI MMHG NSoo SGol SRGP WWEG XSen
'Ed's Blue' (DB) ELan
'Edward' (Reticulata) CBro ECho EPfP EPot GKev LRHS NMin SDeJ
'Edward of Windsor' (TB) ELan GMaP LRHS NLar SRGP WMnd
'Eggnog' (TB) EWoo
'Ego' (Sib) CHel CHid ELon EPfP EPri EWoo GBuc MGos NBro SWat WMoo
'Eileen Louise' (TB) ♀^{H4} WCAu
'Eldorado' (TB) EWoo
'Eleanor Clare' (IB) ♀^{H4} CKel
'Eleanor Roosevelt' (IB) EWoo
'Eleanor's Pride' (TB) CKel ESgI WCAu
'Electrique' (TB) WCAu
elegantissima see *I. iberica* subsp. *elegantissima*
'Elizabeth Arden' (TB) CKel
'Elizabeth of England' (TB) GKev MLHP WWEG
'Elizabeth Poldark' (TB) ESgI XSen
'Ellenbank Sapphire' (Sib) GBin
'Ellesmere' (Sib) EBee NGdn
'Elsa Sass' (TB) ESgI
'Elsie Petty' (IB) SIri
'Elvinhall' CBro
'Emperor' (Sib) CRow CWat NBre NSti SWat
'Encre Bleue' (IB) ESgI
'Endless Love' (TB) EIri
'Enfant Prodige' (SpH) WCAu
'English Charm' (TB) ESgI WCAu XSen
'English Cottage' (TB) COIW ELon GBin GCal LSRN MWat NLar SMrm WCAu WSHC WWEG XSen
'Ennerdale' (TB) SRms
'Enriched' (MTB) ♀^{H4} LMin SIri WCAu
§ ***ensata*** ♀^{H4} CBcs CBro CHEx CHel COIW ELan EPfP GKev LRHS MHer MJak MLHP MMuc MNrw NLar SPlb SRms SWat

– 'Activity' CRow SHar WWEG
– 'Agrippine' SKHP
– 'Alpine Majesty' ♀^{H4} CIri
* – 'Aoigata' CPrp
– 'Apollo' CRow
– 'Asian Warrior' NLar
– 'August Emperor' IPot
– 'Azuma-kagami' CCon ELan EPfP MNrw
– 'Azure' WMoo
– 'Barnhawk Sybil' SKHP
– 'Barr Purple East' ♀^{H4} CRow
– 'Blue Beauty' GAbr
I – 'Blue King' NHol
I – 'Blue Peter' CRow
– 'Butterflies in Flight' CRow
– 'Caprician Butterfly' ♀^{H4} EPfP
– 'Carnival Prince' CCon WMoo
– 'Cascade Crest' SWat
– 'Center of Interest' NBir NCGa
– 'Chitose-no-tomo' CRow
– 'Chiyodajō' CKel
– 'Cry of Rejoice' ECho ECtt SGol SWat WCAu
– 'Crystal Halo' ♀^{H4} CIri EBee WCAu
– 'Dacc' GBin
– 'Dancing Waves' CRow
I – 'Darling' CRow ECho EPfP NLar SWat WMoo WWEG
– 'Diamant' GBin
– 'Dramatic Moment' GBuc WWEG
I – 'Dresden China' CRow
– 'Eden's Blue Pearl' EBee
– 'Eden's Blush' EBee MLHP
– 'Eden's Charm' EPfP GBin
– 'Eden's Paintbrush' ELan EPfP SPer
– 'Eden's Picasso' CCon ELan
– 'Eden's Purple Glory' CHid GBin WCot
– 'Eden's Starship' CCon
– 'Electric Rays' EBee
I – 'Emotion' CMac EBee
– 'Flying Tiger' ♀^{H4} CIri
I – 'Fortune' GBin IKil SHar SMrm
– 'Freckled Geisha' CIri EBee ELon EPfP IPot NBir SGol SPoG WCAu
– 'Frilled Enchantment' ♀^{H4} IPot
I – 'Galatea' CExl CHel CPrp EBee LEdu
– 'Gold Bound' SKHP
– 'Gracieuse' ELan EPfP GBin LRHS NLar SWat WCot WWEG
– 'Gusto' CMHG EBee ELon EPfP EWTr IPot LDai MBri MNrw NCGa SMrm SWat WBor
– 'Haru-no-umi' CKel
– 'Hercule' CExl CHid CRow GAbr NBir
– Higo hybrids LRHS
– Higo white SPer
– 'Hokkaido' CRow
– 'Hoshi-akari' NCGa WBor
– 'Hue and Cry' ♀^{H4} CIri
– hybrids CHel EHon
* – 'Innocence' CKel NBre NLar SWat WMoo
– 'Iso-no-nami' CDes EBee
* – 'Jitsugetsu' CCon NLar
– 'Jocasta' EPfP MBri NCGa
– 'Katy Mendez' ♀^{H4} IPot NLar
* – 'Kiyo-tsura' CKel
* – 'Kiyo-zuru' EPfP
– 'Kogesho' EPfP GBuc MNrw NLar
– 'Koh Dom' SPer
– 'Kongo San' NLar

	– 'Kuma-funjin'	CExl CRow
	– 'Kumo-no-obi'	CExl CHel CMHG EBee GBuc LRHS MCot NHol NPnk SWat
	– 'Lace Ruff'	CMHG MBri
	– 'Lady in Waiting'	CHel CMHG EBee ECtt EPfP MBri NLar NWad SMrm WHil
	– 'Landscape at Dawn'	CRow
	– 'Laughing Lion'	ECtt IKil WCAu WMoo WWEG
	– 'Light at Dawn'	CMHG LDai MBel WMoo
	– 'Lilac Blotch'	SPer
I	– 'Loyalty'	CExl ECho SHar
	– 'Mancunian' YH4	CKel
I	– 'Mandarin'	CRow
	– 'Momozomo'	LLHF
§	– 'Moonlight Waves'	CExl CHid CMHG CPrp CRow EBee ELan EPfP EShb GAbr GBuc GCra GKin GMaP LRHS MCot MWts NGdn NHol SMrm SWat WCAu
	– 'Oase'	ECtt
	– 'Ocean Mist'	CHid EBee ECtt GBuc IKil
	– 'Oku-banri'	CExl CHEx CPrp EBee EShb
	– 'Oriental Eyes'	NGdn NLar
	– pale mauve-flowered	NBir SPer
	– 'Pin Stripe'	CDes CHel EBee GAbr MBri NLar SWat WMoo
	– 'Pink Frost'	CPrp CRow EBee ELan EPfP LBMP LHop LRHS
	– 'Pinkerton'	CIri
	– 'Pleasant Journey'	ECtt
	– 'Prairie Frost'	EBee NLar
	– 'Prairie Noble'	EBee
	– 'Purple Glory'	ELan
	– purple-flowered	SPer
	– 'Queen's Tiara'	ELon
	– 'Rakka-no-utage'	EBee NLar
	– 'Ranpo'	CRow
I	– 'Reveille'	EBee SWat
	– 'Rivulets of Wine'	CIri
§	– 'Rose Queen' YH4	CBAq CExl COlW CPrp CRow CSam EHon ELan EPfP GBin GBuc GCra GKin GMaP LRHS MCot MRav NBir NGdn NHol NLar SMrm SPer WCAu WMoo XLum
	– 'Rowden'	CRow
	– 'Rowden Amir'	CRow
	– 'Rowden Autocrat'	CRow
	– 'Rowden Begum'	CRow
	– 'Rowden Caliph'	CRow
	– 'Rowden Consul'	CRow
	– 'Rowden Dauphin'	CRow
	– 'Rowden Dictator'	CRow
	– 'Rowden Empress'	CRow
	– 'Rowden King'	CRow
	– 'Rowden Knight'	CRow
	– 'Rowden Mikado'	CRow
	– 'Rowden Naib'	CRow
	– 'Rowden Nuncio'	CRow
	– 'Rowden Pasha'	CRow
	– 'Rowden Prince'	CRow
	– 'Rowden Queen'	CRow
	– 'Rowden Shah'	CRow
	– 'Rowden Sirdar'	CRow
	– 'Rowden Sultan'	CRow
I	– 'Royal Banner'	EBee ECtt SHar WWEG
	– 'Royal Crown'	ECho XLum
I	– 'Ruby King'	LEdu
	– 'Ruffled Dimity'	CBcs EBee IPot SMrm
	– 'Sandsation'	CIri

	– 'Sapphire Star'	CKel
	– 'Sennyo-no-hora'	CPrp
I	– 'Sensation'	CWCL ECho ECtt GBin IKil MWts NLar SMrm SWat WWEG
	– 'Snowy Hills'	XLum
	– var. ***spontanea***	SWat
	– – B&SWJ 1103	WCru
	– – B&SWJ 8699	WCru
	– 'Stippled Ripples'	IPot MWts
	– 'Summer Storm' YH4	CKel SPer
	– 'Sylvia's Masquerade'	CHel
	– 'Taketori-hime' (v)	XLum
	– 'The Great Mogul' YH4	CKel CRow
	– 'Umi-kaze'	NLar
	– 'Variegata' (v) YH4	Widely available
	– 'Velvety Queen'	CPrp ECtt WCAu
I	– 'White Ladies'	CSBt SWat WWEG
I	– 'White Pearl'	CRow
	– 'Wine Ruffles'	CHel CMHG LSRN SIri SMrm
	– 'Yako-no-tama'	CRow WMoo
	– 'Yedo-yeman'	EBee
	'Entertainer' (TB)	EWoo
	'Épée Violette' (TB)	ESgI
	'Epicenter' (TB)	ESgI XSen
	'Eramosa Miss' (BB)	WCAu
	'Eramosa Skies' (SDB)	WCAu
	'Erect' (IB)	CKel
	'Eric the Red' (Sib)	EWoo IBlr
	'Erste Sahne' (Sib)	GBin
	'Eternal Bliss' (TB)	EWoo SIri
	'Evening Gown' (TB)	XSen
	'Evening Pond' (MTB)	CKel
	'Ever After' (TB)	EWoo XSen
	'Ever Again' (Sib)	EWoo
	'Everything Plus' (TB)	ESgI WCAu XSen
	'Ewen' (Sib)	CHid CPou CRow EWoo GBin GKin GMaP LEdu MNrw NGdn SMrm SWat WCot WWEG WWlt
	'Exotic Isle' (TB)	ESgI XSen
	'Extra' (BB)	CPBP LLHF
	'Extra Dazzle' (La) **new**	LLWG
	'Extra Innings' (TB)	EWoo
	'Eye Magic' (IB) YH4	CKel XSen
	'Eye of Tiger'	see *I.* 'Tigereye'
	'Eyebright' (SDB) YH4	CBro WCAu
	'Fabuleux' (TB)	SIri
	'Faenelia Hicks' (La)	WMAq
	'Fall Empire' (TB)	EWoo
	'Fall Enterprise' (TB)	CIri
	'Fall Fiesta' (TB)	XSen
	'Fancy Brass' (TB)	SIri
	'Fancy Dress' (TB)	SIri
	'Fancy Woman' (TB)	WCAu
	'Fanfaron' (TB)	ESgI XSen
	'Farleigh Damson' (SDB)	SIri
	'Fashion Holiday' (IB)	SIri
	'Fashion Lady' (MDB)	CBro ECho
	'Fathom' (IB)	WCAu
	'Feminine Charm' (TB)	MRav WCAu
	'Festival's Acadian' (La) **new**	LLWG
	'Festive Skirt' (TB)	CKel
	'Feu du Ciel' (TB) YH4	ESgI EWoo XSen
	'Fierce Fire' (IB) YH4	CKel
	'Fiesta Time' (TB)	CWCL XSen
	'Filibuster' (TB)	WCAu
	filifolia var. ***latifolia***	NMin
	'Film Festival' (TB)	ESgI
	'Finalist' (TB)	WCAu XSen
	'Firebeard' (TB)	CIri

'Firebug' (IB)	ESgI XSen
'Firecracker' (TB)	MRav WCAu
'First Interstate' (TB)	CWCL ESgI XSen
'First Movement' (TB)	ESgI
'First Romance' (SDB)	LSRN
'First Violet' (TB)	ESgI
'Fit the Bill' (TB)	EWoo
'Five Star Admiral' (TB)	XSen
'Flaming Dragon' (TB)	XSen
'Flaming Victory' (TB)	XSen
flavescens	ESgI EWoo WCAu XSen
'Flavours' (BB)	WCAu
'Fleece of White' (BB) **new**	WCAu
'Fleur Collette Louise' (La)	CIri
'Flight of Butterflies' (Sib)	Widely available
'Flight of Fantasy' (La)	CKel
'Flirting Again' (SDB) ♀H4	SIri
'Floorshow' (TB)	XSen
'Flopsy' (TB) **new**	CIri
§ 'Florentina' (IB/TB) ♀H4	CArn CBro CHby COIW EBee ECGP ESgI EWoo GCal GPoy MNHC MRav NBid NBir SEND WCAu WHer WHfH XSen
'Florentine Silk' (TB)	WCAu
'Fluffy Pillows' (TB) **new**	CIri
'Flumadiddle' (IB)	CBro CKel
'Flûte Enchantée' (TB)	CIri XSen
'Focus' (TB)	XSen
foetidissima ♀H4	Widely available
- 'Aurea'	EBee WCot
- ***chinensis***	see *I. foetidissima* var. *citrina*
§ - var. ***citrina***	CBre CCon ECGP EPfP EPri EWld GAbr GCal GCra LEdu NLar SChr SLPl WCot WGwG
- 'Fructu Albo'	GBin NSti
- var. ***lutescens***	CHid EPPr
- 'Variegata' (v) ♀H4	CElw EBee EPfP MSCN NBir NPer
- yellow-seeded	GCal
'Fogbound' (TB)	WCAu
'Foggy Dew' (TB)	LRHS NCGa NPnk
'Fondation Van Gogh' (TB)	XSen
'Foolish Fancy' (TB)	SIri
'Footloose' (TB)	SIri XSen
'For Mary' (TB)	CIri
'Foreign Legion' (TB)	WCAu
'Foreigner' (TB)	WCAu
'Forest Light' (SDB)	CBro ESgI
'Forever Blue' (SDB)	WCAu
'Forever Gold' (TB)	EWoo XSen
'Forge Fire' (TB)	ESgI
formosana	ECho
- B&SWJ 3076	WCru
'Forrest Hills' (TB)	EPfP LRHS
forrestii ♀H4	CAby CBro CCon CExl CHel CHid CMac ECho EWTr GAbr GBin GCal GCra GKev ITim LRHS MBri MHer MMuc NBir NBro SRot WAbe
- SDR 5802 **new**	GKev
'Fort Apache' (TB)	EWes EWoo
'Fortunata' (TB)	XSen
'Fortunate Son'	EWoo WCAu
'Fortune Teller' (TB)	CKel
'Fourfold Blue' (SpH)	GBin
'Fourfold Lavender' (Sib)	EWes MSpe NLar
'Fourfold White' (Sib)	ESgI
'Foxy Lady' (TB)	EWoo
'Framboise' (TB)	XSen
'Frances Iva' (TB)	EWoo
'Francheville' (TB)	EWoo
'Frank Elder' (Reticulata)	ECho EPot ERCP GKev LLHF MRav SDeJ WIce
'Frans Hals' (Dut)	GKev MMHG MNrw
'Freedom Flight' (TB)	CIri
'French Can Can' (TB)	EWoo SIri
'French Horn' (TB)	CIri
'French Rose' (TB)	CKel WCAu
'Fresno Calypso' (TB)	ESgI WCAu XSen
'Frigiya' (Spuria)	CIri
'Frison-roche' (TB)	CWCL
'Frisonnette' (TB)	ESgI
'Fritillary Flight' (IB) ♀H4	CKel
'Frivolité' (TB)	ESgI
'Frontier Lady' (TB)	CIri
'Frontier Marshall' (TB)	XSen
'Frost and Flame' (TB)	CAby EBee ECtt ELan GBin LBuc LRHS MRav NBir NLar SDeJ SPer SPoG SWat WWEG
'Frost Echo' (TB)	EWoo
'Frosted Angel' (SDB)	CBro
'Frosted Biscuit' (TB) ♀H4	CKel
'Frosted Velvet' (MTB)	LMin WCAu
'Frosty Crown' (SDB)	CDes
'Frosty Elegance' (IB)	ESgI
'Frosty Jewels' (TB)	XSen
'Frosty Moonscape' (TB) **new**	CIri
'Fruit Cocktail' (IB)	CKel CRDP XSen
'Full Sun' (Spuria)	EWoo
fulva ♀H3	CRow CSpe EPri GBin GCal LPot MMHG MWts NBir NBro NSti WBor WCot
- 'Marvell Gold' (La)	CRow EBee
× ***fulvala*** ♀H4	CCon EWes GBin NBir NSti
- 'Violacea'	LRHS
'Funambule' (TB)	EWoo
'Furnaceman' (SDB)	CBro
'Futuriste' (TB)	SIri
'Gai Luron' (TB)	WWEG
'Gallant Moment' (TB)	ECtt ESgI EWoo SIri XSen
'Galleon Gold' (SDB)	CKel
'Galway' (IB)	SIri XSen
'Game Plan' (TB)	WCAu
'Gandalf the Grey' (TB)	ESgI
'Gelbe Mantel' (Sino-Sib)	CHid CIri NBir NSti
'Gemstone Walls' (TB)	ESgI
'Gentius' (TB)	WMnd
'George' (Reticulata) ♀H4	CAby CAvo CBro ECho EPfP EPot ERCP GKev LRHS NMin WBor WBrk WCot WHoo
'Gerald Darby'	see *I.* × *robusta* 'Gerald Darby'
'Gerbel Mantel' (Sib)	GBin GKin MSpe WMoo
germanica ♀H4	CHel MMuc SEND WCAu
- var. ***florentina***	see *I.* 'Florentina'
§ - 'Nepalensis'	WCAu
- 'The King'	see *I. germanica* 'Nepalensis'
'Gertrude' (TB)	EWoo
'Ghost Train' (TB)	CIri EWoo SIri
'Gigha' **new**	EBee
'Gingerbread Castle' (TB)	WCAu
'Gingerbread Man' (SDB)	CBro CMea EBee ESgI MBrN SMrm WCAu
'Gingersnap' (TB)	EWoo
'Glacier' (TB)	ECho
'Glacier Gold' (TB)	XSen
'Glad Rags' (TB)	XSen
'Gladys Austin' (TB)	XSen
'Glowing Embers' (TB)	ESgI

'Gnu' (TB)	XSen
'Gnus Flash' (TB)	CIri
'Go Between' (TB)	WCAu
'Goddess of Green' (IB)	EWoo
'Godfrey Owen' (TB)	CKel WCAu
'Godsend' (TB)	CIri CKel
'Going Green' (TB) **new**	CIri
'Going Home' (TB) ♀H4	SIri
'Going My Way' (TB)	ESgI EWoo LSou SIri WCAu WWEG XSen
'Gold Burst' (TB)	XSen
'Gold Country' (TB)	XSen
'Gold for Bold'	WCAu
'Gold of Autumn' (TB)	CKel SMrm
'Goldberry' (IB)	WCAu
'Golden Alien' (TB)	CIri
'Golden Alps' (TB)	SRms WCAu
'Golden Beauty'	GKev SDeJ
'Golden Child' (SDB)	XSen
'Golden Crimping' (Sib)	EWoo
'Golden Ducat' (Spuria) **new**	CIri
'Golden Edge' (Sib)	EWoo GQue LLWG MBel MSCN MWts NLar SMrm
'Golden Encore' (TB)	CKel WCAu
'Golden Forest' (TB)	GBin LRHS
'Golden Immortal' (TB)	EWoo
'Golden Panther' (TB)	CIri WCAu
'Golden Planet' (TB)	CKel
'Golden Violet' (SDB)	ESgI
'Goldfinger' (TB)	LWst
goniocarpa	WAbe
'Good Life'	WCAu
'Good Looking' (TB)	ESgI WCAu
'Good Show' (TB)	ESgI EWoo WCAu XSen
'Good Vibrations' (TB)	SIri XSen
'Goodbye Girl' (TB)	ESgI
'Goodbye Heart' (TB)	EWoo LSRN
'Gordon' (Reticulata)	CAvo CBro ECho EPfP EPot ERCP GKev
gormanii	see *I. tenax*
'Gosh' (SDB)	CKel
'Gossip' (SDB)	CBro ESgI
'Got the Melody' (TB) **new**	WCAu
'Gracchus' (TB)	ESgI EWoo LRHS WCAu
gracilipes	SBrt
gracilipes* × *lacustris	WAbe
graeberiana	ECho EPot GKev SDeJ
- yellow fall	ECho GKev
graminea ♀H4	CAvo CBro CHid CMac CRow EBee ECho ELan EPfP EPri GKev IFro LLWP LRHS MLHP NBir NSti WCAu WCot XEll
- var. ***pseudocyperus***	EBee GCal SDys
graminifolia	see *I. kerneriana*
'Granaat' (Sib)	EBee
'Granada Gold' (TB)	SRms XSen
'Grand Circle' (TB)	CIri EWoo
'Grand Illusion' (Spuria)	EWoo
'Grand Waltz' (TB)	XSen
'Grape Adventure' (TB)	LBuc
'Grapelet' (MDB)	CPBP WCAu
'Grapetizer' (TB)	WCAu
'Great Gatsby' (TB)	CKel
'Great Lakes' (TB)	ESgI EWoo
'Grecian Skies' (TB)	ESgI
'Green Eyed Lady' (TB)	ESgI
'Green Ice' (TB)	CKel LRHS MRav
'Green Prophecy' (TB)	CKel
'Green Spot' (SDB) ♀H4	CAby CBro CKel ECho ECtt ELan GBuc LAst LHop LPio LRHS MNrw MRav NBir NLar SDeJ SPer
'Grooving' (BB)	ESgI
'Guatemala' (TB)	WCAu
'Guess Who I Am' (TB)	WCAu
'Gull's Wing' (Sib)	EWTr LHop LLWG MBel NLar NSti SMrm
'Gurkha's Dance' (SDB) **new**	SIri
'Gwen' (Sib) **new**	GLog
'Gwyneth Evans' (BB) ♀H4	CKel
'Gypsy Beauty' (Dut)	CAvo EPfP GKev MWat SDeJ
'Gypsy Jewels' (TB)	CKel ESgI XSen
'Gypsy Romance' (TB) ♀H4	EIri ESgI EWoo SIri WCAu
'Gypsy Tart' (SDB) **new**	SIri
'Habit' (TB)	EWoo WCAu
'Hafnium' (SDB)	CKel
'Hakuna Matata' (AB)	SDys
'Halloween Halo' (TB) **new**	WCAu
'Halloween Rainbow' (IB) **new**	WCAu
halophila	see *I. spuria* subsp. *halophila*
'Happenstance' (TB)	EWoo WCAu
'Happy Hugs' (TB)	WCAu
'Happy Mood' (IB) ♀H4	NBre WCAu
'Harbor Blue' (TB)	CKel CTsd MWat SWat WCAu WWEG
'Harlow Gold' (IB)	ESgI
'Harmonium' (IB) **new**	WCAu
'Harmony' ambig.	SPer
'Harmony' (Reticulata)	CAby CAvo CBro ECho EPfP EPot GKev LRHS MBri SDeJ
'Harpswell Hallelujah' (Sib)	EBee EWoo SBch
'Harpswell Happiness' (Sib) ♀H4	CPrp EBee EPfP EPri GAbr GBin GCra SBch SWat WMoo
'Harriette Halloway' (TB)	CWGN ECGP EPfP EShb IPot LHop LPio LRHS LSRN NLar NPnk SHar SMrm SRGP WCot
hartwegii	ECho
- subsp. ***hartwegii***	IGor
- subsp. ***pinetorum***	IGor
'Harvest King' (TB)	ESgI XSen
'Harvest of Memories' (TB)	ESgI EWoo WWEG
'Haut les Voiles' (TB)	CWCL
'Haute Couture' (TB)	XSen
'Haviland' (TB)	XSen
'Having Fun' (Sib) **new**	CIri
'Headcorn' (MTB) ♀H4	LMin SIri
'Headline Banner' (BB)	EWoo WCAu
'Headlines' (TB)	WCAu
'Headway' (Spuria)	WCAu
'Heartbeat Away' (TB)	CIri
'Heart's Radiance' (MTB)	SDys
'Heather Carpet' (SDB)	WCAu
'Heather Sky' (TB)	CIri
'Heavenly Blue' (Sib)	SPer
'Heavenly Days' (TB)	WCAu
'Heaven's Edge' (TB)	WCAu
'Helen Astor' (Sib)	CPrp CRow CTri MRav SWat WWEG
'Helen Collingwood' (TB)	ESgI EWoo
'Helen Dawn' (TB) ♀H4	SIri
'Helen McGregor' (TB)	CKel EWoo
'Helen Proctor' (IB)	ESgI WCAu WCot XSen
'Helena Terry' (TB)	ESgI
'Helene C.' (TB)	EWoo XSen
'Helge' (IB)	COIW ECho NBre SWat
'Heliotrope Bouquet' (Sib)	EWoo

	'Hellcat' (IB)	EWoo WCAu
	'Hello Darkness' (TB) ♀H4	ESgI EWoo WCAu WCot XSen
	'Hell's Fire' (TB)	ELon EWoo WCAu
	'Hemstitched' (TB)	EWoo
	'Her Majesty' (TB)	EWoo
	'Her Royal Highness' (TB)	CHel
	'Hercules' (Reticulata)	ECho NMin
	'Heure Bleue' (TB)	EWoo
	'Hever Castle' (Kent Castles Series) (BB) **new**	SIri
	'Hi' (IB)	CIri
	'High Barbaree' (TB)	EWoo
	'High Blue Sky' (TB)	WCAu
	'High Command' (TB)	CKel WCAu
	'High Impact' (TB)	EWoo
	'High Peak'	WCAu
	'Highland Mist' (La) **new**	LLWG
	'Highline Amethyst' (Spuria)	EPri
	'Highline Halo' (Spuria)	EWoo
	'Hildegarde' (Dut)	SDeJ
	'Himmel von Komi' (Sib)	GBin
	'His Royal Highness'	WCAu
	'Hissy-Fit' (IB)	CKel
	histrio	ECho EPot
	- subsp. ***aintabensis***	ECho GKev
	histrioides	ECho
§	- 'Angel's Tears' (Reticulata)	CAvo ECho GKev NMin
	- 'Halkis' (Reticulata)	EPot ERCP GKev NMin
	- 'Lady Beatrix Stanley'	CAvo CBro ECho EPfP EPot ERCP GKev LLHF NMin SBch
N	- 'Major'	CDes ECho GKev
	- 'Michael Tears'	ECho
	- var. ***sophenensis***	ECho
	'Hoar Edge' (Sib)	NChi
	'Hocus Pocus' (SDB)	CHel CPBP CWGN ECho EPfP EWoo GBuc LPio LRHS NSoo
	'Hohe Warte' (Sib) ♀H4	GBin
	'Höhenflug' (Sib)	GBin
	'Holden Clough' (SpH) ♀H4	CExl CHel CPrp EBee ELan EPfP GBin GCra GMaP LEdu MBel MNrw MRav NBir NEgg NGdn NSti WBrk WHer WSHC WWEG
	'Holden's Child'	CWat EBee
	'Hollywood Nights' (TB)	EWoo
	'Holy Night' (TB)	CKel
	'Honey Behold' (SDB)	CKel
	'Honey Glazed' (IB)	ESgI WCAu
	'Honey Mocha Lotta' (Spuria)	EWoo
	'Honey Stars' (La) **new**	LLWG
	'Honeylove' (SDB)	SDys
	'Honeymoon Suite' (TB)	EWoo
	'Honeyplic' (IB) ♀H4	ESgI SIri
	'Honington' (SDB)	WCAu
	'Honky Tonk Blues' (TB)	CKel ESgI LSRN
	'Honky Tonk Hussy' (BB)	CKel
	'Honorabile' (MTB)	ESgI EWoo LMin SMrm WCAu
	hoogiana ♀H3	ECho EPot GKev LRHS LWst
	- 'Purpurea'	ECho
§	***hookeri***	CHel COIW CPBP CPrp EBee ECho ELan EPfP GBin GKev GMaP IGor MGos SBrt SMrm WCAu WIce
	- SDR 2202	GKev
	hookeriana	LBuc LRHS
	'Hope You Dance' (TB) **new**	WCAu
	'Hopelessly Devoted' (La) **new**	LLWG
	'Hoptoit' (TB)	CIri

	'Horizon Bleu' (TB)	EWoo
	'Horned Rosyred' (TB)	EWoo
§	'Hornpipe' (TB)	WCAu
	'Hortensia Rose' (TB)	SIri
	'Hot Gossip' (TB)	WCAu
	'Hot Spiced Wine' (TB)	EWoo
	'Hot to Trot' (TB)	ESgI
	'Howard Weed' (TB)	MNrw
	'Hubbard' (Sib)	EPri EShb LLWG MBel MNrw
	'Huckleberry Fudge' (TB)	XSen
	'Hugh Miller' (TB)	WCAu
	'Hula Hands' (IB)	CIri
	'Hula Moon' (TB)	ESgI
	hyrcana	ECho
	'I Feel Good' (TB) **new**	WCAu
	'I Repeat' (TB)	ESgI XSen
	'I Seek You' (TB)	ESgI
	iberica	ECho
§	- subsp. ***elegantissima***	ECho LWst
	'Ice and Indigo' (SDB)	WCAu
	'Ice Cave' (TB) **new**	WCAu
	'Ice Dancer' (TB) ♀H4	CKel
	'Ice Etching' (SDB) **new**	WCAu
	'Ice Wings' (BB)	WCAu
	'Ida' (Reticulata)	ECho
	'Idol' (TB)	EWoo
	'Ila Crawford' (Spuria) ♀H4	XSen
	'Illini Charm' (Sib)	CHid EBee WMoo
	illyrica	see *I. pallida*
	'I'm Back' (TB)	WCAu
	'Immortality' (TB)	CKel CWGN ESgI LPio WCAu WWEG XSen
	'Imperative' (IB)	EWoo SIri
	'Imperator' (Dut)	ECho
	'Imperial Bronze' (Spuria)	WCAu
I	'Imperial Velvet' (Sib)	EWoo
	'Impersonator' (TB) **new**	CIri
	'Impetuous' (BB) ♀H4	CKel
	'Imprimis' (TB)	EWoo XSen
	'In Concert' (TB)	SMrm
	'In Full Sail' (Sib) **new**	CIri
	'In Limbo' (IB)	CKel
	'In Love' (TB)	XSen
	'In Town' (TB)	EWoo XSen
	'In Your Dreams' (TB) **new**	CIri
	'Incentive' (TB)	EWoo
	'Incognito Too' (TB) **new**	CIri
*	'Incoscente' (TB)	ESgI
	'Indeed' (IB)	ESgI
	'Indian Chief' (TB)	CCCN CWCL EPfP ESgI EWoo IBoy MCot MRav WCAu WWEG
	'Indian Hills' (TB)	EWoo
	'Indian Idyll' (IB)	CKel EWoo
	'Indian Jewel' (SDB)	ECho
	'Indian Pow Wow' (SDB)	CRDP CSev
	'Indiana Sunset' (TB)	CKel
	'Indigo Flight' (IB)	CKel
	'Indigo Princess' (TB)	CKel EWoo XSen
	'Infanta' (SDB)	WCAu
	'Inferno' (TB)	EWoo
	'Infinity Ring' (IB)	WCAu
	'Infrared' (TB)	WCAu
	'Innocent Devil' (TB)	CIri
	'Innocent Heart' (IB) ♀H4	WCAu
	'Innocent Pink' (TB)	ESgI
	innominata	CAvo EBee ECho EPot GAbr GKev LHop LRHS NBir NBro SRms WWEG
	- apricot-flowered	IBlr

	– Ballyrogan hybrids	IBlr
	– yellow-flowered	NRya
	'Inscription' (SDB)	ECho
	'Instant Hit' (TB)	WCAu
	'Intermediary' (IB) **new**	WCAu
	'Interpol' (TB)	ESgI EWoo XSen
	'Invicta Daybreak' (IB)	SIri
	'Invicta Garnet' (SDB)	SIri
	'Invicta Gold' (SDB)	SIri
	'Invisible' (SDB)	WCAu
	'Irish Chant' (SDB)	WCAu
	'Irish Doll' (MDB)	WCAu
	'Irish Harp' (SDB)	ESgI WCAu
	'Irish Tune' (TB)	ESgI
	'Iron Eagle' (TB)	CIri
	'Isabelle' (Sib)	LSRN XSen
	'Island Sun' (SDB) **new**	SIri
	'Island Sunset' (TB)	ESgI SIri
	'Isoline' (TB)	ESgI
	'Italian Ice' (TB) **new**	EIri
	'Italian Velvet' (TB)	WCAu
	'Ivory Queen' (Sib)	EWoo
	'J.S. Dijt' (Reticulata)	CAvo CBro ECho EPfP EPot ERCP GKev LPio MBri MGos SDeJ
	'Jabal' (SDB)	SIri
	'Jack Attack' (La)	CPrp SMrm SPoG WMoo
	'Jacquessiana'	EWoo WCAu
	'Jac-y-do' (Sib)	EWes
	'Jade Mist' (SDB)	ECho
	'Jaguar Blue' (TB)	EWoo WCAu
	'Jane Phillips' (TB) ♀H4	Widely available
	'Jane Taylor' (SDB)	CBro
	'Janet Lane' (BB)	CKel
	'Janine Louise' (TB) ♀H4	CKel
	japonica ♀H3	CExl CHEx ECho EPfP NLar NPer XLum XSen
	– B&SWJ 8921	WCru
	– 'Bourne Graceful'	CExl
	– 'Ledger'	CAby CAvo CExl CHll CMac CPrp EPfP IGor MRav SEND SMad
	– 'Monty'	WWFP
I	– 'Purple Heart'	CAvo
	– 'Rudolph Spring'	EBee GCal WWFP
I	– 'Snowflake'	CAvo
§	– 'Variegata' (v) ♀H3	CAby CBro CHEx CKel CPrp CTsd ECho ELan ESwi MHer NBro NPer NSti SAPC SEND SMad WHil WWFP XSen
	'Jasper Gem' (MDB)	ECho
	'Jazz Festival' (TB)	SIri WCAu XSen
	'Jazzed Up' (TB)	XSen
	'Je l'Adore' (TB)	EWoo
	'Jean Cayeux' (TB)	ESgI
	'Jean Guymer' (TB)	ESgI NBir
	'Jeanne Price' (TB)	ESgI EWoo LSRN WCAu
	'Jelly Belly' (SDB)	EWoo
	'Jeremy Brian' (SDB) ♀H4	WCAu
	'Jeremy Jets On' (TB)	CIri
	'Jesse Lee' (SDB)	CKel
	'Jesse's Song' (TB)	ESgI WCAu XSen
	'Jet-Setter' (TB)	CIri
	'Jeunesse' (TB)	ESgI
	'Jewel Baby' (SDB)	CBro CKel
	'Jewel Bright' (SDB)	WCAu
	'Jeweler's Art' (SDB)	ESgI EWoo
	'Jiansada' (SDB)	CBro
	'Jigsaw' (TB)	ESgI XSen
	'Jive' (SDB)	WCAu
	'Joanna' (TB)	LSRN NLar WWEG
	'John' (IB)	CKel LSRN
	'Joli Coeur' (TB)	EWoo
	'Joseph Henry' (TB)	WCAu
	'Joyce' (Reticulata)	CBro ECho EPfP EPot GKev MBri NLar SDeJ
	'Jubilant Spirit' (Spuria)	EWes
	'Jubilation' (TB)	EWoo
	'Jubilee Gem' (TB)	CKel WCAu
	'Jud Paynter' (TB)	CKel
	'Judy Mogil' (TB)	CIri
	'Julia Vennor' (TB)	CKel
	'Juliet' (TB)	ESgI
	'Jump Start' (IB)	EWoo WCAu
	'Jumping Jupiter' (TB)	CIri
	'June Prom' (IB)	LRHS SRGP WCAu
	'Jungle Fires' (TB)	WCAu
	'Jungle Shadows' (BB)	CIri ESgI EWoo MRav NBir WCAu
	'Jungle Warrior' (SDB)	CKel
	'Jurassic Park' (TB)	ESgI EWoo WCAu XSen
	'Just Before Midnight' **new**	LRHS NPri
	'Just Dance' (IB)	ESgI
	'Just Imagine' (La) **new**	LLWG
	'Just Jennifer' (BB)	WCAu
	kaempferi	see *I. ensata*
	'Karen' (TB)	LSRN
	kashmiriana	ECre
	'Katharine Hodgkin' (Reticulata) ♀H4	CAby CAvo CBro CTca CWCL EBee ECho EHyd EPfP EPot ERCP GAbr GKev ITim LRHS MNrw MRav MWat NBir NHar NLar SDeJ SMrm WAbe WBrk WCot WHoo WIce WSHC
	'Katharine Hodgkin' dark-flowered	NMin
	'Katie-Koo' (IB) ♀H4	CKel
	'Katy Petts' (SDB)	ESgI WCAu
	'Kayleigh-Jayne Louise' (TB)	CKel
	'Keep the Peace' (TB)	WCAu
	'Keeping up Appearances' (TB)	WCAu
	'Kelway Renaissance' (TB)	CKel
	kemaonensis	LRHS
	'Ken's Choice' (TB) ♀H4	CKel
	'Kent Arrival' (Sib)	SIri
	'Kent Blackguard' (IB)	SIri
	'Kent Compote' (IB)	SIri
	'Kent Pride' (TB)	CAby CSBt ECtt EPfP ESgI EWoo GBin LRHS MCot MNHC MNrw MRav MWhi SPer SPoG SWat WCAu WWlt
	Kenta No Se129 (Sib)	EPri
	'Kentish Icon' (SDB)	SIri
	'Kentucky Bluegrass' (SDB)	WCAu
	'Kentucky Derby' (TB)	XSen
§	***kerneriana*** ♀H4	GBuc LRHS MBel NBir
	'Kharput' (IB)	EWoo
	'Kildonan' (TB)	WCAu
	'King's Jester' (TB)	EWoo
	'Kinshizen' (SpH) **new**	CIri WCAu
	'Kirkstone' (TB)	WCAu
	kirkwoodii	ECho LWst
	'Kiss of Summer' (TB) ♀H4	ESgI SDys
	'Kissing Circle' (TB)	ESgI EWoo
	'Kita-no-seiza' (Sib)	CIri EBee GAbr
	'Kiwi Slices' (SDB)	CPBP CWat ESgI
	'Knick Knack' (MDB)	CAby CBro CMea CPBP ECho ELan EPfP GMaP MRav SDeJ SPoG
	'Koi' (TB)	ESgI
	korolkowii	ECho LWst

	'La Meije' (TB)	SIri
	'La Senda' (Spuria)	WCot
	'Lace Legacy' (TB)	EWoo LSRN
	'Laced Cotton' (TB)	WCAu XSen
§	***lactea*** ♀H4	SBrt XEll XSen
	- CC 3768	WCot
	lacustris ♀H4	CBro WAbe XSen
	'Lacy Snowflake' (TB)	LHop LRHS
	'Lad'	WCAu
	'Lady Belle' (MTB) ♀H4	ESgI
	'Lady Essex' (TB)	EWoo
	'Lady Friend' (TB)	WCAu XSen
	'Lady Gale' (IB)	CKel
	'Lady in Red' (SDB)	ESgI WCAu
	'Lady Mohr' (AB)	CKel WCAu
	'Lady Phyllis' (MTB)	CIri
	'Lady R' (SDB)	ECho
	'Lady Vanessa' (Sib)	CHel CPou EBee ELon MRav NSti
	laevigata ♀H4	CBAq CRow ECho EHon ELan EPfP EWay ITim MRav NBro NPer SPer SWat WMAq WMoo WShi WWEG
	- var. ***alba***	CBAq CRow ECho EHon EPfP SWat WMoo
	- 'Atropurpurea'	CRow
	- 'Colchesterensis'	CRow CWat EPri EWay ITim NGdn NPer SWat WMAq WMoo
I	- 'Dorothy'	NGdn
	- 'Dorothy Robinson'	LRHS SWat
	- 'Elegant'	see *I. laevigata* 'Weymouth Elegant'
I	- 'Elegante'	EWay
*	- 'Elgar'	WMAq
	- 'Liam Johns'	CRow
	- 'Midnight'	see *I. laevigata* 'Weymouth Midnight'
	- 'Monstrosa'	CDes EWay
	- 'Plena' (d)	CRow
	- 'Rashomon'	CRow
	- 'Regal'	CWat
	- 'Richard Greaney'	CRow EWay
	- 'Rose Queen'	see *I. ensata* 'Rose Queen'
	- 'Shirasagi'	CRow
I	- 'Snowdrift'	CBAq CRow CWat EWay LRHS NBir NGdn NLar NPer SWat WMAq WMoo
	- 'Variegata' (v) ♀H4	CBAq CRow CWat ECho EHoe ELon EPfP EWay LLWG LRHS MWts NBro NGdn NPer SPer SWat WMAq WMoo
	- 'Violet Garth'	EWay
	- 'Weymouth'	see *I. laevigata* 'Weymouth Blue'
§	- 'Weymouth Blue'	CRow EWay
§	- 'Weymouth Elegant'	CRow
§	- 'Weymouth Midnight'	CMil CRow SWat
	- 'Weymouth Purity'	EWay
§	'Lake Niklas' (Sib)	ELon GBin MHol NCGa
	'Lamia' (TB)	CIri
	'Langport Chapter' (IB)	CKel ESgI
	'Langport Chief' (IB)	CKel
	'Langport Claret' (IB)	CKel ESgI
	'Langport Curlew' (IB)	CKel ESgI SMrm
	'Langport Duchess' (IB)	ESgI
	'Langport Fairy' (IB)	CKel
	'Langport Flame' (IB)	CKel ESgI
	'Langport Hope' (IB)	CKel
	'Langport Jane' (IB)	CKel
	'Langport Lady' (IB)	CKel
	'Langport Lord' (IB)	ESgI
	'Langport Minstrel' (IB)	CKel ESgI
	'Langport Pearl' (IB)	CKel
	'Langport Phoenix' (IB)	CKel
	'Langport Pinnacle' (IB)	CKel
	'Langport Smoke' (IB)	CKel
	'Langport Snow' (IB)	CKel
	'Langport Song' (IB)	CKel
	'Langport Star' (IB)	CKel ESgI
	'Langport Storm' (IB)	CKel ECGP EPfP MRav SBea SDeJ
	'Langport Sun' (IB)	CKel ESgI
	'Langport Swift' (IB)	CKel
	'Langport Sylvia' (IB)	CKel
	'Langport Tartan' (IB)	CKel
	'Langport Violet' (IB)	CKel ESgI
	'Langport Vista' (IB)	CKel
	'Langport Warrior' (IB)	CKel
	'Langport Wren' (IB) ♀H4	CAby CBro CKel EPfP EPri ESgI GBuc GCal LAst LHop LRHS MBri MCot MWhi NBir NGdn SBea WWEG
	'Langthorns Pink' (Sib)	CCse ELan MRav
	'Lark Rise' (TB) ♀H4	CKel
	'Larry Gaulter' (TB)	WCAu
	'Late Liftoff' (TB)	CIri
§	***latifolia*** ♀H4	ECho GKev MMuc NMin SEND WHlf WShi
	- 'Duchess of York'	EBee ECho GKev
	- 'Isabella'	ECho GKev SDeJ WCot
	- 'King of the Blues'	CAvo EBee ECho GKev SDeJ
	- 'Mansfield'	ECho
	- 'Montblanc'	CAvo EBee ECho GKev SDeJ
	- 'Queen of the Blues' (Eng)	ECho SDeJ
	- wild collected	GCal
	'Latin Lark' (TB)	ESgI
	'Latino' (IB) **new**	WCAu
	'Laura Jean' (TB)	EWoo
	'Laura Louise' (La)	LLWG SKHP
	'Laurenbuhl' (Sib)	CExl CHel
	'Lava Moonscape' (TB)	CIri
	'Lavender Bounty' (Sib)	CHid NBre NBro
	'Lavender Fair' (Sib)	CIri
	lazica ♀H4	CBct CBro CHII CMac CPrp CRow EPPr EPfP EPot ESgI GBin IBlr LRHS MRav NBir NCGa NSti SBch SBrt SEND SPer SPlb WCot WGwG
	- 'Joy Bishop'	CJun WCot
*	- 'Richard Nutt'	CJun ELon WCot
	- 'Turkish Blue'	CPrp IBlr
	'Lazuline'	LWor
	'Legato' (TB)	ESgI
*	'Lemon Beauty' (TB)	LHop
	'Lemon Brocade' (TB)	EWoo WCAu
	'Lemon Chiffon Pie' (Spuria) **new**	CIri
	'Lemon Fever' (TB)	ESgI
	'Lemon Flare' (SDB)	EIri MRav SRms
	'Lemon Flurry' (IB)	SBch
	'Lemon Ice' (TB)	EBee EPfP GBin LRHS MCot SDeJ SPer WHoo
	'Lemon Lyric' (TB)	ESgI
	'Lemon on Ice' (SDB) **new**	WCAu
*	'Lemon Peel' (IB)	CKel
	'Lemon Pop' (IB)	WCAu
	'Lemon Puff' (MDB)	CBro LLHF WCAu
	'Lemon Tree' (TB)	WCAu
	'Lemon Veil' (Sib) **new**	WCAu
	'Lemon Whip' (IB)	EWoo
	'Lena' (SDB)	CBro
	'Lenna M' (SDB)	CKel ECho
	'Lenora Pearl' (BB)	XSen
	'Lent A. Williamson' (TB)	GMaP WWEG

'Lenten Prayer' (TB)	SIri WCAu
'Leprechaun's Delight' (SDB)	CKel
'Leprechaun's Purse' (SDB)	WCAu
'Let's Elope' (IB)	ESgI WCAu
'Licorice Stick' (TB)	XSen
'Light Beam' (TB)	XSen
'Light Cavalry' (IB)	ESgI EWoo
'Light Laughter' (IB)	WCAu
'Light Rebuff' (TB)	EWoo
'Lilac Times'	EWoo
'Lilli-white' (SDB)	CAby CHel CKel CWat ELan EPfP LRHS MBNS MRav SPoG WCAu WWEG
'Lilting' (TB)	XSen
'Lima Colada' (SDB)	SMrm
'Limbo' (SpH)	CRow
'Lime Fizz' (TB)	XSen
'Limeheart' (Sib)	CPou LLHF
'Limelight' (TB)	SRms
'Linda Mary' (Sib)	EWoo
'Linda's Child' (TB) **new**	WCAu
'Line Dancing' (Spuria) **new**	CIri
'Little Black Belt' (SDB)	EWoo LRHS
'Little Blackfoot' (SDB)	CDes ESgI WCAu WCot
'Little Blue-eyes' (SDB)	ESgI WCAu
'Little Bluets' (SDB)	ESgI
'Little Dandy' (SDB)	ECho
'Little Dogie' (SDB)	ECho
'Little Dream' (SDB)	WCAu
'Little Firecracker' (SDB)	WCAu
'Little Paul' (MTB)	ESgI LMin
'Little Rosy Wings' (SDB)	CBro CPBP
'Little Shadow' (IB)	MRav SRms WWEG
'Little Sheba' (AB)	WCAu
'Little Showoff' (SDB)	ESgI
'Little Snowman'	LRHS
'Little Twinkle Star' (Sib)	NPro
'Living Waters' (TB)	ESgI
'Local Color' (TB)	ESgI EWoo SIri XSen
'Local Hero' (IB)	WCAu
'Lodore' (TB)	SRms
'Logo' (IB)	WCAu
'Lohengrin' (TB)	EWoo
'Lollipop' (SDB)	ESgI SIri
longipetala	EWes NBir
'Looking Forward' (TB)	ESgI
'Loop the Loop' (TB)	CMac CTsd EWoo NBre NSoo SGol SPoG SWat
'Loose Valley' (MTB) ♀H4	LMin SIri
'Lord Warden' (TB)	ECtt EPfP LDai LRHS MCot WGwG
'Lorilee' (TB)	ESgI WCAu
'Lost in Space' (BB) **new**	CIri
'Lothario' (TB)	WCAu
'Lottie Lou' (TB)	SIri
'Lotus Land' (TB)	WCAu
'Louisa's Song' (TB)	WCAu
'Louvois' (TB)	ESgI EWoo NLar
'Love the Sun' (TB)	ESgI XSen
'Lovely Again' (TB)	LRHS MRav WCAu
'Lovely Dawn' (TB)	WCAu
'Lovely Leilani' (TB)	ESgI
'Lovely Light' (TB)	MBri
'Lovely Señorita' (TB)	WCAu
'Love's Tune' (IB)	CAby LBuc LRHS SRGP SWat
'Low Ho Silver' (IB)	WCAu
'Loyalist' (TB)	CPar EWoo SIri
'Lucky Charm' (MTB)	CMea
'Lucky Devil' (Spuria) ♀H4	CIri
'Lucy's Gift' (MTB) ♀H4	LMin SRGP

'Lugano' (TB)	ESgI EWoo
'Lula Marguerite' (TB)	EWoo
'Luli-Ann' (SDB) ♀H4	CKel
'Lullaby of Spring' (TB)	CKel
'Lullingstone Castle' (Kent Castles Series) (IB) **new**	SIri
'Lumarco' (TB)	EWoo
'Lumière d'Automne' (TB)	ESgI XSen
'Luminosity' (TB)	ESgI
'Lure of Gold' (IB)	WCAu
lutescens ♀H4	ECho GCra WCot
§ - 'Campbellii'	ECho
§ - subsp. ***lutescens***	XSen
'Lyrique' (BB)	CKel
'Mabel Coday' (Sib)	EPri EWoo
macrosiphon	IGor
'Madame Lynn' (Spuria)	EWoo
'Madeira Belle' (TB)	ESgI LRHS
'Madeleine Frances' (SDB)	SIri
'Magharee' (TB)	ESgI
'Magic Kingdom' (TB)	CIri
'Magic Man' (TB)	XSen
'Magical Encounter' (TB)	EWoo
magnifica ♀H3-4	ECho ELon GKev
- 'Agalik'	ECho GKev
- 'Alba'	ECho GKev LWst
'Maid of Orange' (BB)	WCAu
'Maisie Lowe' (TB)	ESgI EWoo
'Majestic Ruler' (TB)	WCAu
'Making Eyes' (SDB)	WCAu
'Man About Town' (TB)	WCAu
'Mandarin Purple' (Sino-Sib)	EBee
mandshurica	CPBP
'Mango Entree' (TB)	WCAu
'Mango Smoothy' (BB)	ESgI
'Mara' (IB)	CKel
'Maranatha'	EWoo
'Margrave' (TB)	EWoo XSen
'Marguérite' (Reticulata/v)	ECho
mariae	LWst
'Marilyn Holmes' (Sib)	GBin GLog GQue WCot
'Mariposa Autumn' (TB)	ESgI EWoo SIri
'Mariposa Skies' (TB)	ESgI
'Marmalade Skies' (BB)	WCAu
'Maroon Caper' (IB)	SBch
'Martyn Rix'	see *I. confusa* 'Martyn Rix'
'Marvelous Magic' (SDB) **new**	MAsh
'Mary Constance' (IB) ♀H4	CKel
'Mary Frances' (TB)	ESgI LSRN WCAu XSen
'Mary McIlroy' (SDB) ♀H4	CBro CKel
'Maslon' (MTB)	LMin
'Master Touch' (TB)	ELon XSen
'Masterwork' (TB)	CIri
'Matinata' (TB)	CKel XSen
'Matt McNames' (TB)	EWoo
'Maui Moonlight' (IB) ♀H4	CKel ESgI EWoo NLar WCAu
'May Melody' (TB)	WCAu
'Maya Mint' (MDB)	LLHF
'Meadow Court' (SDB)	CBro CKel WCAu WWEG
'Medallion' (Spuria)	EWoo
'Media Luz' (Spuria)	WCAu
'Medici Prince' (TB)	EWoo
'Medway Valley' (MTB) ♀H4	LMin SIri WCAu
'Megglethorp' (IB) **new**	WCAu
'Meg's Mantle' (TB) ♀H4	CKel

	'Melbreak' (TB)	ESgI WCAu
	mellita	see *I. suaveolens*
	'Melon Honey' (SDB)	CKel EBee ELon WCAu
	'Melted Butter' (TB) **new**	WCAu
§	'Melton Red Flare' (Sib)	EBee ELan LRHS LSou MBNS MSpe SDys SMrm WWEG
	'Men in Black' (TB)	WCAu
	'Memphis Memory' (Sib)	ELan ELon EWTr GCra MHol MNrw NGdn NLar SBch SPer WWEG
	'Menton' (SDB)	CKel
	'Mer du Sud' (TB) ♀H4	EIri ESgI EWoo LRHS XSen
*	'Merebrook Blue Lagoon' (La)	WMAq
	'Merebrook Jemma J' (La)	WMAq
*	'Merebrook Lemon Maid' (La)	WMAq
	'Merebrook Malvern Shadow' (La)	WMAq
	'Merebrook Purpla' (La)	WMAq
	'Merebrook Rum 'n' Raisin' (La)	WMAq
*	'Merebrook Rusty Red' (La)	WMAq
*	'Merebrook Snowflake' (La)	WMAq
	'Merebrook Sunnyside Up' (La)	WMAq
	'Merebrook Symphony' (La)	WMAq
	'Merit' (MTB)	LMin
	'Merry Dance' (SDB)	CKel
	'Mescal' (TB)	WCAu
	'Mesmerizer' (TB)	ESgI
	'Messire Pierre' (BB) **new**	CIri
	'Messy Jessi' (TB)	CIri
	'Metaphor' (TB)	WCAu
	'Mezza Cartuccia' (IB)	ESgI
	'Miami Beach' (TB) **new**	WCAu
	'Midas Mite' (MDB) **new**	LLHF
I	'Midnight Blue' (MDB)	CBro
	'Midnight Caller' (TB)	ESgI EWoo XSen
	'Midnight Majesty' (TB)	EWoo
	'Midnight Mango'	see *I.* 'Midnight Web'
	'Midnight Oil' (TB)	EWoo WCAu
	'Midnight Shy' (Spuria) **new**	CIri
	'Midnight Treat' (TB)	WCAu
§	'Midnight Web' (IB) ♀H4	CKel
	'Midsummer Night's Dream' (IB)	ESgI EWoo
	'Mighty Mouse'	EWoo
	'Miles Ahead' (TB)	WCAu
	milesii ♀H4	CExl IGor NBir WSHC
	- CC 6839 **new**	GKev
	'Millennium Sunrise' (TB)	WCAu
	'Mini Big Horn' (IB)	CIri
	'Mini-Agnes' (SDB)	CBro
	'Minisa' (TB)	ESgI
	'Miss Carla' (IB)	ESgI NBre
	'Miss Nellie' (BB)	CKel
	'Miss Sunshine' (SDB) **new**	CPBP
	'Missouri Rivers' (Spuria)	CIri
	'Missouri Streams' (Spuria)	EWoo
	missouriensis ♀H4	CAvo CMac IGor
	'Mist Arising' (TB) **new**	CIri
	'Mister Matthew' (TB) ♀H4	CKel
	'Mister Roberts' (SDB)	ESgI
	'Mistress of Camelot' (TB)	SDys
	'Mme Chéreau' (TB)	ESgI EWoo WCAu
	'Monet's Blue' (TB)	EWoo
	'Monsieur-Monsieur' (TB)	ESgI
	Monspur Group	WCot
	'Moon Journey' (TB)	SIri
	'Moon Sparkle' (IB)	CKel
	'Moonbeam' (TB)	CKel
	'Moonlight Waves'	see *I. ensata* 'Moonlight Waves'
	'Moonlit' **new**	CIri
	'Moonlit Waves' (TB)	CKel
	'Moon Silk' (Sib)	CHel EBee ECtt ELon EPri GAbr GBuc LLHF WCot
	'Moonstruck' (TB)	EWoo
	'Morning Show' (IB)	MAvo
	'Morning Splendor' (TB)	EWoo
	'Morwenna' (TB) ♀H4	CKel ESgI
	'Mosaic of Blessing' (TB)	ESgI
	'Mother Earth' (TB)	ESgI EWoo
	'Mountain Lake' (Sib)	EPfP EShb GBin LRHS SWat WCot WPtf
	'Mountain Music'	EWoo
	'Mrs Horace Darwin' (TB)	CCon SWat WMnd
	'Mrs Nate Rudolph' (SDB)	WCAu
	'Mrs Rowe' (Sib)	CCse CPou CRow EIri ELon GBuc LLWP MRav MWat SWat
	'Mrs Tait' (Spuria)	NChi
	'Muggles' (SDB)	SIri
	'Mukaddam' (TB)	CIri
	'Murder Mystery' (TB)	WCAu
	'Muriel Neville' (TB)	WCAu
	'Murmuring Morn' (TB)	WCAu
	'Music' (SDB) **new**	SIri
	'Must Unite' (TB)	WCAu
	'Muted Melody' (TB)	CIri
	'My Honeycomb' (TB)	WCAu
	'My Kayla' (SDB)	ESgI
	'My Love' (Sib)	GBin
	'My Seedling' (MDB)	CBro
	'Myra' (SDB)	XSen
	'Mysterieux' (TB)	SIri
	'Mystic Dragon' (TB)	CIri SDys
	'Naivasha' (TB)	CKel
	'Nancy Hardy' (MDB)	CBro
	'Naples' (TB)	WCAu
	narcissiflora	WCot
	'Nassak' (TB)	EWoo
	'Natascha' (Reticulata)	ECho EPfP EPot NMin SDeJ
	'Natchez Trace' (TB)	EPri XSen
	'Navajo Code' (TB)	CIri
	'Navajo Jewel' (TB)	ESgI EWoo WCAu XSen
	'Navy Brass' (Sib)	EPri
	'Nectar of the Gods' (TB)	WCAu
	'Needlecraft' (TB)	NBre XSen
	'Needlepoint' (TB)	ESgI
	'Negro Modelo' (SDB)	WCAu
	'Neige de Mai' (TB)	ESgI
	'Neil's Choice' (TB)	CIri
*	'Nel Jupe' (TB)	LRHS NLar
	'Neon' (TB)	ESgI
	nertschinskia	see *I. sanguinea*
	'Neutron' (SDB)	WCAu
	'Neutron Dance' (TB)	WCAu
	'New Argument' (J)	LLHF
	'New Centurion' (TB)	EWoo XSen
	'New Creation' (TB)	ESgI
	'New Face' (TB)	WCAu
	'New Flame' (TB)	ESgI
	new hybrids (Sib)	WOut
	'New Idea' (MTB)	ESgI LMin WCAu
	'New Leaf' (TB)	WCAu
	'New Snow' (TB)	WCAu
	'Next in Line'	EWoo
	'Next Millenium' (TB)	EWoo

	'Nibelungen' (TB)	CJun ESgI MNrw NBre WCAu XSen
	'Nicola Jane' (TB) ♀^{H4}	CKel
	nicolai RM 8276	LWst
	- VV QQ.175	LWst
	'Night Breeze' (Sib)	EPri SIri
	'Night Edition' (TB)	CJun ESgI EWoo XSen
	'Night Game' (TB)	EWoo XSen
	'Night Owl' (TB)	CKel ELan ELon ESgI LHop MCot MHer SPoG WHrl
	'Night Ruler' (TB)	ESgI EWoo WCAu
	'Night Shift' (IB)	NBre
	'Nightfall' (TB)	ESgI
	'Nightmare' (TB)	CIri
	'Nights of Gladness' (TB)	ESgI
	nigricans	LWst
	'Niklas Sea'	see *I.* 'Lake Niklas'
	'No Down Payment' (TB) **new**	WCAu
	'Noble Lady' (TB)	CIri
	'Noctambule' (TB)	EWoo
	'Noon Siesta' (TB)	ESgI
	'Nora Eileen' (TB) ♀^{H4}	CKel
	'Nordica' (TB)	ESgI
	× ***norrisii***	EBee EHyd EUJe EWes
	- 'Butterfly Magic'	EBee
	- 'Dazzler'	MBel NLBP
	- 'Heart of Darkness'	EBee
	'North Downs' (BB)	SIri
	'Northern Jewel' (IB)	SIri
	'Northwest Pride' (TB)	EWoo
	'Nottingham Lace' (Sib)	GBin LLHF SWat
	'Now This' (Spuria)	EWoo
	'Nuee d'Orage' (TB)	EWoo
	'Oasis Fuzzy Wuzzy' (TB) **new**	CIri
	'Oasis Sydney' (TB)	CIri
	'Oban' (Sib) ♀^{H4}	ESgI GBuc
	'Obsidian' (TB)	WCAu
	'Ocean Depths' (TB)	ESgI
	'Ocelot' (TB)	ESgI
	'Ochraurea' (Spuria)	SMrm
	'Ochre Doll' (SDB)	CBro CKel
	ochroleuca	see *I. orientalis* Mill.
	'O'Cool' (IB)	CKel
	'Octave' (AB)	WCAu
	'October' (TB)	ESgI
	'October Storm' (IB)	CIri EWoo
	odaesanensis	SBrt
	'Oh Jamaica' (TB)	WCAu XSen
	'Oh So Cool' (MTB)	ESgI LMin
	'Oklahoma' (TB)	EWoo
	'Oktoberfest' (TB)	XSen
	'Ola Kalá' (TB)	EWll GMaP LRHS MCot MWat NBre NLar SHil SPer WCAu WWEG XSen
	'Old Black Magic' (TB)	ESgI EWoo XSen
	'Old Flame' (TB)	XSen
	'Olympiad' (TB)	ESgI XSen
	'Olympic Challenge' (TB)	ESgI MRav WCAu
	'Olympic Torch' (TB)	WCAu
	'Ominous Stranger' (TB)	ESgI WCAu
	'Once Again' (TB)	EWoo XSen
	'One Desire' (TB)	XSen
	'Open Sky' (SDB)	EWoo LRHS SIri XSen
	'Opposing Forces' (TB)	WCAu
	'Orageux' (IB)	CWCL SIri
	'Orange Caper' (SDB)	CAby CMac ECtt EPfP ESgI GBuc MRav NLar NSoo
	'Orange Harvest' (TB)	ESgI EWoo XSen
	'Orange Order' (TB)	WCAu

	'Orchardist' (TB)	CKel
	'Orchidarium' (TB)	CKel
	'Orchidea Selvaggia' (TB)	ESgI
	orchioides misapplied	see *I. bucharica* Foster
§	***orchioides*** Carrière	CAby ECho
	- deep yellow-flowered	LWst
	- dwarf	LWst
	- 'Urungachsai'	EPot
	- yellow	GKev
	'Oregon Skies' (TB)	ESgI EWoo
	'Oreo' (TB)	WCAu
	'Oriental Baby' (IB)	CKel
	'Oriental Beauty' (Dut)	GKev SPhx
	'Oriental Beauty' (TB)	SDeJ
	orientalis Thunb.	see *I. sanguinea*
	orientalis ambig.	CAvo EWes MNrw SLPl WCAu
§	***orientalis*** Mill. ♀^{H4}	CCon GBin GCal LRHS NLar WCru XSen
	'Orinoco Flow' (BB) ♀^{H4}	CKel ESgI WCAu
	'Orloff' (TB)	ESgI
	'Oro Antico' (TB)	CIri
	'Orville Fay' (Sib)	WBor WCot
	'Osage Buff' (TB)	CKel
	'Osay Canuc' (TB)	CIri
	'Ostentatious' (TB) **new**	WCAu
	'Ostrogoth' (TB)	CIri
	'Othello' (TB)	EWoo
	'Ottawa' (Sib)	CPou CRow CWat EHyd LPot LRHS MBNS SWat
	'Oulo' (TB)	ESgI XSen
	'Our House' (TB)	ESgI
	'Out Yonder' (TB)	WCAu
	'Outrage' (SDB)	CIri
	'Outset' (Sib)	ELon WWEG
	'Over Easy' (SDB)	CKel
	'Over in Gloryland' (Sib)	WCAu
	'Overjoyed' (TB)	WCAu XSen
	'Overnight Sensation' (TB)	EWoo
	'O'What' (SDB)	ESgI
	'Ozark Maid' (MTB)	SDys
	'Ozone Alert' (TB)	CIri
	Pacific Coast hybrids	see *I.* Californian hybrids
	'Pacific Gambler' (TB)	SMrm
	'Pacific Mist' (TB)	WCAu
	'Pacific Panorama' (TB)	XSen
	'Pagan Dance' (TB)	EWoo
	'Pagan Goddess' (TB)	EWoo
	'Pagan Pink' (TB)	XSen
	'Pagan Princess' (TB)	WCAu
I	'Pageant' (Sib)	WCot
	'Paint It Black' (TB)	EWoo XSen
	'Painter's Choice' (Spuria)	CIri
	'Pale Shades' (IB) ♀^{H4}	CBro CKel
§	***pallida***	EBee ESgI EWoo GMaP MRav MWat SEND SRms WCAu WMnd XSen
§	- 'Argentea Variegata' (TB/v)	CSBt EHoe EPfP EWoo GBuc GKev GMaP LAst LPio LRHS MAsh MBrN MCot MJak MRav NBir NBro NSoo NSti SPer SPoG WCot WHoo WWEG XSen
	- 'Aurea'	see *I. pallida* 'Variegata' Hort.
	- 'Aurea Variegata'	see *I. pallida* 'Variegata' Hort.
	- subsp. ***cengialtii***	XSen
	- var. ***dalmatica***	see *I. pallida* subsp. *pallida*
§	- subsp. ***pallida*** ♀^{H4}	CArn CExl CKel ELan EPfP GCal LRHS SDix SPer WCFE
	- 'Variegata' misapplied	see *I. pallida* 'Argentea Variegata'
§	- 'Variegata' Hort. (v) ♀^{H4}	CAby CBcs CBro CMac CWat ELan EPfP ESgI GMaP LRHS MAsh MAvo

		MBri MRav NSti SDix SPer SPlb SRot SWvt WWEG XSen
	'Palm Springs' (IB)	LLHF NMin
	'Palomino' (TB)	WCAu
	'Pane e Vino' (TB)	ESgI
	'Pansy Purple' (Sib)	WHil
	'Panther' (SDB) **new**	WCAu
	'Papillon' (Sib)	CAby CTri ECtt ELan ELon EWoo GAbr LHop LRHS MBel MWat NBir NBro NGdn NSti SDeJ SMrm SPer SWat WWEG
	'Paradise' (TB)	CKel
	paradoxa	ECho LWst
	'Paricutin' (SDB)	CBro
	'Paris Lights' (TB)	XSen
	'Parisian Dawn' (TB) **new**	WCAu
	'Parisien' (TB)	CWCL EIri
	'Parts Plus' (IB)	CIri
	'Party Dress' (TB)	CMac EBee ELan EPfP IPot LRHS MRav MWhi NBir NGdn NLar NPnk NWad SPer SPoG SRms SWat WGwG
	'Paso Doble' (TB)	ESgI
	'Pastel Charm' (SDB)	NPnk SMrm WMnd
	'Patina' (TB)	EIri EWoo LRHS WCAu
	'Patterdale' (TB)	NBir NBre
	'Paul Black' (TB) $\mathbb{Y}^{H4}$	CIri WCAu
	'Pauline' (Reticulata)	CAvo CBro ECho EPfP ERCP GKev LRHS MWat
	'Pause' (SDB) **new**	WCAu
	'Peaceful Waters' (TB)	XSen
	'Peach Eyes' (SDB)	CBro CKel
	'Peach Picotee' (TB)	ESgI XSen
	'Peach Spot' (TB)	CJun WCAu
	'Peachy Face' (IB)	ESgI XSen
	'Pearl Queen' (Sib)	MCot
	'Pearls of Autumn' (TB)	WCAu
	'Pearly Dawn' (TB)	ECtt SRGP SWat WWEG
*	'Pêche Melba' (TB)	XSen
	'Peg Edwards' (Sib)	EWoo
	'Pegaletta' (La)	NBro
	'Peggy Chambers' (IB) $\mathbb{Y}^{H4}$	SMrm
	'Pelion Hills'	LBuc LRHS
	'Penny a Pinch' (TB)	WWEG
	'Pepita' (SDB)	EWoo
	'Percheron' (Sib)	EBee EPri ESgI EWoo SIri
	'Perfect Interlude' (TB)	EIri XSen
	'Perfect Vision' (Sib) $\mathbb{Y}^{H4}$	CIri
	'Performer' (MTB)	EIri
	'Perfume Shop' (IB)	CKel
	'Perky' (MDB) **new**	CPBP
	'Perry's Blue' (Sib)	CBcs CMac CSBt EBee EHon EPfP EPri GKin GMaP IKil LRHS MGos MRav MSpe NBir NBro NGdn NPer SBch SPer SRms SWat WMnd
I	'Perry's Favourite' (Sib)	CRow
	'Persian Berry' (TB)	WCAu XSen
	'Persimmon' misapplied	see *I.* 'Tycoon'
	'Persimmon' ambig. (Sib)	CAby CCon CHid ECtt GCra GKin LRHS SWat WMoo WPtf
	'Persuit of Happiness' (TB)	WCAu
*	'Peter Hewitt' (Sib) $\mathbb{Y}^{H4}$	CIri
	'Petite Monet' (MTB)	ESgI LMin
	'Phaeton' (TB)	WCAu
	'Pharaoh's Daughter' (IB)	EWoo SIri
	'Phil Edinger' $\mathbb{Y}^{H4}$ **new**	LLWG
	'Phil Keen' (TB) $\mathbb{Y}^{H4}$	CKel
	'Picadee'	CDes EBee EPfP
	'Picasso Moon' (TB) **new**	WCAu
	'Pigeon' (SDB)	XSen
	'Pilot' (SDB)	WCAu
	'Pinewood Charmer' (CH)	CElw
	'Pinewood Sunshine' (CH)	MAvo
	'Pink Attraction' (TB)	ESgI XSen
	'Pink Bubbles' (BB)	WCAu XSen
	'Pink Charm' (TB)	EPfP LRHS NCGa SDeJ SPlb SPoG
	'Pink Clover' (TB)	ESgI
	'Pink Confetti' (TB)	EWoo XSen
	'Pink Haze' (Sib)	CRow EBee EPfP ESgI GBin WWEG
	'Pink Horizon' (TB)	XSen
	'Pink Invasion' (TB)	WCAu
	'Pink Kitten' (IB)	WCAu WGwG XSen
	'Pink Lavender' (TB)	ELon
	'Pink Parchment' (BB) $\mathbb{Y}^{H4}$	CKel
	'Pink Pele' (IB)	ESgI
	'Pink Pinafore' (TB)	EWoo
	'Pink Pussycat' (TB)	MBri
	'Pink Quartz' (TB)	ESgI
	'Pink Reprise' (BB)	EWoo
	'Pink Swan' (TB)	XSen
	'Pink Taffeta' (TB)	XSen
	'Pinnacle' (TB)	CKel GCal SWat
	'Pipes of Pan' (TB)	ESgI WCAu
	'Pirate Prince' (Sib)	NPer
	'Pirate's Quest' (TB)	ESgI EWoo XSen
	'Piroska' (TB) $\mathbb{Y}^{H4}$	ESgI XSen
*	'Piu Blue' (TB)	ESgI
	'Pixie' (DB)	GKev
	'Pixie' (Reticulata) $\mathbb{Y}^{H4}$	ECho ELan EPot LHop LRHS NLar SDeJ SMrm
	planifolia	ECho GKev
	'Platinum' (TB)	WCAu
	'Pleasures of May' (Sib)	EBee WBor
	'Pledge Allegiance' (TB)	ECtt ESgI EWoo WCAu
	'Plickadee' (SDB)	CBro
	'Plissée' (Sib) $\mathbb{Y}^{H4}$	GBin
	'Plum Lucky' (SDB)	SIri
	'Plum Twist' (SDB) **new**	WCAu
	'Plum Wine' (SDB)	CJun CKel
	'Poem of Ecstasy' (TB)	WCAu
	'Pogo' (SDB)	CHel CMac EBee ECho ECtt ELan EPfP EPot GBuc GMaP LRHS MRav NBir NSoo SBea SDeJ SMrm SRms
	'Pokemon' (MDB) **new**	CIri
	'Poker Chips' (MTB) **new**	LMin
	'Polvere di Stelle' (TB)	ESgI
	'Pookanilly' (IB)	CJun
	'Popsicle' (SDB) **new**	WCAu
	'Port of Call' (Spuria)	EWoo
	'Pounsley Purple' (Sib)	CPou EPri
	'Powder Blue Cadillac' (TB)	CKel WCAu
	'Power Point' (TB)	CIri WCAu
	'Praetorian Guard' (TB)	CIri
	'Prairie Sunset' (TB)	EWoo
	'Prairie Thunder' (AB)	WCAu
	'Precious Heather' (TB) $\mathbb{Y}^{H4}$	CKel
	'Presby's Crown Jewel' (TB)	WCAu
	'Presence' (TB)	SIri
	'Pretender' (TB)	WCAu
	'Pretty Please' (TB)	ESgI
	'Primrose Cream' (Sib)	WCot
	'Primrose Drift' (TB)	ESgI
	'Prince Indigo' (TB)	MRav
	'Prince of Burgundy' (IB) $\mathbb{Y}^{H4}$	WCAu
	'Princess Beatrice' (TB)	WCAu
	'Princess Bride' (BB) $\mathbb{Y}^{H4}$	WCAu

'Princess Sabra' (TB) $\mathbb{Y}^{H4}$	CKel
'Princesse Caroline de Monaco' (TB)	ESgI EWoo
prismatica	GKev
- ***alba***	IGor
'Professor Blaauw' (Dut) $\mathbb{Y}^{H4}$	CAvo EPfP GKev
'Progressive Attitude' (TB)	EPri
'Prosper Laugier' (IB)	WCAu
'Protocol' (IB)	CKel
'Proud Tradition' (TB)	ESgI SIri WCAu XSen
'Provençal' (TB)	CJun CKel CPar CWCL ESgI EWoo WCAu XSen
'Prudy' (BB) $\mathbb{Y}^{H4}$	CKel
'Prussian Blue' (Sib) $\mathbb{Y}^{H4}$	CIri GBin WSHC
pseudacorus $\mathbb{Y}^{H4}$	Widely available
- B&SWJ 5018 from Japan	WCru
- from Korea	CRow
- 'Alba'	CPrp GCal MRav MSKA MWts NGdn SWat
- var. ***bastardii***	CRow CWat ELon EPfP ESgI LLWG MSKA NPer SLon SPer SWat WBrk WCAu WMoo WPnP XLum
- 'Beuron'	CRow
- 'Come in Spinner' new	LLWG
- cream-flowered	NBir SWat
- 'Crème de la Crème'	ELon GBin GQue LLWG NLar NSti WHil
- 'Esk'	GCal
- 'Flore Pleno' (d)	CPrp CRow ECho ESgI GCra LLWG MSKA NLar NPer WBrk WCAu WCot WPnP WWEG
I - 'Golden Fleece'	SPer
- 'Golden Queen'	CRow EWay LLWG
- 'Ilgengold'	CRow
- 'Ivory'	CRow LLWG
- 'Krill'	EBee LLWG WHil
- 'Mandchurica'	XBlo
* - ***nana***	CRow
- 'Roy Davidson' $\mathbb{Y}^{H4}$	CBro CPrp CRow GBin GCal IBlr NLar WCot WHil
- 'Sulphur Queen'	WCot WWEG
- 'Sun Cascade'	CRow GBin
- 'Tiger Brother'	CBro WBrk
- 'Tiggah'	CRow
- 'Turnipseed'	WCot
- 'Variegata' (v) $\mathbb{Y}^{H4}$	Widely available
* ***pseudocapnoides*** (J)	LWst
'Pulse Rate' (SDB)	CBro
pumila	CPBP LRHS MCot MWat
- f. ***atroviolacea***	CKel WMnd
- 'Gelber Mantel'	NBir
- 'Violacea' (DB)	SRms
'Pumpin' Iron' (SDB) $\mathbb{Y}^{H4}$	CJun CKel ESgI
'Punchline' (TB)	CWCL
'Punk' (MDB)	CIri
purdyi	IGor
'Pure and Simple' (TB) new	WCAu
'Pure As Gold' (TB)	CWCL ESgI EWoo XSen
'Purple Gem' (Reticulata)	ECho EPfP EPot GKev LPio
'Purple People Eater' (TB)	CIri
'Purple Pepper' (TB) new	WCAu
'Purple Ritz' (TB) new	WCAu
'Purple Sensation' (Dut)	ECho SDeJ
'Purple Study' (MTB) new	WCAu
'Purr for Mints' (TB)	CIri
'Pussycat Pink' (SDB)	ESgI WCAu
'Quaker Lady' (TB)	ESgI EWoo SIri WCAu
'Qualified' (TB) new	CIri
'Quantum Leap' (TB)	CIri
'Quark' (SDB)	CBro CKel CPBP
'Quechee' (TB)	CWCL EBee EPfP ESgI EWoo GMaP IPot LBuc LDai LRHS LSRN MBri MCot MNrw MRav MSpe MWat NCGa NLar NSoo NWad SDeJ SPer SWat WGwG
'Queen in Calico' (TB)	ESgI WCAu
'Queen of Angels' (TB)	WCAu
'Queen of Hearts' (TB)	XSen
'Queen of May' (TB)	EWoo
'Queen's Circle' (TB) $\mathbb{Y}^{H4}$	CIri WCAu
'Queen's Prize' (SDB)	SIri
'Quito' (TB)	WCAu
'Rabbit's Foot' (SDB)	LSRN SIri
'Radiant Apogee' (TB)	ECtt EIri
'Radiant Burst' (IB)	SIri
'Rain Dance' (SDB) $\mathbb{Y}^{H4}$	ESgI
Rainbow Grand Mixture	SDeJ
'Rainbow Rim' (SDB)	ESgI WCAu
'Rajah' (TB)	ELan EPfP EShb EWoo GMaP LPio LRHS LSRN MCot MLHP MRav NCGa NOrc NSoo SDeJ SPer SPoG WMnd
'Rameses' (TB)	ESgI EWoo WCAu
'Rancho Rose' (TB)	CKel XSen
'Rapture in Blue' (TB)	EWoo
'Rare Edition' (IB)	CKel EWoo NBir NBre XSen
'Rare Quality' (TB)	XSen
'Rare Treat' (TB)	XSen
'Raspberry Acres' (IB)	MRav WCAu
'Raspberry Blush' (IB) $\mathbb{Y}^{H4}$	CAby CKel CPar EIri EPfP GBin LBMP LHop LRHS LSou MRav NCGa SBea SWat WGwG WHoo WWFP XSen
'Razoo' (SDB)	CKel
'Reach for the Sky' (TB) new	CIri
'Real Coquette' (SDB)	SIri
'Realm' (TB)	ESgI
'Rebecca Perret' (TB)	WCAu
'Rebus' (SDB)	SIri
'Red Canyon Glow' (TB)	CIri
'Red Dazzler' (La)	CIri
'Red Echo' (La)	CIri
'Red Flash' (TB)	ESgI
'Red Heart' (SDB)	ESgI MRav WWEG XSen
'Red Orchid' (IB)	ELan ESgI LHop LRHS NBre SRms WCAu WWEG
'Red Revival' (TB)	MRav WCAu
'Red Rum' (TB)	CKel EWes
'Red Zinger' (IB)	CJun ESgI EWoo LRHS
'Redelta' (TB)	XSen
'Redflare'	see *I.* 'Melton Red Flare'
'Redondo' (IB)	EWoo
'Reflets Safran' (TB)	SIri XSen
'Regal Surprise' (SpH) $\mathbb{Y}^{H4}$	CRow EBee LLWG
'Regality' (Sib)	CWCL EBee MHer NBro
'Regards' (SDB)	CBro EBee XSen
'Regency Belle' (Sib) $\mathbb{Y}^{H4}$	EWoo SIri
'Regency Buck' (Sib)	EWoo SBch WCot
§ ***reichenbachii***	EPot LWst WAbe WThu
'Reincarnation' (TB)	CIri EWoo
'Remembering Vic' (Spuria)	EWoo
'Renewal' (TB)	EWoo
'Renown' (TB)	EWoo
'Repartee' (TB)	XSen
'Replicator' (SDB)	EWoo
reticulata $\mathbb{Y}^{H4}$	ECho ELan EPfP LRHS SDeJ SEND SMrm SPer
- KPPZ 90-152	LWst

	– var. ***bakeriana***	ECho LLHF NMin
	– 'Violet Queen'	ECho
	'Return to Elegance' (TB) new	WCAu
	'Return to Sender' (TB)	EWoo
	'Réussite' (TB)	EWoo
	'Reversi' (TB) new	CIri
	'Rhages' (TB)	EWoo
	'Rhapsody' (Reticulata)	SDeJ
	'Rheinfels' (TB)	EWoo
	'Rheingauperle' (TB)	ESgI EWoo
	'Rhett's Surprise' (Spuria) new	CIri
	'Rhythm' (TB) new	CIri
	'Rikugi-sakura' (Sib)	EBee EPri GBin LLHF NLar WCot
	'Rime Frost' (TB)	WCAu
	'Ringdove' (TB)	ESgI
	'Ringo' (TB)	CKel EWoo LSRN MRav
	'Rings of Saturn' (TB)	CIri
	'Rio Rojo' (TB)	WCAu
	'Rip City' (TB)	ESgI
	'Risen in Glory' (TB)	ESgI
	'Rising Moon' (TB)	EWoo SIri
	'Ritz' (SDB)	WWEG
	'Rive Gauche' (TB)	ESgI
	'River Avon' (TB) $\mathbb{Y}^{H4}$	WCAu
	'Riverbuds' (SDB)	SIri WCAu
	'Riverdance' (Sib)	EWoo
	'Roanoke's Choice' (Sib)	CBro CElw EBee ELon EWes GAbr GBin MBel NCGa
	'Roaring Jelly' (Sib)	EBee EPri EWes NLar WCAu WCot
	'Rob Cornell' (TB)	ESgI
	'Robe d'Été' (TB)	CWCL
§	× ***robusta*** 'Dark Aura' $\mathbb{Y}^{H4}$	MAvo WCot
§	– 'Gerald Darby' $\mathbb{Y}^{H4}$	Widely available
	– 'Mountain Brook'	CRow LLWG
*	– 'Purple Fan'	LLWG
	'Rochester Castle' (Kent Castles Series) (IB) new	SIri
§	'Rocket' (TB)	EPfP GMaP LBuc LRHS MCot MRav MSpe NBir SDeJ SMrm SPer
	'Rocket Master' (TB)	ESgI
	'Rocket Randy' (TB)	CIri
	'Roku Oji' (Sib) new	CIri
	'Roman Carnival' (TB)	EWoo
	'Romance' (TB)	EWoo
	'Romano' (Dut)	LRHS
	'Romantic Evening' (TB)	EIri EWoo WCAu XSen
	'Romantic Mood' (TB)	CKel
	'Romney Marsh' (IB)	SIri
	'Rosace' (Sib)	EWoo
	'Rosalie Figge' (TB)	ESgI EWoo WCAu WCot
	'Rosé' (TB)	LSRN
	'Rose Queen'	see *I. ensata* 'Rose Queen'
	'Rose Violet' (TB)	WCAu
	'Rose-Marie' (TB)	EWoo
	'Rosemary's Dream' (MTB)	NBre
	rosenbachiana	ECho LWst
	– 'Darwas'	LWst
	– 'Harangon'	ECho LWst
	– 'Hissar' new	LWst
	– 'Tovil-Dara'	LWst
	– 'Varzob'	LWst
	'Roseplic' (TB)	LRHS
	'Rosette Wine' (TB)	ESgI WCAu
	'Rosy Bows' (Sib) new	WCAu
	'Rosy Veil' (TB)	ESgI EWoo
	'Rosy Wings' (TB)	ECho ESgI EWoo
	'Roucoulade' (TB)	SIri
	'Rouge Gorge' (TB)	SIri
	'Roulette' (TB)	MBri
	'Rowden Starlight'	CRow CWat LLWG
I	'Royal Blue' (Sib)	EBee SWat
	'Royal Crusader' (TB)	CCse CJun WCAu XSen
	'Royal Elegance' (TB)	SIri
	'Royal Intrigue' (TB)	SIri
	'Royal Satin' (TB)	CHid WGwG
	'Royal Snowcap' (TB)	WCAu
	'Royal Tapestry' (TB)	NBre
	'Royalist' (TB)	CKel
	'Rubacuori' (TB)	ESgI EWoo
	'Rubistar' (TB)	EWoo
	'Ruby Chimes' (IB)	ESgI WCAu
	'Ruby Contrast' (TB)	WCAu
	'Ruby Eruption' (SDB)	EIri WCAu
	'Ruby Mine' (TB)	WCAu
	'Ruby Morn' (TB)	WCAu
	'Ruby Wine' (Sib)	CCon EPri LEdu NLar
	rudskyi	see *I. variegata*
	'Ruffled Velvet' (Sib) $\mathbb{Y}^{H4}$	CElw CHid CKel ECho ECtt ELan EPfP EPri ESgI EWoo GBin IPot LPio LRHS MBri MCot MRav NBro NLar SMrm SPer SWat WCAu WWEG
	'Ruffles Plus' (Sib)	EPri MBel
	'Russet Crown' (TB)	CKel
	'Rustic Cedar' (TB)	ESgI WCAu
	'Rustle of Spring' (TB)	WCAu
	'Rustler' (TB)	WCAu
	'Rusty Beauty' (Dut)	GKev SDeJ
	'Rusty Magnificence' (TB)	EWoo
	'Ruth Black' (TB)	WCAu
	'Ruth Rowlands' (TB)	ESgI EWoo
	ruthenica	ECho WCot
	– var. ***nana***	CExl GKev
	'Ryan James' (TB)	CKel
	'Sable' (TB)	ELan EPfP ESgI EWoo GMaP LPio LRHS LSRN MBri MCot MRav MWat MWhi NLar NOrc SDeJ SEND SPer WCAu WWEG
	'Sable Night' (TB)	CKel ESgI
	'Safari Sunset' (TB) new	WCAu
	'Sager Cedric' (TB)	WCAu
	'Saint Crispin' (TB)	EBee EPfP GCra GMaP LRHS MRav SPer SPoG WGwG WWlt
	'Salamander Crossing' (Sib) $\mathbb{Y}^{H4}$	CIri
	'Sally Jane' (TB)	WCAu
	'Salmon Sunset' (Spuria)	EWoo
	'Salonique' (TB)	ESgI MMHG NLar WCAu
	'Saltwood' (SDB)	CBro ESgI NBre SIri
	'Saltwood Castle' (Kent Castles Series) (IB) new	SIri
	'Sam Carne' (TB)	WCAu
	'Samarcande' (TB)	ESgI
	× ***sambucina***	XSen
	'San Diego' (TB)	ESgI
	'San Francisco' (TB)	ESgI
	'San Gabriel' (TB)	EWoo
	'San Leandro' (TB)	MBri
	'Sandling Sunset' (TB)	SIri
	'Sandstone Sentinel' (BB)	CIri
	'Sandy Caper' (IB)	WCAu
	'Sangone' (IB)	ESgI MNrw
	'Sangreal' (IB)	LRHS
§	***sanguinea*** $\mathbb{Y}^{H4}$	CMCN
	– 'Nana Alba'	EWoo GBin
§	– 'Snow Queen'	CAvo CBcs CHel EBee ELan ELon EPfP EPri EWoo GBin GKev GMaP

		IKil LPot LRHS MBri MGos NLar NPri NSti SPer SWat WCAu WCot WHoo WMoo WWEG
	'Sapphire Beauty' (Dut)	GKev SDeJ
	'Sapphire Gem' (SDB)	CKel ESgI EWoo LSRN WCAu
	'Sapphire Hills' (TB)	LRHS WCAu XSen
	'Sarah Taylor' (SDB) 🏆H4	CBro ECho EWoo WCAu
*	'Sarajaavo' (AB)	CKel
	sari	ECho LWst
	'Sasha Borisovich' (TB)	ESgI
	'Sass with Class' (SDB)	CKel
	'Satin Gown' (TB)	WCAu
	'Saturday Night Live' (TB)	WCAu
	'Saturn' (TB)	WCAu
	'Scottish Warrior' (TB)	CIri
	'Scramble' (Sib)	ESwi WCot
	'Scribe' (MDB)	CBro NBir WCAu
	'Sea Double' (TB)	WWEG
	'Sea Fret' (SDB)	CBro
	'Sea Monster' (SDB)	CJun
	'Sea of Joy' (TB)	XSen
	'Sea Wisp' (La)	CHel EWTr NBro SKHP
	'Seakist' (TB)	WCAu
	'Sea Shadows' (Sib)	EPri ESgI NBir
	'Season Ticket' (IB)	XSen
	'Seastone' (SDB)	WCAu
	'Second Look' (TB)	XSen
	'Second Wind' (TB)	EWoo WCAu
	'Secret Melody' (TB)	XSen
	'Secret Service' (TB)	CIri
	'Self Evident' (MDB)	LLHF
	'Semola' (SDB)	ESgI
	'Senlac' (TB)	EPfP NLar WMnd
	'Señor Frog' (SDB)	ESgI
	serbica	see *I. reichenbachii*
	'Serene Moment' (TB)	SIri
	'Serenity Prayer' (SDB)	WCAu
	setosa 🏆H4	CBro CMac CTri CWCL ECho EHyd GCra GKev IGor LEdu LRHS MNrw WAbe
	- ***alba***	NLar
	- var. ***arctica***	GBuc LEdu
I	- 'Baby Blue'	EPfP LRHS MBNS NPri
	- subsp. ***canadensis***	see *I. hookeri*
	- dark violet-flowered	EPri
	- var. ***nana***	see *I. hookeri*
	'Seven Hills' (TB)	ESgI
	'Severn Side' (TB) 🏆H4	CKel
	'Shadow Cast' (IB) **new**	WCAu
	'Shahryar'	LWst
	'Shaker's Prayer' (Sib) 🏆H4	CIri CPrp EWes MBrN
	'Shakespeare's Sonnet' (SDB)	ESgI
	'Shall We Dance' (Sib) 🏆H4	CIri EWes
	'Shampoo' (IB)	CKel SIri WCAu
	'Share the Spirit' (TB)	WCAu
	'Sheila Ann Germaney' (Reticulata)	CBro EBee ECho EPot ERCP GKev LLHF LRHS NMin NWad SBch
	'Shelby Lynne' (TB)	CIri
	'Shelford Giant' (Spuria) 🏆H4	CIri NEgg
	'Sherbet Lemon' (IB) 🏆H4	CKel WCAu
	'Shifnal'	WCAu
	'Shirley Chandler' (IB) 🏆H4	SIri
	'Shirley Pope' (Sib) 🏆H4	COlW EWes EWoo GAbr GBin GBuc LRHS MBri MNFA NCGa NSti WMoo WNew WWEG
	'Shirley's Choice' (Sib)	EBee EPri SIri
	'Short Distance' (IB)	EWoo SIri
	'Showdown' (Sib)	ECtt GMaP SWat
	'Shrawley' (Sib)	EWoo
	shrevei	see *I. virginica* var. *shrevei*
	'Shurton Brook' (TB)	CKel
	'Shurton Inn' (TB)	CKel WCAu
	sibirica 🏆H4	CMHG COlW CTsd CWat EHon ESgI GAbr GBBs GKev LLWP MCot MLHP MMuc NChi SEND SPlb SRot WBrk WHer WMoo WShi
	- grey-flowered	ELon
	'Sibirica Alba'	EPfP EPri GBBs IBoy LLWP SWat WBrk
	sichuanensis	CExl
	'Side Effect'	WCAu
	'Sidney Linnegar' (TB) **new**	WCAu
	sieboldii	see *I. sanguinea*
	'Sierra Blue' (TB)	ESgI
	'Sierra Grande' (TB)	SIri XSen
	'Sierra Nevada' (Spuria)	SMrm XSen
	'Sign of Leo' (TB)	XSen
	'Silence in Heaven' (Spuria) **new**	CIri
	'Silkirim' (TB)	CKel
	'Silver Edge' (Sib) 🏆H4	Widely available
	'Silver Shower' (TB)	EWoo
	'Silverado' (TB)	CKel ESgI EWoo GBin LRHS WCAu
	'Silvery Beauty' (Dut)	MBri NBir SDeJ
	sindjarensis	see *I. aucheri*
	'Sindpers' (J) 🏆H3	LWst
	'Sing to Me' (TB)	WCAu
	'Sinister Desire' (IB)	EWoo SIri
	sintenisii 🏆H4	CBro CPBP ECho XSen
	'Sir Michael' (TB)	ESgI EWoo
	'Siva Siva' (TB)	MRav
	'Six Pack' (TB)	CIri
	'Sixteen Candles' (IB)	EWoo
	'Sixtine C' (TB)	SIri
	'Skating Party' (TB)	CKel ESgI EWoo XSen
	'Sky Beauty' (Dut)	GKev SDeJ
	'Sky Hooks' (TB)	XSen
	'Sky Tracery' (MTB)	SDys
	'Skydancer' (SDB)	WCAu
	'Skyfire' (TB)	ESgI EWoo WWEG
	'Skylark's Song' (TB)	EIri EWoo
	'Sky Wings' (Sib)	CRow EWoo GQue MArl WMoo
	'Slap Bang' (SDB)	ESgI
	'Small Sky' (SDB)	CBro
	'Smart Aleck' (TB)	ESgI EWoo
	'Smart Girl' (TB)	CKel EIri
	'Smart Move' (TB)	CWCL ESgI
	'Smarty Pants' (MTB)	LMin
	'Smash' (MTB)	ESgI LMin
	'Smiling Faces' (TB)	WCAu
	'Smith Named Keith' (TB) **new**	CIri
	'Smitten Kitten' (IB)	LSRN WCAu
	'Smokey Dream' (TB)	CKel
	'Smokey Salmon' (TB)	CKel
	'Smooth' (SDB)	SDys
	'Snow Fiddler' (MTB)	EWoo
	'Snow Plum' (IB)	SIri
	'Snow Prince' (Sib)	EPri
	'Snow Queen'	see *I. sanguinea* 'Snow Queen'
	'Snow Season' (SDB)	ESgI
	'Snow Shoes' (TB) **new**	CIri
	'Snow Tracery' (TB)	LRHS MBri NCGa NPnk
	'Snow Troll' (SDB)	WCAu
	'Snowcone' (IB)	EWoo
	'Snowcrest' (Sib)	CBre MRav

'Snowdrift' (*laevigata*)	see *I. laevigata* 'Snowdrift'
'Snowmound' (TB)	CCCN CKel ESgI EWoo WCAu
'Snowy Owl' (TB) ♀H4	CKel WCAu
'Snugglebug' (SDB)	EWoo
'Social Event' (TB)	ESgI XSen
'Social Graces' (TB)	WCAu
'Socialist' (TB)	WCAu
'Soft Blue' (Sib) ♀H4	NBre
'Soft Rain' (TB) **new**	CIri
'Soft Return'	EWoo
'Solar Fire' (TB)	CIri
'Solar Fusion' (Spuria)	EWoo
'Solid Mahogany' (TB)	MRav
'Soligo' (MDB)	ESgI
'Solo Flight' (TB)	SDys
'Somerset Blue' (TB) ♀H4	CKel
'Somerset Cider' (TB)	SIri
'Somerset Vale' (TB)	SMrm
'Somerton Brocade' (SDB)	CKel
'Somerton Dance' (SDB)	CKel
'Song of Norway' (TB)	EIri EWoo XSen
'Sonoran Sands' (IB)	SDys
'Sopra il Vulcano' (BB)	ESgI EWoo
'Sordid Lives' (TB) **new**	WCAu
'Sostenique' (TB)	ESgI
'Southcombe White' (Sib)	CRow WWEG
'Souvenir de Madame Gaudichau' (TB)	ESgI EWoo
'Spanish Coins' (MTB)	LMin
'Sparkling Rosé' (Sib)	Widely available
'Sparkling Waters' (TB)	ESgI
'Sparkplug' (SDB)	ESgI
'Spartan' (TB)	CKel
'Special Feature' (TB)	CIri
'Speck So' (MTB)	WCAu
'Speeding Star' (Spuria) **new**	CIri
'Spellbreaker' (TB)	SIri
'Spice Lord' (TB)	WCAu
'Spiced Custard' (TB)	CKel EIri ESgI EWoo
'Spiced Tiger' (TB)	ESgI
'Spicy Cajun' (La)	WHil
'Spinning Wheel' (TB)	SIri
'Spirit of Memphis' (TB)	XSen
'Splashacata' (TB)	WCAu XSen
'Splashdown' (Sino-Sib)	SWat
'Splat' (IB)	CIri
'Spot of Tea' (MDB)	LLHF
'Spreckles' (TB)	ESgI
'Spree' (SDB) **new**	WCAu
'Spring Blush' (MTB)	SIri
'Spring Festival' (TB)	WCAu
'Spring Kiss' (TB)	SIri
'Spring Madness' (TB)	WCAu
'Spring Time' (Reticulata)	ECho GKev SDeJ
spuria	CMac CPou WCot
§ - subsp. ***halophila***	EBee GBin GKev
- subsp. ***notha*** CC 725 **new**	WCot
- subsp. ***ochroleuca***	see *I. orientalis* Mill.
'Spy' (BB)	WCAu
'Square Dance Skirt' (TB)	SDys
'St Louis Blues' (TB)	ESgI XSen
'Stairway to Heaven' (TB)	ESgI WCAu
'Stapleford' (SDB)	CBro
'Staplehurst' (MTB) ♀H4	LMin SIri
'Star Rider' (Spuria)	CIri
'Star Shine' (TB)	CKel ESgI WCAu
'Starcrest' (TB)	EWoo
'Stardate' (SDB)	CKel
'Starlette Rose' (TB)	EWoo
'Starring' (TB)	EWoo WCAu
'Starship' (TB)	XSen
'Starship Enterprise' (TB)	CIri
'Starwoman' (IB) ♀H4	SDys WCAu
'Staten Island' (TB)	ESgI SEND SRms WCAu
'Steffie' (MTB) **new**	WCAu
'Stella Polaris' (TB)	COIW ELon
'Stellar Lights' (TB)	EIri EWoo WCAu
'Stephen Wilcox' (Sib)	CIri EPri
'Stepping Out' (TB) ♀H4	CMac CPar EPfP ESgI GBin LDai LRHS MBri NBre NCGa SDeJ WCAu
'Steve' (Sib)	CPar EWes SWat
'Steve Varner' (Sib)	EPri EWoo
'Stinger' (SDB) ♀H4	CIri
'Stingray' (TB)	ESgI
'Stitch in Time' (TB)	EIri EWoo WCAu
'Stockholm' (SDB)	CKel
stolonifera	ECho LWst
- 'Zwanenburg Beauty'	ECho
'Stop the Music' (TB)	XSen
'Storm Center' (TB)	EWoo
'Stormy Circle' (SDB)	WCAu
'Storrington' (TB)	EMal
'Strange Brew' (TB)	WCAu
'Strathmore' (TB)	EMal
'Strawberry Fair' (Sib) ♀H4	CIri
'Strawberry Love' (IB) ♀H4	CKel
'Strictly Jazz' (TB)	WCAu
'Strike it Rich' (TB)	ESgI
'Striking' (TB)	EWoo
'Strozzapreti' (TB)	ESgI
'Strut' (TB)	WCAu
'Study In Black' (TB)	XSen
stylosa	see *I. unguicularis*
§ ***suaveolens***	CPBP CPou ECho NWad
- var. ***flavescens***	see *I. suaveolens* yellow-flowered
§ - purple-flowered	ECho
- var. ***violacea***	see *I. suaveolens* purple-flowered
§ - yellow-flowered	ECho EPot GKev
'Subtle'	WCAu
'Succès Fou' (TB)	SIri
'Suffering Became Beauty' (TB)	ESgI
'Sugar' (IB)	NSti WCAu
'Sugar Magnolia' (TB)	EWoo
'Sultan's Palace' (TB)	CWCL EBee ECho ESgI EWoo LRHS WWEG XSen
'Summer Holidays' (TB)	XSen
'Summer Revels' (Sib)	EPri EWTr LLWG
'Summer Sky' (Sib)	CBre CSpe GBin LEdu MSCN NCGa SWat WCot WWEG
'Summer's Smile' (TB)	ESgI EWoo
'Summertime Blues' (TB)	EWoo
'Sun Ada Beach' (TB)	CIri
'Sun Doll' (SDB) ♀H4	CKel
'Sunblaze' (TB)	WCAu
'Sunny and Warm' (TB)	CKel
'Sunny Dawn' (IB) ♀H4	CKel
'Sunny Disposition' (TB)	XSen
'Sunny Side Up'	ECho LWst
'Sunnyside Delight' (TB)	WCAu
'Sunrise in Sonora' (Spuria) ♀H4	CIri
'Sunset Skies' (TB) **new**	CWCL
'Sunshine Boy' (IB)	CKel
'Superstition' (TB) ♀H4	EIri ELan ESgI EWes EWoo LAst LRHS MRav SMrm WCAu WCot WWEG XSen
'Supreme Sultan' (TB)	CWCL ESgI EWoo WCAu XSen

'Susan Bliss' (TB)	CKel ELan EPfP ESgI WCAu
'Susan Gillespie' (IB) 🏆^{H4}	CKel
'Suspect' (AB)	WCAu
'Suspicion' (TB)	CIri
'Sutton Valence' (Sib)	SIri
'Swain' (TB)	ESgI
'Swan Ballet' (TB)	ESgI
'Swazi Princess' (TB)	CKel ELon ESgI WCAu
'Sweet Kate' (SDB) 🏆^{H4}	WCAu
'Sweet Lena' (TB)	ESgI
'Sweet Musette' (TB)	WCAu
'Sweet Surrender' (Sib)	EPri
'Sweeter than Wine' (TB)	MRav
'Swingtown' (TB)	EWoo WCAu
'Swirling Waters' (La) **new**	LLWG
'Swiss Majesty' (TB)	WCAu
'Swizzle' (IB)	XSen
'Sybil' (TB)	GBin GCra
'Sylvan' (TB)	XSen
'Sylvia Murray' (TB)	WCAu
'Symphony' (Dut)	ECho NBir SDeJ
'Syncopation' (TB)	CKel ESgI WCAu XSen
'Tabac Blond' (TB)	EWoo
'Tact' (IB)	SIri
'Tahitian Pearl' (TB)	CIri
'Take Me Away' (TB)	SDys
'Tall Chief' (TB)	WCAu
'Tamberg' (Sib) **new**	EWoo
'Tamerlan' (TB)	EWoo
'Tan Tingo' (IB)	WCAu XSen
'Tanex'	ECho
'Tangerine Sky' (TB)	EWoo WCAu
'Tangfu' (IB)	ESgI
'Tangled Web' (TB)	ESgI
'Tantara' (SDB)	XSen
'Tantrum' (IB)	WCAu XSen
'Tanz Nochmal' (Sib)	GBin
'Tanzanian Tangerine' (TB)	WCAu
'Tarheel Elf' (SDB)	ESgI
'Tarn Hows' (TB)	ESgI SRms WCAu
taurica RCB UA 17 **new**	WCot
'Teal Velvet' (Sib)	EPfP EPri EWoo GLog LRHS MCot WCAu
'Tealwood' (Sib)	CIri
'Teapot Tempest' (BB)	WCAu
'Teasaucer Hill' (MTB) 🏆^{H4}	LMin SIri
tectorum	CCse LRHS SChr SDix WCot XLum XSen
- BWJ 8191	WCru
- 'Alba'	WThu XSen
- 'Cruella'	EBee EPfP
- 'Variegata' misapplied	see *I. japonica* 'Variegata'
'Tell Fibs' (SDB)	CBro CKel
'Temper Tantrum' (Sib)	CKel CPrp MBNS WCAu
'Temple Gold' (TB)	CKel NPer
'Temple Meads' (IB)	ESgI WCAu
'Templecloud' (IB) 🏆^{H4}	CKel
'Tempting Fate' (TB)	EWoo
§ ***tenax***	ECho GBuc
- subsp. ***tenax***	IGor
'Tennison Ridge' (TB)	WCAu
tenuissima subsp. ***tenuissima***	IGor
'Thaïs' (TB)	ESgI
'That's Red' (MTB)	LMin
'The Black Douglas' (TB)	EWoo
'The Bride'	see *I.* 'Bride'
'The Citadel' (TB)	ELon
'The Red Douglas' (TB)	ESgI
'The Rocket'	see *I.* 'Rocket'
'Theatre' (TB)	ESgI
'Theodolinda' (TB)	EWoo
'Think Spring' (MTB) **new**	WCAu
'Third Charm' (SDB)	CBro
'Third World' (SDB)	CBro
'This and That' (IB)	WCAu
thompsonii	IGor
'Thornbird' (TB) 🏆^{H4}	CIri EIri ESgI EWoo WCAu
'Three Cherries' (MDB)	CBro CPBP ECho SIri
'Thriller' (TB)	ESgI EWoo WCAu XSen
thunbergii	see *I. sanguinea*
'Thunder Echo' (TB)	ESgI SIri
'Thundering Hills' (TB)	CKel
'Tickety Boo' (SDB)	CIri
'Tickle the Ivories' (IB) **new**	CIri
'Tide's In' (TB)	EWoo
'Tiffany' (TB)	EWoo
§ 'Tigereye' (Dut)	EPot ERCP GKev
tigridia	CExl
'Tilgate'	WRHF
'Time Piece' (TB)	CKel
'Time to Shine' (SDB) **new**	WCAu
'Time Traveler' (TB)	CIri
'Time Zone' (TB)	WCAu
'Tinkerbell' (SDB)	CAby CPBP EBee EPfP GMaP LRHS NBir NGdn SDeJ
'Tintinara' (TB) 🏆^{H4}	CKel
'Tishomingo'	EWoo
'Titan's Glory' (TB) 🏆^{H4}	ESgI EWoo LEdu MRav WCAu WCot WHoo
'To the Point' (TB)	CIri
'Toasted Watermelon' (TB)	WCAu
'Tollong' 🏆^{H4}	IKil
'Tom Johnson' (TB) 🏆^{H4}	EWoo
'Tom Tit' (TB)	WCAu
'Tomorrow's Child' (TB)	EWoo
'Toni Lynn' (MDB)	ECho
'Toots' (SDB)	ECho
'Top Flight' (TB)	ELan SPer SRms
'Top Gun' (TB)	CJun ESgI
'Topolino' (TB)	CKel
'Torchlight' (TB)	SEND
'Torero' (TB)	EWoo SIri
'Toro Blanco' (IB) **new**	CIri
'Total Eclipse' (TB)	SRms
'Totally Cool' (SDB)	LSRN SIri
'Touch of Frost' (BB)	ESgI
'Touch of Mahogany' (TB)	WCAu
'Toy Clown' (SDB)	EWoo
'Trails West' (TB)	EWoo
'Trajectory' (SDB)	WCAu
'Trapel' (TB)	ESgI
'Trencavel' (TB)	ESgI
'Trenwith' (TB)	CKel ESgI
'Triffid' (TB)	CIri
'Trillion' (TB)	CIri
'Triple Whammy' (TB)	ESgI XSen
'Tripod' (IB) **new**	CIri
'Tropic Night' (Sib)	CCon CHel CPrp CSam CTri ECtt EIri ELan EPfP EPri EWoo GBin GKin LHop LRHS MBel MCot MRav MWts NGdn NHol NRya NSti SMrm SPer SWat WCot WWEG
tuberosa	CAby CArn CAvo CBro CDes CHid CPrp CTri CWCL ECGP ECho EPfP ERCP GKev MBel NMin SDeJ SMrm WCot
- BS 348	WCot

	Plant	Suppliers
	– MS 76	WCot
	– MS 729	WCot
	– MS 731	WCot
	– MS 821	WCot
	– MS 964	WCot
	– PB	WCot
	'Tulip Festival' (TB) **new**	SGol
	'Tumultueux' (TB)	EWoo
	'Tut's Gold' (TB)	ESgI WCAu
	'Tuxedo' (TB)	XSen
	'Two Sided Coin' (TB)	WCAu
§	'Tycoon' (Sib)	EBee EShb EWoo GQue LRHS SMrm SPer
	'Tyland Blue' (TB)	SIri
	typhifolia	SBrt
	'Tyrian Dream' (IB)	WCAu
	'UFO' (TB)	CIri
	'Ultimate' (SDB)	CIri
	'Uncle Charlie' (TB)	WCAu
	'Unfinished Business' (TB)	WCAu
§	***unguicularis*** ♀H4	Widely available
	– 'Abington Purple'	CBro CJun EIri
	– 'Alba'	CBct CExl ESgI XSen
	– broken form	MAvo
§	– subsp. ***cretensis***	CAby ECho EPot GKev SKHP XSen
	– 'Diana Clare'	CJun
	– 'Kilbroney Marble'	EPri
	– 'Marondera'	CJun
	– 'Mary Barnard' ♀H4	CBro CJun CPou CTca ECGP ECho NBir WHoo
	– 'Oxford Dwarf'	ECho LLHF
	– 'Palette'	ELan
§	– 'Walter Butt'	CJun ECGP NBir
	'Unicorn' (TB) **new**	CIri
	'Ursula Warleggan' (TB)	CKel
	'Vague à l'Ame' (TB)	ESgI EWoo
	'Valda' (Sib)	EBee ELon
	'Val de Loire'	EWoo
	'Valerie Joyce'	WCAu
	'Vamp' (IB)	CKel EWoo SMrm XSen
	'Vandal Spirit' (TB)	ESgI
	'Vanilla Skies' (TB)	WCAu
	'Vanity' (TB) ♀H4	ESgI XSen
	'Vanity's Child' (TB)	WCAu XSen
§	***variegata*** ♀H4	IGor XSen
	'Vegas Heat' (BB)	CIri
	'Velvet Dusk' (TB)	EWoo
	'Velvet King' (TB)	ESgI
	'Velvet Purple'	XBlo
	'Venita Faye' (TB) **new**	WCAu
	'Verity Blamey' (TB)	CKel
	versicolor ♀H4	CArn CBAq CRow EHon GBin GKev GMaP GPoy IBlr MGos MMuc MNHC MWts SEND SPlb SRms SWat WBrk WMAq WMoo WPnP WShi
	– 'Algonquin'	CRow LLWG
	– 'Between the Lines'	CRow LLWG
	– 'China West Lake'	CRow LLWG
	– 'Claret Cup'	CPou EWoo WWEG
	– 'Dottie's Double'	CRow
*	– 'Georgia Bay'	CRow
	– 'Kermesina'	COIW CPrp CRow CWat ELan ESgI GBuc IBlr LLWG MGos MWts NPer NSti SRms SWat WMAq WMoo WPnP
	– 'Mint Fresh' **new**	LLWG
	– 'Mysterious Monique'	CCse CDes CWat LLWG
	– 'Party Line'	SIri
	– purple-flowered	EWay
	– 'Rosea'	CRow EWay
	– 'Rowden Allegro'	CRow
	– 'Rowden Aria'	CRow
	– 'Rowden Cadenza'	CRow EWay LLWG
	– 'Rowden Calypso'	CRow
	– 'Rowden Cantata'	CRow
	– 'Rowden Concerto'	CRow LLWG
	– 'Rowden Descant'	CRow
	– 'Rowden Harmony'	CRow
	– 'Rowden Jingle'	CRow
	– 'Rowden Lullaby'	CRow
	– 'Rowden Lyric'	CRow
	– 'Rowden Mazurka'	CRow
	– 'Rowden Melody'	CRow LLWG
	– 'Rowden Minuet'	CRow
	– 'Rowden Nocturne'	CRow
	– 'Rowden Pastorale'	CRow LLWG
	– 'Rowden Refrain'	CRow
	– 'Rowden Rondo'	CRow
	– 'Rowden Sonata'	CRow LLWG
	– 'Rowden Symphony'	CRow
	– 'Rowden Waltz'	CRow
	– 'Silvington'	CRow
	– 'Whodunit'	CRow
	'Vibrant' (TB)	WCAu
	'Vibrations' (TB)	ESgI WCAu
	vicaria	ECho GKev LWst
	– RM 8269	LWst
	– 'Morgiana'	LWst
*	'Prominence'	LWst
I	– 'Sina'	LWst
	'Victoria Falls' (TB)	ESgI EWoo WCAu
	'Victorian Secret' (Sib)	EBee WCAu
	'Viel Schnee' (Sib)	GBin
	'Vi Luihn' (Sib)	CBcs WMoo
	'Vin Nouveau' (TB)	XSen
	'Vinho Verde' (IB) ♀H4	CKel
	'Vino Rosso' (SDB)	ESgI
	'Violet Beauty' (Reticulata)	ECho ERCP GKev
	'Violet Classic' (TB)	WCAu
	'Violet Fusion' (Spuria)	EWoo
	'Violet Harmony' (TB)	ESgI
	'Violet Icing' (TB) ♀H4	CKel
	'Violet Rings' (TB)	WCAu
	'Violet Skies' (Sib)	GBin
	'Viper' (IB)	CIri EWoo
	virginica	LLWG
	– 'De Luxe'	see *I.* × *robusta* 'Dark Aura'
	– 'Lavender Lustre' **new**	LLWG
	– 'Orchid Purple' **new**	LLWG
	– 'Pale Lavender' **new**	LLWG
	– 'Pink Perfection' **new**	LLWG
	– 'Pond Crown Point'	CRow
	– 'Pond Lilac Dream'	CRow
	– 'Purple Fan'	CRow
§	– var. ***shrevei***	LLWG
	– 'Slightly Daft' **new**	LLWG
	'Vision in Pink' (TB)	WCAu
	'Visual Treat' (Sib)	EWoo SIri
	'Vitafire' (TB)	ESgI EWoo
	'Vitality' (IB)	ELon ESgI
	'Viva Mexico' (TB)	EWoo
	'Vizier' (TB)	WCAu
	'Voilà' (IB)	ESgI
	'Volts' (SDB)	CKel XSen
	'Volute' (TB)	ESgI
I	'Vonnies Wedding Iris'	ELon
	'Voyage' (SDB)	EWoo XSen

'Wabash' (TB)	ELan LRHS WCAu XSen
'Wall Street Blues' (Sib)	EWoo
'Walmer Castle' (Kent Castles Series) (IB) **new**	SIri
'Walter Butt'	see *I. unguicularis* 'Walter Butt'
'War Chief' (TB)	ESgI MRav WCAu
'War Sails' (TB)	EWoo SIri WCAu
warleyensis	ECho LWst
'Warlsind' (J)	LWst
'Warrior King' (TB)	EWoo
'Waters Of Miraba' (BB)	EWoo
wattii	CExl GCal
'Way to Go' (TB)	CIri
'Wealden Butterfly' (Sib) ♀H4	SIri
'Wealden Carousel' (Sib)	SIri
'Wealden Mystery' (Sib)	EPri SIri
'Wealden Skies' (Sib)	SIri
'Wearing Rubies' (TB)	ESgI WCAu
'Webelos' (SDB)	MRav
'Webmaster' (SDB)	SIri
'Wedding Vow' (TB)	CKel EIri
'Wedgwood' (Dut)	NBre
'Welch's Reward' (MTB) ♀H4	CKel ESgI LMin
'Welcome Discovery'	WCAu
'Welcome Return' (Sib)	CElw EWoo GQue MBNS MMuc NBro NLar SWat WMoo
'Welfenfürstin' (Sib)	GBin
'Well Suited' (SDB)	EWoo WCAu
'Wench' (TB)	EWoo
'Westar' (SDB) ♀H4	CKel EIri
'Westpointer' (TB)	CIri
'Westwell' (SDB)	WCAu
'What Again' (SDB)	XSen
'Whispering Spirits' (TB)	WCAu
'White Caucasus' (Reticulata) **new**	EPot
'White City' (TB)	EPfP ESgI EWoo GMaP LRHS MCot MRav MWat MWhi NPer SDeJ SMrm SPer SRms SWat WCAu WMnd
'White Excelsior' (Dut)	ECho
'White Gem' (SDB)	ESgI EWoo
'White Knight' (TB)	EBee ELan EPfP ESgI NBre WHrl WMnd WWEG
I 'White Queen' (Sib)	ESgI SWat
'White Reprise' (TB)	ESgI XSen
I 'White Swan' (Sib)	EPri
'White Swirl' (Sib) ♀H4	CAby CBro CHel CKel CPrp CTri EBee ECtt ELon EPfP EWoo GLog LAst LRHS MBri MCot MWat NBro NLar NSti SPer SWat WBor WCot WPnP
'White Triangles' (Sib)	EWoo
'White van Vliet' (Dut)	SDeJ
'White Wine' (MTB)	LMin WCAu
'White-Wave'	XBlo
'Whole Cloth' (TB)	ESgI
'Widow's Veil' (SDB)	ESgI
'Wild Echo' (TB)	CKel
'Wild Jasmine' (TB)	WCAu
'Wild Ruby' (SDB)	CKel
'Wild West' (TB)	CKel
'Wild Wings' (TB)	EWoo MCot NCGa SGbt
willmottiana	ECho LWst
- 'Alba'	ECho
wilsonii ♀H4	CExl CHel EBee GBin GKev SBrt WCot
'Windjammer Seas' (TB)	SDys
'Winemaster' (TB)	EWoo SIri
'Winesap' (TB)	ESgI EWoo
'Winged Angel' (IB) **new**	CIri
'Wings of Peace' (TB)	CIri
'Winner's Circle' (TB)	SMrm
'Winning Edge' (TB) **new**	WCAu
winogradowii ♀H4	CBro ECho EPot ERCP GKev LLHF WAbe XEll
'Winter Crystal' (TB) ♀H4	CKel
'Winter Olympics' (TB)	CAby EPfP EShb LBuc LRHS MRav SPer WGwG
'Winter Pearl' (IB)	EWoo
'Wise' (SDB)	WCAu
'Wish Upon a Star' (SDB) **new**	WCAu
'Wishful Thinking' (TB)	SIri
'Wisteria Sachet' (IB)	WCAu
'Witch's Wand' (TB)	ESgI EWoo
'Wizard's Return' (SDB) **new**	SIri
'Wonders Never Cease' (TB)	WCAu
'Wondrous' (TB)	ESgI
'World Premier' (TB)	WCAu
'Wrangler' (IB)	EWoo SIri
'Xillia' (IB)	CKel
xiphioides	see *I. latifolia*
xiphium	ECho
'Yaquina Blue' (TB)	WCAu
'Yellow Flirt' (MTB)	LMin WCAu
'Yellow Joy'	EABi
'Yes' (TB)	CJun ESgI
'Yippy Skippy' (SDB)	WCAu
'Yosemite Nights' (TB)	EWoo
'Yosemite Star' (TB)	EWoo
'Youth Dew' (TB)	EWoo
'Zakopane' (Sib) ♀H4	EBee EWes
'Zandria' (TB) **new**	WCAu
'Zantha' (TB)	XSen
zenaidae	ECho
- ARJA 9715	LWst
'Zero' (SDB) ♀H4	CKel

Isatis (*Brassicaceae*)

glauca	CFis
tinctoria	CArn CHab CHby CSev EOHP GAbr GJos GPoy MHer MHoo MNHC NPnk SIde SPav SRms WHfH WJek

Ismene see *Hymenocallis*

Isodon (*Lamiaceae*)

calycinus	SPlb
longitubus B&SWJ 11027	WCru
rubescens	IMou WCot

Isoetes (*Isoetaceae*)

lacustris **new**	CBAq

Isolepis (*Cyperaceae*)

§ ***cernua***	CBAq CWat LHop MBri MSKA MWts NOak SCoo SHDw SPad WMAq

Isoloma see *Kohleria*

Isomeris see *Cleome*

Isoplexis see *Digitalis*

Isopogon (*Proteaceae*)

anemonifolius	SPlb
anethifolius	SPlb

Isopyrum (*Ranunculaceae*)

dicarpon	see *Dichocarpum dicarpon*
nipponicum	CLAP WCot WCru WPGP
stoloniferum	WCru
thalictroides	EBee EPot LLHF SDys WCot

Isotoma (*Campanulaceae*)

sp.	SWvt
'Avant-garde Blue'	SPoG
§ ***axillaris***	CSpe NPer SCoo SPer SPet SPoG
- 'Fairy Carpet'	SRms
fluviatilis	NLar

Itea (*Iteaceae*)

chinensis	CExl
ilicifolia ♀H3	Widely available
* - 'Rubrifolia'	LRHS SLon SPoG
japonica 'Beppu'	SLPl SSpi
virginica	CAbP CBcs CMCN ELan ELon ESwi MRav SLim SLon
§ - 'Henry's Garnet'	CAbP CDoC CEnd CJun CMCN CMac CSBt EBee ECrN EPfP GBin IDee LAst LEdu LRHS MBri MGos NLar NSoo SHil SLim SPer SPoG SRGP SSpi SWvt
- Little Henry = 'Sprich'PBR	CHGN CHel CMac CSBt EBee ELan EPfP IVic LRHS LSRN NLar
- 'Long Spire'	CJun NLar
- 'Merlot'	CJun EBee MBlu NLar
- 'Sarah Eve'	CJun CMCN NLar SRGP
- 'Saturnalia'	NLar
- Swarthmore form	see *I. virginica* 'Henry's Garnet'
yunnanensis	CExl MBlu NLar SSpi WSHC

Ixeris (*Asteraceae*)

stolonifera	XLum

Ixia (*Iridaceae*)

aurea 'Saldanha'	ECho
'Blue Bird'	CCon ECho SDeJ
capillaris 'Citrusdal'	ECho
'Castor'	CPrp ECho
curta	ECho
dubia	ECho
flexuosa	ECho
'Gemini'	ECho
'Giant'	CTca ECho SDeJ WHil
'Hogarth'	CPrp ECho WHil
'Holland Glory'	ECho
latifolia var. ***latifolia***	ECho
longituba 'Citrusdal'	ECho
lutea	ECho
'Mabel'	ECho WCot
maculata	ECho
marginifolia from Komsberg	ECho
'Marquette'	ECho WHil
metelerkampiae	ECho
- 'Goudini'	ECho
mixed	SDeJ
monadelpha	ECho WCot
orientalis	ECho
paniculata	ECho WHil
- 'Eos' new	WHil
'Panorama'	ECho
polystachya	ECho
- var. ***longistylis***	ECho
- var. ***lutea***	ECho
pumilio	WCot
purpureorosea 'Saldanha'	ECho
rapunculoides	ECho
- var. ***rigida***	ECho
- var. ***subpendula***	ECho
'Rose Emperor'	ECho SDeJ WHil
scillaris var. ***subundulata***	ECho
'Spotlight'	ECho WHil
thomasiae	WCot
trifolia	ECho
'Venus'	CCon CTca ECho SDeJ WHil
versicolor	ECho
viridiflora	CDes ECho
- var. ***minor***	ECho WCot
'Vulcan'	CPrp ECho WHil
'Yellow Emperor'	CTca ECho SDeJ WHil

Ixiolirion (*Ixioliriaceae*)

montanum	ECho
pallasii	see *I. tataricum*
§ ***tataricum***	ECho MCot
- Ledebourii Group	CAvo EBee

J

Jaborosa (*Solanaceae*)

integrifolia	CCon CExl EBee ELan LEdu LRHS WCot WPGP XLum

Jacaranda (*Bignoniaceae*)

acutifolia misapplied	see *J. mimosifolia*
§ ***mimosifolia***	CBcs CCCN EShb MREP SPlb

Jacobinia see *Justicia*

Jamesbrittenia (*Scrophulariaceae*)

stellata new	SPlb

Jamesia (*Hydrangeaceae*)

americana	ESwi NLar

Jasione (*Campanulaceae*)

§ ***heldreichii***	LRHS NBir SRms
jankae	see *J. heldreichii*
§ ***laevis***	ECho EPfP GAbr LRHS SRms
§ - 'Blaulicht'	CMHG EPfP LPot LRHS MBNS MHol NEgg NLar SPlb WMoo
- Blue Light	see *J. laevis* 'Blaulicht'
montana	ECho MNHC WPnn
perennis	see *J. laevis*

Jasminum ✿ (*Oleaceae*)

CC 4728	CExl
adenophyllum	MOWG
affine	see *J. officinale* f. *affine*
angulare ♀H1	CExl CRHN EShb MOWG
azoricum ♀H1	CCCN CDoC CHll CRHN EPfP EShb GCal MOWG SPre
beesianum	Widely available

	blinii	see *J. polyanthum*
	dispermum	CRHN
	diversifolium	see *J. subhumile*
	farreri	see *J. humile* f. *farreri*
§	***floridum***	EWes
	fruticans	CMac EBee ELon EPfP LRHS SBrt SEND WCru WGob XLum
	- RCB UA 22 **new**	WCot
	giraldii misapplied	see *J. humile* f. *farreri*
	giraldii Diels	see *J. floridum*
	grandiflorum misapplied	see *J. officinale* f. *affine*
	grandiflorum L.	IDee
	- 'De Grasse' ♀H1	CRHN EShb MOWG
	heterophyllum	see *J. subhumile*
	humile	CExl MBrN SEND WKif
§	- f. ***farreri***	MBri
	- var. ***glabrum***	see *J. humile* f. *wallichianum*
§	- 'Revolutum' ♀H4	CBcs CDul CHel CMac CRHN CSBt CWSG CWib EBee ELan EPfP GCal LAst LHop LRHS MGos MRav NLar SEND SLon SPer SPet SPoG SRms SWvt WHar WSHC WWFP
§	- f. ***wallichianum*** B&SWJ 2559	WCru
	- - PAB 2534 **new**	LEdu
§	***laurifolium*** f. ***nitidum***	MOWG
§	***mesnyi*** ♀H2-3	CCCN CDoy CExl CMac CRHN CTri CWib EBak EBee ELan EPfP IGor LRHS MOWG MRav SEND SPer SVen WSHC
	multiflorum	CCCN MOWG
	multipartitum	EShb
	- bushy	CSpe
	nitidum	see *J. laurifolium* f. *nitidum*
§	***nudiflorum*** ♀H4	Widely available
	- 'Argenteum'	see *J. nudiflorum* 'Mystique'
	- 'Aureum'	ELan LBMP MAsh MBNS MRav NSti SPer SRms WCot
*	- 'Compactum'	MAsh
§	- 'Mystique' (v)	ELan LRHS MRav SLon WCot
	odoratissimum	EShb MOWG
	officinale ♀H4	Widely available
	- CC 1709	WMoo
§	- f. ***affine***	CArn CBcs CCCN CRHN CSPN CTri CWib EBee ELan EPfP LAst LRHS MRav SCoo SDix SLim SPet SRms WCru WHar WPat
§	- 'Argenteovariegatum' (v) ♀H4	CBcs CDul CHel CWGN CWib EBee EHoe ELan EPfP LHop LRHS LSRN MAsh MBri MGos MHer MRav MWat NPri SEND SLim SPer SPet SWvt WCFE WHar WPat WSHC
	- 'Aureovariegatum'	see *J. officinale* 'Aureum'
§	- 'Aureum' (v)	CBcs CDoC CMac CWSG CWib EBee ECtt ELan EPfP IBoy LRHS MAsh MBri MHer MREP NBir SCoo SLim SLon SPer SRms WPat
	- 'Clotted Cream'	see *J. officinale* 'Devon Cream'
	- 'Crûg's Collection'	WCru
§	- 'Devon Cream'PBR	CAby CBcs CCCN CDul CFlo CHel CSBt CWGN CWSG EBee ELon EPfP LAst LBMP LRHS LSRN MBri MGos MREP MRav NHol NLar SCoo SHil SLim SPer SPoG WPat
	- Fiona Sunrise = 'Frojas'PBR	Widely available
	- 'Grandiflorum'	see *J. officinale* f. *affine*
	- 'Inverleith' ♀H4	CCCN CDoC CHel CMac CWSG EBee ELan EPfP EShb IArd LAst LBMP LHop LRHS MAsh MBNS MBri MGos MRav SCoo SHil SLim SMad SPad SPer SPoG WGrn WSHC
	- 'Variegatum'	see *J. officinale* 'Argenteovariegatum'
	parkeri	CBcs CCCN CHel CJun CMac CTri EBee ECho ELon EPfP GCal LRHS MBNS NLar WGob WPat
	- 'Bychan'	WAbe
§	***polyanthum*** ♀H1-2	CArn CBcs CExl CRHN CSBt CTri EBak EBee ELan EPfP MBri MOWG NEgg SEND SLim SPer SPre SRms WHar
	- dark-red-leaved	CExl CHel WPGP
	primulinum	see *J. mesnyi*
	reevesii hort.	see *J. humile* 'Revolutum'
	sambac ♀H1	CArn CCCN CDoC CHll CRHN EAmu ELan EPfP EShb MOWG SPre
	- 'Grand Duke of Tuscany' (d)	MOWG SPre
	- 'Maid of Orleans' (d) ♀H1	SPre
	sieboldianum	see *J. nudiflorum*
§	***simplicifolium*** subsp. ***suavissimum***	CHll CRHN
	stenalobium	MOWG
	× ***stephanense***	Widely available
	suavissimum	see *J. simplicifolium* subsp. *suavissimum*
§	***subhumile***	MOWG

Jatropha (*Euphorbiaceae*)

cinerea **new**	SPlb
integerrima	CCCN
multifida	SPlb

Jeffersonia (*Berberidaceae*)

diphylla	CArn CBro CLAP EBee ECho EPPr EPot EPri GAbr GBin LEdu LRHS MMoz MNrw NBir NLar WAbe WCru
dubia	CBro CCon CLAP ECho EPot EWes LEdu LHop LLHF LRHS MNrw NBir NHar NSla WAbe WCru

jostaberry see *Ribes* × *culverwellii*

Jovellana (*Calceolariaceae*)

punctata	CCCN CDoC CExl CMac EBee GCal IBlr SPlb
- var. ***coerulea*** **new**	IBlr
sinclairii	CExl CHll ECou LLHF SMrm
violacea ♀H3	CAbP CAbb CBcs CCCN CDoC CExl CHel CMac CTsd CWib EPfP GCal IBlr IMou IVic LRHS SAPC SMad SVen WCru WPGP WPat WSHC WWlt

Jovibarba ✿ (*Crassulaceae*)

§	***allionii***	CMea CTri CWil EDAr EPot LBMP MHer MSCN NHol NPri WHal WHoo WIvy
	- 'Oki'	ECho EHyd LRHS
	allionii × ***hirta***	CWil MSCN SDys SFgr WIvy
§	***arenaria***	CWil GAbr XLum
	- from Passo di Monte Croce Carnico, Italy	CWil
	'Autumn Fires'	MSCN
*	***echiniformis***	XLum
	'Emerald Spring'	SFgr

§	***heuffelii***	ECho EHyd LRHS XLum
	- 'Aiolos'	NHol
	- 'Almkroon'	NHol
	- 'Angel Wings'	CWil WHoo
§	- 'Apache'	CWil
	- 'Aquarius'	CWil WIvy
	- 'Be Mine'	CWil WGor
	- 'Beacon Hill'	CWil WIvy
	- 'Belcore'	CWil XLum
	- 'Benjamin'	CWil
	- 'Big Red'	NHol
	- 'Blaze'	CWil
	- 'Brandaris'	SDys
	- 'Brocade'	MSCN NHol
	- 'Bronze Ingot'	CWil WCot
§	- 'Cherry Glow'	CWil
I	- 'Compacta' **new**	CWil
	- 'Copper King'	CWil
	- 'Cover Girl' **new**	CWil
	- 'Elmo's Fire' **new**	CWil
	- 'Fan Joy' **new**	CWil
	- 'Fandango'	CWil MHom
	- 'Geronimo'	NHol
	- 'Giuseppi Spiny'	MHom SPlb
	- var. ***glabra***	WHoo
	- - from Anaba Kanak, Bulgaria	CWil MHom NHol
	- - from Anthoborio, Southern Carpathians	CWil
	- - from Haila, Montenegro/Kosovo	CWil SFgr WIvy
	- - from Jakupica, Macedonia	CWil WIvy
	- - from Ljuboten, Balkans	CWil
	- - from Ošljak, Albania	CWil
	- - from Pasina Glava, Macedonia	CWil
	- - from Rhodope, Bulgaria	CWil MHom
	- - from Treska Gorge, Macedonia	CWil
§	- - 'Cameo'	WIvy
	- 'Gladiator' **new**	CWil
	- 'Gold Rand'	NHol
	- 'Grand Slam'	CWil
	- 'Green Land'	CWil
	- 'Greenstone'	CWil MHom NHol
	- 'Harmony'	CWil NHol
	- 'Henry Correvon'	CWil
	- 'Hot Lips'	CWil
	- 'Idylle' **new**	CWil
	- 'Ikaros'	NHol
	- 'Inferno'	MHom
§	- 'Inge'	MSem
	- 'Ithaca'	NHol
	- 'Iuno'	CWil NHol
	- 'Jade'	CWil
I	- 'Jovi King' **new**	CWil
	- 'Kapo'	WIvy
	- 'King Sunny' **new**	CWil
	- var. ***kopaonikensis***	CWil MHom
	- 'Lucky Bell' **new**	CWil
	- 'Mary Ann'	MHom
	- 'Miller's Violet'	CWil
	- 'Mink'	CWil
	- 'Minuta'	CWil WIvy
	- 'Mystique'	CWil
	- 'Nannette'	CWil
	- 'Orion'	CWil XLum
	- var. ***patens***	CWil
	- 'Pelister' **new**	CWil
	- 'Pink Skies'	CWil WIvy
	- 'Pink Star'	CWil
	- 'Prisma'	CWil
	- 'Purple Haze'	XLum
	- 'Red Rose'	CWil
	- 'Serenade'	CWil WGor
	- 'Springael's Choice'	CWil
	- 'Sungold'	NHol
	- 'Suntan'	CWil
	- 'Sylvan Memory'	CWil WGor
	- 'Tan'	CWil
	- 'Tancredi'	CWil
	- 'Torrid Zone'	MBrN
	- 'Tuxedo'	CWil
	- 'Vesta'	CWil
	- 'Violet'	CWil SDys WIvy
	- 'Wotan' **new**	CWil
§	***hirta***	CWil EDAr EUJe GAbr SFgr XLum
	- from Wintergraben, Austria	SPlb
	- 'Belansky Tatra'	CWil
§	- subsp. ***borealis***	CWil ESem
	- subsp. ***glabrescens***	EPot
	- - from High Tatra, Slovakia/Poland	XLum
	- - from Smeryouka, Southern Carpathians	CWil
I	- 'Glauca'	SFgr
	- 'Hedgehog'	SFgr
	- var. ***neilreichii***	ECho EHyd LRHS MHom
	- 'Purpurea'	XLum
	- 'Rax'	SFgr
	preissiana	SFgr WIvy
§	***sobolifera***	CHEx CWil EDAr EPot GKev SFgr SPlb WHal WIvy XLum
	- 'Bronze Globe'	SFgr
	- 'Green Globe'	ECho EHyd LRHS SDys SFgr
	- 'Miss Lorraine'	SFgr XLum

Juania (*Arecaceae*)

	australis	EAmu

Jubaea (*Arecaceae*)

§	***chilensis***	CBcs CPHo EAmu IDee SBig SPlb
	spectabilis	see *J. chilensis*

Juglans ✿ (*Juglandaceae*)

§	***ailanthifolia***	CBcs CMCN
	- var. ***cordiformis*** 'Brock' (F)	CAgr
	- - 'Campbell Cw3' (F)	CAgr
	- - 'Fodermaier' seedling	CAgr
	- - 'Rhodes' (F)	CAgr
	ailanthifolia* × *cinerea	see *J.* × *bixbyi*
§	× ***bixbyi***	CAgr
	cinerea (F)	CBcs
	- 'Beckwith' (F)	CAgr
	- 'Booth' seedlings (F)	CAgr
	- 'Craxczy' (F)	CAgr
	- 'Kenworthy' seedling	CAgr
	- 'Myjoy' (F)	CAgr
	hindsii	EBtc
	mandshurica (F)	CBcs
	- BWJ 8097 from China	WCru
	- RWJ 9905 from Taiwan	WCru
*	- subsp. ***sieboldiana*** B&SWJ 11026	WCru
	microcarpa	CMCN

nigra (F) ♀^{H4}	CBcs CCVT CDul CLnd CMCN CMac CSBt CTho CWib EBee ECrN ELan EPfP GTwe LAst LRHS MAsh MBri MGos NWea SDea SEND SGol SPer WMou
- 'Bicentennial' (F)	CAgr
- 'Emma Kay' (F)	CAgr
- 'Laciniata'	CDul EBee EPfP ERea GBin MBlu WPat
- 'Purpurea'	ERea
- 'Thomas' (F)	CAgr
- 'Weschke' (F)	CAgr
regia (F) ♀^{H4}	Widely available
- 'Axel' (F)	CAgr
- 'Broadview' (F)	CAgr CDul CEnd CSBt CTho ELan EPom ERea GTwe IVic LBuc LRHS MBlu MBri MCoo MGos NEgg NWea SCoo SDea SEWo SKee SPoG SVic WHar
- 'Buccaneer' (F)	CAgr CDul CMam CTho EPom GTwe SDea SKee WHar
- 'Chandler' (F)	CAgr CMam
- 'Corne du Périgord' (F)	CAgr CMam
- 'Excelsior of Taynton' (F) new	CDul MCoo
- 'Ferjean' (F)	CAgr
- 'Fernette'^{PBR} (F)	CAgr CDul CMam WHar
- 'Fernor' (F)	CAgr CMam WHar
- 'Franquette' (F)	CAgr GTwe MCoo WHar
- 'Hansen' (F)	CAgr
- 'Hartley' (F)	CAgr
- 'Jupiter' (F)	CAgr
- 'Laciniata'	CMCN WPat
- 'Lara' (F)	CAgr GTwe
- 'Mayette' (F)	CAgr
- 'Meylannaise' (F)	CAgr CMam
- number 16 (F)	CAgr WHar
- 'Parisienne' (F)	CAgr SGol
- 'Plovdivski' (F)	CAgr WHar
- 'Proslavski' (F)	CAgr CDul WHar
- 'Purpurea'	CMCN MBlu
- 'Rita' (F)	CAgr LBuc
- 'Ronde de Montignac' (F)	CAgr
- 'Saturn' (F)	CAgr
- 'Soleze' (F)	CAgr
sieboldiana	see *J. ailanthifolia*

jujube see *Ziziphus jujuba*

Juncus (*Juncaceae*)

articulatus	LLWG XLum
bulbosus	CNat
§ ***decipiens*** 'Curly-wurly'	CBAq EPfP LRHS NHol NOak SWat
- 'Spiralis'	see *J. decipiens* 'Curly-wurly'
effusus	CWat EHon MSKA NPer SWat WMAq XLum
- 'Carman's Japanese'	CKno
- 'Curly Gold Strike' (v)	LRHS MSKA
- 'Gold Strike' (v)	CBAq EPPr LLWG
§ - f. ***spiralis***	CBAq CRow CSpe CWat EHoe EHon ELan EPfP GKev LRHS MAsh MBri MJak NBir NLar NOak NWsh SLim SPlb SPoG SVic WHal WMAq WPGP WPnP XLum
§ - - 'Unicorn'^{PBR}	EBee LBMP LRHS SPoG
ensifolius	CBAq CKno CRow CWat EBee EHoe EWay EWes MMHG MSKA MWts NPer
filiformis 'Spiralis'	GAbr LPot WWEG
inflexus	CWat EHon MSKA SEND SWat XLum
- 'Afro'	EBee EPfP NBro NOak NWsh SPlb WHal WWEG
pallidus	EPPr GCal
patens 'Carman's Gray'	CKno CWCL EPPr GCal GQue LRHS MMoz NNor NOak NWad NWsh WMoo WPtf WWEG
- 'Elk Blue'	CKno WWEG
subnodulosus new	LLWG
'Unicorn'	see *J. effusus* f. *spiralis* 'Unicorn'
xiphioides	EHoe

Junellia (*Verbenaceae*)

azorelloides	WAbe
§ ***micrantha***	WAbe
odonnellii	WAbe

Juniperus ✿ (*Cupressaceae*)

chinensis	CMen
- 'Aurea' ♀^{H4}	CBcs CMac EHul LRHS
§ - 'Blaauw' ♀^{H4}	CDoC CMac CMen EHul SGol
- 'Blue Alps'	CJun EHul LRHS MGos MMuc NEgg SCoo SEND SGol SLim
- 'Densa Spartan'	see *J. chinensis* 'Spartan'
- 'Echiniformis'	CKen
- 'Expansa Aureospicata' (v)	CDoC CKen EHul EPfP SEND
§ - 'Expansa Variegata' (v)	CDoC CWib EHul EPfP
- 'Ferngold'	CDoC
- 'Itoigawa'	CMen
§ - 'Kaizuka' ♀^{H4}	EHul SGol SLim
- 'Kaizuka Variegata'	see *J. chinensis* 'Variegated Kaizuka'
- 'Kuriwao Gold'	see *J.* × *pfitzeriana* 'Kuriwao Gold'
- 'Obelisk' ♀^{H4}	EHul
- 'Oblonga'	CDoC EHul
§ - 'Parsonsii'	WCFE
- 'Plumosa Aurea' ♀^{H4}	EHul
- 'Plumosa Aureovariegata' (v)	CKen
- 'Pyramidalis' ♀^{H4}	CDoC EHul EPfP MAsh NPri SCoo
- 'Robust Green'	SEND
- 'San José'	CMen EHul LRHS MAsh
§ - var. ***sargentii***	CMen
- 'Shimpaku'	CKen CMen NLar
§ - 'Spartan'	EHul
- 'Stricta'	CSBt EHul LBee LRHS MGos SGol SLim
- 'Sulphur Spray'	see *J.* × *pfitzeriana* 'Sulphur Spray'
- 'Torulosa'	see *J. chinensis* 'Kaizuka'
§ - 'Variegated Kaizuka' (v)	EHul SCoo
communis	CArn CDul CHab EHul GPoy MNHC NWea SIde WAbe
- (f)	SIde
- 'Arnold Sentinel'	CKen
- 'Atholl'	CKen
- 'Barton'	NLar NWad
- 'Barton Gem'	NWad
- 'Berkshire'	CKen
- 'Brien'	CDoC CKen
- 'Brynhyfryd Gold'	CKen
- 'Compressa' ♀^{H4}	CBcs CDoC CKen CMac CSBt CTri CWib EHul EPfP EPot LAst LBee LRHS MAsh MBri MGos MJak NEgg NHol NWad NWea SLim SPer SPoG WIce WPat
§ - 'Constance Franklin' (v)	EHul
- 'Corielagan'	CKen NLar
- 'Cracovia'	CKen
- var. ***depressa***	GPoy SGol

	- 'Depressa Aurea'	CKen CSBt EHul LBee
	- 'Depressed Star'	EHul MGos SPoG WGor
	- 'Derrynane'	EHul
	- 'Effusa'	CKen
	- 'Gelb'	see *J. communis* 'Schneverdingen Goldmachangel'
	- 'Gold Cone'	CKen EHul ELan EPfP LBee LRHS MAsh MGos NLar SLim SPoG WGor
	- 'Golden Showers'	see *J. communis* 'Schneverdingen Goldmachangel'
	- 'Goldschatz'	CKen LAst SPoG
	- 'Green Carpet' 🏆^{H4}	CDoC CKen CMen EHul ELan EPfP GKin LBuc LRHS MAsh MGos NEgg NLar SCoo SLim SPoG WCFE
	- 'Haverbeck'	CKen
	- 'Hibernica' 🏆^{H4}	CDul CSBt EHul ELan EPfP LAst LRHS MGos MJak NLar NWea SLim SPer SPoG
	- 'Hibernica Aurea'	CMac
	- 'Hibernica Variegata'	see *J. communis* 'Constance Franklin'
	- 'Hornibrookii' 🏆^{H4}	EHul NWea SRms
	- 'Horstmann'	GKin NLar
I	- 'Horstmann's Pendula'	CDoC
	- 'Kenwith Castle'	CKen
	- 'Meyer'	GKin
	- 'Pyramidalis'	SPlb
	- 'Rakete'	IVic
	- 'Repanda' 🏆^{H4}	CBcs CDoC CMac CSBt CWib EHul EPfP EPot LAst LRHS MAsh MGos SCoo SGol SLim SPer SPoG
§	- 'Schneverdingen Goldmachangel'	IBoy LRHS MAsh MGos NLar SLim
	- 'Sentinel'	CDoC EHul LRHS SLim WCFE WMou
	- 'Sieben Steinhauser'	CKen NLar
	- 'Silver Mist'	CKen
	- 'Spotty Spreader' (v)	LRHS SLim SPoG
	- Suecica Group	EHul MGos NWea
	- - 'Suecica Aurea'	EHul
	- 'Zeal'	CKen
	conferta	see *J. rigida* subsp. *conferta*
	- var. ***maritima***	see *J. taxifolia*
	davurica	EHul
	- 'Expansa'	see *J. chinensis* 'Parsonsii'
	- 'Expansa Albopicta'	see *J. chinensis* 'Expansa Variegata'
	- 'Expansa Variegata'	see *J. chinensis* 'Expansa Variegata'
	'Leningrad'	LPot NLar
	excelsa subsp. ***polycarpos***	CMen
	foetidissima	CMen
	× ***gracilis*** 'Blaauw'	see *J. chinensis* 'Blaauw'
	'Grey Owl' 🏆^{H4}	EHul ELan EPfP LRHS NWea SCoo SEND SGol SLim
	horizontalis	CDul NWea
§	- 'Andorra Compact'	NLar SCoo
	- 'Bar Harbor'	CMac EHul
§	- 'Blue Chip'	EHul ELan EPfP LBee LRHS MGos MJak NBir SCoo SPer SPoG
	- 'Blue Moon'	see *J. horizontalis* 'Blue Chip'
	- 'Blue Rug'	see *J. horizontalis* 'Wiltonii'
	- 'Douglasii'	EHul
	- 'Emerald Spreader'	EHul ELan
	- Glauca Group	EHul NWea SPoG
	- 'Golden Carpet'	ELan EPfP LBuc MGos NLar SPoG
	- 'Golden Spreader'	CDoC
	- 'Grey Pearl'	CKen EHul
	- 'Hughes'	EHul LBee MRav
	- Icee Blue = 'Monber'	CKen GKin LRHS MAsh MBri NLar SPoG

	- 'Jade River'	EHul
	- 'Limeglow'	CDoC CKen ELan EPfP LAst LRHS MGos NEgg NLar SCoo SLim SPoG WGor
	- 'Mother Lode'	CKen
	- 'Neumann'	CKen
	- 'Plumosa Compacta'	see *J. horizontalis* 'Andorra Compact'
	- 'Prince of Wales'	EHul MAsh MGos
	- 'Prostrata' **new**	IBoy
	- 'Turquoise Spreader'	CSBt EHul MBri NWea SGol
	- 'Venusta'	see *J. virginiana* 'Venusta'
	- 'Villa Marie'	CKen
§	- 'Wiltonii' 🏆^{H4}	CDul EHul MGos
	- 'Winter Blue'	LBee LRHS SLim
	- 'Yukon Belle'	CKen
N	× ***media***	see *J.* × *pfitzeriana*
§	× ***pfitzeriana***	CMac SGol
	- 'Arctic' **new**	NLar
	- 'Armstrongii'	EHul
	- 'Blaauw'	see *J. chinensis* 'Blaauw'
	- 'Blue and Gold' (v)	CKen EHul
	- 'Blue Cloud'	see *J. virginiana* 'Blue Cloud'
§	- 'Carbery Gold'	CBcs CDoC CDul CMac CSBt EHul GKin LBee LRHS MAsh MBri MGos SCoo SLim SPoG
	- 'Daub's Frosted'	SLim
	- 'Gold Coast'	CDoC CKen CSBt EHul EPfP LBee LRHS MBri MGos SGol SLim SPer
	- Gold Sovereign = 'Blound'^{PBR}	LBee MAsh MGos
	- 'Gold Star'	MBri
*	- 'Golden Joy'	LRHS SPoG
	- 'Goldkissen'	MGos
	- 'King of Spring'	SLim
§	- 'Kuriwao Gold'	CMac EHul GKin LRHS MGos MRav NLar NPri SCoo SEND SGol SPoG
	- 'Mint Julep'	CSBt EHul LRHS MGos MJak SCoo SGol SLim
	- 'Old Gold' 🏆^{H4}	CDul CKen EHul EPfP GKin LBee LRHS MBri MGos MJak NEgg NPri NWea SCoo SEND SGol SLim SPer SPlb WHar
	- 'Old Gold Carbery'	see *J.* × *pfitzeriana* 'Carbery Gold'
	- 'Pfitzeriana'	see *J.* × *pfitzeriana* 'Wilhelm Pfitzer'
	- 'Pfitzeriana Aurea'	CMac EHul EPfP MGos NWea SGol
	- 'Pfitzeriana Compacta' 🏆^{H4}	EHul
	- 'Pfitzeriana Glauca'	EHul LRHS
§	- 'Sulphur Spray' 🏆^{H4}	CDul CWib EHul MAsh MMuc SEND SGol SLim SPer WCFE
§	- 'Wilhelm Pfitzer'	EHul EPfP NWea
§	***pingii*** 'Glassell'	CDoC MAsh NLar
§	- var. ***wilsonii***	CDoC CKen NLar
	procera	WPGP
	procumbens 'Bonin Isles'	LRHS SPoG
	- 'Nana' 🏆^{H4}	CDoC CKen CMac CSBt EHul EPfP LAst LBee LRHS MAsh MGos MJak NEgg NHol NLar SCoo SGol SLim SPoG WCFE
	recurva	CDoC
	- 'Castlewellan'	CDoC NHol NLar
	- var. ***coxii***	CDoC CMac EHul NHol NLar SMad WCFE
§	- 'Densa'	CDoC CKen EHul
	- 'Nana'	see *J. recurva* 'Densa'
	rigida	CMen
§	- subsp. ***conferta***	CMac MGos SEND SGol
*	- - 'Blue Ice'	CKen

- - 'Blue Pacific'	EHul NLar SGol WCFE
- - 'Blue Tosho'	CDul NLar
- - 'Emerald Sea'	EHul
- - 'Schlager'	MGos
- - 'Silver Mist'	CKen
sabina	CArn NWea
§ - 'Blaue Donau'	EHul
- Blue Danube	see *J. sabina* 'Blaue Donau'
- 'Broadmoor'	EHul
- 'Knap Hill'	see *J.* × *pfitzeriana* 'Wilhelm Pfitzer'
- 'Mountaineer'	see *J. scopulorum* 'Mountaineer'
- 'Rockery Gem'	EHul LRHS SLim SPoG
- 'Skandia'	CKen
- 'Tamariscifolia'	CBcs CDul CWib EHul GKin LBee LRHS MAsh MGos MJak NWea SEND SGol SLim SPer SPoG WCFE
- 'Variegata' (v)	EHul
sargentii	see *J. chinensis* var. *sargentii*
scopulorum	CKen
- 'Blue Arrow'	CDoC CDul CKen CSBt CWib ELan EPfP GKin IBoy LAst LBee LRHS MAsh MBri MGos MJak NEgg NHol NLar NPCo NSoo NWea SCoo SGol SLim SPer WBor WHar
- 'Blue Banff'	CKen
- 'Blue Heaven'	EHul
- 'Blue Pyramid'	EHul
- 'Moonglow'	EHul
§ - 'Mountaineer'	EHul
- 'Mrs Marriage'	CKen
- 'Silver Star' (v)	EHul
- 'Skyrocket'	CBcs CCVT CDul CMac CSBt CWib ECrN EHul EPfP EPot GGal LAst MGos MJak MRav NPCo NWea SEND SGol SPlb WCFE WHar WMou
- 'Snow Flurries'	SLim
- 'Springbank'	EHul WCFE
- 'Wichita Blue'	EHul EPfP IVic
squamata 'Blue Carpet' 🏆H4	CBcs CDoC CDul CKen CMac CSBt CWib EHul EPfP LAst LBuc LPot LRHS MAsh MBri MGos MJak NEgg NHol NLar NPri NWea SGol SLim SPer SPoG WCFE WHar
- 'Blue Spider'	CKen LRHS
- 'Blue Star' 🏆H4	CDoC CJun CKen CMac CSBt EHul ELan EPfP EPot LAst LBee LPot LRHS MAsh MBri MGos MJak NEgg NHol NLar NPri NWad NWea SGol SLim SPer SPoG WCFE
- 'Blue Star Variegated'	see *J. squamata* 'Golden Flame'
- 'Blue Swede'	see *J. squamata* 'Hunnetorp'
- 'Chinese Silver'	EHul
- 'Dream Joy'	CKen LRHS NLar SPoG
- 'Filborna'	CKen LBee LRHS
- 'Glassell'	see *J. pingii* 'Glassell'
§ - 'Golden Flame' (v)	CKen
- 'Holger' 🏆H4	CDoC CDul CMac EHul EPfP LAst LBee LRHS MAsh MBri MGos MJak NHol NLar SCoo SGol SLim SPoG
§ - 'Hunnetorp'	MGos
- 'Loderi'	see *J. pingii* var. *wilsonii*
- 'Meyeri'	EHul GKev MGos NWea SCoo SGol
- 'Wilsonii'	see *J. pingii* var. *wilsonii*
§ ***taxifolia***	CSBt
§ ***virginiana*** 'Blue Cloud'	EHul LRHS SLim
- 'Burkii'	EHul
- 'Frosty Morn'	CKen EHul
- 'Glauca'	EHul NWea
- 'Golden Spring'	CKen
- 'Helle'	see *J. chinensis* 'Spartan'
- 'Hetzii'	EHul NLar NWea
- 'Hillspire'	EHul
- Silver Spreader = 'Mona'	CKen EHul
- 'Sulphur Spray'	see *J.* × *pfitzeriana* 'Sulphur Spray'
§ - 'Venusta'	CKen

Jurinea (*Asteraceae*)

glycacantha	LRHS
ledebourii	LRHS

Jurinella see *Jurinea*

Justicia (*Acanthaceae*)

americana	LLWG
aurea	EShb WHil
§ ***brandegeeana*** 🏆H1	CCCN EShb MOWG
- 'Lutea'	see *J. brandegeeana* 'Yellow Queen'
- variegated (v)	EShb WHil
§ - 'Yellow Queen'	EShb
- yellow-flowered	EShb
§ ***carnea***	CHII EBak EShb GCal MOWG SMad WCot
- 'Alba'	CCCN EShb WHil
- dark-leaved	CHII WCot
- 'Radiant'	SMad
guttata	see *J. brandegeeana*
'Penrhosiensis'	EShb WHil
pohliana	see *J. carnea*
rizzinii 🏆H1	CBcs CCCN CHII SMad SRot STPC WHil
scheidweileri	EShb
spicigera	EShb WHil
suberecta	see *Dicliptera sericea*

K

Kadsura (*Schisandraceae*)

coccinea B&SWJ 11793	WCru
japonica	CBcs
- B&SWJ 1027	WCru WPGP
- B&SWJ 4463 from Korea	WCru
- B&SWJ 11109 from Japan	WCru
- from Japan	EPfP WSHC
- 'Fukurin' (v)	NLar
- 'Variegata' (v)	CCCN EBee EPfP LRHS SEND WSHC
- white fruit	CBcs NLar

Kaempferia ✿ (*Zingiberaceae*)

rotunda	CCCN

Kageneckia (*Rosaceae*)

oblonga	SPlb

Kalanchoe (*Crassulaceae*)

beharensis 🏆H1	CAbb CCCN CDTJ EShb EUJe
- 'Fang'	CDTJ
- 'Rusty'	CDTJ CSpe
§ ***delagoensis***	CCCN EShb
fedtschenkoi	EShb
humilis	WCot
laciniata	EShb
orgyalis	EShb
prolifera	EShb
pubescens	EShb

	pumila 🏆H1	EShb EWoo SBch SPet
	rhombopilosa	EShb
	sexangularis	EShb
	'Tessa' 🏆H1	WCot
	thyrsiflora 'Bronze Sculpture'	CAbb CHel EUJe WCot
	tomentosa 🏆H1	EShb WCot
	tubiflora	see *K. delagoensis*

Kalimeris (*Asteraceae*)

§	***incisa***	EBee MMuc MRav WBor
	- 'Alba'	LHop NLar XLum
	- 'Blue Star'	ECtt EWll LHop LRHS MSpe NLar WCAu WPtf WSHC
	- 'Charlotte'	EWes NBre NDov
	- 'Madiva'	CSam EBee LHop LPla NDov
	- 'Nana Blue'	NDov
	'Mon Jardin' **new**	WCot
§	***mongolica***	CDes CMac MMuc WSHC
	- 'Antonia'	NDov WCot
§	***pinnatifida***	EBee LRHS
	- 'Hortensis'	ECtt
§	***yomena*** 'Shogun' (v)	CPrp EBee ECtt EHoc ELan EPfP EShb LEdu MSpe NBir NBre NLar NSti SPer WWEG
	- 'Variegata'	see *K. yomena* 'Shogun'

Kalmia ✿ (*Ericaceae*)

	angustifolia 🏆H4	SRms
	- f. ***rubra*** 🏆H4	CBcs CDoC CDul EBee ELan EPfP IDee LRHS MAsh NLar NPri NSoo SPer
I	- 'Rubra Nana'	CMac
	cuneata	GGGa
	latifolia 🏆H4	CBcs CEnd EBee ELan EPfP LRHS LSou MJak MMuc NPri NWea SPer SWvt
	- 'Bandeau' **new**	GGGa
	- 'Bullseye'	NLar
	- 'Carousel'	CBcs CCCN NLar
	- 'Clementine Churchill'	CMac
	- 'Eskimo' **new**	GGGa
	- 'Freckles' 🏆H4	EPfP NPCo SPoG
	- 'Fresca'	NPCo
	- 'Galaxy'	GGGa IVic
	- 'Ginkona'	GGGa
	- 'Kaleidoscope'	GGGa IVic MGos
	- 'Minuet'	CDes CCCN CEnd EPfP GGGa IVic LRHS MLea NLar NPCo SLim SPoG SSpi SWvt
	- 'Mitternacht'	GGGa
	- 'Moyland' **new**	GGGa
	- f. ***myrtifolia***	LRHS
	- - 'Elf'	CEnd EPfP IVic LRHS MAsh MGos NLar SLim
	- 'Nani' **new**	GGGa
	- 'Nipmuck'	CMac
	- 'Olympic Fire' 🏆H4	CEnd GBin GGGa IVic LRHS NLar SLim SWvt
	- 'Olympic Wedding'	NLar
	- 'Ostbo Red'	CBcs CDoC CDul CEnd CMac EPfP GBin IVic LRHS MLea NCGa NPCo SPoG SSpi SWvt
	- 'Peppermint'	GGGa IVic SLim
	- 'Pink Charm' 🏆H4	IVic
	- 'Pink Frost'	NPCo
	- 'Pinkobello' **new**	GGGa
	- 'Pinwheel'	CEnd NLar SLim
	- 'Quinnipiac'	MJak
	- 'Sarah'	LRHS MLea NPCo
§	***microphylla***	WAbe
	polifolia	CBcs EPfP MJak NHar NSoo SPer WThu
	- var. ***compacta***	WSHC
	- 'Glauca'	see *K. microphylla*
	- f. ***leucantha***	NHar WThu

× *Kalmiothamnus* (*Ericaceae*)

	'Haytor'	WAbe
	ornithomma 'Cosdon'	WAbe
	'Sindelberg'	WAbe

Kalopanax (*Araliaceae*)

	pictus	see *K. septemlobus*
§	***septemlobus***	CBcs ELan EPfP EUJe GBin LEdu NLar
	- var. ***magnificus*** B&SWJ 10900	WCru
	- f. ***maximowiczii***	EPfP IVic MBlu NLar WCot

Keckiella (*Plantaginaceae*)

§	***antirrhinoides***	SBrt
§	***cordifolia***	SBrt
§	***ternata*** **new**	SBrt

Kelleria (*Thymelaeaceae*)

	dieffenbachii **new**	WThu

Kelseya (*Rosaceae*)

	uniflora	WAbe

Kennedia (*Papilionaceae*)

	coccinea	CCCN SVen
	macrophylla	CRHN
	nigricans	CCCN MOWG
	prostrata	SPlb
	rubicunda	CCCN CRHN MOWG

Kentia (*Arecaceae*)

	belmoreana	see *Howea belmoreana*
	forsteriana	see *Howea forsteriana*

Kentranthus see *Centranthus*

Kerria (*Rosaceae*)

	japonica misapplied single	see *K. japonica* 'Simplex'
	japonica (L.) DC. (d)	see *K. japonica* 'Pleniflora'
	- 'Albescens'	WCot
	- 'Golden Guinea' 🏆H4	CExl CMac ECtt ELan EPfP EWTr GGal IFro LRHS MAsh MGos MNrw MRav SCoo SHil SPer SRms SWvt
§	- 'Picta' (v)	CDul CMac CTsd CWib EBee ELan EShb LRHS MGos MRav MSwo SGol SLim SLon SPer SRms WSHC
§	- 'Pleniflora' (d) 🏆H4	Widely available
§	- 'Simplex'	CExl CMac GGal NWea
	- 'Variegata'	see *K. japonica* 'Picta'

Khadia (*Aizoaceae*)

	acutipetala	CCCN

Kirengeshoma (*Hydrangeaceae*)

	palmata 🏆H4	Widely available
	- Koreana Group	Widely available

Kitaibela (*Malvaceae*)

	vitifolia	CExl CSpe ELan MPie NBid SBrt SEND SPav SPlb WPtf

Kitchingia see *Kalanchoe*

kiwi fruit see *Actinidia deliciosa*

Kleinia (*Asteraceae*)

articulata	see *Senecio articulatus*
grantii	CSpe WCot
repens	see *Senecio serpens*

Knautia (*Caprifoliaceae*)

§ ***arvensis***	CArn CHab EHyd EPfP MHer MMuc MNHC NLar NMir SEND SPer WHer WMoo WOut WSFF
- 'Rachael'	CElw
- white-flowered **new**	SPhx
dipsacifolia	SHar
'Jardin d'en Face'	ELan EPfP LRHS
§ ***macedonica***	Widely available
- 'Crimson Cushion'	CSpe ECtt LSou
- 'Mars Midget'	CExl CHel CHll COlW CSpe EHyd ELan ELon EPfP EShb GQue IBoy LAst LBMP LRHS LSRN LSou MGos MLHP MSpe NLar SBea SHil SPhx SPoG SWvt WHoo WPtf WSHC WWEG
- Melton pastels	CExl CHel COlW EBee EHyd ELan EPfP EShb GJos IBoy LRHS LSRN MCot MGos NLar NPer SPer SPet SPoG SRot SWat SWvt WWEG
- pink-flowered	CSam
- 'Red Knight'	EBee EPfP MBNS MCot MSCN
- red-flowered	CWib
- short	ECtt SPad
- tall, pale-flowered	SPhx
- 'Thunder and Lightning' (v)	CBct CWGN EBee ECtt EWes IBoy LBMP LBuc LSou MAvo MHol MNrw MPie MSCN MTis NLar SMrm SPer SPoG WCot WWEG
sarajevensis	MAvo

Knightia (*Proteaceae*)

excelsa	CBcs

Kniphofia ✿ (*Asphodelaceae*)

sp.	SVic
'Ada'	ELon EWes LRHS
albescens	SPlb XLum
'Alcazar'	CBcs CPrp ECtt ELon EPfP IBoy LRHS LSRN MAvo MBri MHer MSCN NSoo SPer SRkn SWvt WCAu WCot WMnd WWEG
'Ample Dwarf'	ECtt WCot
'Amsterdam'	MWat SHar
angustifolia	SPlb
'Apricot'	LRHS
'Apricot Souffle'	EPri WCot
'Atlanta'	LRHS
'Aurora'	XLum
'Barton Fever' ♀H4	WCot
baurii	CExl IGor SPlb
'Bees' Jubilee'	MAvo MNrw
'Bees' Lemon'	Widely available
'Bees' Sunset' ♀H4	CAvo CDes EBee GCra LPla MNFA MNrw WCot WWEG
'Bees' Yellow'	SBch
'Bengal Fire'	LRHS
'Bicolor'	EBee ECtt
'Bitter Chocolate'	WCot
'Bob's Choice'	WCot
'Border Ballet'	CRos EHyd LBMP LRHS NBir NBre NGdn NLar SWat XLum
brachystachya	ELon GAbr GCal SPlb
'Bressingham Comet'	CRos ECtt LEdu LRHS NBir NCGa SHil WWEG
'Bressingham Gleam'	LRHS WCot
Bressingham Sunbeam = 'Bresun'	ECtt LRHS NBir WWEG
'Bressingham Yellow'	EBee ECtt
'Brimstone' Bloom ♀H4	CElw CPrp ECtt EHyd EPPr EPfP GBin LEdu LHop LPio LRHS MSpe NBir NPnk NPri SPer SRkn SWvt WGwG WMnd WWEG
bruceae	EPri
'Buttercup' ♀H4	CAvo LSRN WSHC
'Butterfly' **new**	EBee
'Candlelight'	CCse EBee ECtt EPri LRHS NBre
'Candlemass'	CTca
'Carole's Crush'	WCot
caulescens ♀H3-4	Widely available
- 'Coral Breakers'	CExl CTca EBee ECtt GAbr LRHS MAvo MHol MNFA NEgg SDix SKHP SMad SPer SPoG WCot
- 'John May'	ECtt LRHS MAvo MBri WBrk WCot
'Chichi'	WCot
'Christmas Cheer'	CDes
citrina	CCon EPfP GCra IBoy LAst LRHS MBrN NBre NLar NPri WCot WHil XLum
'C.M. Prichard' misapplied	see *K. rooperi*
'C.M. Prichard' Prichard	EBee WCot
'Cobra'	EBee ECtt GBin GMaP LRHS MTis WCot WHil
I 'Cooperi'	EPri
'Coral Sceptre'	LPla WCot
'Creamsicle' (Popsicle Series) **new**	ECtt NLar
'Dingaan'	CAbb EBee ECtt MNrw NBir NEgg NLar WCot
'Dorset Sentry'	CAbb CAby COlW EBee ECtt ELon EPfP LRHS MGos MNrw NBir NEgg NLar NOrc SKHP SMad SMrm WCAu WCot WWEG
drepanophylla **new**	MHer XLum
'Drummore Apricot'	CMHG COlW ECtt ELan EPfP EWTr GBin GBuc IBoy LRHS LSRN NBir NCGa NEgg WCot WGwG
'Early Buttercup'	CTca
'Ember Glow' (Glow Series) **new**	ECtt
ensifolia	CTca ECtt NGdn WMnd XLum
'Ernest Mitchell'	WCot
Express hybrids	NBre XLum
'Fairyland'	NGBl
'Fiery Fred' ♀H4	EBee ELan LRHS MRav NBre WCot
'Firefly'	LRHS
'First Sunrise'PBR	ECtt NCGa
'Flamenco'	COlW ELon EWll LRHS NBre NGdn NHol SPet WRHF WWEG
'Florence Bedecked'	WCot
foliosa Hochst.	LEdu
'Frances Victoria'	WCot
galpinii misapplied	see *K. triangularis* subsp. *triangularis*
'Gilt Bronze'	WCot
'Gladness'	ECtt MAvo NBir NBre NCGa WCot WWEG
'Gloire d'Orléans'	XLum
'Goldelse'	NBir

'Goldfinch'	CCse CSam
gracilis	LEdu
'Green Jade'	Widely available
'Green Lemon'	NBre
'H.E. Beale'	EBee WCot
'Hen and Chickens'	ECtt ESwi MTis WCot
hirsuta	CCon COIW EBee LRHS WSHC
- JCA 3.461.900	SKHP
- 'Fire Dance'	EHyd LRHS
- 'Traffic Lights'	WHlf
'Hollard's Gold'	WCot
'Ice Queen'	CAvo CCon EBee ECtt ELon EPPr EPri GBin IPot LRHS MAvo MRav MTis NChi NLar NSoo SEND SGol SRms SWvt WCot WWEG
ichopensis	WPGP
'Incandesce' ♀H4	WCot
'Innocence' ♀H4	LRHS NBre
'Jane Henry'	CDes EBee
'Jenny Bloom'	CAvo COIW CPrp CRos EBee ECtt ELan ELon EPfP EWTr GBin GBuc GMaP LAst LEdu LRHS MRav MWat NEgg NLar NSti SMrm SPer WCAu WCot WWEG
'John Benary'	CRos EBee ECtt EHyd GBin GLog GMaP IKil LLWG LRHS MAvo MBel NBir NEgg NGdn NLar SEND SMrm SPer WCot WGwG WKif WWEG
'Jonathan' ♀H4	WCot
laxiflora	EPri WPGP XLum
'Light of the World'	see *K. triangularis* subsp. *triangularis* 'Light of the World'
'Limelight'	WHlf
linearifolia	CExl CPrp EBee GCra MNrw SPlb WCot XLum
'Little Elf'	XLum
'Little Maid'	Widely available
'Lord Roberts'	GCal MAvo MRav SMad WCot WPGP
'Luna'	WCot
macowanii	see *K. triangularis* subsp. *triangularis*
'Maid of Orleans'	ELon LRHS
'Mango Popsicle' (Popsicle Series) **new**	NLar
'Mermaiden'	CCon CMHG CRos ECtt MNrw WCAu WCot
'Minister Verschuur'	ECtt GQue LRHS MBri
'Modesta'	WSHC
'Moonstone' ♀H4	CHVG ECtt LLWG NSti WCot
'Mount Etna'	WCot
multiflora	CTca ECtt
- 'November Glory'	WCot
'Nancy's Red'	Widely available
nelsonii Mast.	see *K. triangularis* subsp. *triangularis*
'New England'	EBee
'Nobilis'	see *K. uvaria* 'Nobilis'
northiae ♀H4	CExl CHid CTca CTsd EAmu EBee ECtt ELan ELon EPri EUJe EWes GCal LEdu LRHS MNrw NLar SAPC SDix SEND SMad SPlb WCot WCru WPGP XLum
- JCA 3.462.600	WCot
'Old Court Seedling'	GGal WCot
§ 'Painted Lady'	CAvo CSam CTca CTri EBee ECtt GAbr GMaP LAst MNFA MNrw NCGa NLar WCot
'Papaya Popsicle' (Popsicle Series) **new**	LSou

parviflora	XLum
pauciflora	WCot
'Percy's Pride'	Widely available
'Pfitzeri'	SRms
'Pineapple Popsicle' (Popsicle Series) **new**	ECtt NLar
× ***praecox***	LRHS
'Primrose Upward' ♀H4	WCot
I 'Primulina' Bloom	LRHS
'Prince Igor' misapplied	see *K. uvaria* 'Nobilis'
'Prince Igor' Prichard	GAbr LRHS MLHP NBir
pumila	LLHF
'Red Rocket'	EBee IBoy NHol WCot
'Rich Echoes' ♀H4	CWGN MTis WCot
ritualis	CExl SKHP WWEG
§ ***rooperi*** ♀H4	Widely available
'Rosea Superba' **new**	EBee
'Royal Castle'	CExl GMaP LRHS NBir NGdn NOrc SEND WWEG XLum
'Royal Standard' ♀H4	CBcs CMac CPrp EBee ECtt ELan ELon EPfP EShb LRHS LSRN NCGa NLar SMrm SPer SWvt WHil WMnd WWEG
rufa Baker	LEdu
'Safranvogel' ♀H4	EBee ECtt SMad WCot
'Samuel's Sensation' misapplied	see *K.* 'Painted Lady'
'Samuel's Sensation' Samuel ♀H4	CCon EBee LRHS NLar SEND SRGP WCot WWEG
sarmentosa	SPlb WCot XLum
'Saturn' **new**	MAvo
'Scorched Corn'	MSpe WCot
'Sherbet Lemon'	ECtt MNrw WCot
'Shining Sceptre'	CSam EBee ECtt LRHS MAvo NLar SMad SWvt WWEG
'Son of Notung' **new**	IBlr
'Springtime'	WCot
'Star of Baden-Baden'	EBee IBlr NBir SEND SMad WCot WWEG
Stark's early perpetual-flowering hybrids	XLum
'Strawberries and Cream'	CAvo CBcs CMac COIW CTsd CWCL ECtt ELon GQue LAst LRHS MBri SGbt SPer SWvt
stricta	XLum
'Sunningdale Yellow' ♀H4	CCse CDes COIW ECtt GMaP MAvo MLHP SRms WWEG
'Tawny King' ♀H4	Widely available
'Tetbury Torch' PBR	CPrp CWGN EBee ECGP ECtt GBin GQue LHop LRHS MAvo MCot NCGa NLar WWEG
thomsonii	CExl GCal NGdn SBod
- Grimshaw's form **new**	GCal
- var. ***snowdenii*** misapplied	see *K. thomsonii* var. *thomsonii*
- var. ***snowdenii*** ambig.	CCon CExl WPGP XLum
§ - var. ***thomsonii*** 'Stern's Trip' ♀H3	CDes WHal
'Timothy' ♀H4	Widely available
'Toffee Nosed' ♀H4	Widely available
'Torchbearer'	NBre WCot
triangularis	EPfP EShb MBlu NCGa XLum
§ - subsp. ***triangularis***	CBro EPfP GBuc GCal LAst LSRN MAvo NBre SPer SRms SWat WCot WWEG XLum
§ - - 'Light of the World'	CBcs CTca ECtt GBin LAst LEdu LLWG LRHS MBel MHer NBir NLar SMad SPer SWvt WCot WGrn WWEG

'Tuckii'	SRms
typhoides	EBee NBir SPlb XLum
tysonii	SPlb XLum
uvaria	CPrp LRHS MJak NBir NSoo SPer SRms WMnd XLum XSen
- 'Grandiflora'	CMac MWhi
§ - 'Nobilis' 🏆H4	CAby CCon CExl CTca EBee ECtt ELan ELon EUJe GAbr GBin GMaP GQue LSRN MAvo MNFA MNrw MSCN NGdn SAPC SEND SMad SPav SPer SPoG SWvt WCAu WCot WMnd WWEG
'Vanilla'	CCon LRHS LSRN MAvo NGdn NLar SEND WWEG
'Vincent Lepage'	EBee LHop NLar
'Wol's Red Seedling'	CBct CBro COlW CSam ECtt ELon EUJe GAbr MCot MNrw NCGa NEgg NGdn NLar NSti SPoG WCot WGrn WGwG WHoo
'Wrexham Buttercup' 🏆H4	CSam EBee ECtt ELan EPfP GAbr GMaP GQue LRHS LSRN MCot MNrw NPri SMad SMrm WCot WHal WHoo WWEG WWlt
'Yellow Cheer'	WCot
'Yellow Hammer' Slieve Donard	CSam NBre SEND WHil

Knowltonia (*Ranunculaceae*)

filia	CExl

Koeleria (*Poaceae*)

cristata misapplied	see *K. macrantha*
glauca	CWib EHoe EPPr EPfP EShb EUJe GMaP LRHS MBNS MJak MWhi NBro NGdn NWsh SAPC SLim SMrm SPlb SWvt WWEG
§ ***macrantha***	NLar XLum
pyramidata	SMea XLum
vallesiana	EHoe LRHS SMea
- 'Mountain Breeze'	EPPr

Koelreuteria (*Sapindaceae*)

paniculata 🏆H4	Widely available
- 'Coral Sun'[PBR]	CExl CMHG EBee EPfP EUJe LRHS MBlu MBri NLar SChF WPGP WPat
- 'Fastigiata'	CDul EBee EPfP MBlu MBri SCoo SSpi WHar
- 'Rosseels'	NLar
- 'September'	EPfP

Kohleria (*Gesneriaceae*)

'Ampallang'	WDib
'An's Nagging Macaws' new	WDib
'Brazil Gem' new	WDib
'Cybele'	EABi WDib
'Dark Velvet'	WDib
eriantha 🏆H1	WDib
'Heartland's Blackberry Butterfly' new	WDib
hirsuta	WDib
'Jester' 🏆H1	EABi WDib
'Manchu' new	WDib
'Marquis de Sade'	EABi
'Red Ryder'	EABi
'Ruby Red'	WDib
'Silver Feather'	WDib
§ 'Sunrise'[PBR]	WDib
'Sunshine'	see *K.* 'Sunrise'
'Texas Rainbow' new	WDib
warscewiczii 🏆H1	EABi WDib

Kolkwitzia (*Caprifoliaceae*)

amabilis	CDoy CExl CSBt CTri ECGP ELan EPfP EWld NWea SGol SPlb SRms WCFE WHar WMoo WRHF
- Dream Catcher = 'Maradco'	CMac EPfP MRav NLar NPro WPat
- 'Pink Cloud' 🏆H4	Widely available

Kosteletzkya (*Malvaceae*)

virginica	EDAr MHol SPhx

kumquat see *Fortunella*

Kunzea (*Myrtaceae*)

ambigua	EBee ECou IDee MOWG SPlb
- pink-flowered	ECou
- prostrate	ECou
baxteri	ECou MOWG
ericifolia	SPlb
§ ***ericoides***	CTsd ECou
- 'Auckland'	ECou
- 'Bemm'	ECou
parvifolia	ECou SPlb
pauciflora new	SPlb

L

Lablab (*Papilionaceae*)

§ ***purpureus***	LSou SHDw
- 'Ruby Moon'	CSpe

+ *Laburnocytisus* (*Papilionaceae*)

'Adamii'	CDul CJun CMac EBee ECrN ELan EPfP GBin IVic LAst LSRN MGos MPkF NLar SMad SPer

Laburnum ✿ (*Papilionaceae*)

alpinum	EPfP NWea SPlb
- 'Pendulum'	CDul CLnd EBee ELan LSRN MAsh MBri MGos NEgg SCrf SGol SLim SPer SPoG
§ ***anagyroides***	CDul CWib MMuc NWea SEND SRms
'Famous Walk'	see *L.* × *watereri* 'Vossii' AGM
vulgare	see *L. anagyroides*
× ***watereri*** new	IBoy
§ - 'Vossii' 🏆H4	Widely available

Lachenalia (*Asparagaceae*)

alba 'Nieuwoudtville'	ECho
algoensis	ECho
§ ***aloides***	CDoC CGrW ECho EPot GKev SDeJ
- var. ***aurea*** 🏆H1	ECho SBch WCot
I - var. ***luteola***	ECho
- 'Nelsonii'	ECho
- 'Pearsonii'	ECho GKev
- var. ***quadricolor*** 🏆H1	CDes CGrW CPrp CTsd ECho WCot
- var. ***vanzyliae*** 🏆H1	WCot

	angelica 'Agterkop'	ECho
	anguinea	ECho
	arbuthnotiae 'Somerset West'	ECho
	attenuata	ECho
	barkeriana	ECho
	bolusii	ECho
§	***bulbifera*** ♀H1	ECho WCot
	- 'George' ♀H1	ECho WCot
	capensis	ECho
	carnosa	ECho
	cernua 'Goudini'	ECho
	comptonii	ECho
	congesta 'Roggeveld'	ECho
	contaminata ♀H1	CGrW CPrp ECho EPfP WCot
	doleritica	ECho
	elegans	ECho
	- var. ***membranacea***	ECho
	- var. ***suaveolens***	ECho
	fistulosa	ECho
	- 'Klein Drakenstein'	ECho
	framesii	ECho
	'Fransie'	ECho
	gillettii	ECho
	glaucophylla	ECho
	hirta	ECho
	juncifolia	ECho
	- var. ***juncifolia***	ECho
	kliprandensis 'Kliprand'	ECho
*	***komsbergensis***	WCot
	lactosa	ECho
	latimerae	ECho
	leipoldtii	ECho
	'Lemon Ripple' (v)	WCot
	liliiflora	CGrW ECho
	longibracteata	ECho
	longituba	WCot
	marginata	ECho
	mathewsii	ECho
	maximilianii 'Cederberg'	ECho
	mediana	ECho
	montana	ECho
	muirii 'Bredasdorp'	ECho
	multifolia	ECho
	mutabilis	ECho WCot
	'Namakwa' (African Beauty Series)	ECho
	namaquensis	ECho
	namibiensis	ECho
	nardoubergensis	ECho
	neilii	ECho
	nervosa	ECho WCot
	obscura	ECho WCot
	orchioides var. ***glaucina***	CDes ECho WCot
	orthopetala	ECho GKev WCot
	pallida	ECho
	peersii 'Betty's Bay'	ECho
	pendula	see *L. bulbifera*
	polyphylla	ECho
	polypodantha 'Varsputs'	ECho
	purpureocoerulea 'Darling'	ECho
	pusilla	ECho WCot
	pustulata ♀H1	ECho EPot WCot
	- blue-flowered	CGrW ECho GKev
	- 'Meerlust'	ECho
	- yellow-flowered	ECho
	reflexa	ECho EPot
	'Robijn'	CPrp ECho
	'Rolina'	ECho
	'Romaud'	ECho WCot
	'Romelia'	ECho WCot
	'Ronina' (African Beauty Series)	CPrp ECho GKev WCot
	'Rosabeth'	ECho WCot
	rosea	ECho EPot
	rubida	CDes CGrW ECho WCot
	'Rupert' (African Beauty Series)	CPrp ECho GKev
	salteri 'Elim'	ECho
	splendida	ECho
	stayneri	CLak
	thomasiae	ECho
	trichophylla	ECho
	tricolor	see *L. aloides*
	unicolor	ECho WCot
	unifolia	ECho
	variegata 'Mamre'	ECho
	violacea	ECho WCot
	- var. ***glauca***	ECho
	viridiflora ♀H1	ECho EPot GKev WCot
	xerophila	ECho
	youngii 'Humansdorp'	ECho
	zebrina	ECho
	- f. ***densiflora*** 'Tanqua'	ECho
	zeyheri	ECho

Lactuca (*Asteraceae*)

	alpina	see *Cicerbita alpina*
	perennis	CPom EPPr LRHS NLar WHer
	virosa	CArn

Lagarostrobos (*Podocarpaceae*)

§	***franklinii***	CBcs CDoC WPGP
	- 'Fota' (f)	WThu
	- 'Picton Castle' (m)	WThu

Lagerstroemia (*Lythraceae*)

	indica ♀H1	CCCN CDul EPfP EShb SEND SPlb SSpi SVen WSHC
	- B&SWJ 12660 **new**	WCru
§	- 'Baton Rouge'	MGos MPkF
	- 'Beverly'	see *L. indica* 'Baton Rouge'
	- 'Cordon Bleu'	MGos MPkF
	- Little Chief hybrids	EShb
	- 'Red Imperator'	CBcs SEND
	- 'Rosea'	CBcs SEND
	subcostata CWJ 12352	WCru

Lagunaria (*Malvaceae*)

	patersonii	CHll WPGP

Lagurus (*Poaceae*)

	ovatus ♀H3	CKno MJak

Lallemantia (*Lamiaceae*)

	canescens	SBrt

Lamiastrum see *Lamium*

Lamium ✿ (*Lamiaceae*)

	album	CArn CHab MWat NMir
	- 'Friday' (v)	NBir WHer WWEG
	flexuosum	EPPr
§	***galeobdolon***	CArn CTri CWib EShb MHer SRms WHer
§	- 'Florentinum' (v)	CMac EBee ELan EPfP MMuc MRav SPer WWEG

- 'Hermann's Pride'	ECtt EHoe ELan ELon EPfP GMaP LBMP LRHS NBir NMir SMrm SPer SPoG SRms SWvt WHoo WMoo WWEG XLum
- 'Kirkcudbright Dwarf'	EBee EPPr EWes GBin NBre XLum
§ - 'Silberteppich'	MRav XLum
- 'Silver Angel'	XLum
- Silver Carpet	see *L. galeobdolon* 'Silberteppich'
- 'Variegatum'	see *L. galeobdolon* 'Florentinum'
garganicum	WSpi
- subsp. ***garganicum***	CCse CPom EWes LPla
luteum	see *L. galeobdolon*
maculatum	MCot MMuc NChi SRms
- 'Album'	ELan EPfP LRHS SHar SPer SRms
- 'Anne Greenaway' (v)	EWes SPet
§ - 'Aureum'	EBee ECtt EHoe ELan SMrm SPet SWvt XLum
- 'Beacon Silver'	CMac CWib EBee ECtt ELan EPfP LRHS MGos MHer MLHP MSCN MWhi NBir SPer SPet SPlb SPoG SRGP SRms SWvt WHar WWEG XLum
- 'Brightstone Pearl'	EWes MAvo
- 'Cannon's Gold'	EBee ECtt ELan EWes LPot LRHS SWvt WMoo WWEG
- 'Chequers' ambig.	EBee ELan SPer
- 'Elisabeth de Haas' (v)	EWes NBre
- 'Forncett Lustre'	EWes
- 'Forncett White Lustre'	NBre
- 'Ghost'	EPPr LBuc
- 'Gold Leaf'	see *L. maculatum* 'Aureum'
- Golden Anniversary = 'Dellam'PBR (v)	ECtt ELan LAst LSRN NBro SWvt
- 'Golden Nuggets'	see *L. maculatum* 'Aureum'
- 'Golden Wedding'	SRms
- 'Ickwell Beauty' (v)	WWEG
- 'James Boyd Parselle'	CMea WHal
- 'Margery Fish'	SRms
- 'Moonglow' **new**	EBee
- 'Orchid Frost'	CHid EBee ECGP ECtt EHoe ELon EWll GQue LHop LRHS MAsh
- Pink Chablis = 'Checkin'PBR	ELon LRHS MHol
- 'Pink Nancy'	SMrm SWvt
- 'Pink Pearls'	CSBt NBre SHar SMrm SPet WMoo WWEG
- 'Pink Pewter'	ECtt EHoe ELan EPfP EShb GMaP LRHS SPer SPlb SPoG WWEG
- 'Purple Winter'	EPPr
- 'Red Nancy'	CFis EBee ELan ELon SWvt XLum
§ - 'Roseum'	CWib EBee ELan EPfP MCot MRav MWat NChi SPer WMoo XLum
- 'Shell Pink'	see *L. maculatum* 'Roseum'
- 'Silver Shield'	EWes
- 'Sterling Silver'	CSam NBre
- 'White Nancy' ♀H4	CSBt ECGP ECtt EHoe ELan ELon EPfP EWTr GMaP LAst LHop LPot LRHS LSRN MCot MHer MWat NBir SMrm SPer SPet SPoG SRGP SWvt WCAu WCFE WHar WMoo WWEG
- 'Wootton Pink'	MHer NBir NLar SWvt
'Marshmallow'	LBuc
orvala	Widely available
- 'Album'	CExl CLAP CPrp EBee ELan EPPr GBin LEdu LRHS NBir NLar SHar SMrm WHer WPGP WPtf
- pink-flowered	CLAP CSpe
- 'Silva'	CCVN CExl CLAP EBee EPfP GBin LEdu LRHS WSHC
purpureum **new**	CArn
sandrasicum	WAbe

Lampranthus (*Aizoaceae*)

aberdeenensis	see *Delosperma aberdeenense*
apricot-flowered **new**	LRHS
aurantiacus	CBcs CHEx SPet
'Bagdad'	CHEx
blandus	CBcs CCCN
'Blousey Pink'	CHEx SVen
§ ***brownii***	CBcs CCCN ECho EHyd ELan EPfP LRHS SPet SPlb WPnn
coccineus	SPet
deltoides	see *Oscularia deltoides*
edulis	see *Carpobrotus edulis*
glaucus	SEND
multiradiatus	SEND
oscularis	see *Oscularia deltoides*
'Pink'	EUJe SPlb WPnn
purple-flowered	EUJe
roseus	CCCN CHEx ECho EHyd LRHS SPet WNew
'Salmon Pink'	SPlb WPnn
'Shanklin'	SPlb SVen
spectabilis	CBcs CCCN CTri SAPC SPet WNew WPnn
- orange-flowered	CAbb EUJe WNew
- purple-flowered	SPlb WNew
- 'Tresco Apricot'	CCCN ECho
- 'Tresco Brilliant'	CCCN CHEx CHVG ELon MSCN SEND SPet WPnn
- 'Tresco Fire'	CAbb CCCN CDoC CExl ELon SPlb SVen
- 'Tresco Orange'	CCCN WPnn
- 'Tresco Peach'	CCCN CHEx
- 'Tresco Purple'	CHEx CWCL
- 'Tresco Red'	CCCN CHEx ELon EUJe SEND WNew WPnn
- white-flowered	CHEx SPlb SVen WPnn
- yellow-flowered	SVen WPnn
stipulaceus **new**	SPlb
'Sugar Pink'	CHEx

Lamprocapnos (*Papaveraceae*)

§ ***spectabilis*** ♀H4	Widely available
- 'Alba' ♀H4	Widely available
- 'Gold Heart'PBR	CBcs EBee ECtt EPfP ESwi IBoy LBMP LRHS MBri MGos MHol MMHG MRav NLar NSti SGol SPoG WCot
- 'Valentine'	CBct CBro ESwi GBin IBoy LHop LLWG LRHS MAsh MBel MBri MHol MPie MSCN NDov NLar NPnk SGol SPoG STPC WCAu WCot

Lamprothyrsus (*Poaceae*)

hieronymi CDPR 3096	EPPr
- RCB RA K2-2	CDes EBee WCot WPGP

Lanaria (*Lanariaceae*)

lanata **new**	CLak

Lancea (*Phrymaceae*)

tibetica	CPBP

Lantana (*Verbenaceae*)

'Calippo Tucano' **new**	LSou
'Calippo Tutti Frutti'	ESwi EUJe LSou
camara	CArn ELan EShb MSCN

- Landmark Sunrise Rose ='Balandrise'PBR (Landmark Series) **new**	LAst
- (Lucky Series) Lucky Red Flame ='Balandimfla' **new**	LAst
- - Lucky Red Hot Improved ='Balucrehot'PBR	SPoG
- - Lucky White ='Balucwite'PBR	SPoG
- - Lucky Yellow Improved ='Balucimyel'PBR	SPoG
- 'Mine d'Or'	EUJe
- orange-flowered	CCCN
- pink-flowered	CCCN EShb
- red-flowered	CCCN
- variegated (v)	EShb
- white-flowered	CCCN EShb
- yellow-flowered	EShb
§ ***montevidensis***	CSam EShb
* ***- alba***	EShb
sellowiana	see *L. montevidensis*
'Spreading Sunset'	MOWG

Lapageria ✿ (*Philesiaceae*)

rosea ♀H3	CBcs CCCN CDoy CExl CFil CRHN CTsd EPfP SChF SWvt WPGP
- var. ***albiflora***	CRHN SChF
- 'Flesh Pink'	CExl CRHN

Lapeirousia (*Iridaceae*)

anceps	ECho
corymbosa	ECho
cruenta	see *Freesia laxa*
divaricata	ECho
fabricii 'Grey's Pass'	ECho
fastigiata	ECho
jacquinii 'Gilberg'	ECho
laxa	see *Freesia laxa*
montana 'Danielskuil'	ECho
plicata 'Nieuwoudtville'	ECho
pyramidalis 'Worcester'	ECho

Lapiedra (*Amaryllidaceae*)

martinezii	ECho

Lapsana (*Asteraceae*)

communis 'Inky'	CNat

Larix ✿ (*Pinaceae*)

decidua ♀H4	CBcs CCVT CDul CMen ECrN ELan EPfP EWTr MGos MMuc NEgg NWea SEND SPer SPlb WHar WMou
- 'Corley'	CKen
- 'Croxby Broom'	CKen
- 'Globus'	LRHS SLim
- 'Horstmann Recurved'	LRHS NLar SCoo SLim
- 'Kornik'	NLar
- 'Krejci'	NLar
- 'Little Bogle'	CKen CMen MAsh MGos NHol NLar
- 'Oberförster Karsten'	CKen NLar
- 'Pendula'	CBcs CMen
- 'Puli'	CEnd LRHS MAsh MBlu NHol NLar SCoo SLim SPer
- 'Schwarzenburg'	NLar SLim
× ***eurolepis***	see *L.* × *marschlinsii*
gmelinii var. ***gmelinii*** **new**	CMen
- var. ***olgensis***	NLar
- 'Tharandt'	CKen LRHS SLim
§ ***kaempferi*** ♀H4	CCVT CDoy CDul CLnd CMen ELan EPfP LBuc LRHS MMuc NWea SCoo SEWo SPer WMou
- 'Bambino'	CKen
- 'Bingman'	CKen
- 'Blue Ball'	CKen NLar SLim
- 'Blue Dwarf'	CKen LRHS MAsh MBri MGos SLim SPoG
- 'Blue Rabbit'	CKen LRHS
- 'Cruwys Morchard'	CKen
- 'Cupido'	LRHS SLim
- 'Diana'	CEnd CKen CMen LRHS MAsh MBlu MGos NHol NLar SLim
- 'Elizabeth Rehder'	CKen
- 'Grant Haddow'	CKen
- 'Grey Green Dwarf'	MAsh
- 'Grey Pearl'	CKen MAsh NLar
- 'Hanna's Broom'	SLim
- 'Hobbit'	CKen
* - 'Jakobsen's Pyramid'	CMen LRHS MAsh MGos
- 'Lobby Dosser'	CMen LRHS SLim
I - 'Nana'	CKen CMen LRHS NHol NLar SLim
I - 'Nana Prostrata'	CKen
- 'Pendula'	CEnd EPfP NLar SPer SPoG
- 'Stiff Weeping'	LRHS MGos MPkF NLar NPCo SLim
- 'Swallow Falls'	CKen
- 'Varley'	CKen
- 'Wehlen'	CKen
- 'Wolterdingen'	CKen LRHS MBlu NLar SLim
- 'Yanus Olieslagers'	CKen
laricina 'Arethusa Bog'	CKen NLar
- 'Bear Swamp'	CKen SLim
- 'Bingman'	CKen
- 'Hartwig Pine'	CKen
- 'Newport Beauty'	CKen
- 'Stubby' **new**	SLim
leptolepis	see *L. kaempferi*
§ × ***marschlinsii***	CCVT MMuc NWea
- 'Domino'	CKen CMen SLim
- 'Gail'	CKen
- 'Julie'	CKen
- 'Snapewood Broom' **new**	SLim
'Varied Directions'	SLim

Larryleachia (*Asclepiadaceae*)

cactiformis	LToo

Laser (*Apiaceae*)

trilobum	LEdu SPhx
- PAB 3382 **new**	LEdu

Laserpitium (*Apiaceae*)

§ ***siler***	CArn CSpe EBee MAvo SPhx SPlb WSHC

Lasiagrostis see *Stipa*

Lasiospermum (*Asteraceae*)

bipinnatum	SPlb

Lastreopsis (*Dryopteridaceae*)

hispida	ESwi

Lathraea (*Orobanchaceae*)

clandestina	CAvo

Lathyrus ✿ (*Papilionaceae*)

§	***articulatus***	CSpe
§	***aureus***	CHid CLAP CPom CSpe GBin GBuc GCal IFro LRHS MCot MHer MNrw NBid NBir NCGa NChi NSti SBch SBrt SKHP WHal WHil WHoo WKif WPGP WWEG
	- 'Cally Variegated' (v)	GCal
	chilensis	LLHF
	chloranthus	SPav
	cirrhosus	CDes EBee WPGP
	clymenum articulatus	see *L. articulatus*
	cyaneus misapplied	see *L. vernus*
	davidii	CPom EBee EWes EWld LLHF SBrt WCot WSHC
	eucosmus	LLHF
	fremontii hort.	see *L. laxiflorus*
	grandiflorus	CSev CTri EBee ECGP NChi NLar SDix SMrm SWat WCot
	heterophyllus	EBee
	incurvus	MPet SPhx
	inermis	see *L. laxiflorus*
	japonicus	NLar SPhx WCot
	subsp. ***maritimus***	
	latifolius ♀H4	CArn CRHN EBee EPfP LAst MHol MWat MWhi NPer SPoG SRms SVic WBor WBrk WHer XLum
§	- 'Albus' ♀H4	CFlo CTri ELan SPav SRms WKif XLum
	- 'Blushing Bride'	CSpe WCot
	- deep pink-flowered	MHer NLar NSti
	- pale pink-flowered	NSti
	- Pink Pearl	see *L. latifolius* 'Rosa Perle'
	- 'Red Pearl'	CBcs CFlo EBee ECtt ELan EPfP GAbr LBuc LRHS LSRN MBri MCot MLHP MNHC MWat NPri SEND SPav SPer SPhx SPlb SPoG SWvt
§	- 'Rosa Perle' ♀H4	CBcs CFlo CTri EBee ECtt LHop LRHS LSRN MAvo MBri MCot MLHP MNHC MRav NBir NLar NPer NPri SMrm SPer SPhx SWvt WMoo WWEG XLum
	- Weisse Perle	see *L. latifolius* 'White Pearl'
	- 'White Pearl' misapplied	see *L. latifolius* 'Albus'
§	- 'White Pearl' ♀H4	CBcs EPfP GAbr LRHS LSRN MAvo MBri MCot MHer MLHP MRav NBir NLar NPer NSti SMrm SPer SPhx SPoG SWvt WSHC WWEG XLum
§	***laxiflorus***	CDes CPom EBee MCot WMoo WPGP WSHC
	linifolius	EBee NLar WCot WHfH WPGP
	montanus	GPoy
	nervosus	CHid CSpe EWes SRms
	neurolobus	CPom
	niger	CSpe EBee EWld LHop LRHS LSou MCot MHer MMHG NLar WKif WWEG
	odoratus	SVic
	- 'Anniversary'	MCot
	- 'Beth Chatto' new	MCot
	- 'Betty Maiden'	MCot
	- 'Blue Medley'	MCot
	- 'Burnished Bronze'	MCot
	- 'Charlie's Angel' ♀H4	MCot
	- 'Clementine Kiss' new	MCot
	- 'Cupani'	SPhx
	- 'Dancing Queen'	MPet
	- 'Dark Passion'	MCot
	- 'Dawn'	MCot
	- 'Ethel Grace' new	MCot
	- 'Evening Glow' ♀H4	MCot
	- 'George Priestley'	MCot
	- 'Honey Pink'	MCot
	- 'Jilly' ♀H4	MCot
	- 'Lord Nelson'	SPhx
	- 'Lucinda Jane'	MPet
	- 'Mammoth Mixed'	MPet
	- 'Marion'	MCot
	- 'Matucana'	CSpe MWat WBrk
	- 'Midnight'	SPhx
	- 'Milly'	MCot
	- 'Misty Mountain'	MCot
	- 'Mollie Rilstone'	MCot
	- 'Mrs Bernard Jones' ♀H4	MCot
	- 'Mrs Collier'	SPhx
	- 'Prima Ballerina' new	CHid
	- 'Promise' new	MCot
	- 'Restormel'	MCot
	- 'Richard and Judy'	MCot
	- 'Tutankhamun's Pea' new	WHfH
	- 'Wedding Day' ♀H4	MCot
	- 'White Frills'	SPhx
	- Winter Elegance Series	MPet
	odoratus × ***belinensis*** 'Erewhon'	MPet
	odoratus × ***belinensis*** 'Navy'	MPet
	palustris	EBee LLWG SPlb
	pisiformis new	EBee
	polyphyllus	MPet NSti
	pratensis	CHab EBee NMir WSFF
	pubescens	MPet
	roseus	EBee GCal WSHC
	rotundifolius ♀H4	CHid GLog NSti SPhx WHoo WSHC
	- 'Tillyperone'	EBee SPhx
	sativus	CHid CSpe ELan MCot
	- f. ***albus***	CHid CSpe
	splendens new	SBrt
	subandinus	SPlb
	sylvestris	EBee WBrk
	transsylvanicus	CPom EBee GBin SPhx
	tuberosus	CArn CHid EBee WCot WSHC
	'Tubro'	EBee
	venetus	EBee EWes GCal MNrw WSHC
§	***vernus*** ♀H4	Widely available
	- 'Albiflorus'	MNrw XEll
	- 'Alboroseus' ♀H4	CLAP CPla EBee ELan EPfP GBuc GCal GCra GMaP IFro LHop MNrw NBir NChi NLar NPnk SPhx SPoG SWat SWvt WCot WHoo
	- var. ***albus***	CLAP CMea CPom MNrw NChi WCot WPGP
	- ***aurantiacus***	see *L. aureus*
	- 'Caeruleus'	CLAP ECGP WHoo WPGP
*	- 'Cyaneus'	SHar SWat WCot
I	- 'Filifolius'	CSpe EBee
	- 'Flaccidus'	CAby CFis MNrw SBrt WCot WKif
*	- 'Gracilis'	EBee LEdu NLar
	- 'Madelaine'	WCot
	- purple-flowered	CHel LRHS MMuc SEND
	- 'Rainbow'	CLAP EPfP GAbr LRHS MMHG SMrm
	- 'Rosenelfe'	CMea GBuc LBMP LEdu MHer SBea SHar SMrm SPhx SPoG WCot WHal WHil WKif WPGP WSHC
	- f. ***roseus***	CHel EBee LRHS MMuc MRav NBir NCGa SEND SRms WBrk WCot

- 'Spring Beauty'	CLAP
- 'Spring Delight'	LRHS
- 'Spring Melody'	EBee MRav SHar WCot
- 'Subtle Hints'	WCot

Laurelia (*Atherospermataceae*)

§ ***sempervirens***	CBcs WPGP
serrata	see *L. sempervirens*

Laureliopsis (*Atherospermataceae*)

philippiana	IArd NLar

Laurentia see *Isotoma*

Laurus (*Lauraceae*)

§ ***azorica***	CBcs
canariensis	see *L. azorica*
nobilis 🏆H4	Widely available
- f. ***angustifolia***	CMac CTsd EBee IDee LRHS MBlu MHer MRav NLar SAPC SEND SPoG
- 'Aurea' 🏆H4	CBcs CDul CMac EBee ELan ELon EPfP LHop LRHS MGos MHer MMuc NEgg NLar SEND SLim SLon SMad SPer SPoG SWvt WMoo
- clipped pyramid	LSRN
- 'Crispa'	MRav
- 'Sunspot' (v)	WCot
- variegated (v)	CMac SRms

Lavandula ✿ (*Lamiaceae*)

'After Midnight'	see *L.* 'Avonview'
'Alba'	see *L. angustifolia* 'Alba', *L.* × *intermedia* 'Alba'
'Alba' ambig	CWib NYoL SIde SPer
'Alexandra' PBR	MWat
§ ***angustifolia***	CArn CBar CCVT CWib EBee ELau EPfP EWTr GPoy LBuc LRHS LSRN MAsh MBri MGos MHer MHol MHoo MWat NGdn NPer NPri NYoL SDow SLim SPlb SPoG SVic XLum XSen
- 'Alba' misapplied	see *L. angustifolia* 'Blue Mountain White'
§ - 'Alba'	EPfP GPoy GQue LBuc LRHS LSRN MHer MHoo MRav MSwo NDov NYoL SBod SLon SPlb SVen WGwG WJek XSen
- 'Alba Nana'	see *L. angustifolia* 'Nana Alba'
- 'Arctic Snow'	CBcs CSev EBee EPfP LRHS LSRN MBri MHer MSwo MWat NGdn NPri NYoL SDow SFai SHil SPoG SRms WLav
- Aromatico Blue = 'Lablusa' PBR	LRHS
- Aromatico Silver = 'Lasila' **new**	LRHS
- 'Ashdown Forest'	CHab GQue LRHS MHer MHoo MLHP MNHC NYoL SBch SDow SFai SPer SRms WHoo WJek WLav
- 'Babelle' **new**	XSen
- 'Backhouse Purple'	SDow
- 'Beechwood Blue' 🏆H4	NYoL SDow WLav
- 'Belle Hélène'	XSen
- 'Betty's Blue'	SDow
- Blue Cushion = 'Lavandula Schola' PBR	LSRN MAsh NYoL SFai SPoG WLav
- Blue Ice = 'Dow3' PBR	EBee LRHS MWat NLar NWad NYoL SDow SFai SGol SLim SPoG SRms WLav
- 'Blue Lance' **new**	MHol
§ - 'Blue Mountain White'	ELMC SDow WLav
- 'Blue Rider'	LRHS NGdn NYoL WGwG WHar WLav
- Blue Scent = 'Syngablusc'	LRHS
§ - 'Bowles's Early'	NYoL
- 'Bowles's Grey'	see *L. angustifolia* 'Bowles's Early'
- 'Bowles's Variety'	see *L. angustifolia* 'Bowles's Early'
- 'Cedar Blue'	ELau MHer MHoo NYoL SDow SHDw SRms WJek WLav
- 'Coconut Ice'	ELMC NYoL WHar WLav
- 'Compacta'	SDow WLav
- 'Dwarf Blue'	ELMC EPfP LSRN NYoL SRms XSen
- 'Elizabeth'	CWCL LRHS LSRN NYoL SDow SFai SPoG WLav
- 'Ellagance Ice'	CWSG LRHS SRms
- 'Ellagance Purple'	LBuc LRHS SHil SRms
- 'Ellagance Sky'	LBMP LBuc LRHS SHil SRms
- 'Folgate'	CArn CHab CWCL ECtt ELau EPfP LSou MHer MHoo MNHC NGdn NYoL SDow SGol SRms WHoo WJek WLav WMnd XSen
- 'Fring A'	SDow
- Garden Beauty = 'Lowmar' PBR (v)	LBuc LRHS NPri SPoG
- Granny's Bouquet = 'Lavang38'	LSRN NYoL
§ - 'Hidcote' 🏆H4	Widely available
- 'Hidcote Pink'	CWCL CWib LSRN LSou MHer MHoo MRav NGdn NYoL SDow SPer SRms SWat WMnd XSen
- 'Hidcote Superior'	LBMP NGdn
- 'Imperial Gem' 🏆H4	Widely available
- 'Jean Davis'	see *L. angustifolia* 'Rosea'
- 'Lady'	MHoo NPer
- 'Lady Ann'	CWCL SDow WLav
- 'Lavenite Petite' PBR	CSev EBee LBMP LLHF LRHS LSRN NLar NYoL SDow SFai SPoG WLav
- Little Lady = 'Batlad'	CMea CSev CWSG EBee ECtt LAst LBMP LRHS LSRN MAsh MNHC MSwo NDov NLar NYoL SFai SGol SRms SWvt WLav
- Little Lottie = 'Clarmo' 🏆H4	CWCL EBee GQue LSRN MHer MHoo NYoL SDow SWvt WLav
- 'Loddon Blue' 🏆H4	EBee EPfP GQue LRHS MAsh MBri MHoo NYoL SDow SFai SHil SRms WLav
§ - 'Loddon Pink' 🏆H4	ELan EPfP GMaP LRHS MAsh MBri MHoo MMuc MRav NGdn NYoL SEND SFai SHil SRms WLav
- 'Luberon'	XSen
- 'Lullaby Blue'	SDow
- 'Lumières des Alpes'	XSen
- 'Maillette'	NGdn NYoL SDow SPet WHar WLav
- 'Matheronne'	XSen
- Melissa Lilac = 'Dow4' PBR	CBcs CHab CSBt CSev EBee LBMP LRHS LSRN MBri MGos MHer MNHC NDov NLar NWad NYoL SDow SFai SHil SRkn SRms WLav
- 'Miss Donnington'	see *L. angustifolia* 'Bowles's Early'
- 'Miss Katherine' PBR 🏆H4	CWCL EBee ECtt ELMC EPfP LRHS LSRN MAsh NLar NYoL SDow WLav
- Miss Muffet = 'Scholmis' 🏆H4	EBee LLHF NYoL SBch SDow SRms WLav
- 'Mont Ventoux'	XSen
- 'Montagne de Lure' **new**	XSen
- 'Munstead'	Widely available
§ - 'Nana Alba' 🏆H4	CArn CMea ELan EPfP GMaP GPoy LRHS MAsh MHer MHoo MWat

		NYoL SBch SDow SPer SRms SWvt WHoo WJek XSen
	- 'Nana Atropurpurea'	SDow
	- 'Nikita'	XSen
	- 'No 9'	SDow
	- 'Pacific Blue'	LRHS MBri SFai SHil
	- 'Perle de Rosée'	XSen
	- 'Peter Pan'	ECtt ELMC ELau GBuc LSRN MHer MHoo NDov NGdn NWad NYoL SBch SDow WLav
	- 'Princess Blue'	EBee ELMC ELan LRHS MAsh MHoo MWat NYoL SDow WLav
§	- 'Rosea'	Widely available
	- 'Royal Purple'	CBcs CHab EWes GQue LSou MWat NGdn NYoL SDow SFai SWvt WLav
	- 'Royal Velvet'	SDow
	- 'Saint Jean'	SDow
	- 'Siesta' **new**	SFai
	- 'Silver Blue'	XSen
	- 'Silver Mist'	CMea EPfP LRHS NYoL SRms WHer
	- 'Sophie' **new**	SFai
	- 'Thumbelina Leigh'PBR	ELMC LBMP NYoL SDow SFai
	- 'Twickel Purple'	CBcs CWCL EBee ELan EPfP LBMP LHop LRHS LSRN MHoo MNHC MRav NGdn NYoL SDow SFai SPer SRms SVen SWat SWvt WLav XSen
	- 'Walberton's Silver Edge'	see *L.* × *intermedia* Walberton's Silver Edge
	- 'Wendy Carlile' ♀H4	CSev
	aristibracteata	MHer WLav
§	'Avonview'	MHer SDow WHoo WLav
	'Ballerina'	CWCL LRHS SDow
§	'Bee Brilliant'PBR	WLav
§	'Bee Cool'PBR	MHer NYoL WLav
§	'Bee Happy'	CWCL NBir NYoL WJek WLav
	'Blue Star'	EBee EPfP LRHS NGdn WGwG
	'Bowers Beauty'	LRHS
	buchii var. ***buchii***	SDow SVen WLav
	'Bulls Cross'	WLav
	canariensis	MHer SDow SVen WLav
	× ***chaytoriae*** 'Gorgeous'	SDow
	- 'Joan Head'	XSen
	- 'Richard Gray' ♀H3-4	CArn EBee EPfP LSRN MHer MNHC NYoL SDow SIgm SLim SPet SRms WAbe WLav WMnd XSen
§	- 'Sawyers' ♀H4	Widely available
	- 'Silver Sands'	EPfP LBMP LSRN LSou NYoL SFai SPoG
	× ***christiana***	CArn LRHS NLar NPri NYoL SDow SFai SHDw SVen WJek WLav
	'Cornard Blue'	see *L.* × *chaytoriae* 'Sawyers'
	dentata	ELan GPoy MHoo MNHC MRav SBod SEND SRms WJek
§	- var. ***candicans***	MHer MNHC NYoL SDow SRms WJek WLav
	- var. ***dentata***	NYoL
	- - 'Dusky Maiden'	SDow WLav
	- - 'Ploughman's Blue'	NYoL SVen
	- - f. ***rosea***	SDow
	- - 'Royal Crown' ♀H2-3	MHer WLav
	- silver-leaved	see *L. dentata* var. *candicans*
	'Devonshire Compact'	CSBt CTsd EBee LRHS SBch SRms WJek
	'Fathead'	CBcs CWCL EBee ECtt ELan EPfP LRHS LSRN LSou MGos MHer MNHC MWat NBir NEgg NGdn NPri NYoL SCoo SDow SFai SGol SLim SPoG WJek WLav
	'Flaming Purple' **new**	LRHS
	× ***ginginsii*** 'Goodwin Creek Grey'	MHer NYoL SDow SGol SRms WGwG WLav
	'Hazel'	CEnd EPfP LRHS
	'Heavenly Blue'	EPfP
	'Helmsdale'PBR	CEnd CSBt CWCL EBee ELan EPfP GAbr GBin GMaP IKil LRHS LSRN LSou MAsh MHer MRav MWat NGdn NYoL SCoo SDow SFai SGol SLim SPer SPoG WJek
	heterophylla misapplied	see *L.* × *heterophylla* Viv. Gaston Allard Group
§	× ***heterophylla*** Viv. Gaston Allard Group	EShb WLav
	- - 'African Pride'	NYoL SVen
	'Hidcote Blue'	see *L. angustifolia* 'Hidcote'
	× ***intermedia*** 'Abrialii'	SDow
§	- 'Alba' ♀H4	CMea EPfP MHer MHoo MMuc MNHC NYoL SDow SEND SPet SVen WKif XSen
	- 'Arabian Night'	see *L.* × *intermedia* 'Impress Purple', 'Sussex'
	- 'Arabian Night' ambig.	SRms
§	- Dutch Group	CSBt CWib EPfP MNHC MRav MSwo MWat NYoL SBod SCoo SDow SFai SLim SPer SPoG SRms SWat XSen
	- 'Edelweiss'	CBar CHab CSBt EPfP LRHS MHoo MNHC MRav NEgg NGdn NYoL SDow SFai SGol SPer SPoG SRms SWvt WLav XSen
	- 'Fragrant Memories'	EPfP MHoo NYoL SDow SIde WLav
	- 'Fred Boutin'	SGol
*	- 'Futura'	XSen
	- Goldburg = 'Burgoldeen' (v)	MWat
	- 'Grappenhall' misapplied	see *L.* × *intermedia* 'Pale Pretender'
	- 'Grey Hedge'	MHoo MNHC NYoL WLav
	- 'Gros Bleu'	SDow WLav XSen
	- 'Grosso'	CArn CCVT CHab CSBt EBee ECrN ELan EPfP GMaP LPio LSRN MHer MHoo MMuc MNHC NYoL SCoo SDow SEND SFai SGol SPer SRms SWvt WHfH WJek WLav XSen
	- 'Hidcote Giant' ♀H4	CArn EPfP LRHS MBri NPer NYoL SDow SHil WKif WLav XSen
§	- 'Impress Purple'	LBuc MNHC NYoL SDow SPet WLav XSen
	- 'Jaubert'	XSen
	- 'Julien'	XSen
	- 'Lullingstone Castle'	MHoo NYoL SDow SRms WJek WLav
	- 'Nizza'	XSen
	- 'Old English' misapplied	see *L.* × *intermedia* 'Seal'
	- 'Old English'	SDow
	- Old English Group	CArn ELau MMuc MNHC NYoL SEND WHoo WJek WLav
§	- 'Pale Pretender'	CSBt GQue MHer MSwo NYoL SDow SPer SRms WJek XSen
	- 'Provence'	LRHS MHoo
§	- 'Seal'	CArn ELau GMaP MHoo MNHC NYoL SDow SRms WJek XSen
	- 'Sumian'	XSen
	- 'Super'	XSen
§	- 'Sussex' ♀H4	ELMC EPfP LRHS NYoL SDow WLav XSen
	- 'Twickel Purple'	CWib ECtt EWes LSRN MCot MHoo NLar NYoL SGol SWat WJek WMnd
§	- Walberton's Silver Edge = 'Walvera' (v)	CSBt EPfP LBuc LRHS MGos MWat NEgg SCoo SDow SFai SPoG SRms
	'Jamboree'	WLav

'Jean Davis'	see *L. angustifolia* 'Rosea'
lanata ♀H3	CArn GPoy SRms WJek WLav
§ ***latifolia***	CArn XSen
I 'Lavender Lace'	LSRN SCoo
'Loddon Pink'	see *L. angustifolia* 'Loddon Pink'
'Madrid Blue'	see *L.* 'Bee Happy'
'Madrid Purple'	see *L.* 'Bee Brilliant'
'Madrid White'	see *L.* 'Bee Cool'
'Marshwood'PBR	CTri SCoo SDow SLim
minutolii	SDow SVen
multifida	CSev LDai MHer WLav
officinalis	see *L. angustifolia*
Passionné = 'Lavsts 08'PBR	CWSG WLav
pedunculata	XSen
§ - subsp. ***pedunculata*** ♀H3-4	Widely available
- - 'James Compton'	CWib LRHS MAsh NGdn NYoL
- - 'Wine'	CBcs
- subsp. ***sampaiana*** 'Purple Emperor'	EPfP LRHS MBri NYoL SHil WLav
pinnata	CSev EPfP LPot LRHS MHer MHoo MNHC SDow
'Pretty Polly'	CBcs CSev EPfP LRHS NYoL SDow SFai SRkn WLav
'Pukehou'	EPfP LRHS SCoo SDow WLav
'Regal Splendour'PBR	CSBt CWCL EBee ECtt ELan EPfP LPio LRHS LSRN LSou MAsh MBri MGos MHer MNHC NPri NYoL SCoo SDow SFai SGol SHil SLim SPoG SRms WLav
Rocky Road = 'Fair09'PBR	LBuc LRHS LSRN NGdn NYoL SFai SRkn WLav
'Rosea'	see *L. angustifolia* 'Rosea'
rotundifolia	SDow
'Roxlea Park'	CWCL
'Russian Anna'	LSRN
'Saint Brelade'	EPfP LRHS SDow
'Silver Edge'	see *L.* × *intermedia* Walberton's Silver Edge
Silver Sands = 'Fair 14' **new**	ELMC
'Somerset Mist'	WLav
N ***spica*** nom. rejic.	see *L. angustifolia*, *L. latifolia*
- 'Hidcote Purple'	see *L. angustifolia* 'Hidcote'
stoechas ♀H3-4	CArn CBcs CDul CMea CSBt CSev EBee ELan ELau EPfP GMaP GPoy LBMP LHop LRHS LSRN MBri MNHC MRav MSwo NYoL SDow SFai SIgm SPer SPet SPlb SWvt WHar WMnd
- from Corsica	LRHS
- var. ***albiflora***	see *L. stoechas* subsp. *stoechas* f. *leucantha*
- 'Anouk'PBR	EBee EPfP LRHS NGdn SPoG
- 'Antibes' (Provençal Series)	LBMP LRHS SRms
- 'Avignon' (Provençal Series)	SRms
- 'Blueberries and Cream'	LSou
- 'Boysenberry Ruffles'PBR (Ruffles Series)	LRHS
- 'Lace'	LSRN WLav
- Lavender Lace = 'Colace'PBR	NYoL
- Lilac Wings = 'Prolil'PBR	CSev EPfP LLHF LRHS MBri SCoo SFai SHil WLav
- (Little Bee Series) Little Bee Deep Purple = 'Florvendula Deep Purple'	LBuc LRHS SHil
- - Little Bee Deep Rose = 'Florvendula Deep Rose'	LBuc LRHS SHil
- - Little Bee Lilac = 'Florvendula Lilac'	LRHS
- - Little Bee Rose = 'Florvendula Rose'	LRHS
- subsp. ***luisieri*** 'Tickled Pink'PBR	CWCL ECtt
- 'Night of Passion'	LRHS SDow
- 'Papillon'	see *L. pedunculata* subsp. *pedunculata*
- subsp. ***pedunculata***	see *L. pedunculata* subsp. *pedunculata*
- 'Purley'	SRms
- 'Raspberry Ruffles' (Ruffles Series)	MWat
- 'Rocky Red'	LSRN
- 'Silver Anouk'PBR	EBee EPfP LRHS
§ - subsp. ***stoechas*** f. ***leucantha***	CWCL CWib EPfP LRHS MSwo MWat SDow SHil SPer
- - - 'Snowman'	CBcs CSBt EPfP LRHS MAsh MHer MWat SCoo SFai SLim SPoG SWvt
- - 'Provençal'	LRHS MBri SCoo SHil
- - 'Purple Wings'	EPfP LRHS LSou MAsh SFai SLim SRkn
- - f. ***rosea***	WHar
- - - 'Kew Red'	CBcs CTri CWCL LBMP LRHS LSRN MGos MHer MNHC NHol NYoL SDow SFai SLim SRms SWvt WGwG WHar WJek WLav
- 'Victory'	LRHS SHil SPoG
- 'White Sparkler' **new**	LRHS
- 'With Love'PBR	LRHS SDow
Tiara = 'Fair 10'PBR	CSBt EPfP LRHS LSRN MBri MGos MWat NPri NYoL SCoo SDow SFai SHil SLim SPoG SRms WLav
'Van Gogh'	SDow
vera misapplied	see *L.* × *intermedia* Dutch Group
vera DC.	see *L. angustifolia*
viridis	CArn CPla ELan ELau EPfP LRHS MHer MHoo NPer SDow SRms WAbe WJek WLav
'Whero Iti'	SDow
'Willow Vale' ♀H3-4	EBee EPfP LBMP LBuc LRHS LSRN MAsh MHer NYoL SDow SFai SRms SWvt WJek
'Willowbridge Calico'PBR	NGdn NYoL WHar

Lavatera (Malvaceae)

arborea	CArn SChr SEND WHer
- 'Rosea'	see *L.* × *clementii* 'Rosea'
- 'Variegata' (v)	ELan NPer SDix SEND WCot
bicolor	see *L. maritima*
cachemiriana	NBir NPer SPhx
Chamallow = 'Inovera'PBR	EPfP LBuc LRHS LSRN SPoG
× ***clementii*** 'Barnsley'	Widely available
- 'Barnsley Baby'	EBee ELon LBuc LRHS MBri MSCN NGdn NHol NLar NPer NPri SPer SRkn SWvt
- 'Blushing Bride'	CDoC ELon EPfP LBMP LRHS LSRN MBri MGos NLar SEND SPer
- 'Bredon Springs' ♀H3-4	CDoC CDul CSBt CWSG EBee EPfP LHop LRHS LSRN MAsh MMuc MSwo MWat NGdn NLar SEND SGol SLim SPer SWvt WHar
- 'Burgundy Wine' ♀H3-4	CBcs EBee ELan EPfP EUJe LRHS MAsh MBri MGos MJak MSwo NBir NEgg NGdn NHol NLar NPer NPri SHil SLim SLon SPer SPoG SWvt WHar
- 'Candy Floss' ♀H3-4	EBee EPfP LBuc LRHS MAsh NBir NLar NPer SGol

	- 'Kew Rose'	CDoC EBee LRHS MMuc MSwo NPer SEND SLim SRms XLum
	- 'Lavender Lady'	LHop NPer SEND
	- 'Lisanne'	LRHS MSwo SGol
	- 'Mary Hope'	EPfP LRHS MAsh MBri SHil
	- Memories = 'Stelav'	EBee LRHS LSRN NLar
	- 'Pavlova'	CExl
§	- 'Rosea' 🏆H3-4	CBcs CMac CWSG EBee ECrN EPfP LAst LRHS LSRN MAsh MGos MWat NBir NEgg NPri NSoo SBod SGol SHil SLon SPer SPoG SWvt WHar
§	- 'Wembdon Variegated' (v)	NPer
	'Grey Beauty'	LHop
§	***maritima*** 🏆H2-3	CDoC CExl CMac EBee ECtt ELan EPfP LHop LRHS MCot NPri SEND SPer SRkn SWvt WKif WSHC
	- 'Princesse de Lignes'	XLum
N	***olbia***	SPlb SRms XSen
	- 'Eye Catcher'	CSBt EBee IVic LRHS MSwo NLar SPer SPoG WHar
	- 'Lilac Lady'	EBee ECrN ELan EPfP LRHS MGos NSoo SLim SPer WHar WKif
§	- 'Pink Frills'	SWvt WCot
	'Peppermint Ice'	see *L. thuringiaca* 'Ice Cool'
	'Pink Frills'	see *L. olbia* 'Pink Frills'
	'Rosea'	see *L.* × *clementii* 'Rosea'
	'Sweet Dreams'PBR	LBuc NLar NSoo
N	***thuringiaca***	GCal NNor
	- 'First Light'	EWll SPhx
§	- 'Ice Cool'	SWvt WKif
	- Red Rum = 'Rigrum'PBR	CMac CSBt EBee EPfP LBuc LLHF LRHS LSRN MAsh MGos MHol NEgg NLar NPri SEND SHar SLim SPoG SWvt
	'Variegata'	see *L.* × *clementii* 'Wembdon Variegated'
	'White Angel'PBR	GBin NLar
	'White Satin'PBR	NHol NLar

Lecanthus (*Urticaceae*)

	peduncularis	CHEx

Ledebouria (*Asparagaceae*)

	adlamii	see *L. cooperi*
	concolor misapplied	see *L. socialis*
§	***cooperi***	CSev ECho ELan EPri LEdu LHop LRHS SBch WPGP
	ovalifolia	ECho
§	***socialis***	CSev ECho LToo MCot SBHP SBch
	violacea	see *L. socialis*

Ledum see *Rhododendron*

Leiophyllum (*Ericaceae*)

	buxifolium 🏆H4	EPfP NLar SSpi WThu
	- var. ***hugeri***	GBin
	- 'Maryfield'	WAbe

Lembotropis see *Cytisus*

Lemna (*Araceae*)

	gibba	NPer
	minor	CWat MSKA NPer SWat
	trisulca	CWat EHon MSKA NPer SWat

lemon see *Citrus limon*

lemon balm see *Melissa officinalis*

lemon grass see *Cymbopogon citratus*

lemon verbena see *Aloysia citrodora*

Leonotis (*Lamiaceae*)

	leonitis	see *L. ocymifolia*
	leonurus	CCCN CDTJ CHGN CHll ECre EPfP EShb EWes LRHS MNrw SLim SLon SMad SMrm SPlb SPoG XLum
	- var. ***albiflora***	CCCN
	nepetifolia	CHll
	- var. ***nepetifolia*** 'Staircase'	CCCN NGBl SPav
§	***ocymifolia***	CCCN CExl LSou WPGP
	- var. ***raineriana***	CHll CSpe

Leontice (*Berberidaceae*)

	albertii	see *Gymnospermium albertii*

Leontochir (*Alstroemeriaceae*)

	ovallei	CCCN

Leontodon (*Asteraceae*)

	autumnalis	CHab NMir
	hispidus	CHab NMir
§	***rigens***	CSpe EBee ELan LRHS MHer MMuc NBid NBir SDix SMrm WMoo
	- B&SWJ 12527 **new**	WCru
	- 'Girandole'	see *L. rigens*

Leontopodium (*Asteraceae*)

	alpinum	CTri CWib ECho EPfP GAbr LRHS MAsh MWat SPlb SPoG SRms XLum
	- 'Everest'	EDAr
	- 'Mignon'	ECho EWes GMaP WAbe WHoo
	coreanum	GKev
	nanum	EPot
§	***ochroleucum*** var. ***campestre***	NLar
	palibinianum	see *L. ochroleucum* var. *campestre*
	souliei	XLum

Leonurus (*Lamiaceae*)

	artemisia	see *L. japonicus*
	cardiaca	CArn GPoy MHer MHoo MNHC SIde SRms WHfH XSen
	- 'Crispa'	SMad
§	***japonicus***	CArn MMuc SHar
	macranthus	EFEx
	- var. ***alba***	EFEx
	sibiricus misapplied	see *L. japonicus*
	sibiricus L.	CArn GCal MHoo
	turkestanicus	EBee

Leopoldia (*Asparagaceae*)

	comosa	see *Muscari comosum*
	tenuiflora	see *Muscari tenuiflorum*

Lepechinia (*Lamiaceae*)

	bella	CSpe SDys
	chamaedryoides	CExl CHll CSpe
	floribunda	CSev
	hastata	CCse CFil CSpe SBHP WJek WPGP WWlt
	salviae	EPri WHil

Lepidium (*Brassicaceae*)

	campestre	CArn CHab

latifolium	CArn LEdu

Lepidothamnus (*Podocarpaceae*)

§ ***laxifolius***	WThu

Lepidozamia (*Zamiaceae*)

peroffskyana	CBrP

Leptinella (*Asteraceae*)

atrata subsp. ***luteola***	EPfP
'County Park'	ECho ECou EDAr
dendyi	ECho ECou EWes MHer NSla WIce
dioica	GBin
filicula	ECou
hispida	see *Cotula hispida* (DC.) Harv.
§ ***minor***	WMoo
§ ***potentillina***	CTri ECho EHoe GBin MBNS NLar SRms WMoo XLum
§ ***pyrethrifolia***	ECho EDAr
- 'Macabe'	ECou
§ ***rotundata***	ECou
§ ***squalida***	ECho EPPr GBin MWat NLar NSti WMoo
§ - 'Platt's Black'	EBee ECho EDAr EHoe EPPr EShb EWes GAbr GBin GKev IBoy LEdu MSCN NLar NSti SBch SMad SPet SWvt WMoo WWFP XLum

Leptocodon (*Campanulaceae*)

gracilis	CSpe EWld
- HWJK 2155	WCru

Leptodactylon (*Polemoniaceae*)

§ ***californicum***	CPBP

Leptospermum ✿ (*Myrtaceae*)

argenteum	CBcs
citratum	see *L. petersonii*
'Confetti'	ECou
'Copper Glow' new	ECou
'Copper Sheen'	CBcs
'County Park Blush'	ECou
cunninghamii	see *L. myrtifolium*
'Electric Red' (Galaxy Series)	CAbb CEnd LRHS SLim
ericoides	see *Kunzea ericoides*
flavescens misapplied	see *L. glaucescens*
flavescens Sm.	see *L. polygalifolium*
§ ***glaucescens***	ECou SPlb
§ ***grandiflorum***	ELan EPfP SSpi SVen WSHC
grandifolium	EBee ECou LRHS
'Havering Hardy'	ECou
humifusum	see *L. rupestre*
juniperinum	SPlb
'Karo Pearl Star'	CBcs
'Karo Spectrobay'[PBR]	CBcs
laevigatum	SVen
- 'Yarrum'	ECou
§ ***lanigerum***	CBcs CExl CMHG CTri CTsd ECou EPfP SPlb SVen
- 'Cunninghamii'	see *L. myrtifolium*
- 'Wellington'	ECou
liversidgei	ECou SPlb
minutifolium	ECou
morrisonii	ECou
§ ***myrtifolium***	CMac CTri ECou EWes SPer
- 'Newnes Forest'	ECou
myrtifolium × ***scoparium***	ECou
nitidum	CBcs ECou SPlb
obovatum	CTsd EBee GGal
§ ***petersonii***	CArn ECou EShb MHer MOWG
- 'Chlorinda'	ECou
phylicoides	see *Kunzea ericoides*
'Pink Surprise'	ECou MOWG
§ ***polygalifolium***	CBcs ECou SPlb
prostratum	see *L. rupestre*
pubescens	see *L. lanigerum*
'Red Cascade'	SWvt
rodwayanum	see *L. grandiflorum*
rotundifolium	ECou SPlb
§ ***rupestre*** ♀^{H4}	CDoC CTri ECou SPlb SVen WSHC
rupestre × ***scoparium***	ECou
scoparium	CArn CHel CTsd ECou ELau GPoy MNHC SPlb SVen WHfH WJek
- 'Adrianne'	EPfP LRHS MRav
- 'Appleblossom'	CEnd EPfP SGol SLim
- 'Autumn Glory'	EBee SLim
- 'Blossom' (d)	CBcs CMac ECou LRHS MOWG
- 'Burgundy Queen' (d)	CBcs CMac CSBt EUJe
- 'Chapmanii'	CMHG
- 'Coral Candy'	CBcs LRHS MMuc SEND
- 'County Park Pink'	ECou
- 'County Park Red'	ECou
- 'Crimson Glory' (d)	CSBt
- 'Essex'	ECou
- 'Gaiety Girl' (d)	CSBt
- var. ***incanum*** 'Keatleyi' ♀^{H3}	MOWG
- 'Jubilee' (d)	CMac
- 'Kerry'	CAbP
- 'Lady Bird'	ECou
- 'Leonard Wilson' (d)	CTri
- 'Martini'	CAbb CBcs CDoC CMac CSBt EBee EPfP LRHS SEND
- (Nanum Group) 'Kea'	ECou MHer MRav
- - 'Kiwi' ♀^{H3}	CAbP CAbb CBcs CCCN CDoC CHel CSBt CWSG EBee ECou ELan ELon EPfP EUJe EWes LRHS MAsh SEND SLim SLon
- - 'Nanum'	ECou
- - 'Tui'	CSBt
- 'Nichollsii' ♀^{H3}	SVen WSHC
- 'Nichollsii Nanum' ♀$^{H2-3}$	WAbe WPat WThu
- 'Pink Cascade'	CAbb CBcs CMac CTri CWib EBee LRHS SLim
- 'Pink Damask'	IVic SLim SWvt
- 'Pink Falls'	ECou
- 'Pink Frills'	ECou
- 'Pink Splash'	ECou
- var. ***prostratum*** hort.	see *L. rupestre*
- 'Red Damask' (d) ♀^{H3}	Widely available
- 'Red Falls'	CExl ECou
- 'Roseum'	MRav
* - 'Ruby Wedding'	ELan EPfP LRHS LSRN MAsh SLon SPoG
- 'Snow Flurry'	EBee EPfP LRHS SGol SLim SVen
- 'Sunraysia'	CHel
- 'Wingletye'	ECou
- 'Winter Cheer' (d)	EPfP LRHS SGol
- 'Wiri Joan' (d)	CBcs CHel
- 'Wiri Linda'	CAbb CBcs CMac
- 'Zeehan'	ECou
sericeum	MOWG
'Silver Sheen' ♀^{H3}	CAbb CDoC CEnd CHel EBee ECou ECre ELan EPfP LHop LRHS MAsh NLar SPlb SPoG SVen WPGP WPat
'Snow Column'	ECou
'Sugar Candy'	CEnd

turbinatum	ECou
- 'Thunder Cloud'	ECou
'Wellington Dwarf'	ECou

Lespedeza (Papilionaceae)

bicolor	CCCN CSpe EBee LRHS MHer MMuc SEND SKHP WCFE WGob WSHC
buergeri	EPfP LRHS MMHG NLar WSHC
japonica	SPlb
thunbergii ♀H4	CBcs CDul CHel CHll CSpe CWib EBee ELan EPfP EPri IVic LHop LRHS MAsh MBlu MBri MGos MOWG SBod SLon SMad SPer SPoG SSpi SSta WCFE WPGP WSHC
- 'Albiflora'	CAbP EBee LRHS SPer WPGP
- 'Avalanche'	NLar
- 'Edo-shibori'	NLar
- 'Summer Beauty'	CBcs EPfP LRHS MGos
- 'White Fountain'	EPfP LRHS SChF SKHP SPoG
tiliifolia	see *Desmodium elegans*

Lesquerella (Brassicaceae)

rubicundula	GKev

Lessertia (Papilionaceae)

diffusa **new**	CPBP

Leucadendron (Proteaceae)

argenteum	CBcs CCCN CHEx EAmu SPlb
daphnoides	SPlb
discolor	SPlb
eucalyptifolium	SPlb
'Inca Gold'	MOWG
laureolum	CCCN
'Safari Sunset'	CBcs CCCN CDoC CHel SBig
salicifolium	SPlb
salignum	CCCN
- 'Fireglow'	CDoC
strobilinum	CDoC

Leucaena (Mimosaceae)

leucocephala	SPlb

Leucanthemella (Asteraceae)

§ ***serotina*** ♀H4	Widely available
- 'Herbststern'	IMou NLar

Leucanthemopsis (Asteraceae)

§ ***alpina***	ECho
hosmariensis	see *Rhodanthemum hosmariense*

Leucanthemum ✿ (Asteraceae)

'Angel'	NPri WGrn
atlanticum	see *Rhodanthemum atlanticum*
catananche	see *Rhodanthemum catananche*
graminifolium	EPfP LRHS
hosmariense	see *Rhodanthemum hosmariense*
mawii	see *Rhodanthemum gayanum*
maximum misapplied	see *L.* × *superbum*
§ ***maximum*** (Ramond) DC.	NBro NPer
- ***uliginosum***	see *Leucanthemella serotina*
nipponicum	see *Nipponanthemum nipponicum*
'Osiris Neige'	ECtt MAvo
'Real Galaxy'	LBuc LRHS
'Sante'	CCVN NPri
'Sunshine Peach'	CFis SRot WGor
§ × ***superbum***	CMac GAbr IBoy MHer MLHP MMuc SEND WBrk
- 'Aglaia' (d) ♀H4	Widely available
- 'Alaska'	CAni CExl CTsd EBee EPfP IBoy LAst LHop LRHS MCot NGdn NLar SPer SWvt WWEG XLum
- 'Amelia'	NBre NLar SRGP
- 'Andernach'	CAni
- 'Anita Allen' (d)	CAni CElw CPrp EBee ECtt MAvo WCot WWEG
- 'Anna Camilla'	CAni
- 'Antwerp Star'	NBre NLar WBrk
- 'Banana Cream' **new**	CCVN CMea MAsh NPri SPoG STPC
- 'Banwell'	CAni
- 'Barbara Bush' (v/d)	NBir SWvt
§ - 'Beauté Nivelloise'	CAni CCVN CElw CHVG COIW CPrp CWCL EBee ECtt EPfP GBin IPot LRHS MAvo NBre NCGa NLar SMad SPoG SRms SWat WPtf WWEG
- 'Becky'	CCse CMac EBee ELan ELon EWes GBin LLHF LRHS LSRN LSou NBre NLar NPro SRGP WCAu WWEG
- 'Bishopstone'	CAni EBee ECtt ELan LBMP LEdu LLHF MSpe NCGa SMrm WWEG
- 'Brightside'	CAby EBee ELan ELon GQue LRHS MWat WMoo
- Broadway Lights = 'Leumayel' PBR	ECtt EPfP GBin IBoy LBMP LRHS MAsh MAvo MBri MRav NBir NPnk SHil SPoG WCAu WCFE WGrn WHil WWEG
- 'Christine Hagemann'	CAni CElw CPrp ECtt EWes GBin IPot MAvo MRav NCGa NLar SHar WCFE WCot WWEG
- 'Cobham Gold' (d)	CAni CWCL NBre NOrc
- 'Coconut Ice'	WWEG
- 'Colwall'	CAni WWEG
- 'Crazy Daisy'	CAni CTri CWib EBee ECtt LRHS NLar SMrm SRot SWvt
- 'Crazy Daisy Butterfly'	LAst
- 'Devon Mist'	CAni
- 'Droitwich Beauty'	CAni CPrp ECtt LLHF MAvo WCFE WHoo WWEG
- 'Duchess of Abercorn'	CAni
- 'Dwarf Snow Lady'	NBre NLar
- 'Easton Lady'	CAni
- 'Eclipse'	CAni MAvo
- 'Edgebrook Giant'	CAni WHil WWEG
- 'Edward VII'	CAni
- 'Eisstern'	CDes EBee LEdu MAvo NCGa
- 'Elworthy Sparkler'	CElw MAvo WWEG
- 'Engelina' **new**	NLar
- 'Esther Read' (d)	CWCL ECtt ELan EPfP GBin GMaP LHop LRHS LSRN MBel MBri MMuc NBro NEgg NLar SPer SPoG SRGP SRms SWat SWvt WCot WMnd WWEG
§ - 'Everest'	CAni SRms WWEG
- 'Exhibition'	NBre WWEG
- 'Fiona Coghill' (d)	CAni CElw CHVG CPrp CWGN EBee ECtt EPfP GBin GBuc IBoy LBMP LHop LRHS LSou MBri MNrw MSpe NBir NCGa NEgg NGdn NLar NPnk WCot WHoo WWEG
- 'Firnglanz'	CAni GBin WWEG
- 'Flore Pleno' (d)	SPlb
- 'Goldrausch' PBR	Widely available
- 'Gruppenstolz'	CAni
- 'H. Seibert'	CAni CPrp MArl MAvo WWEG
- 'Harry'	CAni
- 'Highland White Dream' PBR	LRHS

	- 'Horace Read' (d)	CAni CElw CPrp ECtt NBir SBch SWvt WWEG
	- 'Jennifer Read'	CAni CPrp MAvo WCFE WWEG
§	- 'John Murray' (d)	CAni EWes NBir NWsh SMrm WCot WWEG
	- 'Lacrosse' new	MAvo MBri SHil
	- 'Laspider' new	STPC
	- 'Little Miss Muffet'	CSBt CWGN EBee ECtt LAst LLHF LRHS LSou MAvo MBNS NCGa NWad WWEG
	- 'Little Princess'	see *L.* × *superbum* 'Silberprinzesschen'
	- 'Majestic'	CAni
	- 'Manhattan'	CAni CCse EBee EWes GBin LRHS NBre
	- 'Margaretchen'	CAni EBee MAvo WWEG
	- 'Marion Bilsland'	CAni MAvo MSpe NCGa NChi WBrk
	- 'Marion Collyer'	CAni
	- 'Mayfield Giant'	CAni CTri
	- 'Mount Everest'	see *L.* × *superbum* 'Everest'
	- 'Octopus'	CAni EBee MAvo WBrk
	- 'Old Court'	see *L.* × *superbum* 'Beauté Nivelloise'
	- 'Paladin'^{PBR}	ECtt GBin IPot LRHS SHar
	- 'Phyllis Smith'	CAby CAni COIW EBee ECtt ELan LSRN MAvo MHer MRav MSCN MSpe NCGa NGdn SMad SMrm SPer SPoG WBrk WCAu WCot WMoo WWEG
	- 'Polaris'	EBee MBNS NBre WMoo XLum
	- 'Rags and Tatters'	CAni ECtt EWes MAvo WWEG
	- 'Schwabengruss'	CAni
	- 'Shaggy'	see *L.* × *superbum* 'Beauté Nivelloise'
§	- 'Silberprinzesschen'	CAni CSBt EBee ELon EPfP GJos LPot LRHS NEgg NPri SPlb SRms WHar WMoo WRHF WWEG XLum
	- 'Silver Spoon'	EPfP LRHS
	- 'Snehurka'	CAni LLHF LRHS LSou MAvo WCot WWEG
	- 'Snow Lady'	CAby LRHS NEgg NPer NPri SRms
	- 'Snowcap'	CHid EPfP LRHS MBri MRav NEgg NGdn SBea SPer SPoG SWvt
	- 'Snowdrift'	CAni MAvo NBre NLar WCot WWEG
	- 'Snowstorm'	MAvo
§	- 'Sonnenschein'	Widely available
	- 'Starburst' (d)	ELan SRms
	- 'Stina'	EBee MAvo WWEG
	- 'Summer Snowball'	see *L.* × *superbum* 'John Murray'
	- 'Sunny Killin'	CAni
	- 'Sunny Side Up'^{PBR}	CCVN CHVG CWCL EBee ECtt LHop LRHS MBri NCGa NLar NPnk SHil SMrm SRot WWEG
	- Sunshine	see *L.* × *superbum* 'Sonnenschein'
	- 'T.E. Killin' (d) ♀^{H4}	CPrp EBee ECtt EPfP GBin GBuc LRHS MBri MRav MWat SPoG WCot WHoo WWEG WWlt
	- 'Victorian Secret'	ECtt GBin LBuc LRHS MAsh NLar
	- 'White Iceberg' (d)	CAni
	- White Mountain = 'Gfleuwhmtn' new	NPri STPC
	- 'White Tutu' new	MAvo
	- 'Wirral Pride'	CAni CCVN EBee ELon EPfP MAvo WBrk WMnd WWEG
	- 'Wirral Supreme' (d) ♀^{H4}	CAni CBcs CMac CPrp CSBt CTsd EBee ECtt ELan EPfP GAbr GBBs GMaP IBoy LHop LRHS LSou MBri MNrw MRav MWat NBir SMad SPer SRms SWat SWvt WBrk WMnd WWEG
	'Tizi-n-Test'	see *Rhodanthemum catananche* 'Tizi-n-Test'
§	***vulgare***	CArn CHab CMac EPfP EShb MHer MNHC NMir SEND SIde WHer WJek WMoo WOut WSFF WShi XLum
	- 'Filigran'	EBee EHyd EShb LRHS
§	- 'Maikönigin'	LHop NLar WHrl XLum
	- May Queen	see *L. vulgare* 'Maikönigin'
	- 'Sunny'	CBre EWes
	'White Knight'	LRHS NBre

Leucochrysum (*Asteraceae*)

albicans subsp. ***alpinum***	GKev

Leucocoryne (*Alliaceae*)

	alliacea	ECho
	'Andes'	CCCN ECho
	'Caravelle'	ECho
	coronata new	SPlb
	'Dione' new	ECho SDeJ
	hybrids	CGrW ECho
	ixioides	ECho
*	- ***alba***	ECho
	- 'Blue Ocean'	ECho SDeJ
	purpurea ♀^{H1}	CGrW ECho
	'Spotlight' new	ECho
	'Sunny Stripe' new	ECho
	'White Dream' new	ECho

Leucogenes (*Asteraceae*)

grandiceps	NSla WAbe
leontopodium	NSla WAbe WIce
tarahaoa	WAbe

Leucogenes × *Raoulia* see × *Leucoraoulia*

Leucojum ✿ (*Amaryllidaceae*)

aestivum	CBcs CTri EBee ECGP ECho EPfP GCal ITim LHop MCot NChi NEgg NHol SEND SRms WBor WCot WShi
- 'Gravetye Giant' ♀^{H4}	Widely available
- var. ***pulchellum*** new	CAvo
autumnale	see *Acis autumnalis*
roseum	see *Acis rosea*
tingitanum	see *Acis tingitana*
trichophyllum	see *Acis trichophylla*
valentinum	see *Acis valentina*
vernum ♀^{H4}	CAvo CBro CExl CHel CHid ECho ELan EPfP EPot GBuc GCal GKev LHop MNrw NBir NEgg NHol NPol SDeJ SRms WCot WHer WHil WHoo WShi
- var. ***carpathicum***	CLAP ECho
- var. ***vagneri***	CLAP IGor SDys

Leucophysalis (*Solanaceae*)

sinense BWJ 8093	LHop WCru

Leucophyta (*Asteraceae*)

§	***brownii***	WCot
	- 'Challenge'	EDAr
	- 'Silver Sand'	LAst LSou

Leucopogon (*Ericaceae*)

§	***colensoi***	EBee WThu
	ericoides	GKev

§ ***fraseri***	ECou NHar WThu
§ ***parviflorus***	ECou

× *Leucoraoulia* (*Asteraceae*)

§ ***loganii***	WAbe

Leucosceptrum (*Lamiaceae*)

canum	CExl
- GWJ 9424	WCru
japonicum B&SWJ 10804	WCru
- B&SWJ 10981	WCru
stellipilum	IMou
var. ***formosanum***	
- - B&SWJ 1926	WCru
- - RWJ 9907	SBrt WCru
- var. ***tosaense***	WCru
B&SWJ 8892	

Leucospermum (*Proteaceae*)

conocarpodendron	EBee
'Mardi Gras Ribbons' **new**	
glabrum	SPlb
'Scarlet Ribbon'	CCCN

Leucothoe (*Ericaceae*)

axillaris 'Curly Red'[PBR]	CDoC CWSG ELan EPfP IVic LBuc LRHS MGos MJak MPkF NLar NPnk NSoo SLim SLon SPoG SWvt
Carinella = 'Zebekot'	EPfP LRHS NLar SPoG
davisiae	NLar
§ ***fontanesiana*** ♀H4	CMCN CMac EPfP GGal GKev
- 'Rainbow' (v)	CBcs CDoC CDul CMac CWib EBee ELan EPfP LRHS MAsh MGos NEgg NLar NPnk NPri SGol SHil SLim SPad SPer SPoG SRms SSta SWvt WHar WHil WMoo
- 'Rollissonii' ♀H4	MRav SRms
- Whitewater = 'Howw'[PBR] (v)	LRHS MPkF NPri
keiskei	EPfP
- 'Royal Ruby'	EBee EPfP LRHS MPkF NEgg NLar NSoo SGol SHil SLim SPoG WMoo
Lovita = 'Zebonard'	EPfP LRHS MBri MRav NLar SCoo
Red Lips = 'Lipsbolwi'[PBR]	CDoC ELan EPfP IVic
Scarletta = 'Zeblid'	Widely available
walteri	see *L. fontanesiana*

Leuzea (*Asteraceae*)

centaureoides	see *Stemmacantha centaureoides*

Levisticum (*Apiaceae*)

officinale	CArn CHby CPrp CSev ELau EPfP GAbr GPoy LEdu MHer MHoo MMuc MNHC NPri SDix SEND SIde SPlb SRms SVic SWat WHer WHfH WJek

Lewisia ✿ (*Portulacaceae*)

'Archangel'	NRya
Ashwood Carousel hybrids	CPBP CTri ECho MAsh NHar
Birch strain	CBcs ECho ELan
brachycalyx ♀H2	CPBP ECho EWes LLHF NHar
brachycalyx* × *cotyledon **new**	LLHF
cantelovii	CWCL MAsh
columbiana	ECho MAsh
- subsp. ***columbiana***	GKev
- subsp. ***rupicola***	ITim LLHF
'Constant Comment'	SEND
cotyledon ♀H4	CWCL ECho EHyd GKev ITim LLHF LRHS NSla WIce
- f. ***alba*** 'Snowstorm'	LLHF
- 'Ashwood Ruby'	MAsh
- Ashwood strain	ECho EPfP EWes LRHS MAsh SRms WGor WOld
- 'Bright Eyes'	GKev
- var. ***cotyledon***	LLHF
- double-flowered (d)	GKev
- 'Fransi'	NLar
- var. ***howellii***	LLHF
- hybrid	ECho EPot LHop SPoG WGor
- 'John's Special'	MAsh
- magenta-flowered	ECho
§ - 'Regenbogen'	WGor
- Sunset Group ♀H4	CHel ECho EPfP LAst MHer NLar WHar WNew
'George Henley'	ECho EPfP EWes LLHF MAsh NRya WAbe WGor
'Little Mango' **new**	EDAr
'Little Peach'	CPBP ECho EDAr EPot GBin GKev
'Little Plum'	CMea CPBP ECho EDAr EPot ITim LBMP NLar NRya WGor WHoo
§ ***longipetala***	ECho
§ ***nevadensis***	ECho EDAr EPot ITim LRHS NRya WHoo
I - 'Alba'	GKev
- ***bernardina***	see *L. nevadensis*
- 'Rosea'	NRya NSla
oppositifolia 'Richeyi'	GKev
pygmaea	CPBP CWCL ECho EWes ITim LRHS MAsh MHer NBir NRya NSla XLum
- subsp. ***longipetala***	see *L. longipetala*
pygmaea* × *rediviva **new**	LLHF
Rainbow mixture	see *L. cotyledon* 'Regenbogen'
'Rawreth'	LLHF WAbe
rediviva	CPBP EWes GKev LLHF
- subsp. ***minor***	EPot
'Trevosia'	MAsh
tweedyi ♀H2	ECho EHyd EPfP EPot LHop LRHS MAsh NRya WAbe
- 'Alba'	WAbe
- 'Rosea'	ECho EHyd EPot LHop LRHS WAbe

Leycesteria (*Caprifoliaceae*)

crocothyrsos	CBcs CHEx CWib ELan EPfP NLar
formosa ♀H4	Widely available
- brown-stemmed	IFoB
- 'Gold Leaf'	WHil
- Golden Lanterns = 'Notbruce'[PBR]	CBcs CDoC CMac CSBt EBee ELan EPfP LBuc LRHS LSRN MAsh MBri MGos MMHG MMuc MPkF NEgg NLar SCoo SHil SLim SPoG SWvt WMoo
- 'Golden Pheasant' (v)	EHoe
- from Longstock **new**	SLon
- 'Lydia'	EBee
- 'Purple Rain'	EBee EWes GBin LRHS NLar SHil SLim

Leymus (*Poaceae*)

from Falkland Islands	EPPr
§ ***arenarius***	Widely available
cinereus	WCot
hispidus	see *Elymus hispidus*

Lhotzkya see *Calytrix*

Liatris (*Asteraceae*)

aspera	NLBP SPhx
cylindracea	SPhx
elegans	EBee EPfP NBre NLBP NLar SPlb
ligulistylis	EBee LRHS NLBP SBea SPhx
mucronata	NLBP NLar
punctata	LRHS
pycnostachya	EBee NLBP NLar SRms
scariosa 'Alba'	SMrm
§ ***spicata***	Widely available
- 'Alba'	CHel CMac CPrp CSBt CSpe ECtt ELan EPfP GKev LAst LEdu LSRN MNFA MNrw MSCN NGdn NLar NPri NSoo SPer SPet SPlb XLum
- ***callilepis***	see *L. spicata*
- 'Floristan Violett'	CHel CTri EBee EPfP GMaP LBMP LRHS MBel MHer MJak MWhi NEgg NLBP NLar SCoo SPlb SPoG SWvt WGwG WMnd WMoo WWEG XLum
- 'Floristan Weiss'	CExl CHel CTri EPPr EPfP ERCP GMaP LRHS MBel MHer MRav MWhi NCGa NDov NLar SDeJ SMrm SPoG SWvt WGwG WMnd WMoo WWEG
- Goblin	see *L. spicata* 'Kobold'
§ - 'Kobold'	Widely available
squarrosa	LRHS SPhx

Libanotis (*Umbelliferae*)

montana	see *Seseli libanotis*

Libertia ✿ (*Iridaceae*)

'Amazing Grace'	CDes EBee GCal
'Ballyrogan Blue'	CDes
* ***breunioides***	CDes CExl WPGP
caerulescens	CCCN CExl CHel CMac COIW CTsd ECho EPfP EShb EWll GBBs LRHS NBir NCGa SMad SMrm SPer WMoo
chilensis	see *L. formosa*
elegans	CExl EBee
§ ***formosa***	CBcs CBro CCVN CElw CExl CHel CHid CTri ECho ELan GCal GCra GGal LRHS NChi NSti SAPC SEND SPer SRms SWvt WHer WKif
- brown-stemmed	IFoB
grandiflora ♀H4	Widely available
'Highlander'	ELon LRHS MHol
ixioides	CBcs ECho ECou LEdu WPGP WRHF WSpi
- 'Goldfinger' (v)	Widely available
- hybrid	SDix
- 'Tricolor'	CHel LDai MRav WMoo
ixioides × ***peregrinans***	WSpi
'Nelson Dwarf'	GCal
paniculata	CExl
peregrinans	Widely available
- 'Gold Leaf'	CBcs CCCN CElw CJun CPrp CSpe CTri CTsd EPfP GBuc LAst LHop LRHS NOak SHil SMad SPoG SWvt
- 'Gold Stripe'	LRHS SPad
* ***procera***	CCon CDes CSpe EBee EPfP IVic LEdu LRHS SKHP WKif WPGP WSHC
'Red Devil' **new**	MHol
sessiliflora	CExl NBir
- RB 94073	SMad
'Taupo Blaze'	CBcs CMac EBee LRHS LSRN LSou SKHP SLon SPoG
'Taupo Sunset'PBR	CCCN CExl ELon EPfP EWes LAst LRHS LSou MBNS MPkF NOak NPnk NSoo SKHP SWvt WSpi
tricococca HCM 98.089	WPGP

Libocedrus (*Cupressaceae*)

chilensis	see *Austrocedrus chilensis*
decurrens	see *Calocedrus decurrens*

Libonia see *Justicia*

Ligularia ✿ (*Asteraceae*)

amplexicaulis CC 6829 **new**	GKev
'Britt Marie Crawford'PBR	Widely available
calthifolia	EBee
clivorum	see *L. dentata*
§ ***dentata***	CRow ECtt GGal NBro NLar SBea SRms SWat
- 'Dark Beauty'	MWhi NBre
- dark-leaved	WWEG
- 'Desdemona' ♀H4	Widely available
- 'Enkelrig'	EBee
- 'Midnight Lady'	EHyd ELan LAst MHol NHol NLar SPad WWEG
- 'Orange Princess'	NPer
- 'Osiris Fantaisie' (v)	CAbP CExl ECtt EWes GBee LLHF LPot MAsh MAvo MHol MNrw MWts NLar NMyG NPnk NSti SMad SPoG WBor WCot WPnP WWEG
- 'Othello'	CCon CHel CRow EBee ECtt EHon EPfP EShb LRHS MAsh NBid NCGa NEgg NGdn NLar NWad SMad SPet SPoG SWat SWvt WWEG WWlt
- 'Twilight'	CBct ECtt MBNS
§ ***fischeri***	LEdu NBre
- B&SWJ 2570	WCru
- B&SWJ 4381	WCru
- B&SWJ 4478	WCru
- B&SWJ 5653	WCru
- B&SWJ 8802	WCru
- var. ***megalorhiza*** 'Cheju Charmer'	ELon LEdu WCru WWEG
'Franz Marc'	GCal
'Gold Torch'	CBct ECtt NLar
§ 'Gregynog Gold' ♀H4	ECtt ELan EPfP GAbr GMaP LRHS MRav MWhi NBro NLar NOrc SPer WWEG WWlt
× ***hessei***	GMaP MMuc NLar SWat
hodgsonii	CKno EPPr LEdu LRHS MRav
- B&SWJ 10855	WCru
intermedia B&SWJ 606a	WCru
japonica	CLAP CRow GCra LEdu LRHS MWhi NLar WCot
- B&SWJ 2883	WCru
- 'Rising Sun'	CExl CHel CLAP NLar WCru
'Laternchen'PBR	IBal MBri NLar
'Little Rocket'PBR	CBct CExl CHel ECtt LLWG MBNS MBri MPie MWts NBro NGdn NLar WHil
macrophylla	LRHS
'Osiris Café Noir'	CAbb EBee ECtt IPot NLar WHil
'Osiris Pistache' (v)	EBee ECtt
× ***palmatiloba***	see *L.* × *yoshizoeana* 'Palmatiloba'
§ ***przewalskii*** ♀H4	Widely available
- 'Dragon's Breath'	ECtt
- 'Light Fingered'	NBre

sibirica	CSam EShb GAbr LRHS NLar WMoo WWEG
- B&SWJ 4383	WCru
- B&SWJ 5806	WCru
- B&SWJ 5841	WCru
- var. ***speciosa***	see *L. fischeri*
smithii	see *Senecio smithii*
speciosa	see *L. fischeri*
stenocephala	EBee LRHS MCot NBro NLar SHar SWat XLum
'Sungold'	CMac CSam ECtt LRHS NCGa NGdn
tangutica	see *Sinacalia tangutica*
'The Rocket' 🏆H4	Widely available
tussilaginea	see *Farfugium japonicum*
- 'Aureo-maculata'	see *Farfugium japonicum* 'Aureomaculatum'
veitchiana	CCon CRow CSam EPfP GCal GKev LEdu LRHS NCGa SWat
vorobievii	GAbr GCal NLar
'Weihenstephan'	GCal
wilsoniana	CDoy CRow ECtt LLWG LRHS MMuc MRav NBre SEND SWat
§ × ***yoshizoeana*** 'Palmatiloba'	CHEx ELan ELon EWes GBee GCal LEdu LRHS MRav SPhx SWat WWEG
'Zepter'	CBct CHel ECtt EUJe GBuc GCal GQue IPot LLWG MBNS MWhi MWts NEgg NLar NWad WCot WWEG

Ligusticum (*Apiaceae*)

hultenii	SPhx
lucidum	CMCN EBee EPfP IVic LEdu SPhx WPGP
- 'Curley Whirley' **new**	SPoG
porteri	CArn
§ ***scoticum***	CArn CHid EBee EShb EWTr EWes GPoy LEdu LHop LPio MHer MHoo SRms WHrl WJek WPtf
striatum B&SWJ 7259	WCru

Ligustrum ✿ (*Oleaceae*)

§ ***delavayanum***	EBtc EPfP NLar SAPC STrG
- B&L 12083	CExl
ibota	EBtc NLar
- Musli = 'Muster' (v) **new**	WCot
ionandrum	see *L. delavayanum*
japonicum	ECrN LRHS LSRN SEND SGol SPer
- 'Coriaceum'	see *L. japonicum* 'Rotundifolium'
* - 'Coriaceum Aureum'	LRHS
- 'Macrophyllum'	EPfP
§ - 'Rotundifolium'	CAbP CBcs CDoC CDul CExl CHEx CMac EBee ELan EPfP IVic LBMP LRHS MAsh MRav NLar SMad SPer SPoG WCFE WCot
§ - 'Silver Star' (v)	NLar SEND SGol SLon
§ - 'Texanum'	CDoC EWes NLar WCFE
- 'Texanum Argenteum'	see *L. japonicum* 'Silver Star'
- 'Variegatum' (v)	SGol
lucidum 🏆H4	CBar CCVT CDoC CDul CSBt CTri EBee ELan EWTr IDee LAst LPla MMuc MRav NLar NWea SAPC SEND SGol SPer SWvt
- Guiz 296	CExl
- 'Excelsum Superbum' (v) 🏆H4	CJun CMac ECrN ELan EPfP LHop LSRN SGol SSpi
- 'Golden Wax'	CJun MRav SSpi
- 'Tricolor' (v)	CJun ELan EPfP LRHS MAsh NLar SPer SPoG SSpi SWvt
obtusifolium 'Dart's Perfecta'	SLPl
ovalifolium	Widely available
§ - 'Argenteum' (v)	CBcs CCVT CDoC CDul CMac CTri CWib ECrN EHoe EShb LRHS MMuc MRav MWat NEgg NLar SEND SGol SLim SPer SPoG SWvt
- 'Aureomarginatum'	see *L. ovalifolium* 'Aureum'
§ - 'Aureum' (v) 🏆H4	Widely available
- 'Lemon and Lime' (v)	CDoC EHoe EPfP LRHS LSRN SCoo SHil SWvt WCot WRHF
- 'Variegatum'	see *L. ovalifolium* 'Argenteum'
quihoui 🏆H4	EBee ECre ELan EPfP GKin IDee LHop LRHS SDix SEND SKHP SLon SMad SPer SSpi
sempervirens	EPfP
sinense	CMCN EPfP GLin MRav
- 'Multiflorum'	CWib
- 'Pendulum'	LRHS
- 'Variegatum' (v)	CJun EWes LHop MRav SPer
strongylophyllum	CDoC CExl
texanum	see *L. japonicum* 'Texanum'
undulatum 'Lemon Lime and Clippers'	EShb LRHS MAsh MBNS NLar NPri SDix SLim
'Vicaryi'	CJun EBee ELan EPfP EWTr LRHS NHol NPro SGol SHil SPer
vulgare	CArn CBcs CCVT CDul CHab CMac CTri ECrN EPfP LBuc MMuc MSwo NWea SEND SEWo SWvt WMou WSFF
- 'Aureovariegatum' (v)	CNat
- 'Lodense'	EBtc

Lilium ✿ (*Liliaceae*)

'Acapulco' (VII-/d)	MCri NGdn SDeJ
African Queen Group (VI-/a) 🏆H4	ERCP LRHS NLar SCoo SPer SRms
- 'African Queen' (VIb-c/a)	CBro CHel MCri SDeJ
'Algarve' (VIIIa-b/c)	MBri
'Altari' (VIIIa-b/b)	MCri SDeJ
amabile var. ***luteum*** (IXc/d)	MCri
'Ambergate'	SDeJ
amoenum (IXc/b)	EPot
'Anastasia' (VIIIb-c/b-d)	SDeJ
'Annemarie's Dream' (Ia/c)	SDeJ
'Apeldoorn' (Ia/b)	MCri NNor
'Apollo' (Ia-b) 🏆H4	NNor SDeJ
'Arabian Knight' (IIc/d) **new**	SDeJ
'Arena' (VIIa/b)	EPfP LRHS MCri SCoo
'Ariadne' (Ic-d)	CDes
Asiatic hybrids (I)	NGdn
auratum (IXb/c)	ECho EFEx EPfP GBuc
- 'Gold Band'	see *L. auratum* var. *platyphyllum*
- 'Golden Ray'	GBuc
- 'Perfection' (IXb/c)	LRHS
§ - var. ***platyphyllum*** (IXb/c)	MCri NNor SDeJ
- - B&SWJ 4824	WCru
- - B&SWJ 5041	WCru
- var. ***virginale*** (IXb/c)	MCri SDeJ
'Avignon' (Ia/b)	MCri
'Bach' (VIIIa-b/b)	MBri
'Barbaresco' (VIIa-b/b)	SCoo
'Barcelona' (Ia/b-c)	NNor
'Belgrado'^{PBR} (VIIa/b-c)	SDeJ
'Belladonna'^{PBR} (VIIIb-a/b) **new**	SDeJ
'Belle Epoque' (VIIb/b-c)	SDeJ
'Bergamo' (VIIb/b)	EPfP SCoo SDeJ

'Black Beauty' (VIIIb-c/d)	EPfP GBin LRHS MCri NNor SDeJ
'Black Dragon'	see *L. leucanthum* var. *centifolium* 'Black Dragon'
'Black Pearl'	EPfP
'Black Tie' (VIIa-b/b)	MCri
'Boogie Woogie' (VIIIa-b/b)	SDeJ
'Bracelet' (VIIIa-b/b) **new**	SDeJ
Brasilia = 'Zora' (VII)	SDeJ
Bright Pixie = 'Ceb Bright' (Ia/b)	NSoo SDeJ
'Bright Star' (VIb-c/c)	MCri
brownii (IXb-c/a)	ECho MCri
bulbiferum (IXa/b)	EBee ECho GKev
- var. ***croceum*** (IXa/b)	XEll
'Butter Pixie'PBR (Ia/b)	NNor SDeJ
§ ***canadense*** (IXc/a)	CBro CRDP GBuc WCru XEll
- var. ***coccineum*** (IXc/a)	CRDP GBuc
- var. ***flavum***	see *L. canadense*
'Cancun' (Ia)	SDeJ
candidum (IXb/a) ♀H4	CArn CAvo CBcs CBro CTca CWCL EBee ECho ELan EPfP ERCP GKev MCri MHer NLar SDeJ SEND SRms
'Capuchino' (Ia-b/c)	MCri
carniolicum	see *L. pyrenaicum* subsp. *carniolicum*
'Casa Blanca' (VIIb/b-c) ♀H4	CAvo CBro CSut EPfP MCri NBir NLar NNor SCoo SDeJ WCot
'Cecil' (VIIIa/b) **new**	SDeJ
'Centerfold' (Ia-b/b)	NNor
cernuum (IXc/d)	EBee ECho GKev MCri SDeJ
* - 'Album'	ECho SDeJ
ciliatum	LWst
Citronella Group (Ic/d)	ECho SDeJ
'Claude Shride' (IIc/d)	SDeJ
'Cocktail Twins' (Ia/b) **new**	SDeJ
columbianum (IXc/d)	ECho WHal
- B&SWJ 9564	WCru
'Con Amore' (VIIb/b)	SCoo
'Conca d'Or'PBR (VIIIb/b)	SDeJ
concolor (IXa/c)	LRHS
'Connecticut King' (Ia/b)	MCri
'Corina' (Ia/b)	NNor
'Côte d'Azur' (Ia/b-c)	NNor
'Coulance' (VII-/d)	LRHS
'Creation' (VIa/b)	SDeJ
'Crimson Pixie' (Ia/b)	CBro SDeJ SPet
× ***dalhansonii*** (IIc/d)	CAby SPhx WCot
§ - 'Marhan' (IIc/d)	ECho GBuc
- 'Mrs R.O. Backhouse' (IIc/d)	ECho SDeJ
dauricum var. ***alpinum*** (IX)	MCri
davidii (IXc/d)	CExl EBee ECho GBuc MCri MMoz SDeJ WBor WCru
- var. ***unicolor***	GBuc
§ - var. ***willmottiae*** (IXc/d)	MCri WCru
'Diabora' (Ia/b)	GBuc
'Disco' (Ia)	SDeJ
distichum (IXb-c/d)	WCot
- B&SWJ 794	WCru
- B&SWJ 4465	WCru
'Dizzy' (VIIa-b/b-c)	MCri NNor SDeJ
duchartrei (IXc/d)	CAby CDoy CExl ECho GKev NSla WAbe WCru
'Electric' (Ia/b-c)	MCri NNor
§ 'Electric Yellow' (Ia/b-c)	MCri SDeJ
'Elodie'PBR (Ia/b)	CAvo NLar
'Elusive'	SDeJ
'Enchantment' (Ia/b)	SDeJ
'Expression' (VII)	SDeJ
'Fancy Joy' (Ia/b-c)	MBri
'Fangio' (VIIIa/b)	NNor
fargesii (IXc/d)	GKev
'Fata Morgana' (Ia/b) ♀H4	CSut NNor SCoo SDeJ
'Fire King' (Ib/d)	MCri SCoo SDeJ SRms
'Fopapo'	SDeJ
'Forever Susan' (Ia/b) **new**	SDeJ
formosanum (IXb/a)	LRHS MCri
- RWJ 10005	WCru
- var. ***pricei*** (IXb/a)	EBee ECho EDAr ELan EPot GBin GKev LRHS MHer SHil
- - 'Snow Queen' (Vb/a)	SDeJ
'Garden Party' (VIIb/b) ♀H4	SDeJ
'Gay Lights' (II) **new**	WCot
'Gironde' (Ia/b) **new**	SDeJ
'Glossy Wings' (VIIIa-b/b)	NNor
'Golden Joy' (Ia/-)	MBri
Golden Splendor Group (VIb-c/a) ♀H4	MCri SCoo SDeJ
'Golden Stone' (VIIIa-b/b)	SDeJ
'Gran Paradiso' (Ia/b)	MCri SRms
'Grand Cru' (Ia/b) ♀H4	LRHS MCri NNor SDeJ
grayi (IX)	GBuc
Green Magic Group (VI-/a)	NNor
hansonii (IXb-c/d)	CHel CWCL EBee ECho GBuc GKev MCri SDeJ
- B&SWJ 4756 from Aomori, Japan	WCru
- B&SWJ 8506	WCru
- B&SWJ 8528	WCru
henryi (IXc/d) ♀H4	EBee ECho EPfP GKev MCri NLar NNor SDeJ WCru
'Hit Parade' (VII)	SDeJ
× ***hollandicum*** (Ia/b)	MCri
'Honeymoon' (VIIIa-b/b)	SDeJ
'Hot Lips' (VIIb/b-d)	EPfP
'Ibarra' (Ia/b)	MCri
'Ice Pixie' (Ia/b)	SDeJ
'Italia' (Ia)	LRHS
'Ivory Pixie' (Ia/b)	SDeJ SPet
'Jacqueline'	LRHS
japonicum (IXb/a)	EFEx
'Jo's Choice'	SDeJ
'Josephine' (VIIa/b)	SDeJ
§ 'Joy' (VIIa-b/b) ♀H4	MCri NNor SDeJ
'King Pete' (Ib/b-c) ♀H4	SDeJ
'Kingdom'PBR (VIIIa/b-c)	SDeJ
'Lady Alice' (VI-/d)	SDeJ
§ ***lancifolium*** (IXc/d)	CArn CHid EPot GBin LPio WBrk XLum
- B&SWJ 4352	WCru
- var. ***flaviflorum*** (IXc/d)	CBro EBee GBuc IBoy MCri SDeJ
- 'Flore Pleno' (IXc/d)	CSut EPPr GCal LHop LRHS MHer MMHG NBir NNor SDeJ SMrm WCot WCru WHil XLum
* - var. ***forrestii*** (IX)	MCri
- Forrest's form (IX)	LRHS
- var. ***fortunei*** (IXc/d)	GCal SDix
- - B&SWJ 539	WCru
- pink-flowered	SDeJ
- 'Splendens' (IXc/d) ♀H4	CBro EBee ECGP ECho EPfP MCri NBid NNor SDeJ SPhx
'Landini'PBR (Ia/b)	SDeJ
lankongense (IXc/d)	CWCL EPot GBin GBuc GGGa GKev MCri WCru
- BWJ 7691	WCru
'Latvia' (Ia/b)	MCri SDeJ

'Lazy Lady'	SDeJ
'Le Rêve'	see *L.* 'Joy'
leichtlinii (IXc/d)	CAvo CBro EBee ECho EPot GKev LRHS MCri SDeJ
- B&SWJ 4519	WCru
- 'Iwashimiza' (IXc/d)	MCri
'Lemon Pixie' (Ia/b)	SPet
leucanthum	MCri WCru
var. ***centifolium*** (IXb-c/a)	
- - BWJ 8130	WCru
§ - - 'Black Dragon' (IXb-c/a)	MCri
lijiangense (IXc/d)	MCri
'Linda' (Ia/b)	SDeJ
'Little John' (VIIa-b/b)	MBri SDeJ SPer
'Little Kiss' (Ia/d)	SDeJ
Lollypop = 'Holebibi' (Ia/b)	GBuc MBri NNor SCoo SPet
longiflorum (IXb/a) ♀H2-3	EBee ECho GKev MCri SCoo XLum
- B&SWJ 11376	WCru
- 'Memories'	MBri
- 'Rose'	SDeJ
§ - 'White American' (Vb/a)	CBro ECho LRHS
- 'White Heaven'PBR (Vb/a)	EPfP SPer
lophophorum (IXc/b)	EPot GKev
'Lovely Girl' (VII-/b)	CSut SDeJ
'Luxor' (Ia/b)	MCri NBir
'Luzia' (VII)	NCGa
mackliniae (IXc/a)	CWCL ECho EWes GBuc GCal GCra GGGa GKev NBir WAbe WHal
- from Nagaland, India	GGGa
- deep pink-flowered	GGGa
'Marco Polo' (Ia/-)	SCoo SDeJ
'Marhan'	see *L.* × *dalhansonii* 'Marhan'
martagon (IXc/d) ♀H4	CBro CCon CHel CTca CWCL EBee ECho ELan EPot ERCP GBuc GKev GPoy LRHS NBir NLar NPnk SDeJ SRms WCot WPnP WShi WWFP
- var. ***albiflorum*** (IXc/d)	GBuc
- var. ***album*** (IXc/d) ♀H4	CAvo CBro CWCL ECho ELan EPfP EPot GBin GKev LRHS NBir NChi SDeJ WShi
- var. ***cattaniae*** (IXc/d)	GBuc GKev MCri WCot
* - var. ***rubrum***	CWCL
medeoloides (IXc/d)	ECho EFEx GBuc
'Mediterrannee' (VIIb/d)	NNor
michiganense (IXc/d)	GBuc
'Miss Feya' (VIII)	SDeJ
'Miss France' (VIIb/b-c)	EPfP SDeJ
'Miss Lily'	SDeJ
'Miss Lucy'PBR (VIIa-b/b-c)	CHid SDeJ
'Miss Rio' (VII)	SCoo
'Mister Job' (VIIIa/c)	SDeJ
'Mona Lisa' (VIIb/b-c)	EPfP LRHS MBri MCri NGdn NNor SDeJ
monadelphum (IXc/d)	ECho SDeJ
'Mont Blanc' (Ia)	SDeJ
'Monte Negro' (Ia/b)	LRHS MCri
'Montezuma'PBR (VIIa-b/b)	SDeJ
'Montreux' (Ia/b-c)	SDeJ
'Muscadet'PBR (VIIa-b/b)	NGdn SDeJ
§ ***nanum*** (IXc/b)	ECho WAbe WCru WHal
- from Bhutan (IX)	WCru
- var. ***flavidum*** (IXc/b)	LWst
nepalense (IXc/a)	CAby CBcs CBro CCon CExl CHid CTca EBee ECho EPot ERCP GBin GBuc GKev MCri SDeJ WCot WCru WWFP XLum
- B&SWJ 2985	WCru

'Nerone' (Ia/b)	CHid NNor
'Netty's Pride' (Ia/b-c)	CAvo CBro CHid EPfP ERCP GBuc MCri SDeJ SPer WCot
'New Wave' (Ia/b)	SDeJ
'Night Flyer' (Ib-c/b-c)	SDeJ
nobilissimum (IXa-b/a)	EFEx
'Nove Cento' (Ia/b) ♀H4	MCri SDeJ
'Odeon' (VI-/a)	MCri
'Olivia' (Ia)	MCri
Olympic Group (VI-/a)	MCri
'Orange County' (Ia/b)	SDeJ
'Orange Electric' (Ia/b)	SDeJ
'Orange Marmalade' (IIb/c-d)	SDeJ
'Orange Pixie' (Ia/b)	MCri NNor SCoo SPet
'Orange Twinkle' (Ib-c/b)	SDeJ
'Orania'PBR (VIII)	SDeJ
oriental hybrids (VII)	SDeJ
* Oriental Superb Group	NGdn
§ ***oxypetalum*** (IXb-c/b)	ECho LWst
- var. ***insigne*** (IXb-c/b)	ECho EPot GBin GBuc LWst WAbe WCru WHal
pardalinum (IXc/d) ♀H4	CBro CWCL EBee ECho GKev LWst MMoz WCru WHal
- var. ***giganteum*** (IXc/d)	EPfP MCri MNrw
- subsp. ***pardalinum*** (IX)	GBuc
§ - subsp. ***vollmeri*** (IXc/d)	GBuc WCru
§ - subsp. ***wigginsii*** (IXc/d)	MCri
× ***parkmanii*** 'Rosy Dimple' (VIIa/b)	SDeJ
- 'Sam' (VIIb/c) ♀H4	EPfP
parryi (IXb-c/a)	EBee WHal
parvum (IXa-b/a)	ECho GBuc
'Patricia's Pride' (Ia/b-c)	MCri SDeJ
'Peach Butterflies' (Ic/d)	SDeJ
'Peach Dwarf' (Ia/b-c) **new**	SDeJ
'Peach Pixie' (Ia/b)	NBir SCoo
'Pearl Jennifer' (Ib-a/c)	SDeJ
'Pearl Jessica' (Ib-c/b-c)	SDeJ
'Pearl Loraine' (Ib-c/b-c)	SDeJ
'Pearl Sonja'	SDeJ
'Pearl Stacey' (Ib-c/c)	SDeJ
philippinense (IXa-b/a)	GKev MCri WPGP
'Pimento' (VIIa/b)	NCGa SDeJ
'Pink Flavour'	SDeJ
Pink Perfection Group (VIb/a) ♀H4	CBro EPfP ERCP LRHS MCri NNor SCoo SDeJ SPer
'Pink Pixie'PBR (Ia/b)	NNor NSoo SDeJ SPet
'Pink Tiger' (VIIIb/c)	CAvo MCri NNor
poilanei HWJ 681	WCru
- WWJ 11679	WCru
polyphyllum	GLin
pomponium (IXc/d)	EBee
primulinum (IX)	GKev
- var. ***ochraceum*** (IXc/a)	LWst MCri WCru
§ ***pumilum*** (IXc/d) ♀H4	EBee ECho EPot GKev MCri SDeJ
'Purple Prince' (VIIIa-b/a-b)	SDeJ
pyrenaicum (IXc/d)	CAby ECho GBuc IBlr MCri WPGP WShi
§ - subsp. ***carniolicum*** (IXc/d)	GKev MCri
'Red Carpet' (Ia/b)	MCri NNor SDeJ
'Red County' (Ia/c-b)	SDeJ
'Red Electric' (Ia/b)	SDeJ
'Red Hot' (VIIIc-d/b)	SDeJ
Red Rum = 'Zanlorum' (VIIa-b/b)	MBri
'Red Star'	LRHS
'Red Twinkle'	SDeJ

	'Red Velvet' (Ic/d)	CAvo SDeJ
	regale (IXb/a) ♀H4	CAvo CBro CCon CDoy CMea CTca CWCL EBee ELan EPfP EPot ERCP GKev LRHS MCri NLar NNor SDeJ SPer WCot
	- 'Album' (IXb/a)	CAvo EBee ERCP GKev LRHS MCri NLar NNor SCoo SDeJ WCot XLum
§	- 'Royal Gold' (IXb/a)	MCri
	'Reinesse' (Ia/b)	MBri SDeJ
	'Rina's Twinkle'	LRHS
	'Robert Swanson' (VIIIb-c/b)	SDeJ
	'Robina' (VIIIa-b/b-c)	WCot
	'Roma' (Ia/b)	NBir
	'Rosefire' (Ia/b)	NNor
	'Rosella's Dream' (I)	SDeJ
	'Rosemary North' (Ic/d)	CDes
	'Rosselini'	SDeJ
	rosthornii (IXc/d)	CExl EBee GKev WCru
	'Royal Fantasy' (VIII)	NNor
	'Royal Gold'	see *L. regale* 'Royal Gold'
	rubellum (IXb/a)	EFEx
*	'Rubina'	MCri
	sachalinense (IXa/b) RBS 0235	EPPr
	'Salinas' (VIIa/b)	SDeJ
	'Salmon Star'PBR (VIIa-b/b-c)	NCGa
	'Salmon Tiger'	SDeJ
	'Salmon Twinkle' (Ib-c/c)	LRHS SDeJ
	'San Vincenzo'	EPfP
	sargentiae (IXb-c/a)	GCal MCri WCot WCru
	'Satisfaction' (VIIIa-b/-)	SDeJ
	'Scarlet Delight' (VIIb-c/c-d)	SDeJ
	'Scheherazade' (VIIIc/d)	MCri SDeJ
	'Set Point' (VIIb/b)	SDeJ
	'Silly Girl' (Ia/-)	NNor
	'Smokey Mountain' (VIIIc/d)	SDeJ
§	'Snow Crystal' (Ia/b)	EPfP
	'Souvenir'PBR (VIIa-b/b)	NGdn
	'Spark' (Ia-b/b)	NNor
	speciosum (IXb-c/d) B&SWJ 4847	WCru
	- B&SWJ 4924	WCru
	- var. ***album*** (IXb-c/d)	ECho EPfP GKev LEdu MCri NBir SDeJ
	- var. ***rubrum*** (IXb c/d)	ECho EPfP GKev MCri NBir SDeJ SPer SRms
§	- 'Uchida' (IXb-c/d)	CExl EPfP MCri SDeJ
	'Sphinx' (Ia/d)	CAbP NNor WCot
	'Spring Pink' (Ia)	CSut ERCP SDeJ
	'Staccato' (Ia/c)	MCri
	'Stainless Steel' (Ia/b)	SDeJ
	'Star Gazer' (VIIa/c)	CBro CSut LRHS MCri NNor SCoo SDeJ
	'Starfighter' (VIIa-b/c)	MCri SDeJ
	'Sterling Star' (Ia/b)	MCri NNor
	Stones = 'Holebobo' (Ia/b)	NNor
	'Sulphur King'	WCot
	sulphureum (IXb-c/a)	MCri
	'Sun Ray' (Ia/b)	MCri
	superbum (IXc/d)	EBee GBuc GKev WCru WPGP
	'Sutter's Gold' (I)	MCri
	'Sutton Court' (II)	GBuc
	'Sweet Lord' (Ia/b)	NSoo SDeJ
	'Sweet Surrender' (Ib-c/c-d)	EPfP MCri NNor SDeJ
	'Sweet-kiss' (Ia-b/b)	MBri
	'Tailor Made' (Ia/b)	SDeJ
	taliense (IXc/d)	ECho MCri WCru
	'Tarragona'PBR (VIIIb/b)	SDeJ
	tenuifolium	see *L. pumilum*
	'Tiger Woods' (VII)	EPfP
	tigrinum	see *L. lancifolium*
	'Tom Pouce' (VIIa/b)	EPfP MCri SDeJ
	'Toronto' (Ia-b/b) **new**	SDeJ
	'Toscane' (Ia/b-c)	SDeJ
	'Touch' (VIIb/-)	MCri
	Triumphator = 'Zanlophator'PBR (VIIIb/a-b)	EPfP MCri NNor SDeJ
	tsingtauense (IXa/c)	EBee MCri SDeJ
	- B&SWJ 519	WCru
	- B&SWJ 4263	WCru
	- B&SWJ 4698	WCru
	'Uchida Kanoka'	see *L. speciosum* 'Uchida'
	'Urandi' (VIIIc/b)	SDeJ
	'Val Di Sole'PBR (Ia/b)	SDeJ
	'Venezuela'PBR (VIIa-b/b-c)	SDeJ
	'Venture' (Ia/b)	NNor
	'Vermeer' (Ia-b/b-c)	LRHS
	'Victory Joy'	MBri
	'Visaversa' (VIIIa-b/b)	SDeJ
	'Vivaldi' (Ia/b)	SDeJ
	vollmeri	see *L. pardalinum* subsp. *vollmeri*
	wallichianum (IXb/a)	ECho EPot GKev SDeJ XLum
	wardii (IXc/d)	CExl
	'White American'	see *L. longiflorum* 'White American'
	'White Paradise' (V)	SCoo
	White Pixie	see *L.* 'Snow Crystal'
	'White Present' (Vb/a)	SDeJ
	'White Twinkle' (Ia-b/b)	CAvo SDeJ
	wigginsii	see *L. pardalinum* subsp. *wigginsii*
	willmottiae	see *L. davidii* var. *willmottiae*
	wilsonii var. ***luteum***	MCri
	'Wine Electric' (Ia/c)	SDeJ
	xanthellum var. ***luteum*** (IXb-c/d)	CDes WCru
	'Yellow Electric'	see *L.* 'Electric Yellow'
	'Yellow Eye'	SDeJ
	'Yeti' (Ia/b) **new**	SDeJ

lime see *Citrus aurantiifolia*

lime, djeruk see *Citrus amblycarpa*

lime, Philippine see × *Citrofortunella microcarpa*

Limnanthes (*Limnanthaceae*)

	douglasii ♀H4	CArn EPfP
	- subsp. ***rosea***	CSpe

Limnobium (*Hydrocharitaceae*)

	sp.	LLWG

Limonium (*Plumbaginaceae*)

	bellidifolium	CMea EDAr MWat NSla
	caspium	IFro
	chilwellii	EBee ECGP
	cosyrense	CMea MHer WAbe
	dregeanum	WThu
	dumosum	see *Goniolimon tataricum* var. *angustifolium*
	gmelinii	SPlb
*	- subsp. ***hungaricum***	NLar XLum
	gougetianum	LLHF

latifolium	see *L. platyphyllum*
paradoxum	WAbe
perezii	CCon
§ ***platyphyllum***	CCon CMea EPfP GMaP LAst LHop LRHS MBel MHer MWat NChi NMir SEND SPer SRms WHoo WWEG
- 'Robert Butler'	GCal GQue MRav
- 'Violetta'	EBee ELan EPfP GCal LAst MBel MRav SPer SPoG WHoo
sinuatum	SVic
speciosum	see *Goniolimon incanum*
vulgare	WHer

Linaria (*Plantaginaceae*)

aeruginea	CPBP
- 'Neon Lights'	CSpe EDAr LRHS NGdn SPoG
- subsp. ***nevadensis*** 'Gemstones'	SBch
alpina	CSpe NRya NSla SRms
anticaria 'Antique Silver'	CExl LSou MRav WPtf WWEG
Blue Lace = 'Yalin'	LSou
cymbalaria	see *Cymbalaria muralis*
§ ***dalmatica***	EBee ECGP ELan EPPr IFro MPie NBid NBre SBch SEND SPhx WCot WMoo WWEG
dalmatica* × *purpurea	WCot
× ***dominii*** 'Carnforth'	SBch SHar WCot WWEG
- 'Yuppie Surprise'	CHid NBir
genistifolia subsp. ***dalmatica***	see *L. dalmatica*
hepaticifolia	see *Cymbalaria hepaticifolia*
* ***lobata alba***	ECho SPlb
origanifolia	see *Chaenorhinum origanifolium*
pallida	see *Cymbalaria pallida*
'Peachy'	CSpe WCot
pilosa	see *Cymbalaria pilosa*
purpurea	CTri EHoe ELan EPfP IFoB MHer MNHC NBro NPer NPol NPri NWad SEND SPhx SRms WCot WMoo WSFF XLum
- 'Alba'	see *L. purpurea* 'Springside White'
- 'Brown's White Strain'	CSpe EBee IBoy MHol SPad WCot
- 'Canon Came'	CNat
- 'Canon Went'	CBre CSpe CTri CWib EBee EHoe ELan EPfP EWTr GJos LBMP LPio LRHS MBri MMuc MNHC MSpe NBir NBro NPol SGbt SHil SPer SPet SPhx SRms SWvt WKif WMoo WWEG
- 'Freefolk Piccolo'	SHar
- pink-flowered	CSpe
- 'Radcliffe Innocence'	see *L. purpurea* 'Springside White'
§ - 'Springside White'	ECtt LBMP LRHS NBir NGdn SBch SPer SPhx WSHC WWEG XLum
repens	CPom WCot WHer
× ***sepium***	WCot
triornithophora	CCon LBMP MHol MSpe SPlb WHrl WKif WMoo
- 'Pink Budgies'	LLHF LSou SPad
- purple-flowered	WMoo
- 'Rosea'	CSpe
vulgaris	CArn CHab LDai MHer MHoo MNHC NMir WHer WHfH WJek
- 'Peloria'	CPBP
'Winifrid's Delight'	NBre

Lindelofia (*Boraginaceae*)

anchusoides misapplied	see *L. longiflora*
anchusoides (Lindl.) Lehm.	EPPr NBid
§ ***longiflora***	CAby EBee GCal GCra GMaP LPla WSHC

Lindera (*Lauraceae*)

benzoin	CBcs EPfP LRHS MBlu NLar
erythrocarpa	EPfP
- B&SWJ 6271	WCru
- B&SWJ 8730	WCru
megaphylla	CHEx
obtusiloba ♀H4	CAbP EPfP MBlu
- B&SWJ 8723	WCru
- B&SWJ 11054	WCru
praecox	EPfP
- B&SWJ 10802	WCru
- B&SWJ 10953 from north Japan	WCru
- B&SWJ 11125 from south Japan	WCru
reflexa	NLar
sericea B&SWJ 11123	WCru
- B&SWJ 11141	WCru
- var. ***lancea*** B&SWJ 11071	WCru
- - B&SWJ 11118	WCru
strychnifolia	EPfP
triloba B&SWJ 5570	WCru
- B&SWJ 11121	WCru
- B&SWJ 11466	WCru
umbellata B&SWJ 10881	WCru
- var. ***membranacea*** B&SWJ 6227	WCru
- - B&SWJ 10837	WCru

Lindernia (*Linderniaceae*)

grandiflora	LLWG

Linnaea (*Caprifoliaceae*)

borealis	CExl EPot WAbe
- subsp. ***americana***	NHar WAbe

Linum (*Linaceae*)

alexeenkoanum	XSen
anatolicum new	XSen
arboreum ♀H4	GKev LLHF NBir
campanulatum	WThu
capitatum	NSla
flavum	EPfP XSen
- 'Compactum'	CMea EBee ECho LLHF SRms
'Gemmell's Hybrid' ♀H4	ECho EPot EWes NBir WAbe WThu
grandiflorum 'Rubrum'	CSpe
hirsutum	XSen
leonii	LRHS
monogynum	ECou LLHF
§ - var. ***diffusum***	ECou
- 'Nelson'	see *L. monogynum* var. *diffusum*
narbonense	CCse EWld LDai LRHS SBch SIgm SPhx
- 'Heavenly Blue'	NCGa
§ ***perenne***	CArn CHel ELan EPfP GMaP MHer MNHC NLar SIde SPer SPoG WJek WSHC WWEG
- 'Album'	EBee ELan EPfP NLar SPer WJek
- subsp. ***alpinum*** 'Alice Blue'	WAbe
§ - 'Blau Saphir'	GQue NHol NLar
- Blue Sapphire	see *L. perenne* 'Blau Saphir'
- 'Himmelszelt'	NLar
- subsp. ***lewisii***	NBir
- 'Nanum Diamond'	NLar
- 'Nanum Sapphire'	see *L. perenne* 'Blau Saphir'

- 'White Diamond'	SPoG
sibiricum	see *L. perenne*
suffruticosum	GKev SBrt
subsp. ***salsoloides*** new	
- - 'Nanum'	WThu
tenuifolium	SPhx
uninerve	WAbe
usitatissimum	MHer SIde
- 'Blue Dress'	CSpe SPhx

Lippia (*Verbenaceae*)

sp.	SWvt
canescens	see *Phyla nodiflora* var. *canescens*
chamaedrifolia	see *Verbena peruviana*
citriodora	see *Aloysia citrodora*
dulcis	CArn EOHP
nodiflora	see *Phyla nodiflora*
repens	see *Phyla nodiflora*

Liquidambar ✿ (*Hamamelidaceae*)

acalycina	CDul CJun EBee EBtc ELan EPfP MGos MRav NLar SBir SCoo SGol SLim SPoG SSpi SSta WPGP WPat
- 'Burgundy Flush'	CJun NLar SBir SSta
- 'Spinners'	LRHS SBir SSpi
formosana	CDul CMCN CMac EPfP IArd LAst MSnd NPCo SBir SGol SSta WPGP
- 'Afterglow'	CJun NLar
- 'Ellen'	CJun NLar SSta
- Monticola Group	CJun EPfP NLar SBir SLim SSta
- 'Woodleigh'	SSta
orientalis	CDul CJun CLnd CMCN EBtc EPfP LLHF NPCo SBir SSta WPat
- 'M. Foster'	NLar
styraciflua	Widely available
- 'Andrew Hewson'	CAbP CJun CLnd EPfP IVic LRHS MAsh MBlu NLar SBir SSta WPat
- 'Anja'	CJun MBlu SBir SSta WPat
- 'Anneke'	CJun SBir SSta
- 'Aurea'	see *L. styraciflua* 'Variegata' Overeynder
- 'Aurea Variegata'	see *L. styraciflua* 'Variegata' Overeynder
- 'Aurora'	CJun SBir
- 'Brodsman'	NLar
- 'Burgundy'	CJun CLnd LLHF MBlu SBir SSta WPat
- Cherokee = 'Ward'	MGos
I - 'Corky' new	SSta
- 'Elstead Mill'	CAbP
- 'Emerald Sentinel' new	SSta
- 'Festeri'	CEnd SBir SSta WPat
- 'Festival'	CJun CLnd EUJe MBlu
- 'Frosty' (v)	CJun SBir SSta
- 'Globe'	see *L. styraciflua* 'Gum Ball'
- 'Gold Beacon'	MPkF
- 'Golden Treasure' (v)	CDul CJun CLnd CMCN LRHS MGos NLar SBir SGol SPer SPoG SReu SSta WPat
- 'Goldmember'	CJun SSta
- 'Granary Sunset'	SBir SSta
§ - 'Gum Ball'	CEnd CJun CLnd CMCN EPfP EWes LLHF MGos NLar NPCo SBir SLim SMad SSta SWvt WPat
- Happidaze = 'Hapdell'	CEnd CJun NLar SBir WPat
- 'Jennifer Carol'	CJun NLar SBir SSta
- 'Kia'	CAbP CEnd CJun LLHF NLar SBir WPat
- 'Kirsten'	CJun
- 'Lane Roberts' 🏆^{H4}	CDoC CDul CLnd CMCN CMHG CMac CSBt CTho EBee ELan EPfP IArd LHop LRHS LSRN MAsh MBlu MBri MGos NLar SBir SCoo SEWo SPer SSta SWvt WCFE WPat
- 'Lynn'	SBir SSta
- 'Manon' (v)	CEnd CJun
- 'Midwest Sunset'	CJun MBlu SBir WPat
- 'Moonbeam' (v)	CEnd CJun NLar SBir SLim SSta WPat
- 'Moraine'	CJun SBir
- 'Naree'	CJun NLar SBir SSta WPat
- 'Nina'	SSta
- 'Nyewood' new	SBir
- 'Oconee'	CEnd EPfP LLHF MAsh NLar SSta WPat
- 'Paarl' (v)	CJun CLnd NLar SGol
- 'Palo Alto'	CEnd CJun LLHF LRHS MAsh MBlu NLar SBir SCoo SLim SSta WPGP WPat
- 'Parasol'	CAbP CEnd CJun CLnd EBtc NLar NPCo SBir SSta
- 'Pendula'	CJun CLnd MBlu SBir SSta
- 'Penwood'	CJun NLar SBir SSta WPat
- 'Professor Louwjan'	NLar
- 'Red Sunset'	SSta
- 'Rotundiloba'	CJun CLnd CMCN EPfP LLHF LRHS MAsh MBlu SBir SSta WPat
- 'Savill Torch'	SBir SSta
- 'Schock's Gold'	CJun MAsh SSta WPat
§ - 'Silver King' (v)	CDul CJun CMCN CMac EBee ECrN LRHS MGos MMHG MPkF NHol NLar NPCo SCoo SGol SHil SLim SPer SPoG SReu SSta WPat
- 'Simone'	SBir SGol SSta
- 'Slender Silhouette'	CAbP CDoC CDul CJun CLnd EBee EPfP GKin LLHF LRHS LSRN MAsh MBlu NLar SBir SCoo SGol SLim SPoG SSpi SSta WMou WPat
- 'Stared'	CDul CEnd CJun CLnd EBee EBtc EPfP GQue LRHS MBlu MBri NLar SBir SCoo SLim SPoG SSta WPGP WPat
- 'Thea'	CAbP CJun CLnd EMil EPfP LRHS MAsh MBlu MBri SBir SSta
- 'Variegata' misapplied	see *L. styraciflua* 'Silver King'
§ - 'Variegata' Overeynder (v)	CBcs CJun CLnd CMac EBee ELan EPfP LRHS MAsh SBir SLim SPer SSta
- 'White Star' (v)	CJun
- 'Woorby Rose'	SBir
- 'Worplesdon' 🏆^{H4}	Widely available

Liriodendron ✿ (*Magnoliaceae*)

'Chapel Hill'	MBlu NLar WPat
chinense	CBcs CDul CGHE CMCN EPfP MBlu MPhe SGol WPGP
chinense* × *tulipifera	WPGP
'Doc Deforce's Delight'	MBlu MBri NLar
tulipifera 🏆^{H4}	Widely available
- 'Ardis'	NLar
- 'Arnold'	SGol
- 'Aureomarginatum' (v) 🏆^{H4}	Widely available
- 'Fastigiatum'	CDoC CDul CEnd CMCN CTho EBee ECrN ELan EPfP MAsh MBlu MBri NLar SPer WPat
- 'Glen Gold'	CEnd MBlu NLar

	– 'Heltorf'	NLar
	– 'Integrifolium'	NLar
	– 'Roodhaan'	EBee NLar

Liriope ✿ (*Asparagaceae*)

	'Big Blue'	see *L. muscari* 'Big Blue'
§	***exiliflora***	CEnd CLAP WWEG
	– 'Ariaka-janshige' (v)	LRHS WWEG
	– Silvery Sunproof misapplied	see *L. spicata* 'Gin-ryu', *L. muscari* 'Variegata'
§	***gigantea***	CLAP EPPr
	graminifolia misapplied	see *L. muscari*
	hyacinthifolia	see *Reineckea carnea*
	koreana	EBee EPPr GCal
	– B&SWJ 8821	WCru
	'Majestic'	CBct CLAP MHer WHoo
	'Minnow'	WCot
	minor	CMac
§	***muscari*** Υ^{H4}	Widely available
	– B&SWJ 561	WCru
	– 'Alba'	see *L. muscari* 'Monroe White'
	– Amethyst = 'Liptp'	NPri
§	– 'Big Blue'	CAbb CBct CExl CHel CLAP CMac EBee ECtt ELan ELon EPPr EPfP EPri EShb GBin LEdu LHop LRHS LSRN MBri MRav MSwo NLar SEND SGol SWvt WMoo WWEG
	– 'Christmas Tree'	EPPr WHoo WMoo WWEG
	– 'Evergreen Giant'	see *L. gigantea*
	– 'Gold-banded' (v)	CBct CLAP EPPr EPfP LHop LRHS MBri WCot
	– 'Goldfinger'	CExl EBee SMad WWEG
	– 'Ingwersen'	CExl EBee ECho ELon EPPr EPfP LRHS WWEG XLum
	– Isabella = 'Lirf'	EBee EPPr
	– 'John Burch' (v)	CBct CExl CLAP ECtt ELon EShb LAst LHop NLar NOak SMad WGrn WWEG
	– 'Lilac Wonder'	EPPr
	– 'Majestic' misapplied	see *L. exiliflora*
	– 'Moneymaker'	CHel ECtt EPPr LAst LRHS XEll
§	– 'Monroe White'	CBct CBro CExl CHel CLAP CMac EBee ELan EPPr EPfP EShb LAst LEdu LRHS MBri MRav NBid NLar NOak SPer SPet SWvt WCot WWEG
	– 'Okina' (v)	CKno EBee ECtt ELon LBMP LLHF NLar NSti SMad SPer SPlb WCot WRHF
	– 'Paul Aden'	EPfP WPGP
	– 'Pee Dee Ingot'	EPPr EShb LRHS LSou
	– 'Royal Purple'	CBct CLAP EBee ECtt ELon EPPr LRHS MBri NLar SPer WGrn WWEG
	– 'Silver Ribbon'	CBro CLAP CWGN EPfP LRHS LSRN MGos NOak WWEG
	– 'Super Blue'	EPPr
	– 'Superba'	WCot
§	– 'Variegata' (v)	CCon CDes CExl CLAP EBee ECho ELan EPPr EPfP EWes LAst LEdu LRHS MAsh NBir NOak SMrm SPer SPoG SWvt WPGP WWEG
	– variegated, white-flowered (v)	ECho
	– 'Webster Wideleaf'	CAby EBee WCot WWEG
	platyphylla	see *L. muscari*
	'Samantha'	NOak
	spicata	EBee ECho WWEG XLum
	– 'Alba'	ECho MRav
§	– 'Gin-ryu' (v)	CBct CExl CLAP CMac ECtt ELan ELon EPPr EShb EWes LEdu MBri MRav SGol SLPl SMad SPer WCot WWEG XLum
	– 'Silver Dragon'	see *L. spicata* 'Gin-ryu'
	– 'Small Green'	WWEG

Listera (*Orchidaceae*)

	ovata	WHer

Litchi (*Sapindaceae*)

	chinensis	CCCN

Lithocarpus ✿ (*Fagaceae*)

	edulis	CExl CFil CGHE CHEx EBee SAPC SKHP WPGP
§	***glaber***	CFil

Lithodora (*Boraginaceae*)

§	***diffusa***	ECho SGol SRot
	– 'Alba'	CTri ECho NCGa SPer SPoG
	– 'Cambridge Blue'	NWad SPer
	– 'Compacta'	EWes WAbe
§	– 'Grace Ward' Υ^{H4}	EPfP LLHF MMuc NWad WAbe
§	– 'Heavenly Blue' Υ^{H4}	Widely available
	– 'Inverleith'	ECho
	– 'Pete's Favourite'	ECtt NWad WAbe WHil
	– 'Picos'	CMea ECho NLar NSla NWad SIgm WAbe WThu
	– 'Star'^{PBR}	CHel CHid CMHG ELon EPfP NCGa NLar SCoo SPer SPoG SRot SWvt WIce
	fruticosa	CArn
	× ***intermedia***	see *Moltkia* × *intermedia*
§	***oleifolia*** Υ^{H4}	ECho EPot LLHF LRHS MWat NBir NSla WHil
	rosmarinifolia	WCFE
	zahnii	ECho EPot LHop LLHF LRHS SIgm SVen
	– 'Azureness'	WAbe

Lithophragma (*Saxifragaceae*)

	heterophyllum	EBee
	parviflorum	EWes

Lithospermum (*Boraginaceae*)

	diffusum	see *Lithodora diffusa*
	doerfleri	see *Moltkia doerfleri*
	'Grace Ward'	see *Lithodora diffusa* 'Grace Ward'
	'Heavenly Blue'	see *Lithodora diffusa* 'Heavenly Blue'
	officinale	CArn GPoy NMir WHfH
	oleifolium	see *Lithodora oleifolia*
	purpureocaeruleum	see *Buglossoides purpurocaerulea*

Litsea (*Lauraceae*)

	glauca	see *Neolitsea sericea*
	japonica	SVen

Littonia (*Colchicaceae*)

	modesta	CRHN ECho

Livistona (*Arecaceae*)

	australis	EAmu
	chinensis Υ^{H1}	CPHo EAmu SBig
	decora	EAmu
	nitida	EAmu

Loasa (*Loasaceae*)

	sp.	CArn
	triphylla var. ***volcanica***	EWes WSHC

Lobelia (Campanulaceae)

	angulata	see *Pratia angulata*
	bridgesii	CDTJ CExl CFil EWes GCal NGBl WHil WKif WMoo WPGP
§	***cardinalis*** ♀H3	CArn CBAq CHEx CMac EHon ELon EPfP GMaP MMuc NGBl NLar NPer SMrm SPer SPet SPlb SRms SWat SWvt WHil WMAq
	- 'Bee's Flame'	CCon CPrp CWGN ECtt GBuc LBMP LRHS MRav MSpe NBre NDov NEgg NGdn
§	- 'Elmfeuer'	CMHG ECtt EHoe EPfP EShb IBoy LSou MAsh NLar NPri SPlb SPoG SWvt XLum
	- 'Eulalia Berridge'	ECtt NPnk SMrm
	- subsp. ***graminea*** var. ***multiflora***	CCon
§	- 'Queen Victoria' ♀H3	Widely available
N	- 'Russian Princess' misapplied	CAby CWCL EPfP IBoy LRHS MAsh MHol NGdn NPnk SPoG SWvt WHar WWEG WWlt
	chinensis	LLWG
	'Cinnabar Deep Red'	see *L.* × *speciosa* 'Fan Tiefrot'
	'Cinnabar Rose'	see *L.* × *speciosa* 'Fan Zinnoberrosa'
	Compliment Blue	see *L.* × *speciosa* 'Kompliment Blau'
	Compliment Deep Red	see *L.* × *speciosa* 'Kompliment Tiefrot'
	Compliment Purple	see *L.* × *speciosa* 'Kompliment Purpur'
	Compliment Scarlet	see *L.* × *speciosa* 'Kompliment Scharlach'
	'Compton Pink' **new**	LBuc
	Elizabeth Strangman selection	NDov
	erinus Big Blue = 'Weslobigblue'PBR	LAst
	- Blue Star = 'Wesstar'PBR	LSou
	- 'Crystal Palace' ♀H3	NPri
	- (Fountain Series) 'Fountain Blue' **new**	NPri
	- - 'Fountain Rose' **new**	NPri
	- - 'Fountain White' **new**	NPri
	- Hot Tiger = 'Wesloti'PBR	LAst
	- 'Kathleen Mallard' (d)	CCCN LAst SWvt
	- Purple Star = 'Wespurstar'PBR ♀H3	LBMP LSou
	- 'Richardii'	see *L. richardsonii* hort.
	- Riviera Series **new**	NPri
	- 'Sapphire' **new**	NPri
	- Super Star = 'Weslosu' (Star Series)	LAst LSou
	excelsa	MTPN
	- B&SWJ 9513	WCru
	Fan Deep Red	see *L.* × *speciosa* 'Fan Tiefrot'
	Fan Deep Rose	see *L.* × *speciosa* 'Fan Orchidrosa'
	Fan Salmon	see *L.* × *speciosa* 'Fan Lachs'
	'Flamingo'	see *L.* × *speciosa* 'Pink Flamingo'
	fulgens	see *L. cardinalis*
	- Saint Elmo's Fire	see *L. cardinalis* 'Elmfeuer'
	× ***gerardii***	see *L.* × *speciosa*
	gibberoa	CDTJ CHEx
	'Gladys Lindley'	NLar
	'Hadspen Purple'	see *L.* × *speciosa* 'Hadspen Purple'
	inflata	CArn GPoy
	laxiflora	CFis CHll
	- B&SWJ 9064	WCru
	- var. ***angustifolia***	CAby CDTJ CHEx CPrp CSam ECtt EPfP EWld GCal LRHS SMrm SRms
	linnaeoides	SPlb
	'Lipstick'	WWEG
	montana	EWld
	- B&SWJ 8220	WCru
	pedunculata	see *Pratia pedunculata*
	'Periwinkle Blue'	LAst
	'Pink Passion'	LRHS
	'Queen Victoria'	see *L. cardinalis* 'Queen Victoria'
§	***richardsonii*** hort. ♀H1+3	SWvt WOth
	sessilifolia	CExl LLWG
	- B&SWJ 8875	WCru
	siphilitica	Widely available
	- 'Alba'	CSam EBee EPfP GCal LRHS SBch SPoG SRms SWat SWvt WBor WHrl WMnd WMoo WShi
	- blue-flowered	CSpe NCGa NLar SMrm SWat SWvt
	- 'Rosea'	MNrw
§	× ***speciosa***	IKil NBre SVic SWat WBor WMoo XLum
	- 'Butterfly Blue'	LBMP SGbt SPad
	- 'Butterfly Rose'	SRot
	- 'Cherry Ripe'	CPrp GCra LLHF NHol
	- 'Dark Crusader'	CCon CPrp ECtt ELan EPfP LBMP LRHS NHol SWat WMnd
	- Fan Series	MRav
	- - 'Fan Blau'	EHyd ELan EPfP LPot LRHS MHol NHol WWEG
	- - 'Fan Burgundy'	CPrp EHyd EPfP LRHS MHer NGdn NLar SPet WRHF
§	- - 'Fan Lachs'	EHyd EPfP LRHS MHer SMrm SPet WOut
§	- - 'Fan Orchidrosa' ♀H3-4	CHEx EPfP LRHS NGdn SPet SRot
	- - 'Fan Scharlach' ♀H3-4	EHyd EPfP LRHS NLar SPoG SRot SWvt WShi
§	- - 'Fan Tiefrot' ♀H3-4	LRHS SPet SRms SWvt WOut
§	- - 'Fan Zinnoberrosa' ♀H3-4	SRms SRot SWvt WMoo
	- 'Grape Knee-high'	GCra LLHF LSRN
§	- 'Hadspen Purple'PBR	CAby CHel CMHG CMac CSpe CWGN EBee ECtt ELan EPfP IPot LRHS LSRN MAsh MBri MCot MRav NCGa NDov SHar SRms SWat SWvt
	- 'Kimbridge Beet'	CMac
	- Kompliment Series	WWEG
§	- - 'Kompliment Blau'	CWat SPet SWvt
§	- - 'Kompliment Purpur'	MNrw SPet SWvt
§	- - 'Kompliment Scharlach' ♀H3-4	CAby CWat EPfP MNrw NHol NPer SPet SWvt WMnd WWEG
§	- - 'Kompliment Tiefrot'	EPfP MNrw SMrm SPet SWvt
	- 'Monet Moment'	EBee ECtt EWes SPoG SWvt
	- 'Pauline'	ECtt
	- 'Pink Elephant' ♀H4	ECtt GCra NBre SHar WCFE WWEG
§	- 'Pink Flamingo'	LRHS MBri NLar SHar SPer WMoo WShi
	- 'Red Velvet' **new**	WOut
	- 'Ruby Slippers'	EBee ELan EPfP LRHS LSRN NCGa WWEG
N	- 'Russian Princess' purple-flowered	CCon CPrp ECtt EHoe ELan EWTr LAst LBMP LHop LSou MBel MBri MCot MHer MSpe NCGa NDov NHol SPer WMnd
	- 'Sparkle deVine'	SMrm
	- 'Sparkling Burgundy'	LRHS
	- 'Sparkling Ruby'	CHel EPfP LBuc MCot SWvt
	- 'Tania'	Widely available
§	- 'Vedrariensis'	CMac CSpe CWib ECtt EHon ELan EPfP GBuc LRHS MBel MCot MHer MMuc MNrw NPnk SEND SPer SPoG SRms SWvt WCFE WHoo WMnd XLum

- 'Will Scarlet'	LRHS
'Star Sky'	LSou
'Tania's Sister'	WCot WGrn
treadwellii	see *Pratia angulata* 'Treadwellii'
tupa	Widely available
- JCA 12527	IBlr
- Archibald's form	CExl GCra WCot WPGP
urens	CFil CRDP WPGP
valida	SWvt
- 'True Blue'	CWGN EPfP SWvt
vedrariensis	see *L.* × *speciosa* 'Vedrariensis'
wollastonii	SPlb

Lobularia (*Brassicaceae*)

maritima Easter Bonnet Series ♀H3	NPri
- 'Snow Crystals'	NPri
Snow Princess = 'Inlbusnopr'PBR **new**	NPri

Loeselia (*Polemoniaceae*)

mexicana	CHll

loganberry see *Rubus* × *loganobaccus*

Lomandra (*Asparagaceae*)

confertifolia	ECou
filiformis Savanna Blue = 'Lmf500'	ESwi LSou NOak
hystrix	SPlb
longifolia	ECou GCal LEdu SPlb
- 'Kulnura'	ECou
- Nyalla = 'Lm400'PBR	LHop
- 'Orford'	ECou
- Tanika = 'Lm300'PBR	ESwi NOak

Lomaria see *Blechnum*

Lomatia (*Proteaceae*)

dentata	LRHS MRav
ferruginea	CBcs CDoC CExl CHel CTsd EPfP GGal SAPC SKHP WCru WPGP
fraseri	EBee EPfP LRHS SSpi
hirsuta	SKHP
longifolia	see *L. myricoides*
§ ***myricoides***	CBcs CCCN CExl CTsd EBee ELan EPfP LRHS MAsh MBri NLar SAPC SHil SKHP SLon SPer SSpi
silaifolia	LRHS SPoG
tinctoria	CBcs CDoC CExl CHel CTsd EPfP LRHS MAsh NLar SAPC SSpi

Lomatium (*Apiaceae*)

grayi	SPhx

Lonicera ✿ (*Caprifoliaceae*)

sp.	CMen
B&SWJ 2654 from Sikkim	WCru
KR 291	ELon
SDR 6044	GKev
§ ***acuminata***	CCon EBee LRHS
- B&SWJ 3480	WCru
- B&SWJ 6743	WCru
- B&SWJ 6815	WCru
alberti	EBee MBNS NLar WGob
alseuosmoides	CDul EBee GBin LEdu LRHS NLar SEND SKHP SLon SPoG WCru WPGP WSHC
× ***americana*** misapplied	see *L.* × *italica*
§ × ***americana*** (Miller) K. Koch	CBcs CFlo CRHN EPfP MBri MMuc MRav MSwo MWhi NLar NWea SEND SKHP SLim SRms WBor
§ × ***brownii*** 'Dropmore Scarlet'	Widely available
- 'Fuchsioides' misapplied	see *L.* × *brownii* 'Dropmore Scarlet'
- 'Fuchsioides' K. Koch	WSHC
caerulea	EPPr EPom MRav WHar
- var. ***altaica***	LEdu
- var. ***edulis***	CAgr LBuc LEdu MCoo
- - 'Blue Moon' **new**	CAgr
- var. ***kamtschatica***	CAgr EPom NLar
- - 'Morena'PBR **new**	GGGa
- - 'Nimfa' **new**	GGGa
- 'Kirke' **new**	GBin NLar
* - var. ***longifolia*** **new**	NLar
§ ***caprifolium*** ♀H4	CDoC CFlo CRHN EBee ELan EPfP LRHS NLar SPer
- 'Anna Fletcher'	CRHN CSPN LSRN WCFE
- 'Cornish Cream'	SGol
- f. ***pauciflora***	see *L.* × *italica*
- 'Spring Bouquet'	LRHS
chaetocarpa	CEnd MRav WSHC
'Clavey's Dwarf'	see *L.* × *xylosteoides* 'Clavey's Dwarf'
crassifolia	NLar SBrt
- 'Little Honey'	EPPr MMHG MRav NLar NPnk WCot
deflexicalyx	EPfP NLar
'Early Cream'	see *L. caprifolium*
elisae	CAbP CJun CMac EPfP IMou NLar WSHC
etrusca	CCon MRav
- 'Donald Waterer' ♀H4	CFlo CRHN EBee EPfP LRHS LSRN NLar WGor
- 'Michael Rosse'	ELan IArd LRHS MBNS SKHP
- 'Superba' ♀H4	CFlo CRHN EBee ELan EPfP LEdu LRHS NLar SEND SLim SPer WSHC
'Fire Cracker'	EBee SLon
flexuosa	see *L. japonica* var. *repens*
fragrantissima	Widely available
giraldii misapplied	see *L. acuminata*
giraldii Rehder	EBee EPfP MRav SLim
glabrata	NLar SCoo SLim
- B&SWJ 2150	WCru
glaucescens	WPat
'Golden Trumpet'	CWGN LRHS LSRN
grata	see *L.* × *americana* (Miller) K. Koch
× ***heckrottii***	CDoC CSBt ECtt NLar
§ - 'American Beauty'	MJak
- 'Gold Flame' misapplied	see *L.* × *heckrottii* 'American Beauty'
- 'Gold Flame' ambig.	CFlo GKin LSRN NLar
- 'Gold Flame' hort.	CDul CMac COlW EBee ELan EPfP LBMP LBuc LRHS MAsh MBri MRav SEND SLim SPer SPoG SRms WMoo WSHC
§ ***henryi***	CBcs CDoC CDul CMac CRHN CWib EBee ECtt EPfP GKin IBoy LAst LHop LRHS LSRN MAsh MGos MJak MSwo MWhi SEND SLim SPer SPet SPlb WMoo WSHC
- B&SWJ 8109	WCru
- Sich 1489	WPGP
- 'Copper Beauty'PBR	CCon CEnd EBee ECrN EPPr EPfP EUJe GKin IBoy LBMP LBuc LHop LRHS LSRN LSou MAsh MGos MJak MRav MWat NLar NPri SGol SLon SPoG WHar WPGP
- var. ***subcoriacea***	see *L. henryi*
hildebrandiana	CCCN CExl CFil CHel CHll CRHN MOWG SKHP WPGP

	hispidula new	SBrt
	'Honey Baby'PBR	COIW ELon EPfP LLHF LRHS NHol NWad
	insularis	see *L. morrowii*
	involucrata	CExl CHll CMCN CMHG CWib EPPr GQui LHop MBNS MBlu MMuc NChi SEND SPer WCFE
	- var. ***ledebourii***	CDul EBee ELan EPfP LAst LLHF LRHS MMHG MRav SKHP WGob
	- - 'Vian' new	NLar
	- 'Orange Dwarf'	SKHP
	× ***americana*** ambig.	see *L.* × *italica*
§	× ***italica*** ♀H4	CRHN CSam CTri EBee ECrN ECtt LRHS MAsh MBNS MJak MSwo NEgg NPer SCoo SKHP SPer
§	- Harlequin = 'Sherlite'PBR (v)	CMac CSPN EHoe EPfP GKin LHop LRHS MJak SLim SPlb SRms SWvt
	japonica	CMen IBoy MHoo
§	- 'Aureoreticulata' (v)	CDul CMac CWib EBee ECrN EHoe ELan EPfP EShb LRHS MGos MJak MRav MWhi NPer SGol SPer SPet SRms
	- 'Cream Cascade'	LRHS MSwo NLar SCoo SGol
	- 'Dart's Acumen'	CRHN
	- 'Dart's World'	EBee MBri
	- 'Halliana' ♀H4	Widely available
	- 'Hall's Prolific'	CDoC CDul CSBt EBee ECrN ELan EPfP EWTr LBMP LBuc LRHS LSRN MAsh MBlu MBri MGos MHer MRav MSwo MWat NEgg SGol SLim SPad SPoG SWvt WHar
§	- 'Horwood Gem' (v)	EBee ECtt NLar SCoo SLim
	- 'Maskerade' (v)	LLHF NBro NLar
	- 'Mint Crisp'PBR (v)	CDul CMac CSBt CSPN CWGN EBee ECrN ECtt ELan EPfP LAst LRHS LSRN LSou MBlu MBri MGos MJak NLar SGol SLim SLon SPad SPer SPoG SWvt WHar
	- 'Peter Adams'	see *L. japonica* 'Horwood Gem'
§	- var. ***repens*** ♀H4	CDul CMac COIW CSBt CTri CWSG EBee ECrN ECtt ELan EPfP LAst LRHS MBri MRav MSwo MWat NLar SCoo SGol SLim SLon SPad SPer SRms WMoo
	- 'Variegata'	see *L. japonica* 'Aureoreticulata'
	korolkowii	CFil CJun EPPr EPfP MBNS NBir NLar SEND WCFE WSHC
	- 'Blue Velvet'	CAgr GBin MCoo NLar
	var. ***zabelii*** misapplied	see *L. tatarica* 'Zabelii'
	- var. ***zabelii*** (Rehder) Rehder	ELan
	lanceolata BWJ 7935	WCru
	maackii	CHll CJun CMCN EPPr EPfP IGor MMHG MRav NLar WCFE
	- f. ***podocarpa***	NLar
*	***macgregorii***	CMCN
	macrantha B&SWJ 11687	WCru
	- WWJ 11606	WCru
	'Mandarin'	CDoC CRHN EBee ELan LRHS MBlu NLar SCoo SGol SLim SWvt WPat WSHC
	maximowiczii var. ***sachalinensis***	NLar
§	***morrowii***	CMCN
	myrtillus	NLar
	nitida	CBar CBcs CCVT CDul CMac CMen CSBt CTri ECrN EPfP NWea SAPC SEWo SGol SPer WHar
	- 'Baggesen's Gold' ♀H4	Widely available
	- 'Eden Spring'	NPro
	- Edmée Gold = 'Briloni'	MAsh
	- 'Fertilis'	SPer
	- 'Lemon Beauty' (v)	CDoC CMac EBee ECrN EHoe EPPr EPfP EShb LAst LHop LRHS LSRN MAsh MBNS MGos MWhi NBir NEgg NLar NWad SGol SHil SPer SPoG SWvt WHar WMoo
	- 'Lemon Queen'	CWib ELan MMuc MSwo SEND
	- 'Lemon Spreader'	CBcs
§	- 'Maigrün'	CBar CBcs CCVT CDul EBee EPfP EShb MSwo NPro SHil SPer SWvt
	- Maygreen	see *L. nitida* 'Maigrün'
	- 'Red Tips'	EHoe EPfP GKin SCoo WMoo
	- 'Silver Beauty' (v)	CDul CMac CWib EBee ECrN EHoe EPfP LAst LHop MGos MSwo NEgg SPer SPlb SRms SWvt WMoo
	- 'Tidy Tips' new	EPPr NSoo
	- 'Twiggy' (v)	CDoC CSBt EDAr EHoe LBuc LHop LRHS MAsh NEgg NHol NLar STPC WGrn
	periclymenum	CArn CCVT CTri ECrN GPoy MHer MLHP MRav NLar NMir NWea SPlb WPnn WSFF
	- 'Belgica' misapplied	see *L.* × *italica*
	- 'Belgica'	Widely available
	- 'Florida'	see *L. periclymenum* 'Serotina'
	- 'Fragrant Cloud' new	LBuc
	- 'Graham Thomas' ♀H4	Widely available
	- 'Harlequin'	see *L.* × *italica* Harlequin
	- 'Heaven Scent'	CFlo EBee LBuc LSRN MNHC NLar WPnn
	- 'Honeybush'	CDoC CJun CSPN CWGN EBee LBMP MAsh MBri MGos NHol NWad SLim WMoo
	- 'La Gasnérie'	EBee SLim WPnn
	- 'Munster'	WPnn WSHC
	- 'Red Gables'	CRHN EBee ELon LSRN MBNS MBri MGos NLar SCoo SEND SLim WGor WKif WPat WPnn
	- 'Scentsation'PBR	CFlo CMac CSBt CWCL CWGN EBee ELan EPfP EUJe LBMP LRHS MAsh MBri NCGa NLar SCoo SLon SPoG
N	- 'Serotina' ♀H4	Widely available
	- 'Sweet Sue'	CFlo COIW CRHN CSPN CSpe EBee ELan ELon EPfP EWTr GBin LRHS LSRN MAsh MBNS MBri MGos MLHP MSwo NEgg SCoo SPoG SWvt WMoo
	- yellow-flowered	NEgg
	pileata	CBcs CCVT CDoy CDul CMac CSBt CTri EBee ECrN EHoe ELan EPfP EShb EWTr LBuc LRHS MGos MJak MRav MSwo MWhi NPer NWea SGol SPer SPoG SRms WCFE WHar
	- 'Craibstone Compact'	SLPl
	- 'Loughall Evergreen'	SLPl
	- 'Moss Green'	EBee EShb
	- 'Pilot'	SLPl
	- 'Silver Lining' (v)	WCFE
	- 'Stockholm'	SLPl
	pilosa Willd. F&M 207	CFil WPGP
	- F&M 256	CFil WPGP
	× ***purpusii***	CHll CMac COIW CRHN CTri CWib EBee ECrN EPfP LSRN MBNS MLHP SPer SRms WCFE WSHC
	- 'Spring Romance'	CMac
	- 'Winter Beauty' ♀H4	Widely available

	pyrenaica	WGob
	ramosissima	NLar
	reticulata 'Silver' new	NLar
	saccata	CJun EPfP
	sempervirens ♀H4	CMac CRHN CSBt EBee MBNS MRav WHar WSHC
	- 'Cedar Lane'	CRHN LRHS
	- 'Dropmore Scarlet'	see *L.* × *brownii* 'Dropmore Scarlet'
	- 'Leo'	CWGN
N	- f. ***sulphurea***	EPfP WSHC
	- - 'John Clayton'	EPfP LRHS SKHP
	setifera 'Daphnis'	CJun EPfP
	similis var. ***delavayi*** ♀H4	CFlo CRHN CSPN CWGN EBee ELan EPfP LBMP LRHS MAsh MBri MNHC MRav NEgg NSoo SDix SEND SLPl SRms WCru WPGP WSHC
	splendida	WSHC
	standishii	CTri EBee
	- 'Budapest'	ELon LLHF LRHS MAsh MBlu MBri MRav NLar SPoG WPat
	stenantha	IGor
	subaequalis	CFil CGHE CRHN
	- Og 93.329	CExl SKHP WPGP WSHC
	Sweet Isabel = 'Genbel'PBR	CWGN EBee EPfP SKHP
	syringantha	CArn CDoC CHel COlW CRHN ECrN ELan EPfP EWTr LAst LEdu LHop MBri MMuc MNrw MRav MWhi NEgg NLar NPro NSoo SEND SLPl SPer WBor WCFE WGob WPat WSHC
	- 'Grandiflora'	GQui
	tatarica	CHll CMCN CWib MRav
	- 'Alba'	CJun EPPr EWTr
	- 'Arnold Red'	CBcs ELan EPPr EPfP MBlu MHer NLar SEND WBor
	- 'Hack's Red'	CMCN CWib EBee ELon EPPr EPfP LEdu LHop LRHS MRav NSoo SCoo SKHP SMDP SPer SPoG SVen SWvt WGob
	- 'Rosea'	EPPr
§	- 'Zabelii'	EPfP EWTr MNrw
	× ***tellmanniana***	CBar CBcs CDoC CDul CExl CHel CMac COlW CRHN CWCL EBee ECtt ELan EPfP LRHS LSRN MBlu MBri MJak MSwo NEgg SEND SLim SPer SPet SRms WSHC
	- 'Joan Sayers'	EBee SCoo SLim WCFE
	- 'Pharaoh's Trumpet'	EPfP LRHS SLon
	thibetica	MBlu
	tragophylla ♀H4	CDoC CDoy CSBt EBee ELan EPfP LRHS LSRN MBNS MBri MRav SCoo SEND SLim SPer SSpi SWvt WPat WSHC
	- 'Maurice Foster'	EBee ELan MBNS SMDP WSHC
	webbiana	ELan
§	× ***xylosteoides*** 'Clavey's Dwarf'	EBee EPPr GKin LLHF
	xylosteum	CArn EBtc EPPr NLar

Lophomyrtus (*Myrtaceae*)

§	***bullata***	CAbP CDTJ EBee SPer
	× ***ralphii*** 'Black Pearl'	CWGN EBee EShb LBuc LRHS MBri MPkF NSoo SCoo SHil SLim SPoG SRkn
	- 'Gloriosa' (v)	EPfP
	- 'Kathryn'	CBcs CDoC CTsd EBee ELan EPfP LRHS MPkF NLar SPoG SRGP
	- 'Krinkly'	SVen
	- 'Little Star' (v)	CBcs LRHS WPat
	- Logan's form (v)	CBcs EBee LRHS
	- 'Multicolor' (v)	CBcs EBee EPfP LRHS NPri SLim SVen
	- 'Pixie'	CBcs EBee EPfP LRHS MAsh SLim SPoG SVen WPat
	- 'Purpurea'	MPkF
	- 'Red Dragon'	CAbP CBcs CMac CWSG EBee LRHS LSou MAsh SLim WPat
	- 'Red Wing'	LRHS
§	- 'Traversii' (v)	SPoG
	- 'Wild Cherry'	EBee LRHS

Lophosoria (*Dicksoniaceae*)

	quadripinnata	CBty CCon CDTJ EAmu SBig WPGP

Lophospermum (*Plantaginaceae*)

	'Cream Delight'	CCCN
§	***erubescens*** ♀H2-3	CRHN SBch
	- 'Bridal Bouquet'	CPla
	Lofos Summer Cream = 'Sunasashiro'	LAst
	Lofos Wine Red = 'Sunasaro' new	LAst
§	'Magic Dragon'	CPla LSou SLim SVic WBor
§	'Red Dragon'	CCCN CPla EShb SBch
§	***scandens***	CCCN
	'Wine Red'	LAst WBor

loquat see *Eriobotrya japonica*

Loropetalum (*Hamamelidaceae*)

	chinense	CWib
	- 'Ming Dynasty'	CAbP MAsh SSta WAbe
	- var. ***rubrum***	CBcs CExl CWib
	- - 'Blush'	CJun EBee
	- - 'Burgundy'	MPkF
	- - 'Daybreak's Flame'	CJun LRHS MPkF SSta
	- - 'Fire Dance'	CAbP CBcs CCCN CDoC CExl CHll CJun CTsd EBee ELon EPfP EUJe LRHS MAsh MGos MPkF SPad SPoG SRkn SSpi SWvt WCot WHlf WPat
	- - 'Fire Glow'	LRHS SHil
	- - 'Pipa's Red'	MGos MPkF
	- 'Snowdance'	CAbP
	- 'Tang Dynasty'	ESwi LRHS SSta

Lotus (*Papilionaceae*)

	berthelotii	CCCN CDTJ ECtt ELan EOHP LPot MCot SPet
	- deep red-flowered ♀H1+3	SWvt
	berthelotii × ***maculatus*** ♀H1+3	CCCN MSCN
	corniculatus	CArn CHab MCoo MHer MMuc MNHC NMir SEND SIde WSFF
	germanicus new	SPhx
	'Gold Flash'	LAst
	hirsutus ♀H3-4	CArn CExl CHEx CWSG CWib EHoe ELan EPfP LBMP LHop LPot LRHS MAsh MBri MCot MRav SEND SIgm SLon SPer SPhx SPlb SPoG SRms SWvt WIce XLum XSen
	- 'Brimstone' (v)	CWSG CWib LHop LRHS MRav SPer SPoG SWvt XSen
	- Little Boy Blue = 'Lisbob'PBR	CSBt EBee EPfP LBMP LRHS LSqu SSpi
	- 'Lois'	EPfP LHop LRHS SPoG WPGP
	jacobaeus	LHop MCot
	maculatus	EOHP MOWG SMrm SPet

maritimus	CPom SRot
pedunculatus	CHab MCoo NMir WSFF
pentaphyllus	CArn XSen
tetragonolobus	SPhx SVic

lovage see *Levisticum officinale*

Loxostigma (*Gesneriaceae*)

kurzii GWJ 9342	WCru

Luffa (*Cucurbitaceae*)

aegyptiaca	SVic

Luma (*Myrtaceae*)

§ ***apiculata*** 🏆H3	Widely available
§ - 'Glanleam Gold' (v) 🏆H3	Widely available
- 'Nana'	LEdu WJek
- 'Penlee'	SRms WJek
- 'Saint Hilary' (v)	EPfP LRHS SPoG SRms WJek
- 'Variegata' (v)	CTri SLim
§ ***chequen***	CBcs CDoy CSpe IDee LRHS MHer NLar SRms WJek WMoo

Lunaria (*Brassicaceae*)

§ ***annua***	CArn CWCL MNHC SIde SWat WCot WJek WSFF
- var. ***albiflora*** 🏆H4	MMuc NBir SEND SWat WCot
I - - 'Alba Variegata' (v)	CSpe LBMP WBrk
- 'Chedglow'	CNat
- 'Corfu Blue'	CDes CSpe WCot WSHC
- 'Munstead Purple'	CSpe
- 'Nettleton'	CNat
- purple-leaved **new**	CMea
- 'Variegata' (v)	NBir SWat WCot WHer
- violet-flowered	NBir
biennis	see *L. annua*
rediviva	CSpe EBee ECGP EPPr GAbr GBin GCal GCra IBlr IFro LEdu LPio LRHS MAvo MMuc NBid NChi NPer NPnk NSti WCot WHer WPGP
- 'Partway White'	WCot

Lunathyrium (*Woodsiaceae*)

pycnosorum	ISha

Lupinus ✿ (*Papilionaceae*)

'African Sunset'	CWCL
albifrons var. ***collinus*** **new**	WHil
albus	CArn
'Animal'	CWCL
'Approaching Storm'	SMrm
arboreus 🏆H4	CBcs CDoC CDul CSBt CTri CWCL CWib EBee ELan EPfP EWTr GKev LAst LRHS MAsh MCoo MHer MNHC MRav NBir NChi NLar SPer SPlb SPoG SRms SVic WBor WWEG
- 'Blue Boy'	ELan LSRN
- blue-flowered	CWCL EShb LRHS MCot SBod SPer SPhx SPlb SPoG SWvt WCot
- 'Chelsea Blue'	EPfP LRHS
- 'Rhubarb and Custard'	CWCL
- 'Snow Queen'	CWCL LRHS SPoG
- 'Sulphur Yellow'	SWvt
- white-flowered	CSpe MCot SPlb
- yellow and blue-flowered	NBir SRkn
- yellow-flowered	ELan GKev MCot MLHP SPhx WWEG
arcticus	CSpe EBee
Band of Nobles Series 🏆H4	MAvo
'Beefeater'	CWCL LBuc LLHF MBri
'Bishop's Tipple'	CWCL EWes
'Blossom' PBR	CWCL CWGN IPot LBuc LLHF LRHS LSRN MBri SPoG
'Blue Streak'	CWCL
'Bruiser'	CWCL
'Camelot Blue'	EPfP
'Cashmere Cream'	CWCL MBri
'Chameleon'	CWCL LRHS
chamissonis	CHII CPla CSpe CWCL ELan EWes LHop LRHS SMrm SPer WOut
'Chandelier' (Band of Nobles Series)	Widely available
'Desert Sun'	CWCL MBri
Dwarf Gallery hybrids	IBoy
'Dwarf Lulu'	see *L.* 'Lulu'
'Everest' **new**	CWCL
Gallery Series	CSBt IBoy MAvo SCoo SPlb
- 'Gallery Blue'	ECtt ELan EPfP IBoy LRHS LSRN NLar NPri SCoo SMrm SPer SPoG
- 'Gallery Pink'	EHyd ELan EPfP IBoy LRHS NLar NPri SCoo SMrm SPer SPoG
- 'Gallery Red'	ECtt EHyd ELan EPfP IBoy LRHS NLar NPri SCoo SMrm SPer SPoG
- 'Gallery Rose'	IBoy LSRN SPoG
- 'Gallery White'	ELan EPfP IBoy LRHS NLar NPri SCoo SPer SPoG
- 'Gallery Yellow'	ECtt ELan EPfP IBoy LRHS NLar NPri SPer SPoG
'Gladiator'	CWCL ECtt EWes LLHF MBri SPoG
'Heathcliffe Blue'	WOut
'Imperial Robe'	CWCL
'Inspiration'	CWCL MBri
'Judy Harper' **new**	ECtt
'Jupiter' **new**	CWCL
'King Canute' **new**	CWCL
'Le Gentilhomme' (Band of Nobles Series)	MCot XLum
lepidus	WAbe
'Lindy Lou'	CWCL
§ 'Lulu'	EPfP IBoy LRHS MWat SGbt SPer SPoG STes SWvt WHar WMoo
'Manhattan Lights' PBR	CWCL CWGN EWes IPot LBuc LLHF LRHS MBri
'Masterpiece' PBR	CWCL GBin IPot LBuc LLHF LRHS MBri
Minarette Group	CTri LRHS SPet SRms
montanus	WPGP
'Morello Cherry'	CWCL
'Mrs Perkins'	SMrm
'My Castle' (Band of Nobles Series)	Widely available
'Neptune'	CWCL
'Noble Maiden' (Band of Nobles Series)	CBcs CPrp CSBt CTri ECtt ELan ELon EPfP LBMP LRHS LSRN MBri MCot MNHC MWat NGBl NHol NLar NPri SHil SMrm SPer SPoG SWvt WCAu WHil WMoo XLum
nootkatensis	GLog LDai LRHS SDix
'Pam Ayres'	ECtt
'Pen and Ink'	CWCL
perennis	LRHS SPhx
'Persian Slipper' PBR	CWCL CWGN ECtt EWes GBin IPot LBuc LLHF LRHS LSRN MBri SPoG
'Pluto'	CWCL
'Polar Princess'	CWCL EWes GBin LRHS SWat
propinquus	SPhx
'Purple Swirl' **new**	CWCL
'Red Arrow'	CWCL

	'Red Rum'[PBR]	CWCL CWGN GBin LBuc LRHS LSRN MBri SPoG
	'Redhead'	CWCL
	'Rote Flamme'	CPrp ELon EWes XLum
	Russell hybrids	CSBt EPfP IBoy LAst MHer MLHP MMuc SBod SEND SPet SPlb SRms SVic SWvt WRHF
	'Saffron'[PBR]	CWCL GBin LBuc LRHS LSRN MBri
	'Salmon Star'[PBR]	CWCL GBin LRHS MBri SPoG
	'Sand Pink'	EWes
	'Silver Fleece'	CHid
	'Sparky'	CWCL
	succulentus	WHil
	'Tequila Flame'	CWCL IPot LLHF LRHS MBri
	'Terracotta'	CWCL LBuc SPoG
	texensis	CSpe
	'The Chatelaine' (Band of Nobles Series)	Widely available
	'The Governor' (Band of Nobles Series)	Widely available
	'The Page' (Band of Nobles Series)	CBcs ELan ELon EPfP IBoy LHop LRHS LSRN MAsh MBri MCot MNHC MWat NLar NPri SMrm SPer SPoG SWvt WHar WHil WMoo XLum
	'Thundercloud'	CDes SMrm
	'Towering Inferno'	CWCL EWes MBri
	'Tutti Frutti'	EWTr IBoy
	variicolor	LDai SIgm SMad
	Woodfield hybrids	GAbr SMrm

Luzula (*Juncaceae*)

	alpinopilosa	EPPr GBin
	× ***borreri***	EPPr
	- 'Botany Bay' (v)	EPPr GBin
	forsteri	IMou
	luzuloides	WPtf
	- 'Schneehäschen'	GBin GCal NWsh
	maxima	see *L. sylvatica*
	nivalis	GAbr
	nivea	Widely available
	pedemontana	EPPr SMea
	pilosa	EBee GCal
	- 'Igel'	CKno LEdu NBid SLPl SMad
	purpureosplendens	LEdu NOak
	rufa	ECou
§	***sylvatica***	CHEx CRow ELan EPPr EPfP LRHS MMoz MMuc MRav NBro NMir NOrc SEND WHer WShi WWEG XLum
	- from Tatra Mountains, Slovakia	EPPr
	- 'A. Rutherford'	see *L. sylvatica* 'Taggart's Cream'
	- 'Aurea'	CHEx CKno ELon EPPr EPfP LAst LBMP LRHS MJak MMoz MRav NBid NOak NSti NWsh WCot WGrn WMoo WPat WPtf
	- 'Aureomarginata'	see *L. sylvatica* 'Marginata'
I	- 'Auslese'	EPPr EPfP WMoo
	- 'Bromel'	EPPr
	- 'Engel'	EBee EPPr EWes
	- 'Hohe Tatra'	CElw CPrp CSpe EHoe EPPr EWes GMaP LEdu MBNS MWhi NBro NGdn NOak SLPl SPer SPoG WPnP WWEG
§	- 'Marginata' (v)	CHEx CPrp EBee EHoe EPPr GMaP LBMP MAvo MBNS MMoz MMuc MRav MWhi NBid NBro NGdn NSti NWad SAPC SEND SLPl WCot WHoo WMoo WWEG XLum
	- 'Mariusz' **new**	EPPr
*	- f. ***nova***	ELon EPPr
	- 'Solar Flair'	MWhi WPtf
§	- 'Taggart's Cream' (v)	EBee EHoe MBNS NBid NHol WMoo WWEG
	- 'Tauernpass'	EHoe EPPr GCal SLPl
	- 'Wäldler'	EPPr MBNS NHol
	ulophylla	ECou WThu

Luzuriaga (*Luzuriagaceae*)

	polyphylla HCM 98202	WCru
	radicans	CCCN ECou WCru WSHC
	- RH 0602	WCru

Lychnis (*Caryophyllaceae*)

	alpina	CMac ECho EDAr GKev GMaP MAsh NGdn WHil XLum
	- 'Rosea'	NBir
	- 'Snow Flurry'	EDAr GKev NLar
§	× ***arkwrightii***	ELan LRHS
	- 'Orange Zwerg'	MBNS SGbt
	- 'Vesuvius'	CBcs CMac CWGN EBee LRHS MWat NBir NPnk NSoo SPer SRms STes WGwG WMnd WWEG XLum
	chalcedonica 🏆[H4]	Widely available
	- var. ***albiflora***	EPfP MBel NBro SMrm WHrl WMoo
	- 'Carnea'	EBee LRHS MBNS NBre NGdn SMrm SPhx WWEG
	- 'Dusky Salmon'	WOut
	- 'Flore Pleno' (d)	ELan EShb GCal NLar WCot
	- 'Morgenrot'	LRHS MBel
	- 'Pinkie'	NLar NWad
	- 'Rauhreif'	NBre SPhx
	- 'Rosea'	EPfP LRHS NBir WHrl WMoo
*	- 'Salmonea'	NBir SRms
	cognata B&SWJ 4234	WCru
§	***coronaria*** 🏆[H4]	Widely available
	- MESE 356	MAvo SPhx
	- 'Abbotswood Rose'	see *L.* × *walkeri* 'Abbotswood Rose'
	- 'Alba' 🏆[H4]	Widely available
	- 'Angel's Blush'	NBir SPav SRkn
	- Atrosanguinea Group	CBre CHel EPfP EWTr GMaP IBlr LRHS MBel MHol MRav MSpe NEgg NGdn NPri NSti NWad SMrm SPer WGwG
	- 'Blood Red'	CSpe
	- 'Castle Haven Variegation' **new**	MAvo
	- 'Cerise'	MArl NBir
	- 'Dancing Ladies'	WMnd
	- dark-red-flowered	MAvo
	- Gardeners' World = 'Blych' (d)	CDes CElw CSpe EBee ECtt ELon EWes GBin LRHS LSou MBNS MBel MHol MSpe MTis NGdn NSti SMrm SPer WBrk WCot
	- 'Hutchinson's Cream' (v)	NBir
	- Oculata Group	CElw CSpe EBee ECGP EHyd ELan EPfP EWTr LEdu LPot MAvo NWad SMrm SPav SPet SPlb WKif WMoo WRHF WWEG
§	***coronata*** var. ***sieboldii***	SBrt
	dioica	see *Silene dioica*
	flos-cuculi	CArn CBAq CHab CPom CWat ECho EHon EPfP LEdu LLWG MHer MNHC NLar NMir NPri WHer WMAq WMoo WOut WPnP WSFF WWFP XLum
	- var. ***albiflora***	CBAq CBre CElw MSKA NBro NLar WHer WMnd WMoo WWFP

- var. ***congesta*** new	WAbe
- Jenny = 'Lychjen'PBR (d)	CWCL EBee ECtt ELan ELon GBin GQue LBMP LEdu LLWG LRHS MBNS MBel MHol MNrw MPie MTis NSti SHar SMad SPad SPoG SRkn WBor WCot WGrn WHer WMnd
- 'Little Robin'	LLWG
- 'Nana'	ECho EDAr GAbr MSKA NGdn NLar SBch
- 'White Robin'	CBre CHel EPfP IFro IKil LEdu LRHS MBNS MBel MWat NCGa NDov NGdn NPnk SBea SHar SMrm SPhx WBor WPnP WWEG
flos-jovis ♀H4	EPfP GJos LRHS MBel NBir NLar SRms WMoo XLum
- 'Hort's Variety'	EBee LRHS NBir NSti
- 'Minor'	see *L. flos-jovis* 'Nana'
§ - 'Nana'	LRHS MSCN SBch
- 'Peggy'	EBee EShb LRHS NBre NGdn NLar
fulgens	NBre
× ***haageana***	IFro NLar SRms
- 'Lumina Bronze Leaf Red'	LRHS
'Hill Grounds'	CDes CElw WCot WSHC
lagascae	see *Petrocoptis pyrenaica* subsp. *glaucifolia*
miqueliana	WMoo
'Molten Lava'	ELan EPfP NLar
'Rollie's Favorite'	ECtt MSCN NDov NPri NSti SHar SHil SPoG WBor WHil
sieboldii 'Matsu Moto'	IFro
* ***sikkimensis***	NBre
'Terry's Pink'	NCGa
§ ***viscaria***	CArn GCra GJos LDai WMoo
- 'Alba'	NBre NBro XLum
- ***alpina***	see *L. viscaria*
§ - subsp. ***atropurpurea***	CAby CFis EWes LSou MPie NBre SBHP SRms WHrl WPtf
- 'Feuer'	EBee EWes GJos LRHS NGBl NLar WMoo
- 'Firebird'	EWes NBre
- 'Plena' (d)	NBir SRkn
- 'Schnee'	LRHS NEgg NLar
- 'Snowbird'	CTsd
- 'Splendens'	EPfP SPet XLum
- 'Splendens Plena' (d) ♀H4	NBre NBro XLum
§ × ***walkeri*** 'Abbotswood Rose' ♀H4	IBlr
§ ***yunnanensis***	EBee GKev NBid SBHP SPhx WPtf XLum
- ***alba***	see *L. yunnanensis*

Lycianthes (*Solanaceae*)

quichensis B&SWJ 10395	WCru
§ ***rantonnetii***	CCCN CHll ELan EPfP EShb EUJe IDee MOWG NSoo SEND SPoG WBor WWlt
- 'Royal Robe'	CRHN
- 'Variegatum' (v)	CHll EShb MSCN WCot

Lycium (*Solanaceae*)

afrum new	SVen
barbarum	CAgr CBcs CCCN EBee EPfP EPom EWes IDee LBuc LEdu LRHS MCoo SEND SPlb SPoG SPre SVic SWvt WHar
- 'Big Lifeberry'	CAgr MCoo
- 'Number 1 Lifeberry' new	CAgr
- 'Sweet Lifeberry' new	CAgr
chinense	CArn IBoy NLar

Lycopodium (*Lycopodiaceae*)

clavatum	GPoy

Lycopsis see *Anchusa*

Lycopus (*Lamiaceae*)

americanus	CArn
europaeus	CArn CHab EBee ELau GPoy LLWG WGwG

Lycoris (*Amaryllidaceae*)

albiflora	ECho WCot
aurea	CCon EBee ECho GKev
haywardii	WCot
incarnata	ECho
radiata	CCCN CCon EBee ECho GKev
sanguinea var. ***kiusiana***	GKev
sprengeri	EBee

Lygodium (*Lygodiaceae*)

japonicum	ISha WFib

Lyonia (*Ericaceae*)

mariana	NLar

Lyonothamnus (*Rosaceae*)

floribundus	CCCN CDoC CExl EUJe NLar SAPC
subsp. ***aspleniifolius***	WPGP

Lysichiton (*Araceae*)

sp.	GGal
americanus ♀H4	Widely available
camtschatcensis ♀H4	CBcs CFwr CLAP CRow CTsd CWat EHon EPfP EUJe GBin GBuc IGor LLWG LRHS MWts NLar NOrc NPer NPnk SMad SPer SSpi SWat SWvt WPnP WShi XLum

Lysiloma (*Mimosaceae*)

watsonii new	SPlb

Lysimachia ✿ (*Primulaceae*)

albescens	CExl SPad XLum
§ ***atropurpurea***	CSpe EBee ELan EPfP GJos LPio LRHS SPer WMnd WWEG
- 'Beaujolais'	CExl GAbr GJos IBoy LPot LRHS LSRN MBri MPie NPnk NPri SDix SMrm SPoG WHil
- 'Geronimo'	CSpe
barystachys	CPrp CSam LPla LRHS MRav NPnk SHar WCot WWEG XLum
- 'Huntingbrook' new	WPGP
Candela = 'Innlyscand'	CSpe ECtt GBin LSou MBri MHol NPnk NPri SMrm SPoG WCot WHil
candida	WCot
ciliata	CMHG CMac EHoe ELan GMaP MNrw NBir NGdn SWat WCot
§ - 'Firecracker' ♀H4	Widely available
- 'Purpurea'	see *L. ciliata* 'Firecracker'
clethroides ♀H4	Widely available
- 'Geisha' (v)	EBee EWes WCot
- 'Lady Jane'	CCon MNrw SRms
§ ***congestiflora***	NPer SPet
- 'Golden Falls'	CTsd
- 'Midnight Sun'PBR	ECtt LAst
- 'Outback Sunset'PBR (v)	ECtt LAst
- 'Persian Carpet' new	WCot
- 'Persian Chocolate' new	WCot

	ephemerum	Widely available
	fortunei	EBee EWld LRHS MWat XLum
	hybrida	WCot
	lichiangensis	CExl EBee GKev IMou LRHS NBir WMoo XLum
	lyssii	see *L. congestiflora*
	mauritiana	LRHS WHil
	minoricensis	CCon ELan SWat XLum
	nemorum subsp. ***azorica***	WCot
	- 'Pale Star'	CBre EBee
	nummularia	CBAq COIW CSBt CTri CWat ECtt EHon EPfP GPoy MJak MMuc NBir SGol SWat WBrk WHfH
	- 'Aurea' 🏆H4	Widely available
	paridiformis	WCot
	- var. ***stenophylla***	CExl
	- - DJHC 704	EBee
	punctata misapplied	see *L. verticillaris*
	punctata L.	CBAq CRow CSBt EHon EPfP GMaP MHer MMuc MRav MWat NBro NHol NMir NPer NSoo SEND SPer SPlb SRms SWat WBrk WMAq WMoo WPnP
§	- 'Alexander' (v)	Widely available
	- 'Gaulthier Brousse'	WCot WWEG
	- Golden Alexander = 'Walgoldalex'[PBR] (v)	CExl ELon LBMP LRHS MBNS MBel MBri NHol NLar NPri SPoG
	- 'Golden Glory' (v)	WCot
	- 'Hometown Hero'	EBee
	- 'Irish Butter'	WCot
	- 'Ivy Maclean' (v)	SWvt WCot WWEG
	- 'Variegata'	see *L. punctata* 'Alexander'
	- ***verticillata***	see *L. verticillaris*
	'Purpurea'	see *L. atropurpurea*
	pyramidalis	WPtf WWEG
	Snow Candles = 'L9902'	CCVN COIW EBee
	thyrsiflora	CBAq CWat EBee EHon EWay NPer SWat WCot WMAq
§	***verticillaris***	CTri WCot
	vulgaris	CArn CHab LLWG MSKA WJek WMoo
	- subsp. ***davurica***	WCot
	- - B&SWJ 8632	WCru

Lysionotus (*Gesneriaceae*)

gamosepalus B&SWJ 7241	WCru
aff. ***kwangsiensis*** HWJ 643	WCru
'Lavender Lady'	NCGa WHil
pauciflorus	CDes WAbe WSHC
- B&SWJ 189	WCru
- B&SWJ 303	WCru
- B&SWJ 335	WCru
serratus HWJK 2426	WCru

Lythrum (*Lythraceae*)

	alatum	NDov
	anceps	NBre NLar
	salicaria	CArn CBAq CHab CKno CWat EHon GJos MCot MHer MLHP MMuc MNHC MWts NBro SEND SPlb SRms SWat WBrk WHer WJek WMoo WPnP WSFF WShi XLum
	- 'Augenweide'	XLum
	- 'Blush' 🏆H4	Widely available
§	- 'Feuerkerze' 🏆H4	CAby CKno CMea CPrp EBee ECtt ELan ELon EPfP LAst LBMP LHop LRHS LSou MBel MBri MCot MNFA MRav MSpe MWts NBir NEgg NHol NSti SPer WHil WWEG
	- Firecandle	see *L. salicaria* 'Feuerkerze'
	- 'Happy'	ELon LRHS SMrm
	- 'Lady Sackville'	EBee ECtt ELon EPPr GMaP IPot MCot NLar SMrm WSHC WWEG
	- 'Little Robert'	ECtt IBoy NHol SBea
	- 'Morden Pink'	EBee EHyd EPfP MBri MMuc NLar SEND SPhx
	- 'Prichard's Variety'	CKno EBee WPGP
	- 'Robert'	Widely available
	- 'Robin'	LLHF LRHS MAsh MBri SGbt SRot SWvt
	- 'Rose'	ELan NBir SWvt
	- 'Stichflamme'	SMrm
	- 'Swirl'	ECtt EHyd EPfP LLWG NLar SHar SMrm WHoo
	- 'The Beacon'	EBee NLar SRms
	- Ulverscroft form	WHil
	- 'Zigeunerblut'	CElw CKno CMHG ELon EPPr GQue IPot LHop MRav NLar SMrm SPhx SWat WHil
	virgatum	CMHG NDov SPhx WCFE WMoo WOut WSHC
	- 'Dropmore Purple'	COIW CPrp CSam EBee ECtt ELon EPPr EPfP IPot LAst LHop LLWG LRHS LSRN MAsh MBri MCot MRav MSpe NDov NEgg NPri SPer SPhx SPoG WCAu WCFE WHar WSHC XLum
	- 'Helene' **new**	IMou
	- 'Rosy Gem'	EBee EPfP GMaP IBoy LAst LRHS MWat MWhi NBro SRms SWvt WCFE WWEG
	- 'The Rocket'	CAby CSam CTri EPPr EPfP GBee GQue LAst LRHS MRav NBro NDov SPer SWvt WWlt

Lytocaryum (*Arecaceae*)

§	***weddellianum*** 🏆H1	EAmu

M

Maackia (*Papilionaceae*)

amurensis	CBcs CDul CHGN CMCN ELan EPfP IDee IVic LRHS WSHC
chinensis	MBlu NLar

Macbridea (*Lamiaceae*)

caroliniana	WPGP

mace, English see *Achillea ageratum*

Macfadyena (*Bignoniaceae*)

	uncata	MOWG
§	***unguis-cati***	CCCN CRHN EShb

Machaerina (*Cyperaceae*)

rubiginosa 'Variegata' (v)	EWay LLWG
sinclairii	ECou

Machilus see *Persea*

Mackaya (*Acanthaceae*)

§	***bella*** 🏆H1	CHll EShb WHil

Macleaya (*Papaveraceae*)

cordata misapplied	see *M.* × ***kewensis***

§ ***cordata*** (Willd.) R. Br. ♀H4	EBee ELan EPfP EWTr LHop LRHS MBri MHol NBir NOrc SPer SPlb SRms WCot WMnd WMoo XLum
§ × ***kewensis***	EBee
- 'Flamingo' ♀H4	CExl CHel EBee ECtt GBuc GQue LAst LRHS MBNS MNFA NPnk SWvt WHoo WWEG
§ ***microcarpa***	MHol SWat WWEG
- 'Kelway's Coral Plume' ♀H4	Widely available
- 'Spetchley Ruby'	CExl EBee MRav SPhx WCot WPGP WWEG XLum
'Plum Tassel'	WCot

Maclura (*Moraceae*)

pomifera	CArn CBcs EBee IVic LEdu NLar SPlb

Macrodiervilla see *Weigela*

Macropiper (*Piperaceae*)

§ ***excelsum***	CHEx ECou

Macrozamia (*Zamiaceae*)

communis	CBrP EAmu
diplomera	CBrP
dyeri	see *M. riedlei*
johnsonii	CBrP
lucida	CBrP
moorei	CBrP
§ ***riedlei***	CBrP

Maddenia (*Rosaceae*)

hypoleuca	NLar

Maesa (*Primulaceae*)

japonica	CExl
- CWJ 12371	WCru
montana	CExl

Magnolia ✿ (*Magnoliaceae*)

acuminata	CBcs CDul CMCN EPfP NLar
- 'Blue Opal'	CBcs CJun
* - 'Kinju'	CEnd CJun MBri NLar
- 'Koban Dori'	CBcs CJun
- large yellow-flowered	NLar
- 'Moegi Dori'	NLar
'Patriot'	SKHP
- 'Patriot' × (× ***brooklynensis*** 'Yellow Bird')	CJun MAsh
- 'Seiju'	CJun
§ - var. ***subcordata***	NLar
- - 'Miss Honeybee'	CBcs CJun
- - 'Mister Yellowjacket'	CJun
acuminata × 'Elizabeth'	ERea SEWo
'Advance'	CBcs CJun
'Albatross'	CBcs CDoC CEnd ERea WPGP
'Alex'	CJun
'Alixeed'	CJun
'Amber'	CJun
'Ambrosia'	CJun
amoena	CTho
- 'Multiogeca'	CWib
'Angelica'	CJun
'Anilou'	CJun
'Ann' ♀H4	CExl NLar
'Anna'	CJun
'Anne Rosse'	SKHP WPGP
'Anticipation'	CEnd CJun CMHG
'Apollo'	CBcs CDoC CJun IVic LSRN SKHP SSta WPGP
'Archangel'	CJun
ashei	see *M. macrophylla* subsp. *ashei*
'Asian Artistry'	CJun
'Athene'	CBcs CDoC CEnd CJun CMHG IVic SSta WPGP
'Atlas'	CBcs CDoC CEnd CJun CTho ERea GGGa WPGP
'Aurora'	CBcs CDoC CJun
'Banana Split'	CBcs CJun NLar
'Betty' ♀H4	CDoC CDul CLnd CMac ECrN ELon EPfP LRHS LSRN MGos NLar NPla SKHP SLim SSta
'Big Dude'	CBcs CDoC CEnd CJun EPfP LSRN
biondii	CLnd LSRN NLar
'Black Beauty'	CBcs CJun MBri
Black Tulip = 'Jurmag1'PBR	CBcs ELan EPfP ERea IVic LBuc LRHS MAsh NLar NSoo SCoo SKHP SLon WPGP
'Blushing Belle'	CJun
'Brenda'	CJun
× ***brooklynensis*** 'Evamaria'	CBcs CTho
- 'Golden Joy'	CDoC CJun
- 'Hattie Carthan'	CBcs CJun
- 'Woodsman'	CBcs MBri NLar
- 'Yellow Bird'	CBcs CDoC CDul CEnd CJun CMHG CTho EPfP GKin IArd LSRN MBlu MBri MGos NEgg NHol NLar SHil SKHP
'Butterbowl'	CJun
'Butterflies'	CBcs CDoC CDul CEnd CJun CTho CTsd EBee ELan ELon EPfP GBin GGGa LAst LRHS LSRN MBlu MBri MGos NLar SGol SKHP SSta
'Caerhays Belle'	CBcs CJun IVic NLar SKHP SSta WPGP
'Caerhays New Purple'	CLnd
'Caerhays Surprise'	CBcs CEnd CJun SKHP WPGP
campbellii	CBcs CMCN ELan EPfP IDee LRHS SKHP SSpi
- Alba Group	CBcs CEnd WPGP
- - 'Sir Harold Hillier'	CJun
- 'Ambrose Congreve'	WPGP
- 'Betty Jessel'	CJun CMHG WPGP
- 'Darjeeling'	CBcs CDoC CJun IVic LRHS SKHP
- 'John Gallagher'	SKHP
- 'Lamellan Pink'	CTho
- 'Lamellan White'	CTho
- subsp. ***mollicomata***	CEnd EPfP
- - 'Lanarth'	CBcs CEnd CJun LRHS WPGP
- 'Queen Caroline'	WPGP
- (Raffillii Group) 'Charles Raffill'	CBcs CDoC CDul CTho ELan EPfP MGos WMou WPGP
- - 'Kew's Surprise'	CBcs CDoC CJun WPGP
- 'Sidbury'	MBri
campbellii × ***sprengeri***	WPGP
'Candy Cane'	CBcs CJun
'Carlos'	CBcs CJun
cathcartii B&SWJ 11802	WCru
- HWJ 874	WCru
cavaleriei var. ***platypetala***	CBcs CExl
'Cecil Nice'	CBcs CDoC
Chameleon	see *M.* 'Chang Hua'
§ 'Chang Hua'	CJun NLar
chapensis	CBcs SKHP
'Charles Coates'	CJun EPfP MBri NLar WPGP

chevalieri B&SWJ 11802	WCru
- DJHV 06037	WCru
- HWJ 533	WCru
- HWJ 621	WCru
China Town = 'Jing Ning'	CJun
'Columbus'	CJun SKHP WPGP
'Columnar Pink'	NLar
compressa	EPfP
'Coral Lake'	CJun SKHP
cordata	see *M. acuminata* var. *subcordata*
'Crystal Chalice'	CJun SSta
'Cup Cake'	CJun
'Curly Locks'	CJun
cylindrica misapplied	see *M.* 'Pegasus'
cylindrica ambig.	CBcs CMCN
cylindrica E.H.Wilson	EPfP
- 'Bjuv'	CJun
'Daphne'	CBcs CDul CJun CMHG EPfP IVic
	LMil LRHS LSRN MAsh NLar SKHP
	WPGP
'Darrell Dean'	CJun ERea
'David Clulow'	CBcs CJun ERea LRHS SKHP WPGP
dawsoniana	CBcs CTho EPfP IDee NLar
- 'Barbara Cook'	CJun
- 'Strybing'	GGGa
- 'Valley Splendour'	CJun
'Daybreak'	CBcs CJun MBlu MBri MRav SGol
	SSpi SSta WPGP
dealbata	see *M. macrophylla* subsp. *dealbata*
'Deborah'	CJun
decidua	SKHP
delavayi	CBcs CBrP CDul CFil CHEx CMCN
	EBee EGFP EPfP EUJe IArd SAPC
	SBig SMad SSpi WPGP
§ ***denudata*** 🏆H3-4	CBcs CDul CMCN CTho CWib EPfP
	IArd LMil LRHS MBlu MBri MGos
	NLar SSpi SSta
- 'Double Diamond'	CJun
- 'Forrest's Pink'	CBcs LRHS
- Fragrant Cloud = 'Dan Xin'	CJun CWib MBri NLar WHar
- 'Gere'	CBcs CJun
- 'Ghost Ship'	CJun
- late-flowered	see *M. denudata* 'Sleeping Beauty'
- 'Rubiflora'	SSta
§ - 'Sleeping Beauty'	ERea
- Yellow River = 'Fei Huang'	CBcs CEnd CJun CWib IDee LRHS
	MBri MJak NLar
doltsopa	CBcs CCCN CExl CGHE CHEx
	CHel CTsd EBee EPfP SKHP SSta
	WPGP
- 'Silver Cloud'	CBcs CDoC CExl
'Early Rose'	CJun GGGa
'Eleanor May'	CJun
'Elegance'	CJun
'Elisa Odenwald'	CJun
'Elizabeth' 🏆H4	CBcs CDoC CDul CJun CMCN
	CTho ELan EPfP ERea GGGa IArd
	LAst LMil LRHS LSRN MAsh MBlu
	MGos NLar SKHP SPer SWvt
§ ***ernestii***	CExl CWib
'Eskimo'	CJun SKHP SSpi
'F.J. Williams' **new**	CBcs
Fairy Blush = 'Micjur01' **new**	LBuc NSoo
'Felicity'	CJun
Felix Jury = 'Jurmag2' [PBR]	CBcs ELan EPfP ERea LRHS WPGP
figo	CBcs CCCN CDoC CExl CFil EBee
	ELan EPfP LRHS SKHP SSta WPGP

- var. ***crassipes***	CBcs IDee
figo* × *laevifolia	SKHP
'Fireglow'	CJun CTho
'Flamingo'	CJun
floribunda NJM 09.179 **new**	WPGP
- WWJ 11874 **new**	WCru
- WWJ 11996 **new**	WCru
- WWJ 12003	WCru
- WWJ 12011 **new**	WCru
aff. ***floribunda***	WCru
var. ***tonkinensis*** DJHV06 105	
fordiana	CBcs CExl
§ ***foveolata***	CBcs CWib
- B&SWJ 11749	WCru
- WWJ 11929	WCru
- WWJ 11955	WCru
'Frank Gladney'	CJun CTho
'Frank's Masterpiece'	CJun IArd SKHP
fraseri	SKHP
- var. ***pyramidata***	SKHP
'Galaxy' 🏆H4	CBcs CDoC CDul CEnd CJun CLnd
	CMHG CMac EBee ELon EPfP ERea
	GGGa LMil LRHS MAsh MGos NLar
	SEWo SSpi SSta WGob
'Genie' [PBR]	CBcs CDoC NLar
'George Henry Kern'	CBcs CDoC CDul CLnd EBee EPfP
	IArd IDee LRHS MBri MGos NEgg
	NLar NPCo SEND SHil WGob
'Gladys Carlson'	CJun
globosa	CBcs CExl
'Gold Crown'	CBcs CJun
'Gold Cup' **new**	CBcs
'Gold Star'	CBcs CDoC CEnd CJun CMHG
	CTho EPfP LMil LRHS MBri MGos
	NLar SKHP SSpi SSta
'Golden Endeavour'	CBcs CJun
'Golden Gala'	CJun
'Golden Gift'	CJun LRHS SSpi WPGP
'Golden Pond'	CJun
'Golden Rain'	CJun
'Golden Sun'	CBcs CJun IArd
'Goldfinch'	CJun
I × ***gotoburgensis*** Chollipo clone	WPGP
- clone 2	CJun
grandiflora	CMCN CWib EPfP ESwi LEdu LRHS
	LSRN MGos MRav NEgg NLar NSoo
	SAPC SEWo
- 'Blanchard'	CBcs CJun EUJe NLar
- 'Bracken's Brown Beauty'	CMCN
- 'Charles Dickens'	CJun
- 'Edith Bogue'	CBcs CJun EUJe GKin LMil NEgg
	NPCo WGob
- 'Exmouth' 🏆H3-4	Widely available
- 'Ferruginea'	CBcs CJun EBee EPfP NLar SGol
- 'Flore Pleno' (d) **new**	SGol
- 'François Treyve'	EPfP LRHS LSRN
- 'Galissonnière'	CBcs CCVT CWib EBee EPfP LRHS
	MGos MREP SGol SKHP SSpi SWvt
	WPGP
- 'Goliath'	CBcs CEnd CHEx EBee ELan EPfP
	LRHS SEWo SKHP SPer SSpi WPGP
- 'Harold Poole'	CJun
- 'Kay Parris'	CJun EPfP LRHS SKHP SPoG SSpi
- 'Little Gem'	CBcs CDoC CJun ELan EPfP EUJe
	LRHS MBri MGos SGol SSpi
- 'Mainstreet'	CJun
- 'Monlia'	CJun

	- 'Nannetensis'	CJun LRHS MBri
	- 'Overton'	CJun
	- 'Russet'	CJun
	- 'Saint Mary'	CBcs CJun
	- 'Samuel Sommer'	CBcs CJun SSpi
	- 'Symmes Select'	CJun
	- 'Treyvei'	CJun
	- 'Victoria' ♀$^{H3-4}$	CDoC CDul CJun CTho ELan ELon EPfP LMil LRHS LSRN MAsh MBlu MGos NLar SEND SPer SPoG SReu SSpi SSta WGob WPGP
	'Green Bee'	CBcs CJun
	'Green Mist'	CJun LMil LRHS SSpi
	'Hawk'	WPGP
	'Heaven Scent' ♀^{H4}	Widely available
	'Helen Fogg'	CJun
	heptapeta	see *M. denudata*
	'Honey Flower'	CJun
§	'Hong Yun'	CEnd CJun
	'Hot Flash'	CBcs CJun
	'Hot Lips'	CJun
	hypoleuca	see *M. obovata* Thunb.
	'Ian's Red'	CBcs CDoC CJun IVic WPGP
§	***insignis***	CExl CHEx SKHP WPGP
	'Iolanthe'	CBcs CDoC CEnd CGHE CJun CMCN CMHG CTho ELan EPfP ERea IVic MAsh MBri MGos SHil WPGP
	'Iufer'	CJun SSta
	'J.C. Williams'	CBcs CDoC CJun CTho IVic WPGP
	'Jack Fogg'	MPkF SKHP
	'Jane' ♀^{H4}	CDoC CJun CMac ELan EPfP LMil LRHS MAsh MGos MRav
	'Jersey Belle'	CJun
	'Joe McDaniel'	CBcs CJun ERea IArd NLar SKHP
	'John Congreve'	WPGP
	'Joli Pompom'	CJun
	'Judy'	CBcs
	'Judy Zuk'	ERea SKHP SSta
	'Kate Brook'	NLar
	× ***kewensis*** 'Wada's Memory'	see *M. salicifolia* 'Wada's Memory'
	kobus	CBcs CCVT CDul CLnd CMCN CTho CTsd EPfP ERea GKin IArd IDee MBlu NLar NWea SEWo
	- 'Esveld Select'	CJun MBri
	- 'Janaki Ammal'	CJun
§	- 'Norman Gould'	CDoC CJun EPfP NLar NPla SSta
	- 'Octopus'	CJun
	- pink-flowered	CBcs CJun
	- 'White Elegance'	CJun
	- 'Wisley Star'	SSta
	laevifolia ambig.	CAbP WSHC
§	***laevifolia*** (Y.W.Law R.Y.F.Wu) Noot	CExl CHel CHid EBee ELan EPfP NLar SChF SKHP WPGP
	- arborescent	SKHP
	- 'Dali Velvet'	CExl
	- 'Gail's Favourite'	EBee EPfP LRHS MAsh SKHP SPoG SSpi
	- 'Mini Mouse' <u>**new**</u>	LRHS SPoG
	- 'Velvet and Cream'	IVic
	- 'Willow Leaf'	SKHP
	'Laura Saylor'	CJun
	'Leda'	CJun ERea SSta
	'Legacy'	CJun NLar SKHP WPGP
	'Legend'	CJun EPfP
	'Lennarth Jonsson'	CJun
§	***liliiflora***	GKin
	- 'Darkest Purple'	CJun
§	- 'Nigra' ♀^{H4}	Widely available

	- 'Raven'	SKHP
*	'Limelight'	CJun EPfP SSpi WPGP
	× ***loebneri***	NEgg
	- 'Ballerina'	CBcs CDoC NLar
	- 'Donna'	CJun EPfP LMil LRHS LSRN NLar SKHP SSpi SSta
	- 'Encore'	CJun
	- 'Leonard Messel' ♀^{H4}	Widely available
	- 'Lesley Jane'	CJun
	- 'Merrill' ♀^{H4}	CBcs CDul CJun CLnd CMCN CMHG CMac CTho CWib EBee ELan EPfP ERea LMil LRHS MAsh MBri MGos MMuc MRav NLar NPCo SEND SGol SKHP SPer SReu SSpi SSta
	- 'Neil McEacharn'	CJun
	- 'Pink Cloud'	CJun
	- 'Powder Puff'	CBcs CJun
	- 'Raspberry Fun'	CJun IArd
	- 'Snowdrift'	CJun NLar
	- 'Star Bright'	CJun
	- 'White Stardust'	CJun
	- 'Wildcat'	CJun NLar SKHP
	- 'Willow Wood'	CJun
	'Lois'	CBcs CJun EPfP ERea GGGa LMil LRHS LSRN NLar SKHP SSpi WPGP
	'Lombardy Rose'	NLar
	lotungensis	NLar
	'Lotus'	CBcs CJun LMil
	'Lucy Carlson'	CJun
	macclurei	CBcs
	macrophylla	CBcs CBrP CFil CMac EPfP IArd IDee LRHS MBlu MPkF NLar SAPC SKHP WPGP
§	- subsp. ***ashei***	CBcs CFil CMCN SKHP WPGP
	- subsp. ***ashei*** × ***virginiana***	CJun
§	- subsp. ***dealbata***	CFil
	macrophylla × ***macrophylla*** subsp. ***ashei***	SKHP
	macrophylla × ***sieboldii***	CJun
	'Mag's Pirouette'	SKHP
	'Malin'	CJun
	'Manchu Fan'	CBcs CJun EBee EMil EPfP IArd IVic LRHS LSRN NLar SKHP SSpi
§	'March Til Frost'	CJun NLar SKHP WPGP
	'Margaret Helen'	CBcs CDoC CJun CMHG
	'Marj Gossler'	CJun
	'Marjorie Congreve'	WPGP
	'Mark Jury'	CBcs SKHP WPGP
	martinii	CBcs SKHP
	'Mary Bee'	SKHP
	'Mary Nell'	CJun
	'Maryland'	CJun CWib EPfP GGGa SKHP SSpi
	maudiae	CBcs CDoC CExl EPfP IDee NLar SKHP SSpi WPGP
	'Maxine Merrill'	CJun IDee SSta
	'May to Frost'	see *M.* 'March Til Frost'
	'Milky Way' ♀^{H4}	CBcs CDoC CGHE CJun CMHG CTho EPfP MGos SKHP WPGP
	'Moondance'	CJun
	'Morning Calm'	SKHP
	'Nimbus'	CJun SKHP SSpi
	nitida	CBcs CExl CFil
	obovata Diels	see *M. officinalis*
§	***obovata*** Thunb. ♀^{H4}	CBcs CDul CJun CMCN CTho EPfP IDee MGos NLar NWea SBig SSpi WMou WPGP

	Name	Suppliers
	odora	CWib
§	***officinalis***	CBcs EPfP NLar
	- var. ***biloba***	NLar WPGP
	'Old Port'	CBcs
	'Olivia'	CJun
	'Peachy'	CBcs CJun EPfP NLar
§	'Pegasus'	CBcs CEnd CJun LMil LRHS MBri SKHP SSpi SSta
	'Peppermint Stick'	CBcs
	'Peter Dummer' **new**	SSta
	'Peter Smithers'	CJun
	'Petit Chicon' **new**	CBcs
	'Phelan Bright'	CJun
	'Phillip Tregunna'	CBcs CMHG CTho SKHP
	'Phil's Masterpiece'	CJun
	'Pickard's Stardust'	EPfP
	'Pickard's Sundew'	see *M.* 'Sundew'
	'Piet van Veen'	CJun
	'Pink Delight'	CJun
	'Pink Goblet'	LRHS
	'Pink Surprise'	CJun
	'Pinkie' 🏆H4	CJun EMil LSRN NEgg NLar WGob
	'Pirouette'	CJun EPfP LLHF LRHS SSpi
	'Porcelain Dove'	CJun SKHP SSpi
	'Princess Margaret'	CDoC CJun
	× ***proctoriana***	CAbP CDoC CGHE LMil LRHS NLar SChF SKHP WPGP
	- Gloster form	NLar
	- 'Robert's Dream'	CJun LRHS MAsh SSta
	- 'Slavin's No 44'	CJun
	'Purple Globe'	CJun SKHP
	'Purple Platter'	CBcs
	'Purple Sensation'	CBcs CJun
	quinquepeta	see *M. liliiflora*
	'Randy'	CBcs
	'Raspberry Ice'	CBcs CDoC CMHG CMac CTho EPfP LMil LRHS MAsh NLar SPoG SRms WGob
	'Raspberry Swirl'	SSta
	'Red as Red'	CBcs CDoC
	'Red Baron'	CJun
	'Red Lion'	CBcs CJun
	'Ricki'	CJun EMil EPfP LSRN MBlu NLar
	'Roseanne'	CJun
	rostrata	CBcs CExl CFil SKHP WPGP
	'Rouged Alabaster'	CBcs CDoC
	'Royal Crown'	CBcs CDoC EPfP IDee LRHS MRav NEgg NPCo
	'Ruby'	CJun
	salicifolia 🏆H3-4	CBcs CMCN EPfP SSpi
	- 'Jermyns'	CJun
	- 'Louisa Fete'	CJun
*	- 'Rosea'	CJun
	- upright	WPGP
	- 'Van Veen'	CJun
§	- 'Wada's Memory' 🏆H4	CDoC CExl CHid CJun CMCN CTho ELan EPfP LMil LRHS MAsh MBlu MBri SHil SKHP SSpi SSta
	- 'Windsor Beauty'	CJun SSta
	sapaensis NJM 09.139	WPGP
	- NJM 09.143	WPGP
	- NJM 09.168	WPGP
	sargentiana	CBcs SSta
	- 'Broadleas'	CJun
	- var. ***robusta***	CBcs CEnd CLnd CMCN ELan EPfP MBri NLar SSpi
	- - 'Blood Moon'	CJun
	- - 'Multipetal'	WPGP
	- - 'Trengwainton Glory'	ERea

	Name	Suppliers
	'Satisfaction'	CDul CJun NLar
	'Sayonara' 🏆H4	CBcs CJun ERea SSpi
	'Schmetterling'	see *M.* × *soulangeana* 'Pickard's Schmetterling'
	'Sentinel' **new**	NLar
	'Serene'	CBcs CEnd CJun CMHG EPfP LMil MBri WPGP
	'Shirazz'	CBcs CDoC CJun SKHP WPGP
	sieboldii	CBcs CDul CGHE CJun CLnd CMCN CMac CTho EBee ELan EPfP EWTr GKin IDee LRHS LSRN MBlu MBri MGos NLar SHil SKHP SLim SPad SSpi WPGP
	- B&SWJ 4127	WCru
	- 'Colossus'	CJun IArd IDee MBlu SKHP
	- 'Genesis'	CJun
	- 'Genesis' × ***tripetala***	CJun
	- 'Genesis' × ***virginiana***	CJun
	- 'Michiko Renge' (d)	CJun NLar
	- 'Min Pyong-gal'	CJun
	- 'Pride of Norway'	CJun
	- subsp. ***sinensis***	CDoC CJun CMCN CTho ELan EPfP MBlu NLar WPGP
I	- - 'Grandiflora'	CJun
	'Sir Harold Hillier'	CBcs WPGP
	'Sleeping Beauty'	SKHP
	'Snow Goose'	CJun
	'Solar Flair'	CJun IArd NLar SKHP
	× ***soulangeana***	Widely available
	- 'Alba Superba'	CBcs CDoC CTri EPfP GBin LMil LRHS MBlu MRav NLar SLim
	- 'Alexandrina'	CBcs EPfP MBlu NLar
	- 'Big Pink' **new**	CBcs
	- 'Brozzonii' 🏆H3-4	CBcs CDoC CMac EPfP GCra IArd LMil LRHS NEgg NLar NPCo SSta WGob
	- 'Burgundy'	CBcs CDoC NPCo WGob
	- 'Fukuju'	CJun
	- 'Lennei' 🏆H3-4	CBcs CDoC CMCN CMac CSBt EBee EPfP IArd LAst LRHS MGos MSwo NLar SPer SRms WGob
	- 'Lennei Alba' 🏆H3-4	CBcs CDoC CMCN CMac ELan IArd MBlu NLar
	- 'Nigra'	see *M. liliiflora* 'Nigra'
	- 'Pickard's Ruby'	MBri
§	- 'Pickard's Schmetterling'	CDoC EPfP LMil LRHS MAsh
	- 'Pickard's Snow Queen'	CJun
	- 'Pickard's Sundew'	see *M.* 'Sundew'
	- 'Picture'	CDoC CMac CTri WGob
	- Red Lucky	see *M.* 'Hong Yun'
	- 'Rubra' misapplied	see *M.* × *soulangeana* 'Rustica Rubra'
§	- 'Rustica Rubra' 🏆H3-4	CBcs CDoC CDul CLnd CMCN CMac CTri EBee ELan EPfP LMil LRHS LSRN MAsh SGol SPer SRms SSpi WGob
	- 'San José'	CJun LMil LRHS MAsh NLar
	- 'Speciosa'	SSta
	- 'Superba'	CMac
	- 'Verbanica'	EPfP LMil LRHS MAsh
	'Spectrum'	CBcs CDoC CEnd CJun EMil ERea IArd IDee LMil LRHS MBri MGos NLar SKHP SSpi SSta
	sprengeri	CWib
	- 'Copeland Court'	CJun
	- var. ***diva***	CBcs CEnd CExl EPfP NLar SKHP WPGP
	- - 'Burncoose'	CBcs CDoC
	- - 'Claret Cup'	GGGa

- - 'Dark Diva'	CJun
- - 'Diva'	GGal LMil WPGP
- - 'Eric Savill'	CJun ERea IVic SKHP WPGP
- - 'Lanhydrock'	CJun SKHP SSta WPGP
- - 'Westonbirt'	WPGP
- var. ***elongata***	SKHP
- 'Marwood Spring'	CMHG SKHP SSta WPGP
'Spring Rite'	CJun SKHP
'Star Wars' ♀H4	CBcs CDoC CEnd CExl CJun CLnd CTho CTsd ELan EPfP ERea GGGa LMil LRHS MAsh MBri MGos NLar SKHP SPoG SSpi SSta WPGP
'Stellar Acclaim'	CBcs CJun
stellata ♀H4	Widely available
- 'Centennial'	CDoC CJun CTho MBri NLar
- 'Chrysanthemumiflora'	CJun EPfP ERea SKHP
- 'Dawn'	CJun
- 'Jane Platt'	CJun ELan EPfP LMil LRHS MBri MGos SKHP SSpi SSta WPGP
- f. ***keiskei***	CBcs CEnd CJun EPfP MGos NHol NLar SKHP
- 'Kikuzaki'	CJun
- 'King Rose'	CBcs CDoC CJun CTsd EPfP LRHS MAsh
- 'Massey'	CJun
- 'Norman Gould'	see *M. kobus* 'Norman Gould'
- 'Rosea'	CBar CJun CLnd CMCN CTho EBee ELan ELon EWTr GKev LMil MGos MRav MSwo NEgg NLar NSoo SKHP
- 'Rosea Massey'	CJun
- 'Royal Star'	CBcs CDoC CEnd CJun CMCN CTho CTri CWSG EBee ELon EPfP IVic LAst LMil LRHS MAsh MBlu MBri MGos MRav NLar NPCo SGol SKHP SPer SPoG SSpi SSta WHar
- 'Scented Silver'	CJun LRHS MAsh SKHP
- 'Shi-banchi Rosea'	CJun
- 'Two Stones'	SKHP
- 'Water Lily' ♀H4	CBcs CJun CMCN CMac CTho EBee ELan ELon EPfP LMil LRHS LSRN MAsh MBlu NLar NPCo SHil SKHP SPer SSta WPGP
- 'Wisley Stardust'	LRHS
'Summer Solstice'	CBcs CJun MBri
'Sun Ray'	CBcs CJun
'Sunburst'	CBcs CJun SRms
'Sundance'	CBcs CJun IArd MBlu MBri NLar
§ 'Sundew'	CDoC EPfP NLar NPCo
'Sunsation'	CBcs CDoC CJun SSta
'Sunspire'	CBcs CJun NLar
'Suntown'	CJun
'Susan' ♀H4	Widely available
'Susanna van Veen'	CBcs CDoC CEnd CJun WPGP
'Swedish Star'	CJun
'Sweet Merlot'	CBcs CDoC CJun
'Sweet Valentine'	CBcs CJun
'Sweetheart'	CBcs CJun SSpi
'Theodora'	MBri NLar
× ***thompsoniana***	CBcs CMCN EPfP NLar SSpi
- 'Olmenhof'	IArd
'Thousand Butterflies'	CBcs CJun
'Tina Durio'	CBcs MBri SKHP
'Todd Gresham'	CJun
'Todd's Forty Niner'	CBcs CJun
'Touch of Pink'	CBcs NLar
'Tranquility'	CBcs CJun SKHP
'Trewidden Belle'	CEnd
tripetala	CBcs CExl CLnd CMCN CTho ELan EPfP NLar SBig SKHP SSpi SSta WPGP
- 'Bloomfield'	CJun
- 'Petite'	SKHP
'Ultimate Yellow'	CJun NLar
× ***veitchii***	CBcs EPfP
- 'Peter Veitch'	CTho
virginiana	CBcs CJun CMCN EPfP IDee NLar SBig SKHP SSpi WPGP
- 'Aiken County'	SKHP
- var. ***australis*** 'Green Shadow'	SGol
- - 'Satellite'	CJun MBri
- 'Havener'	SKHP
- 'Henry Hicks'	CJun
- 'Moonglow'	CJun EPfP LRHS MBlu MBri
- 'Pink Halo'	CJun
'Vulcan'	CBcs CDoC CEnd CJun ELan EPfP MBri SCoo
× ***watsonii***	see *M.* × *wieseneri*
'White Mystery'	CJun
§ × ***wieseneri***	CBcs CJun CMCN CMHG EPfP ERea MBlu MBri NLar SKHP SSpi WPGP
- 'Aashild Kalleberg'	CBcs CJun SKHP SSpi
- 'Lupo Osti'	SKHP
wilsonii ♀H4	CBcs CDoC CDul CExl CJun CMCN CTho CTri EBee ELan EPfP GGGa IArd IDee LRHS MBlu MBri MGos MMuc NLar SBrt SEND SKHP SLim SPer SSpi WHCr WPGP
- 'Gwen Baker'	CEnd
- 'Highdownensis'	MBri
'Yaeko'	CJun
'Yellow Fever'	CBcs CJun CTho
'Yellow Garland'	CJun
'Yellow Lantern'	CAbP CBcs CDoC CEnd CJun EPfP EWTr GGGa LMil LRHS LSRN MAsh MBlu NLar SPoG SSpi SSta
'Yellow Sea'	CJun SKHP
Yuchelia No. 1	CBcs
yunnanensis	CCCN CDoC CHII MBri MPkF
zenii	CBcs CMCN
- 'Pink Parchment'	CJun

× *Mahoberberis* (*Berberidaceae*)

aquisargentii	CMac EBee EMil EPfP GCal IVic LRHS MMuc MRav NLar SKHP
'Dart's Desire'	NLar
miethkeana	SRms
neubertii	NLar

Mahonia ✿ (*Berberidaceae*)

§ ***aquifolium***	CAgr CBcs CDul EBee ECrN MGos MMuc MRav NWea SEND SGol SPer SPlb SWvt WHar
- 'Apollo' ♀H4	CBcs CSBt CWib EBee ELan ELon EPfP LAst LHop LRHS LSRN MAsh MGos MJak MRav NEgg NLar SCoo SPoG SWvt
- 'Atropurpurea'	CMac CSBt ELan EPfP LRHS NLar SPer
- 'Cosmo Crawl'	LRHS MBri SHil
- 'Euro'	NLar
- 'Fascicularis'	see *M.* × *wagneri* 'Pinnacle'
- 'Green Ripple'	CJun EPfP NLar
- 'Mirena'	NLar
- 'Orange Flame'	CJun EPfP NLar

	- 'Smaragd'	CDoC CMac EBee ELan EPfP LRHS LSRN MBlu MGos MRav WHar
	- 'Versicolor'	MBlu
	bealei	see *M. japonica* Bealei Group
	bodinieri	WPGP
	'Bokrafoot' PBR	EPfP LLHF LRHS MAsh MBlu SLon
	chochoco	CExl CFil
	conferta new	CFil
	eurybracteata	CDoC CExl CFil CGHE CHEx EPfP LLHF LRHS NLar SKHP WPGP
	eutriphylla	see *M. trifolia*
	fortunei	CBcs IDee NLar
	- 'Winter Prince'	NLar
	gracilipes	CExl CFil CGHE CHEx EBee EPfP EWes GCal IDee MBlu NLar SKHP SLon WCru WHar WPGP WWFP
	gracilis	CFil
	japonica ♀H4	Widely available
§	- Bealei Group	CBcs CDul CSBt EBee ELan ELon EPfP LRHS MAsh MGos MRav MSwo NLar NPer NPla SCoo SGol SKHP SLim SWvt
	- 'Gold Dust'	CMac NLar
	- 'Hiemalis'	see *M. japonica* 'Hivernant'
§	- 'Hivernant'	EBee EPfP NEgg NWea
	lanceolata	CFil WPGP
	leschenaultii B&SWJ 9535	WCru
	× ***lindsayae***	CFil WPGP
	- 'Cantab'	CFil WPGP
	lomariifolia	see *M. oiwakensis* subsp. *lomariifolia*
	longibracteata	GKin
	× ***media*** 'Buckland' ♀H4	CHab CMac EBee EPfP MRav NEgg NLar SDix SPer SRms WPat
	- 'Charity'	Widely available
	- 'Hope'	NLar
	- 'Lionel Fortescue' ♀H4	CBcs CMac CSBt EBee ELan EPfP GKin LAst LHop LRHS MAsh MCoo MRav NEgg SDix SKHP SPer SPoG SSpi SWvt
	- 'Maharajah' new	IArd
	- 'Winter Sun' ♀H4	Widely available
	moranensis	CExl CFil
	- T 292	WPGP
	napaulensis new	CFil
	nervosa	CBcs CMac EPfP MBlu NEgg NLar WCru
	- B&SWJ 9562	WCru
	nitens	CBcs
	- 'Cabaret' PBR	CRos EPfP LBuc LLHF LRHS MAsh MBlu SHil SPoG
	oiwakensis B&SWJ 371	WCru
	- B&SWJ 3660	WCru
§	- subsp. ***lomariifolia*** ♀H3	CExl CFil CHEx EBee EPfP EWes LRHS MBlu SAPC SKHP
	pallida	CExl CFil SKHP SSpi WPGP
	- from Tamazunchale, Mexico new	CFil
	- from Zimapan, Mexico new	CFil
	pinnata misapplied	see *M.* × *wagneri* 'Pinnacle'
	pinnata ambig.	EPfP
	pinnata (Lag.) Fedde 'Ken S. Howard'	NLar
	repens	GCal NLar
	× ***savilliana***	CFil WPGP
	- 'Commissioner'	CWib
	siamensis	CFil
	Sioux = 'Bokrasio' PBR	LLHF LRHS MAsh SPoG
§	***trifolia***	GCal
	trifoliolata var. ***glauca***	CEnd CJun
	× ***wagneri*** 'Fireflame'	GCal
	- 'Hastings Elegant'	CJun NLar
	- 'Moseri'	NLar WPat
§	- 'Pinnacle' ♀H4	ELan EPfP IDee LRHS MAsh NLar SPoG SWvt
	- 'Sunset'	CJun GKin MBlu NLar
	- 'Undulata'	EPfP LRHS MBlu SPer SRms

Maianthemum (*Asparagaceae*)

	amoenum	LEdu
	- B&SWJ 10390	WCru
	atropurpureum	WCru
	bicolor	CDes LEdu SWat
	bifolium	CAvo CBct CCon CDes CHid ECho GCra GLog LEdu MAvo MMoz MNrw NBro NPnk SRms WCru WPtf WWEG XLum
§	- subsp. ***kamtschaticum***	CAvo CLAP EPPr LEdu MAvo NLar NRya WCot WWEG
	- - B&SWJ 4360	WCru
	- - CD&R 2300	WCru
*	- - var. ***minimum***	EBee GCal LEdu WCru
*	- - var. ***pumilum*** new	LEdu
	canadense	EBee ECho EPot GBuc GCal MNrw NBid WCru WHil
	chasmanthum	see *M. bifolium* subsp. *kamtschaticum*
	comaltepecense B&SWJ 10215	WCru
	dilatatum	see *M. bifolium* subsp. *kamtschaticum*
	flexuosum	LEdu
	- B&SWJ 9069	WCru
	- B&SWJ 9079	WCru
	- B&SWJ 9150	WCru
	aff. ***flexuosum*** B&SWJ 9026	WCru
	- B&SWJ 9055	WCru
	formosanum B&SWJ 349	EPPr WCru
	fuscum	WCru
	- var. ***cordatum***	WCru
	gigas B&SWJ 10470	WCru
	henryi	ECho LEdu LWst WCru
	japonicum	LEdu LWst
	- B&SWJ 1179	WCru
	- B&SWJ 4714	WCru
	oleraceum	CBct CExl EBee LEdu LWst MMoz
	- B&SWJ 2148	WCru
	paniculatum	EBee LEdu
	- B&SWJ 9137	WCru
	- B&SWJ 9140	WCru
	- purple-flowered B&SWJ 9139	WCru
	pendent, B&SWJ 10305 from Guatemala	WCru
	purpureum G-W&P 150	EPPr
	racemosum ♀H4	Widely available
	- subsp. ***amplexicaule***	GCal
	- - 'Emily Moody'	CBct CDes CExl CPou EBee EPPr EPfP SKHP WPGP
	- dwarf	ECho
	aff. ***salvinii*** B&SWJ 9000	WCru
	- B&SWJ 9088	WCru
	- B&SWJ 10402	WCru
	scilloideum B&SWJ 10407	WCru
*	- var. ***roseum*** B&SWJ 10335	WCru
	stellatum	CBct CCon CSam EBee ECho EPPr EPfP EPot GBin GBuc GCal LEdu

	LHop LLWG LRHS MAvo NChi NLar NPnk SPoG WCru WHil WPnP
szechuanicum	WCru
tatsienense	CBct CExl LEdu WCru

Maihuenia (*Cactaceae*)

poeppigii	SPlb
- F&W 9670	WCot

Maireana (*Amaranthaceae*)

georgei	SPlb

Malus ✿ (*Rosaceae*)

§ 'Adirondack'	CLnd EBee EPfP LRHS MAsh MBri MMuc NLar SCoo SEND SLim SLon WJas
'Admiration'	see *M.* 'Adirondack'
× ***adstringens*** 'Hopa'	CDul CLnd
- 'Simcoe'	EBee
'Aldenhamensis'	see *M.* × *purpurea* 'Aldenhamensis'
'Amberina'	CLnd
× ***atrosanguinea*** 'Gorgeous'	CDul CLnd CMac CTho EBee GTwe LBuc LHop LRHS LSRN MBri MGos MSwo NLar NWea SCoo SEWo SLim SPer SPoG WJas WMou
baccata	CDul CLnd CMCN CTho GTwe MMuc NWea SCoo SEND SPlb
- 'Dolgo'	EPom NOra SKee WHar
- var. ***mandshurica***	CTho
aff. ***baccata***	NWea
§ ***bhutanica***	CDul CLnd SCrf
- 'Mandarin'	MBri SCoo
brevipes	CLnd LRHS SCoo
- 'Wedding Bouquet'	EBee ERea LBuc LSRN MAsh MBri NLar SPer
'Butterball'	CDoC CDul CLnd CTho CTsd EPfP ERea GQue LAst LBuc NLar NWea SCoo SLim SPer WHar WJas WMou
'Candymint Sargent'	CLnd
'Cave Hill'	CLnd
'Cheal's Scarlet' new	CHab
* 'Cheal's Weeping'	CMac LAst NEgg
Coccinella = 'Courtarou'	MMuc SGol
'Comtessa de Paris'	CLnd EBee EPfP MAsh
'Coralburst'	EBee MAsh MBri
coronaria var. ***dasycalyx*** 'Charlottae' (d)	CDul CLnd EBee EPfP SPer
- 'Elk River'	EBee EPfP MAsh SCoo
'Crimson Brilliant'	CLnd
'Crittenden'	MAsh MRav SLim
'Dartmouth'	CDul CHab CLnd CSBt CTri NEgg NPCo SFam
* 'Directeur Moerlands'	CCVT CDoC ECrN EPfP IArd LAst SEND SPer
domestica 'Acklam Russet' (D)	SKee
- 'Acme' (D)	ECrN SDea
- 'Adams's Pearmain' (D)	CCAT CDoC CTho CTri ECrN ERea GTwe MCoo NOra SDea SFam SKee WHar
- 'Admiral' (D)	ECrN ERea
- 'Akane' (D)	SDea
- 'Alfriston' (C)	CAgr CHab SKee
§ - 'Alkmene' (D) ♀H4	CAgr ECrN NOra SDea
- 'All Doer' (C/D/Cider)	CTho
- 'Allen's Everlasting' (D)	SDea SKee
- 'Allington Pippin' (D)	CHab CSBt CTho CTri ECrN IArd LRHS SDea SFam SKee WHar
- Ambassy = 'Dalil'PBR (D)	IArd
- 'American Mother'	see *M. domestica* 'Mother'
- 'Ananas Reinette' (D)	ECrN
- 'Anna Boelens' (D)	SDea
- 'Annie Elizabeth' (C)	CAgr CCAT CTho CWib ECrN GTwe IArd LAst LRHS MCoo NOra SDea SFam SKee SVic WHar WJas
- 'Anniversary' (D)	SDea
- 'Api' (D)	GQue LSRN SPoG WHar
- 'Ard Cairn Russet' (D)	ECrN IArd SDea SKee
- 'Aromatic Russet' (D)	SKee
- 'Arthur Turner' (C) ♀H4	CCVT CHab CTri ECrN EPom EWTr GTwe IArd LAst LBuc MWat NOra SCrf SDea SFam SKee WHar WJas
- 'Arthur W. Barnes' (C)	SKee
- 'Ashmead's Kernel' (D) ♀H4	CAgr CCAT CHab CMam CSBt CTho CTri CWSG CWib ECrN EPfP EPom ERea GTwe IArd LBuc LRHS MCoo MRav MWat NOra NWea SCrf SDea SFam SKee SLim SVic WHar WJas
- 'Ashton Bitter' (Cider)	CCAT CHab CTho CTri GTwe
- 'Ashton Brown Jersey' (Cider)	CCAT
- 'Askham Pippin' (F)	MCoo
- 'Autumn Pearmain' (D)	SDea WHar
- 'Aynho Scarlet' (F)	LBuc
- 'Baker's Delicious' (D)	ECrN ERea SDea SKee WHar
- 'Ball's Bittersweet' (Cider)	CCAT CTho
- 'Ballyfatten' (C)	IArd
- 'Ballyvaughan Seedling' (D)	IArd
- 'Balsam'	see *M. domestica* 'Green Balsam'
- 'Banana Pippin' (F)	CEnd
- 'Banns' (D)	ECrN ERea
- 'Bardsey' (D)	CAgr CHab EPom WGwG WHar
- 'Barnack Beauty' (D)	CHab CTho CTri SKee
- 'Barnack Orange' (D)	SKee
- 'Bascombe Mystery' (D)	SKee
- 'Baxter's Pearmain' (D)	ECrN SDea SKee
- 'Beauty of Bath' (D)	CAgr CCAT CCVT CDoC CDul CHab CTho CTri CWib ECrN ELan EWTr GTwe LAst LBuc MRav SDea SFam SKee SPer WHar WJas
- 'Beauty of Hants' (C/D)	ECrN
- 'Beauty of Kent' (C)	SDea SKee
- 'Beauty of Moray' (C)	SKee
- 'Bedwyn Beauty' (C)	CTho
- 'Beeley Pippin' (D)	SDea
- 'Bell Apple' (Cider/C)	CCAT CTho
- 'Belle de Boskoop' (C/D) ♀H4	CAgr CCAT CHab ECrN GTwe MCoo NOra SDea SKee
- 'Bembridge Beauty' (F)	CHab SDea
- 'Ben's Red' (D)	CAgr CCAT CDoC CEnd CTho
- 'Bess Pool' (D)	CCAT CHab MCoo SDea SFam
- 'Bewley Down Pippin'	see *M. domestica* 'Crimson King' (Cider/C)
- 'Bickington Grey' (Cider)	CCAT CTho
- 'Billy Down Pippin' (F)	CTho
- 'Bismarck' (C)	CCAT
- 'Black Dabinett' (Cider)	CCAT CEnd CTho
- 'Black Tom Putt' (C/D)	CTho
- 'Black Vallis' (Cider)	CCAT
- 'Blenheim Orange' (C/D) ♀H4	Widely available
- 'Blood of the Boyne' (D)	IArd
- 'Bloody Ploughman' (D)	CHab ECrN GQue GTwe SKee SLon WHar
- 'Blue Pearmain' (D)	SDea
- 'Blue Sweet' (Cider)	CTho

- Bolero	see *M. domestica* 'Tuscan'
- 'Boston Russet'	see *M. domestica* 'Roxbury Russet'
- 'Bountiful' (C)	CAgr CDoC CDul CMac CSBt CTri CWSG CWib ECrN EPom EWTr GTwe IArd LRHS LSRN MBri NLar NOra SDea SKee SPoG WHar
- 'Bow Hill Pippin' (C)	SKee
- 'Box Apple' (D)	CDoC
- 'Braddick's Nonpareil' (D)	SKee
- 'Bradley's Beauty' (C/D) **new**	NWea
- 'Braeburn' (D)	CAgr CDul CMam CSut CTri ECrN EPom ERea LAst LBuc LRHS MWat NOra SCrf SDea SEWo SFam SKee SPer WHar WJas
- 'Braeburn Hillwell' (D)	EPom NOra
- 'Braintree Seedling' (D)	ECrN
- 'Bramley's Seedling' (C) ♀H4	Widely available
- 'Bramley's Seedling' clone 20 (F)	CDoC CMam CTsd ERea LRHS LSRN MBri NLar NOra SCoo SDea SKee SLim SPer SPoG WHar
- 'Bread Fruit' (C/D)	CDoC CEnd CTho
- 'Breakwell's Seedling' (Cider)	CCAT CTho
- 'Bridgwater Pippin' (C)	CCAT CTho
- 'Bright Future' (D)	EPom LBuc MCoo
- 'Broad-eyed Pippin' (C)	SKee
- 'Broadholm Beauty' (C)	EPom WHar
- 'Brookes's' (D)	WHar
- 'Brown Crofton' (D)	IArd
- 'Brown Snout' (Cider)	CCAT CTho
- 'Brownlee's Russet' (D)	CAgr CHab CTho CTri GTwe MCoo NEgg NOra NWea SDea SFam SKee WHar
- 'Brown's Apple' (Cider)	CAgr CCAT CHab GTwe NOra
- 'Broxwood Foxwhelp' (Cider)	CCAT
- 'Burn's Seedling' (D)	CTho
- 'Burrowhill Early' (Cider)	CTho
- 'Bushey Grove' (C)	SDea
- 'Buttery Do' (F)	CCAT CTho
- 'Cadbury' (F)	CCAT
- 'Calville Blanc d'Hiver' (D)	NOra SKee
- 'Cambusnethan Pippin' (D)	SKee
- 'Camelot' (Cider/C)	CCAT
- 'Cap of Liberty' (Cider)	CCAT
- 'Captain Broad' (D/Cider)	CCAT CEnd CTho
- 'Captain Kidd' (D)	EPom NOra SKee WHar
- 'Captain Smith' (F)	CEnd
- 'Carlisle Codlin' (C)	NWea SDea
- 'Caroline' (D)	ECrN ERea
- 'Catherine' (C)	ECrN
- 'Catshead' (C)	CAgr CCAT CHab CTri CTsd ECrN IArd NOra SDea SKee WHar
- 'Cellini' (C)	LRHS SDea
- 'Chacewater Longstem' (F)	CDoC
- 'Charles Ross' (C/D) ♀H4	Widely available
- 'Charlotte'PBR (C/Ball)	SDea
- 'Chaxhill Red' (Cider/D)	CCAT CTho
- 'Cheddar Cross' (D)	CAgr CCVT CTri ECrN
- 'Chelmsford Wonder' (C)	ECrN
- 'Chisel Jersey' (Cider)	CAgr CCAT CTri NOra SKee
- 'Chivers Delight' (D)	CAgr CSBt ECrN ERea GTwe LRHS MCoo NOra SDea SKee WHar WJas
- 'Chorister Boy' (D)	CTho
- 'Christmas Pearmain' (D)	CAgr CTho ECrN GTwe SDea SFam SKee
- 'Christmas Pippin' (D) **new**	CDoC MCoo NOra
- 'Cider Lady's Finger' (Cider)	CCAT SKee
- 'Cissy' (D)	WGwG
- 'Claygate Pearmain' (D) ♀H4	CAgr CCAT CDoC CHab CTho CTri ECrN GTwe LRHS MCoo NOra SDea SFam SKee SVic WHar
- 'Clopton Red' (D)	ECrN
- 'Coat Jersey' (Cider)	CCAT
- 'Cobra' (F)	CAgr CDoC LBuc LRHS MBri MCoo WHar WJas
- 'Cockle Pippin' (D)	CAgr CTho LRHS SDea
- 'Cockpit' (C)	CHab
- 'Coeur de Boeuf' (C/D)	SKee
- 'Coleman's Seedling' (Cider)	CTho
- 'Collogett Pippin' (C/Cider)	CCAT CDoC CEnd CTho
- 'Colonel Vaughan' (C/D)	SKee
- 'Colonel Yate' (D)	LRHS
- 'Cornish Aromatic' (D)	CAgr CCAT CDoC CTho CTri CTsd GTwe NOra SCrf SDea SFam SKee WHar
- 'Cornish Gilliflower' (D)	CAgr CCAT CDoC CDul CHab CTho ECrN MCoo NOra SDea SFam SKee WHar
- 'Cornish Honeypin' (D)	CEnd CTho SKee
- 'Cornish Longstem' (D)	CAgr CDoC CEnd CTho
- 'Cornish Mother' (D)	CDoC CEnd CTho CTsd
- 'Cornish Pine' (D)	CDoC CEnd CTho SDea
- 'Coronation' (D)	SDea
- 'Corse Hill' (D)	CCAT CTho
- 'Costard' (C)	CCAT CHab SKee
- 'Cottenham Seedling' (C)	SKee
- 'Coul Blush' (D)	SKee
- 'Court of Wick' (D)	CAgr CCAT CHab CTho CTri ECrN NOra SKee SVic WHar
- 'Court Pendu Plat' (D)	CAgr CCAT CHab CTho GQue LEdu MWat NOra NWea SDea SFam SKee WHar WJas
- 'Court Royal' (Cider)	CCAT
- 'Cox Cymraeg' (D)	WGwG
- 'Cox's Orange Pippin' (D)	Widely available
- 'Cox's Pomona' (C)	SDea SKee WHar
- 'Cox's Rouge de Flandres' (D)	SKee
- 'Cox's Selfing' (D)	CDoC CDul CTri CWSG CWib EPfP EPom GTwe LBuc MBri MGos MNHC SCrf SDea SKee SPer SPoG WHar WJas
- 'Crawley Beauty' (C)	CAgr CHab GTwe SDea SFam SKee WHar
- 'Crawley Reinette' (D)	CHab
- 'Crimson Beauty' (D) **new**	SKee
- 'Crimson Beauty of Bath' (D)	CAgr
- 'Crimson Bramley' (C)	CCAT IArd
- 'Crimson Cox' (D)	SDea
§ - 'Crimson King' (Cider/C)	CAgr CCAT
- 'Crimson King' (D)	CAgr CHab CTri
- 'Crimson Peasgood' (C)	ECrN
- 'Crimson Queening' (D)	SKee WHar
- 'Crimson Victoria' (Cider)	CTho
- Crispin	see *M. domestica* 'Mutsu'
- 'Croen Mochyn' (D)	WGwG
§ - 'Crowngold' (D)	EPom
- 'Cutler Grieve' (D)	SDea

- Cybèle = 'Delrouval' (D)	LRHS
- 'Dabinett' (Cider)	CAgr CCAT CHab CTho CTri GTwe LBuc NOra SCrf SDea SKee WHar
- 'D'Arcy Spice' (D)	CAgr CCAT CDoC ECrN EPfP ERea GQue MCoo MWat NOra SDea SFam SKee WHar
- 'Deacon's Blushing Beauty' (C/D)	SDea
- 'Deacon's Millennium' (F)	SDea
- 'Decio' (D)	SKee
- Delbarestivale = 'Delcorf' (red) (D) ♀H4	LRHS
- 'Devon Crimson Queen' (D)	CDoC CTho
- 'Devonshire Buckland' (C)	CEnd CTho
- 'Devonshire Crimson Queen' (D)	SDea
- 'Devonshire Quarrenden' (D)	CAgr CCAT CDoC CDul CEnd CHab CTho CTsd NOra SDea SFam SKee SVic WHar
- 'Diamond' (D)	WGwG
- 'Discovery' (D) ♀H4	Widely available
- 'Doctor Harvey' (C)	ECrN ERea SFam SKee
- 'Doctor Kidd's Orange Red'	see *M. domestica* 'Kidd's Orange Red'
- 'Domino' (C)	MCoo
- 'Don's Delight' (C)	CTho
- 'Dove' (Cider)	CCAT
- 'Downton Pippin' (D)	CHab WHar
- 'Dredge's Fame' (D)	CTho
- 'Duchess's Favourite' (D)	LRHS SKee
- 'Dufflin' (Cider)	CCAT CTho
- 'Duke of Cornwall' (C)	CDoC CTho
- 'Duke of Devonshire' (D)	CCAT CSBt CTho CTri SDea SFam SKee
N - 'Dumeller's Seedling'	see *M. domestica* 'Dummellor's Seedling'
§ - 'Dummellor's Seedling' (C) ♀H4	CCAT CTri MCoo NOra SDea SKee WHar
- 'Dunkerton Late Sweet' (Cider)	CCAT CCVT CHab CTho LBuc
- 'Dunn's Seedling' (D)	SDea
§ - 'Dutch Mignonne' (D)	SKee
- 'Dymock Red' (Cider)	CCAT LBuc
- 'Early Blenheim' (D/C)	CCAT CEnd CTho
- 'Early Bower' (D)	CEnd
- 'Early Julyan' (C)	SKee
- 'Early Victoria'	see *M. domestica* 'Emneth Early'
- Early Windsor	see *M. domestica* 'Alkmene'
- 'Early Worcester'	see *M. domestica* 'Tydeman's Early Worcester'
- 'Eccleston Pippin' (D) **new**	SKee
- 'Ecklinville' (C)	SDea SKee
- 'Edith Hopwood' (D)	ECrN
- 'Edward VII' (C) ♀H4	CCAT CHab GTwe SCrf SDea SFam SKee WHar
- 'Egremont Russet' (D) ♀H4	Widely available
- 'Ellis' Bitter' (Cider)	CCAT CTho GTwe LBuc SKee SVic
- 'Ellison's Orange' (D) ♀H4	CAgr CCAT CDul CHab CMac CSBt CTri CWib ECrN EPfP EPom GTwe LAst LBuc MMuc MWat NOra NWea SDea SEND SFam SKee SPer SVic WHar WJas
- 'Elstar' (D) ♀H4	CCVT CWib ECrN EPom GTwe LAst SDea SKee WHar
- 'Elton Beauty' (D)	SDea SKee
§ - 'Emneth Early' (C) ♀H4	CAgr CHab ECrN GTwe SDea SFam SKee WJas

- 'Empire' (D)	LAst SKee
- 'Encore' (C)	SDea
- 'Endsleigh Beauty' (D)	CEnd
- 'English Codlin' (C)	CCAT CTho CTri ERea
- 'Epicure'	see *M. domestica* 'Laxton's Epicure'
- 'Ernie's Russet' (D)	SDea
- 'Eros' (D)	ECrN
- 'Essex Pippin' (D)	ECrN
- 'Evening Gold' (C)	SDea
- 'Eve's Delight' (D)	SDea
- 'Excelsior' (C)	ECrN
- 'Exeter Cross' (D)	CCAT CSBt ECrN SDea SFam
- 'Fair Maid of Devon' (Cider)	CAgr CCAT CEnd CTho
- 'Fairfield' (D)	CTho
- 'Falstaff'PBR (D) ♀H4	CAgr CCAT CDul ECrN EPfP EPom GTwe LSRN MGos NOra SCoo SDea SKee SPer WHar
- 'Farmer's Glory' (D)	CAgr CCAT CTho
- 'Fearn's Pippin' (D)	LRHS
- 'Fiesta'PBR (D) ♀H4	Widely available
- 'Fillbarrel' (Cider)	CCAT
- 'Fillingham Pippin' (C)	CHab
- 'Firmgold' (D)	SDea
- 'Flame' (D)	ECrN
- 'Flamenco'	see *M. domestica* 'Obelisk'
§ - 'Flower of Kent' (C)	CHab SCrf SDea SKee
- 'Flower of the Town' (D)	CHab
- 'Forfar'	see *M. domestica* 'Dutch Mignonne'
- 'Forge' (D)	CAgr CHab SDea SKee
- 'Fortune'	see *M. domestica* 'Laxton's Fortune'
- 'Four Square' (F)	CCAT
- 'Foxwhelp' (Cider)	SKee
- 'Francis' (D)	ECrN
- 'Frederick' (Cider)	CCAT CTho
- 'Freiherr von Berlepsch' (D) **new**	SKee
- 'French Crab' (C)	SDea
- 'Freyberg' (D)	SKee
- 'Fuji' (D)	SDea SKee
- 'Gala' (D)	CMac CSBt EPom NOra SCoo SCrf SDea SFam SKee SLim WHar
- 'Galaxy'PBR (F) **new**	NOra
- 'Galloway Pippin' (C)	GTwe SKee
- 'Gascoyne's Scarlet' (C/D)	CCAT SDea SFam SKee WHar
- 'Gavin' (D)	CAgr SDea
- 'Genesis II' (D/C)	SDea
- 'Genet Moyle' (C/Cider)	CTri MCoo WHar
- 'George Carpenter' (D)	LRHS SDea
- 'George Cave' (D)	CDul CTho ECrN GTwe IArd MCoo NOra SDea SEND SFam SKee WHar WJas
- 'George Neal' (C) ♀H4	CAgr SDea SFam
- 'Gibbon's Russet' (D)	IArd
- 'Gilliflower of Gloucester' (D)	CTho
- 'Gin' (Cider)	CCAT
- 'Gladstone' (D)	CAgr CCAT CTho SKee WHar
- 'Glansevin' (D)	WGwG
§ - 'Glass Apple' (C/D)	CCAT CEnd CTho
- 'Gloria Mundi' (C)	SDea SKee
- 'Gloster '69' (D)	SDea
- 'Gloucester Cross' (D)	SKee
- 'Gloucester Royal' (D)	CTho
- 'Gloucester Underleaf' (F)	CTho
- 'Golden Ball' (Cider)	CCAT CTho
- 'Golden Bittersweet' (D)	CAgr CTho
- 'Golden Delicious' (D) ♀H4	CCVT CDul CMac CSBt CWib ECrN ELan EPfP LAst LBuc MJak MMuc

		NOra SCrf SDea SEND SEWo SKee SVic WHar
	- 'Golden Glow' (C)	SDea
	- 'Golden Harvey' (D)	CAgr CCAT SKee
	- 'Golden Jubilee' (F)	CEnd
	- 'Golden Knob' (D)	CCAT CTho CTri SKee
	- 'Golden Noble' (C) ♀^{H4}	CAgr CCAT CDul CTho CTri ECrN ERea GTwe IArd MCoo NOra SDea SFam SKee
	- 'Golden Nugget' (D)	CAgr SKee
	- 'Golden Pippin' (C)	CAgr CCAT SKee WHar
	- 'Golden Reinette' (D)	SFam SKee
	- 'Golden Russet' (D)	CAgr ECrN SDea SKee WHar
	- 'Golden Spire' (C)	CHab MCoo NOra SDea SKee WHar
	- 'Gooseberry' (C)	SKee
	- 'Goring' (Cider)	CTho
	- 'Grand Sultan' (D)	CCAT
	- 'Grandpa Ailes' (F)	CTho
	- 'Grandpa Buxton' (C)	CHab
	- 'Granny Smith' (D)	CBcs CDul CWib ECrN GTwe LAst LSRN NOra SCrf SDea SKee SPer SVic WHar
	- 'Gravenstein' (D)	CCAT CHab SDea SFam SKee
§	- 'Green Balsam' (D)	CHab CTri
	- 'Greensleeves'^{PBR} (D) ♀^{H4}	CAgr CDul CMac CSBt CTri CWib ECrN EPfP EPom GTwe LAst MGos MMuc NLar NOra SDea SEND SKee SLim SPer SPoG WHar WJas
	- 'Greenup's Pippin' (D)	CHab
	- 'Grenadier' (C) ♀^{H4}	CAgr CDoC CHab CSBt CTri ECrN GTwe MGos MJak MMuc MWat NOra SDea SEND SFam SKee SLon SPer SVic WHar WJas
	- 'Gwell Na Mil' (D)	WGwG
	- 'Halstow Natural' (Cider)	CAgr CTho
	- 'Hambledon Deux Ans' (C)	SDea SFam
	- 'Hangy Down' (Cider)	CCAT CTho
	- 'Harling Hero' (D)	ECrN
	- Harmonie = 'Delorina' (F)	LRHS
§	- 'Harry Master's Jersey' (Cider)	CAgr CCAT CTho CTri MWat NOra SDea SKee WHar
	- 'Harry Pring' (D)	SKee
	- 'Harvester' (D)	CTho
	- 'Harvey' (C)	SDea
	- 'Hawthornden' (C)	CHab GTwe SKee
	- 'Herefordshire Redstreak' (Cider)	CAgr CDul LBuc WHar
	- 'Herefordshire Russet'^{PBR} (D)	CDoC CDul EPom ERea LBuc LRHS MBri MCoo MWat NLar NOra SKee SLim WHar WJas
	- 'Herring's Pippin' (C/D)	CTri SDea
	- 'High View Pippin' (D)	SKee
	- 'Hoary Morning' (C)	CCAT CTho ECrN SDea SKee
	- 'Hocking's Green' (C/D)	CAgr CCAT CEnd CTho CTsd
	- 'Holland Pippin' (C)	WHar
	- 'Hollow Core' (C)	CAgr CTho
	- 'Holstein' (D)	CTho SDea SKee WHar
	- 'Honey Pippin' (D)	ECrN
	- 'Honey String' (F)	CCAT
	- 'Hormead Pearmain' (C)	SKee
	- 'Horsford Prolific' (D)	ECrN
	- 'Hounslow Wonder' (C)	LRHS MWat
	- 'Howgate Wonder' (C)	CAgr CCVT CDul CHab CSBt CWib ECrN EPom GTwe LAst LBuc MMuc NOra SCrf SDea SEND SFam SKee SPer SVic WHar WJas
	- 'Hubbard's Pearmain' (D)	ECrN SKee
	- 'Hunter's Majestic' (D/C)	ECrN
	- 'Hunt's Duke of Gloucester' (D)	CTho
	- 'Hunt's Early' (D)	SKee
	- 'Idared' (D) ♀^{H4}	CCAT CWib ECrN SDea SKee SVic WHar
	- 'Improved Dove' (Cider)	CCAT
	- 'Improved Hangdown' (Cider) **new**	CCAT
	- 'Improved Keswick' (C/D)	CCAT CDoC CEnd CTho
	- 'Improved Lambrook Pippin' (Cider)	CCAT CTho CTri
	- 'Improved Redstreak' (Cider)	CTho
	- 'Ingrid Marie' (D)	SDea SKee
	- 'Irish Peach' (D)	CAgr CCAT CHab CTri ECrN ERea GTwe IArd MCoo NOra SDea SFam SKee WHar
	- 'Isaac Newton's Tree'	see *M. domestica* 'Flower of Kent'
	- 'Isle of Wight Pippin' (D)	SDea
	- 'Isle of Wight Russet' (D)	SDea
	- 'Jackson's'	see *M. domestica* 'Crimson King' (Cider/C)
	- 'James Grieve' (D) ♀^{H4}	Widely available
	- 'Jerseymac' (D)	SDea
	- 'Jester' (D)	ECrN SDea SKee
	- 'Joaneting' (D)	CAgr CHab
	- 'John Broad' (F)	CDoC
	- 'John Standish' (D)	CAgr CCAT CTri ERea SDea
	- 'John Toucher's'	see *M. domestica* 'Crimson King' (Cider/C)
	- 'Johnny Andrews' (Cider)	CAgr CCAT CTho
	- 'Johnny Voun' (D)	CEnd CTho
	- 'Jonagold' (D) ♀^{H4}	CDul CTri CWib ECrN ELan EPom GTwe IArd NLar SCrf SDea SFam SKee SPer SVic
	- 'Jonagold Crowngold'	see *M. domestica* 'Crowngold'
§	- 'Jonagored'^{PBR} (D)	NOra SDea WHar
	- 'Jonared' (D)	GTwe
	- 'Jonathan' (D)	SDea SKee
	- 'Jordan's Weeping' (C)	SDea
	- 'Josephine' (D)	SDea
	- 'Joybells' (D)	LRHS
	- 'Jubilee'	see *M. domestica* 'Royal Jubilee'
	- 'Julie's Late Golden' (F)	CTri
	- 'Jumbo' (C/D)	MBri MCoo SKee WHar WJas
	- 'Jupiter'^{PBR} (D) ♀^{H4}	CAgr CSBt CTri CWib ECrN EWTr GTwe LSRN MJak MRav NOra SDea SKee SLon WHar WJas
	- 'Kapai Red Jonathan' (D)	SDea
	- 'Karmijn de Sonnaville' (D)	SDea SKee
§	- 'Katja' (D)	CAgr CCAT CCVT CDoC CDul CMac CTri CTsd CWib ERea EWTr GKin GTwe IArd LAst LBuc MJak MMuc MRav NEgg NLar NOra SCoo SDea SEWo SKee SPer WHar WJas
	- Katy	see *M. domestica* 'Katja'
	- 'Kent' (D)	ECrN NLar SCrf SDea SKee
	- 'Kentish Fillbasket' (C)	SKee
	- 'Kentish Quarrenden' (D)	SKee
	- 'Kerry Pippin' (D)	IArd SKee
	- 'Keswick Codlin' (C)	CHab CTho ECrN GQue GTwe MBri MCoo NEgg NLar NOra NWea SDea SKee WHar WJas
§	- 'Kidd's Orange Red' (D) ♀^{H4}	CAgr CCAT CDul CMac CTri ECrN EPfP EPom GTwe LBuc LRHS MWat NOra SCrf SDea SEND SFam SKee SLon WHar
	- 'Kilkenny Pearmain' (D)	IArd

	- 'Kill Boy' (F)	CTho
	- 'Killerton Sharp' (Cider)	CTho
	- 'Killerton Sweet' (Cider)	CTho
	- 'King Byerd' (C/D)	CCAT CDoC CEnd CTho
	- 'King Coffee' (D)	WHar
	- 'King Luscious' (D)	SDea
§	- 'King of the Pippins' (D) ♀^{H4}	CCAT CHab CTho CTri ECrN GTwe MCoo NOra SCrf SDea SFam SKee SVic WHar
	- 'King of Tompkins County' (D)	SFam
	- 'King Russet' (D) ♀^{H4}	SDea
	- 'King's Acre Pippin' (D)	SDea SFam WHar
	- 'Kingston Bitter' (Cider)	CTho
	- 'Kingston Black' (Cider/C)	CAgr CCAT CEnd CHab CTho CTri GTwe LBuc NOra SDea SKee
	- 'Kirton Fair' (D)	CTho
	- 'Lady Henniker' (C)	CCAT CDul CHab CTho ECrN SDea SKee WHar
	- 'Lady Lambourne' (C/D)	CHab
	- 'Lady of the Wemyss' (C)	SKee
	- 'Lady Sudeley' (D)	CCAT CDoC CHab CTho SDea SKee
	- 'Lady's Finger' (C/D)	CDoC CEnd
	- 'Lady's Finger of Lancaster' (C/D)	CHab SKee
	- 'Lady's Finger of Offaly' (D)	IArd SDea
	- 'Lake's Kernel' (D)	CTho
	- 'Lane's Prince Albert' (C) ♀^{H4}	CAgr CCAT CHab CSBt ECrN EPfP EWTr GTwe IArd MGos MRav MWat NLar NOra NWea SCoo SCrf SDea SFam SKee SVic WHar WJas
	- 'Langley Pippin' (D)	SDea
§	- 'Langworthy' (Cider)	CCAT CTho
§	- 'Laxton's Epicure' (D) ♀^{H4}	CAgr CDul CHab ECrN GTwe LAst SDea SFam SKee WHar
§	- 'Laxton's Fortune' (D) ♀^{H4}	CCAT CHab CMac CSBt CTri CWib ECrN GTwe IArd LAst NOra SCrf SDea SFam SKee WHar WJas
	- 'Laxton's Pearmain' (D)	MCoo SFam
	- 'Laxton's Royalty' (D)	SDea
§	- 'Laxton's Superb' (D)	Widely available
	- 'Leathercoat Russet' (D)	CAgr CCAT CDoC CTri SKee
	- 'Lemon Pippin' (C)	CCAT ECrN ELan SDea WHar
	- 'Lemon Pippin of Gloucestershire' (D)	CTho
	- 'Liberty' (D)	SDea
	- 'Limberland' (C)	CTho
	- 'Limelight' (D)	CDoC ERea MBri MCoo MWat NLar NOra SCoo SKee WHar
	- 'Link Wonder' (F)	CEnd
	- 'Lodgemore Nonpareil' (D)	SKee
	- 'Lodi' (C)	SDea
	- 'London Pearmain' (D)	ECrN
	- 'London Pippin' (C)	CAgr CTho
	- 'Longkeeper' (D)	CAgr CDoC CEnd CTho
	- 'Longney Russet' (Cider/D)	CCAT
	- 'Longstem' (Cider)	CTho
	- 'Lord Burghley' (D)	SDea
	- 'Lord Derby' (C)	CAgr CCAT CDoC CDul CHab CMac CTho CWib ECrN EPom EWTr GTwe LRHS MRav SDea SEND SFam SKee SVic WHar
	- 'Lord Grosvenor' (C)	SKee WHar
	- 'Lord Hindlip' (D)	CHab NOra SDea SFam
	- 'Lord Lambourne' (D) ♀^{H4}	CAgr CCAT CDoC CDul CHab CMac CSBt CSut CTri CWib ECrN EPfP EWTr GTwe LAst LRHS LSRN MCoo MGos MWat NOra SCrf SDea SFam SKee SPer WHar WJas
	- 'Lord of the Isles' (F)	CAgr CCAT CDoC
	- 'Lord Rosebery' (D)	SKee
	- 'Lord Stradbroke' (C)	ECrN SKee
	- 'Lord Suffield' (C)	CTri ECrN SKee
	- 'Lough Tree of Wexford' (D)	IArd
	- 'Lucombe's Pine' (D)	CAgr CCAT CEnd CTho CTsd ECrN SVic
	- 'Lucombe's Seedling' (D)	CTho
	- 'Lynn's Pippin' (D)	ECrN
	- 'Mabbott's Pearmain' (D)	SDea
	- 'Machen' (D)	WGwG
	- 'Maclean's Favourite' (D)	ECrN
	- 'Madresfield Court' (D)	SDea
	- 'Major' (Cider)	CAgr CCAT
	- 'Maldon Wonder' (D)	ECrN
	- Malini Dulcessa (F) **new**	CSut
	- Malini Fresco (F) **new**	CSut
	- 'Malling Kent' (D)	SDea SFam
	- Maloni Lilly (F) **new**	CSut
	- Maloni Sally (F) **new**	CSut
	- 'Maltster' (D)	MCoo
	- 'Manaccan Primrose' (C/D)	CDoC CEnd
	- 'Margil' (D)	SDea SFam WHar
	- 'Markham Pippin' (D)	MCoo
	- 'Maxton' (D)	ECrN
	- 'May Queen' (D)	SDea SFam
	- 'Maypole'^{PBR} (D/Ball)	SDea
	- 'McIntosh' (D)	SKee
	- 'Médaille d'Or' (Cider)	CCAT SKee
	- 'Melon' (D)	SDea
	- 'Melrose' (D)	ECrN SVic
	- 'Merchant Apple' (D)	CCAT CTho CTri
	- 'Mère de Ménage' (C)	SFam SKee WHar
	- 'Meridian'^{PBR} (D)	CAgr CDoC ECrN LSRN MCoo MWat NOra SDea
	- 'Merton Beauty' (D)	SKee
	- 'Merton Charm' (D) ♀^{H4}	SKee
	- 'Merton Knave' (D)	SDea SFam
	- 'Merton Russet' (D)	SDea
	- 'Merton Worcester' (D)	ECrN SDea SKee
	- 'Michaelmas Red' (D)	GTwe NEgg SKee
	- 'Michelin' (Cider)	CAgr CCAT CTri GTwe LBuc SDea SKee WHar
	- 'Miller's Seedling' (D)	SKee
	- 'Millicent Barnes' (D)	SDea SKee
	- 'Minshull Crab' (C) **new**	SKee
	- 'Mollie's Delicious' (D)	SKee
	- 'Monarch' (C)	CAgr CTri ECrN GTwe SDea SFam SKee
	- 'Montfort' (D)	ECrN
	- 'Morgan's Sweet' (C/Cider)	CCAT CEnd CHab CTho CTri NOra SDea SKee
	- 'Moss's Seedling' (D)	SDea
§	- 'Mother' (D) ♀^{H4}	CAgr CCAT CTri ECrN GTwe SCrf SDea SKee
§	- 'Mutsu' (C/D)	CCAT CTri ECrN MRav NOra SDea SKee SPer
	- 'Nant Gwrtheyrn' (D)	WGwG
	- 'Nettlestone Pippin' (D)	SDea
	- 'Newton Wonder' (C) ♀^{H4}	CAgr CCAT CDoC CDul CHab CSBt CTho CTri CWib ECrN GTwe IArd

	LAst MCoo MGos NOra SCrf SDea SFam SKee WHar WJas
- 'Newtown Pippin' (D)	SDea
- 'Nine Square' (D)	CTho
- 'Nittany Red' (D)	SDea
- 'No Pip' (C)	CTho
- 'Nolan Pippin' (D)	ECrN
- 'Nonpareil' (D)	SKee WHar
- 'Norfolk Beauty' (C)	ECrN ERea SKee
- 'Norfolk Beefing' (C)	CHab ECrN ERea SDea SFam SKee
- 'Norfolk Royal' (D)	CDoC ECrN ERea GTwe NOra SDea
- 'Norfolk Royal Russet' (D)	ECrN ERea LRHS NOra SKee
- 'Norfolk Winter Coleman' (C)	ERea
- 'Northcott Superb' (D)	CTho
- 'Northern Greening' (C)	SKee WHar
§ - 'Northwood' (Cider)	CCAT CTho
- 'Nutmeg Pippin' (D)	CCAT ECrN SDea SFam
- Nuvar Cheerfull Gold (D) **new**	SKee
- Nuvar Freckles (D)	SKee
- Nuvar Golden Elf (D)	SKee
- Nuvar Golden Hills (D)	SKee
- Nuvar Home Farm (D)	SKee
- Nuvar Melody (D)	SKee
- 'Oaken Pin' (D)	CCAT CDoC CTho
§ - 'Obelisk'PBR (D)	SDea SKee
- 'Old Pearmain' (D)	SDea SKee WHar
- 'Old Somerset Russet' (D)	CCAT CTho
- 'Onibury Pippin' (F) **new**	WHar
- 'Opalescent' (D)	SKee
- 'Orkney Apple' (F)	SKee
- 'Orleans Reinette' (D)	CAgr CCAT CTho CTri CWib ECrN GTwe IArd LBuc LRHS MWat NEgg NOra SCrf SDea SFam SKee WHar WJas
- 'Oslin' (D)	SKee
- 'Otava'PBR (C/D)	SKee
- 'Owen Thomas' (D)	CTri
- 'Paignton Marigold' (Cider)	CCAT CTho
- 'Palmer's Rosey' (D)	SKee
- Paradis Myra (F) **new**	CSut
- 'Pascoe's Pippin' (D/C)	CTho
- 'Payhembury' (C/Cider)	CAgr CTho CTri
- 'Pear Apple' (D)	CAgr CCAT CDoC CEnd CTho
- 'Pearl' (D)	SDea
- 'Peasgood's Nonsuch' (C) ♀H4	CAgr CCAT CDoC CHab ECrN ERea GTwe IArd LSRN NEgg NOra SCrf SDea SFam SKee SLon
- 'Pendragon' (D)	CTho
- 'Penhallow Pippin' (D)	CDoC CTho
- 'Pennard Bitter' (Cider)	CCAT
- 'Pépin Shafrannyi' (D)	SKee
- 'Peter Lock' (C/D)	CAgr CCAT CEnd CTho SKee
- 'Peter's Pippin' (D)	SDea
- 'Peter's Seedling' (D)	SDea
- 'Pethyre' (Cider)	CCVT
- 'Pig Aderyn' (C)	CHab WGwG
- 'Pig y Colomen' (C)	WGwG
- 'Pigeonette de Rouen' (D)	SKee
- 'Pig's Nose Pippin' (D)	CEnd SKee
- 'Pig's Nose Pippin' Type III (D)	CAgr CCAT CTho
- 'Pig's Snout' (Cider/C/D)	CCAT CEnd CTho
- 'Pineapple Russet' (C/D)	CAgr ERea
- 'Pinova'PBR (D)	CAgr EPom MCoo WHar
- 'Pitmaston Pine Apple' (D)	CCAT CHab CTho CTri ECrN ERea EWTr IArd LAst MCoo MWat NOra SDea SFam SKee SLon WHar
- 'Pitmaston Russet Nonpareil' (D)	SKee
- 'Pixie' (D) ♀H4	CDoC CWib EPom GTwe LRHS MWat NOra SDea SFam SKee SLon WHar
- 'Plum Vite' (D)	CAgr CTho CTri
- 'Plympton Pippin' (C)	CDoC CEnd CTho CTri
- Polka = 'Trajan'PBR (D/Ball)	SDea SKee
- 'Polly' (C/D)	CDoC CEnd
- 'Polly Whitehair' (C/D)	CCAT CTho SDea
- 'Poltimore Seedling' (D)	CTho
- 'Pomeroy of Somerset' (D)	CCAT CHab CTho CTri
- 'Ponsford' (C)	CAgr CCAT CTho
- 'Port Wine'	see *M. domestica* 'Harry Master's Jersey'
- 'Porter's Perfection' (Cider)	CCAT NOra
- 'Princesse' (F)	ECrN SDea
- 'Profit' (F)	CCAT CTho
- 'Quarry Apple' (C)	CTho
- 'Queen' (C)	CAgr CTho ECrN WHar
- 'Queen Cox' (D)	CTri ECrN EPom EWTr LSRN NOra SDea SKee SLon
- 'Queen Cox' self-fertile (F)	CSut CWib EPom ERea LSRN SDea SWvt WHar
- 'Queenie' (D)	CCAT
- 'Queens' (D)	CTho
- 'Quench' (D/Cider)	CTho
- 'Rafzubin' (F) **new**	NOra
- 'Rajka'PBR (D)	CDoC NOra SKee
- 'Red Alkmene' (D)	MBri NOra
- 'Red Belle de Boskoop' (D)	CAgr
- 'Red Bramley' (C)	CWib ECrN
- 'Red Charles Ross' (C/D)	SDea
- 'Red Delicious' (D)	SCrf SKee
- 'Red Devil' (D)	CAgr CMac CMam CTri CWSG ECrN EPom GTwe LAst LRHS MBri MRav MWat NLar NOra NPri SCoo SDea SEWo SKee SLim SLon WHar WJas
- 'Red Ellison' (D)	CTho CTri ECrN ERea GTwe SDea
- 'Red Elstar' (D)	IArd
- 'Red Falstaff'PBR (D)	CAgr CCAT CCVT CDoC CDul CMac CTri ECrN EPfP ERea GKin LBuc LRHS LSRN MBri MCoo MWat NLar NOra SKee SLim SLon SPer SPoG WHar
- 'Red Fuji' (D)	SDea
- 'Red James Grieve' (D)	LSRN
- 'Red Jersey' (Cider)	CCAT
- 'Red Joaneting' (D)	SKee WHar
- 'Red Jonagold'	see *M. domestica* 'Jonagored'
- 'Red Jonathan' (D)	SDea
- 'Red Miller's seedling' (D)	ECrN SCrf SDea
- 'Red Pixie' (D) **new**	GQue
- 'Red Rattler' (D)	CTho CTri
- 'Red Roller' (D)	CTho
- 'Red Ruby' (F)	CTho
- 'Red Victoria' (C)	GTwe
- 'Red Windsor' (F)	CDoC CDul CMac CMam EPom ERea LBuc LRHS MWat NLar NOra SCoo SKee SLim SPoG WHar WJas
- 'Redcoat Grieve' (D)	SDea
- Redlove Era (C/D)	CSut
- Redlove Sirena (C/D) **new**	CSut

- 'Redsleeves' (D)	CAgr ECrN GTwe IArd SDea
- 'Redstrake' (Cider)	CCAT
- Regali = 'Delkistar'PBR (D)	LRHS
- 'Reine des Reinettes'	see *M. domestica* 'King of the Pippins'
- 'Reinette Descardre' (D)	SVic
- 'Reinette d'Obry' (Cider)	CCAT
- 'Reinette Rouge Etoilée' (D)	SDea
- 'Reverend Greeves' (C)	SDea
- 'Reverend McCormick' (F)	CTho
- 'Reverend W. Wilks' (C)	CAgr CDoC CDoy CHab CSBt CTri ECrN LAst LRHS MBri NOra SCrf SDea SFam SKee SPer WHar WJas
- 'Ribston Pippin' (D) ♀H4	CCAT CTho CTri CWib ECrN ERea GTwe LBuc MCoo MRav MWat NOra SCrf SDea SFam SKee SLon WHar WJas
- 'Rival' (D)	CAgr SDea SKee
- 'Rivers' Nonsuch' (D)	CHab
- 'Rome Beauty' (D)	SDea
- 'Rosemary Russet' (D) ♀H4	CAgr CCAT CDoC CHab CTho ERea GTwe MCoo SCrf SDea SFam SKee WHar
- 'Rosette' (D) **new**	LBuc LRHS
- 'Ross Nonpareil' (D)	CAgr IArd SDea SKee WHar
- 'Rosy Blenheim' (D)	ECrN
- 'Rough Pippin' (D)	CEnd
- 'Roundway Magnum Bonum' (C/D)	CAgr CTho SDea
§ - 'Roxbury Russet' (D)	SKee
- 'Royal Gala' (D) ♀H4	CMac ECrN EPom LBuc MRav SDea SLon
§ - 'Royal Jubilee' (C)	CCAT LRHS
- 'Royal Russet' (C)	CEnd ECrN SDea
- 'Royal Somerset' (C/Cider)	CCAT CTho CTri
- 'Rubinette' (D)	ECrN SDea
- Rubinette Rosso = 'Rafzubex'PBR (F)	NOra
- 'Rubinola'PBR (D)	SKee
- 'Ruby' Thorrington (D)	ECrN
- 'Saint Cecilia' (D)	CHab SDea WGwG
§ - 'Saint Edmund's Pippin' (D) ♀H4	CDul CHab CTho ECrN ELan EPfP ERea GTwe MCoo NOra SCrf SDea SFam SKee
- 'Saint Edmund's Russet'	see *M. domestica* 'Saint Edmund's Pippin'
- 'Saint Everard' (D)	SKee
- 'Sam Young' (D)	CAgr IArd SKee
- 'Sandlands' (D)	SDea
- 'Sandringham' (C)	ECrN
- 'Sanspareil' (D)	CAgr
- 'Santana' (D)	MBri NOra
- 'Saturn' (D)	CAgr CCVT CDoC CTri NOra SDea SKee WHar
- 'Saw Pits' (F)	CAgr CEnd
- 'Scarlet Crofton' (D)	IArd SKee
- 'Scarlet Nonpareil' (D)	LRHS SDea
- 'Scotch Bridget' (C)	CHab GQue NBid NOra SCoo SKee WHar
- 'Scotch Dumpling' (C)	GKin GQue GTwe MCoo NOra SKee WHar
- 'Scrumptious'PBR (D) ♀H4	CAgr CCVT CDoC CDul CMac CMam CTri EMil EPfP EPom GKin LBuc LHop LRHS LSRN MBri MWat NLar NOra NPri NWea SCoo SEWo SKee SLim SLon SPer SPoG WHar WJas
- 'Seaton House' (C)	SKee
- 'Sercombe's Natural' (Cider)	CCAT CTho
- 'Severn Bank' (C)	CCAT CTho
- 'Sheep's Nose' (C)	CCAT CHab CTho IArd SDea
- 'Shenandoah' (C)	SKee
- 'Sidney Strake' (C)	CAgr CEnd
- 'Sir Isaac Newton's'	see *M. domestica* 'Flower of Kent'
- 'Sir John Thornycroft' (D)	SDea
- 'Sisson's Worksop Newtown' (D)	MCoo
- 'Slack Ma Girdle' (Cider)	CCAT CTho
- 'Smart's Prince Arthur' (C)	CHab SDea
- 'Snell's Glass Apple'	see *M. domestica* 'Glass Apple'
- 'Somerset Lasting' (C)	CTri
'Somerset Redstreak' (Cider)	CAgr CCAT CHab CTho CTri GTwe WHar
- 'Sops in Wine' (C/Cider)	CCAT CTho CTsd SVic
- 'Sour Bay' (Cider)	CAgr CTho
- 'Sour Natural'	see *M. domestica* 'Langworthy'
- 'Spartan' (D)	CCAT CCVT CDoC CMac CSBt CTri CWib ECrN ELan EWTr GKin GTwe LAst LRHS MCoo MGos MJak MWat NLar NOra SCrf SDea SFam SKee SPer SVic WHar WJas
- 'Spencer' (D)	CTri ECrN SKee
- 'Spotted Dick' (Cider)	CTho
- 'Stable Jersey' (Cider)	CCAT
- 'Stamford Pippin' (D)	SDea
- 'Stanway Seedling' (C)	ECrN
- 'Star of Devon' (D)	CEnd SDea
- 'Stark' (D)	SDea
- 'Starking' (D)	ECrN
- 'Stark's Earliest' (D)	SVic
- 'Stembridge Cluster' (Cider)	CCAT
- 'Stembridge Jersey' (Cider)	CCAT
- 'Steyne Seedling' (D)	SDea
- 'Stirling Castle' (C)	CAgr GQue NOra SKee
- 'Stobo Castle' (C)	SKee
- 'Stockbearer' (C)	CTho
- 'Stoke Edith Pippin' (D)	WHar
- 'Stoke Red' (Cider)	CCAT CTho SKee
- 'Strawberry Pippin' (D)	CTho
- 'Striped Beefing' (C)	ECrN ERea
- 'Sturmer Pippin' (D)	CCAT CSBt CTri ECrN GTwe MWat NOra SCrf SDea SFam SKee WHar
* - 'Sugar Apple' (F)	CTho
- 'Sugar Bush' (C/D)	CTho
- 'Sugar Loaf'	see *M. domestica* 'Sugar Apple'
- 'Summerred' (D)	ECrN
- 'Sunburn' (D)	ECrN
- 'Sunlight'PBR (F)	MWat
- 'Sunnydale' (D/C)	SDea
- 'Sunrise'PBR (D)	NOra SKee WHar
- 'Sunset' (D) ♀H4	Widely available
- 'Suntan' (D) ♀H4	CCAT CDoC CWib ECrN LAst MWat NOra SDea SKee
- 'Superb'	see *M. domestica* 'Laxton's Superb'
- 'Sure Crop' (D) **new**	SKee
- 'Sussex Mother' (C/D)	CHab
- 'Sweet Alford' (Cider)	CCAT CTho
- 'Sweet Bay' (Cider)	CAgr CTho
- 'Sweet Cleave' (Cider)	CTho
- 'Sweet Coppin' (Cider)	CCAT CTho CTri
- 'Sweet Society' (D)	MCoo NOra SKee WHar WJas
- 'Tale Sweet' (Cider)	CCAT CTho

– 'Tamar Beauty' (F)	CEnd
– 'Tan Harvey' (Cider)	CCAT CEnd CTho
– 'Taunton Cross' (D)	CAgr
– 'Taunton Fair Maid' (Cider)	CCAT CTho
– 'Taylor's' (Cider)	CAgr CCAT SDea
– 'Ten Commandments' (D/Cider)	CCAT SDea
– 'Tewkesbury Baron' (D)	CTho
– 'The Rattler' (F)	CDoC CEnd
– 'Thomas Rivers' (C)	SDea
– 'Thorle Pippin' (D)	SKee
– 'Tidicombe Seedling' (D)	CTho
– 'Tom Putt' (C)	CAgr CCAT CCVT CDul CHab CTho CTri CWib ECrN GTwe LBuc SDea SKee WHar WJas
– 'Tommy Knight' (D)	CAgr CCAT CDoC CEnd CTho
– 'Topaz'^{PBR} (D)	CDoC SKee
– 'Totnes Apple' (D)	CTho
– 'Tower of Glamis' (C)	CHab GQue GTwe SKee
– Town Farm Number 59 (Cider)	CTho
– 'Tregonna King' (C/D)	CCAT CDoC CEnd CTho CTsd
– 'Tremlett's Bitter' (Cider)	CAgr CCAT CHab CTho NOra SDea SKee SVic
– 'Trwyn Mochyn' (C)	WGwG
§ – 'Tuscan'^{PBR} (D/Ball)	MCoo SDea SKee
§ – 'Tydeman's Early Worcester' (D)	CAgr CDul CHab CWib ECrN EWTr GTwe SDea SKee SVic
– 'Tydeman's Late Orange' (D)	CDoC CHab CTri ECrN EMil GTwe IArd LAst MCoo NOra SDea SFam SKee WHar
– 'Uncle John's Cooker' (C)	IArd
– 'Upton Pyne' (C/D)	CCAT CDoC CTho SDea SKee
– 'Vallis Apple' (Cider)	CCAT CTho
– 'Veitch's Perfection' (C/D)	CTho
– 'Veitch's Prolific' (F)	CDoC
– 'Venus Pippin' (C/D)	CEnd
– 'Vicary's Late Keeper' (F)	CTho
– 'Vickey's Delight' (D)	SDea
– 'Vileberie' (Cider)	CCAT
– 'Vista-bella' (D)	ECrN SDea
– 'Wagener' (D)	SDea
– 'Waltham Abbey Seedling' (C)	ECrN
– Waltz = 'Telamon'^{PBR} (D/Ball)	SDea
– 'Warner's King' (C) $\mathbb{Y}^{H4}$	CTho CTri NOra SCrf SDea SKee WHar
– 'Warrior' (F)	CCAT CTho
– 'Wealthy' (D)	SDea
– 'Wellington' (C)	see *M. domestica* 'Dummellor's Seedling'
– 'Wellington' (Cider)	CAgr CTho
– 'Welsh Russet' (D)	SDea
– 'Wern' (C)	WGwG
– 'West View Seedling' (D)	ECrN
– 'White Alphington' (Cider)	CTho
– 'White Close Pippin' (Cider)	CTho
– 'White Jersey' (Cider)	CCAT
– 'White Joaneting' (D)	SKee
– 'White Melrose' (C)	GQue GTwe SDea SKee
– 'White Transparent' (C/D)	SDea
– 'Whitpot Sweet' (F)	CEnd
– 'Wick White Styre' (Cider)	CTho
– 'William Crump' (D)	CCAT CDul CHab CTho ECrN SDea SFam SKee WHar
– 'Willoughby' (D)	MCoo
– 'Winston' (D) $\mathbb{Y}^{H4}$	CAgr CCAT CCVT CMac CSBt CTri ECrN MCoo NWea SDea SFam SVic WHar
– 'Winter Banana' (D)	ECrN GQue MCoo SDea SVic WHar
– 'Winter Gem' (D)	CAgr CCVT CDul ECrN EPom ERea LAst LBuc NOra SDea SKee WHar WJas
– 'Winter Lawrence' (F)	CTho
– 'Winter Peach' (D/C)	CAgr CDoC CEnd CTho ECrN
– 'Winter Pearmain' (D)	WHar
– 'Winter Quarrenden' (D)	SDea
– 'Winter Queening' (D/C)	SDea
– 'Winter Stubbard' (C)	CTho
– 'Wintergreen' (C)	CDoC
– 'Woodbine'	see *M. domestica* 'Northwood'
– 'Woodford' (C)	ECrN
– 'Woolbrook Pippin' (D)	CAgr CEnd CTho
– 'Woolbrook Russet' (C)	CEnd CTho ECrN
– 'Worcester Pearmain' (D) $\mathbb{Y}^{H4}$	Widely available
– 'Wormsley Pippin' (D)	ECrN
– 'Wyatt's Seedling'	see *M. domestica* 'Langworthy'
– 'Wyken Pippin' (D)	CCAT ECrN SDea SFam SKee
– 'Yarlington Mill' (Cider)	CAgr CCAT CHab CTho CTri NOra SDea SKee SVic
– 'Yellow Ingestrie' (D)	CHab ERea MCoo NOra SFam WHar
– 'Yellow Styre' (Cider)	CTho
– 'Yorkshire Greening' (C)	CHab NOra SKee WHar
– 'Zabergäu Renette' (D)	SKee
'Donald Wyman'	CLnd EPfP NLar SCoo
'Echtermeyer'	see *M.* × *gloriosa* 'Oekonomierat Echtermeyer'
'Elise Rathke' **new**	CLnd
'Evelyn'	CLnd EBee
§ 'Evereste'	Widely available
florentina	CTho EPfP LLHF SSpi
– 'Rosemoor'	CLnd EBee
– 'Skopje'	EPfP WMou
floribunda $\mathbb{Y}^{H4}$	Widely available
fusca **new**	CLnd
'Gardener's Gold'	CEnd CTho
§ × ***gloriosa*** 'Oekonomierat Echtermeyer'	SDea SGol
'Golden Gem'	CLnd EBee EPfP GQue MAsh NOra SEWo SLim SPer
'Golden Hornet'	see *M.* × *zumi* 'Golden Hornet'
'Harry Baker'	CCVT CDul CEnd CLnd EBee ECrN EMil EPfP EPom ERea LRHS LSRN MAsh MBlu MBri NLar SCoo SEWo SLim SPoG WHar WJas
× ***hartwigii***	CLnd
'Hillieri'	see *M.* × *scheideckeri* 'Hillieri'
'Honeycrisp'^{PBR} **new**	WHar
hupehensis $\mathbb{Y}^{H4}$	CDoy CDul CEnd CLnd CMCN CSBt CTho EBee EPfP IMou LHop MBlu MGos MRav NWea SCrf SDix SFam SPer
'Hyde Hall Spire'	EBee LRHS SCoo
'Indian Magic'	CLnd EBee LRHS MAsh MBri
'Indian Summer'	CLnd
Jelly King = 'Mattfru'	CLnd LRHS LSRN MBri MWat NLar WHar WMou
'John Downie' (C) $\mathbb{Y}^{H4}$	Widely available
'Kaido'	see *M.* × *micromalus*
kansuensis	CLnd EPfP
'Kemp'	SDea
'Lady Northcliffe'	CDul CLnd SFam

'Laura'	CDul CLnd EPfP EPom ERea LRHS LSRN MAsh MBri NLar SCoo SKee SLim SLon SPer SPoG WHar WJas
'Lisa'	CLnd
'Louisa'	CLnd CWSG LRHS NWea SCoo SGol
× ***magdeburgensis***	CCVT CDul CLnd CSBt
'Mary Potter'	CLnd
§ × ***micromalus***	CLnd NLar
× ***moerlandsii***	CLnd
- 'Liset'	CDul CEnd CSBt CTsd CWib EBee ECrN LHop MRav NEgg NOra SCoo SFam SPer WMou
§ - 'Profusion'	CBcs CDul CMac CTri EBee ELan LAst MGos MJak MMuc MRav MSwo MWat NOra NPri NWea SCrf SEND SGol SPer SWvt WJas
- 'Profusion Improved'	CEnd CSBt CWSG LRHS MAsh MWat NOra SCoo SWvt WHar
'Mokum'	CCVT CLnd
'Molten Lava'	CLnd MAsh
niedzwetzkyana	CLnd CTho
Nuvar Marble	MBri SKee
orthocarpa	CLnd
Perpetu	see *M.* 'Evereste'
'Pink Glow'	CEnd CLnd CSBt EPom ERea MBlu NLar SCoo SEWo SLim SPer SPoG WHar
'Pink Mushroom'	NLar
'Pink Perfection'	CDoC CEnd ECrN NLar NPri NWea
'Pond Red'	CLnd
'Prairie Fire'	CDul CLnd LRHS MAsh MBri SCoo SLim SLon SPoG
prattii	CLnd CTho EPfP
'Pourpre Noir'	CLnd
'Princeton Cardinal'	CLnd CMac EBee EPfP LRHS MAsh MBri SCoo SLim
'Professor Sprenger'	see *M.* × *zumi* 'Professor Sprenger'
'Profusion'	see *M.* × *moerlandsii* 'Profusion'
prunifolia	MBlu
- var. ***rinkii***	CLnd
pumila 'Cowichan'	CLnd ECrN
- 'Montreal Beauty'	CLnd WJas
'Purple Prince'	CLnd
§ × ***purpurea*** 'Aldenhamensis'	CLnd SDea WHar
- 'Eleyi'	CLnd CNWT LAst NWea
- 'Lemoinei'	CDul CLnd
- 'Neville Copeman'	CCVT CDoC CDul CLnd EBee ECrN EPom EWTr WJas WMou
- 'Pendula'	see *M.* × *gloriosa* 'Oekonomierat Echtermeyer'
'R.J. Fulcher'	CLnd CTho
'Ralph Shay'	CLnd
'Red Ace'	CDul
'Red Barron'	CLnd
'Red Glow'	CDul CLnd ECrN MMuc SEND WJas
'Red Jade'	see *M.* × *scheideckeri* 'Red Jade'
Red Obelisk = 'Dvp Obel'	CLnd CWSG LRHS MBri SCoo
'Red Peacock'	CLnd
'Robinson'	CLnd
§ × ***robusta***	CLnd GTwe LSRN NWea SLon
- 'Red Sentinel' 🏆^{H4}	Widely available
- 'Red Siberian'	SDea SPer
- 'Yellow Siberian'	CLnd
'Rosehip'	EBee MAsh MBri
'Royal Beauty' 🏆^{H4}	CDoC CDul CLnd CWib EBee EPfP EWTr LAst LRHS MBri MGos MJak MSwo NPri SCoo SCrf SLon SPer WHar WMou
'Royalty'	CBcs CDul CLnd CSBt EBee ECrN ELan EWTr GTwe LAst LBuc LHop LRHS MGos MRav MSwo MWat NEgg NOra NPla SCrf SEND SEWo SGol SPer SPoG WHar WJas
'Rudolph'	CCVT CDul CLnd CNWT EBee ECrN EWTr GKin LBuc LHop LRHS LSRN MAsh MGos SCoo SEWo SLim SPer SPoG WJas WMou
'Ruth Ann'	CLnd
sargentii	CDul CTho LRHS NOra NWea SFam
- 'Tina'	CLnd CWSG MAsh
'Satin Cloud'	CLnd
§ × ***scheideckeri*** 'Hillieri'	CDul CLnd ECrN SFam
§ - 'Red Jade'	CDul CLnd CTri CWib EBee ELan LAst LRHS MGos MMuc MRav MSwo MWat NEgg NWea SEND SPer WHar WJas
Siberian crab	see *M.* × *robusta*
sieboldii	see *M. toringo*
- 'Wooster'	CLnd
sieversii	CDul
'Silver Drift'	CLnd
'Snowcloud'	CDul CLnd ECrN MAsh SLim SPer
'Snowdrift'	CLnd
'Street Parade'	CLnd
× ***sublobata***	CLnd
Sugar Tyme = 'Sutyzam'	CLnd
'Sun Rival'	CCVT CDoC CDul CEnd CLnd CSBt EBee EPfP GTwe LRHS MAsh MBlu MBri NLar NOra NSoo SCoo SEWo SLim SPoG WHar WJas
sylvestris	CCVT CDul CHab CLnd ECrN EPfP LBuc MJak MMuc MRav NLar NWea SEND SEWo SPer SPre WMou
§ ***toringo***	CLnd CTho EBee ECrN EPfP LEdu MBri NOra WSHC
I - var. ***arborescens***	CLnd CTho
- 'Scarlett'	CLnd EBee EPfP IArd LRHS LSRN MBri NLar NWea SCoo SLim SPoG WHar WMou
- 'Wintergold'	MMuc
toringoides	see *M. bhutanica*
transitoria 🏆^{H4}	CDoC CDul CEnd CLnd CTho EBee ECrN ELan EPfP MBlu MBri MRav NLar NWea SCoo SFam WMou WPGP
- 'Thornhayes Tansy'	CTho EBee LRHS SLim
trilobata	CDul CLnd CTho EBee ELan EPfP LHop MBlu MGos MMuc SCoo SEND
- 'Guardsman'	EBee LRHS MBlu MBri NLar SSpi WMou
tschonoskii 🏆^{H4}	CDoC CDul CLnd CMCN CMac CSBt CTri CWib EBee ELan EPfP EWTr GTwe LAst LRHS MBlu MBri MGos MJak MMuc NPri NWea SEND SPer SWvt WJas WMou
'Van Eseltine'	CDul CLnd CSBt CWib EBee ECrN EPfP MAsh MMuc SFam WHar WJas
'Veitch's Scarlet'	CDoy CDul CHab CLnd CSBt NEgg NPCo SFam
Weeping Candied Apple = 'Weepcanzam'	CLnd
'White Angel' **new**	CLnd
'White Star'	CCVT CDoC CDul CLnd CSBt EBee ECrN LRHS SLon
'Winter Gold'	CDul SCrf SGol
'Wisley Crab'	CLnd LAst SDea SFam SLon WMou
yunnanensis	EPfP

- var. ***veitchii***	CTho
× ***zumi*** var. ***calocarpa***	CLnd
§ - 'Golden Hornet' Y^{H4}	Widely available
§ - 'Professor Sprenger'	CLnd CSam EPfP MBri SCoo

Malva (*Malvaceae*)

alcea var. ***fastigiata***	CMac EBee ECGP NBro SRms
bicolor	see *Lavatera maritima*
'Gibbortello'	LRHS
moschata	CArn CBcs CPrp EBee ECtt ELan EPfP GAbr GJos GPoy MHer MMuc MNHC NLar NMir NWad SIde SPer SPlb SWat WHer WJek WMoo WOut
- f. ***alba*** Y^{H4}	Widely available
- 'Appleblossom'	SEND WTou
- 'Romney Marsh'	see *Althaea officinalis* 'Romney Marsh'
- 'Rosea'	EPfP GMaP LAst LPot NEgg NPer SPoG SWvt
pusilla	CCCN
sylvestris	CArn NBro SRms SWat WHfH WJek WMoo
- 'Blue Fountain' PBR	WKif
- 'Brave Heart'	SPav SWvt
- Marina = 'Dema' PBR	ELan NLar
- var. ***mauritiana***	NPer WMoo
- - 'Mystic Merlin'	SPav
- - 'Primley Blue'	ECtt ELan EPfP GMaP MCot MRav NPer
- - 'Zebrina'	EPfP LDai NGBl NPer SWvt WMoo
- 'Minety Blue' **new**	CNat
- 'Perry's Blue'	NPer
- 'Windsor Castle'	MPie

Malvaviscus (*Malvaceae*)

arboreus	CHII

mandarin see *Citrus reticulata* Mandarin Group

mandarin, Cleopatra see *Citrus reshni*

Mandevilla (*Apocynaceae*)

sp. **new**	CHel
§ × ***amabilis***	CCCN
- 'Alice du Pont' Y^{H1}	CCCN ELan EShb MOWG SPre
× ***amoena***	see *M.* × *amabilis*
'Audrey' **new**	CSpc
boliviensis Y^{H1}	CCCN CRHN MOWG
§ ***laxa*** Y^{H2}	CCCN CHGN CHII CRHN CSpe ECre ELan EShb LRHS MOWG SVen WPGP WSHC
(Rio Series) Rio Deep Red = 'Fisrix Dered' PBR **new**	CCCN
- Rio Pink = 'Fisrix Pinka' PBR **new**	CCCN
sanderi	CCCN EShb SPre
- 'Rosea'	CCCN
splendens Y^{H1}	CCCN CHII MOWG
suaveolens	see *M. laxa*
Sundaville Series	CCCN
- Sundaville Pink = 'Sunmandecripi' PBR	LAst LSou
- Sundaville Red = 'Sunmandecrim' PBR	LAst LSou

Mandragora (*Solanaceae*)

autumnalis	CDes SMad
§ ***officinarum***	CArn CCon CRDP GCal GPoy SMad WCot

Manettia (*Rubiaceae*)

inflata	see *M. luteorubra*
§ ***luteorubra***	CCCN

Manfreda see *Agave*

× *Mangave* see *Agave*

Mangifera (*Anacardiaceae*)

indica (F)	CCCN SPre
- 'Osteen' (F)	NPla
- 'Tommy Atkins' (F)	NPla

Manglietia see *Magnolia*

yunnanensis	see *Magnolia insignis*

mango see *Mangifera indica*

Manihot (*Euphorbiaceae*)

carthaginensis	SPlb
esculenta 'Variegata'	EAmu

Mantisalca (*Asteraceae*)

salmantica	WCot

Mantisia (*Zingiberaceae*)

saltatoria	WCot
- PAB 4208 **new**	LEdu

Maranta (*Marantaceae*)

leuconeura var. ***erythroneura*** Y^{H1}	XBlo
- var. ***kerchoveana*** Y^{H1}	XBlo

Marchantia (*Marchantiaceae*)

polymorpha	CArn

Mariscus see *Cyperus*

marjoram, pot see *Origanum onites*

marjoram, sweet see *Origanum majorana*

marjoram, wild, or oregano see *Origanum vulgare*

Marrubium (*Lamiaceae*)

§ ***bourgaei*** var. ***bourgaei*** 'All Hallows Green'	ECtt LRHS MRav NEgg XSen
candidissimum	see *M. incanum*
* ***cylleneum*** 'Velvetissimum'	WCot XSen
§ ***incanum***	WCot XSen
lutescens **new**	XSen
supinum	CArn
vulgare	CArn GPoy MHer MHoo MNHC SIde SRms WHfH WJek

Marsdenia (*Asclepiadaceae*)

formosana CWJ 12354	WCru
oreophila **new**	CRHN

Marshallia (*Asteraceae*)

grandiflora	CDes
trinerva	ELon

Marsilea (*Marsileaceae*)

angustifolia	LLWG
crennlata **new**	LLWG

mutica EWay
quadrifolia CBAq EWay
– variegated (v) LLWG

Massonia (*Asparagaceae*)

bifolia see *Whiteheadia bifolia*
depressa ECho
– 'Branvlei Dam' ECho
– 'Reitfontein Gamoep' ECho
echinata CAbP ECho LSou WCot
aff. ***echinata*** ECho WCot
jasminiflora ECho
pustulata ECho EUJe WCot
pygmaea subsp. ***kamiesbergensis*** ECho
– subsp. ***pygmaea*** ECho

Mathiasella (*Apiaceae*)

bupleuroides CHid LPio LSou
– 'Green Dream' CAbP CAvo CBcs CBre CMea CSpe EBee ECtt EWll GBin LRHS MBel MNrw NCGa NPnk NSti SDix SLon SMrm SPoG WCot

Matricaria (*Asteraceae*)

chamomilla see *M. recutita*
parthenium see *Tanacetum parthenium*
§ ***recutita*** CArn GPoy MNHC
– 'Bodegold' new WHfH
tchihatchewii XSen
'White Star' EPfP

Matteuccia (*Onocleaceae*)

orientalis CBty CDTJ CDes CKel CLAP EFer EPfP ERod GCal GMaP LRHS NBid NLar NMyG NOrc SHil WMoo WPnP XLum
pensylvanica CLAP MMoz
struthiopteris ♀H4 Widely available
* – 'Depauperata' CLAP
– 'Jumbo' CBty CCCN CLAP ISha LRHS
– 'The King' WCot

Matthiola (*Brassicaceae*)

fruticulosa 'Alba' CAby CDes EPfP LEdu WPGP
– subsp. ***perennis*** NSti WHal
incana EBee LRHS MArl SPad WKif
alba CHid ELan GBBs LSou NCGa SEND SPav WCot WRHF
– 'Legacy' (mixed) NPri
– 'Pillow Talk' SPhx
– purple-flowered SEND
montana LLHF
white-flowered perennial CArn CSev CSpe NPer

Maurandya (*Plantaginaceae*)

§ ***barclayana*** CDTJ WHil
erubescens see *Lophospermum erubescens*
lophantha see *Lophospermum scandens*
lophospermum see *Lophospermum scandens*
'Magic Dragon' see *Lophospermum* 'Magic Dragon'
'Red Dragon' see *Lophospermum* 'Red Dragon'

Maytenus (*Celastraceae*)

boaria CBcs CMCN EPfP GGal IArd IDee LEdu MGos NLar SAPC SEND WSHC
disticha (Hook.f.) Urb. LEdu

Mazus (*Phrymaceae*)

miquelii EBee LLWG
reptans CCon ECho ECtt EPfP EPot MSKA NLBP NLar NPer XLum
– B&SWJ CExl
– 'Albus' CCon ECho ECtt EPfP EWTr LLWG MSKA NLar SPlb
– 'Blue' LLWG

Mecardonia (*Plantaginaceae*)

'Goldflake' CCCN
'Sundona Early Yellow' LAst

Meconopsis ✿ (*Papaveraceae*)

aculeata GCra
§ ***baileyi*** ♀H4 CBcs CGHE CHel CSBt CTri CTsd CWCL EBee ELan EPau EPfP GAbr GBuc GCra GGGa GKin IBoy ITim LRHS MBri MCot NBir NEgg NLar NSum SPoG WMoo WSpi
* – var. ***alba*** EBee ELan GBin GCra GGGa GKev LRHS NGdn NLar NSum
– 'Hensol Violet' GBuc GCra GGGa GKev NLar NSum
– violet-flowered ITim
betonicifolia misapplied see *M. baileyi*
cambrica CCCN CExl CMac CTri EBee ELan EPfP GJos MMuc WBrk WCot WHer WSpi
– 'Anne Greenaway' (d) WCot
– var. ***aurantiaca*** WCot
– double-flowered (d) WCot
– ***flore-pleno*** orange-flowered (d) NBir WCot
§ – 'Frances Perry' GCal GKev WCot
– 'Muriel Brown' (d) GCal WCot
– 'Rubra' see *M. cambrica* 'Frances Perry'
chelidoniifolia EWld GCra IGor NBid WCru
× ***cookei*** GKev NSum
– 'Old Rose' CWCL GBin GBuc GGGa
N Fertile Blue Group EBee ITim
N – 'Blue Ice' see *M.* (Fertile Blue Group) 'Lingholm'
– 'Cally Lingholm' GCal
N – 'Lingholm' Widely available
§ George Sherriff Group GCal GCra NBir
– 'Ascreavie' GBuc GKev GMaP
– 'Barney's Blue' GMaP
– 'Branklyn' ambig. CExl CGHE LRHS WPGP
– 'Dalemain' GBuc GMaP
– 'Huntfield' GBin GGGa GKev GMaP
– 'Jimmy Bayne' GBin GGGa GMaP
– 'Susan's Reward' GMaP
grandis misapplied see *M.* George Sherriff Group
grandis ambig. CPla GLin
– GS 600 see *M.* George Sherriff Group
– 'Alba' WSpi
– Balruddery form GGGa
horridula CPBP GCra GGGa
(Infertile Blue Group) 'Bobby Masterton' GCra GMaP
– 'Crarae' GGGa
– 'Crewdson Hybrid' GBuc GMaP
– 'Dawyck' see *M.* (Infertile Blue Group) 'Slieve Donard'
– 'Mrs Jebb' GBuc GCra GMaP
§ – 'Slieve Donard' ♀H4 GBuc GCal GCra GGGa GKev GKin GMaP LRHS

	integrifolia	CCCN GBin WAbe
N	***napaulensis*** misapplied	CHid EBee GCra GKev ITim LHop NLar
	- from Solukhumbu, Nepal	GCra
	- pink-flowered	LRHS NGdn
	- red-flowered	ITim
	paniculata	EBee GGGa LRHS WPGP
	- from Bhutan	GCra
	- from Ghunsa, Nepal	CLAP
	- ginger foliage	CAby CHid
	- 'Ginger Snap' **new**	LRHS
	pseudointegrifolia	GGGa GKev
	punicea	GGGa GKev WAbe
	quintuplinervia ♀H4	CLAP GBin GCra GKev NHar NSla
	regia hybrids	GGGa
	× ***sheldonii*** misapplied (fertile)	see *M.* Fertile Blue Group
	× ***sheldonii*** misapplied (sterile)	see *M.* Infertile Blue Group
	× ***sheldonii*** ambig.	CBcs CWCL GAbr ITim MCot NBir NLar NPer SPad
	simplicifolia	GGGa GKev
	'Stewart Annand'	GMaP
	superba	EBee GGGa WAbe
	villosa	GCra GGGa GLin
	wallichii misapplied	see *M. wallichii* Hook.
	wallichii ambig.	GLin
§	***wallichii*** Hook.	GGGa
	'Willie Duncan'	GMaP
	wilsonii subsp. ***australis***	GGGa GLin

Medicago (*Papilionaceae*)

	arborea	CArn SEND SPlb
	lupulina	CHab
	sativa	WHer WSFF

Medinilla (*Melastomataceae*)

	magnifica ♀H1	CCCN

medlar see *Mespilus germanica*

Meehania (*Lamiaceae*)

	cordata	CDes EBee
	fargesii	CLAP
	urticifolia	EPPr GCal WSHC
	- B&SWJ 1210	WCru
	- 'Japanblau'	IMou
	- 'Wandering Minstrel' (v)	WCot

Megacarpaea (*Brassicaceae*)

	polyandra	WCot

Megaskepasma (*Acanthaceae*)

	erythrochlamys	SVen

Melaleuca (*Myrtaceae*)

	acerosa	ECou
	acuminata	ECou SPlb
	alternifolia	CArn CBcs CCCN CTsd ECou EOHP GPoy IDee MHer MHoo MOWG SEND SPlb SVen
	armillaris	CCCN CDoC CHel ECou IDee SEND SPlb
	blaeriifolia	ECou
	bracteata	ECou
	cuticularis	SPlb
	decussata	CBcs ECou SPlb
§	***diosmatifolia***	CBcs CExl
	elliptica	MOWG
	ericifolia	CTri CTsd GLin SEND SPlb
	erubescens	see *M. diosmatifolia*
	fulgens	ECou MOWG SPlb
	- apricot-flowered	MOWG
*	- 'Hot Pink'	MOWG
	- purple-flowered	MOWG
	gibbosa	CExl CHel EBee ECou ELan IVic LRHS LSou MOWG SEND SVen WSHC
	hypericifolia	CDoC CExl MOWG SPlb
	incana	MOWG
	lateritia	ECou MOWG
	linariifolia	CCCN ECou SPlb
	nesophila	ECou EShb SPlb
	pentagona var. ***subulifolia***	ECou
	pulchella	ECou MOWG
	pungens	SPlb
	pustulata	ECou
	spathulata	ECou
	squamea	CTsd SEND SPlb
*	***squarmania***	MOWG
	squarrosa	CExl ECou LRHS MOWG SPlb SVen
	tamariscina	ECou
	thymifolia	ECou LRHS MOWG SPlb
	trichophylla	SPlb
	wilsonii	ECou IDee

Melandrium see *Vaccaria*

	rubrum	see *Silene dioica*

Melanoselinum (*Apiaceae*)

§	***decipiens***	CAbb CArn CSpe IMou LEdu LPio SMad WCot WJek WPGP

Melasphaerula (*Iridaceae*)

	graminea	see *M. ramosa*
§	***ramosa***	ECho

Melia (*Meliaceae*)

§	***azedarach***	CArn CBcs CCCN EPfP EShb GPoy SEND SPlb
	- B&SWJ 7039	WCru
	- var. ***japonica***	see *M. azedarach*

Melianthus (*Melianthaceae*)

	comosus	CDTJ EAmu ELan EPri EShb ESwi EWTr EWes NLar NSoo SCoo SPlb WOut WSpi
	major ♀H3	Widely available
	minor	CCon CHid
	villosus	CCon CDes CHGN EWes SPlb WOut WPGP

Melica (*Poaceae*)

	altissima 'Alba'	MLHP
	- 'Atropurpurea'	COIW EHoe EPPr LEdu LHop LLWP LRHS MCot MMoz MNrw MWat MWhi NBid NLar SEND SPlb WMoo WWEG
	californica	EPPr
	ciliata	EHoe EPPr EPfP MMoz MWhi NDov WPtf WWEG XLum
	macra	EPPr
	nutans	CWCL EBee EHoe EPPr EShb MAsh NOak NWsh SMrm WCot
	penicillaris	EPPr
	persica	NDov
	transsilvanica	EPPr

	- 'Atropurpurea'	MMuc SPer
	- 'Red Spire'	CWib MBNS MWhi SGol SHDw SMea SMrm WMoo XLum
	uniflora	IMou MBel NOak
	- f. ***albida***	EHoe GCal LLWP MAvo NDov NOak WCot WSHC
	- 'Variegata' (v)	CBre ECGP EHoe ELon GCal MAvo MMoz NOak WCot WMoo WWEG

Melicytus (*Violaceae*)

	alpinus	ECou WThu
	angustifolius	ECou
	crassifolius	ECou
	obovatus	ECou NLar
	ramiflorus	CHEx ECou

Melilotus (*Papilionaceae*)

	officinalis	CArn CHab GPoy SIde WHer
	- subsp. ***albus***	CArn

Melinis (*Poaceae*)

	nerviglumis 'Savannah'	CWib

Meliosma (*Sabiaceae*)

	cuneifolia	CBcs CExl NLar
	dilleniifolia subsp. ***tenuis***	CExl
	myriantha	SSpi
	oldhamii new	CExl
	simplicifolia subsp. ***pungens***	CExl
	tenuis new	CExl
	veitchiorum	CBcs CExl NLar

Melissa ✿ (*Lamiaceae*)

	officinalis	CArn CHab CPbn CTri ELau GJos GMaP GPoy LPot MBri MHer MHoo MNHC NBir SEND SIde SPlb SRms SVic WBor WHfH WJek XLum
	- 'All Gold'	CArn CBre CPbn CSev EHoe ELan ELau MHoo NBid SPer SPoG SRms
§	- 'Aurea' (v)	CArn CExl CPrp CSev ELan ELau GCra GMaP GPoy MBri MHer MHoo MNHC MRav NBid NBir NBro NPri SEND SIde SPer SPoG SRms WJek WMnd WMoo XLum
*	- 'Compacta'	CPbn GPoy
	- 'Lime Balm'	CPbn MHoo
	- 'Quedlinburger Niederliegende'	CArn CPbn
N	- 'Variegata' misapplied	see *M. officinalis* 'Aurea'

Melittis (*Lamiaceae*)

	melissophyllum	CAby CArn CLAP CMea CPom CRDP CSpe ELon IMou LEdu LRHS LSou MNrw MPnt MRav WCot WOut
	- subsp. ***albida***	MBri WCot
	- pink-flowered	CLAP LEdu WBor WCot WPtf
	- 'Royal Velvet Distinction' PBR	CSpe EBee LBMP MBri MRav MSCN NDov SHar SHil SPoG WCot WHil WPtf

Melliodendron (*Styracaceae*)

	xylocarpum	CBcs CExl

Menispermum (*Menispermaceae*)

	canadense	CTri GPoy
	dauricum	GKin NLar

Menstruocalamus (*Poaceae*)

	sichuanensis	WPGP

Mentha ✿ (*Lamiaceae*)

	sp.	CHab
	from Jamaica	CArn
	angustifolia Corb.	see *M.* × *villosa*
	angustifolia Host	see *M. arvensis*
	angustifolia ambig.	CPbn
	aquatica	CArn CBAq CHab CPbn CRow CWat EHon EPfP GPoy LEdu MHer MHoo MNHC MWts NMir NPer NPol NYoL SIde SPlb SRms SVic SWat WHer WMAq WMoo WPnP WSFF XLum
§	- var. ***crispa***	CPbn NYoL
	- krause minze	see *M. aquatica* var. *crispa*
	- 'Mandeliensis'	CPbn
§	***arvensis***	CArn CPbn ELau MHer NYoL SIde
	- 'Banana'	CPbn LEdu MHer MHoo MNHC NPri NYoL SIde SRms WJek
	- var. ***piperascens***	LEdu MHer SIde WJek
§	- - 'Sayakaze'	CArn ELau
	- var. ***villosa***	CPbn
	asiatica	CPbn ELau MHer
	'Berries and Cream'	LEdu SRms WJek
	'Betty's Slovakian'	CPbn
	Bowles's mint	see *M.* × *villosa* var. *alopecuroides* Bowles's mint
*	***brevifolia***	CPbn
	cervina	CArn CBAq CPbn CWat EHon LEdu MHer MSKA MWts NLar SIde SRms SWat WJek XLum
*	- ***alba***	CBAq CPbn LLWG MHer MSKA MWts NLar NYoL WMAq
I	'Chocolate Peppermint'	GAbr LEdu LLWG MHoo NBir NPri NYoL
	citrata	see *M.* × *piperita* f. *citrata*
	'Clarissa's Millennium'	CPbn
	cordifolia	see *M.* × *villosa*
	corsica	see *M. requienii*
	crispa L. (1753)	see *M. spicata* var. *crispa*
	crispa L. (1763)	see *M. aquatica* var. *crispa*
	crispa ambig. × (× ***piperita***)	CArn CPbn
	cucumber mint	CPbn
	'Dionysus'	CPbn
	× ***dumetorum***	CPbn NYoL
	- wine mint	CPbn
	'Eau de Cologne'	see *M.* × *piperita* f. *citrata*
	eucalyptus mint	CPbn ELau MHer WGwG
	gattefossei	CArn
	× ***gentilis***	see *M.* × *gracilis*
§	× ***gracilis***	CArn CPbn ELau GAbr NPri NYoL SIde
	- 'Aurea'	see *M.* × *gracilis* 'Variegata'
§	- 'Variegata' (v)	CPbn CSev ELau GPoy LEdu MCot MHer MNHC NPri NYoL SPlb SRms WHer XLum
	graveolens	MHoo
	haplocalyx	CArn ELau NYoL
	'Herbert McHale'	LEdu
*	'Hillary's Sweet Lemon'	CPbn ELau MHer NYoL SIde
	'Julia's Sweet Citrus'	CPbn MHer
*	***lacerata***	NYoL SIde
	lavender mint	ELau GPoy LEdu MHer MNHC NYoL WJek
§	***longifolia***	CPbn ELau LEdu MHoo MMuc NYoL SEND SPlb WHer

	- Buddleia Mint Group	CArn CPbn EBee ELau GAbr LEdu MHer MHoo MRav NSti NYoL SIde WJek XLum
	- - variegated (v)	LEdu MHoo WJek
	- dwarf	CPbn
	- 'Habek' **new**	EOHP
	- subsp. ***schimperi***	LEdu NYoL WJek
	- silver-leaved	CArn CPbn ELau GAbr LEdu MHer MHoo MNHC NLar NYoL SEND WJek
*	- 'Variegata' (v)	CPbn ELau GAbr NYoL
	Nile Valley mint	CArn ELau LEdu NYoL SHDw SIde SRms
	× ***piperita***	CArn CHby CPbn CSev EHoe ELau GJos GPoy LHop MBri MHer MNHC NPri NYoL SPlb
	- 'Black Mitcham'	CArn CPbn NYoL XLum
	- black peppermint	CHby CPbn EPfP GAbr LEdu LLWG MHoo MMuc MNHC NBir NLar NYoL SEND SRms WJek
§	- f. ***citrata***	CArn CHby COlW CPbn CTri ELau GJos GMaP GPoy LEdu LLWG MBri MHer MHoo MMuc MNHC MRav NBir NPri NYoL SEND SHDw SIde SPlb SVic WJek
	- - from Portugal	CPbn
*	- - 'Basil'	CPbn ELau GAbr LEdu MHer MHoo MNHC MRav NPri NYoL SHDw SIde SRms WGwG WJek XLum
	- - 'Bergamot'	CPbn XLum
	- - 'Chocolate'	CArn CPbn ELau EPfP GJos LEdu MHer MNHC NYoL SHDw SIde SPlb SRms WGwG WJek XLum
	- - 'Grapefruit'	CPbn GAbr LSou MHer MNHC NYoL SRms WJek
	- - 'Lemon'	CPbn ELau GAbr GPoy LEdu MBri MHer MHoo MNHC NYoL SHDw SIde SRms WJek
	- - 'Lime'	CPbn GAbr LEdu MHer MHoo NYoL SHDw SIde SPlb SRms WGwG WJek
	- - 'Orange'	CPbn LEdu MHer MNHC NYoL SRms WHil WJek
	- - 'Reverchonii'	CPbn
	- - 'Swiss Ricola'	MHer NYoL
	- 'Crispa' **new**	NPol
	- 'Logee's' (v)	CPbn
	- 'Milly Mitcham'	CPbn
	- f. ***officinalis***	CPbn ELau SIde
	- var. ***ouweneellii*** Belgian mint	CPbn
	- 'Persephone'	CPbn
	- 'Reine Rouge'	CPbn
	- 'Swiss'	LEdu MHoo NLar NPri WJek
I	- Swiss mint	CArn CPbn NPri
*	- white-flowered	CArn CPbn
	'Polynesian Mint'	CPbn
	pulegium	CArn CHby CPbn CSev CTri ELau GPoy LLWG MHer MHoo MNHC MSKA NPri SIde SPlb SRms SVic WHer WHfH WJek
	- 'Upright'	CArn CPbn GPoy MHer MHoo SHDw SIde WJek
§	***requienii***	CArn CPbn CPrp CTri ECho ELau GAbr GCal GPoy LEdu LLWG MBri MHer MHoo MNHC NBir NRya NYoL SDix SIde SPlb SRms WGwG WHfH WJek
	rotundifolia misapplied	see *M. suaveolens*
	rotundifolia (L.) Hudson	see *M.* × *villosa*
	rubra var. ***raripila***	see *M.* × *smithiana*
	'Russian' curled leaf	CPbn
	'Russian' plain leaf	CPbn NYoL
	'Sayakaze'	see *M. arvensis* var. *piperascens* 'Sayakaze'
§	× ***smithiana***	CArn CPbn ELau GPoy LEdu MHer MNHC MRav NBir NPri NYoL SRms WJek
	- 'Capel Ulo' (v)	ELau
	'South of France'	CPbn
§	***spicata***	CArn CHby COlW CPbn CPrp CSev CTri CTsd ELau GJos GPoy LPot MBri MCot MHer MHoo MJak MMuc MNHC NPol NPri NYoL SEND SPlb SRms WHer WJek XLum
	- Algerian fruity	CPbn LEdu
	- 'Austrian'	CPbn
*	- 'Brundall'	CPbn ELau NYoL SIde
	- 'Canaries'	CPbn
*	- var. ***crispa***	CArn CPbn ELau LEdu LHop LPot MHer MMuc MNHC NRya NYoL SIde SPlb SRms WJek
	- - 'Moroccan'	CArn CPbn CPrp CSev ELau GAbr GJos GPoy LEdu MHer MHoo MNHC NPri NYoL SEND SHDw SIde SRms WJek
	- - 'Persian'	CPbn
	- 'Crispula'	GAbr XLum
	- 'Guernsey'	CPbn SHDw SIde SRms
	- 'Irish'	CPbn
	- 'Kentucky Colonel'	CPbn LEdu
	- 'Mexican'	CArn CPbn
	- 'Newbourne'	CPbn ELau
	- 'Pharaoh'	CArn CPbn
	- 'Rhodos'	CPbn
	- 'Russian'	CArn LEdu MHer SIde
	- 'Small Dole' (v)	SHDw
	- 'Spanish'	LEdu SRms
	- 'Spanish Furry'	CPbn MHer
	- 'Spanish Pointed'	CPbn ELau WJek
	- 'Tashkent'	CArn CHby CPbn ELau LEdu MHer MHoo MNHC NYoL SHDw SIde SRms WGwG WHer WJek
	- subsp. ***tomentosa***	CPbn
*	- 'Variegata' (v)	CPbn SHDw
	- 'Verte Blanche'	CPbn
§	***suaveolens***	CArn CHby CPbn ELau GJos GMaP GPoy MBri MHer MHoo MLHP MNHC NYoL SIde SPlb SRms SVic WJek WSFF
*	- 'Grapefruit'	LEdu
	- 'Jokka'	CPbn
*	- 'Mobillei'	CPbn
*	- 'Pineapple'	LBuc MHoo WJek
	- subsp. ***timija***	CPbn ELau LEdu MHer WJek
	- 'Variegata' (v)	CArn CPbn CPrp CTri EHoe ELau GMaP GPoy LEdu MBri MCot MHer MNHC MRav NPri SIde SPlb SRms WHer XLum
	'Sweet Pear'	MHer NYoL
	sylvestris L.	see *M. longifolia*
*	***verona***	CPbn NYoL
	× ***verticillata***	WJek
§	× ***villosa***	CArn CPbn MMuc SEND
§	- var. ***alopecuroides*** Bowles's mint	CBre CPbn CPrp ELau GPoy LEdu MHer MNHC NBir NSti NYoL SWat WGwG WHer WJek
	- 'Jack Green'	LEdu

viridis see *M. spicata*

Menyanthes (*Menyanthaceae*)

trifoliata CBAq CRow CWat EHon EWay GPoy LLWG MMuc MSKA MWts NPer WHal WMAq WSFF XLum

Menziesia (*Ericaceae*)

alba see *Daboecia cantabrica* f. *alba*
ciliicalyx 'Honshu Blue' GGGa
- 'Judith' WAbe
- ***lasiophylla*** see *M. ciliicalyx* var. *purpurea*
- var. ***multiflora*** EPfP
- 'Plum Drops' GGGa
§ - var. ***purpurea*** GGGa
- 'Slieve Donard' CMac
- 'Ylva' GGGa
ferruginea IVic
polifolia see *Daboecia cantabrica*
'Spring Morning' WAbe

Mercurialis (*Euphorbiaceae*)

perennis GPoy WHer WHfH WSFF WShi

Merendera (*Colchicaceae*)

attica ECho
eichleri see *M. trigyna*
filifolia ECho
§ ***montana*** CPBP ECho WIvy
pyrenaica see *M. montana*
raddeana see *M. trigyna*
sobolifera WCot
§ ***trigyna*** ECho

Mertensia (*Boraginaceae*)

ciliata CCse SWat
§ ***maritima*** CCon CSpe CWCL ECho EWes EWld GBee GPoy LEdu NBir SMrm SPlb WHoo WWEG
- subsp. ***asiatica*** see *M. maritima*
primuloides LLHF
pterocarpa see *M. sibirica*
pulmonarioides see *M. virginica*
§ ***sibirica*** CLAP CSpe SPlb
§ ***virginica*** ♀H4 CBro CHel CLAP CWCL EBee ECho ECtt ELan EPfP EWTr LEdu LHop LRHS MBel MMoz MNrw NBir NLar NPhk NPri SRms

Merwilla (*Asparagaceae*)

§ ***plumbea*** WCot

Merxmuellera see *Rytidosperma*

Mesembryanthemum (*Aizoaceae*)

'Basutoland' see *Delosperma nubigenum*
brownii see *Lampranthus brownii*

Mespilus ✿ (*Rosaceae*)

germanica (F) CBcs CDul CHab CLnd CMCN CTri EBee ECrN ELan EWTr IDee NEgg NLar SLon WMou
- 'Bredase Reus' (F) NLar SKee
- 'Dutch' (F) SDea SFam SKee
- 'Iranian' (F) SKee
- 'Large Russian' (F) CAgr
- 'Macrocarpa' (F) SKee
- 'Monstrous' (F) SDea
- 'Nottingham' (F) Widely available
- 'Royal' (F) CAgr CMam ERea LRHS MBri MCoo NOra SCoo SKee WHar
- 'Westerveld' (F) CLnd NLar SKee

Metapanax (*Araliaceae*)

davidii CFil SLon
delavayi SBig

Metaplexis (*Apocynaceae*)

japonica B&SWJ 8459 WCru

Metarungia (*Acanthaceae*)

galpinii new WHil

Metasequoia ✿ (*Cupressaceae*)

glyptostroboides ♀H4 Widely available
- 'All Bronze' NLar
- 'Chubby' PBR NLar
- 'Emerald Feathers' SLim
- 'Fastigiata' see *M. glyptostroboides* 'National'
- 'Gold Rush' CBcs CCVT CDoC CDul CEnd CMen CTri ELan EPfP IArd IDee LRHS LSRN MAsh MBlu MBri MGos NEgg NLar NPCo NWea SCoo SEWo SLim SMad SPer SPoG SWvt WHar
- 'Golden Dawn' NLar SLim
- 'Hamlet's Broom' SLim
- 'Little Creamy' NLar
- 'Little Giant' MBlu
- 'Matthaei Broom' LRHS SLim
- 'McCracken's White' (v) NLar SLim
- 'Miss Grace' MAsh NLar SLim
§ - 'National' MBlu
- 'Ogon' SGol
- 'Royal Air' NLar WBor
- 'Schirrmann's Nordlicht' SLim
- 'Sheridan Spire' CEnd MBlu
- 'Waasland' MBlu
- 'White Spot' (v) MBlu NPCo SLim

Metrosideros (*Myrtaceae*)

carminea CCCN CTsd
§ ***excelsa*** CHll CTsd ECou ECre ESwi SAPC
- 'Aurea' ECou
- 'Parnell' CCCN
- 'Vibrance' CCCN
kermadecensis ECou
- 'Radiant' (v) CBcs
- 'Red and Gold' CDoC
- 'Twisty' (v) CBcs
- 'Variegata' (v) CBcs CDoC ECou
lucida see *M. umbellata*
Moonlight = 'Lowmoo' CHel CWGN EBee SLim
robusta CBcs CCCN CHEx MREP
- ***aureovariegata*** CCCN EShb
§ 'Springfire' CCCN
× ***subtomentosa*** 'Mistral' ECou
'Thomasii' see *M.* 'Springfire'
tomentosa see *M. excelsa*
§ ***umbellata*** CBcs CCCN CDoC CHEx CTsd EBee ECou
- Gold Nugget = 'Lownug' MSCN SLim
villosa 'Tahiti' CBcs

Meum (*Apiaceae*)

from Bulgaria new CSpe
athamanticum CArn CSpe EBee GCal GPoy LEdu LHop LPla LRHS MAvo MNFA MRav SPhx

Michauxia (*Campanulaceae*)

campanuloides	CSpe
tchihatchewii	CDTJ CSpe NGBl

Michelia see *Magnolia*

fulgens	see *Magnolia foveolata*
wilsonii	see *Magnolia ernestii*
yunnanensis	see *Magnolia laevifolia* (Y.W.Law R.Y.F.Wu) Noot

Microbiota (*Cupressaceae*)

decussata ♀H4	CBcs CDoC CMac CSBt ECho EHul LBee LRHS MGos NHol NWea SEND SLim
- 'Gold Spot'	CDoC SLim
- 'Jakobsen'	CDoC CKen
- 'Trompenburg'	CKen

Microcachrys (*Podocarpaceae*)

tetragona	CDoC ECou EHul IArd LRHS SCoo WThu

Microcoelum see *Lytocaryum*

Microlepia (*Dennstaedtiaceae*)

speluncae	EShb
strigosa	CBty CCCN CLAP ISha LRHS

Micromeria (*Lamiaceae*)

sp.	SRms
corsica	see *Acinos corsicus*
fruticosa	WJek
graeca	CArn
juliana **new**	XLum
rupestris	see *M. thymifolia*
§ ***thymifolia***	SPlb
viminea	see *Satureja viminea*

Microseris (*Asteraceae*)

ringens hort.	see *Leontodon rigens*

Microsorum (*Polypodiaceae*)

diversifolium	see *Phymatosorus diversifolius*

Microtropis (*Celastraceae*)

petelotii HWJ 719	WCru

Mikania (*Asteraceae*)

araucana	LSou

Milium (*Poaceae*)

effusum 'Aureum' ♀H4	Widely available
- 'Yaffle' (v)	CBre CKno EBee EPPr EShb LEdu MWat WCot WPnP WWEG

Millettia (*Papilionaceae*)

japonica 'Hime Fuji'	NLar
murasaki-natsu-fuji	see *M. reticulata*
§ ***reticulata***	CExl

Mimetes (*Proteaceae*)

chrysanthus **new**	SPlb

Mimosa (*Mimosaceae*)

pudica	CCCN CDTJ WTou

Mimulus (*Phrymaceae*)

sp.	SVic
'Andean Nymph'	see *M. naiandinus*
§ ***aurantiacus*** ♀H2-3	CMac CSpe CTri EBak ECtt LHop LPot LRHS NPer SBch SPlb
× ***bartonianus***	see *M.* × *harrisonii*
§ ***bifidus*** 'Verity Purple'	EDif
- 'Wine'	see *M. bifidus* 'Verity Purple'
× ***burnetii***	ECho SRms
cardinalis ♀H3	EBee ELan EPfP EWes MNrw MSKA NBir WMoo
- 'Red Dragon'	WHrl
cupreus 'Whitecroft Scarlet' ♀H4	ECho EPfP SRms
'Eleanor'	ECtt
glutinosus	see *M. aurantiacus*
- ***atrosanguineus***	see *M. puniceus*
- ***luteus***	see *M. aurantiacus*
§ ***guttatus***	CBAq NMir NPer SRms WMoo WPnP
§ × ***harrisonii***	EWes LSou
'Highland Orange'	ECho EPfP MAsh SPlb SPoG WGor
'Highland Pink'	ECho EPfP MAsh SPlb SPoG WGor
'Highland Red' ♀H4	ECho ECtt EPfP GKev MAsh NPri SPlb SPoG SRms WIce WNew
'Highland Yellow'	ECho ECtt GKev SPlb SPoG WIce
hose-in-hose (d)	NPer
'Inca Sunset'	EWes
langsdorffii	see *M. guttatus*
lewisii ♀H3	CHll EWes MNrw SRms
'Lothian Fire'	CWat
luteus	CBAq CWat EHon GAbr NPer SPlb WBrk WMAq XLum
- 'Variegatus' ambig. (v)	NPer
Magic Series ♀H4	NPri
* 'Major Bees'	MJak
'Malibu Orange'	EPfP
moschatus	CBAq EBee LLWG
§ ***naiandinus*** ♀H3	EWes GKev SPlb
'Orange Glow'	LLWG MJak WHal
orange hose-in-hose (d)	NBir
§ 'Orkney Gold' (d)	ECtt
'Popacatapetl'	CSpe EDif SBHP
'Prairie Buff'	EDif
'Prairie Caramel'	EDif
'Prairie Cerise'	EDif
'Prairie Citron'	EDif
'Prairie Coral'	EDif
'Prairie Dawn'	EDif
'Prairie Frost'	EDif
'Prairie Lilac Frost'	EDif
'Prairie Pink'	EDif
'Prairie Scarlet'	EDif
'Prairie Sunshine'	EDif
primuloides	ECho EWes LLWG SPlb
'Puck'	SPoG
§ ***puniceus***	CTri EDif LHop SBHP SHil SRkn
Red Emperor	see *M.* 'Roter Kaiser'
ringens	CBAq CWat EHon LHop MSKA MWts NBir NPer SPlb SRms WHil WMAq WMoo
§ 'Roter Kaiser'	EPfP
'Threave Variegated' (v)	EBee MRav
'Vortex'	LSou
'Wine Red'	see *M. bifidus* 'Verity Purple'
'Wisley Red'	ECho SRms
yellow hose-in-hose	see *M.* 'Orkney Gold'

Mina see *Ipomoea*

mint, apple see *Mentha suaveolens*

mint, Bowles's see *M.* × *villosa* var. *alopecuroides*

mint, curly see *M. spicata* var. *crispa*

mint, eau-de-Cologne see *M.* × *piperita* f. *citrata*

mint, ginger see *M.* × *gracilis*

mint, horse or long-leaved see *M. longifolia*

mint (pennyroyal) see *M. pulegium*

mint (peppermint) see *M.* × *piperita*

mint, round-leaved see *M. suaveolens*

mint (spearmint) see *M. spicata*

Minuartia (*Caryophyllaceae*)

	capillacea	ECho
	laricifolia	XSen
	parnassica	see *M. stellata*
	saxifraga subsp. ***tmolea***	ITim
§	***stellata***	EPot
§	***verna***	ECho EDAr
	- subsp. ***caespitosa***	CTri ECho
	- - 'Aurea'	see *Sagina subulata* var. *glabrata* 'Aurea'

Mirabilis (*Nyctaginaceae*)

dichotoma	EShb
jalapa	CArn CExl CHel CSpe EPfP LEdu SEND SRms WTou
- 'Buttermilk'	CCCN
- white-flowered	WTou

Miscanthus ✿ (*Poaceae*)

	sp.	MBNS
	capensis	SPlb
	chejuensis B&SWJ 8803	WCru
	'Dronning Ingrid'	CKno EPPr GBin IMou XLum
	'Elfin'	CKno
	flavidus B&SWJ 6749	WCru
	floridulus misapplied	see *M.* × *giganteus*
	floridulus ambig.	CGon MMuc MNrw SEND SPlb XLum
	floridulus (Labill.) Warb. ex K. Schum. & Lauterb. HWJ 522	WCru
§	× ***giganteus***	CKno CSpe EHoe ELon EPPr EUJe GCal GQue IBoy MAsh MMoz MMuc MNrw MWat NDov NWsh SDix SDys SMad SVic WCot WPGP WWEG
	- 'Gilt Edge' (v)	CKno EPPr NWsh
	- 'Gotemba' (v)	EBee EPPr EWes NWsh
	nepalensis	CAby CElw CExl CKno CSam ECre EHoe EUJe EWes GCal LEdu MNrw NOak NWsh SDix SMrm WPGP
	- NJM 09.141	WPGP
	- 'Shikola'	WCru
	oligostachyus	IMou SDys
§	- 'Afrika'	CDes CKno EPPr GBin IMou LHop MAvo MNrw WPGP XLum
I	- 'Nanus Variegatus' (v)	CKno EHoe EWes LEdu WCot WPGP WWEG
§	'Purpurascens'	CKno CWCL EHoe EShb IBoy LBMP LPla LPot LRHS LSRN MAvo MMoz MNrw MWhi NOak SGol SPer WCot WMoo
	sacchariflorus misapplied	see *M.* × *giganteus*
	sacchariflorus ambig.	CBcs CDul CHEx CKno ELan EPfP EShb LRHS MBrN NGdn SPer WMoo XLum
	sacchariflorus (Maxim.) Hack.	LEdu MMuc MWhi WWEG
	sinensis	CHEx CTri LEdu NGBl NOak WHar WMoo WWEG XSen
	- from Yakushima, Japan	LAst
	- 'Abundance'	CKno EPfP LSqu
	- 'Adagio'	CKno EHoe ELon EPPr GBin GQue LRHS MBri MWhi NWad SHDw SLPl SMea WCot XLum
	- 'Afrika'	see *M. oligostachyus* 'Afrika'
	- 'Aldebaran'	EBee IMou
	- 'Andante'	CKno
	- 'Arabesque'	EPPr MMoz WWEG XLum
	- 'Augustfeder'	EPPr SMea WWEG XLum
	- 'Autumn Light'	CKno EPPr MMoz SMea XLum
	- 'Blütenwunder'	CKno XLum
	- 'Bogenlampe' **new**	GBin
	- 'China'	CKno CPar EHoe ELon EPPr EShb EWes GBin LEdu LRHS MAsh MAvo MNrw NCGa NOrc NPnk SDys SHDw SRms SWat WMoo WPGP WWEG XLum
	- 'Cindy' **new**	CKno
	- var. ***condensatus***	LRHS LSou
	- - 'Cabaret' (v)	CHEx CKno EHoe ELon EPPr EUJe GMaP LEdu LHop LRHS LSRN NCGa NOak NPnk NWsh SEND SHDw WCot WHal WMoo WPGP WWEG XLum
	- - 'Central Park'	see *M. sinensis* var. *condensatus* 'Cosmo Revert'
§	- - 'Cosmo Revert'	LEdu MMoz NWsh
	- - 'Cosmopolitan' (v) 🏆H4	Widely available
	- - 'Emerald Giant'	see *M. sinensis* var. *condensatus* 'Cosmo Revert'
	- 'David'	ELon EPPr LEdu MAvo MBNS XLum
	- 'Dixieland' (v)	CKno ELan ELon EPPr EWes IFoB IMou LEdu LRHS WWEG XLum
	- 'Dreadlocks'	EPPr MAvo
	- 'Emmanuel Lepage'	CKno EPPr LRHS XLum
	- 'Etincelle'	CKno EWes NLar XLum
	- 'Federriese'	GBin
	- 'Ferner Osten' 🏆H4	Widely available
	- 'Filigrän' **new**	XLum
	- 'Flamingo' 🏆H4	Widely available
	- 'Gearmella'	EPPr LRHS NWsh XLum
	- 'Gewitterwolke' 🏆H4	EPPr EWes LRHS SMad XLum
	- 'Ghana' 🏆H4	CKno EBee ELon EPPr GBin GQue IMou LHop LRHS MAvo SDys XLum
	- 'Giraffe'	CDTJ CKno EWes LEdu WPGP WWEG XLum
	- 'Gnome'	CKno EHoe EPPr GQue IMou LRHS MAsh MMHG MWhi WWEG
	- 'Gold Bar'[PBR] (v)	CDul CElw CKno CMea CWGN EHoe ELon EPPr EPfP EUJe LRHS LSRN LSou MAsh MBNS NCGa NGdn NWad SBea SGol SPer SPoG WCot WMoo WWEG
	- 'Gold und Silber' 🏆H4 **new**	XLum
	- 'Goldfeder' (v)	XLum
	- 'Goliath'	CKno EHoe ELan ELon EPPr GBin GQue IPot LBMP LEdu LRHS MBNS MMoz NWsh WWEG XLum

	- 'Gracillimus'	Widely available
	- 'Gracillimus Nanus'	CKno
	- 'Graziella'	CEnd CKno CSam CWCL CWib EHoe EPPr EPfP LBMP LRHS MMoz MWhi NGdn NOak NOrc SHil SLPl SPer SRms WBor WPGP XLum
	- 'Grosse Fontäne' ♀H4	CCon CWCL EHoe ELan EPPr LEdu LRHS LSRN MWhi NWsh WCot WMoo WWEG XLum
	- 'Gutenberg Gold'	XLum
	- 'Haiku'	CKno EBee EPPr LEdu LRHS XLum
	- 'Helga Reich'	EWes LRHS
	- 'Hercules'	EBee LRHS MAvo MMoz XLum
	- 'Hermann Müssel'	CKno EBee EPPr EWes GBin GQue IMou LEdu LPla LRHS NOak SMea XLum
§	- 'Hinjo' (v)	CDul CHGN COlW ECGP EHoe ELon EPPr GBin GBuc GQue LRHS LSou MMoz NGdn NLar NWsh WCot WPGP WWEG
	- hybrids	SGol
I	- 'Jubilaris' (v)	EPPr EWes GBin
	- 'Juli'	EBee MMoz XLum
	- 'Kaskade' ♀H4	CKno EHoe EPPr IPot LEdu MMoz MWhi NDov WMoo WWEG XLum
	- 'Kirk Alexander' (v)	EPPr
	- 'Kleine Fontäne' ♀H4	Widely available
	- 'Kleine Silberspinne' ♀H4	CKno CSam CWCL EHoe EHyd EPPr EPfP GCal GKev GMaP LEdu LHop LLWP LRHS LSRN MAsh MGos MJak MSpe MWhi NDov NGdn NWsh SEND SPer WMoo WWEG XLum
	- 'Krater'	CKno EBee EHoe EPPr LPla LRHS MBrN SDys SMea SWat
	- 'Kupferberg'	XLum
	- 'Largo' **new**	XLum
§	- 'Little Kitten'	CKno LEdu SMad SMea WMoo WPGP WWEG
	- Little Nicky	see *M. sinensis* 'Hinjo'
	- 'Little Zebra' PBR (v)	EBee EPPr EPfP EUJe GMaP LHop LSRN NOak SMad SRms
	- 'Malepartus'	Widely available
	- 'Moonlight' **new**	GBin
	- 'Morning Light' (v) ♀H4	Widely available
	- 'Nippon'	CElw CKno CPrp CWCL EHoe EPPr GBin LEdu LPla LRHS MMoz MWhi NBro NGdn NOrc NWsh SDys SMrm SPer WPGP WWEG XLum
	- 'Nishidake'	XLum
	- 'November Sunset'	EPPr EWes MMoz XLum
	- 'Overdam'	IFoB NGdn
	- 'Pagel's Pride'	LRHS
	- 'Poseidon'	EBee EPPr LRHS MAvo NChi SDys SMad XLum
	- 'Positano'	CKno MMoz WPGP XLum
	- 'Professor Richard Hansen'	CKno LRHS XLum
	- 'Pünktchen' (v)	CWCL EAmu EHoe EPPr GBin LEdu LRHS MAsh MAvo NCGa NOak SHDw SMad SRms WMoo WPnP WWEG XLum
	- 'Purple Fall'	CPar CSpe IPot LRHS MAvo STPC
	- var. ***purpurascens*** misapplied	see *M.* 'Purpurascens'
	- 'Red Chief'	EPPr EWes GQue IMou
	- 'Red Meister'	CKno EPfP MAsh
	- 'Red Star'	SRms
	- 'Rigoletto' (v)	EPPr LRHS
	- 'Roland'	CKno EHoe EPPr GBin LRHS MCot XLum
	- 'Roterpfeil'	EPPr
	- 'Rotfeder'	EPPr
	- 'Rotfuchs'	EBee LLWP LPla LRHS XLum
	- 'Rotsilber'	CKno CPrp CSpe CWib EHoe EPPr GBin GMaP IArd LRHS MAvo MMuc MWhi NOak WHoo WMoo WWEG XLum
	- 'Russia'	NWsh
	- 'Samurai'	EPPr GMaP GQue MAvo SMrm XLum
	- 'Sarabande'	EHoe EPPr GQue IPot WMoo XLum
	- 'Septemberrot' ♀H4	CKno CPrp CWCL LEdu MMuc SEND
§	- 'Silberfeder' ♀H4	Widely available
	- 'Silberpfeil' (v)	NWsh
	- 'Silberspinne'	CCse EBee GBin LEdu LHop MWat NGdn SMea SPlb XLum
	- 'Silberturm'	EPPr LPla XLum
	- Silver Feather	see *M. sinensis* 'Silberfeder'
	- 'Silver Stripe'	EPPr MAvo
	- 'Sioux'	EBee EHoe EPPr EPfP EShb GBin GQue LRHS MAvo MBNS MMoz NCGa SPer WWEG
	- 'Sirene'	CCon EHoe EPPr GQue LRHS MBNS MBlu MSpe MWhi XLum
	- 'Spätgrün'	XLum
	- 'Starlight' **new**	CKno
	- 'Strictus' (v) ♀H4	Widely available
	- 'Super Stripe' (v) **new**	EPPr IMou
	- 'Tiger Cub' (v)	CWCL EPPr EWes LRHS MAvo
	- 'Undine' ♀H4	CCon CKno CMea EHoe ELan EPPr EPfP LEdu LRHS MBel MBrN NWsh SLPl WMoo XLum
	- 'Variegatus' (v)	Widely available
	- 'Verneigung' **new**	GBin
	- 'Vorläufer'	EHoe EPPr GBin
	- 'Westacre Wine'	EWes
	- 'Wetterfahne'	LEdu
§	- 'Yaku-jima'	CSam EPPr LHop MWhi SMea
	- 'Yakushima Dwarf'	Widely available
	- 'Zebrinus' (v) ♀H4	Widely available
	- 'Zwergelefant'	MAvo MMoz XLum
	tinctorius 'Nanus Variegatus' misapplied	see *M. oligostachyus* 'Nanus Variegatus'
	transmorrisonensis	CKno EHoe ELan EPPr EUJe LPla LRHS MAvo MBel MMoz NWsh SPhx WCot WWEG XLum
	- B&SWJ 3697	WCru
	yakushimensis	see *M. sinensis* 'Yaku-jima', *M. sinensis* 'Little Kitten'

Mitchella (*Rubiaceae*)

	repens	CBcs EBee EPot GBin LEdu WAbe WCru
	undulata B&SWJ 10928	WCru
*	- f. ***quelpartensis*** B&SWJ 4402	WCru

Mitella (*Saxifragaceae*)

	acerina B&SWJ 11029	WCru
	breweri	CCon CHid CMac EBee GCal GKev MMoz MRav WMoo WOut WPnP
	caulescens	NBro
	diphylla	EPPr
	formosana B&SWJ 125	EPPr WCru
	furusei var. ***subramosa*** B&SWJ 11097	WCru
	× ***inami*** B&SWJ 11122	WCru

japonica B&SWJ 4971	WCru
kiusiana	CLAP
- B&SWJ 5888	WCru
makinoi	CLAP EWld
- B&SWJ 4992	CExl WCru
ovalis	EPPr
pauciflora B&SWJ 6361	WCru
stylosa B&SWJ 5669	WCru
yoshinagae B&SWJ 4893	CExl CHid EPPr WCru WMoo WPtf

Mitraria (*Gesneriaceae*)

coccinea	CBcs CCCN CExl CHll CMac CTsd CWib ECho ELan GAbr GKev IRos LRHS LSou MBlu NLar SEND SLim SLon SPer SPlb SSpi
- Clark's form	EUJe IDee LAst NSoo
- 'Lake Caburgua'	CCCN CSpe EBee ELon EWld GCal GGal IArd NLar WHor
- 'Lake Puyehue'	CAbb CBcs CCCN CDoC CExl CHel EBee EPfP LHop LRHS MAsh SPlb SVen SWvt WCru WSHC

Modiolastrum (*Malvaceae*)

lateritium	CHcl CHll CRHN CSpe CTri ELan EPri LHop LRHS MAvo NBir SMrm SPet SPhx SRms WHal WHar WHil WPGP WSHC XLum

Moehringia (*Caryophyllaceae*)

muscosa	WCot

Moenchia (*Caryophyllaceae*)

mantica new	WCot

Molinia ✿ (*Poaceae*)

altissima	see *M. caerulea* subsp. *arundinacea*
'Autumn Charm'	CKno
caerulea	CKno CWib EPPr LRHS MAsh MBlu NChi NGBl
§ - subsp. ***arundinacea***	CKno CSpe CWCL EPPr NLar SLPl WPtf WWEG XLum
- - 'Bergfreund'	CKno CSam EBee EHoe EPPr GBin LHop MAvo NWsh WMoo
- - 'Breeze'	CKno
- - 'Cordoba'	CKno EBee EPPr GBin GQue NDov SPhx WWEG XLum
- - 'Fontane'	CSam EHoe EPPr GCal GQue LEdu LPla MAsh MAvo NDov NWsh SPhx
- - 'Karl Foerster'	CKno COIW CSpe CWCL EHoe EPPr EPfP GBin GMaP IKil LEdu LHop LRHS MAsh MAvo MBri MMoz MNrw MWat MWhi NBid SGol SPer SPhx SWat WCot WMoo WWEG XLum
- - 'Liebreiz' new	EPPr
- - 'Skyracer'	CCVN CHel CKno COIW CPrp EBee EHoe ELan ELon EPPr GBin GCal GQue LRHS MAsh MAvo MMoz MWhi NWsh SPhx WCot WGrn WMoo WWEG
- - 'Staefa'	EHoe
- - 'Transparent'	Widely available
- - 'Windsaule'	CKno EPPr SPhx
- - 'Windspiel'	CKno CSam CSpe CWCL EBee EHoe EPPr GBin IKil LEdu LRHS MAvo MBri MNrw MSpe MWat MWhi NDov SMrm SPhx WCot WMoo WPGP WPtf XLum
- - 'Zuneigung'	CKno CSam EPPr LPla MAvo SPhx
- subsp. ***caerulea*** 'Carmarthen' (v)	EHoe EPPr WHal WWEG
- - 'Claerwen' (v)	EPPr MAvo SPhx WMoo
- - 'Coneyhill Gold' (v)	EPPr
- - 'Dauerstrahl'	CKno EBee EPPr GCal GQue LPla MAsh MAvo MNrw NDov
- - 'Edith Dudszus'	CKno COIW CWCL EHoe ELan ELon EPPr GBin GQue IPot LHop LPla LRHS MAvo MBel MBrN NDov NGdn NHol NOrc NWsh SPer SPhx WCot WGrn WMoo WWEG
- - 'Heidebraut'	EBee EHoe EPPr GBin GQue IBoy MBel MRav MSpe NBro NDov NOrc NWsh SPhx WMoo WWEG WWlt
- - 'Moorflamme'	CSam EPPr MAvo MSpe NDov SPhx
- - 'Moorhcxc'	CPrp CSam CWCL EBee EHoe EPPr EPfP GBin GMaP IKil IPot LRHS MAvo MBri MSpe NBid NDov NGdn NHol NOak NSti SAPC SLPl SMrm WCot WMoo WPtf WWEG
- - 'Overdam'	MMuc MNrw NDov SEND
- - 'Poul Petersen'	CKno EBee EPPr NDov SPhx WWEG
- - 'Strahlenquelle'	CSam ELan EPPr GCal GQue LPla MAvo MNFA MSpe NBro NDov NHol WWEG
- - 'Variegata' (v) $\mathbb{Y}^{H4}$	Widely available
- 'Dark Defender'	SPhx
- 'Heidezwerg' new	GBin
- 'Showers of Gold'	SPhx
litoralis	see *M. caerulea* subsp. *arundinacea*

Molopospermum (*Apiaceae*)

peloponnesiacum	CAby CSpe GBin GCal IMou LEdu SBrt SPhx WCru WPnP WPtf

Moltkia (*Boraginaceae*)

§ ***doerfleri***	GCal NBir NChi WSHC
§ × ***intermedia*** $\mathbb{Y}^{H4}$	CMea SBch SIgm WThu
petraea	LHop LLHF LRHS MWat WAbe

Moluccella (*Lamiaceae*)

laevis	SVic
- 'Pixie Bells'	CSpe

Monarda (*Lamiaceae*)

'Adam'	GBuc GCal LRHS LSRN MPkF MSpe NBre NLar WSHC
'Amethyst'	ECtt EWes
'Aquarius'	CAby EPPr GQue IKil LRHS MSpe SPet WCAu XLum
austromontana	see *M. citriodora* subsp. *austromontana*
§ 'Balance'	ECtt EPfP GCal LRHS MRav MSpe NBro NDov NGdn NSti SMrm WSHC WWEG
'Beauty of Cobham' $\mathbb{Y}^{H4}$	CAby CPrp CWCL EBee ECtt ELan EPfP GBin GMaP IBoy LEdu MBri MHer MNrw MPie MSpe NDov NHol NLar NPri SBch SMad SPer SWvt WBor WCAu WHlf WWEG XLum
'Blaukranz'	NBre
§ 'Blaustrumpf'	CElw EBee ECtt ELon EPfP EWTr EWes GBBs GQue LPot NLar SPer WSHC XLum
Blue Stocking	see *M.* 'Blaustrumpf'

	Bowman	see *M.* 'Sagittarius'
	bradburyana	NLar SBrt SPhx
	'Cambridge Scarlet' ♀H4	Widely available
	'Capricorn'	NBre WWEG XLum
	citriodora	GPoy LRHS MHoo NSti SIde SRms SWat
§	- subsp. ***austromontana***	NBir SBch
	- - 'Bee's Favourite'	IKil SPad
	'Comanche'	EWes
	'Croftway Pink' ♀H4	Widely available
	didyma	CArn EPfP LPot MHoo NBro SVic SWat WJek
	- 'Coral Reef'	EBee EWes LRHS WWEG
	- 'Cranberry Lace'	EBee ECtt GBin LRHS MBri NLar SGol
	- 'Duddiscombe'	CSam
	- 'Pink Lace' PBR	EBee ECtt IBoy LSou MBri MNrw MSpe NCGa NHol NLar STes
	'Earl Grey'	ECtt GAbr MSpe NDov SCoo
	'Elsie's Lavender'	CAby EBee EPfP LPla MSpe NDov NLar WWEG
	'Elworthy'	CElw
	'Fireball' PBR	CCVN CWCL ECtt ELon GAbr LEdu LHop LLHF LRHS LSRN LSou MHol MNrw MSCN NCGa NHol NLar NOrc NPri SPad SPoG WBor
§	'Fishes'	CExl CMac ECtt ELan EPPr EWTr EWes IKil LEdu LRHS LSou MRav MSpe NDov NGdn NLar SGbt SMrm SPet WPtf WSHC WWEG
	fistulosa	CArn CHby CMac GPoy MHer MHoo MNHC WJek WMoo XLum
	'Gardenview Scarlet' ♀H4	CElw CPrp CSam CWCL ECtt EWes GCra GQue IKil LEdu LRHS MBri MCot MNFA MPie MSpe MWat NDov NHol NLar NSti SMrm SWvt WHoo WWEG WWlt
	Gemini	see *M.* 'Twins'
	'Gewitterwolke'	CSam MSpe MTis NDov SDys WWEG
	'Hartswood Wine'	EBee ECtt EWes SMad SMrm WWEG
	'Heidelerche'	EPPr
	'Jacob Cline'	ECtt EPPr EWes GBin IPot LRHS MSpe MTis NBre NCGa NDov SGbt SPhx WWEG
	'Kardinal'	GBin LPla LRHS MTis NDov NLar WWEG XLum
	Libra	see *M.* 'Balance'
	'Loddon Crown'	COlW CPrp ECtt ELon GQue LRHS MHoo NHol NLar SBea SHar SIde WSHC WWEG
	'Mahogany'	ECtt ELan GBuc GKev GMaP GQue IBoy IKil LPla LRHS MCot MNrw MRav MSpe NHol NSti SPer SPhx WWEG
	'Marshall's Delight' ♀H4	CPrp CSam CWCL EBee ECtt EWes GBee LRHS MRav MSpe MTis NLar SMrm
	'Melissa'	EBee LSRN NBre NLar WSHC
	menthifolia	GCal SMrm SRms
	'Mohawk'	CPrp ECtt EPPr EPfP GQue LRHS MSpe MTis MWat NDov NGdn NOrc SDix WPtf WWEG
	'Mrs Perry'	EWes
	'Neon'	MSpe MTis NDov SPhx
	'Night Rider'	EWes
	'On Parade'	CElw CSam CWCL ECtt LRHS MMHG MSpe MTis NDov NGdn
	'Othello'	CSam MSpe MTis NDov
	'Ou Charm'	EWes GBin LRHS NDov NLar SMad SMrm
	'Panorama'	NLar SPet SPlb WMoo
	'Panorama Red Shades' (Panorama Series)	CWib MNHC SPet WCFE
	'Pawnee'	LRHS MTis NDov WWEG
	Petite Delight = 'Acpetdel'	CBcs EBee ELan LBMP LHop LSou MPkF NLar NPri SMad WWEG
	'Petite Wonder' **new**	EBee
	'Pink Supreme' PBR	ECtt ELon EPfP GAbr LSou MBri MHol MSpe NCGa NHol NLar SCoo WHil
	'Pink Tourmaline'	MSpe MTis NDov SMrm WWEG
	Pisces	see *M.* 'Fishes'
	'Poyntzfield Pink'	GPoy
	Prairie Night	see *M.* 'Prärienacht'
§	'Prärienacht'	CAby CPrp CSBt CSam EBee ELan EPfP LRHS MCot MHer MJak MSpe NBro NGdn NHol NPri NSoo SBch SGol SPer SPlb SRms SWvt WSHC WWEG
	punctata	CArn EPfP MNrw SPhx SWat
	'Raspberry Wine'	EBee ECtt EPPr LEdu LRHS MSpe
	'Ruby Glow'	CAby CSam CWCL LRHS LSRN MBri MMHG SMad SMrm
§	'Sagittarius'	EBee EPPr LRHS MBNS MMHG MSpe NGdn NSti
	'Saxon Purple'	MTis NDov NLar XLum
§	'Schneewittchen'	CAby CWCL ECtt ELan EPfP GBin LRHS MGos MHer MHol MRav NHol NLar NPri NSoo NSti SBea SCoo SGbt SIde SPer SPoG SWvt WCAu WWEG XLum
	'Scorpion'	EBee ECtt ELan EPPr EPfP EWTr GBin LEdu LRHS MRav MSpe NBir NEgg NGdn NLar NOrc SMrm SPet SPhx SWvt WCAu WSHC WWlt XLum
	'Sioux'	EWes LRHS
	'Snow Maiden'	see *M.* 'Schneewittchen'
	'Snow Queen'	EBee ECtt EPPr LRHS MBel MHoo MSpe MWat NPro SMrm
	Snow White	see *M.* 'Schneewittchen'
	'Squaw' ♀H4	CElw CPrp CWCL ECtt ELan ELon EPPr EPfP EWes GMaP LBMP LRHS LSRN MHer MNrw MPie MRav MSpe NBro NDov NEgg NGdn NHol NLar SRkn WWEG XLum
	'Talud' ♀H4	MSpe NDov
§	'Twins'	CWCL EPPr GKev LRHS LSRN NLar SWvt WSHC WWEG
	'Velvet Queen'	LSou
	'Vintage Wine'	CAby CWCL ECtt MTis NDov
	'Violacea'	NHol
	'Violet Queen' ♀H4	CWCL EBee ECtt ELan EWes GQue LEdu LRHS MBel MCot MSpe MTis NBre NPro SCoo SMrm WPtf WWlt
	'Violette'	EBee MSpe SBch
	'Westacre Purple'	EBee EPPr EWes

Monardella (*Lamiaceae*)

	macrantha subsp. ***hallii***	CPBP

Monochoria (*Pontederiaceae*)

§	***hastata***	CBAq LLWG MSKA

Monopsis (*Campanulaceae*)

	Midnight = 'Yagemon'	LAst

Monstera (*Araceae*)

deliciosa (F) ♀H1	MBri XBlo
- 'Variegata' (v) ♀H1	MBri

Montbretia see *Crocosmia*

Montia (*Portulacaceae*)

perfoliata	see *Claytonia perfoliata*
sibirica	see *Claytonia sibirica*

Moraea (*Iridaceae*)

algoensis	WCot
alticola	ECho GCal WHer
§ ***aristata***	CDes ECho WCot
§ ***bellendenii***	ECho WCot
bifida from Roggeveld	ECho
bipartita	WCot
britteniae	ECho
calcicola	ECho
ciliata	ECho WCot
citrina	ECho
§ ***collina***	ECho
comptonii	WCot
crispa from Roggeveld	ECho
elegans	ECho
fergusoniae from Swellendam	ECho
flaccida	ECho
- from Roggeveld	ECho
fugacissima	ECho
§ ***fugax***	WCot
gigandra	ECho WCot
glaucopsis	see *M. aristata*
huttonii	CCCN CCon CSpe CTca ECre EPri GAbr MHer SMad WCot WHil WKif WSHC
- from Eastern Cape	ECho
inclinata from Howick	ECho
incurva	ECho
iridioides	see *Dietes iridioides*
longiaristata from Caledon	ECho
longifolia Sweet	see *M. fugax*
longifolia (Jacq.) Pers. new	MHol
loubseri	WCot
lurida	WCot
- from Bredasdorp	ECho
macronyx from Komsberg	ECho
marlothii	ECho WCot
mediterranea	ECho
neglecta	ECho
ochroleuca	ECho
papilionacea from Gordon's Bay	ECho
pavonia var. ***lutea***	see *M. bellendenii*
polystachya	CGrW ECho
reflexa from Calvinia	ECho
robusta	EBee GCal
serpentina	ECho
setifolia	ECho
sisyrinchium	ECho
- purple-flowered	ECho
spathacea	see *M. spathulata*
§ ***spathulata***	CCon CExl CTca EBee ECho GCal LEdu WCot WKif
speciosa from Tanqua	ECho
tortilis from Nababeep	ECho
tricolor	ECho
trifida from Sentinel Peak	ECho
tripetala from Riverlands	ECho
unibracteata from Sentinel Peak	ECho
vegeta	ECho WCot
versicolor from Paarl	ECho
villosa	ECho WCot

Morella (*Myricaceae*)

californica	NLar
pensylvanica	CArn IVic
rubra	CAgr

Moricandia (*Brassicaceae*)

arvensis	EBee WCot
moricandioides	CSpe

Morina (*Caprifoliaceae*)

* ***afghanica***	GAbr
alba	GCra
longifolia	Widely available
persica	EWes SPhx

Morinda (*Rubiaceae*)

umbellata WWJ 11680	WCru

Morisia (*Brassicaceae*)

hypogaea	see *M. monanthos*
§ ***monanthos***	CPla EPfP MAsh SRot
- 'Fred Hemingway'	ECho ECtt LRHS NSla WAbe

Morus ✿ (*Moraceae*)

alba	CAgr CArn CBcs CCVT CDul CHab CLnd CMCN CTho CWib ECrN ELan EPfP ERea GTwe LBuc LHop SDea SVic
- 'Black Tabor'	CAgr
- 'Chaparral'	LRHS
- 'Issai'	LRHS SHil
- 'Macrophylla'	CMCN NLar
- 'Nana'	NLar
- 'Pakistan' (F) new	ERea
- 'Paradise' new	CAgr
- 'Pendula'	CDoC CDul CEnd CMac CTho CTri ELan LRHS MBlu MBri NLar SCoo SLim
- 'Platanifolia'	MBlu
- 'San Martin' new	ERea
- var. ***tatarica***	CAgr LEdu NLar
'Capsrum' (F)	CAgr
'Carmen' (F)	CAgr
'Illinois Everbearing' (F)	CAgr ERea
'Italian' (F)	CAgr
'Ivory' (F)	CAgr
latifolia 'Spirata'	NLar
nigra (F) ♀H4	Widely available
§ - 'Chelsea' (F)	CDul CEnd CTho CTri EPfP EPom ERea GTwe IVic LRHS MBri MGos NWea SCoo SEWo SKee SLim SPer SPoG WHar
- 'Jerusalem' (F)	CTho EPom LRHS MCoo WHar
- 'King James'	see *M. nigra* 'Chelsea'
- 'Large Black' (F)	EPom
rubra	CAgr NLar
- 'Nana'	NLar
'Wellington' (F)	CAgr CEnd LSRN NPri

Mosla (*Lamiaceae*)

dianthera	EWld GCal MAvo MNrw

Muehlenbeckia (*Polygonaceae*)

	astonii	CDoC EBee ECou LRHS WPGP
	australis	ECou
	axillaris misapplied	see *M. complexa*
§	***axillaris*** Walp.	CBcs CTri ECou SBig XLum
	- 'Mount Cook' (f)	ECou
	- 'Ohau' (m)	ECou
§	***complexa***	CBcs CDoC CFlo CHEx CHel CHll CMac CTri CWib EBee ECou EPfP EShb EUJe GBin LRHS MBlu NLBP SAPC SEND SLim SLon SPer SPoG SWvt WCFE WPGP WSHC XLum
	- (f)	ECou
	- 'Nana'	see *M. axillaris* Walp.
	- 'Spotlight' PBR (v)	EShb
	- var. ***trilobata***	CBcs CHEx EShb ESwi EUJe SSta XLum
	- 'Ward' (m)	ECou
	ephedroides	ECou
	- 'Clarence Pass'	ECou
*	- var. ***muricatula***	ECou
	gunnii	ECou
	platyclados	see *Homalocladium platycladum*

Muhlenbergia (*Poaceae*)

	capillaris	SDix SHDw
	- white-flowered **new**	SPhx
	dubia	WPGP
	dumosa	CKno
	japonica 'Cream Delight' (v)	EHoe SHDw
	lindheimeri	CKno SDix SMea WCot
	mexicana	LEdu SMad SRms
	rigens	CKno WPGP XLum

Mukdenia (*Saxifragaceae*)

	sp. **new**	CCon
	acanthifolia	CDes CLAP WCru
	rossii	CAby CLAP ELon GCal IFro LEdu MBel MNrw NBid NLar NMyG NPnk SHil SMad WCru WPGP WSHC WThu XLum
	- from Japan	GCal
	- 'Crimson Fans'	see *M. rossii* 'Karasuba'
	- dwarf	CDes CLAP GCal MNrw
§	- 'Karasuba'	CLAP CWGN ECtt EPfP LBMP LEdu LSou MAvo MMHG MPnt NLar NMyG NPnk SPoG WHil

mulberry see *Morus*

Murraya (*Rutaceae*)

*	***elliptica***	MOWG
	exotica	see *M. paniculata*
	koenigii	EOHP GPoy SPre WJek
§	***paniculata***	CArn MOWG

Musa ✿ (*Musaceae*)

	from Yunnan, China	see *M. itinerans* 'Yunnan'
	acuminata 'Siam Ruby' (AA Group) (F)	EAmu
§	- 'Dwarf Cavendish' (AAA Group) (F) ♀H1	CDoC EAmu ELan NPla SBst SPlb XBlo
	- 'Williams' (AAA Group) (F)	EAmu XBlo
	- 'Grand Nain' × ***acuminata*** 'Zebrina'	EAmu
	- 'Zebrina' ♀H1+3	CDTJ EAmu LRHS XBlo
	balbisiana	EAmu
	- 'Black Thai'	EAmu
	basjoo ♀H3-4	CAbb CBcs CDoC CDoy CHEx CHel CHll CSBt EAmu ELan EPfP EUJe LEdu LRHS LSRN NPla NSoo SAPC SBst SChr SEND SHil SLim SMad SPer SPlb SPoG
I	- 'Rubra'	CCCN EAmu ESwi
	'Blue Java'	see *M.* 'Ice Cream'
	cavendishii	see *M. acuminata* 'Dwarf Cavendish'
§	***coccinea*** ♀H1	XBlo
	ensete	see *Ensete ventricosum*
	'Ghew-kera'	EAmu
	'Helen'	EAmu
	hookeri	see *M. sikkimensis*
§	'Ice Cream' (ABB Group)	EAmu
	itinerans var. ***xishuangbannaensis*** 'Mekong Giant' **new**	EAmu
§	- 'Yunnan'	EAmu
	lasiocarpa	CDTJ CDoC CHEx CHll EAmu ESwi EUJe LRHS NPla SBig SBst SHil SPlb
	mannii	EAmu
	nana misapplied	see *M. acuminata* 'Dwarf Cavendish'
	'Orange'	EAmu
	ornata ♀H1	CCCN XBlo
	× ***paradisiaca*** 'Hajaré' (ABB Group) (F)	EAmu
	- 'Malbhog' (AAB Group) (F)	EAmu
	- 'Monthan' (ABB Group) (F)	EAmu
	- 'Ney Poovan' (AB Group) (F)	CCCN EAmu SBst
	- 'Orinoco' (ABB Group) (F)	EAmu
	- 'Rajapuri' (AAB Group) (F)	EAmu
§	***sikkimensis***	CDTJ EAmu ELan ESwi EUJe SBig SBst SPlb XBlo
	- 'Red Tiger'	CCCN CDTJ EAmu IDee SBst
	'Tropicana'	XBlo
	uranoscopus misapplied	see *M. coccinea*
	velutina ♀H1+3	CCCN CDoC EAmu SBig SBst

Muscari ✿ (*Asparagaceae*)

	'Aleyna'	ECho NMin
	ambrosiacum	see *M. muscarimi*
	anatolicum	ECho
	armeniacum ♀H4	CBro CTri ECho EPfP LPot LRHS MBri SEND SPer SRms WCot WShi
	- 'Argaei Album'	ECho EPot
	- 'Atlantic'	ECho EPfP LRHS
	- 'Blue Pearl'	ECho GKev
	- 'Blue Spike' (d)	CBro ECho EPfP GKev MBri NBir NEgg SDeJ WCot WGwG
	- 'Bright Eyes'	GKev
	- 'Cantab'	ECho GKev LPio SDeJ XLum
	- 'Christmas Pearl' ♀H4	ECho GKev WCot
	- 'Côte d'Azur'	GKev
	- 'Cupido'	CGrW GKev
	- 'Dark Eyes'	ECho EPfP SPer
	- 'Early Giant'	ECho SDeJ
	- 'Fantasy Creation'	ECho EPot SDeJ
	- 'Gül'	CDes WCot
	- 'Heavenly Blue'	ECho
	- 'New Creation'	ECho
	- 'Peppermint'	CTca ECho EPfP EPot ERCP LPio NMin SPhx WCot
	- 'Saffier' ♀H4	ECho WCot
	- 'Valerie Finnis'	CAby CAvo CBre CBro CHel CTca EBee ECho EPPr EPfP EPot ERCP

MBri NLar SDeJ SMrm SPer SPhx WBor WBrk WCot
aucheri ♀H4 — ECho NRya
* - var. ***bicolor*** — WCot
- 'Blue Magic' — ECho EPot ERCP SDeJ
- 'Ocean Magic' — CBro CHel ECho GBin GKev MBri NLar
§ - 'Tubergenianum' — ECho
- 'White Magic' — CAvo CBro ECho ERCP SDeJ SMrm SPer WCot
§ ***azureum*** ♀H4 — CAvo CBro CTca ECho ELan EPfP ERCP GMaP LPot LRHS NLar SPhx WCot
- 'Album' — ECho SPhx WCot
'Baby's Breath' — see *M.* 'Jenny Robinson'
'Big Smile' — GKev WCot
'Blue Dream' — ECho
'Blue Eyes' — ECho WCot
'Blue Star' — ECho GKev
botryoides — CAvo ECho
- 'Album' — CAvo CBro CTca CTri ECho EPfP LPio LRHS MBri SDeJ SMrm SRms WCot WShi
caucasicum — ECho WCot
chalusicum — see *M. pseudomuscari*
commutatum — ECho
§ ***comosum*** — CArn CBro ECho EPfP ERCP MCot NEgg WCot
- 'Monstrosum' — see *M. comosum* 'Plumosum'
- 'Pinard' — ECho
§ - 'Plumosum' — ECho ELan EPfP EPot GKev LRHS MBri SDeJ
dionysicum — ECho
- HOA 8965 — ECho WCot
grandifolium JCA 689.450 — WCot
inconstrictum — ECho
'Ivor's Pink' — WCot
§ 'Jenny Robinson' ♀H4 — ECho IFoB SDys SMad WCot
latifolium ♀H4 — CAby CAvo CBro CTca ECho EPfP EPot ERCP LPio LRHS MBri NEgg NLar SDeJ SMrm SPhx WBor WCot
* - 'Blue Angels' — NBir
macbeathianum — WCot
§ ***macrocarpum*** — CBro CPom CTca EBee ECho EPot WCot
- 'Golden Fragrance'PBR — CAvo CExl CHid ECho EPot ERCP GKev IFoB MCot MNrw NMin SDeJ WCot WHil
- white-flowered **new** — ECho
mirum — ECho
moschatum — see *M. muscarimi*
'Mount Hood' — CHel ECho ERCP SDeJ WBor
§ ***muscarimi*** — CAvo CBro CTca ECho IFoB NLar SDeJ WCot
- var. ***flavum*** — see *M. macrocarpum*
§ ***neglectum*** — ECho NLar SEND WCot WShi
pallens — ECho NMin WCot
paradoxum — see *Bellevalia paradoxa*
parviflorum — ECho WCot
'Pink Sunrise' **new** — ECho ERCP
§ ***pseudomuscari*** ♀H4 — CDes ECho WCot
racemosum — see *M. neglectum*
'Rosy Sunrise' — WCot
'Sky Blue' — ECho WCot
'Superstar' — CHel ECho WCot
§ ***tenuiflorum*** — ECho WCot
aff. ***tenuiflorum*** JCA 0.691.251 — WCot
tubergenianum — see *M. aucheri* 'Tubergenianum'

'Venus' **new** — WCot
'White Beauty' — ECho SPhx WBor
'Winter Amethyst' — WCot

Muscarimia (*Asparagaceae*)

ambrosiacum — see *Muscari muscarimi*
macrocarpum — see *Muscari macrocarpum*

Musella see *Musa*

Mussaenda (*Rubiaceae*)

'Tropic Snow' — CCCN

Mutisia (*Asteraceae*)

ilicifolia — WCot
retusa — see *M. spinosa* var. *pulchella*
§ ***spinosa*** var. ***pulchella*** — GGal

Myoporum (*Scrophulariaceae*)

acuminatum — see *M. tenuifolium*
debile — see *Eremophila debilis*
laetum — CAbb CBcs CExl IDee SVen
sandwicense — SVen
§ ***tenuifolium*** — SPlb SVen

Myosotidium (*Boraginaceae*)

§ ***hortensia*** — CBcs CBct CExl CGHE CHel CSpe ECre ELan EPfP EUJe EWes GBin GCal IBoy IKil LRHS MCot MPie SChF WCot WPGP
- 'True Blue' — CHid
- white-flowered — IKil
nobile — see *M. hortensia*

Myosotis (*Boraginaceae*)

capitata — CHid
colensoi — ECou
'Malmesbury' **new** — CNat
My Oh My = 'Myomark'PBR — CHel LSou NPri
palustris — see *M. scorpioides*
pulvinaris — WAbe
pygmaea SDR 7257 **new** — GKev
rakiura — SBch
§ ***scorpioides*** — CBAq CHab CWat EHon MMuc MNrw MSKA MWts NMir SCoo SPer SPlb SRms SWat WBrk WMAq WMoo WPnP WTHF XLum
- 'Alba' — CBAq MSKA MWts
- Maytime = 'Blaqua' (v) — LLWG NBir
- 'Mermaid' — CBAq CRow CWat EWay LLWG MWts SBch SDix SWat WPtf
- 'Pinkie' — CWat EWay LLWG SWat
- 'Snowflakes' — CWat EWay SWat
- variegated (v) — MSKA
sylvatica — MMuc NMir
- 'Rosylva' (Sylva Series) ♀H4 **new** — CWCL
- 'Ultramarine' ♀H4 — WMoo
- (Victoria Series) 'Victoria Blue' — CHel
- - 'Victoria Indigo-blue' **new** — CWCL

Myosurus (*Ranunculaceae*)

minimus — CRDP

Myrica (*Myricaceae*)

gale — CAgr GPoy IVic MGos NLar SWat WGwG

Myricaria (*Tamaricaceae*)

germanica	NLar

Myriophyllum (*Haloragaceae*)

propinquum	LLWG
spicatum	EHon MSKA MWts WMAq
verticillatum	CWat EWay MSKA SCoo

Myrrhis (*Apiaceae*)

odorata	CArn CBre CCon CHby CSev CSpe EBee ELau GPoy IFro LHop MHer MHoo MMuc MNHC NPri SIde SPad SPer SRms SWvt WJek WPtf WSFF WWFP
- 'Forncett Chevron'	EBee LEdu

Myrsine (*Primulaceae*)

africana	CBcs CFil CWib EShb
aquilonia	ECou
australis	SVen
divaricata	ECou SVen

Myrteola (*Myrtaceae*)

§ ***nummularia***	GAbr ITim NHar WAbe WThu

Myrtus (*Myrtaceae*)

apiculata	see *Luma apiculata*
bullata	see *Lophomyrtus bullata*
chequen	see *Luma chequen*
communis 🏆H3	Widely available
- 'Flore Pleno' (d)	ELau EOHP MHer
- 'Jenny Reitenbach'	see *M. communis* subsp. *tarentina*
- 'Merion'	WJek
- 'Microphylla'	see *M. communis* subsp. *tarentina*
- 'Nana'	see *M. communis* subsp. *tarentina*
- 'Pyewood Park'	SRms WJek
§ - subsp. ***tarentina*** 🏆H3	Widely available
- - 'Compacta'	LRHS SLon
- - 'Microphylla Variegata' (v)	CBcs EShb LRHS MHer MNHC SPer SRms WHar WJek
I - - 'Variegata' (v)	EOHP EPfP SEND SPoG
- 'Tricolor'	see *M. communis* 'Variegata'
§ - 'Variegata' (v)	CArn CMCN CMac CSBt CTri CWib EBee ELan ELau ELon EPfP EShb LBMP LEdu LHop LRHS MAsh MHer MHoo MSwo NLar SEND SLon SPer SPoG WCFE WJek WMoo WSHC
'Glanleam Gold'	see *Luma apiculata* 'Glanleam Gold'
lechleriana	see *Amomyrtus luma*
luma	see *Luma apiculata*
nummularia	see *Myrteola nummularia*
'Traversii'	see *Lophomyrtus* × *ralphii* 'Traversii'
ugni	see *Ugni molinae*

N

Nandina (*Berberidaceae*)

domestica 🏆H3	Widely available
- B&SWJ 4923	WCru
- B&SWJ 11113	WCru
- 'Filamentosa' new	EPfP
- 'Fire Power' 🏆H3	Widely available
- Flirt = 'Murasaki' new	LRHS
- 'Gulf Stream'	NLar
- 'Harbour Dwarf'	CDoC CEnd EBee LRHS NLar SPoG
- var. ***leucocarpa***	CMCN NLar
- 'Nana'	see *N. domestica* 'Pygmaea'
- Plum Passion = 'Monum'	LRHS MAsh SPoG
§ - 'Pygmaea'	CMen SGol
- 'Richmond'	CDul CEnd EBee ELan EPfP LAst LRHS MAsh MGos NLar NPri SHil SLim SPer SPoG SRkn SWvt
- 'Wood's Dwarf'	CBcs MPkF NLar

Nannorrhops (*Arecaceae*)

ritchiana	SPlb

Napaea (*Malvaceae*)

dioica	WCot

Narcissus ✿ (*Amaryllidaceae*)

'Abba' (4) 🏆H4	CFen CQua
'Abbey Road' (5)	NMin
'Aberfoyle' (2) 🏆H4	CQua
'Abstract' (11a)	CQua
'Accent' (2) 🏆H4	CQua
'Accomplice' (3)	IRhd
'Achduart' (3)	CQua
'Achentoul' (4)	CQua
'Achnasheen' (3)	CQua
'Acropolis' (4)	CQua EPfP SDeJ
'Actaea' (9) 🏆H4	CBro CFen CQua CTca EPfP MBri SDeJ SEND
'Acumen' (2)	CQua
'Admiration' (8)	CQua
'Adorable Lass' (6)	CQua
'Ad-Rem' (2)	CFen
'Advocat' (3)	CQua
'Aflame' (3)	CFen
'African Sunset' (3)	IRhd
'After All' (3)	CFen
'Agnes Mace' (2)	IRhd
'Ahwahnee' (2)	CQua IRhd
'Ainley' (2)	CQua
'Aintree' (3)	CQua
'Aircastle' (3)	CQua
'Airtime' (2)	IRhd
'Akala' (1)	CQua
'Albatross' (3)	CQua GCro
'Albus Plenus Odoratus'	see *N. poeticus* 'Plenus' ambig.
'All Rounder' (3)	IRhd
'Alpine Glow' (1)	CQua
'Alpine Winter' (1)	IRhd
'Alston' (2)	IRhd
'Alto' (2)	IRhd
'Altruist' (3)	CQua ERCP
'Altun Ha' (2)	CQua IRhd
'Altun Ha Gold' (2)	CQua
'Amazing Grace' (2)	IRhd
'Amber Castle' (2)	CQua
'Ambergate' (2)	CQua SDeJ
'Ambergris Caye' (1)	CQua
'American Goldfinch' (7)	CQua
'American Heritage' (1)	CQua IRhd
'American Robin' (6)	CQua
'American Shores' (1)	CQua IRhd
'Amstel' (4)	CQua
'Andalusia' (6)	CQua
'Andrew's Choice' (7) 🏆H4	CQua
'Angel' (3)	CQua
'Angel Face' (3)	CQua IRhd
'Angel Wings'	see *N.* 'Celtic Wings'

'Angelito' (3) ♀H4	IRhd
'Angel's Breath' (5) ♀H4 **new**	NMin
Angel's tears	see *N. triandrus* subsp. *triandrus* var. *triandrus*
'Angel's Whisper' (5) **new**	NMin
'Angel's Wings' (2)	CQua
'Angels Wood' (2) **new**	IRhd
'Angkor' (4)	CQua
'An-gof' (7)	CQua
'Ann Sonia' (4)	IRhd
'Anna Panna' (3)	IRhd
'Annequin' (3)	CQua
'Apollo Gold' (10)	CQua ECho NMin
'Apotheose' (4)	CFen CQua SDeJ
'Applins' (2)	IRhd
'Apricot' (1)	CBro
'Apricot Blush' (2)	CQua
'Apricot Whirl' (11a)	CQua
'April Love' (1)	CQua
'April Snow' (2)	CBro CQua
'April Tears' (5) ♀H4	NMin
'Ara' (6)	CQua
'Aranjuez' (2)	CFen CQua GCro
'Aranka' (2)	CQua
'Arctic Gem' (3)	CQua
'Arctic Gold' (1) ♀H4	CQua
'Ardress' (2)	CQua
'Areley Kings' (2)	CQua
'Argosy' (1)	CQua
'Arid Plains' (3)	IRhd
'Ariel'PBR (8)	GKev
'Arish Mell' (5)	CQua
'Ark Royal' (1) **new**	CFen
'Arkle' (1) ♀H4	CQua SDeJ
'Arleston' (2)	IRhd
'Armada' (2) ♀H4	CFen
'Armidale' (3)	IRhd
'Armoury' (4)	CQua
'Arndilly' (2)	CQua
'Arpege' (2)	CQua
'Arran Isle' (2)	IRhd
'Arrowhead' (6)	NMin
'Arthurian' (1)	CQua IRhd
'Articol' (11a)	CQua
'Arwenack' (11a)	CQua
'Asante' (1)	IRhd
'Ashland' (2) **new**	IRhd
'Ashmore' (2)	CQua IRhd
'Ashton Wold' (2)	CQua
'Asila' (2)	IRhd
'Assertion' (2)	IRhd
§ ***assoanus*** (13)	CBro ECho EPot GKev LLHF NMin SPhx
'Astropink' (11a)	CQua
§ ***asturiensis*** (13) ♀H3-4	ECho GKev NMin
- giant	see *N. asturiensis* 'Wavertree'
§ - 'Wavertree' (1)	CQua NMin
'Atholl Palace' (4)	IRhd
'Atlas Gold'	see *N. romieuxii* 'Atlas Gold'
'Atricilla' (11a)	IRhd
'Auchranie' (2) **new**	IRhd
'Audubon' (2)	CQua SDeJ
'Aunt Betty' (1)	CQua IRhd
'Auspicious' (2)	IRhd
'Avalanche' (8) ♀H3	CFen CQua IRhd NMin SDeJ
'Avalanche of Gold' (8)	CQua
'Avalon' (2)	CQua
'Avril Amour' (1)	IRhd
'Azocor' (1)	IRhd

'Baby Boomer' (7)	NMin
'Baby Moon' (7)	CFen CQua CTca EPfP EPot ERCP GKev MBri NMin SDeJ
'Baccarat' (11a)	CQua
'Back Flash' (2)	CQua
'Badanloch' (3)	CQua
'Badbury Rings' (3) ♀H4	CQua IRhd
'Bailey' (2)	IRhd
'Bala' (4)	CQua
'Balalaika' (2)	CQua
'Baldock' (4)	CQua
'Ballydorn' (9)	IRhd
'Ballygarvey' (1)	CQua
'Ballygowan' (3)	IRhd
'Ballynichol' (3)	CQua
'Ballyrobert' (1)	CQua
'Baltic Shore' (3)	IRhd
'Balvenie' (2)	CQua
'Bandesara' (3)	CQua IRhd
'Bandit' (2)	CQua IRhd
'Banker' (2)	CQua IRhd
'Banstead Village' (2)	CQua
'Bantam' (2) ♀H4	CBro CQua NMin
'Barbary Gold' (2)	CQua IRhd
'Barlow' (6)	CQua
'Barnesgold' (1)	IRhd
'Barnham' (1)	CQua
'Barnsdale Wood' (2)	CQua
'Barnum' (1) ♀H4	IRhd
'Barrett Browning' (3)	SDeJ
'Barrii' (3)	CQua
'Bartley' (6)	CQua
'Bath's Flame' (3)	CAvo CQua GCro WShi
'Bear Springs' (4)	IRhd
'Bear's Gold' (4)	CQua
'Beaulieu' (1)	CQua
'Beautiful Dream' (3)	CQua
'Beauvallon' (4) ♀H4	SDeJ
'Bebop' (7)	CBro
'Bedruthan' (2)	CQua
'Beersheba' (1)	CQua
'Beige Beauty' (3)	CQua
'Belbroughton' (2)	CQua
'Belcanto' (11a)	CQua SDeJ
'Belfast Lough' (1)	IRhd
'Belisana' (2)	SDeJ
'Bell Rock' (1) ♀H4	CQua
'Bell Song' (7)	CAvo CBro CFen CQua EPfP GKev LSou SDeJ WShi
'Bella Estrella' (11a)	ERCP NMin
'Belzone' (2)	CQua
'Ben Aligin' (1)	IRhd
'Ben Hee' (2) ♀H4	CQua IRhd
'Berceuse' (2)	CQua IRhd
'Bere Ferrers' (4)	CQua
'Bergerac' (11a)	CQua
'Bernardino' (2)	CQua GCro
'Beryl' (6)	CBro CQua NMin
'Best Friend' (3)	CQua
'Best Seller' (1)	SPer
'Bethal' (3)	CQua
'Betsy MacDonald' (6)	CQua
'Biffo' (4)	CQua
'Bikini Beach' (2)	IRhd
'Bilbo' (6)	CBro CQua
'Billy Graham' (2)	CQua
'Binkie' (2)	CBro CQua SPer
'Birchwood' (3)	CQua IRhd
'Birdsong' (3)	CQua

	'Birma' (3)	SDeJ
	'Birthday Girl' (2)	IRhd NMin
	'Bishops Light' (2)	CQua
	'Bittern' (12)	CQua SDeJ
	'Blair Athol' (2)	CQua
	'Blarney' (3)	CQua
	'Blisland' (9)	CQua
	'Blossom' (4)	CQua
	'Blue Danube' (1)	CQua IRhd
	'Blushing Maiden' (4)	CQua
	'Bob Spotts' (2)	CQua
	'Bobbysoxer' (7)	CBro CQua NMin
	'Bobolink' (2)	CQua
	'Boconnoc' (2)	CQua
	'Bodelva' (2)	CQua
	'Bodwannick' (2)	CQua
	'Bold Prospect' (1)	CQua
	'Bombay' (2) **new**	CFen
	'Bon Viveur' (11a)	IRhd
	'Bosbigal' (11a)	CQua
	'Boscastle' (7)	CQua
	'Boscoppa' (11a)	CQua
	'Boslowick' (11a) ♀H4	CQua
	'Bosmeor' (2)	CQua
	'Bossa Nova' (3)	CQua
	'Bossiney' (11a)	CQua
	'Bosvale' (11a)	CQua IRhd
	'Bosvigo' (11a)	CQua
	'Boulder Bay' (2) ♀H4	CQua IRhd
	'Bouzouki' (2)	IRhd
	'Bowles's Early Sulphur' (1)	CRow
	'Boyne Bridge' (1)	IRhd
	'Brahms' (2) **new**	CFen
	'Braid Song' (9)	IRhd
	'Braid Valley' (9) **new**	IRhd
	'Brandaris' (11a)	CQua
	'Bravoure' (1) ♀H4	CFen CQua SDeJ
	'Brentswood' (8)	CQua
	'Brian's Favorite' (2)	CQua IRhd
	'Bridal Crown' (4) ♀H4	CFen EPfP LRHS NHol
	'Brideshead' (2) **new**	CFen
	'Bright Flame' (2)	CQua
	'Bright Spangles' (8) **new**	IRhd
	'Bright Spot' (8)	CQua
	'Brilliancy' (3)	CQua GCro
	'Brindaleena' (2)	IRhd
	'Brindle Pink' (2)	IRhd
	'Broadland' (2)	CQua
	'Broadway Star' (11b)	SDeJ
	'Brodick' (3)	CQua IRhd
	'Bronzewing' (1)	IRhd
	'Brooke Ager' (2) ♀H4	IRhd
	'Broomhill' (2) ♀H4	CQua
	'Broughshane' (1)	CQua
	broussonetii (13)	CFil
	- from Morocco	WPGP
	'Brunswick' (2)	CFen CQua SDeJ
	'Bryanston' (2) ♀H4	CQua
	'Bryher' (3)	CQua
	'Buckshead' (4)	CQua
	'Budock Bells' (5)	CQua
	'Budock Water' (2)	CQua
	'Bugle Major' (2)	CQua
	bulbocodium (13) ♀H3-4	CBro GKev LEdu SMrm SRms
§	- subsp. ***bulbocodium*** (13)	CBro
§	- - var. ***citrinus*** (13)	LRHS SSpi
	- - var. ***conspicuus*** (13)	CBro CQua CTca ECho EPfP EPot ERCP GKev SDeJ WCot XLum
	- - var. ***filifolius*** (13)	CBro

	- - var. ***nivalis*** (13)	ECho EPot WShi
§	- - var. ***tenuifolius*** (13)	EPot
§	- Golden Bells Group (10)	CAvo CBro CHid CQua CTri CWCL ECho EPfP EPot GKev LRHS MBri NHol NMin SDeJ
	- 'Ice Warrior' (10)	SKHP
	- var. ***mesatlanticus***	see *N. romieuxii* subsp. *romieuxii* var. *mesatlanticus*
	- subsp. ***obesus*** (13)	ECho EPot WAbe WCot
§	- - 'Diamond Ring' (10)	CQua EPot NMin
	- subsp. ***praecox*** (13)	ECho LRHS
	- - var. ***paucinervis*** (13)	ECho
	- subsp. ***tananicus***	see *N. cantabricus* subsp. *tananicus*
	- subsp. ***vulgaris***	see *N. bulbocodium* subsp. *bulbocodium*
	'Bunchie' (5)	CQua
	'Bunclody' (2)	CQua
	'Bunting' (7) ♀H4	CQua
	'Burning Bush' (3)	IRhd
	'Burning Ring' (3)	IRhd
	'Burravoe' (1)	CQua
	'Burt House' (2)	IRhd
	'Busselton' (3)	IRhd
	'Bute Park' (4)	CQua
	'Butter and Eggs' (4)	CAvo
	'Butterscotch' (2)	CQua
	'Cabernet' (2)	IRhd
	'Cacatua' (11a)	IRhd
	'Cadgwith' (2)	CQua
	'Cairngorm' (2)	SDeJ
	'Cairntoul' (3)	CQua
	'Calamansack' (2)	CQua
	'California Rose' (4)	IRhd
	'Camaraderie' (2)	IRhd
	'Camden' (1)	CQua
	'Camelot' (2) ♀H4	CFen CQua EPfP SDeJ SPer
	'Cameo King' (2)	CQua
	'Cameo Marie' (3)	CQua
	'Camilla Duchess of Cornwall' (2)	CFen CQua
	'Campernelli' (7)	CQua
	'Campernelli Plenus'	see *N.* × *odorus* 'Double Campernelle'
	'Campion' (9)	CQua IRhd
	canaliculatus Gussone	see *N. tazetta* subsp. *lacticolor*
	'Canaliculatus' (8)	CBro CFen CQua CTri ECho EPfP ERCP GKev LPio LRHS MBri SDeJ SPer
	'Canary' (7)	CQua
	'Canarybird' (8)	CQua WShi
	'Canasta' (11a)	CQua
	'Candida' (4)	CQua
	'Canisp' (2)	CQua
	'Cantabile' (9) ♀H4	CQua
	cantabricus (13)	ECho
	- subsp. ***cantabricus*** (13)	CFil NMin
	- - var. ***foliosus*** (13) ♀H2	CFil ECho EPot GKev WAbe
§	- subsp. ***tananicus*** (13)	ECho
	'Cantatrice' (1)	CQua
	'Canterbury' (5)	CQua
	'Canticle' (9)	IRhd
	'Capax Plenus'	see *N.* 'Eystettensis'
	'Cape Cornwall' (2)	CQua
	'Cape Helles' (3)	IRhd
	'Cape Point' (2)	IRhd
	'Capisco' (3)	CQua
	'Carbineer' (2)	CQua GCro SDeJ
	'Cardiff' (2)	CFen CQua

'Cargreen' (9)	CQua
'Carib Gipsy' (2) ♀H4	CQua IRhd
'Caribbean Snow' (2)	CQua
'Carlton' (2) ♀H4	CFen CQua EPfP GKev SDeJ
'Carnearny' (3)	CQua
'Carnkeeran' (2)	CQua
'Carnkief' (2)	CQua
'Carnyorth' (11a)	CQua
'Carole Lombard' (3)	CQua
'Carolina Dale' (2)	IRhd
'Carwinion' (2)	CQua
'Casiah' (2)	CQua
'Cassata' (11a)	EPfP NBir SDeJ
'Castanets' (8)	IRhd
'Casterbridge' (2)	CQua IRhd
'Castle Rings' (4)	CQua
'Castlerock' (2)	CFen
'Catalyst' (2)	IRhd
'Cataract' (1) **new**	IRhd
'Catistock' (2)	CQua
'Causeway Gem' (6) **new**	IRhd
'Causeway Ringer' (3) **new**	IRhd
'Causeway Sunset' (2)	IRhd
'Causeway Sunshine' (1)	IRhd
'Cavalli King' (4)	CQua
'Cavalryman' (3)	IRhd
'Cawdron' (2)	CQua
'Caye Chapel' (3)	CQua
'Cazique' (6)	CQua
'Ceasefire' (2)	IRhd
'Cedar Hills' (3)	CQua
'Cedric Morris' (1)	CDes CLAP EWoo GBuc WCot
'Celestial Fire' (2)	CQua
'Celtic Gold' (2)	CQua
§ 'Celtic Wings' (5) **new**	IRhd
'Centrefold' (3)	CQua IRhd
'Cha-cha' (6)	CBro CQua
'Changing Colors' (11a)	CQua EPfP SDeJ
'Chanson' (1) ♀H4	CQua IRhd
'Chanterelle' (11a)	SDeJ
'Chantilly' (2)	CQua
'Charity May' (6) ♀H4	CQua
'Charlbury' (2) **new**	IRhd
'Charleston' (2)	CQua
'Charlie Connor' (1)	CQua
'Chasseur' (2)	IRhd
'Chaste' (1)	CQua IRhd
'Chat' (7)	CQua
'Chateau Impney' (2) **new**	IRhd
'Cheer Leader' (3)	CQua
'Cheerfulness' (4) ♀H4	CAvo CFen CQua LRHS MBri NPer SDeJ
'Cheesewring' (3)	CQua
'Cheetah' (1)	CQua IRhd
'Chelsea Girl' (2)	CQua IRhd
'Cheltenham' (2)	CQua
'Chérie' (7)	CQua
'Cherish' (2)	CQua
'Cherry Glow' (3)	IRhd
'Cherrygardens' (2)	CQua IRhd
'Chesapeake Bay' (1)	CQua
'Chesterton' (9) ♀H4	CQua
'Chickadee' (6)	CQua
'Chicken Hill' (1)	CQua
'Chickerell' (3)	CQua
'Chief Inspector' (1)	IRhd
'Chiffon' (2)	CFen
'Chiloquin' (1)	CQua
'China Doll' (2)	CQua
'China Gold' (10)	CQua
'Chinchilla' (2)	CQua IRhd
'Chingah' (1)	IRhd
'Chinita' (8)	CQua EPfP GCro
'Chipper' (5)	CQua NMin
'Chippewa' (3) **new**	IRhd
'Chit Chat' (7) ♀H2	CQua EPot NMin SDeJ
'Chiva' (7)	CBro ECho GKev LLHF NMin
'Chobe River' (1)	CQua IRhd
'Chortle' (3) **new**	IRhd
'Chukar' (4) ♀H4	IRhd
'Churchfield Bells' (5)	CQua
'Churston Ferrers' (4)	CQua
'Chy Noweth' (2)	CQua
'Cinco de Mayo' (2)	CQua
'Cinder Hill' (2) **new**	IRhd
'Cisticola' (3)	IRhd
citrinus	see *N. bulbocodium* subsp. *bulbocodium* var. *citrinus*
'Citron' (3)	CQua
'Citronita' (3)	CQua
'Clare' (7)	CBro CQua NMin
'Classic Gold' (10) ♀H4	CQua
'Claverley' (2)	CQua
'Clearbrook' (2)	CQua
'Cloud Nine' (2)	CBro
'Clouded Yellow' (2)	CQua IRhd
'Clouds Hill' (4)	CQua
'Clouds Rest' (2)	IRhd
'Clovelly Ayr' (9)	CQua
'Codlins and Cream'	see *N.* 'Sulphur Phoenix'
'Coker's Frome' (9)	CQua
'Coldbrook' (2)	CQua
'Colin's Joy' (2)	CQua
'Coliseum' (2)	IRhd
'Colleen Bawn' (1)	CQua NMin
'Colley Gate' (3)	CQua
'Colliford' (2)	CQua
'Colorama' (11a)	CQua
'Colorful' (2) **new**	IRhd
'Columbus' (2)	CQua
'Colville' (9)	CQua
'Comal' (1)	CQua
'Compressus'	see *N.* × *intermedius* 'Compressus'
'Compton Court' (3)	IRhd
'Conestoga' (2)	CQua IRhd
'Congress' (11a)	CQua
'Conly' (3)	CQua IRhd
'Conowingo' (11a)	CQua
'Conspicuus' (3)	CAvo
'Contralto' (2) **new**	IRhd
'Cool Autumn' (2)	CQua
'Cool Crystal' (3)	CQua
'Cool Evening' (11a)	CQua IRhd
'Cool Pink' (2)	CQua
'Cool Shades' (2)	CQua
'Coolmaghery' (2)	IRhd
'Coombe Creek' (6)	CQua
'Copper Nob' (2)	IRhd
'Copper Rings' (3)	CQua
'Copperfield' (2)	CQua
'Cora Ann' (7)	CBro
'Coral Fair' (2)	CQua
'Corbiere' (1)	CQua IRhd
'Corbridge' (2)	CQua
'Corky's Song' (2)	CQua
'Cornet' (6)	CQua
'Cornish Chuckles' (12) ♀H4	CBro CFen CQua NMin

'Cornish Pride' (2) **new**	CFen
'Cornish Sun' (2)	CQua
'Cornish Vanguard' (2) ♀H4	CFen CQua
'Corroboree' (2)	IRhd
'Corofin' (3)	CQua
'Coromandel' (2)	IRhd
'Corozal' (3)	CQua
'Cosine' (11a) **new**	IRhd
'Cosmic Dance' (2)	IRhd
'Cotinga' (6)	CQua NMin SDeJ
'Countdown' (2)	CQua
'Court Martial' (2)	CFen
'Coverack Glory' (2)	CQua
'Crackington' (4) ♀H4	CQua IRhd
'Cragford' (8)	MBri SDeJ
'Craig Stiel' (2)	CQua
'Creag Dubh' (2)	CQua
'Creed' (6)	CQua
'Crenver' (3)	CQua GCro
'Crevenagh' (2)	IRhd
'Crewenna' (1)	CAvo CQua
'Crill' (7)	CQua
'Crimson Chalice' (3)	CQua IRhd
'Cristobal' (1)	CQua
'Crock of Gold' (1)	CFen
'Croesus' (2)	CQua GCro
'Crofty' (6)	CQua
'Croila' (2)	CQua
'Crown of Gold' (2) **new**	IRhd
'Crowndale' (4)	CQua IRhd
'Crugmeer' (11a)	CQua
'Cryptic' (1)	CQua IRhd
'Crystal Star' (2)	CQua
'Cudden Point' (2)	CQua
'Cul Beag' (3)	CQua
'Culmination' (2)	CQua
'Cultured Pearl' (2)	CQua IRhd
'Cum Laude' (11a)	ERCP SDeJ
'Curlew' (7) ♀H4	CQua GKev SDeJ
'Curly' (2)	SDeJ
'Curlylocks' (7)	NMin
cyclamineus (13) ♀H4	CBro CDes CExl CFil CRDP GKev LLHF LRHS SKHP SRms
'Cyclope' (1)	CQua
'Cynosure' (2) **new**	GCro
cypri (13)	CQua
'Cyros' (1)	CQua
'Dailmanach' (2)	CQua IRhd
'Dailmystic' (2)	IRhd
'Dallas' (3)	CFen CQua
'Dalmeny' (2)	CQua
'Dambuster' (4)	IRhd
'Damson' (2)	CQua GCro
'Dan du Plessis' (8)	CFen CQua
'Dancing Queen' (2)	IRhd
'Dardanelles' (2)	IRhd
'Darlow Dale' (2)	IRhd
'Dateline' (3)	CQua IRhd
'David Alexander' (1)	CQua
'David Mills' (2)	CQua
'Dawn Brooker' (2)	CQua
'Dawn Call' (2)	IRhd
'Dawn Run' (2)	CQua IRhd
'Dawn Sky' (2)	CQua
'Daydream' (2) ♀H3	CQua
'Daymark' (8)	CQua
'Daymer Bay' (1) **new**	CFen
'Dayton Lake' (2)	CQua
'Dear Love' (11a) **new**	IRhd

'Debutante' (2)	CQua
'December Bride' (11a)	CQua
'Decision' (2)	IRhd
'Defence Corps' (1)	IRhd
'Del Rey' (1)	CQua
'Delia' (6)	IRhd
'Dell Chapel' (3)	CQua
'Delnashaugh' (4)	CQua ERCP NHol SDeJ
'Delos' (3)	CQua
'Delta Flight' (6)	IRhd
'Demand' (2)	CQua
'Demeanour' (3)	IRhd
'Demmo' (2)	CQua IRhd
'Dena' (3)	IRhd
'Denali' (1)	IRhd
'Descant' (1)	IRhd
'Desdemona' (2) ♀H4	CQua SDeJ
'Desert Bells' (7)	CQua NMin
'Desert Orchid' (2)	CQua
'Dewy Dell' (3)	IRhd
'Diamond Ring'	see *N. bulbocodium* subsp. *obesus* 'Diamond Ring'
'Dick Wilden' (4)	CQua
'Dickcissel' (7) ♀H4	CQua ERCP
'Dignitary' (2)	IRhd
'Dimity' (3)	CQua
'Dimple' (9)	CQua IRhd
'Dinkie' (3)	CBro
'Dispatch Box' (1) ♀H4	IRhd
'Disquiet' (1)	CQua IRhd
'Diversity' (11a)	IRhd
'Doctor Hugh' (3) ♀H4	CQua IRhd
'Doctor Jazz' (2)	CQua IRhd
'Doll Baby' (7)	NMin
'Doombar' (1)	CQua
'Dorchester' (4)	CQua IRhd
'Dorneywood' (1)	IRhd
'Double Campernelle' (4)	CAby CQua ECho MBri SDeJ WShi
'Double Itzim' (4)	NMin
double pheasant eye	see *N. poeticus* 'Plenus' ambig.
double Roman	see *N.* 'Romanus'
'Double White' (4)	CQua
'Doubleday' (4)	IRhd
'Doublet' (4)	CQua
'Doubtful' (3)	CQua
'Dove Song' (2) **new**	IRhd
'Dover Cliffs' (2)	CQua
'Downfield' (4) **new**	IRhd
'Downlands' (3)	CQua
'Downpatrick' (1)	CQua
'Dragon Run' (2)	CQua
'Drama Queen' (11a)	IRhd
'Dream Catcher' (2)	IRhd
'Dreamlight' (3)	CQua
'Drumboe' (2)	CQua
dubius (13)	ECho EPot
'Duchess of Westminster' (2)	GCro
'Duiker' (6)	IRhd
'Duke of Windsor' (2)	CFen
'Dulcimer' (9)	CQua
'Dunadry Inn' (4)	IRhd
'Dunkeld' (2)	CQua
'Dunkery' (4)	CQua IRhd
'Dunley Hall' (3)	CQua IRhd
'Dunmurry' (1)	CQua
'Dunskey' (3)	CQua
'Dupli Kate' (4)	IRhd
'Dusky Lad' (2)	IRhd
'Dusky Maiden' (2)	IRhd

	'Dutch Delight' (2)	IRhd
	'Dutch Lemon Drops' (5) ♀H4	CMea CQua EPot NMin
	'Dutch Master' (1) ♀H4	CFen CQua EPfP LRHS SDeJ SPer
	'Early Bride' (2)	CFen CQua
	'Early Splendour' (8)	CQua
	'Earthlight' (3)	CQua
	'Easter Bonnet' (2)	EPfP
	'Easter Moon' (2)	CQua
	'Eastern Dawn' (2)	CFen CQua SDeJ
	'Eastern Promise' (2)	CQua IRhd
	'Eaton Song' (12) ♀H4	CBro CQua NMin
	'Ebony' (1)	CQua
	'Eddy Canzony' (2)	CFen CQua
	'Eden Gold' (2) **new**	CFen
	'Edenderry' (1)	IRhd
	'Edgbaston' (2)	CQua
	'Edge Grove' (2)	CQua
	'Edgedin Gold' (7) **new**	NMin
	'Editor' (2) **new**	IRhd
	'Edward Buxton' (3)	CFen CQua GCro
	'Egard' (11a)	CQua
	'Egmont King' (2)	CQua
	'Eland' (7)	CQua
	'Elburton' (2)	CQua
	'Electrus' (11a)	IRhd
	'Elegance' (2) **new**	CAvo
	elegans (13)	ECho EPot
	'Elegans' Leeds (3)	GCro
	'Elegant Queen' (2) **new**	IRhd
	'Elf' (2)	CQua
	'Elfin Gold' (6)	CQua
	'Elizabeth Ann' (6)	CQua IRhd
	'Elka' (1) ♀H4	CAvo CBro CQua LLHF NMin
	'Elmbridge' (1) **new**	IRhd
	'Elphin' (4)	CQua
	'Elrond' (2)	CQua
	'Elven Lady' (2)	CQua
	'Elvira' (8)	CQua WShi
	'Emcys' (6)	LLHF NMin
	'Emerald City' (3) **new**	IRhd
	'Emerald Pink' (3)	CQua
	'Emily' (2)	NMin
	'Eminent' (3)	CQua
	'Emperor' (1)	CQua GCro
	'Empire' (2)	GCro
	'Empress of Ireland' (1) ♀H4	CQua IRhd
	'English Caye' (1)	CQua IRhd
	'Ensemble' (4)	CQua
	'Epona' (3)	CQua
	'Erin' (3)	CQua
	'Erlicheer' (4)	CQua SDeJ
	'Escapee' (2)	IRhd
	'Estrella' (3)	CQua
	'Ethereal Beauty' (2)	IRhd
	'Ethos' (1)	IRhd
§	***eugeniae*** (13)	CFil WCot
	'Euryalus' (1)	CQua
	'Evangeline' (3)	GCro
	'Eve Robertson' (2)	CQua
	'Evelyn Roberts' (11a)	CQua
	'Evening' (2)	CQua
	'Evesham' (3)	CQua IRhd
	'Eyeglass' (3)	CQua IRhd
	'Eyelet' (3)	CQua IRhd
	'Eype' (4)	IRhd
	'Eyrie' (3)	CQua IRhd
§	'Eystettensis' (4)	CBro CQua CRDP IBlr

	'Fair Head' (9)	CQua
	'Fair Prospect' (2)	CQua
	'Fair William' (2)	CQua
	'Fairgreen' (3)	CFen CQua
	'Fairlawns' (3)	CQua
	'Fairmile' (3)	CQua
	'Fairy Chimes' (5)	CQua
	'Fairy Footsteps' (3)	CQua
	'Fairy Island' (3)	CQua
	'Fairy Magic' (2)	IRhd
	'Fairy Tale' (3)	CQua
I	'Faith' (1)	SDeJ
	'Falconet' (8) ♀H4	CQua EPfP SPer
	'Falmouth Bay' (3)	CQua
	'Falstaff' (2)	CQua
	'Fanline' (11a)	CQua
	'Far Country' (2)	CQua
	'Farro' (1)	IRhd
I	'Fashion' (11b)	CQua
	'Fashion Model' (2)	IRhd
	'Fastidious' (2)	CQua
	'February Gold' (6) ♀H4	CAvo CBro CQua CTri EPfP EPot ERCP GKev LPio LRHS MBri NBir SDeJ SEND SPer SRms WShi
	'February Silver' (1)	CBro EPot ERCP SDeJ
	'Feeling Lucky' (2) ♀H4	CQua
	'Felindre' (9)	CFen CQua EPot
	'Feline Queen' (1)	IRhd
	'Feock' (3)	CQua
	'Ferial Wendy' (2) **new**	CFen
	fernandesii (13)	ECho NMin WAbe WCot WThu
	- var. ***cordubensis*** (13)	CFil ECho
	- var. ***cordubensis*** × ***jonquilla*** (13)	NMin
	'Ferndown' (3)	CQua IRhd
	'Ferral' (4)	IRhd
	'Fertile Crescent' (7)	CQua
	'Ffitch's Ffolly' (2)	CQua
	'Fiery Maiden' (2) **new**	CFen
	'Filoli' (1)	CQua
	'Finchcocks' (2)	CQua
	'Fine Gold' (1)	CQua
	'Fine Romance' (2)	CQua IRhd
	'Finland' (2)	CFen CQua
	'Fiona Linford' (3)	IRhd
	'Fiona MacKillop' (2)	IRhd
	'Firebrand' (3)	CQua
	'Firefighter' (3) **new**	IRhd
	'Firehills' (2) **new**	IRhd
	'Firetail' (3)	WShi
	'First Born' (6)	CQua NMin
	'First Formal' (3)	CQua
	'First Hope' (6)	CFen CQua
	'Flambards Village' (4)	CQua
	'Fletching' (1) **new**	IRhd
	'Flirt' (6)	CQua
	'Flomay' (7)	NMin
	'Florida Manor' (3)	IRhd
	'Flusher' (2)	CQua
	'Flycatcher' (7)	CQua
	'Flying Colours' (4)	IRhd
	'Flying High' (3)	CQua
	'Foff's Way' (1)	CQua
	'Foresight' (1)	CQua
	'Forge Mill' (2)	CQua
	'Forged Gold' (2) **new**	IRhd
	'Fort Mitchell' (1)	CQua
	'Fortescue' (4)	IRhd
	'Fortissimo' (2)	SDeJ SPer

'Fortune' (2)	CQua GCro LPio MBri SDeJ
'Fossie' (4)	CQua
'Foundling' (6) ♀H4	CQua
'Fowey' (3) **new**	CFen
'Foxfire' (2)	CQua
'Foxhunter' (2)	CQua
'Fragrant Breeze' (2)	SDeJ
'Fragrant Rose' (2)	CQua EPfP ERCP IRhd
'Frances Delight' (11a)	CQua
'Francolin' (1)	IRhd
'Frank' (9)	IRhd
'Frank Miles' (2)	GCro
'Freedom Rings' (2)	CQua
'Freedom Stars' (11a) ♀H4	IRhd
'Fresco' (11a)	IRhd
'Fresh Field' (2)	CQua
'Fresh Lime' (1)	CQua
'Fresno' (3)	IRhd
'Frigid' (3)	CQua
'Front Royal' (2)	CQua
'Frosted Pink' (2)	IRhd
'Frostkist' (6)	CBro CQua
'Frosty Morn' (5)	NMin
'Frozen Jade' (1)	CQua IRhd
'Fruit Cup' (7)	CQua SDeJ
'Fuco' (1)	CQua NMin
'Full House' (4)	SDeJ
'Fulwell' (4)	CQua
'Furbelow' (4)	CQua
'Furnace Creek' (2)	IRhd
'Fynbos' (3)	IRhd
'Gabriella Rose' (4)	CQua
gaditanus (13)	CBro
gaditanus* × *rupicola subsp. ***watieri*** **new**	ECho
'Gamebird' (1)	IRhd
'Ganilly' (2) **new**	CFen
'Garden News' (3)	IRhd
'Garden Opera' (7) ♀H4	CFen CQua
'Garden Treasure' (2)	IRhd
'Gatecrasher' (1)	IRhd
'Gay Cavalier' (4)	CQua
'Gay Kybo' (4) ♀H4	CQua
'Gay Song' (4)	CQua
'Gay Time' (4)	CFen SDeJ
gayi (13)	CQua WShi
'Geevor' (4)	CQua
'Gellymill' (2)	CQua
'Gemini Girl' (2)	CQua
'Gentle Giant' (2) **new**	SDeJ
'Geometrics' (2) **new**	IRhd
'George Leak' (2)	CFen CQua
'Georgia Moon'	CFen
'Georgie Girl' (6)	IRhd
'Geranium' (8) ♀H4	CBro CFen CQua EPfP ERCP SDeJ SPer WShi
'Gerry Smith' (2)	CQua
'Gettysburg' (2)	CQua
'Gigantic Star' (2)	CQua
'Gillan' (11a)	CQua
'Gin and Lime' (1) ♀H4	CQua
'Gipsy Moon' (2)	CQua
'Gipsy Queen' (1)	CBro CQua EPot LLHF NMin
'Gironde' (11)	CQua
'Glacier' (1)	CQua
'Glasnevin' (2)	CQua IRhd
'Glen Clova' (2)	CQua
'Glen Lake' (2) **new**	IRhd
'Glendermott' (2)	CQua

'Glenside' (2)	CQua
'Glissando' (2)	CQua IRhd
'Gloriosus' (8)	CQua
'Glover's Reef' (1)	CQua
'Glowing Phoenix' (4)	CQua
'Glowing Red' (4)	CQua
'Goff's Caye' (2)	CQua IRhd
'Golant' (2)	CQua
'Gold Bond' (2)	CQua IRhd
'Gold Cache' (11a)	CQua
'Gold Charm' (2)	CQua
'Gold Convention' (2) ♀H4	CQua IRhd
'Gold Ingot' (2) ♀H4	IRhd
'Gold Medallion' (1)	CQua
'Gold Top' (2)	CQua
'Golden Amber' (2)	CQua
'Golden Anniversary'	CFen
'Golden Aura' (2) ♀H4	CQua
'Golden Bear' (4)	CQua
'Golden Bells'	see *N. bulbocodium* Golden Bells Group
'Golden Cheer' (2)	CFen CQua
'Golden Dawn' (8) ♀H3	CFen CQua EPfP
'Golden Ducat' (4)	CFen CQua LPio MBri NBir SDeJ
'Golden Echo' (7) **new**	EPfP
'Golden Flute' (2)	IRhd
'Golden Gamble' (11a)	IRhd
'Golden Halo' (2)	CQua
'Golden Harvest' (1)	CQua NPer
'Golden Incense' (7)	CQua
'Golden Jewel' (2) ♀H4	CQua
'Golden Joy' (2)	CQua
'Golden Lion' (1)	CFen CQua EPfP
'Golden Marvel' (1)	CQua
§ 'Golden Mary' Leeds (3) **new**	GCro
'Golden Orbit' (4)	CQua
'Golden Peak' (1) **new**	IRhd
'Golden Phoenix' (4)	CQua
'Golden Rain' (4)	CQua
'Golden Rapture' (1) ♀H4	CQua
'Golden Sceptre' (7)	GCro
'Golden Sheen' (2)	CQua
'Golden Splash' (11a)	IRhd
'Golden Spur' (1)	CQua
'Golden Torch' (2)	CQua
'Golden Twins' (7)	CQua
'Golden Vale' (1) ♀H4	CQua
'Goldfinger' (1) ♀H4	CQua IRhd
'Goldhanger' (2)	CQua IRhd
'Golitha Falls' (2)	CQua
'Good Fella' (2)	CQua
'Good Measure' (2)	CQua
'Goonbell' (2)	CQua
'Goose Green' (3)	GKev
'Gorran' (3)	CQua
'Gossmoor' (4)	CQua
'Grace Note' (3)	CQua
'Graduation' (2)	IRhd
'Grand Monarque'	see *N. tazetta* subsp. *lacticolor* 'Grand Monarque'
'Grand Opening' (4)	IRhd
'Grand Primo Citronière' (8)	CQua
'Grand Prospect' (2)	CQua
'Grand Soleil d'Or' (8)	CQua SDeJ
'Great Expectations' (2)	CQua
'Great Warley' (2)	GCro
'Greatwood' (1)	CQua
'Greek Surprise' (4)	IRhd
'Green Chartreuse' (2)	CQua

'Green Island' (2)	CFen SDeJ
'Green Lawns' (9)	CQua
'Green Lodge' (9)	IRhd
'Green Pearl' (3)	NMin
'Greenodd' (3)	CQua
'Greenpark' (9)	IRhd
'Grenoble' (2)	CQua
'Gresham' (4)	CQua
'Gribben Head' (4)	CQua
'Groundkeeper' (3)	IRhd
'Guiding Spirit' (4)	CQua
'Gull' (2)	CQua
'Gulliver' (3)	CQua GCro
'Gunwalloe' (11a)	CQua
'Guy Wilson' (2)	CQua
'Gwennap' (1)	CQua
'Gwinear' (2)	CQua
'Habit' (1) **new**	IRhd
'Hacienda' (1)	CQua
'Half Moon Caye' (2)	CQua
'Halley's Comet' (3)	CQua IRhd
'Halloon' (3)	CQua
'Halzephron' (2)	CQua
'Hambledon' (2) ♀H4	CQua
'Hampton Court' (2)	CQua IRhd
'Hanley Swan' (1) **new**	IRhd
'Happy Dreams' (2)	IRhd
'Happy Fellow' (2)	CQua
'Happy Valley' (2)	IRhd
'Harbour View' (2)	IRhd
'Harmony Bells' (5)	CQua NMin
'Harp Music' (2)	IRhd
'Harpers Ferry' (1)	CQua
'Hartlebury' (3)	CQua
'Havelock' (2)	GCro
'Hawangi' (3)	IRhd
'Hawera' (5) ♀H4	CAvo CBro CFen CQua CTca CTri EPfP EPot ERCP GKev MBri SDeJ SPer WShi
'Heamoor' (4) ♀H4	CQua
hedraeanthus (13)	ECho
'Helford Dawn' (2)	CQua
'Helford Sunset' (2)	CQua
'Helios' (2)	CQua GCro
hellenicus	see *N. poeticus* var. *hellenicus*
henriquesii	see *N. jonquilla* var. *henriquesii*
'Henry Irving' (1)	CQua GCro
'Hero' (1)	CQua
'Heslington' (3)	CQua
'Hexameter' (9)	CQua
'Hexworthy' (3)	CQua
'Hibernian' (4)	IRhd
'Hicks Mill' (1)	CQua
'High Life' (2)	CFen
'High Society' (2) ♀H4	CQua SDeJ
'Highfield Beauty' (8) ♀H4	CQua
'Highgrove' (1)	CQua
'Highlite' (2)	CQua
'Hihitahi' (2)	CQua
'Hilda's Pink' (2)	CQua
'Hill Head' (9)	IRhd
'Hillstar' (7) ♀H4	CQua NHol NMin SDeJ
hispanicus (13)	ECho
'Hocus Pocus' (3)	IRhd
'Holland's Glory' (4)	GCro
'Holly Berry' (2)	CFen
'Hollypark' (3)	IRhd
'Hollywood' (2) **new**	CFen
'Holme Fen' (2)	CQua IRhd

'Home Fires' (2)	CFen CQua
'Homestead' (2) ♀H4	IRhd
'Honey Pink' (2)	CQua
'Honeybird' (1)	CQua
'Honeyorange' (2)	IRhd
'Hoopoe' (8) ♀H4	CQua GKev
'Hope House' (2) **new**	IRhd
'Horace' (9)	CQua
'Horn of Plenty' (5)	CQua
'Hornpipe' (1)	IRhd
'Hors d'Oeuvre' (1)	CBro
'Hospodar' (2)	CQua GCro
'Hot Affair' (2)	IRhd
'Hot Gossip' (2)	CFen CQua
'Hotspur' (2)	CQua
Howick Beauty (2)	GCro
'Hugh Town' (8)	CAvo CQua
'Hugus' (7)	CQua
'Hullabaloo' (2)	IRhd
humilis misapplied	see *N. pseudonarcissus* subsp. *pseudonarcissus* var. *humilis*
'Hummingbird' (6)	EPot NMin
'Hunting Caye' (2)	CQua
'Huntley Down' (1)	CQua
'Hyperbole' (2) **new**	IRhd
'Ice Chimes' (5)	CQua
'Ice Dancer' (2)	CQua IRhd
'Ice Diamond' (4)	CQua
'Ice Emerald' (3) **new**	IRhd
'Ice Follies' (2) ♀H4	CFen CQua EPfP GKev LPio MBri NBir SDeJ SPer
'Ice King' (4)	LRHS NBir SDeJ
'Ice Wings' (5) ♀H4	CAvo CBro CFen CQua EPot NMin SDeJ WShi
'Idless' (1)	CQua
'Idol' (7)	CQua ECho EPot NMin
'Immaculate' (2)	CQua
'Impeccable' (2) **new**	IRhd
'Inara' (4)	CQua
'Inca' (6)	CQua
'Inchbonnie' (2)	CQua
× ***incomparabilis*** (13)	SEND
'Independence Day' (4)	CQua
'Indian Maid' (7) ♀H4	CQua IRhd
'Indian Ruler' (2) **new**	CFen
'Indora' (4)	CQua
'Inner Glow' (2)	IRhd
'Innisidgen' (8)	CQua
'Innovator' (4)	CQua IRhd
'Innuendo' (2)	IRhd
'Inny River' (1)	IRhd
'Interim' (2)	CFen CQua SDeJ
× ***intermedius*** (13)	CBro CQua NMin WAbe
§ - 'Compressus' (8)	CBro CQua
'Intrigue' (7) ♀H4	CQua
'Invercassley' (3)	CQua
'Inverpolly' (2)	CQua
'Irene Copeland' (4)	CQua
'Irish Fire' (2)	CQua
'Irish Light' (2)	CQua
'Irish Luck' (1)	CQua
'Irish Minstrel' (2) ♀H4	CFen CQua
'Irish Mist' (2)	CQua
'Irish Rum' (2)	CQua
'Irish Trip' (7) **new**	IRhd
'Irish Wedding' (2)	CQua
'Isambard' (4)	CQua
'Island Pride' (8)	CQua

'Islander' (4)	CQua
'Ita' (2)	IRhd
'Itsy Bitsy Splitsy' (11a) **new**	IRhd
'Itzim' (6) $\mathbb{Y}^{H4}$	CBro CQua SDeJ
jacetanus (13)	NMin
'Jack Snipe' (6) $\mathbb{Y}^{H4}$	CAvo CBro CQua ECho EPfP EPot ERCP GKev MBri NHol SDeJ SEND WShi
'Jack Wood' (11a)	CQua IRhd
'Jackadee' (2)	CQua IRhd
'Jacob Maurer' (6)	CQua
'Jake' (3)	IRhd
'Jamage' (8)	CQua
'Jamaica Inn' (4)	CQua
'Jamboree' (2)	CQua
'Jammin' (3)	IRhd
'Janelle' (3)	CQua
'Janet's Gold' (2)	IRhd
'Jantje' (11a)	CQua
'Jauno' (1)	IRhd
'Javelin' (2)	CQua
'Jeanine' (2)	CQua
'Jenny' (6) $\mathbb{Y}^{H4}$	CBro CQua ERCP GKev MBri MCot NBir SDeJ SPhx WShi
'Jenny Out' (7) $\mathbb{Y}^{H4}$ **new**	CFen
'Jersey Lace' (2)	CQua
'Jersey Roundabout' (4)	CQua
'Jersey Star' (4)	CQua
'Jersey Torch' (4)	CQua
'Jetfire' (6) $\mathbb{Y}^{H4}$	CQua ECho EPfP EPot ERCP GKev LPot LRHS LSou MBri NHol SDeJ SPer WShi
'Jim Lad' (2) **new**	NMin
'Jimmy Noone' (1)	CQua
'Jodi' (11b)	IRhd
'Jodi's Sister' (11a)	IRhd
'Johanna' (5)	CBro
'John Daniel' (4)	CQua
'John Dickens' (2)	CQua
'John Evelyn' (2)	GCro
'John Lanyon' (3)	CQua
'John Philip Sousa' (2)	CQua
'Johnny Dodds' (1)	CQua
'John's Delight' (3)	CQua
'Joke Fulmer' (2)	CFen
'Jolly Good' (2) **new**	IRhd
jonquilla (13) $\mathbb{Y}^{H4}$	CBro CQua ECho EPot GKev NMin WShi
- 'Flore Pleno' (4) **new**	ECho
§ - var. ***henriquesii*** (13)	CFil CQua ECho GKev NMin
'Joppa' (7)	CQua
'Joybell' (6)	CQua
'Juanita' (2)	CFen NPer SDeJ
'Jules Verne' (2)	CQua
'Julia Jane'	see *N. romieuxii* 'Julia Jane'
'Juliet Firstbrook' (2)	CQua
'Jumblie' (12) $\mathbb{Y}^{H4}$	CBro EPfP EPot LRHS MBri SDeJ
'Jumbo Gold' (1)	CTri
juncifolius Req. ex Lag.	see *N. assoanus*
'June Allyson' (2)	CFen
'June Lake' (2)	CQua IRhd
'Junior Miss' (12)	NMin
'Kabani' (9)	CQua
'Kaka Point' (2)	IRhd
'Kalimna' (1)	CQua
'Kamau' (9)	IRhd
'Kamms' (1)	CQua
'Kamura' (2)	CQua
'Kate' (1) **new**	IRhd
'Kate Davies' (2)	CQua
'Katherine Jenkins' (7)	CQua
'Kathy A' (5)	IRhd
'Kathy's Clown' (6)	CQua
'Katie Heath' (5)	EPfP ERCP MBri SDeJ
'Katrina Rea' (6)	CQua
'Kaydee' (6) $\mathbb{Y}^{H4}$	CQua IRhd SDeJ
'Kea' (6)	CQua
'Keats' (4)	CQua NMin
'Kebaya' (2)	CQua
'Kedron' (7)	ERCP
'Kelly Bray' (1)	CQua
'Kenellis' (10)	EPot
'Kernow' (2)	CQua
'Kidling' (7)	CQua EPot NMin
'Killara' (8)	CQua
'Killearnan' (9)	CQua
'Killigrew' (2)	CQua
'Killivose' (3)	CQua
'Kilmood' (2)	CQua
'Kiltonga' (2)	IRhd
'Kilworth' (2)	CQua
'Kimmeridge' (3)	CQua
'King Alfred' (1)	CQua EPfP SDeJ SEND SPer
'King Size' (11a)	CQua
'Kinglet' (7)	CQua
'King's Grove' (1) $\mathbb{Y}^{H4}$	CQua
'Kings Pipe' (2)	CQua
'Kingscourt' (1) $\mathbb{Y}^{H4}$	CFen CQua
'Kingsleigh' (1)	IRhd
'Kingsmill Lake' (2)	CQua
'Kirklington' (2)	CQua
'Kit Hill' (7)	CQua
'Kitten' (6)	CQua
'Kiwi Magic' (4)	CQua IRhd
'Kiwi Sunset' (4)	CQua IRhd
'Knight of Saint John' (2)	CFen
'Knightsbridge' (1)	CQua
'Knowing Look' (3)	IRhd
'Kokopelli' (7) $\mathbb{Y}^{H4}$	CBro CQua NMin
'Koomooloo' (2)	CQua
'Korora Bay' (1)	IRhd
'La Belle' (7)	LLHF SDeJ
'La Vella' (2)	CQua
'Ladies' Choice' (7)	IRhd
'Lady Alice' (7)	CQua
'Lady Ann' (2)	IRhd
'Lady Be Good' (2)	CQua IRlıd
'Lady Diana' (2)	CQua IRhd
'Lady Emily' (2)	CQua
'Lady Eve' (11a)	IRhd
'Lady Godiva' (3)	GCro
'Lady Hilaria' (2)	CQua
'Lady Margaret Boscawen' (2)	CQua GCro
'Lady Marina Cowdray' (1) **new**	CFen
'Lady Moore' (3)	GCro
'Lady Sainsbury' (2) **new**	CFen
'Lady Serena' (9)	CQua
'Lady's Favorite' (7)	IRhd
'Lake District' (2)	IRhd
'Lake Tahoe' (2)	IRhd
'Lalique' (3)	CQua
'Lamanva' (2)	CQua
'Lamlash' (2)	IRhd
'Lanarth' (7)	GCro
'Lancaster' (3)	CFen CQua
'Landewednack Lady' (4)	CQua

'Langarth' (11a)	CQua
'Lapwing' (5)	IRhd
'Larkelly' (6)	CQua
'Larkhill' (2)	CQua
'Larkwhistle' (6) $\mathbb{Y}^{H4}$	SDeJ
'Las Vegas' (1)	EPfP SDeJ
'Latchley' (2)	CQua
'Latchley Meadows' (2)	CQua
'Laurelbank' (2)	IRhd
'Lauren' (3)	IRhd
'Laurens Koster' (8)	CQua
'Lava Flow' (3)	IRhd
'Lavender Lass' (6)	CQua
'Lavender Mist' (2)	CQua
'Lazy River' (1)	CQua
'Lee Moor' (1)	CQua
'Lemma' (3) **new**	IRhd
'Lemon Beauty' (11b)	CQua SDeJ
'Lemon Drizzle' (2)	CQua
'Lemon Drops' (5)	ECho ERCP SDeJ SPhx
'Lemon Haze' (2)	CQua
'Lemon Silk' (6)	CBro CQua ECho
'Lemon Snow' (2)	IRhd
'Lemonade' (3)	CQua
'Lennymore' (2)	CQua IRhd
'Lewis George' (1)	CQua
'Libby' (2)	IRhd
'Liberty Bells' (5)	CQua ECho MBri
'Liebeslied' (3)	CQua
'Life' (7)	CQua
'Lifeline' (1)	IRhd
'Lighthouse' (3)	CQua
'Lighthouse Reef' (1)	CQua IRhd
'Lilac Charm' (6)	CQua IRhd
'Lilac Hue' (6)	CBro
'Lilac Mist' (2)	CQua IRhd
'Lilliput' ambig.	CQua
'Lilly-May Bostock' (6)	CQua
'Lima's Green Goddess' (8) **new**	IRhd
'Lima's Shooting Stars' (12) **new**	IRhd
'Limbo' (2)	CQua
'Limehurst' (2)	CQua
'Limequilla' (7)	CQua IRhd
'Limpopo' (3)	IRhd
'Lindsay Joy' (2)	CQua
'Lintie' (7)	CQua
'Lisburn' (3) **new**	IRhd
'Lisnamulligan' (3)	IRhd
'Little Alice' (4)	IRhd
'Little Beauty' (1) $\mathbb{Y}^{H4}$	CBro CMea CQua NMin
'Little Dancer' (1)	CBro CQua
'Little Dorr' (4)	IRhd
'Little Flik' (12)	ECho NMin
'Little Jewel' (3)	CQua
'Little Karoo' (3)	IRhd
'Little Meg' (7)	CQua
'Little Rosie' (2)	IRhd
'Little Rusky' (7)	CBro CQua NMin
'Little Sentry' (7)	CBro CQua NMin
'Little Soldier' (10)	CQua NMin
'Little Tyke' (2)	CQua
'Little Witch' (6)	CBro CQua EPfP GCro GKev SDeJ SPhx WShi
'Littlefield' (7)	CQua
'Livelands' (1)	CQua
'Liverpool Festival' (2)	CQua
lobularis misapplied	see *N. nanus*
§ ***lobularis*** (Haw.) Schult. & Schult. f.	CAby CAvo CBro CQua CTca CTri ECho EPot ERCP GKev LRHS MBri SDeJ SPer
'Lobularis'	see *N. lobularis* (Haw.) Schult. & Schult. f.
'Loch Alsh' (3)	CQua IRhd
'Loch Assynt' (3)	CQua
'Loch Brora' (2)	CQua
'Loch Coire' (3)	CQua
'Loch Fada' (2)	CQua
'Loch Hope' (2)	CQua
'Loch Leven' (2)	CQua
'Loch Loyal' (2)	CQua
'Loch Lundie' (2)	CQua
'Loch Maberry' (2)	CQua
'Loch Naver' (2)	CQua
'Loch Owskeich' (2) $\mathbb{Y}^{H4}$	CFen CQua
'Loch Stac' (2)	CQua
'Logan Rock' (7)	CQua
'Longitude' (1)	IRhd
'Lorikeet' (1)	CQua
'Lothario' (2)	EPfP MBri
'Lough Gowna' (1)	IRhd
'Louise de Coligny' (2)	ERCP
'Love Call' (11a)	CQua
'Loveday' (2) **new**	CFen
'Loveny' (2)	CQua
'Lowin' (1)	CFen
'Lubaantun' (1)	CQua
'Lucifer' (2)	CAvo CQua WShi
'Lucky Chance' (11a)	IRhd
'Lulworth' (2)	GCro
'Lundy Light' (2)	CQua
'Lutana' (2) **new**	IRhd
'Lyme Bay' (1) **new**	IRhd
'Lynher' (2)	CQua
'Lyrebird' (3)	CQua
'Lyric' (9)	CQua
'Lysander' (2)	CFen CQua
'Madam Speaker' (4)	CQua
'Madame Plemp' (1)	GCro
'Madison' (4)	CQua
'Magic Moment' (3)	CQua
'Magician' (2)	CQua
'Magna Carta' (2)	CQua IRhd
'Magnet' (1)	NPer
'Magnificence' (1)	CFen CQua
'Majestic Star' (1)	CQua
'Maker's Mark' (1)	CQua
'Mallee' (11a) $\mathbb{Y}^{H4}$	IRhd
'Malpas' (3)	CQua
'Malvern City' (1)	CFen CQua
'Mamma Mia' (4)	IRhd
'Manaccan' (1)	CQua
'Mangaweka' (6)	CQua
'Manly' (4) $\mathbb{Y}^{H4}$	CQua ERCP
'Mantle' (2)	CQua
'Marabou' (4)	CQua
'Margaret Herbert' (7)	CQua
'Maria Pia' (11a)	IRhd
'Marie Curie Diamond' (7) $\mathbb{Y}^{H4}$	CFen CQua
'Marie-José' (11b)	IRhd
'Marieke' (1)	SDeJ
'Marilyn Anne' (2)	CQua
'Marjorie Hine' (2)	CQua
'Marjorie Treveal' (4)	CQua
'Marlborough' (2)	CQua
'Marlborough Freya' (2)	CQua

'Marshfire' (2)	CQua
'Martha Washington' (8)	CQua
'Martinette' (8)	CFen CQua CTca SDeJ
'Martinsville' (8)	CQua
'Mary Copeland' (4)	CQua
'Mary Kate' (2)	CQua
'Mary Lou' (6)	IRhd
'Mary Plumstead' (5)	NMin
'Mary Rosina' (4)	CQua
'Mary Veronica' (3)	CQua
'Marzo' (7)	IRhd
'Masked Light' (2) **new**	CFen
'Matador' (8)	CFen CQua IRhd
'Mawla' (1)	CQua
'Max' (11a)	CQua
'Maximus Superbus' (1)	CQua
'Maya Dynasty' (2)	CQua
'Mayor's Choice' (11a)	CQua
'Maywood' (11a)	CQua
'Mazzard' (4)	CQua
'Media Girl' (2)	IRhd
× ***medioluteus*** (13)	CBro CQua NMin
'Medusa' (8)	GCro
'Melancholy' (1)	CQua
'Melbury' (2)	CQua
'Meldrum' (1)	CQua
'Melen' (2)	CFen
'Memento' (1)	CQua
'Menabilly' (4)	CQua
'Mên-an-Tol' (2)	CQua
'Menehay' (11a) 🏆^{H4}	CQua
'Mer d'Or' (1) **new**	IRhd
'Mereworth' (2)	CQua
'Merlin' (3) 🏆^{H4}	CFen CQua SDeJ
'Merry Bells' (5)	CQua
'Merrymeet' (4)	CQua
'Mersing' (3)	CQua
'Merthan' (9)	CQua
'Michaels Gold' (2)	CQua
'Midas Touch' (1)	CQua
'Midget'	see *N. nanus* 'Midget'
'Midnight' (3) **new**	IRhd
Midtown Aerolite (2)	GCro
Midtown Alfie (1)	GCro
Midtown Autocrat (2)	GCro
Midtown Brigadier (2)	GCro
Midtown Elegance	see *N.* 'Golden Mary'
Midtown Noble (1)	GCro
Midtown Torch (2)	GCro
'Mike Pollock' (8)	CFen CQua
'Milan' (9)	CQua
'Millennium Sunrise' (2)	CQua
'Millennium Sunset' (2)	CQua
'Milly's Magic' (2)	CQua
Minicycla Group (6)	ECho
minimus misapplied	see *N. asturiensis*
'Minnow' (8) 🏆^{H3}	CAvo CBro CFen CHid CMea CQua ECho EPfP EPot ERCP GKev LPot LRHS MBri NBir SDeJ SPer
minor (13) 🏆^{H4}	CBro CQua ECho EPot GKev NMin WCot WShi
- 'Douglasbank' (1)	NMin
- 'Little Gem' (1) 🏆^{H4}	CBro CQua CTri EPfP SPhx
- var. ***pumilus*** 'Plenus'	see *N.* 'Rip van Winkle'
- Ulster form (13)	IBlr
'Mint Julep' (3) 🏆^{H4}	SDeJ
'Minute Waltz' (6)	CQua
'Mirar' (2)	CQua
'Misquote' (1)	CQua
'Miss Klein' (7)	LLHF NMin
'Miss Muffit' (1)	CQua
'Miss Primm' (2)	IRhd
'Mission Bells' (5) 🏆^{H4}	CQua IRhd NMin
'Mission Impossible' (11a)	CQua
'Mist of Avalon' (4)	CQua
'Misty Glen' (2) 🏆^{H4}	CQua EPfP
'Mite' (6) 🏆^{H4}	CAvo CBro CQua EPot LLHF NMin
'Mithrel' (11a)	CQua
'Mitylene' (2)	GCro
'Mitzy' (6)	LLHF NMin
'Modern Art' (2)	CQua
'Modulation' (2)	EPfP
'Mondragon' (11a)	CQua
'Mongleath' (2)	CQua
'Monks Wood' (1)	CQua
'Monksilver' (3)	CQua
'Montclair' (2)	CQua
'Montego' (3)	CQua
'Monterrico' (4) **new**	CFen
'Montroig' (2)	IRhd
'Moon Dream' (1)	CQua
'Moon Ranger' (3)	CQua
'Moon Shadow' (3)	CQua IRhd
'Moon Valley' (2)	IRhd
'Moonstruck' (1)	CQua
'Morab' (1)	CQua
'Moralee' (4)	IRhd
'Morval' (2)	CQua
moschatus (13) 🏆^{H4}	CBro CQua ECho EPot NMin WShi
'Mount Fuji' (2)	CQua
'Mount Hood' (1) 🏆^{H4}	EPfP GKev LRHS NBir NHol SDeJ SEND SPer
'Movie Star' (2)	IRhd
'Mowser' (7)	CQua
'Mr Julian' (6)	CQua
'Mrs Langtry' (2)	WShi
'Mrs R.O. Backhouse' (2)	CQua WShi
'Mullion' (3)	CQua
'Mulroy Bay' (1)	CQua IRhd
'Murlough' (9)	CQua
'Muscadet' (2)	CFen CQua
'My Sunshine' (2)	CQua
'My Sweetheart' (3)	CQua
'My Word' (2)	CFen
'Mystic' (3)	CQua
'Nacre' (2) **new**	IRhd
'Naivasha' (2)	IRhd
'Namraj' (2)	CQua
'Nancegollan' (7)	CBro CQua
'Nangiles' (4)	CQua
'Nanpee' (7)	CQua
'Nanpusker' (2) **new**	CFen
'Nansidwell' (2)	CQua
'Nanstallon' (1)	CQua
§ ***nanus*** (13)	CWCL ECho GBuc
§ - 'Midget' (1)	CBro CQua ECho ERCP GKev SKHP
'Nare Celebration' **new**	CFen
'Narrative' (2)	IRhd
'Navarre' Buckland (2) **new**	CFil
'Nederburg' (1)	IRhd
Nelsonii Group late-flowering clone (2) **new**	GCro
'Neon Light' (2)	CQua
'Nessa' (7)	CQua
'Nether Barr' (2)	CQua
nevadensis (13)	SKHP
'New Hope' (3)	CQua

'New Life' (3)	CQua
'New Paris' (2)	CQua
'New Penny' (3)	CQua IRhd
'New World' (2)	CQua
'New-Baby' (7)	CQua EPfP NMin SDeJ
'Newcastle' (1)	CQua
'Newcomer' (3)	CQua
'Nicole' (2)	EPfP
'Night Music' (4)	CQua IRhd
'Nightcap' (1)	CQua
'Nirvana' (7)	CBro
'Niveth' (5)	CFen CQua
§ ***nobilis*** (13)	CQua EPot
- var. ***leonensis*** (13)	CFil
- var. ***nobilis*** (13)	NMin
'Nonchalant' (3)	CQua IRhd
'Norma Jean' (2)	CQua
'North Liberty' (2)	CQua
'North Rim' (2)	CQua
'Noss Mayo' (6)	CQua
'Notre Dame' (2) ♀H4	CQua IRhd
'Nuage' (2)	CFen
'Numen Rose' (2)	IRhd
Nylon Group (10)	CBro ECho EPot EPri
- yellow-flowered (10)	ECho
'Oakwood Sprite' (1)	NMin
'Obdam' (4)	SDeJ
'Obsession' (2)	CQua
obvallaris (13) ♀H4	CAvo CBro CFen CQua CTca ECho EPfP EPot ERCP GKev LRHS MBri NMin SDeJ SPer SPhx WHer WShi
'Ocarino' (4)	CFen CQua
'Ocean Blue' (2)	IRhd
'Odd Job' (12)	CQua
× ***odorus*** (13)	WShi
- 'Plenus' (d)	ERCP
'Oecumene' (11a)	CQua
'Ohau Lights' (1)	CQua
old pheasant's eye	see *N. poeticus* var. *recurvus*
'Ombersley' (1)	CQua
'Oops' (2) **new**	IRhd
'Orange Tint' (2)	CQua
'Orange Walk' (3)	CQua IRhd
'Orangery' (11a)	SDeJ
'Orbital Pink' (3)	IRhd
'Orchard Place' (3)	CQua
'Oregon Bells' (7)	CQua
'Oregon Pioneer' (2)	IRhd
'Orkney' (2)	CQua
'Ormeau' (2) ♀H4	CQua
'Ornatus Maximus' (9)	NMin
'Oryx' (7) ♀H4	CQua
'Osceola' (2)	CQua
'Osmington' (2)	CQua
'Ouma' (1)	CQua
'Outline' (2)	IRhd
'Ouzel' (6)	CQua
'Owyhee' (2)	CQua
'Oxford Gold' (10)	CQua
'Oykel' (3)	CQua
'Oz' (12)	LLHF
pachybolbus (13)	ECho NMin
'Pacific Coast' (8) ♀H4	CQua EPfP LLHF NMin
'Pacific Mist' (11a)	CQua
'Pacific Rim' (2)	CQua IRhd
'Painted Desert' (3)	CQua
'Palace Pink' (2)	IRhd
'Pale Sunlight' (2)	CQua
'Palmares' (11a)	CQua SDeJ
'Pamela Hubble' (2)	CQua
'Pamela Joan' (2)	CQua
'Pampaluna' (11a)	CQua IRhd
'Panache' (1)	CQua
panizzianus (13)	CFil CQua WPGP
'Panorama Pink' (3)	IRhd
'Paper White'	see *N. papyraceus*
'Paper White Grandiflorus' (8)	CQua EPfP MBri SDeJ SPer
'Papillon Blanc' (11b)	ERCP
'Papua' (4) ♀H4	CFen CQua
§ ***papyraceus*** (13)	CFil CQua NMin
'Paradigm' (4)	IRhd
'Paramour' (4)	IRhd
'Parcpat' (7)	CBro
'Parisienne' (11a)	SDeJ
'Park Springs' (3)	CQua
'Parkdene' (2)	CQua
'Partisan' (2) **new**	IRhd
'Party Time' (2)	IRhd
'Passionale' (2) ♀H4	CQua EPfP NBir
'Pastiche' (2)	CQua
'Pat Brown' (2)	CQua
'Patabundy' (2)	CQua
'Pathos' (3)	IRhd
'Patois' (9)	IRhd
'Patrick Hacket' (1) ♀H4	CQua
'Paula Cottell' (3)	NMin
'Pay Day' (1)	CQua
'Peach Prince' (4)	CQua
'Pearl Wedding' (3)	CQua
'Pearlshell' (11a)	CQua
'Peeping Tom' (6) ♀H4	CBro ECho ERCP GKev SDeJ SRms
'Peggy's Gift' (3)	IRhd
'Pelynt' (3)	CQua
'Pemboa' (1)	CQua
'Pencrebar' (4)	CAvo CQua EPot LRHS NHol NMin SDeJ WShi
'Pend Oreille' (3)	CQua
'Pengarth' (2)	CQua
'Penjerrick' (9)	CQua
'Penkivel' (2) ♀H4	CQua
'Pennance Mill' (2)	CQua
'Pennine Way' (1)	CQua
'Penny Perowne' (7)	CQua
'Pennyfield' (2)	CQua
'Penpol' (7)	CBro CFen CQua
'Penril' (6)	CQua
'Penstraze' (7)	CQua
'Pentewan' (2)	CQua GCro
'Pentille' (1)	CQua
'Pentire' (11a)	CQua
'Penvale' (7)	CQua
'Peppercorn' (6)	CQua
'Pequenita' (7)	NMin
'Percuil' (6)	CQua
'Perdredda' (3)	CQua
perez-chiscanoi (13)	CFil SKHP WPGP
'Perimeter' (3)	CQua
'Peripheral Pink' (2)	CQua
'Perky' 1964 (6)	NMin
'Perlax' (11a)	CQua
'Perpetuation' (7)	CQua
'Personable' (2)	CQua
'Petanca' (5)	IRhd
'Petit Four' (4)	SDeJ
'Petrel' (5)	CBro CQua EPot ERCP GKev NMin SDeJ SPhx WShi
'Phantom' (11a)	CQua

	'Phil's Gift' (1)	CQua
	'Phinda' (2)	IRhd
	'Phoenician' (2)	CQua
	'Picatou' (3)	IRhd
	'Picoblanco' (2)	CBro CQua NMin
	'Pigeon' (2)	CQua
	'Pineapple Prince' (2) ♀H4	CQua
	'Pink Angel' (7)	CQua
	'Pink Champagne' (4)	CQua
	'Pink Charm' (2)	CQua
	'Pink China' (2)	CQua
	'Pink Clover' (2)	CQua
	'Pink Evening' (2)	CQua
	'Pink Formal' (11a)	CQua
	'Pink Gilt' (2)	IRhd
	'Pink Glacier' (11a)	CQua
	'Pink Holly' (11a)	CQua
	'Pink Ice' (2)	CQua
	'Pink Pageant' (4)	CQua IRhd
	'Pink Paradise' (4)	CQua IRhd
	'Pink Parasol' (1)	SDeJ
	'Pink Perry' (2)	IRhd
	'Pink Silk' (1)	CQua
	'Pink Smiles' (2)	CFen
	'Pink Surprise' (2)	CQua
	'Pink Tango' (11a)	CQua
	'Pinza' (2) ♀H4	CQua SDeJ
	'Pipe Major' (2)	CQua EPfP
	'Pipers Barn' (7)	CQua
	'Piper's End' (3)	CQua
	'Piper's Gold' (1)	CQua
	'Pipestone' (2)	CQua
	'Pipit' (7) ♀H4	CAvo CBro CFen CQua ECho EPfP EPot ERCP GKev LPot LRHS MBri NBir NMin SDeJ WShi
	'Piraeus' (4)	IRhd
	'Pismo Beach' (2)	CQua
	'Pitchroy' (2)	CQua
	'Pixie's Sister' (7) ♀H4	CQua LLHF NMin
	'Pledge' (1)	NMin
	poeticus (13)	WHer
§	- var. ***hellenicus*** (13)	CBro CQua IRhd
	- old pheasant's eye	see *N. poeticus* var. *recurvus*
	- var. ***physaloides*** (13)	CFil CQua ECho
	- 'Plenus' misapplied	see *N.* 'Tamar Double White'
§	- 'Plenus' ambig. (4)	CBro CQua EPot ERCP GQui SDeJ WShi
§	- var. ***recurvus*** (13) ♀H4	CAvo CBro CFen CQua CTca ECho EPfP ERCP GKev LRHS MCot NBir SDeJ SEND SPhx WShi
	- white-flowered (13)	SDeJ
	'Poet's Way' (9)	CQua IRhd
	'Pol Crocan' (2)	CQua IRhd
	'Pol Dornie' (2)	CQua
	'Pol Voulin' (2)	CQua IRhd
	'Polar Ice' (3)	CFen CQua SDeJ SPhx
	'Polar Morn' (3)	CQua
	'Polgoon' (2) **new**	CFen
	'Polgooth' (2)	CQua
	'Polly's Pearl' (8)	CQua
	'Polonaise' (2)	CQua
	'Polwheveral' (2)	CQua
	'Pomona' (3)	GCro
	'Pooka' (3)	IRhd
	'Popeye' (4)	EPfP
	'Poppy's Choice' (4)	CQua
	'Pops Legacy' (1)	CQua
	'Port Noo' (3)	IRhd
	'Porthchapel' (7)	CQua

	'Portloe Bay' (3)	CQua
	'Portrait' (2)	CQua
	'Portrush' (3)	CQua
	'Post Horn' (6) **new**	CFen
	'Potential' (1)	CQua
	'Powerstock' (2)	IRhd
	'Praecox' (9)	CBro
	'Prairie Fire' (3)	CQua IRhd
	'Pratincole' (3)	IRhd
	'Preamble' (1)	CQua
I	'Precocious' (2) ♀H4	CQua SDeJ
	'Predator' (1) **new**	IRhd
	'Premiere' (2)	CQua IRhd
	'Presidential Pink' (2)	CQua
	'Pretty Baby' (3)	CQua
	'Pride of Cornwall' (8)	CQua
	'Primegold' (2) **new**	CFen
	'Primrose Beauty' (4)	CFen CQua
	'Princeps' (1)	CAvo CQua GCro
	'Princess Alexandra' (6)	CFen
	'Princess Diana' (6) **new**	CFen
	'Princess Zaide' (3)	CQua
	'Princeton' (3)	CQua
	'Printal' (11a)	SDeJ
	'Priorsford' (2) **new**	IRhd
	'Prism' (2)	CQua
	'Problem Child' (2)	IRhd
	'Probus' (1)	CQua
	'Professor Einstein' (2)	EPfP SDeJ
	'Prologue' (1)	CQua
	'Prototype' (6)	IRhd
	'Proud Fellow' (1)	IRhd
	'Proverbial Pink' (2)	IRhd
	'Prussia Cove' (2)	CQua
	pseudonarcissus (13) ♀H4	CHab CQua CRow LPot MMuc SEND SPhx WHer WShi
	- subsp. ***eugeniae***	see *N. eugeniae*
	- subsp. ***nobilis***	see *N. nobilis*
	- subsp. ***pseudonarcissus*** double-flowered (4)	CQua
§	- - var. ***humilis*** (13)	ECho
	'Ptolemy' (1)	CFen
	'Pueblo' (7)	CQua LPio SDeJ
	'Pukenui' (4)	CQua
	'Pulsar' (2)	IRhd
	pumilus ambig. (13)	CQua ECho LLHF NMin SDeJ
	'Punchline' (7) ♀H4	CQua
	'Punter' (2) **new**	IRhd
	'Puppet' (5)	CQua
	'Purbeck' (3) ♀H4	CQua IRhd
	'Quail' (7) ♀H4	CFen CQua CTca EPfP GKev LSou MBri
	'Quasar' (2) ♀H4	CQua
	Queen Anne's double daffodil	see *N.* 'Eystettensis'
	'Queen Fiona' (1) **new**	IRhd
	'Queen Juliana' (1)	CQua
	'Queen Mum' (1)	CQua
	'Queen of Spain' (10)	CAvo CQua NMin
	'Queen of the North' (3)	GCro
	'Queen's Guard' (1)	IRhd
	'Queensland' (2)	CFen
	'Quick Step' (7)	CQua
	'Quiet Day' (2)	CQua
	'Quiet Hero' (3)	IRhd
	'Quiet Man' (1)	IRhd
	'Radiant Gem' (8)	CQua
	radiiflorus (13)	EPot
	- var. ***poetarum*** (13)	CBro CQua GCro
	- var. ***radiiflorus*** (13)	GCro

	'Radjel' (4)	CQua
	'Rainbow' (2) ♀^{H4}	CQua SPer
	'Rame Head' (1)	CQua
	'Rameses' (2)	CQua
	'Ransom' (4)	IRhd
	'Raoul Wallenberg' (2)	EPfP
	'Rapid Stride' (6)	IRhd
	'Rapture' (6) ♀^{H4}	CBro CQua ERCP IRhd MBri NMin
	'Rashee' (1)	CQua
	'Raspberry Ring' (2)	CQua
	'Rathowen Gold' (1)	CQua
	'Ravenhill' (3)	CQua
	'Rebekah' (4)	CQua
	'Recital' (2)	CQua
	'Red Devon' (2) ♀^{H4}	CFen SDeJ
	'Red Era' (3)	CQua
	'Red Legend' (2)	CQua
	'Red Lips' (2)	CQua
	'Red Marvel' **new**	CFen
	'Red Reed' (1)	IRhd
	'Red Socks' (6)	CQua
	'Red Spartan' (2)	CQua
	'Refrain' (2)	CQua
	'Regal Bliss' (2)	CQua
	'Reggae' (6) ♀^{H4}	CBro CQua EPfP LPio SDeJ WShi
	'Rembrandt' (1)	CFen CQua
	'Rendezvous Caye' (2)	CQua
	'Repertoire' (3)	IRhd
	'Replete' (4)	CQua
	requienii	see *N. assoanus*
	'Resistasol' (1)	IRhd
	'Resolute' (2)	GCro
	'Reverse Image' (11a)	CQua
	'Rheban Red' (2) **new**	IRhd
	'Ribald' (2)	IRhd
	'Ridgecrest' (3)	IRhd
	rifanus	see *N. romieuxii* subsp. *romieuxii* var *rifanus*
	'Right Stuff' (6)	NMin
	'Rijnveld's Early Sensation' (1) ♀^{H4}	CAvo CBro CFen CMea CQua ERCP SDeJ SEND WCot
	'Rikki' (7)	CBro CQua NMin
	'Rima' (1)	CQua
	'Rimmon' (3)	CQua
	'Rimski' (2)	IRhd
	'Ring Fence' (3)	IRhd
	'Ring Flash' (2) **new**	IRhd
	'Ringhaddy' (3)	IRhd
	'Ringing Bells' (5)	CQua
	'Ringleader' (2)	CQua
	'Ringmaster' (2)	CQua
	'Ringmer' (3)	CQua
	'Rio Bravo' (2)	IRhd
	'Rio Gusto' (2)	IRhd
	'Rio Lobo' (2)	IRhd
	'Rio Rondo' (2)	IRhd
	'Rio Rouge' (2)	IRhd
§	'Rip van Winkle' (4)	CAby CBro CFen CQua CTca EPfP EPot ERCP IFro LRHS MBri NHol SDeJ WShi
	'Rippling Waters' (5) ♀^{H4}	CQua
	'Rising Star' (7) ♀^{H4}	IRhd
	'Ristin' (1)	CQua
	'Rival' (6)	CQua
	'River Dance' (2)	IRhd
	'River Queen' (2)	CQua IRhd
	'Roberta'	CFen
	'Roberta Watrous' (7) **new**	IRhd
	'Rock Creek' (3)	IRhd
	'Rockall' (3)	CQua
	'Rocoza' (2)	IRhd
	'Roger' (6)	CQua
	'Rogue' (2)	CBro
§	'Romanus' (4)	CQua
	romieuxii (13) ♀$^{H2-3}$	CBro CDes EPri ITim LRHS WCot
	- JCA 805	CFil EPot
	- SF 370	WCot
	- subsp. ***albidus*** (13)	ECho WCot
	- - SF 110	WCot
§	- - var. ***zaianicus*** (13)	ECho
	- - - SB&L 82	WCot
§	- 'Atlas Gold' (10)	EPot
§	- 'Julia Jane' (10)	ECho EPot GKev NMin WCot
*	- subsp. ***pallidus*** SB&L 237	WCot
	- subsp. ***romieuxii*** (13)	GKev
§	- - var. ***mesatlanticus*** (13)	ECho
§	- - var. ***rifanus*** (13)	ECho GKev
	- - - B 8927	WCot
§	- 'Treble Chance' (10)	EPot
	'Rory's Glen' (2)	CQua
	'Rosannor Gold' (11a)	CQua
	'Roscarrick' (6)	CQua
	'Rose Noble' (2) **new**	CFen
	'Rose of May' (4)	CQua WShi
	'Rose of Tralee' (2)	CQua
	'Rose Royale' (2)	CQua
	'Rose Sheen' (2)	CQua
	'Rose Umber' (2)	IRhd
	'Rose Villa' (2)	CQua
	'Rosemerryn' (2)	CQua
	'Rosemoor Gold' (7) ♀^{H4}	CBro CFen CQua
	'Rosemullion' (4)	CQua
	'Rosevine' (3)	CQua
	'Rosy Wonder' (2)	CQua
	'Round Oak' (1)	CQua
	'Roxton' (4)	IRhd
	'Royal Armour' (1)	CFen
	'Royal Connection' (8)	CQua
	'Royal Marine' (2)	CQua IRhd
	'Royal Princess' (3)	CQua ERCP
	'Royal Regiment' (2)	CQua
	'Ruby Red' (2)	CQua
	'Ruby Rose' (4)	IRhd
	'Ruby Wedding' (2)	IRhd
	'Rubythroat' (2)	CQua
	'Ruddy Duck'	IRhd
	'Ruddy Rascal' (2)	IRhd
	'Rugulosus' (7) ♀^{H4}	CBro CQua ECho
*	'Rugulosus Flore Pleno' (d)	ECho
	'Runkerry' (4)	IRhd
	rupicola (13)	CBro CQua CWCL ECho EPot GKev LLHF NMin SPhx WCot
§	- subsp. ***watieri*** (13)	CQua ECho EPot GKev LLHF NMin SPhx
	'Rustom Pasha' (2)	CQua GCro
	'Rytha' (2)	CQua
	'Saberwing' (5)	CQua
	'Sabine Hay' (3)	CQua ERCP
	'Sabrosa' (7) ♀^{H2}	CBro CQua LLHF LRHS NMin
	'Sacajawea' (2)	CFen
	'Sacré Coeur' (2)	IRhd
	'Sagana' (9)	CQua
	'Sailboat' (7) ♀^{H4}	CQua EPfP MBri SPer
	'Saint Agnes' (8)	CQua
	'Saint Budock' (1)	CQua
	'Saint Day' (5)	CQua
	'Saint Dilpe' (2)	CQua

'Saint Keverne' (2) ♀H4	CFen CQua EPfP SDeJ SEND
'Saint Keyne' (8)	CQua
'Saint Olaf' (3)	GCro
'Saint Patrick's Day' (2)	CFen CQua SDeJ
'Saint Peter' (4)	CFen CQua
'Saint Petroc' (9)	CQua
'Saint Piran' (7)	CQua
'Salakee' (2)	CQua
'Salcey Forest' (1)	CQua
'Salmon Trout' (2)	CQua
'Salome' (2) ♀H4	CQua LRHS NBir NPer SDeJ SEND
'Salute' (2)	CQua
'Samantha' (4)	CQua
'Samsara' (3) **new**	IRhd
'Sandycove' (2)	CQua IRhd
'Sandymount' (2)	CQua
'Sarah' (2)	CFen
'Sarah Dear' (2)	CQua
'Sarah Markillie' (11a)	CQua
'Sarchedon' (9)	GCro
'Sargeant's Caye' (1)	CQua IRhd
'Satchmo' (1)	CQua
'Satin Blanc' (7) **new**	IRhd
'Saturn' (3)	CQua
'Savoir Faire' (2)	IRhd
scaberulus (13)	ECho EPot
'Scarlet Chord' (2)	CQua
'Scarlet Elegance' (2)	CQua
'Scarlet Gem' (8)	SDeJ
'Scarlet Tanager' (2)	IRhd
'Scarlett O'Hara' (2)	CFen CQua
'Scented Breeze' (2)	IRhd
'Scilly Spring' (8)	CAvo
'Scilly White' (8)	CFen CQua
'Scorrier' (2)	CQua
'Scrumpy' (2)	CQua
'Sea Dream' (3)	CQua
'Sea Gift' (7)	CBro
'Sea Green' (9)	CQua
'Sea Legend' (2)	CQua
'Sea Princess' (3)	CQua
'Sea Shanty' (2)	IRhd
'Seagull' (3)	CAvo CQua GCro WShi
'Sealing Wax' (2)	CFen CQua
'Segovia' (3) ♀H4	CBro CQua EPot NMin SDeJ SPhx
'Sempre Avanti' (2)	SDeJ
'Seraglio' (3)	CQua
'Serena Beach' (4)	IRhd
'Serena Lodge' (4) ♀H4	CQua IRhd
serotinus (13)	ECho EPot GKev
'Sextant' (6)	CQua
'Shangani' (2)	IRhd
'Sheelagh Rowan' (2)	CQua IRhd
'Sheer Joy' (6)	CQua
'Shepherd's Hey' (7)	CQua EPfP SDeJ
'Sherborne' (4) ♀H4	CQua
'Sherpa' (1)	CQua IRhd
'Sheskin' (2) **new**	IRhd
'Shindig' (2)	IRhd
'Shining Light' (2)	CQua
'Shockwave' (2)	CQua
'Shortcake' (2)	CQua
'Shrimp Boat' (11a)	IRhd
'Sidley' (3)	CQua IRhd
'Sidney Torch' (2) **new**	CFen
'Signet Ring' (3)	IRhd
'Signorina' (2)	IRhd
'Silent Valley' (1) ♀H4	CQua IRhd
'Silk Cut' (2)	CQua
'Silkwood' (3)	CQua IRhd
'Silver Bells' (5)	CQua IRhd
'Silver Chimes' (8)	CAvo CBro CFen CQua CTca ECho EPfP LPio NBir SDeJ SPhx
'Silver Convention' (1)	CQua
'Silver Crystal' (3)	CQua IRhd
'Silver Kiwi' (2)	CQua
'Silver Minx' (1)	CQua
'Silver Moon' (2)	CFen
'Silver Plate' (11a)	CQua
'Silver Sabre' (2)	IRhd
'Silver Smiles' (7)	SPhx
'Silver Surf' (2)	CQua IRhd
'Silversmith' (2)	CQua
'Silverthorne' (3)	CQua
'Silverwood' (3)	CQua IRhd
'Singing Pub' (3)	IRhd
'Sinopel' (3)	SDeJ
'Sir Samuel' (2)	CQua
'Sir Watkin' (2)	CQua GCro
'Sir Winston Churchill' (4) ♀H4	CQua EPfP SDeJ SPer
'Sirius' (2)	GCro
'Sissy' (6)	CQua
'Skerry' (2)	CQua
'Skilliwidden' (2) ♀H4	CQua
'Skookum' (3)	CQua
'Skywalker' (2)	IRhd
'Slieveboy' (1)	CQua
'Slipstream' (6)	IRhd
'Small Fry' (1)	CQua
'Small Talk' (1) ♀H4	CQua LLHF NMin
'Smiling Twin' (11a)	EPfP
'Smokey Bear' (4)	CQua
'Smooth Sails' (3)	CQua
'Snipe' (6)	CAvo CQua GKev NMin WShi
'Snoopie' (6)	CQua
'Snow Bunting' (7)	CBro
'Snowcrest' (3)	CQua
'Snowshill' (2)	CQua
'Soft Focus' (2)	IRhd
'Solar System' (3)	IRhd
'Solar Tan' (3)	CQua
'Soleil d'Or' (8)	CQua
'Solera' (2)	IRhd
'Solferique' (2)	CQua
'Soloist' (2)	IRhd
'Solveig's Song' (12)	WAbe
'Sonata' (9)	CQua
'Songket' (2)	CQua
'Sophie Girl' (2)	CQua
'Sophie's Choice' (4)	CAvo
'Soprano' (2)	CQua IRhd
'Sorcerer' (3)	CQua
'South Street' (2)	CQua
'Southease' (2)	CQua
'Southern Gem' (2)	GCro
'Spaniards Inn' (4)	CQua
'Sparkling Tarts' (8)	CQua
'Sparnon' (11a)	CQua
'Sparrow' (6)	CQua
'Spartan Gold' (2) **new**	IRhd
'Special Envoy' (2) ♀H4	CQua
'Speenogue' (1)	IRhd
'Spellbinder' (1) ♀H4	CQua SDeJ
'Spencer Tracy' (2)	CFen CQua
'Sperrin Gold' (1)	IRhd
'Spin Doctor' (3)	IRhd
'Spindletop' (3) ♀H4	IRhd

'Spirit of Rame' (3)	CQua
'Split Vote' (11a)	IRhd
'Spoirot' (10) ♀H4 **new**	ERCP SDeJ
'Sportsman' (2)	CQua
'Spring Dawn' (2)	EPfP
'Spring Morn' (2)	CQua IRhd
'Spun Honey' (4)	CQua
'Stadium' (2)	CFen
'Stainless' (2)	SPhx
'Standard Value' (1)	CFen
'Stann Creek' (1)	CQua
'Stanway' (3)	CQua
'Star Glow' (2)	CQua
'Star Quality' (3)	IRhd
'Starfire' (7)	CQua
'State Express' (2)	CQua IRhd
'Statue' (2)	CFen
'Steenbok' (3)	IRhd
'Stella' (2)	GCro GKev WShi
'Stellar Glow' (3) **new**	IRhd
'Stenalees' (6)	CQua
'Step Child' (6)	CQua
'Step Forward' (7)	CQua
'Steve's Favorite' (2)	CQua
'Stilton' (9)	CQua
'Stinger' (2)	CQua
'Stint' (5) ♀H4	CQua SDeJ
'Stocken' (7)	CBro CQua ECho EPri NMin WAbe
'Stoke Charity' (2)	CFen CQua
'Stoke Doyle' (2)	CQua
'Stormy Weather' (1)	CQua
'Stratosphere' (7) ♀H4	CQua NMin SDeJ
'Strines' (2) ♀H4	CQua
'Suave' (3)	CQua
'Subtle Shades' (2)	IRhd
'Sugar and Spice' (3)	CQua
'Sugar Bird' (2)	IRhd
'Sugar Cups' (8)	CQua
'Sugar Loaf' (4)	CQua
'Sugarbush' (7)	WShi
'Suisgill' (4)	CQua
'Sukey' (6)	CQua
§ 'Sulphur Phoenix' (4)	CQua WShi
Sulphur Star (2)	GCro
'Summer Solstice' (3)	IRhd
'Sumo Jewel' (6)	CQua
'Sun Disc' (7) ♀H4	CBro CFen CQua CTri ECho GKev MBri NMin SDeJ WShi
'Sunday Chimes' (5)	CQua
'Sundial' (7)	CBro GKev NMin
'Sunnyside Up' (11a) ♀H4 **new**	SDeJ
'Sunrise' (3)	CQua
'Suntory' (3)	CQua
'Suntrap' (2)	IRhd
'Surfside' (6) ♀H4	CQua LPio NMin
'Surprise Packet' (2)	IRhd
'Surrey' (2)	CQua IRhd
'Suzie Dee' (6)	IRhd
'Suzie's Sister' (6)	IRhd
'Suzy' (7) ♀H4	CBro CFen SDeJ
'Swaledale' (2)	CQua
'Swallow' (6)	CQua SDeJ
'Swallow Wing' (6)	IRhd
'Swanpool' (3)	CQua
'Sweet Blanche' (7)	CQua
'Sweet Lorraine' (2)	CQua
'Sweet Memory' (2)	CQua
'Sweet Sue' (3)	CQua
'Sweetness' (7) ♀H4	CAvo CBro CFen CQua GCro WShi
'Swift Arrow' (6) ♀H4	CQua
'Swing Wing' (6)	CQua
'Swoop' (6) **new**	SDeJ
'Taffeta' (10)	EPri
'Tahiti' (4) ♀H4	CFen CQua EPfP SDeJ
× ***taitii*** (13)	NMin WShi
'Talgarth' (2)	CQua
§ 'Tamar Double White' (4)	CBro CFil
'Tamar Fire' (4) ♀H4	CQua
'Tamar Lad' (2)	CQua
'Tamar Lass' (3)	CQua
'Tamar Snow' (2)	CQua
'Tamara' (2)	CFen CQua EPfP
'Tangent' (2)	CQua
'Tarnished Gold' (2)	CQua
'Tasgem' (4)	CQua
'Taslass' (4)	CQua
tazetta (13)	ECho
§ - subsp. ***lacticolor*** (13)	CFil CQua ERCP SDeJ
§ - - 'Grand Monarque' (8)	CBro CQua
- subsp. ***ochroleucus*** (13)	CQua
* - var. ***odoratus***	CQua NMin
'Teal' (1)	CQua
'Tehidy' (3)	CQua
§ 'Telamonius Plenus' (4)	CBro CQua IGor SEND WCot WShi
'Temba' (1)	IRhd
'Temple Cloud' (4)	IRhd
'Tenedos' (2)	GCro
tenuifolius	see *N. bulbocodium* subsp. *bulbocodium* var. *tenuifolius*
× ***tenuior*** (13)	NMin
'Terminator' (2) **new**	IRhd
'Terracotta' (2)	CQua IRhd
'Terrapin' (3)	IRhd
'Terwegen' (4) **new**	CFen
'Tête-à-tête' (12) ♀H4	CAvo CBro CFen CQua CTca CWCL EPfP EPot ERCP GAbr GKev LPot LRHS LSou MBri MNHC SDeJ SEND SPer
'Texas' (4)	CQua
'Thalia' (5)	CAvo CBro CQua CTca EPfP ERCP GKev LPot LRHS MBri MCot NBir NHol SDeJ SEND SPer SPhx WShi
'The Alliance' (6) ♀H4	CBro CQua
'The Calcy' (2)	CQua
'The Grange' (1)	CQua
'The Knave' (6)	CQua
'The Little Gentleman' (6)	NMin
'The Mount' (2) **new**	IRhd
'Thistin' (1)	IRhd
'Thomas Kinkade' (2)	CQua
'Thoresby' (3)	CQua
'Thoughtful' (5)	CBro CQua
'Three Oaks' (1)	CQua
'Three Trees' (1)	IRhd
'Tibet' (2)	CFen CQua
'Tickled Pink' (11a)	IRhd
'Tideford' (2)	CQua
'Tidy Tippet' (2)	IRhd
'Tiercel' (1)	CQua
'Tiffany Jade' (3)	CQua
'Tiger Moth' (6)	CQua
'Timolin' (3)	CQua
'Tinderbox' (2)	IRhd
'Tinhay' (7)	CQua
'Tiritomba' (11a)	CQua
'Titania' (6)	CQua
'Tittle-tattle' (7)	CFen CQua

'Toby' (2)	SDeJ
'Toby the First' (6)	CQua
'Tommora Gold' (2)	CQua
'Tommy White' (2)	CQua
'Top Hit' (11a)	CQua
'Topolino' (1) $\mathbb{Y}^{H4}$	CAvo CBro CFen CQua EPot GKev LRHS
'Toreador' (3)	CFen
'Toretta' (3)	IRhd
'Torianne' (2) $\mathbb{Y}^{H4}$	CQua
'Torr Head' (9)	IRhd
'Torridon' (2)	CQua
'Toto' (12) $\mathbb{Y}^{H4}$	CBro CQua ERCP MBri SDeJ SPhx
'Tracey' (6) $\mathbb{Y}^{H4}$	CQua IRhd
'Treasure Hunt' (2)	IRhd
'Trebah' (2) $\mathbb{Y}^{H4}$	CQua
'Treble Chance'	see *N. romieuxii* 'Treble Chance'
'Treble Two' (7)	CQua
'Trecara' (3)	CQua
'Trefusis' (1)	CQua
'Treglisson' (2) **new**	CFen
'Trehane' (6)	CQua
'Trelawney Gold' (2)	CFen CQua
'Trelissick' (7)	CQua
'Tremelling' (2) **new**	CFen
'Tremough Dale' (11a)	CQua
'Trena' (6) $\mathbb{Y}^{H4}$	CQua ERCP NMin
'Trendy Trail' (3)	IRhd
'Trentagh' (3)	IRhd
'Trenwith' (1)	CQua
'Trepolo' (11b)	ERCP
'Tresamble' (5)	CBro CQua GCro MBri SDeJ
'Trevaunance' (6)	CQua
'Treverva' (6)	CQua
'Treviddo' (2)	CQua
'Trevithian' (7) $\mathbb{Y}^{H4}$	CAby CBro CQua SDeJ WShi
'Trewarvas' (2)	CQua
'Trewirgie' (6)	CQua
'Trewoon' (4)	CQua
triandrus var. ***albus***	see *N. triandrus* subsp. *triandrus* var. *triandrus*
- subsp. ***pallidulus*** (13) SG 13	WCot
§ - subsp. ***triandrus*** var. ***triandrus*** (13)	CQua
'Tricollet' (11a)	SDeJ
'Trident' (3)	CQua
'Trielfin' (5)	IRhd
'Trigonometry' (11a) $\mathbb{Y}^{H4}$	CQua IRhd
'Tripartite' (11a) $\mathbb{Y}^{H4}$	CQua IRhd NMin SDeJ
'Triple Crown' (3) $\mathbb{Y}^{H4}$	CQua IRhd
'Tristram' (2)	CQua
'Tropic Isle' (4)	CQua
'Tropical Heat' (2)	IRhd
'Trousseau' (1)	CFen CQua
'Troutbeck' (3)	CQua
'Tru' (3)	CQua
'Truculent' (3)	CQua
'Trueblood' (3)	IRhd
'Trumpet Warrior' (1) $\mathbb{Y}^{H4}$	CQua IRhd
'Tryst' (2)	CQua
'Tudor Minstrel' (2)	CQua
'Tuesday's Child' (5) $\mathbb{Y}^{H4}$	CQua
'Tullyroyal' (2)	CQua
'Tunis' (2)	GCro
'Turncoat' (6)	CQua
'Tutankhamun' (2)	CQua
'Tweety Bird' (6)	EPfP
'Twicer' (2)	IRhd
'Twilight Zone' (2) **new**	IRhd
'Twink' (4)	CQua
'Tyee' (2)	CQua
Tyndrum Conspicuus	GCro
'Tyrian Rose' (2)	CQua
'Tyrone Gold' (1) $\mathbb{Y}^{H4}$	CQua IRhd
'Tyrree' (1)	IRhd
'Tywara' (1)	CQua
'Ulster Bank' (3)	CQua
'Ulster Bride' (4)	CQua
'Ultimus' (2)	CQua
'Uncle Bill' (1)	CQua
'Uncle Duncan' (1)	CQua IRhd
'Unique' (4) $\mathbb{Y}^{H4}$	SDeJ
'Unsurpassable' (1)	CFen CQua GCro
'Upalong' (12)	CQua
'Upshot' (3)	CQua
'Urchin' (2)	IRhd
'Utiku' (6)	CQua
'Val d'Incles' (3)	CQua IRhd
'Valdrome' (11a)	CQua
'Valinor' (2)	CQua
'Valley Dew' (2)	CQua
'Van Sion'	see *N.* 'Telamonius Plenus'
'Vanellus' (11a) $\mathbb{Y}^{H4}$	IRhd
'Vaticaan' (1)	SDeJ
'Velvet Spring' (2)	CQua
'Vendell' (3)	IRhd
'Verdin' (7)	CQua
'Verdoy' (2) **new**	IRhd
'Verger' (3)	MBri SDeJ
'Vernal Prince' (3) $\mathbb{Y}^{H4}$	CQua
'Verona' (3) $\mathbb{Y}^{H4}$	CQua
'Verran Rose' (2)	IRhd
'Vers Libre' (9)	CQua
'Version' (1)	IRhd
'Vice-President' (2) $\mathbb{Y}^{H4}$	CQua
'Victoria' (1)	CQua
'Vigil' (1) $\mathbb{Y}^{H4}$	CQua
'Viking' (1) $\mathbb{Y}^{H4}$	CQua
'Village Green' (3)	IRhd
'Violetta' (2)	CQua
'Virginia Waters' (3)	CQua
'Viva Diva' (3) **new**	IRhd
'Volare' (2)	CQua
'Volcanic Rim' (3)	IRhd
'Vulcan' (2) $\mathbb{Y}^{H4}$	CQua
'W.P. Milner' (1)	CAby CAvo CBro CQua EPfP EPot ERCP GKev MBri NMin SDeJ SEND SMrm SPhx WShi
'Walden Pond' (3)	CQua
'Waldorf Astoria' (4)	CQua IRhd
'Walton' (7)	CQua
'War Dance' (3)	IRhd
'Warbler' (6) $\mathbb{Y}^{H4}$	CQua NMin SDeJ
'Warleggan' (2)	CFen
'Warm Day' (2)	IRhd
'Warm Welcome' (2)	IRhd
'Warmington' (3)	CQua
'Warmwell' (3) **new**	IRhd
'Watamu' (3)	IRhd
'Waterperry' (7)	CBro SEND
'Watership Down' (2)	CQua IRhd
'Watersmeet' (4)	CQua
watieri	see *N. rupicola* subsp. *watieri*
'Wave' (4)	CQua
'Wavelength' (3)	IRhd
'Wavertree'	see *N. asturiensis* 'Wavertree'
'Waxwing' (5)	CQua

'Wayward Lad' (3)	IRhd
'Wee Bee' (1)	CQua
'Weena' (2)	CQua
'Welcome' (2)	CFen CQua
'Welsh Rugby Union' (1)	CQua
'Wendron' (1) **new**	CFen
'West Post' (3)	IRhd
'Westward' (4)	CQua
'Whang-hi' (6)	CQua
'Wheal Bush' (4)	CQua
'Wheal Coates' (7) ♀H4	CQua
'Wheal Honey' (1)	CQua
'Wheal Jane' (2)	CQua
'Wheal Kitty' (7)	CQua
'Wheal Rose' (4)	CQua
'Wheatear' (6)	CQua IRhd NMin
'Whetstone' (1)	CQua
'Whipcord' (7) ♀H4	IRhd
'Whisky Galore' (2)	CQua
'Whisky Mac' (2)	CQua
'White Convention' (1) **new**	IRhd
'White Emperor' (1)	CQua GCro
'White Empress' (1)	CQua
'White Giant' (1)	GKev
'White Lady' (3)	CAvo CQua GCro WShi
'White Lion' (4) ♀H4	CFen CQua SDeJ
'White Marvel' (4)	CQua
'White Medal' (4)	SDeJ
'White Nile' (2)	CQua GCro
'White Star' (1)	IRhd
'White Tea' (2)	CQua IRhd
'White Tie' (3)	CQua
'Wicklow Hills' (3)	CQua
'Wild Honey' (2)	CQua
'Wild Rover' (1) **new**	IRhd
'Will Scarlett' (2)	CQua
willkommii (13)	CBro CQua NMin
'Wimbledon County Girl' (2) ♀H4	CQua
'Wind Song' (2)	CQua
'Winged Victory' (6)	CQua
'Winholm Jenni' (3)	CQua
'Winifred van Graven' (3)	CFen
'Winter Waltz' (6)	CQua
'Wisley' (6) ♀H4	ERCP
'Witch Hunt' (4)	IRhd
'Woodcock' (6)	CQua
'Woodcroft Beauty' (2)	GCro
'Woodland Prince' (3)	CQua
'Woodland Star' (3)	CQua
'Woodley Vale' (2)	CQua
'Woolsthorpe' (2)	CQua
'World Class' (5)	CQua
'Xit' (3)	CAvo CBro CQua NMin SPhx
'Xunantunich' (2)	CQua IRhd
'Yellow Belles' (5)	IRhd
'Yellow Cheerfulness' (4) ♀H4	CQua EPfP LPio MBri SDeJ SPer
'Yellow Triumphator' (1) **new**	CFen
'Yellow Xit' (3)	CQua NMin
'Yoley's Pond' (2)	CQua
'York Minster' (1)	CQua
'Young American' (1)	CQua
'Young Blood' (2)	CQua IRhd
'Your Grace' (2)	CQua
'Yum-Yum' (3)	IRhd
zaianicus	see *N. romieuxii* subsp. *albidus* var. *zaianicus*
'Zekiah' (1)	CQua
'Zion Canyon' (2)	CQua
'Ziva' (8)	CAvo SDeJ
'Zwynner' (2)	IRhd

Nardostachys (*Caprifoliaceae*)

grandiflora	GPoy

Nassauvia (*Asteraceae*)

gaudichaudii	WAbe

Nassella (*Poaceae*)

cernua	WPGP
formicarum (Delile) Barkworth	EBee
poeppigiana	see *Stipa poeppigiana*
pulchra	WPGP
tenuissima	see *Stipa tenuissima*
trichotoma	CKno EHoe EPPr LDai SLim SPer WHal WPGP

Nasturtium (*Brassicaceae*)

'Banana Split'	CCCN CHel ELan
officinale	MHoo MSKA SVic SWat

Natal plum see *Carissa macrocarpa*

Nauplius (*Asteraceae*)

sericeus	CSpe

nectarine see *Prunus persica* var. *nectarina*

Nectaroscordum (*Alliaceae*)

§ ***siculum***	CAvo CBre CBro CSpe CTri ECho ELan ERCP GAbr GCra GKev LLWP LPio LRHS MBel MCot NBir NChi NDov NSti SDeJ SMrm SPer WBor WHoo
§ - subsp. ***bulgaricum***	CAby CBro CTca CWCL EBee EPfP EPot IBlr ITim LRHS MMoz MNrw SPhx WCot XLum
tripedale	CAvo CBro CMea ECho

Neillia (*Rosaceae*)

affinis	CDul CExl EBee EPfP EWTr LLHF LRHS NBid NLar SLon SWvt WCot WPat
longiracemosa	see *N. thibetica*
sinensis	NLar
§ ***thibetica***	Widely available
thyrsiflora PAB 3267 **new**	LEdu
- var. ***tunkinensis*** HWJ 505	WCru

Nelumbo (*Nelumbonaceae*)

'Beautiful Dancer' **new**	LLWG
'Carolina Queen' **new**	LLWG
'Chawan Basu'	LLWG
nucifera	XBlo
- 'Alba Striata'	LLWG
'Penelope' **new**	LLWG
'Pink 'n' Yellow' **new**	EWay
'Russian Red' **new**	LLWG
'The President' **new**	LLWG

Nematanthus (*Gesneriaceae*)

'Apres'	WDib
'Black Magic'	WDib
'Christmas Holly'	WDib
'Freckles'	WDib
§ ***gregarius*** ♀H1	WDib

§ - 'Golden West' (v)	WDib
- 'Variegatus'	see *N. gregarius* 'Golden West'
'Lemon and Lime'	WDib
radicans	see *N. gregarius*
'Tropicana' ♀H1	WDib

Nemesia (*Scrophulariaceae*)

§ Amelie = 'Fleurame'PBR	EPfP LBuc SPoG
Angelart Almond = 'Kirine 4' **new**	SPoG
Angelart Pear = 'Kirine 34'PBR **new**	SPoG
Berrie White = 'Fleurow' **new**	NPri
Berries and Cream = 'Fleurbac'PBR	ECtt EPfP LAst LBuc LSou MCot MSCN SPoG
Blue Lagoon = 'Pengoon'PBR (Maritana Series)	LAst LSRN MCot SCoo
'Blueberry Ripple'	LSou
'Bluebird'	see *N.* Bluebird = 'Hubbird'
§ Bluebird = 'Hubbird'PBR	CHll
Candy Girl = 'Pencand' (Maritana Series)	SCoo
§ ***denticulata*** ♀H3-4	CBar CPrp EPfP GBee LHop NEgg SCoo WHlf
- 'Confetti'	see *N. denticulata*
- 'Maggie'	LBuc LRHS
'Fleurie Blue'	EPfP SPoG
'Fragrant Cloud'	LSou
Fragrant Gem = 'Pengem'PBR	LSRN
'Framboise'	EPfP LBuc SPoG
Golden Eye = 'Yateye'PBR	LSRN MPnt SLon
Honey Girl = 'Penhon' (Maritana Series)	LSRN SCoo
Ice Pink = 'Fleuripi'	EPfP LBuc
'Innocence' ♀H3	CPrp SCoo
(Karoo Series) Karoo Blue = 'Innkablue'PBR	SCoo
- Karoo Soft Blue = 'Innkarsofb'PBR	CWGN
- Karoo Violet Ice = 'Innemkavic'PBR	MAvo NPri
- Karoo White = 'Innkarwhi'PBR	LSou
Lagoon White	see *N.* Pure Lagoon
Maritana Sky Lagoon = 'Pensky' (Maritana Series)	SCoo
'Mirabelle'	LBuc SPoG
'Myrtille' **new**	LBuc SPoG
(Nesia Series) Nesia Dark Blue = 'Dannemes6' **new**	LAst
- Nesia Dark Magenta **new**	LAst
(Nuvo Series) 'Nuvo Blue'	WGor
- 'Nuvo Carmine'	WGor
Opal Innocence	see *N.* Amelie
'Provençal Dusky Blue'	EPfP
'Provençal Dusky Pink'	EPfP
§ Pure Lagoon = 'Penpur'PBR	LAst LHop
Raspberries and Cream = 'Fleurrac'	EPfP LBuc SPoG
Sugar Frosted = 'Lowgreg'	SPoG
Sugar Girl = 'Pensug' (Maritana Series)	LSRN
'Sugar Plum'	EPfP LRHS SLon
(Sunsatia Series) Sunsatia Cherry on Ice **new**	NPri
- Sunsatia Blackberry = 'Inuppink'PBR	SCoo
- Sunsatia Cassis = 'Inupspink8'PBR **new**	MAvo
- Sunsatia Cranberry = 'Intraired'PBR	SCoo
- Sunsatia Lemon = 'Intraigold'PBR	SCoo
- Sunsatia Peach = 'Inupcream'	CWGN MAvo SCoo
'Sweet Lady'	LAst LSou
sylvatica	CSpe
'Vanilla Lady'	ECtt LAst LSou NPri
Vanilla Mist = 'Grega'	EPfP LRHS LSou SLon
'Wisley Vanilla'	EPfP EShb LBuc SPoG

Nemophila (*Boraginaceae*)

menziesii 'Penny Black'	CSpe

Neodypsis (*Arecaceae*)

decaryi	see *Dypsis decaryi*

Neolepisorus (*Polypodiaceae*)

lancifolius	CExl

Neolitsea (*Lauraceae*)

glauca	see *N. sericea*
polycarpa KWJ 12309	WCru
§ ***sericea***	CBcs LEdu SSpi WPGP WSHC

Neomarica ✿ (*Iridaceae*)

caerulea	WCot

Neopanax (*Araliaceae*)

§ ***arboreus***	CDoC CHEx CTsd ECou LEdu SBig
§ ***laetus***	CDoC CHEx LEdu SAPC SBig

Neoregelia (*Bromeliaceae*)

carolinae (Meyendorffii Group) 'Meyendorffii'	XBlo
'Hojo Rojo'	XBlo
'Marconfos'	XBlo

Neoshirakia (*Euphorbiaceae*)

japonica	EPfP MBlu WPGP WPat
- B&SWJ 8744	WCru

Neottia (*Orchidaceae*)

ovata	NLAp

Neottianthe (*Orchidaceae*)

cucullata	EFEx

Nepeta ✿ (*Lamiaceae*)

sp.	LAst
from China	EWes
amethystina	XSen
'Blue Beauty'	see *N. sibirica* 'Souvenir d'André Chaudron'
'Blue Dragon'	ECtt GBin MTis NCGa NDov NLar
bucharica	GBuc
* ***buddlejifolium***	MSCN NLar
cataria	CArn CPrp CTri ELau GJos GPoy LAst MHer MHoo MNHC NBro SIde SVic WHfH WJek WMoo
§ - 'Citriodora'	GPoy MHoo SIde SPhx SRms WJek XLum
citriodora Dum.	see *N. cataria* 'Citriodora'

	clarkei	EPPr GMaP IFro MTis NDov SWat WHrl WMoo
	'Dropmore'	EBee LRHS
§	× ***faassenii*** ♀H4	Widely available
	- 'Alba'	COlW EBee ECtt ELan EPfP NBre NLar NRya WJek WWEG XSen
	- 'Kit Cat'	CSpe ECtt GBuc GCal IBoy LHop LRHS LSRN MTis NCGa NDov SBod WCFE WHoo
	- 'Limelight' **new**	IBoy
	- 'Senior' **new**	XLum
	glechoma 'Variegata'	see *Glechoma hederacea* 'Variegata'
	govaniana	Widely available
	granatensis	XSen
	grandiflora	NBre SIde WHrl
	- 'Blue Danube'	GBin MTis NDov WWEG XLum
	- 'Bramdean'	CElw CMea EBee ECtt EPfP EWes GBin LBMP LHop LRHS MCot MTis SBch SPhx WCAu WCot WWEG XLum
	- 'Dawn to Dusk'	Widely available
	- 'Pool Bank'	EBee ECtt EWes GCal LPla MAvo MTis NBre SIde SMrm XLum
	- 'Wild Cat'	EPfP MAvo MTis SPhx
	hederacea 'Variegata'	see *Glechoma hederacea* 'Variegata'
	italica	WOut
*	***kubabiana***	EBee
	kubanica	CSpe IMou LPla WCot
	'Lamendi'	NDov
	lanceolata	see *N. nepetella*
	latifolia 'Super Cat'	EPfP
§	'Leeds Castle'	EBee ECGP EPfP LHop LRHS MHer MNFA NCGa NGdn NSti SMrm SPer SWat WHal WWEG
	'Lilac Cloud'	NBir
	'Limelight' **new**	NLar
	longipes hort.	see *N.* 'Leeds Castle'
	macrantha	see *N. sibirica*
	'Maurice'	MTis NDov WWEG
	melissifolia	SBch
	mussinii misapplied	see *N.* × *faassenii*
	mussinii Spreng.	see *N. racemosa*
§	***nepetella***	NBir
	nervosa	CSpe EBee ELan EPfP EWTr LAst LPio MCot NBro NLar NSti SPer WHar WJek WMnd WSHC WWEG
	- 'Blue Carpet'	CSpe NEgg
	- 'Blue Moon'	EBee EPfP EWes LRHS LSou MBNS MHol MNHC NBid SHil SMrm SRms WCAu
	- 'Forncett Select'	CSam MRav NBre SMrm
	- 'Pink Cat'	EPfP LRHS LSou MHoo MNHC NLar SHil SRkn WWEG
§	***nuda***	EWes SHar WHil WHrl
*	- 'Grandiflora'	NBre NLar WMoo
	- 'Purple Cat'	EPfP LLHF LSou
	- 'Snow Cat'	SPhx
	pannonica	see *N. nuda*
	parnassica	ECtt GQue MBel MCot MHol MMuc MTis NLar SMrm WHil WHrl WMnd WMoo WPtf
	phyllochlamys	CPBP SRms XSen
	Pink Candy	EWll NWad SRms WHil
	'Porzellan'	LPla SMrm
§	***prattii***	CSpe MWat NLar NPro SMrm
	'Purple Haze' **new**	NLar
§	***racemosa*** ♀H4	CArn CHby CMac CPbn CSev ELau EPfP GJos LPot LRHS MCot MHoo MLHP MNHC MSCN SIde WMoo
	- RCB AM 3	WCot
	- ***alba***	MHoo XLum
	- 'Amelia'	MSpe
	- 'Grog'	EBee
	- 'Little Titch'	ECtt EPfP GBuc GCra IPot LRHS LSRN MAsh MCot NLar SMrm SPoG SWat WWEG
	- 'Senior'	MAsh XSen
	- 'Snowflake'	CBcs CHel CMea ECtt ELan ELon EPfP EShb GMaP LRHS MAsh MBel MCot MHer MTis NBir NCGa NDov NLar SMrm SPer SPoG SWvt
	- 'Superba'	NBre
	- 'Toria'	MTis NDov WWEG
	- 'Walker's Low'	Widely available
*	'Rae Crug'	ECtt EWes
	reichenbachiana	see *N. racemosa*
§	***sibirica***	EHyd ELan EPfP MHer MMuc MSCN NBid NBro NLar NPri SBch SRkn WCot WHal WJek WPtf XLum
§	- 'Souvenir d'André Chaudron'	CMHG CSam CWCL ELan EPfP EWTr GBuc GCal GMaP IPot LAst LHop LRHS MCot MRav MTis NLar SBch SPer SPoG WCAu WHil WWEG
	'Six Hills Giant'	Widely available
	stewartiana	LDai LLHF MRav WMoo WWEG
	- BWJ 7999	WCru
	subsessilis	CCVN CMHG ECtt ELan EPfP EShb GMaP IBoy LAst LBMP LRHS MCot MRav MSpe NBid NBir NGdn NSti NWad SPhx SRms WCru WMnd WWEG
	- 'Blue Dreams'	ELon MHol NLar SHar WHil XLum
	- 'Candy Cat'	EPfP IBoy LPot NBre NLar
	- 'Cool Cat'	EBee EPfP LSRN NBre NLar
	- 'Laufen'	IPot
	- Nimbus = 'Yanim'	EBee MPnt
	- 'Pink Dreams'	EPfP GBee GJos LBMP MHer XLum
	- pink-flowered	SMrm SPhx WWEG
	- 'Sweet Dreams'	EPfP LHop LRHS MRav MSpe MTis NCGa NLar NSti WMnd XLum
	- 'Washfield'	CAby IPot LHop NLar
	transcaucasica 'Blue Infinity'	MSCN WMoo WWEG
	troodii	XLum
	tuberosa	CSpe EBee LRHS SBch WCot WMoo XSen
	'Veluwse Wakel'	IMou
	yunnanensis	EBee EPPr LPla SMrm WHil WOut WPGP

Nerine ✿ (*Amaryllidaceae*)

	'Afterglow'	EBee ECho WCot
	alta	see *N. undulata* Alta Group
	'Anna Fletcher'	WCot
	'Aries'	WCot
	'Aurora'	ECho WCot
	'Baghdad'	ECho WCot
	'Belladonna'	WCot
	'Bennett-Poë'	WCot
	'Berlioz'	WCot
	'Blanchefleur'	WCot
	bowdenii ♀H3-4	Widely available
	- 'Alba' ambig.	CCon CPrp CTca EBee ECho ELan EPot ERCP SCoo WCot
	- 'Alba'	CAvo CBro CDes EPri GKev LRHS SDeJ
	- 'Albivetta'	EBee ECho GKev
	- 'Blanca Perla'	GKev WCot

- 'Chris Sanders'	WCot
- 'Codora'	see *N.* 'Codora'
- 'E.B.Anderson'	EBee WCot
- 'Early Light' new	EBee GKev
- 'Elegance Red' new	GKev
- 'Ella K'	EBee EPot EPri ERCP GKev SPer
- Irish clone	WCot
- 'Isabel'	CBro CPrp CTsd EPot EPri ERCP EWes GKev LRHS NWad WHoo
- 'John Crisp' new	WCot
- 'Linda Vista'	WCot
- 'Manina'	CCse
- 'Marjorie'	EMal
- 'Mark Fenwick'	CBro CDes
- 'Marnie Rogerson'	CBro
§ - 'Mollie Cowie' (v)	CCse CPrp GCal IBlr NCGa WCot WCru WHil
- 'Mount Stewart' new	IBlr
- 'Nikita'	EBee ECho EPot EPri ERCP GKev LRHS SDeJ
- 'Ostara'	CPrp EBee EPot EPri ERCP GKev LRHS WCot
- 'Patricia'	EBee EPot EPri GKev NWad
- 'Pink Frostwork'	WCot
- 'Pink Surprise'	CAvo CDes WCot
§ - 'Quinton Wells'	CAby CPrp CTca SPhx WCot
- 'Ras van Roon' new	GKev
- 'Rowie'	CPrp EBee EPri ERCP GKev LRHS
- 'Sofie' new	EBee GKev
- 'Stam 63' new	EPot
- 'Stefanie'	CTsd EPri GKev SDeJ
- 'Variegata'	see *N. bowdenii* 'Mollie Cowie'
- 'Vesta K' new	EPri GKev WCot
- 'Wellsii'	see *N. bowdenii* 'Quinton Wells'
'Canasta'	WCot
'Caryatid'	WCot
'Catkin'	WCot
'Chorister'	WCot
'Clarabel'	WCot
'Clent Charm'	WCot
§ 'Codora'	CCCN ECho EPfP SPer WCot
'Corlette'	WCot
corusca 'Major'	see *N. sarniensis* var. *corusca*
'Cranfield'	WCot
'Cynthia Chance'	WCot
'Daphne'	WCot
'Diana Oliver'	WCot
'Doris Vos'	WCot
'Elspeth'	WCot
'Evelyn Emmett'	WCot
'Exbury Red'	WCot
filamentosa misapplied	see *N. filifolia*
filamentosa ambig.	CBro ECho
§ ***filifolia***	ECho
flexuosa	see *N. undulata* Flexuosa Group
'Fucine'	CDes
gaberonensis	WAbe
gracilis	ECho WCot
'Harlequin'	WCot
'Hera'	CBro
'Hertha Berg'	WCot
* ***hirsuta***	ECho WAbe WCot
humilis	ECho
- Breachiae Group	SBch
huttoniae	ECho
'Iman'	WCot
'Isobel'	EBee XEll
'Janet'	WCot
'Jenny Wren'	CDes WCot
'Kashmir'	CDes WCot
'King Leopold'	WCot
'King of the Belgians'	ECho
'Kinn McIntosh'	CDes WCot
'Kola'	CDes
krigei	ECho
'Lady Cynthia Colville'	WCot
'Lady Downe'	WCot
'Lady Havelock-Allen'	WCot
'Lady Llewellyn'	WCot
'Lady St Aldwyn'	WCot
laticoma	WCot
'Lawlord'	WCot
'Leila Hughes'	WCot
'Lucinda'	CDes WCot
'Lyndhurst Salmon'	WCot
'Maria'	WCot
masoniorum	CBro ECho SBch WCot
'Miss E. Cator'	WCot
'Miss Florence Brown'	WCot
'Miss Frances Clarke'	WCot
'Mrs Cooper'	WCot
'Mrs Dent Brocklehurst'	WCot
'Nena'	WCot
'November Cheer'	ECho
'Oberon'	CDes
peersii	WCot
'Pink Triumph'	CAbP CBcs CTsd EBee ECho EPot ERCP EShb GKev IBlr LRHS SDeJ SPer WCot WHoo
pudica	SBch
- pink-flowered	WCot
pusilla	CLak
'Quivotina'	WCot
'Red Pimpernel'	ECho
'Regina'	WCot
'Rushmere Star'	SChr WCot
'Ruth'	WCot
sarniensis ♀H2-3	CBro ECho EPot EPri GKev SKHP WCot
* - 'Borde Hill White'	WCot
§ - var. ***corusca***	CTsd
- - 'Major'	ECho SChr WCot
- var. ***curvifolia*** f. ***fothergillii***	ECho WCot
- var. ***sarniensis*** new	GKev
Smee 275	CDes
'Snowflake'	WCot
'Stephanie'	CBro CCCN CTca EBee ECho ERCP EShb LHop MNrw WCot WHoo
'Susan Norris'	CDes WCot
undulata	CAby CBro CCCN CTca ECho EPri GCal GKev LSou MPie SDeJ SPer WHil
* - 'Alba'	ECho
§ - Alta Group	WCot
§ - Flexuosa Group	ECho MRav
- - 'Alba'	CBro EBee ECho EPri GKev MRav WAbe WCot
× ***versicolor*** 'Mansellii'	CBro CDes GKev SKHP
'Vestal'	EPot
'Vicky'	WCot
'Virgo'	ECho
'White Swan'	ECho
'Winter Sun' new	LRHS
'Wolsey'	ECho
'Zeal Giant' ♀H3-4	CAvo CBro CPrp ECho GCal WCot
'Zeal Grilse'	CDes WCot
'Zeal Salmon'	CDes

'Zeal Silver Stripe'	CDes

Nerium ✿ (*Apocynaceae*)

oleander L.	CAbb CArn CBcs CHll CTri EBak ELan EShb MMuc SEND SPer SPlb SPoG
- 'Album'	CTri
- 'Album Plenum' (d)	XSen
* - 'Atlas'	XSen
- 'Cavalaire' (d)	XSen
* - 'Claudia'	SEND
- 'Commandant Barthélemy' (d)	XSen
- 'Flavescens Plenum' (d)	EShb XSen
- 'Hardy Red'	XSen
- 'Madame Allen' (d)	EShb
- pink-flowered **new**	SHil
- 'Professeur Granel' (d)	EShb
- 'Provence' (d)	XSen
- 'Red Beauty'	XSen
- red-flowered **new**	SHil
- 'Rosario' (d)	EShb
- salmon-flowered	SEND
- 'Splendens Giganteum' (d)	EShb
- 'Variegatum' (v) ♀H1+3	CHll EShb SHil
- 'Villa Romaine'	XSen
- white-flowered	SEND SHil
- yellow-flowered **new**	SHil

Neviusia (*Rosaceae*)

alabamensis	NLar

Nicandra (*Solanaceae*)

physalodes	CArn CHby ELan GBee NBir SMrm WSFF
- 'Splash of Cream' (v)	CCCN
- 'Violacea'	CSpe SRms SWvt

Nicotiana (*Solanaceae*)

alata	CSpe EPfP WSFF
glauca	CCCN CDTJ CHGN CHll CSpe EShb EUJe LDai SPav SPlb
'Hopleys'	CSpe
knightiana	CDTJ CSpe
langsdorffii ♀H3	CSpe SPav SPhx
- 'Cream Splash' (v)	CPla
- 'Hot Chocolate'	CSpe
'Lime Green' ♀H3	CSpe
mutabilis	CHll CSpe LDai SDys SPhx
'Perfume Deep Purple' (Perfume Series)	CSpe
suaveolens	CBre SPhx
sylvestris ♀H3	CDTJ CSpe ELan EPfP SDys SEND SPav SPoG SWvt WTou
tabacum	CArn
'Tinkerbell'	CSpe

Nidularium (*Bromeliaceae*)

innocentii	XBlo

Nierembergia (*Solanaceae*)

§ ***repens***	CDoy ECho NLar XLum
rivularis	see *N. repens*

Nigella (*Ranunculaceae*)

damascena 'Miss Jekyll' ♀H4	CWCL
- 'Miss Jekyll Alba' ♀H4	CSpe
papillosa 'African Bride'	CSpe
- 'Midnight'	CSpe

Nigritella see *Gymnadenia*

Nipponanthemum (*Asteraceae*)

§ ***nipponicum***	CDes EBee ECho GCal IDee IVic LAst NLar NSti SRms WHil XLum
- 'Homa-giku' **new**	NWad

Noccaea see *Thlaspi*

Nolina (*Asparagaceae*)

bigelovii	WCot XSen
* ***brevifolia***	CFil
durangensis	CFil EGri
- F&M 333	WPGP
lindheimeriana	WCot
longifolia	EAmu EGri SChr
microcarpa	XSen
nelsonii	CFil EAmu EGri SPlb
- F&M 307	WPGP
parviflora	EGri
- NJM 05.010	WPGP
texana	WCot XSen

Nomocharis (*Liliaceae*)

aperta	CExl CWCL EPot GBin GBuc GCra GGGa GLin WCru
- ACE 2271	EBee LWst
- CLD 229	LWst
- CLD 524	LWst
× ***finlayorum***	LWst
mairei	see *N. pardanthina*
meleagrina	EBee EPot LWst NSoo WAbe
nana	see *Lilium nanum*
oxypetala	see *Lilium oxypetalum*
§ ***pardanthina***	GBuc WAbe
- CLD 1490	GBuc LWst
- f. ***punctulata***	GBuc GGGa LWst WCru
saluenensis	GGGa LWst WAbe

Nonea (*Boraginaceae*)

lutea	LSou NOrc NSti WHal

Nothochelone see *Penstemon*

Nothofagus ✿ (*Nothofagaceae*)

§ × ***alpina***	CBcs GBin
antarctica	CBcs CCVT CDul CMCN CNWT CTho ELan EPfP EWTr GKin IVic MBlu MBri MGos NWea SWvt WHar WSHC
- 'Benmore'	NLar
betuloides	CBcs GBin IArd IDee SPlb
cunninghamii	IArd IDee SPlb
dombeyi	CBcs CDoC CFil EBee EPfP GBin IArd IVic MBlu SAPC SWvt WPGP
fusca	IArd
glauca	CBcs GBin IVic
nitida	CBcs GBin IDee
obliqua	CBcs CDul CMCN GAbr IVic SPlb
procera misapplied	see *N.* × *alpina*
pumilio	GBin

Notholaena see *Cheilanthes*

Notholirion (*Liliaceae*)

bulbuliferum	EBee ECho GCra

	- Cox 5074	LWst
	- SDR 2865	GKev
	campanulatum	ECho GKev LWst
	macrophyllum	ECho GKev LWst
	thomsonianum	ECho LWst

Nothoscordum (*Alliaceae*)

	sp.	GCal
	gracile	CCon
	montevidense	LWst
	neriniflorum	see *Caloscordum neriniflorum*
	ostenii	CDes ECho
	strictum	EBee ECho

Nuphar (*Nymphaeaceae*)

	japonica	LLWG
	- var. ***variegata*** (v)	CRow
	lutea	CBAq CHab CRow EHon MSKA SCoo SWat
	pumila	LLWG

Nylandtia (*Polygalaceae*)

	spinosa	SPlb

Nymphaea ✿ (*Nymphaeaceae*)

	alba (H)	CHab CRow CWat EHon GQue MSKA MWts NBir SCoo SVic SWat WMAq
	'Albatros' misapplied	see *N.* 'Hermine'
§	'Albatros' Latour-Marliac (H)	CBAq CWat LLWG MSKA NPer SWat
	'Albatross'	see *N.*'Albatros' Latour-Marliac, *N.*'Hermine'
*	'Albida'	CBAq WMAq XBlo
	'Almost Black' (H)	CBAq LLWG MSKA
	'Amabilis' (H)	CRow EWay MSKA SWat WMAq
	'American Star' (H)	SWat WMAq
	'Andreana' (H)	EWay LLWG MSKA
	'Anna Epple' (H)	LLWG
	'Arc-en-ciel' (H)	LLWG SCoo SWat WMAq
	'Atropurpurea' (H)	LLWG MSKA NPer SWat WMAq
	'Attraction' (H)	CBAq CRow EHon MSKA MWts NPer SCoo SVic SWat WMAq XBlo XLum
	'Augustus McCray' (H) **new**	LLWG
	'Aurora' (H)	CBAq GQue MWts SVic SWat WMAq
	'Barbara Davies' (H)	LLWG MSKA
	'Barbara Dobbins' (H)	EWay LLWG MSKA
	'Bateau' (H)	LLWG
	'Berit Strawn' (H)	EWay
	'Bernice Ikins' (H)	LLWG
	'Black Princess' (H)	CBAq CRow EWay LLWG
	'Brakeleyi Rosea' (H)	MSKA WMAq
	'Burgundy Princess' (H)	CWat EWay LLWG MSKA NPer
	candida (H)	EHon MSKA MWts NPer WMAq
	'Candidissima' (H)	CBAq SWat
§	***capensis*** (T/D)	XBlo
	'Carolina Sunset' (H)	LLWG
	'Caroliniana Nivea' (H)	EHon
	'Caroliniana Perfecta' (H)	MSKA SWat
	'Celebration' (H)	LLWG MSKA
	'Charlene Strawn' (H)	CWat EWay LLWG WMAq
	'Charles' Choice' (H)	EWay
	'Charles de Meurville' (H)	CBAq CRow LLWG MSKA NPer SVic WMAq
	'Château le Rouge' (H)	LLWG
	'Clyde Ikins' (H)	EWay LLWG MSKA
	'Colonel A.J. Welch' (H)	EHon MSKA NPer SCoo SWat WMAq
	'Colorado' (H)	EWay LLWG MSKA NPer
	colorata	see *N. capensis*
	'Colossea' (H)	CWat MSKA NPer
	'Comanche' (H)	MSKA NPer WMAq
	'Conqueror' (H)	LLWG MSKA NPer SCoo SVic SWat
	'Dallas' (H)	LLWG
§	'Darwin' (H)	CWat MSKA NPer SLon SWat WMAq
	× ***daubenyana*** (T/D)	ECho
	'David' (H)	EWay LLWG
	'Debbie June' (H) **new**	LLWG
	'Denver' (H)	EWay LLWG MSKA
	'Ellisiana' (H)	CBAq LLWG MSKA NPer SWat
	'Escarboucle' (H) ♀H4	CBAq CRow CWat EWay LLWG MSKA NPer SCoo SVic SWat WMAq XBlo
§	'Fabiola' (H)	CRow EHon LLWG MSKA NPer SCoo WMAq
	'Fiesta'	MSKA
	'Fire Crest' (H)	CBAq GQue LLWG MSKA NPer SCoo SVic SWat WMAq
	'Froebelii' (H)	CRow CWat EHon EWay MSKA NPer SWat WMAq
	'Fulva' (H)	LLWG
	'Galatée' (H)	MSKA
	'Geisha Girl'	MSKA
	'Georgia Peach' (H)	EWay LLWG MSKA
	'Gladstoniana' (H) ♀H4	CRow EHon MSKA NPer SCoo SWat WMAq
	'Gloire du Temple-sur-Lot' (H)	LLWG NPer SWat WMAq
	'Gloriosa' (H)	LLWG NPer SCoo SWat
	'Gold Medal' (H)	EWay LLWG MSKA
	'Gonnère' (H) ♀H4	CRow CWat EHon EWay MSKA NPer SLon SWat WMAq
	'Graziella' (H)	MSKA WMAq
	'Gypsy' (H)	EWay LLWG
	'Hal Miller' (H)	LLWG
	'Hassell' (H)	LLWG
	'Hazorea Dagan White' (H) **new**	LLWG
	'Helen Fowler' (H)	WMAq
	× ***helvola***	see *N.* 'Pygmaea Helvola'
§	'Hermine' (H)	MSKA NPer SWat WMAq
	'Hidden Violet' (H) **new**	LLWG
§	'Highlight'	LLWG
	'Hilite'	see *N.*'Highlight'
	'Hollandia' misapplied	see *N.* 'Darwin'
	'Hollandia' ambig.	CBAq
	'Hollandia' Koster (H)	SWat
	'Indiana' (H)	MSKA NPer WMAq
	'Inner Light'	EWay LLWG MSKA
	'James Brydon' (H) ♀H4	CBAq CRow CWat EHon EWay MSKA MWts NPer SCoo SLon SVic SWat WMAq
	'Jean de Lamarsalle' (H)	LLWG MSKA
	'Jerusalem Dawn'	LLWG MSKA
	'Joey Tomocik' (H)	CBAq CWat EWay LLWG MSKA SCoo WMAq
	'Lactea' (H)	LLWG
	'Laydekeri Fulgens' (H)	EWay LLWG MSKA SWat WMAq
	'Laydekeri Lilacea' (H)	CRow SWat WMAq
	'Laydekeri Purpurata' (H)	EWay SWat
	'Laydekeri Rosea' misapplied	see *N.* 'Laydekeri Rosea Prolifera'
§	'Laydekeri Rosea Prolifera' (H)	EWay
	'Lemon Chiffon' (H)	CRow MSKA

	'Lemon Mist'	LLWG MSKA
	'Lily Pons' (H)	LLWG MSKA
	'Liou' (H)	LLWG MSKA
	'Little Sue' (H)	CBAq EWay LLWG MSKA
	'Livingstone' (H)	LLWG
	'Lucida' (H)	MSKA SWat WMAq
	'Madame Wilfon Gonnère' (H)	CBAq CWat EHon MSKA NPer SVic SWat WMAq
	'Marliacea Albida' (H)	CWat EHon EWay LLWG MSKA NPer SWat WMAq XBlo XLum
	'Marliacea Carnea' (H)	CRow EHon MSKA NPer SCoo SWat WMAq
§	'Marliacea Chromatella' (H) ♀H4	CBAq CRow CWat EHon EWay GQue MSKA MWts SCoo SVic SWat WMAq XBlo XLum
	'Marliacea Rosea' (H)	MSKA SWat WMAq XBlo XLum
	'Martha' (H)	EWay
	'Mary' (H)	LLWG
	'Masaniello' (H)	CRow EHon MSKA SWat WMAq
	'Maurice Laydeker' (H)	LLWG
	'Maxima'	see *N.* 'Odorata Maxima'
	'Mayla'	CBAq LLWG MSKA NPer
§	'Météor' (H)	EWay MSKA WMAq
	mexicana	LLWG
	'Millennium Pink'	MSKA
	'Moorei' (H)	MSKA SWat WMAq
	'Mrs Richmond' misapplied	see *N.* 'Fabiola'
	'Mrs Richmond' Latour-Marliac (H)	SWat XBlo
	'Munkala Ubon' (H) **new**	LLWG
	'Neptune' (H)	LLWG
	'Newchapel Beauty'	WMAq
	'Newton' (H)	EWay LLWG MSKA SWat WMAq
	'Nigel' (H)	CBAq LLWG MSKA SWat
	'Norma Gedye' (H)	CWat MSKA SWat WMAq
§	***odorata*** (H)	CRow EHon MSKA SCoo WMAq
§	- var. ***minor*** (H)	CRow MSKA SWat WMAq
	'Pumila'	see *N. odorata* var. *minor*
	'Odorata Alba'	see *N. odorata*
§	'Odorata Maxima' (H)	WMAq
	'Odorata Sulphurea' (H)	CBAq SWat
§	'Odorata Sulphurea Grandiflora' (H)	CRow SCoo SWat XBlo
§	'Odorata Turicensis' (H)	MSKA
	'Odorata William B. Shaw'	see *N.* 'W.B. Shaw'
	'Pam Bennett' (H)	LLWG
	'Panama Pacific' (T/D)	XBlo
	'Patio Joe'	LLWG MSKA
	'Paul Hariot' (H)	CWat LLWG MSKA NPer SWat WMAq
	'Peace Lily'	CBAq LLWG MSKA
	'Peach Glow'	EWay LLWG MSKA
	'Peaches and Cream' (H)	LLWG MSKA
	Pearl of the Pool (H)	SWat
	'Perry's Baby Red' (H)	CBAq CWat EWay LLWG MSKA MWts NPer SCoo WMAq
	'Perry's Double White' (H)	MSKA NPer
	'Perry's Double Yellow'	LLWG MSKA
	'Perry's Dwarf Red' (H)	LLWG MSKA
	'Perry's Fire Opal' (H)	LLWG NPer
	'Perry's Orange Sunset'	LLWG MSKA
	'Perry's Pink' (H)	SWat WMAq
	'Perry's Red Bicolor' (H)	LLWG
	'Perry's Red Glow' (H)	LLWG MSKA
	'Perry's Red Star' (H)	EWay MSKA
	'Perry's White Star' (H)	LLWG
	'Peter Slocum' (H)	EWay SWat
	'Phoebus' (H)	SWat
	'Picciola' (H)	LLWG
	'Pink Domino'	MSKA
	'Pink Grapefruit' (H)	LLWG XBlo
	'Pink Opal' (H)	CWat LLWG
	'Pink Peony' (H)	MSKA
	'Pink Pumpkin' (H)	LLWG MSKA
	'Pink Sensation' (H)	EWay LLWG MSKA NPer SLon SWat WMAq
	'Pink Sparkle' (H)	LLWG
	'Pink Sunrise' (H)	MSKA
	'Pöstlingberg' (H)	LLWG MSKA
	'Princess Elizabeth' (H)	EHon LLWG
	'Pygmaea Alba'	see *N. tetragona*
§	'Pygmaea Helvola' (H) ♀H4	CRow CWat EWay MSKA MWts NPer SCoo SLon SVic SWat WMAq
	'Pygmaea Rubis' (H)	CRow SWat WMAq
	'Pygmaea Rubra' (H)	CRow CWat EWay LLWG MSKA MWts NPer SCoo SVic WMAq
	'Radiant Red' (H)	LLWG
	'Ray Davies' (H)	LLWG
	'Red Paradise' (H)	LLWG MSKA
	'Red Spider' (H)	LLWG MSKA NPer SVic
	'Reflected Flame' (H)	LLWG
	'Rembrandt' misapplied	see *N.* 'Météor'
	'René Gérard' (H)	CWat EHon GQue MSKA MWts NPer SWat WMAq
	'Rosanna Supreme' (H)	LLWG SWat
	'Rose Arey' (H)	EWay LLWG MSKA NPer SCoo SVic SWat WMAq
	'Rose Magnolia' (H)	CWat SWat
	'Rosennymphe' (H)	MSKA NPer SWat WMAq
	'Rosy Morn' (H)	LLWG MSKA
	'Seignouretti' (H)	LLWG
	'Shady Lady'	CBAq LLWG MSKA MWts
	'Sioux' (H)	CBAq MSKA NPer SVic WMAq XBlo
	'Sirbangpra' (H) **new**	LLWG
	'Sirius' (H)	LLWG MSKA SWat
	'Snow Princess'	EWay
	'Solfatare' (H)	EWay LLWG
	'Splendida' (H)	WMAq
	'Starbright'	EWay LLWG
	'Starburst' (H)	LLWG MSKA
	'Steven Strawn' (H)	LLWG
	'Sultan' (H)	MSKA
	'Sunny Pink'	LLWG MSKA
	'Sunrise'	see *N.* 'Odorata Sulphurea Grandiflora'
	'Tan-khwan' (H) **new**	LLWG
§	***tetragona*** (H)	CRow CWat EWay NPer WMAq
	- 'Alba'	see *N. tetragona*
	'Texas Dawn' (H)	CWat EWay LLWG MSKA SLon WMAq
	'Thomas O'Brian'	LLWG
	'Tuberosa Flavescens'	see *N.* 'Marliacea Chromatella'
	'Tuberosa Richardsonii' (H)	EHon MSKA NPer
	'Turicensis'	see *N.* 'Odorata Turicensis'
	'Venusta' (H)	EWay
	'Vésuve' (H)	LLWG MSKA SWat
	'Virginalis' (H)	LLWG MSKA NPer SWat WMAq
	'Virginia' (H)	LLWG
§	'W.B. Shaw' (H)	CBAq EHon MSKA NPer SWat WMAq
	'Walter Pagels' (H)	CBAq EWay LLWG MWts WMAq
	'White Sultan' (H)	CWat LLWG MSKA
	'William Doogue' (H)	MSKA
	'William Falconer' (H)	CWat MSKA NPer SWat
	'Wow' (H)	MSKA
	'Yellow Queen' (H)	MSKA
	'Yul Ling' (H)	EWay LLWG
	'Zeus'	MSKA

Nymphoides (*Menyanthaceae*)

indica LLWG XBlo
peltata CBAq CHab CWat EHon EWay MSKA NPer SCoo SVic WMAq XLum

Nyssa ✿ (*Nyssaceae*)

aquatica CBcs
leptophylla NLar SBir
ogeche SSta
sinensis ♀H4 CAbP CBcs CDoy CDul CMCN CMac CTho ELan EPfP IDee LRHS MAsh MBlu MPkF SBir SSpi WPat
- 'Jim Russell' ESwi SBir
- Nymans form LRHS SBir
- Savill form SSta
sylvatica ♀H4 Widely available
- 'Autumn Cascades' EBee EPfP LRHS MAsh MBlu NLar SBir SSpi SSta
- Bulk's form SSta
- 'Dirr' SSpi
- 'Haymen's Red' see *N. sylvatica* Red Rage
- 'Isabel Grace' EPfP LRHS MAsh SBir SSpi
- 'Jermyns Flame' CAbP EPfP LRHS MAsh NLar SBir SSpi
- Jolly = 'Yiping' (v) MPkF NLar
- 'Lakeside Weeper' SBir
- 'Miss Scarlet' (f) NLar SBir SSta
- 'Pendula' SBir
§ - Red Rage = 'Haymanred' EPfP MPkF SBir
- 'Red Red Wine' CGHE EPfP IVic NLar SBir WPGP
- 'Sheffield Park' CAbP LRHS MAsh SBir SLim SPoG
- 'Wildfire' LRHS MPkF SBir SGol SSpi
- 'Windsor' EPfP LRHS MAsh SBir
- 'Wisley Bonfire' (m) CAbP CDoC CGHE EPfP LRHS MAsh NLar SBir SSpi SSta WPGP
ursina CBcs SSta

O

Oakesiella see *Uvularia*

Ochagavia (*Bromeliaceae*)

carnea RCB RA S-2 LSou
§ ***litoralis*** SAPC SMad
* ***rosea*** CHEx SPlb

Ochna (*Ochnaceae*)

serrulata CCCN

Ocimum (*Lamiaceae*)

'African Blue' CArn CSpe ELau EOHP GPoy LSou MHer SPoG SRms
§ ***americanum*** WJek
- 'Meng Luk' see *O. americanum*
basilicum CArn ELau GPoy MHoo NPri SIde SRms SWat WJek
- 'Anise' see *O. basilicum* 'Horapha'
- 'Ararat' ELau
- ***camphorata*** see *O. kilimandscharicum*
- 'Cinnamon' ELau MNHC SHDw WJek
- 'Gecofure' ELau
- 'Genovese' ELau MHer MNHC
- 'Genovese Special Select' ELau
- 'Glycyrrhiza' see *O. basilicum* 'Horapha'
- 'Green Ruffles' ELau EPfP WJek
- 'Holy' see *O. tenuiflorum*
§ - 'Horapha' CArn ELau MHer MNHC SIde WJek
* - 'Horapha Nanum' WJek
- 'Magic Michael' ELau
- 'Magic Mountain' SPoG
- 'Magic White' SPoG
- 'Mexican' ELau
- 'Mrs Burns' WJek
- 'Napolitano' ELau SIde SWat WJek
- 'New Guinea' ELau
- 'Osmin'PBR ELau
- 'Pistou' ELau
- 'Purple Delight' ELau
- var. ***purpurascens*** SIde
- - 'Dark Opal' MNHC SHDw SRms
- - 'Purple Ruffles' EPfP MNHC SIde SWat WJek
- - 'Red Rubin' MHer MNHC WJek
- var. ***purpurascens*** × ***kilimandscharicum*** CSpe GPoy
- 'Queenette' ELau
- 'Sweet Genovase' SVic
- 'Thai' see *O. basilicum* 'Horapha'
canum see *O. americanum*
× ***citriodorum*** MNHC SHDw SIde WJek
- 'Lime' MNHC
- 'Pesto Perpetuo' SRms
- 'Siam Queen' ELau MHer WJek
gratissimum CArn ELau
§ ***kilimandscharicum*** ELau GPoy
minimum ELau MHer MNHC SIde WJek
sanctum see *O. tenuiflorum*
'Spice' ELau
'Spicy Globe' ELau
§ ***tenuiflorum*** CArn ELau GPoy MNHC SHDw SIde WJek

Odontonema (*Acanthaceae*)

schomburgkianum CCCN WHil
tubaeforme CCCN MOWG

Oemleria (*Rosaceae*)

cerasiformis CBcs CHGN CJun CTri EBtc EPfP LRHS NLar WCot WSHC

Oenanthe (*Apiaceae*)

fistulosa LLWG MSKA
javanica 'Flamingo' (v) CBAq CWat EBee ELan EPfP EWay GCal LEdu MSKA MWts NBro WMAq WSHC XLum
lachenalii LLWG SDix
pimpinelloides CHab LLWG

Oenothera ✿ (*Onagraceae*)

§ ***acaulis*** CMea CSpe MNrw WCot WPGP
§ - 'Aurea' GKev XLum
- 'Lutea' see *O. acaulis* 'Aurea'
'Apricot Delight' CHVG EHoe GJos LRHS SGbt SPad WMnd WMoo
§ ***biennis*** CArn CSev ELan GAbr GPoy MHer MHoo MNHC NBro SIde SPhx SRms WBrk WHer WJek WSFF
* ***campylocalyx*** LDai
childsii see *O. speciosa*
cinaeus see *O. fruticosa* subsp. *glauca*
'Colin Porter' WMoo
'Copper Canyon' SPad
'Crown Imperial' CMac LEdu LSou MArl NHol SHar SLon SPer

	Crown of Gold = 'Lishal'	ELan LLHF
§	***elata*** subsp. ***hookeri***	EWes NBre
	erythrosepala	see *O. glazioviana*
	'Finlay's Fancy'	WCru
§	***fruticosa***	NLar SPlb XSen
	- 'African Sun'PBR	SRot
	- 'Camel' (v)	LDai NPro WHrl WWEG XLum
	- Fireworks	see *O. fruticosa* 'Fyrverkeri'
§	- 'Fyrverkeri' ♀H4	CBcs CMea CPrp ECtt ELan GMaP LEdu LHop LRHS MRav NGdn SPer SWvt WMnd WWEG XLum
§	- subsp. ***glauca*** ♀H4	CElw EPfP MHer SMrm SRms WJek
	- - 'Erica Robin' (v)	CMea ECtt EHoe GBin LRHS LSou MAvo MNrw MRav NEgg NGdn SMad SMrm SRot SWvt WCot WHoo WWEG
	- - 'Longest Day'	MBrN
	- - Solstice	see *O. fruticosa* subsp. *glauca* 'Sonnenwende'
§	- - 'Sonnenwende'	CBre CElw LRHS NLar NPro WMoo WWEG XLum
	- Highlight	see *O. fruticosa* 'Hoheslicht'
§	- 'Hoheslicht'	EBee
	- 'Lady Brookeborough'	MRav
	- 'Michelle Ploeger'	NBre
	- 'Silberblatt' (v)	EBee
	- 'Yellow River'	CElw EBee
	- 'Youngii'	EPfP LEdu WJek WWEG
	'Give-me-Sunshine'	SLon
	glabra Miller	see *O. biennis*
	glabra misapplied	NSti
§	***glazioviana***	MNHC NBir NWad
	hookeri	see *O. elata* subsp. *hookeri*
	kunthiana	ECho WMoo
	- 'Glowing Magenta'	SPoG
	lamarckiana	see *O. glazioviana*
	Lemon Drop = 'Innocno131'PBR	MPkF SHil
	'Lemon Sunset'	CCVN LSou WHil WMoo
	linearis	see *O. fruticosa*
§	***macrocarpa*** ♀H4	Widely available
	- subsp. ***fremontii***	XSen
	- - 'Silver Wings'	SMrm SPhx
	- subsp. ***incana***	CMea CSpe SPhx WHoo
	- 'Yellow Queen'	GJos
	missouriensis	see *O. macrocarpa*
	oakesiana	SPhx
	odorata misapplied	see *O. stricta*
	odorata Hook. & Arn.	see *O. biennis*
	odorata Jacquin	XLum
	- cream-flowered	CSpe
	organensis	CDes MNrw
§	***perennis***	NPro SRms WThu XLum
	pilosella 'Yella Fella' **new**	CHVG
	pumila	see *O. perennis*
	rosea	CMea XLum
§	***speciosa***	NBre SEND SPhx SRms WJek XLum
*	- 'Alba'	EBee EWes
	- var. ***childsii***	see *O. speciosa*
	- 'Pink Petticoats'	NPer
	- 'Rosea'	LAst SPlb
	- 'Siskiyou'	CBcs ECtt EHyd EPfP EShb LEdu LRHS MNrw NBro SCoo SMad SMrm SPer SPoG WGwG XLum
	- Twilight = 'Turner01'PBR (v)	LHop SHar
	- 'Woodside White'	SMrm
§	***stricta***	CMea GCal MNrw
	- 'Sulphurea'	CMHG CMea ECGP ELan EWld GCal GMaP IFro MNFA NPer SMrm SPhx WCot
	'Summer Sun'	CHel ECGP LRHS SPer
	taraxacifolia	see *O. acaulis*
	tetragona	see *O. fruticosa* subsp. *glauca*
	- var. ***fraseri***	see *O. fruticosa* subsp. *glauca*
	- 'Glaber' **new**	CPBP
	versicolor	CSev
	- 'Sunset Boulevard'	CSpe CTsd GCal LDai MMuc SPer WMoo XLum

Olea (Oleaceae)

	europaea (F)	Widely available
	- 'Aglandau' (F)	CAgr
	- 'Arbequina' (F)	SBig
	- 'Bouteillan' (F)	CAgr
	- 'Cailletier' (F)	CAgr
	- 'Chelsea Physic Garden' (F)	CDoC
§	- 'Cipressino' (F)	CDoy ESwi MGos SBig
	- 'El Greco' (F)	CBcs
	- 'Fastigiata'	EBee
	- 'Frantoio' (F)	CAgr CDoy SBig
	- 'Hojiblanca' (F)	EBee SBig
	- 'Leccino' (F)	CDoy SBig
	- 'Maurino' (F)	SBig
	- 'Peace'	CDoy
	- 'Pendolino' (F)	SBig
	- 'Picual' (F)	SBig
	- 'Pyramidalis'	see *O. europaea* 'Cipressino'

Olearia ✿ (Asteraceae)

	arborescens	EWld
	argophylla	CBcs CExl ECou
	avicenniifolia	CMac ECou IVic SEND
	bullata	ECou
	× ***capillaris***	CDoC EBee ECou
	chathamica	IVic
§	***cheesemanii***	CBcs CDoC CExl GGal LRHS NLar SVen
	coriacea	ECou
	'County Park'	CWSG ECou
	erubescens × ***ilicifolia***	SVen
	furfuracea	ECou GLin SEND
	glandulosa	ECou
	gunniana	see *O. phlogopappa*
	× ***haastii***	CBar CBcs CDoC CDoy CDul CMac CSBt CTri CTsd EBee ECou ECrN ELan EPfP GKin LAst LRHS MGos MRav MSwo NLar NWea SGol SKHP SLim SPer SRms SWvt WCFE WHar
	- 'McKenzie'	ECou ELon
	'Havering Blush'	ECou
	hectorii	ECou
§	'Henry Travers'	CBcs CCCN CExl EPfP GCal IVic SVen
	ilicifolia	CDoC CTsd EPfP IDee IVic LRHS MAsh
	insignis	see *Pachystegia insignis*
	lacunosa	WHor
	lepidophylla	ECou
	- silver-leaved	ECou
	lirata	ECou
	macrodonta ♀H3	Widely available
	- 'Major'	CCCN GGal NLar
	- 'Minor'	CBcs CCCN CMac ELan EPfP GCal GQui IVic SPlb

	× ***mollis*** (Kirk) Cockayne	CMac EBee GQui LRHS SPer
	- 'Zennorensis' ♀H3	CBcs CCCN CDoC EPfP IDee IVic NLar
	nummularifolia	CBcs CCCN CDoC CHll CTri CTsd EBee ECou ELan EPfP GKin IVic LRHS NLar NSoo SEND SPer SPoG SVen SWvt
	- var. ***cymbifolia***	ECou
	- hybrids	ECou
	- 'Little Lou'	ECou
	odorata	ECou NLar
	oleifolia	see *O.* 'Waikariensis'
	paniculata	CDoC CMHG COlW CTri CTsd EBee EPfP IVic LRHS NSoo SEND SVen
§	***phlogopappa***	CTri ECou EWld GLin SVen
	- 'Comber's Blue'	CBcs CCCN ELan EPfP GGal GKin IVic LRHS MAsh SLim SPer
§	- 'Comber's Pink'	CBcs CCCN CDoC CExl CHid ELan ELon EPfP GKin LRHS MSCN NPer SLim SPer SPoG WGrn WKif
	- 'Rosea'	see *O. phlogopappa* 'Comber's Pink'
I	- var. ***subrepanda*** (DC.) J.H.Willis	GGal
	ramulosa	CCCN CExl
	- 'Blue Stars'	CMac ECou ELan SLon SRms WGrn
	rani misapplied	see *O. cheesemanii*
	× ***scilloniensis*** misapplied	see *O. stellulata* DC.
	× ***scilloniensis*** ambig.	CBcs ELan EWld LAst MAsh SPoG
	× ***scilloniensis*** Dorrien-Smith ♀H3	CCCN CTsd LRHS MRav
	- 'Compacta'	CBcs
	- 'Master Michael'	CCCN CDoC CTri EBee ELon EPfP IVic MOWG NLar SPer SPoG WGrn WPGP
	semidentata misapplied	see *O.* 'Henry Travers'
	solandri	CCCN CDoC CMac CTsd EBee ECou EHoe IDee LRHS SDix SEND
	- 'Aurea'	CBcs
	'Stardust'	LRHS SPlb SVen WCot
	stellulata misapplied	see *O. phlogopappa*
§	***stellulata*** DC.	CExl CMac CSBt CWib ECou EPfP GGal SDix SLim SPer
	- 'Michael's Pride'	CExl
	- var. ***rugosa***	ECou
	traversii	CBcs CCCN CDoC CMHG COlW CSBt EBee EPfP EWld LRHS NWea SEND WHer
	- 'Tweedledum' (v)	CCCN CDoC CWib ECou EHoe
	- 'Variegata' (v)	CBcs SEND
	virgata	CCCN CHEx ECou IDee
	- var. ***laxiflora***	WHer
	- var. ***lineata***	ECou NLar SEND WHer WSHC
	- - 'Dartonii'	CBcs CTsd EBee ECou EPfP GBin LRHS SLPl SPlb SVen
§	'Waikariensis'	CExl CMHG CMac ECou GKin IDee IVic LRHS MAsh MSCN SEND SLon WCFE

Oligoneuron see *Solidago*

Oligostachyum (*Poaceae*)

lubricum	see *Semiarundinaria lubrica*
oedogonatum	WPGP

olive see *Olea europaea*

Olsynium (*Iridaceae*)

§	***douglasii*** ♀H4	CBro GAbr LLHF NRya NSla
	- 'Album'	CWCL ELon EPot GBin LLHF MNrw NHar NRya NSla WHal WWFP
	- var. ***inflatum***	EBee EWes
§	***filifolium***	GAbr
§	***junceum***	CSpe LLHF WPGP
	trinerve B&SWJ 10459	WCru

Omphalodes ✿ (*Boraginaceae*)

	cappadocica ♀H4	CElw EPfP EPot EShb IFoB LEdu LRHS MMuc NBro NPer NSla SRms SWat WBrk
	- 'Anthea Bloom'	NEgg
	- 'Cherry Ingram' ♀H4	Widely available
	- 'Lilac Mist'	CLAP EBee GBuc LLWP MRav NPnk SRms SWvt WWEG
	- 'Starry Eyes'	Widely available
§	***linifolia*** ♀H4	CSpe MCot SPhx
	- ***alba***	see *O. linifolia*
	nitida	CSpe IMou LRHS MNrw NLBP WWEG
	verna	CHel CMac CTri ECho ELan EPPr EPfP GAbr GJos GMaP LHop LLWP LRHS MBel MCot MNFA MNrw NChi NPri SPer SPlb SPoG SWat WCAu WPGP WWEG
	- 'Alba'	Widely available
	- 'Elfenauge'	CDes EBee IMou NBir NLar SMrm WCot WWEG
	- ***grandiflora***	WCot

Omphalogramma (*Primulaceae*)

minus	GKev

Oncostema see *Scilla*

onion see *Allium cepa*

Onixotis (*Colchicaceae*)

stricta	CLak WCot

Onobrychis (*Papilionaceae*)

viciifolia	EBee

Onoclea (*Onocleaceae*)

sensibilis ♀H4	Widely available
- copper-leaved	CHEx CJun CRow WPGP

Ononis (*Papilionaceae*)

repens	CArn
spinosa	IMou MHer SMrm WSpi

Onopordum (*Asteraceae*)

	acanthium	CArn EBee ELan EPfP GAbr GMaP LRHS MHer MWat NBid NEgg NGBl SIde SPhx WCot WOut
	arabicum	see *O. nervosum*
	illyricum	WCot
§	***nervosum*** ♀H4	CSpe SEND

Onosma (*Boraginaceae*)

alborosea	CCse ECre ELan GCal GCra SEND WKif
nana	WAbe

Onychium (*Pteridaceae*)

contiguum	WCot
japonicum	CBty CExl EFer GQui ISha

Ophiopogon ✿ (*Asparagaceae*)

BWJ 8244 from Vietnam	WCru

	from India	GCal
	'Black Dragon'	see *O. planiscapus* 'Nigrescens'
	bodinieri	CBct ECho EShb EWes LEdu
	- B&L 12505	CLAP EBee EPPr
	caulescens B&SWJ 8230	WCru
	- B&SWJ 11813	WCru
	aff. ***caulescens*** HWJ 590	WCru WPGP
	chingii	EPPr EWes GCal WCot
	clarkei	MMoz
	clavatus KWJ 12267	WCru
	formosanus B&SWJ 3659	WCru
	'Gin-ryu'	see *Liriope spicata* 'Gin-ryu'
	graminifolius	see *Liriope muscari*
	'Hosoba Kokuryu' new	GBin
	intermedius	CBct CJun CPBP EPPr EShb WCot
	- GWJ 9387	WCru
§	- 'Argenteomarginatus' (v)	ECho EWes
	- 'Variegatus'	see *O. intermedius* 'Argenteomarginatus'
§	***jaburan***	CMac EBee ECho LEdu NPnk WMoo WPtf
	- 'Variegatus'	see *O. jaburan* 'Vittatus'
§	- 'Vittatus' (v)	ECho EHoe ELan EPfP EWes LEdu MGos MPkF WCot
	japonicus	CMac CTsd ECho EPPr EPfP EShb GPoy LEdu SGol XLum
	- B&SWJ 1871	WCru
	- 'Albus'	CLAP ECho EPri MWat
	- 'Compactus'	CDoC WPGP
	- 'Gyoku-Ryu'	EBee GCal
	- 'Kigimafukiduma'	CExl CMac LRHS MRav SGol
	- 'Kyoto'	EPPr ESwi NOak
	- 'Minor'	CBct CEnd CKno EBee ELon EPPr EPfP LBMP WPGP WWEG XLum
	- 'Nanus Variegatus' (v)	EBee
	- 'Nippon'	ECho EHoe EPPr NGdn
	- 'Silver Dragon' (v)	EPPr MBri WCFE
*	- 'Tama-ryu Number Two'	ECho EPPr
*	- 'Variegatus' (v)	CDTJ CMac ECho LEdu SLPl SPer
	parviflorus GWJ 9387	WCru
	- HWJK 2093	WCru
	planiscapus	CEnd CExl CKno CMHG CSev ECho EPPr NBro SPad WMoo WWEG
*	- 'Albovariegatus' (v)	WMoo
	- 'Black Beard'	CKno EBee EUJe EWTr GBin LRHS MAsh MBri
	- f. ***leucanthus***	EPPr SLPl WCot
	- 'Little Tabby' (v)	CDes CFil CLAP EBee ECho MMoz NPro WCot WGrn WHal WWEG
*	- ***minimus***	ECho
§	- 'Nigrescens' ♀H4	Widely available
	- 'Silver Ribbon'	ECho
	scaber B&SWJ 1842	WCru
	- B&SWJ 3655	WCru
	'Spring Gold'	EShb

Ophrys (*Orchidaceae*)

apifera	CCon NLAp WHer
- subsp. ***trollii***	NLAp
apifera* × *holoserica	NLAp
bombyliflora	NLAp
ferrum-equinum	NLAp
fuciflora	NLAp
fusca	NLAp
heldreichii	NLAp
insectifera	NLAp
lutea	NLAp
omegaifera new	NLAp
reinholdii	NLAp
speculum	NLAp
sphegodes	NLAp
- subsp. ***helenae***	NLAp
- subsp. ***mammosa***	NLAp
strausii	NLAp
tenthredinifera	NLAp

Oplopanax (*Araliaceae*)

horridus	CArn
- B&SWJ 9551	WCru
japonicus	WCru

Opopanax (*Apiaceae*)

sp. new	NChi
chironium	CArn SDix SPhx
- PAB 845 new	LEdu

Opuntia (*Cactaceae*)

	compressa	see *O. humifusa*
	engelmannii	SChr
	erinacea	SChr
	- var. ***utahensis***	WCot
	× ***polycantha*** NNS 99-263	
	ficus-indica	SPlb
	fragilis	SChr SKHP XSen
§	***humifusa***	CDTJ EAmu EGri SChr WCot XLum XSen
	phaeacantha	SChr
§	***polyacantha***	EGri SChr SPlb
	- 'Carmin' new	XSen
	rhodantha	see *O. polyacantha*
	spinosior new	XLum

orange, sour or Seville see *Citrus aurantium*

orange, sweet see *Citrus sinensis*

Orbexilum (*Papilionaceae*)

pedunculatum var. ***psoralioides***	SBrt SPhx

Orchis (*Orchidaceae*)

	anthropophora	EFEx NLAp
	elata	see *Dactylorhiza elata*
	foliosa	see *Dactylorhiza foliosa*
	fuchsii	see *Dactylorhiza fuchsii*
	italica	NLAp
	laxiflora	see *Anacamptis laxiflora*
	maculata	see *Dactylorhiza maculata*
	maderensis	see *Dactylorhiza foliosa*
	majalis	see *Dactylorhiza majalis*
§	***mascula***	ECho NLAp WHer
	militaris	NLAp
	morio	see *Anacamptis morio*
	purpurea	NLAp

oregano see *Origanum vulgare*

Oreocharis (*Gesneriaceae*)

aurea	WCot

Oreomyrrhis (*Apiaceae*)

argentea	CSpe EBee GKev SDix SPhx

Oreopanax (*Araliaceae*)

	floribundus	see *O. incisus*
§	***incisus*** new	WCru

Oreopteris (*Thelypteridaceae*)

§ ***limbosperma***	WCot

Origanum ✿ (*Lamiaceae*)

from Kalamata	SEND
acutidens	XSen
amanum ♀H2-3	CPBP ECho EPot EWes NBir NSla SBch WAbe
- var. ***album***	ECho NSla WAbe
× ***applii***	ELau
'Barbara Tingey'	CRDP CWCL ECho EWes ITim MNrw SRms WCFE
'Bristol Cross'	EBee ECtt LEdu MHer XSen
'Buckland'	CPrp CRDP EBee ECho ECtt ITim WAbe WSHC
caespitosum	see *O. vulgare* 'Nanum'
§ ***calcaratum***	ECho LLHF WAbe XSen
'Carol's Delight'	MHer
creticum	see *O. vulgare* subsp. *hirtum*
dictamnus	CMea ECho GPoy LLHF MHer SHDw SIgm WJek XSen
'Dingle Fairy'	CWCL EBee ECho ECtt EPot EWes MHer MNrw NBir SBch SIde SRot SWvt WMoo XSen
ehrenbergii	XSen
'Emma Stanley'	WAbe
'Frank Tingey'	ECho LLHF
'Gold Splash'	EPfP MHoo SIde WMoo
heracleoticum L.	see *O. vulgare* subsp. *hirtum*
'Hopfenblüte' **new**	EBee
'Hot and Spicy'	CPbn MHer MHoo SRms WJek XSen
'Ingolstadt' (v)	SPhx WCot
'Jekka's Beauty'	WJek
'Kent Beauty'	CKno CMea CSpe CWCL EBee ECho ECtt ELan EPfP EShb GBuc LPio LRHS LSou MCot MHer MHoo MRav NBir SPhx SWvt WAbe WGwG WJek WKif WSHC XSen
'Kent Beauty Variegated' (v)	ECho
laevigatum ♀H3	ECho ELan EPfP EPot MHer NBro NMir NPer SIde SIgm WCot WKif WMoo WSHC XSen
I - 'Aromaticum' **new**	IMou
- 'Herrenhausen' ♀H4	Widely available
- 'Hopleys'	CPrp CTri EBee ELan EPfP LEdu LHop LRHS MBri MCot MHer MHol MHoo MRav MWat NBir NCGa NDov SEND SPer SPhx SRms WHoo WSHC XSen
- 'Purple Charm'	EDAr SRms
'Lynda Windsor'	CRDP
majorana	CArn CHab CPbn CSev ELau GPoy MHer MHoo MNHC SIde SRms SWat WJek
- Pagoda Bells = 'Lizbell'PBR	CWCL SIde SMrm SRot WHoo
'Marchants Seedling'	SPhx
microphyllum	CArn
minutiflorum	ECho LLHF
'Norton Gold'	CBre ECtt LRHS MHer NBre NPer SIde
'Nymphenburg'	LSou
onites	CHby ELau MHer MHoo MNHC SIde SPlb SRms WJek
Overseas Farm hybrid	MHer
'Rosenkuppel'	CMea EBee ECtt ELan EPot LHop LRHS MHer MLHP NDov SBch SPer SPhx SPlb SWvt WCAu WJek WMoo WPnn WWEG XSen
'Rotkugel'	CPrp WCFE WCru WWEG
rotundifolium ♀H4	ECho ELan MHer MHoo NBir SBch WThu XSen
scabrum subsp. ***pulchrum*** 'Newleaze'	SBch
syriacum	CArn
tournefortii	see *O. calcaratum*
vulgare	CArn CHab CPbn CSev CTsd GJos GMaP GPoy MHer MHoo MMuc MNHC NBro NMir NPol NPri SEND SIde SPlb SRms SVic WHer WJek WSFF XLum
- from Israel	ELau
- 'Acorn Bank'	CArn CPrp EBee ECtt ELau EWes LEdu MNHC NLar SIde SPoG SRms WGwG WHer WJek
- var. ***album***	ELau
- 'Aureum' ♀H4	Widely available
- 'Aureum Crispum'	CPrp ELau GPoy NBid SBch SIde SRms SWat WJek
- 'Compactum'	CArn CMea CPrp CSev EBee ELau EPot GCal GPoy LEdu MHer MHoo MNFA MNHC NBir NSla SIde SPlb SRms SWat WAbe WJek XLum XSen
- 'Country Cream' (v)	CElw CPbn CPrp EBee ECtt ELau ELon EPfP EPot EShb EWes LPot LRHS MAsh MHer MHoo MLHP MNHC NBir NGdn SHDw SPer SPlb SPoG SRms SRot SWat WCFE WMnd WWEG
- var. ***formosanum*** B&SWJ 3180	WCru
§ - 'Gold Tip' (v)	CMea CSev ELau MCot MHer MHol MHoo MNHC NWad SIde SPlb SRms SWat WHer WJek WWEG
- 'Golden Shine'	EHoe EWes MHoo SIde
§ - subsp. ***hirtum***	CArn CHby CPbn GPoy SPlb WJek
- - 'Greek'	CPrp ELau LEdu MHer MNHC SEND SRms
§ - 'Nanum'	LHop LRHS SRms WJek
- 'Nyamba'	GPoy
- 'Pink Mist'	MNrw
- 'Polyphant' (v)	CPbn CSev LSou MHoo NBir SRms WJek XSen
- 'Thumble's Variety'	CElw CMea CPrp EBee ECtt EHoe EPfP GCal LHop LRHS MAsh MBri MHer MNFA MRav NWad SWat SWvt WCFE WHer WMnd WMoo WWEG XLum XSen
- 'Tomintoul'	GPoy
- 'Variegatum'	see *O. vulgare* 'Gold Tip'
- 'White Charm'	CPbn EBee MHoo NWad SIde
'Z'Attar'	MHer WJek

Orixa (*Rutaceae*)

japonica	CExl EBee NLar WPGP
- 'Variegata' (v)	LLHF LRHS NLar

Orlaya (*Apiaceae*)

grandiflora ♀H4	CAby CBre CCon CSam CSpe MCot SBch SPhx WCot WHal

Ornithogalum (*Asparagaceae*)

algeriense	ECho
arabicum	CBro CCCN CCon ECho GAbr GKev MBri SDeJ WCot
arianum	ECho

balansae see *O. oligophyllum*
caudatum see *O. longibracteatum*
chionophilum ECho
dubium ♀H1 CBro ECho ELan WBor
- hybrids CGrW
fimbriatum ECho WCot
lanceolatum ECho GKev WCot
§ ***longibracteatum*** CHEx ECho SChr WHer
magnum CAvo CBro CWCL EBee ECho EPot ERCP GBin GBuc GKev MCot MNrw SDeJ SPad SPhx WCot
multifolium ECho
'Loeriesfontein'
'Namib Gold' SDeJ
nanum see *O. sigmoideum*
narbonense ECho EPot GKev SPhx WCot
nutans ♀H4 CAvo CBro CHid CPrp CWCL EBee ECho EPfP EPot GBin GBuc GCal GKev LHop LRHS MAvo MNrw NBir SDeJ SEND WCot
§ ***oligophyllum*** ECho EPfP EPot MNrw
§ ***orthophyllum*** ECho
ponticum ECho
pyramidale CPom EBee ECho EPot MNrw SPhx
pyrenaicum CAvo CSpe WCot WShi XEll
reverchonii EBee ECho EPot ERCP SPhx
saundersiae ECho
sibthorpii see *O. sigmoideum*
§ ***sigmoideum*** EBee GKev
sintenisii ECho
suaveolens 'Saldanha' ECho
tenuifolium see *O. orthophyllum*
- subsp. ***aridum*** ECho
thyrsoides ♀H1 CCCN ECho EPfP GBin LRHS SDeJ
ulophyllum EBee ECho
umbellatum CAvo CBro CHab CTri ECho EPfP GKev GPoy LHop MBri MCot MNrw SDeJ SEND SPer SRms WShi

Ornithoglossum (*Colchicaceae*)

viride CLak

Orontium (*Araceae*)

aquaticum CBAq CWat EHon EWay LLWG MSKA MWts NPer SWat WMAq

Orostachys (*Crassulaceae*)

§ ***spinosa*** EDAr EWes GKev SPlb WAbe WCot

Orthophytum (*Bromeliaceae*)

gurkenii new WCot

Orthrosanthus (*Iridaceae*)

chimboracensis CCon EWld NLar
- JCA 13743 CPou
laxus CCon ECou ECre EWTr LLHF MAvo NBir SMad WMoo WWEG
multiflorus CBro CSpe EBee EPri
polystachyus CCVN CTsd LPla SMrm WSHC

Orychophragmus (*Brassicaceae*)

violaceus CCCN

Oryzopsis (*Poaceae*)

hymenoides LDai
- 'Rimrock' SPhx
lessoniana see *Anemanthele lessoniana*
miliacea CKno CSpe EHoe EPPr LDai MMoz NDov SEND WCot WPGP

Oscularia (*Aizoaceae*)

§ ***deltoides*** ♀H1-2 CCCN CHEx SVen WCot

Osmanthus (*Oleaceae*)

armatus CAbP CBcs CMac EBee EPfP NLar SGol
× ***burkwoodii*** ♀H4 Widely available
§ ***decorus*** CBcs CDoC CMac CTri EBee ELan EPfP MGos MRav NLar NWea SBrt SEND SGol SPer
- 'Angustifolius' NLar
delavayi ♀H4 Widely available
- 'George Gardner' CMac
- 'Latifolius' CExl CJun EPfP LRHS MAsh SLon SPoG SWvt
forrestii see *O. yunnanensis*
× ***fortunei*** CDoC CExl CHel EBee EPfP LLHF LRHS SEND
fragrans CBcs CMCN EBee SLon SWvt
§ ***heterophyllus*** CBcs CDul CMac EBee ECrN ELan EPfP MGos MRav NLar SGol SPer SRms SSta
§ - all gold ELan EPfP LHop SPer
- 'Argenteomarginatus' see *O. heterophyllus* 'Variegatus'
§ - 'Aureomarginatus' (v) CBcs CDoC CMHG CTsd EHoe ELon GKin NLar NWea SLon SPer WCFE
- 'Aureus' misapplied see *O. heterophyllus* all gold
- 'Aureus' Rehder see *O. heterophyllus* 'Aureomarginatus'
§ - 'Goshiki' (v) Widely available
- 'Gulftide' ♀H4 CDul EPfP LRHS MAsh MGos NLar
- 'Kembu' (v) NLar
- 'Latifolius Variegatus' (v) CDoC
- 'Myrtifolius' CMac NLar
- 'Ōgon' EPfP
- 'Purple Shaft' CAbP ELan EPfP LRHS MAsh
- 'Purpureus' CBcs CDoC CDul CMHG CMac CWSG CWib EBee ELon GBin MBri MGos MRav MSwo NHol NLar SCoo SEND SGol SLim SLon SPer SSpi WCFE
- 'Rotundifolius' CBcs CMac NLar
- Tricolor see *O. heterophyllus* 'Goshiki'
§ - 'Variegatus' (v) ♀H4 Widely available
ilicifolius see *O. heterophyllus*
rigidus NLar
serrulatus NLar
suavis NLar
§ ***yunnanensis*** EBee EPfP MBlu MRav NLar SAPC WPGP WPat WSHC

× *Osmarea* see *Osmanthus*

Osmaronia see *Oemleria*

Osmorhiza (*Apiaceae*)

aristata B&SWJ 1607 WCru

Osmunda ✿ (*Osmundaceae*)

sp. CCCN
asiatica WCru
cinnamomea ♀H4 CBty CCCN CKel CLAP CWCL EBee EWes ISha LEdu LRHS NLar NMyG
claytoniana ♀H4 CLAP EBee EFer GLin ISha LRHS NLar NMyG WCru WPnP XLum
japonica CHid CLAP ISha NCGa

regalis ♀H4	Widely available
- from southern USA	CLAP
- 'Cristata' ♀H4	CBty CLAP ELan EPfP LRHS MMoz MRav NBid NLar SWvt WFib
- 'Purpurascens'	CHid CLAP CWCL ELan ELon EPfP ERod GQui LRHS MAvo MGos MRav NBid NBir NHol NLar NPri NWad SGol SHil SMad SWat WFib WMoo WPGP WPnP WWEG XLum
- var. ***spectabilis***	CCCN CLAP ISha LRHS
- 'Undulata'	WFib

Osteospermum (*Asteraceae*)

'African Queen'	see *O.* 'Nairobi Purple'
'Astra Outback Purple' (Astra Series)	LAst
Banana Symphony = 'Sekiin47' (Symphony Series)	CCCN
barberae misapplied	see *O. jucundum*
'Blue Streak'	CCCN CMac
'Buttermilk' ♀H1+3	CCCN ELan
'Cannington John'	CCCN LSRN
'Cannington Roy'	CBar CBcs CCCN CMac CSam EBee ECtt ELan EPfP GAbr GBee LSRN NSoo SPoG
caulescens misapplied	see *O.* 'White Pim'
compact white-flowered	CHEx
ecklonis	CBcs CCCN CDTJ CHll CTri EBee EPfP GMaP NBro NGdn
- var. ***prostratum***	see *O.* 'White Pim'
Flower Power Double Series (d) **new**	LBuc
'Giles Gilbey' (v)	CCCN MBNS
'Gold Sparkler' (v)	SEND
'Gweek Variegated' (v)	CCCN
'Helen Dimond'	LBuc LRHS
'Hopleys' ♀H3-4	MHer SEND
'Iced Gem'	LBuc LRHS
'In the Pink' **new**	SPer
'Irish'	ECtt EPot IGor LBMP LSou SMrm
§ ***jucundum*** ♀H3-4	CTri CWCL EPfP LRHS LSRN MLHP MRav NBir NPer SEND SMrm SPlb SRms WCFE WIce
- 'Blackthorn Seedling' ♀H3-4	CCCN CWGN IVic NGdn
- var. ***compactum***	CHEx CMac CPrp CTsd ELan ELon EPfP GMaP LBMP LRHS LSRN NPer NPri SMrm SPer SPoG SWvt WAbe WHil WHoo WNew WPat
- 'Langtrees' ♀H3-4	SMrm
- 'Nanum'	EDAr
'Keia' (Springstar Series)	CCCN
§ 'Lady Leitrim' ♀H3-4	CBar CCCN CWCL CWGN EBee ECtt ELan ELon EPfP GCra GKev LBMP LHop LSRN MGos MSpe NPer SPad SWvt WAbe WHlf WPtf
'Lemon Symphony'PBR (Symphony Series)	CBcs
Milk Symphony = 'Seiremi' (Symphony Series)	CCCN CWCL
'Mirach' (Springstar Series)	CWCL
§ 'Nairobi Purple'	CBcs CCCN CHEx CHel CPrp ECtt ELan ELon EPfP ESwi LBMP LBuc MAvo MHol NPri NSoo SEND SWvt WBor WCot WHil WNew
Nasinga Cream = 'Aknam'PBR (Cape Daisy Series)	CCCN
Nasinga Purple = 'Aksullo' (Cape Daisy Series)	EPfP
Orange Symphony = 'Seimora'PBR (Symphony Series)	CBcs CCCN MBNS
'Pale Face'	see *O.* 'Lady Leitrim'
'Peggyi'	see *O.* 'Nairobi Purple'
'Pink Whirls' ♀H1+3	CCCN
polygaloides **new**	SPlb
'Port Wine'	see *O.* 'Nairobi Purple'
'Seaside' (Side Series)	EPfP
(Serenity Series) Serenity Lemonade = 'Balserlem'PBR	CWGN
- Serenity Sunset = 'Balserset'PBR	CWGN
'Silver Sparkler' (v) ♀H1+3	CCCN CDTJ ELan MHer SVen
'Snow Pixie'	CWGN ECtt EDAr ELon LPio MHol NPri SWvt
Sonja	see *O.* 'Sunny Sonja'
'Sparkler'	CCCN CHEx
Springstar Series	CHel
'Stardust'PBR	ECtt EPfP LBuc LRHS NPer SCoo SPoG
(Sunny Series) 'Sunny Amanda'PBR	SPoG
- 'Sunny Atila' **new**	WGor
- 'Sunny Bianca'PBR	SPoG
- 'Sunny Dark Florence'	SVen
- 'Sunny Dark Martha'	EPfP
- 'Sunny Davina'	SVen
- 'Sunny Elena'	WGor
- 'Sunny Felix'PBR	SPoG
- 'Sunny Mary'PBR	SPoG WGor
- 'Sunny Sonja'PBR	EPfP
I 'Superbum'	CHEx CWCL
I 'Superbum' × 'Lady Leitrim'	CHEx
'Tauranga'	see *O.* 'Whirlygig'
'Tresco Peggy'	see *O.* 'Nairobi Purple'
'Tresco Pink'	CCCN
'Tresco Purple'	see *O.* 'Nairobi Purple'
Voltage Yellow = 'Balvoyelo'PBR	LSqH
'Weetwood' ♀H3-4	CCCN CWGN ECtt ELan EPot LHop LRHS MHer MLHP SPer SPoG SWvt WAbe
§ 'Whirlygig' ♀H1+3	CCCN
§ 'White Pim' ♀H3-4	CDTJ CHll NPer SDix SEND SMrm
'Wine Purple'	see *O.* 'Nairobi Purple'
'Wisley Pink'	NEgg
Zanzibar Pink Bicolour = 'Akzapib'PBR (Cape Daisy Series) **new**	SPoG
Zanzibar White with Ring = 'Akzawhir'PBR (Cape Daisy Series) **new**	SPoG
'Zaurak' (Springstar Series)	CCCN CWCL
'Zulu' (Cape Daisy Series)	CCCN

Ostrowskia (*Campanulaceae*)

magnifica	LWst

Ostrya (*Betulaceae*)

carpinifolia	CBcs CCVT CDul CLnd CMCN CTho CWib EBee ELan EPfP MBlu MBri MMuc NLar NWea SGol SWvt
japonica	CDul CMCN NLar
virginiana	EPfP

Otatea (Poaceae)

aztecorum	ERod

Othonna (Asteraceae)

cheirifolia	CCCN CMea EHoe ELan EWes NBir SEND SIgm WBrk XLum XSen
coronopifolia new	SVen

Othonnopsis see *Othonna*

Ourisia (Plantaginaceae)

× ***bitternensis*** 'Cliftonville Crimson'	WAbe
- 'Cliftonville Damask'	WAbe
- 'Cliftonville Ling'	WAbe
- 'Cliftonville Old Rose'	WAbe
- 'Cliftonville Pink'	WAbe
- 'Cliftonville Roset'	WAbe
caespitosa var. ***gracilis***	EPot
coccinea	CCon EBee EWes GAbr GCra GKev NBir
'Loch Ewe'	CCon CExl GAbr GKev
macrophylla	LLHF NWad
microphylla	WAbe
- 'Hollowcliffe'	WAbe
modesta	GBin
polyantha 'Cliftonville Scarlet'	WAbe
ruelloides	WAbe
'Snowflake' ♀H4	GAbr GKev NLBP

Oxalis (Oxalidaceae)

from Mount Stewart	WMoo
acetosella	GAbr MHer MMHG NLBP NMir WHer WShi
- var. ***rosea***	IMou
- var. ***subpurpurascens***	IFro WCot
adenophylla ♀H4	CElw CExl CMea CTri ECho ELan EPfP EPot GAbr GKev GMaP LHop LRHS MAsh MAvo MJak NEgg NHol NLar SDeJ SPoG SRms
adenophylla × ***enneaphylla***	CPBP
'Anne Christie'	CPBP
anomala	ECho
§ ***articulata***	LRHS NPer SEND WCot XLum
- 'Alba'	WCot XLum
- f. ***crassipes*** 'Alba'	WCot
§ - subsp. ***rubra***	SDeJ
'Black Velvet' (Xalis Series)	SPoG
bowiei	ECho EPot
- 'Amarantha'	ECho
brasiliensis	ECho EPot
'Dark Eye'	EPot
deppei	see *O. tetraphylla*
§ ***depressa***	CTri ECho EPot EWes GBin LLHF NBir NSla SDeJ SRms
eckloniana	ECho
- var. ***sonderi***	ECho
enneaphylla ♀H4	CElw ECho ELon GAbr GBin LHop LLHF LRHS NRya SBch
- 'Alba'	CElw CMea CPBP ECho NSla
- subsp. ***ibari***	ECho EPot NSla
- 'Minutifolia'	LLHF NRya NSla
* - 'Minutifolia Rosea'	CPBP
- 'Rosea'	ECho EPot GKev LLHF NLar NRya NSla SBch WIce
- 'Sheffield Swan'	CPBP ECho LLHF NSla
'Fanny'	EBee ECho
flava	CGrW ECho
floribunda misapplied	see *O. articulata*
fourcadei	ECho
'Gwen McBride'	CPBP
hedysaroides misapplied	see *O. spiralis* subsp. *vulcanicola*
hedysaroides Kunth	CCCN GCal
'Hemswell Knight'	CPBP SBch
hirta	EPot SBch
- 'Gothenburg'	EBee ECho EPri
imbricata	ECho LLHF
inops	see *O. depressa*
'Ione Hecker' ♀H4	CMea ECho ELon EPot GKev ITim NHar NLar NRya WIce
'Irish Mist' (v)	EBee ECho
* ***karroica***	ECho
§ ***laciniata***	CPBP ECho NHar
- hybrid	NHar
lactea double-flowered	see *O. magellanica* 'Nelson'
lasiandra	CCCN EBee ECho
loricata	ECho
magellanica	CRow CTri ECho GAbr IMou LBee NChi SPlb WMoo
- 'Flore Pleno'	see *O. magellanica* 'Nelson'
§ - 'Nelson' (d)	EBee ECho EWes GCal LBee MMuc NBir NPer WMoo WPtf
mallobolba 'Citrino'	SBch WAbe
massoniana	CSpe ECho EPot WAbe WCot
§ ***megalorrhiza***	CHEx SChr
§ ***melanosticta***	ECho EPot LLHF SDeJ WCot WIce
monophylla	ECho
namaquana	ECho
obtriangulata	ECho
obtusa	ECho
- apricot-flowered	WCot
oregana	CHid CMac CRow EBee ECho ELon EWld SPhx WCot WCru WPGP WSHC
- 'Klamath Ruby'	WSHC
- f. ***smalliana***	EBee EWld IMou LHop WCru
palmifrons	ECho EPot
perdicaria	ECho EHyd EPot EWes LHop LRHS WAbe
pes-caprae	CGrW
polyphylla	EBee ECho
§ ***purpurea***	ECho
- 'Ken Aslet'	see *O. melanosticta*
regnellii	see *O. triangularis* subsp. *papilionacea*
'Ridgeway Jewel'	CPBP
'Ridgeway Sapphire' new	CPBP
rosea misapplied	see *O. articulata* subsp. *rubra*
semiloba	ECho GCal NCGa
Slack Top hybrids	NSla
'Slack's 53' new	NSla
speciosa	see *O. purpurea*
§ ***spiralis*** subsp. ***vulcanicola***	CCCN LSou SDix
- - 'Burgundy'	NPri
squamata	LLHF
squamoso-radicosa	see *O. laciniata*
stipularis	ECho LLHF
succulenta Barnéoud	see *O. megalorrhiza*
succulenta ambig.	CHII CTsd
'Sunny'	EBee ECho
'Sunset Velvet'	EBee WCot
§ ***tetraphylla***	CExl EBee ECho NPer

* - ***alba***	ECho
- 'Iron Cross'	CCVN CHEx CHid ECho ELan EPot GAbr NBir NPnk SDeJ
'Tina'	CPBP
triangularis	CCCN CExl CHEx CHel ECho EOHP MAvo NBir NPer
- 'Birgit'	EBee ECho SDeJ
- Burgundy Wine = 'JR Oxburwi' (Xalis Series)	CWGN EUJe NPer
- 'Cupido'	EBee ECho
- 'Mijke'	EBee ECho
§ - subsp. ***papilionacea*** ♀H1	EBee ECho
- - 'Atropurpurea'	CSpe EBee LHop SDeJ
- subsp. ***triangularis***	CHid EBee ECho EUJe LDai
tuberosa	GPoy LEdu
- 'Polar Bere' new	LEdu
'Ute'	NSla
valdiviensis	GCal NWad
versicolor ♀H1	ECho EPot NBir SDeJ WAbe WCot
I 'Waverley Hybrid'	GBin

Oxycoccus see *Vaccinium*

Oxydendrum ✿ (*Ericaceae*)

arboreum	CAbP CBcs CDoC CEnd CMCN EPfP IDee IVic LRHS MBlu MMuc NLar NSoo NWea SCoo SPer SSpi SSta WBor WHar WPGP
- 'Chameleon'	SSta

Oxypetalum (*Apocynaceae*)

caeruleum	see *Tweedia caerulea*

Oxytropis (*Papilionaceae*)

campestris	EBee
coerulea	CPBP
hailarensis	CPBP
var. ***chankaensis***	
lagopus	CPBP GKev
lazica new	CPBP
podocarpa	SPlb
purpurea	LLHF
sajanensis new	CPBP

Oziroë (*Asparagaceae*)

biflora	LLHF

Ozothamnus (*Asteraceae*)

antennaria	WSHC
§ ***coralloides*** ♀H2-3	ECou WAbe
§ 'County Park Silver'	EWes GKev LHop
§ ***hookeri***	CBcs CDoC MBrN MRav SVen WJek WPat
§ ***ledifolius*** ♀H4	CBcs EBee EPfP SLon SPer WAbe WPat
§ ***rosmarinifolius***	CBcs CDoC CTsd EPfP LRHS MAsh MSwo SPer SVen WPnn
- 'Kiandra'	ECou
- 'Silver Jubilee' ♀H3	CBcs CDoC CEnd CSBt EBee ECrN EPfP GCal LRHS MGos MNHC MRav MSwo SLim SLon SPer SPlb SRkn
scutellifolius	ECou
§ ***selago***	ECou WCot
§ - var. ***tumidus***	WThu
'Sussex Silver'	CDoC
'Threave Seedling'	CDoC EBee ELan EPfP IVic LRHS MAsh SPer

P

Pachyphragma (*Brassicaceae*)

§ ***macrophyllum***	CPom ECGP ELon GCal IBlr IMou LEdu MNFA NLar NSti WCot WCru WPGP WPtf WSHC

Pachyphytum (*Crassulaceae*)

bracteosum	CHel EUJe
glutinicaule RE 477	CDoC
werdermannii	CDoC

Pachypodium (*Apocynaceae*)

bispinosum	LToo
geayi ♀H1	EAmu
lamerei ♀H1	EAmu EUJe SPlb
succulentum	LToo

Pachysandra (*Buxaceae*)

axillaris	CLAP EBee EPPr GCal SKHP WCot
- BWJ 8032	WCru
- 'Crûg's Cover'	EWld WCru
procumbens	CLAP EBee LHop NLar SKHP WCot WCru
- 'Angola' (v)	WCot
stylosa	CHEx MRav SMad
terminalis	CBcs CDul CMac CTri CWib EBee ECrN ELan EPfP LAst LBMP LBuc MCot MGos MJak MRav MSwo NEgg NLar NWea SGol SHil SLim SPer SPlb WCFE WHar
- 'Green Carpet' ♀H4	Widely available
- 'Green Sheen'	EPPr EPfP ESwi SMad
- 'Variegata' (v) ♀H4	Widely available

Pachystachys (*Acanthaceae*)

lutea ♀H1	CCCN

Pachystegia (*Asteraceae*)

§ ***insignis***	LRHS SLim
minor	WThu

Pachystima see *Paxistima*

× *Pachyveria* (*Crassulaceae*)

'Mrs Coombes'	CDoC

Paederota (*Plantaginaceae*)

§ ***bonarota***	WAbe
lutea	WAbe

Paeonia ✿ (*Paeoniaceae*)

'Age of Gold' (S)	GBin WCAu
'Age of Victoria'	GBin
albiflora	see *P. lactiflora*
'America'	GBin
'Angelet'	WCAu
'Anna Marie' (S)	GBin
anomala	CCon GBin GKev MPhe NLar WCot
- var. ***intermedia***	GCal
'Argosy'	WCAu
'Ariadne' (S) new	GBin
arietina	see *P. mascula* subsp. *arietina*
'Athena'	GBin WCAu
'Avant Garde'	WCAu
'Bai Xue Ta' (S)	NTPC

	banatica	see *P. officinalis* subsp. *banatica*
	'Banquet' (S)	GBin
§	'Bartzella' (d)	CKel EBee ELan GBin NLar WCAu WCot
	beresowskii	EBee GKev
	'Black Pirate' (S)	CKel
	'Blaze'	CKel GMaP LRHS NCGa NSti WCAu WCot
	'Border Charm'	GBin
	'Boreas' (S)	GBin
	'Bravura'	GBin
	'Bridal Icing'	GBin WCAu
	'Bride's Dream'	GBin
	'Brocaded Gown' (S)	GBin
	broteroi	SKHP WThu
	'Buckeye Belle' (d)	CKel EBee ELan EPfP EWTr GBin GMaP IBoy LAst LPio LRHS LSRN MBri NCGa SHar SMrm SPer SWat WCAu WCot WWEG
	'Burma Midnight'	GBin
	'Burma Ruby'	GBin WCAu
	californica	CCon
	'Callie's Memory'	CKel GBin WCAu
	cambessedesii ♀H2-3	CBro EHyd EPot GKev LHop LRHS NBir SSpi WAbe WCot WKif
	'Canary Brilliant' PBR	GBin WCAu
	'Cardinal's Robe'	GBin
	'Carina'	GBin
	'Carol'	WCAu
	caucasica	see *P. mascula* subsp. *mascula*
	'Chalice'	GBin
	× ***chamaeleon***	GBin GKev SKHP
	'Cheddar Royal'	GBin
	'Cherry Ruffles'	GBin
	'Chinese Dragon' (S)	CKel
	'Chocolate Soldier'	CKel GBin WCAu
	'Claire de Lune'	CKel GBin SHar WCAu WCot
	'Command Performance'	GBin
	'Copper Kettle'	CKel GBin WCAu
	'Cora Louise'	CKel GBin WCAu
	'Coral Charm'	CKel GBin LSRN MMHG NCGa NLar SDeJ SKHP WCAu WCot
	'Coral Fay'	GBin WCAu
	'Coral 'n' Gold'	WCAu
	'Coral Scout' **new**	GBin
	'Coral Sunset'	CKel CWCL EWTr GBin IBoy NLar SDeJ SMrm WCAu
	'Coral Supreme'	GBin WCot
	corallina	see *P. mascula* subsp. *mascula*
	coriacea	GKev
	- var. ***atlantica***	CBro
	Crimson Red	see *P. suffruticosa* 'Hu Hong'
	'Cytherea'	WCot
	'Daedalus' (S) **new**	GBin
	'Dancing Butterflies'	see *P. lactiflora* 'Zi Yu Nu'
	'Daredevil' (S)	GBin
	daurica	see *P. mascula* subsp. *triternata*
	- subsp. ***coriifolia*** RCB UA 12	WCot
	decomposita	MPhe
	decora	see *P. peregrina*
	delavayi (S) ♀H4	Widely available
	- BWJ 7775	WCru
	- SDR 4327	CHel GKev
	- from China (S)	MPhe
	- var. ***angustiloba*** f. ***alba*** (S)	CExl
§	- - f. ***angustiloba*** (S)	GBin SSpi
	- - - 'Coffee Cream' (S)	CKel
§	- - f. ***trollioides*** (S)	CExl
§	- var. ***delavayi*** f. ***lutea*** (S)	CCVT CDul EBee EPfP GBin IBoy IFro LEdu LRHS MAsh MGos MLHP NBir NEgg NSoo SLon SPhx SPoG SRms WHar WHoo
	- var. ***lutea***	see *P. delavayi* var. *delavayi* f. *lutea*
	- 'Mrs Colville' (S)	GBin GCal
	- 'Mrs Sarson' (S)	ELan EWes NCGa SWat
	- Potaninii Group	see *P. delavayi* var. *angustiloba* f. CSpe
	- Trollioides Group	see *P. delavayi* var. *angustiloba* f. *trollioides*
	delavayi × ***suffruticosa***	LSRN
	'Diana Parks'	GBin
	'Don Richardson' **new**	WCAu
	Drizzling Rain Cloud	see *P. suffruticosa* 'Shiguregumo'
	'Early Bird'	GBin LRHS
	'Early Glow'	GBin WCAu
	'Early Scout'	EBee GBin LRHS MBri WCAu WCot WHil
	'Echt Klasse'	GBin
	'Eden's Perfume'	EBee GBin IKil LRHS MBri MSCN NLar
	'Elizabeth Foster'	GBin WCAu
	'Ellen Cowley'	GBin WCAu
	emodi	CAvo CKel EBee GBin LPio SHar WCAu WCot
	'Etched Salmon'	CKel
	'Ezra Pound' (S)	GBin WCAu
	'F. Koppius'	CKel
	'Fairy Princess'	GBin WCAu
	'Firelight'	GBin WCAu
	'First Arrival'	CKel GBin WCAu
	'First Dutch Yellow'	see *P.* 'Garden Treasure'
	'Flame'	CKel EBee EPfP MNrw NLar NSti SDeJ WCAu WCot
	'Friendship'	WCAu
§	Gansu Group (S)	CKel MPhe NTPC
	- 'Bai Bi Fen Xia' (S)	MPhe
	- 'Bai Bi Lan Xia' (S)	MPhe
	- 'Bing Shan Xue Lian' (S)	MPhe
	- 'Bing Xin Zi' (S)	MPhe
	- 'Cheng Xin' (S)	MPhe
	- 'Fen Die' (S) **new**	NTPC
	- 'Fen He' (S)	MPhe
	- 'Fen Jin Yu Zhu' (S)	MPhe
	- 'Fen Mian Tao Sui' (S)	MPhe
	- 'Feng Xian' (S)	MPhe
	- 'Gu Cheng Xiang Hui' (S)	MPhe
	- 'He Hua Deng' (S)	MPhe
	- 'He Ping Lian' (S)	MPhe
	- 'Hei Feng Die' (S)	MPhe
	- 'Hei Tian E' (S)	MPhe
	- 'Hei Xuan Feng' (S)	MPhe
	- 'Hei Yuan Shuai' (S)	MPhe
	- 'Hong Lian' (S)	MPhe NTPC
	- 'Hong Xia Ying Xue' (S)	MPhe
	- 'Huang He' (S)	MPhe
	- 'Hui He' (S)	MPhe
	- 'Jiao Rong' (S)	MPhe
	- 'Jin Cheng Ming Yue' (S)	MPhe
	- 'Ju Hua Fen' (S)	MPhe
	- 'Lan Hai Yiu Bo' (S)	MPhe
	- 'Lan He' (S)	MPhe
	- 'Lan Tian Meng' (S)	MPhe
	- 'Lan Yu San Cai' (S)	MPhe
	- 'Lan Zhang Cai Wei' (S) **new**	WKif
	- 'Li Xiang' (S)	MPhe

– 'Lian Chun' (S)	MPhe
– 'Long Yuan Hong' (S)	MPhe
– 'Mo Hai Yin Bo' (S)	MPhe
– 'Mo Hai Yin Zhou' (S)	MPhe
– 'Nong Mo Zhong Cai' (S) **new**	WKif
– 'Ren Mian Tao Hua' (S) **new**	NTPC
– 'Ri Yue Tong Hui' (S)	MPhe
– 'Shu Sheng Peng Mo' (S)	MPhe
– 'Tao Hua Nu' (S)	MPhe
– 'Tie Mian Wu Si' (S)	MPhe
– 'Xiang Lu Zi Yan' (S)	MPhe
– 'Xiong Mao' (S)	MPhe NTPC
– 'Xue Hai Bing Xin' (S)	MPhe
– 'Xue Lian' (S)	GBin MPhe NTPC WKif
– 'Xue Yuan Yu Hui' (S)	MPhe
– 'Ye Guang Bei' (S)	MPhe
– 'Yu Ban Xiu Qiu' (S)	MPhe
– 'Yu Guan Lan Dai' (S)	MPhe
– 'Yu Lu Lian Dan' (S)	MPhe
– 'Yu Rong Dan Xin' (S)	MPhe
– 'Yuan Yang Pu' (S)	MPhe
– 'Zi Ban Bai' (S)	NTPC
– 'Zi Die Ying Feng' (S)	MPhe NTPC
– 'Zi Hai Yin Bo' (S)	MPhe
– 'Zi Yan' (S) **new**	NTPC
– 'Zong Ban Bai' (S)	MPhe
Gansu Mudan Group	see *P.* Gansu Group
'Garden Peace' **new**	WCAu
§ 'Garden Treasure'	GBin SDeJ WCAu
'Gold Standard'	GBin
'Golden Bowl'	CKel GBin
'Golden Dream'	see *P.* 'Bartzella'
'Golden Isles'	CKel
'Golden Thunder'	CKel
'Golden Wings'	GBin
'Grace Root'	GBin
'Hei Hua Kui'	see *P. suffruticosa* 'Hei Hua Kui'
'Hephestos' (S)	GBin
'Heritage'	GBin
'Hillary'	CKel GBin WCAu
'Ho-gioku'	GBin
'Hong Bao Shi' (S)	NTPC
'Honor'	WCAu
'Horizon'	GBin WCAu
'Hua Er Qiao' (S)	NTPC
humilis	see *P. officinalis* subsp. *microcarpa*
'Icarus' (S) **new**	GBin
'Ice Storm' (S) **new**	GBin
'Illini Belle'	GBin
'Illini Warrior'	WCAu
'In the Mood'	GBin
intermedia	WCot
'Iphigenia' (S) **new**	GBin
'Isani Gidui'	see *P. lactiflora* 'Isami-jishi'
japonica misapplied	see *P. lactiflora*
japonica (Makino) Miyabe & Takeda B&SWJ 10985	WCru
'Jay Cee'	GBin
jishanensis	MPhe
'Joseph Rock'	see *P. rockii*
'Joyce Ellen'	GBin
'Jubilation'	GBin
'Julia Rose'	CKel GBin WCAu
'Kathryn Ann'	GBin
kavachensis	GCal
'Kinkaku'	see *P.* × *lemoinei* 'Souvenir de Maxime Cornu'
'Kinko'	see *P.* × *lemoinei* 'Alice Harding'
'Kinshi'	see *P.* × *lemoinei* 'Chromatella'
'Koikagura'	CKel
'Kokamon'	CKel
'Kun Shan Ye Guang'	NTPC
§ ***lactiflora***	CArn CHel EBee GCal GKev MBel MPhe MRav WCot
– 'Abalone Pearl'	GBin
– 'Adolphe Rousseau'	CBcs CKel NLar WCAu
* – 'Afterglow'	CKel
– 'Agida'	GBin LRHS MRav
– 'Agnes Mary Kelway'	CKel
– ***alba***	MBel WBor
– 'Albâtre'	CKel
– 'Albert Crousse'	CBcs CKel GBin MRav NBir SWat
– 'Alexander Fleming'	MBNS MBri NBir SMrm SWat WCAu
– 'Algae Adamson'	CKel
– 'Alice Harding'	CKel GBin WCAu
– 'Amalia Olson' (d) **new**	WCAu
– 'Amibilis'	WCAu
– 'Angel Cheeks'	CKel EBee GBin MBri WCAu
– 'Anna Pavlova'	CKel
– 'Antwerpen'	LRHS
– 'Arabian Prince'	CKel
– 'Arcadia'	WCAu
– 'Argentine'	CKel EBee
– 'Armistice' (d)	WCAu
– 'Asa Gray'	CKel
– 'Auguste Dessert'	CKel GBin WCAu WCFE
§ – 'Augustin d'Hour'	CKel
– 'Aureole'	CKel MRav
– 'Avalanche'	CKel EPfP GBin NLar SMrm
– 'Bai Yu Pan'	NTPC
– 'Ballerina'	CKel MRav
– 'Barbara'	CKel GBin NCGa WCAu
– 'Baroness Schröder'	CKel ELan GBin
– 'Barrington Belle'	EPfP GBin LRHS MAvo WCAu WHoo
– 'Barrymore'	CKel
– 'Bayadere' (d) **new**	GBin
– 'Beacon'	CKel
– 'Beatrice Kelway'	CKel
– 'Belle Center'	GBin WCAu
– 'Best Man'	EBee NGdn WCAu
– 'Bethcar'	CKel
– 'Better Times'	WCAu
– 'Bev'	GBin
– 'Big Ben'	CKel GBin NLar SHar STes
– 'Blaze of Beauty'	CKel
– 'Bluebird'	CKel
– 'Blush Queen'	CKel GBin WCAu
– 'Border Gem'	GBin LRHS MRav
– 'Bouchela'	NLar
– 'Boule de Neige'	EWll GBin LHop NLar
– 'Bouquet Perfect'	GBin WCAu
– 'Bower of Roses'	CKel
– 'Bowl of Beauty' Υ^{H4}	Widely available
– 'Bowl of Cream'	CKel EBee GBin SMrm SWat SWvt WCAu
– 'Break o' Day'	WCAu
– 'Bridal Gown'	GBin WCAu
– 'Bridal Veil'	CKel
– 'Bridesmaid'	CKel
– 'Bright Knight'	WCAu
– 'British Beauty'	CKel
– 'Bunker Hill'	CKel GBin IBoy LRHS SWvt WCAu
– 'Bu-te'	GBin
– 'Butter Bowl'	GBin WCAu
– 'Canarie'	CKel

– 'Candeur'	CKel
– 'Candidissima' **new**	GBin
– 'Cang Long'	CKel
– 'Captivation'	CKel
– 'Carnival'	CKel
– 'Caroline Allain'	CKel
– 'Carrara'	GBin
– 'Cascade'	CKel
– 'Catherine Fontijn'	CKel GBin WCAu
– 'Celebrity' **new**	CWCL MBri MSCN
– 'Charles Burgess'	MSCN WCAu
– 'Charles' White'	CKel GBin NLar SDeJ WCAu
– 'Charm'	GBin
– 'Cheddar Charm'	GBin WCAu
– 'Cheddar Cheese'	WCot
– 'Cheddar Supreme'	GBin
– 'Cherry Hill'	GBin WCAu
– 'Chestine Gowdy'	CKel
– 'Chief Wapello'	GBin
– 'Chiffon Parfait' **new**	GBin
– 'Chippewa'	GBin
– 'Circus Circus'	GBin
– 'Claire Dubois'	CKel GBin WCAu
– 'Companion of Serenity' (S) **new**	GBin
– 'Cora Stubbs'	GBin
– 'Cornelia Shaylor'	CKel WCAu
– 'Couronne d'Or'	GBin
– 'Cream Puff'	WCAu
– 'Crimson Glory'	CKel
– 'Crinkles Linens'	GBin
– 'Da Ban Fen' **new**	NTPC
– 'Dawn Crest'	CKel
– 'Dayspring'	CKel
– 'Daystar'	MRav
– 'Dayton'	WCAu
– 'Decorative'	CKel
– 'Dei Xian Jin'	WCAu
– 'Delachei'	CKel GBin
– 'Dinner Plate'	CKel GBin MAsh MBri SPer WCAu
– 'Do Tell'	CWCL EBee EPfP GBin NCGa NGdn NLar SPer WCAu
– 'Docteur H. Barnsby'	CKel
– 'Doctor Alexander Fleming'	CKel GBin LRHS SDeJ SHar SRot STes SWat SWvt
– 'Dominion'	CKel
– 'Don Juan'	CKel
– 'Doreen'	CKel EBee GBin NCGa SHar WCAu WHil
– 'Doris Cooper'	WCAu
– 'Dorothy Welsh'	CKel
– 'Dragon'	CKel
– 'Dresden'	WCAu
– 'Duchesse de Nemours' ♀^{H4}	Widely available
– 'Edouard Doriat'	WCAu
– 'Edulis Superba'	CKel ELan EWTr GBin LEdu LRHS LSRN MBNS MRav NLar NPer
– 'Elaine'	MRav
– 'Eliza Lundy' (d)	GBin WCAu
– 'Elizabeth Stone'	CKel
– 'Ella Christine Kelway'	CKel
– 'Elsa Sass'	EBee GBin MBri SHar WCAu
– 'Emma Klehm'	CKel GBin WCAu
– 'Emperor of India'	CKel
– 'Enchantment'	CKel
– 'English Princess'	CKel
– 'Ethereal'	CKel
– 'Evelyn Tibbets'	GBin

– 'Evening Glow'	CKel
– 'Evening World'	CKel
– 'Fairy's Petticoat'	CKel GBin WCAu
– 'Fancy Nancy' **new**	GBin
– 'Fashion Show'	CKel
– 'Félix Crousse' ♀^{H4}	CBcs CKel CMac CTri ELan GBin GMaP IBoy LHop LRHS LSRN MBNS MBri MRav NBir SDeJ SPer SWat WCAu
– 'Felix Supreme'	GBin
– 'Festiva Maxima' ♀^{H4}	CKel CSBt CTri EBee ELan EPfP GBin LRHS NBir NEgg NLar SPer SRkn SRot SWat SWvt WCAu WHil WHoo WWEG
– 'Festiva Supreme'	GBin
– 'Fiesta Posey'	WCAu
– 'Fiona' (d)	WCAu
– 'Firebelle'	WCAu
– 'Florence Ellis'	WCAu
– 'Florence Nicholls'	CKel GBin
– 'Foxtrot'	WCAu
– 'France'	CKel
– 'Fuchsia Dragonfly' **new**	GBin
– 'Fuji-no-mine'	GBin
– 'Garden Lace'	GBin SDeJ WCAu
– 'Gardenia'	CKel EBee GBin IBoy NLar SDeJ WCAu WCot
– 'Gay Paree'	CKel CWCL GBin NCGa NLar SHar WCAu
– 'Gayborder June'	CKel
– 'Général Joffre'	MRav
– 'Général MacMahon'	see *P. lactiflora* 'Augustin d'Hour'
– 'General Wolfe'	CKel
– 'Germaine Bigot'	CKel GBin MRav WCAu
– 'Gertrude Allen' **new**	GBin
– 'Gilbert Barthelot'	CKel WCAu
– 'Gladys McArthur'	GBin
– 'Gleam of Light'	CKel
– 'Globe of Light'	CKel GBin
– 'Glory Hallelujah'	WCAu
– 'Glowing Candles'	WCAu
– 'Go-Daigo'	GBin
– 'Golden Fleece'	WCAu
– 'Goldilocks' **new**	WCAu
– 'Great Sport'	MRav
– 'Guidon'	WCAu
– 'Gypsy Girl'	CKel
– 'Hakodate'	CKel
– 'Hansina Brand' (d) **new**	GBin
– 'Happy Days'	WCAu
– 'Heartbeat'	CKel
– 'Helen Hayes'	WCAu
– 'Henri Potin'	GBin
– 'Henry Bockstoce'	GBin NLar
– 'Her Grace'	CKel
– 'Herbert Oliver'	CKel
– 'Hermione'	CKel GBin WCAu
– 'Highlight'	WCAu
– 'Hit Parade'	WCAu
– 'Honey Gold'	CKel GBin WCAu
– 'Hot Chocolate'	GBin WCAu
– 'Huang Jin Lun' **new**	NTPC
– 'Hyperion'	CKel
– 'Immaculée'	CKel CWCL EBee GBin IBoy LHop LRHS LSRN NCGa SPoG
– 'Inspecteur Lavergne'	CKel EUJe GBin IBoy LRHS MBri NGdn SGol SPer WCAu WCot WHil WWEG
– 'Instituteur Doriat'	CKel GBin WCAu

§	- 'Isami-jishi'	GBin
	- 'Jacorma'	CCon GBin
	- 'Jacques Doriat'	CKel
	- 'Jadwigha'	EBee
	- 'James Kelway'	CKel GBin
	- 'Jan van Leeuwen'	CKel EBee EPfP EWTr GBin GMaP LPio MBri SPer WCAu WCot
	- 'Jappensha-ikhu'	GBin
	- 'Jeanne d'Arc'	CKel
	- 'John Howard Wigell'	WCAu
	- 'Johnny' **new**	GBin
	- 'Joseph Christie' (d) **new**	EBee
	- 'Joy of Life'	CKel
	- 'Judith Eileen'	GBin
	- 'June Morning'	CKel
	- 'June Rose'	WCAu
	- 'Kakoden'	GBin
	- 'Kansas'	CKel CWCL EBee ELan EPfP GBin IBoy LRHS MBri MHol NBir NGdn NLar SPoG WCAu WCot
	- 'Karen Gray'	GBin WCAu
	- 'Karl Rosenfield'	CKel CSBt EPfP GBBs GBin IBoy LAst LPio LRHS LSRN MJak MNrw MRav NEgg NLar SGol SHar SPer SPoG SRms SRot SWvt WCAu WHoo WWEG XSen
	- 'Kathleen Mavoureen'	CKel
	- 'Kelway's Betty'	CKel
	- 'Kelway's Brilliant'	CKel
	- 'Kelway's Circe'	CKel
	- 'Kelway's Daystar'	CKel
	- 'Kelway's Exquisite'	CKel
	- 'Kelway's Glorious'	CKel EBee EPfP GBin LRHS MAvo MBNS MRav NLar WCAu WGwG
	- 'Kelway's Lovely'	CKel GBin
	- 'Kelway's Lovely Lady'	CKel
	- 'Kelway's Majestic'	CKel MRav
	- 'Kelway's Scented Rose'	CKel
	- 'Kelway's Supreme'	CKel SWat
	- 'King of England'	GBin
	- 'Knighthood'	CKel
	- 'Königswinter'	GBin
§	- 'Koningin Wilhelmina'	EBee GBin MBri MNrw
	- 'Krekler's Red'	WCAu
	- 'Krinkled White'	CKel EBee EPfP GBBs GBin GMaP LPio LRHS LSRN MRav NCGa NLar NSti SDeJ SHar SKHP WCAu WHil WWEG
	- 'La Belle Hélène'	CKel
	- 'La Lorraine'	CKel
	- 'Lady Alexandra Duff' ♀H4	CKel EPfP GBin LRHS MRav NBir NGdn SWvt WCAu WHil WWEG
	- 'Lady Ley'	CKel
	- 'Lady Mayoress'	CKel
	- 'Lady Orchid'	EPfP MBri NGdn WCAu
	- 'Lancaster Imp'	GBin WCAu
	- 'Langport Triumph'	CKel
	- 'Largo'	WCAu
	- 'Laura Dessert' ♀H4	CKel GBin LRHS NCGa NLar WCAu
	- 'Laura Shaylor'	WCAu
	- 'Lavender Whisper'	WCAu
	- 'Le Cygne'	GBin
	- 'Le Jour'	WCAu
	- 'L'Éclatante'	CKel GBin LRHS WGwG
	- 'Legion of Honor'	CKel
	- 'Lemon Ice'	CKel
	- 'Lemon Queen'	GBin
	- 'L'Étincelante'	GBin
	- 'Lian Dai'	WCAu
	- 'Liebchen'	WCAu
	- 'Lights Out'	GBin
	- 'Lilac Times' **new**	CKel
	- 'Lillian Wild'	GBin
	- 'Little Medicineman'	EBee GBin
	- 'Lois Kelsey'	GBin WCAu
	- 'Lollipop' (d)	GBin WCAu
	- 'Longfellow'	CKel GBin
	- 'Lord Kitchener'	CKel GBin LRHS
	- 'Lorna Doone'	CKel
	- 'Lotus Queen'	GBin NLar WCAu
	- 'Louis van Houtte'	CKel NEgg
	- 'Love's Touch' (d)	GBin WCAu
	- 'Lyric'	CKel WCAu
	- 'Madame Calot'	LRHS WCAu
	- 'Madame Claude Tain'	MBri
	- 'Madame de Verneville'	WCAu
	- 'Madame Ducel'	CKel WCAu
	- 'Madame Emile Debatène'	CKel EBee MAsh MBNS WCAu
	- 'Madame Gaudichau'	WCot
	- 'Madame Jules Dessert'	WCAu
	- 'Madelon'	CKel WCAu
	- 'Maestro'	GBin
	- 'Magenta Moon'	WCAu
	- 'Magic Orb'	CKel
	- 'Mandarin's Coat'	GBin
	- 'Margaret Clark'	WCAu
	- 'Margaret Truman'	CKel EBee WCAu
	- 'Marguérite Gerard'	WCAu
	- 'Marie Crousse'	WCAu
	- 'Marie Lemoine'	CKel GBin LRHS WCAu WCot
	- 'Marietta Sisson'	WCAu
	- 'Mary Brand'	WCAu
	- 'Masterpiece'	CKel
	- 'May Treat'	WCAu
	- 'Merry Mayshine'	GBin WCAu
	- 'Midnight Sun'	WCAu
	- 'Minnie Shaylor'	WCAu
	- 'Mischief'	MRav WCAu
	- 'Miss America'	EPfP GBin MBri WCAu WCot
	- 'Miss Eckhart'	CKel GBin WCAu
	- 'Miss Mary'	EBee
	- 'Missie's Blush'	GBin
	- 'Mister Ed'	GBin WCAu
	- 'Mistral'	CKel
	- 'Monsieur Jules Elie' ♀H4	CKel EBee EPfP GBin IBoy LRHS MBri NGdn NLar SPer WCAu WHoo WWEG
	- 'Monsieur Martin Cahuzac'	CKel GBin LRHS WCAu
	- 'Moon of Nippon'	LRHS
	- 'Moon River'	EPfP GBin LPio MBri SMrm WCAu WHoo
	- 'Moonstone'	CKel GBin
	- 'Morning Kiss' **new**	MBri
	- 'Mother's Choice'	CKel GBin LSRN NGdn NLar WCAu WCot
	- 'Mr G.F. Hemerik'	CKel GBin WCAu WCot
	- 'Mr Thim'	WCAu
	- 'Mrs Edward Harding'	CKel WCAu
	- 'Mrs Franklin D. Roosevelt'	GBin WCAu
	- 'Mrs J.V. Edlund'	GBin WCAu
	- 'My Pal Rudy'	GBin WCAu
	- 'My Petite Cherie'	GBin WCAu
	- 'Myrtle Gentry'	CKel GBin WCAu
	- 'Nancy Nicholls'	WCAu
	- 'Nancy Nora'	SPer WCAu
	- 'Neomy Demay'	CKel GBin
	- 'Neon'	GBin NCGa
	- 'Nice Gal'	GBin WCAu

- 'Nick Shaylor'	GBin WCAu
- 'Nippon Beauty'	CKel GBin LRHS MMHG NCGa NLar SDeJ SHar SKHP
- 'Nippon Gold'	WCAu
- 'Noemie Demay'	LRHS
- 'Norma Volz'	GBin WCAu
- 'Nymphe'	CKel EBee MRav NLar SDeJ WCAu
- 'Orlando Roberts'	GBin
- 'Ornament'	CKel
- 'Orpen'	CKel
- 'Paola'	CKel
- 'Paul Bunyan'	GBin
- 'Paul M. Wild'	NLar WCAu
* - 'Pecher'	CKel LRHS NLar NPer
- 'Peter Brand'	CKel EBee GBin LSRN NLar
- 'Petite Porcelain'	GBin WCAu
- 'Philippe Rivoire'	CKel WCAu
- 'Philomèle'	WCAu
- 'Pico'	WCAu
- 'Picotee'	WCAu
- 'Pillow Cases' **new**	WCAu
- 'Pillow Talk'	CKel EBee GBin LRHS NLar SPer WCAu
- 'Pink Cameo'	EBee NLar WCAu WCot
- 'Pink Dawn'	EBee EPfP SPer WCAu
- 'Pink Delight'	GBin WCAu
- 'Pink Giant'	GBin WCAu
- 'Pink Parfait'	GBin LRHS SPer WCAu
- 'Pink Princess'	GBin WCAu
- 'Plainsman'	GBin
- 'Polar King'	WCAu
- 'President Franklin D. Roosevelt'	LRHS SWat
- 'President Lincoln'	WCAu
- 'Président Poincaré'	CKel MRav SWat WCAu
- 'President Taft'	see *P. lactiflora* 'Reine Hortense'
- 'President Wilson'	GBin
- 'Primevère'	CKel EBee GBin LAst MSCN NBir NLar SPer SPoG WCAu WWEG
- 'Princess Margaret'	WCAu
- 'Qi Hua Lu Shuang'	NTPC
- 'Queen of Sheba'	WCAu
- 'Queen Victoria'	GBin
- 'Queen Wilhelmina'	see *P. lactiflora* 'Koningin Wilhelmina'
- 'Raoul Dessert'	WCAu
- 'Raspberry Sundae'	CKel ELan GBin LRHS MRav NLar SPer STes WCAu WCot
- 'Ray Payton'	GBin
- 'Red Dwarf'	CKel
- 'Red Emperor'	WCAu
- 'Red Sarah Bernhardt'	CKel MBri SDeJ WWEG
§ - 'Reine Hortense'	CKel GBin LRHS MRav
- 'Renato'	EBee GBin MBri WCAu
- 'Richard Carvel'	WCAu
- 'Ruth Cobb'	WCAu
- 'Salmon Dream' **new**	CKel
- 'Sante Fe'	CKel EBee EPfP MSCN WCAu
- 'Sarah Bernhardt' ♀H4	Widely available
- 'Scarlet O'Hara'	CMac GBin SPer SPoG WCAu
- 'Schaffe'	GBin
- 'Sea Shell'	EBee EPfP GBin GMaP LRHS WCAu
- 'Serene Pastel'	GBin WCAu
- 'Shawnee Chief'	GBin
- 'Shimmering Velvet'	CKel
- 'Shirley Temple' (d)	CKel EBee ELan EPfP GBin GBuc IBoy IKil LBMP LRHS MBNS MBel MBri MRav NBir NGdn SDeJ SMrm SPoG WCAu WCot WWEG
- 'Silver Flare'	CKel
- 'Sir Ernest Shackleton' (d)	MRav
- 'Soft Salmon Joy'	GBin
- 'Solange'	CKel GBin IKil LRHS NLar WCAu
- 'Sorbet'	CKel EBee EPfP LHop LPio NBir NCGa NLar NPer SMrm WBor WWEG
- 'Starlight'	CKel EBee GBin LRHS SHar WCAu WCot
- 'Strephon'	CKel
- 'Super Gal'	WCAu
- 'Sweet Melody'	GBin WCAu
- 'Sweet Sixteen'	WCAu
- 'Sword Dance'	CKel EWll GBBs GBin SDeJ
- 'Tamate-boko'	WCAu
- 'The Mighty Mo'	GBin
- 'The Nymph'	LRHS NBir WWEG
- 'Thérèse'	WCAu
- 'Tom Eckhardt'	CKel GBin SPer WCAu
- 'Top Brass'	CKel EBee GBin MRav NLar WCAu WWEG
- 'Topeka Garnet'	GBin
- 'Toro-no-maki'	WCAu
- 'Translucient'	CKel
- 'Twitterpated' **new**	MAsh
- 'Victoire de la Marne'	CKel
- 'Victoria Blush' (d) **new**	WCAu
- 'Violet Dawson'	GBin
- 'Vivid Rose'	WCAu
- 'Vogue'	CKel GBin LRHS MRav NCGa SWvt WCAu
- 'W.F. Turner'	CKel
- 'Walter Faxon'	GBin
- 'West Elkton'	GBin
- 'Westerner'	GBin
- 'White Cap' **new**	GBin MMHG WCAu
- 'White Grace'	WCAu
- 'White Rose of Sharon'	CKel
- 'White Sands'	GBin
- 'White Sarah Bernhardt' **new**	MBri SMrm SPer
- 'White Wings'	CBcs CKel CMac CTri EBee ELan EPfP GBin LRHS NLar STes SWat SWvt WCAu WCot WWEG
- 'Whitleyi Major' ♀H4	WCot
- 'Wilbur Wright'	CKel GBin
- 'Wine Red'	GBin
- 'Wladyslawa'	GBin LRHS NLar SHar WCot
- 'Xue Feng'	NTPC
- 'Zi Hong Kui' **new**	NTPC
§ - 'Zi Yu Nu'	EBee LRHS LSRN
- 'Zuzu'	GBin WCAu
'Lafayette Escadrille' (S)	WCAu
'Late Windflower'	CKel GBin GCra WCAu
'Leda' (S)	GBin
'Legion of Honour'	GBin
× ***lemoinei*** (S)	WHal
§ - 'Alice Harding' (S)	CKel GBin
§ - 'Chromatella' (S)	CKel
- 'High Noon' (S)	CKel GBin MPhe SKHP SWat
- 'Marchioness' (S)	CKel GBin
§ - 'Souvenir de Maxime Cornu' (S)	CKel EPfP SKHP SPer
'Lilith' (S)	GBin
lithophila	see *P. tenuifolia* subsp. *lithophila*
'Little Joe'	WCAu
'Little Red Gem'	GBin
lobata 'Fire King'	see *P. peregrina*
'Lovebirds'	GBin WCAu
'Lovely Rose' **new**	GBin WCAu

	ludlowii (S) ♀H4	Widely available
	lutea	see *P. delavayi* var. *delavayi* f. *lutea*
	macrophylla	MPhe
	'Magenta Gem'	GBin
	'Mai Fleuri'	GBin WCAu
	mairei	CExl GGGa MPhe
	'Many Happy Returns'	CKel GBin
	mascula	CBro EPfP GKev LHop LLHF LPio NBir SHar
§	- subsp. ***arietina***	EBee GKev MWat
	- - 'Northern Glory'	LRHS
	- 'Immaculata' **new**	MHol
§	- subsp. ***mascula***	GKev
§	- subsp. ***russoi***	WCot WThu
	- - 'Picotee'	GBin
§	- subsp. ***triternata***	CKel GKev NLar NSla WCot
	'May Apple' **new**	WCAu
	'Mikuhino-akebono'	CKel
	mlokosewitschii ♀H4	CAvo CBcs CBro CExl CFil CMea CPBP EBee ECho EHyd ELan EPPr GBin GMaP LHop LPio LRHS MAvo MCot MNrw NBir SDix SLon SWvt WAbe WCAu WCot WHoo WKif
	- hybrids	EBee GKev
	mollis	see *P. officinalis* subsp. *villosa*
	'Moonrise'	WCAu
	'Morning Lilac'	WCAu
	'Murad of Hershey Bar' (S)	GBin WCAu
	'Normie' (d)	WCAu
	'Nosegay'	WCAu
	'Nova'	CKel GBin
	obovata ♀H4	CCon LRHS MPhe
	- var. ***alba*** ♀H4	CExl GBin GKev LLHF WAbe WCot
	- 'Grandiflora'	LRHS
	- var. ***willmottiae***	CExl MPhe
	officinalis	CArn GCra GKev
	- WM 9821 from Slovenia	MPhe
	- 'Alba Plena' (d)	CKel CPou EBee GMaP LRHS MRav NEgg NLar SWvt WCAu WWEG
	- 'Anemoniflora Rosea' ♀H4	LRHS NLar SWvt
§	- subsp. ***banatica***	GKev MPhe WCAu WCot
	- 'China Rose'	GBin
	- subsp. ***humilis***	see *P. officinalis* subsp. *microcarpa*
	- 'James Crawford Weguelin'	WCot
	- 'Lize van Veen'	GBin
§	- subsp. ***microcarpa***	WCot
	- 'Mutabilis Plena' (d)	IBlr
	- 'Rosea Plena' (d) ♀H4	CKel CMac EBee ECtt EPfP GMaP LAst LRHS NEgg SPer SWat SWvt WCAu WWEG
	- 'Rubra Plena' (d) ♀H4	CKel CPou CTri EBee ECtt EPfP GAbr GBin GCra GMaP LAst LBMP LHop LRHS MBri MHol MLHP MRav NEgg NGdn NLar SEND SPer SRms SWat SWvt WCAu WCot
§	- subsp. ***villosa***	CKel ELan GKev LRHS
	'Old Rose Dandy'	GBin
	'Oriental Gold'	CKel EBee
	ostii (S)	CExl CKel EPfP MPhe SKHP
§	- 'Feng Dan Bai' (S)	CKel GBin MPhe
	'Pageant'	GBin
	'Paladin'	GBin
	papaveracea	see *P. suffruticosa*
	paradoxa	see *P. officinalis* subsp. *microcarpa*
	'Paramount' **new**	GBin
	'Pastel Splendor'	CKel GBin WCAu
	'Paula Fay'	CKel EBee EPfP GBin MBri MRav SDeJ STes WCAu WCot
	Peony with the Purple Roots	see *P. suffruticosa* 'Shou An Hong'
§	***peregrina***	CBro CKel ECho MPhe SKHP SSpi WCAu WCot
	- 'Fire King'	CKel GBin NLar
§	- 'Otto Froebel' ♀H4	CKel GBin GCra NLar WCot
	- 'Sunshine'	see *P. peregrina* 'Otto Froebel'
	'Picotee' **new**	WCAu
	'Pink Hawaiian Coral'	CKel GBin NLar WCot
	'Postilion'	GBin
	potaninii	see *P. delavayi* var. *angustiloba* f. *angustiloba*
	'Prairie Charm'	GBin WCAu
	'Prairie Moon'	EBee GBin NLar WCAu
	'Prince Charming'	WCAu
	qiui	MPhe
	'Raspberry Charm'	WCAu
	'Red Charm'	CKel CWCL EBee GBin IBoy MBri NCGa WCAu
	'Red Glory'	GBin
	'Red Magic'	EBee
	'Red Red Rose'	GBin WCAu
	'Renown' (S)	CKel
	'Requiem'	GBin WCAu
§	***rockii*** (S)	CBcs CKel CSpe EPfP GBin MPhe NLar WCot
	- from Tianshui, Gansu	MPhe
	- from Wenshian, Gansu	MPhe
	- hybrid	see *P.* Gansu Group
	- subsp. ***linyanshanii*** (S)	MPhe
	'Roman Gold'	CKel GBin
	romanica	see *P. peregrina*
	'Rose Flame' (S)	WCAu
	'Rose Garland'	GBin
	'Rosedale'	WCAu
	'Roselette'	GBin WCAu
	'Roselette's Child'	GBin
	'Roy Pehrson's Best Yellow'	GBin
	'Ruffled Pink Petticoats' (S) **new**	GBin
	ruprechtiana	GKev
	russoi	see *P. mascula* subsp. *russoi*
	'Savage Splendour' **new**	GBin
	'Scarlet Heaven'	CKel GBin WCAu
	'Serenade'	WCAu
	'Shimano-fuji'	CKel
	'Shining Light'	GBin NLar
	'Show Girl'	GBin WCAu
	'Showanohokori'	CKel
	'Silver Dawn'	GBin
	sinensis	see *P. lactiflora*
	'Sonoma Kaleidoscope' **new**	GBin
	'Soshi'	GBin NLar
	'Spring Carnival' (S)	GBin
	'Squirt'	GBin
	steveniana	WCot
§	***suffruticosa*** (S)	CWib ELan GKev MGos SSpi
	- 'Akashigata' (S)	CKel
	- 'Alice Palmer' (S)	CKel
	- 'Bai Yu' (S)	GBin
I	- 'Better than Snow Tower' (S)	LRHS
	- Bird of Rimpo	see *P. suffruticosa* 'Rimpo'
	- Black Dragon Brocade	see *P. suffruticosa* 'Kokuryū-nishiki'
	- Black Flower Chief	see *P. suffruticosa* 'Hei Hua Kui'
	- Brocade of the Naniwa	see *P. suffruticosa* 'Naniwa-nishiki'
	- 'Burgundy Wine' (S)	GBin
	- 'Cardinal Vaughan' (S)	CKel
	- 'Chu Wu' (S) **new**	NTPC

- 'Dan Lu Yan' (S) **new** SPer
- 'Duchess of Kent' (S) CKel
- 'Duchess of Marlborough' (S) CKel
- Eternal Camellias see *P. suffruticosa* 'Yachiyo-tsubaki'
- 'Feng Dan Bai' (S) **new** SPer
- Flight of Cranes see *P. suffruticosa* 'Renkaku'
- Floral Rivalry see *P. suffruticosa* 'Hana-kisoi'
- Fragrant Jade see *P.* 'Xiang Yu'
- 'Frost on Peach Blossom' (S) LRHS
* - 'Glory of Huish' (S) CKel
- 'Godaishu' (S) CKel GBin SKHP
- 'Guardian of the Monastry' (S) GBin
- 'Hai Huang' (S) NTPC WKif
§ - 'Hakuo-jisi' (S/d) CKel EPfP
§ - 'Hana-kisoi' (S) CKel GBin
- 'Haru-no-akebono' (S) CKel
- 'Hei Hai Sa Jin' (S) **new** NTPC
§ - 'Hei Hua Kui' (S) NTPC
§ - 'Higurashi' (S) EPfP
- 'Hinode-sekai' (S/d) **new** GBin
§ - 'Hu Hong' (S) SPer
§ - 'Huang Hua Kui' (S) NTPC
- 'Hu's Family Red' (S) LRHS
- Jewel in the Lotus see *P. suffruticosa* 'Tama-fuyo'
- Jewelled Screen see *P. suffruticosa* 'Tama-sudare'
- 'Jin Zhi' (S) **new** NTPC SPer
- 'Jing Ge' (S) NTPC SPer WKif
- 'Jitsugetsu-nishiki' (S) CKel
- 'Joseph Rock' see *P. rockii*
- Kamada Brocade see *P. suffruticosa* 'Kamada-nishiki'
§ - 'Kamada-nishiki' (S) CKel GBin
§ - 'Kaow' (S) CKel
- King of Flowers see *P. suffruticosa* 'Kaow'
- King of White Lions see *P. suffruticosa* 'Hakuo-jisi'
- 'Kinkaku' see *P.* × *lemoinei* 'Souvenir de Maxime Cornu'
- 'Kinshi' see *P.* × *lemoinei* 'Alice Harding'
- 'Kokucho' (S) CKel
§ - 'Kokuryū-nishiki' (S) CKel LRHS SKHP
- 'Koshi-no-yuki' (S) CKel
- 'Lan Bao Shi' (S) GBin NTPC WKif
- 'Lu Yu' (S) **new** NTPC
- 'Ming Xing' (S) **new** NTPC
- 'Mo Sa Jin' (S) **new** NTPC
- 'Montrose' (S) CKel
* - 'Mrs Shirley Fry' (S) CKel
- 'Mrs William Kelway' (S) CKel
§ - 'Naniwa-nishiki' (S) CKel
- 'Nigata Akashigata' (S) CKel
- Pride of Taisho see *P. suffruticosa* 'Taisho-no-hokori'
- 'Princess Chiffon' (S) GBin
- 'Reine Elisabeth' (S) CKel
§ - 'Renkaku' (S) CKel SKHP
§ - 'Rimpo' (S) CKel EPfP GBin SKHP
- 'Sai Xue Ta' (S) SPer
§ - 'Shiguregumo' (S) CKel
- 'Shimadaigin' (S) CKel
- 'Shimane-chōjuraku' (S) CKel GBin
- 'Shimane-hakugan' (S) CKel
- 'Shimane-otone-mai' (S/d) **new** GBin
- 'Shimane-seidai' (S) CKel
- 'Shimanishiki' (S) CKel SKHP SPer
- 'Shin Shima Kagayaki' (S) CKel
- 'Shintoyen' (S) CKel
§ - 'Shou An Hong' (S) NTPC
- 'Sumi-no-ichi' (S) CKel
- 'Superb' (S) CKel
§ - 'Taisho-no-hokori' (S) CKel
§ - 'Taiyo' (S) CKel EPfP SKHP SPer
§ - 'Tama-fuyo' (S) CKel
§ - 'Tama-sudare' (S) CKel GBin
- The Sun see *P. suffruticosa* 'Taiyo'
- 'Toichi Ruby' (S) **new** GBin
- Twilight see *P. suffruticosa* 'Higurashi'
- 'White Snow' (S) **new** LRHS
- 'Wu Long Peng Sheng' (S) CKel GBin SPer
- 'Xue Lian' (S/d) **new** SPer
- 'Xue Ta' (S) CKel LRHS
§ - 'Yachiyo-tsubaki' (S) CKel SKHP
- 'Yin Hong Qiao Dui' (S) CKel NTPC SPer
- 'Ying Ri Hong' (S) WKif
- 'Yoshinogawa' (S) CKel EPfP
- 'Yu Ban Bai' (S) NTPC WKif
- 'Zhao Fen' (S) LRHS NPer NTPC

'Sugar n' Spice' WCAu
'Sunny Girl' **new** GBin WCAu
'Sunshine' see *P. peregrina* 'Otto Froebel'
* ***szowitsianum*** GKev
'Taiheko' CKel
'Tango' WCAu
'Ten' i' CKel
tenuifolia CAby EWll GBin GCal GKev LRHS NLar NSla SKHP SMad WCot
- RCB UA 11 WCot
- subsp. ***biebersteiniana*** GKev
§ - subsp. ***lithophila*** MPhe
- 'Plena' (d) EPot
- 'Rosea' GBin
'Terpsichore' (S) **new** GBin
'Tria' (S) GBin
veitchii CKel EPfP GCal GKev GMaP NLar SSpi WCot
- SDR 6020 **new** GKev
- from China MPhe
- pale-flowered GCal
- var. ***woodwardii*** CCon ECho GAbr GBin GCra GKev SSpi WCot WThu
'Vesuvian' CKel
'Viking Full Moon' GBin
'White Emperor' GBin
White Phoenix see *P. ostii* 'Feng Dan Bai'
'Wings of the Morning' (S) **new** GBin
wittmanniana CKel GBin GCal GKev NLar WCot
- PAB 3673 **new** LEdu
§ 'Xiang Yu' (S) LRHS
§ 'Yao Huang' (S) GBin SPer
Yao's Yellow see *P.* 'Yao Huang'
'Yellow Crown' CKel GBin WCAu
'Yellow Dream' GBin
'Yellow Emperor' GBin
Yellow Flower of Summer see *P. suffruticosa* 'Huang Hua Kui'
'Yellow Gem' GBin
'Yellow Heaven' **new** GBin
'Yokohama' **new** GBin
I 'Zephyrus' (S) **new** GBin

Paesia (*Dennstaedtiaceae*)

scaberula CLAP NBir WFib

Paliurus (*Rhamnaceae*)

spina-christi CArn CBcs SLon

Pallenis (Asteraceae)

§	***maritima***	CCCN

Panax (Araliaceae)

	ginseng	EBee GPoy
	japonicus	WCru
	- BWJ 7932	WCru

Pancratium (Amaryllidaceae)

	maritimum	CArn ECho GKev SDeJ

Pandanus (Pandanaceae)

	utilis	EAmu

Pandorea (Bignoniaceae)

	jasminoides	CCCN CDoC CHll CRHN CSpe CTri EBak ECou EShb MOWG
	- 'Alba'	CRHN SPer
§	- 'Charisma' (v)	CCCN CHel CHll EPfP EShb LSou MOWG SEND SLim SPer SPoG
	- 'Lady Di'	CCCN MOWG
	- 'Rosea'	CCCN CHel
	- 'Rosea Superba' 🏆H1	CBcs CHEx CRHN LHop SEND SLim SPer
	- 'Variegata'	see *P. jasminoides* 'Charisma'
	lindleyana	see *Clytostoma calystegioides*
	pandorana	CHll CRHN EBee SLim
	- 'Golden Showers'	CCCN CDoC CHel CRHN EBee MOWG MRav SEND SLim

Panicum (Poaceae)

	amarum 'Dewey Blue'	CKno EPPr MAvo
	bulbosum	CKno EHoe EPPr
	clandestinum	EHoe EPPr EWes IMou MWhi SMea
§	'Fibre Optics'	CSpe
	miliaceum	LRHS
	- 'Purple Majesty'	CWib SPhx
	- 'Violaceum'	CSpe SPhx
	oligosanthes var. ***scribnerianum*** new	SPhx
	virgatum	MAsh SMrm WMnd WWEG XLum
	- 'Blue Tower'	CKno ELon MAvo SMea XLum
	- 'Cardinal'	EPPr
	- 'Cloud Nine'	CKno EPPr MAvo NOak SMrm WHal WRHF
	- 'Dallas Blues'	CKno CPrp EBee EHoe EPPr EWes LAst LHop LRHS MAvo MRav MWhi NOak NWsh SHDw SMrm WMoo WPGP XLum
	- 'Emerald Chief' new	MWhi
	- 'Farbende Auslese'	MAvo WWEG
	- 'Hänse Herms'	CKno EHoe ELon EPPr LRHS MAvo MBri MWhi SMea WWEG
	- 'Heavy Metal'	Widely available
	- 'Heiliger Hain'	CKno CSpe EPPr LHop MAvo WCot
I	- 'Kupferhirse'	CKno EPPr
	- 'Nican' new	EPPr
	- 'Northwind'	CKno EBee EPPr LRHS MAvo SHDw
	- 'Prairie Fire' new	LRHS
	- 'Prairie Sky'	CKno CPrp CWCL EBee EHoe ELon EPPr EUJe GBin LEdu LRHS MAsh MAvo MNFA NBro NLar SDix SGbt SMea WMoo WPGP
	- 'Purple Haze'	EHoe EPPr LRHS
	- 'Red Cloud'	CKno MAvo
	- 'Rehbraun'	EBee EHoe EPPr EPfP LEdu LHop LRHS NOak NWsh SGol WWEG XLum
	- 'Rotstrahlbusch'	CKno CPrp CWib EBee EHoe EPPr GMaP MAvo MWhi NOak SPer WCot WMoo WPGP WWEG XLum
	- 'Rubrum'	EHoe ELan EPPr MAvo MWat SDix WMoo
	- 'Shenandoah'	Widely available
	- 'Squaw'	CKno CMac CPrp CWCL CWib EHoe EPPr EPfP IPot LRHS MAsh MJak MMuc MNFA NOak NOrc NWsh SBea SEND SMad WCot WMoo WWEG
	- 'Strictum'	EHoe EPPr EWes GQue LEdu LPla LRHS MAvo SPhx WMoo
	- 'Warrior'	CKno CPrp CWCL EHoe ELan ELon EPPr EPfP GBin LHop LRHS MAsh MAvo MCot MRav MWhi NCGa NWsh WPGP WWEG
	- 'Wood's Variegated' (v)	WCot

Papaver ✿ (Papaveraceae)

	aculeatum	CTca
	alboroseum	LLHF LRHS
	'Alpha Centauri' (SPS)	LLHF SWat
	alpinum	CSpe GJos LRHS MAsh NGdn SPet SWat
	- album	GKev
	amurense	SWat
	atlanticum	LDai NBro NGdn SPlb
	- 'Flore Pleno' (d)	CSpe IFro NBro NGdn WCot
	'Aurora'	SWat
	'Beyond Red' (SPS)	SWat
	bracteatum	see *P. orientale* var. *bracteatum*
	'Bright Star' (SPS)	CDes GBin SWat
	burseri	SRot
	'Cathay' (SPS)	SWat
	commutatum 🏆H4	CSpe ELan SPhx SWat
	- 'Ladybird' 🏆H4	CCVN NPri
	corona-sancti-stephani	SWat
	'Danish Flag'	NNor
	degenii	CPBP
	'Eccentric Silk' (SPS)	SWat
	fauriei	GKev
§	'Fire Ball' (d)	GCal LHop NBid NBro SWat WRHF WWEG
	'Harlequin' (SPS)	ELon
	'Heartbeat' PBR (SPS)	EBee IPot LRHS MAvo MBel SWat
	heldreichii	see *P. pilosum* subsp. *spicatum*
	hybridum 'Flore Pleno' (d)	NSti SWat
	'Jacinth' (SPS)	CDes EBee GBin LLHF SWat WCot
	lateritium	CHid CPou SRms
	- 'Nanum Flore Pleno'	see *P.* 'Fire Ball'
	'Lauffeuer'	ELon SWat
	'Matador' PBR 🏆H4	CWCL EBee MBel NNor WCot
	'Medallion' (SPS)	CDes EBee EPri GBin LLHF LRHS SWat
	microcarpum	EDAr LLHF
§	***miyabeanum***	CSpe ECho EDAr ELan LRHS MJak MMuc SRot
	- tatewakii	see *P. miyabeanum*
	'Moondance'	NPri
	nanum 'Flore Pleno'	see *P.* 'Fire Ball'
	nudicaule 'Aurora Borealis'	CSpe
	- Champagne Bubbles Group	NNor SPet SWat
	- var. ***croceum*** 'Flamenco'	NNor
	- Garden Gnome Group	see *P. nudicaule* Gartenzwerg Group

§	– Gartenzwerg Group ♀H4	CSpe EHyd EPfP LRHS MBri NGdn SPet SPlb SPoG SRot SWvt WGor WRHF WWEG
	– 'Matador'	NPri
	– 'Pacino'	EWll LRHS SPet
	– 'Party Fun' (mixed)	CSpe
	– 'Solar Fire Orange' ♀H4	LHop LRHS MBel WGwG
	– 'Summer Breeze'	SPet
	– 'Summer Breeze Orange' ♀H4	NPri
	– 'Summer Breeze Yellow'	NPri
	– Wonderland Series	NNor SPet
	– – 'Wonderland Orange'	ELan NPri
	– – 'Wonderland Pink Shades'	NPri
	– – 'Wonderland White'	ELan NPri
	– – 'Wonderland Yellow'	ELan NPri
	orientale	CBcs EPfP MJak SRms SWat WHar
	– 'Abu Hassan'	IPot SWat
	– 'Aglaja' ♀H4	CElw CKno CWCL ECtt ELon LRHS MBel MHol MPie NEgg NGdn NSti SMrm SPad SWat WCot
	– 'Aladin'	SWat
	– 'Ali Baba'	GCra SWat
	– 'Alison'	SWat
	– 'Allegro'	CSBt ELon EPfP GMaP IBoy LRHS MBNS MBri MRav NGdn SPer SPlb SVic SWat SWvt WWEG
	– 'Allegro Vivace'	LRHS
	– 'Arwide'	SWat
	– 'Aslahan'	ELon MRav SWat
	– 'Atrosanguineum'	SWat
	– 'Avebury Crimson'	MWat SWat
	– 'Baby Kiss'[PBR]	ECtt MBri NLar SWat
	– 'Ballkleid'	ELon SWat
	– 'Beauty Queen'	MRav NGdn SDix SWat
	– 'Bergermeister Rot'	SWat
	– 'Big Jim'	SWat
	– 'Black and White' ♀H4	CMac ELan EPfP GMaP MNrw MRav NEgg NPri SEND SMrm SWat
	– 'Blackberry Queen'	SWat
	– 'Blickfang'	SWat
	– 'Bolero'	ECtt NLar
	– 'Bonfire'	GAbr LRHS MBri MHol
	– 'Bonfire Red'	SWat
§	– var. ***bracteatum*** ♀H4	NBir SWat
	– 'Brilliant'	EPfP GJos LRHS MWat NBre NGdn SWat WMoo
	– 'Brooklyn' (New York Series)	ECtt LRHS LSRN SWat
	– 'Burning Heart'	CPar CWGN ECtt IBoy IPot LRHS MBri MSCN NLar SPer SPoG SWat
	– 'Carmen'[PBR]	ECtt ELon GAbr MNrw WCot
*	– 'Carneum'	LRHS NBre NLar WWEG
	– 'Carnival'	EBee NBre SWat
	– 'Casino'[PBR]	EBee GAbr NLar SPer
	– 'Catherina'	NBre SWat
	– 'Cedar Hill'	EBee ECtt ELon EWes GCal MRav NBre SWat WCAu
	– 'Cedric Morris' ♀H4	ELan MRav SWat WCot WHoo WMnd
	– 'Central Park' (New York Series)	EBee ELon MBri SWat
I	– 'Charming' pink-flowered	CAby CMac ECtt MWat NCGa NGdn SMrm SPhx SWat WGwG
	– 'Charming' red-flowered	LRHS
	– 'China Boy'	SWat
	– 'Clochard'	CElw ECtt ELon SWat WCot
	– 'Coral Reef'	ECtt EPfP MHer MLHP NPri SWat WHar WMoo
	– 'Corrina'	SWat
	– 'Curlilocks'	ECtt ELan ELon EPfP IBoy LRHS MRav MWat NGdn SPer SRms SWat SWvt WCot WWEG
	– 'Derwisch'	ELon SWat
*	– 'Diana'	SWat
	– 'Distinction'	WCot
	– 'Double Pleasure'	ECtt NBre SWat
	– double red shades (d)	NGdn
	– 'Doubloon' (d)	EBee NBre SWat
	– 'Dwarf Allegro Vivace'	LRHS
	– 'Earl Grey'	SWat
	– 'Effendi' ♀H4	CWCL EBee ECtt SWat WCot
	– 'Elam Pink'	SWat WCot
	– 'Erste Zuneigung'	ELon SWat
	– 'Eskimo Pie'	SWat
	– 'Eyecatcher'	ELon NLar NSoo SGol
	– 'Fancy Feathers'[PBR]	ECtt MBri NLar SWat WHil
	– 'Fatima'	CAby SWat
	– 'Feuerriese'	SWat
	– 'Feuerzwerg'	SWat
	– 'Fiesta'	CAby ELon SWat
	– 'Firefly'[PBR]	SWat
	– 'Flamenco'	CBcs IBoy SWat
	– 'Flamingo'	ELon SWat
*	– 'Flore Pleno' (d)	NGdn
	– 'Forncett Summer'	CPar ECtt ELon MRav NBre NLar NSoo SPer SWat WCAu WCot WHoo WWEG
	– 'Frosty' (v)	SHar
	– 'Fruit Punch'	MNHC
	– 'Garden Glory'	CAby ECtt ELon GCra LRHS LSRN MArl NBre SWat WCAu
	– 'Glowing Embers'	ECtt SWat
	– 'Glowing Rose'	ELon NBre SWat
	– Goliath Group	ELan ELon LHop LRHS MAvo MRav NBro SDix SRms SWat WMnd WWEG
	– – 'Beauty of Livermere'	Widely available
§	– – 'Beauty of Livermere' clonal	ECtt WCot
	– 'Graue Witwe'	ELon SWat
	– 'Guardsman'	see *P. orientale* (Goliath Group) 'Beauty of Livermere' clonal
	– 'Halima'	SWat
	– 'Harlem' (New York Series)	CElw MSCN NLar NPnk SMrm SWat
	– 'Harvest Moon' (d)	ECtt NPer SWat WHal WWEG
	– 'Heidi'	SWat
	– 'Hewitt's Old Rose'	NBre
	– 'Hula Hula'	ELon SWat
	– 'Indian Chief'	MHol NLar NPer SRot WWEG
	– 'Inferno'[PBR]	ECtt
	– 'John III' ♀H4	CAby SMrm SPhx SWat
	– 'John Metcalf'	EBee ECtt LHop LRHS NBre NSti SWat
	– 'Juliane'	CAby ECtt ELon NSti SWat
	– 'Karine' ♀H4	CElw CSam ELan EPPr EPfP GMaP IBoy LHop LRHS MAvo MNrw NLar SGol SPoG SWat WCAu WHoo
	– 'Khedive' (d) ♀H4	CWCL EBee SWat
	– 'King George'	SWat
	– 'King Kong'	CPar ECtt NLar SWat WCot
	– 'Kleine Tänzerin'	CSam ECtt LRHS MBel MHer MMuc MRav NBre NSti SWat WCAu WCot
	– 'Kollebloem'	SWat
	– 'Lady Frederick Moore'	LHop LRHS NBre NLar SWat WWEG

- 'Lady Roscoe'	NBre SWat
- 'Ladybird'	EPfP LRHS NBre
- 'Lambada'	SWat
- 'Lauren's Lilac'	CAby ECtt ELon LSRN NBre NCGa SWat
- 'Leuchtfeuer' ♀H4	CAby LRHS NBre SWat
- 'Lighthouse' ♀H4	EBee SWat
- 'Lilac Girl'	ECtt ELon GMaP NLar SWat WCAu
- 'Little Candyfloss' PBR	MSCN SWat
- 'Little Patty Plum' PBR **new**	NLar
- 'Louvre' (Parisienne Series)	ECtt ELon MBri SPoG SWat WCot
- 'Maiden's Blush'	ECtt NBre NSti SWat
- 'Mandarin' PBR	LRHS
- 'Manhattan' (New York Series)	CElw CSam CSpe ECtt ELon EPfP EWes MBri MNrw MSCN NEgg NGdn NPnk NSti SGbt SPer SPoG SWat WHoo
- 'Marcus Perry'	ECtt EWes GMaP LRHS MAvo NEgg NGdn SGol SPoG SWat WCAu
- 'Marlene'	IPot LRHS MSCN SWat
- 'Mary Finnan'	CTca SWat
- 'Master Richard'	SWat
- 'May Queen' (d)	ECtt ELon EWes IBlr MRav NBro NLar NSti SWat WCot WPnn
- 'May Sadler'	NLar SWat
- 'Midnight'	ELon NBre SWat
- 'Miss Piggy' PBR	EBee ECtt IKil LLHF MBri NLar NSoo SGbt SMrm SPer SWat WCot WHil
- 'Mrs H.G. Stobart'	SWat
- 'Mrs Marrow's Plum'	see *P. orientale* 'Patty's Plum'
- 'Mrs Perry'	CMac CMea CSBt ECtt ELan GMaP IFro LRHS MBel MWat NGdn NHol NPer SGbt SPer SRms SWat WBrk WCAu WMnd
- 'Nanum Flore Pleno'	see *P.* 'Fire Ball'
- 'Noema'	SWat
- 'Orange Glow'	SWat WMoo
- 'Orangeade Maison'	SWat
- 'Oriana'	SWat
- 'Oriental'	SWat
- 'Pagode'	NCGa
- 'Pale Face'	SWat
- 'Papillon' PBR	NLar NPri WCot WHar
- 'Paradiso'	EPfP LPio MAsh MAvo MBri NCGa NSoo NSti SMrm
§ - 'Patty's Plum'	Widely available
- 'Perry's White'	CBcs CSBt ECtt ELan ELon EPfP GMaP IBoy LHop LRHS MCot MMuc MRav NHol NLar SGol SMrm SPer SPoG SRkn SWat SWvt WCAu WMnd WWEG
- 'Persepolis' **new**	SGol
- 'Peter Pan'	CAby ELon NBre SWat
- 'Petticoat'	ECtt ELon NBre SWat
- 'Picotée'	CAby EBee ECtt ELan ELon EShb LRHS MBri MRav NEgg NLar SPer SPoG SRot SWat SWvt WMoo WWEG
- 'Pink Lassie'	SWat
- 'Pink Panda'	CAby SWat
- 'Pink Pearl' PBR	NCGa SWat
- 'Pink Ruffles' PBR	CBcs ECtt NLar SGbt SPoG SWat WCot
- 'Pinnacle'	SWat
- 'Pizzicato'	CWib EPfP LRHS NNor NPer SPet SWat WHar WMoo WWEG
- 'Place Pigalle' (Parisienne Series)	EBee ECtt ELon EPfP LHop MAsh MAvo MBri NEgg SPer SPoG SWat
- 'Polka'	SWat
- 'Prince of Orange'	MBri SWat SWvt WWEG
- Princess Victoria Louise	see *P. orientale* 'Prinzessin Victoria Louise'
- 'Prinz Eugen'	ELon GMaP LRHS NBre SWat
§ - 'Prinzessin Victoria Louise'	EPfP GMaP IBoy LAst LRHS NGdn NLar NNor SEND SMrm SWat WBrk WHar WWEG
- 'Prospero'	NBre SWat
- 'Queen Alexandra'	ITim LBMP NGdn NLar WWEG
- 'Raspberry Queen'	CCon CDes CMac CMea ECtt ELan ELon EPri EWTr GMaP IBoy MArl MAvo MBel MRav NLar NSti SWat WCAu WCot WHal WHoo WMnd WWEG
- 'Raspberry Ruffles'	CAby NBre SWat
- 'Rembrandt'	CAby SWat
- 'Rose Queen'	NBre
- 'Rosenpokal'	SWat
- 'Roter Zwerg'	ELon SWat
- 'Royal Chocolate Distinction'	CAby CElw CSpe EBee ECtt ELan ELon EPPr EPfP GBin LRHS LSRN MAvo NLar NSti SRot SWat WWlt
- 'Royal Wedding'	CAby CSpe CTri CWCL EBee ELon EPfP EShb IBoy LAst LBMP LHop LRHS MBel MCot MHer MLHP NEgg NGdn NLar NPri NSoo SGbt SMrm SPer SPoG SWat WJek WMoo WWEG
- 'Ruffled Patty' PBR	EBee ECtt EPfP NCGa NSti SGbt SWat
- 'Ruffled Princess of Orange' PBR	SWat
* - 'Saffron'	SWat
- 'Salmon Glow' (d)	SWat WWEG
- 'Salome'	SWat
- 'Scarlet King'	CMac LRHS SWat
- scarlet-flowered	SEND
- 'Scarlett O'Hara' PBR (d)	CPar ECtt EPfP GAbr LLHF LRHS MBri SWat WBor
- 'Showgirl'	ELon NBre SWat
* - 'Silberosa'	IPot SWat
- 'Sindbad'	ELon NEgg SWat
- 'Snow Goose'	CAby CMea CWGN ECtt ELon ESwi IPot LLHF LRHS MAsh MAvo MBel MCot MHol NPnk NPri SMad SWat WCot WHoo WKif WRHF
- 'Snow Queen'	GAbr
- 'Spätzünder'	NBre SWat
- 'Springtime'	ELon EWes LAst MRav SWat
- 'Staten Island' (New York Series)	ECtt
- Stormtorch	see *P. orientale* 'Sturmfackel'
§ - 'Sturmfackel'	NBre SWat
- 'Suleika'	SWat
- 'Sultana'	CAby ELon MArl SWat
- 'Sunset' PBR	SWat
- 'The Promise'	NBre SWat
- 'Tiffany'	CMac ECtt ELon GAbr LSRN MCot NEgg SMrm SWat WCot WWEG
- 'Trinity'	SWat
- 'Türkenlouis'	EBee ECGP ECtt ELon EPfP GAbr GCra GMaP IBoy LAst LRHS NGdn NLar NSoo SMrm SWat WCAu WCot WHoo WWEG
- 'Turkish Delight'	CAby ECtt ELon EWTr GCra GMaP LRHS MBel MMuc MRav NBir NLar NSoo SMrm SWat SWvt WCAu WMnd WWEG

	- 'Tutu'	SWat
	- 'Victoria Dreyfuss'	SWat
	- 'Viola'	SWat
	- 'Violetta'	SWat
	- 'Walking Fire'	MNrw
	- 'Water Babies'	SWat
	- 'Watermelon'	ECtt LRHS NLar SPer SWat
	- 'White Ruffles' PBR	EBee ECtt IKil MAvo NCGa SGbt SPoG SWat WCot
	- 'Wild Salmon'	NBre
	- 'Wisley Beacon'	CAby ELon SWat
	- 'Wunderkind'	ECtt LRHS SWat
	pilosum	SWat
§	- subsp. ***spicatum***	CCon CMea CSpe EBee ELon GBin LHop LPla NBir WCot WHer WMoo
	pseudocanescens	EDAr
	'Rhapsody in Red' (SPS)	SWat
	rhoeas	CArn CHab GJos GPoy MNHC NNor WJek
	- Angels' Choir Group (d)	NNor SWat
	- 'Bridal White' new	SPhx
	- Mother of Pearl Group	CSpe MCot SPhx SWat
	- Shirley Group	CWCL NNor
	rupifragum	GAbr WCot WPnn
	- 'Double Tangerine Gem'	see *P. rupifragum* 'Flore Pleno'
§	- 'Flore Pleno' (d)	CSpe GBin LAst NCGa SVic WBrk WMoo
	- 'Tangerine Dream'	SPet
	'Serena' (SPS)	SWat
	'Shasta' (SPS)	CDes ELon GBin LLHF MAvo SWat
	'Snow White' (SPS)	SWat
	somniferum	CArn ELau GPoy SVic SWat
	- var. ***album***	CArn
	- 'Blackcurrant Fizz' (d)	SPhx
	- 'Boudoir Babe' (d)	CSpe
	- (Laciniatum Group) 'Crimson Feathers'	NNor
	- - 'Swansdown' (d)	CSpe
	- 'Lauren's Grape'	CSpe SPhx
	- Paeoniiflorum Group (d)	SWat
	- - 'Black Beauty' (d)	CSpe SDcJ SVic SWat
	- 'Pink Chiffon'	SWat
	- 'Ragged Red' (d)	CSpe
	- subsp. ***setigerum***	NNor
	- single white-flowered	CSpe
	- 'White Cloud' (d)	SWat
	'Tequila Sunrise' (SPS)	CDes EBee SWat
	'The Cardinal'	NBre
	'The Falklands' (SPS)	SWat
	triniifolium	CSpe GCal LRHS SPhx WCot
	'Vesuvius' (SPS)	GBin SWat
	'Viva' (SPS)	SWat

papaya (pawpaw) see *Carica papaya*

Parabenzoin see *Lindera*

Parachampionella see *Strobilanthes*

Paradisea (*Asparagaceae*)

	liliastrum ♀H4	CHid CPBP CPrp EBee ECho EPri GCal IGor NBid NChi
	- 'Major'	ECho SPhx
	lusitanica	CAvo CDes CHid CMHG CPom CSam CSpe CTca ECho EPri GBin GCal IBlr IBoy LEdu MCot WPGP

Parahebe (*Plantaginaceae*)

	'Angela'	MSCN
	× ***bidwillii***	GJos MHer SRms SRot
	- 'Kea'	SRot
	canescens	ECou
§	***catarractae***	CExl CTri CWib ECho ECou EPfP GAbr GCra MLHP MRav MWat NBir NBro SRms WKif WMnd
	- blue-flowered	CDoC SPer
	- 'County Park'	ECou
	- 'Cuckoo'	ECou
§	- 'Delight' ♀H3	CExl ECou EWes GCal GMaP GQue LHop LRHS MHer NPer SDix SRot
	- subsp. ***diffusa***	NPer
	- 'Miss Willmott'	SPer SPlb
	- 'Porlock'	CHel GKev WHoo
	- 'Porlock Purple'	see *P. catarractae* 'Delight'
	- 'Rosea'	ECho SRms
	- white-flowered	CSpe MLHP SRms
	decora	NSla
§	***formosa***	SPlb SVen
	'Greencourt'	see *P. catarractae* 'Delight'
	linifolia	CTri
§	***lyallii***	ECho EPfP GJos GMaP MCot MHer MMuc MRav MSwo MWat NLBP SPlb SRms WKif
	- 'Julie-Anne' ♀H3	GCal LRHS
	- 'Rosea'	CTri
	- 'Summer Snow'	ECou
	'Mervyn'	CTri
§	***perfoliata*** ♀H3-4	CExl CMac CMea EBee ELan EPfP EPri GCal GCra GGal GMaP LEdu LHop MAsh MCot MMuc MNrw MRav NChi SDix SEND SPer SRms WWFP XLum
	'Snow Clouds'	CHel CMea EPfP LHop LRHS SBch SDix SRot
	'Snowcap'	CDoC LRHS MRav SPlb SRms

Parajubaea (*Arecaceae*)

	sunkha	EAmu
	torallyi var. ***torallyi***	EAmu

Parakmeria see *Magnolia*

Paranomus (*Proteaceae*)

	reflexus	SPlb

Paraquilegia (*Ranunculaceae*)

§	***anemonoides***	CExl WAbe
	grandiflora	see *P. anemonoides*

Parasenecio (*Asteraceae*)

	delphiniifolius B&SWJ 5789	WCru
	- B&SWJ 10885	WCru
	- B&SWJ 11189	WCru
	- B&SWJ 11415	WCru
	farfarifolius new	WCru
	- var. ***acerinus*** B&SWJ 11549	WCru
	- - B&SWJ 11554	WCru
	- var. ***bulbifer***	WCru
	hastatus	see *P. maximowiczianus* var. *farfarifolius*
	kiusianus B&SWJ 11460	WCru
§	***maximowiczianus*** B&SWJ 11468	WCru

mortonii GWJ 9419	WCru
- HWJK 2214	WCru
tebakoensis B&SWJ 11167	WCru
- B&SWJ 11536	WCru
aff. ***yatabei*** B&SWJ 11117	WCru

Paraserianthes (*Mimosaceae*)

distachya	see *P. lophantha*
§ ***lophantha*** ♀H1	CExl CHEx EBak EShb SPlb

Parasyringa see *Ligustrum*

Parathelypteris (*Thelypteridaceae*)

§ ***novae-boracensis***	ISha

Parietaria (*Urticaceae*)

judaica	CArn GPoy WHer WSFF

Paris ✿ (*Melanthiaceae*)

chinensis	WCru
- B&SWJ 265 from Taiwan	WCru
delavayi	WCru
fargesii	WCru
- var. ***brevipetalata***	WCru
- var. ***petiolata***	WCru
forrestii	WCru
incompleta	CLAP EPot GCal WCru
japonica	WCru
lancifolia B&SWJ 3044 from Taiwan	WCru
mairei	WCru
polyphylla ♀H4	CArn CBct CBrO CCon CHel CLAP ECho LRHS MAvo MNrw NBid NLar NWad SKHP WCru WPnP WSHC WShi
- B&SWJ 2125	WCru
- Forrest 5945	GCal
- HWJCM 475	WCru
- var. ***alba***	CCon
- var. ***stenophylla***	CCon EBee WCru
- var. ***yunnanensis***	ECho
* - - ***alba***	GCal
quadrifolia	CLAP CSpe ECho EPfP EWld GCal GKev GPoy NLar NMyG SKHP SPhx SSpi WBor WCru WHer WPGP WPnP WShi
- SDR 2828	GKev
tetraphylla	WCru
thibetica	CBct CCon EBee NBid SKHP WCru
- var. ***apetala***	WCru
verticillata	CLAP WCru
- 'Ryokutei' (d)	WCru

Parnassia (*Celastraceae*)

CC 6173 **new**	GKev
SDR 5128	EBee
palustris	GKev WHer

Parochetus (*Papilionaceae*)

§ ***africanus*** ♀H2	CHid ECre
* - 'Blue Gem'	CCCN CSpe
communis misapplied	see *P. africanus*
communis ambig.	CCon CExl MSCN NPer WHil
communis Buch.-Ham. ex D. Don from Himalaya	EBee GCra

Paronychia (*Caryophyllaceae*)

§ ***capitata***	CTri SRms WHoo
kapela	SPlb XSen
- 'Binsted Gold' (v)	XLum XSen
§ - subsp. ***serpyllifolia***	GBin XLum
nivea	see *P. capitata*
serpyllifolia	see *P. kapela* subsp. *serpyllifolia*

Parrotia (*Hamamelidaceae*)

persica ♀H4	Widely available
- 'Biltmore'	CJun NLar SSta
- 'Burgundy'	CJun NLar
- 'Felicie'	CJun EPfP NLar
- 'Globosa'	NLar
- 'Het Plantsoen'	NLar
- 'Jodrell Bank'	CJun MBlu NLar
§ - 'Lamplighter' (v)	CJun
- 'Pendula'	CJun CMCN EPfP SSta
- 'Persian Carpet'	NLar
- 'Summer Bronze'	LRHS LSRN MAsh SBir SSpi SSta
- 'Vanessa'	CBcs CDoC CDul CJun CLnd CMCN CMac EBee EPfP EWes GBin GKin IArd LRHS MAsh MBlu MGos NLar SBir SGol SLPl SPoG SSta WMou
- 'Variegata'	see *P. persica* 'Lamplighter'
subaequalis	MBri

Parrotiopsis (*Hamamelidaceae*)

jacquemontiana	CBcs CJun GBin IVic MBlu NLar SSpi

Parrya (*Brassicaceae*)

menziesii	see *Phoenicaulis cheiranthoides*

parsley see *Petroselinum crispum*

Parsonsia (*Apocynaceae*)

capsularis	ECou
heterophylla	ECou

Parthenium (*Asteraceae*)

integrifolium	CArn GPoy IMou LRHS SPhx

Parthenocissus (*Vitaceae*)

§ ***henryana*** ♀H4	Widely available
himalayana	CBcs
- 'Purpurea'	see *P. himalayana* var. *rubrifolia*
§ - var. ***rubrifolia***	CBcs CWCL EBee ELan EUJe GBin LRHS MAsh MRav NLar SLim SLon SPoG WCru
inserta misapplied	see *P. quinquefolia*
inserta ambig.	CMac CTsd NLar
laetevirens	NLar
§ ***quinquefolia*** ♀H4	Widely available
- var. ***engelmannii***	CBcs EBee LAst LBuc SPer WCFE
- 'Guy's Garnet'	WCru
- Star Showers = 'Monham' (v)	EBee EPfP NLar
semicordata B&SWJ 6551	WCru
striata	see *Cissus striata*
thomsonii	see *Cayratia thomsonii*
§ ***tricuspidata*** ♀H4	CCVT CDul EBee EHoe EPfP IBoy MAsh MGos MMuc SGol SPer
- 'Beverley Brook'	EBee LBuc LRHS LSRN MBri NLar SBod SPer SRms
- 'Crûg Compact'	WCru
- 'Fenway Park'	CFlo EBee ELan MRav NLar
- 'Green Spring'	CBcs EBee IArd MGos NLar SPer
- 'Lowii'	CMac EBee EPfP LBuc LRHS MBlu MGos MRav NLar SLon SPer
- 'Minutifolia'	EBee
- 'Robusta'	CHEx EBee

§	- 'Veitchii'	Widely available

Pasithea (*Hemerocallidaceae*)

	caerulea	CAbP CAvo EBee ECGP ESwi GAbr MHol SPer WCot

Paspalum (*Poaceae*)

	glaucifolium	MNrw
	quadrifarium	CKno LDai
	- RCB RA S-5	WCot

Passiflora ✿ (*Passifloraceae*)

	actinia	CCCN CRHN SPlb
	'Adularia'	CCCN
	alata (F) ♀H1	CCCN
	× ***alatocaerulea***	see *P.* × *belotii*
	'Allardii'	CCCN
	ambigua	CCCN
§	'Amethyst' ♀H1	CCCN CFlo CRHN CSBt CSPN EAmu EShb LHop LSRN MRav SAPC SPoG WPGP
	amethystina misapplied	see *P.* 'Amethyst'
§	***amethystina*** Mikan	CBcs ECre
	'Anastasia'	CCCN
	'Andy'	CCCN
	'Anemona'	CCCN
	'Angelo Blu'	CCCN
	'Annika'	CCCN
	antioquiensis misapplied	see *P.* × *exoniensis*
	antioquiensis ambig.	CBcs CCCN CDoC CHel CSPN MOWG SEND
	antioquiensis ambig. × (× ***exoniensis*** 'Hill House')	CHll
	antioquiensis Karst ♀H2	CHll GGal
	'Ariane'	CCCN
	× ***atropurpurea***	CCCN
§	***aurantia***	CCCN
	banksii	see *P. aurantia*
§	× ***belotii***	CCCN CRHN
	'Impératrice Eugénie'	see *P.* × *belotii*
	'Betty Myles Young'	CCCN CRHN
	'Blue Bird'	CCCN
	'Blue Crown'	CCCN
	'Blue Moon'	CCCN
	'Blue Stripper'	CCCN
	'Blue Velvet'	CCCN
	'Byron Beauty'	CCCN
	'Byte'	CCCN
§	***caerulea*** ♀H3	Widely available
	- 'Clear Sky'PBR	CCCN CFlo CSPN ELan EPfP LHop LRHS NLar
	- 'Constance Eliott'	CAgr CBcs CCCN CDoC CFlo CHel CMac CRHN CSBt CSPN CWib EAmu EBee ELan EPfP LBMP LHop LRHS MAsh MBri MOWG MRav MWat NLar NPri SGol SPer SWvt
	- ***rubra***	CSBt
	× ***caeruleoracemosa***	see *P.* × *violacea*
	× ***caponii***	CCCN
	- 'John Innes'	CCCN
	'Celine'	CCCN
	chinensis	see *P. caerulea*
	citrifolia	CCCN
	citrina	CCCN MOWG SLim
	× ***colvillii***	CCCN CHll
	'Coordination'	CCCN
§	***coriacea***	CCCN
	'Crimson Tears'	CCCN EBee
	'Daylight'	CCCN
	'Debby'	CCCN LSRN
	× ***decaisneana*** (F)	CCCN
	'Divertido' **new**	CCCN
	Eden = 'Hil Pas Eden'	CCCN CFlo CSPN EAmu EBee LRHS MBri NLar SCoo SLim SPoG SRkn
	edulis (F)	CCCN ELau SPre SVic
	- f. ***flavicarpa*** (F)	CCCN
	- 'Norfolk' (F)	CCCN
	- 'Parati' (F)	CCCN
	'Elizabeth' (F)	CCCN
	'Empress Eugenie'	see *P.* × *belotii*
*	'Evatoria'	CCCN
§	× ***exoniensis*** ♀H1	CCCN CHll CRHN CSBt ECre
	'Fairylights'	CCCN
	'Fantasma'	CCCN
	'Fata Confetto'	CCCN
	'Fledermouse'	CCCN
	'Flying V'	CCCN
	'Grand Duchess'	CCCN
	gritensis	CCCN
	'Heidi'	CCCN
	'Hetty Nicolaas' **new**	CCCN
	'Hildegard' **new**	CCCN
	incarnata (F)	CArn GPoy SPlb
	'Incense' (F) ♀H1	CCCN SPlb
	'Inspiration'	CCCN
	'Jelly Joker'	CCCN
	'Justine Lyons'	CCCN CRHN
	karwinskii	CCCN
	× ***kewensis***	CCCN
	'Lady Margaret'	CCCN
	'Lambiekins'	CCCN CRHN
§	***ligularis*** (F)	CCCN
	'Lilac Lady'	see *P.* × *violacea* 'Tresederi'
	'Livie'	CCCN
	lowei	see *P. ligularis*
	lutea	CCCN
	'Luzmarina'	CCCN
	manicata (F)	CCCN
	'Maria'	CCCN
	'Mary Jane'	CCCN
I	***matthewsii*** 'Alba'	CRHN
	'Mavis Mastics'	see *P.* × *violacea* 'Tresederi'
	mayana	see *P. caerulea*
	membranacea (F)	CCCN
	'Michael'	CCCN
	'Minal'	CCCN
	'Mini Lamb'	CRHN
	mixta (F)	CCCN SEND
	- red-flowered **new**	CCCN
	mollissima misapplied	see *P. tarminiana*
	mollissima ambig. (F)	CBcs CCCN CHll MOWG SPlb
	mollissima (Kunth) L.H. Bailey (F) ♀H1	CRHN
	'Monika Fischer' **new**	CCCN
	mucronata	CCCN
	murucuja	CCCN
	'New Incense'	CCCN
	'Nightshift'	CCCN
	obtusifolia	see *P. coriacea*
	onychina	see *P. amethystina* Mikan
	'Panda'	CCCN
	'Pink Festival'	CCCN
	'Pink Nightmare'	CCCN
	'Pinky'	CCCN
	× ***piresiae***	CCCN
	'Precioso'	CCCN

	'Pura Vida'	CCCN
	'Purple Haze'	CCCN CSPN CWib EBee LRHS NEgg NLar
	'Purple Rain'	CCCN
	quadrangularis (F) ♀H1	CCCN CHll
	quinquangularis	CBcs CCCN
	racemosa ♀H2	CCCN
	- 'Buzios'	CCCN
	'Red Inca'	CCCN
	reitzii	CCCN
	riparia	CCCN
	rubra	CCCN EBee SLim
	sexocellata	see *P. coriacea*
	'Silvie' **new**	CCCN
	'Simply Red'	CCCN
	'Star of Bristol' ♀H2	CSPN EBee SLim
	'Star of Kingston'	CCCN
	'Star of Surbiton'	CCCN CRHN
	'Sunburst'	CCCN
	'Surprise'	CCCN
§	***tarminiana*** (F)	CCCN CRHN CSBt
	- white-flowered **new**	CCCN
	'Temptation'	CCCN
	tetrandra	CExl ECou
	× ***tresederi***	see *P.* × *violacea* 'Tresederi'
	trifasciata	CCCN
	tucumanensis	CCCN
	tetraploid **new**	
	tulae	CCCN
§	***variolata*** from French Guiana	CCCN
§	× ***violacea*** ♀H1	CBcs CCCN CRHN
	- 'Eynsford Gem'	CCCN EAmu
	- 'Lilac Lady'	see *P.* × *violacea* 'Tresederi'
	- 'Sabin'	CCCN LHop NLar
§	- 'Tresederi'	CCCN SEND
	- 'Twin Star'	CCCN
	- 'Victoria'	CCCN CSBt EUJe NLar
	vitifolia (F)	CCCN
	'White Lightning'	CCCN CFlo CSPN CWSG EBee LBuc LRHS LSqu NPri SLim SPoG SWvt
	'White Queen' **new**	CCCN
	'White Wedding'	CCCN
	'Wilgen Heintje'	CCCN
	'Winterland'	CCCN
	wurdackii	see *P. variolata* from French Guiana

passion fruit see *Passiflora*

passion fruit, banana see *Passiflora mollissima* (Kunth) L.H. Bailey

Pastinaca (*Apiaceae*)

sativa	CHab SVic

Patersonia (*Iridaceae*)

occidentalis	LRHS SPlb

Patrinia ✿ (*Caprifoliaceae*)

gibbosa	CSam CSpe LRHS MLHP MMHG NLar SPhx WMoo WPnP WWFP
- B&SWJ 874	WCru
rupestris B&SWJ 12654 **new**	WCru
scabiosifolia	CHll CKno CSpe ECtt LPio LRHS MHer MNFA NBir NLar SPhx WHoo WMoo WPGP
- B&SWJ 8740	WCru
- 'Nagoya'	MNrw
triloba	CPla CRDP CSpe ECho GCal LRHS LSou MMHG WMoo
* - 'Minor'	ECho
- var. ***palmata***	EBee GKev WMoo
villosa	CExl GCal IMou LRHS NGdn

Paulownia (*Paulowniaceae*)

catalpifolia	LLHF MBri NLar
elongata	NLar
fortunei	IVic MBlu NLar SPlb
- Fast Blue = 'Minfast'	CExl CHGN EBee EPfP ESwi LLHF LSRN SGol WHar WMou
kawakamii	EBee WPGP
- RWJ 9909	WCru
tomentosa ♀H3	Widely available
- 'Coreana'	CHll WCru

Pavonia (*Malvaceae*)

multiflora ambig.	CCCN
strictiflora	CCCN
* ***volubilis***	CCCN

pawpaw (false banana) see *Asimina triloba*

pawpaw (papaya) see *Carica papaya*

Paxistima (*Celastraceae*)

canbyi	WThu

peach see *Prunus persica*

pear see *Pyrus communis*

pear, Asian see *Pyrus pyrifolia*

pecan see *Carya illinoinensis*

Pedicularis (*Orobanchaceae*)

SDR 7126 **new**	GKev

Peganum (*Nitrariaceae*)

harmala	CArn

Pelargonium (*Geraniaceae*)

	'A.M. Mayne' (Z/d)	WFib
	'Abba' (Z/d)	WFib
	Abelina = 'Pacabel' (Z) **new**	WGor
	abrotanifolium (Sc)	EWoo LPio MHer SSea SVen WFib WGwG
	'Abundance' (Sc)	CSev
	acetosum	CSev EWoo GCal LPio MHer SMrm SPet SPhx WCot
*	- 'Variegatum' (v)	LPio
	'Ada Green' (R)	WFib
	'Ade's Elf' (Z/St)	NFir
	'Ainsdale Beauty' (Z)	WFib
	'Ainsdale Duke' (Z)	NFir
	'Alan West' (Z/St)	SSea
	album	LAst
	alchemilloides	CRHN LPio
	'Alde' (Min)	NFir
	'Aldwyck' (R)	WFib
	'Alex Kitson' (Z)	WFib
	'Algenon' (Min/d)	WFib
I	'Alice' (Min)	WFib
	'Alice Greenfield' (Z)	NFir
	'Allesley Shadow' (Dw/d) **new**	WFib
	alpinum	MHer

	'Amari' (R)	WFib
	'Ambrose' (Min/d)	WFib
	Amelit = 'Pacameli'^{PBR} (I/d)	LAst MCot NPri SSea
	'American Prince of Orange' (Sc)	MBPg
	Ameta = 'Pacmeta'^{PBR} (Z)	LAst
	'Amethyst' (R)	SCoo SPet WFib
	(Angeleyes Series) Angeleyes Bicolor = 'Pacbicolor'^{PBR} (A)	LAst NPri
	- Angeleyes Burgundy = 'Pacburg'^{PBR} (A)	LAst SSea
	- Angeleyes Orange = 'Paccrio'^{PBR} (A)	EWoo LAst LSou
	- Angeleyes Randy (A)	SSea
	'Angelique' (Dw/d)	WFib
	'Ann Hoystead' (R) ♀$^{H1+3}$	NFir WFib
	'Annsbrook Aquarius' (St)	NFir
	'Annsbrook Beauty' (A/C)	NFir WFib
	'Annsbrook Jupitor' (Z/St)	NFir
	Anthony = 'Pacan'^{PBR} (Z/d)	LAst
	'Antoine Crozy' (Z × I/d)	WFib
	'Apache' (Z/d) ♀$^{H1+3}$	WFib
	appendiculatum	CLak MHer WCot
	'Apple Betty' (Sc)	EWoo MBPg WFib
	'Apple Blossom Rosebud' (Z/d) ♀$^{H1+3}$	CHel ECtt EShb MBri MHer NEgg SMrm SSea WFib
	'Appleblossom' (Angeleyes Series)	LAst
	'Apricot' (Z/St)	LAst
	'April Hamilton' (I)	CWCL WFib
	'April Showers' (A)	WFib
	'Arctic Frost'	WFib
§	'Arctic Star' (Z/St)	CSpe NFir WBrk WFib
	'Ardens'	CHll CSev CSpe EUJe EWoo LPio LSou MCot MHer NFir SSea SWvt WCot WFib WWFP
	'Ardwick Cinnamon' (Sc)	EWoo MBPg MHer NFir WDib WFib
	(Aristo Series) Aristo Apricot = 'Regapri' (R)	LAst
	- Aristo Darling = 'Regdar'^{PBR} (R) **new**	LAst
	- Aristo Red Velvet = 'Regvel'^{PBR} (R)	LAst
	- Aristo Schoko = 'Regschoko' (R)	LAst
	'Arnside Fringed Aztec' (R)	MHer WFib
	'Aroma' (Sc)	EWoo MBPg
	'Ashby' (U/Sc)	CWCL EWoo MBPg MHer NFir SBch SSea
	'Ashfield Jubilee' (Z/C)	NFir
	'Ashfield Monarch' (Z/d) ♀$^{H1+3}$	NFir
	'Ashfield Serenade' (Z) ♀$^{H1+3}$	WFib
	'Askham Fringed Aztec' (R) ♀$^{H1+3}$	WFib
	asperum Ehr. ex Willd.	see *P.* 'Graveolens'
	'Atlantic Burgundy'	CWCL MCot
§	'Atomic Snowflake' (Sc/v)	MCot MNHC SPet WDib WFib
	'Atrium' (U)	MHer WFib
	'Attar of Roses' (Sc) ♀$^{H1+3}$	CArn CHby CRHN ECtt MBPg MCot MHer NFir NPri SBch SIde SPet SSea WBrk WFib WGwG
	'Aurora' (Z/d)	LAst
	australe	CRHN CSpe EWoo LPio MCot SBch SVen WFib
	'Australian Mystery' (R/Dec)	CSpe NFir WFib
	'Aztec' (R) ♀$^{H1+3}$	NFir WFib
	'Baby Bird's Egg' (Min)	WFib
	'Baby Harry' (Dw/v)	WFib
	'Balcon Lilas'	see *P.* 'Roi des Balcons Lilas'
	'Balcon Rose'	see *P.* 'Hederinum'
	'Balcony Red'^{PBR} (I) **new**	ECtt
	'Ballerina' (R)	see *P.* 'Carisbrooke'
I	'Ballerina' (Min)	WFib
§	'Barbe Bleu' (I/d)	NFir WFib
	'Barking' (Min/Z)	NFir
	'Barnston Dale' (Dw/d)	NFir
	'Bath Beauty' (Dw)	CSpe
	'Beatrice Cottington' (I/d)	WFib
	Beau Jangles Tom (I)	NPri
	'Beauty of Eastbourne' misapplied	see *P.* 'Lachskönigin'
	'Belinda Adams' (Min/d) ♀$^{H1+3}$	NFir
	Belladonna = 'Fisopa' (I/d)	SCoo
	'Bembridge' (Z/St/d)	WFib
	'Ben Franklin' (Z/d/v) ♀$^{H1+3}$	NFir
	'Ben Matt' (R)	WFib
	'Berkswell Lace' (A)	MHer
	Bernardo = 'Guiber'^{PBR} (I/d)	LAst
	'Beromünster' (Dec)	EWoo MHer NFir WFib
	'Bert Pearce' (R)	WFib
	'Beryl Reid' (R)	CWCL WFib
	'Bette Shellard' (Z/d/v)	NFir
	'Betty Catchpole' (Z)	EWoo
	betulinum	WFib
	'Betwixt' (Z/v)	SSea
	'Big Apple' (Sc)	MBPg
	'Bird Dancer' (Dw/St) ♀$^{H1+3}$	CSpe MCot MHer MNHC NFir SBch SSea WBrk
	(Birdbush Series) 'Birdbush Andy Pandy' (Sc)	MBPg
	- 'Birdbush Beautiful' (Sc)	MBPg
	- 'Birdbush Belinda' (Sc)	MBPg
	- 'Birdbush Betty' (Sc)	MBPg
	- 'Birdbush Big Ears' (Sc)	MBPg
	- 'Birdbush Blanco' (Sc)	MBPg
	- 'Birdbush Blossom' (Sc) **new**	MBPg
	- 'Birdbush Blush' (Sc)	MBPg
	- 'Birdbush Blythe' (Sc) **new**	MBPg
	- 'Birdbush Bob' (Sc) **new**	MBPg
	- 'Birdbush Bobby' (Sc)	MBPg
	- 'Birdbush Bold and Beautiful' (Sc)	MBPg
	- 'Birdbush Bolero' (Sc)	MBPg
	- 'Birdbush Bountiful' (Sc)	MBPg
	- 'Birdbush Brilliant' (Sc)	MBPg
	- 'Birdbush Chloe' (St)	MBPg
	- 'Birdbush Dawndew' (Sc)	MBPg
	- 'Birdbush Eleanor' (Z)	MBPg WFib
	- 'Birdbush Julie Anne' (Sc)	MBPg WDib
	- 'Birdbush Lemonside' (Sc)	MBPg
	- 'Birdbush Limey' (Sc)	MBPg
	- 'Birdbush Linda Creasey' (Sc)	MBPg
	- 'Birdbush Matty'	MBPg
	- 'Birdbush Miriam' (Sc)	WDib
	- 'Birdbush Suzy' (Sc)	MBPg
	- 'Birdbush Sweetness' (Sc)	MBPg
	- 'Birdbush Too Too O' (Sc)	MBPg
	- 'Birdbush Victoria' (Sc)	MBPg
	'Birthday Girl' (R)	CWCL WFib

'Bitter Lemon' (Sc)	ECtt EWoo MBPg
'Black Butterfly'	see *P.* 'Brown's Butterfly'
'Black Knight' (A)	NFir
'Black Knight' Lea (Dw/d/C)	NFir
'Black Knight' (R)	CSpe EWoo MHer
'Black Prince' (R/Dec)	CSpe EWoo NFir WFib
'Black Velvet' (R)	EWoo MCot
'Black Vesuvius'	see *P.* 'Red Black Vesuvius'
'Blackcurrant Yhu' (Dec)	NFir
'Blackdown Delight' (Z)	NFir
'Blackdown Sensation' (Dw/Z)	NFir
Blanca = 'Penwei'PBR (Dark Line Series) (Z/d)	LAst LBMP
Blanche Roche = 'Guitoblanc' (I/d)	LAst LBMP LSou NPri SCoo
§ 'Blandfordianum' (Sc)	EWoo LPio MHer
'Blandfordianum Roseum' (Sc)	EWoo MHer
'Blazonry' (Z/v)	WFib
(Blizzard Series) Blizzard Blue = 'Fisrain'PBR (I)	SCoo
- Blizzard Dark Red = 'Fisblizdark' (I)	CWCL EWoo
- Blizzard Red = 'Fizzard' (I)	SCoo
- Blizzard White = 'Fisbliz'PBR	SCoo
'Blue Beard'	see *P.* 'Barbe Bleu'
Blue Sybil = 'Pacblusy'PBR (I/d)	LAst LSou MCot NPri
Blue Wonder = 'Pacbla'PBR (Z/d)	LAst
'Bob Newing' (Min/St)	WFib
'Bobberstone' (Z/St)	WFib
'Bold Appleblossom' (Z)	WFib
'Bold Carmine' (Z/d)	NFir
'Bold Carousel' (Z/d)	WFib
'Bold Flame' (Z/d)	WFib
'Bold Limelight' (Z/d)	WFib
'Bold Minstrel' (Z/d)	WFib
'Bold Pixie' (Dw/d)	WFib
'Bold Princess' (Z/d)	WFib
'Bold Special' (Z) **new**	WFib
'Bold Sunrise' (Z/d)	NFir
'Bold Sunset' (Z/d)	NFir WFib
'Bold White' (Z)	NFir
'Bolero' (U) ♀H1+3	NFir WFib
'Bon Bon' (Min/St)	WFib
'Bontrosai'PBR (Sc)	MCot
'Bosham' (R)	WFib
'Both's Snowflake' (Sc/v)	MBPg WDib
bowkeri	WFib
'Brackenwood' (Dw/d) ♀H1+3	NFir
Bravo = 'Fisbravo' (Z/d)	WFib
'Brenda' (Min/d)	WFib
'Brenda Hyatt' (Dw/d)	WFib
'Brian West' (Min/St/C)	WFib
'Brian West Butterfly' (Z/St)	WFib
'Bridesmaid' (Dw/d)	NFir
'Brightstone' (Z/d)	WFib
'Brilliant' (Dec)	WFib
'Brilliantine' (Sc)	CSev EWoo MBPg MHer WFib WGwG
'Bristol' (Z/v)	SSea
'Brixworth Pearl' (Z)	WFib
'Bronze Corinne' (Z/C/d)	SPet

'Brook's Purple'	see *P.* 'Royal Purple'
'Brookside Flamenco' (Dw/d)	WFib
'Brookside Primrose' (Min/C/d)	WFib
'Brookside Serenade' (Dw)	WFib
§ 'Brown's Butterfly' (R)	ECtt WFib
'Brunswick' (Sc)	EWoo LPio MHer SMrm WFib
BullsEye Series (Z) **new**	SPet
- 'BullsEye Cherry' (Z) **new**	SMrm
'Burgundy' (R)	LBMP
'Burns Country' (Dw)	NFir
'Bushfire' (R) ♀H1+3	EWoo WFib
Butterfly = 'Fisam'PBR (I)	NFir SCoo
caffrum	LPio
'Cal'	see *P.* 'Salmon Irene'
Calais = 'Paclai'PBR	LAst
'California Brilliant' (U)	MHer
'Calignon' (Z/St)	WFib
'Camphor Rose' (Sc)	MBPg NFir
'Can-can' (I/d)	WFib
canescens	see *P.* 'Blandfordianum'
'Cape Beauty'	EWoo
'Cape Town' (Dw/z/v)	WFib
capitatum	MHer MNHC WFib
'Capri' (Sc)	WFib
'Captain Starlight' (A)	EWoo MHer NFir WFib
'Cardinal'	see *P.* 'Kardinal'
'Carefree' (U)	NFir WFib
§ 'Carisbrooke' (R) ♀H1+3	WFib
'Carmel' (Z)	WFib
carnosum	MHer
'Carol Gibbons' (Z/d)	NFir
'Caroline Schmidt' (Z/d/v)	LAst MCot NFir SSea WBrk WFib
'Carolyn Dean' (St)	NFir
'Carolyn Hardy' (Z/d)	WFib
Cascade Lilac	see *P.* 'Roi des Balcons Lilas'
Cascade Pink	see *P.* 'Hederinum'
'Cathay' (Z/St)	NFir
'Cathy' (R)	NFir
caucalifolium subsp. ***caucalifolium***	MHer
- subsp. ***convolvulifolium***	WFib
'Cézanne' (R)	MCot
'Charity' (Sc) ♀H1+3	MBPg MCot MHer NFir WDib WFib
'Charlotte Bronte' (Dw/v)	WFib
'Charmay Snowflake' (Sc/v)	MBPg
'Chelsea Gem' (Z/d/v) ♀H1+3	SSea WFib
'Chelsea Morning' (Z/d)	WFib
'Cherie Maid' (Z/v)	SSea
'Cherry' (Min)	WFib
'Cherry Baby' (Dec)	MHer NFir
'Cherry Orchard' (R)	WFib
'Chew Magna' (R)	WFib
'Chieko' (Min/d)	WFib
'Chinz' (R)	NFir
§ 'Chocolate Peppermint' (Sc)	CSev EWoo MBPg MCot MHer NFir SEND WDib WFib
'Chocolate Tomentosum'	see *P.* 'Chocolate Peppermint'
'Chocolate Twist' (St/C)	LAst
'Chrissie' (R)	WFib
'Cindy' (Dw/d)	WFib
'Citriodorum' (Sc) ♀H1+3	MBPg MCot MHer WFib
'Citronella' (Sc)	CRHN MBPg WFib WGwG
'Claret Rock Unique' (U)	EWoo SSea WFib
'Clatterbridge' (Dw/d)	NFir
'Clorinda' (U/Sc)	CRHN EShb EWoo MBPg MCot MHer MNHC SBch SPet SSea WFib WGwG

	'Coddenham' (Dw/d)	WFib
	'Cola Bottles'	NPer NPri
§	'Colonel Baden-Powell' (I/d)	WFib
	'Colwell' (Min/d)	WFib
	'Concolor Lace'	see *P.* 'Shottesham Pet'
	'Contrast' (Z/C/v)	CWCL MBri NEgg SCoo SPoG WFib
	'Cook's Peachblossom'	WFib
	'Copthorne' (U/Sc) Υ^{H1+3}	CRHN EWoo MBPg MCot MHer SSea WFib
	cordifolium	CRHN EWoo WFib
	- var. ***rubrocinctum***	NFir
I	- 'Valentine'	CSpe
	coriandrifolium	see *P. myrrhifolium* var. *coriandrifolium*
	'Cornell' (I/d)	WFib
	cortusifolium	MHer
	'Cottenham Beauty' (A)	NFir
	'Cottenham Delight' (A)	NFir
	'Cottenham Glamour' (A)	MHer NFir
	'Cottenham Jubilee' (A)	MHer
	'Cottenham Surprise' (A)	NFir
	'Cottenham Wonder' (A)	NFir
	cotyledonis	CSpe WFib
	'Countess of Scarborough'	see *P.* 'Lady Scarborough'
	'Country Girl' (R)	SPet
	'Cover Girl' (Z/d)	WFib
	'Covina' (R)	WFib
	'Cramdon Red' (Dw)	WFib
	'Cream 'n' Green' (R/v)	NFir
	'Creamery' (d)	WFib
	'Creamy Nutmeg' (Sc/v)	EShb EWoo MHer NFir SEND SSea
	'Crimson Fire' (Z/d)	MBri
	'Crimson Unique' (U) Υ^{H1+3}	CSpe EWoo MCot MHer WFib
§	***crispum*** (Sc)	GPoy MBPg NEgg SBch
§	- 'Golden Well Sweep' (Sc/v)	MBPg WFib
	- 'Major' (Sc)	WFib
	- 'Peach Cream' (Sc/v)	MBPg WFib
	- 'Prince Rupert' (Sc)	MBPg
	- 'Variegatum' (Sc/v) Υ^{H1+3}	CRHN GBin GPoy MBPg MHer NFir SBch SIde SPet SSea WCot WFib
	crithmifolium	MHer
	'Crocketta' (I/d/v)	NFir
	'Crocodile' (I/C/d)	ECtt EShb MHer NFir WFib
	'Crystal Palace Gem' (Z/v)	SSea WFib
	cucullatum	WFib
	- 'Flore Pleno' (d)	MHer WFib
	- subsp. ***strigifolium***	EWoo
	'Cupid' (Min/Dw/d)	WFib
§	'Czar' (Z/C)	SCoo
	'Dainty Maid' (Sc)	CSpe NFir
	'Dale Queen' (Z)	WFib
	'Dark Gigette' (Min)	NFir
	'Dark Red Irene' (Z/d)	WFib
	'Dark Secret' (R)	CSpe SMrm WFib
	'Dark Venus' (R)	EWoo WFib
	'Darmsden' (A) Υ^{H1+3}	NFir
	'Davina' (Min/d)	WFib
	'Dawn Star' (Z/St)	NFir
	'Deacon Avalon' (Dw/d)	WFib
	'Deacon Barbecue' (Z/d)	WFib
	'Deacon Birthday' (Z/d)	WFib
	'Deacon Bonanza' (Z/d)	WFib
	'Deacon Clarion' (Z/d)	WFib
	'Deacon Coral Reef' (Z/d)	WFib
	'Deacon Fireball' (Z/d)	WFib
	'Deacon Gala' (Z/d)	WFib
	'Deacon Golden Bonanza' (Z/C/d)	WFib
	'Deacon Golden Lilac Mist' (Z/C/d)	WFib
	'Deacon Lilac Mist' (Z/d)	WFib
	'Deacon Mandarin' (Z/d)	WFib
	'Deacon Minuet' (Z/d)	NFir WFib
	'Deacon Peacock' (Z/C/d)	WFib
	'Deacon Picotee' (Z/d)	WFib
§	'Deacon Summertime' (Z/d)	WFib
	'Deborah Miliken' (Z/d)	NFir WFib
	'Decora Lavender'	see *P.* 'Decora Lilas'
§	'Decora Lilas' (I)	ECtt LAst SPet
	'Decora Mauve'	see *P.* 'Decora Lilas'
	'Decora Pink'	see *P.* 'Decora Rouge'
	'Decora Red'	see *P.* 'Decora Rouge'
§	'Decora Rose' (I)	ECtt SPet
§	'Decora Rouge' (I)	ECtt LAst SPet
	'Deerwood Darling' (Min/v/d)	WFib
	'Deerwood Lavender Lad' (Sc)	CSev EWoo MBPg MHer SSea WDib WFib
	'Deerwood Lavender Lass'	LPio MBPg MCot MHer
	'Deerwood Pink Puff' (St/d)	WFib
	'Delightful' (R)	WFib
	'Delli' (R)	CWCL MHer NFir NPer SMrm WFib
	'Dennis Hunt' (Z/C)	NFir
	denticulatum	MHer SSea
§	- 'Filicifolium' (Sc)	CRHN EShb MBPg MCot MHer NFir SSea WFib
	Designer Peppermint Twist = 'Baldespep' (Designer Series) (Z) **new**	LAst
	'Dibbinsdale' (Z)	NFir
	dichondrifolium (Sc)	CSev MBPg MHer NFir SSea WFib
	dichondrifolium × ***reniforme*** (Sc)	NFir
	'Display' ambig. (Dw/v)	WFib
	'Distinction' (Z)	NFir SPoG WFib
	'Dolly Varden' (Z/v) Υ^{H1+3}	NFir SSea WFib
	'Donatella Love' (R/Dec) **new**	NFir
	'Don's Helen Bainbridge' (Z/C)	NFir
	'Don's Mona Noble' (Z/C)	NFir
	'Don's Richard A. Costain' (Z/C)	NFir
	'Don's Southport' (Z/v)	NFir
	'Dorcus Bingham' (Sc)	MBPg
	'Doris Hancock' (R)	WFib
	'Double Pink' (R/d)	WFib
	'Dovedale' (Dw/C)	WFib
	'Dovepoint' (Dw/2)	NFir
	'Downlands' (Z/d)	WFib
	'Dresden White' (Dw)	WFib
	Dresdner Apricot = 'Pacbriap'^{PBR} (I/d)	NPri
	'Duchess of Devonshire' (U)	WFib
	'Duke of Edinburgh'	see *P.* 'Hederinum Variegatum'
	'Dunkery Beacon' (R)	WFib
	'E. Dabner' (Z/d)	WFib
	echinatum	EWoo MHer
	- 'Album'	WFib
	'Eden Gem' (Min/d)	WFib
	'Edmond Lachenal' (Z/d)	WFib
	'Eileen Nancy' (Z)	NFir
	'Eileen Postle' (R) Υ^{H1+3}	WFib

Elbe Silver = 'Pensil' (I)	NFir SCoo
'Elmsett' (Dw/C/d)	NFir WFib
'Els' (Dw/St)	WBrk
'Elsi' (I × Z/d/v)	WFib
'Elsie Gillam' (St)	WFib
'Embassy' (Min)	WFib
Emilia = 'Pactina'^{PBR}	LAst
'Emma Hössle'	see *P.* 'Frau Emma Hössle'
'Emma Jane Read' (Dw/d)	WFib
endlicherianum	SPhx WCot
'Erwarton' (Min/d)	NFir
'Eskay Gold' (A)	WFib
'Eskay Jewel' (A)	WFib
'Eskay Ruby' (A)	MHer
'Eskay Sugar Candy' (A)	WFib
'Eskay Verglo' (A)	WFib
Evening Glow = 'Bergpalais'^{PBR}	LAst
'Evka'^{PBR} (I/v)	CWCL LAst SCoo SSea
exhibens	WCot
exstipulatum	EShb EWoo SSea SVen
'Fair Ellen' (Sc)	MBPg MHer WFib
'Fairlee' (DwI)	WFib
'Fairy Lights' (Dw/St)	NFir
'Fairy Orchid' (A)	WFib
'Fandango' (Z/St)	NFir SMrm WFib
'Fanny Eden' (R)	EWoo WFib
'Fantasia' white-flowered (Dw/d) ♀$^{H1+3}$	WFib
'Fareham' (R) ♀$^{H1+3}$	WFib
'Fenton Farm' (Dw/C)	NFir
'Fiat Queen' (Z/d)	WFib
'Fieldings Unique' (U)	EWoo NFir
'Fifth Avenue' (R)	WFib
'Filicifolium'	see *P. denticulatum* 'Filicifolium'
'Fir Trees Audrey B' (St)	NFir
'Fir Trees Betty' (U)	NFir
'Fir Trees Catkins' (A) **new**	NFir
'Fir Trees Echoes of Pink' (A)	EWoo
'Fir Trees Eileen' (St)	NFir SMrm
'Fir Trees Ele' (A/v)	NFir
'Fir Trees Fantail' (Min)	NFir
'Fir Trees Fiesta' (R)	NFir
'Fir Trees Flamingo' (Dw)	NFir
'Fir Trees Jack' (Z/Dw)	NFir
'Fir Trees Janet' (Dw)	NFir
'Fir Trees Jennifer' (R/Dec)	NFir
'Fir Trees John Grainger' (Z/v)	NFir
'Fir Trees Mark' (R/Dec/v)	NFir
'Fir Trees Nan' (R/Dec)	NFir
'Fir Trees Pink Pom-Pom' (Dw/St/C/d)	NFir
'Fir Trees Ruby Wedding' (C)	NFir
'Fir Trees Silver Wedding' (Z/C/d)	NFir
'Fir Trees Sparkler' (Min/C)	NFir
'Fir Trees Val' (Z)	NFir
Fireworks Cherry-white = 'Fiwocher'^{PBR} (Fireworks Series) (Z)	SSea
'First Blush' (R)	WFib
'First Love' (Z)	NFir
First Yellow = 'Pacyell'^{PBR}	LAst
'Flaming Katy' (Min)	NFir
'Fleurisse' (Z)	WFib
'Florence Hunt' (R)	NFir
'Floria Moore' (Dec)	EWoo NFir SSea
'Flower Basket' (R/d)	EWoo
(Flower Fairy Series) Flower Fairy Berry = 'Sweberry'^{PBR}	LAst
- Flower Fairy Rose = 'Swero'^{PBR} (Z)	LAst LSou
- Flower Fairy White Splash = 'Swewhi'^{PBR} (Z)	LAst LSou
'Flower of Spring' (Z/v) ♀$^{H1+3}$	SSea
Foxy = 'Pacfox'^{PBR} (Z)	LAst LSou
fragrans	WDib
Fragrans Group (Sc)	CRHN CSev EWoo GPoy MBPg MCot MHer SPet SSea WFib WGwG
§ - 'Fragrans Variegatum' (Sc/v)	CSev LPio MBPg NFir WFib
- 'Snowy Nutmeg'	see *P.* (Fragrans Group) 'Fragrans Variegatum'
'Fraiche Beauté' (Z/d)	WFib
'Francis Gibbon' (Z/d)	WFib
'Francis Parmenter' (MinI/v)	LAst
'Francis Parrett' (Min/d) ♀$^{H1+3}$	WFib
'Frank Hazel' (Dw/Z)	NFir
'Frank Headley' (Z/v) ♀$^{H1+3}$	CHel LAst MCot NPer SCoo SMrm SSea WFib WOld
§ 'Frau Emma Hössle' (Dw/d)	WFib
'Freak of Nature' (Z/v)	MHer NFir WFib
'Frensham' (Sc)	MBPg MHer WFib
'Freshfields Suki' (Dw)	NFir
'Freshwater' (St/C)	WFib
'Friary Wood' (Z/C/d)	NFir WFib
'Friesdorf' (Dw/Fr)	MCot MHer NFir WBrk WFib
'Fringed Aztec' (R) ♀$^{H1+3}$	CWCL NFir SPet WFib
'Fringed Jer-Ray' (A)	SSea
'Frosty' misapplied	see *P.* 'Variegated Kleine Liebling'
'Frosty Petit Pierre'	see *P.* 'Variegated Kleine Liebling'
'Fruity' (Sc)	MBPg
frutetorum	MHer
fruticosum	EWoo WFib
'Fuji' (R)	NFir
fulgidum	EWoo LPio MCot WFib
'Gabriel' (A)	EWoo
'Galway Star' (Sc/v) ♀$^{H1+3}$	MBPg MHer WFib
'Ganther' (Dec)	WFib
'Garnet Rosebud' (Min/d)	NFir WFib
'Gartendirektor Herman' (Dec)	EWoo NFir WFib
'Gatwig'	LAst
'Gaudy' (Z)	WFib
'Gemini' (Z/St/d)	CWCL NFir WFib
'Gemma' (R)	NFir
'Gemstone' (Sc) ♀$^{H1+3}$	CSev MBPg MHer
'Genie' (Z/d)	WFib
'Gentle Georgia' (R)	WFib
'Georgia' (R)	WFib
'Georgia Peach' (R)	WFib
'Georgina Blythe' (R) ♀$^{H1+3}$	WFib
'Gerainbow Neon' (Gerainbow Series) (I)	LAst
'Gesa'	LAst
'Giant Oak' (Sc)	MBPg
gibbosum	CSpe EWoo MHer SSea WFib WHer
'Ginger Frost' (Sc/v)	WFib
'Ginger Rogers' (Z)	NFir

'Glacis'PBR (Quality Series) (Z/d)	LSou SSea
'Gladys Evelyn' (Z/d)	WFib
'Gladys Weller' (Z/d)	NFir WFib
glaucum	see *P. lanceolatum*
§ ***glutinosum***	WFib
Golden Angel	see *P.* 'Sarah Don'
'Golden Brilliantissimum' (Z/v)	WFib
'Golden Chalice' (Min/v)	WFib
'Golden Clorinda' (U/Sc/C)	CRHN MBPg NFir SEND
'Golden Ears' (Dw/St/C)	NFir NPer WFib
'Golden Edinburgh' (I/v)	WFib
'Golden Harry Hieover' (Z/C) 𝕐H1+3	MBri SSea
'Golden Lilac Gem' (I/d)	WFib
'Golden Princess' (Min/C)	WFib
'Golden Square' (Dw/St)	WFib
'Golden Staphs' (Z/St/C)	MHer NFir
'Golden Tears' (MinI/C/d)	ECtt
'Golden Wedding' (Z/d/v)	NFir
'Golden Well Sweep'	see *P. crispum* 'Golden Well Sweep'
'Gooseberry Leaf'	see *P. grossularioides*
'Gordano Midnight' (R)	EWoo
'Gordon Quale' (Z/d)	WFib
'Grace Thomas' (Sc) 𝕐H1+3	CSev MBPg MHer WFib
'Grace Wells' (Min)	WFib
'Grand Slam' (R)	CWCL NFir WFib
'Grandad Mac' (Dw/St)	NFir SSea
grandiflorum	EWoo LPio MCot MHer WFib
graveolens L'Hér.	see *P.* 'Graveolens'
graveolens ambig.	SEND
graveolens sensu J.J.A. van der Walt	SBch WFib
§ 'Graveolens' (Sc)	GPoy MBPg MHer SVen WBrk WDib WFib
'Graveolens Minor' (Sc)	EWoo
'Great Glemham Lemon' (Sc)	EWoo
'Green Eyes' (I/d)	MHer
'Greetings' (Min/v)	MBri WFib
'Grey Lady Plymouth' (Sc/v)	MBPg MCot MHer WFib
'Grey Sprite' (Min/v)	WFib
§ ***grossularioides***	MBPg MHer
- 'Coconut'	MBPg
'Guernsey Flair' (Z)	LSou
'Gwen' (Min/v)	NFir
§ 'Hannaford Star' (Z/St)	WFib
'Hansen's Pinkie' (R)	EWoo
'Happy Anniversary' (Dw/C)	NFir
'Happy Appleblossom' (Z/v/d)	NFir
(Happy Face Series) Happy Face Mex = 'Pacvet'PBR (I)	NPri
- Happy Face Velvet Red = 'Pachafvel'PBR (I)	NPri
'Happy Thought' (Z/v) 𝕐H1+3	MBri MCot NFir SCoo SSea WFib
'Harbour Lights' (R)	WFib
'Harewood Slam' (R)	WFib
'Harlequin Pretty Girl' (I × Z/d)	WFib
'Harlequin Rosie O'Day' (I)	WFib
'Harvard' (I/d)	WFib
havlasae	ECou
'Hazel' (R)	WFib
'Hazel Cherry' (R)	WFib
'Hazel Choice' (R)	NFir
'Hazel Perfection' (R)	NFir
'Hazel Star' (R)	WFib
'Hazel Stardust' (R)	NFir
§ 'Hederinum' (I)	LSou
§ 'Hederinum Variegatum' (I/v)	ECtt SPet WFib
'Helen Christine' (Z/St)	NFir WFib
'Henry Weller' (A)	NFir WFib
'Hermione' (Z/d)	WFib
'Highfields Attracta' (Z/d)	WFib
'Highfields Candy Floss' (Z/d)	NFir
'Highfields Delight' (Z)	WFib
'Highfields Fancy' (Z/d)	NFir
'Highfields Festival' (Z/d)	NFir WFib
'Highfields Melody' (Z/d)	WFib
'Highfields Pride' (Z)	WFib
'Highfields Symphony' (Z)	WFib
'Hilbre Island' (Z/C/d)	NFir
'Hills of Snow' (Z/v)	MBri MHer SSea WFib
'Hindoo' (R × U)	CSpe EWoo LPio MCot NFir SBch WFib
hispidum	MHer
'Hitcham' (Min/d)	WFib
'Holbrook' (Dw/C/d)	NFir WFib
'Holt Beauty'	EWoo
'Hope Valley' (Dw/C/d) 𝕐H1+3	NFir
'House and Garden' (R)	NFir
'Hula' (R × U)	EWoo
'Hunter's Moon' (Z/C)	NFir
'Icing Sugar' (I/d)	WFib
ignescens	NFir
'Immaculatum' (Z)	WFib
'Imperial'PBR (R)	LAst
'Imperial Butterfly' (A/Sc)	CRHN NFir WFib
ionidiflorum	CSpe EShb MCot MHer MNHC
'Irene' (Z/d) 𝕐H1+3	WFib
'Irene Toyon' (Z) 𝕐H1+3	WFib
'Islington Peppermint' (Sc)	NFir SBch SPet WFib
'Isobel Eden' (Sc)	MBPg
'Ivalo' (Z/d)	WFib
'Ivory Snow' (Z/d/v)	NFir WFib
'Jack of Hearts' (I × Z/d)	WFib
'Jack Wood' (Z/d)	NFir
§ 'Jackie' (I/d)	MBri WFib
'Jackie Davies' (R)	EWoo
'Jackie Gall'	see *P.* 'Jackie'
'Jackie Totlis' (Z/St)	WFib
'Jackpot Wild Rose' (Z/d)	WFib
'Janet Hofman' (Z/d)	WFib
'Janet Kerrigan' (Min/d)	WFib
'Jayne Eyre' (Min/d)	WFib
'Jean Caws' (Z/St)	WFib
'Jeanie Hunt' (Z/C/d)	NFir
§ 'Jeanne d'Arc' (I/d)	WFib
'Jellow' (Sc) **new**	LPio
'Jer-Ray' (A)	EWoo NFir WFib
'Jessel's Unique' (U)	SPet
'Jip's Bunjy'	NFir
'Jip's Desert Dawn' (Z/Min)	WFib
'Jip's Desert Poppy' (Z/Min)	WFib
'Jip's Eleanor Renton' (Dw/d) **new**	WFib
'Jip's Freda Burgess' (Z/C/d)	NFir
'Jip's Pip' (Z/C/d)	NFir

	'Jip's Proud Sentinel' (Dw/d) **new**	WFib
	'Jip's Rosy Glow' (Min/d)	NFir
	'Joan Fontaine' (Z)	WFib
	'Joan Morf' (R)	EWoo NFir WFib
	'Joan of Arc'	see *P.* 'Jeanne d'Arc'
	'John's Pride' (Dw)	MBri NFir
	'Joy' (I)	SPet
	'Joy' (R) 🏆H1+3	CSpe NFir WFib
	'Joy Lucille' (Sc)	MBPg
	'Juliana' (R)	LAst
	'Julie Smith' (R)	WFib
	'Juniper' (Sc)	MBPg
	'Just Bella' (d)	NFir
	'Just Beth' (Z/C/d)	NFir
	'Just Joss' (Dw/d)	NFir
	'Just William' (Min/C/d)	WFib
	'Kamahl' (R)	WFib
§	'Kardinal' (Z/d)	SPet
	'Karen' (Dw/C)	LAst LSou
	'Karl Hagele' (Z/d)	WFib
	'Karmin Ball'	WFib
	'Karrooense'	see *P. quercifolium*
	'Katie' (R)	EWoo
	'Katrine'	CWCL NPri
	'Keepsake' (Min/d)	WFib
	'Keith Vernon' (Z)	NFir
	'Kenny's Double' (Z/d)	WFib
	'Kerensa' (Min/d)	WFib
	'Kesgrave' (Min/d)	WFib
	'Kewense' (Z)	EShb
	'Kimono' (R)	NFir
	'Kinder Gaisha' (R)	NFir
	'King Edmund' (R)	NFir
	'King of Balcon'	see *P.* 'Hederinum'
	'King of Denmark' (Z/d)	WFib
	'King Solomon' (R)	WFib
§	'Kleine Liebling' (Min)	WFib
	'Kyoto' (R)	NFir
	'La France' (I/d) 🏆H1+3	MCot WFib
	'La Paloma' (R)	WFib
	Laced Red Mini Cascade = 'Achspen' (I)	NFir
§	'Lachskönigin' (I/d)	SPet WFib
	'Lady Ilchester' (Z/d)	WFib
	'Lady Love Song' (R)	NFir WFib
	'Lady Mary' (Sc)	EWoo MHer
	'Lady Mavis Pilkington' (Z/d)	WFib
	'Lady Plymouth' (Sc/v) 🏆H1+3	CRHN EPfP EShb EWoo GLog MBPg MCot MHer MSCN NEgg NFir SEND SPet WFib WGwG
§	'Lady Scarborough' (Sc)	EWoo MBPg MHer WFib
	laevigatum	MHer
	'Lancastrian' (Z/d)	WFib
§	***lanceolatum***	MHer
	'Lara Ballerina'	NFir SBch
	'Lara Beacon' **new**	EWoo
	'Lara Candy Dancer' (Sc) 🏆H1+3	CRHN MBPg SBch SPet WFib
	'Lara Jester' (Sc)	EWoo WFib
	'Lara Rajah' (R)	EWoo
	'Lara Starshine' (Sc) 🏆H1+3	EWoo MHer NFir SPet WFib
	'Lara Waltz' (R/d)	WFib
N	'Lass o' Gowrie' (Z/v)	NFir
	'Laurel Hayward' (R)	WFib
	'Lauren Alexandra' (Z/d)	WFib
	'Lavender Grand Slam' (R) 🏆H1+3	NFir
	'Lavender Lindy' (Sc) **new**	EWoo
	'Lavender Mini Cascade'	see *P.* Lilac Mini Cascade
	'Lavender Sensation' (R)	WFib
	'Lawrenceanum'	WFib
	'L'Élégante' (I/v) 🏆H1+3	CHel EWoo MCot MHer WFib
	'Lemon Crisp'	see *P. crispum*
	'Lemon Fancy' (Sc)	MBPg MHer NFir SPet WDib WFib
	'Lemon Kiss' (Sc)	CSpe EWoo MBPg
	'Lemon Toby' (Sc)	MBPg
	'Leslie William Burrows'	EWoo
	Lila Compakt-Cascade	see *P.* 'Decora Lilas'
	Lilac Cascade	see *P.* 'Roi des Balcons Lilas'
	'Lilac Gem' (Min/I/d)	MCot
§	Lilac Mini Cascade = 'Lilamica'PBR (I)	NFir
	'Lilian Pottinger' (Sc)	CRHN CSev EWoo MBPg MHer NFir SSea
	'Lilian Woodberry' (Z)	WFib
	Lilly = 'Paclill'PBR	LAst NPri
	'Limoneum' (Sc)	CSev MBPg MHer
	'Lipstick' (St)	WFib
	'Lisa Jo' (St/v/Dw/d)	WFib
	'Little Alice' (Dw/d) 🏆H1+3	NFir WFib
	'Little Gem' (Sc)	MBPg MHer WFib
	'Little Jim' (Min/d)	NFir
	'Little Jip' (Z/d/v)	NFir WFib
	'Little Spikey' (St/Min/d)	WFib
	'Lord Baden-Powell'	see *P.* 'Colonel Baden-Powell'
	'Lord Bute' (R) 🏆H1+3	CSpe ECtt EWoo LAst MCot MHer MSCN NFir NPer SMrm SPet SSea SVen WFib WGwG
	'Lord de Ramsey'	see *P.* 'Tip Top Duet'
	'Lord Roberts' (Z)	WFib
	Lorena = 'Pacdala'PBR (Dark Line Series) (Z/d)	LAst
	'Lotus' (R) **new**	LAst
	'Lotusland' (Dw/St/C)	NFir WFib
I	'Louise' (R)	NFir
	'Love Song' (R/v)	NFir WFib
	'Lucy Gunnett' (Z/d/v)	NFir
	'Lyewood Bonanza' (R)	CWCL WFib
	'Mabel Grey' (Sc) 🏆H1+3	CRHN CSev CSpe EWoo MBPg MHer MNHC NFir NPer SBch SSea WFib
§	'Madame Auguste Nonin' (U/Sc)	MHer NFir SBch WFib
	'Madame Butterfly' (Z/d/v)	NFir
	'Madame Crousse' (I/d) 🏆H1+3	EWoo WFib
	'Madame Layal' (A)	EWoo MHer NFir SBch WFib
	'Madame Margot'	see *P.* 'Hederinum Variegatum'
	'Madame Salleron' (Min/v) 🏆H1+3	LSou WBrk
	'Madge Taylor' (R)	NFir
	'Magaluf' (I/C/d)	SSea
	'Magic Lantern' (Z/C)	NFir
	'Magnum' (R)	WFib
	'Mangles' Variegated' (Z/v)	WFib
	'Manx Maid' (A)	NFir
	'Maple Leaf' (Sc)	EWoo MBPg
	'Marble Sunset'	see *P.* 'Wood's Surprise'
	'Margaret Soley' (R) 🏆H1+3	WFib
	'Margaret Waite' (R)	WFib
	'Margery Stimpson' (Min/d)	WFib
	'Marie Thomas' (Sc)	MBPg SBch
	Marimba = 'Fisrimba'PBR	SCoo
	'Marion Saunders' (Dec) **new**	WFib
	'Mariquita' (R)	WFib
	'Mark' (Dw/d)	WFib

'Marquis of Bute' (R/v) NFir SPet
'Martin Parrett' (Min/d) WFib
'Mary Harrison' (Z/d) WFib
'Masquerade' (R) SPet
I 'Maureen' Hoddinott (Z/d) MHer
'Mauve Beauty' (I/d) WFib
(Maverick Series) 'Maverick Appleblossom' (Z) **new** LAst
- 'Maverick Orange' (Z) **new** LAst
- 'Maverick Red' (Z) LAst
- 'Maverick Violet' (Z) LAst
- 'Maverick White' (Z) LAst
'Maxime Kovalevski' (Z) WFib
'Maxine' (Z/C) NFir
'May Day' (R) WFib
'May Magic' (R) NFir WFib
'Meadowside Dark and Dainty' (St) NFir WFib
'Meadowside Harvest' (Z/St/C) NFir
'Meadowside Julie Colley' (Dw) NFir
'Meadowside Midnight' (St/C) WFib
'Medley' (Min/d) WFib
'Megan Hannah' (Dw/c/d) NFir
'Melanie Day' (St) NFir
'Memento' (Min/d) WFib
'Mendip' (R) WFib
'Mendip Anne' (R) NFir
'Mendip Barbie' (R) NFir
'Mendip Blanche' (R) NFir
'Mendip Lorraine' (R) NFir
'Mendip Louise' (R) NFir
'Mendip Sarah' (R) NFir
'Meon Maid' (R) SMrm WFib
'Mere Casino' (Z) WFib
'Mexica Tomcat' (I/d) LAst
'Mexican Beauty' (I) WFib
'Mexicana' see *P.* 'Rouletta'
'Mexicanerin' see *P.* 'Rouletta'
'Michael' (A) MHer NFir
'Michelle West' (Min) WFib
'Milden' (Dw/Z/C) NFir
'Millfield Gem' (I/d) WFib
'Millfield Rose' (I/d) EWoo
'Mini-Czech' (Min/St) ECtt WBrk
'Minnie' (Z/d/St) WBrk
'Minstrel Boy' (R) EWoo WFib
'Minx' (Min/d) WFib
'Miss Burdett Coutts' (Z/v) MHer SSea WFib
'Miss McKinsey' (Z/St/d) NFir
'Miss Muffett' (Min/d) WFib
§ 'Miss Stapleton' EWoo MHer WFib
'Misterioso' (R) EWoo WFib
'Misty Morning' (R) EWoo WFib
'Modesty' (Z/d) WFib
'Mohawk' (R) NFir WFib
'Mole' see *P.* 'The Mole'
mollicomum WCot
'Monkwood Rose' (A) NFir
'Monkwood Sprite' (R) SMrm
'Monsieur Ninon' misapplied see *P.* 'Madame Auguste Nonin'
§ 'Monsieur Ninon' (U) CRHN WFib
'Mont Blanc' (Z/v) WFib
'Montague Garabaldi Smith' (R) WFib
'Moon Maiden' (A) EWoo WFib
Moonlight Violino (Moonlight Series) (Z) **new** LAst
Morning Sun = 'Pacmorsu'PBR (Green Leaf Series) (Z) LAst
'Morval' (Dw/C/d) ♀H1+3 WFib
'Morwenna' (R) LPio MHer NFir SMrm WCot WFib
'Mosaic Gay Baby' (I/v/d) WFib
'Mr Henry Cox' (Z/v) ♀H1+3 MHer NFir WFib
'Mr Wren' (Z) WFib
'Mrs Cannell' (Z) WFib
'Mrs Farren' (Z/v) MCot
'Mrs G.H. Smith' (A) MBPg NFir WFib
'Mrs Kingsbury' (U) WFib
'Mrs Martin' (I/d) WFib
'Mrs McKenzie' (Z/St) WFib
'Mrs Parker' (Z/d/v) NFir WFib
'Mrs Pat' (Dw/St/C) NFir
'Mrs Pollock' (Z/v) CHel EUJe LAst MCot NEgg SCoo SSea WBrk WFib
'Mrs Quilter' (Z/C) ♀H1+3 MBri SMrm SSea WBrk WFib
'Mrs Strang' (Z/d/v) SSea
'Mrs W.A.R. Clifton' (I/d) WFib
mutans WFib
§ 'Mutzel' (I/v) NFir
'My Chance' (Dec) NFir WFib
§ ***myrrhifolium*** var. ***coriandrifolium*** MHer NFir WFib
'Mystery' (U) ♀H1+3 LPio NFir WFib
'Narina' (I) SCoo
Nealit 2 = 'Pennea'PBR (I/d) NPri
'Nellie Nuttall' (Z) WFib
'Nervosum' (Sc) MBPg
'Nervous Mabel' (Sc) ♀H1+3 MHer WFib
'New Gypsy' (R) CWCL
'New Life' (Z) NFir
'Nicola Buck' (R) NFir
'Nicor Star' (Min) WFib
'Night' (I) **new** EWoo
'Noche' (R) SMrm
'Noele Gordon' (Z/d) WFib
'Occold Profusion' (Dw/d) NFir
'Occold Shield' (Dw/C/d) NEgg NFir SMrm SSea WBrk WFib
'Occold Tangerine' (Z) WFib
'Occold Volcano' (Dw/C/d) WFib
'Octavia Hill' (Z) LAst
odoratissimum (Sc) EWoo GPoy MBPg MHer NFir SSea WFib WGwG
'Odyssey' (Min) WFib
'Old Rose' (Z/d) WFib
'Old Spice' (Sc/v) EWoo MBPg MCot NFir WFib
'Oldbury Duet' (A/v) LAst MHer NFir
'Olga Shipstone' (Sc) MBPg
'Olivia' (R) WFib
'Onalee' (Dw) WFib
'Opera House' (R) WFib
'Orange Fizz' (Sc) EWoo MHer NFir
'Orange Parfait' (R) WFib
I 'Orange Princeanum' (Sc) MBPg
'Orangeade' (Dw/d) WFib
'Orchid Clorinda' (Sc) MBPg WFib
'Orion' (Min/d) WFib
'Orsett' (Sc) ♀H1+3 GLog
'Otto's Red' (R) NFir
'Our Amy' (Z/d) SSea

'Our Flynn' (Z/St)	WFib
'Our Gynette' (Dec)	EWoo
'Overchurch' (Dw)	NFir
PAC cultivars	see under selling name
'Pagoda' (Z/St/d)	MHer WFib
'Paisley Red' (Z/d)	NFir WFib
'Pam Tutcher' (St)	NFir
'Pamela Vaughan' (Z/St)	WFib
'Pampered Lady' (A)	NFir
panduriforme	WFib
papilionaceum	CHEx CRHN EWoo MCot MHer NFir SSea WFib
'Parisienne' (R)	EWoo WFib
'Party Dress' (Z/d)	WFib
'Pat Hannam' (St)	WFib
'Paton's Unique' (U/Sc) ♀H1+3	CRHN EWoo MCot MHer NFir SPet SVen WCot WFib
'Patricia Andrea' (T)	NFir NPer WFib
'Paul Crampel' (Z)	MCot MHer WFib
'Paul West' (Min/d)	SBch
'Peace' (Min/C)	WFib
'Peach Princess' (R)	NFir
'Peaches and Cream' (R)	MBPg WDib
Pearl Necklace	see *P.* 'Perlenkette'
PELFI cultivars	see under selling name
peltatum	WFib
'Penny' (Z/d)	WFib
'Penny Dixon' (R)	NFir
'Penny Lane' (Z)	WFib
'Pensby' (Dw)	NFir
'Peppermint Lace' (Sc)	CSev EWoo LPio
'Peppermint Scented Rose' (Sc)	MBPg MSCN
'Percy Hunt' (R)	NFir
'Perfect' (Z)	WFib
§ 'Perlenkette' (Z/d)	MHer
'Pershore Princess'	WBrk
'Peter Godwin' (R)	WFib
'Peter's Choice' (R)	WFib
'Petit Pierre'	see *P.* 'Kleine Liebling'
'Philomel' (I/d)	SPet
'Phyllis' (U/v)	EWoo MBPg MHer NFir
'Phyllis Variegated' (v)	MSCN WCot
'Picotee' (Z)	MHer
'Pink Aurore' (U)	WFib
'Pink Bonanza' (R)	NFir WFib
'Pink Capitatum'	see *P.* 'Pink Capricorn'
§ 'Pink Capricorn' (Sc)	CRHN EWoo WFib
'Pink Cascade'	see *P.* 'Hederinum'
'Pink Champagne' (Sc)	CRHN MCot MHer
'Pink Dolly Varden' (Z/v)	WFib
'Pink Fondant' (Min/d)	WFib
'Pink Gay Baby'	see *P.* 'Sugar Baby'
'Pink Happy Thought' (Z/v)	WFib
'Pink Hindoo' (Dec)	EWoo
'Pink Ice' (Min/d)	NFir
'Pink Mini Cascade'	see *P.* 'Rosa Mini-cascade'
'Pink Needles' (Min/St)	WFib
'Pink Pet' (U)	NFir
'Pink Rambler' (Z/d)	WFib
'Pink Rosebud' (Z/d)	WFib
Pink Sybil = 'Pacpisyb'^{PBR} (I/d)	NPri
'Pippa' (Min/Dw)	NFir
'Playmate' (Min/St)	WFib
'Plum Rambler' (Z/d)	EShb WBrk WFib
'Polka' (U)	EWoo NFir SPet WFib
'Pompeii' (R)	LPio NFir WFib
'Poquita' (Sc)	MBPg
'Porchfield' (Min/St)	WBrk
'Preston Park' (Z/C)	WFib
'Pretty Girl' (I)	MCot
'Pretty Polly' (Sc)	WFib
'Prim' (Dw/St/d)	WFib
'Prince of Orange' (Sc)	CSev EWoo GPoy MBPg MCot MHer NFir SBch SIde SPet WFib WGwG
'Princeanum' (Sc) ♀H1+3	MBPg WFib
'Princess Abigail' (Dw/d)	NFir
'Princess Josephine' (R)	WFib
'Princess of Balcon'	see *P.* 'Roi des Balcons Lilas'
'Princess of Wales' (R)	WFib
'Princess Virginia' (R/v)	WFib
'Priory Salmon' (St/d)	EShb
'Priory Star' (St/Min/d)	WFib
'Proud Sentinel' (Dw) **new**	WFib
pseudoglutinosum	WFib
'Purple Heart' (Dw/St/C)	NFir
'Purple Rogue' (R)	WFib
Purple Sybil = 'Pacpursyb'^{PBR}	LAst NPri
'Purple Unique' (U/Sc)	EWoo MCot MHer NFir SVen WFib
'Pygmalion' (Z/d/v)	WFib
'Quantock' (R)	WFib
'Quantock Angelique' (A)	NFir
'Quantock Candy' (A)	EWoo NFir
'Quantock Clare' (A)	NFir
'Quantock Classic' (A)	NFir
'Quantock Darren' (A)	NFir
'Quantock Double Dymond' (A)	NFir
'Quantock Kendy' (A)	NFir
'Quantock Kirsty' (A)	EWoo NFir
'Quantock Louise' (A)	NFir
'Quantock Marjorie' (A)	NFir
'Quantock Matty' (A)	NFir
'Quantock May' (A)	NFir
'Quantock Mr Nunn' (A)	NFir
'Quantock Perfection' (A)	NFir
'Quantock Sally' (A/d)	NFir
'Quantock Star' (A)	NFir
'Quantock Ultimate' (A)	NFir
'Queen of Denmark' (Z/d)	WFib
'Queen of Hearts' (I × Z/d)	WFib
'Queen of the Lemons'	EWoo
N ***quercifolium*** (Sc)	CRHN CSev GPoy MBPg WFib
- variegated (v)	MBPg WDib
quinquelobatum	CSpe LPio
radens (Sc)	WFib
'Rads Star' (Z/St)	NFir
'Radula' (Sc) ♀H1+3	CSev MBPg MHer SBch SSea WFib
'Radula Roseum' (Sc)	EWoo WFib
'Raspberry Ripple' (A)	NFir
'Ray Bidwell' (Min)	NFir WFib
§ 'Red Black Vesuvius' (Min/C)	LPio WFib
'Red Cactus' (St)	NFir
'Red Cascade' (I) ♀H1+3	LAst WFib
'Red Gables'	CSpe
'Red Ice' (Min/d)	NFir
'Red Pandora' (Z)	NFir WFib
'Red Rambler' (Z/d)	WBrk WFib
'Red Robin' (R)	WCot
'Red Silver Cascade'	see *P.* 'Mutzel'
'Red Spider' (Dw/Ca)	WFib
'Red Startel' (Z/St/d)	WFib
'Red Susan Pearce' (R)	WFib
Red Sybil = 'Pensyb'^{PBR} (I/d)	NPri

	'Red Velvet' (R)	LBMP
	'Red Witch' (Dw/St/d)	MHer WBrk WFib
	'Reflections' (Z/d)	WFib
	'Reg 'Q'' (Z/C)	NFir
	'Regalia Lavendel' (R) **new**	LAst
	'Regalia Lilac' (R) **new**	LAst
	'Regalia Red' (R) **new**	LAst
	'Regina' (Z/d)	WFib
	'Rembrandt' (R)	WFib
	'Renate Parsley'	MHer NFir SSea WFib
	reniforme	GPoy MBPg MHer SSea WFib
	'Reverend David Harley' (Z)	NFir
	'Richard Gibbs' (Sc)	MBPg MHer
	'Richard Key' (Z/d/C)	WFib
	Ricky = 'Pacric'^{PBR}	LAst
	'Rietje van der Lee' (A)	WFib
	'Rigel' (Min/d)	NFir
	'Rigi' (I/d)	MBri
	'Rimey' (St)	NFir
	'Rimfire' (R)	CWCL EWoo LPio MHer NFir WFib
	'Rio Grande' (I/d)	MHer NFir SPet WFib
	'Rober's Lemon Rose' (Sc)	CRHN MBPg MHer SEND SSea WBrk
	'Robert Fish' (Z/C)	SCoo
	'Robert McElwain' (Z/d)	WFib
	'Robin' (Sc)	MBPg
	'Robin's Unique' (U)	WFib
	'Robyn Hannah' (St/d)	NFir
	rodneyanum	CDes
	'Rogue' (R)	WFib
	'Roi des Balcons'	see *P.* 'Hederinum'
§	'Roi des Balcons Lilas' (I) 🏆$^{H1+3}$	LAst
	'Roi des Balcons Rose'	see *P.* 'Hederinum'
	'Roller's Echo' (A)	WFib
	'Roller's Pioneer' (I/v)	EWoo
	'Roller's Satinique' (U) 🏆$^{H1+3}$	MHer
	'Rollison's Unique' (U)	MHer WFib
	'Romeo' (R)	EWoo
	'Rookley' (St/d)	NFir
§	'Rosa Mini Cascade' (Mini Cascade Series) (I)	NFir
	'Rose of Amsterdam' (Min/d)	WFib
	'Rose Paton's Unique' (U/Sc)	SMrm
	'Rose Silver Cascade' (I)	MCot MHer
	'Rosebud Supreme' (Z/d)	WFib
	'Rosmaroy' (R)	WFib
	'Rosy Dawn' (Min/d)	WFib
§	'Rouletta' (I/d)	LAst WFib
	'Royal Ascot' (R)	NFir SPet SSea
	'Royal Norfolk' (Min/d)	NFir
	'Royal Oak' (Sc) 🏆$^{H1+3}$	CRHN CSev MBPg MCot MHer MNHC SBch SPet SVen WFib
§	'Royal Purple' (Z/d)	WFib
	'Royal Surprise' (R)	EWoo NFir
	'Ruben' (d)	LSou
	'Ruben' (Z/d) **new**	LAst
	'Ruby' (Min/d)	WFib
	'Ruffled Velvet' (R)	EWoo
	'Rushmere' (Dw/d)	WFib
	'Rushmoor Golden Rosebud' (Z)	WFib
	'Rushmoor Mrs Eve Scott' (Z/d)	WFib
	'Saint Elmo's Fire' (St/Min/d)	MHer WFib
	Saint Malo = 'Guisaint' (I)	NFir
	'Salmon Beauty' (Dw/d)	WFib
§	'Salmon Irene' (Z/d)	WFib
	Salmon Princess = 'Pacsalpri'^{PBR}	LAst LSou
	'Salmon Queen'	see *P.* 'Lachskönigin'
	'Samantha' (R)	WFib
	'Samantha Stamp' (Dw/d/C)	WFib
	Samelia = 'Pensam'^{PBR} (Dark Line Series) (Z/d)	LAst LBMP WGor
	'Sancho Panza' (Dec) 🏆$^{H1+3}$	CSpe WFib
	'Sandra Lorraine' (I/d)	WFib
	'Sanguineum'	CSev CSpe
§	'Sarah Don' (A/v)	ECtt LAst WFib
	'Sarah Hunt' (Min/d)	NFir
	'Sarah Jane' (Sc)	MBPg
	'Sassa'^{PBR} (Quality Series) (Z/d)	LAst
	'Satsuki' (R)	NFir
	'Scarborough Fair' (A)	NFir
	'Scarlet Gem' (Z/St)	WBrk WFib
	'Scarlet Pet' (U)	MBPg NFir SMrm
	'Scarlet Rambler' (Z/d)	EShb SMrm WFib
	'Scarlet Unique' (U)	CRHN EWoo LPio MCot SSea WFib
	schizopetalum	WFib
	'Schottii'	LPio MHer NFir WFib
	'Scilly Robin' (Sc) **new**	WDib
	'Scottow Star' (Z/C)	WFib
	'Seale Star' (Dw/St/C)	SSea
	'Seaview Silver' (Min/St)	WFib
	'Seaview Sparkler' (Z/St)	WFib
	'Secret Love' (Sc)	MBPg
	'Seeley's Pansy' (A)	EWoo MHer
	'Sefton' (R) 🏆$^{H1+3}$	WFib
	'Shan Hoy' (Dw)	NFir
	'Shanks' (Z)	NFir
	'Shannon'	EWoo SBch WFib
	Shocking Orange = 'Pacshorg'^{PBR} (Quality Series)	LAst
	Shocking Pink = 'Pensho'^{PBR} (Quality Series) (Z/d)	LAst
	'Shogan' (R)	NFir
§	'Shottesham Pet' (Sc)	EWoo MHer MNHC SPet
	'Shrubland Pet' (U/Sc)	LPio
	sidoides	CDes CSpe EWoo GPoy LPio MBPg MCot MHer NFir SBch SMrm SPhx SSea SVen WFib WHer
	- black-flowered	CTca SBrt
	- 'Sloe Gin Fizz'	CSpe LPio
	Sidonia = 'Pensid'^{PBR} (Dark Line Series) (Z/d)	LAst WGor
	'Sienna' (R)	NFir
	'Sil Falko'^{PBR} (I)	LSou WGor
	'Sil Frauke'^{PBR} (Z)	LAst
	'Sil Friesia'^{PBR} (Z)	LAst
	'Sil Hero'^{PBR} (Z)	LAst WGor
	'Sil Lenja'^{PBR} (Z)	LAst
	'Sil Linus'^{PBR} (Z)	LSou
	'Sil Liske'^{PBR} (Z)	LAst
	'Sil Magnus'^{PBR} (Z)	LAst
	'Sil Malaika'^{PBR} (I)	LSou
	'Sil Pia'^{PBR} (I)	LAst LSou
	'Sil Quirin'^{PBR} (I)	LAst
	'Sil Raiko'^{PBR}	LAst
	'Sil Sören'	LAst
	'Sil Teske'^{PBR} (I)	LAst

	'Sil Tomke'^{PBR} (I)	LAst LSou
	'Sil Wittje'^{PBR} (I)	LAst
	'Silver Anne' (R/v)	NFir
	'Silver Blazon' (Z/Dw/C/v)	WFib
	'Silver Delight' (v/d)	WFib
	'Silver Kewense' (Dw/v)	WFib
	'Silver Leaf Rose' (Sc)	MBPg
	'Silver Snow' (Min/St/d)	WFib
	'Silver Wings' (Z/v)	NFir
	'Sir Colin' (Z)	SSea
	'Skelly's Pride' (Z)	WFib
	'Skies of Italy' (Z/C/d)	MBri WFib
	'Sneezy' (Min)	NFir
	'Snow Cap' (MinI)	NFir
	'Snowbaby' (Min/d)	WFib
	'Snowdrift' (I/d)	WFib
	'Snowflake' (Min)	see *P.* 'Atomic Snowflake'
	'Snowstorm' (Z)	WFib
	'Sofie'	see *P.* 'Decora Rose'
	Solidor (I/d) ♀$^{H1+3}$	NFir
	'Something Special' (Z/d)	NFir WFib
	Sophie Casade	see *P.* 'Decora Rose'
	'Sophie Dumaresque' (Z/v)	MBri NFir WFib
	'Sophie Emma' (Z)	NFir
	'South American Bronze' (R) ♀$^{H1+3}$	SMrm WFib
	'Souvenir de Prue'	EWoo
	'Spanish Angel' (A) ♀$^{H1+3}$	CWCL MHer NFir WFib
	'Spellbound' (R)	WFib
	'Spital Dam' (Dw/d)	NFir
	'Spitfire' (Z/Ca/d/v)	WFib
§	'Splendide'	CSpe EPfP LPio MBPg MHer NFir SSea SWvt WFib
	'Spot-on-bonanza' (R)	NFir WFib
	'Springfield Black' (R)	MCot
	'Springtime' (Z/d)	WFib
	'Stadt Bern' (Z/C)	MBri NFir
	× ***stapletoniae***	see *P.* 'Miss Stapleton'
	'Star Flecks' (St)	NFir
	'Startel Salmon' (Z/St)	MHer
	'Stella Ballerina'	SMrm
	'Stellar Arctic Star'	see *P.* 'Arctic Star'
	'Stellar Hannaford Star'	see *P.* 'Hannaford Star'
	'Strawberries and Cream' (Z/St)	NFir
	'Strawberry Fayre' (Dw/St)	WFib
§	'Sugar Baby' (DwI)	ECtt MBri MHer WFib
	'Summer Cloud' (Z/d)	WFib
	'Summertime' (Z/d)	see *P.* 'Deacon Summertime'
	'Sun Rocket' (Dw/d)	WFib
	'Sundridge Moonlight' (Z/C)	NFir WFib
	'Sundridge Surprise' (Z)	WFib
	'Sunraysia' (Z/St)	WFib
	'Sunset Snow' (R)	WFib
	'Sunspot' (Min/C)	NFir
	'Sunspot Petit Pierre' (Min/v)	WFib
	'Sunstar' (Min/d)	WFib
	'Super Rose' (I)	SPet
	'Supernova' (Z/St/d)	WFib
	'Surcouf' (I)	CWCL WFib
	'Susan Payne' (Dw/d)	MHer
	'Sussex Delight' (Min)	SPet
	'Sussex Gem' (Min/d)	WFib
	'Sussex Lace'	see *P.* 'White Mesh'
	'Swanland Lace' (I/d/v)	WFib
	'Swedish Angel' (A)	NFir WFib
	'Sweet Lady Mary' (Sc)	MBPg
	'Sweet Mimosa' (Sc) ♀$^{H1+3}$	CRHN EWoo LAst LPot MCot MHer NEgg NFir SBch WFib WGwG
	'Sweet Miriam' (Sc)	MBPg WDib
	'Sweet Sixteen' (R)	WFib
	'Sybil Holmes' (I/d)	MBri SPet WFib
	'Tamie' (Dw/d)	NFir
	tetragonum	CRHN EWoo MBPg MHer WFib
	'The Boar' (Fr) ♀$^{H1+3}$	EWoo MCot WFib
	'The Culm' (A)	EWoo WFib
	'The Czar'	see *P.* 'Czar'
	'The Joker' (I/d)	WFib
	'The Kenn-Lad' (A)	EWoo
	'The Marchioness of Bute' (R)	MHer NFir WFib
§	'The Mole' (A)	WFib
	'The Tamar' (A)	EWoo MHer
	'The Yar' (Z/St)	WFib
	'Thomas' (Sc)	MBPg
	'Thomas Earle' (Z)	WFib
	'Tilly' (Min)	NFir
	'Tinker West' (Z/St/Dw)	WFib
§	'Tip Top Duet' (A) ♀$^{H1+3}$	EWoo MHer NFir SMrm WFib
	'Tirley Garth' (A)	WFib
	'Tomcat'^{PBR} (I/d)	LAst
	tomentosum (Sc) ♀$^{H1+3}$	CHEx CSev CSpe EShb EWoo GLog GPoy LPio MBPg MCot MHer MNHC NFir SSea WDib WFib
	- 'Chocolate'	see *P.* 'Chocolate Peppermint'
	'Tomgirl' (A)	NPri
	Tomgirl = 'Pactomgi'^{PBR} (I × Z/d)	LAst
	Tommy = 'Pactommy' (I)	NPri
	'Topscore' (Z/d)	WFib
	'Tornado' (R)	NFir WFib
	'Torrento' (Sc)	MBPg MHer WFib
	'Tortoiseshell' (R)	WFib
	'Toscana Okka' (Toscana Series) (I)	LAst LSou SPet
	'Tracy' (Min/d)	NFir
	transvaalense	NFir
	tricolor misapplied	see *P.* 'Splendide'
	tricolor Curt.	NFir
	tricuspidatum	EWoo LPio WCot
	trifidum	EWoo MBPg WFib
	'Triomphe de Nancy' (Z/d)	WFib
	triste	EWoo LPio MCot MHer WCot WFib
	'Trudie' (Dw/Fr)	MHer WFib
	'Turkish Coffee' (R)	WFib
	'Turkish Delight' (Dw/C)	NFir WFib
	'Turtle's Surprise' (Z/d/v)	WBrk
	'Tweenaway' (Dw)	NFir
	'Tyabb Princess' (R)	EWoo
	'Unique Aurore' (U)	LPio MHer
	'Unique Mons Ninon'	see *P.* 'Monsieur Ninon'
	'Urchin' (Min/St)	NFir WFib
	'Ursula Key' (Z/c)	WFib
	'Ursula's Choice' (A)	WFib
	'Val Merrick' (Dw/St)	WFib
	'Valentine' (Z/C)	WFib
	'Vancouver Centennial' (Dw/St/C) ♀$^{H1+3}$	MBri MCot MHer NEgg NFir SCoo WFib
	'Vandersea'	EWoo MCot
	'Variegated Clorinda' (Sc/v)	WFib
	'Variegated Fragrans'	see *P.* (Fragrans Group) 'Fragrans Variegatum'
	'Variegated Joy Lucille' (Sc/v)	MBPg
§	'Variegated Kleine Liebling' (Min/v)	SSea WFib

'Variegated Petit Pierre' (Min/v)	MHer WFib
'Vectis Blaze' (I)	EWoo
'Vectis Cascade'	EWoo
'Vectis Finery' (St/d)	NFir
'Vectis Glitter' (Z/St)	NFir WBrk WFib
'Vectis Pink' (Dw/St)	WFib
'Vectis Purple' (Z/d)	WFib
'Vectis Sparkler' (Dw/St)	NFir
'Vectis Starbright' (Dw/St)	WFib
'Vectis Volcano' (Z/St)	WFib
'Velvet Duet' (A) ♀H1+3	NFir
'Verona' (Z/C)	MBri
'Verona Contreras' (A)	NFir
'Vesuvius' (Z)	LPio
'Vic Claws' (Dw/St)	NFir
'Vicki' (R)	EWoo
'Vicki Town' (R)	WFib
Vicky = 'Pacvicky'PBR (I)	LAst NPri
'Vicky Claire' (R)	EWoo NFir SMrm WFib
Victor = 'Pacvi'PBR (Quality Series) (Z/d)	LBMP LSou
Victoria = 'Pacvica'PBR (Quality Series) (Z/d) new	LAst
Ville de Dresden = 'Pendresd'PBR (I)	EWoo
'Ville de Paris'	see *P.* 'Hederinum'
'Vina' (Dw/C/d)	WFib
Vinco = 'Guivin'PBR (I/d)	WGor
violareum misapplied	see *P.* 'Splendide'
'Virginia' (R)	SPet
'Viscossisimum' (Sc)	MHer
viscosum	see *P. glutinosum*
'Vivat Regina' (Z/d)	WFib
'Voodoo' (U) ♀H1+3	CSpe EWoo LPio MCot MHer NFir SMrm SPet WCot WFib
'Wantirna' (Z/v)	NFir
'Warrenorth Coral' (Z/C/d)	NFir WFib
'Washbrook' (Min/d)	NFir
'Wedding Royale' (Dw/d)	WFib
'Welling' (Sc)	MHer NFir
'Wendy Jane' (Dw/d)	WFib
'Wendy Read' (Dw/d)	WFib
'Westdale Appleblossom' (Z/d/C)	WFib
'Westside' (Z/d)	WFib
'Westwood' (Z/St)	WFib
'Whisper' (R)	EWoo WFib
'White Bird's Egg' (Z)	WFib
'White Boar' (Fr)	CSpe EShb EWoo WFib
'White Bonanza' (R)	WFib
'White Eggshell' (Min)	WFib
'White Feather' (Z/St)	MHer
'White Glory' (R) ♀H1+3	NFir
§ 'White Mesh' (I/v)	MBri NFir
'White Unique' (U)	SBch SPet WFib
Wico = 'Guimongol'PBR (I/d)	CWCL LAst WGor
'Wilhelm Kolle' (Z)	WFib
'Wilhelm Langath'	SCoo WBrk
'Willa' (Dec)	WFib
'Winner'	LAst
'Wolverton' (Z)	WFib
§ 'Wood's Surprise' (Min/I/d/v)	SPet
'Wootton's Unique'	CSev CSpe EWoo
'Wychwood' (A/Sc)	EWoo
'Yale' (I/d) ♀H1+3	MBri WFib
'Yan la Grouch' (Z/s/C) new	WFib
'Yhu' (R)	NFir SMrm WFib
'Yvonne' (Z)	WFib
'Zama' (R)	NFir
'Zinc' (Z/d)	WFib
'Zofia Pope' (R)	NFir
zonale	WFib
'Zulu King' (R)	WFib
'Zulu Warrior' (R)	WFib

Peliosanthes (*Asparagaceae*)

arisanensis B&SWJ 3639	WCru
caesia B&SWJ 5183	WCru
teta subsp. ***humilis*** RWJ 10044	WCru

Pellaea (*Pteridaceae*)

ovata	SPlb
rotundifolia ♀H2	CBty CLAP ISha LRHS
viridis	WPGP

Pellionia see *Elatostema*

Peltandra (*Araceae*)

alba	see *P. sagittifolia*
§ ***sagittifolia***	CRow EWay
undulata	see *P. virginica* (L.) Schott
§ ***virginica*** (L.) Schott	CBAq CRow EWay NPer SWat
- 'Snow Splash' (v)	CRow EWay

Peltaria (*Brassicaceae*)

alliacea	CSpe LEdu WCot
* ***dumulosa*** new	WCot

Peltiphyllum see *Darmera*

Peltoboykinia (*Saxifragaceae*)

§ ***tellimoides***	CLAP EBee GCal GKev NBir WMoo WPnP
watanabei	CDes CLAP CSpe EBee IMou LEdu LRHS NLar WCru WMoo WPGP WPtf

Pennantia (*Pennantiaceae*)

baylisiana	ECou
corymbosa	ECou
- 'Akaroa'	ECou
- 'Woodside'	ECou

Pennellianthus see *Penstemon*

Pennisetum ✿ (*Poaceae*)

§ ***alopecuroides***	CEnd EHoe EPfP LRHS MJak MWat NGdn SAPC SLim SPer SPlb SWat SWvt WWEG XLum XSen
- B&SWJ 11434	WCru
- Autumn Wizard	see *P. alopecuroides* 'Herbstzauber'
- 'Black Beauty'	CSpe
- 'Cassian's Choice'	CKno EHoe ELon EWes SMrm
- 'Caudatum'	CKno
- f. ***erythrochaetum*** 'Ferris'	WCru
- 'Foxtrot'	IPot MAvo
- 'Gelbstiel'	EPPr
- 'Hameln'	Widely available
§ - 'Herbstzauber'	CCon CKno EHoe EPfP LHop LRHS MAvo NWsh WGwG XLum
- 'Little Bunny'	CKno CWib EBee EHoe ELan EPPr EPfP GCal IVic LRHS LSRN MBri

		NGdn NLar SMea SMrm SWvt WWEG
	- 'Little Honey' (v)	CKno MBNS NLar XLum
	- 'Magic'	ELon EPPr MAvo WWEG
	- 'Moudry'	CExl CKno EBee EHoe ELon EPPr EPfP LRHS MAvo MBri SHDw XLum
	- 'National Arboretum'	CKno EBee EHoe EPPr LEdu WCot
	- 'Reborn'	MAvo
	- 'Red Head'	CAbP CKno CMea ELon EUJe EWes IPot LRHS LSou MAvo MBNS MSCN WCot
	- f. ***viridescens***	CKno EHoe ELan EPPr EPfP EShb LEdu LRHS MRav MWhi NWsh SDix SMrm WPnP WPtf WWEG XLum
	- 'Weserbergland'	CKno EBee EHoe ELon EPPr LRHS WWEG
	- 'Woodside'	CKno CWCL EHoe EPPr LEdu MBNS SMad XLum
	compressum	see *P. alopecuroides*
	'Fairy Tails'	CKno EPfP LRHS LSqu MAsh SPoG
	flaccidum	EPPr
	glaucum 'Purple Baron'	EPfP MAsh
	- 'Purple Majesty'	CSpe MNrw SMrm SWvt
	incomptum	EHoe XLum
	- purple-flowered	CCon MMoz
	longistylum misapplied	see *P. villosum*
	macrourum	CCVN CElw CKno CSam CSpe CWCL EHoe ELon EPPr GCal LEdu LHop LRHS MAvo MNrw MSpe MWhi NDov NWsh SMad SMrm SPhx WMoo WPGP
	- 'Short Stuff'	CKno
	massaicum 'Red Bunny Tails'	ELon EUJe EWTr LRHS
	- 'Red Buttons'	see *P. thunbergii* 'Red Buttons'
	orientale ♀H3	CHel CKno COlW CPrp CSpe CWCL EHoe EPfP LHop LRHS MNrw MRav NBir NWsh SEND SPer SRkn SWvt WCot WHoo WKif WWEG XLum
	- 'Karley Rose'PBR	CKno CPar EHoe EWes IBoy IPot LHop LRHS MAvo MWhi NDov NOak NPnk NWsh SWvt WWEG
I	- 'Robustum'	EPPr MAvo WPGP
	- 'Shogun'	CKno CSam EPPr EPfP LRHS MAvo SPoG
	- 'Tall Tails'	CKno ECGP EHoe EPPr EWes LRHS MWhi NPnk NSti SMea WWEG XLum
	'Paul's Giant'	CKno XLum
	rueppellii	see *P. setaceum*
§	***setaceum*** ♀H3	CWib EPfP NWsh SHDw SWvt
	- 'Emelia Mae'	SHDw
	- 'Fireworks' (v)	EBee EPfP EUJe LLWG LRHS MAsh MSCN NSti SLon SPad SPoG SWvt WCot
	- 'Rubrum' ♀H4	CBcs CExl CKno CSam CWCL EShb LSRN MAsh NSti NWsh SCoo SHDw SMad SPoG SRot SWvt WCot
	- 'Skyrocket' **new**	LRHS
	- 'Summer Samba' **new**	LRHS
	thunbergii	CAby LRHS
§	- 'Red Buttons'	CKno EHoe ELon EPPr EPfP LEdu LRHS LSqu MAsh MAvo MBri NOak SDix SHDw SMea SPhx WHoo
§	***villosum*** ♀H3	Widely available
	- 'Cream Falls'	LRHS

pennyroyal see *Mentha pulegium*

Penstemon ✿ (*Plantaginaceae*)

	sp.	SVic
	NJM 09.028	WPGP
	'Abberley'	MBNS
	'Abbey Dore'	SLon
	'Abbotsmerry'	ECtt EPfP LLHF MBNS MCot SLon
	'Agnes Laing'	MBNS SPlb
	albertinus	see *P. humilis*
§	'Alice Hindley' ♀H3	Widely available
	alpinus	EDAr
§	'Andenken an Friedrich Hahn' ♀H4	Widely available
	antirrhinoides	see *Keckiella antirrhinoides*
	'Apple Blossom' misapplied	see *P.* 'Thorn'
	'Apple Blossom' ♀H3-4	Widely available
	arizonicus	see *P. whippleanus*
	'Ashton'	MBNS
	attenuatus var. ***attenuatus*** NNS 08-285 **new**	GKev
	- subsp. ***militaris*** **new**	SPlb
	'Audrey Cooper'	CMac MBNS
	'Axe Valley Penny Mitchell'	ECtt
	azureus	CCon GKev
	'Baby Lips'	LLHF
	'Barbara Barker'	see *P.* 'Beech Park'
§	***barbatus***	SBrt SRms
	- 'Cambridge Mixed'	LAst
	- subsp. ***coccineus***	CCon GBin MBNS MNFA NLar SPhx XLum
	- 'Iron Maiden'	LRHS
	- 'Jingle Bells'	EPfP SPav
	- orange-flowered	SPlb
	- 'Peter Catt'	CMea SMrm
	- Pinacolada Series	LRHS
	- - 'Pinacolada Blue' **new**	MHol
	- var. ***praecox***	EPfP MBNS SRot
	- - f. ***nanus*** 'Rondo'	LRHS NLar
	barrettiae	LLHF
	'Beckford'	EPfP LLHF MBNS
§	'Beech Park' ♀H3	EHyd ELan EPfP EWes MBNS
	'Bisham Seedling'	see *P.* 'White Bedder'
	'Blackbird'	Widely available
	'Blue Spring'	see *P. heterophyllus* 'Blue Spring'
	'Blueberry Fudge' (Ice Cream Series)	LSou WCot WNPC WSpi
	'Bodnant'	LAst LLHF LSou MBNS WHoo
	bradburii	see *P. grandiflorus*
	'Bredon'	MBNS
	bridgesii	see *P. rostriflorus*
	'Bubblegum' (Ice Cream Series)	MHol WCot WNPC
	'Burford Purple'	see *P.* 'Burgundy'
	'Burford Seedling'	see *P.* 'Burgundy'
	'Burford White'	see *P.* 'White Bedder'
§	'Burgundy'	CCon CMac CPrp CWCL ECtt GMaP LLWP LRHS MCot MHol NBir NPer NPri SPer SPoG SRms XLum
	caespitosus subsp. ***suffruticosus***	see *P. tusharensis*
§	***campanulatus***	EPfP EPot EWes SBch SRms
	- PC&H 148	SDys
	- ***pulchellus***	see *P. campanulatus*
	- 'Roseus' misapplied	see *P. kunthii*
	'Candy Pink'	see *P.* 'Old Candy Pink'
	cardwellii	EWes ITim
	cardwellii × ***davidsonii***	WAbe

	'Castle Forbes'	GMaP MBNS SRms
	'Cathedral Rose'	EHyd EPfP
	'Catherine de la Mare'	see *P. heterophyllus* 'Catherine de la Mare'
	'Centra'	MBNS XLum
	'Charles Rudd'	COIW CWCL ECtt ELon EPfP LSRN MBNS NLar SBod SEND SRGP SRms SWvt
§	'Cherry' ♀H3	ECtt GBee MBNS SHar SMrm SPlb WWEG
	'Cherry Ripe' misapplied	see *P.* 'Cherry'
§	'Chester Scarlet' ♀H3	ECtt MBNS MRav SDix SLon WCFE WKif XLum
	'Choirboy'	EWes
	cinicola	LLHF
	cobaea	GLog
	comarrhenus new	SBrt
	'Comberton'	MBNS
	confertus	CTri ECho EPot MBNS NChi SBrt XLum
	- RCB/MO A-7	WCot
	'Connie's Pink' ♀H3	ECtt MBNS SLon SRms WWEG
	cordifolius	see *Keckiella cordifolia*
	'Cottage Garden Red'	see *P.* 'Windsor Red'
§	'Countess of Dalkeith'	CBcs COIW ECtt ELan EWes GBin LLWP MBel MCot MRav SHar SPlb SRms SWvt WCFE
§	***crandallii*** subsp. ***taosensis***	LPio MBNS
	cristatus	see *P. eriantherus*
*	***cyananthus*** var. ***utahensis***	WCot
	aff. ***cyananthus*** new	SBrt
	cyaneus	GKev
	'Dark Towers'PBR new	ECtt IPot SPoG
	davidsonii	ECho EPot EWes NSla WAbe WThu
	- var. ***davidsonii***	CPBP WAbe
	- var. ***menziesii*** ♀H4	LRHS
	- - 'Microphyllus'	EPot LLHF NHar NSla NWad WAbe
	'Dazzler'	MBNS SWvt
	'Devonshire Cream'	CWCL ECtt MBNS
	diffusus	see *P. serrulatus*
	digitalis	GCal LRHS MBNS
§	- 'Husker Red'	Widely available
	- 'Husker Lilac'	CHel WSpi
	- 'Joke'	IPot
	- 'Mystica'	EDif EWll LHop MBri SPad
	- 'Purpureus'	see *P. digitalis* 'Husker Red'
	- 'Ruby Tuesday'	CDes EWes WPGP
	- white-flowered	EBee
	discolor pale lavender-flowered	NBir
§	'Drinkstone Red'	EPfP MBNS SDix SDys
	'Drinkwater Red'	see *P.* 'Drinkstone Red'
	eatonii	GKev
	(Elgar Series) 'Elgar Crown of India'	ELon MHol WCot WSpi
	- 'Elgar Enigma'	EBee ELon LLHF MHol WCot WSpi
	- 'Elgar Firefly'	ELon MHol WCot
	- 'Elgar Light of Life' new	MHol WCot WSpi
	- 'Elgar Nimrod'	ELon MHol WCot WSpi
	'Ellenbank Amethyst'	SDys
	'Ellwood Red Phoenix'	MBNS
	'Elmley'	EPfP MBNS
§	***eriantherus***	LLHF SPlb
	- dwarf new	GKev
	Etna = 'Yatna'	ECtt EPfP LHop LPio LRHS MBNS MBri NEgg SAll SRms WHlf
	euglaucus	EBee GKev LLHF
	- NNS 07-397	GKev
§	'Evelyn' ♀H4	CMea CTri ELan EPfP IBoy LHop LRHS LSRN MBNS MCot MHer MRav NEgg SEND SPer SPet SPoG SRGP SRms SWvt WCot WKif WSHC WWEG XLum
	'Firebird'	see *P.* 'Schoenholzeri'
	'Flame'	MBNS SLon WWEG
	'Flamingo'	CHel CWCL EBee ELon EPfP EWes GBin LAst LRHS LSRN MBNS MBri NLar SGbt SMrm SPet SPoG SRms SWvt WHoo WMnd WWEG
	franklinii new	CPBP
§	***fruticosus*** var. ***scouleri*** ♀H4	MAsh
	- - f. ***albus*** ♀H4	CSpe WAbe
	- - 'Amethyst'	SRms WAbe
	Fujiyama = 'Yayama'PBR	CSam CWGN ECtt EPfP LHop LPot LRHS MBri SAll SLon SMrm SRms SWvt WHlf
	'Garden Red'	see *P.* 'Windsor Red'
	'Garnet'	see *P.* 'Andenken an Friedrich Hahn'
	gentianoides B&SWJ 10271	WCru
	'Geoff Hamilton'	ECtt EPfP LSRN MBNS SLon SPoG
	'George Elrick'	LLHF WHoo
§	'George Home' ♀H3	EWes MBNS SMrm SRms
	'George Moon'	EPfP SPad
	'Gilchrist'	ECtt SLon
	glaber	CMHG CMea EWld GBee LHop LLWP LSRN SPlb WKif
	- 'Roundway Snowflake'	SHar SPhx
	'Gloire des Quatre Rues'	MBNS XLum
	gormanii	WHil
§	***grandiflorus***	CCon EBee
	- 'Prairie Snow'	EBee
	- 'War Axe'	EDAr
	hallii	EPot EWes SBrt
	hartwegii 'Albus'	LHop SBch SHar SRms
	- 'Picotee Red'	CWCL LRHS
	- 'Tubular Bells Rose'	SPet
	'Helenetti'	SDys
§	***heterophyllus***	LRHS MNrw MSCN NBir NGBl SPet SRkn SRms
	- 'Blue Eye'	MBrN
	- 'Blue Gem'	CElw CTri
§	- 'Blue Spring'	CSpe EPfP LRHS MAvo MRav NLar SPhx SPoG WAbe
§	- 'Catherine de la Mare' ♀H4	CKno EBee ELan GBBs GBin LHop LRHS LSRN MHer MMuc MWat NBir NLar SBch SPer SRGP SWvt WHrl WKif XLum
	- 'Electric Blue'	CWCL LRHS SMrm
	- 'Heavenly Blue'	CAby CPrp CSBt CWCL EBee ECtt EPfP GMaP LAst LPio LRHS MBNS MCot MLHP MSwo MWat NEgg NLar SAll SGbt SPer SPet SPoG SWat SWvt WHil WHoo
	- 'Jeanette'	CMea
	- 'Misty Blue Shades'	LRHS
	- subsp. ***purdyi***	EPyc
	- 'Roundway White'	WCot
	- 'True Blue'	see *P. heterophyllus*
	- 'Züriblau'	CCon SPhx SPlb
§	'Hewell Pink Bedder' ♀H3	COIW EPfP GBin GBuc LPot LRHS MBNS MRav NCGa NPri SMrm SRms SWvt WHil WMnd
	'Hewitt's Pink'	CBcs SLon

	hidalgensis	CDes
	'Hidcote Pink' ♀H3-4	Widely available
	'Hidcote Purple'	SHar WHoo XLum
	'Hidcote White'	LPot MHer SWvt WWEG
	'Hillview Pink'	SLon XLum
	'Hillview Red'	MBNS
§	***hirsutus***	LRHS XLum
	- var. ***pygmaeus***	CMea CPBP ECho EDAr EShb GKev MHer NRya SBrt SPlb WHoo WIce
*	- - f. ***albus***	WHoo
	'Hopleys Variegated' (v)	LRHS MBNS SWvt
§	***humilis***	SBrt
	isophyllus ♀H3-4	LPot
	'James Bowden'	MBNS
	jamesii	EBee
	Jean Grace = 'Penbow'	CSpe NDov WHlf
	'Jessica'	CWGN
	'Jingle Bells'	NLar
	'John Booth'	MBNS
	'John Nash' misapplied	see *P.* 'Alice Hindley'
	'John Nash'	MHer SRms
	'John Spedan Lewis'	SLon
	'Joy'	MBNS
	'Juicy Grape' (Ice Cream Series)	SAll WCot WHil WSpi
	'June'	see *P.* 'Pennington Gem'
	'Kate Gilchrist'	SLon
	Kilimanjaro = 'Yajaro'	EPfP LRHS MBri SLon SRms
	'King George V'	Widely available
	'Knight's Purple'	ECtt MBNS
	'Knightwick'	MBNS
§	***kunthii***	CAby
§	***laetus*** subsp. ***roezlii***	ECho EPot
	'Lane Fox' **new**	WCot
§	'Le Phare'	MBNS XLum
	'Lilac and Burgundy'	MBNS MBel SMrm SRms SWvt WWEG
	'Lilac Frost'	LLHF MCot WMoo
	'Lilliput'	CMea ELon EPot GBin SLon WHil WHoo
	linarioides 'Marilyn Ross'	ECtt MBNS
	'Lord Home'	see *P.* 'George Home'
	'Louise Wilson'	WHlf
	'Lucinda Gilchrist'	SLon
	lyallii	CCon ELan GKev SRms WCot
	'Lynette'	MBNS SBch SPlb
	'Macpenny's Pink'	CMac MBNS
	'Madame Golding'	MBNS XLum
	'Malvern Springs'	MBNS
	'Margery Fish' ♀H3	CElw CFis ECtt EPyc EWes WWEG
	'Maurice Gibbs' ♀H3	CBcs CWCL ECtt EPfP EWes LHop LSRN LSqH MBNS MBel SBod SRGP SRms WMnd WWEG
	'Melting Candy' (Ice Cream Series)	WCot WSpi
	mensarum	EDAr
	× ***mexicanus*** 'Sunburst Amethyst'	LRHS SPad SPhx SRms XLum
	- 'Sunburst Ruby'	CPla LRHS SLon SPhx
	'Midnight'	ECtt ELan EPfP GBin LPot MBNS MRav MSwo SEND SHar SWvt WCFE WWEG XLum
	'Modesty'	EPfP MBNS SRms
	'Mother of Pearl'	CBcs CCon EBee EPfP EShb GBin GMaP LHop LRHS LSRN MBNS MBel MCot MSwo MWat SPad SPer SRms SWvt WWEG WWlt
	'Mrs Miller'	MBNS
	'Mrs Morse'	see *P.* 'Chester Scarlet'
	'Mrs Oliver'	EWes
§	'Myddelton Gem'	MWat SRms
	'Myddelton Red'	see *P.* 'Myddelton Gem'
	newberryi ♀H4	WIce
	- f. ***humilior***	EPot
§	- subsp. ***sonomensis***	NSla SRms WAbe
*	'Newbury Gem'	MBNS SRGP SWvt
	'Oaklea Red'	GBin
§	'Old Candy Pink'	MBNS SWvt
	'Osprey' ♀H3	CHel CMac CMea CWCL EBee ECtt EHyd ELan EPfP EShb EWes GBin LAst LRHS MAsh MBNS NBir SMrm SRms SWvt WMnd WWEG
	ovatus	CCon CMac CSpe EBee ELan NBre SPhx SRms
	'Overbury'	ECtt MBNS SRms
	'Papal Purple'	LLWP MAsh MBNS MHer NBir NCGa SLon SPhx SRms XLum
	'Patio Bells Pink'	MLHP
	'Patio Bells Shell'	SLon
	'Patio Wine'	MBel
	'Peace'	GBin MBNS SLon WHoo
§	'Pennington Gem' ♀H3	CPrp ELan LRHS MHer NBir SRms SWvt
	'Pensham Amelia Jane'	CWGN ECtt ELon EPfP LHop LRHS LSRN LSou MAsh MBNS MBri MHol NCGa NLar NPri SAll SHil SLon SMrm SPer SRkn SRms SWvt WCot WHil
	'Pensham Arctic Fox'	ECtt LRHS SBch SLon
	'Pensham Arctic Sunset'	SLon WHrl
	'Pensham Avonbelle'	MBNS SRms
	'Pensham Bilberry Ice'	EPyc MBNS SWvt WMnd
	'Pensham Blackberry Ice'	ECtt EPfP EPyc LSou MBNS SAll SLon SRms
	'Pensham Blueberry Ice'	ECtt EPyc LSou MBNS SWvt
	'Pensham Capricorn Moon'	ECtt NLar SLon SRGP
	'Pensham Charlotte Louise'	ECtt ELon LRHS MAsh NLar SAll SRms
	'Pensham Czar'	CAby ECtt ELon EPfP LHop LRHS LSou MAsh MBNS MBri MCot NCGa NPri SAll SGbt SHil SLon SMrm SPer SPoG SRkn SRms SWvt WHil WHrl
	'Pensham Dorothy Wilson'	EPyc MBri SMrm
	'Pensham Edith Biggs'	EPfP SMrm
	'Pensham Eleanor Young'	ECtt LRHS LSou MBNS NCGa SAll SLon SRkn SWvt
	'Pensham Freshwater Pearl'	SRms WHlf WHoo
	'Pensham Great Expectations'	ECtt
	'Pensham Jessica Mai'	ECtt ELon LRHS LSou MAsh SPer SRms SWvt WHil
	'Pensham Just Jayne'	ECtt ELon EPfP EPyc LRHS LSRN MBNS SAll SLon SRGP SRms SWvt WHoo WMnd XLum
	'Pensham Kay Burton'	EPfP EPyc SRGP WMnd
	'Pensham Laura'	CAby CSam CWGN EBee ECtt EPfP LHop LRHS LSRN MAsh MBNS MBel MBri MHol NLar NPri SAll SHil SLon SMrm SPer SRGP SRkn SWvt WBor WHlf WHoo
	'Pensham Loganberry Ice'	LSou MBNS NCGa SLon
	'Pensham Marilyn'	WHlf
	'Pensham Marjorie Lewis'	WMnd
	'Pensham Miss Wilson'	SRms
	'Pensham Plum Jerkum'	CAby CWGN ECtt ELon EPfP EPyc EWTr LHop LRHS LSou MBNS MBri MCot NLar SAll SHil SLon SMrm SPad SPer SRkn SWvt WHoo WMnd

'Pensham Princess' **new**	ECtt
'Pensham Raspberry Ice'	MBNS SLon WMnd
'Pensham Saint James's'	WHlf
'Pensham Skies'	WHlf
'Pensham Son of Raven'	MWhi
'Pensham Tayberry Ice'	ECtt EPyc MBNS SLon WMnd
'Pensham Victoria Plum'	CElw SHar WHoo
'Pensham Wedding Bells'	SRms
'Pensham Wedding Day'	CMea CWCL EPfP LHop LRHS LSRN LSou MBNS MBri MCot NLar NPri SAll SLon SPer SPoG SRGP WHlf WHoo WMnd
'Pensham Westminster Belle' **new**	ECtt
'Pershore Carnival'	SRms WHrl
'Pershore Fanfare'	WHrl
'Pershore Pink Necklace'	CWCL ECtt LRHS SRms SWvt WHlf WWEG
'Phare'	see *P.* 'Le Phare'
(Phoenix Series) Phoenix Appleblossom 09 = 'Peni Ablos09' **new**	SHil
- Phoenix Lavender = 'Peni Laver' **new**	SHil
- Phoenix Magenta 09 = 'Peni Mag09' **new**	SHil
- Phoenix Pink 09 = 'Peni Pina09' **new**	SHil
- Phoenix Red = 'Pheni Reeda'PBR	EBee LRHS SHil WCFE
- Phoenix Violet 09 = 'Peni Vio09' **new**	EPfP SHil
'Phyllis'	see *P.* 'Evelyn'
pinifolius ♀H4	CCon CMea CTri EBee ECho EDAr ELon EPot GKev LHop LRHS MAsh MBel NHar SPhx SPoG XLum XSen
- 'Mersea Yellow'	CCon CMea ECho EDAr EPfP EPot GKev LHop LRHS MAsh NHar SBch SLon SPhx SPlb SPoG XLum XSen
- 'Wisley Flame' ♀H4	ECho EPfP EPot EWes MBNS MHer MSCN MWat
'Pink Bedder'	see *P.* 'Hewell Pink Bedder', 'Sutton's Pink Bedder'
'Pink Endurance'	MBNS WHal
'Polaris Red'	EPfP
'Pomegranate' (Ice Cream Series) **new**	WHlf
'Port Wine' ♀H3	CMea CTri ELon EPfP GMaP LHop LPot LRHS LSRN MCot MWat NBir SPoG SWvt WKif WMnd WWEG
'Powis Castle'	EWes
'Pretty Petticoat'	IPot MBri
'Priory Purple'	MBNS WHrl
procerus	GKev
var. ***brachyanthus***	
§ - var. ***formosus***	WAbe
- 'Hawkeye'	CPBP
§ - 'Roy Davidson' ♀H4	CMea EPot NHar WAbe
- var. ***tolmiei***	EPot GCal
pubescens	see *P. hirsutus*
pulchellus Greene	see *P. procerus* var. *formosus*
pulchellus Lindl.	see *P. campanulatus*
'Purple and White'	see *P.* 'Countess of Dalkeith'
'Purple Bedder'	CMac COIW EPfP GBin LRHS LSRN MBri MLHP MWat NBir SPoG SRkn SRms SWvt WGor XLum
'Purple Passion'	CElw EHyd ELan EPfP EWes LRHS
'Purple Sea'	MAsh

'Purpureus Albus'	see *P.* 'Countess of Dalkeith'
'Raspberry Ripple' (Ice Cream Series) **new**	LSou
'Raven' ♀H3	CBar CMac CSam CWCL ECtt EShb EWTr GBin GCra LAst LBMP LHop LLWP LPio LRHS MCot MHer SAll SEND SRms SWvt WHal WHar WHil WWEG
'Razzle Dazzle'	MBNS SPlb WCot
'Red Emperor'	WWEG
'Red Knight'	GCra MBNS
'Red Riding Hood'PBR	EPfP LRHS MPie
'Red Rocks'	GBin LRHS WCot
'Red Sea'	MAsh
'Rich Purple'	EPyc MBNS SPlb XLum
'Rich Ruby'	CAby COIW CWCL CWGN ELan EPfP EWes LLWP LRHS MWhi NBir SPlb SRGP SWvt WWEG
'Ridgeway Red'	MBNS
(Riding Hood Series) 'Riding Hood Lavender' **new**	LRHS
- 'Riding Hood Marbled Cream' **new**	LRHS
- 'Riding Hood Purple' **new**	LRHS
roezlii Regel	see *P. laetus* subsp. *roezlii*
roezlii ambig.	MAsh SBrt
'Ron Sidwell'	SLon
§ ***rostriflorus***	LLHF
'Rosy Blush'	MBNS SPlb
'Roy Davidson'	see *P. procerus* 'Roy Davidson'
'Royal White'	see *P.* 'White Bedder'
'Rubicundus' ♀H3	CWCL EBee EHyd ELan EPfP GBin LRHS LSRN MBNS MWhi SMrm SWvt WBor WMnd
'Ruby' misapplied	see *P.* 'Schoenholzeri'
'Ruby Field'	EPyc
rupicola ♀H4	EPot LHop
- 'Albus'	EPot
- 'Conwy Lilac'	SRms WAbe
- 'Conwy Rose'	EPot WAbe WThu
- 'Puyallup Pink'	GKev
'Russian River'	CPrp ECtt EPfP EWes LHop LRHS LSRN MBNS SPlb SWvt XLum
rydbergii	SPlb
'Samsong'	WCFE
Saskatoon hybrids	LHop
- rose-flowered	SLon
Scarlet Queen	see *P.* 'Scharlachkönigin'
§ 'Scharlachkönigin'	ECtt
§ 'Schoenholzeri' ♀H4	Widely available
scouleri	see *P. fruticosus* var. *scouleri*
§ ***serrulatus***	EPot EWes SBrt XLum
- 'Albus'	SPhx
'Sherbourne Blue'	LPot WCot
'Sissinghurst Pink'	see *P.* 'Evelyn'
'Six Hills'	CMea EPot SDys WAbe
'Skyline'	EPfP
smallii	EDAr EPPr EPfP EWes LRHS LSRN MHer SPhx SRkn WPGP
'Snow Storm'	see *P.* 'White Bedder'
'Snowflake'	see *P.* 'White Bedder'
sonomensis	see *P. newberryi* subsp. *sonomensis*
'Sour Grapes' misapplied	see *P.* 'Stapleford Gem'
'Sour Grapes' ambig.	CAby CHVG COIW EHyd IBoy LPot MBel MCot MJak NGdn SAll SMrm WWEG
§ 'Sour Grapes' M. Fish ♀H3-4	CHel CMac CPrp CSpe CWCL EBee ELan EPfP EShb GBin IBoy LAst LRHS LSRN MBri MHer MSwo NLar

		SEND SHar SPer SPoG WCot WHil WHoo WKif WMnd
	'Southgate Gem'	GBee GKcv MBNS MWat SRms SWvt
	'Souvenir d'Adrian Regnier'	MBNS
	'Souvenir d'André Torres' misapplied	see *P.* 'Chester Scarlet'
	speciosus	SBrt
	spectabilis	SBrt
	'Spitfire' **new**	WCFE
§	'Stapleford Gem' ♀H3	CWCL ECtt ELan EUJe GBuc LRHS MBel MBri MRav NPri SMrm SPet SRms SWvt WHar WHoo WMnd WWEG
	'Strawberries and Cream' (Ice Cream Series)	ELon EWTr NLar SAll SRkn WCot WHil WSpi
	strictus	CCon EPPr GKev LRHS MBNS MNFA
	Stromboli = 'Yaboli'	LRHS
§	'Sutton's Pink Bedder'	MBNS
	'Sweet Cherry' (Ice Cream Series)	ECtt LSou WCot WHlf WSpi
	tall pink-flowered	see *P.* 'Welsh Dawn'
	taosensis	see *P. crandallii* subsp. *taosensis*
	'Ted's Purple'	WCFE WHlf
	ternatus	see *Keckiella ternata*
	teucrioides	EPot
	- JCA 1717050	CPBP
	'The Juggler'	ECtt EPfP MBNS SMrm SWvt
§	'Thorn'	ECtt EShb LRHS MWat NBir SPhx SRms SWvt WWEG
	'Threave Pink'	ECtt LLWP MBNS MRav SEND SHar SMrm SPer SWvt WWEG
	'Thundercloud'	ECtt
	'Torquay Gem'	LLHF MBNS SDys
	'True Sour Grapes'	see *P.* 'Sour Grapes' M. Fish
§	***tusharensis***	GKev
	utahensis	GBee LRHS
	'Vanilla' (Ice Cream Series) **new**	WHlf
	'Vanilla Plum' (Ice Cream Series)	LSou WHil
	Vesuvius = 'Yasius'	ECtt EPfP LRHS MBri NEgg SLon SRms WHlf
	virens	CPBP EBee
	virgatus **new**	EBee
	- 'Blue Buckle'	IPot MHol SPlb
	'Wallington Pink'	LRHS
	watsonii	EDAr
§	'Welsh Dawn'	MBNS
§	***whippleanus***	CAby EDAr LRHS SPhx SPlb
§	'White Bedder' ♀H3	Widely available
I	'Whitethroat' purple-flowered	WCot
	'Whitethroat' Sidwell	MBNS
	'Willy's Purple'	ECtt MBNS
§	'Windsor Red'	COlW CTri ECtt EPfP LRHS MBNS SLon SRms SWvt WCot
	'Woodpecker'	ECtt MAvo MBNS SRms

Pentaglottis (*Boraginaceae*)

§	***sempervirens***	CArn EPfP WSFF

Pentapanax see *Aralia*

Pentapterygium see *Agapetes*

Pentas (*Rubiaceae*)

	lanceolata	CCCN ELan EShb

Penthorum (*Saxifragaceae*)

	sedoides	LLWG

pepino see *Solanum muricatum*

peppermint see *Mentha* × *piperita*

Pericallis (*Asteraceae*)

	aurita	CRHN
	× ***hybrida*** Senetti Series	MGos NPer NPri SPoG
	- - Senetti Blue = 'Sunsenebu'PBR	SPoG
	- - Senetti Blue Bicolor = 'Sunseneribuba'PBR	LAst MGos SPoG
	- - Senetti Magenta = 'Sunsenere'PBR	SPoG
	- - Senetti Magenta Bicolor = 'Sunsenereba'PBR	LAst MGos SPoG
§	***lanata*** (L'Hér.) B. Nord.	CHll EShb
	- Kew form	CSpe

Perilla (*Lamiaceae*)

§	***frutescens*** var. ***crispa*** ♀H2	CSpe SHDw
	- green-leaved	ELau
	- var. ***japonica***	GPoy
	- var. ***nankinensis***	see *P. frutescens* var. *crispa*
	- var. ***purpurascens***	CArn ELau WJek

Periploca (*Apocynaceae*)

	graeca	CBcs CMac CRHN EBee SLon
	purpurea B&SWJ 7235	WCru
	sepium	CExl

Peristrophe (*Acanthaceae*)

	cernua **new**	WHil

Pernettya see *Gaultheria*

N	***mucronata***	see *Gaultheria mucronata*

Perovskia (*Lamiaceae*)

	abrotanoides	LRHS XLum
	atriplicifolia	CArn CBcs CMea EHyd ELan MHer MNHC NSti WKif WMnd XSen
	- 'Blue Shadow'	EBee EWTr LHop LRHS STPC
	- Lacey Blue = 'Lisslitt'PBR	EPfP MAsh SPoG
	- 'Little Spire'PBR	CBar CMac CSBt CSpe EBee EHoe ELon EPfP EWes GMaP GQue IBoy LRHS LSRN MAsh MJak NBid NDov NLar SGol SPer SPoG SRkn WHil
	'Blue Haze'	GCal LRHS
	'Blue Spire' ♀H4	Widely available
	'Filigran'	EBee ELan EUJe GBin GBuc LRHS LSou MWhi SPoG WGrn WHoo WPat XSen
	'Hybrida'	LRHS
	'Longin'	EBee LHop NDov

Persea (*Lauraceae*)

	americana	CCCN
	indica	CCCN
	japonica B&SWJ 8410	WCru
	lingue	CBcs
	thunbergii	CBcs CFil CHEx

Persicaria (*Polygonaceae*)

	B&SWJ 11268 from Sumatra	WCru

§	***affinis***	CBcs CSBt EBee GAbr MWhi NBro NSti SWat WBrk WMoo
	- 'Darjeeling Red' ♀H4	Widely available
	- 'Dimity'	see *P. affinis* 'Superba'
	- 'Donald Lowndes' ♀H4	CHVG CMac CTri EBee ELan ELon EPfP GBin GMaP IVic LAst LHop LPot LRHS LSRN MCot MHer MNrw MRav MWat NPri SPer SRms SWat SWvt WMoo WWEG
	- 'Kabouter'	GBin IPot NLar WBor
	- 'Ron McBeath'	LRHS
§	- 'Superba' ♀H4	Widely available
	alata	see *P. nepalensis*
	alpina	CDes EBee ELan EPPr GBin GCal GMaP IPot LEdu LRHS MAvo MCot MNFA SBch SDix WCot WMoo WWEG
	amphibia	LLWG MSKA SWat XLum
§	***amplexicaulis***	CBre CKno CPrp CRow CSpe ELan EWes GMaP MBel MCot MHer MMuc NOrc WBor WGwG WMoo WRHF XLum
	- 'Alba'	Widely available
	- 'Anouk'	EBee
	'Arun Gem'	see *P. amplexicaulis* var. *pendula*
	- 'Atrosanguinea'	CKno CMac CRow CTri EBee ELan LRHS MMuc MNFA MRav MSpe MWat NBir NLar SEND SMrm SPer SRms SWat SWvt WOld WWEG XLum
	- 'Baron'	CRow
	- 'Betty Brandt'	GBin
	- 'Blackfield'[PBR]	CBct CKno CSpe EBee ECtt ELon EPPr EWes GBin GQue IKil IPot LRHS LSou MBNS NDov NLar STPC WCot WHil
	- 'Blush Clent'	WHoo
	- 'Clent Charm'	NChi WOut WWEG
	- 'Cottesbrooke Gold'	CRow ECtt MAvo
	- 'Dikke Floskes'	CRow IPot WCot
	- 'Eastfield' (v)	WCot
	- 'Fascination'	WCot
	- 'Fat Domino'[PBR]	CKno GBin GQue IPot NDov NLar
	- 'Firedance'	CKno EHoe ELon EPPr GQue IPot MSpe NDov SPhx SWat WCot
	- 'Firetail' ♀H4	CKno CMac CRow CSam CSpe ECtt ELon EPfP GAbr GCra IFro LAst LLWP LPio LRHS MHol MLHP NBid NLar NPri SPer SPoG SWat WHil WHoo WMnd WMoo WPtf WSFF WWEG
	- 'Golden Arrow' (v)	LBuc LRHS
	- 'High Society'	GBin IPot
	- 'Inverleith'	CBct CBre CKno CRow EBee ECGP ECtt EPPr GBin GBuc GMaP GQue LBMP LRHS MBel MMuc MNFA MSpe NBir SPhx WCot WMoo WOut WPGP WPnP
I	- 'Jo and Guido's Form'	CHVG ELon NLar WCAu
	- 'JS Caliente'[PBR]	CHVG CKno CMea EBee ECtt ELon GBin GQue LLWG LRHS MBel MHol NBir NCGa WCot
	- 'Lisan' **new**	GBin
	- Orange Field = 'Orangofield'[PBR]	CKno ECtt ELon EPPr GBin GQue LHop LRHS NCGa NDov
*	- var. ***pendula***	EBee EPPr GQue NBir WMoo
	- - HWJK 2255	WCru
	- 'Pink Elephant'	CSam EBee EPPr GBin GQue MAvo NDov NLar STPC WWEG

	- 'Pink Lady'	CRow ECGP MPie NLar
	- 'Rosea'	Widely available
	- 'Rowden Gem'	CRow WMoo WOut
	- 'Rowden Jewel'	CRow
	- 'Rowden Rose Quartz'	CRow
	- 'Sangre' **new**	GBin MAvo
	- 'September Spires'	IPot NDov
	- 'Seven Oaks Village' **new**	GBin
	- 'Summer Dance'	CKno EBee ECtt EPPr GQue IPot LPla NLar
	- Taurus = 'Blotau'	CElw CHVG CKno CSam EBee ECtt EPPr GBin GBuc GQue IPot LRHS MBri NCGa NLar NSti WCAu WHoo WPGP WPnP WWEG
§	***bistorta***	CArn ELau GPoy MHer MMuc MWhi NBir NLar SEND SRms SWat WOut
	- subsp. ***carnea***	EBee EHoe ELon EPPr GBin LPla LRHS MBNS MMuc MSpe NBir NBro NDov WCot WMoo
	- 'Hohe Tatra'	CDes EBee EPPr GMaP LRHS NDov
	- 'JS Calor'[PBR] **new**	GBin GQue
	- 'Superba' ♀H4	Widely available
	campanulata	CElw CRow ECtt EHoe GAbr GMaP IFro LPot MMuc MRav MSpe MWhi NBro NEgg NOrc SEND SPer WMoo WOut
	- Alba Group	CElw CFis GBin NBro WMoo
	- var. ***lichiangense***	GBin
	- 'Madame Jigard'	CRow GBin
	- 'Rosenrot'	CBre CRow GBin LRHS NBir SWat WOld
	- 'Southcombe White'	CRow GBin LRHS WWEG
§	***capitata***	CHVG LLWG XLum
	- 'Pink Bubbles'	EHoe NBir SWvt
	chinensis B&SWJ 11268	WCru
	emodi	GKev
	hydropiper 'Fastigiata'	CArn
*	- var. ***rubra*** **new**	WJek
*	***kahil***	GBin WCot
*	***macrophylla***	EBee LDai LRHS
	- CC 5790	GKev
	microcephala	CRow EWes
	- 'Purple Fantasy' **new**	NSoo
	- 'Red Dragon'[PBR]	Widely available
	milletii	EBee GBuc NLar WCot WCru
§	***mollis***	EBee LRHS WPGP
	nakaii	EBee
	neofiliformis	EShb MWhi
§	***nepalensis***	CExl CRow EPPr EShb IMou MPie MSpe MTPN
	'October Pink'	CSam
§	***odorata***	CArn ELau EOHP GPoy MHer MHoo MNHC SHDw SRms WJek
	orientalis	CSpe SMrm
	polystachya	see *P. wallichii*
	'Red Baron'	EPPr
§	***runcinata***	CRow EBee MMuc NBir WMoo
	- Needham's form	CRow CSpe
	scoparia	see *Polygonum scoparium*
	sphaerostachya Meisn.	see *P. macrophylla*
	tenuicaulis	CBre GBin MNFA NLar SBch WCru WMoo
§	***tinctoria***	EOHP WSFF
§	***vacciniifolia*** ♀H4	CBcs COIW CPrp CSBt CTri EBee ECho ECtt EHoe GAbr GBin IPot LAst LHop MHer MLHP MMuc MWat NBid NBir NRya SDix SPlb SRms SWat SWvt WAbe WMoo WWEG

§ ***virginiana***	CRow EPPr GCal LRHS WMoo
- f. ***albiflora***	CKno EPPr
- 'Brushstrokes' **new**	MWhi
- var. ***filiformis***	CHEx CSpe EBee ECtt ELan LBMP LPla MMoz MPie SRkn SWvt WCot WHil
- - 'Ballet'	WCot
- - 'Batwings'	ESwi LRHS
- - 'Compton's Red'	CHEx CRow ECtt EShb GCal LDai LHop LPla LRHS MMoz SBrt WCot WHil
- - 'Lance Corporal'	CMac CRow EHoe EPPr EShb GBin MAvo NLar SMrm
- - 'Moorland Moss'	WMoo
- Variegated Group (v)	CRow EShb MBNS WCot WMoo WOld
- - 'Painter's Palette' (v)	CHEx CMac CRow EBee ECtt EHoe ELan EPPr EPfP EShb EUJe GBuc LRHS MRav MSpe NBid NSti SMad SPer SWvt WCot WCru WMoo XLum
vivipara	MMHG NLar
§ ***wallichii***	CSpe MMuc NLar SDix SWat WCot WMoo WPtf WWEG XLum
§ ***weyrichii***	EPPr GCal NBir NBro NLar WMoo XLum

persimmon see *Diospyros virginiana*

persimmon, Japanese see *Diospyros kaki*

Petalostemon see *Dalea*

Petamenes see *Gladiolus*

Petasites (*Asteraceae*)

albus	GPoy LLWG MHer NLar
fragrans	EBee SWat WHer XLum
§ ***frigidus*** var. ***palmatus***	NLar
- - JLS 86317CLOR	SMad
- - 'Golden Palms'	CHid EUJe WBor
hybridus	EBee LEdu MSKA SWat
* - 'Variegatus' (v)	XLum
japonicus	CBcs GPoy
- var. ***giganteus***	CArn CHEx CHid CMac CRow EPfP EUJe LEdu MBel SWat WCru
§ - - 'Nishiki-buki' (v)	CHEx CMac CRow EBee EPPr EUJe EWld GQue MBel MHer MSKA NBir NEgg NSti SMad WBor WWEG XLum
- - 'Variegatus'	see *P. japonicus* var. *giganteus* 'Nishiki-buki'
- f. ***purpureus***	EBee EPPr
palmatus	see *P. frigidus* var. *palmatus*
paradoxus	CDes CLAP EPPr EWld LEdu MBel WCot

× *Petchoa* (*Solanaceae*)

SuperCal Terracotta = 'Kakegawa S91'PBR (SuperCal Series)	LSou

Petrea (*Verbenaceae*)

volubilis	CCCN

Petrocallis (*Brassicaceae*)

lagascae	see *P. pyrenaica*
§ ***pyrenaica***	WAbe
- white-flowered	WAbe

Petrocoptis (*Caryophyllaceae*)

pyrenaica	SRms
§ - subsp. ***glaucifolia***	ITim

Petrocosmea (*Gesneriaceae*)

begoniifolia	WAbe
cryptica	WThu
formosa 'Crûg's Capricious'	WCru
forrestii	WAbe
grandiflora	WAbe
- 'Crème de Crûg'	WCru
kerrii	CDes WCot
minor	CPBP WAbe
sericea	WAbe

Petrophytum (*Rosaceae*)

caespitosum	EPot WAbe
§ ***hendersonii***	WAbe WThu

Petrorhagia (*Caryophyllaceae*)

illyrica PAB 4871 **new**	LEdu
'Pink Starlets'	EPfP LHop
saxifraga ♀H4	CSpe ECho SRms WMoo XLum

Petroselinum (*Apiaceae*)

§ ***crispum***	CArn GPoy LPot MHoo MNHC SIde SPoG SRms WJek
- 'Bravour' ♀H4	ELau MHer MHoo
- 'Champion Moss Curled'	SVic
- 'Darki'	ELau MHoo NPri
- French	CArn ELau MHer MHoo MNHC NPri SPoG SRms WJek
- 'Italian'	see *P. crispum* var. *neapolitanum* plain-leaved
- 'Moss Curled' ♀H4	MHoo SRms
§ - var. ***neapolitanum*** plain-leaved	ELau MHoo SIde SPoG SRms SVic
§ - var. ***tuberosum***	MHer MNHC SIde SRms SVic
hortense	see *P. crispum*
tuberosum	see *P. crispum* var. *tuberosum*

Petteria (*Papilionaceae*)

ramentacea	EBtc

Petunia (*Solanaceae*)

Black Velvet = 'Balpevac'	LAst NPri
Candyfloss = 'Kercan'PBR (Tumbelina Series) (d)	LSou NPri
(Cascadias Series) Cascadias Bicolor Pastel = 'Dancasbipas'	NPri
- Cascadias Rim Violet	LAst NPri
Cherry Ripple = 'Kerripcherry'PBR (Tumbelina Series) (d)	LSou
Conchita Doble Lavender = 'Condost177'PBR (Conchita Doble Series) (d)	LAst
(Corona Series) 'Corona Amethyst'	NPri
- 'Corona Rose Rim'	NPri
Daddy Series **new**	CWCL
(Fanfare Series) 'Fanfare Blue' **new**	NPri
- 'Fanfare Crème de Cassis'	NPri
- 'Fanfare Hot Rose'	NPri
- 'Fanfare Red' **new**	NPri

– 'Fanfare White' **new**	NPri
– 'Fanfare Yellow'	NPri
'Happy Copper' **new**	LAst
Inga (Tumbelina Series) (d)	LSou
Joanna (Tumbelina Series)	LAst LSou
Katrina = 'Kerkat'PBR (Tumbelina Series) (d)	LAst
(Littletunia Series) Littletunia Bicolour Illusion	LAst
– Littletunia Blue Vein	NPri
– Littletunia Rachel **new**	NPri
Melissa = 'Kermelis'PBR (Tumbelina Series) (d)	LAst LSou
multiflora (Frenzy Series) 'Frenzy Mid Blue' **new**	NPri
– – 'Frenzy Plum Bicolour'	NPri
– – 'Frenzy Red Frost' **new**	NPri
patagonica	WAbe
Phantom = 'Balpephan' **new**	NPri
'Pink Star' (Designer Series) **new**	LAst
(Potunia Series) Potunia Blackberry Ice **new**	LAst
– Potunia Papaya	LAst
Priscilla = 'Kerpril'PBR (Tumbelina Series) (d)	LAst LSou NPri
'Stardust' (Designer Series) **new**	LAst
Supercascade Series **new**	CWCL
(Surfinia Series) Surfinia Blue Picotee	LSou
– Surfinia Blue = 'Sunblu'	LAst LSou NPri WGor
– Surfinia Blue Vein = 'Sunsolos'PBR	LAst WGor
– Surfinia Burgundy = 'Keiburtel'PBR	LAst WGor
– Surfinia Double Blue Star = 'Sunsurfelevi'PBR (d)	LAst
– Surfinia Double Red = 'Keidoreral'PBR (d)	LAst
– Surfinia Hot Pink 06 = 'Sunrovein'PBR	LAst
– Surfinia Hot Pink = 'Marrose'PBR	LSou WGor
– Surfinia Hot Red = 'Sunhore'PBR	NPri
– Surfinia Impulz Yellow = 'Sunpatiki'PBR	LAst NPri
– Surfinia Lime = 'Keiyeul'PBR	LAst WGor
– Surfinia Pastel 2000 = 'Sunpapi'PBR	WGor
– Surfinia Pink Ice = 'Hakice'PBR (v)	LAst NPri WGor
– Surfinia Purple = 'Shihi Brilliant' ♀H3	LAst LSou NPri WGor
– Surfinia Red = 'Keirekul'PBR	LAst WGor
– Surfinia Rose Vein = 'Sunrove'PBR	LAst WGor
– Surfinia Sky Blue = 'Keilavbu'PBR ♀H3	LAst NPri WGor
– Surfinia Sweet Pink = 'Sunsurfmomo'PBR	LSou
– Surfinia Vanilla = 'Sunvanilla'PBR	LSou
– Surfinia White = 'Kesupite'	LAst
Susanna (Tumbelina Series)	LAst
Sweetunia Mystery **new** (Sweetunia Series)	LAst
Victoria = 'Kervic'PBR (Tumbelina Series)	LAst LSou

Peucedanum (*Apiaceae*)

* ***aromaticum***	IMou
caffrum	SPlb
japonicum B&SWJ 8816B	WCru
officinale	CSpe GBin LRHS NLar
ostruthium	GPoy LEdu NCGa WPtf
– 'Daphnis' (v)	CDes CSpe EBee LEdu LPla MAvo MMoz NChi NLar NPro WCFE WCot WHrl WWFP XLum
verticillare	CArn CSam CSpe EBee IMou ITim LPio LRHS MAvo MBel MNFA SDix SKHP SMrm SPhx WSHC WWEG

Peumus (*Monimiaceae*)

boldus	CBcs

Phacelia (*Boraginaceae*)

bolanderi	GKev LDai
tanacetifolia	SPhx

Phaedranassa (*Amaryllidaceae*)

BKBlount 2623	WCot
carmiolii	WCot
cinerea	ECho WCot
dubia	ECho WCot
* ***montana***	ECho
tunguraguae	ECho
viridiflora	ECho WCot

Phaenocoma (*Asteraceae*)

prolifera	SPlb

Phaenosperma (*Poaceae*)

globosa	CSam CSpe EBee EHoe EPPr GQue LRHS NWsh SPoG WCot WPGP XLum

Phaiophleps see *Olsynium*

nigricans	see *Sisyrinchium striatum*

Phalaris (*Poaceae*)

arundinacea	CDAq LPot MDKP MSKA SPlb SVic SWat
– cream-flowered	WWEG
– 'Elegantissima'	see *P. arundinacea* var. *picta* 'Picta'
– var. ***picta***	CDul CHEx CTri CWCL CWib EWTr MJak MSKA NBir NPer SPoG XLum XSen
– – 'Arctic Sun' (v)	CKno EBee ELon EPPr GBin LLWG SDix SPoG STPC WWEG
– – 'Aureovariegata' (v)	CBcs MRav NPer SWat WMoo XLum
– – 'Feesey' (v)	CBAq CMac COIW CPrp CSBt CWCL EBee ECtt EHoe ELon EWes LLWG LRHS MAsh MMuc MWhi NBid NBro NWsh SEND SGbt SHil SLim SMad SMrm SPoG WMoo WWEG XLum
– – 'Luteopicta' (v)	EHoe EPPr MMuc SEND WWEG XLum
§ – – 'Picta' (v) ♀H4	COIW ELan EPfP LBMP LLWG LRHS MMuc SPer SWat WMoo
– – 'Streamlined' (v)	EPPr LLWG NWsh SLPl
– – 'Tricolor' (v)	EHoe LLWG

Phanerophlebia (*Dryopteridaceae*)

caryotidea — see *Cyrtomium caryotideum*
falcata — see *Cyrtomium falcatum*
fortunei — see *Cyrtomium fortunei*

Pharbitis see *Ipomoea*

Phaseolus (*Papilionaceae*)

caracalla — see *Vigna caracalla*
vulgaris 'Yin Yang' — LSou

Phedimus see *Sedum*

Phegopteris (*Thelypteridaceae*)

§ ***connectilis*** — EFer
decursive-pinnata — CBty CDes CLAP LRHS NLar NMyG WFib WPnP

Phellodendron (*Rutaceae*)

amurense — CBcs CCCN CDul CLnd CMCN EBee ELan EPfP EWTr GBin IDee IVic LEdu SEND WBor WPGP
- B&SWJ 11000 — WCru
- var. ***sachalinense*** — LEdu
japonicum B&SWJ 11175 — WCru

Phenakospermum (*Strelitziaceae*)

guianense — XBlo

Pherosphaera (*Podocarpaceae*)

fitzgeraldii — CKen WThu

Philadelphus ✿ (*Hydrangeaceae*)

SDR 2823 — CExl
SDR 4202 **new** — GKev
SDR 4945 — GKev
SDR 4946 — CExl GKev
SDR 5111 — GKev
'Atlas' (v) — NLar
'Avalanche' — CExl NLar SPer SRms
'Beauclerk' $\mathbb{Y}^{H4}$ — CDoC CDul CTri EBee EPfP GGal GQui IVic LRHS MBri MGos MRav NBro NEgg NWea SHil SKHP SLim SPer SPoG SRms SWvt WHar WPat
'Belle Etoile' $\mathbb{Y}^{H4}$ — Widely available
'Bicolore' — NLar WHar
'Boule d'Argent' (d) — WHar
'Bouquet Blanc' — MRav NLar SRms WCFE WPat
brachybotrys — MRav
'Buckley's Quill' (d) — EBee ECrN EPfP EWes LRHS MRav SGol SWvt WGrn
'Burfordensis' — CWSG EPfP LAst MRav SEND
calcicola **new** — CFil
§ ***calvescens*** — MRav
aff. ***calvescens*** — MRav
- BWJ 8005 — WCru
caucasicus — CFil
coronarius — CBcs CDul EBee EPfP LBuc MLHP MMuc MRav NWea SEND SPer
- 'Aureus' $\mathbb{Y}^{H4}$ — Widely available
- 'Bowles's Variety' — see *P. coronarius* 'Variegatus'
§ - 'Variegatus' (v) $\mathbb{Y}^{H4}$ — Widely available
coulteri — WPGP
'Coupe d'Argent' — MRav
'Dainty Lady' — LBuc LRHS SLon
'Dame Blanche' (d) — EPfP EWTr MRav
delavayi — CFil CGHE EBee EPfP GBin GGal NLar SKHP WPGP
- var. ***calvescens*** — see *P. calvescens*
- f. ***melanocalyx*** — EBee EPfP GCra MRav WPGP WPat
- - B&L 12168 — CFil WPGP
- 'Nymans' — CExl CFil EPfP SKHP WKif WPGP
cf. ***delavayi*** **new** — CAbb
'Enchantement' (d) — MRav SDix
'Erectus' — CHel CSBt CWib EBee ELon EPfP LRHS MRav NLar SKHP SLim SPer SPoG WPat
'Etoile Rose' — WMoo
'Falconeri' — MRav
'Frosty Morn' (d) — CBcs EPfP LRHS MBlu MMuc MRav NBro NLar SEND SPer
incanus B&SWJ 8616 — WCru
§ 'Innocence' (v) — CExl CMac EBee EHoe ELan EPfP LAst LRHS MAsh MBri MGos MMuc MRav MSwo NPro SEND SKHP SLim SPad SPer SPoG SRms WPat
'Innocence Variegatus' — see *P.* 'Innocence'
§ ***insignis*** — MRav
karwinskianus **new** — CFil
'Kelmarsh' — SLPl
× ***lemoinei*** — CBcs CDul CTri EBee EWTr MGos NLar NSoo WGrn WHar
I - 'Lemoinei' — NWea
'Lemon Hill' — NLar
lewisii — CExl
- L 1896 — CExl
'Limestone' — MRav NLar
maculatus — CFil WPat
- 'Mexican Jewel' — CExl CFil CGHE EBee ELon NLar SKHP WKif WPGP WPat WSHC
- 'Scented Storm' — CHel CMHG CSam
- 'Sweet Clare' — LRHS MBri
madrensis — CGHE LHop MRav
- F&M 326 — CFil WPGP
'Manteau d'Hermine' (d) $\mathbb{Y}^{H4}$ — Widely available
'Marjorie' — NLar
mexicanus — CFil GCal
- B&SWJ 10253 — WCru
- 'Rose Syringa' — CExl CFil CGHE EBee SKHP WPGP
mexicanus × ***palmeri*** — WPGP
microphyllus — CDul CHel CMCN CTri EBee ELan ELon EPfP LAst MAsh MGos MRav MWhi SKHP SLon SPer SPhx SPoG SSpi WKif WPGP WPat WSHC
'Miniature Snowflake' (d) — MAsh WPat
'Minnesota Snowflake' (d) — CBcs EBee EWes LRHS LSRN LSqu MMuc MRav NEgg NLar NPro SGol WGob
'Mont Blanc' — CBcs EBee GKin MRav NLar WGob
'Mrs E.L. Robinson' (d) — CMac EBee ELon LAst LLHF LRHS MAsh MGos NEgg NLar SHil WBor WCFE WPat
myrtoides B&SWJ 10436 — WCru
'Natchez' (d) — CMac ELon LLHF NLar WHar WPat
'Oeil de Pourpre' — MRav
palmeri — CFil CGHE WPGP WPat
pekinensis — CExl
'Perryhill' — MRav
'Polar Star' — ELon GBin NLar WKif
purpurascens — CExl EBee EPfP EWes GBin GQui LLHF MRav NLar SChF SKHP WGob WPGP WPat
- BWJ 7540 — WCru
× ***purpureomaculatus*** — ELon LLHF MAsh MRav WPat
sargentianus **new** — CFil

satsumi	SLPl
- B&SWJ 10811	WCru
- B&SWJ 11004	WCru
schrenkii	CFil NLar
- B&SWJ 8465	WCru
§ 'Silberregen'	CDul CHel CMac CSam EBee ELon EPfP LRHS MAsh MGos MMuc MRav NLar NPro SRms SWvt WGrn WPat
Silver Showers	see *P.* 'Silberregen'
'Snow Velvet'	EBee EPfP LLHF LRHS
'Snowbelle' (d)	EBee EPfP LBMP LRHS MAsh MBri MWat NBro NHol NLar SKHP SWvt
'Snowflake'	WMoo
'Souvenir de Billiard'	see *P. insignis*
'Starbright'	LRHS
subcanus	CExl
- L 524	CExl CFil WPGP
'Sybille' ♀H4	CDul CHel EBee EPfP LHop LRHS MAsh MRav MSwo SDix SKHP SPer SRms SSpi WKif WPat WSHC
tenuifolius	SLPl
tomentosus	CExl
- AC 3678 new	MSnd
- B&SWJ 2707	WCru
- GWJ 9215	WCru
'Virginal' (d)	Widely available
'Voie Lactée'	MRav WGob
White Icicle = 'Bialy Sopel'	CCCN
White Rock = 'Pekphil'	CMac EBee EPfP IVic LLHF LRHS LSRN MRav NLar SKHP SLim SPer
'Yellow Cab'	NEgg
'Yellow Hill'	CMac EPfP LRHS NEgg SKHP
zeyheri	SLPl

Philesia (*Philesiaceae*)

buxifolia	see *P. magellanica*
§ ***magellanica***	CExl CFil GGGa IBlr ITim SSpi WAbe WCru WSHC
- 'Rosea'	CWib EPfP IBlr SSpi

Phillyrea (*Oleaceae*)

angustifolia	CDul CFil CGHE CMCN EBee ELan EPfP EUJe EWTr IVic LRHS MBri MGos MRav NLar SBig SEND SPer SSpi WPGP XSen
- f. ***rosmarinifolia***	CCCN CExl ELan EPfP NLar SLPl
- - 'French Fries'	WPGP
decora	see *Osmanthus decorus*
§ ***latifolia***	CDul CFil CTsd EBee ELan EPfP EShb EUJe LRHS NLar SAPC SEND SSpi WPGP XSen
media	see *P. latifolia*

Philodendron (*Araceae*)

'Angra dos Reis'	see *P. cordatum*
§ ***angustisectum*** ♀H1	XBlo
bipinnatifidum ♀H1	EAmu SEND XBlo
corcovadense new	XBlo
§ ***cordatum*** new	XBlo
elegans	see *P. angustisectum*
erubescens 'Red Emerald'	XBlo
* ***radiatum***	XBlo
var. ***pseudoradiatum*** 'Simmonds' new	
* ***rubrum***	XBlo
scandens 'Green Emerald' new	XBlo
- 'Mica'	XBlo
tripartitum new	XBlo
xanadu	XBlo

Phlebodium (*Polypodiaceae*)

§ ***aureum*** ♀H1	CSpe
pseudoaureum	ISha WCot

Phleum (*Poaceae*)

phleoides	LRHS MMHG
pratense	EHoe MAvo NMir WSFF

Phlomis (*Lamiaceae*)

* ***anatolica***	LRHS NLar XSen
I - 'Lloyd's Variety'	CAbP CSam ELan LRHS MAsh NLar SPer
angustifolia	LRHS XSen
anisodonta white flowered	XSen
armeniaca	XSen
atropurpurea BWJ 7922	WCru
bourgaei	XSen
bovei subsp. ***maroccana***	SEND WHal WOut XLum XSen
breviflora HWJCM 250 new	WCru
capitata	XSen
cashmeriana	CCon CSam EHoe EPfP LAst LDai LSou MMuc NLar SBea SKHP SMad SPhx WCFE WWEG
chrysophylla ♀H3	CAbP ELan EPfP LRHS MAsh MRav NLar SDix SPer XSen
cretica	XSen
crinita	EBee XSen
cypria	XSen
× ***cytherea*** new	XSen
'Edward Bowles'	CDul CHel EBee LRHS LSRN MRav NLar SEND SIgm SKHP SLPl SWvt XSen
* 'Elliot's Variety'	CExl
fruticosa ♀H4	Widely available
grandiflora	SEND XSen
herba-venti	XSen
italica	Widely available
- 'Pink Glory'	CMac
lanata ♀H3-4	CAbP ELan EPfP LAst LRHS NLar SBrt SPer WCFE WKif XSen
- 'Pygmy'	CHVG XSen
'Le Sud'	XSen
leucophracta	SVen
longifolia	CHel EBee EPfP LHop LRHS MNrw NLar SEND SKHP SPer WGrn WPGP XSen
- var. ***bailanica***	CSam EPfP LRHS XLum
lunariifolia	XSen
lychnitis	XSen
lycia	XSen
macrophylla	SPhx
× ***margaritae*** new	XSen
monocephala	XSen
nissolei	XSen
platystegia	XSen
purpurea	CAbP CArn CExl ELan EPfP LRHS MAsh MNrw NBir SEND WGrn XSen
- ***alba***	EPfP LRHS SKHP XSen
- subsp. ***almeriensis***	CCse CPom XSen
- subsp. ***caballeroi***	XSen
§ ***russeliana*** ♀H4	Widely available
- 'Dappled Shade' (v)	WCot
- 'Mosaic' (v)	MAvo XSen
samia Boiss.	see *P. russeliana*

samia L. CKno CMac CSpe EBee LBMP LDai LHop LRHS NBir NGdn NLar SEND SKHP WOut WPtf XSen
sieheana new XSen
taurica EPfP LRHS SEND SPhx
× ***termessi*** new XSen
tuberosa CArn CBcs CCon CKno CMac CPou EPfP EWTr LEdu LRHS LSRN MMuc NGdn NLar SDix SPet WPtf XLum XSen
- 'Amazone' CKno CSev EBee EPfP GBin LHop MBel MRav NBid NCGa NDov NOrc NPnk NSti SMad SMrm WMnd WSHC XSen
- 'Bronze Flamingo' CKno ECGP EPfP GMaP LAst LBMP LPio LRHS LSou MNrw MPnt MRav NOrc SKHP WMnd WWEG
viscosa misapplied see *P. russeliana*

Phlox ✿ (*Polemoniaceae*)

adsurgens ♀H4 WAbe
- 'Alba' WAbe
- 'Red Buttes' ECho
- 'Wagon Wheel' CMea EBee ECho ECtt EPot EWes GBuc LBMP LHop LPio LRHS NHar SPlb SRms SRot WAbe WIce
amplifolia NBre XLum
× ***arendsii*** 'Aureole' LSou
- 'Autumn's Pink Explosion' WCot
- 'Babyface' LSou NGdn SPet
- 'Casablanca' EBee NDov SMrm
- 'Dougal' WCot
- 'Dylan' WCot
- 'Early Star' EBee LSou
- 'Eyecatcher' NBro
- 'Gary' WCot
- 'Hesperis' CAby EBee ELon GBin GQue IPot MAvo NDov NLar SMrm SPhx WHil
- 'Lilac Girl' NBre
- 'Luc's Lilac' CAby CPrp ECtt EPPr GBin LLHF LRHS MCot MSpe NBro NCGa NDov NEgg NGdn NSti SGbt SMrm SPhx WCAu WWlt
§ - 'Miss Jill' (Spring Pearl Series) EBee ELan EPfP SPet WCot
§ - 'Miss Karen' (Spring Pearl Series) ELan NBro
§ - 'Miss Margie' (Spring Pearl Series) LEdu
§ - 'Miss Mary' (Spring Pearl Series) ECtt ELan EPfP GMaP MSpe
§ - 'Miss Wilma' (Spring Pearl Series) ELan EPfP
- 'Neon Flare Blue' (Neon Series) LSou
- 'Paul' WCot
- 'Ping Pong' LDai SGbt
- 'Pink Attraction' MNrw NBro NCGa
- 'Purple Star' EBee
- 'Roger' WCot
- 'Rosa Star' NBre
- 'Sweet William' MSpe NEgg
- 'Utopia' CDes CSam EBee ELon IPot LPla NLar SMrm SPhx WCot
austromontana EPot GKev NWad
bifida ECho
- 'Alba' ECho LLHF MWat
- blue-flowered ECho
- 'Colvin's White' ECho
- 'Frohnleiten' NHar
- 'Minima Colvin' ECho EPot
- 'Ralph Haywood' CMea CPBP CWCL ECtt EPot
- 'Starcleft' NHol
- 'Thefi' EWes MNrw WIce
borealis see *P. sibirica* subsp. *borealis*
* - ***arctica*** EPot
bryoides see *P. hoodii* subsp. *muscoides*
caespitosa CMea ECho EWes
- subsp. ***pulvinata*** see *P. pulvinata*
- 'Zigeunerblut' CMea CPBP EPot ITim NHar NWad WAbe
canadensis see *P. divaricata*
carolina 'Bill Baker' ♀H4 CSam ECtt ELon EPPr EPfP LRHS LSRN MAsh MNrw NBir NCGa NGdn NLar NSti WCFE WKif WPtf WSHC WWEG XLum
- 'Magnificence' EWes NLar SMad SPhx WCot WSHC
- 'Miss Lingard' ♀H4 CSam ECtt ELon LRHS LSou MCot NBir NGdn NLar NSti SMrm WCot WWEG WWlt
'Charles Ricardo' LRHS WHoo
'Chattahoochee' see *P. divaricata* subsp. *laphamii* 'Chattahoochee'
§ ***condensata*** WAbe
Coral Flame (Flame Series) CMac LRHS LSou NPri SRkn
covillei see *P. condensata*
'Daniel's Cushion' see *P. subulata* 'McDaniel's Cushion'
diffusa EPot
§ ***divaricata*** ♀H4 SPlb
- 'Blue Dreams' CCon ECtt LRHS MNrw WHal WWlt
- 'Blue Perfume' ECtt NBro NGdn NLar
- 'Charles' XLum
- 'Clouds of Perfume' CWCL ECtt EPfP GBuc GMaP LLWG LRHS LSRN LSou MSCN MSpe NDov NEgg NLar NPnk SGbt SMrm SPoG STes SWvt WWEG
- 'Dirigo Ice' ECho LHop LRHS WSHC
- 'Eco Texas Purple' CPrp ECtt MSCN NCGa WSHC WWlt
- 'Fuller's White' CWCL ECtt LRHS
- subsp. ***laphamii*** EBee EWes
§ - - 'Chattahoochee' ♀H4 Widely available
- 'May Breeze' ECho ECtt GCra GMaP LHop LRHS MNrw MSCN NCGa NPnk WSHC WWEG WWlt
- 'Plum Perfect' ECtt LLHF
* - 'White Perfume' CPrp CWCL EWes LRHS LSou NBro NCGa NLar SMrm SPet WWEG XLum
douglasii SRms
- 'Alba' GJos
- 'Apollo' CTri ECho ECtt LLHF
- 'Boothman's Variety' ♀H4 CPBP ECho ECtt EDAr ELan EPfP EPot ITim MLHP MWat SRms
- 'Crackerjack' ♀H4 CMea CTri ECho ECtt EDAr ELan ELon EPfP EPot GAbr GJos GMaP ITim LRHS MAsh MHer MLHP MWat NBir NEgg NHol NSla SPoG WIce
- 'Eva' ECho ECtt EDAr ELon EPot GMaP ITim LHop LRHS LSRN MAsh MSCN NBir NLar NPri NSla NWad WNew
- 'Georg Arends' ECtt GJos
- 'Ice Mountain' CMea ECho ECtt ELan EPot GMaP NEgg NHol NWad SPoG SRot WNew

– 'Iceberg' ΨH4	GJos
– 'J.A. Hibberson'	EPot
– 'Lilac Cloud'	ECho ECtt EDAr GJos NPro NRya
– Lilac Queen	see *P. douglasii* 'Lilakönigin'
– 'Lilac Wonder'	CPBP
§ – 'Lilakönigin'	CTri
– 'Napoleon'	ECho ECtt EPot ITim LLHF NWad
– 'Ochsenblut'	ECho LLHF LRHS MHer MLHP MSCN NHar NLar
– 'Red Admiral' ΨH4	ECho ECtt EPfP EWes GMaP NLar NWad WCFE
– 'Rose Cushion'	ECho EDAr EWes MHer
– 'Rose Queen'	ECho
– 'Rosea'	ECho EDAr ELan MAsh WNew
– 'Silver Rose'	ECho ECtt MWat WRHF
– 'Sprite'	SRms
– 'Tycoon'	see *P. subulata* 'Tamaongalei'
– 'Violet Queen'	ECho EWes
– 'Waterloo'	CMea ECho ECtt EPot LRHS
I – 'White Admiral'	CTri ECho ECtt LHop LSRN
drummondii 'Classic Cassis'	LSou SPoG
I – 'Phlox of Sheep' ΨH3 **new**	CWCL
'Fancy Feelings' (Feelings Series)	NBro NLar
Flame White Edge **new**	STPC
glaberrima 'Morris Berd'	CDes EBee WSHC
hendersonii	WAbe
§ ***hoodii*** subsp. ***muscoides***	WAbe
idahoensis	SPhx
'Jeff's Pink'	MSCN WHlf
'Junior Surprise' PBR	GBin
'Kelly's Eye' ΨH4	CPBP ECho ECtt EPot LRHS NBir NHar SPoG
kelseyi	WAbe
– 'Lemhi Purple'	CPBP WAbe
– 'Rosette'	ECho
Light Pink Flame = 'Bareleven' PBR	ECtt EPfP NPri SPoG WHil
Lilac Flame = 'Barten' PBR	EPfP SPoG WHil
longifolia subsp. ***brevifolia***	CPBP WAbe
maculata	NOrc
– 'Alba'	WCAu
– 'Alpha' ΨH4	CPrp CSam CWCL EBee ECtt EPfP GBuc GCra GMaP LRHS MSpe MWhi NLar NOrc SGbt SKHP SPer SWvt WSHC XLum
– Avalanche	see *P. maculata* 'Schneelawine'
– 'Delta'	EBee EPPr GBuc LRHS NLar SGbt SPer SRkn SWvt
– 'Natascha'	Widely available
– 'Omega' ΨH4	CExl CMac CPrp EBee ECtt EWTr GAbr GBuc LHop LRHS MCot MNrw NGdn NLar NPnk SGbt SKHP SPer SWvt WCAu WWEG
– 'Princess Sturdza' ΨH4	SDix WCot
– 'Reine du Jour'	CSam ELon IVic LPla MSpe NDov SMrm SPhx WSHC
– 'Rosalinde'	CPrp ECtt ELon GAbr GBuc LRHS NHol NLar SWvt WCAu WSHC WWEG XLum
§ – 'Schneelawine'	SPer SPlb
'Matineus'	SPhx
'Millstream Blue'	EPfP
'Millstream Jupiter'	ECho
'Minnie Pearl'	EWes SKHP WCot
muscoides	see *P. hoodii* subsp. *muscoides*
'Mystic Green' **new**	LAst
nana 'Arroya'	WAbe
– 'Mary Maslin'	WAbe
nivalis 'Nivea'	GJos
– 'Jill Alexander'	SBch
paniculata	GCra NBid NDov SDix WCot
– 'A.E. Amos'	ELon
– 'Aida'	EBee
– var. ***alba***	MAvo SDix WCot
– 'Alba Grandiflora' ΨH4	GMaP MAvo MNrw WCot WHrl
– 'Albert Leo Schlageter' ΨH4	WHil
– 'Alexandra' PBR	MSCN
– 'All in One'	EBee ECtt LSou
– 'Amethyst' misapplied	see *P. paniculata* 'Lilac Time'
– 'Amethyst' Foerster	CCon CSam GQue LRHS NBir NLar NOrc SPet SWat WCAu
– 'Anne'	CSam
I – 'Aureovariegata Undulata' (v)	WCot
– 'Auslese D. Bach'	CSam
– 'Balmoral'	CMac EBee ECtt GCra LRHS MLHP NEgg NSti SMrs SWat SWvt WWEG
– 'Barnwell'	SWat
– 'Becky Towe' PBR (v)	CAby ECtt LLHF LRHS LSou MBri MNrw NEgg NHol NLar
– 'Betty Margarite'	NDov
– 'Blauer Morgen'	IPot
– 'Blue Boy'	COIW EBee ECtt ELan ELon EPfP GMaP LAst LRHS MJak NBir NBro NEgg NLar SKHP SMrm SRms SWvt WMnd
– 'Blue Evening'	MCot
– 'Blue Ice' ΨH4	NBro
– 'Blue Paradise'	Widely available
– 'Blushing Bride'	MSpe SRms
– 'Border Gem'	CAby CBcs CMac EBee ECtt ELon LAst LRHS MAvo MCot MRav MSpe MTis MWat NChi NHol NLar SDix SWat SWvt WBrk WHrl WSHC WWEG WWlt
– 'Branklyn'	GCra LRHS
– 'Brigadier' ΨH4	CPrp CTri EBee ECtt ELan ELon GMaP LRHS MCot MSpe MWat NEgg NGdn SMrm SPer SRms WWFP
– 'Bright Eyes' ΨH4	Widely available
– 'Burgi'	SDix
– 'Candy Floss'	ELon LLHF
– 'Cardinal'	MTis NDov
– 'Caroline van den Berg'	SRms
– 'Cecil Hanbury'	NLar
– 'Chintz'	MRav SRms
– 'Cinderella'	ECtt MTis
– 'Cool Best'	NDov
§ – 'Cool of the Evening'	EBee WKif
– 'Coral Queen'	MSpe
– 'Cosmopolitan' PBR	LSou MBri MNrw NCGa NLar
– Count Zeppelin	see *P. paniculata* 'Graf Zeppelin'
– 'Crème de Menthe' (v)	CWGN
– 'Danielle'	CSBt LSou MSCN SGol SPet WHil
– 'Darwin's Choice'	see *P. paniculata* 'Norah Leigh'
– 'David'	Widely available
– 'David's Lavender'	ELon
– 'Delilah' PBR	MAsh
– 'Discovery'	EWes MCot MRav MSpe NEgg SWat
– 'Doghouse Pink'	SDix
– 'Dresden China'	MTis SWat
§ – 'Düsterlohe'	CSBt CSam EBee ECtt GBin GBuc GQue MTis NBir NLar NSoo SGol SMrm SPer SWat WCot WHoo XLum

	- 'Early Light Pink'	IPot
	- 'Early Velvet'	IPot
	- 'Eclaireur' misapplied	see *P. paniculata* 'Düsterlohe'
	- 'Eclaireur' Lemoine	SWat
	- 'Eden's Crush'	NBre
	- 'Eden's Flash'	CElw ECtt LRHS MSpe NBre
	- 'Eden's Glow'	WHil
	- 'Eden's Smile'	ECtt
	- 'Elisabeth' (v)	EPfP LSRN WHil
	- 'Elizabeth Arden'	ECtt MAvo NLar SWat
	- 'Elizabeth Campbell'	GCal
	- 'Empty Feelings' (Feelings Series)	NBro
	- 'Etoile de Paris'	see *P. paniculata* 'Toits de Paris' Symons-Jeune
	- 'Europa'	EBee ECtt ELan MCot NBir NGdn NLar SPer WCAu
	- 'Eva Cullum'	CSam EBee ECtt ELan ELon EPfP GCra GMaP LHop LRHS MArl MBri MCot MSpe NHol NLar SPer SPet SWat WCAu WCot WWEG WWlt
	- 'Eva Foerster'	XLum
	- 'Eventide' ♀H4	CMac CSam ECtt EPfP LHop LPot LRHS MArl MCot MNrw MRav MSpe MWat SPer SPet SWat WPtf
	- 'Excelsior'	MRav
	- 'Ferris Wheel'	LSou MBri NCGa SRot
	- 'Flamingo'	EBee ECtt LRHS NLar SWvt XLum
	- 'Fondant Fancy' PBR	LSou MBri NLar SPoG
	- 'Franz Schubert'	CAby CSam EBee ECtt ELan EPfP EWTr GBin GCra LPot LRHS MBel MBri MCot MLHP MSpe MWat NBir NGdn NLar NSti SPer SWat SWvt WCot WKif WWEG WWlt
§	- 'Frau Alfred von Mauthner'	COlW SMrm
	- 'Frosted Elegance' (v)	EBee MAvo WWEG
	- 'Fujiyama'	see *P. paniculata* 'Mount Fuji'
	- 'Giltmine' (v)	EBee
	- 'Goldmine' PBR (v)	LSou MNrw NSti SPoG WCot
§	- 'Graf Zeppelin'	ECtt ELan MTis NHol SRms XLum
	- 'Grenadine Dream' PBR	EBee LAst LSou MBri SPoG
	- 'Harlequin' (v)	CBcs CMac CWGN ECtt ELon GMaP LRHS MAvo MHol NBro NEgg NLar NSti SPer SPoG WCot WWEG WWlt
	- 'Irene Mast'	CSam
	- 'Iris'	MNrw SMrm SRms WCot
	- 'Jade'	CWGN EBee ECGP ECtt ELon GQue LBMP LRHS MAvo MBel MCot MHol MNrw MPie NLar NSti WCot WHlf XLum
	- 'Judy'	LSRN NBro NCGa NLar
	- 'Jules Sandeau'	LRHS
§	- 'Juliglut'	SWat WCot
	- July Glow	see *P. paniculata* 'Juliglut'
	- 'Junior Bouquet'	NLar
	- 'Junior Dance'	NLar NSoo
	- 'Junior Dream'	LRHS NLar SPad
	- 'Junior Fountain'	NLar
	- 'Katarina'	CElw ECtt NLar
	- 'Katherine'	NLar
	- 'Kirchenfürst'	CElw IPot LPla LRHS NBir SMrm XLum
	- 'Kirmesländler'	ECtt GBin IPot NLar SWat
	- 'Lads Pink'	SDix
	- 'Lady Clare'	SRms
	- 'Landhochzeit'	EBee
	- 'Laura'	ECtt ELon EPfP GBin IPot LHop LRHS MTis NBro NCGa NHol NPri SGol SMrm SPet SRkn SRms STes SWvt WBor WHoo WMnd WSHC XLum
§	- 'Lavendelwolke'	CSam GCal NBir NLar SWat
	- Lavender Cloud	see *P. paniculata* 'Lavendelwolke'
	- 'Le Mahdi' ♀H4	MTis SRms SWat
	- 'Lichtspel'	LPla NDov SPhx
	- 'Lila Miniatur'	NDov
§	- 'Lilac Time'	CElw EBee ECtt ELon EPfP GKev LRHS LSRN MMuc NLar NSoo SWat SWvt WWEG
	- 'Little Boy'	CElw ECtt ELon LRHS MNrw NLar NSoo SGbt WHil
	- 'Little Laura'	CElw CWGN ECtt EWTr LRHS LSRN MSpe NHol NLar NOrc NPri NWad SDix SPoG WCot WWlt
	- 'Little Princess'	ELon LLHF NLar SMrm WHil WMnd
	- 'Little Sara'	NDov
	- 'Lizzy' PBR	NLar
	- 'Logan Black'	EBee GCal MAvo
	- 'Magic Blue'	LSou SPoG
	- 'Manoir d'Hézèques'	WCot
	- 'Mary Christine' (v)	CDes NBid
	- 'Maude Stella Dagley'	MSpe
	- 'Mia Ruys'	MArl MLHP
	- 'Midnight Feelings' (Feelings Series)	NBro NLar
	- 'Milly van Hoboken'	WKif
	- 'Miss Elie'	NBre
	- 'Miss Holland'	NGdn SGbt SPet WWEG XLum
	- 'Miss Jill'	see *P.* × *arendsii* 'Miss Jill'
	- 'Miss Karen'	see *P.* × *arendsii* 'Miss Karen'
	- 'Miss Kelly'	LRHS LSou MSpe NLar WHoo WWlt
	- 'Miss Margie'	see *P.* × *arendsii* 'Miss Margie'
	- 'Miss Mary'	see *P.* × *arendsii* 'Miss Mary'
	- 'Miss Pepper'	CWCL ECtt ELon LSou MMuc MSpe NGdn NLar SEND SGol SMrm SRkn WBor WHil
	- 'Miss Universe'	NBre WWEG
	- 'Miss Wilma'	see *P.* × *arendsii* 'Miss Wilma'
	- 'Monica Lynden-Bell'	Widely available
	- 'Mother of Pearl' ♀H4	ECtt GQue IPot LRHS MAvo MSpe MWat NEgg SPer WWEG
§	- 'Mount Fuji' ♀H4	Widely available
	- 'Mount Fujiyama'	see *P. paniculata* 'Mount Fuji'
	- 'Mrs A.E. Jeans'	SRms
	- 'Mystique Black'	LSou WPtf
	- 'Natural Feelings' PBR (Feelings Series)	NBro NLar WWlt
	- 'Newbird'	ECtt EPfP IBoy LRHS SRms WWEG
	- 'Nicky'	see *P. paniculata* 'Düsterlohe'
	- 'Nirvana'	CSam
§	- 'Norah Leigh' (v)	Widely available
	- 'Orange Perfection'	see *P. paniculata* 'Prince of Orange'
	- 'Othello'	CSam ECGP ECtt LRHS MSpe NSti SMrs WMnd WWlt
	- 'Otley Choice'	CSam EBee ECtt LRHS MRav MWat NLar NSti SWat WHrl
	- 'Otley Purple'	MHer
	- 'P.D. Williams'	WCot
	- 'Pallas Athene' **new**	IPot
	- 'Pastorale'	WCot
	- Peacock Lilac (Peacock Series) **new**	EPfP
	- 'Peppermint Twist'	CWCL CWGN EBee ELon GKev LRHS LSou MAsh MBri MHol MMuc MNrw MTis NEgg NHol NLar SMad SPad SPoG SWvt WCot WHil
	- 'Picasso'	EBee ECtt LSou

	– 'Pina Colada'PBR	CWGN LSou MAvo NLar SPoG WHil
	– Pink Eye Flame = 'Barthirtyfive'PBR	EPfP LBMP LRHS LSou NPri SKHP SPoG WHil
	– 'Pink Lady' **new**	LAst MSCN
	– Pink Red Eye Flame	EPfP LRHS LSou NPri SPoG
	– 'Pinky Hill'	CElw CSBt EBee
	– 'Pleasant Feelings'PBR (Feelings Series)	NBro
	– 'Popeye'	LPla NLar
	– 'Prime Minister'	ELon
§	– 'Prince of Orange' ♀H4	Widely available
	– 'Prospero' ♀H4	CSam CSpe LRHS MCot MRav NBid SWat
	– Purple Eye Flame = 'Barthirtythree'PBR	LLHF LRHS LSou NPri SHar SKHP SWvt WHil
	– 'Purple Kiss'PBR	CWGN LSou MAvo MHer WHil
	– 'Rainbow'	ELon
	– 'Rectory Pink'	MSpe
	– 'Red Caribbean'	LSou
	– 'Red Feelings' (Feelings Series)	NBro
	– 'Red Flame'	CBct CWGN EBee ECtt EPfP GBin LRHS LSou MHol SKHP WHil
	– 'Red Indian'	MCot
	– 'Red Riding Hood'	ECtt EWTr IBoy LAst LRHS LSou MAsh MBri MSCN SPet SRkn
I	– 'Reddish Hesperis'	MAvo NDov
	– 'Rembrandt'	CExl ELon EPfP LRHS MTis XLum
	– 'Rijnstroom'	CBcs ECtt ELon LRHS MArl MSpe NLar SMrm SRot WBrk
	– 'Robert Poore'	ELon
	– 'Rosa Goliath'	CSam
	– 'Rosa Pastell'	CAby CElm CSpe EBee EGGP ECtt ELon GQue IPot ITim LHop LPla MAvo MBel MCot MHol MSCN MTis NDov SMrm SPer SPoG WCot WWlt
	– 'Rosanne'	MAvo
	– 'Rowie'	NBid
	– 'Rubymine' (v)	LLHF
	– 'Sandringham'	LRHS MArl MLHP MRav MSpe NBir NHol SPer SPoG SWvt
§	– 'Schneerausch'	LPla SPhx
	– 'Septemberglut'	EBee EPfP LRHS MTis NLar
	– 'Sir Malcolm Campbell'	IPot
	– 'Skylight'	LSRN NBre NBro SDix
	– 'Snow White'	NBre
	– Snowdrift	see *P. paniculata* 'Schneerausch'
	– 'Speed Limit 45'	WCot
	– 'Spitfire'	see *P. paniculata* 'Frau Alfred von Mauthner'
	– 'Starburst'	NBro
	– 'Starfire' ♀H4	Widely available
	– 'Starlight'	NHar
	– 'Steeple Bumpstead'	WCot
	– 'Sternhimmel'	LPla
	– 'Strawberry Daiquiri'	LSou MAsh NCGa SPoG
	– Sweet Summer Candy = 'Ditosdre'PBR **new**	MAsh
	– Sweet Summer Dream = 'Ditomdre'PBR **new**	MAsh
	– Sweet Summer Melody = 'Ditosmel'PBR **new**	MAsh
	– Sweet Summer Surprise = 'Ditomsur'PBR **new**	MAsh
	– Sweet Summer Temptation = 'Ditostem'PBR **new**	MAsh
	– 'Swizzle'	CWGN LSou MAsh MBri MHer NCGa SMrm SPoG WBor
	– 'Tempest'	LRHS
	– 'Tenor'	CAby CCon CMac CTri ECtt ELon EPfP GBuc IBoy LAst LRHS MCot NHol NLar SPet SPoG SWvt WGwG WSHC WWEG
	– 'Tequila Sunrise'	MBri
	– 'The King'	EBee ECtt LRHS MAvo NBro NLar SWat WHlf WSHC
	– 'Tiara' (d)	EBee ECtt ELon IPot LRHS LSou MBri MHol MPie MTis NCGa NLar SPer SWvt WCot
	– 'Toits de Paris' misapplied	see *P. paniculata* 'Cool of the Evening'
§	– 'Toits de Paris' Symons-Jeune	MAvo WSHC
	– 'Twister'	LSou MAsh MAvo
	– 'Uspekh'	CAby COlW CSam EBee ECtt EPPr EWes LRHS MCot MRav MSpe MWhi NBro NLar NOrc NSti SMrs SPer WCAu WGwG WHrl WWEG
	– 'Van Gogh'	CCse
	– 'Velvet Flame'	CAbP EPfP LBMP LSou MBel NPri SKHP WHil
	– 'Vintage Wine'	MNrw
	– 'Violetta Gloriosa'	ELon LPla SMrm
	– 'Visions'	WHil
	– 'Watermelon Punch'	LSou MBri MHer NLar
	– 'Wendy House'	EBee ECtt LEdu LLHF MNrw NHol
	– 'White Admiral' ♀H4	Widely available
	– White Flame = 'Bartwentynine'PBR	CBct ECtt EPfP GBin LBMP LRHS LSou NPri SKHP SWvt WCot WHil
	– 'Wilhelm Kesselring'	EBee ECtt ELon NBre WBor
	– 'Windsor' ♀H4	EBee ECtt ELon EPfP LRHS MSpe NDov NEgg NHol NLar SPoG SRms SWvt WCAu WWEG
	– 'Younique White' **new**	MAsh
	'Petticoat'	CMea CPBP ECtt EPot MWat NHar SBch WIce
	Pink Flame = 'Bartwelve'PBR	CBct EPfP GBin LLHF LRHS LSou NPri SPoG
	'Pride of Rochester'	ECtt GJos LHop LRHS
	× ***procumbens*** 'Variegata' (v)	ECho ECtt SRot
§	***pulvinata***	WAbe
	Purple Flame = 'Barfourteen'PBR	CBct EPfP GBin LBMP LSou NPri SPoG
	× ***rugelii***	LPot
	'Sherbet Cocktail'PBR	CWGN EBee NHol NLar WCot WHil WPtf
§	***sibirica*** subsp. ***borealis***	EDAr
	stolonifera	IFro MNrw
I	– 'Alba'	EBee EPfP NSoo
	– 'Ariane'	ECtt EWld IPot LSou MCot SBch
	– 'Blue Ridge' ♀H4	CExl ECtt EPfP EWld LRHS LSRN MCot MHol NSoo SRms
	– 'Fran's Purple'	ECtt EWld MNrw NBro SBch WCFE
	– 'Home Fires'	ECho ECtt EPfP LEdu LRHS MCot NBro SMrm SPlb WHil XLum
	– 'Montrose Tricolor' (v)	NBro
	– 'Pink Ridge'	SBch
	– 'Purpurea'	EPfP LEdu LSou
	– 'Violet Vere'	LRHS
	subulata 'Alexander's Surprise'	CMea ECho ECtt EDAr EPfP EPot LBee LRHS MAsh NBir NLar SPlb
	– 'Amazing Grace'	CTri CWCL ECho EDAr EPfP EPot EWes IPot LAst LHop LRHS NWad SPoG WIce
	– 'Apple Blossom'	NHol SPet SPoG SRms
	– 'Atropurpurea'	EDAr EPfP LRHS SPoG XLum

	- 'Bavaria'	CMea IPot LLHF
	- Beauty of Ronsdorf	see *P. subulata* 'Ronsdorfer Schöne'
	- 'Blue Eyes'	see *P. subulata* 'Oakington Blue Eyes'
	- 'Bonita'	CPBP ECho ECtt EPot GJos LRHS MAsh MMuc NLar WHoo WIce XLum
	- 'Bressingham Blue Eyes'	see *P. subulata* 'Oakington Blue Eyes'
	- 'Candy Stripe'	see *P. subulata* 'Tamaongalei'
	- 'Cavaldes White'	SPoG
	- 'Drumm'	see *P. subulata* 'Tamaongalei'
	- 'Emerald Cushion'	CMea CTri CWCL ECho ECtt EDAr ELon LAst MHol MWat NHol NLar SGbt WCFE WHil WNew WRHF
	- 'Emerald Cushion Blue'	CExl CTri ECho ECtt EPfP GJos LAst LRHS MAsh NBir NPnk NPri NPro SBch SPlb SPoG WAbe
	- 'G.F. Wilson'	see *P. subulata* 'Lilacina'
*	- 'Holly'	ECtt EPot ITim LLHF NHol NWad
	- 'Jupiter'	ECho
	- 'Kimono'	see *P. subulata* 'Tamaongalei'
§	- 'Lilacina'	CMea ECho ECtt MAsh WIce
§	- 'Maischnee'	CPBP CTri ECho ECtt MAsh MWat SPlb
	- 'Marjorie'	ECho ECtt GJos LBee MHer NBir SPoG WNew
	- May Snow	see *P. subulata* 'Maischnee'
§	- 'McDaniel's Cushion' ♀H4	CExl CHel ECho ECtt EDAr ELan ELon EPfP EPot GAbr GJos LAst LBee LHop LRHS MAsh MHol MLHP MMuc MSCN NHar NLar NPnk SPlb SPoG WCFE WHil WHoo WIce
	- 'Mikado'	see *P. subulata* 'Tamaongalei'
	- 'Millstream Daphne'	ECho
	- 'Moonlight'	ECtt EDAr GJos
	- 'Nettleton Variation' (v)	ECho ECtt EDAr ELon EPfP EPot EWes GKev LHop LRHS NLar NRya SPoG WIce
§	- 'Oakington Blue Eyes'	CTri SRms
	- 'Pink Pearl'	EWes
	- 'Purple Beauty'	CMea ECho ECtt EHyd EPot GJos LAst LHop LLHF LRHS NHar NWad SBch SPoG STes WCFE WSHC XLum
	- 'Red Wings' ♀H4	CMea ECho ECtt EPfP SRms
§	- 'Ronsdorfer Schöne'	EPot LBee LLHF NBir
	- 'Samson'	EDAr LSRN MMuc
	- 'Sarah'	LLHF
	- 'Scarlet Flame'	CBar CMea ECho ECtt EDAr EPfP EPot MAsh NHol SBch WHil WHoo WRHF
	- 'Snow Queen'	see *P. subulata* 'Maischnee'
	- 'Snowflake'	MSCN
§	- 'Tamaongalei'	CMea CTri ECtt EDAr ELon EPfP EPot EWes GJos GKev GMaP LAst LRHS MHol MMuc MSCN NWad SEND SPet STes WCFE WHil WHoo WIce WNew
	- 'Temiskaming'	CTri ECho ECtt EDAr EWes LHop LRHS MLHP SRms WSHC
	- 'Tschernobyl'	EPot
	- 'White Delight'	CMea ECho ECtt EDAr EPfP GJos LAst LBee LRHS MAsh SPet SPoG STes WHil
	- 'Winifred'	NEgg
	'Swirly Burly'	GQue NLar
	'Tiny Bugles'	CPBP
	Violet Flame = 'Barsixtyone'	EPfP LRHS MAvo NPri STPC WCot
	White Eye Flame = 'Barsixty'	CHel EPfP LRHS
	'White Kimono'	ECho LHop LRHS
	'Zwergenteppich'	LLHF

Phoenicaulis (*Brassicaceae*)

§	***cheiranthoides***	LLHF

Phoenix (*Arecaceae*)

acaulis new	EAmu
canariensis ♀H1+3	CBcs CExl CWib EAmu EGri EPfP EUJe IVic MBri MMuc MREP NPri NSoo SAPC SBst SEND SPlb SPoG STrG
dactylifera (F)	EAmu SBig
reclinata	EAmu XBlo
roebelenii ♀H1+3	CDTJ CDoC MBri SBig
- 'Multistem'	XBlo
rupicola	EAmu
sylvestris	EAmu
theophrasti	CPHo EAmu

Phormium ✿ (*Hemerocallidaceae*)

§	'Alison Blackman'PBR	CBcs CDoC CKno COIW EBee EPfP ESwi GBin IVic LHop LRHS LSRN MAsh MBri MGos MJak MRav NPla NSoo SCoo SEND SHil SPoG SRkn SWvt
	'Amazing Red'	EBee
	'Apricot Queen' (v)	CAbb CBcs CCCN CDoC CSBt CWib EBee EPfP LRHS LSRN MBri MGos NEgg NLar SBod SEND SEWo SHil SPer SPoG
	Back in Black = 'Seilack'PBR	NPri NSoo
	'Black Edge'	MRav
	'Black Rage'	CBcs EPfP LRHS
	Black Velvet = 'Seivel'	IBoy LBuc MSwo NPla NPri NSoo
	'Bronze Baby'	CBcs CCCN CDoC CEnd COIW CSBt EBee ECtt EHoe ELan ELon EPfP LRHS LSRN MAsh MGos MRav MSwo MWat NSoo SLim SPer SPoG SWvt
	'Buckland Ruby'	CDoC
	'Chocolate Fingers'	CBcs
	'Chocomint'PBR	CBcs
	colensoi	see *P. cookianum*
§	***cookianum***	CHEx EPfP GGal SAPC
	- 'Alpinum Purpureum'	see *P. tenax* 'Nanum Purpureum'
	- 'Black Adder'PBR	CBcs ELon EPfP EUJe IBoy LBuc LPio LRHS LSRN MAsh SEND SPoG
	- dwarf	SLPl
	- 'Flamingo' (v)	CBcs CCCN CDTJ CSBt EBee ELan ELon EPfP LRHS LSou MBri MGos MHol NLar SEWo SLim SPer SPoG SRkn
	- subsp. ***hookeri*** 'Cream Delight' (v) ♀H3-4	CAbb CBcs CCCN CDoC CEnd COIW CSBt CWib EBee EHoe EPfP EUJe LRHS LSRN MAsh MGos MRav MSwo NPri SCoo SGol SHil SPer SWvt WGrn
	- - 'Tricolor' (v) ♀H3-4	CBcs CDTJ CDoC CDul CSBt CWib EAmu EBee EHoe ELan ELon EPfP EUJe GBuc LRHS MGos MRav MWat NPla SAPC SEND SGol SHil SLPl SLim SPer SPoG SRms SWvt WGrn
	'Crimson Devil'	CBcs LRHS NPri SHil SLim

	Dark Avocado = 'Westado'PBR	EBee MAsh SLim
	'Dark Delight'	CBcs CDoC
	'Dazzler' (v)	CDoC
	'Duet' (v) ♀H3	CCCN CDoC CWib EHoe EPfP LRHS SEND SEWo SWvt
	'Dusky Chief'	CSBt EPfP LRHS
	'Dusky Princess'	LRHS
	'Emerald Isle'	CDoC
	'Evening Glow' (v)	CBcs CCCN CSBt EBee ELan ELon EPfP EUJe LRHS LSRN MBri MGos NLar NPri SEND SEWo SPoG SRkn SWvt WGrn
	'Firebird'	EUJe LSRN SWvt
	'Glowing Embers'	CBcs COIW EAmu ELon
	'Gold Ray'	CBcs EBee LRHS MBri NPri SCoo SHil SWvt
	'Gold Sword' (v)	CCCN CDoC CSBt EBee EPfP LRHS MAsh NEgg
	'Golden Alison'	see *P.* 'Alison Blackman'
	'Golden Ray' (v)	EUJe LRHS NSoo
	'Green Sword'	CBcs CCCN
	'Jack Spratt' (v)	CBcs ECou EHoe SWvt
	'Jester' (v)	Widely available
	'Limelight'	SWvt
§	'Maori Chief' (v)	CSBt EPfP LRHS SWvt
§	'Maori Maiden' (v)	CBcs CCCN CDoC CDul CTri EBee EHoe ELon EPfP MGos MRav MSwo SWvt
§	'Maori Queen' (v)	CBcs CCCN CDTJ CDoC COIW CSBt EBee ELan ELon EPfP LRHS MBri MGos MSwo NLar NPri NSoo SCoo SEND SHil SLPl SPer SPoG SWvt
§	'Maori Sunrise' (v)	CBcs CCCN CDoC EBee ELon EPfP IArd LRHS LSRN MGos MRav NPla SCoo SLim SPer SWvt
	'Margaret Jones'PBR	CCCN CKno LSRN SLim
	'Merlot'PBR	NPri
	'Moonraker'	CBcs MHol
	'Pink Panther' (v)	CAbb CBcs CCCN CDoC CWib EBee ELan ELon EPfP LRHS LSRN MBri MGos MRav MSwo NGdn NPla NPri SCoo SHil SPer SPoG
	'Pink Stripe' (v)	CBcs CDoC CSBt EAmu EBee LRHS MAsh MBri MGos MJak NPri NSoo SHil SPoG SWvt WCot
	'Platt's Black'	CBcs CCCN CDoC EAmu EPfP EUJe EWes IBoy LAst LRHS LSRN MBri MGos MJak MRav MSwo NBir NPla SCoo SHil SLim SPer SPoG SRkn SWvt WGrn
	'Rainbow Chief'	see *P.* 'Maori Chief'
	'Rainbow Maiden'	see *P.* 'Maori Maiden'
	'Rainbow Queen'	see *P.* 'Maori Queen'
	'Rainbow Sunrise'	see *P.* 'Maori Sunrise'
	'Red Fingers'	CBcs
	'Red Sensation'	ELon EPfP LRHS SEWo
I	'Rubrum'	EUJe LRHS
	'Sundowner' (v) ♀H3	CBcs CCCN CDoC CDul CSBt CTsd EBee EHoe ELan EPfP LHop LRHS MAsh MBri MGos MJak MRav NBir NEgg NLar SCoo SEND SHil SLim SPer SPlb SPoG SWvt WGrn
	'Sunset' (v)	CBcs CCCN CSBt EUJe NPri SWvt
	'Surfer' (v)	CBcs MBel MBri WGrn
	'Surfer Bronze'	CBcs CCCN CSBt LSou
	'Surfer Green'	CCCN
	'Sussex Velvet'	SCoo SLim
	'Taya'	CBcs
	tenax ♀H4	Widely available
	- 'All Black'PBR	LRHS MBri MGos SCoo SHil
	- 'Bronze'	CTsd SWvt
	- 'Chocolate Dream'	EPfP
	- 'Co-ordination'	CBcs CCCN EPfP
	- 'Deep Purple'	CHEx
	- dwarf	CSpe SLPl
I	- 'Giganteum'	CHEx
	- In The Red = 'Seied'PBR **new**	MHol
	- 'Joker' (v)	CBcs ELon
*	- ***lineatum***	MMuc SEND
§	- 'Nanum Purpureum'	SAPC
	- Purpureum Group ♀H3-4	CBar CDoC CDul CHEx COIW CSBt CWib EBee ELan ELon EPfP LRHS MMuc MRav MSwo MWat NEgg NGdn NLar NSoo SEND SEWo SGol SLim SLon SPer SPlb SPoG WPGP
	- Sweet Mist = 'Phos2'PBR	NOak
	- 'Tiny Tiger' **new**	EPfP
	- 'Variegatum' (v) ♀H3-4	CDTJ CDoy EBee ELon EPfP EUJe LRHS MGos MJak MMuc MWat NPri NSoo SAPC SEND SEWo SPer SRms
	- 'Veitchianum' (v)	EUJe SPer
	'Thumbelina'	CBcs CCCN
	'Tom Thumb'	CBcs
	'Yellow Wave' (v) ♀H3	Widely available

Photinia ✿ (*Rosaceae*)

	beauverdiana var. ***notabilis***	EPfP
	Corallina = 'Bourfrits'PBR	NLar
	davidiana	CDul CMac CTri ELan EPfP MRav NLar SRms SVen
	- 'Palette' (v)	CBcs CDul CEnd CMac CWib EBee EHoe ELan ELon EPfP LAst LHop LRHS MAsh MGos MMuc MSwo NEgg NPri SGol SLim SPer SPoG SRms SWvt WMoo
	- var. ***undulata*** 'Fructu Luteo'	CAbP GGal MMuc MRav SEND
	- - 'Prostrata'	CMac CTri MRav NLar
	× ***fraseri*** 'Allyn Sprite'PBR	NEgg
I	- 'Atropurpurea Nana'	EPfP LBMP MGos
	- 'Birmingham'	CMac EBee EWes
	- 'Camilvy'	CEnd EBee EWes IVic LRHS MBri SGol SHil
	- Cracklin' Red = 'Parred'	ELon MBri MPkF WMoo
	- Dynamo Red = 'Parsur'	MBri
	- Fireball Red = 'Parbri'	CWSG MBri
*	- 'Ilexifolium'	ESwi
	- 'Little Red Robin'	Widely available
	- Pink Marble = 'Cassini' (v)	CBcs CEnd EBee ELan EPfP EUJe LBuc LRHS MAsh MBri MJak MPkF NPri NSoo SGol SHil SLim SLon SPer SPoG SRms
	- 'Purple Peter'	CEnd
	- 'Red Robin' ♀H4	Widely available
	- 'Red Select'	NPri WPat
	- 'Robusta'	CMac EPfP LRHS SWvt
	glabra	SAPC
§	- 'Parfait' (v)	CAbP LRHS MAsh SLon
	- 'Pink Lady'	see *P. glabra* 'Parfait'
	- 'Rubens'	EPfP LRHS MAsh MRav WPat
	- 'Variegata'	see *P. glabra* 'Parfait'
	integrifolia HWJ 946	WCru
	lasiogyna	CMCN
	lucida	WCru

	microphylla B&SWJ 11837	WCru
	- HWJ 564	WCru
	niitakayamensis	IGor MSnd
	parvifolia	EPfP
	'Redstart'	CAbP CMac EBee ELan EPfP LRHS LSou NEgg NLar NPro SEND SLon SPer SWvt WMoo
§	***serratifolia***	CAbP CBcs CDul CHEx EBee ELan EPfP NLar SAPC SBrt SEND SPer
	- Curly Fantasy = 'Kolcurl' PBR	EBee IVic LRHS MRav NLar NSoo SPoG
	- 'Jenny'	LRHS NEgg NLar
	serrulata	see *P. serratifolia*
§	Super Hedge = 'Branpara' PBR	EShb LRHS LSou MSwo
	'Super Red'	CSBt EBee NLar SLim
	villosa ♀H4	CAbP CTho MSnd SPoG
	- B&SWJ 8665	WCru
	- var. ***coreana*** B&SWJ 8789	WCru
	- var. ***laevis***	CExl EPfP MBri
	- - B&SWJ 8877	WCru
	- f. ***maximowicziana***	EPfP MBri
*	- var. ***zollingeri*** B&SWJ 8903	WCru

Phragmites (*Poaceae*)

	sp.	CHab
	from Sichuan, China	EPPr
§	***australis***	CBAq CHab CWat MSKA NLar NMir SEND SVic SWat WMAq WPnP XLum
	- subsp. ***australis*** var. ***striatopictus***	EPPr
	- - 'Variegatus' (v)	CKno CWat EBee EPPr EShb LLWG LRHS MMuc MWhi NBir NLar NWsh SEND SMad WWEG XLum
	- subsp. ***humilis***	CHab
	- subsp. ***pseudodonax***	EBee EPPr MMoz
	communis	see *P. australis*
	karka	EPPr
	- 'Candy Stripe' (v)	EPPr MSKA

Phuopsis (*Rubiaceae*)

§	***stylosa***	CHVG CTri EBee ELan ELon EPfP EUJe GAbr GBin GMaP IFoB LRHS LSou MHer MLHP MMuc NBid NBir NBro NChi SPoG SRms SWvt WMoo WPtf XLum
	- 'Purpurea'	ECGP MNrw MRav NChi NDov

Phygelius ✿ (*Scrophulariaceae*)

	aequalis	CTca MRav WMoo
	- ***albus***	see *P. aequalis* 'Yellow Trumpet'
	- 'Aureus'	see *P. aequalis* 'Yellow Trumpet'
	- 'Cream Trumpet'	see *P. aequalis* 'Yellow Trumpet'
	- 'Indian Chief'	see *P.* × *rectus* 'African Queen'
	- 'Pink Trumpet'	SMrm SPet
	- 'Sani Pass'	CPrp ELon EPfP GMaP MHer SPet SPlb SWvt
	- 'Trewidden Pink' ♀H4	CWib EBee ELan ELon EPfP GBin LHop MSCN SLim SWvt WMnd WMoo WWEG XLum
§	- 'Yellow Trumpet' ♀H3-4	CBcs CSBt CTca CWib EBee ELan ELon EPfP GMaP IBoy LSRN MAsh MLHP SEND SLim SPet SWvt WMnd WMoo WWEG XLum
	(Candy Drops Series) Candy Drops Peach = 'Kerphypeach' PBR	SVic
	- Candy Drops Salmon Orange = 'Kerphysalm' PBR	LRHS
	- Candy Drops Tangerine = 'Kerphytan' PBR	SVic
§	***capensis*** ♀H3-4	CDoy CHll CWib ELan GCra GGal MHer SPet SRms WMnd WOut
	- ***coccineus***	see *P. capensis*
	- orange-flowered	LHop
	'Golden Gate'	see *P. aequalis* 'Yellow Trumpet'
	Logan form	GBin
	'Midas Touch'	CHel ELon NLar SPad
	New Sensation = 'Blaphy' PBR	EPfP LRHS MRav SWvt
	'Passionate' PBR	NLar
§	× ***rectus*** 'African Queen' ♀H3-4	ELan EPfP LPot MLHP MRav MSwo NBir NGdn SEND SMad SPlb SWvt WKif WMnd WMoo WWEG XLum
	- 'Devil's Tears' ♀H4	CBcs CPrp ELan GKev LPot LRHS NEgg NLar SEND SLim SWvt WHil WMnd WMoo
	- 'Ivory Twist'	ELon LHop LRHS NLar
	- 'Jodie Southon'	ELon LSou SDys WCot
	- 'Moonraker'	CHll CPrp CTri EBee ELan EPfP GBin LHop LRHS MAsh MBri MHer MRav NEgg NGdn NLar SEND SMrm SPlb SRms WHil WKif WMoo XLum
	- 'Raspberry Swirl'	ELon LRHS
	- 'Salmon Leap' ♀H4	CTri EBee ELan EPfP GBin GBuc LRHS LSRN MBNS MGos MRav NEgg NLar SBod SEND SLim SMrm SPlb SWvt WMnd WMoo WWEG
	- Somerford Funfair Series **new**	IBoy
	- - Somerford Funfair Apricot = 'Yapapr'	SWvt
	- - Somerford Funfair Coral = 'Yapcor' PBR	CPrp EBee EPfP GKev LPot LRHS MAsh MBri NEgg NLar SLim SRkn SWvt
	- - Somerford Funfair Cream = 'Yapcre' PBR	CHel EBee EPfP LBMP LRHS MAsh NEgg NLar SLim SWvt WPtf
	- - Somerford Funfair Orange = 'Yapor' PBR	EBee EPfP LBMP LRHS MAsh MBri NLar NPri SLim SPoG SWvt
	- - Somerford Funfair Wine = 'Yapwin'	EBee ELan EPfP EShb LBMP LPot LRHS MAsh MBNS MBri NEgg NLar NPri SLim SMrm SPoG SWvt WPtf
	- - Somerford Funfair Yellow = 'Yapyel' PBR	EBee EPfP LRHS MAsh SLim SPoG SWvt
	- 'Sunshine'	EBee
	- 'Sweet Dreams'	LRHS
§	- 'Winchester Fanfare'	CSBt ELan GBin GMaP LBMP LRHS MGos MRav SEND SLim SMrm SWvt WKif WMoo WWEG
	- 'Winton Fanfare'	see *P.* × *rectus* 'Winchester Fanfare'
	'Rory' PBR	SRms

Phyla (*Verbenaceae*)

	lanceolata	LLWG
§	***nodiflora***	SRms WJek
	- 'Alba'	MMuc SEND
§	- var. ***canescens***	WHal XLum

× *Phylliopsis* (*Ericaceae*)

	'Coppelia' ♀H4	NHar WPat
	hillieri 'Askival'	WThu
	- 'Pinocchio'	GKev NHar WAbe WPat WThu
	'Hobgoblin'	WAbe

'Mermaid'	ITim NHar WAbe WThu
'Sprite'	CWSG WPat
'Sugar Plum'	CCCN LRHS NHar NLar SWvt WAbe WThu
'Swanhilde'	WAbe WThu
'Titania' new	WThu

Phyllitis see *Asplenium*

scolopendrium	see *Asplenium scolopendrium*

Phyllocladus (*Podocarpaceae*)

alpinus	CDoC CDul ECou EUJe

Phyllodoce (*Ericaceae*)

aleutica	ECho NHar SRms WThu
§ - subsp. ***glanduliflora*** 'Flora Slack'	WThu
- - white-flowered	see *P. aleutica* subsp. *glanduliflora* 'Flora Slack'
caerulea $\mathbb{Y}^{H4}$	ECho ITim
- ***japonica***	see *P. nipponica*
- 'Murray Lyon'	NHar WAbe WThu
- 'W.M. Buchanan's Peach Seedling'	NHar
empetriformis	ECho SRms WThu
§ ***nipponica*** $\mathbb{Y}^{H4}$	NHar WThu
'Peach'	WThu

Phyllostachys ✿ (*Poaceae*)

angusta	ERod MWht SBig
arcana	WJun
- 'Luteosulcata'	CEnt CFil ERod MMoz MMuc MWht NLar WJun
§ ***atrovaginata***	ERod SGol WJun
aurea $\mathbb{Y}^{H4}$	Widely available
- 'Albovariegata' (v)	CDTJ ENBC EPfP ERod LRHS MWht WJun
- 'Flavescens Inversa'	ERod MWht WJun
- 'Holochrysa'	CDTJ CFil ERod MMuc MWht WJun
- 'Koi'	CDTJ CEnt ERod MMoz MWht SBig SGol WJun WPGP
aureocaulis	see *P. aureosulcata* f. *aureocaulis*, *P. vivax* f. *aureocaulis*
aureosulcata	CWib ERod MMoz MWht WJun WMoo
- f. ***alata***	see *P. aureosulcata* f. *pekinensis*
§ - f. ***aureocaulis*** $\mathbb{Y}^{H4}$	CAbb CBcs CDoC CEnt CFil CJun CTsd ELon ENBC EPfP EUJe GCal LAst LBMP LHop LRHS LSRN MBri MGos MMoz MREP MWht NGdn SAPC SGol SPer SPoG SWvt WJun
- 'Harbin'	ERod
- 'Harbin Inversa'	CDTJ ERod
- 'Lama Tempel'	CDTJ CFil WPGP
§ - f. ***pekinensis***	MMoz SBig
- f. ***spectabilis*** $\mathbb{Y}^{H4}$	Widely available
bambusoides	CDTJ ERod SBig SDix WJun
- 'Allgold'	see *P. bambusoides* 'Holochrysa'
- 'Castilloni Inversa'	EAmu ERod EWes LEdu MMoz MWht WJun
- 'Castillonii'	CBcs CEnt EAmu ENBC ERod EUJe EWes LEdu MMoz MMuc MWht NLar SAPC SBig SDix SEND WJun WPGP
- 'Castillonis Inversa Variegata' (v)	WJun
- 'Castillonis Variegata' (v)	ERod
§ - 'Holochrysa'	CDTJ CDoC CEnt ERod MMoz MMuc MWht SEND WJun WPGP
- 'Kawadana' (v)	ERod WJun
- f. ***lacrima-deae***	CAgr CDTJ EPfP EUJe
- 'Marliacea'	ERod SBig WJun
- 'Sulphurea'	see *P. bambusoides* 'Holochrysa'
- 'Tanakae'	CDTJ ENBC MMoz SBig
- 'Violascens'	SBig
bissetii	CAbb CAgr CBcs CCVT CDoC CDul CEnt CWSG EAmu ENBC EPfP ERod EUJe GBin LRHS MAvo MBrN MBri MCoo MGos MMoz MMuc MSwo MWht SEND SGol SPer SPoG WJun WPGP
congesta misapplied	see *P. atrovaginata*
decora	ERod MMoz MMuc MWht SEND WJun
dulcis	CEnt EPfP ERod MWht SBig WJun
§ ***edulis***	CAgr CDTJ ELon ERod MMoz MWht SAPC SBig SBst SPlb WJun
- 'Bicolor'	WJun
§ - 'Heterocycla'	XBlo
- f. ***pubescens***	see *P. edulis*
fimbriligula	WJun
flexuosa	CBcs CEnt LRHS MWht SGol WJun
glauca	CDTJ EPfP ERod MMoz MWht SBig
- f. ***yunzhu***	ERod MWht WJun
heteroclada	CAgr CDTJ CEnt WJun
- 'Solid Stem' misapplied	see *P. purpurata* 'Straight Stem'
heterocycla	see *P. edulis* 'Heterocycla'
- f. ***pubescens***	see *P. edulis*
humilis	CEnt ENBC ERod EUJe MMoz MMuc MWht SBig SEND WJun
incarnata	WJun
iridescens	ERod SBig WJun
lithophila	ERod
makinoi	ERod
mannii	ERod MWht
nidularia	ERod MMoz SBig WJun
nigra $\mathbb{Y}^{H4}$	Widely available
- 'Boryana'	CCVT CDoC CEnt EAmu EPfP ERod EUJe MGos MMoz MMuc MWht SBig SEND SWvt WJun WMoo
- 'Hale'	MWht
- f. ***henonis*** $\mathbb{Y}^{H4}$	EAmu ENBC ERod MMoz MMuc MREP MWht SBig SEND SGol WJun WPGP
- 'Megurochiku'	ERod MWht WJun
- f. ***nigra***	CFil
- f. ***punctata***	CDoC ENBC ERod MAvo MMuc MWht SEND WJun WMoo
- 'Tosaensis'	ERod
nuda	EAmu ERod MMoz MMuc MWht WJun
- f. ***localis***	ERod MWht
parvifolia	CEnt ERod MWht WJun
platyglossa	ERod
praecox	WJun
- f. ***viridisulcata***	EAmu ERod WJun
prominens	ERod
propinqua	CDoC EAmu ERod MMoz MMuc MWht WJun
pubescens	see *P. edulis*
§ ***purpurata*** 'Straight Stem'	MWht
rubicunda	WJun
rubromarginata	CDTJ CEnt ERod MMuc MWht WJun
'Shanghai 3'	EAmu ERod
stimulosa	ERod MWht WJun
sulphurea	CDTJ
- 'Houzeau'	ERod MMuc SEND
§ - f. ***sulphurea***	ERod WJun

	- 'Sulphurea'	see *P. sulphurea* f. *sulphurea*
§	- f. ***viridis***	ERod SBig
	violascens	CEnt ERod EUJe MMoz MWht SBig WJun
	viridiglaucescens	CDTJ ERod MBrN MMoz MMuc MWht SBig SEND WJun
	viridis	see *P. sulphurea* f. *viridis*
	vivax	EPfP ERod EUJe MMoz MWht NLar SBig WJun
§	- f. ***aureocaulis*** 🏆H4	CAbb CAgr CBcs CCVT CDoC CEnt CHEx CWSG EAmu ENBC EPPr EPfP ERod EUJe IBoy LEdu LRHS LSRN MGos MMoz MMuc MREP MWht NLar SAPC SBig SEND SGol WJun WPGP
	- - 'Huanwenzii'	CDTJ EAmu ERod EUJe MMoz MWht NPla WJun
	- 'Katrin'	LEdu
*	- 'Sulphurea'	XBlo

× *Phyllothamnus* (*Ericaceae*)

	erectus	WPat

Phymatosorus (*Polypodiaceae*)

§	***diversifolius***	WCot WPGP

Phymosia (*Malvaceae*)

§	***umbellata***	MOWG WPGP

Phyodina see *Callisia*

Physalis (*Solanaceae*)

	alkekengi 🏆H4	CTri NBir NLar SWvt
	- var. ***franchetii***	CArn CDoy CMac CSBt EBee EHyd ELan EPfP LAst LRHS MHer NBir NBro NEgg NGdn NPri SMad SPer SPoG SRms WMnd WOld
	- - dwarf	LRHS NLar
	- - 'Gigantea'	ECGP MNHC NLar SPlb XLum
	- - 'Gnome'	see *P. alkekengi* var. *franchetii* 'Zwerg'
	- - 'Variegata' (v)	EWes LEdu MMuc NPro SEND
§	- - 'Zwerg'	EWll LRHS
	- 'Halloween King'	LRHS NLar NPri
	- 'Halloween Queen'	LRHS NLar
	angulata B&SWJ 7016	LLHF
	campanula B&SWJ 10409	WCru
	edulis	see *P. peruviana*
§	***peruviana*** (F)	CCCN SHDw SPlb SVic

Physaria (*Brassicaceae*)

	alpina	CPBP GKev SPlb
	rollinsii new	GKev

Physocarpus (*Rosaceae*)

	'Burning Embers'	LBuc SRms
	Little Devil	see *P. opulifolius* 'Donna May'
	malvaceus	EWes
	monogynus	NLar
	opulifolius	CDul
	- 'Angel Gold'	ELan EMil EPfP MAsh NPri
	- Coppertina	see *P. opulifolius* Diable D'Or
	- 'Dart's Gold' 🏆H4	Widely available
§	- Diable D'Or = 'Mindia'PBR	CHel EMil EPfP LBuc LRHS LSRN MAsh MBlu MBri MPkF NEgg NPla SGol SHil WMoo
	- 'Diabolo'PBR 🏆H4	Widely available
§	- 'Donna May'	EPfP SLon
§	- Lady in Red = 'Tuilad'PBR	Widely available
§	- 'Luteus'	CWib MRav WMoo
	- 'Nugget'	LBuc LRHS MBri SHil
	- Ruby Spice	see *P. opulifolius* Lady in Red
	- Summer Wine = 'Seward'PBR	EBee EPfP EWes LHop LRHS MAsh
	- 'Tilden Park'	EBee SGol
	ribesifolius 'Aureus'	see *P. opulifolius* 'Luteus'

Physochlaina (*Solanaceae*)

	orientalis	SPhx

Physoplexis (*Campanulaceae*)

§	***comosa*** 🏆H2-3	EPot NSla WAbe

Physostegia (*Lamiaceae*)

	angustifolia	GQui NBre
I	'Aquatica'	LLWG
§	***virginiana***	CBAq CSBt CTri GMaP LHop LRHS MBel SPoG SRms SWat WCFE
	- 'Alba'	CSBt CTri EBee ELon GAbr GJos GMaP LEdu LRHS NChi SBod SMrm SPet SPlb WHrl XLum
§	- 'Crown of Snow'	CCon EBee EPfP MHer MRav MWat MWhi NPri SBea SPoG SWvt WHil WMoo WWEG
	- 'Grandiflora'	CCon
	- 'Miss Manners'	CHel CMac ECGP ECtt LRHS MBri NBre NCGa NGdn NLar SRGP
	- 'Pink Manners' new	STPC
	- 'Rose Crown'	SPer
	- 'Rose Queen'	CTri MWat NBre NChi NPri
	- 'Rosea'	EBee EPfP GJos IFoB LPio MMuc MWhi NBre NGdn SHar SPoG SWvt WHrl WWEG
	- Schneekrone	see *P. virginiana* 'Crown of Snow'
	- 'Snow Queen'	see *P. virginiana* 'Summer Snow'
§	- var. ***speciosa*** 'Bouquet Rose'	CHel CMac CPrp ECGP EPfP LEdu LRHS MCot MRav NBir NLar SGbt SPer SWvt WBrk WCAu WMoo WRHF WWEG XLum
	- - Rose Bouquet	see *P. virginiana* var. *speciosa* 'Bouquet Rose'
	- - 'Variegata' (v)	CMac CSBt EBee ECtt EHoe ELan ELon EPfP LHop MRav NBir NGdn NHol NLar NPnk SBea SPer SRms SWat WCAu WCot WHoo WMnd WWEG XLum
§	- 'Summer Snow' 🏆H4	CBcs CPrp ELan EPfP LHop LRHS NGBl NLar SPer SRms SWat WCAu WCot WMnd
	- 'Summer Spire'	LRHS
	- 'Vivid' 🏆H4	CKno CMac ELan ELon EPfP LAst LBMP LRHS LSou MBri MCot MHer MNrw MRav NCGa NEgg NHol NLar SDix SPer SPet SPlb SRms WCAu WCot WHil WHoo WMnd WWEG XLum
	- 'Wassenhove'	SMrm

Phyteuma (*Campanulaceae*)

	balbisii	see *P. cordatum*
	comosum	see *Physoplexis comosa*
§	***cordatum***	GJos
	hemisphaericum	ECho
	humile	LRHS WThu
	nigrum	ECho LLHF NBid WBor WPGP
	scheuchzeri	CSpe EBee ECho EPfP EWld GBin NSla SMad SRms WIce WPGP XLum
	spicatum	CDes NBro

Phytolacca (*Phytolaccaceae*)

	acinosa	GPoy SWat
	- HWJ 647	WCru
§	***americana***	CArn CHel CSev EBee ELan EPfP ESwi EUJe GPoy MBNS MHer MNHC MPie NLar SRms SWat WJek WMnd
	- B&SWJ 1000	WCru
	- B&SWJ 8817A	WCru
	- 'Silberstein' (v)	CBct EBee ECtt ESwi LDai MBNS MPie NLar WCot
	clavigera	see *P. polyandra*
	decandra	see *P. americana*
	dioica	CExl SPlb
	esculenta	LEdu SEND
	icosandra B&SWJ 8988	WCru
	- B&SWJ 9033	WCru
	- Purpurascens Group B&SWJ 11251	SRms WCru
	japonica B&SWJ 3005	NBid WCru
	- B&SWJ 3522	WCru
	'Laka Boom'	LHop
	octandra B&SWJ 9514	WCru
	- B&SWJ 10151	WCru
§	***polyandra***	NBid NBro SRms
	rivinoides B&SWJ 10264	WCru
	rugosa B&SWJ 10263	WCru

Picea (*Pinaceae*)

§	***abies***	CCVT CDul CLnd CMac CSBt CTho CTri CWib EHul EPfP LBuc MJak MMuc NEgg NWea SCoo SEND SLim SPer SPoG WHar WMou
	- 'Acrocona'	MGos NLar
	- 'Archer'	CKen
	- 'Argenteospica' (v)	NPCo
	- 'Aurea'	ELan NPCo
	- 'Capitata'	CKen NLar
	- 'Clanbrassiliana'	CKen ELan NLar NWad WGor
	- Compacta Group	NPCo
I	- 'Congesta'	CKen
	- 'Crippsii'	CKen
I	- 'Cruenta'	CKen SLim
	- 'Cupressina'	CKen
	- 'Decumbens'	NLar
	- 'Diffusa'	CKen NLar
	- 'Dumpy'	CKen NHol NLar NWad WGor
	- 'Ellwangeriana'	NLar
	- 'Excelsa'	see *P. abies*
	- 'Fahndrich'	CKen CMen
	- 'Finedonensis'	NLar
	- 'Formanek'	CDoC CMen
	- 'Four Winds'	CKen
	- 'Frohburg'	CKen MJak NLar NSoo
	- 'Gold Drift'	NLar
	- 'Gregoryana'	CKen CMac
	- 'Heartland Gem'	CKen
	- 'Himfa'	NLar
	- 'Horace Wilson'	CKen CMen
	- 'Humilis'	CKen
	- 'Hystrix'	CMen NHol NLar NWad
	- 'Inversa'	CDul CKen MBlu NLar SLim
	- 'J.W. Daisy's White'	see *P. glauca* 'J.W. Daisy's White'
	- 'Jana'	CKen
	- 'Kral'	CKen
	- 'Little Gem' ♀H4	CDoC CKen CMen EHul ELan LBee LRHS MAsh MGos NHol NLar NWad NWea SCoo SLim SPer SPoG
	- 'Marcel'	CKen
	- 'Maxwellii'	EHul
	- 'Mini Kalous' **new**	CKen
	- 'Nana Compacta'	CKen CMen EHul MAsh WGor
	- 'Nidiformis' ♀H4	CDoC CKen CMac CMen CSBt CTri EHul LPot LRHS MGos NLar NPCo NWea SCoo SGol SLim SPer SRms
	- 'Norrköping'	CKen
	- 'Ohlendorffii'	CKen EHul MGos NLar
	- 'Pachyphylla'	CKen
	- 'Pumila Nigra'	EHul LRHS SLim WGor
	- 'Pusch'	CKen CMen NLar SLim
	- 'Pygmaea'	CKen WGor
	- 'Reflexa'	MGos NPCo
	- 'Remontii'	NWea
	- 'Rydal'	CBcs CDoC CDul CKen MAsh MBri NLar NWea SLim
	- 'Saint James'	CKen
	- 'Spring Fire' **new**	CKen
	- 'Tompa'	LRHS NLar SLim
	- 'Typner' **new**	CKen
	- 'Vermont Gold'	CKen NLar
	- 'Walter Bron'	NLar
	- Will's Dwarf	see *P. abies* 'Wills Zwerg'
§	- 'Wills Zwerg'	SGol
§	***alcoquiana*** var. ***alcoquiana***	NWea SLim
	- var. ***reflexa***	MPkF
	asperata	NWea
	bicolor	see *P. alcoquiana* var. *alcoquiana*
	breweriana ♀H4	CCVT CDoC CDul CMac CTho EHul EPfP GKin IDee LEdu LRHS MBlu MGos MJak MMuc NEgg NLar NPCo NTri NWea SLim SSta WCFE WMou
	- 'Kohout's Dwarf'	CKen
	chihuahuana	SLim
	engelmannii	NWea
	- 'Compact'	SLim
	- subsp. ***engelmannii***	CKen NPCo
	- 'Jasper'	NLar
	- 'Lace'	SLim
	glauca	CDul NWea
	- Alberta Blue = 'Haal'PBR	CKen EUJe LRHS
	- var. ***albertiana*** 'Alberta Globe'	CDoC CSBt EHul EPot GKin LBee LRHS MAsh MBri MGos NEgg NHol NWad SCoo SLim SPoG
	- - 'Conica'	CBcs CDoC CMac CMen CSBt EHul EPfP EUJe LBee MAsh MBri MGos MJak NEgg NHol NWad NWea SEND SGol SLim SPer SPoG SRms WCFE
	- - 'Gnome'	CKen
	- - 'Laurin'	CKen NPCo NWad WGor
	- - 'Tiny'	CKen NWad WGor
	- 'Arneson's Blue Variegated' (v)	CDoC CKen LRHS MAsh MBri SLim
	- 'Biesenthaler Frühling'	CKen SLim
	- 'Blue Planet'	CKen IVic
	- 'Coerulea'	NPCo
	- 'Cy's Wonder'	CKen
	- 'Echiniformis' ♀H4	CKen GKin NLar
	- 'Goldilocks'	CKen
§	- 'J.W. Daisy's White'	CBcs CDoC CKen EHul EPfP GKin LAst LRHS MAsh MGos MJak NEgg NHol NLar NWad NWea SBod SCoo SLim SPer SPoG WGor
	- 'Jean Dilly'	NLar
I	- 'Julian Potts Monstrosa'	NLar

	- 'Lilliput'	CKen EHul NLar NWad NWea WGor
§	- 'Nana'	CKen
	- 'Pendula' **new**	CKen
	- 'Piccolo'	CBcs CKen LRHS NLar SLim
	- 'Pixie'	CKen
	- 'Rainbow's End' (v)	CKen LRHS NLar SLim
	- 'Sander's Blue'	CKen EHul EPfP GKin LBee LRHS MBri SLim SPoG WGor
	- 'Spring Surprise'	CKen
	- 'Zuckerhut'	GKin LRHS NLar
	glehnii 'Sasanosei'	CKen
	- 'Shimezusei'	CKen
	jezoensis	CKen CMen NLar NWea
	- 'Aurea'	SLim
	- subsp. ***hondoensis***	CMen
	- 'Marianbad'	CKen
	- 'Yatsabusa'	CKen CMen
	koraiensis	CDul NLar NWea
	kosteri 'Glauca'	see *P. pungens* 'Koster'
	koyamae 'Bedgebury Blue' **new**	SLim
	- 'Bedgebury Cascade'	NLar SLim
	likiangensis	CDul CMCN CTho EPfP NLar NWea
	- var. ***balfouriana***	see *P. likiangensis* var. *rubescens*
§	- var. ***rubescens***	LRHS NLar NSoo SLim
	mariana	CDul EPfP NWea
	- 'Austria Broom'	CKen
	- 'Bill Archer'	NWad
	- 'Blue Teardrop' **new**	CKen
	- 'Doumetii'	NLar
	- 'Fastigiata'	CKen
	- 'Nana' ♀H4	CDoC CKen CMac CMen EHul EPfP EPot LRHS MAsh MGos MMuc NHol NWad NWea SCoo SEND SLim SPoG
I	- 'Pygmaea'	CKen NWad
	morrisonicola	CKen
	omorika ♀H4	CBcs CCVT CDul CJun CMCN CMac CTho EPfP EWTr MMuc NWea SEND SEWo WCFE WHar
	- 'de Ruyter'	IVic
	- 'Frohnleiten'	CKen
	- 'Frondenberg'	CKen
	- 'Halone' **new**	CKen
	- 'Karel'	CKen
	- 'Minimax'	CKen
	- 'Nana' ♀H4	LRHS NPCo SCoo SLim WCFE
	- 'Pendula' ♀H4	CDoC LRHS MBlu NLar SLim SSta
	- 'Pendula Bruns'	LRHS NLar SLim SMad
	- 'Peve Tijn'	LRHS NLar
	- 'Pimoko'	CKen LRHS MBri NPCo SLim
	- 'Pimpf'	IVic
	- 'Pygmy'	CKen
	- 'Schneverdingen'	CKen
	- 'Tijn'	CKen SLim
	- 'Treblitsch'	CKen
	- 'Tremonia'	NLar
	orientalis ♀H4	CDul NWea WThu
	- 'Aurea' (v) ♀H4	CMac EHul ELan MBri MGos MJak NLar NPri NSoo SCoo SLim SMad
	- 'Aureospicata'	CDoC CTho MAsh MBlu NLar NPCo SCoo
	- 'Bergman's Gem'	CKen
	- 'Golden Start'	LRHS NLar SLim
	- 'Juwel'	CKen NLar
	- 'Kenwith'	CKen
	- 'Mount Vernon'	CKen
	- Nana Group	GKin
	- 'Professor Langner'	CKen MAsh SLim
	- 'Reynolds'	NHol
	- 'Shadow's Broom' **new**	CMen
	- 'Skylands'	CKen ELan LRHS MAsh MBri MGos NHol NLar SLim SPoG
	- 'Tom Thumb'	CKen SLim
	- 'Wittboldt'	CKen MBri
	pungens 'Blaukissen'	CKen SLim
	- 'Blue Pearl'	CKen NLar
	- 'Blue Trinket'	WGor
	- 'Edith'	CKen LRHS NLar NPCo SLim SPer WGor
	- 'Erich Frahm'	MAsh MBri NLar
	- 'Fat Albert'	LRHS NEgg NLar NPCo NWea SLim
	- 'Frieda'	LRHS SLim
	- Glauca Group	CDul CLnd CMac MMuc NWea SCoo SPoG WMou
	- - 'Glauca Pendula'	EUJe
	- - 'Glauca Procumbens'	CMen NLar NWea
§	- - 'Glauca Prostrata'	CMac EHul SLim
	- 'Glauca Globosa'	see *P. pungens* 'Globosa'
	- 'Globe'	CKen CMen
I	- 'Globosa' ♀H4	CBcs CKen CSBt EHul EPfP LRHS MAsh MBri NHol NPCo NPri NSoo NWea SCoo SLim SPer SPoG WCFE
	- 'Gloria'	CKen SLim
	- 'Hoopsii' ♀H4	CDoC CDul CSBt EHul EPfP GKin IVic LAst LRHS MAsh MBri MGos MJak NEgg NLar NPCo NPri NWea SEWo SLim SPoG SWvt
	- 'Hoto'	EHul
	- 'Hunnewelliana'	EPfP
	- 'Iseli Fastigiate'	GKin MAsh NLar NPCo SCoo SLim SPer SPoG
	- 'Iseli Foxtail'	LAst
§	- 'Koster' ♀H4	CSBt EHul EPfP LAst LRHS MAsh NEgg NPri NSoo NWea SLim SPoG WMou
	- 'Koster Fastigiata'	NEgg
	- 'Lucky Strike'	CKen NLar
	- 'Maigold' (v)	CKen IVic NLar SLim
	- 'Moerheimii'	EHul NLar
	- 'Montgomery'	CKen NLar
	- 'Mrs Cesarini'	CKen NLar SLim
	- 'Niemitz'	SLim
	- 'Nimetz'	CKen
	- 'Oldenburg'	NEgg NLar NPCo NWea SLim
	- 'Procumbens'	CKen
	- 'Prostrata'	see *P. pungens* 'Glauca Prostrata'
	- 'Rovelli's Monument'	NLar
	- 'Saint Mary's Broom'	CKen NLar NPCo
	- 'Schovenhorst'	EHul
	- 'Snowkiss'	NPCo
	- 'The Blues' **new**	CKen
	- 'Thomsen'	EHul
	- 'Thuem'	EHul EPfP NLar NPCo
	- 'Waldbrunn'	CKen
	- 'Wendy'	CKen
	- 'Yvette'	NLar
	retroflexa	NWea
	rubens	NLar
	schrenkiana	CMCN
	sitchensis	CDul MAsh NWea
	- 'Christine Berkau' **new**	NLar
	- 'Nana'	NLar
	- 'Papoose'	see *P. sitchensis* 'Tenas'
	- 'Pévé Wiesje'	NLar
	- 'Silberzwerg'	CKen LRHS NLar SLim
	- 'Strypemonde'	CKen

§	- 'Tenas'	CKen LRHS NLar SLim
	smithiana	CDul CTho EPfP NLar
	- 'Sunray'	LRHS SLim
	wilsonii	CKen NLar

Picrasma (*Simaroubaceae*)

	ailanthoides	see *P. quassioides*
§	***quassioides***	CMCN EBee EPfP WPGP

Picris (*Asteraceae*)

	echioides	WHer

Picrorhiza (*Plantaginaceae*)

	kurrooa	GPoy

Pieris (*Ericaceae*)

	'Balls of Fire'	CMac
	'Bert Chandler'	CMac GKin
	'Firecrest' ♀H4	CMHG MMuc NLar SSpi
	'Flaming Silver' (v) ♀H4	Widely available
	'Forest Flame' ♀H4	Widely available
	formosa B&SWJ 2257	WCru
	- var. ***forrestii***	CWib GLin
	- - 'Charles Michael'	CExl
	- - 'Jermyns'	CMac MRav
	- - 'Wakehurst' ♀H3	CAbP CDul CExl CMac CTri EPfP GKin LRHS MAsh MGos MRav MSnd SPer SSpi
	Havila = 'Mouwsvila' (v)	CMac MAsh NWad
	japonica	CMac GGal
	- 'Astrid'	IVic
	- 'Bisbee Dwarf'	WThu
	- 'Bolero' **new**	NSoo
	- 'Bonfire'	CCCN CEnd ELan IVic LRHS MBri MGos MMuc NEgg NLar NSoo SHil SLim SPoG WHar
	- 'Carnaval' (v)	CCCN CEnd CMac CSBt CWCL CWib ELan ELon IBoy IVic LBuc LRHS LSRN MAsh MBri MGos MMuc MRav NLar NPCo NPri NSoo SCoo SHil SLim SPer SPoG SWvt
	- 'Cavatine' ♀H4	CMHG IVic
§	- 'Christmas Cheer'	CMac LSRN WMoo
	- 'Compacta'	WAbe
	- 'Cupido'	IVic MAsh MGos NLar SLim SPoG
	- 'Debutante' ♀H4	CBcs CWib ELan GBin GKin IVic LRHS MAsh MBri MGos NLar NPCo NPri NSoo SCoo SHil SSpi SWvt WHar
	- 'Don'	see *P. japonica* 'Pygmaea'
	- 'Dorothy Wyckoff'	MAsh NLar SSta
	- 'Flaming Star'	SWvt
	- 'Flamingo'	CMac
	- 'Fuga' **new**	CWSG
I	- 'Katsura'	CDoC CMac CSBt ELan EPfP GBin GKin IBoy IVic LBuc LRHS LSRN LSqu MAsh MBlu MBri MGos MJak NEgg NHol NLar SCoo SHil SLim SPer SPoG SSpi SWvt
	- 'Little Heath' (v) ♀H4	Widely available
	- 'Little Heath Green' ♀H4	CDoC CMac ELon GKin IBoy MAsh MGos MMuc NEgg NPCo SPer SPoG SWvt WMoo
	- 'Minor'	GKev NWad WThu
	- 'Mountain Fire' ♀H4	Widely available
	- 'Passion'PBR	CEnd IVic MPkF NLar NSoo
	- 'Pink Delight' ♀H4	CAbP LRHS LSRN MRav NEgg SRms
	- 'Prelude' ♀H4	CSBt CWCL LRHS MAsh NLar NSoo WAbe WHar
	- 'Purity' ♀H4	CBcs CDoC CHel CMHG CMac LRHS MAsh MGos NEgg NLar SLim SPer SWvt WGwG WHar
§	- 'Pygmaea'	CMac GKev NWad SSta WThu
	- 'Ralto'PBR	MBri MRav NSoo
	- Red Mill = 'Zebris'	CEnd IVic MAsh NSoo SLim SPer SSpi
	- 'Rokujo's Dwarf'	WAbe
	- 'Rondo'	IVic
	- 'Rosalinda'	MAsh MGos
	- 'Sarabande' ♀H4	GKin IVic MAsh MJak MMuc MPkF NHol
	- 'Scarlett O'Hara'	CSBt NSoo
	- 'Select'	NSoo
	- Taiwanensis Group	GKin LRHS MMuc NLar SRms
	- 'Temple Bells'	CSBt
	- 'Valley Rose'	CGHE CSBt ELan GKin IVic LLHF MGos NLar SPoG SSpi
	- 'Valley Valentine' ♀H4	CBcs CDoC CEnd CMac CSBt CWib EPfP IVic LRHS LSRN MAsh MBri MGos MMuc MPkF NPCo NSoo SCoo SHil SLim SPer SPoG SWvt
	- 'Variegata' misapplied	see *P. japonica* 'White Rim'
	- 'Variegata' ambig.	NLar SPer
	- 'Variegata' (Carrière) Bean (v)	CMHG EPfP LRHS MGos MRav NHol NSoo WHar
	- 'Wada's Pink'	see *P. japonica* 'Christmas Cheer'
	- 'White Pearl'	CAbP CMac EPfP IVic MAsh NSoo
§	- 'White Rim' (v) ♀H4	CDul CMac MAsh SPlb
	- 'William Buchanan'	WThu
	- var. ***yakushimensis***	NLar
	nana	WThu
	'Tilford'	CMac

Pilea (*Urticaceae*)

§	***microphylla***	EBak EShb
	muscosa	see *P. microphylla*
	peperomioides ♀H1	CHel CSev

Pileostegia (*Hydrangeaceae*)

	viburnoides ♀H4	Widely available
	- B&SWJ 3565	WCru
	- B&SWJ 3570 from Taiwan	WCru
	- B&SWJ 7132	WCru

Pilosella (*Asteraceae*)

§	***aurantiaca***	CArn ELan IRos LEdu MHer MNHC NBid NOrc SIde WCot WHer WMoo WOut WSFF
§	- subsp. ***carpathicola***	MMuc
	hoppeana **new**	WCot
§	***officinarum***	NRya
	tardans	CFis

Pilularia (*Marsileaceae*)

	globulifera	MSKA

Pimelea (*Thymelaeaceae*)

	coarctata	see *P. prostrata*
	ferruginea	ECou WAbe
	- 'Magenta Mist'	MOWG
	filiformis	ECou
	oreophila	WThu
§	***prostrata***	CTri ECho ECou WThu
	- f. ***parvifolia***	ECou
	tomentosa	ECou LRHS

Pimpinella (*Apiaceae*)

	anisum	CArn SVic

	bicknellii	WPGP
	major	LEdu
	- 'Rosea'	CDes CExl CMea CPom CSam CSpe ECtt GCal IPot LDai LEdu LHop LRHS LSou MBel MHer MSCN NCGa NChi NDov NGdn NPnk SMrm SPer SPhx WCot WHal WOut WPGP
	saxifraga	CHab

pineapple see *Ananas comosus*

pineapple guava see *Acca sellowiana*

Pinellia (*Araceae*)

	cordata	CPom LEdu WCru
	pedatisecta	CCon CDes EBee WCot
	pinnatisecta	see *P. tripartita*
	ternata	EBee NLar WCot WPnP
	- B&SWJ 3532	WCru
§	***tripartita***	CExl ECho EPPr WCot
	- B&SWJ 1102	WCru
	- 'Dragon Tails' (v)	SKHP
	- 'Purple Face'	WCru

Pinguicula (*Lentibulariaceae*)

	ehlersiae	EFEx
	esseriana	EFEx
	grandiflora	EECP EFEx NRya
	longifolia subsp. ***longifolia***	EFEx
	moranensis var. ***caudata***	EFEx
	- ***moreana***	EFEx
	- ***superba***	EFEx
	vulgaris	EFEx WHer

pinkcurrant see *Ribes rubrum* (P)

Pinus ✿ (*Pinaceae*)

	albicaulis 'Flinck'	CKen
	- 'Nana'	see *P. albicaulis* 'Noble's Dwarf'
	- 'No 3'	CKen
§	- 'Noble's Dwarf'	CKen
	aristata	CDul CLnd CMen EHul
	- 'Bashful' **new**	CKen
	- 'Cecilia'	CKen
	- 'Kohout's Mini'	CKen
	- 'Sherwood Compact'	CKen MAsh NLar SLim
	- 'So Tight'	CKen
	armandii	CDoC CDul CMCN WPGP
	- 'Gold Tip'	CKen
	austriaca	see *P. nigra* subsp. *nigra*
N	***ayacahuite***	CKen
	- var. ***veitchii***	WPGP
	balfouriana dwarf	CKen
	banksiana	CDul
	- 'Chippewa'	CKen
I	- 'Compacta'	CKen
	- 'H.J. Welch'	CKen
	- 'Manomet'	CKen
	- 'Neponset'	CKen
	- 'Schneverdingen'	CKen
	- 'Schoodic'	LRHS SLim
	- 'Wisconsin'	CKen
	bhutanica	WPGP
	brutia	IGor
	bungeana	CDul CLnd EPfP MBlu
	- 'Diamant'	CKen
	- 'June's Broom'	CKen
	cembra	CAgr CDul CLnd NWea SEND
	- 'Aurea'	see *P. cembra* 'Aureovariegata'
§	- 'Aureovariegata' (v)	LRHS NPCo
	- 'Barnhourie'	CKen
	- 'Blue Mound'	CKen
	- 'Chalet'	CKen
	- Glauca Group	MGos
	- 'Inverleith'	CKen
	- 'Jermyns'	CKen
	- 'King's Dwarf'	CKen
	- 'Ortler'	CKen
	- 'Roughills'	CKen
	- 'Stricta'	CKen
	- witches' broom	CKen
	cembroides NJM 09.022A	WPGP
	contorta	CBcs CDoC CDul NWea SPlb
	- 'Asher'	CKen
	- 'Chief Joseph'	CKen MAsh NLar SLim
	- var. ***latifolia***	CDul CLnd
	- 'Spaan's Dwarf'	CKen LRHS MBri NLar SCoo SLim
	- 'Taylor's Sunburst'	CKen MAsh NLar
	coulteri ♀^{H4}	EPfP SBig SKHP WPGP
	densiflora	CDul CMCN EUJe IGor
	- 'Alice Verkade'	CDoC CMen LRHS MAsh MBri NLar SCoo
	- 'Aurea'	LRHS NLar
	- 'Golden Ghost'	MAsh NLar
	- 'Jane Kluis'	CMen LAst LRHS MGos NLar SLim
	- 'Jim Cross'	CKen
	- 'Low Glow'	CKen LRHS NLar NPCo SLim
	- 'Oculus-draconis' (v)	LRHS NEgg NLar SLim
	- 'Pendula'	CKen LRHS NEgg SCoo SLim
	- 'Umbraculifera'	CMen GKin MAsh NLar NPCo SSta
§	***devoniana***	LRHS
	edulis 'Juno'	CKen
	elliottii	SBig
	- var. ***densa***	CKen
	fenzeliana	CKen
	flexilis	CDul IGor
	- 'Firmament'	LRHS NLar NSoo SLim
	- 'Glenmore Dwarf'	CKen
	- 'Nana'	CKen
	- 'Ririe' **new**	CKen
	- 'Tarryall'	CKen
	- 'Vanderwolf's Pyramid'	MAsh NLar
	- WB No 1	CKen
	- WB No 2	CKen
	funebris	IGor
	greggii	CDul
	- NJM 09.014	WPGP
	griffithii	see *P. wallichiana*
	halepensis	CDul SEND
§	***hartwegii*** NJM 09.029	WPGP
§	***heldreichii*** ♀^{H4}	CDoC GKin NWea
	- 'Aureospicata'	NLar
	- 'Compact Gem'	CDoC CKen LRHS MBri NLar SLim
	- 'Dolce Dorme'	CKen NLar
	- 'Groen'	CKen
	- 'Kalous'	NLar
	- var. ***leucodermis***	see *P. heldreichii*
	- - 'Irish Bell'	NLar
	- - 'Pirin 7'	NLar
	- 'Malink'	CKen IVic LRHS SLim
	- 'Ottocek'	CKen
	- 'Pygmy'	CKen
	- 'Pyramid'	NLar
	- 'Satellit'	CKen LRHS MAsh NLar NPCo SLim
	- 'Schmidtii'	see *P. heldreichii* 'Smidtii'

§	- 'Smidtii' ♀^{H4}	CDoC CKen CMen LRHS MAsh MBri NLar SLim WGor
	- 'Zwerg Schneverdingen'	CKen NLar NPCo
	× ***holfordiana***	CDoC WPGP
	jeffreyi ♀^{H4}	CDul CMCN CTho NWea
	- 'Joppi'	CKen SLim
	koraiensis	GKin LRHS
	- 'Bergman'	CKen
	- 'Blue Ball' **new**	CKen
	- 'Dragon Eye'	CKen SLim
	- 'Jack Corbit'	CKen
	- 'Shibamichi' (v)	CKen
	- 'Silver Lining'	NPCo
	- 'Silveray'	NLar
	- 'Silvergrey'	CKen
	- 'Spring Grove'	CKen NLar
	- 'Winton'	CKen NLar
	leucodermis	see *P. heldreichii*
	magnifica	see *P. devoniana*
	massoniana	NLar
	monophylla 'Tioga Pass'	NLar
	montezumae misapplied	see *P. hartwegii*
	montezumae Lamb.	SAPC
	- NJM 09.016	WPGP
	- 'Sheffield Park'	SLim
	monticola 'Pendula'	CKen
	- 'Pygmy'	see *P. monticola* 'Raraflora'
§	- 'Raraflora'	CKen
	- 'Skyline'	NLar
	'Windsor Dwarf'	CKen
	mugo	CArn CBcs CDul CMac EHul MGos MJak NWea SEND WBor
	- 'Allgäu'	CKen
	- 'Amber Glow'	NLar
	- 'Benjamin'	CKen NLar
	- 'Bisley Green'	NLar
	- 'Brownie'	CKen
	- 'Carsten'	CKen ELan SCoo SLim WGor
	- 'Carsten's Wintergold'	CDoC LRHS MAsh MBri NLar SPoG
	- 'Chameleon'	NLar
	- 'Columbo'	NLar
	- 'Corley's Mat'	CKen LAst MGos NLar
	- 'Devon Gem'	NPCo
	- 'Dezember Gold'	IVic LRHS NLar SLim
	- 'Flanders Belle'	LRHS SLim
	- 'Gnom'	CDul EHul GKin MAsh MBri MGos NEgg NLar NPCo SCoo
	- 'Gold Star'	CMen SLim
	- 'Golden Glow'	CKen LRHS NLar SCoo SLim
	- 'Hesse'	SCoo
	- 'Hoersholm'	CKen
	- 'Hulk'	CKen
	- 'Humpy'	CKen CMen LRHS MAsh MBri NPCo SCoo SLim WCFE
	- 'Ironsides'	CKen
	- 'Jacobsen'	CKen NLar
	- 'Janovsky'	CKen
	- 'Kamila'	NLar
	- 'Kissen'	CKen EPfP MBri NHol NLar SLim
	- 'Klosterkötter'	NLar
	- 'Kobold'	NEgg
	- 'Krauskopf'	CKen
	- 'Laurin'	CKen
	- 'Little Lady'	NLar
	- 'Marand'	NLar
	- 'March'	CKen
	- 'Mini Mops'	CKen NLar
	- 'Minikin'	CKen MBri
	- 'Mops' ♀^{H4}	CMac CMen EHul EPfP LAst LRHS MAsh MBlu MBri MGos NHol NPCo NWea SCoo SLim SPer SPoG SSta
	- 'Mops Midget'	CMen MAsh MBri NPCo
	- 'Mops Sněžná'	NLar
	- var. ***mughus***	see *P. mugo* subsp. *mugo*
§	- subsp. ***mugo***	NWea SGol
	- 'Mumpitz'	CKen
	- 'Northern Lights'	CKen
	- 'Ophir'	CBcs CDul CKen CMen EHul EPfP LAst LRHS MAsh MBri MGos MJak NLar SCoo SLim SPer SSta
	- 'Pal Maleter' (v)	LRHS NLar NPCo SCoo SLim
	- 'Paul's Dwarf'	CKen
	- 'Picobello'	LRHS MAsh NHol NLar SLim
	- 'Piggelmee'	CKen IVic NLar
	Pumilio Group ♀^{H4}	CDoC CDul CLnd EHul EPfP GQue LAst MGos MMuc NWea WMoo WRHF
	- var. ***rostrata***	see *P. mugo* subsp. *uncinata*
	- 'Rushmore'	CKen
	- 'Spaan'	CKen
	- 'Sunshine' (v)	CKen NLar
	- 'Suzi'	CKen
	- 'Trompenburg'	NPCo
	- 'Tuffet'	CKen NHol NLar SLim
	- 'Uelzen'	CKen NLar
§	- subsp. ***uncinata***	NWea
	- - 'Grüne Welle'	CKen SLim
	- - 'Heideperle' **new**	NLar
	- - 'Paradekissen'	CKen NPCo
	- 'Varella'	CKen LRHS NLar SCoo SLim
	- 'White Tip'	CKen
	- 'Winter Gold'	CKen EHul ELan EPfP LAst MGos MJak NHol NLar NPCo NWea SSta WGor
	- 'Winter Sun'	MAsh NLar
	- 'Winzig'	CKen
	- 'Yellow Tip' (v)	NHol
	- 'Zundert'	CKen NLar SPoG
	- 'Zwergkugel'	CKen
	muricata ♀^{H4}	CDoC CDul CLnd NWea
	nigra ♀^{H4}	CBcs CDul CLnd CMac CTri LRHS MAsh MGos SGol WMou
	- var. ***austriaca***	see *P. nigra* subsp. *nigra*
	- 'Bambino'	CKen
	'Black Prince'	CKen GQue LRHS NLar NPCo SLim
	- 'Hobo' **new**	CKen
	- var. ***calabrica***	see *P. nigra* subsp. *laricio*
	- var. ***caramanica***	see *P. nigra* subsp. *pallasiana*
N	- 'Cebennensis Nana'	CKen
	- var. ***corsicana***	see *P. nigra* subsp. *laricio*
*	- 'Fastigiata'	NPCo
	- 'Frank'	CKen LRHS NLar SLim
	- 'Green Tower'	NLar
	- 'Hornibrookiana'	CKen NLar
	- 'Komet'	IVic NLar SCoo SLim
§	- subsp. ***laricio*** ♀^{H4}	CCVT CDoC CDul CMac ECrN IVic LRHS MMuc NWea SEND
	- - 'Aurea'	MBlu
	- - 'Bobby McGregor'	CKen
	- - 'Globosa Viridis'	NEgg NPCo
	- - 'Goldfingers'	NLar
	- - 'Moseri'	CKen
	- - 'Pygmaea'	CKen
	- - 'Spingarn'	CKen
	- - 'Wurstle'	CKen
	- subsp. ***maritima***	see *P. nigra* subsp. *laricio*
	- 'Nana'	MBri NLar

§	– subsp. ***nigra***	CCVT CDoC CJun CLnd CTho LBuc MMuc NLar NWea SEND SEWo SGol
	– – 'Birte'	CKen
	– – 'Bright Eyes'	NLar
	– – 'Helga'	CKen NLar
	– – 'Schovenhorst'	CKen
	– – 'Skyborn'	CKen
	– – 'Strypemonde'	CKen NPCo
	– – 'Yaffle Hill'	CKen NLar
	– 'Obelisk'	CKen NLar
	– 'Oregon Green' **new**	CKen
§	– subsp. ***pallasiana***	CDul
	– – 'Pyramidalis'	CDoC NLar
	– 'Pierrick Brégeon'PBR	LRHS
	– 'Richard'	CKen LRHS NLar
	– 'Rondello'	NLar
	– 'Spielberg'	NLar
	palustris	CDoC CLnd IVic SBig SKHP SSpi
	parviflora	CDul SPlb
	– 'Aaba-jo'	CKen
	– 'Adcock's Dwarf' ♀H4	CDoC CKen LRHS MBri NLar NPCo SLim
	– 'Al Fordham'	CKen
	– 'Aoi'	CKen CMen NLar
	– 'Ara-kawa'	CKen CMen
	– 'Atco-goyo'	CKen
	– Azuma-goyo Group	CKen CMen
I	– 'Baasch's Form'	CKen NLar
	– 'Bergman'	CDoC MAsh NLar
	– 'Blauer Engel'	CDoC MBlu NLar
	– 'Blue Giant'	MBlu NLar
	– 'Blue Lou'	NLar
	– 'Bonnie Bergman'	CDoC CKen EPfP NHol NLar
	– 'Brevifolia'	NLar
	– 'Chikusa Goten'	IArd NLar
	– 'Dai-ho'	CKen
	– 'Daisetsusan'	CKen
	– 'Doctor Landis Gold'	CKen SLim
	– 'Dougal'	CKen
	– 'Fukai' (v)	CKen NHol NLar WBor
	– 'Fukiju'	CKen
	– Fukushima-goyo Group	CKen CMen
	– 'Fuku-zu-mi'	CKen IVic NLar
	– 'Fu-shiro'	CKen
	– 'Gimborn's Ideal'	IVic NLar
	– 'Gin-sho-chuba'	CKen
	– Glauca Group	EHul MAsh MBlu MBri NPCo SGol SKHP
I	– 'Glauca Nana'	CKen
	– 'Goldilocks'	CKen MAsh NLar
	– 'Green Wave'	CKen
	– 'Gyok-ke-sen'	CKen
	– 'Gyo-ko-haku'	CKen
	– 'Gyokuei'	CKen
	– 'Gyokusen Sämling'	CKen NLar
	– 'Gyo-ku-sui'	CKen CMen
	– 'H2'	CKen
	– 'Hagaromo Seedling'	CKen CMen NLar
	– 'Hakko'	CKen
	– 'Hatchichi'	CKen
	– 'Hatsumari'	NLar
	– 'Hobbit' **new**	NLar
	– 'Ibo-can'	CKen CMen
	– 'Ichi-no-se'	CKen
	– 'Iri-fune'	CKen
	– Ishizuchi-goyo Group	CKen
	– 'Jim's Mini Curls' **new**	CKen
	– 'Ka-ho'	CKen
	– 'Kanrico'	CKen
	– 'Kanzan'	CKen
	– 'Kin-po'	NLar
	– 'Kiyomatsu'	CKen NLar
	– 'Kobe'	CKen NLar
	– 'Kokonoe'	CKen CMen
	– 'Kokuho'	CKen NLar
	– 'Kusu-dama'	CKen
	– 'Marika' **new**	NLar
	– 'Masami' **new**	CKen
	– 'Meiko'	CKen CMen
	– 'Michinoku'	CKen
	– 'Momo-yama'	CKen
	– 'Myo-jo'	CKen
	– Nasu-goyo Group	CKen
	– 'Negishi'	CDoC CKen CMen LRHS MAsh NLar SCoo SLim
	– 'Nellie D.'	NLar
	– 'Ogon-goyo' **new**	CKen
	– 'Ogon-janome'	CKen MAsh SLim
	– 'Ossorio Dwarf'	CKen
	– var. ***pentaphylla***	IVic
	– 'Regenhold'	CKen
	– 'Richard Lee'	CKen
	– 'Ryo-ku-ho'	CKen
	– 'Ryu-ju'	CKen IArd NLar
	– 'Sa-dai-jin'	CKen
	– 'San-bo'	CKen
§	– 'Saphir'	CKen
	– 'Schoon's Bonsai'	CDoC NHol NLar
	– 'Setsugekka'	CKen NLar
	– 'Shika-shima'	CKen
	– 'Shimada'	CKen
	– 'Shin Sen' **new**	NLar
	– Shiobara-goyo Group	CKen
	– 'Shirobana'	NLar
	– 'Shizukagoten'	CKen
	– 'Shu-re'	CKen NLar
	– 'Sieryoden'	CKen
	– 'Smout'	CKen
	– 'Tani-mano-uki'	CKen NHol
	– 'Tempelhof'	MGos NLar NPCo
	– 'Tenysu-kazu'	CKen
	– 'Tokyo Dwarf'	CKen NLar
	– 'Tribune'	NLar
	– 'Walker's Dwarf'	CKen
	– 'Watnong'	CKen
	– 'Zelkova'	CMen
	– 'Zui-sho'	CKen
	patula ♀H2-3	CBcs CCCN CDoC CDul CHll CLnd CMCN EPfP EUJe IDee IVic LAst LRHS NSoo SAPC SBig SCoo SLim SPlb WPGP
	peuce	GLin IGor NWea
	– 'Arnold Dwarf'	CKen
	– 'Cesarini'	CKen
	– 'Daniel' **new**	CKen
	– 'Thessaloniki Broom'	CKen
	pinaster ♀H4	CBcs CDoC CDul CLnd EPfP GQue IVic MMuc SEND
	pinea ♀H4	CAgr CArn CCVT CDoC CDul CLnd CTho ELau EPfP EUJe IVic LRHS MGos MMuc SAPC SCoo SEND SEWo SGol SLim SPlb
	– 'Queensway'	CKen
	ponderosa ♀H4	CDul CLnd NLar
	– var. ***scopulorum***	NWea
	pseudostrobus	WPGP
	– NJM 09.009A	WPGP
	pumila 'Buchanan'	CKen

	- 'Draijer's Dwarf'	LRHS SCoo SLim
	- 'Dwarf Blue'	NHol NLar
	- 'Glauca' ♀H4	CDoC CKen MAsh NLar
	- 'Globe'	MAsh SLim
	- 'Jeddeloh'	CKen
	- 'Knightshayes'	CKen
	- 'Pinocchio'	CKen
	- 'Säntis'	CKen
	- 'Saphir'	see *P. parviflora* 'Saphir'
	radiata ♀H3-4	CBcs CCVT CDoC CDul CLnd CMac CTri ECrN ELan EPfP EUJe LRHS MMuc NSoo NWea SAPC SCoo SEND
	- Aurea Group	CDoC CDul EPfP MAsh NEgg NPCo SCoo SLim SPoG
	- 'Bodnant'	CKen
	- 'Isca'	CKen
	- 'Marshwood' (v)	CKen SLim
	resinosa 'Don Smith'	CKen
	- 'Joel's Broom'	CKen
	- 'Quinobequin'	CKen
	× ***schwerinii***	CDoC CKen
	- 'Wiethorst'	CKen IDee LRHS NLar SLim
	sibirica 'Blue Smoke'	CKen
	- 'Mariko'	CKen
	strobiformis 'Coronado'	CKen
	- 'Loma Linda'	CKen SLim
	strobus	CBcs CCVT CDul CLnd CMen EPfP MGos MMuc NWea SEND SLim
§	- 'Alba'	SLim
	- 'Amelia's Dwarf'	CKen
	- 'Angel Falls' new	CKen
	- 'Anna Fiele'	CKen MBri
	- 'Bergman's Mini'	CKen NLar
	- 'Bergman's Pendula Broom'	CKen
I	- 'Bergman's Sport of Prostrata'	CKen
	- 'Beth'	CKen
	- 'Bloomer's Dark Globe'	CKen
	- 'Blue Shag'	LRHS NLar SCoo SLim SPer SPoG
	- 'Brevifolia'	CKen
	- 'Cesarini'	CKen
	- 'Compacta'	NPCo
	- 'Contorta'	CDoC
	- 'Densa'	CKen
	- 'Diggy' new	NLar
	- 'Ed's Broom'	CKen
	- 'Elkins Dwarf'	CKen NLar
	- 'Fastigiata'	CKen
	- 'Golden Showers'	NLar
	- 'Green Curls'	CKen
	- 'Green Twist'	MAsh SLim
	- 'Greg'	CKen
	- 'Hershey'	CKen
	- 'Hillside Gem'	CKen
	- 'Himmelblau'	EUJe IDee MBlu NLar SLim
	- 'Horsford'	CDoC CKen LRHS SLim
	- 'Horsford Sister'	CKen
	- 'Julian Pott'	CKen
	- 'Julian's Dwarf'	CKen
	- 'Krügers Lilliput'	LRHS NLar SLim
	- 'Louie'	CKen LRHS NLar
	- 'Macopin'	NLar
	- 'Mary Butler'	CKen NLar
	- 'Merrimack'	CKen
	- 'Minima'	CDoC CDul CKen LRHS MBlu NLar NPCo NWea SLim SPoG WGor
	- 'Minuta'	CKen
	- 'Nana'	see *P. strobus* Nana Group
	- 'Nana Compacta'	LRHS
§	- Nana Group	NPri SEWo WGor
	- 'Nivea'	see *P. strobus* 'Alba'
	- 'Northway Broom'	CKen LRHS SLim
	- 'Pacific Sunrise' new	NLar
	- 'Pendula'	CKen IDee
I	- 'Pendula Broom'	CKen
	- 'Radiata'	CTri MBri NLar
I	- 'Radiata Aurea'	LRHS
	- 'Reinshaus'	CKen
	- 'Sayville'	CKen
	- 'Sea Urchin'	CKen LRHS SLim
	- 'Secrest'	LRHS NLar
	- 'Stowe Pillar'	NLar SLim
	- 'Tiny Kurls'	CKen MAsh SLim
	- 'Torulosa'	MBlu
	- 'Uncatena'	CKen
	- 'Verkade's Broom'	CKen
	sylvestris ♀H4	CBcs CCVT CDoC CDul CHab CMac CTho CTri ECrN EHul ELan EPfP LAst LBuc LRHS MGos MJak MMuc NEgg NLar NWea SEND SEWo SGol SPer SPlb SPoG WHar WMou
	- 'Abergeldie'	CKen
	- 'Alderly Edge'	CMen
	- 'Andorra'	CKen
§	- 'Argentea'	CMen SLim
	- 'Aurea'	see *P. sylvestris* Aurea Group
§	- Aurea Group ♀H4	CDul CKen CMac CMen EHul EUJe MAsh MBlu MJak NEgg NLar NPCo NPri NWea SCoo SLim SPer SPoG SSta
	- 'Avondene'	CKen
	- 'Bergfield'	CMen NLar
	- 'Beuvronensis' ♀H4	CMen MGos NEgg NLar NPCo
	- 'Blue Sky'	NLar
	- 'Bonna'	LRHS
	- 'Buchanan's Gold'	CKen
	- 'Burghfield'	CMen
	- 'Chantry Blue'	CMen EHul LRHS MAsh MBri MGos NEgg NLar NPCo SCoo SLim
	- 'Clumber Blue'	CKen
	- 'Dereham'	CKen
	- 'Doone Valley'	CKen NEgg NPCo
	- 'Edwin Hillier'	see *P. sylvestris* 'Argentea'
	- Fastigiata Group	CDoC CDul CEnd CKen CMac CMen GQue IDee LRHS NPCo SCoo SLim SPoG WCFE
	- 'Frensham'	CKen MAsh MBri MGos NLar NPCo
	- 'Globosa'	NPCo
	- 'Gold Coin'	CDoC CKen CMen EPfP LRHS MAsh NEgg NHol NLar NPCo SCoo SLim SPoG
	- 'Gold Medal'	CKen SLim
	- 'Grand Rapids'	CKen
	- 'Gwydyr Castle'	CKen
	- 'Hesley Dwarf'	NLar
	- 'Hillside Creeper'	CKen LRHS NLar SLim
	- 'Humble Pie'	CKen
	- 'Inverleith' (v)	EHul
	- 'Jeremy'	CKen NEgg NPCo
	- 'John Boy'	CMen
	- 'Kelpie'	LRHS
	- 'Kenwith'	CKen
	- 'Lakeside Dwarf'	CMen
	- 'Lodge Hill'	CMen LRHS MAsh NPCo SLim
	- 'Longmoor'	CKen NLar

	- 'Martham'	CKen CMen
	- 'Mitsch Weeping'	CKen
*	- 'Moseri'	MAsh NPCo
	- 'Munches Blue'	CKen
	- 'Nana' misapplied	see *P. sylvestris* 'Watereri'
	- 'Nana Compacta'	CMen
§	- 'Nisbet's Gem'	CKen CMen
	- 'Padworth'	CMen NLar
	- 'Perkeo' new	NLar
	- 'Peve Miba'	NLar
I	- 'Pine Glen'	CKen
	- 'Piskowitz'	CKen
	- 'Pixie'	CKen NLar
I	- 'Prostrata'	NPCo
	- 'Repens'	CKen
	- 'Saint George'	CKen
	- 'Saxatilis'	CKen CMen
	- subsp. ***scotica***	GQue NWea
	- 'Scott's Dwarf'	see *P. sylvestris* 'Nisbet's Gem'
	- 'Scrubby'	NLar
	- 'Sentinel'	CKen NLar
	- 'Skjak I'	CKen
	- 'Skjak II'	CKen LRHS
	- 'Slimkin'	CKen
	- 'Spaan's Slow Column'	CKen LRHS SCoo SLim
	- 'Tage'	CKen
	- 'Tanya'	CKen
	- 'Tilhead'	CKen
	- 'Treasure'	CKen MBri
	- 'Trefrew Quarry'	CKen
	- 'Troll Guld'	NLar
	- 'Vargguld'	CKen
§	- 'Watereri'	CNWT EHul LAst LRHS MBri MJak NLar NPri SCoo SLim
	- 'Westonbirt'	CKen CMen MAsh
	tabuliformis	CDul
	taeda	CDul EPfP WPGP
	taiwanensis	CDoC CDul EPfP
	thunbergii	CDul CLnd CMCN CMen ELan GQue MMuc NSoo
	- 'Akame'	CKen CMen
	- 'Akame Yatsabusa'	CMen
	- 'Aocha-matsu' (v)	CKen CMen NLar
	- 'Arakawa-sho'	CKen CMen
	- 'Banshosho'	CKen CMen LRHS NLar
	- 'Beni-kujaku'	CKen CMen
	- 'Compacta'	CKen CMen
	- var. ***corticosa*** 'Fuji'	CMen
	- - 'Iihara'	CMen
	- 'Dainagon'	CKen CMen
	- 'Eechee-nee'	CKen
	- 'Hayabusa'	CMen
	- 'Iwai'	CMen
	- 'Janome'	CMen
	- 'Katsuga'	CMen
	- 'Kotobuki'	CKen CMen NLar NPCo
	- 'Koyosho'	CMen
	- 'Kujaku'	CKen CMen
	- 'Kyokko'	CKen CMen
	- 'Kyushu'	CKen CMen
	- 'Maijima'	NLar
	- 'Mikawa'	CMen MBlu
	- 'Miyajuna'	CKen CMen
	- 'Nishiki-ne'	CKen CMen
	- 'Nishiki-tsusaka'	CMen
	- 'Oculus-draconis' (v)	CMen NPCo
	- 'Ōgon'	CMen LRHS NLar SLim
	- 'Porky'	CKen CMen
§	- 'Sayonara'	CMen LRHS MAsh NLar
	- 'Senryu'	CKen CMen
	- 'Shinsho'	CKen CMen
	- 'Shio-guro'	CKen CMen
	- 'Suchiro'	NEgg NPCo
	- 'Suchiro Yatabusa'	CKen CMen
	- 'Sunsho'	CKen CMen
	- 'Taihei'	CKen CMen
I	- 'Thunderhead'	CDoC CKen CMen LRHS NLar NSoo SLim
	- 'W.B.'	CKen
	- 'Yatsubusa'	see *P. thunbergii* 'Sayonara'
	- 'Ye-i-kan'	CKen
	- 'Yoshimura'	CMen
	- 'Yumaki'	CKen CMen
	uncinata	see *P. mugo* subsp. *uncinata*
	- 'Etschtal'	CKen
	- 'Grünne Welle'	SLim
	- 'Jezek'	CKen
	- 'Kostelnicek'	CKen
	- 'Leuco-like'	CKen
	- 'Offenpass'	CKen
	- 'Süsse Perle'	CKen
	virginiana 'Wate's Golden'	CKen NLar SLim
§	***wallichiana*** ♀H4	CCVT CDoC CDul CGHE CJun CKen CMCN CTho EHul EPfP IDee LRHS MBlu MGos MJak MMuc NEgg NHol NLar NPCo NWad NWea SBir SEND SEWo SGol SLim SPoG WPGP
	- 'Densa'	NLar
	- 'Densa Hill'	LRHS
	- 'Frosty'	CKen
	- 'Nana'	CKen LRHS NLar SCoo SLim SPoG
	- 'Umbraculifera'	MBri
	- var. ***wallichiana***	EUJe
	- 'Zebrina' (v)	MBlu NHol NLar
	yunnanensis	CDoC

Piper (*Piperaceae*)

	auritum	GPoy LEdu
	excelsum	see *Macropiper excelsum*

Piptanthus (*Papilionaceae*)

	forrestii	see *P. nepalensis*
	laburnifolius	see *P. nepalensis*
§	***nepalensis***	CBcs CDul CSpe EBee EGri ELan EPfP LAst LHop LRHS MGos MPie MSCN NBid NLar NSoo SBrt SPer SPhx SPoG SRms
	aff. ***nepalensis***	SWvt
	tomentosus	CFil

Pistacia (*Anacardiaceae*)

	chinensis	CBcs EBtc EPfP WPGP
	lentiscus	CArn CBcs EBee EUJe SEND SVen XSen
	terebinthus	XSen

Pistia (*Araceae*)

	stratiotes	CBAq MSKA NPer SCoo

Pitcairnia (*Bromeliaceae*)

	bergii	CHII
	heterophylla	WCot
	recurvata new	WCot
	ringens new	WCot

Pittosporum ✿ (*Pittosporaceae*)

	anomalum	CCCN CDoC ECou MOWG
	- (f)	ECou

- (m)	ECou
- 'Falcon'	ECou
- 'Raven' (f)	ECou
- 'Starling' (m)	ECou
* ***argyrophyllum***	MGos
'Arundel Green'	CDoC EPfP EUJe LRHS LSRN MAsh MBri SHil SLim SWvt
bicolor	CTsd GQui WPGP
buchananii	SVen
colensoi	ECou
- 'Cobb' (f)	ECou
- 'Wanaka' (m)	ECou
'Collaig Silver'	EPfP LRHS MAsh SLim
crassifolium	CCCN CHEx CTsd ECou
- 'Havering Dwarf' (f)	ECou
- 'Napier' (f)	ECou
- 'Variegatum' (v)	CCCN WPat
'Crinkles' (f)	ECou SVen
daphniphylloides	CHEx EBee ELan WPGP
- B&SWJ 6789	WCru
- RWJ 9913	WCru
'Dark Delight' (m)	ECou
'Essex' (f/v)	ECou
eugenioides	CHEx CSam ESwi
- 'Platinum' (v)	CBcs CCCN EBee LRHS
- 'Variegatum' (v) ♀H3	CBcs CCCN CDoC CDul CHEx CHel CMac EBee EHoe EPfP EUJe EWTr GQui IArd IDee LAst LHop LRHS MBri MGos NLar SEND SHil SKHP SLim SPoG SVen
'Garnettii' (v) ♀H3	Widely available
glabratum B&SWJ 11685	WCru
heterophyllum	ECou ECrN ELan EWes SEND
- variegated (v)	EBee EBtc ECou LRHS WSHC
'Holbrook' (v)	CSam
'Humpty Dumpty'	ECou
illicioides	WCru
var. ***angustifolium*** B&SWJ 6771	
- - RWJ 9846	WCru
- var. ***illicioides*** B&SWJ 6712	WCru
× ***intermedium***	CWib ECou SWvt
- 'Craxten' (f)	CCCN EBee ECou
michiei	ECou
- (f)	ECou
- (m)	ECou
- 'Jack' (m)	ECou
- 'Jill' (f)	ECou
'Nanum Variegatum'	see *P. tobira* 'Variegatum'
obcordatum	ECou
- var. ***kaitaiaense***	ECou
oblongilimbum DJHV 06137	WCru
'Oliver Twist'	LRHS LSRN SCoo
omeiense	ECou EWes SKHP
pimeleoides var. ***reflexum*** (m)	ECou
ralphii	CCCN CTsd EBee ECou
- 'Green Globe'	SKHP
- 'Variegatum' (v)	CCCN CGHE LRHS SKHP WPGP
ralphii* × *tenuifolium	ECou
'Saundersii' (v)	SCoo
tenuifolium ♀H3	Widely available
- 'Abbotsbury Gold' (f/v)	CAbb CBcs CCCN CDoC CMac CTri EBee ECou EHoe ELan EPfP EUJe EWes LAst LRHS MGos MREP MSwo MWat NSoo SEND SGol SLim SPer SWvt WHar WSHC
- 'Atropurpureum'	ELan
- 'Brockhill Compact'	EBee LRHS
- 'Cornish Mist' **new**	CTsd
- 'County Park'	CCCN EUJe
- 'County Park Dwarf'	ECou
- 'Deborah' (v)	ECou
- 'Dixie'	ECou
§ - 'Eila Keightley' (v)	CMHG
- 'Elizabeth' (m/v)	CAbP CBcs CDoC CMac EBee ECou EHoe EPfP EUJe IArd LRHS LSRN MAsh MBri MGos MREP MRav NLar SEND SHil SLim SPoG
- 'French Lace'	CBcs CCCN EBee ECou ELan NLar SEND
- 'Gold Star'	CDoC EBee ECou EHoe ELan ELon EPfP LAst LBMP LRHS MAsh MBri MGos SCoo SLim SPer SPoG SWvt WMoo
- 'Golden Cut'	NLar
- 'Golden King'	CCCN CDoC CMHG CMac CSBt EBee EPfP LRHS MAsh MGos NEgg NPla SHil SLim SPoG SRms
- 'Golden Princess' (f)	ECou
- 'Golf Ball' PBR	CBcs CDoC EPfP EUJe LRHS
- 'Green Elf'	ECou
- 'Green Thumb'	CMac ELan
- 'Irene Paterson' (m/v) ♀H3	Widely available
- 'James Stirling'	CCCN ECou EPfP
- 'John Flanagan'	see *P. tenuifolium* 'Margaret Turnbull'
- 'Limelight' (v)	CBcs CSBt EBee EBtc EPfP LHop LRHS LSRN MGos SLim SPoG
- 'Loxhill Gold'	CCCN EBee IArd LRHS NPla SEND SGol
§ - 'Margaret Turnbull' (v)	CBcs EBee ECou ELan EPfP EWes GKin LHop LRHS LSRN MGos SGol
- 'Marjory Channon' (v)	ELan EPfP LRHS LSRN
- 'Mellow Yellow'	CAbP
- 'Moonlight' (v)	CBcs EHoe LRHS MRav
- 'Mountain Green'	CMac
- 'Nutty's Leprechaun'	CCCN
- 'Pompom'	CCCN EBee IVic LRHS
- 'Purpureum' (m)	CCCN CMac CSBt CSam CTri EHoe EPfP EUJe LAst LRHS LSRN MAsh MWat NEgg NLar SCoo SEND SHil SLim SPer SPoG SRms
- 'Silver Magic' (v)	CBcs EPfP LRHS NLar
- 'Silver Princess' (f)	ECou
- 'Silver Queen' (f/v) ♀H3	Widely available
- 'Silver Sheen' (m)	CBcs CJun CMac ECou LRHS
- 'Stevens Island'	CBcs CJun LRHS
- 'Stirling Gold' (f/v)	ECou EPfP EWes
- 'Sunburst'	see *P. tenuifolium* 'Eila Keightley'
- 'Tandara Gold' (v)	CBcs CCCN CSBt EBee ECou EHoe ELan ELon EPfP EUJe LBMP LRHS LSRN MAsh MBri MGos SCoo SLim SPoG WCot
- 'Tiki' (m)	CBcs CCCN ECou
- 'Tom Thumb' ♀H3	Widely available
- 'Tresederi' (f/m)	CCCN CTsd ECou
- 'Variegatum' (m/v)	CBcs CDoC CSBt EBee ECou LRHS LSRN MGos MSwo SAPC SHil SLim SPer SPoG SWvt WGob WHar
- 'Victoria' (v)	CBcs CCCN LRHS LSRN MGos SLim SPoG
- 'Warnham Gold' (m) ♀H3	CBcs CDoC CMac CWib EBee ECou ELan EPfP GKin IVic LHop LRHS

		MAsh MGos SLim SPer SPoG SSpi SVen WCot
	- 'Wendle Channon' (m/v)	CBcs CCCN CMHG CMac CSBt EBee ECou EHoe EPfP LRHS MAsh SGol SLim SPer WSHC
	- 'Wrinkled Blue'	CBcs EBee EPfP LRHS MAsh MRav SPoG
	tobira ♀H3	Widely available
*	- 'Cuneatum'	CCCN CDoC CExl ELan EPfP LHop LRHS SKHP
*	- 'Nanum'	CBcs CCCN CDoC CHel CMac EBee ELan EPfP EUJe LRHS MGos MOWG SAPC SLim SPer SPoG
§	- 'Variegatum' (v) ♀H2-3	CBcs CCCN CHll CMac EBee ELan EPfP EUJe IVic LHop LRHS LSRN MGos NLar SAPC SEND SKHP SLim SLon SPer SPoG SSta WSHC
	'Trim's Hedger'	CTho
	undulatum	CHEx
	viridiflorum	EShb

Pityrogramma (*Pteridaceae*)

	trifoliata new	WCot

Plagianthus (*Malvaceae*)

	betulinus	see *P. regius*
	divaricatus	CBcs
	lyallii	see *Hoberia lyallii*
§	***regius***	CBcs SBig

Plagiorhegma see *Jeffersonia*

Plantago (*Plantaginaceae*)

	asiatica 'Variegata' (v)	NBro
	coronopus	ELau
	holosteum	GKev
	lanceolata	CArn CHab NMir WHfH WSFF
	- 'Freaky'	WHer
	- 'Golden Spears'	EBee
	major	CArn GPoy WSFF
	- 'Atropurpurea'	see *P. major* 'Rubrifolia'
	- 'Bowles's Variety'	see *P. major* 'Rosularis'
	- 'Brenda' new	CNat
§	- 'Rosularis'	CArn CFis CRow CSpe EBee LEdu MHer NBro NChi SPav SRms WHer
§	- 'Rubrifolia'	CArn CHid CSpe EShb LDai LLWG MBNS MHer NBid NBro NChi NDov NLBP WHer WMoo WSFF XLum
	maritima	WHer
	media	CHab MHer
	psyllium L.	CArn
	rosea	see *P. major* 'Rosularis'
	subulata	MHer
	triandra 'Wanaka'	IMou

Platanthera (*Orchidaceae*)

	bifolia	NLAp
	chlorantha	NLAp
	hologlottis	EFEx
	metabifolia	EFEx

Platanus ✿ (*Platanaceae*)

	× ***acerifolia***	see *P.* × *hispanica*
§	× ***hispanica*** ♀H4	CBcs CCVT CDul CLnd CMCN EBee ECrN ELan EPfP EWTr LAst LBuc MGos MMuc NWea SEND SEWo SGol SPer WMou
	- 'Alphen's Globe'	SEWo
	- 'Bloodgood'	CTho
	- 'Suttneri' (v)	WMou
	orientalis ♀H4	CCVT CDul CLnd CMCN CTho EPfP SLPl
	- PAB 346	LEdu
	- 'Cuneata'	ECrN
§	- f. ***digitata*** ♀H4	CCVT CDul CLnd CMCN CTho EBee EPfP ERod MBlu
	- var. ***insularis***	WPGP
	- 'Laciniata'	see *P. orientalis* f. *digitata*
	- 'Minaret'	CDul
	- 'Mirkovec'	IArd MBri

Platycarya (*Juglandaceae*)

	strobilacea	CBcs CMCN LEdu

Platycerium (*Polypodiaceae*)

	alcicorne misapplied	see *P. bifurcatum*
§	***bifurcatum*** ♀H1	CCCN XBlo

Platycladus (*Cupressaceae*)

§	***orientalis*** 'Aurea Nana' ♀H4	CKen CMac CSBt CWib EHul ELan EPfP LBee LRHS MGos MJak NWea SGol SLim SPoG
	- 'Autumn Glow'	CKen WGor
	- 'Beverleyensis'	NLar
	- 'Collen's Gold'	EHul
	- 'Conspicua'	CKen CSBt CWib EHul SPoG
	- 'Elegantissima' ♀H4	EHul LRHS
	- 'Franky Boy'	CDoC LAst LRHS NHol NLar SLim SPoG
	- 'Golden Pygmy'	CKen
	- 'Juniperoides'	EHul
	- 'Kenwith'	CKen
	- 'Magnifica'	EHul
	- 'Meldensis'	CDoC CTri EHul
	- 'Minima'	EHul WGor
	- 'Minima Glauca'	CKen
	- 'Morgan'	NLar
I	- 'Pyramidalis Aurea'	LBee
	- 'Raffles'	WBor
	- 'Rosedalis'	CKen CSBt EHul EPfP LBee LRHS
	- 'Sanderi'	WCFE
	- 'Sieboldii'	EHul
	- 'Southport'	LBee
	- 'Summer Cream'	CKen EHul
	- 'Westmont' (v)	NLar

Platycodon ✿ (*Campanulaceae*)

	grandiflorus ♀H4	CArn CTri ELau EPfP GKev LHop LRHS MHer SRms WHar WHoo
	- 'Albus'	EPfP LRHS SPer SWvt WHar WHoo
	- Apoyama Group ♀H4	WHoo WThu
	- - 'Fairy Snow'	CHel EShb EWTr NBre WHoo WSHC
	- (Astra Series) 'Astra Blue'	EPfP LHop LRHS SPoG SRot
	- - 'Astra Pink'	LRHS SPoG
	- - 'Astra White'	EBee SPoG
	- 'Blue Pearl'	WHoo
	- 'Fuji Blue'	WHoo XLum
	- 'Fuji Pink'	ELan EPfP LAst LHop LRHS MRav SWvt WHoo WWEG XLum
	- 'Fuji White'	ELan GKev WWEG XLum
	- 'Hakone'	MRav WHoo
	- 'Hakone Blue'	CHel EPfP NBre
*	- 'Hakone Double Blue' (d)	ELan MBNS SRms
	- 'Hakone White'	EPfP MRav WHoo
	- 'Mariesii' ♀H4	CDoy CSBt EPfP LAst LRHS MHol MNHC MRav NBir NEgg SEND SPer SPlb SRms SWvt WHoo WWlt

- 'Miss Tilly' new	MHol
- Mother of Pearl	see *P. grandiflorus* 'Perlmutterschale'
§ - 'Perlmutterschale'	EBee EPfP MRav
- 'Pink Star'	EBee
- ***pumilus***	WHoo
- 'Sentimental Blue'	CWib XLum
- 'Shell Pink'	see *P. grandiflorus* 'Perlmutterschale'
- 'Willy'	XLum
- 'Zwerg'	EShb NBre

Platycrater (*Hydrangeaceae*)

arguta	WCru
- B&SWJ 6266	WCru

Plectranthus (*Lamiaceae*)

sp.	LAst
from Puerto Rico	CArn
ambiguus	EOHP
- 'Manguzuku'	EOHP
- 'Nico'	EOHP SBch
- 'Umigoye'	EOHP
amboinicus	CArn EOHP MNHC WJek
* - 'Variegatus' (v)	EOHP
- 'Well Sweep Wedgewood' (v)	EOHP
argentatus ♀^{H2}	CDoC CSpe EOHP EShb EUJe GCal IDee MCot SDix SEND SRkn WKif WWlt
- 'Hill House' (v)	CHll EOHP
- 'Silver Shield'	MPie
australis misapplied	see *P. verticillatus*
barbatus	EOHP
behrii	see *P. fruticosus*
Blue Angel = 'Edelblau' (Cape Angels Series)	EOHP
caninus	SPoG
ciliatus	EOHP EShb EUJe SRkn
- 'Easy Gold' (v)	EOHP EUJe
- 'Sasha' (v)	CCCN CDoC CHll ECtt EShb SPet
'Cloud Nine'	EOHP
coleoides 'Marginatus'	see *P. forsteri* 'Marginatus'
- 'Variegatus'	see *P. madagascariensis* 'Variegated Mintleaf'
Cuban oregano	EOHP
ecklonii	EOHP
'Medley Wood'	EOHP
ernstii	EOHP
excisus	CDes EBee IMou WPGP
forskohlii new	EOHP
§ ***forsteri*** 'Marginatus'	EOHP
'Frills'	EOHP
§ ***fruticosus***	EOHP EUJe SBch
- 'Behr's Pride'	EOHP
- 'James'	EOHP EUJe
hadiensis var. ***tomentosus*** 'Carnegie'	EOHP
- - green-leaved	EOHP
- - 'Penge' (v)	EOHP
- var. ***woodii***	EOHP
madagascariensis	EOHP
- gold-leaved	EOHP
- 'Lothlorien' (v)	EOHP
§ - 'Variegated Mintleaf' (v) ♀^{H1}	EOHP MNHC SRms WJek
'Marble Ruffles'	EOHP
menthol-scented, large-leaved	EOHP
menthol-scented, small-leaved	EOHP
Mona Lavender = 'Plepalila'^{PBR}	EOHP
mutabilis	EOHP
neochilus	CSpe
§ ***oertendahlii*** ♀^{H1}	EBak EOHP
- silver-leaved	EOHP
ornatus	EOHP NPla
- 'Pee Off'	EOHP
- variegated (v)	EOHP
prostratus	EOHP
purpuratus small-leaved	EOHP
rehmannii	EOHP
rotundifolius new	LEdu
saccatus	EOHP
subsp. ***longitubus***	
- subsp. ***pondoensis***	EOHP
sinensis	LRHS
spicatus	EOHP
- 'Nelspruit'	EOHP
strigosus	EOHP
Swedish ivy	see *P. verticillatus*, *P. oertendahlii*
§ ***thyrsoideus***	EOHP
§ ***verticillatus***	EOHP
- 'Barberton'	EOHP
- 'Pink Surprise'	EOHP
Vick's plant	EOHP
zatarhendii	EOHP
zuluensis	CArn CDoC EOHP EShb EUJe SBch SDix SRkn WBor
- dark-leaved	EOHP
- 'Sky'	EOHP

Pleioblastus (*Poaceae*)

akebono	see *P. argenteostriatus* 'Akebono'
§ ***argenteostriatus*** 'Akebono'	ERod
§ - f. ***pumilus***	CDoC EHoe ERod MBlu MMuc MWht SPlb
auricomus	see *P. viridistriatus*
- 'Vagans'	see *Sasaella ramosa*
chino f. ***aureostriatus*** (v)	MMoz
- f. ***elegantissimus***	CCon CDoC CEnt EPfP ERod EShb MMoz MMuc NLar SBig SEND WJun WMoo
- var. ***hisauchii***	ERod MWht WJun
- 'Kimmei'	MMuc
fortunei	see *P. variegatus* 'Fortunei'
'Gauntlettii'	see *P. argenteostriatus* f. *pumilus*
glaber 'Albostriatus'	see *Sasaella masamuneana* 'Albostriata'
§ ***hindsii***	ERod MMoz MMuc
§ ***humilis***	ENBC MWhi SEND
- var. ***pumilus***	see *P. argenteostriatus* f. *pumilus*
linearis	EAmu ERod LRHS MMoz MWht NLar SBig WJun WMoo
§ ***pygmaeus***	CDoC CDul CTri CTsd EHoe ELan ENBC MBrN MJak MMuc MWhi NBro NGdn NLar SGol SRms WMoo
§ - 'Distichus'	CEnt ENBC EPPr MJak MMuc MWht NLar WMoo
§ - 'Mirrezuzume'	CExl
* - var. ***pygmaeus*** 'Mini'	SEND
§ ***simonii***	LRHS MMuc MWht NLar SEND XBlo
- 'Variegatus' (v)	LRHS SPer
§ ***variegatus*** (v) ♀^{H4}	CBcs CDoC CDul CEnt EHoe ELan ELon ENBC EPfP LEdu LPot LRHS MBrN MJak MWht NSoo SAPC SDix SLim SPlb SWvt WJun WMoo XBlo

§ – 'Fortunei' (v)	CTsd MMuc SEND SGol
– 'Tsuboii' (v)	CAbb CDTJ CDoC ERod GQui MBrN MBri MJak MMoz MWhi MWht NLar SGol WJun WMoo
§ ***viridistriatus*** ♀H4	CBcs CDoC CDul CEnt CExl CWib EHoe ELon EPfP ERod GMaP LEdu LHop LRHS MBri MJak MMoz MMuc MRav MWht NLar NWsh SDix SEND SGol SPer SRms WJun WMoo XBlo
– f. ***variegatus*** (v)	CTsd SWvt WMoo

Pleione ✿ (*Orchidaceae*)

sp.	NDav
Adams gx	LYaf
Alishan gx 'Merlin'	LYaf
– 'Mother's Day'	LYaf
– 'Mount Fuji'	LYaf
Asama gx 'Red Grouse'	LYaf
aurita	EPot LYaf
Bandai-san gx 'Sand Grouse'	LYaf
× ***barbarae***	EPot IFoB LYaf
Barcena gx	EPot LYaf
Berapi gx 'Purple Sandpiper'	EPot LEdu LYaf
Betty Arnold gx	LYaf
Brigadoon gx	EPot
– 'Stonechat'	EPot LYaf
Britannia gx 'Doreen'	EPot LYaf
§ ***bulbocodioides***	CExl CFil EPot LYaf
§ – 'Yunnan'	IFoB
Captain Hook gx	LYaf
Caroli gx 'Cape Robin'	LYaf
chunii	EFEx LYaf
Danan gx	LYaf
Deriba gx	EPot LYaf
Eastfield gx 'Purple Emperor'	LYaf
Eiger gx	LYaf
El Pico gx 'Pheasant'	EPot LYaf
Erebus gx 'Redpoll'	LYaf
formosana ♀H2	CCon CFil CTsd ECho EFEx EPot LEdu WPGP
– Alba Group	ECho
– – 'Claire'	IFoB LEdu LYaf
– – 'Snow Bunting'	LEdu LYaf
– 'Blush of Dawn'	GLin LYaf
– 'Cairngorm'	IFoB
– 'Greenhill'	LYaf
– Hyb 8001	IFoB
– 'Iris'	IFoB
– 'Pitlochry'	LYaf
– (Pricei Group) 'Oriental Grace'	IFoB LYaf
– – 'Oriental Splendour'	LYaf
– 'Snow White'	CExl CFil LEdu LYaf WPGP
forrestii	ECho EFEx EPot
Fuego gx	IFoB
Gerry Mundey gx 'Tinney's Firs'	LYaf
§ ***grandiflora***	LYaf
Harlequin gx 'Norman'	LYaf
Hekla gx	IFoB
– 'Partridge'	LYaf
humilis	LYaf
Irazu gx	IFoB
Jorullo gx 'Long-tailed Tit'	LYaf
Keith Rattray gx 'Kelty'	LYaf
Kenya gx	LYaf
– 'Bald Eagle'	LYaf
Krakatoa gx 'Wheatear'	LYaf
Lascar gx 'Dipper'	LYaf
– 'Purple Finch'	LYaf
Leda gx	LYaf
Lhasa gx 'Blushes'	LYaf
limprichtii ♀H2	ECho EFEx EPot IFoB LEdu LYaf
Lyn Butterfield gx	LYaf
maculata	EFEx
Mandalay gx 'Purple Rain' new	LYaf
– 'Strawberry Fields' new	LYaf
Marion Johnson gx	LYaf
Mauna Loa gx	LYaf
– 'Glossy Starling'	LYaf
Mawenzi gx	LYaf
Michael Butterfield gx new	LYaf
Novarupta gx 'Goshawk'	LYaf
– 'Raven'	LYaf
Orizaba gx	LYaf
– 'Fish Eagle'	LYaf
Paricutin gx	LYaf
pinkepankii	see *P. grandiflora*
Piton gx	EPot LYaf
§ ***pleionoides***	EPot LYaf
pogonioides misapplied	see *P. pleionoides*
pogonioides (Rolfe) Rolfe	see *P. bulbocodioides*
Quizapu gx 'Peregrine'	LYaf
Rakata gx	EPot IFoB
– 'Locking Stumps'	EPot
– 'Redwing'	LYaf
– 'Shot Silk'	LYaf
– 'Skylark'	LYaf
Salek gx 'Eagle Owl' new	LYaf
San Salvador gx	LYaf
Sangay gx	LYaf
Santorini gx	LYaf
– 'Yellow Wagtail'	LYaf
saxicola	LYaf
scopulorum	EFEx LYaf
Shantung gx	CCon EPot
Shantung gx 'Ducat'	EPot LYaf
– 'Gerry Mundey'	LYaf
– 'Ridgeway'	LYaf
– 'Silver Anniversary'	LYaf
Sharon Ann Winter gx	LYaf
Shasta gx new	LYaf
Sirena gx new	LYaf
Soufrière gx	LYaf
speciosa Ames & Schltr.	see *P. pleionoides*
Stromboli gx 'Fireball'	CExl CFil EPot
Surtsey gx	EPot
Taal gx 'Red-tailed Hawk'	LYaf
× ***taliensis***	LYaf
Tarawera gx	LYaf
Tibesti gx	LYaf
Toff gx	LYaf
Tolima gx 'Moorhen'	LEdu LYaf
Tongariro gx	CPBP EPot
Versailles gx	EPot
– 'Bucklebury' ♀H2	EPot LYaf
Vesuvius gx	EPot
– 'Grey Wagtail'	LYaf
– 'Leopard'	LYaf
– 'Phoenix'	EPot LYaf
– 'Tawny Owl'	LYaf
Volcanello gx 'Honey Buzzard'	LYaf

- 'Song Thrush'	LYaf
Whakari gx	LYaf
Wharfedale gx 'Pine Warbler'	LYaf
yunnanensis misapplied	see *P. bulbocodioides* 'Yunnan'
Zeus Weinstein gx	IFoB LYaf WCot

Pleomele see *Dracaena*

Pleurospermum (*Apiaceae*)

sp. new	CSpe
from Nepal	WCot
aff. ***album*** KWJ 12281	WCru
aff. ***amabile*** BWJ 7886	WCru
benthamii B&SWJ 2988	WCru
calcareum B&SWJ 8008	WCru
yunnanense BWJ 7952A	WCru

plum see *Prunus domestica*

Plumbago (*Plumbaginaceae*)

§ ***auriculata*** ♀H1-2	CBcs CCCN CDoC CHEx CSBt CTri CWCL EBak ELan EPfP EPri EShb EUJe MOWG MRav SEND SMrm SPer SPoG SRms SVic
- f. ***alba*** ♀H1-2	CBcs CCCN CHEx CRHN CSev EPfP EShb MOWG SEND
- 'Crystal Waters'	CCCN CSam EShb
- dark blue-flowered	CRHN CSpe
- 'Escapade Blue' (Escapade Series)	CWGN SPre
capensis	see *P. auriculata*
larpentiae	see *Ceratostigma plumbaginoides*

Plumeria (*Apocynaceae*)

sp.	WSFF
rubra ♀H1	XBlo
- 'Golden Glow'	XBlo
- 'Velvet Red'	XBlo

Poa (*Poaceae*)

alpina	SMea XLum
chaixii	EHoe EPPr
cita	IMou
colensoi	EHoe GAbr
× ***jemtlandica***	EHoe EPPr
labillardierei	CKno CWCL EBee EHoe EPPr IMou MAvo MMuc NWsh SEND SPer WMoo XLum
pratensis	CHab

Podalyria (*Papilionaceae*)

calyptrata	SPlb
sericea	SPlb

Podocarpus ✿ (*Podocarpaceae*)

acutifolius	CBcs CDoC ECou IGor
- (f)	ECou
- (m)	ECou
alpinus R. Br. ex Hook. f.	CDul
andinus	see *Prumnopitys andina*
'Autumn Shades' (m)	ECou NLar
'Blaze' (f)	CBcs CDoC ECou LEdu LRHS MBrN NLar SCoo SLim SPoG
chilinus	see *P. salignus*
'Chocolate Box' (f)	ECou MAsh NLar SLim
'County Park Fire' PBR (f)	CBcs CDoC ECou EHul EPfP ESwi LRHS MAsh MGos NEgg NHol NLar SCoo SLim SPoG SWvt WGor
'County Park Treasure'	ECou
cunninghamii	ECou
- 'Kiwi' (f)	ECou
- 'Roro' (m)	CBcs CDoC ECou
cunninghamii × ***nivalis*** (f)	ECou
dacrydioides	see *Dacrycarpus dacrydioides*
elongatus 'Blue Chip'	CBcs
ferrugineus	see *Prumnopitys ferruginea*
'Flame'	CDoC ECou EHul MAsh NLar NPCo
'Guardsman'	ECou
'Havering' (f)	CDoC ECou
'Jill' (f)	ECou
latifolius	ECou
lawrencei	EHul WThu
- (f)	ECou
- 'Alpine Lass' (f)	ECou
- 'Blue Gem' (f)	CDoC ECou LRHS MAsh MGos MMuc SCoo SLim
- 'Kiandra'	ECou
- 'Kosciuszko'	ECou
- 'Pine Lake'	ECou
- 'Red Tip'	CDoC CMen LRHS MGos SCoo SLim
'Lucky Lad'	ECou
'Macho' (m)	ECou
macrophyllus	CDoC SAPC
- (m)	ECou
- 'Aureus'	CBcs
'Maori Prince' (m)	CDoC ECou NLar
matudae new	CFil
nivalis	CBcs CDul CMac ECou GCal SRms WThu
- 'Arthur' (m)	ECou
- 'Bronze'	CDoC ECou GCal
- 'Christmas Lights' (f)	ECou
- 'Clarence' (m)	ECou
- 'Cover Girl'	LRHS
- 'Green Queen' (f)	ECou
- 'Hikurangi'	CDoC
- 'Jack's Pass' (m)	ECou
- 'Kaweka' (m)	ECou
- 'Kilworth Cream' (v)	CBcs CDoC CMen ECou ESwi LRHS NHol NLar SLim SPoG SWvt WGor
- 'Little Lady' (f)	ECou
- 'Livingstone' (f)	ECou
- 'Lodestone' (m)	ECou
- 'Moffat' (f)	CDoC ECou
- 'Otari' (m)	CDoC ECou MAsh NLar
- 'Park Cover'	ECou
- 'Princess' (f)	ECou MBrN
- 'Ruapehu' (m)	CDoC ECou
- 'Trompenburg'	NLar
nubigenus	CBcs
'Orangeade' (f)	CBcs NLar
'Red Embers' (f)	CDoC ECou EPfP ESwi NEgg SCoo WGor
§ ***salignus*** ♀H3	CBcs CDoC CDul CExl CHEx CHel CTsd EPfP EUJe GGal IDee LRHS SAPC SLim WSHC WThu
- (f)	ECou
- (m)	ECou
'Soldier Boy'	ECou
spicatus	see *Prumnopitys taxifolia*
'Spring Sunshine' (f)	CBcs ECou NLar
totara	CBcs CBrP ECou LEdu
- 'Aureus'	CBcs CDoC ECou
- 'Pendulus'	CDoC ECou

	'Young Rusty' (f)	CBcs CDoC ECou MAsh NLar

Podophyllum (*Berberidaceae*)

	aurantiocaule	CExl GGGa
§	***delavayi***	CBct CCon CExl CLAP NLar SKHP WCot WCru
	difforme	CBct CLAP SKHP WCru
	emodi	see *Sinopodophyllum hexandrum* var. *emodi*
	- var. ***chinense***	see *Sinopodophyllum hexandrum* var. *chinense*
	hexandrum	see *Sinopodophyllum hexandrum*
	- var. ***chinense***	see *Sinopodophyllum hexandrum* var. *chinense*
	'Kaleidoscope' (v)	CBct CLAP ESwi EUJe NCGa NPnk WCot
	peltatum	CAby CArn CBct CBro CHel CHid CLAP CWCL EBee ECho EWTr EWld GAbr GBBs GBin GPoy LEdu LWst NLar NMyG NSti SPhx WBor WCot WCru WPGP WPnP
	pleianthum	CAby CBct CLAP ECho LRHS WCru
	- B&SWJ 282 from Taiwan	WCru
	- short	WCru
	veitchii	see *P. delavayi*
	versipelle	CLAP LEdu LWst SKHP WCru
	- 'Spotty Dotty'PBR (v)	CBct CExl CLAP ECtt ESwi EUJe IBoy ITim LEdu LRHS MAvo MHol MMHG MMoz MNrw NLar NPnk NSti SHeu SKHP SMad WCot

Podranea (*Bignoniaceae*)

§	***ricasoliana***	CRHN EBee MOWG SPoG WBor

Pogonatherum (*Poaceae*)

*	***distichum***	XBlo

Pogonia (*Orchidaceae*)

	sp.	NDav

Pogostemon (*Lamiaceae*)

	from An Veleniki Herb Farm, Pennsylvania	CArn
§	***cablin***	EOHP GPoy
	patchouly	see *P. cablin*

Polemonium ✿ (*Polemoniaceae*)

	ambervicsii	see *P. pauciflorum* subsp. *hinckleyi*
	'Apricot Beauty'	see *P. carneum* 'Apricot Delight'
N	***archibaldiae*** ♀H4	NBir SRms
	'Blue Pearl'	CMea ELan GJos LRHS MNrw NBro NGdn NLar SPer WPtf
§	***boreale***	LRHS NPol SWvt WMoo
	- 'Heavenly Habit'	GJos LRHS NGdn WJek
	brandegeei misapplied	see *P. pauciflorum*
§	***brandegeei*** Greene	CCVN GBin
	- subsp. ***mellitum***	see *P. brandegeei* Greene
§	***caeruleum***	CArn CSBt CSev EBee ELan EPfP GMaP GPoy IBoy IFro LHop LPot MHer MLHP MMuc MNHC NBro NLar NPol SEND SIde SPer SPlb SPoG SRms SWvt WJek WMoo
	- subsp. ***amygdalinum***	see *P. occidentale*
	- 'Bambino Blue'	EBee LRHS SWvt WHar
	- Brise d'Anjou = 'Blanjou'PBR (v)	CMac CMea ECtt ELan EPfP EShb EWes IBoy LRHS MAsh MBri NBir NGdn NLar NPol SMad SPer SWvt WWEG
	- subsp. ***caeruleum***	GKev
	- - f. ***albiflorum***	CBre CSBt CWCL ELan EPfP GAbr MBNS MBel MHer MRav NBro SGbt SPer SPoG SRms STes WMoo
I	- f. ***dissectum***	NPol
	- 'Filigree Clouds'	LRHS NGdn NLar
	- 'Filigree Skies'	LRHS NGdn NLar
	- var. ***grandiflorum***	see *P. caeruleum* subsp. *himalayanum*
§	- subsp. ***himalayanum***	CSpe GAbr WJek WMoo
	- 'Humile'	see *P.* 'Northern Lights'
	- 'Idylle'	NPol
	- 'Larch Cottage' (v)	NPol
	- 'Pam' (v)	NPol
	- 'Sky Blue'	MBel
	- 'Snow and Sapphires' (v)	EBee ECtt LSou MPnt NLar NPer NPol SWvt
	- 'Southern Skies'	NPol
	- subsp. ***vulgare***	NPol
	- white-flowered	GJos IBoy MMuc
	carneum	CTri EBee GMaP LRHS MCot MNrw NLar NPol WMoo
§	- 'Apricot Delight'	EDAr GJos MNHC MNrw NGdn NLar NPol SGbt SPer STes WHer WJek WPtf WWEG
	cashmerianum	see *P. caeruleum* subsp. *himalayanum*
	chartaceum	LLHF
	chinense new	GKev
	'Churchills'	CBre EBee NPol WPGP WSHC
	'Dawn Flight'	NPol
	'Eastbury Purple'	CElw MAvo NPol
	'Elworthy Amethyst'	CElw EBee NPol SBch WPGP
	eximium	ECho LLHF
	flavum	see *P. foliosissimum* var. *flavum*
	foliosissimum misapplied	see *P. archibaldiae*
	foliosissimum A. Gray	NPol
	- var. ***albiflorum***	see *P. foliosissimum* var. *alpinum*
§	- var. ***alpinum***	NPol
	- 'Bressingham'	NPol
	- 'Cottage Cream'	CDes NPol WCot WPGP
§	- var. ***flavum***	NPol
	- var. ***foliosissimum***	EWes NPol
	- 'Scottish Garden'	NPol
	- 'White Spirit'	NPol
	'Glebe Cottage Lilac'	GCra NBir NPol WPGP
	'Glebe Cottage Violet'	NPol
	'Hannah Billcliffe'	CDes CElw ECtt EWes MBrN MTis NPol SBch WPGP
	'Heaven Scent'	EBee MBri NDov NLar
	'Heavenly Blue'	IBoy
§	'Hopleys'	GCal LHop MNrw
	× ***jacobaea***	EBee EWes WCot WPGP
	'Katie Daley'	see *P.* 'Hopleys'
	'Lambrook Mauve' ♀H4	Widely available
	'Mary Mottram'	NPol
	mellitum	see *P. brandegeei* Greene
	'North Tyne'	NChi NPol
§	'Northern Lights'	Widely available
	'Norwell Mauve'	MAvo MNrw NPol
§	***occidentale***	NPol
§	***pauciflorum***	ECtt EDAr IFro LRHS NBir WJek WMoo WTou
§	- subsp. ***hinckleyi***	GKev LRHS NLBP NPol
§	- subsp. ***pauciflorum***	NPol SPav
	- silver-leaved	see *P. pauciflorum* subsp. *pauciflorum*
	- 'Sulphur Trumpets'	SPad SWvt
	- subsp. ***typicum***	see *P. pauciflorum* subsp. *pauciflorum*

'Pink Beauty'	EBee ELan EPfP EWTr GBuc NBre NGdn NPol WWEG
pulchellum Salisb.	see *P. reptans*
pulchellum Turcz.	see *P. caeruleum*
pulcherrimum misapplied	see *P. boreale*
- 'Tricolor'	see *P. boreale*
pulcherrimum Hook.	ECho NBro
- subsp. ***pulcherrimum***	LLHF
'Rainbow Magic'	NLar
§ ***reptans***	CArn GPoy MHer NBro NPol WMoo WPtf
- 'Album'	see *P. reptans* 'Virginia White'
- 'Blue Ice'	NPol
- 'Firmament'	EBee MAvo WPGP
* - 'Sky Blue'	NBro
- 'Stairway to Heaven'PBR (v)	Widely available
- 'Touch of Class'PBR (v)	LSou NLar SPoG
§ - 'Virginia White'	CBre CElw CMea CSev EBee EWes MAvo MTis NChi NPol SBch WPGP
- 'White Pearl'	MBel MHol NPri
'Ribby'	NPol
× ***richardsonii*** misapplied	see *P.* 'Northern Lights'
richardsonii Graham	see *P. boreale*
'Sapphire'	CBre LRHS
'Sonia's Bluebell'	CDes CElw CWCL EBee ECGP ECtt EPPr EWes MAvo MNrw MPie MTis NDov NLar NPol NSti SBch STes WPGP WWFP
'Sunnyside Storm' **new**	NPol
'Theddingworth'	EBee NPol
viscosum	LLHF NPol SPlb
- f. ***leucanthum***	NPol
yezoense	NBre NPol
- var. ***hidakanum***	NPol NWad
- - Bressingham Purple = 'Polbress'	CHel EBee ECtt ELan EWes GBin LHop LRHS MAsh MBNS MBri NCGa NDov NHol NLar NOrc NPol NPri NSti NWad SGbt SPer SPoG
- - 'Purple Rain'	Widely available

Polianthes (*Agavaceae*)

elongata	WCot
§ ***geminiflora***	WCot
tuberosa ♀H1-2	CBcs CCCN EPfP SPer WCot XLum
- 'The Pearl' (d)	SDeJ WCot WPGP XLum

Poliomintha (*Lamiaceae*)

bustamanta	CAby NBir SPhx WSHC

Poliothyrsis (*Salicaceae*)

sinensis ♀H4	CBcs EPfP IArd IDee MBri NLar WPGP

Pollia (*Commelinaceae*)

japonica	EShb ESwi EWes SBrt SPad

Polygala (*Polygalaceae*)

calcarea Bulley's form	EPot
- 'Lillet' ♀H4	CPBP ECho EHyd EWes LHop LLHF LRHS WAbe WThu
chamaebuxus ♀H4	CBcs GKev LLHF MAsh MGos NLar NSla SRms WThu
I - ***alba***	LBee NLar SChF WAbe
§ - var. ***grandiflora*** ♀H4	CBcs CCon ECho EPfP EPot GAbr GKev IVic LBee LHop MAsh MGos MWat NSla SChF SPoG WAbe WIce
- 'Kamniski'	EPot
- 'Loibl'	EPot
- 'Purpurea'	see *P. chamaebuxus* var. *grandiflora*
- 'Rhodoptera'	see *P. chamaebuxus* var. *grandiflora*
§ × ***dalmaisiana*** ♀H1	CAbb CCCN CHEx CHel CHll CRHN CSpe CTsd CWGN EBee ECre ELan EPri SEND SMrm SPlb WAbe WCFE
myrtifolia	CCCN ELan GFai MGos SPlb
- Bibi Pink = 'Polylap'	LBuc LHop SPoG
- 'Grandiflora'	see *P.* × *dalmaisiana*
'Purple Passion'	WHlf
virgata	CCCN

Polygonatum ✿ (*Asparagaceae*)

B&SWJ 8246 **new**	WCru
HWJ 551 **new**	WCru
HWJ 567 **new**	WCru
HWJ 573 **new**	WCru
HWJ 588 **new**	WCru
Og 94047	CDes LEdu
altelobatum B&SWJ 286	WCru
- B&SWJ 1886	WCru
arisanense B&SWJ 271	WCru
- B&SWJ 3839	WCru
§ ***biflorum***	Widely available
canaliculatum	see *P. biflorum*
cathcartii B&SWJ 2429	WCru
cirrhifolium	CCon CCse CDes CLAP CPom EBee EPot LWst MMoz MNrw SKHP WCru WPGP
- ARGS 320 **new**	EPPr
- red-flowered	EBee NLar
commutatum	see *P. biflorum*
'Corsley'	CPou
cryptanthum	WCru
curvistylum	CAvo CBct CCon CLAP CPom EPPr IFoB IGor IMou MNFA NLar NRya SPhx WCru WSHC
- pink-flowered	SBch
cyrtonema misapplied	see *Disporopsis pernyi*
cyrtonema Hua	CDes WCru
- B&SWJ 271 **new**	LEdu
* ***desoulavyi*** var. ***yezoense*** B&SWJ 764	WCru
falcatum misapplied	see *P. humile*
falcatum A. Gray	NRya
- B&SWJ 1077	WCru
- 'Shikoku Silver'	CLAP
- silver-striped	see *P. falcatum* 'Shikoku Silver'
- 'Variegatum'	see *P. odoratum* var. *pluriflorum* 'Variegatum'
'Falcon'	see *P. humile*
filipes	EPPr WCru
fuscum	WCru
geminiflorum	CBct CLAP CPom IGor LRHS WCru
- McB 2448	CLAP
giganteum	see *P. biflorum*
glaberrimum	CBct WCot
§ ***graminifolium***	CAby CBct CLAP CPBP CPom ECho EPPr GKev LRHS WCot WCru WThu
- G-W&P 803	ECho IPot
§ ***hirtum***	CBct CLAP CPom CPrp ECho EPPr IFoB LEdu MMoz NMyG WCru
- BM 7012	ECho
- 'Robustum'	LWst
hookeri	CAby CBct CExl ECho EPPr GBin IBal ITim LEdu LRHS LWst NBid NCGa NLar NMyG NRya NSla SPhx WCru WWEG

§	***humile***	CBct CDes CLAP ECho ELan EPPr EPfP GCal IBal LHop LWst MAvo MHer NGdn NLar NMyG NPnk SWvt WBor WCru WHil XLum
I	- 'Variegatum' (v)	CMac
§	× ***hybridum*** 🏆H4	Widely available
	- 'Betberg'	CAvo CBct CCon CLAP CPom CRow EPPr IFoB IMou MAvo NBir WCot
	- 'Flore Pleno' (d)	CBct ELon WHer
	- 'Nanum'	CBct CHid WCot
	- 'Purple Katie'	MAvo NMyG
§	- 'Striatum' (v)	Widely available
	- 'Variegatum'	see *P.* × *hybridum* 'Striatum'
	- 'Weihenstephan'	GCal IPot
	- 'Welsh Gold' (v)	CAvo
	inflatum	ECho WCru
	- B&SWJ 922	WCru
	involucratum	ECho WCru
	- B&SWJ 4285	WCru
	japonicum	see *P. odoratum*
	kingianum yellow-flowered B&SWJ 6545	WCru
	- - B&SWJ 6562	WCru
	'Langthorn's Variegated' (v)	ELan
	lasianthum	CPom LWst WCru
	- B&SWJ 671	NMyG WCru
	latifolium	see *P. hirtum*
	maximowiczii	CDes CPom EBee EPPr GCal WCru
	'Multifide'	EBee
	multiflorum misapplied	see *P.* × *hybridum*
	multiflorum L.	CBcs CElw CHab CHel CMac CPrp CRow CSBt CWCL ECho EPot GAbr GCal MRav NGdn NLar NMyG NPnk SGol SKHP SPlb SRms SWvt WBor WCAu WHer WMoo WWEG XLum
	- C 4572	WCot
	- ***giganteum*** hort.	see *P. biflorum*
*	***nanum*** 'Variegatum' (v)	CBcs ECho
	nodosum	WCru
§	***odoratum*** 🏆H4	CAvo CBct CBro CPom CRow CTsd EBee ECho GMaP NBid NLar NMyG NPnk NRya WCru WHil WWEG
	- 'Angel's Wings'	MAvo
§	- dwarf	ECho LEdu
	- 'Flore Pleno' (d) 🏆H4	CAvo CDes CLAP CPom CRDP ECho LEdu MMoz NMyG WCot WHoo
	- 'Grace Barker'	see *P.* × *hybridum* 'Striatum'
	- Kew form	EPot
	- var. ***pluriflorum***	EBee
§	- - 'Variegatum' (v) 🏆H4	Widely available
	- 'Red Stem'	ECho MAvo WCru
	- 'Silver Wings' (v)	CBct CLAP NBir NLar
	- var. ***thunbergii***	WCru
	- 'Ussuriland'	EPPr GCal MAvo
	- 'Ussuriland Roundleaf'	GCal
	officinale	see *P. odoratum*
	oppositifolium B&SWJ 2537	WCru
§	***orientale***	CBct CLAP ECho ELau LWst
	pluriflorum	see *P. graminifolium*
	polyanthemum	see *P. orientale*
	prattii	ECho LWst WCru
	pubescens	CBct ECho LEdu LWst WCru WThu
	pumilum	see *P. odoratum* dwarf
	punctatum	CBct CRDP LEdu NBid
	- B&SWJ 2395	CBct WCru
	racemosum	IMou
	roseum	CLAP CPom EPPr LLHF MAvo MMoz WCot WCru
	sewerzowii	EPPr
	sibiricum	CAvo CBct CPom CRDP IGor WCru
	- DJHC 600	CDes WPGP
	stenanthum	CPom LWst
	- B&SWJ 5727	LEdu WCru
	stenophyllum	CAvo IMou WCru
	stewartianum	CLAP EPPr NRya
	aff. ***tessellatum*** B&SWJ 9752	WCru
	'Variegatum' ambig. (v)	LPio
	verticillatum	CBct CBro CGHE CHel CHid CRow EPPr EPfP IFoB LEdu LRHS MNFA MNrw MRav SKHP SMad WCot WCru WPGP
	- CLD 1308	EPPr
	- PAB 2455 **new**	LEdu
	- 'Giant One'	EBee IMou MAvo
	- 'Himalayan Giant'	CHid ECho EPPr IPot LWst WPnP
	- 'Krynica' **new**	LEdu
*	- 'Roseum'	CAvo
	- 'Rubrum'	CAby CArn CBct CDes CLAP CRow EBee EPPr IGor LEdu LHop LRHS MAvo NBid NChi NLar WCot WCru WHil WWEG
	- 'Serbian Dwarf'	CBct CHid ECho EPot IPot LEdu
	aff. ***verticillatum***	CSpe IFoB
	wardii	WCot
	aff. ***wardii***	WCot
	- B&SWJ 6599	WCru
	white-flowered HWJ 861 **new**	WCru
	zanlanscianense	CBct CPom EBee IGor LWst WCru

Polygonum (*Polygonaceae*)

	affine	see *Persicaria affinis*
	amplexicaule	see *Persicaria amplexicaulis*
	aubertii	see *Fallopia baldschuanica*
	aviculare	CArn
	baldschuanicum	see *Fallopia baldschuanica*
	bistorta	see *Persicaria bistorta*
	capitatum	see *Persicaria capitata*
	compactum	see *Fallopia japonica* var. *compacta*
	equisetiforme misapplied	see *P. scoparium*
	filiforme	see *Persicaria virginiana*
	forrestii	GKev
	molle	see *Persicaria mollis*
	multiflorum	see *Fallopia multiflora*
	odoratum	see *Persicaria odorata*
	polystachyum	see *Persicaria wallichii*
	runciforme	see *Persicaria runcinata*
§	***scoparium***	EHoe ESwi EWes SDys SVen WOld XLum
	tinctorium	see *Persicaria tinctoria*
	vacciniifolium	see *Persicaria vacciniifolia*
	weyrichii	see *Persicaria weyrichii*

Polylepis (*Rosaceae*)

	australis	CSpe ESwi LEdu SEND SMad
	- tall	WPGP

Polymnia (*Asteraceae*)

	sonchifolia	see *Smallanthus sonchifolius*
	uvedalia	see *Smallanthus uvedalius*

Polypodium ✿ (*Polypodiaceae*)

	sp. **new**	MLHP
	aureum	see *Phlebodium aureum*

	- 'Glaucum'	CSpe
	australe	see *P. cambricum*
§	***cambricum***	EFer WCot WFib
	- 'Barrowii'	CLAP WAbe WFib
I	- 'Cambricum' ♀[H4]	CLAP GCal WAbe
	- 'Conwy'	WFib
	- 'Cristatum'	CLAP WFib
	- (Cristatum Group) 'Grandiceps Forster'	CLAP
	- - 'Grandiceps Fox' ♀[H4]	MRav WFib
	- 'Hornet'	WFib
	- 'Macrostachyon'	CLAP GBin NBid WFib
	- 'Oakleyae'	MMoz WCot
	- 'Omnilacerum Oxford'	CLAP
	- 'Prestonii'	CDes WCot WFib
	- Pulcherrimum Group	CLAP SDys WAbe
	- - 'Pulcherrimum Addison'	CDes WCot WFib WPGP
	- - 'Pulchritudine'	CLAP GBin LLWG WCot
	- 'Richard Kayse'	CDes CLAP MMoz WAbe WCot WFib WPGP
	- Semilacerum Group	EFer
	- - 'Carew Lane'	WFib
	- - 'Robustum'	WFib
	- 'Whilharris' ♀[H4]	CLAP CRDP
I	× ***coughlinii*** bifid	WFib
	glycyrrhiza	CLAP GPoy WFib
	- bifid	see *P.* × *coughlinii* bifid
	- 'Longicaudatum' ♀[H4]	CLAP MWhi NMyG WCot WFib
	- 'Malahatense'	CLAP
	- 'Malahatense' (sterile)	CDes WAbe WPGP
	interjectum	CLAP EFer LRHS MMoz MRav
	- 'Cornubiense' ♀[H4]	CHVG CLAP ECGP GBin MMoz NBid NBir WAbe
	- 'Glomeratum Mullins'	WFib
	× ***mantoniae***	WFib WIvy
	- 'Bifidograndiceps'	GBin NBid WFib
	scouleri	CBty CFil CLAP EFer ISha NBro WPGP
	vulgare	CHel CWCL ELon EPfP ERod EShb GAbr GMaP GPoy LRHS MBlu MBri MGos MMuc MRav MWat NBro NOrc SEND SGol SPer SPlb SPoG SRms WCot WFib WMoo WWEG
	- 'Bifidocristatum'	see *P. vulgare* 'Bifidomultifidum'
	- 'Bifidomulticeps'	WCot
§	- 'Bifidomultifidum'	CBty CLAP CWCL ELon EWTr GCal ISha LLWP LRHS MGos MRav NLar WCot WMoo WWEG
*	- 'Congestum Cristatum'	SRms
	- 'Cornubiense Grandiceps'	GCal SRms WIvy
*	- 'Cornubiense Multifidum'	EBee WCot
	- 'Elegantissimum'	NBid WFib
	- 'Parsley'	WCot
	- 'Trichomanoides Backhouse'	CLAP GCal WAbe WFib
	'Whitley Giant'	EBee ESwi GBin LLWG NMyG WCot

Polypompholyx see *Utricularia*

Polyspora (*Theaceae*)

§	***axillaris***	CCCN CHII EBee
	- CWJ 12363	WCru
	longicarpa DJHV 06041	WCru
	- WWJ 11604	WCru
	speciosa B&SWJ 11750	WCru
	- WWJ 11934	WCru

Polystichum ✿ (*Dryopteridaceae*)

	acrostichoides	CBty CDTJ CKel CLAP EBee ERod LRHS MBri NCGa NLar NMyG WPGP XLum
	aculeatum ♀[H4]	CLAP EFer ELan EPfP ERod EShb GMaP LAst LHop LRHS MBri MCot MGos MMuc NBid NCGa NEgg NLar NOrc SEND SRms SWvt WFib WMoo WWEG XLum
	- 'Cristatum Wollaston' new	CBcs
I	- Densum Group	EFer
	- Grandiceps Group	EFer
	- 'Portia'	WFib
	andersonii	CLAP
	bissectum	CExl
	braunii	CBcs CMac CWCL GBin GMaP IKil LRHS MMoz MMuc NBid NLar WFib WPnP WWEG XLum
	caryotideum	see *Cyrtomium caryotideum*
	× ***dycei***	CBty ISha LRHS
	falcatum	see *Cyrtomium falcatum*
	falcinellum	GLin
	fortunei	see *Cyrtomium fortunei*
	imbricans	CLAP SAPC
	interjectum	MRav
	makinoi	CBty CCCN CLAP EPPr GBin ISha LRHS NBid SPlb WFib WMoo
	munitum ♀[H4]	Widely available
	neolobatum	WFib
	- BWJ 8182	WCru
	polyblepharum ♀[H4]	Widely available
	- 'Jade'	CMac EBee LRHS
	proliferum misapplied	see *P. setiferum* Acutilobum Group
	proliferum ambig.	CBty EAmu EUJe WPtf
	proliferum (R. Br.) C. Presl	CLAP GCal SBig WFib WPGP
*	- ***plumosum***	LAst SPad SWvt
	richardii	SBig
	rigens	CBty CLAP EFer ISha LRHS LSou NLar SRms SRot WCru WFib WWEG
	setiferum ♀[H4]	CMac CWCL EBee EFer ELan EPPr EPfP ERod GAbr LAst LBMP LLWP LRHS MCot MMuc MWat NBid NHol NOrc SAPC SGol SPer SPlb SRms SWvt WFib WPGP WWEG XLum
§	- Acutilobum Group	CLAP CWCL GMaP LRHS NHol SDix SGol SPer SRms WBor WMoo WPGP XLum
	- Congestum Group	MMoz NCGa NEgg NHol NLar SPer SRms WFib WPat
	- - 'Congestum'	CBty CHel CLAP CWCL ELan EPPr EPfP ERod IKil ISha LBMP LRHS MRav MWhi NBir NGdn NHol SPoG WGor WMoo XLum
	- - 'Congestum Cristatum'	LAst
	- 'Cristatopinnulum'	CGHE CLAP NHar WPGP
	- Cristatum Group	CLAP SRms
	- Cruciatum Group	CLAP
	- Divisilobum Group	CBcs CLAP EFer ELan MCot MGos MLHP MMoz MWat MWhi SPer SRms WFib WHoo WPGP
	- - 'Caernarfon'	CLAP
	- - 'Dahlem'	CBty CDoC CLAP EBee EFer ELan ELon EPfP GBin GMaP LRHS LSRN MMoz SPer SPoG WFib WMoo WPnP WWEG XLum

	- - 'Divisilobum Densum' ♀H4	CLAP EPfP MMuc MRav NBir NOrc
	- - 'Divisilobum Iveryanum' ♀H4	CLAP EFer SRms WFib
	- - 'Divisilobum Laxum'	CLAP
	- - 'Divisilobum Wollaston'	CDTJ CKel CLAP CWCL LRHS MRav NBid NLar SHil WMoo
	- - 'Herrenhausen'	Widely available
	- - 'Madame Patti'	MMoz
	- - 'Mrs Goffey'	WFib
	- Foliosum Group	CLAP EFer
	- 'Gracile'	MRav NBir
	- 'Grandiceps'	CGHE CLAP EFer ELan
	- 'Hamlet'	WFib
	- 'Helena'	WFib
	- 'Hirondelle'	SRms
	- Lineare Group	WFib
	- Multilobum Group	CLAP SRms WFib
	- 'Othello'	WFib
	- Perserratum Group	NBid WFib
	- 'Plumo-Densum'	see *P. setiferum* Plumosomultilobum Group
	- 'Plumosodensum'	see *P. setiferum* Plumosomultilobum Group
	- Plumosodivisilobum Group	CLAP LSou NBid WFib
	- - 'Baldwinii'	CLAP WFib
	- - 'Bland'	WFib
§	- Plumosomultilobum Group	CBty CGHE CLAP CWCL EBee EPfP GBin ISha MCot MGos MMoz NBir NCGa NLar WCot WFib WHoo WMoo WPat WRHF
I	- - 'Plumosomultilobum Densum'	CHVG CMea LRHS MBel MJak WCot WWEG XLum
*	- ***plumosum grande*** 'Moly'	SRms
	- Plumosum Group	CGHE CLAP CMac CSpe EFer ELon MJak NOrc SAPC SRot
	- - dwarf	CSBt MMuc
	- Proliferum Group	see *P. setiferum* Acutilobum Group
*	- 'Proliferum Wollaston'	CBty ELon ISha LRHS MMoz MMuc WWEG
	- 'Pulcherrimum Bevis' ♀H4	CAby CBty CHid CLAP EBee ELon ESwi EUJe GBin LBMP LLWG MAvo MCot MRav MSCN NGdn SDix SWvt WCot WFib WPGP WPat WPnP WSpi
	- Rotundatum Group	CLAP
	- - 'Cristatum'	CLAP ISha
	- - 'Rotundatum Ramosum'	CLAP
	- 'Smith's Cruciate'	CLAP LLHF MRav WFib
	- 'Wakeleyanum'	EFer SRms
	tsussimense ♀H4	CDoC CLAP CWCL EAmu ELon EPfP ERod EShb GBin LAst LBMP LRHS MRav MWat NBir NEgg NHol NLar NPri SBch SPer SPlb SPoG SRms SRot WFib WMoo WPat WPnP XLum
	vestitum	CLAP MMoz SBig

Polyxena (*Asparagaceae*)

*	***brevifolia***	ECho
	corymbosa	ECho
§	***ensifolia***	CPBP ECho LLHF WCot WHil
	longituba	CPBP ECho WCot
	odorata	ECho NRya
	paucifolia	ECho
	pygmaea	see *P. ensifolia*

Pomaderris (*Rhamnaceae*)

	apetala	CExl
	elliptica	CExl ECou

pomegranate see *Punica granatum*

Poncirus (*Rutaceae*)

§	***trifoliata***	CAgr CArn CBcs CCCN CDoC CDul EBee ELan EPfP IDee LRHS MBlu MRav NEgg SAPC SMad SPer SPlb SPoG SVic WSHC
	- 'Flying Dragon'	IVic SMad

Pontederia (*Pontederiaceae*)

	cordata ♀H4	CBAq CHEx CRow CWat EHon ELan EPfP EWay MSKA MWts NPer SCoo SPlb SWat WMAq XLum
	- f. ***albiflora***	CBAq CRow CWat EPfP EWay MWts WMAq XLum
	- - 'White Pike' **new**	LLWG
	- 'Blue Spires'	MSKA
§	- var. ***lancifolia***	CRow EWay LLWG MNrw MSKA MWts NPer SWat
	- 'Pink Pons'	CRow EWay
	- pink-flowered **new**	LLWG
	dilatata	see *Monochoria hastata*
	lanceolata	see *P. cordata* var. *lancifolia*

Populus ✿ (*Salicaceae*)

	× ***acuminata***	WMou
	alba	CBcs CCVT CDul CLnd CMac CSBt CTho CTri CWib EBee ECrN LBuc NWea SEWo SGol SPer WMou
	- 'Bolleana'	see *P. alba* f. *pyramidalis*
	- 'Nivea'	MMuc SEND
§	- f. ***pyramidalis***	SRms WMou
§	- 'Raket'	CCVT CTho ECrN ELan SPer
	- 'Richardii'	EBtc EGFP WCot WMou
	- Rocket	see *P. alba* 'Raket'
§	'Balsam Spire' (f) ♀H4	CDul CLnd CTho WMou
§	***balsamifera***	CCVT CLnd CSBt CTri MGos SPer WCot
	- 'Vita Sackville West'	MBlu
	× ***canadensis***	CMam
§	- 'Aurea' ♀H4	CDul CLnd CTho CWib EBee ECrN MRav NEgg SPer WMou
	- 'Columbia'	WMou
	- 'Eugenei' (m)	WMou
	- 'Robusta' (m)	CCVT CDul CLnd CTri LBuc NWea WMou
	- 'Serotina' (m)	CDul WMou
	× ***canescens***	CLnd NWea
	deltoides 'Fuego'	SGol
	- 'Purple Tower'	ELan EPfP MBlu SMad WCot
	× ***generosa*** 'Beaupré'	WMou
	× ***jackii*** 'Aurora' (f/v)	CBcs CCVT CDul CLnd CMac CSBt ELan LBuc LPot MGos MMuc NPri NWea SGol SPer WHar WMou
	lasiocarpa ♀H4	CExl CMCN EBee EPfP IArd IDee MBlu SGol SLPl WMou WPGP
	nigra	CHab CLnd CMac CTho CTri CTsd EBee EPfP NWea WSFF
	- (f)	ECrN
	- subsp. ***betulifolia***	CCVT CDul CHab CLnd NWea WMou
	- - (f)	EBtc WMou
	- - (m)	EBtc WMou

§	- 'Italica' (m) 🏆H4	CCVT CDul CLnd CMac CTho CTri CWib ECrN ELan LBuc MGos NWea SEWo SPer WMou
	- 'Pyramidalis'	see *P. nigra* 'Italica'
	'Serotina Aurea'	see *P.* × *canadensis* 'Aurea'
	simonii 'Fastigiata'	WMou
	szechuanica	WMou
§	- var. ***tibetica***	WMou
	tacamahaca	see *P. balsamifera*
	'Tacatricho 32'	see *P.* 'Balsam Spire'
	tremula 🏆H4	CCVT CDul CHab CLnd CMac CTho CTri CWib EBee ECrN ELan EWTr GAbr LBuc MJak NWea SEND SEWo SPer WHar WMou WSFF
§	- 'Erecta'	CDul CEnd CTho EBee MBlu WMou
	- 'Fastigiata'	see *P. tremula* 'Erecta'
	- 'Pendula' (m)	CEnd CTho ECrN IDee WMou
	trichocarpa	SPer
	- 'Fritzi Pauley' (f)	CDul CTho WMou
	- 'Trichobel'	CMam
	violascens	see *P. szechuanica* var. *tibetica*
	× ***wilsocarpa*** 'Beloni' **new**	WPGP
	wilsonii	WPGP
	yunnanensis	WMou

Porophyllum (*Asteraceae*)

ruderale	CArn ELau

Portulaca (*Portulacaceae*)

oleracea	CArn MHer MNHC SVic WJek
- var. ***aurea***	MNHC WJek

Potamogeton (*Potamogetonaceae*)

crispus	CBAq CWat EHon MSKA MWts WMAq WSFF
natans	LLWG MSKA XLum

Potentilla ✿ (*Rosaceae*)

	alba	CTri ECho ELan GCal MLHP MNFA MRav MWat NChi NSti NWad
	alchemilloides	CMac LRHS
	ambigua	see *P. cuneata*
	andicola	EBee
	anglica	CArn
	anserina	CArn MHer NMir WHer XLum
	- 'Golden Treasure' (v)	EBee WHer
	anserinoides	WMoo
	arbuscula misapplied	see *P. fruticosa* 'Elizabeth'
	- 'Beesii'	see *P. fruticosa* 'Beesii'
	'Arc-en-ciel'	Widely available
	argentea	SPlb XLum
	arguta	EBee
	argyrophylla	see *P. atrosanguinea* var. *argyrophylla*
	- 'Alfred Salter'	LRHS
	atrosanguinea	Widely available
	- CC 6871 **new**	GKev
§	- var. ***argyrophylla***	CCon COlW CSam CWCL EBee ELan EPfP GCal ITim LRHS MMuc MWat NBir NBro NLar SRms WMoo XLum
	- - CC 6945 **new**	GKev
	- - 'Golden Starlit'	LRHS
§	- - 'Scarlet Starlit'	EDAr EPfP IBoy LRHS NCGa
	- 'Fireball' (d)	EPfP GJos
	- var. ***leucochroa***	see *P. atrosanguinea* var. *argyrophylla*
*	- 'Sundermannii'	LLHF
	aurea	ECho ECtt EPfP GBin WNew
	- 'Aurantiaca'	EWes NLar NPro
§	- 'Goldklumpen'	ECtt MRav NPro
	- 'Plena' (d)	NRya
	'Blazeaway'	EBee ECtt LRHS LSou MArl MAvo MBNS NGdn NPro
	calabra	EWes WHer
§	***cinerea***	CTri ECho LLHF
	collina	LLHF
	'Coronation Triumph' **new**	NLar
§	***crantzii***	CMea SRms
	- 'Nana'	see *P. crantzii* 'Pygmaea'
§	- 'Pygmaea'	ECho ECtt EPfP NBir
§	***cuneata*** 🏆H4	ECho GAbr GKev MMuc SEND
	davurica 'Abbotswood'	see *P. fruticosa* 'Abbotswood'
	delavayi	LRHS MNrw
	detommasii	LLHF
	dombeyi	IMou
	'Emilie' (d)	CSpe CWCL ECtt GAbr GBuc GCal IKil LRHS MAvo MBNS MBel MCot MNrw NHol NLar NPro SWvt WBor WCot WHil WWlt
§	***erecta***	GPoy MNHC WHfH
	eriocarpa	ECho EPau NSla WAbe WIce
	- var. ***tsarongensis***	WAbe
	'Esta Ann'	CMac ECtt GBuc IPot LHop LRHS MArl MAvo MBNS MCot MNrw NCGa NLar NPro SRGP
	'Etna'	CHel CWCL ECtt ELan GBuc LRHS MAvo MLHP MNFA MNrw NBir NLar NPnk SPad WHrl WMoo WPtf
	'Everest'	see *P. fruticosa* 'Mount Everest'
	'Fireflame'	NLar WMoo
	fissa	MNrw NBir NLar SPhx
	'Flambeau' (d)	CWCL ECtt EShb GBuc GKin IPot LAst LDai LHop LPla LRHS MArl MAvo MNFA MRav NGdn NLar NPro WCAu WMoo
	'Flamenco'	CSam CTri ECtt MArl MAvo MBNS MBri MLHP MNrw MRav NBir NCGa WMoo
	fragariiformis	see *P. megalantha*
	fruticosa	LBuc NWea
§	- 'Abbotswood' 🏆H4	Widely available
	- 'Abbotswood Silver' (v)	MSwo WMoo
	- 'Annette'	CMac MBrN NPro WRHF
	- 'Apple Blossom'	CWib
	- var. ***arbuscula*** hort.	see *P. fruticosa* 'Elizabeth'
	- 'Argentea Nana'	see *P. fruticosa* 'Beesii'
	- 'Baby Bethan'PBR (d)	LLHF
§	- 'Beesii'	EPfP MAsh SIgm
	- 'Bewerley Surprise'	LBuc
	- 'Chelsea Star' 🏆H4	CDoC CMac LBuc LRHS LSRN MAsh MGos SHil
	- 'Chilo' (v)	NEgg WMoo
	- var. ***dahurica*** 'Hersii'	see *P. fruticosa* 'Snowflake'
	- 'Dakota Sunrise' **new**	NSoo
	- 'Dart's Cream'	MBri
	- 'Dart's Golddigger'	CTri NWad
	- 'Daydawn'	CBcs CDul CMac CTri CWSG EBee ELan EPfP LBMP LHop LRHS MAsh MLHP MRav MSwo NBir NEgg NHol NLar NWad SGol SLim SPer SWvt WHar WMoo
§	- 'Elizabeth'	CBar CBcs CDul CWib EBee ECrN ELan EPfP LAst LBMP LRHS LSRN MGos MJak MMuc MNHC MSwo NHol NWea SGol SLim SPer SRms SWvt WCFE WHar WMoo
	- 'Farreri'	see *P. fruticosa* 'Gold Drop'

	- 'Floppy Disc'	ELan EPfP
	- 'Glenroy Pinkie'	MRav NLar
§	- 'Gold Drop'	CMac
	- 'Golden Spreader'	LRHS
	- 'Goldfinger'	CMac CSBt EBee ELan EPfP IBoy LHop LRHS MAsh MGos MJak MMuc MRav MSwo MWat NEgg NSoo SCoo SEND SLim SPer SPlb SPoG WHar WMoo
	- Goldkugel	see *P. fruticosa* 'Gold Drop'
	- 'Goldstar'	CWSG IArd LRHS MBri NPri SCoo SEND SLim SLon SRms
	- 'Goldteppich'	LBuc
	- 'Grace Darling'	ELan EPfP EWes NBir NEgg NHol NLar SRGP SWvt WHar WMoo
	- 'Groneland' 🏆H4	EPfP LRHS MAsh SCoo SPoG
	- Happy Face White	see *P. fruticosa* 'White Lady'
	- 'Haytor's Orange'	CWib
	- 'Hopleys Orange' 🏆H4	CDoC CSBt CWSG EBee ELon EPfP EWes LHop LRHS MBri MMuc MWat NHol NPri NSoo SCoo SEND SGol SHil SRms WGor WMoo
	- 'Hurstbourne'	NPro
	- 'Jackman's Variety' 🏆H4	CDoC CWib EPfP IBoy LRHS MAsh SRms
	- 'Katherine Dykes'	CDul CTri CWib EBee EPfP GKin LAst LBMP LRHS LSRN MAsh MGos MNHC MWat NEgg NSoo NWea SCoo SLim SPer SRms WHar WMoo
	- 'King Cup' 🏆H4	EPfP LRHS MAsh
§	- 'Klondike'	CBcs CSBt MMuc NEgg NWea
	- 'Kobold'	MBri
*	- 'Lemon and Lime'	LRHS NPro
	- 'Limelight' 🏆H4	CDoC CSBt EBee ELan EPfP GKin LHop LRHS MAsh MBri MRav MSwo NSoo SHil SRms WHar
	- 'Longacre Variety'	CMac CTri IArd MSwo NWea
	- 'Lovely Pink'	see *P. fruticosa* 'Pink Beauty'
§	- 'Maanelys'	CSBt ELan MWat NHol NWea SPer WMoo
	- 'Macpenny's Cream'	CMac
§	- 'Manchu'	CMac MRav MWat SPer WPat
	- Mango Tango = 'Uman'PBR	CSBt EBee EPfP LHop LRHS LSRN MBri NSoo SPoG STPC
§	- Marian Red Robin = 'Marrob'PBR 🏆H4	CDoC CSBt CWib EBee ELan EPfP GKin IBoy LAst LRHS MAsh MBri MRav MSwo MWat NEgg NHol NPri NWea SCoo SHil SLim SLon SPer SPoG SWvt
	- 'McKay's White'	NLar
	- 'Medicine Wheel Mountain' 🏆H4	ELan EWes IArd LRHS MAsh MPkF MRav NHol NLar NPro NWad SCoo SGol SHil SLim SPer SPoG
	- Moonlight	see *P. fruticosa* 'Maanelys'
§	- 'Mount Everest'	CTri MMuc NWea SEND SLon
	- 'Nana Argentea'	see *P. fruticosa* 'Beesii'
	- 'New Dawn'	GKin LBuc MBri
	- 'Orangeade'	EPfP LRHS MAsh MBri NLar SCoo SPoG
*	- 'Peachy Proud'	NPro
§	- 'Pink Beauty'PBR 🏆H4	Widely available
	- 'Pink Pearl'	WMoo
	- 'Pink Queen'	NLar
	- 'Pink Whisper'	NPro
	- 'Pretty Polly'	ELan LAst LBMP LRHS MSwo NHol NLar WMoo WRHF
	- 'Primrose Beauty' 🏆H4	CDoC CDul CMac EBee ELan ELon EPfP IBoy LAst LBMP LPot LRHS LSRN MAsh MBri MMuc MRav MSwo NEgg NHol SCoo SEND SHil SLPl SLim SPer SPlb SPoG WMoo
§	- Princess = 'Blink'	CBcs CDul EBee ELan EPfP LBMP LRHS MAsh MRav NEgg SCoo SGol SLim SRms WMoo
	- 'Red Ace'	Widely available
	- 'Red Lady' **new**	EPfP LRHS SHil SPoG STPC WMoo
	- Red Robin	see *P. fruticosa* Marian Red Robin
	- 'Setting Sun'	LBuc
	- 'Snowbird'	EBee EPfP NPro SLim
§	- 'Snowflake'	CBcs WMoo
	- 'Sommerflor' 🏆H4	CDoC EPfP LRHS MAsh NCGa
	- 'Sophie's Blush'	MRav NWea WSHC
	- 'Summer Dawn'	LBuc
	- 'Summer Sorbet'	LRHS
	- 'Sunset'	CBcs CMac CWib ELan GKin LSRN MJak NBir NEgg NWea SCoo SLim SPer SRms WMoo
	- 'Tangerine'	Widely available
	- 'Tilford Cream'	CSBt CTri EBee ELan EPfP GKin IBoy LAst LRHS LSRN MJak MRav MSwo MWat NBir NEgg NHol SGol SLim SPer SPoG SRms WHar WMoo
	- 'Tom Conway'	CMac NLar
	- var. ***veitchii***	CDoy CSBt
	- 'Vilmoriniana'	CTri ELan EPfP GCal LRHS MAsh MLHP MRav SPer SPoG SWvt WPat
	- 'Whirligig'	CMac
§	- 'White Lady' **new**	MPkF
	- 'Wickwar Beauty'	CWib
	- 'William Purdom'	WHar
	- 'Yellow Bird' 🏆H4	LRHS MAsh
	'Gibson's Scarlet' 🏆H4	Widely available
§	***glandulosa*** subsp. ***nevadensis***	CTri ECho EWld MAsh SRms
	'Gloire de Nancy' (d)	CWCL EBee GBuc IKil LBMP MRav NBir NChi NLar WCot
	'Gold Clogs'	see *P. aurea* 'Goldklumpen'
	'Helen Jane'	EPfP EWld GBuc GJos GQue LRHS MBNS MHer NBir NLar WPtf WWFP
	'Herzblut'	NLar
	× ***hopwoodiana***	CMea CSpe CWCL EBee ECtt ELan EPPr GCal GJos GMaP LAst LHop MCot MNrw MRav NBir NCGa NChi NDov NLar NPnk WCAu WMoo WWEG
	× ***hybrida*** 'Jean Jabber'	EBee GLog MRav NLar NPro SRGP
	'Jack Elliot'	NPro
	kurdica	XLum
	leuconota	LRHS
	'Light My Fire'	ECtt LLHF MAvo MBNS NCGa WWlt
§	'Majland'	EBee NDov
	'Mandshurica'	see *P. fruticosa* 'Manchu'
	'Maynard's'	see *P.* 'Majland'
§	***megalantha*** 🏆H4	Widely available
	- 'Gold Sovereign'	EPfP LRHS LSou NPro SPoG
	'Melton'	MNrw
*	'Melton Fire'	ECtt EPfP GBee GJos GKin GQue LBMP MNHC MNrw NBir WMoo WPnP
	'Monarch's Velvet'	see *P. thurberi* 'Monarch's Velvet'
	'Monsieur Rouillard' (d)	CFis CMac CSam CWCL ECtt GCra IPot LRHS MArl MCot MNrw MRav MWat NGdn NLar WHoo WMnd
	'Mont d'Or'	MRav NLar
	nepalensis	EHoe GKev MLHP NBro NChi NPro XLum
	- 'Helen Jane'	NHol SBea

- 'Master Floris' WHal
§ - 'Miss Willmott' 🏆H4 Widely available
- 'Ron McBeath' CCon CHel CKno COIW CWCL ECtt ELan EPfP GBin GCra ITim LAst LHop MRav MSCN NHol NLar NSti SGol SPer SPoG SRGP SWvt WHoo WMoo WPtf WWEG
- 'Roxana' CCon ELan MRav NBro NLar SRGP WMoo
- 'Shogran' COIW GJos GQue LAst LBMP MBNS NHol NLar WPtf
§ ***neumanniana*** NBir NPri
- 'Goldrausch' LEdu MRav
§ - 'Nana' ECho ECtt EPot MHer MWat NRya NWad SPlb SRms WIce WMoo XLum
nevadensis see *P. glandulosa* subsp. *nevadensis*
nitida EPot MAsh SRms WAbe
- 'Alba' ECho EPot
- 'Rubra' CMea CPBP ECho EDAr MWat NBir NSla SRms WAbe
nivalis ECho
ovina var. ***ovina*** LLHF
- - NNS 08-374 GKev
palustris CWat EBee EWay LLWG MWts NLar NMir WMoo XLum
parvifolia 'Klondike' see *P. fruticosa* 'Klondike'
pedata LLWP NChi XLum
peduncularis GKev
CC 5717 new
pensylvanica LLHF
'Pink Panther' see *P. fruticosa* Princess
aff. ***polyphylla*** CHP&W 314 GKev
porphyrantha new SBrt
recta COIW NPri WTou XLum
- 'Alba' GMaP LDai NBre NEgg WPtf
- 'Citrina' see *P. recta* var. *sulphurea*
- 'Macrantha' see *P. recta* 'Warrenii'
§ - var. ***sulphurea*** CAby CMea GAbr GKev LAst MCot MHer MLHP MMuc MNFA MNrw NBir NBre NLar NSti NWad SBch SPhx WBrk WHal WHil WHoo WHrl WMnd WMoo WPtf XLum
§ - 'Warrenii' CSBt EPfP GMaP LAst LRHS MRav NBir NEgg SPer SRms WHal WHrl WMoo XLum
reptans CArn CBAq
'Roxanne' (d) LRHS MHer
rupestris CMea EWTr MHer NLar NSti WCAu WHal WMoo WOut WPtf
'Scarlet Starlet' see *P. atrosanguinea* var. *argyrophylla* 'Scarlet Starlit'
speciosa EWes WMoo
sterilis CHid LEdu WHer WSFF
* ***sundermanii*** WHrl
tabernaemontani see *P. neumanniana*
thurberi LRHS MCot MNrw NLar SPhx WMoo XLum
§ - 'Monarch's Velvet' Widely available
tommasiniana see *P. cinerea*
× ***tonguei*** 🏆H4 Widely available
tormentilla see *P. erecta*
'Twinkling Star' CHel EBee SPad WHlf WPtf
verna misapplied see *P. neumanniana*
- 'Pygmaea' see *P. neumanniana* 'Nana'
'Versicolor Plena' (d) NLar
villosa see *P. crantzii*
'Volcan' CWCL ECtt EWes GBuc GQue MAvo MNFA NPro WCAu WHal
'White Queen' GLog MRav NBre SHar
'William Rollisson' 🏆H4 Widely available
willmottiae see *P. nepalensis* 'Miss Willmott'
'Yellow Queen' CBcs CMac CTri GKin GMaP LHop LPot MNrw MRav NLar SBod WCAu

Poterium see *Sanguisorba*

sanguisorba see *Sanguisorba minor*

Pratia (*Campanulaceae*)

§ ***angulata*** CDoy
- 'Jack's Pass' NEgg
§ - 'Treadwellii' ECho EPfP SPlb WHal
§ ***pedunculata*** CBar CTri ECho ECou ECtt EDAr ELan EPfP EWTr GAbr LLWG MAsh NChi SPet SPlb SRms SRot WMoo WPtf
I - 'Alba' EWes
- 'County Park' CBar CExl CHel CMea CSpe CTri ECho ECou ECtt EDAr ELan EWTr GAbr LLWG MAsh MMuc SPlb SPoG SRms SRot WIce WMoo XLum
- 'Tom Stone' ECtt
- 'White Stars' ECho LLWG

Preslia see *Mentha*

Primula ✿ (*Primulaceae*)

sp. SVic
- (Si) new MAsh
* ***abyssinica*** LEdu
acaulis see *P. vulgaris*
'Adrian Jones' (Au) IPen
advena var. ***euprepes*** see *P. euprepes*
agleniana (Cy) IPen
'Alan Robb' (Pr/Prim/d) ECtt EPfP NGdn SPer
albenensis (Au) IPen
'Alexina' (*allionii* hybrid) (Au) MFie NHar
algida (Al) ECho GKev
- 'Sibirica' GKev
§ ***allionii*** (Au) 🏆H2 IPen NSum WAbe
- HNG 12 IPen ITim
- 'Agnes' (Au) IPen ITim MFie WAbe
- 'Aire Waves' see *P.* × *loiseleurii* 'Aire Waves'
- 'Alan Burrow' (Au) IPen
- var. ***alba*** (Au) IPen
- 'Allen Queen' (Au) IPen
- 'Andrew' (Au) IPen WAbe
- 'Anna Griffith' (Au) CPBP IPen MFie WAbe
- 'Anne' (Au) IPen
- 'Aphrodite' (Au) IPen NHar
- 'Apple Blossom' (Au) GKev
- 'Archer' (Au) IPen ITim NWad
- 'Ares' (Au) NHar
- 'Aries Violet' (Au) IPen NHar
- 'Austen' (Au) EPot MFie
- 'Avalanche' (Au) IPen WAbe
- 'Beryl' (Au) IPen
- 'Biddy' (Au) IPen
- 'Bill Martin' (Au) IPen ITim NWad
- 'Blood Flake' (Au) IPen ITim
- 'Broadwell No 4' new CPBP
- Burnley form (Au) NWad
- 'Cherry' (Au) WAbe
- 'Chivalry' (Au) CPBP MFie
- 'Circe's Flute' (Au) NHar
- 'Cissie' (Au) IPen ITim
- 'Claude Flight' (Au) IPen MFie

– 'Crystal' (Au)	MFie
– 'Daniel Burrow' (Au)	IPen
– 'David Burrow' (Au)	IPen
– 'David Philbey' **new**	CPBP IPen
§ – 'Edinburgh' (Au)	GKev IPen NWad
– 'Edrom' (Au)	IPen ITim NWad
– 'Ekli Weib' (Au) **new**	IPen
– 'Elizabeth Baker' (Au)	EPot IPen ITim MFie
– 'Elizabeth Burrow' (Au)	IPen WAbe
– 'Elizabeth Earle' (Au)	IPen ITim
– 'Elliott's Large'	see *P. allionii* 'Edinburgh'
– 'Elliott's Variety'	see *P. allionii* 'Edinburgh'
– 'Emily Jane' (Au)	IPen
– 'Eureka' (Au)	CPBP WAbe
– 'Eveline Burrow' (Au)	CPBP WAbe
– 'Fanfare' (Au)	IPen NHar
– 'Flute' (Au)	IPen
– 'Frank Barker' (Au)	IPen
– 'Gabriele' (Au)	MFie
– 'Gavin Brown' (Au)	IPen
– 'Gilderdale Glow' (Au)	CPBP IPen MFie
– 'Giuseppi's Form'	see *P. allionii* 'Mrs Dyas'
– 'Grace Burrow' (Au)	IPen
– 'Grandiflora' (Au)	ITim
– 'Hannah' (Au)	IPen
– 'Hartside' (Au)	NWad
– 'Hartside 6' (Au)	IPen ITim NHar
– 'Hartside 12' (Au)	EPot IPen
– 'Hazey' (Au)	ITim
– 'Hocker Edge' (Au)	EPot GKev ITim MFie NWad
– 'Horwood' (Au)	ITim
– 'Huntsman' (Au)	MFie
– 'Hythe Dorothy' (Au) **new**	IPen
– 'Imp' (Au)	IPen
– 'Io 2' (Au)	NHar
– 'Ion's Amethyst' (Au)	NHar
– 'Isobel' (Au)	IPen
– 'Jacqueline' (Au) **new**	IPen
– 'James' (Au)	IPen WAbe
– 'Jan' (Au)	IPen
– 'Jenny' (Au)	IPen
– 'Joe Elliott' (Au)	IPen ITim
– 'Joseph Collins' (Au)	IPen
– 'Julia' (Au)	IPen
– KRW	see *P. allionii* 'Ken's Seedling'
– 'Kate Evans' (Au) **new**	IPen
§ – 'Kath Dryden' (Au)	IPen LLHF
§ – 'Ken's Seedling' (Au)	IPen MFie
– 'Laura Louise' (Au)	IPen
– 'Lepus' (Au) **new**	IPen
– 'Lindisfarne' (Au)	IPen
– 'Lindum Prima' (Au)	IPen
– 'Lismore 81/19/2' (Au)	EPot MFie
– 'Lismore 87/3/2' (Au)	MFie
– 'Little O' (Au)	NWad WAbe
– 'Louise' (Au)	IPen
– 'Lucy' (Au)	IPen NHar
– 'Malcolm' (Au)	IPen ITim WAbe
– 'Margaret Earle' (Au)	IPen
– 'Marion' (Au)	IPen ITim
– 'Marjorie Wooster' (Au)	IPen ITim MFie
– 'Martin' (Au)	IPen ITim
– 'Mary Anne' (Au)	WAbe
– 'Mary Berry' (Au)	IPen MFie NWad
– 'Maurice Dryden' (Au)	IPen WAbe
– 'Megan' (Au)	IPen
– 'Molly' (Au)	IPen
§ – 'Mrs Dyas' (Au)	IPen MFie NWad WAbe
– 'Neon' (Au)	IPen
– 'Neptune's Wave' (Au)	NHar
– 'New Dawn' (Au)	ITim MFie NHar
– 'Pale Venus' (Au)	IPen NHar
– 'Peace' (Au)	MFie
– 'Peggy Wilson' (Au)	EWld IPen NWad WThu
– 'Pennine Pink' (Au)	IPen
– 'Perkie' (Au)	IPen
– 'Phoebe's Moon' (Au)	IPen NHar
– 'Pink Ice' (Au)	EBee ITim
– 'Pinkie' (Au)	IPen WAbe
– 'Praecox' (Au)	EPot IPen
– 'Quip' (Au)	IPen
– RAH form	MFie
– 'Raymond Wooster' (Au)	GKev IPen NWad
– 'Roger Bevan' (Au)	IPen
– 'Saint Dalmas' (Au)	IPen
– 'Scimitar' (Au)	IPen MFie
– 'Serendipity' (Au)	IPen
– 'Snowflake' (Au)	CPBP GKev IPen WAbe
– 'Stanton House' (Au)	MFie
– 'Stephen' (Au)	IPen MFie
– 'Tranquillity' (Au)	CPBP ITim NHar
– 'Travellers' (Au)	IPen
– 'Viscountess Byng' (Au)	IPen WAbe
– white-flowered, thrum-eyed (Au)	IPen
– 'William Earle' (Au)	CPBP GKev IPen ITim WAbe
allionii* × *auricula 'Old Red Dusty Miller' (Au)	ECho NWad
allionii* × *auricula 'Blairside Yellow' (Au)	ECho IPen NSum WThu
allionii* × *clusiana (Au)	ECho
allionii* × *hirsuta (Au)	NWad
allionii × 'Lismore Jewel' (Au)	ITim
allionii × 'Lismore Treasure' (Au)	CPBP
allionii* × *pedemontana	see *P.* × *sendtneri*
allionii* × *pubescens (Au)	ECho
allionii* × *pubescens 'Harlow Car' (Au)	GAgs
allionii × 'Snow Ruffles' (Au)	IPen ITim
allionii × 'White Linda Pope' (Au)	IPen MFie NHar NWad
alpicola (Si) ♀H4	CAby CLAP CWCL GAbr GKev IPen LRHS NBid NBro NCGa NGdn NSum NWad WAbe
– var. ***alba*** (Si)	CAby CPla GBuc GKev IPen LRHS MNrw NBid
§ – var. ***alpicola*** (Si)	CLAP EBee GBin GBuc GCra GKev IPen MMuc MNrw WAbe
– hybrids (Si)	WMoo
– 'Kevock Sky' (Si)	GKev
– 'La Luna' (Si)	MMuc
– var. ***luna***	see *P. alpicola* var. *alpicola*
– mixed	ECho
– var. ***violacea*** (Si)	CAby CCVN CCon CLAP CPla EBee GAbr GBin GCra GKev IPen LRHS MMuc MNrw NBid WAbe WHil
'Altaica'	see *P. elatior* subsp. *meyeri*
altaica grandiflora	see *P. elatior* subsp. *meyeri*
amoena	see *P. elatior* subsp. *meyeri*
'Amy Smith'	GAbr
anisodora	see *P. wilsonii* var. *anisodora*
'Annemijne'	WCot
'April Rose' (Pr/Prim/d)	NBid
× ***arctotis***	see *P.* × *pubescens*
'Arduaine' (Pe)	LLHF

aurantiaca (Pf) CCon CPla EBee GBin GKev IPen
- SDR 6713 GKev
aureata (Pe) IPen
auricula ambig. (Au) CTsd NSla
auricula L. (Au) ♀H4 EDAr IPen MFie NBro SPer SPet SPlb SPoG WAbe WRHF
auricula misapplied '2nd Vic' (Au/S) SPop
- A74 (Au) SEND
- K85 (Au/S) SPop
- 'A.C. Hadfield' (Au) **new** MFie
- 'Abdor' (Au/St) SPop
- 'Abrigde' (Au/d) WAln
- 'Abundance' (Au/A) NDro SPop
- 'Achates' (Au/A) IPen WAln
- 'Admiral' (Au/A) EWoo WAln WCre
- 'Adrian' (Au/A) GAbr GAgs IPen MFie NBro NDro SPop WBla WCre WHil
- 'Adrian's Cross' (Au/A) **new** EWoo
- 'Adrienne' (Au/A) SPop
- 'Adrienne Ruan' (Au/A) NDro WAln
- 'Aga Khan' (Au/A) WAln
- 'Agamemnon' (Au/A) EWoo MFie WAln WCre
- 'Airy Fairy' (Au/S) **new** SPop
- 'Alamo' (Au/A) MFie WCre
- 'Alan Ball' (Au) WAln WCre
- 'Alan Ravenscroft' (Au/A) MFie SPop
- 'Albert Bailey' (Au/d) EWoo GAgs IPen ITim MFie NDro NEgg SPop WCre WHil
- 'Albury' (Au/d) IPen
- 'Alchemist' (Au/S) IPen SPop WAln WCre
- 'Alexandra Georgina' (Au/A) MFie NDro WAln
- 'Alf' (Au/A) IPen MFie NDro SPop WHil
- 'Alfred Charles' (Au/A) WAln
- 'Alfred Niblett' (Au/S) IPen
- 'Alice' (Au/d) IPen
- 'Alice Haysom' (Au/S) CWCL ELan EWoo GAbr GAgs IPen ITim MAsh NDro SPop WCre WHil
- 'Alicia' (Au/A) EWoo GAbr MFie NDro SPop WCre
- 'Alison Jane' (Au/A) CPBP GAgs IPen MFie WCre WHil
- 'Alison Rose' (Au/B) **new** NDro
- 'Alison Telford' (Au/A) WHil
- 'Allard' (Au/A) WAln
- 'Allegro' (Au/A) WAln
- 'Allensford' (Au/A) WCre
- 'Alloway' (Au/d) WAln
- 'Almand' (Au/d) WAln
- 'Almondbury' (Au/S) NDro SPop
- alpine mixed (Au/A) EPfP SRms
- 'Amber Light' (Au/S) SPop WAln
- 'Amber Waves' (Au) GAbr
- 'Amethyst' (Au/S) WAln
- 'Amicable' (Au/A) EWoo GAgs IPen MFie NDro NSum SPop WCre WHil
- 'Amore' (Au/St) **new** SPop WAln
- 'Ancient Order' (Au/A) IPen WAln
- 'Ancient Society' (Au/A) EWoo GAbr IPen MFie NDro SPop WHil
- 'Andrea Julie' (Au/A) GAgs IPen MFie NDro SPop WCre WHil
- 'Andrew Hunter' (Au/A) IPen MFie NDro SPop WCre
- 'Andy Cole' (Au/A) EWoo IPen NDro SPop WAln
- 'Angel Eyes' (Au/St) EWoo IPen SPop
- 'Angel Islington' (Au/S) NDro
- 'Angela Gould' (Au) GAbr MFie
- 'Angela Short' (Au/St) IPen SPop WAln
- 'Angostura' (Au/d) EWoo IPen SPop

- 'Ann Brookes' (Au/d) **new** WAln
- 'Ann Taylor' (Au/A) IPen WAln
- 'Anne Hyatt' (Au/d) GAbr NDro SPop
- 'Anne Swithinbank' (Au/d) IPen WAln
- 'Annie Tustin' (Au/S) SPop
- 'Ansells' (Au/S) **new** WAln
- 'Antoc' (Au/S) EWoo SPop
- 'Anwar Sadat' (Au/A) EWoo MFie NDro WCre WHil
- 'Apple Blossom' (Au/B) NDro
- 'Applecross' (Au/A) IPen NDro SPop WCre WHil
- 'April Moon' (Au/S) MFie NDro SPop WCre
- 'April Tiger' (Au/St) EWoo WAln
- 'Aquarius' (Au/d) SPop
- 'Arab Prince' (Au/A) WAln
- 'Arab Queen' (Au/A) WAln
- 'Arabian Night' (Au/A) WAln
- 'Arapaho' (Au/A) WAln
- 'Arctic Fox' (Au) MFie WAln
- 'Argus' (Au/A) EWoo GAbr GAgs IPen MFie NDro SPop WCre WHil
- 'Arlene' (Au/A) WAln
- 'Arthur Delbridge' (Au/A) MFie NDro SPop WHil
- 'Arundel Cross' (Au) IPen NEgg
- 'Arundell' (Au/S/St) CPBP CWCL EBee GAgs IPen ITim MAsh MFie NDro SPop WCre WHil
- 'Arwen' (Au/A) IPen MFie SPop
- 'Ascot Gavotte' (Au/S) WAln
- 'Ashcliffe Gem' (Au/A) IPen NDro WAln
- 'Astolat' (Au/S) EBee EWoo GAbr GAgs GKev IPen ITim NDro SPop WCre WHil
- 'Athene' (Au/S) IPen ITim NDro SPop WAln
- 'Atlantic' (Au/S) NDro NEgg
- 'Aubergine' (Au/B) NDro
- 'Audacity' (Au/d) IPen WAln
- 'Audrey' (Au/S) SPop
- 'Aurora' (Au/A) EDAr MFie WAln WCre
- 'Austin' (Au/A) IPen NDro SPop WAln
- 'Autumn Fire' (Au/A) EWoo GAgs SPop
- 'Autumn Glow' (Au/d) SPop
- 'Aviemore' (Au/A) WCre
- 'Avon Carrier' (Au/d) SPop
- 'Avon Citronella' (Au) SPop
- 'Avon Eclipse' (Au/d) **new** SPop
- 'Avon Khaki' (Au/d) **new** SPop
- 'Avon Tan' (d) **new** WCre
- 'Avon Twist' (Au/d) EWoo SPop
- 'Avril' (Au/A) IPen NDro SPop WAln WCre
- 'Avril Hunter' (Au/A) EWoo GAgs IPen ITim MFie NDro SPop WCre WHil
- 'Awesome' (Au/St) SPop
- 'Aztec' (Au/d) WAln
- 'Bacchante' (Au/d) SPop WAln
- 'Bacchus' (Au/A) MFie NDro SPop
- 'Baggage' (Au) EWoo IPen MAsh WBla
- 'Balbithan' (Au/B) EWoo GAbr
- 'Baltic Amber' (Au) EWoo GAbr GAgs MFie SPop WAln WCre
- 'Bank Error' (Au/S) IPen NDro SPop WAln
- 'Barbara Mason' WAln
- 'Barbara Weinz' (Au/S) **new** WAln
- 'Barbarella' (Au/S) IPen MFie NDro SPop WCre
- Barnhaven doubles (Au/d) CWCL GAbr NSum
- 'Barnhaven Gold' (Au) IPen
- 'Barr Beacon' (Au/A) IPen ITim NDro
- 'Basilio' (Au/S) NDro WAln
- 'Basuto' (Au/A) GAbr IPen ITim MFie NDro SPop WCre WHil

- 'Beatrice' (Au/A) CTri EWoo GAbr IPen MFie NDro SPop WCre WHil WIce
- 'Beauty of Bath' (Au/S) WAln
- 'Beckminster' (Au/A) WAln
- 'Bedford Lad' (Au/A) NDro WCre
- 'Beechen Green' (Au/S) EWoo GAbr IPen ITim MAsh SPop WCre
- 'Behold' (Au) WCre
- 'Belgravia Gold' (Au/B) NDro
- 'Bella' (Au/d) **new** WAln
- 'Bellamy Pride' (Au/B) EWoo GAbr IPen NDro SPop WCre
- 'Belle Zana' (Au/S) EWoo GAgs IPen MFie NDro SPop
- 'Ben Lawers' (Au/S) SPop WBla
- 'Ben Wyves' (Au/S) SPop WBla WCre
- 'Bendigo' (Au/S) EWoo MFie SPop WAln
- 'Bengal Rose' (Au/S) SPop
- 'Benny Green' (Au/S) IPen SPop WCre
- 'Beppi' (Au) WHil
- 'Best Wishes' (Au/F) **new** WAln
- 'Bethan McSparron' (Au/B) NDro
- 'Betty Stewart' (Au/A) WAln
- 'Bewitched' (Au/A) MFie NDro WAln
- 'Bilbao' (Au/A) WAln
- 'Bilbo Baggins' (Au/A) NDro SPop WAln WCre
- 'Bill Bailey' (Au/d) EWoo GAbr NDro SPop WCre
- 'Bilton' (Au/S) SPop WCre
- 'Bingley Folk' (Au/B) NDro SPop
- 'Bisto' (Au/S) **new** WAln
- 'Bitterne Beauty' (Au/d) **new** SPop
- 'Bitterne Bounty' (Au/d) **new** SPop
- 'Bitterne Buttercup' (Au/d) **new** SPop
- 'Bizarre' (Au) GAgs WCre
- 'Black Adder' (Au/S) **new** SPop WAln
- 'Black Diamond' (Au/d) MFie WHil
- 'Black Ice' (Au/S) WAln
- 'Black Jack'PBR (Au/d) GBin GKin LBMP MHol NDov NLar NPri SMrm
- 'Blackcurrant' (Au) GAbr
- 'Blackfield' (Au/S) SPop
- 'Blackhill' (Au/S) ITim MFie SPop
- 'Blackpool Rock' (Au/St) CWCL MFie WAln WBla
- 'Blairside Yellow' (Au/B) ECho EWes LLHF NDro WAbe
- 'Blakeney' (Au/d) MFie NDro
- 'Blossom' (Au/A) GAbr MFie SPop WBla
- 'Blossom Dearie' (Au/St) **new** SPop
- 'Blue Bonnet' (Au/A/d) EWoo GAbr GAgs ITim MFie NDro WAln WCre
- 'Blue Boy' (Au/S) NDro WAln WBla
- 'Blue Chip' (Au/S) EWoo GAgs MAsh MFie NDro SPop WCre WHil
- 'Blue Cliff' (Au/S) IPen SPop WAln
- 'Blue Fire' (Au/S) MFie SPop
- 'Blue Frills' (Au) WAln
- 'Blue Heaven' (Au/A) IPen NDro SPop WCre
- 'Blue Jean' (Au/S) GAbr IPen MFie NDro SPop
- 'Blue Lace' (Au) WAln
- 'Blue Merle' (Au/B) **new** NDro
- 'Blue Mist' (Au/B) NDro
- 'Blue Night' (Au/B) ITim
- 'Blue Nile' (Au/S) SPop WCre
- 'Blue Ridge' (Au/A) WAln
- 'Blue Skies' (Au/St) SPop
- 'Blue Steel' (Au/S) WAln
- 'Blue Velvet' (Au/B) EWoo GAbr GAgs IPen LLHF MFie NBro NDro WCre
- 'Blue Wave' (Au/d) MSCN SPop
- 'Blue Yodeler' (Au/A) GAbr GAgs MFie NDro NSum SPop WBla WCre WHil
- 'Blue Yonder' (Au/S) **new** WAln
- 'Blush Baby' (Au/St) EWoo GAbr GAgs NDro SPop WBla WCre
- 'Blusher' (Au/St) **new** WAln
- 'Blyth Spirit' (Au/A) SPop WAln
- 'Bob Dingley' (Au/A) IPen SPop WCre
- 'Bob Lancashire' (Au/S) CWCL GAbr GAgs IPen ITim MFie NDro SPop WBla WCre
- 'Bokay' (Au/d) WAln
- 'Bold Tartan' (Au/St) IPen NDro WAln
- 'Bolero' (Au/A) SPop WAln
- 'Bollin Tiger' (Au/St) WAln
- 'Bonafide' (Au/d) SPop WAln
- 'Bonanza' (Au/S) SPop WAln
- 'Bookham Firefly' (Au/A) GAbr GAgs IPen MFie NDro SPop WBla WCre WHil
- 'Bookham Star' (Au/S) SPop
- 'Border Bandit' (Au/B) MFie SPop WAln
- 'Border Beauty' (Au/St) NDro
- 'Border Blue' (Au/B) WAln
- 'Border Patrol' (Au/B) WAln
- 'Border Tawny' (Au/B) NDro
- 'Boromir' (Au/A) EWoo MFie NDro WAln
- 'Bournebrook' (Au/A) WAln
- 'Bowen's Blue' (Au/B) **new** EWoo NDro SPop
- 'Bradford City' (Au/A) CFis CWCL NDro SPop WHil
- 'Bradmore Bluebell' (Au) NDro
- 'Bramley Rose' (Au/B) SPop
- 'Bran' (Au/B) NDro
- 'Brandaris' (Au/A) WAln
- 'Branno' (Au/S) WAln
- 'Brass Dog' (Au/S) WAln
- 'Brasso' (Au) IPen MFie NDro SPop WAln
- 'Brazen Hussy' (Au/d) WAln
- 'Brazil' (Au/S) EBee GAbr IPen MFie NDro SPop WCre WHil
- 'Brazos River' (Au/A) EWoo IPen MFie WAln WHil
- 'Breckland Joy' (Au/A) NDro WAln
- 'Brenda's Choice' (Au/A) EWoo IPen MFie NDro SPop WBla WCre
- 'Brentford Bees' (Au/St) WAln
- 'Bright Eyes' (Au/A) IPen MFie NDro WCre
- 'Bright Ginger' (Au/S) EWoo WAln
- 'Brimstone and Treacle' (Au/d) SPop WAln
- 'Broad Gold' (Au/A) MFie SPop WBla WCre
- 'Broadwell Gold' (Au/B) GAbr NDro SPop WCre
- 'Brompton' (Au/S) SPop
- 'Brookfield' (Au/S) GAgs IPen ITim MFie NDro SPop WBla WCre
- 'Broughton' (Au/S) SPop
- 'Brown Ben' (Au) EWoo IPen MFie WHil
- 'Brown Bess' (Au/A) GAbr GAgs IPen MFie WCot WCre WHil
- 'Brown Tan Double' (Au/d) **new** EWoo
- 'Brownie' (Au/B) CWCL GAbr NBir NDro SPop WHil
- 'Brownie Point' (Au/B) **new** NDro
- 'Bucks Green' (Au/S) GAbr NDro SPop
- 'Bunty' (Au/A) MFie
- 'Buoyance' (Au/A) WAln
- 'Burnished Gold' (Au/d) **new** WAln
- 'Bush Baby' (Au/B) NDro
- 'Buttermere' (Au/d) **new** WAln

- 'Butternut' (Au/S) WAln
- 'Butterwick' (Au/A) EWoo GAbr GAgs GMaP IPen MFie NDro NEgg SPop WBla WCre
- 'C.G. Haysom' (Au/S) GAbr NDro SPop WCre
- 'C.W. Needham' (Au/A) IPen MFie NDro SPop WCre
- 'Cadiz Bay' (Au/d) WAln
- 'Calypso' (Au/d) NDro SPop WAln
- 'Cambodunum' (Au/A) IPen MFie NDro SPop WCre WHil
- 'Camelot' (Au/d) ELan EWoo GAgs MFie NBro NDro SPop WCre WHil
- 'Cameo' (Au/A) WCre
- 'Cameo Beauty' (Au/d) NDro SPop
- 'Camilla' (Au/A) WAln
- 'Candida' (Au/d) EWoo IPen MFie SPop WBla WCre
- 'Candy Stripe' (Au/St) SPop WBla
- 'Cappela' (Au/d) WAln
- 'Caramel' (Au/A) IPen WAln
- 'Cardinal Red' (Au/d) NDro SPop
- 'Cardington' (Au/A) WAln
- 'Carioca' (Au/A) WAln
- 'Carl Andrew' (Au/S) WAln
- 'Carmel' (Au/d) EWoo SPop WAln
- 'Carnival' (Au/A) WAln
- 'Carole' (Au/A) MFie SPop WBla WCre
- 'Carreras' (Au) MFie NDro
- 'Carsa Wakes' (Au/d) **new** WAln
- 'Carzon' (Au/A) NDro
- 'Catherine Butler' (Au/S) **new** NDro
- 'Catherine Wheel' (Au/St) SPop WAln
- 'Catta Ha' (Au/d) **new** NDro
- 'Celtic One' (Au/St) SPop
- 'Ceri Nicolle' (Au/B) NDro
- 'Chadwick End' (Au/S) WAln
- 'Chaffinch' (Au/S) EWoo GAbr GAgs IPen NDro SPop WBla
- 'Chamois' (Au/B) EWoo GAbr IPen MFie NDro WHil
- 'Chanel' (Au/S) SPop WAln WCre
- 'Chantilly Cream' (Au/d) WAln
- 'Charles Bronson' (Au/d) GAbr MFie NDro WAln
- 'Charles Rennie' (Au/B) EWoo MFie NDro SPop WAln WHil
- 'Charlie's Aunt' (Au/A) WAln
- 'Charlotte Brookes' (Au/d) **new** WAln
- 'Checkmate' (Au) EWoo MFie SPop WAln WCre
- 'Cheeky' (Au/d) **new** SPop
- 'Chelsea Bridge' (Au/A) EWoo IPen MFie NDro SPop WBla WCre
- 'Cheops' (Au/A) IPen MFie NDro NEgg
- 'Cherry' (Au/S) GAbr GAgs IPen SPop WCre
- 'Cherry Picker' (Au/A) MFie NDro SPop WCre
- 'Cheyenne' (Au/S) EWoo GAbr GAgs MFie NDro SPop WCre
- 'Chiffon' (Au/S) CPBP EWoo IPen NDro SPop
- 'Chiquita' (Au/d) SPop
- 'Chirichua' (Au/S) WAln
- 'Chloë' (Au/S) IPen NDro SPop
- 'Chloris' (Au/S) MFie SPop
- 'Choir Boy' (Au/A) WAln
- 'Chorister' (Au/S) CPBP EBee GAbr GAgs IPen ITim MFie NDro WCre WHil
- 'Chyne' (Au) EWoo
- 'Cicero' (Au/A) MFie SPop WAln
- 'Cinders' (Au/St) **new** SPop
- 'Cindy' (Au/A) NDro
- 'Cinnamon' (Au/d) EWoo GAgs ITim MFie NDro SPop WBla WCre
- 'Cinnamon' (Au/S) GAbr WHil
- 'Ciribiribin' (Au/A) WAln
- 'Citron-Ella' (Au/d) SPop
- 'Clara' (Au/d) SPop
- 'Clare' (Au/S) IPen MFie NDro SPop WCre
- 'Clarish' (Au) ITim
- 'Classic' (Au/A) WAln
- 'Clatter-Ha' (Au/d) SPop WHil
- 'Claud Wilson' (Au/St) **new** WAln
- 'Claudia Taylor' (Au) EWoo SPop
- 'Cleft Stick' (Au) IPen
- 'Clipper' (Au/S) WAln
- 'Cloth of Gold' (Au/A) **new** NDro
- 'Clotted Cream' (Au/B) NDro
- 'Cloud Nine' (Au/S) WCre
- 'Clouded Yellow' (Au/S) SPop WBla WHil
- 'Cloudy Bay' (Au) NDro WCot
- 'Cloverdale' (Au/d) WAln
- 'Clunie' (Au/S) IPen MFie NDro WCre
- 'Clunie II' (Au/S) GAgs IPen
- 'Cobden Meadows' (Au/A) WAln WCre
- 'Cockle' (Au/S) SPop
- 'Coffee' (Au/S) IPen ITim MFie NDro SPop WCre
- 'Colbury' (Au/S) NDro SPop WCre
- 'Colonel Champney' (Au/S) EWoo NDro SPop WCre
- 'Comet' (Au/S) IPen NDro
- 'Confederate' (Au/S) WAln
- 'Connaught Court' (Au/A) EWoo IPen NDro WCre
- 'Conquistador' (Au/A) IPen NDro WAln
- 'Conservative' (Au/S) EWoo IPen
- 'Consett' (Au/S) EWoo IPen MFie SPop WHil
- 'Cooks Hill' (Au/d) **new** WAln
- 'Cooper's Gold' (Au/B) NDro
- 'Coop's Green' (Au/S) **new** EWoo
- 'Copper King' (Au/B) WAln
- 'Coppi' (Au/A) EWoo IPen NDro SPop WCre
- 'Coral' (Au/S) EWoo GAgs SPop
- 'Cornish Cream' (Au/B) IPen NDro
- 'Cornmeal' (Au/S) GAgs ITim MFie NDro SPop WAln WCre WHil
- 'Corntime' (Au/S) IPen SPop WAln WCre
- 'Corona' (Au/S) WAln
- 'Corporal Jones' (Au/S) SPop WCre
- 'Corporal Kate' (Au/St) WAln WCre
- 'Corrie Files' (Au/d) MFie SPop WAln
- 'Cortez Silver' (Au/S) SPop WAln
- 'Cortina' (Au/S) CPBP ECho EWoo GAbr GAgs IPen ITim MFie NDro SPop WCre WHil
- 'Country Maid' (Au/A) WAln
- 'County Park Red' (Au/B) NDro
- 'Coventry Street' (Au/S) MFie NDro SPop
- 'Crackley Tagetes' (Au/d) ECho
- 'Craig Nordie' (Au/B) NDro
- 'Craig Vaughan' (Au/A) MFie NDro SPop
- 'Cranborne' (Au/A) SPop WAln
- 'Crecy' (Au/A) MFie SPop WAln
- 'Cressida' (Au/d) SPop
- 'Crimple' (Au/S) NDro SPop WAln
- 'Crimson Black' (Au/B) **new** SPop
- 'Crimson Glow' (Au/d) EWoo GAbr GAgs MFie NDro NSum SPop WBla WCre
- 'Crinoline' (Au/S) NDro SPop
- 'Cuckoo Fair' (Au/S) EWoo GAbr IPen NDro SPop WCre
- 'Cuddles' (Au/A) EWoo MFie WAln
- 'Curly Wurlie' (Au) GAbr
- 'Curry Blend' (Au/B) GAbr IPen NDro SPop
- 'Cutie Pie' (Au/St) IPen WCre
- 'Cuttlefish' (Au/St) SPop

- 'Daftie Green' (Au/S)	EWoo GAbr GAgs IPen NDro WCre
- 'Dakota' (Au/S)	EWoo MFie
- 'Dales Red' (Au/B)	EWoo GAbr GAgs IGor IPen MFie NDro NSum SPop WCre WHil
- 'Dan Tiger' (Au/St)	EWoo MFie NDro SPop WAln WHil
- 'Daniel' (Au/A)	EWoo NDro SPop WAln
- 'Daniel T. Taylor' (Au/A) **new**	NDro WAln
- 'Daphnis' (Au/S)	GAbr SPop WAln
- 'Dark Eyes' (Au/d)	EWoo GAbr GAgs MFie NDro SPop
- 'Dark Lady' (Au/A)	WAln
- 'Dark Red' (Au/S)	IPen
- 'David Beckham' (Au/d)	SPop WAln
- 'Day by Day' (Au/St) **new**	SPop
- 'Decaff' (Au/St)	WAln
- 'Deckchair' (Au/St)	MFie NDro SPop
- 'Dedham' (Au/d)	WAln
- 'Del Boy' (Au/A)	SPop WAln
- 'Delilah' (Au/d)	GAbr GAgs MFie NDro SPop WHil
- 'Denise' (Au/S)	WAln
- 'Denna Snuffer' (Au/d)	GAbr NDro
- 'Derrill' (Au/B)	NDro SPop
- 'Devon Cream' (Au/d)	ECho MFie SPop
- 'Diamond' (Au/d)	WAln
- 'Diane' (Au/A)	MFie
- 'Dick Rogers' (Au/B)	NDro
- 'Digby' (Au/d)	EWoo NDro WAln
- 'Digit' (Au/d)	NDro WAln
- 'Dilemma' (Au/A)	SPop
* - 'Dill' (Au/A)	IPen MFie NDro SPop WAln WHil
- 'Dilly Dilly' (Au/A)	MFie NDro SPop WCre
- 'Divint Dunch' (Au/A)	GAgs IPen MFie NDro SPop WCre WHil
- 'Doctor Duthie' (Au/S)	SPop WAln
- 'Doctor Lennon's White' (Au/B)	GAbr IPen MFie NDro SPop WCre WHil
- 'Doctor Woolhead' (Au/S) **new**	SPop
- 'Dolly Viney' (Au/d)	GAbr WAln
- 'Donhead' (Au/A)	ITim MFie NDro SPop WCre WHil
- 'Donn' (Au/d) **new**	SPop WAln WCre
- 'Donna Clancy' (Au/S)	EWoo MFie SPop WCre
- 'Dorado' (Au/d)	WAln
- 'Doris Jean' (Au/A)	MFie
- 'Dorothy' (Au/S)	WAln
- 'Doublet' (Au/d)	ECho GAbr GAgs IPen MFie NDro SPop WCre WHil
- 'Doubloon' (Au/d)	ECho
- 'Doublure' (Au/d)	EWoo GAbr GAgs NDro SPop WCre WHil
- 'Douglas Bader' (Au/A)	EWoo GAbr MFie NDro SPop WCre WHil
- 'Douglas Black' (Au/S)	EWoo GAbr IPen MFie SPop WCre WHil
- 'Douglas Green' (Au/S)	EWoo IPen NDro
- 'Douglas White' (Au/S)	MFie SPop
- 'Dovedale' (Au/S)	NDro SPop WAln
- 'Dowager' (Au/A)	MFie
- Downtown Doubles (Au/d)	SPop
- 'Doyen' (Au/d)	EWoo IPen ITim MFie NDro WAln
- 'Drax' (Au/A)	SPop WAln
- 'Dream' (Au/St)	SPop
- 'Dubarii' (Au/A)	MFie WAln
- 'Duchess of Malfi' (Au/S)	SPop WAln
- 'Duchess of York' (Au)	LLHF
- 'Duke of Edinburgh' (Au/B)	NDro WAln
- 'Dusky Girl' (Au/A)	NDro WAln
- 'Dusky Maiden' (Au/A)	EWoo GAbr GAgs MFie NDro SPop WBla WCre WHil
- 'Dusky Yellow' (Au/B)	ECho NDro
- 'Dusty Miller' (Au/B)	EBee ECho NBir
- 'Eastern Promise' (Au/A)	EWoo GAgs MFie NDro SPop WBla WHil
- 'Eaton Dawn' (Au/S) **new**	SPop
- 'Ed Spivey' (Au/A)	NDro WBla WCre
- 'Eddy Gordon' (Au/A)	WAln
- 'Eden Alexander' (Au/B)	MFie NDro
- 'Eden Blue Star' (Au/B)	EWoo NDro SPop
- 'Eden Carmine' (Au/B)	MFie NDro SPop
- 'Eden Cynthia' (Au/B)	MFie
- 'Eden David' (Au/B)	MFie NDro SPop WHil
- 'Eden Ensign' (Au/B) **new**	SPop
- 'Eden Fanfare' (Au/B) **new**	NDro
- 'Eden Goldfinch' (Au/B)	SPop WBla
- 'Eden Greenfinch' (Au/B)	EWoo GAgs MFie NDro SPop WCre
- 'Eden Moonlight' (Au/B)	MFie NDro WAln WHil
- 'Eden Sunrise' (Au/B)	NDro
- 'Edinburgh' (Au/A)	WAln
- 'Edith Allen' (Au/A)	WAln
- 'Edith Major' (Au/d)	CPBP MFie SPop
- 'Edith Mather' (Au/S)	WAln
- 'Edward Sweeney' (Au/S)	WAln
- 'Eglinton' (Au)	WCre
- 'Eileen K' (Au/S)	NDro
- 'Elf Star' (Au/A)	SPop WAln
- 'Eli Jenkins' (Au)	WAln
- 'Elizabeth Ann' (Au/A)	NDro SPop
- 'Ellen Thompson' (Au/A)	EWoo GAbr GAgs IPen MFie NDro SPop WCre WHil
- 'Elsie' (Au/A)	WCre
- 'Elsie May' (Au/A)	EWoo ITim MFie NDro SPop WCre WHil
- 'Elsinore' (Au/S)	IPen WCre
- 'Emberglow' (Au/d)	WAln
- 'Embley' (Au/S)	NDro SPop WCre
- 'Emery Down' (Au/S)	NDro SPop WBla
- 'Emily' (Au/d)	IPen
- 'Emma Louise' (Au)	IPen
- 'Emmett Smith' (Au/A)	NBro NDro WAln
- 'Emorydown' (Au/S)	WCre
- 'Enigma' (Au/S)	SPop WAln
- 'Enlightened' (Au/A)	MFie
- 'Envy' (Au/S)	MFie WAln
- 'Erica' (Au/A)	GAbr IPen MFie NDro SPop WCre WHil
- 'Erjon' (Au/S)	MFie NDro SPop
- 'Error' (Au/S)	MFie WAln
- 'Esso' (Au/S)	WAln
- 'Ethel' (Au)	NDro WCre
- 'Ethel Wild' (Au/d)	SPop
- 'Ethel Wilkes' (Au/d)	WAln
- 'Etna' (Au/S)	WAln
- 'Ettrick' (Au/S)	WAln
- 'Europa' (Au/d)	SPop
- 'Eve Guest' (Au/A)	EWoo NDro SPop WAln
- 'Eventide' (Au/S)	SPop
- 'Everest Blue' (Au/S)	GAbr MAsh SPop WCre
- 'Everest Flush' (Au/S) **new**	WAln
- 'Excalibur' (Au/d)	EWoo GAbr GAgs NDro SPop
- 'Eye Candy' (Au/St) **new**	SPop
- 'Eyeopener' (Au/A)	IPen MFie NDro SPop WCre WHil
- 'Fabuloso' (Au/St)	EWoo SPop WBla
- 'Fairy' (Au/A)	WAln
- 'Fairy Light' (Au/S)	WAln
- 'Fairy Moon' (Au/S)	IPen WAln
- 'Fairy Queen' (Au/S)	WAln

- 'Falcon' (Au/S) SPop WAln
- 'Faliraki Fanciful' (Au) EWoo
- 'Falstaff' (Au/d) WAln
- 'Fanciful' (Au/S) EWoo MFie NDro WHil
- 'Fancy Free' (Au) SPop
- 'Fancy Pants' (Au/S) **new** SPop
- 'Fandancer' (Au/A) WAln
- 'Fandango' **new** WBla
- 'Fanfare' (Au/S) EWoo MAsh MFie NDro SPop WBla
- 'Fanny Meerbeck' (Au/S) GAbr IPen MFie NDro SPop WBla WHil
- 'Fantasia' (Au/d) WAln
- 'Faro' (Au/S) NDro SPop WBla WCre
- 'Favourite' (Au/S) EWoo GAbr GAgs IPen ITim MAsh MFie NDro SPop WBla WCre WHil
- 'Fearless' (Au/S) WAln
- 'Fen Tiger' (Au/St) SPop WAln
- 'Fenby' (Au/S) **new** SPop
- 'Fennay' (Au/S) EWoo WAln
- 'Ferrybridge' (Au/A) IPen NDro WAln
- 'Fiddler's Green' (Au/d) CPBP EWoo GAbr GAgs IPen NDro SPop
- 'Figaro' (Au/S) EWoo MFie NDro SPop WCre
- 'Figurine' (Au/d) WAln
- 'Finchfield' (Au/A) GAbr IPen MFie NDro WAln
- 'Finley' (Au/B) **new** NDro
- 'Firecracker' (Au) IPen WAln
- 'Firenze' (Au/A) MFie SPop
- 'Firsby' (Au/d) NDro SPop WAln WBla WCre WHil
- 'First Lady' (Au/A) IPen SPop WAln WBla WCre
- 'First Light' (Au/B) NDro SPop
- 'Fishtoft' (Au/d) MFie
- 'Fitzroy' (Au/d) SPop
- 'Fleet Street' (Au/S) MFie NDro
- 'Fleminghouse' (Au/S) GAbr MAsh MFie NDro SPop WCre
- 'Florence Brown' (Au/S) IPen
- 'For You' (Au/St) SPop
- 'Foreign Affairs' (Au/S) **new** SPop
- 'Forest Beech' (Au/d) **new** SPop
- 'Forest Bracken' (Au/d) **new** SPop
- 'Forest Burgundy' (Au/d) SPop
- 'Forest Cappuccino' (Au/d) EWoo SPop
- 'Forest Duet' (Au/d) EWoo SPop
- 'Forest Fire' (Au/d) EWoo SPop
- 'Forest Lemon' (Au/d) EWoo SPop
- 'Forest Lime' (Au/d) **new** SPop
- 'Forest Pines' (Au/S) SPop WAln
- 'Forest Shade' (Au/d) SPop
- 'Forest Sunburst' (Au/d) **new** SPop
- 'Forest Sunlight' (Au/d) SPop
- 'Forest Twilight' (Au/d) EWoo MFie SPop
- 'Foxfire' (Au/A) WAln
- 'Fradley' (Au/A) IPen MFie NDro WAln WCre WHil
- 'Frank Bailey' (Au/d) MFie SPop WAln
- 'Frank Crosland' (Au/A) MFie NDro WCre WHil
- 'Frank Faulkner' (Au/A) WAln
- 'Frank Jenning' (Au/A) NDro WAln
- 'Frank Taylor' (Au/S) EWoo
- 'Fred Booley' (Au/d) EWoo GAbr IPen MFie NDro SPop WCre WHil
- 'Fred Livesley' (Au/A) NDro WAln
- 'Fresco' (Au/A) SPop WAln
- 'Freya' (Au/S) SPop
- 'Friskney' (Au/d) EWoo SPop WAln
- 'Frittenden Yellow' (Au/B) GAbr SPop
- 'Frosty' (Au/S) NDro SPop WBla WCre
- 'Fuller's Red' (Au/S) ITim NDro SPop WCre WHil
- 'Funny Valentine' (Au/d) EWoo IPen MFie SPop
- 'Fuzzy' (Au/St) WAln
- 'G.L. Taylor' (Au/A) IPen NDro
- 'Gaia' (Au/d) SPop WCre
- 'Gail Atkinson' (Au/A) SPop WAln WBla
- 'Galatea' (Au/S) WAln
- 'Galator' (Au/A) WAln
- 'Galen' (Au/A) GAbr WCre
- 'Ganymede' (Au/d) SPop WAln
- 'Gary Pallister' (Au/A) WAln WBla
- 'Gavin Ward' (Au/S) WAln
- 'Gay Crusader' (Au/A) GAbr IPen MFie NDro SPop WCre WHil
- 'Gazza' (Au/A) WAln
- 'Gee Cross' (Au/A) GAbr IPen MFie
- 'Geldersome Green' (Au/S) ITim NDro SPop WCre
- 'Gemini' (Au/S) NDro
- 'General Champney' (Au) WCre
- 'Generosity' (Au/A) MFie WCre WHil
- 'Geoffrey Bick' (Au/A) **new** SPop
- 'Geordie' (Au/A) WAln
- 'George Edge' (Au/B) NDro
- 'George Harrison' (Au/B) GAbr NDro SPop
- 'George Jennings' (Au/A) MFie NDro
- 'George Swinford's Leathercoat' (Au/B) GAbr NDro
- 'Geronimo' (Au/S) GAbr IPen MFie NDro SPop WBla WCre
- 'Ghost Grey' (Au) WBla WCre
- 'Gimli' (Au/A) WAln
- 'Girl Guide' (Au/S) WHil
- 'Gizabroon' (Au/S) CHis CPBP CWCL EWoo GAbr GAgs MFie NDro NEgg NLar SPop WBla WCre WHil
- 'Glasnost' (Au/S) WAln
- 'Glazebrook' (Au/S) **new** SPop
- 'Gleam' (Au/S) CWCL EBee ECho EDAr IPen LLHF MFie NDro SPop WBla WCre WHil
- 'Glencoe' (Au/S) EWoo
- 'Gleneagles' (Au/S) EWoo IPen NDro SPop WAln WBla WCre
- 'Glenelg' (Au/S) EWoo GAbr ITim MFie NDro SPop WBla WCre WHil
- 'Glenluce' (Au/S) EWoo SPop
- 'Gnome' (Au/B) GAbr IPen NDro
- 'Goeblii' (Au/B) MFie NDro SPop WHil
- 'Gold Seal' (Au/d) SPop
- 'Gold Seam' (Au/A) EWoo MFie WAln
- 'Golden Boy' (Au/A) MFie NDro SPop WAln
- 'Golden Chartreuse' (Au/d) EWoo GAbr NDro SPop
- 'Golden Fleece' (Au/S) EWoo GAbr MAsh MFie NDro SPop
- 'Golden Girl' (Au/A) WAln
- 'Golden Glory' (Au/A) WAln
- 'Golden Harvest' (Au/A) SPop
- 'Golden Hill' (Au/S) EWoo ITim SPop
- 'Golden Hind' (Au/d) EWoo GAbr MFie NBro NDro SPop WBla WCre
- 'Golden Splendour' (Au/d) EWoo GAgs IPen ITim MFie NDro NSum SPop WBla WCre WHil
- 'Golden Wedding' (Au/A) IPen MFie SPop WAln WBla WCre WHil
- 'Goldie' (Au/S) NDro
- 'Goldthorn' (Au/A) WCre
- 'Gollum' (Au/A) MFie NDro SPop WAln WBla

- 'Good Report' (Au/A) GAgs MFie NDro SPop WBla WHil
- 'Goody Goody' (Au/St) SPop
- 'Googie' (Au/d) SPop
- 'Gordon Files' (Au/S) **new** WAln
- 'Gorey' (Au/A) MFie WCre WHil
- 'Gorgeous George' (Au/St) SPop
- 'Grabley' (Au/S) SPop
- 'Grace' (Au/S) WAln
- 'Grace Ellen' (Au/S) WAln
- 'Grand Slam' (Au/D) **new** MFie
- 'Grandad's Favourite' (Au/B) NDro SPop
- 'Green Abundance' (Au/B) EWoo
- 'Green Café' (Au/S) **new** SPop
- 'Green Finger' (Au/S) MFie SPop
- 'Green Frill' (Au) GAgs NDro
- 'Green Goddess' (Au/St) EWoo WAln
- 'Green Heart' (Au/S) EWoo SPop
- 'Green Isle' (Au/S) EWoo GAbr IPen MFie NDro SPop WCre
- 'Green Jacket' (Au/S) IPen SPop WCre
- 'Green Meadows' (Au/S) SPop WAln
- 'Green Mouse' (Au/S) WAln
- 'Green Mustard' (Au/S) SPop
- 'Green Parrot' (Au/S) GAbr NDro SPop WCre WHil
- 'Green Shank' (Au/S) EWoo GAgs IPen NDro SPop WHil
- 'Greenfield's Fancy' (Au) EBee
- 'Greenfinch' (Au/S) EWoo
- 'Greenfinger' (Au/S) WAln
- 'Greenheart' (Au/S) EWoo SPop
- 'Greenpeace' (Au/S) EWoo GAbr NDro SPop WAln WBla
- 'Greswolde' (Au/d) EWoo SPop WAln
- 'Greta' (Au/S) CWCL ECho EWoo GAbr IPen MFie NDro SPop WHil
- 'Gretna Green' (Au/S) EWoo SPop
- 'Grey Bonnet' (Au/S) SPop WAln
- 'Grey Cloud' (Au/B) **new** NDro
- 'Grey Dawn' (Au/S) WAln
- 'Grey Edge' (Au) ECho
- 'Grey Friar' (Au/S) WAln
- 'Grey Hawk' (Au/S) IPen SPop WAln
- 'Grey Lady' (Au/S) WAln
- 'Grey Lag' (Au/S) SPop WHil
- 'Grey Monarch' (Au/S) GAbr IPen MFie SPop WAln WCre WHil
- 'Grey Owl' (Au/S) SPop WAln
- 'Grey Ridge' (Au/S) WAln
- 'Grey Shrike' (Au/S) WAln
- 'Grizedale' (Au/S) SPop
- 'Groupie' (Au/St) SPop
- 'Grüner Veltliner' (Au/S) NDro SPop WCre
- 'Guinea' (Au/S) EWoo GAbr IPen ITim MFie SPop WCre
- 'Gwai Loh' (Au) NDro
- 'Gwen' (Au/A) MFie NDro SPop WAln WCre
- 'Gwen Baker' (Au/d) MFie NDro WAln WCre
- 'Gwenda' (Au/A) SPop WAln WHil
- 'Gypsy Rose Lee' (Au/A) MFie
- 'Habanera' (Au/A) MFie NDro SPop WCre
- 'Haffner' (Au/S) NDro SPop
- 'Hallmark' (Au/A) MFie NDro WAln
- 'Handsome Lass' (Au/St) EWoo IPen MFie SPop WAln WCre
- 'Hannah' (Au/A) WAln
- 'Harlequin' (Au/B) NDro
- 'Harmony' (Au/B) EWoo MFie NBro
- 'Harry Hotspur' (Au/A) EWoo IPen MFie NDro SPop WHil
- 'Harry 'O'' (Au/S) MFie NDro SPop WCre
- 'Harthorpeburn' (Au/B) NDro
- 'Harvest Glow' (Au/S) IPen NDro SPop WHil
- 'Havana' (Au/d) SPop WAln
- 'Hawkwood' (Au/S) CPBP CWCL GAbr GAgs IPen MFie NDro NEgg SPop WBla WHil
- * – 'Hazel' (Au/A) IPen MFie NDro SPop WCre WHil
- 'Headdress' (Au/S) EWoo GAbr IPen MFie SPop WCre
- 'Heady' (Au/A) CWCL EWoo MFie NDro WHil
- 'Heart of Gold' (Au/A) MFie SPop WAln
- 'Hebers' (Au) NDro SPop WAln
- 'Helen' (Au/S) GAbr IPen MFie NDro SPop WCre WHil
- 'Helen Barter' (Au/S) NDro SPop WHil
- 'Helen Ruane' (Au/d) EBee EWoo GAgs GKev SPop WCre
- 'Helena' (Au/S) IPen MFie NDro SPop WAln WHil
- 'Helena Brown' (Au/S) SPop WAln
- 'Helena Dean' (Au/d) SPop WAln
- 'Henry's Bane' (Au/St) **new** SPop
- 'Hermia' (Au/A) MFie SPop
- 'Hetty Woolf' (Au/S) GAbr NDro SPop WCre
- 'Hew Dalrymple' (Au/S) NDro SPop WAln
- 'High Hopes' (Au) NDro WAln
- 'Highland Park' (Au/A) NDro SPop
- 'Hillhook' (Au/A) WAln
- 'Hinton Admiral' (Au/S) EWoo GAbr IPen NDro SPop
- 'Hinton Fields' (Au/S) CPBP CSev EBee EShb GAbr GAgs IPen MFie NDro NEgg SPop WBla WCre WHil
- 'Hobby Horse' (Au) EWoo ITim NDro
- 'Holyrood' (Au/S) EWoo GAbr IPen NDro SPop WAln
- 'Honey' (Au/d) GAbr NBro NDro NEgg NSum SPop
- 'Honeydawn' (Au/B) **new** NDro
- 'Hopleys Coffee' (Au/d) EWoo GAbr NDro SPop WAln WCre
- 'Hopton Gem' (Au/B) NDro
- 'Howard Telford' (Au/A) MFie NDro SPop
- 'Hughie' (Au/A) WAln
- 'Humphrey' (Au/S) WAln
- 'Hurstwood Midnight' (Au) MFie WAln
- 'Iago' (Au/S) NDro SPop WAln
- 'Ian Greville' (Au/A) IPen MFie NDro SPop WBla WCre
- 'Ibis' (Au/S) WAln WCre
- 'Ice Cap' (Au/d) **new** SPop
- 'Ice Maiden' (Au/A) EWoo GAbr IPen MFie NDro SPop WBla WCre WHil
- 'Icon' (Au/St) SPop
- 'Ida' (Au/A) IPen
- 'Idmiston' (Au/S) CWCL EWoo GAbr IPen NDro SPop WCre WHil
- 'Ilona' (Au/d) SPop
- 'Imari Stripe' (Au/St) MAsh WBla
- 'Immaculate' (Au/A) MFie SPop WBla WCre WHil
- 'Impassioned' (Au/A) MFie SPop WBla WCre
- 'Impeccable' (Au/A) IPen MFie
- 'Imperturbable' (Au/A) IPen MFie NDro SPop
- 'Indian Love Call' (Au/A) GAbr GAgs IPen ITim MFie NDro SPop WBla WCre WHil
- 'Innsworth' (Au/A) WAln
- 'Iris Scott' (Au/A) NDro
- 'Isabel' (Au/S) WAln
- 'Isabella' (Au/A) NDro WAln
- 'Jac' (Au/S) **new** SPop
- 'Jack Dean' (Au/A) EWoo MFie SPop WCre WHil
- 'Jack Horner' (Au) WAln
- 'Jack Redfern' (Au/A) NDro
- 'Jaffa' (Au/A) EWoo NDro WAln WCre
- 'James Arnot' (Au/S) GAbr IPen SPop WAln
- 'James Watham' (Au/S) WAln
- 'Jane' (Au/S) WAln
- 'Jane Myers' (Au/d) WAln WHil

– 'Janet' (Au)	ECho
– 'Janet Watts' (Au)	GAgs WCre
– 'Janie Hill' (Au/A)	MFie SPop WBla WCre
– 'Jean Fielder' (Au/A)	NDro SPop WAln
– 'Jean Jacques' (Au/A)	WAln
– 'Jeanne' (Au/A)	EWoo MFie
– 'Jeannie Telford' (Au/A)	MFie NDro SPop WCre WHil
– 'Jeff Scruton' (Au/A)	SPop WAln
– 'Jenny' (Au/A)	EWoo IPen MFie SPop WCre
– 'Jersey Bounce' (Au/A)	EWoo GAbr NDro WAln WCre
– 'Jesmond' (Au/S)	WAln
– 'Jessie' (Au/d)	EWoo
– 'Jilting Jessie' (Au/St)	IPen NDro SPop
– 'Joan Butler' (Au)	WAln
– 'Joan Curtis' (Au/d)	SPop
– 'Joan Elliott' (Au/A)	GAbr
– 'Joanne' (Au/A)	EWoo GAbr MFie NDro SPop WCre
– 'Joe Perks' (Au/A)	EWoo IPen MFie NBro NDro SPop WCre WHil
– 'Joel' (Au/S)	EWoo GAgs IPen ITim MFie NDro SPop WBla WCre WHil
– 'Johann Bach' (Au/B)	EWoo SPop
– 'John Kerridge' (Au/A) **new**	WAln
– 'John Stewart' (Au/A)	MFie SPop
– 'John Wayne' (Au/A)	EWoo GAbr MFie NDro WBla WCre
– 'John Woolf' (Au/S)	NDro
– 'Jonathon' (Au/A)	EWoo NDro WAln
– 'Jorvik' (Au/S)	NDro SPop
– 'Joy' (Au/A)	IPen LLHF MFie NDro SPop WCre WHil
– 'Joyce' (Au/A)	EWoo GAbr GAgs IPen MFie NDro SPop WCre WHil
– 'Judith' (Au/B)	NDro
– 'Judith Dorman' (Au/d)	GAgs NDro
– 'Julia' (Au/S)	NDro SPop WAln
– 'Julia Jane' (Au/B) **new**	NDro
– 'Julie Nuttall' (Au/B)	NDro
– 'June' (Au/A)	NDro SPop WCre
– 'Jungfrau' (Au/d)	NDro SPop WAln
– 'Jupiter' (Au/S)	NDro SPop WAln
– 'Jupp' (Au)	EBee
– 'Jura' (Au/A)	WAln
– 'Just Steven' (Au/A)	SPop WAln
– 'K S' (Au/S)	NDro
– 'Karen Cordrey' (Au/S)	EBee ECho EWoo GAbr GAgs GKev IPen ITim MAsh MFie NDro SPop WBla WCre WHil
– 'Karen McDonald' (Au/A)	MFie NDro SPop
– 'Kate Haywood' (Au/B)	NDro WHil
– 'Kath Dryden'	see *P. allionii* 'Kath Dryden'
– 'Kelso' (Au/A)	MFie
– 'Ken Chilton' (Au/A)	MFie SPop WCre WHil
– 'Kenco' (Au/d) **new**	SPop
– 'Kentucky Blues' (Au/d)	MFie SPop WAln
– 'Kercup' (Au/A)	EWoo MFie SPop WCre
– 'Kerry'	EBee WAln
– 'Kersey' (Au/S) **new**	SPop
– 'Kevin' (Au/A)	SPop WAln
– 'Kevin Keegan' (Au/A)	MFie NDro SPop WHil
– 'Key West' (Au/A)	NDro SPop WAln
– 'Khachaturian' (Au/A)	MFie NDro WAln
– 'Kilby' (Au/A)	SPop WBla
– 'Kim' (Au/A)	GAbr IPen MFie NDro SPop WCre
– 'Kimberworth Boy' (Au/A) **new**	NDro
– 'Kincraig' (Au/S)	WAln WBla
– 'King George' (Au/d) **new**	WAln
– 'King Kong' (Au)	WAln
– 'Kingcup' (Au/A)	GAbr MFie NDro SPop WCre
– 'Kingfisher' (Au/A)	EWoo GAbr IPen ITim MFie NDro SPop WHil
– 'Kingpin' (Au/St)	NDro
– 'Kintail' (Au/A)	MFie
– 'Kiowa' (Au/S)	SPop
– 'Kirklands' (Au/d)	EWoo ITim MFie NDro SPop
– 'Kohinoor' (Au)	MFie NDro WHil
– 'Königin der Nacht' (Au/St)	MFie NDro SPop WCre
– 'Lady Daresbury' (Au/A)	MFie NDro SPop WCre
– 'Lady Day' (Au/d)	SPop WAln
– 'Lady Diana' (Au/S)	EWoo NDro
– 'Lady Emma Monson' (Au/S)	EWoo NDro SPop
– 'Lady Joyful' (Au/S)	WCre
– 'Lady of the Vale' (Au/A)	NDro WAln
– 'Lady Penelope' (Au/S)	WAln
– 'Lady Zoë' (Au/S)	EWoo MAsh MFie NDro SPop WCre
– 'Lambert's Gold' (Au)	GAbr SPop
– 'Lamplugh' (Au/d)	IPen SPop WHil
– 'Lancelot' (Au/d)	EWoo SPop
– 'Landy' (Au/A)	MFie NDro SPop WCre
– 'Langley Park' (Au/A)	GAgs IPen MFie NDro SPop WCre WHil
– 'Laphroaigh' (Au/S) **new**	WAln
– 'Laptop' (Au/St)	SPop WBla
– 'Lara' (Au/A)	MFie NDro
– 'Laredo' (Au/A)	EWoo NDro WAln
– 'Larry' (Au/A)	EWoo GAgs MFie NDro SPop WCre
– 'Late Romantic' (Au)	ECtt GBin NDov NLar NPnk SMrm WIce
– 'Lavender Lady' (Au/B)	IPen NDro NEgg
– 'Lavender Ridge' (Au/B)	WAln
– 'Lavenham' (Au/S)	WAln
– 'Laverock' (Au/S)	MFie NBir NBro NEgg WBla WCre WHil
– 'Laverock Fancy' (Au/S)	GAbr IPen ITim NDro
– 'Lazy River' (Au/A)	EWoo NDro WAln WCre
– 'Leather Jacket' (Au)	GAbr WHil
– 'Leathercoat' (Au)	EWoo SPop
– 'Lechistan' (Au/S)	GAbr GAgs IPen MAsh MFie NDro SPop WCre WHil
– 'Lee' (Au/A)	IPen MFie NDro WAln WCre
– 'Lee Clark' (Au/A)	MFie WAln
– 'Lee Paul' (Au/A)	EWoo GAbr GAgs IPen MFie NDro SPop WAln WBla WCre WHil
– 'Lee Sharpe' (Au/A)	EWoo IPen MFie NDro SPop WAln
– 'Legolas' (Au/A)	SPop WAln
– 'Lemon Drizzle' (Au/S)	WAln
– 'Lemon Drop' (Au/S)	EWoo ITim MFie NBro NDro SPop
– 'Lemon Ice' (Au/S)	WAln
– 'Lemon Sherbet' (Au/B)	EWoo GAbr GAgs NDro SPop WHil
– 'Lemon Zest' (Au/d) **new**	WAln
– 'Lemonade' (Au)	GAgs
– 'Lepton Jubilee' (Au/S)	EWoo GAbr NDro WAln
– 'Leroy Brown' (Au/A)	WAln
– 'Lester' (Au/d)	SPop WAln
– 'Leverton' (Au/d)	EWoo SPop
– 'Lewis Telford' (Au/A)	SPop
– 'Lich' (Au/S)	NDro
– 'Lichfield' (Au/A/d)	EWoo IPen SPop WCre
– 'Light Hearted' (Au/A)	CWCL MFie NDro
– 'Light Music' (Au/d)	WAln
– 'Likely Lad' (Au/St)	EWoo SPop
– 'Lila' (Au/S)	EWoo NDro SPop WAln
– 'Lilac Domino' (Au/S)	EWoo GAbr GAgs IPen MFie NDro NEgg SPop WCre WHil

- 'Lilac Ladywood' (Au/d) MFie SPop
- 'Lillian Hill' (Au/A) EWoo MFie WAln WBla
- 'Lillibet' (Au/A) NDro
- 'Lima' (Au/d) IPen MFie WAln
- 'Limaki' (Au/d) **new** SPop
- 'Lime Ridge' (Au) WAln
- 'Limelight' (Au/A) EWoo IPen NDro SPop
- 'Limelight' (Au/S) IPen SPop
- 'Lincoln Bullion' (Au/d) EWoo NDro SPop
- 'Lincoln Charm' (Au/d) GAbr SPop
- 'Lincoln Chestnut' (Au/d) EWoo NDro SPop
- 'Lincoln Consort' (Au/d) **new** SPop
- 'Lincoln Gem' (Au/d) **new** SPop
- 'Lincoln Glow' (Au/d) SPop
- 'Lincoln Halo' (Au/d) **new** SPop
- 'Lincoln Imperial' (Au/d) SPop
- 'Lincoln Whisper' (Au/d) **new** NDro
- 'Linda' (Au/A) WAln
- 'Lindley' (Au/S) ITim NDro SPop
- 'Lindsey Moreno' (Au/S) WAln
- 'Ling' (Au/A) MFie NDro SPop WCre
- 'Linnet' (Au/B) NDro
- 'Lintz' (Au/B) MFie NDro SPop WCre
- 'Linze 2' (Au/S) NDro
- 'Lisa' (Au/A) EWoo IPen MFie NDro SPop WCre WHil
- 'Lisa Clara' (Au/S) EWoo GAbr GAgs IPen ITim MFie NDro SPop WCre
- 'Lisa's Smile' (Au/S) EWoo MFie NDro SPop WHil
- 'Little Bo Peep' (Au) WAln
- 'Little Rosetta' (Au/d) GAbr MFie NDro WHil
- 'Lizzie Files' (Au/A) SPop WAln
- 'Lockyer's Gem' (Au/B/St) IPen NDro NEgg
- 'Lockyer's Green' (Au) EWoo
- 'Lofty' (Au/St) MAsh
- 'Lolita' (Au/St) EWoo SPop WHil
- 'Lord Saye and Sele' (Au/St) CWCL EWoo GAbr IPen ITim MAsh MFie NCGa NDro NEgg SPop WBla WCre WHil
- 'Lothlorien' (Au/A) WAln
- 'Louisa Woolhead' (Au/d) EWoo SPop
- 'Lovebird' (Au/S) CPBP EWoo GAbr MAsh MFie NDro SPop
- 'Lucky Strike' (Au) WAln
- 'Lucy Locket' (Au/B) EWoo GAbr IPen NDro NEgg WCre
- 'Ludlow' (Au/S) GAbr SPop WCre
- 'Lune Tiger' (Au/St) MFie
- 'Lupy Minstrel' (Au/S) IPen NDro SPop WAln
- 'Lusty Lad' (Au/St) SPop
- 'Lynn' (Au/A) WAln
- 'Lynn Cooper' (Au) SPop WBla
- 'MacWatt's Blue' (Au/B) GAbr IGor IPen NDro SPop WCre WHil
- 'Madelaine Palmer' (Au/d) SPop
- 'Maggie' (Au/S) GAbr NDro SPop WCre
- 'Magnolia' (Au/B) WCre
- 'Mandarin' (Au/A) CWCL GAbr GAgs MFie NDro SPop WBla WCre WHil
- 'Mandy' (Au/S) **new** MFie
- 'Manka' (Au/S) SPop
- 'Mardi Gras' (Au/d) WAln
- 'Margaret' (Au/S) EWoo GAbr
- 'Margaret Faulkner' (Au/A) GAbr MFie NDro WBla WCre
- 'Margaret Irene' (Au/A) IPen SPop WCre
- 'Margaret Martin' (Au/S) IPen MFie NDro SPop WCre
- 'Margaret Merril' (Au) GAbr
- 'Margot Fonteyn' (Au/A) EWoo GAbr IPen MFie SPop WAln WBla WHil
- 'Marie Crousse' (Au/d) CFis CMea CPBP EWoo GMaP IPen MFie NDro SPop WCre
- 'Marion Howard Spring' (Au/A) MFie WCre
- 'Marion Tiger' (Au/St) NDro SPop WAln
- 'Mark' (Au/A) IPen MFie NBro NDro SPop WCre
- 'Marmion' (Au/S) EWoo GAbr IPen MFie NDro SPop WBla WCre WHil
- 'Martha Livesley' (Au/A) WAln
- 'Martha's Choice' (Au/A) WAln
- 'Martin Fish' (Au) WCre
- 'Martin Luther King' (Au/S) EWoo NDro WHil
- 'Mary' (Au/d) GAbr NDro SPop WAln
- 'Mary Poppins' (Au/S) **new** NDro
- 'Mary Taylor' (Au/S) WAln
- 'Mary Zach' (Au/S) EWoo MFie NDro SPop WAln WHil
- 'Matthew Yates' (Au/d) CMea GAbr IPen MFie NDro SPop WCot WCre WHil WWFP
- 'Maureen Millward' (Au/A) IPen MFie NDro SPop WCre
- 'May' (Au/A) EWoo NDro WCre
- 'Mazetta Stripe' (Au/S/St) GAbr MFie NBro NDro SPop WBla WHil
- 'Meadow Sweet' (Au/S) WAln
- 'Meadowlark' (Au/A) EWoo ITim MFie NDro SPop WCre WHil
- 'Mease Tiger' (Au/St) GAbr
- 'Megan' (Au/d) WAln
- 'Mehta' (Au/A) IPen MFie NDro SPop WAln
- 'Mellifluous' (Au) MFie WBla WCre WHil
- 'Melody' (Au/S) IPen SPop
- 'Menin' (Au/d) **new** SPop
- 'Mere Green' (Au/S) WAln
- 'Mere Peppermint' (Au) EWoo WAln
- 'Merlin' (Au/A) IPen
- 'Merlin' (Au/S) MFie
- 'Merlin Stripe' (Au/St) CWCL IPen MAsh NDro SPop WBla WCre WHil
- 'Mermaid' (Au/d) GAbr IPen NDro
- 'Merridale' (Au/A) GAbr MFie WCre WHil
- 'Mersey Tiger' (Au/S) EWoo GAbr ITim MAsh MFie NDro SPop WCre WHil
- 'Metis' (Au/d) SPop
- 'Mexicano' (Au/A) WAln
- 'Michael' (Au/S) MFie SPop WAln
- 'Michael Wattam' (Au/S) SPop WAln
- 'Mick' (Au/A) MFie WCre WHil
- 'Midland Marvel' (Au/St) SPop WBla
- 'Midnight' (Au/A) WAln
- 'Mikado' (Au/S) IPen MFie SPop WBla WCre WHil
- 'Milkmaid' (Au/A) MFie WMAq
- 'Millicent' (Au/A) MFie WHil
- 'Minley' (Au/S) CPBP GAbr MFie NBir NBro NDro NEgg SPop WCre WIce
- 'Minstead' (Au/S) SPop
- 'Minstrel' (Au/S) MFie NDro SPop WCre
- 'Minty' (Au/St) **new** SPop
- 'Mipsie Miranda' (Au/d) SPop
- 'Mirabella Bay' (Au/A) WAln
- 'Miranda' (Au/d) **new** EWoo
- 'Mirandinha' (Au/A) MFie
- 'Miriam' (Au/A) EWoo SPop WAln
- 'Mish Mish' (Au/d) GAbr NDro WHil
- 'Miss Bluey' (Au/d) EWoo NDro SPop WAln WCre
- 'Miss Jones' (Au/St) **new** SPop
- 'Miss Muffet' (Au/S) WAln

- 'Miss Newman' (Au/A) SPop
- 'Miss Pinky' (Au) EWoo NDro SPop
- 'Mist' (Au/S) **new** WAln
- 'Mojave' (Au/S) EWoo GAbr GAgs IPen MFie NDro NEgg SPop WCre WHil
- 'Mollie Langford' (Au/A) MFie NDro SPop WHil
- 'Mondeo' (Au/A) **new** WAln
- 'Monet' (Au/S) WAln
- 'Moneymoon' (Au/S) EWoo GAgs IPen NDro SPop WCre WHil
- 'Monica' (Au/A) MFie
- 'Monk' (Au/S) EWoo MFie NDro SPop WAln WBla WHil
- 'Moon Fairy' (Au/S) NDro SPop WAln WCre
- 'Moonglow' (Au/S) EWoo MAsh
- 'Moonlight' (Au/S) WAln
- 'Moonrise' (Au/S) EWoo MFie NDro
- 'Moonriver' (Au/A) EWoo NDro SPop WCre WHil
- 'Moonshadow' (Au/d) WAln
- 'Moonshine' (Au/d) **new** SPop
- 'Moonstone' (Au/d) SPop
- 'Morven' (Au) **new** GAbr
- 'Moscow' (Au/S) SPop
- 'Moselle' (Au/S) MAsh MFie NDro SPop WAln
- 'Mossy Vale' (Au/S) **new** SPop
- 'Mr A' (Au/S) EWoo NDro WHil
- 'Mr Bojangles' (Au/d) SPop WAln
- 'Mr Greenfingers' (Au) WCre
- 'Mrs Cairn's Blue' (Au/B) NDro
- 'Mrs Dargan' (Au/d) NDro
- 'Mrs J.H. Watson' (Au) WCre
- 'Mrs L. Hearn' (Au/A) EWoo GAbr IPen ITim MFie NDro SPop WHil
- 'Mrs R. Bolton' (Au/A) WCre
- 'Mrs Robinson' (Au/St) SPop
- 'Mrs Wilson' (Au) GAbr
- 'Murray Lakes' (Au/A) EWoo NDro SPop WAln
- 'Mustard Sauce' (Au/B) NDro
- 'My Buddy' (Au/St) SPop
- 'My Delight' (Au/d) **new** SPop
- 'My Fair Lady' (Au/A) MFie NDro SPop
- 'My Friend' (Au/B) NDro SPop
- 'Myoleboots' (Au/B) **new** SPop
- 'Myrtle Park' (Au/A) WAln
- 'Mystery' (Au) GAbr
- 'Nancy Dalgetty' (Au/B) NDro
- 'Naniconan' (Au/A) NDro
- 'Nankenan' (Au/S) NDro WBla
- 'Nantenan' (Au/S) **new** GAbr MFie SPop
- 'Neat and Tidy' (Au/S) EWoo GAbr GAgs MAsh MFie NDro SPop WBla WCre
- 'Nefertiti' (Au/A) EWoo IPen MFie NDro SPop WCre WHil
- 'Nessun Dorma' (Au/A) EWoo NDro SPop WAln
- 'Neville Telford' (Au/S) GAbr IPen MFie NDro SPop WHil
- 'Newbottle' (Au/S) SPop WAln
- 'Newsboy' (Au/A) **new** WAln
- 'Newton Harcourt' (Au/A) SPop
- 'Nicholas Loakes' (Au/S) **new** WAln
- 'Nick Drake' (Au/d) SPop
- 'Nickity' (Au/A) GAbr GAgs IPen ITim MFie NDro SPop WAln WCre WHil
- 'Nicola Jane' (Au/A) EWoo SPop WAln
- 'Nigel' (Au/d) EWoo GAbr MFie NDro
- 'Night and Day' (Au/St) SPop WAln
- 'Nightwink' (Au/S) MFie WAln
- 'Nil Amber' (Au) GAbr SPop
- 'Nina' (Au/A) NDro SPop WAln
- 'Nita' (Au/d) SPop WAln
- 'No 21' (Au/S) NDro SPop
- 'Nocturne' (Au/S) EWoo IPen NBro NDro SPop WBla WCre
- 'Noelle' (Au/S) EWoo IPen
- 'Nona' (Au/d) EWoo MFie NDro SPop
- 'Nonchalance' (Au/A) MFie NDro SPop WHil
- 'Norma' (Au/A) EWoo MFie NDro SPop
- 'Northern Lights' (Au/S) **new** WAln
- 'Nureyev' (Au/A) EWoo SPop
- 'Nymph' (Au/d) EWoo GAbr MFie NDro SPop WBla WHil
- 'Oakie' (Au/S) SPop WAln
- 'Oban' (Au/S) EWoo MFie NDro SPop WBla
- 'Odette' (Au) IPen MFie SPop
- 'O'er the Moon' (Au/S) **new** WAln
- 'Oikos' (Au/B) NDro SPop
- 'Ol' Blue Eyes' (Au/St) SPop WAln
- 'Old Black Isle Dusty Miller' (Au/B) NDro
- 'Old Buffer' (Au/St) **new** SPop
- 'Old Clove Red' (Au/B) EWoo GAbr GAgs MFie NDro WCre WHil
- 'Old Cottage Blue' (Au/B) GAbr NDro
- 'Old Dublin Blue' (Au/B) NDro
- 'Old England' (Au/S) EWoo GAbr MFie NDro SPop WBla
- 'Old Gold' (Au/S) GAbr IPen NDro SPop WAln WBla
- 'Old Gold Double' (Au/d) **new** EWoo
- 'Old Gold Dusty Miller' (Au/B) NDro
- 'Old Irish Blue' (Au/B) ITim NDro NEgg WCre
- 'Old Irish Green' (Au/B) EWoo GAbr NDro
- 'Old Irish Scented' (Au/B) EWoo GAbr IPen MFie NBro NDro WHil
- 'Old Irish Yellow' (Au/B) NDro NEgg
- 'Old Mustard' (Au/B) COIW NDov NDro
- 'Old Pink Dusty Miller' (Au/B) GAbr IPen
- § 'Old Purple Dusty Miller' (Au/B) GAbr
- 'Old Red Dusty Miller' (Au/B) GAbr LLHF NDro SPop WHil
- 'Old Red Elvet' (Au/S) GAbr SPop
- 'Old Smokey' (Au/A) EWoo MFie NDro SPop WHil
- 'Old Suffolk Bronze' (Au/B) GAbr GAgs ITim NDro WCre WHil
- 'Old Timer' (Au/S) SPop
- 'Old Yellow Dusty Miller' (Au/B) EWes EWoo GAbr IGor IPen NBro NDro NRya WCre WHil
- 'Old-Fashioned' (Au/B) NDro
- 'Olivia' (Au/d) SPop
- 'Olton' (Au/A) IPen MFie
- 'Optimist' (Au/St) EWoo IPen NDro SPop WCre
- 'Opus One' (Au/A) EWoo WAln
- 'Orb' (Au/S) IPen MAsh MFie NDro SPop WBla WCre WHil
- 'Ordvic' (Au/S) WAln
- 'Orlando' (Au/S) MFie NDro SPop WAln
- 'Orwell Tiger' (Au/St) EWoo GAgs IPen MFie NDro SPop WCre
- 'Osbaston Bullseye' (Au/St) SPop
- 'Osborne Green' (Au/B) GAbr GAgs GBin IGor NDov NDro SPop WCre WHil
- 'Ossett Sapphire' (Au/A) NDro SPop
- 'Otto Dix' (Au/A) SPop WAln

- 'Our Sophie' (Au/B) **new**	NDro
- 'Overdale' (Au/A)	NDro WAln
- 'Paddlin' Madeleine' (Au/A)	EWoo NDro WAln
- 'Pageboy' (Au/A) **new**	WAln
- 'Paleface' (Au/A)	EWoo IPen MFie NDro WBla WCre
- 'Pam Tiger' (Au/St)	WAln WCre
- 'Panache' (Au/S)	WAln
- 'Pang Tiger' (Au/St) **new**	WAln
- 'Papageno' (Au/St)	WAln
- 'Paphos' (Au/d)	IPen SPop
- 'Paradise Yellow' (Au/B)	EWoo GAbr MFie NDro NEgg SPop
- 'Paragon' (Au/A)	IPen ITim MFie WAln WHil
- 'Parakeet' (Au/S)	WAln
- 'Paris' (Au/S)	WAln
- 'Party Time' (Au/S)	IPen SPop WBla
- 'Pass Me By' (Au)	IPen
- 'Passchendaele' (Au/d) **new**	SPop
- 'Passing Cloud' (Au/d)	WAln
- 'Pastiche' (Au/A)	MFie WCre
- 'Pastures New' (Au)	WAln
- 'Pat' (Au/S)	SPop
- 'Pat Barnard' (Au)	IPen
- 'Pat Mooney' (Au/d)	NDro
- 'Patience' (Au/S)	ITim NDro SPop WHil
- 'Patricia Barras' (Au/S)	EWoo WAln
- 'Pauline' (Au/A)	EWoo MFie
- 'Pavarotti' (Au/A)	NDro SPop
- 'Peewit' (Au/S)	WAln
- 'Pegasus' (Au/d)	EWoo NDro SPop
- 'Peggy' (Au/A)	GAbr WHil
- 'Pequod' (Au/A)	MFie NDro WBla
- 'Perdito' (Au/S)	WAln
- 'Perito Moreno' (Au/d) **new**	SPop
- 'Perseus' (Au/S)	WAln
- 'Phantom' (Au/d)	EWoo SPop WAln
- 'Pharaoh' (Au/A)	CWCL EWoo GAbr GAgs MFie NDro SPop WBla WCre
- 'Phoenix' (Au/A)	WAln
- 'Phyllis Douglas' (Au/A)	EWoo IPen MFie NDro NEgg SPop WCre WHil
- 'Piccadilly' (Au/S)	MFie
- 'Pierot' (Au/A)	IPen MFie NDro SPop WCre WHil
- 'Piers Telford' (Au/A)	CPBP CWCL EWoo GAbr GAgs IPen MFie NDro NEgg NSum SBch SPop WCre WHil
- 'Piglet' (Au/d)	EWoo GAbr GAgs NDro SPop
- 'Pikey' (Au/S) **new**	SPop
- 'Pimroagh' (Au/A)	EWoo NDro
- 'Pink Floyd' (Au/A) **new**	SPop
- 'Pink Fondant' (Au/d)	GAbr NDro
- 'Pink Hint' (Au/B)	NDro
- 'Pink Lady' (Au/A)	GAbr MFie NBro SPop WHil
- 'Pink Lilac' (Au/A/S)	NDro
- 'Pinkerton' (Au/d)	EWoo SPop WAln
- 'Pinkie' (Au/A)	WHil
- 'Pinkie Dawn' (Au/B)	IPen NDro WCre
- 'Pinstripe' (Au)	EWoo GAbr GAgs IPen NDro SPop WCre WHil
- 'Pioneer Stripe' (Au/S)	GAbr GAgs IPen SPop WCre
- 'Pippin' (Au/A)	CPBP CWCL GAgs IPen MFie NBro NDro SPop WCre WHil
- 'Pixie' (Au/A)	EWoo IPen MFie SPop
- 'Plain Jane' (Au)	MAsh
- 'Playboy' (Au/A)	NDro SPop WAln
- 'Plum Pudding' (Au/d)	SPop WAln
- 'Polestar' (Au/A)	MFie NDro SPop WBla WCre WHil
- 'Polly' (Au/B)	EBee GAgs GKev NDro WCre
- 'Pop's Blue' (Au/S/d)	EWoo NEgg SPop
- 'Portree' (Au/S)	GAbr SPop
- 'Post Master' (Au/S) **new**	WAln
- 'Pot o' Gold' (Au/S)	CPBP EBee ECho EWoo GAgs IPen MFie NDro NEgg SPop WBla WCre WHil
- 'Powder and Paint' (Au/A)	WAln
- 'Powder Puff' (Au/B)	NDro SPop
- 'Prague' (Au/S)	GAbr IPen MFie NBir NDro SPop WCre
- 'Pretender' (Au/A)	MFie SPop
- 'Pretty Prop' (Au/St) **new**	SPop
- 'Pride of Poland' (Au/S)	SPop
- 'Prince Bishops' (Au/S)	SPop WAln
- 'Prince Charming' (Au/S)	GAgs IPen ITim MFie SPop
- 'Prince Igor' (Au/A)	SPop
- 'Prince John' (Au/A)	MFie NBro NDro SPop WBla WCre WHil
- 'Proctor's Yellow' (Au/B)	NDro
- 'Prometheus' (Au/d)	EWoo MFie NDro SPop WCre WHil
- 'Prosperine' (Au/S)	SPop WAln WCre
- 'Psyche' (Au/S)	SPop WAln
- 'Ptarmigan' (Au)	WAln
- 'Puppy Love' (Au/St) **new**	SPop
- 'Purbeck' (Au/B) **new**	SPop
- 'Purple Dusty Miller'	see *P. auricula* 'Old Purple Dusty Miller'
- 'Purple Emperor' (Au/A)	MFie
- 'Purple Frills' (Au)	MFie
- 'Purple Glow' (Au/d)	WAln
- 'Purple Haze' (Au)	SPop
- 'Purple Knight' (Au/S) **new**	WAln
- 'Purple Lovely' (Au)	MFie SPop
- 'Purple Orient' (Au/d)	SPop
- 'Purple Patch' (Au/d)	SPop
- 'Purple Promise' (Au)	GAbr ITim SPop
- 'Purple Prose' (Au/St)	MFie SPop
- 'Purple Royale' (Au/B)	NDro
- 'Purple Sage' (Au/S)	EWoo ITim MFie NDro SPop WHil
- 'Purple Star' (Au/d)	SPop
- 'Purple Velvet' (Au/S)	CWCL IPen NDro SPop
- 'Quatro' (Au/d)	EWoo SPop
- 'Queen Alexandra' (Au/B)	EWoo GAbr NDro WHil
- 'Queen Bee' (Au/S)	GAbr MFie NDro SPop WBla WCre
- 'Queen's Bower' (Au/S)	SPop WCre
- 'Queenswood' (Au/S)	WCre
- 'Quintessence' (Au/A)	MFie WCre WHil
- 'R.L. Bowes' (Au/A)	NDro
- 'Rab C. Nesbitt' (Au/A)	SPop WAln
- 'Rabley Heath' (Au/A)	GAbr ITim MFie NDro SPop WCre WHil
- 'Rachel' (Au/A)	EWoo WAln WCre
- 'Rachel de Thame' (Au/S)	WAln
- 'Rachel Labouchere' (Au/S)	WAln
- 'Radiant' (Au/A)	IPen
- 'Rag Doll' (Au/S)	NDro WAln
- 'Ragnald the Magnificent' (Au/S)	WAln
- 'Rainy Days' (Au/B)	NDro
- 'Rajah' (Au/S)	ECho EWoo GAbr GAgs IPen ITim MFie NDro NEgg SPop WBla WCre WHil
- 'Raleigh Stripe' (Au/St)	EWoo GAbr GAgs IPen ITim WAln WBla WCre
- 'Rameses' (Au/A)	IPen MFie NDro WCre
- 'Rebecca Baker' (Au/d)	SPop
- 'Red Admiral' (Au)	NDro SPop WAln

- 'Red Arrows' (Au) SPop WAln
- 'Red Baron' (Au/S) WAln
- 'Red Beret' (Au/S) SPop
- 'Red Bordeaux' (Au/S) NDro
- 'Red Carpet' (Au/S) SPop
- 'Red Diamond' (Au/d) WAln
- 'Red Embers' (Au/S) SPop WAln
- 'Red Ensign' (Au/B) NDro
- 'Red Gauntlet' (Au/S) EWoo GAbr GKev IPen MFie NDro SPop WCre
- 'Red King' (Au/S) **new** WAln
- 'Red Mark' (Au/A) MFie SPop WHil
- 'Red Rum' (Au/S) MFie SPop WAln
- 'Red Sonata' (Au/S) SPop
- 'Red Vulcan' (Au) WCre
- 'Red Wire' (Au/St) EWoo NDro SPop
- 'Redcar' (Au/A) MFie NDro WCre
- 'Reddown Apricot' (Au/B) **new** NDro
- 'Reddown Barley Meal' (Au/B) **new** NDro
- 'Reddown Bat' (Au/d) SPop
- 'Reddown First Swallow' (Au/B) **new** NDro
- 'Reddown Rainman' (Au/B) **new** NDro
- 'Reddown Tickled Pink' (Au/B) **new** NDro
- 'Redstart' (Au/B) GKev ITim
- 'Redstart' (Au/S) EBee EWoo GAgs IPen ITim WHil
- 'Regency' (Au/A) NDro WAln
- 'Regency Dandy' (Au/St) SPop
- 'Regency Denja' (Au) IPen
- 'Regency Emperor' (Au/St) EWoo IPen SPop
- 'Regency Saint Clements' (Au/St) SPop WAln
- 'Remus' (Au/S) CPBP ECho ELan EWoo GAbr IPen ITim LLHF MFie NDro NEgg SPop WCre WHil
- 'Rene' (Au/A) EWoo GAbr IPen MFie WCre
- 'Renown' (Au/A) IPen NDro WAln WCre
- 'Requiem' (Au/d) WAln
- 'Resi' WHil
- 'Respectable' (Au/A) WAln
- 'Reverie' (Au/d) SPop WAln
- 'Reynardyne' (Au/d) SPop WAln
- 'Rhubarb Rock' (Au/B) **new** NDro
- 'Riatty' (Au/d) GAbr MFie NDro SPop
- 'Richard Shaw' (Au/A) IPen NDro SPop
- 'Ring of Bells' (Au/S) SPop WAln
- 'Risdene' (Au) IPen WAln WCre
- 'Rivendell' (Au/A) WAln
- 'Robbo' (Au/B) EWoo NDro
- 'Robert Green' (Au/S) EWoo SPop WAln
- 'Robert Lee' (Au/A) WAln
- 'Roberto' (Au/S) MAsh NDro WAln
- 'Robin Hood Stripe' (Au/St) EWoo NDro SPop WBla
- 'Robinette' (Au/d) GAbr IPen SPop
- 'Rock Sand' (Au/S) EWoo GAbr MFie NDro SPop WBla WCre WHil
- 'Rodeo' (Au/A) EWoo GAbr IPen SPop
- 'Rolts' (Au/S) ECho EWoo GAbr GAgs IPen NBro NDro SPop WBla WCre WHil
- 'Romanza' (Au/S) **new** NDro
- 'Romsley' (Au/S) **new** WAln
- 'Rondy' (Au/S) ITim MFie SPop WAln
- 'Ronnie Johnson' (Au) WAln
- 'Ronny Simpson' (Au) WCre
- 'Rosalie' (Au) SPop
- 'Rosalie Edwards' (Au/S) EWoo MFie SPop WCre
- 'Rose Conjou' (Au/d) EWoo GAbr IPen MFie NDro SPop
- 'Rose Kaye' (Au/A) GAbr IPen WCre
- 'Rosebud' (Au/S) EWoo GAbr ITim SPop
- 'Rosemarket Rackler' (Au/B) NDro
- 'Rosemary' (Au/S) EWoo MAsh MFie SPop WCre WHil
- 'Rosewood' (Au) SPop WAln WCre
- 'Rosie' (Au/S) NDro
- 'Rostock' (Au/B) NDro
- 'Rothesay Robin' (Au/A) WAln
- 'Rowena' (Au/A) IPen MFie NBro NDro SPop WCre WHil
- 'Roxborough' (Au/A) EWoo GAgs IPen
- 'Roxburgh' (Au/A) MFie NDro SPop WCre
- 'Roy Keane' (Au/A) IPen MFie SPop WAln WBla
- 'Royal Mail' (Au/S) MFie NDro SPop WAln WBla WCre
- 'Royal Marine' (Au/S) MFie SPop WAln
- 'Royal Scot' (Au/S) SPop WCre
- 'Royal Velvet' (Au/S) GAbr GAgs IPen NDro WHil
- 'Ruby Hyde' (Au/B) EWoo GAbr NDro
- 'Ruby Sutton' (Au/d) EWoo
- 'Ruddy Duck' (Au/S) SPop WAln WBla WCre
- 'Runwell' (Au/B) **new** NDro
- 'Rusty Dusty' (Au) EWoo GAbr
- 'Rusty Red' (Au/B) NDro
- 'Ryecroft' (Au/A) WAln
- 'Sabrina' (Au/A) WAln
- 'Saginaw' (Au/A) EWoo WAln
- 'Sailor Boy' (Au/S) MFie NDro SPop WAln
- 'Saint Boswells' (Au/S) GAbr SPop
- 'Saint Elmo' (Au/A) MFie SPop
- 'Saint Quentin' (Au/S) WAln
- 'Salad' (Au/S) GAbr
- 'Sale Green' (Au/S) MFie SPop
- 'Sally' (Au/A) MFie
- 'Sam Brown' (Au/S) WAln
- 'Sam Gamgee' (Au/A) NDro WAln WCre
- 'Sam Hunter' (Au/A) NDro SPop
- 'Samantha' (Au/A) EWoo WAln WCre
- 'Samantha' (Au/d) MFie SPop WAln
- 'San Gabriel' (Au/A) **new** WAln
- 'Sanctuary Wood' (Au/d) **new** SPop
- 'Sandhills' (Au/A) MFie WCre WHil
- 'Sandmartin' (Au/S) MFie
- 'Sandra' (Au/A) ELan GAbr GAgs IPen MFie NDro SPop WBla WCre WHil
- 'Sandra's Lass' (Au/A) EWoo SPop
- 'Sandwood Bay' (Au/A) EWoo GAbr GAgs MFie NBro NDro NEgg SPop WCre WHil
- 'Sappho' (Au/S) WAln
- 'Sarah Gisby' (Au/d) MFie NDro SPop WBla
- 'Sarah Grey' (Au/d) **new** WAln
- 'Sarah Humphries' (Au/d) WAln
- 'Sarah Lodge' (Au/d) EWoo GAbr IPen NDro SPop WCre WHil
- 'Sarah Suzanne' (Au/B) **new** NDro
- 'Saruman' (Au/A) WAln
- 'Sasha Files' (Au/A) WAln
- 'Satchmo' (Au/S) SPop
- 'Satin Doll' (Au/d) MFie SPop
- 'Satsuma' (Au/d) **new** SPop WAln
- 'Scaraben' (Au) GAbr
- 'Schaumburg' (Au/B) **new** NDro

- 'Scipio' (Au/S) NDro SPop WAln
- 'Scorcher' (Au/S) IPen MFie NDro SPop WBla
- 'Sea Lavender' (Au/d) WAln
- 'Sea Mist' (Au/d) WAln
- 'Searchlight' (Au) WCre
- 'Second Victory' (Au) CPBP NDro WCre WHil
- 'Serenity' (Au/S) MFie NDro SPop WBla WCre WHil
- 'Sergeant Wilson' (Au) SPop WAln
- 'Shalford' (Au/d) EWoo GAbr MFie NDro SPop WCre WHil
- 'Sharmans Cross' (Au/S) MFie WAln
- 'Sharon Louise' (Au/S) IPen SPop WCre
- 'Shaun' (Au/d) ECtt GAbr MHol NDov NLar NPnk NPri WIce
- 'Sheila' (Au/S) GAbr MAsh NDro SPop WCre WHil
- 'Shere' (Au/S) EWoo MFie NDro SPop WCre
- 'Shergold' (Au/A) MFie WCre
- 'Sherwood' (Au/S) CWCL EWoo GAbr IPen MFie NDro SPop WHil
- 'Shining Hour' (Au/St) **new** SPop
- 'Shirley' (Au/S) SPop WAln
- 'Shotley' (Au/A) ITim MFie SPop
- 'Show Bandit' (Au/St) SPop
- 'Showtime' (Au/S) NDro SPop
- 'Sibsey' (Au/d) NDro SPop WHil
- 'Sidney' (Au/A) WAln
- 'Silas' (Au/B) NDro
- 'Silmaril' (Au) SPop WAln
- 'Silver City' (Au/S) WAln
- 'Silver Rose' (Au) WCre
- 'Silver Surfer' (Au/St) **new** WAln
- 'Silverway' (Au/S) EWoo ITim SPop WAln WCre WHil
- 'Simply Red' (Au) EWoo IPen MFie NDro SPop WAln WBla
- 'Sir John' (Au/A) MFie WHil
- 'Sir John Hall' (Au) MFie
- 'Sir Robert' (Au/d) WAln
- 'Sir Titus Salt' (Au/S) **new** WAln
- 'Sirbol' (Au/A) EWoo IPen MFie NDro SPop WBla WCre WHil
- 'Sirius' (Au/A) CWCL EWoo GAbr IPen MFie NDro SPop WBla WCre
- 'Skylark' (Au/A) EWoo GAbr GAgs IPen ITim NDro SPop WBla WCre WHil
- 'Skyliner' (Au/A) NDro
- 'Slack Top Red' (Au) NSla
- 'Sleeping Beauty' (Au/d) **new** SPop
- 'Slim Whitman' (Au/A) NDro SPop WAln WBla
- 'Slioch' (Au/S) EWoo GAbr GAgs IPen MAsh SPop WCre WHil
- 'Slip Anchor' (Au/A) WAln
- 'Smart Tar' (Au/S) WAln WCre
- 'Smoothy' (Au/St) SPop
- 'Snooty Fox' (Au/A) GAbr IPen MFie SPop WCre
- 'Snooty Fox II' (Au/A) MFie NDro WBla
- 'Snow Maiden' (Au/d) WAln
- 'Snowstorm' (Au/S) **new** SPop
- 'Snowy Owl' (Au/S) GAbr MFie NDro SPop WCre
- 'Solario' (Au/F) **new** WAln
- 'Solero' (Au/St) **new** SPop
- 'Soncy Face' (Au/A) MFie SPop WBla WCre WHil
- 'Sonia Nicolle' (Au/B) NDro
- 'Sonny Boy' (Au/A) SPop WAln
- 'Sooty' (Au/d) IPen SPop
- 'Sophie' (Au/d) NDro SPop WAln
- 'South Barrow' (Au/d) GAbr SPop WCre WHil
- 'Southease Jane' (Au) WAln
- 'Southport' (Au) EWoo GAbr NDro
- 'Sparky' (Au/A) MFie NDro WAln
- 'Spartan' (Au) WAln
- 'Spitfire' (Au/S) MFie
- 'Spokey' (Au) IPen
- 'Spring Meadows' (Au/S) EWoo GAbr MFie NDro NEgg SPop
- 'Springtime' (Au/A) SPop
- 'Standish' (Au/d) GAbr ITim
- 'Stant's Blue' (Au/S) IPen MFie NBro NDro SPop WCre
- 'Star Spangle' (Au/St) NDro
- 'Star Wars' (Au/S) GAbr MFie NDro SPop WAln WCre
- 'Star Wars II' (Au) GAgs
- 'Stardust' (Au/S) WCre
- 'Starling' (Au/B) EWoo GAbr IPen NDro SPop
- 'Starry' (Au/S) NDro
- 'Starsand' (Au/S) WAln WCre
- 'Stella' (Au/S) SPop
- 'Stella Coop' (Au/d) EWoo NDro WAln
- 'Stella North' (Au/A) **new** WAln
- 'Stella South' (Au/A) IPen SPop WCre
- 'Stetson' (Au/A) WAln
- 'Stoney Cross' (Au/S) SPop WAln
- 'Stonnal' (Au/A) MFie NDro SPop WHil
- 'Stormin' Norman' (Au/A) EWoo MFie NDro SPop WHil
- 'Stormy Weather' (Au/St) SPop
- 'Strawberry Fields' (Au/S) **new** SPop
- 'Stripe Tease' (Au/St) SPop
- 'Striped Ace' (Au/St) NDro SPop WCre WHil
- 'Stripey' (Au/d) IPen WCre
- 'Stromboli' (Au/d) MFie NDro SPop WBla WCre
- 'Stuart West' (Au/A) WCre
- 'Stubb's Tartan' (Au/S) MFie WAln
- 'Sue' (Au/A) MFie SPop WCre
- 'Sue Ritchie' (Au/d) SPop
- 'Suede Shoes' (Au/S) SPop
- 'Sugar Plum Fairy' (Au/S) EWoo GAbr NDro SPop WHil
- 'Sultan' (Au/A) WAln
- 'Summer Sky' (Au/A) NDro SPop WCre
- 'Summer Wine' (Au/A) EWoo MFie NDro SPop
- 'Sumo' (Au/A) EWoo GAbr GAgs MFie NDro SPop WBla WCre WHil
- 'Sunflower' (Au/A/S) EWoo GAbr ITim MAsh MFie NDro SPop WCre
- 'Sunlight' (Au/A) WAln
- 'Sunlit Tiger' (Au/S) EWoo WAln
- 'Sunray' (Au/St) **new** SPop
- 'Sunsplash' (Au) WBla WCre
- 'Sunspot' (Au/A) EWoo IPen WAln
- 'Sunstar' (Au/S) NDro
- 'Super Para' (Au/S) EWoo GAbr IPen MFie NDro SPop WBla
- 'Superb' (Au/S) MFie WAln WBla
- 'Surething' (Au/A) WAln
- 'Susan' (Au/A) GAbr MFie NDro WCre
- 'Susannah' (Au/d) EWoo GAgs GMaP IPen MFie NDro SPop WCre WHil
- * - 'Sweet Chestnut' (Au/S) WAln
- 'Sweet Georgia Brown' (Au/A) MFie SPop WAln
- 'Sweet Pastures' (Au/S) CPBP GAbr IPen MFie NDro SPop WCre
- 'Swiss Royal Velvet' (Au/B) NDro
- 'Sword' (Au/d) CPBP EWoo GAbr GAgs IPen ITim MFie NDro SPop WCre WHil
- 'Symphony' (Au/A) EWoo ITim MFie NDro SPop WBla WCre WHil
- 'T.A. Hadfield' (Au/A) EWoo GAgs MFie NDro SPop WBla WHil

- 'Taffeta' (Au/S) EWoo GAbr LHop NDro SPop WCre WHil
- 'Tall Purple Dusty Miller' (Au/B) SPop
- 'Tally-ho' (Au/A) WAln
- 'Tamar Gold' (Au/d) SPop WAln
- 'Tamar Mist' (Au) WAln
- 'Tamino' (Au/S) IPen NDro SPop WAln
- 'Tango' (Au/d) WAln
- 'Tarantella' (Au/A) GAbr MFie NDro SPop WCre
- 'Tawny Owl' (Au/B) GAbr NBro
- 'Tay Tiger' (Au/St) EWoo GAbr MFie SPop WHil
- 'Taylor's Grey' (Au/S) **new** SPop
- 'Teawell Pride' (Au/d) EWoo ITim SPop WHil
- 'Ted Gibbs' (Au/A) EWoo MFie NDro SPop WBla WCre WHil
- 'Ted Roberts' (Au/A) EWoo ITim MFie NDro SPop WBla WCre WHil
- 'Teem' (Au/S) GAbr IPen MAsh NDro SPop WCre
- 'Telesto' (Au/d) SPop
- 'Telford's Surprise' (Au/A) WAln
- 'Temeraire' (Au/A) MFie
- 'Tenby Grey' (Au/S) SPop WCre
- 'Tender Trap' (Au/A) IPen WAln
- 'Terpo' (Au/A) MFie WAln WBla WCre WHil
- 'Tess' (Au/A) ITim
- 'The Argylls' (Au/St) SPop
- 'The Baron' (Au/S) GAbr GAgs GKev IPen MFie SPop WBla WCre WHil
- 'The Bishop' (Au/S) GAbr IPen MFie SPop WAln WHil
- 'The Bride' (Au/S) MFie NDro SPop WCre
- 'The Cardinal' (Au/d) EWoo WAln
- 'The Czar' (Au/A) MFie NDro SPop
- 'The Egyptian' (Au/A) IPen MFie NDro SPop WBla WHil
- 'The Few' (Au/St) SPop
- 'The Hobbit' (Au/A) WAln
- 'The Lady Galadriel' (Au/A) NDro
- 'The Maverick' (Au/S) MFie SPop
- 'The President' (Au/d) WAln
- 'The Raven' (Au/S) GAbr GAgs ITim MAsh MFie SPop WAln WBla WCre
- 'The Sheep' (Au/A) EWoo IPen ITim MFie NDro SPop WBla WCre
- 'The Snods' (Au/S) EWoo IPen MFie NDro SPop WBla WCre
- 'The Wrekin' (Au/S) SPop
- 'Thetis' (Au/A) EWoo MFie SPop WCre
- 'Thisbe' (Au/A) NDro
- 'Three Way Stripe' (St) EWoo GAbr GAgs NDro WBla WCre WHil
- 'Thutmoses' (Au/A) NDro WAln
- 'Tiger Tim' (Au/St) EWoo WAln
- 'Tim' (Au) GAbr IPen NDro SPop
- 'Tim's Fancy' (Au/S) NDro
- 'Tinker' (Au/S) WAln
- 'Tinkerbell' (Au/S) EWoo IPen MFie SPop WCre
- 'Tiptoe' (Au/St) SPop
- 'Tirpo' (Au) **new** EWoo
- 'Titania' (Au) SPop
- 'Toddington Green' (Au/S) WAln
- 'Toffee Crisp' (Au/A) EWoo IPen NDro SPop WBla
- 'Toffee Nosed' (Au/St) **new** SPop
- 'Tom Farmer' (Au) WCre
- 'Tomboy' (Au/S) EWoo IPen MFie NDro SPop WBla
- 'Tony Bray' (Au/A) **new** SPop
- 'Toolyn' (Au/S) EWoo GAgs NDro WAln
- 'Top Cat' (Au/d) WAln
- 'Top Style' (Au/d) SPop WAln
- 'Tosca' (Au/S) CWCL GAbr IPen NDro SPop WBla WCre WHil
- 'Trafalgar Square' (Au/S) EWoo GAbr GAgs MFie NDro SPop WBla WCre
- 'Trident' (Au/d) WAln
- 'Trish' (Au) GAbr
- 'Trojan' (Au/S) GKev WCre
- 'Trouble' (Au/d) EWoo GAbr GMaP IPen MFie NDro SPop WCre WHil
- 'Troy Aykman' (Au/A) MFie NDro SPop WAln
- 'Trudy' (Au/S) EWoo GAbr IPen ITim NDro SPop WCre WHil
- 'True Briton' (Au/S) IPen MFie NDro SPop WBla WCre
- 'Trumpet Blue' (Au/S) MFie SPop WAln WHil
- 'Tudor Rose' (Au/S) NDov WAln
- 'Tumbledown' (Au/A) EWoo MFie SPop
- 'Tummel' (Au/A) EWoo NDro SPop WBla WHil
- 'Tupelo Honey' (Au/d) WAln
- 'Turnberry' (Au/S) SPop
- 'Tut Tut' (Au/A) **new** SPop
- 'Twiggy' (Au/S) NDro NSum SPop
- 'Two Steeples' (Au/A) **new** SPop
- 'Typhoon' (Au/A) EWoo IPen MFie SPop WHil
- 'Uncle Arthur' (Au/A) MFie WAln WHil
- 'Unforgettable' (Au/A) MFie
- 'Upper Crust' (Au/St) SPop WBla
- 'Upton Belle' (Au/S) IPen MAsh MFie NDro SPop WAln WCre
- 'Ursula' (Au/d) WAln
- 'Ushba' (Au/d) SPop
- 'V2 Green' (Au/S) WCre
- 'Valerie' (Au/A) IPen MFie SPop WCre
- 'Valerie Clare' (Au) MFie SPop WAln
- 'Vee Too' (Au/A) GAbr MFie NDro SPop WCre WHil
- 'Vega' (Au/A) EWoo SPop WAln
- 'Velvet Moon' (Au/A) EWoo MFie WAln
- 'Venetian' (Au/A) MFie NDro SPop WAln WBla WHil
- 'Venus' (Au/A) WAln
- 'Vera' (Au/A) SPop WAln
- 'Vera Eden' (Au) WAln
- 'Vera Hill' (Au/A) WAln
- 'Verdi' (Au/A) EWoo SPop WAln
- 'Vesuvius' (Au/d) IPen NDro SPop
- 'Victoria' (Au/S) SPop WAln
- 'Victoria de Wemyss' (Au/A) IPen MFie NDro WBla WCre WHil
- 'Victoria Jane' (Au/A) WAln
- 'Victoria Park' (Au/A) WAln
- 'Violet Surprise' (Au/St) NDro
- 'Vulcan' (Au/A) MFie NBro WCre
- 'W. Muller' (Au) NBro
- 'Walhampton' (Au/S) SPop
- 'Walter Lomas' (Au/S) WAln
- 'Walton' (Au/A) CPBP GAbr IPen MFie NDro SPop WCre
- 'Walton Heath' (Au/d) GAbr GAgs IPen MFie NDro SPop WBla WCre
- 'Waltz Time' (Au/A) MFie
- 'Wanda's Moonlight' (Au/d) SPop WAln
- 'Warpaint' (Au/St) NDro NSum
- 'Warwick' (Au/S) MFie NDro SPop
- 'Wayward' (Au/S) WAln WCre
- 'Wedding Day' (Au/S) EWoo ITim MFie NDro WBla
- 'Wentworth' (Au/A) IPen WAln
- 'Werner Müller' (Au/B) NDro
- 'Wheal' (Au) **new** EWoo
- 'Whistlejacket' (Au/S) MFie NDro SPop WBla

- 'White Ensign' (Au/S)	EWoo GAbr IPen ITim MFie NDro SPop WCre
- 'White Pyne' (Au/B) **new**	NDro
- 'White Satin' (Au/S)	SPop WAln WCre
- 'White Water' (Au/A)	EWoo MFie NDro SPop WCre WHil
- 'White Wings' (Au/S)	EWoo GAgs IPen ITim MFie NDro NSum SPop WCre
- 'Whitecap' (Au/S)	WAln
- 'Whoopee' (Au/A)	WAln
- 'Whorton's Claret' (Au/S) **new**	WAln
- 'Wichita Falls' (Au/A)	NDro WAln
- 'Wide Awake' (Au/A)	MFie SPop
- 'Wild and Grey' (Au/S)	NDro
- 'Wilf Booth' (Au/A)	MFie SPop WBla
- 'William Gunn' (Au/d)	MFie SPop WAln
- 'Willow Tree' (Au/S)	WAln
- 'Wincha' (Au/S)	ITim MFie NDro NEgg SPop WBla WCre
- 'Windways Mystery' (Au/B)	GAbr NDro
- 'Windways Pisces' (Au/d)	WAln
- 'Windy Goldtop' (Au/A) **new**	WAln
- 'Winifrid' (Au/A)	EWoo GAbr GAgs MFie NDro SPop WCre
- 'Witchcraft' (Au)	IPen SPop WCre
- 'Woodlands Lilac' (Au/B)	NDro
- 'Woodmill' (Au/A)	EWoo IPen MFie NDro SPop WBla WHil
- 'Wookey Hole' (Au/A)	MFie NDro SPop
- 'Wor Jackie' (Au/S)	SPop
- 'Wycliffe Harmony' (Au/B)	NDro
- 'Wycliffe Midnight' (Au/B)	EWoo GAbr ITim NDro WAln
- 'Wye Hen' (Au/St)	SPop WAln
- 'Wye Lemon' (Au/S)	EWoo SPop
- 'X2' (Au)	WBla WHil
- 'Xavier' (Au)	EBee
- 'Yellow Ace' (Au) **new**	GAbr
- 'Yellow Hammer' (Au/S)	WAln
- 'Yellow Isle' (Au/S)	WAln
- 'Yellow Muff' (Au/S)	WAln
- 'Yellow Ribbon'	WAln
- 'Yes Indeed' (Au/St) **new**	SPop
- 'Yitzhak Rabin' (Au/A)	WHil
- 'Yorkshire Grey' (Au/S)	GAbr IPen NBro NDro SPop WAln WCre
- 'Zambia' (Au/d)	GAbr IPen MFie NDro WCre
- 'Ziggy' (Au/St) **new**	SPop
- 'Zimmer' (Au/St)	SPop
- 'Zircon' (Au/S)	SPop WAln
- 'Zodiac' (Au/S)	WAln
- 'Zoe' (Au/A)	WAln
- 'Zoe Ann' (Au/S)	WAln
- 'Zorro' (Au/St)	WAln
auriculata (Or)	COIW GKev
- subsp. ***olgae*** (Or)	GKev
§ ***balbisii*** (Au)	GKev
'Barbara Midwinter' (Pr)	CDes CJun EBee GAbr LLHF NHar SHar WAbe
Barnhaven Blues Group (Pr/Prim) 🏆H4	NCGa NSum WHil
Barnhaven doubles (Pr/Prim/d)	CWCL
Barnhaven Gold-laced Group	see *P.* Gold-laced Group Barnhaven
Barnhaven hybrids	NSum
'Beatrice Wooster' (Au)	GAbr GAgs IPen MFie
'Beeches' Pink'	GAbr NHar NSum
beesiana (Pf)	Widely available
(Belarina Series) Belarina Butter Yellow = 'Kerbelbut'[PBR] (Pr/Prim/d)	CExl CWCL EPfP EWll LLHF MBNS MFie MHol NDov NLar NPnk SMrm SRot WHil
- 'Belarina Cobalt Blue' (Pr/Prim/d)	CExl CWCL EWll GAbr LLHF MBNS MFie MHol NLar NPnk SRot WHil
- Belarina Cream = 'Kerbelcrem'[PBR] (Pr/Prim/d)	CAby CExl CWCL ELon EWll LLHF MFie NPnk SRot WBor WCot WHil
- 'Belarina Pink Ice' (Pr/Prim/d)	CHel CWCL ELon EPot EWll MBNS MFie MHol NLar NPnk SMrm WBor WHil
- 'Belarina Rosette Nectarine' (Pr/Prim/d)	CExl CWCL ECtt ELon EPot EWll MBNS MFie MHol NLar NPnk SMrm WHil
bellidifolia (Mu)	IPen NGdn
§ - subsp. ***hyacinthina*** (Mu)	WAbe
beluensis	see *P.* × *pubescens* 'Freedom'
§ × ***berninae*** 'Windrush' (Au)	WAbe
'Bewerley White'	see *P.* × *pubescens* 'Bewerley White'
bhutanica	see *P. whitei* 'Sherriff's Variety'
bileckii	see *P.* × *forsteri* 'Bileckii'
§ ***blinii*** (Y)	GKev LLHF
'Blue Julianas' (Pr)	NCGa NSum
'Blue Riband' (Pr/Prim)	CDes LLHF SIgm
'Blue Ribbon'	IGor
'Blue Sapphire' (Pr/Prim/d)	CDes GAbr GBin NCGa WHil
'Blutenkissen' (Pr/Prim)	GAbr
'Bon Accord Cerise' (Pr/Poly/d)	GAbr
'Bon Accord Purple' (Pr/Poly/d)	WRHF
boothii 'Alba' (Pe)	LLHF
- subsp. ***repens*** (Pe)	MNrw
'Boothman's Ruby'	see *P.* × *pubescens* 'Boothman's Variety'
boreiocalliantha	GKev
bracteata (Bu)	WAbe
§ ***bracteosa*** (Pe)	GKev
brevicula (Cy) SDR 4452	GKev
'Broadwell Milkmaid'	CPBP IPen WAbe
'Broadwell Oliver' (Au)	IPen
'Broadwell Pink' (Au)	IPen
'Broadwell Ruby' (Au)	WAbe
'Broadwell Violet'	IPen ITim
'Broxbourne'	MFie
'Buckland Wine' (Pr/Prim)	CElw GAbr
× ***bulleesiana*** (Pf)	CAby CWCL EPfP GBin GBuc GKev LBMP LRHS MBri MCot MFie MSCN MWts NBro NChi NEgg NGdn NHol NLar NSum SMrm SPet SWat WHar WMoo WPnP WWEG
bulleyana (Pf) 🏆H4	Widely available
- ACE 2484	SWat
burmanica (Pf)	CPla GBuc GKev IPen MMuc SWat WMoo
- SDR 5801	GKev
'Butter's Bronze' (Pr/Prim)	WOut
'Butterscotch' (Pr/Prim)	NCGa NSum WHil
'Caerulea Plena' (Pr/Prim)	NBid
calderiana subsp. ***calderiana*** (Pe)	GKev
- subsp. ***strumosa*** (Pe)	GKev
Candelabra hybrids (Pf)	CBre CBro CHVG ECho GAbr IPen ITim LSou NBir NGdn SMrm SPet SWat WOut

- orange-flowered (Pf) SMrm
Candy Pinks Group (Pr/Prim) NCGa NSum WHil
capitata (Ca) CMac ECho EPfP EPot EWld GKev IBoy IPen SPer
- CC 3843 GKev
- CC 6536B **new** GKev
- CC 6542 **new** GKev
- subsp. ***mooreana*** (Ca) CCon CExl CHid CLAP CPrp CTsd EDAr EPfP GKev IPen LRHS NGdn NSum SPet SPhx SPlb SRot WAbe XLum
- subsp. ***sphaerocephala*** (Ca) GKev
'Captain Blood' (Pr/Prim/d) EPfP IPot
'Carmen' (Pr/Prim/d) EPfP
carniolica (Au) GKev WCot
cernua (Mu) GKev IPen NSum
'Charlotte' (Pr/Prim) IPen
'Cheshire Life' **new** CMea
§ ***chionantha*** (Cy) ♀H4 CLAP CWCL ECho EPfP GBin GBuc GCra GKev MFie MMuc NBir NCGa NGdn NLar NSum SPer WAbe
- SDR 4426 GKev
- SDR 4847 GKev
- subsp. ***chionantha*** (Cy) GBuc GKev IPen
- cream-flowered MMuc
- subsp. ***melanops*** see *P. melanops*
§ - subsp. ***sinoplantaginea*** (Cy) NLar
- - SDR 4563 GKev
§ - subsp. ***sinopurpurea*** (Cy) CLAP EBee EPfP GBin GBuc GKev IPen MFie MMuc NBir NCGa NLar NSum WAbe WHil
- - SDR 2747 GKev
- - SDR 4418 GKev
- - SDR 6845 **new** GKev
chungensis (Pf) CHel CLAP CWCL EBee EPfP GBin GCra GKev GLog IPen MFie MMuc NGdn NHol NSum SWvt WAbe WHil WMAq WMoo
§ ***chungensis* × *pulverulenta*** (Pf) CHid CLAP NLar WWEG
× *chunglenta* see *P. chungensis* × *P. pulverulenta*
'Cisca' WCot
'Clarence Elliott' (Au) CPBP IPen MFie MPnt NHar NWad WAbe WThu
clarkei (Or) WAbe
clusiana (Au) WAbe
- 'Murray-Lyon' (Au) NDro
cockburniana (Pf) ♀H4 GKev GQui IPen LRHS NCGa NGdn SWat WAbe
- SDR 1967 EBee
- SDR 5939 GKev
- hybrids (Pf) SWat
- 'Kevock Sunshine' (Pf) EBee GKev IPen
concholoba (Mu) GKev
'Corporal Baxter' (Pr/Prim/d) EPfP LLHF
cortusoides (Co) CLAP EPfP GCra GKev IPen WBor
Cowichan Amethyst Group (Pr/Poly) CDes CWCL NCGa
Cowichan Blue Group (Pr/Poly) NCGa NSum
Cowichan Garnet Group (Pr/Poly) CDes EWoo NCGa NSum
Cowichan strain (Pr/Poly) CElw
Cowichan Venetian Group (Pr/Poly) NCGa NSum
Cowichan Yellow Group (Pr/Poly) NCGa NSum
'Coy' (Au) WAbe
'Craddock White' (Pr/Prim) CFis
'Craven Gem' (Pr/Poly) GBuc
Crescendo Series (Pr/Poly) GAbr
- 'Crescendo Blue Shades' (Pr/Poly) ♀H4 LSou
- 'Crescendo Bright Red' (Pr/Poly) ♀H4 LSou
- 'Crescendo Lemon Yellow' (Pr/Poly) LSou
- 'Crescendo White' (Pr/Poly) LSou
'Crimson Velvet' (Au) GAbr IPen WThu
crispa see *P. glomerata*
cuneifolia (Cu) GKev
- subsp. ***heterodonta*** (Cu) GKev
daonensis (Au) GAgs GKev
darialica (Al) GKev LLHF
'Dark Rosaleen' (Pr/Poly) CExl CHVG CWGN EBee ECtt GAbr GBuc IGor ITim LLHF MAvo MBNS MBri MFie MHol MNrw MPie NCGa NDov WCot
'David Valentine' (Pr) GAbr GBuc WAbe WCot
'Dawn Ansell' (Pr/Prim/d) CWCL ECtt EPfP EPot GAbr GBuc IGor MBNS MHol MNrw MRav NBir NCGa NDov NPnk NSum SPer WHer WHil
Daybreak Group (Pr/Poly) CWCL NCGa
deflexa (Mu) IPen
denticulata (De) ♀H4 Widely available
- CC 4629 GKev
- var. ***alba*** (De) CBcs CTri EBee ECho EPfP GAbr GBin GCra GMaP MBel MFie MWat NGdn NHol NLar NPri SGbt SMrm SPer SPoG WBor WGwG WMoo WWEG
- blue-flowered (De) CWCL ECho GAbr NLar NPri WBor
- 'Bressingham Beauty' (De) EBee LRHS
- 'Glenroy Crimson' (De) CLAP EBee LLHF
- 'Karryann' (De/v) WHil
- lilac-flowered (De) ECho EHon MWat NHol SMrm WWEG
- purple-flowered (De) ECho WMoo
- red-flowered (De) ECho MFie NBir WMoo
- 'Robinson's Red' (De) GBuc
- 'Ronsdorf' (De) ELon NLar
- 'Rubin' (De) CWCL CWat EBee ECho EHon GAbr GBin GMaP LLWG MBrN MLHP NChi NLar NRya SPer SPoG SRms WWEG XLum
- 'Rubinball' (De) NHol WCot
'Desert Sunset' (Pr/Poly) CWCL NCGa WHil
'Devon Cream' (Pr/Prim) NDro
dickieana (Am) GKev
'Don Keefe'PBR CMHG ECtt GAbr GBin LLHF LSou MBNS MFie MHol MNrw NGdn NLar NPnk SPoG WCot WWlt
'Dorothy' (Pr/Poly) MRav
'Double Lilac' see *P. vulgaris* 'Lilacina Plena'
'Drumcliffe' **new** ECtt LLHF MBel NSti WCot
dubernardiana **new** WAbe
'Duchess of York' (Pr/Poly) GAbr LLHF LLWP NLar WCot
'Duckyls Red' (Pr/Prim) WHal
'Dusky Lady' CLAP
'Early Bird' (*allionii* hybrid) (Au) IPen ITim MFie
'Easter Bonnet' (Pr/Prim) NBid

	edgeworthii	see *P. nana*
§	***elatior*** (Pr) 🏆H4	CArn CMac CPla CRow CSev ECho EWTr GKev MHer MHol MNHC MNrw NChi NEgg NLar NPnk NPri SPer SPoG SWvt WBrk WCot
	- hose-in-hose (Pr/d)	NBid
	- hybrids (Pr)	EPfP SPlb
§	- subsp. ***meyeri*** (Pr)	EBee GKev LLHF
	- subsp. ***pseudoelatior*** (Pr)	WAbe
	'Elizabeth Browning'	GAbr WCot
	'Elizabeth Killelay'PBR (Pr/Poly/d)	CBct CCVN CExl CWCL CWGN EBee ECtt ELan GBin GBuc LDai LSou MAvo MFie MHol MNrw NBir NEgg NGdn NLar NPnk NSti NSum SPer SPoG WBor WCot
	'Ellen Page' (Au)	MFie
	'Ethel Barker' (Au)	IPen MFie NWad
	'Eugénie' (Pr/Prim/d)	ECtt LLHF MRav NCGa
§	***euprepes***	GKev
	'Fairy Rose' (Au)	IPen NWad
	farinosa (Al)	GKev IPen NGdn WAbe
	fasciculata (Ar)	GKev
	- CLD 345	WAbe
	- SDR 3092	GKev
	'Feuerkönig' (Au) **new**	NDro
	'Fire Opal'	EBee LRHS
	Firefly Group (Pr/Poly)	NCGa WCot
§	***firmipes*** (Si)	EWes GKev IPen LPot
§	***flaccida*** (Mu)	ECho GKev IPen NSum WAbe
	Flamingo Group (Pr/Poly)	NCGa WHil
	florida	see *P. blinii*
	florindae (Si) 🏆H4	Widely available
	- SDR 4626	GKev
	- bronze-flowered (Si)	GQui NBir
	- hybrids (Si)	CMac EDAr GAbr GMaP MLHP NCGa SMrm WHar WHil
	- Keillour hybrids (Si)	CLAP IBoy NGdn NHol NLar SMrm
	- 'Muadh' (Si)	MMuc SEND
	- orange-flowered (Si)	CSam IPen LLWG MNrw WMoo
	- peach-flowered (Si)	CSpe
	- 'Ray's Ruby' (Si)	CLAP MNrw NBir NGdn WCot
	- red-flowered (Si)	CSpe GBin IPen LLWG MFie MMuc NBid NLar NSum
	- terracotta-flowered (Si)	NGdn
	Footlight Parade Group (Pr/Prim)	NCGa
	forbesii (Mo) CC 4084	CExl
	forrestii (Bu)	GKev IPen WAbe
	- SDR 4304	CExl GKev
§	× ***forsteri*** (Au)	NLar
§	- 'Bileckii' (Au)	GMaP LLHF NBir NHar NSla
	- 'Dianne' (Au)	EDAr GAbr GKev LLHF NBro NRya WAbe WThu
	- 'Dianne' hybrids (Au)	NHar
	'Francesca' (Pr/Poly) **new**	LBMP WHer XLum
	'Francisca' (Pr/Poly)	Widely available
	frondosa (Al) 🏆H4	ECho GCra GKev IPen MFie MHol MLHP MPnt SBch WAbe
	Fuchsia Victorians Group (Pr/Poly)	CWCL
	'Garnet' (*allionii* hybrid) (Au)	MFie
	'Garryarde Crimson'	LLHF
	'Garryarde Guinevere'	see *P.* 'Guinevere'
	gemmifera (Ar)	ECho GKev LLHF
	- SSSE 242	GKev
	- var. ***monantha*** (Ar)	GKev
	geraniifolia (Co)	CLAP EBee GCra GKev
§	'Gigha' (Pr/Prim)	CLAP CWCL GBin GCal GKev MNrw
	'Gilded Ginger'	CWCL NCGa
	'Ginger Spice' (Au)	NDro
§	***glomerata*** (Ca)	GKev IPen
	- CC 6748	GKev
	- SDR 3924	GKev
	'Glowing Embers' (Pf)	EBee LLHF MSCN NBir
	glutinosa All.	see *P. allionii*
	Gold-laced Group (Pr/Poly)	CBre CMea CPla CSpe CWCL ECtt ELon EPfP EWoo IPen LBMP LRHS LSRN MAsh MAvo MCot NDov NEgg NGdn NLar NPri NSla NSum NWad SPer SPet SPoG WHil WIce WNew
§	- Barnhaven (Pr/Poly)	GBuc MFie NBir
	- Beeches strain (Pr/Poly) 🏆H4	CWCL IPen
	- red-flowered (Pr/Poly)	IPen LBMP XEll
	gracilipes (Pe)	CLAP LLHF
	- L&S 1166	CLAP
	- early-flowering (Pe)	GCra
	- late-flowering (Pe)	CLAP GCra
	- 'Major'	see *P. bracteosa*
	- 'Minor'	see *P. petiolaris* Wall.
	graminifolia	see *P. chionantha*
	Grand Canyon Group (Pr/Poly)	CWCL NCGa
	grandis (Sr)	GKev IPen
	'Groenekan's Glorie' (Pr/Prim)	CFis GAbr GBuc NBir NLar NSum
§	'Guinevere' (Pr/Poly) 🏆H4	CElw CExl CHel CSam CSpe EBee ECtt EHoe GAbr GBuc GMaP IGor LSou MCot MFie MHol MNFA MNrw NBid NBir NBro NDov NLar NSla NSum SPer SPlb WAbe WCot WHil
	'Hall Barn Blue' (Pr/Prim)	CSam GAbr GMaP NHar NMyG WCot
§	***halleri*** (Al)	GKev IPen MFie WAbe
	- 'Longiflora'	see *P. halleri*
	handeliana	EPot GKev
	Harbinger Group (Pr/Prim)	CWCL WHil
	Harbour Lights mixture (Pr/Poly)	CWCL NCGa
	Harlow Carr hybrids (Pf)	EPfP GQui NCGa NLar NSla WHil WMoo
	Harvest Yellows Group (Pr/Poly)	CWCL NCGa
	'Hazel's White'	GAbr GKev
	'Hemswell Abbey' (Au)	GAgs GKev
	helodoxa	see *P. prolifera*
	'Hemswell Blush' (Au)	CSpe EPot GKev ITim LLHF NHar WCre
	'Hemswell Ember' (Au)	CPBP GAgs NRya NWad
	heucherifolia (Co)	IPen
	- SDR 3224	GKev
	'High Point' (Au)	WAbe
	hirsuta (Au)	GAgs IPen SEND WAbe
	- 'Lismore Snow' (Au)	NHar NWad WAbe
	- red-flowered (Au)	EBee GAgs GKev MMuc
	hirsuta* × *minima	see *P.* × *forsteri*
	hose-in-hose (Pr/Poly/d)	MNrw
	'Hyacinthia' (Au)	EWoo GAgs IPen MFie
	hyacinthina	see *P. bellidifolia* subsp. *hyacinthina*
	ianthina	see *P. prolifera*
	'Ilana'	IPen
	incana (Al)	GKev

	Indian Reds Group (Pr/Poly)	CWCL WHil
	'Ingram's Blue' (Pr/Poly)	CDes CDoC EBee GAbr MHol
	'Innisfree' **new**	CBct ECtt MBel NSti WCot
	Inshriach hybrids (Pf)	CMHG LRHS
§	'Inverewe' (Pf) $\mathbb{Y}^{H4}$	CRow GBin GBuc GCra GKev GQui NBir
	involucrata	see *P. munroi*
	ioessa (Si)	EWes GCra GKev NGdn WAbe
	- var. ***hopeana*** (Si)	GKev
	- hybrids (Si)	WAbe
	'Iris Mainwaring' (Pr/Prim)	ECtt GAbr GCra LLHF MCot
	irregularis (Pe)	WAbe
	'Jackie Richards' (Au)	MFie NWad
	Jack-in-the-Green Group (Pr/Poly)	CLAP CWCL MNrw NSla WBor WMoo
	- red-flowered (Pr/Poly)	WHil
	- white-flowered (Pr/Poly)	IFro
	jaffreyana (Pu)	GKev
	'Janet Aldrich' **new**	CPBP
	japonica (Pf)	CMHG CSam GQui IPen LRHS MSCN NBro NGdn SPer SWat WAbe WMoo
	- 'Alba' (Pf)	CPrp CTri ECho EPfP GBuc GCal IPen MFie NGdn NWad WAbe WHil WWEG
	- 'Apple Blossom' (Pf)	Widely available
*	- 'Atropurpurea' (Pf)	IPen
	'Carminata' (Pf) **new**	IPen
*	- 'Carminea' (Pf)	CHid GKev IPen MFie MSCN NBro NGdn NLar NWad WHil WPnP
	- 'Cherry Red' (Pf)	IPen
	- 'Fuji' (Pf)	NBro
	- - hybrids (Pf)	NLar
	- hybrids (Pf)	CMac GCra MRav
	'Jim Saunders' (Pf)	SLon
	- 'Merve's Red' (Pf)	CAby
	- 'Miller's Crimson' (Pf) $\mathbb{Y}^{H4}$	Widely available
	'Oriental Sunrise' (Pf)	CMil EBee GBuc GKev IPen LLHF MSCN
	- pale pink-flowered (Pf)	ITim NSum
	- 'Peninsula Pink' (Pf)	IPen
	- 'Pink Pagoda' (Pf)	EBee WHil
	- 'Pinkie' (Pf)	IPen
	- 'Postford White' (Pf) $\mathbb{Y}^{H4}$	CBcs CHel CLAP CPla CRow CWCL EBee ELan EPfP GAbr GBuc GCra GKev GMaP ITim LHop LLWG LRHS NBir NCGa NLar NPnk SHil SPer SPoG SWat SWvt WMoo WTin
	- 'Purpurascens' (Pf) **new**	IPen
	- Redfield strain (Pf)	IPen
	- red-flowered (Pf)	IPen WAbe
	- 'Splendens' (Pf)	IFro IPen
	- 'Valley Red' (Pf)	IPen ITim LRHS
	jesoana (Co)	GKev LLHF
	- B&SWJ 618	WCru
	'Joan Hughes' (*allionii* hybrid) (Au)	WAbe
	'Joanna'	ECou GBuc MPnt
	'Johanna' (Pu)	GAbr GKev NGdn NHar NPnk NSum WAbe
	'John Fielding' (Sr × Pr)	CBro CElw EBee GAbr MCot
	'Jo-Jo' (Au)	EPot MFie WAbe
	juliae (Pr)	ECho EDAr LRHS NBid NHar NPnk NSum SPlb WAbe
I	- 'Millicent' (Pr)	WCot
	- white-flowered (Pr)	NSum
	'Juliana's Fireflies' (Pr/Poly)	CWCL

	'Ken Dearman' (Pr/Prim/d)	ECtt EPfP MRav NBir SPer
	kialensis (Y)	WAbe
	'Kinlough Beauty' (Pr/Poly)	CFis ECtt GAbr GBuc GMaP LLHF LRHS NPnk
§	***kisoana*** (Co)	CExl CLAP EBee GKev IPen LLHF LRHS WCru
	- var. ***alba*** (Co)	CLAP
	- var. ***shikokiana***	see *P. kisoana*
	- 'Velvet' (Co)	CLAP
	'Koblenz' (Au) **new**	NHar
	'Kusum Krishna'	GBin MBNS NHar NSti WCot
	'Lady Greer' (Pr/Poly) $\mathbb{Y}^{H4}$	CMac CSam EBee ECtt EPfP GAbr GBuc GKev GMaP IGor LHop LLWP MCot MHer NChi NGdn NHar NLar NSum WHer
	'Lambrook Mauve' (Pr/Poly)	CElw CFis GAbr
§	***latifolia*** (Au)	GKev
	latisecta (Co)	IPen
§	***laurentiana*** (Al)	GKev WAbe
	'Lea Gardens' (*allionii* hybrid) (Au)	IPen MFie NWad
	'Lee Myers' (*allionii* hybrid) (Au)	IPen MFie
	'Lemon and Lime'	CMea
	leucophylla	see *P. elatior*
	'Lilac Domino' (Au)	IPen
	lilacina	GKev IPen
	- SDR 3088	GKev
	- SDR 6832 **new**	GKev
	limbata (Cy)	GKev
	'Lindum Buttermilk'	IPen
	'Lindum Crepes Suzette'	IPen MFie
	'Lindum Finale' (Au)	IPen
	'Lindum First Kiss'	IPen
	'Lindum Frosty Moon'	IPen
	'Lindum Lace'	IPen
	'Lindum Malcolm's Mate'	CPBP IPen
	'Lindum Moonlight'	IPen LLHF MFie
	'Lindum Pixie' **new**	IPen
	'Lindum Rapture' (Au)	IPen
	'Lindum Serenade' (Au)	IPen
	'Lindum Smoke'	IPen
	'Lindum Snowdrift' (Au)	IPen
	'Lindum Wedgwood' (Au)	IPen MFie
	'Lingwood Beauty' (Pr/Prim)	CFis CSam GAbr LLHF WAbe
	'Lipstick' **new**	CHid
	'Lismore' (Au)	GAgs
	'Lismore 79/7' (Au)	NWad
	'Lismore Bay' (Au)	GKev
	'Lismore Pink Ice' (Au)	WThu
	'Lismore Sunshine'	NHar WThu
	'Lismore Treasure' (Au)	MFie
	'Lismore Yellow' (Au)	CPBP NHar WAbe
	Lissadel hybrids (Pf)	NCGa NLar
	'Little Egypt' (Pr/Poly)	CWCL NCGa
	littledalei (Cf) **new**	GKev
	littoniana	see *P. vialii*
	× ***loiseleurii*** 'Aire Mist' (Au)	IPen NHar NRya NSla NSum NWad WAbe WThu
§	- 'Aire Waves' (Au)	CWCL ITim NHar NWad
	- 'White Waves' (Au)	IPen
	longiflora	see *P. halleri*
	luteola (Or)	ECho GKev LLHF NGdn NSum
	macrocalyx	see *P. veris*
	macrophylla (Cy)	GKev
	- CC 6986 **new**	GKev
	- var. ***moorcroftiana*** (Cy)	GKev

	- - CC 6990 **new**	GKev
	'MacWatt's Claret' (Pr/Poly)	GAbr GBuc LLWP
	'MacWatt's Cream' (Pr/Poly)	CFis EBee GAbr GCra LLHF LRHS NLar WHil
	magellanica (Al)	WAbe
	'Maisie Michael'	LHop LLHF WAbe
	marginata (Au) ♀H4	ECho EWoo IPen LHop LRHS MFie MMuc NSla NSum SBch SEND WAbe WBla
	- 'Adrian Evans' (Au)	ITim SBch
	- 'Adrian Jones' (Au)	ITim
	- 'Alba' (Au)	MFie NBro NRya NWad WThu
	- 'Ardfearn' (Au)	GAgs
	- 'Baldock's Purple' (Au)	IPen
	- 'Barbara Clough' (Au)	IPen MFie NRya NWad
	- 'Beamish' (Au) ♀H4	NBro NRya NSla NWad
	- 'Beatrice Lascaris' (Au)	MFie NRya WAbe WThu
	- 'Caerulea' (Au)	ITim MFie NWad
	- 'Clear's Variety' (Au)	GKev IPen ITim LLHF
	- 'Doctor Jenkins' (Au)	IPen NLar NRya NWad
	- 'Drake's Form' (Au)	IPen NLar NRya
	- dwarf (Au)	ECho LRHS MFie NRya
	- 'Earl L. Bolton'	see *P. marginata* 'El Bolton'
§	- 'El Bolton' (Au)	IPen NRya NWad
	- 'Elizabeth Fry' (Au)	IPen MFie
	- 'F.W. Millard' (Au)	CWCL
	- 'Grandiflora' (Au)	IPen NWad
	- 'Herb Dickson' (Au) **new**	ITim
	- 'Highland Twilight' (Au)	IPen NSla WAbe
	- 'Holden Variety' (Au)	GKev IPen ITim MFie NRya NWad
	- 'Ivy Agee' (Au)	IPen NRya
	- 'Janet' (Au)	LLHF NWad WBla
	- 'Jenkins Variety' (Au)	ECho
	- 'Johannes Holler' (Au) **new**	ITim
	- 'Kesselring's Variety' (Au)	CMea ECho IPen ITim LLHF MFie NWad WAbe
	- 'Laciniata' (Au)	ECho IPen LRHS
	- 'Lemon Sorbet' (Au)	IPen
	- lilac-flowered (Au)	IPen
	- 'Linda Pope' (Au) ♀H4	GAgs GKev IPen NBir NHar NSum WAbe WThu
	- maritime form (Au)	IPen
	- 'Millard's Variety' (Au)	IPen ITim NWad
	- 'Miss Fell' (Au)	IPen
	- 'Mrs Carter Walmsley' (Au)	NRya
	- 'Nancy Lucy' (Au)	WAbe
	- 'Napoleon' (Au)	IPen ITim MFie MSCN NWad
	- 'Prichard's Variety' (Au) ♀H4	ECho IPen ITim LLHF MFie MSCN NLar NRya WAbe
	- 'Rosea' (Au)	IPen
	- 'Sheila Denby' (Au)	IPen
	- 'The President' (Au)	GAgs
	- violet-flowered (Au)	ECho
	- 'Waithman's Variety' (Au)	IPen NRya
	- wild-collected (Au)	MFie NWad
	'Maria Talbot' (*allionii* hybrid) (Au)	IPen
	'Marianne Davey' (Pr/Prim/d)	WKif
	'Marie Crousse' (Pr/Prim/d)	EPfP WHal
	Marine Blues Group (Pr/Poly)	CWCL NCGa NSum
	'Maris Tabbard' (Au)	IPen MFie NLar WAbe
	'Mark Viette'	EBee
	'Mars' (*allionii* hybrid) (Au)	IPen MFie NRya NWad
	'Marven' (Au)	IPen
	'Mary Anne'	GAbr
	maximowiczii (Cy)	ECho EDAr EPot GBin GBuc IPen LLHF MMHG NGdn NHar NSum
	- Red-flowered Group	GBuc GKev IPen
	megaseifolia (Pr)	GBuc GKev IPen
	melanodonta (Pf) **new**	GKev
§	***melanops*** (Cy)	GKev
	× ***meridiana*** (Au)	NWad
§	- 'Miniera' (Au)	IPen MFie
	Midnight Group	CWCL NCGa
	'Mike Smith'	IPen
	'Miniera'	see *P.* × *meridiana* 'Miniera'
	minima (Au)	GKev NBro NLar WAbe
	- var. ***alba*** (Au)	NLar
	minor (Cy)	GKev
	'Miss Indigo' (Pr/Prim/d)	CAby CTsd ECtt ELon EPfP EPot EWll GBin GMaP MBNS MFie MRav NPnk NSum SPer WHil
	mistassinica (Al)	GKev WAbe
	- var. ***macropoda***	see *P. laurentiana*
	miyabeana (Pf)	GKev IPen
	modesta var. ***faurieae*** (Al)	GKev IPen
	- - f. ***leucantha*** (Al)	GKev
	monticola	EBee GKev
	'Moorland Apricot'	WMoo
	moupinensis (Pe)	CExl CLAP LLHF
	- subsp. ***barkamensis*** (Pe)	GKev
*	'Mrs Eagland'	GAbr
	'Mrs Frank Neave' (Pr/Prim)	IPen
	'Mrs Marjorie Banks' (Pr)	GKev
	'Mrs McGillivray' (Pr/Prim)	GAbr
§	***munroi*** (Ar)	CDes GKev IPen NHar WAbe
	- CC 5311	GKev
	- CC 6907 **new**	GKev
	- CC 6908 **new**	GKev
	- white-flowered (Al)	WAbe
§	- subsp. ***yargongensis*** (Al)	EBee GKev IPen
	- - SDR 3096	GKev
	- - SDR 6121	GKev
	muscarioides (Mu)	GKev IPen
	Muted Victorians Group (Pr/Poly)	NCGa NSum WHil
§	***nana*** (Pe)	IPen
	nanobella (Mi)	GKev
	'Netta Dennis' (Pe)	LLHF NHar
	neurocalyx	GKev
	New Pinks Group (Pr/Poly)	CWCL NCGa NSum
	nivalis Pallas	see *P. chionantha*
	nivalis ambig.	NSum
	nutans Delavay ex Franch.	see *P. flaccida*
	obconica (Ob) SDR 6730 **new**	GKev
	'Oberau'	IPen
	obtusifolia (Cy)	GKev
	'Old Port' (Pr/Poly)	CSam EBee GKev NSum SBch
	Old Rose Victorians Group (Pr/Poly)	NSum
	orbicularis (Cy)	ECho EWTr GKev LLHF
	Osiered Amber Group (Pr/Prim)	NSum
*	'Page'	IPen MFie
	palinuri (Au)	IPen
	palmata (Co)	GKev NHar
	'Pamilata'	EBee
	pamirica (Ar)	GKev
	'Paris '90' (Pr/Poly)	CWCL NCGa NSum WHil
	parryi (Pa)	EBee EPfP GKev
	pedemontana 'Alba' (Au)	LLHF MFie WBla WThu
	'Perle von Bottrop' (Pr/Prim)	GAbr NHar WCot

	petelotii (Ch)	WAbe
	'Peter Klein' (Or)	GBuc GKev LLHF WAbe
	petiolaris misapplied	see *P.* 'Redpoll'
§	***petiolaris*** Wall. (Pe)	GCra NHar NSum
	- Sherriff's form	see *P.* 'Redpoll'
	'Petticoat'	EPfP
	'Pink Aire' (Au)	MFie NRya
	'Pink Cabbage' (Poly) **new**	CDes
	'Pink Fairy' (Au)	IPen
	'Pink Ice' (*allionii* hybrid) (Au)	CPBP GKev MFie NHar NRya NWad
	poissonii (Pf)	CTri EBee ELan EPfP GAbr GBin GCra GKev GQui IPen LRHS NGdn NLar NSum WAbe WShl
	- SDR 5126	GKev
	- SDR 5959	GKev
	polyneura (Co)	ECho GKev IPen MSnd NGdn WBor
	'Port Wine' (Pr)	GAbr GCra
	'Powdery Pink'	LRHS
	prenantha (Pf)	GKev
	- SDR 3909	GKev
	Primlet Series (Pr/Prim)	SMrm
§	***prolifera*** (Pf) ♀H4	CHel CMHG CWCL EPfP GBuc GCra GKev GQui IPen LHop LRHS MMuc NCGa NGdn SPer SWat WAbe WMoo
§	× ***pubescens*** (Au) ♀H4	IPen MHer NDro NGdn
	- 'A.E. Matthews' (Au)	NWad
	- 'Apple Blossom' (Au)	EWoo GAgs IPen MFie
§	- 'Bewerley White' (Au)	EBee ECho EPfP GAgs IPen NDro
	- 'Blue Wave' (Au)	IPen MFie SPop
§	- 'Boothman's Variety' (Au)	CTri ECho EPfP EWoo ITim MFie NSla WHoo
	- 'Carmen'	see *P.* × *pubescens* 'Boothman's Variety'
	- 'Chamois' (Au)	MFie
	- 'Christine' (Au)	CDes CMea EBee GAgs GKev IPen NBir NSum WCot
	- 'Cream Viscosa' (Au)	EWoo
	- 'Deep Mrs Wilson' (Au)	MFie
	- 'Faldonside' (Au)	IPen MFie NPnk NSum WBla WThu
§	- 'Freedom' (Au)	CTri ECho EWoo GAgs GKev IPen MFie NBir NLar NSla
	- 'George Harrison' (Au)	MFie
	- 'Harlow Car' (Au)	CMea GQui IPen MFie MPnt NSum
	- 'Hazel's White' (Au)	GAgs
	- 'Joan Danger' (Au)	IPen NDro
	- 'Joan Gibbs' (Au)	IPen ITim MFie
	- 'Joan Stead' (Au) **new**	GKev
	- 'Kath Dryden' (Au)	ITim
	- 'Lilac Fairy' (Au)	IPen ITim NPnk NWad WThu
	- 'Moonlight' (Au)	NDro
	- 'Mrs J.H. Wilson' (Au)	MFie NRya
	- 'Pat Barwick' (Au)	IPen MFie NDro NRya NWad
	- 'Peggy Fell' (Au)	NWad WHil
	- 'Rufus' (Au)	EWes GAbr GAgs NDro WThu
	- 'Sid Skelton' (Au)	IPen
	- 'Snowcap' (Au)	IPen ITim
	- 'Sonya' (Au)	IPen
	- 'The General' (Au)	CTri IPen MFie
§	- 'Wedgwood' (Au)	GAbr IPen MFie WHil
	- 'Winnifred' (Au)	NDro
	- yellow-flowered (Au)	IPen
	pulchella (Pu)	EPot GKev
	pulverulenta (Pf) ♀H4	Widely available
	- Bartley hybrids (Pf) ♀H4	GAbr GKev ITim LRHS NSum NWad WMoo
	- 'Bartley Pink' (Pf)	CPla GBuc
	purdomii	GKev
	'Quaker's Bonnet'	see *P. vulgaris* 'Lilacina Plena'
	'Rachel Kinnen' (Au)	GAbr IPen MFie
	'Ramona' (Pr/Poly)	CWCL NCGa
	'Ravenglass Vermilion'	see *P.* 'Inverewe'
	'Red Ruffles' (Pr/Poly/d)	ECtt EWll WHil
§	'Redpoll' (Pe)	CLAP GBuc LLHF NHar
	reidii (So)	GKev
	- var. ***williamsii*** (So)	IPen
	'Reverie' (Pr/Poly)	NCGa
	'Rheniana' (Au)	IPen MFie NLar NRya
	'Rick Lupp'	IPen
	'Romeo' (Pr/Prim)	CLAP LLHF WCot
	rosea (Or) ♀H4	CElw CWCL EBee ECho EPfP GKev GLog IPen MAsh MFie MMuc NBid NBir NRya WWFP
	- CC 5260	GKev
	- 'Gigas' (Or)	EDAr GAbr LRHS NRya WBor WMAq
	- 'Grandiflora' (Or)	CMac CPrp ECho EPfP GKev LHop LRHS NCGa NLar SPoG SRms SWat WHil XLum
	'Rosemary Cottage'	GAbr
	Rosie Series (Pr/Poly/d) **new**	EDAr
§	***rotundifolia*** (Cf) CC 6537	GKev
	'Rowallane Rose' (Pf)	IPen
I	'Rowena'	GAbr GCra LLHF WCot
	roxburghii	see *P. rotundifolia*
	'Roy Cope' (Pr/Prim/d)	EPfP NBir
	rubra	see *P. firmipes*
	'Ruby Tuesday' (Au) **new**	NDro
	rusbyi (Pa)	EBee GKev WHil
	- subsp. ***ellisiae*** (Pa)	GKev IPen
	sachalinensis (Al) **new**	GKev
	'Saracen'	IPen MFie
	saxatilis ambig. (Co)	MFie
§	'Schneekissen' (Pr/Prim)	CSam CWCL GAbr GBuc GCra LLHF LRHS MHer NBro NChi NPro WHil
	scotica (Al)	GAbr GKev GPoy NSla WAbe WHil
	secundiflora (Pf)	CCon CLAP CWCL EBee ECho ELan EWTr GBin GBuc GCra GKev LLWG MMuc NBir NSum SBrt SPer SPlb SWat WAbe WHoo WMoo WPtf WWFP
	- SDR 4401	GKev
	- SDR 4435	GKev
§	× ***sendtneri*** (Au)	MFie
	serratifolia (Pf)	GKev
	- SDR 5165	GKev
	'Shizuko Hara'	IPen
	sibthorpii	see *P. vulgaris* subsp. *sibthorpii*
	sieboldii (Co) ♀H4	ECho EWld GKev IPen MCot MLHP MNrw NSla SBch SRms WAbe WBla
	- Beeches seedling C (Co) **new**	WHil
	- Beeches seedling D (Co) **new**	WHil
	- 'Bide-a-Wee Blue' (Co)	NBid
I	- 'Blue Lagoon' (Co)	CDes EBee LLHF LRHS NLar WHil
	- 'Blue Shades' (Co)	IPen
	- blue-flowered (Co)	CLAP CWCL
	- 'Blush' (Co)	CAby CLAP WHil WWEG
	- 'Carefree' (Co)	CLAP IPen LLHF NBro NLar
	- 'Cherubim' (Co)	CAby CLAP EBee GCra LLHF LRHS WHil
	- 'Daiminnisiki' (Co)	NHar
	- 'Dancing Ladies' (Co)	CLAP IPen NBro NHar WHil
	- 'Dart Rapids' (Co)	CDes WSHC
	- 'Duane's Choice' (Co)	CAby CDes CLAP MNrw

- 'Frilly Blue' (Co)	EBee LRHS WWEG
- 'Galaxy' (Co)	NBro
- 'Geisha Girl' (Co)	CCon CLAP CSpe EBee LRHS MRav NLar WAbe WHil WWEG
- 'Hatusugato' (Co)	NHar
- 'Lacewing' (Co)	WHil
- f. ***lactiflora*** (Co)	CLAP IPen NBro SRot
- 'Lilac Sunbonnet' (Co)	CLAP EPfP LLHF NHar SBch
- 'Manakoora' (Co)	CLAP EBee IPen NBro NSum
- 'Mikado' (Co)	CLAP EBee IPen WHil WWEG
- 'Our White' (Co) **new**	WHil
- 'Pago-Pago' (Co)	CDes CLAP EBee IPen MNrw NBro WHil
- pink-flowered (Co)	CWCL GKev NBir
- 'Senyuu' (Co)	WHil
- 'Seraphim' (Co)	CLAP EBee MMHG NLar WWEG
- 'Snowdrop' (Co)	LHop LSou MHol MNrw MPie NCGa NMyG WCot WHil WMoo
- 'Snowflake' (Co)	CAby CDes CLAP EBee GKev NLar NSla SBch WAbe
- 'Tah-ni' (Co)	NBro NSum
- 'Winter Dreams' (Co)	CAby CLAP CWCL GKev NBid NBro NHar NSum WHil
sikkimensis (Si) ♀H4	EBee ECho GKev IPen LRHS MSnd NGdn NSum SPoG
- CC 5730	GKev
- CC 5986	GKev
- CC 6397	GKev
- CC 6771 **new**	GKev
- SDR 5933	GKev
- 'Claret' (Si)	WHil
- var. ***pseudosikkimensis*** (Si)	GKev IPen
- - SDR 4528	GKev
- var. ***pudibunda*** (Si)	GKev
- - SDR 3099	GKev
- - SDR 4919	GKev
- 'Tilman Number 2' (Si)	GBuc
aff. ***sikkimensis*** (Si)	IPen NCGa NGdn
'Silver Lace Charlotte'	WIce
Silver-laced Group (Pr/Poly)	EPfP LBMP NLar SPoG SWvt WIce
- black-flowered (Pr/Poly)	XEll
simensis (Sp)	GKev
sinoplantaginea	see *P. chionantha* subsp. *sinoplantaginea*
sinopurpurea	see *P. chionantha* subsp. *sinopurpurea*
'Sir Bedivere' (Pr/Prim)	CDes EBee GAbr GBuc NHar WCot
smithiana	see *P. prolifera*
'Snow Carpet'	see *P.* 'Schneekissen'
'Snow White' (Pr/Poly)	GBin MRav
Snowcushion	see *P.* 'Schneekissen'
'Snowruffles'	ITim
sonchifolia (Pe)	CCon CLAP GKev
- subsp. ***emeiensis***	GKev
- subsp. ***sonchifolia***	GKev
sorachiana	see *P. yuparensis*
'Sparkling Eyes'	WCot
spectabilis (Au)	GBin GKev
Spice Shades Group (Pr/Poly)	CHid NCGa
× ***steinii***	see *P.* × *forsteri*
stenocalyx (Pu)	GKev
'Stonewash'	LRHS
'Stradbrook Charm' (Au)	CPBP CWCL EPot MFie WThu
'Stradbrook Dainty' (Au)	MFie NWad
'Stradbrook Dream' (Au)	ITim MFie
'Stradbrook Lilac Lustre' (Au)	MFie
'Stradbrook Lucy' (Au)	IPen ITim NWad
'Stradbrook Mauve Magic' (Au)	MFie
stricta (Al)	GKev
Striped Victorians Group (Pr/Poly)	NCGa NSum WHil
'Strong Beer' (d)	EBee ECtt LSou MHol MNrw MPie NMyG NSum WCot
'Sue Jervis' (Pr/Prim/d)	CWCL EPfP MRav NBir WHal
suffrutescens (Su)	WAbe
'Sunshine Susie' (Pr/Prim/d)	EPfP GMaP SPer
szechuanica (Cy)	GKev IPen
'Tango' (Pr/Prim)	NCGa
tangutica (Cy)	GKev IPen
tanneri (Pe)	GKev
'Tantallon' (Pe)	CLAP LLHF NHar
Tartan Reds Group (Pr/Prim)	CWCL
'Tawny Port' (Pr/Poly)	CElw CLAP NBro
'Theodora' (Pr)	GAbr
tibetica (Ar)	EPot
'Tie Dye' (Pr/Prim)	EBee LLHF MHol MNrw MPie WCot
'Tipperary Purple' (Pr/Prim)	GAbr
'Tomato Red' (Pr/Prim)	CDes CFis EBee GAbr LHop LLHF WCot
'Tony' (Au)	CPBP IPen MFie WAbe
'Top Affair' (Au/d)	IPen WAln
'Torchlight' (Pr/Prim/d)	IGor
'Tortoiseshell' (Pr/d)	CHid
'Val Horncastle' (Pr/Prim/d)	ECtt EPfP GAbr GMaP MFie SPer
Valentine Victorians Group (Pr/Poly)	NCGa
× ***venusta*** (Au)	GKev
'Vera Maud' (Pr)	NCGa NSum
§ ***veris*** (Pr) ♀H4	Widely available
- PAB 3777 **new**	LEdu
- subsp. ***columnae*** (Pr)	EBee EDAr
I - 'Coronation Cowslips' (Pr)	GBuc
- hybrids (Pr)	LBMP MBel
- 'Katy McSparron' (Pr/d)	CExl CMea ECtt GAbr GCra LSou MFie MHol MNrw MPie SPer SPoG WBor WCot
- subsp. ***macrocalyx*** (Pr)	EPot GKev WCot
- orange-flowered (Pr)	MHer WMoo
- red flowered (Pr)	CAby NBid NGdn SPer WMoo
- 'Sunset Shades' (Pr)	ECGP GBuc LBMP MHoo NGdn NLar SPet XEll
vernalis	see *P. vulgaris*
verticillata (Sp)	IPen
§ ***vialii*** (So) ♀H4	Widely available
'Vicky'	IPen
Violet Victorians Group (Pr/Poly)	NCGa
viscosa	see *P. latifolia*
§ ***vulgaris*** (Pr/Prim) ♀H4	Widely available
- var. ***alba*** (Pr/Prim)	CRow NSla WBrk
- 'Alba Plena' (Pr/Prim/d)	GAbr GCal NSum
- Belarina Buttermilk = 'Kerbelmilk'PBR (Belarina Series) (d) **new**	NPnk WHil
- green-flowered	see *P. vulgaris* 'Viridis'
- hybrids (Pr/Prim)	MBel
§ - 'Lilacina Plena' (Pr/Prim/d)	CCon EBee EPfP GAbr GCal IFro IGor LLHF MRav NCGa NSum WHer

	- var. ***pulchella*** (Pr/Prim) new	CDes
§	- subsp. ***sibthorpii*** (Pr/Prim) ♀H4	CAby CMHG CSam EBee ECho ELon EPfP GBuc IPen LLWP LRHS MCot MFie MHer MLHP MNrw MRav NBro NChi NDov SBch SKHP SRms WHil
	- - pale-flowered (Pr/Prim)	GBuc
	- 'Taigetos' (Pr/Prim)	CBro CExl CHid
§	- 'Viridis' (Pr/Prim/d)	CCon CDes EOHP MNrw
	- subsp. ***vulgaris*** (Pr/Prim/d) ♀H4 new	WMAq
	waltonii (Si)	CCVN CLAP CWCL EPfP GBin GKev IPen MMuc MNrw NCGa NLar NSum WHil
	- hybrids (Si)	ELon
	'Wanda' (Pr/Prim) ♀H4	CBcs CDoC CTri ECho GAbr GCra LBMP LLWP MBel MCot MHer MMuc NBid NDov NPnk SEND SRms WBrk WCFE WCot WHil
	Wanda Group (Pr/Prim)	CHVG ECho LBMP LRHS SPet SVic
	- 'Wanda Grace'	NPnk
	- 'Wanda Hose-in-hose' (Pr/Prim/d)	GCra LLWP MMHG NBir WHer WHil
	- 'Wanda Jack-in-the-Green' (Pr/Prim)	CLAP WCot
	wardii	see *P. munroi*
	warshenewskiana (Or)	CLAP EBee EWes GBuc GKev NHar NRya WAbe WGwG
	watsonii (Mu)	EWes GKev NHar SWat
	- ACE 1402	IPen
	'Wedgwood'	see *P.* × *pubescens* 'Wedgwood'
	'Welsh Blue'	CSpe
	'Wharfedale Bluebell' (Au)	IPen NBir NHar WThu
	'Wharfedale Buttercup' (Au)	IPen NHar NWad WAbe
	'Wharfedale Butterfly' (Au)	NWad
	'Wharfedale Crusader' (Au)	IPen
	'Wharfedale Gem' (*allionii* hybrid) (Au)	EPot MFie NSla NWad
	'Wharfedale Ling' (*allionii* hybrid) (Au)	CPBP GKev MFie NHar NWad
	'Wharfedale Sunshine' (Au)	CPBP GKev IPen NWad
	'Wharfedale Superb' (*allionii* hybrid) (Au)	MFie
	'Wharfedale Village' (Au)	IPen MPnt NHar WAbe WThu
	'White Linda Pope' (Au)	GAgs NWad WThu
	'White Wanda' (Pr/Prim)	GAbr
	'White Waves' (*allionii* hybrid) (Au)	ITim
§	***whitei*** 'Sherriff's Variety' (Pe)	CLAP
	'William Genders' (Pr/Poly)	LLHF
	wilsonii (Pf)	CTri CTsd CWCL LDai LLWG NGdn SWat
§	- var. ***anisodora*** (Pf)	CLAP GBin GKev GLog IPen NGdn
	- var. ***wilsonii*** (Pf)	GKev
	'Windrush'	see *P.* × *berninae* 'Windrush'
	'Winter White'	see *P.* 'Gigha'
	'Wisley Crimson'	see *P.* 'Wisley Red'
§	'Wisley Red' (Pr/Prim)	CElw LRHS
	'Woodland Walk' (Pr/Prim)	EPfP
	woodwardii (Cy)	GKev
	wulfeniana (Au)	EBee GKev
	yargongensis	see *P. munroi* subsp. *yargongensis*
§	***yuparensis*** (Al)	EBee GBuc GKev IPen WHil
	- white-flowered (Al)	GKev
	zambalensis (Ar)	EPot GKev IPen
	- SDR 1611	GKev
	'Zenobia'	WCre

Prinsepia (*Rosaceae*)

	sinensis	CArn MBlu NLar SLon WSHC

Pritchardia (*Arecaceae*)

	affinis	XBlo
	pacifica	XBlo

Pritzelago (*Brassicaceae*)

	alpina	NSla

Prosartes (*Liliaceae*)

§	***hookeri***	CLAP EBee ECho LLHF LWSt MNrw WCru
§	- var. ***oregana***	EBee EPPr IBlr IFoB LRHS WCru
§	***lanuginosa***	CBct EBee EPPr LRHS LWSt MAvo WCru
§	***maculata***	CBct CDes CLAP IFoB LEdu MNrw WCru
§	***smithii***	CBct EBee ECho EPfP GKev GLog LEdu NBir WCot WCru WPGP
§	***trachycarpa***	CLAP

Prostanthera (*Lamiaceae*)

	'Alpine Gold'	MAsh
	aspalathoides	CCCN CTsd EWes MOWG
	'Badja Peak'	CTsd EBee EWes LEdu LRHS MAsh MOWG SLim
	baxteri	ECou MOWG
	- 'Silver Ghost'	SLim
	cuneata ♀H4	Widely available
	- 'Alpine Gold'	CMHG CTsd LRHS
	- Kew form	WPGP
	- 'Sense' new	CWSG
*	***digitiformis***	CTsd ECou
	incisa	CTsd
	- 'Rosea'	EOHP
	lasianthos	CBcs CCCN CDoC CHII CTsd EWes LRHS MOWG SHDw SLim SPlb SVen WJek
	- 'Kallista Pink'	CTsd MOWG
	- var. ***subcoriacea***	CExl
	latifolia	CTsd
	magnifica	MOWG
	melissifolia	CArn CTsd ECre
§	- var. ***parvifolia***	CBcs CCCN CTsd
	'Mint Delight'	SLim
	'Mint Royale'	CCCN LBuc LEdu LRHS MNHC SLim
	'Mint-ice'	SLim SPoG
	nivea	ECou
	ovalifolia ♀H2	CCCN ECou MOWG WJek
I	- 'Variegata' (v)	CBcs CCCN CExl CHGN CHel CMac CTsd EBee ECou LRHS MOWG SPoG WGrn WWFP
	phylicifolia	CTsd MOWG
	'Poorinda Ballerina'	CTsd EBee ECou EOHP LRHS MAsh SLim SPer SPoG SRkn
	'Poorinda Petite'	CCCN CTsd EBee LRHS
	rotundifolia ♀H2	CAbb CCCN CHEx CSev CSpe CTri CTsd EBee ECho EOHP ESwi MHoo MOWG MSCN SPer SVen WGrn
	- 'Chelsea Girl'	see *P. rotundifolia* 'Rosea'
§	- 'Rosea' ♀H2	CCCN CDoC CTsd ECou EPfP LHop LRHS MOWG SEND
	scutellarioides 'Lavender Lady'	ECou
	sericea	LRHS
	sieberi misapplied	see *P. melissifolia* var. *parvifolia*

sieberi Benth.	CTsd MOWG
spinosa new	CTsd MOWG
walteri	CCCN CTsd LRHS MOWG

Protea (*Proteaceae*)

aurea	SPlb
burchellii	SPlb
coronata	SPlb
cynaroides	CBcs CCCN CHEx EAmu IDee SBig SPlb
effusa	SPlb
eximia	CBcs CCCN EAmu SPlb
grandiceps	CCCN SPlb
lacticolor	SPlb
laurifolia	SPlb
nana	SPlb
neriifolia	CCCN SPlb
obtusifolia	SPlb
repens	SPlb
scolymocephala	SPlb
subvestita	SPlb
susannae	SPlb

Prumnopitys (*Podocarpaceae*)

§ ***andina***	CBcs CDoC IArd IDee LRHS SLim
elegans	see *P. andina*
§ ***ferruginea***	IGor
§ ***taxifolia***	CDoC ECou

Prunella (*Lamiaceae*)

§ ***grandiflora***	CHby CPrp SPer SRms SWat WWEG
- 'Alba'	CBre EBee EPfP GMaP LRHS MSCN NLar SPer
- 'Blue Loveliness'	GBee SWvt
- 'Carminea'	EBee SPer
- 'Freelander' new	EWll
- 'Freelander Blue' new	WOut
- light blue-flowered	WOut
- 'Loveliness' 🏆H4	CDoC CMac CPrp GMaP MBel MRav NBro NGdn NSti SPer SPlb SRGP WCAu
- 'Pagoda'	CSpe NLar
- 'Pink Loveliness'	CPrp SRms
- 'Rosea'	EBee
- 'Rubra'	GAbr NLar
- violet-flowered	EPfP LRHS
- 'White Loveliness'	CMac CPrp WWEG
hyssopifolia	XSen
'Icing Sugar' new	EBee
incisa	see *P. vulgaris*
Summer Daze = 'Binsumdaz'PBR	LSou NSti SPoG
§ ***vulgaris***	CArn CHab GPoy MHer MHoo MNHC NMir WHer WHfH WJek WMoo WOut
- f. ***leucantha***	WHer
- 'Rose Pearl'	EWll LRHS
× ***webbiana***	see *P. grandiflora*

Prunus ✿ (*Rosaceae*)

'Accolade' (d) 🏆H4	Widely available
§ 'Amanogawa' 🏆H4	Widely available
americana	EUJe
amygdalus	see *P. dulcis*
aprium (F) new	ERea
armeniaca 'Alfred' (F)	CDul ERea GTwe SDea SFam SKee WHar
- var. ***ansu*** 'Flore Pleno' (d)	LAst
- 'Blenheim' (F)	ERea
- 'Bredase' (F)	CWib ERea SDea
- 'De Nancy'	see *P. armeniaca* 'Gros Pêche'
- 'Early Moorpark' (F)	CAgr CWib EPfP GTwe MBri SDea SEND SLon WHar
- 'Farmingdale' (F)	SDea
- Flavorcot = 'Bayoto'PBR (F)	CAgr CMam CSut EPfP EPom ERea GTwe MCoo SKee SPer WHar
- 'Garden Aprigold' (F)	SPoG
- 'Goldcot' (F)	CAgr CTho ERea MBri MCoo SDea SKee SPoG WHar
- 'Golden Glow' (F)	CAgr CTho EPom ERea MBri MCoo SKee WHar
- 'Goldrich' (F)	CAgr
§ - 'Gros Pêche' (F)	SVic WHar
- 'Hargrand' (F)	CAgr SVic
- 'Harogem' (F)	CAgr
- 'Hemskirke' (F)	ERea SKee
- 'Hongaarse' (F)	SDea
- 'Isabella' (F)	CAgr ERea
- 'Moniqui' (F)	ERea
- 'Moorpark' (F) 🏆H3	CDul CEnd CHab CSBt CTri CWib ELan EWTr GTwe LAst MMuc MRav SDea SKee SPer
- 'New Large Early' (F)	ERea SDea SEND SKee
- 'Petit Muscat' (F)	ERea SKee
- 'Tomcot' (F)	CAgr CDul CTho CTri EPfP EPom GTwe LBuc LRHS LSRN MBri MCoo SFam SKee SPoG WHar
- 'Tross Orange' (F)	CWib SDea
'Asano'	see *P.* 'Geraldinae'
avium 🏆H4	Widely available
- 'Amber Heart' (F)	SKee
- 'Archduke' (F)	SKee
- 'Bigarreau de Schrecken' (F)	SKee
- 'Bigarreau Gaucher' (F)	SKee WHar
§ - 'Bigarreau Napoléon' (F)	ELan EPom GTwe LSRN SCrf SKee SVic
- 'Birchenhayes'	see *P. avium* 'Early Birchenhayes'
- 'Black Glory' (F)	SKee
- 'Black Heart' (F)	CWib ELan MMuc SEND
- 'Black Tartarian' (F)	SKee
- 'Bottlers'	see *P. avium* 'Preserving'
- 'Bradbourne Black' (F)	SCrf SKee WHar
- 'Bullion' (F)	CEnd CTho
- 'Burcombe' (F)	CEnd CTho
- Celeste = 'Sumpaca'PBR (D)	CAgr CMac CTri EMil ERea GTwe LRHS MBri MCoo NLar NOra SDea SFam SKee SLim SPoG WHar
- 'Cherokee'	see *P. avium* 'Lapins'
- 'Colney' (F) 🏆H4	CDul ERea GTwe IArd NLar NOra SFam SKee WHar WJas
- 'Dun' (F)	CHab CTho
§ - 'Early Birchenhayes' (F)	CEnd CTho
- 'Early Rivers' (F)	CDul CLnd CSBt CWib GTwe IArd LSRN NLar SDea SKee SVic WHar
- 'Elton Heart' (F)	SKee
- 'Emperor Francis' (F)	SKee
- 'Fastigiata'	WHar
- 'Fice' (F)	CEnd CTho
- 'Florence' (F)	SKee
- 'Governor Wood' (F)	SKee
- 'Grandiflora'	see *P. avium* 'Plena'
- 'Greenstem Black' (F)	CTho
- 'Hannaford' (D/C)	CHab CTho
- 'Hertford' (F) 🏆H4	NOra SFam SKee WHar
- 'Inga' (F)	SFam SKee
- 'Ironsides' (F)	SKee
- 'Kentish Red' (F)	SKee

	– 'Kordia' (D)	EPom GTwe NOra SFam SKee WHar
§	– 'Lapins' (F)	CAgr CDul CLnd CSut CTho CTri ECrN EPfP EPom EWTr GTwe MBri MRav NLar NOra SDea SFam SKee WHar WJas
	– 'May Duke'	see *P.* × *gondouinii* 'May Duke'
	– 'Merchant' (F) ♀H4	SKee
	– 'Mermat' (F)	SKee
	– 'Merpet' (F)	SKee
	– 'Merton Bigarreau' (F)	GTwe WHar
	– 'Merton Crane' (F)	SKee
	– 'Merton Favourite' (F)	SKee
	– 'Merton Glory' (F)	CAgr CDul CSBt EPfP GTwe IArd SCrf SEND SEWo SFam SKee SLim WHar
	– 'Merton Late' (F)	SKee
	– 'Merton Marvel' (F)	SKee
	– 'Merton Premier' (F)	ELan SKee SVic
	– 'Merton Reward'	see *P.* × *gondouinii* 'Merton Reward'
	– 'Nabella' (F)	IArd WJas
	– 'Napoléon'	see *P. avium* 'Bigarreau Napoléon'
	– 'Noble' (F)	SKee
	– 'Noir de Guben' (F)	IArd SKee WHar
	– 'Noir de Meched' (D)	SKee
	– 'Old Black Heart' (F)	SKee
	– 'Penny'[PBR] (F)	CAgr CDul EPom GTwe NOra SKee WHar
	– 'Petit Noir' (F) **new**	GTwe MCoo
§	– 'Plena' (d) ♀H4	CBcs CCVT CDul CLnd CMac CSBt CTho EBee ECrN ELan EPfP LBuc LRHS LSRN MAsh MBri MGos MMuc MRav MSwo NEgg NLar NWea SEND SEWo SGol SPer WHar WJas WMou
§	– 'Preserving' (F)	CTho
	– 'Regina' (F)	CSut NLar NOra SFam WHar
	– 'Ronald's Heart' (F)	SKee
	– 'Roundel Heart' (F)	SKee WHar
	– 'Small Black' (F)	CHab CTho
	– 'Stella' (F) ♀H4	Widely available
	– 'Stella Compact' (F)	CWib ECrN EWTr LAst LSRN SDea WHar
	– 'Summer Sun' (D) ♀H4	CAgr CDul CSut CTho CTri EPfP EPom ERea GTwe LBuc LRHS MBri MCoo MGos NLar NOra SCoo SDea SFam SKee SLim SPoG WHar
	– 'Summit' (F)	SKee
	– 'Sunburst' (D)	CAgr CCVT CDul CEnd CMac CMan CTho CTri CWib ECrN GTwe IArd LBuc LRHS LSRN MBri MGos NOra SCoo SDea SEWo SFam SKee SLim SPer SPoG SVic SWvt WHar WJas
	– 'Sweetheart' (F)	CAgr CDul EPom GTwe LRHS LSRN MBri NOra SKee SLim SPoG WHar
	– 'Sylvia' (F)	CAgr SFam WHar
	– 'Turkish Black' (F)	SKee
	– 'Van' (F)	CSBt GTwe IArd NOra SFam WHar
	– 'Vega' (F)	CAgr ERea GTwe IArd SKee WHar WJas
	– 'Waterloo' (F)	SKee
	– 'White Heart' (F)	CWib ECrN SKee
	'Beni-yutaka'	CCVT CTsd EPfP LAst MAsh MBri MRav MSwo SCoo SLim SPoG WHar
	besseyi	CAgr
	'Blaze'	see *P. cerasifera* 'Nigra'
	× ***blireana*** (d) ♀H4	CDul CEnd CLnd CTri EBee EPfP LAst MAsh MBri MGos MMuc MRav MSwo MWat NLar NWea SCoo SPer SPoG WHar

	'Blushing Bride'	see *P.* 'Shōgetsu'
	campanulata 'Felix Jury'	EBee
	Candy Floss	see *P.* 'Matsumae-beni-murasaki'
	cerasifera	CDul CHab CTri ECrN EPfP EPom GAbr LBuc NWea SPer SVic
	– 'Cherry Plum' (F)	CHab CTri ECrN MMuc SDea SKee
	– 'Crimson Dwarf'	MBri SCoo SWvt
	– 'First' (F)	CAgr
	– 'Golden Sphere' (F)	CAgr CDul CLnd CTho CTri EPom LRHS NOra SPer WHar
	– 'Gypsy' (F)	CAgr CDul CLnd CTho LRHS NOra SEWo SPer WHar
	– 'Hessei' (v)	EBee MBri MRav NLar
	– 'Kentish Red' (F)	SEND
§	– Myrobalan Group (F)	ECrN MRav SDea SPre SVic
	– – 'Magda Jensen' (C)	CAgr
§	– 'Nigra' ♀H4	Widely available
	– 'Pendula'	ECrN SWvt
§	– 'Pissardii'	CWib ECrN EPfP LSRN MMuc NWea SCoo SFam SLon SWvt WJas WMou
	– 'Rosea'	NLar
	– 'Ruby'	CAgr EPom MBri
	cerasus 'Maynard'	LSRN
	– 'Montmorency' (F)	SKee
	– 'Morello' (C) ♀H4	Widely available
	– 'Nabella' (F)	SKee
	– 'Rhexii' (d)	CDul ECrN MAsh MBri NEgg NPCo
	– 'Semperflorens' **new**	CLnd
	'Cheal's Weeping'	see *P.* 'Kiku-shidare-zakura'
	Chocolate Ice	see *P.* 'Matsumae-fuki'
§	× ***cistena*** ♀H4	CDul CSBt EBee ELan EPfP LAst LRHS MAsh MBri MGos MSwo SCoo SGol SHil SPoG SWvt
	– 'Crimson Dwarf'	see *P.* × *cistena*
	'Collingwood Ingram'	EBee LRHS MBlu MBri MWat SLim
	conradinae	see *P. hirtipes*
	'Daikoku'	EBee
	davidiana	SPlb
	'Delma'[PBR] (F) **new**	WHar
	domestica (D/C) **new**	SPre
	– 'Allgroves Superb' (D)	ERea
	– 'Angelina Burdett' (D)	CHab SDea SKee
	– 'Anna Späth' (C/D)	SKee
	– 'Ariel' (C/D)	SDea SKee
	– 'Autumn Compote' (C)	SKee
	– 'Avalon' (D)	CAgr CCAT CCVT CLnd GTwe IArd LBuc NOra SDea SFam SKee WHar
	– 'Beauty' (D)	CSut
	– 'Belgian Greengage' (F)	CHab
	– 'Belgian Purple' (C)	SKee
	– 'Belle de Louvain' (C)	CDul CHab CLnd CTho CTri GTwe NOra SDea SKee WHar
	– 'Birchenhayes' (F)	CEnd
	– 'Black Diamond'	see *P. salicina* 'Black Diamond'
	– 'Blaisdon Red' (C)	CTho GTwe SKee WHar
	– 'Blue Rock' (C/D) ♀H4	SKee
	– 'Blue Tit' (C/D) ♀H4	CAgr CTho EPom ERea GTwe LSRN NOra SDea SEND SKee WHar
	– 'Bonne de Bry' (D)	SKee
	– 'Brandy Gage' (C/D)	SKee
	– 'Bryanston Gage' (D)	CTho SKee
	– 'Burbank's Giant'	see *P. domestica* 'Giant Prune'
	– 'Burcombe' (F)	CEnd
	– 'Cambridge Gage' (D) ♀H4	Widely available
	– 'Chrislin' (F)	CAgr CTho

	- 'Coe's Golden Drop' (D)	CHab CLnd ECrN ERea GTwe IArd LAst MBri MGos MRav NOra SDea SFam SKee SPer WHar
	- 'Count Althann's Gage' (D)	CHab ERea GTwe NEgg SDea SFam SKee
	- 'Cox's Emperor' (C)	SKee
	- 'Crimson Drop' (D)	ERea SKee
	- 'Cropper'	see *P. domestica* 'Laxton's Cropper'
	- 'Curlew' (C)	SDea SKee
	- 'Czar' (C) 🏆H4	Widely available
	- 'Delicious'	see *P. domestica* 'Laxton's Delicious'
	- 'Denbigh Plum' (D)	CHab WGwG
	- 'Denniston's Superb'	see *P. domestica* 'Imperial Gage'
	- 'Diamond' (C)	SKee
	- 'Dittisham Black' (C)	CAgr CTho
	- 'Dittisham Ploughman' (C)	CTho SKee
	- 'Dunster Plum' (F)	CAgr CTho CTri CWib
	- 'Early Green Gage' (D)	NEgg
	- 'Early Laxton' (C/D) 🏆H4	CDul CHab LAst SDea SEND SFam SKee
	- 'Early Prolific'	see *P. domestica* 'Early Rivers'
§	- 'Early Rivers' (C)	CAgr CCAT CDul CHab CSBt CTho CTri ELan EPom ERea GTwe LRHS LSRN NOra NWea SCoo SDea SFam SKee WHar
	- 'Early Transparent Gage' (C/D)	CMac CSBt CTho ERea GTwe IArd LAst LBuc LRHS MBri MCoo NOra SCoo SDea SFam SKee WHar
	- 'Early Victoria' (C/D)	SDea
	- 'Edda' (D)	WHar
	- 'Edwards' (C/D) 🏆H4	CTri CWib EMil GTwe NEgg SDea SKee
	- 'Excalibur' (D)	CAgr EPom GTwe IArd LBuc LSRN NOra SDea SFam SKee WHar
§	- German Prune Group (C)	SKee
§	- 'Giant Prune' (C)	CDul ECrN GTwe MMuc SDea SEND SFam SKee WHar
I	- 'Godshill Big Sloe' (F)	SDea
	- 'Godshill Blue' (C)	SDea
	- 'Godshill Minigage' (F)	SDea
	- 'Gold Dust' (F)	SPoG
	- 'Golden Transparent' (D)	LAst MCoo SFam SKee
	- 'Goldfinch' (D)	MCoo SKee
	- 'Gordon Castle'	GQue NLar WHar
	- Green Gage Group	see *P. domestica* Reine-Claude Group
	- 'Grey Plum' (F)	CAgr CTho
	- 'Guinevere' (C)	CAgr LRHS MBri MCoo NOra WHar
	- 'Guthrie's Late Green' (D)	SKee
	- 'Haganta' PBR (F)	CAgr ERea NOra WHar
	- 'Herman' (D)	CAgr CLnd EPom GTwe LRHS MBri MCoo NOra SDea SFam SKee WHar
	- 'Heron' (C)	GTwe NOra SKee WHar
	- 'Impérial Epineuse' (D)	SKee
§	- 'Imperial Gage' (D) 🏆H4	CAgr CCAT CLnd CSBt CTho CTri EPom GTwe NLar SDea SEND SFam SKee WHar
	- 'Italian Prune' (F)	CLnd
	- 'Jan James' (F)	CEnd
	- 'Jefferson' (D) 🏆H4	CAgr CHab CLnd GTwe IArd NLar NOra SDea SFam SKee SVic WHar
*	- 'Jubilaeum' (D)	CAgr CLnd EPom GTwe LRHS NOra SCoo SEWo SFam SKee WHar
	- 'Kea' (C)	CAgr CLnd CTho SKee
	- 'Kirke's' (D)	CTho ERea GTwe LAst SDea SFam SKee WHar
	- 'Landkey Yellow' (F)	CAgr CTho
	- 'Langley Gage' (D)	CAgr ERea SDea
	- 'Late Muscatelle' (D)	SKee
	- 'Late Transparent Gage' (D)	SKee
§	- 'Laxton's Cropper' (C)	CHab GTwe LAst SKee WHar
§	- 'Laxton's Delicious' (D)	CHab
	- 'Laxton's Gage' (D)	SDea SKee
	- 'Laxton's Jubilee' (C/D)	CSBt
I	- 'Liegel's Apricot'	SKee
	- 'Mallard' (D) 🏆H4	SKee WHar
	- 'Manaccan' (C)	CAgr CTho
	- 'Marjorie's Seedling' (C) 🏆H4	Widely available
	- 'McLaughlin' (D)	SKee
	- 'Merton Gage' (D)	SKee
	- 'Merton Gem' (D)	SKee
	- 'Monarch' (C)	SKee
	- Old English gage	CMac ECrN EPom ERea LAst
	- 'Olympia' (C/D)	SKee
	- 'Opal' (D) 🏆H4	Widely available
	- 'Orleans' (C)	SKee
	- 'Oullins Gage' (C/D) 🏆H4	Widely available
	- 'Pershore' (C) 🏆H4	CAgr CHab CWib ERea GTwe LRHS MBri NEgg SDea SFam SKee WHar
	- 'Pond's Seedling' (C)	CSBt SDea SKee
	- 'President' (C)	CHab SDea SEND SKee
	- 'Priory Plum' (D)	SDea
	- 'Purple Pershore' (C)	CAgr CHab CTri CWib GTwe IArd LAst NEgg NOra SDea SFam SKee WHar
	- 'Quetsche d'Alsace'	see *P. domestica* German Prune Group
	- 'Reeves' (C) 🏆H4	GTwe IArd NOra SFam SKee WHar
	- 'Reine-Claude Dorée'	see *P. domestica* Reine-Claude Group
§	- Reine-Claude Group (D)	CLnd CSBt ELan GTwe SDea SFam SKee SLim SPer
	- - 'Old Green Gage'	see *P. domestica* (Reine-Claude Group) 'Reine-Claude Vraie'
	- - 'Reine-Claude de Bavais' (D)	CCAT CTho CTri GTwe NOra SDea SFam SKee WHar
	- - 'Reine-Claude de Vars' (D)	SVic
	- - 'Reine-Claude Violette' (D)	SKee
§	- - 'Reine-Claude Vraie' (C/D)	CAgr CLnd CMac CSBt CTsd CWib EPfP LBuc LRHS LSRN NPri SPoG WJas
§	- - 'Willingham Gage' (C/D)	GTwe LRHS LSRN SKee WHar
	- 'Royale de Vilvoorde' (D)	SKee
	- 'Sanctus Hubertus' (D) 🏆H4	CTri GTwe IArd SDea SKee WHar
	- 'Seneca' (D)	EPom NOra WHar
	- 'Severn Cross' (D)	GTwe SKee
	- 'Stanley' (C/D)	SVic
	- 'Stella'	CCVT ELan LAst LSRN NEgg NPri SLim WHar
	- 'Stella's Star'	LBuc MCoo
	- 'Stint' (C/D)	SKee
	- 'Swan' (C)	GTwe IArd NOra SKee WHar
	- 'Syston White'	MGos
	- 'Thames Cross' (D)	CLnd SKee
	- 'Transparent Gage' (D)	SKee
	- 'Upright' (F)	CEnd
	- 'Utility' (D)	SKee
	- 'Valor' (D) 🏆H4	NOra WHar
	- 'Verity' (C/D)	SKee
	- 'Victoria' (D) 🏆H4	Widely available
	- 'Violetta' PBR (D)	CAgr GTwe SFam WHar

	- 'Wangenheimer Frühzwetsche' (F)	SKee
	- 'Warwickshire Drooper' (C)	CAgr CHab CTho CWib GTwe IArd LAst NEgg NLar NOra SDea SFam SKee SLon SPer WHar
	- 'Washington' (D)	SDea SKee
	- 'White Magnum Bonum' (C)	SDea
	- 'Willingham'	see *P. domestica* (Reine-Claude Group) 'Willingham Gage'
	- 'Zimmers Frühzwetsche' (F)	SKee
§	***dulcis***	CDul CHab CLnd CTri CWib ELan EPfP EPom EWTr LAst LRHS MGos MWat NWea SCoo SCrf SDea SEND SFam SWvt WMou
	- 'Ai' (F)	CAgr
	- 'Ardechoise' (F)	CAgr
	- 'Ferraduel' (F)	CAgr
	- 'Ferragnes' (F)	CAgr
	- 'Lauranne' (F)	CAgr
	- 'Mandaline' (F)	CAgr
*	- 'Phoebe' (F)	CAgr
	- 'Supernova' (F)	CCCN
	- 'Tuono' (F)	CCCN
	Easter Bonnet = 'Comet'^{PBR}	CTri EPfP LRHS
	Fragrant Cloud	see *P.* 'Shizuka'
	Frilly Frock = 'Fpmspl' (v) **new**	LRHS LSRN SPoG
	'Fugenzō'	CDoy CSBt EBee
§	'Geraldinae'	CLnd
	glandulosa 'Alba Plena' (d)	CEnd CMac CSBt LBMP MAsh SGol SPlb SRms SWvt
	- 'Rosea Plena'	see *P. glandulosa* 'Sinensis'
§	- 'Sinensis' (d)	CEnd CLnd CSBt SRms
§	× ***gondouinii*** 'May Duke' (F)	SKee SVic WHar
§	- 'Merton Reward' (F)	SKee
	'Gyoikō'	CEnd CLnd EBee
	'Hally Jolivette'	CEnd EBee ELan GKin MAsh MBlu SPoG
	'Hillieri Spire'	see *P.* 'Spire'
	'Hilling's Weeping'	EBee SLon
	himalaica	NLar
§	***hirtipes***	CLnd
	'Hokusai'	CDul EPfP LRHS SGol
	Hollywood	see *P.* 'Trailblazer'
	'Horinji'	EBee MBri SCoo
	'Ichiyo' (d) 🏆^{H4}	CDul CLnd EBee ECrN EPfP LAst MAsh MBri SCoo SCrf
	× ***incam*** 'Okamé' 🏆^{H4}	CDoC CDul CLnd CMac CTho EBee ECrN ELon EPfP EWTr IVic LAst LHop LRHS LSRN MAsh MGos MMuc MRav NSoo NWea SCoo SEND SEWo SLPl SLim SPer SPoG WMou
	incisa	CTri NEgg NWea
	- 'Beniomi'	MRav
	- 'Cunera' **new**	NSoo
	- 'February Pink'	CJun SGol
	- 'Fujima'	LAst
	- 'Kojo-no-mai'	Widely available
	- 'Lotte' **new**	NLar
	- 'Mikinori'	CEnd CMac CSBt EBee EPfP LBMP MAsh MBlu MJak NLar SCoo
	- 'Oshidori' (d)	CMac CSBt ELon EPfP LRHS MBri MRav NEgg NLar SLim SRms
	- 'Pendula'	SCoo

	- 'Praecox' 🏆^{H4}	CHGN CSBt CTho EPfP LRHS MWat SCoo
§	- f. ***yamadae***	CJun LBMP NLar
	insititia 'Black Bullace' (F)	ERea
	- 'Blue Violet Damson' (F)	CAgr ERea GTwe MCoo NLar WHar
§	- 'Bradley's King Damson' (C)	GQue MCoo NLar NOra SKee WHar
	- bullace (C)	ERea LEdu SDea
	- 'Countess' (C)	CTri
	- 'Dittisham Damson' (C)	CTho
	- 'Farleigh Damson' (C) 🏆^{H4}	CAgr CHab CWib EPfP ERea GTwe IArd LAst LBuc MJak MMuc NOra NWea SDea SFam SKee SPer SVic WHar WJas
	- 'Godshill Damson' (C)	SDea
	- 'Golden Bullace'	see *P. insititia* 'White Bullace'
	- 'King of Damsons'	see *P. insititia* 'Bradley's King Damson'
	- 'Langley Bullace' (C)	CAgr CDul ERea GTwe NLar NOra SKee WHar
	- 'Lisna' (C)	CTri
	- 'Merryweather Damson' (C)	Widely available
	- 'Mirabelle de Nancy' (C)	CAgr CDul CLnd CTho EPom GTwe LAst NOra SDea SEWo SFam SKee WHar
	- 'Mirabelle de Nancy' red (C)	SDea
	- 'Mirabelle Ruby' (C)	LRHS NOra
§	- 'Prune Damson' (C) 🏆^{H4}	CAgr CDoC CDul CHab CLnd CTho CTri EPom ERea GTwe IArd LBuc LRHS MBri MMuc MWat NLar NOra NPri SDea SEND SFam SKee SPer WHar WJas
	- 'Shepherd's Bullace' (C)	CAgr CTho ERea
	- 'Shropshire Damson'	see *P. insititia* 'Prune Damson'
	- 'Small Bullace' (C)	CAgr
§	- 'White Bullace' (C)	CAgr ERea
	- 'Yellow Apricot' (C)	ERea
§	***jamasakura***	CDul
	'Jō-nioi'	CDul CEnd CLnd CTho MBri
§	'Kanzan' 🏆^{H4}	Widely available
§	'Kiku-shidare-zakura' 🏆^{H4}	Widely available
	Korean hill cherry	see *P. verecunda*
	'Kuboko-zakura'	EBee
	'Kulilensis Ruby'	LSRN SLPl
	'Kursar' 🏆^{H4}	CDoC CDul CLnd CSBt CTho CTri EBee EPfP GKin LRHS LSRN MAsh MBri NLar NWea SCoo SCrf SLim SLon SPer SPoG SWvt WMou
	laurocerasus 🏆^{H4}	CBcs CCVT CDul CMac CWSG EBee ECrN ELan EPfP EShb GKin IBoy LAst MGos MMuc MRav NPri NWea SAPC SEND SGol SPer SPoG WMoo WMou
	- 'Angustifolia'	IBoy
	- 'Aureovariegata'	see *P. laurocerasus* 'Taff's Golden Gleam'
	- 'Camelliifolia'	CMac CTri MBlu
N	- 'Castlewellan' (v)	CDoC CDul CTri EPfP EShb LHop LRHS MGos MRav MSwo NLar NWad SDix SPer SPoG SSta WHar WMoo
	- 'Caucasica'	CEnd NLar SGol
	- 'Cherry Brandy'	MRav SGol SLPl
	- Dart's Lowgreen	see *P. laurocerasus* Low 'n' Green
	- Etna = 'Anbri'^{PBR}	CMac EPfP LBuc LRHS LSou MAsh MBri NPri SWvt WMou
	- 'Gajo'^{PBR}	SPer

	- Genolia = 'Mariblon'PBR	SGol
	- 'Green Marble' (v)	CTri EBee EHoe
	- 'Herbergii'	MAsh
§	- 'Latifolia'	CHEx EUJe SLPl
§	- Low 'n' Green = 'Interlo'	MRav
	- 'Magnoliifolia'	see *P. laurocerasus* 'Latifolia'
	- 'Marbled White'	see *P. laurocerasus* 'Castlewellan'
	- 'Miky'	CJun
	- 'Mischeana'	SLPl
	- 'Mount Vernon'	CTri LBuc MBlu
	- 'Novita'	CWSG EPfP NSoo
	- 'Otto Luyken' ♀H4	CBcs CCVT CDul CMac CTri EBee EHoe ELan EPfP LAst LBMP LBuc LHop LRHS LSRN MAsh MGos MJak MRav MSwo MWhi NBir NEgg NWea SGol SPer SPlb WHar
	- 'Reynvaanii'	CJun MBri SLPl
	- 'Rotundifolia'	Widely available
	- 'Schipkaensis'	SLPl
§	- 'Taff's Golden Gleam' (v)	CJun
	- 'Van Nes'	CJun MAsh
	- 'Variegata' misapplied	see *P. laurocerasus* 'Castlewellan'
	- 'Variegata' ambig. (v)	CWib SRms
	- 'Whitespot'	MMuc
	- 'Zabeliana'	CDul CMac CTri EBee EPfP MJak MSwo NEgg NWad NWea SBod SPer SRms WHar
	litigiosa	CLnd EBee SCoo
	'Little Pink Perfection'	MBri SCoo SPoG
	lusitanica ♀H4	Widely available
	- subsp. ***azorica***	CDoC CExl EBee LRHS MRav WPGP
	- 'Myrtifolia'	CBar CTri EPfP EShb LRHS MBri MRav SGol SHil SLon SWvt WCFE WMoo
	- 'Variegata' (v)	CBar CDul CMac CTri CWib ELan ELon LHop MGos MLHP MMuc MRav MSwo SDix SEND SGol SPer SPoG SSta SWvt WMoo
	maackii	MMuc SEND
	- 'Amber Beauty'	CBcs CDul EBee EPfP GBin GKin LSRN MRav SGol SLon
	mahaleb	CNWT
	maritima	LEdu
§	'Matsumae-beni-murasaki'	NLar SCoo WHar
§	'Matsumae-beni-tamanishiki'	LRHS
§	'Matsumae-fuki'	CWSG EBee LRHS LSRN MBri NLar NWea SLim WHar
§	'Matsumae-hanagasa'	CEnd EBee LRHS MBri NLar WMou
	maximowiczii B&SWJ 10967	WCru
	'Mount Fuji'	see *P.* 'Shirotae'
	mume	CMCN CMen
	- 'Beni-chidori'	CEnd CMac CWib ELan EPfP EWTr IVic LRHS MBlu MBri NLar SCoo SLim SPoG WCot WJas
§	- 'Omoi-no-mama' (d)	CEnd CMen
	- 'Omoi-no-wac'	see *P. mume* 'Omoi-no-mama'
	myrobalana	see *P. cerasifera* Myrobalan Group
	nipponica var. ***kurilensis*** 'Brilliant'	CBcs CSBt GBin LRHS MBri NLar NSoo SHil
	- - 'Ruby'	CBcs LSRN MBri NEgg NSoo
	'Okumiyako' misapplied	see *P.* 'Shōgetsu'
	padus	CCVT CDul CHab CLnd CMac CSBt CTri ECrN EWTr LBuc MGos MJak MMuc MSwo NLar NWea SEND SEWo WMou
	- 'Albertii'	CCVT MBri SCoo
	- 'Colorata' ♀H4	CDul CEnd CMac CTho EBee ECrN ELan EWTr LHop MAsh MGos MRav NLar SCoo SGol SPer SWvt
	- 'Grandiflora'	see *P. padus* 'Watereri'
	- 'Purple Queen'	ECrN SGol
§	- 'Watereri' ♀H4	CCVT CDul CEnd CLnd CMCN CMac CTho CWib EBee ELan EPfP EWTr GBin LAst LHop NWea SCoo SEWo SGol SPer SPoG WMou
	'Pandora' ♀H4	CCVT CDoC CDul CLnd EBee ECrN EPfP LAst LHop LRHS MAsh MBri MGos MMuc MRav MSwo NPCo NWea SCoo SEND SEWo SPer SPoG
	pendula	SCrf
	- var. ***ascendens*** 'Rosea'	LRHS
§	- 'Pendula Rosea' ♀H4	CDoC CDul CEnd CLnd CTri CWib EPfP MAsh SCrf SPer WJas
§	- 'Pendula Rubra' ♀H4	CCVT CDoC CLnd CMac CSBt CWib EBee EPfP EWTr LAst LHop MBri MJak MSwo SCoo SLim SPer SPoG WMou
§	- 'Stellata'	LRHS MAsh MBri NLar
	persica **new**	SPre
	- 'Amsden June' (F)	CLnd CWib EBtc GTwe LEdu MWat NLar SDea SFam SKee WHar
	- 'Avalon Pride' (F)	CAgr CSut EPfP EPom ERea LBuc MCoo SKee
	- 'Barrington' (F)	ERea
	- 'Bellegarde' (F)	ERea SDea SFam
	- 'Black' (F) **new**	ERea
	- 'Bonanza' (F)	EPom ERea LSRN
	- 'Champion' (F)	CLnd
	- 'Darling' (F)	SVic
	- 'Dixi Red' (F)	CAgr ERea
	- 'Doctor Hogg' (F)	ERea SDea
	- 'Duke of York' (F) ♀H3	CTri ERea GTwe SDea SFam
	- 'Dymond' (F)	ERea
	- 'Early Alexander' (F)	ERea
	- 'Foliis Rubris' (F)	CDul LRHS
	- 'Francis' (F)	SKee
	- 'Frost' (F) **new**	ERea
	- 'Garden Lady' (F)	CMam GTwe SLim WHar
	- 'Hale's Early' (F)	GTwe MRav MWat SFam SKee SLim SPer WHar
	- 'Harken' (F) **new**	ERea
	- 'Hylands' (F)	SDea
	- 'Jalousia' (F) **new**	EPom
	- 'Johnny Brack' (F)	ERea
	- 'Kestrel' (F)	ERea
	- 'Madison' (F)	ERea
	- 'Mesembrine'PBR (F)	EPom
	- 'Natalia' (F)	SDea
	- var. ***nectarina*** Crimson Gold (F)	SDea
	- - 'Early Gem' (F)	ERea SDea
	- - 'Early Rivers' (F) ♀H3	ERea GTwe LAst LSRN SDea
	- - 'Elruge' (F)	ERea SDea
	- - 'Fantasia' (F)	EPfP SDea
	- - 'Fire Gold' (F)	ERea SDea
	- - 'Flavortop' (F)	EPfP ERea SPer
	- - 'Garden Beauty' (F/d)	SPoG
	- - 'Humboldt' (F)	CAgr CDul ERea GTwe SDea SFam SKee SPoG WHar
	- - 'John Rivers' (F)	SDea
	- - 'Lord Napier' (F) ♀H3	CAgr CDoC CDul CSBt CTri CWSG CWib EPfP EPom ERea EWTr LAst LBuc LRHS MGos MMuc MWat SDea SEND SFam SKee SLim SPer SPoG SVic WHar

	- - 'Nectared' (F)	CWib
	- - 'Nectarella' (F)	CMam EPom ERea LSRN SLim WHar
	- - 'Pineapple' (F)	CAgr CTri ERea GTwe SDea SFam SKee WHar
	- - 'Ruby Gold' (F)	SDea
	- - 'Terrace Ruby' (F)	SPoG
	- 'Pallas' (F) **new**	ERea
	- 'Peregrine' (F) ♀^{H3}	CAgr CDul CLnd CSBt CTri CWSG CWib EPfP EPom ERea EWTr GTwe LAst LBuc LRHS LSRN MBri MGos MMuc MWat NLar SDea SEND SFam SKee SLim SPer SPoG WHar WJas
	- 'Pink Peachy' (F)	NLar
	- 'Purpurea'	GKin
	- 'Raritan Rose' (F) **new**	ERea
	- 'Red Haven' (F)	CAgr CWib ERea GTwe SDea SKee SVic WHar
	- 'Red Top' (F)	EPfP
	- 'Redwing' (F)	CAgr
	- 'Reliance' (F)	SDea
	- 'Robin Redbreast' (F)	CAgr SDea
	- 'Rochester' (F) ♀^{H3}	CAgr CMam CSBt CTri CWSG CWib EPom ERea GTwe LAst LSRN MBri MMuc NLar SDea SEND SFam SKee SLim SPer SPoG WHar
	- 'Royal George' (F)	SFam
	- 'Saturne' (F)	CLnd EPom ERea SKee WHar
	- 'Springtime' (F)	SDea
	- 'Terrace Amber' (F)	SPoG
	- 'Terrace Diamond' (F)	SPoG
	- 'White Peachy' (F)	NLar
	× ***persicoides*** 'Ingrid' (F)	CAgr CDul CMam EBtc ECrN LBuc LRHS MBri MCoo NLar SCoo WHar
	- 'Pollardii' (F)	MMuc NWea WJas
	- 'Robijn' (F)	CAgr CDul EPom LBuc LEdu SVic
	- 'Spring Glow' (F)	CCVT CDoC CDul CEnd EBee EPfP LAst MBri MMuc MSwo NWea SCoo SEND SLim SLon WJas
	'Petite Noir'	CLnd
	'Pink Parasol'	see *P.* 'Matsumae-hanagasa'
	'Pink Perfection' ♀^{H4}	CBcs CDul CLnd CSBt CWib EBee EPfP LAst LRHS MAsh MBri MGos MSwo MWat NLar NSoo SPer WHar WJas
	'Pink Shell' ♀^{H4}	CLnd EBee EPfP MAsh MBri
	pissardii	see *P. cerasifera* 'Pissardii'
	'Pissardii Nigra'	see *P. cerasifera* 'Nigra'
*	***prostrata*** var. ***discolor***	NLar
	pumila var. ***depressa***	MRav NLar NPro
	'Royal Burgundy' (d)	CCVT CEnd CLnd CMac CWGN EBee ECrN EMil EPfP LAst LRHS LSRN MAsh MBri MGos MJak MWat NLar NSoo SCoo SEWo SGol SLim SPer SPoG WHar
	rufa	CDul CJun CLnd CTho EBee EBtc GKin SKHP SLon WPat
	salicina 'Abundance' (F) **new**	ERea
	- 'Beauty'	ERea
§	- 'Black Diamond' (F)	SDea
	- 'Howard Miracle' (F) **new**	ERea
	- 'Lizzie'	EPom
	- 'Mariposa' (F) **new**	ERea
	- 'Methley' (D)	CAgr ERea NOra SPoG WHar
	- 'Ozark Premier' (F) **new**	ERea
	- 'Santa Rosa' (F) **new**	ERea
	- 'Satsuma' (F)	ERea
	- 'Shiro' (D)	ERea
	- 'Sierra' (F) **new**	ERea
	- 'Sorriso di Primavera' (F) **new**	ERea
	sargentii ♀^{H4}	Widely available
	- 'Charles Sargent'	EBee GBin LRHS
	- 'Columnaris'	MBri
	- 'Rancho'	CLnd EBee MAsh SCoo SPer SPoG
	× ***schmittii***	CCVT ECrN MMuc SCoo SEND SPer WJas
	'Sekiyama'	see *P.* 'Kanzan'
	serotina	CDul NLar
§	***serrula*** ♀^{H1}	Widely available
	- Branklyn form	MGos
	- Dorothy Clive form	EBee LSRN
	- 'Princesse Sturdza'	MBlu
	- var. ***tibetica***	see *P. serrula*
	serrula × ***serrulata***	CBcs CTho
	serrulata 'Erecta'	see *P.* 'Amanogawa'
	- 'Grandiflora'	see *P.* 'Ukon'
	- 'Longipes'	see *P.* 'Shōgetsu'
	- 'Miyako' misapplied	see *P.* 'Shōgetsu'
N	- var. ***pubescens***	see *P. verecunda*
	- 'Rosea'	see *P.* 'Kiku-shidare-zakura'
	- var. ***spontanea***	see *P. jamasakura*
	'Shidare-zakura'	see *P.* 'Kiku-shidare-zakura'
	'Shimizu-zakura'	see *P.* 'Shōgetsu'
	'Shirofugen' ♀^{H4}	CBcs CDoC CDul CLnd CMCN CMac CSBt CTho CWib EBee ECrN EPfP EWTr GKin LBuc LRHS LSRN MAsh MBri MMuc MRav MWat SEND SGol SPer WHar WJas
§	'Shirotae' ♀^{H4}	Widely available
§	'Shizuka'	CWib EBee LRHS MBri MSwo NLar NSoo SCoo SLim SPer SPoG WHar
§	'Shōgetsu' ♀^{H4}	CBcs CDul CEnd CLnd CMac CSBt CTho EBee ELan EPfP EWTr LAst LRHS MAsh MBri MMuc MRav NEgg NLar SEND SEWo SFam SLim SPer WHar
	'Shosar'	CEnd CWib EBee ECrN SCoo SPer
	× ***sieboldii*** 'Caespitosa'	see *P.* × *sieboldii* 'Takasago'
§	- 'Takasago'	EBee MBri SCoo
	'Snow Goose'	CDoC EBee ELan LAst LHop LRHS NEgg SCoo SEND SGol
	'Snow Showers'	CCVT CDoC CEnd CMac ELan LRHS LSRN MAsh MBri MGos MMuc NSoo NWea SEND SEWo SLim SPer SPoG
	spinosa	CCVT CDoC CDul CHab CMac CTri ECrN EPfP EPom EShb GAbr LAst LBuc LSRN MAsh MBlu MJak NLar NWea SEWo SPer SPoG SVic WHar WMou WSFF
	- 'Plena' (d)	CEnd CTho MBlu
	- 'Purpurea'	CDul CTho EGFP MAsh MBlu MBri NLar WMou
§	'Spire' ♀^{H4}	CCVT CDoC CDul CLnd CMCN CMac CSBt CTho CWib EBee ELon EPfP EWTr LAst LBuc LRHS MAsh MBlu MGos MJak MMuc MSwo NWea SCoo SEND SGol SPer WJas WMou
	'Spring Snow'	see *P.* 'Matsumae-beni-tamanishiki'
	× ***subhirtella*** var. ***ascendens***	see *P. pendula* var. *ascendens*
	- 'Autumnalis' ♀^{H4}	Widely available

	- 'Autumnalis Rosea' 🏆H4	Widely available
	- 'Falling Stars'	EBee SLon
	- 'Fukubana'	CLnd CMac EBee EPfP MAsh MBri NLar
	- 'Pendula' misapplied	see *P. pendula* 'Pendula Rosea'
	- 'Pendula Rosea'	see *P. pendula* 'Pendula Rosea'
	- 'Pendula Rubra'	see *P. pendula* 'Pendula Rubra'
N	- 'Rosea'	CLnd MRav
	- 'Stellata'	see *P. pendula* 'Stellata'
	'Sunset Boulevard'	EBee LRHS LSRN MBri MGos
	'Taihaku' 🏆H4	Widely available
	'Taoyame'	CLnd EBee
	tenella	CAgr ELan SEND WCot
	- 'Fire Hill'	CJun CWib ECho ELan EPfP LRHS LSRN MGos MRav SKHP SPer WCFE WCot WJas
	'The Bride'	CDul CEnd EBee LRHS MAsh MBri SCoo
	tibetica	see *P. serrula*
	'Tiltstone Hellfire'	EBee MBri
	tomentosa	CAgr LLHF SEND
§	'Trailblazer' (C/D)	CDul CEnd CLnd CMac CSBt ECrN IVic LAst MRav MSwo SLon WMou
	triloba	CBcs CWib ECrN LAst MBlu NWea
	- 'Multiplex' (d)	SPoG SRms WJas
§	'Ukon' 🏆H4	CBcs CDoC CDul CLnd CMCN CMac CTho CTri EBee ECrN EPfP EWTr LRHS MAsh MBri MGos MMuc MRav NEgg NLar NWea SCrf SEND SGol SLim SPer WHar
	'Umineko'	CCVT CLnd CWib ECrN MGos MMuc SEND SEWo SLPl SPer WHar
§	***verecunda***	CLnd NWea WJas
	- 'Autumn Glory'	CTho
	virginiana 'Schubert'	CDul EBee ECrN SCoo WMou
	'White Cloud'	CDul
	yamadae	see *P. incisa* f. *yamadae*
	× *yedoensis*	CCVT CDoC CDul EBee MBri MRav SLon SPer WHar WMou
	- 'Ivensii'	CBcs CDul CSBt CWib EBee LHop MAsh MMuc NEgg NWea SCoo SEND SPer
	- 'Pendula'	see *P.* × *yedoensis* 'Shidare-Yoshino'
	- 'Perpendens'	see *P.* × *yedoensis* 'Shidare-Yoshino'
§	- 'Shidare-Yoshino'	CCVT CDoC CDul CLnd CSBt EBee ECrN LRHS MAsh MBri MGos MRav MSwo MWat NWea SLim SLon SPoG
§	- 'Somei-Yoshino' 🏆H4	CCVT CLnd CTho CTri EPfP MBri NWea SLim SPer WHar WJas
	'Yoshino'	see *P.* × *yedoensis* 'Somei-Yoshino'
	'Yoshino Pendula'	see *P.* × *yedoensis* 'Shidare-Yoshino'

Psacalium (*Asteraceae*)

	pinetorum B&SWJ 10269	WCru

Pseuderanthemum (*Acanthaceae*)

	carruthersii var. ***atropurpureum*** 'Rubrum'	LSou

Pseudocydonia (*Rosaceae*)

§	***sinensis***	CAgr CBcs CMen NLar WHil

Pseudofumaria see *Corydalis*

	alba	see *Corydalis ochroleuca*

Pseudogynoxys (*Asteraceae*)

§	***chenopodioides***	CCCN CRHN CSpe SVen

Pseudolarix (*Pinaceae*)

§	***amabilis*** 🏆H4	CDoC CMen CTho EPfP GBin LRHS MBlu MBri MMuc MPkF NPCo NPnk NWea SCoo SKHP SLim SPoG
	kaempferi	see *P. amabilis*

Pseudomuscari see *Muscari*

	azureum	see *Muscari azureum*

Pseudopanax (*Araliaceae*)

	(Adiantifolius Group) 'Adiantifolius'	CBcs CDoC CHEx ESwi SVen
	- 'Cyril Watson' 🏆H1	CBcs CDoC CHEx ELan IDee LRHS SBig SLim SVen
	arboreus	see *Neopanax arboreus*
	chathamicus	CDoC CHEx SAPC
	crassifolius	CAbb CBcs CBct CBrP CCCN CDTJ CHEx EAmu EBee ELon ESwi EUJe GBin IDee LRHS SAPC SBig SMad SPoG WCot
	- var. ***trifoliolatus***	CHEx
	discolor	ECou IDee LEdu
	ferox	CAbb CBcs CBct CBrP CDTJ CTsd EAmu ESwi EUJe GBin LRHS SAPC SBig SLim SMad SVen
	'Forest Gem'	CDoC LRHS
	laetus	see *Neopanax laetus*
	lessonii	CBcs CBrP CHEx ECou ELan
	- 'Black Ruby'	ECou
	- 'Gold Splash' (v) 🏆H1	CBcs CDoC CHEx ELan IDee IVic LRHS SBig SEND SLim SVen
	- 'Rangitira'	CBcs CDoC IDee LRHS SBig SLim
	'Linearifolius'	CHEx IDee LEdu
	'Purpureus' 🏆H1	CDoC CHel ESwi SEND SVen
	'Sabre'	CBcs CDoC CHEx EUJe IDee LRHS SLim
	'Trident'	CDoC CHEx ECou IDee LRHS SBig SLim SVen

Pseudosasa (*Poaceae*)

	amabilis misapplied	see *Arundinaria gigantea*
§	***japonica*** 🏆H4	CAbb CBcs CDoC CEnt CHEx CTsd CWib ENBC EPfP LRHS MMoz MMuc MWhi MWht NGdn NLar SAPC SEND SEWo SPer SPoG WCFE WJun WMoo
§	- 'Akebonosuji' (v)	CEnt MWht WJun WPGP
I	- var. ***pleioblastoides***	MWht
	- 'Tsutsumiana'	CHEx ELon ERod EUJe MMoz MWht NLar SBig WJun
	- 'Variegata'	see *P. japonica* 'Akebonosuji'
	usawai	WJun
	viridula	ERod MWht

Pseudotsuga (*Pinaceae*)

§	***menziesii*** 🏆H4	CBcs CDul CLnd EPfP MBlu MMuc NWea SEND
	- 'Bhiela Lhota'	CKen
	- 'Blue Wonder'	CKen
	- 'Densa'	CKen
	- 'Fastigiata'	CKen
	- 'Fletcheri'	CKen
	- 'Geijsteren'	NLar
	- var. ***glauca***	CDul CTho
	- 'Glauca Pendula'	CKen
I	- 'Gotelli's Pendula'	CKen
	- 'Graceful Grace'	CKen
	- 'Idaho Gem'	CKen

- 'Julie'	CKen
- 'Little Jamie'	CKen
- 'Lohbrunner'	CKen
- 'McKenzie'	CKen
- 'Nana'	CKen
- 'Oudemansii'	NLar
- Pendula Group	NPCo
- 'Stairii'	CKen
- 'Uwes Golden'	NLar
taxifolia	see *P. menziesii*

Pseudowintera (*Winteraceae*)

§ ***colorata***	CBcs CDoC CExl CHel CMac CPla CTsd CWib GAbr GKin IVic MPkF MRav NLar NPnk
- 'Marjorie Congreve'	IVic LRHS
- 'Moulin Rouge'	CBcs LRHS
- 'Mount Congreve'	CBcs GKin IArd NLar
- 'Red Leopard'	CDoC LRHS NLar NPnk NSoo

Psidium (*Myrtaceae*)

cattleyanum	see *P. littorale* var. *longipes*
guajava (F)	CCCN SPlb XBlo
§ ***littorale*** var. ***longipes*** (F)	CCCN EDif XBlo

Psilotum (*Psilotaceae*)

nudum	ECou

Psoralea (*Papilionaceae*)

* ***fleta***	SPlb
glabra	SPlb
glandulosa	SBrt SPlb WSHC
* ***macrothyrsa***	EBee
oligophylla	SPlb
onobrychis	SPhx
pinnata	CExl

Psychotria (*Rubiaceae*)

capensis	CExl

Ptelea (*Rutaceae*)

trifoliata	CArn CBcs CDul CLnd CMac CWib ELan EPfP MBlu SChF SPer SRms WPGP
- 'Aurea' ♀H4	CAbP CBcs CEnd CExl CJun CLnd CMac CTho EBee ELan EPfP EWTr GBin LHop LRHS MAsh MBlu MBri NLar SPer SPoG SSpi WBor WPGP
- 'Fastigiata'	EPfP

Pteracanthus see *Strobilanthes*

Pteridophyllum (*Papaveraceae*)

racemosum	EFEx WCru

Pteris (*Pteridaceae*)

from Yunnan	CLAP
§ ***actiniopteroides***	WCot
angustipinna B&SWJ 6738	WCru
cretica ♀H1+3	CHEx SAPC
- var. ***albolineata*** ♀H1	CBty LRHS XBlo
- 'Mayi' (v)	CBty
- 'Ouvradii'	CBty
- 'Rowei'	CBty LRHS XBlo
- 'Wimsettii'	CBty LRHS
ensiformis	CBty
'Evergemiensis' (v)	
gallinopes	CLAP
henryi	see *P. actiniopteroides*
* ***staminea***	XBlo
tricolor	CBty
wallichiana	CBty CGHE CHEx EBee SMad WPGP

Pterocactus (*Cactaceae*)

hickenii F&W 10240	WCot

Pterocarya ✿ (*Juglandaceae*)

fraxinifolia ♀H4	CBcs CCVT CDul CLnd CMCN CTho EBee ECrN EPfP GQui IArd IDee LRHS MBlu MMuc MRav SEND
macroptera var. ***insignis***	CExl CFil WPGP
× ***rehderiana***	CTho MBlu WMou
stenoptera	CBcs CDTJ CLnd CMCN CTho EGFP NLar
- 'Fern Leaf'	CExl CFil EBee EPfP MBlu MBri WMou WPGP

Pterocephalus (*Caprifoliaceae*)

parnassi	see *P. perennis*
§ ***perennis***	CMea ECho MHer NBir NRya SRms WAbe WHoo XSen
pinardii	WAbe XSen

Pterodiscus (*Pedaliaceae*)

aurantiacus	LToo
luridus	LToo
ngamicus	LToo

Pterostylis (*Orchidaceae*)

coccina	ECho
curta	ECho LLHF

Pterostyrax (*Styracaceae*)

corymbosa	CBcs CJun CMCN MBri NLar SSpi
hispida ♀H4	CAbP CBcs CDoC CDul CHGN CJun CMCN CTsd CWib EBee EPfP GBin IDee IVic LRHS MBlu MBri MRav NLar SChF SHil SPoG WHar
psilophyllus	WPGP

Ptilostemon (*Asteraceae*)

§ ***diacantha***	ELan EPfP IFoB LRHS WCot
niveus new	WCot

Ptilotrichum see *Alyssum*

Ptilotus (*Amaranthaceae*)

exaltatus	SPlb

Pueraria (*Papilionaceae*)

montana var. ***lobata***	CArn

Pulicaria (*Asteraceae*)

§ ***dysenterica***	CArn CHab LLWG NMir WHer WSFF

Pulmonaria (*Boraginaceae*)

angustifolia ♀H4	CMac EPfP GKev GMaP MNrw NOrc SRms
- 'Azurea'	CElw CHVG CTca EBee ELan EPPr EPfP GAbr GMaP IGor LRHS MCot MMuc MRav NBro NLar SRms
- 'Blaues Meer'	EBee ECtt GAbr SGbt
- 'Munstead Blue'	CElw CLAP CMac GBuc MCot MRav NRya SRms
'Apple Frost'	LRHS SGol WWEG

	'Barfield Regalia'	EBee IGor LLHF NSti WWEG
	'Benediction'	CDes LLHF MNrw NSti WCot
	'Beth Chatto' **new**	CElw
	'Beth's Pink'	GAbr
	'Blake's Silver' **new**	EBee ECtt MBel NSti SMrm WCot WRHF
	'Blauer Hügel'	LLHF NSti
	'Blauhimmel'	GCra
	'Blue Buttons'	CCon ECtt WWEG
	'Blue Crown'	CElw CSev EWes
	'Blue Ensign'	Widely available
	'Blue Moon'	see *P. officinalis* 'Blue Mist'
	'Blueberry Muffin'	CSpe
	'Bubble Gum' PBR	EBee MBri SHeu
	Cally hybrid	CLAP GCal
	'Cedric Morris'	CElw
	'Chintz'	MAvo
	'Coral Springs'	GBuc LLHF NLar
	'Cotton Cool'	Widely available
	'Crawshay Chance'	CElw
	'Dark Vader'	ECtt GBin SHeu
	'Diana Clare'	Widely available
	'Elworthy Carnival' **new**	CElw
	'Elworthy Rubies'	CElw
	'Emerald Isles'	SWvt
	'Excalibur'	EBee ECtt NLar SHeu
	'Fiona'	WWEG
	'Glacier'	CTca EBee ELan EPfP MNrw WCot WWEG
	'Hazel Kaye's Red'	CElw LLWP
	'High Contrast'	ECtt SHeu
	'Highdown'	see *P.* 'Lewis Palmer'
	'Ice Ballet' (Classic Series)	CLAP CPrp EBee ECtt EPfP MAvo NLar WCAu
§	'Lewis Palmer' ♀H4	CBro CSam CTca EBee GCal GMaP LPot LRHS MBri MNrw NBir NLar SRGP SRms WHoo WWEG
	'Little Star'	CElw EBee ECtt GBuc LRHS MAvo SRGP WWEG
	longifolia	EHoe ELan EPfP GAbr GBin GKev LLWG LRHS NBir NLar NOrc NSti WBrk
§	- 'Ankum'	CElw CLAP NBir WCot WSHC WWEG
	- 'Ballyrogan Blue'	IBlr
	- 'Bertram Anderson'	CTca EBee ECtt GMaP IBoy LRHS NBir NLar SPer SPoG SRGP SRms SWvt WBrk WMnd WWEG
	- subsp. ***cevennensis***	CLAP EBee LRHS MBel NCGa NLar NSti WPtf WWEG
	- 'Coen Jansen'	see *P. longifolia* 'Ankum'
	- 'Dordogne'	CLAP EBee NBir NLar
	- 'Howard Eggins'	WWEG
	'Mado'	WWEG
	'Majesté'	CLAP CWib EBee ELan EPfP EWes GBuc GMaP IFro LRHS MBel MBri MRav NBir NEgg NOrc NSti SHeu SPer SPoG WBor WBrk WCot WMnd WWEG
	'Margery Fish' ♀H4	CLAP CSam EPfP LRHS MWhi SPer WMnd
	'Mary Mottram'	CElw ECtt NBir NSti SMrm WMnd
	'Mawson's Blue'	CLAP EWes MRav NBir NChi SWvt WBrk WMoo WSHC
	'May Bouquet'	LLHF
	'Melancholia'	IBlr
	'Merlin'	CLAP SKHP
§	'Milchstrasse'	EBee
	Milky Way	see *P.* 'Milchstrasse'
	'Milky Way'	ECtt SHeu

	mollis	GCal IMou MNrw NSti
	- 'Royal Blue'	MRav
	'Monksilver'	CElw
	'Moonshine' PBR	ECtt SHeu
	'Moonstone'	CElw
	'Mountain Magic' PBR	LRHS
	'Mrs Kittle'	CCon CElw CSam EBee GQue LRHS MRav NBir NIIol NSti WBrk WMnd WWEG
	'Netta Statham'	EBee LLHF NSti
	'Nürnberg'	CElw WWEG
	officinalis	CArn CBro CHby IFoB MHoo MLHP NChi SIde WBrk
	- 'Alba'	WBrk
	- 'Bamberg'	EBee
§	- 'Blue Mist'	CBro CLAP ELan GMaP MBel NBir WBrk WCot WHoo WMnd WMoo
	- 'Bowles's Blue'	see *P. officinalis* 'Blue Mist'
	- Cambridge Blue Group	LRHS MRav MWat NBir WCot
	- 'Marjorie Lawley'	LRHS
	- 'Stillingfleet Gran'	LLHF
	- 'White Wings'	CLAP NLar
	'Oliver Wyatt's White'	CLAP SRGP
	Opal = 'Ocupol'	Widely available
	'Open Skies' (v)	CDes
	'Pink Haze' PBR	EBee ECtt ITim LPla LRHS MBel MHol MPie NLar NSti SPoG SWvt WCAu WCot WRHF
	'Polar Splash'	LRHS
	'Raspberry Splash' PBR	CLAP COIW ECtt GBin GKev LRHS NLar SGol SHeu SIde SMrm SPoG
*	'Rowlatt Choules'	MAvo
	'Roy Davidson'	CLAP CSam CTca ECGP ECtt EPfP IGor LHop LRHS MBel MCot NBir NCGa NSti SRms SWvt WPtf WWEG
	rubra ♀H4	CBcs CElw CHab CPom ELan EShb GAbr LBMP LLWP MLHP MMuc MNrw NBid NOrc NSti SEND SRms WCAu
	- var. ***alba***	see *P. rubra* var. *albocorollata*
§	- var. ***albocorollata***	CBre CElw EBtc GAbr GBin MBel NBid WBrk WWEG
	- 'Barfield Pink'	CBro ELan GCal IFro MBel NBir NLar
	- 'Bowles's Red'	CHel CMac EBee EPfP IFoB LRHS MNrw MRav NBir NCGa NGdn NLar NPnk SPer WGwG WHoo WMnd
	- 'David Ward' (v)	CCon CMac CPla EBee ECtt ELan EPfP GCra GMaP LHop LRHS MPnt MRav MSCN NBir NLar NPnk SMrm SPer WBrk WCFE WMnd WPtf WSHC WWEG
	- 'Rachel Vernie' (v)	CElw CLAP CPou MAvo WBrk WWEG
	- 'Redstart'	CBro CMac CSBt CSam CTca ECtt EPfP GKev IGor LEdu LHop LLWP LRHS MNrw MRav NBir NEgg NGdn NLar SGol SPer SRms SWvt WBrk WMnd WMoo WWEG
§	***saccharata***	ELan GMaP IFro MMuc NEgg NPnk SEND SRms
	- 'Alba'	CBro CElw IFro MMuc SRms
	- Argentea Group ♀H4	CBro CSev CTri ELan EPfP GMaP LRHS MRav NGdn WBrk WWEG
	- 'Clent Skysilver'	NLar
	- 'Dora Bielefeld'	CLAP EBee EPPr EPfP GBuc GMaP LLWP LRHS MBri MNrw MRav NBir NCGa NChi NGdn NHol NOrc

	NSoo SMrm SPer SRGP SWvt WHoo WMnd WWlt
- 'Frühlingshimmel'	CBro CElw EBee ECtt EPfP LRHS MNrw MRav NSti WPtf
- 'Glebe Cottage Blue'	CElw ECGP
- 'Leopard'	CLAP CMac CMea CPrp CSam CTca CWCL ECtt GBin GBuc GMaP LRHS MBel NBir NLar NSti SHeu WCot WHoo WWEG
- 'Mrs Moon'	CTri CWib EBee ECtt ELon EPfP GMaP IKil LRHS NLar NOrc SGol SPer SWvt WCAu WMnd WWEG
- 'Old Rectory Silver'	NBir
- 'Picta'	see *P. saccharata*
- 'Pink Dawn'	CMHG
- 'Reginald Kaye'	EWes
- 'Silverado'PBR	ECtt LRHS MBel MBri NLar NOrc
- 'Stanhoe'	EWes
'Saint Ann's'	EBee LLHF LRHS NSti
'Samurai'	EBee GBin LRHS MBri NSti
'Silver Bouquet'PBR	CElw ECtt GBin LSou SHeu
'Silver Sabre'	IBlr
'Silver Shimmers'PBR	SHeu
'Silver Surprise'	WCot
'Sissinghurst White' ♀H4	Widely available
'Smoky Blue'	CLAP ECtt EPfP LHop MRav SWat WWEG
'Spilled Milk'	NLar
'Stillingfleet Meg'	CHel CLAP ECtt LRHS MBNS NLar NSti NWad SRGP WPtf
'Trevi Fountain'	CHid CLAP COIW CWCL EBee ECtt EShb GBin GJos LRHS NPri SHeu SIde SMrm SPoG WCot WPtf
'Victorian Brooch'PBR	CLAP COIW CSam CWCL ECtt GBin GKev IBoy LRHS LSou MNrw NEgg NLar NPri SHeu SIde SMrm SPoG WWEG
'Weetwood Blue'	CBre CLAP CTca EBee EPfP MNrw
'Wisley White'	EBee

Pulsatilla (*Ranunculaceae*)

alba	CBro
albana	CBro ECho EHyd LHop LLHF LRHS
- 'Lutea'	EBee LLHF NSla
alpina	NGdn SRms
§ - subsp. ***apiifolia*** ♀H4	EBee IFro
- subsp. ***sulphurea*** misapplied	see *P. alpina* subsp. *apiifolia*
ambigua	CPBP GKev LLHF
campanella	LLHF
caucasica	CBro ECho LRHS
cernua	LHop LRHS
georgica	WIce
halleri ♀H4	CHel EBee GKev
- subsp. ***slavica*** ♀H4	EPot LLHF
- subsp. ***taurica***	LRHS
lutea	see *P. alpina* subsp. *apiifolia*
montana	LLHF SPlb
§ ***patens***	EDAr LLHF NGdn WIce
pratensis	GPoy SRms
- subsp. ***nigricans***	GKev LHop NSla
I - 'Semiplena'	MMoz
red-flowered **new**	CHel
rubra	GKev NGdn SPad SRot
* ***serotina***	EBee GKev
turczaninovii	LLHF LPla LRHS
§ ***vernalis*** ♀H2	NLar NSla WAbe
violacea	CBcs
§ ***vulgaris*** ♀H4	Widely available
- 'Alba' ♀H4	Widely available
- 'Barton's Pink'	CBro ECho EPot EWes LHop LLHF LRHS SRot
- 'Blaue Glocke'	EPot LRHS MCot NPri SHar SMrm SWvt XSen
- 'Eva Constance'	CBro ECho EHyd LHop LLHF LRHS WAbe
- 'Gotlandica'	LLHF
- subsp. ***grandis***	LRHS NSla
- - 'Budapest'	CRDP
- - 'Papageno'	CSpc ECho EPot LBMP LRHS MAvo MBel MHol NCGa NHol NLar NSla SMrm WHil WIce
- Heiler hybrids	CPrp LLHF MRav NCGa NDov NEgg NGdn NSla
- 'Perlen Glocke'	EBee EDAr EWTr MHer
- pink-flowered	CHel CMea LLHF NSla
- Red Clock	see *P. vulgaris* 'Röde Klokke'
- red-flowered **new**	CTsd SGbt
§ - 'Röde Klokke'	ECtt LRHS MCot MNrw MWhi NPri NWad SHar SMrm SWvt WCot WHil XLum XSen
- ***rosea***	GAbr
- Rote Glocke	see *P. vulgaris* 'Röde Klokke'
- var. ***rubra***	CHel CMea ECho EHyd ELan EPPr EPfP GMaP LRHS MBri MHer MNHC MRav NBir NLar NSla SPer SPet SPoG SRms SRot WHoo WIce
§ - 'Weisse Schwan'	EPfP GMaP SRot
- 'White Bells'	NHol
- White Swan	see *P. vulgaris* 'Weisse Schwan'

Pultenaea (*Papilionaceae*)

juniperina	SPlb

pummelo see *Citrus maxima*

Punica (*Lythraceae*)

granatum	CArn CBcs CHEx CMen CTsd EAmu ELan EPfP IDee MOWG MREP SPre SVic SWvt WSHC
- 'Fina Tendral' (F)	CCCN
- var. ***nana*** ♀H3	CAgr CCCN CMen EBee EBtc ELau EOHP EPfP EShb LEdu LRHS MREP SMrm SRms SVen WPat
- f. ***plena*** (d)	CBcs LRHS MRav WCFE WPat
- - 'Chico' (d)	CBcs SEND
- - 'Legrelleae' (F/d)	SEND SLPl WPat
- - 'Maxima Rubra' (d)	EShb XSen
- - 'Flore Pleno Luteo' (d)	LRHS
- 'Provence' (F)	XSen
* - 'Striata'	MOWG

Puschkinia (*Asparagaceae*)

scilloides	ECho NBir
- 'Aragat's Gem'	ECho LWst
- var. ***libanotica***	CHel ECho EPfP EPot ERCP GKev LEdu LPio LRHS SDeJ SMrm SPer WRHF WShi
- - 'Alba'	CHel ECho EPot GKev SDeJ SPer WCot
- 'Snowdrift'	LWst

Puya (*Bromeliaceae*)

RH 1809 **new**	WCot
RH 2910A **new**	WCot
RH 2961C **new**	WCot
alpestris	CCCN CFil EAmu EBee EShb SAPC SBig SPlb WCot WPGP

assurgens **new**	WCot
berteroana	CAbb CBcs CCCN CDTJ CDoC CHEx EGri EShb EUJe SPlb WCot
boliviensis **new**	WCot
castellanosii	WCot
chilensis	CAbb CBcs CCCN CDTJ CDoC CHEx CHel EAmu LRHS SAPC SPlb WCot
coerulea	CCCN CCon CDTJ CTsd SPlb
- var. ***monteroana*** **new**	WCot
dyckioides **new**	WCot
- red-bracted **new**	WCot
ferruginea	EUJe SPlb WCot
gilmartiniae	WCot
F&W 8697 **new**	
laxa	EGri EUJe WCot
mirabilis	CDTJ EGri ESwi GBin WHil
- RCB/Arg L-3	WCot
raimondii	WCot WPGP
venusta	CCCN CDTJ EGri SPlb WCot
yakespala **new**	WCot

Pycnanthemum (*Lamiaceae*)

montanum	GBin
muticum	CArn LEdu
pilosum	CArn ELau MHer NLar XLum
tenuifolium	NLar
virginianum	GCal SPhx

Pycnostachys (*Lamiaceae*)

reticulata	EOHP
urticifolia	EOHP EWes

Pygmea see *Chionohebe*

Pyracantha (*Rosaceae*)

Alexander Pendula = 'Renolex'	LHop MRav MSwo SRms
angustifolia	WCFE
§ ***atalantioides***	SPlb WCFE
'Brilliant'	EPfP SCoo
§ ***coccinea*** 'Lalandei'	CMac
- 'Red Column'	Widely available
- 'Red Cushion'	MJak MRav SRms
Dart's Red = 'Interrada'	CSBt SLim WHar
'Fiery Cascade'	LRHS SHil SPoG
gibbsii	see *P. atalantioides*
'Golden Charmer' 🏆H4	CDul CMac EPfP IBoy LRHS MBri MGos MSwo NEgg NLar NWea SCoo SGol SLPl SPer SPoG SRms SWvt WGwG WRHF
'Golden Glow'	SLim
'Golden Sun'	see *P.* 'Soleil d'Or'
'Harlequin' (v)	SGol
'Knap Hill Lemon'	MBlu
'Mohave'	CMac CTri EBee ECrN ELan ELon IBoy LRHS MAsh MWat SCoo SGol SLim SRms SWvt
'Mohave Silver' (v)	CMac CWSG ELan EShb LBMP LRHS MAsh NHol
'Monrovia'	see *P. coccinea* 'Lalandei'
'Navaho'	SEWo
'Orange Charmer'	CMac CTri ELan LHop LRHS MBri MGos MWat NHol NLar NWea SPer SPlb WHar
'Orange Glow' 🏆H4	CSBt CTri CWib EBee ECrN EPfP IBoy LAst LBMP LBuc LPot LRHS MAsh MGos MJak MMuc MSwo NWea SEND SEWo SGol SHil SLim SPer SPoG SRms SWvt WGwG WHar
'Red Charmer' **new**	NHol
'Renault d'Or'	SLPl
rogersiana 🏆H4	CDul MRav
- 'Flava' 🏆H4	CDul CSBt EPfP LRHS MAsh NEgg SPoG SWvt
'Rosedale'	LRHS WHar
Saphyr Jaune = 'Cadaune'PBR	CBcs CCVT CDoC CEnd CSBt CWSG EBee ECrN EMil EPfP LRHS MBri MGos MRav NCGa NHol NLar NPri SCoo SGol SPer WHar
Saphyr Orange = 'Cadange'PBR 🏆H4	CBcs CCVT CDoC CEnd CMac CSBt CWSG EBee EMil EPfP LRHS MBri MGos MRav NEgg NLar NPri SCoo SGol SPer WHar
Saphyr Panache = 'Cadvar'PBR (v)	EBee
Saphyr Rouge = 'Cadrou'PBR 🏆H4	CBcs CCVT CDoC CEnd CMac CSBt CWSG EBee ELan EMil EPfP LRHS MBri MGos MMuc MRav NLar NPri SCoo SEND SGol SPer SWvt WHar
'Shawnee'	CMac CWib MSwo MWat
§ 'Soleil d'Or'	CTri CWib EBee ECrN ELan EPfP IBoy LAst LBuc LRHS MAsh MBri MJak MMuc MRav NLar SEND SEWo SGol SHil SLPl SLim SLon SPer SPlb SWvt WHar
'Sparkler' (v)	CMac EHoe SMad
'Teton' 🏆H4	CMac ELan EPfP LAst LRHS MAsh MJak MSwo NEgg NWea SGol SHil SPoG SRms
'Ventoux Red'	SCoo
'Watereri'	NWea SLPl
'Yellow Sun'	see *P.* 'Soleil d'Or'

Pyrethropsis see *Rhodanthemum*

Pyrethrum see *Tanacetum*

Pyrola (*Ericaceae*)

rotundifolia	LEdu WHer

Pyrostegia (*Bignoniaceae*)

venusta	MOWG

Pyrrocoma (*Asteraceae*)

clementis	EBee

Pyrrosia (*Polypodiaceae*)

hastata	CMen
linearifolia 'Urakoryu Jishi' **new**	CMen
lingua	CMen WPGP
polydactyla	CMen
sheareri	CBty ISha

Pyrus ✿ (*Rosaceae*)

amygdaliformis var. ***cuneifolia***	CLnd EBee SCoo
calleryana 'Chanticleer' 🏆H4	Widely available
- 'Chanticleer' variegated (v)	CDul MAsh
communis (F)	CCVT CDul CTri ECrN LBuc NWea SPer SPlb WMou
- 'Abbé Fétel' (D)	SKee
- 'Bambinella' (D)	SKee
- 'Barland' (Perry)	CHab SKee

- 'Barnet' (Perry)	CHab
- 'Baronne de Mello' (D)	CTho SFam SKee
- 'Beech Hill' (F)	CDul EBee ECrN SGol SPer
- 'Belle Guérandaise' (D)	SKee
- 'Belle Julie' (D)	SKee
- 'Bergamotte Esperen' (D)	SKee
- 'Beth' (D) ♀H4	CAgr CDoC CHab CMac CSBt CTri CWib ECrN EPfP EPom ERea GTwe IArd LAst LBuc LRHS MBri MGos NLar NOra SDea SFam SKee SLim SPer WHar
- 'Beurré Alexandre Lucas' (D)	SKee
- 'Beurré Bedford' (D)	SKee
- 'Beurré Clairgeau' (C)	SKee
- 'Beurré d'Amanlis' (D)	SKee
- 'Beurré d'Anjou' (F) **new**	SKee
- 'Beurré d'Avalon' (D)	SKee
- 'Beurré de Beugny' (D)	SKee
- 'Beurré Diel' (D)	SKee
- 'Beurré Dumont' (D)	CAgr SFam
- 'Beurré Giffard' (D)	CAgr
- 'Beurré Hardy' (D) ♀H4	Widely available
- 'Beurré Mortillet' (D)	SKee
§ - 'Beurré Precoce Morettini' (D)	SDea
- 'Beurré Six' (D)	SKee
- 'Beurré Superfin' (D) ♀H4	CDul GTwe SFam SKee WHar
- 'Bianchettone' (D)	SKee
- 'Bishop's Thumb' (D)	SDea SKee
- 'Black Worcester' (C)	CDul GTwe SDea SFam SKee WHar WJas
- 'Blakeney Red' (Perry)	CHab SDea SKee WHar
- 'Blickling' (D)	SKee
- 'Brandy' (Perry)	CAgr CTho IArd NOra SDea SKee WHar
- 'Bristol Cross' (D)	CAgr CHab SKee
- 'Butt' (Perry)	CHab
- 'Calebasse Bosc' (D)	SKee
- 'Canal Red' (F) **new**	SKee
- 'Catillac' (C) ♀H4	CAgr CHab GTwe SFam SKee WHar
- 'Chaumontel' (D)	SKee
- 'Clapp's Favourite' (D)	CTho ECrN ELan SKee SVic
- 'Concorde'PBR (D) ♀H4	Widely available
- 'Conference' (D) ♀H4	Widely available
- 'Deacon's Pear' (D)	SDea
- Delbardélice = 'Delété'	LRHS
- 'Devoe' (D)	SDea
- 'Docteur Jules Guyot' (D)	CAgr SDea SKee
- 'Double de Guerre' (C/D)	SKee
- 'Doyenné Blanc' (F)	SKee
- 'Doyenné d'Été' (D)	ERea MCoo SFam SKee
- 'Doyenné du Comice' (D) ♀H4	Widely available
- 'Doyenné Georges Boucher' (D)	SKee
- 'Duchesse d'Angoulême' (D)	SKee
- 'Durondeau' (D)	ERea GTwe SDea SFam SKee
- 'Easter Beurré' (D)	SKee
- 'Emile d'Heyst' (D)	GQue GTwe MCoo SKee WHar
- 'Fertility' (D)	CLnd
- 'Fertility Improved'	see *P. communis* 'Improved Fertility'
- 'Fondante d'Automne' (D)	CAgr CTho SKee WHar
- 'Forelle' (D)	ERea SKee
- 'Gansel's Bergamot' (D)	SKee
- 'Gin' (Perry)	CHab
- 'Glou Morceau' (D)	CAgr ECrN ERea GTwe MCoo MWat SDea SFam SKee WHar
- 'Glow Red Williams' (D)	SFam
- 'Gorham' (D) ♀H4	CAgr CTho GTwe SFam SKee WHar
- 'Green Horse' (Perry)	CCAT CHab
- 'Hacon's Imcomparable' (D)	SKee
- 'Harley Gum' (F)	WHar
- 'Harrow Delight' (D)	SDea
- 'Harvest Queen' (D/C)	CAgr SDea
- 'Hellen's Early' (Perry)	CHab ERea IArd SKee WHar
- 'Hendre Huffcap' (Perry)	CAgr CCAT CHab CTho WHar
- 'Hessle' (D)	CAgr CHab GTwe NWea SDea SFam SKee
- 'Highland' (D)	SKee
- Humbug = 'Pysanka' (F)	EPom GQue LBuc MBri NOra WHar
§ - 'Improved Fertility' (D)	CAgr ERea SDea
- Invincible = 'Delwinor' (D/C)	CAgr CDul CSut CTho EPom LBuc LRHS MBri MCoo NOra SLim WHar
- 'Jargonelle' (D)	CAgr CDul CHab CTho GTwe SDea SFam SKee WHar
- 'Jeribasma' (F) **new**	SKee
- 'Joséphine de Malines' (D) ♀H4	CAgr ERea GTwe IArd SDea SFam SKee WHar
- 'Judge Amphlett' (Perry)	CTho WHar
- 'Kieffer' (C)	CAgr
- 'Laxton's Foremost' (D)	CAgr SKee
- 'Laxton's Satisfaction' (D)	SFam
- 'Légipont' (F)	CAgr
- Löffelbirne (F) **new**	CSut
- 'Louise Bonne of Jersey' (D) ♀H4	CAgr CMac CTri ECrN EPom ERea GTwe IArd LAst MGos NOra SDea SFam SKee WHar
- 'Marguérite Marillat' (D)	SDea SKee
- 'Marie-Louise' (D)	SKee WHar
- 'Merrylegs' (Perry) **new**	CHab
- 'Merton Pride' (D)	CAgr CLnd CTho GTwe IArd MCoo MWat SDea SFam SKee WHar
- 'Merton Star' (D)	SKee
- 'Moonglow'	CAgr ERea SDea
- 'Moorcroft' (Perry)	SKee
- 'Morettini'	see *P. communis* 'Beurré Precoce Morettini'
- 'Nouveau Poiteau' (C/D)	CAgr ECrN SKee
- 'Nuvar Celebration' (F)	SKee
- 'Nye Russet Bartlett' (F)	CAgr
- 'Oldfield' (Perry)	CHab
- 'Olivier de Serres' (D)	SKee
- 'Onward' (D) ♀H4	CAgr CDul CHab CLnd CTho CTri CWib ECrN EPom GTwe IArd LRHS MBri NEgg NLar NOra NWea SDea SFam SKee WHar
- 'Ovid' (D)	CAgr
§ - 'Packham's Triumph' (D)	CAgr CDoC CTri CWib ECrN GTwe LAst SDea SKee SVic WHar
- 'Parsonage' (Perry)	CHab
- 'Passe Crassane' (D)	SKee
- 'Pear Apple' (D)	SDea
- 'Penrhyn' (D)	WGwG
- 'Pero Nobile' (D)	SKee
I - 'Petite Poire' (F) **new**	CSut
- 'Pitmaston Duchess' (C/D) ♀H4	ECrN GTwe MCoo SDea SFam SKee WHar
- 'Précoce de Trévoux' (D)	WHar
- 'Red Comice' (D/C)	GTwe SKee
- 'Red Pear' (Perry)	CHab
- 'Red Sensation Bartlett' (D/C)	GTwe LBuc SKee
- 'Robin' (C/D)	ERea IArd SDea SKee

- 'Santa Claus' (D)	SDea SFam SKee
- 'Seckel' (D)	SFam SKee
- 'Shipova' (F)	CAgr WHar
- 'Sierra' (D)	CAgr
- 'Snowdon Queen' (D)	CHab WGwG
- 'Souvenir du Congrès' (D)	CAgr
- 'Swan's Egg' (D)	SKee
- 'Terrace Pearl' (D)	SPoG
- 'Tettenhall Dick' (C/D)	WHar
- 'Thompson's' (D)	SFam
- 'Thorn' (Perry)	CAgr CHab SKee WHar
- 'Triomphe de Vienne' (D)	SFam
- 'Triumph'	see *P. communis* 'Packham's Triumph'
- 'Uvedale's St Germain' (C)	SFam SKee
- 'Verbelu'	SKee
- 'Vicar of Winkfield' (C)	GTwe SDea SKee
- 'Williams' Bon Chrétien' (D/C) ♀H4	Widely available
- 'Williams' Red' (D/C)	GTwe LHop SKee
- 'Williams' Rouge Delbard' (F) new	EPom
- 'Winnal's Longdon' (Perry)	WHar
- 'Winter Nelis' (D)	CAgr CHab CTri CWib ECrN GTwe LRHS SDea SFam SKee WHar
cordata	CDul CTho
elaeagnifolia	MAsh
- var. ***kotschyana***	CDul SLim
- 'Silver Sails'	CLnd EMil MBri SCoo SSpi
fauriei	CTho
nivalis	CDul CEnd CLnd CTho EBee ECrN EPfP LRHS MBri MRav SCoo SPer
- 'Catalia'	CEnd MAsh MBri SCoo
pashia	EBee NLar
pyraster	CDul CHab WCot
pyrifolia '20th Century'	see *P. pyrifolia* 'Nijisseiki'
- 'Chojuro' (F)	LEdu
- 'Hosui' (F)	CAgr SVic
- 'Kosui' (F)	SVic
- 'Kumoi' (F)	ERea LRHS MCoo SDea WHar
§ - 'Nijisseiki' (F)	CDul SVic
- 'Shinko' (F)	CAgr
- 'Shinseiki' (F)	CAgr CLnd ERea SDea SKee WHar
- 'Shinsui' (F)	SDea SKee
* ***salicifolia*** var. ***orientalis***	CTho
- 'Pendula' ♀H4	Widely available
ussuriensis	CTho

Q

Qiongzhuea see *Chimonobambusa*

Quercus ✿ (*Fagaceae*)

NJM 09.181	WPGP
acerifolia	EPfP
acherdophylla	SBir WPGP
§ ***acuta***	CBcs
acutifolia	SBir
acutifolia × mexicana	SBir
acutissima	CBcs CDul CLnd CMCN EPfP SBir SGol
aegilops	see *Q. ithaburensis* subsp. *macrolepis*
affinis	EPfP SBir
agrifolia	CDul CMCN EBtc
alba	CDul CMCN
aliena	CDul CMCN SBir
alnifolia	CDul
arkansana	CMCN SBir
× ***atlantica***	SBir
austrina	CMCN SBir
× ***beadlei***	see *Q.* × *saulii*
× ***benderi***	SBir
berberidifolia	CMCN SBir
bicolor	CDul CLnd CMCN EPfP MBlu
× ***bimundorum***	SBir
§ - 'Crimschmidt'	CLnd EPfP MBlu MBri SGol
borealis	see *Q. rubra*
breweri	see *Q. garryana* var. *breweri*
buckleyi	CMCN SBir
× ***bushii***	CMCN EPfP MBlu MBri SBir WPat
- 'Seattle Trident'	EPfP MBlu
canariensis ♀H4	CLnd CMCN CTho EPfP SGol WMou WPGP
candicans	SBir
× ***capesii*** new	SBir
castanea	WPGP
castaneifolia	CDul CMCN
- 'Green Spire' ♀H4	CDul CMCN EBee EPfP IArd MBlu SBir SEND
cerris	CBcs CCVT CDoC CDul CLnd CMCN EBee ECrN EPfP MGos MMuc NWea SEND SGol SPer
- 'Afyon Lace'	MBlu SBir
§ - 'Argenteovariegata' (v)	CBcs CDul CEnd CMCN EBee ELan EPfP IArd MAsh MBlu MBri SBir SEND SMad WCot WPat
- 'Athena'	MBlu
- 'Curly Head'[PBR] new	SMad
- 'Marmor Star'	SEND
- 'Variegata'	see *Q. cerris* 'Argenteovariegata'
- 'Wodan'	MBlu
chenii	CDul CMCN SBir
chrysolepis	CMCN EGFP EPfP SBir
coccifera	CMCN SGol SSpi SVen WCot WPGP
- subsp. ***calliprinos***	SBir
coccinea	CBcs CDul CMCN CTho CTri EBee EPfP MBlu MMuc MWht NEgg NWea SBir SEWo SPer WPat
- 'Splendens' ♀H4	CDoC CDul CEnd CHll CJun CMCN CTri EBee ELan EPfP IArd MAsh MBlu MBri NLar SGol SMad SPer WPat
conspersa	SBir
crassifolia	WPGP
crassipes	SBir
Crimson Spire	see *Q.* × *bimundorum* 'Crimschmidt'
crispipilis	SBir
dalechampii	CMCN SBir
dentata	CMCN
- 'Carl Ferris Miller'	CBcs CDul CMCN EPfP LLHF MBlu MBri SBir WCot WMou WPGP WPat
- 'Pinnatifida'	CMCN EPfP IDee MBlu MPkF SMad WCot WPat
- 'Sir Harold Hillier'	MBlu MBri
- subsp. ***yunnanensis***	SBir
dolicholepis	CMCN SBir
'Doring's Zweizack'	SBir
douglasii	CMCN SSpi
- G 261	WPGP
dumosa	CMCN
- G 315	WPGP
- G 316	WPGP
durifolia	SBir

	× ***dysophylla***	CFil EBee WPGP
	elliottii	SBir
	ellipsoidalis	CDul CMCN SBir SGol
	– 'Hemelrijk'	EPfP IDee MBlu MBri SBir WPGP WPat
	emoryi	SBir
	× ***exacta***	SBir
	fabrei	CMCN SBir
	faginea	CDul CMCN EGFP WPGP
	– subsp. ***broteroi*** **new**	CMCN
	falcata	CMCN EBtc SBir
	– var. ***pagodifolia***	see *Q. pagoda*
	× ***fernaldii***	CMCN EPfP MBlu
	frainetto	CDul CMCN CTho EBee ECrN EPfP NWea SEND SGol SPer WMou
	– 'Hungarian Crown' ♀H4	CMCN EPfP MBlu MMuc SBir
	– 'Tortworth'	SMad WMou
	– 'Trump'	CMCN MBri
	franchetii	SBir
	gambelii	CBcs CMCN EBtc EGFP MPkF
	gambelii × ***macrocarpa***	EGFP
	garryana	CBcs CMCN WPGP
§	– var. ***breweri***	CMCN
	– var. ***fruticosa***	see *Q. garryana* var. *breweri*
	georgiana	CDul CMCN EPfP SBir
	gilva	CMCN SBir
	glabra	see *Lithocarpus glaber*
	glabrescens	WPGP
	glandulifera	see *Q. serrata* Thunb.
§	***glauca***	CBcs CDul CMCN EPfP NLar SAPC SBir WPGP
	graciliformis	SBir
	gravesii	CMCN EPfP SBir
	greggii	WPGP
	× ***hastingsii***	CMCN SBir
	× ***hawkinsiae***	SBir
	× ***haynaldiana***	SBir
	hemisphaerica	CMCN EPfP SBir
	× ***heterophylla***	CMCN EPfP SBir
	× ***hickelii***	CMCN EPfP SBir
	– 'Giesselhorst'	CDul
	hirtifolia	WPGP
	× ***hispanica*** 'Ambrozyana'	CDul CMCN
	– 'Bloemendaal'	MBri
	– 'Diversifolia'	CMCN EPfP MBlu
	– 'Fulhamensis'	CDul CMCN MBlu MBri SBir SEND WMou
§	– 'Lucombeana' ♀H4	CBcs CDul CHGN CMCN CSBt CTho EBee ELan EPfP IDee MBlu SBir SEND SPer
§	– 'Pseudoturneri'	CBcs CDul EBee ELan MBlu SEND
	– 'Suberosa'	CTho
	– 'Waasland Select'	IArd MBri NLar SBir WMou
	– 'Wageningen'	CDul CMCN MBri SBir
	hypoleucoides	CDul CMCN EPfP SBir
	ilex ♀H4	Widely available
	– 'Fordii'	SBir
	ilicifolia	CMCN EPfP SBir WPGP
	imbricaria	CDul CMCN EGFP EPfP SBir WPat
	incana Roxb.	see *Q. leucotrichophora*
§	***ithaburensis*** subsp. ***macrolepis***	CMCN LEdu SBir
	– – 'Hemelrijk Silver'	MBlu SBir WPat
	× ***jackiana***	EPfP
	john-tuckeri G 271	WPGP
	kelloggii	CBcs CDul CLnd CMCN EPfP WPGP
	× ***kewensis***	CMCN SBir WMou
	laevigata	see *Q. acuta*
	laevis	CDul CMCN EPfP SBir
	'Langtry'	SBir
§	***laurifolia***	CDul CMCN EPfP SBir
	laurina	SBir WPGP
§	***leucotrichophora***	CMCN LEdu SBir WPGP
	liaotungensis	see *Q. wutaishanica*
	× ***libanerris***	SBir
	– 'Rotterdam'	CMCN SBir
	libani	CMCN EPfP
	lobata	CMCN LEdu
	× ***lucombeana*** 'William Lucombe'	see *Q.* × *hispanica* 'Lucombeana'
	× ***ludoviciana***	CDul CMCN EPfP SBir
	lyrata	CDul CMCN SGol
	macranthera	CMCN EPfP SBir
	macrocarpa	CDul CMCN EGFP EPfP
	macrocarpa × ***robur***	EGFP
	macrolepis	see *Q. ithaburensis* subsp. *macrolepis*
	marilandica	CEnd CMCN EPfP IDee MBlu SBir
	'Mauri'	CDul MBlu MBri SBir
	mexicana	IArd SBir WPGP
§	***michauxii***	CDul CMCN EPfP MBlu SBir
	mongolica	CBcs MBlu
	– subsp. ***crispula*** var. ***grosseserrata***	CMCN
	muhlenbergii	CMCN MBlu MPkF SBir
	× ***mutabilis***	SBir
	myrsinifolia	see *Q. glauca*
	myrtifolia	SBir
	nigra	CDul CMCN NLar SBir
	– 'Beethoven'	MBlu SBir
I	– 'Nyewoodii'	SBir
	nuttallii	see *Q. texana*
	obtusa	see *Q. laurifolia*
	oglethorpensis	SBir
	oxyodon	SBir
	pacifica G 301	WPGP
	– G 305	WPGP
	– G 313	WPGP
§	***pagoda***	CMCN IGor SBir
	palustris ♀H4	CCVT CDoC CDul CLnd CMCN CTho ELan EPfP EWTr MAsh MBlu MMuc NEgg NLar NWea SBir SEWo SGol SPer WMou
	– 'Green Dwarf'	CMCN MBlu NLar SEWo SLim
	– Green Pillar = 'Pringreen' **new**	SGol
	– 'Isabel'	EPfP
	– 'Pendula'	CEnd CMCN
	– 'Silhouette'	CJun SBir
	– 'Swamp Pygmy'	CMCN EPfP MBlu
	– 'Windischleuba'	MBlu
	pannosa	SBir
	parvula var. ***parvula***	SBir
§	× ***pauciloba***	CMCN
	pedunculata	see *Q. robur*
	pedunculiflora	see *Q. robur* subsp. *pedunculiflora*
§	***petraea*** ♀H4	CDoC CDul CHab CLnd CTri ECrN EPfP GAbr MBlu NLar NWea SGol WMou
	– 'Acutiloba'	SBir
§	– 'Insecata'	CDul CEnd CMCN EPfP MBlu
	– 'Laciniata'	see *Q. petraea* 'Insecata'
	– Mespilifolia Group	CDul
§	– 'Purpurea'	CMCN MBlu NLar
	– 'Rubicunda'	see *Q. petraea* 'Purpurea'
§	***phellos***	CDul CLnd CMCN EBee EBtc EPfP MBlu NLar SBir SLPl

	phillyreoides	CBcs CDul CMCN EPfP SBir SLPl
	polymorpha	CMCN MPkF
	Pondaim Group	CMCN WMou
	pontica	CDul CMCN EPfP LLHF MBlu MPkF WPat
	prinus misapplied	see *Q. michauxii*
§	***prinus*** L.	CMCN EGFP EPfP WPGP
	pubescens	CDul CMCN SEND
	pumila Michx.	see *Q. prinus* L.
	pumila Walt.	see *Q. phellos*
	pungens	CMCN
	pyrenaica	CLnd CMCN CTho EBtc SEND
	- 'Pendula'	CMCN EPfP
	Regal Prince	see *Q.* × *warei* 'Long'
	rhysophylla	CDul CMCN EPfP IDee MBlu SBir WPGP
	- 'Maya'	CDul EBee ELan EPfP EUJe IArd MBri NLar SBir WMou WPat
	× ***riparia***	SBir
§	***robur*** ♀H4	Widely available
	- 'Argenteomarginata' (v)	CDul CMCN MBlu WPat
	- 'Atropurpurea'	EBee MPkF NWea
	- 'Compacta'	MBlu
	- 'Concordia'	CEnd CLnd CMCN EBtc ELan EPfP MBlu MPkF NLar SKHP
	- 'Dissecta'	CMCN
	- 'Facrist'	SBir
	- f. ***fastigiata***	CDoC CDul CLnd CTho EBee EPfP IArd IVic LHop MGos NWea SBir SGol SLPl SLim SPer
	- - 'Koster' ♀H4	CDul CMCN CMac CNWT CTri EPfP MBlu SBir SPoG
	- 'Filicifolia' misapplied	see *Q. robur* 'Pectinata'
	- 'Filicifolia'	CEnd WPat
	- var. ***haas***	CDul
	- - 'Cankiri'	SBir
	- 'Irtha'	EPfP
	- 'Menhir'	LLHF MAsh MBlu WCot WPat
§	- 'Pectinata'	EPfP MBlu
§	- subsp. ***pedunculiflora***	CMCN
	- 'Pendula'	CEnd CMCN MBlu
	- 'Purpurascens'	CDul CEnd CMCN
	- 'Purpurea'	MBlu
	- 'Raba'	CMCN
§	- 'Salfast'	CDul MBlu
	- 'Salicifolia Fastigiata'	see *Q. robur* 'Salfast'
	- 'Strypemonde'	CMCN
	- 'Timuki'	IArd MBlu WPat
	- f. ***variegata*** (v)	CJun
	- - 'Fürst Schwarzenburg' (v)	MBlu
	- 'Zeeland'	SBir
	robur × ***macrocarpa*** × ***virginiana***	SBir
	rotundifolia	CAgr CMCN EBee EPfP WPGP
§	***rubra*** ♀H4	Widely available
	- 'Aurea'	CEnd CJun CMCN EBee EPfP MBlu
	- 'Boltes Gold'	CJun MBlu MBri
	- 'Cyrille'	SBir
	- 'Magic Fire'	CMCN EBee EPfP MBlu SBir
	- 'Red Queen'	MBlu
*	- 'Sunshine'	CDul CMCN MBlu WPat
	× ***rudkinii*** new	EPfP
	rugosa	SBir
	× ***runcinata***	SBir
	salicina	WPGP
	× ***sargentii*** 'Thomas'	CDul EPfP MBri
	sartorii	SBir WPGP
§	× ***saulii***	CMCN SBir
	× ***schochiana***	EPfP MBlu MBri
	× ***schuettei***	SBir
	semecarpifolia	MBlu
§	***serrata*** Thunb.	CDul CMCN EPfP LEdu MBri SBir WPGP
	sessiliflora	see *Q. petraea*
	shumardii	CDul CMCN EPfP MBlu MBri NLar SBir SGol
	sinuata subsp. ***breviloba***	SBir
	stellata	CDul CMCN EGFP EPfP SBir
	suber	CAgr CBcs CDoC CDul CFil CMCN CTho EBee ELan EPfP IArd LEdu MGos MMuc MREP SAPC SEND WPGP
	- 'Sopron'	EPfP MBlu
§	***texana***	CMCN EPfP SBir
	- New Madrid Group	CDul EBee EPfP MBlu MBri SBir
	tomentella	SBir
	trojana	CMCN SBir
	tuberculata	WPGP
	turbinella	CMCN
	× ***turneri***	CDoC CMCN CTho EPfP MBri WMou
	- 'Pseudoturneri'	see *Q.* × *hispanica* 'Pseudoturneri'
	undulata Torr.	see *Q.* × *pauciloba*
	vacciniifolia	CMCN
	variabilis	CDul CMCN EPfP MPkF SGol
	velutina	CDul CJun CMCN CTho EGFP EPfP IVic NLar SBir
	- 'Albertsii'	CJun MBlu
	- 'Oakridge Walker'	MBlu
	- 'Rubrifolia'	CJun CMCN EPfP
	'Vilmoriana'	CMCN IArd IDee
	virginiana	CBcs CMCN EGFP SBir
	× ***warburgii***	EPfP
	× ***warei*** 'Chimney Fire'	EPfP MBri
§	- 'Long'	EBee EPfP MBlu MBri MPkF
	- 'Windcandle'	MBlu MBri SBir
	wislizeni	CDul CMCN NLar SBir
	- G 265	CBcs
§	***wutaishanica***	CBcs

Quillaja (*Quillajaceae*)

	saponaria	CArn CBcs CCCN IDee SPlb

quince see *Cydonia oblonga*

Quisqualis (*Combretaceae*)

	indica	CCCN MOWG

R

Racosperma see *Acacia*

× *Ramberlea* (*Gesneriaceae*)

	sp. new	GKev
	'Inchgarth'	WAbe

Ramonda (*Gesneriaceae*)

§	***myconi*** ♀H4	CLAP ECho EWes LLHF NSla SChF SRms WAbe
	- var. ***alba***	CLAP ECho WThu
	- 'Jim's Shadow'	WAbe
	- 'Rosea'	LLHF
	nathaliae ♀H4	CPBP ECho WAbe WThu
	- 'Alba'	CLAP NSla WAbe
	pyrenaica	see *R. myconi*

	serbica	WThu

Ranunculus (*Ranunculaceae*)

	abnormis	WAbe
	aconitifolius	ECho GCra GMaP NLar SHar SWat WHal WMnd WMoo
	- 'Flore Pleno' (d) ♀^{H4}	CCon CMac CSpe EBee ECho EPPr EPfP GAbr GBBs GBin GCal GMaP IFoB IGor IPot LEdu LRHS MLHP MRav NBir NPnk SRms WBor WCot WHer WMoo WPnP WSHC
	acris	CHab NBir NMir NPer WSFF
	- subsp. ***acris*** 'Stevenii'	EPPr IGor LPla SDix WHal
	- 'Citrinus'	CElw LLWG LRHS MHol NCGa WCot WHal WMoo WPtf
	- 'Flore Pleno' (d) ♀^{H4}	CElw CWCL EBee ECho ELan EPfP GAbr GBin GQue LEdu LLWG LPot LRHS MCot MRav NBid NBro NGdn NRya NWad SEND SPoG SRms WHil WMoo WSHC XLum
	- 'Hedgehog'	ECho EPPr MMHG
	- 'Sulphureus'	CBre WHal
	alpestris	ECho LLHF NRya NSla
	amplexicaulis	EBee ELon GMaP NHar NSla
	aquatilis	CBAq CWat EHon MSKA MWts SWat WMAq WSFF
	× ***arendsii*** 'Moonlight'	CElw CRDP LRHS
	asiaticus	ERCP
	baurii	ECho
	bilobus	WAbe
§	***bulbosus*** 'F.M. Burton'	GBuc NRya WCot
	- ***farreri***	see *R. bulbosus* 'F.M. Burton'
	- 'Speciosus Plenus'	see *R. constantinopolitanus* 'Plenus'
	bullatus new	WCot
	calandrinioides ♀$^{H2-3}$	ECho EWes IFoB NBir WAbe WCot
	SF 137	WCot
§	***constantinopolitanus***	GCal MNrw MRav NBid NBro WCot
	'Plenus' (d)	WMoo
	cortusifolius	SWat
	crenatus	ECho NRya
	creticus	ECho
	ficaria	CArn CTri ESwi MHer SEND WHer WOut WSFF WShi
	- 'Aglow in the Dark'	CDes CHid
	- var. ***albus***	CHid CSam ELon LEdu NRya WOut
	- anemone-centred	see *R. ficaria* 'Collarette'
	- 'Art Nouveau'	CDes
	- 'Ashen Primrose'	EBee
§	- var. ***aurantiacus***	ECho MHer NLar NRya SPhx SRms
	'Bowles's Double'	see *R. ficaria* 'Double Bronze', 'Picton's Double'
	- 'Brambling'	CBre CHid CLAP ECho LEdu NLar SBch
	- 'Brazen Child'	SHar
	- 'Brazen Daughter'	ECho
	- 'Brazen Hussy'	Widely available
	- 'Broadleas Black'	ECho
	- subsp. ***bulbilifer*** 'Chedglow'	WCot
	- 'Chocolate Cream'	ECho
§	- subsp. ***chrysocephalus***	CDes ELon IFro SBch WCot
	- - 'Pencarn' new	CFis
§	- 'Collarette' (d)	CHid ECho ELon GBuc IGor LEdu MHer NBir NLar NRya WOut
	- 'Coppernob'	CHid ECho ELon SBch WCot
	- 'Cupreus'	see *R. ficaria* var. *aurantiacus*
	- 'Damerham' (d)	CHid
§	- 'Double Bronze' (d)	CHid ECho GBuc LEdu MHer NBir NLar NRya SHar

§	- 'Double Mud' (d)	CHid CLAP ECho GAbr GBuc IFro LEdu NLar NRya SHar WHal
	- double, cream-flowered	see *R. ficaria* 'Double Mud'
	- - yellow-flowered	see *R. ficaria* Flore Pleno Group
	- - green-eyed (d)	CHid LEdu
	- 'Dusky Maiden'	ECho NLar SBch
	- 'E.A. Bowles'	see *R. ficaria* 'Collarette'
	- 'Elan' (d)	CDes EBee MMoz
§	- Flore Pleno Group (d)	CHid CTri ECho ELan ELon EPPr GAbr NRya NSti SBch SRms WCot
	- 'Fried Egg'	ECho
	- 'Granby Cream'	ECho
	- 'Green Mantle'	ECho
	- 'Green Petal'	CHid ECho EPPr GBuc LEdu MCot MHer NBir NRya WHal WHer
	- 'Holly'	see *R. ficaria* 'Holly Green'
§	- 'Holly Green'	ECho
	- 'Hyde Hall'	ECho NLar SBch
	- 'Jake Perry'	EBee MNrw
	- 'Jane's Dress'	CHid
	- 'Ken Aslet Double' (d)	CDes EBee LEdu MHer NLar WHal
	- 'Lambrook Black'	WHer
	- 'Lambrook Variegated' (v)	CFis EPPr
	- 'Lemon Queen'	CHid
	- 'Leo'	MNrw
	- subsp. ***major***	see *R. ficaria* subsp. *chrysocephalus*
	- 'Mobled Jade'	CHid
	- 'Monksilver'	IFro
	- 'Newton Abbot'	CBre
	- 'Old Master'	NCGa WCot
	- 'Orange Sorbet'	LEdu MNrw
§	- 'Picton's Double' (d)	MNrw
	- 'Primrose'	CHid NRya
	- 'Primrose Elf'	EBee
	- 'Ragamuffin' (d)	CDes EBee
	- 'Randall's White'	CFis EBee EPfP NCGa SHar
	- 'Richard and Val'	WCot
	- 'Salad Bowl' (d)	ECho
	- 'Salmon's White'	CBre ECho ELon EPPr NBir NLar NRya SHar WHal
	- 'Sheldon Silver'	CHid
	- 'Silver Collar'	LEdu
	- 'Single Cream'	MNrw
	- 'Tortoiseshell'	CHid EPPr
	- 'Wisley Double'	see *R. ficaria* 'Double Bronze'
	- 'Wisley White'	NSti
	- 'Witchampton'	CDes EBee
	- 'Yaffle'	CFis CHid EBee ECho
	flammula	CBAq CHab CRow CWat EHon EWay MSKA MWts SWat WPnP
	- subsp. ***minimus***	CRow
	gouanii	NRya
	gramineus ♀^{H4}	CCon CSpe ECho GBin GMaP LRHS NRya SMrm SRms XEll
	- 'Pardal'	WCot
	hederaceus	LLWG
	illyricus	EPPr LRHS NRya WAbe WHal
	kochii	ECho EPot MNrw WCot
	lanuginosus	EPPr
	lingua	SPlb
	- 'Grandiflorus'	CBAq CRow EHon MSKA NPer SWat WHal WMAq WPnP
	lyallii	EBee GKev
	millefoliatus	CPBP ECho GBuc WAbe
	montanus double-flowered (d)	SHar WCot
	- 'Molten Gold' ♀^{H4}	EBee ECho GMaP MMHG MRav
	nivicola	WCot
	parnassiifolius	LLHF MNrw WAbe

platanifolius	EBee LPla
'Purple Heart' (d)	EPfP
repens 'Buttered Popcorn' (v)	CRow EBee LLWG NLar WMoo
- 'Cat's Eyes' (v)	EBee
- 'Gloria Spale'	CBre CRow
- var. ***pleniflorus*** (d)	CBre CRow LLWG SRot
- 'Snowdrift' (v)	EBee
- 'Timothy Clark' (d)	CBre
seguieri	ECho LHop LLHF LRHS WAbe
serbicus	WSHC
speciosus 'Flore Pleno'	see *R. constantinopolitanus* 'Plenus'

Ranzania (*Berberidaceae*)

japonica	WCru

Raoulia (*Asteraceae*)

australis misapplied	see *R. hookeri*
australis ambig.	NSla SMad
australis Hook.f. ex Raoul	EDAr EPot GKev ITim MAsh MWat
§ - Lutescens Group	ECho
haastii	ECou
§ ***hookeri***	CMea ECho EPot ITim MAsh SPlb SRms WAbe
- var. ***laxa***	EWes
× ***loganii***	see × *Leucoraoulia loganii*
lutescens	see *R. australis* Lutescens Group
petriensis	WAbe
× ***petrimia*** 'Margaret Pringle'	WAbe
subsericea	EWes
tenuicaulis	SPlb

raspberry see *Rubus idaeus*

Ratibida (*Asteraceae*)

columnifera	EPfP SPet SPhx
- f. ***pulcherrima***	CSpe EPfP LRHS SPet SPhx XLum
- - 'Red Midget'	CSpe LHop LRHS SPet SPhx
pinnata	CSam EPfP LSRN MNFA NBir SMad SPet SPhx SPlb WCot WMnd WSHC XLum

Ravenala (*Strelitziaceae*)

madagascariensis	EAmu SPlb XBlo

Ravenea (*Arecaceae*)

rivularis	CCCN EAmu XBlo

Rechsteineria see *Sinningia*

redcurrant see *Ribes rubrum* (R)

Rehderodendron (*Styracaceae*)

macrocarpum	CBcs WPGP

Rehmannia (*Plantaginaceae*)

angulata misapplied	see *R. elata*
§ ***elata*** ♀H2	CCon CHel CSam CSpe CWCL ELan EPfP LAst LBMP LHop LLWP LRHS MHer MNHC NOrc SDys SMrm SRms WHil XLum
glutinosa ♀H3	CSpe
piasezkii	WPGP

Reineckea (*Asparagaceae*)

§ ***carnea***	CCon CExl CHel CHid CHll ELan EPPr GBin GCal GKev IMou LEdu LRHS MMuc MPie NSti SDys SEND SPlb WCot WCru WPGP WPtf XLum
- B&SWJ 4808	ELon WCru
- SDR 330	EPPr GKev
- 'Baoxing Booty'	IMou WCru
- 'Crûg's Broadleaf'	WCru
- 'Variegata' (v)	EShb WCot
aff. ***carnea*** from Sichuan	WCot

Reinwardtia (*Linaceae*)

§ ***indica***	CCCN CExl CHll EShb
trigyna	see *R. indica*

Remusatia (*Araceae*)

hookeriana	GBin
- B&SWJ 2529	WCru

Reseda (*Resedaceae*)

alba	MHer
lutea	SIde SRms
luteola	CHab CHby GPoy MHer MNHC WHer WHfH WSFF

Restio (*Restionaceae*)

paniculatus	CCCN CDTJ
subverticillatus	CHEx
tetraphyllus	CCon CHel CHid CTsd EBee SPlb SPoG

Reynoutria see *Fallopia*

Rhamnus (*Rhamnaceae*)

alaternus	XSen
§ - 'Argenteovariegata' (v) ♀H4	Widely available
- 'Variegata'	see *R. alaternus* 'Argenteovariegata'
cathartica	CCVT CDul CHab CLnd CTri ECrN EPfP EShb LBuc NLar NWea SEWo WMou WSFF
frangula	see *Frangula alnus*
imeretina	EBee WCot WPGP WPat
pallasii	NLar
taquetii	NLar

Rhaphidophora (*Araceae*)

decursiva new	XBlo

× *Rhaphiobotrya* (*Rosaceae*)

§ 'Coppertone'	EPfP SAPC SEND

Rhaphiolepis (*Rosaceae*)

× ***delacourii***	CWib EBee ECrN ELan EPfP LAst SEND SRms
- 'Coates' Crimson'	CDoC CTsd EBee ELan EPfP IVic LHop LRHS MAsh WPat WSHC
- Enchantress = 'Moness'	CTsd ELan EPfP LRHS MAsh MRav SLon
- 'Pink Cloud'	EPfP LRHS
- 'Spring Song'	SLon
indica	CBcs SEND
- B&SWJ 8405	WCru
- 'Coppertone'	see × *Rhaphiobotrya* 'Coppertone'
- Springtime = 'Monme'	CBcs EPfP IVic LRHS
umbellata ♀H2-3	CBcs CDoy CHEx CTri CWib EBee ELan EPfP LAst LHop LRHS MAsh SBrt SEND SHil SLon SVen WPGP WPat WSHC
- f. ***ovata***	WCot
- - B&SWJ 4706	WCru

Rhaphithamnus (*Verbenaceae*)

	cyanocarpus	see *R. spinosus*
§	***spinosus***	CBcs CMCN EBee EPfP GAbr LEdu LRHS

Rhapidophyllum (*Arecaceae*)

	hystrix	CBrP

Rhapis ✿ (*Arecaceae*)

§	***excelsa*** ♀H1	CCCN EAmu XBlo
	- 'Variegata' (v)	EAmu

Rhazya (*Apocynaceae*)

	orientalis	see *Amsonia orientalis*

Rheum ✿ (*Polygonaceae*)

	GWJ 9329 from Sikkim	WCru
	SDR 5004	GKev
§	'Ace of Hearts'	Widely available
	'Ace of Spades'	see *R.* 'Ace of Hearts'
	acuminatum	CSpe
	- HWJCM 252	WCru
	- HWJK 2354	WCru
	- PAB 2487	LEdu WPGP
	alexandrae	ESwi EWTr EWes GBin GCal GKev LEdu MMHG NLar SBHP SDix
	- SDR 2924	EBee
	- SDR 6031	GKev
	altaicum PAB 1055 new	LEdu
§	***australe***	CAgr CArn CCon CSpe EBee GCal LEdu NBro NLar WCot
	'Cally Dwarf'	GCal
	'Cally Giant'	EBee GCal
	× ***cultorum***	see *R.* × *hybridum*
	delavayi	GCal NLar
	emodi	see *R. australe*
§	× ***hybridum***	SEND
	- from Burston Hall	LRHS
	- from Gledhill	LRHS
	- from Hartley	LRHS
	- from Holt	LRHS
	- from Isle of Ely Horticultural Institute	LRHS
	- from Maldon, Essex	LRHS
	- from Ramsden	LRHS
	- from Sherburn Park	LRHS
	- 'Amerikanske Kaempe'	LRHS
	- 'Amstel Seedling'	LRHS
	- 'Appleton's Forcing'	LRHS
	- 'Baker's All Season'	LRHS
	- 'Bedford Scarlet'	LRHS
	- 'Brandy Carr Scarlet'	MRav
	- 'Brown's Crimson'	LRHS
	- 'Brown's Red'	LRHS
	- 'Canada Red'	GTwe LRHS
	- 'Carter's Forcing'	LRHS
	- 'Cawood Advance'	LRHS
	- 'Cawood Castle'	LRHS
	- 'Cawood Delight'	GTwe LRHS
	- 'Cawood Ensign'	LRHS
	- 'Cawood Oak'	LRHS
	- 'Champagne'	CAgr EPfP EPom GTwe LBuc LRHS NPri SPer
*	- 'Champagne Rood'	LRHS
	- 'Collis's Ruby'	LRHS
	- 'Coutt's Red Stick'	LRHS
	- 'Crimson Queen'	LRHS
	- 'Crimson Wine'	LRHS
	- 'Cutbush's Seedling'	LRHS
	- 'Dawe's Challenge'	LRHS
	- 'Daw's Champion'	GTwe LRHS
	- 'Donkere Bloedrede Zoet'	LRHS
	- 'Drust's Red'	LRHS
	- 'Early Champagne'	LRHS
	- 'Early Cherry'	LRHS
	- 'Early Devon'	LRHS
	- 'Early Mitchell'	LRHS
	- 'Early Superb'	LRHS
	- 'Early Victoria'	LRHS
	- 'Exhibition Red'	LRHS
	- 'Fenton's Special'	CTri GTwe LRHS MCoo MRav
*	- 'Frambozenrood Limburg'	LRHS
	- 'Fulton's Strawberry Surprise' ♀H4	GTwe LRHS
	- 'German Wine'	LRHS
	- 'Giant Grooveless Crimson'	LRHS
	- 'Glaskin's Perpetual'	CAgr CWib EPfP LBuc LRHS NPri WHar
	- 'Goliath'	LRHS MCoo
	- 'Grandad's Favorite' ♀H4	LRHS
	- 'Green Jam'	LRHS
	- 'Greengage'	GTwe LRHS
	- 'Guardsman'	LRHS
	- 'Hammond's Early'	GTwe LRHS
	- 'Harbinger'	GTwe LRHS
	- 'Hawke's Champagne' ♀H4	GTwe LRHS WCot
	- 'Holsteiner Blut'	EPfP LRHS NLar SPoG
	- 'Irish Apple'	LRHS
	- 'Kentville'	LRHS
	- 'Larne'	LRHS
	- 'Laxton's No 1'	LRHS
	- 'Linnaeus'	LRHS
	- 'Livingstone' PBR	LRHS
	- 'Mac Red' ♀H4	GTwe
	- 'Marshall's Early'	LRHS
	- 'McDonald'	LRHS
	- 'Merton's Banner'	LRHS
	- 'Merton's Broadleaf'	LRHS
	- 'Merton's Foremost'	LRHS
	- 'Merton's Yardstick'	LRHS
	- 'Mikoot'	LRHS
	- 'Mira'	LRHS
	- 'Mitchell's Early Albert'	LRHS
	- 'Mitchell's Royal Albert'	LRHS
	- 'Mrs McKenzie'	LRHS
	- 'Perpetual'	LRHS
	- 'Pink Champagne'	EPfP GQue
	- 'Prince Albert'	GTwe LRHS NEgg
*	- 'Ras Versteeg'	LRHS
	- 'Raspberry Red'	EPfP EPom LBuc LRHS NPri
	- 'Red Champagne'	ELan EPfP LBuc LRHS
	- 'Red Prolific'	GTwe
	- 'Red Victoria'	LRHS
	- 'Reed's Champagne'	LRHS
	- 'Reed's Early Superb' ♀H4	GTwe LRHS
	- 'Reed's Red'	LRHS
	- 'Riverside Giant'	LRHS
	- 'Rosenhagen'	LRHS
	- 'Ruby'	LRHS
	- 'Saint Kevin'	LRHS
	- 'Seedling Le Grice'	LRHS
	- 'Seedling Piggot'	LRHS
	- 'Stein's Champagne' ♀H4	GTwe LRHS
	- 'Stockbridge'	LRHS
	- 'Stockbridge Arrow'	CMac CSut CTri EMil GTwe LRHS NEgg

– 'Stockbridge Bingo'	GTwe LRHS
– 'Stockbridge Cropper'	LRHS
– 'Stockbridge Emerald'	GTwe LRHS
– 'Stockbridge Guardsman'	GTwe
– 'Stockbridge Harbinger'	LRHS
– 'Stockbridge Smith'	LRHS
– 'Stott's Monarch'	LRHS
– 'Strawberry'	GTwe LRHS NBir
– 'Strawberry Taylor'	LRHS
– 'Sutton's Cherry Red'	GTwe LRHS
– 'The Appleton'	LRHS
– 'The Sutton'	CWib EPfP GTwe LRHS
– 'Timperley Early' ♀^{H4}	CDoC CMac CSBt CTri CWib ELan EMil EPfP EPom GTwe IBoy LRHS LSRN MGos MMuc MRav NEgg NPri SCoo SDea SEND SKee SLim SPer SPoG WHar
– 'Tingley Cherry'	GTwe
– 'Valentine'	LRHS
– 'Victoria'	CAgr CDoC CMac CSBt CTri CWib ELan ELau EMil EPfP EPom GTwe LBuc LRHS LSRN MCoo MGos MHer MNHC NPri SDea SLim SPoG SVic WGwG WHar
– 'Victoria 2'	LAst
– 'Vinrabarber Svenborg'	LRHS
– 'Vroege Engelse'	LRHS
– 'Zwolle Seedling'	GTwe
kialense	CBct EBee LEdu NBid NSti WPGP WWEG
nobile	CHid
officinale	CArn CBct CHEx GCal LRHS MBri SIde SWat
palmatum	CArn CBcs CHel EBee ELan EPfP EWTr GCra LRHS MGos MRav NGdn SWat
– 'Atropurpureum'	see *R. palmatum* 'Atrosanguineum'
– 'Atropurpureum Dissectum' **new**	IBoy
§ – 'Atrosanguineum' ♀^{H4}	CBct CCon CMac CMea ELan EPfP EShb EUJe GCal IFro LBMP LRHS MBri MGos MMuc MRav NBid NBro NEgg NWad SEND SPlb SWat WCru WMnd
– 'Bowles's Crimson'	CBct LRHS MBri MGos MRav NBid WCot
– 'Hadspen Crimson'	CBct WCot
– 'Red Herald'	CBct LRHS WCot WWEG
– 'Rubrum'	CBct LRHS NBir
– 'Savill'	LRHS MBri MRav WWEG
– var. ***tanguticum***	Widely available
rhaponticum	NLar
ribes	WCot WCru
spiciforme	CFil WPGP
tataricum	EBee LEdu

Rhinanthus (*Orobanchaceae*)

minor	CHab

Rhodanthemum (*Asteraceae*)

'African Eyes'	ECho ELan EPfP LRHS MBrN MBri MGos MHol NPri SPoG SRot SVen WNew
Agadir	LBuc SPoG
§ ***atlanticum***	ECho EWes
§ ***catananche***	CCCN ECho EPot EWes MBNS SRot WAbe
§ – 'Tizi-n-Test'	ECho
– 'Tizi-n-Tichka'	CPBP ECho EHyd EWes LHop LRHS
§ ***gayanum***	CCCN ECho EWes
– 'Flamingo'	see *R. gayanum*
– 'Pretty in Pink' **new**	WHlf
§ ***hosmariense*** ♀^{H4}	CCCN ECho EHyd ELan EPfP EPot GMaP LHop LPio LRHS MCot MHol MWat SCoo SEND SPer SPoG SRms SRot WAbe WHoo WIce
Marrakech	see *R.* Moondance
§ Moondance = 'Usrhod0701'	LBuc NPri SPoG
Tangier	SPoG

Rhodiola (*Crassulaceae*)

CC 5344	GKev
crassipes	see *R. wallichiana*
cretinii HWJK 2283	WCru
§ ***fastigiata***	GCal WCot WThu
– BWJ 7544	SKHP WCru
§ ***heterodonta***	ELan LRHS MRav WCot
himalensis misapplied	see *R.* 'Keston'
himalensis (D. Don) Fu	CTri
integrifolia	EDAr
subsp. ***integrifolia***	
§ ***ishidae***	CTri
§ 'Keston'	CTri
kirilovii var. ***rubra***	EBee
§ ***pachyclados***	ECho ECtt EDAr EHyd EUJe GBin GJos GKev GMaP LBee LRHS MHer MMuc NBir NRya NWad SEND SPlb SRot SWvt WAbe XLum
aff. ***purpureoviridis*** BWJ 7544	WCru
§ ***rosea***	CArn CElw EBee ECho EDAr ELan EPfP GCal GJos GPoy LRHS MCot MHer MLHP MNHC MRav NBid NBir NDov NGdn NLar SPer SPoG SRms WCAu WCFE WCot
semenovii	NLar
sinuata HWJK 2318	WCru
– HWJK 2326	WCru
§ ***trollii***	ECho EHyd EPot LHop LRHS SPlb WAbe
§ ***wallichiana***	MLHP NBid
– GWJ 9263	WCru
– HWJK 2352	WCru
§ ***yunnanensis*** BWJ 7941 **new**	WCru

Rhodochiton (*Plantaginaceae*)

§ ***atrosanguineus*** ♀$^{H1-2}$	CBcs CCCN CEnd CHll CSpe CWCL ELan EPfP GBee LBuc LRHS MPie NPri SLon SPer SPoG
volubilis	see *R. atrosanguineus*

Rhodocoma (*Restionaceae*)

arida	CCCN
capensis	CAbb CCCN CCon CTsd GCal LRHS
gigantea	CCCN CCon CPrp SPlb

Rhododendron ✿ (*Ericaceae*)

sp.	GKin SEWo
'A.J. Ivens'	see *R.* 'Arthur J. Ivens'
'Abegail'	SLdr
aberconwayi	LMil
– 'His Lordship'	GGGa LMil MSnd
acrophilum (V)	GGGa
'Addy Wery' (EA) ♀$^{H3-4}$	CDoC ECho GKin MGos SPer
adenogynum	GGGa LMil MSnd

§	- Adenophorum Group F 20444	SLdr
	adenophorum	see *R. adenogynum* Adenophorum Group
	adenopodum	GGGa MSnd
	adenosum	GGGa
	'Admiral Piet Hein'	SReu SSta
	'Adonis' (EA/d)	CBcs CMac LMil NLar SLdr
	'Adriaan Koster' (hybrid)	SHea
	'Advance' (EA)	MSnd SLdr
	aeruginosum	see *R. campanulatum* subsp. *aeruginosum*
	aganniphum	MSnd
	- var. ***flavorufum***	MSnd
	- 'Rusty'	MSnd
	'Aksel Olsen'	CTri LRHS MAsh
	'Aladdin' (EA)	CMac ECho NEgg SLdr
	'Aladdin' (*auriculatum* hybrid)	GGGa SSta
	Aladdin Group	SReu
	'Albatross'	SSta
	Albatross Group	SReu
	'Albatross Townhill Pink'	LMil
	'Albert Schweitzer' ♀H4	CDoC CWri LMil NLar NSoo SLdr SLim
	albertsenianum	GGGa MSnd
	albrechtii (A)	GGGa IVic LMil
	- Whitney form (A)	LMil WMoo
	'Alexander' (EA) ♀H4	IVic LMil LSRN MGos NLar
	'Alfred'	GGGa
	'Alice' (EA)	SLdr
	'Alice' (hybrid) ♀H4	CMac CWri LMil SHea SLdr
	'Alison Johnstone'	GGGa GGal SHea WThu
	Alison Johnstone Group	CBcs LMil MSnd SLdr SReu
	'All Gold' **new**	GGGa
	'Alpine Gem'	IVic
	Alpine Gem Group	GQui
	'Altaclerense'	LMil
	'Altair' (K)	SHea
§	***alutaceum*** var. ***alutaceum*** Globigerum Group	GGGa
§	- var. ***iodes***	MSnd
§	- var. ***russotinctum***	MSnd
	- - R 158	SLdr
§	- - Triplonaevium Group	GGGa
	amagianum (A)	LMil
	'Amalfi' **new**	LMil
	Amalfi Group	LMil
	'Amber Rain' (A)	SHea
	ambiguum	LMil MSnd
I	- 'Crosswater'	LMil
	- 'Golden Summit'	GGGa
	- 'Jane Banks'	LMil
	'Ambrosia' (EA)	CSBt
	'Ambush'	SHea
	'America'	MJak SHea
	'Amethyst' (EA) **new**	GGal
	'Amity'	CWri ECho LMil MAsh MBri MLea MMuc MSnd NPCo SLdr WGwG
	'Amoenum Coccineum' (EA/d)	CBcs MSnd SLdr SReu
	Amor Group	SHea SLdr
	'Amoretto'	IVic
	'Anah Kruschke'	MAsh SPoG
	'Analin'	see *R.* 'Anuschka'
	'Anatta Gold' (V)	GGGa
	'Anchorite' (EA)	SLdr
	'Androcles'	LMil
	'Angelo'	LMil SSta
	Angelo Group	CWri LMil SReu
	Anita Group	SHea SLdr
	'Anna Baldsiefen'	ELon GKin MGos SLim SPoG
	'Anna Kauser'	MSnd
	'Anna Rose Whitney'	CBcs CTri CWri LRHS MAsh MGos MJak NEgg SLim SPer
	'Annabella' (K) ♀H4	NLar SReu SSta
	annae	GGGa LMil
	'Anne Frank' (EA)	MGos SPoG
	'Anne Teese'	GGGa LMil
	'Annegret Hansmann'	GGGa
	'Anneke' (A)	EPfP LMil NHol NLar SPer SPoG SReu SSta
	anthopogon	LMil
	- from Marpha Meadow, Nepal	WThu
	- 'Betty Graham'	GGGa
	- subsp. ***hypenanthum*** 'Annapurna'	GGGa ITim WAbe
§	***anthosphaerum***	GGGa
	'Antilope' (Vs)	CBcs CWri ECho LMil MAsh MGos MLea MMuc NEgg NLar SHea SLdr SPer SReu SSta
	'Antonio'	LMil
§	'Anuschka'	MAsh MMuc
	anwheiense	GGGa SHea
	aperantum	GGGa
	apodectum	see *R. dichroanthum* subsp. *apodectum*
	'Apple Blossom' ambig.	CMac GKin
	'Apple Blossom' Wezelenburg (M)	SLdr
N	'Appleblossom' (EA)	see *R.* 'Ho-o'
	'Apricot Blaze' (A)	NHol SReu SSta
	'Apricot Fantasy'	LMil
	'Apricot Surprise'	CTri MAsh
	'April Chimes'	WThu
	'April Showers' (A)	LMil
	'Aquamarin'	IVic
	'Arabesk' (EA)	GKin LMil MAsh MBri MGos SHil SLdr
	araiophyllum	LMil
	- KR 7483	LMil
	arborescens (A)	GGGa LMil
	- pink-flowered (A)	LMil
	arboreum	CDoC CHEx GGGa IDee LMil MSnd SReu
	- B&SWJ 2244	WCru
	- subsp. ***arboreum***	MSnd
	- subsp. ***cinnamomeum***	CDoC GGGa IDee LMil MSnd SLdr
	- - var. ***album***	GGGa MSnd SReu
	- - 'Everest Reunion'	LMil
	- - var. ***roseum***	GGGa
	- - - 'Tony Schilling'	GKin LMil SReu SSta
	- subsp. ***delavayi***	GGGa LMil MSnd
	- - var. ***delavayi***	GLin
	- - var. ***peramoenum*** AC 5577	GLin
	- 'Heligan'	SReu
§	- subsp. ***nilagiricum***	GLin
	- var. ***roseum***	SHea
§	- subsp. ***zeylanicum***	GGGa
	'Arctic Fox' (EA)	GGGa
	'Arctic Regent' (K)	GQui
	'Arctic Tern' ♀H4	CDoC CSBt CTri ECho EPot GQui LMil MGos MLea NLar NSoo SLdr SPer WThu
	'Ardeur' **new**	NSoo
§	***argipeplum***	GGGa MSnd

	'Argosy' ♀H4	LMil SReu
	argyrophyllum	MSnd SLdr
	- subsp. ***argyrophyllum***	GGGa SLdr
§	- subsp. ***hypoglaucum***	GGGa MSnd
	- subsp. ***nankingense***	GGGa
	- - 'Chinese Silver' ♀H4	CDoC GGGa LMil MSnd SLdr SReu
	arizelum	GGGa LMil MSnd
	- subsp. ***arizelum*** Rubicosum Group	GGGa LMil
	'Arkona'	IVic
	armitii (V)	GGGa
	'Arneson Gem' (M)	CDoC GGGa LMil MMuc NLar SLdr
	'Arneson Ruby' (K)	GGGa
	'Arpege' (Vs)	LMil NLar SLdr SReu
	'Arthur Bedford'	CBcs CSBt SLdr SReu
§	'Arthur J. Ivens'	SLdr
	'Arthur Osborn'	SLdr
	'Arthur Stevens'	MSnd SLdr
	'Asa-gasumi' (Kurume) (EA)	SLdr
	asterochnoum	GGGa MSnd
	'Astrid'	IVic LMil LSRN
	'Astronaut' (K)	SHea
	atlanticum (A)	GGGa LMil SLdr SReu SSta
	- 'Seaboard' (A)	LMil
	Augfast Group	CHel
	augustinii	CWri GGGa GGal LMil MLea MSnd NLar SLdr SSpi SSta
§	- subsp. ***chasmanthum***	GGGa
	- compact EGM 293	LMil
§	- 'Electra' ♀H3-4	GGGa
	- Electra Group	CDoC LMil MLea SLdr
	- Exbury form	GGGa LMil SReu
§	- subsp. ***hardyi***	GGGa
*	- 'Trewithen'	GGGa LMil
I	- 'Werrington'	CExl SLdr SReu
§	***aureum***	GGGa WThu
	auriculatum	GGGa LMil MSnd SLdr SSta
	- Reuthe's form	SReu
	auriculatum × ***hemsleyanum***	GGGa
	auritum	SLdr
	'Aurora' (K)	SLdr
	austrinum (A)	LMil NLar
	- yellow-flowered (A)	LMil
	Autumn Magic	see *R.* 'Herbstzauber'
	'Avalanche' ♀H4	LMil
	Avocet Group	LMil
	'Award'	LMil
	'Ayah'	LMil
	'Aya-kammuri' (EA)	SLdr
	'Ayton'	LMil
	Azor Group	SHea
	Azrie Group	SLdr
§	'Azuma-kagami' (Kurume) (EA)	LMil LSRN MJak
	'Azurika'	IVic NSoo
	'Azurro'	GGGa LMil NLar
	B.B.C. Group	LMil
	'Babuschka'	LMil NLar
	'Baden-Baden'	CMac CTri ECho GKin LMil MAsh MGos MSnd NEgg SLdr SPoG
	'Bagshot Ruby'	SHea
	baileyi	MSnd
	'Bakkarat' (K)	SHea
	balangense	GGGa
	balfourianum	GGGa
	'Ballerina' (K)	SHea
	'Balzac' (K)	CDoC ECho GKin MAsh MBri MGos NEgg SHea SPer
	'Bambi'	MJak
	'Bandoola'	SReu
	'Barbara Coats' (EA)	SLdr
	'Barbara Reuthe'	SSta
	'Barbarella'	GGGa IVic
	barbatum	CDoC CHEx GGGa LMil MSnd
	- B&SWJ 2160	WCru
	- B&SWJ 2237	WCru
	- B&SWJ 2624	WCru
	'Barbecue' (K)	LMil
	'Barmstedt'	CWri MAsh WMoo
	'Barnaby Sunset'	GGGa LMil LRHS MAsh
	'Bartholo Lazzari' (G)	SReu SSta
	'Bashful' ♀H4	CBcs CSBt ECho EPfP MGos MJak SLdr
§	***basilicum***	CDoC GGGa LMil SLdr
	- AC 616	MSnd
	- KR 7532	LMil
	- KR 7540	LMil
	× ***bathyphyllum***	GGGa
	bauhiniiflorum	see *R. triflorum* var. *bauhiniiflorum*
	beanianum	GGGa
	- APA 60	GGGa
	- KC 0122	GGGa
	- compact	see *R. piercei*
	'Beatrice Keir'	LMil MSnd SReu SSta
	'Beau Brummell'	LMil
	'Beaulieu' (K)	SHea
	'Beaulieu Manor'	GQui
	'Beaver' (EA)	MMuc
	'Beefeater' × ***yakushimanum***	SLdr
	beesianum	GGGa
	- AC 1528 **new**	MSnd
	'Beethoven' (EA) ♀H3-4	MSnd SLdr
	'Belkanto'	CDoC GKin MJak
	'Belle Heller'	SLdr
	'Ben Cruachan' (K)	GGGa
	'Ben Lawers' (K)	GGGa
	'Ben Lomond' (K)	GGGa
	'Ben Vorlich' (K)	GGGa
	'Ben Vrackie' (K)	GGGa
	'Bengal'	ECho LRHS LSRN MAsh NLar SLdr SLim
	'Bengal Beauty' (EA)	SLdr
	'Bengal Fire' (EA)	CMac SLdr
	'Beni-giri' (EA)	CMac
	'Bergensiana'	SReu SSta
	'Bergie Larson'	CBcs ECho IVic LMil MLea MMuc SLdr
	'Berg's 10'	MLea
	'Berg's Yellow'	CWri ECho LMil MGos MLea MMuc MSnd SLdr
	'Bernard Shaw'	SSta
	'Bernstein'	LMil MAsh MJak
	'Berryrose' (K) ♀H4	CBcs CMac CSBt CTri CWri ECho EPfP GKin LMil MAsh MBri MGos MJak MMuc MSnd NSoo SLdr SPer SReu
	'Beryl Taylor'	GGGa
	'Betty Anne Voss' (EA)	ECho LRHS LSRN MAsh MBri MGos SCoo SLdr
	'Betty Wormald'	CDul CMac CWri ECho MGos MLea MMuc SHea SLdr SPer
	bhutanense	GGGa
	- KR 8233	LMil
	Bibiani Group	LMil SHea
	'Bijou de Ledeberg' (EA)	CMac

	'Billy Budd'	SLdr
	'Birthday Girl'	CBcs CSBt ECho ELon LMil LSRN MAsh MLea SLdr
	'Biskra'	GGGa LMil
	'Blaauw's Pink' (EA) 🏆$^{H3-4}$	CDoC CMac CSBt ECho ELon EPfP GKin GQui LMil MBri MGos MMuc MSnd NSoo SGol SLdr SPer SPlb SPoG SReu
	'Black Knight' (EA)	SLdr
	'Black Magic'	CDoC CWri GKin LMil
	'Black Sport'	MLea
	Blaue Donau	see *R.* 'Blue Danube'
	'Blaue Jungs' **new**	GGGa
	'Blazecheck'	SCoo
	'Blewbury' 🏆^{H4}	LMil SLdr SReu
	'Blue Bell'	SHea
	'Blue Boy'	CDoC LMil
	'Blue Chip'	SLdr
§	'Blue Danube' (EA) 🏆$^{H3-4}$	CDoC CDul CHel CMac CSBt CTri ECho ELon EPfP GGGa GKin IVic LMil LRHS MAsh MBri MGos MJak MMuc MSnd NPCo NPri NSoo SGol SLdr SLim SPer SPoG SReu SSta
	'Blue Diamond'	CMac CSBt ECho ELon LRHS LSRN MAsh MGos MJak NPCo SLdr SPer WGwG
	Blue Diamond Group	CBcs ECho EPfP MGos MSnd SReu
	'Blue Monday' (EA)	SLdr
	'Blue Moon' (EA)	ELon LMil NLar SLdr
	'Blue Peter' 🏆^{H4}	CBcs CSBt CWri ECho ELon LMil LRHS MAsh MGos MLea NHol NLar SLdr SPer SReu SSta
	'Blue Pool'	LMil
	'Blue Silver'	GGGa IVic LMil MAsh NSoo
	'Blue Steel'	see *R. fastigiatum* 'Blue Steel'
	Blue Tit Group	CBcs CDoC EPfP GGGa LRHS MAsh MSnd NLar SLdr SLim SReu SSta
	Bluebird Group	CMac CSBt MGos SLdr
	'Blurettia'	CDoC CWri MMuc
	'Blutopia'	LMil
	Bobolink Group	LMil
	'Boddaertianum'	SHea SLdr SReu
	'Bodnant Yellow'	LMil
	Bohlken's Juditha **new**	GGGa
	Bohlken's Kronjewel **new**	GGGa
	Bohlken's Laura	GGGa LMil
	Bohlken's Lupinenberg	GGGa
	Bohlken's Snow Fire **new**	GGGa
	'Bonfire'	SHea SReu
	boothii	GGGa
	HECC 10077	GGGa
	'Bo peep'	GQui LMil SLdr
	Bo-peep Group	CBcs
	'Boskoop Ostara'	CBcs LMil MGos
	'Bouquet de Flore' (G) 🏆^{H4}	CDoC EPfP LMil NLar SReu
	'Bow Bells' 🏆^{H4}	ECho EPfP LMil LRHS MAsh MBri MSnd NHol NLar NPri SHea SLdr
	Bow Bells Group	MLea
	'Bow Street'	SHea
	'Bowjingles'	GGGa
	brachyanthum subsp. ***hypolepidotum***	GGGa
	brachycarpum	GKev GLin
	- 'Roseum Dwarf'	GGGa
	'Brambling'	GGGa
	'Brazier' (EA)	SLdr
	'Brazil' (K)	SHea
	'Bremen'	LMil
	brevinerve	MSnd
	'Briane' (EA)	GGGa
	'Bric-à-brac'	SLdr WThu
	Bric-à-brac Group	CBcs
	'Bright Forecast' (K)	CWri IVic MBri MLea SLdr
	'Brigitte'	CWri IVic LMil LSRN MAsh SLdr
	'Brilliant Blue' (EA)	MAsh
	'Britannia'	CSBt CWri EPfP LMil MJak NHol SReu SSta
	'Brocade'	MSnd SHea SLdr
	'Bronze Fire' (A)	NHol SLdr SReu SSta
	'Brown Eyes'	ECho GKin MMuc SLdr
	'Bruce Brechtbill' 🏆^{H4}	CDoC CWri ECho GGGa GKin LMil MAsh MBri MGos MMuc NPCo SEND SLdr SReu
	'Bruce Hancock' (Ad)	ECho ELon MMuc SLdr
§	'Bruns Gloria'	LMil
	'Bruns Schneewitchen'	SPoG SReu
	'Buccaneer' (EA)	SLdr
	bullatum	see *R. edgeworthii*
	'Bungo-nishiki' (EA/d)	CMac WThu
	bureavii 🏆^{H4}	CBcs GGGa GLin IDee LMil MGos MSnd NLar SReu SSta
	- 'Berg'	GGGa
	bureavii × ***yakushimanum***	SReu
	bureavioides	LMil MSnd
	'Burletta'	IVic LMil
	burmanicum	CBcs GGGa GGal SLdr
	'Busuki'	GGGa LMil
	'Butter Brickle'	LMil MLea SLdr
	'Butter Yellow'	ECho
	'Butterfly'	SHea
	'Buttermint'	ECho MGos
	calendulaceum (A)	GGGa LMil
	- red-flowered (A)	LMil
	- yellow-flowered (A)	LMil
	'Calfort'	GGGa
	Calfort Group	SLdr
	callimorphum	GGGa LMil
	- var. ***myiagrum***	MSnd
	calophytum 🏆^{H4}	GGGa IDee LMil LRHS MSnd SLdr
	calostrotum	WAbe
	- 'Gigha' 🏆^{H4}	GGGa IDee LMil MAsh MGos SLdr WAbe
§	- subsp. ***keleticum*** 🏆^{H4}	CDoC EPot GGGa GKev ITim NSla
	- - R 58	GGGa LMil
§	- - Radicans Group	GGGa IVic MLea NSla WAbe WThu
	- - - USDAPI 59182/R11188	MLea
	- - - mound form	ITim
	- subsp. ***riparium***	GLin ITim
	- - Calciphilum Group	GGGa WThu
§	- - Nitens Group	CDoC GGGa WAbe
	caloxanthum	see *R. campylocarpum* subsp. *caloxanthum*
	'Calsap'	GGGa
	Calstocker Group	LMil
	camelliiflorum	GGGa
	campanulatum	GGGa IDee LMil MSnd SReu WAbe
	- CC 5124	GKev
§	- subsp. ***aeruginosum***	GGGa LMil MSnd SLdr SReu
	'Campfire' J.B. Gable (EA) **new**	SLdr
	campylocarpum	GGGa LMil MSnd
	- KR 8212	LMil
§	- subsp. ***caloxanthum***	GGGa LMil
§	- - Telopeum Group	MSnd
	campylogynum 🏆^{H4}	GGGa LMil WAbe
	- SBEC 0519	GGGa
	- 'Album'	see *R.* 'Leucanthum'

- black-flowered	IVic
- Charopoeum Group	WThu
- - 'Patricia'	ECho EPot LLHF LMil NLar NSla SLdr
- (Cremastum Group) 'Bodnant Red'	GGGa WThu
- Myrtilloides Group	CDoC ECho GGGa GQui LMil MAsh MSnd WAbe WThu
- plum-flowered	WAbe
- salmon pink-flowered	ECho WAbe
camtschaticum	GGGa LMil WThu
- var. ***albiflorum***	GGGa
- red-flowered	GGGa
canadense (A)	GGGa
- f. ***albiflorum*** (A)	GGGa LMil
- dark-flowered (A)	LMil
'Candy Striped Pink'	IVic
canescens (A)	LMil
'Cannon's Double' (K/d) ♀H4	CBcs CWri GKin LMil MAsh MBri MGos MLea NLar SLdr SPer
'Canzonetta' (EA) ♀H4	ECho ELon EPfP GGGa LMil LRHS MAsh MBri MGos MMuc
'Captain Jack'	GGGa
'Caractacus'	MJak
'Carat' (A)	NLar
cardiobasis	see *R. orbiculare* subsp. *cardiobasis*
Carita Group	SHea
'Carita Charm'	LMil
'Carita Golden Dream'	LMil
'Carita Inchmery'	SHea SLdr
'Carmen'	ECho ELon GGGa GKev GKin LMil MAsh MGos MLea NPCo SLdr SReu
'Carmine'	MSnd
carneum	GGGa
'Carnival' (EA)	CBcs
'Caroline Allbrook' ♀H4	CWri ECho ELon GGGa MAsh MGos MLea NEgg NLar NSoo SLdr
'Caruso'	IVic SPoG
'Cary Ann'	CTri LMil LRHS MAsh SLdr SReu
'Casablanca' (EA)	SLdr
'Cassata'	LMil
'Cassley' (Vs)	LMil
catacosmum	GGGa
catawbiense	GKev GLin SLdr
'Catawbiense Album'	CTri MAsh
'Catawbiense Boursault'	SLdr
'Catawbiense Grandiflorum'	CWri MAsh NSoo
caucasicum	GGGa
'Caucasicum Pictum'	LMil MSnd SLdr
'Cayenne' (EA)	SLdr
'Cecile' (K) ♀H4	CBcs CDoC CMac CWri ECho GBin GKin LMil LSRN MAsh MBri MGos MMuc NLar SEND SLdr SPer SReu
'Celestial' (EA)	CMac
'Centennial'	see *R.* 'Washington State Centennial'
cephalanthum	GGGa LMil
- subsp. ***cephalanthum*** SBEC 0751	WThu
- - Crebreflorum Group	GGGa LMil WAbe WThu
- - - Week's form	ITim
- - Nmaiense Group	GGGa
- subsp. ***platyphyllum***	GGGa
- - AC 1926 **new**	MSnd
cerasinum	LMil MSnd
- 'Cherry Brandy'	GGGa MSnd
- 'Coals of Fire'	GGGa MSnd
'Cetewayo' ♀H4	CWri LMil SReu
chaetomallum	see *R. haematodes* subsp. *chaetomallum*

	chamaethomsonii	GGGa
	- var. ***chamaethomsonii***	MSnd
	- - Rock form	GGGa
§	'Champagne' ♀H3-4	CBcs CSBt EPfP LMil LRHS MAsh SHea SReu
	championae	GGGa
	'Chanel' (Vs)	SReu SSta
	changii	GGGa
	'Chanticleer' (EA)	SLdr
	chapaense	see *R. maddenii* subsp. *crassum*
	'Chariots of Fire' (EA)	LMil
	charitopes	LMil
	- F 25570	GGGa LMil
§	- subsp. ***tsangpoense***	GGGa GQui
*	'Charlotte de Rothschild' (A)	SLdr
	'Charlotte Megan' (A)	LMil
	'Charme La'	GGGa
	chasmanthum	see *R. augustinii* subsp. *chasmanthum*
	'Cheer'	CWri MAsh MMuc NEgg SEND SLdr SLim SPer
	'Chelsea Reach' (K/d)	SHea SLdr
	'Chelsea Seventy'	MSnd SLdr
	'Chenille' (K/d)	SHea SLdr
	'Cherokee' (EA)	MSnd SLdr
	'Cherries and Cream'	LMil
	'Cherry Cheesecake'	NLar
	'Cherry Drops' (EA)	EPfP LRHS MAsh
	'Chetco' (K)	LMil NLar
	'Chevalier Félix de Sauvage' ♀H4	LMil SHea SReu
	'Chikor'	CBcs ECho GBin GGGa GKin MAsh MBri MGos MSnd WThu
	'Chinchilla' (EA)	GQui NLar
	'Chink'	MSnd SLdr
	'Chionoides'	CMac SLdr
	'Chipmunk' (EA/d)	GGGa LRHS MAsh MBri
	'Chippewa' (EA)	CTri IVic LMil
	'Chocolate Ice' (K/d)	SHea
	'Choremia' ♀H3	LMil MLea SHea SLdr
	christi (V)	GGGa
	'Christina' (EA/d)	LMil MMuc SLdr
	'Christmas Cheer' (EA/d)	see *R.* 'Ima-shojo'
	'Christmas Cheer' (hybrid)	CBcs CDoC CMac CSBt CWri GBin GGGa GGal GKin LMil MAsh MGos MLea MSnd NLar SLdr SReu
	chrysanthum	see *R. aureum*
	chrysodoron	LMil
	'Chrysomanicum'	CHel
	ciliatum	CBcs GGGa LMil SLdr
	ciliicalyx	CBcs
	'Cilpinense' ♀H3-4	CMac CSBt CWri ECho EPfP LMil LRHS MAsh MMuc NPri SEND SHea SLdr WGwG
	Cilpinense Group	CBcs GGGa MSnd SPer
	cinnabarinum	LMil MSnd SLdr
	- subsp. ***cinnabarinum*** BL&M 234	LMil
	- - Blandfordiiflorum Group	GGGa LMil MSnd
§	- - 'Conroy'	CTsd LMil
	- - 'Nepal'	LMil
	- - Roylei Group	GGGa LMil
	- - - 'Vin Rosé'	LMil
§	- subsp. ***xanthocodon***	GGGa LMil MSnd
§	- - Concatenans Group	GGGa LMil MSnd SLdr
	- - - KW 5874	LMil
	- - - 'Amber'	LMil

- - Purpurellum Group	GGGa MSnd
Cinzan Group	LMil
circinnatum	GGGa
citriniflorum	LMil
- R 108	LMil
- Brodick form	LMil
- var. ***citriniflorum***	LMil MSnd
- var. ***horaeum***	GGGa MSnd
'Clarice' (K)	SHea
'Claudine'	IVic
clementinae	GGGa MSnd
- F 25705	LMil
- subsp. ***aureodorsale*** new	GKev
'Cliff Garland'	GQui LMil
'Coccineum Speciosum' (G) ♀H4	CDoC CMac CSBt GKin LMil SLdr SReu SSta
coeloneuron	GGGa LMil
- EGM 334	LMil
collettianum	GGGa
'Colonel Coen'	CWri ELon GBin GKin LMil MBri MGos MLea MMuc SLdr
Colonel Rogers Group	SLdr SReu
'Colyer' (EA)	SLdr
comisteum C 6541	GGGa
concatenans	see *R. cinnabarinum* subsp. *xanthocodon* Concatenans Group
concinnoides new	GGGa
concinnum	CWri GGGa SLdr
- Pseudoyanthinum Group	GGGa GQui SLdr
'Connie' (EA)	NSoo
'Conroy'	see *R. cinnabarinum* subsp. *cinnabarinum* 'Conroy'
'Contina'	LMil
'Conversation Piece' (EA)	SLdr
'Conyan Apricot'	SLdr
cookeanum	see *R. sikangense* var. *sikangense* Cookeanum Group
'Cool Haven'	LMil
'Coral Mist'	GGGa
'Coral Reef'	SLdr
'Coral Sea' (EA)	SLdr SReu
'Coral Seas' (V)	GGGa
coriaceum	GGGa LMil MSnd SLdr
'Corinna'	GGGa
'Corneille' (G/d) ♀H4	CSBt LMil SReu
'Corona'	SHea
'Coronation Day'	LMil
'Coronation Lady' (K)	SHea
coryanum 'Chelsea Chimes'	MSnd
'Cosmopolitan'	CWri ELon LMil MGos MMuc SEND SPer SPoG WMoo
Cote Group (A)	SLdr
'Countess of Derby'	SHea SLdr
'Countess of Haddington' ♀H2	CBcs LMil SLdr
'Cowslip'	LRHS
Cowslip Group	CTri LMil MAsh MGos MLea MSnd
coxianum	GGGa
'Craig Faragher' (V)	GGGa
'Crane' ♀H4	EPfP GGGa GQui IVic LLHF LMil LRHS MAsh SLdr
crassum	see *R. maddenii* subsp. *crassum*
'Cream Crest'	GKin GQui LMil NLar SLdr SLim WMoo
'Creamy Chiffon'	CWri ECho MGos MLea WGwG
§ 'Creeping Jenny'	ECho GGGa GGal MSnd SLdr
crenulatum	GGGa
'Crest' ♀H3-4	CWri GGGa LMil SSta
'Crete' ♀H4	LMil
'Crimson Pippin'	LMil
crinigerum	GGGa IDee LMil
- var. ***crinigerum***	MSnd
- var. ***euadenium***	MSnd
'Crinoline' (EA)	SLdr
Crossbill Group	CBcs SLdr
'Crossroads'	MSnd
'Crosswater Belle'	LMil NLar
'Crosswater Red' (K)	LMil
'Csárdás'	GGGa IVic
cubittii	see *R. veitchianum* Cubittii Group
cucullatum	see *R. roxieanum* var. *cucullatum*
cumberlandense (A)	GGGa LMil LRHS NLar
- 'Sunlight' (A)	LMil
'Cunningham's Blush'	SGol
'Cunningham's White'	CBcs CTri CWri ELan EPfP GBin GGGa LMil LRHS MAsh MGos MMuc NHol NPri NSoo SEND SLdr SLim SPer SPoG SReu SSta
'Cupcake'	GGGa
'Curlew' ♀H4	CBcs CMac GKin LMil MAsh MBri MGos MJak MSnd NHol NLar SLdr SReu SSpi
cyanocarpum	GGGa MSnd
'Cynthia' ♀H4	CBcs CMac CSBt CWri ECho ELon EPfP GGGa LMil LSRN MBri MGos MSnd NEgg SLdr SPer SReu SSta
'Dagmar'	IVic
dalhousiae	GGGa
- LS&T 6694 new	MSnd
§ - var. ***rhabdotum***	GGGa
'Damozel'	LMil SHea SLdr
'Danger' (K)	SHea SLdr
'Danuta'	IVic
'Daphne Daffarn'	SHea
'Daphne Millais'	SHea SLdr
'Dartmoor Pixie'	WThu
dasycladum	see *R. selense* subsp. *dasycladum*
dauricum 'Album'	see *R. dauricum* 'Hokkaido'
§ - 'Hokkaido'	GGGa
- 'Mid-winter' ♀H4	GGGa LMil
'David' ♀H4	SHea
davidii	GGGa LMil
davidsonianum ♀H3-4	GGGa GGal LMil MSnd SLdr
- Bodnant form	LMil
- 'Caerhays Blotched'	GGGa SLdr
- 'Caerhays Pink'	SLdr
- 'Ruth Lyons'	LMil
'Daviesii' (G) ♀H4	CBcs CDoC CSBt CTri CWri ECho ELan EPfP GGGa GKin GQui LMil MAsh MBri MLea MMuc MSnd NLar NPCo NPri SLdr SPer SPoG SReu SSpi WMoo
'Day Dream'	SHea SLdr
N 'Daybreak' (EA/d)	see *R.* 'Kirin'
'Daybreak' (K)	GQui SHea
'Dear Barbara'	LMil LSRN
'Dear Grandad' (EA)	CTri LMil LSRN SCoo
'Dear Grandma'	LMil LSRN
'Dearest' (EA)	LMil LRHS MAsh NPri
'Debutante'	SHea
decorum ♀H4	CDoC GGGa IDee LLHF LMil MSnd SLdr SSpi
- KR 2496	LMil
- SDR 4208	GKev
- SDR 5026	GKev
- SDR 5805	GKev

- subsp. ***cordatum*** C&H 7132	GGGa
- 'Cox's Uranium Green'	SReu
§ - subsp. ***diaprepes***	MSnd
- late-flowering	LMil
- pink-flowered	GGGa
decorum × ***yakushimanum***	SLdr SReu
§ ***degronianum*** subsp. ***degronianum***	GGGa LMil MSnd
- subsp. ***heptamerum*** 'Ho Emma'	LMil
- - 'Oki Island'	LMil
- 'Rae's Delight'	IDee LMil
dekatanum	GGGa
deleiense	see *R. tephropeplum*
'Delicatissimum' (O)	CBcs CDoC CTsd CWri ECho GGGa GKin GQui MBri MGos MLea MMuc MSnd NEgg NPCo SHea SLdr SPer WGwG
'Delta'	NLar SLdr SLim
dendrocharis	LMil
- Cox 5016	GGGa WAbe
- Glendoick Gem = 'Gle002'	GGGa
'Denise'	IVic
* 'Denny's Rose' (A)	LMil SReu
'Denny's Scarlet'	NHol SReu SSta
'Denny's White' (A)	LMil NHol SReu SSta
denudatum	GLin LMil MSnd
- EGM 294	LMil
desquamatum	see *R. rubiginosum* Desquamatum Group
'Diabolo' (K)	SHea
Diamant Group lilac-flowered (EA)	ECho LMil MLea
- pink-flowered (EA)	ECho MLea
§ - purple-flowered (EA)	ECho MLea SLdr
§ - red-flowered (EA)	ECho MLea SLdr
- rosy red-flowered (EA)	ECho
- white-flowered (EA)	ECho
'Diamant Purpur'	see *R.* Diamant Group purple-flowered
'Diamant Rot'	see *R.* Diamant Group red-flowered
'Diane'	CMac
diaprepes	see *R. decorum* subsp. *diaprepes*
dichroanthum	GGGa LMil
§ - subsp. ***apodectum***	GGGa LMil MSnd
- subsp. ***dichroanthum***	MSnd
- - AC 1079 **new**	MSnd
§ - subsp. ***scyphocalyx***	GGGa LMil MSnd NSoo
- subsp. ***septentrionale***	GGGa
didymum	see *R. sanguineum* subsp. *didymum*
'Diorama' (Vs)	GKin SReu SSta
discolor	see *R. fortunei* subsp. *discolor*
diversipilosum 'Milky Way'	GGGa
'Doc'	CMac EPfP MGos SLdr SReu
'Doctor A. Blok'	SLdr
'Doctor M. Oosthoek' (M) ♀H4	CSBt GKin SReu
'Doctor Reiger'	NLar
'Doctor Stocker'	LMil MSnd
'Dopey' ♀H4	CBcs CDul CSBt CWri ECho ELon EPfP GGGa LMil LRHS MAsh MBri MGos MJak MLea MSnd NEgg NHol NLar SLdr SLim SReu SSta
'Dora Amateis' ♀H4	CDoC ECho GGGa IVic LMil LRHS MAsh MBri MGos MMuc NSoo SLdr SLim SReu WThu
Dormouse Group	CBcs ECho LMil MAsh MMuc SLdr SReu SSta
'Dorothy Corston' (K)	SHea
'Dörte Reich'	GGGa
'Dotella'	GGGa
'Double Beauty' (EA/d)	SReu SSta
'Double Damask' (K/d) ♀H4	SLdr
'Double Date' (d)	SLdr
'Double Dots' (d)	LMil
double yellow-flowered (A/d)	SLdr
'Douglas McEwan'	SLdr
Dragonfly Group	SReu SSta
'Dreamland' ♀H4	CBcs CDoC CSBt CWri ECho EPfP LMil LRHS MAsh MGos MLea MSnd NLar NSoo SLdr SLim SPoG SReu SSta
'Drury Lane' (K)	GQui LMil
dryophyllum misapplied	see *R. phaeochrysum* var. *levistratum*
'Dufthecke'	see *R.* White Dufthecke
'Dusky Dawn'	SLdr
'Düsselfeuer'	IVic
'Dusty Miller'	LRHS MAsh MBri MGos MJak MSnd NSoo SLdr
'Earl of Donoughmore'	SReu
'Easter Parade' (EA) **new**	SLdr
eastmanii (A)	GGGa
ebianense NN 904 **new**	GGGa
'Ebony Pearl'	CBcs ECho ELon MGos MMuc SLdr WGwG
eclecteum	GGGa LMil MSnd
§ ***edgeworthii*** ♀H2-3	GGGa WAbe
'Edith Bosley'	NLar SLdr
'Edna Bee' (EA)	LMil SLdr
'Egret' ♀H4	CDoC ECho EPot GGGa LMil MBri MGos MLea MSnd NSla SLdr
'Eider'	GGGa MAsh SLdr
'Eileen'	LMil
N 'Eisenhower' (K)	SHea
'El Camino'	ECho LMil MBri MMuc MSnd SEND SLdr
'El Greco'	SLdr
Eldorado Group	GQui
'Eleanore'	SLdr
'Electra'	see *R. augustinii* 'Electra'
elegantulum	LMil MSnd
'Elisabeth Hobbie' ♀H4	LMil NLar
'Eliska'	IVic
N 'Elizabeth' (EA)	CMac CSBt EPfP SLdr
'Elizabeth'	CTri CTsd CWri GBin LRHS LSRN MGos MSnd NHol SHea
Elizabeth Group	CBcs LMil MAsh SLdr SPer SReu
'Elizabeth Jenny'	see *R.* 'Creeping Jenny'
'Elizabeth Lockhart'	ECho GQui
'Elizabeth Red Foliage'	CTri GGGa LMil LRHS MAsh MBri SPer
'Else Frye'	GGGa
'Elsie Lee' (EA/d) ♀H3-4	CSBt CTrh ECho LMil MAsh MMuc NLar SLdr SPer
'Elsie Pratt' (A)	NHol SHea
'Emasculum'	LMil SLdr
'Emma Williams'	CBcs
'Endsleigh Pink'	CBcs CWri LMil MMuc
'English Roseum'	LMil
eriogynum	see *R. facetum*

eritimum	see *R. anthosphaerum*
'Ernest Inman'	LMil SLdr
erosum	MSnd
'Eruption'	IVic
'Esmeralda'	CMac
'Ethel' **new**	SLdr
'Etna' (EA)	SLdr
'Etta Burrows'	CWri GGGa
'Euan Cox'	GGGa
euchroum	MSnd
eudoxum	MSnd
'Europa'	LMil SReu SSta
'Eurydice'	LMil
eurysiphon	GGGa MSnd
'Eva Goude' (K)	SHea
'Evelyn Hyde' (EA)	SLdr
'Evening Fragrance' (A)	LMil
'Everbloom' (EA)	SLdr
'Everest' (EA)	SLdr
'Everestianum'	SHea
Everred = '851C'^{PBR}	GGGa WCot
exasperatum	GGGa
Exburiense Group	MMuc
'Exbury Calstocker'	LMil
'Exbury Late Red' **new**	MSnd
'Exbury Naomi'	LMil
'Exbury White' (K)	GQui
excellens	GGGa IDee LMil
eximium	see *R. falconeri* subsp. *eximium*
'Explorer' (EA) **new**	MJak
exquisitum	see *R. oreotrephes* Exquisitum Group
'Exquisitum' (O) ♀^{H4}	CBcs CDoC CWri ECho EPfP GGGa GKin LMil MBri SLdr
'Extraordinaire'	GGGa SReu SSta
faberi	GGGa LMil
'Fabia' ♀^{H3}	CBcs CMac GGGa GGal GKin LMil MSnd SHea SLdr
Fabia Group	CWri
§ 'Fabia Tangerine'	CMac MLea NHol
'Fabia Waterer'	LMil
§ ***facetum***	GGGa LMil
- KR 7593	LMil
'Faggetter's Favourite' ♀^{H4}	LMil SHea SReu SSta
Fairy Light Group	LMil
faithae CGG 14142 **new**	GGGa
falconeri ♀$^{H3-4}$	CDoC CHEx CHll GGGa LMil MGos MSnd NPCo SLdr
§ - subsp. ***eximium***	CDoC GGGa GKev LMil MSnd NLar
'Falling Snow'	IVic
'Fanal' (K)	NLar
'Fanny'	see *R.* 'Pucella'
'Fantastica' ♀^{H4}	CDoC CWri ELan ELon EPfP GGGa IDee LMil LRHS MAsh MBri MGos MLea NLar NPri SLdr SLim SPoG
fargesii	see *R. oreodoxa* var. *fargesii*
'Fashion' (EA)	SLdr
fastigiatum	EPot LMil MSnd NSla SLdr
- SBEC 804/4869	GGGa WThu
§ - 'Blue Steel' ♀^{H4}	CBcs CTri ECho ELon GKin IVic LMil LRHS MAsh MGos NPCo SLdr SPlb SReu
- 'Indigo Steel'	GGGa
'Fastuosum Flore Pleno' (d) ♀^{H4}	CBcs CDul CMac CSBt CWri EPfP GGGa LMil MGos MLea MSnd SHea SLdr SPer SReu SSta
'Fatima'	LMil
faucium	GGGa
'Favor Major' (K)	SHea
'Favorite' ambig. (EA)	SLdr
'Fawley' (K)	SHea SLdr
'Fedora' (EA)	SLdr
'Feenkissen' (EA)	IVic
ferrugineum	GGGa LMil
'Feuerwerk' (K)	GGGa IVic NLar SHea
fictolacteum	see *R. rex* subsp. *fictolacteum*
Fire Bird Group	CHel SHea SLdr
'Fire Rim'	LRHS MAsh
'Fireball' (K) ♀^{H4}	CBcs CDoC CTri CWri EPfP GBin GGGa GKev GKin LMil LRHS MAsh MBri MGos MLea MMuc NLar SEND SLdr SPer SPoG
'Fireball' (hybrid)	MJak
'Firecracker' (A) **new**	LRHS
'Fireglow' (EA)	GKin LMil LRHS
'Firelight' (hybrid)	GKin LMil NLar SPer
'Firetail'	SHea
'Flaming Gold'	EPfP LRHS LSRN MAsh NPri
§ ***flammeum*** (A)	LMil
'Flanagan's Daughter'	LMil MAsh
'Flautando'	IVic
Flava Group	see *R.* Volker Group
flavidum	GGGa
- 'Album'	WThu
fletcherianum 'Yellow Bunting'	GGGa
aff. ***flinckii*** AC 5441	GLin
floccigerum	LMil MSnd
- AC 1863 **new**	MSnd
- bicolored	GGGa
'Floriade' × ***yakushimanum***	SLdr
floribundum	GGGa LMil SLdr
'Florida' (EA/d) ♀$^{H3-4}$	CMac LMil NSoo SLdr SReu
'Flower Arranger' (EA)	LMil LRHS MAsh MBri SCoo
formosanum	GGGa
formosum	CBcs GGGa SLdr
§ - var. ***formosum*** Iteaphyllum Group	GGGa
- - 'Khasia'	GGGa
- var. ***inaequale***	GGGa
forrestii	GKev
- KR 6113	LMil
- subsp. ***forrestii***	LMil
- - Repens Group	LMil
- - - 'Seinghku'	GGGa WThu
- Tumescens Group	GGGa WThu
Fortune Group	SLdr
fortunei	GGGa IDee LMil SLdr
§ - subsp. ***discolor*** ♀^{H4}	LMil MSnd SLdr
- - (Houlstonii Group) 'John R. Elcock'	IDee LMil LRHS
- - 'Hummeltanz'	IVic
- - var. ***kwangfuense*** AC 5208	LMil
- 'Mrs Butler'	see *R. fortunei* 'Sir Charles Butler'
§ - 'Sir Charles Butler'	LMil
'Fox Hunter'	SLdr
fragariiflorum	GGGa
'Fragrant Star' (A)	GGGa
'Fragrantissimum' ♀$^{H2-3}$	CBcs CEnd CHel CMac CSBt CTsd CWri ECre GGGa GGal IDee LMil MRav NLar SKHP SLdr
'Frank Galsworthy' ♀^{H4}	LMil SReu
'Fraseri' (M)	LMil
'Fred Peste'	CDoC ECho GKin LMil MAsh MBri MGos MLea MMuc MSnd NLar SLdr SLim

	'Fred Wynniatt'	LMil MSnd SLdr
	'Fred Wynniatt Stanway'	see *R.* 'Stanway'
	'Freda' (EA)	SLdr
	'Freya' (R/d)	LMil LSRN
	'Fridoline' (EA)	IVic
	'Frigate' (EA)	SLdr
	'Frills' (K/d)	SHea
	'Frome' (K)	SHea
	'Frosted Orange' (EA)	LMil MAsh NSoo
	'Frosthexe'	WAbe
	'Frühlingsbeginn'	IVic
	'Frühlingsglühen'	IVic
	'Fulbrook'	LMil
	fulgens	GGGa GLin LMil MSnd
	- KR 8204	LMil
	fulvum ♀^{H4}	CDoC GGGa GKin IDee LMil MSnd NLar SReu SSta
	- KR 7614	LMil
	- subsp. ***fulvoides***	GGGa LMil MSnd
§	'Fumiko' (EA)	CBcs CSBt ELon LRHS MAsh MGos MLea MMuc
	'Furnivall's Daughter' ♀^{H4}	CMac CSBt CWri ECho EPfP GBin GGGa LMil MBri MGos MMuc MSnd NHol SEND SHea SLdr SReu SSta
	'Fusilier'	SHea
	'Gabrielle Hill' (EA)	MAsh SLdr
	'Gaiety' (EA)	LMil SLdr SReu
	galactinum	GGGa LMil
	'Galathea' (EA)	MMuc
	'Gallipoli' (K)	SHea
	'Gandy Dancer'	CWri MLea SLdr
	'Garden State Glow' (EA/d)	SLdr
	'Garibaldi'	SHea
	'Garnet'	SHea
	'Gartendirektor Glocker'	CWri ECho GGGa IVic MAsh MSnd SLim
	'Gartendirektor Rieger' ♀^{H4}	CWri GGGa IVic LMil SHea SReu
	'Gauche' (A)	GQui SLdr
	'Gaugin'	GQui
	'Geisha' (EA)	SGol
	'Geisha Lilac'	see *R.* 'Hanako'
	'Geisha Orange'	see *R.* 'Satschiko'
	'Geisha Pink'	see *R.* 'Momoko'
	'Geisha Purple'	see *R.* 'Fumiko'
	'Gena Mae' (A/d)	GGGa SLdr
	'General Eisenhower'	SHea
	'General Eric Harrison'	SLdr
	'General Practitioner'	MSnd SLdr
	'General Wavell' (EA)	CMac GGal SLdr
	'Gene's Favourite'	SReu SSta
	genestierianum	GGGa
	'Geoffroy Millais'	LMil
	'Georg Arends' (Ad)	EPfP LRHS MAsh SLdr
	'George Hyde' (EA)	LRHS LSRN MAsh SCoo
	'George Johnstone'	SLdr
	'George Reynolds' (K)	MLea
	'George's Delight'	MSnd
§	× ***geraldii***	SLdr
	'Germania'	LMil LRHS MAsh NLar NPri NSoo SPoG SReu SSta
	Gertrud Schäle Group	CDoC CTri SHea
	'Gibraltar' (K) ♀^{H4}	CBcs CDoC CMac CSBt CTri CWri EPfP GGGa GKin LMil LRHS MAsh MGos MJak NHol NLar SLdr SLim SPer SReu SSta WMoo
	Gibraltar Group	LMil
	'Gilbert Mullie' (EA)	LMil NSoo SLim
	'Gill's Crimson'	SHea SReu
	'Ginger' (K)	CSBt CWri GKin LMil
	'Ginny Gee' ♀^{H4}	CBcs CDoC CSBt CWri ECho EPfP EPot GGGa GKin IVic LMil LRHS MAsh MBri MGos MLea MMuc MSnd NEgg NLar NSla SReu SSta
§	'Girard's Hot Shot' (EA)	ECho MAsh MGos SReu
	'Girard's Hot Shot' variegated (EA/v)	ECho GGGa LMil LRHS MAsh MMuc
	glanduliferum	GGGa
	- EGM 347	LMil
	glaucophyllum	GGGa LMil MSnd
	- B&SWJ 2638	WCru
	- Borde Hill form	LMil
	- var. ***glaucophyllum***	MSnd
§	- subsp. ***tubiforme***	GGGa
	Glendoick Butterscotch = 'Gle003'	GGGa
	Glendoick Crimson = 'Gle004' (EA)	GGGa
	Glendoick Dream = 'Gle005' (EA)	GGGa
	Glendoick Ermine = 'Gle006' (EA)	GGGa
	Glendoick Frolic = 'Gle007'	GGGa
	Glendoick Garnet = 'Gle008' (EA)	GGGa
	Glendoick Glacier = 'Gle009' (EA)	GGGa
	Glendoick Goblin = 'Gle010' (EA)	GGGa
	Glendoick Gold = 'Gle011'	GGGa
	Glendoick Ice Cream = 'Gle013'	GGGa
	Glendoick Mystique = 'Gle014'	GGGa
	Glendoick Petticoats = 'Gle015'	GGGa
	Glendoick Rosebud = 'Gle022' (EA)	GGGa
	Glendoick Ruby = 'Gle016'	GGGa
	'Glendoick Silver'	GGGa
	Glendoick Snowflakes = 'Gle001' (EA)	GGGa
	'Glendoick Tanager' **new**	GGGa
	Glendoick Vanilla = 'Gle017'	GGGa
	Glendoick Velvet = 'Gle018'	GGGa
	'Glenna'	GGGa
	'Gletschernacht'	IVic
	glischrum	GGGa
	- subsp. ***glischroides***	GGGa LMil
§	- subsp. ***rude***	GGGa MSnd
	globigerum	see *R. alutaceum* var. *alutaceum* Globigerum Group
	'Glockenspiel' (K/d)	SHea SLdr
	'Gloria'	see *R.* 'Bruns Gloria'
	'Gloria Mundi' (G)	SHea
	'Glory of Littleworth' (Ad)	LMil
	'Glowing Embers' (K)	CDoC CMac CTri CWri ECho GKin MAsh MBri MLea NHol NLar NSoo SHea SLdr SLim SPer SReu SSta
	'Goblin'	MSnd SLdr
	'Gog' (K)	CSBt SHea
§	'Goldbukett'	GGGa
	'Goldcrest' (A)	SHea

'Golden Belle'	MAsh
Golden Bouquet	see *R.* 'Goldbukett'
'Golden Coach'	CWri ECho MGos MLea MSnd SBod SLdr
'Golden Eagle' (K)	CBcs CDoC ECho GKin LMil MAsh MGos MJak MSnd NLar NSoo SHea SPer SReu SSta WMoo
'Golden Flare' (A)	CBcs CDoC CSBt CWri ECho GBin GKin LRHS MAsh MGos MLea MMuc NEgg NPCo SLdr
'Golden Gate'	CDoC CSBt ECho MLea MMuc NLar SLdr
'Golden Hind' (A)	SHea
'Golden Horn'	SLdr
'Golden Horn' (K)	GQui SHea
'Golden Lights' (A)	CWri ECho GKin LMil MBri MGos MLea NEgg NLar NPCo
(Golden Oriole Group) 'Talavera'	LMil SSpi
'Golden Princess'	LMil
'Golden Ruby'	ECho MLea SLdr SPer
'Golden Splendour'	LMil
'Golden Sunset' (K)	CMac ECho EPfP LMil MAsh MGos MLea NHol NLar SHea SLdr
'Golden Torch' $\mathbb{Y}^{H4}$	CBcs CDoC CDul CWri ECho EPfP LMil LRHS MAsh MBri MGos MJak MLea MSnd NLar NSoo SLdr SLim SPoG SReu
'Golden Wedding'	CBcs CDul CSBt CWri ECho ELon LMil LRHS LSRN MAsh MBri MGos MJak MMuc MSnd SBod SLdr
'Golden Wit'	MAsh MMHG MMuc NEgg
'Goldfinch' (K)	SHea
'Goldflimmer' (v)	CDoC EPfP GGGa GKin LMil LRHS MAsh MBri MGos MJak MMuc NLar NPri SLim SPoG
'Goldfort'	SReu
'Goldika'	LMil
'Goldinetta' **new**	LMil
'Goldkollier'	IVic
'Goldkrone' $\mathbb{Y}^{H4}$	CWri ELon EPfP GGGa LMil MAsh MGos MLea SLdr SPer SPoG SReu SSta
'Goldpracht' (K)	IVic
Goldschatz = 'Goldprinz'	IVic LMil SPoG
'Goldshine' **new**	NSoo
'Goldsworth Orange'	CWri ECho LMil MGos MSnd SBod SLdr
'Goldsworth Yellow'	CSBt
'Goldtopas' (K)	GGGa GKin LMil NLar
'Golfer'	LMil
'Gomer Waterer' $\mathbb{Y}^{H4}$	CBcs CDoC CDul CMac CSBt CWri ECho EPfP GGGa LMil LRHS MAsh MBri MGos MJak MMuc MSnd NLar SLdr SPer SPoG SReu SSta
'Gorbella'	NSoo SReu
Gowenianum Group (Ad)	LMil
'Grace Seabrook'	CDul CSBt CTri CWri ECho ELon GGGa MGos MMuc MSnd NPCo SBod SLdr SPer SReu
'Graf Lennart'	GGGa
'Graffito'	GGGa IVic LMil
'Graham Thomas'	LMil
'Grand Slam'	ECho MLea MSnd
grande	GGGa LMil MSnd SLdr
– pink-flowered	MSnd
gratum	see *R. basilicum*
'Graziella'	GGGa LMil NPri
'Greensleeves'	LMil
'Greenway' (EA)	CBcs SLdr
'Grenadier'	LMil SHea
griersonianum	CBcs GGGa LMil
griersonianum* × *yakushimanum	SLdr
griffithianum	MSnd SLdr
'Gristede' $\mathbb{Y}^{H4}$	ECho LMil LRHS MGos MLea SReu
groenlandicum	MLea NLar SPer WSHC
– 'Compactum'	GKin NLar
– 'Helma'	IVic NLar
– 'Lenie'	NLar
'Grosclaude'	CMac SHea
'Grouse' × ***keiskei*** var. ***ozawae*** 'Yaku Fairy'	ECho
'Grumpy'	CBcs CSBt CWri ECho EPfP GBin LMil LRHS MAsh MGos SLdr SReu
'Gumpo' (EA)	CMac SLdr
'Gumpo Pink' (EA)	SLdr
'Gumpo White' (EA)	LRHS MAsh MGos
'Gundula'	LMil
'Gunter Dinger'	IVic
'Gwenda' (EA)	CTri SLdr
'Gwendoline' (A)	SReu SSta
habrotrichum	GGGa LMil
'Hachmann's Anastasia'	LMil
'Hachmann's Brasilia'	SSta
'Hachmann's Charmant'	GGGa SPoG
'Hachmann's Constanze'	LMil
'Hachmann's Diadem'	LMil
'Hachmann's Eskimo'	LMil
'Hachmann's Junifeuer'	SSta
'Hachmann's Kabarett'	LMil NLar
'Hachmann's Marlis' $\mathbb{Y}^{H4}$	LMil SPoG SReu
'Hachmann's Picobello'	GGGa SPoG
§ 'Hachmann's Polaris' $\mathbb{Y}^{H4}$	CDoC LMil MBri MJak NLar NSoo SLdr
'Hachmann's Porzellan' $\mathbb{Y}^{H4}$	LMil
§ 'Hachmann's Rokoko' (EA)	LMil
'Hachmann's Sunny Boy' **new**	LRHS
haematodes	GGGa LMil SLdr
§ – subsp. ***chaetomallum***	GGGa LMil MSnd
– subsp. ***haematodes***	LMil
'Halfdan Lem'	CBcs CDoC ECho GGGa GKin LMil MAsh MBri MGos MMuc MSnd NLar SLdr SLim SPer SReu SSta
'Hallelujah'	IVic
'Halopeanum'	SHea SLdr
'Hamlet' (M)	LMil
'Hammondii'	LMil
'Hampshire Belle'	LMil SReu
'Hana-asobi' (EA)	MSnd SLdr
§ 'Hanako' (EA)	MLea
hanceanum	SLdr
– 'Canton Consul'	GGGa
– Nanum Group	GGGa
'Hanger's Flame' (A)	LMil
'Hansel'	CDoC CWri ECho GQui LMil MAsh MMuc SLdr
Happy Group	ECho
'Hardijzer Beauty' (Ad)	MSnd SLdr
'Hardy Gardenia' (EA/d)	SReu SSta
hardyi	see *R. augustinii* subsp. *hardyi*
'Harkwood Red' (EA)	SLdr
'Harry Tagg'	SLdr
Harry White's hybrid (A)	SReu SSta
'Harvest Moon' (K)	MBri NLar SCoo SHea SLdr SPer SSta

'Harvest Moon' (hybrid)	MMuc
'Hatsu-giri' (EA)	CMac LMil MSnd SLdr SPer SReu
'Heather Macleod' (EA)	SLdr
heatheriae	GGGa LMil
- KR 6176	LMil
- KR 6187	LMil
'Heidi'PBR (EA)	SLdr
'Helen Close' (EA)	SLdr
'Helena Evelyn' (A)	LMil
'Helene Schiffner' ♀H4	LMil SReu
heliolepis	GGGa LMil
- var. ***fumidum***	see *R. heliolepis* var. *heliolepis*
§ - var. ***heliolepis***	GGGa
hemidartum	see *R. pocophorum* var. *hemidartum*
hemsleyanum	LMil MSnd
'Herbert' (EA)	CMac NSoo SLim
§ 'Herbstzauber'	LMil LRHS
'Heureuse Surprise' (G)	SLdr
'High Summer'	LMil SLdr
'Hilda Margaret'	SReu
'Hille'	LMil
'Himmelberg'	GGGa
'Hinamayo'	see *R.* (Obtusum Group) 'Hinomayo'
'Hino-crimson' (EA) ♀H3-4	CBcs CDoC CHel CMac CSBt CTri ELon GKin LMil LRHS MAsh MBri MGos MMuc NHol NLar NSoo SGol SLdr SPoG SReu SSta
'Hinodegiri' (EA)	CMac CSBt SLdr SReu
'Hino-scarlet' (EA)	CBcs
hippophaeoides	LMil MSnd SLdr
- 'Bei-ma-shan'	see *R. hippophaeoides* 'Haba Shan'
- Glendoick Iceberg ='Gle019'	GGGa
§ - 'Haba Shan' ♀H4	GGGa LMil WThu
hirsutum	LMil
- 'Flore Pleno' (d)	ECho
hirtipes	GGGa MSnd
hodgsonii	LMil MSnd SLdr
* 'Hogi-kasane' (A) **new**	NLar
'Homebush' (K/d) ♀H4	CBcs CDoC CMac CTri CWri EPfP GBin LMil MAsh MBri MGos MJak NLar NPCo NSoo SLdr SPer SPoG SReu SSta WMoo
'Honey Butter'	LMil NLar SLim
'Honeysuckle' (K)	NHol SHea SReu SSta
§ 'Ho-o' (EA)	CBcs SLdr
hookeri	LMil
- Tigh-na-Rudha form	GGGa
'Hoppy'	CBcs CWri LMil MAsh MGos MLea MMuc MSnd NLar SLdr SLim SPer
'Horizon Monarch' ♀H3-4	CDoC CWri GGGa GKin IVic LMil LRHS MBri MLea NLar SLdr SLim SPer SReu SSta
horlickianum	GGGa
'Hortulanus H. Witte' (M)	CSBt SReu
'Hot Shot'	see *R.* 'Girard's Hot Shot'
'Hot Shot Variegated' (EA/v)	CDoC GGGa NEgg SLdr
'Hotei' ♀H4	CSBt ECho EPfP GKin LMil LRHS MAsh MGos NEgg NHol NPCo SLdr SPer SReu
'Hotspur' (K)	CWri ECho GBin MGos NLar SLdr
'Hotspur Red' (K) ♀H4	CDoC GKev GKin LMil MAsh NEgg NPCo SHea WMoo
huanum	GGGa LMil
- EGM 316	LMil
'Hugh Koster'	SLdr
aff. ***huidongense***	LMil

- KR 7315	LMil
'Hullaballoo'	LMil
Humming Bird Group	CMHG LMil SLdr
hunnewellianum	MSnd
'Hussar'	CWri LMil
'Hyde and Seek'	GQui
'Hydon Dawn' ♀H4	CBcs CDoC CWri LMil MBri MGos MLea MSnd SHea SLdr SReu SSta
'Hydon Hunter' ♀H4	MSnd SHea SLdr SReu SSta
'Hydon Pink'	SHea
'Hydon Velvet'	LMil SReu WMoo
hylaeum	MSnd
Hyperion Group	SReu
hyperythrum	GGGa LMil MSnd
hypoglaucum	see *R. argyrophyllum* subsp. *hypoglaucum*
'Ice Cube'	ECho MLea MMuc SEND SLdr SPer
'Iceberg'	see *R.* 'Lodauric Iceberg'
'Idealist'	LMil
'Ightham Gold'	SReu
'Ightham Peach'	SReu
'Ightham Purple'	SReu
'Ightham Yellow'	SHea SReu
'Ilam Carmen' (K)	SHea
§ 'Ilam Melford Lemon' (A)	LMil
§ 'Ilam Ming' (A)	LMil
'Ilam Violet'	LMil
'Imago' (K/d)	LMil SLdr
§ 'Ima-shojo' (EA/d)	CMac LRHS LSRN MGos SPer
impeditum	CBcs CSBt CWib ECho GBin GQui MGos MJak MLea MMuc MSnd NSoo SLdr SPer SReu SSta
- 'Blue Steel'	see *R. fastigiatum* 'Blue Steel'
- 'Indigo'	GKin LLHF MGos NPCo SLdr SReu WAbe
- 'Pygmaeum'	NHar WAbe WThu
- Reuthe's form	SReu
imperator	see *R. uniflorum* var. *imperator*
§ ***indicum*** 'Macranthum' (EA)	SLdr
'Ingrid Mehlquist'	GGGa
Inkarho Lilac Dufthecke ='Rhodunter 149'PBR	LMil
insigne ♀H4	GGGa GLin LMil MSnd
- Reuthe's form	SReu
insigne* × *yakushimanum	SReu
Intrifast Group	GGGa
iodes	see *R. alutaceum* var. *iodes*
'Irene Koster' (O) ♀H4	CDoC CSBt CWri EPfP GGGa GKin LMil MBri MLea NEgg NLar SLdr SLim SPer
'Irohayama' (EA) ♀H3-4	CMac ELon EPfP GQui LMil LRHS MAsh MMuc NPri SLdr
irroratum	LMil
- subsp. ***irroratum***	MSnd
* - subsp. ***kontumense*** var. ***ningyuenense***	GGGa GLin
- 'Polka Dot'	GGGa LMil
- subsp. ***yiliangense*** EGM 339	LMil
'Isabel'	NPri
'Isabel' (EA)	LRHS MAsh
'Isola Bella'	GGGa
iteaphyllum	see *R. formosum* var. *formosum* Iteaphyllum Group
'Ivette' (EA)	CMac
'Izabelle' (EA)	MBri
'Izumi-no-mai' (EA) **new**	SLdr
'J.C. Williams'	CBcs
'J.G. Millais'	SLdr

	'J.M. de Montague'	see *R.* 'The Hon. Jean Marie de Montague'
	'Jack A. Sand' (K)	GGGa
	'Jalisco Eclipse'	LMil
	'Jalisco Elect'	CWri SLdr
	'Jalisco Janet'	LMil SHea
	'James Burchett' ♀H4	LMil SLdr SReu
	'James Gable' (EA)	MAsh SLdr
	'Janet Blair'	CWri
	'Janet Rhea' (EA)	SLdr
	'Janet Ward'	SReu
	japonicum (A. Gray) Valcken	see *R. molle* subsp. *japonicum*
	- var. ***pentamerum***	see *R. degronianum* subsp. *degronianum*
	jasminiflorum (V)	GGGa
	javanicum (V)	GGGa
	'Jean Marie Montague'	see *R.* 'The Hon. Jean Marie de Montague'
	'Jeff Hill' (EA)	ECho MMuc SLdr
	'Jenny'	see *R.* 'Creeping Jenny'
	'Jeremy Davies'	SReu
	'Jessica Rose' (A)	LMil
	'Jim Russell' (*ciliicalyx* hybrid)	GGGa
	'Jingle Bells'	GGGa
	'Joan Paton' (A)	SLdr
	'Joanna'	MMuc
	'Jocelyne'	LMil
	'Jock'	SLdr
	Jock Group	CBcs CMHG
	'Jock Brydon' (O)	GGGa LMil SHea
	'Johanna' (EA) ♀H4	CDoC CTri EPfP LMil LRHS MAsh NHol NLar NPri SLdr SPer SReu
	'John Cairns' (EA)	CMac MSnd SLdr
	'John Walter'	SHea
	'John Waterer'	SHea
	'Johnny Bender'	SLdr
	johnstoneanum	CBcs GGGa LMil SLdr
	- KW 7732	SLdr
	- 'Double Diamond' (d)	IDee LMil
	'Jolie Madame' (Vs)	CWri ECho GKin LMil LRHS MAsh MBri MLea MMuc NLar NPri SLdr SPer SReu SSta
	'Joseph Baumann' (G)	SLdr
	'Joseph Hill' (EA)	ECho ELon MGos MMuc NLar SLdr
	'Jubilant'	LMil SHea
	'Jubilee'	SLdr
	'Juliette' (EA)	IVic
	'June Fire' (A)	GGGa SReu
	kaempferi (EA)	CBcs LMil SLdr
	- 'Damio'	see *R. kaempferi* 'Mikado'
§	- 'Mikado' (EA)	LMil NSoo SReu
	- orange-flowered (EA)	CMac
	'Kali' **new**	GGGa
	'Kalinka'	LMil MAsh NLar SLdr SPoG
	'Karen Triplett'	LMil
	'Karin'	MJak SLdr
	'Kasane-kagaribi' (EA)	SLdr
	'Kate Waterer' ♀H4	CWri SReu
N	'Kathleen' de Rothschild (K)	SHea
	'Kathleen' van Nes (EA)	SLdr
	'Katisha' (EA)	SLdr
	'Katy Watson'	SReu SSta
	'Keija' (EA)	SLdr
	keiskei Cordifolium Group	WAbe
	- var. ***ozawae*** 'Yaku Fairy' ♀H4	LMil WAbe WThu

	keleticum	see *R. calostrotum* subsp. *keleticum*
	'Kelsay's Double'	MLea
	'Ken Janeck' ♀H4	GGGa
§	***kendrickii***	GGGa
	'Kentucky Colonel'	SLdr
	'Kermesinum' (EA)	CTri MAsh MGos NWad SLdr SLim SReu
I	'Kermesinum Rosé' (EA)	CSBt ECho ELon LMil MGos MLea SLdr SLim SReu
	kesangiae	GGGa LMil
	- AC 5343	LMil
	- var. ***album***	GGGa
	Kewense Group	CWri
	keysii	GGGa
	- EGM 064	LMil
	'Kilimanjaro'	LMil SReu
	'Kimbeth'	GGGa
	'King George' Loder	see *R.* 'Loderi King George'
	kingianum	see *R. arboreum* subsp. *zeylanicum*
§	'Kirin' (Kurume) (EA/d)	CBcs CMac LMil NLar SLdr
	'Kirsten Begeer'	IVic
	kiusianum (EA) ♀H4	LMil MSnd SReu
I	- 'Album' (EA)	LMil SReu WAbe
	- 'Hillier's Pink' (EA)	LMil
	'Klondyke' (K) ♀H4	CBcs CSBt CTri EPfP GGGa GKin LMil LRHS MAsh MGos NLar NPri SHea SLdr SPoG SReu
	'Kluis Sensation' ♀H4	CMac CSBt MSnd SLdr SReu
	'Kluis Triumph'	SReu
	'Knap Hill Apricot' (K)	LMil SHea
	'Knap Hill Red' (K)	CDoC LMil SHea
	'Knap Hill Yellow' (K)	SHea
	'Kobold' (EA)	SLdr
	'Koichiro Wada'	see *R. yakushimanum* 'Koichiro Wada'
	'Kokardia'	LMil
	'Kokette'	IVic
	kongboense	GGGa WAbe
	'Königstein' (EA)	IVic LMil
§	'Koningin Emma' (M)	GKin LMil NLar
	'Konsonanz'	IVic
	'Koromo-shikibu' (EA)	GGGa
	'Koromo-shikibu White' (EA)	GGGa
	'Koster's Brilliant Red' (M)	CSBt EPfP MGos SReu SSta
	'Kranenfee' (A) **new**	GGGa
§	'Kure-no-yuki' (EA/d)	LMil MMuc
	kyawii	GGGa
	'Lackblatt'	see *R.* (Volker Group) 'Lackblatt'
	lacteum	GGGa LMil
	'Lady Alice Fitzwilliam' ♀H2-3	CBcs CMHG CMac ECre GGGa GKin IDee LMil SLdr
	'Lady Chamberlain Salmon Trout'	see *R.* 'Salmon Trout'
	'Lady Clare' (K)	SHea
	'Lady Clementine Mitford' ♀H4	CSBt CWri ECho EPfP LMil MAsh MBri MGos MLea MMuc SEND SHea SLdr SPer SReu
	'Lady Eleanor Cathcart'	SHea SLdr
	'Lady Louise' (EA)	SLdr
	'Lady Montagu'	LMil
	'Lady Robin' (EA)	SLdr
	'Lady Romsey' ♀H4	LMil MSnd SLdr
	laetum (V)	GGGa
	Lamellen Group	LMil
	'Lamplighter'	SReu
	lanatoides	GGGa LMil
§	***lanatum***	ECho GGGa LMil
	- Flinckii Group	see *R. lanatum*

	'Langworth'	CWri ECho MGos MLea MMuc MSnd SLdr SReu
	lanigerum	LMil SReu
	'Lanzette'	IVic
	lapponicum Parviflorum Group	GGGa
	'Lapwing' (K)	NLar SLdr
	'Laramie'	GGGa
	'Late Love' (EA)	CDoC
*	***laterifolium***	GGGa
	Laura Aberconway Group	SHea SLdr
	'Lavender Brilliant' (EA)	SLdr
	'Lavender Girl' ♀H4	CMac LMil MSnd SLdr SReu SSta
	'Lavender Queen'	SLdr
	'Lea Rainbow'	MLea
	'Ledifolium'	see *R.* × *mucronatum*
	'Ledifolium Album'	see *R.* × *mucronatum*
	'Lee's Dark Purple'	CWri LMil
	'Lee's Scarlet'	LMil
	'Lemon Dream'	LMil LRHS MAsh NLar NPri SLdr SLim
*	'Lemon Drop' (A)	GGGa
	'Lemon Meringue'	LMil
	'Lemonora' (M)	CBcs GKin
	'Lem's 45'	CBcs CWri ECho MBri SLdr
	'Lem's Cameo' ♀H3	GGGa LMil SReu SSta
	'Lem's Monarch' ♀H4	CBcs CDoC CWri ELon GGGa LMil MBri MGos MLea MMuc SLdr SReu SSta
	'Lem's Tangerine'	CDoC LMil
	'Lemur' (EA)	ECho GGGa LMil MLea NLar WThu
	'Leni'	LRHS MAsh
	'Leo' (EA)	MSnd SLdr
	'Leonardslee Giles'	SLdr
	'Leonardslee Primrose'	SLdr
	'Leonore'	LMil
	lepidostylum	CMac CWri GGGa LMil SReu
	lepidotum	GGGa
	- var. ***album***	GGGa
	- yellow-flowered McB 110	WThu
§	***leptocarpum***	GGGa
§	'Leucanthum'	GGGa WThu
	leucaspis	GGal SLdr
	'Leuchtpolster'	IVic
	'Lewis Monarch'	GQui
	'Lila Pedigo'	CWri ECho MGos SLdr SPer
	'Lilactina'	SLdr
	'Lily Marleen' (EA)	CTri SCoo
	'Limetta' (K)	GGGa
	'Linda' ♀H4	CBcs CTri CWri ECho EPfP GGGa LMil LSRN MAsh MBri MGos MJak MMuc SLdr
	'Linda Stuart' (EA)	GGGa
	lindleyi	CBcs GGGa
	- 'Dame Edith Sitwell'	LMil
	- 'Geordie Sherriff'	GGGa
	'Linearifolium'	see *R. stenopetalum* 'Linearifolium'
	'Linnet' (K/d)	SHea SLdr
	'Lionel's First'	LMil
	Lionel's Triumph Group	LMil
	'Lisetta' **new**	WMoo
	'Little Beauty' (EA)	SLdr
	'Little Ben'	ECho
	'Loch Arkaig'	GGGa
	'Loch Awe'	GGGa
	'Loch Earn'	GGGa
	'Loch Faskally' **new**	GGGa
	'Loch Laggan'	GGGa
	'Loch Leven'	GGGa
	'Loch Linnhe'	GGGa
	'Loch Lomond'	GGGa
	'Loch Morar'	GGGa
	lochiae (V)	GGGa
	'Lochinch Spinbur'	GQui
	Lodauric Group	SReu
§	'Lodauric Iceberg' ♀H3-4	LMil MSnd SReu
	'Lodbrit'	SReu
	Loderi Group	SLdr SPer
	'Loderi Fairy Queen'	SLdr
	'Loderi Game Chick' ♀H3-4	SLdr
	'Loderi Georgette'	SLdr
	'Loderi Helen'	SLdr
	'Loderi Julie'	SSta
§	'Loderi King George' ♀H3-4	CBcs CDoC CDul CHll CWri ECho GGGa GKin IVic LMil MGos MLea MSnd SLdr SReu SSta WGwG
	'Loderi Patience'	SLdr
	'Loderi Pink Coral'	LMil SLdr
	'Loderi Pink Diamond' ♀H3-4	CDoC CWri LMil SLdr
	'Loderi Pink Topaz' ♀H3-4	SLdr
	'Loderi Pretty Polly'	SLdr
	'Loderi Princess Marina'	SLdr
	'Loderi Sir Edmund'	MSnd SLdr
	'Loderi Sir Joseph Hooker'	MSnd SLdr
	'Loderi Titan'	SLdr SReu SSta
	'Loderi Venus' ♀H3-4	MSnd SLdr SReu SSta
	'Loderi White Diamond'	SLdr
	'Loder's White' ♀H3-4	LMil MLea SHea SLdr SReu SSta
	longesquamatum	GGGa MSnd
	longipes	GGGa LMil MSnd SLdr
	- EGM 336	LMil
	- var. ***chienianum***	LMil MSnd
	lopsangianum	GGGa
	'Lord Roberts' ♀H4	CBcs CDoC CDul CMac CSBt CTri CWri ECho EPfP GBin GGGa LMil LRHS MAsh MGos MJak MLea MMuc MSnd NEgg NHol NLar SHea SLdr SLim SPer SReu SSta WMoo
	'Louis Pasteur'	SReu
	'Louisa' (EA)	MAsh NLar
	'Louise Dowdle' (EA)	SLdr
	'Lovely William'	CMac LMil MSnd SLdr
	lowndesii	WAbe
	'Lucy Lou'	GGGa
	ludlowii	GGGa
	'Luisella'	IVic
	'Lullaby' (EA)	SLdr
	'Lunar Queen'	SLdr
	luteiflorum	GGGa
	- KW 7833 **new**	MSnd
	lutescens	CBcs CTsd LMil MSnd SLdr SReu WAbe WThu
	- 'Bagshot Sands' ♀H3-4	GGGa IDee LMil LRHS NLar SLdr
	- 'Exbury'	CExl
	luteum (A) ♀H4	Widely available
	- 'Golden Comet' (A)	GGGa
	lyi	GGGa
*	'Mac Ovata'	CMac
	macabeanum ♀H3-4	CBcs CDoC GBin GGGa GKev GKin LMil MLea MMuc MSnd NPCo SLdr SPer SReu SSpi SSta
	- NAPE 052	GGGa
	- Reuthe's form	SReu
	'Macarena'	IVic
	maccabeanum × ***wardii***	GGGa
	macgregoriae (V)	GGGa
	macranthum	see *R. indicum* 'Macranthum'

	macrosmithii	see *R. argipeplum*
	maculiferum	GGGa
	'Madame Ad. van Hecke' (EA)	CTri GKin IVic LMil MAsh MBri MMuc NLar NSoo SLdr SLim
	'Madame Galle'	NSoo
	'Madame Masson'	CDoC CDul CTri CWri ECho ELan LMil LRHS MAsh MBri MGos MLea MMuc MSnd NLar NPri SPer SReu SSta
	maddenii	CDoC LMil
§	- subsp. ***crassum***	CBcs CExl GGGa GLin IVic MSnd SKHP SLdr
§	- subsp. ***maddenii*** Polyandrum Group	CBcs GGGa GGal GQui
	'Madeleine' (K)	SHea
	'Maggie'	IVic
	'Maggie Brown' (A)	GGGa
	'Magic Flute' (EA)	MAsh MBri
I	'Magic Flute' (V)	LMil SCoo
	'Magnificum' (O)	SHea SLdr
	magniflorum	GGGa
	'Maharani'	GGGa
	'Mai-ogi' (EA)	IVic
	'Maischnee' (EA)	GGGa
	'Maja' (G)	SReu SSta
§	***makinoi*** ♀H4	GGGa LLHF LMil SReu SSpi SSta WAbe
	- 'Fuju-kaku-no-matsu'	MGos
	'Makiyak'	LMil
	'Malahat'	MSnd
	malayanum	GGGa
	mallotum	GGGa IDee LMil MSnd SReu
	'Manda Sue'	MMuc
	Mandalay Group	SHea
	'Mandarin Lights' (A)	LMil NLar
	'Manderley'	LMil
	maoerense	GGGa
	'Maraschino' (EA)	GGGa IVic
	'Marcel Ménard'	CDoC CDul GGGa LMil LRHS MAsh NLar NPri SLdr SReu SSta
	'Marchioness of Lansdowne'	CWri SHea SLdr
	'Mardi Gras'	CDoC MLea NEgg NLar SLdr
	'Margaret Blain' **new**	SReu
	Margaret Dunn Group	CWri
	'Margaret Falmouth'	SReu
	'Maria Elena' (EA/d)	LMil
	'Marie Curie'	LMil
	'Marie Hoffman'	LMil
	'Marilee' (EA)	CDoC ECho ELon IVic LRHS MAsh MGos NLar SLdr
	Mariloo Group	LMil MSnd
	'Marina' (K)	SHea
	'Marion Merriman' (K)	SHea
	'Marion Street' ♀H4	LMil SReu
	'Markeeta's Prize' ♀H4	CDoC CWri ECho EPfP GGGa LMil LRHS MAsh MBri MGos MLea MMuc NLar NPri SHea SLdr SLim SReu
	'Marlies' (A)	MBri NLar
	'Marmot' (EA)	ECho MLea NLar
	'Mars'	SLdr
	'Marsalla'	LMil
	'Martha Isaacson' (Ad) ♀H4	CWri LMil MGos MLea SLdr SReu
	'Martha Wright'	GGGa LMil MAsh NPri
	martinianum	GGGa SLdr
	'Maruschka' (EA)	GGGa IVic LMil LRHS MAsh SPoG
	'Mary Claire' (K)	SHea
	'Mary Fleming'	SLdr
	'Mary Forte'	NSoo
	'Mary Helen' (EA)	LRHS MAsh MBri SCoo SLdr SLim SPoG
	'Mary Poppins' (K)	GKin LMil LSRN MAsh NLar SCoo SLdr SLim WMoo
	'Master of Elphinstone' (EA)	SLdr
	'Matador'	GGGa LMil MSnd SHea SLdr
	Matador Group	SReu
	maximum	GGGa
§	'Maxwellii' (EA)	CMac SLdr
	'May Day' ♀H3-4	CMac MAsh NEgg SHea SLdr
	May Day Group	CBcs CWri MGos MSnd
	'Mayor Johnstone'	CTri MAsh NPri
	'Mazurka' (K)	IVic SHea SLdr
	Medusa Group	SHea SLdr
	megacalyx	GGGa
	'Megan' (EA)	ECho ELon LSRN MAsh MGos MMuc SLdr WGwG
	megaphyllum	see *R. basilicum*
	megeratum	GGGa SLdr
	- 'Bodnant'	GGGa ITim WAbe WThu
	mekongense	see *R. viridescens* Rubroluteum Group
	var. ***mekongense*** Rubroluteum Group	
	- - Viridescens Group	see *R. viridescens*
	'Melford Lemon'	see *R.* 'Ilam Melford Lemon'
	'Melina' (EA/d)	LMil
	'Melville'	SReu SSta
	'Mendosina'	IVic
	mengtszense	MSnd
	'Mephistopheles' (K)	SHea
	'Merganser' ♀H4	GGGa LMil MLea
	'Merlin' (EA)	LMil SLdr
	metternichii var. ***pentamerum***	see *R. degronianum* subsp. *degronianum*
	'Mi Amor'	GGGa LMil
	'Miami' (A)	SLdr
	'Michael Hall' **new**	LMil
	'Michael Hill' (EA)	MAsh
	'Michael Waterer'	MSnd SLdr
	'Michael's Pride'	CBcs GQui LMil
	'Michiko' (EA)	IVic
	microgynum	GGGa MSnd
	- Gymnocarpum Group	MSnd
	microleucum	see *R. orthocladum* var. *microleucum*
	micromeres	see *R. leptocarpum*
	'Midnight Mystique'	GGGa SReu SSta
	'Midnight Ruby'	GGGa
	'Midsummer'	IVic SHea
	'Midsummer Mermaid' (A)	LMil
	'Mikado' (EA)	see *R. kaempferi* 'Mikado'
	'Milton' (R)	LMil
	'Mimi' (EA)	CMac
	'Mindy's Love'	LMil
	'Ming'	see *R.* 'Ilam Ming'
	miniatum	GGGa
	- CER 9927	GGGa
	'Minikin' (K)	SHea
	minus var. ***minus*** (Carolinianum Group) 'Epoch'	LMil
	'Miss Muffet' (EA)	SLdr
	'Moerheim' ♀H4	CBcs CWri ECho LRHS MAsh MGos MMuc NPCo NPri SLdr SLim SReu
§	'Moerheim's Pink'	LMil MSnd SLdr
	'Moidart' (Vs)	LMil NLar
	'Moira Salmon' (EA)	SLdr

§ ***molle*** subsp. ***japonicum*** (A)	LMil
– subsp. ***molle*** (A)	LMil
Mollis, orange-flowered (M)	GKin SRms
– pink-flowered (M)	GKin SRms
– red-flowered (M)	GKin
– salmon-flowered (M)	GQui
– yellow-flowered (M)	GKin GQui SRms
'Molly Ann'	ECho LSRN MBri MGos MSnd NLar SLdr
'Molten Gold' (v)	GGGa LMil LRHS MAsh
§ 'Momoko' (EA)	MAsh
monanthum	GGGa
monosematum	see *R. pachytrichum* var. *monosematum*
montroseanum	GGGa LMil MSnd SLdr
'Moon Maiden' (EA)	ECho ELon GGal GQui MMuc
Moonstone Group	MLea
'Moonstone Pink'	MSnd SLdr
'Moonstone Yellow'	MSnd SLdr
'Moonwax'	SLdr
§ 'Morgenrot'	NLar
morii	GGGa SLdr
'Morning Cloud' ♀H4	ECho EPfP LRHS MAsh NHol NLar SLdr SLim SReu
Morning Red	see *R.* 'Morgenrot'
'Moser's Maroon'	CBcs CWri ECho GGGa MGos SLdr SPoG
'Motet' (K/d)	SHea
'Mother's Day' (EA) ♀H4	CBcs CDoC CDul CMac CSBt CTri ECho EPfP EPot GKin GQui LMil LRHS LSRN MAsh MBri MGos MMuc NEgg NHol NPCo NPri SLdr SLim SPer SPoG SReu SSta
Moulten Gold = 'Blattgold'	LMil
'Mount Everest'	LMil SReu SSta
'Mount Rainier' (K)	SLdr
'Mount Saint Helens' (A)	LMil SLdr SLim
'Mount Seven Star'	see *R. nakaharae* 'Mount Seven Star'
moupinense	GGGa GLin MSnd SLdr
– 'Fulmar'	GGGa
'Mrs A.C. Kenrick'	SHea SLdr
'Mrs A.T. de la Mare' ♀H4	LMil SHea SReu SSta
'Mrs Betty Robertson'	CMac ECho GBin MBri MGos MMuc SLdr
'Mrs Charles E. Pearson' ♀H4	CDul CSBt LMil MSnd SHea SLdr
'Mrs Davies Evans' ♀H4	SReu SSta
'Mrs Emil Hager' (EA)	SLdr
'Mrs Furnivall' ♀H4	CBcs CDoC CWri ECho GGGa MBri MGos MLea MMuc SLdr SReu
'Mrs G.W. Leak'	CDul CSBt CWri GGGa LMil MLea SHea SReu
'Mrs J.C. Williams' ♀H4	LMil
'Mrs J.G. Millais'	LMil SHea
'Mrs James Horlick'	CWri
'Mrs Kingsmill'	SLdr
'Mrs Lionel de Rothschild' ♀H4	CWri SReu
'Mrs P.D. Williams'	SReu
'Mrs Peter Koster' (M)	SLdr
'Mrs R.S. Holford' ♀H4	MSnd SHea SLdr
'Mrs T.H. Lowinsky' ♀H4	CDoC CDul CMac ECho ELon GGGa GKin LMil MAsh MGos MLea MMuc MSnd NLar SEND SHea SLdr SLim SPer SReu
'Mucronatum'	see *R.* × *mucronatum*
§ × ***mucronatum*** (EA)	CBcs MSnd
mucronulatum	CBcs MSnd SLdr
– B&SWJ 786	WCru
– var. ***chejuense***	see *R. mucronulatum* var. *taquetii*
– 'Cornell Pink' ♀H4	GGGa
§ – var. ***taquetii***	GGGa
– – B&SWJ 4486	WCru
'Mulroy Cream'	LMil
'Muneira' (EA)	IVic
'Nabucco' (A)	EPfP GGGa LMil MMuc SEND WMoo
nakaharae (EA)	MSnd SLdr SReu WAbe
– 'Mariko' (EA)	WAbe WThu
§ – 'Mount Seven Star' (EA) ♀H4	ECho GGGa LMil MGos NWad SLdr WAbe WPat WThu
§ – orange-flowered (EA)	ECho LMil LRHS MAsh MGos MMuc SLdr SReu
– pink-flowered (EA)	ECho MGos MMuc SLdr SReu
– red-flowered (EA)	ECho
'Nakahari Orange'	see *R. nakaharae* orange-flowered
nakotiltum	MSnd
'Nancy Buchanan' (K)	SLdr
'Nancy Evans' ♀H3-4	CDoC CSBt ECho EPfP GGGa GGal GKin LMil LSRN MAsh MLea NLar NPCo NPri SLdr SLim SReu SSpi SSta
'Nancy of Robinhill' (EA)	SReu
'Nancy Waterer' (G) ♀H4	EPfP LMil NLar SReu
'Nanki Poo' (EA)	SLdr
'Naomi' (EA)	GQui MSnd SLdr
Naomi Group	MSnd
'Naomi Hope'	LMil
'Naomi Nautilus'	LMil
'Naomi Pink Beauty'	LMil
'Naomi Stella Maris'	LMil
'Narcissiflorum' (G/d) ♀H4	CSBt EPfP GKin LMil SReu SSta
'Naselle'	GGGa SReu
'Ne Plus Ultra' (V)	GGGa
neoglandulosum SIN 1828	GLin
neriiflorum	GGGa LMil MSnd
– subsp. ***neriiflorum*** AC 1356 new	MSnd
§ – – Phoenicodum Group	GGGa
– – – Farrer 877	MSnd
§ – subsp. ***phaedropum***	GGGa LMil
'Netty Koster'	SLdr
'Newcomb's Sweetheart'	LMil
'Niagara' (EA) ♀H3-4	CMac LMil MGos NLar SLdr SPer
'Nichola' (EA)	LSRN
'Nico' (EA)	CMac LRHS MAsh
'Nicoletta'	LMil
'Night Sky'	CDoC ECho GGGa LMil LRHS MAsh MGos MMuc MSnd NLar NPCo SLdr
'Nightingale'	SReu
nigroglandulosum	GGGa
nilagiricum	see *R. arboreum* subsp. *nilagiricum*
'Ninotschka'	IVic
nipponicum	GGGa
'Nishiki' (EA)	CMac
nitens	see *R. calostrotum* subsp. *riparium* Nitens Group
nitidulum var. ***omeiense***	GGGa MSnd
nivale subsp. ***boreale*** Ramosissimum Group	GGGa
§ – subsp. ***nivale***	GKev ITim
niveum ♀H4	GGGa LMil MSnd SReu
– B&SWJ 2611	WCru
– B&SWJ 2659	WCru
– B&SWJ 2675	WCru

	nobleanum	see *R.* Nobleanum Group
§	Nobleanum Group	GGGa LMil MSnd SLdr SSta
	'Nobleanum Album'	GGGa LMil SReu SSta
	'Nobleanum Coccineum'	SLdr SReu
	'Nobleanum Venustum'	CWri LMil SReu SSta
	'Nordlicht' (EA)	SLdr
	'Norfolk Candy'	LMil LRHS
	'Noriko' (EA)	SLdr
N	'Norma' (R/d) ♀H4	SReu
	'Northern Hi-Lights' (A)	GKin LMil NLar SLdr SLim
	'Nova Zembla'	CBcs CDoC CTri ECho ELon EPfP GGGa LMil LRHS MAsh MGos MMuc NEgg SLim SPer SPoG SReu SSta
	nudiflorum	see *R. periclymenoides*
	nudipes	LMil
	nuttallii	GGGa LMil
	nymphaeoides CGG 14027 **new**	GGGa
	'Oban'	EPot ITim NSla WAbe WThu
	Obtusum Group (EA)	MSnd SLdr
	- 'Amoenum' (EA/d)	CBcs CDoC CMac CSBt ECho LMil MGos MSnd SLdr SPer
§	- 'Hinomayo' (EA) ♀H3-4	CMac CTri EPfP GKin GQui LMil MSnd SLdr SPer SReu
	occidentale (A) ♀H4	CDul GGal GKin LMil SHea
	- SIN 1830	GGGa GLin
	ochraceum	GGGa LMil
	'Odee Wright'	CTri CWri LRHS MAsh SLdr
	'Odoratum' (Ad)	MLea
	'Oh! Kitty'	CWri ECho MLea NPCo SLdr
	'Old Gold' (K)	ECho SHea SLdr
	'Old Port' ♀H4	CWri LMil
	'Olga' ♀H4	LMil SHea SReu SSta
	'Olga Niblett' (EA)	NSoo SReu SSta
	oligocarpum	GGGa
	'Olive'	SLdr
	'Olympic Sunrise'	LMil
I	'Olympic Torch' **new**	LMil
§	'One Thousand Butterflies'	MSnd SLdr
	'Ophelia' (EA)	SLdr
	'Opossum' (EA)	GGGa
	'Orange Beauty' (EA) ♀H3-4	CBcs CDoC CMac ECho GGGa MAsh MGos MSnd SGol SLdr SReu
	'Orange King' (EA)	LMil SLdr SPoG
	'Orangeade' (K)	SHea
	orbiculare ♀H3-4	GGGa LMil MSnd
§	- subsp. ***cardiobasis***	GGGa MSnd
	'Orchid Lights'	MAsh
	'Oregon' (EA)	SLdr
	Oregonia Group	LMil
	oreodoxa	LMil
§	- var. ***fargesii*** ♀H4	GGGa LMil MSnd
	- - AC 4052 **new**	MSnd
	- var. ***oreodoxa***	GGGa LMil
	oreotrephes	GKev IDee LMil MSnd NLar SHea SLdr
	- 'Bluecalyptus'	GGGa
§	- Exquisitum Group	SLdr
	- 'Pentland'	GGGa IDee LMil LRHS NLar
	'Orient' (K)	SHea
§	***orthocladum*** var. ***microleucum***	GGGa GKev WThu
	'Oryx' (O)	SHea SLdr
	'Osaraku Seedling' (EA)	EPfP LRHS
	'Osmar' ♀H4	GGGa MSnd
	'Ostara'	MGos
	'Osterschnee'	IVic
	'Oudijk's Favorite'	SLdr
	'Oudijk's Sensation'	CBcs CWri ECho GQui MAsh MGos MMuc NPCo SEND SHea SLdr
	'Oxydol' (K)	IVic MMuc SHea SLdr
§	***pachypodum***	GGGa
	pachysanthum ♀H4	CDoC GGGa GKin IDee LMil LRHS MSnd NLar SLdr SReu SSpi
	- 'Crosswater'	LMil
	pachysanthum × ***yakushimanum***	SReu
	pachytrichum	GGGa SLdr
§	- var. ***monosematum***	MSnd
	'Palestrina' (EA) ♀H3-4	CBcs CMac CSBt ECho EPfP GBin GKin MAsh MGos MJak MMuc NLar NPCo SGol SLdr SPer SReu SSta
	'Pallas' (G)	GKin
	paludosum	see *R. nivale* subsp. *nivale*
	'Pancake'	CMac
	'Panda' (EA) ♀H4	CSBt CTri ECho EPfP EPot GGGa LMil LRHS MAsh MLea NPri
	'Paprika Spiced'	ECho MGos MLea NPCo SLdr
	'Parfait' (EA)	LMil NLar SPer
	'Parkfeuer' (A)	GGGa IVic
	parmulatum	LMil
	- KW 5876	LMil
	- 'Ocelot'	GGGa
	parryae AM (roseatum)	GGGa
	'Patty Bee' ♀H4	CBcs CSBt CTri CWri ECho EPfP EPot GBin GGGa GKev IDee LMil LRHS MAsh MBri MGos MLea NPri NSla SLdr SLim SReu SSpi SSta
	patulum	see *R. pemakoense* Patulum Group
	'Pavane' (K)	SHea
	'Peep bo' (EA)	SLdr
	'Peeping Tom'	NHol
	pemakoense	GGGa MSnd SLdr WThu
§	- Patulum Group	SLdr
	'Pemakofairy'	WThu
	pendulum	GGGa
	Penelope Group	SReu
	'Penheale Blue' ♀H4	GKin LMil
	'Penjerrick'	GGGa
	'Penny Tomlin'	SReu SSta
	pentaphyllum (A)	GGGa
	'Peppina'	GGGa
	'Percy Wiseman' ♀H4	CBcs CDoC CDul CHel CSBt CWri ECho EPfP GBin GGGa GKin LMil LRHS MAsh MBri MGos MJak MMuc MSnd NEgg NLar SLdr SLim SPer SReu SSta
	'Perfect Lady'	LMil
§	***periclymenoides*** (A)	GGGa GKev LMil
	'Persil' (K) ♀H4	CBcs CMac CSBt CTri CWri ECho EPfP GGGa GKin LMil LRHS MAsh MBri MGos MJak MLea MMuc NHol NLar SCoo SLdr SPer SReu SSta WMoo
	'Peter Chapell'	GGGa
	'Peter Gable' (EA)	SLdr
	'Peter Koster' (M)	SHea
	'Peter Koster' (hybrid)	GKin SLdr
	petrocharis	GGGa
	'Petrouchka' (K)	SHea
	'Pfauenauge'	GGGa
	phaedropum	see *R. neriiflorum* subsp. *phaedropum*
	phaeochrysum	MSnd SLdr
	- var. ***agglutinatum***	GKev
§	- var. ***levistratum***	MSnd SLdr
	- var. ***phaeochrysum***	GKev
	- - C 12529 **new**	GGGa

	'Phalarope'	SLdr SReu
	phoenicodum	see *R. neriiflorum* subsp. *neriiflorum* Phoenicodum Group
	'Phyllis Korn'	CWri IVic LMil SLdr
	'Picotee' (EA) **new**	SPer
	'Picotee' (K)	LMil
§	***piercei***	GGGa LMil MSnd
	'Pilgrim'	LMil
	'Pine Marten' (EA)	GGGa
	pingianum	GGGa SLdr
	'Pink Bride'	SLdr
	'Pink Cameo'	CWri
	'Pink Cherub' ♀H4	ECho ELon LMil MAsh SLdr
	'Pink Delight'	MAsh
I	'Pink Delight' (K)	GKin MBri MGos SHea SLdr
	'Pink Delight' (V)	MMuc
	'Pink Drift'	CSBt ECho LMil MGos MMuc NPCo NSla SLdr SPer WThu
	'Pink Gin'	LMil LRHS NLar
	'Pink Mimosa' (Vs)	SLdr
	'Pink Pancake' (EA) ♀H4	ECho ELon EPfP GKin LMil MAsh MGos MMuc NPri SLdr
	'Pink Pearl' (EA)	see *R.* 'Azuma-kagami'
	'Pink Pearl' (hybrid)	CBcs CMac CSBt CTri CWri ECho EPfP GGGa LMil MAsh MBri MGos MJak MMuc MSnd NPri SHea SLdr SPer SPoG SReu SSta
	'Pink Pebble' ♀H3-4	CBcs CExl CHel ELon MAsh MLea SLdr
	'Pink Perfection'	CMac MGos MSnd SHea SLdr
	'Pink Polar Bear'	GKin LMil
	'Pink Ruffles' (K)	SHea SLdr
	'Pinkerton'	LMil
	'Pintail'	GGGa LMil LRHS MAsh
	'Pipit'	GGGa
	'Pippa' (EA)	CMac
	'PJM Elite'	NLar
	'PJM Regal'	IVic
	platypodum CGG 14005 **new**	GGGa
	'Pleasant White' (EA)	LMil
	'Plover'	GGGa
	pocophorum	MSnd
§	- var. ***hemidartum***	MSnd
	- var. ***pocophorum***	GGGa
	'Point Defiance'	CWri ECho MSnd
	'Polar Bear' ♀H3-4	CBcs CHll CSBt GGGa GKin IVic LMil MGos SLdr SReu
	Polar Bear Group	CWri ECho LMil MLea
	'Polaris'	see *R.* 'Hachmann's Polaris'
	'Polaris' (EA)	NLar
	'Polarnacht'	CDoC GGGa GKin IVic LMil
	poluninii	GGGa
	- KR 8231	LMil
	polyandrum	see *R. maddenii* subsp. *maddenii* Polyandrum Group
§	***polycladum*** Scintillans Group	GGGa SLdr
	polylepis	MSnd
	'Polyroy'	GGGa
	'Pomegranate Splash'	GGGa
	ponticum	CDul CMac CTri CWri MGos NHol
	- 'Filigran'	IVic
	- 'Roseum'	SGol
§	- 'Variegatum' (v)	CBcs CMac EPfP LRHS MAsh MBri MGos MLea NPri NSoo SLdr SPer SPoG SRms SSta
	'Popocatapetl'	SReu
	populare	GGGa
	- KC 0126 **new**	GGGa
	'Praecox' ♀H4	CBcs CHel CSBt ECho ELon EPfP GGGa GKev GKin LMil LRHS MAsh MGos MMuc NLar NPri SLdr SLim SPoG SReu
	praestans	GGGa GKin IDee LMil LRHS MSnd SLdr
	prattii	GGGa
	- 'Perry Wood'	LMil
	preptum	GGGa SLdr
	'President Roosevelt' (v)	CSBt EPfP GKin MAsh MGos MJak NPri NSoo SPoG SReu
	'Pridenjoy'	LMil
	primuliflorum	GKev MSnd WAbe
	- 'Doker-La'	GGGa LMil WAbe
	'Prince Camille de Rohan'	LMil SHea
	'Princess Alice'	CBcs
	'Princess Anne' ♀H4	CBcs CMHG ECho ELon EPot LMil LRHS MAsh MGos MLea NSoo SHea SLdr SLim SPer SPoG SReu SSta
	'Princess Galadriel'	SLdr
	'Princess Juliana'	ECho MMuc SLdr
	'Princess Margaret of Windsor' (K)	GQui LMil
	principis	GGGa LMil SLdr
	- 'Lost Horizon'	CDoC LMil MSnd SLdr
§	- Vellereum Group	SLdr
§	***prinophyllum*** (A)	GGGa GKin IDee LMil NLar
	'Prins Bernhard' (EA)	MAsh SLdr
	'Prinses Juliana' (EA)	MMuc SLdr SReu
	'Professor Hugo de Vries' ♀H4	SHea SLdr
	pronum	GGGa
	- R.B. Cooke form	GGGa
	- Towercourt form	GGGa
	prostratum	see *R. saluenense* subsp. *chameunum* Prostratum Group
	proteoides	GGGa
	protistum	GGGa
	pruniflorum	GGGa
	prunifolium (A)	GGGa LMil
	przewalskii	GGGa MSnd
	pseudochrysanthum ♀H4	GGGa LMil MSnd SReu
	- dwarf	GGGa
	pseudociliipes	GGGa
	'Ptarmigan' ♀H3-4	ECho GGGa LMil MAsh MGos MMuc MSnd NPri NSoo SLdr SReu WPat WThu
	pubicostatum	GLin
	- AC 2051	MSnd
§	'Pucella' (G) ♀H4	CWri SLdr
	pudorosum	GGGa
	'Pulchrum Maxwellii'	see *R.* 'Maxwellii'
	pumilum	GGGa WAbe WThu
	'Pumuckl'	IVic
	'Puncta'	SLdr
	'Purple Cushion' (EA)	EPfP LRHS MAsh NPri
	'Purple Diamond'	see *R.* Diamant Group purple-flowered
	purple Glenn Dale (EA)	SLdr
	'Purple Passion'PBR	NLar SLdr
	'Purple Queen' (EA/d)	MAsh
	'Purple Splendor' (EA)	CMac MMuc SGol SLdr
	'Purple Splendour' ♀H4	CBcs CSBt CWri ECho ELon EPfP LMil MBri MGos MLea MMuc NEgg NPCo SPer SReu SSta WMoo

'Purple Triumph' (EA) ♀H3	LMil NLar SLdr
'Purpurtraum' (EA) ♀H4	LMil
'Pyari' **new**	GGGa
qiaojiaense NN 0903	GGGa
'Quail'	GGGa LMil SLdr
'Queen Anne's'	GGGa
Queen Emma	see *R.* 'Koningin Emma'
'Queen Louise' (K)	SHea
'Queen Mary'	SReu SSta
'Queen of Hearts'	SHea SLdr
'Queen Souriya'	SReu
'Quentin Metsys' (R)	SLdr SReu SSta
quinquefolium (A)	GGGa LMil MSnd
Rabalz = 'Hachraba'	GGGa IVic LMil
racemosum ♀H4	GKev LMil MSnd SLdr
- 'Rock Rose' ♀H3-4	IDee LMil
'Racine' (G)	SLdr SReu
'Racoon' (EA) ♀H4	GGGa
radicans	see *R. calostrotum* subsp. *keleticum* Radicans Group
'Raimunde' (K)	IVic
'Ramapo' ♀H4	CDoC ECho EPfP GGGa LMil LRHS MAsh MBri MGos MSnd NSoo SLdr SLim SReu
'Rangoon'	LMil
'Raoul Millais'	LMil
'Raphael de Smet' (G/d)	SReu
'Razorbill' ♀H4	CDoC ECho GGGa GKin LMil MGos SLim
recurvoides	GGGa LMil MSnd SLdr SReu
- Keillour form	GGGa
'Red and Gold'	GGGa
'Red Dawn'	LRHS
'Red Delicious'	CWri LMil MBri SLdr
'Red Diamond'	see *R.* Diamant Group red-flowered
'Red Fountain' (EA)	ECho MMuc SLdr
'Red Jack'	CWri LMil MBri SReu SSta
'Red Panda' (EA)	GGGa
'Red Pimpernel' (EA)	SLdr
'Red Sunset' (A)	SLdr
'Red Velour'	MSnd SLdr
'Red Wood'	GGGa
'Redwing' (EA)	CDoC MAsh SLdr
'Rennie' (A)	ECho GKin MGos MLea MMuc SHea
'Renoir' ♀H4	CSBt LMil SLdr SReu
reticulatum (A)	LMil MSnd SReu
'Reuthe's Purple'	SReu WAbe WThu
'Rêve d'Amour' (Vs)	SReu SSta
rex	CDoC GGGa GKin LMil SLdr
- EGM 295	LMil
§ - subsp. ***fictolacteum*** ♀H3-4	CDoC GGGa GKin LMil MSnd SLdr SReu
- - Miniforme Group	MSnd
- subsp. ***rex*** ♀H3-4	MSnd
rex* × *yakushimanum	SReu
'Rex' (EA)	MAsh SLdr
rhabdotum	see *R. dalhousiae* var. *rhabdotum*
'Ria Hardijzer'	LMil
rigidum	GGGa GLin MSnd
* - ***album***	LMil
'Ring of Fire'	CWri ECho ELon IVic LMil MBri MGos MLea MSnd SLdr
'Ripe Corn'	MSnd
'Ripples' (EA)	CTrh
ririei	GGGa LMil SLdr SReu
- AC 2036	LMil
'Robert Croux'	MSnd SLdr

'Robert Seleger'	EPfP GGGa GKin LMil LRHS MAsh MMuc NSoo SReu
'Robin Hill Frosty' (EA)	SLdr
'Robin Hill Gillie' (EA)	SLdr
Robin Hood Group	LMil
'Robinette'	CBcs CWri ECho MAsh MBri SLdr
'Rocket'	CDoC CTri ECho ELon LMil MAsh MGos MLea MMuc SHea SLdr SLim SPer SPoG
'Roehr's Peggy Ann' (EA)	LMil
'Rokoko'	see *R.* 'Hachmann's Rokoko'
(Romany Chai Group) 'Romany Chai'	SHea
'Romany Chal'	SHea
'Rosa' (EA)	LMil NSoo
Rosalind Group	CMac
'Rosalinda' (EA)	SLdr
'Rosata' (Vs) ♀H4	GGGa GKin SReu SSta
'Rose Bud'	CSBt CTri
'Rose Elf'	WThu
'Rose Glow' (A)	SReu
'Rose Gown'	SReu
'Rose Greeley' (EA)	CDoC ECho SLdr SLim SPer SReu WGwG
'Rose Haze' (Vs)	SLdr SReu
'Rose Torch' (A)	SReu
'Rosebud' (EA/d) ♀H3-4	CBcs CMac MGos SLdr SReu
roseum	see *R. prinophyllum*
'Roseum Elegans'	CDoC LMil MAsh SLim
'Rosevallon'	MSnd
Rosinetta = 'Hachrosi' (EA)	GGGa
'Rosy Dream'	CWri ECho MAsh MBri MMuc MSnd
'Rosy Fire' (A)	LMil SReu
'Rosy Lea'	MLea
'Rosy Lights' (A)	LMil NLar SLdr
'Rotglocke'	IVic
'Rothenburg'	SLdr
rothschildii	CDoC GGGa IDee LMil MSnd SLdr
'Rotkäppchen'	IVic
'Rouge'	SHea
rousei (V)	GGGa
roxieanum	GGGa LMil MSnd SLdr
- AC 1753 **new**	MSnd
§ - var. ***cucullatum***	GGGa
- var. ***oreonastes*** ♀H4	GGGa IVic LMil MSnd SSta
- - Nymans form	SReu
- var. ***parvum***	GGGa
'Royal Command' (K)	CTri CWri GKin LMil MAsh SHea
'Royal Lodge' (K)	SHea
'Royal Mail'	SHea
'Royal Ruby' (K)	CWri ECho MBri MGos MMuc SHea SLdr
'Roza Stevenson'	LMil
'Rubicon'	CWri ECho GGGa MAsh MMuc SLdr
rubiginosum	CBcs GGGa IDee LMil MSnd
- SDR 5142	GKev
§ - Desquamatum Group	CBcs SLdr
- pink-flowered	LMil
rubroluteum	see *R. viridescens* Rubroluteum Group
'Ruby Glow' (EA) **new**	GGal
'Ruby Hart'	GGGa LSRN MMuc
'Ruddy Duck' (K)	SHea
rude	see *R. glischrum* subsp. *rude*
rufum	GGGa
rugosum Sinclair 240 (V)	GGGa
'Rumba' (K)	SHea

	rushforthii	GGGa
	russatum 🏆^{H4}	EPfP GGGa IDee LMil MSnd SLdr SSpi WAbe
	- blue-black-flowered	GKin IDee LMil
*	- 'Collingwood Ingram'	GGGa
	- 'Purple Pillow'	NSoo
	Russautinii Group	MSnd SLdr
	Russellianum Group	GGal
	russotinctum	see *R. alutaceum* var. *russotinctum*
	'Ryde Heron' (EA)	SLdr
	'Sabina' (EA)	SLdr
	'Sacko'	CWri GGGa LLHF LMil NLar SLim
	'Saffron Queen'	CBcs CHel MMuc SLdr
	'Sahara' (K)	LMil SHea
	'Saint Breward'	GQui MSnd SLdr
	'Saint Merryn' 🏆^{H4}	CBcs CWri ECho MBri MMuc NSla SLdr
	'Saint Minver'	SLdr
	'Saint Tudy'	SLdr
	'Saint Valentine' (V)	GGGa
	'Salmon Sander' (EA)	SLdr
§	'Salmon Trout'	LMil LSRN
	'Salmon's Leap' (EA/v)	CMac CSBt ELan LMil LRHS MAsh MBri SLdr SReu SSta
	saluenense	LMil MSnd SLdr WThu
§	- subsp. ***chameunum*** Prostratum Group	GGGa
	'Sammetglut'	CWri
	'Samuel Taylor Coleridge' (M)	GKin
	sanguineum	LMil MSnd SLdr
§	- subsp. ***didymum***	GGGa MSnd SLdr
	- subsp. ***sanguineum*** var. ***haemaleum***	GGGa LMil MSnd
	- - var. ***sanguineum*** F 25521	LMil
	'Santa Maria' (EA)	ECho ELon LMil LSRN MBri MGos NSoo SReu
	santapaui (V)	GGGa
	'Sapphire'	WThu
	'Sappho'	CBcs CMac CWri ECho ELon EPfP GGGa GKin LMil MBri MGos MLea NEgg NPCo SLdr SPer SReu SSta WGwG
	sargentianum	GGGa NHar WAbe WThu
	- 'Whitebait'	GGGa
	'Sarled' 🏆^{H4}	GGGa ITim LMil NHar SHea WThu
	Sarled Group	WAbe
	'Saroi' (EA)	SLdr
	'Saskia' (K)	IVic
	'Satan' (K) 🏆^{H4}	LMil MBri NLar NSoo SHea SReu
§	'Satschiko' (EA) 🏆^{H4}	CBcs CSBt GGGa LRHS MAsh MGos MJak NPri NSoo SLdr
	'Satsop Surprise'	SLdr
	Satsuki type (EA)	ECho SLdr
	'Saturnus' (M)	GKin
§	***scabrifolium*** var. ***spiciferum***	SLdr WAbe
	'Scandinavia'	SHea
	'Scarlet Pimpernel' (K)	SHea
	'Scarlet Wonder' 🏆^{H4}	CBcs CDoC CMHG CSBt CWri ECho EPfP EPot GGGa GKev GKin LMil LRHS MAsh MBri MGos MJak NPri NSoo SHea SLdr SPer SReu
	'Sceptre' (K)	SHea
	schistocalyx F 17637	MSnd
	schlippenbachii (A)	GGGa GKev IDee LMil MSnd
	- 'Sid's Royal Pink' (A)	LMil

	'Schneekrone' 🏆^{H4}	GGGa MBri
	'Schneeperle' (EA)	IVic LMil
	'Schneespiegel'	GGGa
	scintillans	see *R. polycladum* Scintillans Group
	'Scintillation'	CBcs CWri GGGa LMil MAsh MBri MGos MLea MMuc MSnd SLdr
	scopulorum	GGGa MMuc SLdr
	'Scotian Bells'	GGGa
	scottianum	see *R. pachypodum*
	'Scottish Marmalade' **new**	GGGa
	'Scout' (EA)	MAsh SLdr
	scyphocalyx	see *R. dichroanthum* subsp. *scyphocalyx*
	searsiae	MSnd
	'Seaview Sunset'	GGGa LMil
	'Seb'	SLdr
	'Second Honeymoon'	CBcs CWri ECho MLea MSnd SLdr
	'Seikai' (EA)	SLdr
	seinghkuense	GGGa LMil
	- CCH&H 8106	GGGa LMil
§	***selense*** subsp. ***dasycladum***	MSnd
	- subsp. ***jucundum***	GGGa
	semibarbatum	GLin
	semnoides	GGGa LMil SLdr
	'Sennocke'	LMil
	'September Song'	CBcs CMac CWri ECho ELon GGGa LMil MAsh MGos MLea MMuc NHol NPCo SLdr SPer
	serotinum	GGGa GLin LMil
	serpyllifolium (A)	SLdr
	'Sesterianum'	CMHG SLdr
	'Seta'	CAbP SHea SLdr WThu
	Seta Group	SReu
	'Seville'	SHea
	'Shamrock'	CDoC EPfP LRHS MAsh MBri MGos MLea NEgg NLar NSla NSoo SLdr SLim SPoG WThu
	'Shanty' (K/d)	SHea
	'Sheila' (EA)	CSBt LRHS MAsh NPri
	'Shelley' (EA)	LMil LSRN
	shepherdii	see *R. kendrickii*
	sherriffii	GGGa MSnd
	'Shiko' (EA)	MAsh
	'Shiko Lavender' (A)	SPoG
	Shilsonii Group	LMil
	'Shi-no-noe' (EA)	SLdr
	'Shrimp Girl'	GKin MSnd
	sichotense	GGGa
	sidereum	GGGa
	siderophyllum	GGGa GLin MSnd
	sikangense	GGGa MSnd SLdr
	- var. ***exquisitum***	GGGa GLin
§	- var. ***sikangense*** Cookeanum Group	SLdr
	'Silbervelours'	IVic
§	'Silberwolke' 🏆^{H4}	IVic LMil MAsh
	'Silkeborg Silence'	GGGa
	Silver Cloud	see *R.* 'Silberwolke'
	'Silver Edge'	see *R. ponticum* 'Variegatum'
	'Silver Glow' (EA)	CMac
	'Silver Jubilee' 🏆^{H4}	LMil
	'Silver Moon' (EA)	SLdr
	'Silver Queen' (EA)	ECho ELon MGos NEgg NSoo SLdr
	'Silver Sixpence'	CBcs ECho EPfP LRHS LSRN MAsh MBri MGos MJak MMuc MSnd NPCo SLdr
	'Silver Skies'	LMil

'Silver Slipper' (K) ♀H4	CBcs GKin LMil MBri MLea NHol NLar SHea SLdr SReu SSta
'Silver Sword' (EA/v)	EPfP NSoo
'Silver Thimbles' (V)	GGGa
'Silverwood' (K)	LMil
'Silvester' (EA)	CTri LMil LRHS MAsh MBri MGos SLdr SReu
'Simona'	LMil
simsii (EA)	CMac LMil SLdr
'Simson' <u>**new**</u>	LMil
sinofalconeri	GGGa LMil MSnd
- KR 7342	LMil
- SEH 229	LMil
sinogrande ♀H3	CBcs CDoC CHEx CHll CWri ELon GBin GGGa GKev GKin IDee LMil MMuc NLar NPCo SLdr SPer
- KR 4027	LMil
'Sir Charles Lemon' ♀H3-4	CDoC CWri ECho GGGa LMil MAsh MGos MLea NPCo SHea SLdr SPer
'Sir Robert' (EA)	LRHS MAsh
'Sleeping Beauty'	WAbe
'Sleepy'	CBcs CSBt ECho MAsh MGos MLea MSnd NHol SLdr
smirnowii	GGGa IDee LMil LRHS MSnd
smithii	see *R. argipeplum*
'Sneezy'	CBcs CSBt CWri ECho EPfP GGGa LMil LRHS MAsh MGos MJak MSnd SLdr SLim
'Snipe'	CTri ECho GBin LMil LRHS MAsh MBri MGos NLar SLdr SLim SReu WThu
'Snow' (EA)	SLdr
'Snow Crown' (*lindleyi* hybrid)	MAsh
'Snow Hill' (EA)	LMil MGos NLar SLdr
'Snow Lady'	CBcs CHel ECho EPfP EPot GKin GQui MAsh MGos MMuc SLdr SReu
'Snow Pearl'	EPfP MAsh
'Snow Queen'	LMil
Snow Queen Group	LMil SReu
'Snowbird' (A)	GGal SLdr
'Snowflake' (EA/d)	see *R.* 'Kure-no-yuki'
'Snowstorm'	MMuc
'Soft Lips' (K)	SHea
'Soho' (EA)	GQui
'Soir de Paris' (Vs)	CSBt GGGa GKin IVic LMil MBri MLea MMuc NHol SLdr SReu SSta WGwG
'Soldier Sam'	SReu
'Solidarity'	ECho MBri MGos MLea SLdr SReu
'Solway' (Vs)	LMil
'Sommerduft' (A)	IVic
'Son de Paris' (A)	GQui
'Sonata'	CWri GBin GGGa GGal SReu
'Sonatine'	LMil
'Songbird'	LMil MSnd SLdr
'Sophie Hedges' (K/d)	SLdr
sororium (V)	GGGa LMil
- KR 3085	LMil
souliei	LMil SSpi
- deep pink-flowered	GGGa
'Southern Cross'	SLdr
'Souvenir de D.A. Koster'	SLdr
'Souvenir de Doctor S. Endtz' ♀H4	SHea SLdr
'Souvenir of Anthony Waterer' ♀H4	SHea SReu
'Souvenir of W.C. Slocock'	SReu

'Spätlese'	IVic
speciosum	see *R. flammeum*
'Spek's Orange' (M) ♀H4	GGGa GKin
sperabile	GGGa LMil
- var. ***weihsiense***	LMil MSnd SLdr
sphaeranthum	see *R. trichostomum*
sphaeroblastum	GGGa MSnd
- var. ***wumengense***	GGGa GLin
- - KR 1481	MSnd
spiciferum	see *R. scabrifolium* var. *spiciferum*
'Spicy Lights' (A)	LMil
spilotum	LMil
'Spinner's Glory'	MAsh
spinuliferum	CBcs GGGa
'Spitfire'	NHol SReu
'Spring Beauty' (EA)	CMac MSnd SLdr SReu
'Spring Magic'	MSnd SLdr
'Spring Pearl'	see *R.* 'Moerheim's Pink'
'Spring Rose'	SLdr
'Spring Sunshine'	LMil LRHS
'Springday'	CMac
'Squirrel' (EA) ♀H4	CDoC ECho GGGa GKin LMil MAsh MGos MLea SLdr SLim SReu
'Staccato'	IVic
Stadt Essen Group	LMil SLdr
'Stadt Westerstede'	LMil
stamineum	GGGa
§ 'Stanway'	LMil
'Starbright Champagne'	GGGa MAsh
'Statuette'	IVic
§ ***stenopetalum*** 'Linearifolium' (EA)	CMac LMil SLdr WAbe
stenophyllum	see *R. makinoi*
stewartianum	GGGa LMil SLdr
'Stewartstonian' (EA)	CMac ELon MJak SReu
'Stoat' (EA)	GQui NLar
'Stopham Girl' (A)	LMil
'Stopham Lad' (A)	LMil
'Stour' (K)	SHea
'Strategist'	SHea SLdr
'Strawberry Cream'	GGGa LRHS MAsh
'Strawberry Ice' (K) ♀H4	CDoC CSBt CWri ECho ELan EPfP GBin GGGa GKin LMil LRHS MAsh MBri MGos MMHG MMuc NEgg SLdr SPer SReu WMoo
'Strawberry Sundae'	MMuc NEgg SLdr
strigillosum	GGGa GLin MSnd
- Reuthe's form	SReu
subansiriense	GGGa
suberosum	see *R. yunnanense* Suberosum Group
succothii	GGGa SLdr
'Suga-no-ito' (EA)	SLdr
sulfureum	GGGa
'Summer Blaze' (A)	SLdr SReu
'Summer Dawn'	LMil
'Summer Flame'	SReu
'Summer Fragrance' (O) ♀H4	LMil SReu SSta
'Summer Snow'	IVic
'Summer Sorbet'	LMil
'Sun Chariot' (K)	CBcs MAsh MMHG
'Sun Fire'	LMil
'Sun of Austerlitz'	SHea SLdr
Sunkist Group	SLdr
(Sunrise Group) 'Sunrise'	MSnd SLdr
'Sunset Pink' (K)	ELan SLdr
'Sunte Nectarine' (K) ♀H4	ECho GKin GQui LMil MBri MLea MMuc NLar SHea SLdr

suoilenhensis NVD 18 **new**	GGGa
'Surprise' ambig. (EA)	CDoC CTri SLdr
'Surrey Heath'	CBcs CDoC CDul CWri ECho EPfP LMil MAsh MGos MJak MMuc MSnd NSoo SLdr SLim
'Susan' (EA)	MSnd
'Susan' J.C. Williams ♀H4	LMil SReu
'Susannah Hill' (EA)	CDoC SLdr
sutchuenense	GGGa LMil MSnd
- var. ***geraldii***	see *R.* × *geraldii*
'Swamp Beauty'	CWri ECho MAsh MGos MLea MMuc MSnd SLdr WGwG
'Swansong' (EA)	CMac SLdr
'Sweet Simplicity'	CWri SHea SLdr
'Sweet Sue'	MSnd SLdr
'Swift'	ECho GBin GGGa GQui LLHF LMil LRHS MAsh MBri MMuc NPCo SLdr
'Sylphides' (K)	CMac
'T.S. Black' (EA)	SLdr
taggianum	GGGa
'Taka-no-tsukasa' (EA)	SLdr
taliense	GGGa LMil
- SBEC 0350	GGGa
Tally Ho Group	SHea
'Tama-no-utena' (EA)	SLdr
'Tanager' (EA/k)	SLdr
'Tangerine'	see *R.* 'Fabia Tangerine'
'Tangiers' (K)	SHea SLdr
tapetiforme	GGGa
'Tarantella'	NEgg
'Taurus' ♀H4	CDoC CWri ECho ELon GKin IVic LMil LRHS MAsh MBri MGos MMuc MSnd NPCo SLdr SReu WMoo
taxifolium (v)	GGGa
'Tay' (K)	SLdr
'Teal'	ECho
'Ted Millais'	LMil
'Teddy Bear'	CWri LMil MLea
telopeum	see *R. campylocarpum* subsp. *caloxanthum* Telopeum Group
'Temple Belle'	ECho SLdr
'Tender Heart' (K)	SLdr
'Teniers' (R)	SReu SSta
§ ***tephropeplum***	GGGa MSnd WAbe
- Deleiense Group	see *R. tephropeplum*
'Tequila Sunrise'	LMil
'Terra-cotta'	LMil
'Terra-cotta Beauty' (EA)	NWad WThu
'Tessa'	CBcs ECho ELon MMuc SLdr
Tessa Group	LMil
'Tessa Roza' (EA) ♀H4	GKev GQui
thayerianum	GGGa MSnd
§ 'The Hon. Jean Marie de Montague' ♀H4	CWri EPfP GGGa GKin LMil MAsh MGos MLea MMuc MSnd NLar SLdr SPer SReu
'Thomas David' (A)	LMil
thomsonii	CDoC GGGa GKin LMil MSnd SLdr SReu
- AC 113	MSnd
'Thor'	GGGa SReu
'Thousand Butterflies'	see *R.* 'One Thousand Butterflies'
'Thunderstorm'	SReu
'Tibet' ♀H3-4	GQui LMil
'Tidbit' ♀H4	CMac GGGa LMil MGos MLea MSnd SLdr
'Tinkerbird'	GGGa LMil LRHS MAsh NPri
'Tinsmith' (K)	SLdr

titapuriense	GGGa
'Titian Beauty'	CBcs CDoC CSBt CWri ECho ELon EPfP GGGa LMil LRHS MAsh MGos MMuc MSnd NEgg NPCo NPri SLdr SLim SPer SPoG WMoo
'Titness Delight'	SLdr
'Tit-Willow' (EA)	MAsh SCoo
'Tolkien'	SReu
'Tom Hyde' (EA)	LSRN
tomentosum	WThu
'Top Banana'	SLdr
'Torchlight' (EA)	LMil
'Toreador' (EA)	MSnd SLdr
'Torridon' (Vs)	LMil
'Tortoiseshell Champagne'	see *R.* 'Champagne'
'Tortoiseshell Orange' ♀H3-4	CBcs CSBt CWri LMil MBri NLar SHea SLim SReu SSta
'Tortoiseshell Salome'	SHea
'Tortoiseshell Wonder' ♀H3-4	CWri EPfP LMil LRHS MAsh NPri SHea
'Toucan' (K)	CSBt SHea SLdr
'Tower Beauty' (A)	SHea SLdr
'Tower Dainty' (A)	SHea
'Tower Daring' (A)	SHea
'Tower Dragon' (A)	LMil SHea SLdr
traillianum	LMil MSnd
'Treecreeper'	GGGa GKin LMil SLdr
'Tregedna Red'	SReu
'Trewithen Orange'	SLdr
'Trewithen Purple'	GGGa
trichanthum	GGGa
- 'Honey Wood'	LMil SLdr
§ ***trichostomum***	GGGa GKev SSpi WAbe
- Ledoides Group	LMil
- - 'Collingwood Ingram' (EA) ♀H4	IDee LRHS
triflorum	GGGa LMil
§ - var. ***bauhiniiflorum***	CBcs GGGa SLdr
- var. ***triflorum*** Mahogani Group	GGGa MSnd
trilectorum	GGGa
'Trill' (EA)	SLdr
triplonaevium	see *R. alutaceum* var. *russotinctum* Triplonaevium Group
'Tromba'	LMil
'Troupial' (K)	SHea
tsangpoense	see *R. charitopes* subsp. *tsangpoense*
tsariense	GGGa LMil MSnd
- var. ***trimoense***	GGGa LMil
- - KW 8288	LMil
- 'Yum Yum'	GGGa
tubiforme	see *R. glaucophyllum* subsp. *tubiforme*
'Tuffet' (EA)	SLdr SReu
'Tunis' (K)	LRHS MAsh NPri
'Turaço'	GGGa LMil SLdr
'Turnstone'	GGGa
'Twilight Pink'	SLdr
'Umpqua Queen' (K)	SLdr
ungernii	GGGa MSnd SLdr
§ ***uniflorum*** var. ***imperator***	GGGa
'Unique' (G)	ECho EPfP GGGa MGos MMuc SPer
'Unique' (*campylocarpum* hybrid) ♀H4	MAsh MBri MSnd SHea SLdr SReu
'Unique Marmalade'	ECho LMil LRHS MAsh MMuc SLdr
'Ursine'	IVic
uvariifolium var. ***griseum***	LMil MSnd
- 'Reginald Childs'	LMil

	'Valencia'	IVic
	valentinianum	CBcs GGGa MSnd SLdr WAbe
	- F 24347	MSnd
	- var. ***oblongilobatum***	GGGa
	'Van'	LMil SLim
	'Van Houttei Flore Pleno' (G/d)	SLdr SReu SSta
	'Van Nes Sensation'	LMil
	Vanessa Group	GGal LMil
	'Vanessa Pastel' ♀$^{H3-4}$	CMac GGGa LMil SReu
	vaseyi (A) ♀$^{H3-4}$	CBcs GGGa GLin LMil
	- 'White Find'	GGGa
	- white-flowered (A)	LMil
	'Vayo' (A)	SLdr
§	***veitchianum*** Cubittii Group	CBcs GGGa SLdr
	- KNE Cox 9001	GGGa
	vellereum	see *R. principis* Vellereum Group
	venator	GGGa MSnd
	aff. ***venator*** KC 0104	GGGa
	'Venetian Chimes'	CSBt ECho MGos MSnd SLdr
	vernicosum	GGGa MSnd
	- AC 1901 **new**	MSnd
	- AC 4102 **new**	MSnd
	'Victoria Hallett'	SLdr
	'Vida Brown' (EA/d)	CMac SLdr SReu WThu
	'Vinecourt Dream' (M)	GKin MBri MLea MMuc NLar SLdr
	'Vinecourt Duke' (R/d)	CWri ECho GKin MAsh MMuc NEgg NLar NPCo
	'Vinecourt Troubador' (K/d)	MAsh NPCo
	'Vineland Dream' (K/d)	CWri ECho GKin
	'Vineland Fragrance'	SLdr
	'Vintage Rosé' ♀^{H4}	LMil MLea SLdr
	'Violetta' (EA)	SLdr
	'Violette Funken'	LMil
	'Virginia Richards'	LRHS SLdr
	Virginia Richards Group	CWri MAsh MGos
§	***viridescens***	MSnd
	- 'Doshong La'	GGGa LMil
§	- Rubroluteum Group	SLdr
	viscidifolium	GGGa
	'Viscosepalum' (G)	SHea SLdr
	viscosum (A) ♀^{H4}	CBcs GGGa GQui LMil MBri MLea MMHG NLar SHea SReu
	- 'Grey Leaf' (Vs)	LMil
	- f. ***rhodanthum*** (A)	LMil
	- 'Roseum' (Vs)	LMil SHea
	'Viscount Powerscourt'	SLdr
	'Viscy' ♀^{H4}	CDul CWri ECho EPfP GKin GQui LMil MGos MMuc MSnd NLar SLdr
§	Volker Group	CWri EPfP LMil MAsh SSta
§	- 'Lackblatt'	MGos MSnd
	'Vollblut'	SReu SSta
	'Vulcan' ♀^{H4}	GGGa LMil MLea
	'Vuyk's Rosyred' (EA) ♀^{H4}	CBcs CDoC CDul CMac CTri GKin LMil MAsh MGos NHol NWad SGol SLdr SPer SPoG SReu
	'Vuyk's Scarlet' (EA) ♀^{H4}	CBcs CDoC CMac CSBt CTri EPfP GKin LRHS MAsh MGos MMuc MSnd NHol NPri NWad SGol SLdr SPer SPlb SReu SSta
	'W.E. Gumbleton' (M)	SReu
	'W.F.H.' ♀^{H4}	CWri IDee LMil MSnd SLdr
	'Wagtail'	GGGa
	'Walküre'	LMil
	wallichii	GGGa LMil MSnd SLdr
	- KR 8227	LMil
	- Heftii Group	GGGa GLin
	'Wallowa Red' (K)	ECho LMil MBri MLea MMHG MMuc SEND SLdr
	'Wally Miller'	ECho MAsh SReu
	walongense	GGGa
	'Wanna Bee' **new**	LMil
	wardii	GGGa GKev IDee LMil MSnd SHea
	- L&S 5679	GGGa MSnd
	- var. ***puralbum***	GGGa
	- var. ***wardii*** AC 3425 **new**	MSnd
	- - AC 3469 **new**	MSnd
	'Ward's Ruby' (EA)	CTrh
§	'Washington State Centennial' (A)	GGGa
	wasonii	LMil MSnd
	- SIN 1852	GLin
	- f. ***rhododactylum***	MSnd
	- var. ***wenchuanense***	GGGa
	- yellow-flowered	GGGa
	'Water Baby' (A)	LMil
	'Water Girl' (A)	GGGa LMil
	'Waterfall'	SLdr
	watsonii	MSnd
	'Waxwing'	SHea
	websterianum	SLdr
	'Wee Bee' ♀^{H4}	CDoC ECho EPfP GKin LLHF LMil LRHS MAsh MLea NLar NPCo SLdr SLim SReu
	'Wendy'	MAsh
	'Westminster' (O)	LMil
	'Weston's Pink Diamond' (d)	LMil
	'What a Dane'	GGGa
	'Whidbey Island'	LMil
	'Whisperingrose'	LMil
	'White Brocade'	SSta
§	White Dufthecke = 'Rhodunter 48'PBR	LMil
	'White Frills' (EA)	ECho NLar SLdr
	'White Glory'	SLdr
	'White Gold'	GGGa
	'White Grandeur' (EA)	CTrh
	'White Jade' (EA)	SLdr
	'White Lady' (EA)	SLdr
	'White Lights' (A) ♀^{H4}	EPfP LMil NLar
	'White Pearl' (EA)	LSRN
	'White Perfume' (A)	SReu SSta
	'White Rosebud' (EA)	SReu
	'White Swan' (K)	GKin MGos MMuc SHea SLdr
	'White Swan' (hybrid)	CBcs SReu
	'White Wings'	GQui
	'Whitethroat' (K/d) ♀^{H4}	CWri ECho EPfP GQui LMil LRHS MAsh MBri MMHG MMuc NEgg SEND SLdr SPer SReu SSta
	'Whitney's Dwarf Red'	SLdr
	'Wigeon'	LMil
	wightii	GGGa GLin MSnd
	'Wilgen's Ruby'	CDoC CSBt LMil MGos MSnd SLdr SLim SPer
	'Willbrit'	CBcs CWri ECho MAsh MGos SLdr
	'William III' (G)	SLdr
	williamsianum ♀^{H4}	CBcs CMac ECho EPot GBin GGGa GKev LMil MLea MSnd SLdr SReu
	- 'Andrea'	IVic
	- Caerhays form	CExl
	'Willy' (EA)	LMil SLdr
	wiltonii ♀^{H4}	GGGa IDee LMil SLdr
	'Windlesham Scarlet'	SLdr
	'Windsor Hawk'	CWri
	'Windsor Lad'	SReu

	'Windsor Sunbeam' (K)	CWri
	'Wine and Roses'PBR	GGGa
	'Winsome' (hybrid) ♀H3	CBcs GGal GKin MJak NLar NPri SHea SLdr
	Winsome Group	CMac CWri GGGa MAsh MSnd
	'Winston Churchill' (M)	SReu SSta
I	'Winter Green' (EA)	MMuc
	'Winter Spice'	GGGa
	'Wintergreen' (EA)	MMuc
	'Winterpurpur'	IVic
	'Wishmoor'	SReu
	'Witchery'	GGGa
	'Wombat' (EA) ♀H4	CTri EPfP GGGa LMil LRHS MAsh MGos NLar NPri SLdr SReu
	wongii	GGGa GQui MSnd SLdr
	'Woodcock'	SHea SLdr
	'Wren'	ECho EPot GBin GGGa GKev IVic LMil LRHS MAsh MGos MLea MMuc NSoo SLdr SReu WThu
	'Wryneck' (K)	SHea SLdr
	'Wye' (K)	SLdr
	xanthocodon	see *R. cinnabarinum* subsp. *xanthocodon*
	xanthostephanum	GGGa
	'XXL'	SReu
	'Yaku Angel'	IVic
	'Yaku Incense'	ECho LMil MAsh MLea MMuc MSnd NLar SLdr
	'Yaku Prince'	ECho MAsh MGos MLea MMuc SLdr
	'Yaku Princess'	CBcs
	yakushimanum	CBcs CMHG CWri ECho GKin LMil MBri MGos MLea MMuc MSnd NHol NLar SLdr SPer SReu SSta
	- 'Edelweiss' ♀H4	IDee LMil LRHS NLar
	- Exbury form	CMac SReu
	- FCC form	see *R. yakushimanum* 'Koichiro Wada'
§	- 'Koichiro Wada' ♀H4	CExl CMac EPfP GGGa IDee IVic LMil LRHS MGos NLar SLdr SReu
	yaoshanense	GGGa
	'Yaye' (EA)	SLdr
	'Yellow Cloud' (A)	ECho MLea NPCo
	'Yellow Cloud' (K)	MBri MMuc
	'Yellow Hammer' ♀H4	CMac ECho ELan GGGa GKin LMil MBri NLar SLdr
	Yellow Hammer Group	CWri MGos MSnd SPer SReu SSta
	'Yellow Petticoats'	SReu
	'Yoga' (K)	SHea
	'Yol'	SLdr
	yuefengense	GGGa
	yunnanense	GGGa GGal GKev LMil MSnd SLdr SSpi
	- SDR 4217	GKev
	- SDR 4957	GKev
	- SDR 4960	GKev
	- 'Openwood' ♀H3-4	LMil
	- pink-flowered	GGGa
	- 'Red Throat'	SLdr
	- red-blotched	LMil
§	- Suberosum Group	SLdr
	- white-flowered	GGGa
	aff. ***yunnanense***	IDee
	zaleucum	GGGa LMil
	- Flaviflorum Group	GGGa
	- var. ***zaleucum***	MSnd
	zeylanicum	see *R. arboreum* subsp. *zeylanicum*
	ziyuanense AC 4211	MSnd

Rhodohypoxis ✿ (*Hypoxidaceae*)

	'1000 Cranes'	IBal
	'Andromeda'	EWes
	'Ann Brazier' **new**	NWad
	baurii ♀H4	CAby CAvo CCCN CMea ECho IBal LRHS MAsh MBel NBir NSla SPoG WAbe WIce XLum
	- 'Abigail'	EWes
	- 'Alba'	CRDP ECho IBal LPio
	- 'Albrighton'	CRDP CTri ECho EWes IBal NBir NHol NWad WAbe WPat
	- 'Apple Blossom'	CTca ECho EWes IBal LBee LPio NHol NWad WAbe
	- 'Badger'	NWad WAbe
	- var. ***baurii***	ECho EWes GKev
	- var. ***baurii*** × ***baurii*** var. ***platypetala***	ECho
	- 'Bridal Bouquet' (d)	EWes IBal NHol WAbe
	- 'Coconut Ice'	EWes IBal LEdu
	- var. ***confecta***	ECho EWes GKev NHol
	- 'Daphne Mary'	EWes
	- 'David Scott'	EWes
	- 'Dawn'	ECho EPot EWes GKev IBal LRHS WAbe
	- 'Douglas'	ECho EPfP EPot EWes GKev IBal LEdu NBir NHol
	- 'Dulcie'	ECho EWes GKev WAbe
	- 'Emily Peel'	ECho EPot EWes GKev IBal LLHF WAbe
	- 'Eva-Kate'	ECho EWes GKev IBal WAbe WPat
	- 'Fred Broome'	CTca ECho EPot EWes GKev IBal NHol NWad WPat
	- 'Goliath'	EWes
	- 'Harlequin'	ECho EWes GKev IBal NHol NWad
§	- 'Helen'	ECho EWes GKev IBal LEdu NHol WAbe
	- 'Kitty'	EWes
	- 'Lily Jean' (d)	CRDP CTri ECho EPfP EPot EWes GKev IBal ITim LRHS NWad WCot
	- 'Luna'	EWes
	- 'Margaret Rose'	CTca ECho EWes GKev IBal LLHF NHol
	- 'Mars'	EWes LEdu NBir NHol
	- 'Monique'	EWes
	- 'Pearl'	ECho
	- 'Perle'	ECho EWes IBal NHol NSla NWad
	- 'Pictus' (v)	CRDP ECho EPot EWes GKev IBal LRHS NHol NWad WPat
	- 'Pink Pearl'	EWes IBal NHol WAbe
	- pink-flowered	ECho MMuc
	- var. ***platypetala***	CRDP ECho EPfP EPot EWes GKev IBal NHol NWad WAbe XLum
	- - Burtt 6981	EWes
	- var. ***platypetala*** × ***milloides***	IBal LLHF NHol NWad WAbe
	- 'Rebecca'	ECho EWes
	- 'Red King'	EWes IBal
	- red-flowered	ECho MMuc SPlb
	- 'Ruth'	ECho EPfP EWes GKev IBal NHol SDeJ WAbe
	- 'Susan Garnett-Botfield'	ECho EWes IBal WAbe
	- 'Tetra Red'	ECho EWes GKev LRHS NHol NWad SDeJ WAbe
	- 'The Bride'	EWes
	- white-flowered	CTca ECho EPot
	'Betsy Carmine'	CCCN IBal NWad WAbe
	'Blush'	ECho IBal
	'Bright Eyes' (d)	CRDP EWes

'Butterfly Wings' **new**	NWad
'Candy Stripe'	ECho EWes LRHS NWad
'Carina'	ECho EWes
'Cayasan'	ECho WAbe
'Confusion'	EWes LEdu NHol NWad WAbe
'Dainty Dee' (d)	EWes
deflexa	CRDP CWCL ECho EPot EWes GKev IBal ITim LRHS NHol NSla NWad
'Donald Mann'	ECho EWes LLHF NHol WAbe
'Dusky'	ECho EWes
'E.A. Bowles'	ECho EWes IBal NSla
'Ellicks'	IBal
'Flashing Rubies' **new**	IBal
'Garnett'	ECho EWes IBal WAbe
'Goya' (d)	ECho IBal WPat
'Great Scot'	ECho EPot EWes GKev IBal LRHS
'Hebron Farm Biscuit'	see *Hypoxis parvula* var. *albiflora* 'Hebron Farm Biscuit'
'Hebron Farm Cerise'	see × *Rhodoxis* 'Hebron Farm Cerise'
'Hebron Farm Pink'	see × *Rhodoxis hybrida* 'Hebron Farm Pink'
'Holden Rose' (d)	ECho NHol NWad
'Hope' **new**	IBal
hybrids	CWCL ELan
'Jupiter'	NWad
'Kiwi Joy' (d)	CRDP EPot EWes GKev IBal LLHF NHol NWad SDeJ WAbe
'Knockdolian Red'	NHol NWad
'Louise' **new**	IBal
'Midori'	ECho EWes NWad
milloides	CAby CPla CRDP CTca ECho EPot EWes GKev IBal ITim LBee LEdu LRHS NHol NWad
– 'Claret'	CAby CRDP CSam ECho EPot EWes GKev ITim LLHF LRHS NHol WPat
– 'Damask'	CRDP ECho EPot EWes GKev
– 'Donaldson' **new**	GKev
– 'Drakensberg Snow'	EWes
– giant	ECho
'Monty'	ECho EWes NWad WAbe
'Mystery'	EWes NHol
'Naomi'	ECho EWes
'New Look'	ECho EWes GKev IBal LLHF NWad
'Ori Zuru'	ECho
'Origami'	IBal LEdu
'Pearl White'	ECho
'Pink Ice'	IBal NBir NWad
'Pinkeen'	ECho EWes IBal LLHF WAbe
'Pinkie'	IBal
'Pintado'	ECho EWes LEdu NWad
'Pretty in Pink' **new**	IBal
'Raspberry Ice'	ECho NHol NWad
'Rosie Lee'	EWes
'Shell Pink'	EWes IBal NHol NWad
'Snow'	EWes
'Snow White'	EWes NHol
'Starlett'	EWes IBal NHol
'Starry Eyes' (d)	CRDP ECho EWes
'Stella'	CCCN ECho EPot EWes GKev IBal NHol NWad
'Sunburst' **new**	NWad
'Telios'	IBal
'Tetra Pink'	ECho EWes IBal LRHS NHol NWad
'Tetra White'	see *R. baurii* 'Helen'
thodiana	CRDP ECho EWes GKev IBal NHol NWad WAbe
'Twinkle Star Mixed'	ECho LRHS SPoG
'Two Tone'	EWes
'Venetia'	CMea ECho IBal NHol NWad
'Westacre Picotee'	EWes
'Wild Cherry Blossom'	ECho EWes IBal

Rhodohypoxis × *Hypoxis* see × *Rhodoxis*

R. baurii × ***H. parvula***	see × *Rhodoxis hybrida*

Rhodoleia (*Hamamelidaceae*)

aff. ***henryi*** B&SWJ 11782	WCru
parvipetala **new**	WCru

Rhodophiala (*Amaryllidaceae*)

rhodolirion	SPlb

Rhodora see *Rhododendron*

Rhodothamnus (*Ericaceae*)

sessilifolius	WThu

Rhodotypos (*Rosaceae*)

kerrioides	see *R. scandens*
§ ***scandens***	CDul CExl CHel CTri CWib EBee ELan EPfP EShb EWTr GKin IGor LEdu LHop LRHS MMHG MMuc MNrw NHol NLar NSoo SEND SLon SPoG SSpi WCru WHar WPat WSHC

× *Rhodoxis* ✿ (*Hypoxidaceae*)

'Anne Crock'	EWes IBal
'Aurora'	EWes
'Bloodstone'	EWes IBal NHol NWad
'Hebron Farm Biscuit'	see *Hypoxis parvula* var. *albiflora* 'Hebron Farm Biscuit'
§ 'Hebron Farm Cerise'	CCCN ECho EWes GKev LEdu
'Hebron Farm Rose'	LLHF
§ ***hybrida***	ECho EWes IBal WAbe XLum
– 'Aya San'	EWes GKev IBal
§ – 'Hebron Farm Pink'	CBro ECho EWes GKev IBal NHol WAbe
– 'Hebron Farm Red Eye'	CCCN EWes GKev IBal
– 'Pink Stars'	IBal LRHS
– 'White Stars'	EWes
'Little Pink Pet'	EWes

Rhoeo see *Tradescantia*

Rhopalostylis (*Arecaceae*)

baueri	EAmu
sapida	CBrP
– 'East Cape'	SBig

rhubarb see *Rheum* × *hybridum*

Rhus (*Anacardiaceae*)

ambigua	ESwi
– B&SWJ 3656	WCru
– large-leaved B&SWJ 10884	WCru
§ ***aromatica***	CArn CDul EBtc LRHS NLar
chinensis	CMCN
– var. ***roxburghii***	SSpi
copallinum	EBtc
coriaria	CArn EPfP NLar
cotinus	see *Cotinus coggygria*
glabra	CArn CBcs CDoC EBtc EPfP MGos SPer
– 'Laciniata' misapplied	see *R.* × *pulvinata* Autumn Lace Group
– 'Laciniata' ambig.	MMuc
– 'Laciniata' Carrière	NLar

	glauca	EShb
N	***hirta***	see *R. typhina*
	incisa	SPlb
	krebsiana	WHil
	magalismontana	EShb
	potaninii	EPfP LRHS MAsh
§	× ***pulvinata*** Autumn Lace Group	EBee EPfP
	- - 'Red Autumn Lace' Υ^{H4}	LBuc LRHS MBlu MBri MRav SHil SPer
	punjabensis	EGFP
§	***radicans***	CArn GPoy WHer
	succedanea	CDTJ
	toxicodendron	see *R. radicans*
	trilobata	see *R. aromatica*
N	***typhina*** Υ^{H4}	CBcs CDoC CDul CHEx CMac EBee ELan EPfP GKin LBMP LRHS MAsh MGos MMuc MRav NEgg NHol NLar NWea SAPC SEND SGol SPer SSta
§	- 'Dissecta' Υ^{H4}	CBcs CDoC CDul CMac ELan EPfP LAst LRHS MBri MGos MJak MRav MWat NEgg NLar NPri SEND SGol SPer
	- 'Laciniata' hort.	see *R. typhina* 'Dissecta'
	- Radiance = 'Sinrus'	LRHS MAsh MBlu SPoG
	- Tiger Eyes = 'Bailtiger'^{PBR}	EBee ELan EMil EPfP GKin LBuc LRHS MAsh MBri MGos NPri NSoo SCoo SGol SHil SPoG SWvt
§	***verniciflua***	NLar SSpi

Rhynchelytrum see *Melinis*

Rhynchospora (*Cyperaceae*)

	colorata	LLWG NPer
	latifolia	CKno SDix SHDw

Ribes ✿ (*Grossulariaceae*)

	alpinum	CExl ELan EPfP MRav MWht NWea SPer SRms WOut
	- 'Aureum'	CAbP EHoe NEgg
	americanum 'Variegatum' (v)	EHoe NLar WPat
	aureum misapplied	see *R. odoratum*
	aureum Pursh. subsp. ***gracillimum*** **new**	SBrt
	× ***beatonii***	Widely available
	'Ben Hope'^{PBR} (B)	CAgr EPom MCoo MJak SCoo SWvt WHar
	'Black Velvet' (D)	CAgr MCoo
	californicum	SBrt
	cereum **new**	SBrt
§	× ***culverwellii*** (F)	CAgr CCCN CWib EMil EPom GTwe LBuc LEdu LSRN NLar SDea SPoG SVic WHar
	divaricatum	CAgr GPri LEdu
	gayanum	NLar
	glaciale	NLar
	griffithii	LEdu
	- GWJ 9331	WCru
	jostaberry	see *R.* × *culverwellii*
	'Kathleen'	EPfP
	laurifolium	CBcs CDoC CDul CEnd CExl CHGN CMHG CPla CTri EBee ELan EWTr EWes LAst MRav NLar SBrt SPer WCFE WKif WSHC
	- (f)	CMac EPfP SBrt SRms
	- (m)	EPfP SBrt
	- 'Mrs Amy Doncaster'	CMac WCot WPGP WPat
	- Rosemoor form	CDoC CSam EBee ELan EPfP LRHS SKHP WCot
	longeracemosum	GGGa
	menziesii	CHII EWes GBin NLBP WCot
	nigrum PAB 3755 **new**	LEdu
	- 'Baldwin' (B)	CTri EPfP LRHS MAsh NLar SDea SKee SLim SPer SPoG WHar
	- 'Barchatnaja' (B)	CAgr
	- 'Ben Alder'^{PBR} (B)	CAgr CWib LRHS MAsh SCoo SDea
	- 'Ben Connan'^{PBR} (B) Υ^{H4}	CAgr CMac CSBt CWib EPfP EPom ERea GPri GTwe LBuc LHop LRHS LSRN MAsh MBri MGos MMuc NLar NWea SCoo SDea SKee SLim SPer SPoG SRms SWvt WHar
	- 'Ben Gairn'^{PBR} (B)	CAgr CSBt MCoo WHar
	- 'Ben Lomond'^{PBR} (B) Υ^{H4}	CAgr CMac CSBt CTri CWib ECrN EPfP GTwe LBuc LRHS LSRN MAsh MGos MJak MRav NEgg NLar NPri NWea SDea SEND SKee SPer SRms SVic WHar
	- 'Ben More' (B)	CAgr CWib MBri MJak
	- 'Ben Nevis' (B)	CAgr CTri CWib SDea SKee SPer
	- 'Ben Sarek' (B) Υ^{H4}	Widely available
	- 'Ben Tirran'^{PBR} (B)	CAgr CDoC CSBt CWib ERea LBuc LRHS LSRN MAsh MBri MGos NLar SCoo SPoG SRms SWvt WHar
	- 'Big Ben'^{PBR} (B)	CSut EPom LBuc LSRN NPri
	- 'Black Reward' (B)	CAgr
	- 'Boskoop Giant' (B)	CAgr ELan NEgg SLim SPer WHar
*	- 'Byelorussian Sweet' (B)	CAgr
	- 'Consort' (B)	CAgr
	- 'Ebony' (B)	CMac EMil EPom ERea NPri SLon SVic
*	- 'Hystawneznaya' (B)	CAgr
	- 'Jet' (B)	CAgr NEgg
	- 'Karaka Black' (B) **new**	ERea
*	- 'Kosmicheskaya' (B)	CAgr
	- 'Loch Ness' (B)	ERea WHar
	- 'Noiroma' (B) **new**	CSut
	- 'Pilot Alexander Mamkin' (B)	CAgr
	- 'Seabrook's' (B)	CAgr
	- 'Titania' (B)	LRHS MBri NLar SPoG
	- 'Wellington XXX' (B)	CAgr EMil GTwe LBuc NWea SPer
§	***odoratum***	CBcs CDoC CDul CRHN CSBt CWib EBee ECrN ELan ELon EPfP EWTr GBin LHop LRHS MGos MJak MMuc MNrw MRav NCGa NLar NWea SEND SKHP SPer SPoG SRms SSpi WHar
	- 'Crandall'	CAgr LEdu
	'Pink Perfection'	CMCN
	praecox	CBcs MMuc SEND
	rubrum 'Blanka' (W)	CAgr CMac CSut ERea
	- 'Cascade' (R)	CAgr
	- 'Cherry' (R)	CAgr
	- 'Hollande Rose' (P)	GTwe
	- 'Jonkheer van Tets' (R) Υ^{H4}	CAgr CSBt CWib EMil EPfP EPom GTwe IArd LRHS LSRN MAsh MBri MCoo MMuc NLar NWea SDea SEND SKee SLim SPer SRms WHar
	- 'Junifer' (R)	CAgr ERea GTwe LRHS SKee
	- 'Laxton's Number One' (R)	CAgr CTri GTwe LRHS LSRN MBri MNHC NLar NWea SDea SLim SPer SPoG SRms WGwG WHar
	- 'Lisette' (R) **new**	CSut
	- 'Red Lake' (R) Υ^{H4}	CAgr CTri CWib ELan EPfP ERea GTwe LBuc LRHS MGos MJak NEgg NLar NPri SDea SKee SPer SPoG

- 'Redstart' (R)	CAgr CSBt CTri CWib GTwe LBuc MAsh MBri NLar SKee SPoG WHar
- 'Rondom' (R)	CAgr SDea SVic
- 'Rovada' (R)	CAgr CMac CSBt CSut CWib EPom ERea GTwe LBuc LRHS LSRN MAsh MBri SKee SVic WHar
- 'Roxby Red' (R)	LEdu MCoo
- 'Stanza' (R) ♀H4	CAgr EMil GTwe MMuc SDea SEND
- 'Transparent' (W)	GTwe
§ - 'Versailles Blanche' (W/C)	CAgr CSBt CTri CWib EPfP EPom GTwe LBuc LRHS LSRN MBri MGos MMuc NPri SDea SKee SLim SPer SPoG WHar
- 'White Pearl' (W)	ELan EMil SDea SVic
- White Versailles	see *R. rubrum* 'Versailles Blanche'
- 'Wilson's Long Bunch' (R)	GTwe
sanguineum	CDul NEgg WMoo
- 'Albescens'	EPfP
- 'Brocklebankii'	CExl CMac EBee LRHS MGos MRav MWat NLar SChF SPer SRms WCFE WSHC
- 'Carneum'	LRHS
- double-flowered	see *R. sanguineum* 'Plenum'
- 'Elkington's White'	EPfP ESwi EWTr LBuc LRHS LSRN MBri SHil SLon WBor
- 'Flore Pleno'	see *R. sanguineum* 'Plenum'
- 'Icecrystal' **new**	ESwi
- 'King Edward VII'	Widely available
- 'Koja'	GBin LRHS LSRN MGos SHil SPoG WCot WPat
- 'Lombartsii'	EPfP MRav
- 'Pink Rain' **new**	MGos
§ - 'Plenum' (d)	EPfP
- 'Poky's Pink'	CMac LLHF LRHS MRav SPoG
- 'Pulborough Scarlet' ♀H4	Widely available
- 'Red Bross'	LBuc SWvt
- 'Red Pimpernel'	EBee EPfP LRHS LSRN MAsh MBNS MGos SCoo SPoG SWvt
- 'Tydeman's White'	CExl CSBt ELan EPfP MGos NLar NWea WSHC
- var. ***variegata***	CMac
- White Icicle = 'Ubric' ♀H4	CBcs CDoC CDul CEnd CTri CWib EBee EPfP EWTr GBin LAst LBMP LRHS MAsh MBlu MHer MRav MSwo MWat NBir NLar NPri SLim SPer SPoG SRms SWvt WPat
speciosum ♀H3	Widely available
uva-crispa 'Achilles' (D)	GTwe
- 'Admiral Beattie' (F)	GTwe NEgg
- 'Annelii' (F)	CAgr
- 'Aston Red'	see *R. uva-crispa* 'Warrington'
- 'Bedford Red' (C/D)	GTwe
- 'Bedford Yellow' (C/D)	GTwe
- 'Beech Tree Nestling' (D)	GTwe
- 'Blucher' (D)	GTwe
- 'Bright Venus' (D)	GTwe
- 'Broom Girl' (D)	GTwe
- 'Captivator' (C)	CSBt GTwe LBuc MCoo NEgg NLar SDea SPoG WHar
- 'Careless' (C/D) ♀H4	CMac CSBt EMil GTwe LRHS LSRN MAsh MGos MJak NLar SDea SKee SPer WGwG WHar
- 'Cook's Eagle' (C)	GTwe
- 'Cousen's Seedling' (D)	GTwe
- 'Criterion' (D)	GTwe
- 'Crown Bob' (C/D)	GTwe
- 'Dan's Mistake' (D)	GTwe
- 'Early Sulphur' (D)	ELan GTwe LEdu SDea
- Easycrisp Late Lady (F) **new**	CSut
- 'Espera' (D)	CSut
- 'Firbob' (D)	GTwe NEgg
- 'Forester' (D)	GTwe
- 'Freedom' (C)	GTwe
- 'Gipsy Queen' (D)	GTwe
- 'Glenton Green' (D)	GTwe
- 'Golden Drop' (D)	GTwe
- 'Green Gem' (C/D)	GTwe
- 'Green Ocean' (D)	GTwe
- 'Greenfinch' (C) ♀H4	CAgr
- 'Guido' (F)	GTwe
- 'Gunner' (C/D)	GTwe NEgg
- 'Heart of Oak' (F)	GTwe
- 'Hedgehog' (D)	GTwe
- 'Hero of the Nile' (D)	GTwe
- 'High Sheriff' (D)	GTwe
- 'Hinnonmäki' (F)	CAgr LBuc NPri SPer
- 'Hinnonmäki Grön' (F)	CSBt EMil EPfP LRHS LSRN MAsh MRav NPri WHar
- 'Hinnonmäki Gul' (D)	CAgr CSBt CSut CTri EMil EPfP EPom ERea GTwe LBuc LEdu LRHS MAsh MGos NLar SDea SKee SPer SPoG SVic WHar
- 'Hinnonmäki Röd' (C/D)	CAgr CMac CTri EMil EPfP EPom ERea GTwe LBuc LRHS LSRN MAsh MBri MCoo MRav NLar SDea SPer SPoG SVic WHar
- 'Howard's Lancer' (C/D)	GTwe SDea
- 'Invicta' (C/D) ♀H4	Widely available
- 'Ironmonger' (D)	GTwe
- 'Jubilee' (C/D)	LBuc
- 'Keen's Seedling' (D)	GTwe
- 'Keepsake' (C/D)	GTwe SDea
- 'King of Trumps' (F)	GTwe
- 'Lady Sun' (F)	CSut
- 'Lancashire Lad' (C/D)	GTwe
- 'Langley Gage' (D)	GTwe MCoo NEgg
- 'Laxton's Amber' (D)	GTwe
- 'Leveller' (D) ♀H4	CTri GTwe LAst LBuc MCoo MGos SDea SPer WHar
- 'London' (C/D)	GTwe
- 'Martlet' (F)	CAgr GTwe MCoo SLim
- 'May Duke' (C/D)	SDea
- 'Pax'PBR (D)	CAgr CSut EMil EPfP GTwe LRHS NLar SDea SKee SLim
- 'Peru' (D)	GTwe
- 'Pitmaston Green Gage' (D)	GTwe
- 'Plunder' (C)	GTwe
- 'Queen of Trumps' (D)	GTwe
- 'Red Champagne' (D)	GTwe
- 'Rifleman' (D)	GTwe
- 'Rokula'PBR (C/D)	ELan LRHS MBri MCoo SLim
- 'Rosebery' (D)	GTwe
- 'Scotch Red Rough' (D)	GTwe
- 'Scottish Chieftan' (D)	GTwe
- 'Snow' (F)	EPfP SCoo
- 'Snowdrop' (D)	GTwe
- 'Spinefree' (C)	GTwe
- 'Surprise' (D)	GTwe
- 'Victoria' (C/D)	GTwe
§ - 'Warrington' (F)	GTwe
- 'Whinham's Industry' (C/D) ♀H4	CSBt CTri ELan GTwe LAst LBuc LHop LRHS LSRN MGos MMuc NEgg SDea SEND SPer WHar
- 'White Lion' (C/D)	GTwe
- 'White Transparent' (C)	GTwe
- 'Whitesmith' (C/D)	CTri GTwe LSRN MCoo SDea

- 'Woodpecker' (D)	GTwe NEgg
- 'Xenia' (D)	EPom LBuc
- 'Yellow Champagne' (D)	GTwe
valdivianum	WCot
viburnifolium	NLar
'Worcesterberry' (C)	SDea SPer

Ricinocarpos (*Euphorbiaceae*)

pinifolius	ECou

Ricinus (*Euphorbiaceae*)

communis	CDTJ ELan MBel SPlb
- 'Carmencita' ♀H3	NGBl SDys
- 'Carmencita Bright Red'	CWCL
- 'Carmencita Pink'	CDTJ
- 'Carmencita Red'	CDTJ
- 'Dominican Republic'	CDTJ
- 'Gibsonii'	CDTJ SBst
- 'Impala'	CDTJ SBst
- 'New Zealand Black'	CDTJ CSpe
- 'Zanzibariensis'	CDTJ

Rigidella see *Tigridia*

Riocreuxia (*Apocynaceae*)

torulosa	CCCN SPlb

Robinia (*Papilionaceae*)

× ***ambigua***	EBee SKHP
§ ***boyntonii***	LSRN
§ ***hispida***	CDul CEnd CWib ECrN ELan EPfP EWTr MBlu NLar SPer
- 'Macrophylla'	CEnd NLar
- 'Rosea' misapplied	see *R. boyntonii*, *R. hispida*
- 'Rosea' ambig.	CBcs EBee SPoG
kelseyi	CDul EBee EWes
× ***margaretta*** Casque Rouge	see *R.* × *margaretta* 'Pink Cascade'
§ - 'Pink Cascade'	CDul CEnd CTri EPfP LAst MAsh MBlu MGos SCoo SCrf SEND SEWo SGol SLim SPer
pseudoacacia	CCVT CDul CHab CLnd CNWT ELan LBuc MCoo NEgg SEND SGol SPlb
- 'Bessoniana'	CDul EBee EPfP LAst
- 'Frisia' ♀H4	Widely available
- 'Inermis' hort.	see *R. pseudoacacia* 'Umbraculifera'
§ - 'Lace Lady'PBR	CSBt CWSG ELan EPfP EUJe LRHS MAsh MBri MGos NLar NSoo SCoo SLim SPoG
- 'Rozynskiana'	CDul
- 'Tortuosa'	CEnd EBee EBtc MBlu SPer
- 'Twisty Baby'	see *R. pseudoacacia* 'Lace Lady'
§ - 'Umbraculifera'	CDul CLnd MBri MGos SCoo
× ***slavinii*** 'Hillieri' ♀H4	CDul CEnd EBee ECrN ELan EPfP EUJe EWTr LSRN MAsh MBlu MBri NLar SCrf SEND SLon SPer SPoG

Rochea see *Crassula*

Rodgersia (*Saxifragaceae*)

ACE 2303	SDix
CLD 1432	CExl
aesculifolia ♀H4	Widely available
- green bud	IBlr
- var. ***henrici***	CLAP GBin GCal GLog IBoy MRav NBro NMyG SGbt SWat WHoo WMoo
- - hybrid	CHid EWTr ITim IVic NLar WWEG XLum
- pink-flowered	SSpi
- 'Red Dawn'	IBlr
- 'Red Leaf'	GCal IFoB
'Blickfang'	IBlr
'Bloody Mary'	CElw ECtt EPPr LLWG SKHP
'Borodin'	EBee
Cally strain	GCal
'Dark Pokers'	MBri NLar
'Die Anmutige'	CLAP CRow
'Die Schöne'	CLAP EBee NLar
'Die Stolze'	GBin LEdu LLWG MBrN
'Elfenbeinturm'	IBlr
'Fascination'	IBlr
'Herkules'	EBee ECtt EHoe ELon GBin GCal GMaP IFoB LEdu LHop LSou MBNS MMuc NEgg NLBP NLar SKHP SSpi WCot WPnP WWEG
'Irish Bronze' ♀H4	CLAP CPrp ECtt ELan EPfP GBin GQue IVic LBMP LEdu LLWG LRHS LSRN MWts NPnk WMoo WPnP WWEG
'Koriata'	IBlr
'Kupfermond'	CRow IBlr NBir
'La Blanche'	CMil EBee ECtt ELon LEdu LRHS MHol NCGa NEgg NGdn NLar SPer WCot WPnP WWEG
'Maigrün'	IBlr
nepalensis	CLAP LRHS
- EMAK 713	IBlr WPGP
- HWJK 2140	WCru
'Parasol'	CBro CLAP CMac IBlr NBir NHol SKHP SSpi WPGP
pinnata	Widely available
- B&SWJ 7741A	CBcs WCru
- L 1670	CExl CLAP ELan IBlr SSpi WPGP
- SDR 3301	GKev
- 'Alba'	GCal IBlr NHol
- 'Buckland Beauty'	CDes EBee IBlr LRHS SSpi WMoo WPGP
- 'Cally Coffee'	GCal
- 'Cally Coral'	EBee GCal
- 'Cally Salmon'	EBee EWes GBin GCal IBlr
- 'Chocolate Wing'	Widely available
- 'Crûg Cardinal'	GCal WCru
- 'Elegans'	CCon EBee EHoe ELan EPfP GKev GMaP IBlr LAst LBMP LEdu LRHS MRav NEgg NHol NOrc SPer SWvt WGwG WHil
- 'Fireworks'PBR	CCon CHid CLAP EBee ECtt ELan GBin IMou IPot LEdu LSou NLar SMrm SPer WHil
- 'Jade Dragon Mountain'	CDes GCal IBlr SKHP
- 'Maurice Mason'	CExl CLAP EBee ECtt GKev IBlr NLar WWEG
- 'Mont Blanc'	IBlr
- Mount Stewart form	IBlr
- 'Panache'	IBlr
- 'Perthshire Bronze'	IBlr
- pink-flowered	WCru
- 'Rosea'	IBlr
- 'Superba' ♀H4	Widely available
- white-flowered	GAbr SWat WCru
pinnata × ***sambucifolia***	IBlr
podophylla ♀H4	Widely available
- B&SWJ 10818	WCru
- B&SWJ 10823	WCru
- 'Braunlaub'	CLAP GBuc GQue LLWG NBro WMoo WPnP WWEG

- 'Bronceblad'	IBlr
- Donard selection	IBlr MBri
- 'Rotlaub'	CAby CLAP CRow EBee IBlr IMou IPot IVic WBor WMoo
- 'Smaragd'	CLAP CRow GCal IBlr LRHS MRav NBir NLar
purdomii hort.	GCal WCot WPGP
'Reinecke Fuchs'	IBlr
'Rosenlicht'	CRow
'Rosenzipfel'	IBlr
sambucifolia	CBcs CLAP CMac CRow EWTr GBBs GBee GBin GCal LEdu LLWG LRHS MLHP MMuc NBir NEgg NLar NSti SEND SWat WMoo WPnP WWEG XLum
- B&SWJ 7899	WCru
- dwarf, pink-flowered	IBlr
- dwarf, white-flowered	IBlr
- large, red-stemmed	NBir
- 'Mountain Select'	EBee GCal
tabularis	see *Astilboides tabularis*

Roemeria (*Papaveraceae*)

hybrida	CSpe

Rohdea (*Asparagaceae*)

japonica	CHEx LRHS WCot WPGP
- B&SWJ 4853	WCru
- B&SWJ 5091	WCru
- 'Godaishu' (v)	WCot
- 'Gunjaku' (v)	WCot
- 'Lance Leaf'	LEdu
- long-leaved	WCot
- 'Miyakonojo' (v)	WCot
'Talbot Manor' (v)	CDes WCot
- 'Tama-jishi' (v)	WCot
- 'Tuneshige Rokujo' (v)	WCot
tonkinensis HWJ 562	WCru
watanabei B&SWJ 1911	WCru

Romanzoffia (*Boraginaceae*)

§ ***sitchensis***	CTri
suksdorfii Greene	see *R. sitchensis*
tracyi	CDes NRya
unalaschcensis	EBee SRms

Romneya (*Papaveraceae*)

coulteri ♀H4	Widely available
§ - var. ***trichocalyx***	CCon
§ - 'White Cloud' ♀H4	CExl EBee SChF WPGP WSpi
× ***hybrida***	see *R. coulteri* 'White Cloud'
trichocalyx	see *R. coulteri* var. *trichocalyx*

Romulea (*Iridaceae*)

amoena 'Nieuwoudtville'	ECho
austinii 'Komsberg'	ECho
§ ***autumnalis***	ECho
barkerae 'Paternoster'	ECho
biflora 'Vanrhynsdorp'	ECho
bulbocodium	CBro ECho WAbe
- var. ***clusiana***	ECho
- var. ***crocea***	ECho
- var. ***leichtliniana***	CDes
citrina from Tweerivier	ECho
- 'Kamiesberg'	ECho
columnae	ECho
- subsp. ***columnae***	ECho
cruciata var. ***cruciata*** 'Riverlands'	ECho
- var. ***intermedia*** 'Somerset West'	ECho
dichotoma	ECho
discifera 'Grasberg'	ECho
diversiformis 'Komsberg'	ECho
eximia	ECho
flava var. ***minor*** 'Dassenberg'	ECho
- 'Rawsonville'	ECho
hirsuta var. ***cuprea*** 'Rawsonville'	ECho
- var. ***hirsuta*** 'Klipheuwel'	ECho
- var. ***zeyheri*** 'Malmesbury'	ECho
hirta	ECho
kamisensis	ECho
leipoldtii	ECho
linaresii	ECho
longipes 'Coega'	ECho
longituba	see *R. macowanii*
* ***luteoflora*** var. ***sanguinea***	ECho
§ ***macowanii***	CPBP ECho GKev
montana	ECho
namaquensis	ECho
nivalis	ECho
obscura var. ***blanda***	ECho
- var. ***obscura***	ECho
- var. ***subtestacea***	ECho
pratensis	ECho
ramiflora	CExl ECho
rosea	ECho
- var. ***rosea*** 'Caledon'	ECho
- var. ***speciosa***	see *R. autumnalis*
sanguinalis from Tweerivier	ECho
setifolia var. ***aggregata*** 'Rawsonville'	ECho
sladenii 'Gifberg'	ECho
stellata 'Nardouwsberg'	ECho
subfistulosa from Roggeveld	ECho
tabularis	ECho
tempskyana	ECho
tetragona var. ***flavandra*** 'Matjiesfontein'	ECho
tortuosa subsp. ***aurea*** 'Komsberg'	ECho
- var. ***tortuosa*** 'Botuin'	ECho
toximontana 'Gifberg'	ECho
triflora 'Riverlands'	ECho

Rondeletia (*Rubiaceae*)

amoena	MOWG

Rorippa (*Brassicaceae*)

amphibia	LLWG MSKA
nasturtium-aquaticum	WMAq

Rosa ✿ (*Rosaceae*)

A Shropshire Lad = 'Ausled'PBR (S)	EHyd LBuc LRHS LStr MAus MBri NEgg SMrm SPer SSea SWCr
A Whiter Shade of Pale = 'Peafanfare'PBR (HT)	EBee ECnt ESty GCoc LRHS LStr MAus MJak MRav SPer SWCr
Abbeyfield Gold = 'Korquelda'PBR (F)	SWCr
Abbeyfield Rose = 'Cocbrose' (HT) ♀H4	GCoc MRav SPer
Abigaile = 'Tanelaigib' (F)	LSRN
Abracadabra = 'Korhocsel' (HT)	ESty

Abraham Darby = 'Auscot' (S)	CTri EBee EPfP GCoc IBoy LRHS LSRN LStr MAsh MAus MBri MJak MRav MWat NEgg NLar SEND SLon SMrm SPer SWCr
Absent Friends = 'Dicemblem'PBR (F)	ESty IBoy SRGP WBor
Absolutely Fabulous = 'Wekvossutono'PBR (F)	CGro CSBt CWSG ECnt EPfP ESty GCoc LBuc LRHS LSRN LShp LStr MAsh MBri MJak MRav NPri SCoo SMrm SPer SPoG SWCr
abyssinica	LEdu
'Adam' (ClT)	LSRN
'Adam Messerich' (Bb)	SLon
Adam's Rose = 'Wekromico' (F)	LSRN
'Adélaïde d'Orléans' (Ra) 𝕐H4	CRHN LBuc LRHS MAus MBri MRav NLar SEND SFam SPer
Agatha Christie = 'Kormeita'PBR (ClF)	LBuc MAsh
'Aglaia' (Ra)	CPou EBee MAus
'Agnes' (Ru) 𝕐H4	CGro EHyd EPfP EWTr GCoc IArd LRHS MAus MCot MRav NLar SPer SRGP
'Aimée Vibert' (N)	MAus MRav NLar SEND SPer SRGP
'Alain Blanchard' (G)	CPou EBee MAus
Alan Titchmarsh = 'Ausjive'PBR (S)	CSBt CWSG LRHS LSRN MAus MBri SCoo SPer
§ × ***alba*** 'Alba Maxima' (A)	CArn EWTr GCoc MAus MRav NLar SEND SPer WHer
§ - 'Alba Semiplena' (A) 𝕐H4	EPfP GCoc LRHS MAus NLar SPer SWCr WHer
- Celestial	see *R.* 'Céleste'
- 'Maxima'	see *R.* × *alba* 'Alba Maxima'
'Albéric Barbier' (Ra) 𝕐H4	CRHN CSBt CSam CTri ECnt EHyd ELan EPfP EWTr LRHS LStr MAus MBri MRav MWat NLar NWea SEND SMrm SPer SPoG SSea SWCr WHer
'Albertine' (Ra) 𝕐H4	Widely available
'Alchymist' (S/Cl)	CPou EPfP ESty LRHS MAsh MAus MBri MRav NLar SPer WBor
Alec's Red = 'Cored' (HT)	CBcs CTri CWSG GCoc IBoy LBuc LRHS LSRN LStr MAsh MAus MJak MRav MWat SPer SPoG SRGP SWCr
Alexander = 'Harlex' (HT) 𝕐H4	CGro GCoc IBoy LSRN LStr MAus MRav SEND SPer SSea SWCr
Alexander's Issie = 'Dicland'PBR (F)	IDic
'Alexandre Girault' (Ra)	CRHN LBuc LRHS MAus MBri SPer SWCr WHer
'Alfred de Dalmas' misapplied	see *R.* 'Mousseline'
Alfred Sisley = 'Delstrijor'PBR (S)	ESty MRav NLar
'Alfresco'PBR (ClHT)	MBri SSea
Alibaba = 'Chewalibaba' (Cl)	ECnt ESty LSRN MAsh SMrm SWCr
'Alida Lovett' (Ra)	LRHS MAus
Alison = 'Coclibee'PBR (F)	GCoc LSRN SWCr
Alissar, Princess of Phoenicia = 'Harsidon'	ESty
§ 'Alister Stella Gray' (N)	EPfP EWTr MAus MBri MCot MMuc NEgg NLar SLon SPer SSea WBor
All American Magic = 'Meiroylear' (HT)	ESty
Alleluia = 'Delatur' (HT) **new**	ESty
'Allen Chandler' (ClHT)	MAus
§ Alnwick Castle	see *R.* The Alnwick Rose
'Aloha' (ClHT) 𝕐H4	CBcs CGro CTri EBee EHyd ELan EPfP ESty LRHS LStr MAsh MAus MCot MJak MRav NLar SEND SMrm SPer SPoG SSea SWCr
alpina	see *R. pendulina*
'Alpine Sunset' (HT)	CTri ELon ESty MAsh MBri MRav SPer SPoG SWCr
altaica misapplied	see *R. spinosissima* 'Grandiflora'
altaica Willd.	see *R. spinosissima*
Altissimo = 'Delmur' (Cl)	EBee EWTr LRHS MAus SEND SPer SSea SWCr
'Amadis' (Bs)	MAus
Amanda = 'Beesian' (F)	ESty LSRN
Amber Abundance = 'Harfizz'PBR (Abundance Series) (S)	ESty
Amber Nectar = 'Mehamber'PBR (F)	MAsh
Amber Queen = 'Harroony' (F) 𝕐H4	CSBt CTri GCoc IArd IBoy LBuc LStr MAsh MAus MBri MRav NLar SPer SWCr
Amber Sun	see *R.* County of Staffordshire
Amber Sweet Dream = 'Fryritz' (Patio) **new**	ECnt
amblyotis RBS 0262	GBin NLar
Ambridge Rose = 'Auswonder' (S)	LRHS MAus
'Amélia'	see *R.* 'Celsiana'
Amelia = 'Poulen011'PBR (Renaissance Series) (S)	ECnt LSRN SWCr
'American Pillar' (Ra)	CGro CSBt CTri CWSG EBee ECnt ELan EPfP IBoy LAst LRHS LStr MAsh MAus MBri MMuc MRav NLar SPer SPoG SSea SWCr WBor
Anabell = 'Korbell' (F)	LSRN
'Anaïs Ségalas' (G)	MAus
'Andersonii' (*canina* hybrid)	MAus
§ 'Anemone' (Cl)	EWTr MAus
anemoniflora	see *R.* × ***beanii***
anemonoides	see *R.* 'Anemone'
Angela = 'Grifgela'	LSRN
Angela Rippon = 'Ocaru' (Min)	CSBt SPer
'Angela's Choice' (F)	LSRN
Anisley Dickson = 'Dickimono' (F) 𝕐H4	SPer
Ann = 'Ausfete'PBR (S)	LSRN MAus
Ann Henderson = 'Fryhoncho' (F)	LSRN SMad
Anna Ford = 'Harpiccolo' (Min/Patio) 𝕐H4	LStr SPer
Anna Livia = 'Kormetter'PBR (F) 𝕐H4	EBee ECnt
Anne Boleyn = 'Ausecret'PBR (S)	EPfP IBoy LBuc LRHS MAus MBri NEgg SCoo
'Anne Dakin' (ClHT)	MAus
Anne Harkness = 'Harkaramel' (F)	MAus SPer
Antique '89 = 'Kordalen'PBR (ClF)	MAsh
Antique = 'Antike' (F)	CPou EBee
Aphrodite = 'Tan00847'PBR (S)	ESty MRav SWCr
apothecary's rose	see *R. gallica* var. *officinalis*
'Apple Blossom' (Ra)	SMrm
'Apricot Nectar' (F)	GCoc MAus
'Apricot Silk' (HT)	CTri SPer
Apricot Sunblaze = 'Savamark' (Min)	CSBt
'Archiduc Joseph' misapplied	see *R.* 'Général Schablikine'

	Name	Suppliers
	Art Nouveau = 'Pejamark' (F)	SWCr
	'Arthur Bell' (F) ♀H4	CGro CSBt CTri ELon EPfP ESty IArd IBoy LAst LRHS LSRN LStr MAsh MAus MBri MJak MRav MWat NEgg NPri SMrm SPer SPoG SRGP SSea SWCr WBor
	'Arthur de Sansal' (DPo)	MAus
	Artistic Licence = 'Guesmarble' (HT)	SWCr
	arvensis	CCVT CHab LBuc MAus NWea
	'Assemblage des Beautés' (G)	MAus
	'Astra Desmond' (Ra)	MNrw
	Audrey Wilcox = 'Frywilrey' (HT)	ESty
	'Auguste Gervais' (Ra)	MAus
	Austrian copper rose	see *R. foetida* 'Bicolor'
	Austrian yellow	see *R. foetida*
	'Autumn' (HT)	LSRN
	Autumn Fire	see *R.* 'Herbstfeuer'
	'Autumnalis'	see *R.* 'Princesse de Nassau'
	Avon = 'Poulmulti'PBR (GC) ♀H4	ELan EPfP GCoc MRav SPer
	Awakening = 'Probuzeni' (ClHT)	EWTr NLar SWCr
	'Ayrshire Splendens'	see *R.* 'Splendens'
	'Baby Bio' (F/Patio)	ESty SWCr
	'Baby Faurax' (Poly)	MAus
	Baby Love = 'Scrivluv'PBR (Min/Patio) ♀H4	MAus
	Baby Masquerade = 'Tanba' (Min)	MRav MWat SMrm SPer
	Babyface = 'Rawril'PBR (Min)	ESty
	'Ballerina' (HM/Poly) ♀H4	CDul CGro CSBt CTri EBee ECnt EHyd ELan EPfP GCoc IBoy LRHS LSRN LStr MAsh MAus MRav MWat NEgg NLar NPri SHil SMad SMrm SPer SSea SWCr WBor WKif
	Ballindalloch Castle = 'Cocneel'PBR (F)	GCoc
	'Baltimore Belle' (Ra)	CRHN EBee MAus
	banksiae (Ra)	CHel CPou SRms
	- ***alba***	see *R. banksiae* var. *banksiae*
§	- var. ***banksiae*** (Ra/d)	CDul CHll CPou CRHN CSBt CSPN CTri ELan EPfP GQui LRHS LStr MAus SEND SLon SPer XSen
	- 'Lutea' (Ra/d) ♀H3	Widely available
	- 'Lutescens' (Ra)	CHll
	- var. ***normalis*** (Ra)	CSBt CSam MAus SKHP SLon WCot WHer WPGP
I	- 'Rosea'	MWat NLar
	banksiae × gigantea	WPGP
	'Bantry Bay' (ClHT)	CSBt ELan LSRN LStr SLon SPer SSea SWCr
	Barbara Austin = 'Austop'PBR (S)	MAus
	Barbara Windsor = 'Ganleon'PBR (F)	SWCr
	Barkarole = 'Tanelorak'PBR (HT)	CSBt ESty LStr SWCr
	'Baron Girod de l'Ain' (HP)	ELon LAst LRHS MAsh MAus MMuc MRav NEgg NLar SPer SWCr
	'Baroness Rothschild' ambig.	see *R.* Climbing Baronne Edmond de Rothschild
	'Baronne Prévost' (HP)	MAus SFam
	Baroque Floorshow = 'Harbaroque'PBR (S)	MRav
	Barry Stephens = 'Horcabellero' (HT)	LSRN
§	× ***beanii*** (Ra)	IFro
	Beatrix Potter (S)	ESty MCot
	'Beau Narcisse' (G)	MAus
	Beautiful Britain = 'Dicfire' (F)	LStr MRav SWCr
	Beautiful Sunrise = 'Bostimebide'PBR (ClPatio)	SWCr
	'Belinda' (HM)	LSRN
§	Bella = 'Pouljill'PBR (Renaissance Series) (S)	CPou
	'Belle Amour' (A × D)	CPou MAus
	'Belle de Crécy' (G) ♀H4	CPou CSam CTri EHyd LRHS LStr MAsh MAus MBri MMuc MNrw NLar NPri SFam SKHP SPer SWCr
	'Belle des Jardins' misapplied	see *R. × centifolia* 'Unique Panachée'
	Belle Epoque = 'Fryyaboo'PBR (HT)	GCoc LStr SMad SMrm SWCr
	'Belle Isis' (G)	MAus SPer
	'Belle Portugaise' (ClT)	MAus
	Belmonte = 'Harpcarl'PBR (F)	GCoc
§	'Belvedere' (Ra)	CPou EBee IBoy MAus SPer WBor
	Benita = 'Dicquarrel' (HT)	IDic
	Benjamin Britten = 'Ausencart'PBR (S)	CSBt EPfP ESty IBoy LBuc LRHS MAus MBri NEgg
	Berkshire = 'Korpinka'PBR (GC) ♀H4	LStr SSea SWCr
	Beryl Joyce = 'Tan96145'PBR (HT)	ESty MRav SWCr
	Best of Friends = 'Pouldunk'PBR (HT)	LSRN
	Best Wishes = 'Chessnut'PBR (ClHT/v)	LBuc LSRN SRGP
	'Betty Prior' (F)	GCoc
	'Betty's Smile' (HT)	LSRN
	'Bewitched' (HT)	LSRN
§	Bewitched = 'Poulbella'PBR (Castle Series) (F)	LBuc MAsh SWCr
	Bianco = 'Cocblanco' (Patio/Min)	GCoc MAus MRav MWat SPoG
	Big Purple = 'Stebigpu'PBR (HT)	ECnt ESty
	Birthday Boy = 'Tan97607'PBR (HT)	ESty LSRN LStr MRav SWCr
	Birthday Girl = 'Meilasso'PBR (F)	CGro CSBt ESty LBuc LSRN LStr MAsh MBri MJak MRav MWat NPri SCoo SMrm SRGP SVic SWCr
	Birthday Wishes (Patio)	see *R.* Shrimp Hit (Patio)
	Birthday Wishes = 'Guesdelay' (HT)	CTri LRHS LSRN SSea
	Bishop Elphinstone = 'Cocjolly' (F)	GCoc
	Black Baccara = 'Meidebenne'PBR (HT)	ESty SMrm SWCr
	Black Beauty = 'Korfleur' (HT)	MAus
	'Black Ice' (F)	SPer SWCr
	'Black Jack' (Ce)	see *R.* 'Tour de Malakoff'
	'Blairii Number Two' (ClBb) ♀H4	CSam EBee EPfP MAus MRav NEgg NLar SEND
	'Blanche de Vibert' (DPo)	EBee
	'Blanche Double de Coubert' (Ru) ♀H4	CDul CSBt CSam CTri EBee ECnt ELan EPfP EWTr GBin GCoc LBuc LSRN LStr MAus NEgg NLar SEND SMrm SPer SSea SWCr

	'Blanche Moreau' (CeMo)	MAus SKHP SLon SPer
	'Blanchefleur' (Ce × G)	CPou MAus
	'Blesma Soul' (HT)	CSBt
	'Blessings' (HT) ♀H4	CBcs CSBt CTri GCoc LBuc LSRN LStr MAus MBri MGos MJak MRav NPri SPer SWCr
	'Bleu Magenta' (Ra) ♀H4	IArd MAus MCot MRav NLar SEND SMrm SWCr WKif
	'Bloomfield Abundance' (Poly)	CPou EPfP MAus NLar SPer SWCr WHer
	'Blossomtime' (Cl)	SMad SPer
	Blue for You = 'Pejamblu'PBR (F)	CGro ECnt ESty GCoc LBuc LRHS LStr MAsh MAus SCoo SMad SPoG SWCr
	Blue Moon = 'Tannacht' (HT)	CTri ELan EPfP GCoc IBoy MGos MRav SPer SPoG SRGP
	Blue Peter = 'Ruiblun' (Min)	ESty IBoy MBri
	'Blush Excelsior'	SMrm
	'Blush Hip' (A)	MAus
	'Blush Noisette'	see *R.* 'Noisette Carnée'
	'Blush Rambler' (Ra)	CSBt EBee EPfP EWTr LBuc MAus MMuc SPer
	'Blushing Lucy' (Ra)	MTPN SMrm
	Blythe Spirit = 'Auschool'PBR (S)	LRHS MAus MBri NEgg
	'Bobbie James' (Ra) ♀H4	CTri EHyd EPfP EWTr GCoc LBuc LRHS LStr MAus MBri MRav NEgg NLar SPer SPoG SSea SWCr
	'Bobby Charlton' (HT)	LSRN
	Bonica = 'Meidomonac' (GC) ♀H4	CSam CTri EBee ECnt EHyd ELan EPfP ESty GCoc IBoy LRHS LSRN LShp LStr MAsh MAus MBri MRav MWat NEgg NLar SEND SMrm SPer SPoG SSea SWCr WKif
§	Bonita = 'Poulen009'PBR (Renaissance Series) (S)	ECnt
	Boogie-Woogie = 'Poulyc006'PBR (Courtyard Series) (ClHT)	ECnt LBuc MAsh SWCr
	Born Again	see *R.* Renaissance
	'Botzaris' (D)	SFam
	'Boule de Neige' (Bb)	CBcs CTri ECnt ELan EPfP GCoc IBoy LRHS LSRN LStr MAus MBri MRav MWat NLar SFam SMrm SPer SWCr
	'Bouquet d'Or' (N)	MAus NLar
	'Bouquet Tout Fait' misapplied	see *R.* 'Nastarana'
	'Bouquet Tout Fait' (N)	EBee
	Bow Bells = 'Ausbells' (S)	MAus
	Bowled Over = 'Tandolgnil'PBR (F)	ESty SWCr
§	***bracteata***	CRHN EWes GQui MAus SSea
	Brass Ring	see *R.* Peek-a-boo
	Brave Heart = 'Horbondsmile' (F)	MAus MRav SPoG
	Breath of Life = 'Harquanne'PBR (ClHT)	ELan EPfP LStr MAus MRav SPer SWCr
	Breathtaking = 'Hargalore'PBR (HT)	ESty SWCr
	Bredon = 'Ausbred' (S)	MAus
	'Brenda Colvin' (Ra)	MAus
	'Brian's Star' (F)	LSRN
	Bride and Groom = 'Smi10-98' (HT)	ESty GCoc
	Bride = 'Fryyearn'PBR (HT)	GCoc LSRN LStr MBri MRav
	Bridge of Sighs = 'Harglowing'PBR (Cl)	ECnt ESty LBuc LShp LStr MAsh SPoG SSea SWCr
	Bright and Breezy = 'Dicjive' (F) **new**	ECnt GCoc IDic
	Bright as a Button = 'Chewsumsigns' (S) **new**	ESty
	Bright Fire = 'Peaxi'PBR (ClHT)	SSea
	Bright Future = 'Kirora'PBR (Cl)	ECnt ESty
	Bright Smile = 'Dicdance' (F/Patio)	MAus
	Brilliant Pink Iceberg = 'Probril' (F)	LStr SWCr
	Britannia = 'Frycalm'PBR (HT)	ECnt
	Broadlands = 'Tanmirsch'PBR (GC)	EBee GCoc NLar SLon SWCr
	Brooklands = 'Tananaistrua'PBR (F) **new**	SHil
	Brother Cadfael = 'Ausglobe'PBR (S)	CRos EHyd ELon LRHS LStr MAus MBri NEgg NLar SCoo SLon SMrm SPer SSea SWCr
	Brown Velvet = 'Maccultra' (F)	ESty SWCr
	Brownie = 'Simstripe' (Cl) **new**	ESty
§	***brunonii*** (Ra)	CExl EWes MAus
	- 'Betty Sherriff' (Ra)	CDoC
§	- 'La Mortola' (Ra)	MAus MRav NLar
	Brush-strokes = 'Guescolour' (F)	ESty SWCr
	'Buff Beauty' (HM) ♀H4	CSBt CSam CTri CWSG EBee ECnt EHyd ELan EPfP GCoc IBoy LRHS LSRN LStr MAsh MAus MCot MRav MWat NEgg NLar SFam SMad SPer SSea SWCr WCFE
	'Bullata'	see *R.* × *centifolia* 'Bullata'
§	'Burgundiaca' (G)	MAus
	Burgundian rose	see *R.* 'Burgundiaca'
§	Burgundy Ice = 'Prose'PBR (F)	CGro CSBt EBee ECnt ELon EPfP ESty GCoc LBuc LRHS LShp LStr MAsh MBri MRav SCoo SMad SMrm SPoG SSea SWCr
	'Burgundy Iceberg'	see *R.* Burgundy Ice
	'Burgundy Rose'	see *R.* 'Burgundiaca'
	'Burma Star' (F)	GCoc
	burnet	see *R. spinosissima*
	Buttercup = 'Ausband'PBR (S)	EHyd LBuc LRHS MAus
	Buxom Beauty = 'Korbilant'PBR (HT)	EPfP ESty GCoc LRHS MAsh MBri MWat SCoo SWCr
	'C.F. Meyer'	see *R.* 'Conrad Ferdinand Meyer'
	californica (S)	MAus
	- 'Plena'	see *R. nutkana* 'Plena'
	'Callisto' (HM)	MAus
§	Calypso = 'Poulclimb'PBR (ClHT)	ECnt SWCr
	'Camayeux' (G)	CPou ECnt MAus NLar SPer
	Cambridgeshire = 'Korhaugen'PBR (GC)	CTri LStr MAus NLar SPer SSea SWCr
	'Canary Bird'	see *R. xanthina* 'Canary Bird'
	Canary Showground = 'Chewpatyel'PBR (GC) **new**	SHil
	canina (S)	CArn CCVT CDul CHab CLnd CTri ECrN EPfP LBuc MAus MRav NLar NWea SEWo SPer WHar WMou WOut

	'Cantabrigiensis' (S) ♀H4	EPfP LRHS MAus NLar SLon SPer SSea
	'Capitaine Basroger' (CeMo)	MAus
	'Capitaine John Ingram' (CeMo) ♀H4	MAus NLar SEND SLon
	'Captain Christy'	see *R.* 'Climbing Captain Christy'
	'Captain Scarlet' (ClMin)	ESty
	Caramella = 'Korkinteral'PBR (HT)	MAsh
	'Cardinal de Richelieu' (G) ♀H4	CBcs CPou CSam CTri EHyd EPfP GCoc GCra IBoy LRHS LSRN LShp LStr MAsh MAus MBri MCot MRav MWat NEgg NLar NPri SEND SFam SPer SPoG SWCr
	Cardinal Hume = 'Harregale' (S)	EBee ESty
	Carefree Days = 'Meirivouri' (Patio)	EPfP IBoy LBuc LRHS MAsh MBri NPri SMrm SPoG SSea
	Cariad = 'Auspanier' (HM)	LBuc LRHS MAus
	Caribbean Dawn = 'Korfeining'PBR (Patio)	MAsh
	Caring for You ambig.	LSRN
	Caring for You = 'Coclust'PBR (HT)	GCoc
	'Carol' (F)	see *R.* 'Carol Amling'
§	'Carol Amling' (F)	LSRN
	carolina	SLPl
	'Caroline Testout'	see *R.* 'Madame Caroline Testout'
	Caroline Victoria = 'Harprior'PBR (HT)	LSRN SWCr
	Carris = 'Harmanna'PBR (HT)	ESty
§	Casino = 'Macca' (ClHT)	CTri ELon LBuc MRav SPer
	'Castle Apricot'	see *R.* Lazy Days
	'Castle Cream'	see *R.* Perfect Day
	'Castle Fuchsia Pink'	see *R.* Bewitched = 'Poulbella'
	Castle of Mey = 'Coclucid' (F)	GCoc
	'Castle Peach'	see *R.* Imagination = 'Pouldron'
	'Castle Shrimp Pink'	see *R.* Fascination = 'Poulmax'
	'Castle Yellow'	see *R.* Summer Gold
	'Catherine Mermet' (T)	MAus
§	'Cécile Brünner' (Poly) ♀H4	CSam CTri EHyd ELan EWTr GCoc LRHS LSRN LStr MAus MCot NLar SMrm SPer SSea
	Celebration 2000 = 'Horcoffitup'PBR (S)	MAus
	Celebration Time	see *R.* Cinco de Mayo
§	'Céleste' (A) ♀H4	EPfP GCoc LStr MAus MRav NLar SEND SFam SPer SSea
	'Célina' (CeMo)	LSRN
	'Céline Forestier' (N) ♀H3	CPou EWTr MAus MRav NLar SEND SPer SPoG
§	'Celsiana' (D)	CPou CSam EBee EWTr LSRN MAus SFam SPer
	Centenary = 'Koreledas'PBR (F) ♀H4	MAsh
§	× ***centifolia*** (Ce)	CArn LRHS MAus MRav SMad SPer
§	- 'Bullata' (Ce)	MAus
§	- 'Cristata' (Ce) ♀H4	ECnt ELon LRHS LStr MAus MRav NLar SFam SPer WBor
§	- 'De Meaux' (Ce)	MAus NLar SPer
§	- 'Muscosa' (CeMo)	LRHS LStr MAus MRav MWat SFam
	- 'Parvifolia'	see *R.* 'Burgundiaca'
§	- 'Shailer's White Moss' (CeMo)	MAus SFam
	- 'Spong' (Ce)	MAus
§	- 'Unique' (Ce)	MAus NLar
§	- 'Unique Panachée' (Ce)	CPou MAus

	'Centifolia Variegata'	see *R.* × *centifolia* 'Unique Panachée'
	Centre Stage = 'Chewcreepy'PBR (S/GC)	MAsh MAus
	'Cerise Bouquet' (S) ♀H4	GGal MAus MRav NLar SPer WKif
	César = 'Meisardan'PBR (ClHT)	SSea
§	Champagne Moments = 'Korvanaber'PBR (F)	CBcs CSBt EBee ECnt ELan EPfP ESty GCoc LRHS LSRN LStr MAsh MAus MBri MGos MJak MRav MWat NPri SPer SRGP SSea SWCr
	'Champneys Pink Cluster' (China hybrid)	LRHS MAus
	Chandos Beauty = 'Harmisty'PBR (HT)	CGro ECnt ELon ESty GCoc LRHS LSRN LStr MAsh MRav SSea SWCr
	'Chanelle' (F)	SDix SPer
	Chantal Merieux = 'Masmaric' (Generosa Series) (S)	MRav
	Chapeau de Napoléon	see *R.* × *centifolia* 'Cristata'
	Charles Austin = 'Ausles' (S)	MAus MRav SMrm
	Charles Darwin = 'Auspeet'PBR (S)	CWSG EHyd EPfP LBuc LRHS MAsh MAus MBri NEgg SCoo SMrm SPer
	Charles de Gaulle	see *R.* Katherine Mansfield
	'Charles de Mills' (G) ♀H4	CSam CTri ECnt ELan EPfP GCra LRHS LShp LStr MAsh MAus MBri MCot MRav MWat NLar SFam SKHP SPer SWCr WHer
	Charles Rennie Mackintosh = 'Ausren'PBR (S)	CSBt LBuc MAsh MAus MBri NEgg
	Charlie's Rose = 'Tanellepa' (HT)	ESty LSRN SWCr
	Charlotte = 'Auspoly'PBR (S) ♀H4	CGro CRos ECnt EPfP ESty LRHS LSRN MAsh MAus MBri NEgg SCoo SEND SMrm SPer SSea SWCr
	Charlotte Vieli = 'Diclooker' (F) **new**	IDic
	Charmant = 'Korpeligo'PBR (Min)	MAsh
	Charmian = 'Ausmian' (S)	MAus
	Charming Cover = 'Poulharmu'PBR (Towne & Country Series) (GC/S)	MAsh
	Chartreuse de Parme = 'Delviola' (S)	ESty MRav NLar SLon
	'Château de Clos-Vougeot' (HT)	IArd
	Chatsworth = 'Tanotax'PBR (Patio/F)	MRav SPer SSea
	Chaucer = 'Auscer' (S)	MAus
§	Cheek to Cheek = 'Poulslas'PBR (Courtyard Series) (ClMin)	LBuc MAsh SWCr
	Cheerful Charlie = 'Cocquimmer'PBR (F)	LSRN MRav
	Cherie	see *R.* Songs of Praise
	Cherry Brandy '85 = 'Tanryrandy'PBR (HT)	CSBt
	Cheshire = 'Fryelise'PBR (HT)	GCoc
	Cheshire = 'Korkonopi'PBR (County Rose Series) (S)	LRHS MAus SWCr
	'Cheshire Life' (HT)	MAus
	Chianti = 'Auswine' (S)	EBee MAus NLar
	Chicago Peace = 'Johnago' (HT)	SWCr

Child of Achievement	see *R.* Bella
Childhood Memories = 'Ferho' (ClHM)	SWCr
Chilterns = 'Kortemma'^{PBR} (GC)	SWCr
'Chinatown' (F/S) 🏆^{H4}	CGro CTri IBoy LRHS LStr MAsh MAus MBri MRav SPer SSea SWCr
chinensis misapplied	see *R.* × *odorata*
- 'Minima' *sensu stricto* hort.	see *R.* 'Pompon de Paris'
- 'Mutabilis'	see *R.* × *odorata* 'Mutabilis'
- 'Old Blush'	see *R.* × *odorata* 'Pallida'
- var. ***spontanea***	WPGP
Chloe = 'Poulen003'^{PBR} (Renaissance Series) (S)	CPou ECnt LSRN SLon SWCr
'Chloris' (A)	EWTr MMuc
Chris Beardshaw = 'Wekmeredoc'^{PBR} (HT)	SWCr
Chris = 'Kirsan'^{PBR} (ClHT)	EBee ECnt ESty GCoc LSRN MAus MBri SWCr WGor
Christopher = 'Cocopher' (HT)	GCoc SWCr
Christopher Columbus = 'Meinronsse' (HT)	IArd MMuc
Christopher Marlowe = 'Ausjump'^{PBR} (S)	MAus MBri SCoo
§ 'Chromatella' (N)	MAus
Cider Cup = 'Dicladida'^{PBR} (Min/Patio) 🏆^{H4}	IBoy IDic LStr MAus
§ Cinco de Mayo = 'Wekcobeju'^{PBR} (F) **new**	MAsh
'Cinderella' (Min)	CSBt EWTr NLar
Cinderella = 'Korfobalt' (ClS)	CPou MAsh SWCr
City Lights = 'Poulgan'^{PBR} (Patio)	CSBt
City of Carlsbad	see *R.* Hanky Panky
'City of Leeds' (F)	SPer
City of London = 'Harukfore'^{PBR} (F)	CSBt SWCr
City of York = 'Direktör Benschop' (Cl/HT)	MCot
Clair Matin = 'Meimont' (ClS)	CPou MAus
Claire Austin = 'Ausprior'^{PBR} (S)	CGro CWSG EPfP ESty LBuc LRHS MAsh MAus MBNS MBri SSea SWCr
'Claire Jacquier' (N)	CSam EPfP EWTr MAus MMuc SPer SWCr
Claire Marshall = 'Harunite' (F) **new**	ESty
Claire Rose = 'Auslight'^{PBR} (S)	LSRN MAus MRav SMrm
Claret = 'Frykristal'^{PBR} (HT)	ECnt ESty GCoc LRHS MAsh MBri MRav SPoG SSea SWCr
Clarinda = 'Cocsummery'^{PBR} (F)	GCoc
Claude Monet = 'Jacdesa' (HT)	ESty MRav
'Clementina Carbonieri' (T)	CPou EBee NLar
Cleo = 'Beebop' (HT)	LSRN
Cleopatra = 'Korverpea'^{PBR} (HT)	MAsh
'Cliff Richard' (F)	ESty LBuc LSRN SWCr
'Climbing Alec's Red' (ClHT)	ELon
'Climbing Allgold' (ClF)	SLon
'Climbing Arthur Bell' (ClF) 🏆^{H4}	CSBt CTri ESty IBoy LAst LBuc SPer SPoG SSea SWCr
'Climbing Ballerina' (Ra)	CSBt SWCr
§ Climbing Baronne Edmond de Rothschild = 'Meigrisosar' (ClHT)	CSBt
'Climbing Blue Moon' (ClHT)	GCoc LBuc SWCr
§ 'Climbing Captain Christy' (ClHT)	MAus
'Climbing Cécile Brünner' (ClPoly) 🏆^{H4}	CSBt CTri EBee ECnt EPfP LSRN LStr MAus MBri MCot MRav NLar SEND SPer SSea SWCr
'Climbing Château de Clos-Vougeot' (ClHT)	MAus
'Climbing Christine' (ClHT)	MAus
§ 'Climbing Columbia' (ClHT)	EShb EWTr SPer
'Climbing Crimson Glory' (ClHT)	CPou GCoc LBuc MAus MBri
§ 'Climbing Devoniensis' (ClT)	CPou
'Climbing Ena Harkness' (ClHT)	CTri GCoc MAus MRav SEND SPer SPoG SSea SWCr
'Climbing Etoile de Hollande' (ClHT) 🏆^{H4}	CSBt CSam CTri CWSG EPfP GCoc IBoy LStr MAus MBri MRav NPri SEND SFam SMad SPer SPoG SSea SWCr
Climbing Fragrant Cloud = 'Colfragrasar' (ClHT)	CBcs ELan
'Climbing Home Sweet Home' (ClHT)	LSRN
'Climbing Iceberg' (ClF) 🏆^{H4}	CGro CSBt CTri EBee ELan EPfP ESty GCoc IArd LEdu LSRN LStr MAus MBri MCot MJak MMuc MRav NEgg NLar SMrm SPer SPoG SSea SWCr
'Climbing Jazz'	see *R.* That's Jazz
'Climbing la France' (ClHT)	MRav
§ 'Climbing Lady Hillingdon' (ClT) 🏆^{H3}	EBee EPfP LAst LRHS MAus MBri MRav NEgg NLar SEND SPer WBor
'Climbing Lady Sylvia' (ClHT)	CSBt EBee EPfP LRHS MAus SPer
'Climbing Little White Pet'	see *R.* 'Félicité Perpétue'
'Climbing Madame Abel Chatenay' (ClHT)	MAus
'Climbing Madame Butterfly' (ClHT)	MAus NLar SPer
'Climbing Madame Caroline Testout' (ClHT)	CPou CTri MAus MRav SPer
§ 'Climbing Madame Edouard Herriot' (ClHT)	MAus
'Climbing Masquerade' (ClF)	CTri LBuc MAus MRav NEgg SPer SSea SWCr
'Climbing Mrs Herbert Stevens' (ClHT)	EPfP LRHS MAus MRav SEND SMrm SPer
'Climbing Mrs Sam McGredy' (ClHT) 🏆^{H4}	CSBt MAus NLar
'Climbing Niphetos' (ClT)	MAus
'Climbing Ophelia' (ClHT)	MAus SPer
§ 'Climbing Paul Lédé' (ClT)	LRHS MAus
'Climbing Peace' (ClHT)	SPer
§ 'Climbing Pompon de Paris' (ClMinCh)	CTri LRHS MAus MNrw SEND SLPl SMrm SPer
'Climbing Ruby Wedding' (ClHT)	LSRN
'Climbing Shot Silk' (ClHT) 🏆^{H4}	CSam SPer SWCr
§ 'Climbing Souvenir de la Malmaison' (ClBb)	CPou MAus SPer
'Climbing White Cloud'	see *R.* White Cloud = 'Korstacha'
'Cloth of Gold'	see *R.* 'Chromatella'

	Cloud Nine = 'Fryextra'PBR (HT)	ECnt GCoc
	Coco = 'Korferse' (F) **new**	LSRN
	Colchester Beauty = 'Cansend' (F)	ECnt
§	'Colonel Fabvier' (Ch)	MAus NLar
	colonial white	see *R.* 'Sombreuil'
	'Columbia' (HT)	CPou
	'Columbian'	see *R.* 'Climbing Columbia'
	'Commandant Beaurepaire' (Bb)	CPou MAus
	common moss	see *R.* × *centifolia* 'Muscosa'
	Commonwealth Glory = 'Harclue'PBR (HT)	SWCr
	'Compassion' (ClHT) ♀H4	Widely available
*	'Compassionate' (F)	MRav
	'Complicata' (G) ♀H4	CPou CSam CTri EPfP EWTr LRHS LStr MAus MBri MCot MRav NLar SEND SKHP SPer SSea SWCr
	'Comte de Chambord' misapplied	see *R.* 'Madame Boll'
	Comte de Champagne = 'Ausufo'PBR (S)	LBuc LRHS MAus MBri SCoo
	'Comtesse Cécile de Chabrillant' (HP)	CPou EBee MAus
	'Comtesse de Lacépède' misapplied	see *R.* 'Du Maître d'Ecole'
§	'Comtesse de Murinais' (DMo)	MAus SFam
§	'Comtesse du Caÿla' (Ch)	MAus
	Concert	see *R.* Calypso
	'Conditorum' (G)	SFam
	Congratulations = 'Korlift' (HT)	CSBt ECnt IArd IBoy LBuc LSRN LStr MAus MGos MRav NPri SMrm SPer SSea SVic SWCr
§	'Conrad Ferdinand Meyer' (Ru)	EBee SPer
	Conservation = 'Cocdimple' (Min/Patio)	GCoc MBri MJak SMrm SWCr
	'Constance Spry' (ClS) ♀H4	CTri EBee EHyd EPfP LRHS LStr MAus MBri MCot MMuc MRav MWat NEgg NLar SEND SMrm SPer
§	'Cooperi' (Ra)	CAbP CSam CWib EWTr LRHS MAus MCot SPer SSea WPGP
	Cooper's Burmese	see *R.* 'Cooperi'
	'Coral Cluster' (Poly)	MAus
	Coral Palace	see *R.* Imagination = 'Pouldron'
	Cordelia = 'Ausbottle'PBR (S)	MAus MBri
	'Cornelia' (HM) ♀H4	CBcs CSam CTri EHyd EPfP GCoc IArd LRHS LSRN LStr MAsh MAus MBri MCot MRav MWat NLar SFam SPer SRGP SWCr WBor
	Coronation Street = 'Wekswetrup' (F)	LSRN
	Corvedale = 'Ausnetting'PBR (S)	MAus
	cottage maid	see *R.* × *centifolia* 'Unique Panachée'
	Cottage Maid = 'Poulspan' (S)	MAus
	Cottage Rose = 'Ausglisten'PBR (S)	LSRN MAus MBri MRav SMrm
	Countess Celeste	see *R.* Imagination = 'Pouldron'
§	County of Staffordshire = 'Korsoalgu'PBR (S) **new**	LRHS
	County of Yorkshire = 'Korstarnow'PBR (GC) **new**	ELan ESty LRHS

	'Coupe d'Hébé' (Bb)	MAus
	Courage = 'Poulduf'PBR (HT)	ECnt
	Courvoisier = 'Macsee' (F)	CSBt
	'Cramoisi Picotée' (G)	MAus
	'Cramoisi Supérieur' (Ch)	MAus
	Crathes Castle = 'Cocathes' (F)	GCoc
	Crazy for You = 'Wekroalt'PBR (F)	ECnt ESty LSRN MAsh SWCr
	Cream Abundance = 'Harflax'PBR (Abundance Series) (F)	LStr SSea SWCr
	Crème Brûlée = 'Ganbru'PBR (Cl)	GCoc
	Crème de la Crème = 'Gancre'PBR (ClHT)	CSBt EBee ECnt ELon ESty GCoc LRHS MAsh MAus MRav SPer SPoG SRGP SSea SWCr WBor
	'Crépuscule' (N)	EWTr MAus NLar
	Cressida = 'Auscress' (S)	MAus
	crested moss	see *R.* × *centifolia* 'Cristata'
	Cricri = 'Meicri' (Min)	MAus
	Crimson Cascade = 'Fryclimbdown'PBR (ClHT)	CGro ESty LRHS MAsh MBri MRav SMad SPer SPoG SSea SWCr
	crimson damask	see *R. gallica* var. *officinalis*
	'Crimson Descant' (ClHT)	ECnt
	'Crimson Glory' (HT)	GCoc
	'Crimson Shower' (Ra) ♀H4	CSam CTri LRHS MAus MBNS MBri MMuc MRav NEgg NLar SEND SMrm SPer WHer
	'Cristata'	see *R.* × *centifolia* 'Cristata'
	Crocus Rose = 'Ausquest'PBR (S)	EHyd EPfP LAst LRHS LStr MAsh MAus MBri MRav NEgg SMrm SPer SWCr
	Crown Princess Margareta = 'Auswinter'PBR (S)	CRos ECnt EPfP ESty LRHS MAus MBri NEgg SCoo SMad SMrm SPer SSea SWCr
	cuisse de nymphe	see *R.* 'Great Maiden's Blush'
	Cumberland = 'Harnext'PBR (Cl) **new**	ESty
	'Cupid' (ClHT)	EBee EWTr MAus SPer
I	'Cutie' (Patio)	ESty SWCr
	Dacapo = 'Poulcy012'PBR (Courtyard Series) (ClPatio)	ECnt
	'D'Aguesseau' (G)	EBee MAus
	'Daily Mail'	see *R.* 'Climbing Madame Edouard Herriot'
	'Dainty Bess' (HT)	EWTr MAus SMrm SSea
	'Dale Farm' (F/Patio)	ESty
	× ***damascena*** var. ***bifera***	see *R.* × *damascena* var. *semperflorens*
§	– var. ***semperflorens*** (D)	MAus MRav NLar SSea SWCr
	– 'Trigintipetala' misapplied	see *R.* 'Professeur Emile Perrot'
§	– 'Versicolor' (D)	MAus SPer SSea SWCr
	Dame Wendy = 'Canson' (F)	MAus
	'Danaë' (HM)	CSam MAus
	Dancing Queen = 'Fryfeston' (ClHT)	ECnt ESty GCoc LBuc LRHS LSRN LShp MAsh MBri MRav SPoG SWCr
	Danny Boy = 'Dicxcon'PBR (Patio)	IDic LSRN WGor
	'Danse du Feu' (ClF)	CBcs CSBt CTri ELan EPfP IBoy LAst LRHS LStr MAsh MAus MRav SPer SWCr
	Dapple Dawn = 'Ausapple' (S)	MAus

Darcey Bussell = 'Ausdecorum'PBR (S)	CGro CRos CSBt EHyd EPfP ESty LBuc LRHS LSRN MAsh MAus MBri SSea SWCr
'Darling Jenny' (HT)	LSRN
'Dart's Defender' (Ru)	SLPl
David Whitfield = 'Gana'PBR (F)	LSRN
davidii	MAus
Dawn Chorus = 'Dicquasar'PBR (HT) ♀H4	CGro CSBt CWSG EPfP ESty IBoy LStr MAsh MBri MJak MRav MWat SPer SPoG SSea SWCr
'Daybreak' (HM)	CTri EBee MAus NLar
'De Meaux'	see *R.* × *centifolia* 'De Meaux'
'De Meaux, White'	see *R.* 'White de Meaux'
§ 'De Resht' (DPo) ♀H4	CPou CTri ECnt EPfP EWTr GCoc LRHS MAsh MAus MCot MRav MWat NLar NPri SMrm SPer SWCr WKif
'Dear Daughter' (F)	ESty
'Dearest' (F)	CBcs SPer SWCr
'Debbie Thomas' (HT)	LSRN
Deb's Delight = 'Legsweet'PBR (F)	LSRN
'Debutante' (Ra)	CSam EBee EWTr LRHS MAus
'Deep Secret' (HT) ♀H4	CBcs CSBt CTri CWSG EBee ECnt ELon EPfP ESty GCoc LBuc LRHS LStr MAsh MBri MJak MRav SPer SRGP SSea SWCr
'Deidre Hall' (HT)	LSRN
'Delambre' (DPo)	MAus
Della Balfour = 'Harblend'PBR (ClHT)	SWCr
Dentelle de Malines = 'Lenfiro' (S)	MAus
Desert Island = 'Dicfizz'PBR (F)	ELon GCoc
'Designer Sunset' (Patio)	LBuc MAsh
§ 'Desprez à Fleur Jaune' (N)	EBee IArd LRHS MAus MRav NEgg SEND SFam SMrm SPer SWCr
'Devoniensis' (ClT)	see *R.* 'Climbing Devoniensis'
Diamond Anniversary = 'Morsixty' (Min)	LSRN
'Diamond Celebration' (HT)	LSRN SWCr
Diamond Days Forever = 'Fryjess'PBR (F)	LSRN
'Diamond Jubilee' (HT)	CSBt SWCr
Diamond = 'Korgazell'PBR (Patio)	CGro EPfP ESty LSRN LStr MAsh NSoo SPoG
'Diamond Wishes'	see *R.* Misty Hit
Diamonds Forever = 'Mattdiafor' (HT)	CWSG
Diana = 'Tananaid'PBR (HT)	LSRN
Diana, Princess of Wales = 'Jacshaq' (HT)	MJak
Dick's Delight = 'Dicwhistle' (GC)	LSRN
Dizzy Heights = 'Fryblissful'PBR (ClHT)	GCoc MAus MRav SPer
'Docteur Grill' (T)	MAus
Doctor Goldberg = 'Gandol' (HT)	GCoc
Doctor Jackson = 'Ausdoctor' (S)	MAus
Doctor Jo = 'Fryatlanta'PBR (F)	SWCr
'Doctor W. Van Fleet' (Ra/Cl)	MAus
Dolly = 'Poulvision' (F) **new**	LSRN
'Don Charlton' (HT)	NEgg
'Don Juan' (ClHT)	SWCr
'Doncasteri'	MAus
Donna = 'Pekcoupamaple' (HT) **new**	LSRN
'Doreen' (HT)	LSRN
'Doris Tysterman' (HT)	CTri LBuc LStr MAus SPer
Dorothy = 'Cocrocket'PBR (F)	GCoc LSRN MRav
'Dorothy Perkins' (Ra)	CGro CTri LRHS MAus MBri MRav MWat NPer SPer SRGP WHer
'Dortmund' (S) ♀H4	EPfP GCoc MAus NLar SPer SWCr
Double Delight = 'Andeli' (HT)	ESty GCoc IBoy LSRN MAsh SPer SSea SWCr
Douglas = 'Cocfresco' (F)	GCoc
Dream Lover = 'Peayetti'PBR (Patio)	ESty MBri SWCr
'Dreaming Spires' (Cl)	SPer SWCr
§ 'Du Maître d'Ecole' (G)	ELon LRHS MAus WHer
Dublin Bay = 'Macdub' (ClF) ♀H4	CSBt CSam CTri EBee ECnt ELan ELon EPfP GCoc IArd IBoy LAst LRHS LSRN LStr MAsh MBri MCot MRav MWat NLar SEND SMrm SPer SPoG SSea SWCr WBor
'Duc de Guiche' (G) ♀H4	CSam EHyd MAus MMuc NLar SEND SFam SLon SPer WHer
Duchess of Cornwall = 'Tan97157' (HT)	CSBt MRav SWCr
'Duchess of Portland'	see *R.* 'Portlandica'
Duchess of York	see *R.* Sunseeker
'Duchesse d'Angoulême' (Ce × G)	MAus SFam
'Duchesse de Buccleugh' (G)	MAus MRav
§ 'Duchesse de Montebello' (G) ♀H4	CPou CSam EBee LRHS MAus NLar SFam SLon SPer
'Duchesse de Verneuil' (CeMo)	MAus SFam
Duke of EdinburghPBR (Patio)	see *R.* The Gold Award Rose
'Duke of Edinburgh' (HP)	MAus
'Duke of Wellington' (HP)	CPou
'Duke of Windsor' (HT)	SPer
'Dundee Rambler' (Ra)	MAus
§ 'Duplex' (S)	MAus
'Dupontii' (S)	GCoc LRHS MAus MMuc NLar SFam SKHP SPer
Durrell = 'Tan02876' (F)	SWCr
'Dusky Maiden' (F)	MAus MCot SWCr
Dusty Springfield = 'Horluvdust' (F)	LBuc
'Dutch Gold' (HT)	MAus SPer
'E.H. Morse'	see *R.* 'Ernest H. Morse'
'Easlea's Golden Rambler' (Ra) ♀H4	EPfP LRHS MAus MRav NEgg NLar SLon
East Park = 'Harjope' (HT) **new**	ECnt ESty
'Easter Morning' (Min)	SPer
Easy Does It = 'Harpageant' (F)	EBee ECnt ESty
Easy Going = 'Harflow'PBR (F)	IArd LBuc MAsh MRav SWCr
§ Ebb Tide = 'Weksmopur'PBR (F) **new**	ECnt ESty
ecae	MAus
'Éclair' (HP)	ELon WBor
'Eddie's Crimson' (*moyesii* hybrid) **new**	LSRN
'Eddie's Jewel' (*moyesii* hybrid)	LSRN MAus

	'Eden Rose' (HT)	GCoc
	Eden Rose '88 = 'Meiviolin'PBR (ClHT)	CPou SPer SWCr
	Edward's Rose = 'Smi73/7/97' (F)	ESty
	eglanteria	see *R. rubiginosa*
	Eglantyne = 'Ausmak'PBR (S) ♀H4	CNec CSBt EHyd ELan ELon EPfP GCoc LAst LRHS MAsh MAus MBri MRav SMrm SPer SPoG SSea SWCr
	'Eleanor' (Patio)	LSRN
	Eleanor Masson = 'Cocdesire' (F)	GCoc
	Eleanor = 'Poulberin'PBR (S)	CPou ECnt LSRN SLon SWCr
§	***elegantula*** 'Persetosa' (S)	LRHS MAus NLar SKHP
§	Elina = 'Dicjana' (HT) ♀H4	ECnt ELon LStr MAus MJak MRav SPer SPoG SWCr
	Elizabeth = 'Coctail'PBR (F)	GCoc
	'Elizabeth Harkness' (HT)	MAus SPer
	Elizabeth of Glamis = 'Macel' (F)	CTri GCoc SPer SWCr
	Elizabeth Stuart = 'Maselstu' (Generosa Series) (S)	LSRN MRav
	Elle = 'Meibderos'PBR (HT)	ESty LSRN SWCr
	Ellen = 'Auscup' (S)	LSRN MAus
	'Ellen Willmott' (HT)	EWTr MAus SPer
	'Elmshorn' (S)	CBcs
	Elspeth Marshall = 'Coczefma' (HT)	GCoc
	Emilien Guillot = 'Masemgui' (Generosa Series) (S)	MRav
	Emily = 'Ausburton' (S)	LSRN
	'Emily Gray' (Ra)	CPou EBee ECnt LBuc LSRN LStr MAsh MAus MRav SPer
	Emily Victoria = 'Boshipeacon' (F)	LSRN
	'Emma Wright' (HT)	MAus
	'Emmerdale' (F)	LBuc
	'Empereur du Maroc' (HP)	IBoy MAus MRav
	'Ena Harkness' (HT)	CRos CTri ELan GCoc LBuc LRHS MAsh SRGP
§	'Enfant de France' (HP)	LSRN
	England's Rose = 'Auslounge' (S)	EHyd ESty LBuc MAus
§	England's Rose = 'Ausrace' (S)	LRHS
	English Elegance = 'Ausleaf' (S)	MAus
	English Garden = 'Ausbuff' (S)	CTri EPfP LRHS LSRN MAus MRav SMrm SPer
	'English Miss' (F) ♀H4	CPou EBee ECnt ELon EPfP ESty IBoy LBuc LRHS LStr MAsh MAus MBri MJak MRav SPer SPoG SWCr
	English Sonnet	see *R.* Samaritan
	'Eos' (*moyesii* hybrid)	MAus
	'Erfurt' (HM)	EBee EWTr MAus SPer
§	'Ernest H. Morse' (HT)	CSBt CTri GCoc IBoy MBri MRav SPer SPoG SWCr
	Escapade = 'Harpade' (F) ♀H4	MAus
	Especially for You = 'Fryworthy'PBR (HT)	CSBt ESty GCoc LSRN LStr SCoo SSea SWCr
	Essex = 'Poulnoz'PBR (GC)	MRav SPer SPoG
	'Etain' (Ra)	EBee ECnt
§	'Étendard' (ClHT)	EBee MRav NLar SMrm SPer SPoG SWCr
	Eternal Flame = 'Korassenet'PBR (F)	LBuc LRHS MAsh MBri
	Eternally Yours = 'Macspeego'PBR (HT)	ESty
	Eternity = 'Twoetern' (HT) **new**	MAsh
	'Ethel' (Ra)	CPou LSRN
	'Étoile de Hollande' (HT)	EBee EHyd ELan GBin LRHS MAsh MBNS MBri NEgg NLar SLon
	'Eugénie Guinoisseau' (Mo)	CPou EBee EWTr
	Euphoria = 'Intereup'PBR (GC/S)	LBuc SWCr
	'Euphrosyne' (Ra) **new**	MAus
	'Europeana' (F)	GCoc
	'Evangeline' (Ra)	MAus
	Evelyn = 'Aussaucer'PBR (S) ♀H4	CNec CSBt EPfP ESty GCoc LRHS LSRN MAsh MAus MBri MRav MWat NEgg NLar SLon SMrm SPer SWCr
§	Evelyn Fison = 'Macev' (F)	CSBt CTri ELan GCoc IBoy LSRN MAus MBri MWat SPer
	'Excelsa' (Ra)	CSBt CSam CTri EPfP IArd IBoy MAsh MRav NWea SPoG WBor
	Eye Paint = 'Maceye' (F)	MAus SMrm
	Eyes for You = 'Pejbigeye' (F)	CSBt ESty LStr SMad SWCr WKif
	'F.E. Lester'	see *R.* 'Francis E. Lester'
§	'F.J. Grootendorst' (Ru)	IBoy NEgg SPer
	Fabulous at 50 = 'Rawfabsal' (F) **new**	LSRN
	'Fabvier'	see *R.* 'Colonel Fabvier'
	Fair Bianca = 'Ausca' (S)	MAus
	Fairy Prince = 'Harnougette' (GC)	ESty
	Fairy Queen = 'Sperien' (Poly/GC)	LBuc
	'Fairy Rose'	see *R.* 'The Fairy'
	Fairy Snow = 'Holfairy' (S)	SWCr
	Faithful Friend = 'Beachallenge' (S)	LSRN
	Falstaff = 'Ausverse'PBR (S)	CRos CSBt EHyd ELon EPfP IBoy LRHS LSRN LStr MAus MBNS MBri MJak MRav NEgg SMrm SPer SPoG SSea SWCr
	'Fantin Latour' (*centifolia* hybrid) ♀H4	CTri ECnt EHyd ELan EPfP GCoc GCra IBoy LAst LRHS LStr MAus MBri MRav MWat NEgg NLar SEND SFam SMad SPer SSea SWCr
	farreri var. ***persetosa***	see *R. elegantula* 'Persetosa'
	Fascination = 'Jacoyel' (Castle Series) (HT)	LStr SCoo
§	Fascination = 'Poulmax'PBR (F) ♀H4	EPfP IBoy LBuc LRHS MAsh MBri MRav SPer SWCr
	Father's Favourite = 'Gandoug'PBR (F)	GCoc LSRN SWCr
	fedtschenkoana misapplied	MAus SPer
	fedtschenkoana Regel	SLPl
	Fée des Neiges	see *R.* Iceberg
	'Felicia' (HM) ♀H4	CSBt CSam CTri EBee ECnt ELan EPfP EWTr GCoc LRHS LStr MAsh MAus MBri MCot MRav MWat NLar SEND SFam SKHP SMrm SPer SPoG SWCr WKif
	'Félicité Parmentier' (A × D) ♀H4	LRHS MAus MBri MRav MWat NLar SFam SPer SWCr
§	'Félicité Perpétue' (Ra) ♀H4	CBcs CTri EHyd ELan EPfP EWTr GCoc IBoy LRHS LShp LStr MAus MBri MRav NEgg NLar SEND SFam SPer SPoG SSea SWCr
	'Fellemberg' (ClCh)	EBee MAus

Fellowship = 'Harwelcome'PBR (F) ♀H4	GCoc LStr MAus MRav SCoo SSea SWCr
'Ferdinand Pichard' (Bb) ♀H4	CPou CRos CSBt CSam CTri ECnt ELon EPfP ESty GCoc LAst LRHS MAsh MAus MBri MCot MRav NEgg NLar SEND SKHP SPer SSea SWCr WKif
Ferdy = 'Keitoli'PBR (GC)	SPer
ferruginea	see *R. glauca* Pourr.
Festival = 'Kordialo'PBR (Patio)	ESty IBoy MRav SPer SPoG SWCr
Fetzer Syrah Rosé = 'Harextra'PBR (S)	ESty
Fiery Hit = 'Poulfiry'PBR (PatioHit Series) (Min/Patio)	MAsh
Fighting Temeraire = 'Austrava' (S) **new**	CRos EHyd MAus SSea
§ ***filipes*** 'Kiftsgate' (Ra) ♀H4	Widely available
§ 'Fimbriata' (Ru)	CPou MAus NLar SPer WBor
Financial Times Centenary = 'Ausfin' (S)	MAus
Fiona = 'Meibeluxen' (S/GC)	LSRN
First Great Western = 'Oracharpam'PBR (HT)	ESty SMrm SWCr
'Fisher and Holmes' (HP)	MAus
Fisherman's Friend = 'Auschild'PBR (S)	MAus SPer
Flashdance = 'Poulyc004'PBR (ClMin)	ECnt SWCr
Flirt = 'Korkopapp'PBR (F)	LBuc
'Flora' (HT)	MAus
'Flore' (Ra)	CRHN
'Florence Mary Morse' (S)	SDix
Florence Nightingale = 'Ganflor'PBR (F)	GCoc SPer
'Flower Carpet Amber' (GC)	CGro CSBt GCoc IBoy LBuc LRHS MAsh SCoo SPoG SWCr
'Flower Carpet Coral'PBR (GC)	CSBt GCoc LBuc LRHS MAsh MBri SCoo SWCr
Flower Carpet Gold = 'Noalesa'PBR (GC)	CGro ECnt GCoc IBoy LBuc LRHS MAsh NPri SPoG
Flower Carpet Pink	see *R.* Pink Flower Carpet
Flower Carpet Red Velvet = 'Noare'PBR (GC/S)	CGro ELan EPfP GCoc IBoy LBuc LRHS LStr MAsh MBri NLar NPri SCoo SPer SPoG SWCr
Flower Carpet Ruby (GC)	LBuc LRHS SCoo SPoG
Flower Carpet Scarlet = 'Noa83100b'PBR (GC)	LBuc LRHS MAsh
§ Flower Carpet Sunshine = 'Noason'PBR (GC)	ELan LRHS LStr MAsh NLar SCoo SPer
Flower Carpet White = 'Noaschnee'PBR (GC) ♀H4	CGro CTri EBee ECnt ELan EPfP GCoc IBoy LRHS LStr MAsh MAus NPri SCoo SPer SPoG SWCr
Flower Power = 'Frycassia'PBR (Patio)	CSBt ECnt ELon ESty GCoc IBoy LRHS LStr MAsh MAus MBri MRav SPoG SWCr
Flower Power Gold = 'Fryneon' (Patio)	ECnt ESty LStr
§ ***foetida*** (S)	EBee MAus SPer
§ - 'Bicolor' (S)	MAus NLar SPer
§ - 'Persiana' (S)	LRHS MAus
foliolosa	SLPl
Fond Memories = 'Kirfelix'PBR (Patio)	ESty LSRN LStr MBri SWCr
For You With Love = 'Fryjangle' (Patio)	GCoc LBuc LSRN

Forever Royal = 'Franmite' (F)	ESty
Forget Me Not = 'Coccharm'PBR (HT)	ESty GCoc
forrestiana	LRHS MAus
Fortune's double yellow	see *R.* × *odorata* 'Pseudindica'
'Fountain' (HT)	MAus
Fragrant Cloud = 'Tanellis' (HT)	CTri CWSG EPfP ESty GCoc IBoy LRHS LStr MAsh MAus MGos MRav NPri SMrm SPer SPoG SSea SWCr
'Fragrant Delight' (F) ♀H4	CSBt ELan ELon GCoc LStr MAus MBri MRav MWat SPer SPoG SSea
Fragrant Dream = 'Dicodour'PBR (HT)	ESty IBoy LStr MRav SMrm SSea
Fragrant Memories = 'Korpastato'PBR (HT)	CSBt SCoo SKHP
'Francesca' (HM)	EWTr LRHS LSRN MAus SFam SPer
Francine Austin = 'Ausram'PBR (S/GC)	LRHS MAus MBri NEgg SPer
§ 'Francis E. Lester' (HM/Ra) ♀H4	CRHN CSam EHyd ELan EPfP LRHS MAus MBri MMuc NLar SEND SMrm SPer SRGP SSea SWCr WBor
× ***francofurtana*** misapplied	see *R.* 'Impératrice Joséphine'
'François Juranville' (Ra) ♀H4	CPou CRHN EBee EPfP GGal IBoy LRHS LShp LStr MAus MBri MMuc MRav NLar SEND SLon SPer WHer
§ 'Frau Karl Druschki' (HP)	EBee MAus
'Fred Loads' (F) ♀H4	MAus
Freddie Mercury = 'Batmercury' (HT)	ESty LSRN NEgg
Free Spirit = 'Fryjeru'PBR (F)	ECnt GCoc MBri
Free Spirit = 'Pixiree' (Min) **new**	EBee
Freedom = 'Dicjem' (HT) ♀H4	CTri ECnt GCoc LStr MAus MBri MJak MRav SPer SSea SVic
'Frensham' (F)	GCoc SSea SWCr
Friend for Life = 'Cocnanne'PBR (F) ♀H4	GCoc LSRN MRav
Friends Forever = 'Korapriber' (F)	EPfP GCoc MAsh NPri
'Fritz Nobis' (S) ♀H4	CPou GCoc LStr MAus NLar SPer
Frothy = 'Macfrothy'PBR (Patio)	ECnt ESty
'Fru Dagmar Hastrup' (Ru) ♀H4	CDul CSBt CTri EBee ECnt ELan EMil EPfP EWTr GCoc IBoy LBuc LRHS LStr MAsh MAus NEgg NLar NWea SEND SMad SPer SWCr
'Frühlingsgold' (SpH) ♀H4	CBcs ELan GCoc LRHS LStr MAus NLar NWea SPer
'Frühlingsmorgen' (SpH)	GCoc LStr MAus SLon SMad SPer
Fulton Mackay = 'Cocdana'PBR (HT)	GCoc
Fyvie Castle = 'Cocbamber' (HT)	GCoc
§ ***gallica*** var. ***officinalis*** (G) ♀H4	CArn CPrp CSam CTri EHyd EPfP GCoc GPoy LRHS MAsh MAus MBri MHer MRav NLar SFam SKHP SPer SSea SWCr
§ - 'Versicolor' (G) ♀H4	Widely available
Galway Bay = 'Macba' (ClHT)	CPou IBoy LRHS MAsh MRav SPer SWCr
Garden of Roses	see *R.* Joie de Vivre
'Gardeners Glory'PBR (ClHT)	ECnt ESty LAst LRHS MAsh SMad
'Gardenia' (Ra)	EWTr LRHS MAus MMuc NLar SPer
'Garnette Carol'	see *R.* 'Carol Amling'

	Name	Suppliers
	'Garnette Pink'	see *R.* 'Carol Amling'
	'Gaujard'	see *R.* Rose Gaujard
	'Gelbe Dagmar Hastrup'	see *R.* Yellow Dagmar Hastrup
	'Général Jacqueminot' (HP)	MAus
	'Général Kléber' (CeMo)	MAus SFam
§	'Général Schablikine' (T)	MAus NLar
	Genesis = 'Fryjuicy'PBR (Patio)	ECnt ESty LBuc MRav SWCr
N	***gentiliana*** misapplied	see *R.* 'Polyantha Grandiflora'
N	***gentiliana*** H. Lév. & Variot	see *R. multiflora* var. *cathayensis*
	Gentle Hermione = 'Ausrumba'PBR (S)	CRos ELan EPfP IBoy LRHS MAus MBri SWCr
	Gentle Touch = 'Diclulu' (Min/Patio)	CSBt LBuc MRav SPer SPoG
	Geoff Hamilton = 'Ausham'PBR (S)	EHyd EPfP IBoy LRHS LSRN LStr MAus MBNS MBri NEgg SCoo SMrm SPer SSea
	'Geoffrey Smith' (Cl)	LSRN
	'Georg Arends' (HP)	MAus
	George Best = 'Dichimanher'PBR (Patio)	ESty IDic LBuc LSRN SWCr
	'George Dickson' (HT)	MAus
	'Georges Vibert' (G)	MAus
	'Geranium' (*moyesii* hybrid) ♀H4	CBcs CDul CSam CTri ELan EPfP EWTr GCoc IArd IBoy LRHS LStr MAus MBri MCot MRav MWat NLar SEND SPer SSea SWCr WKif
	Gerbe d'Or	see *R.* Casino
	'Gerbe Rose' (Ra)	MAus
	Gertrude Jekyll = 'Ausbord'PBR (S) ♀H4	Widely available
	'Ghislaine de Féligonde' (Ra/S)	CPou CSam EPfP GCoc LRHS LStr MAus MBri MCot NLar SEND SMrm SPer SWCr
	Ghita	see *R.* Millie
	Giardina = 'Tan97286' (Cl)	ESty SWCr
	gigantea* × *longicuspis	WPGP
	Giggles = 'Frynoodle' (Patio) new	ECnt
	Ginger Syllabub = 'Harjolina'PBR (ClHT)	EBee ECnt ELon ESty GCoc MRav SPoG SRGP SWCr
	Gingernut = 'Coccrazy'PBR (Patio)	SWCr
	Gipsy Boy	see *R.* 'Zigeunerknabe'
	Glad Tidings = 'Tantide'PBR (F)	IBoy MRav SPer SWCr
	Glamis Castle = 'Auslevel'PBR (S)	CBcs CTri EPfP IBoy LRHS LStr MAus MBri NEgg SCoo SMrm SPer SWCr
	glauca ambig.	GCra MHer NLar
§	***glauca*** Pourr. (S) ♀H4	CMea CPom CSBt CTri EBee ECnt EPfP GCoc GGal LBuc LHop LRHS LStr MAus MLHP MMuc MRav NEgg NSti NWea SEND SGol SKHP SMrm SPer SPoG SSea SWCr WMoo
	'Glenfiddich' (F)	CSBt CTri CWSG GCoc MAus MRav SPer
	Glenshane = 'Dicvood' (GC/S)	MRav
	Global Beauty = 'Tan 94448' (HT)	MRav SWCr
	'Gloire de Dijon' (ClT)	CGro CSBt CTri CWSG ECnt ELan EPfP IBoy LRHS LSRN LStr MAus MBri MCot MRav NEgg NLar NPri SPer SPoG SRGP SSea SWCr
	'Gloire de Ducher' (HP)	MAus
	'Gloire de France' (G)	MAus MRav WHer
	'Gloire de Guilan' (D)	MAus
	'Gloire des Mousseuses' (CeMo)	LRHS MAus SFam
	'Gloire du Midi' (Poly)	MAus
	'Gloire Lyonnaise' (HP)	MMuc SLon
	'Gloria Mundi' (Poly)	NEgg SMrm
	Gloriana = 'Chewpope'PBR (ClMin)	CGro ECnt ESty LRHS MAsh MAus MBri MRav MWat SCoo SKHP SMrm SPer SPoG SSea SWCr
	Glorious = 'Interictira'PBR (HT)	ESty SWCr
	'Glory of Seale' (S)	SSea
	Glowing Amber = 'Manglow' (Min)	ESty
	Gold Charm = 'Chewalbygold' (Cl) new	ECnt ESty
	Gold Rush = 'Jacrebin'PBR (F)	ESty GCoc
	Gold Symphonie = 'Macfraba' (Min)	LBuc
	'Golden Anniversary' (Patio)	IBoy LStr NSoo SPer SSea SWCr
	'Golden Autumn' (HT)	LSRN
	Golden Beauty = 'Korberbeni'PBR (F)	CPou ESty MAsh MBri
	Golden Celebration = 'Ausgold'PBR (S) ♀H4	CRos CSBt CSam CTri CWSG ECnt EHyd EPfP ESty GCoc IBoy LAst LRHS LSRN LStr MAsh MAus MBri MJak MRav NLar SLon SMad SMrm SPer SPoG SSea SWCr
	'Golden Chersonese' (S)	MAus
	'Golden Dawn' (HT) new	MAsh
	Golden Future = 'Horanymoll'PBR (ClHT)	MAus SWCr
	Golden Gate = 'Korgolgat'PBR (ClHT)	ECnt EPfP ESty LStr MAsh MAus SSea
	Golden Jewel = 'Tanledolg'PBR (F/Patio)	ESty
	Golden Jubilee = 'Cocagold' (HT)	GCoc MRav SWCr
	Golden Memories = 'Korholesea'PBR (F)	CBcs CSBt ESty GCoc MAsh MBri MGos MJak MRav SCoo SPer SWCr
	Golden Moment = 'Smi-99-2-04' (HT)	ESty
	'Golden Rambler'	see *R.* 'Alister Stella Gray'
	'Golden Showers' (Cl) ♀H4	CGro CSBt CTri CWSG ELan EPfP GCoc GGal IBoy LRHS LSRN LStr MAsh MAus MBri MRav MWat NEgg NLar NPri SMrm SPer SPoG SSea SWCr WBor
	Golden Smiles = 'Frykeyno'PBR (F)	ECnt ESty GCoc MBri
	Golden Symphonie = 'Meitoleil' (Min/Patio)	ELon
	Golden Trust = 'Hardish'PBR (Patio)	LStr MBri MWat
	Golden Wedding Anniversary (F)	LSRN
	Golden Wedding = 'Arokris'PBR (F)	Widely available
	'Golden Wedding Celebration' (F)	ESty LSRN MAsh SWCr
	'Golden Wings' (S) ♀H4	CPou CTri ELan EPfP GCoc IBoy LRHS LStr MAus MRav NLar SKHP SPer SWCr
	'Goldfinch' (Ra)	CRos ELan EPfP LRHS LStr MAus MBri MRav NEgg NLar SEND SPer SPoG SWCr WBor
	Goldstar = 'Candide' (HT)	ECnt

Good as Gold = 'Chewsunbeam'^{PBR} (ClMin)	CSBt ECnt ESty LStr SMrm SPer SSea SWCr
Good Life = 'Cococircus'^{PBR} (HT)	GCoc SCoo
Gordon Snell = 'Dicwriter' (F)	IDic
Gordon's College = 'Cocjabby'^{PBR} (F) ϒ^{H4}	GCoc
'Grace Abounding' (F)	LSRN
Grace = 'Auskeppy'^{PBR} (S)	CRos CSBt EHyd EPfP ESty LRHS LSRN LStr MAus MBri NEgg SMrm SPer SSea SWCr
Gracious Queen = 'Bedqueen' (HT)	GCoc SWCr
'Graciously Pink' (Min)	LBuc MAsh
Graham Thomas = 'Ausmas' (S) ϒ^{H4}	Widely available
Grande Amore = 'Korcoluma'^{PBR} (HT)	CSBt LRHS LSRN
'Grandma' (F)	LSRN
'Grandpa Dickson' (HT)	CBcs GCoc IBoy LBuc MAsh MAus MBri MRav SPer
Granny's Favourite (Patio/F)	LSRN
Great Expectations = 'Jacdal' (F)	SPoG
Great Expectations = 'Lanican' (HT)	CBcs
Great Expectations = 'Mackalves'^{PBR} (F)	EPfP ESty GCoc IArd LBuc LRHS LStr MAsh MRav SCoo SPer SWCr
§ 'Great Maiden's Blush' (A)	GCoc MRav NLar SFam
'Great News' (F)	MAus
Greenall's Glory = 'Kirmac'^{PBR} (F/Patio)	MAus MRav
Greetings = 'Jacdreco'^{PBR} (F)	ELon LBuc MAsh MJak MRav
Grenadine = 'Poulgrena'^{PBR} (HT)	ECnt
'Grootendorst'	see *R.* 'F.J. Grootendorst'
Grouse 2000 = 'Korteilhab'^{PBR} (GC)	CTri MAus
Grouse = 'Korimro' (S/GC) ϒ^{H4}	EPfP MAus NLar SEND SLon SPer
'Gruss an Aachen' (Poly)	EPfP EWTr LStr MAus NLar SPer SWCr
'Gruss an Teplitz' (China hybrid)	MAus NLar SPer
'Guinée' (ClHT)	CSBt EBee ELan EPfP EWTr LAst LRHS MAsh MAus MCot MRav NLar NPri SMrm SPer SRGP SSea WCot
'Gustav Grünerwald' (HT)	MAus
Guy Savoy = 'Delstrimen'^{PBR} (F)	ESty MRav SLon
Guy's Gold = 'Harmatch'^{PBR} (HT)	ESty
Gwen Mayor = 'Cocover'^{PBR} (HT)	GCoc
Gwent = 'Poulurt'^{PBR} (GC)	CSBt ELan LSRN LStr SEND SPer SSea
§ ***gymnocarpa*** var. ***willmottiae***	SSea
Gypsy Boy	see *R.* 'Zigeunerknabe'
'Hakuun' (F/Patio) ϒ^{H4}	MAus
Hampshire = 'Korhamp'^{PBR} (GC)	MAus
Hand in Hand = 'Haraztec'^{PBR} (Patio/Min)	MWat
Händel = 'Macha' (ClHT) ϒ^{H4}	CGro CSBt CTri CWSG ELan EPfP IBoy LBuc LRHS LStr MAsh MRav MWat NEgg NLar SMrm SPer SPlb SPoG SSea SWCr
§ Hanky Panky = 'Wektorcent'^{PBR} (F)	CGro ESty GCoc MAsh MRav SCoo SWCr
Hannah Gordon = 'Korweiso' (F)	MAsh SPer SWCr
'Hansa' (Ru)	EBee EMil EWTr GCoc LBuc MAus SPer SWCr
Happy Anniversary ambig.	SSea
Happy Anniversary = 'Bedfranc'^{PBR} (F)	LSRN MBri SWCr
Happy Anniversary = 'Delpre' (F)	CGro CTri LRHS LStr MAsh MRav SPoG
'Happy Birthday' (Min/Patio)	CWSG ESty IBoy LBuc LSRN LStr SSea SWCr
Happy Child = 'Auscomp'^{PBR} (S)	LRHS MAus
Happy Retirement = 'Tantoras'^{PBR} (F)	CGro ESty GCoc LBuc LSRN LStr MAsh MRav SCoo SPoG SSea SWCr
Happy Times = 'Bedone'^{PBR} (Patio/Min)	MBri
§ × ***harisonii*** 'Harison's Yellow' (SpH)	MAus
§ - 'Lutea Maxima' (SpH)	MAus
§ - 'Williams Double Yellow' (SpH)	EWTr MAus
Harlow Carr = 'Aushouse'^{PBR} (S)	CRos EHyd EPfP IBoy LRHS MAus MRav SCoo SMrm SPer
Harlow Carr = 'Kirlyl' (F)	MBri
'Harry Edland' (F)	SSea SWCr
'Harry Wheatcroft' (HT)	CGro IBoy MAus MBri SPer
Harvest Fayre = 'Dicnorth'^{PBR} (F)	SPer
Havana Hit = 'Poulpah032'^{PBR} (Patio)	EPfP LBuc MAsh
'Headleyensis' (S)	MAus SLon
Heart of Gold = 'Coctarlotte'^{PBR} (HT)	ECnt ESty GCoc MRav
Heather Austin = 'Auscook'^{PBR} (S)	MAus
Heavenly Rosalind = 'Ausmash'^{PBR} (S)	MAus
§ 'Hebe's Lip' (D × RH)	MAus
'Helen Knight' (*ecae* hybrid) (S)	ESty LRHS MAsh MAus SSea
helenae	CTri MAus NLar SPer
Helen's Trust = 'Taytrust' (HT) **new**	LSRN
hemisphaerica (S)	MAus
§ 'Henri Martin' (CeMo)	IBoy LEdu LRHS MAus NEgg NLar SKHP SLon SMrm SPer
Henri Matisse = 'Delstrobla' (HT)	ESty MRav SPoG
'Henry Nevard' (HP)	MAus
§ 'Herbstfeuer' (RH)	CPou EBee NLar
Heritage = 'Ausblush' (S)	CTri EBee ELan EPfP LStr MAus MBri MRav MWat NEgg NLar SLon SMrm SPer SPoG SSea
'Hermosa' (Ch)	EWTr LRHS MAus MRav
Hero = 'Aushero' (S)	MAus
Hertfordshire = 'Kortenay'^{PBR} (GC) ϒ^{H4}	ELan LRHS MAus MRav SEND SPer SWCr
× ***hibernica***	MAus
'Hidcote Gold' (S)	MAus

	Name	Suppliers
§	'Hidcote Yellow' (Cl)	LRHS MAus SPer
	High Flier = 'Fryfandango'PBR (ClHT)	MBri MWat SWCr
	High Hopes = 'Haryup'PBR (ClHT) ♀H4	CGro EPfP GCoc IBoy LStr MAsh MAus SPer SPoG SSea SWCr
	'Highdownensis' (*moyesii* hybrid) (S)	ELan MAus
	Highfield = 'Harcomp' (ClHT)	MAus
	Hilda Murrell = 'Ausmurr' (S)	MAus
	'Hillieri' (*moyesii* hybrid)	MAus
	'Hippolyte' (G)	MAus
	Hole-in-one = 'Horeagle' (F)	LSRN
	holy rose	see *R.* × *richardii*
	'Homère' (T)	MAus
	Hommage à Barbara = 'Delchifrou'PBR (HT)	ESty MRav SMrm WKif
	Honey Bunch = 'Cocglen'PBR (F)	ELon MRav SPer SRGP
	Honey Dijon = 'Weksproulses'PBR (F)	CSBt ECnt ESty SWCr
	Honeybun = 'Tan98264'PBR (Patio)	ESty SWCr
	'Honorine de Brabant' (Bb)	CPou LRHS MAus MCot NLar SPer SWCr
	Hot Chocolate = 'Wekpaltez' (F)	CGro CSBt EBee ECnt ELan ELon EPfP ESty GCoc IBoy LBuc LRHS LShp LStr MAsh MBri MJak MRav NPri SCoo SMad SMrm SPer SPoG SRGP SSea SWCr WBor WCot
	Hot Stuff = 'Maclarayspo' (Min)	SWCr
	House Beautiful = 'Harbingo' (Patio)	MRav
	'Hugh Dickson' (HP)	CPou LSRN MAus NLar
	hugonis	see *R. xanthina* f. *hugonis*
	- 'Plenissima'	see *R. xanthina* f. *hugonis*
	Humanity = 'Harcross'PBR (F)	MRav SMrm
	Hydo Hall = 'Ausbosky'PBR (S)	CRos EHyd MAus SCoo
	I Love You = 'Geelove' (HT)	LBuc
	Ice Cream = 'Korzuri'PBR (HT) ♀H4	CGro CSBt CWSG ECnt ESty GCoc IBoy LStr MAus MRav MWat SPoG SWCr
§	Iceberg = 'Korbin' (F) ♀H4	CBcs CGro CNec CRos CSBt CTri CWSG EBee ECnt EHyd EPfP ESty GCoc IBoy LRHS LStr MAsh MAus MBri MGos MJak MRav MWat NPri NWea SMrm SPer SPoG SSea SWCr
	'Illusion' (ClF)	SWCr
§	Imagination = 'Pouldron'PBR (F)	MAsh
§	'Impératrice Joséphine' (Gn) ♀H4	CSam EWTr IBoy LRHS MAus MRav NLar SFam
	In Memory Of	LSRN
	Indian Summer = 'Harwigwam' (ClMin) **new**	MBri MJak
	Indian Summer = 'Peaperfume'PBR (HT) ♀H4	CSBt CWSG ELon GCoc MAsh MRav MWat SMrm SPoG SWCr
	'Indigo' (DPo)	CPou EWTr MAus SMrm
	Ingrid Bergman = 'Poulman'PBR (HT) ♀H4	CTri ECnt ELon EPfP GCoc IBoy LBuc LRHS LSRN LStr MAsh MGos MRav SMrm SPer SPoG SWCr
	Innocence = 'Cocoray'PBR (Patio)	CGro GCoc
	Intrigue = 'Korlech' (F)	LStr
	Invincible = 'Runatru' (F)	LBuc
	'Ipsilanté' (G)	MAus
	'Irène Watts' (Ch)	CPou ECre EPfP LSRN NLar SKHP SWCr
	'Irene's Delight' (HT)	LSRN
	Iris = 'Coczero' (HT)	LSRN
	Iris = 'Ferecha' (HT)	LSRN SWCr
	Irish Eyes = 'Dicwitness'PBR (F)	CBcs CGro CWSG EPfP ESty IArd IBoy LBuc LStr MAsh MBri MJak MRav MWat SCoo SPer SSea SWCr
	Irish Hope = 'Harexclaim'PBR (F)	SWCr
	Irish Wonder	see *R.* Evelyn Fison
	Isabel Rose = 'Hortickle' (HT) **new**	SMrm
	Isabella = 'Poulisab'PBR (Renaissance Series) (S)	CPou CTri ECnt SLon SWCr
	Isis (HT)	see *R.* Silver Anniversary = 'Poulari'
	Isn't She Lovely = 'Diciluvit'PBR (HT)	EBee ECnt ESty GCoc IDic LBuc LSRN SMrm SWCr
	'Ispahan' (D) ♀H4	EPfP LRHS MAsh MAus MBri MCot NEgg NLar SFam SLPl SLon SPer
	Ivory Castle = 'Guesoverlay' (HT)	SWCr
	Jack's Wish = 'Kirsil' (HT)	LSRN
§	× ***jacksonii*** 'Max Graf' (GC/Ru)	LRHS MAus NLar
	- Red Max Graf	see *R.* Rote Max Graf
§	- White Max Graf = 'Korgram'PBR (GC/Ru)	SHil
	'Jacky's Favorite' (F) **new**	LSRN
	Jacobite rose	see *R.* × *alba* 'Alba Maxima'
	Jacqueline du Pré = 'Harwanna'PBR (S) ♀H4	EBee ECnt EPfP ESty GCoc LSRN MAus MCot MRav MWat NLar SLon SPer SSea SWCr
	Jacquenetta = 'Ausjac' (S)	MAus
N	'Jacques Cartier' misapplied	see *R.* 'Marchesa Boccella'
	James Galway = 'Auscrystal'PBR (S)	CSBt IBoy LRHS LStr MAus MBri NEgg SCoo SSea
	'James Mason' (G)	MAus
	'James Mitchell' (CeMo)	MAus
	'James Veitch' (DPoMo)	MAus
	Janet = 'Auspishus'PBR (S)	LRHS LSRN MAus MBri SSea SWCr
	'Janet's Pride' (RH)	MAus
§	'Japonica' (CeMo)	EBee MAus
§	Jardins de Bagatelle = 'Meimafris' (HT)	LSRN MRav SMrm
	Jasmina = 'Korcentex'PBR (ClHT)	CPou EPfP ESty MAsh NPri SWCr
	'Jaune Desprez'	see *R.* 'Desprez à Fleur Jaune'
	Jayne Austin = 'Ausbreak'PBR (S)	CSBt LRHS MAus SPer
	Jazz (ClF)	see *R.* That's Jazz
	'Jazz' (F)	LSRN
	Jean = 'Cocupland'PBR (Patio)	GCoc LSRN
	'Jean Mermoz' (Poly)	MAus
	'Jeanne de Montfort' (CeMo)	MAus
	'Jenny Duval' misapplied	see *R.* 'Président de Sèze'
	Jenny's Rose = 'Cansit' (F)	ECnt GCoc LSRN SWCr
	Jill's Rose = 'Ganjil'PBR (F)	GCoc LSRN SWCr
	John Clare = 'Auscent'PBR (S)	MAus
	'John Hopper' (HP)	EWTr MAus SWCr

§	Joie de Vivre = 'Korfloci 01'[PBR] (Patio/S)	CGro CPou CSBt CWSG ECnt EPfP ESty GCoc IBoy LBuc LRHS LStr MAsh MRav MWat NLar NPri SCoo SMad SMrm SPoG SWCr
	'Josephine Bruce' (HT)	CBcs LSRN
	'Joseph's Coat' (ClS)	IArd LAst LBuc LStr SWCr
	Joy Vieli = 'Dickaramel' (F) **new**	IDic
	'Jubilee Celebration' (F)	EPfP
	Jubilee Celebration = 'Aushunter'[PBR] (S)	CRos CSBt EPfP LRHS MAsh MAus MBri SMrm SPer SSea
	Jude the Obscure = 'Ausjo'[PBR] (S)	CNec CSBt EHyd EPfP ESty LRHS MAus MBri NEgg SWCr
	'Julia's Rose' (HT)	LSRN LStr MAus SPer SWCr
	Julio Iglesias = 'Meistemon'[PBR] (F)	ESty LSRN
	'Juno' (Ch)	CPou MAus
	Just for You = 'Moryou' (Min)	LSRN
	'Just Jenny' (Min)	LSRN
	'Just Joey' (HT) Υ^{H4}	CBcs CGro CSBt CWSG ECnt ELan ELon EPfP GCoc IArd IBoy LSRN LStr MAus MBri MJak MRav MWat NEgg SMrm SPer SPoG SRGP SSea SWCr
	'Just Steve' **new**	LSRN
	'Katharina Zeimet' (Poly)	CTri MAus
§	Katherine Mansfield = 'Meilanein' (HT)	CSBt
	'Kathleen' (HM)	LSRN
	'Kathleen Harrop' (Bb)	ELon LRHS LStr MAus MMuc NLar SEND SFam SPer SRGP SWCr
	Kathleen Jane = 'Horcoed' (S/F)	LSRN
	Kathleen's Rose = 'Kirkitt' (F)	LSRN
	Kathryn Morley = 'Ausclub'[PBR] (F)	MAus
	'Katie' (ClF)	LSRN SWCr
N	'Kazanlik' misapplied	see *R.* 'Professeur Emile Perrot'
	Keep Smiling = 'Fryflorida' (HT)	GCoc LBuc LStr MAsh MBri MRav MWat SWCr
§	Kent = 'Poulcov'[PBR] (Towne & Country Series) (S/GC) Υ^{H4}	CSBt ECnt ELan EPfP ESty EWTr GCoc IBoy LBuc LSRN LStr MRav MWat NLar SEND SMrm SPer SPoG SSea SWCr
	Kew Gardens = 'Ausfence'[PBR] (S)	EPfP GGal LRHS MAus SSea
	'Kew Rambler' (Ra)	CRHN CSam EBee MAus MMuc SFam SLon
	'Kiftsgate'	see *R. filipes* 'Kiftsgate'
	'Kim' (Patio)	LSRN
	Kind Regards = 'Peatiger' (F)	LSRN
	King's Macc = 'Frydisco'[PBR] (HT)	LRHS MAsh MAus MWat SPoG SWCr
	'King's Ransom' (HT)	CSBt MRav SPer SPoG SWCr
	Knirps = 'Korverlandus'[PBR] (GC)	LRHS
	Knock Out = 'Dadler' (F)	MAsh
§	'Königin von Dänemark' (A) Υ^{H4}	ECnt EPfP GCoc IBoy LRHS MAsh MAus MBri MRav MWat NEgg NLar SKHP SPer SSea SWCr
§	'Kordes' Magenta' (S/F)	MAus
	'Korresia' (F)	CSBt CTri ECnt ELon EPfP ESty GCoc IBoy LBuc LStr MAsh MAus MBri MRav MWat SPer SPoG SWCr
	'Kronprinzessin Viktoria von Preussen' (Bb)	MAus
	L.D. Braithwaite = 'Auscrim'[PBR] (S) Υ^{H4}	CBcs EHyd ELan EPfP GCoc IBoy LRHS LStr MAsh MAus MBNS MBri MRav NLar SLon SMrm SPer SSea
	'La Belle Distinguée' (RH)	EBee
	'La Belle Sultane'	see *R.* 'Violacea'
	'La France' (HT)	MAus
	'La Mortola'	see *R. brunonii* 'La Mortola'
	La Parisienne = 'Delpartricol' (F) **new**	ESty
	'La Perle' (Ra)	CRHN
	'La Reine Victoria'	see *R.* 'Reine Victoria'
	La Rose de Molinard = 'Delgrarose' (S)	CPou ESty NLar
	La Rose de Petit Prince = 'Delgramau' (F)	EBee ESty MRav
	'La Rubanée'	see *R.* × *centifolia* 'Unique Panachée'
	La Sévillana = 'Meigekanu' (F/GC)	SPer WCot
	'La Ville de Bruxelles' (D) Υ^{H4}	CSam EHyd LRHS MAus NLar SLon SPer
	Lady Emma Hamilton = 'Ausbrother'[PBR] (S)	CGro CRos EPfP ESty IBoy LRHS MAus MBri SCoo SPer SSea SWCr
	'Lady Gay' (Ra)	WBor
	'Lady Godiva' (Ra)	MAus
	'Lady Hillingdon' (ClT)	see *R.* 'Climbing Lady Hillingdon'
	'Lady Hillingdon' (T)	CRos MAsh MAus
	'Lady Iliffe' (HT)	GCoc SWCr
	Lady MacRobert = 'Coclent' (F)	GCoc
	Lady Mitchell = 'Haryearn' (HT)	ECnt
	Lady of Megginch = 'Ausvolume'[PBR] (S)	CWSG EPfP LRHS MAus MBri
	Lady of Shalott = 'Ausnyson'[PBR] (S)	CRos EHyd LRHS MAsh MAus MBri SSea
	Lady Penelope = 'Chewdor'[PBR] (ClHT)	CSBt
§	'Lady Penzance' (RH) Υ^{H4}	CBcs CHab MAus
	Lady Rose = 'Korlady' (HT)	MAsh
	Lady Salisbury = 'Auscezed' (S) **new**	CRos EHyd LRHS MAsh MAus
	'Lady Sylvia' (HT)	CTri LSRN MAus NEgg SPer
	Lady Taylor = 'Smitling' (F/Patio)	ESty
	'Lady Waterlow' (ClHT)	EWTr MAus NLar
	laevigata (Ra)	MAus MMuc NLar SSea
	- 'Anemonoides'	see *R.* 'Anemone'
	Laguna = 'Koradigel'[PBR] (Cl)	LRHS MAsh NPri
	L'Aimant = 'Harzola'[PBR] (F) Υ^{H4}	CGro CSBt ELon ESty GCoc LStr MAus MRav SWCr
	'Lamarque' (N)	CPou EWTr MAus SSea
	Lancashire = 'Korstesgli'[PBR] (GC) Υ^{H4}	ECnt ESty GCoc LRHS LSRN LStr MAus MRav SMrm SSea SWCr
§	'Lanei' (CeMo)	EBee
	Laura Ford = 'Chewarvel'[PBR] (ClMin) Υ^{H4}	CGro CTri IBoy LRHS LStr MAsh MAus MBri MGos MRav MWat SPer SPoG SSea
	'Laure Davoust' (Ra)	CPou MMuc NLar
	Lavender Ice = 'Tan04249' (F)	ESty GCoc LStr SWCr
	'Lavender Jewel' (Min)	MAus
	'Lavender Lassie' (HM) Υ^{H4}	CPou CSam EBee MAus NLar SPer SSea
	Lavender Symphonie = 'Meiptima' (Patio)	ESty SMrm
	Lavinia	see *R.* Lawinia

§	Lawinia = 'Tanklewi' (ClHT) ♀H4	CSBt EBee EPfP LRHS LStr MBri MRav SPer
	'Lawrence Johnston'	see *R.* 'Hidcote Yellow'
§	Lazy Days = 'Poulkalm'PBR (F)	ECnt MAsh
	'Le Rêve' (Cl)	EWTr
	Le Rouge et le Noir = 'Delcart' (HT) **new**	ESty
	'Le Vésuve' (Ch)	CPou MAus
	Lea = 'Poulren019'PBR (ClS)	ECnt
	Leander = 'Auslea' (S)	MAus
	Leaping Salmon = 'Peamight'PBR (ClHT)	CGro CSBt EBee ELan ELon ESty GCoc LSRN LStr MAus MRav SPer SRGP SWCr
	'Leda' (D)	ELon MAus NLar SFam SPer
	'Lemon Pillar'	see *R.* 'Paul's Lemon Pillar'
	Léonardo de Vinci = 'Meideauri'PBR (F)	CSBt
	'Léontine Gervais' (Ra)	CRHN LRHS MAus MBri
	'Leo's Eye'	CPou EPfP
	Leslie's Dream = 'Dicjoon' (HT)	IDic
	Let's Celebrate = 'Fryraffles' (F) **new**	SMad
	'Leverkusen' (ClF) ♀H4	EWTr LRHS MAus MCot MRav NLar SEND SMrm SPer SWCr
	Lichfield Angel = 'Ausrelate'PBR (S)	EHyd EPfP LRHS MAus MBri SCoo
	Lichtkönigin Lucia = 'Korlillub' (S)	SSea
	Life Begins at 40! = 'Horhohoho' (F)	LSRN SWCr
	Light Fantastic = 'Dicgottago' (F)	GCoc IDic MAsh
	'Lilac Dream' (F)	SWCr
	Lilac Rose = 'Auslilac' (S)	MAus
	Lilian Austin = 'Ausli' (S)	MAus
	Liliana = 'Poulsyng'PBR (S)	CPou ECnt SLon SMrm SWCr
	Lilli Marlene = 'Korlima' (F)	CSBt GCoc IBoy SPer
	Lincoln Cathedral = 'Glanlin'PBR (HT)	MJak SPer
	Lincolnshire Poacher = 'Glareabit' (HT)	NEgg
	'Lincolnshire Yellow Belly' (F)	ESty
	Lion's Fairy Tale	see *R.* Champagne Moments
	Lisa = 'Kirdisco' (F)	LSRN
	Little Amy = 'Battamy' (Min)	LSRN
	'Little Buckaroo' (Min)	SPer
	'Little Flirt' (Min)	MAus
	'Little Gem' (DPMo)	MAus
	Little Jackie = 'Savor' (Min)	LSRN
	Little Miss Sunshine = 'Dicgungho' (F)	IDic
	Little Rambler = 'Chewramb'PBR (MinRa) ♀H4	CSBt EBee ECnt ESty LStr MAus MBri MGos MMuc MRav MWat SCoo SMrm SPer SSea SWCr
	'Little White Pet'	see *R.* 'White Pet'
	Lochinvar = 'Ausbilda'PBR (S)	LRHS MAus
	'Lolabelle'	CPou EBee
	'Long John Silver' (Cl)	MAus SSea
	longicuspis misapplied	see *R. mulliganii*
	longicuspis Bertol. (Ra)	EBee EWTr
§	- var. ***sinowilsonii*** (Ra)	GCal MAus
	aff. ***longicuspis***	EWTr SWCr
	Lord Byron = 'Meitosier' (ClHT)	ESty LStr SSea SWCr
	'Lord Penzance' (RH)	NLar SPer

	Lorna = 'Cocringer' (F)	GCoc LSRN
	'L'Ouche' misapplied	see *R.* 'Louise Odier'
	'Louis Gimard' (CeMo)	MAus SFam
	'Louis XIV' (Ch)	MCot
§	'Louise Odier' (Bb)	CTri ECnt ELon EPfP EWTr GCoc IArd LRHS LSRN LStr MAsh MAus MBri MRav MWat NLar SFam SPer SRGP SSea SWCr
	Love & Peace = 'Baipeace'PBR (HT)	ESty MAsh SPoG SWCr
	Love Knot = 'Chewglorious'PBR (ClMin)	CSBt ECnt EPfP ESty LRHS MAsh MBri MRav MWat SCoo SMrm SSea SWCr WGor
§	Lovely Bride = 'Meiratcan'PBR (Patio)	EPfP LRHS MAsh SPoG
	Lovely Fairy = 'Spevu'PBR (Poly/GC)	ELon WMoo
	Lovely Lady = 'Dicjubell'PBR (HT) ♀H4	CSBt ECnt ESty GCoc LBuc LSRN LStr MAus MBri MRav MWat SMrm SSea SWCr
	Lovely Meidiland	see *R.* Lovely Bride
	'Lovers' Meeting' (HT)	GCoc MJak MRav SPer SWCr
	Loving Memory = 'Korgund81' (HT)	CGro CSBt CWSG ECnt ESty GCoc IArd LRHS LSRN LStr MAsh MGos MRav NPri SPer SPoG SSea SVic SWCr
	Lucetta = 'Ausemi' (S)	MAus
	'Lucky' (F)	CGro CWSG EBee EPfP ESty LRHS LShp LStr NPri SMrm SPer
	Lucky! = 'Frylucy' (F)	CSBt ECnt ELon GCoc LBuc LSRN MAsh MBri MRav SCoo SPoG SWCr
	Lucy = 'Kirlis' (F)	LSRN
	Ludlow Castle	see *R.* England's Rose = 'Ausrace'
	Luscious Lucy = 'Tucklucy' (Patio)	LSRN
	'Lutea Maxima'	see *R.* × *harisonii* 'Lutea Maxima'
	'Lykkefund' (Ra)	EBee MAus
	'Mabel Morrison' (HP)	MAus
	Macartney rose	see *R. bracteata*, *R.* The McCartney Rose
	Macmillan Nurse = 'Beamac' (S)	ESty MCot
	'Macrantha' (Gallica hybrid)	LRHS MAus
	macrophylla	MAus
	- B&SWJ 2603	WCru
	- CC 6259	GKev
§	- 'Master Hugh' ♀H4	MAus
	'Madame Abel Chatenay' (HT)	MAus
	'Madame Alfred Carrière' (N) ♀H4	Widely available
	'Madame Alice Garnier' (Ra)	CPou MMuc SPer
	'Madame Antoine Mari' (T)	CPou
§	'Madame Boll' (DPo) ♀H4	CPou CSam ECnt ELon EPfP ESty LRHS MAsh MCot MRav SMrm SPer SSea SWCr
	'Madame Bravy' (T)	MAus
	'Madame Butterfly' (HT)	LRHS MAus
§	'Madame Caroline Testout' (HT)	CTri EBee LRHS SPoG SRGP
	'Madame de la Roche-Lambert' (DPMo)	CPou MAus
	'Madame de Sancy de Parabère' (Bs)	EWTr IArd MAus
	'Madame Driout' (ClT)	CPou
	'Madame Ernest Calvat' (Bb)	CPou
	'Madame Eugène Résal' misapplied	see *R.* 'Comtesse du Caÿla'

	Name	Suppliers
	Madame Figaro = 'Delrona' (S)	MRav
§	'Madame Grégoire Staechelin' (ClHT) Υ^{H4}	CTri ECnt EHyd ELan EPfP IBoy LRHS LSRN LStr MAsh MAus MBri MRav NEgg SPer SPlb SPoG SWCr
	'Madame Hardy' (ClD) Υ^{H4}	CPou CSBt ECnt EHyd EPfP GCoc LRHS LStr MAus MBri MCot MRav NChi NEgg NLar SFam SMrm SPer SSea SWCr
	'Madame Isaac Pereire' (ClBb) Υ^{H4}	CSBt CTri ECnt EPfP GCoc IBoy LRHS LStr MAsh MAus MBri MCot MRav MWat NLar NPri SFam SMad SMrm SPer SPoG SSea SWCr WBor
	'Madame Jules Gravereaux' (ClT)	MAus
	'Madame Knorr' misapplied	see *R.* 'Madame Boll'
	'Madame Laurette Messimy' (Ch)	CPou
	'Madame Lauriol de Barny' (Bb)	MAus MRav NLar SFam SLon
	'Madame Legras de Saint Germain' (A × N)	CPou EWTr LRHS MAus NLar SFam SPer
	'Madame Louis Lévêque' (DPMo)	CPou
	'Madame Pierre Oger' (Bb)	CTri ECnt EWTr LStr MAus MCot MRav SKHP SPer SWCr
	'Madame Plantier' (A × N)	CPou LRHS MAus MRav NLar SEND SPer WBor
	'Madame Scipion Cochet' (HP)	CPou
	'Madame Zöetmans' (D)	MAus
	'Madge' (HM)	SDix
	'Magenta' (S/F)	see *R.* 'Kordes' Magenta' (S/F)
	Magic Carpet = 'Jaclover'^{PBR} (S/GC) Υ^{H4}	CWSG GCoc IBoy LBuc MAus MBri MGos MRav MWat SHil SMrm SPer SSea SWCr
	'Magnifica' (RH)	MAus
	Maid Marion = 'Austobias' (HM)	EPfP LRHS MAus
	Maid of Honour = 'Jacwhink'^{PBR} (F)	IDic
	'Maid of Kent'^{PBR} (Cl)	EBee LSRN MAus SCoo SPer SWCr
	'Maiden's Blush' (A) Υ^{H4}	CArn CTri ELan EWTr LRHS MAsh MAus SFam SPer SWCr WHer
	'Maiden's Blush, Great'	see *R.* 'Great Maiden's Blush'
	'Maigold' (ClPiH) Υ^{H4}	CBcs CGro CTri ELan ELon EPfP GCoc LRHS LStr MAsh MAus MBri MCot MRav MWat NLar SEND SMad SPer SWCr
	Make a Wish = 'Mehpat'^{PBR} (Min/Patio)	ESty
	Maltese rose	see *R.* 'Cécile Brünner'
	Malvern Hills = 'Auscanary'^{PBR} (Ra)	CSBt EPfP LRHS MAsh MAus MBri SPer SWCr
	'Maman Cochet' (T) **new**	MAus
	Mamma Mia = 'Poulcy013' (Courtyard Series) (Ra) **new**	LRHS
	Mamma Mia! = 'Fryjolly'^{PBR} (HT)	EBee ECnt ESty GCoc LBuc MAsh MBri MRav NPri SPoG SWCr
	'Mandarin' (F)	SSea
	Mandarin = 'Korcelin'^{PBR} (Min)	ESty IBoy LStr MRav
	Many Happy Returns = 'Harwanted'^{PBR} (F) Υ^{H4}	CBcs CGro CSBt CWSG ECnt ELan EPfP GCoc IBoy LRHS LSRN LStr MAsh MBri MGos MJak MRav MWat NPri SPer SPoG SSea SVic SWCr
	'Marbrée' (DPo)	MAus
	'Märchenland' (F)	MAus
§	'Marchesa Boccella' (DPo) Υ^{H4}	CPou CSam CTri EPfP GCoc LRHS MAsh MAus MBri NLar NPri SEND SPer SPoG SSea SWCr WBor WHer
	'Maréchal Davoust' (CeMo)	MAus SFam
	'Maréchal Niel' (N)	EShb MAus SPer
	'Margaret' (HT)	GCoc LSRN
	Margaret Merril = 'Harkuly' (F) Υ^{H4}	CBcs CGro CSBt CTri CWSG EBee ECnt ELan EPfP ESty GCoc IArd IBoy LAst LRHS LSRN LStr MAsh MAus MJak MRav MWat NPri SPer SPoG SRGP SSea SWCr
	'Marguerite Hilling' (S) Υ^{H4}	CTri EPfP MAus MCot MRav NLar SPer
	'Mariae-Graebnerae'	SLPl
	'Marie Louise' (D)	EBee MAus SFam
	'Marie Pavič' (Poly)	CPou MAus
	'Marie van Houtte' (T)	MAus
	'Marie-Jeanne' (Poly)	MAus
	Marigold Sweet Dream = 'Fryprospa' (Patio) **new**	ECnt
	Marinette = 'Auscam'^{PBR} (S)	MAus
	Marjorie Fair = 'Harhero' (Poly/S) Υ^{H4}	EPfP GCoc MAus MRav SWCr
	'Marlena' (F/Patio)	GCoc MAus
	Marry Me = 'Dicwonder'^{PBR} (Patio) Υ^{H4}	ESty IDic LBuc
	'Martha' (Bb)	LSRN
	'Martin Frobisher' (Ru)	MAus
I	'Mary' (Poly)	LSRN LStr
	Mary Magdalene = 'Ausjolly'^{PBR} (S)	MAus
	Mary Rose = 'Ausmary' (S) Υ^{H4}	CNec CSBt CTri CWSG EBee EHyd ELan ELon EPfP GCoc IBoy LRHS LSRN LStr MAus MBri MJak MRav MWat NLar NPri SLon SMrm SPer SPoG SSea SWCr WKif
	'Mary Wallace' (Cl)	MAus
	Mary Webb = 'Auswebb' (S)	MAus
	'Masquerade' (F)	CTri CWSG ELan EPfP GCoc MRav SMrm SPer SSea SWCr
	'Master Hugh'	see *R. macrophylla* 'Master Hugh'
	Matawhero Magic	see *R.* Simply the Best
	'Max Graf'	see *R.* × *jacksonii* 'Max Graf'
	'Maxima'	see *R.* × *alba* 'Alba Maxima'
	'May Queen' (Ra)	CPou LRHS MAus MRav NLar SEND SFam SPer SWCr
	Mayor of Casterbridge = 'Ausbrid'^{PBR} (S)	LRHS MAus
	'McCartney Rose'	see *R.* The McCartney Rose
	'Meg' (ClHT)	LRHS LSRN MAus MCot MMuc SPer SRGP
	'Meg Merrilies' (RH)	MAus NLar
	Melody Maker = 'Dicqueen'^{PBR} (F)	IBoy
	Memory Lane = 'Peavoodoo'^{PBR} (F)	LSRN SWCr
	'Mermaid' (Cl) Υ^{H3-4}	CBcs CDul CSBt EBee ECnt EHyd ELon EPfP LEdu LHop LRHS LStr MAus MBri NLar SEND SMrm SPer SSea SWCr
§	'Mevrouw Nathalie Nypels' (Poly) Υ^{H4}	CTri LRHS LStr MAus MMuc MRav NLar SPer SWCr
	'Michèle Meilland' (HT)	MAus
	× ***micrugosa***	MAus
	- 'Alba'	MAus
	Middlesborough Football Club = 'Horflame' (HT)	LSRN
§	Millie = 'Poulren013'^{PBR} (Renaissance Series) (S)	ECnt EPfP ESty LRHS LSRN NPri SPoG SWCr

	Millie Rose = 'Wekblunez'PBR (HT)	SWCr
	Millionaire = 'Peazara' (F)	LSRN
	Mind Games = 'Dickylie' (F) **new**	IDic
	'Minnehaha' (Ra)	MAus SSea
	mirifica stellata	see *R. stellata* var. *mirifica*
	Mischief = 'Macmi' (HT)	LSRN SPer
	Miss Alice = 'Ausjake'PBR (S)	LSRN MAus MBri SWCr
	'Miss Edith Cavell' (Poly)	EBee MAus
§	'Mister Lincoln' (HT)	SPer
	Mistress Quickly = 'Ausky'PBR (S)	MAus
§	Misty Hit = 'Poulhi011'PBR (PatioHit Series) (Patio)	ECnt LRHS LSRN LStr MAsh SWCr
	Mitsouko = 'Delnat' (HT) **new**	ESty
	Molineux = 'Ausmol'PBR (S) ♀H4	CRos EHyd EPfP LRHS MAsh MAus MBri SMrm SPer SWCr
§	***mollis***	MAus
	Moment in Time = 'Korcastrav'PBR (F)	CGro EBee ECnt EPfP ESty GCoc LShp LStr MAsh NPri NSoo SCoo SMrm SPoG SWCr
	Monsieur Pélisson	see *R.* 'Pélisson'
	Moody Blue = 'Fryniche' (HT)	CGro ECnt ELon ESty GCoc IBoy LRHS LShp MRav SWCr
	Moonbeam = 'Ausbeam' (S)	MAus
	'Moonlight' (HM)	CSam CTri EBee ELan EWTr LRHS MAus MRav SPer SWCr
	Moonshine = 'Tan97123'PBR (HT)	ESty
	'Morgengruss' (Cl)	SPer
	'Morletii' (Bs)	MMuc MRav
	'Morning Jewel' (ClF) ♀H4	GCoc SPer SWCr
	Morning Mist = 'Ausfire' (S)	LRHS MAus SSea
§	'Morsdag' (Poly/F)	LSRN LStr MJak SVic
	Mortimer Sackler = 'Ausorts'PBR (S)	CWSG EHyd ELon LRHS MAus MBri SCoo
	moschata (Ra)	MAus MRav NLar SSea
	- 'Autumnalis'	see *R.* 'Princesse de Nassau'
	- var. ***nepalensis***	see *R. brunonii*
I	'Mother's Day'	SRGP
	Mother's Day	see *R.* 'Morsdag'
	Mother's Joy = 'Horsiltrop' (F)	LSRN
	Mountain Snow = 'Aussnow' (Ra)	LRHS MAus MBri
	Mountbatten = 'Harmantelle' (F) ♀H4	ELan EPfP LBuc LRHS LStr MAus MRav SPer SPoG SSea SWCr
§	'Mousseline' (DPoMo)	CPou MAus MCot NLar SFam SPer
	'Mousseuse du Japon'	see *R.* 'Japonica'
	moyesii (S)	CTri ELan GCra GKev LAst MAus NEgg NWea SKHP SPer
	'Mr Bluebird' (MinCh)	MAus
	'Mr Lincoln'	see *R.* 'Mister Lincoln'
	'Mrs Anthony Waterer' (Ru)	EBee MAus SPer
	'Mrs Arthur Curtiss James' (ClHT)	MMuc
	Mrs Doreen Pike = 'Ausdor'PBR (Ru)	LRHS MAus
	'Mrs Honey Dyson' (Ra)	CPou EBee EWTr
	'Mrs John Laing' (HP)	EPfP EWTr LRHS MAus NLar SFam SLon SPer SWCr
	'Mrs Oakley Fisher' (HT)	EBee EWTr MAus MCot SDix SMad SMrm SPer SWCr WCot
	'Mrs Paul' (Bb)	MAus
	'Mrs Sam McGredy' (HT)	CPou LRHS NEgg SSea
	'Mullard Jubilee' (HT)	SWCr
§	***mulliganii*** (Ra) ♀H4	EPfP GKin MAus SPer
	multibracteata (S)	MAus
	multiflora (Ra)	LBuc MAus
§	- var. ***cathayensis*** (Ra)	WBor
§	- 'Grevillei' (Ra)	EBee MAus MMuc SPer
	- 'Platyphylla'	see *R. multiflora* 'Grevillei'
	- wild-collected	GCal
	Mum in a Million	see *R.* Millie
	Mummy	see *R.* Newly Wed
	Mum's Blessing = 'Guesimage' (F)	SWCr
	mundi	see *R. gallica* 'Versicolor'
	Munstead Wood = 'Ausbernard'PBR (S)	CRos EHyd EPfP ESty LRHS LSRN MAus MBri SSca
	'Muscosa Alba'	see *R.* × *centifolia* 'Shailer's White Moss'
	'Mutabilis'	see *R.* × *odorata* 'Mutabilis'
	My Dad = 'Boselftay'PBR (F)	GCoc LSRN NPri SWCr
	'My Darling Husband' (F) **new**	LSRN
	'My Darling Wife' (F) **new**	LSRN
	My Everything = 'Coccastle'PBR (F)	GCoc
	My Girl = 'Tan00798'PBR (HT)	ESty
	'My Joy' (HT)	LSRN
	My Mum = 'Webmorrow'PBR (F)	CGro ESty GCoc LBuc LSRN MBri NPri SWCr
	My Valentine = 'Mormyval' (Min)	LRHS LSRN MAsh NPri SPoG SWCr
	Myriam = 'Cocgrand' (HT)	GCoc LSRN
	Mystery Girl = 'Dicdothis'PBR (HT)	EBee ECnt ELon GCoc LBuc
	Nahéma = 'Deléri' (ClHT)	SWCr
	Nancy = 'Poulninga'PBR (Renaissance Series) (S)	CPou EBee LSRN
	'Naomi' (HT) **new**	CPou
	'Narrow Water' (Ra)	CPou NLar SWCr
§	'Nastarana' (N)	NLar
	Natalie = 'Poulren014' (Renaissance Series) (S) **new**	LSRN
	'Nathalie Nypels'	see *R.* 'Mevrouw Nathalie Nypels'
	'National Trust' (HT)	CBcs CTri IArd IBoy MAsh MBri SPer
	'Nestor' (G)	EBee MAus
	'Nevada' (S) ♀H4	CSBt CTri ECnt EHyd ELan EPfP EWTr GCoc IArd IBoy LRHS LStr MAsh MAus MRav NLar SPer SSea SWCr
	Never Forgotten = 'Gregart' (HT)	LSRN
	New Arrival	see *R.* 'Red Patio'
	New Beginnings = 'Korprofko'PBR (F)	GCoc MAsh
§	'New Dawn' (Cl) ♀H4	Widely available
	'New Home'	LSRN
	New Life = 'Cocwarble'PBR (F)	GCoc
	New Zealand = 'Macgenev'PBR (HT)	SWCr
§	Newly Wed = 'Dicwhynot'PBR (Patio)	LBuc LSRN LStr SSea
	News = 'Legnews' (F)	MAus
	Nice Day = 'Chewsea'PBR (ClMin) ♀H4	CGro ELon EPfP ESty IBoy LRHS LStr MAsh MRav MWat SPer SPoG SSea SWCr
	'Nicola' (F)	LSRN
	Night Light = 'Poullight'PBR (Courtyard Series) (Cl)	ECnt MRav

	Name	Suppliers
	Nina = 'Mehnina'PBR (S)	LSRN SWCr
	Nina = 'Poulren018'PBR (Renaissance Series) (S)	ECnt
	nitida	MAus NWea SEND SLPl SPer WHer
	Noble Antony = 'Ausway'PBR (S)	CWSG EPfP LRHS LStr MAus MBri SMrm SSea
§	'Noisette Carnée' (N)	CSam EPfP GCra LRHS LStr MAus MBNS MBri MCot MRav NLar SLPl SPer SSea SWCr
	Norfolk = 'Poulfolk'PBR (GC)	CTri ESty EWTr SMrm SPer
	'Northern Lights' (HT)	GCoc
	'Norwich Pink' (S)	MAus
	Nostalgia = 'Savarita' (Min)	LRHS MAsh MAus
	Nostalgie = 'Taneiglat'PBR (HT)	CGro CSBt ECnt ELon ESty GCoc LStr MBri MRav SPoG SSea SWCr
	'Nozomi' (ClMin/GC) ♀H4	CTri ELan EPfP ESty EWTr GCoc MAus MRav NLar SMrm SPer
	'Nuits de Young' (CeMo) ♀H4	EHyd GCoc LRHS MAus MBri NLar SEND SFam SKHP WHer
	'Nur Mahal' (HM)	MAus
	Nurse Tracey Davies = 'Frykookie'PBR (F)	ESty
	nutkana (S)	MAus
§	- 'Plena' (S/D) ♀H4	EPfP MAus MCot NLar SKHP WHer
	'Nymphenburg' (HM)	SPer
	'Nyveldt's White' (Ru)	MAus
	Octavia Hill = 'Harzeal'PBR (F)	CWSG EBee MBri MRav NLar SMrm SPer SWCr
§	**× *odorata***	CPou SVic
	- 'Fortune's Double Yellow'	see *R.* × *odorata* 'Pseudindica'
§	- 'Mutabilis' (Ch) ♀H3-4	CPou CRHN CTri ECre ELan EPfP EWTr GBin GCoc GGal LRHS MAus MCot MRav NLar SEND SKHP SMrm SPer SPoG SSea SWCr WCFE WCot XSen
§	- 'Pallida' (Ch)	EPfP LRHS MAsh MAus MCot MRav NLar SPer SSea SWCr
§	- 'Pseudindica' (ClCh)	MAus
§	- Sanguinea Group (Ch)	SEND XSen
	- - 'Bengal Crimson' (Ch)	EBee EPfP EWTr LPla LRHS LSRN SKHP SLon WCot WKif
	- - 'Bob's Beauty' (Ch)	WCot
§	- 'Viridiflora' (Ch)	CPou EBee LRHS MAus SLon SPer SSea WCot WHer
	Odyssey = 'Franski'PBR (F)	ESty SWCr
	'Oeillet Flamand'	see *R.* 'Oeillet Parfait'
§	'Oeillet Parfait' (G)	MAus
	officinalis	see *R. gallica* var. *officinalis*
	Oh Wow = 'Wekspitrib' (F) **new**	ESty
	'Oklahoma' (HT)	ELon
	old blush China	see *R.* × *odorata* 'Pallida'
	old cabbage	see *R.* × *centifolia*
	Old John = 'Dicwillynilly' (F)	IDic
	old pink moss rose	see *R.* × *centifolia* 'Muscosa'
	Old Port = 'Mackati'PBR (F)	ESty IArd
	old red moss	see *R.* 'Henri Martin', *R.* 'Lanei'
	old velvet moss	see *R.* 'William Lobb'
	'Old Velvet Rose'	see *R.* 'Tuscany'
	old yellow Scotch (SpH)	see *R.* × *harisonii* 'Williams Double Yellow'
	Olivia = 'Wekquahofa' (HT)	LSRN
	'Olympic Flame' (F)	EPfP LRHS MAsh
	Olympic Spirit = 'Peaprince' (F)	LRHS MAsh
	'Omar Khayyám' (D)	MAus MRav NLar
	omeiensis	see *R. sericea* subsp. *omeiensis*
	Open Arms = 'Chewpixcel'PBR (ClMin) ♀H4	ESty MAus SMad SMrm SPer SSea SWCr
	'Ophelia' (HT)	LRHS MAus
	'Orange Sensation' (F)	CTri MAus
§	Orange Sunblaze = 'Meijikatar'PBR (Min)	CSBt SMrm SPer
	Oranges and Lemons = 'Macoranlem'PBR (S/F)	CGro CSBt ESty IBoy LBuc LStr MAus SSea SWCr
	Othello = 'Auslo'PBR (S)	LAst MAus
	'Our Beth' (S)	LSRN
	'Our Dream' (Patio)	MAsh
	Our George = 'Kirrush' (Patio)	LSRN
	Our Hilda = 'Lancoro' (F) **new**	LSRN
	Our Jubilee = 'Coccages' (HT)	ESty LBuc SVic
	Our Molly = 'Dicreason' (GC/S)	IDic LSRN SPer SWCr
	Oxfordshire = 'Korfullwind'PBR (GC) ♀H4	LRHS LStr MRav MWat SSea
	Paddy Stephens = 'Macclack'PBR (HT)	SWCr
	Painted Moon = 'Dicpaint' (HT)	ESty
	Panache = 'Poultop'PBR (Patio/Min)	ECnt IBoy LBuc LStr MAsh SWCr
	'Papa Gontier' (T)	MAus
	Papa Meilland = 'Meisar' (HT)	CSBt GCoc MAus SPer SSea
	Paper Anniversary (Patio)	LSRN
	Papi Delbard = 'Delaby' (ClHT)	ESty MRav SMrm
§	'Para Ti' (Min)	MAus
I	'Parade' (Cl) ♀H4	MAus MRav NLar SMad SWCr
	'Parkdirektor Riggers' (F)	CSam GBin LStr MAus MBri NLar SPer SWCr
	Parson's pink China	see *R.* × *odorata* 'Pallida'
	Partridge = 'Korweirim' (GC)	MAus SPer
	parvifolia	see *R.* 'Burgundiaca'
	Pas de Deux = 'Poulhult'PBR (Courtyard Series) (ClF)	MAsh
	Pascali = 'Lenip' (HT)	CTri ELon GCoc IBoy LBuc MAus MJak SMrm SPer
	Pat Austin = 'Ausmum'PBR (S) ♀H4	CNec CRos CSBt CTri EBee EHyd EPfP IBoy LRHS LSRN LStr MAsh MAus MBNS MBri MRav MWat NEgg NLar SEND SMrm SPer SWCr
	Patricia = 'Korpatri' (F)	SWCr
	'Paul Lédé' (ClT)	see *R.* 'Climbing Paul Lédé'
	Paul McCartneyPBR (HT)	see *R.* The McCartney Rose
	'Paul Neyron' (HP)	MAus MCot SPer
	'Paul Noël' (Ra)	CRos MAus
	'Paul Ricault' (Ce × HP)	MAus
	Paul Shirville = 'Harqueterwife'PBR (HT) ♀H4	MAus SPer SWCr
	'Paul Transon' (Ra) ♀H4	CPou CRHN EPfP LRHS MBri MMuc NEgg NLar SEND SPer SRGP SWCr WHer
§	'Paulii' (Ru/GC)	MAus
	'Paulii Alba'	see *R.* 'Paulii'
	'Paulii Rosea' (Ru/GC)	MAus
	'Paul's Himalayan Musk' (Ra) ♀H3-4	CExl CRHN CSBt CTri ECnt EHyd EPfP GKin IArd IBoy LRHS LStr MAsh MAus MBri MCot MRav NEgg

	NLar SEND SFam SMad SMrm SPer SPoG SRGP SSea SWCr WBor WKif
§ 'Paul's Lemon Pillar' (ClHT)	LRHS MAus NLar SMad SMrm SPer SSea
'Paul's Scarlet Climber' (Cl/Ra)	ELan IBoy LStr MAsh MAus MRav NPri SEND SPer SRGP
'Paul's Single White Perpetual' (Ra)	CTri EWTr MMuc NLar
'Pax' (HM)	CPou MAus WKif
Peace = 'Madame A. Meilland' (HT) Y^{H4}	CGro CSBt CTri ECnt ELan EPfP ESty GCoc IBoy LRHS LSRN LStr MAsh MAus MRav MWat NEgg NPri SMrm SPer SPoG SRGP SSea SWCr
Peacekeeper = 'Harbella'^{PBR} (F)	CSBt
Peach Blossom = 'Ausblossom' (S)	MAus
'Peach Grootendorst' (Ru)	CPou EWTr
Peachy = 'Macrelea' (HT)	MAsh SPoG
§ Pearl Abundance = 'Harfrisky'^{PBR} (F)	ESty SWCr
Pearl Anniversary = 'Whitston'^{PBR} (Min/Patio)	CSBt ESty LSRN LStr MRav SSea SWCr
Pearl Drift = 'Leggab' (S)	MAus MCot MWat SMrm SPer SWCr
Pearl = 'Korterschi'^{PBR} (F)	MAsh MRav SWCr
Peaudouce	see *R.* Elina
§ Peek-a-boo = 'Dicgrow' (Min/Patio)	SPer
Peer Gynt = 'Korol' (HT)	SWCr
Pegasus = 'Ausmoon'^{PBR} (S)	MAus
§ 'Pélisson' (CeMo)	SFam
§ ***pendulina***	LBuc MAus WOut
- 'Nana'	NWad
'Penelope' (HM) Y^{H4}	CSBt CSam CTri EBee ECnt EHyd ELan EPfP EWTr GCoc IBoy LRHS LSRN LStr MAsh MAus MBri MCot MRav MWat NLar SEND SFam SPer SRGP SSea SWCr
Penny Lane = 'Hardwell'^{PBR} (ClHT) Y^{H4}	CSBt EBee ECnt EPfP GCoc IBoy LAst LRHS LStr MAsh MAus MBri MRav MWat NLar NPri SCoo SPer SPoG SSea SWCr
× ***penzanceana***	see *R.* 'Lady Penzance'
Peppermint Splash	see *R.* Rachel Louise Moran
Perception = 'Harzippee'^{PBR} (HT)	SWCr
Perdita = 'Ausperd' (S)	LRHS MAus
Perennial Blue = 'Mehr9601' (Ra)	ESty MBri MRav SSea SWCr
Perennial Blush = 'Mehbarbie'^{PBR} (Ra)	ESty MRav SSea SWCr
§ Perfect Day = 'Poulrem' (F)	ECnt
Perfect Harmony = 'Tangustedv' (HT) **new**	ESty
'Perle des Jardins' (T)	MAus
§ 'Perle d'Or' (Poly) Y^{H4}	LRHS MAus MMuc NLar SDix SLon SMad SPer
Perpetually Yours = 'Harfable'^{PBR} (Cl)	CGro LStr MBri MRav MWat SCoo
Persian yellow	see *R. foetida* 'Persiana'
Peter Pan = 'Chewpan'^{PBR} (Min)	MAus MBri MWat SWCr
Peter Pan = 'Sunpete' (Patio)	EPfP MAsh SPoG
'Petite de Hollande' (Ce)	MAus NLar SPer
'Petite Lisette' (Ce × D)	MAus NLar
'Petito' (F)	SMrm

Phab Gold = 'Frybountiful'^{PBR} (F)	ESty GCoc MAsh
Pheasant = 'Kordapt'^{PBR} (GC)	MAus SPer SWCr
Phillipa = 'Poulheart'^{PBR} (S)	LSRN
Phoebe (Ru)	see *R.* 'Fimbriata'
'Phyllis Bide' (Ra) Y^{H4}	EBee EHyd EPfP EWTr IArd LPot LRHS LStr MAus MBri MCot NLar SEND SPer SRGP SSea SWCr WKif
Piccadilly = 'Macar' (HT)	CGro CSBt CTri GCoc IBoy MRav SPer SWCr
Piccolo = 'Tanolokip' (F/Patio)	LStr SWCr
'Picture' (HT)	MAus SPer
Pigalle '84 = 'Meicloux' (F)	SWCr
'Pilgrim'	see *R.* The Pilgrim
pimpinellifolia	see *R. spinosissima*
- 'Altaica'	see *R. spinosissima* 'Grandiflora'
- double yellow-flowered	see *R.* × *harisonii* 'Williams Double Yellow'
- 'Harisonii'	see *R.* × *harisonii* 'Harison's Yellow'
- 'Lutea'	see *R.* × *harisonii* 'Lutea Maxima'
Pink Abundance = 'Harfrothy'^{PBR} (Abundance Series) (F)	LStr MBri
Pink Bells = 'Poulbells' (GC)	CGro SPer
'Pink Bouquet' (Ra)	CRHN
'Pink Favorite' (HT)	SPer
Pink Fizz = 'Poulycool' (ClPatio)	ECnt
§ Pink Flower Carpet = 'Noatraum'^{PBR} (GC) Y^{H4}	CGro CSBt CTri ECnt ELan GCoc IBoy LRHS LStr MAsh MBri NLar NPri SCoo SEND SPer SPoG SWCr
'Pink Garnette'	see *R.* 'Carol Amling'
'Pink Grootendorst' (Ru) Y^{H4}	EPfP LRHS MAus NEgg NLar SPer SWCr
§ Pink Hit = 'Poultipe'^{PBR} (Min/Patio)	ECnt LRHS LSRN LStr MAsh SWCr
Pink Knock Out = 'Radcon' (S)	MAsh
'Pink Leda' (D)	EBee
pink moss	see *R.* × *centifolia* 'Muscosa'
'Pink Parfait' (F)	SPer
Pink Peace = 'Meibil' (HT)	SWCr
Pink Perfection = 'Korpauvio'^{PBR} (HT)	ESty SWCr
'Pink Perpétué' (Cl)	CBcs CSBt CTri ECnt ELan ELon EPfP GCoo IBoy LAst LBuc LRHS LStr MAsh MAus MBri MRav SMrm SPer SPoG SSea SWCr
'Pink Prosperity' (HM)	MAus
Pirouette = 'Poulyc003'^{PBR} (ClS)	ECnt MAsh SWCr
'Plaisanterie' (HM)	LRHS
'Playboy' (F)	GCoc
Playtime = 'Morplati' (F)	MAus
Pleine de Grâce = 'Lengra' (S)	GGal MAus
Poetry in Motion = 'Harelan'^{PBR} (HT)	MBri
Polar Star = 'Tanlarpost' (HT)	CSBt ECnt LBuc LStr MRav MWat SPer SWCr
× ***polliniana***	SLPl
'Polly' (HT)	GCoc LSRN
§ 'Polyantha Grandiflora' (Ra)	MAus
'Pompon Blanc Parfait' (A)	MAus
'Pompon de Bourgogne'	see *R.* 'Burgundiaca'

'Pompon de Paris' (ClMinCh)	see *R.* 'Climbing Pompon de Paris'
§ 'Pompon de Paris' (MinCh)	ITim WAbe
'Pompon Panaché' (G)	MAus
Pomponella = 'Korpompan' PBR (F)	ESty
Port Sunlight = 'Auslofty' PBR (HM)	IBoy LRHS MAus MBri SSea
Portland rose	see *R.* 'Portlandica'
§ 'Portlandica' (Po)	CTri LRHS MAsh SPer
Portmeirion = 'Ausguard' PBR (S)	MAus SCoo
Pot o' Gold = 'Dicdivine' (HT)	SWCr
Pour Toi	see *R.* 'Para Ti'
prairie rose	see *R. setigera*
'Precious Amber' (F) **new**	MAsh
'Precious Memories' (Min)	LSRN
Precious Memories = 'Dichello' PBR (F)	ESty GCoc IDic
'Precious Platinum' (HT)	MJak SPer
§ 'Président de Sèze' (G) ♀H4	CPou CSam MAus NLar SFam SPer
Pretty in Pink = 'Dicumpteen' PBR (GC)	ECnt LBuc SWCr
Pretty Jessica = 'Ausjess' (S)	CGro LRHS LSRN MAus MRav SMrm SPer
Pretty Lady = 'Scrivo' PBR (F) ♀H4	MAus
Pretty Polly = 'Meitonje' PBR (Min) ♀H4	CGro EPfP ESty IBoy LRHS LStr MAsh MBri MRav MWat SMrm SPer SPoG SSea SWCr
Pretty Sunrise = 'Meipelmel' PBR (S)	LBuc
Pride of England = 'Harencore' PBR (HT)	GCoc
Pride of Scotland = 'Macwhitba' (HT)	GCoc
'Prima Ballerina' (HT)	CTri GCoc LBuc LRHS MAsh MBri SPer SSea
primula (S) ♀H3-4	EShb EWTr GCoc MAus NLar SPer
'Prince Camille de Rohan' (HP)	EBee MAus
'Prince Charles' (Bb)	MAus NLar WKif
Prince Jardinier = 'Meitroni' PBR (HT)	ESty
Princess Alexandra of Kent = 'Ausmerchant' PBR (S)	EHyd EPfP ESty LRHS MAsh MAus MBri SSea
Princess Alexandra = 'Pouldra' PBR (Renaissance Series) (S)	CTri ECnt EPfP NLar SWCr
Princess Anne = 'Auskitchen' (S)	EHyd EPfP LRHS MAus MBri
Princess = 'Korspobux' PBR (HT)	ECnt
Princess Nobuko = 'Coclistine' PBR (HT)	GCoc
'Princess of Wales' (HP)	EPfP
Princess of Wales = 'Hardinkum' PBR (F) ♀H4	EPfP GCoc LStr MAsh MRav SCoo SPer SWCr
Princess Royal = 'Dicroyal' PBR (HT)	IDic
§ 'Princesse de Nassau' (Ra)	MAus SKHP
'Princesse Louise' (Ra)	CRHN LRHS SFam
'Princesse Marie' misapplied	see *R.* 'Belvedere'
'Pristine' (HT)	MAus
§ 'Professeur Emile Perrot' (D)	LEdu MAus MCot
'Prolifera de Redouté' misapplied	see *R.* 'Duchesse de Montebello'
Proper Job = 'Tan02733' (HT)	ESty SWCr
'Prosperity' (HM) ♀H4	CSam CTri EPfP EWTr GCoc LRHS MAus MCot MRav NLar SLon SMrm SPer SWCr
Prospero = 'Auspero' (S)	MAus NLar
Pure Bliss = 'Dictator' PBR (HT)	ELon SWCr
Pure Gold = 'Harhappen' PBR (F)	CSBt
'Purezza' (Ra)	NLar
Purple Eden	see *R.* Ebb Tide
Purple Skyliner = 'Franwekpurp' PBR (ClS)	ESty SMrm
Purple Tiger = 'Jacpurr' PBR (F)	ESty LStr SMrm SSea SWCr
Quaker Star = 'Dicperhaps' (F)	IDic
quatre saisons	see *R.* × *damascena* var. *semperflorens*
'Quatre Saisons Blanche Mousseuse' (DMo)	NLar SMrm
Queen Anne = 'Austruck' (S) **new**	EHyd EPfP ESty MAus MBri
Queen Elizabeth	see *R.* 'The Queen Elizabeth'
Queen Mother = 'Korquemu' PBR (Patio) ♀H4	CSBt ELan EPfP GCoc LStr MAus MJak MRav SPer SPoG SWCr
'Queen of Bourbons' (Bb)	MAus NLar
Queen of Denmark	see *R.* 'Königin von Dänemark'
Queen of Sweden = 'Austiger' PBR (S)	CRos ECnt EPfP LBuc LRHS MAsh MAus MBri SMrm SPer SWCr
'Rachel' (HT)	EWTr LSRN MAsh
Rachel = 'Booyol' (S) **new**	SMrm
§ Rachel Louise Moran = 'Jacdrama' PBR (HT)	ESty
Rachel = 'Tangust' PBR (HT)	CSBt ESty LStr MRav SPoG SSea SWCr
Rainbow Magic = 'Dicxplosion' PBR (Patio)	MJak
'Rambling Rector' (Ra) ♀H4	Widely available
Rambling Rosie = 'Horjasper' PBR (Ra)	CRos CSBt ECnt EPfP ESty GCoc LSRN MAsh MAus MBri SMrm SWCr
'Raspberry Royale' (F/Patio)	LBuc LRHS MAsh NPri
'Raubritter' ('Macrantha' hybrid)	EPfP MAus MMuc SPer SWCr
Ray of Hope = 'Cocnilly' PBR (F)	GCoc
Ray of Sunshine = 'Cocclare' PBR (Patio)	GCoc
Raymond Blanc = 'Delnado' (HT)	MRav SLon SMrm
'Raymond Chenault' (S)	SWCr
Rebecca (Patio)	ESty LSRN
'Rebecca Claire' (HT)	LSRN
Rebecca Mary = 'Dicjury' PBR (F)	IDic
Reconciliation = 'Hartillery' PBR (HT)	SWCr
Red Abundance	see *R.* Songs of Praise
Red Blanket = 'Intercell' (S/GC)	LAst MAus SPer
Red Coat = 'Auscoat' (F)	MAus
Red Devil = 'Dicam' (HT)	ESty GCoc IBoy MBri SCoo

Red Drift = 'Meigalpio' (GC)	LBuc
Red Eden Rose = 'Meidrason'^{PBR} (Cl)	ESty SSea SWCr
Red Finesse = 'Korvillade'^{PBR} (F)	ECnt EPfP LBuc MAsh MBri
'Red Grootendorst'	see *R.* 'F.J. Grootendorst'
'Red Max Graf'	see *R.* Rote Max Graf
Red Medley = 'Noapu'^{PBR} (Min)	LBuc
red moss	see *R.* 'Henri Martin'
Red New Dawn	see *R.* 'Étendard'
§ 'Red Patio' (F/Patio)	LSRN
Red Rascal = 'Jacbed'^{PBR} (S/Patio)	CSBt
red rose of Lancaster	see *R. gallica* var. *officinalis*
Redouté = 'Auspale'^{PBR} (S)	LRHS MAus
Reflections = 'Simref' (F)	SWCr
Regensberg = 'Macyoumis'^{PBR} (F/Patio)	IBoy MAus SPer SWCr
'Reine des Centfeuilles' (Ce)	SFam
'Reine des Violettes' (HP)	CPou ELon EPfP IArd LRHS LSRN LStr MAsh MAus MBri MRav MWat NLar SPer SRGP SWCr
§ 'Reine Victoria' (Bb)	EPfP LStr MAus MBri MRav NLar SPer SWCr
§ Remember = 'Poulht001'^{PBR} (HT)	ECnt EPfP LRHS MAsh SWCr
Remember Me = 'Cocdestin' (HT) ♀^{H4}	CGro CSBt CWSG ECnt EPfP ESty GCoc IArd IBoy LSRN LStr MAsh MAus MBri MGos MRav NEgg NPri SPer SPoG SWCr
Remembrance = 'Harxampton'^{PBR} (F) ♀^{H4}	CTri CWSG ESty GCoc LBuc LRHS LSRN LStr MAsh MBri MJak MRav NPri SPer SPoG SSea SWCr
§ Renaissance = 'Harzart'^{PBR} (HT)	CSBt ELon GCoc MJak MRav SWCr
'René André' (Ra)	CPou CRHN MAus NLar
'René d'Anjou' (CeMo)	MAus
'Rescht'	see *R.* 'De Resht'
'Rêve d'Or' (N)	MAus SLon SPer
'Réveil Dijonnais' (ClHT)	MAus
Rhapsody in Blue = 'Frantasia'^{PBR} (S)	Widely available
§ × ***richardii***	GCoc MAus NLar
Rick Stein = 'Tan96205'^{PBR} (HT)	LSRN LStr
'Rival de Paestum' (T)	MAus
'River Gardens'	NPer
Rob Roy = 'Cocrob' (F)	GCoc SPer
Robbie Burns = 'Ausburn' (SpH)	MAus
'Robert le Diable' (Ce × G)	EBee MAus NLar SPer
Rock & Roll = 'Wekgobnez' (HT)	ESty
Rockabye Baby = 'Dicdwarf' (Patio)	ESty SWCr
'Roger Lambelin' (HP)	MAus
Romance = 'Tanezamor'^{PBR} (S)	IBoy LSRN MBri MRav
'Rosa Mundi'	see *R. gallica* 'Versicolor'
Rosabell = 'Cocceleste'^{PBR} (F/Patio)	GCoc
'Rose à Parfum de l'Haÿ' (Ru)	CTri
'Rose de Meaux'	see *R.* × *centifolia* 'De Meaux'
'Rose de Meaux White'	see *R.* 'White de Meaux'
'Rose de Rescht'	see *R.* 'De Resht'
Rose des Cisterciens = 'Delarle' (HT)	ESty MRav
'Rose des Maures' misapplied	see *R.* 'Sissinghurst Castle'
'Rose du Maître d'Ecole'	see *R.* 'Du Maître d'Ecole'
'Rose du Roi' (HP/DPo)	ELon LRHS MAus NLar
§ Rose Gaujard = 'Gaumo' (HT)	LAst MAsh MBri
Rose of Picardy = 'Ausfudge' (S)	LRHS MAus MBri
'Rose-Marie Viaud' (Ra)	CPou CSam MAus MMuc
Rosemary Harkness = 'Harrowbond' (HT)	ESty LStr MJak MRav SMrm SPer SRGP
Rosemoor = 'Austough'^{PBR} (S)	CRos CSBt EHyd LBuc LRHS MAus MBri
'Roseraie de l'Haÿ' (Ru) ♀^{H4}	Widely available
Rosie = 'Benros' (Min)	LSRN
Rosy Cushion = 'Interall' (S/GC) ♀^{H4}	EWTr GCoc LBuc LRHS MAsh MAus MCot NLar SLon SPer WKif
Rosy Future = 'Harwaderox' (F/Patio)	SWCr
'Rosy Mantle' (ClHT)	CSBt SPer SWCr
§ Rotary Sunrise = 'Fryglitzy' (HT)	CSBt
§ Rote Max Graf = 'Kormax' (GC/Ru)	CDul NLar
Rouge Royale = 'Meikarouz' (HT)	ESty
roxburghii (S)	CBcs EPfP LEdu MAus SKHP
- 'Plena'	see *R. roxburghii* f. *roxburghii*
§ - f. ***roxburghii*** (d/S)	MAus
'Royal Albert Hall' (HT)	GCoc
Royal Copenhagen	see *R.* Remember
'Royal Occasion' (F)	SPer
Royal William = 'Korzaun'^{PBR} (HT) ♀^{H4}	CSBt ELan ELon GCoc LRHS LSRN LStr MAsh MAus MBri MGos MJak MRav NPri SMrm SPer SSea SWCr
§ ***rubiginosa***	CArn CCVT CDul EPfP GPoy IFro LBuc MAus MRav NWea SFam SPer WMou
rubrifolia	see *R. glauca* Pourr.
'Rubrotincta'	see *R.* 'Hebe's Lip'
rubus (Ra)	MAus
Ruby Anniversary = 'Harbonny'^{PBR} (Patio)	CSBt CWSG ELon ESty LBuc LRHS LSRN LStr MAsh MBri MRav MWat NSoo SCoo SMrm SPoG SSea SVic SWCr
Ruby Celebration = 'Peawinner'^{PBR} (F)	ESty MRav SWCr
Ruby Rambler = 'Chewrubyramb' (Ra)	LBuc
Ruby Ruby	see *R.* Ruby Slippers
§ Ruby Slippers = 'Weksactrumi' (Min)	LBuc LRHS MAsh SPoG
'Ruby Wedding' (HT)	CBcs CGro CSBt CTri CWSG EBee ECnt ELan EPfP GCoc IArd IBoy LRHS LSRN LStr MAsh MAus MBri MGos MJak MRav NPri NSoo SMrm SPer SPoG SSea SVic SWCr
'Ruby Wedding Anniversary' (F)	LSRN
rugosa (Ru)	CDul CLnd CTri CTsd ECrN EHyd EPfP EPom LBuc LRHS MAus MBri MHer MRav NWea SGol SPlb SVic SWCr WHar WMou
- 'Alba' (Ru) ♀^{H4}	CBcs CCVT CDul CHab CTri EBee ECnt ELan EPfP GBin GCoc LAst

	LBuc LRHS LStr MAus MRav NWea SGol SMrm SPer SSea SVic SWCr WHar
- 'Rubra' (Ru) ♀H4	CBcs CCVT CHab CTri CWib ELan EPfP EPom GCoc LAst LBuc LStr SEWo SMrm SPer SPoG SSea SVic WHar
'Rugosa Atropurpurea' (Ru)	EPom
'Rumba' (F)	ELan
Rushing Stream = 'Austream' (GC)	MAus
'Russelliana' (Ra)	MAus MMuc NLar SFam
Safe Haven = 'Jacreraz'PBR (F)	LBuc
Saint Alban = 'Auschesnut'PBR (S)	MAus
Saint Boniface = 'Kormatt' (F/Patio)	CSBt
Saint Cecilia = 'Ausmit'PBR (S)	MAus
Saint Edmunds Rose	see *R.* Bonita
Saint Ethelburga = 'Beabimbo' (S)	MCot
Saint John's rose	see *R.* × *richardii*
'Saint Nicholas' (D)	MAus
Saint Swithun = 'Auswith'PBR (S)	EPfP LRHS MAus MBri SSea
'Salet' (DPMo)	CPou MAus WHer
'Sally Holmes' (S) ♀H4	EBee ECnt EPfP EWTr GCoc LRHS MAus MRav MWat NLar SEND SLon SMad SPer SWCr
Sally Kane = 'Frygroovy'PBR (HT)	CGro MRav
Sally's Rose = 'Canrem' (HT)	EBee ECnt GCoc LSRN
Salsa	see *R.* Cheek to Cheek
Salvation = 'Harlark'PBR (F)	ESty SWCr
§ Samaritan = 'Harverag'PBR (HT)	CSBt ESty MRav SWCr
sambucina	WPGP
sancta	see *R.* × *richardii*
'Sander's White Rambler' (Ra) ♀H4	CRHN CSam CTri EBee EPfP EWTr LRHS MAus MBri MRav NLar SPer SWCr
Sandra = 'Carsandra'	EPfP SLon
Sandra = 'Koreinek' (HT)	LSRN
Sandra = 'Poulen055'PBR (Renaissance Series) (S)	LSRN
'Sanguinea'	see *R.* × *odorata* Sanguinea Group
Sarah (HT)	see *R.* Jardins de Bagatelle
'Sarah van Fleet' (Ru)	CTri ELon EPfP GCoc IArd IBoy LStr MAus MBri MMuc MRav MWat NEgg NLar SPer WBor
Sarah, Duchess of York	see *R.* Sunseeker
Savoy Hotel = 'Harvintage'PBR (HT) ♀H4	ECnt EPfP GCoc LStr MAus MBri MRav SPer SWCr
'Scabrosa' (Ru) ♀H4	ECnt EPfP GCoc LRHS MAsh MAus NLar SLon SPer SPoG
Scarborough Fair = 'Ausoran' (S)	LBuc MAus
Scarlet Fire	see *R.* 'Scharlachglut'
Scarlet Glow	see *R.* 'Scharlachglut'
Scarlet Hit = 'Poulmo'PBR (PatioHit Series) (Min/Patio)	ECnt IBoy LBuc LRHS LSRN LStr SWCr
Scarlet Patio = 'Kortingle'PBR (Patio)	ESty LBuc MAsh MBri MWat SSea
Scarlet Queen Elizabeth = 'Dicel' (F)	CBcs LBuc MRav
'Scented Air' (F)	SPer
Scented Carpet = 'Chewground'PBR (GC)	ECnt MAus SHil SWCr
Scented Memory = 'Poulht002'PBR (HT)	ECnt
Scentimental = 'Wekplapep'PBR (F)	ESty LStr MAsh MBri MRav SCoo SSea SWCr
Scent-sation = 'Fryromeo'PBR (HT)	CGro CWSG ELon GCoc LStr MRav SCoo SPoG SWCr
Scepter'd Isle = 'Ausland'PBR (S) ♀H4	CSBt EPfP LBuc LRHS MAsh MAus MBri SCoo SPer SWCr
§ 'Scharlachglut' (ClS) ♀H4	CPou EPfP GGal LRHS SPer
Schneewittchen	see *R.* Iceberg
§ 'Schneezwerg' (Ru) ♀H4	GCoc MAus MRav NLar SSea
'Schoolgirl' (ClHT)	CBcs CTri CWSG ELan ELon EPfP GCoc IBoy LBuc LRHS LStr MAsh MBri MRav MWat NEgg SPer SPoG SSea SWCr
'Scintillation' (S/GC)	MAus
Scotch rose	see *R. spinosissima*
Scotch yellow (SpH)	see *R.* × *harisonii* 'Williams Double Yellow'
'Sea Foam' (S)	WMoo
'Seagull' (Ra) ♀H4	CTri CWSG EBee ECnt EPfP EWTr IBoy LAst LRHS LSRN LStr MAsh MAus MRav MWat NLar NWea SLon SMad SMrm SPer SPoG SWCr WHer
'Seale Pink Diamond' (S)	SSea
'Sealing Wax' (*moyesii* hybrid)	EBee NLar
'Semiplena'	see *R.* × *alba* 'Alba Semiplena'
sericea (S)	MAus
- var. ***morrisonensis*** B&SWJ 7139	WCru
§ - subsp. ***omeiensis*** BWJ 7550	WCru
- - f. ***pteracantha*** (S)	CBcs CDul CSBt ELan EPfP EWTr GCoc LRHS MAus MRav NLar NWea SPer
- - - 'Atrosanguinea' (S)	CArn
§ ***setigera***	MAus
setipoda (S)	MAus
seven sisters rose	see *R. multiflora* 'Grevillei'
Seventh Heaven = 'Fryfantasy'PBR (HT)	GCoc SWCr
Sexy Rexy = 'Macrexy' (F) ♀H4	CGro EPfP GCoc IBoy LRHS LSRN LStr MAsh MAus MBri MRav SMrm SPer SRGP SWCr
'Shailer's White Moss'	see *R.* × *centifolia* 'Shailer's White Moss'
Sharifa Asma = 'Ausreef'PBR (S)	CSBt ELan EWTr LStr MAus MBri MRav NEgg NLar SLon SMrm SPer SWCr
Sheila's Perfume = 'Harsherry' (F)	CGro EBee ECnt ESty GCoc IBoy LRHS LSRN LStr MAsh MRav SPer SPoG SWCr
Shine On = 'Dictalent'PBR (Patio) ♀H4	CSBt ECnt IBoy LBuc LStr MBri MWat SWCr
Shining Light = 'Cocshimmer'PBR (Patio)	GCoc MRav SCoo
Shona = 'Dicdrum' (F)	IDic
Showmee Music = 'Chewdaybell' (GC) **new**	ECnt
Showmee Sunshine = 'Kenveron' (GC)	ECnt ESty
Showtime = 'Baitime' (ClS)	LBuc MAsh

§	Shrimp Hit = 'Poulshrimp'PBR (Patio)	ECnt LBuc LStr MAsh
	'Shropshire Lass' (S)	MAus
	Silver Anniversary ambig.	LSRN
	Silver Anniversary = 'Jaclav' (HT)	MBri MJak NSoo
§	Silver Anniversary = 'Poulari'PBR (HT) ♀H4	CSBt CTri CWSG ECnt ELan GCoc LRHS LSRN LStr MAsh MAus MGos MRav MWat NPri SCoo SMrm SPer SPoG SSea SVic SWCr
	'Silver Cushions' (S) **new**	MAsh
	Silver Ghost = 'Kormifari'PBR (S)	LBuc LRHS
	'Silver Jubilee' (HT) ♀H4	EPfP GCoc IArd IBoy LBuc LRHS LStr MAsh MAus MRav SPer SPoG SVic SWCr
	'Silver Lining' (HT)	SRGP
	'Silver Wedding' (HT)	ELan GCoc IArd MAus MJak MRav NEgg SPer SVic SWCr
	'Silver Wedding Celebration' (F)	CTri ESty LSRN
	Silver Wishes	see *R.* Pink Hit
	Simba = 'Korbelma' (HT)	LSRN
	'Simplex Multiflora'	CWib
	Simply Heaven = 'Diczombie'PBR (HT)	GCoc
	Simply Sally = 'Harpaint'PBR (Patio) **new**	LSRN
§	Simply the Best = 'Macamster'PBR (HT)	CGro CSBt CWSG ECnt ELan ESty GCoc LRHS LSRN LStr MAsh MAus MGos MJak MRav MWat NPri SCoo SMrm SPer SPoG SWCr
	sinowilsonii	see *R. longicuspis* var. *sinowilsonii*
	'Sir Cedric Morris' (Ra)	NLar SSea
	Sir Clough = 'Ausclough' (S)	MAus
	Sir Edward Elgar = 'Ausprima'PBR (S)	MAus
I	'Sir Galahad' white-flowered (F)	MRav SMrm
	Sir John Betjeman = 'Ausvivid'PBR (S)	CWSG EHyd EPfP IBoy LRHS MAus MBri
	'Sir Joseph Paxton' (Bb)	CPou MAus
	Sir Walter Raleigh = 'Ausspry' (S)	MAus MRav MWat SMrm
§	'Sissinghurst Castle' (G)	MAus
	Sister Elizabeth = 'Auspalette'PBR (S)	LBuc LSRN MAsh MAus MBri SCoo
	Skylark = 'Ausimple'PBR (S)	LBuc LRHS MAsh MAus MBri
	'Skyrocket'	see *R.* 'Wilhelm'
	Smarty = 'Intersmart' (S/GC)	MAus SPer
	Snow Carpet = 'Maccarpe' (Min/GC)	MAus
	'Snow Dwarf'	see *R.* 'Schneezwerg'
	Snow Goose = 'Auspom'PBR (ClS)	CSBt EPfP LBuc LRHS MAus MBri SSea
	Snow Hit = 'Poulsnows'PBR (Min/Patio)	ECnt SWCr
	'Snow Queen'	see *R.* 'Frau Karl Druschki'
	Snow Sunblaze = 'Meigovin' (Min)	CSBt SPer
	Snowball = 'Macangeli' (Min/GC)	LSRN
	Snowcap = 'Harfleet'PBR (Patio)	ESty SMrm
	'Snowdon' (Ru)	LRHS MAsh MAus
	Soeur Emmanuelle = 'Delamo'PBR (S)	MRav SLon SMrm
	Soft Cover = 'Poultco10' (Min)	LBuc LRHS MAsh
	'Soldier Boy' (Cl)	CPou
§	Solo Mio = 'Poulen002'PBR (Renaissance Series) (S)	CTri ECnt NLar
§	'Sombreuil' (ClT)	EPfP IArd LRHS MAsh MAus MBri MRav NEgg NLar SPer SWCr
	Something Special = 'Macwyo'PBR (HT)	ESty SWCr
	Song and Dance = 'Frydishy'PBR (HT)	GCoc SWCr
§	Songs of Praise = 'Harkimono'PBR (Abundance Series) (F)	ESty LBuc SWCr
	'Sophia'	see *R.* Solo Mio = 'Poulen002'
	'Sophie's Perpetual' (ClCh)	CPou CTri EWTr GCoc LRHS MAus SLon SPer
	Sophy's Rose = 'Auslot'PBR (S)	CRos EHyd LRHS LSRN MAus MBNS MBri NEgg SMrm SPer SWCr
	Sorbet Fruité = 'Meihestries'PBR (Cl)	SSea
	soulieana (Ra/S) ♀H3-4	MAus
	'Soupert et Notting' (DPoMo)	CPou LRHS MAus MRav SPer
	'Southampton' (F) ♀H4	LSRN LStr MAus SPer SSea SWCr
	'Souvenir de Claudius Denoyel' (ClHT)	CPou CSam SPer
	'Souvenir de Jeanne Balandreau' (HP)	CPou EBee
	'Souvenir de la Malmaison' (ClBb)	see *R.* 'Climbing Souvenir de la Malmaison'
	'Souvenir de la Malmaison' (Bb)	EPfP EWTr GCoc LRHS MAus MRav MWat NLar SPer
	'Souvenir de Madame Léonie Viennot' (ClT)	MAus MRav
	'Souvenir de Saint Anne's' (Bb)	EWTr MAus
	'Souvenir di Castagneto' (HP)	MRav
	'Souvenir du Docteur Jamain' (ClHP)	CPou CSBt EBee ELan ELon EPfP ESty GCoc GGal LRHS LSRN LStr MAus MCot MRav NLar SFam SMrm SPer SPoG SSea SWCr WKif
	'Spanish Beauty'	see *R.* 'Madame Grégoire Staechelin'
	Sparkle = 'Frymerlin' (HT)	ECnt ESty GCoc MAsh
	Sparkler	see *R.* Kent
	Sparkling Scarlet = 'Meihati' (ClF)	MAsh
	Special Anniversary = 'Whastiluc'PBR (HT)	CGro CSBt EPfP ESty GCoc LRHS LSRN LShp MAsh MBri MJak MRav MWat NPri SCoo SMrm SPoG SSea SWCr
	Special Child = 'Taniripsa'PBR (F/Patio)	ECnt LStr MRav SSea SWCr
	Special Event = 'Meibrelon' (HT)	ESty
	Special Friend = 'Kirspec'PBR (Patio)	CWSG ESty GCoc LSRN LStr MWat SWCr
	Special Occasion = 'Fryyoung'PBR (HT)	GCoc MAsh MRav SMrm SWCr
	Special Son (F)	ESty
	'Spectabilis' (Ra)	CPou EWTr SKHP
	'Spencer' misapplied	see *R.* 'Enfant de France'
	Spice of Life = 'Diccheeky'PBR (F/Patio)	IDic
§	***spinosissima***	CDul ECrN LBuc LRHS MAus NWea SGol SPer SSea WCot

	– 'Andrewsii' ♀H4	MAus MRav
	– double, pink-flowered	SKHP WBor
	– – white-flowered	GCoc IGor MAus SSea
	– 'Dunwich Rose'	CSam EPfP GCoc LRHS MAus NLar SKHP SPer WCot
	– 'Falkland'	GCra MAus
	– 'Glory of Edzell'	MAus
§	– 'Grandiflora'	LRHS
	– 'Marbled Pink'	MAus
	– 'Mary, Queen of Scots'	MAus SRms
	– 'Mrs Colville'	MAus
	– 'Ormiston Roy'	MAus
	– 'Single Cherry'	MAus SSea
	– 'William III'	EWes GCra MAus MCot SLPl
	Spirit of Freedom = 'Ausbite'PBR (S)	EPfP ESty LBuc LRHS MAsh MAus MBri NEgg SSea
§	'Splendens' (Ra)	EBee MMuc SLPl
	St Helena = 'Canlish' (F)	ECnt
	'Stanwell Perpetual' (SpH)	CSam ELan EPfP GCoc IBoy LStr MAus MRav MWat SEND SFam SPer SSea SWCr
	Star Dust = 'Morstar' (Min)	ELon
	'Star Performer'PBR (ClPatio)	CSBt ECnt EPfP ESty LBuc LRHS MAsh MBri SPoG SSea SWCr
	Stardust = 'Devstar' (HT) **new**	WBor
	Stardust = 'Peavandyke'PBR (Patio/F)	CPou ESty
	Starlight Express = 'Trobstar'PBR (Cl)	IBoy LBuc LRHS MAsh MBri MRav SCoo SPer
	Starry Eyed = 'Horcoexist' (Patio)	SWCr
	'Stars 'n' Stripes' (Min)	MAus
	Stella (HT)	GCoc LSRN
	stellata	MAus
§	– var. ***mirifica***	MAus
	Strawberries and Cream = 'Geestraw' (Min/Patio)	ELan ESty LBuc
	Strawberry Fayre = 'Arowillip'PBR (Min/Patio)	ESty MRav SPoG
	Strawberry Hill = 'Ausrimini'PBR (S)	CSBt EBee ECnt ESty LRHS MAus MBri SCoo
	Strike It Rich = 'Wekbepmey'PBR (HT)	ECnt ESty GCoc
§	Sue Hipkin = 'Harzazz'PBR (HT)	ESty MRav SWCr
	Suffolk = 'Kormixal'PBR (S/GC)	CSBt ELan GCoc LRHS LStr MAus MRav SEND SHil SPer SSea
	Sugar and Spice = 'Peaallure'PBR (Patio)	SPoG
	Sugar Baby = 'Tanabagus'PBR (Patio)	ESty SWCr
	Sugar 'n' Spice = 'Tinspice' (Min)	MRav
	Suma = 'Harsuma' (GC)	ESty SMrm
	Summer Beauty = 'Kororbe'PBR (F)	EBee ESty MAsh
	Summer Breeze = 'Korelasting'PBR (ClS)	MAsh
	Summer Fever = 'Tan99106' (Patio)	SWCr
	Summer Fragrance = 'Tanfudermos'PBR (Castle Series) (HT)	ELon
§	Summer Gold = 'Poulreb'PBR (F)	MAsh SWCr
	Summer Love = 'Franluv' (F)	CBcs
	Summer Song = 'Austango'PBR (S)	EPfP ESty IBoy LRHS LSRN MAus MBri SWCr
	Summer Wine = 'Korizont'PBR (Cl) ♀H4	CSBt EBee ECnt EPfP LRHS MGos SCoo SPer SPoG SWCr
	Summertime = 'Chewlarmoll'PBR (ClPatio)	CGro CSBt EBee ECnt ELan EPfP GCoc IBoy LRHS LStr MAsh MAus MBri MRav MWat NPri SCoo SMrm SPer SPoG SSea
	Sun Hit = 'Poulsun'PBR (PatioHit Series) (Min/Patio)	CGro CSBt ECnt LBuc LRHS LStr MAsh MRav
	'Sunblaze'	see *R.* Orange Sunblaze
	Sunblest = 'Landora' (HT)	MAsh MRav
	Sunfire = 'Jacko' (F)	EBee ECnt
	Sunrise = 'Kormarter'PBR (S)	CGro EPfP ESty LBuc MAsh MBri MWat SWCr
§	Sunseeker = 'Dicracer'PBR (F/Patio)	EPfP LBuc MAsh MRav SPoG SWCr
	Sunset Boulevard = 'Harbabble'PBR (F) ♀H4	GCoc LStr MAsh MAus MBri MRav SCoo SPer SWCr
	Sunset Celebration	see *R.* Warm Wishes
	Sunshine Abundance	SWCr
	Super Dorothy = 'Heldoro' (Ra)	LRHS LSRN MAus SSea SWCr
	Super Elfin = 'Helkleger'PBR (Ra) ♀H4	CRos LBuc LRHS LStr MAus MRav SMrm SPer SSea SWCr
	Super Excelsa = 'Helexa' (Ra)	ESty IBoy LRHS LStr MAus SSea SWCr
	Super Fairy = 'Helsufair'PBR (Ra)	EBee ECnt LStr MAus MRav SMad SPer SSea SWCr
	Super Sparkle = 'Helfels'PBR (Ra)	LStr SSea
§	Super Star = 'Tanorstar' (HT)	GCoc LStr MAus MBri MRav MWat SSea SWCr
	Super Trouper = 'Fryleyeca' (F)	CGro CSBt ECnt ESty GCoc IBoy LStr MAsh MRav SCoo SWCr WBor
	'Surpasse Tout' (G)	MAus
	Surrey = 'Korlanum'PBR (GC) ♀H4	CSBt CTri EBee ELan EPfP ESty GCoc LSRN LStr MAus MRav MWat NLar SPer SSea SWCr
	Susan = 'Poulsue' (S)	EBee ECnt LSRN NLar SLon SWCr
	Susan Williams-Ellis = 'Ausquirk' (S)	EHyd EPfP LRHS MAus MBri
	Sussex = 'Poulave'PBR (GC)	CSBt GCoc LStr MRav SMrm SPer SSea
	Swan = 'Auswhite' (S)	MAus
	Swan Lake = 'Macmed' (Cl)	CPou ECnt ELan EPfP IBoy LBuc LStr MBri MRav NLar SMrm SPer
	Swany = 'Meiburenac' (Min/GC) ♀H4	ECrN ESty LSRN MAus SPer SWCr
	'Sweet Ballymaloe'	IBoy
	Sweet Caroline = 'Micaroline' (Min)	LSRN
	Sweet Child of Mine (HT)	CWSG ESty
	Sweet Cover = 'Poulweeto'PBR (F) (Towne & Country Series)	LBuc MAsh
	Sweet Dream = 'Fryminicot'PBR (Patio) ♀H4	CGro CSBt CTri ECnt ELan EPfP GCoc IBoy LRHS LSRN LStr MAsh MAus MBri MJak MRav NPri SMad SMrm SPer SPoG SRGP SSea SWCr
	Sweet Dream Cream = 'Fryniggle' (F) **new**	ECnt
	'Sweet Fairy' (Min)	CSBt
	Sweet Haze = 'Tan97274'PBR (F)	CSBt EPfP GCoc IBoy LRHS LStr MAsh MRav SCoo SPer SWCr

	Sweet Juliet = 'Ausleap'^{PBR} (S)	CSBt ECnt IBoy LRHS MAus MCot SMrm SPer SWCr
*	'Sweet Lemon Dream' (Patio)	CTri
	Sweet Magic = 'Dicmagic'^{PBR} (Min/Patio) ♀^{H4}	CTri ELon EPfP IBoy LBuc LStr MBri MRav SPoG
	Sweet Memories = 'Whamemo' (Patio)	CTri ECnt ELon EPfP ESty IBoy LRHS LStr MAsh MBri MRav NPri SCoo SMrm SPer SSea SWCr
	Sweet Parfum de Provence = 'Meiclusif'^{PBR} (HT)	ESty
	Sweet Remembrance = 'Kirr' (HT)	LStr SCoo
	'Sweet Revelation'	see *R.* Sue Hipkin
	'Sweet Wonder' (Patio)	EPfP LBuc LRHS SPoG
N	Sweetheart = 'Cocapeer' (HT)	GCoc
	'Sweetie' (Patio)	ESty SWCr
	sweginzowii	MAus
	'Sydonie' (HP)	CPou EBee
	'Sylvia Dot' (F)	LSRN
	'Sympathie' (ClHT)	SPer SSea SWCr
	Tall Story = 'Dickooky' (F) ♀^{H4}	MRav SWCr
	Tam O'Shanter = 'Auscerise'^{PBR} (S)	EPfP LRHS MAus
	Tamora = 'Austamora' (S)	MAus
	Tango Showground = 'Chewpattens'^{PBR} (GC)	ESty SHil SSea
	Tatton = 'Fryentice'^{PBR} (F)	ESty MAus MRav SMrm SWCr
	Tawny Tiger = 'Frygolly'^{PBR} (F)	CGro GCoc MBri SWCr
	Tea Clipper = 'Ausrover'^{PBR} (S)	CSBt LRHS MAus MBri SCoo SSea
	Tear Drop = 'Dicomo'^{PBR} (Min/Patio)	LStr SSea SWCr
	Teasing Georgia = 'Ausbaker'^{PBR} (S)	CRos ECnt EHyd ELon EPfP ESty IBoy LRHS LSRN MAus MBri SCoo SSea SWCr
	Temptress = 'Korramal' (ClS)	CPou EPfP LBuc MAsh SMrm
	Tenacious = 'Macblackpo'^{PBR} (F)	ESty LStr SWCr
	Tequila Sunrise = 'Dicobey'^{PBR} (HT) ♀^{H4}	CGro CTri ELan EPfP ESty IBoy LStr MAsh MAus MBri MJak MRav SMrm SPer SSea SWCr
	Terracotta = 'Meicobuis' (HT)	ESty SWCr
	Tess of the d'Urbervilles = 'Ausmove'^{PBR} (S)	CNec CRos EHyd ESty IBoy LRHS LSRN LStr MAsh MAus MBri NEgg SCoo SMrm SPer SSea SWCr
	'Tessa' (F)	LSRN
	Thank You = 'Chesdeep'^{PBR} (Patio)	ESty LBuc LStr SMrm SWCr
§	That's Jazz = 'Poulnorm'^{PBR} (Courtyard Series) (ClF)	EBee ECnt MBri MWat SWCr
	The Alexandra Rose = 'Ausday'^{PBR} (S)	EPfP GGal LRHS MAsh MAus SEND SSea
	The Alnwick Rose = 'Ausgrab'^{PBR} (S)	EPfP LRHS LStr MAus MBri NLar SCoo SPer SSea
I	'The Anniversary Rose'	EPfP LBuc MAsh
	'The Bishop' (Ce × G)	MAus
	'The Bishop of Bradford' (ClPiH)	EBee
	The Compass Rose = 'Korwisco'^{PBR} (S)	EPfP
	The Countryman = 'Ausman'^{PBR} (S)	IBoy LRHS LStr MAus SSea
	The Coventry Cathedral Rose = 'Smi72-02' (F) **new**	ESty
	The Dark Lady = 'Ausbloom'^{PBR} (S)	MAus MBri NEgg SPer
	The Diamond Wedding Rose (HT) **new**	LSRN MAsh
	'The Ednaston Rose' (Cl)	WHil
§	'The Fairy' (Poly) ♀^{H4}	CSBt CTri EBee ECnt ELan EPfP EWTr GCoc IBoy LAst LEdu LRHS LStr MAsh MAus MRav MWat NLar SEND SHil SMad SMrm SPer SSea SWCr WBor WCFE WMoo
	'The Garland' (Ra) ♀^{H4}	CRHN EPfP LRHS MAus MBri MMuc NLar SFam SPer SWCr
	The Generous Gardener = 'Ausdrawn'^{PBR} (S)	CRos CWSG EHyd EPfP ESty LBuc LRHS MAus MBri SCoo SPer SSea SWCr
§	The Gold Award Rose = 'Poulac008' (Palace Series) (Patio)	ECnt
	The Herbalist = 'Aussemi' (S)	LRHS MAus SSea
	The Hilda Ogden Rose = 'Korchason' (Patio)	LBuc NPri NSoo
	The Ingenious Mr Fairchild = 'Austijus'^{PBR} (S)	EPfP LRHS MAus MBri SCoo
	The Jack Duckworth Rose = 'Korlutmag'^{PBR} (Patio)	LBuc NPri NSoo
	The Jubilee Rose = 'Poulbrido'^{PBR} (F)	EBee ECnt SCoo
	The Lady's Blush = 'Ausoscar' (S)	EHyd EPfP LRHS MAus MBri
	The Maidstone Rose = 'Kordauerpa' (S)	SCoo
	'The Margaret Coppola Rose'	see *R.* White Gold
	The Mayflower = 'Austilly'^{PBR} (S)	CSBt ELon IBoy LBuc LRHS LStr MAus MBri SMrm
§	The McCartney Rose = 'Meizeli'^{PBR} (HT)	CWSG SPer SWCr
	'The New Dawn'	see *R.* 'New Dawn'
	The Nun = 'Ausnun' (S)	LRHS MAus
	The Painter = 'Mactemaik'^{PBR} (F)	LSRN LStr
§	The Pilgrim = 'Auswalker'^{PBR} (S)	CRos CSBt EHyd EPfP LRHS LStr MAsh MAus MBri MJak SMrm SPer SSea SWCr
	The Prince = 'Ausvelvet'^{PBR} (S)	LRHS MAus NLar SPer
	The Prince's Trust = 'Harholding'^{PBR} (Cl)	LBuc LStr MAsh MAus SPoG
	'The Prioress' (S)	MAus
§	'The Queen Elizabeth' (F)	CBcs CSBt CTri GCoc IBoy LSRN LStr MAsh MAus MBri MRav MWat NPri SPer SPoG SRGP SWCr WBor
	The Reeve = 'Ausreeve' (S)	MAus
§	The Rita Sullivan Rose = 'Korzweenu'^{PBR} (Patio)	LBuc NPri NSoo
	The Rotarian	see *R.* Rotary Sunrise
I	'The Rugby Rose' (HT)	LSRN
	The Sheikh Khalifa Rose = 'Dickoolrid' (Patio) **new**	IDic
	The Shepherdess = 'Austwist'^{PBR} (S)	IBoy LBuc LRHS MAus MBri SMrm
	The Soham Rose	see *R.* Pearl Abundance
	The Squire = 'Ausquire' (S)	MAus
	The Times Rose = 'Korpeahn' (F) ♀^{H4}	ECnt LStr MAus MRav SPer SWCr

	The Wedgwood Rose = 'Ausjosiah'PBR (ClS)	EHyd EPfP LBuc LRHS MAus MBri SKHP SMrm SPer SSea SWCr WBor WHer WKif
	The Wren = 'Kormamtiza'PBR (F/Patio)	EPfP
	'Thelma' (Ra)	MAus
	'Thérèse Bugnet' (Ru)	MAus
	Thinking of You = 'Frydandy'PBR (HT)	ESty GCoc IBoy LRHS LStr MAsh MAus NPri SRGP SVic SWCr
	'Thisbe' (HM)	CPou EBee MAus SPer
	Thomas Barton = 'Meihirvin' (HT)	LStr
	'Threave' (Bb)	CPou
	Three Wishes = 'Poulpak038' (Patio)	LBuc
	threepenny bit rose	see *R. elegantula* 'Persetosa'
	Tickled Pink = 'Fryhunky'PBR (F)	CSBt EPfP ESty GCoc LRHS LSRN LShp MAsh MBri MRav MWat SCoo SPer SPoG SWCr
	Times Past = 'Harhilt'PBR (ClHT)	ELon ESty GCoc LStr MRav SPoG SRGP SWCr
	'Tina Turner' (HT)	LSRN
	Tintinara = 'Dicuptight'PBR (HT)	ECnt
	Tip Top = 'Tanope' (F/Patio)	SPer
	'Tipo Ideale'	see *R.* × *odorata* 'Mutabilis'
	Together Forever = 'Dicecho'PBR (F)	IDic MAsh
	'Tom Marshall'	EBee LSRN
	'Tony Jacklin' (F)	LSRN
	Top Marks = 'Fryministar'PBR (Min/Patio)	CGro CSBt EPfP GCoc LStr MJak MRav MWat SCoo SPer SWCr
	Topaz Jewel	see *R.* Yellow Dagmar Hastrup
	Toprose = 'Cocgold'PBR (F)	GCoc LBuc
	'Topsi' (F/Patio)	SPer
§	'Tour de Malakoff' (Ce)	CPou IBoy LRHS MAus MRav NLar SFam SPer
	Tradescant = 'Ausdir'PBR (S)	MAus
	Tradition	see *R.* Tradition '95
§	Tradition '95 = 'Korkeltin'PBR (ClHT) ♀H4	MAsh
	'Treasure Trove' (Ra)	CRHN LRHS MAus SMrm SWCr
	Trevor Griffiths = 'Ausold'PBR (S)	MAus
	'Tricolore de Flandre' (G)	MAus
	'Trier' (Ra)	CPou MAus
	'Trigintipetala' misapplied	see *R.* 'Professeur Emile Perrot'
	'Triomphe de l'Exposition' (HP)	MAus
	'Triomphe du Luxembourg' (T)	MAus
	triphylla	see *R.* × *beanii*
I	'Trish's Rose' **new**	LSRN
	Troika = 'Poumidor' (HT) ♀H4	CSBt GCoc IBoy LRHS LStr MAsh MAus MRav SMrm SPer SPoG SWCr
	Troilus = 'Ausoil' (S)	MAus
	'Tropicana'	see *R.* Super Star
	Truly Scrumptious = 'Smi35-4-02' (HT) **new**	ESty
	Trumpeter = 'Mactru' (F) ♀H4	CTri EBee ECnt GCoc IArd IBoy LBuc LStr MAsh MAus MBri MRav MWat SPer SPoG SSea SWCr WCot
§	'Tuscany' (G)	GCoc MAus SPer
	'Tuscany Superb' (G) ♀H4	CPou CSBt CSam CTri EBee EHyd ELan EPfP EWTr LRHS MAus MBri MCot MRav NChi NLar SEND SFam SKHP SMrm SPer SSea SWCr WBor WHer WKif
	Twenty-one Again! = 'Meinimo'PBR (HT)	LSRN
	Twice in a Blue Moon = 'Tan96138'PBR (HT)	CGro CSBt ECnt ELon ESty GCoc IBoy LBuc MBri MJak MRav MWat SCoo SMrm SPoG SSea SWCr
	Twist = 'Poulstri'PBR (Courtyard Series) (ClPatio)	CGro ECnt ESty MBri
	Tynwald = 'Mattwyt' (HT)	LStr SPer
	'Ulrich Brünner'	see *R.* 'Ulrich Brünner Fils'
§	'Ulrich Brünner Fils' (HP)	MAus
	'Unique Blanche'	see *R.* × *centifolia* 'Unique'
	Valencia = 'Koreklia'PBR (HT) ♀H4	MAus
	Valentine Heart = 'Dicogle'PBR (F) ♀H4	CSBt CWSG ESty IArd LSRN MAsh MAus MBri MRav SPoG SWCr
	'Vanity' (HM)	MAus
	'Variegata di Bologna' (Bb)	EPfP EWTr LRHS MAsh MAus MMuc MRav SLon SSea SWCr
	'Vatertag' (Min)	LSRN
	'Veilchenblau' (Ra) ♀H4	CRHN CRos CSBt CSam CTri ECnt EHyd ELan EPfP LRHS LStr MAus MCot MRav NEgg NLar SEND SMrm SPer SPoG SSea SWCr WBor WKif
	Velvet Fragrance = 'Fryperdee'PBR (HT)	CSBt ECnt ELon EPfP ESty GCoc LStr MAus MBri MRav MWat SPoG SSea SWCr
	'Venusta Pendula' (Ra)	MAus
	'Verschuren' (HT/v)	ESty
	versicolor	see *R. gallica* 'Versicolor'
	'Vick's Caprice' (HP)	MAus NLar
	'Vicomtesse Pierre du Fou' (ClHT)	MAus
	Victoria Joy = 'Diciwill' (F)	IDic
	Viking Princess	see *R.* Imagination = 'Pouldron'
	'Village Maid'	see *R.* × *centifolia* 'Unique Panachée'
	villosa misapplied	see *R. mollis*
§	'Violacea' (G)	EBee MAus
	'Violette' (Ra)	CPou CRHN EHyd LRHS MAus SPer WHer WKif
	virginiana ♀H4	GCal MAus NWea
	- 'Harvest Song'	SPer
	'Viridiflora'	see *R.* × *odorata* 'Viridiflora'
	Waltz = 'Poulkrid'PBR (Courtyard Series) (ClPatio)	ECnt
	wardii var. ***culta***	MAus
	Warm Welcome = 'Chewizz'PBR (ClMin) ♀H4	CGro CWSG ECnt ELan EPfP ESty GCoc IBoy LRHS LSRN LStr MAsh MAus MGos MRav SMad SMrm SPer SPoG SSea SWCr WCot
§	Warm Wishes = 'Fryxotic'PBR (HT) ♀H4	CSBt ECnt GCoc IBoy LBuc LRHS LSRN LStr MAsh MAus MBri MGos MJak MRav MWat SPoG SSea SWCr
	'Warrior' (F)	GCoc
	Warwick Castle = 'Auslian' (S)	MAus
	webbiana	MAus SKHP
	Wedding Celebration = 'Poulht006'PBR (HT)	ECnt LRHS
	'Wedding Day' (Ra)	Widely available
	Wee Cracker = 'Cocmarris'PBR (Patio)	ESty GCoc
	Wee Jock = 'Cocabest' (F/Patio)	GCoc IBoy
	'Weetwood' (Ra)	CRHN

	Name	Suppliers
	Weisse Wolcke	see *R.* White Cloud = 'Korstacha'
	Well-Being = 'Harjangle'PBR (S)	CSBt ELon SWCr
	'Wendy Cussons' (HT)	CTri GCoc MRav SPer SWCr
	Wenlock = 'Auswen' (S)	MAus SPer
	Westerland = 'Korwest' (S) ♀H4	GCoc MRav NLar SWCr WCot
	Where the Heart Is = 'Cocoplan'PBR (HT)	ESty
	Whisky Mac = 'Tanky' (HT)	CBcs CSBt CTri ELan GCoc LBuc LSRN MRav NPri SMrm SPer SRGP
	'White Bath'	see *R.* × *centifolia* 'Shailer's White Moss'
	'White Cécile Brünner' (Poly)	LAst
	'White Christmas' (HT)	GCoc
§	White Cloud = 'Korstacha'PBR (S/ClHT) ♀H4	EPfP ESty LRHS MWat SKHP SWCr
	'White Cockade' (Cl)	CPou ESwi GCoc SPer SWCr
	White Cover	see *R.* Kent
§	'White de Meaux' (Ce)	LRHS MAus
	White Diamond = 'Interamon'PBR (S)	EBee ECnt LBuc
	White Eden = 'Meiviowit'PBR (Cl) **new**	ESty
§	White Gold = 'Cocquiriam'PBR (F)	CSBt GCoc
	'White Grootendorst' (Ru)	LRHS
	White Max Graf	see *R.* × *jacksonii* White Max Graf
	White Meidiland = 'Meicoublan'PBR (S/GC)	MAsh
	white moss	see *R.* 'Comtesse de Murinais', *R.* × *centifolia* 'Shailer's White Moss'
	White Parfum de Provence = 'Meidiaphaz' (HT)	CSBt ESty
	'White Patio' (Min/Patio)	LRHS MAsh
§	'White Pet' (Poly) ♀H4	CSBt CTri EBee ECnt ELan EPfP GCoc LRHS LStr MAus MCot MRav SEND SMrm SPer SSea SWCr WKif
	white Provence	see *R.* × *centifolia* 'Unique'
	white rose of York	see *R.* × *alba* 'Alba Semiplena'
	White Star = 'Harquill' (ClHT)	ECnt ESty
	'White Wings' (HT)	IBoy SPer WKif
N	***wichurana*** (Ra)	CBcs EWTr GCal GLin MAus SKHP
*	- 'Variegata Nana' (Ra/v)	MRav
	'Wickwar' (Ra)	EWTr GCal GGal
	Wife of Bath = 'Ausbath' (S)	MAus
	Wild Edric = 'Aushedge'PBR (Ru)	LBuc LRHS MAus SCoo
	Wild Rover = 'Dichirap'PBR (F)	ESty GCoc IDic LRHS MAsh
	Wild Thing = 'Jactoose'PBR (S)	IDic LBuc LRHS MAsh
	Wildeve = 'Ausbonny'PBR (S)	LBuc LRHS MAus MBri
	Wildfire = 'Fryessex' (Patio)	ECnt ESty IBoy LRHS MAsh MAus MBri MWat SPoG SWCr
§	'Wilhelm' (HM)	CPou MAus SPer
	'Will Scarlet' (HM)	MAus
	'William Allen Richardson' (N)	MAus
	William and Catherine = 'Ausrapper' (S) **new**	CRos EHyd LRHS MAus SSea
	'William Cobbett' (F)	SSea
§	'William Lobb' (CeMo) ♀H4	CPou CRHN EHyd EPfP EWTr IBoy LRHS LStr MAus MBri MNrw MRav NEgg NLar SPer SWCr WHer WKif
	William Morris = 'Auswill'PBR (S)	CRos CSBt LBuc LRHS MAus MBri NEgg SSea SWCr
	William Shakespeare 2000 = 'Ausromeo'PBR (S)	CRos CSBt EBee ECnt EHyd EPfP ESty IBoy LRHS LStr MAsh MAus MBNS MBri NEgg SCoo SSea SWCr
	William Shakespeare = 'Ausroyal'PBR (S)	CGro CWSG IBoy MCot SPer
	'William Tyndale' (Ra)	CPou EBee
	'Williams' Double Yellow'	see *R.* × *harisonii* 'Williams Double Yellow'
	willmottiae	see *R. gymnocarpa* var. *willmottiae*
	Wilton = 'Eurosa' (GC)	SHil
	Wiltshire = 'Kormuse'PBR (S/GC) ♀H4	CSBt CTri ECnt ELan ESty IBoy LRHS LSRN LStr MRav SEND SLon SSea SWCr
	Winchester Cathedral = 'Auscat'PBR (S)	CGro CRos CSBt CTri ECnt EHyd ELan EPfP IBoy LRHS LSRN LStr MAsh MAus MBri MRav MWat NEgg NLar SLon SMad SMrm SPer SPoG SSea SWCr
	Windflower = 'Auscross' (S)	MAus
	Windrush = 'Ausrush' (S)	MAus
	Wise Portia = 'Ausport' (S)	MAus
	Wisley 2008 = 'Ausbreeze'PBR (S)	CGro CSBt ECnt EHyd EPfP IBoy LRHS MAus MBri
	Wisley = 'Ausintense'PBR (S)	SCoo
	With All My Love = 'Coczodiac'PBR (HT)	CSBt GCoc LStr
	With Love = 'Andwit' (HT)	SWCr
	With Thanks = 'Fransmoov'PBR (HT)	MJak SWCr
	Wizard (HT)	ESty
	Wollerton Old Hall = 'Ausblanket' (S) **new**	EHyd ESty MAsh MAus MBri SSea
	'Wolley-Dod'	see *R.* 'Duplex'
	Wonderful = 'Poulpmt005'PBR (HT)	EBee ECnt SWCr
	Wonderful News = 'Jonone'PBR (Patio)	CGro ESty
§	***woodsii***	MAus
	- var. ***fendleri***	see *R. woodsii*
	Worcestershire = 'Korlalon'PBR (GC)	GCoc LRHS MAus MRav SPer SSea SWCr
§	***xanthina*** 'Canary Bird' (S) ♀H4	Widely available
§	- f. ***hugonis*** ♀H4	CTri ELan EWTr LRHS MAus NLar SKHP SPer
	'Yellow Beauty' (Min) **new**	NLar
	'Yellow Cécile Brünner'	see *R.* 'Perle d'Or'
	Yellow Charles Austin = 'Ausyel' (S)	MAus
§	Yellow Dagmar Hastrup = 'Moryelrug'PBR (Ru)	CPou EBee EWTr SPer
	Yellow Floorshow = 'Harfully'PBR (GC)	MRav
	Yellow Flower Carpet	see *R.* Flower Carpet Sunshine
	'Yellow Patio' (Min/Patio)	LBuc LRHS LStr MAsh NPri SPoG SSea SWCr
	yellow Scotch	see *R.* × *harisonii* 'Williams Double Yellow'
	Yellow Sunblaze = 'Meitrisical' (Min)	CSBt
	'Yesterday' (Poly/F/S) ♀H4	MAus NLar
	'Yolande d'Aragon' (HP)	EWTr
	York and Lancaster	see *R.* × *damascena* 'Versicolor'
	Yorkshire = 'Korbarkeit'PBR (GC)	GCoc LStr MRav
	'Yorkshire Lady' (HT)	NEgg

You Are My Sunshine = 'Frykwango' PBR (HT)	ECnt GCoc LBuc LRHS MAsh MJak
Young Lycidas = 'Ausvibrant' PBR (S)	CSBt EPfP ESty IBoy LRHS MAus MBri SSea
You're Beautiful = 'Fryracy' (F) **new**	ECnt ESty GCoc LStr
'Yvonne Rabier' (Poly) ♀H4	MAus MRav NLar SLon SPer
'Zéphirine Drouhin' (Bb)	Widely available
§ 'Zigeunerknabe' (S)	ECnt GCoc MAus MRav NLar SKHP SPer
Zwergenfee 09	see *R.* The Rita Sullivan Rose

Roscoea ✿ (*Zingiberaceae*)

alpina	CAby CBro CExl CLAP EBee ECho GBuc LWst WCru XLum
- CC 3667	EPPr
- 'Leaping Salmon'	CCon
- pink-flowered	IBlr
- purple-flowered	IBlr
- short	WCru
alpina* × *cautleyoides **new**	IBlr
§ ***auriculata***	CAby CAvo CBct CBro CCon CLAP EBee ECho EPfP EPot EShb GBuc GCal IBlr IFoB LWst MPie NHar NPnk NSoo SChF SDeJ SKHP SPer SPoG WCru WHar WSHC
- B&SWJ 2594	WCru
- 'Anorexia' **new**	IBlr
- brown-stemmed × ***purpurea***	IBlr
- early-flowering	IBlr WCru
- 'Floriade'	CDes CLAP GBuc IBlr LRHS LWst WHil WSHC
- green-stemmed × ***purpurea***	IBlr
- late-flowering	WCru
- 'Special'	CLAP
- 'White Cap'	LWst
auriculata* × *australis	IBlr
auriculata* × *capitata	IBlr
australis	CCon CSam ELon GBuc MNrw WCru WThu
- pink-flowered KW 22124	IBlr
- purple-flowered KW 22124	IBlr
australis* × *humeana	IBlr
'Ballyrogan Lavender'	IBlr
× ***beesiana*** **new**	CAvo
- 'Ballyrogan Purple'	IBlr
- Cream Group	CBct CDes CLAP EPfP GBuc IBlr LEdu MMHG NBir NPnk SKHP WCru WPGP
- Dark Group	IBlr
- Gestreept Group	CBro CCon CHEx CLAP CMea CTsd EPot GBuc IBlr MPie NHar SKHP WCru WHar WHil WWEG
- 'Lemon and Lavender'	IBlr
- 'Monique'	CDes EBee IBlr LWst NHar WHil WPGP
- 'Moonlight'	IBlr
- 'Petite Purple'	IBlr
Blackthorn strain	IBlr
brandisii misapplied	see *R. tumjensis*
capitata	CLAP IBlr
cautleyoides ♀H4	CAby CAvo CBro CMea CWCL EBee ECho ELon EPot GBuc IBlr IFoB LHop LRHS MNrw NBid NCGa NGdn NPnk NSoo SPer SPoG SRot WCru WHar WKif XEll
- CLD 772	IBlr
- var. ***cautleyoides*** f. ***atropurpurea***	IBlr
- - - 'Giraffe'	IBlr
- - white-flowered	CRDP
- cream-flowered × ***humeana***	LWst
- 'Crûg's Late Lemon'	WCru
- 'Doge Purple'	IBlr
- dwarf, from Kew	LRHS
- 'Early Purple'	CDes CLAP ECho GBuc WPGP
- 'Early Yellow'	LWst
- 'Himalaya'	LWst
- 'Jeffrey Thomas'	CBct CLAP CSam ECho ELan EPPr EPot GBuc GCal IBlr LWst MLHP SRGP WHil
- 'Kew Beauty' ♀H4	CAby CCon CDes CExl CLAP CMea CRDP EPfP EUJe GBuc GCal LLWG LRHS MMoz NGdn SKHP WCot WPGP
- late, lavender-flowered	IBlr
- late, yellow-flowered	IBlr NCot
- 'Lemon Giraffe'	IBlr
- 'Pennine Purple'	IBlr NHar
- plum-flowered	IBlr
- var. ***pubescens***	IBlr
- 'Purple Giant'	CLAP EBee SKHP
- purple-flowered	CAby IBlr NHar
- 'Reinier'	CLAP EBee GCal IBlr LWst SKHP
- f. ***sinopurpurea***	GKev IBlr
- 'Vanilla'	LEdu SKHP
- 'Vien Beauty' **new**	WHil
- 'Washfield Purple'	IBlr
- 'Wine Red' **new**	WHil
- 'Yeti'	LWst SKHP
cautleyoides* × *humeana	CLAP IBlr LWst WHar
cautleyoides* × *praecox **new**	IBlr
cautleyoides* × *scillifolia f. ***atropurpurea***	IBlr
debilis var. ***debilis***	IBlr
forrestii f. ***forrestii***	IBlr
- - pubescent **new**	IBlr
- 'Ice Maiden' **new**	IBlr
- f. ***purpurea***	IBlr
- f. ***purpurea* × *humeana***	IBlr
humeana ♀	CAby CBct CBro CLAP ECho EHyd EPot GBuc GKev LRHS LWst SPoG WThu
- ACE 2539	IBlr
- CC 1820	IBlr
- f. ***alba***	IBlr
- from Cruickshank Botanic Garden **new**	IBlr
- Forrest's form	IBlr
- 'Guincho White Stripe' **new**	IBlr
- 'Harvington Raw Silk' **new**	NHar
- 'Harvington Royale' **new**	NHar
- lavender-flowered	IBlr
- 'Long Acre Sunrise'	CDes CLAP WHil WPGP
- f. ***lutea***	CLAP IBlr
- pink-flowered	IBlr
- 'Purple Streaker'	CDes WPGP
- 'Rosemoor Plum'	CDes CLAP EBee WHil WPGP
- 'Two Tone'	IBlr
- f. ***tyria***	EBee IBlr
- - 'Inkling'	GBuc
'Ice Maiden'	IBlr

'Lavender Mist' **new**	IBlr
'Pallid Sun' **new**	IBlr
praecox	IBlr
- BWJ 7848	WCru
procera misapplied	see *R. auriculata*
procera Wall.	see *R. purpurea*
'Purple King'	LWst
§ ***purpurea***	CAvo CBro CHEx ELan ELon EPPr EPfP EPot EUJe GCal IBlr IFoB LEdu LLWG LRHS NBir NGdn SPer WCru WHer WHil WKif WWEG
- CC 1757	IBlr
- CC 3628	CExl IBlr
- HWJK 2020	WCru
- HWJK 2169	WCru
- HWJK 2175	WCru
- HWJK 2400	WCru
- HWJK 2407	WCru
- KW 13755	IBlr
- MECC 2	IBlr
- MECC 10	IBlr
- 'Bronzed Albino' **new**	IBlr
- bronze-leaved	CAby
- 'Brown Peach'	LRHS
- 'Brown Peacock'	CDes CFil CLAP GBuc IBlr LWst SKHP WCru WPGP
- 'Cinnamon Stick'	NHar
- 'Dalai Lama'	LWst
- var. ***gigantea*** CC 1757	IBlr
- 'Himalayan Delight'	IBlr
- 'Late Lavender' **new**	IBlr
- 'Nico'	ELan IBlr LRHS LWst SKHP WCot
- 'Niedrig'	EBee IBlr SKHP
- 'Peacock'	CLAP EBee IBlr LWst SKHP
- 'Peacock Eye'	IBlr LRHS LWst SKHP
- var. ***procera***	see *R. purpurea*
- 'Purple Dwarf' **new**	IBlr
- 'Purple Tower' **new**	IBlr
- Rosemoor form	CLAP
- f. ***rubra***	CAby CDes CLAP IBlr LLHF LRHS NHar SPoG
- short	CLAP IBlr
- 'Slender Wisp' **new**	IBlr
- tall	CLAP WCru WPGP
- 'Twin Towers'	EBee
- 'Typico'	IBlr
- 'Vannin'	LEdu WCru
- 'Vincent'	LWst
- 'Wisley Amethyst'	CLAP EBee IBlr LLHF LRHS NCot SKHP SPoG
schneideriana	IBlr WThu
- robust form	IBlr
scillifolia	CBro CCon CPBP ECho EHyd GBuc GKev LHop LRHS NBir SDeJ WHar
- f. ***atropurpurea***	CAby CDes GBuc GCal IBlr WCru WPGP WThu WWEG
- f. ***scillifolia***	CDes EBee IBlr IFoB WCru WHar WHil WThu
aff. ***scillifolia*** purple-flowered	IBlr
'Summer Deep Purple' **new**	LRHS
tibetica	CCon EBee GKev IBlr WCru WThu
- ACE 2538	IBlr WCru
- BWJ 7878	WCru
- f. ***atropurpurea*** BWJ 7640	WCru
aff. ***tibetica***	IBlr
aff. ***tibetica*** f. ***albo-purpurea***	IBlr
§ ***tumjensis***	IBlr WPGP
wardii	CExl IBlr

rosemary see *Rosmarinus officinalis*

Rosenia (Asteraceae)

humilis	CPBP

Rosmarinus ✿ (*Lamiaceae*)

sp.	CHab
corsicus 'Prostratus'	see *R. officinalis* Prostratus Group
lavandulaceus misapplied	see *R. officinalis* Prostratus Group
× ***noeanus***	XSen
officinalis	Widely available
- var. ***albiflorus***	CArn CSev EBee ELau EPfP GPoy LEdu LRHS MHer MNHC SDow SEND SHDw SLim SPlb SRms WGwG WJek XSen
- - 'Lady in White'	CSBt ELan EPfP LRHS SDow SLim SPer SPoG SRms WGwG WJek
- 'Alderney'	MHer SDow SRms
§ - var. ***angustissimus*** 'Benenden Blue' ♀H4	CSBt CWib EBee ELan EPfP GPoy MHoo SDix SDow SEND SPer SPlb SPoG SRms WGwG WJek
- - 'Corsican Blue'	CArn ELan EPfP GPoy MHer MHol MNHC MRav SGol SHDw SPer SRms
- - 'Corsicus Prostratus'	SHil
- 'Arp' **new**	CArn LHop
- 'Aureovariegatus'	see *R. officinalis* 'Aureus'
§ - 'Aureus' (v)	CPla SRms WJek
- 'Baby P.J.'	EOHP
- 'Baie d'Audierne'	XSen
- 'Barbecue' PBR	ELan ELau LRHS SRms
- 'Blue Lagoon'	ELau LRHS MHer MHoo MNHC SIde SPer SRms WGwG WHer WJek
- 'Blue Rain'	CHel EPfP MHer MJak MSwo WHfH WPnn
- 'Boule'	CArn ELau MHer SDow SRms WGwG WJek XLum XSen
- 'Capercaillie'	SDow
- 'Collingwood Ingram'	see *R. officinalis* var. *angustissimus* 'Benenden Blue'
- 'Cottage White'	WGwG WHer
- dwarf, blue-flowered	ELau
- 'Farinole'	CArn ELau MNHC SRms
- 'Fastigiatus'	see *R. officinalis* 'Miss Jessopp's Upright'
- 'Fota Blue'	CArn CSpe CTsd CWib ELau LAst LGor LRHS MHer MHoo MNHC SDow SEND SGol SHDw SIde SRms SVen SWvt WGwG WJek WPnn
- 'Foxtail'	LBuc LRHS SRms WJek
- 'Frimley Blue'	see *R. officinalis* 'Primley Blue'
- 'Genges Gold' (v)	MHer
- 'Golden Rain'	see *R. officinalis* 'Joyce DeBaggio'
- 'Gorizia'	CArn EHoe SDow SLim SRms WGwG WPnn
- 'Green Ginger'	CArn CHel CPrp EBee ELan ELau EPfP GBin LHop LRHS MAsh MHer MHoo MNHC MRav MSCN NPer SDow SPer SPoG SRms SVen WGwG WJek WPnn
- 'Guilded'	see *R. officinalis* 'Aureus'
- 'Haifa'	EBtc ELau LRHS MHoo NLBP SRms WJek WPnn
- 'Henfield Blue'	SHDw
- 'Iden Blue Boy'	CSpe
§ - 'Joyce DeBaggio' (v)	MHer SDow WGwG WHer

- 'Knightshayes Blue'	LRHS
- 'Lady in Blue'	WGwG
- ***lavandulaceus***	see *R. officinalis* Prostratus Group
- 'Lilies Blue'	GPoy
- 'Lockwood Variety'	see *R. officinalis* (Prostratus Group) 'Lockwood de Forest'
- 'Logee Blue' **new**	CArn
- 'Majorca Pink'	CBcs CHab CSBt CSpe EBee ELau LRHS MHer MNHC MSCN NPri SDow SPer WGwG WJek XLum
- 'Marenca'	CHll ELau MNHC SRms
- 'McConnell's Blue' 🏆H4	CArn CDoC CPrp EBee ELan ELau IGor LHop LRHS MAsh MGos MNHC SDow SHDw SHil SRms WGwG WHer WHoo WJek WPGP
§ - 'Miss Jessopp's Upright' 🏆H4	Widely available
- 'Pointe du Raz'	CAbP CArn CPrp ELan EPfP LRHS MAsh SChF SLim SRms
§ - 'Primley Blue'	CBcs CMea CSev CTsd EBee ECtt ELau MHoo MNHC MRav SGol SIde SRms WJek
§ - Prostratus Group	Widely available
- - 'Capri'	CAbP CSBt EBee ELau EPfP LRHS MHer SPoG SRms WJek
- - 'Gethsemane'	CArn WGwG
- - 'Jackman's Prostrate'	CHab
§ - - 'Lockwood de Forest'	WGwG WHer
- - 'Sheila Dore'	SPlb SVen
- f. ***pyramidalis***	see *R. officinalis* 'Miss Jessopp's Upright'
- ***repens***	see *R. officinalis* Prostratus Group
- 'Rex'	ELau
- 'Roman Beauty'^{PBR}	CBcs CSBt CSev EBee EHoe LAst LRHS LSRN MAsh MHol SLim SRms SWvt WHer
- 'Roseus'	CArn CHVG CPrp CWib EBee ELan ELau EPfP GPoy LHop LRHS MAsh MHoo MNHC NEgg SDow SEND SLim SPoG SRms SVen WGwG WHer WJek WPnn
- 'Salem'	MHer
- 'Sea Level'	ELau MHer WGwG
- 'Severn Sea' 🏆H4	CArn CBcs CSBt CTri EBee ECtt ELan ELau EPfP GPoy LRHS MAsh MGos MHer MNHC MRav MSwo SDow SIde SLon SPer SRms SVen WCFE WGwG WHoo WJek
- 'Shimmering Stars'	SDow
- 'Silver Sparkler'	WPat
- Silver Spires = 'Wolros'	MNHC
- 'Sissinghurst Blue' 🏆H4	CArn CWCL EBee ECrN ELan ELau EPfP LRHS MAsh MHer MLHP MNHC MRav SDow SGol SLim SPer SPlb SRms SWvt WGwG WJek
- 'Sissinghurst White'	MMuc WGwG
- 'Sorcerer's Apprentice'	WGwG
- 'South Downs Blue'	SHDw
- 'Spanish Snow'	WGwG
- 'Spice Island' **new**	SPer
- 'Sudbury Blue'	ELau EPfP MHer MHoo SDow SHDw SPad SRms WJek XSen
- 'Sunkissed'	LBuc LRHS SLim SPoG SRms
- 'Trusty'	ELan
- 'Tuscan Blue'	CArn CBcs CDoC CExl CPrp EBee ECtt ELan ELau EPfP LRHS MHer MHoo MNHC MSwo NEgg NPri SDow SGol SPer SRms WGwG WHfH WJek WPGP WPnn XSen
- 'Variegatus'	see *R. officinalis* 'Aureus'
- 'Vicomte de Noailles'	XSen
repens	see *R. officinalis* Prostratus Group
Salcombe form	CHll
'Sappho'	CHll

Rostrinucula (*Lamiaceae*)

dependens	ECre ELon EPfP ESwi EWes MTPN NLar SBrt WCFE WWFP
sinensis	CExl

Rosularia ✿ (*Crassulaceae*)

from Sandras Dag, Turkey	CWil LBee
§ ***aizoon***	ECho EHyd LRHS
alba	see *R. sedoides* var. *alba*
alpestris from Rhotang Pass, Himalaya	WThu
§ ***chrysantha***	ECho EDAr EHyd EPot LRHS SPlb
crassipes	see *Rhodiola wallichiana*
libanotica RCB RL 20	WCot
pallida A. Berger	see *R. chrysantha*
pallida Stapf	see *R. aizoon*
pallida ambig.	EPot SFgr
sedoides	CWil MMuc
§ - var. ***alba***	ECho EDAr EPot WNew
sempervivum	CWil ECho EWes
§ - subsp. ***glaucophylla***	CWil EHyd MSCN WAbe WThu
spatulata hort.	see *R. sempervivum* subsp. *glaucophylla*

Rotala (*Lythraceae*)

indica	LLWG

Rubia (*Rubiaceae*)

peregrina	CArn GPoy
tinctorum	CArn CHab CHby EOHP GPoy MNHC SWat WHfH WSFF

Rubus ✿ (*Rosaceae*)

RCB/Eq C-1	WCot
SDR 4635	GKev
alceifolius Poir.	SDys
arcticus	EBee ECtt EPPr GPri NHar NLar SRot WCru WPat WThu XLum
- subsp. ***stellatus***	NHar
× ***barkeri***	ECou
'Benenden' 🏆H4	Widely available
'Betty Ashburner'	CAgr CBcs CDoC CDul COIW EBee EPPr EWTr GQui LAst MGos MRav MWhi SPer WHar WMoo XLum
biflorus 🏆H4	EWes LEdu MBlu MMuc NLar SEND WPGP
'Boatsberry'	SDea
'Boysenberry' (F)	LRHS
boysenberry, thornless (F)	CMac EMil GPri GTwe LBuc LSRN NPri SDea SPer
buergeri B&SWJ 5555	WCru
caesius	WCot
calophyllus	WPGP
calycinoides Hayata	see *R. rolfei*
calycinoides Kuntze	EBtc GKev SGol
chamaemorus	GPoy
- 'Nyby' **new**	GPri
cockburnianus (F)	CArn CBcs CTri CWib EBee ELan EPfP GCra GKin IFoB LBuc MRav MSwo NLar NSti NWea SPer SPlb SRms WHar
- 'Goldenvale' 🏆H4	CDoC CDul EBee EHoe ELon EPfP EWTr GQui IFro LBMP LHop LRHS

	MAsh MBlu MGos MMuc MRav MSwo MWhi NBir NEgg NLar NSti SEND SLon SPer SPoG
crataegifolius	MRav WPat
'Emerald Spreader'	WMoo
fockeanus misapplied	see *R. rolfei*
formosensis B&SWJ 1798	ESwi WCru
N ***fruticosus*** agg.	NWea WSFF
- 'Adrienne' (F)	CAgr CSBt LRHS MAsh MBri SPoG WHar
- 'Apache' (F) **new**	GPri NPri SPer
- 'Ashton Cross' (F)	GTwe LBuc
- 'Bedford Giant' (F)	CSBt GTwe LRHS LSRN MAsh MGos MMuc SEND SKee SLim SPoG WHar
- 'Black Butte' (F)	EPom GPri LRHS SDea SLon SVic
- 'Black Satin' (F)	CAgr ECrN GPri LRHS NLar NPri SDea SVic
- 'Čačanska Bestrna' (F) **new**	MCoo
- 'Chester' (F)	EPom ERea LRHS SKee SPer
- 'Godshill Goliath' (F)	SDea
- 'Helen' (F)	CAgr CSut GPri MAsh MCoo SDea
- 'Himalayan Giant' (F)	MRav NEgg NLar SDea
- 'John Innes' (F)	GPri
- 'Karaka Black'PBR (F)	ERea GPri LBuc LRHS SVic
- 'Kotata' (F)	MRav
- 'Loch Maree' (F/d)	CMac EPom GPri LRHS MCoo SLon
- 'Loch Ness'PBR (F) ♀H4	CAgr CWib EPom GPri GTwe IArd LBuc LRHS LSRN SCoo SDea SKee SVic WHar
- 'Loch Tay'PBR (F)	CMac EPom GPri LRHS
- 'Merton Thornless' (F)	CSBt CWib LAst LEdu LSRN MBri MGos MJak SPlb SRms WHar
- 'Natchez' (F)	GPri NPri
- 'Navaho' (F) **new**	GPri
- 'Navaho Big and Early' (F)	CSut
- 'No Thorn' (F)	SDea
- 'Oregon Thornless' (F)	CAgr CDoC CSBt CWib ECrN EPfP GPri GTwe LRHS LSRN MAsh MBri MJak MRav NEgg NLar SCoo SDea SKee SLim SPoG SRms SVic WHar
- 'Ouachita' (F)	GPri NPri SPer
- 'Parsley Leaved' (F)	SDea
- 'Reuben' (F) **new**	EPom SPer
- 'Silvan' (F) ♀H4	GPri MCoo MMuc SEND
- 'Thornfree' (F)	CAgr CDoC CTri LRHS MBri MMuc NLar SDea SKee SLim
- 'Triple Crown' (F) **new**	CMac MCoo
- 'Variegatus' (v)	CMac CRDP MBlu WCot
- 'Waldo' (F)	CAgr CSBt CWib GPri LBuc LSRN MAsh MBri MGos NPri SDea SRms WHar
aff. ***gachetensis*** B&SWJ 10603	WCru
'Glencoe'	GPri MCoo
'Golden Showers'	CWib
henryi	ESwi IGor LRHS MAsh MRav WCot
- var. ***bambusarum***	ESwi MRav WCru
'Hildaberry' (F)	GPri
ichangensis	CBcs ESwi LEdu
idaeus	GPoy
- 'All Gold' (F) ♀H4	CAgr EMil EPom ERea GPri LRHS MAsh MCoo NPri SCoo SPer SVic WHar
- 'Aureus' (F)	ELan LEdu MRav NBid WCot
- 'Autumn Bliss' (F) ♀H4	Widely available
- 'Autumn Treasure' (F)	CSut EPom ERea GTwe LRHS MCoo NPri SLon
- 'Cascade Delight' (F)	CSut EPom LBuc MAsh
- 'Erika'PBR (F)	LBuc NPri
- 'Fallgold' (F)	CWib EPfP LSRN MMuc SEND SKee SPoG
- 'Glen Ample'PBR (F) ♀H4	CAgr CMac CSBt CTri CWSG CWib EMil EPfP EPom ERea GTwe LBuc LRHS LSRN MAsh MBri MCoo MNHC NPri NWea SCoo SDea SEND SKee SLim SPer SPoG SVic WHar
- 'Glen Clova' (F)	CAgr CSBt CTri CWib ELan GTwe LRHS LSRN MAsh MGos MRav NLar SKee SLim SPer SPoG SVic WHar
- 'Glen Doll'PBR (F)	CAgr GTwe LBuc LRHS MAsh MCoo SCoo SPoG WHar
- 'Glen Fyne'PBR (F)	GTwe SPer
- 'Glen Lyon'PBR (F)	CWib GKin LAst LBuc MAsh MBri MJak SCoo WHar
- 'Glen Magna'PBR (F) ♀H4	CAgr CMac CSBt CWib ERea GKin LRHS MAsh MBri NLar SCoo SDea SKee SLim WHar
- 'Glen Moy'PBR (F) ♀H4	CAgr CSBt CTri CWib ECrN EPfP GTwe LAst LRHS LSRN MAsh MGos MJak NEgg NWea SCoo SDea SKee SLim WHar
- 'Glen Prosen'PBR (F) ♀H4	CAgr CSBt CWib EPfP GKin GTwe LRHS LSRN MAsh MBri MGos MRav NEgg NPri SCoo SDea SKee SLim SPer SPlb WHar
- 'Glen Rosa' (F)	ERea MCoo
- 'Heritage' (F)	CWib ELan MAsh SCoo
- 'Joan J'PBR (F) ♀H4	CMac CSut EMil EPom ERea GPri GTwe LRHS LSRN MCoo
- 'Leo'PBR (F) ♀H4	CSBt CTri CWib GTwe LSRN MAsh SCoo SKee SPer WHar
- 'Malling Admiral' (F) ♀H4	CSBt CTri CWib EPom LSRN MAsh NWea SCoo SKee SPer WHar
- 'Malling Delight' (F)	CSBt CWib ELan SCoo SPlb WHar
- 'Malling Jewel' (F) ♀H4	CAgr CSBt CWib EPom GTwe LBuc LSRN MAsh MJak SDea SKee SPer WHar
- 'Malling Promise' (F)	CWib MJak
- 'Octavia'PBR (F)	CAgr CSBt EMil EPom GTwe LBuc LRHS MCoo NLar NWea SLim SPoG WHar
- 'Polka'PBR (F) ♀H4	EPom GPri LBuc LRHS LSRN MAsh MCoo MRav SCoo SKee SLim SVic WHar
- 'Sanibelle' (F) **new**	CSut
- 'Summer Gold' (F)	GTwe
- 'Tadmor'PBR (F) **new**	SPer
- 'Tulameen' (F) ♀H4	CAgr CSBt CWSG CWib ECrN ELan EMil EPom GPri LRHS LSRN MAsh MBri NLar SCoo SKee SLim SPer SPoG SVic WHar
- Twotimer Sugana = 'Sugana'PBR (F) **new**	CSut LBuc MAsh
- Twotimer Sugana Yellow (F) **new**	CSut
- 'Valentina' (F)	GPri SVic
- 'Zeva Herbsternte' (F)	CWib MAsh
illecebrosus (F)	XLum
irenaeus	LEdu LRHS SEND
Japanese wineberry	see *R. phoenicolasius*
'Kenneth Ashburner'	CDoC NLar
lineatus	CDTJ CWib EBee EPfP EWes GBin LHop LRHS MCot MMuc SKHP WCru WPGP

– B&SWJ 11261 from Sumatra	WCru
– HWJ 892 from Vietnam	ESwi WCru
– HWJK 2045 from Nepal	GQui WCru
– from Nepal	GCra
× ***loganobaccus*** (F)	LRHS
– 'Brandywine' (F)	GPri SDea
– 'Ly 59' (F) ♀H4	ECrN EPfP GTwe MMuc MRav SDea SKee SRms
– 'Ly 654' (F) ♀H4	CSBt EPom ERea GTwe LBuc MBri NEgg NPri SDea SPer WHar
– thornless (F)	CAgr CTri CWib EPom GPri GTwe LEdu SDea SPoG SVic
'Malling Minerva' (F)	CAgr CMac CSut
'Margaret Gordon'	MRav
microphyllus 'Variegatus' (v)	MRav
§ ***nepalensis***	CAgr CDoC GCra GKev LEdu
nutans	see *R. nepalensis*
occidentalis 'Ebony'	LRHS
– 'Haut'	GPri
– 'Jewel'	GPri
odoratus	CExl ELan EPPr EPfP EWTr LEdu MBlu MRav NBid SPer
palmatus var. ***coptophyllus***	MMuc
parviflorus	CArn GPri
– 'Bill Baker' **new**	LEdu
– double-flowered (d)	EPPr
– 'Sunshine Spreader'	EHoe GPri LEdu WPat
parvus	LEdu
pectinellus var. ***trilobus***	WCot
– – B&SWJ 1669B	NLar WCru
peltatus	CFil NLar WPGP
pentalobus	see *R. rolfei*
§ ***phoenicolasius***	CAgr CCCN CDul CHGN CMac ELan EMil EPPr EPfP EWTr GPri GTwe LEdu LHop LRHS MBlu MCoo MHer MRav NLar SDea SPer SPoG SVic WPGP
§ ***rolfei***	CTri XLum
– B&SWJ 3546 from Taiwan	WCru
– B&SWJ 3878 from the Philippines	WCru
– 'Emerald Carpet'	CAgr NLar
rosifolius 'Coronarius' (d)	CSpe LSou NLar NPro WCot
sanctus	CNat
saxatilis	GPri LEdu
– PAB 3912 **new**	LEdu
setchuenensis	CMCN EPPr NLar
spectabilis	CBcs CPom CWib ELan EPPr EWTr LEdu MMuc MRav WSHC
– 'Flore Pleno'	see *R. spectabilis* 'Olympic Double'
§ – 'Olympic Double' (d)	Widely available
splendidissimus B&SWJ 2361	ESwi WCru
squarrosus	ECou
'Sunberry' (F)	CCCN GPri GTwe SDea
swinhoei B&SWJ 1735	WCru
taiwanicola B&SWJ 317	ESwi LHop WCru
– CWJ 12400	WCru
Tayberry Group (F) ♀H4	CSBt CTri GTwe LRHS LSRN MGos NLar NPri SPer SRms SVic WHar
– 'Buckingham' (F)	CSut EMil EPom ERea GPri GTwe LBuc LRHS SVic
– 'Medana Tayberry' (F)	CAgr EPfP GPri LEdu LRHS MBri SDea SKee SPoG WHar
§ ***thibetanus*** ♀H4	Widely available
– 'Silver Fern'	see *R. thibetanus*
treutleri B&SWJ 2139	WCru
tricolor	CAgr CBcs CDul COlW CSBt CTri CWib EBee ECrN EPfP GKev GKin GPri MBlu MCoo MMuc MRav MSwo MWhi NEgg NLar SDix SGol SPer WMoo
aff. ***tricolor*** **new**	WHar
trilobus B&SWJ 9096	WCru
'Tummelberry' (F)	EMil GPri GTwe LRHS SVic
ulmifolius 'Bellidiflorus' (d)	MBlu MRav
'Veitchberry' (F)	CDoy GPri
xanthocarpus	NLar XLum
'Youngberry' (F)	SDea
'Youngberry' thornless (F)	GPri

Rudbeckia ✿ (*Asteraceae*)

Autumn Sun	see *R. laciniata* 'Herbstsonne'
'Berlin'	CWGN ECtt LRHS LSRN LSou MAvo MHol MTis SMrm SPer SPoG WCot WGrn
deamii	see *R. fulgida* var. *deamii*
'Dublin'	CWGN ECtt IPot LRHS LSRN LSou MAvo MHol MTis SPoG WCot
fulgida	SWvt
– 'City Garden'	CKno ECtt GBin NCGa NLar SRms
§ – var. ***deamii*** ♀H4	Widely available
– 'Early Bird Gold'	CWGN EBee ECtt GBin MTis NDov NLar WCot
– var. ***fulgida***	CMea EBee EPfP LEdu SMrm SPoG
§ – var. ***speciosa*** ♀H4	CKno CPrp EBee ECtt ELan EPfP GAbr MMuc SBch SEND SPhx SPlb SRms SWvt WMoo WOut WPtf WWEG XLum
– var. ***sullivantii*** 'Goldsturm' ♀H4	Widely available
– – 'Pot of Gold'	EBee LSou NLar
– Viette's Little Suzy = 'Blovi'	EBee SRms
gloriosa	see *R. hirta*
'Golden Jubilee'	LRHS
grandiflora 'Sundance'	EBee LRHS SPhx WPtf
§ ***hirta***	LRHS NBir SVic
– 'Autumn Colours' (mixed)	CMea SPhx
– 'Cappuccino'	MSCN
– 'Cherokee Sunset' (d)	CSpe EPfP
– 'Cherry Brandy'	LHop LRHS NPri NSoo SGol SLon SPhx
– 'Chim Chiminee'	NGBl
– 'Goldilocks'	SVic
– 'Indian Summer' ♀H3	EPfP MHol MNHC SPav SPhx
– 'Irish Eyes'	SPav SVic
– 'Marmalade'	EPfP LRHS NGBl SVic
– 'Prairie Sun'	ELon EPfP LRHS MBel NGBl SPhx
– 'Sonora'	NGBl
– 'Tiger Eye'	LRHS SPoG
– 'Toto' ♀H3	SPav SWvt
July Gold	see *R. laciniata* 'Juligold'
laciniata	CElw CHVG CKno CMac CSpe EBee ELan GCal GQue LEdu MMuc MSpe NCGa NDov NGBl NLar NOrc SPhx WCot WMoo WOld WWEG XLum
– var. ***digitata***	IMou
– 'Golden Glow'	see *R. laciniata* 'Hortensia'
– 'Goldkugel' (d) ♀H4	MSpe
– 'Goldquelle' (d) ♀H4	CNec ECtt EHyd ELan EPfP GMaP IVic LHop LRHS MSpe NGdn NOrc NPnk NPri NSoo SBea SMad SMrm SPer SPoG SRms SRot SWvt WMnd WWEG XLum

§ – 'Herbstsonne' 🏆^{H4}	Widely available
§ – 'Hortensia' (d)	EBee GQue MBel MRav WBrk WCot WHoo WOld WWEG
§ – 'Juligold'	CPrp EBee ECtt LBMP LRHS MBNS MCot NBre NDov NEgg NGdn NPnk SMrm SPoG WWEG WWFP
– 'Starcadia Razzle Dazzle'	WCot WWEG
'Little Gold Star'	CKno EBee ECtt ELon LRHS MHol MPie MTis NDov NPnk NPri SPoG WCot
maxima	CAby CKno CSpc EBee ELon GBin IFoB LEdu LHop LRHS MBel MHol MSpe NCGa NLar NSti SKHP SMad SMrm SPhx SPlb WCot WWEG XLum
missouriensis	EBee LRHS
mollis	EBee NBre
newmannii	see *R. fulgida* var. *speciosa*
nitida	IBoy
occidentalis	LRHS NBre NLar
– 'Black Beauty'[PBR]	ECtt EPfP
– 'Green Wizard'	CMac CWib EBee ECtt ELan EPfP GBin IBoy LRHS MCot MLHP NLar NSti SMad SMrm SPav SPer SRms WHar WMnd WWEG
* ***paniculata***	EBee LLHF NBre WCot
'Peking'	CWGN ECtt LRHS LSRN MTis SMrm SPoG WCot WGrn
purpurea	see *Echinacea purpurea*
speciosa	see *R. fulgida* var. *speciosa*
subtomentosa	CSam EBee EWes GCal LEdu LPla MSpe MTis NBre NDov NPnk NSti WCot WOld XLum
– 'Henry Eilers'	CKno EBee ECtt ELan EPPr EPfP GBin GQue IBoy IKil IPot LBMP LEdu LRHS LSou MBel MCot MMHG MNrw MTis NPnk NSoo SGol SKHP SPoG SRms SWvt WCot
triloba 🏆^{H4}	CDes CMea CSpe EBee ELon EPfP EShb IBoy LRHS MBel MNrw NGdn NPnk SMad SPhx WCAu WMoo WPGP
– 'Prairie Glow'	CAby IPot LHop MNrw NPnk NSoo SGol SMrm SPhx WHil
'Vitamin C'	EBee

rue see *Ruta graveolens*

Ruellia (*Acanthaceae*)

amoena	see *R. brevifolia*
§ ***brevifolia***	ECre EShb
humilis	EBee EPPr EShb SPhx WHil
macrantha	CCCN EShb WHil
makoyana 🏆^{H1}	CSev EShb WHil
– white-flowered	WHil
strepens	EBee
tweediana	EShb WHil
– 'Katie'	WHil

Rulingia (*Sterculiaceae*)

hermanniifolia	ECou MOWG

Rumex (*Polygonaceae*)

acetosa	CArn CHab CHby CSev ELau GPoy MCoo MHer MHoo MMuc MNHC NBir SEND SIde SRms WHer WJek WSFF
– 'Abundance'	ELau LEdu
– subsp. ***acetosa*** 'Saucy' (v)	LEdu WCot
– 'De Belleville'	CPrp
– 'Profusion'	GPoy MHer
acetosella	CArn CHab NMir WSFF
alpinus	EBee LEdu SPhx WCot
crispus	ELau
flexuosus	CElw CSpe EPPr GCal LPot NLar WJek WOut
hydrolapathum	CArn CBAq CHab MMuc MSKA SEND SPlb WCot WSFF
patientia	CArn CHab ELau
sanguineus	CBAq CTri EShb LEdu MSKA NLBP NLar SRms XLum
– var. ***sanguineus***	CArn CElw CHby CRow CSev ELan GBin IFoB MHer MNHC NBro NPri WHer WJek
scutatus	CArn CHby CSev ELau GPoy MHoo MNHC SIde SPlb SRms WHer WHfH WJek
– 'Silver Shield'	CRow ELau LEdu MHer SRms WJek

Rumohra (*Dryopteridaceae*)

adiantiformis 🏆^{H1}	CCCN ISha LRHS SEND WFib WPGP
– RCB/Arg D-2	WCot

Ruschia (*Aizoaceae*)

tumidula **new**	SPlb

Ruscus ✿ (*Asparagaceae*)

aculeatus	CArn CBcs CDul CMac CTsd ELan EPfP GPoy IDee LEdu MGos MRav NLar SAPC SPlb SRms SWvt WBor WPGP WRHF
– hermaphrodite	EPfP GCal SEND SMad WPGP WPat WThu
– var. ***aculeatus*** 'Lanceolatus' (f)	GCal
– var. ***angustifolius*** PAB 254	LEdu
– 'Christmas Berry'	EPfP
– 'John Redmond'[PBR]	ELan ELon EPfP EShb EWes LHop LLHF LRHS LSqu MAsh MMuc NHol NLar NWad SCoo SKHP SLon SPer SPoG SSpi SWvt WBor WCot WPGP
* – 'Wheeler's Variety' (f/m)	CJun MRav WPGP
hypoglossum	MMuc SEND WPGP
racemosus	see *Danae racemosa*

Ruspolia (*Acanthaceae*)

hypocrateriformis	CCCN
seticalyx	EShb

Russelia (*Plantaginaceae*)

§ ***equisetiformis*** 🏆^{H1}	CAbb EShb MOWG
– 'Lemon Falls'	EShb MOWG
– 'Tangerine Falls' **new**	MOWG
juncea	see *R. equisetiformis*

Ruta (*Rutaceae*)

chalepensis	CArn XLum XSen
corsica	CArn XLum
graveolens	CArn CHab EPfP GPoy MHoo MNHC SIde WJek WSpi XLum
– 'Jackman's Blue'	CBcs CSev CTri EHoe ELan EPfP GMaP GPoy MGos MHer MRav MSwo NLar SRms SWvt WMnd WSpi XLum
– 'Variegata' (v)	MNHC NPer SRms

Ruttya (*Acanthaceae*)

fruticosa	CCCN
- 'Scholesii'	EShb
ovata new	WHil

× *Ruttyruspolia* (*Acanthaceae*)

lutea	CCCN
'Phyllis van Heerden'	CCCN

Rytidosperma (*Poaceae*)

* ***arundinaceum***	EShb

S

Sabal (*Arecaceae*)

§ ***bermudana***	EAmu
§ ***mexicana***	EAmu
minor	CHEx CPHo EAmu MREP SBig SPlb
palmetto	CDoC EAmu
princeps	see *S. bermudana*
texana	see *S. mexicana*

Saccharum (*Poaceae*)

arundinaceum	CKno
ravennae	EBee EPPr SMad SMrm SPlb WCot XLum

sage see *Salvia officinalis*

sage, annual clary see *Salvia viridis*

sage, biennial clary see *Salvia sclarea*

sage, pineapple see *Salvia elegans*

Sageretia (*Rhamnaceae*)

§ ***thea***	CMen
theezans	see *S. thea*

Sagina (*Caryophyllaceae*)

subulata	ECho EHoe LRHS SVic XLum
- var. ***glabrata*** new	MAsh
§ - - 'Aurea'	CMea CTri ECho ECtt EDAr GMaP SPoG

Sagittaria (*Alismataceae*)

australis new	EWay
'Bloomin' Babe'	CRow EWay
graminea	LLWG
- 'Crushed Ice' (v)	CRow EWay MWts
japonica	see *S. sagittifolia*
lancifolia new	EWay
latifolia	LLWG MWts NPer
§ ***sagittifolia***	CBAq CRow CWat EHon LLWG MSKA MWts WMAq XLum
- 'Flore Pleno' (d)	CBAq CWat EWay WMAq XLum
- var. ***leucopetala***	WMAq
* - - 'Flore Pleno' (d)	NLar NPer

Saintpaulia (*Gesneriaceae*)

'Aca's Pink Delight'	WDib
'Aca's Red Ember' (v)	WDib
'Allegro Appalachian Trail'	WDib
'Always Pink'	WDib
'Aly's Rosy Baby'	WDib
'Anouk'	WDib
'Arctic Frost' (d)	WDib
'Baby Brian'	WDib
'Baby's Breath'	WDib
'Beacon Trail'	WDib
'Beatrice Trail'	WDib
'Betty Stoehr'	WDib
'Blackie Bryant'	WDib
'Blue Dragon' (d)	WDib
'Blue Tail Fly'	WDib
'Blushing Trail'	WDib
'Bob Serbin' (d)	WDib
brevipilosa new	WDib
'Buffalo Hunt' (d)	WDib
'Candy Swirls'	WDib
'Cathedral'	WDib
'Chantaspring'	WDib
'Cherries 'n' Cream'	WDib
'Chiffon Fiesta'	WDib
'Chiffon Moonmoth'	WDib
'Chiffon Vesper'	WDib
'Coral Sparkle Trail'	WDib
'Crimson Ice'	WDib
'Cupid's Jewel'	WDib
'Deer Trail'	WDib
'Delft' (d)	WDib
'Desir'	WDib
'Dibley's Beate'	WDib
'Dibley's Kaarina' new	WDib
'Dibley's Lis'	WDib
'Dibley's Mercedes' new	WDib
'Electric Dreams'	WDib
'Emerald Love'	WDib
'Falling Raindrops'	WDib
'Favorite Child'	WDib
'Fire Mountain'	WDib
'Flashy Angel' (v)	WDib
'Flower Drum'	WDib
'Fun Trail'	WDib
'Genetic Blush'	WDib
'Gillian' (d)	WDib
'Golden Eye'	WDib
'Golden Glow' (d)	WDib
'Grandmother's Halo'	WDib
'Green Ice'	WDib
'Green Lace' (d)	WDib
'Halo's Aglitter'	WDib
'Happy Cricket'	WDib
'Indigo Ruffles'	WDib
ionantha	WDib
subsp. ***rupicola*** new	
'Irish Flirt' (d)	WDib
'Jolly Cutie Pie'	WDib
'King's Trail' (d)	WDib
'Kostina Fantaziya'	WDib
'Lemon Drop' (d)	WDib
'Lemon Whip' (d)	WDib
'Little Axel'	WDib
'Lollipop'	WDib
'Looking Glass'	WDib
'Louisiana Lagniappe'	WDib
'Louisiana Lullaby' (d)	WDib
'Love Spots'	WDib
'Lucky Lee Ann' (d)	WDib
'Luminescence'	WDib
'Lyon's Paprika'	WDib
'Lyon's Plum Pudding'	WDib
'Mac's Black Jack'	WDib
'Mac's Carnival Clown'	WDib

'Mac's Cheery Cherry'	WDib
'Mac's Circus Clown'	WDib
'Mac's Coral Cutie'	WDib
'Mac's Exquisite Extravaganza'	WDib
'Mac's Just Jeff' (d/v)	WDib
'Mac's Nocturne' (d)	WDib
'Mac's Strawberry Sundae'	WDib
'Mair'	WDib
'Ma's Corsage'	WDib
'Ma's Easter Parade'	WDib
'Ma's Lily Pad'	WDib
'Midget Lilian' (v)	WDib
'Midnight Flame' (d)	WDib
'Midnight Magic'	WDib
'Midnight Rascal' (d)	WDib
'Midnight Waltz' (d)	WDib
'Milky Way Trail'	WDib
'Minnie Mine'	WDib
'Minstrel's Mary Ruth'	WDib
'Motley Crew'	WDib
'Ness' Antique Red'	WDib
'Ness' Bangle Blue'	WDib
'Ness' Cherry Smoke'	WDib
'Ness' Crinkle Blue' (d)	WDib
'Ness' Dynomite'	WDib
'Ness' Midnight Fantasy'	WDib
'Ness' Satin Rose'	WDib
'Ness' Sheer Peach'	WDib
'Ness' Sno Fun'	WDib
'Ness' Viking Maiden'	WDib
'Newtown Ohio'	WDib
nitida	WDib
'Ode to Beauty'	WDib
'Okie Easter Bunny'	WDib
'Oksana'	WDib
'Optimara Little Seneca'	WDib
'Otoe' (d)	WDib
'Petite Blarney' **new**	WDib
'Pink Wink'	WDib
'Pirate's Treasure'	WDib
'Pixie Blue'	WDib
'Pixie Pink'	WDib
'Pixie Show-off'	WDib
'Powder Keg' (d)	WDib
'Powwow' (d/v)	WDib
'Purple Passion'	WDib
'Rain Man'	WDib
'Rainbow's Limelight' (d)	WDib
'Rainbow's Quiet Riot'	WDib
'Ramblin' Amethyst'	WDib
'Ramblin' Angel' (d)	WDib
'Ramblin' Dots'	WDib
'Ramblin' Lassie'	WDib
'Ramblin' Magic' (d)	WDib
'Ramblin' Sunshine'	WDib
'Rare Tapestry'	WDib
'Raspberry Crisp'	WDib
'Red Lantern' (d)	WDib
'Red Summit'	WDib
'Rhapsodie Clementine'	WDib
'Rhapsodie Rosalie'	WDib
'Robert Mayer'	WDib
'Rob's Bamboozle' (d)	WDib
'Rob's Blue Cat'	WDib
'Rob's Blue Socks'	WDib
'Rob's Boo Hoo'	WDib
'Rob's Chilly Willy' (d/v)	WDib
'Rob's Cloudy Skies' (d)	WDib
'Rob's Dandy Lion' (d/v)	WDib
'Rob's Denim Demon' (d/v)	WDib
'Rob's Dust Storm' (d)	WDib
'Rob's Gundaroo' (d)	WDib
'Rob's Hallucination'	WDib
'Rob's Heebie Jeebie'	WDib
'Rob's Hopscotch' (d)	WDib
'Rob's Hot Tamale'	WDib
'Rob's Ice Ripples' (d)	WDib
'Rob's Jitterbug'	WDib
'Rob's June Bug' (d/v)	WDib
'Rob's Love Bite' (d)	WDib
'Rob's Peedletuck'	WDib
'Rob's Pink Buttercups' (v)	WDib
'Rob's Rinky Dink' (d)	WDib
'Rob's Ruff Stuff'	WDib
'Rob's Sarsparilla' (d)	WDib
'Rob's Scarecrow'	WDib
'Rob's Scrumptious'	WDib
'Rob's Seduction' (d/v)	WDib
'Rob's Shadow Magic' (d/v)	WDib
'Rob's Smarty Pants' (d)	WDib
'Rob's Sticky Wicket' (d)	WDib
'Rob's Toorooka' (d)	WDib
'Rob's Twinkle Blue' (d)	WDib
'Rob's Vanilla Trail' (d)	WDib
'Rob's Wooloomooloo' (d)	WDib
'Roll Along Blue' (d)	WDib
'Santa Anita'	WDib
shumensis	WDib
'Silly Girl'	WDib
'Sky Bells' (v)	WDib
'Snow Leopard'	WDib
'Sweet Amy Sue' (d)	WDib
'Taffeta Blue' (d)	WDib
'Taffeta Petticoats'	WDib
'Teen Thunder'	WDib
'The Madam'	WDib
'Tula'	WDib
'Twist 'n' Shout'	WDib
'Warm Sunshine'	WDib
'Whirligig Star'	WDib
'Wisteria' (d)	WDib
'Witch Doctor' (d)	WDib
'Yesterday's Child'	WDib

Salicornia (*Amaranthaceae*)

europaea	SVic

Salix ✿ (*Salicaceae*)

acutifolia 'Blue Streak' (m) Y^{H4}	CEnd CWiW EPfP EWes MBlu NBir NLar SWat WMou
- 'Pendulifolia' (m)	SGol
'Aegma Brno' (f)	WMou
aegyptiaca	EBtc MBlu NWea WMou
alba	CCVT CDul CHab CLnd CWiW LBuc NWea SEWo SGol WJPR WMou
- f. ***argentea***	see *S. alba* var. *sericea*
- 'Aurea'	CTho WIvy WMou
- var. ***caerulea***	CDul CLnd NWea WMou
- - 'Wantage Hall' (f)	CWiW
- 'Cardinalis' (f)	CWiW SWat
- 'Chermesina'	see *S. alba* var. *vitellina* 'Britzensis'
- 'Dart's Snake'	ELan EPfP MAsh MBrN MRav NLar WCot
- 'Golden Ness'	LRHS MAsh MBlu SPoG
- 'Hutchinson's Yellow'	CTho ECrN NLar
- 'Liempde' (m)	NWea

	- 'Raesfeld' (m)	CWiW
§	- var. ***sericea*** ♀H4	CBcs CDul CLnd CTho EPfP MBlu MRav MWat NLar NWea SPer WCot WMou
	- 'Splendens'	see *S. alba* var. *sericea*
	- 'Tristis' misapplied	see *S.* × *sepulcralis* var. *chrysocoma*
§	- 'Tristis' ambig.	CLnd CTri ELan IBoy MBri MGos MRav MSwo NLar NWea SEND SEWo SWat WHar
	- 'Tristis' Gaudin	MMuc
	- var. ***vitellina*** ♀H4	CDul CTri EPfP GQue LBuc MBNS MBrN NLar NWea SGol SLon SWat
§	- - 'Britzensis' (m) ♀H4	Widely available
	- - 'Nova'	SWat
§	- - 'Yelverton'	EPfP GQue MAsh SPoG SWat
	- 'Vitellina Pendula'	see *S. alba* 'Tristis' ambig.
	- 'Vitellina Tristis'	see *S. alba* 'Tristis' ambig.
§	***alpina***	ECho NHar
	'Americana'	CWiW
	amplexicaulis 'Pescara' (m)	CWiW
	amygdaloides	CWiW
	'Aokautere'	see *S.* × *sepulcralis* 'Aokautere'
§	***arbuscula***	ECho NLar
	arenaria	see *S. repens* var. *argentea*
	aurita	NLar NWea
	babylonica	CDul CEnd WMou
	- 'Annularis'	see *S. babylonica* 'Crispa'
	- 'Bijdorp'	NLar
§	- 'Crispa'	ELan LHop LRHS MTPN MWts SMad SPoG
	- 'Pan Chih-kang'	CWiW NLar
	- var. ***pekinensis*** 'Pendula'	IArd
§	- - 'Tortuosa' ♀H4	CDul CLnd CSBt CWib ECrN ELan EPfP IBoy IVic LRHS MGos MMuc MWat NBir NPer NWea SEND SGol SLon SPer SPlb SPoG SRms SWat WGwG WHar
*	- 'Tortuosa Aurea'	IBoy SGol SWvt
	× ***balfourii***	SDix
	bicolor	NWea
	'Blackskin' (f)	CWiW
	bockii	EBee EBtc ELan LLHF LRHS MMuc SDys SKHP SPhx
§	'Bowles's Hybrid'	CMam WMou
	'Boydii' (f) ♀H4	ECho EPfP GAbr GBin ITim LEdu LRHS MGos NBir NRya NSla WAbe WPat WThu WWFP
§	'Boyd's Pendulous' (m)	CWib
	caesia	WIvy
	candida	CMam
	caprea	CBcs CCVT CDul CHab CLnd CTri EPfP LBuc NWea SEWo SPer WMou WSFF
	- 'Black Stem'	CDul
§	- 'Kilmarnock' (m)	Widely available
	- 'Mas' (m) new	CNWT
	- var. ***pendula*** (m)	see *S. caprea* 'Kilmarnock' (m)
	capusii	WPGP
*	***caspica rubra nana***	SWat
	'Chrysocoma'	see *S.* × *sepulcralis* var. *chrysocoma*
	cinerea	CBcs CTri LBuc NWea SEWo WJPR WMou
	- 'Tricolor' (v)	NPro
	cordata	SLPl
	daphnoides	CCVT CDul CLnd CMac EBee EPPr EPfP LRHS MGos MMuc MSwo NWea SEND SGol SPer SRms SWat WMou WSFF
	- 'Aglaia' (m)	CBcs CDul GQue WIvy
	- 'Meikle' (f)	CWiW SWat
	- 'Netta Statham' (m)	CWiW
	- 'Ovaro Udine' (m)	CWiW
	- 'Oxford Violet' (m)	NWea WIvy
	- 'Sinker'	WIvy
	- 'Stewartstown'	CWiW
	× ***dasyclados*** 'Grandis'	NWea
§	× ***doniana*** 'Kumeti'	CWiW
	'E.A. Bowles'	see *S.* 'Bowles's Hybrid'
	× ***ehrhartiana***	CNat
§	***elaeagnos***	CCVT CTho CTri ECrN EPfP MBrN MMuc NWea SLon SPer SWat WMou
§	- subsp. ***angustifolia*** ♀H4	CBcs CDul ELan EPfP MMuc MRav MSwo NLar NPCo NWea SEND SRms WIvy
	'Elegantissima'	see *S.* × *pendulina* var. *elegantissima*
	eriocephala 'American Mackay' (m)	CWiW
	- 'Kerksii' (m)	CWiW
	- 'Mawdesley' (m)	CWiW
	- 'Russelliana' (f)	CWiW
§	'Erythroflexuosa'	CBcs CDoC CDul CEnd ELan EPPr EPfP LAst LBMP LHop MGos MMuc MRav NWea SGol SPer SPoG SWat WCFE WHer
	exigua	CBcs CDul CLnd CTho EBee ELan EPfP EWes LAst LBuc MBlu MBrN MGos MLHP MMuc MSwo NBir NLar NWea SCoo SLPl SMad SPer WMou WPGP WPat
	fargesii	CAbP CDoC CDul CEnd CExl CFil CMac EBee ELan EPfP EUJe GBin GCal IDee LEdu LHop LRHS MBlu MGos MRav NBid NEgg NPCo SBrt SKHP SMad SSpi WCot WCru WPat
	fargesii × ***magnifica***	CFil
§	× ***finnmarchica***	WAbe
	formosa	see *S. arbuscula*
	fragilis	CCVT CDul CHab CLnd MRav NWea WMou
§	- var. ***furcata***	CTri GKev
	- 'Legomey'	WIvy
	× ***fruticosa*** 'McElroy' (f)	CWiW
	fruticulosa	see *S. fragilis* var. *furcata*
	'Fuiri-koriyanagi'	see *S. integra* 'Hakuro-nishiki'
	furcata	see *S. fragilis* var. *furcata*
	glauca	CNat
	'Golden Curls'	see *S.* 'Erythroflexuosa'
	gracilistyla	CTho NWea SCoo SLPl WMou
§	- 'Melanostachys' (m)	CDul CTho EBee ECrN ELan EPfP EWTr GAbr LHop LRHS MAsh MBNS MBlu MBrN MGos MMuc MRav NBir NEgg NLar NSoo NWea SBrt SGol SRms SWat WBor
	× ***greyi***	NPro
	hastata (f)	SWat
	- 'Wehrhahnii' (m) ♀H4	CBcs CDul EBee ECho ELan EPfP GCra IVic LEdu MBlu MJak MMuc MRav MSwo NBir NLar NWea SPer SWat
	helvetica ♀H4	CBcs CDul CMac EBee ECho ELan EPfP GAbr IVic MBlu MMuc MRav NBir NEgg NHol NLar NWea SEND SPer
	herbacea	ECho WAbe

hibernica	see *S. phylicifolia*
hookeriana	CDul CExl CFil ELan MBlu MBrN MBri NLar SLPl SSpi WCFE WIvy WMou
incana	see *S. elaeagnos*
integra 'Albomaculata'	see *S. integra* 'Hakuro-nishiki'
- 'Flamingo'PBR	CBcs ELan SPoG
§ - 'Hakuro-nishiki' (v)	Widely available
- 'Pendula' (f)	CEnd MAsh MBri
irrorata	CDul CLnd EBee EPfP LRHS MBlu MSwo NLar SWat
'Jacquinii'	see *S. alpina*
kinuyanagi (m)	LHop WIvy
§ ***koriyanagi***	CWiW
'Kumeti'	see *S.* × *doniana* 'Kumeti'
'Kuro-me'	see *S. gracilistyla* 'Melanostachys'
lanata ♀H4	CBcs CMac CMea EBee ECho ELan ELon EPfP EWTr GAbr GKev MAsh MGos MJak MRav NBir NEgg NLar NWea SBrt SPer SWat
lapponum	LEdu NLar NWea SRms
- compact	GKev
magnifica ♀H4	CDul CEnd CExl CFil CGHE CLnd EBee ELan EPfP EWTr IArd IDee LEdu LRHS MSnd NWea SKHP SSpi SWat WMou WPGP
'Mark Postill' (f)	CDoC EBee ELon LRHS MBNS MMuc NLar
matsudana 'Tortuosa'	see *S. babylonica* var. *pekinensis* 'Tortuosa'
- 'Tortuosa Aureopendula'	see *S.* 'Erythroflexuosa'
'Melanostachys'	see *S. gracilistyla* 'Melanostachys'
× ***meyeriana***	WIvy
- 'Lumley' (f)	CWiW
miyabeana	CMam
× ***mollissima*** var. ***hippophaifolia*** 'Jefferies' (m)	CWiW
- - 'Notts Spaniard' (m)	CWiW
- - 'Trustworthy' (m)	CWiW
- 'Q83'	CMam
- var. ***undulata*** 'Kottenheider Weide' (f)	CWiW
moupinensis	EPfP
aff. ***moupinensis*** from Vietnam	CFil
§ ***myrsinifolia***	EBee ELan LHop MBlu MMuc NLar WGrn
- 'Black Knight' new	EPfP
myrsinites var. ***jacquiniana***	see *S. alpina*
myrtilloides 'Pink Tassels' (m)	ECho NLar SBrt
myrtilloides × ***repens***	see *S.* × *finnmarchica*
nakamurana var. ***yezoalpina***	EBee ELan EPot EWes GKev GQui IVic LRHS MBlu MMuc MRav NHar NLar WPat
nigricans	see *S. myrsinifolia*
nivalis	see *S. reticulata* subsp. *nivalis*
§ × ***pendulina*** var. ***elegantissima***	SWat
pentandra	CDul CLnd NWea WJPR WMou
- 'Patent Lumley'	CWiW
§ ***phylicifolia***	NWea WJPR WMou
- 'Malham' (m)	CWiW
§ ***purpurea***	CCVT CDul NWea WJPR WMou
- 'Brittany Green' (f)	CWiW
- 'Continental Reeks'	CWiW
- 'Dark Dicks' (f)	CWiW NLar WSFF

- 'Dicky Meadows' (m)	CWiW
- 'Goldstones'	CWiW NLar
- f. ***gracilis***	see *S. purpurea* 'Nana'
- 'Green Dicks'	CWiW
- 'Helix'	see *S. purpurea*
- 'Howki' (m)	WMou
- 'Irette' (m)	CWiW
- 'Jagiellonka' (f)	CWiW
- var. ***japonica***	see *S. koriyanagi*
- subsp. ***lambertiana***	CWiW
- 'Lancashire Dicks' (m)	CWiW
- 'Leicestershire Dicks' (m)	CWiW
- 'Light Dicks'	CWiW
- 'Lincolnshire Dutch' (f)	CWiW
§ - 'Nana'	EPfP MMuc NLar NWea SLPl SLon WCot
- 'Nancy Saunders' (f)	CTho CWiW EHoe GBin MBNS MBlu MBrN MRav NBir NLar NPro NSti WCot WIvy
- 'Pendula' ♀H4	CCVT CEnd ECrN MAsh MBri MGos MSwo NPri NWea
- 'Read' (f)	CWiW
- 'Reeks' (f)	CWiW
- 'Richartii' (f)	CWiW
- 'Uralensis' (f)	CWiW
pyrenaica	EWes
pyrenaica × ***retusa***	ECho
pyrifolia	NWea
repens	NLar NWea SRms SWat
§ - var. ***argentea***	CDul ELan EPfP EWes LRHS MMuc MRav NWea SPer
- 'Armando'PBR	NLar
- 'Iona' (m)	NLar
- ***pendula***	see *S.* 'Boyd's Pendulous' (m)
- 'Voorthuizen' (f)	ECho
reticulata ♀H4	ECho EPot NBir NSla WAbe
§ - subsp. ***nivalis***	EPot
retusa	CTri NBir
rosmarinifolia misapplied	see *S. elaeagnos* subsp. *angustifolia*
rosmarinifolia L. new	NLar
× ***rubens*** 'Basfordiana' (m)	CDul CLnd CTho CWiW MBNS SWat WMou
- 'Bouton Aigu'	CWiW
- 'Farndon'	CWiW
- 'Flanders Red' (f)	CWiW
- 'Fransgeel Rood' (m)	CWiW
- 'Glaucescens' (m)	CWiW
- 'Golden Willow'	CWiW
- 'Jaune de Falaise'	CWiW
- 'Jaune Hâtive'	CWiW
- 'Laurina'	CWiW
- 'Natural Red' (f)	CWiW
- 'Parsons'	CWiW
- 'Rouge Ardennais'	CWiW
- 'Rouge Folle'	CWiW
- 'Russet' (f)	CWiW
× ***rubra***	CWiW
- 'Abbey's Harrison' (f)	CWiW
- 'Continental Osier' (f)	CWiW
- 'Eugenei' (m)	CDul GQui MBlu SWat
- 'Fidkin' (f)	CWiW
- 'Harrison's' (f)	CWiW
- 'Harrison's Seedling A' (f)	CWiW
- 'Mawdesley'	CWiW
- 'Mawdesley Seedling A' (f)	CWiW
- 'Pyramidalis'	CWiW
Scarlet Curls = 'Scarcuzam'	WPat
schwerinii × ***viminalis***	CMam
× ***sepulcralis***	NWea

§	– 'Aokautere'	CWiW
	– 'Caradoc'	CWiW
§	– var. ***chrysocoma***	CBcs CDoC CDul CMac CSBt CWib EBee ECrN EPfP EWTr LAst LBuc LSRN MAsh MBlu MGos MJak MWat NEgg NLar NPCo NPri NWea SCoo SEWo SGol SLim SPer SPoG SWat
	serpyllifolia	CTri NHar WThu
	– 'Chamonix'	NSla
	serpyllum	see *S. fragilis* var. *furcata*
	'Setsuka'	see *S. udensis* 'Sekka'
	sitchensis	NWea
	× ***smithiana***	CLnd NWea
	× ***stipularis*** (f)	NWea
	subopposita	EBee EBtc ELan MMuc WAbe
	triandra	CDul WMou
	– 'Black German' (m)	CWiW
	– 'Black Hollander' (m)	CWiW NLar
	– 'Black Maul'	CWiW GQue
	– 'Grisette de Falaise'	CWiW
	– 'Grisette Droda' (f)	CWiW
	– 'Long Bud'	CWiW
	– 'Noir de Challans'	CWiW
	– 'Noir de Touraine'	CWiW
	– 'Noir de Villaines' (m)	CWiW
	– 'Rouge d'Orléans'	EBtc
	– 'Sarda d'Anjou'	CWiW
	– 'Semperflorens' (m)	NLar
	– 'Whissander'	CWiW
	× ***tsugaluensis*** 'Ginme' (f)	SLPl
	udensis	NWea
§	– 'Sekka' (m)	ELan EPfP MBlu MMuc NBir NWea SWat WIvy WMou
	uva-ursi	WAbe
	viminalis	CCVT CLnd CMac CMam EPfP LBuc NWea SEWo SVic WJPR WMou WSFF
	– 'Gigantea' (m)	CMam
	– 'Green Gotz'	CWiW
	vitellina 'Pendula'	see *S. alba* 'Tristis' ambig.
	'Yelverton'	see *S. alba* var. *vitellina* 'Yelverton'

Salsola (*Amaranthaceae*)

	soda	CArn ELau

Salvia ✿ (*Lamiaceae*)

	sp.	CHab
	ACE 2172	SPin
	CD&R 1162	CAby EPyc SPhx
	CD&R 1458	SPin
	CD&R 1495	SPin
	CD&R 3071	SPin
	PC&H 226	SPin
	from Catamarca, Argentina	EPyc SDys
	acerifolia new	SPin
	acetabulosa	see *S. multicaulis*
	adenophora	EPyc SDys SPin XSen
	aerea	CPom
	aethiopis	EWes SPav SPin XSen
I	'African Sky' new	SDys SPin
§	***africana***	CSpe SPin WHil XSen
	africana-caerulea	see *S. africana*
	africana-lutea	see *S. aurea*
	agnes	EPyc SPin
	algeriensis	EPyc SBch
	'Allen Chickering'	XSen
	amarissima	EPyc SPin XSen
	'Amber'	LHop SBrt SPin XSen
	ambigens	see *S. guaranitica* 'Blue Enigma'
	'Amistad'	LRHS NPri SDys STPC WHlf WWlt
	ampelophylla	SDys
	– B&SWJ 10751	SPin
§	***amplexicaulis***	EPyc NLar SMrm SPin SRms WHrl XSen
	amplifrons	EPyc SPin
	angustifolia Cav.	see *S. reptans*
	angustifolia Mich.	see *S. azurea*
	'Anna'	SDys
	'Anthony Parker'	WOut XSen
	'Anthony Waterer'	EWld
	apiana	CArn CHel EOHP EPyc MHer MOWG SPin SPlb SRms SVen WHfH XSen
	arenaria	SPin
	argentea 🏆H3	CBcs CHel CSpe EBee ELan EPfP GKev GMaP LHop LPio LRHS MSpe NSoo SMrm SPer SPin SRkn SWat WCAu WJek WKif WWEG XLum XSen
	– 'Artemis'	EBee
	arizonica	EPyc EWld GCal LHop LPio LPla MAsh SDys SPin XSen
	aspera	SPin XSen
	atrocyanea	CAby CSam CSpe ECre EPyc EWes EWld LPio MAsh SBHP SDys SPin WHal WKif WWlt XSen
	aucheri	SPin
§	***aurea***	CHll CSev CSpe ELan MOWG SPin SPlb SVen XLum XSen
	– 'Kirstenbosch'	CAby CSev ECtt EPyc EWld MRav SDys SPin WKif XSen
	aurita	EPyc SPin
	– var. ***galpinii***	SPin XSen
	austriaca	SPin XSen
§	***azurea***	EPyc LPio LRHS SMrm SPhx SPin XSen
	– var. ***grandiflora***	SPin WCot
	bacheriana	see *S. buchananii*
§	***barrelieri***	ESwi SPin WHil XSen
	'Bee's Bliss'	XSen
	'Belhaven'	GCal LPio SPin
	bertolonii	see *S. pratensis* Bertolonii Group
	bicolor	see *S. barrelieri*
	'Black Knight'	CSpe CWGN EPyc LPio SDys SPin WPGP
	blancoana	see *S. lavandulifolia* subsp. *blancoana*
	blepharophylla	CAby CMea CPrp ECtt EPyc EUJe LHop LPio MCot MHer MSCN SPin SRkn XSen
	– 'Diablo'	ECtt SPin
	– 'Painted Lady'	CSpe CWGN ECtt MAsh SDys SPin WWlt
	'Blue Chiquita'	SPin
	'Blue Sky'	EWld
	bracteata	XSen
	brandegeei	SPin
	broussonetii	SPin XSen
§	***buchananii*** 🏆H1+3	CHel CSam ECtt EPyc LHop LPio MAsh MCot MHer MHoo MRav SDys SPin SRkn XSen
	bulleyana misapplied	see *S. flava* var. *megalantha*
	bulleyana Diels	CExl EWes EWld MHoo WCru XSen
	– 'Blue Lips'	MBri
	bullulata	SPin
	cacaliifolia 🏆H1+3	CExl CRHN ECtt EPyc EWld GCal LPio MAsh MHer MSCN SDys SPer SPin SRkn WWlt XSen

	cadmica	SPin WHil
	caerulea misapplied	see *S. guaranitica* 'Black and Blue'
	caerulea L.	see *S. africana*
	caespitosa	SPin XSen
	campanulata	CPom EWld SPin
	- B&SWJ 9232	WCru
	- DJHC C394	SPin
	- GWJ 9294	SPin WCru
	- aff. var. ***hirtella*** GWJ 9397	WCru
	canariensis	IDee SPin WOut XSen
	- f. ***albiflora***	SVen XSen
	- f. ***candidissima***	SPin XSen
	candelabrum ♀H3-4	CAbP CSpe ECre EWes GCal LPio MHer SBch SPav SPhx SPin SVen WCot WKif WPnn WWlt XSen
	candidissima	SPin XSen
	canescens	XSen
	cardinalis	see *S. fulgens*
	cardiophylla	SPin
	carnea	EWld SPin
	- from Valle de Bravo, Mexico	EPyc SDys
	- var. ***carnea*** new	SDys
	castanea	CDes EWld LRHS SPin
	caudata	SPin XSen
	caymanensis new	SPin
§	***chamaedryoides***	CFil CSev EPyc MHom SBrt SPet SPhx SPin XLum XSen
	- var. ***isochroma***	EPyc MAsh SDys SPin WPGP XSen
	- 'Marine Blue'	MAsh MCot
	- silver-leaved	CAby CSpe SPin XLum
	aff. ***chamaedryoides*** B&SWJ 9032 from Guatemala	SPin
	chamelaeagnea	EPyc GFai MCot SDys SPin XSen
	chapalensis	SPin
	chiapensis	EPyc MAsh SDys SPin WWlt XSen
	chinensis	see *S. japonica*
	chionophylla	SPin
	'Christine Yeo'	CAby CElw CSev EBee ECtt ELon EPfP EPri EPyc MAsh SBch SDys SEND SPin WHil WHoo WMnd WPGP WSHC XSen
	cinnabarina	SPin
	cleistogama misapplied	see *S. glutinosa*
	clevelandii	EWes MHer SPav SPin WJek XSen
	- 'Winnifred Gilman'	SDys
	clinopodioides	CDes EBee SDys SPin
	'Clotted Cream'	EWld
	coahuilensis misapplied	see *S. greggii* × *serpyllifolia*
	coahuilensis ambig.	CAby EPyc LSou MAsh SKHP SLon SMrm SPin SPoG SRkn WSHC XLum
	coahuilensis Fernald	LHop
	coccinea	SPin
	- 'Brenthurst'	SPin WHlf
	- 'Forest Fire'	EPyc
	- (Nymph Series) 'Coral Nymph'	EPyc LDai SPav SPin
	- - 'Lady in Red' ♀H3	SPav
*	- - 'Snow Nymph'	EPyc
	columbariae	CArn
	concolor misapplied	see *S. guaranitica*
	concolor Lamb. ex Benth.	EPyc EWld GCal GGal MHom SDys SPin WSHC XSen
	confertiflora	CCon CDes CExl CHEx CHel CSam CSpe CWCL ECre ECtt ELan EPyc EShb GCal LPio MAsh MHer MHom MSCN SDys SPin SPlb SRkn SVen WKif WOth WPGP WWlt XSen
	corrugata	CBcs CCon CDes CElw EBee ECtt EPyc EWld GBin GCal LPio LRHS MAsh MHer SDys SPhx SPin SRkn WPGP WWlt XSen
	'Crème Caramel'	CWGN ECtt EPyc MAsh MHom SDys WWlt
	cruickshanksii	SPin
	cryptantha	XSen
	aff. ***curtiflora*** B&SWJ 10356	WCru
	curviflora	CSpe EPyc MAsh SBch SDys SPin WOth XSen
	- 'Tubular Bells' new	WHlf
	cyanescens	CMea CPBP EPot EPyc SBch SPhx SPin XSen
	cyanicalyx	EPyc SDys SPin XSen
	cyclostegia	CExl
	daghestanica	GKev SPin XSen
	'Dancing Dolls' new	CWGN
I	***dangitalis*** SDR 4332	CExl
	darcyi misapplied	see *S. roemeriana*
	darcyi J. Compton	CAby CExl CHll CSpe EPyc EWes EWld MCot SDys SPin WOth WSHC WWlt XLum XSen
	davidsonii	SPin
	dentata	SPin
	desoleana	SPin WHil WOut XSen
	dichlamys new	SPin
	'Didi'	NDov
	digitaloides	GBin XSen
	- BWJ 7777	SPin WCru
	'Dinah'	WWlt
	discolor ♀H1	CHel CHll CSev CSpe ECtt ELan EPyc EWld GCal LDai MAsh MBel MCot MHer SDys SEND SPet SPin WWlt XSen
*	- ***nigra***	CArn CCse
	disermas	SPin SPlb XSen
	- pink-flowered	SPin
	disjuncta	CElw SPin XSen
	- 'Chimbango'	SPin
	divinorum	CArn EOHP GPoy LEdu XSen
	dolichantha	CCVN CCon CTsd EPyc LRHS MCot MMuc NBir NLar SPin WHer WMoo XSen
	dolomitica	SPav SPin
	dombeyi	CAby CSam EPyc SDys SPin
	dominica	CArn SPin XSen
	dorisiana	MAsh SDys SPin SVen XSen
	'Dorset Wonder'	NDov
	durifolia	SPin
	'Dyson's Crimson'	CAby MCot SDys
	'Dyson's Joy' new	SDys
	eigii	SHar SPin XSen
	eizi-matudae	EPyc SDys SPin
	elegans	ELau EWes GCal GCra MHom MHoo WOth XSen
	- 'Golden Delicious'	ECtt EWes LHop MHer SPin SRms WOut
	- 'Honey Melon'	CAby EPyc MAsh SDys
§	- 'Scarlet Pineapple'	CAby CArn CExl COlW CPrp CSev ECtt ELan ELau EPfP EShb EWTr GPoy MCot MHer MNHC SDys SPad SPin SRms SVen WJek WWlt XSen
	- 'Sonoran Red'	SDys
	- 'Tangerine'	CArn CPrp ELau EPyc LSou MHer MHoo MNHC NLBP SPin SRms WJek

	'Endless Love'	EBee LSou MBri NDov
	eremostachya	XSen
	euphratica	XSen
	evansiana	SPin XSen
	'Eveline'	CHel CSev CWGN EBee ECtt EPfP GBin LBMP LRHS MBri MCot MTis NLar SPoG STPC
	excelsa	SPin XSen
	fallax	see *S. roscida*
	farinacea	EPfP SPin
	- 'Victoria' ♀H3	LRHS
	firma **new**	SPin
§	***flava*** var. ***megalantha***	CFis CHel LSRN SPin WOut XSen
	- - BWJ 7974	WCru
	florida	SPin XSen
	forreri	EBee EPyc MAsh NDov SBHP SPin WPGP XSen
	- 'Karen Dyson'	SDys
§	***forsskaolii***	CArn CCon CElw CExl CHel CSam CSev CSpe ECtt ELan LLWP LRHS MNrw MRav NLBP NLar NSti SEND SPav SPin WCot WGwG WKif WMnd WMoo WPtf XLum XSen
	- white-flowered	SPin XSen
§	***fruticosa***	CArn ELau EPyc LRHS SLon SPin SRms XSen
§	***fulgens*** ♀H3	EPyc EWld GCal MAsh SBHP SDys SPin SRkn WWlt XSen
	- from Mt Popocatepetl, Mexico	SDys
	gesneriiflora	ECtt EPyc EWld SDys SPin WOth WPGP XSen
	- mountain form	SDys WPGP
	- 'Tequila'	SPin WOut WWlt
	gilliesii	SPin
	glabrescens	SPin
	- B&SWJ 11152	WCru
*	- var. ***robusta***	LHop
	- - B&SWJ 11147	WCru
	glechomifolia	EPyc SPin XSen
§	***glutinosa***	CArn CMac CSpe EBee EPyc EWld GCal IMou LDai LRHS MCot MNrw NBro NLar SPav SPin WCAu WCot XLum XSen
	graciliramulosa	SPin XSen
	gracilis	SPin
	grahamii	see *S. microphylla* var. *microphylla*
	gravida	SPin
	'Great Comp'	SDys
	greggii	ECtt EPfP EPyc EWes LRHS MHer XLum XSen
	- CD&R 1148	MCot SDys
	- 'Alba'	CAby LPio SPin XLum XSen
	- 'Blush Pink'	see *S. microphylla* 'Pink Blush'
	- 'Caramba' (v)	CHel ESwi LHop LRHS SPet
	- 'Devon Cream'	see *S. greggii* 'Sungold'
	- 'Diane'	WHil
	- 'Flame' **new**	CWGN
	- 'Icing Sugar'PBR	CCVN CHel CWGN ECtt ELan EPyc LHop LPio LRHS MAsh MCot NDov NPri SDys SPet SPoG SRkn WBor WSHC WWFP
	- 'Lara'	WHlf WWlt
	- 'Lipstick'	CExl ECtt MAsh
	- 'Magnet'	SPin
	- (Navajo Series) 'Navajo Bright Red'	EPyc
*	- - 'Navajo Cream'	EPyc
*	- - 'Navajo Dark Purple'	EPyc

	- - Navajo Pink = 'Rfds019'	SVen
*	- - 'Navajo Purple'	EPyc
	- - Navajo Salmon Red = 'Rfds016'	EPyc
*	- - 'Navajo White'	EPyc
	- 'Peach' misapplied	see *S.* × *jamensis* 'Pat Vlasto'
	- 'Peach'	CAby CWGN ELau EPfP EPyc MAsh MHer SEND SPet SPoG WPGP WWlt XLum XSen
	- 'Pink Preference'	MAsh SDys
	- 'Purple Pastel' **new**	CWGN
	- 'Raspberry Red'	XLum
	- 'Sierra San Antonio'	see *S.* × *jamensis* 'Sierra San Antonio'
	- 'Sparkler' (v)	ELan EPfP LRHS MAsh SLon SPoG
	- 'Stormy Pink'	CDes CHll CPrp CSam CSpe EPyc LRHS MAsh MCot NDov SPoG WIvy WPGP WSHC WWlt XSen
§	- 'Sungold'	CWGN ECtt EPfP EPyc LRHS MAsh MHoo NDov SDys SPin WWlt XSen
	- variegated (v)	XSen
	- yellow-flowered	CAby XLum
	greggii* × *lycioides	see *S. greggii* × *serpyllifolia*
§	***greggii* × *serpyllifolia***	CAbP CAby CSpe EPyc MAsh MCot MHoo NDov NPri SDys SPin SVen
	grewiifolia	SPin
	guadalujarensis	SPin
§	***guaranitica***	CBcs CHEx ECtt EShb EWld LRHS MHer SPin WKif WPGP WWlt XLum XSen
	- 'Argentina Skies'	CAby CHGN CSpe EPPr EPyc SDys SMrm SPin WWlt XSen
§	- 'Black and Blue'	CCon CExl CRHN CWCL CWGN EBee ECre ECtt EPfP EPyc GCal GGal LHop LPio LRHS LSRN MBri MSpe SDys SMad SMrm SPin SVen WPGP WSHC XSen
§	- 'Blue Enigma' ♀H3-4	CAby CArn CExl CSev CSpe CWGN EBee ECtt ELan EPfP EShb GCal LHop LPio LRHS MAsh MGos MRav MSpe SDix SDys SMrm SPhx SPin WWlt XLum XSen
	- 'Brazil'	LRHS
	- 'Costa Rica Blue'	EPyc SDys
	- 'Indigo Blue'	ECtt EPfP MAsh SPin WWlt
	- 'Omaha' **new**	SPin
	- 'Omaha Gold' (v) **new**	EPyc
	- 'Purple Emperor'	LHop
	- 'Purple Splendor'	EShb MHer
	- purple-flowered	CSam SDys
	haematodes	see *S. pratensis* Haematodes Group
	haenkei	CElw SPin XSen
	- 'Prawn Chorus'	CSpe CWGN LRHS MAsh WWlt
	hayatae **new**	SPin
	heerii	SPin
	heldreichiana	SPin XSen
	henryi	SPin
	hians	CPom EWld GCal GCra NLar SRms XLum
	- CC 1787	CExl
	hierosolymitana	CHid LRHS XSen
	hirtella	SPin
	hispanica misapplied	see *S. lavandulifolia*
	hispanica L.	CSam SPin
	holwayi	EPyc SPin XSen
	horminum	see *S. viridis* var. *comata*
	huberi	XSen
	hydrangea	SPin
	hypargeia	XSen

	'Ice Blue'	MHom
	inconspicua	SPin
	indica	XSen
	'Indigo Spires'	CAby CExl CHel CHll CSam CSpe CWGN ECre ECtt EPfP EPyc EShb EUJe EWld LPio MAsh MCot NDov SDys SMrm SPhx SPin WOth WSHC WWlt XLum XSen
	interrupta	EWld MCot MHer SPin XSen
	involucrata ♀H3	CCon CSev EPyc EWld GCra LPio MCot MHom NBro SDys SPin SVen WSHC XSen
	- 'Bethellii' ♀H3-4	CArn CCon CHel CMHG ECtt ELan EPfP EPyc LRHS MAsh MHer SDix SDys SKHP SMrm SPin SRkn WGrn WKif WWlt XLum XSen
	- 'Boutin' ♀H3	EPyc LPio MAsh MHom SDys WWlt
§	- 'Hadspen'	CCon CDes CHll CRHN CSam CSpe EPyc EWes GCal SBch SPin XLum XSen
	- 'Joan'	CWGN EPyc MAsh SBch SDys SPet SPin WSHC WWlt
	- 'Mrs Pope'	see *S. involucrata* 'Hadspen'
	- 'Pink Icicles'	SDys
*	- var. ***puberula***	MHom SPin XSen
	iodantha	SDys SPin
	- 'Louis Saso'	SPin
	iodochroa B&SWJ 10252	SPin WCru
	× ***jamensis***	ELau EWes MAsh SPin
	- 'Blue Amor' **new**	MPkF
	- 'California Sunset'	EWld MAsh SDys
	- 'Cherry Queen'	CWGN EPyc MAsh SPin SPoG WWlt XSen
	- 'Dark Dancer'	MAsh SDys SPhx WHil WWlt XSen
	- 'Desert Blaze' (v)	CWGN ECtt EPyc LBuc MCot MHer NCGa SDys SMrm SPin WGrn WPGP WWlt XLum
	- 'Devantville'	NDov XLum
	- 'Dysons' Orangy Pink'	CSpe NDov
	- 'Flammenn'PBR **new**	MPkF
§	- 'Hot Lips'	Widely available
	- 'James Compton'	EPyc SIgm SMrm
	- 'Javier'	SDys SPin
	- 'Kentish Pink'	EPyc SDys
	- 'La Luna'	CPrp CSam CSpe ECtt EPyc LHop MAsh MCot MHer MRav MSCN NDov SPin WIvy WPGP WSHC WWlt XLum XSen
	- 'La Siesta'	EPyc MAsh MHoo XSen
	- 'La Tarde'	CTri EPyc MAsh MHom WWlt XSen
	- 'Los Lirios' ♀H3-4	CPom CSpe CTri EPyc GCal SPin WHil WWlt
	- 'Maraschino'	EPfP EPyc LHop LRHS MAsh SDys SPin SPoG SRms WHil WMnd WWlt XLum XSen
*	- 'Mauve'	EPyc NDov
	- 'Melen'PBR **new**	MBri SPin
	- 'Moonlight Over Ashwood' (v)	EPyc MAsh SPin WSHC WWlt
	- 'Moonlight Serenade'	CAby EPyc MAsh SDys
	- 'Nachtvlinder'	CSpe EPyc NDov SDys SPin
§	- 'Pat Vlasto'	EPyc SPin WWlt
	- 'Peter Vidgeon'	CWGN EPyc LHop LPio MAsh MCot SDys SPhx SPin SPoG WHil WWlt
	- 'Pleasant Pink'	EPyc MAsh XSen
	- 'Pluenn'PBR **new**	MPkF
	- 'Plum Wine'	WHil WWlt
	- 'Raspberry Royale' ♀H3-4	CPom ECtt EPfP EPyc LHop LRHS MAsh MHer MHoo SBch SDys SMrm SPin WHil WIvy WMnd WSHC WWlt XLum XSen
	- 'Red Velvet'	CAby EBee ECtt ELon EPyc EWld GGal LPio MAsh MHom SDys WHrl WSHC WWlt XSen
	- 'Señorita Leah'	CWGN EPyc MAsh MCot SDys WWlt
§	- 'Sierra San Antonio'	CDes CPom CWGN EPPr EPfP EPyc LRHS MAsh MHom NDov SDys SMrm WHil WPGP XLum XSen
	- 'Stormy Sunrise'	EPyc SDys
§	- 'Trebah'	CHel CSpe ECre EPyc EShb LHop LRHS MAsh MCot MHom SDys SPin SPoG SRot WHil WIvy WKif WSHC WWlt XSen
	- 'Trenance'	CHel CSpe ECre ELon EPyc LHop LRHS MHer MHom SBch SPin SRot WHil WWlt XSen
§	***japonica***	SPin XSen
	- 'Alba'	SPin
	'Jean's Purple Passion'	EPyc SDys SPin
	judaica	CMac SPin WGrn XSen
	jurisicii	CWib EPyc LRHS MAsh SBrt SEND SPav SPin WJek WSHC XLum XSen
	- 'Alba'	XSen
	- pink-flowered	CSpe SPin XSen
	karwinskyi	SPin XSen
	- B&SWJ 9081	WCru
	keerlii	SPin XSen
	koyamae	LRHS MBri SPin
	- B&SWJ 10919	WCru
	kronenburgii	XSen
	'Lady Strybing'	SPin
	'Lalarsha'	CElw EPyc SDys
	lanceolata	CSpe EPyc LHop SPin WWlt XSen
	lanigera	WHil
	'Lararsha'	MCot
	lasiantha	SPin XSen
§	***lavandulifolia***	CArn EBee ECho ELan ELau EPfP EWes GPoy LRHS MAsh MHer MHoo MLHP MNHC MRav SMrm SPer SPin SRms WHoo WJek WKif WWlt XLum XSen
§	- subsp. ***blancoana***	CMea ELau EPyc MHer SPin XSen
	- subsp. ***pyrenaeorum***	XSen
	- subsp. ***vellerea***	XSen
	lavanduloides	SPin
	lemmonii	see *S. microphylla* var. *wislizeni*
	'Lemon Pie'	WHil WWlt
	leptophylla	see *S. reptans*
	leucantha ♀H1	CArn CSpe ECre ELan EPyc LPio MAsh MCot MHer MOWG MRav MSCN SPin SPlb SRkn SVen XSen
	- 'Eder' (v)	MAsh SDys SPin
	- 'Midnight'	CSam LHop
	- 'Purple Velvet'	ECtt EPyc MAsh MHer MHom SDix SDys SPin WWlt XSen
	- 'San Marcos Lavender'	EPyc SPin
	- 'Santa Barbara'	CDes CHll LRHS MAsh SDys XSen
	leucocephala	EPyc SDys SPin XSen
	leucophylla	XSen
	- NNS 01-375	SPin
	limbata	XSen
	littae	SPin XSen
	longispicata	SPin
	longistyla	CFil SDys SPin SVen WPGP XSen
	lycioides misapplied	see *S. greggii* × *serpyllifolia*

	lycioides A. Gray	CAbP CHll EPyc LRHS SEND SPhx SPin
	lyrata	XSen
	- 'Burgundy Bliss'	see *S. lyrata* 'Purple Knockout'
§	- 'Purple Knockout'	EPfP NLBP SMrm SPin XSen
	- 'Purple Vulcano'	see *S. lyrata* 'Purple Knockout'
	macellaria misapplied	see *S. microphylla*
	macellaria Epling	CSam
	macrophylla	GCal SDys SPin WPGP XSen
	- Cally selection	SPin
	- upright **new**	CSpe
	- 'Wendy's Surprise'	WWlt
	macrosiphon	SPin
	'Madeline' PBR	CWGN EPfP GBin IBoy LBMP LRHS LSou MBri STPC
	madrensis	EPyc SPin XSen
	- 'Dunham'	GCal LPio WWlt
	'Magic Potion'	CWGN
	melissodora	SPin
	mellifera	CArn XSen
	merjamie 'Mint-sauce'	LRHS
	mexicana	SPin
	- B&SWJ 10288	WCru
	- 'Limelight'	EPyc
	- 'Lollie Jackson'	WWlt
	- var. ***mexicana***	XSen
	- var. ***minor***	EPyc SDys SPin
	- 'Snowflake'	XSen
	meyeri	EPyc GGal MHom SPin WWlt
	- CDPR 3071 **new**	WPGP
I	***miahuatlanensis*** **new**	SPin
§	***microphylla***	CArn CMHG CMac CPom CPrp CTri ELau EWes LAst LHop MAsh MHer MHoo MSCN SPet SVen XLum
	- CD&R 1141	SPin
	- 'Belize'	CPrp MAsh NDov SBri WHil WWlt
	- 'Cerro Potosi'	CCse CElw CPrp CSpe ELon EPfP EPyc LPio MAsh MCot MHer SDys SPin WCFE WIvy WWlt XLum
	- 'Hot Lips'	see *S.* × *jamensis* 'Hot Lips'
	- 'Huntington'	EPyc SPin XSen
	- 'Kew Red' ♀H3-4	CCon CHVG EWld MHoo MNrw SBch SPin WHil WHoo WPGP
	- 'La Trinidad'	XSen
I	- 'Lutea'	LPio MAsh
	- 'Maroon'	CWGN EPyc SDys
§	- var. ***microphylla***	CRHN CSev CTri CWib ECtt ELan EPfP EPyc LSRN MCot MHer MHoo MNHC MRav SEND SPin SRkn WHfH WJek XLum XSen
	- - 'La Foux'	EPyc MCot SMrm SPhx XSen
	- - 'Newby Hall' ♀H3-4	CAby CDes CPom ECtt EPyc EShb EWes MHoo SPhx WPGP XSen
	- var. ***neurepia***	see *S. microphylla* var. *microphylla*
	- 'Orange Door'	EPyc SDys XSen
	- orange-red-flowered	MRav
	- 'Oregon Peach'	EPfP LRHS
	- 'Oxford'	SPin
§	- 'Pink Blush' ♀H3-4	CAby EABi ECtt ELan EPfP EPyc LRHS MAsh MCot MHer MHom MHoo SEND SMrm SPin SPoG SRkn WHil WHoo WIvy WKif WPGP WSHC WWlt XSen
	- 'Pleasant View' ♀H3-4	EPyc WHil WWlt XSen
	- 'Ribambelle' **new**	XLum
	- 'Robin's Pride'	EPyc SDys
	- 'Rodbaston Current Purple'	WWlt
	- 'Rodbaston Red'	WHil WWlt
	- 'Rosy Cheeks'	WOut
	- 'San Carlos Festival'	CAby EPyc NCGa NDov SBch SDys SPhx SPin WPGP WWlt XSen
	- 'Trelawny Rose Pink'	see *S.* 'Trelawney'
	- 'Trelissick Creamy Yellow'	see *S.* 'Trelissick'
	- 'Trewithen Cerise'	see *S.* 'Trewithen'
	- 'Violette'	EPfP EPyc
	- 'Wild Watermelon'	CPrp CWGN EBee EPfP EPyc LHop MAsh MCot SDys WHil WWFP WWlt XSen
§	- var. ***wislizeni***	CElw CPom EPyc SPhx SPin
	- 'Zaragoza'	SPin
	microstegia	XSen
	miltiorhiza	CArn MHoo SPhx SPin XLum XSen
	miniata	EPyc SPin XSen
	misella	SPin
	mocinoi **new**	SPin
	mohavensis	XSen
	moorcroftiana	EPyc
	moschata	SPin
	'Mrs Beard'	XSen
	muelleri misapplied	see *S. greggii* × *serpyllifolia*
	muelleri ambig.	NDov WWFP
	muelleri Epling	EPyc
	muirii	SPin
	'Mulberry Jam'	CAby CCse CDes CHGN CHll CSev CSpe ECtt EPfP EPyc EWes LHop LPio MAsh MCot MHom SDys SPin SRkn WHil WKif WPGP WSHC WWlt XSen
§	***multicaulis*** ♀H4	EPyc MAsh SPin XSen
	munzii	SDys SPin XSen
*	***murrayi***	CAbP SPin
	Mystic Spires Blue = 'Balsalmisp' PBR	CSpe CWGN EPyc NDov SPoG
	namaensis	CSev SPin XSen
	nana B&SWJ 10272	SPin WCru WHil
	napifolia	EBee LPot LRHS NLar SPav SPin XSen
	- 'Baby Blue'	EBee LRHS
	'Nazareth'	MAsh SPin XSen
	'Nel'	LHop
	nemorosa	EPyc LRHS SPin SRms XLum XSen
	- 'Amethyst' ♀H4	EBee ELon EPfP GQue IKil LPio LPot LRHS MBel MBri MHol MPie MRav MSpe NDov SDys SMrm SPhx SPin SRms WCAu WCot WHoo WKif WWEG WWlt XSen
	- 'Blaureiter'	LRHS
	- Blue Mound	see *S.* × *sylvestris* 'Blauhügel'
	- 'Caradonna'	Widely available
	- East Friesland	see *S. nemorosa* 'Ostfriesland'
	- 'Lubecca' ♀H4	ECtt EPfP LHop LRHS MAsh MCot MSpe NDov NEgg NGdn NLar SPer WMnd WWEG XSen
	- Marcus = 'Haeumanarc' PBR	CWGN EBee ECtt ELan EPfP EUJe LAst LBMP LRHS LSRN LSou MBNS MBri MRav MSpe MWhi NDov NLar SDys SPoG WSHC
	- 'Midsummer'	EWld
	- 'New Dimension Blue'	EPfP
	- 'New Dimension Rose'	EBee
§	- 'Ostfriesland' ♀H4	Widely available
	- 'Pink Beauty'	MWat
	- 'Pink Friesland' PBR	ECtt ELon GQue LRHS LSou MGos MSpe NDov NSti SMrm WCAu
	- 'Plumosa'	see *S. nemorosa* 'Pusztaflamme'
	- 'Porzellan' ♀H4	ECtt

§	– 'Pusztaflamme' ♀H4	EBee ECtt ELon EPfP GQue LRHS LSou MRav MSpe NOrc SMrm WWEG XSen
	– 'Rose Queen'	CHel ELon EWTr LAst MWat NBir SWat WCot XLum XSen
	– 'Rosenwein'	LDai LRHS NGdn SGbt SMrm SPhx XSen
	– 'Royal Distinction'	ECtt
	– 'Schneekönig'	LSou
	– 'Schwellenburg'	CMea ECGP ECtt ELon GBin GBuc GQue LBMP LHop LRHS LSou MHol MTis NLar SPad WCot WMnd XSen
I	– (Sensation Series) 'Sensation Blue'	MBri
	– – 'Sensation Blue Improved'	LRHS
	– – 'Sensation Deep Blue'	ELon
I	– – 'Sensation Deep Rose Improved'	LRHS SPoG
	– – 'Sensation Rose'	CCVN LAst LBMP LLHF LRHS LSou MBri SHil SMrm
	– – 'Sensation Sky Blue'	LRHS
	– – 'Sensation White'	CSev CWGN MHol
§	– subsp. ***tesquicola***	CHel EPyc LSRN MWhi NGdn SMrm SPhx
	– 'Wesuwe'	ELon NDov XSen
	neurepia	see *S. microphylla* var. *microphylla*
*	***nevadensis***	SPin
	'Newe Ya'ar'	EPfP
	nilotica	LRHS SPin XSen
	nipponica B&SWJ 5829	SPin WCru
	– 'Fuji Snow' (v)	EBee MBri
	– var. ***trisecta***	SPin
	nubicola	CExl GPoy SPin WOut XSen
	– BWJ 7639	WCru
	– CC 4607	EBee
	– CC 4762	NLar
	'Nuchi'	SPin
	nutans	CHVG SBrt SPin XSen
	officinalis	Widely available
	– 'Albiflora'	CArn CSev SPin WJek XSen
N	– 'Aurea' ambig.	CWib GPoy MHoo
	– 'Berggarten'	CArn CPrp ELau EPfP GBin GCal LEdu LHop LPio MCot MHer MRav SDix SPhx SPin WHer WJek WMnd XLum XSen
§	– broad-leaved	ELau MHer SWat WJek
	– 'Crispa'	SPin XSen
	– 'Extrakta'	SPhx
	– 'Grete Stolze'	LHop SEND XSen
	– 'Grower's Friend'	CTsd LAst LBMP
§	– 'Icterina' (v) ♀H4	Widely available
	– 'Kew Gold'	MRav
	– ***latifolia***	see *S. officinalis* broad-leaved
	– narrow-leaved	see *S. lavandulifolia*
	– 'Nazareth' PBR	ELau WJek XSen
	– ***prostrata***	see *S. lavandulifolia*
	– 'Purpurascens' ♀H4	Widely available
	– 'Robin Hill'	ECGP LRHS LSou NDov
	– 'Rosea'	CArn WJek XSen
	– 'Tricolor' (v)	CTri EBee ECho ELan ELau EPfP EShb GPoy LAst LBMP MAsh MBri MHer MHoo MLHP MNHC MRav NGdn NPri SGol SPer SPin SPlb SPoG SRms WHil WJek WMnd XSen
	– 'Variegata'	see *S. officinalis* 'Icterina'
	– variegated (v)	ECho MHer
	– 'Würzburg'	XSen

	ombrophila	SPin
	omeiana BWJ 8062	SPin WCru
	– 'Crûg Thundercloud'	LHop WCru
	oppositiflora misapplied	see *S. tubiflora*
	oppositiflora ambig.	EPyc SDys SPin XSen
	orbignaei	SPin XSen
	orthostachys	SPin
	'Out of the Mist' **new**	WOut
	oxyphora	EPyc MOWG SDys SPin XSen
	pachyphylla	SPin XSen
	'Pakhuis Pass' **new**	SPin
	palaestina	XSen
	pallida	EPyc SDys SPin
	'Pam's Purple'	MAsh
§	***patens*** ♀H3	Widely available
	– 'Alba' misapplied	see *S. patens* 'White Trophy'
	– 'Blue Angel'	CHel EHyd EPfP EWes NSoo SPet WIvy WWEG
	– 'Cambridge Blue' ♀H3	CExl CHel CPrp CSpe CWGN EBee ECtt ELan EPfP LHop LRHS MAsh MBel MCot MHer MHoo MRav MSpe NLar NPer SDys SIgm SMrm SPer SPhx SPin WOth WSHC WWlt XSen
	– 'Chilcombe'	EPyc MHer SDys SPin WOut WWlt XSen
	– 'Dot's Delight'	CExl CHel CPrp CSpe ECtt EPyc EWes LHop LRHS MAsh MHol NCGa SBch SDys SMrm SPer SPin
	– 'Guanajuato'	CBcs CExl CHel CSam ECtt EPyc EWes MAsh MBel MCot MHer NLar SDys SMad SMrm SPin SRkn SRot WBor WSHC
	– large	CSpe
	– lavender-flowered	MBel
	– light blue-flowered	CHel EPfP
	– 'Oxford Blue'	see *S. patens*
	– (Patio Series) 'Patio Deep Blue'	CHel CWGN EPfP MHoo SPoG
	– – 'Patio Sky Blue'	CHel SPet
	– 'Pink Ice'	CPom EPyc WOut
	– pink-flowered	SPin
	– 'Royal Blue'	see *S. patens*
§	– 'White Trophy'	CExl CHel ECtt ELan EPyc EWld LRHS MHoo SDys SMrm SPer SPin WIvy WOut
	pauciserrata	SPin
	'Peach Cobbler' **new**	WWlt
	pennellii	SPin
	'Penny's Smile'	EPyc LBuc LPio MAsh SDys SPin WHoo WWlt
	'Peru Blue'	CSpe EPyc SDys
	'Peter Vider' **new**	EPfP
	'Phyllis' Fancy'	CSam CSpe CWGN EPyc LPio MAsh MHer NDov SDys SPlb WSHC XSen
	pinguifolia	SPin XSen
	'Pink Icing'	SPin
	pinnata	SPin
	pisidica	SPin XSen
	plectranthoides	SPin XSen
	pogonochila	XSen
	polystachya	SPin XSen
	– B&SWJ 8985	WCru
	pomifera	SPin XSen
*	'Powis Castle'	MHom
	pratensis	CArn CWib EHyd ELan EPfP EPyc GJos MHer MNHC SPin WCot WHer WOut XSen

	- 'Albiflora'	CDes
§	- Bertolonii Group	EPyc SPin XSen
	- 'Dear Anja'	see *S.* × *sylvestris* 'Dear Anja'
§	- Haematodes Group ♀H4	ELan EPyc LDai MNrw NLar SPin SRms
	- 'Indigo' ♀H4	CDes ECtt ELon EPfP GMaP LRHS LSou MCot MRav NCGa NEgg NLar SPhx SPin SPoG WCot WMnd WPGP
	- 'Lapis Lazuli'	EBee EPyc EWes LPio
	- 'Pink Delight' PBR	EBee ECtt EPfP LRHS NCGa NDov NLar SMrm SPoG
	- 'Rose Rhapsody' (Ballet Series)	CAby EBee EPPr EPfP EPyc LDai LRHS SPhx WHil XSen
	- 'Rosea'	SPhx SPin
	- 'Swan Lake' (Ballet Series)	CAby CPom EBee EPPr EPfP EPyc LRHS NLar SPhx SPin SPlb WHil XSen
	- 'Sweet Esmeralda' (Ballet Series)	EBee EPyc LRHS NGdn NLar SPhx WOut XSen
	- 'Tenorei'	LRHS
	- 'Twilight Serenade' (Ballet Series)	CAby EBee ECtt EPfP EPyc IPot LRHS NCGa WHil XSen
	- 'White Swan'	MCot
	pratensis* × *transylvanica	GJos
	procurrens	EBee EPyc SPin XSen
	prunelloides	SPin
	przewalskii	CCon CExl EBee EPyc EWld LRHS SPhx SPin XSen
	- ACE 1157	WCru
	- BWJ 7920	SPin WCru
	- var. ***mandarinorum***	LRHS
I	***pseudonutans*** **new**	SPin
	pubescens	SPin
	pulchella	SPin
	'Purple Majesty'	CHll CSam ECtt EPyc EShb LHop SDys SMrm SPhx SPin SRkn WKif WWlt XLum
	'Purple Queen'	CAbP CAby EBee EPyc LRHS LSou SDys SPoG WWlt
	purpurea	LBMP LSRN SPin
	radula	EPyc SPin
	ranzaniana	SPin XSen
	raymondii subsp. ***mairanae***	SPin WHil
	recognita	SPin WSHC XSen
	recurva	SPin
	reflexa	SPin
	regeliana misapplied	see *S. virgata* Jacq.
	regeliana Trautv.	LRHS NBir XSen
	regla	EPyc LRHS MAsh SPin WHil WPGP XSen
	- 'Jame'	SPin
	- 'Mount Emory'	SPin
	- 'Royal'	SPin
	repens	EPyc SPin XSen
§	***reptans***	EPyc SBrt SPin XSen
	- from western Texas	CWGN SDys WCot
	retinervia	SPin
	rhinosima	EPyc
	'Ribbon Belle'	MAsh WWlt
	ringens	SPin XSen
	riparia misapplied	see *S. rypara*
	roborowskii	SPin
§	***roemeriana*** ♀H3	CSpe EPyc IFoB WPGP
	- 'Bordeaux Steel Blue'	LRHS SRms
	'Rolando'	SDys SPin
§	***roscida***	SPin XSen
	'Rose Queen' ambig.	MSCN WMnd
	rosifolia	ECtt XSen
	'Royal Bumble'	CSpe ECtt EPfP EPyc IPot LHop LRHS MAsh MBri MCot NDov WHoo WPGP WWlt XLum XSen
	'Royal Crimson Distinction' PBR	EBee ECtt EPPr LSou MBri
	rubescens	SPin XSen
	rubiginosa	SPin XSen
	runcinata	EPyc SPin
	rutilans	see *S. elegans* 'Scarlet Pineapple'
§	***rypara***	CPom SPin XSen
	sagittata	CSpe EPyc GCal LPio SPin WWlt XSen
	(Savannah Series) 'Savannah Purple'	LRHS SRot
	- 'Savannah Red'	EPfP LRHS
	- 'Savannah Salmon Rose'	LRHS SRot
	scabra	EPyc SPin WOut XSen
	schlechteri	SPin
	sclarea	CArn CHab CHby ECtt GPoy LRHS MHer MHol MHoo MNHC SPin SRms WHfH WJek XLum XSen
	- 'Mojito' **new**	MHol
	- var. ***turkestanica*** hort.	CPom CSev CSpe ECtt ELan EPfP LRHS LSRN MCot MHoo MRav NEgg NGdn SEND SMad SMrm SPav SPer SPhx SRkn SWat WBrk WKif WMnd XSen
	- var. ***turkestaniana*** Mottet	MSpe
§	- 'Vatican White'	CHel CSpe EBee ELan EPfP LDai LPio LRHS MHoo MNHC MSpe SMrm SPad WJek XSen
	- white-bracted	CWib NLar SPin SWvt
*	***scordifolia***	SPin
	scutellarioides	SPin XSen
	semiatrata misapplied	see *S. chamaedryoides*
	semiatrata ambig.	EPyc
	semiatrata Zucc.	CSpe SPin XSen
	serboana	WCru
	- B&SWJ 10236	SPin WCru
	'Serenade'	LRHS NDov SPhx
	serpyllifolia	SPin XSen
	- white-flowered	SPin
	sessei	SPin XSen
	setulosa	SPin XSen
	'Shame'	NDov
	'Silas Dyson'	CAby CDes CFil CSpe ECre ECtt EPfP EPyc IPot LPio LRHS MBel MHom NDov SBch SDys SPet SPhx SPin SPoG WPGP WWlt
	'Silke's Dream'	CAby CDes CFil CPom CWGN ECtt EPfP EPyc LPio LRHS MAsh SDys SPin SPoG WPGP WWlt XSen
	sinaloensis	MAsh SPin XSen
	smithii	SPin
	somalensis	CHVG SPin SVen XSen
	sonomensis	XSen
	'Southern Belle'	SPin
	spathacea ♀H3-4	SBrt SPhx SPin WOut
	- 'Avis Keedy'	SPin
	spinosa	XSen
	splendens	SPin
	- 'Dancing Flame' (v)	EPyc
	- 'Helen Dillon'	CSpe EPyc SPin WWlt
	- 'Jimi's Good Red'	CSpe LHop LPio SDys WOth
	- 'Peach'	SPin
	- 'Red Indian' **new**	SDys

	Name	Suppliers
	- 'Sao Borja' new	SDys
	- 'Vanguard' 🏆^{H3}	LAst NPri
§	- 'Van-Houttei' 🏆^{H3}	CSam ECre EPyc EShb EWld SDys SPin SVen WWlt
	- 'Vista Purple'	LAst
	sprucei	SPin XSen
	squalens	SPin
	stachydifolia	EPyc SPin WPGP XSen
§	***staminea***	LRHS SDys
	stenophylla	WHil XSen
	'Stephanie'	EPyc SDys SPin
	stolonifera	CAby EPyc MAsh SDys SPin XSen
	striata	EPyc SPin WHil XSen
	- red-flowered	SPin
	styphelus	SDys SPin
	subpalmatinervis	SPin
	subrotunda	EPyc SDys SPin
	summa	XSen
	× ***superba*** 🏆^{H4}	CSBt EBee ECtt ELan EPfP EPyc LRHS LSRN MWat SDix SRms WCAu WHar WHoo
	- 'Adora Blue'	LRHS SHil
	- 'Adrian'	EBee ECtt EPfP LRHS LSRN LSou MSpe SPoG
	- 'Merleau'	LRHS
	- 'Merleau Rose'	EBee LPot MRav SRms WGor
*	- 'Rosea'	EBee
	- 'Rubin' 🏆^{H4}	ECtt MBNS NBre SMrm
I	- 'Superba'	CSev ECtt MRav SMrm SPhx SRkn
	× ***sylvestris***	LSRN SPin
§	- 'Blauhügel' 🏆^{H4}	CSam ECtt ELan EPfP EShb LPio LRHS LSou MArl MRav MSpe NDov NLar NPri SHil SMrm SPhx WGwG WHoo WMnd WPtf WWEG XSen
§	- 'Blaukönigin'	ELon EPfP GBin GMaP LAst LRHS MWat NGBl NLar SPad SPer SPet SPlb SPoG SRms SWvt WCot WWEG XSen
	- Blue Queen	see *S.* × *sylvestris* 'Blaukönigin'
§	- 'Dear Anja'	EBee IPot LHop LPla MTis NCGa NDov NLar SPhx WHlf
	- 'Lye End'	MRav MWat WCot
§	- 'Mainacht' 🏆^{H4}	Widely available
	- May Night	see *S.* × *sylvestris* 'Mainacht'
	- 'Negrito'	EBee ECtt ELon EWll GQue NGdn NLar SMrm XSen
	- 'Rhapsody in Blue' PBR	CAbP LRHS MBNS MBri MTis NDov NLar
	- 'Rose Queen'	ECtt ELan ELon EPfP LHop LRHS MHol MJak MRav NGBl NOrc SCoo SPet SPhx SPoG SWvt WHar WWEG XSen
	- 'Rügen'	ELon GQue XSen
	'Schneehügel'	CMac CSBt EBee ECtt EHoe ELan ELon EPPr EPfP GMaP LRHS MBNS MRav MSpe MTis NBre NEgg NLar NPri NPro NSoo SHil SMrm SPer WCAu WHil WMnd WWEG XSen
	- 'Superba'	GBuc
	- 'Tänzerin' 🏆^{H4}	EBee ECtt ELon LPla LRHS MTis NDov NLar WHlf XSen
	- 'Viola Klose'	EBee ECtt ELan GBuc LRHS LSRN MBri MCot MSpe NCGa NDov NGdn NLar NSti SRms XSen
	tachiei	see *S. forsskaolii*
	taraxacifolia	LHop SPhx SPin XSen
	tarayensis	SPin
	tesquicola	see *S. nemorosa* subsp. *tesquicola*
	thymoides	SPin WHil
	tianschanica	SPin
	tiliifolia	SPav SPin SRms
	tingitana	SPin XSen
	tomentosa	SPin XSen
	tortuosa	SPin
	transcaucasica	see *S. staminea*
	transsylvanica	GAbr IMou LDai MSpe SMrm SPav SPhx SPin XSen
	- 'Baumgartenii'	LRHS WHfH
	- 'Blue Spire'	CHel CMea MCot MWhi SRkn
	'Trebah Lilac White'	see *S.* × *jamensis* 'Trebah'
§	'Trelawney'	CHel EPPr EPyc LRHS MCot MHom SRot WWlt XSen
§	'Trelissick'	CHel ECre EPPr EPyc LHop LRHS MAsh MCot MHom SEND SPet SPin SRkn SRot WHil WWlt
§	'Trewithen'	CExl CHel ECre EPyc LRHS MHom SPin SPoG SRot WHil XSen
	trijuga	EPyc SPin
	triloba	see *S. fruticosa*
	tubifera	SPin
§	***tubiflora*** 🏆$^{H1+3}$	EPyc MAsh SPin XSen
	uliginosa 🏆$^{H3-4}$	Widely available
	- 'African Skies'	IPot SPin WHlf WWlt
	- 'Ballon Azul'	CSpe MAsh SDys WSHC
	univerticillata	SPin
	urica	SPin XSen
	- short	SDys
	'Valerie'	CAby EPyc SDys
	'Van-Houttei'	see *S. splendens* 'Van-Houttei'
	variana	SPin
	vaseyi	XSen
	'Vatican City'	see *S. sclarea* 'Vatican White'
	verbenaca	CArn EPyc LRHS MHer SPin WOut XSen
	- pink-flowered	SPhx
	verticillata	EPfP EPyc LEdu NLar SPin XSen
§	- 'Alba'	CAbP EBee ECtt EPfP GJos GQue LRHS MCot MRav NGdn NLar SPer SPin WCAu XSen
	- 'Hannay's Blue'	EPPr EPyc MTis SMrm
	- 'Hannay's Purple'	ECtt EPPr
	- 'Purple Rain'	CKno CMac CSam CSpe EBee ECtt ELan EPfP GBuc GJos GMaP LAst LHop LRHS LSRN MArl MCot MRav NEgg NLar SMad SMrm SPer SPhx SRms WCAu WHoo WMnd WWEG XSen
I	- 'Rosea' new	LRHS
	- 'Smouldering Torches'	EBee LHop LPla MTis NDov SPhx
	- 'White Rain'	see *S. verticillata* 'Alba'
	villicaulis	see *S. amplexicaulis*
	villosa	WHil
§	***virgata*** Jacq.	EBee SPin WOut XSen
	viridis	CHby MNHC SPin
§	- var. ***comata***	MCot WJek
	- 'Marble Arch Blue' (Marble Arch Series)	CSpe
	- var. ***viridis***	WHrl
	viscosa ambig.	EPyc
	viscosa Jacq.	SPin WHil WOut XSen
	vitifolia	CSpe EPyc SDys
	wagneriana	SPin
	'Waverly'	CSam EPyc EWld LPio MAsh MCot MHer SDys WWlt XSen
	'Wendy's Wish'	CMea CSam CWGN ECtt EPyc LHop LPio MAsh MHol NLar NPri SPin SPoG SRkn WHil

	× ***westerae***	SPin XSen
	– 'Petra' new	SDys
	xalapensis	SPin
	yunnanensis	SPin
	– BWJ 7874	WCru
	aff. ***yunnanensis***	SPin

Salvinia (*Salviniaceae*)

	natans	LLWG MSKA

Sambucus ✿ (*Adoxaceae*)

	adnata	SDix
	caerulea	see *S. nigra* subsp. *caerulea*
	callicarpa	NLar WCot
	chinensis	WCot
	coraensis	see *S. williamsii* subsp. *coreana*
	ebulus	LEdu SMad WCot
	formosana	WCot
	gaudichaudiana	ECou
*	***himalayensis***	WCot
	mexicana B&SWJ 10349	WCot WCru
	miquelii	WCot
	nigra	CArn CBcs CCVT CDul CHab EPom GPoy IBoy LBuc NWea SEWo SPer WMou WSFF
	– 'Albomarginata'	see *S. nigra* 'Marginata'
	– 'Albovariegata' (v)	CMac WCot WMoo
*	– 'Ardwall'	CAgr GCal WCot
N	– 'Aurea' ♀H4	CBcs CDul CMac CSBt ELan EPfP MRav NWea SPer WCot WMoo
	– 'Aureomarginata' (v)	ECrN ELan EPPr EPfP LPot MRav NLar WCot
	– 'Bradet'	CAgr NLar WCot
	– 'Broadway' (v) new	WCot
	– 'Cae Rhos Lligwy'	CAgr WCot WHer
§	– subsp. ***caerulea***	EPfP
	– subsp. ***canadensis***	CDul
	– – 'Adams' (F)	WCot
	– – 'Aurea'	CWib WCot WHar
	– – 'Goldfinch'	MAsh
	– – 'John's'	CAgr WCot
	– – 'Maxima'	SMad WCot
	– – 'Rubra'	WCot
	– – 'York' (F)	CAgr WCot
	– 'Castledean'	WCot
	– 'Dolomite' (v)	WCot
	– 'Donau'	CAgr WCot
	– 'Frances' (v)	EPPr WCot
	– 'Franzi'	CAgr WCot
	– 'Fructu Luteo'	NLar WCot
	– 'Godshill' (F)	CAgr SDea WCot
	– 'Haschberg'	CAgr WCot
	– 'Heterophylla'	see *S. nigra* 'Linearis'
	– 'Hillier's Dwarf'	WCot
	– 'Ina'	CAgr WCot
	– 'Körsör' (F)	NLar WCot
	– f. ***laciniata*** ♀H4	CDul EBee ELan EPPr EPfP GCal LPot LRHS MBlu MMuc MRav NLar NWea SDix SLon SPer SPoG WCFE WCot WPGP WPat
§	– 'Linearis'	ELan NLar WCot
	– 'Long Tooth'	CDul WCot
	– 'Lutea Punctata'	WCot
	– 'Madonna' (v)	CMac LEdu MBlu MGos MRav NLBP NLar NPol SMad SPer WCot
§	– 'Marginata' (v)	CDul CWib EHoe MHer MRav SDix SPoG WCot
	– 'Marion Bull' (v)	CDul NLar WCot
I	– 'Marmorata'	WCot
	– 'Mint Julep'	WCot
I	– 'Monstrosa'	WCot
	– 'Nana'	WCot
	– 'Naomi'	WCot
	– 'Norfolk Speckled' (v)	WCot
	– 'Pingo Trail'	WCot
	– 'Plena' (d)	WCot
	– f. ***porphyrophylla*** 'Black Beauty'	see *S. nigra* f. *porphyrophylla* 'Gerda'
	– – 'Black Lace'	see *S. nigra* f. *porphyrophylla* 'Eva'
	– – 'Black Tower'	CHid CSBt CWSG EAmu ELon GBin LRHS MAsh MMHG MPkF NSoo
	– – 'Dart's Greenlace'	WCot
§	– – 'Eva'^{PBR}	Widely available
§	– – 'Gerda'^{PBR} ♀H4	Widely available
§	– – 'Guincho Purple'	CBcs CDul CMac CTri ELan EPPr EPfP MHer MRav NLar NWea SGol SPlb WCot WMoo
	– – 'Purple Pete'	CDul WCot
	– – 'Thundercloud'	CDul CMHG ECrN ELon EPPr EWes GBin GCal MAsh MMHG MNrw NChi NLar NPro WCot WMoo
	– 'Pulverulenta' (v)	CWib EPPr GCal LHop MRav NLBP NLar SPer SVen WCot
	– 'Purpurea'	see *S. nigra* f. *porphyrophylla* 'Guincho Purple'
	– 'Pyramidalis'	MRav WCot
	– 'Riese aus Vossloch'	WCot
	– 'Robert Piggin' (v)	WCot
	– var. ***rotundifolia***	WCot
	– 'Sambu' (F)	CAgr WCot
	– 'Samdal' (F)	CAgr WCot
	– 'Samidan' (F)	CAgr WCot
	– 'Samnor' (F)	CAgr WCot
	– 'Sampo' (F)	CAgr WCot
	– 'Samyl' (F)	CAgr WCot
	– 'Urban Lace'	CAgr WCot
	– 'Variegata'	see *S. nigra* 'Marginata'
	– f. ***viridis***	CAgr WCot
	palmensis	WCot
	racemosa	EPfP NWea WCot
	– 'Aurea'	EHoe
	– 'Crûg Lace'	WCru
	– 'Goldenlocks'	EWes MSwo NLar WCot
	– subsp. ***kamtschatica***	WCot
	– 'Plumosa Aurea'	CBcs CSBt CWib ELan EPfP GCra LRHS MRav MSwo NLar NWea SLim
	– var. ***pubens***	WCot
§	– var. ***sieboldiana***	WCot
	– 'Sutherland Gold' ♀H4	CBcs CDul CSBt EBee ELan ELon EPfP EUJe IBoy LAst LBMP LRHS LSRN MAsh MGos MRav MSwo NEgg NHol NLar NPri NSoo SGol SLim SPer SPoG SWvt WCot WMoo WPat
	– 'Tenuifolia'	EPfP WCot
	– 'Welsh Gold'	LRHS MAsh SPoG
	sieboldiana	see *S. racemosa* var. *sieboldiana*
	tigranii	WCot
§	***williamsii*** subsp. ***coreana***	WCot

Samolus (*Primulaceae*)

	repens	ECou LLHF
	valerandi	LLWG

Sandersonia (*Colchicaceae*)

	aurantiaca	ECho EPot SDeJ

Sanguinaria (*Papaveraceae*)

	canadensis	CArn CAvo CBct CBro CCon CHel EBee ECho EHyd EPfP EPot EWTr GKev GPoy LEdu LRHS MHoo NHol NLar NOrc NRya SDeJ SPer SWat WAbe WCru WPGP WShi WWFP
	- f. ***multiplex*** (d)	CLAP ECho EPot IFro NBir SPhx
	- - 'Plena' (d) 🏆H4	CBct CBro CHel CSpe CWCL EBee ECho ELon EPfP GBin GBuc GCra GKev GPoy LRHS MNrw NHar NHol NLar NRya NSla SDeJ SKHP WAbe WCot WHil WKif WPGP

Sanguisorba ✿ (*Rosaceae*)

	DJHC 535 **new**	MAvo
§	***albiflora***	CCVN CDes CKno EBee ELan EShb GBuc LBMP LEdu LPla MAvo MRav NGdn NLar NPro SMrm SPhx SWat WHil WMoo WOut WPGP
	'All Time High'	MAvo NDov
	applanata	MAvo WCot
	armena	CElw EBee EWes MAvo MBel MNrw MPie XEll
	'Autumn Bliss'	EBee MAvo
	benthamiana	CHEx
	'Blacksmith's Burgundy'	MAvo
	'Blackthorn'	CKno ECtt MAvo MTis NDov NLar SPhx WCot
	'Burr Blanc'	MAvo SPhx
	canadensis	CDes CKno CMac CRow EBee ECtt EPPr EPfP GCal GMaP GPoy LPla MAvo MNrw MRav NBir NLar NSti SPhx SWat WCot WMoo WOld WWEG XEll
	- hybrid	MAvo
	'Cangshan Cranberry'	MAvo NLar WCot WWEG
*	***caucasica***	EWes GBee LEdu LPla MAvo NBre SPhx
	'Chocolate Tip'	EBee ECtt IPot LHop MAvo NBro
	dodecandra	CDes MAvo
	hakusanensis	CKno EBee GBBs GCal IFro IPot LEdu MAvo MNFA MNrw NBir NBre NBro NChi NLar NPro SMad WCot WPGP WSHC WWEG
	- B&SWJ 8709	MAvo WCru
	- 'Lilac Squirrel'	ECtt MAvo NLar
	'John Coke'	MAvo NLar
	magnifica	EWes GCal LEdu MAvo WCot WPGP
	- ***alba***	see *S. albiflora*
	menziesii	Widely available
	- 'Dali Marble' (v)	EBee ECtt MAvo MTis NLar SPoG WMoo WWEG
	- 'Wake Up'	MAvo
§	***minor***	CArn CHby CPrp EBee ELau GPoy LEdu MHer MHoo MJak MNHC NBro NMir SIde SPhx SPlb SRms WHer WHfH WJek WMoo WOut XLum
	- subsp. ***minor***	CHab
	obtusa	Widely available
	- 'Chatto'	MAvo
	- silver-leaved	MNrw
	- white-flowered	CDes EBee MAvo MMuc WPGP
	officinalis	CArn CHab CKno COIW EHoe GQue MHer MHoo MNFA NMir NPro SPer SPhx SWat WCAu WMoo WOut WWEG
	- CDC 262	EPPr
	- CDC 282	CSpe SPhx
	- CDC 292	GQue MAvo WCot
	- 'Arnhem'	CCse CKno EBee ECtt EPPr LEdu LPla LRHS MAvo MTis NDov SMrm SPhx WCot WPGP WWEG
	- 'Crimson Queen'	EBee GQue MAvo MTis
	- dark-flowered	MAvo
	- early-flowering	CDes
	- 'False Tanna'	CWib
	- 'Lemon Splash' (v)	EBee LEdu MAvo WCot WWEG
	- 'Martin's Mulberry'	CDes EBee EWes GCal MAvo NDov
	- 'Morning Select'	EBee ECtt EPPr NLar
	- 'Red Thunder'	CDes CKno CSpe ECtt EPPr GBin IPot LEdu LPla LPot LRHS MAvo NCGa NDov NLar NOrc WCAu WWEG
	- 'Shiro-fukurin' (v)	EBee EWes LEdu LLWG MAvo MBel MSCN MTis NLar WCot WHer WOut WSHC
	- 'Tsetseguun' **new**	LEdu MAvo
	parviflora	see *S. tenuifolia* var. *parviflora*
	pimpinella	see *S. minor*
	'Pink Brushes'	IMou IPot LPla MAvo MTis NCGa NDov NLar WCAu
	'Pink Tanna'	CDes CElw CHel CKno CPrp EBee EPPr GBBs GBin GBuc LEdu LHop LRHS MAvo MCot MGos MMuc MTis NBid NBro NSti SMrm SPhx WCAu WCot WHoo WMoo WWEG
	'Raspberry Coulis' **new**	MAvo
	'Raspberry Mivvi'	SPhx
	'Rock and Roll'	CHel ECtt EPPr GQue MAvo MTis NLar SBea
	sitchensis	see *S. stipulata*
§	***stipulata***	EBee GCal LEdu LPla LRHS MAvo MNrw WCAu WWEG
	- var. ***riishirensis***	EBee MAvo
	'Tanna'	Widely available
	'Tanna' seedling	EPPr EShb
	tenuifolia	CCon GCal IFro LRHS MCot MHer NChi NLar SBHP SMrm SPhx
	- var. ***alba***	CKno COIW CPrp CWCL EBee EPPr EPfP EWes EWll GQue IMou MAvo MCot NDov NPro SMrm SPhx WCot WHoo WMoo WOld WWEG WWFP XLum
	- - CDC	GCal MRav
	- - 'Korean Snow'	CCse MAvo MNFA NDov SMad SPhx
	- 'Big Pink'	GCal MAvo MNrw
	- 'Henk Gerritsen'	MAvo
§	- var. ***parviflora***	CDes EBee LEdu MAvo MNrw NLar WPGP
	- 'Pink Elephant'	CKno EBee ECtt EPPr EWTr GBin GQue LDai LEdu LHop MAvo NCGa NDov NLar SMad WMoo WPGP WWFP
	- 'Pink Tickler'	MAvo
	- var. ***purpurea***	CDes EBee WCAu
	- 'Purpurea'	CKno EBee EPPr LEdu MAvo NLar SPhx WCot WPGP
	- 'Stand Up Comedian'	EBee GBin IMou LEdu MAvo NLar WWEG
	- 'Sturdy Guard'	MAvo
	- 'White Tanna'	EBee EPPr GQue MAvo MTis

Sanicula (*Apiaceae*)

	europaea	CArn GPoy

Santolina (*Asteraceae*)

'Apple Court' **new**	LRHS
benthamiana	XSen
§ ***chamaecyparissus*** ♀H4	Widely available
- var. ***corsica***	see *S. chamaecyparissus* 'Nana'
- 'Double Lemon'	EPfP
- subsp. ***insularis***	XSen
- 'Lambrook Silver'	CDoC CFis EBee ECtt EPfP LRHS MAsh NLar SCoo SLim SPoG WJek
- 'Lemon Queen'	CDoC EPfP LRHS MAsh MGos MNHC MSwo MWat NBir NLar SRms SWat WJek XSen
§ - 'Nana' ♀H4	CBar CMHG EBee EPfP LRHS MAsh MHer MNHC MRav MSwo SPoG SRms SWat XSen
- 'Pretty Carroll'	EBee ECtt ELan EPfP LRHS LSRN MAsh MBri NLar WJek
- 'Small-Ness'	CMea ECho ELan EPfP EWes LRHS MHer SWvt WHer WJek
- 'Weston'	ECho
incana	see *S. chamaecyparissus*
* ***lindavica***	XSen
pectinata	see *S. rosmarinifolia* subsp. *canescens*
pinnata	CArn CTri MHer MLHP
§ - subsp. ***neapolitana*** ♀H4	CArn CSBt CSev CWib ELan EPfP MBri MMuc MRav SDix SEND WMnd WWEG
- - cream-flowered	see *S. pinnata* subsp. *neapolitana* 'Edward Bowles'
§ - - 'Edward Bowles'	Widely available
- - 'Sulphurea'	CArn CMea EBee EPfP LRHS MAsh SPer SPhx WKif XSen
rosmarinifolia	CArn CDoC CDul GPoy LRHS MMuc MRav SEND SLon SPlb SPoG SRms
§ - subsp. ***canescens***	EPfP XSen
- 'Lemon Fizz'	EBee ECrN EHoe ELan EMil EPfP LBMP LHop LRHS LSou MAsh MAvo MHer MSCN NBir NPri SCoo SHil SPer SPoG SRms SWvt WHar WHer WPnn
§ - subsp. ***rosmarinifolia***	CSev ECrN ELan EPfP MHer MHoo MRav NSoo SDix SIgm SPer SRms SWvt WHoo WJek XLum XSen
- - 'Primrose Gem' ♀H4	CBcs CDoC CPrp CSBt CSam CTri EBee EPfP LHop LRHS MMuc MNHC MRav MSwo MWat NLar NPri SBod SEND SGbt SPer SRms SWvt WHoo WJek XSen
- - white-flowered	WHer XSen
Shades of Jade = 'Sant101'	WRHF
tomentosa	see *S. pinnata* subsp. *neapolitana*
virens	see *S. rosmarinifolia* subsp. *rosmarinifolia*
viridis	see *S. rosmarinifolia* subsp. *rosmarinifolia*

Sanvitalia (*Asteraceae*)

Aztekengold = 'Starbini'PBR	LAst WGor
'Little Sun'	SPet
procumbens 'Irish Eyes'	CSpe
'Sunbini'PBR	CCCN CSpe LSou NPri

Saponaria (*Caryophyllaceae*)

× ***boissieri***	EPot
'Bressingham' ♀H4	ECho ECtt EDAr EPfP EPot MHol WAbe WIce
Bressingham hybrid	MAsh
caespitosa	EDAr EPot EWes
× ***lempergii*** 'Fritz Lemperg' **new**	WCot
- 'Max Frei'	CSam EBee ELon EPPr LSou MCot MRav SBch SPhx WCot XLum
ocymoides ♀H4	CMea EBee ECho ECtt EDAr EHon EPfP LAst MAsh MLHP MMuc MNHC MSpe SEND SPlb SPoG SRms SRot XLum
- 'Alba'	EBee
- 'Snow Tip'	ECho EDAr MSpe NGdn NLar XLum
officinalis	CArn CBre CPbn GPoy MHer MHoo MLHP MNHC SIde SPlb SRms WHer WHfH WJek WMoo WPtf
- 'Alba Plena' (d)	CBre LRHS MMuc NLar SEND WPtf XLum
- 'Betty Arnold' (d)	CAby EBee ECtt EWes MHer WCot
§ - 'Dazzler' (v)	WWEG
- 'Flore Pleno' (d)	GAbr
- 'Rosea Plena' (d)	CAby CBre CMac COIW ECtt ELan EPfP GCra LEdu LLWP LPio MHer MLHP MMuc NBid NBir NGdn NOrc SEND SIde SMrm SPer WGwG WHlf WMoo
- 'Rubra Plena' (d)	CPrp ELan EWes MMuc MSCN MWhi SHar WHer
- 'Variegata'	see *S. officinalis* 'Dazzler'
× ***olivana*** ♀H4	CPBP ECho ECtt MAsh XLum
'Rosenteppich'	ECtt
zawadskii	see *Silene zawadskii*

Saposhnikovia (*Apiaceae*)

divaricata	CArn SPhx

Sarcocapnos (*Papaveraceae*)

enneaphylla	LSRN

Sarcococca ✿ (*Buxaceae*)

confusa ♀H4	Widely available
hookeriana ♀H4	ELon EPfP GKin IFoB LBMP LPio LSRN MBlu MSwo NLar NPri NWad SWvt WPGP
- B&SWJ 2585	WCru
- HWJK 2393	WCru
- Sch 1160	CJun CExl WCru
- Sch 2396	CExl
- var. ***digyna*** ♀H4	Widely available
- - 'Purple Stem'	CExl CJun CTri EBee EPfP EUJe GKin LAst LRHS MGos MNrw MRav NLar NPnk SCoo SPer SPoG SWvt WCru
- var. ***hookeriana***	CJun LSRN
- - GWJ 9369	WCru
- - HWJK 2102	WCru
- var. ***humilis***	Widely available
orientalis	CAbP CExl CHel CJun CMCN EBee ELan ELon EPfP IDee LRHS MAsh MGos NLar SPoG SSpi WPGP WPat
'Roy Lancaster'	see *S. ruscifolia* var. *chinensis* 'Dragon Gate'
'Rudolph' **new**	EPfP LLHF
ruscifolia	CBcs CDoy CDul CExl CHab CJun CMCN CMac CSBt EBee ECrN ELan ELon EPfP GKin LEdu LHop LPio LRHS MAsh MGos MRav NEgg NSoo SLim SLon SPer SRms SSpi WCru

- var. ***chinensis*** ♀H4 CJun CSam EPfP SLon WCru WPGP
§ - - 'Dragon Gate' CDoC CExl CGHE CJun EBee ELan EPfP LHop LLHF LRHS LSRN MAsh NLar SLim SLon SPoG SWvt WCru WPGP WPat
saligna CBcs CJun EBee EBtc ELan EPfP LRHS MRav NLar SLon WCru
- MF P2056 WCru
trinervia B&SWJ 9500 WCru
vagans B&SWJ 7285 WCru
wallichii CDoC CExl CGHE EBee ELon MBlu SPoG WPGP WPat
- B&SWJ 2291 CJun WCru
- GWJ 9427 WCru
- HWJK 2425 **new** WCru
- HWJK 2428 **new** WCru
'Winter Gem' **new** STPC
zeylanica **new** WCru
- var. ***brevifolia*** GWJ 9480 WCru

Sarmienta (*Gesneriaceae*)

repens ♀H2 CExl CFil CGHE WAbe WPGP

Sarothamnus see *Cytisus*

Sarracenia ✿ (*Sarraceniaceae*)

× ***ahlesii*** CHew
alata CHew EECP WSSs
- 'Black Tube' WSSs
- heavily veined WSSs
- pubescent EECP WSSs
- 'Red Lid' EECP WSSs
- 'Red Lid' × ***flava*** red pitcher EECP
- wavy lid WSSs
- white-flowered WSSs
alata × ***flava*** var. ***maxima*** WSSs
× ***areolata*** CHew WSSs
× ***catesbyi*** ♀H1 CHew WSSs
'Eva' **new** WSSs
× ***excellens*** ♀H1 WSSs
× ***exornata*** SPlb
× ***farnhamii*** EECP
flava ♀H1 MREP WSSs
- all green giant see *S. flava* var. *maxima*
- var. ***atropurpurea*** EECP WSSs
- 'Burgundy' WSSs
- 'Claret' WSSs
- var. ***cuprea*** WSSs
- var. ***flava*** CHew EECP WSSs
§ - var. ***maxima*** CHew EECP WSSs
- var. ***ornata*** CHew EECP WSSs
- var. ***rubricorpora*** CHew EECP WSSs
- var. ***rugelii*** CHew EECP WSSs
'Juthatip Soper' WSSs
leucophylla ♀H1 CHew SPlb WSSs
- green WSSs
- green and white WSSs
- pubescent WSSs
- 'Schnell's Ghost' WSSs
- 'Tarnok' WSSs
leucophylla × ***oreophila*** EECP
leucophylla × (× ***popei***) EECP
'Lynda Butt' WSSs
× ***miniata*** EECP WSSs
minor EECP WSSs
- var. ***minor*** CHew
§ - 'Okee Giant' WSSs
- 'Okefenokee Giant' see *S. minor* 'Okee Giant'
- var. ***okefenokeensis*** CHew WSSs
× ***mitchelliana*** ♀H1 WSSs
× ***moorei*** CHew WSSs
- 'Brook's Hybrid' CHew EECP WSSs
oreophila CHew WSSs
× ***popei*** WSSs
psittacina CHew EECP WSSs
purpurea MREP SPlb
- subsp. ***purpurea*** CHew WSSs
- - f. ***heterophylla*** WSSs
- subsp. ***venosa*** CHew WSSs
- - var. ***burkii*** WSSs
× ***readii*** WSSs
rubra EECP WSSs
- subsp. ***alabamensis*** CHew WSSs
- subsp. ***gulfensis*** CHew WSSs
* - - f. ***heterophylla*** WSSs
- subsp. ***jonesii*** EECP WSSs
* - - f. ***heterophylla*** WSSs
- subsp. ***rubra*** CHew WSSs
- subsp. ***wherryi*** CHew EECP WSSs
- - giant WSSs
- - yellow-flowered WSSs
'Vogel' **new** WSSs
× ***wrigleyana*** ♀H1 MREP

Saruma (*Aristolochiaceae*)

henryi CAby CDes CLAP CPom ESwi EWld LEdu MAvo WCot WCru WPGP WSHC

Sasa (*Poaceae*)

disticha 'Mirrezuzume' see *Pleioblastus pygmaeus* 'Mirrezuzume'
glabra f. ***albostriata*** see *Sasaella masamuneana* 'Albostriata'
kagamiana NLar
kurilensis MWhi MWht WJun
§ - 'Shima-shimofuri' (v) EPPr EPfP ERod EShb MMoz MWht WJun
- 'Shimofuri' see *S. kurilensis* 'Shima-shimofuri'
nana see *S. veitchii* f. *minor*
§ ***palmata*** CDul CWSG CWib EHoe MMuc MWhi SEND WHer
- f. ***nebulosa*** CBcs CCon CDoC CHEx ENBC EPfP EWes MBrN MMoz MWht NLar SAPC WJun WMoo
quelpaertensis MWht
tessellata see *Indocalamus tessellatus*
tsuboiana CBcs CDoC LRHS MJak MMoz MWht NLar SBig SGol WMoo WPnP
§ ***veitchii*** CBcs CDoy EHoe ENBC MJak MMoz MMuc MRav MWht NLar SEND SGol SPer WJun WMoo
§ - f. ***minor*** WMoo

Sasaella (*Poaceae*)

§ ***masamuneana*** 'Albostriata' (v) CDoC CEnt ENBC EPPr ERod LEdu LRHS MMoz MMuc MWht SBig WJun WMoo WPGP
- f. ***aureostriata*** (v) MMoz
§ ***ramosa*** CHEx MWht

Sassafras (*Lauraceae*)

albidum CArn CBcs CMCN EBee ELan EPfP LRHS MAsh NLar SChF SKHP SLon SPoG SSpi

satsuma see *Citrus unshiu*

Satureja ✿ (*Lamiaceae*)

	coerulea ♀H4	EWes NBir XSen
	douglasii	EOHP SHDw WJek
	- 'Indian Mint'PBR	CArn MHer
	hortensis	ELau GPoy MHer MHoo MNHC SIde SRms WJek
	intricata	XSen
	macedonica	LLWP
	montana	CArn CHby ELau GKev GPoy LLWP MBri MHer MHoo MNHC SDix SEND SIde SRms SVic WHfH WJek XSen
*	- ***citriodora***	GPoy LLWP MHer MHoo XSen
§	- subsp. ***illyrica***	CPBP MHoo SPhx WJek XLum XSen
	- 'Purple Mountain'	GPoy LLWP MHer
	- ***subspicata***	see *S. montana* subsp. *illyrica*
	obovata	XSen
	parnassica	LLWP
	repanda	see *S. spicigera*
	seleriana	SDys
§	***spicigera***	CArn CPrp ELau EPot LEdu LLWP MHer MHoo NBir SPhx SRms WJek XLum
	spinosa	XSen
	thymbra	CArn SHDw XSen
§	***viminea***	EOHP

Saurauia (*Actinidiaceae*)

	subspinosa	CHEx

Sauromatum (*Araceae*)

	gaoligongense new	CDes
	guttatum	see *S. venosum*
§	***venosum***	CArn CCon CExl EAmu EBee ECho EShb LEdu LRHS MMoz SBig SBst WCru WPGP XLum

Saururus (*Saururaceae*)

	cernuus	CArn CBAq CHEx CRow CWat EHon ELan LLWG MSKA MWts SRms SWat WMAq XLum
	chinensis	CRow LLWG

Saussurea (*Asteraceae*)

	costus	GPoy
	japonica new	WCru
	nepalensis	CArn

savory, summer see *Satureja hortensis*

savory, winter see *Satureja montana*

Saxegothaea (*Podocarpaceae*)

	conspicua	CBcs CDoC IArd IDee NLar

Saxifraga ✿ (*Saxifragaceae*)

	McB 1377/1 (7)	NWad
	McB 1377/2 (7)	NWad
	SEP 22	CPBP
	aizoides (9)	ECho
	- SDR 5497	GKev
	- var. ***atrorubens*** (9)	ECho GKev
	aizoon	see *S. paniculata* subsp. *paniculata*
	'Alan Hayhurst' (8)	CPBP WAbe
	'Alan Martin' (× *boydilacina*) (7)	ECho EPot
	'Alba' ambig.	EHyd LRHS
	'Alba' (× *apiculata*) (7)	ECho MHer NRya SPlb WIce WPat
	'Alba' (*oppositifolia*) (7)	ECho ELan EWes ITim NWad WAbe
	'Albertii' (*callosa*)	see *S.* 'Albida'
§	'Albida' (*callosa*) (8)	ECho WAbe
	'Albrecht Dürer' (Lasciva Group) (7)	EPot WAbe
	'Alfons Mucha' (7)	WPat
	'Allendale Argonaut' (7)	WAbe
	'Allendale Beauty' (7)	CPBP
	'Allendale Betty' (× *lismorensis*) (7)	EPot
	'Allendale Bonny' (7)	EPot WAbe
	'Allendale Bravo' (× *lismorensis*) (7)	WAbe
	'Allendale Cabal' (7)	CPBP ITim
	'Allendale Carol' (7)	WAbe
	'Allendale Charm' (Swing Group) (7)	ITim WAbe WHoo
	'Allendale Chick' (7)	NHar
	'Allendale Desire' (7)	WAbe
	'Allendale Divine' (7)	WAbe
	'Allendale Dream' (7)	EPot
	'Allendale Duo' (7)	WAbe
	'Allendale Elegance' (7)	WAbe
	'Allendale Elf' (7)	WAbe
	'Allendale Elite' (7)	WAbe
	'Allendale Envoy' (7)	ITim WAbe
	'Allendale Epic' (7)	NHar
	'Allendale Fairy' (7)	ITim NHar
	'Allendale Ghost' (7)	WAbe
	'Allendale Goblin' (7)	WAbe
	'Allendale Grace' (7)	WAbe
	'Allendale Hobbit' (7)	NHar WAbe
	'Allendale Host' (7)	WAbe
	'Allendale Icon' (× *polulacina*) (7)	WAbe
	'Allendale Imp' (7)	WAbe
	'Allendale Ina' (7)	NHar WAbe
	'Allendale Jinn'	WAbe
	'Allendale Jo'	EPot WAbe
	'Allendale Ruby' (7)	WAbe
	'Allendale Snow' (× *rayei*) (7)	EPot
	alpigena (7)	WAbe
	× ***andrewsii*** (8 × 11)	XLum
	angustifolia Haw.	see *S. hypnoides*
	'Anne Beddall' (× *goringiana*) (7)	WAbe
	'Antonio Vivaldi' (7)	WAbe
	'Apfelblüten' (*oppositifolia*) (7) new	WHoo
	× ***apiculata*** (7)	MAsh
	× ***apiculata*** *sensu stricto* hort.	see *S.* 'Gregor Mendel'
	'Apple Blossom' (Mossy Group) (15)	ECtt EPfP NPro NRya WGor
	'Arabella' (× *edithae*) (7)	ECho
	× ***arendsii*** purple-flowered (15)	SPlb
	'Asahi' (*fortunei*) (5)	IVic
	aspera (10) new	EDAr WAbe
	'Assimilis' (× *petraschii*) (7)	EPot
	'Atropurpurea' (*paniculata* subsp. *cartilaginea*) (8)	NHar NHol WIce XLum
	'Aufheiter von Eri' (*fortunei*) (5)	IVic
	'Aurea Maculata' (*cuneifolia*)	see *S.* 'Aureopunctata'
	'Aurea' (*umbrosa*)	see *S.* 'Aureopunctata'

§ 'Aureopunctata' (× *urbium*) (11/v)	CBct CMac CTri ECho ELan EPfP GKev GMaP LPot LRHS MHer MLHP MRav SPer SPlb SPoG SRms WMoo XLum
'Autumn Tribute' (*fortunei*) (5)	CBct CLAP WAbe
'Ayer's Rock' (7)	WAbe
'Balcana' (*paniculata*) (8)	WAbe
'Baldensis'	see *S. paniculata* var. *minutifolia*
'Beatles' (Beat Group) (7)	EPot
§ 'Beatrix Stanley' (× *angelica*) (7)	ECho LRHS MAsh MHer NWad WGor
× ***biasolettoi*** *sensu stricto* hort.	see *S.* 'Phoenix'
× ***bilekii*** (7)	ECho
'Black Beauty' (15)	ECtt LPot MHer
Black Ruby (*fortunei*) (5)	Widely available
'Blackberry and Apple Pie' (*fortunei*) (5)	CBct CExl CHel CLAP EBee ECtt EPfP IBal LRHS MBrN MHol MLHP MNrw NHar NMyG SBch SPet SWvt WCot WMoo WWEG
'Bob Hawkins' (Mossy Group) (15/v)	NHol NWad
§ 'Bodensee' (× *hofmannii*) (7)	WPat
'Bohemia' (7)	ECho EPot NLar
× ***borisii*** *sensu stricto* hort.	see *S.* 'Sofia'
'Boston Spa' (× *elisabethae*) (7)	ECho ECtt EPot LRHS MAsh MHer NLar SPlb WPat
'Bridget' (× *edithae*) (7)	ECho LRHS
'Brimstone' (7)	WAbe
'Brno' (× *elisabethae*) (7)	EPot
'Brookside' (*burseriana*) (7)	EPot
brunoniana	see *S. brunonis*
§ ***brunonis*** (1) CC 5315	GKev
'Bryn Llwyd'	WAbe
bryoides (10)	ECho
* 'Buckland' (*fortunei*) (5)	WCot
'Bürgel' (× *poluanglica*) (7)	EPot GKev
× ***burnatii*** (8)	EHyd LRHS NSla WGor
burseriana (7)	ECho SBch WAbe WGor
× ***caesia*** misapplied (× *fritschiana*)	see *S.* 'Krain'
× ***caesia*** L. (8)	SRms WAbe
§ ***callosa*** (8) ♀H4	ECho EDAr MHer MLHP WAbe WPat
- subsp. ***callosa*** (8)	ECho
§ - - var. ***australis*** (8)	GJos NBro
- var. ***lantoscana***	see *S. callosa* subsp. *callosa* var. *australis*
- ***lingulata***	see *S. callosa*
'Camyra' (7)	WAbe
× ***canis-dalmatica***	see *S.* 'Canis-dalmatica'
§ 'Canis-dalmatica' (× *gaudinii*) (8) ♀H4	ECho ECtt EPot GJos GKev LRHS NHar NWad WGor
§ 'Carmen' (× *elisabethae*) (7)	WAbe
'Carniolica' (× *engleri*) (8)	WAbe
§ 'Carniolica' (*paniculata*) (8)	NBro NHol
carolinica	see *S.* 'Carniolica' (*paniculata*)
cartilaginea	see *S. paniculata* subsp. *cartilaginea*
'Caterhamensis' (*cotyledon*) (8)	NHar
caucasica (7)	ECho WAbe
cebennensis (15) ♀H2	NRya
- dwarf (15)	WAbe
'Cecil Davies' (8)	NHar
'Celebration'	WAbe
cespitosa (15)	WAbe

'Chambers' Pink Pride'	see *S.* 'Miss Chambers'
'Charles Chaplin' (7)	ECho
'Charles Darwin' (7)	CPBP
Cheap Confections (*fortunei*) (4)	CBct CLAP ECtt IFoB LLHF NMyG SBch WBor WMoo WOld WPGP WWEG
§ ***cherlerioides*** (10)	NRya
Cherry Pie (*fortunei*) (5)	CBct LLHF LRHS NBir NHar NMyG
'Chodov' (Holenka's Miracle Group) (× *megaseiflora*) (7)	EPot
'Christine' (× *anglica*) (7)	ECho
cinerea (7)	WAbe
- McB 1376	NWad
'Cio-Cio-San' (Vanessa Group) (7)	CPBP WAbe
'Citronella' (7)	ECho WAbe
'Clare' (× *anglica*) (7)	ECtt NHol
§ 'Clarence Elliott' (London Pride Group) (*umbrosa*) (11) ♀H4	CMea CTri ECho EWes GAbr GBin GCal GKev GMaP LPio MHer NDov NLar NRya WIce WPat WWEG
'Claude Monet' (Impressio Group) (7)	CPBP
'Cloth of Gold' (*exarata* subsp. *moschata*) (15)	ECho ECtt EHyd ELan GMaP LRHS MAsh MHer NHol NRya NWad SPlb SPoG SRms WAbe WIce
cochlearis (8)	CTri LRHS MAsh NBro NSla SBch WAbe
'Cockscomb' (*paniculata*) (8)	ECho EPot NHar NWad WAbe
columnaris (7)	WAbe
'Conwy Snow' (*fortunei*) (5)	CDes CLAP NHar WAbe WMoo
'Conwy Star' (*fortunei*) (5)	CLAP NHar WAbe
'Coolock Gem' (7)	EPot WAbe
'Coolock Kate' (7)	WAbe
'Corennie Claret'	see *S.* 'Glowing Ember'
'Correvoniana' misapplied	see *S.* 'Lagraveana'
'Correvoniana' Farrer (*paniculata*) (8)	EDAr EPot MHer MSCN XLum
cortusifolia (5)	CLAP EBee ECho
- B&SWJ 5879	WCru
- var. ***stolonifera*** (5)	CBct ECho GCal XLum
B&SWJ 6205	WCru
§ ***corymbosa*** (7)	EPot
Cotton Crochet (*fortunei*) (5/d)	CAbP CBct CHel EBee ECtt ESwi LRHS MNrw NHar NMyG SHeu WBor WCot WMoo WOld
cotyledon (8)	ECho WAbe WCFE
§ 'Cranbourne' (× *anglica*) (7) ♀H4	CMea ECho LRHS MAsh WPat
'Cream' (*paniculata*) (8)	ECho
'Cream Seedling' (× *elisabethae*) (7)	ECho
'Crenata' (*burseriana*) (7)	EPot
'Crimson Rose' (*paniculata*)	see *S.* 'Rosea' (*paniculata*)
§ ***crustata*** (8)	CPBP ECho NHar WAbe WThu XLum
- var. ***vochinensis***	see *S. crustata*
Crystal Pink (*fortunei*) (5/v)	CAbP CBct CExl CHel EBee ECtt IFoB LBMP LRHS MHol MNrw NHar NMyG NPnk WCot WGrn WOld
'Crystalie' (× *biasolettoi*) (7)	LRHS WPat
'Cultrata' (*paniculata*) (8)	NBro
'Cumulus' (7) ♀H4	EDAr EPot GKev WAbe
§ ***cuneifolia*** (11)	ECho IMou LBee MHer MLHP MWat NWad WMoo XLum
- var. ***capillipes***	see *S. cuneifolia* subsp. *cuneifolia*
§ - subsp. ***cuneifolia*** (11)	ECtt GJos

* - var. ***subintegra*** (11)	ECho
'Cuscutiformis' (*stolonifera*) (5)	CAby CElw CExl CHid EWld GBuc LRHS MAvo MBel MRav MSCN SBch SMrm SRms WBor WCru WPGP XLum
cymbalaria (2)	WHil
dahurica	see *S. cuneifolia*
'Dainty Dame' (× *arco-valleyi*) (7)	WAbe
'Dawn Frost' (7)	EPot WIce
'Delia' (× *hornibrookii*) (7)	ITim
densa	see *S. cherlerioides*
'Dentata' (× *geum*)	see *S.* 'Dentata' (× *polita*)
'Dentata' (× *urbium*)	see *S.* 'Dentata' (× *polita*)
§ 'Dentata' (× *polita*) (London Pride Group) (11)	ECho GCal MAvo WMoo WWEG
diapensioides (7)	WAbe
dinnikii (7)	WAbe
'Doctor Clay' (*paniculata*) (8)	EHyd GKev LRHS NHar NHol NRya SPlb WAbe
'Doctor Ramsey' (8)	ECho EHyd EWes LRHS NBro NWad WAbe WGor WPnn
'Don Giovanni' (7)	WAbe
'Donald Mann' (15)	EWes
'Drakula' (*ferdinandi-coburgi*) (7)	ECho EHyd LRHS
'Edith' (× *edithae*) (7)	ECho LRHS
'Elf' (7)	see *S.* 'Beatrix Stanley'
'Elf' (*exarata* subsp. *moschata*) (15)	ECtt SRms WGor
× ***elisabethae*** *sensu stricto* hort.	see *S.* 'Carmen'
× ***elisabethae*** Sünd. (7)	EDAr
'Elizabeth Sinclair' (× *elisabethae*) (7)	EPot
'Elliott's Variety'	see *S.* 'Clarence Elliott' (*umbrosa*)
epiphylla (5) BWJ 8177	WCru
'Esther' (× *burnatii*) (8)	CMea ECho EHyd GKev LRHS SRGP WAbe WHoo WPnn
§ 'Eulenspiegel' (× *geuderi*) (7)	EPot NWad
'Eva Hanzliková' (× *izari*) (7)	WAbe
exarata (15)	WAbe
§ - subsp. ***moschata*** (15)	GAbr
'Excellent' (Exclusive Group) (7)	EPot
fair maids of France	see *S.* 'Flore Pleno'
'Fairy' (*exarata* subsp. *moschata*) (15)	CMea ECtt NBir
'Faldonside' (× *boydii*) (7) ♀H4	MAsh WAbe WPat
'Falstaff' (*burseriana*) (7)	WAbe
× ***farreri*** (15)	WIce
§ ***federici-augusti*** subsp. ***grisebachii*** (7) ♀H2-3	ECho LRHS NSla WAbe
ferdinandi-coburgi (7) ♀H4	ECtt SBch WAbe
§ - subsp. ***chrysosplenifolia*** var. ***rhodopea*** (7)	ECho LRHS
- var. ***pravislavii***	see *S. ferdinandi-coburgi* subsp. *chrysosplenifolia* var. *rhodopea*
- var. ***radoslavoffii***	see *S. ferdinandi-coburgi* subsp. *chrysosplenifolia* var. *rhodopea*
'Findling' (Mossy Group) (15)	EPfP NWad SPoG WAbe
'Firebrand' (× *kochii*) (7)	CPBP WAbe
Five Color (*fortunei*)	see *S.* 'Go-nishiki'
§ ***flagellaris*** (1)	WAbe
'Flavescens' misapplied	see *S.* 'Lutea' (*paniculata*)
§ 'Flore Pleno' (*granulata*) (15/d)	CRDP EWes NBir
'Flowers of Sulphur'	see *S.* 'Schwefelblüte'
fortunei (5) ♀H4	CHEx CLAP CMac ECho GMaP LEdu NBir NPnk SRms WAbe
- B&SWJ 6346	WCru
- from John Fielding (5) **new**	WCot
- f. ***alpina*** (5)	CLAP
- - from Hokkaido (5)	CLAP WCru
- var. ***koraiensis*** (5) B&SWJ 8688	WCru
- var. ***obtusocuneata*** (5)	CLAP ECho LLHF WAbe
- f. ***partita*** (5)	CLAP WCot WCru
- var. ***pilosissima*** (5) B&SWJ 8557	WCru
- pink-flowered (5)	CLAP WAbe
- var. ***suwoensis*** (5)	CLAP
'Four Winds' (Mossy Group) (15)	EPfP EWes MBrN SPoG
'Francis Cade' (8)	GAbr WAbe
'Franz Liszt' (7)	WAbe
'Freckles'	GKev
'Frederik Chopin' (7)	EPot WAbe
'Friar Tuck' (× *boydii*) (7)	NWad
'Friesei' (× *salmonica*) (7)	EPot
'Fumiko' (*fortunei*) (5)	CLAP WAbe WCru
'Gaiety' (15)	ECho EHyd LRHS SPoG
'Ganymede' (*burseriana*) (7)	EPot WAbe
× ***gaudinii*** (8) **new**	XLum
'Gelber Findling' (7)	WAbe
'Gelbes Monster' (*fortunei*) (5)	IVic
'Gem' (× *irvingii*) (7)	EPot WIce
'General Joffre' (15)	see *S.* 'Maréchal Joffre'
'Geoff Wilson' (× *biasolettoi*) (7)	EPot
georgei (7)	WAbe
× ***geuderi*** *sensu stricto* hort.	see *S.* 'Eulenspiegel'
§ × ***geum*** (11)	CHid MRav WMoo
- Dixter form (11)	WWEG
'Gleborg' (Mossy Group) (15)	EWes SPoG
'Gloria' (*burseriana*) (7) ♀H4	ECho LRHS MAsh WIce WPat
× ***gloriana*** *sensu stricto* hort. (7)	see *S.* 'Godiva'
'Gloriana'	see *S.* 'Godiva'
'Gloriosa' (× *gloriana*) (7)	see *S.* 'Godiva'
§ 'Glowing Ember' (Mossy Group) (15)	EWes
'Glückliches Mädchen' (*fortunei*) (5)	IVic
§ 'Godiva' (× *gloriana*) (7)	WAbe
'Gold Dust' (× *eudoxiana*) (7)	ECho NRya
'Gold Mound'	WNew
'Golden Falls' (Mossy Group) (15/v)	EWes SPlb SPoG
Golden Prague (× *pragensis*)	see *S.* 'Zlatá Praha'
'Golem' (7)	WAbe
§ 'Go-nishiki' (*fortunei*) (5)	CBct LLHF NHar NMyG
'Gorges du Verdon' (8)	GKev
'Gothenburg' (7)	EPot WAbe WPat
'Grace Farwell' (× *anglica*) (7)	ECho NLar

granulata (15)	ECho GJos MHer NMir NSla WAbe
'Gregor' (× *poluanglica*) (7)	WAbe
§ 'Gregor Mendel' (× *apiculata*) (7) 🏆H4	CMea ECho ECtt EHyd LRHS NLar SBch SIgm SRms WAbe WHoo
grisebachii	see *S. federici-augusti* subsp. *grisebachii*
'Haagii' (× *eudoxiana*) (7)	CTri ECho GKev NLar
'Harbinger' (7)	WAbe
'Hare Knoll Beauty' (8)	CPBP ECho EHyd ITim LRHS NHar NHol NSla WAbe
'Harlow Car' (× *anglica*) (7)	NSla
'Harry Marshall' (× *irvingii*) (7)	NWad
'Harvest Moon' (*stolonifera*) (5)	CHEx WBor WHer
'Hedwig' (× *malbyana*) (7)	WAbe
'Heisel Kurenai' (*fortunei*) (5)	IVic
'Hi-Ace' (Mossy Group) (15/v)	ECtt MHer SPlb
'Hime' (*stolonifera*) (5)	WCru
'Hindhead Seedling' (× *boydii*) (7)	LRHS WAbe
hirsuta (11)	EWTr EWld LEdu LRHS MMuc WCru
'Hirsuta' (× *geum*)	see *S.* × *geum*
'Hirtella' Ingwersen (*paniculata*) (8)	EPot
'Hirtifolia' (*paniculata*) (8)	GJos
'His Majesty' (× *irvingii*) (7)	EPot
'Hiten' (*fortunei*) (5)	GKev
'Hocker Edge' (× *arco-valleyi*) (7)	WAbe
'Holden Seedling' (Mossy Group) (15)	ECtt
hostii (8)	ECho EDAr GKev NWad XLum
- subsp. ***hostii*** (8)	XLum
- - var. ***altissima*** (8)	XLum
- subsp. ***rhaetica*** (8)	NBro XLum
'Hsitou Silver' (*stolonifera*) (5)	EPPr
§ ***hypnoides*** (15)	NMir SPoG WAbe
hypostoma (7)	WAbe
'Iceland' (*oppositifolia*) (7)	EWes WAbe
'Ignaz Dörfler' (× *doerfleri*) (7)	WAbe
imparilis (5)	CLAP WCru
'Ingeborg' (Mossy Group) (15)	CElw
× ***irvingii*** (7)	ECho EPot
× ***irvingii*** *sensu stricto* hort.	see *S.* 'Walter Irving'
'James' (7)	NSla
'Jan Neruda' (× *megaseiflora*) (7)	CPBP
'Jaromir' (8)	NHar
'Jenkinsiae' (× *irvingii*) (7) 🏆H4	CMea ECho EPot LRHS MAsh NRya NWad WAbe WIce WPat
§ 'Johann Kellerer' (× *kellereri*) (7)	EPot
'Johann Wolfgang Goethe' (7)	WAbe
'John Byam-Grounds' (Honor Group) (7)	WAbe
'Jorg' (× *biasolettoi*) (7)	EPot
'Joy'	see *S.* 'Kaspar Maria Sternberg'
'Joy Bishop' (7)	WAbe
'Judith Shackleton' (× *abingdonensis*) (7)	CPBP WAbe

'Juliet'	see *S.* 'Riverslea'
§ ***juniperifolia*** (7)	ECho GAbr SRms XLum
'Jupiter' (Holenka's Miracle Group) (× *megaseiflora*) (7)	CPBP
'Kanna' (*fortunei*) (5)	IVic
'Karel Čapek' (Prichard's Monument Group) (× *megaseiflora*) (7)	ECho EPot LRHS WAbe
'Karlštejn' (× *borisii*) (7)	EPot
§ 'Kaspar Maria Sternberg' (× *petraschii*) (7)	LRHS WPat
'Kath Dryden' (7)	ECho ECtt NWad
'Kathleen' (× *polulacina*) (7)	EPot
'Kathleen Pinsent' (8) 🏆H4	ECho
'Kath's Delight' (8)	GKev
× ***kellereri*** *sensu stricto* hort.	see *S.* 'Johann Kellerer'
'Ken McGregor' (7)	WAbe
'Kew Gem' (× *petraschii*) (7)	ECho
'Kewensis' (× *kellereri*) (7)	WAbe
'King Lear' (× *bursiculata*) (7)	ECho LRHS
'Kinki Purple' (*stolonifera*) (5)	CBct EShb EWld LHop WCru WPGP
'Knapton Pink' (Mossy Group) (15)	ECtt EDAr EPfP NPro SPoG WAbe WIce
'Knebworth' (8)	ECho
'Kokaku' (*fortunei*) (5)	LLHF
* 'Kosumosu' (*fortunei*) (5)	WOld
kotschyi × ***wendelboi***	EPot
'Koukan' (*fortunei*) (5)	IVic
§ 'Krain' (× *fritschiana*) (8)	ECho
'Labe' (× *arco-valleyi*) (7)	EPot WAbe
'Lady Beatrix Stanley'	see *S.* 'Beatrix Stanley'
§ 'Lagraveana' (*paniculata*) (8) 🏆H4	ECho EDAr EHyd LRHS WGor
'Laka' (7)	EPot WAbe
× ***landaueri*** *sensu stricto* hort.	see *S.* 'Leonore'
'Lantoscana Superba' (*callosa* subsp. *callosa* var. *australis*) (8)	GKev
'Le Bourg d'Oisans' (*oppositifolia*) (7)	WAbe
'Lemon Spires' (7)	EPot
'Lenka' (× *byam-groundsii*) (7)	WAbe
'Leo Gordon Godseff' (× *elisabethae*) (7)	ECho LRHS
'Leonardo da Vinci' (7)	WAbe
§ 'Leonore' (× *landaueri*) (7)	ECho LRHS SIgm WAbe
'Letchworth Gem' (London Pride Group) (× *urbium*) (11)	ECho GCal LPio
'Licht des Cerise' (*fortunei*) (5)	IVic
'Lidice' (7)	EPot WAbe WHoo
'Lilac Time' (× *youngiana*) (7)	EPot
lilacina (7)	WAbe WPat WThu
'Limelight' (*callosa* subsp. *callosa* var. *australis*) (8)	NWad
'Lincoln Foster' (8)	NHar
lingulata	see *S. callosa*
'Lismore Carmine' (× *lismorensis*) (7)	EPot
'Lismore Gem' (× *lismorensis*) (7)	ECho

'Lismore Mist' (× *lismorensis*) (7)	CPBP
'Lissadell' (*callosa*) (8)	GKev IFoB
* 'Little Piggy' (*epiphylla*) (5)	CDes WCru
'Lizzy' (7)	EPot
llonakhensis	WAbe
'Lohengrin' (× *hoerhammeri*) (7)	EPot
'Lohmuelleri' (× *biasolettoi*) (7)	GKev
lolaensis (7)	WAbe
'Long Acre Pink' (*fortunei*) (5)	CLAP
longifolia (8)	ECho EPot NSla
- var. ***aitanica*** new	WAbe
- hybrids	GKev WAbe
'Louis Armstrong' (Blues Group) (7)	EPot WAbe
Love Me	see *S.* 'Miluj Mne'
lowndesii (7)	WAbe
'Lutea' (*aizoon*)	see *S.* 'Lutea' (*paniculata*)
'Lutea' ambig.	GJos
§ 'Lutea' (*paniculata*) (8) 🏆^{H4}	ECho EDAr EHoe EPot GMaP NBro NHol NRya NSla NWad
luteoviridis	see *S. corymbosa*
macedonica	see *S. juniperifolia*
'Maigrün' (*fortunei*) (5)	NHar
'Major' (*cochlearis*) (8) 🏆^{H4}	WGor
'Marc Chagall' (Decora Group) (7)	WAbe
§ 'Maréchal Joffre' (15)	NEgg
marginata (7)	WAbe
- subsp. ***marginata*** var. ***boryi*** (7)	EPot WAbe
- - var. ***coriophylla*** (7)	WAbe
'Maria Callas' (× *poluanglica*) (7)	WAbe WGor
'Maria Luisa' (× *salmonica*) (7)	CPBP WAbe WPat
'Marie Stivínová' (× *borisii*) (7)	EPot
'Maroon Beauty' (*stolonifera*) (5)	CCVN EBee ECtt EPPr LPot NBid NBre WCot WWEG
'Marshal Joffre' (15)	see *S.* 'Maréchal Joffre' (15)
'Mary Golds' (Swing Group) (7)	GKev ITim NLar WGor
× ***megaseiflora*** *sensu stricto* hort.	see *S.* 'Robin Hood'
mertensiana (6)	NBir WCru WSHC
'Meteor' (7)	NHol NRya
micranthidifolia (4)	CLAP
'Mikuláš Koperník' (× *zenittensis*) (7)	WAbe
'Millstream Cream' (× *elisabethae*) (7)	ECho
§ 'Miluj Mne' (× *poluanglica*) (7)	ECho WHoo
'Minnehaha' (× *elisabethae*) (7)	WAbe
'Minor' (*cochlearis*) (8) 🏆^{H4}	ECho EHyd GKev LRHS NHar NWad WGor WPat
'Mirko Webr' (Harmonia Group) (7)	WAbe
§ 'Miss Chambers' (London Pride Group) (11)	GCal WCot WMoo WSHC WWEG
'Momo Sekisui' (*fortunei*) (5)	IVic
'Mona Lisa' (× *borisii*) (7)	NWad SIgm
'Monarch' (8) 🏆^{H4}	GAbr GKev NWad WAbe WIce
'Moonlight' (× *boydii*)	see *S.* 'Sulphurea'
moorcroftiana (1) CC 6939 new	GKev
moschata	see *S. exarata* subsp. *moschata*
Mossy Group (15)	LRHS
* 'Mossy Pink'	SPoG
'Mossy Red'	SPoG WNew
'Mossy Triumph'	see *S.* 'Triumph'
'Mossy White'	GAbr WNew
'Mother of Pearl' (× *irvingii*) (7)	ECho WIce
'Mother Queen' (× *irvingii*) (7)	WPat
'Mount Nachi' (*fortunei*) (5)	CBct CDes EPfP EWes GAbr GMaP IBal LRHS MLHP NBro NMyG SPlb WAbe WMoo WPGP WWEG
'Mrs Helen Terry' (× *salmonica*) (7)	EPot WIce
'Musgrove Pink' (*fortunei*) (5)	CLAP
mutata (9)	GKev
'Myra' (× *anglica*) (7)	ECho WHoo WPat
'Myra Cambria' (× *anglica*) (7)	NWad
'Nancye' (× *goringiana*) (7)	ITim
'Nicholas' (8)	GKev
'Nisi' (*fortunei*) (5)	IVic
'Norvegica' (*cotyledon*) (8)	ITim WThu
'Nottingham Gold' (× *boydii*) (7)	EPot NWad
§ ***obtusa*** (7)	EPot MHer
'Omar Khayyám'	WAbe
oppositifolia (7)	MAsh MWat NHol NSla SPlb SRms WAbe
I - 'Holden Variety' (7)	NRya NWad
- subsp. ***oppositifolia*** var. ***latina*** (7)	ECho GAbr
'Pablo Picasso' (Conspecta Group) (7)	WAbe
paniculata (8)	ECho EDAr EHoe GKev GMaP MHer MWat NSla SPlb SRms WAbe WHoo WNew
§ - subsp. ***cartilaginea*** (8)	GKev
- subsp. ***kolenatiana***	see *S. paniculata* subsp. *cartilaginea*
§ - var. ***minutifolia*** (8)	CPBP CTri ECho EHyd LRHS MSCN NBro NHar NRya NSla SPlb WAbe
§ - subsp. ***paniculata*** (8) new	MAsh
'Pankrác' (7)	GKev
paradoxa (15)	ECho EHyd LRHS NHol NWad WGor
'Parcevalis' (× *finnisiae*) (7 × 9)	EPot WAbe
'Paul Gaughin'	WAbe
'Paul Rubens' (7) new	WAbe
'Peach Melba' (7)	CPBP EPot NLar WAbe WHoo
* 'Peachy Head'	WAbe
'Pearl Rose' (× *anglica*) (7)	EPot
'Pearly King' (Mossy Group) (15)	ECtt GKev GMaP WAbe
× ***pectinata*** Schott, Nyman & Kotschy	see *S.* 'Krain'
pedemontana from Mount Kazbek, Georgia (15)	WAbe
'Penelope' (× *boydilacina*) (7)	ECho EPot LRHS NLar WHoo WPat
pensylvanica (4)	GCal GCra IMou WCot
'Peter Burrow' (× *poluanglica*) (7) 🏆^{H4}	ECho ITim WIce

	'Peter Pan' (Mossy Group) (15)	EDAr EPfP GJos GMaP LRHS MAsh MHer NHol NWad SPoG WNew WPat WSHC
	'Petra' (7)	EPot
§	'Phoenix' (× *biasolettoi*) (7)	ECho LRHS
	'Pink Cloud' (*fortunei*) (5)	CLAP NHar WAbe
	'Pink Haze' (*fortunei*) (5)	CLAP NHar WAbe
	'Pink Mist' (*fortunei*) (5)	CLAP NHar WAbe WMoo
	'Pink Pagoda' (*nipponica*) (5)	CDes CLAP EBee WCot WCru WPGP
	'Pink Pearl' (7)	SBch
	'Pink Ray' (*fortunei*) (5)	LLHF
	'Pink Star' (× *boydilacina*) (7)	NLar
	'Pixie' (15)	CTri ECtt MAsh NHol NRya NWad SPoG SRms
	'Pixie Alba'	see *S.* 'White Pixie'
	'Plena' (*granulata*)	see *S.* 'Flore Pleno'
	'Polar Drift'	NHar NSla WAbe
	'Pollux' (× *boydii*) (7)	EPot
	poluniniana (7)	WAbe
	poluniniana × 'Winifred' (× *poluanglica*) (7)	ECho EPot
	'Pompadour' (15)	NPro
	'Popelka' (subsp. *marginata* var. *rocheliana*) (7)	LRHS
	porophylla var. ***thessalica***	see *S. sempervivum* f. *stenophylla*
	'Portae' (× *fritschiana*) (8)	XLum
	'Precious Piggy' (*epiphylla*) (5)	WCru
	'Primrose Bee' (× *apiculata*) (7)	ITim
	'Primrose Dame' (× *elisabethae*) (7)	ECho WIce
	'Primulaize Salmon' (9 × 11)	NHar WHoo
	'Primuloides' (*umbrosa*) (11) ♀H4	ECho EDAr MMuc SEND SRms SWvt
	'Prince Hal' (*burseriana*) (7)	ECho EPot LRHS
	'Princess' (*burseriana*) (7)	ECho LRHS
	'Probynii' (*cochlearis*) (8)	CPBP MWat NWad WAbe
	× ***prossenii*** *sensu stricto* hort.	see *S.* 'Regina'
	× ***proximae*** 'Květy Coventry' (7)	EPot
	'Pseudo-valdensis' (*cochlearis*) (8)	WAbe
	'Psycho' (7)	WAbe
	pubescens (15)	WAbe
	- subsp. ***iratiana*** (15)	EPot
	'Punctatissima' (*paniculata*) (8)	NHar
*	***punctissima***	NWad
	'Purple Piggy' (*epiphylla*) (5)	CLAP WCru
	'Purpurea' (*fortunei*)	see *S.* 'Rubrifolia'
§	'Pygmalion' (× *webrii*) (7)	WGor
	'Pyramidalis' (*cotyledon*) (8)	EPfP EWTr XLum
	'Pyrenaica' (*oppositifolia*) (7)	ECho
	quadrifaria (7)	WAbe
	'Radvan Horný' (× *cullinanii*) (7)	WAbe
	'Rainsley Seedling' (8)	GKev NBro
	'Red Poll' (× *poluanglica*) (7)	NRya
*	'Regent'	WAbe
§	'Regina' (× *prossenii*) (7)	EPot MHer
	'Rembrandt van Rijn' (7)	WAbe
	retusa (7)	WAbe
	'Rex' (*paniculata*) (8)	NWad
	rhodopetala (7)	ECho
§	'Riverslea' (× *hornibrookii*) (7)	WAbe
§	'Robin Hood' (× *megaseiflora*) (7)	EPot WHoo WPat
	'Rokujō' (*fortunei*) (5)	CLAP EBee IVic NLar NPnk NPro SHeu
	'Rosa Tubbs'	GKev
	'Rosea' (*cortusifolia*) (5)	CLAP MHol NHar
§	'Rosea' (*paniculata*) (8) ♀H4	GMaP LBMP NBro NRya NSla SEND SRms
	'Rosemarie' (7)	ECho EPot
	'Rosina Sündermann' (× *rosinae*) (7)	ECho LRHS
	'Rote Stadt' (*fortunei*) (5)	IVic
	rotundifolia (12)	EBee EWTr
	'Rubella' (× *irvingii*) (7)	EPot
	'Rubra' (*aizoon*)	see *S.* 'Rosea' (*paniculata*)
§	'Rubrifolia' (*fortunei*) (5)	CLAP CMac CSpe ECtt EHoe GAbr IBal LBMP LRHS NMyG NPnk SMad SPet SWvt WBor WCot WCru WMoo WWEG
*	'Ruby Red'	NPro
*	'Ruby Wedding' (*cortusifolia*) (5)	CLAP WCru
	rufescens (5) BWJ 7510	WCru
	- BWJ 7684	WCru
	'Russell V. Prichard' (× *irvingii*) (7)	NWad
	'Ruth Draper' (*oppositifolia*) (7)	WAbe
	'Ruth McConnell' (15)	CMea SBch
	'Saint John's' (8)	ECho GKev
	'Saint Kilda' (*oppositifolia*) (7)	ITim
	× ***salmonica*** *sensu stricto* hort.	see *S.* 'Salomonii'
§	'Salomonii' (× *salmonica*) (7)	EPot SRms
	sancta (7)	ECho EHyd LRHS SRms
	- subsp. ***pseudosancta***	see *S. juniperifolia*
	- - var. ***macedonica***	see *S. juniperifolia*
	'Sara Sinclair' (× *arco-valleyi*) (7)	CMea
	sarmentosa	see *S. stolonifera*
	'Sartorii'	see *S.* 'Pygmalion'
	scardica (7)	EPot NBro WAbe
	- var. ***dalmatica***	see *S. obtusa*
§	'Schelleri' (× *petraschii*) (7)	EPfP
	'Schöne Mädchen' (*fortunei*) (5)	IVic
§	'Schneeblüte' (15)	ECho EPfP GMaP LRHS WPat
	sempervivum (7)	NGdn WAbe
§	- f. ***stenophylla*** (7)	ECho MHer
	sendaica (5)	WCru
	'Sherlock Holmes' (7)	WAbe
	'Shimmy'	WAbe
	'Shinkunomai' (*fortunei*) (5)	IVic
	'Shiragiku' (*fortunei*) (5)	WCot
	'Silver Beads' (*paniculata*) (8)	NHar
§	'Silver Cushion' (15/v)	CMea CTri ECho ELan LRHS MHol NEgg SPlb SPoG WAbe WNew
	'Silver Edge' (× *arco-valleyi*) (7)	WAbe
	'Silver Maid' (× *engleri*) (8)	NSla WAbe
	'Silver Mound'	see *S.* 'Silver Cushion'
	'Silver Velvet' (*fortunei*) (5)	CAbP CBct CLAP CSpe ECtt ESwi IFoB LRHS MHol MSCN NMyG NWad SHeu WBor WCot

	'Sir Douglas Haig' (15)	NWad
	'Sissi' (7)	EPot WAbe
	'Slack's Ruby Southside' (Southside Seedling Group) (8) 🏆H4	NSla NWad WIce
	'Slack's Sensation'	NSla
	'Slack's Supreme'	NHar NSla
	'Slzy Coventry' (× *proximae*) (7)	EPot WAbe
	'Snowcap' (*pubescens*) (15)	EPot WAbe
	'Snowflake' (Silver Farreri Group) (8) 🏆H4	WAbe
§	'Sofia' (× *borisii*) (7)	EPot
	'Southside Red'	EPot
	Southside Seedling Group (8) 🏆H4	CMea ECho EDAr EHyd EPfP EPot GAbr GJos GKev GMaP LHop LRHS MAsh MHer MMuc NBro NHol NRya NWad SEND SPoG SRms WAbe WCot WHoo WIce WPat XLum
	'Southside Star' (Southside Seedling Group) (8) 🏆H4	WAbe
	spathularis (11)	WCot
	'Splendens' (*oppositifolia*) (7) 🏆H4	ECho EPfP GAbr NHar SIgm SRms WAbe WPat
	'Spotted Dog'	see *S.* 'Canis-dalmatica'
	'Sprite' (15)	SPoG
	spruneri (7)	ECho LRHS
	'Stansfieldii' (*rosacea*) (15)	SPlb SPoG
	'Star Dust' (7)	EPot
	'Štásek' (*dinnikii*) (7) **new**	EPot
	stellaris (4)	WAbe
	stenophylla subsp. ***stenophylla***	see *S. flagellaris*
§	***stolonifera*** (5) 🏆H2	CArn CCVN CHEx CSpe ECho EShb EWTr LDai NBro NPnk SDix SWvt WCot WMoo WPnn
	– large-flowered (5)	WCot WGrn
	'Strawberry Melba' (7) **new**	EPot
	'Sturmiana' (*paniculata*) (8)	SRms
	'Sue Drew' (*fortunei*) (5)	LLHF
	'Sue Tubbs'	GKev
	'Suendermannii' (× *kellereri*) (7)	ECho LRHS
	'Suendermannii Major' (× *kellereri*) (7)	ECho EHyd LRHS
	'Sugar Plum Fairy' (*fortunei*) (5)	EBee ECtt EShb ESwi IVic LRHS MHol SPer WCot
§	'Sulphurea' (× *boydii*) (7)	ECho LRHS MAsh NSla NWad WPat
	'Symons-Jeunei' (8)	NWad WAbe
	'Tenerife' (Swirly Group) (7)	EPot WAbe
	'Theoden' (*oppositifolia*) (7) 🏆H4	CMea CPBP ECho EWes NHar WAbe
	'Theresa Cooper' (7)	EPot WAbe
	tolmiei (3)	WAbe
	tombeanensis (7)	EPot
	Touran Deep Red = 'Rockred' (Mossy Group) (15) **new**	LRHS
	Touran Large White = 'Rocklarwhi'PBR (Mossy Group) (15) **new**	LRHS
	'Tricolor' (*stolonifera*) (5) 🏆H2	EBak
§	'Triumph' (× *arendsii*) (15)	ECtt EPfP EPot GMaP MAsh NEgg SPoG
	'Tully' (× *elisabethae*) (7)	WGor WPat
	'Tumbling Waters' (8) 🏆H4	ECho EHyd EPot GAbr LHop LRHS MRav NHol NSla WAbe WGor
§	'Tvoje Píseň' (× *poluanglica*) (7)	GKev WHoo WThu
§	'Tvůj Polibek' (× *poluanglica*) (7)	EPot
§	'Tvůj Úsměv' (× *poluanglica*) (7)	NLar
§	'Tvůj Úspěch' (× *poluanglica*) (7)	EPot WAbe
	'Tycho Brahe' (× *doerfleri*) (7)	WAbe
	umbrosa (11)	CMac CTri ECho EDAr LAst LEdu LRHS MMuc MRav SEND SPlb SPoG SRms STes SWvt WMoo XLum
	'Unique'	see *S.* 'Bodensee'
	× ***urbium*** (11) 🏆H4	CHEx CTri ECho ELan EPfP GMaP LEdu MBel NPri SPer SRms WBrk WCAu WWEG
	'Vaccariana' (*oppositifolia*) (7)	ECho EPot
	'Valborg'	see *S.* 'Cranbourne'
	'Valentine'	see *S.* 'Cranbourne'
I	'Variegata' (*cuneifolia*) (11/v)	ECho ECtt EPfP LRHS NHol NRya NWad SPet SPlb SPoG WMoo
I	'Variegata' (*exarata* subsp. *moschata*) (15/v)	GMaP
	'Variegata' (*umbrosa*)	see *S.* 'Aureopunctata'
I	'Variegata' (× *urbium*) (11/v)	EBee ECho EPfP LRHS MBel MSpe NLar SRms WNew WWEG
	'Večerní Hvězda' (7)	WAbe
	veitchiana (5)	NBro XLum
	'Verona' (× *caroli-langii*) (7)	WAbe
	'Vladana' (× *megaseiflora*) (7)	CPBP ECho LRHS WAbe
	'Vltava' (7)	EPot
	'Vreny' (8)	GKev
	'Vysoké Mýto' (7)	WAbe
	'Wada' (*fortunei*) (5)	CAbP CCon CDes CHel CLAP CSpe ECtt ELon EPri GAbr GBuc LAst LBMP LRHS MCot MHol MNrw MSpe NBir NMyG NPri SPer WBor WCot WOld WPGP WSHC WWEG
	'Walter Ingwersen' (*umbrosa*) (11)	SRms
§	'Walter Irving' (× *irvingii*) (7)	WAbe
	'Warmes Herz' (*fortunei*) (5)	IVic
	'Wartosque' (*callosa*) (8)	EPot
	'Welsh Dragon' (15)	WAbe
	'Welsh Red' (15)	WAbe
	'Welsh Rose' (15)	WAbe
	wendelboi (7)	EPot WAbe
	'Wendy' (× *wendelacina*) (7)	WAbe
	'Wheatley Rose' (7)	ECho LRHS
§	'White Pixie' (15)	ECtt EDAr EPfP MAsh MHer NHol NPro NRya NWad SPlb SPoG SRms WIce WNew
	'White Star' (× *petraschii*)	see *S.* 'Schelleri'
	'Whitehill' (8) 🏆H4	CMea CPBP ECho ELan EPot GJos GMaP LRHS NBro NHol NRya NSla NWad SBch SPet WHoo WNew
	'William Boyd' (× *boydii*) (7)	WAbe
	'William Shakespeare' (Blues Group) (7)	EPot WAbe
	'Winifred' (× *anglica*) (7)	ECho EPot WAbe
	'Winifred Bevington' (8 × 11) 🏆H4	CPBP ECho EDAr EHyd LHop LRHS MMuc NBro NLar NRya NWad WAbe WHoo WPnn
	'Winston Churchill' (15)	CTri ECho ECtt EHyd LRHS NHol NWad

I	'Winston Churchill Variegata' (15/v)	ECtt NHol NWad
	'Wisley' (*federici-augusti* subsp. *grisebachii*) (7) ♀H2-3	WPat
	'Woodside Ross' (15)	ECtt
	'Yellow Rock' (7)	NRya
	'Youkuy' (*fortunei*) (5)	IVic
	Your Good Fortune	see *S.* 'Tvůj Úspěch'
	Your Kiss	see *S.* 'Tvůj Polibek'
	Your Smile	see *S.* 'Tvůj Úsměv'
	Your Song	see *S.* 'Tvoje Píseň'
	Your Success	see *S.* 'Tvůj Úspěch'
	'Yunagi' (*fortunei*) (5)	IVic WOld
	× ***zimmeteri*** (8 × 11)	ECho
§	'Zlatá Praha' (× *pragensis*) (7)	WAbe

Scabiosa (*Caprifoliaceae*)

	africana	EWes SHar
	- 'Jocelyn'	EBee EWes IPot SHar
	alpina L.	see *Cephalaria alpina*
	argentea	EWes LEdu
	atropurpurea	SPav
	- 'Ace of Spades'	CWCL ELan EPfP MCot SMad SPav SPhx
	- 'Beaujolais Bonnets'	EPfP LRHS MCot SHil SPer WHrl
	- 'Black Knight' **new**	CSpe SPav
§	- 'Chile Black'	CBcs CHab CHel EBee EHoe ELan EPfP EUJe EWes GCal IBoy LAst LHop LRHS MWat NPri SMrm SPav SPet SPhx SRkn SWvt WGwG WMnd WWlt XLum
§	- 'Chilli Pepper'	CWCL EBee EPfP LHop LRHS
§	- 'Chilli Sauce'	EBee EPfP LHop LRHS
	- 'Derry's Black'	CSpe
	- 'Fata Morgana' **new**	SPav
	- 'Night and Day' **new**	LRHS
	- 'Nona'	LLHF
	- 'Peter Ray'	WWlt
	- 'Snowmaiden' **new**	SPav
	banatica	see *S. columbaria*
	'Barocca'	CSpe EPfP LRHS WHil
	'Blue Diamonds'	EWTr IBoy LPio LRHS MHer MHol
	Burgundy Bonnets = 'Scabon'PBR	CHel EPfP LRHS
§	'Butterfly Blue'	CHel CMHG EBee ECtt ELon EPPr EPfP GAbr GBin LRHS LSRN LSou MAsh MBri MHol MPie NDov NHol NLar SCoo SEND SPer SPoG SWvt WBrk WCAu WCot WHoo WWEG
	'Cambridge Blue' **new**	EPfP
	canescens **new**	MSpe
	caucasica	CMac EPfP GKev LAst LEdu WHoo
	- var. ***alba***	CBcs CKno EPfP NGBl WHoo
	- 'Blauer Atlas'	EBee
	- 'Blausiegel'	CMac MRav NBre NDov SPet
	- 'Clive Greaves' ♀H4	CWCL EBee ECtt EPfP GBuc GMaP IBoy MBNS MSpe NDov NPri SGbt SPad SRms SWvt WCAu WCot
	- 'Deep Waters'	CSpe LRHS WPtf
	- 'Fama'	CSpe CWib NBir NGBl NLar SMrm SPlb SRms WWEG
	- 'Fama Deep Blue' **new**	SMrm
	- 'Fama White' **new**	SMrm
	- 'Goldingensis'	CWCL NGdn NPri WHil
	- House's hybrids	CSBt MHol NGdn SRms
	- 'Isaac House'	NLar XLum
	- 'Kompliment'	NBre NLar SMrm WWEG
	- 'Miss Willmott' ♀H4	CMac CSam EBee ECtt EHoe EPfP GBin IBoy IPot LAst LHop LRHS MBri MHer MLHP MRav NCGa NPri SGbt SPad SWvt WCAu WMnd
	- 'Moerheim Blue'	EBee
	- Perfecta Series	CWib LRHS MMHG NGdn NLar SPoG SWat
	- - 'Perfecta Alba'	CAby CHel CWCL CWib ELan GMaP LAst LRHS MHer MSpe MWat NLar NOrc NPri NSoo SPad SPer SPoG SWat WWEG XLum
	- - 'Perfecta Blue'	CAby ELan GMaP MHer MSpe NSoo WCot XLum
	- - 'Perfecta Lilac Blue'	CWib EPfP SPer WWEG
	- 'Stafa'	EBee GBee GBin LRHS MBri MCot MRav MSpe NCGa NEgg NLar WMnd
	- 'Thorp's Variegated' (v)	WCot
	'Chile Black'	see *S. atropurpurea* 'Chile Black'
	'Chile Pepper'	see *S. atropurpurea* 'Chilli Pepper'
	'Chile Sauce'	see *S. atropurpurea* 'Chilli Sauce'
	cinerea	SPhx
§	***columbaria***	CHab EBee ECGP LRHS MLHP MMuc NEgg NMir SMrm WHer WJek WSFF WWEG
*	- ***alpina***	GKev WAbe
	- 'Blue Note'PBR **new**	SMrm
	- 'Misty Butterflies'	CCVN ECtt EPfP GBin LBMP LHop LPio LSou NEgg NGdn NLar SMrm WWEG
	- 'Nana'	CCse CMea EBee EHyd GBin LRHS NBir NGdn NLar SBch SBea WCFE WWFP XLum
	- 'Nana Pink'	EHyd
§	- subsp. ***ochroleuca***	CKno CSpe GBBs GLin LRHS MCot MSpe NBir NLar SHar SPhx SPoG SRms WHil WPGP
	MESE 544	EBee
	- - 'Moon Dance'	CCon CMea EWll GBin LLHF LRHS MSpe NCGa NPri SBea SGbt SMad WHoo
	- 'Pincushion Blue'	EDAr MSpe
	- 'Pincushion Pink'	EDAr MSpe NGdn SBea WWEG
	- pink-flowered	LRHS
	cretica	XLum XSen
	drakensbergensis	CHid ELan EWTr EWes GAbr IKil LRHS MTPN SLon WCot WPtf
	farinosa	MMuc WAbe
	gigantea	see *Cephalaria gigantea*
	graminifolia	ECho GKev NBir SBch SRms WWEG XLum
	[illegible]	EWes
	'Helen Dillon'	EWes LSou WWEG
	'Irish Perpetual Flowering'	see *S.* 'Butterfly Blue'
	japonica var. ***acutiloba***	SPhx
	- var. ***alpina***	CPrp EBee EPfP GAbr GKev MMuc MWat NGdn SPet SPhx WHoo WNew WWFP XLum
	- - 'Blue Star'	EBee NBre NCGa SGbt
	- 'Ritz Blue'	EPfP SPad
	lachnophylla	EBee GCal SPhx WCot
	- 'Blue Horizon'	EBee WHil
	'Little Emily'	ELon LSou
	lucida	ECho ECtt EPfP IPot LRHS MRav WPGP XLum
	'Midnight'	CMea
	'Miss Havisham'	EBee EWes
	montana Mill.	see *Knautia arvensis*
	ochroleuca	see *S. columbaria* subsp. *ochroleuca*

parnassi	see *Pterocephalus perennis*
'Perpetual Flowering'	see *S.* 'Butterfly Blue'
Pink Buttons = 'Walminipink'	CCon EBee LSou NDov SMrm
'Pink Diamonds'	CMac EBee ELan EPfP MHol
'Pink Mist'PBR	EBee ECtt ELan EPfP IBoy LRHS MBri NBir NDov NLar SCoo SPer SPoG SRms WCAu
pterocephala	see *Pterocephalus perennis*
rhodopensis	EBee
'Rosie's Pink'	ECtt
rumelica	see *Knautia macedonica*
'Satchmo'	see *S. atropurpurea* 'Chile Black'
succisa	see *Succisa pratensis*
tatarica	see *Cephalaria gigantea*
tenuis	SPhx
triandra	LHop
'Vivid Violet'	CAbP CSpe CWGN EBee ECtt IPot LSRN LSou MBNS MHol MNrw NDov NLar SHil SMrm WBor WCot

Scadoxus ✿ (*Amaryllidaceae*)

multiflorus	CCCN ECho SDeJ WHil
§ - subsp. ***katherinae*** ♀H1	WCot
§ - subsp. ***multiflorus*** ♀H1	WCot
natalensis	see *S. puniceus*
§ ***puniceus***	CLak WCot

Scaevola (*Goodeniaceae*)

aemula 'Blue Fan'	see *S. aemula* 'Blue Wonder'
§ - 'Blue Wonder'PBR	NPer SWvt
- 'Purple Fan'	LAst
- 'Sparkling Fan' new	LAst
- 'Suntastic' new	LAst
- White Wonder = 'Scax0226'	LHop
- 'Zig Zag'PBR	CCCN
Blauer Facher = 'Saphira'PBR	CCCN LHop
'Brillant'PBR	LAst LSou
crassifolia	SPlb
'Mini Blue'	CCCN
'Topaz Pink'	LHop LSou

Sceletium (*Aizoaceae*)

tortuosum	SPlb

Schefflera (*Araliaceae*)

alpina	IVic
- B&SWJ 8247	WCru
- B&SWJ 11827	WCru
- HWJ 936	WCru
arboricola ♀H1	SEND XBlo
- 'Gold Capella' ♀H1	SEND XBlo
- 'Kalahari'	XBlo
brevipedicellata HWJ 870	WCru
- KWJ 12224	WCru
§ ***chapana*** B&SWJ 11848	WCru
- HWJ 983	WCru
delavayi	CFil CHEx WPGP
elegantissima ♀H1	EShb
enneaphylla B&SWJ 11727	WCru
- HWJ 1018	WCru
fantsipanensis B&SWJ 11666	WCru
- B&SWJ 11671	WCru
- NJM 09.123 new	WPGP
fengii	GLin
gracilis HWJ 622	WCru
- HWJ 878	WCru
hoi B&SWJ 11747	WCru
kornasii B&SWJ 11830	WCru
- HWJ 918	WCru
lenticellata B&SWJ 9762	WCru
macrophylla B&SWJ 8210	WCru
- B&SWJ 9788	WCru
- PAB 2788 new	LEdu
microphylla B&SWJ 3872	WCru
multinervia B&SWJ 11727	WCru
aff. ***myriocarpa*** B&SWJ 11828	WCru
rhododendrifolia	CExl CFil CHEx CMHG WPGP
- GWJ 9375	WCru
taiwaniana	CHEx IVic
- B&SWJ 3575	WCru
- B&SWJ 7096	WCru
- RWJ 10000	WCru
- RWJ 10016	WCru
vietnamensis	see *S. chapana*

Schima (*Theaceae*)

wallichii	CExl
- subsp. ***noronhae*** var. ***superba***	CCCN CExl EPfP
- subsp. ***wallichii*** var. ***khasiana***	CBcs

Schinus (*Anacardiaceae*)

latifolius	CBcs
lentiscifolius	SPlb
molle	SPlb
polygamus	CBcs SPlb

Schisandra (*Schisandraceae*)

sp.	LAst
arisanensis B&SWJ 3050	WCru
aff. ***bicolor***	WPGP
- BWJ 8151	WCru
chinensis	CAgr CArn CBcs GPoy LEdu MSwo NLar SBrt
- B&SWJ 4204	WCru
grandiflora	CBcs CDoC EBee ELan EPfP ESwi LEdu LRHS MBlu NLar SKHP SPer WGwG
- B&SWJ 2245	WCru WSHC
- var. ***cathayensis***	see *S. sphaerandra*
- 'Jamu' (m)	WCru
- 'Lahlu' (f/F)	WCru
grandiflora × ***rubriflora***	WCru
henryi subsp. ***yunnanensis*** B&SWJ 6546	WCru
incarnata × ***rubriflora***	WCru
nigra	see *S. repanda*
aff. ***plena*** HWJ 664	WCru
propinqua	CMac LEdu MBlu NLar
subsp. ***sinensis***	
- - BWJ 8148	WCru
§ ***repanda*** B&SWJ 5897	WCru
- B&SWJ 11455	WCru
rubriflora	CBcs CTri CWSG EBee EPfP IDee LRHS MBlu MGos SKHP SLon SMDP SSpi
- BWJ 7557	WCru
- (f)	WSHC
- (m)	NHol
§ ***sphaerandra*** BWJ 7739	WCru
sphenanthera	LRHS NLar WSHC
- BWJ 8151 new	WCru

Schivereckia (*Brassicaceae*)

	doerfleri	MWat

Schizachyrium (*Poaceae*)

§	***scoparium***	CKno EBee ECGP EHoe EPPr LBMP LRHS MWhi SPhx WCot XLum
	- 'Blaze'	EPPr
	- 'Prairie Blues'	CKno EPfP EShb LRHS SMea SMrm SPhx WCot

Schizocarphus (*Asparagaceae*)

	nervosus	ECho WCot

Schizocodon see *Shortia*

Schizophragma (*Hydrangeaceae*)

	corylifolium	NLar
	- BWJ 8150	WCru WPGP
	aff. ***elliptifolium*** WWJ 11905	WCru
	hydrangeoides	CBcs CDoC CDul CHel EBee ELan EPfP EWTr GKin LAst LRHS MBlu MGos SGol SLim SLon SPer SWvt
	- B&SWJ 5489	WCru
	- B&SWJ 5732	WCru
	- B&SWJ 5954	WCru
	- B&SWJ 6119 from Yakushima, Japan	WCru
	- B&SWJ 8505 from Ulleungdo, Korea	WCru
	- B&SWJ 8522 from Ulleungdo, Korea	WCru
	- 'Brookside Littleleaf'	see *Hydrangea anomala* subsp. *petiolaris* var. *cordifolia* 'Brookside Littleleaf'
	- 'Cheju's Early'	WCru
	- 'Iwa Garami'	NLar
	- 'Moonlight'	Widely available
*	- f. ***quelpartensis*** B&SWJ 8771	WCru
	- 'Rose Sensation' **new**	LRHS LSqu
	- 'Roseum' ♀H4	CDoC CMac CSPN EBee ELan EPfP EWes GBin GKin IArd LRHS MBlu MBri MGos NCGa NLar SGol SKHP SPer SPoG SSpi SWvt WCru WPGP
	integrifolium ♀H4	CBcs CHel CMac EBee ELan EPfP LRHS MBlu NLar SKHP SPer SSpi WKif WPGP WSHC
	- var. ***fauriei***	NLar WSHC
	- - B&SWJ 1701	WCru
	- - B&SWJ 7052	WCru
	- - CWJ 12433	WCru

Schizostachyum (*Poaceae*)

§	***funghomii***	MMuc

Schizostylis see *Hesperantha*

	coccinea 'Gigantea'	see *Hesperantha coccinea* 'Major'
	- 'Grandiflora'	see *Hesperantha coccinea* 'Major'
	- 'Pink Princess'	see *Hesperantha coccinea* 'Wilfred H. Bryant'
	- 'Sunset'	see *Hesperantha coccinea* 'Sunrise'

Schoenoplectus (*Cyperaceae*)

§	***lacustris***	CBAq CWat MMuc MSKA SEND
§	- subsp. ***tabernaemontani***	CBAq CSpe
	- - 'Albescens' (v)	CBAq CWat MNrw MSKA MWts SWat WHal XLum
	- - 'Zebrinus' (v)	CBAq CWat ELan EPfP MMuc MNrw MSKA MWts NPla SPlb SWat WHal WMAq WPnP XLum

Schoenus (*Cyperaceae*)

	pauciflorus	CWCL EHoe EWes LLWG NOak WMoo

Sciadopitys (*Sciadopityaceae*)

	verticillata ♀H4	CBcs CDoC CDoy CDul CKen CMac CSBt CTho EHul EPfP GKin IDee LRHS MBlu MBri MGos MJak MMuc NHol NWea SCoo SLim SPoG SSpi SWvt WHar
I	- 'Compacta'	LRHS
	- 'Firework'	CKen
	- 'Globe'	CKen
	- 'Gold Star'	CKen
	- 'Golden Rush'	CKen NLar
	- 'Goldmahne'	CKen
	- 'Grüne Kugel'	CKen NLar
	- 'Jeddeloh Compact'	CKen
	- 'Kupferschirm'	CKen
	- 'Mecki'	CKen
	- 'Megaschirm'	CKen
	- 'Ossorio Gold'	CKen
	- 'Perlenglanz'	CKen
	- 'Picola'	CKen
	- 'Pygmy'	CKen
	- 'Richie's Cream'	CKen
	- 'Richie's Cushion'	CKen
	- 'Shorty'	CKen
	- 'Speerspitze'	CKen
	- 'Star Wars'	CKen
	- 'Starburst'	CKen
	- 'Sternschnuppe'	CKen NLar
	- 'Wintergreen'	CKen

Scilla (*Asparagaceae*)

	adlamii	see *Ledebouria cooperi*
	× ***allenii***	see × *Chionoscilla allenii*
	amethystina	see *S. litardierei*
	amoena	ECho WCot
	aristidis from Algeria	ECho
	autumnalis	CAvo CDes ECho EPot GKev LLHF WShi WThu
	bifolia ♀H4	CAby CAvo CBro CPom CTca ECho EPot GKev LLWP SBch SDeJ SPhx WShi
	- RB 136/85	ECho
	- 'Alba'	ECho EPot SPhx
	- 'Rosea'	ECho EPot GKev LLWP SDeJ
	bithynica ♀H4	WCot WShi
I	- 'Alba' **new**	CAvo
	campanulata	see *Hyacinthoides hispanica*
	chinensis	see *S. scilloides*
	cilicica	ECho SPhx
	greilhuberi	ECho EPPr EPot LLHF WCot
	hohenackeri	ECho EPot LLHF SPhx WThu
	- BSBE 811	CDes WCot
§	***hughii***	CDes ECho
	hyacinthoides	CDes ECho ERCP WCot
	ingridiae	ECho
	- var. ***taurica***	ECho
	italica	see *Hyacinthoides italica*
	japonica	see *S. scilloides*
	latifolia from Morocco	ECho
	liliohyacinthus	CBro CRow ECho IBlr MMHG WSHC WShi

lingulata	ECho LLHF WCot
- S&F 253	CDes
- var. ***ciliolata***	CBro ECho EPot SBch
- var. ***lingulata***	ECho
§ ***litardierei*** ♀H4	CPom CTca ECho EPPr EPot ERCP GKev SBch SDeJ SEND SPhx WShi
lutea hort.	see *Ledebouria socialis*
madeirensis	CLak WCot
melaina	WCot
messeniaca	CPom
- MS 38 from Greece	WCot
mischtschenkoana ♀H4	CAby CAvo CBro CHid ECho EPot IFro MBri SDeJ WShi
§ - 'Tubergeniana' ♀H4	CMea ECho GKev SPhx WCot
- 'Zwanenburg'	ECho
monophyllos	ECho WCot
natalensis	see *Merwilla plumbea*
non-scripta	see *Hyacinthoides non-scripta*
nutans	see *Hyacinthoides non-scripta*
obtusifolia	ECho WCot
persica ♀H4	CDes ECho SPhx WCot
peruviana	Widely available
- S&L 285	WCot
- SB&L 20/1	WCot
- 'Alba'	CBro CDes CTca ECho WCot WHil XLum
* - var. ***ciliata***	WCot
- var. ***elegans***	CDes WCot
- 'Hughii'	see *S. hughii*
- 'Paul Voelcker'	CDes
- var. ***venusta***	CDes
- - S&L 311/2	WCot
pratensis	see *S. litardierei*
puschkinioides	ECho
reverchonii	ECho
- from Spain	WCot
rosenii	ECho
§ ***scilloides***	ECho GKev
- B&SWJ 8812	WCru
* - 'Alba'	SDeJ
siberica ♀H4	CAby CAvo CBro CTca ECho ELan EPfP GAbr GKev LRHS MMuc SPer SPhx WBor WShi
- 'Alba'	CTca ECho EPfP EPot GKev SDeJ SMrm WShi
- 'Spring Beauty'	CMea ECGP ECho EPot ERCP GKev MBri SDeJ SMrm SPhx SRms
'Tubergeniana'	see *S. mischtschenkoana* 'Tubergeniana'
verna	ECho WShi WThu
vicentina	see *Hyacinthoides vincentina*
violacea	see *Ledebouria socialis*

Scirpoides (*Cyperaceae*)

§ ***holoschoenus***	EBee

Scirpus (*Cyperaceae*)

cernuus	see *Isolepis cernua*
holoschoenus	see *Scirpoides holoschoenus*
lacustris	see *Schoenoplectus lacustris*
- 'Spiralis'	see *Juncus effusus* f. *spiralis*
maritimus	see *Bolboschoenus maritimus*
tabernaemontani	see *Schoenoplectus lacustris* subsp. *tabernaemontani*

Scleranthus (*Caryophyllaceae*)

biflorus	ECho EDAr EUJe EWes GBin LEdu NSla SPlb XLum
uniflorus	ECho EShb IDee LEdu SMad SPlb XLum

Sclerochiton (*Acanthaceae*)

harveyanus	EShb WHil

Scoliopus (*Liliaceae*)

bigelowii	WHal
hallii	EBee LEdu LWst WCru

Scolopendrium see *Asplenium*

Scopolia (*Solanaceae*)

anomala	EBee
carniolica	CArn CAvo CCon EBee ELan EWld GPoy LEdu MPhe NChi NLar NSti SPlb WCru WPGP WSHC XLum
- from Poland	LEdu
- from Slovenia	WCot
§ - var. ***brevifolia***	EPPr EWld LEdu MNrw SPhx
- - WM 9811	MPhe
- subsp. ***hladnikiana***	see *S. carniolica* var. *brevifolia*
- 'Zwanenburg'	EPPr EWes LEdu NLar SPhx XLum
japonica new	IMou
lurida	see *Anisodus luridus*

Scorzonera (*Asteraceae*)

hispanica	SVic

Scrophularia (*Scrophulariaceae*)

aquatica	see *S. auriculata*
§ ***auriculata***	CHab MHer NMir NPer WHer
§ - 'Variegata' (v)	CBAq CBcs EHoe ELan EPfP EShb GCal LLWG LRHS NEgg NSti SPer SPoG WSHC
buergeriana 'Lemon and Lime' misapplied	see *Teucrium viscidum* 'Lemon and Lime'
- 'Lemon and Lime' (v)	NEgg
canina	GKev
nodosa	CArn EBee GPoy NMir WHer WHfH
- ***variegata***	see *S. auriculata* 'Variegata'
scopolii	EBee

Scutellaria ✿ (*Lamiaceae*)

albida	EBee WOut
§ ***alpina***	ECho GJos SPlb SRms SRot WGor
- 'Arcobaleno'	LLHF SMrm
- 'Moonbeam'	LRHS
altissima	CFis ELan LRHS MMuc NBro SPlb WOut WPtf XSen
'Amazing Grace'	EWes
baicalensis	CArn CDes EBee GJos GPoy LHop MHoo SMrm WPtf
canescens	see *S. incana*
columnae	EBee
galericulata	CHab GPoy MHer WHer
hastata	see *S. hastifolia*
§ ***hastifolia***	CTri ECtt
hypericifolia new	XSen
§ ***incana***	EBee ECGP ELan EPPr GMaP LHop LPla MAvo MHol MPie WCot WMnd
indica	EWld
- var. ***japonica***	see *S. indica* var. *parvifolia*
§ - var. ***parvifolia***	ECho EWes GJos LRHS SRot WAbe
- - 'Alba'	ECho LLHF
lateriflora	CArn GPoy LRHS SMrm WJek
- PAB 3921 new	LEdu
maekawae	EBee WPGP
- B&SWJ 557a	WCru

'Mood Indigo'	EPPr LRHS
nana var. ***sapphirina***	CPBP
novae-zelandiae	ECou
orientalis	ECtt SBch
- subsp. ***bicolor***	ECtt
- subsp. ***pinnatifida***	XSen
pontica	CDes CPBP SBch WIce
scordiifolia	CMea ECho IMou LHop LRHS NRya NWad SBHP SRms WHal
- 'Seoul Sapphire'	CDes CSpe EWes GAbr GBin LEdu LHop LRHS WPtf
sevanensis	EBee LHop MNrw WCot WIce
'Sherbert Lemon'	CMea ELon SRot WHil
suffrutescens	EDAr
- 'Texas Rose'	CFis CMea CSpe EBee LHop LLHF LRHS SBch SRot WHil
supina	see *S. alpina*
tournefortii	ECtt LLWP XSen
* ***zhongdianensis***	MAvo WPtf

seakale see *Crambe maritima*

Sebaea (*Gentianaceae*)

rehmanii	SPlb
thomasii	WAbe
- 'Bychan'	WAbe

Securigera (*Papilionaceae*)

§ ***varia***	CArn EPfP LHop MMuc NPri SEND SRms XLum

Sedastrum see *Sedum*

× *Sedeveria* (*Crassulaceae*)

'Darley Dale'	CDoC CSuc
'Fanfare' new	CSuc
'Letizia'	EUJe

Sedum ✿ (*Crassulaceae*)

'Abbey Dore'	ECtt ELan EPfP GCal LPio LPla LRHS LSou MTis NCGa SPhx WCAu WPGP
acre	CTri ECho EHyd EPfP GPoy LEdu LRHS MAsh MHer MNHC NMir SEND SPlb XLum
- 'Aureum'	ECho EDAr EHoe ELan EPfP LAst MAsh NLar NPri NRya SPer SPoG XLum
- 'Golden Queen'	ECho EHyd EPot LRHS MSCN SPlb SPoG
- 'Helvetica'	WCot
- 'Minus'	ECho
§ - subsp. ***neglectum*** var. ***majus***	EPfP NLar
adolphi	EPfP
aizoon	ECho GCal LAst NBre SPlb XLum
'Aurantiacum'	see *S. aizoon* 'Euphorbioides'
§ - 'Euphorbioides'	ECtt ELan LDai LPot MHer MMuc MRav NLar SEND SHar SPer SPlb
albescens	see *S. forsterianum* f. *purpureum*
alboroseum	see *S. erythrostictum*
§ ***album***	ECho EHyd LRHS MMuc NBro NMir SEND XLum
- 'Coral Carpet'	ECho ECtt EDAr EPPr EPfP EPot GAbr GJos GKev MAsh MRav MWat NRya SFgr SPoG WCot XLum
- subsp. ***teretifolium*** var. ***micranthum*** 'Chloroticum'	XLum
§ - - var. ***murale***	CTri XLum
alpestre	XLum
altissimum	see *S. sediforme*
* ***altum***	NBre
anacampseros	MHer SEND XLum
'Aquarel' new	GBin
athoum	see *S. album*
atlanticum	see *S. dasyphyllum* subsp. *dasyphyllum* var. *mesatlanticum*
'Autumn Charm'	see *S.* (Herbstfreude Group) 'Lajos'
Autumn Joy	see *S.* Herbstfreude Group
beauverdii	WCru
subsp. ***vietnamense*** HWJ 824 new	
'Bertram Anderson' ♀H4	Widely available
beyrichianum misapplied	see *S. glaucophyllum*
bithynicum 'Aureum'	see *S. hispanicum* var. *minus* 'Aureum'
Black Beauty = 'Florseblab'	LRHS MBri MNrw NLar SHil
'Blade Runner'	LRHS LSou
brevifolium	NHol
§ - var. ***quinquefarium***	WIce
burrito	EShb
'Carl'	CKno COIW CPrp ECtt ELan ELon EPfP EShb GBin GMaP LHop LPio LRHS LSRN MHol MRav MTis NBro NOrc NSti NWsh SBch SMrm SRGP WCot WHoo WMnd WMoo WWEG XLum
cauticola ♀H4	CSpe ECho EDAr EPot GBuc GCal LPio MAsh MAvo MBrN MHer MRav NBre SRms SRot WAbe WIce XLum
- from Lida, Belarus	ECho
- 'Coca-Cola'	CCVN CHel CMac CWGN ECtt EHoe GBin GJos LAst LBMP LRHS MAsh MCot NDov NPri SPhx SPoG SWvt WHoo WNew
- 'Lidakense' ♀H4	CMea CSpe CWCL ECho ECtt EPot GBuc MAsh MBri MLHP MSCN NHol NSla SBch SPlb SRot WCot XLum
- 'Purpurine'	ECho
- 'Robustum'	see *S.* 'Ruby Glow'
'Chocolate Drop'	ECtt NLar
chrysicaulum	EPot
'Class Act'PBR ♀H4	ECtt MNrw NLar
'Cloud Walker'PBR	CAbP ECtt LRHS MNrw NCGa
confusum Hemsl.	SEND
crassipes	see *Rhodiola wallichiana*
crassularia	see *Crassula setulosa* 'Milfordiae'
'Crazy Ruffles'	ECtt WCot
cryptomerioides B&SWJ 054	WCru
'Dark Jack'	ECtt MAvo MNrw NCGa NGdn SMrm WCot
dasyphyllum	ECho MWat NRya SPlb SRms
§ - subsp. ***dasyphyllum*** var. ***mesatlanticum***	NBir
- ***mucronatis***	see *S. dasyphyllum* subsp. *dasyphyllum* var. *mesatlanticum*
'Diamond Edge' (v)	EBee ECtt
divergens	XLum
douglasii	see *S. stenopetalum* 'Douglasii'
drymarioides	LRHS NBre WHil
'Dudley Field'	MHer
'Eleanor Fisher'	see *S. telephium* subsp. *ruprechtii*
ellacombeanum	see *S. kamtschaticum* var. *ellacombeanum*
'Elworthy Rose'	CElw

§	***erythrostictum***	XLum
	– 'Frosty Morn' (v)	Widely available
§	– 'Mediovariegatum' (v)	EBee ELan LRHS MHer MNrw MRav NLar NPnk SWvt WMnd WMoo WWEG XLum
	ewersii	ECho ECtt EDAr GKev MAsh MMuc NBro NLar NSla SPhx SPlb XLum
	– CC 5288	ITim
	– var. ***homophyllum*** 'Rosenteppich'	EPPr LBuc LRHS MBrN SWvt WMoo
	fabaria	see *S. telephium* subsp. *fabaria*
	fastigiatum	see *Rhodiola fastigiata*
	floriferum	see *S. kamtschaticum* var. *floriferum*
	forsterianum subsp. ***elegans***	SPlb XLum
§	– f. ***purpureum***	NRya
	'Frosted Fire'	EBee LSou MAsh MBri NSti
	furfuraceum	WAbe
	Garnet Brocade = 'Garbro'PBR	CCVN ECtt WMoo
§	***glaucophyllum***	EDAr XLum
	'Gold Mound'	EPfP LAst NLar
	'Goldie'	CDoC
	'Green Expectations'	ECtt GBin MNFA MRav MWat NBre
	hakonense 'Chocolate Ball'	EBee ECtt LHop
	Herbstfreude Group	EHyd NWad NWsh
	– 'Autumn Fire'	EBee MAsh
	– 'Beka' (v)	LSou WHil
	– 'Elsie's Gold' (v)	EBee ECtt LRHS MAsh MBri NLar SPoG WHil
§	– 'Herbstfreude' ♀H4	Widely available
	– 'Jaws'PBR	CAby CKno EBee ECtt IKil NLar SMrm WCot
§	– 'Lajos' (v)	LSou MAsh NPro
	– 'Mini Joy'	GKev LRHS MBri MNrw WRHF
	heterodontum	see *Rhodiola heterodonta*
	hidakanum	ECtt EHoe EPot GMaP NBro NHol NWad WHoo
	himalense misapplied	see *Rhodiola* 'Keston'
	hispanicum	ECho NBre SPlb
	– 'Blue Carpet' **new**	EPPr
	– ***glaucum***	see *S. hispanicum* var. *minus*
§	– var. ***minus***	ECho ECtt MMuc MSCN SEND SPlb WMoo
§	– – 'Aureum'	ECho
§	***hybridum***	XLum
	– 'Czar's Gold'	NGdn
	'Ice Ruffles' (v) **new**	MAvo
	'Indian Chief'	see *S.* (Herbstfreude Group) 'Herbstfreude'
	ishidae	see *Rhodiola ishidae*
	'James Windsor'	CRDP
	'José Aubergine'PBR	CKno CPrp EBee ECtt IPot LRHS MAvo MBri MTis NCGa NDov NHol NLar NSoo NSti SGol SPoG WPGP
	'Joyce Henderson'	ECtt EHyd ELan EPfP LHop LRHS MCot MRav MTis NChi NLar SPer SRGP WBrk WCot WMoo WWEG
	kamtschaticum ♀H4	ECho EDAr GJos
	– B&SWJ 10870	WCru
§	– var. ***ellacombeanum*** ♀H4	MMuc SEND WCot XLum
	– – B&SWJ 8853	WCru
§	– var. ***floriferum*** **new**	XSen
§	– – 'Weihenstephaner Gold'	CTri ECho ECtt EDAr EPfP GAbr GKev GMaP LPot MAsh MHer MMuc MRav MSCN MWat NBir SPlb SPoG SRms WAbe XLum
	– var. ***kamtschaticum*** 'Variegatum' (v) ♀H4	CMea ECho EDAr EHoe EHyd EPfP LBMP LRHS MHer MJak MMuc MWat NPri SPoG SRms SRot SWvt XLum
	lanceolatum	NBre
	lineare 'Variegatum' (v)	XLum
	'Little Dove' **new**	SBch
§	***lydium***	CTri ECho MHer SFgr SPlb
	– 'Aureum'	see *S. hispanicum* var. *minus* 'Aureum'
	– 'Bronze Queen'	see *S. lydium*
I	'Marchants Best Red' ♀H4	LPio SPhx WCot
	'Matrona' ♀H4	Widely available
	maweanum	see *S. acre* subsp. *neglectum* var. *majus*
	middendorffianum	ECho MBrN MHer MWat SEND SRms SRot XLum
	– 'Striatum'	EDAr
	'Moonglow'	ECtt
	moranense	MMuc SEND XLum
	morganianum ♀H1	EBak EShb
	morrisonense B&SWJ 7078	WCru
	'Mr Goodbud'PBR ♀H4	CAby CPrp ECtt GBin LRHS MHol MNrw NDov NLar WCot WWEG
	'Munstead Red'	COIW CPrp CWCL EBee ECtt EPfP GAbr GBin LAst LDai LRHS MAsh MRav MTis MWat NLar SMrm SPer SPhx SPoG WKif WMnd WMoo
	murale	see *S. album* subsp. *teretifolium* var. *murale*
	nevii misapplied	see *S. glaucophyllum*
	nevii ambig.	SPlb
	nicaeense	see *S. sediforme*
	'Novem'PBR	MBri
	obtusatum misapplied	see *S. oreganum*
§	***obtusatum*** A. Gray	NBro NSla
	obtusifolium var. ***listoniae***	EDAr
	ochroleucum	MMuc NBre SEND
	oppositifolium	see *S. spurium* 'Album'
§	***oreganum***	ECho EDAr GAbr GKev GMaP MHer MSCN MWat SPlb SRms SRot XLum
	– 'Procumbens'	see *S. oreganum* subsp. *tenue*
§	– subsp. ***tenue***	EPot NHol NRya NWad WAbe
§	***oregonense***	ECho EHyd LRHS MHer
	pachyclados	see *Rhodiola pachyclados*
	pachyphyllum	EPfP WNew
	palmeri	CHEx LSou MRav NBir SChr SEND XLum
	'Parish Plum'	SBch
	'Pewter'	ECho
	'Pink Dove'	SBch
§	***pluricaule***	ECho EHyd LRHS NSla SPlb SRms
	populifolium	GCal GJos IMou MHer NLar SPhx XLum
	praealtum	SChr SEND
	pulchellum	ECtt SMad
	'Purple Leaf'	LAst
	quinquefarium	see *S. brevifolium* var. *quinquefarium*
	'Red Cauli' ♀H4	Widely available
	'Red Rum'	GBin LPla SPhx
	'Red Setter'	WPGP
	reflexum L.	see *S. rupestre* L.
	reptans	ECho
	rhodiola	see *Rhodiola rosea*
	rosea	see *Rhodiola rosea*
	rubroglaucum misapplied	see *S. oregonense*

	rubroglaucum Praeger	see *S. obtusatum* A. Gray
	× ***rubrotinctum***	CHEx
	- 'Aurora'	SChr
§	'Ruby Glow' ♀H4	Widely available
	'Ruby Port'	CSpe
§	***rupestre*** L.	ECho GJos LAst MBNS MMuc MNHC MWat SEND SPlb XLum
	- 'Angelina'	CKno ECtt EPPr EWes IMou LRHS MGos MHer NBir NDov NHol NPri NPro NWad SPoG SRGP WCot WGrn XLum
	- 'Monstrosum Cristatum'	NBir SMad XLum
	ruprechtii	see *S. telephium* subsp. *ruprechtii*
	sarcocaule hort.	see *Crassula sarcocaulis*
	sarmentosum	ECho XLum
§	***sediforme***	EDAr EPot GAbr LRHS XSen
	- B&F MA 25	WCot
	- ***nicaeense***	see *S. sediforme*
	selskianum	GJos NBre SBch XLum
	sempervivoides	ECho
	sexangulare	ECho EDAr EPot MHer MMuc NRya SEND SFgr SPlb SRms XLum
	sibiricum	see *S. hybridum*
	sieboldii	CFis ECho
	- 'Dragon'	LRHS
	- 'Mediovariegatum' (v) ♀H2-3	CFis CHEx COIW ECho EHoe LPot MHer NPri NWsh SPlb XLum
	'Silvermoon'	ECtt NWad
	spathulifolium	CTri ECho
	- 'Aureum'	ECho ECtt MWat WAbe
	- 'Cape Blanco' ♀H4	Widely available
	- 'Purpureum' ♀H4	COIW ECho ECtt EDAr EHoe EHyd EPfP GAbr GKev GMaP LAst LBee LPot LRHS MBel MHer MMuc MSem MWat NHol NPri NRya NWad SPer SPlb SPoG WAbe WMoo WNew XLum
	- subsp. ***yosemitense*** 'Red Raver'	CPBP
	spectabile ♀H4	CArn CHEx CHab CPrp CTri ELan EPfP GJos GMaP LRHS MCot MHer MRav NGdn SPer SPlb SRms WBor WBrk WCAu WSFF WWEG
	- 'Album'	CHEx
	- Brilliant Group	CBar CHab LAst LBMP WCAu
	- - 'Brilliant' ♀H4	CBcs CHel CKno CSBt CTri EBee ECtt ELan EPfP LAst LRHS MAsh MBri MGos MMuc MRav NGdn NOrc SPer SPoG SWvt WMoo WWEG
	- - 'Carmen'	LRHS XLum
	- - 'Hot Stuff'	ECtt ELon EPfP LRHS LSRN NPri SRot WCot
	- - 'Lisa'	GBin MTPN NLar
	- - 'Meteor'	CPrp LPla MWat NLar SMrm SPhx WWEG
	- - 'Neon'	EBee LRHS MAsh MBel NCGa NDov
	- - 'Pink Fairy'	WHil
	- - 'Rosenteller'	CKno EBee GBin NBre SMrm
§	- - 'Septemberglut'	NBre XLum
	- - 'Steven Ward'	CKno EWes SRGP WCot
	- 'Crystal Pink'	MNrw NLar
	- 'Humile'	XLum
	- 'Iceberg'	CMea COIW CSev EBee ECtt EHyd EPfP EShb LAst LRHS MAvo MCot MGos MRav MWat MWhi NCGa NGdn NLar SPer SPhx SWvt WCAu WHil WMnd WMoo WWEG XLum
*	- 'Mini'	MRav
	- 'Nordlicht' **new**	GBin
	- 'Pink Chablis'PBR (v)	NLar WCot
	- September Glow	see *S. spectabile* (Brilliant Group) 'Septemberglut'
	- 'Stardust'	CKno CPrp CTri EBee EPfP GBin GMaP LAst LRHS LSou MRav MTis NCGa NLar NSoo SGol SPer SPet WGor WWEG XLum
	- 'Variegatum'	see *S. erythrostictum* 'Mediovariegatum'
	- Walberton's Pizazz **new**	EPfP
	spinosum	see *Orostachys spinosa*
	spurium	CHEx ECho GAbr GJos MMuc SEND SRms XSen
§	- 'Album'	NRya XLum
	- 'Atropurpureum'	ECho WMoo XLum
	- 'Coccineum'	ECho GJos MMuc MNHC SEND
	- Dragon's Blood	see *S. spurium* 'Schorbuser Blut'
	- 'Fuldaglut'	CTri EBee ECho EHoe EHyd EPfP GMaP GQue IPot LRHS MNrw NRya SMrm WMoo WNew WPnn WRHF
	- 'Green Mantle'	EBee ECho EPfP LRHS
	- Purple Carpet	see *S. spurium* 'Purpurteppich'
	- 'Purpureum'	SRms
§	- 'Purpurteppich'	ECho ECtt GJos MJak MRav NBro NLar NWad SBod SRms SVen
	- 'Roseum'	SRms
	- 'Ruby Mantle'	EWll GKev MSCN MWat NBro NPro SBch SPoG SWvt WMoo XLum
§	- 'Schorbuser Blut' ♀H4	CMea EBee ECho ECtt EPau EPfP GJos GKev MCot MLHP MWat NBir NRya NSla SPlb SRGP SRms WHoo WIce XLum
I	- 'Splendens Roseum'	XLum
	- 'Summer Glory'	NLar
§	- 'Tricolor' (v)	CHel CTri EBee ECho EHoe EPfP GJos GKev MAsh MHer MLHP MRav NHol NRya SPlb SPoG WMoo XLum
	- 'Variegatum'	see *S. spurium* 'Tricolor'
	- 'Voodoo'	ECtt EPfP EWes LBMP LPot MBel MHer MWat NBro NGdn XLum
	stefco	XLum
	stenopetalum	SPlb
§	- 'Douglasii'	MHer SRms
	'Stewed Rhubarb Mountain'	CHel CKno CPrp EBee ECtt EHyd ELan EPfP LDai LHop LRHS MBNS MCot MNFA MRav NBro NCGa NLar NOrc SGbt WCAu WMoo WWEG
	stoloniferum	ECho
	stribrnyi	see *S. urvillei* Stribrnyi Group
	'Sunset Cloud'	CHEx CMHG EBee ECtt EWes GCal IPot LPla LPot MRav NBre
	takesimense	XLum
	- B&SWJ 8518	WCru
	telephium	CArn IFro NBir SRms XLum
§	- Atropurpureum Group ♀H4	ELan EPfP MRav SWvt WWEG
	- - 'African Pearl'	EBee GBin WCFE WCot WWEG
	- - 'Arthur Branch'	CPrp EBee GBin LRHS WWEG
I	- - 'Atropurpureum Nanum'	WWEG
	- - 'Bon Bon'	CPrp LRHS MBNS MBel NLar SPoG
	- - 'Bressingham Purple'	EBee EPPr
	- - 'Chocolate'	EBee ECtt EPPr LPio LRHS MAvo NLar
	- - 'Dark Knight'	LRHS

	- - 'El Cid'	EWes
	- - 'Hester'	WWEG
	- - 'Karfunkelstein' 🏆H4	CKno ECtt EPPr GBin GLog LPio MAsh MAvo MHol MTis NDov SPhx WCot
	- - 'Leonore Zuuntz'	NBre
	- - 'Lynda et Rodney'	EWes
	- - 'Lynda Windsor'	ECtt EPfP GAbr NLar NPnk NPro SWvt
	- - 'Möhrchen'	GBin GMaP LRHS MHer MRav MTis NGdn NLar NPnk NWsh SMrm SPhx SPoG WMnd WMoo
	- - 'Picolette'	EBee ECtt EPfP LBuc LRHS LSou MNrw NCGa SPoG WCot WMoo
	- - 'Postman's Pride' PBR	CHel CKno CWGN EBee ECtt EPfP GBin LPio LPla LRHS LSou MSCN MWat NGdn NLBP SPad WCot
§	- - 'Purple Emperor' 🏆H4	Widely available
	- - 'Purple Moon' **new**	SPhx
	- - 'Ringmore Ruby'	MHer WCot WPGP WWEG
	- - 'Xenox' PBR 🏆H4	CWGN EBee ECtt EPfP EWll GBin IPot LPio LRHS MAsh MAvo MBNS MBri MCot MNrw MTis NLar SHar SMrm WCAu WHil WPGP
	- 'Bronco' PBR	MBri
	- 'Coral Reef' PBR	MBri WMoo
	- Emperor's Waves Group	NGdn
§	- subsp. ***fabaria***	ECtt MRav NWsh SMrm WCot WWEG
	- - var. ***borderei***	CElw LBMP LPla SBch SPhx
	- 'Jennifer'	EBee ECtt MBel MHol SBch WCot WHoo
	- subsp. ***maximum*** 'Atropurpureum'	see *S. telephium* Atropurpureum Group
	- - 'Gooseberry Fool'	CAby CFis CMea COIW CPrp EBee ECGP ECtt ELan EPfP GMaP SBch SPhx WWEG
	- 'Moonlight Serenade' PBR	EBee ECtt MAsh MBri MTis
	- 'Rainbow Xenox' PBR	LSou MAsh MBri
	- 'Roseum'	WWEG
§	- subsp. ***ruprechtii***	CPrp ECtt EHoe EPPr EPfP GMaP LRHS LSou MCot MRav NSti SDix SPer SPet SPhx WMoo
	- - 'Citrus Twist'	EBee ECtt LRHS MRav NPnk
	- - 'Hab Gray'	COIW CSpe EBee ECtt EWes GBin GQue LRHS MAvo MTis NLar SBch SMrm WCot
	- 'Strawberries and Cream'	Widely available
	- 'Sunkissed' PBR	EBee ECtt MBri NCGa NLar STPC
	- subsp. ***telephium***	GCra
	- 'Twinkling Star' PBR	MBri MNrw
	- 'Yellow Xenox' PBR	ECtt LSou MBri WHil
	ternatum	MHer
	tetractinum	LRHS
	'Thundercloud' **new**	LRHS
	trollii	see *Rhodiola trollii*
	'Twinkle Stars' **new**	MAsh
	urvillei Sartorianum Group	MHer XLum
§	- Stribrnyi Group	XLum
	ussuriense	EPfP GCal NBir
	- 'Chuwangsan'	EWld WCru
	'Veluwse Wakel'	ECtt GBin
	'Vera Jameson' 🏆H4	CHEx CMac CPrp ECtt EHoe EPfP EShb GKev LAst LRHS LSRN MBel MBrN MCot MNFA MRav NHol NSti NWsh SBch SBod SMrm SPer SWvt WHoo WMoo WWEG
	viviparum B&SWJ 8662	WCru
	Walberton's Pink Whisper **new**	EPfP
	'Washfield Purple'	see *S. telephium* 'Purple Emperor'
	'Weihenstephaner Gold'	see *S. kamtschaticum* var. *floriferum* 'Weihenstephaner Gold'
	weinbergii	see *Graptopetalum paraguayense*
	'Winky'	CWGN LSou MBel
	yezoense	see *S. pluricaule*
	yunnanense	see *Rhodiola yunnanensis*

Seemannia see *Gloxinia*

Selaginella (*Selaginellaceae*)

	braunii	CLAP WCot
	erythropus var. ***sanguinea***	LRHS
	helvetica	IMou
	kraussiana 🏆H1	CLAP EDAr EShb
	- 'Aurea'	CBty CCCN ISha LRHS
	- 'Brownii' 🏆H1	CBty CCCN ISha LRHS
	- 'Gold Tips'	CBty CCCN ISha LRHS
	lepidophylla	SVic
	moellendorfii	CBty ISha LRHS
	tamariscina	WAbe
	uncinata 🏆H1	CBty CLAP ISha

Selago (*Scrophulariaceae*)

	thunbergii	LHop

Selinum (*Apiaceae*)

	CC 6869 **new**	EWld
	carvifolium	CSpe EShb LDai LEdu LRHS
	- PAB 2676 **new**	LEdu
	tenuifolium	see *S. wallichianum*
§	***wallichianum***	CCon CDes CHid COIW CPom CSam CSpe ELan EPri EShb GBin GBuc GCra LBMP LRHS MAvo MWat NCGa NDov NLar SPer SPhx SWvt WPtf WSHC WWEG
	- EMAK 886	EBee GPoy SDix
	- HWJK 2224	WCru
	- HWJK 2347	WCru
	- PAB 3579	LEdu

Selliera (*Goodeniaceae*)

	radicans	ECou EDAr GAbr GBin

Semele (*Asparagaceae*)

	androgyna	CHEx CRHN

Semiaquilegia (*Ranunculaceae*)

	'Early Dwarf'	EDif
§	***ecalcarata***	CAby CDes CPom CWCL ECho GCal GJos GKev LDai MNrw NGdn SBea SRms WCru WHal WPGP WTou
	- Australian	CDes
*	- f. ***bicolor***	CPom WCru
	- 'Flore Pleno' (d)	WTou
	- 'Snowbell'	WCru
	simulatrix	see *S. ecalcarata*
	'Sugar Plum Fairy'	EPfP LBuc LRHS SPoG

Semiarundinaria (*Poaceae*)

§	***fastuosa*** 🏆H4	CBcs CDoC CEnt CHEx CJun CTsd EAmu ENBC EPfP ERod EUJe IMou MJak MMoz MMuc MWht SAPC SEND SPlb WJun

	– var. ***viridis***	CEnt ERod MWht SBig WCru WJun
	kagamiana	CDoC ENBC EPfP IMou MMoz MMuc MWhi MWht SBig SEND WJun
§	***lubrica***	MWht
	makinoi	EAmu MWht SLPl WJun
	nitida	see *Fargesia nitida*
§	***okuboi***	CEnt ERod MMoz MWht
	villosa	see *S. okuboi*
	yamadorii	ERod MMoz MWht WJun
	yashadake	CEnt ERod WJun
	– f. ***kimmei***	CDoC CEnt ERod LRHS MMoz MMuc MWht NLar SBig SEND WJun WMoo WPGP
I	– – 'Inversa'	CEnt

Semnanthe see *Erepsia*

Sempervivella see *Rosularia*

Sempervivum ✿ (*Crassulaceae*)

	sp.	SVic
	from Sierra Nova	ESem
	'Aaroundina'	CWil
	'Abba'	CMea EDAr WHal
	'Adelaar'	CWil MSem
	'Adelmoed'	CWil SFgr
	'Ageet'	CWil
	'Aglow'	ESem MHom
	'Aladdin'	CWil ESem MSCN SRms WIvy
	'Albernelli'	SFgr
	'Alchimist'	XLum
	'Aldo Moro'	CWil EDAr ESem GAbr LBee MHom SFgr WIce WIvy XLum
	'Alice'	MSCN
	'Alidae'	ESem
	allionii	see *Jovibarba allionii*
	'Allison'	CWil
	'Alluring'	ESem GAbr
	'Alpha'	CMea ESem LBee SFgr SRms WHal XLum
	altum	CWil EHyd ESem LRHS MHom SPlb XLum
	'Amanda'	CWil EDAr ESem MBrN SRms WHoo
	'Ambergreen'	MSem
	andreanum	see *S. tectorum* var. *alpinum*
	'Andrenor' **new**	ESem MSem
	– sport **new**	MSem
	'Anna Marie' **new**	ESem MSem
	'Apache' Payne	see *Jovibarba heuffelii* 'Apache'
	'Apache' Haberer	ESem
	'Apollo'	SFgr XLum
	'Apple Blossom'	CMea ESem MSem
	arachnoideum ♀H4	Widely available
	– from Massif du Canigou, France **new**	MSem
	– from the Abruzzi, Italy	MSem
	– 'Ararat'	SDys
	– 'Boria'	ESem
	– var. ***bryoides***	CWil ESem LLHF LRHS MSem WIvy
	– 'Cebennense'	ESem
	– 'Clärchen'	EPot ESem MSCN MSem NSla SFgr WAbe
	– cristate	CWil
*	– ***densum***	EDAr EPPr WAbe
	– subsp. ***doellianum***	see *S. arachnoideum* subsp. *tomentosum* var. *glabrescens*
	– form No 1	ECho
	– 'Laggeri'	see *S. arachnoideum* subsp. *tomentosum* (C.B. Lehm. & Schnittsp.) Schinz & Thell.
	– 'Red Wings'	XLum
	– 'Rubrum'	CHEx ECho EHyd EUJe GMaP LRHS SPlb XLum
	– 'Sultan'	ESem
	– subsp. ***tomentosum*** misapplied	see *S.* × *barbulatum* 'Hookeri'
§	– subsp. ***tomentosum*** (C.B. Lehm. & Schnittsp.) Schinz & Thell. ♀H4	CHEx CWil ECho EHyd LRHS MSCN MSem NPer NWad SFgr SPlb SRms WAbe WGor
	– – GDJ 92.04	CWil
§	– – var. ***glabrescens***	SDys
§	– – 'Stansfieldii'	ECho EPPr LRHS MSem WHal
§	– 'White Christmas'	CWil MHer
	– 'Yukon Snow'	MSem
	arachnoideum* × *calcareum	CWil WIvy
	arachnoideum* × *montanum	see *S.* × *barbulatum*
	arachnoideum* × *nevadense	CWil SDys
	arachnoideum* × *pittonii	CWil WAbe
	arenarium	see *Jovibarba arenaria*
	'Arlet'	EDAr
	armenum	ESem
	'Arondina'	CWil
	'Aross'	CMea ESem MSem
	'Artist'	CWil ESem MSem SFgr
	'Ashes of Roses'	EPot ESem MHom NHol WAbe WGor XLum
	'Asteroid'	CWil ESem
	'Astrid'	CWil
	'Atlantic' **new**	MSem
	atlanticum	ESem MHom NSla SFgr SRot
	– from Atlas Mountains, Morocco	CWil ESem
	– from Oukaïmeden, Morocco	CWil ESem GAbr MSem SRms
	– 'Edward Balls'	CWil ESem SDys SFgr
	'Atropurpureum' ambig.	CHEx CWil EDAr MBrN WGor
	'Attraction' **new**	CWil
	'Aureum'	see *Greenovia aurea*
	'Averil'	CWil
	'Aymon Correvon'	ESem
	'Baby Skrocki'	CWil
	balcanicum	CWil EDAr MSem WIvy XLum
	ballsii	ECho EHyd LLHF LRHS
	– from Kambeecho, Greece	MHom
	– from Smólikas, Greece	CWil MHom
	– from Tschumba Petzi, Greece	CWil MHom SDys XLum
	'Banyan'	ECho LRHS
	'Barbarosa'	CWil
§	× ***barbulatum***	ESem LBee SDys SFgr WHoo
§	– 'Hookeri'	CTri CWil EPot ESem MSem NLar SFgr WAbe WHoo XLum
	'Bascour Zilver'	CMea CWil LBee MSCN SRms WHal
	'Be Mine' **new**	MSCN
	'Beaute'	ESem
	'Beautiful' **new**	MSem
	'Bedivere'	CWil LBee MSem SRms
*	'Bedley Hi'	MHom
	'Bella Donna'	CWil ESem MHom
	'Bella Meade'	CWil EDAr ESem SFgr SRms
	'Bellotts Pourpre'	CWil ESem
	'Benny Hill'	CWil

	'Bernstein'	CWil EDAr EPot ESem MHer NWad SFgr WHal XLum
	'Beta'	ESem MHom MSem WAbe XLum
	'Bethany'	CMea CWil ESem NWad WHal
	'Bicolor' ambig.	EPfP
	'Big Slipper'	ESem
	'Bijou' **new**	CWil
	'Binstead'	ESem
	'Birchmaier'	SFgr
	'Black Cap'	ESem
	'Black Knight'	ECho LRHS MHer SPlb SRms WHal
	'Black Mini'	CWil EPot GAbr GKev MSem NBir SRms
	'Black Mountain'	CHEx CWil ESem GKev LBee
	'Black Prince'	ESem
	'Black Velvet'	WIvy
	'Blood of Winter'	WGor
	'Blood Sucker'	WGor
	'Blood Tip'	CHEx CMea CWil ECho EHyd EPfP ESem GAbr GCra LAst LRHS MHer MSCN NHol NRya NWad SBch SPlb SPoG SRms WGor WHal WHoo
	'Bloodgood'	ECho
	'Bloody Goose'	ESem
	'Blue Boy'	CWil ECho EHyd EPPr EPot GAbr LBee LRHS MSCN MSem SFgr SRms WIvy
	'Blue Moon'	ESem
	'Blue Time'	EPot LLHF SFgr WHoo XLum
	'Blush'	EDAr
	'Boissieri'	see *S. tectorum* subsp. *tectorum* 'Boissieri'
	'Bombardier'	EDAr
	'Booth's Red'	CHEx WGor
	'Boreale'	see *Jovibarba hirta* subsp. *borealis*
	borisii	see *S. ciliosum* var. *borisii*
	borissovae	EPot MHom SDys
	'Boromir'	CWil EDAr MSem XLum
	'Boule de Neige'	MSem NRya
	'Braune Maus'	ESem SFgr
I	'Braunella' **new**	CWil
	'Britta'	ESem SDys
	'Brock'	ECho LLHF LRHS MHer MHom
	'Bronco' ♀H4	CDes CHEx CWil ECho ESem GAbr GBin LBee MHom NHol NRya NWad SRms WCot WHfH WPGP XLum
	'Bronze Beauty'	EDAr
	'Bronze Pastel'	CWil EDAr MHom MSCN MSem NSla SFgr SRms SRot WGor
	'Brown Owl'	CWil ECho ESem SRms
	'Brownii'	ESem
	'Brunette'	ECho GAbr
	bungeanum hort.	ESem
	'Bunny Girl' **new**	SFgr
	'Burnatii'	see *S. montanum* subsp. *burnatii*
	'Burning Desire'	WGor
	'Burnished Bronze'	CWil
	'Butterfly'	ESem MAsh
	'Café'	CWil MSCN MSem NHol NWad SFgr SRms WIvy
*	***calabricum***	NHol
	× ***calcaratum***	EDAr EPot
	calcareum	CMea CWil ECho EHyd EPfP EUJe EWll GKev LBMP LRHS MAsh MMuc NBro NEgg NHol SAPC SEND SPlb SPoG SRms SRot WHoo XLum
	- from the Alps, France	CWil ESem
	- from Calde la Vanoise, France	CWil MSem
	- from Ceüze, France	CWil ESem WIvy
	- from Cleizé, France	see *S. calcareum* 'Limelight'
	- from Col Bayard, France	CWil ESem GAbr
	- from Colle St Michel, France	CWil ESem SFgr SRms
	- from Gorges supérieures du Cians, France	CWil ESem
	- from Mont Ventoux, France	CWil ESem MSem
	- from Petite Ceüse, France	ESem SRot
	- - GDJ 92.15	CWil
	- - GDJ 92.16	CWil SRms
	- from Queyras, France	CWil ESem
	- from Route d'Annôt, France	CWil ESem
	- from Triora, Italy	CWil ESem MSem
	- 'Benz'	ESem SDys
	- 'Extra' ♀H4	CHEx CWil ESem GAbr MSCN MSem SFgr SRot
	- 'Greenii'	CWil ECho EHyd ESem GKev LRHS MMuc MSem SEND SPlb
§	- 'Grigg's Surprise'	SPlb WHil
	- 'Guillaumes' ♀H4	CWil ESem LBee MSem SFgr SRot WHoo
§	- 'Limelight'	CMea CWil EDAr EHyd LBee LRHS MSem WHal WHoo WIvy
	- 'Monstrosum'	see *S. calcareum* 'Grigg's Surprise'
	- 'Mrs Giuseppi'	CWil ECho ESem GAbr LBee LRHS SFgr SRms WAbe WIce XLum
	- 'Nigricans' **new**	MSem
	- 'Pink Pearl'	CWil MSCN MSem SDys SFgr WIvy XLum
	- 'Sir William Lawrence' ♀H4	CMea CWil ECho EDAr ESem LBee MSem SFgr SRms WAbe WHal WHoo WIvy WThu XLum
	'Cameo'	see *Jovibarba heuffelii* var. *glabra* 'Cameo'
	'Canada Kate'	CWil
	'Cancer'	XLum
	'Candy Floss'	CWil WGor
	cantabricum	CWil ESem MMuc SEND WThu XLum
	- from Cuevas del Sil, Spain	CWil
	- from Navafria, Spain	CWil
	- from Riaño, Spain	CWil GAbr
	- from San Glorio, Spain	CWil GAbr
	- from Ticeros	XLum
	- subsp. ***cantabricum*** from Leitariegos, Spain	CWil GAbr MHom
	- - GDJ 93.13 from Peña de Llesba, Spain	CWil
	- - from Pico del Lobo, Spain	CWil
I	- subsp. ***gredense*** GDJ 95.04 **new**	CWil
	- subsp. ***guadarramense***	see *S. vicentei* subsp. *paui*
	- - from Pico del Lobo, Spain, No 1	SRms SRot
	- - from Valvanera, Spain, No 1	CWil
	- subsp. ***urbionense***	CWil SRms
	- - from El Gatón, Spain	CWil
	- - from Picos de Urbión, Spain	CWil ESem
	cantabricum × ***montanum*** subsp. ***stiriacum***	ESem
	cantabricum × ***montanum*** subsp. ***stiriacum*** 'Lloyd Praeger'	CWil
	'Carmen'	CWil ESem GAbr SFgr
	'Carnival'	CWil ESem

caucasicum	CWil EHyd MHom MSem XLum
'Cavo Doro'	CWil SFgr
'Celon'	CWil
'Centennial'	ESem
charadzeae	CWil ESem LBee MSem XLum
'Charolensis'	ESem
'Chartbury'	EDAr
'Cherry Frost'	ECho ESem MSem NHol SFgr XLum
'Cherry Glow'	see *Jovibarba heuffelii* 'Cherry Glow'
'Cherry Tart'	MSem WIvy
'Chivalry'	ESem
'Chocolate'	ESem WAbe
'Christmas Time'	SFgr
chrysanthum	ESem
ciliosum ♀H4	CMea CPBP CWil ECho ESem NRya SPlb
- from Alí Butús, Bulgaria	SDys
- from Ochrid, Macedonia	CWil MSem
- from Pestani, Macedonia	ESem
§ - var. ***borisii***	CFis EPPr EPfP ESem GCal GKev MSem NRya WAbe WHal
- var. ***ciliosum*** × ***ciliosum*** var. ***borisii***	CTri
- var. ***galicicum*** 'Mali Hat'	ESem MSem
ciliosum × ***grandiflorum***	CWil ESem
ciliosum × ***marmoreum***	ESem
'Cindy'	ESem SRms
'Circlet'	CWil
'Clara Noyes'	MSem
'Clare'	ESem MHer
'Claudine'	ESem
'Clemanum'	MSem
'Cleveland Morgan'	ESem MHom MSem NBro XLum
'Climax' ambig.	ECho EPfP ESem MHom
'Cobweb Capers'	ESem MHom
'Cochise'	MSem
'Collage'	ESem
'Collecteur Anchisi'	ESem SDys SFgr
'Commander Hay' ♀H4	CHEx CMea EDAr EPfP EWes GBin GCra GKev MHom MSCN NPer SRGP SRms WHal WIvy WJek XLum
'Concorde'	LBee
'Congo'	ESem SFgr XLum
'Cornstone'	ESem
'Corona'	CWil ESem MSem SFgr
'Corsair'	CWil EPPr ESem MBrN SFgr WGor WIvy
'Cotopaxi'	CWil
'Cranberry'	ESem
'Cresta'	MSem
'Crimson King'	SFgr
'Crimson Velvet'	CHEx CMea ESem LBee MSem SFgr XLum
§ 'Crispyn' ♀H4	CWil EPot ESem LBee MHer MHom MSCN MSem SFgr
'Crucify'	ESem
'Cupream'	CWil ESem MSem SRms
'Dakota'	CWil EDAr SFgr
'Dallas'	CWil MSem SRms
'Damask'	CWil LBee MSem SFgr
'Dancer's Veil'	MSem
'Darjeeling'	CWil ESem MSem
'Dark Beauty'	CWil ECho EHyd ESem LRHS MSCN MSem NHol SFgr WAbe WCot WGor WHal
'Dark Cloud'	CWil ESem GAbr LBee MSem WHoo WIvy XLum
'Dark Point'	CWil MHom MSCN SFgr

'Dark Velvet'	CMea
'Darkie'	CWil ESem SFgr
'Deep Fire'	CWil ESem SRms WIvy
× ***degenianum***	GAbr SFgr XLum
'Delta' ♀H4	MHom WHoo
densum	see *S. tectorum*
'Devon Glow'	MSCN
'Devon Jewel'	WGor
'Diane'	CWil ESem MSem SFgr
'Director Jacobs'	CWil EDAr ESem MSem SFgr
'Dolle Dina's' **new**	MSem
dolomiticum	XLum
dolomiticum × ***montanum***	NBro SFgr
'Donarrose'	ESem MSem SFgr
'Downland Queen'	CWil ESem
'Dragoness'	ESem
'Dream Catcher'	CWil
'Duke of Windsor'	SFgr
'Dusky'	ESem
'Dyke'	CTri CWil EDAr GAbr MSem SFgr WHal
dzhavachischvilii	CWil XLum
'Edge of Night'	CWil
'Eefje'	CWil ESem
'El Greco'	ESem
'El Toro'	MHom MSCN
'Elgar'	WIvy
'Elvis'	CWil GAbr MHom SFgr
'Emerald Giant'	CWil ESem MSem SFgr
'Emerson's Giant'	CWil ESem MSem
'Eminent'	ESem
'Emmchen'	CWil MSem SFgr
'Engle's'	CMea CTri ECho LRHS MHer MSCN MSem SEND SPlb SRms WHal
'Engle's 13-2'	MSem NBro
'Engle's Rubrum'	CPBP EPot LBee
erythraeum	ECho EHyd LLHF LRHS MHom SPlb WAbe WHal
- 'Red Velvet'	MSem
'Eureka' **new**	MSem
'Excalibur'	ESem MSem WIvy
'Exhibita'	CWil EPPr SDys
'Exorna'	CWil EDAr ESem MHom SFgr WIvy
'Fair Lady'	CWil MHom
'Fairy'	EPot
'Fame'	CWil ESem WGor
'Fat Jack'	CWil
× ***fauconnetii***	CWil EDAr ESem
'Thompsonii'	CWil ESem
'Feldmaier'	GAbr
'Festival'	EDAr
'Fiery Furness'	ESem MSem
'Fiesta' ambig.	MSem WHal
fimbriatum	see *S.* × *barbulatum*
'Finerpointe'	ESem
'Fire Glint'	CWil ESem SRms WIvy
'Firebird'	SFgr
'Firefly'	ESem
'Firgrove Silver'	SFgr
'First Try'	ESem MSem
flagelliforme	XLum
'Flaming Heart'	CWil EDAr ESem MBrN WGor
'Flamingo'	ESem
'Flanders Passion'	LBee SRms
'Flasher'	MSem
'Fluweel'	MSCN
'Forden'	CHEx SFgr WGor

	'Ford's Amiability'	SDys
	'Ford's Giant'	XLum
	'Ford's Shadows'	SDys
	'Ford's Spring'	CWil ESem MSem WIvy
	'Frolic'	ESem
	'Fronika'	CWil MSem
	'Frosty'	CWil ESem MSem SFgr SRms
	'Fuego' ♀H4	CWil MHom MSem SFgr
	× ***funckii***	CHEx CWil EDAr ESem MBrN SDys SFgr XLum
	'Furryness'	ESem
	'Fuzzy Wuzzy'	EDAr ESem
	'Gallivarda' ♀H4	CWil ESem MSCN MSem SFgr
	'Gambol'	NWad
	'Gamma'	CHEx CWil ESem LBee
	'Garnet'	ECho WGor WIvy
	'Gay Jester'	CTri CWil SFgr WHoo
	'Gazelle'	ESem WIvy XLum
	'Genevione'	CWil
	'Georgette'	CWil ESem MSem XLum
	'Gilosum'	EDAr
	'Ginnie's Delight'	CWil MSem
	giuseppii ♀H4	ECho ESem GKev LBee MHer MSem
	- GDJ 93.04 from Cumbre de Cebolleda	CWil
	- GDJ 93.17 from Coriscao, Spain	CWil
	- from Coriscao, Spain	LBee
	- from Peña Espigüete, Spain	CWil SDys
	- from Peña Prieta, Spain	CWil
	'Gizmo'	CWil SFgr
	globiferum	XLum
	subsp. ***globiferum*** 'Minor' new	
	- subsp. ***hirtum*** new	SFgr
	'Gloriosum' ambig.	EDAr ESem MSCN SFgr
	'Glowing Embers'	CWil ESem MHom MSem WHal XLum
	'Godaert'	SEND XLum
	'Goldie'	ESem SFgr
	'Grammens'	ESem
	'Granada'	EDAr ESem
	'Granat'	CPBP ESem LBee MHer SRms WIvy XLum
	'Granby'	CWil ECho ESem LBee SDys
	grandiflorum	CWil ESem WThu XLum
	- from Valpine	ESem
	- 'Fasciatum'	ESem
	- 'Keston'	ESem
	'Grape Idol'	CWil
	'Grapetone'	ESem MHom MSem SDys WHal
	'Graupurpur'	CWil XLum
	'Green Apple'	CWil MHom MSem SDys
	'Green Disk'	SRms
	'Green Dragon'	ECho EHyd ESem LRHS MSCN SRms WOut
	'Green Gables'	EDAr ESem
	'Green Ice'	CWil ESem SFgr
	'Greenwich Time'	EDAr
	'Grey Dawn'	ECho EHyd ESem LRHS MHom XLum
	'Grey Ghost'	ESem WIvy
	'Grey Green'	CWil
	'Grey Lady'	CWil MSem
	'Grey Owl'	ECho EHyd LRHS MSCN MSem SRms
	'Grey Velvet'	CWil LBee
	'Greyfriars'	CMea ECho EDAr EHyd EPot ESem LBee LRHS SFgr WGor
	'Greyolla'	CWil ESem
	'Grünschnabel'	XLum
	'Gulle Dame'	CWil ESem MHom SFgr
	'Halemaumau'	CWil ESem
I	'Hall's Hybrid'	CWil GAbr MSCN MSem NBro
	'Happy'	CWil ESem MSem SFgr SRms WGor WIvy WThu
	'Hart'	CWil MSem
	'Havana'	CWil ESem
	'Hayling'	ECho ESem LRHS MSem SRms XLum
	'Heigham Red'	CWil ECho EHyd EPPr ESem GKev LBee LRHS WIce
	'Heike'	CWil
	'Helen'	EDAr
	'Heliotroop'	ESem MSem SDys SRot
	helveticum	see *S. montanum*
	'Hester'	CHEx CWil ECho ESem MBrN MSem NBro
	'Hey-hey'	ECho EHyd EPot GBin LBee LRHS MBrN SPlb XLum
	'Hidde'	CWil ESem MSem SFgr
	'Hirsutum'	see *Jovibarba allionii*
	hirtum	see *Jovibarba hirta*
	'Hookeri'	see *S.* × *barbulatum* 'Hookeri'
	'Hopi'	CWil
	'Hortulanus Smit'	XLum
	'Hot Peppermint'	ESem
	'Huggable Helen'	GKev
	'Hullabaloo'	EDAr ESem SFgr
	'Hurricane'	CWil ESem MSem WIvy
	'Icicle'	CHEx CMea ECho EHyd ESem LRHS MSCN NBro NHol SRms WAbe WGor
	imbricatum	see *S.* × *barbulatum*
	'Imperial'	CWil MHom SPlb
	'Inge'	see *Jovibarba heuffelii* 'Inge'
	ingwersenii	ESem MHom XLum
	ingwersenii × ***pumilum***	CWil MSem
	'Iophon'	LBee
	iranicum	MSem
	'Irazu'	CWil EHyd ESem GAbr LRHS MSCN MSem SDys SFgr SRms
	'Irene'	ESem SFgr
	'Irish Mist' new	CMea
	'Isaac Dyson'	SDys SRot
	'Isabelle'	CWil
	italicum	MHom XLum
	'Iwo'	CHEx SFgr
	'Jack Frost'	ESem NBro SFgr XLum
	'Jacquette'	CWil ESem
	'Jadestern'	CWil
	'Jamie's Pride'	WGor
	'Jelly Bean'	CWil SFgr
	'Jet Stream' ♀H4	CWil ECho EHyd ESem LRHS MHom MSem SDys SPlb SRms WGor
	'Jewel Case'	CWil ECho LRHS
I	'John Hobbs Seedling No. 2'	ESem
	'John T.'	ESem
	'Jolly Green Giant'	MHom
	'Jubilee'	CMea CWil ECho EDAr ELan ESem MAsh MSem XLum
	'Jubilee Tricolor'	ESem NHol SFgr WAbe
	'Jungle Fires'	CMea CWil EPot ESem MSem SDys SRms WHoo
	'Jungle Shadows'	EDAr ESem XLum

	'Jupiter'	GKev XLum
	'Jurrina' **new**	MSem
	'Justine's Choice'	CWil ESem SRms
	'Kalinda'	MHom
	'Kappa'	CTri CWil ESem MSem NBro SDys SRot
	'Katmai'	CWil ESem
	'Kaya'	CWil
	'Keiko' **new**	MSem
	'Kelly Jo'	CWil ESem NBro SFgr
	'Kelut'	ESem
	'Kermit'	ESem MHom
	'Kia'	CWil
	'Kiara'	CWil
	'Kibo'	ESem WIvy
	'Kimba'	CWil
	'Kimble'	ESem
	'Kimono'	MSem NWad
	kindingeri	CWil ESem MHom MSem XLum
	'King George'	CTri CWil ESem GKev LBee MSem SFgr SRms WHal WHoo XLum
	'King Lear'	ESem GBin
	'Kip'	CMea MSem
	'Koko Flanel'	CWil ESem MSem SFgr
	'Korspelsegietje'	CWil GAbr MSem SRms
	kosaninii	ESem MSem SFgr
	- from Koprivnik, Slovenia	MSCN SDys WAbe XLum
	'Kramer's Spinrad'	CHEx CMea CPBP CWil EPPr EPot ESem GAbr LBee MBel MSem SDys SFgr SPlb SRms WHoo WIvy
	'Krater'	CWil
	'Kubi'	ESem
	'Lady Kelly'	WIvy
	'Laura Lee'	SEND
	'Lavender and Old Lace'	CHEx CWil ECho EHyd GAbr LBee LRHS MSCN SFgr SPlb SRms WIce
	'Laysan'	CWil
	'Legolas' **new**	MSem
	'Lemon and Lime'	ESem
	'Leneca'	MSem
	'Lennik's Glory'	see *S.* 'Crispyn'
	'Lennik's Glory No.2'	ESem
	'Lentezon'	ESem MSem
	'Les Yielding'	ESem
	leucanthum	XLum
	'Lilac Queen' **new**	MSem
	'Lilac Time' ♀H4	CMea CWil ECho EHyd EPPr ESem LRHS MBrN MHer MSCN MSem SFgr SPlb SRms WHal WIvy XLum
	'Lion King'	CWil ESem MSCN
	'Lipari'	WCot XLum
	'Lipstick'	MSem
	'Little Coffee Cup' **new**	SFgr
	'Little Flirt'	MSCN
	'Lively Bug'	CWil ECho EDAr EPPr ESem LBee LRHS MSCN MSem SDys SEND SRms WGor
	'Lloyd Praeger'	see *S. montanum* subsp. *stiriacum* 'Lloyd Praeger'
	'Long Shanks'	MSCN SFgr
	'Lonzo'	ESem MSem SRms
	'Louisse-Marie' **new**	MSem
	'Lynn's Choice'	CWil GAbr SFgr WHal WIvy
	macedonicum	WIvy XLum
	- from Ljuboten, Macedonia/Kosovo	CWil
	'Madeleine'	CWil ESem
	'Magic Spell'	CWil ESem MSem
	'Magical'	CWil MSem
	'Magnificum'	CWil ESem MSem WGor
	'Mahogany'	CHEx CTri CWil ECho EDAr ESem GKev LBee MHer MSCN NHol SFgr SRms WGor WHal WIvy WNew XLum
	'Maigret'	CWil MSem
	'Majestic'	CWil ESem LBee
	'Major White'	CHEx
	'Malby's Hybrid'	see *S.* 'Reginald Malby'
	'Marella'	ESem
	'Maria Laach'	CWil ESem MMuc MSem
	'Marijntje'	CWil ESem
	'Marjorie Newton'	CWil ESem
	'Marmalade'	CMea
§	***marmoreum***	ECho EPot LBee SRms WHal
	- from Kanzan Gorge, Bulgaria	ESem XLum
	- from Monte Tirone, Italy	SDys
	- 'Brunneifolium'	CWil GAbr LBee WIvy XLum
	- subsp. ***marmoreum*** var. ***dinaricum***	MHer
§	- - 'Rubrifolium'	XLum
	'Mate'	ESem
	'Maubi'	CHEx
	'Mauna Kea'	ESem
	'Mauvine'	XLum
	'Mayfair'	EDAr
	'Meisse'	ECho
	'Melanie'	CWil ESem MBrN WIvy
	'Memorial Merit'	ESem
	'Mercury'	CWil ECho EHyd ESem GAbr LRHS NBro SRms
	'Merlin'	ESem MSCN MSem
	'Midas'	CWil ECho EHyd ESem LRHS MSem SFgr
	'Milá'	CWil
	'Mini Frost'	CWil ESem
	'Mixed Spice'	CMea CWil
	'Moerkerk's Merit'	CWil ESem GAbr MSem XLum
	'Mohair'	MSem
	'Mona Lisa' **new**	MSem
	'Mondstein'	CWil ESem MSem WIvy
	'Monseigneur Desmet'	ESem
	'Montage'	CWil MSem
§	***montanum***	ESem
	- from Arbizion, France	CWil
	- from Monte Tirone, Italy	LBee
	- from Monte Tonale, Italy	CWil
	- from Windachtal, Germany	CWil
§	- subsp. ***burnatii***	CWil ESem MHom WIvy
	'Caesar'	MSCN
	- subsp. ***carpaticum***	CWil XLum
	- - 'Cmiral's Yellow'	MSCN SFgr WAbe WIvy
*	- Fragell form	SFgr
	- subsp. ***montanum***	CWil
	- 'Rubrum'	see *S.* 'Red Mountain'
	- subsp. ***stiriacum***	CWil ESem SFgr XLum
§	- - 'Lloyd Praeger'	CWil ESem LBee MSem SDys SFgr WIvy
	montanum* × *tectorum var. ***boutignyanum*** GDJ 94.15	CWil
	'Moondrops'	CWil
	'More Honey'	CWil
	'Morning Glow'	CMea ESem WGor WHal
	'Mount Hood'	ECho EHyd ESem LRHS WHal
	'Mulberry Wine'	CWil ESem LBee LRHS SRms WGor WHoo
	'Mystic'	CWil ESem MBrN

'Neon'	CWil MSem
nevadense	CWil EPot MSem SRms
- GDJ 96A-07 from Calar de Santa Barbara, Spain	CWil
- from Puerto de San Francisco	CWil ESem
'Nico'	CWil MSem NWad SRms
'Night Raven'	WIvy
'Nigrum'	see *S. tectorum* 'Nigrum'
'Niobe'	CWil SFgr WHal
'Noellie'	CWil
'Noir'	CWil EDAr ESem GKev LAst MSCN NBro WAbe WGor
'Norbert'	CWil EDAr SRms WIvy XLum
'Nörtofts Beauty'	MSem
'Nouveau Pastel'	CFis CMea CWil ESem WHal XLum
'Octet'	CWil
octopodes	NBir XLum
- var. ***apetalum***	CWil EPPr ESem GAbr MSCN MSem SRms WHoo WIvy
'Oddity'	CWil GBin MBrN MHer WHal
'Oh My' **new**	MSem
'Ohio Burgundy'	ECho EHyd ESem LRHS MSem SRms WAbe
'Old Copper'	ESem
'Old Rose'	SFgr
'Olivette'	ESem MSem XLum
'Omega'	ESem
'Ornatum'	EPot ESem MHer MHom MWat WHal WIvy
ossetiense	CWil EDAr GAbr XLum
'Othello' ♀H4	CDes CTri CWil EPfP GAbr GCra MSem NBir WPGP XLum
'Pacific Charm' **new**	MSem
'Pacific Hep'	CWil MSem
'Pacific Opal'	CWil
'Pacific Purple Shadows'	CWil MSem
'Pacific Spring Frost'	SFgr
'Packardian'	CWil ESem GKev NWad SFgr WIvy
'Painted Lady'	ESem
'Palissander'	EDAr SFgr XLum
'Pam Wain'	MHom
'Passionata'	CWil SFgr
'Pastel'	CWil ESem MHer
patens	see *Jovibarba heuffelii*
'Patrician'	CWil LBee SRms
'Peggy'	CWil MSem WGor
'Pekinese'	ECho EDAr EHyd EPot ESem LRHS MBrN MSem NBro SFgr SRms WGor XLum
'Peridot' **new**	SFgr
'Peterson's Ornatum'	SDys
'Petite Renée' **new**	MSem
'Petsy'	ESem SRms
'Pilatus'	MSCN SRms XLum
× ***piliferum*** 'Hausmannii'	MSem
'Pine Cone'	WGor
'Pink Astrid'	CWil
'Pink Cloud'	CWil
'Pink Dawn'	ESem
'Pink Delight'	MSCN
'Pink Lemonade'	CWil MHom
'Pink Mist'	SRms
'Pink Puff'	CWil MHom MSem SFgr
'Pippin'	CMea CWil ESem MSem SRms
'Piran'	CWil
pittonii ♀H4	CMea CWil EPot ESem MSem WHal XLum
'Pixie'	CPBP CWil MSem SFgr
'Plum Frosting'	ESem MSCN WGor
'Plum Mist'	NWad
'Plumb Rose'	CWil ESem WIvy
'Pluto'	CWil ESem LBee XLum
'Poke Eat'	ESem
'Polaris'	CWil ESem MHom
'Ponderosa'	CWil
'Pottsii'	CWil ESem
'President Arsac'	XLum
'Procton'	ESem MSem
'Proud Zelda'	CWil EDAr ESem MSem
'Průhonice'	CWil
'Pseudo-ornatum'	LBee SRms
'Pumaros'	SDys
pumilum	CWil ECho EHyd LRHS
- from Adyl-Su, Chechnya, No 1	CWil
- from Armkhi, Ingushetia	SDys
- from El'brus, Russia, No 1	CWil ESem
- from Techensis, Caucasus Mtns	CWil
- 'Sopa'	CWil MSCN
'Purdy'	MHom MSCN WAbe
'Purdy's 50-6'	CWil
'Purdy's 70-40'	MSem
'Purdy's Big Red' **new**	MSem
'Purple Beauty'	EPot GKev
'Purple King'	CMea MHom SDys
'Purple Passion'	ESem
'Purple Queen'	CWil EDAr EHyd EPPr LRHS SFgr
'Pygmalion'	CWil ESem
'Queen Amalia'	see *S. reginae-amaliae*
'Quintessence'	CWil MSCN SFgr SRms
'Racey'	ESem
'Ramses'	ESem SDys
'Raspberry Ice'	CFis CMea ESem LBee MSCN MSem NBro
'Rauer Kulm'	CWil
'Rauhreif'	XLum
'Red Ace'	CWil MBel MSem NBro SFgr
'Red Beam'	CWil MSCN
'Red Chips'	EDAr MHom
'Red Delta'	CDes CWil NBir SFgr WCot WPGP
'Red Devil'	CMea CWil ECho EHyd ESem LLHF LRHS SFgr SPlb WHoo
'Red King'	GBin
'Red Lion'	CWil MSem SFgr
'Red Lynn'	CWil ESem
§ 'Red Mountain'	CWil ESem LBee MSem SRms
'Red Pink'	CWil MSem
'Red Pluche' **new**	MSem
'Red Robin'	EDAr
'Red Shadows'	LBee
'Red Spider'	CWil EPPr EPot MHom MSem NBro
'Red Summer'	ESem
'Regal'	ESem
reginae	see *S. reginae-amaliae*
§ ***reginae-amaliae***	CWil EPot GKev XLum
- from Kambeecho, Greece, No 2	SDys
- from Mavri Petri, Greece	CWil SDys
- from Sarpun, Turkey	CWil SDys
- from Vardusa, Serbia	CWil SDys
§ 'Reginald Malby'	CTri ECho EHyd ESem GMaP LRHS MSem SFgr SRms WIvy
'Reinhard' ♀H4	CMea CWil ECho EDAr EHyd EPot ESem LRHS MAsh MBrN MHer MSCN MSem NRya SPlb SRms WHal WHoo WIvy

	'Remus'	CWil ELan ESem MSem SDys SFgr WGor
	'Rhône'	CWil LBee MSem
	'Rich 'n' Fruity'	MSCN
	'Risque'	CWil LBee
	'Rita Jane'	CWil ESem MHom SFgr
	'Robin'	LBee MSem NBro NHol SFgr
	'Rocknoll Rosette' **new**	MSem
	'Ronny'	CWil ESem MSem
	'Roosemaryn'	EDAr ESem
	× ***roseum***	ESem
	'Rosie'	CMea CPBP CWil ECho EHyd EPot ESem GAbr GMaP LBee LRHS MAsh MSCN NHol SRms WHal WHoo WIce
	'Rotkopf' ♀H4	CWil ESem MSCN SFgr XLum
	'Rotmantel'	MSem SDys
	'Rotund'	CWil ESem MSCN
	'Royal Opera'	CWil EDAr ESem
	'Royal Ruby'	LBee WIvy
	'Royale'	SFgr
	'Rubellum Mahogany'	SFgr
	'Rubin'	CMea CTri EPfP GBin GKev LBMP MAsh MSCN MSem NBir NEgg SPoG SRms WAbe WHoo WIce WNew XLum
I	'Rubra Ash'	CWil ESem WAbe
I	'Rubra Ray'	CWil EDAr MSem
	'Rubrifolium'	see *S. marmoreum* subsp. ***marmoreum*** 'Rubrifolium'
*	'Ruby Glow'	EDAr
	'Ruby Heart'	EDAr
	'Russian River'	CMea WHoo
	'Rusty'	CWil ESem SFgr
	ruthenicum	ECho EHyd LLHF LRHS MHom MSem NRya XLum
	- 'Regis-Fernandii'	ECho XLum
	'Safara'	ESem
	'Saga'	MHom
	'Sarah'	EDAr
	'Sarotte'	CWil MSem
	'Saturn'	ESem MSem SRms
	schlehanii	see *S. marmoreum*
	schnittspahnii	XLum
	'Sea Breeze' **new**	SFgr
	'Sea Urchin' **new**	SFgr
	'Seminole'	CWil ESem
	'Serendipity'	EDAr
	'Sharon's Pencil'	CWil MSem
	'Sheila'	GAbr
	'Shirley Moore'	CWil EDAr ESem MSem SFgr
	'Shirley's Joy'	ESem XLum
	'Sigma'	ESem
	'Silberkarneol' misapplied	see *S.* 'Silver Jubilee'
	'Silberspitz'	CWil ECho EHyd LRHS MHer MHom NBro SPlb
	'Silver Andre' **new**	MSem
	'Silver Crows' **new**	MSem
	'Silver Cup'	CWil SFgr WIvy
§	'Silver Jubilee'	CMea CWil ECho EDAr EHyd ESem GAbr GBin LRHS NBro NRya SPlb SRms WGor XLum
	'Silver Queen'	CWil ESem SFgr
	'Silver Shadow'	MSCN WGor
	'Silver Thaw'	CWil EDAr MSem SFgr
	'Silverine'	CWil EDAr
	'Silvertone'	CWil ESem
	'Simonkaianum'	see *Jovibarba hirta*
	'Sioux'	CWil ESem LBee MBrN NHol WHal WIvy

	'Sirius' **new**	MSem
	'Skrocki's Bronze'	GAbr
	'Slabber's Seedling'	CWil MSem
	'Smaragd'	LBee XLum
	'Smit's Seedling' **new**	MSem
	'Smokey Jet'	ESem SFgr
	'Smokey Quartz'	WGor
	'Snowberger'	CMea CWil EPot ESem MSCN SFgr SRms WGor WHal WIvy
	'Soarte'	ESem
	soboliferum	see *Jovibarba sobolifera*
	'Soothsayer'	CWil
	sosnowskyi	CWil MSem XLum
	'Soul Sister'	ESem
	'Spangle' **new**	MSem
	- sport **new**	MSem
	'Speciosum'	ESem
	'Spherette'	CWil EDAr ESem MBrN MSCN WAbe
	'Spider's Lair' ♀H4	EDAr MHom
	'Spinellii'	WThu
	'Spiver's Velvet'	ESem
	'Springmist'	ECho EHyd EPot ESem GAbr LRHS SFgr SRms WGor
	'Sprite'	CWil MBel MSem SDys WIvy
	'Squib'	CWil ESem MSCN
	stansfieldii	see *S. arachnoideum* subsp. *tomentosum* 'Stansfieldii'
	'Starburst'	CWil
	'Starion'	CWil MSem
	'Starshine'	ESem SFgr
	'State Fair'	CWil EDAr MSem
*	***stoloniferum***	GAbr
	'Strawberry Fields'	ESem
	'Strawberry Sundae'	ESem
	'Strider'	CWil GAbr
	'Stuffed Olive'	CWil SDys SRms SRot
	'Sun Waves'	CWil ESem SDys
	'Sunray Desire'	WGor
	'Sunray Magic'	WGor
	'Super Dome'	CWil MSem
	'Superama'	ESem
	'Supernova'	ESem
	'Tamberlane'	EDAr
	'Tarita'	CWil MSem
§	***tectorum*** ♀H4	CArn CHby CTri ECho EDAr ELan EPfP GKev GPoy LBee LPot MHer MHoo MNHC SIde SPlb WJck XLum
	- from Eporn	CWil
§	- var. ***alpinum***	CWil ECho EHyd LRHS MHom NBro SRms
	- - from Sierra del Cadi, Spain	MSem
	- var. ***andreanum***	CWil XLum
	- 'Atropurpureum'	ECho ELan
	- 'Atroviolaceum'	EDAr MSem NLar SPlb WIvy XLum
*	- 'Aureum'	SFgr
	- var. ***boutignyanum*** from Route de Tuixén, Spain	ESem
	- - GDJ 94.02 from Sant Joan de Caselles, Andorra	CWil
	- - GDJ 94.03	CWil
	- - GDJ 94.04	CWil SRms
	- var. ***calcareum***	ECho ESem
	- 'Marin' **new**	MSem
§	- 'Nigrum'	ESem LBee MHer NBro SDys WGor
	- 'Red Flush'	CWil EDAr EPPr MBrN SDys SFgr
	- 'Royanum' ♀H4	ESem GAbr MSCN
*	- subsp. ***sanguineum***	EDAr
	- 'Sunset'	CMea EDAr ESem GAbr SDys WHal

	- subsp. ***tectorum***	ESem
§	- - 'Boissieri'	CWil WIvy
	- - 'Triste'	CHEx CWil LBee XLum
	- 'Tokajense'	ESem
	- 'Val Minera' **new**	MSem
	- 'Violaceum'	MHom SPlb SRms WGor
	'Tederheid'	MSem
	'Telfan'	MSem
	'Terlamen'	CWil
	'Terracotta Baby'	CWil ESem MSem SFgr
	'The Platters'	CWil
	'The Rocket'	CWil
	× ***thompsonianum***	CWil LBee SFgr
	'Thunder'	CWil
	'Tip Top'	CWil MSem SFgr
	'Titania'	CWil MSem NBro WHal
	'Topaz'	CWil LBee SRms XLum
	'Tordeur's Memory'	CWil ESem MSCN MSem SEND
I	'Tourmalyi' **new**	MSem
	'Tracy Sue'	EDAr XLum
	'Trail Walker'	CWil LBee SRms
	transcaucasicum	CWil XLum
	'Tree Beard'	CWil
	'Trine'	CWil
	'Tristesse' 🏆^{H4}	CWil EDAr GAbr LBee MBrN MSem SFgr WGor WIvy
	'Truva'	CWil ESem MSem SFgr
	'Twilight Blues'	CWil ECho ESem LRHS SFgr SRms
	'Twizzler'	MSCN
	'Undine'	CWil ESem SFgr
	'Unicorn'	ESem MSem
	'Uranus' **new**	MSem
	'Urmina' **new**	MSem
	'Utopian'	ESem
	× ***vaccarii***	CWil XLum
	'Van der Steen'	GAbr
	'Vanbaelen'	CWil GAbr MSem SDys
	'Velanovsky' **new**	MSem
	'Veughelen'	MSem
	vicentei	ESem MHom
	- from Gaton, Spain	ESem LBee
§	- subsp. ***paui***	NHol NSla
	'Victorian'	ESem
	'Video'	CWil ESem MHom SFgr
	'Vignola'	CWil
	'Violet Queen'	ESem MSem
	'Virgil'	CWil EDAr ESem MBrN MSCN MSem NWad SDys WAbe WCot WGor WIce
I	'Virginius'	CWil
	'Waldalina'	CWil
	'Warrior'	EDAr
	'Wasti'	CWil
	'Watermelon Rind'	ESem MSem
	webbianum	see *S. arachnoideum* L. subsp. *tomentosum* (C.B. Lehm. & Schnittsp.) Schinz & Thell.
	'Webby Flame'	CWil MSem
	'Webbyola'	ESem
	'Weirdo'	CWil ESem
	'Wendy'	ESem MSem SFgr
	'Westerlin'	CWil ESem MSem
	'White Christmas'	see *S. arachnoideum* 'White Christmas'
	'Whitening'	EDAr GAbr
	'Whitney' **new**	ESem MSem
	'Winter Beauty' **new**	MSem
I	'Woolcott's Variety'	CWil ECho ESem MSCN MSem NBir
	wulfenii	CWil
*	- ***roseum***	EDAr
	'Xaviera'	CWil MSem
	'Yanisha'	CWil
	'Yarnton'	ESem
	'Yolanda' **new**	CWil
	'Yvette'	CWil
	'Zaza'	CWil
	zeleborii	SDys WHal
	'Zenith'	CWil EDAr ESem GAbr SFgr SRms
	'Zenobia'	MHom
	'Zenocrate'	NHol WHal
	'Zepherin'	CWil MSCN MSem
	'Zilver Moon'	CWil ESem
	'Zilver Snowflake'	CWil
	'Zilver Suzanna'	CWil
	'Zircon'	EDAr
	'Zone'	CHEx ESem
	'Zorba'	MSem
	'Zulu'	SFgr

Senecio (*Asteraceae*)

	aquaticus	LLWG
§	***articulatus***	EShb
	aschenbornianus	CFil
	bidwillii	see *Brachyglottis bidwillii*
	candicans misapplied	see *S. cineraria*
	cannabinifolius **new**	GCal
	chrysanthemoides	see *Euryops chrysanthemoides*
§	***cineraria***	CWCL LPot SEND
	- 'Silver Dust' 🏆^{H3}	EPfP
	cinerascens **new**	SVen
*	***coccinilifera***	SBch
	compactus	see *Brachyglottis compacta*
	confusus	see *Pseudogynoxys chenopodioides*
	crassissimus	EShb
	cristobalensis	WCot
	doria	EBee EShb LRHS WHil WHrl
	ficoides	EShb
	formosoides B&SWJ 10736	WCru
	formosus B&SWJ 10700	WCru
	- B&SWJ 10746	WCru
	gerberifolius B&SWJ 10357	WCru
	- B&SWJ 10361	WCru
	glastifolius	LRHS
	grandifolius	see *Telanthophora grandifolia*
	'Gregynog Gold'	see *Ligularia* 'Gregynog Gold'
	greyi misapplied	see *Brachyglottis* (Dunedin Group) 'Sunshine'
	greyi Hook.	see *Brachyglottis greyi* (Hook. f.) B. Nord.
	heritieri DC.	see *Pericallis lanata* (L'Hér.) B. Nord.
	hoffmannii	EShb
	integrifolius subsp. ***capitatus***	SPlb
	kleiniiformis	EShb
	laxifolius hort.	see *Brachyglottis* (Dunedin Group) 'Sunshine'
	leucostachys	see *S. viravira*
	macroglossus	CHll CRHN EShb
	- 'Variegatus' (v) 🏆^{H1}	EShb
	maritimus	see *S. cineraria*
	monroi	see *Brachyglottis monroi*
	petasitis	CBcs CFil CHEx SDix WCot
	polyodon	CCCN CDes CSpe EDAr EPPr EShb EWll GAbr GBin GLog MHol MNrw MPie MSpe NDov NLar SPhx WCAu WCFE WMoo WPGP WSHC WWEG

- S&SH 29	EBee NCGa
- subsp. ***subglaber***	EWes
przewalskii	see *Ligularia przewalskii*
pulcher	CDTJ CDes MNrw NCGa SBch SHar WPGP
reinholdii	see *Brachyglottis rotundifolia*
rowleyanus	EBak
scandens	CCCN CExl EShb MNrw WPGP
§ ***serpens***	CDoC EShb EUJe MSCN SEND
§ ***smithii***	ELan GBee NBid WCot
squalidus	WHer
subnivalis new	XLum
subulatus var. ***subulatus*** CC 6515	GKev
- - CC 6516	EBee
'Sunshine'	see *Brachyglottis* (Dunedin Group) 'Sunshine'
talinoides subsp. ***cylindricus*** 'Himalaya'	EShb
tanguticus	see *Sinacalia tangutica*
§ ***viravira*** ♀H3-4	EPfP EUJe MCot SDix SMrm SPer WSHC

Senna (*Caesalpiniaceae*)

alata B&SWJ 9772	WCru
alexandrina	CCCN EShb LRHS WPGP
§ ***corymbosa***	CBcs CCCN CHEx CRHN CTri EAmu ECre SMrm
hebecarpa	LRHS SBrt SPhx
§ ***marilandica***	CArn EBee ELan GBin LRHS
multiglandulosa	CBcs WPGP
retusa	CHEx
septemtrionalis	CCCN EBee LRHS SEND

Sequoia (*Cupressaceae*)

sempervirens ♀H4	CBcs CDoC CDul CLnd CMCN CMen CTho ECrN EHul EPfP EWTr GKin LRHS MBlu MMuc NWCa SAPC SEND SGol SPoG WMou
- 'Adpressa'	CDoC CDul CTho EHul LRHS MAsh MBri MGos SCoo SLim
- 'Cantab'	CDoC SLim WMou
- 'Glauca' new	MAsh
- 'Henderson Blue'	SLim
- 'Prostrata'	CDoC LRHS MMuc SEND SLim
- 'Simpson's Silver'	SLim

Sequoiadendron (*Cupressaceae*)

giganteum ♀H4	CBcs CCVT CDoC CDul CMCN CTho CTri EHul ELan EPfP EWTr LRHS MAsh MBlu MBri MGos MMuc NEgg NSoo NWCa SEND SEWo SGol SPer SPlb WMou
- 'Barabits Requiem'	IArd LRHS MBlu NLar SLim SMad
- 'Blauer Eichzwerg'	NLar
- 'Bultinck Yellow'	MBlu NLar
- 'Curly Green'	NLar
- 'French Beauty'	NLar
- 'Glaucum'	CDoC CTho LRHS MBlu MBri NLar SLim SPoG WMou
* - 'Glaucum Compactum'	MBlu
- 'Greenpeace'	MBlu NLar
- 'Little Stan'	NLar
- 'Pendulum'	CCVT CDoC CDul CKen ERod MBlu NLar SLim SMad
- 'Philip Curtis'	NLar
- 'Pierie'	NLar
- 'Pirat'	NLar

- 'Powdered Blue'	LRHS NLar SLim WPGP
- 'Von Martin'	NLar

Serapias (*Orchidaceae*)

lingua	CDes SChF

Serenoa (*Arecaceae*)

repens	EAmu

Seriphidium see *Artemisia*

Serratula (*Asteraceae*)

bulgarica	WCot
coronata	LRHS
- subsp. ***insularis*** B&SWJ 8698	WCru
- - f. ***alba***	GAbr
§ ***seoanei***	CKno CMea CPom CSam EBee EDAr ELan LHop LPla LRHS MHer MLHP MMuc MNrw MPie MRav MWat NBid SBch SDix SPhx SRms WCot WPGP
shawii	see *S. seoanei*
tinctoria	CArn NLar NMir SPhx
- subsp. ***macrocephala***	EBee

Serruria (*Proteaceae*)

florida	SPlb
phylicoides	SPlb

Sesamum (*Pedaliaceae*)

indicum	CArn

Sesbania (*Papilionaceae*)

punicea	CCCN

Seseli (*Apiaceae*)

elatum	LPio
gummiferum	CHid CSam CSpe EBee LDai LPio SBrt SKHP SPhx WHil WPtf
hippomarathrum	EBee LEdu LPio SPhx WCot WHrl WPGP
§ ***libanotis***	CSam GBin LEdu LPio LPla NDov NLar SDix SPhx WCot WPtf
montanum	CSpe EBee IMou LHop MNFA WPGP
varium new	CArn

Sesleria (*Poaceae*)

§ ***argentea***	EHoe EPPr
autumnalis	CKno EBee IMou LEdu LPla SPhx XLum
caerulea	CKno CSam EHoe ELan EPfP GQue IMou LEdu MBrN MWhi SPoG WPtf XLum
- 'Malvern Mop'	EBee WHrl WPGP WWEG
* ***candida***	EPPr
cylindrica	see *S. argentea*
glauca	EHoe NLar NOak
'Greenlee'	CKno NDov
heufleriana	CWCL EHoe EPPr IMou MBel NLar SMea SPhx SPlb WCot WWEG
insularis	EPPr EShb
'Morning Dew'	EBee GCal
nitida	CKno EBee EHoe IMou LEdu MBrN MMoz SDix SPhx WCot WPGP XLum
rigida	EHoe
sadleriana	EBee EPPr EWes

Setaria (*Poaceae*)

macrostachya 🏆^{H3}	CKno LLWP SPhx
palmifolia	CHEx CHll CKno EUJe SPlb WCot
- BWJ 8132	WCru
viridis	CSpe WCot

Setcreasea see *Tradescantia*

shaddock see *Citrus maxima*

Sharon fruit see *Diospyros kaki*

Shepherdia (*Elaeagnaceae*)

argentea	CBcs NLar

Shibataea (*Poaceae*)

chinensis	CBcs
kumasaca	CAbb CBcs CDoC CEnt ENBC EPfP ERod GCal LEdu LRHS MBrN MJak MMoz MWht SBig SGol SLPl WJun WPGP
lancifolia	WJun

Shortia (*Diapensiaceae*)

galacifolia	GKev
soldanelloides	GKev
uniflora	NHar WAbe
- var. ***kantoensis***	GKev

Sibbaldia (*Rosaceae*)

procumbens	GKev

Sibbaldiopsis (*Rosaceae*)

tridentata 'Lemon Mac'	NHar
- 'Nuuk'	CCon EPPr

Sibthorpia (*Plantaginaceae*)

europaea	CExl CHEx

Sida (*Malvaceae*)

hermaphrodita	EBee

Sidalcea (*Malvaceae*)

'Brilliant'	CBcs EBee EPfP GBin IBoy LAst LRHS MJak MNrw MSCN NBir NPri NSoo SHar SPer WCAu WMoo WWEG
campestris from Oregon, USA	EPPr
candida	CHel CPrp CSam EBee ECtt ELan EPfP GCra GMaP LAst LHop LRHS MAsh MBNS MBel MCot MMuc MRav MTis NEgg NGdn NLar NSoo NSti SEND SMrm SPer WCAu WCot
- 'Bianca'	EBee EPfP NGBl NLar WHal WMoo WOut WWEG
'Candy Girl'	EBee
'Croftway Red'	CCon EBee ELan EPfP GCra LRHS MBel MCot NBro NGdn NHol NWad SPet SWvt
'Elsie Heugh' 🏆^{H4}	Widely available
'Interlaken'	LRHS
'Little Princess'^{PBR}	CCon EBee EPfP EWes LBuc LRHS LSou MAsh NDov NGdn NLar NSoo SPoG
'Loveliness'	EBee ECtt ELan EShb LHop LSou MRav NBro NCGa NGdn NHol NLar NWad
malviflora	SRms WBrk
'Moorland Rose Coronet'	WMoo
'Mr Lindbergh'	EBee EPfP NLar
'Mrs Borrodaile'	CMac CPrp MRav NBro NGdn NPro SMrm WMoo WWEG
'Mrs T.Alderson'	EBee
'My Love'	EBee NDov SMrm
'Oberon'	EBee MRav
oregana	NGdn
- subsp. ***spicata***	WMoo
'Party Girl'	CHel CMac CSBt ECtt EHyd ELan EPfP GJos IBoy LRHS LSRN LSqH MCot MRav NBro NGdn NHol NLar NOrc NPri SMrm SPlb SPoG WMnd WMoo WWEG XLum
'Purpetta'	EBee ELan EPfP NGBl NGdn NLar NPro SPad
reptans	CDes WWFP
'Reverend Page Roberts'	MRav WCot WWEG
'Rosaly'	EWll IFoB LRHS MPie NLar WGor WHal
'Rosanna'	GMaP LAst LRHS NLar WHal WPtf WWFP
'Rose Bud'	CPrp EBee ELan
'Rose Queen'	EBee LHop MCot MRav NBro NHol SPer SRms
'Rosy Gem'	ECtt NBre
Stark's hybrids	LRHS SRms
'Sussex Beauty'	CPrp CSam EBee MBel MCot MLHP MRav NCGa NEgg NGdn NHol SMrm WMoo WWlt
'Wensleydale'	CDes EBee
'William Smith' 🏆^{H4}	CPrp CSam EBee ECtt EPfP EWes GBuc LRHS LSRN MBel MMuc MRav MWat NBir NCGa NChi NGdn NLar NOrc SEND WMnd WMoo WPtf WWEG
'Wine Red'	CCon CMHG CPrp EBee EShb LRHS MCot NEgg NGdn SPoG SWvt WWEG WWFP

Sideritis (*Lamiaceae*)

RCB UA 2 new	WCot
clandestina	XSen
cypria	XSen
hyssopifolia	EBee
- subsp. ***guillonii*** new	XSen
perfoliata	XSen
phlomoides	XSen
phrygia	XSen
scardica	XSen
stachydioides new	XSen
syriaca	CArn NBre XSen
taurica	XSen

Sieversia (*Rosaceae*)

§ ***pentapetala***	WAbe
reptans	see *Geum reptans*

Silaum (*Apiaceae*)

silaus	NMir

Silene (*Caryophyllaceae*)

RBS	EPPr
SDR 6174	GKev
from Uzbekistan	GCal
acaulis	ECho EDAr GJos MAsh MMuc NLar SRms WAbe
§ - subsp. ***acaulis***	ECho SPlb SRms

	- 'Alba'	ECho EDAr EWes NLar WAbe WThu
	- 'Blush'	NSla WAbe
§	- subsp. ***bryoides***	NLar
	- 'Correvoniana'	NLar
	- subsp. ***elongata***	see *S. acaulis* subsp. *acaulis*
	- subsp. ***exscapa***	see *S. acaulis* subsp. *bryoides*
	- 'Frances'	CPBP ITim NRya NSla WAbe
	- 'Francis Copeland'	ECho
	- 'Helen's Double' (d)	ECho GJos
	- 'Mount Snowdon'	ECho ECtt EPfP EWes GMaP MMuc NLar SPlb SPoG SRms SRot WHoo
	- 'Pedunculata'	see *S. acaulis* subsp. *acaulis*
	alba	see *S. latifolia* subsp. *alba*
§	***alpestris***	NLar SBch SRms SRot WMoo WThu
	- 'Flore Pleno' (d) ♀H4	CMea CPBP EWes NSla SBch WIce WWFP
	uraralica	ITim WAbe
	argaea	WAbe
	× *arkwrightii*	see *Lychnis* × *arkwrightii*
	armeria	SDys
	- 'Aphrodite'	CSpe
	- 'Electra'	CAby CSpe
	asterias	GCal GCra MNrw NSti SBrt WWFP
	- MESE 429	GBin
	atropurpurea	see *Lychnis viscaria* subsp. *atropurpurea*
	bolanthoides	LLHF WAbe
§	***compacta***	NLar WCot
	'Confetti'	EDif
	'Country Comet'	NChi
§	***davidii***	EBee EPot GKev
	delavayi	LRHS
	dinarica	WAbe
§	***dioica***	CArn CHab CMac EWTr LEdu MHer MNHC NLar NMir SPoG SWat WMoo WOut WSFF WShi
	- 'Clifford Moor' (v)	EBee ECtt MSCN NSti SCoo
	- 'Compacta'	see *S. dioica* 'Minikin'
	'Firefly' PBR (d)	CMac CWCL EBee ECtt LBMP NSti SHar SPoG SRkn SWvt WWlt
§	- 'Flore Pleno' (d)	GCra MRav NBid NBro NChi NGdn SMrm WHoo
§	- 'Graham's Delight' (v)	NWad
	- 'Inane'	CDes EBee WBor WPGP WRHF WSHC WWFP
	- 'Innocence'	NChi
	- f. ***lactea***	MHer
§	- 'Minikin'	MAvo MSCN MTis NGdn
	- 'Purple Prince'	CMea NChi SEND SMrm WMoo WPtf
I	- 'Ray's Golden Campion'	NWad WOut WTou
	- 'Rubra Plena'	see *S. dioica* 'Flore Pleno'
	'Stella' new	NChi
	- 'Thelma Kay' (d/v)	ECtt NBre NGdn WMoo WWFP
	- 'Underdine'	EWes
	- 'Valley High' (v)	ECtt EWes MHol MMuc WHer WHil
	- 'Variegata'	see *S. dioica* 'Graham's Delight'
	elisabethae	EWld LSou
§	***fimbriata***	CCon CSpe ELan EPPr EPyc EShb LPla MCot MMHG MNFA MNrw MRav NLar NSti SBri SMrm WBor WCot WKif WMoo WPGP WPtf WRHF
	hookeri	GKev
	- Ingramii Group	WAbe
	kantzeensis	see *S. davidii*
	keiskei	CPBP
	- var. ***akaisialpina***	ITim
	- var. ***minor***	ECho EWes LRHS WAbe
	laciniata 'Jack Flash'	GJos MSCN
	latifolia	CArn CHab MMuc MNHC NMir WOut
§	- subsp. ***alba***	SEND
	maritima	see *S. uniflora*
	multifida	see *S. fimbriata*
	noctiflora	CHab WSFF
	nutans	CArn SRms WSFF
	orientalis	see *S. compacta*
	pharnaceifolia	CPBP
	pusilla	CPBP ITim NLar
	quadridentata	see *S. alpestris*
	regia	SPhx
	rubra	see *S. dioica*
	saxifraga	NLar
	schafta ♀H4	CTri ECho ECtt EPfP GKev MAsh MMuc MRav NBid NHol SRms WHoo XLum
	- 'Abbotswood'	see *Lychnis* × *walkeri* 'Abbotswood Rose'
	- 'Persian Carpet'	MCot SBch
	- 'Robusta'	LRHS NDov
	- 'Shell Pink'	CPBP EPot EWes GJos LRHS NBid NDov SBch WHoo
	sieboldii	see *Lychnis coronata* var. *sieboldii*
§	***uniflora***	CHab ECho ECtt EPfP MMuc MSCN MWat NBro SBch SEND SPlb SRms SRot WMoo WOut
	- 'Alba Plena'	see *S. uniflora* 'Robin Whitebreast'
I	- 'Compacta'	ECho WMoo
§	- 'Druett's Variegated' (v)	CMea CTri ECho ECtt EHyd ELon EPot EWes GJos LHop LRHS MAsh MHer MHol NBid NPri SPet SPlb SPoG SRms WIce XLum
	- 'Flore Pleno'	see *S. uniflora* 'Robin Whitebreast'
§	- 'Robin Whitebreast' (d)	CMea ECho ECtt EPfP NBid NBro SRms SRot WMoo WSHC XLum
	- 'Rosea'	CMea ECho EPfP MMuc SPlb SRot
	- 'Variegata'	see *S. uniflora* 'Druett's Variegated'
	- Weisskehlchen	see *S. uniflora* 'Robin Whitebreast'
	- 'White Bells'	CTri WKif WSHC
	viridiflora	SPhx
§	***vulgaris***	CArn CHab ELau LEdu MHer MNHC NMir SEND WHer WOut
	- subsp. ***maritima***	see *S. uniflora*
	wallichiana	see *S. vulgaris*
	'Wisley Pink'	ECtt
	yunnanensis	SPhx WSHC
§	***zawadskii***	GKev LRHS NWad SBrt

Siler (*Umbelliferae*)

montanum	see *Laserpitium siler*

Silphium (Asteraceae)

integrifolium	EBee NBre SMad SPhx WCot WOld XLum
laciniatum	CArn LEdu NBre SBrt SMad SPhx WCot XLum
perfoliatum ♀H4	CArn CFis EBee GPoy IMou NBre NDov NLar SMrm SPhx WCot WOld WWEG XLum
- var. ***connatum***	SPhx
terebinthinaceum	SPhx WCot XLum
trifoliatum	WCot

Silybum (Asteraceae)

marianum	CArn ELan EPfP GAbr GPoy LRHS MCot MHoo MNHC SIde SPav WHer WHfH WOut WTou

Simmondsia (*Simmondsiaceae*)

chinensis	CArn

Sinacalia (*Asteraceae*)

§ ***tangutica***	CSam EShb GQue LHop MBel NBid NBro NLar SDix WCot

Sinarundinaria (*Poaceae*)

anceps	see *Yushania anceps*
jaunsarensis	see *Yushania anceps*
maling	see *Yushania maling*
murielae	see *Fargesia murielae*
nitida	see *Fargesia nitida*

Sinningia (*Gesneriaceae*)

sp.	EABi
* ***caerulea***	WDib
calcaria	WDib
canescens 🏆H1	WDib
§ ***cardinalis***	EBak WDib
- 'Innocent'	WDib
conspicua	WDib
nivalis	WDib
speciosa 'Blanche de Méru'	SDeJ
- 'Hollywood'	SDeJ
- 'Kaiser Friedrich'	SDeJ
- 'Kaiser Wilhelm'	SDeJ
- 'Mont Blanc'	SDeJ
tubiflora	CSpe WCot WKif XLum

Sinobambusa (*Poaceae*)

tootsik	WJun

× *Sinocalycalycanthus* (*Calycanthaceae*)

raulstonii 'Hartlage Wine'	CJun EPfP EUJe GBin GKin IArd IDee LLHF LRHS MBlu MBri NLar SHil SPoG SSpi
'Venus'	EPfP LLHF LRHS MBlu SPoG SSpi

Sinocalycanthus (*Calycanthaceae*)

chinensis	CArn CBcs CHll CJun CMCN CMac EBee ELan EPfP EUJe GKin LRHS MBlu MPkF NLar SHil SMad

Sinofranchetia (*Lardizabalaceae*)

chinensis	CBcs CFil CRHN LEdu WPGP

Sinojackia (*Styracaceae*)

xylocarpa	CBcs NLar

Sinopodophyllum (*Berberidaceae*)

§ ***hexandrum***	CArn CBct CBro CHel EBee ECho EPot GAbr GBBs GBuc GCra GPoy LRHS MNrw MRav NBid NBir NChi SKHP SPhx SPlb WCot WPnP
§ - var. ***chinense***	CLAP EBee ECho EWld GCal LEdu LRHS WCru
- - BWJ 7908	WCru
- - SDR 4409	CExl
- 'Chinese White'	CExl WCot
§ - var. ***emodi***	CArn GBuc ITim
- - 'Majus'	CCon CLAP EBee GBin WHal

Sinowilsonia (*Hamamelidaceae*)

henryi	NLar

Siphocampylus (*Campanulaceae*)

foliosus RCB RA S4	WCot

Siphocranion (*Lamiaceae*)

§ ***macranthum***	CDes EBee EWes WPGP

Sison (*Apiaceae*)

amomum	CBre

Sisymbrium (*Brassicaceae*)

§ ***luteum***	WHil

Sisyrinchium ✿ (*Iridaceae*)

× ***anceps***	see *S. angustifolium*
§ ***angustifolium***	CMHG EDAr MCot NBir NChi NLar SChF SPlb SRms WBrk
- f. ***album***	EDAr MCot NChi NLar
§ ***arenarium***	CWCL MAvo SPet
atlanticum	NBro
bellum hort.	see *S. idahoense* var. *bellum*
bermudiana	see *S. angustifolium*
- 'Album'	see *S. graminoides* 'Album'
'Biscutella'	CKno CPrp CTri ECho ECtt EPfP GMaP LEdu LHop SPad SPlb WHal WHoo WKif
'Blue Ice'	CMea CWCL LRHS MWat WAbe WMoo
boreale	see *S. californicum*
brachypus	see *S. californicum* Brachypus Group
'Californian Skies'	CAby CBro CElw CExl CKno CTri ECho ECtt GMaP LHop LRHS MAvo MNrw MWhi NBir NDov NSla SMrm SWvt WKif WMoo
§ ***californicum***	CBAq ECho EDAr EHon LLWG LRHS NBro WMAq WNew XLum
§ - Brachypus Group	ECho EPfP LPot MAsh MMuc MWat NBir NLar SPlb SWvt WMoo
- 'Yellowstone' **new**	EPfP
* ***capsicum***	CExl
coeruleum	see *Gelasine coerulea*
convolutum	NDov
- B&SWJ 9117	WCru
cuspidatum	see *S. arenarium*
depauperatum	MNrw
'Devon Skies'	CElw CWCL ECho ECtt EHyd LRHS MNrw SBch SWvt WAbe WIce
'Doctor Bailey'	GKev
douglasii	see *Olsynium douglasii*
'Dragon's Eye'	CElw CKno CMea ECtt EWes MBrN MHer SMrm WIce
'E.K. Balls'	COIW CPBP CPrp ECho ECtt EDAr EHoe EHyd ELan EPfP GMaP LAst LBMP LBee LHop LRHS MAsh NBro NRya NSla SMad SMrm SPad SPoG SRms SWvt WAbe WIce WMoo WNew
filifolium	see *Olsynium filifolium*
graminoides	IFoB NBro
§ - 'Album'	NBro
grandiflorum	see *Olsynium douglasii*
'Hemswell Sky'	EHoe GAbr NRya
'Iceberg'	CElw MAvo MWat SMrm
idahoense	ECtt EDAr GAbr GKev LSou MHer NRya SPlb SRms
§ - var. ***bellum***	CKno ECho EDAr EPfP SPet SRms SVen WMoo XLum
- - pale-flowered	CKno
- - 'Rocky Point'	CElw EBee EPfP EWes GJos LRHS SPoG
- var. ***macounii***	SPlb

§	- - 'Album' $\mathbb{Y}^{H4}$	CAby CElw CMea ECho GAbr GKev LPot MWat SPet SPlb WAbe
	iridifolium	see *S. micranthum*
	'Janet Denman' (v) **new**	ECho
	junceum	see *Olsynium junceum*
	littorale	CExl NLar
	macrocarpon misapplied	see *S. macrocarpum*
	macrocarpon E.P. Bicknell $\mathbb{Y}^{H2-3}$	EBee MNrw
§	***macrocarpum***	ECho
	'Marion'	CElw CMea CPBP ECtt MAvo MBrN NLar SMrm SPet
	'May Snow'	see *S. idahoense* var. *macounii* 'Album'
§	***micranthum***	ECho
	montanum × ***nudicaule***	ECho GAbr MNrw NSla SRot
	'Mrs Spivey'	MHer NBir
	palmifolium	CDes CSpe EBee LEdu MHer MNrw SBch SPoG WSHC XLum
	patagonicum	CExl EBee
	'Quaint and Queer'	CAvo CExl COIW CWCL ECtt EHoe LPot MBrN MLHP MNrw NBir NBro NChi WMnd WSHC
	'Raspberry'	CMea
	'Sapphire'	CPrp CSpe ECtt EHoe EPot GJos LPot LRHS MHol NPri SPoG STes WBor WGrn WMoo
	'Sisland Blue'	EWes
§	***striatum***	Widely available
§	- 'Aunt May' (v)	CBcs CMac CSBt EBee ECho EHoe ELan EPfP GMaP LAst LRHS LSRN MGos MRav NLar NSti SBea SMrm SPer SPoG SRms SWat SWvt WMnd WPGP WWEG
	- 'Variegatum'	see *S. striatum* 'Aunt May'
	aff. ***unispathaceum*** B&SWJ 10683	WCru

Sium (*Apiaceae*)

	sisarum	CArn ELau GPoy MHer

Skimmia ✿ (*Rutaceae*)

	anquetilia	CMac
	- (f)	IVic WCru
	- (m)	WCru
	arborescens B&SWJ 11799	WCru
	- subsp. ***nitida*** B&SWJ 8239	WCru
	arisanensis B&SWJ 7114	WCru
	- CWJ 12417	WCru
	black-fruited B&SWJ 8259 from northern Vietnam (f/m)	WCru
	× ***confusa*** 'Kew Green' (m) $\mathbb{Y}^{H4}$	Widely available
	'Daddy's Dream' **new**	NSoo
	japonica	CDul CMHG CMac CWib MGos NPla SSta
	- (f)	CDoy CMac CTri ELan EPfP GGal SRms
	- (m)	GGal
	- B&SWJ 5053 (f) and (m)	WCru
	- 'Alba'	see *S. japonica* 'Wakehurst White'
	- 'Bowles's Dwarf Female' (f)	CDoC CMHG ELan EPfP MGos MRav MWht SLim SLon
	- 'Bowles's Dwarf Male' (m)	CMHG ELan NWad SLim
*	- 'Bronze Beauty'	MAsh
	- 'Bronze Knight' (m)	CMac EBee IVic MGos MRav NWad
	- 'Carberry' (f)	IVic
	- 'Chameleon' (f)	NHol NLar
	- compact (f)	GGal
	- 'Dad's Red Dragon' (f)	MAsh MGos NHol
	- 'Emerald King' (m)	MAsh
	- 'Finchy'PBR (m)	MBri
N	- 'Foremanii'	see *S. japonica* 'Veitchii'
§	- 'Fragrans' (m) $\mathbb{Y}^{H4}$	CDoC CMac CRos CSBt CTri CWib EBee EPfP LRHS LSRN MAsh MGos MJak MRav NHol NLar NPnk NPri NSoo NWea SEWo SHil SLim SPer SPoG SWvt WGwG
	- 'Fragrant Cloud'	see *S. japonica* 'Fragrans'
	- 'Fructu Albo'	see *S. japonica* 'Wakehurst White'
	- 'Godrie's Dwarf' (m)	CRos EPfP LRHS NLar SHil
	- 'Hot Chocolate' **new**	NSoo
	- var. ***intermedia*** f. ***repens*** B&SWJ 5560	LAst WCru
	- - B&SWJ 11165	WCru
	- 'Kew White' (f)	CAbP CDoC CWib EBee ELan EPfP IArd LAst LRHS MAsh MGos NHol NLar NWad SLon SPer SSta SWvt WCFE WCot
	- Luwian = 'Wanto' (m)	LRHS SHil WCFE
	- 'Magic Marlot'PBR (m/v)	EBee EPfP LRHS MAsh MGos MRav NLar SHil SPoG
	- 'Marlot' (m)	EPfP LRHS NLar SPoG
	- 'Nymans' (f) $\mathbb{Y}^{H4}$	CDoC CEnd CRos CSam EBee ELan EPfP LPot LRHS MAsh MGos MRav SHil SLim SPoG SRms SSpi WGob
	- Obsession = 'Obsbolwi'PBR	LBuc LRHS MAsh NPri SHil
	- 'Olympic Flame' (f)	EPfP IArd LRHS MBlu MJak NPri NSoo SHil SPoG
	- 'Pigmy' (f)	CExl
	- 'Red Dragon' (f)	CMac
	- 'Red Princess' (f)	MAsh
	- 'Red Riding Hood' (f)	CRos ELan ELon LRHS MAsh NHol SHil SLon SPer
	- 'Redruth' (f)	CBcs CDoC CMac CSBt CTsd ELon LRHS MAsh MGos NLar SEND
§	- subsp. ***reevesiana***	CBcs CDoC CDul CMHG CMac CSBt CTri CWSG CWib ELan EPfP IVic LRHS MBri MGos MRav MSwo NLar NSoo SHil SPoG SSpi SWvt
	- - B&SWJ 3763	MAsh WCru
	- - var. ***reevesiana***	MJak SPer
	- - - B&SWJ 3544	WCru
§	- Rogersii Group	CMac CTri
	- - 'George Gardner' (m)	EPfP LRHS
	- - 'Nana Mascula' (m)	CTri
	- - 'Snow Dwarf' (m)	NHol
	- 'Rubella' (m) $\mathbb{Y}^{H4}$	Widely available
	- 'Rubinetta' (m)	EPfP IArd MAsh
	- 'Ruby Dome' (m)	MAsh
	- 'Ruby King' (m)	CDoC CSBt IArd LSRN NHol NLar
	- 'Scarlet Dwarf' (f)	MAsh NHol WHar
	- 'Snow White'PBR (m)	MAsh
	- 'Tansley Gem' (f)	LRHS MAsh MWht SPoG
	- 'Temptation'PBR (f)	ELan EPfP LRHS SHil
	- 'Thereza'PBR (m)	EPfP LBuc NLar NPri
§	- 'Veitchii' (f)	CBar CBcs CDoy CDul CMac CSBt CTri EBee ELan EPfP IArd LRHS LSRN MGos MJak MMuc MRav NHol NLar SEND SLim SPer SPoG SWvt
§	- 'Wakehurst White' (f)	CBcs CMHG CMac CSBt CTri EPfP IVic LRHS MRav NLar SLim SLon SPoG
	- 'White Bella' (m) **new**	LRHS SHil
	- 'Winifred Crook' (f)	LHop LRHS
	- 'Wisley Female' (f)	CTri

laureola	CDoC CExl CSam MRav SRms WSHC
- GWJ 9364	WCru
- subsp. ***laureola*** HWJK 2095	WCru
- subsp. ***multinervia*** GWJ 9374	WCru
reevesiana	see *S. japonica* subsp. *reevesiana*
rogersii	see *S. japonica* Rogersii Group

Smallanthus (*Asteraceae*)

sonchifolius	LEdu
§ ***uvedalius***	CArn

Smilacina see *Maianthemum*

Smilax (*Smilacaceae*)

sp.	WBor
B&SWJ 6628 from Thailand	WCru
aspera	CArn CMac EShb LEdu WCru WPGP
china B&SWJ 4427	WCru
discotis	CBcs SEND
glaucophylla B&SWJ 2971	WCru
nipponica B&SWJ 4331	WCru
rotundifolia	LEdu
sieboldii	LEdu MRav
- B&SWJ 744	WCru

Smithiantha (*Gesneriaceae*)

'Extra Sassy'	EABi
'Little One'	WDib
'Multiflora'	EABi
'Santa Clara'	EABi
I 'Temple Bells'	EABi

Smyrnium (*Apiaceae*)

olusatrum	CArn CHab CSev CSpe MHer MNHC SRms SWat WHer WSFF
perfoliatum	CHid CSpe ELan EWes LEdu NBir SDix SMrm WCot WHal WSHC
rotundifolium	WCot

Solandra (*Solanaceae*)

grandiflora misapplied	see *S. maxima*
hartwegii	see *S. maxima*
§ ***maxima***	CCCN WCot

Solanum (*Solanaceae*)

atropurpureum	CDTJ CSpe SPlb
betaceum (F)	CCCN EShb SVic
capsicastrum	SPlb
conchifolium hort.	see *S. linearifolium*
crispum	NBir
- 'Autumnale'	see *S. crispum* 'Glasnevin'
- 'Elizabeth Jane Dunn' (v)	WCot
§ - 'Glasnevin' ♀H3	Widely available
dulcamara	CArn GPoy WHfH
- var. ***album***	EHoe LSRN
- 'Variegatum' (v)	CMac EBee EHoe MAsh
elaeagnifolium new	WCru
incanum	LEdu
jasminoides	see *S. laxum*
laciniatum	CCCN CDTJ CExl CHEx CSev CSpe EShb SBig SBst SEND SPav SPlb WOut WWlt
§ ***laxum***	EBee EShb GGal LRHS SPer SRms SWvt WSHC
- 'Album' ♀H3	Widely available
- 'Album Variegatum' (v)	CWib LRHS WSHC
* - 'Aureovariegatum' (v)	CMac EShb LBMP NEgg SLim SPlb
- 'Coldham'	EShb GCal
§ ***linearifolium***	CSpe EBee LBMP SKHP WCot WOut WPGP WSHC
muricatum (F)	CCCN CHll EShb SPlb
pinnatum new	SPlb
pseudocapsicum 'Thurino'	EPfP
- variegated (v)	WCot
pyracanthum	CDTJ SPlb WCot
quitoense (F)	CDTJ SBig
rantonnetii	see *Lycianthes rantonnetii*
sisymbriifolium	SBst SPlb WWlt
aff. ***stenophyllum*** B&SWJ 10744	WCru
wendlandii	CCCN CHll

Solaria (*Alliaceae*)

sp.	GCal

Soldanella (*Primulaceae*)

alpicola	GJos
alpina	CCon CPBP EBee ECho GBin GCra GKev LLHF SRms WAbe
- SDR 6332	GKev LEdu
I - 'Alba'	ECho WAbe
carpatica	EBee ECho GKev LEdu LLHF NSla WAbe
- 'Alba'	NHar WAbe
carpatica* × *pusilla	CPBP ECho ITim MNrw NHar NRya NWad WAbe
carpatica* × *villosa	ECho LEdu
cyanaster	EBee ECho GBin GJos GKev LEdu LLHF NLBP NRya WAbe
dimoniei	EBee ECho GKev ITim LEdu WAbe
hungarica	ECho WAbe
minima	EBee ECho GJos GKev LEdu NSla
montana	CFis EBee ECho GBin GJos LEdu LLHF NLar SBch
pindicola	ECho EWes WAbe
pusilla	GKev NWad
'Spring Symphony'	LEdu LLHF
'Sudden Spring'	LEdu WAbe
villosa	CCon EBee ECho GAbr GBin GKev LEdu NRya NWad SBch WAbe WMoo WPtf WSHC WThu

Soleirolia (*Urticaceae*)

soleirolii	CHEx CHel CTri EUJe MWhi SBHP SMad SPer SVic SWvt WHer XLum
- 'Argentea'	see *S. soleirolii* 'Variegata'
§ - 'Aurea'	CTri SVic SWvt
- 'Golden Queen'	see *S. soleirolii* 'Aurea'
- 'Silver Queen'	see *S. soleirolii* 'Variegata'
§ - 'Variegata' (v)	SVic WHer

Solenopsis (*Campanulaceae*)

axillaris	see *Isotoma axillaris*

Solenostemon ✿ (*Lamiaceae*)

'Autumn Rainbow'	WDib
'Beauty' (v)	WDib
'Beauty of Lyons'	WDib
'Black Heart'	WDib
'Black Prince'	WDib
'Brilliant' (v)	WDib
'Bronze Pagoda'	WDib
'Buttercup'	WDib

	'Chamaeleon' (v)	WDib
	'City of Sunderland'	WDib
	'Combat' (v)	ECtt WDib
	'Crimson Ruffles' (v) ♀H1	WDib
	'Crimson Velvet'	NPri
	'Dazzler' (v)	WDib
	'Display'	WDib
	'Durham Gala'	WDib
	'Firelight'	WDib
	'Flamingo' **new**	WDib
	'Freckles' (v)	WDib
	'Gay's Delight'	NPri
	'Gingernut'	EUJe NPri
	'Illumination'	WDib
	'Inky Fingers' (v)	WDib
	'Juliet Quartermain'	EUJe WDib
	'Jupiter'	WDib
	'Kentish Fire' (v)	WDib
	'Kiwi Fern' (Stained Glassworks Series) (v)	WDib
	'Lemon Chiffon'	WDib
	'Lord Falmouth' ♀H1	WDib
	'Midnight'	EUJe
	'Mrs Pilkington' (v)	WDib
	'Muriel Pedley' (v)	WDib
	'Paisley Shawl' (v) ♀H1	WDib
	'Palisandra'	CSpe
	'Peter Wonder' (v)	WDib
	'Picturatus' (v) ♀H1	WDib
	'Pineapple Beauty' (v) ♀H1	WDib
	'Pineapplette' ♀H1	WDib
	'Pink Chaos'	WDib
	'Red Angel'	WDib
	'Red Velvet'	WDib
	Redhead = 'Ufo646'PBR **new**	LSqH NPri
	'Rose Blush' (v)	WDib
	'Roy Pedley'	WDib
	'Royal Scot' (v) ♀H1	WDib
	'Salmon Plumes' (v)	WDib
	'Saturn'	WDib
	scutellarioides Henna = 'Balcenna'PBR	ECtt NPri
	'The Flume'	WDib
	thyrsoideus	see *Plectranthus thyrsoideus*
	'Timotei'	WDib
	Trusty Rusty = 'Ufo6419'PBR	NPri SMrm
	'Walter Turner' (v) ♀H1	ECtt WDib
	'Winsome' (v)	WDib
	'Winter Sun' (v)	WDib
	'Wisley Flame'	WDib
	'Wisley Tapestry' (v) ♀H1	WDib

Solidago (Asteraceae)

	sp.	MJak
	Babygold	see *S.* 'Goldkind'
	brachystachys	see *S. cutleri*
	caesia	EBee EWes NBir WOld
	canadensis	CTri ELan MBel MMuc SPlb WHer XLum
	– var. ***salebrosa***	EBee LRHS
	– var. ***scabra***	WOld
	'Citronella'	ECtt EWll GQue
	'Cloth of Gold'	CMac ECtt EPfP LRHS NHol NPro NSoo SPoG SWvt WGwG WMnd
§	'Crown of Rays'	CPrp EBee ECtt EHyd EPfP LRHS MRav WMnd WWEG
§	***cutleri***	EBee ECho MWat NLar SBch SPlb SRms WThu
I	– ***nana***	ECho
	'Early Bird'	NLar
	'Featherbush'	LRHS
§	***flexicaulis***	GMaP XLum
	– 'Variegata' (v)	EBee ECtt ELan GMaP NLar WHer WMoo WWEG XLum
	glomerata	NLar SMrm
	Golden Baby	see *S.* 'Goldkind'
§	'Golden Dwarf'	CWCL WPtf WWEG XLum
	'Golden Falls'	LRHS
	'Golden Fleece'	see *S. sphacelata* 'Golden Fleece'
	Golden Gate = 'Dansolgold'	LRHS
	'Golden Rays'	see *S.* 'Goldstrahl'
	'Golden Thumb'	see *S.* 'Queenie'
	'Golden Wings'	CBre MWat
	'Goldenmosa' ♀H4	CAby CMac CSBt EBee EPfP EWes GKev GMaP LRHS SPer
	'Goldilocks'	NPri SRms
§	'Goldkind'	CAby COIW CSBt CTri EBee ECtt ELan EPfP GAbr IBoy LPot LRHS MCot MMuc MWhi NEgg NOrc SEND SWvt WBrk WWEG XLum
§	'Goldstrahl'	LRHS
	Goldzwerg	see *S.* 'Golden Dwarf'
	'Harvest Gold'	CAby CElw
	hybrida	see *S.* × *luteus*
	latifolia	see *S. flexicaulis*
	'Laurin'	LRHS NLar XLum
	'Ledsham'	ECtt EWll LEdu LRHS MCot NBre SPoG WMnd
	'Lena'	SRms
	'Linner Gold'	NBre
	'Little Lemon'PBR	EBee ELan
§	× ***luteus***	EBee SRms WHil WOut XLum
	– 'Lemore' ♀H4	CMea CPrp EBee ELan EPfP GBuc GMaP GQue LAst LDai LHop LRHS LSou MSpe MWat NCGa NSti SMrm SPer SPhx SRms WCot WWEG XLum
	ohioensis	XLum
§	***ptarmicoides***	EBee XEll XLum
§	'Queenie'	MHer MLHP NBre WWEG
	rigida	LRHS WCot
	rugosa	MBNS MMuc SPhx WCot
	– 'Fireworks'	CAby CBre CHVG CMHG CMac CMea COIW CPrp CSam EBee ECtt ELon GQue IBoy LHop MAvo MNFA MSpe NLar SDys SPhx WBrk WCot WHoo WOld WWEG WWlt XLum
	sempervirens	EBee IMou WOld
	'Septembergold'	CSam
	'Sonnenschein'	NBre
	speciosa	LRHS SPhx
	spectabilis var. ***confinis***	EBee
§	***sphacelata*** 'Golden Fleece'	CBcs EHyd ELan IMou NBre SRms WMnd WWEG
	spiraeifolia	EBee
	Strahlenkrone	see *S.* 'Crown of Rays'
	'Summer Sunshine'	WWEG
	'Super'	CAby CPrp
	'Tom Thumb'	CMac MRav NBir SRms
	uliginosa	EShb XLum
	ulmifolia	EBee
	virgaurea	CArn GPoy MHer MNHC NLar SRms WHer
	– var. ***cambrica***	see *S. virgaurea* subsp. *minuta*
§	– subsp. ***minuta***	GBin

§ – 'Variegata' (v)	CBre EHoe NPro
vulgaris 'Variegata'	see *S. virgaurea* 'Variegata'
'Yellow Stone' **new**	EBee EHyd

× *Solidaster* see *Solidago*

hybridus	see *Solidago* × *luteus*

Sollya (*Pittosporaceae*)

fusiformis	see *S. heterophylla*
§ ***heterophylla*** $\mathbb{Y}^{H1}$	Widely available
– 'Alba'	CBcs CCCN CFlo CHel CSPN EBee ELan EPfP GCal LRHS SLim SLon SWvt WSHC
– mauve-flowered	ECou
– 'Pink Charmer'	CBcs EBee ELan LRHS SLon SPoG
– pink-flowered	CCCN CHll CSPN LBMP LRHS SLim SWvt

Sonchus (*Asteraceae*)

arboreus **new**	WCot
fruticosus	CHEx IDee
giganteus	CHll
pinnatus	SPlb

Sophora (*Papilionaceae*)

cassioides NJM 08.008	WPGP
§ ***davidii***	CBcs CExl CWGN CWib EBee EPfP LRHS MBlu MGos MMuc MOWG SBrt SEND SPoG SSpi WPGP WSHC
flavescens	SBrt
fulvida	ECou WPGP
howinsula	ECou
japonica	see *Styphnolobium japonicum*
§ 'Little Baby'	CAbP CWib EBee ELan EPfP EUJe LRHS LSRN MGos SPoG SWvt WGrn
longicarinata	ECou
macrocarpa	CBcs
microphylla	CHEx CTri ECou EPfP EUJe LHop SEND WPGP
molloyi	ECou
– 'Dragon's Gold'	CBcs EBee ECou ELan EPfP LRHS MAsh SCoo SPoG SSpi SSta WPGP
– 'Early Gold'	WPGP
prostrata misapplied	see *S.* 'Little Baby'
prostrata ambig.	CBcs
prostrata Buch.	CMac ECou
Sun King = 'Hilsop'PBR $\mathbb{Y}^{H4}$	CBcs CWGN EBee ELan EPfP EWes LRHS LSRN MBlu MGos SCoo SHil SLim SLon SPoG SWvt
tetraptera $\mathbb{Y}^{H3}$	CAbP CBcs CDul CTsd EBee ECou EPfP LRHS SEND WCFE WPGP
viciifolia	see *S. davidii*

Sorbaria (*Rosaceae*)

aitchisonii	see *S. tomentosa* var. *angustifolia*
arborea	see *S. kirilowii*
aff. ***assurgens*** BWJ 8185	WCru
§ ***kirilowii***	CExl CMac MRav NLar SMad WOut
– AC 3433	MSnd
sorbifolia	CAbP CBcs CCVT CMCN ELan GAbr MLHP MMuc NLar NPro SBrt SEND SPer SPlb
– 'Sem'PBR	Widely available
– var. ***stellipila***	SLPl
– – B&SWJ 776	WCru
§ ***tomentosa*** var. ***angustifolia*** $\mathbb{Y}^{H4}$	CBcs CDul CTri ELan EPfP IDee LRHS MMuc MRav NBid NPro SEND SLon SPer WHer

× *Sorbaronia* (*Rosaceae*)

fallax 'Ivan's Beauty' **new**	ECrN

× *Sorbopyrus* (*Rosaceae*)

auricularis	MCoo
– 'Shipova' (F)	CAgr

Sorbus ✿ (*Rosaceae*)

sp.	CMen
adamii	CMCN
alnifolia	CJun CLnd CMCN EPfP MBlu SLPl
– B&SWJ 8461	WCru
– B&SWJ 10948	WCru
– 'Red Bird'	EPfP MBlu MBri
americana	CLnd NWea
anglica	CDul CNat CTho
'Apricot'	CEnd
'Apricot Queen'	CDul CLnd EBee ECrN LAst MJak MMuc NEgg SGol
aria	CCVT CDul CHab CLnd CSBt CTri ECrN IBoy LBuc MGos MMuc NWea SEND SEWo SGol WHar WMou
– 'Aurea'	CLnd SPer
– 'Chrysophylla'	CDul CSBt ECrN NWea
– 'Decaisneana'	see *S. aria* 'Majestica'
– 'Lutescens' $\mathbb{Y}^{H4}$	Widely available
– 'Magnifica'	ECrN ELan NEgg SCoo SEWo WJas
§ – 'Majestica' $\mathbb{Y}^{H4}$	CCVT CDoC CDul CLnd CMac EBee ECrN LHop MAsh MRav NWea SCoo SPer WHar WJas
– 'Mitchellii'	see *S. thibetica* 'John Mitchell'
arnoldiana 'Golden Wonder'	see *S.* 'Lombarts Golden Wonder'
aronioides misapplied	see *S. caloneura*
arranensis	CLnd WPat
§ ***aucuparia***	Widely available
– 'Aspleniifolia'	CBcs CCVT CDul CLnd CMCN CMac CSBt EBee ECrN GBin IBoy LAst LRHS MGos MJak MRav MWat NPCo NWea SLim SPer WJas
§ – 'Beissneri'	CAgr CDul MGos MRav NLar NWea SCoo SLon WHCr
– Cardinal Royal = 'Michred'	CCVT CDoC CLnd ECrN MMuc NEgg SCoo SEWo SLon WJas
– 'Dirkenii'	EBee MAsh SGol WJas
§ – var. ***edulis*** (F)	CBcs CDul CLnd CTho EBee ECrN LBuc MCoo MGos SPer
– – 'Rossica' misapplied	see *S. aucuparia* var. *edulis* 'Rossica Major'
§ – – 'Rossica Major'	CDul ECrN GQui SEWo
§ – 'Fastigiata'	CEnd CTri ELan EPfP GKin LAst MBlu MGos NPCo
– 'Hilling's Spire'	CTho
– 'Pendula'	ELan
– ***pluripinnata***	see *S. scalaris* Koehne
– var. ***rossica*** Koehne	see *S. aucuparia* var. *edulis*
– 'Sheerwater Seedling' $\mathbb{Y}^{H4}$	CBcs CCVT CDoC CDul CMCN CSBt EBee ECrN ELan EPfP GKin IBoy LAst LHop MGos MMuc MRav MSwo SEND SEWo SGol SPer
– var. ***xanthocarpa*** $\mathbb{Y}^{H4}$	ECrN ELan EPfP
Autumn Spire = 'Flanrock'	CDoC CLnd CTsd ELan IBoy LRHS LSRN MAsh MBri MGos NLar SCoo SLim SLon SPoG SWvt WHar
bakonyensis	IGor
bissetii	WPat
brevipetiolata B&SWJ 11771	WCru
§ ***caloneura***	EBee EPfP MBlu WPGP WPat

	- Guiz 80	WCru
	carmesina B&L 12545	GKev WCru
	cashmiriana Hedl. ♀H4	Widely available
	aff. ***cashmiriana***	MJak NHol
	- B 751	WCru
	'Chamois Glow'	WJas
	'Chinese Lace'	Widely available
§	***commixta***	CBcs CDul CEnd CLnd CMCN CSto CTho EBee ECrN EWTr IBoy LAst MBlu MGos MJak MMuc MSwo NLar SGol SLim SPer WJas
	- B&SWJ 10839	WCru
	- B&SWJ 11043	WCru
	- 'Embley' ♀H4	CBcs CCVT CDul CMCN CSBt CTho CTri EBee ECrN ELan EPfP LHop MBlu MGos MMuc MRav NEgg NLar NPCo NWea SEND SGol SPer SPoG
	- Olympic Flame = 'Dodong'	EBee EPfP IArd IDee LRHS LSRN MBri NLar SCoo SEWo SLim SPer WHar
	- 'Ravensbill'	EBee EPfP NLar SCoo WHCr WHar WMou
	- var. ***rufoferruginea***	GQui
	- - B&SWJ 11486	WCru
	- var. ***sachalinensis*** B&SWJ 8496	WCru
	- - B&SWJ 8515	WCru
	aff. ***commixta*** new	MSnd
	conradinae misapplied	see *S. pohuashanensis* (Hance) Hedlund
	conradinae Koehne	see *S. esserteauana*
	'Copper Kettle'	EBee EPfP MAsh MBri NLar SCoo WHar
	'Coral Beauty'	CLnd
	corymbifera WWJ 11860	WCru
	'Covert Gold'	CEnd
	croceocarpa	CDul
	'Croft Coral'	MAsh WHar
	cuspidata	see *S. vestita*
*	***decora*** 'Grootendorst'	CDul
	- var. ***nana***	see *S. aucuparia* 'Fastigiata'
	devoniensis	CDoC CDul CNat CTho
	- 'Devon Beauty'	CAgr
	discolor misapplied	see *S. commixta*
	discolor (Maxim.) Maxim.	EBee MBlu MJak NWea WJas
	- MF 96172	MAsh
	domestica	CDul EPfP MMuc NWea SEND
	- 'Maliformis'	see *S. domestica* f. *pomifera*
§	- f. ***pomifera***	CLnd LEdu WThu
§	- f. ***pyrifera***	CLnd
	- 'Pyriformis'	see *S. domestica* f. *pyrifera*
	- 'Rosie'	CAgr
	'Eastern Promise'	EBee EPfP GBin MAsh MBri MSwo MWat NLar NWea SCoo SLim WHCr WHar WMou
§	***eburnea*** Harry Smith 12799	GQui
	eminens	CDul CNat
	epidendron WWJ 11930	WCru
§	***esserteauana***	CLnd CTho EPfP WPat
	'Fastigiata'	see *S. aucuparia* 'Fastigiata', *S.* × *thuringiaca* 'Fastigiata'
	aff. ***filipes*** KR 6453	WCru
	folgneri	CEnd CJun
	- 'Emiel'	EPfP MBlu MBri
	- 'Lemon Drop'	CDul CEnd CJun CLnd CWSG EBee EPfP MAsh NLar SCoo SMad WHar
§	***foliolosa***	CLnd
	forrestii	CBcs CMCN EPfP GKev LRHS MBri
*	***fortunei***	CLnd
*	***fosteri*** new	EBee
§	***frutescens***	CEnd EPfP NWea WPGP
	fruticosa Crantz	EBee GKev NSla
	- 'Koehneana'	see *S. koehneana* C.K. Schneid.
	'Ghose'	CEnd EBee MBri SCoo
	glabrescens	CSto
	glabriuscula	EBee GKev
	'Glendoick Gleam'	GGGa
	'Glendoick Glory'	GGGa
	'Glendoick Ivory'	GGGa
	'Glendoick Pearl'	GGGa
	'Glendoick Ruby'	GGGa
	'Glendoick Spire'	GGGa
	'Glendoick White Baby'	GGGa
	glomeruluta	LLHF
	'Golden Wonder'	see *S.* 'Lombarts Golden Wonder'
	gonggashanica	EPfP GKev WPGP WPat
*	***gorrodini***	CLnd
§	***graeca***	WPat
	granulosa HWJ 1041	WCru
	harrowiana	GCal WPGP WPat
	hazslinszkyana	IGor
	hedlundii	CExl EBee EBtc EPfP NLar NWea SKHP WPGP
	- KR 1687	WPGP
	- KR 1810	WPGP
	hemsleyi	CBcs CDul CExl EPfP WPGP WPat
	- 'John Bond'	CDoC EBee LRHS NLar SPoG
	× ***hostii***	CLnd
	hugh-mcallisteri CLD 310	GKev
	hupehensis C.K. Schneid. ♀H4	CBcs CDul CEnd CLnd CMCN CMac CTho CTri EBee EPfP LAst LHop MMuc MRav NWea SEND SGol SLPl SPer WHar WJas WMou
	- MF 96170	EPfP
	- 'November Pink'	see *S. hupehensis* 'Pink Pagoda'
§	- var. ***obtusa*** ♀H4	CCVT CDoC CDul CLnd EPfP NEgg NPCo
§	- 'Pink Pagoda'	CDoC CLnd EBee EPfP EWTr GBin IArd LHop LRHS LSRN MAsh MBlu MGos MMuc MRav MWat NLar NPri NWea SCoo SEWo SLim SLon SPer SPoG WHCr WMou
	- 'Rosea'	see *S. hupehensis* var. *obtusa*
	× ***hybrida*** misapplied	see *S.* × *thuringiaca*
	hybrida L.	ECrN
	- 'Gibbsii' ♀H4	CDoC EBee ELan EPfP EWTr SPoG WHar
	insignis	EPfP WPGP WPat
	intermedia	CBcs CCVT CDul CLnd CSBt CTho CTri CWib ECrN ELan MGos NWea SEND SGol WHar WMou
	- 'Brouwers'	CLnd ELan WMou
	japonica B&SWJ 10813	WCru
	- B&SWJ 11048	WCru
	'Joseph Rock'	Widely available
§	× ***kewensis***	CDul CLnd NWea SPlb
	'Kirsten Pink'	CWib EBee ECrN SPer
	koehneana misapplied	see *S. frutescens*
§	***koehneana*** C.K. Schneid. ♀H4	CBcs CLnd EBee ELan GKev GQui IDee NWea
	aff. ***koehneana***	see *S. eburnea*
	lanata misapplied	see *S. vestita*
	lancastriensis	CNat
	latifolia	CLnd NWea
	- 'Henk Vink'	CCVT
	'Leonard Messel'	CDoC EBee EPfP MAsh MBri NLar SCoo WHCr
	'Leonard Springer'	EPfP

	'Likjornaja'	EPfP MBri
§	'Lombarts Golden Wonder'	CBcs CDul MMuc NWea SEND
	macrantha new	GKev
	maderensis	WPat
	matsumurana misapplied	see *S. commixta*
	megalocarpa	CDoC CDul CJun EPfP SKHP SSpi WPGP
	meliosmifolia B&SWJ 11709	WCru
	microphylla	CMCN
	- GWJ 9252	WCru
	minima	WPat
	monbeigii (Card.) Yü	CLnd GKev
	moravica 'Laciniata'	see *S. aucuparia* 'Beissneri'
	aff. ***ovalis*** H 1948	EBee
	'Pearly King'	CTho MAsh WJas
§	'Pink Pearl'	CDul EPfP
	'Pink-Ness'	EBee MBlu SCoo
	pohuashanensis misapplied	see *S.* × *kewensis*
§	***pohuashanensis*** (Hance) Hedlund	WPat
	porrigentiformis	CDul
	poteriifolia	NHar WPat
	prattii Koehne	CTho EBee GKev MBri MMuc
*	***pseudobalsomnensis***	CBcs
	pseudohupehensis	MSnd
	pseudovilmorinii	CDul CPom EBee LRHS MBri SSpi
	- CLD 1437	GKev
	- MF 93044	SSpi
	- SDR 82	GKev
	randaiensis	CSto EBee GKev GQui MBri SPlb
	- B&SWJ 3202	EPfP NWad SSpi WCru
	'Red Robin'	IBoy
	'Red Tip'	CDul
	reducta ♀H4	CBcs CEnd GAbr GBin GCal GKev GQui MMuc NHar NHol NSla SPer WPat
	aff. ***reducta*** new	MSnd
	reflexipetala misapplied	see *S. commixta*
	rehderiana misapplied	see *S. aucuparia*
	rehderiana Koehne	CDul CLnd
	- AC 3459 new	MSnd
	rosea	GKev
	- SEP 492	WCru
	- 'Rosiness'	CLnd EBee EPfP MBri SCoo WHar
	rushforthii KR 3412 new	GKev
	'Salmon Queen'	CLnd
	sambucifolia	SKHP
	sargentiana ♀H4	CCVT CDul CEnd CLnd CMCN CTho CTri EBee ECrN ELan EPfP GQui MBlu MBri MGos MRav MSwo NLar NWea SLim SPer SPoG WMou
	scalaris ambig.	CMCN ELan IDee MAsh MGos MSwo NWea WHar WMou
§	***scalaris*** Koehne	CBcs CCVT CDul CEnd CLnd CTho CTri EBee EPfP IDee LHop MBlu MGos SPer SPoG WJas
	'Schouten'	ECrN
	scopulina misapplied	see *S. aucuparia* 'Fastigiata'
	simonkaiana	IGor
	subulata HWJ 925	WCru
	- KWJ 12272	WCru
	'Sunshine'	CCVT CDoC CDul CLnd MAsh MBri MGos MMuc SEND WJas
	thibetica AGS/ES 347	WPGP
§	- 'John Mitchell' ♀H4	CAgr CDul CEnd CLnd CMCN CWib EBee ECrN EPfP MBlu MBri MGos MRav NWea SLim SPer WMou
	aff. ***thibetica*** BWJ 7757a	WCru
	thomsonii GWJ 9363	WCru
	- HWJ 984	WCru
	- WWJ 12004	WCru
§	× ***thuringiaca*** 'Fastigiata'	CBcs CCVT CDul CLnd CSBt EPfP MMuc NEgg SCoo WJas
	× ***tomentella***	CLnd WMou
	torminalis	CBcs CCVT CDul CHab CLnd CMCN CMac CTho CTri EBee ELan EPfP LEdu MBri MGos MMuc MRav MSnd NLar NWea SCoo SEWo SLPl SPer SPoG WHar WMou
	umbellata var. ***cretica***	see *S. graeca*
	ursina	see *S. foliolosa*
§	***vestita***	CLnd CTho EPfP WCru
	vexans	CDul GBin
	vilmorinii ♀H4	Widely available
	- 'Robusta'	see *S.* 'Pink Pearl'
	aff. ***vilmorinii***	GKin IBoy MJak
	wardii	CBcs CDul CLnd CTho EPfP MBlu MBri WPat
	'White Swan'	MAsh NLar
	'White Wax'	CDul EPfP LAst MGos SPer SPoG
	'Wilfrid Fox'	EBee SLPl
	wilmottiana	CDul WPat
	wilsoniana	CLnd GGGa GQui
	'Wisley Gold'	EBee LRHS MAsh SCoo SLim SPoG WMou
	yuana new	WPGP

Sorghastrum (*Poaceae*)

	avenaceum	see *S. nutans*
§	***nutans***	CKno SMad
	- 'Indian Steel'	EBee GQue SDix XLum

sorrel, common see *Rumex acetosa*

sorrel, French see *Rumex scutatus*

Souliea see *Actaea*

soursop see *Annona muricata*

Sparaxis (*Iridaceae*)

	auriculata 'Vanrhynsdorp'	ECho
	bulbifera	ECho
	elegans 'Coccinea'	WCot
	fragrans 'Napier'	ECho
	grandiflora subsp. ***acutiloba***	ECho
	- subsp. ***fimbriata***	ECho
	- subsp. ***grandiflora***	CGrW ECho
	- subsp. ***violacea*** 'Botriver'	ECho
	meterlekampiae 'Piekenierskloof'	ECho
	- 'Rawsonville'	ECho
	mixed	SDeJ
	parviflora	ECho
	'Red Reflex'	ECho
	tricolor	CGrW ECho SDeJ
	variegata (v)	ECho
	villosa	ECho

Sparganium (*Sparganiaceae*)

	RCB RA G-1 new	WCot
§	***erectum***	CBAq CRow CWat EHon NMir NPer SWat WMAq WSFF XLum
	ramosum	see *S. erectum*

Sparrmannia (*Malvaceae*)

africana ♀H1	CHEx CHll EAmu ELan EShb MBri SEND SVen
- 'Flore Pleno' (d)	CBcs

Spathipappus see *Tanacetum*

Spartina (*Poaceae*)

pectinata	SGol XLum
- 'Aureomarginata' (v)	CHEx CPrp CWCL EBee EHoe ELan EPPr EPfP GMaP LBMP LRHS MBri MLHP MMoz MMuc MWhi NLar NOak NWsh SEND SMrm SPer WMoo WWEG

Spartium (*Papilionaceae*)

junceum ♀H4	CArn CBcs CDoC CDul CEnd EBee ECrN ELan ELon EPfP GCal LAst MGos MMuc SDix SEND SPer SPoG SRms WBor XSen
- 'Brockhill Compact'	CDoC EBee ELan EPfP LRHS

Spartocytisus see *Cytisus*

Spathantheum (*Araceae*)

orbignyanum	WCot

Spathiphyllum (*Araceae*)

wallisii	SPre

Spathodea (*Bignoniaceae*)

campanulata	SPlb

spearmint see *Mentha spicata*

Speirantha (*Asparagaceae*)

§ ***convallarioides***	CDes CGHE CLAP CPom EBee ECho ELon EPPr EPfP LEdu LWst MNrw WCot WCru WHil WPGP
gardenii	see *S. convallarioides*

Sphacele see *Lepechinia*

Sphaeralcea (*Malvaceae*)

ambigua	SPlb XSen
'Childerley'	CSpe CWGN ECtt LHop MCot MHol SMrm SPad WCot
coccinea	SPlb
fendleri	CHll
- subsp. ***venusta***	LHop XSen
grossulariifolia	XSen
'Hopleys Lavender'	LAst LHop LSou SWvt
'Hyde Hall'	MHom
incana	CSpe LHop LSou
- 'Sourup'	CSpe EBee ECtt ELan MCot MHol MPie WCot
laxa new	XSen
malviflora	CDTJ
miniata	CCCN CHll SMrm
munroana	CDTJ CPom CSev ECtt ELan SRkn WSHC
- pale pink-flowered	CSam ECtt
'Newleaze Coral'	CWGN ECtt ELan LAst LBMP LHop LSou MAsh MHom MNrw SPoG SRkn SWvt WCot WWFP
'Newleaze Pink'	LHop SRkn
remota	CExl EBee SPhx SPlb
rivularis	EBee LPla
umbellata	see *Phymosia umbellata*

Sphaeromeria (*Asteraceae*)

§ ***capitata***	CPBP

Sphenomeris (*Dennstaedtiaceae*)

chinensis B&SWJ 6108	WCru

Spigelia (*Loganiaceae*)

marilandica	CDes EBee SKHP
- 'Red Feather'	NLar
- 'Wisley Jester'	SKHP

Spilanthes (*Asteraceae*)

acmella misapplied	see *Acmella oleracea*
oleracea	see *Acmella oleracea*

Spiloxene (*Hypoxidaceae*)

canaliculata 'Kamiesberg'	ECho
capensis 'Somerset West'	ECho
minuta 'Nay'	ECho
serrata 'Saldanha'	ECho

Spiraea (*Rosaceae*)

SDR 6047	GKev
'Abigail'	CDoC
albiflora	see *S. japonica* var. *albiflora*
arborea	see *Sorbaria kirilowii*
arcuata	MJak
§ 'Arguta' ♀H4	Widely available
aff. 'Arguta'	SHil
× ***arguta*** 'Bridal Wreath'	see *S.* 'Arguta'
bella	SLon
betulifolia	EBee GKin MRav
- var. ***aemiliana***	ECtt MAsh MMuc SLPl
- 'Tor'	EPPr MBri
- 'Tor Gold' new	EPPr
× ***billardii*** misapplied	see *S.* × *pseudosalicifolia*
× ***bumalda*** 'Wulfenii'	see *S. japonica* 'Walluf'
callosa 'Alba'	see *S. japonica* var. *albiflora*
canescens	CExl GKin
- AC 1354	MSnd
§ ***cantoniensis*** 'Flore Pleno' (d)	SLon
- 'Lanceata'	see *S. cantoniensis* 'Flore Pleno'
× ***cinerea*** 'Grefsheim' ♀H4	CDoC CSBt EBee ELan MBri MGos MJak SEND SGol SLim SPer SPlb
crispifolia	see *S. japonica* 'Bullata'
douglasii	CMac
formosana B&SWJ 1597	CExl WCru
§ × ***foxii***	SLPl
fritschiana	CMac SLPl SLon
hayatana	SLon
- RWJ 10014	WCru
hendersonii	see *Petrophytum hendersonii*
§ ***japonica*** var. ***albiflora***	CBcs CDoC CDul CMac CSBt CTri CWib ELan ELon EPfP LRHS MAsh MGos MMuc MRav MSwo MWat NEgg NSoo NWad SGol SLim SPad SPer SRms SWvt WMoo
- 'Alpina'	see *S. japonica* 'Nana'
- 'Alpine Gold'	NPro
- 'Anthony Waterer' (v)	Widely available
- 'Barkby Gold'	MGos
- 'Blenheim'	SRms
§ - 'Bullata'	CMac NLar NSla SRms WAbe WPat
- 'Candlelight' ♀H4	CDoC CSBt ELan EPfP GKin LAst LRHS MAsh MBri MGos NEgg NLar SCoo SGol SLim SPer SPoG SWvt WMoo
- 'Crispa'	EPfP NPro NSoo WGrn WMoo

	- 'Dart's Red' ♀H4	CDul ELan GKin IVic MBri MWat WMoo
	- 'Firelight'	CSBt EBee EHoe ELan ELon EPfP EShb GKin IBoy LAst LRHS MAsh MBri MGos MSwo NEgg NHol NLar NSoo NWad SCoo SGol SHil SLim SPer SSta STes SWvt WHar WMoo
§	- 'Genpei'	CMac EBee MJak SEND SGol SPer SPoG
	- 'Gold Mound'	CBar CExl CMac CWSG CWib EBee EHoe ELan EPfP LAst LRHS MAsh MGos MJak MMuc MRav MSwo NLar SCoo SEND SLim SPlb SRms WHar
	- Golden Princess = 'Lisp' ♀H4	CDoC CMac CTri ELan EPfP IBoy LBuc LRHS MAsh MGos NEgg NPri SCoo SGol SHil SRms SSta WMoo
	- 'Goldflame'	Widely available
	- 'Little Princess'	CBar CBcs CDoC CDul CMac CWib EBee ELan EShb LRHS MAsh MRav MSwo MWat NSoo NWea SCoo SGol SHil SLim SPer SRGP SRms SSta SWvt WHar WMoo
§	- 'Macrophylla'	WPat
	- Magic Carpet = 'Walbuma' PBR (v) ♀H4	CDoC EPfP GBin LBuc LRHS MAsh MBri MMuc NLar SCoo SEND SPoG
	- 'Magnifica'	see *S. japonica* 'Macrophylla'
§	- 'Nana' ♀H4	CMac CSBt ECho MAsh MRav SRms
	- 'Nyewoods'	see *S. japonica* 'Nana'
	- 'Shiburi'	see *S. japonica* var. *albiflora*
N	- 'Shirobana' misapplied	see *S. japonica* 'Genpei'
N	- 'Shirobana'	see *S. japonica* var. *albiflora*
	- 'Snow Cap'	CWib
§	- 'Walluf'	CMac CTri CWib
	- 'White Gold' PBR	CDoC CSBt EBee ELan EPfP LAst LRHS LSqu MAsh MBri NHol NPro NWad SCoo SLim SPer SPoG SWvt WHar WMoo
	latifolia	MMuc SEND
	'Margaritae'	SPer SWvt
	micrantha	CExl
	nipponica	CBcs
	- 'Halward's Silver'	MBri MRav NPro SLPl
	- 'June Bride'	MBri
§	- 'Snowmound' ♀H4	Widely available
	- var. ***tosaensis*** misapplied	see *S. nipponica* 'Snowmound'
	- var. ***tosaensis*** (Yatabe) Makino	LHop
	palmata 'Elegans'	see *Filipendula purpurea* 'Elegans'
	prunifolia (d)	CMac ELan EPfP LRHS MRav SPer WCFE WGrn WPat
	× ***pseudosalicifolia*** 'Triumphans'	MMuc SEND SPer
	salicifolia	MMuc
	'Sparkling Champagne'	CWSG LBuc LRHS SLim SLon SPoG WNPC
	'Summersnow'	SLPl
	Sundrop = 'Bailcarol' **new**	LBuc
	'Superba'	see *S.* × *foxii*
	thunbergii ♀H4	CDul CTri CWib EBee EPfP MMuc MRav NWea SCoo SEND SGol SLim SRms
	- 'Golden Times'	LRHS SPoG
	- 'Mount Fuji'	CMac CWib EHoe MMuc MRav NPro
	ulmaria	see *Filipendula ulmaria*
	× ***vanhouttei***	CBcs CTri EBee ELan EPfP MMuc MRav MSwo SEND SLim SPer SRms WMoo
	- 'Gold Fountain'	EBee ELan EMil EPfP EShb GBin NHol SCoo SPer SPoG WMoo
	- 'Pink Ice' (v)	CDoC CDul CWib EBee EHoe EPfP LAst LBMP LHop LRHS MAsh MGos MMuc MRav SPer SPlb SPoG SWvt
	veitchii	MRav
	venusta 'Magnifica'	see *Filipendula rubra* 'Venusta'

Spiranthes (*Orchidaceae*)

	aestivalis	NLAp
	cernua	NGdn
	- var. ***odorata***	LSou
	- - 'Chadd's Ford' ♀H4	CBcs CBro CExl EBee ECho ECtt IKil LHop LRHS MNrw NBir NCGa NLar NPnk SEND WCot WPnP WSHC WWEG
	spiralis	NLAp WHer

Spodiopogon (*Poaceae*)

	sibiricus	CKno EBee EHoe EPPr LDai SMad XLum
	- 'West Lake'	IMou

Sporobolus (*Poaceae*)

	airoides	CKno EBee EHoe EPPr EShb LPla SMad WCot WHrl
	heterolepis	CKno EBee EHoe EShb LPio MAvo NDov SMad SMea SPhx
	- 'Cloud'	GBin
I	- 'Wisconsin Strain'	EBee EPPr IMou LPla SPhx
	wrightii	EPPr MWhi SMad SPhx

Sprekelia (*Amaryllidaceae*)

	formosissima	CCon CSpe ECho LEdu SDeJ SPav

Stachys ✿ (*Lamiaceae*)

	aethiopica 'Danielle'	see *S. thunbergii* 'Danielle'
§	***affinis***	CArn CCon GPoy LEdu SPlb SVic XLum
	albens	IFro XSen
	alpina	EBee
	balcanica	CDes
	- MESE	EBee WPGP
	betonica	see *S. officinalis*
§	***byzantina***	Widely available
§	- 'Big Ears'	CAby EBee ELan EPfP EWTr GMaP LHop LSRN MBri MCot MGos MMuc MNFA MRav MWat SMrm SPer SPhx SPoG SRms SWvt WBor WCAu WCFE WCot WHoo WMnd WWEG
§	- 'Cotton Boll'	COIW GCal SPer WWEG
	- 'Countess Helen von Stein'	see *S. byzantina* 'Big Ears'
	- gold-leaved	see *S. byzantina* 'Primrose Heron'
	- large-leaved	see *S. byzantina* 'Big Ears'
	- 'Limelight'	WCot XLum
§	- 'Primrose Heron'	EBee GKev LRHS MRav NBid NLar NOrc SMrm SPer SPoG SWvt XLum
	- 'Sheila McQueen'	see *S. byzantina* 'Cotton Boll'
	- 'Silky Fleece'	EBee ELan EPfP EShb GKev LRHS NBre SRms WWEG XSen
	- 'Silver Carpet'	CBcs COIW EBee EHoe ELon EPfP GMaP LRHS LSRN MBel MCot MRav NOrc NPri NSti SPer SRms SWat SWvt WCAu WCot WHoo WMnd WWEG XLum
	chamissonis var. ***cooleyae***	EBee
	citrina	CMea GCal WAbe XSen
	coccinea	CPla ECtt MNrw SBch WMoo

	cretica	XSen
	- subsp. ***salviifolia***	XSen
	densiflora	see *S. monieri* (Gouan) P.W. Ball
§	***discolor***	CFis CMea EBee IKil NLar SPhx
	germanica	NBre WHfH
	- subsp. ***bithynica***	SMrm
	glutinosa	XSen
	grandidentata	WPGP
	grandiflora	see *S. macrantha*
	heraclea	LRHS
	'Hidalgo'	CSpe
	lanata	see *S. byzantina*
	lavandulifolia	WAbe XSen
§	***macrantha***	CKno CMac CTri GLog LEdu LRHS LSRN MCot MLHP MMuc MWat NBir NChi NOrc NSti SPhx SRms SWat WCFE WCot WWEG
	- 'Hummelo'	see *S. officinalis* 'Hummelo'
*	- 'Nivea'	CSam ELan NBir
	- 'Robusta' ♀H4	ELan GCal LEdu LRHS MMuc NBro NGdn SMrm WCot WRHF WWEG
	- 'Rosea'	CElw CMHG ELan GBee GMaP LLWP LRHS MArl MAvo MLHP SPlb SWat
	- 'Superba'	CPrp CSpe ECtt EPfP GCra GKev GMaP IBoy LEdu MAvo MRav MWhi NEgg NSoo SPer SWvt WBor WCot WMnd WMoo XLum
	- 'Violacea'	CDes EBee GKev LRHS MBrN NChi WCot WOut
	mexicana misapplied	see *S. thunbergii*
	monieri misapplied	see *S. officinalis*
	monieri ambig.	CPom CPrp EHyd EShb LBMP NLar NSti WOut
	- white-flowered	GKev
§	***monieri*** (Gouan) P.W. Ball	LEdu LRHS
*	- 'Rosea'	EBee LEdu NBre NDov NLar
	nivea	see *S. discolor*
	obliqua	NBre WOut
§	***officinalis***	CArn CCVN CHab CPrp CSev EBee GPoy LEdu MHer MHoo MMuc MNHC MWhi NMir WCFE WCot WHer WHfH WJek WOut
	- SDR 3554	GKev
	- 'Alba'	CArn CPrp EBee LEdu MMuc NBro
	- dwarf	LRHS
	- dwarf, white-flowered	GCal
§	- 'Hummelo'	CAby CKno CPrp CSam EBee ECtt ELon EPPr EPfP GAbr GBin GQue IKil IPot LDai LHop LPla LRHS LSou MBel MRav NDov NLar SMrm SPhx WHoo WPtf WWEG XLum
	- 'Pink Cotton Candy' **new**	STPC
	- 'Powder Puff'	EBee
	- 'Rosea'	CCVN GCal GQue NBro WSHC WWEG
	- 'Rosea Superba'	NBre WCAu WCot
	- 'Saharan Pink'	CMHG EPfP LSRN LSou MMuc NLar WOut WWEG
	- 'Wisley White'	CAby EBee GQue LRHS NPri SRms WCot WHfH
	olympica	see *S. byzantina*
	ossetica	CDes CFis EBee
	palustris	CArn CHab LLWG MMuc NLar NMir SEND
	- pale-flowered	WOut
	recta	EBee
	setifera	NBre XLum
	spicata	see *S. macrantha*
	stricta	LRHS
	- 'Alba'	LRHS
	swainsonii	XSen
	sylvatica	CArn CHab NMir WHer WOut WSFF
	thirkei	XSen
§	***thunbergii***	CDes LEdu MBrN SBch WPGP
§	- 'Danielle'	CMac LAst LHop LRHS NLar SDys SRkn SRms WOut
	tuberifera	see *S. affinis*
	tymphaea **new**	XSen

Stachyurus (*Stachyuraceae*)

	chinensis	CBcs CJun CMCN CTri CWib IArd MGos NLar SMad
	- 'Celina'	CJun EPfP GKin LRHS NLar SHil SPoG
	- 'Goldbeater'	NLar
	- 'Joy Forever' (v)	CBcs CDoC CEnd CMac EBee EMil EPfP IArd IDee IVic LLHF LRHS LSRN MBri MGos NLar SHil SKHP SLim SSpi SSta SWvt
	- 'Senna'	LRHS NLar
	- 'Wonderful Image'	NLar
	himalaicus	CBcs NLar
	- HWJCM 009	WCru
	- HWJK 2035	WCru
	- 'Dolly'	NLar
	aff. ***himalaicus*** HWJK 2052	WCru
	'Magpie' (v)	CJun EPfP MBri NLar
	praecox ♀H4	Widely available
	- B&SWJ 8898	WCru
	- B&SWJ 10899	EWTr LHop WCru
	- var. ***leucotrichus***	CJun NLar
	- var. ***matsuzakii***	CJun NLar
	- - B&SWJ 2817	WCru
	- - B&SWJ 11229	WCru
	- - 'Issai'	LRHS SHil SSta
	- 'Oriental Sun'	MBri
	- 'Petra'	CJun
	retusus	CExl
	'Rubriflorus'	CJun EPfP LRHS MAsh MBri SChF WPGP
	salicifolius	CBcs CExl CFil CGHE CJun EBee EPfP IDee MBri SKHP WPGP WPat
	sigeyosii	CBcs CExl CFil
	- B&SWJ 6915	WCru
	- CWJ 12420	WCru
	- RWJ 10094	WCru
	aff. ***szechuanensis***	CExl
	- RWJ 8153	WCru
	yunnanensis	CBcs CFil CJun IArd IDee

Stanleya (*Brassicaceae*)

	pinnata	SBrt

Staphylea ✿ (*Staphyleaceae*)

	bolanderi	CBcs
	bumalda	CJun LEdu NLar
	- B&SWJ 11053	WCru
	colchica	CBcs CDul CHll CJun CMCN EBee ELan EPfP EWTr EWes LEdu LRHS MBri MGos MMHG MRav SPer WKif WSHC
	holocarpa	CJun EPfP MBri
	- 'Innocence'	NLar
N	- var. ***rosea***	CJun EPfP SMad SWvt
N	- 'Rosea'	CBcs CJun MBlu NLar SSpi

pinnata	CAgr CBcs CJun EBtc EPfP IVic NLar SEND
trifolia	CBcs CJun NEgg

Statice see *Limonium*

Stauntonia (*Lardizabalaceae*)

B&SWJ 8223	WCru
NJM 09.081	WPGP
aff. ***chinensis*** DJHV 06175	WCru
hexaphylla	CBcs CHEx CHel CHll CTri CWGN EBee EPfP ESwi EUJe LEdu LRHS MAsh NLar SKHP SPer SPoG SSpi SSta WSHC
- B&SWJ 4858	WCru
leucantha KWJ 12218	WCru
obovatifoliola B&SWJ 3685	WCru
- CWJ 12353	WCru
purpurea	NLar
- B&SWJ 3690	WCru
yaoshanensis B&SWJ 8223	WCru
- HWJ 1024	NLar WCru

Stegnogramma (*Thelypteridaceae*)

pozoi	EFer

Stellaria (*Caryophyllaceae*)

graminea	CHab
holostea	CHab NBir NMir WShi

Stemmacantha (*Asteraceae*)

carthamoides	CArn
§ ***centaureoides***	CDes EBee ECGP EPPr GAbr GCal GQue IBoy IPot LPla MAvo NBid WCAu WCot

Stenanthium (*Melanthiaceae*)

gramineum	CFil EWes WPGP

Stenomesson (*Amaryllidaceae*)

§ ***miniatum***	WCot
pearcei	ECho WCot
variegatum	WCot
- yellow-flowered	WCot

Stenotaphrum (*Poaceae*)

secundatum	EShb
- 'Variegatum' (v) ♀H1	EShb LSou XLum

Stephanandra (*Rosaceae*)

chinensis	SLon
incisa	CBcs CExl
§ - 'Crispa'	CDoC CDul CMac CTri EBee ELan EPfP EWTr GKin LAst LHop MBlu MJak MRav NEgg NHol NLar NSoo SPer WCFE WCot WHar WMoo
- 'Dart's Horizon'	SLPl
- 'Prostrata'	see *S. incisa* 'Crispa'
tanakae	CBcs CDoC CDul CExl CMac CTri EBee ELan EPfP EWTr LAst MBlu MRav NEgg SLon SPer

Stephania (*Menispermaceae*)

japonica CWJ 12823 new	WCru
longa KWJ 12163	WCru
rotunda B&SWJ 2396	WCru
sinica BWJ 8094	WCru
aff. ***tetrandra*** WWJ 11896	WCru

Stephanotis (*Asclepiadaceae*)

floribunda ♀H1	CBcs CCCN CSpe MBri

Sternbergia (*Amaryllidaceae*)

'Autumn Gold'	ECho
candida	CBro
fischeriana	CBro
greuteriana	ECho EPot LWst
lutea	CAby CAvo CBro ECho EPfP EPot ERCP EWes LHop LRHS SDeJ SDix WHoo XLum
- Angustifolia Group	CBro CMea ECho WCot
sicula	CBro ECho EPot GKev
- from Dodona, Greece	LWst
- 'Arcadian Sun'	ECho GKev LWst
- var. ***graeca***	ECho
- - from Crete	ECho
- 'John Marr'	WThu

Stevia (*Asteraceae*)

rebaudiana	CArn EOHP EUJe GPoy MHoo SHDw SRms WCot WJek

Stewartia ✿ (*Theaceae*)

gemmata	see *S. sinensis*
'Korean Splendor'	see *S. pseudocamellia* Koreana Group
koreana	see *S. pseudocamellia* Koreana Group
malacodendron ♀H4	EPfP LRHS
monadelpha	CBcs CMen IArd IDee LLHF MPkF NLar SSpi
ovata	LRHS SSpi
pseudocamellia ♀H4	Widely available
- B 322 new	GKev
- B&SWJ 11044 from North Japan	WCru
§ - Koreana Group ♀H4	CDul CEnd CMCN EPfP GKin LRHS MBri NLar SHil SSpi WPGP
pteropetiolata	CMHG IVic
- B&SWJ 11726	WCru
- WWJ 11939	WCru
rostrata	CBcs CJun ELan EPfP GBin IDee MPkF NLar SSpi WCru
serrata	CJun CMen GBin MPkF NLar
§ ***sinensis*** ♀H4	CBcs CJun EBee EPfP IArd IDee MPkF NLar SSpi

Stigmaphyllon (*Malpighiaceae*)

ciliatum	CCCN
littorale	CCCN

Stipa (*Poaceae*)

F&M 248	CDes WPGP
arundinacea	see *Anemanthele lessoniana*
barbata	CKno CSpe ELon EPPr EWes WKif
- 'Silver Feather'	WPtf
brachytricha	see *Calamagrostis brachytricha*
§ ***calamagrostis***	Widely available
- 'Allgäu'	WCot
- 'Lemperg'	IMou NDov
capillata	COIW EBee EPPr GCal LPio MNrw MWhi SDix
- 'Brautschleier'	CWib
* - 'Lace Veil'	MBel
elegantissima	CKno EHoe SHDw

extremiorientalis	CKno EPPr SMad
gigantea ♀H4	Widely available
- 'Gold Fontaene'	CElw CKno EBee EPPr EWes LRHS LSqu MAvo MMoz MNrw NDov SMad WCot WMoo WPGP WWEG
- 'Pixie'	WWEG
grandis	EPPr WMoo
ichu	CKno CSpe MAvo SDix SPoG
- F&M 32	CFil WPGP
joannis	EBee GCal
lasiagrostis	see *S. calamagrostis*
leptostachya	WCot
lessingiana	CExl EBee EHoe EPPr LRHS SEND WMoo
offneri	EPPr LRHS
pennata	EPPr LRHS
§ ***poeppigiana***	EBee
pseudoichu	CFil CSpe ESwi LBMP MAvo MBel WCot
- RCB/Arg Y-1	EBee ELon NCGa
pulcherrima	EBee EPPr GCal LRHS
- 'Windfeder'	CCon
ramosissima	CKno
robusta	EPPr SPhx
splendens misapplied	see *S. calamagrostis*
stenophylla	see *S. tirsa*
tenacissima	CDul IBoy MAsh
tenuifolia misapplied	see *S. tenuissima*
tenuifolia Steud.	CMea EBee EPfP LRHS MBri MRav NBir NBro NOak NSti WHal WMoo XLum XSen
§ ***tenuissima***	Widely available
- 'Wind Whispers'	CSpe EUJe EWTr GBin LEdu LHop MBel
§ ***tirsa***	EPPr
turkestanica	SWat
ucrainica	EPPr

Stoebe (*Asteraceae*)

alopecuroides	SPlb

Stokesia ✿ (*Asteraceae*)

cyanea	see *S. laevis*
§ ***laevis***	CHel CPrp EBee ECGP EPfP LRHS MMuc NLar NPnk SBea SMrm SPlb WMoo WPGP WWEG XLum
- 'Alba'	CCVN COIW ELan EPfP EPri LEdu LRHS MRav NPnk SPer
- 'Blue Star'	Widely available
- 'Klaus Jelitto'	IPot LEdu LRHS MBri NPnk SPoG
- 'Mary Gregory'	CCon CHel CMac CPrp CSam ECtt ELan EPfP IKil LEdu LHop LRHS LSRN LSou MBel MBri MNrw MRav NCGa NHol NLar NPnk SMrm SPer SPhx SRGP SWvt WHrl WPGP WWEG
- mixed	CPou
- 'Omega Skyrocket'	CPou NHol NLar SBea SMrm
- 'Peach Melba'	ECtt NCGa WMoo
- 'Peachie's Pick'	ECtt
- 'Purple Parasols'	CCVN COIW CWGN EBee ECtt EPfP EShb GBin IKil LHop LRHS LSou MBel MBri MWat NCGa NPnk SMrm SPoG STPC STes SWvt WHrl WMoo WWEG
- 'Purple Pixie'PBR **new**	ECtt
- 'Silver Moon'	CAbP CHel EBee ECtt EPfP GBin LRHS MTPN NBir NHol NPnk STPC WMoo WWEG
§ - 'Träumerei'	CWGN EBee ECtt EPfP LPio LRHS NLar NPnk SMrm WMnd WMoo WWEG XLum
- 'White Star'	see *S. laevis* 'Träumerei'

Stranvaesia see *Photinia*

× *Stranvinia* see *Photinia*

Stratiotes (*Hydrocharitaceae*)

aloides	CBAq CWat EHon EWay MWts NPer SVic SWat WMAq WPnP

strawberry see *Fragaria*

Strelitzia (*Strelitziaceae*)

alba	CCCN EAmu
juncea	XBlo
nicolai	CAbb EAmu NPer SPlb XBlo
reginae ♀H1	CAbb CBcs CCCN ELan EShb EUJe MREP NPer NPla SAPC SBig SEND SPlb XBlo
- 'Kirstenbosch Gold'	EAmu XBlo

Streptocarpella see *Streptocarpus*

Streptocarpus ✿ (*Gesneriaceae*)

'Albatross' ♀H1	CTsd WDib
'Alissa'PBR	WDib
'Amanda' Dibley ♀H1	WDib
'Amanda'PBR Fleischle (Marleen Series)	WDib
'Anne'	CTsd WDib
'Athena'	WDib
'Awena'	WDib
baudertii	WDib
'Bethan' ♀H1	CTsd WDib
'Bianca'	WDib
'Black Gardenia'	CTsd WDib
'Black Panther'	CTsd WDib
'Blue Bird'	SBrm
'Blue Gem'	WDib
'Blue Moon'	WDib
'Blue Nymph'	WDib
'Blushing Bride' (d)	WDib
* 'Boysenberry Delight'	WDib
'Branwen'	CTsd WDib
'Brimstone'	SBrm
'Bristol's Black Bird'	WDib
'Bristol's Very Best'	WDib
'Buttons'	SBrm
caeruleus	WDib
'Caitlin'	CTsd WDib
candidus	WDib
'Carol'	WDib
'Carolyn Ann'	SBrm
'Carys' ♀H1	CTsd WDib
caulescens	WDib
- var. ***pallescens***	WDib
'Charlotte'	SBrm WDib
'Chloe'	WDib
'Chorus Line' ♀H1	CTsd WDib
'Christine'	SBrm
'Concord Blue'	WDib
'Constant Nymph'	WDib
'Copper Knob'	SBrm
'Crystal Beauty'	WDib
'Crystal Blush'	WDib
'Crystal Charm'	WDib

'Crystal Dawn'	WDib
'Crystal Ice'PBR ♀H1	WDib
'Crystal Snow'	WDib
'Crystal Wonder'	WDib
cyaneus	WDib
- subsp. ***polackii***	WDib
'Cynthia' ♀H1	WDib
'Dainty Lady'	SBrm
'Daphne' ♀H1	WDib
'Dark Eyes Mary'	SBrm
'Denim'	WDib
denticulatus	WDib
'Diana'	WDib
'Dinas'	WDib
'Dreamtime'	SBrm
dunnii	WDib
'Elegance'	SBrm
'Elizabeth'	SBrm
'Ella'	SBrm
'Ella Mae'	SBrm
'Ellie'	WDib
'Elsi'	CTsd WDib
'Emily'	WDib
'Emma'	WDib
'Eve'	WDib
'Falling Stars' ♀H1	CTsd WDib
'Festival Wales'	WDib
'Fiona'	WDib
floribundus hort.	WDib
'Frances'	SBrm
'Franken Alison'	SBrm
'Franken Jenny'	SBrm
'Franken Kelly'	SBrm
'Franken Misty Blue'	SBrm
'Franken Texas Sunset'	SBrm
'Frosty Diamond'	CTsd WDib
gardenii	WDib
'Gillian'	SBrm
glandulosissimus ♀H1	WDib
'Gloria' ♀H1	CSpe CTsd WDib
'Gwen'	WDib
'Hannah'	WDib
'Hannah Ellis'	SBrm
'Happy Snappy' ♀H1	WDib
'Harlequin Blue'	WDib
'Harlequin Lace' **new**	WDib
'Harlequin Purple' **new**	WDib
'Harriet'	WDib
'Hayley' **new**	WDib
'Heidi' ♀H1	CTsd WDib
'Helen' ♀H1	CTsd WDib
'Hope'	WDib
'Ida'	SBrm
'Inky Fingers'	SBrm
'Iona'	WDib
'Isabella'	WDib
'Izzy'	SBrm
'Jacquie'	WDib
'Jane Elizabeth'	SBrm
'Jennifer' ♀H1	WDib
'Jessica'	WDib
'Joanna'	CTsd WDib
johannis	WDib
'Josie'	SBrm
'Joy' **new**	WDib
'Judith'	SBrm
'Karen'	WDib
'Katie'PBR	WDib
kentaniensis	WDib
'Kerry's Gold'	SBrm
'Kim' ♀H1	CSpe WDib
kirkii	WDib
'Kisie'	SBrm
'Lady Lavender'	SBrm
'Largesse'	SBrm
'Laura' ♀H1	WDib
'Leyla'PBR	WDib
'Louise'	WDib
'Lucy'	WDib
'Lyndee' **new**	WDib
'Lynne'	WDib
'Maassen's White' ♀H1	WDib
'Magpie'	SBrm
'Margaret' Gavin Brown	WDib
'Marie'	WDib
'Mary'	SBrm
'Megan'	WDib
'Melanie' Dibley ♀H1	WDib
meyeri	WDib
'Midnight Flame'	CTsd WDib
'Mini Nymph'	WDib
'Misty Pink'	SBrm
'Modbury Lady'	SBrm
modestus	WDib
'Molly'	SBrm
'Monica's Magic'	SBrm
'Moonlight'	WDib
'Myfanwy'	WDib
'Neptune'	WDib
'Nerys'	CTsd WDib
'Nia'	CTsd WDib
'Nicola'	CTsd WDib
'Olga'	WDib
'Olivia' **new**	WDib
'Olwen'	WDib
'Padarn'	WDib
'Pale Rider'	SBrm
'Party Doll'	WDib
'Patricia'	SBrm
'Paula' ♀H1	WDib
'Pearl' **new**	WDib
pentherianus	WDib
'Pink Leyla'PBR	WDib
'Pink Souffle'	WDib
polyanthus subsp. ***dracomontanus***	WDib
primulifolius	WDib
- subsp. ***formosus***	WDib
'Princesse' (Marleen Series)	WDib
prolixus	WDib
'Raspberry Dream'	SBrm
rexii	WDib
'Rhiannon'	CTsd WDib
'Rose Halo'	WDib
'Rosebud'	WDib
'Rosemary' (d)	WDib
(Roulette Series) 'Roulette Azur'	WDib
- 'Roulette Cherry'	WDib
'Rubina'PBR	WDib
'Ruby' ♀H1	CTsd WDib
'Ruby Anniversary'	SBrm
'Ruffles'	SBrm
'Sally'	WDib
'Sandra'	WDib
'Sarah'	WDib
saxorum ♀H1	CCCN WDib
- compact	CCCN WDib

'Scarlett'	WDib
'Seren'[PBR]	WDib
'Shannon'	SBrm
'Sian'	WDib
silvaticus	WDib
'Sioned'	WDib
'Snow White' 🏆H1	CSpe WDib
'Sophie'	WDib
'Southshore'	WDib
'Spirit'[PBR]	WDib
'Stacey'	SBrm
'Stella'[PBR] 🏆H1	WDib
'Stephanie'	WDib
stomandrus	WDib
'Strawberry Fondant'	SBrm
'Susan' 🏆H1	CTsd WDib
'Swaybelle'	SBrm
'Sweet Melys' new	WDib
'Targa' (Marleen Series)	WDib
'Tatan Blue'	SBrm
'Teleri'	WDib
'Terracotta'	SBrm
'Texas Hot Chili'	CTsd WDib
'Texas Sunrise'	SBrm
thompsonii	WDib
'Tina' 🏆H1	WDib
'Tracey'	WDib
vandeleurii	WDib
'Vanessa'	SBrm
variabilis	WDib
'Velvet Underground'	SBrm
'Vera'	SBrm
'Watermelon Wine'	WDib
wendlandii	WDib
'Wendy'	WDib
'White Butterfly'	WDib
'White Wings'	SBrm
'Wiesmoor Red'	WDib
'Winifred'	WDib

Streptopus (*Liliaceae*)

amplexifolius	EBee ECho MNrw NMyG WCru
roseus	ECho
streptopoides	EBee EPPr LRHS MMHG

Streptosolen (*Solanaceae*)

jamesonii 🏆H1	CHll EBak EShb IDee MOWG SWvt

Strobilanthes (*Acanthaceae*)

sp.	WBor
CC 4071	CExl
CC 4573	CExl
anisophylla	EShb SDys WCot WHil
atropurpurea misapplied	see *S. attenuata*
atropurpurea Nees	see *S. wallichii*
§ ***attenuata***	CCon EBee ECGP ECtt EPfP GCal GCra IVic LHop LRHS MBel MCot MRav NCGa NChi NDov NSti WCru WMoo WWlt
- 'Blue Carpet'	NDov
- subsp. ***nepalensis***	CHll CLAP XLum
dyeriana 🏆H1	EAmu EBak EShb WCot WHil
flexicaulis	WPGP
- B&SWJ 354	WCru
aff. ***inflata*** B&SWJ 7754	WCru
lactata new	WHil
nutans	CPou EBee NSti SBrt XLum
aff. ***pentstemonoides*** HWJK 2019	WCru
rankanensis	CCon EPPr SBch SDys XLum
- B&SWJ 1771	WCru
violacea	CHVG CPrp EShb EWTr LHop
§ ***wallichii***	CMac CSam EBee EWes EWld LLWP NSti WCot WCru WMoo WSHC WWEG
'Wollerton'	WWlt

Stromanthe (*Marantaceae*)

sanguinea 'Triostar'[PBR] (v)	XBlo

Strongylodon (*Papilionaceae*)

macrobotrys	MOWG

Strophanthus (*Apocynaceae*)

speciosus	CCCN CHll EShb

Strumaria (*Amaryllidaceae*)

aestivalis	ECho
chaplinii	ECho
discifera subsp. ***bulbifera***	WCot
karooica 'Komsberg'	ECho
leipoldtii 'Vanrhynsdorp'	ECho
massoniella 'Reitfontein'	ECho
salteri 'Nardouwsberg'	ECho
truncata	ECho WCot
- 'Garies'	ECho

Stuartia see *Stewartia*

Stylidium (*Stylidiaceae*)

adnatum	ECou
graminifolium	SPlb
- Little Saphire = 'St116'	NOak SRot
- 'Tiny Trina'	LRHS NOak

Stylophorum (*Papaveraceae*)

diphyllum	CPou EWld IMou MRav WCru WPnP
lasiocarpum	CExl CPom CSpe EWes EWld IGor MMHG NBid WCot WCru

Stypandra (*Phormiaceae*)

glauca new	CLak

Styphelia (*Epacridaceae*)

colensoi	see *Leucopogon colensoi*

Styphnolobium (*Leguminosae*)

§ ***japonicum*** 🏆H4	CAbP CDul CHab CTho CWib EPfP MGos MMuc SPer SPlb
- 'Pendulum'	ELan

Styrax (*Styracaceae*)

americanus	NLar
faberi	CExl
formosanus	CBcs CGHE EBee
- var. ***formosanus***	CExl CFil CJun EPfP WPGP
- - B&SWJ 3803	WCru
- - B&SWJ 6786	WCru
- var. ***hayatiana*** B&SWJ 6823	WCru
hemsleyanus 🏆H4	CAbP CBcs CExl CTho EBee EPfP GBin IDee MBlu MMuc NLar SPer SSpi
hookeri	CExl
japonicus 🏆H4	CBcs CDoC CDul CEnd CExl CMCN CTho CTri CWib EBee ELan EPfP GKin IDee LRHS MAsh MBlu

MGos MMuc MRav SChF SPer SReu SSpi WPGP WPat
- B&SWJ 4405 WCru
- B&SWJ 8770 WCru
- Guiz 216 CExl WPGP
- (Benibana Group) 'Pink Chimes' CBcs CEnd CExl CJun CMac ELan EPfP GBin GKin MBlu MPkF NLar SCoo SPer SSpi WPat
- 'Carillon' CJun
- 'Fargesii' CBcs CDoC CDul CExl CJun CTho EPfP GBin IVic SCoo SKHP SSpi
- 'Fragrant Fountain' MBlu
- 'Hyme' NLar
- 'Issai' NLar
- 'Masaku' **new** SSpi
- 'Pendulus' WPGP
- 'Purple Dress' CJun MBlu MBri NLar
- 'Snowfall' CJun NLar
- 'Sohuksan' CExl CJun MBlu NLar SSpi WPGP
limprichtii **new** CExl CFil
obassia 🏆H4 CBcs CDul CLnd CMCN CTho EPfP GBin IDee IVic LRHS MBlu MBri NLar SSpi
- B&SWJ 6023 WCru
- B&SWJ 10890 WCru
odoratissimus CExl
officinalis CBcs
platanifolius CFil
var. ***mollis*** **new**
serrulatus CExl
shiraiana **new** CFil
suberifolius WWJ 11868 WCru
* ***taiwanensis*** SKHP
wilsonii CExl
wuyuanensis NLar

Succisa (*Caprifoliaceae*)

§ ***pratensis*** CAby CArn CHab CMac CRDP EBee EPri LEdu LHop LLWG LRHS MAvo MHer MPie NLar SBch SPhx WHer WHoo WPtf WSFF WWFP XLum
- 'Alba' EWes
- 'Buttermilk' CRDP
- 'Cassop' NRya
- 'Derby Purple' CSpe
- 'Peddar's Pink' EBee EWes LEdu LLWG SPhx

Succisella (*Caprifoliaceae*)

inflexa LEdu MSpe SPhx
- 'Frosted Pearls' CFis CMHG EBee EDif LEdu LLWP WHil WWFP

Sullivantia (*Saxifragaceae*)

sullivantii dwarf WThu

sunberry see *Rubus* 'Sunberry'

Sutera (*Scrophulariaceae*)

(Abunda Series) Abunda Blue Improved = 'Balabimblu' LAst
- Abunda Colossal Sky Blue = 'Balabolav' NPri
- Abunda Colossal White = 'Balabowite'PBR NPri
Cabana Trailing White = 'Sutcatrwhi' (Cabana Series) WGor
(Copia Series) Copia Dark Pink = 'Dancop19'PBR LAst
- Copia Double White (d) LAst
- Copia Gulliver White = 'Dangul14'PBR LAst
cordata 'Blizzard' LSou
- 'Olympic Gold' (v) SCoo
- 'Pink Domino' SPet
- Scopia Double Pink Pearl (Scopia Series) LAst
§ - 'Snowflake' LAst NPer SCoo SPet SPoG SWvt
Great Purple = 'Dancop21'PBR (Scopia Series) LSou
'Lime Delight' LAst
microphylla CPBP
neglecta SPlb WPGP
(Scopia Series) Scopia Golden Leaves = 'Dancopgoleav' NPri
- Scopia Great Pink Beauty = 'Dancop35' **new** NPri
(Secrets Series) 'Secrets Blue Delight' LSou
- 'Secrets Central Pink' LSou
- 'Secrets Silver Sky' LSou

Sutherlandia ✿ (*Papilionaceae*)

frutescens CArn CSpe SPlb WJek
montana CSpe SBrt WHil

Swainsona (*Papilionaceae*)

galegifolia CHll
- 'Albiflora' MOWG WWlt

sweet cicely see *Myrrhis odorata*

Swietenia (*Meliaceae*)

mahogani **new** SPlb

Syagrus (*Arecaceae*)

botryophora XBlo
§ ***romanzoffiana*** EAmu XBlo
- 'Santa Caterina' EAmu
weddelliana see *Lytocaryum weddellianum*

× *Sycoparrotia* (*Hamamelidaceae*)

semidecidua CBcs CJun MBlu NLar SLPl
- 'Purple Haze' CJun NLar

Sycopsis (*Hamamelidaceae*)

sinensis CAbP CBcs CExl CHel CWib EBee EMil EPfP LHop LRHS NLar SKHP SPoG SSpi SWvt WHor WPGP WSHC

Symphoricarpos (*Caprifoliaceae*)

albus CDul CMac EBee MSwo NWea
- 'Constance Spry' SRms
§ - var. ***laevigatus*** EPfP LBuc
§ - 'Taff's White' (v) WMoo
- 'Variegatus' see *S. albus* 'Taff's White'
× ***chenaultii*** 'Brain de Soleil'PBR EBee
- 'Hancock' CBar CDul CMac EBee ECrN ELan EPfP MGos MMuc MRav MSwo SGol SLim SPer WCFE
× ***doorenbosii*** 'Magic Berry' MRav NWea SGol
- 'Mother of Pearl' EBee ELan EPfP MMuc MRav NWea SPer

- 'White Hedge'	EBee ELan LBuc MMuc NWea SPer SPlb
guatemalensis B&SWJ 1016	WCru
Magical Candy = 'Kolmcan'PBR	ELan EPfP LRHS
Magical Galaxy = 'Kolmgala'PBR	ELan EPfP LRHS MBri
Magical Sweet = 'Kolmaswet'PBR	MBri
orbiculatus	EBee SLon
- 'Albovariegatus'	see *S. orbiculatus* 'Taff's Silver Edge'
- 'Argenteovariegatus'	see *S. orbiculatus* 'Taff's Silver Edge'
- 'Bowles's Golden Variegated'	see *S. orbiculatus* 'Foliis Variegatis'
§ - 'Foliis Variegatis' (v)	CMac CTri EHoe ELan EPfP MGos MRav SGol SPer WSHC
- 'George Gardiner'	CMac
§ - 'Taff's Silver Edge' (v)	EHoe SGol
- 'Variegatus'	see *S. orbiculatus* 'Foliis Variegatis'
rivularis	see *S. albus* var. *laevigatus*

Symphyandra see *Campanula*

asiatica	see *Hanabusaya asiatica*

Symphyotrichum see *Aster*

Symphytum (*Boraginaceae*)

'Angela Whinfield'	CDes CMea
asperum	CSev MRav NLar WMoo
* ***azureum***	EBee NChi NLar WMnd
'Belsay'	GBuc
'Belsay Gold'	NBid NBir SDix
bulbosum Schimp. PAB 4886 **new**	LEdu
caucasicum ♀H4	CElw CMHG GPoy GQue IFro LEdu SEND SIde WHer WHil WMoo WOut XLum
- 'Norwich Sky'	CExl CKno EWld
cordatum	EBee EPPr LEdu MNrw SKHP
'Denford Variegated' (v)	NBid
§ 'Goldsmith' (v)	CMea CSam EBee ELan EPfP LAst LBMP LRHS LSou MBri MCot MMuc MSCN NBid NBir NEgg NLar NOrc NPer SPer WBrk WHoo WJek WMnd WWEG
grandiflorum	CArn CMac CTri GPoy LEdu
* - 'Sky-blue-pink'	IFro
'Grandiflorum' variegated (v)	LRHS
'Hidcote Blue'	CBar CBre CPrp CTri ECtt EPPr EPfP LBMP LRHS MHoo MMuc NBro NEgg NOrc SEND SLPl SPer SPoG WCru WGwG WMoo WOut WPtf WWEG
§ 'Hidcote Pink'	CWCL ECtt EPPr LBMP LPot LRHS MHoo MMuc MNrw NBir NEgg SEND SLPl SPer SPoG WGwG WMoo WPnP WWEG XLum
'Hidcote Variegated' (v)	CMac
ibericum	CArn CSam EWTr GKev GMaP GPoy LHop LRHS MHoo MLHP MMuc NSti SEND SRms WGwG WJek WMoo WOut
- 'All Gold'	MHer MNrw WMoo
- 'Blaueglocken'	CSev LPla WMoo
- dwarf	IFro WMoo
- 'Gold in Spring'	NLar
- 'Jubilee'	see *S.* 'Goldsmith'
- 'Lilacinum'	CFis LRHS WHer
- variegated (v)	MHoo
- 'Variegatum'	see *S.* 'Goldsmith'
- 'Wisley Blue'	CBcs CHab CPrp EPfP WMoo WWEG
'Lambrook Gold'	LHop
'Lambrook Sunrise'	CFis CMac EBee LEdu NBro WCot WMoo WWEG
'Langthorns Pink'	CPom ELan GCal
'Mereworth'	see *S.* × *uplandicum* 'Mereworth'
officinale	CArn CHab CSev GJos GPoy MHer MHoo MNHC MNrw NPer NPri SIde SPoG SRms WHer WHfH WJek XLum
- blue-flowered	MHoo SEND
- 'Bohemicum'	ECho
- var. ***ochroleucum***	WHer
orientale	CPom GCal MBel
peregrinum	see *S.* × *uplandicum*
'Roseum'	see *S.* 'Hidcote Pink'
'Rubrum'	CDes ELan EPfP EWes GBin GCra LEdu LRHS NBro NOrc SPer WCAu WGwG WPGP XLum
'Sera Howys'	WOut
tuberosum	CArn CBre CElw CPom CSam EPPr GPoy LEdu MHer MMuc SEND WBor WCot WHer
§ × ***uplandicum***	CSev CTri ELan GCra GPoy SVic WJek
- 'Axminster Gold' (v)	CMea EWes WCot
- 'Bocking 14'	CAgr CHby CPbn CPrp EOHP EShb GAbr LEdu MNHC SIde WSFF XLum
- 'Droitwich' (v)	WCot
§ - 'Mereworth' (v)	CBct LRHS MMuc SEND
- 'Moorland Heather'	CDes MHer MHoo WMoo
- purple-flowered	MMuc SEND
- 'Variegatum' (v) ♀H4	EBee ECtt ELan EPfP EWes GBuc LAst NBir NGdn NSti SDix SPoG WMoo

Symplocarpus (*Araceae*)

renifolius	WCru

Symplocos (*Symplocaceae*)

paniculata	see *S. sawafutagi*
§ ***sawafutagi***	CBcs NLar WPGP WPat

Syncarpha (*Asteraceae*)

vestita **new**	SPlb

Syneilesis (*Asteraceae*)

aconitifolia	MNrw WCot
- B&SWJ 879	CDes LEdu WCru
palmata	WCot
- B&SWJ 1003	CDes WCru
- B&SWJ 11226	WCru
subglabrata B&SWJ 298	WCru
aff. ***tagawae*** B&SWJ 11191	WCru

Syngonium (*Araceae*)

podophyllum ♀H1	XBlo

Synnotia see *Sparaxis*

Synthyris (*Plantaginaceae*)

laciniata	EBee
missurica	CLAP
- subsp. ***missurica***	EBee GBuc

- var. ***stellata***	CLAP EBee ECre EPfP EPri EWes GBuc GCal LEdu LLWG LRHS MMHG NCGa NSti SPoG WGwG WHal WMoo WPGP WPtf WWEG
reniformis	CLAP GBuc WPGP WWEG

Syringa ✿ (*Oleaceae*)

	afghanica misapplied	see *S. protolaciniata*
	afghanica C.K. Schneid.	IVic WSHC
	'Alexander's Pink'	WGob
	× ***chinensis*** 'Alba'	see *S.* 'Correlata'
	- 'Bicolor' **new**	WGob
	- 'Saugeana'	NLar SLPl SPer
§	'Correlata' (graft-chimaera)	EBee
	emodi 'Aurea'	NLar
	- 'Aureovariegata'	see *S. emodi* 'Elegantissima'
§	- 'Elegantissima' (v)	CBcs CDoC CEnd CMac EBee EBtc ELan EPfP GQui LLHF LRHS MAsh NEgg SKHP SPoG SSpi
	- 'Variegata' (v)	LRHS
	'Hagny'	WGob
	× ***hyacinthiflora*** 'Clarke's Giant'	NLar
	- 'Esther Staley' ♀H4	CLnd EPfP MRav SKHP
	- 'Maiden's Blush'	EWTr
	- 'Pocahontas'	EBee GBin NLar
	Josée = 'Morjos 060f'	CDoC EBee ELon EPfP LBMP MAsh NLar SPoG SWvt WGob WPat
	× ***josiflexa***	CExl
	- 'Agnes Smith'	MMuc NLar
	- 'Anna Amhoff'	NLar
	- 'Bellicent' ♀H4	CEnd CMac EBee ELan EPfP LRHS MAsh MMuc MRav NLar NSti SKHP SMad SPer SPlb SPoG SRms SWvt WCFE WPat
	- 'James MacFarlane'	NLar WGob
	- 'Lynette'	NPro
	- 'Redwine'	NLar SKHP
§	- 'Royalty'	NLar SKHP WGob
	josikaea	CMCN CSBt NLar SPer WGob
	'Kim'	MRav
	komarowii	GGGa
§	- subsp. ***reflexa***	CDul EPfP EWTr IDee LLHF SLon
§	× ***laciniata*** Mill.	CJun EBee ELan EPfP LRHS MGos MMuc MRav NLar SPer SPoG SSpi WCFE WGor WHar WPGP
	meyeri **new**	SVen
§	- 'Palibin' ♀H4	Widely available
	microphylla	see *S. pubescens* subsp. *microphylla*
	'Minuet'	CBcs NLar SKHP WGob
	'Miss Canada'	NLar
	oblata	CMCN
	palibiniana	see *S. meyeri* 'Palibin'
	patula misapplied	see *S. meyeri* 'Palibin'
	patula (Palibin) Nakai	see *S. pubescens* subsp. *patula*
	pekinensis	see *S. reticulata* subsp. *pekinensis*
	× ***persica*** ♀H4	CDul CExl CJun CTri EPfP EWTr IDee MGos MRav NLar SLon SPer WGob
	- 'Alba' ♀H4	CJun MRav WGob WSHC
	- var. ***laciniata***	see *S.* × *laciniata* Mill.
	pinnatifolia	CBcs GBin NLar
	× ***prestoniae*** 'Desdemona'	EBtc LRHS MMuc SKHP SSta
	- 'Donald Wyman'	WGob
	- 'Elinor' ♀H4	CMHG ELan EPfP MRav NSti SKHP
	- 'Nocturne'	WGob
	- 'Royalty'	see *S.* × *josiflexa* 'Royalty'
§	***protolaciniata***	NLar SKHP SLim
	- 'Kabul'	EPfP NLar
	pubescens subsp. ***julianae*** 'George Eastman'	MRav WGob
§	- subsp. ***microphylla***	EWTr
	- - 'Superba' ♀H4	Widely available
§	- subsp. ***patula***	CMac ECho LRHS MMuc MRav NWea SEND SVen
	- - 'Miss Kim' ♀H4	CDoC CMac CSBt EBee ELan ELon GAbr IArd LAst LRHS LSRN MAsh MBri MGos MJak MRav MSwo NEgg NHol NLar SCoo SKHP SLim SPoG SSta WGob WPat
	'Red Pixie'	CHll CMac ELon EPfP LBuc LRHS MBri MGos MMHG NLar SCoo SHil SKHP WGob
	reflexa	see *S. komarowii* subsp. *reflexa*
	reticulata	MBlu
	- 'Ivory Silk'	EPfP LLHF NLar SKHP
§	- subsp. ***pekinensis***	CMCN GBin
	- - China Snow = 'Morton'	SKHP
	- - 'Yellow Fragrance'	NLar
	× ***swegiflexa***	CDul CExl NLar
	sweginzowii	GKin SPer
	tomentella	NWea SRms WPGP
	velutina	see *S. pubescens* subsp. *patula*
	villosa	SPlb WGob
	vulgaris	CDul EPfP EWTr LBuc NWea WHlf
	- 'Albert F. Holden'	WGob
§	- 'Andenken an Ludwig Späth' ♀H4	Widely available
	- 'Aurea'	LBuc MGos MRav NPro
	- Beauty of Moscow	see *S. vulgaris* 'Krasavitsa Moskvy'
	- 'Belle de Nancy' (d)	CCCN CDul CLnd CMac CWib EBee ELan ELon LAst MAsh MMuc MRav NEgg SEND SGol SWvt WGob
	- 'Charles Joly' (d) ♀H4	Widely available
	- 'Comtesse d'Harcourt'	WGob
	- 'Congo'	LSRN MRav
	- 'Edith Cavell' (d)	WGob
	- 'Edward J. Gardner' (d)	ELon SEND
	- 'Firmament' ♀H4	EBee ELan EPfP MRav NEgg SEND SPer WGob
	- 'Hope'	see *S. vulgaris* 'Nadezhda'
	- 'Hugo de Vries' **new**	IArd
	- 'Katherine Havemeyer' (d) ♀H4	Widely available
§	- 'Krasavitsa Moskvy' (d)	CDoC EPfP EWes GBin LRHS MAsh MBri MRav NLar SHil
	- 'Lee Jewett Walker'	SSta
	- 'Lila Wonder' PBR	EPfP
	- 'Madame Florent Stepman'	CMac NLar WGob
	- 'Madame Lemoine' (d) ♀H4	Widely available
	- 'Masséna'	MRav SPer WGob
	- 'Michel Buchner' (d)	CBcs CDul CWib EBee ELan MBlu MGos MJak MRav NLar NSoo SCoo SLim SPer WGob
	- 'Miss Ellen Willmott' (d)	IArd MRav NLar
	- 'Mrs Edward Harding' (d) ♀H4	EPfP LBuc MRav NLar NWea SCoo WGob
§	- 'Nadezhda' (d)	WGob
	- 'Olivier de Serres' (d)	NLar
	- 'Pat Pesata'	WGob
	- 'Paul Deschanel' (d)	ELan NLar
	- 'Paul Thirion' (d)	WGob
	- 'Pavlinka' (d) **new**	IArd
	- 'Président Grévy' (d)	CBar CDoC CMac EBee EMil EPfP MAsh SLim

- 'Primrose'	CBcs CCCN CDul CMac CWib EBee ELan ELon EPfP GBin IArd LRHS MAsh MGos MJak MMuc MSnd NEgg NLar SCoo SEND SHil SKHP SPer WGob
- 'Prince Wolkonsky' (d)	EBee EMil EPfP LSRN SPer WGob
- 'Princesse Sturdza'	EMil
- 'Professor Hoser'	IArd WGob
- 'Ruhm von Horstenstein'	MBri
- 'Sensation'	Widely available
- 'Souvenir d'Alice Harding' (d)	MBri
- 'Souvenir de Louis Spaeth'	see *S. vulgaris* 'Andenken an Ludwig Späth'
- 'Ukraina'	WGob
- variegated (v)	EWes
- variegated double (d/v)	WCot
- 'Vesper' **new**	IArd
- 'Vestale' ♀H4	MRav
- 'Victor Lemoine' (d)	WGob
- 'Viviand-Morel' (d)	CMac LLHF NEgg SKHP WGob
- 'William Robinson' (d)	SPer
- 'Wonderblue' **new**	WGob
wolfii	CArn EBtc
yunnanensis	CExl GGGa LLHF
- 'Prophecy'	WGob

Syringodea (*Iridaceae*)

longituba 'Perdekraal'	ECho

Syzygium (*Myrtaceae*)

australe	EShb
paniculatum	CExl EShb IDee

T

Tabernaemontana (*Apocynaceae*)

coronaria	see *T. divaricata*
§ ***divaricata***	CCCN

Tacca (*Taccaceae*)

chantrieri	CCCN EAmu GKev
- 'Green Isle'	GKev
integrifolia	GKev

Tacitus see *Graptopetalum*

Tagetes (*Asteraceae*)

'Cinnabar'	SDix
lemmonii	SDix SHDw WJek
'Lemon Gem'	WJek
lucida	CArn LEdu SRms WJek
patula Durango Series	NPri
- - 'Durango Bee'	NPri
- - 'Durango Flame'	NPri
- - 'Durango Orange'	NPri
- - 'Durango Yellow'	NPri
- - 'Durango Yellow Fire'	NPri
- 'Harlequin'	see *T. patula* 'Old Scotch Pride'
§ - 'Old Scotch Pride' **new**	SPav

Taiwania (*Cupressaceae*)

cryptomerioides	IArd IDee

Talinum (*Portulacaceae*)

'Zoe'	CPBP

tamarillo see *Solanum betaceum*

tamarind see *Tamarindus indica*

Tamarindus (*Caesalpiniaceae*)

indica (F)	SPlb

Tamarix (*Tamaricaceae*)

chinensis	CSBt
gallica	CMen CSBt NWea SAPC SEND WSHC
hampeana	SEND
§ ***parviflora***	CDul CMac EPfP IVic LRHS SPoG
pentandra	see *T. ramosissima*
§ ***ramosissima***	CCCN CMac CTri ECrN ELan EPfP MAsh MWhi SEWo SLim SLon SRms WHar
- 'Hulsdonk White'	EBee
- 'Pink Cascade'	CBcs CCCN CDul CSBt ELon EPfP LRHS MBlu MBri MGos MMuc MREP MRav NEgg NSoo SBod SEND SGol SPer SPoG SWvt WBor
- 'Rosea'	CBcs
§ - 'Rubra' ♀H4	CDoC CWSG EPfP IVic NLar SLon
- 'Summer Glow'	see *T. ramosissima* 'Rubra'
tetrandra ♀H4	CBcs CCVT CDul CMac CSBt CWib EBee ELan EPfP LRHS MBlu MBri MGos MMuc MRav MSwo MWat NLar NPer SEND SGol SHil SPer SPlb SRms SWvt WHar
- var. ***purpurea***	see *T. parviflora*

Tamus (*Dioscoreaceae*)

communis	CArn

Tanacetum ✿ (*Asteraceae*)

§ ***argenteum***	ECho MRav SIde
- subsp. ***canum***	ECho LRHS SLon
§ ***balsamita***	CArn CHby CPrp EBee ELan ELau GPoy LEdu MHer MHoo MNHC SRms WHer WHfH WJek XLum XSen
§ - subsp. ***balsamita***	GPoy SIde
§ - subsp. ***balsamitoides***	CHby CPrp MHer WJek
- var. ***tanacetoides***	see *T. balsamita* subsp. *balsamita*
- ***tomentosum***	see *T. balsamita* subsp. *balsamitoides*
capitatum	see *Sphaeromeria capitata*
§ ***cinerariifolium***	CArn CPrp GPoy MNHC WJek
coccineum 'Alfred'	EBee
- 'Aphrodite' (d)	NEgg
- 'Beauty of Stapleford'	NEgg
- 'Bees' Pink Delight'	LRHS MBNS NEgg
- 'Brenda'	EPfP
- 'Duro'	LRHS
- 'Eileen May Robinson' ♀H4	EBee EPfP LSRN MBNS MMHG NGdn
- 'Evenglow'	EPfP
- 'Garden Treasure' **new**	LBuc
- 'H.M. Pike'	MMHG
- 'James Kelway' ♀H4	EBee EPfP MRav NBir
- Robinson's giant-flowered	CTsd SRms
- Robinson's pink-flowered	EBee EHyd ELan EPfP EWll GMaP MHol WWEG XLum
- Robinson's red-flowered	CSBt EHyd EPfP EUJe GMaP LPio MHol MLHP SPlb SWvt WWEG XLum

	- 'Scarlet Glow'	EWll
	- 'Snow Cloud'	EBee ECtt EPfP WWEG
	- 'Vanessa'	LRHS MNrw
§	***corymbosum***	GCal WCot
	- 'Festtafel'	LPla
	densum	ECho WCFE
	- subsp. ***amani***	ECho GMaP LRHS MWat SEND XSen
	- - 'Beth Chatto' **new**	XSen
	- subsp. ***sivasicum***	XSen
§	***haradjanii***	ECho MCot SBch WKif
	huronense	EBee
	macrophyllum misapplied	see *Achillea grandifolia* Friv.
§	***macrophyllum*** (Waldst. & Kit.) Sch.Bip.	CPrp EBee ECtt EPPr LPla SPhx
	- 'Cream Klenza'	WCot
	niveum	WCot
	- 'Jackpot'	CFis CWib EBee EPfP EWes SWvt
§	***parthenium***	CArn CHab CHby CPbn ELau GPoy MHer MHoo MNHC NPer SIde SRms SVic WHer WJek XLum
	- 'Aureum'	CHid CPbn CPrp CRow ELan ELau EWes GPoy LEdu LPot MBri MHer MLHP MNHC MRav SPer SPlb SRms SWvt WCot WHer WJek WMoo XLum
	- double white-flowered (d)	MHoo NPer SRms
	- 'Golden Ball'	EPfP
	- 'Golden Moss'	XLum
	- 'Plenum' (d)	MNrw
§	- 'Rowallane' (d)	MMuc SEND WCot
	- 'Sissinghurst White'	see *T. parthenium* 'Rowallane'
	- 'Snowball' (d)	EPfP
	poteriifolium	EBee LRHS MAvo
	ptarmiciflorum 'Silver Feather'	SRms SVen WJek
*	***tommansii***	EBee LRHS
	vulgare	CArn CHab CHby CMac CSev ECtt ELau GPoy MHer MHoo MNHC SIde SRms SVic WJek WMoo WSFF XSen
	- 'All Gold'	CSev SMad SRms
	- var. ***crispum***	CPrp EBee ELau MHer MNHC MRav SIde SMad SRms WJek
	- 'Golden Fleece'	EBee ECtt EWes LEdu LLWG LRHS LSou NSti SPer WCot WGrn
	- 'Isla Gold' (v)	ECtt EWes GMaP LDai LEdu LHop LPla MHer MMuc MRav SEND SMrm WCot WJek WMoo
	- 'Silver Lace' (v)	CBre EBee EWes NBid WHer WJek WMoo

Tanakaea (*Saxifragaceae*)

radicans	WCru

tangelo see *Citrus* × *tangelo*

tangerine see *Citrus reticulata*

tangor see *Citrus* × *nobilis* Tangor Group

Taraxacum (*Asteraceae*)

albidum	GLin
faeroense	WCot
officinale agg.	CArn CHab
- 'Nettleton'	CNat
rubrifolium	CBre CSpe EPPr

tarragon see *Artemisia dracunculus*

Tasmannia see *Drimys*

Taxodium (*Cupressaceae*)

	ascendens 'Nutans'	see *T. distichum* var. *imbricarium* 'Nutans'
	distichum 🏆H4	Widely available
	- 'Cascade Falls'[PBR]	LRHS MBlu MBri MGos NLar SLim
	- 'Cave Hill'	SLim
	- 'Falling Waters'	CBcs SGol SKHP WMou
	- 'Gee Whiz'	SLim
	- 'Hursley Park'	NLar
	- var. ***imbricarium***	CMCN EPfP LRHS
§	- - 'Nutans' 🏆H4	CBcs CEnd EPfP IArd LRHS MBlu NLar SCoo SGol SLim
	- 'Little Leaf'	NLar SMad
	- 'Minaret'	MBlu
*	- 'Pendulum'	IDee
	- 'Peve Minaret'	CDoC CMen LRHS MBri MGos NLar SGol SKHP SLim SMad
	- 'Peve Yellow'	MBlu
	- 'Schloss Herten'	LRHS NLar SLim
	- 'Secrest'	MBlu SLim
	- Shawnee Brave = 'Mickelson'	MBlu
	mucronatum	CDoC CExl CFil
	- NJM 09.037	WPGP

Taxus ✿ (*Taxaceae*)

	baccata 🏆H4	Widely available
	- 'Adpressa Aurea' (v)	GKin
	- 'Adpressa Variegata' (m/v) 🏆H4	CDoC
	- 'Aldenham Gold'	CKen
	- 'Amersfoort'	CDoC GKin LRHS NLar
	- Aurea Group	CDul ELan SRms
I	- 'Aureomarginata' (v)	CBcs MAsh NEgg SWvt WGor
	- 'Autumn Shades'	CBcs NLar
	- 'Bridget's Gold'	CKen
	- 'Corleys Coppertip'	CKen EBtc LRHS MBri MRav NLar SCoo SLim
	- 'Cristata'	CKen NLar
	- 'David'	IArd MBri MGos NLar SPoG SWvt WGor
	- 'Dovastoniana' (f) 🏆H4	CMac NLar NWea WMou
	- 'Dovastonii Aurea' (m/v) 🏆H4	CBcs EPfP GKin MBlu MBri NEgg NLar NPCo NWea SGol SLim
	- 'Elegantissima' (f/v)	CTho EHul EPfP LRHS NPCo NWea SCoo WGor
§	- 'Fastigiata' (f) 🏆H4	CBcs CDul CMac CNWT CSBt CTho CTri CWib EHul ELan EPfP LAst MGos MJak MRav MSwo NEgg NPCo NWea SEWo SGol SPer SPoG SRms SWvt WHar
	- Fastigiata Aurea Group	CLnd CMac CWib EPfP GKev IArd MAsh MGos NSoo SGol SRms WHar
	- 'Fastigiata Aureomarginata' (m/v) 🏆H4	CDoC CDul CMac CSBt CTri EHul EPfP LBee LRHS MBri MGos MJak NWea SCoo SLim SLon SPer SPoG SWvt
	- 'Fastigiata Robusta' (f)	CDoC CSBt EBtc ELan EPfP LRHS MAsh MBri NLar NPCo SCoo SLim SPoG
	- 'Goud Elsje'	NLar
	- 'Gracilis Pendula'	IArd
	- 'Grayswood Hill'	NLar
	- 'Green Column'	CKen
	- 'Green Diamond'	CKen NLar

- 'Green Rocket'	CDul NLar
- 'Hibernica'	see *T. baccata* 'Fastigiata'
- 'Icicle'	CBcs LRHS MAsh NHol NLar NWad SLim
- 'Itsy Bitsy'	CKen
- 'Ivory Tower'	CBcs CDoC CKen ELan NEgg NHol NLar NPCo NWad SLim WGor
- 'Klitzeklein'	CKen
- 'Litfass'	NLar
- 'Lutea' (f)	SLim
- 'Micro' **new**	CKen
- 'Nutans'	CDoC CKen
- 'Pendula'	MRav
- 'Prostrata'	CMac
- 'Pygmaea'	CKen
- 'Repandens' (f) ♀H4	EHul IArd MGos NWea
I - 'Repens Aurea' (v) ♀H4	CDoC CDul CKen CMac EHul LAst MBri NEgg SCoo
- 'Rushmore'	MBri
- 'Semperaurea' (m) ♀H4	CBcs CDoC CMac EHul LBuc MAsh MBri NWea SCoo SGol SLim SPoG
- 'Silver Spire' (v)	CKen
- 'Standishii' (f) ♀H4	CBcs CDoC CDul CKen CMac CSBt EHul ELan EPfP GKin IArd LAst LBee LRHS MAsh MBri MGos MRav NEgg NHol NLar NPCo NWad NWea SEND SLim SPer SPoG SWvt
- 'Stove Pipe'	CKen
- 'Summergold' (v)	EHul ELan EPfP LRHS MAsh MGos MRav NBir NEgg NHol NLar SCoo SLim
- 'White Icicle'	WGor
brevifolia	NLar
cuspidata	CMen
- 'Aurescens' (v)	CKen
- 'Minuet'	CKen
- 'Straight Hedge'	LRHS SLim
× ***media*** 'Hicksii' (f) ♀H4	CDul LBuc LRHS NLar NWea SCoo SGol
- 'Hillii'	LBMP LBuc MGos
- 'Lodi'	LBee
- 'Nixe'	SLim
wallichiana **new**	IDee

tayberry see *Rubus* Tayberry Group

Tecoma (*Bignoniaceae*)

capensis ♀H1	CHII CRHN EBee SVen
cochabambensis RCB RA L-8	WCot
ricasoliana	see *Podranea ricasoliana*
stans	EUJe

Tecomanthe (*Bignoniaceae*)

speciosa	ECou

Tecomaria see *Tecoma*

Tecophilaea (*Tecophilaeaceae*)

cyanocrocus ♀H2	ECho EPot GKev LLHF LRHS NMin
- 'Leichtlinii' ♀H2	CAvo ECho EPot GKev LLHF LRHS SDeJ
- 'Purpurea'	see *T. cyanocrocus* 'Violacea'
- Storm Cloud Group	ECho EPot GKev LLHF
§ - 'Violacea'	CAvo ECho EPot GKev LLHF LRHS
violiflora	ECho GKev

Telanthophora (*Asteraceae*)

§ ***grandifolia***	CHEx

Telekia (*Asteraceae*)

§ ***speciosa***	CCon CMac CSam CSpe EBee ELan EPPr EPfP GAbr GLog LRHS MBel MMuc MRav NBro NChi NLar SDix SLPl SPlb WBrk WCFE WHer WHoo WMoo WWEG

Telesonix see *Boykinia*

Teline see *Genista*

Tellima (*Saxifragaceae*)

grandiflora	CBcs CTri EHon ELan EPfP GAbr GCra GKev GMaP LAst LHop LRHS MBel MCot MMuc MWhi NEgg NHol NOrc NPri SEND SMrm SPer SWvt WBrk WCot WHar WMoo XLum
- 'Bob's Choice'	WCot
- 'Delphine' (v)	EBee EPPr WCot XLum
- 'Forest Frost'	CBct CFis CMac EBee EHoe ELan EPPr EShb LHop LRHS MBNS MPnt NBre NDov NLar NOrc SWvt WCot WGwG WHoo WMoo WOut WWEG
- Odorata Group	CBre MRav WCot WMoo
- 'Purpurea'	see *T. grandiflora* Rubra Group
- 'Purpurteppich'	EBee EPPr LHop LRHS MPnt MRav NDov WCot WMnd WMoo WPtf WWEG
§ - Rubra Group	CBre CBro CMac CPrp CTri EBee EHoe ELan EPfP LBMP LRHS MCot MLHP MRav MWat NEgg NLar NPer NSti SPer SPlb SRms SWvt WCAu WCot WHoo WMnd WMoo WWEG
- 'Silver Select'	EPPr

Telopea (*Proteaceae*)

'Emperor's Torch' **new**	MPkF
oreades	GGal SPlb
speciosissima	CCCN SPlb
truncata	CCCN GGal SPlb WCru

Templetonia (*Papilionaceae*)

retusa	ECou

Temu see *Blepharocalyx*

Tetracentron (*Trochodendraceae*)

sinense	CBcs EPfP IArd NLar

Tetradenia (*Lamiaceae*)

riparia	EOHP

Tetradium (*Rutaceae*)

austrosinense NJM 09.215	WPGP
§ ***daniellii***	CBcs CCVT CMCN EBee EPfP IArd IDee LEdu LRHS SSpi WHar WPGP
* - ***henryi***	NLar
§ - Hupehense Group	CMCN CTho GBin MBri MSnd NLar SEND WPGP
glabrifolium B&SWJ 6882	WCru
- CWJ 12364	WCru
ruticarpum	LEdu WPGP
- B&SWJ 3541	WCru

Tetragonia (*Aizoaceae*)

tetragonoides	CArn

Tetragonolobus see *Lotus*

Tetraneuris (*Asteraceae*)

§	***grandiflora***	SPlb WIce
	scaposa	EPot

Tetrapanax (*Araliaceae*)

§	***papyrifer*** ♀$^{H2-3}$	CBrP CDTJ CHEx CHGN ELan ESwi MBri SAPC SBig SBst SVen XBlo
	- B&SWJ 7135	EUJe WCru
	- 'Di-Sue-Shan'	WCru
	- 'Empress'	WCru
	- 'Rex'	CAbb CDTJ CExl CHEx CHid CSpe CTsd CWGN EAmu EExo EGri EPfP ESwi EUJe LRHS MAvo MSCN NLar SDix SKHP SMad SPad SPoG WCot WCru WGrn WHer WPGP
	- 'Steroidal Giant'	CDTJ SBig SKHP

Tetrapathaea see *Passiflora*

Tetrastigma (*Vitaceae*)

	obtectum	CCCN EBee ECre ESwi EWes SEND WCFE
	voinierianum ♀^{H1}	WCot

Tetratheca (*Elaeocarpaceae*)

	'Bicentennial Belle'	LBuc LRHS
	ciliata var. ***alba***	MOWG
	thymifolia pink-flowered	MOWG

Teucridium (*Lamiaceae*)

	parvifolium	ECou MPie

Teucrium (*Lamiaceae*)

*	***ackermannii***	CMea ECho SBch SIgm WAbe WHoo XSen
	arduinoi	XSen
	aroanium	ECho EPot MWat SIgm XSen
	asiaticum	XSen
	botrys	MHer
	canadense	XSen
	chamaedrys misapplied	see *T.* × *lucidrys*
	chamaedrys L.	CBar CPom CPrp CWib ELon EWTr GMaP GPoy LAst LRHS LSRN MCot MHoo MNHC MSwo NWad SEND SLim SPlb SRms SVen SWvt WBrk WHfH WJek WWEG XSen
	- 'Nanum'	ECho
	divaricatum	XSen
	dunense	XSen
	flavum	CArn EDAr EPPr NBre WJek XSen
	fruticans	Widely available
	- 'Azureum' ♀^{H3}	CBcs CHel COIW CTsd CWSG EBee ELan EPfP LAst LHop LRHS LSRN MGos MRav NSoo SEND SMad SPer SPoG SWvt WCFE WKif XSen
	- 'Compactum'	CDoC EBee ELan EWTr LAst LRHS LSRN MGos SLim SLon SPer SPoG SWvt WCFE WPGP WPnn
	- 'Drysdale'	CDoC CSBt EBee ELan LRHS SLim SWvt
	gnaphalodes	XSen
	hircanicum	CAby CArn CSam CSev ECtt ELan EPfP GAbr IFro LLWP LRHS LSRN MMuc MNrw MWhi NBir NLar SEND SMrm SPhx SRkn WCFE WCot WJek WMoo WPtf WWFP XSen
	- 'Paradise Delight'	ECtt IKil NLar NPnk WBor
	- 'Purple Tails'	COIW CPrp CSpe CTsd CWib EPfP GQue LSou MCot MNHC NBir SMad SPad WWEG
§	× ***lucidrys***	CArn CMea CSev ECrN ELan EPfP LRHS MGos MHer MMuc MNHC MPie MRav SPer SPoG SRms SWvt WCFE WHar WHoo WJek WPnn XSen
	lucidum	GCal SLon
	marum	CArn CMea CTri LEdu SRms WJek XSen
	massiliense misapplied	see *T.* × *lucidrys*
	massiliense L.	XSen
	montanum	WJek XSen
	musimonum	EPot SIgm
	orientale	EBee XSen
	polium	MWat WJek WThu XSen
	- subsp. ***aureum***	XSen
	pseudochamaepitys	XSen
	pyrenaicum	CMea CPBP CPom EPot EWes SBch SIgm XSen
	- subsp. ***guarense***	XSen
	scordium	CNat
	scorodonia	CArn CHab GPoy MCot MHer MNHC NLar NMir WHer WJek XSen
	- 'Binsted Gold'	EBee LDai MMoz NSti
	- 'Crispum'	LEdu LRHS MHer MMuc NBro NLar SBch SBod SPer SRms WGrn WGwG WJek WKif WMnd WMoo
	- 'Crispum Marginatum' (v)	CFis EBee ECGP EHoe EPPr EPfP LEdu LSou MNrw MRav WWEG
	- 'Spring Morn'	EBee
	- 'Winterdown' (v)	EBee SBch
	subspinosum	ECho LLHF MWat SVen WHoo WThu
§	***viscidum*** 'Lemon and Lime' (v)	EBee LSou
	webbianum	ECho XSen

Thalia (*Marantaceae*)

	dealbata	CBAq CHEx EAmu EUJe EWay LLWG MSKA NLar SBig SDix SLon WMAq XLum

Thalictrum (*Ranunculaceae*)

	CC 4576	CExl
	Cox 6118 **new**	ITim
	from Afghanistan	see *T. isopyroides*
	actaeifolium	CLAP CWib
	- B&SWJ 4664	WCru
	- B&SWJ 6310	WCru
	- var. ***brevistylum*** B&SWJ 8819	CDes WCru
	- - 'Twinkling Star'	ECtt
	- 'Perfume Star'	CPar ECtt GBin
	adiantifolium	see *T. minus* 'Adiantifolium'
	alpinum	EDAr EPPr
	angustifolium	see *T. lucidum*
	'Anne'[PBR]	CSpe EBee ECtt IPot NLar
	aquilegiifolium	Widely available
	- SDR 5463 **new**	GKev
	- 'Album'	CMea CSpe EBee ELan EPfP GBin GCra IPot LAst LHop LRHS MMuc MNFA NBid SEND SKHP SPhx SWvt WBor WMnd WPtf WSHC WWEG
*	- 'Hybridum'	WMoo
	- var. ***intermedium*** B&SWJ 10965	WCru
	- 'Purpureum'	CPom CSev LRHS NLar WHoo

	- 'Roseum'	ITim
	- var. ***sibiricum***	IMou
	- - B&SWJ 11007	WCru
	- 'Small Thundercloud'	GCal
	- 'Thundercloud' ♀H4	Widely available
	baicalense	CPom
	'Black Stockings'	CExl CKno CMac ECtt ELan EShb GBin IPot LRHS LSou MBel NCGa NDov NLar NPnk NSti SKHP SPoG SRkn WHil WWlt
	'Blizzard' **new**	NWad
	calabricum	NLar
	chelidonii	GMaP LRHS
	- HWJK 2216	WCru
	clavatum	CLAP CPom WPGP
	coreanum	see *T. ichangense*
	cultratum	CDes EBee WPGP
	dasycarpum	NBre NLar WCot WPnP
§	***delavayi*** ♀H4	Widely available
	- BWJ 7903	WCru
	- var. ***acuminatum*** BWJ 7535	WCru
	- - BWJ 7971	WCru
	- 'Album'	Widely available
	- 'Ankum'	EBee NLar
	- var. ***decorum***	CElw CLAP CPom CWCL EPPr MNFA NCGa NPnk WCot WCru WPGP WSHC
	- - BWJ 7770	WCru
	aff. var. ***decorum***	CExl
	- 'Gold Laced'	NLar WCot
	- 'Hewitt's Double' (d) ♀H4	Widely available
	- 'Hinkley'	IPot NLar
	- var. ***mucronatum***	WCru
	- - DJHC 473	WCru
	- purple-stemmed BWJ 7748	WCru
	- 'White Cloud' **new**	GBin WCAu
	diffusiflorum	IMou WCru WSHC
	dipterocarpum misapplied	see *T. delavayi*
	dipterocarpum Franch.	CMac LRHS WMnd XLum
	'Elin'	Widely available
	fendleri	GBin
	- var. ***polycarpum***	WOut
	filamentosum	EPPr IMou
	- B&SWJ 777	WCru
	- B&SWJ 4145	WCru
	- var. ***yakusimense*** B&SWJ 6094	WCru
	aff. ***finetii*** DJHC 473	CLAP
	flavum	CHab CMac EHon ELan LPio LRHS MSCN NBro NMir SMrm SPhx SWat WShi WTou WWEG
	- 'Chollerton'	see *T. isopyroides*
§	- subsp. ***glaucum*** ♀H4	Widely available
	- - dwarf	WPGP
	- - 'True Blue'	NDov SGbt
	- 'Illuminator'	CElw CTri EPfP IBoy LRHS MArl MRav NLar SDix SMad SMrm SPoG WCot
	flexuosum	see *T. minus* subsp. *minus*
	foetidum	NBre
	grandidentatum	WCot
	honanense	SKHP
	- BWJ 7962	WCru
	- 'Marble Leaf'	SKHP
§	***ichangense***	CPom CSpe IPot LBMP LRHS MBel MPie MSCN MTis NMyG NWad WCot WSHC
	- B&SWJ 8203	WCru
	- Evening Star strain (v)	CSpe ECtt MHol WCot
	- var. ***minus*** 'Chinese Chintz'	WCru
	- 'Purple Marble'	CWGN EBee LEdu NCGa SHar WCot
§	***isopyroides***	CCon CPom EBee GCal GKev LAst MMuc MNFA MRav NLar NPnk SMrm WCot
	javanicum	LEdu
	- B&SWJ 9506	WCru
	- var. ***puberulum*** B&SWJ 6770	WCru
	johnstonii B&SWJ 9127	WCru
	kiusianum	CDes EBee ECho EHoe ELan EWes GCra GMaP ITim LBMP LRHS MBel MHol MMuc MPie NBir NEgg NLar NPnk NSla SKHP SRot SWvt WAbe WCot WWEG XEll
	- Kew form	WSHC
	koreanum	see *T. ichangense*
§	***lucidum***	CDes CElw CExl EBee ECtt ELan EShb GBin GCal LRHS MHol MMuc MPie MTis NBre NLar NSti SKHP SPhx WCot
	minus	CArn GBin LEdu LRHS MBel MMuc NBre SEND
§	- 'Adiantifolium'	GBin IPot MBel MRav NBre NGdn NLar SHar SRms XLum
	- var. ***hypoleucum*** B&SWJ 8634	WCru
	- subsp. ***kemense***	EBee
§	- subsp. ***minus***	NBre
	- var. ***sipellatum*** B&SWJ 5051	WCru
	morisonii	LRHS NBid
	omeiense	CPom
	- BWJ 8049	WCru
	- DJHC 762	CDes
	orientale	EWes
	osmundifolium	WCru
	petaloideum	EPPr GCal NLar
	platycarpum B&SWJ 2261	WCru
	polygamum	see *T. pubescens* Pursh
	przewalskii	WCru
§	***pubescens*** Pursh	EBee ECtt GBin GMaP LRHS NDov WCot
	punctatum B&SWJ 1272	WCru
	ramosum BWJ 8126	WCru
	reniforme	CCon CSpe IGor WCot
	- B&SWJ 2610	WCru
	- GWJ 9311	WCru
	- HWJK 2403	WCru
	rochebrunianum	Widely available
	rubescens B&SWJ 10006	WCru
*	***rugosum***	LRHS
	sachalinense	CCon WOut WPGP
	- RBS 0279	EBee EPPr NLar
	shensiense	CExl
	simplex var. ***brevipes*** B&SWJ 4794	WCru
	speciosissimum	see *T. flavum* subsp. *glaucum*
*	***sphaerostachyum***	CElw EBee ECtt MNrw MWhi SMrm WHal WHil
	'Splendide'	CExl CSpe ECGP ECtt ELan ELon EPfP GBin IPot MBel MBri MHol MNrw MTis NCGa NDov NLar STPC WCot WHil
	'Splendide White' **new**	CSpe IPot STPC

squarrosum LRHS WPGP
tenuisubulatum BWJ 7929 WCru
tuberosum CElw CRDP CSpe LLHF SHar WCot
tubiferum B&SWJ 10999 WCru
'Tukker Princess' ECtt IKil NLar WCot
uchiyamae CDes EBee GBin LRHS WPGP
yunnanense WCru

Thamnocalamus (*Poaceae*)

aristatus EPfP
crassinodus SBig
- 'Gosainkund' CEnt ERod MMoz MWht
- 'Kew Beauty' CAbb CDTJ CDoC CEnt EPfP ERod MBrN MMoz MWht SBig WJun WPGP
- 'Lang Tang' CEnt ERod MMoz MWht WJun WPGP
- 'Merlyn' CDoC CEnt EPfP ERod MMoz MWht WJun WPGP

falconeri see *Himalayacalamus falconeri*
funghomii see *Schizostachyum funghomii*
khasianus see *Drepanostachyum khasianum*
maling see *Yushania maling*
spathaceus misapplied see *Fargesia murielae*
§ ***spathiflorus*** CEnt WJun
- subsp. ***nepalensis*** ERod MMuc MWht SBig WPGP

§ ***tessellatus*** ERod MMuc MWht SEND WJun

Thamnochortus (*Restionaceae*)

insignis SPlb
lucens SPlb
rigidus CCCN

Thapsia (*Apiaceae*)

decipiens see *Melanoselinum decipiens*
villosa CArn

Thea see *Camellia*

Thelypteris (*Thelypteridaceae*)

kunthii ISha
limbosperma see *Oreopteris limbosperma*
noveboracensis see *Parathelypteris novae-boracensis*
ovata var. ***lindheimeri*** ISha
palustris CKel EBee MMoz NLar SRms WFib WPnP WShi XLum
phegopteris see *Phegopteris connectilis*

Themeda (*Poaceae*)

triandra SMad

Thermopsis (*Papilionaceae*)

caroliniana see *T. villosa*
chinensis EBee SBea WHil
fabacea see *T. lupinoides*
lanceolata CMea CTri EBee EPfP EWTr LRHS NSti SHar SMrm WHrl WKif
§ ***lupinoides*** LRHS MHer
mollis CExl NBid
montana see *T. rhombifolia* var. *montana*
§ ***rhombifolia*** var. ***montana*** CWCL EBee ELan ELon EPfP GAbr GCra GMaP LHop LRHS MSpe NBir NCGa NLar NOrc NPol NSti NWad SPer SPoG WBor WWEG
§ ***villosa*** CAbP CWCL ELon LRHS MRav NDov NGdn NLar WCot WHoo WWEG WWFP

Therorhodion see *Rhododendron*

Thladiantha (*Cucurbitaceae*)

dubia EBee SDix WCot

Thlaspi (*Brassicaceae*)

sp. NGdn
biebersteinii see *Pachyphragma macrophyllum*
zaffranii new GKev

Thryptomene (*Myrtaceae*)

baeckeacea CCCN
saxicola ECou

Thuja ✿ (*Cupressaceae*)

'Extra Gold' see *T. plicata* 'Irish Gold'
§ ***koraiensis*** IDee
occidentalis NWea SEND
- 'Amber Glow' CDoC CKen CSBt LRHS MAsh NHol NLar NWad SCoo SLim SPoG WBor
- Aurea Group MJak
- 'Aureospicata' EHul
- 'Bateman Broom' CKen
- 'Beaufort' (v) CKen EHul
- 'Brabant' CDul MGos MJak NLar SCoo SLim WMou
- 'Brobecks Tower' CDoC CKen LRHS NLar SLim
- 'Caespitosa' CKen WGor
- 'Cristata Aurea' CKen
- 'Danica' ♀H4 CMac EHul GKin IBoy MAsh MBri MGos MJak MMuc NWea SCoo SLim SRms WBor WCFE
- 'Degroot's Spire' CKen LRHS NLar SLim
- 'Douglasii Aurea' (v) CKen
- Emerald see *T. occidentalis* 'Smaragd'
- 'Ericoides' CDoC EHul SRms
- 'Europa Gold' CDoC EHul NLar SGol
- 'Filiformis' CKen
- 'Globosa' ELan

I - 'Globosa Variegata' (v) CKen
- 'Gold Drop' CKen
- 'Golden Globe' CDoC EHul IBoy LRHS MGos MJak SCoo SLim
- 'Golden Minaret' EHul
- 'Golden Tuffet' CDoC CKen EHul ELan GKin LBee LRHS MBri MPkF SCoo SLim SPer WGor
- 'Hetz Midget' CKen EHul GKin IBoy LAst LRHS NLar NWad SCoo SLim SPlb
- 'Holmstrup' ♀H4 CDoC CMac CWib EHul MAsh MGos MJak SCoo SGol SLim SPoG SRms
- 'Holmstrup's Yellow' EHul LRHS
- 'Hoveyi' CTri EHul
- 'Linesville' CKen
- 'Little Champion' EHul IBoy NLar
- 'Little Gem' EHul NLar SRms
- 'Lutea Nana' ♀H4 EHul WCFE
- 'Malonyana' NLar
- 'Malonyana Holub' SLim
- 'Marrisen's Sulphur' CDoC EHul
- 'Meineke's Zwerg' (v) CKen
- 'Miky' CKen
- 'Mr Bowling Ball' CDoC LRHS NLar SLim SPoG
- 'Ohlendorffii' CDoC CKen EHul

I - 'Pygmaea' CKen
- 'Pyramidalis Compacta' EHul WGor
- 'Recurva Nana' EHul NWad
- 'Rheingold' ♀H4 Widely available

§	– 'Smaragd' 🏆H4	CCVT CDoC CDul CSBt CWib EHul ELan EPfP IBoy LAst LBuc LRHS MAsh MGos MJak NLar NWea SCoo SGol SLim SPer SPoG SWvt WCFE WMou
*	– 'Smaragd Variegated' (v)	CKen
	– 'Smokey'	CKen
	– 'Southport'	CKen
	– 'Spaethii'	EHul
	– 'Spiralis'	EHul NLar WCFE
§	– 'Stolwijk' (v)	EHul
	– 'Sunkist'	CKen CMac CWib EHul LAst MAsh MBri MGos MJak NEgg SCoo SGol SLim
	– 'Teddy'	CDoC EHul EPfP LBee LRHS MAsh MBri MGos NHol NWad SCoo SPoG WGor
	– 'Tiny Tim'	CDoC CMac CWib EHul IBoy MGos SGol WGor
	– 'Trompenburg'	CDoC EHul NLar
	– 'Wansdyke Silver' (v)	CMac EHul SCoo
	– 'Wareana'	CMac
	– 'Wareana Aurea'	see *T. occidentalis* 'Wareana Lutescens'
§	– 'Wareana Lutescens'	CWib EHul
	– 'Waterfield'	NWad
	– 'Yellow Ribbon'	CKen CSBt EHul LRHS MGos MJak NLar SCoo SGol WBor
	orientalis	see *Platycladus orientalis*
	– 'Lemon 'n' Lime' (v)	LRHS
	– 'Miller's Gold'	see *Platycladus orientalis* 'Aurea Nana'
	plicata	CCVT CDoy CDul CMac CTho EHul ELan EPfP NWea SPer WHar WMou
	– 'Atrovirens' 🏆H4	CDul CTri LBee LBuc MAsh MBri MGos MJak MMuc SCoo SEND SEWo SGol SRms SWvt WHar WMou
	– 'Aurea' 🏆H4	EHul LRHS MAsh SLim SPoG SRms
	– 'Brooks Gold'	CKen
	– 'Can-can' (v)	ELan MAsh NLar SCoo
I	– 'Cole's Variety'	CDul CWib
	– 'Collyer's Gold'	CDul EHul SRms
	– 'Copper Kettle'	CKen EHul GKin LRHS SCoo SLim WGor
	– 'Cuprea'	CKen EHul
	– 'Doone Valley'	CKen EHul
	'Emerald'[PBR]	EUJe
	– 'Excelsa'	CDul
	– 'Fastigiata' 🏆H4	CDul
	– 'Gelderland'	EHul ELan LRHS NEgg NLar SCoo
	– Goldy = '4ever'[PBR]	CDoC MBri SPoG
	– 'Gracilis Aurea'	EHul
	– 'Hillieri'	CDoC CDul
§	– 'Irish Gold' (v) 🏆H4	CDul CMac LRHS SMad
	– 'Martin'	CJun SWvt
	– 'Rogersii'	CDoC CKen CMac EHul MAsh NHol SCoo SPoG SRms
	– 'Semperaurescens' (v)	CMac
	– 'Stolwijk's Gold'	see *T. occidentalis* 'Stolwijk'
	– 'Stoneham Gold' 🏆H4	CDoC CMac EHul GKin LRHS MAsh MGos MMuc NPCo SPer SRms
	– 'Sunshine'	CKen
	– Verigold = 'Courtapli'	CCVT MMuc SEND
	– 'Whipcord'	CBcs CKen EHul ELan EPfP LRHS MPkF NHol NLar SCoo SLim SPer SPoG WBor
*	– 'Windsor Gold'	EHul
	– 'Winter Pink' (v)	CKen
	– 'Zebrina' (v)	CBcs CDoC CDul CMac CTri CWib EHul ELan EPfP LRHS MGos MJak MMuc NEgg NLar NPri NWea SCoo SEND SLim SMad SPer SPoG SWvt WHar
	plicata* × *standishii	CDul

Thujopsis (*Cupressaceae*)

	dolabrata 🏆H4	CBcs CDul EHul GKin MJak MMuc NEgg NLar NWea SWvt
	– 'Aurea' (v)	CDoC CKen EHul LRHS NLar SCoo SLim
	– var. ***hondae*** new	IArd
	– 'Laetevirens'	see *T. dolabrata* 'Nana'
	– 'Melbourne Gold'	NLar
§	– 'Nana'	CDoC CKen CMac EHul LRHS MGos NLar SCoo SLim SRms
	– 'Variegata' (v)	CMac EHul GKin LRHS NLar SCoo SLim
	koraiensis (Nakai) hort.	see *Thuja koraiensis*

Thunbergia (*Acanthaceae*)

	alata	EPfP SPoG
	– 'African Sunset'	CSpe
	– 'Lemon Queen'	CHll SWvt
	– 'Orange Beauty'	LSou SWvt WBor
*	***arborea***	CCCN
	battiscombei	CCCN EShb MOWG
	coccinea	CCCN
	erecta	CCCN MOWG
	fragrans GWJ 9441	WCru
	grandiflora 🏆H1	CCCN CHll MOWG
	– 'Alba'	CCCN CHll
	gregorii 🏆H1+3	CCCN CHll EShb MOWG
	– 'Mango'	SPoG
	laurifolia B&SWJ 7166	WCru
	'Moonglow'	CCCN
	mysorensis 🏆H1	SVen
	natalensis	CCCN EShb
	'Orange Wonder'	CCCN

Thymbra (*Lamiaceae*)

	spicata	CArn

thyme, caraway see *Thymus herba-barona*

thyme, garden see *Thymus vulgaris*

thyme, lemon see *Thymus citriodorus*

thyme, wild see *Thymus serpyllum*

Thymus ✿ (*Lamiaceae*)

	from Albania	CArn
	from Turkey	EWes LEdu SHDw
	'A Touch of Frost'	SHDw
	'Anderson's Gold'	see *T. pulegioides* 'Bertram Anderson'
	'Aureus' ambig.	MJak
	azoricus	see *T. caespititius*
	'Bressingham'	CArn CMea CPrp CTri ECtt EDAr ELau GMaP LEdu LLWP LRHS MHer MHoo MMuc MNHC NYoL SEND SPlb SRms WIce WJek WWEG
	'Caborn Fragrant Cloud'	LLWP
	'Caborn Grey Lady'	LLWP
	'Caborn Lilac Gem'	LLWP SHDw

	'Caborn Pink Beauty'	LLWP
	'Caborn Pink Carpet'	LLWP
	'Caborn Rosanne'	LLWP
	'Caborn Royale' new	LLWP
	'Caborn Wine and Roses'	LLWP SRms
§	***caespititius***	CArn ELau GMaP GPoy MHer NRya NYoL SPlb SRot WHer WJek WWEG
	caespitosus	CTri LEdu
	camphoratus	CArn ELau ESwi EWes MHer MHoo SPhx WWEG
	capitatus	CArn
§	***carnosus*** Boiss.	MHer NYoL XSen
	'Carol Ann' (v)	ELau EWes MNHC NYoL SRms WWEG
	ciliatus	XSen
	cilicicus misapplied	see *T. caespititius*
	cilicicus ambig.	MNHC SRms WWEG
	cilicicus Boiss. & Bail.	WAbe
	citriodorus misapplied	see *T.* 'Culinary Lemon'
	citriodorus ambig.	CTsd SRms WCFE XLum
	citriodorus (Pers.) Schreb.	LEdu NYoL
	- 'Archer's Gold'	see *T. pulegioides* 'Archer's Gold'
	- 'Aureus'	see *T. pulegioides* 'Aureus'
	- 'Bertram Anderson'	see *T. pulegioides* 'Bertram Anderson'
	- 'Silver Posie'	see *T.* 'Silver Posie'
	'Coccineus'	see *T.* Coccineus Group
§	Coccineus Group ♀H4	CArn CPrp CTri ECtt ELan ELau GMaP LBMP LLWP LRHS MBri MHer MHoo MMuc MNHC NPri NRya NSla NWad NYoL SEND SPer SPoG SRms SRot WAbe WHoo WIce WJek
	- 'Atropurpureus' Schleipfer	see *T.* 'Purple Beauty'
§	- 'Purple Beauty'	EPot MHer SHDw WWEG
§	- 'Red Elf'	GAbr MHer NYoL WWEG
	'Coccineus Major'	CMea EDAr LRHS MHer MNHC WJek
	comosus misapplied	NYoL SHDw WJek
	'Creeping Lemon' misapplied	see *T. pulegioides* 'Kurt'
§	'Culinary Lemon'	CArn CHby EDAr ELau GPoy LLWP MBrN MHer MNHC NPri NYoL WJek XLum XSen
	'Dark Eyes'	SHDw
	'Dartmoor'	LLWP SHDw WJek WWEG
	'Desboro'	see *T. serpyllum* 'Desborough'
	doerfleri	NYoL XSen
	'Doone Valley' (v)	Widely available
	drucei	see *T. polytrichus* subsp. *britannicus*
	'E.B. Anderson'	see *T. pulegioides* 'Bertram Anderson'
	'Eastgrove Pink'	SHDw
	'Emma's Pink'	LLWP
	erectus	see *T. carnosus*
	'Fragrantissimus'	CArn CMea ELau GPoy LLWP MHer MHoo MNHC MWat NPri SIde SPlb WJek WOut XSen
	'Golden King' (v)	EDAr ELan LHop LSRN MAsh MBri MHer SRms WWEG
	'Golden Lemon' misapplied	see *T. pulegioides* 'Aureus'
	'Golden Lemon' (v)	WJek
	'Golden Queen' (v)	EDAr MHol MWat NPri NYoL SRms
	'Gratian'	SHDw
§	'Hartington Silver' (v)	CSam ECho ECtt EPot EWes GKev LAst LBMP LEdu LHop LRHS MHer MHoo NRya NYoL SPlb SPoG SRms WHoo WJek WWEG
	herba-barona	CArn CMea CPrp CTri EDAr ELau GPoy LEdu LLWP MHer MHoo MMuc MNHC MWat NYoL SIde SRms WJek WWEG
	- ***citrata***	see *T. herba-barona* 'Lemon-scented'
§	- 'Lemon-scented'	GPoy LEdu LLWP MHer NYoL SHDw SRms WJek
	'Highdown'	ECtt SHDw
	'Highdown Adur'	SHDw
	'Highdown Lemon'	SHDw
	'Highdown Red'	SHDw
	'Highdown Stretham'	SHDw
	'Highland Cream'	see *T.* 'Hartington Silver'
	hyemalis	GPoy
§	'Iden'	WJek WWEG
	'Jekka'	SRms WJek
	'Kurt'	see *T. pulegioides* 'Kurt'
	'Lavender Sea'	EWes LLWP
	'Lemon Caraway'	see *T. herba-barona* 'Lemon-scented'
	'Lemon Curd'	CPrp ELau LLWP MHoo MNHC NHol NYoL SHDw SPlb SPoG SRms WJek WWEG
	'Lemon Sorbet'	SHDw
*	'Lemon Variegated' (v)	EDAr ELau EPfP MHoo MNHC NYoL SPer SPoG WWEG
	leucotrichus	XSen
	'Lilac Time'	ECtt EWes LLWP MHer SHDw SPlb SRms WJek WWEG
	'Lime'	LEdu
	'Lindisfarne'	LLWP
	linearis	XSen
	longicaulis	CArn ELau LLWP MHer SRms
	'Magic Carpet'	SPhx
	'Marjorie'	LLWP
	marschallianus	see *T. pannonicus*
§	'Massa'	LLWP SHDw
	mastichina	CArn MHoo XSen
	- 'Didi'	MHer
	micans	see *T. caespititius*
	minus	see *Calamintha nepeta*
	'Mountain Select'	LLWP SHDw
	neiceffii	CMea ELau LLWP SBch WWEG XSen
§	'Nettleton Pink Carpet'	LLWP
	'Orange'	LEdu SRms
§	Orange Spice = 'Tm95'	LLWP SHDw XSen
	pallasianus	ELau SHDw
§	***pannonicus***	MHer NYoL
	'Peter Davis'	LHop LRHS LSRN MHer MHoo NBir NYoL SIde SPoG SRms WAbe WIce XSen
§	'Pinewood'	LEdu MHer WJek XSen
	'Pink Ripple'	CMea ECtt ELau EPot EWes LEdu LLWP MHer MNHC SBch SHDw SIgm SRms WHal WHoo WJek WWEG
	polytrichus misapplied	see *T. praecox*
§	***polytrichus*** A. Kern. ex Borbás subsp. ***britannicus***	CArn CHab CTri EPot GJos GMaP GPoy LEdu MBNS MBri MHer MLHP MMuc MNHC NBir NYoL SHDw SPlb SRms WHoo WJek WWEG
	- - 'Minor'	see *T.* 'Nettleton Pink Carpet'
§	- - 'Thomas's White' ♀H4	CTri NYoL
	'Porlock'	CMea CPrp CTri ELau EPfP GPoy MHer NYoL SRms WAbe WHoo WJek WWEG

§	***praecox***	GJos MHer NMir
	– 'Albiflorus'	EPot
	– subsp. ***arcticus***	see *T. polytrichus* subsp. *britannicus*
	– – 'Albus'	see *T. polytrichus* subsp. *britannicus* 'Thomas's White'
	pulegioides	CArn CHby ELau GPoy LLWP MBri MHer MNHC NYoL SBch SHDw SIde SRms WJek
§	– 'Archer's Gold'	CBar CTri ECtt EDAr EHoe ELau EPfP EPot GAbr GJos GKev LEdu LHop LLWP LPot LRHS LSRN MAsh MBri MHer MHoo MRav NBir NHol NWad NYoL SRms WJek WWEG
§	– 'Aureus' ℽH4	GMaP LLWP LRHS MAsh MBri MHer SPer SPlb SRms WHoo WJek
§	– 'Bertram Anderson' ℽH4	CMea ECtt ELau EPfP GMaP LAst LLWP MAsh MHer MHoo NBir NPri NRya NYoL SPer SPoG SRms WAbe WHoo WJek WWEG
	– 'Foxley' (v)	EHoe ELau EPfP GAbr LLWP MHer MHoo MNHC NPri NYoL SHDw SIde SPlb SPoG SRms WHer WJek WWEG
§	– 'Kurt'	ELau LLWP MHer SHDw WJek WNew WWEG
	– 'Sir John Lawes'	MHer
	– 'Tabor'	MNHC NYoL SHDw SRms
	'Rainbow Falls' (v)	EPfP MHoo MNHC NYoL SHDw WWEG
	'Rasta' (v)	LLWP MHer
§	'Red Glow'	LLWP
	'Redstart'	ECtt ELau EPot LEdu LLWP MHer NYoL SBch SHDw SRms WJek WWEG
	richardii subsp. ***nitidus*** 'Compactus Albus'	see *T. vulgaris* 'Snow White'
	'Rosa Ceeping'	LLWP SHDw
	'Rosalicht'	see *T.* 'Rosedrift'
§	'Rosedrift'	SHDw
	rotundifolius misapplied	see *T. vulgaris* 'Elsbeth'
	'Ruby Glow'	ECtt ELau EWes MHer SHDw SIgm WWEG
	serpyllum ambig.	SVic XLum
	serpyllum L.	CArn GJos LLWP MBri MMuc SPlb SRms WJek WOut
	– var. ***albus***	CPrp ELau GMaP GPoy LAst LLWP LRHS MNHC SPer SRms WAbe WHoo WJek WWEG
	– 'Albus Variegatus'	see *T.* 'Hartington Silver'
	– 'Annie Hall'	CPrp EDAr ELau EPfP EPot LHop LLWP LRHS MHer MNHC SRms WJek
	– 'Atropurpureus'	see *T.* (Coccineus Group) 'Purple Beauty'
	– ***coccineus*** 'Minor' misapplied	see *T.* Coccineus Group
	– 'Conwy Rose'	CPBP WAbe
§	– 'Desborough'	MHer WWEG
	– 'East Lodge'	LLWP MNHC SRms
	– 'Elfin'	ECho EWes MBri SPlb WAbe WThu WWEG
	– 'Goldstream' (v)	CPrp ELau EPfP LEdu LHop LLWP LRHS MBri MHer NYoL SPlb SRms WJek
	– 'Iden'	see *T.* 'Iden'
	– 'Minimalist'	see *T. serpyllum* 'Minor'
	– 'Minimus'	see *T. serpyllum* 'Minor'
§	– 'Minor'	CArn CMea CPBP CTri ECtt ELau EPot LLWP LRHS MBri MHer MHoo MLHP MMuc MNHC NRya NSla NYoL SEND SHDw SPlb SRms SRot WAbe WHoo WJek WNew WWEG
	– 'Minus'	see *T. serpyllum* 'Minor'
	– 'Petite'	LLWP
	– 'Pink Chintz' ℽH4	CArn CMea ECtt EDAr ELau EPfP EPot GMaP GPoy LLWP LRHS MBri MHer MHoo MNHC NYoL SPer SPlb SPoG SRms WHoo WIce WJek WWEG
	– 'Posh Pinky'	LLWP
	– 'Purple Beauty'	see *T.* (Coccineus Group) 'Purple Beauty'
	– 'Red Carpet'	ECtt NWad NYoL
	– 'Red Elf'	see *T.* (Coccineus Group) 'Red Elf'
	– 'Red Glow'	see *T.* 'Red Glow'
	– 'Russetings'	CPrp CTsd ECtt ELau EPfP EPot MHer MHoo MNHC NYoL SIde SPoG SRms WJek WNew WWEG
	– 'September'	MHer
	– 'Snowdrift'	CArn CMea ECtt ELau EPfP EPot LLWP MHer MNHC MWat NWad SIde SPlb SRms WCFE WJek WWEG
	– 'Variegatus'	see *T.* 'Hartington Silver'
	– 'Vey'	CPBP EPot EWes GMaP LHop LLWP LRHS MHer SHDw SRms WJek WWEG
	sibthorpii	CArn
§	'Silver Posie'	Widely available
	'Silver Queen' (v) ℽH4	CBcs EDAr ELan EPfP GKev GMaP LAst LLWP MHer MHoo MNHC NHol NPri NYoL SPlb SRms WJek WNew WWEG
	'Snowdonia Isolde'	LLWP
	'Snowdonia Pryderi'	LLWP
	'Snowdonia Pwyll'	LLWP
	'Snowdonia Rhiannon'	LLWP
	'Snowdonia Rowena'	LLWP
	'Spicy Orange'	see *T* Orange Spice
	valesiacus	see *T.* 'Massa'
§	***vulgaris***	Widely available
	– 'Aranjuez'	LLWP
	– 'Château Queribus'	LLWP
*	– 'Compactus'	GPoy LEdu LLWP MHer MNHC MRav SRms WJek
	– 'Deutsche Auslese'	see *T. vulgaris*
	– 'Dorcas White'	MHer
§	– 'Elsbeth'	ELau LLWP MHer SHDw
	– French	see *T. vulgaris*
	– 'Golden Pins'	MHer
	– 'Lemon Queen'	ELau
	– 'Lucy'	LLWP MHer
	– 'Pinewood'	see *T.* 'Pinewood'
§	– 'Snow White'	ELau EWes SHDw WJek
	'Widecombe' (v)	LLWP SHDw
	zygis	SPhx

Tiarella (*Saxifragaceae*)

'Appalachian Trail'	CHVG ECtt GBin LSou MAsh MPnt NPnk NSoo NWad SHeu WCot WNPC
'Black Snowflake'	MPnt SHeu
'Black Velvet'	MBel MPnt SHeu
'Braveheart'	EPfP LHop MPnt SHeu WNPC WWEG
'Butter and Sugar'	MPnt
'Butterfly Wings'	MPnt
'Candy Striper'	MPnt SHeu

'Cascade Creeper'	ECtt LRHS LSou MPnt NPnk SHeu WNPC
collina	see *T. wherryi*
cordifolia ♀H4	Widely available
- 'Glossy'	CCon MPnt
- 'Milk Chocolate'	MMoz MPnt
- 'Oakleaf'	CCon MBel MPnt NBro SHeu
- 'Rosalie'	see × *Heucherella alba* 'Rosalie'
- 'Running Tapestry'	MPnt SHeu
- 'Slick Rock'	EPPr
'Crow Feather'PBR	LSou MPnt SHeu WNPC
'Cygnet'	CLAP COlW ECtt MPnt NPnk SHeu SRot
'Dunvegan'	MPnt
'Elizabeth Oliver'	EBee MPnt
'Freckles'	MRav
'Happy Trails'	MPnt NPnk SHeu WNPC
'Hidden Carpet'	CHid
'Inkblot'	ELan LRHS MPnt NBro SHeu WMoo
'Iron Butterfly'PBR (v)	CLAP CMac CWCL EBee ECtt EHoe EPfP GBin GMaP LHop LRHS LSRN MBel MNrw MPnt MRav NBro NPnk SGbt SMrm SPer SPoG SRot STes WPGP
'Iron Cross'	SPlb
'Jeepers Creepers'PBR	CHid ECtt MHol MPnt NCGa NPnk NWad SHeu WNPC
'Martha Oliver'	CLAP EBee MPnt SBch WPGP
'Mint Chocolate'	CLAP ECtt EHoe ELan EPfP GMaP LPot MBel MNrw MPnt MRav MWhi NBir NGdn NLar NPnk SHeu SPer SWvt WPGP
Morning Star = 'Tntia042'PBR	CHel CHid COlW CWCL ECtt EWll LRHS MBri MPnt NPnk SHeu SMrm SRkn SRot WHoo
'Mystic Mist'PBR (v)	CHid ECtt LSou MPnt NLar NPnk SHeu SPoG WNPC
'Neon Lights'PBR	CHid ECGP ELan EWes MAsh MPnt NBir NCGa NPnk NSoo NWad SHeu SPer SWvt WCot WNPC
§ 'Ninja'	CHid ECtt ELan EUJe GMaP LRHS MPnt MRav NBir NLar NSti SPer SWvt WCot
'Oregon Trail'	ECtt GBin MBel MPnt NPnk NSoo NWad SHeu WCot WNPC
'Pacific Crest'	ECtt MPnt SHeu WNPC
'Pink Bouquet'	CAbP CLAP CMac CSpe CWGN ECtt ELan GJos LRHS MBel MBri MNFA MPie MPnt NBro NDov NLar NPnk SBch SHeu WCot WMoo WPnP
'Pink Brushes'PBR	CLAP MPnt SHeu WPnP
'Pink Skyrocket'PBR	CAbP CLAP CWGN EBee ECtt ELan LLHF LLWG LRHS LSRN MBel MPnt NBir NGdn NHol NPnk NWad SHar SHeu SPer WCot
'Pinwheel'	LRHS MPnt MRav
'Pirate's Patch'PBR	LLHF MPnt SHeu WNPC
polyphylla	MPnt NLar SHeu WCru
- 'Baoxing Pink'	CFis CLAP LAst MPnt WCru
- 'Filigran'	EPfP MPnt NLar NWad SHeu WPtf
- 'Moorgrün'	GCal LRHS SHeu
- pink-flowered	CLAP
'Running Tiger'	MPnt
'Sea Foam'	MPnt NPnk SHeu
'Simsalabim'	MPnt
'Skeleton Key'	MPnt
'Skid's Variegated' (v)	ECtt LBMP LLWG LRHS MHol MNrw MPie MPnt NSti SHeu SWvt WCot WNPC
'Skyrocket'	ECtt MCot NLar
'Spanish Cross'	EBee MPnt SHeu
'Spring Symphony'PBR	CLAP CWCL EBee ECtt EShb GBin GBuc LRHS LSou MBel MBri MPnt MWat NCGa NLar NPer NPnk NWad SHil
Starburst = 'Tntia041'PBR	ECtt MPnt NPnk SHeu WNPC
'Sugar and Spice'PBR	LRHS MBrN MPnt NCGa NDov NHol NPnk NWad SHeu SMad WNPC
'Sunset Ridge'	ECtt MPnt SHeu WNPC
'Tiger Stripe'	EPfP MPnt MRav NBro NPnk SHeu
'Timbuktu'	ECtt MAsh MPnt SHeu WNPC
trifoliata	MPnt MRav
- var. ***unifoliata***	MPnt WWEG
'Viking Ship'	see × *Heucherella* 'Viking Ship'
§ ***wherryi*** ♀H4	CBcs CSpe CWCL EBee ELan ELon EPfP GMaP IBoy LAst LPot LRHS MPnt NBir NBro NOrc NPri NRya SBch SPer SPlb SRot SWvt WHar WPnP XLum
- 'Bronze Beauty'	CLAP GBuc IGor MPnt MRav SBch SHeu WPGP
- 'Green Velvet'	MPnt SHeu
- 'Heronswood Mist' (v)	CAbP CBct CCon ECtt ELan MHol MMoz MNrw MPnt SHeu SWvt WCot
- 'Montrose'	WPGP

Tibouchina (*Melastomataceae*)

grandifolia	CCCN
granulosa	MOWG
heteromalla	CCCN
'Jules'	MOWG
organensis	CCCN CHll MOWG SHeu SWvt WPGP
paratropica	CRHN
- RCB/Arg X-4	WCot
semidecandra hort.	see *T. urvilleana*
§ ***urvilleana*** ♀H1	CBcs CCCN CDoC CEnd CHEx CHel CRHN CSBt CTri CTsd EBak ELan EPfP EUJe MCot MMuc MOWG NCGa SPer SRkn WCot
- 'Compacta'	CCCN
- 'Edwardsii'	SMrm WCot
- 'Nana'	CDoC
- variegated (v)	CCCN EMil LSou SPer WCot

Tigridia ✿ (*Iridaceae*)

catarinensis	SDeJ
§ ***immaculata*** B&SWJ 10393	WCru
lutea	ECho
orthantha 'Red-Hot Tiger'	WCru
pavonia	CBro CExl ECho EWll SDeJ
- 'Alba'	ECho
- 'Alba Grandiflora'	WHil
- 'Alba Immaculata'	CSpe
- 'Aurea'	EBee ECho WHil
- 'Canariensis'	CTca ECho WHil
- lemon-flowered **new**	CSpe
- 'Lilacea'	ECho SDeJ WHil
- red-flowered **new**	ECho
- 'Speciosa'	CTca SDeJ WHil
- yellow-flowered **new**	ECho

Tilia ✿ (*Malvaceae*)

HRS 2808	WPGP
americana	CLnd CMCN
- 'Dentata'	CDul

- 'Nova'	CDoC
amurensis	CMCN
argentea	see *T. tomentosa*
begoniifolia	see *T. dasystyla*
chenmoui	CMCN EPfP MBlu WPGP
chinensis	CMCN EBee NPCo WPGP
- F 30558	WPGP
chingiana	CDul CMCN SLon
cordata ♀H4	CBcs CCVT CDul CHab CLnd CMac CSBt CTho CTri EBee ECrN ELan EPfP LBuc LPot MAsh MJak MMuc MSwo NLar NWea SCoo SEND SEWo SPer WHar WMou
§ - 'Böhlje'	CDul ECrN SLPl
- 'Dainty Leaf'	CDul
- 'Erecta'	see *T. cordata* 'Böhlje'
- 'Greenspire' ♀H4	CCVT CDoC CDul CLnd CWib ECrN EPfP IBoy MRav SEWo WMou
- 'Len Parvin'	EBee WPGP
- 'Roelvo'	CDul
- 'Swedish Upright'	CDul
- 'Winter Orange'	CDul CEnd EBee ECrN EPfP GQue LAst MBlu MBri NPCo SBir SCoo SEWo
§ ***dasystyla***	CMCN EBee
- subsp. ***caucasica***	CMCN WPGP
endochrysea	WPGP
× ***euchlora*** ♀H4	CBcs CCVT CDul CLnd CMCN EBee ECrN EPfP NWea SEWo SPer
§ × ***europaea***	CBcs CDul CLnd ELan EWTr MMuc NWea SEND
- 'Koningslinde'	CDul
- 'Pallida'	CDul CLnd MBlu NWea
- 'Wratislaviensis' ♀H4	CDul CLnd EBee EPfP MAsh MBlu NLar NWea
§ 'Harold Hillier'	MBlu
henryana	CBcs CDoC CDul CEnd CLnd CMCN CTho CWib EBee ELan EMil EPfP ERod IArd IDee LRHS MBlu MBri MMuc MREP NWea SBir SCoo WPGP
- 'Arnold Select'	WMou
§ ***heterophylla***	CMCN EBee ELan EPfP MBlu MBri WPGP
'Hillieri'	see *T.* 'Harold Hillier'
insularis misapplied	see *T. japonica* 'Ernest Wilson'
intonsa	CMCN
japonica	CDul CMCN WPGP
§ - 'Ernest Wilson'	CMCN MBlu
kiusiana	CDul CMCN EBee MBlu MBri WMou WPGP
mandshurica	CDul CMCN EBee WPGP
maximowicziana	WPGP
mexicana	WPGP
- CD&R 1318	WPGP
miqueliana	CMCN
'Moltkei'	CMCN EBee IArd WPGP
mongolica	CBcs CDul CMCN EBee EPfP MBlu MMuc SCoo WMou WPGP
monticola	see *T. heterophylla*
nobilis KR 226	WPGP
oliveri	CDul CMCN EBee MBlu NWea WMou WPGP
paucicostata	WPGP
'Petiolaris' ♀H4	CBcs CCVT CDoC CDul CEnd CLnd CMCN EBee ECrN ELan EPfP MBlu MSwo NWea SEND SPer WMou
platyphyllos	CCVT CDul CHab CLnd CMCN CSBt CTho CTri ECrN EPfP LAst LBuc MMuc NWea SCoo SEND SPer WMou
- 'Aurea'	CDul CTho ECrN MBlu
- 'Corallina'	see *T. platyphyllos* 'Rubra'
- 'Erecta'	see *T. platyphyllos* 'Fastigiata'
§ - 'Fastigiata'	CDul
- 'Laciniata'	CDul CMCN CTho MBlu
§ - 'Rubra' ♀H4	CCVT CDoC CDul CLnd CTho EPfP IBoy LBuc MGos NWea SEWo
- 'Tortuosa'	MBlu WMou
§ ***tomentosa***	CDul CLnd CMCN ELan MMuc NWea SCoo WMou
- 'Brabant' ♀H4	CDul ELan EPfP MBri
tuan	CMCN WPGP
× ***vulgaris***	see *T.* × *europaea*

Tilingia (*Apiaceae*)

ujanensis B&SWJ 11202	WCru

Tillaea see *Crassula*

Tillandsia (*Bromeliaceae*)

sp.	XBlo
aeranthos	SChr

Tinantia (*Commelinaceae*)

pringlei	EShb LEdu MNrw MPie SBrt SDys WPGP WSHC
- AIM 77	EBee WCot
- variegated (v)	WCot

Tinnea (*Lamiaceae*)

barbata **new**	GFai

Titanopsis (*Aizoaceae*)

calcarea ♀H1	CCCN EPfP

Tithonia (*Asteraceae*)

rotundifolia	CSpe
- 'Torch'	CSpe SMrm

Tofieldia (*Tofieldiaceae*)

coccinea	GCal WCru

Tolmiea (*Saxifragaceae*)

menziesii	CMac EWld MCot XLum
- 'Goldsplash'	see *T. menziesii* 'Taff's Gold'
- 'Maculata'	see *T. menziesii* 'Taff's Gold'
§ - 'Taff's Gold' (v) ♀H4	EHoe EShb GMaP NBld SPlb WHoo XLum
- 'Variegata'	see *T. menziesii* 'Taff's Gold'

Toona (*Meliaceae*)

§ ***sinensis***	CArn CBcs CDul CEnd CTho CWib EBee ELan EPfP LEdu MMuc SEND WPGP
- 'Flamingo' (v)	CBcs EBee EPfP ESwi EUJe GKin IVic LEdu LRHS MAsh MGos NLar SChF SHil SMad SPoG WCot

Tordylium (*Apiaceae*)

apulum **new**	WCot

Torenia (*Linderniaceae*)

'Lovely White' **new**	LAst
(Moon Series) Blue Moon = 'Dantmoon'	LAst

- Purple Moon = 'Dantopur'[PBR]	LAst LSou
- Rose Moon = 'Dantoromoon'	LAst
- Yellow Moon = 'Danmoon20'[PBR]	LAst
Summer Wave Series	CCCN SCoo

Torilis (*Apiaceae*)

japonica	CBre CHab

Townsendia (*Asteraceae*)

alpigena	GKev
§ - var. ***alpigena***	CPBP
condensata	WAbe
formosa	ECho
hookeri	CPBP
incana	WAbe
leptotes	CPBP
montana	see *T. alpigena* var. *alpigena*
nuttallii	CPBP
§ ***rothrockii***	GKev
spathulata	CPBP
wilcoxiana misapplied	see *T. rothrockii*

Toxicodendron (*Anacardiaceae*)

vernicifluum	see *Rhus verniciflua*

Trachelium (*Campanulaceae*)

§ ***asperuloides***	WAbe
caeruleum 'Black Knight'	CSpe
lanceolatum new	WCot

Trachelospermum ✿ (*Apocynaceae*)

from Nanjing, China	EShb
§ ***asiaticum*** ♀H2-3	Widely available
- B&SWJ 4814	WCru
- 'Golden Memories'	CExl CSPN CWGN EBee ELan ELon EPfP LRHS LSRN LSqu NLar SKHP SLon SPoG SSpi SSta SWvt WCot WPat
- 'Goshiki' (v)	EShb WPat
- var. ***intermedium***	WPGP
* - 'Kiejiu Chirimen'	SKHP
- 'Kulu Chirimen'	WCot
- 'Nagaba' (v)	SKHP
- 'Ōgon-nishiki' (v)	LRHS SKHP
- 'Pink Showers'	SKHP
- 'Shirofu Chirimen' (v)	SKHP
- 'Summer Sunset'	EPfP MPkF WCot
- 'Theta'	SKHP WCot WPGP WPat
'Chameleon'	SKHP
jasminoides ♀H3-4	Widely available
- B&SWJ 5117	WCru
- 'Big White Star'	EPfP
§ - 'Japonicum'	CRHN CSPN LRHS NPri SLon SPer SPoG WBor WSHC
- 'Major'	CMac CSPN EBee ELan MAsh SEND SSpi
* - 'Oblanceolatum'	GCal
- 'Star of Toscana'	EPfP LRHS
- 'Tricolor' (v)	CBcs EBee LRHS NSoo SGol SLim SWvt WCot
- 'Variegatum' (v) ♀H3-4	Widely available
- 'Waterwheel'	EBee ELan LRHS SKHP WPGP WSHC
- 'Wilsonii'	CDul CExl CMac CSPN EBee ELan EPfP EUJe LRHS LSRN NLar SEND SKHP SLim SPer SPoG SWvt WCot WCru WHar WPGP WPat
majus misapplied	see *T. jasminoides* 'Japonicum'
majus Nakai	see *T. asiaticum*

Trachycarpus (*Arecaceae*)

sp.	EAmu
from Manipur	CPHo EAmu
§ ***fortunei*** ♀H3-4	Widely available
fortunei × ***wagnerianus***	EBee WPGP
latisectus	EAmu SBig
martianus	EAmu SBig
nanus	CDTJ
'Nova'	EAmu
princeps	CBrP
takil Becc.	EAmu
wagnerianus	CBrP CDTJ CExl CGHE CPHo EAmu EPfP NPla SAPC SBig SChr SMad WPGP

Trachymene (*Apiaceae*)

coerulea	CSpe

Trachyspermum (*Apiaceae*)

ammi	CArn

Trachystemon (*Boraginaceae*)

orientalis	CBre CExl CHEx CMac CSev ELan EPfP IKil LEdu LHop MAvo MCot MRav NBid NLar SBig SKHP WBrk WCot WCru WHer WMoo XLum

Tradescantia ✿ (*Commelinaceae*)

albiflora	see *T. fluminensis*
× ***andersoniana*** W. Ludwig & Rohw. nom. inval.	see *T.* Andersoniana Group
§ Andersoniana Group	CWib SPet
- 'Angelic Charm' (Charm Series) new	SHeu
- 'Baby Doll'	XLum
- 'Bilberry Ice'	CHel CMac CPrp CWCL ECtt EPfP GJos GKev GMaP IKil LBMP LHop LRHS MBel MWhi NBir NBro NCGa NGdn NLar NPnk SGbt SMrm SPoG SWvt WHoo WMnd WWEG XLum
- 'Blanca'	WWEG
- 'Blue and Gold'	CBcs EBee ECtt ELon EPfP EUJe LAst LHop MHol MRav NHol NLar NSti WCot WWEG
- 'Blue Stone'	CCse CMea CSBt ECtt IKil MAvo MRav SPad SRkn SRms WHoo XLum
- 'Bridal Veil'	CHll
- 'Caerulea Plena'	see *T. virginiana* 'Caerulea Plena'
- Carmine Glow	see *T.* (Andersoniana Group) 'Karminglut'
- 'Charlotte'	ECtt ELan LRHS LSRN NBre NBro NGdn NLar SMrm WCAu WMnd WWEG XLum
- 'Chedglow'	WWEG
- 'Concord Grape'	Widely available
- 'Danielle'	EBee EPfP
- 'Domaine de Courson'	ECtt XLum
- 'In the Navy'	LDai NLar
- 'Innocence'	CMHG CSBt CTri ECtt ELan EPfP GCra GJos GMaP IBoy LAst LHop LRHS MBel MMuc NBir NCGa NGdn NPnk NSti SEND SPer SWvt WMnd XLum
- 'Iris Prichard'	CPrp EBee ELan EPfP GCra GLog GMaP LAst NCGa NLar

- 'Isis' ♀H4	CPrp CTri EBee ECtt ELan EPfP GCra LBMP LRHS MMuc MNFA MRav NBir NCGa NGdn NOrc SEND SPer SWvt WKif WMnd WWlt
- 'J.C.Weguelin' ♀H4	EPfP LPot NBir NPnk NSoo SRms WCAu WMnd WWEG XLum
§ - 'Karminglut'	EBee ECtt ELan EPfP GLog GMaP NBir NGdn NPnk WCAu WHoo WWEG XLum
- 'Leonora'	EPfP LRHS MMuc NLar SEND XLum
- 'Little Doll'	CHel CWCL ECtt EPfP GLog LAst LRHS NBro NLar WWEG XLum
- 'Little White Doll'	CPrp ECtt EPfP LAst MNFA NLar WWEG
- 'Mariella'	EBee
- 'Melissa' **new**	XLum
- 'Mrs Loewer'	MAvo
- 'Ocean Blue' **new**	WWlt
- 'Osprey' ♀H4	CBcs CTri ECtt ELan EPfP GCal LRHS MLHP MRav MWhi NCGa NGdn NLar NPri NSoo NSti SMrm SPer SPoG SRms WCAu WHoo WKif WWEG XLum
- 'Pauline'	ECtt ELon LAst MRav NBir NLar WHoo WWEG XLum
- 'Perinne's Pink'	CWCL EBee ECtt EPfP LRHS NLar NPnk NSti SPoG
- 'Pink Chablis'	CWCL ECtt IKil MNFA NBro NLar
- 'Purewell Giant'	CMac CTri GLog LHop LRHS NBro NLar SPer SWvt WGor WKif WMnd
- 'Purple Dome'	ECtt EPfP GMaP LAst LRHS MAvo MMuc MRav NBir NBro NCGa NGdn SEND SPoG WMnd
- 'Red Grape'	ECtt EWll LPot LRHS MBel MWhi NPro NSti WWEG
- 'Regal Charm' (Charm Series) **new**	SHeu
- 'Rosi'	EBee
- 'Rubra'	CPrp NOrc SRms XLum
- 'Satin Doll'PBR	CBcs COtW ECtt EPfP
- 'Snowbank'	EBee
- 'Sunshine Charm'PBR (Charm Series)	CWCL NLar SHeu WHil
- 'Sweet Kate'	CMac CWCL ECtt LBMP LRHS LSRN MBNS NBro SGbt SHil SPoG SRGP XLum
- 'Sylvana'	EBee
- 'Temptation'	ECtt
- 'Valour'	CSBt EBee EPfP
- 'Zwanenburg Blue'	ECtt ELan GLog LAst LRHS MLHP NCGa NPnk SPlb SPoG WMnd WWEG XLum
'Angel Eyes'	EBee ECtt
'Blushing Bride' (v)	MPkF
crassifolia	CFil
- F&M 258	WPGP
crassula	EOHP
§ ***fluminensis***	SChr
- 'Albovittata'	EShb
§ - 'Aurea' ♀H1	EShb SChr
- 'Maiden's Blush' (v)	CSpe EShb SPlb SRms
- 'Quicksilver' (v) ♀H1	EShb
- 'Variegata'	see *T. fluminensis* 'Aurea'
'Gold Mound'	WRHF
'Lucky Charm'	NLar SHeu
pallida 'Kartuz Giant'	CSpe EShb WCot
§ - 'Purpurea' ♀H2-3	EOHP EShb
pendula	see *T. zebrina*
'Purple Sabre'	CBcs LAst MWhi NHol SMrm SPlb
purpurea	see *T. pallida* 'Purpurea'
sillamontana ♀H1	EShb
spathacea	EShb
- 'Vittata' ♀H1	WCot
tricolor	see *T. zebrina*
virginiana	LPot MWhi
- 'Alba'	CMac GCal
* - 'Brevicaulis'	EBee ECtt NBro WWEG
§ - 'Caerulea Plena' (d)	ELan EPfP MRav SPer SRms WWEG
- 'Rubra'	SPlb
§ ***zebrina*** ♀H1	EShb
- ***pendula***	see *T. zebrina*
- 'Purpusii' ♀H1	SRms

Tragopogon (*Asteraceae*)

crocifolius	CCVN CSpe SPhx
porrifolius	CFis GCal MCot SVic WCot
pratensis	CArn NMir

Trapa (*Lythraceae*)

natans	CBAq

Trautvetteria (*Ranunculaceae*)

carolinensis **new**	IMou
- var. ***japonica***	CLAP WCru
- - B&SWJ 10861	WCru
- var. ***occidentalis***	CBct EBee LEdu WCru

Triadica (*Euphorbiaceae*)

sebifera	LEdu WCru

Trichodiadema (*Aizoaceae*)

intonsum	SPlb

Trichopetalum (*Asparagaceae*)

§ ***plumosum***	CBro

Trichostema (*Lamiaceae*)

dichotomum RCB RL 15	WCot

Tricuspidaria see *Crinodendron*

Tricyrtis (*Liliaceae*)

B&SWJ 3229 from Taiwan	WCru
'Adbane'	CAby CBct CHel CLAP EBee ELan EPPr EWes GBuc GKev IKil LRHS MMoz NGdn SMrm WGwG WWEG
affinis B&SWJ 2804	CLAP WCru
- B&SWJ 5645	WCru
- B&SWJ 6182	WCru
- B&SWJ 11169	WCru
- B&SWJ 11442	WCru
- 'Early Bird'	WCru
'Amanagowa'	CLAP
bakeri	see *T. latifolia*
'Blue Wonder'	LRHS LSou NLar SPer SPet
dilatata	see *T. macropoda*
'Empress'	CBct CExl CHel ELon EPfP EThi EWes GBuc IBal LAst LEdu LRHS LSou MTis NEgg NPnk NSoo SMrm SPet SPoG SRkn SRot WHil WWEG
flava	LRHS WCru
formosana ♀H4	CAby CAvo CPom CTri ECho ELan EPfP GKev GLog GMaP IBoy LEdu LPot LRHS MCot MMuc MNrw NCGa NLar NPnk SBea SDys SPet SRms SRot WCAu WKif
- B&SWJ 306	CLAP MNrw
- B&SWJ 355	WCru

	- B&SWJ 3073	WCru
	- B&SWJ 3616	CExl WCru
	- B&SWJ 3635	CLAP
	- B&SWJ 3712	WCru
	- B&SWJ 6705	CLAP
	- B&SWJ 6741	WCru
	- B&SWJ 6970	WCru
	- RWJ 10109	WCru
	- 'Dark Beauty'	CDes CExl CLAP CWCL EBee ECtt ELan GBuc MAvo MBel MBri MNrw MTis MWat SMrm SPad WPGP
	- dark-flowered	CHel GAbr NCGa
	- 'Emperor' (v)	ESwi LPio
	- 'Gilt Edge' (v)	CBct CExl CWCL ECtt ELan ELon EPfP EPri EThi GBuc IBal LRHS LSou MBNS MBel MTis NBro NEgg NLar NPnk NSoo NSti SMrm SWvt WHil WWEG
	- f. ***glandosa*** B&SWJ 7084	WCru
	- aff. f. ***glandosa*** 'Blu-Shing Toad'	WCru
	- var. ***grandiflora*** 'W-Ho-ping Toad'	WCru
	- 'Kestrel' (v)	WCot
	- pale-flowered	CBct EThi WWEG
	- 'Purple Beauty'	LSou MNrw MPkF NPnk
	- 'Samurai' (v)	CHel CWCL EWes NPnk
	- 'Shelley's'	CBct CLAP NBro WWEG
	- 'Small Wonder'	WCru
	- 'Spotted Toad'	LEdu WCru
§	- Stolonifera Group	CBcs CMac ELan EPfP LEdu LRHS MCot MWat NWad SDix WMnd
	- - B&SWJ 7046	WCru
	- 'Taiwan Toad'	CExl
	- 'Taroko Toad'	WCru
	- 'Tiny Toad'	WCru
	- 'Variegata' (v)	CBct CHel LEdu NBir WCru
	- 'Velvet Toad'	WCru
	'Golden Leopard'	EBee EPfP LSou NCGa SPer
	'Harlequin'	LEdu WWEG
§	***hirta***	CBcs CDes CHel CHid CMac CPrp CTri CTsd ECho EPfP GAbr ITim LRHS MCot MMuc NBro NHol SEND SGbt SPet SPlb SWvt WWEG
	- B&SWJ 5971	WCru
	- B&SWJ 11182	WCru
	- B&SWJ 11227	WCru
	- 'Alba'	CMac
	- 'Albomarginata' (v)	CMac CPrp EPPr EPfP GCra LLWG LPio LRHS NEgg NLar NSti SWvt WPGP
	- 'Golden Gleam'	LRHS WCot
	- var. ***masamunei***	WCru
	- 'Matsukaze'	CExl CLAP CPom EWes
	- 'Miyazaki'	CCon CLAP CMac EBee ECtt EPfP GBuc IFoB LBMP LRHS MHer MNrw MPkF MTis NCGa NLar WWEG XLum
	- 'Taiwan Atrianne'	CHel ECtt ELan LDai LRHS MNrw NBro NCGa NEgg NWad SGbt
	- 'Variegata' (v)	CBct CTri ELon EWes GCra GKev WCot WWEG
N	Hototogisu	CBct CBro CExl CHel CLAP CPom ECtt ELan GAbr LHop LRHS MWat NBir NEgg NHol NLar NPnk WMnd WWEG
	'Imperial Banner' (v)	MAvo WCot
	ishiiana	CLAP MMoz WCot WCru WPGP WSHC
	- var. ***surugensis***	LEdu WCru
	japonica	see *T. hirta*
	'Kohaku'	CLAP EBee ELan EThi GKev WPGP WWEG
	lasiocarpa	LEdu MAvo XLum
	- B&SWJ 3635	CExl WCru
	- B&SWJ 6861	WCru
	- B&SWJ 7013	CBct WCru
	- B&SWJ 7103	WCru
	- 'Royal Toad'	WCru
§	***latifolia***	CHel ELan GLog GMaP LEdu LRHS NLar WCru WWEG
	- B&SWJ 10996 from Japan	WCru
	- 'Yellow Sunrise'	ECtt EPPr NSti
	'Lemon Lime' (v)	NPro WWEG
	'Lightning Strike' (v)	CHel ECtt EWes LEdu NHol NPnk WCot
	'Lilac Towers'	WCru WWEG
	macrantha	GAbr GKev GLog WCru WSHC
§	- subsp. ***macranthopsis***	CBct CExl CLAP GBuc LHop WCot WCru
	- - 'Juro' (d)	WCru
	macranthopsis	see *T. macrantha* subsp. *macranthopsis*
*	***macrocarpa***	XLum
N	***macropoda***	ELan GKev GLog LEdu LHop LRHS NGdn WMnd WWEG
	- B&SWJ 1271 from Korea	WCru
	- B&SWJ 5013	WCru
	- B&SWJ 5556	WCru
	- B&SWJ 5847 from Japan	WCru
	- B&SWJ 6209	WCru
	- B&SWJ 8700	WCru
	- B&SWJ 8829 from Korea	WCru
	- from Yungi Temple, China	CLAP EPPr NCGa
	- 'Tricolor'	WCot
	maculata HWJCM 470	WCru
	- HWJK 2010	WCru
	- HWJK 2411	WCru
	- PAB 3188 new	LEdu
	'Moonlight Treasure' PBR	CExl CLAP EBee NHol WCot
	nana	WCru
	- B&SWJ 11399	WCru
	ohsumiensis	CAby CLAP CPom GBuc LRHS WCru WPGP
	perfoliata	CLAP LEdu WCru
	- 'Spring Shine' (v)	WCru
	pilosa	EBee
	Pink Freckles = 'Innotripf' PBR	CBct CHel ELon ESwi EThi LRHS LSou MPnt NPri SPoG SRot SWvt WHil
	'Raspberry Mousse'	CLAP CWCL EPfP IFoB LHop LSou MBNS NSti SMrm WPGP
	ravenii B&SWJ 3229	WCru
	setouchiensis	WCru
	'Shimone'	CExl CHid CLAP CPom NCGa
	'Sinonome'	MAvo MPkF
	stolonifera	see *T. formosana* Stolonifera Group
	suzukii RWJ 10111	WCru
	'Taipei Silk' PBR	ESwi IFoB LSou NCGa NLar NPri NSti
	'Tojen'	CBct ECtt ELon EPPr EPfP EThi EWTr EWes LEdu LHop LRHS MNrw MSCN NBid NBir NCGa NEgg NLar SPer SPet SPoG WPGP WWEG XPou
	'Variegata' (*affinis* hybrid) (v)	WWEG
	'Washfields'	WPGP
	'White Towers'	CExl CHid CLAP CWCL EBee EPPr EPfP GBuc IFoB LRHS MBel MRav

	NCGa NEgg NLar NPnk NSti SPer SRms XLum

Trifolium (*Papilionaceae*)

angustifolium	CArn
dubium	SPre
incarnatum	CSpe MHer
nanum	LLHF
ochroleucon	CHab EPPr GMaP LEdu LPio LRHS MAvo MCot MMuc MNFA MPie MSCN NPnk NSti SBch SMad SPhx WMoo WWEG
pannonicum	CCVN CMea GCal MNrw WOut
pratense	CHab MHer NMir WSFF
- 'Dolly North'	see *T. pratense* 'Susan Smith'
- 'Ice Cool'	see *T. repens* 'Green Ice'
§ - 'Susan Smith' (v)	CCCN EBee EPfP LEdu WHer
repens	SVic WSFF
- 'Douglas Dawson'	LDai
- 'Dragon's Blood'	CDes CMea LEdu LLWG MHol MPie MSpe NSla SMrm SPer SPoG WPGP
- 'Gold Net'	see *T. pratense* 'Susan Smith'
§ - 'Green Ice'	CBre EBee LLWG LRHS MSpe NPnk NSti WHal
- 'Harlequin' (v)	MHer WCot WMoo WOut
- 'Hullavington'	CNat
- 'Purpurascens'	CArn CBre EPfP LLWG LRHS MAsh MBNS MHer MPie MSpe NEgg NSla NSti SPoG WNew
§ - 'Purpurascens Quadrifolium'	CMea EBee EHoe EPau EWes GAbr MCot NEgg NMir NPer SPer SPlb WHer
- 'Quadrifolium'	WWFP
- 'Tetraphyllum Purpureum'	see *T. repens* 'Purpurascens Quadrifolium'
- 'Wheatfen'	CNat NDov NPer
- 'William'	CBre ECGP LEdu NDov WCot WOut
rubens	CAby CArn CCVN CMea CWCL ELan EPPr EShb GCal LEdu LPio LRHS MAvo MHol MMHG MMuc MNFA MNHC MNrw MSCN SPer SPhx SPlb WCAu WMoo WSHC
- 'Drama'	MNrw
- 'Peach Pink'	CSpe ELon EPPr LHop MBel MMHG SBch SPhx WCot
- 'Red Feathers'	ELon EPPr LPio LRHS MCot SMad SMrm WWEG
trichocephalum	EPPr
variegatum	WOut
var. ***variegatum*** new	

Trigonella (*Papilionaceae*)

foenum-graecum	CArn

Trillidium see *Trillium*

Trillium ✿ (*Melanthiaceae*)

albidum	ECho GBin GBuc LLHF LRHS LWst MNrw SKHP SSpi WHal
angustipetalum	LWst
camschatcense	CExl
- from Japan	LWst
§ ***catesbyi***	CCon CExl CWCL ECho EPot GKev LLHF LWst MNrw NWad
cernuum	CWCL ECho GCra LRHS WCru WSHC
chloropetalum	CBro GBBs GBin GBuc SChF SSpi WPGP
- var. ***chloropetalum***	GBuc
- var. ***chloropetalum*** × ***parviflorum***	SKHP
§ - var. ***giganteum*** 🏆^{H4}	CExl GBuc LWst SPhx SSpi WCru
- var. ***rubrum***	see *T. chloropetalum* var. *giganteum*
- white-flowered	GKev
cuneatum	CArn CBcs CBct CBro CExl CHel CWCL ECho EHyd EPot GBBs GBuc GMaP LEdu LRHS LWst MBri MCot MNrw NBir NHol NWad SChF SDeJ SKHP SSpi WCru WPnP
- 'Ghost'	SKHP
- 'Moonshine'	SKHP
decipiens	LWst
decumbens	LWst SKHP
discolor	LWst
erectum 🏆^{H4}	Widely available
- f. ***albiflorum***	CCon EBee ECho GBuc LWst MMoz MNrw SKHP SSpi WCru
- 'Beige'	GKev
- f. ***luteum***	LWst SKHP
- red-flowered	ECho GKev
erectum × ***flexipes***	EBee ECho GBuc LWst MNrw NBir SKHP SSpi
flexipes	CWCL ECho GAbr GKev LWst MNrw NHol SKHP SSpi
- erect	LWst
I - 'Harvington Selection'	LRHS LWst SKHP
foetidissimum	LWst SKHP
govanianum	LWst
gracile	LWst
grandiflorum 🏆^{H4}	Widely available
- f. ***polymerum*** 'Flore Pleno' (d)	CAvo CWCL ECho LLHF LWst SKHP
- - 'Snowbunting' (d)	CWCL EWes GKev LWst MMHG NHar WThu
- 'Quicksilver'	SKHP
- f. ***roseum***	LWst
- white-flowered	MAvo
kurabayashii	CBct CExl ECho ELan EPot EWld GBin GBuc LRHS LWst MNrw SChF SKHP SSpi WCru WHal WPGP
lancifolium	LWst
ludovicianum	LWst
luteum 🏆^{H4}	CBcs CBro CCon CExl CWCL ECho EPfP EPot EWTr GBBs GBuc GGGa GKev GMaP LRHS LWst MAvo MBri MCot MNrw NBid NHar NHol NPnk NWad SDeJ SKHP SSpi WCru WThP
maculatum	LWst
nivale	NHar
ovatum	SSpi
- f. ***hibbersonii***	GBuc GCra
- 'Roy Elliott'	CExl MNrw
parviflorum	ECho LWst MNrw SKHP
pusillum	CExl CWCL ECho EPot GBBs GKev LLHF LWst MBri MNrw NHol
* - var. ***alabamicum***	SKHP
I - var. ***georgianum***	SKHP
recurvatum	CBcs CCon CWCL EBee ECho EPot GBBs GKev LEdu LWst MBri NHol NPnk SKHP WCru WPnP
reliquum	LWst
rivale 🏆^{H3}	CExl ECho GBBs GBuc GKev LLHF
- pink-flowered	GKev
rugelii	EBee ECho EWes LWst MNrw SKHP SSpi
- Askival hybrids	EBee ECho GBuc LWst MNrw SKHP SSpi

- 'Orchard Pink'	LWst MNrw
rugelii* × *vaseyi	EBee EWes LWst MNrw SKHP SSpi
sessile	CExl CWCL EBee ECho EWTr GBBs GBuc GKev LRHS LWst MAvo MBri NBir NPnk NWad SDeJ SKHP SMrm WCot WKif WSHC WShi
- 'Rubrum'	see *T. chloropetalum* var. *giganteum*
simile	ECho LLHF LRHS MNrw SKHP SSpi
smallii	WCru
stamineum	ECho
stylosum	see *T. catesbyi*
sulcatum	CExl CWCL EBee ECho GBuc GGGa GMaP LRHS LWst MBri MNrw SKHP SSpi WCot
- cream-flowered	LWst
taiwanense B&SWJ 3411	WCru
texanum	SKHP
tschonoskii	ECho
underwoodii	LWst
undulatum	ECho LWst MNrw
vaseyi	CWCL EBee ECho EWes GAbr GBBs GKev LRHS LWst MNrw SKHP SSpi
viride	GBBs
viridescens	ECho LWst

Triosteum (*Caprifoliaceae*)

erythrocarpum	EBee
himalayanum	GCal GKev WSHC
- BWJ 7907	CLAP WCru
pinnatifidum	CLAP CPom EBee GCal IMou

Tripsacum (*Poaceae*)

dactyloides	EPPr

Tripterospermum (*Gentianaceae*)

* aff. ***chevalieri*** B&SWJ 8359	WCru
cordifolium B&SWJ 081	WCru
distylum B&SWJ 11491	WCru
fasciculatum B&SWJ 7197	WCru
- B&SWJ 11297	WCru
hirticalyx B&SWJ 11725	WCru
- B&SWJ 11786	WCru
japonicum	LLHF WCot
- B&SWJ 8920	WCru
- B&SWJ 10876	WCru
lanceolatum B&SWJ 085	WCru
- RWJ 9918	WCru
volubile B&SWJ 11774	WCru

Tripterygium (*Celastraceae*)

doianum B&SWJ 11467	WCru
regelii B&SWJ 5453	WCru
- B&SWJ 10921	WCru
wilfordii BWJ 7852 from China	WCru
- WWJ 12009	WCru

Tristagma (*Alliaceae*)

nivale	EBee

Triteleia (*Asparagaceae*)

'4U'	CAvo CBro EBee ECho GKev WCot
bridgesii	ECho
californica	see *Brodiaea californica*
§ 'Corrina'	CAvo CBro EBee ECho EPot
'Crystal Pink' **new**	SDeJ
grandiflora	ECho WCot
hyacinthina	EBee ECho GKev WCot
ixioides	ECho
- 'Splendens'	EBee ECho
- 'Starlight'	CAvo CBro CTri ECho EPot ERCP GKev SDeJ SMrm WHil
§ ***laxa***	ECho
- NNS 00-743	WCot
- 'Allure'	EBee ECho
- 'Dexter'	CAbP WCot
§ - 'Koningin Fabiola'	CBro CMea CSpe CTri EBee ECho EPot GKev MLHP MNrw NBir SDeJ SEND SPer WCot WRHF
- Queen Fabiola	see *T. laxa* 'Koningin Fabiola'
lilacina	ECho
'Ocean Queen'	CHid CMea EBee ERCP
§ ***peduncularis***	ECho WCot
'Royal Blue'	ERCP
'Rudy'	CAvo CBro CHid CMea CWCL EBee ECho ERCP SDeJ WCot
'Silver Queen' **new**	CMea ECho ERCP
× ***tubergenii***	ECho
uniflora	see *Ipheion uniflorum*
'White Sweep' **new**	ECho
'www' PBR **new**	ECho

Trithrinax (*Arecaceae*)

brasiliensis	EAmu SBig
campestris	CBrP EAmu SBig

Tritoma see *Kniphofia*

Tritonia (*Iridaceae*)

crocata ♀H2-3	CPrp ECho
- 'Baby Doll'	EBee LEdu WHil
- 'Bridal Veil'	EBee
- 'Pink Sensation'	CDes CSpe EBee ECho WHil
- 'Plymouth Pastel'	CDes
- 'Prince of Orange'	CDes EBee
- 'Princess Beatrix'	CDes
- 'Riversdale'	ECho
- 'Serendipity'	CDes EBee EPri
- 'Tangerine'	CDes EBee
deusta	CDes EPri
§ ***disticha***	Widely available
subsp. ***rubrolucens***	
- - short, red-pink-flowered	CDes
- - tall, clear pink-flowered	CDes CTca
flabellifolia	ECho
florentiae 'Tanqua Karoo'	ECho
karooica 'Middlepos'	ECho
laxifolia	CDes CTca ECho EPot LEdu
lineata	CDes CTca EBee ECho EPri WPGP
- 'Parvifolia'	EBee
pallida	ECho SPlb
rosea	see *T. disticha* subsp. *rubrolucens*
securigera	CDes ECho LEdu WCot
squalida	ECho EPri

Trochocarpa (*Ericaceae*)

clarkei	WThu
gunnii	WThu
thymifolia	WThu
- white-flowered	WThu

Trochodendron (*Trochodendraceae*)

aralioides	Widely available
- B&SWJ 1651 from Taiwan	WCru
- CWJ 12357 from Taiwan	WCru
- RWJ 9845 from Taiwan	WCru

Trollius (*Ranunculaceae*)

ACE 1187	CExl
SDR 4816	GKev
acaulis	ECho EWes
asiaticus	GKev
§ ***chinensis***	CHVG GCal GKev SWat
- 'Golden Queen' ♀H4	Widely available
- 'Imperial Orange'	GBin LLWG
× ***cultorum***	CAby
- 'Alabaster'	Widely available
- 'Baudirektor Linne'	ECtt MRav NGdn
- 'Byrne's Giant'	ECtt
- 'Canary Bird'	ELan EPfP GCal NGdn SRms
- 'Cheddar'	CWCL ECtt ELon EPPr EPfP GBin GCal GMaP LHop LSou MBNS MBel MBri MCot MMHG MRav MWts NBro NEgg NLar NOrc NPnk NPro SKHP SPoG SWvt WBor WWEG
- 'Commander-in-Chief'	EBee
- 'Earliest of All'	CSam CWCL NGdn SPer WWEG
- 'Etna'	GBin SHar WWEG
§ - 'Feuertroll'	ECtt LLWG LRHS MRav NEgg NGdn NPro
- Fireglobe	see *T.* × *cultorum* 'Feuertroll'
- 'Golden Cup'	NBir NGdn
- 'Goldquelle' ♀H4	EBee GBuc
- 'Helios'	CSam GBin GBuc LLHF LRHS
- 'Lemon Queen'	CMac CWCL CWat ECtt EPfP GBin GKev GMaP LRHS MBri MNFA MRav NLar NPnk NSoo SGol SMrm SPer SWat WHil
- 'New Moon' **new**	EShb GBin IKil LLWG NPnk
- 'Orange Crest'	ECtt GCal LSou MBri WHal WWEG
- 'Orange Glow'	LLWG SMad
- 'Orange Princess' ♀H4	CWCL CWat EPfP GMaP LLWG NBro NLar NSoo SPer SRms
- 'Orange Queen'	SWvt
- 'Prichard's Giant'	CMHG ECtt ELan ELon NBro NEgg NGdn NLBP WCFE WWEG
§ - 'Superbus' ♀H4	CAby CCon CDes ELan EPfP GMaP NGdn SPer
- 'T. Smith'	NBro WWEG
- 'Taleggio'	LEdu
europaeus	CWCL ELan GCal LAst LBMP LEdu LHop MLHP MMuc MRav NGdn NHol SBrt SPet SPhx SRot SWat WCFE WHoo WWEG
- SDR 5473	CHel
- SDR 6306	GKev
- 'Lemon Supreme'	GKev
- 'Superbus'	see *T.* × *cultorum* 'Superbus'
hondoensis	EBee LLHF NLar NPro
ircuticus	GKev
laxus	EWes
- 'Albiflorus'	CExl CHel
ledebourii misapplied	see *T. chinensis*
pumilus	ECho ELan EPfP GKev LRHS NLar SPer WAbe
- ACE 1818	CExl GCal MHer NHol
- 'Wargrave'	ECho
ranunculinus	EBee
riederianus	LRHS
stenopetalus	CDes CWCL EBee EWes MBri MNrw MRav NPnk
vaginatus	EBee
yunnanensis	EBee GBin
- orange-flowered	CExl GKev

Tropaeolum ✿ (*Tropaeolaceae*)

azureum	CCCN CExl CFil CPla WPGP
beuthii	ECho WCot
brachyceras	CCCN EBee ECho EPot GKev WCot
ciliatum ♀H1	CCCN CCon CFil CGHE CPla ECho GKev NBid NLar WCot WCru WPGP
- subsp. ***austropurpureum***	CDes CExl CFil CGHE
- subsp. ***hookerianum***	CExl CFil
incisum	CCCN CWCL EBee WCot
lepidum	CPla
majus	MHoo SVic
- Alaska Series (v) ♀H3	CPrp CWCL MNHC NPri SEND SIde WJek
- 'Apricot Twist'	GBee
- 'Crimson Beauty'	CSpe
§ - 'Darjeeling Double' (d) ♀H4	WCot
- 'Darjeeling Gold'	see *T. majus* 'Darjeeling Double'
- 'Empress of India'	CPrp MNHC WJek
- 'Hermine Grashoff' (d) ♀H2-3	CSpe GBee GCal NPer
- Jewel of Africa Group (v) **new**	CWCL
- 'Margaret Long' (d)	CSpe GCal WCot
* - 'Peaches and Cream'	WJek
- 'Red Wonder'	CCCN CHel CSpe EPfP NPri
- 'Sunset Pink'	CPrp
- Tom Thumb mixed	MNHC WJek
nubigenum × ***polyphyllum***	CFil
pentaphyllum	CExl CFil CSpe EBee ECho GCal GKev WCot WPGP
peregrinum	ECho
polyphyllum	CCCN CSpe CWCL EBee ECho EPfP EPot GBuc GGGa LHop NBir WCot WPGP
sessilifolium	CFil EBee ECho
smithii	GCal
speciosum ♀H4	Widely available
tricolor ♀H1	CAvo CCCN CFil ECho GKev WBor XEll
tuberosum	CEnd ECho GPoy SDeJ WHer
- var. ***lineamaculatum*** 'Ken Aslet' ♀H3	CBcs CBro CCCN CSpe CWCL EBee ECho ELan EPfP EPot SPer SPoG

Tsuga ✿ (*Pinaceae*)

canadensis	CDul EPfP NWea
- 'Abbott's Dwarf'	CDoC CKen MGos NHol WGor
§ - 'Abbott's Pygmy'	CKen
- 'Arnold Gold Weeper'	CKen
- 'Aurea' (v)	NLar
- 'Bacon Cristate'	CKen
- 'Betty Rose' (v)	CKen
- 'Birkett's White'	CKen
- 'Brandley'	CKen
§ - 'Branklyn'	CKen
- 'Cappy's Choice'	CKen
- 'Cinnamonea'	CKen
- 'Coffin'	CKen
- 'Cole's Prostrate'	CKen MAsh NLar SLim
- 'Creamey' (v)	CKen
- 'Curley'	CKen
- 'Curtis Ideal'	CKen
- 'Dr Hornbeck'	see *T. canadensis* 'Hornbeck'
- 'Eisburg'	SLim
- 'Essex'	CKen NWad

*	– 'Everitt's Dense Leaf'	CKen
	– 'Everitt's Golden'	CKen
	– 'Fantana'	LRHS MAsh NHol NLar SCoo SLim
	– 'Gentsch White' (v)	NLar
	– 'Gracilis'	WThu
	– 'Greenwood Lake'	WThu
	– 'Hedgehog'	CDoC NLar
§	– 'Hornbeck'	CKen
	– 'Horsford'	CKen NLar NWad
	– 'Horstmann' No 1	CKen
	– 'Hussii'	CKen NHol NLar
	– 'Jacqueline Verkade'	CKen MAsh NLar
	– 'Jeddeloh' 🏆H4	CDoC CMac EPot LRHS MAsh MGos NEgg NHol SCoo SGol SLim
	– 'Jervis'	CKen NHol NLar NWad
	– 'Julianne'	CKen
	– 'Kingsville Spreader'	CKen
	– 'Little Joe'	CKen
	– 'Little Snow'	CKen
I	– 'Lutea'	CKen
	– 'Many Cones'	CKen
	– 'Minima'	CKen
	– 'Minuta'	CDoC CKen MGos NHol NLar NWad WGor
	– 'Moon Frost'	MAsh
	– 'Palomino'	CKen
	– 'Pendula' 🏆H4	CKen EPfP LRHS MAsh MBri SLim
	– 'Pincushion'	CKen
	– 'Prostrata'	see *T. canadensis* 'Branklyn'
	– 'Pygmaea'	see *T. canadensis* 'Abbott's Pygmy'
	– 'Rugg's Washington Dwarf'	CKen
	– 'Snowflake'	CKen
	– 'Stewart's Gem'	CKen
	– 'Verkade Petite'	CKen
	– 'Verkade Recurved'	CKen NLar
	– 'Vermeulen's Wintergold'	NLar
	– 'Von Helms' Dwarf'	CKen
	– 'Warnham'	CKen MAsh
	caroliniana 'La Bar Weeping'	CKen NLar
	– 'Planting Fields Broom' **new**	CKen
	chinensis	CKen
	diversifolia 'Gotelli'	CKen
	dumosa	CKen
	heterophylla 🏆H4	CBcs CCVT CDul EPfP LBuc NWea SEWo SGol SMad
	– 'Iron Springs'	CKen
	– 'Laursen's Column'	CKen
	– 'Thorsens Weeping'	CKen
	menziesii	see *Pseudotsuga menziesii*
	mertensiana 'Blue Star'	CKen MAsh
	– 'Elizabeth'	CKen
	– 'Glauca'	CKen
I	– 'Glauca Nana'	CKen
I	– 'Horstmann'	CKen
	– 'Quartz Mountain'	CKen
	sieboldii 'Baldwin'	CKen
	– 'Green Ball'	CKen
	– 'Honeywell Estate'	CKen
	– 'Nana'	CKen

Tuberaria (*Cistaceae*)

	lignosa	WAbe

Tulbaghia ✿ (*Alliaceae*)

	acutiloba	CTca EBee LEdu MHom
	alliacea	CAvo CDes ECho EShb LEdu WCot
	alliacea* × *violacea	ECho
*	***allioides***	CBro
	'Bob Brown'	CDes
	capensis	CDes CPou LEdu NBir SMrm WCot
	'Cariad'	LEdu
	cernua	EBee
	– CD&R 199	CDes
	– hybrid	EPri
§	***coddii***	LEdu MHom
	cominsii	CExl EPri SBch
	cominsii* × *violacea	CAvo CExl CTca MHom
	'Cosmic'	CDes CPou EPri LEdu
	'Fairy Star'	CDes CTca EPri EShb LEdu WCot WPGP
	fragrans	see *T. simmleri*
	– 'Alba'	ELan EPot NLar SDeJ
	'Hazel'	CDes CPou MHer
	'John May's Special'	CDes CKno EShb LEdu MHom SMrm WCot WHoo WPGP
	leucantha	CDes CTca LEdu MHom NWad WPGP
	– H&B 11996	CDes
	maritima	see *T. violacea* var. *maritima*
	Marwood seedling	MHer MHom MTPN
	montana	EBee LEdu MHer
	natalensis	CBro CPou CPrp ECho LEdu
	– B&V 421	EBee EPri
	– clone 2 pink B&V 421	CDes
	– pink-flowered	CTca ECho MHom
	– white-flowered	CTca
	poetica	see *T. coddii*
	'Purple Eye'	CHel CKno CSpe GBin LEdu MCot NSti
§	***simmleri***	CPou EBee ECho EPot EPri EShb EWes LEdu NLar SDeJ
	– 'Cheryl Renshaw'	WCot
	– pink-flowered	CTca
	– 'Snow Queen'	CPrp
	– white-flowered	CPou CPrp CTca
	verdoorniae	LEdu WHil
	violacea	CBcs CBro CGHE CKno CMHG CMea CPou CPrp CSpe CTca ECho EPot EPri ERCP EShb LEdu LPio LRHS MCot MHom MMuc MSCN SEND SMrm SWat WHoo WPGP XLum XSen
	– from RBGE	MHom
*	– 'Alba'	EBee EPri GCal MHer SWat WKif
I	– 'Fine Form'	CKno WKif
*	– ***grandiflora***	CAvo
	– 'John Rider'	EPri
*	– var. ***maritima***	EShb LEdu MHom SMrm WCot
	– 'Pallida'	CAvo CBro CCse CDes CPou CTca ECho LEdu WPGP
	– 'Pearl'	CPou
	– 'Peppermint Garlic'	CDes CTca LEdu WPGP
	– var. ***robustior***	CPou CTca EWes
§	– 'Silver Lace' (v)	Widely available
	– 'Variegata'	see *T. violacea* 'Silver Lace'
	– 'White Goddess'	CPou

Tulipa ✿ (*Liliaceae*)

	'Abba' (2)	EPfP SDeJ
	'Absalon' (9)	GKev
	'Abu Hassan' (3)	CAby CAvo CMea ERCP MBri SDeJ
	acuminata (15)	CAvo CBro CTca ECho ERCP NMin SDeJ SPhx
	'Ad Rem' (4)	MBri
	'Air' (10) **new**	ERCP

aitchisonii	see *T. clusiana*
'Aladdin' (6)	SDeJ
'Aladdin's Record' (6)	CAvo CBro SDeJ
'Albert Heijn' (13)	SDeJ
albertii (15)	ECho NMin
'Aleppo' (7)	SDeJ
'Alfred Cortot' (12) ♀H4	SDeJ
'Allegretto' (11)	MBri
altaica (15) ♀H4	ECho
amabilis	see *T. hoogiana*
'American Eagle' (7)	SDeJ
'Ancilla' (12) ♀H4	CBro
'Angélique' (11) ♀H4	CAvo CTca CWCL EPfP ERCP GKev LPio MBri NBir SDeJ SPer
'Angel's Wish' (3) new	CAvo MCot
'Annie Schilder' (3)	ERCP
'Antraciet' (11) new	ERCP
'Apeldoorn' (4)	GKev MBri SDeJ SPer
'Apeldoorn's Elite' (4) ♀H4	MBri SDeJ
'Apricot Beauty' (1) ♀H4	CAby CHid CTca CWCL ERCP MBri MCot NBir SDeJ
'Apricot Emperor' (13)	MCot
'Apricot Jewel'	see *T. linifolia* (Batalinii Group) 'Apricot Jewel'
'Apricot Parrot' (10) ♀H4	CAvo CWCL MBri SDeJ
'Aquilla' (11) new	SDeJ
'Arabian Mystery' (3)	CAvo ERCP NHol SDeJ
'Aria Card' (7)	SDeJ
'Artist' (8) ♀H4	EPfP ERCP SDeJ
'Atlantis' (5)	MBri
'Attila' (3)	CAvo
aucheriana (15) ♀H4	CBro ECho EPot LLHF NMin
australis (15)	ECho
aximensis (15)	ECho NMin
bakeri	see *T. saxatilis* Bakeri Group
'Ballade' (6) ♀H4	CAvo ERCP MCot SDeJ
Ballade Dream = 'Sonnet' (6)	SDeJ
'Ballerina' (6) ♀H4	CAby CAvo CBro CMea CTca ECho EPfP ERCP IFro LPio MBri MCot SDeJ SPer SPhx
'Banja Luka' (4)	SDeJ
'Barbados' (7)	CAby
'Barcelona' (3) ♀H4	ERCP
'Baronesse' (5)	SDeJ
'Bastogne Parrot'PBR (10)	EPfP
batalinii	see *T. linifolia* Batalinii Group
'Beau Monde' (3) ♀H4	SDeJ
'Beauty of Apeldoorn' (4)	MBri
'Beauty Queen' (1)	SDeJ
'Bellona' (3)	SDeJ
'Berlioz' (12)	SDeJ
'Bestseller' (1)	SDeJ
biebersteiniana (15)	ECho NMin
§ ***biflora*** (15)	CAby CAvo ECho EPot GKev SDeJ SPhx WShi
bifloriformis (15)	ECho LLHF
I - 'Maxima' (15)	ECho NMin SPhx
- 'Starlight' (15) ♀H4	ECho NMin SPhx
'Black Hero' (11)	CAby CAvo EPfP ERCP MCot SDeJ
'Black Jewel' (7)	ERCP SDeJ
'Black Parrot' (10) ♀H4	CAby CAvo CBro CHid CWCL EPfP ERCP MBri SDeJ SPer
'Black Swan' (5)	SDeJ
'Bleu Aimable' (5)	CAvo ERCP MCot SDeJ
'Blue Diamond' (11)	CAvo ERCP SDeJ
'Blue Heron' (7) ♀H4	CAvo ERCP SDeJ
'Blue Parrot' (10)	EPfP ERCP SDeJ SPer
'Blue Ribbon' (3)	CAvo
Blueberry Ripple	see *T.* 'Zurel'
'Blushing Beauty' (5)	SDeJ
'Blushing Bride' (5)	SDeJ
'Blushing Lady' (5)	MCot
'Boutade' (14)	NPer
'Brown Sugar' (3) new	EPfP ERCP SPer
'Burgundy' (6)	CTca ERCP SDeJ
'Burgundy Lace' (7)	SDeJ
'Burning Heart' (4) ♀H4	SDeJ
'Buttercup' (14) ♀H4	SDeJ
'Café Noir' (5)	ERCP NHol
'Cairo' (3)	MCot
'Calgary' (3) ♀H4	CAvo EPfP
'Calibra' (7)	CAvo
'Calypso' (14) ♀H4	LRHS
'Canasta' (7)	SDeJ
'Candela' (13) ♀H4	SDeJ
'Candy Prince'PBR (1)	EPfP SDeJ
'Canova' (7)	SDeJ
'Cardinal Mindszenty' (2)	ERCP LRHS SDeJ
carinata (15)	ECho NMin
'Carlton' (2)	MCot
'Carnaval de Nice' (11/v) ♀H4	CBro CTca ERCP MBri SDeJ SPer
'Carrousel' (7)	SDeJ
'Cartouche' (11) new	ERCP SDeJ
'Cassini' (3)	SDeJ
§ ***celsiana*** (15)	ECho
'China Lady' (14) ♀H4	ECho SDeJ
'China Pink' (6) ♀H4	CAvo CBro CMea CTca EPfP ERCP MBri MCot SDeJ
'China Town' (8) ♀H4	ERCP MBri SDeJ
'Chopin' (12)	NHol
'Christmas Dream' (1)	SDeJ
chrysantha Boiss. ex Baker	see *T. montana*
'Cistula' (6)	SDeJ
'City of Vancouver' (5)	EPfP
'Claudia' (6)	SPer
'Cloud Nine' (5)	ECho
§ ***clusiana*** (15)	CBro ECho ERCP MBri NMin SPhx WHer
- var. ***chrysantha*** (15) ♀H4	CAby CAvo CExl ECho SPhx WHoo WShi
- - 'Tubergen's Gem' (15)	ECho EPot GKev MBri NMin SPhx
- 'Cynthia' (15) ♀H4	CTca ECGP ECho EPot ERCP GKev MBri NMin SDeJ SPhx
- 'Sheila' (15)	CBro ECho IFro NMin SPhx
§ - var. ***stellata*** (15)	ECho
'Colour Spectacle'PBR (5)	CAby
'Columbine' (5)	ECho
'Concerto' (13)	CBro MBri NPer SDeJ
'Coquette' (1)	SDeJ
'Corona' (12)	ECho SDeJ
'Corsage' (14) ♀H4	SDeJ
'Cortina' (9)	SDeJ
'Couleur Cardinal' (3)	CBro ERCP SDeJ
'Creme Upstar' (11)	ERCP MBri SDeJ
cretica (15)	ECho NMin
'Crispion Dark' (7)	ERCP
'Cummins' (7)	CAvo ERCP
'Curly Sue' (7)	CAvo ERCP SPer
'Czaar Peter' (14) ♀H4	CAvo EPfP MBri NPer
'Dance' (13)	SDeJ
'Dancing Queen' (2)	MBri
dasystemon (15)	ECho EPot LLHF
dasystemonoides (15)	ECho
'Davenport' (7)	ERCP
'David Teniers' (2)	ERCP SDeJ
'Daytona' (7)	CAvo

	'Doll's Minuet' (8)	EPfP ERCP
	'Don Quichotte' (3) ♀H4	MBri SDeJ
	'Donald Duck' (14) ♀H4	MBri
	'Donauperle' (14)	SDeJ
	'Donna Bella' (14) ♀H4	EPfP SDeJ
	'Dordogne' (5) ♀H4	SDeJ
	'Double Price' (2)	ERCP
	'Double Red Riding Hood' (14v)	SDeJ
	'Dragon King' (3) **new**	SDeJ
	'Dreamboat' (14)	MBri
	'Dreaming Maid' (3)	MBri
	'Dreamland' (5) ♀H4	MBri SDeJ
	'Duc van Tol Red and Yellow' (1)	GKev WHer
	'Dutch Gold' (3)	MBri
	'Dynasty' (3)	SPer
	'Early Harvest' (12) ♀H4	CAvo SDeJ
	'Easter Surprise' (14) ♀H4	MBri SDeJ
	eichleri	see *T. undulatifolia*
	'Electra' (5)	MBri NHol
	'Elegant Lady' (6)	CAvo CWCL MCot SDeJ
	'Esperanto' (8/v) ♀H4	CAby SDeJ
	'Estella Rijnveld' (10)	ERCP SDeJ
	'Exotic Emperor' (13)	CAby
	'Fancy Frills' (7) ♀H4	ERCP SDeJ
	'Fashion' (12)	SDeJ
	ferganica (15)	ECho NMin
	'Fidelio' (3) ♀H4	SDeJ
*	'Finola' (11)	MCot
	'Fire Queen' (3) ♀H4	ERCP
	'Fire Wings' (6) **new**	CMea
	'Flair' (1)	SDeJ
	'Flamenco' (7) **new**	SDeJ
	'Flaming Parrot' (10)	CAby CAvo CWCL ERCP GKev MBri
I	'Flaming Purissima' (13)	CAvo MBri SDeJ
	'Flaming Springgreen' (8)	CAvo CWCL ERCP SDeJ
	'Flashback' (10)	ERCP MCot
	'Flig Flag' (3)	ERCP
	'Florosa' (8)	ERCP SDeJ
	'Foxtrot'^{PBR} (2)	EPfP ERCP
	'Françoise' (3)	SDeJ
	'Franz Léhar' (12)	SDeJ
	'Fringed Family' (7)	SDeJ
	'Fritz Kreisler' (12)	SDeJ
	'Fulgens' (6)	ECho
	'Für Elise' (14)	SDeJ
	'Gaiety' (12)	SDeJ
	'Garden Party' (3) ♀H4	SDeJ
	'Gavota' (3) ♀H4	CAvo CBro EPfP MCot NHol SDeJ SPer
	'Generaal de Wet' (1)	SDeJ
	'Georgette' (5)	MBri
	'Gerbrand Kieft' (11) ♀H4	ERCP
	'Girlfriend' (15)	ECho
	'Giuseppe Verdi' (12)	LRHS MBri
	'Glück' (12) ♀H4	ECho EPfP LRHS
	'Golden Apeldoorn' (4)	MBri SDeJ
	'Golden Artist' (8)	EPfP MBri SDeJ
	'Golden Emperor' (13)	SDeJ
	'Golden Melody' (3)	SDeJ
	'Goldwest' (14)	SDeJ
	'Gordon Cooper' (4)	SDeJ
	'Grand Perfection'^{PBR} (3) ♀H4	EPfP LPio
	'Green Eyes' (8)	SDeJ
	'Green River' (8)	SDeJ
	'Green Wave' (10)	ERCP SDeJ
	'Greenstar' (6) **new**	ERCP
	grengiolensis (15)	ECho NMin
	'Groenland' (8)	CAvo CBro CWCL MBri MCot SDeJ
	hageri (15)	ECho LLHF MBri
	- 'Red Cup' (13)	NMin
	- 'Splendens' (15)	ECho EPot SPhx
	'Hamilton' (7) ♀H4	SDeJ
	'Happy Generation' (3)	MBri
	'Happy Hour' (7) ♀H4	ERCP
	'Havran' (3)	CAvo ERCP
	'Heart's Delight' (12)	CBro ECho MBri SDeJ
	'Helmar' (3)	SDeJ
	'Hemisphere' (3)	EPfP ERCP SDeJ
	'Hermitage' (3)	CWCL ERCP
	heweri (15)	ECho NMin
	hissarica (15)	ECho
	'Hocus Pocus' (5)	SDeJ
	'Holland Baby' (2)	SDeJ
	'Holland Chic' (6)	MCot SDeJ
	'Hollandia' (3)	MBri
	'Hollands Glorie' (4) ♀H4	SDeJ
	'Honky Tonk' (15) ♀H4	CAvo ECho GKev LPio MBri NMin
§	***hoogiana*** (15)	ECho
	'Hotpants' (3)	SPer
§	***humilis*** (15)	CBro ECho GKev MBri WShi
	- 'China Carol' (15)	ECGP ECho LLHF SDeJ
	- 'Eastern Spice' (15)	ECho NMin
	- 'Eastern Star' (15)	ECho GKev MBri NMin
	- 'Helene' (15)	ECho
§	- 'Lilliput' (15)	CBro CMea ECho EPot GKev LRHS NMin SPhx
	- 'Magenta Queen' (15)	ECho
	- 'Odalisque' (15)	ECho EPot ERCP GKev NMin
	- 'Pegasus' (15)	NMin
	- 'Persian Pearl' (15)	CAby CAvo ECho EPfP EPot ERCP GKev MBri NMin SDeJ SMrm
*	- 'Pink Charm' (15)	ECho
	- var. ***pulchella*** Albocaerulea Oculata Group (15)	CTca ECho EPot ERCP GKev LLHF MCot NMin
I	- 'Rosea Coerulea Oculata' (15) **new**	NMin
§	- Violacea Group (15)	CAvo CMea ECho MBri
	- - black base (15)	CBro ECho EPot ERCP GKev MBri NMin SBch
	- - yellow base (15)	ECho EPot GKev
	- 'Zephyr' (15)	NMin
	'Ice Cream' (11) **new**	SDeJ
	'Ile de France' (5)	ERCP SDeJ
	iliensis (15)	CMea ECho EPot LLHF NMin
	'India' (3)	ERCP
	'Indian Summer' (3)	MCot
	ingens (15)	ECho NMin
	'Inzell' (3)	EPfP
	'Ivory Floradale' (4) ♀H4	SDeJ
	'Jan Reus' (3)	CAby CAvo ERCP
	'Jazz' (6)	ERCP
	'Joffre' (1)	MBri
	'Johann Strauss' (12)	ECho MBri SPer
	'Juan' (13) ♀H4	MBri
	julia (15)	ECho NMin
	kaufmanniana (12)	ECho EPot
§	'Kees Nelis' (3)	MBri
	'Keizerskroon' (1) ♀H4	SDeJ
	'Kingsblood' (5) ♀H4	SDeJ
	kolpakowskiana (15) ♀H4	ECho EPfP EPot ERCP LLHF MBri NMin WShi
	kurdica (15)	ECho SPhx
	- purple-flowered (15)	ECho

	'Lac van Rijn' (1)	GKev
*	'Lady Diana' (14)	MBri
	'Lady Jane' (15) ♀H4	CAvo CBro CMea ECho EPfP ERCP MBri NMin SPer SPhx WShi
	lanata (15)	NMin
	'Latvian Gold' (15)	ECho NMin
	'Leen van der Mark' (3)	MBri
	'Libretto Parrot' (10)	SDeJ
	'Lilac Perfection' (11)	CTca ERCP MBri SDeJ
	'Lilac Wonder'	see *T. saxatilis* (Bakeri Group) 'Lilac Wonder'
	'Lilliput'	see *T. humilis* 'Lilliput'
	'Lilyfire' (6)	ECGP SDeJ
	linifolia (15) ♀H4	CAvo ECho EPfP EPot ERCP GKev MBri NMin SDeJ SPhx WShi
§	- Batalinii Group (15) ♀H4	ECho MBri SPhx
§	- - 'Apricot Jewel' (15)	CBro ECho EPot ERCP GKev
	- - 'Bright Gem' (15) ♀H4	CAby CBro ECho EPot GKev MBri NPer SPhx WHoo
	- - 'Bronze Charm' (15)	CAvo CMea ECGP ECho EPot MBri NMin SDeJ SPhx
	- - 'Red Gem' (15)	ECho GKev SPhx
	- - 'Red Hunter' (15) ♀H4	CBro CMea ECho EPfP ERCP GKev MBri SPer
	- - 'Red Jewel' (15)	ECho
	- - 'Salmon Gem' (15)	ECho
	- - 'Yellow Jewel' (15)	ECho GKev
§	- Maximowiczii Group (15)	ECho EPot
	'Lipgloss' (3)	NHol
	'Little Beauty' (15) ♀H4	CAby CAvo CBro CMea ECho EPfP GKev MBri SDeJ SPhx WHoo
	'Little Princess' (15) ♀H4	CAvo CBro CTca ECho ERCP GKev SPhx
	'Little Star' (15)	NMin
	'Lovely Surprise' (14)	SDeJ
	'Lucky Strike' (3)	MBri
§	'Lustige Witwe' (3)	SDeJ
§	'Madame Lefeber' (13)	MBri SDeJ
	'Madonna' (10)	EPfP
	'Magier' (5)	MBri
	'Maja' (7)	CAvo MBri
	'March of Time' (14)	MBri
	'Marie José' (14)	SDeJ
	'Mariette' (6)	CBro MBri SDeJ SPer
	'Marilyn' (6)	ERCP SDeJ
	marjolletii (15)	CBro ECho NMin
	'Maroon' (7)	ERCP
	'Matchpoint' (7/d)	ERCP SDeJ
	'Maureen' (5) ♀H4	ERCP SDeJ
	mauritiana 'Cindy' (15)	ECho NMin
	maximowiczii	see *T. linifolia* Maximowiczii Group
	'Maytime' (6)	MBri MCot SDeJ
	'Maywonder' (11) ♀H4	MBri MCot
	'Menton' (5) ♀H4	ERCP SDeJ
	'Menton Exotic' (11)	ERCP
	Merry Widow	see *T.* 'Lustige Witwe'
	'Mickey Mouse' (1)	MBri
	'Miskodeed' (14)	SDeJ
	'Miss Holland' (3)	MBri
	'Mona Lisa' (6)	SDeJ
	'Moneymaker' (6)	ERCP
§	***montana*** (15)	CTca ECho EPot NMin
	- yellow-flowered	ECho GKev NMin
	'Monte Carlo' (2) ♀H4	CBro MBri NHol SDeJ
	'Montreux' (2)	ECho
	'Moonlight Girl' (6) ♀H4 **new**	MCot
	'Mount Tacoma' (11)	CAvo CBro EPfP ERCP MBri SDeJ SPer
	'Mr Van der Hoef' (2)	MBri SDeJ
	'Mrs John T. Scheepers' (5) ♀H4	SDeJ
	'Muriel' (10)	ERCP
	'Negrita' (3)	ERCP MBri MCot SDeJ
	neustruevae (15)	ECho EPot NMin SPhx
	'New Design' (3/v)	CWCL MBri
	'Nightrider' (8)	CAvo ERCP MCot
	'Ollioules' (4) ♀H4	SDeJ
	'Olympic Flame' (4) ♀H4	SDeJ
	'Orange Bouquet' (3) ♀H4	MBri
	'Orange Elite' (14)	MBri
	'Orange Emperor' (13) ♀H4	CAvo MBri MCot SDeJ
	'Orange Favourite' (10)	ERCP
	'Orange Princess' (11) ♀H4	CTca ERCP SDeJ
	'Orange Sun'	see *T.* 'Oranjezon'
	'Orange Triumph' (11)	MBri
	'Oranje Nassau' (2) ♀H4	MBri
§	'Oranjezon' (4) ♀H4	ERCP
	'Oratorio' (14) ♀H4	MBri SDeJ
	'Oriental Beauty' (14) ♀H4	EPfP
	orithyioides	NMin
	orphanidea (15)	ECho NMin
	- 'Flava' (15)	ECho EPot
§	- Whittallii Group (15) ♀H4	CAvo ECho EPot ERCP GKev NMin SPhx
	'Oscar' (3)	NHol
	ostrowskiana (15)	ECho NMin
	'Page Polka' (3)	MBri SDeJ
	'Palestrina' (3)	EPfP SPer
	'Pandour' (14)	MBri
	'Parade' (4) ♀H4	MBri
	'Passionale' (3) ♀H4	EPfP SDeJ SPer
	'Paul Scherer' (3) ♀H4	ERCP SDeJ
	'Peach Blossom' (2)	ERCP MBri SDeJ SPer
	'Peppermintstick' (15) ♀H4	CAvo CTca ECho NMin SDeJ
	'Perestroyka' (3)	MBri SDeJ
	persica	see *T. celsiana*
	'Picture' (5) ♀H4	ERCP SDeJ
	'Pieter de Leur' (6)	EPfP MBri SPer
	'Pimpernel' (8/v)	SDeJ
	'Pink Diamond' (5)	CAvo EPfP ERCP NHol SDeJ
	'Pink Dwarf' (12)	SDeJ
	'Pink Impression' (4) ♀H4	MBri SDeJ
	'Pink Sensation' (14) ♀H4	SDeJ
	'Pinocchio' (14)	CAby LPio LRHS MBri SDeJ
	'Pirand' (13) ♀H4 **new**	ERCP SDeJ
	'Plaisir' (14) ♀H4	MBri
	platystigma (15)	ECho NMin
	'Poco Loco' (13)	SDeJ
	polychroma	see *T. biflora*
	praestans (15)	ECho SPer WShi
	- 'Bloemenlust' (15)	GKev
	- 'Fusilier' (15) ♀H4	CBro CExl ECGP ECho EPfP EPot MBri NBir SDeJ
	- 'Red Sun' (15)	ECho GKev
	- 'Shogun' (15)	ECho ERCP
	- 'Unicum' (15/v)	ECho ERCP MBri NMin SDeJ
	- 'Van Tubergen's Variety' (15)	ECho NPer
	- 'Yari' (15)	ECho GKev
	- 'Zwanenburg Variety' (15)	ECho
	'Princeps' (13)	MBri SDeJ
	'Princesse Charmante' (14) ♀H4	MBri
	'Prinses Irene' (3) ♀H4	CAby CAvo CBro CMea CTca CWCL EPfP ERCP LRHS MBri MCot NBir NHol SDeJ
	'Prinses Margriet' (3)	ERCP
	'Professor Röntgen' (10)	ERCP SDeJ

	pulchella humilis	see *T. humilis*
§	'Purissima' (13) 🏆H4	CAvo CBro EPfP MBri MCot SDeJ SPer
	'Purple Bouquet' (3)	SDeJ
	'Purple Prince' (5)	CBro LRHS SDeJ
	'Quebec' (14)	SDeJ
	'Queen of Marvel' (2)	SDeJ
	'Queen of Night' (5)	CAby CAvo CBro CMea CTca EPfP ERCP GKev MBri MCot SPer SPhx
	'Queen of Sheba' (6) 🏆H4	CMea
	'Queensland' (7) **new**	ERCP
	'Rai' (10)	ERCP MCot
	'Recreado' (5)	CAvo ERCP SDeJ
	'Red Emperor'	see *T.* 'Madame Lefeber'
	'Red Georgette' (5) 🏆H4	CAby MBri NBir
	'Red Princess' (11) 🏆H4	ERCP
	'Red Riding Hood' (14) 🏆H4	CAby CAvo CBro EPfP GKev LRHS MBri NBir SDeJ SPer
	'Red Shine' (6) 🏆H4	CAby CAvo CBro MBri SDeJ
	'Red Springgreen' (8)	SDeJ
	'Red Wing' (7) 🏆H4	SDeJ
	Rembrandt mix (9)	MBri
	'Rems Favourite' (3) **new**	CAvo
	'Renown' (5)	SDeJ
	rhodopea	see *T. urumoffii*
	'Ringo'	see *T.* 'Kees Nelis'
	'Rococo' (10)	CBro ERCP MBri SDeJ
	'Ronaldo' (3)	EPfP ERCP
*	'Rose Emperor' (13)	MBri
	'Rosy Dream' (13)	SDeJ
	'Ruby Red' (1)	CAby
	'Salmon Impression'[PBR] (4)	MBri
	'Sapporro' (6)	ERCP
	saxatilis (15)	CBro CMea ECho EPfP GKev MBri SDeJ WShi
§	- Bakeri Group (15)	ECho SEND
§	- - 'Lilac Wonder' (15) 🏆H4	CAby CAvo CBro CExl ECho EPot ERCP GKev MBri NPer SPhx
	'Scarlet Baby' (12)	EPfP MBri
	'Schoonoord' (2)	MBri
	schrenkii (15)	CMea ECho ERCP NMin
	'Sensual Touch' (7) 🏆H4	SDeJ
	'Shakespeare' (12)	CBro SDeJ
	'Shirley' (3)	CAby CAvo EPfP ERCP MBri MCot SDeJ SPer
	'Shirley Dream' (3)	SDeJ
	'Showtime' (14)	SDeJ
	'Showwinner' (12) 🏆H4	CAvo CBro MBri NHol
	'Snow Parrot' (10)	ERCP
	sogdiana (15)	ECho LLHF NMin
	'Sorbet' (5) 🏆H4	SDeJ
	sprengeri (15) 🏆H4	CAvo CBro CExl CLAP CRDP CTca ECGP ECho EPot ERCP LLHF SDix WHal WIvy WShi
	- Trotter's form (15)	WCot
	'Spring Green' (8) 🏆H4	CAby CAvo CBro EPfP ERCP GKev LPio MBri MCot SDeJ SPer SPhx
	'Spryng' (3) 🏆H4	SDeJ
	'Starfighter' (7)	SDeJ
	stellata	see *T. clusiana* var. *stellata*
	'Stresa' (12) 🏆H4	CBro LRHS SDeJ
	'Sunny Prince'[PBR] (1) **new**	CBro
	'Swan Wings' (7)	ERCP SDeJ
	'Sweet Harmony' (5) 🏆H4	MBri
	'Sweetheart' (13)	MBri SDeJ
	sylvestris (15)	CAby CAvo CBro CTca ECho EPfP EPot ERCP MBri NBir NMin SDeJ SPer SPhx WCot WHer WShi
	systola (15)	ECho NMin
	'Taco' (15)	ECho MBri NMin
	tarda (15) 🏆H4	CAvo CBro CExl ECho EPfP ERCP GKev LPot LRHS MBri NSla SDeJ SPhx
	'Temple of Beauty' (5) 🏆H4	SDeJ
	'Temple's Favourite' (5)	MBri
	tetraphylla (15)	ECho NMin
	'Texas Flame' (10)	MBri SDeJ
	'Texas Gold' (10)	SDeJ
	'The First' (12)	CAvo
	'Tinka' (15) 🏆H4	ECho EPfP LSou NMin
	'Tiny Timo' (15) **new**	LLHF NMin
	'Toplips' (11)	SDeJ
	'Topparrot' (10)	SDeJ
	'Toronto' (14) 🏆H4	CTca MBri SDeJ
	'Toronto Double' (2)	SDeJ
	'Toulon' (13) 🏆H4	MBri
	'Très Chic' (6)	CAvo CTca EPfP MBri SPer
	'Tricolored Beauty' (8) **new**	ERCP
	tschimganica (15)	ECho
	turkestanica (15) 🏆H4	CAby CBro CExl CHid CSpe CTca ECho EPfP EPot ERCP GKev LPio LPot MBri NPer SDeJ SPhx WHoo
	'Turkish Delight' (14)	NPer
	'Uncle Tom' (11)	ERCP MBri SDeJ
§	***undulatifolia*** (15)	ECho
	- 'Clare Benedict' (15)	ECho NMin
	- 'Excelsa' (15)	ECho NMin
	'United States' (14)	NPer
	urumiensis (15) 🏆H4	CBro CHid ECho EPot GKev LPot MBri NMin SDeJ SPhx
§	***urumoffii*** (15)	ECho
	'Valentine' (3) 🏆H4	SDeJ
	'Valery Gergiev' (7)	ERCP
	'Van der Neer' (1)	SDeJ
	'Velvet Lily' (6)	NMin
	'Verona' (2)	SDeJ
	'Véronique Sanson' (3)	ERCP SDeJ
	violacea	see *T. humilis* Violacea Group
	'Violet Beauty' (5) **new**	SDeJ
	'Violet Bird' (8)	SDeJ
	'Virichic' (8)	ERCP MCot
	vvedenskyi (15)	ECho EPot GKev
	- 'Tangerine Beauty' (15) 🏆H4	ECho GKev MBri
	'Wallflower' (5) **new**	ERCP
	'Warbler' (7)	SDeJ
*	'Water Lily'	ECho
	'Weber's Parrot' (10)	ERCP MBri MCot
	'Weisse Berliner' (3)	CBro
	'West Point' (6) 🏆H4	CAvo CBro CTca MBri SDeJ
	'White Dream' (3)	CAvo EPfP MBri SDeJ
	'White Emperor'	see *T.* 'Purissima'
	'White Parrot' (10)	CAvo CWCL ERCP SDeJ
	'White Triumphator' (6) 🏆H4	CAvo CBro CMea ERCP GKev MBri NBir SDeJ SPhx
	whittallii	see *T. orphanidea* Whittallii Group
	'Wildhof' (3) 🏆H4	ERCP
	'Willemsoord' (2)	MBri SDeJ
	'William of Orange'	SDeJ
	wilsoniana	see *T. montana*
	'Wisley' (5)	MBri
	'World Expression' (5) 🏆H4	SDeJ
	'Yellow Emperor' (5)	MBri
	'Yellow Flight' (3)	SDeJ
	'Yellow Pompenette'[PBR] (11) 🏆H4	SDeJ
I	'Yellow Purissima' (13) 🏆H4	EPfP

'Yellow Springgreen' (8)	CBro ERCP
'Yokohama' (3)	SDeJ
'Zampa' (14) 🏆H4	MBri
zenaidae (15)	ECho
§ 'Zurel' (3)	EPfP ERCP MCot

tummelberry see *Rubus* 'Tummelberry'

Tunica see *Petrorhagia*

Tupistra (*Asparagaceae*)

sp. new	WCot
aurantiaca B&SWJ 2267	WCot WCru
- B&SWJ 2401	WCru
chinensis 'Eco China Ruffles'	WCot
fimbriata	WCot
grandistigma	WCot
jinshanensis new	WCot
urotepala HWJ 562	WCru
wattii B&SWJ 8297	WCru

Turnera (*Passifloraceae*)

ulmifolia	CArn

Tussilago (*Asteraceae*)

farfara	CArn GPoy MHer NMir WHer WHfH WSFF

Tweedia (*Asclepiadaceae*)

§ ***caerulea*** 🏆H2	CBcs CCCN CDTJ CFlo CHll CSPN CSpe EShb SChF SPad SWvt

Typha (*Typhaceae*)

angustifolia	CBAq CKno CRow CWat EHon LLWG MMuc MSKA NPer SPlb SWat WPnP
latifolia	CRow CWat EHon MSKA NBir NPer SVic SWat WHer WMAq WPnP XLum
- 'Variegata' (v)	CRow ELan LLWG MSKA MWts NPla WMAq
§ ***laxmannii***	CBAq CRow EHon LLWG MSKA WPnP XLum
lugdunensis	MWts
minima	CBAq CRow CWat EHoe EHon ELan EPfP MSKA MWts NPer SWat WMAq WPnP XLum
shuttleworthii	CRow LLWG
stenophylla	see *T. laxmannii*

Typhonium (*Araceae*)

alpinum	EBee WCot
giganteum	SKHP WCot
roxburghii	EBee
venosum	EUJe

Typhonodorum (*Araceae*)

lindleyanum	XBlo

U

Uapaca (*Euphorbiaceae*)

kirkiana (F)	XBlo

ugli see *Citrus* × *tangelo* 'Ugli'

Ugni (*Myrtaceae*)

candollei	SVen
§ ***molinae***	CAgr CBcs CCon CDoy CDul CExl CHel CHll CPrp CTsd EBee ELan ELon EShb GGal IDee IVic LEdu LRHS MGos MHer MOWG SLPl SPoG SWvt WGwG WHar WJek WMoo
- PAB 1347 new	LEdu
- 'Butterball'	EPfP LRHS SWvt
- 'Flambeau' (v)	CAgr CBcs CExl CHel CMac EBee ELan EPfP EShb IVic LBMP LEdu LHop LRHS MAsh MGos NLar SHil SLon SPoG SRkn SWvt WGrn
- orange-leaved	WJek
- 'Variegata' (v)	LEdu WJek

Ulex (*Papilionaceae*)

europaeus	CArn CBcs CCVT CDoC CDul CHab CMac CTri ECrN ELan EPfP LBuc MCoo MGos MMuc NEgg NWea SEWo SPer WHar
§ - 'Flore Pleno' (d) 🏆H4	CBcs CDoC CMac CSBt CTri ELan ELon EPfP GCal IArd MBlu MGos MMuc NLar NWea SEND SPer WHer
- 'Plenus'	see *U. europaeus* 'Flore Pleno'
gallii	NLar
- 'Mizen Head'	GCal MWhi SLon

Ulmus ✿ (*Ulmaceae*)

alata	EGFP
americana 'Princeton'	SGol
- 'Valley Forge'	SGol
carpinifolia	CDul
var. ***suberosa*** new	
'Dodoens'	IArd SCoo
'Frontier' new	SGol
§ ***glabra***	CDul EPfP NWea SCoo
- 'Camperdownii'	CMac EBee ECrN ELan LAst WMou
- 'Exoniensis'	CTho IVic
- 'Gittisham'	CTho
- 'Horizontalis'	see *U. glabra* 'Pendula'
- 'Lutescens'	CEnd CTho CTri NLar NWea SCoo SEWo
§ - 'Pendula'	CMac
§ × ***hollandica*** 'Dampieri Aurea'	CDul CTho EBee ELan EPfP LBuc MAsh MBlu MGos MRav NLar NWea SPer SPoG WPat
- 'Jacqueline Hillier'	CDul CMac CSpe EBee ECho ELan LAst LBuc MMuc MRav NLar SEND SGol WCFE WPat
- 'Wredei'	see *U.* × *hollandica* 'Dampieri Aurea'
laevis	CDul EGFP
'Lobel'	CCVT
Lutèce = 'Nanguen'	CDoC CDul EBee SGol
minor	CDul
- 'Dampieri Aurea'	see *U.* × *hollandica* 'Dampieri Aurea'
montana	see *U. glabra*
parvifolia	CMCN CMen WPGP
- Everclear = 'Bsnupf'	SGol
- 'Frosty' (v)	ECho
- 'Geisha' (v)	ECho ELan MAsh MRav WPat

§ - 'Hokkaido' CMen EWes LLHF WAbe WPat WThu
- 'Pygmaea' see *U. parvifolia* 'Hokkaido'
- 'Yatsubusa' ECho MRav NLar
procera CDul LBuc MCoo MGos SLon WSFF
pumila 'Beijing Gold' ELan NLar
rubra CArn
'Sapporo Autumn Gold' CCVT EBee LBuc MRav SGol WCFE
Vada = 'Wanoux'PBR SGol

Umbellularia (*Lauraceae*)

californica CArn CMCN EPfP SSpi

Umbilicus (*Crassulaceae*)

rupestris CArn SChr WHer WShi

Uncinia (*Cyperaceae*)

* ***cyparissias*** from Chile NBir
divaricata ECou
egmontiana EBee ECou EPfP LRHS SHil SPoG WGrn WMoo
N ***rubra*** Widely available
§ - 'Belinda's Find'PBR CKno CWGN EBee ELan IBoy LLWG LRHS MAsh MNrw NSti SPoG WCot
- Everflame see *U. rubra* 'Belinda's Find'
uncinata CBcs SDix
* - ***rubra*** CCon CKno CTri CWCL ELon IFro LBMP LRHS MAsh SLim SMrm SRms SWvt

Uniola (*Poaceae*)

latifolia see *Chasmanthium latifolium*

Urceolina (*Amaryllidaceae*)

miniata see *Stenomesson miniatum*
peruviana see *Stenomesson miniatum*

Urginea (*Asparagaceae*)

capitata 'Sentinel Peak' ECho
fugax EBee
macrocentra ECho
maritima CArn EBee ECho WCot
ollivieri ECho
undulata ECho

Urospermum (*Asteraceae*)

dalechampii CSam LRHS

Ursinia (*Asteraceae*)

alpina WHil

Urtica (*Urticaceae*)

from Casa Meca **new** CNat
dioica 'Chedglow 2' (v) CNat
- 'Dog Trap Lane' CNat
- 'Judith' CNat
- OGG mutant CNat
- 'Winter Yellow' CNat

Utricularia (*Lentibulariaceae*)

sp. EECP
australis EFEx
biloba CHew
bisquamata 'Betty's Bay' CHew
dichotoma CHew EFEx
exoleta R. Brown see *U. gibba*
§ ***gibba*** EFEx
heterosepala CHew
intermedia EFEx
lateriflora CHew EFEx
livida CHew EECP EFEx
menziesii EFEx
microcalyx CHew
monanthos CHew EFEx
nephrophylla CHew
novae-zelandiae CHew
ochroleuca EFEx
paulineae CHew
praelonga CHew
prehensilis CHew
reniformis EFEx
- ***nana*** EFEx
sandersonii CHew EECP
- blue-flowered EECP
simplex CHew
subulata EFEx
tricolor CHew
uniflora CHew
vulgaris CBAq EFEx
warburgii CHew
welwitschii CHew

Uvularia (*Colchicaceae*)

§ ***caroliniana*** ECho
disporum ECho
grandiflora ♀H4 Widely available
- dwarf ECho
- gold-leaved CAby MAvo
- 'Lynda Windsor' CDes CRDP SKHP
- orange-flowered SKHP
- var. ***pallida*** CAby CAvo CBct CLAP CPom EBee ECho EPPr EPfP EPot GBin GCal IBlr LEdu LRHS MNFA MRav NCGa NHar NPnk WCru WPnP
- 'Susie Lewis' WCru
grandiflora × ***perfoliata*** ECho NBir WWEG
perfoliata CBct CExl CHel CLAP EBee ECho EPPr EPfP EPot EWTr GBuc IBlr IMou LEdu MRav NBir NPnk WCru
- tall EPPr
pudica see *U. caroliniana*
sessilifolia CBct CExl CLAP CRDP EBee ECho EPot IMou LEdu LRHS MMHG WCru
- 'Cobblewood Gold' (v) EPPr WCru

V

Vaccinium ✿ (*Ericaceae*)

alaskaense **new** GPri
angustifolium **new** GPri
- var. ***laevifolium*** GLin
arctostaphylos NLar SWvt
'Berkeley' (F) CAgr CCCN CWib GKin LBuc LSRN MAsh MBlu NPla SDea SPoG SPre WHar
'Bluecrop' (F) Widely available
'Bluejay' (F) CWib ELan LAst LRHS MAsh SCoo SLon WHar

'Blueray' (F)	CWib GKin GPri
'Brigitta' (F)	CTrh EMil GTwe LRHS NPla SPoG SPre
chaetothrix	WAbe WThu
'Chandler' (F)	CAgr CMac CTrh EMil EPom EWTr GKin GPri LRHS LSRN MCoo NPla SKee SPoG
consanguineum B&SWJ 10486	WCru
corymbosum (F) ♀H4	CBcs MGos MNHC SCoo SSta
- 'Blauweiss-Goldtraube' (F)	CAgr CSBt CWSG CWib EPfP ESwi GKin LSRN MAsh NLar NPri SDea SPoG SVic WGwG WHar
- 'Blue Duke' (F)	LSRN
- 'Bluegold' (F)	CTrh EMil LRHS MAsh
- 'Bluetta' (F)	CAgr CTri CWib ELan GPri GTwe SCoo SPoG
- 'Coville' (F)	CWib NLar
- 'Darrow' (F)	CAgr GTwe LRHS
- 'Dixie' (F)	CSBt MSCN NPla
- 'Duke' (F) ♀H4	CTrh CWib ELan EPfP EPom GPri LRHS MGos NPla NWea SDea SPre WHar
- 'Elizabeth' (F)	GPri
- 'Elliott' (F)	LRHS LSRN
- 'Grover' (F)	NLar
- 'Hannah's Choice' (F)	GPri
- 'Hardyblue' (F)	CAgr
- 'Ivanhoe' (F)	GKin
- 'Jersey' (F)	CAgr CWib EPfP LAst LRHS MAsh MGos MMuc NLar SCoo SDea SPer SVic WHar
- 'Legacy' (F)	CTrh
- 'Nelson' (F)	GPri LRHS NPla SCoo
- 'Nui' (F)	EPom LSRN
- 'Patriot' (F)	CAgr CSBt CTrh CWib GKin GPri GTwe LBuc LRHS MBri MGos MPkF MRav NPla NPri SCoo SDea SHBl SPoG SPre
- 'Reka' (F)	CAgr
- 'Sierra' (F)	GPri
- 'Spartan' (F) ♀H4	CTrh CWib EPom GTwe LRHS LSRN MAsh MGos NPla SKee
- 'Stanley' (F)	ELan EPfP LRHS MAsh
- 'Toro' (F)	GPri GTwe LRHS MAsh SPre
- 'Weymouth' (F)	SDea
crassifolium	LRHS MAsh SPoG
subsp. ***sempervirens*** 'Well's Delight' (F)	
cylindraceum ♀H4	CBcs EPfP NLar WPat
delavayi	GPri LRHS MAsh NHar WAbe WPat WThu
deliciosum (F) new	GPri
donianum	see *V. sprengelii*
dunalianum	CBcs MMuc
- var. ***caudatifolium*** B&SWJ 1716	WCru
- var. ***megaphyllum*** HWJ 515	WCru
'Earliblue' (F)	CAgr CSBt GKin MBri SDea
floribundum	CBcs CDoC CMHG GPri LRHS MAsh NLar SSpi
glaucoalbum ♀H3-4	CAbP CDoC CMac EBee EPfP LRHS MAsh MBlu MRav SMad SPoG WPGP WPat
'Goldtraube 71'	LRHS MAsh NPla
* ***grandiflorum***	ECho
griffithianum	SSta
'Herbert' (F)	CAgr CMac EPom LBuc
macrocarpon (F)	CArn ECho ELan GTwe LRHS MAsh MMuc NHar SDea SPoG SPre SRms
- 'Centennial' (F)	NHar
- 'CN' (F)	CAgr NLar
- 'Early Black' (F)	ELan EPom GKin GPri SVic
- 'Franklin' (F)	CAgr
- 'Hamilton'	LLHF WThu
- 'Howes' (F)	NHar
- 'Langlois' (F)	NLar
- 'Olson's Honkers' (F)	CAgr NLar
- 'Pilgrim' (F)	CAgr CMac GKin GPri LEdu LRHS MAsh NHar WHar
- 'Red Star' (F)	CTrh
- 'Stevens' (F)	CAgr CTrh
'Misty' (F)	CAgr
moupinense	GPri IDee LRHS MAsh WThu
- 'Variegatum' (v)	LLHF
myrtillus	CAgr EPom GPoy GPri NLar SVic
'Northland' (F)	CSBt CWib EPfP GTwe LRHS MBri NLar NPla NPri SCoo SDea SPoG
nummularia	ECho LRHS MMuc NHar SSpi WAbe WThu
ovatum	CBcs CMHG CMac CTsd GPri IDee WThu
- 'Thundercloud'	CAbP GPri LRHS MAsh
§ ***oxycoccos*** (F)	CAgr CArn GPoy GPri MCoo NHar WThu
'Ozarkblue' (F)	CTrh EPom GTwe LSRN MCoo
pallidum	IBlr
palustre	see *V. oxycoccos*
'Poppins'	CTrh
'Rubel' (F)	NPri
§ ***sprengelii***	CFil
'Spring Surprise' new	WAbe
'Sunrise' (F)	GTwe
'Sunshine Blue' (F)	CAgr CTrh EPom LBuc LRHS SDea SPoG
'Tophat' (F)	CCCN LEdu MPkF
vitis-idaea	CArn EPfP EWes GPoy NWea SVic
- 'Autumn Beauty'	NLar
- 'Compactum'	EWes LLHF
- 'Ida'	LBuc
- Koralle Group ♀H4	CAgr EPfP GKin MBri MCoo NLar NWad
- subsp. ***minus***	GPri NLar WAbe WThu
- 'Red Candy'	ELan EPfP NWad
- 'Red Pearl'	CSBt EPfP EPom LRHS MAsh NLar

Vagaria (*Amaryllidaceae*)

ollivieri	ECho

Valeriana (*Caprifoliaceae*)

'Alba'	see *Centranthus ruber* 'Albus'
alliariifolia	EBee GCal NBro WCot
- PAB 3001 new	LEdu
'Coccinea'	see *Centranthus ruber*
dioica	CHab LLWG
jatamansi	CArn GPoy WJek
montana	NBro NRya SRms SWat
officinalis	CAby CArn CHab CHby ELau GPoy LEdu LLWG MHer MHoo MLHP MMuc MNHC NBro NLar NPri SEND SIde SPhx SRms SWat WHer WHfH WJek WMoo WSFF WShi XLum
- subsp. ***sambucifolia***	EPPr GCal MNrw MSpe SHar WHil
phu 'Aurea'	CArn CHby CMac EBee EHoe ELan EPfP GKin LHop LRHS MBri

MCot MLHP MRav NBid NBir NBro NEgg NSti NWad SMrm SPer SRms WMoo

pyrenaica — EBee EPPr GCal LPla LRHS MMHG MMuc MNrw SDix SEND SPhx WCot WMoo
saxatilis — NLar NRya
supina — CPBP
wallrothii — WCot

Valerianella (*Caprifoliaceae*)

§ ***locusta*** — GPoy SVic
olitoria — see *V. locusta*

Vallea (*Elaeocarpaceae*)

stipularis — CHll CTsd IGor

Vallota see *Cyrtanthus*

Vancouveria (*Berberidaceae*)

chrysantha — CCon CExl CFil CLAP CMil CPom EBee EPPr GLog MRav NLar NRya SKHP SMad WMoo WPGP
hexandra — CBct CCon CExl CFil CGHE CLAP CMac EPPr EPfP GAbr GKev GLog LEdu NSti SKHP SPhx WCru WMoo WPGP WWEG
planipetala — CLAP IMou WCru

Vania see *Thlaspi*

veitchberry see *Rubus* 'Veitchberry'

Veltheimia ✿ (*Asparagaceae*)

§ ***bracteata*** 🏆H1 — CCse CHll CLak EBak ECho LToo WCot
viridifolia Jacq. — see *V. bracteata*

× *Venidioarctotis* see *Arctotis*

Venidium see *Arctotis*

Veratrum ✿ (*Melanthiaceae*)

album 🏆H4 — CBct CCon EBee ECho GPoy LEdu LWst MNrw MRav NBid WCru WWFP
- PAB 537 **new** — LEdu
- var. ***flavum*** — LPla MNrw SPhx WCot WCru
- subsp. ***lobelianum*** — GCal
- 'Lorna's Green' — GCal MNrw WCot
- var. ***oxysepalum*** — WCru

californicum — CHGN EBee GCal MNrw NBid WCot
dolichopetalum B&SWJ 4195 — WCru
formosanum — CDes EWld MNrw
- B&SWJ 1575 — WCru
- RWJ 9806 — WCru

grandiflorum B&SWJ 4416 — WCru
longebracteatum — WCru
maackii — MNrw
- var. ***japonicum*** — MNrw WCru
- var. ***maackii*** — MNrw
- - B&SWJ 5831 — WCru

nigrum 🏆H4 — CBct CHel GAbr GCal GMaP IKil LEdu LPla LWst MLHP MNrw MRav NBid NBir NCGa NLar SMad SPhx SPlb WCot WCru WPnP WSHC WSpi
- B&SWJ 4450 from South Korea — WCru

schindleri — MNrw
- B&SWJ 4068 — WCru

stamineum — WCru
viride — CBct EBee EWes GCal MNrw NBid

Verbascum (*Scrophulariaceae*)

acaule — EPot
'Annie May' — LSRN NOrc
'Arctic Summer' — see *V. bombyciferum* 'Polarsommer'
'Bill Bishop' — ECho
blattaria — NBir SPav SWat WHer WWEG
- f. ***albiflorum*** — CSpe GBBs IFro LLWP NDov SPlb WHer WMoo
- yellow-flowered — SPav SWat

'Blue Lagoon' **new** — GBin STPC
'Blushing Bride'PBR — LLHF
§ ***bombyciferum*** — CBre CSev ELan GMaP NGBl
* - 'Arctic Snow' — SPav SPoG
§ - 'Polarsommer' — CSpe EPfP MBri NBir SMad SPer SPet SWat WWEG
- 'Silver Lining' — NLar NPer

'Broussa' — see *V. bombyciferum*
'Buttercup' — ECtt LRHS
'Caribbean Crush' — CBcs EBee ECtt ELan ELon EPfP EWll GBin IBoy LPio LRHS NLar SPer
chaixii — CHel CSam MBel MMHG NBir WMoo
- 'Album' 🏆H4 — Widely available
- 'Sixteen Candles' — GJos LRHS MBNS NLar WHil WPtf
- 'Wedding Candles' — ELan IPot NGdn NLar SBea WHil

'Cherry Helen'PBR — ECtt LRHS LSRN MBri NEgg NGdn NLar NPnk SPer
'Christo's Yellow Lightning' 🏆H4 — WCot
'Clementine' — ECtt ELan LPla MBri SPhx
'Coneyhill Yellow' — EPPr
(Cotswold Group) 'Cotswold Beauty' 🏆H4 — CHel CSam CSpe ECtt EPfP LPio LRHS MBel MCot MRav MWat NGdn SBea SPer WHoo WMnd
- 'Cotswold Gem' — ECtt
- 'Cotswold Queen' — CBcs CHel ECtt ELan EPPr EPfP GBBs LBMP LPio LRHS MRav MWat NGdn SBea SGol SPer SWvt WCAu
- 'Gainsborough' 🏆H4 — COlW CSBt EBee ECtt ELan EPfP GMaP LHop LPio LRHS LSRN MBri MJak MRav NGdn NLar NPri NSoo NSti SGbt SPer SWat SWvt WCAu WHil
- 'Mont Blanc' — LRHS SWat
- 'Pink Domino' 🏆H4 — CBcs CSam ECtt ELan EPPr EPfP GMaP LRHS MJak MLHP MRav MWat NGdn NSoo SBea SPer SWvt WMnd WWFP WWlt
- 'Royal Highland' — CHel EBee ECtt ELan EPfP LPio NGdn NLar SWvt
- 'White Domino' — EBee ECtt

'Cotswold King' — see *V. creticum*
§ ***creticum*** — CSpe IKil WCot
'Dark Eyes'PBR — CWGN ECtt
§ ***densiflorum*** — CArn WWEG
- BSSS 232 — WCru

epixanthinum ♀	CPla CSpe LRHS
'Flower of Scotland'	MBNS MBri
'Golden Wings' ♀H2-3	CPla WAbe
'Helen Johnson'	CBcs CHel CWCL ECtt ELan EPfP GMaP LHop LPio LRHS LSRN MGos MRav NLar NPnk NPri SCoo SHil SPer SRkn SWvt WMnd
× ***hybridum*** 'Banana Custard'	NGBl
- 'Snow Maiden'	CTri EPfP MHer
- 'Wega'	NLar
'Hyde Hall Sunrise'	EPfP
'Jackie'	CBcs CHel ECtt ELan GBBs LBMP LRHS LSRN MBri NGdn SCoo SPer SPoG WHil
'Jackie in Pink'	ELan LRHS MBri NGdn SHil
'Jackie in Yellow' PBR	LLHF MBri NGdn
'Jester'	ECtt MBNS MHol SPoG WHil
'Jolly Eyes'	ECtt GBBs
'June Johnson'	ECtt LRHS WWlt
'Kynaston'	IPot MBNS
'Letitia' ♀H3	CMea CPla ECho ECtt EHyd ELan EWes GCal ITim LRHS SWvt WAbe
'Linda'	ECtt
longifolium var. ***pannosum***	see *V. olympicum*
lychnitis	CArn SPhx
'Megan's Mauve'	LRHS
'Merlin' PBR	ECtt LRHS LSRN LSou MBNS NSti SPoG WMnd WPtf
nigrum	CArn CHab LHop NGdn NLar WHer WMoo
- var. ***album***	NChi NGdn NLar WMoo WOut
'Norfolk Dawn'	ECtt
§ ***olympicum***	EBee ELan EPfP GJos LBMP LPot LRHS MBNS NGBl NSti SDix SEND SMrm WCot WWEG
'Pandora'	LRHS
'Petra'	LPla SPhx
phlomoides white-flowered **new**	SPhx
phoeniceum	ELan EPfP GBBs GJos GKev LRHS NBid NBro SPlb SPoG WMoo
* - 'Album'	CSpe
- 'Antique Rose'	WHrl
- 'Flush of White'	ECtt EPfP GBin GQue MSCN NGBl NGdn NLar NPnk WHil WMoo WWEG WWFP
- hybrids	CTri GMaP NEgg NGdn SRms SWat WWEG
- 'Rosetta'	EPfP MCot NGBl NGdn SPad SPla
- 'Violetta'	CArn CCVN CSpe ECtt EPPr EPfP EWll LBMP MCot MHol MLHP MNFA MWat NEgg NGBl NGdn NSti SGbt SPav SPer SPhx WCFE WCot WHrl WMoo WPtf
'Phoenix'	CTsd
'Pink Kisses'	LLHF LRHS LSRN MBNS
'Pink Petticoats'	LBuc LRHS SPoG
(Pixie Series) 'Pixie Apricot'	ECtt MBri
- 'Pixie Blue'	ECtt LSou
- 'Pixie Pink'	LSou MBri
- 'Pixie White'	ECtt MBri
'Plum Smokey' PBR	ECtt IBoy LLHF LRHS
'Primrose Path'	EBee ECtt ELon EPfP LRHS NPri
'Purple Prince'	ECtt
pyramidatum	SPhx
'Raspberry Ripple'	ECtt LLHF SPer STPC
'Rosie'	EBee
'Sierra Sunset'	ECtt EPfP
'Southern Charm'	EPfP EWll GJos GMaP MHer NLBP NPnk SPoG WPtf
'Spica'	NLar
'Sugar Plum' PBR	ECtt ELon EWll LBuc LLHF MHol SPoG
'Summer Sorbet'	EBee ECtt EPfP LRHS NSti
Sunset shades	GJos WOut
thapsiforme	see *V. densiflorum*
thapsus	CHab GPoy MHer MHoo MNHC NBir NMir SEND WOut
'Twilight'	LRHS
undulatum	CArn

Verbena (*Verbenaceae*)

(Aztec Series) Aztec Blue Velvet = 'Balazvelu' (G)	NPri
- Aztec Cherry Red = 'Balazcherd' PBR (G)	NPri
- Aztec Coral = 'Balazcoral' PBR (G)	NPri
- Aztec Dark Pink Magic = 'Balazdapima' (G)	NPri
- Aztec Pearl = 'Balazpearl' PBR (G)	SCoo
- Aztec Plum Magic = 'Balazplum' PBR (G)	NPri
- Aztec Red = 'Balazred' (G)	SCoo
- Aztec Silver Magic = 'Balazsilma' PBR (G) ♀H3	NPri SCoo
'Bampton' **new**	LHop
'Betty Lee' (G)	ECtt
'Blue Prince' (G)	CSpe
§ ***bonariensis*** ♀H3-4	Widely available
- 'Lollipop'	CKno CSpe ELan EPfP GBin IBal LHop MAsh MBel NPnk NSti SGbt SPer SPoG SWvt WCot
brasiliensis misapplied	see *V. bonariensis*
canadensis 'Perfecta' (G)	CSpe
'Candy Carousel' (G)	SPet
chamaedrifolia	see *V. peruviana*
§ 'Claret' (G) ♀H3	CCVN CMac CSev CSpe ECtt EHyd ELan EPfP LAst LRHS LSRN LSou MCot MGos MNrw SCoo SHil SMrm SPet SPhx SPoG WWEG
corymbosa	CHid CHII EBee ECGP LRHS MMuc MSpe NLar SMrm SPhx WMoo
- 'Gravetye'	CPrp LPot
'Diamond Merci' (G)	WHoo
(Donalena Series) Donalena Pink Heart (G) ♀H3 **new**	LAst
- Donalena Twinkle Pink (G)	NPri
- Donalena Twinkle Purple (G)	NPri
'Edith Eddleman' (G)	CMac CWGN EPfP LRHS LSqH SPoG
'Empress Peach Flair'	LAst
'Fiesta' (G)	LRHS
'Hammerstein Pink'	EBee EHyd EPfP
hastata	CSpe ECtt EPfP LAst LEdu LRHS MNrw NDov NSti SPhx SPlb SRms SWat SWvt WBor WMnd WMoo WSHC

* - 'Alba'	CTsd ELan EPfP GBin LDai NLar WMoo WWFP
- 'Blue Spires'	CAby EPfP WWEG
- f. ***rosea***	CElw CMea CPom CSpe EHoe ELan EPfP GKev LRHS MCot MLHP MNrw MRav NBid NDov SPhx SWat WCAu WMoo WSHC WWEG WWFP
- - 'Pink Spires'	ECtt ELan EPfP LHop WWEG
- 'White Spires'	CMea EPfP WWEG
'Homestead Purple' (G)	CBar CMac COIW CPrp CSev ECtt EHyd ELan EPfP LDai LRHS LSRN MCot MGos MNrw NDov SMrm SPer SPet SWvt WHoo WWEG
'Jenny's Wine'	see *V.* 'Claret'
'La France' (G)	CHGN EPfP LRHS SDix SMrm SPhx SPoG WMnd WSHC
Lanai Blue Denim = 'Bludena'PBR **new**	MCot
lasiostachys	EBee
'Lavender Spires'	MCot SPhx
'Lois' Ruby'	see *V.* 'Claret'
macdougalii	LHop SPhx
officinalis	CArn GPoy MHer MNHC SIde SRms WHer WJek
patagonica	see *V. bonariensis*
§ ***peruviana*** (G)	EBee ECho EHyd ELan EPfP LBMP LHop LRHS SChF SRms XLum
'Pink Bouquet'	see *V.* 'Silver Anne'
'Pink Parfait' (G)	EPfP
Quartz Series 🏆H3	LAst NPri
- 'Quartz Red Polka Dot'	ELan EPfP
- 'Quartz Waterfall' (mixed)	LAst
'Red Cascade'	SPet
§ ***rigida*** 🏆H3	Widely available
- f. ***lilacina***	LSRN NLar
- - 'Lilac Haze'	CMac EHyd EPfP LBMP LRHS NSti SRkn
- - 'Polaris'	CSam EBee EHyd ELan ELon EPfP EWTr GCal LHop LRHS MMuc MNrw MRav SHar SMrm SPet SPhx SPoG WSHC
Seabrook's Lavender = 'Sealav'PBR	CPrp CSev EBee EPfP ESwi LHop LRHS LSRN LSqH MNrw SCoo SHar SPer SPoG SRkn SWvt WSHC
serpyllifolia	see *Junellia micrantha*
§ 'Silver Anne' (G) 🏆H3	LDai MCot SMrm
§ 'Sissinghurst' (G) 🏆H2-3	CSam ECtt SMrm SRms
'Sissinghurst Pink'	SPer
stricta	EBee LRHS NLar SPhx
(Tapien Series) Tapien Compact Velvet = 'Suntapikovel' (G)	LSou
- Tapien Pink Parfait = 'Suntapipipa'PBR (G)	LSou
- Tapien Pink = 'Sunver'PBR (G)	LAst
- Tapien Red (G)	LAst
- Tapien Salmon = 'Suntapiro'PBR (G) 🏆H3	LAst LSou WGor
- Tapien Sky Blue = 'Suntapilabu'PBR (G) 🏆H3	LAst
- Tapien Violet = 'Sunvop'PBR (G)	LAst LHop LSou WGor
- Tapien White = 'Suntapipurew'PBR (G)	LAst
(Temari Series) Temari Blue = 'Sunmariribu'PBR (G)	LAst
- Temari Coral Pink = 'Sunmariripi'PBR (G)	LAst LSou
- Temari Neon Red = 'Sunmarineopi'PBR (G) 🏆H3	LAst
- Temari Patio Red = 'Sunmaribisu'PBR (G)	LAst
- Temari Vanilla = 'Sunmarivani'PBR (G)	LAst LSou
'Tenerife'	see *V.* 'Sissinghurst'
'Vegas Appleblossom' (Vegas Series) (G)	WGor
venosa	see *V. rigida*
'White Cascade'	SPet

Verbesina (*Asteraceae*)

alternifolia	CArn
- 'Goldstrahl'	EPPr

Vernicia (*Euphorbiaceae*)

fordii	SPlb

Vernonia (*Asteraceae*)

angustifolia* × *missurica	WCot
§ ***arkansana***	CHGN EBee EPPr EWes IPot LEdu LRHS MMuc NLar SDix SMad WWEG
- 'Betty Blindeman'	LEdu
- 'Mammuth'	CDes EBee EWes GQue LEdu LHop LRHS SPhx
crinita	see *V. arkansana*
fasciculata	CSpe EShb EWes LEdu LPla MRav NLar SPhx WCot
gigantea	EBee ELon EWes MMuc MNrw NLar SBHP SMad SPhx WHrl
glauca	WCot
lindheimeri	WCot
missurica	EBee SPhx
noveboracensis	LEdu NLar SMad SPhx XLum
- 'Albiflora'	EPPr EWes

Veronica (*Plantaginaceae*)

amethystina	see *V. spuria* L.
anagallis-aquatica	LLWG
'Anna'PBR	NDov
armena	ECho EDAr EWes MHer MWat SBch SRot WIce XSen
'Atomic Blue'	LSou
'Atomic Lilac'	LSou
'Atomic Pink'	LSou MBri
'Atomic Red Ray' **new**	MAsh
'Atomic Silvery Pink Ray' **new**	MAsh
'Atomic Sky Ray'PBR	LSou MAsh
'Atomic Violet'	MBri
'Atomic Violet Ray'PBR	LSou MBri
§ ***austriaca***	NBre NChi WMoo
- dark blue-flowered	NChi
- var. ***dubia***	see *V. prostrata*
- 'Ionian Skies'	CElw CTri ECho ECtt EPPr EWTr EWes MMuc NEgg NWad SIgm SMrm SPer WIce WKif WSHC WWEG
§ - subsp. ***teucrium***	CArn CSam CTri ECho SRms WKif

- - 'Crater Lake Blue' ♀H4	CAby EBee ECtt ELan EPfP EShb LEdu LHop LRHS MCot MRav NBre NGdn SMrm SPlb SRms WCot WMnd WSHC
- - 'Kapitän'	ECho GBuc LHop LRHS MNrw NGdn
- - 'Knallblau'	EBee SMrm
- - 'Royal Blue' ♀H4	CCVN EBee EPfP EShb GMaP LRHS MJak MWhi NCGa NSti SBch SPer SRms WKif WMnd WMoo XLum XSen
'Baby Blue'PBR	CHel
'Baby Doll'PBR	LRHS LSou MBNS MBri NCGa NLar
beccabunga	CArn CBAq CHab CWat EHon EWay GPoy MSKA MWts NMir NPer SWat WHer WMAq WSFF
'Bergen's Blue'	NLar SHar WSHC
Blue Bouquet	see *V. longifolia* 'Blaubündel'
'Blue Indigo'	MNrw MTis NBre NGdn
'Blue Spire'	SWat
bombycina	ECho ITim WAbe
bonarota	see *Paederota bonarota*
caespitosa	CPBP
- subsp. ***caespitosa***	WAbe
candida	see *V. spicata* subsp. *incana*
× ***cantiana*** 'Kentish Pink'	WCFE WMoo WOut WWEG XLum
caucasica	XSen
chamaedrys	ECho NMir XLum
- 'Pam' (v)	ECtt
'Charlotte' (v) **new**	WCot
Christy = 'Henslerone'PBR	EPfP LBuc LRHS
cinerea ♀H4	GMaP MLHP SBch SBrt WHoo WSHC XSen
dabneyi	CDes EBee WPGP
'Dark Martje'	IPot WSHC
'Darwin's Blue'PBR	NGdn NLar NOrc WHrl
'Ellen Mae'	CElw ECtt EWes WCAu WMnd
'Eveline'PBR	EBee ECtt EPfP MBri MSpe NDov NLar
exaltata (d)	LRHS NChi SMrm WCot
'Fairytale'PBR	EPfP LPio LRHS LSou MBNS MBel MBri NCGa NGdn NSti SMrm WHil
'Fantasy'	NDov
filiformis	XLum
'First Love'	LSou MAsh MBri NGdn
formosa	see *Parahebe formosa*
§ ***fruticans***	ECho GJos
fruticulosa	LLHF
gentianoides ♀H4	Widely available
- 'Alba'	CMea GCal LEdu LRHS NBre NChi NSti
- 'Barbara Sherwood'	EBee LRHS NBre NGdn WWEG
- 'Blue Streak'	LRHS XLum
- 'Lilacina'	EBee ECho LRHS
- 'Nana'	EBee
- 'Pallida'	EPfP GAbr GKev MBrN MMuc MRav SPlb WBor WWEG XLum
- 'Robusta'	ECtt GKev LRHS NCGa NEgg NGdn SBea WHoo WMnd
- 'Tissington White'	CMHG EBee ECtt EHyd EPfP GMaP LAst LEdu LHop LRHS MBri MCot MLHP MNFA MPie MSpe NBir NBro NEgg NGdn NLar NWad SBea SHar SMrm SPoG SWat WCAu WWEG
- 'Variegata' (v)	EBee ECtt ELan EPfP GCra GMaP LAst LBMP MHer MRav MSCN MSpe NBir NEgg NPnk NWad SPer SWat WWEG
gigantea	MMuc
'Giles van Hees'	ECtt WCot
grandis	EBee GAbr IFro LEdu MMuc MWhi NChi NLar SEND SMad WHrl WMoo WPtf XLum
× ***guthrieana***	SRms
hendersonii	see *V. subsessilis hendersonii*
incana	see *V. spicata* subsp. *incana*
* - 'Candidissima'	GCal
'Ink'	SPhx
'Inspiration'	CCse CMea NBre NDov SMrm
'Inspire Blue'	EPfP LBMP LSou MPnt
'Inspire Pink'	LBMP LSou MPnt
kellereri	see *V. spicata*
kiusiana	CMHG EBee IFro LPla LRHS NLar NWad SPhx WHrl
* - var. ***maxima***	WPtf
kotschyana	XSen
'Lavender Plume'	CWGN EPfP MAsh WHil
liwanensis	ECho
- Mac&W 5936	EPot
longifolia	CMac CMea CSBt ELan GCra LRHS MAvo MBel MLHP MNFA NSti WMoo XLum
- 'Alba'	ELan MMuc NLar SEND WMoo
- 'Antarctica'	MTis
- 'Blaubart'	XLum
§ - 'Blaubündel'	CCse EHyd NGdn
- 'Blauer Sommer'	EBee EPfP MCot NDov NEgg NGdn
§ - 'Blauriesin'	CTri ECtt ELan EPfP GMaP LRHS MAvo NBre NPnk NSti SPer
- Blue Giantess	see *V. longifolia* 'Blauriesin'
- 'Blue John'	ECtt EPfP LSou MPie MTis NBre NSti WCot WHoo WRHF
- 'Charming Pink'	LRHS MAsh SMrm
- 'Fascination'	ECtt LAst NGdn NPro
- 'Foerster's Blue'	see *V. longifolia* 'Blauriesin'
- 'Joseph's Coat' (v)	NBre
- 'Lilac Fantasy'	LHop MBri MRav MSCN WWlt
- 'Oxford Blue'	CBar WBor WHoo
- 'Pacific Ocean'PBR	ECtt
- 'Pink Eveline'PBR	MSpe NDov STPC
- pink-flowered	EShb
- 'Rose Tone'	GJos NLar WMoo
- 'Rosea'	LPio
- 'Schneeriesin'	CPrp EBee EPfP GMaP LEdu MAvo MRav NBir NLar NPnk SPer
lyallii	see *Parahebe lyallii*
macrostachya	SKHP
'Martje'	SMrm XLum
montana 'Corinne Tremaine' (v)	EBee NBir NLar SRms WHer
officinalis	CArn XLum XSen
oltensis	CPBP ECho EPot ITim LLHF MHer WAbe
orchidea	LRHS SRms
ornata	WOld
pectinata 'Rosea'	ECho ECtt EWes XSen
peduncularis 'Oxford Blue'	see *V. umbrosa* 'Georgia Blue'
perfoliata	see *Parahebe perfoliata*
petraea 'Madame Mercier'	SMrm XLum
'Pink Damask'	CSpe ECtt ELan ELon EPfP GMaP MAvo MCot MRav MTis NEgg

		NGdn NLar NSti SDys SMrm SPhx WHoo WMnd WWEG
	'Pink Harmony' **new**	MAsh NSti
	***pinnata* new**	SBrt
	- 'Blue Feathers'	EDAr
	porphyriana	EBee EDAr MMuc
	prenja	see *V. austriaca*
§	***prostrata*** ♀H4	CMea CSpe CTri ECho ECtt EDAr EPfP GJos LAst LBee LRHS MAsh MHol MLHP NEgg NHar NPri SRms WHoo WIce WMoo WNew XLum
	- 'Alba'	MLHP MWat
	- 'Aztec Gold'PBR	CMac MSCN NLar NPro
§	- 'Blauspiegel'	CPBP SIgm
	- 'Blue Ice'	SMrm
	- Blue Mirror	see *V. prostrata* 'Blauspiegel'
	- 'Blue Sheen'	ECho ECtt EPfP LRHS NBir
	- 'Goldwell'	ECtt EPPr LBMP SRot
	- 'Lilac Time'	ECho ECtt GMaP LHop LRHS NBir NHol NLar SRms WHil WIce
	- 'Loddon Blue'	ECho SRms WCot
	- 'Miss Willmott'	see *V. prostrata* 'Warley Blue'
	- 'Mrs Holt'	ECho ECtt LHop LRHS NBir NWad SRms WBrk WHoo XLum
	- 'Nana'	ECho ECtt EPot EWes MWat WAbe
	- 'Nestor'	CTri ECtt NGdn WPtf XLum
	- 'Rosea'	ECho MWat
	- 'Spode Blue' ♀H4	CBar CMac CMea ECho ECtt GMaP LBMP LHop LRHS MHer SPoG SRms WWEG
	- 'Trehane'	ECho ECtt EDAr EPfP LEdu LHop LRHS MAsh MHer NEgg NRya SPlb SPoG SRms WIce WNew
§	- 'Warley Blue'	ECho
	'Purpleicious Harmony'PBR	EPfP LRHS LSou MAsh MBri NPri SMrm WHil WOut
	repens	ECho EPfP GJos NPro SPlb
	- 'Sunshine'	LRHS
	'Rosalinde'	NGdn
	'Royal Pink'	CPrp LAst MRav NLar
	rupestris	see *V. prostrata*
	saturejoides	CPBP SRms
	saxatilis	see *V. fruticans*
	schmidtiana 'Nana'	GKev
	selleri	see *V. wormskjoldii*
	'Shirley Blue' ♀H4	CPrp CWib ELan EPfP LPot LSRN MCot MHer MMuc MWat SRms WCAu WCFE WWEG
§	***spicata***	CSam EBee ELan EPfP GJos LRHS NBid NPnk SMrm SRms WBrk WMoo WOut WShi XLum
	- 'Alba'	CHel EBee EPfP GJos LPot LRHS MRav NLar WWEG XLum
	- 'Barcarolle'	EBee EPfP
§	- 'Blaufuchs'	CSam
	- 'Blue Bouquet'	NLar NPri
	- 'Blue Candles'	GQue
	- Blue Fox	see *V. spicata* 'Blaufuchs'
§	- 'Erika'	CPrp CSam ECtt EPfP GBin IBoy LPio LSou MBri MNrw MWat NBid NBir NBre NGdn WHil
§	- 'Glory'PBR	CPrp ECtt ELan ELon EPfP LRHS LSou MGos MPie MTis NBre NEgg NPri NSoo SMrm SPer SPoG WCot WHil WMnd WRHF
	- 'Heidekind'	CHel ECho ECtt EDAr ELan EPfP EPot GKev LAst LHop MWat NBir NGdn SRms SRot SWat WCAu WGrn WHil WHoo XLum
	- 'High Five'PBR	EBee
	- subsp. ***hybrida***	WHer
	- - 'Elaine's Form'	WCot
§	- 'Icicle'	EBee WCAu
§	- subsp. ***incana***	CMea ECho EHoe ELan EPfP GJos MMuc SEND SPlb SRms SWat WMoo WWEG XSen
	- - 'Nana'	MLHP NBir SRms
	- - 'Silbersee'	MAvo MLHP
	- - 'Silver Carpet'	CPrp ECtt LAst LHop MRav SPer WGwG WMnd
	- - 'Wendy'	EWes GCal LPla SPhx WSHC
	- 'Minuet'	LRHS
	- 'Nana Blauteppich'	CPBP EDAr EPfP LRHS NBre NLar
	- 'Pink Goblin'	ECtt EDAr ELan EPfP NBre SMrm
	- 'Pink Panther'PBR	LSou WCot
	- Red Fox	see *V. spicata* 'Rotfuchs'
	- 'Romiley Purple'	EBee NBre SPer
	- 'Rosalind'	NLar
	- ***rosea***	see *V. spicata* 'Erika'
	- 'Rosenrot'	ECho
§	- 'Rotfuchs'	CPrp EBee ECtt EHoe EHyd ELan ELon EPfP LAst LSou MBel MCot MMuc MRav NBid NBir NGdn NOrc NSoo SPad SPer SPoG SRms WCAu WCFE WWEG
	- 'Royal Candles'	see *V. spicata* 'Glory'
	- 'Sightseeing'	CWib GJos NBir NBre SRms WRHF
	- subsp. ***spicata*** 'Nana'	XSen
	- 'Total Eclipse'PBR	EBee LSou NCGa NSti
	- 'Twilight'PBR	ECtt EPfP MBri NCGa
	- 'Ulster Blue Dwarf'	EBee EPfP IBoy LRHS LSou MAsh MAvo MBri MCot NBid NGdn
§	***spuria*** L.	MMuc SEND
	stelleri	see *V. wormskjoldii*
	subsessilis 'Blaue Pyramide'	NBre
*	- ***hendersonii***	NBre
	'Sunny Border Blue'	EPfP NBre NLar NSoo SPoG WCAu WCot
	tauricola	XSen
	telephiifolia	EWes
	teucrium	see *V. austriaca* subsp. *teucrium*
§	***umbrosa*** 'Georgia Blue'	Widely available
	urticifolia	SBrt
	virginica	see *Veronicastrum virginicum*
	'Waterperry Blue'	ECtt
	'White Icicle'	see *V. spicata* 'Icicle'
	'White Jolanda'	NSti
	whitleyi	MMuc
§	***wormskjoldii***	EBee ECho GBin MAvo MBrN NLar NWad SBch SRms
	- 'Alba'	MLHP

Veronicastrum (*Plantaginaceae*)

'Adoration'	LPla MAvo NCGa NDov SPhx
axillare	IMou
brunonianum	GCal WSHC
japonicum var. ***australe*** B&SWJ 11009	WCru
latifolium	CDes EBee WCot
- BWJ 8158	WCru
sibiricum	CKno EShb GCal GQue LRHS MMuc NBre WMoo WSpi XLum
- BWJ 6352	LEdu NLar WCru

	– 'Red Arrows'	CPrp EBee ECtt GBin IPot LSou MAsh MAvo MBel MHol MSCN MTis NDov NLar NOrc NSti SHar SMrm SPer SPhx WCot
	– var. ***yezoense*** RBS 0290	NPro
	villosulum	CPom EBee EWes IMou NBid NBro WCru WSHC
§	***virginicum***	CArn CKno EBee ECtt GCra GPoy LPio LRHS MBrN MHoo MLHP MMuc MWhi NBir SRms WMoo WWEG XLum
	– 'Album'	Widely available
	– 'Apollo'	CBct CBre EBee ECtt EPPr EPfP EWll GAbr GBin GMaP IBoy LEdu LPio LPla LRHS LSou MBri MTis NBro NDov NLar NOrc NSti SMrm SPhx SWvt WHrl WSpi WWEG
	– 'Cupid' **new**	GBin STPC
	– 'Diane'	EBee IPot LPla NBre NDov SPhx SWvt WCAu WSpi
	– 'Erica'	CCVN CKno ECtt EPPr EPfP GBin GMaP GQue IKil IPot LPla LRHS LSou MAvo MBri MNrw MTis NCGa NDov NPnk NSti SMrm SPhx SWvt WBor WCot WHil WWEG WWlt
	– 'Fascination'	Widely available
	– var. ***incarnatum***	see *V. virginicum* f. *roseum*
	– 'Lavendelturm'	CDes CKno CMea CSam ECtt ELon EPPr EWll GMaP IPot LEdu LHop LRHS MAvo MCot MNrw MTis NCGa NDov NLar NSti SMrm SPer SPhx SWvt WCot
	– light blue-flowered	MMuc SEND
	– 'Pointed Finger'	CMea GCal GMaP IPot LEdu NBre [illegible] SMrm SPhx
§	– f. ***roseum***	CAby CPrp ELan GMaP LPla LRHS MAvo MBel MHol MRav MTis NBro NDov SGbt SPad SPer SPhx SWvt WBor WCot WKif WMoo WSpi XLum
	– – 'Pink Glow'	Widely available
	– 'Spring Dew'	CBre EBee EPfP LEdu LPla NBid NBro NPro SPhx WMnd
	– 'Temptation'	EBee EWll GMaP IPot LEdu LPla MRav NBre NBro NCGa NPro SPhx WCAu

Verschaffeltia (*Arecaceae*)

	splendida	XBlo

Vestia (*Solanaceae*)

§	***foetida*** ♀H1	CBcs CCCN CExl CTsd CWib EBee ELan EMil EPfP IDee LRHS MNrw SBig SBrt SEND WSHC
	lycioides	see *V. foetida*

Viburnum ✿ (*Adoxaceae*)

	acerifolium	LLHF NWad WPat
	alnifolium	see *V. lantanoides*
	atrocyaneum	CExl CGHE CJun EBee MBlu NLar NWad SKHP WPat
	– B&SWJ 7272	EPfP MRav WCru
	– HIRD 113	WPGP
§	***awabuki***	CExl CHEx ELon EPfP EUJe LRHS MAsh MBlu MGos NLar SEND SLim SMad WPGP WPat
	– B&SWJ 8404	WCru
	– B&SWJ 11374 from Wabuka, Japan	WCru
	– 'Emerald Lustre'	CHEx EBee WPGP
	betulifolium	CAbP CBcs CExl CHel CJun EBee ELan EPfP EWes GGGa GKin NLar SMad SPer WPGP
	– PAB 3877 **new**	LEdu
	– f. ***aurantiacum***	CJun
	– 'Hohuanshan'	WCru
	bitchiuense	CJun MRav NLar
	× ***bodnantense***	CHel CMac CTri EBee WHar
	– 'Charles Lamont' ♀H4	EBee ECrN ELan EPfP GBin GCal LAst LBMP LHop LRHS LSRN MAsh MBri MGos MMuc MRav MSwo NEgg NLar NSoo SCoo SGol SHil SLim SPer WPat
	– 'Dawn' ♀H4	Widely available
	– 'Deben' ♀H4	EPfP MMHG NLar SPer SPoG WPat
	brachyandrum B&SWJ 5784	WCru
	bracteatum	NLar
	buddlejifolium	CMac EBee EBtc EPfP EWes MMuc SKHP WCru WPGP
	× ***burkwoodii***	Widely available
	– 'Anika'	NLar
	– 'Anne Russell' ♀H4	Widely available
	– 'Chenaultii'	MRav
	– 'Compact Beauty'	CJun WCFE WPat
	– 'Conoy'	CJun ELon MAsh WPat
	– 'Fulbrook' ♀H4	CAbP EPfP LEdu LRHS MAsh NLar WHar WPat
	– 'Mohawk'	CAbP CDoC CEnd CJun EBee ELan ELon EPfP LRHS MAsh NLar SCoo SHil SKHP SWvt WPat
	– 'Park Farm Hybrid' ♀H4	CAbP CDoC CExl CJun CMac CSam CTri CWib EBee ECrN ELan ELon EPfP LAst LEdu LRHS MAsh MGos MRav NLar SLPl SPer SPoG SRms WPat
	calvum	CExl
	aff. ***calvum*** WWJ 12012	WCru
	× ***carlcephalum*** ♀H4	Widely available
	– 'Cayuga'	ELon MAsh NLar WPat
	– 'Van der Maat' **new**	NLar
*	– 'Variegatum' (v)	CJun
	carlesii	CBcs CMac CTri CWib EBee EPfP GKin LSRN MBlu MGos MRav MSwo SCoo SEWo SGol SLim SPer
	B&SWJ 0038	WCru
	– 'Aurora' ♀H4	Widely available
	– 'Charis'	CJun CSBt LRHS NLar WKif
	– 'Compactum'	CJun MAsh WCot WPat
	– 'Diana'	CDoC CEnd CJun CMHG CMac EPfP LHop LRHS LSRN MAsh MBlu MRav NLar SPer SPoG SSta WCFE WPat
	– 'Marlou'	CJun NLar WPat
	cassinoides	CJun
	– 'Bullatum'	EPfP
	– 'Sear Charm'	WPGP
	'Chesapeake'	CDul CJun EWes MMuc SEND
	chingii	CJun SLon WCru WPGP WPat
	'Chippewa'	CJun
	cinnamomifolium ♀H3	CAbP CDoy CExl CHEx EBee ELan EPfP GBin LRHS MAsh MMuc NLar NSoo SAPC SBrt SEND SLon SPer SPoG SSpi WHor WPGP WSHC

	Name	Suppliers
	cotinifolium	CExl
	- CC 4541	CExl NLar
	- CC 6267 **new**	GKev
	cylindricum	CGHE EBee EPfP EWTr LHop LRHS NLar SKHP WCru WPGP WPat
	- B&SWJ 6479 from Thailand	WCru
	- B&SWJ 7239	WCru
	- B&SWJ 9719 from Vietnam	WCru
	- HWJCM 434 from Nepal	WCru
	- NJM 09.127 from Vietnam	WPGP
	dasyanthum	NLar
	davidii YH4	Widely available
	- (f)	CBcs CDoC CMac CSBt ELan EPfP EWTr LAst MAsh MGos SPer SPoG SRms WHar WPat
	- (m)	CBcs CDoC CMac CSBt ELan EPfP MGos MRav SPer SPoG SRms WHar WPat
	- 'Angustifolium'	CJun EBee WPGP
	dentatum	EBtc MAsh WPat
	- Autumn Jazz	see *V. dentatum* 'Ralph Senior'
	- Blue Muffin = 'Christom'	WPat
	- Chicago Lustre	see *V. dentatum* 'Synnestvedt'
§	- 'Ralph Senior'	NLar
§	- 'Synnestvedt'	NLar
	- 'White and Blue'	CJun NLar
	dilatatum B&SWJ 4456	WCru
	- B&SWJ 5844	WCru
	- B&SWJ 8734	WCru
	- B&SWJ 10894	WCru
	- 'Erie'	NLar
	- 'Inneke'	NLar
	- 'Iroquois'	EPfP
	- 'Michael Dodge'	EPfP MBri NLar
	- 'Sealing Wax'	NLar
	'Emerald Triumph'	CJun
	erosum B&SWJ 3585	WCru
	- B&SWJ 8735	WCru
	- B&SWJ 8893	WCru
	- B&SWJ 10880	WCru
	erubescens	CAbP CJun EPfP NLar
	- HWJK 2163	WCru
	- var. ***gracilipes***	CJun EPfP LLHF MAsh WPat
	- 'Ward van Teylingen'	EPfP NLar
	'Eskimo'	CAbP CBcs CJun CMac CSBt EBee ELan EPfP GBin LRHS MAsh MBNS MGos MRav SCoo SKHP SLim SPoG SSta SWvt
	fansipanense B&SWJ 8302 **new**	WCru
	- KWJ 12239 **new**	WCru
§	***farreri*** YH4	CBcs CDoC CDoy CDul CSBt CTri CWib EBee ELan EPfP GGal LBuc LRHS LSRN MGos MRav MSwo NLar NSoo SGol SHil SPer SPoG SWvt WHar
	- 'Album'	see *V. farreri* 'Candidissimum'
§	- 'Candidissimum'	CDul CExl CMac EBee ELan EPfP EWTr IArd LHop LRHS MAsh MRav NLar SGol SPer
	- 'December Dwarf'	CJun NLar
	- 'Farrer's Pink'	CAbP CExl CJun NLar
	- 'Fioretta'	NLar
	- 'Nanum'	CJun CMac EBee EBtc ELan ELon EPfP LRHS MAsh MBrN MRav MWat NLar SKHP WPat
	foetens	see *V. grandiflorum* f. *foetens*
	foetidum var. ***ceanothoides***	NLar
	- var. ***rectangulatum*** B&SWJ 1888	WCru
	- - B&SWJ 3451	WCru
	fragrans Bunge	see *V. farreri*
	'Fragrant Cloud'	ECrN
	furcatum YH4	EPfP GKin MAsh NLar SKHP WPat
	- B&SWJ 5939	WCru
	× ***globosum*** 'Jermyns Globe'	CAbP CCVT CDoC CJun CMHG CMac EBee EPfP MRav NLar SEND SLon SPoG
	grandiflorum	CJun CMac EPfP NLar
	- 'De Oirsprong'	NLar
§	- f. ***foetens***	CJun EPfP LRHS NLar
	- - GWJ 9227	WCru
	- 'Snow White'	CJun
	aff. ***griffithianum*** GWJ 9388	WCru
	harryanum	CAbP CDoy EBtc EPfP MBNS NLar WCru WSHC
	henryi	CAbP CJun EPfP NLar SBrt WPat
	× ***hillieri***	CHGN
	- 'Winton' YH4	CAbP CDoC CJun CMac CWib EBee EPfP GBin IDee LHop LRHS LSRN MBri NLar SHil SKHP SLon SPoG SSpi SVen WPGP
	hoanglienense B&SWJ 8281 **new**	WCru
	'Huron'	EPfP NLar
	ichangense	CJun NLar
	japonicum	CExl EBee EPfP NLar SLon WPGP
	- B&SWJ 5968	WCru
	× ***juddii*** YH4	CBcs CDul CExl CJun CMHG CMac CWib EBee ECrN ELan ELon EPfP EWTr GKin LAst LEdu LHop LRHS MAsh MBlu MBri MGos MRav MSwo NLar SLon SPer SWvt WHar WPat
	kansuense	CExl
	- BWJ 7737	WCru
	koreanum B&SWJ 4231	WCru
	lantana	CBcs CCVT CDul CHab CLnd CTri CWib ELan EShb LAst LBuc NLar NWea SEND SEWo SPer SVic WMou
	- 'Aureum'	CMHG EHoe EPfP MAsh MBlu NLar SDix
	- var. ***discolor***	NLar
	- 'Mohican'	NLar
	- 'Variefolium' (v)	CJun
§	***lantanoides***	EPfP NLar SSpi
	latifolium 'Chino-Crûg'	WCru
	aff. ***lautum*** B&SWJ 10290	WCru
	'Le Bois Marquis'[PBR]	CDoC EBee EMil EPfP
	lentago	CAbP CMac NLar
	lobophyllum	EPfP NLar
	luzonicum B&SWJ 3930	WCru
	- var. ***formosanum*** B&SWJ 3585	WCru
	- var. ***oblongum*** B&SWJ 3549	WCru
	- var. ***sinuatum*** B&SWJ 4009	WCru
	macrocephalum	CJun SLon
	- 'Sterile'	LHop

	mariesii	see *V. plicatum* f. *tomentosum* 'Mariesii'
	nervosum B&SWJ 2251a	WCru
	nudum	ECrN EPfP IDee NLar
	- 'Pink Beauty'	CJun EBee EPfP LRHS LSRN MBri MMHG NLar SHil WPGP WPat
	- 'Winterthur'	CJun NLar
	odoratissimum misapplied	see *V. awabuki*
	odoratissimum Ker Gawl.	EBee LEdu
	- RWJ 10046	WCru
	- aff. 'Arboricolum'	WCru
	aff. ***odoratissimum*** B&SWJ 3913	WCru
	- from the Philippines	MAsh
	'Oneida'	CJun NLar
	opulus	Widely available
	- var. ***americanum*** 'Bailey's Compact'	MAsh
	- - 'Hans'	NLar
	- - 'Phillips'	CAgr
	- - 'Spring Red'	NLar
	- - 'Wentworth'	CAgr
	- 'Amy's Magic Gold' **new**	NLar
	- 'Apricot'	NLar
	- 'Aureum'	CHel CMac CWib EHoe ELan EPfP LBMP MAsh MGos MMuc MRav NEgg NLar SPer WMoo
	- var. ***calvescens*** B&SWJ 10544	WCru
	- 'Compactum' ♀H4	Widely available
N	- 'Fructu Luteo'	SGol
*	- 'Harvest Gold'	SCoo SLim SPoG
	- 'Nanum'	CAbP CBcs ECrN ELan ELon EPfP EShb MRav NHol NLar WPat
	- 'Notcutt's Variety' ♀H4	EPfP MAsh WPat
	- 'Park Harvest'	CDul EBee EBtc EPfP LRHS MAsh NLar SKHP SLPl WPat
§	- 'Roseum' ♀H4	Widely available
	- 'Sterile'	see *V. opulus* 'Roseum'
*	- 'Sterile Compactum'	LAst SWvt
N	- 'Xanthocarpum' ♀H4	CBcs CDoC CDul CExl CMac EBee ELan EPfP GBin GKin LAst LHop LRHS MAsh MBlu MGos MMuc MRav MSwo NLar SEND SKHP SLPl SLon SPer SRms SWvt WPat
	parvifolium	NLar
	- B&SWJ 6768	WCru
	phlebotrichum B&SWJ 11058	WCru
	pichinchense B&SWJ 10660	WCru
N	***plicatum***	CTri CWib NLar
	- 'Kilimanjaro' **new**	GBin MBlu NPnk NSoo
	- 'Mary Milton'	CJun GBin NLar
	- 'Nanum'	see *V. plicatum* f. *tomentosum* 'Nanum Semperflorens'
	- 'Pink Sensation'	CJun GBin NCGa
§	- f. ***plicatum***	EWTr NSoo SChF
	- - 'Grandiflorum'	CAbP CDoC CNec EPfP LRHS NLar SPer WMoo
	- 'Popcorn'	CAbP CDoC CExl CJun CMac ELon EPfP EWTr LEdu LRHS LSRN MAsh MRav NLar SLim SPoG SSta WPat
	- 'Rosace'	EPfP LRHS MBlu NLar SSpi WPat
N	- 'Sterile'	see *V. plicatum* f. *plicatum*
	- f. ***tomentosum***	EPfP
	- - 'Cascade'	EBee EWTr LRHS NEgg NLar SSpi
	- - 'Dart's Red Robin'	ECtt LLHF MAsh NLar WPat
	- - 'Elizabeth Bullivant'	LLHF LRHS
	- - 'Igloo'	NLar
	- - 'Lanarth'	CBar CBcs CDoC CDul CExl CMac CSBt CTri CWib EBee ELan EPfP GBin LEdu LHop LRHS LSRN MAsh MBlu MGos MJak MMuc NLar NSti SCoo SGol SKHP SLim SPer SWvt
§	- - 'Mariesii' ♀H4	Widely available
	- - 'Molly Schroeder'	CJun NLar
§	- - 'Nanum Semperflorens'	CDoC CMac ECtt MGos NLar SPoG WPat WSHC
	- - Newport = 'Newzam'	NLar
	- - 'Pink Beauty' ♀H4	Widely available
	- - 'Rotundifolium'	IArd LRHS MAsh MRav NLar SHil WPat
	- - 'Rowallane'	EPfP WPat
	- - 'Saint Keverne'	GKin
	- - 'Shasta'	CDoC CMCN EPfP EWTr LEdu NLar SKHP
	- - 'Shoshoni'	GBin NLar
	- - 'Summer Snowflake'	CDoC CEnd CWGN EBee ECrN EPfP LRHS MAsh MSwo NLar SKHP SLim SPer SPoG
	- - 'White Beauty'	EPfP MAsh
	- Triumph = 'Trizam'	NLar
	- 'Watanabe'	see *V. plicatum* f. *tomentosum* 'Nanum Semperflorens'
	'Pragense' ♀H4	CAbP CBcs CDul CMCN EBee EPfP GBin LRHS MGos NHol NLar SEND SLon SPer
	propinquum	CAbP NLar
	- CWJ 12426	WCru
	prunifolium	EBtc NLar SGol WCru
	- 'Mrs Henry's Large'	CJun NLar
*	'Regenteum'	CWib
	× ***rhytidophylloides***	IBoy
	- 'Alleghany'	NLar
	- Dart's Duke = 'Interduke'	WPat
	- 'Willowwood'	EBee ELan LRHS MAsh NLar WPat
	rhytidophyllum	CBcs CDoC CDoy CDul CHEx CMac CNWT EBee ECrN EPfP LAst LHop LRHS MGos MJak MMuc MSCN MSwo NEgg NWea SEND SGol SPer SRms WCFE WHar WMoo WSFF
	- 'Aldenham'	GCal LSRN
	- 'Roseum'	CExl SLPl SWvt
	- 'Variegatum' (v)	CJun NLar WPat
	- 'Wisley Pink'	LRHS MAsh SSpi
	'Royal Guard'	CJun LLHF NLar
	sambucinum HWJ 838	WCru
	- var. ***tomentosum*** HWJ 733	WCru
	sargentii B&SWJ 8695	WCru
	- f. ***flavum***	NLar
	- 'Onondaga' ♀H4	Widely available
	- 'Susquehanna'	EPfP NLar
	semperflorens	see *V. plicatum* f. *tomentosum* 'Nanum Semperflorens'
§	***setigerum***	EPfP NLar SLPl WPat
	- 'Aurantiacum'	NLar
	sieboldii B&SWJ 2837	WCru
	- 'Seneca'	EPfP NLar
	subalpinum	NLar
	taiwanianum B&SWJ 3009	WCru
	ternatum	EPfP
	theiferum	see *V. setigerum*
	tinoides B&SWJ 10612	WCru
	tinus	Widely available

	- 'Bewley's Variegated' (v)	EBee MRav SPer
I	- 'Compactum'	SWvt
	- 'Eve Price' ♀H4	Widely available
	- 'French White' ♀H4	CDoC CDul CMac EBee ELan EPfP LRHS MGos MRav NLar SCoo SLim SPoG SWvt WHar WRHF
	- 'Gwenllian' ♀H4	Widely available
	- 'Israel'	MBNS SPer
	- 'Little Bognor'	NLar
	- 'Lucidum'	CBcs CJun EPfP NLar SGol
	- 'Lucidum Variegatum' (v)	CJun CMac SLim
*	- 'Macrophyllum'	EPfP LRHS NLar SPoG SWvt
	- 'Purpureum'	CBar CBcs CJun CNec CSBt EBee ECrN EHoe ELon EPfP LRHS MAsh MGos MSwo MWat NEgg NLar SCoo SGol SLPl SLim SPer SPoG WMoo WPat
	- Spirit = 'Anvi'^PBR	CAbP CSBt CWSG EBee ELan LRHS LSou MAsh MBri NLar SCoo SPoG
	- 'Spring Bouquet'	MAsh NLar SPoG
	- subsp. ***subcordatum*** B&SWJ 12544 **new**	WCru
	- 'Variegatum' (v)	CDul CMac CTri CWib EBee EHoe ELan ELon EPfP LAst LRHS MAsh MGos NEgg NLar NPol SEND SGol SLim SPlb SPoG SRms SWvt WPat
	tomentosum	see *V. plicatum*
	triphyllum B&SWJ 5784	WCru
	urceolatum B&SWJ 6988	WCru
	utile	WPat WThu
	aff. ***venustum*** B&SWJ 10477	WCru
	wrightii	IArd MRav NLar
	- B&SWJ 5871	WCru
	- 'Hessei'	WPat
	- var. ***stipellatum*** B&SWJ 5856	WCru
	- - B&SWJ 8780A	WCru

Vicia (*Papilionaceae*)

	americana	EBee
	cracca	CHab NMir WSFF
	oroboides	LRHS
	sativa	CHab

Vigna (*Papilionaceae*)

§	***caracalla***	CCCN

Viguiera (*Asteraceae*)

	multiflora	EBee

Villaresia see *Citronella*

Vinca (*Apocynaceae*)

	balcanica	IMou XLum
	difformis ♀H3-4	COIW CPom CTri LLWP LRHS MGos SBri SDix WHer XLum
*	- 'Alba'	CPom SBch
	- Greystone form	CExl EPPr EPfP NLar SEND WGwG
	- 'Jenny Pym'	CExl COIW CPom EBee EPPr EWes LHop MBNS NLar SEND SPoG WBor WRHF
	- 'Ruby Baker'	EWes LRHS NChi WHrl
	- 'Snowmound'	EBee EWTr LRHS MRav NLar SPoG SWvt
	herbacea RCB UA 21	WCot
	'Hidcote Purple'	see *V. major* var. *oxyloba*
	major	CBcs CDul CMac CSBt CWib ELan EPfP EShb GPoy LBuc LRHS MGos MJak MSwo NPol NPri NWea SGbt SGol SHil SLim SPer SRms WGwG WMoo XLum XSen
	- 'Alba'	CMac CWib
	- 'Elegantissima'	see *V. major* 'Variegata'
	- 'Expoflora' (v)	COIW NLar
	- var. ***hirsuta*** hort.	see *V. major* var. *oxyloba*
§	- subsp. ***hirsuta*** (Boiss.) Stearn	CMac LPla WCot XLum
§	- 'Maculata' (v)	CDoC CSBt EBee EHoe EShb LRHS LSou MRav NPri SEND SLim SPer SPoG SWvt WMoo
§	- var. ***oxyloba***	CExl CFis CMac COIW CTri ELan EPri LHop LPot LRHS MBel MRav NLar SPoG SRms WBor WHer XSen
	- var. ***pubescens***	see *V. major* subsp. *hirsuta* (Boiss.) Stearn
	- 'Surrey Marble'	see *V. major* 'Maculata'
§	- 'Variegata' (v) ♀H4	Widely available
	- 'Wojo's Jem' (v)	CDoC CMac EBee ELan EPfP EWes LBuc LRHS MBri MGos NLar NPri SCoo SHil SLim SPoG SWvt WBor WCot
	minor	CArn CBar CBcs CDoC CDul CMac CSBt ELan EPfP GAbr GKin GPoy LAst LRHS MAsh MGos MJak NPri NSoo NWea SLim SVic XLum
	- f. ***alba*** ♀H4	CBcs CDoC CMac EPPr EPfP LRHS LSRN MAsh NEgg NLar NPri SPer WCot WPtf XLum
§	- - 'Alba Variegata' (v)	CExl EHoe LSRN NPro SPer SRms WCot WHoo WOut
	- - 'Gertrude Jekyll' ♀H4	Widely available
	- 'Alba Aureovariegata'	see *V. minor* f. *alba* 'Alba Variegata'
§	- 'Argenteovariegata' (v) ♀H4	CBcs CDoC CDul CMac CSBt CSam CTri EBee ELan ELon EPfP LAst LBMP LBuc LRHS MBri MGos MJak MMuc NEgg NPri NWea SEND SGol SHil SLim SPer SPoG SRms WGwG
§	- 'Atropurpurea' ♀H4	Widely available
§	- 'Aureovariegata' (v)	CBcs CMac ELan EPPr EPfP GAbr LRHS MGos MRav NPri SGol SHil SLim SPer SPlb WRHF
	- 'Azurea'	CHid
§	- 'Azurea Flore Pleno' (d) ♀H4	Widely available
*	- 'Blue and Gold'	ECGP ELon MAvo NBre NHol
	- 'Blue Drift'	EWes MSwo
	- 'Bowles's Blue'	see *V. minor* 'La Grave'
	- 'Bowles's Purple'	CTsd WBor
	- 'Bowles's Variety'	see *V. minor* 'La Grave'
	- 'Burgundy'	SRms
	- 'Caerulea Plena'	see *V. minor* 'Azurea Flore Pleno'
	- 'Dartington Star'	see *V. major* var. *oxyloba*
	- 'Double Burgundy'	see *V. minor* 'Multiplex'
	- 'Halstenbek' **new**	XLum
	- 'Hawaii'	ELon
	- 'Illumination' (v)	Widely available
	- 'Josephine' **new**	MHol
§	- 'La Grave' ♀H4	CDoC CExl COIW CSBt CSev CTri EBee ECGP ELan EPfP EShb LRHS LSRN MAsh MBri MGos MHol MRav NEgg NLar NPri SGol SHil SLim SPer SPoG SRms SWvt XLum
	- 'Marie'	EPPr
	- 'Mrs Betty James' (d)	WCot

§	– 'Multiplex' (d)	EBee EPPr LBuc SLim SRms WPtf
	– 'Purpurea'	see *V. minor* 'Atropurpurea'
	– 'Ralph Shugert'	CExl EBee ELon EPPr EPfP EWes LHop LRHS LSqu MAsh NLar NPri SCoo SGol SHil SPoG
	– 'Rubra'	see *V. minor* 'Atropurpurea'
	– 'Sabinka'	CHid EPPr
	– 'Silver Service' (d/v)	CHid MRav
	– 'Snowdrift' **new**	EPPr
	– 'Variegata'	see *V. minor* 'Argenteovariegata'
	– 'Variegata Aurea'	see *V. minor* 'Aureovariegata'
	– 'White Gold'	NPro
	sardoa	COlW EBee EPPr EWes LRHS

Vincetoxicum (*Apocynaceae*)

	cretaceum PAB 3432	LEdu
	forrestii	CExl
§	***hirundinaria***	EBee EPPr GPoy LEdu
	– CC 6289	EWld
	nigrum	CArn EBee GCal LEdu NChi NMyG WCot WTou
	officinale	see *V. hirundinaria*

Viola ✿ (*Violaceae*)

	'Ada Segre' (Vt)	CGro
	'Admiration' (Va)	WGoo
	adunca* var. *minor	see *V. labradorica* ambig.
§	***alba***	EWes
	'Alethia' (Va)	SDys WGoo
	'Alice' (Vt)	CLAP
	'Alice Kate'	WGoo
	'Alice Witter' (Vt)	LLHF
*	'Alison' (Va)	WGoo
	'Amelia' (Va)	WGoo
	'Annette Ross' (Va)	NDov WGoo
I	'Annie' (Vt)	CGro CLAP LLHF
	'Ardross Gem' (Va)	ECho ECtt NDov WGoo WKif
	arenaria	see *V. rupestris*
	arvensis	CHab
	'Ashvale Blue' (PVt)	CGro
	'Aspasia' (Va) 🏆H4	EWoo MNFA WGoo
	'Avril Lawson' (Va)	GKev SHar WGoo
	(Balconita Series) Balconita Cheeky Yellow **new**	LSou
	– Balconita Deep Red **new**	LSou
	– Balconita Meridian Blue **new**	LSou
	– Balconita Rose **new**	LSou
	– Balconita Spring **new**	LSou
	– Balconita White Surprise **new**	LSou
	'Barbara' (Va)	WGoo
	'Baroness de Rothschild' ambig. (Vt)	CGro CLAP
§	'Baronne Alice de Rothschild' (Vt)	NLar WCot
	'Beatrice' (Vtta)	WGoo
	'Becky Groves' (Vt)	CGro CLAP
	'Beetroot' (Vt)	CGro
§	'Belmont Blue' (C)	CSam CSpe CTri EBee ELon EWes EWoo GCal GMaP IFro LRHS MCot MHer MMuc MNFA MRav MSCN NBir NCGa SMrm SPer SPhx WCot WGoo
§	***bertolonii***	WGoo
	'Beshlie' (Va) 🏆H4	MNFA WGoo
	biflora	CMHG CPla MNrw
	'Blue Butterfly' (C)	EWoo
	'Blue Horns' (C)	ELon
	'Blue Moon' (C)	MNFA WGoo
	'Blue Moonlight' (C)	CElw MMuc
	'Blue Tit' (Va)	ECtt
	'Boughton Blue'	see *V.* 'Belmont Blue'
	'Bournemouth Gem' (Vt)	CGro
§	'Bowles's Black' (T)	CSpe EPfP EShb LBMP LEdu NBro NChi NWad SRms WJek
	'Boy Blue' (Vtta)	ECtt
	'Bruneau' (dVt)	CBre EBee ECtt EWll MPie NLar SMrm WCot
*	'Bryony' (Vtta)	NDov WGoo
	'Bullion' (Va)	WGoo
	'Burncoose Yellow'	WGoo
	'Buttercup' (Vtta)	ECtt LSRN MHol NEgg SDys SPoG WGoo
	'Butterpat' (C)	WGoo
	'Buxton Blue' (Va)	WGoo
	Can Can Series	CWCL
	canina	NBro NMir
	'Catalina'	CLAP
	'Charles William Groves' (Vt)	CLAP ELon
	'Charles Winston Groves' (Vt)	CGro
	'Charlotte'	EDAr WGoo WJek
	'Chloe' (Vtta)	CGro
	'Christie's Wedding' (Vt)	CGro
	'Christmas' (Vt)	CGro
	'Clementina' (Va) 🏆H4	MRav WGoo
	'Cleo' (Va)	WGoo
	'Clive Farrell' (Vt)	CGro
	'Clive Groves' (Vt)	CGro CLAP ELon
	'Coeur d'Alsace' (Vt)	CGro CLAP CPBP EBee ECtt GMaP NLar WHal XLum
	'Colette' (Va)	WGoo
	'Colombine' (Vt)	MAsh
	'Columbine' (Va)	ECtt EPfP GMaP LRHS MHer MHol NBir NDov NEgg SPer SPoG WCot WGoo WJek
	'Connigar'	CSam
§	'Conte di Brazza' (dPVt)	CGro NLar SHar
	'Cordelia' (Vt)	CLAP ECtt
	cornuta 🏆H4	CElw CMea CPla CSpe ECho EPot MLHP MNrw MWat NBir NBro SRms WGoo WHoo WTou
	– Alba Group 🏆H4	Widely available
	– 'Alba Minor'	ECho EPfP EWes EWoo IGor MNFA NBro NPri NSla
	– blue-flowered	ECho MHer MLHP WMoo
	– 'Clouded Yellow'	EWoo
	– 'Gypsy Moth' (C)	EWoo
	– 'Icy But Spicy'	MCot MNFA MRav NDov SMrm WCot WGoo
	– Lilacina Group (C)	MRav SWat WMnd WPtf
	– 'Mark's Dainty' **new**	MPie
	– 'Minor' 🏆H4	CPla CSam EWoo NBro NDov NPri NSla WGoo
	– 'Netta Statham'	EWoo MPie NDov WGoo
	– Purpurea Group	CMea WMnd
	– 'Spider'	MPie SDys WGoo
	– 'Victoria's Blush' (C)	CElw CSpe ELon GMaP MCot MMuc MPie NBir NDov WGoo
	– 'Violacea'	EWoo
	corsica	CMea CSpe NChi SBch
§	***cucullata*** 🏆H4	ECho SRms
§	– 'Alba' (Vt)	CBro ECho LLWP NBir SRms
	– ***rosea***	EWes
*	– 'Striata Alba'	NBro
	'Czar'	see *V.* 'The Czar'

	'Daisy Smith' (Va)	WGoo
	'Dancing Geisha' (Vt)	EPfP
	'Danielle Molly'	WGoo
	'Dawn' (Vtta)	CAby CMea ECtt EPfP GMaP MCot NEgg SPoG WGoo
	'Delicia' (Vtta)	NDov WGoo
	'Des Charentes' (Vt)	CGro
	'Desdemona' (Va)	EWoo NDov WGoo
	'Devon Cream' (Va)	WGoo
	dissecta	WCot
	'Donau' (Vt)	WCot
	'Double White' (dVt)	CGro
	'Duchesse de Parme' (dPVt)	IFro SRms
	'D'Udine' (dPVt)	CBre ECtt SRms WCot
	'Dusk'	WGoo
	'E.A. Bowles'	see *V.* 'Bowles's Black'
	'Eastgrove Blue Scented' (C)	EWoo SDys WGoo WOut WPtf
	'Eastgrove Ice Blue' (C)	MCot WGoo WOut
	'Elaine Quin'	CElw ECtt MCot MHol NDov NEgg NPri SPoG WGoo WKif
§	***elatior***	CPla EPPr EWTr MNrw WHil WPtf
	'Elizabeth' (Va)	ECtt WGoo
	'Elizabeth Lee'	WCot
	'Elliot Adam' (Va)	WGoo
	'Emperor Blue Vein'	EBee EPfP
	erecta	see *V. elatior*
	'Eris' (Va)	WGoo
	'Etain' (Va)	CAby ECho ECtt ELan EPfP EWoo GBuc GMaP LRHS MAsh MHol NDov NEgg NPri SMrm SPoG WGoo WIce
	'Fabiola' (Vtta)	EWoo NDov
	'Famecheck Apricot'	CPom
*	'Fantasy'	WGoo
	'Ferndale' (Vt)	CGro
	'Fiona' (Va)	EWoo MCot WGoo
	'Fiona Lawrenson' (Va)	WGoo
	'Fiona Mark' (Va) **new**	WCot
	'Florence' (Va)	WGoo
	'Foxbrook Cream' (C)	WGoo
	'Francesca' (Va)	WGoo
	'Freckles'	see *V. sororia* 'Freckles'
	'Fred Morey' (Vt)	CGro
	Friolina Creamy Pink (Friolina Series)	LAst
	glabella	SBch
	'Gladys Findlay' (Va)	WGoo
	'Glanmore' **new**	WCot
*	'Glenda'	WGoo
	'Glenholme'	EWoo NDov
	'Gloire de Verdun' (PVt)	CGro
	'Governor Herrick' (Vt)	CGro CLAP EBee ECtt LLHF NLar WCot WHer
§	***gracilis***	NBir
	- 'Lutea'	CSam
	- 'Major'	WGoo
	'Green Goddess' PBR	MHol SMrm
	'Green Jade' (v)	CPla
	'Grey Owl' (Va)	WGoo
	'Grovemount Blue' (C)	CElw CMea
	grypoceras var. ***exilis*** 'Sylettas'	LEdu
	'Gustav Wermig' (C)	WGoo
	'Haslemere'	see *V.* 'Nellie Britton'
	'Heartthrob' **new**	ECtt
*	'Heaselands'	SMrm
§	***hederacea***	CExl CPom ECou EWoo GQui IFoB MBNS SRms

	'Helena' (Va)	WGoo
	'Hespera' (Va)	WGoo
	heterophylla subsp. ***epirota***	see *V. bertolonii*
*	'Hetty Gatenby'	WGoo
	'Hudsons Blue'	CElw
	'Huntercombe Purple' (Va) ♀H4	ECho EHyd LHop LRHS NBir WGoo WHal WKif
	'Iden Gem' (Va)	WGoo
	'Inverurie Beauty' (Va) ♀H4	EWoo GBin GMaP NDov SDys WGoo WKif
	'Irish Elegance'	see *V.* 'Sulfurea'
	'Irish Molly' (Va)	CSpe ECho ECtt ELan EPfP GBuc LRHS MAsh MHer MHol NDov NEgg NPri SPer SPoG SRms WGoo WIce
	'Isabel'	NDov SRms WGoo
	'Isabella' (Vt)	CGro CLAP
	'Ivory Queen' (Va)	EWoo MNFA MRav NDov WGoo
	'Jack Sampson' (Vt)	CGro
	'Jackanapes' (Va) ♀H4	CHVG EBee ECho ECtt ELan EPfP LBMP LRHS MHol NEgg SPer SPoG SRms WGoo WIce
	'Jane Mott' (Va)	EWoo
	'Janet' (Va)	EBee ECtt LSRN MHol NPri SDys SPoG
	'Jeannie Bellew' (Va)	WGoo
	'Jennifer Andrews' (Va)	WGoo
	'Joanna' (Va)	WGoo
	'Joker Violet Gold' (Joker Series) **new**	CWCL
	jooi	CPBP EPfP GKev NBir SPhx WAbe WPtf
	'Josephine' (Vt)	CGro
	'Josie' (Va)	WGoo
	'Joyce Gray' (Va)	WGoo
	'Judy Goring' (Va)	EWoo NDov
	'Julian' (Va)	EWoo WGoo
	'Juno' (Va)	EWoo
	'Katerina' (Va)	WGoo
	'Kim'	CLAP
	'Kitten'	EWoo SDys WGoo
	'Kitty White' (Va)	EWoo SDys
§	'Königin Charlotte' (Vt)	COlW EPfP GBin GMaP LRHS MCot MHer NEgg WCot WMoo
	'Kristina' (Vt)	CGro
N	***labradorica*** misapplied	see *V. riviniana* Purpurea Group
N	- ***purpurea***	see *V. riviniana* Purpurea Group
§	***labradorica*** ambig.	EWTr GQui MCot NPri SMrm
	'Lady Jane' (Vt)	CGro
	'Lady Saville'	see *V.* 'Sissinghurst'
	'Lavender Lady' (Vt)	CGro
	'Lees Peachy Pink' (Vt)	CGro CLAP ELon
	'Letitia' (Va)	MCot SDys WGoo
	'Lianne' (Vt)	CGro CLAP LLHF WCot
	'Lindsay'	WGoo
	'Lisa Tanner' (Va)	WGoo
	'Little David' (Vtta) ♀H4	CSam CTri ECtt MCot MNFA NDov WGoo
	'Lizzy Wootten' (Va)	EWoo
	'Lord Plunket' (Va)	WGoo
	'Lorna Cawthorne' (C)	SDys WGoo
	'Louisa' (Va)	EWoo NDov WGoo WOut
	'Lucy' (Va)	CElw
§	***lutea***	WGoo
	- subsp. ***elegans***	see *V. lutea*
	'Lydia Groves' (Vt)	CGro CLAP ECtt ELon LLHF LSou SRms WCot
	'Lydia's Legacy' (Vt)	CGro

	'Madame Armandine Pagès' (Vt)	CGro
	'Maggie Mott' (Va) ♀H4	ECho ECtt EWoo GKev LHop MCot WGoo
	'Magic'	NDov WGoo
	mandshurica 'Fuji Dawn' (v)	CPla
	– f. ***hasegawae***	EPPr
	'Margaret' (Va)	WGoo
	'Marie-Louise' (dPVt)	ECtt NLar SHar
I	'Mars'	CAbP LSRN LSou MSCN
	'Mars' (Va)	LEdu SMrm
	'Martin' (Va) ♀H4	CAby EPfP EWoo GMaP LHop LSRN MAsh MAvo MBrN MHer MHol MNFA NDov SPer SPoG WGoo
	'Mary Mouse'	NDov WGoo
	'Mauve Haze' (Va)	WGoo
	'Mauve Radiance' (Va)	ECtt EWoo MNFA WGoo
	'May Mott' (Va)	WGoo
	'Melinda' (Vtta)	WGoo
	'Melting Moments' (Va)	NEgg
	'Mercury' (Va)	CElw MCot NDov WGoo
	'Midnight' (Va)	EWoo
	'Milkmaid' (Va)	ELon EWoo GBin NBir
	(Miracle Series) 'Miracle Bride White' (Vt)	SHar
	– 'Miracle Classy Pink' (Vt)	SHar
	– 'Miracle Ice White' (Vt)	SHar
	– 'Miracle Intense Blue' (Vt)	SHar
	– 'Miracle Vanilla White' (Vt)	SHar
	'Miss Brookes' (Va)	WGoo
	'Mistress Mallory' (Vt)	CGro
	'Misty Guy' (Vtta)	CElw WGoo
	'Molly Sanderson' (Va) ♀H4	CMea CSpe ECho ECtt EHyd ELan EPfP EWoo GMaP LHop LRHS MHer MHol MMuc NEgg NPri SPer SPlb SPoG WGoo WIce WNew
	'Moonlight' (Va) ♀H4	ECho EHyd ELan LHop LRHS MHer MMuc WGoo
	'Moonraker'	NBir
	'Morwenna' (Va)	ECtt MCot NDov WGoo WKif
	'Mrs Lancaster' (Va)	CAby EBee ECtt ELan EWoo GMaP LHop LSRN MCot MHol NBir NPri SDys SPoG WGoo
	'Mrs Pinehurst' (Vt)	CGro EBee GMaP
	'Mrs R. Barton' (Vt)	CGro CLAP ELon SHar
	'Myfawnny' (Va)	ECho EHyd LRHS MCot NDov SDys SRms WGoo
	'Neapolitan'	see *V.* 'Pallida Plena'
§	'Nellie Britton' (Va) ♀H4	ECho SRms
	'Netta Statham'	see *V.* 'Belmont Blue'
	'Nora'	NDov WGoo
	'Norah Church' (Vt)	CGro CLAP
	'Norah Leigh' (Va)	NDov WGoo
	obliqua	see *V. cucullata*
	odorata (Vt)	CArn CBcs CGro CHab EPfP GPoy MHoo MRav NMir NPri SIde SPer SRms SVic WJek WOut
	– 'Alba' (Vt)	CPom EBee ECho ELan EPfP GBin LEdu MHer NPri SEND SRms WMoo
	– 'Alba Plena' (dVt)	LSou
	– 'Albiflora' (Vt)	CLAP CPBP EPfP
	– apricot-flowered	see *V.* 'Sulfurea'
	– 'Bethan Davies' (d/Vt)	WCot
	– 'Dawnie' (Vt)	CGro
	– var. ***dumetorum***	see *V. alba*
	– 'Ellie' (Vt)	CGro
	– 'Elsmeer' (Vt)	ECtt LSou WCot

	– 'Empress Augusta' (Vt) **new**	CGro
	– 'Francis Lee' (Vt) **new**	CGro
	– 'Hungarian Beauty' (Vt)	EBee
	– 'Katy' (Vt)	CLAP CPom ELon
	– 'King of Violets' (dVt)	CBre EBee ECtt EWll LSou MAvo NEgg SHar SPer WCot
	– 'Melanie' (Vt)	WCot
	– 'Mrs R.O. Barlow' (Vt) **new**	WCot
	– 'Perky' (Vt)	CGro
	– pink-flowered	see *V. odorata* Rosea Group
	– 'Port Breedy' (Vt)	CGro
	– ***rosea***	see *V. odorata* Rosea Group
§	– Rosea Group (Vt)	CGro CPom EWll GBin IFoB LLWG LSou MPie MRav NEgg SEND SIde SPer SRms WCot WSHC
*	– subsp. ***subcarnea*** (Vt)	SEND
	– 'Sulphurea'	see *V.* 'Sulfurea'
	– 'Vin d'André Thorp' (Vt)	ECtt LEdu WCot
I	– 'Violett Charm' (Vt)	WCot
	– 'Weimar' (Vt)	GBin
	– 'Wismar' (Vt)	WCot
	'Olive Edwards'	WGoo
	'Opéra' (Vt)	CGro CLAP LLHF
	'Orchid Pink' (Vt)	CLAP EBee GMaP
§	'Pallida Plena' (dPVt)	CGro
	palustris	LLWG WHer WSFF WShi
	'Pamela Zambra' (Vt)	CGro CLAP WSHC
	'Papilio'	MHol
	papilionucea	see *V. sororia*
	'Parchment' (Vt)	CGro
	'Parme de Toulouse' (dPVt)	XLum
	'Pasha' (Va)	EWoo SDys
	'Pat Creasy' (Va)	NDov WGoo
	'Pat Kavanagh' (C)	NDov WGoo
	'Patience'	NDov WGoo
	'Pearl Rose'	ELon
	pedata	CBro EBee WAbe
	– f. ***alba***	MHer
	– 'Bicolor'	WAbe
	pedatifida	IFoB
	pensylvanica	see *V. pubescens* var. *eriocarpa*
	'Perle Rose' (Vt)	CLAP
	'Perry's Pride'	NDov
	'Petra' (Vtta)	EWoo NDov WGoo
	'Phyl Dove' (Vt)	CLAP EBee WCot
	'Pickering Blue' (Va)	WGoo
	'Primrose Dame' (Va)	MHer WCot WGoo
	'Primrose Pixie' (Va)	WGoo
	'Prince Henry' (T)	MNHC
	'Prince John' (T)	MNHC
	'Princess Mab' (Vtta)	WGoo
	'Princess of Prussia' (Vt)	CGro WCot
	'Princess of Wales'	see *V.* 'Princesse de Galles'
§	'Princesse de Galles' (Vt)	CTri
§	***pubescens*** var. ***eriocarpa***	SRms
	'Purple Wings' (Va)	WGoo
	'Putty'	ECou
	Queen Charlotte	see *V.* 'Königin Charlotte'
	'Queen Victoria'	see *V.* 'Victoria Regina'
	'Raven'	WGoo
	'Rebecca' (Vtta)	CAby CPla CSam ECho ECtt ELan EPfP GBuc GMaP LBMP LRHS LSRN MAsh MCot MHer MHol NBir NDov NEgg NPri SDys SMrm SPer SPoG SRms WGoo WIce
	'Red Giant' (Vt)	LEdu MBNS NEgg
	'Red Queen' (Vt)	CGro CLAP
	reichenbachiana	CRDP

	'Reine des Blanches' (dVt)	EBee ECtt ELon GBin LEdu LLWP LPla MAvo MBel MPie NEgg NGdn NLar SMrm SPer SRms WCot
	reniforme	see *V. hederacea*
	riviniana	CArn MHer MMuc WHer WOut WSFF WShi
	- dark pink-flowered	MMuc
	- 'Ed's Variegated' (v)	EPPr WCot
§	- Purpurea Group	Widely available
	- white-flowered	EWes MMuc
	'Roscastle Black'	CMea EPfP EWoo MHol NDov SMrm WGoo WKif
	'Rosine' (Vt)	CGro
	'Royal Elk' (Vt)	CGro
	'Rubra' (Vt)	EPfP XLum
§	***rupestris***	CTri
*	- ***rosea***	CPla CPom EBee IFro LLWP MHer WHer WPtf
	sagittata **new**	LPot
	'Saint Helena' (Vt)	WCot
	selkirkii Pursh ex Goldie	CPla WThu
	seoulensis	LLHF
	septentrionalis	see *V. sororia*
	'Serena' (Va)	WGoo
	'Sherbet Dip'	WGoo
	'Sidborough Poppet'	CRDP EWes
§	'Sissinghurst' (Va)	MHer NBir
	'Sisters' (Vt)	CGro
	'Smugglers' Moon'	WGoo
	somchetica	WCot
	'Sophie' (Vtta)	WGoo
	'Sorbet Series'	NPri
§	***sororia***	EBee ECho EPPr EWoo MLHP MNrw NBir NBro SPhx WPtf
*	- 'Albiflora' ♀H4	CHid ECho EPPr EPfP EWll EWoo LEdu LLWG MRav SPhx WCFE WHil WJek XLum
	- 'Dark Freckles'	ECho LHop NRya SPhx XLum
§	- 'Freckles'	Widely available
	- 'Priceana'	ECGP EPri EWTr LEdu NBir SPlb WCot WGwG WPtf
	- 'Sorority Sisters' **new**	NChi
	- 'Speckles' (v)	WCot
	- 'Sweet Emma'	SPhx
*	'Spencer's Cottage'	WGoo
	'Steyning' (Va)	WGoo
	stojanowii	CSpe ECho EPfP LLHF
§	'Sulfurea' (Vt)	CLAP CPBP EBee LLWP MMHG NRya WCot
	'Susan Chilcott' (Vt)	CGro
	'Susie' (Va)	WGoo
	'Swanley White'	see *V.* 'Conte di Brazza'
	'Sybil' (SP)	NDov WGoo
§	'The Czar' (Vt)	CBre CLAP ELon SBch WCot
	'Tiger Eyes' (Va)	EPfP SPoG
	'Tom Tit' (Va)	ECtt WGoo
	'Tony Venison' (C/v)	ELon EPfP MHol NEgg SPoG WGoo WHer
	tricolor	CArn CHab CPrp ECho EPfP GPoy MHer MNHC SIde SRms WJek
	velutina	see *V. gracilis*
	verecunda	WSHC
	- B&SWJ 604a	EWld WCru
§	- var. ***yakusimana***	CRDP WThu
	'Victoria Cawthorne' (C)	EWoo GBuc MHer MNFA NDov WGoo
§	'Victoria Regina' (Vt)	EPfP
	'Violacea' (C)	EWoo
	'Virginia' (Va)	WGoo
	'Vita' (Va)	EWoo SRms WGoo
	'Wasp' (Va)	NDov
	'White Ladies'	see *V. cucullata* 'Alba'
	'White Pearl' (Va)	SPhx WGoo
	'Winifred Jones' (Va)	WGoo
	'Winona Cawthorne' (C)	EWoo NDov
	'Wisley White'	LHop LPla
	× ***wittrockiana*** (Frizzle Sizzle Series) 'Frizzle Sizzle Orange' **new**	NPri
	- - 'Frizzle Sizzle Yellow' **new**	NPri
	- Matrix Series	NPri
	'Woodlands Cream' (Va)	MHer WGoo
	'Woodlands Lilac' (Va)	WGoo
	yakusimana	see *V. verecunda* var. *yakusimana*
	'Zara' (Va)	NDov WGoo
	'Zoe' (Vtta)	ECtt EPfP MHol NEgg NPri SPoG WGoo

Viscaria (*Caryophyllaceae*)

	vulgaris	see *Lychnis viscaria*

Vitaliana (*Primulaceae*)

§	***primuliflora***	ECho EDAr GKev NRya NSla
	- subsp. ***chionantha***	WAbe
	- subsp. ***cinerea***	GKev
	- subsp. ***praetutiana***	CPBP NWad WAbe WPat WThu

Vitex (*Lamiaceae*)

	agnus-castus	CArn CBcs CHel EPri EShb GPoy LEdu LRHS MRav NLar SEND SLon SPer WSHC XSen
	- 'Alba'	CDul CWib EPfP
	- var. ***latifolia***	CWib EBee ELan EPfP LRHS LSRN MGos MHer NLar SPoG WPGP XSen
I	- 'Rosea'	NLar XSen
	- 'Silver Spire'	CDul EBee ELan EPfP LRHS SPoG WPGP
	chinensis	see *V. negundo* var. *heterophylla*
	incisa	see *V. negundo* var. *heterophylla*
	negundo	CArn LEdu
§	- var. ***heterophylla***	EWes XSen

Vitis ✿ (*Vitaceae*)

	'Abundante' (F)	WSuV
	'Alden' (O/B)	WSuV
	'Amandin' (G/W)	WSuV
	amurensis	EPfP
	- B&SWJ 4138	WCru
	- B&SWJ 4299	WCru
	- B&SWJ 12568 **new**	WCru
	'Atlantis' (O/W)	WSuV
§	'Aurore' (W)	CAgr WSuV
	'Baco Noir' (O/B)	CAgr GTwe SDea WSuV
	betulifolia	EPfP
	'Bianca' (O/W)	WSuV
	'Birstaller Muscat' (W)	WSuV
	Black Hamburgh	see *V. vinifera* 'Schiava Grossa'
*	'Black Strawberry' (B)	CAgr SDea WSuV
	'Blanc Seedless' (W/S)	SDea
§	'Boskoop Glory' (O/B) ♀H4	CMac ERea LBuc NLar SCoo SDea WHar WSuV
	'Brant' (O/B) ♀H4	Widely available
	'Brilliant' (B)	WSuV
	'Buffalo' (B)	WSuV
	californica (F)	NLar
	'Canadice' (O/R/S)	SDea WSuV

	'Cascade'	see *V.* Seibel 13053
	Castel 19637 (B)	WSuV
	'Chambourcin' (B)	WSuV
	coignetiae ♀H4	Widely available
	- B&SWJ 4550 from Korea	WCru
	- B&SWJ 4744	WCru
	- B&SWJ 8553 from Korea	WCru
	- B&SWJ 10882 from Japan	WCru
	- B&SWJ 10908 from Japan	WCru
	- Claret Cloak = 'Frovit'PBR	ELan EPfP EUJe LRHS LSRN MAsh MBlu NLar SCoo SPer SSpi WPGP
	- cut-leaved	CMac
	- var. ***glabrescens*** B&SWJ 8537	WCru
	- Sunningdale form	COIW NLar WGrn
	'Dalkauer' (W)	WSuV
I	'Diamond' (B)	WSuV
	'Dutch Black' (O/B)	WSuV
	'Edwards No 1' (O/W)	WSuV
	'Eger Csillaga' (O/W)	WSuV
	'Einset' (B/S)	WSuV
	ficifolia	see *V. thunbergii*
	flexuosa B&SWJ 5568	WCru
	- var. ***choii*** B&SWJ 4101	WCru
N	'Fragola' (O/R)	CAgr CMac CTri EPfP GTwe LRHS MRav NLar SDea SLim SPer SPoG SRms WSuV
	'Gagarin Blue' (O/B)	CAgr EPom GTwe SDea SVen WSuV
	'Glenora' (F/B/S)	CAgr WSuV
	'Hecker' (O/W)	WSuV
	henryana	see *Parthenocissus henryana*
	'Himrod' (O/W/S)	CCCN ELan ERea GTwe SDea WSuV
	'Horizon' (O/W)	WSuV
	inconstans	see *Parthenocissus tricuspidata*
	'Interlaken' (O/W/S)	CAgr WSuV
	'Johanniter' (W)	SPre WSuV
	'Kempsey Black' (O/B)	CAgr WSuV
	'Kozmapalme Muscatoly' (O/W)	WSuV
	'Kuibishevski' (O/R)	WSuV
	Landot 244 (O/B)	WSuV
	Landot 3217 (O/B)	WSuV
	'L'Arcadie Blanche' (W)	WSuV
	'Léon Millot' (O/G/B)	CAgr CSBt LSRN SDea WSuV
	'Lucy Kuhlman' (B)	WSuV
	'Maréchal Foch' (O/B)	WSuV
	'Maréchal Joffre' (O/R)	CAgr GTwe WSuV
	'Mars' (O/B/S)	WSuV
	'Merzling' (O/W)	WSuV
	'Munson R.W.' (O/R)	WSuV
	'Muscat Bleu' (O/B)	CCCN CMam EPom LRHS NLar SLim SPoG WSuV
	'Nero'PBR	CAgr
	'New York Muscat' (O/B) ♀H4	ECrN WSuV
	'New York Seedless' (O/W/S)	WSuV
	'Niagara' (O/W)	WSuV
	'Niederother Monschrebe' (O/R)	WSuV
	Oberlin 595 (O/B)	WSuV
	'Orion' (O/W)	LRHS MAsh WSuV
	'Paletina' (O/W)	WSuV
	parsley-leaved	see *V. vinifera* 'Ciotat'
	parvifolia	WPat
	- B&SWJ 1946	WCru

	'Perdin' (O/W)	WSuV
	'Phönix' (O/W)	CAgr CCCN EPom GTwe LRHS LSRN MAsh MBri MGos NLar NPla SKee SLim SPoG SPre SVic WSuV
	piasezkii	WCru
*	'Pink Strawberry' (O)	WSuV
	'Pirovano 14' (O/B)	GTwe SDea WSuV
§	'Plantet' (O/B)	WSuV
	'Poloske Muscat' (W)	CCCN CMam EPom WSuV
	purpurea 'Spetchley Park' (O/B)	CAgr WSuV
	quinquefolia	see *Parthenocissus quinquefolia*
	'Ramdas' (O/W)	WSuV
	Ravat 51 (O/W)	WSuV
	'Rayon d'Or' (O/W)	WSuV
	'Regent'PBR (O/B)	CAgr CCCN EPom GTwe LRHS MBri MCoo MGos NLar SKee SLim SPoG SPre WSuV
	'Reliance' (O/R/S)	CAgr ERea WSuV
	'Rembrant' (R)	CAgr WSuV
	riparia	CArn NLar
	'Romulus' (O/G/W/S)	WSuV
	'Rondo' (O/B)	CAgr NPla SPre SVic WSuV
	'Saturn' (O/R/S)	CAgr WSuV
	'Schuyler' (O/B)	CAgr WSuV
	Seibel (F)	GTwe SDea
	Seibel 5279	see *V.* 'Aurore'
	Seibel 5409 (W)	WSuV
	Seibel 5455	see *V.* 'Plantet'
	Seibel 7053	WSuV
	Seibel 9549	WSuV
§	Seibel 13053 (O/B)	CMac LRHS MAsh MMuc SDea SEND WSuV
	Seibel 138315 (R)	WSuV
	'Seneca' (W)	WSuV
	'Serena' (O/W)	WSuV
§	'Seyval Blanc' (O/W)	CAgr GTwe MAsh MMuc SDea SEND SVic WSuV
	Seyve Villard 5276	see *V.* 'Seyval Blanc'
	Seyve Villard 12.375	see *V.* 'Villard Blanc'
	Seyve Villard 20.473 (F)	NPer
	Seyve Villard ambig.	LRHS NPer
	'Sirius' (B)	WSuV
	'Solaris' (O/W)	WSuV
	'Stauffer' (O/W)	WSuV
	'Suffolk Seedless' (B/S)	ERea GTwe WSuV
	'Tereshkova' (O/B)	CAgr SDea WSuV
	'Thornton' (O/S)	WSuV
§	***thunbergii*** B&SWJ 4702	WCru
	'Triomphe d'Alsace' (O/B)	CAgr CSBt NPer SDea WSuV
	'Trollinger'	see *V. vinifera* 'Schiava Grossa'
	'Vanessa' (O/R/S)	SDea WSuV
§	'Villard Blanc' (O/W)	WSuV
	vinifera	EAmu EUJe MGos MREP
	- EM 323158B	WSuV
	- 'Abouriou' (O/B)	WSuV
	- 'Acolon' (O/B)	WSuV
	- 'Adelheidtraube' (O/W)	WSuV
	- 'Albalonga' (W)	WSuV
§	- 'Alicante' (G/B)	CBcs CMac GTwe SDea WSuV
	- 'Apiifolia'	see *V. vinifera* 'Ciotat'
	- 'Augusta Louise' (O/W)	WSuV
	- 'Auxerrois' (O/W)	WSuV
	- 'Bacchus' (O/W)	CAgr CMam LRHS MBri NLar SDea SLim SVic WSuV
	- 'Baresana' (G/W)	NPla WSuV
	- 'Beauty'	CAgr
	- 'Black Alicante'	see *V. vinifera* 'Alicante'

	– 'Black Frontignan' (G/O/B)	WSuV
	– Black Hamburgh	see *V. vinifera* 'Schiava Grossa'
	– 'Black Monukka' (G/B/S)	WSuV
	– 'Black Prince' (G/B)	CAgr WSuV
	– 'Blue Portuguese'	see *V. vinifera* 'Portugieser'
§	– 'Bouvier' (W)	WSuV
	– 'Bouviertraube'	see *V. vinifera* 'Bouvier'
	– 'Buckland Sweetwater' (G/W)	GTwe LRHS SDea SLim WSuV
	– 'Cabernet Sauvignon' (O/B)	EPfP LRHS MAsh MGos NPer SDea SVic WSuV
	– 'Cardinal' (O/R)	LRHS SHil WSuV
	– 'Carla' (O/R)	WSuV
	– 'Centennial' (O/N/S)	WSuV
	– 'Chardonnay' (O/W)	CAgr CCCN LRHS LSRN MAsh NPer SDea SPer SPre SVic WSuV
§	– 'Chasselas' (G/O/W)	LRHS SDea WSuV
	– 'Chasselas Blanc' (O/W)	SVic
	– 'Chasselas de Fontainebleau' (F)	SVic
	– 'Chasselas d'Or'	see *V. vinifera* 'Chasselas'
	– 'Chasselas Rosé' (G/R)	CAgr SVic WSuV
	– 'Chasselas Rosé Royal' (O/R)	CCCN SVic
	– 'Chasselas Vibert' (G/W)	WSuV
	– 'Chenin Blanc' (O/W)	SVic WSuV
§	– 'Ciotat' (F)	ERea EShb IDee MRav SDea WSuV
	– 'Cot Précoce de Tours' (O/B)	WSuV
	– 'Crimson Seedless' (R/S)	ERea WSuV
	– 'Csabyongye' (O/W)	WSuV
	– 'Dattier de Beyrouth' (G/W)	WSuV
	– 'Dattier Saint Vallier' (O/W)	SVic WSuV
	– 'Dolcetto' (O/B)	WSuV
	– 'Dornfelder' (O/R)	CCCN NLar SLim SPoG SVic WSuV
	– 'Dunkelfelder' (O/R)	WSuV
	– 'Early Van der Laan' (F)	CMac
	– 'Ehrenfelser' (O/W)	WSuV
	– 'Elbling' (O/W)	WSuV
	– 'Exalta' (G/W/S)	CCCN WSuV
	– 'Excelsior' (W)	WSuV
	– 'Faber' (O/W)	WSuV
	– 'Fiesta' (W/S)	WSuV
	– 'Findling' (W)	WSuV
	– 'Flame'	CAgr LRHS NPla WHar
	– 'Flame Red' (O/D)	CCCN EPom
	– 'Flame Seedless' (G/O/R/S)	CMac EPom GTwe SPoG WSuV
	– 'Forta' (O/W)	WSuV
	– 'Foster's Seedling' (G/W)	SDea SVic WSuV
	– 'Freisamer' (O/W)	WSuV
	– 'Frühburgunder' (O/B)	WSuV
	– 'Gamay Hâtif des Vosges'	WSuV
	– 'Gamay Noir' (O/B)	SVic WSuV
	– Gamay Teinturier Group (O/B)	WSuV
	– 'Gewürztraminer' (O/R)	LRHS MAsh SDea SVic WSuV
	– 'Glory of Boskoop'	see *V.* 'Boskoop Glory'
	– 'Golden Chasselas'	see *V. vinifera* 'Chasselas'
	– 'Goldriesling' (O/W)	WSuV
	– 'Gros Colmar' (G/B)	WSuV
	– 'Grüner Veltliner' (O/W)	WSuV
	– 'Gutenborner' (O/W)	WSuV
	– 'Helfensteiner' (O/R)	WSuV
	– 'Huxelrebe' (O/W)	WSuV
	– 'Incana' (O/B)	ELon GCal LRHS MRav SVen WCFE WCot WPGP WSHC
	– 'Italia' (O/W)	LRHS NPla SHil
	– 'Juliaumsrebe' (O/W)	WSuV
	– 'Kanzler' (O/W)	WSuV
	– 'Kerner' (O/W)	WSuV
	– 'Kernling' (F)	WSuV
	– 'King's Ruby' (F/S)	WSuV
	– 'Lakemont' (O/W/S)	CAgr CCCN CMac CMam ELan EPfP GTwe LRHS MBri MGos NLar NPla SDea SKee SLim SPoG SPre WHar WSuV
	– 'Lival' (O/B)	WSuV
	– 'Madeleine Angevine' (O/W)	CAgr EPfP GTwe LRHS LSRN MAsh NPer SDea SPoG SVen SVic WSuV
	– 'Madeleine Celine' (B)	WSuV
	– 'Madeleine Royale' (G/W)	WSuV
	– 'Madeleine Silvaner' (O/W)	CSBt GTwe LRHS MAsh NPer SDea SPoG WSuV
	– 'Madresfield Court' (G/B)	GTwe SLim WSuV
	– 'Merlot' (G/B)	LRHS SDea SVic WSuV
§	– 'Meunier' (B)	SVic WSuV
	– 'Mireille' (F)	SDea WSuV
	– 'Morio Muscat' (O/W)	WSuV
§	– 'Müller-Thurgau' (O/W)	GTwe LRHS LSRN MAsh MGos NPri SDea SPer SVic WSuV
	– 'Muscat Blanc à Petits Grains' (O/W)	SWvt WSuV
	– 'Muscat de Lierval' (O/B)	WSuV
	– 'Muscat de Saumur' (O/W)	WSuV
	– 'Muscat Hamburg' (G/B)	LHop LRHS LSRN MAsh MGos NPri SDea SWvt WSuV
	– 'Muscat of Alexandria' (G/W)	CBcs CCCN CMac CRHN ERea LRHS MRav SDea SLim SPer SVic WHar
	– 'Muscat Ottonel' (O/W)	WSuV
	– 'Muscat Saint Laurent' (W)	WSuV
	– 'Nebbiolo' (O/B)	WSuV
	– 'No 69' (W)	WSuV
	– 'Noblessa' (W)	WSuV
	– 'Noir Hâtif de Marseille' (O/B)	WSuV
	– 'Olive Blanche' (O/W)	WSuV
	– 'Oliver Irsay' (O/W)	WSuV
	– 'Optima' (O/W)	WSuV
	– 'Ora' (O/W/S)	WSuV
	– 'Ortega' (O/W)	CCCN WSuV
	– 'Perle' (O/W)	WSuV
	– 'Perle de Czaba' (G/O/W)	WSuV
	– 'Perlette' (O/W/S)	CCCN EPom GTwe NPri WSuV
	– 'Petit Rouge' (R)	WSuV
	– 'Pinot Blanc' (O/W)	CCCN LRHS MAsh SVic WSuV
	– 'Pinot Gris' (O/B)	SDea SVic WSuV
	– 'Pinot Noir' (O/B)	CCCN SVic WSuV
§	– 'Portugieser' (O/B)	WSuV
	– 'Précoce de Bousquet' (O/W)	WSuV
	– 'Précoce de Malingre' (O/W)	CAgr SDea
	– 'Prima' (O/B)	WSuV
	– 'Primavis Frontignan' (G/W)	WSuV
	– 'Purpurea' (O/B) 🏆H4	Widely available
	– 'Queen of Esther' (B)	GTwe MBri NLar SKee SLim WSuV
	– 'Regner' (O/W)	WSuV
	– 'Reichensteiner' (O/G/W)	CAgr SDea WSuV
	– 'Riesling' (O/W)	CCCN LRHS MAsh SVic WSuV
	– Riesling-Silvaner	see *V. vinifera* 'Müller-Thurgau'

	- 'Rotberger' (O/G/B)	WSuV
	- 'Royal Muscadine' (G/O/W)	WSuV
	- 'Saint Laurent' (G/O/W)	SVic WSuV
	- 'Sauvignon Blanc' (O/W)	CCCN LRHS SVic WSuV
	- 'Scheurebe' (O/W)	WSuV
§	- 'Schiava Grossa' (G/B/D)	CMac CRHN CTri ELan EPfP EPom GTwe LRHS LSRN MAsh MBri NPer NPla NPri SDea SLim SPer SPoG SPre SVic SWvt WHar WMoo WSuV
	- 'Schönburger' (O/W)	SDea SVic WSuV
	- 'Schwarzriesling'	see *V. vinifera* 'Meunier'
	- 'Sémillon'	LRHS LSRN MAsh SVic
	- 'Senator' (O/W)	WSuV
	- 'Septimer' (O/W)	WSuV
	- 'Shiraz' (B)	WSuV
	- 'Siegerrebe' (O/W/D)	CAgr GTwe LRHS MAsh NPer SDea SVic WSuV
	- 'Silvaner' (O/W)	WSuV
	- 'Spetchley Red' (O/B)	CRHN EBee GCal NLar WCot WCru WPGP WPat
	- strawberry grape	see *V.* 'Fragola'
§	- 'Sultana' (W/S)	CAgr GTwe NPla NPri SDea WSuV
	- 'Theresa' (O/W)	MBri NLar SLim WSuV
	- 'Thompson Seedless'	see *V. vinifera* 'Sultana'
*	- 'Triomphe' (O/B)	SVic
	- 'Triomphrebe' (W)	WSuV
	- 'Vitalis Gold' (F)	CWSG
	- 'Vitalis Ruby' (F)	CWSG
	'Vroege van der Laan' (O/W)	NLar
	- 'Wrotham Pinot' (O/B)	SDea WSuV
	- 'Würzer' (O/W)	WSuV
	- 'Zweigeltrebe' (O/B)	WSuV
*	'White Strawberry' (O/W)	WSuV
	'Zalagyöngye' (W)	CAgr WSuV

Vriesea (*Bromeliaceae*)

imperialis	EAmu
splendens ♀H1	XBlo

W

Wachendorfia (*Haemodoraceae*)

multiflora new	CLak
paniculata	CLak
thyrsiflora	CAbb CCon CDes CExl CHEx EBee EShb IGor LEdu WPGP WSHC

Wahlenbergia (*Campanulaceae*)

albomarginata	ECho GBin
- 'Blue Mist'	ECho
congesta	ECho
gloriosa	ECou MOWG WAbe
matthewsii	WThu
pumilio	see *Edraianthus pumilio*
serpyllifolia	see *Edraianthus serpyllifolius*
undulata 'Melton Bluebird'	GJos

Waldsteinia (*Rosaceae*)

	fragarioides	GKev
	geoides	EBee EPPr EPfP LAst LRHS NPro SPer WMoo WWEG XLum
	ternata	Widely available
§	- 'Mozaick' (v)	EBee EShb EWes NBir NPro
	- 'Variegata'	see *W. ternata* 'Mozaick'

walnut, black see *Juglans nigra*

walnut, common see *Juglans regia*

Wasabia (*Brassicaceae*)

wasabi	CArn CExl CFil GPoy LEdu

Washingtonia (*Arecaceae*)

'Filibusta'	EAmu
filifera ♀H1	CAbb CCCN CDoC CPHo EAmu LRHS SAPC SBig SEND SPlb
robusta	EAmu EGri SHil SPlb

Watsonia (*Iridaceae*)

	aletroides	CDes EBee ECho GCal SDeJ
	amatolae	IBlr
	angusta	CDes CExl CPrp EBee IBlr SPlb WPGP
	ardernei	see *W. borbonica* subsp. *ardernei* (Sander) Goldblatt 'Arderne's White'
	beatricis	see *W. pillansii*
§	***borbonica***	CDes CPrp
	- subsp. ***ardernei*** misapplied	see *W. borbonica* subsp. *ardernei* (Sander) Goldblatt 'Arderne's White'
§	- subsp. ***ardernei*** (Sander) Goldblatt 'Arderne's White'	CAby CBre CCon CExl CPrp ECho GCal IBlr LRHS WPGP
	- subsp. ***borbonica***	IBlr WPGP
	- 'Paarl'	ECho
	brevifolia	see *W. laccata*
	brick red-flowered	CDes EBee WPGP
	coccinea 'Somerset West'	ECho
	'Dart Sea Trout' new	CDes
	densiflora	IBlr
	fourcadei	GCal
	fulgens	LEdu
	galpinii	CCon
	- lavender-flowered	IBlr
	- pink-flowered	IBlr
	galpinii* × *knysnana	IBlr
§	***humilis***	CDes EBee GCal SKHP
	knysnana	CDes IBlr WPGP
§	***laccata***	CCon CPrp EBee
	- orange-flowered	CDes
	- pink-flowered	CDes
	latifolia	IBlr
	lepida	EBee ECho IBlr SPlb
	marginata	CPrp EBee ECho
	- ***alba***	SKHP
	meriana	CHel ERCP GBin IBlr
	- var. ***bulbillifera***	CPrp EBee ECho GCal GCra GGal IBlr
	'Peachy Pink Orphan'	CDes EBee WPGP
§	***pillansii***	CAbb CCon CExl CHEx CHel CPrp EBee EPri IBal IBlr LRHS NCGa
	- 'Cathcart'	ECho
	- peach-flowered	CExl
	- pink-flowered	CExl CPrp IVic
	- red-flowered	CExl IVic
	- soft pink-flowered	EPri
	pink-flowered	CDes
	pyramidata	see *W. borbonica*
	roseoalba	see *W. humilis*
	'Stanford Scarlet'	CAby CCon CDes CExl CPrp ELon IBlr SChF SChr WPGP
	stenosiphon	IBlr
	strubeniae	IBlr

'Tresco Dwarf Pink'	CCon CDes CExl CPrp EBee IBlr LEdu WPGP
Tresco hybrids	CAbb CBcs CExl EPri GGal SRkn
vanderspuyae	CExl CPrp IBlr
wilmaniae	CExl CPrp EBee IBlr WPGP
- JCA 3.955200	SKHP
- 'Ice Angel'	SKHP
wordsworthiana	GCal
zeyheri	EBee

Wattakaka see *Dregea*

Wedelia (*Asteraceae*)

trilobata **new**	LLWG

Weigela ✿ (*Caprifoliaceae*)

CC 1231	CExl
'Abel Carrière'	CMac CTri ECtt EPfP EWes GKin MGos NWea WCFE
'Avalanche' misapplied	see *W.* 'Candida'
'Avalanche' Lemoine	see *W. praecox* 'Avalanche'
'Avant Garde'	MAsh WCot WPat
Black and White = 'Courtacad1'	CWGN EBee LRHS LSRN SGol SPoG
'Boskoop Glory'	GQui SPer
'Bouquet Rose'	LPot
§ Briant Rubidor = 'Olympiade' (v)	CDoC CMac EBee EHoe EPfP LRHS MAsh MGos MMuc MRav NEgg NLar SGol SHil SLim SPer SPlb SPoG WHar
'Bristol Ruby'	CBar CDul CMac CTri CWib EBee ELan EPfP GKin LRHS MGos MHer MJak MMuc MSwo NBir NPri NSoo NWea SEND SGol SHil SLon SPer SPlb SRms WHar WMoo
§ 'Candida'	CTri ELan EWes MRav NLar NSoo SGol SPer
Cappuccino = 'Verweig 2'[PBR]	LBuc MBlu MJak NBro NEgg NLar SGol
Carnaval = 'Courtalor'[PBR]	CBcs CWib EBee LRHS NLar
'Chameleon' **new**	MPkF
'Conquête'	SLon
coraeensis	CHll MBlu MMHG SBrt SPer WCot WPat
- 'Alba'	CHll
decora	GQui
- B&SWJ 10834	WCru
'Eva Rathke'	GKin NBir NLar NWea
'Evita'	GKin IBoy MBlu
floribunda B&SWJ 10831	WCru
florida	CDul CMac EPfP
- B&SWJ 8439	WCru
- f. ***alba***	CBcs
* - 'Albovariegata' (v)	CExl
- 'Bicolor'	CMac ELan
- 'Bristol Snowflake'	CDul CMac EPPr EPfP EWTr MBlu MHer MMuc MSwo NBir NLar SLon
- 'Foliis Purpureis' ♀H4	Widely available
- Magical Fantasy	see *W. florida* Sunny Fantasy
- Magical Rainbow = 'Kolmagira'[PBR]	MPkF SGol
- 'Milk and Honey'	GKin LRHS MBri
- Minor Black = 'Verweig 3'[PBR]	CHel CWSG EBee EPfP GBin LRHS MBri MPkF NBro NHol NLar SPoG WMoo
- Monet = 'Verweig'[PBR] (v)	Widely available
- Moulin Rouge = 'Brigela'[PBR]	CBcs CDoC EBee ELan EPfP LBuc LRHS MAsh MBri MGos SLim
- 'Pink Princess'	EBee LRHS MSwo WHar
- Rubigold	see *W.* Briant Rubidor
§ - Sunny Fantasy = 'Kolsunn'	MPkF
- 'Suzanne' (v)	NPro
- 'Tango'	CJun LRHS MAsh NPro
'Florida Variegata' (v) ♀H4	Widely available
florida 'Versicolor'	CExl CMHG CMac CWib GQui SLon SMrm WGor
- Wine and Roses = 'Alexandra'[PBR]	Widely available
'Gold Rush'	NLar
'Golden Candy'	NPro
'Gustave Malet'	CMCN GQui
hortensis	CExl
japonica 'Dart's Colourdream'	EHoe EWes LAst MMuc SEND SLim
- 'Variegated Dart's Colourdream' (v)	ELon
'Jean's Gold'	ELan MBlu MRav
'Kosteriana Variegata' (v)	CSBt EBee EPfP EWTr LRHS MAsh MMuc NEgg SHil SLon
'Little Red Robin'	ELon MPkF NSoo
'Looymansii Aurea'	CExl CMHG CTri ELan EPfP NLar SGol SPer WHar
Lucifer = 'Courtared'[PBR]	CDoC
maximowiczii	CExl GQui
§ ***middendorffiana***	Widely available
'Minuet'	EPfP LRHS MRav MSwo NPro
'Mont Blanc'	MAsh MMHG
Nain Rouge = 'Courtanin'[PBR]	CBcs CTri LRHS MBri
'Nana Variegata' (v)	CExl ECrN ELon EPfP LRHS MBri MJak NSoo SLPl
Naomi Campbell = 'Bokrashine'[PBR]	EShb GBin GKin MMHG NEgg NHol NLar NSoo WHar WMoo
'Newport Red'	GKin MBNS MWat NWea WHar
Pink Poppet = 'Plangen'[PBR]	CAbP CSBt EBee EPfP GKin LBMP LRHS LSRN MAsh MPkF NLar SCoo SHil SLim SPoG SRkn SWvt
praecox	ECrN
- B&SWJ 8705	WCru
§ - 'Avalanche'	EPfP
'Praecox Variegata' (v) ♀H4	CMac CTri EPfP LAst LRHS MAsh MRav NBir SDix SPer SPoG SRms WCFE WPat
'Red Prince' ♀H4	CWCL EBee ELan EPPr EPfP LBuc LRHS MGos MJak MSwo NEgg NLar SGol SHil SPoG
Rubidor	see *W.* Briant Rubidor
Rubigold	see *W.* Briant Rubidor
'Ruby Anniversary'	CWSG LBuc NSoo SLon
'Ruby Queen'[PBR]	CMac EPfP
Ruby Wedding	LSRN
'Rumba'	CMac MRav
sessilifolia	see *Diervilla sessilifolia*
'Snowflake'	ECrN LPot SRms
'Stelzneri'	MMuc
'Styriaca'	NSoo
subsessilis B&SWJ 1056	WCru
- B&SWJ 4206	WCru
'Victoria'	CDul CMac CWSG CWib ECrN EHoe ELan EPPr EPfP LBMP LRHS MGos MSwo NBir NWad SGol SPer WGor WHar WMoo

Weinmannia (*Cunoniaceae*)

racemosa	IVic
trichosperma	CBcs EUJe IDee SAPC

Weldenia (*Commelinaceae*)

	candida	ECho IBlr LLHF NHar

Westringia (*Lamiaceae*)

	angustifolia	MOWG
	brevifolia	ECou
	- var. ***raleighii***	ECou
§	***fruticosa*** 🏆^{H1}	CBcs CCCN CHll CTsd SRms SVen WJek
	- 'Smokie' (v)	CCCN CPBP CTsd MOWG
	- 'Variegata' (v)	CCCN SRms SVen WJek
	longifolia	CCCN ECou
	rosmariniformis	see *W. fruticosa*
	'Wynyabbie Gem'	CAbb CCCN EBee EWTr LRHS SEND SVen

whitecurrant see *Ribes rubrum* (W)

Whiteheadia (*Asparagaceae*)

	bifolia 'Nardonwsberg'	ECho

Wigandia (*Boraginaceae*)

	caracasana	CHll

Wikstroemia (*Thymelaeaceae*)

	gemmata	LRHS

wineberry see *Rubus phoenicolasius*

Wisteria ✿ (*Papilionaceae*)

	'Betty's Dwarf Blue' **new**	NLar
§	***brachybotrys***	CCVT SLau
§	- Murasaki-kapitan	CEnd CTri CWGN EBtc EPfP LRHS SKHP
	- 'Okayama'	EPfP SKHP
	- 'Pink Chiffon'	EPfP LRHS SKHP
	- 'Shiro-beni'	CTri MMuc
§	- 'Shiro-kapitan'	CBcs CEnd CFlo CSPN CTri CWGN EBee EPfP IArd LRHS LSRN MBri MGos MRav NHol NLar SEND SHil SKHP SLau SLim SPer WPGP WPat WSHC
	- 'Showa-beni'	CDoC CEnd CFlo CSPN CWGN EPfP LHop MGos SCoo SEND SKHP SLau SLim WPGP
*	- 'White Silk'	CBcs EPfP LRHS LSRN MGos NPla SLon
§	'Burford'	CEnd CFlo CSPN CWGN EBee EPfP LRHS LSRN MAsh MBri MWat NHol NLar SCoo SEND SKHP SLau SLim WHar WPGP
	'Caroline'	CBcs CCCN CDoC CFlo CHab CSPN CWGN EBee EBtc EPfP LRHS LSRN MAsh MGos MRav NEgg NPCo SHil SLau SPer SPoG SRms SSpi WPGP WSHC
	floribunda	CBcs CCVT CRHN CWib ELan EPfP IBoy MMuc NPCo SEWo SGol
§	- 'Alba' 🏆^{H4}	Widely available
	- 'Black Dragon'	see *W. floribunda* 'Yae-kokuryū'
	- 'Burford'	see *W.* 'Burford'
*	- 'Cascade'	CBcs LRHS MBri NEgg SHil
§	- 'Domino'	CBcs CCVT CMac CWGN ELon EPfP IArd LRHS LSRN MAsh MGos MRav MSwo MWat NLar NPla SCoo SEND SGol SKHP SLau SLim SPer SPoG SSta
	- 'Ed's Blue Dragon' (d) **new**	LBuc LRHS SHil
	- 'Fragrantissima'	see *W. sinensis* 'Jako'
	- 'Geisha'	CBcs CEnd CFlo CHel EBee SEND SKHP
	- 'Golden Dragon'	EPfP
	- 'Harlequin'	CBcs CFlo CSPN EBee ELon LRHS MJak NPCo NPla SEND SKHP
	- 'Hocker Edge'	SLau
	- 'Hon-beni'	see *W. floribunda* 'Rosea'
	- 'Honey Bee Pink'	see *W. floribunda* 'Rosea'
	- 'Honko'	see *W. floribunda* 'Rosea'
	- 'Issai Perfect'	LRHS LSRN NLar SCoo SLon
	- 'Issai-naga' **new**	NLar
	- 'Jakohn-fuji'	see *W. sinensis* 'Jako'
§	- 'Kuchi-beni'	CBcs CCVT CEnd CSPN EBee ELan GBin IBoy LRHS LSRN MBri MGos MJak MRav NEgg NHol NLar NPCo SEND SHil SKHP SLau SPer SPoG SRms
	- 'Lawrence'	CBcs CCVT CDoC CEnd CFlo CSPN CWGN EBtc LRHS NLar SKHP SLau
	- 'Lipstick'	see *W. floribunda* 'Kuchi-beni'
	- 'Longissima'	see *W. floribunda* 'Multijuga'
	- 'Longissima Alba'	see *W. floribunda* 'Alba'
	- 'Macrobotrys'	see *W. floribunda* 'Multijuga'
	- 'Magenta'	LRHS NPla
§	- 'Multijuga' 🏆^{H4}	Widely available
	- Murasaki-naga	see *W. floribunda* 'Purple Patches'
	- 'Nana Richin's Purple'	CEnd SLau
	- 'Peaches and Cream'	see *W. floribunda* 'Kuchi-beni'
	- 'Pink Ice'	see *W. floribunda* 'Rosea'
§	- 'Purple Patches'	EBee SEND
	- Reindeer	see *W. sinensis* 'Jako'
§	- 'Rosea' 🏆^{H4}	Widely available
	- 'Royal Purple'	CEnd EPfP IArd LRHS MBri NLar SPoG WGor
	- 'Russelliana'	CBcs CFlo EBee GBin NLar
	- 'Shiro-naga'	see *W. floribunda* 'Alba'
	- 'Shiro nagi'	see *W. floribunda* 'Alba'
	- 'Shiro-noda'	see *W. floribunda* 'Alba'
	- 'Snow Showers'	see *W. floribunda* 'Alba'
	- 'Variegata' (v)	CWGN
N	- 'Violacea Plena' (d)	CBcs CDoC CMac EPfP NLar SKHP SWvt
N	- 'Yae-kokuryū' (d)	Widely available
	× ***formosa***	CEnd SLau SLim
	- 'Black Dragon'	see *W. floribunda* 'Yae-kokuryū'
	- 'Domino'	see *W. floribunda* 'Domino'
	- 'Issai' Wada *pro parte*	see *W. floribunda* 'Domino'
	- 'Kokuryū'	see *W. floribunda* 'Yae-kokuryū'
	- 'Yae-kokuryū'	see *W. floribunda* 'Yae-kokuryū'
	frutescens	EBee EPfP NLar
	- 'Amethyst Falls'^{PBR}	CEnd CWCL CWGN IArd LRHS LSRN MGos SCoo SLon SPer SPoG WMoo
	- 'Longwood Purple'	LRHS
	Kapitan-fuji	see *W. brachybotrys*
	'Lavender Lace'	EBee EPfP LRHS LSRN MAsh MJak NEgg NLar SLau
	macrostachya 'Aunt Dee' **new**	NLar
	- 'Blue Moon'	MGos WHar
	- 'Clara Mack'	IArd
	multijuga 'Alba'	see *W. floribunda* 'Alba'
	sinensis 🏆^{H4}	CBcs CCVT CTri CWCL EBee ELan EPfP IBoy LAst LRHS LSRN MGos MJak MNHC MRav MSwo MWat NCGa NLar NPri NWea

SEWo SGol SLim SPoG SRms SSta SWvt WMoo WPat
- 'Alba' ♀H4 CBcs CDoC CDul CMen CWib EBee ELan EPfP IBoy LAst LRHS LSRN MAsh MGos MSwo MWat NEgg NPla SLau SPer SPoG
- 'Amethyst' CBcs CEnd CHab CSPN EPfP LRHS LSRN MAsh MBri MGos MRav MWat NPla SHil SKHP SLau SLim SPoG WPat
- 'Blue Sapphire' CBcs CHab CSPN CWGN EBee EBtc LSRN NEgg NLar NPCo SLau SRms
- 'Consequa' see *W. sinensis* 'Prolific'
- 'Cooke's Special' CWGN
§ - 'Jako' CEnd NHol
- 'Oosthoek's Variety' see *W. sinensis* 'Prolific'
I - 'Pink Ice' EWTr NEgg NPCo
- 'Prematura' see *W. floribunda* 'Domino'
- 'Prematura Alba' see *W. brachybotrys* 'Shiro-kapitan'
§ - 'Prolific' CDul CMac CSam CTri CWGN CWib EBee ELan EPfP IBoy LBuc LRHS MBri MGos MMuc MRav MSwo MWat NHol NLar SCoo SGol SKHP SLim SPer SPoG SSpi SWvt WPGP WPat
- 'Rosea' LSRN SWvt
- 'Shiro-capital' see *W. brachybotrys* 'Shiro-kapitan'
'Tiverton' CBcs EBee EUJe NPla
venusta see *W. brachybotrys* 'Shiro-kapitan'
- 'Alba' see *W. brachybotrys* 'Shiro-kapitan'
- var. ***violacea*** misapplied see *W. brachybotrys* Murasaki-kapitan

Withania (*Solanaceae*)
somnifera CArn GPoy

Wittsteinia (*Alseuosmiaceae*)
vacciniacea SBrt WCru

Wodyetia (*Arecaceae*)
bifurcata EAmu XBlo

Wollemia (*Araucariaceae*)
nobilis CDTJ CDoC CHel CTho EAmu EPfP ESwi EUJe GBin MGos SAPC WMou

Woodsia (*Woodsiaceae*)
obtusa CBty CDTJ CKel CLAP CWCL EBee EFer ISha LRHS MBri NBro NLar SGol SPoG SRot WWEG XLum
polystichoides ♀H4 SRms

Woodwardia (*Blechnaceae*)
from Emei Shan, China CLAP
areolata SKHP
fimbriata CBty CCCN CCon CLAP CWCL EAmu EFer ELon EPfP ERod EWTr GCal LEdu LRHS NBro NHol NLar SBig SEND SPer SPoG WFib WMoo WPGP WWEG XLum
orientalis CBty ESwi LEdu LRHS WFib
- var. ***formosana*** B&SWJ 6865 ESwi WCru
radicans ♀H3 CHEx CHid CLAP EWes SAPC WCot WFib
unigemmata CHEx CLAP EFer EWes SAPC SKHP WAbe WFib WHal
virginica CBty CLAP ISha

Worcesterberry see *Ribes* 'Worcesterberry'

Wulfenia (*Plantaginaceae*)
baldaccii GKev
carinthiaca EBee ECho GAbr GKev LEdu NBir NLar NWad XLum
- 'Alba' EBee
× ***schwarzii*** CDes EBee IMou LEdu WPGP WSHC

Wurmbea (*Colchicaceae*)
dioica new CLak
pusilla 'Sentinel Peak' ECho
recurva ECho
spicata 'Rawsonville' ECho
stricta WCot

X

Xanthium (*Asteraceae*)
sibiricum CArn

Xanthoceras (*Sapindaceae*)
sorbifolium ♀H3-4 CAgr CBcs CLnd CMCN CWib EBee ELan EPfP MBlu NLar SSpi WBor

Xanthocyparis (*Cupressaceae*)
nootkatensis 'Glauca' MGos NWea
- 'Green Arrow' CKen LRHS NLar SCoo SLim WHar
- 'Jubilee' LRHS NPCo SCoo SLim WCFE WHar
- 'Kanada' NLar
- 'Lutea' MGos NWea
- 'Nordkroken' NLar
- 'Pendula' ♀H4 CCVT CDoC CDul CKen ELan EPfP GKin LRHS MBlu MBri MMuc NEgg NPCo NWea WCFE
- 'Strict Weeper' CKen NLar SLim

Xanthorhiza (*Ranunculaceae*)
simplicissima CArn CBcs CDoC CDul CGHE CRow EPfP GCal IVic LEdu MBri NLar SDys SSpi WPGP

Xanthorrhoea (*Xanthorrhoeaceae*)
australis SPlb
fulva SPlb
glauca CCCN EAmu
johnsonii SPlb
preisii GBin SPlb

Xanthosoma (*Araceae*)
sagittifolium CDTJ
violaceum CDTJ

Xerochrysum (*Asteraceae*)
§ ***bracteatum*** 'Coco' CMHG CSpe WWlt
§ - 'Dargan Hill Monarch' CHll CSpe WWlt
§ - 'Skynet' WWlt
- 'Wollerton' WWlt
subundulatum WAbe

Xeronema (*Xeronemataceae*)
callistemon CBcs CBrP

Xerophyllum (*Melanthiaceae*)

tenax	GCal

Xylotheca (*Flacourtiaceae*)

kraussiana	SPlb

Y

Youngberry see *Rubus* 'Youngberry'

Ypsilandra (*Melanthiaceae*)

cavaleriei	CExl EBee WCot
thibetica	CCon CDes CExl CGHE CLAP CPrp ELon EPfP LEdu LLHF LRHS NLar SMad WCot WCru WPGP WSHC

Yucca ✿ (*Asparagaceae*)

SDR 3701	GKev
aloifolia	CCCN CDoC CHEx EAmu EGri MREP SAPC SBig SEND SPlb
§ - f. ***marginata*** (v)	EAmu EGri MREP SBig
- 'Purpurea'	SPlb
- 'Tricolor' (v)	EGri MREP
- 'Variegata'	see *Y. aloifolia* f. *marginata*
angustifolia	see *Y. glauca*
baccata	CCCN EAmu EGri SPlb XSen
- NNS 99-510	WCot
brevifolia	EGri
campestris	EGri
carnerosana	EAmu EGri WCot
constricta	EGri
decipiens	EGri
§ ***elata***	CCCN EGri WPGP XSen
§ ***elephantipes*** ♀H1	CDTJ EAmu SEND
- 'Jewel' (v)	EAmu MMuc SEND
- 'Puck' (v)	SEND
- variegated (v)	SEND
faxoniana	EAmu EGri SPlb
filamentosa ♀H4	CBcs CCCN CDul CMac CTri CWib EBee ELan EPfP EUJe EWTr GKev LAst LEdu LRHS MBlu MCri MGos MJak MMuc SBod SEND SGol SLim SPer SPlb SRms XLum
- 'Antwerp'	GCal
- 'Bright Edge' (v) ♀H3	CBcs CDoC CDul CMHG CMac CTri ELan ELon EPfP EUJe LAst LEdu LHop LRHS LSRN MAvo MBri MJak MRav MSwo SChu SEND SLim SPer SWvt WBrk
- 'Color Guard' (v)	LAst LRHS MAsh MBri NLar SChr WCot
- 'Garland's Gold' (v)	CCCN CDoC MAsh MJak SBig
- 'Variegata' (v) ♀H3	CBcs SRms
filifera	EAmu EGri EUJe SPlb
flaccida	MMuc SDix
- 'Golden Sword' (v) ♀H3	CBcs CDoC CMac CTsd EBee ELan EPfP GMaP LAst LRHS LSRN MAsh MGos MSCN MSwo NLar SGol SLim SPer SPoG SWvt WHar
- 'Ivory' ♀H3-4	CDoC CEnd CTsd ELan ELon EPfP GCal GMaP LSRN MBlu MBri MRav NLar SLPl SPer SRms
× ***floribunda***	SAPC
§ ***glauca***	EGri EPfP LEdu LRHS MBri SAPC WCot
gloriosa ♀H4	CDoC CHEx CMac CTri EAmu EUJe LRHS MREP NPla SAPC SEND SPer SPlb SPoG SWvt WBrk
- 'Aureovariegata'	see *Y. gloriosa* 'Variegata'
- Bright Star = 'Walbristar'PBR	LBuc LRHS NSoo SPer WCot
§ - 'Variegata' (v) ♀H4	Widely available
guatemalensis	see *Y. elephantipes*
harrimaniae	XSen
jaliscensis	EGri
linearifolia	EAmu WCot
linearis	see *Y. thompsoniana*
madrensis	EGri
'Nobilis'	CHEx SDix
pallida	EGri WPGP
queretaroensis new	EAmu
radiosa	see *Y. elata*
recurvifolia ♀H4	CHEx EAmu EPfP SAPC
- Banana Split = 'Monvil' (v)	EPfP LRHS SPoG
- 'Gold Stream' (v)	WCot
reverchonii	EGri
rigida	CDTJ EAmu WCot WPGP
rostrata	CCCN CDTJ EAmu EGri EUJe SAPC SPlb WCot
- 'Sapphire Skies'	MAvo WCot
rupicola	EGri WCot
schidigera	EAmu EGri
schottii	WCot
§ ***thompsoniana***	CDTJ EAmu EGri XSen
- blue leaved	EAmu
torreyi	EAmu
treculeana	EAmu EGri
'Vittorio Emanuele II'	SMad
whipplei	CBcs CCCN CDoC EBee EGri IGor LRHS SBig WCot WPGP
- subsp. ***caespitosa***	WPGP

Yushania (*Poaceae*)

KR 7698	ERod MWht
§ ***anceps***	CBcs CDoC CEnt CExl CHEx ENBC EPfP MMoz MMuc MWht SAPC SBig SEND WMoo
- 'Pitt White'	CEnt CExl MWht WJun
- 'Pitt White Rejuvenated'	ERod WPGP
brevipaniculata	ERod WJun
chungii	CEnt CExl ERod MWht WJun WPGP
* ***equatus***	WJun
maculata	CEnt CExl ERod MMoz MWht SBig WJun
§ ***maling***	CExl EPfP ERod MMoz WJun
Yunnan 5	CExl

Z

Zaluzianskya (*Scrophulariaceae*)

JCA 15665	WAbe
elongata	SPlb
'Katherine'	SRot
microsiphon	SPlb
'Orange Eye'	GKev NSla WAbe WIce
ovata	CElw CPBP EPfP EPot EWld GKev LPio MHer MSCN NSla SBch SPet SPlb SPoG WAbe WHlf WIce
pulvinata	SPlb
'Semonkong'	GCal LPio SWvt

Zamia (Zamiaceae)

pumila	SPlb

Zamioculcas (Araceae)

zamiifolia	CCCN

Zantedeschia (Araceae)

§ ***aethiopica*** ♀H3	Widely available
- 'Apple Court Babe'	CAby CElw CRow ELon MNrw SMrm
- 'Crowborough' ♀H3	Widely available
- 'Gigantea'	CHEx
- 'Glow'	CExl CMac ECtt MRav WGwG
- 'Green Goddess' ♀H3	Widely available
- 'Little Gem'	SMad
- 'Luzon Lovely'	WCru
- 'Marshmallow'	ECtt ELan EPfP SPet
- 'Mr Martin'	CCCN CMac EBee ECtt ELon SBig SMad SWvt WCot
- 'Pershore Fantasia' (v)	CExl EBee WCot WWEG
- 'Snow White' PBR	LRHS
- 'White Gnome'	WCot
- 'White Sail'	ECtt ELan LRHS MRav NGdn SWat WGwG
albomaculata	CHel CTca SPlb
'Anneke'	CCCN EPfP
'Apricot Glow'	CHll
'Ascari' PBR	CCCN
'Auckland' PBR	SDeJ
'Black Magic'	CCCN CMac EPfP
'Black Star'	see *Z.* 'Edge of Night'
'Cameo'	CCCN SDeJ
'Captain Tendens' PBR (Captain Series)	SDeJ
'Chianti'	SDeJ
'Crystal Blush'	SDeJ
§ 'Edge of Night'	CCCN ERCP EUJe SDeJ
'Elegant Swan' PBR **new**	LRHS
elliottiana ♀H1	CBcs CCon CHEx CTri
'Flame'	CCCN SPad
'Flamingo' PBR **new**	WCot
'Garnet Glow'	WCot
'Helen O'Connor'	CExl CHel
'Hercules' **new**	ESwi
'Kiwi Blush'	CBAq CBro CCCN CCon CExl CHEx CHel CSpe EBee EHyd ELan ELon EPfP EWll LHop SEND SKHP SPer SPet SRkn SWat WGwG
'Lime Lady'	EWay
'Mango'	EPri WCot
'Mozart'	CCCN
'Picasso' PBR	CCCN ERCP SDeJ SPad WCot
'Pink Mist'	SMad
'Purple Sensation'	EPfP
'Red Sox' PBR	CCCN SDeJ
rehmannii ♀H1	NLar SDeJ SRms
'Schwarzwalder' PBR	EHyd
'Sunshine'	WCot
'White Giant'	WPGP
'White Pixie'	EPfP

Zanthorhiza see *Xanthorhiza*

Zanthoxylum (Rutaceae)

acanthopodium GWJ 9287	WCru
ailanthoides B&SWJ 11115	WCru
- B&SWJ 11394 from Japan	WCru
- f. ***inermis*** RWJ 10048	WCru
americanum	ELan LEdu
armatum	CAgr
- HWJK 2178	WCru
bungeanum BWJ 8040 **new**	WCru
fauriei B&SWJ 11080	WCru
aff. ***fauriei*** B&SWJ 11371	WCru
- B&SWJ 11523	WCru
laetum WWJ 11678	WCru
- WWJ 11914	WCru
myriacanthum B&SWJ 11844	WCru
oxyphyllum HWJK 2131 **new**	WCru
- HWJK 2199	WCru
piperitum	CAgr CBcs GPoy
- B&SWJ 8543	WCru
- B&SWJ 11377	WCru
- B&SWJ 11433	WCru
- purple-leaved	CExl CFil WPGP
schinifolium	CAgr LEdu
- B&SWJ 8593	WCru
- B&SWJ 11080	WCru
- B&SWJ 11391	WCru
simulans	CAgr CArn CBcs CDul CExl GBin IGor IVic LEdu MBlu NLar

Zauschneria (Onagraceae)

arizonica	see *Z. californica* subsp. *latifolia*
§ ***californica***	CFis CHll CSam CTri ECho MBrN SLon SWat SWvt WHrl WPnn XLum
§ - subsp. ***cana***	SWat
- - 'Sir Cedric Morris'	EPfP LRHS
§ - 'Dublin' ♀H3	CBcs EBee ECho ECtt EPfP EPot LBMP LHop LRHS MHer MMuc MSCN MWat NSla SEND SPer SPhx SPlb SPoG SRkn SWvt WHoo WKif WSHC XLum
- 'Ed Carman'	ECtt ESwi LSou SEND XLum
§ - subsp. ***garrettii***	ECho SDys SWat
- 'Glasnevin'	see *Z. californica* 'Dublin'
§ - subsp. ***latifolia***	XLum
§ - subsp. ***mexicana***	MHer SRms
- 'Olbrich Silver'	EBee ECtt EWes LRHS SIgm WKif XLum
- 'Western Hills' ♀H4	CCon CSpe CTri EBee ECho EPfP LHop LRHS LSou MMuc MRav SPhx SWvt WHoo XLum
cana villosa	see *Z. californica* subsp. *mexicana*
I 'Pumilio'	EPot NSla
§ ***septentrionalis***	WAbe

Zebrina see *Tradescantia*

Zelkova ✿ (Ulmaceae)

abelicea	MBri
carpinifolia	CDul CLnd CMCN SPlb
'Kiwi Sunset'	CDul CEnd EBee EPfP NWea
schneideriana	CMCN
serrata ♀H4	CBcs CCVT CDul CLnd CMCN CMen CTho EBee ECrN ELan EPfP MGos MMuc NWea SEND SGol WMou
- B&SWJ 8491 from Korea	WCru
- 'Goblin'	CJun MBlu NLar WPat
- 'Green Vase'	MBlu

- 'Kiwi Sunset'[PBR]	LRHS
- 'Musashino'	SGol
- 'Ogon'	SGol
- 'Urban Ruby'	NLar
- 'Variegata' (v)	CJun CMac MBlu NLar SGol SMad
sinica	CMCN CMen
× ***verschaffeltii***	EPfP MBlu

Zenobia (*Ericaceae*)

pulverulenta	CAbP CBcs CDoC CMac CSBt ELan EPfP IVic LRHS MAsh MBlu MGos NLar SHil SLon SSpi SSta WAbe WPat WSHC
- 'Blue Sky'	CAbP CBcs CDoC CMCN EBee EPfP GBin GKin IDee LRHS MBlu MBri MGos MPkF NLar SPer SPoG SSpi SSta
- f. ***nitida***	CMac NLar
- 'Raspberry Ripple'	CBcs GKin MBri NLar SSta
- 'Viridis'	NLar

Zephyranthes ✿ (*Amaryllidaceae*)

atamasca	SKHP
'Big Dude'	SKHP
candida	CBro EBee ECho EPot EShb LPot LRHS SDeJ
citrina	CDoy CExl EBee ECho EPot SDeJ WCot
drummondii	ECho
flavissima	CDes ECho
'Krakatau' **new**	WCot
La Bufa Rosa Group	CExl WCot
lindleyana	WHil
mexicana	EBee
minima	ECho
robusta	see *Habranthus robustus*
rosea	EBee EPot SDeJ

Zigadenus (*Melanthiaceae*)

elegans	EBee ECGP EPri GCal LEdu MAvo MHer SMad WCot WSHC
fremontii	WCot
nuttallii	CRDP ECho WCot
venenosus NNS 03-605	WCot

Zingiber ✿ (*Zingiberaceae*)

malaysianum	EAmu
mioga	CCon CFil CMac GPoy IMou LEdu SChr SPlb WPGP
- 'Crûg's Zing'	LEdu WCru
- 'Dancing Crane' (v)	CFil CMac EUJe IFro LEdu
officinale	CTsd SRms
zerumbet	SBst

Zinnia (*Asteraceae*)

elegans	SVic
'Envy' (d) **new**	CSpe
'Profusion Cherry' **new**	CWCL
'Red Spider'	CSpe
'Swizzle Scarlet and Yellow' **new**	CWCL

Zizia (*Apiaceae*)

aptera	LRHS SPhx
aurea	SDix SPhx WSHC XLum

Ziziphus (*Rhamnaceae*)

§ ***jujuba*** (F)	CAgr CBcs
- 'Lang' (F)	CAgr
- 'Li' (F)	CAgr
- var. ***spinosa***	CArn
sativa	see *Z. jujuba*

Bibliography

This is by no means exhaustive but lists some of the more useful works used in the preparation of the *RHS Plant Finder*. The websites of raisers of new plants (not listed here) are also an invaluable source of information.

General

Allan, H.H., et al. 2000. *Flora of New Zealand.* Wellington. http://floraseries.landcareresearch.co.nz

Ball Colegrave. 2007. *Plant Catalogue 2008 & Seed Catalogue 2008.* West Adderbury, Oxon: Ball Colegrave.

Bean, W.J. 1988. *Trees and Shrubs Hardy in the British Isles.* (8th ed.) Sir George Taylor, D.L. Clarke (eds). Supp. D.L. Clarke (ed.). London: John Murray.

Beckett, K. (ed.). 1994. *Alpine Garden Society Encyclopaedia of Alpines.* Pershore, Worcs.: Alpine Garden Society.

Boufford, D.E., et al. (eds). 2003. *Flora of Taiwan Checklist.* A checklist of the vascular plants of Taiwan. Taipei, Taiwan: NTU. http://tai2.ntu.edu.tw

Bramwell, D. & Bramwell, Z.I. 2001. *Wild Flowers of the Canary Islands.* (2nd ed.). Madrid: Editorial Rueda, S.L.

Brickell, C. (ed.). 2008. *The Royal Horticultural Society A-Z Encyclopedia of Garden Plants.* (3rd ed.) London: Dorling Kindersley.

Brickell, C.D. et al (eds.). 2009. *International Code of Nomenclature for Cultivated Plants* (8th ed.). ISHS.

Brummitt, R.K. (comp.). 1992. *Vascular Plant Families and Genera.* Kew: Royal Botanic Gardens. http://data.kew.org

Castroviejo, S. et al. (eds). *Flora Iberica.* 1987-2007. (Vols 1-8, 10, 14, 15, 21). Madrid: Real Jardín Botánico, C.S.I.C.

Cave, Y. & Paddison, V. 1999. *The Gardener's Encyclopaedia of New Zealand Native Plants.* Auckland: Godwit.

Cooke, I. 1998. *The Plantfinder's Guide to Tender Perennials.* Newton Abbot, Devon: David & Charles.

Cronquist, A., Holmgren, A.H., Holmgren, N.H., Reveal, J.L. & Holmgren, P.H. et al. (eds). *Intermountain Flora: Vascular Plants of the Intermountain West, USA.* (1986-97). (Vols 1, 3-6). New York: New York Botanical Garden.

Davis, P.H., Mill, R.R. & Tan, K. (eds). 1965-88. *Flora of Turkey and the East Aegean Island.* (Vols 1-10). Edinburgh University Press.

Goldblatt, P. & Manning, J. 2000. *Cape Plants. A Conspectus of the Cape Flora of South Africa.* South Africa/USA: National Botanical Institute of South Africa/Missouri Botanical Garden.

Greuter, W., Brummitt, R.K., Farr, E., Kilian, N., Kirk, P.M. & Silva, P.C. (comps). 1993. *NCU-3.*

Grierson, A.J.C., Long, D.G. & Noltie, H.J. et al. (eds). 2001. *Flora of Bhutan.* Edinburgh: Royal Botanic Garden.

Grimshaw, J. & Bayton, R. 2009. *New Trees. Recent Introductions to Cultivation.* Kew: Royal Botanic Gardens.

Güner, A., Özhatay, N., Ekîm, T., Baser, K.H.C. & Hedge, I.C. 2000. *Flora of Turkey and the East Aegean Islands.* Supp. 2. Vol. 11. Edinburgh: Edinburgh University Press.

Hickman, J.C. (ed.). 1993. *The Jepson Manual. Higher Plants of California.* Berkeley & Los Angeles: University of California Press. Jan 2010. http://ucjeps.berkeley.edu/interchange.html

Hillier, J. & Coombes, A. (eds). 2002. *The Hillier Manual of Trees & Shrubs.* (7th ed.). Newton Abbot, Devon: David & Charles.

Hirose, Y. & Yokoi, M. 1998 & 2001. *Variegated Plants in Colour.* Vols 1 & 2. Iwakuni, Japan: Varie Nine.

Hoffman, M. (ed.). 2005. *List of Woody Plants. International Standard ENA 2005-2010.* Netherlands: Applied Plant Research.

Huxley, A., Griffiths, M. & Levy, M. (eds). 1992. *The New RHS Dictionary of Gardening.* London: Macmillan.

Iwatsuki, K., et al. 1995. *Flora of Japan.* Vols I-IIIb. Tokyo, Japan: Kodansha Ltd.

Jelitto, L. & Schacht, W.R., Simon, H. 2002. *Die Freiland-Schmuchstauden.* Germany: Verlag Eugen Ulmer.

Krüssmann, G. & Epp, M.E. (trans.). 1986. *Manual of Cultivated Broad-leaved Trees and Shrubs.* London: Batsford (3 vols).

Leslie, A.C. (trans.). *New Cultivars of Herbaceous Perennial Plants 1985-1990.* Hardy Plant Society.

Mabberley, D.J. 2008. *Mabberley's Plant Book. A Portable Dictionary of Plants, their Classification and Uses.* (3rd ed.). Cambridge: Cambridge University Press.

McNeill, J. et al. (eds). 2006. *International Code of Botanical Nomenclature (Vienna Code).* Ruggell, Liechtenstein: A.R.G. Gantner Verlag. Jan 2010. http://ibot.sav.sk.

Metcalf, L.J. 1987. *The Cultivation of New Zealand Trees and Shrubs.* Auckland: Reed Methuen.

Nelson, E.C. 2000. *A Heritage of Beauty: The Garden Plants of Ireland: An Illustrated Encyclopaedia.* Dublin: Irish Garden Plant Society.

Ohwi, J. 1965. *Flora of Japan.* Washington DC: Smithsonian Institution.

Phillips, R. & Rix, M. 1997. *Conservatory and Indoor Plants.* London: Macmillan. (2 vols).
Platt, K. (comp.). 2002. *The Seed Search.* (5th ed.). Sheffield: Karen Platt.
Press, J.R. & Short, M.J. (eds). 1994. *Flora of Madeira.* London: Natural History Museum/HMSO.
Rehder, A. 1940. *Manual of Cultivated Trees and Shrubs Hardy in North America.* (2nd ed.). New York: Macmillan.
Rice, G. (ed.), 2006. *Encyclopedia of Perennials.* London: Dorling Kindersley.
Stace, C. 2010. *New Flora of the British Isles.* (3rd ed.). Cambridge: Cambridge University Press.
Stearn, W.T. 1992. *Botanical Latin.* (4th ed.). Newton Abbot, Devon: David & Charles.
Stearn, W.T. 1996. *Stearn's Dictionary of Plant Names for Gardeners.* London: Cassell.
Thomas, G.S. 1990. *Perennial Garden Plants. A Modern Florilegium.* (3rd ed.). London: Dent.
Trehane, P. (comp.). 1989. *Index Hortensis. Vol. 1: Perennials.* Wimborne: Quarterjack
Tutin, T.G., et al. (ed.). 1993. *Flora Europaea. Vol. 1. Psilotaceae to Platanaceae.* (2nd ed.). Cambridge University Press.
Tutin, T.G., et al. 1964. *Flora Europaea.* Cambridge University Press. Vols 1-5. http://rbg-web2.rbgc.org.uk
Walter, K.S. & Gillett, H.J. (eds). 1998. *1997 IUCN Red List of Threatened Plants.* Gland, Switzerland and Cambridge, UK: IUCN.
Walters, S.M. & Cullen, J. et al. (eds). 2000. *The European Garden Flora.* Cambridge: Cambridge University Press. (6 vols).

General Periodicals

Dendroflora
New, Rare and Unusual Plants.
The Hardy Plant Society. *The Hardy Plant.*
The Hardy Plant Society. *The Sport.*
Internationale Stauden-Union. *ISU Yearbook.*
Royal Horticultural Society. *Hanburyana.*
Royal Horticultural Society. *The Garden*
Royal Horticultural Society. *The Plantsman.*
Royal Horticultural Society. *The New Plantsman.*
Royal Horticultural Society. *The Plantsman* (new series).

General Websites

Annotated Checklist of the Flowering Plants of Nepal. Jan 2010 www.efloras.org/flora_page-aspx?_id=110
Australian Cultivar Registration Authority. Jan 2010. www.anbg.gov.au/acra
Australian Plant Breeders Rights: Database Search. Jan 2010. http://pbr.ipaustralia.optus.com.au
Australian Plant Names Index. Australian National Botanic Gardens (comp.). Jan 2010. www.anbg.gov.au/apni/index.html
Bolivia Checklist. Jan 2010. www.efloras.org/flora_page.aspx?flora_id=40
Botanical Expedition in Myanmar Checklist. Jan 2010. http://botany.si-edu/myanmar/checklistNames.cfm
Brand, H. UConn Plant Database of Trees Shrubs and Vines. Jan 2010. www.hort.uconn.edu
Canadian Ornamental Plant Foundation. Jan 2010. www.copf.org
Canadian Plant Breeders Rights Office: Canadian Food Inspection Agency. Jan 2010. www.inspection.gc.ca
Catálogo de las Plantas Vasculares de las República Argentina. Jan 2010. www.darwin.edu.ar/Publicaciones/catalogoVaseII/CatalogoVaseII.asp
Catalogue of the Vascular Plants of Madagascar: www.efforas.org/flora_page.aspx?flora_id+12
Darwin Checklist of Moroccan Vascular Plants www.herbarium.rdg.ac.uk/
DEFRA Plant Varieties and Seeds Gazette. Jan 2010. www.defra.gov.uk
Flora Himalaya Database. Jan 2010. www.leca.univ-savoie.fr
Flora Mesoamericana Internet Version (W3FM). Jan 2010. Missouri Botanical Garden. www.mobot.org/MOBOT/FM/intro.html
Flora of Australia Online. Jan 2010. Australian Biological Resources Study. www.environment.gov.au/biodiversity/abrs/online-resources/flora/index.html
Flora of Chile. Jan 2010. www.efloras.org/flora_page.aspx?flora_id=60
Flora of China Checklist. Jan 2010. http://flora.huh.harvard.edu/china
Flora of Pakistan. Jan 2010. www.efloras.org/flora_page.aspd?flora_id=5
Flora of North America Website. Jan 2010. Morin, N.R., et al. www.efloras.org-page.aspx/flora_id=1
GRIN (Germplasm Resources Information Network) Taxonomy. Jan 2010. www.ars-grin.gov
Hatch, D. Jan 2010. New Ornamentals Society Database. http://members.tripod.com/~Hatch_L/nos.html
International Plant Names Index. Jan 2010. www.ipni.org
International Plant Names Index: Author Query. Jan 2010. www.ipni.org/ipni
IOPI Provisional Global Plant Checklist. Jan 2010. www.bgbm.fu-berlin.de/iopi/gpl/query.asp
Manaaki Whenua: Landcare Research in New Zealand Plants Database Jan 2010. http://nzflora.landcareresearch.co.nz
Manual de plantas de Costa Rica. Jan 2010. www.mobot.org/manual.plantas
Plant List, The. A working list of all plant species www.theplantlist.org.

Plants Database. USDA, NRCS. Jan 2010. http://plants.usda.gov
Plants of Southern Africa: an Online Checklist. Jan 2010. http://posa.sanbi.org
PLUTO: Plant Variety Database www.upov.int/pluto/en
New Zealand Plant Variety Rights Office www.iponz.govt.nz/cms/pvr
Royal Horticultural Society. www.rhs.org.uk/plants/RHS-Publications/Plant-registers
Synonymized Checklist of the Vascular Flora of the United States, Puerto Rico and the Virgin Isles. BIOTA of North America Program. Jan 2010. www.bonap.org
Tropicos. Jan 2010. www.tropicos.org
US Patent Full-Text Database. US Patent and Trademark Office, (comp.). Jan 2010. www.uspto.gov/patft
World Checklist of Selected Families. 2010. apps.kew.org/wcsp

GENERA AND OTHER PLANT GROUPINGS

Acer
Gregory, P. & Angus, H. 2008. *World Checklist of Maple Cultivar Names*. Forestry Commission National Arboreta.
Harris, J.G.S. 2000. *The Gardener's Guide to Growing Maples.* Newton Abbot, Devon: David & Charles.
Van Gelderen, C.J. & Van Gelderen, D.M. 1999. *Maples for Gardens.* A Color Encyclopedia. Portland, Oregon: Timber Press.
Vertrees, J.D. 2001. *Japanese Maples.* Momiji and Kaede. (3rd ed.). Portland, Oregon: Timber Press.
Actaea
Compton, J.A., Culham, A. & Jury, S.L. 1998. Reclassification of *Actaea* to Include *Cimicifuga* and *Souliea (Ranunculaceae). Taxon* 47:593-634.
Adiantum
Goudey, C.J. 1985. *Maidenhair Ferns in Cultivation.* Melbourne: Lothian.
Agapanthus
Snoeijer, W. 2004. *Agapanthus. A Revision of the Genus*. Portland, Oregon: Timber Press.
Agavaceae
Irish, M. & Irish, G. 2000. *Agaves, Yuccas and Related Plants.* A Gardener's Guide. Portland, Oregon: Timber Press.
Aizoaceae
Burgoyne, P. et al. 1998. *Mesembs of the World. Illustrated Guide to a Remarkable Succulent Group.* South Africa: Briza Publications.
Allium
Davies, D. 1992. *Alliums. The Ornamental Onions.* London: Batsford
Gregory, M., et al. 1998. *Nomenclator Alliorum.* Kew: Royal Botanic Gardens.
Mathew, B. 1996. *A Review of Allium Section Allium.* Kew: Royal Botanic Gardens.
Androsace
Smith, G. & Lowe, D. 1997. *The Genus Androsace.* Pershore, Worcs.: Alpine Garden Society.
Anemone, Japanese
McKendrick, M. 1990. Autumn Flowering Anemones. *The Plantsman* 12(3):140-151.
McKendrick, M. 1998. Japanese Anemones. *The Garden* (RHS) 123(9):628-633.
Anthemis
Leslie, A. 1997. Focus on Plants: *Anthemis tinctoria. The Garden* (RHS) 122(8):552-555.
Apiaceae
Pimenov, M.G. & Leonov, M.V. 1993. *The Genera of the Umbelliferae.* Kew: Royal Botanic Gardens.
Aquilegia
Munz, P.A. 1946. *Aquilegia:* the Cultivated and Wild Columbines. *Gentes Herb.* 7(1):1-150.
Araceae
Govaerts, R. & Frodin, D.G. 2002. *World Checklist and Bibliography of Araceae (and Acoraceae).* Kew:Royal Botanic Gardens
Araliaceae
Govaerts, R. & Frodin, D.G. 2002. *World Checklist and Bibliography of Araliaceae.* Kew:Royal Botanic Gardens
Arecaceae (palms)
Craft, P. & Riffle, R.L. 2003. *Encyclopedia of Cultivated Palms.* Portland, Oregon: Timber Press.
Uhl, N.W. & Dransfield, J. 1987. *Genera Palmarum.* A Classification of Palms Based on the Work of Harold E. Moore Jr. Lawrence, Kansas: Allen Press.
Argyranthemum
Humphries, C.J. 1976. A Revision of the Macaronesian Genus *Argyranthemum. Bull. Brit. Mus. (Nat. Hist.) Bot.* 5(4):145-240.
Arisaema
Gusman, G. & Gusman, L. 2002. *The Genus Arisaema: A Monograph for Botanists and Nature Lovers.* Ruggell, Leichtenstein: A.R. Gantner Verlag Kommanditgesellschaft.
Pradhan, U.C. 1997. *Himalayan Cobra Lilies* (Arisaema). Their Botany and Culture. (2nd ed.). Kalimpong, West Bengal, India: Primulaceae Books.
Arum
Bown, D. 2000. *Plants of the Arum Family.* (2nd ed.). Portland, Oregon: Timber Press.
Boyce, P. 1993. *The Genus Arum.* London: HMSO.
Asclepiadaceae
Eggli, U. (ed.). 2002. *Illustrated Handbook of Succulent Plants: Asclepiadaceae*. Heidelberg, Germany: Springer-Verlag.
Aster
Picton, P. 1999. *The Gardener's Guide to Growing Asters.* Newton Abbot: David & Charles.
Asteraceae
Bremer, K. et al. 1994. *Asteraceae: Cladistics and Classification*. Portland, Oregon: Timber Press.

Cubey, J. & Grant, M. 2004. *Perennial Yellow Daisies: RHS Bulletin No 6.* Wisley, Surrey: RHS.

Astilbe

Noblett, H. 2001. *Astilbe.* A Guide to the Identification of Cultivars and Common Species. Cumbria: Henry Noblett.

Aubrieta

1975. *International Registration Authority Checklist.* Weihenstephan, Germany: (Unpublished).

Bamboos

Ohrnberger, D. 1999. *The Bamboos of the World.* Amsterdam: Elsevier.

Begonia

American Begonia Society Astro Branch Begonia Data Base. Jan 2010. http://absastro.tripod.com

American Begonia Society Registered Begonias. Jan 2010. http://www.begonias.org

Ingles, J. 1990. *American Begonia Society Listing of Begonia Cultivars.* Revised Edition Buxton Checklist. American Begonia Society.

Tebbitt, M.C. 2005. *Begonias: Cultivation, Identification and Natural History.* Portland, Oregon: Timber Press.

Berberidaceae

Stearn, W.T. & Shaw, J.M.H. 2002. *The Genus Epimedium and Other Herbaceous Berberidaceae including the Genus Podophyllum.* Kew: Royal Botanic Gardens.

Betula

Ashburner, K.B. 1980. *Betula* – a Survey. *The Plantsman* 2(1):31-53.

Hunt, D. (ed.) 1993. *Betula: Proceedings of the IDS Betula Symposium 1992.* Richmond, Surrey: International Dendrology Society.

Boraginaceae

Bennett, M. 2003. *Pulmonarias and the Borage Family.* London: Batsford.

Bougainvillea

Gillis, W.T. 1976. Bougainvilleas of Cultivation *(Nyctaginaceae). Baileya* 20(1):34-41.

Iredell, J. 1990. *The Bougainvillea Grower's Handbook.* Brookvale, Australia: Simon & Schuster.

Iredell, J. 1994. *Growing Bougainvilleas.* London: Cassell.

MacDaniels, L.H. 1981. A Study of Cultivars in *Bougainvillea (Nyctaginaceae). Baileya* 21(2):77-100.

Singh, B., Panwar, R.S., Voleti, S.R., Sharma, V.K. & Thakur, S. 1999. *The New International Bougainvillea Check List.* (2nd ed.). New Delhi: Indian Agricultural Research Institute.

Bromeliaceae

Beadle, D.A. 1991. *A Preliminary Listing of all the Known Cultivar and Grex Names for the Bromeliaceae.* Corpus Christi, Texas: Bromeliad Society.

Bromeliad Cultivar Registry Online Databases. Bromeliad Society International. Jan 2010. www.bsi.org

Brugmansia

Wreggitt, L. et al. (comp.). Jan 2010. *Register of Brugmansia Cultivars and Checklist of Names in Use.* American Brugmansia and Datura Society. www.abads.org

Buddleja

Stuart, D.D. 2006. *Buddlejas: Royal Horticultural Society Collector Guide.* Portland, Oregon: Timber Press.

Bulbs

Leeds, R. 2000. *The Plantfinder's Guide to Early Bulbs.* Newton Abbot, Devon: David & Charles.

KAVB Online registration pages. Jan 2010. http://kavb.back2p.soft-orange.com

Buxus

Batdorf, L.R. 1995. *Boxwood Handbook. A Practical Guide to Knowing and Growing Boxwood.* Boyce, VA, USA: The American Boxwood Society. Jan 2010. www.boxwoodsociety.org

Cactaceae

Hunt, D. et al. 2006. *New Cactus Lexicon.* (2 vols.) Sherborne, Dorset: DH Books.

Camellia

Trujillo, D. J. (ed.). 2002. *Camellia Nomenclature.* (24th revd ed.). Southern California Camellia Society.

Savige, T.J. (comp.). 1993. *The International Camellia Register.* (Vol 1 2). Supp. 1997. The International Camellia Society.

Campanula

Lewis, P. & Lynch, M. 1998. *Campanulas.* A Gardeners Guide. (2nd ed.). London: Batsford.

Lewis, P 2002. *Campanulas in the Garden.* Pershore, Worcs.: Hardy Plant Society.

Campanulaceae

Lammers, T.G. 2007. *World Checklist and Bibliography of Campanulaceae.* Kew Publishing.

Canna

Cooke, I. 2001. *The Gardener's Guide to Growing Cannas.* Newton Abbot, Devon: David & Charles.

Gray, J. & Grant, M. 2003. Canna: RHS Bulletin No 3. Wisley, Surrey: RHS.

Hayward, K. Jan 2010. www.hartcanna.com

Carnivorous Plants

Schlauer, J. (comp.). Jan 2010. Carnivorous Plant Database. www.omnisterra.com

Ceanothus

Fross, D. & D. Wilken. 2006. *Ceanothus.* Portland, Oregon: Timber Press.

Cercidiphyllum

Dosmann, M.S. 1999. Katsura: a Review of *Cercidiphyllum* in Cultivation and in the Wild. *The New Plantsman* 6(1):52-62.

Dosmann, M., Andrews, S., Del Tredici, P. & Li, J. 2003. Classification and Nomenclature of Weeping Katsuras. *The Plantsman* 2(1):21-27.

Chaenomeles
Weber, C. 1963. Cultivars in the Genus *Chaenomeles. Arnoldia (Jamaica Plain)* 23(3):17-75.
Chrysanthemum
Brummitt, D. 1997. *Chrysanthemum* Once Again. *The Garden* (RHS) 122(9):662-663.
Gosling, S.G. (ed.). 1964. *British National Register of Chrysanthemums*. Whetstone, London: National Chrysanthemum Society.
National Chrysanthemum Society. 2000. *British National Register of Names of Chrysanthemums Amalgamated Edition 1964-1999*. Tamworth, Staffordshire: National Chrysanthemum Society. Cultivar database. Jan 2010. www.nationalchrysanthemumsociety.org.uk
Cistus
Page, R.G. Feb 2007. Cistus and Halimium Website. www.cistuspage.org.uk
Citrus
Davies, F.S. & Albrigo, L.G. 1994. *Citrus*. Wallingford, Oxon: Cab International.
Page, M. 2008. *Growing Citrus*. London: Timber Press
Saunt, J. 1990. *Citrus Varieties of the World*. An Illustrated Guide. Norwich: Sinclair
Clematis
Clematis on the Web. Jan 2008. www.clematis.hull.ac.uk
Grey-Wilson, C. 2000. *Clematis: the Genus*. London: Batsford
HelpMeFind Clematis. Nov 2006. www.helpmefind.com/clematis
Johnson, M. 2001. *The Genus Clematis*. Södertälje, Sweden: Magnus Johnsons Plantskola AB & Bengt Sundström.
Matthews, V. (comp.). 2002. *The International Clematis Register and Checklist 2002* & Supps 1-3. 2004-2009. London: RHS.
Toomey, M. & Leeds, E. 2001. *An Illustrated Encyclopedia of Clematis*. Portland, Oregon: Timber Press.
Conifers
den Ouden, P. & Boom, B.K. 1965. *Manual of Cultivated Conifers*. The Hague: Martinus Nijhof.
Eckenwalder, J.E. 2009. *Conifers of the World*. China:Timber Press
Farjon, A. 1998. *World Checklist and Bibliography of Conifers*. Kew: Royal Botanic Gardens.
Knees, S.G. & Springate, L.S. 2009. *The International Conifer Register, Pt 5*. London: RHS.
Krüssmann, G. & Epp, M.E. (trans.). 1985. *Manual of Cultivated Conifers*. London: Batsford.
Lewis, J. & Leslie, A.C. 1987-1998. *The International Conifer Register. Pts 1-4*. London: RHS.
Welch, H.J. 1979. *Manual of Dwarf Conifers*. New York: Theophrastus.
Welch, H.J. 1991. *The Conifer Manual*. Vol. 1. Dordrecht, Netherlands: Kluwer Academic Publishers.
Welch, H.J. 1993. *The World Checklist of Conifers*. Bromyard, Herefordshire: Landsman's Bookshops Ltd.
Cornus
Cappiello, P. & Shadow, D. 2005. *Dogwoods*. Portland, Oregon: Timber Press.
Howard, R.A. 1961. Registration Lists of Cultivar Names in *Cornus L. Arnoldia (Jamaica Plain)* 21(2):9-18.
Corydalis
Lidén, M. & Zetterlund, H. 1997. *Corydalis. A Gardener's Guide and a Monograph of the Tuberous Species*. Pershore, Worcs.: Alpine Garden Society Publications Ltd.
Corylus
Crawford, M. 1995. *Hazelnuts: Production and Culture*. Dartington, Devon: Agroforestry Research Trust.
Cotoneaster
Fryer, J. & Hylmö, B. 1998. Seven New Species of *Cotoneaster* in Cultivation. *The New Plantsman* 5(3):132-144.
Fryer, J. & Hylmö, B. 2001. Captivating Cotoneasters. *The New Plantsman* 8(4):227-238.
Fryer, J. & Hylmö, B. 2009. *Cotoneasters. A Comprehensive Guide to Shrubs for Flowers, Fruit and Foliage*. Portland, Oregon: Timber Press.
Crassulaceae
Rowley, G. 2003. *Crassula: A Grower's Guide*. Venegono superiore, Italy: Cactus & Co.
Eggli, U. (ed.) 2003. *Illustrated Handbook of Succulent Plants*. Springer.
Crocosmia
Goldblatt, P., Manning, J.C. & Dunlop, G. 2004. *Crocosmia and Chasmanthe*. Portland, Oregon: Timber Press.
Crocus
Jacobsen, N., van Scheepen, J. & Ørgaard, M. 1997. The *Crocus chrysanthus – biflorus* Cultivars. *The New Plantsman* 4(1):6-38.
Mathew, B. 1982. *The Crocus. A Review of the Genus Crocus (Iridaceae)*. London: Batsford.
Mathew, B. 2002. *Crocus* Up-date. *The Plantsman* 1(1):44-56.
Cyclamen
Clennett, C. Jan. 2003. Register of Cultivar Names. www.cyclamen.org
Grey-Wilson, C. 2003. *Cyclamen. A Guide for Gardeners, Horticulturists & Botanists*. London: Batsford.
Grey-Wilson, C. 2002 Sprenger's Alpine Cyclamen. *The Plantsman* 1(3):173-177.
Cypripedium
Cribb, P. 1997. *The Genus Cypripedium*. Portland, Oregon: Timber Press.
Dahlia
American Dahlia Society website. Jan 2010. www.dahlia.org
Bates, D. Dahlia Plant Finder 2007. Jan 2010. www.dahliaworld.co.uk

National Dahlia Society. 2005. *Classified Directory and Judging Rules*. (28th ed.) Aldershot, Hants: National Dahlia Society.

RHS & Hedge, R. (comps). 1969. *Tentative Classified List and International Register of Dahlia Names 1969* & Supps 1-13. Supps 13-20. 2002-09. London: RHS.

Winchester Growers Ltd English National Dahlia Collection website. Jan 2010. www.national-dahlia-collection.co.uk

Daphne

Brickell, C.D. & Mathew, B. 1976. *Daphne. The Genus in the Wild and in Cultivation*. Woking, Surrey: Alpine Garden Society.

Grey-Wilson, C. (ed.). 2001. *The Smaller Daphnes. The Proceedings of 'Daphne 2000', a Conference held at the Royal Horticultural Society*. Pershore, Worcs.: Alpine Garden Society.

White, R. 2006. *Daphnes: A Practical Guide for Gardeners*. Portland, Oregon: Timber Press.

Delphinium

1949. *A Tentative Check-list of Delphinium Names*. London: RHS.

1970. *A Tentative Check-list of Delphinium Names*. Addendum. London: RHS.

Bassett, D. & Wesley, W. 2004. *Delphinium: RHS Bulletin No 5*. Wisley, Surrey: RHS.

Leslie, A.C. 1996. *The International Delphinium Register Cumulative Supp. 1970-1995*. London: RHS.

Leslie, A.C. 1996-2005. The International Delphinium Register Supp. 1994-99. *The Delphinium Society Year Book 1996-2005*. London: RHS.

Dianthus

Galbally, J. & Galbally, E. 1997. *Carnations and Pinks for Garden and Greenhouse*. Portland, Oregon: Timber Press.

Leslie, A.C. *The International Dianthus Register*. 1983-2002. (2nd ed. & Supps 1-19). Supps 19-27, 2002-11. London: RHS.

Dierama

Hilliard, O.M. & Burtt, B.L. 1991. *Dierama. The Harebells of Africa*. Johannesburg; London: Acorn Books

Dionysia

Grey-Wilson, C. 1989. *The Genus Dionysia*. Woking, Surrey: Alpine Garden Society.

Douglasia

Mitchell, B. 1999. Celebrating the Bicentenary of David Douglas: a Review of *Douglasia* in Cultivation. *The New Plantsman* 6(2):101-108.

Dracaena

Bos, J.J., Graven, P., Hetterscheid, W.L.A. & van de Wege, J.J. 1992. Wild and cultivated *Dracaena fragrans*. *Edinburgh J. Bot.* 49(3):311-331.

Echeveria

Schulz, L. & Kapitany, A. *Echeveria Cultivars*. Teesdale, Australia: Schulz Publishing.

Episcia

Dates, J.D. 1993. *The Gesneriad Register 1993*. Check List of Names with Descriptions of Cultivated Plants in the Genera *Episcia* & *Alsobia*. Galesburg, Illinois: American Gloxinia & Gesneriad Society, Inc.

Erica (see also **Heathers**)

Baker, H.A. & Oliver, E.G.H. 1967. *Heathers in Southern Africa*. Cape Town: Purnell.

Schumann, D., Kirsten, G. & Oliver, E.G.H. 1992. *Ericas of South Africa*. Vlaeberg, South Africa: Fernwood Press.

Erodium

Clifton, R. 1994. *Geranium Family Species Checklist. Pt 1 Erodium*. (4th ed.). The Geraniaceae Group.

Leslie, A.C. 1980. The Hybrid of *Erodium corsicum* with *Erodium reichardii*. *The Plantsman* 2:117-126.

Toomey, N., Cubey, J. & Culham, A. 2002. *Erodium × variabile*. *The Plantsman* 1(3): 166-172

Victor, D.X. (comp.). 2000. *Erodium: Register of Cultivar Names*. The Geraniaceae Group.

Erythronium

Mathew, B. 1992. A Taxonomic and Horticultural Review of *Erythronium* L. (*Liliaceae*). *J. Linn. Soc., Bot.* 109:453-471.

Mathew, B. 1998. The Genus *Erythronium*. *Bull. Alpine Gard. Soc. Gr. Brit.* 66(3):308-321.

Eupatorium sensu lato

Hind, D.J.N. 2006. Splitting *Eupatorium*. *The Plantsman* (n.s.) 5(2):185-189.

Euonymus

Brown, N. 1996. Notes on Cultivated Species of *Euonymus*. *The New Plantsman* 3(4):238-243.

Lancaster, C.R. 1981. An Account of *Euonymus* in Cultivation and its Availability in Commerce. *The Plantsman* 3(3):133-166.

Lancaster, C.R. 1982. *Euonymus* in Cultivation – Addendum. *The Plantsman* 4:61-64, 230-234.

Euphorbia

Govaerts, R., Frodin, D.G. & Radcliffe-Smith, A. 2000. *World Checklist and Bibliography of Euphorbiaceae*. Kew: Royal Botanic Gardens.

Turner, R. 1995. *Euphorbias. A Gardeners Guide*. London: Batsford.

Witton, D. 2000. *Euphorbias*. Pershore, Worcs.: Hardy Plant Society.

Fagales

Gocaerts, R. & Frodin, D.G. 1998. *World Checklist and Bibliography of Fagales*. RBG Kew.

Fagus

Dönig, G. 1994. *Die Park-und Gartenformen der Rotbuche Fagus sylvatica L.* Erlangen, Germany: Verlag Gartenbild Heinz Hansmann.

Wyman, D. 1964. Registration List of Cultivar Names of *Fagus* L. *J. Arnold Arbor.* 24(1):1-8.

Fascicularia

Nelson, E.C. & Zizka, G. 1997. *Fascicularia* (*Bromeliaceae*): Which Species are Cultivated and

Naturalized in Northwestern Europe. *The New Plantsman* 4(4):232-239.
Nelson, E.C., Zizka, G., Horres, R. & Weising, K. 1999. Revision of the Genus *Fascicularia* Mez (*Bromeliaceae*). *Botanical Journal of the Linnean Society* 129(4):315-332.

Ferns

Checklist of World Ferns. Jan 2010. http://homepages.caverock.net.nz/nbj/fern
Johns, R.J. 1996. *Index Filicum.* Supplementum Sextum pro annis 1976-1990. Kew:Royal Botanic Gardens.
Johns, R.J. 1997. *Index Filicum.* Supplementum Septimum pro annis 1991-1995. Kew:Royal Botanic Gardens.
Jones, D.L. 1987. *Encyclopaedia of Ferns.* Melbourne, Australia: Lothian.
Kaye, R. 1968. *Hardy Ferns.* London: Faber & Faber
Rickard, M.H. 2000. *The Plantfinder's Guide to Garden Ferns.* Newton Abbot, Devon: David & Charles.
Rush, R. 1984. *A Guide to Hardy Ferns.* London: British Pteridological Society.

Forsythia

INRA Forsythia website. Jan 2010. www.angers.inra.fr/forsy

Fritillaria

Clark, T. & Grey-Wilson, C. 2003. Crown Imperials. *The Plantsman* 2(1):33-47.
Mathew, B., et al. 2000. *Fritillaria* Issue. *Bot. Mag.* 17(3):145-185.
Pratt, K. & Jefferson-Brown, M. 1997. *The Gardener's Guide to Growing Fritillaries.* Newton Abbot: David & Charles.
Turrill, W.B. & Sealy, J.R. 1980. *Studies in the Genus Fritillaria (Liliaceae).* Hooker's Icones Plantarum Vol. 39 (1 & 2). Kew: Royal Botanic Gardens.

Fruit

Brogdale Horticultural Trust National Fruit Collection. Jan 2010. www.nationalfruitcollection.org.uk
Bowling, B.L. 2000. *The Berry Grower's Companion.* Portland, Oregon: Timber Press.
Hogg, R. 1884. *The Fruit Manual.* (5th ed.). London: Journal of Horticulture Office.

Fuchsia

American Fuchsia Society Registration Database. Jan 2010. www.americanfuchsiasociety.org
Bartlett, G. 1996. *Fuchsias – A Colour Guide.* Marlborough, Wilts: Crowood Press.
Boullemier, Leo.B. (comp.). 1991. *The Checklist of Species, Hybrids and Cultivars of the Genus Fuchsia.* London, New York, Sydney: Blandford Press.
Boullemier, Leo.B. (comp.). 1995. *Addendum No 1 to the 1991 Checklist of Species, Hybrids and Cultivars of the Genus Fuchsia.* Dyfed, Wales: The British Fuchsia Society.
Goulding, E. 1995. *Fuchsias: The Complete Guide.* London: Batsford.
Johns, E.A. 1997. *Fuchsias of the 19th and Early 20th Century.* An Historical Checklist of Fuchsia Species & Cultivars, pre-1939. Kidderminster, Worcs.: British Fuchsia Society
Jones, L. & Miller, D.M. 2005. *Hardy Fuchsias: RHS Bulletin No 12.* Wisley, Surrey: RHS.
Stevens, R. Jan 2010. Find That Fuchsia. www.findthatfuchsia.info

Galanthus

Bishop, M., Davis, A. & Grimshaw, J. 2001. *Snowdrops. A monograph of cultivated Galanthus.* Maidenhead: Griffin Press.
Davis, A.P., Mathew, B. (ed.) & King, C. (ill.). 1999. *The Genus Galanthus. A Botanical Magazine Monograph.* Oregon: Timber Press.

Gentiana

Bartlett, M. 1975. *Gentians.* Dorset: Blandford Press.
Halda, J.J. 1996. *The Genus Gentiana.* Dobré, Czech Republic: Sen.
Ho T.N. & Liu S. 2001. *Worldwide Monograph of Gentiana.* Beijing: Science Press.

Geranium

Armitage, J. 2005-2007. *Hardy Geraniums – Stages 1-3: RHS Bulletin Nos 10 , 14 & 18.* Wisley, Surrey: RHS.
Bath, T. & Jones, J. 1994. *The Gardener's Guide to Growing Hardy Geraniums.* Newton Abbot, Devon: David & Charles.
Bendtsen, B.H. 2005. *Gardening with Hardy Geraniums.* Portland, Oregon: Timber Press.
Clifton, R.T.F. 1995. *Geranium Family Species Check List Pt 2.* Geranium. (4th ed. issue 2). Dover: The Geraniaceae Group.
Jones, J., et al. 2001. *Hardy Geraniums for the Garden.* (3rd ed.). Pershore, Worcs.: Hardy Plant Society.
Victor, D.X. 2004. *Register of Geranium Cultivar Names.* (2nd ed.). The Geraniaceae Group.
Yeo, P.F. 2002. *Hardy Geraniums.* (3rd ed.). Kent: Croom Helm.

Gesneriaceae

The Gesneriad Society. Listing of registered gesneriads. Jan 2010. www.aggs.gesneriadsociety.org
Dates, J.D. 1986-1990. *The Gesneriad Register 1986-1987 & 1990.* Galesburg, Illinois: American Gloxinia & Gesneriad Society, Inc.

Gladiolus

British Gladiolus Society List of Cultivars Classified for Show Purposes 1994. Mayfield, Derbyshire: British Gladiolus Society.
1997-1998. British Gladiolus Society List of European, New Zealand & North American Cultivars Classified for Exhibition Purposes 1997 & 1998. Mayfield, Derbyshire: British Gladiolus Society.
Goldblatt, P. & Manning, J. 1998. *Gladiolus in Southern Africa.* Vlaeberg, South Africa: Fernwood Press.

Goldblatt, P. 1996. *Gladiolus in Tropical Africa.* Systematics Biology and Evolution. Oregon: Timber Press.

Lewis, G.J., Obermeyer, A.A. & Barnard, T.T. 1972. A Revision of the South African Species of *Gladiolus. J. S. African Bot.* (Supp. Vol. 10)

Gleditsia

Santamour, F.S. & McArdle, A.J. 1983. Checklist of Cultivars of Honeylocust (*Gleditsia triacanthos* L.). *J. Arboric.* 9:271-276.

Grevillea

Olde, P. & Marriott, N. 1995. *The Grevillea Book.* (3). Kenthurst, NSW: Kangaroo Press.

Haemanthus

Snijman, D. 1984. A Revision of the Genus *Haemanthus. J. S. African Bot.* (Supp. Vol. 12).

Hamamelis

Lane, C. 2005. *Witch Hazels.* Portland, Oregon: Timber Press.

Heathers

Nelson, E.C. Aug 2007. International Cultivar Registration Authority for Heathers. www.heathersociety.org.uk

Hebe

Chalk, D. 1988. *Hebes and Parahebes.* Bromley, Kent: Christopher Helm (Publishers) Ltd.

Hutchins, G. 1997. *Hebes: Here and There.* A Monograph on the Genus *Hebe.* Caversham, Berks: Hutchins & Davies.

Metcalf, L.J. 2001. *International Register of Hebe Cultivars.* Canterbury, New Zealand: Royal New Zealand Institute of Horticulture (Inc.).

Metcalf, L.J. 2006. *Hebes: A Guide to Species, Hybrids and Allied Genera.* Portland, Oregon: Timber Press.

Hedera

Jury, S. et al. 2006. *Hedera algeriensis*, a Fine Species of Ivy. *Sibbaldia* 4: 93-108.

McAllister, H. 1988. Canary and Algerian Ivies. *The Plantsman* 10(1):27-29.

McAllister, H.A. & Rutherford, A. 1990. *Hedera helix and H. hibernica* in the British Isles. *Watsonia* 18:7-15.

Rose, P.Q. 1996. *The Gardener's Guide to Growing Ivies.* Newton Abbot, Devon: David & Charles.

Rutherford, A., McAllister, H. & Mill, R.R. 1993. New Ivies from the Mediterranean Area and Macaronesia. *The Plantsman* 15(2):115-128.

Heliconia

Berry, F. & Kress, W.J. 1991. *Heliconia.* An Identification Guide. Washington: Smithsonian Institution Press.

Helleborus

Burrell, C.C. & Tyler, J.K. 2006. *Hellebores: A Comprehensive Guide.* Portland, Oregon: Timber Press.

Mathew, B. 1989. *Hellebores.* Woking: Alpine Garden Society.

Rice, G. & Strangman, E. 1993. *The Gardener's Guide to Growing Hellebores.* Newton Abbot, Devon: David & Charles.

Hemerocallis

Baxter, G.J. (comp.). American Daylily Society Registry of Daylily Cultivars. Jan 2010. www.daylilies.org

Herbs

Phillips, R. & Foy, N. 1990. *Herbs.* London: Pan Books Ltd.

Heuchera **and ×** ***Heucherella***

Heims, D. & Ware, G. 2005. *Heucheras and Heucherellas: Coral Bells and Foamy Bells.* Portland, Oregon: Timber Press.

Hibiscus

Noble, C. Apr 2007. Australian Hibiscus Society Database Register. www.australianhibiscus.com/

Hosta

Hosta Library. Aug 2006. www.hostalibrary.org

Grenfell, D. & Shadrack, M. 2004. *The Color Encyclopedia of Hostas.* Portland, Oregon: Timber Press.

Schmid, W.G. 1991. *The Genus Hosta.* London: Batsford.

Hyacinthaceae **pro parte *(Asparagaceae)***

Dashwood, M. & Mathew, B. 2006. *Hyacinthaceae – little blue bulbs: RHS Bulletin No 11.* Wisley, Surrey: RHS.

Mathew, B. 2005. *Hardy Hyacinthaceae* Pt 1: *Muscari. The Plantsman* 4(1):40-53.

Mathew, B. 2005. *Hardy Hyacinthaceae* Pt 2: *Scilla, Chionodoxa* and × *Chinoscilla. The Plantsman* 4(2):110-121.

Hydrangea

Dirr, M.A. 2004. *Hydrangeas for American Gardens.* Portland, Oregon: Timber Press.

Haworth-Booth, M. 1975. *The Hydrangeas.* London: Garden Book Club.

Van Gelderen, C.J. & Van Gelderen, D.M. 2004. *Encyclopedia of Hydrangeas.* Portland, Oregon: Timber Press.

Hypericum

Lancaster, R. & Robson, N. 1997. Focus on Plants: Bowls of Beauty. *The Garden* (RHS) 122(8):566-571.

Ilex

Bailes, C. 2006. *Hollies for Gardeners.* Portland, Oregon: Timber Press.

Dudley, T.R. & Eisenbeiss, G.K. 1973 & 1992. *International Checklist of Cultivated Ilex, Pts 1 & 2.* Washington DC: United States Dept of Agriculture.

Galle, F.C. 1997. *Hollies: the Genus Ilex.* Portland, Oregon: Timber Press.

Impatiens

Morgan, R.J. 2007. *Impatiens: The Vibrant World of Busy Lizzies, Balsams and Touch-me-nots.* Portland, Oregon: Timber Press.

Iris

Austin, C. 2005. *Irises: A Gardener's Encyclopedia.* Oregon:Timber Press.

Hoog, M.H. 1980. Bulbous Irises . *The Plantsman* 2(3):141-64.

Keppel, K. (ed.) 2001. *Iris Check List of Registered Cultivar Names 1990-1999.* Hannibal, New York: the American Iris Society.

Mathew, B. 1981. *The Iris.* London: Batsford.

Mathew, B. 1993. The Spuria Irises. *The Plantsman* 15(1):14-25.

Service, N. 1990. *Iris unguicularis. The Plantsman* 12(1):1-9.

Stebbings, G. 1997. *The Gardener's Guide to Growing Iris.* Newton Abbot: David & Charles.

The Species Group of the British Iris Society, (ed.). 1997. *A Guide to Species Irises.* Their Identification and Cultivation. Cambridge: Cambridge University Press.

Jovibarba see under ***Sempervivum***

Kalmia

Jaynes, R.A. 1997. *Kalmia. Mountain Laurel and Related Species.* Portland, Oregon: Timber Press.

Kniphofia

Taylor, J. 1985. *Kniphofia* – a Survey. *The Plantsman* 7(3):129-160.

Kohleria

Dates, J.D. (ed.) & Batcheller, F.N. (comp.). 1985. *The Gesneriad Register 1985. Check List of Names with Descriptions of Cultivated Plants in the Genus Kohleria.* Lincoln Acres, California: American Gloxinia and Gesneriad Society, Inc.

Lachenalia

Duncan, G.D. 1988. *The Lachenalia Hand Book.* Kirstenbosch, South Africa: National Botanic Gardens.

Lantana

Howard, R.A. 1969. A Check List of Names Used in the Genus *Lantana. Arnoldia.* 29(11):73-109.

Lathyrus

Norton, S. 1996. *Lathyrus. Cousins of Sweet Pea.* Surrey: NCCPG.

Lavandula

Upson, T. & Andrews, S. 2004. *The Genus Lavandula.* Kew: Royal Botanic Garden.

Legumes

ILDIS. International Legume Database and Information Service. Jan 2010. Version 10.01. www.ildis.org/LegumeWeb

Leptospermum

Check List of *Leptospermum* Cultivars. 1963. *J. Roy. New Zealand Inst. Hort.* 5(5):224-30.

Dawson, M. 1997. A History of *Leptospermum scoparium* in Cultivation – Discoveries from the Wild. *The New Plantsman* 4(1):51-59.

Dawson, M. 1997. A History of *Leptospermum scoparium* in Cultivation – Garden Selections. *The New Plantsman* 4(2):67-78.

Lewisia

Davidson, B.L.R. 2000. *Lewisias.* Portland, Oregon: Timber Press.

Elliott, R. 1978. *Lewisias.* Woking: Alpine Garden Society.

Mathew, B. 1989. *The Genus Lewisia.* Bromley, Kent: Christopher Helm.

Liliaceae sensu lato

Mathew, B. 1989. Splitting the *Liliaceae. The Plantsman* 11(2):89-105.

Lilium

Leslie, A.C. *The International Lily Register 1982-2002.* (4th ed. & 1st supp.). Supps 1-2, 2008-2010. London: RHS.

Online Lily Register. Jan 2010. www.lilyregister.com

Lonicera

Blahník, Z. 2006. *Lonicera* Cultivar Names: The First World List. *Acta Pruhoniciana* 81:59-64.

Magnolia

Callaway, D.J. Sep 2001. Magnolia Cultivar Checklist. www.magnoliasociety.org

Frodin, D.G. & Govaerts, R. 1996. *World Checklist and Bibliography of Magnoliaceae.* Kew: Royal Botanic Garden.

Maianthemum

Cubey, J.J. 2005 *The Incorporation of Smilacina within Maianthemum. The Plantsman* N.S.4(4).

Malus

Crawford, M. 1994. *Directory of Apple Cultivars.* Devon: Agroforestry Research Trust.

Fiala, J.L. 1994. *Flowering Crabapples.* The genus *Malus.* Portland, Oregon: Timber Press.

Rouèche, A. Oct 2007. Les Crets Fruits et Pomologie. www.pomologie.com

Spiers, V. 1996. *Burcombes, Queenies and Colloggetts.* St Dominic, Cornwall: West Brendon.

Meconopsis

Grey-Wilson, C. 1992. A Survey of the Genus *Meconopsis* in Cultivation. *The Plantsman* 14(1): 1-33.

Grey-Wilson, C. 2002. The True Identity of *Meconopsis napaulensis. Bot. Mag.* 23(2): 176-209.

Meconopsis Group website. Jan 2010. www.meconopsis.org

Stevens, E. & Brickell, C. 2001. Problems with the Big Perennial Poppies. *The New Plantsman* 8(1):48-61.

Stevens, E. 2001. Further Observations on the Big Perennial Blue Poppies. *The New Plantsman* 8(2):105-111.

Miscanthus

Jones, L. 2004. Miscanthus: RHS Bulletin No 7. Wisley, Surrey: RHS.

Moraea

Goldblatt, P. 1986. *The Moraeas of Southern Africa.* Kirstenbosch, South Africa: National Botanic Gardens.

Musa

Banana and Plantain Section of Biodiversity International 2001. http://bananas.bioversityinternational.org

INIBAP *Musa* Germplasm Information System. Jan 2010. www.crop-diversity.org/banana

Narcissus

Blanchard, J.W. 1990. *Narcissus – A Guide to Wild Daffodils.* Woking, Surrey: Alpine Garden Society.

Kington, S. (comp.). 2008. *The International Daffodil Register and Classified List 2008* (4th ed. & Supps 1-3. 2008-2011. London: RHS.

Nematanthus

Arnold, P. 1978. *The Gesneriad Register 1978.* Check List of *Nematanthus.* American Gloxinia and Gesneriad Society, Inc.

Nerium

Pagen, F.J.J. 1987. *Oleanders. Nerium L. and the Oleander Cultivars.* Wageningen, The Netherlands: Agricultural University Wageningen.

Nymphaea

Knotts, K. & Knotts, B. Victoria Adventure Website. Checklist of Waterlily Cultivars. Jan 2010. www.victoria-adventure.org

Orchidaceae

Shaw, J.M.H. Jan 2010. The International Orchid Register. http://apps.rhs.org.uk/horticulturaldatabase/orchidregister/orchidregister.asp

Origanum

Paton, A. 1994. Three Membranous-bracted Species of *Origanum. Kew Mag.* 11(3):109-117.

White, S. 1998. *Origanum. The Herb Marjoram and its Relatives.* Surrey: NCCPG.

Paeonia

HelpMeFind Peonies. Jan 2010. www.helpmefind.com/peony/index.php

Jakubowski, R. American Peony Society Peony Checklist. www.americanpeonysociety.org

Jakubowski, R. 2008. *Peonies 1997-2007. Registered Peony Cultivars, with a Checklist of Peony Names, References and Originators.* Missouri: American Peony Society.

Osti, G.L. 1999. *The Book of Tree Peonies.* Turin: Umberto Allemandi.

Wang, L., et al. 1998. *Chinese Tree Peony.* Beijing: China Forestry Publishing House.

Papaver

Grey-Wilson, C. 1998. Oriental Glories. *The Garden* (RHS) 123(5):320-325.

Papaveraceae

Grey-Wilson, C. 2000. *Poppies. The Poppy Family in the Wild and in Cultivation.* London: Batsford.

Tebbitt, M. Liden, M. Zetterlund, H. 2008. *Bleeding Hearts, Corydalis and their Relatives.* Portland, Oregon: Timber Press

Passiflora

King, L.A. Jan 2008. Passiflora online passion flower cultivar register. www.passionflow.co.uk

Pelargonium

Abbott, P.G. 1994. *A Guide to Scented Geraniaceae.* Angmering, West Sussex: Hill Publicity Services.

Anon. 1978 & 1985. *A Checklist and Register of Pelargonium Cultivar Names.* Pts 1 & 2. Australian Pelargonium Society.

Bagust, H. 1988. *Miniature and Dwarf Geraniums.* London: Christopher Helm.

Clifford, D. 1958. *Pelargoniums.* London: Blandford Press.

Clifton, R. 1999. *Geranium Family Species Checklist, Pt 4: Pelargonium.* The Geraniaceae Group.

Complete Copy of the Spalding Pelargonium Checklist. (Unpublished). USA.

Key, H. 2000. *1001 Pelargoniums.* London: Batsford.

Miller, D. 1996. *Pelargonium.* A Gardener's Guide to the Species and Cultivars and Hybrids. London: Batsford.

Pelargonium Palette: The Geranium and Pelargonium Society of Sydney Incorporated. Varieties – Alphabetical List. July 2010. www.elj.com/geranium

Van der Walt, J.J.A., et al. 1977. *Pelargoniums of South Africa.* (1-3). Kirstenbosch, South Africa: National Botanic Gardens.

Penstemon

Lindgren, D.T. & Davenport, B. 1992. List and description of named cultivars in the genus *Penstemon.* University of Nebraska.

Nold, R. 1999. *Penstemons.* Portland, Oregon: Timber Press.

Way, D. & James, P. 1998. *The Gardener's Guide to Growing Penstemons.* Newton Abbott, Devon: David & Charles.

Way, D. 2006. *Penstemons.* Pershore, Worcs.: Hardy Plant Society.

Phlomis

Mann Taylor, J. 1998. *Phlomis: The Neglected Genus.* Wisley: NCCPG.

Phlox

Harmer, J. & Elliott, J. 2001. *Phlox.* Pershore, Worcs.: Hardy Plant Society.

Stebbings, G. 1999. Simply Charming. *The Garden* (RHS) 124(7):518-521.

Wherry, E.T. 1955. *The Genus Phlox.* Philadelphia, Pennsylvania: Morris Arboretum.

Phormium

Heenan, P.B. 1991. *Checklist of Phormium Cultivars.* Royal New Zealand Institute of Horticulture.

McBride-Whitehead, V. 1998. Phormiums of the Future. *The Garden* (RHS) 123(1):42-45.

Pieris

Bond, J. 1982. *Pieris* – a Survey. *The Plantsman* 4(2):65-75.

Wagenknecht, B.L. 1961. Registration Lists of Cultivar Names in the Genus *Pieris* D. Don. *Arnoldia (Jamaica Plain)* 21(8):47-50.

Pittosporum
Miller, D.M. 2006. RHS Plant Assessments: *Pittosporum tenuifolium* hybrids & cultivars.
Plectranthus
Addink, Wouter. Jan 2010. Coleus Finder. http://coleusfinder.org
Miller, D. & Morgan, N. 2000. Focus on Plants: A New Leaf. *The Garden* (RHS) 125(11):842-845.
Shaw, J.M.H. 1999. Notes on the Identity of Swedish Ivy and Other Cultivated *Plectranthus. The New Plantsman* 6(2):71-74.
Van Jaarsveld, E.J. 2006. *South African Plectranthus*. Vlaeberg, South Africa: Fernwood Press.
Pleione
Cribb, P. & Butterfield, I. 1999. *The Genus Pleione.* (2nd ed.). Kew: Royal Botanic Gardens.
Shaw, J.M.H. (comp.). Oct 2002. Provisional List of *Pleione* Cultivars. RHS.
Poaceae (grasses)
Clayton, W.D., Harman, K.T. & Williamson, H. Jan 2010. GrassBase : The Online World Grass Flora. www.kew.org/data/grasses-syn
Clayton, W.D. & Renvoize, S.A. 1986. *Genera Graminum.* Grasses of the World. London: HMSO.
Darke, R. 2007. *Encyclopedia of Grasses for Livable Landscapes*. Portland, Oregon: Timber Press.
Govaerts, R. & Simpson, D.A. 2007 *World Checklist of Cyperaceae: Sedges*. Richmond, Surrey: RBG Kew
Grounds, R. 1998. *The Plantfinder's Guide to Ornamental Grasses.* Newton Abott, Devon: David & Charles.
Wood, T. 2002. *Garden Grasses, Rushes and Sedges*. (3rd ed.). Abingdon, Oxon: John Wood.
Polemonium
Nichol-Brown, D. 2000. *Polemonium.* Wisley: NCCPG.
Potentilla
Davidson, C.G., Enns, R.J. & Gobin, S. 1994. *A Checklist of Potentilla fruticosa: the Shrubby Potentillas.* Morden, Manitoba: Agriculture & Agri-Food Canada Research Centre.
Miller, D.M. 2002. *Shrubby Potentilla: RHS Bulletin No 1.* Wisley, Surrey: RHS.
Primula
Richards, J. 2002 (2nd ed.). *Primula.* London: Batsford.
Primula allionii
Archdale, B. & Richards, D. 1997. *Primula allionii Forms and Hybrids.* National Auricula & Primula Society, Midland & West Section.
Primula auricula
Baker, G. *Double Auriculas.* National Auricula & Primula Society, Midland & West Section.
Baker, G. & Ward, P. 1995. *Auriculas*. London: Batsford.
Guest, A. 2009. *The Auricula History, Cultivation and Varieties*. Woodbridge, Suffolk: Garden Art Press
Hawkes, A. 1995. Striped Auriculas. National Auricula & Primula Society, Midland & West Section.
Nicholle, G. 1996. *Border Auriculas.* National Auricula & Primula Society, Midland & West Section.
Robinson, M.A. 2000. *Auriculas for Everyone.* How to Grow and Show Perfect Plants. Lewes, Sussex: Guild of Master Craftsmen Publications.
Telford, D. 1993. *Alpine Auriculas.* National Auricula & Primula Society, Midland & West Section.
Ward, P. 1991. *Show Auriculas.* National Auricula & Primula Society, Midland & West Section.
Proteaceae
International *Proteaceae* Register. July 2002. (7th ed.).
Rebelo, T. 1995. *Proteas.* A Field Guide to the Proteas of Southern Africa. Vlaeberg: Fernwood Press/National Botanical Institute.
Prunus
Crawford, M. 1996. *Plums.* Dartington, Devon: Agroforestry Research Trust.
Crawford, M. 1997. *Cherries: Production and Culture.* Dartington, Devon: Agroforestry Research Trust.
Jacobsen, A.L. 1992. *Purpleleaf Plums.* Portland, Oregon: Timber Press.
Jefferson, R.M. & Wain, K.K. 1984. *The Nomenclature of Cultivated Flowering Cherries (Prunus).* The Sato-Zakura Group. Washington DC: USDA.
Kuitert, W. 1999. *Japanese Flowering Cherries.* Portland, Oregon: Timber Press.
Pulmonaria
Bennett, M. 2003. *Pulmonarias and the borage family*. London: B.T. Batsford.
Hewitt, J. 1994. *Pulmonarias.* Pershore, Worcs.: Hardy Plant Society.
Hewitt, J. 1999. Well Spotted. *The Garden* (RHS) 124(2):98-103.
Pyracantha
Egolf, D.R. & Andrick, A.O. 1995. *A Checklist of Pyracantha Cultivars.* Washington DC: Agricultural Research Service.
Pyrus
Crawford, M. 1996. *Directory of Pear Cultivars.* Totnes, Devon: Agroforestry Research Institute.
Smith, M.W.G. 1976. *Catalogue of the British Pear.* Faversham, Kent: MAFF.
Quercus
International Oak Society. Oak Name Checklist. www.oaknames.org.
Miller, H.A. & Lamb, S.H. 1985. *Oaks of North America.* Happy Camp, California: Naturegraph Publishers.
Mitchell, A. 1994. The Lucombe Oaks. *The Plantsman* 15(4):216-224.

Rhododendron

Argent, G., Fairweather, C. & Walter, K. 1996. *Accepted Names in Rhododendron section Vireya.* Edinburgh: Royal Botanic Garden.

Argent, G., Bond, J., Chamberlain, D., Cox, P. & Hardy, A. 1997. *The Rhododendron Handbook 1998.* Rhododendron Species in Cultivation. London: RHS.

Chamberlain, D.F. & Rae, S.J. 1990. A Revision of *Rhododendron* IV. Subgenus *Tsutsusi. Edinburgh J. Bot.* 47(2).

Chamberlain, D.F. 1982. A Revision of *Rhododendron* II. Subgenus *Hymenanthes. Notes Roy. Bot. Gard. Edinburgh* 39(2).

Chamberlain, D., Hyam, R., Argent, G., Fairweather, G. & Walter, K.S. 1996. *The Genus Rhododendron.* Edinburgh:Royal Botanic Garden.

Cullen, J. 1980. A Revision of *Rhododendron* I. Subgenus *Rhododendron* sections *Rhododendron* and *Pogonanthum. Notes Roy. Bot. Gard. Edinburgh* 39(1).

Davidian, H.H. 1982-1992 *The Rhododendron Species* (Vols 1-4). London: Batsford.

Galle, F.C. 1985. *Azaleas.* Portland, Oregon: Timber Press.

Leslie, A. C. (comp.). 1980. *The Rhododendron Handbook 1980.* London: RHS.

Leslie, A.C. (comp.) 2004. *The International Rhododendron Register and Checklist* (2nd ed. & Supps 1-5). Supps 1-6, 2004-2011. London: RHS.

Tamura, T. (ed.). 1989. *Azaleas in Kurume.* Kurume, Japan: International Azalea Festival '89.

Ribes

Crawford, M. 1997. *Currants and Gooseberries: Production and Culture.* Dartington, Devon: Agroforestry Research Trust.

Rosa

Beales, P., Cairns, T., et al. 1998. *Botanica's Rose: The Encyclopedia of Roses.* Hoo, Kent: Grange Books.

Cairns, T. (ed.). 2000. *Modern Roses XI. The World Encyclopedia of Roses.* London: Academic Press.

Dickerson, B.C. 1999. *The Old Rose Advisor.* Portland, Oregon: Timber Press.

Haw, S.G. 1996. Notes on Some Chinese and Himalayan Rose Species of Section *Pimpinellifoliae. The New Plantsman* 3(3):143-146.

HelpMeFind Roses. Jan 2010. www.helpmefind.com

McCann, S. 1985. *Miniature Roses.* Newton Abbot, Devon: David & Charles.

Pawsey, Angela (ed.) 2012. *Find That Rose! 2012-2013.* (30th ed.) Colchester, Essex.

Quest-Ritson, C. 2003. *Climbing Roses of the World.* Portland, Oregon: Timber Press.

Quest-Ritson, C. & Quest-Ritson, B. 2003. *The Royal Horticultural Society Encyclopedia of Roses: The Definitive A-Z Guide.* London: Dorling Kindersley.

Thomas, G.S. 1995. *The Graham Stuart Thomas Rose Book.* London: John Murray.

Verrier, S. 1996. *Rosa Gallica.* Balmain, Australia: Florilegium.

Roscoea

Cowley, J. 2007. *The Genus Roscoea.* Kew Publishing.

Rosularia

Eggli, U. 1988. A Monographic Study of the Genus *Rosularia. Bradleya* (Supp.) 6:1-118.

Saintpaulia

Goodship, G. 1987. *Saintpaulia Variety List* (Supp.). Slough, Bucks: Saintpaulia & Houseplant Society.

Moore, H.E. 1957. *African Violets, Gloxinias and Their Relatives.* A Guide to the Cultivated Gesneriads. New York: Macmillan.

Salix

Newsholme, C. 1992. *Willows.* The Genus *Salix.* London: Batsford.

Stott, K.G. 1971 *Willows for Amenity, Windbreaks and Other Uses.* Checklist of the Long Ashton Collection of Willows, with Notes on their Suitability for Various Purposes. Long Ashton Research Station: University of Bristol.

Salvia

Clebsch, B. 2003. *A Book of Salvias.* (2nd ed.). Portland, Oregon: Timber Press.

Compton, J. 1994. Mexican Salvias in Cultivation. *The Plantsman* 15(4):193-215.

Middleton, R. *Robin's Salvias.* www.robinssalvias.com

Saxifraga

Bland, B. 2000. *Silver Saxifrages.* Pershore, Worcs.: Alpine Garden Society.

Dashwood, M. & Bland, B. 2005. Silver Saxifrages: RHS Bulletin No 9. Wisley, Surrey: RHS.

McGregor, M. Jan 2010. Saxbase. Saxifrage Society. www.saxifraga.org

McGregor, M. 1995. *Saxifrages: The Complete Cultivars & Hybrids: International Register of Saxifrages.* (2nd ed.). Driffield, E. Yorks: Saxifrage Society.

Webb, D.A. & Gornall, R.J. 1989. *Saxifrages of Europe.* Bromley, Kent: Christopher Helm.

Sedum

Evans, R.L. 1983. *Handbook of Cultivated Sedums.* Motcombe, Dorset: Ivory Head Press.

Lord, T. 2006. *Sedum* up for assessment. *The Plantsman* 5(4):244-252.

Stephenson, R. 1994. *Sedum.* The Cultivated Stonecrops. Portland, Oregon: Timber Press.

Sempervivum

Diehm, H. Jan 2010. www.semperhorst.de

Miklánek, M. 2002. *The List of Cultivars: Sempervivum and Jovibarba v. 7.01.* Pieštany, Slovakia: M. Miklánek (private distribution).

Miklánek, M. 2000. *List of Cultivars: Sempervivum and Jovibarba* v. 15.1. http://miklanek.tripod.com

Sinningia

Dates, J.D. 1988. *The Gesneriad Register 1988. Check List of Names with Descriptions of Cultivated Plants in the Genus Sinningia.* Galesburg, Illinois: American Gloxinia and Gesneriad Society, Inc.

Solenostemon
Pedley, W.K. & Pedley, R. 1974. *Coleus – A Guide to Cultivation and Identification*. Edinburgh: Bartholemew.
Sorbus
McAllister, H. 2005. *The Genus Sorbus: Mountain Ash and Other Rowans*. Kew: Royal Botanical Gardens.
Snyers d'Attenhoven, C. 1999. *Sorbus* Lombarts hybrids *Belgische Dendrologie*: 76-81. Belgium.
Wright, D. 1981. Sorbus – a Gardener's Evaluation. *The Plantsman* 3(2):65-98.
Spiraea
Miller, D.M. 2003. *Spiraea japonica with coloured leaves: RHS Bulletin No 4*. Wisley, Surrey: RHS
Streptocarpus
Arnold, P. 1979. *The Gesneriad Register 1979: Check List of Streptocarpus*. Binghamton, New York: American Gloxinia & Gesneriad.
Dibleys Nurseries Online Catalogue. Jan 2010. www.dibleys.com.
Succulents
Eggli, U. (ed.) 2002. *Illustrated Handbook of Succulent Plants*. Heidelberg, Germany: Springer-Verlag.
Eggli, U. & Taylor, N. 1994. *List of Names of Succulent Plants other than Cacti Published 1950-92*. Kew: Royal Botanic Gardens.
Grantham, K. & Klaassen, P. 1999. *The Plantfinder's Guide to Cacti and Other Succulents*. Newton Abbot, Devon: David & Charles.
Jacobsen, H. 1973. *Lexicon of Succulent Plants*. London: Blandford.
Syringa
Vrugtman, F. 2000. *International Register of Cultivar Names in the Genus Syringa L. (Oleaceae)*. (Contribution No 91). Hamilton, Canada: Royal Botanic Gardens.
Thymus
Easter, M. 2009. *International* Thymus *Register and Checklist*. UK: Owl Prints.
Tiliaceae pro parte (***Malvaceae***)
Wild, H. 1984. *Flora of Southern Africa 21 (1: Tiliaceae)*. Pretoria: Botanical Research Institute, Dept of Agriculture.
Tillandsia
Kiff, L.F. 1991. *A Distributional Checklist of the Genus Tillandsia*. Encino, California: Botanical Diversions.
Trillium
Case, F.W.J. & Case, R.B. 1997. *Trilliums*. Portland, Oregon: Timber Press.
Jacobs, D.L. & Jacobs, R.L. 1997. *American Treasures*. Trilliums in Woodland Garden. Decatur, Georgia: Eco-Gardens.
Tulipa
KAVB Online registration pages. http://kavb.back2p.soft-orange.com
Ulmus
Green, P.S. 1964. Registratration of Cultivar Names in *Ulmus*. *Arnoldia (Jamaica Plain)* 24:41-80.
Vaccinium
Trehane, J. 2004. *Blueberries, Cranberries and Other Vacciniums*. Portland, Oregon: Timber Press.
Vegetables
Official Journal of the European Communities. Oct 2007. Common catalogue of varieties of agricultural plant species: consolidated version. http://ec.europa.eu/food
Viburnum
Dirr, M.A. 2007. *Viburnums: Flowering Shrubs for Every Season*. Portland, Oregon: Timber Press.
Viola
Coombes, R.E. 2003. *Violets*. (2nd ed.). London: Batsford.
Fuller, R. 1990. *Pansies, Violas & Violettas*. The Complete Guide. Marlborough: The Crowood Press.
Perfect, E.J. 1996. *Armand Millet and his Violets*. High Wycombe: Park Farm Press.
Robinson, P.M. & Snocken, J. 2003. Checklist of the Cultivated Forms of the Genus *Viola* including the Register of Cultivars. American Violet Society. http://americanvioletsociety.org
Zambra, G.L. 1950. *Violets for Garden and Market*. (2nd ed.). London: Collingridge.
Vitis
Robinson, J. 1989. *Vines, Grapes and Wines*. London: Mitchell Beazley.
Watsonia
Goldblatt, P. 1989. *The Genus Watsonia*. A Systematic Monograph. South Africa: National Botanic Gardens.
Weigela
Howard, R.A. 1965. A Checklist of Cultivar Names in *Weigela*. *Arnoldia (Jamaica Plain)* 25:49-69.
Wisteria
Valder, P. 1995. *Wisterias*. A Comprehensive Guide. Balmain, Australia: Florilegium.
Yucca
Smith, C. 2004. *Yuccas: Giants among the Lilies*. NCCPG.
Zauschneria
Raven, P.H. 1977. Generic and Sectional Delimitation in *Onagraceae*, Tribe *Epilobieae*. *Ann. Missouri Bot. Gard.* 63(2):326-340.
Robinson, A. 2000. Focus on Plants: Piping Hot (*Zauschneria* Cultivars). *The Garden* (RHS) 125(9):698-699.
Zingiberaceae
Branney, T.M.E. 2005. *Hardy Gingers. Including Hedychium, Roscoea and Zingiber*. Cambridge: Timber Press.

NURSERIES

THE FOLLOWING NURSERIES BETWEEN THEM STOCK AN UNRIVALLED CHOICE OF PLANTS. BEFORE MAKING A VISIT, PLEASE REMEMBER TO CHECK WITH THE NURSERY THAT THE PLANT YOU SEEK IS CURRENTLY AVAILABLE.

Nursery Codes and Symbols

The first letter of each nursery code represents the area of the country in which the nursery is situated.

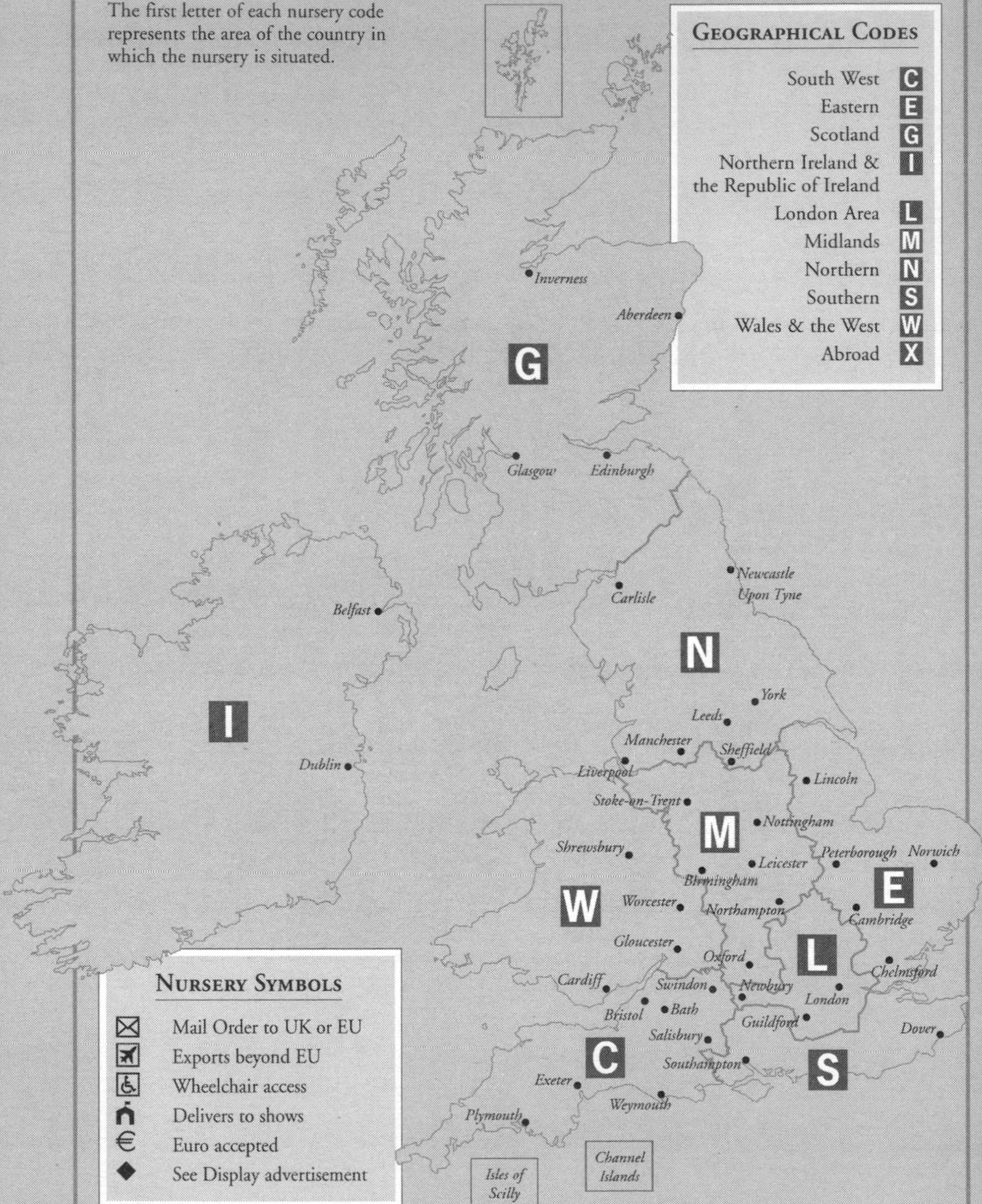

Geographical Codes

South West	C
Eastern	E
Scotland	G
Northern Ireland & the Republic of Ireland	I
London Area	L
Midlands	M
Northern	N
Southern	S
Wales & the West	W
Abroad	X

Nursery Symbols

- ☒ Mail Order to UK or EU
- Exports beyond EU
- Wheelchair access
- Delivers to shows
- € Euro accepted
- ◆ See Display advertisement

USING THE NURSERY LISTINGS

Your main reference from the Plant Directory is the Nursery Details by Code listing, which includes all relevant information for each nursery in order of nursery code. The Nursery Index by Name is an alphabetical list for those who know a nursery's name but not its code and wish to check its details in the main list.

1 NURSERY DETAILS BY CODE

Once you have found your plant in the Plant Directory, turn to this list to find out the name, address, opening times and other details of the nurseries whose codes accompany the plant.

KEY
- ⊠ Mail order to UK or EU
- Exports beyond EU
- Accessible by wheelchair
- Delivers to shows
- € Euro accepted
- ◆ See Display advertisement

A geographical code is followed by three letters reflecting the nursery's name

Refer to the box at the base of each right-hand page for a key to the symbols

WHil **HILLVIEW HARDY PLANTS** ⊠ €
(off B4176), Worfield, Nr Bridgnorth, Shropshire WV15 5NT
Ⓣ (01746) 716454
Ⓜ 07974 391608
Ⓕ (01746) 716454
Ⓔ hillview@onetel.net
Ⓦ www.hillviewhardyplants.com
Contact: Ingrid, John & Sarah Millington
Opening Times: 0900-1700 Mon-Sat Mar-mid Oct. At other times, please phone first.
Min Mail Order UK: £10.00 + p&p
Min Mail Order EU: £10.00 + p&p
Cat. Cost: Online only.
Credit Cards: All major credit/debit cards
Specialities: Choice herbaceous perennials incl. *Acanthus* & *Acanthaceae*, *Albuca*, *Aquilegia*, auricula, *Primula*, *Canna*, *Crocosmia*, *Eucomis*, *Ixia*, South African bulbs. Nat. Collections of *Acanthus* & *Albuca*.
Notes: Also sells wholesale.
Map Ref: W, B4 **OS Grid Ref:** SO772967

Other information about the nursery

A brief summary of the plants available

The map letter is followed by the map square in which the nursery is located

The Ordnance Survey national grid reference for use with OS maps

2 NURSERY INDEX BY NAME

If you are looking for a particular nursery, use this alphabetical index to find it, note its code and then turn to the Nursery Details by Code listing for full information.

Highdown Nursery	SHDw
Hill House Nursery Ltd	CHll
Hillier Garden Centres	SHil
Hillview Hardy Plants	WHil
Hoecroft Plants	EHoe
Holden Clough Nursery Ltd	NHol
Hollies Farm Plant Centre	MHol
Homestead Plants	MHom

How to Use the Nursery Listings

The details given for each nursery have been compiled from information supplied to us in answer to a questionnaire. In some cases, because of constraints of space, the entries have been slightly abbreviated.

Nurseries are not charged for their entries and inclusion in no way implies a value judgement.

Nursery Details by Code (*page 804*)

Each nursery is allocated a code, for example GPoy. The first letter of each code indicates the main area of the country in which the nursery is situated. In this example, G=Scotland. The remaining three letters reflect the nursery's name, in this case Poyntzfield Herb Nursery.

In this main listing the nurseries are given in alphabetical order of codes for quick reference from the Plant Directory. All of the nurseries' details, such as address, opening times, mail order service etc., will be found here.

Opening Times

Although opening times have been published as submitted and where applicable, **it is always advisable, especially if travelling a long distance, to check with the nursery first**. The initials NGS indicate that the nursery is open under the National Gardens Scheme.

Mail Order ⊠

Many nurseries provide a mail order service. **This is, however, often restricted to certain times of the year or to particular genera**. Please check the **Notes** section of each nursery's entry for any restrictions or special conditions.

In some cases, the mail order service extends to all members of the European Union. Where this is offered, the minimum charge to the EU will be noted in the Nursery entry.

Where **'No minimum charge' (Nmc)** is shown, please note that to send even one plant may involve the nursery in substantial postage and packing costs. Some nurseries may not be prepared to send tender or bulky plants.

Where a nursery offers a **mail order only** service, this will be noted under **Opening Times** in the nursery entry. Many nurseries also offer an online mail order facility.

Export ✈

Export refers to mail order beyond the European Union. Nurseries that are prepared to consider exporting are indicated. There is usually a substantial minimum charge and, in addition, all the costs of Phytosanitary Certificates and Customs have to be met by the purchaser.

Catalogue Cost

Some nurseries may not charge for their printed catalogues or may ask for a few stamps to bear the cost of postage, although a large (at least A5) stamped address envelope is always appreciated. Overseas customers should use an equivalent number of International Reply Coupons (IRC) in place of stamps.

If catalogues (or plant lists) are available in an electronic format, some nurseries have indicated that they will email them to enquirers.

There is a growing trend for nurseries to publish their catalogues only on the internet as this is more cost-effective than producing a printed copy.

Wheelchair Access ♿

Nurseries are asked to indicate if their premises are suitable for wheelchair users. Where only partial access is indicated, this is noted in the **Notes** field and the nursery is not marked with the symbol.

The assessment of ease-of-access is entirely the responsibility of the individual nursery.

Specialities

Nurseries list here the plants or genera that they supply and any National Collections of plants they may hold. Please note that some nurseries may charge an entry fee to visit a National Collection. Always enquire before visiting.

Nurseries will also note here if they only have small quantities of individual plants available for sale or if they will propagate to order.

Notes

In this section, you will find notes on any restrictions to mail order or export; on limited wheelchair access; or the nursery site address, if this differs from the office address; together with any other non-horticultural information.

Delivery to Shows

Many nurseries will deliver pre-ordered plants to flower shows for collection by customers. These are indicated by a marquee symbol. Contact the nursery for details of shows they attend.

Payment in Euros €

A number of UK nurseries have indicated that they will accept payment in Euros. You should, however, check with the nursery concerned before making such a payment, as some will only accept cash and some only cheques, whilst others will expect the purchaser to pay bank charges.

Maps

If you wish to visit any of the nurseries you can find its approximate location on the relevant map (following p.901), unless the nursery has requested this is not shown. Nurseries are also encouraged to provide their Ordnance Survey national grid reference for use with OS publications such as the Land Ranger series.

Nursery Index by Name

For convenience, an alphabetical index of nurseries is included (*page 895*). This gives the names of all nurseries listed in the book in alphabetical order of nursery name together with their code.

Deleted Nurseries

Every year some nurseries ask to be removed from the book. This may be a temporary measure because, for example, they are relocating or because their plant stocks are low due to adverse growing conditions, or it may be permanent following closure, sale, retirement or a change in the way they trade.

Occasionally, nurseries are unable to meet the closing date and may ask to re-enter the book in the following edition.

Some nurseries simply do not respond at all and, as we have no current information on them, they are not included in the book.

Please, never use an out of date edition

NURSERY DETAILS BY CODE

Please note that all these nurseries are listed in alphabetical order by their code. All nurseries are listed in alphabetical order by their name in the **Nursery Index by Name** on page 895.

SOUTH WEST

CAbb **ABBOTSBURY SUB-TROPICAL GARDENS** ⊠ ♿
Abbotsbury, Nr Weymouth, Dorset
DT3 4LA
Ⓣ (01305) 871344
Ⓕ (01305) 871344
Ⓔ info@abbotsburygardens.co.uk
Ⓦ www.abbotsburyplantsales.co.uk
Contact: David Sutton
Opening Times: 1000-1800 daily, mid Mar-1st Nov. 1000-1500, Nov-mid Mar.
Min Mail Order UK: Nmc
Cat. Cost: £2.00 + A4 sae
Credit Cards: Access, Visa, MasterCard, Switch
Specialities: Less common & tender shrubs incl. palms, tree ferns, bamboos & plants from Australia, New Zealand & S. Africa.
Map Ref: C, C5

CAbP **ABBEY PLANTS** ⊠ ♿
Chaffeymoor, Bourton, Gillingham, Dorset
SP8 5BY
Ⓣ (01747) 840841
Contact: K Potts
Opening Times: 1000-1300 & 1400-1700 Wed-Sat, Mar-Nov. Dec-Feb by appt.
Min Mail Order UK: Nmc
Cat. Cost: 2 × 2nd class.
Credit Cards: None
Specialities: Flowering trees & shrubs.
Map Ref: C, B4 **OS Grid Ref:** ST762304

CAby **THE ABBEY NURSERY** ♿
Forde Abbey, Chard, Somerset TA20 4LU
Ⓣ (01460) 220088
Ⓕ (01460) 220088
Ⓔ TheAbbeyNursery@btconnect.com
Contact: Paul Bygrave
Opening Times: 1000-1700 7 days, 1st Mar-31st Oct. Please phone first to check opening times in Mar.
Cat. Cost: None issued.
Credit Cards: All major credit/debit cards
Specialities: Hardy herbaceous perennials.
Map Ref: C, C4 **OS Grid Ref:** ST359052

CAgr **AGROFORESTRY RESEARCH TRUST** ⊠
46 Hunters Moon, Dartington,
Totnes, Devon
TQ9 6JT
Ⓕ (01803) 840776
Ⓔ mail@agroforestry.co.uk
Ⓦ www.agroforestry.co.uk
Contact: Martin Crawford
Opening Times: Not open. Mail order only.
Min Mail Order UK: Nmc
Min Mail Order EU: Nmc
Cat. Cost: 4 × 1st class.
Credit Cards: All major credit/debit cards
Specialities: Top & soft fruit, nut trees including *Castanea*, *Corylus*, *Juglans*, *Pinus*. Also seeds. Some plants in small quantities only.

CAni **ANITA ALLEN** ⊠
Shapcott Barton Estate,
East Knowstone, South Molton,
Devon EX36 4EE
Ⓣ (01398) 341664
Ⓕ (01398) 341664
Contact: Anita Allen
Opening Times: By appt. only. Garden open under NGS.
Min Mail Order UK: Nmc
Cat. Cost: 5 × 1st class & state which catalogue: Shasta daisies or *Buddleja*.
Credit Cards: None
Specialities: Nat. Collections of *Leucanthemum* × *superbum* & *Buddleja davidii* & hybrids, 70+ cvs. 80+ accurately named Shasta daisies, a few in very short supply. Also many hardy perennials.
Map Ref: C, B3 **OS Grid Ref:** SS846235

C

CArn **ARNE HERBS** ⊠ € ♿
Limeburn Nurseries, Limeburn Hill,
Chew Magna, Bristol
BS40 8QW
Ⓣ (01275) 333399
Ⓔ anthony@arneherbs.co.uk
Ⓦ www.arneherbs.co.uk
Contact: A Lyman-Dixon & Jenny Thomas
Opening Times: 1000-1600 most weekdays, prior telephone call advisable.
Min Mail Order UK: Nmc
Min Mail Order EU: Nmc
Cat. Cost: Detailed illustrated catalogue online or A4 sae for free non-descriptive plantlist. Separate Classical-early Renaissance (c.1520) list available.
Credit Cards: Maestro, Visa, MasterCard
Specialities: Herbs, some very rare. North American, Mediterranean & UK wild flowers. Also plants for research, conservation projects & historical recreations.
Notes: Also sells wholesale.
Map Ref: C, A5 **OS Grid Ref:** ST563638

CAvo **AVON BULBS** ⊠ ⛺
Burnt House Farm, Mid-Lambrook,
South Petherton, Somerset
TA13 5HE
Ⓣ (01460) 242177 or 249060
Ⓕ (01460) 249025
Ⓔ info@avonbulbs.co.uk
Ⓦ www.avonbulbs.co.uk
Contact: C Ireland-Jones
Opening Times: Mail order only. Open Thu, Fri, Sat, mid-Sep to end Oct & mid-Feb to end Mar, for collection of pre-booked orders.
Min Mail Order UK: £10.00 + p&p
Min Mail Order EU: £20.00 + p&p
Cat. Cost: 4 × 2nd class.
Credit Cards: All major credit/debit cards
Specialities: Some special snowdrops are only available in small quantities.
Map Ref: C, B5 **OS Grid Ref:** ST422187

CBAq **BOW GARDEN (AQUATICS) CENTRE** ♿
Bow, Crediton, Devon EX17 6LA
Ⓣ (01363) 82438
Ⓔ peter@bowaquatics.co.uk
Ⓦ www.bowaquatics.co.uk
Contact: Peter Muggeridge
Opening Times: 0900-1700 Mon-Sat, 1000-1600 Sun.
Credit Cards: All major credit/debit cards
Specialities: Pond plants (incl. water lilies) and plants for damp places. Garden centre with adjoining nursery (not open to public but supplies garden centre). Established 1984.
Map Ref: C, C3 **OS Grid Ref:** SS713018

CBar **BARTERS PLANT CENTRE & NURSERY** ♿
Chapmanslade, Westbury, Wiltshire BA13 4AL
Ⓣ (01373) 832694
Ⓕ (01373) 832677
Ⓔ plantcentre@barters.co.uk
Ⓦ www.barters.co.uk
Contact: Giles Hall
Opening Times: 0900-1700 Mon-Thu, 0900-1730 Fri & Sat, summer. 0900-1630 Mon-Thu, 0900-1700 Fri & Sat, winter. 1030-1630 Sun.
Cat. Cost: None issued.
Credit Cards: All, except American Express
Specialities: Wide range of shrubs. Ground cover, container trees, ferns, half-hardy perennials, grasses, herbaceous & climbers. Hedging, fruit trees, old fashioned roses & bare-root stock.
Notes: Also sells wholesale.
Map Ref: C, B5 **OS Grid Ref:** ST830480

CBcs **BURNCOOSE NURSERIES** ⊠ ⛺ ♿
Gwennap, Redruth, Cornwall TR16 6BJ
Ⓣ (01209) 860316
Ⓕ (01209) 860011
Ⓔ burncoose@eclipse.co.uk
Ⓦ www.burncoose.co.uk
Contact: C H Williams
Opening Times: 0830-1700 Mon-Sat & 1100-1700 Sun.
Min Mail Order UK: Nmc
Min Mail Order EU: Individual quotations for EU sales.
Cat. Cost: Free
Credit Cards: Visa, Switch, MasterCard, Maestro
Specialities: Extensive range of over 3500 ornamental trees & shrubs and herbaceous. Rare & unusual *Magnolia*, *Rhododendron*. Conservatory plants. 30 acre garden.
Notes: Also sells wholesale.
Map Ref: C, D1 **OS Grid Ref:** SW742395

CBct **BARRACOTT PLANTS** ⊠ ⛺ € ♿
Old Orchard, Calstock Road, Gunnislake, Cornwall PL18 9AA
Ⓣ (01822) 832234
Ⓜ 07811 207186
Ⓔ geoffandthelma@barracott.eclipse.co.uk
Ⓦ www.barracottplants.co.uk
Contact: Geoff & Thelma Turner
Opening Times: 0900-1700 Thu & Fri, Mar-end Sep. Other times by appt.
Min Mail Order UK: Nmc
Cat. Cost: 1st class stamp.

KEY
⊠ Mail order to UK or EU ⛺ Delivers to shows
✈ Exports beyond EU € Euro accepted
♿ Accessible by wheelchair ◆ See Display advertisement

C

Credit Cards: None
Specialities: Herbaceous plants: shade-loving, foliage & form. *Acanthus, Aspidistra, Astrantia, Bergenia, Convallaria, Disporum, Liriope, Maianthemum, Polygonatum, Roscoea, Trillium* & *Uvularia.*
Notes: Also sells wholesale.
Map Ref: C, C3 **OS Grid Ref:** SX436702

CBgR **Beggar's Roost Plants** ⊠ €
Lilstock, Bridgwater, Somerset TA5 1SU
Ⓣ (01278) 741519
Ⓔ ro@lilstock.eclipse.co.uk
Ⓦ www.beggarsroostplants.co.uk
Contact: Rosemary FitzGerald
Opening Times: Not open. Mail order only.
Min Mail Order UK: £10.00
Min Mail Order EU: £15.00
Cat. Cost: 3 × large 2nd class.
Credit Cards: None
Specialities: *Hemerocallis* (incl. heritage) grown in British conditions. *Galanthus* (incl. West Country variants).
Notes: Mail order for specialities *Hemerocallis* & *Galanthus*. Ask for lists.
Map Ref: C, B4 **OS Grid Ref:** ST168450

CBot **The Botanic Nursery** ⊠ ⌂ €
Atworth, Nr Melksham, Wiltshire SN12 8NU
Ⓜ 07850 328756
Ⓕ (01225) 700953
Ⓔ botanicnursery@botanicguru.co.uk
Ⓦ www.botanicguru.co.uk
Contact: T. Baker
Opening Times: 1000-1700 Tue-Sat, Mar-Oct. Please avoid lunch time if possible.
Min Mail Order UK: £11.00 for 24hr carriage service. At cost for Royal Mail.
Min Mail Order EU: Nmc
Cat. Cost: Online only.
Credit Cards: All major credit/debit cards
Specialities: Nursery propagates from large range of lime-tolerant plants in varying quantities, all peat free. Nat. Collection of *Digitalis.*
Notes: If travelling, please phone first to confirm specific plant availability. Only partially suitable for wheelchairs as not all areas are accessible.
Map Ref: C, A5 **OS Grid Ref:** ST852655

CBre **Bregover Plants** ⊠ ⌂
Middlewood, North Hill, Nr Launceston, Cornwall PL15 7NN
Ⓣ (01566) 782661
Ⓔ bregoverplants@gmail.com
Contact: Jennifer Bousfield
Opening Times: 1100-1700 Wed, Mar-mid Oct and by appt.
Min Mail Order UK: Nmc
Min Mail Order EU: Nmc
Cat. Cost: 3 × 1st class. Plant list available as PDF download.
Credit Cards: None
Specialities: Unusual hardy perennials grown in small garden nursery. Available in small quantities only.
Notes: Mail order Oct-Mar only.
Map Ref: C, C2 **OS Grid Ref:** SX273752

CBro **Broadleigh Gardens** ⊠ ⌂ € ♿
Bishops Hull, Taunton, Somerset TA4 1AE
Ⓣ (01823) 286231
Ⓕ (01823) 323646
Ⓔ info@broadleighbulbs.co.uk
Ⓦ www.broadleighbulbs.co.uk
Contact: Lady Skelmersdale
Opening Times: 0900-1600 Mon-Fri for viewing only (charity donation). Orders collected if notice given.
Min Mail Order UK: Nmc
Min Mail Order EU: Nmc
Cat. Cost: 2 × 1st class.
Credit Cards: All major credit/debit cards
Specialities: Jan catalogue: bulbs in growth (*Galanthus, Cyclamen* etc.) & herbaceous woodland plants (trilliums, hellebores etc). Extensive list of *Agapanthus*. June catalogue: dwarf & unusual bulbs, *Iris* (DB & PC). Nat. Collection of Alec Grey hybrid daffodils.
Notes: Euro payment accepted as cash only.
Map Ref: C, B4 **OS Grid Ref:** ST195251

CBrP **Brooklands Plants** ⊠ €
25 Treves Road, Dorchester, Dorset DT1 2HE
Ⓣ (01305) 265846
Ⓔ cycads@btinternet.com
Contact: Ian Watt
Opening Times: By appt. only for collection of plants.
Min Mail Order UK: £25.00 + p&p
Cat. Cost: 2 × 2nd class or by email.
Credit Cards: None
Specialities: Cycad nursery specialising in the more cold-tolerant species of *Encephalartos, Dioon, Macrozamia* & *Cycas*. Also specialist in cold-tolerant palms as well as plants from New Zealand. Some species available in small quantities only.
Map Ref: C, C5 **OS Grid Ref:** SY682897

CBty **Bentley Plants** ⊠ ⌂ € ♿
1 Bentley Wood Cottages, West Tytherley, Salisbury, Wiltshire SP5 1QB
Ⓣ (01794) 340775
Ⓕ (01794) 340775
Ⓔ john@bentleyplants.fsnet.co.uk

Ⓦ www.bentleyplants.co.uk
Contact: John Wilson
Opening Times: By appt. only.
Min Mail Order UK: Nmc
Cat. Cost: Online only.
Credit Cards: All major credit/debit cards
Specialities: Tree ferns & ground ferns.
Notes: Mail order Oct-Mar.
Map Ref: C, B6 **OS Grid Ref:** SU258306

CBur **BURNHAM NURSERIES** ⊠ ☒ ⌂ € ♿
Forches Cross, Newton Abbot, Devon
TQ12 6PZ
Ⓣ (01626) 352233
Ⓕ (01626) 362167
Ⓔ mail@orchids.uk.com
Ⓦ www.orchids.uk.com
Contact: Any member of staff
Opening Times: 1000-1600 Mon-Sun.
Min Mail Order UK: Nmc
Min Mail Order EU: £100.00 + p&p
Cat. Cost: A4 sae + 2nd large stamp.
Credit Cards: Visa, MasterCard, Maestro
Specialities: All types of orchid except British native types.
Notes: Please ask for details on export beyond EU.
Map Ref: C, C4 **OS Grid Ref:** SX841732

CCAT **CIDER APPLE TREES** ⊠ € ♿
Kerian, Corkscrew Lane, Woolston, Nr North Cadbury, Somerset BA22 7BP
Ⓣ (01963) 441101
Ⓦ www.ciderappletrees.co.uk
Contact: Mr J Dennis
Opening Times: By appt. only.
Min Mail Order UK: £9.50
Min Mail Order EU: £9.50
Cat. Cost: Free.
Credit Cards: None
Specialities: *Malus* (speciality standard trees).
Notes: Also sells wholesale.
Map Ref: C, B5

CCCN **CROSS COMMON NURSERY** ⊠ ◆
The Lizard, Helston, Cornwall TR12 7PD
Ⓣ (01326) 290722 or 290668
Ⓔ info@crosscommonnursery.co.uk
Ⓦ www.crosscommonnursery.co.uk
Contact: Kevin Bosustow
Opening Times: 1000-1700 7 days, Apr, May & Jun. Reduced hours Jul-Sep, please phone for opening times.
Min Mail Order UK: Nmc
Cat. Cost: Online only.
Credit Cards: All major credit/debit cards
Specialities: Tropical/sub-tropical, coastal plants & conservatory plants. Wide range of grapevines and citrus trees. Some plants available in small quantities only.
Map Ref: C, D1 **OS Grid Ref:** SW704116

CCha **CHAPEL FARM HOUSE NURSERY** € ♿
Halwill Junction, Beaworthy, Devon
EX21 5UF
Ⓣ (01409) 221594
Ⓕ (01409) 221594
Contact: Robin or Toshie Hull
Opening Times: 1000-1600 Tue-Sat, 1000-1600 Sun & B/hol Mons.
Cat. Cost: None issued.
Credit Cards: None
Specialities: Plants from Japan. Also herbaceous. Japanese garden design service offered.
Notes: Newly designed & built Japanese garden. Open for NGS, see "Yellow Book" for details.
Map Ref: C, C3

CCon **CONSTANTINE GARDEN NURSERY (FORMERLY FIR TREE FARM)** ⊠ ⌂ € ♿
Tresahor, Constantine, Falmouth, Cornwall
TR11 5PL
Ⓣ (01326) 340593
Ⓔ plants@cornwallgardens.com
Ⓦ www.cornwallgardens.com
Contact: Sorcha Hitchcox
Opening Times: 1000-1700 Wed-Sat, 1100-1600 Sun, Feb-Sep. By appt. Oct-Jan.
Min Mail Order UK: £25.00 + p&p
Min Mail Order EU: £40.00 + p&p
Cat. Cost: 6 × 1st class.
Credit Cards: Visa, Access, Delta, Switch
Specialities: Over 4000 varieties of cottage garden & rare perennials with many specialities. Also 80 varieties of *Clematis*. Some rare varieties available in small quantities only.
Notes: Display gardens. Free planting plans. Dogs welcome. Refreshments available. Plenty of car parking.
Map Ref: C, D1

CCse **CHASE PLANTS (FORMERLY MEADOWS NURSERY)** ⊠ ⌂
Hookswood Cottage, Farnham, Blandford Forum, Dorset DT11 8DQ
Ⓣ (01725) 516394
Ⓔ sales@chaseplants.co.uk
Contact: Sue Lees & Eddie Wheatley
Opening Times: By appt. only.

KEY		
	⊠ Mail order to UK or EU	⌂ Delivers to shows
	☒ Exports beyond EU	€ Euro accepted
	♿ Accessible by wheelchair	◆ See Display advertisement

C

Min Mail Order UK: £10.00
Credit Cards: None
Specialities: Hardy perennials, shrubs & some conservatory plants.

CCVN **Culm View Nursery** ⊠ ☒ ⌂
Waterloo Farm, Clayhidon, Devon EX15 3TN
Ⓣ (01823) 680698
Ⓔ plants@culmviewnursery.co.uk
Ⓦ www.culmviewnursery.co.uk
Contact: Brian & Alison Jacobs
Opening Times: By appt. only for collection.
Min Mail Order UK: Nmc
Min Mail Order EU: Nmc
Credit Cards: Paypal
Specialities: Hebaceous perennials grown in peat-free compost.
Notes: Mail order seed & some plants.

CCVT **Chew Valley Trees** ⊠ ♿
Winford Road, Chew Magna, Bristol BS40 8HJ
Ⓣ (01275) 333752
Ⓕ (01275) 333746
Ⓔ info@chewvalleytrees.co.uk
Ⓦ www.chewvalleytrees.co.uk
Contact: S Scarth
Opening Times: 0800-1700 Mon-Fri all year. 0900-1600 Sat. Closed Sun. Closed B/hols & Sats Jul & Aug.
Min Mail Order UK: Nmc
Cat. Cost: Free.
Credit Cards: All major credit/debit cards
Specialities: Native British & ornamental trees, shrubs, fruit trees & hedging.
Notes: Also sells wholesale.
Map Ref: C, A5 **OS Grid Ref:** ST558635

CDes **Desirable Plants** ⊠ ⌂
(Office) Pentamar, Crosspark, Totnes, Devon TQ9 5BQ
Ⓣ (01803) 864489 evenings
Ⓔ sutton.totnes@lineone.net
Ⓦ www.desirableplants.com
Contact: Dr J J & Mrs S A Sutton
Opening Times: Not open. Mail order only.
Min Mail Order UK: £15.00
Cat. Cost: 4 × 2nd class.
Credit Cards: None
Specialities: Eclectic range of choice & interesting herbaceous perennials & bulbs by mail order.
Notes: Nursery not at this address.

CDob **Dobies of Devon** ⊠
Long Road, Paignton, Devon TQ4 7SX
Ⓣ 0844 701 7623
Ⓕ 0844 701 7624
Ⓦ www.dobies.co.uk
Contact: Customer Services
Opening Times: Not open. Mail order only. Phone line open 0830-1700 Mon-Fri (office). Also answerphone.
Min Mail Order UK: Nmc
Min Mail Order EU: £5.00
Cat. Cost: Free.
Credit Cards: Visa, MasterCard, Switch, Delta
Specialities: Wide selection of popular flower & vegetable seeds. Also incl. young plants, summer-flowering bulbs & garden sundries.
Notes: Mail order to UK & Rep. of Ireland only.

CDoC **Duchy of Cornwall** ⊠ ◆
Cott Road, Lostwithiel, Cornwall PL22 0HW
Ⓣ (01208) 872668
Ⓕ (01208) 872835
Ⓔ sales@duchyofcornwallnursery.co.uk
Ⓦ www.duchyofcornwallnursery.co.uk
Contact: Jim Stephens
Opening Times: 0900-1700 Mon-Sat, 1000-1700 Sun & B/hols.
Min Mail Order UK: £10.00
Cat. Cost: None issued.
Credit Cards: All major credit/debit cards
Specialities: *Camellia*, *Fuchsia*, conifers & *Magnolia*. Also a huge range of garden plants incl. trees, shrubs, roses, perennials, fruit & conservatory plants.
Notes: Nursery partially accessible to wheelchair users.
Map Ref: C, C2 **OS Grid Ref:** SX112614

CDoy **Caradoc Doy** ⊠ €
PO Box 28, Exeter, Devon EX3 0WY
Ⓣ (01392) 877225
Ⓜ 07918 684750
Ⓕ (01392) 877225
Ⓔ info@caradocdoy.co.uk
Ⓦ www.caradocdoy.co.uk
Contact: Caradoc Doy
Opening Times: Open by appt. only.
Min Mail Order UK: Nmc
Cat. Cost: Online.
Credit Cards: All major credit/debit cards
Specialities: Olive trees. Plants introduced by the Veitch Nurseries. Some varieties only available in small quantities.
Notes: Nursery located at Poppleford's, Exeter Road, Newton Poppleford, Devon EX10 0DE
Map Ref: C, C4 **OS Grid Ref:** SY065895

CDTJ **Desert to Jungle** ⊠ ⌂ ♿
Henlade Garden Nursery, Lower Henlade, Taunton, Somerset TA3 5NB
Ⓣ (01823) 443701
Ⓕ (01458) 250521

Ⓔ plants@deserttojungle.com
Ⓦ www.deserttojungle.com
Contact: Rob Gudge, Dave Root
Opening Times: 1000-1700 Mon, Tues & Thu-Sun (closed Wed), 1st Mar-31st Oct. Thu, Fri & Sat only Nov-Feb, or phone first.
Min Mail Order UK: Nmc
Credit Cards: All major credit/debit cards
Specialities: Exotic-looking plants giving a desert or jungle effect in the garden. Incl. *Canna*, aroids, succulents, tree ferns & bamboos.
Notes: Nursery shares drive with Mount Somerset Hotel. Also sells wholesale.
Map Ref: C, B4 **OS Grid Ref:** ST273232

CDul **Dulford Nurseries** ⊠ ♿
Cullompton, Devon EX15 2DG
Ⓣ (01884) 266361
Ⓕ (01884) 266663
Ⓔ dulford.nurseries@virgin.net
Ⓦ www.dulford-nurseries.co.uk
Contact: Paul Rawlings
Opening Times: 0730-1630 Mon-Fri.
Min Mail Order UK: Nmc
Min Mail Order EU: Nmc
Cat. Cost: Free.
Credit Cards: All major credit/debit cards
Specialities: Native, ornamental & unusual trees, hedging & shrubs incl. oaks, maples, beech, birch, chestnut, ash, lime, *Sorbus* & pines.
Map Ref: C, C4 **OS Grid Ref:** SY062062

CEls **Elsworth Herbs** ⊠
Farthingwood, Broadway, Sidmouth, Devon EX10 8HS
Ⓣ (01395) 578689
Ⓔ john.twibell@btinternet.com
Contact: Drs J D & J M Twibell
Opening Times: By appt. only.
Min Mail Order UK: £10.00
Cat. Cost: 3 × 1st class or email.
Credit Cards: None
Specialities: Nat. Collection of *Artemisia*. Wide range of *Artemisia*. Stock available in small quantities only. Orders may require propagation from Collection material, for which we are the primary reference source.
Notes: Partially accessible for wheelchairs. Mail order spring & autumn only.
Map Ref: C, C4 **OS Grid Ref:** SY119881

CElw **Elworthy Cottage Plants** 🚚 ♿
Elworthy Cottage, Elworthy, Nr Lydeard St Lawrence, Taunton, Somerset TA4 3PX
Ⓣ (01984) 656427
Ⓔ mike@elworthy-cottage.co.uk
Ⓦ www.elworthy-cottage.co.uk
Contact: Mrs J M Spiller
Opening Times: 1000-1600 Thu, late Mar-end Aug. Also by appt. Feb-Nov.
Cat. Cost: 3 × 2nd class.
Credit Cards: None
Specialities: Unusual herbaceous plants esp. hardy *Geranium*, *Geum*, *Crocosmia*, *Monarda*, *Phlox*, *Pulmonaria*, *Astrantia* & *Viola*. Some varieties only available in small quantities. *Galanthus* available by mail order in Feb.
Notes: Nursery on B3188, 5 miles north of Wiveliscombe, in centre of Elworthy village.
Map Ref: C, B4 **OS Grid Ref:** ST084349

CEnd **Endsleigh Gardens** ⊠ ♿ ◆
Milton Abbot, Tavistock, Devon PL19 0PG
Ⓣ (01822) 870235
Ⓕ (01822) 870513
Ⓔ info@endsleigh-gardens.com
Ⓦ www.endsleigh-gardens.com
Contact: Michael Taylor
Opening Times: 0800-1700 Mon-Sat. 1000-1700 Sun.
Min Mail Order UK: Nmc
Cat. Cost: 2 × 1st class.
Credit Cards: Visa, Access, Switch, MasterCard
Specialities: Choice & unusual trees & shrubs incl. *Acer* & *Cornus* cvs. Old apples & cherries. *Wisteria*. Grafting service.

CEnt **Entwood Farm Plants** 🚚
Harcombe, Lyme Regis, Dorset DT7 3RN
Ⓣ (01297) 444034
Ⓔ jennyhlyme@hotmail.co.uk
Contact: Jenny & Ivan Harding
Opening Times: By prior arrangement only.
Credit Cards: None
Specialities: Bamboo specialist. Selection of grasses, shrubs & perennials. Some stock in small quantities.
Map Ref: C, C4 **OS Grid Ref:** SY335953

CExl **Exclusive Plants Nursery** ⊠ €
Tretawn, High Cross, Constantine, Falmouth, Cornwall TR11 5RE
Ⓣ (01326) 341496
Ⓜ 07775 811385
Ⓕ (01326) 341496
Ⓔ info@exclusiveplants.com
Ⓦ www.exclusiveplants.com
Contact: Paul Bonavia & Alison Jones
Opening Times: By appt. only.

KEY
⊠ Mail order to UK or EU 🚚 Delivers to shows
✈ Exports beyond EU € Euro accepted
♿ Accessible by wheelchair ◆ See Display advertisement

C

Min Mail Order UK: Nmc
Min Mail Order EU: £25.00
Cat. Cost: 2 × 1st class.
Credit Cards: All major credit/debit cards
Specialities: A plantsperson's nursery, offering rare & unusual plants from around the world. Also new introductions & the best form of our better known plants.
Map Ref: C, D1 **OS Grid Ref:** SW175131

CFen **FENTONGOLLAN FARM** ⊠ ♿ € ♿
Merther Lane, St Michael Penkivel, Tresillian, Truro, Cornwall TR2 4AQ
Ⓣ (01872) 520209
Ⓕ (01872) 520606
Ⓔ admin@flowerfarm.co.uk
Ⓦ www.flowerfarm.co.uk
Contact: James Hosking
Opening Times: 0900-1700 7 days, Aug-end Nov.
Min Mail Order UK: Nmc
Min Mail Order EU: Nmc
Cat. Cost: Free.
Credit Cards: All major credit/debit cards
Specialities: *Narcissus.*
Notes: Also sells wholesale.
Map Ref: C, D2

CFil **FILLAN'S PLANTS** ⊠
Tuckermarsh Gardens, Yelverton, Devon PL20 7HN
Ⓣ (01822) 841551 Fri only, please.
Ⓜ 07813 161276 Fri only, please.
Ⓕ (01822) 841551
Ⓔ fillansplants@yahoo.co.uk
Ⓦ www.fillansplants.co.uk
Contact: Mark Fillan
Opening Times: 1000-1700 Fri, Mar-Oct. By appt. at other times.
Min Mail Order UK: Nmc
Min Mail Order EU: Nmc
Cat. Cost: 4 x 1st class
Credit Cards: None
Specialities: Bamboos, *Hydrangea* & unusual woody plants. Some plants available in small quanitities only.
Notes: Also sells wholesale.
Map Ref: C, C3 **OS Grid Ref:** SX444678

CFis **MARGERY FISH PLANT NURSERY** ♿
East Lambrook Manor Gardens, East Lambrook, South Petherton, Somerset TA13 5HH
Ⓣ (01460) 240328
Ⓜ 07710 484745
Ⓔ enquiries@eastlambrook.com
Ⓦ www.eastlambrook.com
Contact: Tom Wild
Opening Times: 1000-1700 Feb & May-Jul 7 days. 1000-1700 Tue-Sat & B/hol Mons Mar-Apr & Aug-Oct. Nov-Jan by appt.
Cat. Cost: None issued.
Credit Cards: All major credit/debit cards
Specialities: Hardy geraniums & cottage garden herbaceous plants. Stock available in small quantities only. Major collection of hardy geraniums on site.
Map Ref: C, B5 **OS Grid Ref:** ST431188

CFlo **FLOYDS CLIMBERS AND CLEMATIS** ⊠ ♿ €
36 Dowding Drive, Lower Compton, Calne, Wiltshire SN11 8QL
Ⓣ (01249) 823200
Ⓜ 07762 499416
Ⓔ sales@floydsclimbers.co.uk
Ⓦ www.floydsclimbers.co.uk
Contact: Marcel Floyd
Opening Times: Open w/ends twice a year. See website or phone for dates.
Min Mail Order UK: Nmc
Credit Cards: Paypal
Specialities: *Clematis* and climbers.
Notes: Also sells wholesale.
Map Ref: C, A6

CFwr **THE FLOWER BOWER** ⊠
Woodlands, Shurton, Stogursey, Nr Bridgwater, Somerset TA5 1QE
Ⓣ (01278) 732134
Ⓔ theflowerbower@yahoo.co.uk
Ⓦ www.theflowerbower.co.uk
Contact: Sheila Tucker
Opening Times: By appt. only.
Min Mail Order UK: Nmc
Min Mail Order EU: Nmc
Cat. Cost: 2 × 1st class.
Credit Cards: None
Specialities: *Hemerocallis,* esp. newer varieties & spiders. *Epiphyllum* 700+ varieties
Notes: Daylilies can also be pre-ordered for Autumn delivery. Newer & rarer varieties mostly available in small quantities.
Map Ref: C, B4 **OS Grid Ref:** ST203442

CGHE **GARDEN HOUSE ENTERPRISES** ♿
The Garden House, Buckland Monachorum, Yelverton, Devon PL20 7LQ
Ⓣ (01822) 854769
Ⓔ office@thegardenhouse.org.uk
Ⓦ www.thegardenhouse.org.uk
Contact: Jo Selman
Opening Times: 1030-1700 7 days 1st Mar-31st Oct.

C

Cat. Cost: None issued.
Credit Cards: All major credit/debit cards
Specialities: Choice woodland plants.
Map Ref: C, C3 **OS Grid Ref:** SX496683

CGro **C W Groves & Son Ltd** ⊠ ♿
West Bay Road, Bridport, Dorset
DT6 4BA
Ⓣ (01308) 422654
Ⓕ (01308) 420888
Ⓔ garden@grovesnurseries.co.uk
Ⓦ www.grovesnurseries.co.uk
Contact: Becky Groves
Opening Times: 0830-1700 Mon-Sat, 1030-1630 Sun.
Min Mail Order UK: Nmc
Min Mail Order EU: £15.00 + p&p
Cat. Cost: 2 × 1st class.
Credit Cards: Visa, Switch, MasterCard
Specialities: Nursery & garden centre specialising in Parma & hardy *Viola*. Nat. Collection of *Viola odorata* cvs & Parma Violets. Also roses.
Notes: Mainly violets by mail order. Main display at nursery in Feb, Mar & Apr. Roses when dormant (Nov-Mar).
Map Ref: C, C5 **OS Grid Ref:** SY466918

CGrW **The Great Western Gladiolus Nursery** ⊠ €
17 Valley View, Clutton, Bristol
BS39 5SN
Ⓣ (01761) 452036
Ⓔ clutton.glads@btinternet.com
Ⓦ www.greatwesterngladiolus.co.uk
Contact: G F Hazell
Opening Times: Mail order only. Open by appt. only.
Min Mail Order UK: Nmc
Min Mail Order EU: Nmc
Cat. Cost: 4 × 1st class (2 catalogues).
Credit Cards: None
Specialities: *Gladiolus* species & hybrids, corms & seeds. Other South African bulbous plants. Only available in small quantities.
Notes: Also sells wholesale.

CHab **Habitat Aid Ltd** ⊠ ⌂
Hookgate Cottage, South Brewham, Somerset
BA10 0LQ
Ⓣ (01749) 812355
Ⓜ 07973 776613
Ⓔ info@habitataid.co.uk
Ⓦ www.habitataid.co.uk
Contact: Nick Mann
Opening Times: Not open. Mail order only.
Min Mail Order UK: £50.00, incl. p&p.
Cat. Cost: None issued.
Credit Cards: All major credit/debit cards
Specialities: British trees, plants and seeds. Local provenance seed mixes in small quantities only. Cottage garden perennials. Non-native trees for bees. Heritage fruit trees.
Notes: Also sells wholesale.

CHby **The Herbary** ⊠ €
161 Chapel Street, Horningsham, Warminster, Wiltshire BA12 7LU
Ⓣ (01985) 844442
Ⓔ info@beansandherbs.co.uk
Ⓦ www.beansandherbs.co.uk
Contact: Pippa Rosen
Opening Times: May-Sep strictly by appt. only.
Min Mail Order UK: Nmc
Min Mail Order EU: Nmc
Cat. Cost: 4 × 1st class or online.
Credit Cards: None
Specialities: Culinary, medicinal & aromatic herbs organically grown in small quantities.
Notes: Mail order for seed only and all year for organic vegetable seed & large variety of organic bean & herb seed. Also sells wholesale.

CHel **Heligan Nursery & Plant Centre** ⊠ ♿
The Lost Gardens of Heligan, Pentewan, St Austell, Cornwall PL26 6EN
Ⓣ (01726) 845100
Ⓕ (01726) 845101
Ⓔ nursery@heligan.com
Ⓦ www.heligan.com
Contact: Claire Wood
Opening Times: 1000-1800 Mon-Sat & 1200-1800 Sun, Apr-Oct. 1000-1700 Mon-Sat & 1100-1700 Sun, Nov-Mar.
Min Mail Order UK: Nmc
Min Mail Order EU: Nmc
Credit Cards: All, except American Express
Specialities: Less common trees, shrubs & perennials. Collection holders of Pre 1920 *Rhododendron* & *Camellia*, incl. Tremayne hybrids and rare Heligan camellias. Further information on request.

CHew **Hewitt-Cooper Carnivorous Plants** ⊠ ⌂ €
The Homestead, Glastonbury Road, West Pennard, Somerset BA6 8NN
Ⓣ (01458) 832844
Ⓕ (01458) 832712

KEY
⊠ Mail order to UK or EU ⌂ Delivers to shows
✈ Exports beyond EU € Euro accepted
♿ Accessible by wheelchair ◆ See Display advertisement

C

Ⓔ sales@hccarnivorousplants.co.uk
Ⓦ www.hccarnivorousplants.co.uk
Contact: Nigel Hewitt-Cooper
Opening Times: By appt.
Min Mail Order UK: £10.00 + p&p
Min Mail Order EU: £30.00
Cat. Cost: 1 × 1st class/1× IRC.
Credit Cards: All major credit/debit cards
Specialities: Carnivorous plants.
Notes: Mail order May-Nov.
Map Ref: C, B5

CHEx **HARDY EXOTICS** ⊠ ♿
Gilly Lane, Whitecross, Penzance, Cornwall
TR20 8BZ
Ⓣ (01736) 740660
Ⓕ (01736) 741101
Ⓔ contact@hardyexotics.co.uk
Ⓦ www.hardyexotics.co.uk
Contact: C Shilton/J Smith
Opening Times: 1000-1700 7 days Apr-Oct. 1000-1600 Mon-Sat, Nov-Feb. Please phone first in winter months if travelling a long way.
Min Mail Order UK: £25 carriage.
Credit Cards: All major credit/debit cards
Specialities: Largest selection in the UK of trees, shrubs & herbaceous plants for exotic & desert effects. Hardy & half-hardy plants for gardens, patios & conservatories. Mature plants & plantings to inspire.
Map Ref: C, D1 **OS Grid Ref:** SW524345

CHGN **HIGH GARDEN NURSERIES** ♿
Chiverstone Lane, Kenton, Exeter, Devon
EX6 8NJ
Ⓣ (01626) 899106
Ⓔ highgarden@highgarden.co.uk
Ⓦ www.highgarden.co.uk
Contact: Chris Britton
Opening Times: 0900-1700 Tue-Fri
Cat. Cost: None issued.
Credit Cards: None
Specialities: Quality shrubs, trees & perennials, some unusual & different.
Map Ref: C, C4 **OS Grid Ref:** SX957836

CHid **HIDDEN VALLEY NURSERY** ⌂ €
Umberleigh, Devon EX37 9BU
Ⓣ (01769) 560567
Ⓜ 07899 788789
Ⓔ plalindley@itsosbroadband.co.uk
Contact: Linda & Peter Lindley
Opening Times: Daylight hours, but please phone first.
Cat. Cost: None issued.
Credit Cards: None
Specialities: Hardy perennials esp. shade lovers & Chatham Islands forget-me-nots (*Myosotidium hortensia*).
Notes: Nursery not easy to find using Sat Nav or Google Street Map.
Map Ref: C, B3 **OS Grid Ref:** SS567205

CHII **HILL HOUSE NURSERY LTD** ⊠ € ♿
Landscove, Nr Ashburton, Devon
TQ13 7LY
Ⓣ (01803) 762273
Ⓕ (01803) 158218
Ⓔ bluebird@hillhousenursery.com
Ⓦ www.hillhousenursery.com
Contact: Raymond, Sacha & Matthew Hubbard
Opening Times: 1100-1700 7 days, all year. Open all B/hols incl. Easter Sun. Closed 24th Dec-7th Jan. Tearoom open 1st Mar-30th Sep.
Min Mail Order UK: Nmc
Cat. Cost: None issued.
Credit Cards: Delta, MasterCard, Switch, Visa, Paypal
Specialities: 3000+ varieties of plants, most propagated on premises, many rare or unusual. The garden, open to the public, was laid out by Edward Hyams. Pioneers of glasshouse pest control by beneficial insects.
Map Ref: C, C3 **OS Grid Ref:** SX774664

CHVG **HIDDEN VALLEY GARDENS** € ♿
Treesmill, Nr Par, Cornwall
PL24 2TU
Ⓣ (01208) 873225
Ⓔ hiddenvalleygardens@yahoo.co.uk
Ⓦ www.hiddenvalleygardens.co.uk
Contact: Mrs P Howard
Opening Times: 1000-1800 Thu-Mon (closed Tue & Wed), 20th Mar-15th Oct. Please phone for directions. Garden open as nursery.
Cat. Cost: None issued.
Credit Cards: All major credit/debit cards
Specialities: Cottage garden plants, *Dahlia* & many perennials which can be seen growing in the garden. Some stock available in small quantities. Display garden.
Notes: Award-winning Garden In Cornwall, 2010 & 2011.
Map Ref: C, D2 **OS Grid Ref:** SX094567

CIri **THE IRIS GARDEN** ⊠ € ·
Yard House, Pilsdon, Bridport, Dorset
DT6 5PA
Ⓣ (01308) 868797
Ⓔ info@theirisgarden.co.uk
Ⓦ www.theirisgarden.co.uk
Contact: Clive Russell

Opening Times: Show garden open by appt. only. Please email or phone for details.
Min Mail Order UK: £15.00 + p&p
Min Mail Order EU: £25.00 + p&p
Cat. Cost: 6 × 1st class.
Credit Cards: American Express, Visa
Specialities: Modern bearded & beardless *Iris* from breeders in UK, USA, France, Italy & Australia. Nat. Collection of Space Age *Iris*. Collection of 6-fall & novelty bearded *Iris* in preparation for ratification in 2012.
Notes: Orders for bearded iris & sibiricas must be received by end Jun & by end Aug for spurias & ensatas.
Map Ref: C, C5 **OS Grid Ref:** SY421988

CJas **Jasmine Cottage Gardens**
26 Channel Road, Clevedon, Somerset BS21 7BY
Ⓣ (01275) 871850
Ⓔ margaret@bologrew.net
Ⓦ jasminecottage.bologrew.net
Contact: Mr & Mrs M Redgrave
Opening Times: May to Aug, daily by appt. Garden open at the same times.
Cat. Cost: None issued.
Credit Cards: None
Specialities: *Rhodochiton*, *Lophospermum*, *Maurandya*, *Dicentra macrocapnos*, *Salvia*, *Isotoma*, half-hardy geraniums.
Map Ref: C, A4 **OS Grid Ref:** ST405725

CJun **Junker's Nursery Ltd (formerly P M A Plant Specialities)** ⊠
Higher Cobhay, Milverton, Somerset TA4 1NJ
Ⓣ (01823) 400075
Ⓔ karan@junker.co.uk
Ⓦ www.junker.co.uk
Contact: Karan or Nick Junker
Opening Times: Strictly by appt. only.
Min Mail Order UK: Nmc
Min Mail Order EU: Nmc
Cat. Cost: 6 × 1st class.
Credit Cards: None
Specialities: Choice & unusual shrubs & trees incl. grafted *Acer palmatum*, *Cornus*, *Daphne*, *Magnolia*. Many available in larger, more mature sizes. Small quantities only of some hard to propagate plants, esp. daphnes.
Notes: Extensive planted areas showing how the plants look growing in "real world" conditions. We propagate & grow all our own plants with an increasing number grown naturally in open ground as well as in pots, incl. larger sizes. Ltd wheelchair access.
Map Ref: C, B4

CKel **Kelways** ⊠ ⊠̸ ⌂ € ♿
Langport, Somerset TA10 9EZ
Ⓣ (01458) 250521
Ⓕ (01458) 253351
Ⓔ sales@kelways.co.uk
Ⓦ www.kelways.co.uk
Contact: Dave Root, Andy Martin
Opening Times: 0900-1700 Mon-Fri, 0900-1700 Sat, 1000-1600 Sun.
Min Mail Order UK: £4.00 + p&p
Min Mail Order EU: £8.00 + p&p
Cat. Cost: Online only.
Credit Cards: All major credit/debit cards
Specialities: *Paeonia*, *Iris*, *Hemerocallis* & herbaceous perennials. Nat. Collection of *Paeonia lactiflora*. Wide range of trees, shrubs & herbaceous. Hardy ferns & tree ferns.
Notes: Also sells wholesale.
Map Ref: C, B5 **OS Grid Ref:** ST434273

CKen **Kenwith Conifer Nursery (Gordon Haddow)** ⊠ ♿ ◆
Blinsham, Nr Torrington, Beaford, Winkleigh, Devon EX19 8NT
Ⓣ (01805) 603274
Ⓕ (01805) 603663
Ⓔ info@kenwithconifernursery.co.uk
Ⓦ www.kenwithconifernursery.co.uk
Contact: Gordon Haddow
Opening Times: 1000-1630 Tue-Sat all year. Closed all B/hols. If travelling a long distance, please phone previous day to ensure nursery will be open.
Min Mail Order UK: £20 + p&p
Min Mail Order EU: £50 + p&p
Cat. Cost: Online only.
Credit Cards: Visa, MasterCard
Specialities: All conifer genera. Grafting a speciality.
Map Ref: C, B3 **OS Grid Ref:** SS518160

CKno **Knoll Gardens** ⊠ ⌂ ♿
Hampreston, Nr Wimborne, Dorset BH21 7ND
Ⓣ (01202) 873931
Ⓕ (01202) 870842
Ⓔ enquiries@knollgardens.co.uk
Ⓦ www.knollgardens.co.uk
Contact: N R Lucas
Opening Times: 1000-1700 Tue-Sat, Feb-Dec. Open B/hol Mons. See website for further details.
Min Mail Order UK: Nmc

KEY		
	⊠ Mail order to UK or EU	⌂ Delivers to shows
	⊠̸ Exports beyond EU	€ Euro accepted
	♿ Accessible by wheelchair	◆ See Display advertisement

C

Min Mail Order EU: Nmc
Cat. Cost: £2.00 + 50p postage.
Credit Cards: Visa, MasterCard
Specialities: Grasses (main specialism). Select perennials. Nat. Collection of *Pennisetum*.
Notes: Also sells wholesale.
Map Ref: C, C6

CLak **Lakka Bulbs** ⊠
(Office) 127 Mill Street, Torrington, North Devon EX38 8AW
Ⓣ (01805) 625071
Ⓔ lakkabulbs@talktalk.net
Contact: Jonathan Hutchinson
Opening Times: Not open. Mail order only.
Min Mail Order UK: Nmc
Min Mail Order EU: Nmc
Cat. Cost: None issued.
Credit Cards: None
Specialities: Nat. Collections of *Urginea*, *Veltheimia* & *Scadoxus*. Other South African bulbs of families *Amaryllidaceae* & *Hyacinthaceae*. All available in small quantities only.

CLAP **Long Acre Plants** ⊠ ♿
South Marsh, Charlton Musgrove, Nr Wincanton, Somerset BA9 8EX
Ⓣ (01963) 32802
Ⓕ (01963) 32802
Ⓔ info@plantsforshade.co.uk
Ⓦ www.plantsforshade.co.uk
Contact: Nigel & Michelle Rowland
Opening Times: 0900-1300 & 1330-1600 Thu & Fri only, Feb-Jun, Sep & Oct.
Min Mail Order UK: £20.00 + p&p
Min Mail Order EU: Nmc
Cat. Cost: 3 × 1st class.
Credit Cards: MasterCard, Visa, Maestro, American Express, JCB
Specialities: Ferns, woodland bulbs & perennials. Marginal/bog plants.
Notes: Some plants available in small numbers only and only seasonally available. Ship to EU in autumn and winter only.
Map Ref: C, B5

CLnd **Landford Trees** €
Landford Lodge, Landford, Salisbury, Wiltshire SP5 2EH
Ⓣ (01794) 390808
Ⓕ (01794) 390037
Ⓔ trees@landfordtrees.co.uk
Ⓦ www.landfordtrees.co.uk
Contact: C D Pilkington
Opening Times: 0800-1700 Mon-Fri.
Cat. Cost: Free.
Credit Cards: All, except American Express
Specialities: Deciduous ornamental trees.
Notes: Also sells wholesale.
Map Ref: C, B6 **OS Grid Ref:** SU247201

CLng **Longcombe Nursery and Garden Centre** ⊠ ♿
Longcombe, Totnes, Devon TQ9 6PL
Ⓣ 0844 335 6915
Ⓔ info@simplyclematis.co.uk
Ⓦ www.simplyclematis.co.uk
Contact: Linda Clarke
Opening Times: 0900-1700 Mon-Sat, 1000-1600 Sun.
Min Mail Order UK: Nmc
Cat. Cost: Online only.
Credit Cards: All major credit/debit cards
Specialities: *Clematis*.
Notes: Also sells wholesale.
Map Ref: C, C3 **OS Grid Ref:** SX834601

CLoc **C S Lockyer (Fuchsias)** ⊠ € ◆
Lansbury, 70 Henfield Road, Coalpit Heath, Bristol BS36 2UZ
Ⓣ (01454) 772219
Ⓕ (01454) 772219
Ⓔ sales@lockyerfuchsias.co.uk
Ⓦ www.lockyerfuchsias.co.uk
Contact: C S Lockyer
Opening Times: 1000-1300, 1430-1700 most days, please ring.
Min Mail Order UK: 6 plants + p&p
Min Mail Order EU: £12.00 + p&p
Cat. Cost: 4 × 1st class.
Credit Cards: All major credit/debit cards
Specialities: *Fuchsia*.
Notes: Many open days & coach parties. Partial wheelchair access. Also sells wholesale.
Map Ref: C, A5

CMac **Mac Pennys Nurseries** ⊠
154 Burley Road, Bransgore, Christchurch, Dorset BH23 8DB
Ⓣ (01425) 672348
Ⓕ (01425) 673917
Ⓔ office@macpennys.co.uk
Ⓦ www.macpennys.co.uk
Contact: T & V Lowndes & S Lowndes
Opening Times: 0900-1700 Mon-Sat, 1000-1700 Sun & B/hols, except closed Xmas-New Year.
Min Mail Order UK: Nmc
Cat. Cost: A4 sae with 4 × 1st class.
Credit Cards: All major credit/debit cards
Specialities: General. Plants available in small quantities only.
Notes: Mail order available Sep-Mar, UK only. Nursery partially accessible for wheelchairs. Also sells wholesale.
Map Ref: C, C6

C

CMam **MAMMOTH TREES**
Wrangaton Road, South Brent, Devon
TQ10 9JE
Ⓜ 07847 329314
Ⓔ giles@mammothtrees.co.uk
Ⓦ www.MammothTrees.co.uk
Contact: Giles Nicholson
Opening Times: Not open. Mail order only. Office open 0930-1700 for phone & email enquiries.
Min Mail Order UK: Nmc
Min Mail Order EU: Nmc
Cat. Cost: 80p.
Credit Cards: All major credit/debit cards
Specialities: *Salix* & *Populus*. Fruit & nut trees.
Notes: Credit cards accepted online only. Trees may be collected from above address. Also sells wholesale.
Map Ref: C, C3 **OS Grid Ref:** SX688587

CMCN **MALLET COURT NURSERY**
Marshway, Curry Mallet, Taunton, Somerset
TA3 6SZ
Ⓣ (01823) 481493
Ⓕ (01823) 481493
Ⓔ malletcourtnursery@btinternet.com
Ⓦ www.malletcourt.co.uk
Contact: J G S & P M E Harris F.L.S.
Opening Times: 0930-1700 Mon-Fri summer, 0930-1600 winter. Sat & Sun by appt.
Min Mail Order UK: Nmc
Min Mail Order EU: Nmc
Cat. Cost: £1.50
Credit Cards: All major credit/debit cards
Specialities: Maples, oaks, *Magnolia*, hollies & other rare and unusual plants including those from China & South Korea.
Notes: Mail order Oct-Mar only. Also sells wholesale.
Map Ref: C, B4

CMea **THE MEAD NURSERY**
Brokerswood, Nr Westbury, Wiltshire
BA13 4EG
Ⓣ (01373) 859990
Ⓔ info@themeadnursery.co.uk
Ⓦ www.themeadnursery.co.uk
Contact: Steve & Emma Lewis-Dale
Opening Times: 0900-1700 Wed-Sat & B/hol Mons, 1200-1700 Sun, 1st Feb-10th Oct. Closed Easter Sun.
Cat. Cost: 5 × 1st class.
Credit Cards: All major credit/debit cards
Specialities: Perennials, alpines, pot-grown bulbs and grasses.
Map Ref: C, B5 **OS Grid Ref:** ST833517

CMen **MENDIP BONSAI STUDIO**
Byways, Back Lane, Downside, Shepton Mallet, Somerset BA4 4JR
Ⓣ (01749) 344274
Ⓜ 07711 205806
Ⓔ john@mendipbonsai.co.uk
Ⓦ www.mendipbonsai.co.uk
Contact: John Trott
Opening Times: Private nursery. Visits by appt. only.
Min Mail Order UK: £15.00
Cat. Cost: Large sae for plant & workshop lists
Credit Cards: All major credit/debit cards
Specialities: Bonsai, Potensai, accent plants & garden stock. Acers, conifers, incl. many *Pinus thunbergii* species, *Aciphylla*, *Davallia* & *Pyrrosia*. Many plants available in small numbers only. Young trees for garden or bonsai culture.
Notes: Education classes, lectures, demonstrations & club talks on bonsai. Stockist of most bonsai sundries. Mail orders will normally be despatched late Mar/early Apr-late Sep/Oct.
Map Ref: C, B5

CMHG **MARWOOD HILL GARDENS**
Marwood, Barnstaple, Devon
EX31 4EB
Ⓣ (01271) 342528
Ⓕ (01271) 342528
Ⓔ info@marwoodhillgarden.co.uk
Ⓦ www.marwoodhillgarden.co.uk
Contact: Malcolm Pharoah
Opening Times: 1100-1630, 7 days. Closed Nov-Feb.
Cat. Cost: 3 × 1st class
Credit Cards: Visa, Delta, MasterCard, Switch, Solo
Specialities: Large range of unusual trees & shrubs. *Eucalyptus*, alpines, *Camellia*, *Astilbe*, bog plants & perennials. Nat. Collections of *Astilbe*, *Tulbaghia* & *Iris ensata*.
Map Ref: C, B3 **OS Grid Ref:** SS545375

CMil **MILL COTTAGE PLANTS**
Henley Mill, Henley Lane, Wookey, Somerset
BA5 1AW
Ⓣ (01749) 676966
Ⓜ 07851 698759
Ⓔ millcottageplants@googlemail.com
Ⓦ www.millcottageplants.co.uk
Contact: Sally Gregson
Opening Times: By appt. only. Phone for directions.

KEY
- Mail order to UK or EU
- Delivers to shows
- Exports beyond EU
- € Euro accepted
- Accessible by wheelchair
- ◆ See Display advertisement

C

Min Mail Order UK: Nmc
Min Mail Order EU: £25.00 + p&p
Credit Cards: All major credit/debit cards
Specialities: Rare *Hydrangea serrata* cvs, *H. aspera* cvs, *Epimedium*, shade & damp-loving plants.
Map Ref: C, B5

CMus **MUSGROVE WILLOWS** ⊠ ☒ ♿
Willowfields, Lakewall, Westonzoyland, Bridgwater, Somerset TA7 0LP
Ⓣ (01278) 691105
Ⓕ (01278) 699107
Ⓔ info@musgrovewillows.co.uk
Ⓦ www.musgrovewillows.co.uk
Contact: Ellen Musgrove
Opening Times: 0900-1700 Mon-Fri.
Min Mail Order UK: £12.50
Min Mail Order EU: Nmc
Credit Cards: All major credit/debit cards
Specialities: *Salix* (willow). A family nursery for over 65 years.
Map Ref: C, B4

CNat **NATURAL SELECTION** ⊠ €
1 Station Cottages, Hullavington, Chippenham, Wiltshire SN14 6ET
Ⓣ (01666) 837369
Ⓜ 07800 583999
Ⓔ martin@worldmutation.demon.co.uk
Ⓦ www.worldmutation.demon.co.uk
Contact: Martin Barber
Opening Times: Please phone first.
Min Mail Order UK: £9.00 + p&p
Cat. Cost: 2 × 2nd class.
Credit Cards: None
Specialities: Unusual British natives & others. Also seed. Only available in small quantities.
Map Ref: C, A5

CNec **NECTAR PLANTS GARDEN NURSERY**
646 Dorchester Road, Upwey, Weymouth, Dorset
DT3 5LG
Ⓣ (01305) 855988
Ⓔ martinyoung100@btinternet.com
Ⓦ www.nectarplants.co.uk
Contact: Martin Young
Opening Times: 1000-1700 Thu-Sun, mid-March to mid-Oct.
Cat. Cost: A5 sae.
Credit Cards: None
Specialities: Small scale nursery specialising in plants for bees & butterflies; cottage garden favourites & coastal plants. Wide selection of *Buddleja davidii*, *B. weyeriana* & hardy geraniums. Good selection of David Austin roses & many flowering shrubs.
Notes: Nursery is on old Dorchester-Weymouth road. Follow signs to Upwey. Large copper beech tree next to green gate.
Map Ref: C, C5 **OS Grid Ref:** SY674838

CNMi **NEWPORT MILLS NURSERY** ⊠ €
Wrantage, Taunton, Somerset
TA3 6DJ
Ⓣ (01823) 490231
Ⓜ 07940 872800
Ⓔ newportmillsnursery@live.co.uk
Ⓦ www.newportmillsnursery.farming.officelive.com
Contact: John Barrington
Opening Times: Not open. Mail order only.
Min Mail Order UK: Nmc free p&p
Min Mail Order EU: Nmc. EU postal rate per order.
Cat. Cost: Free.
Credit Cards: All major credit/debit cards
Specialities: *Delphinium elatum* hybrids. English scented perpetual flowering carnations. Pinks, Exhibition, Modern & Old World.
Notes: Mail order Apr-Sep for young delphiniums in 7cm pots. Dormant plants can be sent out in autumn/winter if requested.
Map Ref: C, B4

CNWT **NEW WOOD TREES** ⌂
Oldwood House, Aish Road, Stoke Gabriel, Totnes, Devon TQ0 6PX
Ⓣ (01803) 782666
Ⓕ (05601) 262999
Ⓔ info@newwoodtrees.co.uk
Ⓦ www.newwoodtrees.co.uk
Contact: Philip Nieuwoudt
Opening Times: 0900-1700 Mon-Fri.
Credit Cards: None
Specialities: Trees. Multi-stem ornamentals; small to medium sized trees and large shrubs.
Notes: Specialises in specimen trees so when a species is sold out it takes a while to replenish stocks. Also sells wholesale.
Map Ref: C, C3 **OS Grid Ref:** SX8448057908

COIW **THE OLD WITHY GARDEN NURSERY** ⊠
Grange Fruit Farm, Gweek, Helston, Cornwall
TR12 6BE
Ⓣ (01326) 221171
Ⓔ sales@theoldwithygardennursery.co.uk
Ⓦ www.theoldwithygardennursery.co.uk
Contact: Sheila Chandler or Nick Chandler
Opening Times: 0930-1700 7 days, Feb-end Sep. 0930-1700 Mon-Sat, Oct. 1000-1600 Tue-Fri, Nov.
Min Mail Order UK: £15.00
Cat. Cost: Online.
Credit Cards: Maestro, MasterCard, Visa, Delta

Specialities: Cottage garden plants, perennials, some biennials & grasses. Some varieties in small quantities only. Small range of shrubs.
Notes: Partially accessible for wheelchairs (gravel paths).
Map Ref: C, D1 **OS Grid Ref:** SW688255

CPar **PARKS PERENNIALS** ⛫
242 Wallisdown Road, Wallisdown, Bournemouth, Dorset BH10 4HZ
Ⓣ (01202) 524464
Ⓔ parks.perennials@ntlworld.com
Contact: S. Parks
Opening Times: Apr-Oct most days. Please phone first.
Cat. Cost: None issued.
Credit Cards: None
Specialities: Hardy herbaceous perennials.
Map Ref: C, C6

CPbn **PENBORN GOAT FARM** ⊠ ♿
Penborn, Bounds Cross, Holsworthy, Devon EX22 6LH
Ⓣ (01288) 381569
Ⓔ penborngoats@btinternet.com
Ⓦ www.penborngoats.com
Contact: P R Oldfield
Opening Times: By appt. only.
Min Mail Order UK: £10.00
Min Mail Order EU: £10.00
Cat. Cost: Online.
Credit Cards: None
Specialities: *Mentha, Melissa.* Available in small quantities only.
Map Ref: C, C2 **OS Grid Ref:** SS290021

CPBP **PARHAM BUNGALOW PLANTS** ⊠ ⛫ €
Parham Lane, Market Lavington, Devizes, Wiltshire SN10 4QA
Ⓣ (01380) 812605
Ⓔ jjs@pbplants.freeserve.co.uk
Contact: Mrs D E Sample
Opening Times: Please ring first.
Min Mail Order UK: Nmc
Min Mail Order EU: Nmc
Cat. Cost: Sae.
Credit Cards: None
Specialities: Alpines.
Map Ref: C, B6

CPen **PENNARD PLANTS** ⊠ ⊠ ⛫ €
3 The Gardens, East Pennard, Shepton Mallet, Somerset BA4 6TU
Ⓣ (01749) 860039
Ⓕ 07043 017270
Ⓔ sales@pennardplants.com
Ⓦ www.pennardplants.com
Contact: Chris Smith
Opening Times: By appt. only.
Min Mail Order UK: Nmc
Min Mail Order EU: Nmc
Cat. Cost: 3 × 1st class.
Credit Cards: All major credit/debit cards
Specialities: *Agapanthus.*
Notes: Nursery at The Walled Garden at East Pennard.
Map Ref: C, B5

CPhi **ALAN PHIPPS CACTI** ⊠ €
62 Samuel White Road, Hanham, Bristol BS15 3LX
Ⓣ (0117) 9607591
Ⓦ www.cactus-mall.com/alan-phipps/index.html
Contact: A Phipps
Opening Times: 1000-1700 but prior phone call essential to ensure a greeting.
Min Mail Order UK: £5.00 + p&p
Min Mail Order EU: £20.00 + p&p
Cat. Cost: Sae or 2 × IRC (EC only).
Credit Cards: None
Specialities: *Mammillaria, Astrophytum* & *Ariocarpus.* Species & varieties will change with times. Ample quantities exist in spring. Limited range of *Agave.*
Notes: Euro accepted as cash only. Specimen-size plants not available by mail order.
Map Ref: C, A5 **OS Grid Ref:** ST644717

CPHo **THE PALM HOUSE** ⊠
8 North Street, Ottery St Mary, Devon EX11 1DR
Ⓣ (01404) 815450
Ⓜ 07815 673397
Ⓔ george@thepalmhouse.co.uk
Ⓦ www.thepalmhouse.co.uk
Contact: George Gregory
Opening Times: Mail order only. Open by appt. only.
Min Mail Order UK: £15.00
Min Mail Order EU: £10.00
Cat. Cost: 2 × 1st class.
Credit Cards: All major credit/debit cards
Specialities: Palms.
Notes: Also sells wholesale.

CPla **PLANT WORLD BOTANIC GARDENS** ⊠ ⊠ € ♿
St Marychurch Road, Newton Abbot, Devon TQ12 4SE
Ⓣ (01803) 872939
Ⓕ (01803) 875018

KEY		
	⊠ Mail order to UK or EU	⛫ Delivers to shows
	⊠ Exports beyond EU	€ Euro accepted
	♿ Accessible by wheelchair	◆ See Display advertisement

C

Ⓔ raybrown@plant-world-seeds.com
Ⓦ www.plant-world-seeds.com
Contact: Ray Brown
Opening Times: 0930-1700 7 days a week, Apr (Easter if earlier)-Oct.
Min Mail Order UK: Nmc
Min Mail Order EU: Nmc
Cat. Cost: 3 x 1st class or 2 x IRC.
Credit Cards: Visa, Access, EuroCard, MasterCard
Specialities: Alpines & unusual herbaceous plants.
Notes: Mail order for seed only. 4 acre garden correctly planted out as the map of the world. Tea room. Also sells wholesale.
Map Ref: C, C4

CPom **Pomeroy Plants**
Tower House, Pomeroy Lane, Wingfield, Trowbridge, Wiltshire BA14 9LJ
Ⓣ (01225) 769551
Ⓜ 07895 096564
Ⓔ drsimonyoung@yahoo.co.uk
Contact: Simon Young
Opening Times: Feb-Nov. Please phone first.
Cat. Cost: 2 × 1st class.
Credit Cards: None
Specialities: Hardy, mainly species, herbaceous perennials. Many unusual and often small numbers. Specialities *Allium*, *Salvia* & shade-lovers, esp. *Epimedium*.
Map Ref: C, B5 **OS Grid Ref:** ST817569

CPou **Pounsley Plants** ⊠ ♿ € ♿
Pounsley Combe, Spriddlestone, Brixton, Plymouth, Devon PL9 0DW
Ⓣ (01752) 402873
Ⓜ 07770 758501
Ⓕ (01752) 406682
Ⓔ pou599@aol.com
Ⓦ www.pounsleyplants.com
Contact: Mrs Jane Hollow
Opening Times: Normally 1000-1600 Mon-Sat but please phone first.
Min Mail Order UK: £10.00 + p&p
Min Mail Order EU: €20.00 + p&p
Cat. Cost: 2 × 1st class.
Credit Cards: None
Specialities: Unusual herbaceous perennials & *Clematis*. Comprehensive range of Old Roses & large selection of modern roses.
Notes: Mail order Nov-Feb only. Mail order roses bare root only. Also sells wholesale.
Map Ref: C, D3 **OS Grid Ref:** SX521538

CPrp **ProperPlants.com** ⊠ ⊠ ♿
Penknight, Edgcumbe Road, Lostwithiel, Cornwall PL22 0JD
Ⓣ (01208) 872291
Ⓔ info@ProperPlants.com
Ⓦ www.ProperPlants.com
Contact: Sarah Wilks
Opening Times: 1000-1800 or dusk if earlier, Tue & B/hols mid-Mar to end-Sep & by appt.
Min Mail Order UK: Nmc
Min Mail Order EU: Nmc
Cat. Cost: 4 × 1st class.
Credit Cards: All major credit/debit cards
Specialities: Wide range of unusual & easy herbaceous perennials, esp. of South African origin. Grasses. Less common herbs.
Notes: Partially accessible for wheelchair users.
Map Ref: C, C2 **OS Grid Ref:** SX093596

CQua **Quality Daffodils** ⊠ ⊠ € ◆
14 Roscarrack Close, Falmouth, Cornwall TR11 4PJ
Ⓣ (01326) 317959
Ⓜ 07989 243450
Ⓕ (01326) 317959
Ⓔ rascamp@daffodils.uk.com
Ⓦ www.qualitydaffodils.com
Contact: R A Scamp
Opening Times: Not open. Mail order only. Viewing by appt. only.
Min Mail Order UK: Nmc
Min Mail Order EU: Nmc
Cat. Cost: 4 × 1st class.
Credit Cards: All major credit/debit cards
Specialities: *Narcissus* hybrids & species. Some stocks are less than 100 bulbs.
Notes: Also sells wholesale.
Map Ref: C, D1

CRDP **R D Plants** ♿ ♿
Homelea Farm, Chard Road (A358), Tytherleigh, Axminster, East Devon EX13 7BG
Ⓣ (01460) 220206
Ⓕ (01460) 220206
Contact: Rodney Davey & Lynda Windsor
Opening Times: 1000-1600 most days, 1st Mar-end May. Open 1st Feb for hellebores.
Cat. Cost: None issued.
Credit Cards: None
Specialities: Double & anemone-centred hellebores. Choice plants for moist shade. Established garden-worthy plants in flower for most situations.
Map Ref: C, C4 **OS Grid Ref:** ST3203

CRHN **Roseland House Nursery** ⊠ ♿
Chacewater, Truro, Cornwall TR4 8QB
Ⓣ (01872) 560451
Ⓔ clematis@roselandhouse.co.uk
Ⓦ www.roselandhouse.co.uk

C

Contact: C R Pridham
Opening Times: 1300-1700 Tue & Wed, Apr-Sep. Other times by appt.
Min Mail Order UK: Nmc
Min Mail Order EU: Nmc
Cat. Cost: Online only.
Credit Cards: All major credit/debit cards
Specialities: Climbing & conservatory plants. Nat. Collections of *Clematis viticella* & *Lapageria rosea*. Named *Lapageria* in short supply but occasionally available.
Notes: Garden open to the public. Credit cards accepted from mail order customers only.
Map Ref: C, D1 **OS Grid Ref:** SW752445

CRos **ROSEMOOR GARDEN PLANT CENTRE (RHS)** ♿ ◆
RHS Garden, Rosemoor,
Torrington, Devon
EX38 8PH
Ⓣ (01805) 624067
Ⓕ (01805) 622422
Ⓔ rosemooradmin@rhs.org.uk
Ⓦ www.rhs.org.uk/rosemoor
Contact: Emma Van-Huysse or Sam Smith
Opening Times: 1000-1800 Mon-Sat, 11.30-1730 Sun, Apr-Sep. 1000-1700 Mon-Sat, 1030-1630 Sun, Oct-Mar.
Cat. Cost: None issued
Credit Cards: All major credit/debit cards
Specialities: Wide range of shrubs, herbaceous plants, climbers, alpines & seasonal lines, trying, where possible, to reflect the diversity of planting in the Garden. National Collection of *Ilex*.
Notes: Plants subject to seasonal availability but will help to source plants required.
Map Ref: C, B3 **OS Grid Ref:** SS500176

CRow **ROWDEN GARDENS** ⊠ ✈ ♿
Brentor, Nr Tavistock, Devon
PL19 0NG
Ⓣ (01822) 810275
Ⓔ rowdengardens1@btinternet.com
Ⓦ www.rowdengardens.com
Contact: John R L Carter
Opening Times: By appt only.
Min Mail Order UK: Nmc
Min Mail Order EU: Nmc
Cat. Cost: 6 × 1st class.
Credit Cards: None
Specialities: Aquatics, damp loving & associated plants incl. rare & unusual varieties. Nat. Collections of Water Iris. Some stock available in small quantities only.
Notes: Also sells wholesale.
Map Ref: C, C3

CRWN **THE REALLY WILD NURSERY** ⊠ ✈ €
19 Hoopers Way, Torrington, Devon
EX38 7NS
Nursery closing spring 2012
Ⓣ (01805) 624739
Ⓕ (01805) 624739
Ⓔ thereallywildnursery@yahoo.co.uk
Ⓦ www.thereallywildnursery.co.uk
Contact: Kathryn Moore
Opening Times: Not open. Mail order only.
Min Mail Order UK: £10.00 + p&p
Min Mail Order EU: £20.00 + p&p
Credit Cards: Paypal
Specialities: Wildflowers, bulbs & seeds.
Notes: Mail order all year round, grown to order (plants in pots or plugs). Credit card payment accepted via Paypal online only. Also sells wholesale.

CSam **SAMPFORD SHRUBS** ⊠ € ♿
Sampford Peverell, Tiverton, Devon
EX16 7EN
Ⓣ (01884) 821164
Ⓔ via website
Ⓦ www.samshrub.co.uk
Contact: M Hughes-Jones & S Proud
Opening Times: 1000-1700 Wed-Fri, 28th Mar-14th Sep incl.
Min Mail Order UK: Nmc
Cat. Cost: Free online or A5 sae.
Credit Cards: All major credit/debit cards
Specialities: Plants particularly suitable for naturalistic gardening.
Notes: Mail order only via dedicated ecommerce website. Despatched Oct-Mar.
Map Ref: C, B4 **OS Grid Ref:** ST043153

CSBt **ST BRIDGET NURSERIES LTD** ⊠ ⌂ ♿
Old Rydon Lane, Exeter, Devon
EX2 7JY
Ⓣ (01392) 873672
Ⓕ (01392) 876710
Ⓔ sales@stbridgetnurseries.co.uk
Ⓦ www.stbridgetnurseries.co.uk
Contact: Sales Dept
Opening Times: 0900-1700 Mon-Sat, 1030-1630 Sun. Closed Xmas Day, Boxing Day, New Year's Day & Easter Sunday.
Min Mail Order UK: Nmc
Cat. Cost: Free.
Credit Cards: All major credit/debit cards
Specialities: Large general nursery, with two garden centres.

KEY
⊠ Mail order to UK or EU ⌂ Delivers to shows
✈ Exports beyond EU € Euro accepted
♿ Accessible by wheelchair ◆ See Display advertisement

C

Notes: Mail order available, please contact for prices & carriage charges. Also sells wholesale.
Map Ref: C, C4 **OS Grid Ref:** SX955905

CSev **Lower Severalls Nursery** ⊠ ♿
Crewkerne, Somerset TA18 7NX
Ⓣ (01460) 73234
Ⓜ 07769 273829
Ⓔ mary@lowerseveralls.co.uk
Ⓦ www.lowerseveralls.co.uk
Contact: Mary R Pring
Opening Times: 1000-1700 Tue, Wed, Fri, Sat, Mar-end Sep. Closed Aug.
Min Mail Order UK: £20.00
Cat. Cost: 4 × 1st class.
Credit Cards: Visa, MasterCard
Specialities: Herbs, herbaceous.
Notes: Mail order perennials only.
Map Ref: C, B5 **OS Grid Ref:** ST457111

CSil **Silver Dale Nurseries** €
Shute Lane, Combe Martin, Devon EX34 0HT
Ⓣ (01271) 882539
Ⓔ silverdale.nurseries@virgin.net
Contact: Roger Gilbert
Opening Times: 1000-1700 7 days. Closed Nov-Jan.
Cat. Cost: 4 × 1st class.
Credit Cards: Visa, MasterCard, EuroCard
Specialities: Nat. Collection of *Fuchsia*. Hardy fuchsias (cultivars and species).
Map Ref: C, B3

CSna **Snape Cottage** ⊠
Chaffeymoor, Bourton, Dorset SP8 5BZ
Ⓣ (01747) 840330 (evenings only).
Ⓔ ianandangela@snapecottagegarden.co.uk
Ⓦ www.snapestakes.com
Contact: Mrs Angela Whinfield
Opening Times: 1400-1700 last w/end (Sat & Sun) in months Feb-Aug incl.
Min Mail Order UK: Nmc
Cat. Cost: Sae.
Credit Cards: None
Specialities: 'Old' forms of many popular garden plants. Plantsman's garden open same time as nursery. Stock available in small quantities. Snape Stakes plant supports.
Notes: Mail order *Galanthus* only. List issued in Feb. Group visits welcome all year.
Map Ref: C, B5 **OS Grid Ref:** ST762303

CSpe **Special Plants** ⊠ ⌂ €
Hill Farm Barn, Greenways Lane, Cold Ashton, Chippenham, Wiltshire SN14 8LA
Ⓣ (01225) 891686
Ⓔ derry@specialplants.net
Ⓦ www.specialplants.net
Contact: Derry Watkins
Opening Times: 1000-1700 7 days Mar-Oct. Other times please ring first to check.
Min Mail Order UK: £10.00 + p&p
Cat. Cost: 2 × 1st class for seed list.
Credit Cards: All major credit/debit cards
Specialities: Tender perennials, *Pelargonium*, *Salvia*, *Streptocarpus*, hardy geraniums, *Anemone*, *Erysimum*, *Papaver*, *Viola* & grasses. Many varieties propagated in small numbers only.
Notes: Mail order Sep-Mar only.
Map Ref: C, A5 **OS Grid Ref:** ST749726

CSPN **Sherston Parva Nursery** ⊠ ⊠ ⌂ € ♿
Malmesbury Road, Sherston, Wiltshire SN16 0NX
Ⓣ (01666) 840348
Ⓜ 07887 814843
Ⓔ sherstonparva@aol.com
Ⓦ www.sherstonparva.com
Contact: Martin Rea
Opening Times: 1000-1700 7 days 1st Feb-31th Dec. Closed Jan.
Min Mail Order UK: Nmc
Min Mail Order EU: Nmc
Cat. Cost: Free.
Credit Cards: MasterCard, Delta, Visa, Switch
Specialities: *Clematis*, wall shrubs & climbers.
Map Ref: C, A5

CSto **Stone Lane Gardens** ⊠
Stone Farm, Chagford, Devon TQ13 8JU
Ⓣ (01647) 231311
Ⓔ paul.bartlett@stonelanegardens.com
Ⓦ www.stonelanegardens.com
Contact: Paul Bartlett
Opening Times: 0900-1700 Mon-Fri. Collection at w/ends possible. Please phone first if travelling a long distance.
Min Mail Order UK: Nmc
Min Mail Order EU: Nmc
Cat. Cost: 6 × 1st class for colour catalogue with photos or online.
Credit Cards: All major credit/debit cards
Specialities: Comprehensive selection of wild origin *Betula* & *Alnus*, both bare-root & in pots. Choice selection of specially grafted cvs. Nat. Collection of Birch & Alder.
Notes: Arboretum open all year with summer sculpture exhibition (charges apply). Planting service available in West Country, details on request. Credit cards accepted online only. Also sells wholesale.
Map Ref: C, C3 **OS Grid Ref:** SX708908

C

CSuc **SURREAL SUCCULENTS** ⊠ € ◆
(Office) 5 Cober Crescent, Reawla, Hayle, Cornwall TR27 5HB
Ⓜ 07707 314823
Ⓔ info@surrealsucculents.co.uk
Ⓦ www.surrealsucculents.co.uk
Contact: Daniel Michael
Opening Times: Mail order only. Open by appt.
Min Mail Order UK: £1.99
Min Mail Order EU: £2.50
Cat. Cost: Online only.
Credit Cards: All major credit/debit cards
Specialities: Hardy & half-hardy succulents. *Aeonium*, *Echeveria*. Some in small quantities only. National Collection of *Aeonium* applied for.
Notes: Nursery located at Clowance Wood Nursery, Praze-an-Beeble, Cornwall TR14 0NW.
Map Ref: C, D1 **OS Grid Ref:** SW625344

CSut **SUTTONS SEEDS** ⊠
Woodview Road, Paignton, Devon TQ4 7NG
Ⓣ 0844 922 2899
Ⓕ 0844 922 2265
Ⓦ www.suttons.co.uk
Contact: Customer Services
Opening Times: Office: 0830-1700 Mon-Fri. Also answerphone.
Min Mail Order UK: Nmc
Min Mail Order EU: £5.00
Cat. Cost: Free.
Credit Cards: Visa, MasterCard, Switch, Delta
Specialities: Over 1,000 varieties of flower & vegetable seed, bulbs, plants & sundries.

CTca **TRECANNA NURSERY** ⊠ ✈ ⋒
Rose Farm, Latchley, Nr Gunnislake, Cornwall PL18 9AX
Ⓣ (01822) 834680
Ⓜ 07785 242148
Ⓔ mark@trecanna.com
Ⓦ www.trecanna.com
Contact: Mark Wash
Opening Times: Please note nursery is now open by prior appt.only, so please phone in advance. Nursery will be relocating during 2012/13.
Min Mail Order UK: £22.00
Min Mail Order EU: £45.00
Cat. Cost: £2.50
Credit Cards: All major credit/debit cards
Specialities: Hardy South African plants. Good collections of *Crocosmia*, *Eucomis*, *Kniphofia*, *Watsonia*, *Crinum*, *Albuca*, nerines, *Zantedeschia*, *Lachenalia* & *Moraea*. Wide range of dry bulbs from around the globe.
Notes: Talks to garden societies.
Map Ref: C, C3 **OS Grid Ref:** SX247733

CTho **THORNHAYES NURSERY** ⊠ €
St Andrews Wood, Dulford, Cullompton, Devon EX15 2DF
Ⓣ (01884) 266746
Ⓕ (01884) 266739
Ⓔ trees@thornhayes-nursery.co.uk
Ⓦ www.thornhayes-nursery.co.uk
Contact: K D Croucher
Opening Times: 0800-1600 Mon-Fri. 0930-1400 Sat.
Min Mail Order UK: £100
Min Mail Order EU: £100
Credit Cards: All major credit/debit cards
Specialities: A broad range of forms of ornamental, amenity & fruit trees incl. West Country apple varieties.
Notes: Limited wheelchair access. Also sells wholesale.
Map Ref: C, C4

CTrh **TREHANE NURSERY** ⊠ ⋒ ♿
Stapehill Road, Hampreston, Wimborne, Dorset BH21 7ND
Ⓣ (01202) 873490
Ⓕ (01202) 873490
Ⓔ nursery@trehane.co.uk
Ⓦ www.trehane.co.uk
Contact: Lorraine Keets
Opening Times: 0830-1630 Mon-Fri all year (excl. Xmas & New Year). 1000-1600 Sat Sun in spring & by special appt.
Min Mail Order UK: Nmc
Cat. Cost: £1.50 cat./book.
Credit Cards: All major credit/debit cards
Specialities: Extensive range of *Camellia* species, cultivars & hybrids. Many new introductions. Evergreen azaleas, *Pieris* & blueberries.
Notes: Also sells wholesale.
Map Ref: C, C6 **OS Grid Ref:** SU059000

CTri **TRISCOMBE NURSERIES** ⊠ ♿ ◆
West Bagborough, Nr Taunton, Somerset TA4 3HG
Ⓣ (01984):
Ⓔ triscombe.nurseries2000@virgin.net
Ⓦ www.triscombenurseries.co.uk
Contact: S Parkman

KEY
⊠ Mail order to UK or EU ⋒ Delivers to shows
✈ Exports beyond EU € Euro accepted
♿ Accessible by wheelchair ◆ See Display advertisement

C

Opening Times: 0900-1730 Mon-Sat. 1400-1730 Sun & B/hols.
Min Mail Order UK: Nmc
Cat. Cost: 1 × 1st class.
Credit Cards: None
Specialities: Trees, shrubs, roses, fruit, *Clematis*, herbaceous & rock plants.
Map Ref: C, B4

CTsd **TRESEDERS** ⊠ ♿
Wallcottage Nursery, Lockengate, St. Austell, Cornwall PL26 8RU
Ⓣ (01208) 832234
Ⓔ Treseders@btconnect.com
Ⓦ www.treseders.co.uk
Contact: James Treseder
Opening Times: 0900-1700 Mon-Sat, 1000-1600 Sun. Closed Wed.
Min Mail Order UK: Nmc
Min Mail Order EU: Nmc
Cat. Cost: Plant list available on request.
Credit Cards: All major credit/debit cards
Specialities: A wide range of choice & unusual plants grown in peat-free compost. Establishing collection of *Prostanthera*.
Notes: Plants sometimes only available in small quantities. Also sells wholesale.
Map Ref: C, C2 **OS Grid Ref:** SX034620

CTuc **EDWIN TUCKER & SONS** ⊠
Brewery Meadow, Stonepark, Ashburton, Newton Abbot, Devon TQ13 7DG
Ⓣ (01364) 652233
Ⓕ (01364) 654211
Ⓔ seeds@edwintucker.com
Ⓦ www.edwintucker.com
Contact: Geoff Penton
Opening Times: 0800-1700 Mon-Fri, 0800-1600 Sat.
Min Mail Order UK: Nmc
Min Mail Order EU: Nmc
Cat. Cost: Free.
Credit Cards: All major credit/debit cards
Specialities: Nearly 120 varieties of seed potatoes, incl. 50 organic varieties. Wide range of vegetables, flowers & green manures in packets. None treated. Nearly 200 varieties of organically produced seeds.
Notes: Also sells wholesale.
OS Grid Ref: SX756697

CWat **THE WATER GARDEN** ⊠ ♿
Hinton Parva, Swindon, Wiltshire SN4 0DH
Ⓣ (01793) 790558
Ⓕ (01793) 791298
Ⓔ mike@thewatergarden.co.uk
Ⓦ www.thewatergarden.co.uk
Contact: Mike & Anne Newman
Opening Times: 1000-1700 Wed-Sun.
Min Mail Order UK: £10.00 + p&p
Cat. Cost: 4 × 1st class.
Credit Cards: Visa, Access, Switch
Specialities: Water lilies, marginal & moisture plants, oxygenators & alpines.
Notes: Also sells wholesale.
Map Ref: C, A6

CWCL **WESTCOUNTRY NURSERIES** ⊠ ♿
Donkey Meadow, Woolsery, Devon EX39 5QH
Ⓣ (01237) 431111
Ⓔ info@westcountry-nurseries.co.uk
Ⓦ www.westcountry-nurseries.co.uk
Contact: Sarah Conibear
Opening Times: 1000-1600 Mar-Jul. Closed for lunch 1300-1330.
Min Mail Order UK: Nmc
Cat. Cost: 2 × 1st class + A5 sae for full colour cat.
Credit Cards: All major credit/debit cards
Specialities: *Lupinus*, *Lewisia*, *Hellebore*, *Clematis*, cyclamen, acers, lavender, select perennials, grasses, ferns & climbers. Nat. Collection of Lupins.
Map Ref: C, B2 **OS Grid Ref:** SS351219

CWGN **WALLED GARDEN NURSERY** ⊠ ♿
Brinkworth House, Brinkworth, Nr Malmesbury, Wiltshire SN15 5DF
Ⓣ (01666) 826637
Ⓔ f.wescott@btinternet.com
Ⓦ www.clematis-nursery.co.uk
Contact: Fraser Wescott
Opening Times: 1000-1700, 7 days Mar-Oct. 1000-dusk, Mon-Fri Nov & Feb. Closed Dec & Jan.
Min Mail Order UK: Nmc
Credit Cards: All major credit/debit cards
Specialities: *Clematis* & climbers, with a selection of unusual perennials & shrubs.
Map Ref: C, A6 **OS Grid Ref:** SU002849

CWib **WIBBLE FARM NURSERIES** ⊠ ♿
Wibble Farm, West Quantoxhead, Nr Taunton, Somerset TA4 4DD
Ⓣ (01984) 632303
Ⓕ (01984) 633168
Ⓔ sales@wibblefarmnurseries.co.uk
Ⓦ www.wibblefarmnurseries.co.uk
Contact: Mrs M L Francis
Opening Times: 0800-1700 Mon-Fri, 1000-1600 Sat. 1400-1600 Sun (open Sun Mar-Sep only). All year incl. some B/hols.
Min Mail Order UK: Nmc
Min Mail Order EU: Nmc
Cat. Cost: 3 × 1st class.
Credit Cards: All major credit/debit cards

Specialities: Growers of a wide range of hardy plants, many rare & unusual. Display gardens.
Notes: Also sells wholesale.
Map Ref: C, B4

CWil **Fernwood Nursery** ⊠ ✈ €
Peters Marland, Torrington, Devon EX38 8QG
Ⓣ (01805) 601446
Ⓔ hw@fernwood-nursery.co.uk
Ⓦ www.fernwood-nursery.co.uk
Contact: Howard Wills & Sally Wills
Opening Times: Any time by appt. Please phone or email first.
Min Mail Order UK: Nmc
Min Mail Order EU: Nmc
Cat. Cost: Sae for list.
Credit Cards: Paypal
Specialities: Nat. Collection of *Sempervivum*, *Jovibarba* & *Rosularia*.
Notes: Mail order for *Sempervivum*, *Jovibarba* & *Rosularia* only. 5 miles from RHS Rosemoor.
Map Ref: C, C3 **OS Grid Ref:** SS479133

CWiW **Windrush Willow** ⊠ €
Higher Barn, Sidmouth Road, Aylesbeare, Exeter, Devon EX5 2JJ
Ⓣ (01395) 233669
Ⓕ (01395) 233669
Ⓔ windrushw@aol.com
Ⓦ www.windrushwillow.com
Contact: Richard Kerwood
Opening Times: Mail order only. Open by appt.
Min Mail Order UK: Nmc
Min Mail Order EU: Nmc
Cat. Cost: 2 × 1st class.
Credit Cards: All major credit/debit cards
Specialities: *Salix*. Unrooted cuttings available Dec-Mar.
Notes: Also sells wholesale.

CWri **Nigel Wright Rhododendrons** ♿
The Old Glebe, Eggesford, Chulmleigh, Devon EX18 7QU
Ⓣ (01769) 580632
Ⓔ wrightrhodos@aol.com
Ⓦ www.wrightrhodos.com
Contact: Nigel Wright
Opening Times: By appt. only. 7 days.
Cat. Cost: 2 × 1st class.
Credit Cards: None
Specialities: *Rhododendron* & deciduous azaleas. 200 varieties field grown, root-balled, some potted. For collection only. Specialist grower. Free advice & planting plans.
Notes: Also sells wholesale.
Map Ref: C, B3 **OS Grid Ref:** SS684106

CWSG **West Somerset Garden Centre** ⊠ ♿
Mart Road, Minehead, Somerset TA24 5BJ
Ⓣ (01643) 703812
Ⓕ (01643) 706476
Ⓔ wsgc@btconnect.com
Ⓦ www.westsomersetgardencentre.co.uk
Contact: Ms J K Webber
Opening Times: 0800-1700 Mon-Sat, 1000-1600 Sun.
Min Mail Order UK: Nmc
Cat. Cost: None issued.
Credit Cards: Visa, Solo, Maestro, MasterCard
Specialities: Wide general range. *Ceanothus*. *Clematis* & rose varieties change throughout the season.
Map Ref: C, B4

CWVF **White Veil Fuchsias** ⊠ ♿
Verwood Road, Three Legged Cross, Wimborne, Dorset BH21 6RP
Ⓣ (01202) 813998
Contact: A. C. Holloway
Opening Times: 0900-1300 & 1400-1700 Mon-Sat, 1000-1300 & 1400-1600 Sun, Jan-Aug. Closed Sat & Sun, Sep-Dec.
Min Mail Order UK: 8 plants of your choice.
Cat. Cost: 4 × 1st class.
Credit Cards: None
Specialities: Fuchsias. Small plants grown from Jan-Apr. Available in small quantities only.
Map Ref: C, C6

Eastern

EABi **Alison Bilverstone** ⊠ €
22 Kings Street, Swaffham, Norfolk PE37 7BU
Ⓣ (01760) 725026
Ⓔ a.bilverstone@tiscali.co.uk
Contact: Alison Bilverstone
Opening Times: Not open. Mail order only.
Min Mail Order UK: Nmc
Min Mail Order EU: Nmc
Cat. Cost: A4 sae.
Credit Cards: None
Specialities: *Achemene*, *Kohleria* & *Smithiantha* rhizomes, available Dec to mid-Apr. Stocked in small quantities.

EACa **Alpine Campanulas (Bellflower Nursery)** ⊠ ⛟
Langham Hall Walled Garden, Langham, Nr Bury St Edmunds, Suffolk IP31 3EE
Ⓜ 07879 644958

KEY
⊠ Mail order to UK or EU ⛟ Delivers to shows
✈ Exports beyond EU € Euro accepted
♿ Accessible by wheelchair ◆ See Display advertisement

Ⓔ campanulas@btinternet.com
Ⓦ www.bellflowernursery.co.uk
Contact: Sue Wooster
Opening Times: 1000-1700 Thu & Fri, 1000-1300 Sat, Mar-Oct. Other times by appt.
Min Mail Order UK: £10.00
Cat. Cost: 1 × 1st class sae.
Credit Cards: None
Specialities: *Campanula*. Nat. Collection of Alpine Campanulas. Most stock in small numbers only.
Notes: Hardy plant nursery within the Walled Garden, Langham Hall, Nr Bury St Edmunds, Suffolk. Groups welcome by appt.
Map Ref: E, C3 **OS Grid Ref:** TL978691

EAmu **Amulree Exotics** ⊠ ♿
The Turnpike, Norwich Road (B1113), Fundenhall, Norwich, Norfolk NR16 1EL
Ⓣ (01508) 488101
Ⓕ (01508) 488101
Ⓔ SDG@exotica.fsbusiness.co.uk
Ⓦ www.turn-it-tropical.co.uk
Contact: S Gridley
Opening Times: 0930-1730 7 days spring-autumn, 1000-1630 7 days autumn-spring.
Min Mail Order UK: Nmc
Min Mail Order EU: Nmc
Cat. Cost: 2 × 1st class.
Credit Cards: Visa, MasterCard, Electron, Solo, Switch
Specialities: Hardy & half-hardy plants for home, garden & conservatory. Palms, bamboos, bananas, tree ferns, cannas, gingers, cacti, succulents & much more.
Notes: Also sells wholesale.
Map Ref: E, B3 **OS Grid Ref:** DX123740

EBak **B & H M Baker** ♿
Bourne Brook Nurseries, Greenstead Green, Halstead, Essex CO9 1RB
Ⓣ (01787) 476369
Contact: Clive Baker
Opening Times: 0800-1600 Mon-Fri, 0900-1200 & 1400-1600 Sat & Sun, Mar-30th Jun.
Cat. Cost: 2 × 1st class + 33p.
Credit Cards: All major credit/debit cards
Specialities: *Fuchsia* & conservatory plants.
Notes: Also sells wholesale.
Map Ref: E, C2

EBee **Beeches Nursery** ⊠ ♿
Village Centre, Ashdon, Saffron Walden, Essex CB10 2HB
Ⓣ (01799) 584362
Ⓕ (01799) 584421
Ⓔ sales@beechesnursery.co.uk
Ⓦ www.beechesnursery.co.uk
Contact: Alan Bidwell/Kevin Marsh
Opening Times: 0830-1700 Mon-Sat, 1000-1700 Sun & B/hols.
Min Mail Order UK: £15.00
Min Mail Order EU: £20.00
Cat. Cost: Online only.
Credit Cards: All major credit/debit cards
Specialities: Herbaceous specialists & extensive range of other garden plants. Rarieties available in ltd. numbers only.
Notes: Plants dispatched Oct-Feb only. Orders accepted throughout the year. No trees by mail order.
Map Ref: E, C2 **OS Grid Ref:** TL586420

EBtc **Botanica** ⊠
Chantry Farm, Campsea Ashe, Wickham Market, Suffolk IP13 0PZ
Ⓣ (01728) 747113
Ⓜ 07887 423964
Ⓕ (01728) 747725
Ⓔ sales@botanica.org.uk
Ⓦ www.botanica.org.uk
Contact: Daniel Everett
Opening Times: 1000-1700 6 days, summer. 1000-1700 5 days, August. 1000-1600 7 days, winter.
Min Mail Order UK: £15 + p&p
Cat. Cost: Online only.
Credit Cards: All, except American Express
Specialities: Range of rare & unusual hardy plants. All stock is English grown at our nursery and in non-peat based compost.
Notes: Also sells wholesale.
Map Ref: E, C3 **OS Grid Ref:** TM328550

ECGP **Cambridge Garden Plants** € ♿
The Lodge, Clayhithe Road, Horningsea, Cambridgeshire CB25 9JD
Ⓣ (01223) 861370
Ⓔ kit@cambridgegardenplants.co.uk
Contact: Kit Buchdahl
Opening Times: 1100-1730 Thu-Sun mid Mar-31st Oct. Other times by appt.
Cat. Cost: 4 × 1st class.
Credit Cards: None
Specialities: Hardy perennials incl. wide range of *Geranium*, *Allium*, *Euphorbia*, *Cyclamen*, *Digitalis*.
Map Ref: E, C2 **OS Grid Ref:** TL497637

ECho **Choice Landscapes** ⊠ ☒ ♿
Priory Farm, 101 Salts Road, West Walton, Wisbech, Cambridgeshire PE14 7EF
Ⓣ (01945) 585051
Ⓔ info@choicelandscapes.org
Ⓦ www.choicelandscapes.org

Contact: Michael Agg & Jillian Agg
Opening Times: By appt.
Min Mail Order UK: £12.00
Min Mail Order EU: £15.00 + p&p
Cat. Cost: 6 × 1st class or 6 IRC
Credit Cards: Visa, MasterCard
Specialities: Alpines, rhododendrons, bulbs, lilies & South African bulbs & seed.
Map Ref: E, B1

ECnt **Cants of Colchester Ltd** ⊠ ✈
Nayland Road, Mile End, Colchester, Essex CO4 5HA
Ⓣ (01206) 844008
Ⓕ (01206) 855371
Ⓔ finder@cantsroses.co.uk
Ⓦ www.cantsroses.co.uk
Contact: Angela Pawsey
Opening Times: 0900-1300, 1400-1630 Mon-Fri. Sat varied, please phone first. Sun closed.
Min Mail Order UK: Nmc
Min Mail Order EU: Nmc
Cat. Cost: Free
Credit Cards: Visa, MasterCard, Delta, Solo, Switch
Specialities: Roses. Unstaffed rose field can be viewed dawn-dusk every day from end Jun-end Sep.
Notes: Bare-root mail order end Oct-end Mar, containers Apr-Aug. Partial wheelchair access.
Map Ref: E, C3

ECou **County Park Nursery**
Essex Gardens, Hornchurch, Essex RM11 3BU
Ⓣ (01708) 445205
Ⓦ www.countyparknursery.co.uk
Contact: G Hutchins
Opening Times: 1000-1700 Mon-Sat excl. Wed, 1000-1700 Sun, Mar-Oct. Nov-Feb by appt. only.
Cat. Cost: Online only.
Credit Cards: None
Specialities: Alpines & rare and unusual plants from New Zealand, Tasmania & the Falklands. Many plants in small quantities only.
Map Ref: E, D2

ECrc **The Crocosmia Gardens** ⊠ ✈ €
9 North Street, Caistor, Lincolnshire LN7 6QU
Ⓣ (01472) 859269
Ⓜ 07506 441205
Ⓔ mark@thecrocosmiagardens.net
Ⓦ www.thecrocosmiagardens.net
Contact: Mark Fox
Opening Times: 1000-1700 Mon-Sun.
Min Mail Order UK: £5.00
Min Mail Order EU: Nmc
Credit Cards: None
Specialities: Nat. Collection of *Crocosmia*.
Map Ref: E, A1

ECre **Creake Plant Centre** ♿
Leicester Road, South Creake, Fakenham, Norfolk NR21 9PW
Ⓣ (01328) 823018
Ⓜ 07760 762499
Ⓔ trevor-harrison@btconnect.com
Ⓦ www.creakeplantcentre.co.uk
Contact: Mr T Harrison
Opening Times: 1000-1300 & 1400-1730 7 days excl. Xmas.
Cat. Cost: None issued
Credit Cards: All major credit/debit cards
Specialities: Unusual shrubs, herbaceous, conservatory plants, old roses. Hellebores.
Map Ref: E, B1 **OS Grid Ref:** TF864353

ECrN **Crown Nursery** ⊠ ♿
High Street, Ufford, Suffolk IP13 6EL
Ⓣ (01394) 460755
Ⓕ (01394) 460142
Ⓔ enquiries@crown-nursery.co.uk
Ⓦ www.crown-nursery.co.uk
Contact: Jill Proctor
Opening Times: 0900-1700 (1600 in winter) Mon-Sat.
Min Mail Order UK: Nmc
Credit Cards: All major credit/debit cards
Specialities: Mature & semi-mature native, ornamental & fruit trees. Heritage fruit varieties.
Notes: Mail order for small/young stock only. Also sells wholesale.
Map Ref: E, C3 **OS Grid Ref:** TM292528

ECtt **Cottage Nurseries** ⊠ ♿
Thoresthorpe, Alford, Lincolnshire LN13 0HX
Ⓣ (01507) 466968
Ⓕ (01507) 463409
Ⓔ bill@cottagenurseries.net
Ⓦ www.cottagenurseries.net
Contact: W H Denbigh
Opening Times: 0900-1700 7 days, 1st Mar-31st Oct. 1000-1500 w/ends only Nov-Feb.
Min Mail Order UK: £15.00
Cat. Cost: 3 × 1st class.

KEY
⊠ Mail order to UK or EU — Delivers to shows
✈ Exports beyond EU — € Euro accepted
♿ Accessible by wheelchair — ◆ See Display advertisement

Credit Cards: Visa, MasterCard, Maestro
Specialities: Hardy perennials. Wide general range.
Map Ref: E, A2 **OS Grid Ref:** TF423716

E

EDAr **D'ARCY & EVEREST** ⊠ ⌂ € ♿
(Office) PO Box 78, St Ives, Huntingdon, Cambridgeshire PE27 6ZA
Ⓣ (01480) 497672 answerphone
Ⓜ 07715 374440
Ⓕ (01480) 466042
Ⓔ angela@darcyeverest.co.uk
Ⓦ www.darcyeverest.co.uk
Contact: Angela Whiting, Richard Oliver
Opening Times: Mon-Fri, last week of Mar-Sep, except show dates. Winter by appt. Coach parties welcome by appt.
Min Mail Order UK: £15.00 + p&p
Min Mail Order EU: £30.00 + p&p
Cat. Cost: 6 × 1st class.
Credit Cards: None
Specialities: Alpines & sempervivums.
Notes: Nursery is at Pidley Sheep Lane (B1040), Pidley, Huntingdon, Cambs PE28 3FL.
Map Ref: E, C2 **OS Grid Ref:** TL338762

EDel **DELFLAND NURSERIES LTD** ⊠ ♿
Benwick Road, Doddington, March, Cambridgeshire PE15 0TU
Ⓣ (01354) 740553
Ⓕ (01354) 741200
Ⓔ info@delfland.co.uk
Ⓦ www.organicplants.co.uk
Contact: Jill Vaughan
Opening Times: 0900-1600 Mon-Fri, 0900-1300 Sat, all year. Additionally, at peak season, 0900-1600 Sat & 1000-1600 Sun.
Min Mail Order UK: £1.85
Cat. Cost: Free or online.
Credit Cards: All major credit/debit cards
Specialities: Vegetables. Bedding & container plants.
Notes: Mail order mainly veg. plants. Organic & peat-free for mail order plants only. Also sells wholesale.
Map Ref: E, C2 **OS Grid Ref:** TL386908

EDif **DIFFERENT PLANTS** ♿
The Mellis Stud, Gate Farm, Cranley Green, Eye, Suffolk IP23 7NX
Ⓣ (01379) 870291
Ⓔ rickwtrs@talktalk.net
Contact: Fleur Waters
Opening Times: Sat-Thu by appt. only.
Cat. Cost: 4 × 1st class.
Credit Cards: None
Specialities: *Mimulus aurantiacus* & hybrids.
Map Ref: E, C3

EECP **ESSEX CARNIVOROUS PLANTS** ⊠ ⌂
12 Strangman Avenue, Thundersley, Essex SS7 1RB
Ⓣ (01702) 551467
Ⓔ Mark@essexcarnivorousplants.com
Ⓦ www.essexcarnivorousplants.com
Contact: Mark Haslett
Opening Times: By appt. only.
Min Mail Order UK: Nmc
Min Mail Order EU: Nmc
Cat. Cost: 2 × 1st class or online.
Credit Cards: None
Specialities: Good range of carnivorous plants. *Sarracenia*, *Dionaea*. Some stock available in small quantities only.
Notes: Also sells wholesale.
Map Ref: E, D2 **OS Grid Ref:** TQ797875

EExo **THE EXOTIC GARDEN COMPANY** ♿
Saxmundham Road, Aldeburgh, Suffolk IP15 5JD
Ⓣ (01728) 454456
Ⓦ www.theexoticgardencompany.com
Contact: Matthew Couchy
Opening Times: 1000-1700 Mon-Sat, 1000-1600 Sun, Mar-Oct. 1000-dusk Nov-Dec. Closed Jan-Feb.
Cat. Cost: None issued.
Credit Cards: All major credit/debit cards
Specialities: General range of choice & some unusual perennials, shrubs, ferns, tree ferns, olives, palms, bamboos, herbs.
Map Ref: E, C3

EFar **FARNDALE PLANTS** ⊠
145 Fields Farm North, Sutton Bridge, South Lincolnshire PE12 9SN
Ⓣ (01406) 350969 evenings
Ⓜ 07722 389465
Ⓔ farndaleplants@btinternet.com
Contact: Allan Robinson
Opening Times: Mail order only.
Min Mail Order UK: 4 plants.
Cat. Cost: Sae or email for current list.
Credit Cards: None
Specialities: Small specialist nursery concentrating on hardy *Erodium* (species & hybrids) & *Geranium* (mostly species) plus various scarce dwarf perennials.
Notes: Plants usually despatched between Sep-Mar.

EFer **THE FERN NURSERY** ⊠ € ♿
Grimsby Road, Binbrook, Lincolnshire LN8 6DH
Ⓣ (01472) 398092
Ⓔ rtimm@fernnursery.co.uk
Ⓦ www.fernnursery.co.uk

Contact: R N Timm
Opening Times: 0900-1700 Fri, Sat & Sun Apr-Oct or by appt.
Min Mail Order UK: Nmc
Min Mail Order EU: Nmc
Cat. Cost: 2 × 1st class.
Credit Cards: None
Specialities: Ferns. Display garden.
Notes: Only plants listed in the mail order part of the catalogue will be sent mail order. Also sells wholesale.
Map Ref: E, A1 **OS Grid Ref:** TF212942

EFEx **FLORA EXOTICA** ⊠ ✈ €
Pasadena, South-Green, Fingringhoe, Colchester, Essex CO5 7DR
Ⓣ (01206) 729414
Ⓜ 07972 068679
Contact: J Beddoes
Opening Times: Not open. Mail order only.
Min Mail Order UK: Nmc
Min Mail Order EU: Nmc
Cat. Cost: 4 × 1st class.
Credit Cards: None
Specialities: Exotica flora incl. orchids.

EFly **THE FLY TRAP PLANTS** ⊠ ∩ € ♿
Cooke Road, Berghapton, Norwich, Norfolk NR15 1BA
Ⓣ (01508) 480348
Ⓜ 0776 92556
Ⓔ sales@tftplants.co.uk
Ⓦ www.tftplants.co.uk
Contact: Pauline Steward
Opening Times: By appt. only.
Min Mail Order UK: Nmc
Cat. Cost: 1 × 1st class sae
Credit Cards: None
Specialities: All kinds of carnivorous plants, from *Sarracenia*, *Drosera*, *Pinquicula*, to *Utricularia* aquatic plants.
Map Ref: E, C3

EGFP **GRANGE FARM PLANTS** ⊠ € ♿
Grange Farm, 38 Fishergate Road, Sutton St James, Spalding, Lincolnshire PE12 0EZ
Ⓣ (01945) 440240
Ⓜ 07742 138760
Ⓕ (01945) 440355
Ⓔ ellis.family@tinyonline.co.uk
Contact: M C Ellis
Opening Times: Mail order only. Open by appt. only.
Min Mail Order UK: Nmc
Min Mail Order EU: Nmc
Cat. Cost: 1 × 1st class.
Credit Cards: None
Specialities: Rare trees & shrubs, esp. *Juglans*, *Fraxinus*. Some species available in small quantities only.
Map Ref: E, B2 **OS Grid Ref:** TF382186

EGol **GOLDBROOK PLANTS** ⊠ ✈
Hoxne, Eye, Suffolk IP21 5AN
Ⓣ (01379) 668770
Ⓕ (01379) 668770
Contact: Sandra Bond
Opening Times: 1000-1700, Thu-Sun Apr-Sep, or by appt. Other times by appt.
Min Mail Order UK: £15.00 + p&p
Min Mail Order EU: £100.00 + p&p
Cat. Cost: 2 × 1st class.
Credit Cards: None
Specialities: Very large range of *Hosta*, esp. miniature & small varieties. Some small hostas available in ltd quantities. Larger hostas being phased out & sold off cheaply.
Notes: Also sells wholesale.
Map Ref: E, C3

EGri **D GRIFFIN**
Alafin, Langford Road, Maldon, Essex CM9 4SU
Ⓣ (01621) 858384
Ⓜ 07725 876187
Contact: D Griffin
Opening Times: Open by appt. only (not Wed.). Please phone mobile number for appt.
Credit Cards: None
Specialities: *Yucca*, *Agave*. All plants available in small numbers.
Map Ref: E, D2

EHoe **HOECROFT PLANTS** ⊠ € ♿
Severals Grange, Holt Road, Wood Norton, Dereham, Norfolk NR20 5BL
Ⓣ (01362) 684206
Ⓔ hoecroft@hotmail.co.uk
Ⓦ www.hoecroft.co.uk
Contact: Jane Lister
Opening Times: 1000-1600 Thu-Sun, 1st Apr-31st Oct or by appt.
Min Mail Order UK: Nmc
Min Mail Order EU: Nmc
Cat. Cost: 5 × 2nd class.
Credit Cards: None
Specialities: An extensive range of coloured & variegated-leaved shrubs & herbaceous perennials. 260 ornamental grasses. Free entry to display gardens.

KEY
⊠ Mail order to UK or EU ∩ Delivers to shows
✈ Exports beyond EU € Euro accepted
♿ Accessible by wheelchair ◆ See Display advertisement

Notes: Nursery 2 miles north of Guist on B1110.
Map Ref: E, B3 **OS Grid Ref:** TG008289

E

EHon **Honeysome Aquatic Nursery** ⊠
The Row, Sutton, Nr Ely, Cambridgeshire CB6 2PB
Ⓣ (01353) 778889
Ⓕ (01353) 777291
Ⓔ info@honeysomeaquaticnursery.co.uk
Ⓦ www.honeysomeaquaticnursery.co.uk
Contact: Mrs L S Bond
Opening Times: At all times by appt. only.
Min Mail Order UK: Nmc
Cat. Cost: 2 × 2nd class.
Credit Cards: Paypal
Specialities: Hardy aquatic, bog & marginal.
Notes: Also sells wholesale.
Map Ref: E, C2

EHul **Hull Farm** ⊠
Spring Valley Lane, Ardleigh, Colchester, Essex CO7 7SA
Ⓣ (01206) 230045
Ⓜ 07900 298366
Ⓔ jackfryer1@tiscali.co.uk
Ⓦ www.fryersfarmshop.co.uk
Contact: Jack Fryer
Opening Times: By appt. only. Please phone for appt.
Min Mail Order UK: £50.00 + p&p
Cat. Cost: 5 × 2nd class.
Credit Cards: MasterCard, Visa
Specialities: Conifers.
Notes: Also sells wholesale.
Map Ref: E, C3 **OS Grid Ref:** GR043274

EHyd **Hyde Hall Garden (RHS)** ♿ ◆
RHS Garden Shop & Plant Centre, Rettenden, Chelmsford, Essex CM3 8ET
Ⓣ (01245) 402113
Ⓕ (01245) 400013
Ⓦ www.rhs.org.uk
Contact: Alex Jobber
Opening Times: 0930-1600 Mon-Sat, 1000-1600 Sun, Nov-Feb. 0930-1800 Mon-Sat, 1100-1700 Sun, Mar-Oct. Closed Xmas Day & Easter Sun.
Credit Cards: All major credit/debit cards

EIri **Irisesonline** ⊠
Slade Cottage, Petts Lane, Little Walden, Essex CB10 1XH
Ⓣ (01799) 526294
Ⓔ sales@irisesonline.co.uk
Ⓦ www.irisesonline.co.uk
Contact: Clare Kneen
Opening Times: By appt. only.
Min Mail Order UK: Nmc
Cat. Cost: 3 × 1st class or online.
Credit Cards: None
Specialities: *Iris.* Small family-run nursery. Some varieties available in small quantities only.
Map Ref: E, C2 **OS Grid Ref:** TL546416

ELan **Langthorns Plantery** ⊠ ♿
High Cross Lane West, Little Canfield, Dunmow, Essex CM6 1TD
Ⓣ (01371) 872611
Ⓕ 0871 661 4093
Ⓔ info@langthorns.com
Ⓦ www.langthorns.com
Contact: E Cannon
Opening Times: 1000-1700 or dusk (if earlier) 7 days excl. Xmas fortnight.
Min Mail Order UK: £15.00
Cat. Cost: £1.50
Credit Cards: Visa, Access, Switch, MasterCard, Delta
Specialities: Wide general range with many unusual plants.
Notes: Mail order anything under 4ft tall. Mail order not available during spring & summer months.
Map Ref: E, D2 **OS Grid Ref:** TL592204

ELar **Larkspur Nursery** ⊠
Fourways, Dog Drove South, Holbeach Drove, Spalding, Lincolnshire PE12 0SD
Ⓣ (01406) 330830
Ⓔ info@larkspur-nursery.co.uk
Ⓦ www.larkspur-nursery.co.uk
Contact: Ashley Ramsbottom
Opening Times: Mail order only. Open by prior arrangement. See website for details of nursery Open Days in Jun.
Min Mail Order UK: Nmc
Min Mail Order EU: Nmc
Cat. Cost: 2 × 1st class.
Credit Cards: None
Specialities: Delphiniums & Abutilons. Also rare *Delphinium* seed for sale. Some varieties in small quantities. Order early to avoid disappointment.

ELau **Laurel Farm Herbs** ⊠ ♿
Main Road (A12), Kelsale, Saxmundham, Suffolk IP17 2RG
Ⓣ (01728) 668223
Ⓔ laurelfarmherbs@aol.com
Ⓦ www.laurelfarmherbs.co.uk
Contact: Chris Seagon
Opening Times: Please phone or check website for opening hours as times can vary.
Min Mail Order UK: 1 plant + p&p

Min Mail Order EU: 1 plant + p&p
Cat. Cost: Online only.
Credit Cards: Visa, MasterCard, Switch, Delta
Specialities: Herbs esp. rosemary, thyme, mint & sage.
Notes: Mail orders accepted by email, phone or post. Also sells wholesale.
Map Ref: E, C3

ELMC **L.M.C. Nurseries Ltd** ⊠
Somersham Road, Colne, Huntingdon, Cambridgeshire PE28 3NG
Ⓣ (01487) 842917
Ⓕ (01487) 842917
Ⓔ lmcnurseries@aol.com
Contact: Lynne Carter
Opening Times: Mon-Fri by appt. only. Please phone.
Min Mail Order UK: Nmc
Cat. Cost: A5 sae (letter rate postage) for list
Credit Cards: None
Specialities: *Clematis*, lavender, climbers, shrubs & hardy ferns. All in small quantities of 25 or less.
Notes: Phone or email for mail order enquiries and plant availability. Also sells wholesale.
Map Ref: E, C2 **OS Grid Ref:** TL3776

ELon **Long House Plants** ♿
The Long House, Church Road, Noak Hill, Romford, Essex RM4 1LD
Ⓣ (01708) 371719
Ⓕ (01708) 346649
Ⓔ tim@longhouse-plants.co.uk
Ⓦ www.longhouse-plants.co.uk
Contact: Tim Carter
Opening Times: 1000-1700 Fri, Sat & B/hols, 1000-1600 Sun, beginning Mar-end Sep, or by appt.
Cat. Cost: None issued.
Credit Cards: All major credit/debit cards
Specialities: Interesting range of choice shrubs, grasses & herbaceous perennials. Many unusual varieties.
Map Ref: E, D2 **OS Grid Ref:** TQ554194

EMal **Marshall's Malmaisons** ⊠ ♿
Hullwood Barn, Shelley, Ipswich, Suffolk IP7 5RE
Ⓣ (01473) 822400
Ⓜ 07768 454875
Ⓔ jim@malmaisons.plus.com
Ⓦ www.malmaisonsandiris.co.uk
Contact: J M Marshall/Sarah Cook
Opening Times: By appt. only.
Min Mail Order UK: £30.00 incl. p&p
Min Mail Order EU: £35.00 incl. p&p
Cat. Cost: 1st class sae.
Credit Cards: None
Specialities: Nat. Collections of Malmaison Carnations & Cedric Morris Irises. *Iris* stock only available in small quantities.
Notes: Also sells wholesale.
Map Ref: E, C3 **OS Grid Ref:** TM006394

EMic **Mickfield Hostas** ⊠ ⌂ € ♿
The Poplars, Mickfield, Stowmarket, Suffolk IP14 5LH
Ⓣ (01449) 711576
Ⓕ (01449) 711576
Ⓔ mickfieldhostas@btconnect.com
Ⓦ www.mickfieldhostas.co.uk
Contact: Mr & Mrs R L C Milton
Opening Times: For specified dates see catalogue or website.
Min Mail Order UK: Nmc
Min Mail Order EU: Nmc
Cat. Cost: 4 × 1st class.
Credit Cards: All, except American Express
Specialities: Holders of Nat. Collection of *Hosta* containing over 2000 varieties. See website for details of cvs held & latest availability. Will split parent plants for customers if practical. Also operates a waiting list for rarities.
Map Ref: E, C3 **OS Grid Ref:** TM136619

EMil **Mill Race Garden Centre** ⊠ ♿
New Road, Aldham, Colchester, Essex CO6 3QT
Ⓣ (01206) 242521
Ⓔ plantdesk@millracegardencentre.co.uk
Ⓦ www.millracegardencentre.co.uk
Contact: Annette Bayliss
Opening Times: 0900-1730 Mon-Sat, 1000-1630 Sun.
Min Mail Order UK: £9.00
Credit Cards: All major credit/debit cards
Specialities: Stock available in small quantities only.
Notes: Trees & large shrubs not sent by mail order.
Map Ref: E, C2 **OS Grid Ref:** TL918268

ENBC **Norfolk Bamboo Company** ⊠
Vine Cottage, The Drift, Ingoldisthorpe, King's Lynn, Norfolk PE31 6NW
Ⓣ (01485) 543935
Ⓜ 07970 310880
Ⓕ (01485) 543314

KEY
⊠ Mail order to UK or EU ⌂ Delivers to shows
☒ Exports beyond EU € Euro accepted
♿ Accessible by wheelchair ◆ See Display advertisement

E

Ⓔ Lewdyer@hotmail.com
Ⓦ www.norfolkbamboo.co.uk
Contact: Lewis Dyer
Opening Times: 1000-1600 Fri & 1000-1400 Sat, Apr-Sep, or by appt.
Min Mail Order UK: £10.00 + p&p
Cat. Cost: 1 × 1st class sae for price list.
Credit Cards: None
Specialities: Bamboos.
Map Ref: E, B2 **OS Grid Ref:** TF684334

EOHP **OLD HALL PLANTS** ⊠
1 The Old Hall, Barsham, Beccles, Suffolk NR34 8HB
Ⓣ (01502) 717475
Ⓔ info@oldhallplants.co.uk
Ⓦ www.oldhallplants.co.uk
Contact: Janet Elliott
Opening Times: By appt. only. Please phone first.
Min Mail Order UK: Nmc
Min Mail Order EU: Nmc
Cat. Cost: 4 × 1st class.
Credit Cards: Paypal
Specialities: A variety of rare herbs, house plants, *Plectranthus*. Some plants available in small quantities.
Notes: Partial wheelchair access. Paypal accepted for overseas orders only.
Map Ref: E, C3 **OS Grid Ref:** TM396904

EPau **PAUGERS PLANTS** ⊠ ♿
Bury Road, Depden, Bury St Edmunds, Suffolk IP29 4BU
Ⓣ (01284) 850527
Ⓜ 07906 618603
Ⓔ geraldine.arnold@btinternet.com
Ⓦ www.paugers-plants.co.uk
Contact: Geraldine Arnold
Opening Times: 0900-1730 Wed-Sat, 1000-1700 Sun & B/hols, 1st Mar-30th Nov.
Min Mail Order UK: Nmc
Cat. Cost: None issued.
Credit Cards: None
Specialities: Hardy shrubs & perennials in large or small quantities.
Notes: Also sells wholesale.
Map Ref: E, C2 **OS Grid Ref:** TL783568

EPfP **THE PLACE FOR PLANTS** ⊠ ⌂ € ♿
East Bergholt Place, East Bergholt, Suffolk CO7 6UP
Ⓣ (01206) 299224
Ⓕ (01206) 299229
Ⓔ sales@placeforplants.co.uk
Ⓦ www.placeforplants.co.uk
Contact: Rupert & Sara Eley
Opening Times: 1000-1700 (or dusk if earlier) 7 days. Closed Easter Sun. Garden open Mar-Oct.
Min Mail Order UK: Nmc
Cat. Cost: 2 × 1st class.
Credit Cards: All major credit/debit cards
Specialities: Wide range of specialist & popular plants. Nat. Collection of Deciduous *Euonymus*. 20 acre mature garden with free access to RHS members during season.
Notes: Mail order from Sep-Feb only.
Map Ref: E, C3

EPom **POMONA FRUITS LTD** ⊠
Pomona House, 12 Third Avenue, Walton-on-the-Naze, Essex CO14 8JU
Ⓣ 0845 676 0607
Ⓕ 0845 676 0608
Ⓔ Info@PomonaFruits.co.uk
Ⓦ www.PomonaFruits.co.uk
Contact: Ming Yang/Claire Higgins
Opening Times: Not open. Mail order only.
Min Mail Order UK: Nmc
Cat. Cost: Free.
Credit Cards: All major credit/debit cards
Specialities: Fruit stock.

EPot **POTTERTONS NURSERY** ⊠ ⊠ ⌂ € ♿
Moortown Road, Nettleton, Caistor, Lincolnshire LN7 6HX
Ⓣ (01472) 851714
Ⓕ (01472) 852580
Ⓔ sales@pottertons.co.uk
Ⓦ www.pottertons.co.uk
Contact: Robert Potterton
Opening Times: 1000-1600 Tue-Sun. Closed Mon except B/hols. By appt. only Nov-Feb.
Min Mail Order UK: Nmc
Min Mail Order EU: Nmc
Cat. Cost: £2.00 in stamps
Credit Cards: MasterCard, Visa
Specialities: Alpines, dwarf bulbs & woodland plants. Hardy orchids & *Pleione*.
Notes: External talks nationally & internationally to garden clubs & societies. Group nursery tours by arrangement.
Map Ref: E, A1 **OS Grid Ref:** TA091001

EPPr **THE PLANTSMAN'S PREFERENCE** ⊠ ⌂ ♿
Church Road, South Lopham, Diss, Norfolk IP22 2LW
Ⓣ Office (evenings): (01953) 681439
Ⓜ Nursery (day): 07799 855559
Ⓕ (01953) 688194
Ⓔ tim@plantpref.co.uk
Ⓦ www.plantpref.co.uk
Contact: Tim Fuller
Opening Times: 0930-1700 Fri, Sat & Sun Mar-Oct. Other times by appt.

Min Mail Order UK: Nmc
Min Mail Order EU: £30.00
Cat. Cost: Online only.
Credit Cards: All major credit/debit cards
Specialities: Hardy geraniums & ornamental grasses. Unusual & interesting perennials incl. shade/woodland. Some choice shrubs esp. *Caprifoliaceae*. Nat. Collection of *Molinia*.
Map Ref: E, C3 **OS Grid Ref:** TM041819

EPri **Priory Plants** ⊠ ♠ ♿
1 Covey Cottages, Hintlesham, Nr Ipswich, Suffolk IP8 3NY
Ⓣ (01473) 652656
Ⓕ (01473) 652656
Ⓔ sue.mann3@btinternet.com
Ⓦ www.prioryplants.co.uk
Contact: Sue Mann
Opening Times: By appt. only. Please ring first to avoid disappointment.
Min Mail Order UK: £15.00 + p&p
Min Mail Order EU: £25.00
Cat. Cost: Online only.
Credit Cards: None
Specialities: Cottage garden perennials, as well as increasing range of South African plants. *Agapanthus*, *Astrantia*, *Dierama*, *Geum*, Siberian *Iris*, *Kniphofia*, *Nerine*, *Tritonia*, *Tulbaghia* & *Watsonia*.
Notes: Sells at plant fairs & agricultural shows.
Map Ref: E, C3 **OS Grid Ref:** TM070448

EPts **Potash Nursery** ⊠ ♠ ♿
Cow Green, Bacton, Stowmarket, Suffolk IP14 4HJ
Ⓣ (01449) 781671
Ⓔ enquiries@potashnursery.co.uk
Ⓦ www.potashnursery.co.uk
Contact: M W Clare
Opening Times: Pre-ordered plants can be collected by appt. only.
Min Mail Order UK: £18.00
Cat. Cost: 4 × 1st class.
Credit Cards: Visa, Delta, MasterCard
Specialities: *Fuchsia*.
Map Ref: E, C3 **OS Grid Ref:** TM0565NE

EPyc **Pennycross Plants** ⊠ ♠
Earith Road, Colne, Huntingdon, Cambridgeshire PE28 3NL
Ⓣ (01487) 841520
Ⓔ salvias@pennycrossplants.co.uk
Ⓦ www.pennycrossplants.co.uk
Contact: Janet M Buist
Opening Times: 1000-1600 Mon-Fri, 1st Apr-31st Jul. Sep by appt.
Min Mail Order UK: Nmc
Cat. Cost: 1 × 2nd class for *Salvia* list only.
Credit Cards: None
Specialities: Hardy perennials. Salvias. Some plants available in ltd. quantities only. Will propagate salvias to order.
Notes: Mail order for young *Salvia* plants only.
Map Ref: E, C2 **OS Grid Ref:** TL378759

ERCP **Rose Cottage Plants** ⊠ ♠
Bay Tree Farm, Epping Green, Essex CM16 6PU
Ⓣ (01992) 573775
Ⓕ (01992) 561198
Ⓔ anne@rosecottageplants.co.uk
Ⓦ www.rosecottageplants.co.uk
Contact: Anne & Jack Barnard
Opening Times: By appt. & for special events (see website for details).
Min Mail Order UK: Nmc
Min Mail Order EU: £20.00
Cat. Cost: Online only
Credit Cards: All major credit/debit cards
Specialities: Bulbs.
Notes: Mail order, bulbs only.
Map Ref: E, B1 **OS Grid Ref:** TL435053

ERea **Reads Nursery** ⊠
Douglas Farm, Bungay, Suffolk NR35 2JG
Ⓣ (01986) 895555
Ⓔ plants@readsnursery.co.uk
Ⓦ www.readsnursery.co.uk
Contact: Stephen Read
Opening Times: Not open. Mail order only.
Min Mail Order UK: Nmc
Min Mail Order EU: Nmc
Cat. Cost: Free.
Credit Cards: All major credit/debit cards
Specialities: Unusual fruit trees. *Magnolia*.
Notes: Also sells wholesale.

ERod **The Rodings Plantery** ⊠ ♠ € ♿
Anchor Lane, Abbess Roding, Essex CM5 0JW
Ⓣ (01279) 876421
Ⓜ 07790 020940
Ⓔ janeandandy@therodingsplantery.co.uk
Ⓦ www.therodingsplantery.co.uk
Contact: Jane & Andy Mogridge
Opening Times: By appt. only. Occasional open days, please phone for details.
Min Mail Order UK: Nmc
Min Mail Order EU: £500.00 + p&p

KEY
⊠ Mail order to UK or EU ♠ Delivers to shows
✈ Exports beyond EU € Euro accepted
♿ Accessible by wheelchair ◆ See Display advertisement

E

E

Cat. Cost: 3 × 1st class.
Credit Cards: None
Specialities: Bamboos. Rare & unusual trees.
Map Ref: E, D2

ESem **Semps by Post** ⊠
28 Mill Road, Newbourne, Woodbridge, Suffolk IP12 4NP
Ⓣ (01473) 736440
Ⓔ Tricia@sempsbypost.co.uk
Ⓦ www.sempsbypost.co.uk
Contact: Tricia Newell
Opening Times: Not open.
Min Mail Order UK: Nmc
Min Mail Order EU: Nmc
Cat. Cost: Online only.
Credit Cards: Paypal
Specialities: *Sempervivum*. Some stock available in small quantities.

ESgI **Seagate Irises** ⊠ ✈ € ♿
A17 Long Sutton By-Pass, Long Sutton, Lincolnshire PE12 9RX
Ⓣ (01406) 365138
Ⓜ 07887 856389
Ⓔ sales@irises.co.uk
Ⓦ www.irises.co.uk
Contact: Julian Browse or Wendy Browse
Opening Times: 1000-1700 daily Apr-mid Jul. Please phone for appt. mid-Jul to Mar.
Min Mail Order UK: Nmc
Min Mail Order EU: Nmc. Carriage at cost.
Cat. Cost: £3.50 or €8.00.
Credit Cards: Maestro, Visa, MasterCard
Specialities: Different types of *Iris*, bearded, beardless & species hybrids with about 1000 varieties in all, both historic & modern. Nat. Collection of Historic Tall Bearded Irises (pre-1965). Some only available in small quantities. Many container-grown available to callers.
Map Ref: E, B1 **OS Grid Ref:** TF437218

EShb **Shrubland Park Nurseries** ⊠ ♠
Maltings Farm, Whatfield Road, Elmsett, Ipswich, Suffolk IP7 6LZ
Ⓣ (01473) 657012
Ⓜ 07890 527744
Ⓔ gill@shrublandparknurseries.co.uk
Ⓦ www.shrublandparknurseries.co.uk
Contact: Gill & Catherine Stitt
Opening Times: By prior arrangement only. Please phone/email before visiting or check website for details.
Min Mail Order UK: Nmc
Min Mail Order EU: £30.00
Cat. Cost: 6 × 2nd class or free by email.
Credit Cards: All major credit/debit cards, Nochex, Paypal
Specialities: Conservatory plants, succulents, hardy perennials, climbers, shrubs, ferns & grasses.
Map Ref: E, C3 **OS Grid Ref:** TM0534146646

ESty **Style Roses** ⊠ ✈ ♠ ♿
10 Meridian Walk, Holbeach, Spalding, Lincolnshire PE12 7NR
Ⓣ (01406) 424089
Ⓜ 07932 044093 or 07780 860415
Ⓕ (01406) 490006
Ⓔ info@styleroses.co.uk
Ⓦ www.styleroses.co.uk
Contact: Margaret Styles
Opening Times: Vary. Nursery address is different from office, so please make an appt. before visiting.
Min Mail Order UK: Nmc
Min Mail Order EU: Nmc
Cat. Cost: Free in UK.
Credit Cards: MasterCard, Visa, Maestro
Specialities: Standard & bush roses.
Notes: Export to EU during bare-root season Nov-Mar. Also sells wholesale.
Map Ref: E, B1

ESwi **Swines Meadow Farm Nursery** ⊠ ♠ € ♿ ◆
47 Towngate East, Market Deeping, Peterborough PE6 8LQ
Ⓣ 01778 343340
Ⓜ 07432 627766
Ⓔ ceveandsons@btconnect.com
Ⓦ www.swinesmeadowfarmnursery.co.uk
Contact: Colin Ward
Opening Times: 0900-1700 Mon-Sat, 1000-1600 Sun (summer); 0900-1600 Mon-Sat, 1000-1600 Sun (winter).
Min Mail Order UK: £10.00
Min Mail Order EU: £10.00
Credit Cards: All, except American Express
Specialities: Hardy exotics, tree ferns, bamboos & phormiums. Wollemi pine stockist. Many specialities available in small quantities only.
Map Ref: E, B1 **OS Grid Ref:** TF150113

EThi **Thistlefield Plants and Design** ⊠ ♠
65 Westgate Street, Shouldham, Kings Lynn, Norfolk PE33 0BL
Ⓣ (01366) 347365
Ⓜ 07899 994071
Ⓕ (01366) 347365
Ⓔ paul@thistlefieldplants.co.uk
Ⓦ www.thistlefieldplants.co.uk
Contact: Paul Welford

Opening Times: Not open. Sells at plant fairs & shows only.
Min Mail Order UK: Nmc
Cat. Cost: Online only.
Credit Cards: None
Specialities: Perennials. *Tricyrtis* available in small quantities only.

ETho **THORNCROFT CLEMATIS** ✉ ✈ ⌂ ♿
The Lings, Reymerston, Norwich, Norfolk NR9 4QG
Ⓣ (01953) 850407
Ⓕ (01953) 851788
Ⓔ sales@thorncroftclematis.co.uk
Ⓦ www.thorncroftclematis.co.uk
Contact: Peter Skeggs-Gooch
Opening Times: 1000-1600 Tue-Sat, Oct-Feb (closed Sun & Mon). 0900-1700 Tue-Sun, Mar-Sep, closed most Mondays but open B/hol Mon.
Min Mail Order UK: Nmc
Min Mail Order EU: Nmc
Cat. Cost: 6 × 2nd class.
Credit Cards: All major credit/debit cards
Specialities: *Clematis*.
Notes: Does not export to USA, Canada or Australia.
Map Ref: E, B3 **OS Grid Ref:** TG039062

EUJe **URBAN JUNGLE** ✉ ⌂
Ringland Lane, Old Costessey, Norwich, Norfolk NR8 5BG
Ⓣ (01603) 744997
Ⓕ (0709) 2366869
Ⓔ lizzy@urbanjungle.uk.com
Ⓦ www.urbanjungle.uk.com
Contact: Elizabeth Browne
Opening Times: 1000-1700 1st Feb-31st Oct 7 days incl B/hols. 1000-1600 Nov-Dec Thu, Fri, Sat, Sun. Closed Jan.
Min Mail Order UK: Nmc
Min Mail Order EU: Nmc
Credit Cards: All major credit/debit cards
Specialities: Wide range of choice plants from exotic bedding to hardy evergreens.
Notes: Display gardens & living walls. Limited wheelchair access.
Map Ref: E, B3 **OS Grid Ref:** TG1593612782

EWay **WAYSIDE AQUATICS** ✉
Blackmore Road, Doddinghurst, Brentwood, Essex CM15 0HU
Ⓣ (01277) 823603
Ⓔ sales@waysideaquatics.co.uk
Ⓦ www.waysideaquatics.co.uk
Contact: Anna Robinson
Opening Times: 1000-1700 Wed-Sun.
Min Mail Order UK: Nmc
Min Mail Order EU: Nmc
Cat. Cost: Online.
Credit Cards: All major credit/debit cards
Specialities: Range of water garden plants: waterlilies; floating plants; oxygenating plants; marginals; marsh plants. Some stock in small quantities.
Map Ref: E, D2 **OS Grid Ref:** TQ585995

EWes **WEST ACRE GARDENS** ⌂ ♿
West Acre, King's Lynn, Norfolk PE32 1UJ
Ⓣ (01760) 755562
Ⓔ info@westacregardens.co.uk
Ⓦ www.westacregardens.co.uk
Contact: J J Tuite
Opening Times: 1000-1700 7 days 1st Feb-30th Nov. Other times by appt.
Cat. Cost: None issued.
Credit Cards: Visa, MasterCard, Delta, Switch
Specialities: Very wide selection of herbaceous & other garden plants incl. *Rhodohypoxis* & *Primula auricula*.
Map Ref: E, B1 **OS Grid Ref:** TF792182

EWld **WOODLANDS**
Peppin Lane, Fotherby, Louth, Lincolnshire LN11 0UW
Ⓣ (01507) 603586
Ⓜ 07866 161864
Ⓔ annbobarmstrong@uwclub.net
Ⓦ www.woodlandsplants.co.uk
Contact: Ann Armstrong
Opening Times: Flexible, but please phone or email to avoid disappointment.
Cat. Cost: None issued.
Credit Cards: None
Specialities: Small but interesting range of unusual plants, esp. woodland and *Salvia*, all grown on the nursery in limited quantity.
Notes: Mature garden, art gallery & refreshments.
Map Ref: E, A2 **OS Grid Ref:** TF322918

EWll **THE WALLED GARDEN** ♿ ◆
Park Road, Benhall, Saxmundham, Suffolk IP17 1JB
Ⓣ (01728) 602510
Ⓕ (01728) 602510
Ⓔ sales@thewalledgarden.co.uk
Ⓦ www.thewalledgarden.co.uk
Contact: Jim Mountain

KEY
✉ Mail order to UK or EU ⌂ Delivers to shows
✈ Exports beyond EU € Euro accepted
♿ Accessible by wheelchair ◆ See Display advertisement

Opening Times: 0930-1700 Tue-Sun Mar-Nov, 0930-dusk Tue-Sat Nov-mid Feb.
Specialities: Tender & hardy perennials. For current information see website.
Map Ref: E, C3 **OS Grid Ref:** TM371613

G

EWoo WOOTTENS PLANTS ⊠ ♿
Wenhaston, Blackheath, Halesworth, Suffolk IP19 9HD
Ⓣ (01502) 478258
Ⓕ (01502) 478888
Ⓔ sales@woottensplants.co.uk
Ⓦ www.woottensplants.co.uk
Contact: M Loftus
Opening Times: 0930-1700 7 days.
Min Mail Order UK: Nmc
Min Mail Order EU: Nmc
Cat. Cost: Online only.
Credit Cards: All, except American Express
Specialities: *Pelargonium*, *Hemerocallis*, *Primula auricula*, *Iris*, *Chrysanthemum* & *Clivia*.
Notes: Also sells wholesale.
Map Ref: E, C3 **OS Grid Ref:** TM42714375

EWTr WALNUT TREE GARDEN NURSERY ⊠
Flymoor Lane, Rocklands, Attleborough, Norfolk NR17 1BP
Ⓣ (01953) 488163
Ⓔ info@wtgn.co.uk
Ⓦ www.wtgn.co.uk
Contact: Jim Paine & Clare Billington
Opening Times: 0900-1800 Tue-Sun Feb-Nov & B/hols.
Min Mail Order UK: Nmc
Cat. Cost: Online.
Credit Cards: All major credit/debit cards
Map Ref: E, B1 **OS Grid Ref:** TL978973

SCOTLAND

GAbr ABRIACHAN NURSERIES ⊠ ⌂ ♿
Loch Ness Side, Inverness, Inverness-shire IV3 8LA
Ⓣ (01463) 861232
Ⓔ info@lochnessgarden.com
Ⓦ www.lochnessgarden.com
Contact: Mr & Mrs D Davidson
Opening Times: 0900-1900 daily (dusk if earlier) Feb-Nov.
Min Mail Order UK: Nmc
Cat. Cost: 4 × 1st class.
Credit Cards: All major credit/debit cards
Specialities: Herbaceous perennials, old-fashioned *Primula*, *Helianthemum*, hardy geraniums, *Sempervivum* & *Primula auricula*.
Notes: Wheelchair access to nursery only.
Map Ref: G, B2 **OS Grid Ref:** NH571347

GAgs ANGUSPLANTS ⊠ ♿
3 Balfour Cottages, Menmuir, By Brechin, Angus DD9 7RN
Ⓣ (01356) 660280
Ⓜ 07972 026109
Ⓔ alison@angusplants.co.uk
Ⓦ www.angusplants.co.uk
Contact: Dr Alison S. Goldie & Mark A. Hutson
Opening Times: By appt. only. Please phone first. Light refreshments provided.
Min Mail Order UK: Nmc
Min Mail Order EU: Nmc
Cat. Cost: A5 sae
Credit Cards: None
Specialities: Predominantly *Primula auricula*, although other *Primula* species are offered. A few available in small quantities only.
Notes: Mail order available all year.
Map Ref: G, B3 **OS Grid Ref:** NO528643

GBBs BORDER BELLES ⊠ ♿
Old Branxton Cottages, Innerwick, Nr Dunbar, East Lothian EH42 1QT
Ⓣ (01368) 840325
Ⓔ mail@borderbelles.com
Ⓦ www.borderbelles.com
Contact: Gillian Moynihan
Opening Times: Open by appt. only.
Min Mail Order UK: Nmc
Min Mail Order EU: On request
Cat. Cost: Online only.
Credit Cards: All major credit/debit cards
Specialities: Hardy perennials & woodland plants.
Notes: Also sells wholesale.
Map Ref: G, C3

GBee BEECHES COTTAGE NURSERY ♿
High Boreland, Lesmahagow, South Lanarkshire ML11 9PY
Ⓣ (01555) 893369
Ⓜ 07930 343131
Ⓔ thebeeches.nursery@talktalk.net
Ⓦ www.beechescottage.co.uk
Contact: Margaret Harrison, Steven Harrison
Opening Times: 1000-1630 7 days incl. Apr-end Jun. 1000-1630 Wed-Sat, Jul-end Sep.
Cat. Cost: None issued.
Credit Cards: None
Specialities: Traditional & unusual hardy cottage garden perennials which can be seen growing in display gardens at 850ft. Some plants available in small quantities only. Hanging basket specialists. Cottage gardens designed and planted.
Notes: Wheelchair access to nursery only. Also sells wholesale.
Map Ref: G, C2 **OS Grid Ref:** NS837403

GBin **BINNY PLANTS** ⊠ € ♿
West Lodge, Binny Estate, Ecclesmachan Road, Nr Broxbourn, West Lothian EH52 6NL
Ⓣ (01506) 858931
Ⓜ 07753 626117
Ⓔ contact@binnyplants.com
Ⓦ www.binnyplants.com
Contact: Billy Carruthers
Opening Times: 1000-1700 7 days. Closed mid-Dec to mid-Jan.
Min Mail Order UK: £25.00
Min Mail Order EU: £25.00
Cat. Cost: £2.50 refundable on ordering.
Credit Cards: Visa, MasterCard, EuroCard, Maestro
Specialities: Perennials incl. *Astilbe*, *Geranium*, *Hosta*, *Paeonia* & *Iris*. Plus large selection of grasses & ferns.
Notes: Mail order Sep-Apr only. Also sells wholesale.
Map Ref: G, C3 **OS Grid Ref:** NT050732

GBuc **BUCKLAND PLANTS** ⊠ € ♿
Whinnieliggate, Kirkcudbright, Kirkcudbrightshire DG6 4XP
Ⓣ (01557) 331323
Ⓕ (01557) 331323
Ⓔ via website
Ⓦ www.bucklandplants.co.uk
Contact: Rob or Dina Asbridge
Opening Times: 1000-1700 Thu-Sun 1st Mar-1st Nov & B/hols.
Min Mail Order UK: £20.00 + p&p
Min Mail Order EU: £50.00 + p&p
Cat. Cost: 3 × 1st class.
Credit Cards: All major credit/debit cards
Specialities: A very wide range of scarce herbaceous, woodland plants & larger alpines incl. *Anemone*, *Cardamine*, *Erythronium*, *Helleborus*, *Lilium*, *Meconopsis*, *Nomocharis*, *Primula*, *Tricyrtis* & *Trillium*.
Notes: Assisted wheelchair access.
Map Ref: G, D2 **OS Grid Ref:** NX719524

GCal **CALLY GARDENS** ⊠ ♿
Gatehouse of Fleet, Castle Douglas, Kirkcudbrightshire DG7 2DJ
Ⓣ (01557) 815029 recorded information only.
Ⓔ info@callygardens.co.uk
Ⓦ www.callygardens.co.uk
Contact: Michael Wickenden
Opening Times: 1000-1730 Sat-Sun, 1400-1730 Tue-Fri. Easter Sat-last Sun in Sept.
Min Mail Order UK: £15.00 + p&p
Cat. Cost: 3 × 1st class.
Credit Cards: None
Specialities: Unusual perennials & grasses. Some rare shrubs, climbers & conservatory plants. 3500 varieties growing in an 2.7 acre walled garden built in the 1760s.
Notes: Also sells wholesale.
Map Ref: G, D2 **OS Grid Ref:** NX604549

GCoc **JAMES COCKER & SONS** ⊠ ♿
Whitemyres, Lang Stracht, Aberdeen, Aberdeenshire AB15 6XH
Ⓣ (01224) 313261
Ⓕ (01224) 312531
Ⓔ sales@roses.uk.com
Ⓦ www.roses.uk.com
Contact: Alec Cocker
Opening Times: 0900-1700 Mon-Fri.
Min Mail Order UK: Nmc
Min Mail Order EU: £7.70 + p&p
Cat. Cost: Free
Credit Cards: Visa, MasterCard, Delta, Maestro
Specialities: Roses.
Notes: Also sells wholesale.
Map Ref: G, B3

GCra **CRAIGIEBURN GARDEN** ♿
Craigieburn House, by Moffat, Dumfriesshire DG10 9LF
Ⓣ (01683) 221758
Ⓜ 07899 055114
Ⓔ ajmw1@aol.com
Ⓦ www.craigieburngarden.com
Contact: Janet & Andrew Wheatcroft
Opening Times: 1030-1800 daily, Easter-31st Oct. Other times by appt.
Specialities: *Meconopsis* plants for damp gardens, herbaceous perennials.
Map Ref: G, D3

GCro **CROFT 16 DAFFODILS** ⊠
16 Midtown of Inverasdale, Poolewe, Achnasheen, Ross-shire IV22 2LW
Ⓣ (01445) 781717
Ⓔ sales@croft16daffodils.co.uk
Ⓦ www.croft16daffodils.co.uk
Contact: Duncan & Kate Donald
Opening Times: By appt. only. Please phone or email first.
Min Mail Order UK: Nmc
Min Mail Order EU: Nmc
Cat. Cost: Online. Customers without internet access send 4 × 1st for Sales List.
Credit Cards: Paypal
Specialities: Daffodils bred pre-1930.

KEY
⊠ Mail order to UK or EU | Delivers to shows
Exports beyond EU | € Euro accepted
♿ Accessible by wheelchair | ◆ See Display advertisement

Awarded full Nat. Collection status (2010).
Notes: Please order by Jul if possible as limited availability. Orders unfulfilled in one season will take priority the following year. Customers outside the EU should contact nursery.
Map Ref: G, A1 **OS Grid Ref:** NG822851

GFai **Fairholm Plants** ⊠ €
Fairholm, Larkhall, Lanarkshire ML9 2UQ
Ⓣ (01698) 881671
Ⓕ (01698) 888135
Ⓔ fairholm.plants@stevenson-hamilton.co.uk
Contact: Mrs J M Hamilton
Opening Times: Apr-Oct by appt.
Min Mail Order UK: Nmc
Cat. Cost: 1 × 2nd class for descriptive list.
Credit Cards: None
Specialities: *Abutilon* & unusual half-hardy perennials esp. South African. Nat. Collection of *Abutilon* cvs. Plants & rooted cuttings available in small quantities only.
Notes: Mail order for young/small plants.
Map Ref: G, C2 **OS Grid Ref:** NS754515

GGal **Galloway Plants** ⊠ ♿
Claymoddie, Whithorn, Newton Stewart, Dumfries & Galloway DG8 8LX
Ⓣ (01988) 500422
Ⓔ gallowayplants@aol.com
Ⓦ www.gallowayplants.co.uk
Contact: Robin & Mary Nicholson
Opening Times: 1400-1700 Fri, Sat & Sun, 2nd Apr-12th Sep 2010, other times by prior appt.
Min Mail Order UK: £50.00 + p&p
Min Mail Order EU: £50.00 + p&p
Cat. Cost: 2 × 1st class.
Credit Cards: None
Specialities: Southern hemisphere *Hydrangea*. Available in small quantities only.
Notes: Also sells wholesale.
Map Ref: G, D2 **OS Grid Ref:** NX450377

GGGa **Glendoick Gardens Ltd** ⊠ ✈ ♿
Glendoick, Perth, Perthshire PH2 7NS
Ⓣ (01738) 860205
Ⓕ (01738) 860630
Ⓔ orders@glendoick.com
Ⓦ www.glendoick.com
Contact: Kenneth Cox
Opening Times: Nursery not open to the public. Garden centre open 0900-1730 (summer), 0900-1700 (winter) 7 days. Gardens open Apr & May, details on website.
Min Mail Order UK: £40.00
Min Mail Order EU: £100.00
Cat. Cost: £1.00.
Credit Cards: All, except American Express
Specialities: Rhododendrons, azaleas and ericaceous, *Primula* & *Meconopsis*. Plants from wild seed. Many catalogue plants available at garden centre. 3 Nat. Collections.
Notes: Wheelchair access to Garden Centre.
Map Ref: G, C3

GJos **Jo's Garden Enterprise** ♿
Easter Balmungle Farm, Eathie Road, by Rosemarkie, Ross-shire IV10 8SL
Ⓣ (01381) 621006
Ⓔ jos_garden_enterprise@hotmail.co.uk
Contact: Joanna Chance
Opening Times: 1000 to dusk, 7 days.
Cat. Cost: None.
Credit Cards: None
Specialities: Alpines & herbaceous perennials. Selection of native wild flowers.
Map Ref: G, B2 **OS Grid Ref:** NH600742

GKev **Kevock Garden Plants** ⊠ ⌂ €
Kevock Road, Lasswade, Midlothian EH18 1HT
Ⓣ 0131 454 0660
Ⓜ 07811 321585
Ⓕ 0131 454 0660
Ⓔ info@kevockgarden.co.uk
Ⓦ www.kevockgarden.co.uk
Contact: Stella Rankin
Opening Times: Not open. Mail order & plant stalls only.
Min Mail Order UK: £25.00
Min Mail Order EU: £25.00
Cat. Cost: 4 × 1st class.
Credit Cards: Visa, MasterCard, Switch
Specialities: Chinese & Himalayan plants. *Androsace, Daphne, Paeonia, Primula, Meconopsis, Iris,* woodland plants, alpines, rock, marginal, bog & bulbs.
Notes: Also sells wholesale.

GKin **Kinlochlaich Garden Plant Centre**
Appin, Argyll PA38 4BB
Ⓣ (01631) 730342
Ⓜ 07881 525754
Ⓔ fiona@kinlochlaich.plus.com
Ⓦ www.kinlochlaichgardencentre.co.uk
Contact: Fiona Hutchison
Opening Times: 0900-1730, 7 days.
Cat. Cost: None issued
Credit Cards: All major credit/debit cards
Specialities: Hardy shrubs, trees, azaleas, perennials. Also Gulf Stream plants such as *Tropaeolum, Embothrium, Eucryphia, Drymis* & more. Good selection of hardy seaside plants.

Notes: Do not offer mail order but will post where possible.
Map Ref: G, C2

GLin **Linn Botanic Gardens** € ♿
Cove, Helensburgh, Dunbartonshire G84 0NR
Ⓣ (01436) 842084
Ⓜ 07747 416342
Ⓔ jamie@linnbotanicgardens.org.uk
Ⓦ www.linnbotanicgardens.org.uk
Contact: Jamie Taggart
Opening Times: 1100-1700, 7 days.
Cat. Cost: 4 × 1st class or by email.
Credit Cards: None
Specialities: Small plant sales area offering diverse range of plants. Botanic Gardens open (charges apply).
Notes: Wheelchair access to plant sales area but not gardens.
Map Ref: G, C2 **OS Grid Ref:** NS223827

GLog **Logie Steading Plants** ♿
Forres, Moray IV36 2QN
Ⓣ (01309) 611222 or 611278
Ⓕ (01309) 611300
Ⓔ panny@logie.co.uk
Ⓦ www.logie.co.uk
Contact: Mrs Panny Laing
Opening Times: 1030-1700 hours, 7 days, April-end Oct.
Credit Cards: All major credit/debit cards
Specialities: Unusual hardy plants, grown in Scotland for Scottish gardens. Large range of hardy geraniums, bold herbaceous plants, grasses & marginal plants.
Notes: Logie House Garden open every day. Café, farm shop, gallery, secondhand books, antiques, river walk, heritage centre.
Map Ref: G, B2 **OS Grid Ref:** NJ006504

GMaP **Macplants** ✉ 🚚 ♿
Berrybank Nursery, 5 Boggs Holdings, Pencaitland, East Lothian EH34 5BA
Ⓣ (01875) 341179
Ⓕ (01875) 340842
Ⓔ sales@macplants.co.uk
Ⓦ www.macplants.co.uk
Contact: Gavin McNaughton
Opening Times: 1030-1700, 7 days, Mar-end Sep.
Min Mail Order UK: Nmc
Cat. Cost: 4 × 2nd class.
Credit Cards: MasterCard, Switch, Visa
Specialities: Herbaceous perennials, alpines, hardy ferns, violas & grasses. *Meconopsis*. National Collection of *Sanguisorba*.
Notes: Also sells wholesale.
Map Ref: G, C3 **OS Grid Ref:** NT447703

GPoy **Poyntzfield Herb Nursery** ✉ ✈ ♿
Nr Balblair, Black Isle, Dingwall, Ross-shire IV7 8LX
Ⓣ (01381) 610352
Ⓕ (01381) 610352
Ⓔ info@poyntzfieldherbs.co.uk
Ⓦ www.poyntzfieldherbs.co.uk
Contact: Duncan Ross
Opening Times: 1300-1700 Mon-Sat 1st Mar-30th Sep, 1300-1700 Sun May-Aug.
Min Mail Order UK: £10.00 + p&p
Min Mail Order EU: £10.00 + p&p
Cat. Cost: 4 × 1st class.
Credit Cards: All major credit/debit cards
Specialities: Over 400 popular, unusual & rare herbs esp. medicinal. Also seeds.
Notes: Phone between 1200-1300 & 1800-1900 Mon-Sat only.
Map Ref: G, B2 **OS Grid Ref:** NH711642

GPPs **POGS Penstemons** ✉ €
Drumterlie Farmhouse, Newton Stewart, Wigtownshire DG8 6QG
Ⓣ (01671) 401666
Ⓜ 07905 825818
Ⓔ pogspenstemons@yahoo.co.uk
Ⓦ www.pogspenstemons.co.uk
Contact: Allison Fitz-Earle
Opening Times: Not open. Mail order only.
Min Mail Order UK: Nmc
Min Mail Order EU: Nmc
Cat. Cost: Free.
Credit Cards: All major credit/debit cards
Specialities: Penstemons.
Notes: Mail order plants available all year. Also sells wholesale.

GPri **Privick Mill Nursery** ✉ ♿
Privick Mill Road, Annbank, Ayr KA6 5JA
Ⓣ (01292) 521003
Ⓔ jackie.jess@yahoo.com
Ⓦ www.privickmillnursery.co.uk
Contact: Jackie Jess
Opening Times: By appt. only for collection of plants.
Min Mail Order UK: Nmc
Min Mail Order EU: Nmc
Cat. Cost: None.
Credit Cards: None
Specialities: Soft fruit bushes. Blueberries. Black raspberries. *Rubus* hybrids. Available in small quantities only. All plants organically grown but not certified by Soil Assoc.

KEY
✉ Mail order to UK or EU 🚚 Delivers to shows
✈ Exports beyond EU € Euro accepted
♿ Accessible by wheelchair ◆ See Display advertisement

Notes: Also sells wholesale.
Map Ref: G, D2 **OS Grid Ref:** NS405224

GQue **QUERCUS GARDEN PLANTS** ♿
Rankeilour Gardens, Rankeilour Estate, Springfield, Fife KY15 5RE
Ⓣ (01337) 810444
Ⓔ colin@quercus.uk.net
Ⓦ www.quercus.uk.net
Contact: Colin McBeath, Alyson Yorkston
Opening Times: 1000-1700 Wed-Sun, 1st w/end Apr-mid Oct. 1000-1400 Sat only, mid Oct-end Mar. Closed Xmas fortnight.
Cat. Cost: 4 × 1st class.
Credit Cards: All major credit/debit cards
Specialities: Easy & unusual plants for contemporary Scottish gardens.
Notes: Delivery service available on large orders at nursery's discretion.
Map Ref: G, C3 **OS Grid Ref:** NO330118

GQui **QUINISH GARDEN NURSERY** ⊠
Dervaig, Isle of Mull, Argyll PA75 6QL
Ⓣ (01688) 400344
Ⓕ (01688) 400344
Ⓔ quinishplants@aol.com
Ⓦ www.Q-gardens.org
Contact: Nicholas Reed
Opening Times: By appt. only.
Min Mail Order UK: Nmc
Min Mail Order EU: Nmc
Cat. Cost: 2 × 1st class.
Credit Cards: None
Specialities: Choice garden shrubs & conservatory plants.
Map Ref: G, C1

GSPN **SPRING PARK NURSERY** ⊠ €
Drumterlie Farmhouse, Newton Stewart, Wigtownshire DG8 6QG
Ⓣ (01671) 401666
Ⓜ 07905 825818
Ⓔ julianfitzearle@aol.com
Ⓦ www.springparknursery.co.uk
Contact: Julian Fitz-Earle
Opening Times: Not open. Mail order only.
Min Mail Order UK: Nmc
Min Mail Order EU: Nmc
Cat. Cost: Free.
Credit Cards: All major credit/debit cards
Specialities: Heathers.
Notes: Mail order plants available all year. Also sells wholesale.

GTwe **J TWEEDIE FRUIT TREES** ⊠
Maryfield Road Nursery, Nr Terregles, Dumfriesshire DG2 9TH
Ⓣ (01387) 720880
Contact: John Tweedie
Opening Times: Please ring for times. Collections by appt.
Min Mail Order UK: Nmc
Cat. Cost: Sae
Credit Cards: None
Specialities: Fruit trees & bushes. A wide range of old & new varieties.
Map Ref: G, D2

N. IRELAND & REPUBLIC

IArd **ARDCARNE GARDEN CENTRE** € ♿
Ardcarne, Boyle, Co. Roscommon, Republic of Ireland
Ⓣ (353) 7196 67091
Ⓕ (353) 7196 67341
Ⓔ ardcarne@indigo.ie
Ⓦ www.ardcarneplantsplus.ie
Contact: James Wickham, Mary Frances Dwyer, Kirsty Ainge
Opening Times: 0900-1800 Mon-Sat, 1300-1800 Sun & B/hols.
Credit Cards: Access, Visa, American Express
Specialities: Native & unusual trees, perennials, roses, plants for coastal areas, fruit trees & vegetable plants, specimen plants & semi-mature trees. Wide general range.
Map Ref: I, B1

IBal **BALI-HAI MAIL ORDER NURSERY** ⊠ ☒ €
42 Largy Road, Carnlough, Ballymena, Co. Antrim, N. Ireland BT44 0EZ
Ⓣ 028 2888 5289
Ⓜ 07708 257164
Ⓕ 028 2888 5289
Ⓔ balihainursery@btinternet.com
Ⓦ www.mailorderplants4me.com
Contact: Mrs M E Scroggy
Opening Times: Mon-Sat by appt. only.
Min Mail Order UK: Nmc
Min Mail Order EU: Nmc
Cat. Cost: Online only.
Credit Cards: All major credit/debit cards
Specialities: Nat. Collection of *Hosta*, part planted in 1.5 acres, open to the public by appt. *Agapanthus*, *Crocosmia*, *Rhodohypoxis*, tree ferns & other perennials.
Notes: Exports beyond EU restricted to bare root perennials, no grasses. *Hostas* grown to order. Also sells wholesale.
Map Ref: I, A3 **OS Grid Ref:** D287184

IBlr **BALLYROGAN NURSERIES** ⊠ € ♿
The Grange, Ballyrogan, Newtownards, Co. Down, N. Ireland BT23 4SD
Ⓣ 028 9181 0451 (evenings)

Ⓔ gary.dunlop@btinternet.com
Contact: Gary Dunlop
Opening Times: Only open by appt.
Min Mail Order UK: £10.00 + p&p
Min Mail Order EU: £20.00 + p&p
Cat. Cost: 2 × 1st class.
Credit Cards: None
Specialities: Choice herbaceous. *Agapanthus, Celmisia, Crocosmia, Rodgersia, Iris, Dierama, Erythronium* & *Roscoea.*
Notes: Also sells wholesale.

IBoy **BOYNE GARDEN CENTRE** €
Ardcalf, Slane, Co. Meath,
Republic of Ireland
Ⓣ 00353 (0)419 824350
Ⓕ 00353 (0)419 824350
Ⓔ boynegardencentre@eircom.net
Ⓦ www.boynegardencentre.com
Contact: Aileen Muldoon Byrne
Opening Times: 0930-1800 Mon-Sat, 1400-1800 Sun, Mar-Sep. 0930-1800 B/hols. W/ends only Oct-Feb.
Credit Cards: All major credit/debit cards
Specialities: Hardy herbaceous perennials. David Austin roses. Trees, shrubs, climbers, grasses, bamboos & ferns.
Notes: Pre-ordered plants delivered to shows.
Map Ref: I, B3

IDee **DEELISH GARDEN CENTRE** ⊠ €
Skibbereen, Co. Cork,
Republic of Ireland
Ⓣ 00 (353) 28 21374
Ⓕ 00 (353) 28 21374
Ⓔ deel@eircom.net
Ⓦ www.deelish.ie
Contact: Bill & Rain Chase
Opening Times: 1000-1800 Mon-Sat, 1400-1800 Sun.
Min Mail Order EU: €50 (Ireland only).
Cat. Cost: Sae
Credit Cards: Visa, Access
Specialities: Unusual plants for the mild coastal climate of Ireland. Conservatory plants. Sole Irish agents for Chase Organic Seeds.
Notes: No mail order outside Ireland.
Map Ref: I, D1

IDic **DICKSON NURSERIES LTD** ⊠
Milecross Road, Newtownards,
Co. Down, N. Ireland
BT23 4SS
Ⓣ 028 9181 2206
Ⓜ 07522 222161
Ⓕ 028 9181 3366
Ⓔ mail@dickson-roses.co.uk
Ⓦ www.dickson-roses.co.uk
Contact: Colin Dickson
Opening Times: 0800-1230 & 1300-1515 Mon-Thu. 0800-1230 Fri.
Min Mail Order UK: Nmc
Min Mail Order EU: £25.00 + p&p
Cat. Cost: Free
Credit Cards: None
Specialities: Roses esp. modern Dickson varieties. Limited selection, check website. Most varieties available in small quantities only.
Notes: Glasshouses accessible for wheelchairs. Also sells wholesale.
Map Ref: I, B3

IFoB **FIELD OF BLOOMS** ⊠ € ♿
Ballymackey, Lisnamoe, Nenagh,
Co. Tipperary, Republic of Ireland
Ⓣ (353) 67 29974
Ⓜ (353) 8764 06044
Ⓔ guy2002@eircom.net
Ⓦ www.fieldofblooms.com
Contact: Guy de Schrijver
Opening Times: Strictly by appt.
Min Mail Order UK: Nmc
Min Mail Order EU: Nmc
Cat. Cost: Online only.
Credit Cards: None
Specialities: Hellebores, herbaceous, hardy perennials, ornamental grasses, woodland plants & some alpines.
Map Ref: I, C2

IFro **FROGSWELL NURSERY** €
Cloonconlan, Straide,
Foxford, Co. Mayo,
Republic of Ireland
Ⓣ (353) 94 903 1420
Ⓜ (353) 8621 06166
Ⓔ frogswell@gmail.com
Ⓦ www.frogswell.eu
Contact: Celia Graebner
Opening Times: Feb-Oct by appt. Please phone first. Also Garden Open Days & occasional workshops; see website for details.
Cat. Cost: Online only.
Credit Cards: None
Specialities: A small garden-based nursery specialising in shade & woodland plants incl. hybrid hellebores & hardy geraniums, plus unusual flowering & food plants for the Irish climate, all raised on site & without chemical inputs. Some in very small quantities.

KEY
⊠ Mail order to UK or EU — Delivers to shows
Exports beyond EU — € Euro accepted
♿ Accessible by wheelchair — ◆ See Display advertisement

Notes: Group visits & talks by arrangement. See website for location map. Partial disabled access.
Map Ref: I, B1 **OS Grid Ref:** M2497

IGor **Gortkelly Castle Nursery** ⊠ ♠ €
Upperchurch, Thurles, Co. Tipperary, Republic of Ireland
Ⓣ (353) 504 54441
Ⓔ clarevbeumer@ireland.com
Contact: Clare Beumer
Opening Times: Mail order only. Not open to the public.
Min Mail Order UK: Nmc
Min Mail Order EU: Nmc
Cat. Cost: 5 × 1st class (UK), 5 × 55c (Rep. of Ireland).
Credit Cards: None
Specialities: Choice perennials. Cultivars of Irish origin. Alpines.
Map Ref: I, C2

IKil **Kilmurry Nursery** ⊠ ♠ € ♿
Gorey, Co. Wexford, Republic of Ireland
Ⓣ (353) 53 948 0223
Ⓜ (353) 8681 80623
Ⓕ (353) 53 948 0223
Ⓔ info@kilmurrynursery.com
Ⓦ www.kilmurrynursery.com
Contact: Paul & Orla Woods
Opening Times: 0900-1700 Mon-Fri, Mar-Sep. Wintertime by appt.
Min Mail Order UK: Nmc
Min Mail Order EU: Nmc
Cat. Cost: Online only.
Credit Cards: None
Specialities: Herbaceous perennials and grasses.
Notes: Also sells wholesale.
Map Ref: I, C3 **OS Grid Ref:** 3C

IMou **Mount Venus Nursery** ⊠ ♠ € ♿
The Walled Garden, Mutton Lane, Dublin 16, Republic of Ireland
Ⓣ (353) 1 493 3813
Ⓜ (353) 8632 18789
Ⓔ schurmann@ireland.com
Ⓦ www.mountvenusnursery.com
Contact: Oliver & Liat Schurmann
Opening Times: 1000-1800 Mon-Sat, Feb-Nov.
Min Mail Order UK: €20
Min Mail Order EU: €35
Credit Cards: All major credit/debit cards
Specialities: Specialist perennials. Grasses & bamboos. Unusual woodland plants.
Notes: Also sells wholesale.
Map Ref: I, C3

IPen **Peninsula Primulas** ⊠ ♠ €
72 Ballyeasborough Road, Kircubbin, Co. Down, N. Ireland BT22 1AD
Ⓣ 028 4277 2193
Ⓜ 07714 465834
Ⓔ peninsula.primulas@btinternet.com
Ⓦ www.primulasandauriculas.com
Contact: Philip Bankhead
Opening Times: Mail order only. Not open.
Min Mail Order UK: Nmc
Min Mail Order EU: Nmc
Cat. Cost: Free
Credit Cards: Paypal
Specialities: Extensive selection of *Primula* species, plus auriculas. Also *P. allionii* cvs and European hybrid alpines.
Notes: Also sells wholesale.
Map Ref: I, B3

IPot **The Potting Shed** ⊠ ♠ € ♿
Bolinaspick, Camolin, Enniscorthy, Co Wexford, Republic of Ireland
Ⓣ (353) 5393 83629
Ⓔ sricher@iol.ie
Ⓦ www.camolinpottingshed.com
Contact: Susan Carrick
Opening Times: 1300-1800, Thu-Sat (incl.), Mar-Sep 2011. Other times by appt.
Min Mail Order UK: Nmc
Min Mail Order EU: Nmc
Cat. Cost: 3 × 1st class.
Credit Cards: MasterCard, Visa
Specialities: We grow a wide range of unusual, hard to find and new introductions of herbaceous perennials, ornamental grasses and *Clematis*, many of which can be seen growing to their full potential in our many display beds.
Notes: Member of the Irish Specialist Nursery Assoc. (ISNA).
Map Ref: I, C3

IPPN **Perennial Plants Nursery** ⊠ ♠ €
Nr Ballymaloe, Barnabrow, Midleton, Co. Cork, Republic of Ireland
Ⓣ (353) 21 465 2122
Ⓔ perennialplants@eircom.net
Ⓦ www.perennialplants.biz
Contact: Sandy McCarthy
Opening Times: Please ring for times.
Min Mail Order UK: Nmc
Min Mail Order EU: Nmc
Cat. Cost: None issued.
Credit Cards: None
Specialities: Many unusual herbaceous, ornamental grasses, tender perennials. Some available in small quantities only.
Notes: Will accept payment in sterling.
Map Ref: I, D2 **OS Grid Ref:** W9568

IRhd **Ringhaddy Daffodils** ⊠ ✈ €
Ringhaddy Road, Killinchy,
Co. Down, N. Ireland
BT23 6TU
Ⓣ 028 9754 1007
Ⓜ 07762 337534
Ⓔ info@ringhaddy-daffodils.com
Ⓦ www.ringhaddy-daffodils.com
Contact: Nial Watson
Opening Times: Mail order only. Not open.
Min Mail Order UK: £20.00 + p&p
Min Mail Order EU: £50.00 + p&p
Cat. Cost: £2.50.
Credit Cards: Paypal
Specialities: Daffodil bulbs, some varieties only available in small numbers.

IRos **Ros Ban Wildlife Garden** € ♿
Common, Raphoe, Co. Donegal, Republic of Ireland
Ⓣ (353) 74 914 5336
Ⓜ (353) 8608 05214 or (353) 8511 91016
Ⓔ Rosbangarden@gmail.com
Contact: Ann Kavanagh
Opening Times: Garden open all year, morning to evening.
Credit Cards: None
Notes: Plants available in season from the garden. Please check plant availability with nursery before travelling.
Map Ref: I, A2 **OS Grid Ref:** C254037

ISha **Shady Plants** ⊠ ⌂ € ♿
Coolbooa, Clashmore, Youghal, Co. Cork, Republic of Ireland
Ⓣ (353) 024 96735
Ⓜ (353) 08605 42171
Ⓔ mike@shadyplants.ie
Ⓦ www.shadyplants.net
Contact: Mike Keep
Opening Times: 1300-1700, Tue-Sat.
Min Mail Order UK: Nmc
Min Mail Order EU: Nmc
Cat. Cost: €5.00
Credit Cards: Paypal
Specialities: Specialist fern nursery based near the south coast of Ireland.
Map Ref: I, D2 **OS Grid Ref:** 613,585

ISsi **Seaside Nursery** ⊠ € ♿
Claddaghduff, Co. Galway, Republic of Ireland
Ⓣ (353) 95 44687
Ⓜ (353) 8633 91555
Ⓔ Tom@seasidenursery.biz
Ⓦ www.seasidenursery.biz
Contact: Tom Dyck
Opening Times: 1000-1300 & 1400-1800 Mon-Sat, 1400-1800 Sun. Closed Sun 1st Oct-31st Mar.
Min Mail Order UK: Nmc
Min Mail Order EU: Nmc
Cat. Cost: €3.50
Credit Cards: Visa, MasterCard
Specialities: Plants & hedging suitable for seaside locations. Rare plants originating from Australia & New Zealand esp. *Phormium*, *Astelia*.
Notes: Also sells wholesale.

ITim **Timpany Nurseries & Gardens** ⊠ ⌂ ♿
77 Magheratimpany Road, Ballynahinch,
Co. Down, N. Ireland
BT24 8PA
Ⓣ 028 9756 2812
Ⓕ 028 9756 2812
Ⓔ s.tindall@btconnect.com
Ⓦ www.timpanynurseries.com
Contact: Susan Tindall
Opening Times: 1000-1730 Tue-Sat, Sun by appt.
Min Mail Order UK: Nmc
Min Mail Order EU: £30.00 + p&p
Cat. Cost: £2.00
Credit Cards: Visa, MasterCard
Specialities: *Celmisia*, *Androsace*, *Primula*, *Saxifraga*, *Dianthus*, *Meconopsis*, *Cassiope*, *Rhodohypoxis*, *Cyclamen* & *Primula auricula*.
Notes: Also sells wholesale.
Map Ref: I, B3

IVic **Victoria's Nursery & Garden** €
Upper Kells, Kells, Cahirceveen, Co Kerry, Republic of Ireland
Ⓣ (353) 66 947 7605
Ⓜ (353) 8791 11465
Ⓔ kellshouse@eircom.net
Contact: Victoria Vogel
Opening Times: 1000-1700 Wed-Sun all year except Xmas. Closed Mon & Tue, except B/hols & by arrangement.
Cat. Cost: None issued.
Credit Cards: None
Specialities: *Rhododendron*, azaleas, *Acer*, tree ferns, seaside & woodland plants, *Saxifraga fortunei* forms.
Notes: Drive along Ring of Kerry, at Kells follow signs to Kells Bay Garden towards Kells Beach, nursery to left after little bridge.
Map Ref: I, D1

KEY
⊠ Mail order to UK or EU ⌂ Delivers to shows
✈ Exports beyond EU € Euro accepted
♿ Accessible by wheelchair ◆ See Display advertisement

L

LONDON AREA

LAma **JACQUES AMAND INTERNATIONAL LTD** ⊠ ⊠ ⌂ € ♿
The Nurseries, 145 Clamp Hill, Stanmore, Middlesex HA7 3JS
Ⓣ (020) 8420 7110
Ⓕ (020) 8954 6784
Ⓔ bulbs@jacquesamand.co.uk
Ⓦ www.jacquesamand.com
Contact: John Amand & Stuart Chapman
Opening Times: 0900-1700 Mon-Fri, 1000-1400 Sat.
Min Mail Order UK: Nmc
Min Mail Order EU: Nmc
Cat. Cost: 1 × 1st class.
Credit Cards: All major credit/debit cards
Specialities: Rare and unusual species bulbs esp. *Arisaema*, *Trillium*, *Fritillaria*, tulips.
Notes: Also sells wholesale.
Map Ref: L, B3

LAst **ASTERBY & CHALKCROFT NURSERY** ⊠ ♿
The Ridgeway, Blunham, Bedfordshire MK44 3PH
Ⓣ (01767) 640148
Ⓔ sales@asterbyplants.co.uk
Ⓦ www.asterbyplants.co.uk
Contact: Simon & Eva Aldridge
Opening Times: 1000-1700 7 days. Closed Xmas & Jan.
Min Mail Order UK: Nmc
Credit Cards: All major credit/debit cards
Specialities: Hardy shrubs, herbaceous & trees.
Notes: Please ring for mail order information.
Map Ref: L, A3 **OS Grid Ref:** TL151497

LAyl **AYLETT NURSERIES LTD** ♿ ◆
North Orbital Road, St Albans, Hertfordshire AL2 1DH
Ⓣ (01727) 822255
Ⓕ (01727) 823024
Ⓔ info@aylettnurseries.co.uk
Ⓦ www.aylettnurseries.co.uk
Contact: Julie Aylett
Opening Times: 0830-1730 Mon-Fri, 0830-1700 Sat, 1030-1630 Sun.
Cat. Cost: Free.
Credit Cards: All major credit/debit cards
Specialities: *Dahlia*. 2-acre trial ground adjacent to garden centre.
Map Ref: L, B3 **OS Grid Ref:** TL169049

LBee **BEECHCROFT NURSERY** ♿
127 Reigate Road, Ewell, Surrey KT17 3DE
Ⓣ 0208 393 4265
Ⓕ 0208 393 4265
Ⓔ enquiries@beechcroft-nursery.co.uk
Ⓦ www.beechcroft-nursery.co.uk
Contact: C Kimber
Opening Times: 1000-1600 Mon-Sat, 1000-1400 Sun and B/hols. Closed Xmas-New Year week.
Cat. Cost: None issued.
Credit Cards: All major credit/debit cards
Specialities: Conifers.
Map Ref: L, C3

LBMP **BLOOMING MARVELLOUS PLANTS** ⌂
Korketts Farm, Aylesbury Road, Winslow, Buckinghamshire MK18 3JL
Ⓣ (01296) 714714
Ⓜ 07963 747305
Ⓔ alex@bmplants.co.uk
Ⓦ www.bmplants.co.uk
Contact: Alexia Ballance
Opening Times: 0900-1700 Tue-Sat & 1000-1600 Sun, 7th Feb-28th Oct 2012. Closed Mon (except B/hols). By appt. only Nov-Jan.
Credit Cards: All major credit/debit cards
Specialities: A mixture of unusual and familiar perennials, shrubs, grasses, ferns & bedding plants, most in more generous sizes than usually found in nurseries. Some more unusual plants available in small quantities only.
Notes: Located on the A413 just outside Winslow (heading in the Aylesbury direction). Partial wheelchair access.
Map Ref: L, A2 **OS Grid Ref:** SP777271

LBuc **BUCKINGHAM NURSERIES** ⊠ € ♿ ◆
14 Tingewick Road, Buckingham MK18 4AE
Ⓣ (01280) 822133
Ⓕ (01280) 815491
Ⓔ enquiries@buckingham-nurseries.co.uk
Ⓦ www.buckingham-nurseries.co.uk
Contact: R J & P L Brown
Opening Times: 0830-1730 (1800 in summer) Mon-Sat, 1030-1630 Sun.
Min Mail Order UK: Nmc
Min Mail Order EU: Nmc
Cat. Cost: Free.
Credit Cards: Visa, MasterCard
Specialities: Bare rooted and container grown hedging. Fruit trees, soft fruit, trees, shrubs, herbaceous perennials, alpines, grasses & ferns.
Map Ref: L, A2 **OS Grid Ref:** SP675333

LCla **CLAY LANE NURSERY** ⊠ ⌂
3 Clay Lane, South Nutfield, Nr Redhill, Surrey RH1 4EG
Ⓣ (01737) 823307

Ⓔ claylane.nursery@btinternet.com
Ⓦ www.claylane-fuchsias.co.uk
Contact: K W Belton
Opening Times: Variable opening times. Please phone before travelling.
Min Mail Order UK: £8.00
Cat. Cost: 3 × 2nd class.
Credit Cards: None
Specialities: *Fuchsia*. Many varieties in small quantities only.
Notes: Mail order by telephone pre-arangement only.
Map Ref: L, C4

LCtg **Cottage Garden Nursery** ◆
127 Barnet Road, Arkley, Barnet, Hertfordshire EN5 3JX
Ⓣ (020) 8441 8829
Ⓕ (020) 8531 3178
Ⓔ nurseryinfo@cottagegardennursery-barnet.co.uk
Ⓦ www.cottagegardennursery-barnet.co.uk
Contact: David and Wendy Spicer
Opening Times: 0930-1700 Tue-Sat Mar-Oct, 0930-1600 Tue-Sat Nov-Feb, 1000-1600 Sun & B/hol Mon all year.
Cat. Cost: None issued.
Credit Cards: All major credit/debit cards
Specialities: General range of hardy shrubs, trees, fruit trees & bushes, perennials. Architectural & exotics, *Fuchsia*, seasonal bedding, patio plants.
Map Ref: L, B3 **OS Grid Ref:** TQ226958

LDai **Daisy Roots** ⊠ ⛫
(Office) 8 Gosselin Road, Bengeo, Hertford, Hertfordshire SG14 3LG
Ⓣ (01992) 582401
Ⓜ 07958 563355
Ⓕ (01992) 582401
Ⓔ anne@daisyroots.com
Ⓦ www.daisyroots.com
Contact: Anne Godfrey
Opening Times: 1000-1600 Fri & Sat Mar-Oct, or by appt.
Min Mail Order UK: £15.00
Cat. Cost: Online only.
Credit Cards: All major credit/debit cards
Specialities: Ever-increasing range of choice & unusual perennials, particularly *Agastache*, *Anthemis*, *Centaurea*, *Digitalis*, *Erysimum*, *Salvia* & *Sedum*. Some plants available in small quantities only.
Notes: Nursery is at Jenningsbury, London Road, Hertford Heath, SG13 7NS. Also sells wholesale.
Map Ref: L, B4

LEdu **Edulis** ⊠ ⛫ € ♿
(Office) 1 Flowers Piece, Ashampstead, Reading, Berkshire RG8 8SG
Ⓣ (01635) 578113
Ⓜ 07802 812781
Ⓔ edulisnursery@gmail.com
Ⓦ www.edulis.co.uk
Contact: Paul Barney
Opening Times: By appt. only.
Min Mail Order UK: £15.00 + p&p
Min Mail Order EU: £50.00 + p&p
Cat. Cost: 5 × 1st class.
Credit Cards: All, except American Express
Specialities: Unusual edibles, architectural plants, permaculture plants.
Notes: Nursery is at Bere Court Farm, Tidmarsh Lane, Pangbourne, RG8 8HT. Also sells wholesale.
Map Ref: L, B2 **OS Grid Ref:** SU615747

LHel **Herts Hellebores** ⊠ € ♿
Green Lane Farm, Levens Green, Nr Ware, Hertfordshire SG11 1HD
Ⓣ (01920) 438458
Ⓔ lorna@herts-hellebore.co.uk
Ⓦ www.herts-hellebore.co.uk
Contact: Lorna Jones
Opening Times: 1000-1600 Wed & Sat only, 1st Feb-31st Mar 2012. Other times Jan-Apr by appt. only. Check with nursery for 2013 opening times.
Min Mail Order UK: £18
Min Mail Order EU: £18
Cat. Cost: Free.
Credit Cards: All major credit/debit cards
Specialities: Hellebore hybrids. Specialising in developments of double & anemone centred hybrids. Seed-raised plants offered by colour. Some available in small quantities only.
Map Ref: L, A4 **OS Grid Ref:** TL357224

LHop **Hopleys Plants Ltd** ⊠ ⛫ ♿
High Street, Much Hadham, Hertfordshire SG10 6BU
Ⓣ (01279) 842509
Ⓕ (01279) 843784
Ⓔ plants@hopleys.co.uk
Ⓦ www.hopleys.co.uk
Contact: Mr Aubrey Barker
Opening Times: 0900-1700 Mon & Wed-Sat, 1400-1700 Sun. Closed Nov, Jan, Feb except by appt.

KEY
⊠ Mail order to UK or EU ⛫ Delivers to shows
✈ Exports beyond EU € Euro accepted
♿ Accessible by wheelchair ◆ See Display advertisement

Min Mail Order UK: Nmc
Cat. Cost: 5 × 1st class.
Credit Cards: Visa, Access, Switch
Specialities: Wide range of hardy & half-hardy shrubs & perennials.
Notes: Also sells wholesale.
Map Ref: L, A4 **OS Grid Ref:** TL428196

LLHF **LITTLE HEATH FARM (UK)** ⌂
Little Heath Lane, Potten End, Berkhamsted, Hertfordshire HP4 2RY
Ⓣ (01442) 864951
Ⓔ lhfnursery@gmail.com
Ⓦ www.littleheathfarmnursery.co.uk
Contact: John Spokes
Opening Times: 1000-1700 or dusk if earlier, 7 days.
Cat. Cost: Online only.
Credit Cards: Visa, MasterCard
Specialities: Large range of alpines, herbaceous, shrubs, many available in small quantities only.
Map Ref: L, B3

LLWG **LILIES WATER GARDENS** ⊠ ♿
Broad Lane, Newdigate, Surrey RH5 5AT
Ⓣ (01306) 631064
Ⓜ 07801 166244
Ⓕ (01306) 631693
Ⓔ mail@lilieswatergardens.co.uk
Ⓦ www.lilieswatergardens.co.uk
Contact: Simon Harman
Opening Times: 0900-1700 Wed-Sat, Mar-Aug. By appt. only Sep-Feb.
Min Mail Order UK: Nmc but flat rate £6.50 delivery charge.
Min Mail Order EU: Nmc
Cat. Cost: Online only.
Credit Cards: All major credit/debit cards
Specialities: Waterlilies, moist perennials, bog-garden plants, primulas, marginal plants, ferns, oxygenating plants. Pond, incl. submerged & free-floating, aquatic, water iris, water-garden, floating, stream & deep-water plants. Alpine, rock & creeping plants. Rushes & grasses.
Map Ref: L, C3

LLWP **LW PLANTS** ⊠ ⌂
23 Wroxham Way, Harpenden, Hertfordshire AL5 4PP
Ⓣ (01582) 768467
Ⓔ lwplants@waitrose.com
Ⓦ www.thymus.co.uk
Contact: Mrs Margaret Easter
Opening Times: 1000-1700 most days, but please phone first.
Min Mail Order UK: Nmc
Cat. Cost: Online only.
Credit Cards: None
Specialities: Plants from a plantsman's garden, esp. *Geranium*, grasses & *Thymus*. Some available in small quantities only. Nat. Collections of *Thymus* (Scientific), *Hyssopus* & *Satureja*. Brickell award 2011. *Thymus* ICRA (provisional). *Thymus* propagated to order.
Notes: Mail order *Thymus* only.
Map Ref: L, B3 **OS Grid Ref:** TL141153

LMil **MILLAIS NURSERIES** ⊠ ♿
Crosswater Farm, Crosswater Lane, Churt, Farnham, Surrey GU10 2JN
Ⓣ (01252) 792698
Ⓕ (01252) 792526
Ⓔ sales@rhododendrons.co.uk
Ⓦ www.rhododendrons.co.uk
Contact: David Millais
Opening Times: 1000-1700 Mon-Fri all year. Daily in spring. Please phone or see website for w/end opening in spring.
Min Mail Order UK: Nmc
Min Mail Order EU: Nmc
Cat. Cost: Free list on request. Full catalogue Online.
Credit Cards: All major credit/debit cards
Specialities: Rhododendrons, azaleas, magnolias, camellias & acers. Garden open in spring.
Notes: Mail order all year. Also sells wholesale.
Map Ref: L, C3 **OS Grid Ref:** SU856397

LMin **NATIONAL COLLECTION OF MINIATURE TALL BEARDED IRIS** ⊠
3 Bower Street, Bedford, Bedfordshire MK40 3RD
Ⓔ iris@rosewarnegardens.com
Ⓦ www.miniaturetallbeardediris.wordpress.com
Contact: Rosalind Rosewarne
Opening Times: Not open. Mail order only.
Min Mail Order UK: £5.00 + p&p
Cat. Cost: Online only.
Credit Cards: None
Specialities: Provisional National Coll. of Miniature Tall Bearded *Iris*.
Notes: Plants available in small quantities only.

LPio **PIONEER PLANTS** ⊠ € ♿
Baldock Lane, Willian, Letchworth Garden City, Hertfordshire SG6 2AE
Ⓣ (01462) 675858
Ⓔ milly@pioneerplants.com
Ⓦ www.pioneerplants.com
Contact: Nick Downing & John Hoyland

Opening Times: 0900-1700 Wed-Sat, Mar-Oct. Other times by appt.
Min Mail Order UK: £15.00
Min Mail Order EU: £25.00
Cat. Cost: Online only.
Credit Cards: All major credit/debit cards
Specialities: *Clematis*, *Salvia*, tender perennials, species *Pelargonium*. Wide range of hard-to-find perennials & bulbs.
Notes: Mail order via internet only. Also sells wholesale.
Map Ref: L, A3 **OS Grid Ref:** TL224307

LPla **The Plant Specialist**
7 Whitefield Lane, Great Missenden, Buckinghamshire HP16 0BH
Ⓣ (01494) 866650
Ⓕ (01494) 866650
Ⓔ higwal@supanet.com
Ⓦ www.theplantspecialist.co.uk
Contact: Sean Walter
Opening Times: 1000-1700 Wed-Sat, 1000-1600 Sun, Apr-Oct.
Cat. Cost: None issued.
Credit Cards: All major credit/debit cards
Specialities: Herbaceous perennials, grasses, half-hardy perennials, bulbs.
Notes: Limited wheelchair access.

LPot **Potash Plants** ♠ ♿
Potash Nursery, Drayton Parslow, Buckinghamshire MK17 0JE
Ⓣ (01296) 720578
Ⓔ info@potashplants.co.uk
Ⓦ www.potashplants.co.uk
Contact: Gill Gallon
Opening Times: 0900-1730 Mon-Sat. 1030-1630 Sun.
Cat. Cost: Online.
Credit Cards: All, except American Express
Specialities: Wide range of traditional and unusual hardy perennials, grasses, trees & shrubs. Some available in small quantities only.
Notes: Nursery on B4032 mid-way between Aylesbury and Milton Keynes. Also sells wholesale.
Map Ref: L, A3 **OS Grid Ref:** SP834279

LRHS **Wisley Plant Centre (RHS)** ♿ ◆
RHS Garden, Wisley, Woking, Surrey GU23 6QB
Ⓣ (01483) 211113 or 0845 060 9800
Ⓕ (01483) 212372
Ⓔ wisleyplantcentre@rhs.org.uk
Ⓦ www.rhs.org.uk/wisleyplantcentre
Opening Times: 0930-1700 Mon-Sat, Oct-Feb. 0930-1800 Mon-Sat, Mar-Sep. 1100-1700 Sun all year, browsing from 1030.
Cat. Cost: Online only.
Credit Cards: All major credit/debit cards
Specialities: Over 9,000 plants, many rare or unusual, reflecting the range of the RHS flagship garden at Wisley. Plants subject to seasonal availability. For plants not in stock, we operate a reservation service by phone & in person.
Notes: Programme of free plant events throughout the year. Please ring or check website for details.
Map Ref: L, C3

LShp **Squire's Garden Centre, Shepperton** ♿
Halliford Road, Upper Halliford, Shepperton, Middlesex TW17 8SG
Ⓣ (01932) 784121
Ⓕ (01932) 785386
Ⓔ shepp.plants@squiresgardencentres.co.uk
Ⓦ www.squiresgardencentres.co.uk
Contact: Plant Area Manager
Opening Times: 0900-1800 Mon-Sat, 1030-1630 Sun.
Cat. Cost: None issued.
Credit Cards: All major credit/debit cards
Specialities: Roses.
Notes: Other garden centres in Middlesex, Surrey, Berkshire and West Sussex.
Map Ref: L, C3

LSou **Southon Plants** ✉ ♿
Mutton Hill, Dormansland, Lingfield, Surrey RH7 6NP
Ⓣ (01342) 870150
Ⓔ lyn@southon-plants.co.uk
Ⓦ www.southonplants.com
Contact: Mr Southon
Opening Times: 0900-1730 Feb-Oct. For Nov, Dec & Jan please phone first.
Min Mail Order UK: Nmc
Cat. Cost: Online only.
Credit Cards: All major credit/debit cards
Specialities: New & unusual hardy & tender perennials, specialising in *Agapanthus* (over 30 varieties), *Coreopsis*, *Euphorbia* & *Heuchera* (over 40 varieties).
Notes: Mail order Sep-Mar only. Please phone/email for details.
Map Ref: L, C4

KEY
✉ Mail order to UK or EU ♠ Delivers to shows
☒ Exports beyond EU € Euro accepted
♿ Accessible by wheelchair ◆ See Display advertisement

L

L

LSqH **Squire's Garden Centre, West Horsley** ♿
Epsom Road, West Horsley,
Leatherhead, Surrey
KT24 6AR
Ⓣ (01483) 282911
Ⓕ (01483) 281380
Ⓔ hors.plants@squiresgardencentres.co.uk
Ⓦ www.squiresgardencentres.co.uk
Contact: Plant Area Manager
Opening Times: 0900-1800 Mon-Sat, 1030-1630 Sun.
Cat. Cost: None issued.
Credit Cards: All major credit/debit cards
Specialities: Herbaceous.
Notes: Other garden centres in Middlesex, Surrey, Berkshire and West Sussex.
Map Ref: L, C3

LSqu **Squire's Garden Centre, Twickenham** ♿
Sixth Cross Road, Twickenham, Middlesex
TW2 5PA
Ⓣ 0208 977 9241
Ⓕ 0208 943 4024
Ⓔ twic.plants@squiresgardencentres.co.uk
Ⓦ www.squiresgardencentres.co.uk
Contact: Plant Area Manager
Opening Times: 0900-1800 Mon-Sat, 1030-1630 Sun.
Credit Cards: All major credit/debit cards
Specialities: *Clematis*.
Notes: Other garden centres in Middlesex, Surrey, Berkshire and West Sussex.
Map Ref: L, B3

LSRN **Spring Reach Nursery** ⊠ ♿
Long Reach, Ockham, Guildford, Surrey
GU23 6PG
Ⓣ (01483) 284769
Ⓜ 07884 432666
Ⓕ (01483) 284769
Ⓔ info@springreachnursery.co.uk
Ⓦ www.springreachnursery.co.uk
Contact: Nick & Lissa Hourhan
Opening Times: 7 days. 1000-1700 Mon-Sat, 1030-1630 Sun. Open B/hols.
Min Mail Order UK: Nmc
Min Mail Order EU: Nmc
Credit Cards: All major credit/debit cards
Specialities: Shrubs, evergreen climbers, *Clematis*, perennials, roses, grasses, ferns, bamboos, trees, hedging, soft fruit & top fruit. Plants for chalk & clay. Deer & rabbit proof plants. Specimen & acid-loving plants.
Notes: Please ring for mail order details. Also sells wholesale.
Map Ref: L, C3

LStr **Henry Street Nursery** ⊠ ♿
Swallowfield Road, Arborfield,
Reading, Berkshire
RG2 9JY
Ⓣ (0118) 9761223
Ⓕ (0118) 9761417
Ⓔ info@henrystreet.co.uk
Ⓦ www.henrystreet.co.uk
Contact: Mr M C Goold
Opening Times: 0900-1730 Mon-Sat, 1030-1630 Sun.
Min Mail Order UK: Nmc
Min Mail Order EU: Nmc
Cat. Cost: Free
Credit Cards: All major credit/debit cards
Specialities: Roses.
Notes: Also sells wholesale.
Map Ref: L, C3

LToo **Toobees Exotics** ⊠ €
20 Inglewood, St Johns, Woking, Surrey
GU21 3HX
Ⓣ (01483) 722600
Ⓜ 07836 334011
Ⓕ (01483) 751995
Ⓔ bbpotter@woking.plus.com
Ⓦ www.toobees-exotics.com
Contact: Bob Potter
Opening Times: Not open. Mail order & online shop only. Visits by appt. only.
Min Mail Order UK: Nmc
Min Mail Order EU: Nmc
Cat. Cost: Sae
Credit Cards: All major credit/debit cards
Specialities: South African & Madagascan succulents, many rare & unusual species, *Euphorbia* & *Pachypodium*. Stock varies constantly.
Notes: Credit cards accepted online only.
Map Ref: L, C3

LTop **Topiary Arts** ⊠
(Office) 224 Hospital Bridge Road, Whitton, Twickenham, Middlesex TW2 6LF
Ⓣ 020 8893 9579
Ⓜ 07775 602704
Ⓔ jcb@topiaryarts.com
Ⓦ www.topiaryarts.com
Contact: James Crebbin-Bailey
Opening Times: By appt. only.
Min Mail Order UK: £30
Cat. Cost: Online only.
Credit Cards: None
Specialities: Topiary Small quantities of *Buxus*, *Philyrea*, *Taxus* & *Ligustrum*.
Notes: Nursery is at Copped Hall Walled Garden, Upshire, Epping, Essex CM16 5HS. Also sells wholesale.

LWst **Westonbirt Plants** ⊠ ⛫ €
17 Stanley Road, Carshalton, Surrey SM5 4LE
Ⓜ 07788 676079
Ⓔ office@westonbirtplants.co.uk
Ⓦ www.westonbirtplants.co.uk
Contact: Tony Dickerson
Opening Times: Not open. Mail order & shows only.
Min Mail Order UK: Nmc
Min Mail Order EU: Nmc
Cat. Cost: 4 × 2nd class.
Credit Cards: All major credit/debit cards
Specialities: Bulbs & woodland plants incl. *Anemone nemorosa, Anemonella, Arisaema, Arum, Colchicum, Corydalis, Crocus, Erythronium, Fritillaria, Galanthus, Helleborus, Iris* (Juno & Oncocyclus), *Lilium, Nemocharis, Paeonia, Roscoea, Trillium* & hardy orchids (*Calanthe, Cypripedium* & *Epipactis*). Many rare plants in ltd. numbers.

LYaf **Yaffles** ⊠ ⛫ ♿
Harvest Hill, Bourne End, Buckinghamshire SL8 5JJ
Ⓣ (01628) 525455
Contact: I Butterfield
Opening Times: 0900-1300 & 1400-1700. Please phone beforehand in case we are attending shows.
Min Mail Order UK: Nmc
Min Mail Order EU: £30.00 + p&p
Cat. Cost: 2 × 2nd class.
Credit Cards: None
Specialities: Nat. Collection of *Pleione*. *Dahlia* for collection only.
Notes: Only *Pleione* by mail order.
Map Ref: L, B3

Midlands

MAJR **A J Robinson** ⊠
Sycamore Farm, Foston, Derbyshire DE65 5PW
Ⓣ (01283) 815635
Ⓔ argyspot@aol.com
Contact: A J Robinson
Opening Times: By appt. for collection of plants only.
Min Mail Order UK: £15.00
Cat. Cost: 2 × 1st class for list.
Credit Cards: None
Specialities: Nat. Collection of *Argyranthemum*.
Map Ref: M, B2

MArl **Arley Hall Nursery** ♿
Arley Hall Nursery, Northwich, Cheshire CW9 6NA
Ⓣ (01565) 777479 or 777231
Ⓕ (01565) 777465
Ⓦ www.arleyhallandgardens.com
Contact: Jane Foster, Rosie Jackson
Opening Times: 1100-1730 Tue-Sun Apr-end Sep. Also B/hol Mons.
Cat. Cost: 4 × 1st class.
Credit Cards: All major credit/debit cards
Specialities: Wide range of herbaceous incl. many unusual varieties, some in small quantities. Wide range of unusual pelargoniums.
Notes: Nursery is beside car park at Arley Hall Gardens.
Map Ref: M, A1 **OS Grid Ref:** SJ673808

M

MAsh **Ashwood Nurseries Ltd** ⊠ ♿ ◆
Ashwood Lower Lane, Ashwood, Kingswinford, West Midlands DY6 0AE
Ⓣ (01384) 401996
Ⓕ (01384) 401108
Ⓔ mailorder@ashwoodnurseries.com
Ⓦ www.ashwoodnurseries.com
Contact: Karrina Gilbert & Rachel Kendall
Opening Times: 0900-1700 Mon-Sat & 0930-1700 Sun excl. Xmas & Boxing Day.
Min Mail Order UK: Nmc
Min Mail Order EU: Nmc
Cat. Cost: 6 × 1st class.
Credit Cards: All major credit/debit cards
Specialities: Large range of hardy plants, shrubs & dwarf conifers. Roses, alpines & herbaceous plants. Also specialises in *Auricula, Cyclamen, Galanthus*, hellebores, *Hepatica, Hydrangea* & *Salvia*. Nat. Collection of *Lewisia*.
Notes: Tea room overlooking display garden. Ample parking. Regular events. Groups by appt. to visit private garden.
Map Ref: M, C2 **OS Grid Ref:** SO865879

MAus **David Austin Roses Ltd** ⊠ ✈ € ♿ ◆
Bowling Green Lane, Albrighton, Wolverhampton, West Midlands WV7 3HB
Ⓣ (01902) 376300
Ⓕ (01902) 375177
Ⓔ retail@davidaustinroses.co.uk
Ⓦ www.davidaustinroses.com
Contact: Customer Services Dept
Opening Times: 0830-1800 Mon-Fri, 0830-1630 Sat, 1000-1400 Sun.
Min Mail Order UK: Nmc
Min Mail Order EU: Nmc
Cat. Cost: Free.

KEY
⊠ Mail order to UK or EU ⛫ Delivers to shows
✈ Exports beyond EU € Euro accepted
♿ Accessible by wheelchair ◆ See Display advertisement

Credit Cards: Switch, Visa, MasterCard, Maestro, Access
Specialities: Roses. Nat. Collection of English Roses.
Notes: Also sells wholesale.
Map Ref: M, B2 **OS Grid Ref:** SJ798042

MAvo **Avondale Nursery** ⌂ ♿
(Office) 3 Avondale Road, Earlsdon, Coventry, Warwickshire CV5 6DZ
Ⓣ (024) 766 73662
Ⓜ 07979 093096
Ⓕ (024) 766 73662
Ⓔ enquiries@avondalenursery.co.uk
Ⓦ www.avondalenursery.co.uk
Contact: Brian Ellis
Opening Times: 1000-1230, 1400-1700 Mon-Sat, 1030-1630 Sun, Mar-Sep. Other times by appt.
Cat. Cost: 4 × 1st class.
Credit Cards: All major credit/debit cards
Specialities: Rare & unusual perennials esp. *Aster, Eryngium, Leucanthemum, Geum, Crocosmia, Sanguisorba* & grasses. Nat. Collections of *Aster novae-angliae, Anemone nemorosa* & *Sanguisorba*. Display garden open. Groups welcome.
Notes: Nursery is at Russell's Nursery, Mill Hill, Baginton, Nr Coventry, CV8 3AG.
Map Ref: M, C2 **OS Grid Ref:** SP339751

MBel **Bluebell Cottage Nursery (formerly Lodge Lane Nursery)** ⊠ ♿
Lodge Lane, Dutton, Cheshire WA4 4HP
Ⓣ (01928) 713718
Ⓔ info@bluebellcottage.co.uk
Ⓦ www.bluebellcottage.co.uk
Contact: Sue Beesley
Opening Times: 1000-1700 Wed-Sun & B/hols, mid Mar-end Sep. By appt. only outside these dates.
Min Mail Order UK: £10.00
Cat. Cost: Online, or by email.
Credit Cards: All major credit/debit cards
Specialities: Hardy perennials incl. *Achillea, Astrantia, Campanula, Digitalis, Penstemon, Geranium, Heuchera, Kniphofia, Nepeta, Papaver, Salvia* & ornamental grasses.
Notes: Mail order Mar/Apr & Sep/Oct only, subject to plant size.
Map Ref: M, A1 **OS Grid Ref:** SJ586779

MBlu **Bluebell Arboretum & Nursery** ⊠ ⌂ ♿
Annwell Lane, Smisby, Nr Ashby de la Zouch, Derbyshire LE65 2TA
Ⓣ (01530) 413700
Ⓕ (01530) 417600
Ⓔ sales@bluebellnursery.com
Ⓦ www.bluebellnursery.com
Contact: Robert & Suzette Vernon
Opening Times: 0900-1700 Mon-Sat & 1030-1630 Sun Mar-Oct, 0900-1600 Mon-Sat (not Sun) Nov-Feb. Closed 24th Dec-1st Jan incl. & Easter Sun.
Min Mail Order UK: £9.50
Min Mail Order EU: Nmc
Cat. Cost: £1.50 + 3 × 1st class.
Credit Cards: Visa, Access, Switch, MasterCard
Specialities: Uncommon trees & shrubs. Rare *Acer, Betula, Cornus, Fagus, Magnolia, Liquidambar, Quercus* & *Tilia*. Woody climbers.
Notes: Display garden & arboretum. 9-acre woodland garden with unusual trees. Guide dogs only. Working nursery, so wear appropriate clothing & sturdy footwear when visiting.
Map Ref: M, B1 **OS Grid Ref:** SK344187

MBNS **Barnsdale Gardens** ⊠ ⌂ ♿
Exton Avenue, Exton, Oakham, Rutland LE15 8AH
Ⓣ (01572) 813200
Ⓔ info@barnsdalegardens.co.uk
Ⓦ www.barnsdalegardens.co.uk
Contact: Nick Hamilton
Opening Times: 0900-1700 Mar-May & Sep-Oct, 0900-1900 Jun-Aug, 1000-1600 Nov-Feb, 7 days. Closed 24th & 25th Dec.
Min Mail Order UK: Nmc
Min Mail Order EU: Nmc
Cat. Cost: Online only.
Credit Cards: All major credit/debit cards
Specialities: Wide range of choice & unusual garden plants. Over 160 varieties of *Penstemon*, over 250 varieties of *Hemerocallis*.
Notes: Mail order from website or by telephone ordering only.
Map Ref: M, B3 **OS Grid Ref:** SK912108

MBPg **Barnfield Pelargoniums** ⊠
Barnfield, off Wilnecote Lane, Belgrave, Tamworth, Staffordshire B77 2LF
Ⓣ (01827) 250123
Ⓕ (01827) 250123
Ⓔ brianandjenniewhite@hotmail.com
Contact: Brian White
Opening Times: Open by appt. only.
Min Mail Order UK: £6.00
Cat. Cost: 4 × 2nd class.
Credit Cards: None
Specialities: Over 150 varieties of scented leaf pelargoniums.

MBri **Bridgemere Nursery & Garden World** ⊠ € ♿
Bridgemere, Nr Nantwich, Cheshire
CW5 7QB
Ⓣ (01270) 521100
Ⓕ (01270) 520215
Ⓔ bridgemere.plantinfo@thegardencentregroup.co.uk
Ⓦ www.bridgemere.co.uk
Contact: Keith Atkey, Roger Pierce
Opening Times: 0900-1800 7 days. Closed 25th & 26th Dec.
Min Mail Order UK: Nmc
Cat. Cost: None issued.
Credit Cards: Visa, Access, MasterCard, Switch
Specialities: Huge range outdoor & indoor plants, many rare & unusual. Specimen shrubs.
Notes: Mail order restricted to "click & collect" & home delivery service available on www.thegardencentregroup.co.uk
Map Ref: M, B1 **OS Grid Ref:** SJ727435

MBrN **Bridge Nursery** € ♿
Tomlow Road, Napton-on-the-Hill,
Nr Rugby, Warwickshire
CV47 8HX
Ⓣ (01926) 812737
Ⓔ pemartino@tiscali.co.uk
Ⓦ www.Bridge-Nursery.co.uk
Contact: Christine Dakin & Philip Martino
Opening Times: 1000-1600 Mon-Sun mid Feb-mid Nov. Other times by appt.
Cat. Cost: Online only.
Credit Cards: All major credit/debit cards
Specialities: Ornamental grasses, sedges & bamboos. Also range of shrubs & perennials. Display garden.
Notes: Also sells wholesale.
Map Ref: M, C2 **OS Grid Ref:** SP463625

MCms **Chrysanthemums Direct** ⊠ ⛺
Holmes Chapel Road,
Over Peover, Knutsford,
Cheshire WA16 9RA
Ⓣ 0800 046 7443
Ⓜ 07977 312593
Ⓔ sales@chrysanthemumsdirect.co.uk
Ⓦ www.chrysanthemumsdirect.co.uk
Contact: Martyn Flint
Opening Times: Not open. Mail order only.
Min Mail Order UK: Nmc
Min Mail Order EU: Nmc
Cat. Cost: 4 × 1st class.
Credit Cards: All major credit/debit cards
Specialities: Chrysanthemums. Young plants grown to order. Delivery within 14 days.

MCoo **Cool Temperate** ⊠ ✈
(Office) 45 Stamford Street,
Awsworth, Nottinghamshire
NG16 2QL
Ⓣ (0115) 916 2673
Ⓕ (0115) 916 2673
Ⓔ phil.corbett@cooltemperate.co.uk
Ⓦ www.cooltemperate.co.uk
Contact: Phil Corbett
Opening Times: 0900-1700, 7 days. Please ring/write first.
Min Mail Order UK: £30.00
Min Mail Order EU: £50.00
Cat. Cost: 3 × 1st class.
Credit Cards: None
Specialities: Tree fruit, soft fruit, nitrogen-fixers, hedging, own-root fruit trees. Many species available in small quantities only.
Notes: Nursery at Trinity Farm, Awsworth Lane, Cossall, Notts. Also sells wholesale.
Map Ref: M, B2 **OS Grid Ref:** SK482435

MCot **Coton Manor Garden** ♿
Guilsborough, Northampton,
Northamptonshire NN6 8RQ
Ⓣ (01604) 740219
Ⓔ nursery@cotonmanor.co.uk
Ⓦ www.cotonmanor.co.uk
Contact: Caroline Tait
Opening Times: 1200-1730 Tue-Sat, 3rd April-29th Sep. Also Sun Apr, May & B/hol w/ends. Other times in working hours by appt.
Cat. Cost: None issued.
Credit Cards: All major credit/debit cards
Specialities: Wide-range of herbaceous perennials (3000+ varieties), some available in small quantities only. Also many tender perennials & selected shrubs.
Notes: Garden open. Tea rooms. Garden School. Partial wheelchair access.
Map Ref: M, C3 **OS Grid Ref:** SP675715

MCri **Crin Gardens** ⊠ €
79 Partons Road, Kings Heath, Birmingham
B14 6TD
Ⓣ 0121 443 3815
Ⓜ 07805 591475
Ⓕ 0121 443 3815
Ⓔ cringardens@tiscali.co.uk
Ⓦ www.cringardens.co.uk
Contact: M Milinkovic
Opening Times: Not open. Mail order only.

KEY
⊠ Mail order to UK or EU ⛺ Delivers to shows
✈ Exports beyond EU € Euro accepted
♿ Accessible by wheelchair ◆ See Display advertisement

M

Min Mail Order UK: Nmc
Min Mail Order EU: Nmc
Cat. Cost: 2 × 1st class + 1× 2nd.
Credit Cards: None
Specialities: Lilies. Limited stock available on first come, first served basis.

MFie **Field House Nursery** ⊠ ♠ € ♿
Leake Road, Gotham, Nottinghamshire
NG11 0JN
Ⓣ (01159) 830278
Ⓜ 07504 125209
Ⓔ val.woolley@btinternet.com
Contact: Valerie A Woolley & Bob Taylor
Opening Times: 0900-1600 Fri-Wed or by appt.
Min Mail Order UK: 4 plants.
Min Mail Order EU: £30.00
Cat. Cost: 4 × 1st class or 4 × IRC (auriculas/primulas). 2 x 1st class (astrantias).
Credit Cards: Visa, MasterCard, Electron, Maestro, Solo
Specialities: *Primula auricula* & seed, *Astrantia*, herbaceous perennials. Nat. Collections of *Primula auricula* (show & alpine) & *Astrantia*.
Notes: Mail order for *Astrantia*, *Auricula*, small *Primula*, & seeds.
Map Ref: M, B3

MGos **Goscote Nurseries Ltd** ♿ ◆
Syston Road, Cossington, Leicestershire
LE7 4UZ
Ⓣ (01509) 812121
Ⓕ (01509) 814231
Ⓔ sales@goscote.co.uk
Ⓦ www.goscote.co.uk
Contact: James Toone
Opening Times: 7 days, year round, apart from between Xmas & New Year.
Cat. Cost: Online only.
Credit Cards: Visa, Access, MasterCard, Delta, Switch
Specialities: Japanese maples, rhododendrons & azaleas, *Magnolia*, *Camellia*, *Pieris* & other *Ericaceae*. Ornamental trees & shrubs, conifers, fruit, heathers, alpines, roses, *Clematis* & unusual climbers. Show Garden to visit.
Notes: Design & landscaping service available. Also sells wholesale.
Map Ref: M, B3 **OS Grid Ref:** SK602130

MHer **The Herb Nursery** ♿
Thistleton, Oakham, Rutland LE15 7RE
Ⓣ (01572) 767658
Ⓔ herbnursery@southwitham.net
Ⓦ www.herbnursery.co.uk
Contact: Peter Bench
Opening Times: 0900-1800 (or dusk) 7 days excl. Xmas-New Year.
Cat. Cost: A5 sae.
Credit Cards: All major credit/debit cards
Specialities: Herbs, wild flowers, cottage garden plants, scented-leaf pelargoniums. *Thymus*, *Mentha*, *Lavandula*.
Map Ref: M, B3

MHol **Hollies Farm Plant Centre**
Uppertown, Bonsall, Nr Matlock, Derbyshire
DE4 2AW
Ⓣ (01629) 822734
Ⓔ rbrt.wells@gmail.com
Ⓦ www.holliesfarmplantcentre.co.uk
Contact: Robert or Linda Wells
Opening Times: 0900-1700 every day except Wed.
Credit Cards: None
Specialities: Range of rare & unusual herbaceous perennials.
Notes: Also sells wholesale.
Map Ref: M, B2

MHom **Homestead Plants** ⊠
The Homestead, Normanton, Bottesford, Nottingham NG13 0EP
Ⓣ (01949) 842745
Ⓦ www.homesteadplants.com
Contact: Mrs S Palmer
Opening Times: By appt.
Min Mail Order UK: Nmc
Cat. Cost: 2 × 2nd class.
Credit Cards: None
Specialities: Unusual hardy & half-hardy perennials, esp. *Argyranthemum*, *Galanthus*, *Hosta*, *Jovibarba*, *Salvia*, *Sempervivum* & Heliotrope. Drought-tolerant asters. Most available only in small quantities. Nat. Collection of *heliotropium* cultivars.
Notes: Mail order not offered year round. Please check with nursery for details.
Map Ref: M, B3 **OS Grid Ref:** SK812407

MHoo **Hooksgreen Herbs Ltd** ⊠ ♠ €
Hooksgreen Farm, Oulton Heath,
Stone, Staffordshire
ST15 8TN
Ⓜ 07977 883810
Ⓔ sales@hooksgreenherbs.com
Ⓦ www.hooksgreenherbs.com
Contact: Malcolm Dickson
Min Mail Order UK: £10.00
Min Mail Order EU: £10.00
Credit Cards: All major credit/debit cards
Specialities: Culinary, medicinal & scented herbs.

MJac **JACKSON'S NURSERIES**
Clifton Campville, Nr Tamworth, Staffordshire B79 0AP
Ⓣ (01827) 373307
Contact: N Jackson
Opening Times: 0900-1800 Mon & Wed-Sat, 1000-1700 Sun.
Cat. Cost: 2 × 1st class.
Credit Cards: None
Specialities: *Fuchsia*.
Notes: Also sells wholesale.
Map Ref: M, B1

MJak **JACKSON'S NURSERIES** ⊠
Thorney Edge Road, Bagnall, Stoke-on-Trent, Staffordshire ST9 9LE
Ⓣ (01782) 502741
Ⓕ (01782) 504932
Ⓔ sales@jacksonsnurseries.co.uk
Ⓦ www.jacksonsnurseries.co.uk
Contact: Sherrie Davison
Opening Times: 0800-1700 7 days, Mar-Oct. 0800-1630, Nov-Feb.
Credit Cards: MasterCard, Visa
Specialities: Good general range.
Notes: Family-run nursery, established for over 50 years, a short distance from the Peak District. Tea room. Also sells wholesale.
Map Ref: M, B2

MLea **LEA RHODODENDRON GARDENS LTD** ⊠ ✈ ♿
Lea, Matlock, Derbyshire DE4 5GH
Ⓣ (01629) 534380 or 534260
Ⓕ (01629) 534260
Ⓦ www.leagarden.co.uk
Contact: Peter Tye
Opening Times: 1000-1730 7 days 20 Mar-30 Jun. Out of season by appt.
Min Mail Order UK: £15.00 + p&p
Min Mail Order EU: £15.00 + p&p
Cat. Cost: 30p + sae.
Credit Cards: All major credit/debit cards
Specialities: Rhododendrons & azaleas.
Map Ref: M, B1 **OS Grid Ref:** SK324571

MLHP **LONGSTONE HARDY PLANT NURSERY** ♿
Station Road, Great Longstone, Nr Bakewell, Derbyshire DE45 1TS
Ⓣ (01629) 640136
Ⓜ 07762 083674
Ⓔ lucyinlongstone@hotmail.com
Ⓦ www.longstonehardyplants.co.uk
Contact: Lucy Wright
Opening Times: 1000-1700 Wed-Mon (closed Tue), Mar-Oct.
Credit Cards: None
Specialities: Peat-free nursery displaying all our own hardy perennials, ornamental grasses, herbs & shrubs, incl. many unusual varieties. Some stock available in small quantities only. Can propagate to order.
Notes: Turn into Station Road between the White Lion Pub & the Cripin Inn. Nursery 100 yds on right.
Map Ref: M, A2 **OS Grid Ref:** SK198717

MLod **LODGE FARM PLANTS & WILDFLOWERS** ⊠ 🚚 € ♿
Case Lane, Fiveways, Hatton, Warwickshire CV35 7JD
Ⓣ (01926) 484649
Ⓜ 07977 631368
Ⓔ lodgefarmplants@btinternet.com
Ⓦ www.lodgefarmplants.com
Contact: Janet Cook & Nick Cook
Opening Times: Open 7 days all year, except Xmas Day & Boxing Day.
Min Mail Order UK: Nmc
Cat. Cost: Availability list online.
Credit Cards: All major credit/debit cards
Specialities: All forms of fruit trees: bush; espalier; fan; stepovers; cordons. Soft fruit. Wildflower plants. Native trees & hedging.
Notes: Courier service to all UK. Also sells wholesale.
Map Ref: M, C2 **OS Grid Ref:** SP223700

MMHG **MORTON NURSERIES LTD** ⊠ 🚚 ♿
Morton Hall, Ranby, Retford, Nottinghamshire DN22 8HW
Ⓣ (01777) 702530
Ⓜ 07940 434398
Ⓔ enquiries@morton-nurseries.com
Ⓦ www.morton-nurseries.co.uk
Contact: Gill McMaster
Opening Times: By appt.only
Min Mail Order UK: £5.00 + p&p
Cat. Cost: 3 × 1st class.
Credit Cards: None
Specialities: Shrubs & perennials.
Map Ref: M, A3

MMoz **MOZART HOUSE NURSERY GARDEN** 🚚
84 Central Avenue, Wigston, Leicestershire LE18 2AA
Ⓣ (0116) 288 9548
Contact: Des Martin
Opening Times: Please phone for appt.
Cat. Cost: Phone for list.
Credit Cards: None

KEY
⊠ Mail order to UK or EU — 🚚 Delivers to shows
✈ Exports beyond EU — € Euro accepted
♿ Accessible by wheelchair — ◆ See Display advertisement

M

Specialities: Bamboos, ornamental grasses, rushes & sedges, ferns. Shade & woodland plants. Some stock available in small quantities.
Map Ref: M, C3

MMuc **Mucklestone Nurseries** ⊠ ♿ ◆
Rock Lane, Mucklestone, Nr Market Drayton, Shropshire TF9 4DN
Ⓣ (01630) 674284
Ⓜ 07714 241668
Ⓔ info@botanyplants.co.uk
Ⓦ www.botanyplants.co.uk
Contact: William & Louise Friend
Opening Times: 1000-1700 Mon-Sat, winter times may vary, please phone first.
Min Mail Order UK: Nmc
Cat. Cost: Online.
Credit Cards: All major credit/debit cards
Specialities: Trees, shrubs, grasses & perennials for acid & damp soils of the north & west UK.
Notes: Any plants on website or listed under nursery code SEND can be collected to order. Contact nursery manager Martyn Jolly on 07704 874194 (working hours). Credit cards not accepted by phone. Also sells wholesale.
Map Ref: M, B2 **OS Grid Ref:** SJ728373

M

MNFA **The Nursery Further Afield** ⊠ ♿
Evenley Road, Mixbury, Nr Brackley, Northamptonshire NN13 5YR
Ⓣ (01280) 848808
Ⓔ sinclair@nurseryfurtherafield.co.uk
Ⓦ www.nurseryfurtherafield.co.uk
Contact: Gerald & Mary Sinclair
Opening Times: 1000-1700 Wed-Sat, Apr-mid Sep. Other times by appt.
Min Mail Order UK: £15.00
Cat. Cost: 3 × 1st class.
Credit Cards: None
Specialities: Worthwhile hardy perennials, many unusual. Large selection of *Geranium* & *Hemerocallis*. Nat. Collection of *Hemerocallis* on display 1400-1700 14th & 15th Jul 2012.
Notes: Mail order for *Hemerocallis* only.
Map Ref: M, C3 **OS Grid Ref:** SP608344

MNHC **The National Herb Centre** ⊠ ♿
Banbury Road, Warmington, Nr Banbury, Oxfordshire OX17 1DF
Ⓣ (01295) 690999
Ⓕ (01295) 690034
Ⓔ info@herbcentre.co.uk
Ⓦ www.herbcentre.co.uk
Contact: Plant Centre Staff
Opening Times: 0900-1730 Mon-Sat, 1030-1700 Sun.
Min Mail Order UK: Nmc but carriage charge of £10.00 for orders valued up to £50, more for larger orders.
Credit Cards: All major credit/debit cards
Specialities: Herbs, culinary & medicinal. Extensive selection of rosemary, thyme & lavender, in particular.
Notes: Next day delivery. UK mainland only. Signature required.
Map Ref: M, C2 **OS Grid Ref:** SP413471

MNrw **Norwell Nurseries** ⊠ ⌂ ♿ ◆
Woodhouse Road, Norwell, Newark, Nottinghamshire NG23 6JX
Ⓣ (01636) 636337
Ⓔ wardha@aol.com
Ⓦ www.norwellnurseries.co.uk
Contact: Dr Andrew Ward
Opening Times: 1000-1700 Mon, Wed-Fri & Sun (Wed-Mon May & Jun). By appt. Aug & 20th Oct-1st Mar.
Min Mail Order UK: £15.00 + p&p
Min Mail Order EU: £40.00
Cat. Cost: 3 × 1st class or online.
Credit Cards: None
Specialities: A large collection of unusual & choice herbaceous perennials esp., hardy geraniums, *Geum*, pond & bog plants, cottage garden plants, *Hemerocallis*, grasses, hardy chrysanthemums & woodland plants. Over 2500 different species & cvs grown. One acre garden open.
Notes: Talks given. Also sells wholesale.
Map Ref: M, B3 **OS Grid Ref:** SK767616

MOld **Old Hall Nursery** ♿
Winkhill, Leek, Staffordshire ST13 7PN
Ⓣ (01538) 308257
Ⓜ 07866 175881
Ⓔ oldhallnursery@hotmail.co.uk
Contact: Sandra Henshall
Opening Times: 1000-1600, 7 days.
Cat. Cost: Not available.
Credit Cards: None
Specialities: Large selection of herbaceous, herbs & alpines. Also shrubs, climbers & fruit trees. All hardy.
Map Ref: M, B2 **OS Grid Ref:** SK051521

MOWG **The Old Walled Garden** ⊠ ⌂ ♿
Honeybourne Road, Pebworth, Stratford-upon-Avon, Warwickshire CV37 8XP
Ⓣ (01789) 720788
Ⓕ (01789) 721162
Ⓔ Heather@oldwalledgarden.com
Ⓦ www.oldwalledgarden.com
Contact: Heather Godard-Key
Opening Times: 0900-1700 Mon-Sat, 1st Mar-31st Aug. 0900-1600 Mon-Fri,

1st Sep-28th Feb. 1030-1600 Sat & Sun, 2nd Apr-31st Jul. Closed last 2 weeks of Dec-1st week Jan, Easter Sun & Aug B/hol Mon.
Min Mail Order UK: Nmc
Min Mail Order EU: £30
Cat. Cost: 3 × 1st class
Credit Cards: Switch, MasterCard, Visa, Maestro
Specialities: Many rare & unusual shrubs. Wide range of conservatory plants esp. Australian. *Callistemon* & *Hibiscus*.
Map Ref: M, C2 **OS Grid Ref:** SP133458

MPet **PETER GRAYSON (SWEET PEA SEEDSMAN)** ⊠ ☒ €
34 Glenthorne Close, Brampton, Chesterfield, Derbyshire S40 3AR
Ⓣ (01246) 278503
Ⓕ (01246) 278503
Contact: Peter Grayson
Opening Times: Not open. Mail order only.
Min Mail Order UK: Nmc
Min Mail Order EU: Nmc
Cat. Cost: C5 sae, 1 × 2nd class.
Credit Cards: None
Specialities: *Lathyrus* species & cvs. Large collection of old-fashioned sweet peas & over 100 Spencer sweet peas incl. own cultivars and collection of old-fashioned cottage garden annuals & perennials.
Notes: Mail order for seeds only. Also sells wholesale.

MPhe **PHEDAR NURSERY** ⊠ ☒ €
42 Bunkers Hill, Romiley, Stockport, Cheshire SK6 3DS
Ⓣ (0161) 430 3772
Ⓔ mclewin@phedar.com
Ⓦ www.phedar.com
Contact: Will McLewin
Opening Times: Frequent but irregular. Please phone to arrange appt.
Min Mail Order UK: Nmc
Min Mail Order EU: Nmc
Cat. Cost: A5 sae + 4 × 1st class, or email for email version.
Credit Cards: None
Specialities: *Helleborus*, *Paeonia*. Limited stock of some rare items.
Notes: Non-EU exports subject to destination & on an ad hoc basis only. Please contact nursery for details. Also sells wholesale.
Map Ref: M, A2 **OS Grid Ref:** SJ936897

MPie **PIECEMEAL PLANTS** ♿
Whatton House Gardens, Nr Kegworth, Loughborough, Leicestershire LE12 5BG
Ⓣ (01509) 672056
Ⓔ nursery@piecemealplants.co.uk
Ⓦ www.piecemealplants.co.uk
Contact: Mary Thomas
Opening Times: 1300-1600 (1700 in summer) 2nd Mar-12th Oct, most Fri & some Sun. For up to date details, please ring or see website. Also by arrangement.
Cat. Cost: Online only.
Credit Cards: None
Specialities: Interesting range of herbaceous perennials, some half-hardy or tender. Many in small quantities.
Notes: Nursery located at entrance to Whatton Gardens, off A6. Car parking in front of Whatton House at top of drive.
Map Ref: M, B3 **OS Grid Ref:** SK494242

MPkF **PACKHORSE FARM NURSERY** ⌂ ♿
Sandyford House, Lant Lane, Tansley, Matlock, Derbyshire DE4 5FW
Ⓣ (01629) 57206
Ⓜ 07974 095752
Ⓕ (01629) 57206
Contact: Hilton W Haynes
Opening Times: 1000-1700 Tues & Wed, 1st Mar-31st Oct. Any other time by appt. only.
Cat. Cost: 2 × 1st class for plant list.
Credit Cards: None
Specialities: *Acer*, rare stock is limited in supply. Other more unusual hardy shrubs, trees & conifers.
Map Ref: M, B2 **OS Grid Ref:** SK322617

MPnt **PLANTAGOGO.COM** ⊠ ⌂ ♿
Jubilee Cottage Nursery, Snape Lane, Englesea Brook, Crewe, Cheshire CW2 5QN
Ⓣ (01270) 820335
Ⓜ 07713 518271
Ⓔ info@plantagogo.com
Ⓦ www.plantagogo.com
Contact: Vicky & Richard Fox
Opening Times: By appt. only. Also Open Days 1000-1600, 13th & 14th Oct 2012.
Min Mail Order UK: £8.95 single payment.
Min Mail Order EU: Price on application or see website.
Cat. Cost: 4 × 1st class.
Credit Cards: All major credit/debit cards
Specialities: *Heuchera*, *Heucherella*, *Tiarella*, also large selection of perennials. Nat. Collections of *Heuchera* & *Heucherella*. Nat. Collection of *Tiarella* applied for. Plants listed in *RHS Plant Finder* are available in good quantities. Others, not listed here, are

KEY
⊠ Mail order to UK or EU ⌂ Delivers to shows
☒ Exports beyond EU € Euro accepted
♿ Accessible by wheelchair ◆ See Display advertisement

M

available from our collections on request.
Notes: Also sells wholesale.
Map Ref: M, B1 **OS Grid Ref:** SJ750516

MRav **RAVENSTHORPE NURSERY** ⊠ ♿
6 East Haddon Road, Ravensthorpe, Northamptonshire NN6 8ES
Ⓣ (01604) 770548
Ⓕ (01604) 770548
Ⓔ ravensthorpenursery@hotmail.com
Contact: Jean & Richard Wiseman
Opening Times: 1000-1800 (or dusk if earlier) Tue-Sat. B/hol w/ends in May. Easter Mon.
Min Mail Order UK: Nmc
Min Mail Order EU: Nmc
Cat. Cost: None issued.
Credit Cards: Visa, MasterCard, Delta
Specialities: Over 3000 different trees, shrubs & perennials with many unusual varieties.
Notes: Search & delivery service for large orders, winter months only.
Map Ref: M, C3 **OS Grid Ref:** SP665699

MREP **RARE AND EXOTIC PLANTS AT WOODSHOOT NURSERIES** ⊠ ♿
King's Bromley, Burton-upon-Trent, Staffordshire DE13 7HN
Ⓣ (01543) 472233
Ⓜ 07802 737676
Ⓕ (01543) 472115
Ⓔ sales@rareandexoticplants.com
Ⓦ www.rareandexoticplants.com
Contact: Richard Flint
Opening Times: 0900-1700, 7 days.
Min Mail Order UK: £20.00 + p&p
Cat. Cost: 1 × 1st class.
Credit Cards: All major credit/debit cards
Specialities: *Acacia*, *Agave*, *Arbutus*, *Bamboo*, *Citrus*, *Cordyline*, *Dicksonia*, *Pittosporum*, palms, olives, *Yucca*, topiary & specimens.
Notes: Also sells wholesale.
Map Ref: M, B2 **OS Grid Ref:** SK127164

MSCN **STONYFORD COTTAGE NURSERY** ⊠ ♿
Stonyford Lane, Cuddington, Northwich, Cheshire CW8 2TF
Ⓣ (01606) 888970/888128 (answerphone)
Ⓜ 07714 205177
Ⓔ stonyfordcottage@yahoo.co.uk
Ⓦ www.stonyfordcottagenursery.co.uk
Contact: Andrew Overland
Opening Times: 1000-1700 Tue-Sun & B/hol Mons 1st Feb-31st Oct.
Min Mail Order UK: Nmc
Min Mail Order EU: Nmc
Cat. Cost: Not available this year
Credit Cards: All major credit/debit cards
Specialities: Wide range of herbaceous perennials, *Iris*, hardy *Geranium*, moisture-loving & bog plants. *Sempervivum*, *Paeonia*, candelabra *Primula*.
Notes: Also sells wholesale.
Map Ref: M, A1 **OS Grid Ref:** SJ580710

MSem **SEMPERVIVUM NURSERY** ⊠
(Office) 208 Park Lane, New Duston, Northamptonshire NN5 6QW
Ⓔ via website
Ⓦ www.sempervivumnursery.co.uk
Contact: Andrew Whelan
Opening Times: Not open. Mail order only.
Min Mail Order UK: £10.00
Min Mail Order EU: £30.00
Cat. Cost: Online.
Credit Cards: All major credit/debit cards
Specialities: *Sempervivum*.

MSKA **SWEET KNOWLE AQUATICS** ⊠ ♿
Wimpstone-Ilmington Road, Stratford-upon-Avon, Warwickshire CV37 8NR
Ⓣ (01789) 450036
Ⓕ (01789) 450036
Ⓔ sweetknowleaquatics@hotmail.com
Ⓦ www.sweetknowleaquatics.co.uk
Contact: Zoe Harding
Opening Times: 0930-1700 Sun-Fri, closed Sat. Open B/hols.
Min Mail Order UK: Nmc
Min Mail Order EU: Nmc
Cat. Cost: By email only.
Credit Cards: All major credit/debit cards
Specialities: Aquatics. Hardy & tropical water lilies, marginals & oxygenators. 2-acre display garden open to the public (no charge).
Map Ref: M, C2 **OS Grid Ref:** SP207480

MSnd **SOUND GARDEN RHODODENDRONS** ⊠ ⌂
(Office) 7 Lumber Lane, Burtonwood, Warrington, Cheshire WA5 4AS
Ⓣ (01925) 229100
Ⓜ 07931 340836
Ⓔ tim@sound-garden-design.com
Ⓦ www.sound-garden-designs.co.uk
Contact: Tim Atkinson
Opening Times: By appt. only.
Min Mail Order UK: £50.00
Min Mail Order EU: £100.00
Cat. Cost: 2 × 1st class
Credit Cards: None
Specialities: Species *Rhododendron* & hardy hybrids. Species *Sorbus*.
Notes: Nursery at Middledale Farm, Dale Road, Marple, Cheshire SK6 6NL.
Map Ref: N, B1 **OS Grid Ref:** SJ948901

M

MSpe **SPECIALPERENNIALS.COM** ⊠ ⌂ ♿
Yew Tree House, Hall Lane, Hankelow, Crewe, Cheshire CW3 0JB
Ⓣ (01270) 811443
Ⓜ 07716 990695
Ⓔ plants@specialperennials.com
Ⓦ www.specialperennials.com
Contact: Janet & Martin Blow
Opening Times: Nursery only open when garden open for NGS & Nat. Collection of *Helenium* & *Centaurea* Open Days. See website or phone for details.
Min Mail Order UK: Nmc
Min Mail Order EU: Nmc
Cat. Cost: Online or send A5 large letter sae.
Credit Cards: Paypal
Specialities: Herbaceous perennials. Nat. Collection of *Helenium* cvs (100+ varieties for sale). Nat. Collection of *Centaurea* (50+ varieties). Also *Geum*, border *Phlox*, *Hemerocallis*, *Monada* & *Persciaria*. All plants available in small quantities only.
Notes: All plants grown in garden nursery. Garden open for NGS. Talks given. Group visits to garden & nursery welcomed. See website or send sae for details. Some plants sell out quickly.
Map Ref: M, B1 **OS Grid Ref:** SJ699452

MSwo **SWALLOWS NURSERY** ⊠ ♿
Mixbury, Brackley, Northamptonshire NN13 5RR
Ⓣ (01280) 847721
Ⓕ (01280) 848611
Ⓔ enq@swallowsnursery.co.uk
Ⓦ www.swallowsnursery.co.uk
Contact: Chris Swallow
Opening Times: 0900-1300 & 1400-1700 (earlier in winter) Mon-Fri, 0900-1300 Sat.
Min Mail Order UK: £15.00
Cat. Cost: 3 × 1st class (plus phone number).
Credit Cards: All major credit/debit cards
Specialities: Growing a wide range, particularly shrubs, climbers, trees & roses.
Notes: Trees not for mail order unless part of larger order. Nursery transport used where possible, esp. for trees. Also sells wholesale.
Map Ref: M, C3 **OS Grid Ref:** SP607336

MTis **TISSINGTON NURSERY** ⊠ ⌂ ♿
The Old Kitchen Gardens, Tissington, Ashbourne, Derbyshire DE6 1RA
Ⓣ (01335) 390650
Ⓜ 07929 720284
Ⓔ info@tissington-nursery.co.uk
Ⓦ www.tissington-nursery.co.uk
Contact: Mairi Longdon
Opening Times: 1000-1700 daily, end Mar-end Sep.
Min Mail Order UK: Nmc
Cat. Cost: 4 × 1st class.
Credit Cards: All major credit/debit cards
Specialities: Choice & unusual perennials esp. *Achillea*, *Geranium*, *Geum*, *Helenium*, *Helianthus*, *Nepeta*, *Salvia*, *Sanguisorba* & *Sedum*.
Map Ref: M, B1 **OS Grid Ref:** SK176521

MTPN **SMART PLANTS** ⊠ ⌂
Sandy Hill Lane, off Overstone Road, Moulton, Northampton NN3 7JB
Ⓣ (01604) 454106
Ⓜ 07519 339508
Ⓔ smartplants@hotmail.co.uk
Contact: Stuart Smart
Opening Times: 1000-1500 Thu & Fri, 1000-1700 Sat. Other times by appt.
Min Mail Order UK: Nmc
Cat. Cost: 3 × 1st class
Credit Cards: None
Specialities: Wide range of herbaceous, alpines, shrubs, grasses, hardy *Geranium*. Some plants available in small quantities only
Notes: Limited wheelchair access.
Map Ref: M, C3

MWat **WATERPERRY GARDENS LTD** ⊠ ♿
Waterperry, Nr Wheatley, Oxfordshire OX33 1JZ
Ⓣ (01844) 339226/254
Ⓕ (01844) 339883
Ⓔ management@waterperrygardens.co.uk
Ⓦ www.waterperrygardens.co.uk
Contact: Mr R Jacobs
Opening Times: 1000-1730 summer. 1000-1700 winter.
Min Mail Order UK: £30.00
Cat. Cost: Online only.
Credit Cards: All major credit/debit cards
Specialities: General, large range of herbaceous esp. *Aster*, also Nat. Collection of *Saxifraga* (subsect. *Kabschia* & *Engleria*).
Map Ref: M, D3 **OS Grid Ref:** SP630064

MWhi **WHITEHILL FARM NURSERY** ⊠ € ♿
Whitehill Farm, Burford, Oxfordshire OX18 4DT
Ⓣ (01993) 823218
Ⓕ (01993) 822894
Ⓔ a.youngson@virgin.net
Ⓦ www.whitehillfarmnursery.co.uk
Contact: P J M Youngson

KEY
⊠ Mail order to UK or EU ⌂ Delivers to shows
✈ Exports beyond EU € Euro accepted
♿ Accessible by wheelchair ◆ See Display advertisement

M

Opening Times: 0900-1800 (or dusk if earlier) daily except Mon, Mar-Nov. Dec-Feb & Mons by appt.
Min Mail Order UK: £15 + p&p
Min Mail Order EU: £25 + p&p
Cat. Cost: 4 × 1st class.
Credit Cards: All major credit/debit cards
Specialities: Grasses & bamboos, less common shrubs & perennials. Some available in small quantities only.
Notes: £1.00 of catalogue cost refunded on 1st order.
Map Ref: M, D2 **OS Grid Ref:** SP268113

N

MWht **WHITELEA NURSERY** ⊠ ♿
Whitelea Lane, Tansley, Matlock, Derbyshire DE4 5FL
Ⓣ (01629) 55010
Ⓔ sales@uk-bamboos.co.uk
Ⓦ www.uk-bamboos.co.uk
Contact: David Wilson
Opening Times: By appt.
Min Mail Order UK: Nmc
Cat. Cost: Online only. Price list available 2 × 1st class.
Credit Cards: None
Specialities: Bamboos. Substantial quantities of 45 cvs & species of bamboo, remainder stocked in small numbers only. Ltd stocks of grasses, trees & shrubs.
Notes: Mail order limited by carrier restrictions, please contact nursery or see website for details. Also sells wholesale.
Map Ref: M, B1 **OS Grid Ref:** SK325603

MWts **WATERSIDE NURSERY** ⊠ ♿
Sharnford, Leicestershire
Ⓣ (01455) 273730
Ⓜ 07931 557082
Ⓔ watersidenursery@yahoo.co.uk
Ⓦ www.watersidenursery.co.uk
Contact: Linda Smith
Opening Times: By appt. only.
Min Mail Order UK: Nmc
Cat. Cost: Online only.
Credit Cards: All major credit/debit cards
Specialities: Aquatics, marginal pond plants, miniature water lilies, waterlilies, bog garden plants & moisture-loving plants.

NORTHERN

NAbi **ABI AND TOM'S GARDEN PLANTS** ♿
Halecat Nurseries, Witherslack, Grange Over Sands, Cumbria LA11 6RT
Ⓣ (01539) 552946
Ⓜ 07904 522665
Ⓔ info@halecatplants.co.uk
Ⓦ www.halecatplants.co.uk
Contact: Tom & Abi Attwood
Opening Times: 0900-1700 Mon-Sat, 1000-1600 Sun.
Cat. Cost: Online.
Credit Cards: All major credit/debit cards
Specialities: Hardy herbaceous perennials.
Map Ref: N, C1 **OS Grid Ref:** SD433838

NBid **BIDE-A-WEE COTTAGE GARDENS** ⊠ ♿
Stanton, Netherwitton, Morpeth, Northumberland NE65 8PR
Ⓣ (01670) 772238
Ⓕ (01670) 772238
Ⓔ info@bideawee.co.uk
Ⓦ www.bideawee.co.uk
Contact: Mark Robson
Opening Times: 1330-1700 Sat & Wed, 21st Apr-29th Aug 2012. Group visits at other times, except Sun.
Min Mail Order UK: £20.00
Cat. Cost: Online only.
Credit Cards: All major credit/debit cards
Specialities: Unusual herbaceous perennials, *Agapanthus*, *Primula*, ferns, grasses. Nat. Collection of *Centaurea*.
Map Ref: N, B2 **OS Grid Ref:** NZ132900

NBir **BIRKHEADS SECRET GARDENS & NURSERY** ♿
Nr Hedley Hall Woods, Sunniside, Gateshead, Tyne & Wear NE16 5EL
Ⓣ (01207) 232262
Ⓜ 07778 447920
Ⓕ (01207) 232262
Ⓔ birkheadsnursery@gmail.com
Ⓦ www.birkheadssecretgardens.co.uk
Contact: Mrs Christine Liddle
Opening Times: 1000-1700 Wed-Sun (closed Mon & Tues) Mar-Oct. Open B/hol Mons. Coach groups by appt.
Cat. Cost: None issued.
Credit Cards: All major credit/debit cards
Specialities: Hardy herbaceous perennials, grasses, bulbs & herbs. *Allium*, *Digitalis*, *Euphorbia*, *Galanthus* & *Geranium*. Max. 30 of any plant propagated each year.
Map Ref: N, B2 **OS Grid Ref:** NZ220569

NBre **BREEZY KNEES NURSERIES** ♿
Common Lane, Warthill, York YO19 5XS
Ⓣ (01904) 488800
Ⓦ www.breezyknees.co.uk
Contact: Any member of staff
Opening Times: 1000-1700 7 days (open 1100 Sun), 1st Apr-30th Sep.
Credit Cards: All major credit/debit cards
Specialities: Very wide range of perennials.

All can be viewed in 14-acre gardens (open 22nd May-30th Sep).
Map Ref: N, C3 **OS Grid Ref:** SE675565

NBro **BROWNTHWAITE HARDY PLANTS** ⊠ ♁ ♿
Fell Yeat, Casterton, Kirkby Lonsdale, Lancashire LA6 2JW
Ⓣ (01524) 271340 (after 1800 hours).
Ⓦ www.hardyplantsofcumbria.co.uk
Contact: Chris Benson
Opening Times: 1000-1700, 1st Apr-30th Sep.
Min Mail Order UK: Nmc
Cat. Cost: 4 × 1st class for *Hydrangea* catalogue. Sae for auricula list.
Credit Cards: None
Specialities: Herbaceous perennials incl. *Geranium*, *Hosta*, also *Tiarella*, *Heucherella* & *Primula auricula*.
Notes: Follow brown signs from A65 between Kirkby Lonsdale & Cowan Bridge. Mail order for *Hydrangea* & *P. auricula*.
Map Ref: N, C1 **OS Grid Ref:** SD632794

NCGa **CATHS GARDEN PLANTS** ⊠ ♁ ♿ ◆
The Walled Garden, Heaves Hotel, Heaves, Levens, Cumbria LA8 8EF
Ⓣ (01539) 561126
Ⓕ (01539) 561126
Ⓔ cath@cathsgardenplants.co.uk
Ⓦ www.cathsgardenplants.co.uk
Contact: Bob Sanderson
Opening Times: 1030-1700 7 days, Mar-Oct. 1030-1600 Mon-Fri, Nov-Feb. Closed Xmas & New Year weeks.
Min Mail Order UK: £15.00 + p&p
Min Mail Order EU: £25.00
Cat. Cost: Online only.
Credit Cards: All major credit/debit cards
Specialities: Wide variety of perennials, incl. uncommon varieties & selections of grasses, ferns, shrubs & climbing plants.
Notes: On A590 follow signs for Heaves (not in Levens village).
Map Ref: N, C1 **OS Grid Ref:** SD497867

NChi **CHIPCHASE CASTLE NURSERY** ⊠ ♁ ♿
Chipchase Castle, Wark, Hexham, Northumberland NE48 3NT
Ⓣ (01434) 230083
Ⓜ 07881 630398
Ⓔ info@chipchaseplants.co.uk
Ⓦ www.chipchaseplants.co.uk
Contact: Joyce Hunt & Alison Jones
Opening Times: 1000-1700 Thu-Sun & B/hol Mons Easter (or 1st Apr)-end Aug.
Min Mail Order UK: Nmc
Min Mail Order EU: Nmc
Cat. Cost: A5 sae for list
Credit Cards: All major credit/debit cards
Specialities: Unusual herbaceous esp. *Eryngium*, *Geum* & *Geranium*. Some plants only available in small quantities.
Notes: Suitable for accompanied wheelchair users.
Map Ref: N, B2 **OS Grid Ref:** NY880758

NChl **CHILTERN SEEDS** ⊠ ☒ €
Bortree Stile, Ulverston, Cumbria LA12 7PB
Ⓣ (01229) 581137 (24 hrs)
Ⓕ (01229) 584549
Ⓔ info@chilternseeds.co.uk
Ⓦ www.chilternseeds.co.uk
Opening Times: Mail order only. Normal office hours, Mon-Fri.
Min Mail Order UK: Nmc
Min Mail Order EU: Nmc
Cat. Cost: 3 × 2nd class.
Credit Cards: All major credit/debit cards
Specialities: Over 4,500 items of all kinds - wild flowers, trees, shrubs, cacti, annuals, houseplants, vegetables & herbs.

NCot **COTTAGE GARDEN PLANTS** ⊠ ♁
1 Kelton Croft, Kirkland, Cumbria CA26 3YE
Ⓣ (01946) 862664
Ⓔ expressplants@aol.com
Ⓦ http://simplesite.com/hardy_geraniums
Contact: Mrs J Purkiss
Opening Times: Open by appt. only for collecting orders & viewing garden. Consult local press & radio for charity openings.
Min Mail Order UK: £10.00
Min Mail Order EU: £15.00
Cat. Cost: 4 × 1st class sae.
Credit Cards: Paypal
Specialities: Hardy perennials incl. *Crocosmia*, *Galanthus*, *Geranium*, *Primula*, *Schizostylis* & bog plants. Small quantities only. Nat. Collection of *Geranium phaeum* Group. Viewing by appt. & on specified Open Days (check local press & radio).

NCro **CROSTON CACTUS** ⊠ € ♿
43 Southport Road, Eccleston, Chorley, Lancashire PR7 6ET
Ⓣ (01257) 452555
Ⓕ (01257) 452555
Ⓔ sales@croston-cactus.co.uk

KEY		
	⊠ Mail order to UK or EU	♁ Delivers to shows
	☒ Exports beyond EU	€ Euro accepted
	♿ Accessible by wheelchair	◆ See Display advertisement

N

Ⓦ www.croston-cactus.co.uk
Contact: John Henshaw
Opening Times: 0930-1700 by appt. only.
Min Mail Order UK: £5.00 + p&p
Min Mail Order EU: £10.00 + p&p
Cat. Cost: 2 × 1st class or 2 × IRCs.
Credit Cards: All major credit/debit cards
Specialities: Mexican cacti, *Echeveria* hybrids & some bromeliads & *Tillandsia*. Some items held in small quantities only. See catalogue.
Notes: Credit card payment accepted for online orders only.
Map Ref: N, D1 **OS Grid Ref:** SD522186

NDar **Dargem Carnations** ⊠

(Office) 167 Doncaster Lane, Woodlands, Doncaster, South Yorkshire DN6 7LH
Ⓣ (01302) 808326
Ⓜ 07506 012003
Ⓔ dargemcarnations1@gmail.co.uk
Ⓦ www.dargemcarnations.co.uk
Contact: Daryl Harris
Opening Times: By appt. only.
Min Mail Order UK: Nmc
Cat. Cost: None issued.
Credit Cards: None
Specialities: *Dianthus*.
Notes: Collection by appt. only from Markham Grange Nursery DN5 7XB (we use some of their greenhouses).
Map Ref: N, D2 **OS Grid Ref:** SE540082

N

NDav **Dave Parkinson Plants** ⊠

4 West Bank, Carlton, Goole, East Yorkshire DN14 9PZ
Ⓣ (01405) 860693
Ⓜ 07773 564945
Ⓕ (01405) 860693
Ⓦ www.daveparkinsonplants.co.uk
Contact: Mary Parkinson
Opening Times: Not open. Mail order only.
Min Mail Order UK: £12 + p&p
Min Mail Order EU: Nmc
Cat. Cost: 1st class stamp.
Credit Cards: None
Specialities: Hardy orchids. Terrestrial South African *Disa* orchids, species & hybrids.

NDov **Dove Cottage Nursery & Garden** ⊠

Shibden Hall Road, Halifax, West Yorkshire HX3 9XA
Ⓣ (01422) 203553
Ⓔ info@dovecottagenursery.co.uk
Ⓦ www.dovecottagenursery.co.uk
Contact: Stephen & Kim Rogers
Opening Times: 1000-1700 Wed-Sat, Mar-Oct. 1100-1600 Sun & B/hols Mar-Jun.
Min Mail Order UK: £20.00
Cat. Cost: 6 × 2nd class.
Credit Cards: All major credit/debit cards
Specialities: Herbaceous perennials & selected grasses, many displayed in adjoining naturalistic garden.
Map Ref: N, D2 **OS Grid Ref:** SE115256

NDro **Drointon Nurseries** ⊠

Plaster Pitts, Norton Conyers, Ripon, North Yorkshire HG4 5EF
Ⓣ (01765) 641849
Ⓜ 07909 971529
Ⓔ info@auricula-plants.co.uk
Ⓦ www.auricula-plants.co.uk
Contact: Robin & Annabel Graham
Opening Times: Open days in spring, otherwise by appt. only.
Min Mail Order UK: Nmc
Min Mail Order EU: Nmc
Cat. Cost: 4 × 1st class.
Credit Cards: All major credit/debit cards
Specialities: *Primula auricula*. More than 800 cvs of show, alpine, double & border auriculas. Ltd stocks of any one cultivar. Nat. Collection of *Primula auricula* (borders).
Map Ref: N, C2 **OS Grid Ref:** SE315753

NEgg **Eggleston Hall Gardens** €

Eggleston, Barnard Castle, Co. Durham DL12 0AG
Ⓣ (01833) 650230
Ⓔ mbhock@btinternet.com
Ⓦ www.plantsmanscorner.co.uk
Contact: Malcolm Hockham
Opening Times: 1000-1700 7 days. Closed 24th Dec to 6th Jan each year.
Cat. Cost: Online only.
Credit Cards: All major credit/debit cards
Notes: Collection from nursery only.
Map Ref: N, C2 **OS Grid Ref:** NY997233

NEqu **Equatorial Plant Co.** ⊠ €

7 Gray Lane, Barnard Castle, Co. Durham DL12 8PD
Ⓣ (01833) 690519
Ⓕ (01833) 690519
Ⓔ equatorialplants@teesdaleonline.co.uk
Ⓦ www.equatorialplants.com
Contact: Dr Richard Warren
Opening Times: Mail order only. Open by appt. only.
Min Mail Order UK: Nmc
Min Mail Order EU: Nmc
Cat. Cost: Free.
Credit Cards: Visa, Access, Paypal
Specialities: Laboratory-raised orchids only.
Notes: Also sells wholesale.

NFir **Fir Trees Pelargonium Nursery** ⊠ ⌂ ♿

Stokesley, Middlesbrough, Cleveland TS9 5LD
Ⓣ (01642) 713066
Ⓕ (01642) 713066
Ⓔ mark@firtreespelargoniums.co.uk
Ⓦ www.firtreespelargoniums.co.uk
Contact: Helen Bainbridge
Opening Times: 1000-1600 7 days 1st Apr-31st Aug, 1000-1600 Mon-Fri 1st Sep-31st Mar.
Min Mail Order UK: £4.00 + p&p
Cat. Cost: 4 × 1st class or £1.00 coin.
Credit Cards: All major credit/debit cards
Specialities: All types of *Pelargonium*, fancy leaf, regal, decorative regal, oriental regal, angel, miniature, zonal, ivy leaf, stellar, scented, dwarf, unique, golden stellar & species.
Map Ref: N, C2

NGBl **Garden Blooms** ⊠ ⌂ ♿

Fieldgate, Mill Field Road, Fishlake, Doncaster, Yorkshire DN7 5GH
Ⓣ 0845 5440964
Ⓔ info@gardenblooms.co.uk
Ⓦ www.gardenblooms.co.uk
Contact: Liz Webster
Opening Times: Not open, except by appt.
Min Mail Order UK: Nmc
Cat. Cost: Online only.
Credit Cards: None
Specialities: Hardy & tender perennials. Available in small quantities only.
Notes: Credit cards accepted online only.
Map Ref: N, D2 **OS Grid Ref:** SE659148

NGdn **Garden House Nursery** ♿

The Square, Dalston, Carlisle, Cumbria CA5 7LL
Ⓣ (01228) 710297
Ⓜ 07595 219082
Ⓔ stephickso@hotmail.co.uk
Ⓦ www.gardenhousenursery.co.uk
Contact: Stephen Hickson
Opening Times: 0900-1700 7 days Mar-Oct.
Cat. Cost: Plant list online only.
Credit Cards: None
Specialities: *Geranium*, *Hosta*, *Hemerocallis*, *Iris*, grasses & bamboos.
Notes: Also sells wholesale.
Map Ref: N, B1 **OS Grid Ref:** NY369503

NHal **Halls of Heddon** ⊠

West Heddon Nurseries, Heddon-on-the-Wall, Northumberland NE15 0JS
Ⓣ (01661) 852445
Ⓕ (01661) 852398
Ⓔ enquiry@hallsofheddon.co.uk
Ⓦ www.hallsofheddon.co.uk
Contact: David Hall
Opening Times: 0900-1700 Mon-Sat 1000-1700 Sun.
Min Mail Order UK: £10.00
Min Mail Order EU: £25.00
Cat. Cost: 3 × 2nd class
Credit Cards: MasterCard, Visa, Switch, Delta
Specialities: *Chrysanthemum* & *Dahlia*.
Notes: Also sells wholesale.
Map Ref: N, B2 **OS Grid Ref:** NZ122679

NHar **Hartside Nursery Garden** ⊠ ⌂

Nr Alston, Cumbria CA9 3BL
Ⓣ (01434) 381372
Ⓕ (01434) 381372
Ⓔ enquiries@plantswithaltitude.co.uk
Ⓦ www.plantswithaltitude.co.uk
Contact: S L & N Huntley
Opening Times: 1130-1630 Mon Fri, 1230-1600 w/ends & B/hols, Mar-Jun (incl.). 1130-1630 Tue-Fri, 1230-1600 B/hols, w/ends by appt., Jul-Oct (incl.). Winter months by appt. Times may vary during show season, so please phone before travelling.
Min Mail Order UK: Nmc
Min Mail Order EU: £50.00 + p&p
Cat. Cost: 4 × 1st class or 3 × IRC
Credit Cards: All major credit/debit cards
Specialities: Alpines grown at altitude of 1100 feet in Pennines. *Primula*, ferns, *Gentian* & *Meconopsis*.
Map Ref: N, B1 **OS Grid Ref:** NY708447

NHaw **The Hawthornes Nursery** ⊠ ♿

Marsh Road, Hesketh Bank, Nr Preston, Lancashire PR4 6XT
Ⓣ (01772) 812379
Ⓔ richardhaw@talktalk.net
Ⓦ www.hawthornes-nursery.co.uk
Contact: Irene & Richard Hodson
Opening Times: 0900-1800 7 days 1st Mar-30th Jun, Thu-Sun July-Oct. Gardens open for NGS. National Collection Open Day Thu 26th Jul 2012.
Min Mail Order UK: £10.00
Min Mail Order EU: Nmc
Cat. Cost: None issued.
Credit Cards: None
Specialities: *Clematis*, honeysuckle, choice selection of shrub & climbing roses, extensive

KEY
⊠ Mail order to UK or EU ⌂ Delivers to shows
☒ Exports beyond EU € Euro accepted
♿ Accessible by wheelchair ◆ See Display advertisement

N

range of perennials, mostly on display in the garden. Nat. Collection of *Clematis viticella*.
Map Ref: N, D1

NHer **HERTERTON HOUSE GARDEN NURSERY**
Hartington, Cambo, Morpeth,
Northumberland NE61 4BN
Ⓣ (01670) 774278
Contact: Mrs M Lawley & Mr Frank Lawley
Opening Times: 1330-1730 Mon, Wed, Fri-Sun 1st Apr-end Sep. (Earlier or later in the year weather permitting.)
Cat. Cost: None issued.
Credit Cards: None
Specialities: Country garden flowers.
Map Ref: N, B2 **OS Grid Ref:** NZ022880

NHol **HOLDEN CLOUGH NURSERY LTD** ⊠ ✈ ń ♿
Holden, Bolton-by-Bowland, Clitheroe,
Lancashire BB7 4PF
Ⓣ (01200) 447615
Ⓔ info@holdencloughnursery.co.uk
Ⓦ www.holdencloughnursery.co.uk
Contact: John Foley
Opening Times: 0900-1630 Mon-Fri Mar-Oct & B/hol Mons, 0900-1630 Sat all year. Nov-Feb by appt. only.
Min Mail Order UK: Nmc
Min Mail Order EU: Nmc
Cat. Cost: Free
Credit Cards: All major credit/debit cards
Specialities: Large general list incl. perennials, esp. *Crocosmia*, *Astilbe* & *Hosta*, shrubs, dwarf conifers, alpines, heathers, grasses & ferns.
Notes: Seasonal mail order on some items. Also sells wholesale on some items.
Map Ref: N, C2 **OS Grid Ref:** SD773496

NLAp **LANESIDE HARDY ORCHID NURSERY** ⊠ ń € ♿
74 Croston Road, Garstang, Preston,
Lancashire PR3 1HR
Ⓣ (01995) 605537
Ⓜ 07946 659661
Ⓔ jcrhutch@aol.com
Ⓦ www.lanesidehardyorchids.com
Contact: Jeff Hutchings
Opening Times: By telephone appt. only. Details of Open Days on website.
Min Mail Order UK: £35.00
Min Mail Order EU: £35.00
Cat. Cost: Sae or lists updated every month online.
Credit Cards: All major credit/debit cards
Specialities: 150+ species of hardy terrestrial orchids plus composts & cultivation notes. Species suitable for garden, cold or frost-free greenhouse.
Notes: Mail order for orchids during appropriate dormancy period as plants only sent bare-rooted. Also hardy orchid composts & pumice from the nursery or from Shows if ordered. See website for shows & talks. Also sells wholesale.
Map Ref: N, D1

NLar **LARCH COTTAGE NURSERIES** ⊠ € ♿ ◆
Melkinthorpe, Penrith, Cumbria
CA10 2DR
Ⓣ (01931) 712404
Ⓕ (01931) 712727
Ⓔ plants@larchcottage.co.uk
Ⓦ www.larchcottage.co.uk
Contact: Peter Stott & Joanne McCullock
Opening Times: Daily from 1000-1730 (or dusk in winter), all year round.
Min Mail Order UK: Nmc
Min Mail Order EU: Nmc
Cat. Cost: £7.00
Credit Cards: All major credit/debit cards
Specialities: Comprehensive plant collection in unique garden setting. Rare & unusual plants; particularly shrubs, trees, perennials, dwarf conifers & Japanese maples. *Acer*, *Hamamelis*, *Magnolia* & *Cornus kousa* cvs. Old-fashioned roses, bamboo & alpines.
Notes: Terraced restaurant & art gallery.
Map Ref: N, C1 **OS Grid Ref:** NY315602

NLBP **L.B. PLANTS** ⊠ ń ♿
Whitworth Hall Country Park, Spennymoor,
Co. Durham DH16 7QX
Ⓜ 079321 59204 or 07747 895096
Ⓔ enquiries@lbplants.co.uk
Ⓦ www.lbplants.co.uk
Contact: Howard Leslie & Sharon Bartle
Opening Times: 1000-1800 (or sunset in winter), 7 days.
Min Mail Order UK: Nmc
Cat. Cost: 3 × 1st class.
Credit Cards: None
Specialities: Hardy herbaceous & shrubby perennials, incl. lesser known and harder to find plants.
Notes: Also sells wholesale.
Map Ref: N, B2

NMin **MINIATURE BULBS & WILDFLOWER BULBS** ⊠ ń €
The Warren Estate, 9 Greengate Drive,
Knaresborough, North Yorkshire
HG5 9EN
Ⓣ (01423) 542819
Ⓕ (01423) 542819

Ⓦ www.miniaturebulbs.co.uk
Contact: Ivor Fox
Opening Times: Not open. Mail order only.
Min Mail Order UK: £15.00
Min Mail Order EU: £15.00
Cat. Cost: 1 × 1st class.
Credit Cards: All major credit/debit cards
Specialities: Rare & unusual miniature & wildflower bulbs, incl. *Narcissus*, *Tulipa*, *Iris*, *Crocus*, *Fritillaria* & others. Spring bulb list sent out in April. Some stock in small quantities.
Map Ref: N, C2 **OS Grid Ref:** SE350584

NMir MIRES BECK NURSERY ⊠ ♿
Low Mill Lane, North Cave, Brough, East Riding, Yorkshire HU15 2NR
Ⓣ (01430) 421543
Ⓕ (01430) 421543
Ⓔ admin@miresbeck.co.uk
Ⓦ www.miresbeck.co.uk
Contact: Judy Burrow & Martin Rowland
Opening Times: 1000-1600 Mon-Sat, 1st Mar-30th Sep. 1000-1500 Mon-Fri, 1st Oct-30th Nov & by appt.
Min Mail Order UK: Nmc
Cat. Cost: 3 × 1st class.
Credit Cards: None
Specialities: Wildflower plants of Yorkshire provenance.
Notes: Mail order for wildflower plants & plugs only. Also sells wholesale.

NMyG MARY GREEN ⊠ ⌂ ♿
The Walled Garden, Hornby, Lancaster, Lancashire LA2 8LD
Ⓣ (01524) 221989
Ⓜ 07778 910348
Ⓕ (01524) 221989
Ⓔ Marygreenplants@aol.com
Contact: Mary Green
Opening Times: By appt. only.
Min Mail Order UK: £10.00
Cat. Cost: 4 × 1st class.
Credit Cards: None
Specialities: Hostas, ferns & other shade-loving perennials.
Map Ref: N, C1 **OS Grid Ref:** SD588688

NNor NORCROFT NURSERIES ⊠ € ♿
Roadends, Intack, Southwaite, Carlisle, Cumbria CA4 0LH
Ⓣ (01697) 473933
Ⓔ stellagbell@btinternet.com
Contact: Keith Bell
Opening Times: Every afternoon excl. Mon (open B/hol), Apr-Jul, or ring for appt.
Min Mail Order UK: Nmc
Cat. Cost: 2 × 2nd class
Credit Cards: None
Specialities: Hardy herbaceous, *Dianthus*, *Aquilegia*, hostas, *Lilium*, *Papaver*.
Map Ref: N, B1 **OS Grid Ref:** NY474433

NOaD OAK DENE NURSERIES ⊠
10 Back Lane West, Royston, Barnsley, South Yorkshire S71 4SB
Ⓣ (01226) 722253
Contact: J Foster or G Foster
Opening Times: 0900-1230 & 1330-1800 1st Apr-30th Sep, 1000-1230 & 1330-1600 1st Oct-31st Mar. (Closed all day Wed.)
Min Mail Order UK: Phone for details.
Min Mail Order EU: Phone for details.
Cat. Cost: 1 × 2nd class for *Lithops* list.
Credit Cards: None
Specialities: Cacti, succulents (*Lithops*) & South African bulbs.
Notes: Also sells wholesale.
Map Ref: N, D2

NOak OAK TREE NURSERY ⊠ ⌂ ♿
Mill Lane, Barlow, Selby, North Yorkshire YO8 8EY
Ⓣ (01757) 618409
Ⓜ 07706 505688
Ⓔ gill@oaktreenursery.plus.com
Ⓦ www.oaktreenursery.com
Contact: Gill Plowes
Opening Times: By appt. only.
Min Mail Order UK: £10.00 + p&p
Min Mail Order EU: Nmc
Cat. Cost: 4 × 1st class.
Credit Cards: All major credit/debit cards
Specialities: Ornamental grasses & grass-like plants.
Notes: Will export seeds only beyond the EU. Also sells wholesale.
Map Ref: N, D3 **OS Grid Ref:** SE640285

NOra ORANGE PIPPIN LTD ⊠ ✈
(Office) 33 Algarth Rise, Pocklington, York, Yorkshire YO42 2HX
Ⓣ (01759) 392007
Ⓔ trees@orangepippin.com
Ⓦ www.orangepippinshop.com
Contact: Maureen Borrie
Opening Times: Not open. Mail order online only.
Min Mail Order UK: Nmc
Min Mail Order EU: Nmc

KEY
⊠ Mail order to UK or EU ⌂ Delivers to shows
✈ Exports beyond EU € Euro accepted
♿ Accessible by wheelchair ◆ See Display advertisement

N

Cat. Cost: Online only.
Credit Cards: MasterCard, Visa
Specialities: Wide range of many types of fruit tree, incl. traditional & modern varieties. Wide choice of rootstocks. Fruit tree expert available most days & at w/ends.
Notes: Order online all year round, deliveries from end Aug-end Mar. Website incl. extensive tasting notes & variety comparisons.

NOrc **ORCHARD HOUSE NURSERY** ♿
Orchard House, Wormald Green,
Nr Harrogate, North Yorkshire HG3 3NQ
Ⓣ (01765) 677541
Ⓕ (01765) 677541
Contact: Mr B M Corner
Opening Times: 0800-1630 Mon-Fri. Closed B/hols.
Cat. Cost: 4 × 1st class.
Credit Cards: None
Specialities: Herbaceous perennials, ferns, grasses, bog plants & unusual cottage garden plants.
Notes: Also sells wholesale.
Map Ref: N, C2

NPCo **PLANTSMAN'S CORNER**
Sunniside, Barningham, Richmond, Yorkshire
DL11 7DW
Ⓜ 07707 694310
Ⓔ plantsmanscorner@btinternet.com
Ⓦ www.plantsmanscorner.co.uk
Contact: Malcolm Hockham
Opening Times: Not yet fully open. Visits by appt. only. Plant orders can be collected by prior arrangement or from Eggleston Hall Gardens (see nursery NEgg for opening hours). Pls contact nursery for details.
Credit Cards: All major credit/debit cards
Specialities: *Cornus*, *Ilex*, & Japanese maples. Variable stock levels.

NPer **PERRY'S PLANTS** € ♿
The River Garden, Sleights, Whitby,
North Yorkshire YO21 1RR
Ⓜ 07879 498623
Ⓔ sharon.perry@virgin.net
Ⓦ www.perrysplants.co.uk
Contact: Sharon & Richard Perry
Opening Times: 1000-1700 mid-March to Oct.
Cat. Cost: None published.
Credit Cards: None
Specialities: *Lavatera*, *Malva*, *Erysimum*, *Euphorbia*, *Anthemis*, *Osteospermum* & *Hebe*. Uncommon hardy & container plants & aquatic plants.
Map Ref: N, C3 **OS Grid Ref:** NZ869082

NPla **THE PLANT DIRECTORY** ✉
Scawsby Hall Nurseries, Barnsley Road,
Scawsby, Doncaster, South Yorkshire
DN5 7UB
Ⓣ (01302) 783434
Ⓔ mail@the-plant-directory.co.uk
Ⓦ www.the-plant-directory.co.uk
Contact: David Lawson
Opening Times: Not open. Mail order only.
Min Mail Order UK: Nmc
Cat. Cost: None issued
Credit Cards: Visa, MasterCard, Paypal
Specialities: A wide range of herbaceous perennials, hardy trees, shrubs & indoor plants. Some indoor & aquatic plants in small quantities only.
Map Ref: N, D3

NPnk **PRIMROSE BANK** ✉ ⌂ ♿
Redroofs, Dauby Lane, Kexby, Yorkshire
YO41 5LH
Ⓣ (01759) 380220
Ⓜ 07774 944447
Ⓔ suegoodwill@yahoo.co.uk
Ⓦ www.primrosebank.co.uk
Contact: Sue Goodwill
Opening Times: 1000-1700, Thu-Sun, 1st Apr-30th Jun. Every day in Dec. By appt. only at other times.
Min Mail Order UK: Nmc
Cat. Cost: 6 × 1st class
Credit Cards: All major credit/debit cards
Specialities: Unusual hardy perennials, woodland garden & shade-tolerant plants. *Astrantia*, *Echinacea* & *Heuchera*.
Map Ref: N, C3 **OS Grid Ref:** SE695508

NPol **POLEMONIUM PLANTERY** ✉ ⌂
28 Sunnyside, Trimdon Grange, Co. Durham
TS29 6HF
Ⓣ (01429) 881529
Ⓔ dandd@polemonium.co.uk
Ⓦ www.polemonium.co.uk
Contact: David or Dianne Nichol-Brown
Opening Times: By appt. only.
Min Mail Order UK: £10.00
Cat. Cost: 3 × 1st class
Credit Cards: None
Specialities: Nat. Collections of *Polemonium*, *Collomia*, *Gilia*, *Leptodactylon* (*Polemoniaceae*) & *Hakonechloa*.
Notes: Also sells wholesale.
Map Ref: N, B2 **OS Grid Ref:** NZ369353

NPri **PRIMROSE COTTAGE NURSERY** ♿
Ringway Road, Moss Nook, Wythenshawe,
Manchester M22 5WF
Ⓣ (0161) 437 1557

Ⓔ info@primrosecottagenursery.co.uk
Ⓦ www.primrosecottagenursery.co.uk
Contact: Caroline Dumville
Opening Times: 0830-1730 Mon-Sat, 0930-1730 Sun (summer). 0830-1700 Mon-Sat, 0930-1700 Sun (winter).
Cat. Cost: Plant lists can be sent by email.
Credit Cards: All major credit/debit cards
Specialities: Hardy herbaceous perennials, alpines, herbs, roses, patio & hanging basket plants. Shrubs, ornamental trees, fruit trees, soft fruit bushes & vegetable plants.
Notes: Coffee shop open daily.
Map Ref: N, D2

NPro **ProudPlants** ⊠ ♠ ♿
East of Eden Nurseries, Ainstable, Carlisle, Cumbria CA4 9QN
Ⓣ (01768) 896604
Ⓜ 07788 142969
Ⓔ rogereastofeden@hotmail.com
Contact: Roger Proud
Opening Times: By appt. only, Mar-Oct.
Min Mail Order UK: £10.00
Cat. Cost: None issued
Credit Cards: None
Specialities: Interesting & unusual shrubs, perennials & alpines, esp. astilbes and geums.
Notes: Mail order available Sep-Mar on geums & astilbes only.
Map Ref: N, B1 **OS Grid Ref:** NY467504

NRib **Ribblesdale Nurseries** ♿
Newsham Hall Lane, Woodplumpton, Preston, Lancashire PR4 0AS
Ⓣ (01772) 863081
Ⓕ (01772) 861884
Ⓔ philsd@btinternet.com
Ⓦ www.ribblesdalenurseries.co.uk
Contact: Mr & Mrs Dunnett
Opening Times: 0900-1800 Mon-Sat Apr-Sep, 0900-1700 Mon-Sat Oct-Mar. 1030-1600 Sun.
Credit Cards: Visa, MasterCard, Delta, Switch
Specialities: Trees, shrubs & perennials. Conifers, hedging, alpines, fruit, climbers, herbs, aquatics, ferns & wildflowers. Own grown plants in peat-free compost.
Map Ref: N, D1 **OS Grid Ref:** SD515351

NRob **W Robinson & Son (Seeds & Plants) Ltd** ⊠ ✈ ♠ € ♿
Sunny Bank, Forton, Nr Preston, Lancashire PR3 0BN
Ⓣ (01524) 791210
Ⓕ (01524) 791933
Ⓔ info@mammothonion.co.uk
Ⓦ www.mammothonion.co.uk
Contact: Miss Robinson
Opening Times: 1000-1600 7 days Mar-Jun, 0800-1700 Mon-Fri Jul-Feb.
Min Mail Order UK: Nmc
Min Mail Order EU: Nmc
Cat. Cost: Free.
Credit Cards: Visa, Access, American Express, Switch
Specialities: Mammoth vegetable seed. Onions, leeks, tomatoes & beans. Range of vegetable plants in the spring.
Notes: Also sells wholesale.

NRya **Ryal Nursery** ♠ ♿
East Farm Cottage, Ryal, Northumberland NE20 0SA
Ⓣ (01661) 886562
Ⓔ alpines@ryal.freeserve.co.uk
Contact: R F Hadden
Opening Times: Mar-Jul by appt., please phone.
Cat. Cost: Sae.
Credit Cards: None
Specialities: Alpine & woodland plants. Mainly available in small quantities only. Nat. Collection of *Primula marginata*.
Notes: Also sells wholesale.
Map Ref: N, B2 **OS Grid Ref:** NZ015744

NSla **Slack Top Nurseries** ⊠ ♠ € ♿
1 Waterloo House, 24 Slack Top, Hebden Bridge, West Yorkshire HX7 7HA
Ⓣ (01422) 845348
Ⓜ 07508 953804
Ⓔ enquiries@slacktopnurseries.co.uk
Ⓦ www.slacktopnurseries.co.uk
Contact: Michael & Allison Mitchell
Opening Times: 1000-1700 Fri-Sun 1st Mar-31st Aug & B/hols. Other times by appt.
Min Mail Order UK: £30.00
Min Mail Order EU: £50.00
Cat. Cost: 2 × 1st class A5 sae or online.
Credit Cards: None
Specialities: Alpine, rockery & woodland plants.
Notes: Some areas of garden inaccessible for wheelchairs. Talks given to gardening clubs & other groups by appt.
Map Ref: N, D2 **OS Grid Ref:** SD977286

NSoo **Sooty's Plants** ♿
113a Southport New Road, Tarleton, Preston, Lancashire PR4 6HX
Ⓣ (01772) 816901

KEY
⊠ Mail order to UK or EU ♠ Delivers to shows
✈ Exports beyond EU € Euro accepted
♿ Accessible by wheelchair ◆ See Display advertisement

N

Ⓔ sales@sootysplants.co.uk
Ⓦ www.sootysplants.co.uk
Contact: Paul Milbourn
Opening Times: 0900-1700 Mon-Sat, 1000-1600 Sun. Closed 25th Dec-mid Feb.
Cat. Cost: None issued.
Credit Cards: All, except American Express
Specialities: Wide range of common & unusual plants. Some varieties available in small quantities only.
Map Ref: N, D1 **OS Grid Ref:** SD441196

NSti Stillingfleet Lodge Nurseries ♿
Stewart Lane, Stillingfleet, North Yorkshire YO19 6HP
Ⓣ (01904) 728506
Ⓔ vanessa.cook@stillingfleetlodgenurseries.co.uk
Ⓦ www.stillingfleetlodgenurseries.co.uk
Contact: Vanessa Cook
Opening Times: 1300-1700 Wed & Fri 2nd Apr-30th Sep. 1300-1700, 1st & 3rd Sat & Sun in each month.
Cat. Cost: Online only.
Credit Cards: None
Specialities: Foliage & unusual perennials. Hardy geraniums, *Pulmonaria*, variegated plants & grasses, interesting climbers.
Map Ref: N, C2

NSue Sue Proctor Plants ⊠ ⌂ €
69 Ing Mill Avenue, Clayton West, Huddersfield, West Yorkshire HD8 9QG
Ⓣ (01484) 866189
Ⓜ 07917 006636
Ⓔ sueproctor@talktalk.net
Ⓦ www.sueproctorplants.co.uk
Contact: Richard Proctor
Opening Times: By appt. only. Please phone first.
Min Mail Order UK: £3.50
Min Mail Order EU: £3.50
Cat. Cost: Large 1st sae.
Credit Cards: All major credit/debit cards
Specialities: *Hosta*, especially miniature hostas.
Notes: Garden & nursery open under the NGS (3rd and 19th Aug 2012), see NGS Yellow Book for details.

NSum Summerdale Garden Nursery ⊠ ⌂
Summerdale House, Cow Brow, Lupton, Carnforth, Lancashire LA6 1PE
Ⓣ (01539) 567210
Ⓔ sheals@btinternet.com
Ⓦ www.summerdalegardenplants.co.uk
Contact: Gail Sheals
Opening Times: 0930-1630 Thu, Fri & Sat, 1st Apr-30th Sep. Other times by appt. only.
Min Mail Order UK: £25.00
Cat. Cost: Online only.
Credit Cards: None
Specialities: Wide variety of perennials, large collection of *Primula*. Many moist and shade-loving plants incl. *Meconopsis* & hellebores.
Notes: Mail order for primulas only.
Map Ref: N, C1 **OS Grid Ref:** SD545819

NTay Taylors Clematis Nursery ⊠ ⌂ ♿
Sutton Road, Sutton, Nr Askern, Doncaster, South Yorkshire DN6 9JZ
Ⓣ (01302) 700716
Ⓕ (01302) 708415
Ⓔ info@taylorsclematis.co.uk
Ⓦ www.taylorsclematis.co.uk
Contact: Chris & Suzy Cocks
Opening Times: Open by appt. only. Please ring for details.
Min Mail Order UK: Nmc
Min Mail Order EU: Nmc
Cat. Cost: 4 × 2nd class.
Credit Cards: All major credit/debit cards
Specialities: *Clematis* (over 350+ varieties).
Map Ref: N, D2 **OS Grid Ref:** SE552121

NTPC Tree Peony Company ⊠ ⌂
Willow Cottage, Rillington, Malton, North Yorkshire YO17 8JU
Ⓣ (01944) 758280
Ⓔ info@treepeony.co.uk
Ⓦ www.treepeony.co.uk
Contact: Thelma Scruton, Roger Scruton
Min Mail Order UK: Nmc
Cat. Cost: None.
Credit Cards: None
Specialities: Tree peonies. *Paeonia suffruticosa*. *P.* Gansu Group. *P. rockii*.
Notes: Also sells wholesale.

NTre Treetyme ⊠
Prospect Hill House, Kirkoswald, Penrith, Cumbria CA10 1ER
Ⓣ (01768) 800238
Ⓕ (01768) 897138
Ⓔ sales@treetyme.co.uk
Ⓦ www.treetyme.co.uk
Contact: Hugh Povey
Opening Times: Not open. Mail order via website only.
Min Mail Order UK: Nmc
Cat. Cost: Online only.
Credit Cards: All major credit/debit cards
Specialities: *Cercis*. Stock available in small quantities only. National Collection of *Cercis* (Provisional).

NWad **Waddow Lodge Garden** ⊠ ♿
Clitheroe Road, Waddington, Clitheroe, Lancashire BB7 3HQ
Ⓣ (01200) 429145
Ⓔ peterfoleyhcn@hotmail.co.uk
Ⓦ www.gardentalks.co.uk
Contact: Peter Foley
Opening Times: By appt. only all year.
Min Mail Order UK: Nmc
Min Mail Order EU: Nmc
Cat. Cost: Online only.
Credit Cards: None
Specialities: A developing plantsman's garden with a wide-ranging, interesting plant collection.
Notes: Open for group visits by appt., incl. evenings. Also open under NGS 27th May & 29th Jul 2012 with plant sales for Plant Heritage NW Group.
Map Ref: N, C1 **OS Grid Ref:** SD732434

NWea **Weasdale Nurseries Ltd** ⊠
Newbiggin-on-Lune, Kirkby Stephen, Cumbria CA17 4LX
Ⓣ (01539) 623246
Ⓕ (01539) 623277
Ⓔ sales@weasdale.com
Ⓦ www.weasdale.com
Contact: Andrew Forsyth
Opening Times: 0830-1300 & 1400-1730 Mon-Fri. Closed w/ends, B/hols, Xmas through to the New Year.
Min Mail Order UK: Nmc
Min Mail Order EU: Nmc
Cat. Cost: Free of charge in UK or £2.00 to EU.
Credit Cards: All major credit/debit cards
Specialities: Hardy forest trees, hedging, broadleaved & conifers. Specimen trees & shrubs grown at 850 feet (260 metre) elevation.
Notes: Mail order a speciality. Mail order Nov-Apr only. Also sells wholesale to VAT registered customers.
Map Ref: N, C1 **OS Grid Ref:** NY690039

NWit **D S Witton** ⊠
26 Casson Drive, Harthill, Sheffield, Yorkshire S26 7WA
Ⓣ (01909) 771366
Ⓔ donshardyeuphorbias@btopenworld.com
Ⓦ www.euphorbias.co.uk
Contact: Don Witton
Opening Times: By appt. only. Open Day, 1300-1600, Sun 6th May 2012.
Min Mail Order UK: Nmc
Cat. Cost: 1 × 1st class + sae.
Credit Cards: None
Specialities: Nat. Collection of Hardy *Euphorbia*. Over 130 varieties.
Notes: Mail order seed only, Oct-June.
Map Ref: N, D2 **OS Grid Ref:** SK494812

NWsh **Westshores Nurseries** ⊠
82 West Street, Winterton, Lincolnshire DN15 9QF
Ⓣ (01724) 733940
Ⓜ 07875 732535
Ⓔ westshnur@aol.com
Ⓦ www.westshores.co.uk
Contact: Gail & John Summerfield
Opening Times: 1st Mar-31st Oct by appt. only.
Min Mail Order UK: £15.00
Credit Cards: All major credit/debit cards
Specialities: Ornamental grasses.
Map Ref: N, D3 **OS Grid Ref:** SE927187

NYoL **Yorkshire Lavender** ⊠ ♿
Terrington, York, North Yorkshire YO60 6PB
Ⓣ (01653) 648008
Ⓦ www.yorkshirelavender.com
Contact: Julia Snowball
Opening Times: 1000-1700 7 days, 17th Mar-28th Oct 2012.
Min Mail Order UK: £10.00
Cat. Cost: None issued
Credit Cards: All major credit/debit cards
Specialities: *Lavandula, Mentha, Thymus.* Herbs.
Map Ref: N, C3 **OS Grid Ref:** SE655710

Southern

SAll **Allwoods** ⊠ ♿
London Road, Hassocks, West Sussex BN6 9NB
Ⓣ (01273) 844229
Ⓔ info@allwoods.net
Ⓦ www.allwoods.net
Contact: David & Emma James
Opening Times: Office: 0900-1630 Mon-Fri. Answer machine all other times. Nursery: open to visitors 7 days. Check website for detailed opening times.
Min Mail Order UK: Nmc
Min Mail Order EU: Nmc
Cat. Cost: 2 × 1st class.
Credit Cards: Access, Visa, MasterCard, Switch, Maestro

S

KEY
⊠ Mail order to UK or EU | Delivers to shows
✈ Exports beyond EU | € Euro accepted
♿ Accessible by wheelchair | ◆ See Display advertisement

Specialities: *Dianthus* incl. hardy border carnations, pinks, perpetual flowering & spray carnations, Malmaisons & *D. allwoodii*, some available as seed. Certain lavender varieties. Penstemons.
Notes: All listed varieties available as plugs but choice varies depending on time of year. Please phone before travelling to avoid disappointment and/or to ensure order is ready for collection.
Map Ref: S, D4 **OS Grid Ref:** TQ303170

SAPC **ARCHITECTURAL PLANTS (CHICHESTER) LTD** ⊠ ♠ € ♿
Lidsey Road Nursery, Westergate, Nr Chichester, West Sussex PO20 6SU
Ⓣ (01243) 545008
Ⓕ (01243) 545009
Ⓔ chichester@architecturalplants.com
Ⓦ www.architecturalplants.com
Contact: Rebecca Carter
Opening Times: 0900-1700 Mon-Sat & B/hols. Closed Sun.
Min Mail Order UK: Nmc
Min Mail Order EU: £150.00
Cat. Cost: Free.
Credit Cards: All major credit/debit cards
Specialities: Architectural plants & hardy exotics esp. rare evergreen broadleaved trees & seaside exotics, spiky plants, yuccas/agaves, climbers & bamboos.
Notes: Second nursery near Horsham. Also sells wholesale.
Map Ref: S, D3 **OS Grid Ref:** SU937040

SBch **BIRCHWOOD PLANTS** ⊠ ♠ ♿
(Office) 10 Westering, Romsey, Hampshire SO51 7LY
Ⓣ (01794) 502192 or (02380) 814345
Ⓔ info@birchwoodplants.co.uk
Ⓦ www.birchwoodplants.co.uk
Contact: Lesley Baker
Opening Times: Not open. Plants can be collected by arrangement from nursery or from sales & shows as posted on website.
Min Mail Order UK: £15 + p&p
Cat. Cost: Online only.
Credit Cards: Paypal
Specialities: Good selection of hardy geraniums & *Dianthus*, esp. old-fashioned pinks. Scented plants & those to attract bees & butterflies. Increasing number of alpines & drought-tolerant plants. National Collection of *Geranium nodosum*. Most stock only available in small quantities unless ordered in advance.
Notes: Nursery at Silverwood House, Gardener's Lane, Nr Romsey, SO51 6AD. Mostly accessible for wheelchairs. Mail order considered for small plants. No mail order sent Dec-Jan.
Map Ref: S, D2 **OS Grid Ref:** SU333190

SBea **BEAN PLACE NURSERY** ⊠ ♠
Watersfield, Bletchenden Road, Headcorn, Kent TN27 9JB
Ⓜ 07841 484822
Ⓔ beanplacenursery@googlemail.com
Ⓦ www.beanplace.co.uk
Contact: Anita or Tim Waters
Opening Times: By appt. only.
Cat. Cost: Online.
Credit Cards: None
Specialities: Ornamental grasses, herbaceous perennials & cottage garden plants.
Notes: Only sells at shows. Contact nursery for details of shows attended. Also sells wholesale.
Map Ref: S, C5

SBHP **BLEAK HILL PLANTS** ♿
Braemoor, Bleak Hill, Harbridge, Ringwood, Hampshire BH24 3PX
Ⓣ (01425) 652983
Ⓔ tracy@bleakhillplants.co.uk
Contact: Tracy Netherway
Opening Times: 0900-1800, Mon, Tue, Fri, Sat & 1000-1600 Sun, Mar-Oct. Closed Wed & Thu.
Cat. Cost: 2 × 1st class.
Credit Cards: None
Specialities: Hardy & half-hardy herbaceous perennials. Stock available in small quantities.
Map Ref: S, D1 **OS Grid Ref:** SU132111

SBig **BIG PLANT NURSERY** ⊠ ♠ ♿ ◆
Hole Street, Ashington, West Sussex RH20 3DE
Ⓣ (01903) 891466
Ⓜ 07957 262845
Ⓕ (01903) 892829
Ⓔ info@bigplantnursery.co.uk
Ⓦ www.bigplantnursery.co.uk
Contact: Bruce Jordan
Opening Times: 0900-1700 Mon-Sat, 1000-1600 Sun & B/hols.
Min Mail Order UK: Please phone for further info.
Cat. Cost: A5 sae with 2 × 1st class.
Credit Cards: All major credit/debit cards
Specialities: Bamboos, hardy exotics & palms, *Ginkgo*, *Betula*.
Notes: Programme of events & propagation tuition, see nursery website for details. Also sells wholesale.
Map Ref: S, D3 **OS Grid Ref:** TQ132153

S

SBir **BIRCHFLEET NURSERIES** ♿ ◆
Greenfields Close, Nyewood, Petersfield, Hampshire GU31 5JQ
Ⓣ (01730) 821636
Ⓕ (01730) 821636
Ⓔ gammoak@aol.com
Ⓦ www.birchfleetnurseries.co.uk
Contact: John & Daphne Gammon
Opening Times: By appt. only. Please phone.
Cat. Cost: 2 × 1st class.
Credit Cards: None
Specialities: Oaks. Beech. *Nyssa*. Nat. Collection of *Liquidambar*.
Notes: Nursery accessible for wheelchairs in dry weather. Also sells wholesale.
Map Ref: S, C3

SBod **BODIAM NURSERY**
Bodiam, Robertsbridge, East Sussex TN32 5RA
Ⓣ (01580) 830811
Ⓜ 07971 419302
Ⓔ enquiries@bodiamnursery.co.uk
Ⓦ www.bodiamnursery.co.uk
Contact: Jill Kaye
Opening Times: 1000-1700 (or dusk in winter) 7 days, 18th Feb-30th Jun. Closed Mon, 1st Jul-30th Nov. Closed from 1st Dec until new season.
Cat. Cost: None issued
Credit Cards: All major credit/debit cards
Specialities: Wide range of *Acer palmatum*, available in small quantities only. Coastal & Mediterranean plants. *Euphorbia*.
Notes: Opposite Bodiam Castle, between Great Dixter & Merriments Gardens.
Map Ref: S, C5

SBri **BRICKWALL COTTAGE NURSERY** ✉ ♿
1 Brickwall Cottages, Frittenden, Cranbrook, Kent TN17 2DH
Ⓣ (01580) 852425
Ⓜ 07714 529946
Ⓔ sue.martin@talktalk.net
Ⓦ www.geumcollection.co.uk
Contact: Sue Martin
Opening Times: By appt. only.
Min Mail Order UK: Nmc
Min Mail Order EU: Nmc
Credit Cards: None
Specialities: Hardy perennials. Stock available in small quantities only. Nat. Collection of *Geum*.
Map Ref: S, C5 **OS Grid Ref:** TQ815410

SBrm **BRAMBLY HEDGE** ✉
Mill Lane, Sway, Hampshire SO41 8LN
Ⓣ (01590) 683570
Contact: Kim Williams
Opening Times: By appt. only in Jul & Aug.
Min Mail Order UK: Nmc
Cat. Cost: Sae for descriptive list.
Credit Cards: None
Specialities: Nat. Collections of *Streptocarpus* & *Begonia rex* cvs. Plants available in small quantities only.
Notes: Mail order Mar-Aug, small quantities only.
Map Ref: S, D2 **OS Grid Ref:** SZ294973

SBrt **BRIGHTON PLANTS** ✉ 🚚 € ♿
New Hall Lane, Small Dole, Sussex BN5 9YJ
Ⓜ 07807 594209
Ⓔ peganum1@yahoo.co.uk
Ⓦ www.brightonplants.blogspot.com/
Contact: Steve Law
Opening Times: 1000-1700 w/ends, May-Oct. Please email/phone first.
Min Mail Order UK: Nmc
Min Mail Order EU: Nmc
Cat. Cost: 2 × 1st class.
Credit Cards: None
Specialities: Hardy herbaceous and woody plants. Drought-tolerant plants.
Map Ref: S, D3 **OS Grid Ref:** TQ208132

SBst **BEAST PLANTS**
24 Arundel Road, Boyatt Wood, Eastleigh, Hampshire SO50 4PQ
Ⓜ 07887 997263 or 07887 997433
Ⓔ beastplants@tiscali.co.uk
Contact: Toni & Steve Newell
Opening Times: By appt. only.
Cat. Cost: Free.
Credit Cards: None
Specialities: Exotic, sub-tropical & unusual plants.

SCac **CACTI & SUCCULENTS** ✉
Hammerfield, Crockham Hill, Edenbridge, Kent TN8 6RR
Ⓣ (01732) 866295
Contact: Geoff Southon
Opening Times: Flexible. Please phone first.
Min Mail Order UK: Nmc
Cat. Cost: None issued.
Credit Cards: None
Specialities: *Echeveria* & related genera & hybrids. Haworthias & gasterias. A large range of aeoniums, both species & hybrids. A large range of plants available in small quantities.

KEY
✉ Mail order to UK or EU — 🚚 Delivers to shows
✈ Exports beyond EU — € Euro accepted
♿ Accessible by wheelchair — ◆ See Display advertisement

S

SCam **Camellia Grove Nursery** ⊠ ⊠ ⌂ € ♿
Market Garden, Lower Beeding, West Sussex RH13 6PP
Ⓣ (01403) 891412
Ⓔ sales@camellia-grove.com
Ⓦ www.camellia-grove.com
Contact: Chris Loder
Opening Times: 1000-1600 Mon-Sat, please phone first so we can give try to give you our undivided attention.
Min Mail Order UK: Nmc
Min Mail Order EU: Nmc
Cat. Cost: 2 × 1st class.
Credit Cards: All, except American Express
Specialities: *Camellia japonica*, *C. williamsii*, *C. sasanqua* & *C. reticulata*, from the purest white to richest red flowers.
Notes: Also sells wholesale.
Map Ref: S, C3 **OS Grid Ref:** TQ221255

S

SCan **Canna Man** ⊠ €
(Office) 4 Newland Road,
Upper Beeding, Steyning, West Sussex BN44 3JJ
Ⓣ (01903) 813780
Ⓔ clivethecannaman@gmail.com
Ⓦ www.cannaman.co.uk
Contact: Clive Parker
Opening Times: Not open. Mail order only.
Min Mail Order UK: Nmc
Min Mail Order EU: Nmc
Cat. Cost: Online only.
Credit Cards: Paypal
Specialities: A wide range of disease-free *Canna*, many only available in very small numbers. All plants grown in own peat-free compost without the use of chemical pesticides. Will propagate to order.
Notes: Plants only available from May-Oct.

SChF **Charleshurst Farm Nursery** ⊠ ⌂ €
Loxwood Road, Plaistow, Billingshurst, West Sussex RH14 0NY
Ⓣ (01403) 752273
Ⓜ 07736 522788
Ⓔ Charleshurstfarm@aol.com
Ⓦ www.charleshurstplants.co.uk
Contact: Clive Mellor
Opening Times: Normally 0900-1730 Fri, Sat, Sun, Feb-Oct, but please ring first before travelling.
Min Mail Order UK: Nmc
Min Mail Order EU: Nmc
Cat. Cost: 2 × 1st class.
Credit Cards: All major credit/debit cards
Specialities: Shrubs including some more unusual species. Good range of daphnes & Japanese maples.
Map Ref: S, C3 **OS Grid Ref:** TQ015308

SChr **John Churcher** ⊠ ⊠
47 Grove Avenue, Portchester, Fareham, Hampshire PO16 9EZ
Ⓣ (023) 9232 6740
Ⓜ 07917 350928
Ⓔ johnchurcher47@btinternet.com
Contact: John Churcher
Opening Times: By appt. only. Please phone or email.
Min Mail Order UK: Nmc
Min Mail Order EU: Nmc
Cat. Cost: None issued.
Credit Cards: None
Specialities: Hardy exotics for the Mediterranean-style garden, incl. palms, tree ferns, *Musa*, hedychiums, cycads, *Agave*, *Aloe*, *Opuntia* & echiums. Stock available in small quantities only.
Map Ref: S, D2 **OS Grid Ref:** SU614047

SCmr **Cromar Nursery** ⊠ ♿
39 Livesey Street, North Pole, Wateringbury, Maidstone, Kent ME18 5BQ
Ⓣ (01622) 812380
Ⓔ CromarNursery@aol.com
Ⓦ www.cromarnursery.co.uk
Contact: Debra & Martin Cronk
Opening Times: 0930-1700 daily except Wed. Winter opening 0930-1630 Thu, Fri, Sat, Sun. Please check website or phone if travelling far.
Min Mail Order UK: Nmc
Min Mail Order EU: Nmc
Cat. Cost: 2 × 1st class.
Credit Cards: All major credit/debit cards
Specialities: Ornamental & fruit trees.
Map Ref: S, C4 **OS Grid Ref:** TQ697547

SCog **Coghurst Camellias** ⊠ ⌂ € ♿
Ivy House Lane, Near Three Oaks, Hastings, East Sussex TN35 4NP
Ⓣ (01424) 756228
Ⓔ rotherview@btinternet.com
Ⓦ www.rotherview.com
Contact: R Bates & W Bates
Opening Times: 1000-1530 7 days, all year.
Min Mail Order UK: Nmc
Min Mail Order EU: Nmc
Cat. Cost: 6 × 1st class.
Credit Cards: All major credit/debit cards
Specialities: *Camellia*.
Notes: Nursery is on the same site as Rotherview Nursery. Also sells wholesale.
Map Ref: S, D5

SCoo **COOLING'S NURSERIES LTD** ♿
Rushmore Hill, Knockholt, Sevenoaks, Kent TN14 7NN
Ⓣ (01959) 532269
Ⓕ (01959) 534092
Ⓔ Plantfinder@coolings.co.uk
Ⓦ www.coolings.co.uk
Contact: Mark Reeve or Toby Davies
Opening Times: 0900-1700 Mon-Sat & 1000-1630 Sun.
Cat. Cost: None issued
Credit Cards: All, except American Express
Specialities: Large range of perennials, conifers & bedding plants. Many unusual shrubs & trees. Third generation family business.
Notes: Display garden. Coffee shop.
Map Ref: S, C4 **OS Grid Ref:** TK477610

SCrf **CROFTERS NURSERIES** € ♿
Church Hill, Charing Heath, Near Ashford, Kent TN27 0BU
Ⓣ (01233) 712798
Ⓔ croftersnursery@yahoo.co.uk
Contact: John & Sue Webb
Opening Times: 1000-1700. Closed Sun-Tue. Please check first.
Cat. Cost: 3 × 1st class.
Credit Cards: None
Specialities: Fruit, ornamental trees. Old apple varieties. Small number of *Prunus serrula* with grafted ornamental heads.
Map Ref: S, C5 **OS Grid Ref:** TQ923493

SDay **A LA CARTE DAYLILIES** ⊠ €
Little Hermitage, St Catherine's Down, Nr Ventnor, Isle of Wight PO38 2PD
Ⓣ (01983) 730512
Ⓔ andy@alacartedaylilies.co.uk
Ⓦ www.alacartedaylilies.co.uk
Contact: Jan & Andy Wyers
Opening Times: Mail order only. Open by appt. only. Difficult to find on an unmade private road.
Min Mail Order UK: Nmc
Min Mail Order EU: Nmc
Cat. Cost: 3 × 1st class.
Credit Cards: None
Specialities: *Hemerocallis*. Nat. Collections of Miniature & Small Flowered *Hemerocallis* & Large Flowered *Hemerocallis* (post-1960 award-winning cultivars).
Map Ref: S, D2 **OS Grid Ref:** SZ499787

SDea **DEACON'S NURSERY** ⊠ ✈ € ◆
Moor View, Godshill, Isle of Wight PO38 3HW
Ⓣ (01983) 840750 (24 hrs) or (01983) 522243
Ⓕ (01983) 523575
Ⓔ info@deaconsnurseryfruits.co.uk
Ⓦ www.deaconsnurseryfruits.co.uk
Contact: G D & B H W Deacon
Opening Times: 0800-1600 Mon-Fri May-Sep, 0800-1700 Mon-Fri 0800-1200 Sat Oct-Apr.
Min Mail Order UK: Nmc
Min Mail Order EU: Nmc
Cat. Cost: Free.
Credit Cards: All major credit/debit cards
Specialities: Over 300 varieties of apple, old & new, pears, plums, gages, damsons, cherries. Modern soft fruit, grapes, hops, nuts & family trees.
Notes: Also sells wholesale.
Map Ref: S, D2

SDeJ **P. DE JAGER & SONS LTD** ⊠ ✈ € ♿ ◆
Church Farm, Ulcombe, Maidstone, Kent ME17 1DN
Ⓣ (01622) 840229
Ⓕ (01622) 844073
Ⓔ flowerbulbs@dejager.co.uk
Ⓦ www.dejager.co.uk
Contact: George Clowes
Opening Times: Mail order only. Orders taken from 0900-1700 Mon-Fri
Min Mail Order UK: Nmc
Min Mail Order EU: Nmc
Cat. Cost: Free
Credit Cards: All major credit/debit cards
Specialities: Complete range of all flower bulbs.
Notes: Also sells wholesale.

SDix **GREAT DIXTER NURSERIES** ⊠ ♿
Northiam, Rye, East Sussex TN31 6PH
Ⓣ (01797) 254044
Ⓕ (01797) 252879
Ⓔ nursery@greatdixter.co.uk
Ⓦ www.greatdixter.co.uk
Contact: Michael Morphy
Opening Times: 0900-1700 7 days, Apr-Oct. 0900-1630 Mon-Fri, 0900-1230 Sat, closed Sun, Nov-Mar.
Min Mail Order UK: Nmc
Min Mail Order EU: Nmc
Cat. Cost: 5 × 1st class.
Credit Cards: All major credit/debit cards
Specialities: *Clematis*, shrubs and plants. Gardens open.
Notes: Plants dispatched Sep-Mar only. Partially accessible for wheelchairs.
Map Ref: S, C5

KEY
⊠ Mail order to UK or EU — Delivers to shows
✈ Exports beyond EU — € Euro accepted
♿ Accessible by wheelchair — ◆ See Display advertisement

S

SDow **Downderry Nursery** ⊠ ✈ € ♿
Pillar Box Lane, Hadlow, Nr Tonbridge, Kent TN11 9SW
Ⓣ (01732) 810081
Ⓕ (01732) 811398
Ⓔ info@downderry-nursery.co.uk
Ⓦ www.downderry-nursery.co.uk
Contact: Dr Simon Charlesworth
Opening Times: 1000-1700 Tue-Sun 1st May-30th Sep & B/hols. Other times by appt.
Min Mail Order UK: Nmc
Min Mail Order EU: Nmc
Cat. Cost: 3 × 1st class.
Credit Cards: Delta, MasterCard, Maestro, Visa
Specialities: Nat. Collections of *Lavandula* and *Rosmarinus*.
Map Ref: S, C4 **OS Grid Ref:** TQ625521

SDys **Dysons Nurseries** ⊠ ⌂ ♿
Great Comp Garden, Platt, Sevenoaks, Kent TN15 8QS
Ⓣ (01732) 885094
Ⓜ 07887 997663
Ⓔ dysonsorders@greatcompgarden.co.uk
Ⓦ www.greatcompgarden.co.uk
Contact: William T Dyson
Opening Times: 1100-1700 7 days 1st Apr-31st Oct. Other times by appt.
Min Mail Order UK: £24.00
Cat. Cost: Online only.
Credit Cards: All major credit/debit cards
Specialities: Salvias & an eclectic range of choice and uncommon plants.
Map Ref: S, C4

SEND **East Northdown Farm Nursery** ⊠ € ♿ ◆
George Hill Road (B2052), Margate, Kent CT9 3TS
Ⓣ (01843) 862060
Ⓜ 07714 241668 or 241667
Ⓔ friend.northdown@btinternet.com
Ⓦ www.botanyplants.co.uk
Contact: Louise & William Friend
Opening Times: 1000-1700 7 days, all year except Sun in Nov & Jan. Closed Xmas week.
Min Mail Order UK: Nmc
Cat. Cost: Online only.
Credit Cards: Visa, Switch, MasterCard
Specialities: Chalk & coast-loving plants. Specimen shrubs & bamboos available.
Notes: Credit cards not accepted over the phone. Plant from our other nursery MMuc available to order. Small quanitities only, larger numbers propagated to order. Also sells wholesale.
Map Ref: S, B6 **OS Grid Ref:** TR383702

SEWo **English Woodlands** ⊠ ♿
Burrow Nursery, Herrings Lane, Cross-in-Hand, Heathfield, East Sussex TN21 0UG
Ⓣ (01435) 862992
Ⓕ (01435) 867742
Ⓔ sales@englishwoodlands.com
Ⓦ www.englishwoodlands.com
Contact: Joanne Carter
Opening Times: 0800-1700 Mon-Fri. 0800-1630 Sat. Closed Sun & B/hols.
Min Mail Order UK: £25.00
Cat. Cost: Free.
Credit Cards: All, except American Express
Specialities: Trees, shrubs, hedging.
Notes: Also sells wholesale.
Map Ref: S, C4 **OS Grid Ref:** TQ567222

SFai **Fairweather's Garden Centre** ⊠ € ♿
High Street, Beaulieu, Hampshire SO42 7YB
Ⓣ (01590) 612307
Ⓕ (01590) 612519
Ⓔ info@fairweathers.co.uk
Ⓦ www.fairweathers.co.uk
Contact: Sue Greaves
Opening Times: 0900-1700 7 days.
Min Mail Order UK: Nmc
Min Mail Order EU: £100.00
Cat. Cost: None issued.
Credit Cards: Visa, MasterCard
Specialities: *Agapanthus*, *Heuchera* & *Lavandula*.
Notes: Nursery located at Aline Fairweather Ltd., Hilltop, Beaulieu, SO42 7YR. Also sells wholesale.
Map Ref: S, D2

SFam **Family Trees** ⊠ ♿
Sandy Lane, Shedfield, Hampshire SO32 2HQ
Ⓣ (01329) 834812
Ⓦ www.familytreesnursery.co.uk
Contact: Philip House
Opening Times: 0930-1230 Tue, Wed, Fri & Sat (closed 20th Dec-10th Jan).
Min Mail Order UK: £10.00
Cat. Cost: Online.
Credit Cards: None
Specialities: Fruit & ornamental trees. Trained fruit tree specialists: standards, espaliers, cordons. Other trees, old-fashioned & climbing roses, evergreens. Trees, except evergreens, sold bare-rooted. Also herbaceous plants & roses.
Map Ref: S, D2

SFgr **Firgrove Plants** ⊠
24 Wykeham Field, Wickham, Fareham, Hampshire PO17 5AB
Ⓣ (01329) 835206 after 1900 hours.

Ⓔ jenny@firgroveplants.demon.co.uk
Ⓦ www.firgroveplants.demon.co.uk
Contact: Jenny MacKinnon
Opening Times: Not open. Mail order only.
Min Mail Order UK: £7.00
Cat. Cost: Sae.
Credit Cards: None
Specialities: Wide range of houseleeks & smaller range of other alpines in small quantities.
Notes: Houseleeks by mail order Apr-mid Oct.

SGbt **GILBERT'S NURSERY** ⊠ ♠ ♿
Dandy's Ford Lane, Sherfield English, Romsey, Hampshire
SO51 6DT
Ⓣ (01794) 322566
Ⓔ gilbertsnursery@aol.com
Ⓦ www.gilbertsnursery.co.uk
Contact: Nick Gilbert
Opening Times: 0900-1700 Tue-Sat, 10.00-16.30 Sun.
Min Mail Order UK: Nmc
Min Mail Order EU: Nmc
Cat. Cost: 2 × 1st class
Credit Cards: All, except American Express
Specialities: *Dahlia*.
Notes: *Dahlia* field open Aug to first frosts. Talks for groups on or off site.
Map Ref: S, C2

SGol **GOLDEN HILL NURSERIES** ⊠ € ♿
Lordsfield, Goudhurst Road, Marden, Kent
TN12 9LT
Ⓣ (01622) 833218
Ⓜ 07826 523655
Ⓕ (01622) 832528
Ⓔ enquiries@goldenhillplants.com
Ⓦ www.goldenhillplants.com
Contact: Roger Butler
Opening Times: 0900-1700 Mon-Sat, 1st Mar-31st Oct. 0900-1600 Mon-Sat, 1st Nov-28th Feb. 1100-1600 Sun from 3rd Sun in Feb until Xmas.
Min Mail Order UK: Nmc
Cat. Cost: Online only.
Credit Cards: All major credit/debit cards
Specialities: Specimen plants, shrubs, grasses, bamboos, Japanese maples, conifers & trees.
Notes: Also sells wholesale.

SHaC **HART CANNA** ⊠ ♠ € ♿
25-27 Guildford Road West, Farnborough, Hampshire GU14 6PS
Ⓣ (01252) 514421
Ⓜ 07762 950000
Ⓔ sales@hartcanna.com
Ⓦ www.hartcanna.co.uk
Contact: Keith Hayward
Opening Times: By arrangement.
Min Mail Order UK: Nmc
Min Mail Order EU: Nmc
Cat. Cost: Sae.
Credit Cards: All major credit/debit cards
Specialities: *Canna*. Nat. Collection of *Canna*.
Notes: Also sells wholesale.
Map Ref: S, C3

SHal **HALL'S COURT NURSERY** ♿
Pluckley Road, Bethersden, Ashford, Kent
TN26 3ET
Ⓣ (01233) 820828
Ⓔ info@hallscourt.co.uk
Ⓦ www.hallscourt.co.uk
Contact: Jeanette Jahnz
Opening Times: 0900-1700 every w/end, end Mar-beginning Oct. Weekdays by appt.
Cat. Cost: Online only.
Credit Cards: None
Specialities: Around 90 varieties of hardy geraniums & around 50 varieties of pelargoniums, incl. some species. Also alpines, herbs, some succulents, perennials & hardy fuchsias. Some plants available in small quantities only.
Notes: Small nursery, situated midway between Ashford and Tenterden in rural Kent.
Map Ref: S, C5 **OS Grid Ref:** TQ91931 41525

SHar **HARDY'S COTTAGE GARDEN PLANTS** ⊠ ♠ ♿
Priory Lane Nursery, Freefolk Priors, Whitchurch, Hampshire
RG28 7NJ
Ⓣ (01256) 896533
Ⓔ info@hardys-plants.co.uk
Ⓦ www.hardys-plants.co.uk
Contact: Rosemary Hardy
Opening Times: 1000-1700 7 days, 1st Mar-30th Sep. 1000-1600 Mon-Fri, 1st Oct-31st Oct, 1000-1500 Mon-Fri, 1st Nov-28th Feb. Closed 23rd Dec-4th Jan 2011.
Min Mail Order UK: Nmc
Cat. Cost: 10 × 1st class.
Credit Cards: Visa, Access, Electron, Switch, Solo
Specialities: Wide range of herbaceous perennials incl. *Achillea*, *Alstroemeria*,

KEY
⊠ Mail order to UK or EU ♠ Delivers to shows
✈ Exports beyond EU € Euro accepted
♿ Accessible by wheelchair ◆ See Display advertisement

S

Geranium, Hemerocallis, Heuchera, Paeonia, Penstemon & *Salvia*.
Notes: Accepts HTA Gift Tokens. Offers trade discount.
Map Ref: S, C2

SHDw **Highdown Nursery** ⊠ ⌂ €
New Hall Lane, Small Dole, Nr Henfield, West Sussex BN5 9YH
Ⓣ (01273) 492976
Ⓜ 07900 956456
Ⓕ (01273) 492976
Ⓔ highdown.herbs@btopenworld.com
Ⓦ www.highdownnursery.com
Contact: A G & J H Shearing
Opening Times: 0900-1700 7 days.
Min Mail Order UK: £10.00 + p&p
Cat. Cost: 3 × 1st class.
Credit Cards: None
Specialities: Herbs. Grasses.
Notes: Partial wheelchair access. Also sells wholesale.
Map Ref: S, D3 **OS Grid Ref:** TV214134

SHea **Heaselands Garden Nursery** ⊠ €
The Old Lodge, Isaacs Lane, Haywards Heath, West Sussex RH16 4SA
Ⓣ (01444) 458084
Ⓜ 07743 939490
Ⓕ (01444) 458084
Ⓔ headgardener@heaselandsnursery.co.uk
Ⓦ www.heaselandsnursery.co.uk
Contact: Stephen Harding
Opening Times: 0800-1700, Mon-Fri by appt. only so please phone first.
Min Mail Order UK: Nmc
Min Mail Order EU: Nmc
Cat. Cost: Online only. Monthly availability lists.
Credit Cards: None
Specialities: *Rhododendron* hybrids and deciduous azaleas, home-produced from cuttings. Some varieties in small quantities. Nat. Collection of Mollis Azaleas & Knaphill/Exbury Azaleas. Also *Hydragea, Hebe* & *Camellia*.
Notes: Also sells wholesale.
Map Ref: S, C4 **OS Grid Ref:** TQ314230

SHeu **Heucheraholics** ⊠ ⌂ ♿
(Office) The Paddock, Pilley Street, Pilley, Lymington, Hampshire SO41 5QP
Ⓣ (01590) 670581
Ⓜ 07973 291062
Ⓔ jooles.heucheraholics@googlemail.com
Ⓦ www.heucheraholics.co.uk
Contact: Julie Burton/Sean Atkinson
Opening Times: Visits to nursery by appt. only. Please phone first.
Min Mail Order UK: Nmc
Credit Cards: All major credit/debit cards
Specialities: *Heuchera, Heucherella, Pulmonaria* & *Tiarella*. Other foliage plants.
Notes: Nursery is located at Boldre Nurseries, Southampton Road, Boldre, Lymington, Hants.
Map Ref: S, D2 **OS Grid Ref:** SZ310934

SHil **Hillier Garden Centres** ⊠
Ampfield House, Ampfield, Romsey, Hampshire SO51 9PA
Ⓣ (01794) 368944
Ⓕ (01794) 367830
Ⓔ info@hillier.co.uk
Ⓦ www.hillieronline.co.uk
Contact: Mark Pitman
Opening Times: Office 0830-1700 Mon-Fri. Garden Centres: 0900-1730 Mon-Sat, 1000-1630 Sun.
Min Mail Order UK: Nmc
Min Mail Order EU: £250
Cat. Cost: None issued.
Notes: Other nursery branches in the south of England.

SHyH **Hydrangea Haven** ⊠ ☒ ⌂ € ♿
Market Garden, Lower Beeding, West Sussex RH13 6PP
Ⓣ (01403) 891412
Ⓔ sales@hydrangea-haven.com
Ⓦ www.hydrangea-haven.com
Contact: Chris Loder
Opening Times: 1000-1600 Mon-Sat, please phone first, so we can give you our undivided attention.
Min Mail Order UK: Nmc
Min Mail Order EU: Nmc
Cat. Cost: 2 × 1st class.
Credit Cards: All, except American Express
Specialities: *Hydrangea* : mophead, lacecap & panicle.
Notes: Also sells wholesale.
Map Ref: S, C3 **OS Grid Ref:** TQ221255

SIde **Iden Croft Herbs** ⊠ ♿
Frittenden Road, Staplehurst, Kent TN12 0DH
Ⓣ (01580) 891432
Ⓔ idencroftherbs@yahoo.co.uk
Ⓦ www.uk-herbs.com
Contact: Tracey Connors-Parry
Opening Times: 0900-1700 Mon-Sat & 1100-1700 Sun & B/hols, Mar-Sep. Closed Oct-Feb.
Min Mail Order UK: £10.00
Min Mail Order EU: £25.00
Cat. Cost: 4 × 1st class.

S

Credit Cards: All major credit/debit cards
Specialities: Herbs, aromatic & wildflower plants & plants for bees & butterflies. Nat. Collections of *Mentha*, *Nepeta* & *Origanum*.
Notes: Wheelchairs available at nursery.
Map Ref: S, C5

SIgm **TIM INGRAM** ⌂ ♿
Copton Ash, 105 Ashford Road, Faversham, Kent ME13 8XW
Ⓣ (01795) 535919
Ⓔ coptonash@yahoo.co.uk
Ⓦ coptonash.plus.com
Contact: Dr T J Ingram
Opening Times: 1400-1800 Fri Apr-Oct. Other times by appt.
Credit Cards: None
Specialities: Small, specialised nursery, offering mainly alpines and spring plants.
Map Ref: S, C5 **OS Grid Ref:** TR015598

SIri **IRIS OF SISSINGHURST** ⊠ €
Roughlands Farm, Goudhurst Road, Marden, Kent TN12 9NH
Ⓣ (01622) 831511
Ⓔ orders@irisofsissinghurst.com
Ⓦ www.irisofsissinghurst.com
Contact: Sue Marshall
Opening Times: Contact nursery or see website for opening times.
Min Mail Order UK: Nmc
Min Mail Order EU: Nmc
Cat. Cost: 2 × 1st class.
Credit Cards: None
Specialities: *Iris*, short, intermediate & tall bearded, *ensata*, *sibirica* & many species.
Map Ref: S, C4 **OS Grid Ref:** TQ735437

SKee **KEEPERS NURSERY** ⊠
Gallants Court, Gallants Lane, East Farleigh, Maidstone, Kent ME15 0LE
Ⓣ (01622) 726465
Ⓕ 0870 705 2145
Ⓔ info@keepers-nursery.co.uk
Ⓦ www.keepers-nursery.co.uk
Contact: Hamid Habibi
Opening Times: Only on a limited number of Open Days & for collection of trees & plants by arrangement.
Min Mail Order UK: Nmc
Cat. Cost: Online only.
Credit Cards: Visa, MasterCard, Switch, Maestro
Specialities: A very large range of fruit trees incl. old & rare as well as modern varieties. Soft fruit plants & nut trees.
Map Ref: S, C4

SKHP **KEVIN HUGHES PLANTS** ⊠ ✈ € ♿
(Office) 89 Ladysmith, East Gomeldon, Salisbury, Wiltshire SP4 6LE
Ⓣ (01722) 782504
Ⓜ 07720 718671
Ⓔ info@kevinsplants.co.uk
Ⓦ www.kevinsplants.co.uk
Contact: Kevin Hughes
Opening Times: 1000-1700 Wed-Sun, 1st Feb-31st Oct. Other times by appt. only.
Min Mail Order UK: £10.00
Min Mail Order EU: £20.00
Cat. Cost: 3 × 1st class
Credit Cards: All, except American Express
Specialities: Less common & new hardy garden plants with a particular emphasis on *Magnolia*, *Trillium*, climbers, *Philadelphus*, *Viburnum* & *Syringa*. We try to select plants that are garden-worthy & attract wildlife. Many plants are slow to propagate & will always be in short supply. None are from wild-dug sources.
Notes: Nursery at Heale Garden, Middle Woodford, Salisbury, SP4 5NT.
Map Ref: S, C1 **OS Grid Ref:** SU125363

SKin **KINGS BARN TREES** ⊠
Kings Barn Farm, Kent Street, Cowfold, West Sussex RH13 8BB
Ⓣ (01403) 865405
Ⓔ contact@kingsbarntrees.co.uk
Ⓦ www.kingsbarntrees.co.uk
Contact: Adrian Rumble
Opening Times: Not open. Mail order via website only.
Min Mail Order UK: £9.95
Min Mail Order EU: £9.95
Cat. Cost: Not available.
Specialities: Mainly grow containerised trees, specialising in *Eucalyptus*. Also grow willow for sale as whips & setts during the winter/early spring. *Eucalyptus* available in small quantities only.

SLau **THE LAURELS NURSERY** ⊠ € ♿
Benenden, Cranbrook, Kent TN17 4JU
Ⓣ (01580) 240463
Ⓦ www.thelaurelsnursery.co.uk
Contact: Peter or Sylvia Kellett
Opening Times: 0800-1600 Mon-Fri, 0900-1200 Sat, Sun by appt. only.
Min Mail Order UK: £28.00
Cat. Cost: Free.

KEY
⊠ Mail order to UK or EU ⌂ Delivers to shows
✈ Exports beyond EU € Euro accepted
♿ Accessible by wheelchair ◆ See Display advertisement

S

Credit Cards: All major credit/debit cards
Specialities: Open ground & container ornamental trees, shrubs & climbers especially birch, beech & *Wisteria*.
Notes: Mail order of small *Wisteria* only. Also sells wholesale.
Map Ref: S, C5 **OS Grid Ref:** TQ815313

SLay **LAYHAM GARDEN CENTRE & NURSERY** ✉ € ♿
Lower Road, Staple, Nr Canterbury, Kent CT3 1LH
Ⓣ (01304) 813267
Ⓕ (01304) 814007
Ⓔ info@layhamgardencentre.co.uk
Ⓦ www.layhamgardencentre.co.uk
Contact: Ellen Wessel
Opening Times: 0900-1700 7 days.
Min Mail Order UK: Nmc
Min Mail Order EU: £25.00 + p&p
Cat. Cost: Free.
Credit Cards: Visa, MasterCard, Maestro
Specialities: Roses, herbaceous, shrubs, trees & hedging plants.
Notes: Mail order roses only. Also sells wholesale.
Map Ref: S, C6 **OS Grid Ref:** TR276567

SLBF **LITTLE BROOK FUCHSIAS** ♿
Ash Green Lane West, Ash Green, Nr Aldershot, Hampshire GU12 6HL
Ⓣ (01252) 329731
Ⓔ carol.gubler@ntlbusiness.com
Ⓦ www.littlebrookfuchsias.co.uk
Contact: Carol Gubler
Opening Times: 1000-1700 Wed-Sun 1st Jan-3rd Jul.
Cat. Cost: 50p + sae.
Credit Cards: All major credit/debit cards
Specialities: Fuchsias, old & new.
Notes: Nursery located off White Lane in Ash Green.
Map Ref: S, C3 **OS Grid Ref:** SU901496

SLdr **LODER PLANTS** ✉ ☒ ♁ € ♿
Market Garden, Lower Beeding, West Sussex RH13 6PP
Ⓣ (01403) 891412
Ⓔ sales@rhododendrons.com
Ⓦ www.rhododendrons.com
Contact: Chris Loder
Opening Times: 1000-1600 Mon-Sat, please ring first so we can try to give you our undivided attention.
Min Mail Order UK: Nmc
Min Mail Order EU: Nmc
Cat. Cost: 2 × 1st class.
Credit Cards: All, except American Express
Specialities: Rhododendrons & azaleas in all sizes. Some in very ltd. quantities only.
Notes: Also sells wholesale.
Map Ref: S, C3 **OS Grid Ref:** TQ221255

SLim **LIME CROSS NURSERY** ✉ ♿
Herstmonceux, Hailsham, East Sussex BN27 4RS
Ⓣ (01323) 833229
Ⓕ (01323) 833944
Ⓔ info@limecross.co.uk
Ⓦ www.limecross.co.uk
Contact: Jonathan Tate, Anita Green
Opening Times: 0830-1700 Mon-Sat & 1000-1600 Sun.
Min Mail Order UK: Nmc
Min Mail Order EU: £50.00
Cat. Cost: Free of charge.
Credit Cards: All major credit/debit cards
Specialities: Conifers, trees & shrubs, climbers.
Notes: Also sells wholesale.
Map Ref: S, D4 **OS Grid Ref:** TQ642125

SLon **LONGSTOCK PARK NURSERY** ✉ ♿
Longstock, Stockbridge, Hampshire SO20 6EH
Ⓣ (01264) 810894
Ⓕ (01264) 810924
Ⓔ longstocknursery@leckfordestate.co.uk
Ⓦ www.longstocknursery.co.uk
Contact: David Roberts
Opening Times: 0830-1630 Mon-Sat all year excl. Xmas & New Year, & 1100-1700 Sun Mar-Oct, 1000-1600 Sun, Nov-Feb.
Min Mail Order UK: Nmc
Cat. Cost: 2 × 1st class or email for lists of *Buddleja*, *Penstemon*, roses & fruit
Credit Cards: All major credit/debit cards
Specialities: A wide range, over 2000 varieties, of trees, shrubs, perennials, climbers, aquatics & ferns. Extensive collection of *Penstemon*. Nat. Collections of *Buddleja* & *Clematis viticella*.
Notes: Mail order for *Buddleja* only.
Map Ref: S, C2 **OS Grid Ref:** SO365389

SLPl **LANDSCAPE PLANTS** ✉ ☒ ♿
Stocks Studio, Grafty Green, Maidstone, Kent ME17 2AP
Ⓣ (01622) 850245
Ⓕ (01622) 858063
Ⓔ landscapeplants@aol.com
Contact: Tom La Dell
Opening Times: 0800-1600 Mon-Fri, by appt. only.
Min Mail Order UK: £100.00 + p&p
Min Mail Order EU: £200.00 + p&p

S

Cat. Cost: By email.
Credit Cards: None
Specialities: Garden & landscape shrubs & perennials.
Notes: Also sells wholesale.
Map Ref: S, C5 **OS Grid Ref:** TQ772468

SMad **MADRONA NURSERY** ⛫ € ♿
Pluckley Road, Bethersden, Kent TN26 3DD
Ⓣ (01233) 820100
Ⓕ (01233) 820091
Ⓔ madrona@hotmail.co.uk
Ⓦ www.madrona.co.uk
Contact: Liam MacKenzie
Opening Times: 1000-1700 Sat-Tue 17th Mar-30th Oct. Other times by appt.
Cat. Cost: Free
Credit Cards: All major credit/debit cards
Specialities: Unusual shrubs, conifers & perennials. Eryngiums, *Pseudopanax*.
Map Ref: S, C5 **OS Grid Ref:** TQ918419

SMDP **MARCUS DANCER PLANTS** ⊠ ⛫
Kilcreggan, Alderholt Road, Sandleheath, Fordingbridge, Hampshire SP6 1PT
Ⓣ (01425) 652747
Ⓜ 07709 922730
Ⓔ marcus.dancer@btopenworld.com
Ⓦ www.clematisplants.co.uk
Contact: Marcus Dancer
Opening Times: By appointment only.
Min Mail Order UK: Nmc
Cat. Cost: 4 × 1st class.
Credit Cards: None
Specialities: Wide range of *Clematis*, smaller range of *Daphne*. Some varieties available in small quantities only.
Map Ref: S, D1

SMea **MEADOWGATE NURSERY** ⊠ ⛫
Street End Lane, Sidlesham, Chichester, West Sussex PO20 7RG
Ⓣ (01243) 641997
Ⓜ 07736 523262
Ⓔ meadowgatenursery@tiscali.co.uk
Ⓦ www.meadowgatenursery.co.uk
Contact: David Allen
Opening Times: 1000-1700 Sat-Wed.
Min Mail Order UK: Nmc
Credit Cards: All major credit/debit cards
Specialities: Ornamental grasses and complimentary perennials.

SMor **MOREHAVENS** ⊠ € ♿
Stocks Lane, Meonstoke, Hampshire SO32 3NQ
Ⓣ (01489) 878501
Ⓔ morehavens@hotmail.co.uk
Ⓦ www.camomilelawns.co.uk
Contact: E. Clements
Opening Times: Mail order only. Open only for collection.
Min Mail Order UK: £15.00
Min Mail Order EU: £15.00 + p&p
Cat. Cost: Free.
Credit Cards: Paypal
Specialities: *Camomile nobile* 'Treneague' and *C. nobile* dwarf.
Notes: Accepts payment in euros by Paypal only. Also sells wholesale.

SMrm **MERRIMENTS GARDENS** ♿
Hawkhurst Road, Hurst Green, East Sussex TN19 7RA
Ⓣ (01580) 860666
Ⓕ (01580) 860324
Ⓔ shop@merriments.co.uk
Ⓦ www.merriments.co.uk
Contact: Taryn Murrells
Opening Times: 0900-1730 Mon-Sat, 1030-1730 Sun (or dusk in winter).
Cat. Cost: Online only.
Credit Cards: Visa, Access, American Express
Specialities: Extensive range of unusual perennials, tender perennials, grasses & annuals. Also large selection of roses & seasonal shrubs. 4 acre show garden.
Map Ref: S, C4

SMrs **MRS MITCHELL'S KITCHEN & GARDEN** ⛫ € ♿
2 Warren Farm Cottages, The Warren, West Tytherley, Salisbury, Wiltshire SP5 1LU
Ⓣ (01980) 863101
Ⓔ julianm05@aol.com
Ⓦ www.mrsmitchellskitchenandgarden.co.uk
Contact: Louise Mitchell
Opening Times: 1400-1700 Fri & Sat, Apr, May & Aug, Sep. All other times by appt. only.
Cat. Cost: Online only.
Credit Cards: None
Specialities: Family-run nursery stocking less usual cottage garden plants, esp. hardy geraniums, oriental poppies, *Phlox*, Michaelmas daisies & *Chrysanthemum*. Some items in small quantities. Most plants grown in peat-free compost.
Notes: Despite postal designation, nursery is in Hampshire. Accessible but difficult for wheelchairs because of deep gravel. Sells

KEY
⊠ Mail order to UK or EU ⛫ Delivers to shows
✈ Exports beyond EU € Euro accepted
♿ Accessible by wheelchair ◆ See Display advertisement

S

mostly at plant shows & farmers' markets. See website for details of these.
Map Ref: S, C2 **OS Grid Ref:** SU261333

SPad **PADDOCK PLANTS** ⊠ ⌂
The Paddock, Upper Toothill Road, Rownhams, Southampton, Hampshire SO16 8AL
Ⓣ (023) 8073 9912
Ⓜ 07763 386717
Ⓔ rob@paddockplants.co.uk
Ⓦ www.paddockplants.co.uk
Contact: Robert Courtney
Opening Times: By appt. only. Please telephone in advance.
Min Mail Order UK: Nmc
Cat. Cost: Online only.
Credit Cards: All major credit/debit cards
Specialities: Family-run nursery offering interesting range of perennials, grasses, ferns & shrubs, incl. some more unusual varieties. Some varieties grown in small quantities.
Notes: Credit cards only accepted for online orders. Local delivery by our own transport.
Map Ref: S, D2 **OS Grid Ref:** SU383177

SPav **PAVILION PLANTS** ⊠
18 Pavilion Road, Worthing, West Sussex BN14 7EF
Ⓣ (01903) 821338
Ⓔ rewrew18@hotmail.com
Contact: Andrew Muggeridge
Opening Times: Mail order only. Please phone for details.
Min Mail Order UK: Nmc
Cat. Cost: 4 × 1st class.
Credit Cards: None
Specialities: Perennials and bulbs. *Digitalis*.
Map Ref: S, D3

SPer **PERRYHILL NURSERIES LTD** ⊠ ♿
Edenbridge Road, Hartfield, East Sussex TN7 4JP
Ⓣ (01892) 770377
Ⓕ (01892) 770929
Ⓔ sales@perryhillnurseries.co.uk
Ⓦ www.perryhillnurseries.co.uk
Contact: P J Chapman
Opening Times: 0900-1700 7 days 1st Mar-31st Oct. 0900-1630 1st Nov-28th Feb.
Min Mail Order UK: Nmc
Cat. Cost: Online only.
Credit Cards: Maestro, Visa, Access, MasterCard
Specialities: Wide range of trees, shrubs, perennials, roses, fruit trees, soft fruit. Unusual & rare plants may be available in small quantities.
Notes: Mail order despatch depends on size & weight of plants.
Map Ref: S, C4 **OS Grid Ref:** TQ480375

SPet **PETTET'S NURSERY** ⌂ ♿
Poison Cross, Eastry, Sandwich, Kent CT13 0EA
Ⓣ (01304) 613869
Ⓜ 07961 998354
Ⓕ (01304) 613869
Ⓔ pettets.nursery@btconnect.com
Ⓦ www.pettetsnursery.co.uk
Contact: Terry & Evelyn Pettet
Opening Times: 0900-1700 daily Mar-Jun. 1000-1600 Jul-Oct weekdays only.
Credit Cards: None
Specialities: Climbers, fuchsias, herbaceous perennials, pelargoniums.
Map Ref: S, C6

SPhx **PHOENIX PERENNIAL PLANTS** ⌂ ♿
Paice Lane, Medstead, Alton, Hampshire GU34 5PR
Ⓣ (01420) 560695
Ⓕ (01420) 563640
Ⓔ marina@phoenixperennialplants.co.uk
Ⓦ www.phoenixperennialplants.co.uk
Contact: Marina Christopher
Opening Times: 1100-1700 Fri & Sat 30th Mar-27th Oct 2012. Other times by appt. only.
Cat. Cost: 4 × 1st class.
Credit Cards: All major credit/debit cards
Specialities: Perennials, many uncommon. *Achillea*, *Agastache*, *Centaurea*, hardy chrysanthemums, *Monarda*, *Phlox*, *Sanguisorba*, *Sedum*, *Thalictrum*, *Verbascum*, bulbs, prairie plants, grasses, especially *Molinia* & late-flowering perennials.
Notes: Co-located with Select Seeds SSss. Also sells wholesale.
Map Ref: S, C2 **OS Grid Ref:** SU657362

SPin **JOHN AND LYNSEY'S PLANTS** ♿
2 Hillside Cottages, Trampers Lane, North Boarhunt, Fareham, Hampshire PO17 6DA
Ⓣ (01329) 832786
Contact: Mrs Lynsey Pink
Opening Times: By appt. only. Open under NGS.
Cat. Cost: None issued.
Credit Cards: None
Specialities: Mainly *Salvia* with a wide range of other unusual perennials. Stock is only available in small quantities but we are happy to try & propagate anything that we have. Nat. Collection of species *Salvia*.
Map Ref: S, D2 **OS Grid Ref:** SU603109

SPlb **Plantbase** ⊠ ⛺ € ♿
Sleepers Stile Road, Cousley Wood, Wadhurst, East Sussex TN5 6QX
Ⓣ (01892) 785599
Ⓜ 07967 601064
Ⓔ graham@plantbase.freeserve.co.uk
Ⓦ www.plantbase.co.uk
Contact: Graham Blunt
Opening Times: 1000-1700, 7 days all year (appt. advisable).
Min Mail Order UK: Nmc
Min Mail Order EU: Nmc
Cat. Cost: Online only.
Credit Cards: All major credit/debit cards
Specialities: Wide range of alpines, perennials, shrubs, climbers, waterside plants, herbs, Australasian, South African & South American plants in particular. Some available in small quantities only.
Map Ref: S, C5

SPoG **The Potted Garden Nursery** ♿
Ashford Road, Bearsted, Maidstone, Kent ME14 4NH
Ⓣ (01622) 737801
Ⓦ www.thepottedgarden.co.uk
Contact: Any staff member
Opening Times: 0900-1730 (dusk in winter) 7 days. Xmas/New Year period opening times on website or answerphone.
Credit Cards: All major credit/debit cards
Notes: Mail order not available.
Map Ref: S, C5 **OS Grid Ref:** TQ810550

SPol **Pollie's Perennials and Daylily Nursery** ⊠ € ♿
Lodore, Mount Pleasant Lane, Sway, Lymington, Hampshire SO41 8LS
Ⓣ (01590) 682577
Ⓜ 07415 682288
Ⓕ (01590) 682577
Ⓔ terry@maasz.fsnet.co.uk
Ⓦ www.polliesdaylilies.co.uk
Contact: Pollie Maasz
Opening Times: 1000-1730 w/ends & 1400-1730 Mon-Fri during the daylily season, late-May to mid-Aug. Other times by appt. only.
Min Mail Order UK: Nmc
Min Mail Order EU: £20.00
Cat. Cost: 2 × 1st class.
Credit Cards: None
Specialities: *Hemerocallis*, also less commonly available hardy perennials. Stock available in small quantities only. Nat. Collection of Spider & Unusual Form *Hemerocallis*. 1700+ different cvs can be viewed, mid Jun-mid Sep.
Notes: Mail order, daylilies only.
Map Ref: S, D2

SPop **Pops Plants** ⊠ ☒ ⛺ €
Pops Cottage, Barford Lane, Downton, Salisbury, Wiltshire SP5 3PZ
Ⓣ (01725) 511421
Ⓔ mail@popsplants.com
Ⓦ www.popsplants.com
Contact: Lesley Roberts
Opening Times: By appt. only, please.
Min Mail Order UK: 5 plants.
Min Mail Order EU: 5 plants.
Cat. Cost: £2.00
Credit Cards: Paypal
Specialities: *Primula auricula*. Some varieties in ltd. numbers. Nat. Collection of show, alpine, double & striped auriculas.
Notes: Credit cards accepted online only. Min. mail order outside EU, 10 plants.

SPre **Plants4Presents** ⊠ ◆
The Glasshouses, Fletching Common, Newick, Lewes, East Sussex BN8 4JJ
Ⓣ (01825) 721162
Ⓔ plants@4presents.co.uk
Ⓦ www.plants4presents.co.uk
Contact: Emily Rae
Opening Times: Not open. Mail order only.
Min Mail Order UK: Nmc
Min Mail Order EU: Nmc
Cat. Cost: Online only.
Specialities: Well-established nursery offering a range of unusual flowering and fruiting plants, incl. citrus trees.

SRea **Really Wild Flowers** ⊠
H V Horticulture Ltd, Glenwood, 55 Balcombe Road, Haywards Heath, West Sussex RH16 1PE
Ⓣ (01444) 413376
Ⓕ 0844 443 2503
Ⓔ info@reallywildflowers.co.uk
Ⓦ www.reallywildflowers.co.uk
Contact: Grahame Dixie
Opening Times: Not open. Mail order only.
Min Mail Order UK: £40.00 + p&p
Cat. Cost: 3 × 1st class.
Credit Cards: All major credit/debit cards
Specialities: Native wild flowers for grasslands, woodlands & wetlands. Seeds & bulbs. Hedge plants & trees. Advisory & soil analysis services.
Notes: Credit card payment accepted for online orders only. Also sells wholesale.

KEY
⊠ Mail order to UK or EU ⛺ Delivers to shows
☒ Exports beyond EU € Euro accepted
♿ Accessible by wheelchair ◆ See Display advertisement

S

SReu **G REUTHE LTD** ⊠
Crown Point Nursery, Sevenoaks Road, Ightham, Nr Sevenoaks, Kent TN15 0HB
Ⓣ (01732) 865614
Ⓕ (01732) 862166
Ⓔ reuthe@hotmail.co.uk
Contact: C & P Tomlin
Opening Times: 0900-1600 Thu-Sat. Closed Jan, Feb, Jul & Aug. Please phone before visiting as we are sometimes closed due to circumstances beyond our control.
Min Mail Order UK: £30.00 + p&p
Min Mail Order EU: £500.00
Credit Cards: Visa, Access
Specialities: Rhododendrons & azaleas, trees, shrubs & climbers.
Notes: Mail order certain plants only to EU.
Map Ref: S, C4

S

SRGP **ROSIE'S GARDEN PLANTS** ⊠ ✈ ⌂
Fieldview Cottage, Pratling Street, Aylesford, Kent ME20 7DG
Ⓣ (01622) 715777
Ⓜ 07740 696277
Ⓕ (01622) 715777
Ⓔ jcaviolet@aol.com
Ⓦ www.rosiesgardenplants.biz
Contact: J C Aviolet
Opening Times: Not open. Mail order only.
Min Mail Order UK: Nmc
Min Mail Order EU: Nmc
Cat. Cost: Online only.
Specialities: Hardy *Geranium*, *Buddleja* & *Aster*. Herbaceous & shrubs. Roses. Grows & sells asters, hardy geraniums, roses, plants & shrubs with people's names.
Notes: Check web for dates of shows, talks & Farmers Markets.
Map Ref: S, C5

SRiv **RIVER GARDEN NURSERIES** ⊠ ⌂ €
Troutbeck, Otford, Sevenoaks, Kent TN14 5PH
Ⓣ (01959) 525588
Ⓕ (01959) 525810
Ⓔ box@river-garden.co.uk
Ⓦ www.river-garden.co.uk
Contact: Jenny Alban Davies
Opening Times: By appt. only.
Min Mail Order UK: £10.00 + p&p
Min Mail Order EU: £50.00 + p&p
Cat. Cost: 2 × 1st class.
Credit Cards: All major credit/debit cards
Specialities: *Buxus* species, cultivars & *Buxus* hedging. *Buxus* topiary.
Notes: Also sells wholesale.
Map Ref: S, C4 **OS Grid Ref:** TQ523593

SRkn **RAPKYNS NURSERY** ⊠ ⌂ ♿
Street End Lane, Broad Oak, Heathfield, East Sussex TN21 8UB
Ⓣ (01825) 830065
Ⓜ 07771 916933
Ⓕ (01825) 830065
Ⓔ rapkyns@homecall.co.uk
Ⓦ www.rapkynsnursery.co.uk
Contact: Steven Moore
Opening Times: 1000-1700 Tue, Thu & Fri, Mar-Oct incl.
Min Mail Order UK: Nmc
Min Mail Order EU: Nmc
Cat. Cost: 2 × 1st class or online.
Credit Cards: None
Specialities: Unusual shrubs, perennials & climbers. Asters, campanulas, *Ceanothus*, geraniums, lavenders, *Clematis*, penstemons & grasses. New collections of *Crocosmia*, *Anemone*, *Heuchera*, *Heucherella*, *Echinacea*, *Phlox*, *Coreopsis*, *Helleborus* & *Kniphofia*. Extensive range of salvias.
Notes: Nursery next door to Scotsford Farm, TN21 8UB. Mail order Sep-Apr incl. Also sells wholesale.
Map Ref: S, C4 **OS Grid Ref:** TQ604248

SRms **RUMSEY GARDENS** ⊠ ♿
117 Drift Road, Clanfield, Waterlooville, Hampshire PO8 0PD
Ⓣ (023) 9259 3367
Ⓔ info@rumsey-gardens.co.uk
Ⓦ www.rumsey-gardens.co.uk
Contact: Mrs M A Giles
Opening Times: 0900-1700 Mon-Sat & 1000-1600 Sun & B/hols. Closed Sun Nov-Feb.
Min Mail Order UK: £15.00
Cat. Cost: Online only.
Credit Cards: American Express, Visa, MasterCard
Specialities: Wide general range. Herbaceous, alpines, heathers & ferns. Nat. & International Collection of *Cotoneaster*.
Map Ref: S, D2

SRot **ROTHERVIEW NURSERY** ⊠ ⌂ € ♿
Ivy House Lane, Three Oaks, Hastings, East Sussex TN35 4NP
Ⓣ (01424) 756228
Ⓔ rotherview@btinternet.com
Ⓦ www.rotherview.com
Contact: Ray & Wendy Bates
Opening Times: 1000-1700 Mar-Oct, 1000-1530 Nov-Feb, 7 days.
Min Mail Order UK: Nmc
Min Mail Order EU: Nmc
Cat. Cost: 6 × 1st class.

Credit Cards: All major credit/debit cards
Specialities: Alpines. Ferns. *Camellia.*
Notes: Nursery is on same site as Coghurst Camellias. Also sells wholesale.
Map Ref: S, D5

SSea **SEALE NURSERIES** ♿
Seale Lane, Seale, Farnham, Surrey GU10 1LD
Ⓣ (01252) 782410
Ⓔ catherine@sealenurseries.demon.co.uk
Ⓦ www.sealenurseries.co.uk
Contact: David & Catherine May
Opening Times: 1000-1600 Tue-Sat incl. Other times by appt. Closed 25th Dec-mid Jan.
Cat. Cost: None issued.
Credit Cards: Visa, Access, Delta, MasterCard
Specialities: Roses & *Pelargonium.* Some varieties in short supply, please phone first.
Map Ref: S, C3 **OS Grid Ref:** SU887477

SSpi **SPINNERS GARDEN** ☒ ♿
School Lane, Boldre, Lymington, Hampshire SO41 5QE
Ⓣ (01590) 675488
Ⓜ 07545 432090
Ⓔ info@spinnersgarden.co.uk
Ⓦ www.spinnersgarden.co.uk
Contact: Andrew Roberts
Opening Times: 1000-1700 Mon-Sat, Mar-Oct. By appt. only Nov, Dec, Jan & Feb.
Min Mail Order UK: £50.00
Cat. Cost: Sae for plant list or available online.
Credit Cards: All major credit/debit cards
Specialities: Less common trees & shrubs esp. *Acer, Magnolia,* species & lacecap *Hydrangea.* Bog & woodland plants.
Notes: Ltd mail order.
Map Ref: S, D2 **OS Grid Ref:** SZ323981

SSss **SELECT SEEDS** ☒ Ⴖ ♿
Paice Lane, Medstead, Nr Alton, Hampshire GU34 5PR
Ⓣ (01420) 560695
Ⓕ (01420) 563640
Ⓔ marina@phoenixperennialplants.co.uk
Contact: Marina Christopher
Opening Times: Not open. Mail order only.
Min Mail Order UK: £10.00
Cat. Cost: 3 × 1st class.
Credit Cards: All major credit/debit cards
Specialities: Seeds. Unusual hardy perennial seed selection incl. many prairie plants & ornamental umbellifers. Genera incl. *Agastache, Angelica, Centaurea, Seseli, Sanguisorba* & *Silphium.*
Notes: Only sells seed by mail order. Credit cards not accepted by phone. Co-located with Phoenix Perennial Plants SPhx.
Map Ref: S, C2 **OS Grid Ref:** SU657362

SSta **STARBOROUGH NURSERY** ☒ ♿
Starborough Road, Marsh Green, Edenbridge, Kent TN8 5RB
Ⓣ (01732) 865614
Ⓕ (01732) 862166
Ⓔ starborough@hotmail.co.uk
Contact: C & P Tomlin
Opening Times: 0900-1600 Thu, Fri & Sat. Closed Jan, Jul & Aug.
Min Mail Order UK: £30.00 + p&p
Min Mail Order EU: Certain plants only to EU.
Cat. Cost: £2.50
Credit Cards: Visa, Access
Specialities: Rare and unusual shrubs esp. *Daphne, Acer, Cercis,* rhododendrons & azaleas, *Magnolia* & *Nyssa.*
Notes: Mail order only between Oct & Apr.
Map Ref: S, C4

STes **TEST VALLEY NURSERY** ☒ Ⴖ
Stockbridge Road, Timsbury, Romsey, Hampshire SO51 0NG
Ⓣ (01794) 368881
Ⓔ george@testvalleynursery.co.uk
Ⓦ www.testvalleynursery.co.uk
Contact: George Benn
Opening Times: Not open. Mail order only.
Min Mail Order UK: Nmc
Specialities: Large range of herbaceous perennials, incl. unusual & new varieties. Some varieties available in small quantities only.
Map Ref: S, C2

STPC **THE PLANT COMPANY** ☒ Ⴖ ♿
Coolham Road, West Chiltington, Pulborough, West Sussex RH20 2LH
Ⓣ (01403) 740100
Ⓔ sales@theplantco.co.uk
Ⓦ www.theplantco.co.uk
Contact: Tim Ricketts
Opening Times: 0900-1730 Mon-Sat.
Min Mail Order UK: Nmc
Min Mail Order EU: Nmc
Credit Cards: Visa, MasterCard
Specialities: A range of herbaceous, shrubs and grasses.

KEY
☒ Mail order to UK or EU Ⴖ Delivers to shows
✈ Exports beyond EU € Euro accepted
♿ Accessible by wheelchair ◆ See Display advertisement

S

Notes: Also sells wholesale.
Map Ref: S, C3 **OS Grid Ref:** TQ111196

STrG **Terrace Gardener** ⊠ €
8 Foxbush, Hildenborough, Kent
TN11 9HT
Ⓣ (01732) 832762
Ⓔ johan@terracegardener.com
Ⓦ www.terracegardener.co.uk
Contact: Mr J Hall
Opening Times: Not open. Mail order only, incl. online & by phone. Telephone orders 0930-1500 Mon-Fri.
Min Mail Order UK: Nmc
Cat. Cost: Free
Credit Cards: All major credit/debit cards
Specialities: Patio plants & topiary trees. Container gardening. Architectural & hardy exotics.

S

SVen **Ventnor Botanic Garden** ⊠ ♿
Undercliff Drive, Ventnor, Isle of Wight
PO38 1UL
Ⓣ (01983) 855397
Ⓕ (01983) 856756
Ⓔ sales@botanic.co.uk
Ⓦ www.botanic.co.uk
Contact: Chris Kidd
Opening Times: 1000-1700 7 days, Mar-Oct.
Min Mail Order UK: Nmc
Min Mail Order EU: Nmc
Cat. Cost: None issued
Credit Cards: All, except American Express
Specialities: Coastal, drought-tolerant, Mediterranean & southern hemisphere plants. Some of the more unusual plants may only be available in small numbers.
Map Ref: S, D2 **OS Grid Ref:** SZ548768

SVic **Victoriana Nursery Gardens** ⊠ ♿
Challock, Ashford, Kent
TN25 4DG
Ⓣ (01233) 740529
Ⓕ 0203 292 1529
Ⓔ For email, use contact form on website.
Ⓦ www.victoriananursery.co.uk
Contact: Serena Shirley
Opening Times: 0930-1630 (or dusk if sooner) Mon-Fri, 1030-1500 (or dusk if sooner) Sat.
Min Mail Order UK: Nmc
Cat. Cost: Free by post or online.
Credit Cards: All major credit/debit cards
Specialities: Heritage & unusual vegetable plants, seeds, fruit trees & bushes. Also 600+ varieties of *Fuchsia*.
Notes: Also sells wholesale.
Map Ref: S, C5 **OS Grid Ref:** TR018501

SWat **Water Meadow Nursery** ⊠ ☒ ⌂ ♿
Cheriton, Nr Alresford, Hampshire
SO24 0QB
Ⓣ (01962) 771895
Ⓔ plantaholic@talktalk.net
Ⓦ www.plantaholic.co.uk
Contact: Mrs Sandy Worth
Opening Times: 1000-1700 Fri & Sat, 23rd Mar-28th Jul. Other times by prior telephone appt. only.
Min Mail Order UK: £10.00 + p&p
Min Mail Order EU: £50.00 + p&p
Cat. Cost: Full catalogue online only. 2 × 1st class for individual plant lists, please indicate with application.
Credit Cards: All major credit/debit cards
Specialities: Water lilies, extensive water garden plants, unusual herbaceous perennials, aromatic herbs & wildflowers. New Super Poppy range. Nat. Collection of *Papaver orientale* Group & the re-blooming *Papaver* Super Poppy Series.
Notes: Mail order by 24 or 48 hour courier service only. Also sells wholesale.
Map Ref: S, C2

SWCr **Wych Cross Nurseries** ⊠ ♿
Wych Cross, Forest Row, East Sussex
RH18 5JW
Ⓣ (01342) 822705
Ⓕ (01342) 828246
Ⓔ jp@wychcross.co.uk
Ⓦ www.wychcross.co.uk
Contact: J Paisley
Opening Times: 0900-1730 Mon-Sat.
Min Mail Order UK: Nmc
Cat. Cost: Free
Credit Cards: All major credit/debit cards
Specialities: Roses.
Map Ref: S, C4 **OS Grid Ref:** TQ420320

SWhi **John Hall Plants Ltd** ⊠ ☒ € ♿
Whitehall Nursery, Red Lane (off Churt Road), Headley Down, Hampshire
GU35 8SR
Ⓣ (01428) 715505
Ⓜ 07714 344327
Ⓔ info@johnhallplants.com
Ⓦ www.johnhallplants.com
Contact: John Hall
Opening Times: 0900-1630 Mon-Fri, 0900-1300 Sat, by appt. only.
Min Mail Order UK: Nmc
Min Mail Order EU: Nmc
Cat. Cost: By email only.
Credit Cards: None
Specialities: *Erica* and *Calluna*.
Notes: Also sells wholesale.

SWvt **WOLVERTON PLANTS LTD** € ♿ ◆
Wolverton Common, Tadley, Hampshire RG26 5RU
Ⓣ (01635) 298453
Ⓕ (01635) 299075
Ⓔ Julian@wolvertonplants.co.uk
Ⓦ www.wolvertonplants.co.uk
Contact: Julian Jones
Opening Times: 0900-1800 (or dusk Nov-Feb), 7 days. Closed Xmas/New Year.
Cat. Cost: Online only.
Credit Cards: All major credit/debit cards
Specialities: Wide range of herbaceous perennials & shrubs grown on a commercial scale for the public.
Notes: Horticultural club visits welcome by prior arrangement. Also sells wholesale.
Map Ref: S, C2 **OS Grid Ref:** SU555589

WALES AND THE WEST

WAba **ABACUS NURSERIES** ⊠
Drummau Road, Skewen, Neath, West Glamorgan SA10 6NW
Ⓣ (01792) 817994
Ⓔ plants@abacus-nurseries.co.uk
Ⓦ www.abacus-nurseries.co.uk
Contact: David Hill
Opening Times: Not open to the public. Collection by arrangement.
Min Mail Order UK: Nmc
Cat. Cost: 2 × 2nd class.
Credit Cards: None
Specialities: *Dahlia*.
Map Ref: W, D3

WAbe **ABERCONWY NURSERY** ñ
Graig, Glan Conwy, Colwyn Bay, Conwy LL28 5TL
Ⓣ (01492) 580875
Contact: Keith & Tim Lever
Opening Times: 1000-1600 Tue-Sun Mar-Sep incl.
Cat. Cost: 2 × 2nd class.
Credit Cards: Visa, MasterCard
Specialities: Alpines, including specialist varieties, esp. gentians, dionysias, dwarf *Dianthus*, *Primula*, *Saxifraga* & dwarf ericaceous plants. Some choice shrubs & woodland plants incl. smaller ferns.
Map Ref: W, A3 **OS Grid Ref:** SH799744

WAln **L. A. ALLEN** ⊠
Windy Ridge, Llandrindod Wells, Powys LD1 5NY
Ⓔ leslie.allen@mypostoffice.co.uk
Contact: Les Allen
Opening Times: By prior appt.
Min Mail Order UK: Nmc
Min Mail Order EU: Nmc
Cat. Cost: 6 × 1st class.
Credit Cards: None
Specialities: All sections of *Primula auricula*: alpine auricula, show-edged, show-self, doubles, show-stripe. Surplus plants from private collection so available in small quantities. Occasionally only 1 or 2 available of some cvs.
Notes: Also sells wholesale.

WBla **BLACK MOUNTAIN AURICULAS** ⊠ ñ € ♿
Whitegrove Nurseries, Fferm Gelliwen, Llanedi, Pontardulais, Swansea, West Glamorgan SA4 0FR
Ⓣ (01269) 832509
Ⓜ 07967 488782
Ⓕ (01269) 832509
Ⓔ whitegrovenurseries@tiscali.co.uk
Contact: Richard Williams
Opening Times: By prior appt. only.
Min Mail Order UK: Nmc
Min Mail Order EU: £50
Cat. Cost: 2 x 1st class
Credit Cards: None
Specialities: *Primula auricula*. Many cultivars available in very small quantities only.
Map Ref: W, D3 **OS Grid Ref:** SN573083

WBor **BORDERVALE PLANTS** ⊠ ñ ♿
Nantyderi, Sandy Lane, Ystradowen, Cowbridge, Vale of Glamorgan CF71 7SX
Ⓣ (01446) 774036
Ⓔ lonytwod@gmail.com
Ⓦ www.bordervale.co.uk
Contact: Claire E Jenkins
Opening Times: 1000-1700 Fri-Sun & B/hols Mar-early Oct. Often open Mon-Thu but please make an appt. on these days if travelling some distance.
Min Mail Order UK: £20.00 + p&p
Cat. Cost: 3 × 1st class.
Credit Cards: None
Specialities: Unusual herbaceous perennials, trees & shrubs, as well as cottage garden plants, many displayed in the 2-acre garden.
Notes: Mail order available for smaller items, subject to season. Garden open May-Sep when nursery open. Also open for NGS. See website for details.
Map Ref: W, D3 **OS Grid Ref:** ST022776

KEY
⊠ Mail order to UK or EU ñ Delivers to shows
✈ Exports beyond EU € Euro accepted
♿ Accessible by wheelchair ◆ See Display advertisement

W

WBrk **BROCKAMIN PLANTS** ♿
Brockamin, Old Hills, Callow End,
Worcestershire WR2 4TQ
Ⓣ (01905) 830370
Contact: Margaret Stone
Opening Times: By appt. only.
Cat. Cost: Free.
Credit Cards: None
Specialities: Nat. Collections of *Aster novae-angliae*, *Erigeron* cvs, *Geranium sanguineum*, *G. macrorrhizum* & *G.* × *cantabrigiense*. Plants available in small quantities only.
Map Ref: W, C5 **OS Grid Ref:** SO830488

WBuc **BUCKNELL NURSERIES** ⊠ ♿
Bucknell, Shropshire SY7 0EL
Ⓣ (01547) 530606
Ⓕ (01547) 530699
Ⓔ nickcoull@yahoo.co.uk
Contact: A N Coull
Opening Times: 0800-1700 Mon-Fri & 1000-1300 Sat.
Min Mail Order UK: Nmc
Cat. Cost: Free
Credit Cards: All major credit/debit cards
Specialities: Bare-rooted hedging conifers & forest trees.
Notes: Also sells wholesale.
Map Ref: W, C4 **OS Grid Ref:** SO356736

W

WCas **CASTREE'S GARDEN PLANTS**
Bromsash (B4224), Ross-on-Wye,
Herefordshire HR9 7PL
Ⓣ (01989) 750315
Ⓔ castrees@btconnect.com
Contact: Susan and Richard Edwards
Opening Times: 0900-1700 7 days, 1st Mar-1st Dec.
Credit Cards: All major credit/debit cards
Specialities: *Paeonia*. *Fuchsia*. Good general range. Perennials & seasonal bedding plants.

WCAu **CLAIRE AUSTIN HARDY PLANTS** ⊠ €
White Hopton Farm, Wern Lane,
Sarn, Newtown, Powys
SY16 4EN
Ⓣ (01686) 670432
Ⓔ enquiries@claireaustin-hardyplants.co.uk
Ⓦ www.claireaustin-hardyplants.co.uk
Contact: Claire Austin
Opening Times: Mail order only. Open during Jun when *Iris* field is in flower. See website for details.
Min Mail Order UK: Nmc
Min Mail Order EU: Nmc
Cat. Cost: UK free; Europe €5.00
Credit Cards: MasterCard, Visa, Switch
Specialities: *Paeonia*, *Iris*, *Hemerocallis* & hardy plants. Nat. Collections of Bearded *Iris* & Hybrid Herbaceous *Paeonia*.

WCFE **CHARLES F ELLIS** ⊠ €
Oak Piece Nurseries, Stanton,
Nr Broadway, Worcestershire
WR12 7NQ
Ⓣ (01386) 584077
Ⓕ (01386) 584491
Ⓔ ellisplants@cooptel.net
Ⓦ www.ellisplants.co.uk
Contact: Charles Ellis
Opening Times: 1000-1600 7 days 1st Apr-30th Sep. Other times by appt.
Min Mail Order UK: Nmc
Cat. Cost: None issued.
Credit Cards: None
Specialities: Wide range of shrubs, conifers & climbers, some of them unusual. Some available in small quantities only.
Map Ref: W, C5

WChG **CHENNELS GATE GARDENS & NURSERY** ♿
Eardisley, Herefordshire HR3 6LT
Ⓣ (01544) 327288
Contact: Mark Dawson
Opening Times: 1000-1700 7 days Mar-Oct.
Cat. Cost: None issued.
Credit Cards: None
Specialities: Interesting & unusual cottage garden plants, grasses & shrubs.
Map Ref: W, C4

WCot **COTSWOLD GARDEN FLOWERS** ⊠ ⌂ €
Sands Lane, Badsey, Evesham, Worcestershire
WR11 7EZ
Ⓣ nursery (01386) 833849 or mail order (01386) 422829
Ⓜ 07812 833849
Ⓕ nursery: (01386) 49844
Ⓔ info@cgf.net
Ⓦ www.cgf.net
Contact: Bob Brown
Opening Times: 0900-1730 Mon-Fri, 1000-1730 Sat & Sun mid Mar-Sep. 0900-1630 Mon-Fri, w/ends by appt. only Oct-mid March
Min Mail Order UK: Nmc
Min Mail Order EU: Nmc
Cat. Cost: £1.50 or 6 × 1st class.
Credit Cards: MasterCard, Access, Visa, Switch
Specialities: A very wide range of easy & unusual perennials.
Notes: Ltd wheelchair access. Also sells wholesale.
Map Ref: W, C5 **OS Grid Ref:** SP077426

WCra **Cranesbill Nursery** ⊠
Greenhayes, Upper Westmancote, Tewkesbury, Gloucestershire GL20 7ES
Ⓜ 07970 103168
Ⓔ john@cranesbillnursery.com
Ⓦ www.cranesbillnursery.com
Contact: John Dilks
Opening Times: Not open. Mail order only. Visitors by appt.
Min Mail Order UK: Nmc
Min Mail Order EU: Nmc
Cat. Cost: 4 × 1st class. Current availability list on request.
Credit Cards: MasterCard, Visa, Maestro, Delta
Specialities: Specialist nursery offering a wide range of hardy geraniums.

WCre **Crescent Plants** ⊠ ♿
Stoney Cross, Marden, Hereford, Herefordshire HR1 3EW
Ⓣ (01432) 880262
Ⓜ 07990 970539
Ⓔ crescent@btinternet.com
Ⓦ www.auriculas.co.uk
Contact: June Poole
Opening Times: Open by appt. only. Essential to phone first.
Min Mail Order UK: Nmc
Min Mail Order EU: Nmc
Cat. Cost: Free
Credit Cards: Paypal
Specialities: Named varieties of *Primula auricula* incl. show, alpine, double, striped & border types.
Notes: Payment by Paypal via website or cheque with order. Orders dispatched post free.
Map Ref: W, C4 **OS Grid Ref:** SO525477

WCru **Crûg Farm Plants** ⊠ ⌂ ♿
Griffith's Crossing, Caernarfon, Gwynedd LL55 1TU
Ⓣ (01248) 670232
Ⓔ mailorder@crug-farm.co.uk
Ⓦ www.mailorder.crug-farm.co.uk
Contact: B and S Wynn-Jones
Opening Times: 1000-1700 Thu-Sat, last Thu in Mar to 3rd Sat in Sep, incl. Fri B/hol. Or all year Mon-Fri by appt.
Min Mail Order UK: Nmc
Min Mail Order EU: Nmc
Cat. Cost: 5 × 2nd class or online.
Credit Cards: All major credit/debit cards
Specialities: Unusual & rare inc. trees, shrubs, herbaceous & bulbous, mostly self-collected new introductions from the Far East & the Americas. Rare woody & climbers esp. *Acer*, *Araliaceae*, *Carpinus*, *Hydrangeaceae* & *Magnolia* with many other extraordinary introductions. Shade plants esp. *Convallariaceae*, *Liliaceae*, *Ranunculaceae* & *Saxifragaceae*. Many supplied bare rooted. Nat. Collections of *Coriaria*, *Paris* & *Polygonatum*.
Notes: Delivery by overnight carrier for UK & Ireland. Courier for rest of EU.
Map Ref: W, A2 **OS Grid Ref:** SH509652

WDib **Dibley's Nurseries** ⊠ ⌂ € ♿ ◆
Llanelidan, Ruthin, Denbighshire LL15 2LG
Ⓣ (01978) 790677
Ⓕ (01978) 790668
Ⓔ sales@dibleys.com
Ⓦ www.dibleys.com
Contact: R Dibley
Opening Times: 1000-1700 7 days, Apr-Aug. 1000-1700 Mon-Fri, Mar, Sep & Oct.
Min Mail Order UK: Nmc
Min Mail Order EU: Nmc
Cat. Cost: Free
Credit Cards: Visa, Access, Switch, Electron, Solo
Specialities: *Streptocarpus*, *Columnea*, *Solenostemon*, *Saintpaulia* & other gesneriads & *Begonia*. Nat. Collection of *Streptocarpus*.
Notes: Also sells wholesale.
Map Ref: W, A3

WFib **Fibrex Nurseries Ltd** ⊠ ⌂ ♿
Honeybourne Road, Pebworth, Stratford-on-Avon, Warwickshire CV37 8XP
Ⓣ (01789) 720788
Ⓕ (01789) 721162
Ⓔ sales@fibrex.co.uk
Ⓦ www.fibrex.co.uk
Contact: U Key-Davis & R L Godard-Key
Opening Times: 0900-1700 Mon-Fri, 1st Mar-31st Aug. 0900-1600 Mon-Fri 3rd Sep-28th Feb. 1030-1600 Sat & Sun 31st Mar-29th Jul. Closed last 2 weeks Dec & 1st week Jan. Closed Easter Sun & Aug B/hol Mon.
Min Mail Order UK: £10.00 + p&p
Min Mail Order EU: £20.00 + p&p
Cat. Cost: 3 × 1st class.
Credit Cards: Switch, MasterCard, Visa, Maestro
Specialities: *Hedera*, ferns, *Pelargonium*. Nat. Collections of *Pelargonium* & *Hedera*. Plant collections subject to time of year, please check by phone.

KEY
⊠ Mail order to UK or EU — ⌂ Delivers to shows
✈ Exports beyond EU — € Euro accepted
♿ Accessible by wheelchair — ◆ See Display advertisement

Notes: Also sells wholesale.
Map Ref: W, C5 **OS Grid Ref:** SP133458

WGob **The Gobbett Nursery** ⊠ ⌂
Farlow, Kidderminster, Worcestershire
DY14 8TD
Ⓣ (01746) 718647
Ⓕ (01746) 718647
Ⓔ christine.link@lineone.net
Ⓦ www.thegobbettnursery.co.uk
Contact: C H Link
Opening Times: 1030-1700, Mon-Sat.
Min Mail Order UK: £10.00
Min Mail Order EU: £50.00
Cat. Cost: 3 × 1st class.
Credit Cards: None
Specialities: *Syringa*, *Magnolia*, *Camellia* & *Cornus*. Some varieties available in small quantities only.
Map Ref: W, B4 **OS Grid Ref:** SO648811

W

WGoo **Wildegoose Nursery home of Bouts Violas** ⊠ ⌂ €
Lower Farm Cottage, Holdgate,
Much Wenlock, Shropshire
TF13 6LW
Ⓣ (01746) 712708
Ⓜ 07717 265212
Ⓔ flowers@boutsviolas.co.uk
Ⓦ www.boutsviolas.co.uk
Contact: Laura Crowe
Opening Times: Mail order only. Open strictly by appt. only.
Min Mail Order UK: Nmc
Min Mail Order EU: Nmc
Cat. Cost: 1st class sae.
Credit Cards: None
Specialities: *Viola.*
Notes: Taken over *Viola* stock from Bouts Cottage Nursery.

WGor **Gordon's Nursery** ⊠ ⌂ ♿
1 Cefnpennar Cottages, Cefnpennar,
Mountain Ash, Mid-Glamorgan CF45 4EE
Ⓣ (01443) 474593
Ⓕ (01443) 475835
Ⓔ sales@gordonsnursery.co.uk
Ⓦ www.gordonsnursery.co.uk
Contact: D A Gordon
Opening Times: 1000-1800 7 days Mar-Jun. 1000-1700 7 days Jul-Oct. 1100-1600 weekends only Nov & Feb. Closed Dec-Jan.
Min Mail Order UK: Nmc
Cat. Cost: 3 × 1st class.
Credit Cards: All major credit/debit cards
Specialities: Shrubs, perennials, alpines & dwarf conifers. Some plants available in small quantities only.
Notes: Mail order only available in some cases, please check for conditions in catalogue.
Map Ref: W, D3 **OS Grid Ref:** SO037012

WGrn **Green's Leaves** ⊠ ⌂ ♿
36 Ford House Road, Newent, Gloucestershire
GL18 1LQ
Ⓣ (01531) 820154
Ⓜ 07890 413036
Ⓔ r.paul.green@hotmail.co.uk
Ⓦ www.greensleavesnursery.co.uk
Contact: Paul Green
Opening Times: By appt. only. Please phone to arrange.
Min Mail Order UK: £10.00 + p&p
Cat. Cost: 4 × 2nd class.
Credit Cards: None
Specialities: Range of rare & choice shrubs, also some perennials. Ornamental grasses, sedges & phormiums.
Notes: Also sells wholesale.
Map Ref: W, C4 **OS Grid Ref:** SO732273

WGwG **Gwynfor Growers** ⊠ ⌂
Gwynfor, Pontgarreg, Llangranog,
Llandysul, Ceredigion
SA44 6AU
Ⓣ (01239) 654151
Ⓔ info@gwynfor.co.uk
Ⓦ www.gwynfor.co.uk
Contact: Steve & Angie Hipkin
Opening Times: 1000 to 2000 or sunset if earlier, Wed, Thu & Sun, all year round.
Min Mail Order UK: Nmc
Cat. Cost: PDF list available by email.
Credit Cards: Paypal
Specialities: Welsh fruit trees. *Rosmarinus.* Classic & contemporary plants to intrigue & delight plantsmen & garden designers alike. Some plants available in small quantities only. Rarities propagated to order.
Notes: Plants also available at local farmers' markets, plant fairs & some NGS Open Gardens.
Map Ref: W, C2 **OS Grid Ref:** SN331536

WHal **Hall Farm Nursery** ⊠ ⌂ € ♿
Vicarage Lane, Kinnerley, Nr Oswestry,
Shropshire SY10 8DH
Ⓣ (01691) 682135
Ⓕ (01691) 682135
Ⓔ info@hallfarmnursery.co.uk
Ⓦ www.hallfarmnursery.co.uk
Contact: Christine & Nick Ffoulkes-Jones
Opening Times: 1000-1700 Tue-Sat 1st Mar-27th Oct 2011.
Min Mail Order UK: £20.00
Cat. Cost: Online only.

Credit Cards: Visa, MasterCard, Electron, Maestro
Specialities: Unusual herbaceous plants, grasses, bog plants, late-flowering perennials, foliage plants, woodland plants, scree alpine plants.
Notes: Nursery partially accessible for wheelchairs.
Map Ref: W, B4 **OS Grid Ref:** SJ333209

WHar **HARLEY NURSERY** ⊠ ♿
Harley, Shrewsbury, Shropshire SY5 6LN
Ⓣ (01952) 510241
Ⓔ plants@harleynursery.co.uk
Ⓦ www.harleynursery.co.uk
Contact: Nick Murphy & Debbie Plant
Opening Times: 0900-1730 Mon-Sat, 1000-1600 Sun & B/hols. Winter hours 0830-1630 Mon-Sat, 1000-1600 Sun & B/hols.
Min Mail Order UK: Nmc
Cat. Cost: Online only.
Credit Cards: All major credit/debit cards
Specialities: Wide range of trees & shrubs. Large selection of fruit trees & bushes, many old & unusual varieties. Seasonal selection of conifers, climbing & herbaceous plants. Wide range of hedging & forestry plants, many available bare root.
Map Ref: W, B4 **OS Grid Ref:** SJ598020

WHCr **HERGEST CROFT GARDENS**
Kington, Herefordshire HR5 3EG
Ⓣ (01544) 230160
Ⓜ 07968 435627
Ⓕ (01544) 232031
Ⓔ gardens@hergest.co.uk
Ⓦ www.hergest.co.uk
Contact: Stephen Lloyd
Opening Times: 1200-1730, 7 days, Apr-Oct.
Cat. Cost: None issued
Credit Cards: All major credit/debit cards
Specialities: *Acer*, *Betula* & unusual woody plants.
Notes: Limited wheelchair access.
Map Ref: W, C4 **OS Grid Ref:** SO284566

WHer **THE HERB GARDEN & HISTORICAL PLANT NURSERY** ⊠
Ty Capel Pensarn, Pentre Berw, Anglesey, Gwynedd LL60 6LG
Ⓣ (01248) 422208 or (01545) 580893
Ⓜ 07751 583958
Ⓕ (01248) 422208
Ⓔ corinnetremaine@gmail.com
Ⓦ www.HistoricalPlants.co.uk
Contact: Corinne & David Tremaine-Stevenson
Opening Times: By appt. only.
Min Mail Order UK: £15.00 + p&p
Min Mail Order EU: £50.00 + p&p sterling only.
Cat. Cost: Online, or £3.00 by post in the spring.
Credit Cards: None
Specialities: Rarer herbs, rare natives & wild flowers; rare & unusual & historical perennials & old roses.
Map Ref: W, A2

WHfH **HERBS FOR HEALING** ⊠ ⛫ € ♿
Barnsley Herb Garden, Barnsley, Nr Cirencester, Gloucestershire GL7 5EE
Ⓜ 07773 687493
Ⓔ herbs@herbsforhealing.net
Ⓦ www.herbsforhealing.net
Contact: Davina Wynne-Jones
Opening Times: 1000-1700 Wed. 1400-1700 Fri & Sun.
Min Mail Order UK: Nmc
Credit Cards: Paypal
Specialities: Medicinal & some culinary herbs. Display garden.
Notes: Courses and workshops on use of herbs. Sells at local farmers markets. Nursery in Clapton's Lane, Barnsley, behind Barnsley House Hotel. See web for directions.
Map Ref: W, D5 **OS Grid Ref:** SP048177

WHil **HILLVIEW HARDY PLANTS** ⊠ ☒ ⛫ € ♿
(off B4176), Worfield, Nr Bridgnorth, Shropshire WV15 5NT
Ⓣ (01746) 716454
Ⓜ 07974 391608
Ⓕ (01746) 716454
Ⓔ hillview@onetel.net
Ⓦ www.hillviewhardyplants.com
Contact: Ingrid, John & Sarah Millington
Opening Times: 0900-1700 Mon-Sat Mar-mid Oct. At other times, please phone first.
Min Mail Order UK: £10.00 + p&p
Min Mail Order EU: £10.00 + p&p
Cat. Cost: Online only.
Credit Cards: All major credit/debit cards
Specialities: Choice herbaceous perennials incl. *Acanthus* & *Acanthaceae*, *Albuca*, *Aquilegia*, auricula, *Primula*, *Canna*, *Crocosmia*, *Eucomis*, *Ixia*, South African bulbs. Nat. Collections of *Acanthus* & *Albuca*.
Notes: Also sells wholesale.
Map Ref: W, B4 **OS Grid Ref:** SO772969

KEY
⊠ Mail order to UK or EU ⛫ Delivers to shows
☒ Exports beyond EU € Euro accepted
♿ Accessible by wheelchair ◆ See Display advertisement

W

WHlf **Hayloft Plants** ⊠
Manor Farm, Pensham, Pershore, Worcestershire WR10 3HB
Ⓣ (01386) 554440 or (01386) 562999
Ⓕ (01386) 553833
Ⓔ info@hayloftplants.co.uk
Ⓦ www.hayloftplants.co.uk
Contact: Yvonne Walker
Opening Times: Not open. Mail order only.
Min Mail Order UK: Nmc
Min Mail Order EU: Nmc
Cat. Cost: Free.
Credit Cards: All major credit/debit cards

WHoo **Hoo House Nursery** € ◆
Hoo House, Gloucester Road, Tewkesbury, Gloucestershire GL20 7DA
Ⓣ (01684) 293389
Ⓕ (01684) 293389
Ⓔ nursery@hoohouse.co.uk
Ⓦ www.hoohouse.co.uk
Contact: Robin & Julie Ritchie
Opening Times: 1000-1700 Mon-Sat, 1100-1700 Sun.
Cat. Cost: 3 × 1st class.
Credit Cards: All major credit/debit cards
Specialities: Wide range of herbaceous & alpines grown peat-free. *Aster*, *Cyclamen*, *Geranium*, *Penstemon* & many later-flowering varieties. Nat. Collections of *Platycodon* & *Gentiana asclepiadea* cvs.
Notes: Partially accessible for wheelchairs. Also sells wholesale.
Map Ref: W, C5 **OS Grid Ref:** SO893293

W

WHor **Horticultural Sales** ⊠ €
Upper Brockington, Berrington Street, Bodenham, Herefordshire HR1 3HT
Ⓣ (01568) 797747
Ⓜ 07966 635005
Ⓕ (01568) 797013
Ⓔ pdavies@hortsales.fsnet.co.uk
Contact: Peter Davies
Opening Times: By appt. only.
Min Mail Order UK: Nmc
Min Mail Order EU: Nmc
Cat. Cost: Free but available by email only.
Credit Cards: None
Specialities: *Acer*, *Pinus* & grafted conifers, plus wide selection of less commonly grown shrubs, available in small quantities only.
Notes: Offers plant finding service. Also sells wholesale, 35 years experience in trade.

WHrl **Harrells Hardy Plants** ⊠
(Office) 15 Coxlea Close, Evesham, Worcestershire WR11 4JS
Ⓣ (01386) 443077
Ⓜ 07799 577120 or 07733 446606
Ⓔ mail@harrellshardyplants.co.uk
Ⓦ www.harrellshardyplants.co.uk
Contact: Liz Nicklin & Kate Phillips
Opening Times: By appt. only. Please telephone.
Min Mail Order UK: Nmc
Cat. Cost: 4 × 2nd class.
Credit Cards: None
Specialities: Display gardens showcase wide range of hardy perennials, esp. *Hemerocallis* & grasses.
Notes: Nursery located off Rudge Rd, Evesham. Please phone for directions or see catalogue. Partial wheelchair access. Mail order Nov-Mar only.
Map Ref: W, C5 **OS Grid Ref:** SP033443

WIce **Ice Alpines** ⊠ ♿
Lyehead, Bewdley, Worcestershire DY12 2UW
Ⓣ (01299) 269219
Ⓕ (01562) 510003
Ⓔ icealpines@gmail.com
Ⓦ www.Icealpines.co.uk
Contact: Mark Lagomarsino
Opening Times: Mail order. Open by appt. only.
Min Mail Order UK: Nmc
Min Mail Order EU: £18
Credit Cards: Paypal
Specialities: British grown alpine & rockery plants.

WIvy **Ivycroft Plants** ⊠ € ♿
Upper Ivington, Leominster, Herefordshire HR6 0JN
Ⓣ (01568) 720344
Ⓔ ivycroft@homecall.co.uk
Ⓦ www.ivycroftgarden.co.uk
Contact: Roger Norman
Opening Times: 0900-1600 Thu, Apr-Sep. Feb & other times by appt., please phone.
Min Mail Order UK: Nmc
Min Mail Order EU: Nmc
Cat. Cost: Sae for specialist lists.
Credit Cards: None
Specialities: *Cyclamen*, *Galanthus*, *Salix*, alpines, herbaceous & ferns.
Notes: Mail order for *Galanthus* & *Salix* only.
Map Ref: W, C4 **OS Grid Ref:** SO464562

WJas **Paul Jasper Trees** ⊠
(Office) The Lighthouse, Bridge Street, Leominster, Herefordshire HR6 8DX
Ⓕ (01568) 616499 for orders.
Ⓔ enquiries@jaspertrees.co.uk
Ⓦ www.jaspertrees.co.uk
Contact: Paul Jasper
Opening Times: Not open. Mail order only.

Min Mail Order UK: £40.00 + p&p
Cat. Cost: Online only.
Credit Cards: All major credit/debit cards
Specialities: Full range of fruit & ornamental trees. Over 100 modern and traditional fruit tree varieties plus 100 ornamental tree varieties, all direct from the grower. Many unusual varieties of *Malus domestica* & *Prunus*.
Notes: Regular catalogue updates & notes on website. Also sells wholesale.
Map Ref: W, C4 **OS Grid Ref:** SO495595

WJek **JEKKA'S HERB FARM** ⊠ ♠ ♿
Rose Cottage, Shellards Lane, Alveston, Bristol, South Gloucestershire BS35 3SY
Ⓣ (01454) 418878
Ⓕ (01454) 424907
Ⓔ sales@jekkasherbfarm.com
Ⓦ www.jekkasherbfarm.com
Contact: Jekka McVicar
Opening Times: 5 times a year. Please check website for dates.
Min Mail Order UK: £10.00
Min Mail Order EU: Charges per order on application.
Cat. Cost: 4 × 1st class.
Credit Cards: Visa, MasterCard, Delta, Maestro
Specialities: Culinary, medicinal, aromatic, decorative herbs. Soil Association licensed G5869.
Notes: Only seeds mail order. Plants can be ordered for collection from the farm with 24 hours notice or from RHS Shows. Please check website for dates.
Map Ref: W, D4

WJPR **JPR ENVIRONMENTAL** ⊠
(Office) Unit 2, Breadstone Business Centre, Breadstone, Berkeley, Gloucestershire GL13 9HF
Ⓣ (01453) 811537
Ⓕ (01453) 810646
Ⓔ enquiries@jprenvironmental.co.uk
Ⓦ www.jprwillow.co.uk
Contact: John Robinthwaite
Opening Times: Mail order only. 0900-1700.
Min Mail Order UK: £6.00
Credit Cards: All, except American Express
Specialities: *Salix*.
Notes: Also sells wholesale.
Map Ref: W, D4 **OS Grid Ref:** SO712009

WJun **JUNGLE GIANTS** ⊠ ✈ € ♿
Ferney, Onibury, Craven Arms, Shropshire SY7 9BJ
Ⓣ (01584) 856200
Ⓕ (01584) 856663
Ⓔ bamboo@junglegiants.co.uk
Ⓦ www.junglegiants.co.uk
Contact: Michael Brisbane
Opening Times: 7 days. By appt. only please.
Min Mail Order UK: £25.00 + p&p
Min Mail Order EU: £100.00 + p&p
Cat. Cost: Online only.
Credit Cards: Access, MasterCard, Visa
Specialities: Bamboos.
Notes: Also sells wholesale.
Map Ref: W, C4 **OS Grid Ref:** SO430779

WKif **KIFTSGATE COURT GARDENS** ♿
Kiftsgate Court, Chipping Camden, Gloucestershire GL55 6LN
Ⓣ (01386) 438777
Ⓕ (01386) 438777
Ⓔ anne@kiftsgate.co.uk
Ⓦ www.kiftsgate.co.uk
Contact: Mrs J Chambers
Opening Times: 1200-1800 Sat-Wed, May, Jun & Jul. 1400-1800 Sat-Wed, Aug. 1400-1800 Sun, Mon & Wed, Apr & Sep.
Cat. Cost: None issued
Credit Cards: All, except American Express
Specialities: Small range of unusual plants.
Map Ref: W, C5 **OS Grid Ref:** SP170430

WLav **THE LAVENDER GARDEN** ⊠ ♠ €
Ashcroft Nurseries, Nr Ozleworth, Kingscote, Tetbury, Gloucestershire GL8 8YF
Ⓣ (01453) 860356 or 549286
Ⓜ 07837 582943
Ⓔ Andrew007Bullock@aol.com
Ⓦ www.TheLavenderG.co.uk
Contact: Andrew Bullock
Opening Times: 1100-1700 Sat & Sun. Weekdays variable, please phone. 1st Nov-1st Mar by appt. only.
Min Mail Order UK: £10.00 + p&p
Min Mail Order EU: £20.00 + p&p
Cat. Cost: 2 × 1st class.
Credit Cards: All major credit/debit cards
Specialities: *Lavandula*, *Buddleja*, plants to attract butterflies, Herbs, wildflowers. Nat. Collection of *Buddleja*.
Notes: Also sells wholesale.
Map Ref: W, D5 **OS Grid Ref:** ST798948

WMAq **MEREBROOK WATER PLANTS** ⊠
Kingfisher Barn, Merebrook Farm, Hanley Swan, Worcestershire WR8 0DX
Ⓣ (01684) 310950
Ⓜ 07876 777066

KEY
⊠ Mail order to UK or EU ♠ Delivers to shows
✈ Exports beyond EU € Euro accepted
♿ Accessible by wheelchair ◆ See Display advertisement

Ⓔ enquiries@pondplants.co.uk
Ⓦ www.pondplants.co.uk
Contact: Roger Kings & Biddi Kings
Opening Times: Not open. Mail order only.
Min Mail Order UK: Nmc
Min Mail Order EU: £25.00
Cat. Cost: Online only.
Credit Cards: All major credit/debit cards
Specialities: *Nymphaea*, Louisiana irises & other aquatic plants. International Waterlily & Water Gardening Soc. accredited collection.
Map Ref: W, C5 **OS Grid Ref:** SO802425

WMnd **Mynd Hardy Plants** ♿
Delbury Hall Estate, Diddlebury, Craven Arms, Shropshire SY7 9DH
Ⓣ (01584) 841222
Ⓔ myndhardyplants@aol.com
Ⓦ www.myndplants.co.uk
Contact: Mark Zenick
Opening Times: 1300-1700 Wed-Fri, 1000-1700 Sat, 24th Mar-15th Sep. 1300-1700 B/Hol Mons. 1300-1700 Sun May-Jul. Other times, phone for appt.
Cat. Cost: 4 × 2nd class.
Credit Cards: All major credit/debit cards
Specialities: Herbaceous plants, specialising in American bred, British grown, *Hemerocallis*. Home to New Hope Garden's *Hemerocallis* plants.
Notes: Also sells wholesale.
Map Ref: W, B4 **OS Grid Ref:** SO510852

W

WMoo **Moorland Cottage Plants** ✉ ♿
Rhyd-y-Groes, Brynberian, Crymych, Pembrokeshire SA41 3TT
Ⓣ (01239) 891363
Ⓦ www.moorlandcottageplants.co.uk
Contact: Jennifer Matthews
Opening Times: 1030-1730 daily excl. Wed 1st Mar-30th Sep.
Min Mail Order UK: See cat. for details.
Cat. Cost: 4 × 1st class.
Credit Cards: All major credit/debit cards
Specialities: Traditional & unusual hardy perennials. Many garden-worthy rarities. Cottage garden plants, ferns & many shade plants, moisture lovers, ornamental grasses & bamboos, colourful ground cover.
Notes: Display garden open for NGS from mid-May.
Map Ref: W, C2 **OS Grid Ref:** SN091343

WMou **Mount Pleasant Trees** ✉ ♿
Rockhampton, Berkeley, Gloucestershire GL13 9DU
Ⓣ (01454) 260348
Ⓔ info@mountpleasanttrees.com
Ⓦ www.mountpleasanttrees.com
Contact: Tom Locke & Elizabeth Murphy
Opening Times: 0830-1630 Mon-Fri, 0830-1230 Sat, Oct-Apr.
Min Mail Order UK: Nmc but p&p quoted on individual basis.
Cat. Cost: Free.
Credit Cards: All major credit/debit cards
Specialities: Wide range of trees for forestry, hedging, woodlands & gardens esp. *Populus*, *Salix*, *Tilia* & *Quercus*.
Notes: Mail order available for plants under 1m in height, quotes on request. Also sells wholesale.
Map Ref: W, D4 **OS Grid Ref:** ST654929

WNew **Newbridge Nursery** ✉ ♿
Crundale, Haverfordwest, Pembrokeshire SA62 4EJ
Ⓣ (01437) 731678
Ⓕ (01437) 731678
Ⓔ newbridgenursery@btinternet.com
Ⓦ www.newbridgeplantcentre.co.uk
Contact: Phil & Jane Davies
Opening Times: 1000-1730 daily throughout year.
Min Mail Order UK: Nmc
Cat. Cost: 2 × 1st class.
Credit Cards: All major credit/debit cards
Specialities: Wide range of herbaceous perennials & alpines from the common to the more unusual. Also a selection of coastal & acid-loving shrubs.
Notes: Credit cards not accepted for mail order. Plants also sold at Haverfordwest Farmers Market.
Map Ref: W, D2 **OS Grid Ref:** SM991196

WNHG **New Hope Gardens** ✉ ♿
The Old Chapel, Cefn Einion, Nr Bishops Castle, Shropshire SY9 5LF
Ⓣ office (01588) 630750 or nursery (01584) 841222
Ⓔ Newhopegardensmz@aol.com
Ⓦ www.newhopegardens.com
Contact: Mark Zenick
Opening Times: 1300-1700 Wed-Fri, 1000-1700 Sat, 24th Mar-15th Sep. 1300-1700 B/hol Mons during season. 1300-1700 Sun, May-Jul. Other times phone nursery for appt. Daylily Open W/ends 30th Jun/1st Jul, 7th/8th, 14th (NGS Open Day)/15th, 21st/22nd Jul.
Min Mail Order UK: Nmc
Min Mail Order EU: Nmc
Cat. Cost: Online only. Plant list on request.
Credit Cards: All major credit/debit cards

Specialities: American bred, British grown, *Hemerocallis*. Ships bare-rooted plants.
Notes: Nursery co-located with Mynd Hardy Plants (code WMnd).
Map Ref: W, B4 **OS Grid Ref:** SO510852

WNPC **NEWENT PLANT CENTRE** ⌂ ♿
Ledbury Road, Newent, Gloucestershire
GL18 1DL
Ⓣ (01531) 828488
Ⓕ (01531) 828488
Ⓔ markmoir999@btinternet.com
Ⓦ www.newentplantcentre.co.uk
Contact: Mark Moir
Opening Times: 0900-1700 Mon-Sat, 1000-1600 Sun. Closed Jan.
Credit Cards: All major credit/debit cards
Specialities: Extensive range of *Heuchera* & *Euphorbia*. Herbaceous perennials, climbers, shrubs, trees, alpines, herbs, roses & fruit.
Map Ref: W, C4 **OS Grid Ref:** SO 718279

WOld **OLD COURT NURSERIES** ⊠
Colwall, Nr Malvern, Worcestershire
WR13 6QE
Ⓣ (01684) 540416
Ⓔ paulpicton@btinternet.com
Ⓦ www.autumnasters.co.uk
Contact: Paul, Meriel or Helen Picton
Opening Times: 1400-1700 Wed-Sat, May-Aug. 1200-1700 Wed-Sun, Aug. 1100-1700 7 days, 1st week Sep-2nd week Oct. Also by appt. May to Oct.
Min Mail Order UK: Nmc
Min Mail Order EU: Nmc
Credit Cards: None
Specialities: Nat. Collection of Michaelmas Daisies. Herbaceous perennials.
Notes: Mail order for *Aster* only. Display garden open Aug-Oct.
Map Ref: W, C4 **OS Grid Ref:** SO759430

WOth **OTHER FELLOW FUCHSIAS** ⊠ ✈ €
25 Spring Meadow Road, Lydney, Gloucestershire GL15 5LF
Ⓣ (01594) 844452
Ⓜ 07564 357637
Ⓔ info@otherfellow.co.uk
Ⓦ http://otherfellow.co.uk
Contact: Nick Egginton
Opening Times: Not open. Mail order only.
Min Mail Order UK: Nmc
Min Mail Order EU: Nmc
Credit Cards: All major credit/debit cards
Specialities: Expanding collection of *Fuchsia*, esp. unusual, single & exhibition varieties. Small selection of *Salvia* & other tender perennials.
Notes: Some stock available in small quantities only. Can propagate to order.

WOut **OUT OF THE COMMON WAY** ⊠ ⌂ €
(Office) Penhyddgan, Boduan, Pwllheli, Gwynedd
LL53 8YH
Ⓣ office (01758) 721577 or nursery (01407) 720431
Ⓔ ziggymen22@hotmail.co.uk
Contact: Joanna Davidson (nursery) Margaret Mason (office & mail order)
Opening Times: By arrangement.
Min Mail Order UK: Nmc
Min Mail Order EU: Nmc
Cat. Cost: A5 sae large letter rate postage.
Credit Cards: None
Specialities: *Labiates*, esp. *Nepeta* & *Salvia*. *Aster*, *Geranium* & *Crocosmia*. Native plants. Some plants propagated in small quantities only. Will propagate salvias to order.
Notes: Nursery is at Pandy Treban, Bryngwran, Anglesey. Partially accessible for wheelchairs.
Map Ref: W, A2 **OS Grid Ref:** SH370778

WPat **CHRIS PATTISON** ⊠ € ♿
Brookend, Pendock, Gloucestershire
GL19 3PL
Ⓣ (01531) 650480
Ⓕ (01531) 650480
Ⓔ cp@chris-pattison.co.uk
Ⓦ www.chris-pattison.co.uk
Contact: Chris Pattison
Opening Times: 0900-1700 Mon-Fri. W/ends by appt. only.
Min Mail Order UK: £10.00 +p&p
Cat. Cost: 3 × 1st class.
Credit Cards: None
Specialities: Choice rare shrubs & alpines. Grafted stock esp. Japanese maples & *Liquidambar*. Wide range of *Viburnum* & dwarf/miniature trees & shrubs suitable for bonsai or rockery.
Notes: Mail order Nov-Feb only. Also sells wholesale.
Map Ref: W, C5 **OS Grid Ref:** SO781327

WPGP **PAN-GLOBAL PLANTS** ♿
The Walled Garden, Frampton Court, Frampton-on-Severn, Gloucestershire
GL2 7EX
Ⓣ (01452) 741641

KEY
⊠ Mail order to UK or EU ⌂ Delivers to shows
✈ Exports beyond EU € Euro accepted
♿ Accessible by wheelchair ◆ See Display advertisement

W

Ⓜ 07801 275138
Ⓔ info@panglobalplants.com
Ⓦ www.panglobalplants.com
Contact: Nick Macer
Opening Times: 1100-1700 Wed-Sun 1st Feb-31st Oct. Also B/hols. Closed 2nd Sun in Sep. Winter months by appt., please phone first.
Cat. Cost: 6 × 1st class.
Credit Cards: Maestro, MasterCard, Visa, Solo, Delta
Specialities: A plantsman's nursery offering a very wide selection of rare & desirable trees, shrubs, herbaceous, bamboos, exotics, climbers, ferns etc. Specialities incl. *Magnolia*, *Hydrangea*, *Bamboo* & *Agavaceae*.
Map Ref: W, D5 **OS Grid Ref:** SO750080

WPnn **The Perennial Nursery** ⊠
Rhosygilwen, Llanrhian Road, St Davids, Haverfordwest, Pembrokeshire
SA62 6DB
Ⓣ (01437) 721954
Ⓜ 07891 982230
Ⓔ theperennialnursery@tesco.net
Ⓦ www.droughttolerantplants.co.uk
Contact: Mrs Philipa Symons
Opening Times: 1030-1630 Mar-Oct. Closed Sun & Mon.
Min Mail Order UK: Nmc
Min Mail Order EU: Nmc
Cat. Cost: Online only.
Credit Cards: Visa, MasterCard
Specialities: *Rosmarinus*, *Lampranthus*, wind & drought-tolerant plants.
Map Ref: W, C1 **OS Grid Ref:** SM775292

WPnP **Penlan Perennials** ⊠ €
Wern Rhos, Newchapel, Boncath, Pembrokeshire
SA37 0EN
Ⓣ (01239) 842260
Ⓜ 07857 675312
Ⓕ (01239) 842260
Ⓔ info@penlanperennials.co.uk
Ⓦ www.penlanperennials.co.uk
Contact: Richard Cain
Opening Times: Mail order only. Open for collection of orders only.
Min Mail Order UK: Nmc
Min Mail Order EU: Nmc
Cat. Cost: Online, or sae for CD-ROM.
Credit Cards: All major credit/debit cards
Specialities: Aquatic, marginal & bog plants. Shade-loving & woodland perennials, ferns & hardy geraniums, all grown peat-free.
Notes: Mail order all year, next day delivery. Secure online web ordering. Nursery has relocated so please note new phone number (above). Also sells wholesale.
Map Ref: W, C2

WPtf **Pantyfod Garden Nursery** ⊠
Llandewi Brefi, Tregaron, Ceredigion
SY25 6PE
Ⓣ (01570) 493564
Ⓔ sales@pantyfodgarden.co.uk
Ⓦ www.pantyfodgarden.co.uk
Contact: Susan Rowe
Opening Times: Mail order only. Not open to visitors. Garden occasionally open under the National Gardens Scheme, when plants are offered for sale. Please check with NGS for Open Days.
Min Mail Order UK: Nmc
Min Mail Order EU: Nmc
Cat. Cost: Online only.
Credit Cards: Paypal
Specialities: Unusual hardy perennials, hardy geraniums, black plants, woodland plants, grasses, plants for moist soil. All plants grown largely peat-free. Many plants available in small quantities.
Notes: Stock changes throughout the year. See website for regular updates or phone/email. Email to enquire about plants not listed on website.
Map Ref: W, C3 **OS Grid Ref:** SN654540

WRHF **Red House Farm** ♿
Flying Horse Lane, Bradley Green, Nr Redditch, Worcestershire
B96 6QT
Ⓣ (01527) 821269
Ⓕ (01527) 821674
Ⓔ redhousenursery@googlemail.com
Ⓦ www.redhousefarmgardenandnursery.co.uk
Contact: Mrs Maureen Weaver
Opening Times: 0900-1700 Mon-Sat all year. 1000-1700 Sun & B/hols.
Cat. Cost: 2 × 1st class.
Credit Cards: None
Specialities: Cottage garden perennials.
Map Ref: W, C5 **OS Grid Ref:** SO986623

WRou **Roualeyn Nurseries** ⊠ ⌂
Trefriw, Conwy LL27 0SX
Ⓣ (01492) 640548
Ⓔ roualeynnursery@btinternet.com
Ⓦ www.roualeynfuchsias.co.uk
Contact: Doug Jones
Opening Times: 1000-1600 Fri, Sat & Sun.
Min Mail Order UK: £14.00
Cat. Cost: 2 x 1st class sae.
Credit Cards: All major credit/debit cards
Specialities: Fuchsias, incl. species.

Notes: Orders may be collected from any of the flower shows listed in current catalogue.
Map Ref: W, A3 **OS Grid Ref:** SH632778

WSFF SAITH FFYNNON WILDLIFE PLANTS ⊠ € ♿
Whitford, Holywell, Flintshire CH8 9EQ
Ⓣ (01352) 711198
Ⓕ (01352) 716777
Ⓔ jan@7wells.org
Ⓦ www.7wells.co.uk
Contact: Jan Miller
Opening Times: By appt. only.
Min Mail Order UK: Nmc
Min Mail Order EU: Nmc
Cat. Cost: 2 × 1st class (list only) or full catalogue online.
Credit Cards: All major credit/debit cards
Specialities: Plants and seeds to attract butterflies and moths. Natural dye plants. Nat. Collection of *Eupatorium*. Stock available in small quantities unless ordered well in advance.
Notes: Percentage of profits go to conservation. Credit cards accepted via website only. Also sells wholesale.
Map Ref: W, A3 **OS Grid Ref:** SJ154775

WSHC STONE HOUSE COTTAGE NURSERIES ♿
Stone, Nr Kidderminster, Worcestershire DY10 4BG
Ⓣ (01562) 69902
Ⓔ louisa@shcn.co.uk
Ⓦ www.shcn.co.uk
Contact: L N Arbuthnott
Opening Times: 1000-1700 Wed-Sat. By appt. only early Sep-late Mar.
Cat. Cost: Sae
Credit Cards: None
Specialities: Small general range esp. wall shrubs, climbers & unusual plants.
Map Ref: W, C5 **OS Grid Ref:** SO863750

WShi SHIPTON BULBS ⊠ ⌂ €
Y Felin, Henllan Amgoed, Whitland, Carmarthenshire SA34 0SL
Ⓣ (01994) 240125
Ⓕ (01994) 241180
Ⓔ admin@shiptonbulbs.co.uk
Ⓦ www.shiptonbulbs.co.uk
Contact: John Shipton & Astra Shipton
Opening Times: By appt. only.
Min Mail Order UK: Nmc
Min Mail Order EU: Nmc
Cat. Cost: Sae.
Credit Cards: All major credit/debit cards
Specialities: Native British bulbs. Bulbs & plants for naturalising.
Map Ref: W, D2 **OS Grid Ref:** SN188207

WSpi SPINNEYWELL NURSERY ⊠ ⌂ ◆
Spinneywell Farm, Waterlane, Oakridge, Stroud, Gloucestershire GL6 7PH
Ⓣ (01452) 770092
Ⓜ 07986 887158
Ⓕ (01452) 770151
Ⓔ wendy.spinneywell@virgin.net
Ⓦ www.spinneywellplants.co.uk
Contact: Wendy Asher
Opening Times: 0900-1600 Mon-Fri, Apr-Sep. 1000-1500 Mon-Fri, Oct-Mar.
Min Mail Order UK: £10.00 + p&p
Min Mail Order EU: £30.00 + p&p
Cat. Cost: Online only.
Credit Cards: All major credit/debit cards
Specialities: *Buxus*, *Taxus* & unusual herbaceous & shrubs. Hellebores, euphorbias, *Ceanothus*, hardy geraniums.
Notes: Plant sourcing service available. Mail order only after Jul 2011. Also sells wholesale.
Map Ref: W, D5 **OS Grid Ref:** SO921044

W

WSSs SHROPSHIRE SARRACENIAS ⊠ ☒ ⌂ € ♿
5 Field Close, Malinslee, Telford, Shropshire TF4 2EH
Ⓣ (01952) 501598
Ⓔ mike@carnivorousplants.uk.com
Ⓦ www.carnivorousplants.uk.com
Contact: Mike King
Opening Times: By appt. only.
Min Mail Order UK: Nmc
Min Mail Order EU: Nmc
Cat. Cost: 2 × 1st class.
Credit Cards: Paypal
Specialities: *Sarracenia*. *Dionaea muscipula* & forms. Some stock available in small quantities only. Nat. Collections of *Sarracenia* & *Dionaea*.
Map Ref: W, B4 **OS Grid Ref:** SJ689085

WSuV SUNNYBANK VINE NURSERY (NATIONAL VINE COLLECTION) ⊠ ☒
Cwm Barn, King Street, Ewyas Harold, Rowlestone, Herefordshire HR2 0EE
Ⓣ (01981) 240256
Ⓔ Sarah@sunnybankvines.co.uk
Ⓦ www.sunnybankvines.co.uk
Contact: Sarah Bell
Opening Times: Not open. Mail order only.
Min Mail Order UK: £10.00 incl. p&p
Min Mail Order EU: £15.00 incl. p&p
Cat. Cost: Online only.
Credit Cards: None
Specialities: Vines. Nat. Collection of *Vitis*

KEY
⊠ Mail order to UK or EU ⌂ Delivers to shows
☒ Exports beyond EU € Euro accepted
♿ Accessible by wheelchair ◆ See Display advertisement

vinifera (hardy, incl. dessert & wine). 70 varieties available as rooted plants, the entire Collection usually available as bare wood cuttings for own propagation.
Notes: EU sales by arrangement.
Map Ref: W, C4

WTan **Tan-y-Llyn Nurseries** ⊠
Meifod, Powys SY22 6YB
Ⓣ (01938) 500370
Ⓔ info@tanyllyn-nursery.co.uk
Ⓦ www.tanyllyn-nursery.co.uk
Contact: Callum Johnston
Opening Times: 1000-1700 Tue-Sat Mar-Jun and at other times by appt.
Min Mail Order UK: Nmc
Cat. Cost: 2 × 1st class or online.
Credit Cards: Paypal
Specialities: Herbs, alpines, perennials.
Map Ref: W, B3 **OS Grid Ref:** SJ167125

W

WThu **Thuya Alpine Nursery** ⊠
Glebelands, Hartpury, Gloucestershire GL19 3BW
Ⓣ (01452) 700548 (after dark)
Contact: S W Bond
Opening Times: 1000-dusk Sat & B/hols. 1100-dusk Sun, Weekdays appt. advised.
Min Mail Order UK: £6.00 + p&p
Min Mail Order EU: £12.00 + p&p
Cat. Cost: 4 × 2nd class.
Credit Cards: None
Specialities: Wide and changing range including rarities, available in smallish numbers.
Notes: Partially accessible for wheelchair users. Will deliver plants to AGS shows.
Map Ref: W, C5

WTou **Touchwood Plants** ⊠ ☒
4 Clyne Valley Cottages, Killay, Swansea, West Glamorgan SA2 7DU
Ⓣ (01792) 522443
Ⓔ Carrie.Thomas@ntlworld.com
Ⓦ www.touchwoodplants.co.uk
Contact: Carrie Thomas
Opening Times: Most reasonable days/times. Please phone first.
Min Mail Order UK: Nmc
Min Mail Order EU: Nmc
Cat. Cost: 1 × 2nd class large sae.
Credit Cards: Paypal, All major credit/debit cards
Specialities: Seeds & plants. Nat. Collection of *Aquilegia vulgaris* cvs & hybrids. Plant stocks held in small quantities. Main stock is seed. Garden & *Aquilegia* Collection open.
Notes: Plants sent bare-rooted at relevant times of the year. Beyond the UK only seeds exported. Credit cards accepted online only.
Map Ref: W, D3 **OS Grid Ref:** SS600924

WWEG **World's End Garden Nursery** ⊠
♿ ◆
Moseley Road, Hallow, Worcester, Worcestershire WR2 6NJ
Ⓣ (01905) 640977
Ⓕ (01905) 641373
Ⓔ info@worldsendgarden.co.uk
Ⓦ www.worldsendgarden.co.uk
Contact: Kristina & Robin Pearce
Opening Times: 1000-1700, Mon-Fri. Other times strictly by appt. only.
Min Mail Order UK: £20.00
Min Mail Order EU: £20.00
Cat. Cost: Online only.
Credit Cards: All major credit/debit cards
Specialities: Wide range of herbaceous perennials, hardy ferns & ornamental grasses. Especially *Hosta*, *Geum*, *Leucantheum*, *Helenium*.
Notes: Also sells wholesale.
Map Ref: W, C5 **OS Grid Ref:** SO815597

WWFP **Whitehall Farmhouse Plants** ⊠
Sevenhampton, Cheltenham, Gloucestershire GL54 5TL
Ⓣ (01242) 820772
Ⓜ 07711 021034
Ⓕ (01242) 821226
Ⓔ info@wfplants.co.uk
Ⓦ www.wfplants.co.uk
Contact: Victoria Logue
Opening Times: By appt. only.
Min Mail Order UK: Nmc
Cat. Cost: 2 × 1st class.
Credit Cards: None
Specialities: A small nursery producing a range of interesting & easy hardy perennials for the garden. Some plants held in small quantities only.
Map Ref: W, C5 **OS Grid Ref:** SP018229

WWlt **Wollerton Old Hall Garden** ♿
Wollerton, Market Drayton, Shropshire TF9 3NA
Ⓣ (01630) 685760
Ⓔ info@wollertonoldhallgarden.com
Ⓦ www.wollertonoldhallgarden.com
Contact: Mr John Jenkins
Opening Times: 1200-1700 Fri, Sun & B/hols Easter-end Aug, Fri only in Sep.
Cat. Cost: None issued
Credit Cards: All, except American Express
Specialities: Perennials, hardy & half-hardy.
Map Ref: W, B4 **OS Grid Ref:** SJ624296

Abroad

XBlo **Table Bay View Nursery** ⊠ ✈ €
(Office) 60 Molteno Road, Oranjezicht, Cape Town, 8001 South Africa
Ⓣ (27) 21 683 5108
Ⓕ (27) 21 683 5108
Ⓔ info@tablebayviewnursery.co.za
Contact: Terence Bloch
Opening Times: Mail order only. No personal callers.
Min Mail Order UK: £15.00 + p&p
Min Mail Order EU: £15.00
Cat. Cost: £3.40 (postal order)
Credit Cards: None
Specialities: Tropical & sub-tropical ornamental & fruiting plants. Self-harvested seed, predominently from our own inventory of mother stock plants.
Notes: Due to high local bank charges, can no longer accept foreign bank cheques, only undated postal orders. To comply with UK import regulations, prospective buyers must register with DEFRA before placing an order.

XEll **Ellebore** ⊠ €
La Chamotière, 61 360 Saint-Jouin-de-Blavou, France
Ⓣ (33) 2 3383 3772
Ⓜ (33) 6802 28674
Ⓕ (33) 2 3383 3773
Ⓔ pepiniere.ellebore@orange.fr
Ⓦ www.pepiniere-ellebore.fr
Contact: Nadine Albouy & Christian Geoffroy
Opening Times: 1000-1800 Wed-Sat, mid-Feb to late Jun & Sep-Dec. 1500-1800 Thu, Fri & Sat, Jul, Aug & Jan to mid-Feb.
Min Mail Order UK: Nmc
Min Mail Order EU: Nmc
Cat. Cost: Free.
Credit Cards: All major credit/debit cards
Specialities: *Helleborus*. Bulbs. *Clematis*.
Notes: Also sells wholesale.

XFro **Frosch Exclusive Perennials** ⊠ ✈ €
Ziegelstadelweg 5, D-83623 Dietramszell-Lochen, Germany
Ⓣ (49) 172 842 2050
Ⓕ (49) 8027 904 9975
Ⓔ info@cypripedium.de
Ⓦ www.cypripedium.de
Contact: Michael Weinert
Opening Times: Not open. Mail order only. Orders taken between 0700-2200 hours.
Min Mail Order UK: £350.00 + p&p
Min Mail Order EU: £350.00 + p&p
Cat. Cost: Online only.
Credit Cards: None
Specialities: *Cypripedium* hybrids. Hardy orchids.
Notes: Also sells wholesale.

XLum **Lumen Plantes Vivaces** ⊠ ✈ ⌂ €
Les Coutets, 24100 Creysse-Bergerac, Occitania, France
Ⓣ (33) 5 5357 6215
Ⓕ (33) 5 5358 5488
Ⓔ lumenviva@aol.com
Ⓦ www.lumen.fr
Contact: Michel Lumen
Opening Times: 0900-1200 & 1300-1630 Mon-Thu, 0900-1200 & 1300-1530 Fri. Closed Sat, Sun & B/hols. 0900-1200 & 1300-1830 Mon-Sat, Mar-Jun.
Min Mail Order UK: Nmc
Min Mail Order EU: Nmc
Cat. Cost: Online only.
Credit Cards: Visa, MasterCard
Specialities: Hardy perennials. French Nat. Collection of *Miscanthus*.
Notes: Also sells wholesale.
OS Grid Ref: N44 51.789 E0 32.0518

XPde **Pépinière de l'Île** ⊠ ✈ ⌂ €
Keranroux, 22870, Ile de Brehat, France
Ⓣ (33) 2 96 200384
Ⓜ (33) 06861 28609
Ⓕ (33) 2 96 200384
Ⓔ contact@pepiniere-brehat.com
Ⓦ www.pepiniere-brehat.com
Contact: Laurence Blasco & Charles Blasco
Opening Times: 1400-1800 spring & summer. Other times by appt. incl. Aug.
Min Mail Order UK: Nmc
Min Mail Order EU: Nmc
Cat. Cost: Online only.
Credit Cards: None
Specialities: *Agapanthus* & *Echium*. Plants from South Africa, Madeira, Canary Islands & New Zealand.

XPou **Koen Van Poucke** ⊠ ⌂ € ♿
Heistraat 106, Sint-Niklaas, Oost-Vlaanderen, 9100 Belgium
Ⓣ (32) 0377 77642
Ⓕ (32) 0376 61698
Ⓔ kvanpoucke@skynet.be
Ⓦ www.koenvanpoucke.be
Contact: Koen Van Poucke

KEY
⊠ Mail order to UK or EU ⌂ Delivers to shows
✈ Exports beyond EU € Euro accepted
♿ Accessible by wheelchair ◆ See Display advertisement

X

Opening Times: 0900-1230 & 1300-1800, Tue-Sat. Closed Sun & Mon. Closed Jul. Check website before travelling a long distance.
Min Mail Order UK: €80
Min Mail Order EU: €80
Credit Cards: None
Specialities: *Epimedium*. Also rare Asian shade plants. *Dahlias*.
Notes: Mail order Sep-Apr. Collector's garden open to the public.

XSen **Les Senteurs Du Quercy** ⊠ € ♿
Mas de Fraysse, Escamps, Lot, 46230 France
Ⓣ (33) 5 652 10167
Ⓔ melie.fred@aliceadsl.fr
Ⓦ www.senteursduquercy.com
Contact: Frédéric Prévot
Opening Times: 1400-1800 spring & summer (excl. Aug). Other times, incl. Aug by appt.
Min Mail Order UK: Nmc
Min Mail Order EU: Nmc
Cat. Cost: €5.00
Specialities: *Salvia*, *Iris*, *Phlomis*, *Teucrium*, *Lavandula* and drought tolerant plants. French Nat. Coll. of *Salvia* species.

XTur **Etablissements Pierre Turc** ⊠ ☒ ⌂ € ♿ ◆
63 Route de Seiches, 49630 Mazé, France
Ⓣ (33) 2 418 06408
Ⓜ (33) 06475 63327
Ⓕ (33) 2 418 02696
Ⓔ export@turcieflor.com
Ⓦ www.turcieflor.com
Contact: Mark Hodson
Opening Times: 0800-1215 & 1400-1700 Mon-Fri.
Min Mail Order UK: Nmc + p&p
Min Mail Order EU: Nmc + p&p
Credit Cards: None
Specialities: *Alstroemeria*, *Agapanthus* & *Canna*. Also *Arum*, *Begonia*, *Dahlia*, *Fuchsia* & *Hippeastrum*.
Notes: Also sells wholesale.

X

NURSERY INDEX BY NAME

Nurseries that are included in the *RHS Plant Finder* for the first time this year (or have been reintroduced) are marked in **bold type**. Full details of the nurseries will be found in **Nursery Details by Code** on page 804. For a key to the geographical codes, see the start of **Nurseries**.

Great Dixter Nurseries	SDix
Great Western Gladiolus Nursery, The	CGrW
Green, Mary	NMyG
Green's Leaves	WGrn
Griffin, D.	EGri
Groves, C.W. & Son Ltd	CGro
Gwynfor Growers	WGwG
Habitat Aid Ltd	CHab
Hall Farm Nursery	WHal
Halls of Heddon	NHal
Hall's Court Nursery	**SHal**
Hardy Exotics	CHEx
Hardy's Cottage Garden Plants	SHar
Harley Nursery	WHar
Harrells Hardy Plants	WHrl
Hart Canna	SHaC
Hartside Nursery Garden	NHar
Hawthornes Nursery, The	NHaw
Hayloft Plants	WHlf
Heaselands Garden Nursery	SHea
Heligan Nursery & Plant Centre	**CHel**
Henry Street Nursery	LStr
Herb Garden & Historical Plant Nursery, The	WHer
Herb Nursery, The	MHer
Herbary, The	CHby
Herbs for Healing	WHfH
Hergest Croft Gardens	WHCr
Herterton House Garden Nursery	NHer
Herts Hellebores	LHel
Heucheraholics	SHeu
Hewitt-Cooper Carnivorous Plants	CHew
Hidden Valley Gardens	CHVG
Hidden Valley Nursery	CHid
High Garden Nurseries	CHGN
Highdown Nursery	SHDw
Hill House Nursery Ltd	CHll
Hillier Garden Centres	SHil
Hillview Hardy Plants	WHil
Hoecroft Plants	EHoe
Holden Clough Nursery Ltd	NHol
Hollies Farm Plant Centre	**MHol**
Homestead Plants	MHom
Honeysome Aquatic Nursery	EHon
Hoo House Nursery	WHoo
Hooksgreen Herbs Ltd	MHoo
Hopleys Plants Ltd	LHop
Horticultural Sales	WHor
Hull Farm	EHul
Hyde Hall Garden (RHS)	**EHyd**
Hydrangea Haven	SHyH
Ice Alpines	WIce
Iden Croft Herbs	SIde
Ingram, Tim	**SIgm**
Iris Garden, The	CIri
Iris of Sissinghurst	SIri
Irisesonline	EIri
Ivycroft Plants	WIvy
JPR Environmental	WJPR
Jackson's Nurseries, Bagnall	**MJak**
Jackson's Nurseries, Tamworth	MJac
Jacques Amand International Ltd	LAma
James Cocker & Sons	GCoc
Jasmine Cottage Gardens	CJas
Jekka's Herb Farm	WJek
Jo's Garden Enterprise	GJos
John and Lynsey's Plants	SPin
John Hall Plants Ltd	SWhi
Jungle Giants	WJun
Junker's Nursery Ltd (formerly PMA Plant Specialities)	CJun
Keepers Nursery	SKee
Kelways	CKel
Kenwith Conifer Nursery (Gordon Haddow)	CKen
Kevin Hughes Plants	SKHP
Kevock Garden Plants	GKev
Kiftsgate Court Gardens	WKif
Kilmurry Nursery	IKil
Kings Barn Trees	**SKin**
Kinlochlaich Garden Plant Centre	GKin
Knoll Gardens	CKno
Koen Van Poucke	**XPou**
L.B. Plants	NLBP
L.M.C. Nurseries Ltd	**ELMC**
LW Plants	LLWP
Lakka Bulbs	CLak
Landford Trees	CLnd
Landscape Plants	SLPl
Laneside Hardy Orchid Nursery	NLAp
Langthorns Plantery	ELan
Larch Cottage Nurseries	NLar
Larkspur Nursery	ELar
Laurel Farm Herbs	ELau
Laurels Nursery, The	SLau
Lavender Garden, The	WLav
Layham Garden Centre & Nursery	SLay
Lea Rhododendron Gardens Ltd	MLea
Lilies Water Gardens	**LLWG**
Lime Cross Nursery	SLim
Linn Botanic Gardens	GLin
Little Brook Fuchsias	SLBF
Little Heath Farm (UK)	LLHF
Lockyer, C.S. (Fuchsias)	CLoc
Loder Plants	SLdr
Lodge Farm Plants & Wildflowers	**MLod**
Logie Steading Plants	GLog
Long Acre Plants	CLAP
Long House Plants	ELon
Longcombe Nursery and Garden Centre	CLng
Longstock Park Nursery	SLon
Longstone Hardy Plant Nursery	MLHP
Lower Severalls Nursery	CSev
Lumen Plantes Vivaces	XLum
Mac Pennys Nurseries	CMac

Rapkyns Nursery	SRkn
Rare and Exotic Plants at Woodshoot Nurseries	MREP
Ravensthorpe Nursery	MRav
Reads Nursery	**ERea**
Really Wild Flowers	SRea
Really Wild Nursery, The	CRWN
Red House Farm	WRHF
G. Reuthe Ltd	SReu
Ribblesdale Nurseries	NRib
Ringhaddy Daffodils	**IRhd**
River Garden Nurseries	SRiv
Robinson, A. J.	**MAJR**
Robinson, W. & Son (Seeds & Plants) Ltd	NRob
Rodings Plantery, The	ERod
Ros Ban Wildlife Garden	IRos
Rose Cottage Plants	ERCP
Roseland House Nursery	CRHN
Rosemoor Garden Plant Centre (RHS)	**CRos**
Rosie's Garden Plants	SRGP
Rotherview Nursery	SRot
Roualeyn Nurseries	**WRou**
Rowden Gardens	CRow
Rumsey Gardens	SRms
Ryal Nursery	NRya
St Bridget Nurseries Ltd	CSBt
Saith Ffynnon Wildlife Plants	WSFF
Sampford Shrubs	CSam
Seagate Irises	ESgI
Seale Nurseries	SSea
Seaside Nursery	ISsi
Select Seeds	SSss
Sempervivum Nursery	**MSem**
Semps by Post	ESem
Senteurs Du Quercy, Les	XSen
Shady Plants	ISha
Sherston Parva Nursery	CSPN
Shipton Bulbs	WShi
Shropshire Sarracenias	WSSs
Shrubland Park Nurseries	EShb
Silver Dale Nurseries	CSil
Slack Top Nurseries	NSla
Smart Plants	MTPN
Snape Cottage	CSna
Sooty's Plants	**NSoo**
Sound Garden Rhododendrons	MSnd
Southon Plants	LSou
Special Plants	CSpe
SpecialPerennials.com	MSpe
Spinners Garden	SSpi
Spinneywell Nursery	WSpi
Spring Park Nursery	GSPN
Spring Reach Nursery	LSRN
Squire's Garden Centre, Shepperton	LShp
Squire's Garden Centre, Twickenham	LSqu
Squire's Garden Centre, West Horsley	LSqH
Starborough Nursery	SSta
Stillingfleet Lodge Nurseries	NSti
Stone House Cottage Nurseries	WSHC
Stone Lane Gardens	CSto
Stonyford Cottage Nursery	MSCN
Style Roses	ESty
Sue Proctor Plants	**NSue**
Summerdale Garden Nursery	NSum
Sunnybank Vine Nursery (National Vine Collection)	WSuV
Surreal Succulents	**CSuc**
Suttons Seeds	CSut
Swallows Nursery	MSwo
Sweet Knowle Aquatics	MSKA
Swines Meadow Farm Nursery	ESwi
Table Bay View Nursery	XBlo
Tan-y-Llyn Nurseries	WTan
Taylors Clematis Nursery	NTay
Terrace Gardener	STrG
Test Valley Nursery	STes
Thistlefield Plants and Design	EThi
Thorncroft Clematis	ETho
Thornhayes Nursery	CTho
Thuya Alpine Nursery	WThu
Timpany Nurseries & Gardens	ITim
Tissington Nursery	MTis
Toobees Exotics	LToo
Topiary Arts	LTop
Touchwood Plants	WTou
Trecanna Nursery	CTca
Tree Peony Company	**NTPC**
Treetyme	**NTre**
Trehane Nursery	CTrh
Treseders	CTsd
Triscombe Nurseries	CTri
Tweedie, J., Fruit Trees	GTwe
Urban Jungle	EUJe
Ventnor Botanic Garden	**SVen**
Victoriana Nursery Gardens	SVic
Victoria's Nursery & Garden	IVic
Waddow Lodge Garden	NWad
Walled Garden Nursery	CWGN
Walled Garden, The	EWll
Walnut Tree Garden Nursery	EWTr
Water Garden, The	CWat
Water Meadow Nursery	SWat
Waterperry Gardens Ltd	MWat
Waterside Nursery	MWts
Wayside Aquatics	EWay
Weasdale Nurseries Ltd	NWea
West Acre Gardens	EWes
West Somerset Garden Centre	CWSG
Westcountry Nurseries	CWCL
Westonbirt Plants	LWst
Westshores Nurseries	NWsh
White Veil Fuchsias	CWVF
Whitehall Farmhouse Plants	WWFP
Whitehill Farm Nursery	MWhi

INDEX MAP

The maps on the following pages show the approximate location of the nurseries whose details are listed in this directory.

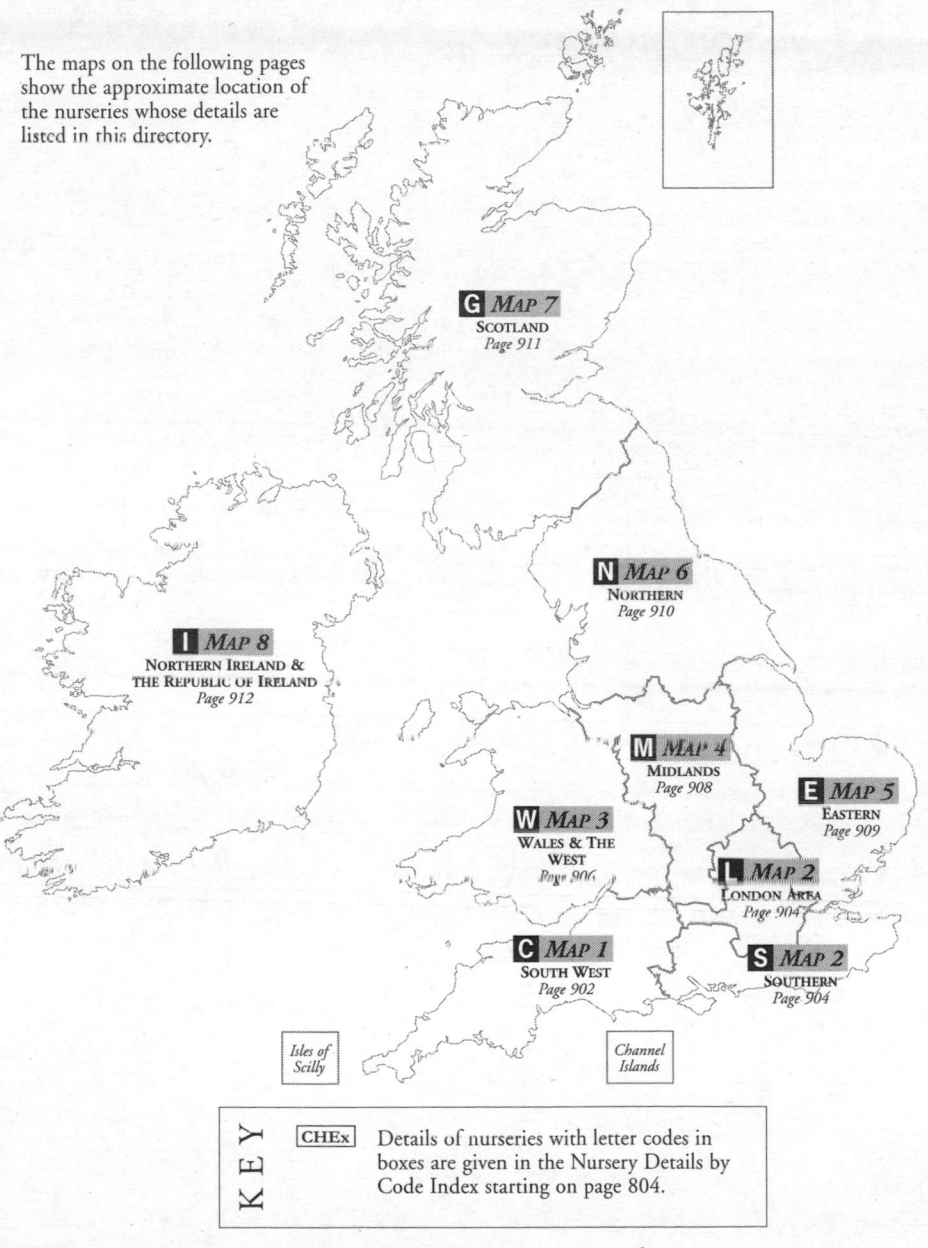

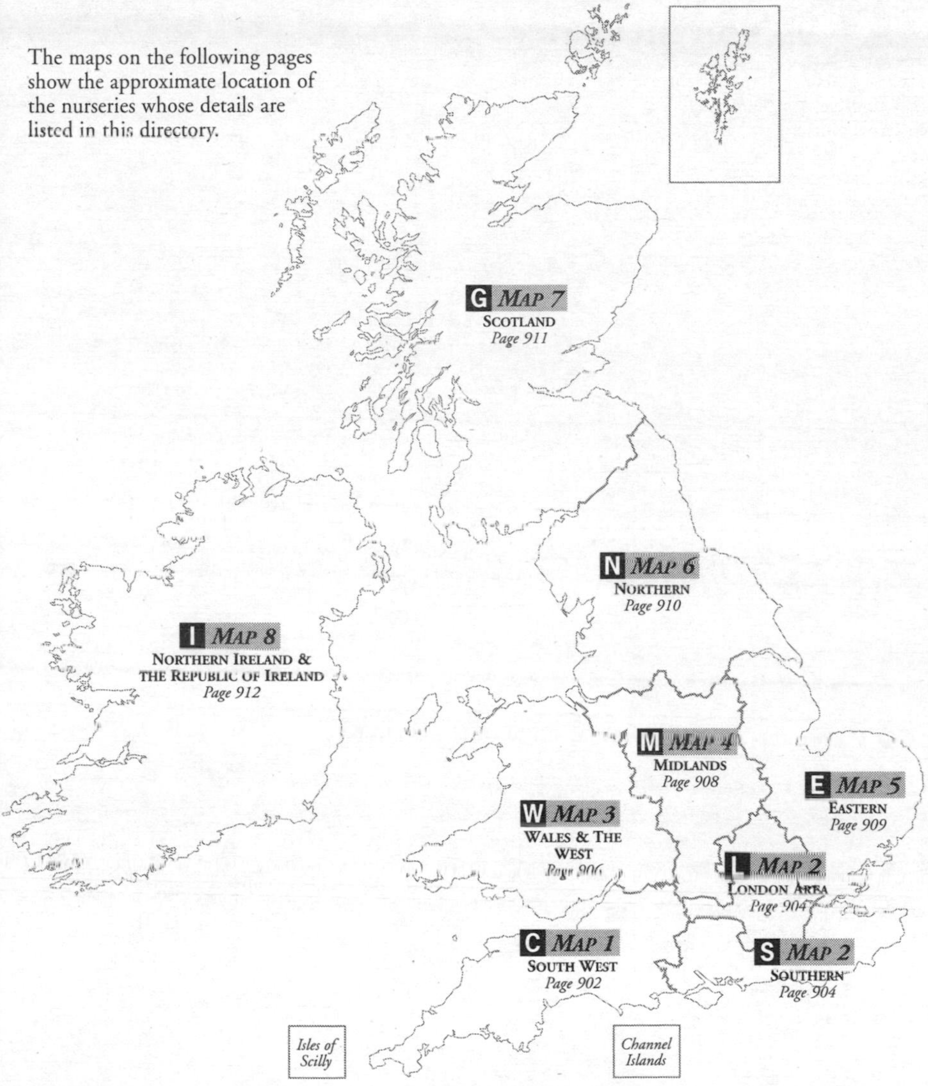

KEY

CHEx Details of nurseries with letter codes in boxes are given in the Nursery Details by Code Index starting on page 804.

C
MAP ONE
SOUTH WEST
1
2
3
A
B
C
D
Llanelli
M4
Neath
Swansea
Port Talbo
Bridgen
CSil
Ilfracombe
Combe Martin
CMHG
Barnstaple
CAni
Bideford
CHid
CWCL
CRos
CKen
CWri
A377
Bude
CWil
CBAq
A39
CCha
CPbn
Okehampton
CSto
Launceston
CBre
CRow
Tavistock
Newton Abbott
CBct
CNW
Wadebridge
CTca
CGHE
CHll
CTsd
Bodmin
Liskeard
CFil
A38
CLng
CDoC
Newquay
CPrp
Plymouth
CMam
A30
CHVG
CPou
CRHN
St Austell
Truro
St Ives
CSuc
CFen
Redruth
CHEx
Camborne
CBcS
Penzance
Falmouth
Helston
COlW
CCon
CExl
CCCN
CQua

4
5
6
A
B
C
D
Stroud
Cirencester
Pontypool
Cwmbran
Newport
M4
M5
CARDIFF
Bristol
CSPN
CWGN
Swindon
CWat
CLoc
CPhi
CSpe
Chippenham
CFlo
Marlborough
Calne
CJas
Clevedon
CBot
Newbury
Weston
Super
Mare
CArn
CCVT
Bath
Melksham
Devizes
Trowbridge
CPom
CPBP
CMea
Burnham on Sea
CWSG
CFwr
Minehead
CWib
CMil
CMen
Frome
Wells
Warminster
Andover
Williton
CBgR
A36
CTri
Bridgwater
Glastonbury
CSna
CMus
CElw
CPcn
CAbP
CBty
Salisbury
CBro
Wincanton
CKel
CLAP
A303
Taunton
CJun
CNMi
Shaftesbury
M3
CDTJ
CCAT
CMCN
CFis
CLnd
Wellington
CSam
Yeovil
A354
Southampton
Tiverton
Chard
CSev
Ringwood
Blandford Forum
CTho
CKno
CTrh
Lymington
CDul
CAby
CIri
CMac
Winborne Minster
CEnt
Bridport
Lyme Regis
A35
Dorchester
CSBt
CBrP
CPar
Bournemouth
Poole
CGro
CDoy
CNec
CEls
Exmouth
CBur
Teignmouth
CPla
Torquay

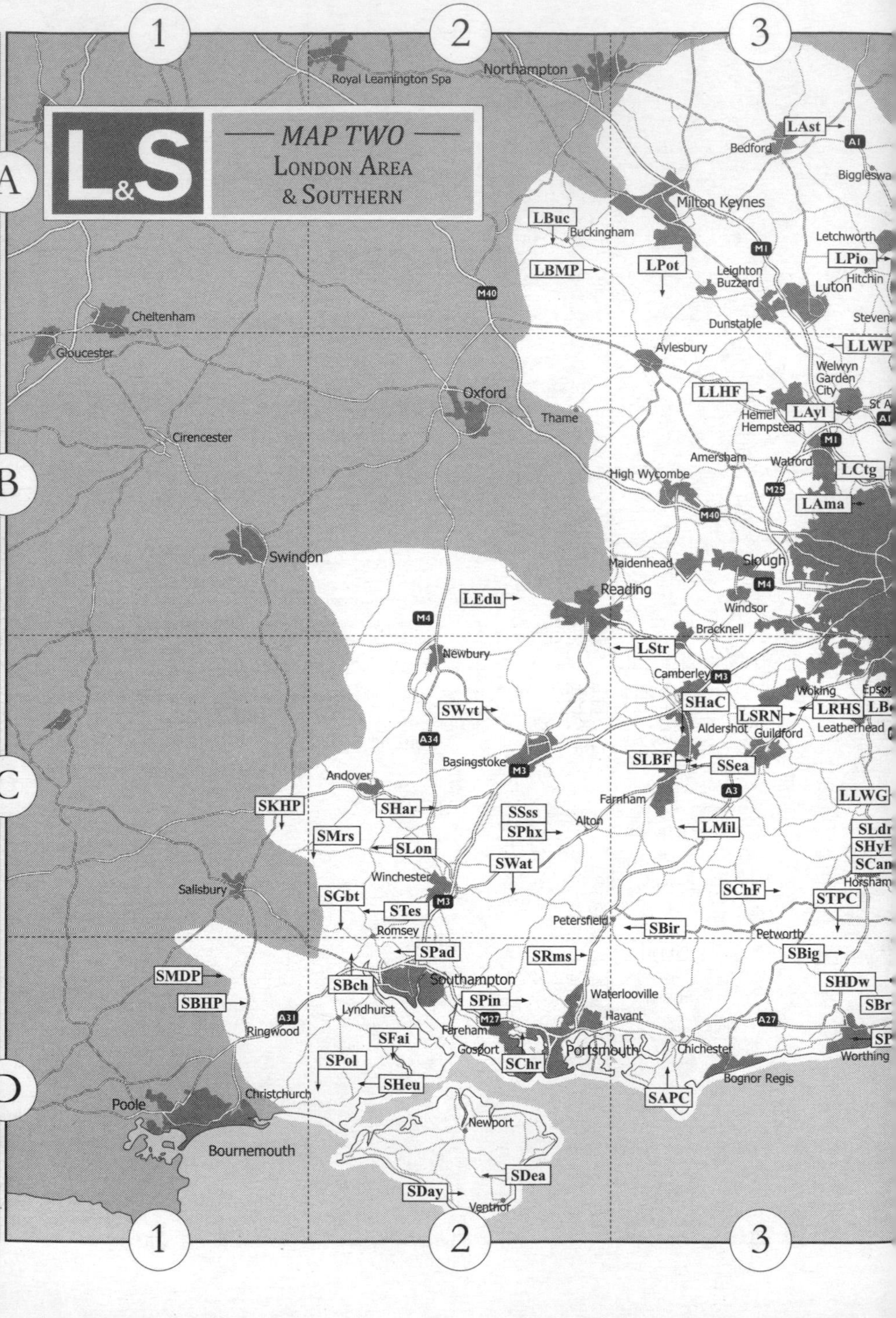
1
2
3
A
B
C
D
L&S
MAP TWO
London Area
& Southern
Royal Leamington Spa
Northampton
Bedford
LAst
A1
Biggleswa
Milton Keynes
LBuc
Buckingham
LBMP
M1
Letchworth
LPio
Hitchin
LPot
Leighton Buzzard
Luton
M40
Cheltenham
Dunstable
Steven
Gloucester
Aylesbury
LLWP
Welwyn Garden City
Oxford
LLHF
Hemel Hempstead
LAyl
St A
Thame
Cirencester
M1
Amersham
Watford
LCtg
High Wycombe
M25
LAma
M40
Swindon
Maidenhead
Slough
M4
LEdu
Reading
Windsor
M4
Bracknell
Newbury
LStr
Camberley
M3
Woking
Epso
SHaC
SWvt
LSRN
LRHS
LB
Aldershot
Guildford
Leatherhead
A34
Basingstoke
M3
SLBF
SSea
Andover
Farnham
A3
LLWG
SKHP
SHar
SSss
SPhx
Alton
LMil
SMrs
SLon
SLdr
SHyH
SWat
SCan
Winchester
Horsham
Salisbury
SChF
SGbt
STes
M3
STPC
Petersfield
SBir
Romsey
Petworth
SPad
SRms
SBig
SMDP
SBch
Southampton
SHDw
SBHP
SPin
Waterlooville
SBr
A31
Lyndhurst
M27
Havant
A27
SP
Ringwood
Fareham
SFai
Gosport
Portsmouth
Chichester
Worthing
SPol
SChr
Bognor Regis
SHeu
Christchurch
SAPC
Poole
Newport
Bournemouth
SDea
SDay
Ventnor
1
2
3

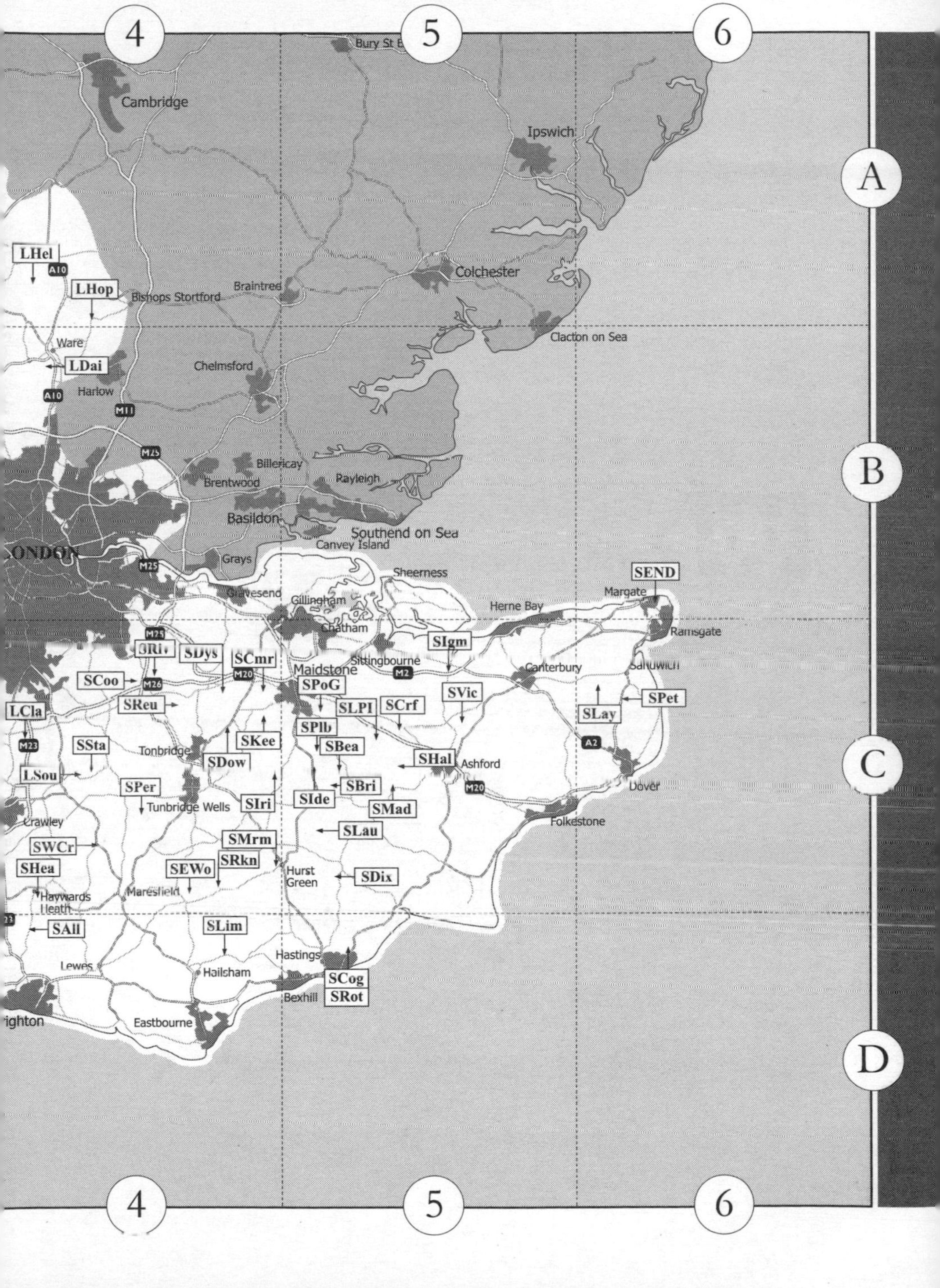
4
5
6
A
B
C
D
Bury St E
Cambridge
Ipswich
Colchester
Braintree
Bishops Stortford
Clacton on Sea
Ware
Harlow
Chelmsford
Billericay
Brentwood
Rayleigh
Basildon
Southend on Sea
Canvey Island
LONDON
Grays
Sheerness
Gravesend
Gillingham
Chatham
Herne Bay
Margate
Ramsgate
Maidstone
Sittingbourne
Canterbury
Sandwich
Tonbridge
Ashford
Dover
Tunbridge Wells
Folkestone
Crawley
Hurst Green
Haywards Heath
Maresfield
Lewes
Hailsham
Hastings
Bexhill
Eastbourne
righton
A10
M11
M25
M26
M20
M2
A2
M23
LHel
LHop
LDai
LCla
LSou
SEND
SIgm
SVic
SPet
SLay
SDys
SCmr
SCoo
SReu
SPoG
SLPI
SCrf
SPlb
SBea
SKee
SDow
SSta
SHal
SPer
SIri
SIde
SBri
SMad
SLau
SMrm
SRkn
SEWo
SWCr
SHea
SDix
SAll
SLim
SCog
SRot

1
2
3
A
B
C
D
W
MAP THREE
Wales & The West
Holyhead
WOut
WHer
Bangor
WAbe
Llandudno
A55
WCru
Caernarvon
A470
A5
Betws-y-coed
Ruthin
WDib
Porthmadog
A470
A494
Dolgellau
WTan
A458
A470
Machynlleth
Newtown
Aberystwyth
A44
Llangurig
A483
A487
Aberaeron
A470
Llandrindod Wells
WPtf
Builth Wells
A470
WGwG
Cardigan
WMoo
A483
Fishguard
Llandovery
WPnn
St David's
Llandeilo
WNew
WShi
Carmarthen
Haverfordwest
A40
St Clears
A48
Merthyr Tydfil
Milford Haven
Pembroke Dock
Tenby
WBla
WGor
Llanelli
Neath
Swansea
Port Talbot
WTou
WBor
Bridgend
Barry

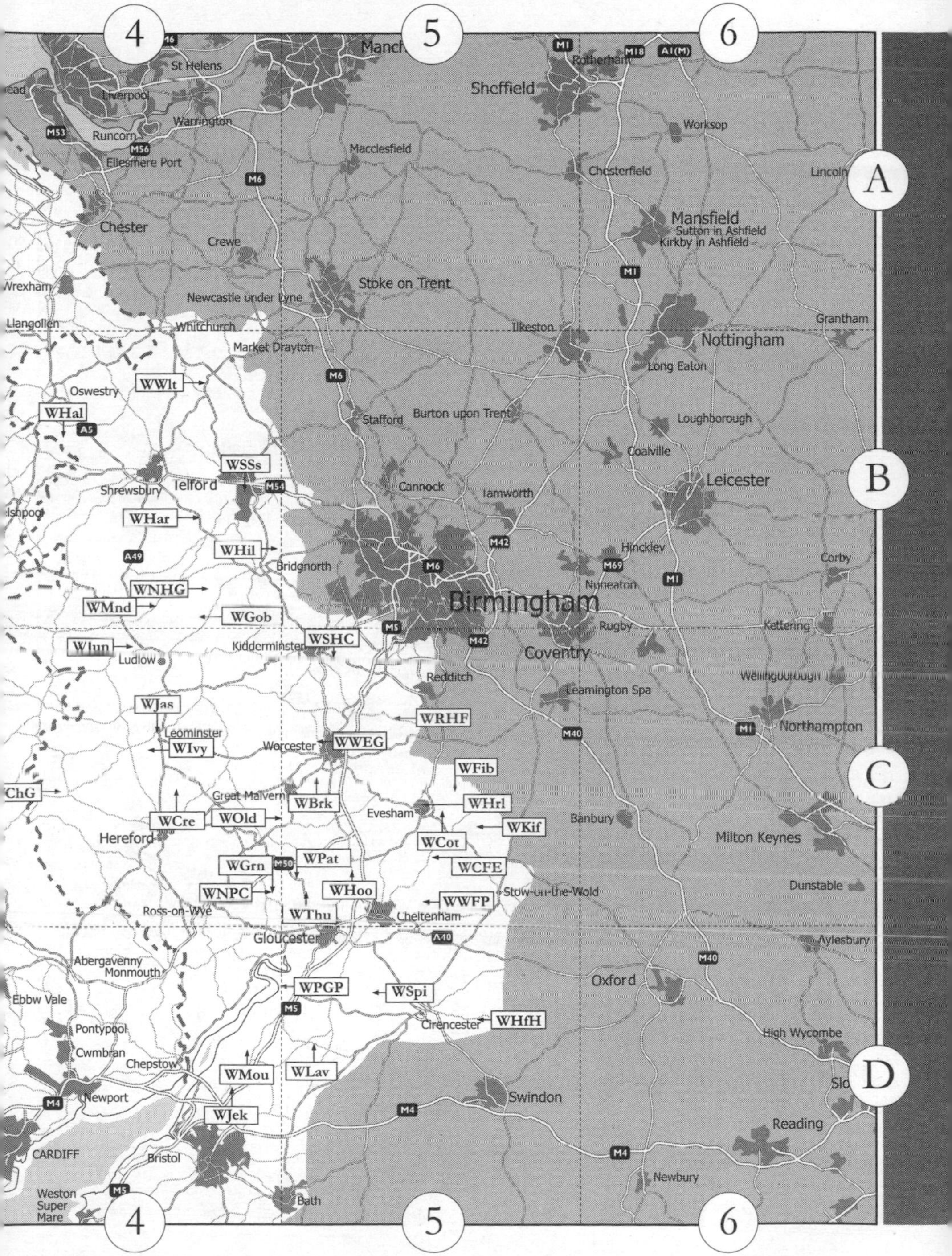
4
5
6
A
B
C
D
Manch
St Helens
Liverpool
Runcorn
Warrington
Ellesmere Port
Chester
Crewe
Wrexham
Llangollen
Whitchurch
Market Drayton
Oswestry
Macclesfield
Stoke on Trent
Newcastle under Lyne
Sheffield
Rotherham
Worksop
Chesterfield
Lincoln
Mansfield
Sutton in Ashfield
Kirkby in Ashfield
Grantham
Ilkeston
Nottingham
Long Eaton
Loughborough
Coalville
Leicester
Stafford
Burton upon Trent
Cannock
Tamworth
Hinckley
Nuneaton
Corby
Shrewsbury
Telford
Bridgnorth
Birmingham
Rugby
Kettering
Coventry
Kidderminster
Ludlow
Redditch
Leamington Spa
Wellingborough
Northampton
Leominster
Worcester
Great Malvern
Evesham
Banbury
Hereford
Milton Keynes
Stow-on-the-Wold
Dunstable
Ross-on-Wye
Cheltenham
Gloucester
Aylesbury
Abergavenny
Monmouth
Oxford
Ebbw Vale
Pontypool
Cwmbran
Cirencester
High Wycombe
Chepstow
Newport
Swindon
Reading
CARDIFF
Bristol
Newbury
Weston Super Mare
Bath
M6
M1
M18
A1(M)
M53
M56
A5
M54
A49
M42
M69
M5
M40
M50
A40
M4
WWlt
WHal
WSSs
WHar
WHil
WNHG
WMnd
WGob
WSHC
WIun
WJas
WIvy
WRHF
WWEG
WFib
ChG
WHrl
WBrk
WCre
WOld
WKif
WCot
WPat
WGrn
WCFE
WHoo
WNPC
WWFP
WThu
WPGP
WSpi
WHfH
WMou
WLav
WJek

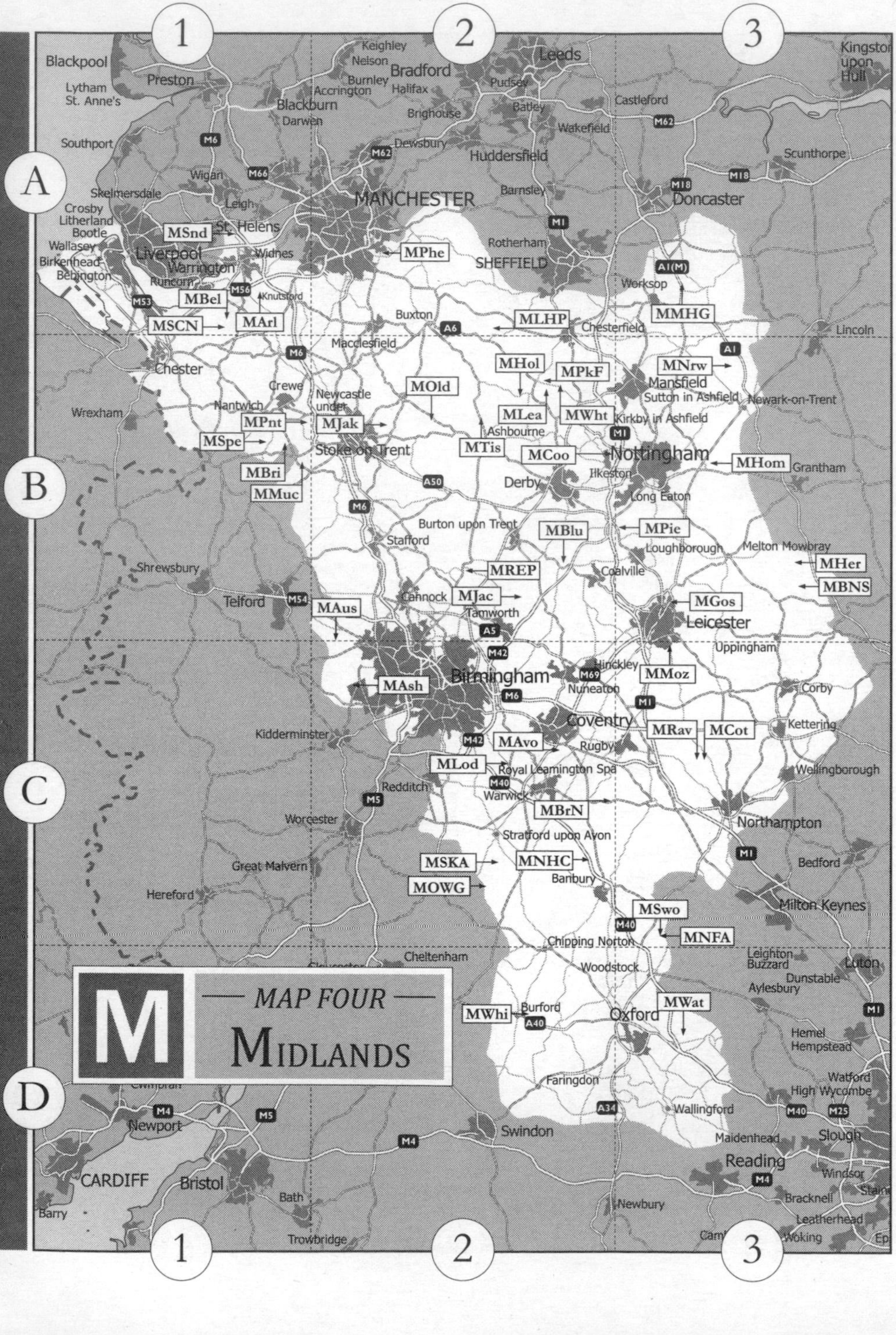

1
2
3
A
B
C
D
MAP FOUR
M
MIDLANDS
Blackpool
Preston
Lytham St. Anne's
Keighley
Nelson
Burnley
Accrington
Bradford
Halifax
Leeds
Pudsey
Batley
Castleford
Kingston upon Hull
Blackburn
Darwen
Brighouse
Wakefield
Southport
Dewsbury
Huddersfield
Scunthorpe
Wigan
Skelmersdale
Leigh
MANCHESTER
Barnsley
Doncaster
Crosby
Litherland
Bootle
Wallasey
Birkenhead
Bebington
St. Helens
Liverpool
Warrington
Widnes
Runcorn
Knutsford
Rotherham
SHEFFIELD
Worksop
Buxton
Chesterfield
Lincoln
Macclesfield
Chester
Crewe
Mansfield
Sutton in Ashfield
Kirkby in Ashfield
Newark-on-Trent
Wrexham
Nantwich
Newcastle under
Stoke on Trent
Ashbourne
Nottingham
Ilkeston
Derby
Long Eaton
Grantham
Burton upon Trent
Stafford
Loughborough
Melton Mowbray
Coalville
Shrewsbury
Telford
Cannock
Tamworth
Leicester
Uppingham
Birmingham
Hinckley
Nuneaton
Corby
Coventry
Kettering
Kidderminster
Rugby
Royal Leamington Spa
Warwick
Wellingborough
Redditch
Worcester
Northampton
Stratford upon Avon
Great Malvern
Banbury
Bedford
Hereford
Milton Keynes
Chipping Norton
Cheltenham
Woodstock
Leighton Buzzard
Luton
Dunstable
Aylesbury
Burford
Oxford
Hemel Hempstead
Watford
High Wycombe
Faringdon
Wallingford
Newport
Swindon
Maidenhead
Slough
Reading
Windsor
CARDIFF
Bristol
Bath
Bracknell
Newbury
Barry
Leatherhead
Trowbridge
Woking
M6
M62
M66
M18
M1
A1(M)
M56
M53
A6
A1
A50
M54
A5
M42
M69
M40
M5
A40
A34
M4
M25
MSnd
MPhe
MBel
MArl
MSCN
MLHP
MMHG
MHol
MPkF
MNrw
MOld
MLea
MWht
MPnt
MJak
MSpe
MTis
MCoo
MHom
MBri
MMuc
MBlu
MPie
MREP
MHer
MBNS
MJac
MGos
MAus
MMoz
MAsh
MRav
MCot
MAvo
MLod
MBrN
MSKA
MNHC
MOWG
MSwo
MNFA
MWhi
MWat

E
MAP FIVE
EASTERN
1
2
3
A
B
C
D
Kingston upon Hull
Winterton
Scunthorpe
Grimsby
Cleethorpes
ECrc
Caistor
EPot
EFer
EWld
Louth
Gainsborough
ECtt
Lincoln
Horncastle
Skegness
Newark-on-Trent
Sleaford
Boston
Grantham
Spalding
ESty
ESgl
ENBC
ECre
Fakenham
EHoe
Cromer
King's Lynn
ESwi
EGFP
EWes
EUJe
Great Yarmouth
Stamford
Wisbech
Swaffham
ETho
Norwich
Leicester
ECho
Downham Market
EWTr
EAmu
Lowestoft
Peterborough
Mundford
EPPr
Beccles
EDel
Corby
EPyc
EHon
Thetford
EOHP
Kettering
Ely
EGol
EWoo
EDif
Huntingdon
Mildenhall
EAca
Wellingborough
EDAr
ELMC
ELau
St Neots
Newmarket
Bury St Edmunds
EPts
EMic
Northampton
ECGP
EShb
Bedford
Cambridge
EPau
Ipswich
EBtc
EWil
EPri
ECrN
EExo
Milton Keynes
Royston
EIri
EBee
Saffron Walden
EMal
EHul
EPfP
Letchworth
Hitchen
EMil
Leighton Buzzard
EBak
ECnt
Stevenage
ELan
Braintree
Colchester
Dunstable
Luton
ERod
Clacton on Sea
Welwyn Garden City
Aylesbury
Hemel Hempstead
St Albans
ERCP
Chelmsford
Harlow
EGri
EWay
Sth Benfleet
Southminster
Watford
ELon
EECP
High Wycombe
Brentwood
ECou
Slough
Grays
Southend
Reading
London
Gravesend
Gillingham
M62
M18
A16
A17
A1
A47
A10
A11
A12
A14
M11
M1
A1(M)
M25
M40
M4
M3

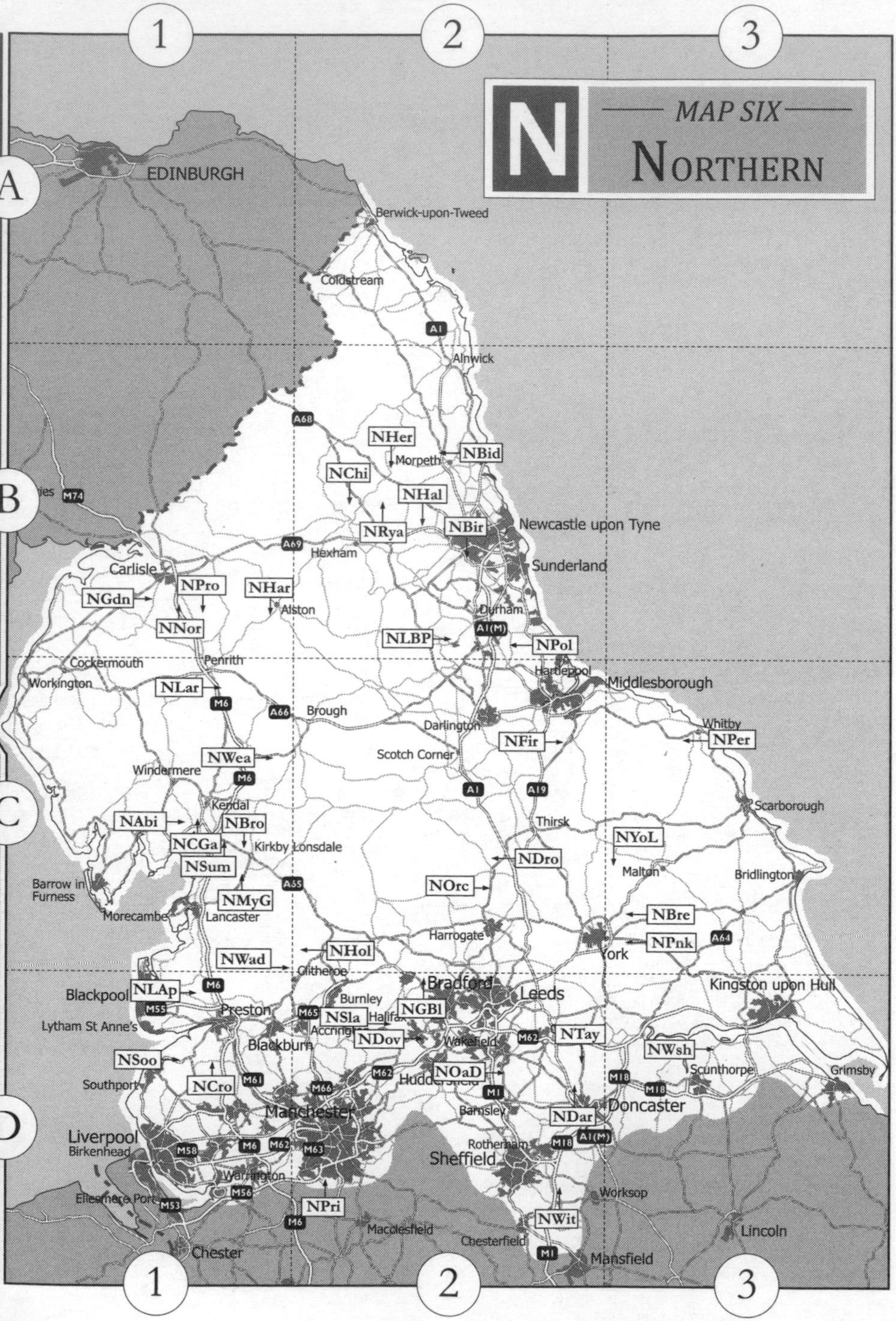
1
2
3
A
B
C
D
N
MAP SIX
NORTHERN
EDINBURGH
Berwick-upon-Tweed
Coldstream
A1
Alnwick
A68
NHer
NBid
Morpeth
NChi
NHal
M74
NRya
NBir
Newcastle upon Tyne
A69
Hexham
Sunderland
Carlisle
NPro
NHar
NGdn
Alston
NNor
Durham
A1(M)
NLBP
NPol
Penrith
Cockermouth
Workington
Hartlepool
Middlesborough
NLar
M6
A66
Brough
Darlington
Whitby
NFir
NPer
Scotch Corner
NWea
Windermere
M6
A1
A19
Scarborough
Kendal
NAbi
NBro
Thirsk
NYoL
NCGa
Kirkby Lonsdale
NDro
NSum
Malton
Bridlington
Barrow in Furness
A55
NOrc
NMyG
Morecambe
Lancaster
NBre
Harrogate
York
A64
NPnk
NHol
NWad
Clitheroe
Bradford
Kingston upon Hull
Blackpool
NLAp
M6
Leeds
Burnley
M55
Preston
M65
NSla
Halifax
NGBl
Lytham St Anne's
Accrington
NTay
NDov
Wakefield
M62
NWsh
Blackburn
NSoo
M62
NOaD
Scunthorpe
Grimsby
Southport
NCro
M61
M66
Huddersfield
M18
M18
M1
Doncaster
Manchester
Barnsley
NDar
Liverpool
Birkenhead
M58
M6
M62
M63
M18
A1(M)
Rotherham
Sheffield
Warrington
M56
Worksop
Ellesmere Port
M53
NPri
M6
Macclesfield
NWit
Lincoln
Chesterfield
M1
Chester
Mansfield

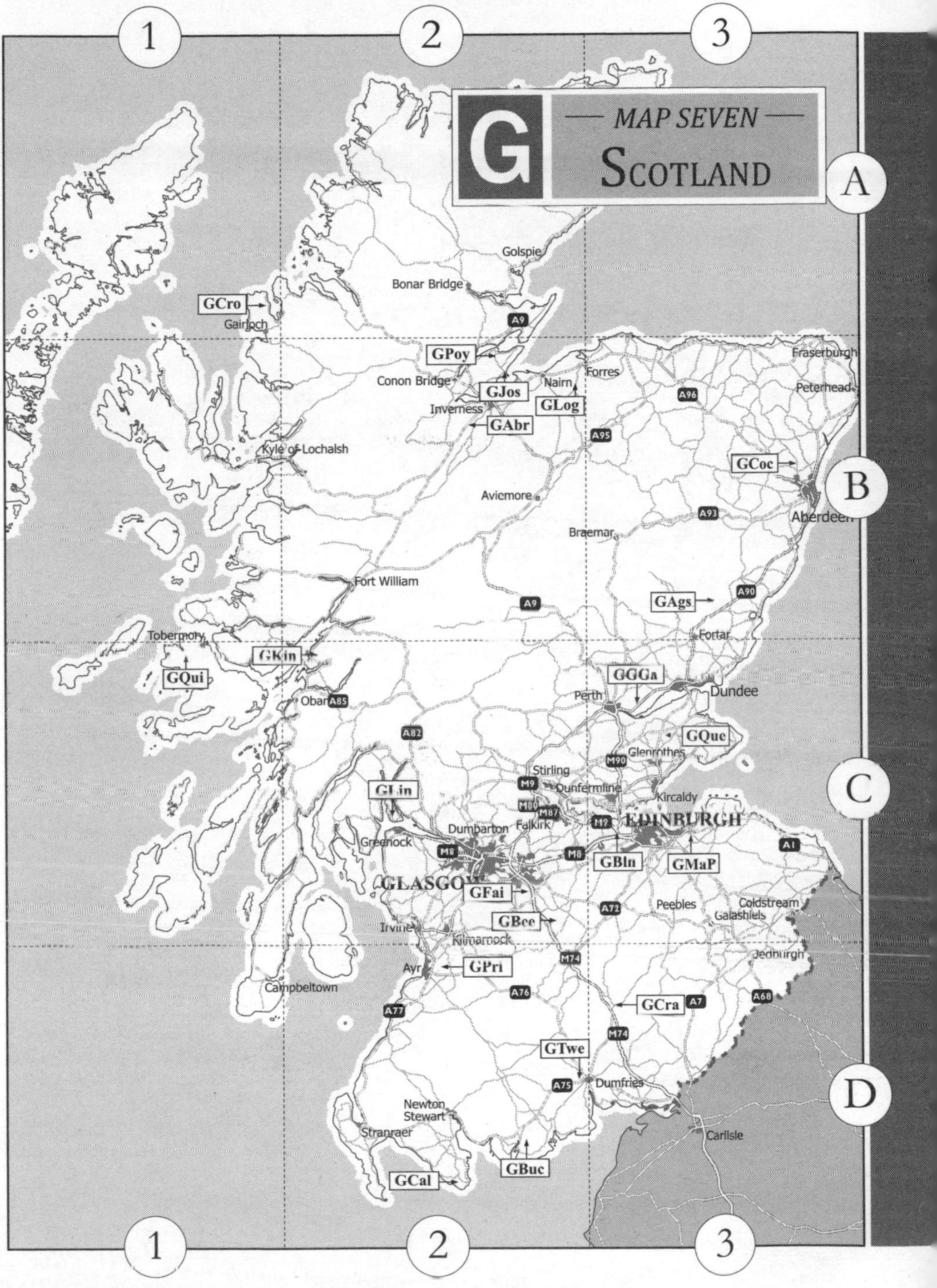
G
MAP SEVEN
SCOTLAND
1
2
3
A
B
C
D
Golspie
Bonar Bridge
GCro
Gairloch
A9
GPoy
Conon Bridge
GJos
Nairn
Forres
Inverness
GLog
GAbr
Fraserburgh
Peterhead
A96
A95
Kyle of Lochalsh
GCoc
Aviemore
A93
Aberdeen
Braemar
Fort William
A9
GAgs
A90
Tobermory
Forfar
GKin
GQui
GGGa
Dundee
Perth
Oban
A85
A82
GQue
Glenrothes
M90
Stirling
M9
Dunfermline
GLin
Kircaldy
M80
M87
Falkirk
M9
EDINBURGH
Dumbarton
Greenock
M8
M8
GBln
GMaP
A1
GLASGOW
GFai
Peebles
Coldstream
Galashiels
A72
GBee
Irvine
Kilmarnock
Jedburgh
Ayr
GPri
M74
Campbeltown
A76
GCra
A7
A68
A77
M74
GTwe
A75
Dumfries
Newton Stewart
Stranraer
Carlisle
GBuc
GCal

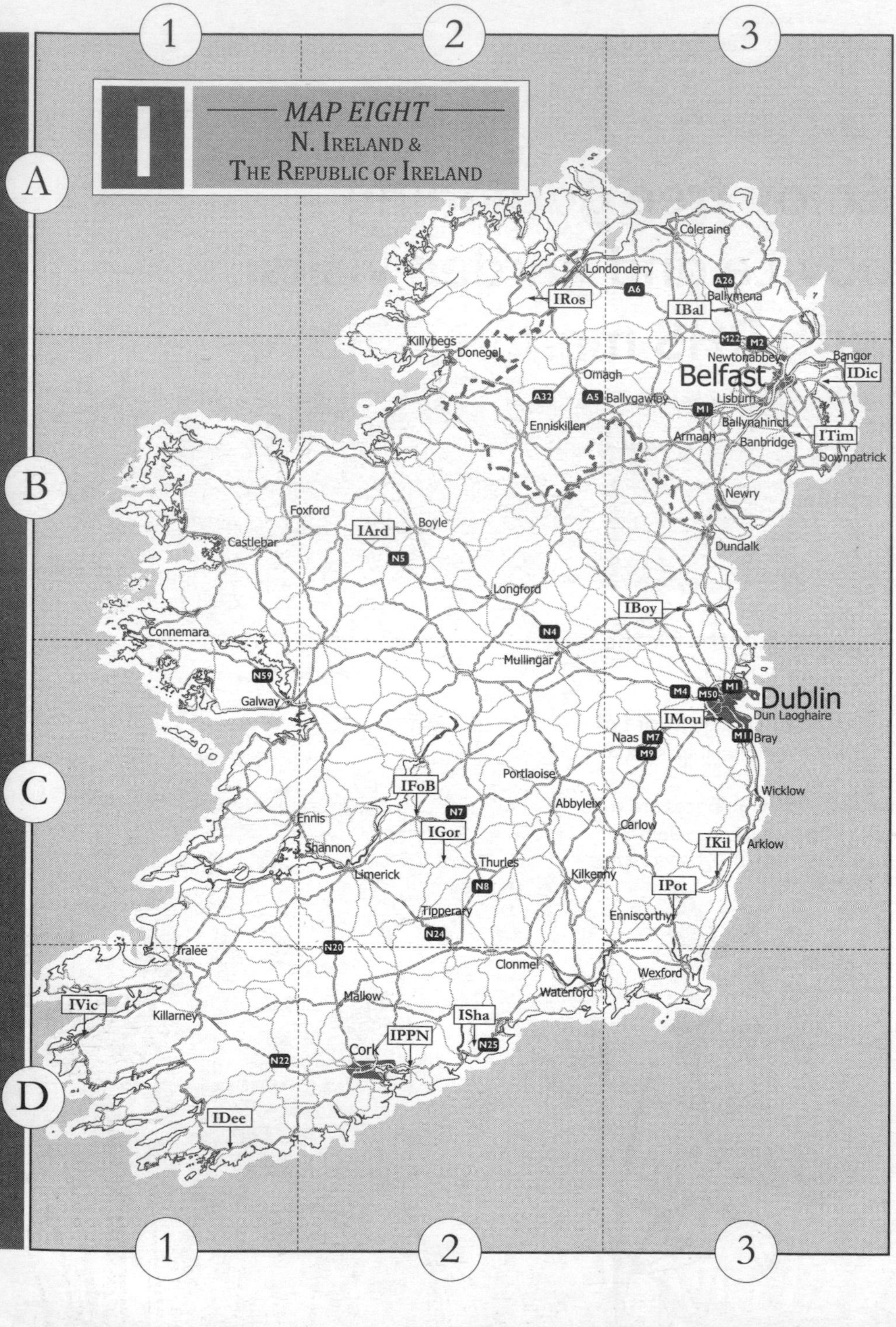
1
2
3
A
B
C
D
I
MAP EIGHT
N. Ireland &
The Republic of Ireland
Coleraine
Londonderry
A26
A6
IRos
IBal
Ballymena
Killybegs
Donegal
M22
M2
Newtonabbey
Bangor
Belfast
IDic
Omagh
A32
A5
Ballygawley
Lisburn
M1
Enniskillen
Ballynahinch
Armagh
Banbridge
ITim
Downpatrick
Newry
Foxford
IArd
Boyle
Castlebar
N5
Dundalk
Longford
IBoy
Connemara
N4
Mullingar
N59
M4
M50
M1
Dublin
Galway
IMou
Dun Laoghaire
Naas
M7
M11
Bray
M9
Portlaoise
IFoB
N7
Wicklow
Ennis
Abbyleix
IGor
Carlow
IKil
Arklow
Shannon
Thurles
Limerick
Kilkenny
N8
IPot
Tipperary
Enniscorthy
N24
N20
Tralee
Clonmel
Wexford
Mallow
Waterford
IVic
Killarney
ISha
IPPN
N25
Cork
N22
IDee

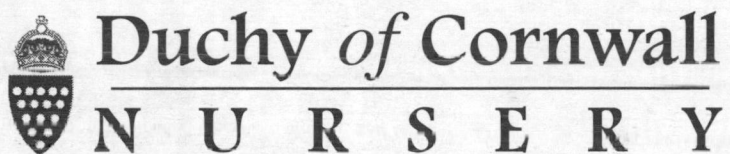

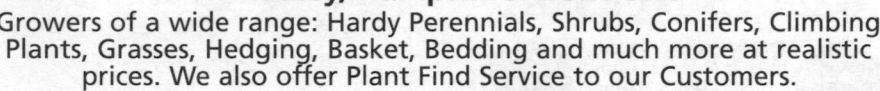

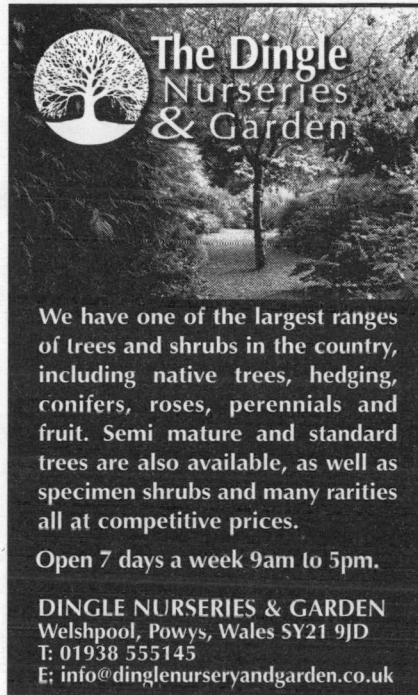

INDEX OF ADVERTISERS